POCKET
SCHOOL
&
OFFICE
DICTIONARY

The indispensable guide for everyone who needs to know the right word, in the right place, at the right time . . .

For easy reference, every word included in this dictionary receives a separate entry and indication of its pronunciation. The pronunciations are recorded in the simplest key consistent with accurate transcription. The definitions are written in a clear, simple style and individual parts of speech are clearly distinguished.

Slang words are designated *(Slang)*, and words of foreign origin that are not yet fully naturalized in English are marked with the language of origin.

In addition, *The Pocket Webster School & Office Dictionary* contains an up-to-date gazetteer, a perpetual calendar, and other lists and tables on a variety of subjects, making this book a valuable volume of general information.

THE
POCKET
WEBSTER
SCHOOL
&
OFFICE
DICTIONARY

POCKET BOOKS

New York London Toronto Sydney Tokyo Singapore

POCKET BOOKS, a division of Simon & Schuster Inc.
1230 Avenue of the Americas, New York, New York 10020

ISBN 0-671-70016-2

First Pocket Books printing February 1990

10 9 8 7 6 5 4 3 2

POCKET and colophon are registered trademarks of
Simon & Schuster Inc.

Printed in the U.S.A.

CONTENTS

CONTENTS

INTRODUCTION

The dictionary you now hold in your hands is a total revision and resetting of the WEBSTER'S NEW SCHOOL & OFFICE DICTIONARY that for several decades served as a helpful, economical reference book on language. In bringing that work up to date and in making it even more useful, the editors compiled a list of over 63,000 vocabulary entries, more than in any other pocket-sized paperback dictionary, that includes the basic word list of English, as well as many specialized terms in the sciences and arts. Newer terms frequently encountered in newspapers, magazines, and books are also well represented here—such terms as *sky marshal, audiophile, dermabrasion, Afro, minibus, sexism,* and *Ms.*

Conciseness is an essential feature of any good pocket-sized dictionary, but precision must never be sacrificed to brevity. In this dictionary, the definitions are brief, but never to the point of distorting the meanings. And to make it easier for the user to find the precise sense he is looking for, the individual meanings are numbered after each identified part of speech. As a further aid, irregular inflections of verbs, comparisons of adjectives and adverbs, and plurals of nouns are shown in full or in a truncated form.

Words and meanings that are slang, informal, obsolete, dialectal, or the like are identified by the proper label, and words of foreign borrowing that are not yet fully naturalized in English are marked with the language of origin. The pronunciations, recorded in a simple, but precise key, are those prevailing at the present time in American speech, and the key itself appears in a shortened form on every two-page spread of the book.

To increase the value of this book as a volume of general information, a number of supplements have been appended, including a gazetteer, tables of weights and measures, a perpetual calendar, and a listing of U.S. and Canadian holidays.

The full key to pronunciation will be found on the following page, along with a list of the abbreviations used in the definitions of this dictionary.

The editors responsible for this revision are: *Supervising Editor:* Thomas Layman; *Editors:* Roslyn Block, Jonathan Goldman, Christopher Hoolihan, Ruth Kent, Paul Murry; *Assistants:* Virginia Becker, Cynthia Sadonick, Gertrude Tullar; *Proofreader:* Joy Walworth.

KEY TO PRONUNCIATION

a: in cap, act, pad
ā: in cane, age, save
ä: in father, ah, mark
å: in abet, suitable, diploma
ch: in chair, archer, rich
e: in met, end, peril
ē: in be, equal, regal
ê: in baker, maker, allergy
ė: in regent, adequate, elephant
g: in get, ogre, log
i: in pit, in, taxi
ī: in fine, isle, rabbi
i: in manifest, attitude, politics
j: in joy, injure, jet
kh: in loch (a foreign sound, like a breathy k)
l: in loot, rule, apple
n: in no, tune, sudden
ng: in ring, long, tongue

o: in hot, odd, pond
ō: in bone, old, hero
ô: in horse, off, gong
ọ: in dragon, occur, apology
oi: in boil, oil, coin
ōō: in tool, ooze, moo
oo: in wool, book, good
ou: in house, out, sour
sh: in shall, cashier, ash
th: in thin, ether, tooth
th: in sheathe, then, other
u: in cup, us, bud
ū: in cure, use, menu
û: in turn, urn, burn
ů: in focus, circus, circumstance
w: in wood, wit, when
y: in yet, yarn, yolk
zh: in azure, measure, vision

NOTES

Although only the symbol w is shown for words that begin with wh (as for when), the sound "hw" is also often used.

COMPOUND WORDS: For variant pronunciations see the base word; thus, see **operative** for a variant pronunciation of **postoperative**.

FOREIGN WORDS: Foreign words have the source language in brackets after the part-of-speech label. The pronunciations for these words show only approximate English equivalents of the foreign sounds. Example: ge·müt·lich (gẽ-mēt´lich), adj. [German].

ABBREVIATIONS USED IN THIS DICTIONARY

adj.	adjective	Fr.	French	prep.	preposition
adv.	adverb	indef. art.	indefinite article	pron.	pronoun
alt.	alternate	indic.	indicative	p.t.	past tense
Brit.	British	interj.	interjection	sing.	singular
c.	circa	masc.	masculine	sp.	spelled; spelling
cent.	century	n.	noun	v.	verb
cf.	compare	Obs.	obsolete	var.	variant
conj.	conjunction	pl.	plural	v.aux.	auxiliary verb
Dial.	dialectal	poss.	possessive	v.i.	intransitive verb
fem.	feminine	p.p.	past participle	v.t.	transitive verb

A

A, a (ā), *n.*, *pl.* **A's, a's,** 1. the first letter of the English alphabet. 2. any of the various sounds of this letter, as in *cap, cane, father,* and *abet.* 3. a type or impression of *A* or *a*.

A (ā), *adj.* 1. shaped like *A*. 2. superior: see **A one:** *n.* 1. an object shaped like *A*. 2. a school mark or rating signifying excellence. 3. in *Music, a)* the sixth tone in the scale of C major. *b)* the key having this tone for a basic note.

a (å, stressed ā), *adj. & indef. art.* 1. one. 2. any; some. 3. each: used before consonants; *an* is used before vowels or mute *h*.

a-, a prefix meaning *not, of, off, in, on, in the state of.*

aard-vark (ärd'värk), *n.* an ant-eating African mammal with a long, sticky tongue: it burrows in the ground.

Ab (ab), *n.* the eleventh month of the Jewish year.

a-back (å-bak'), *adv.* 1. [Archaic], backward. 2. by surprise: used only in *taken aback.*

ab-a-cus (ab'å-kůs, å-bak'ůs), *n.*, *pl.* **-cus-es, -ci** (-sī), 1. a frame with beads that slide on rods, for doing arithmetic. 2. the slab forming the top of a column.

a-baft (å-baft'), *adv.* toward, or in the direction of, the stern of a ship; astern: *prep.* behind.

ab-a-lo-ne (ab-å-lō'ni), *n.* a large, ear-shaped, edible sea mollusk: its shell is lined with mother-of-pearl.

a-ban-don (å-ban'dŏn), *n.* a surrender of one's self to impulses: *v.t.* 1. to desert; forsake. 2. to give up all claim to. **—a-ban'don-ment,** *n.*

a-ban-doned (-dŏnd), *adj.* 1. given up entirely. 2. shamelessly profligate.

a-base (å-bās'), *v.t.* **a-based', a-bas'ing,** to humble or degrade. **—a-base'ment,** *n.*

a-bash (å-bash'), *v.t.* to embarrass or make ashamed. **—a-bash'ment,** *n.*

a-bate (å-bāt'), *v.t.* **a-bat'ed, a-bat'ing,** 1. to lessen. 2. to deduct. 3. to suppress: *v.i.* to decrease; moderate; subside.

a-bate-ment ('mĕnt), *n.* 1. an abating, or lessening. 2. a deduction; amount by which a sum or quantity is reduced. 3. suppression, as of a nuisance.

ab-a-tis, ab-at-tis (ab'å-tis), *n.*, *pl.* **-tis,** a barricade of felled trees with sharpened branches pointing outward.

ab-at-toir (ab-å-twär'), *n.* a slaughterhouse.

ab-ba-cy (ab'å-si), *n.*, *pl.* **-cies,** the office and jurisdiction of an abbot.

ab-bé (å-bā'), *n.* a French title of respect given to an ecclesiastic.

ab-bess (ab'ĕs), *n.* a woman who is the superior of a convent or nunnery.

ab-bey (ab'i), *n.* 1. a monastery or convent. 2. a place of worship belonging to an abbey.

ab-bot (ab'ŏt), *n.* a man who is the head of an abbey for men.

ab-bre-vi-ate (å-brē'vi-āt), *v.t.* **-at-ed, -at-ing,** to shorten; especially, to contract a word by the omission of letters. **—ab-bre'vi-a-tor,** *n.*

ab-bre-vi-a-tion (-å'shůn), *n.* 1. the act of shortening. 2. the state of being abbreviated. 3. the word, phrase, or title contracted, as M.D. for Doctor of Medicine.

A B C (ā-bē-sē'), *n.*, *pl.* **A B C's,** 1. *usually pl.* the alphabet. 2. a rudiment; fundamental.

ab-di-cate (ab'dī-kāt), *v.t. & v.i.* **-cat-ed, -cat-ing,** 1. to give up or withdraw from. 2. to renounce. **—ab-di-ca'tion,** *n.* **—ab'di-ca-tor,** *n.*

ab-do-men (ab'dŏ-měn, ab-dō'-), *n.* 1. the belly; cavity of the body containing digestive organs and other viscera. 2. the posterior division of the body of an insect. **—ab-dom-i-nal** (ab-dom'ĭ-nl), *adj.*

ab-duct (ab-dukt'), *v.t.* to carry off by stealth or force; kidnap. **—ab-duc'tion,** *n.*

ab-duc-tor (-duk'tēr), *n.* 1. one who abducts; kidnapper. 2. a muscle that pulls (a body part) away from the median axis.

a-beam (å-bēm'), *adv.* at right angles to the keel of a ship.

a-be-ce-dar-i-an (å-bi-si-der'i-ăn), *adj.* belonging to the alphabet: *n.* one learning the alphabet.

a-bed (å-bed'), *adv.* in bed.

ab-er-rant (a-ber'ănt), *adj.* departing from the usual path, type, or standard. **—ab-er'rance, ab-er'ran-cy,** *n.*

ab-er-ra-tion (ab-ēr-ā'shůn), *n.* 1. the act of departing from the usual path, type, or standard. 2. mental derangement. 3. the unequal refraction of rays of light from a lens so that they do not converge to a single point.

a-bet (å-bet'), *v.t.* **a-bet'ted, a-bet'ting,** to aid or assist in the performance of an act, usually of a criminal nature; incite. **—a-bet'ment,** *n.* **—a-bet'tor, a-bet'ter,** *n.*

a-bey-ance (å-bā'åns), *n.* a state of suspension.

ab-hor (ab-hŏr'), *v.t.* **-horred', -hor'ring,** to hate; loathe; execrate; abominate. **—ab-hor'-rence,** *n.*

ab-hor-rent ('ĕnt), *adj.* detestable; hateful; repulsive.

a-bide (å-bīd'), *v.t.* **a-bode** (å-bōd') or **a-bid'ed, a-bid'ing,** 1. to await. 2. to endure; withstand; tolerate: *v.i.* 1. [Archaic], to dwell; reside. 2. to continue; stand firm.

a-bid-ing ('ing), *adj.* remaining; steadfast.

a-bil-i-ty (å-bil'ĭ-ti), *n.*, *pl.* **-ties,** 1. power to perform; skill to achieve. 2. talents or gifts.

ab-i-o-gen-e-sis (ab-i-ō-jen'ě-sis), *n.* spontaneous generation.

ab-ject (ab'jekt), *adj.* 1. low; miserable. 2. despicable; degraded. **—ab-ject'ness,** *n.*

ab-ju-ra-tion (ab-jū-rā'shůn), *n.* an oath of

renunciation, as of allegiance; act of renouncing.

ab·jure (ab-joor'), v.t. -jured', -jur'ing, 1. to renounce upon oath; forswear allegiance to. 2. to repudiate or recant.

ab·late (ab-lāt'), v.t. -lat'ed, -lat'ing, 1. to remove. 2. to wear away, as rock: v.i. to be worn away, as the shield on a spacecraft as it reenters the earth's atmosphere. —ab·la'tion, n.

ab·la·tive (ab'lā-tiv), n. one of the grammatical cases of Latin, expressing chiefly separation and instrumentality.

ab·laut (äb'lout), n. the changing of a vowel in the root of a word, indicating modification of meaning or use, as get, got.

a·blaze (ā-blāz'), adj. 1. on fire. 2. eager; inflamed with desire. 3. resplendent.

a·ble (ā'bl), adj. 1. possessed of power, means, or ability. 2. qualified; competent.

-a·ble (ā-bl), a suffix signifying able to, tending to, worthy or capable of, with qualities of.

a·ble-bod·ied (ā'bl-bod-id), adj. possessed of physical strength; capable or efficient.

a·bloom (ā-blōōm'), adj. in bloom.

ab·lu·tion (ab-lōō'shŭn), n. a washing or cleansing of the body, as in a religious ceremony to achieve moral purification.

ab·ne·gate (ab'nē-gāt), v.t. -gat·ed, -gat·ing, to refuse; deny; reject; abjure.

ab·ne·ga·tion (ab-nē-gā'shŭn), n. an act of self-denial or renunciation.

ab·nor·mal (ab-nôr'mäl), adj. irregular; departing from a type, standard, or rule. —ab·nor'mal·ly, adv.

ab·nor·mal·i·ty (ab-nôr-mal'ĭ-tĭ), n. 1. the state or condition of being abnormal or irregular. 2. pl. -ties, a thing that is abnormal.

a·board (ā-bōrd'), adv. on or within a ship, airplane, etc.: prep. into a ship, airplane, etc.

a·bode (ā-bōd'), n. a place of continued residence; dwelling; habitation.

a·bol·ish (ā-bol'ish), v.t. to do away with; put an end to. —a·bol'ish·ment, n.

ab·o·li·tion (ab-ō-lish'ŭn), n. 1. the act of abolishing or the state of being abolished; annulment or abrogation. 2. the abolishing of slavery.

ab·o·li·tion·ist (-ist), n. one who is in favor of the repeal or abolition of some existing law or custom, as slavery. —ab·o·li'tion·ism, n.

A-bomb (ā'bom), n. same as atomic bomb.

a·bom·i·na·ble (ā-bom'ĭ-nā-bl), adj. 1. hateful; odious. 2. unpleasant to the senses; offensive.

a·bom·i·nate (ā-bom'ĭ-nāt), v.t. -nat·ed, -nat·ing, to abhor; regard with feelings of disgust or hatred.

a·bom·i·na·tion (ā-bom-ĭ-nā'shŭn), n. 1. the act of abominating; excessive hatred. 2. the thing abominated.

ab·o·rig·i·nal (ab-ō-rij'ĭ-nl), adj. original; primitive; existing from the beginning: n. a species of animals or plants presumed to have originated within a given area.

ab·o·rig·i·ne (ab-ō-rij'ĭ-nē), n., pl. -nes, 1. one of the first or primitive inhabitants of a country. 2. pl. the native or indigenous animals or plants of any geographical area.

a·born·ing (ā-bôrn'ing), adv. while in the process of being born, produced, or created.

a·bort (ā-bôrt'), v.i. 1. to miscarry; have a miscarriage in giving birth. 2. to remain undeveloped: v.i. 1. to cause to have a miscarriage in giving birth. 2. to shorten, as the flight of a missile due to a malfunctioning of its apparatus.

a·bor·ti·cide (ā-bôr'tĭ-sīd), n. the destruction of the fetus in the womb.

a·bor·ti·fa·cient (ā-bôr-tĭ-fā'shĕnt), n. a drug or device used to kill a fetus or cause abortion.

a·bor·tion (ā-bôr'shŭn), n. 1. premature birth of a fetus so that it does not survive; miscarriage. 2. that which falls short of maturity due to arrest of development. —a·bor'tion·ist, n.

a·bor·tive ('tiv), adj. 1. causing abortion. 2. failing in effect; unsuccessful. 3. arrested in development.

a·bound (ā-bound'), v.i. 1. to have in plenty or abundance. 2. to exist in great numbers or quantity (followed by in or with).

a·bout (ā-bout'), adv. 1. around; on every side. 2. near. 3. to an opposite position. 4. almost: prep. 1. concerned with. 2. around. 3. near to. 4. with. 5. on the verge of.

a·bout-face (ā-bout'fās), n. 1. a reversal of physical position. 2. a change of opinion: v.i. -faced', -fac'ing, to move so as to be facing in the opposite direction.

a·bove (ā-buv'), adv. 1. in a higher place; overhead. 2. in heaven. 3. before: prep. 1. superior to. 2. beyond. 3. over; in excess of.

a·bove-board ('bōrd), adj. & adv. in open sight; without trickery.

ab·ra·ca·dab·ra (ab-rā-kā-dab'rā), n. 1. a mystical combination of letters written or inscribed on amulets and charms and supposed to ward off evils. 2. talk without meaning.

ab·rade (ā-brād'), v.t. & v.i. -rad'ed, -rad'ing, to wear or rub away; remove as by friction or abrasion. —ab·rad'er, n.

ab·ra·sion (ā-brā'zhŭn), n. 1. the act of wearing or rubbing away. 2. a chafed area.

ab·ra·sive ('siv), adj. causing abrasion: n. a substance used to grind or polish.

a·breast (ā-brest'), adv. & adj. 1. side by side; in line with. 2. with information; aware (followed by of).

a·bridge (ā-brij'), v.t. a·bridged', a·bridg'ing, 1. to curtail; shorten. 2. to use fewer words in expressing; condense. —a·bridg'a·ble, a·bridge'a·ble, adj.

a·bridg·ment, a·bridge·ment ('mĕnt), n. 1. the act of abridging or the state of being abridged. 2. something abridged, as a book.

a·broad (ā-brôd'), adv. 1. widely; expansively. 2. beyond the limits of house or country. 3. circulating; current.

ab·ro·gate (ab'rō-gāt), v.t. -gat·ed, -gat·ing, to abolish, annul, or repeal by authority. —ab'ro·ga·tor, n.

ab·ro·ga·tion (ab-rō-gā'shŭn), n. the act of abrogating; repeal or annulling of a law.

a·brupt (ā-brupt'), adj. 1. ending suddenly. 2. steep; precipitous. 3. rough; unceremonious. —a·brupt'ness, n.

---

a-brupt-ly ('li), adv. in an abrupt or sudden manner.

ab-scess (ab'ses), n. a collection of pus in the tissues of the body with attendant swelling and inflammation: v.i. to become inflamed and pus-filled. —ab'scessed, adj.

ab-scis-sa (ab-sis'å), n., pl. -sas, -sae ('ē), in Mathematics, the horizontal distance of a point, represented by a coordinate, from the vertical axis.

ab-scond (ăb-skond'), v.i. to flee one's residence or duty, especially in an effort to avoid arrest; leave in secret.

ab-sence (ab'sĕns), n. 1. the state of being absent. 2. the period of being absent. 3. a lack or a being without.

ab-sent (ab'sĕnt), adj. 1. not present; away. 2. wanting; lacking. 3. abstracted: v.t. (absent'), to retire or keep away from.

ab-sen-tee (ab-sĕn-tē'), n. one who is absent or absents himself purposely from home or duty: adj. denoting a landowner who lives away from his real estate.

ab-sen-tee-ism ('izm), n. the state or habit of being away from one's property, work, etc.

ab-sent-ly (ab'sĕnt-li), adv. in an abstracted manner.

ab-sent-mind-ed (-mīn'did), adj. 1. preoccupied. 2. forgetful. —ab'sent-mind'ed-ly, adv. —ab'-sent-mind'ed-ness, n.

ab-sinthe, ab-sinth (ab'sinth), n. 1. wormwood. 2. a bitter, aromatic liqueur of anise and wormwood.

ab-so-lute (ab'sŏ-lōōt), adj. 1. free as to condition. 2. perfect in itself. 3. unlimited in power. 4. fixed; irrevocable. 5. positive. 6. with nothing added; pure. 7. with no uncertainty; actual. —ab'so-lute-ness, n.

absolute pitch, the ability to sing or identify an isolated tone.

absolute temperature, temperature with absolute zero as its base.

absolute zero, the hypothetical temperature at which a substance has neither heat nor motion, theoretically −273.15°C or −459.67°F.

ab-so-lu-tion (ab-sŏ-lōō'shŭn), n. 1. the act of absolving from the consequences of sin. 2. the actual release from sin and its consequences.

ab-so-lut-ism (ab'sŏ-lōō-tizm), n. 1. the state of being absolute. 2. the principle or system of absolute government.

ab-so-lut-ist (-lōōt-ist), n. a supporter or advocate of despotic or absolute government.

ab-solve (ăb-zolv', -solv'), v.t. -solved', -solv'ing, 1. to release or acquit; free of crime, guilt, duty, etc. 2. to forgive or remit sin.

ab-sorb (ăb-sôrb'), v.t. 1. to drink in; imbibe; suck or swallow up. 2. to engross or engage wholly. 3. to assimilate. 4. to take in (light, shock, etc.) without reflection or reaction. —ab-sorb'a-ble, adj.

ab-sorb-ent (ăb-sôrb'nt), adj. that can absorb: n. anything which absorbs. —ab-sorb'en-cy, n.

ab-sorb-ing ('ing), adj. taking one's complete attention.

ab-sorp-tion (ăb-zôrp'shŭn, -sôrp'-), n. 1. the process or act of absorbing. 2. the state of

being absorbed. 3. the entire occupation of the mind.

ab-sorp-tive (ăb-zôrp'tiv, -sôrp'-), adj. having capacity for absorption. —ab-sorp-tiv'i-ty, n.

ab-stain (ăb-stān'), v.i. to forbear; refrain; keep away from.

ab-stain-er ('ĕr), n. one who abstains, especially from intoxicants.

ab-ste-mi-ous (ăb-stē'mi-ŭs), adj. moderate in the use of food and drink; not indulgent.

ab-sten-tion (ăb-sten'shŭn), n. the act of holding off or abstaining. —ab-sten'tious, adj.

ab-sterge (ab-stürj'), v.t. -sterged', -sterg'ing, 1. to cleanse; purify. 2. to purge.

ab-ster-gent (-stür'jĕnt), adj. possessing cleansing or purging properties: n. that which cleanses or purges.

ab-ster-sion (-stür'shŭn), n. 1. the act of cleansing. 2. the act of purging.

ab-ster-sive ('siv), adj. same as abstergent.

ab-sti-nence (ab'sti-nĕns), n. the act or practice of abstaining; self-denial; partial or total abstaining from food, drink, etc.

ab-sti-nent (ab'sti-nĕnt), adj. refraining from overindulgence; practicing abstinence.

ab-stract (ab-strakt', ab'strakt), adj. 1. considered or conceived apart from its concrete or material nature. 2. expressing such a quality. 3. not put into practice; theoretical. 4. in Art, not realistically representing objects: n. (ab'strakt), a summary comprising the essence or principal parts of a larger work: v.t. (ab-strakt'), 1. to take or draw away. 2. (ab'strakt), to epitomize; summarize. 3. to separate from and consider apart.

ab-stract-ed (ab-strakt'id), adj. 1. separated; disjoined. 2. preoccupied; mentally absent. —ab-stract'ed-ly, adv.

abstract expressionism, a form of painting emphasizing self-expression in compositions which do not represent natural objects.

ab-strac-tion (ab-strak'shŭn), n. 1. the act of separating or drawing away. 2. the state of being withdrawn. 3. preoccupation; absentmindedness. 4. something that is abstract, as an idea. 5. an abstract quality. 6. a painting or sculpture that is abstract.

ab-strac-tion-ist (-ist), n. one who deals with abstractions, especially in art. —ab-strac'tion-ism, n.

ab-strac-tive (ab-strak'tiv), adj. pertaining to or having the quality of abstraction.

abstract of title, a brief history of the ownership of a piece of real estate.

ab-struse (ab-strōōs'), adj. hidden; difficult to comprehend; profound. —ab-struse'ly, adv. —ab-struse'ness, n.

ab-surd (ăb-sürd'), adj. contrary to reason or sense; ridiculous. —ab-surd'ly, adv. —ab-surd'ness, n.

ab-surd-i-ty (ăb-sür'di-ti), n. 1. the state of being absurd. 2. pl. -ties, that which is absurd.

a-bu-li-a (å-bōō'li-å), n. loss of willpower; inability to act for one's self.

a-bun-dance (å-bun'dåns), n. 1. a great supply; overflowing quantity. 2. affluence; wealth.

a-bun-dant (å-bun'dånt), adj. plentiful; fully sufficient; abounding. —a-bun'dant-ly, adv.

a-buse (å-būz'), v.t. a-bused', a-bus'ing, 1. to use badly. 2. to treat rudely or wrongfully;

hurt or mistreat. 3. to use violent or abusive language to or about; vituperate: n. (á-būs'), 1. excessive or injudicious use of anything. 2. mistreatment. 3. a corrupt custom or practice. 4. an insult or insults.

a-bu-sive (á-bū'siv), *adj.* 1. practicing abuse; hurtful. 2. insulting or scolding; vituperative. —a-bu'sive-ly, *adv.* —a-bu'sive-ness, *n.*

a-but (á-but'), *v.i.* a-but'ted, a-but'ting, to border upon; touch at one end; terminate (followed by *on*, *upon*, or *against*): *v.t.* to end at or touch upon.

a-but-ment (á-but'mĕnt), *n.* 1. that which borders upon something else. 2. the solid structure which supports the extremity of a bridge or arch.

a-but-tals (á-but'álz), *n.pl.* parts of land that touch; boundaries.

a-but-ter (á-but'ēr), *n.* the owner of an abutting, or adjacent, piece of land.

a-buzz (á-buz'), *adj.* 1. filled with buzzing sounds. 2. full of bustle or activity.

a-bysm (á-bizm'), *n.* [Poetic], an abyss, or bottomless gulf.

a-bys-mal (á-biz'ml), *adj.* 1. pertaining to an abyss; bottomless. 2. wretched; very bad. —a-bys'mal-ly, *adv.*

a-byss (á-bis'), *n.* 1. a bottomless gulf. 2. that which is unfathomable. 3. in *Theology,* the void before the Creation.

a-ca-cia (á-kā'shá), *n.* 1. an ornamental tree or shrub with white or yellow flower clusters. 2. the flower. 3. the locust tree.

ac-a-deme (ak'á-dēm), *n.* [Poetic], 1. a school. 2. a college or university. 3. the academic or scholarly world.

ac-a-dem-ic (ak-á-dem'ik), *n.* a college student or a teacher at a university: *adj.* 1. belonging or pertaining to a college or university. 2. following a fixed set of rules; pedantic. 3. having no practical application; theoretical.

ac-a-dem-i-cal ('i-kl), *adj.* same as academic.

ac-a-dem-i-cal-ly ('ik-li), *adv.* 1. in an academic manner. 2. after the fashion of an academy.

ac-a-dem-i-cals ('ik-lz), *n.pl.* the cap and gown worn by graduates and undergraduates at a university or a college.

academic freedom, freedom within a school or university to express views without fear of administrative interference or reprisal.

a-cad-e-mi-cian (á-kad-ē-mish'án), *n.* a member of an academy or society for promoting the arts, sciences, and literature.

ac-a-dem-i-cism (ak-á-dem'á-sizm), a-cad-e-mism (á-kad'ē-mizm), *n.* formal or pedantic quality, spirit, etc.

a-cad-e-my (á-kad'ē-mi), *n.* 1. a private school or seminary for the teaching of the higher branches of education. 2. a school for instruction in special subjects. 3. an association or society of persons eminent in literature, science, and art. 4. a building devoted to academic purposes.

Academy Award, any of the annual awards presented in the U.S. by the Academy of Motion Picture Arts and Sciences.

ac-a-leph (ak'á-lef), *n.* an invertebrate animal, as the jellyfish.

a-can-thine (á-kan'thin), *adj.* of or pertaining to the acanthus plant.

a-can-thoid ('thoid), *adj.* spiny; formed like a spine.

a-can-thus (á-kan'thŭs), *n., pl.* -thus-es, -thi ('thī), 1. a plant having lobed or sharp-toothed leaves. 2. ornamentation in the capitals of the Corinthian order of architecture, resembling the foliage of the acanthus.

a cap-pel-la (ä kä-pel'á), [Italian], in *choral music,* sung without accompaniment.

ac-a-ri-a-sis (ak-á-rī'á-sis), *n.* the state of being affected with acarids, as in scabies.

ac-a-rid (ak'á-rid), *n.* any of a number of mites and ticks.

a-cau-dal (á-kô'dl), a-cau-date ('dāt), *adj.* without a tail; tailless.

ac-cede (ak-sēd'), *v.i.* -ced'ed, -ced'ing, 1. to come at or attain. 2. to agree or yield. (Followed by *to*).

ac-cel-er-an-do (ak-sel-ē-ran'dō), *adv. & adj.* in *Music,* with faster tempo.

ac-cel-er-ate (ăk-sel'ē-rāt), *v.t.* -at-ed, -at-ing, 1. to hasten; cause to move or progress faster. 2. to quicken the speed of. 3. to bring nearer in time: *v.i.* to move faster. —ac-cel-er-a'tion (-rā'shŭn), *n.*

ac-cel-er-a-tive (-rāt-iv), *adj.* of, causing an increase in, or tending to increase velocity.

ac-cel-er-a-tor (-ēr), *n.* 1. that which quickens or accelerates. 2. a device that increases the speed of a machine; especially, the foot throttle attached to an internal-combustion engine. 3. in *Photography,* a chemical that speeds up the developing process.

ac-cel-er-om-e-ter (ăk-sel-ē-rom'ē-tēr), *n.* an instrument for determining acceleration or vibration.

ac-cent (ak'sent), *n.* 1. the stress laid by the voice upon a particular syllable, so as to make it more prominent than the rest. 2. the mark or character used in writing and printing to indicate stress. 3. a peculiarity of utterance or expression distinguishing the language of different parts or districts of the same or a foreign country. 4. the emphasis placed upon certain notes of a bar of music. 5. any special emphasis or attention: *v.t.* (also ak-sent'), 1. to express the accent, or denote the vocal division, of a word with the voice. 2. to mark or accent a word in writing by use of a sign. 3. to dwell upon or emphasize.

ac-cen-tu-al (ak-sen'choo-wál), *adj.* 1. of or pertaining to accent. 2. rhythmical. —ac-cen'tu-al-ly, *adv.*

ac-cen-tu-ate (-wāt), *v.t.* -at-ed, -at-ing, 1. to speak, pronounce, or mark with an accent. 2. to lay stress upon; emphasize.

ac-cen-tu-a-tion (ak-sen-choo-wā'shŭn), *n.* 1. the act of accentuating by stress or accent. 2. the act of emphasizing.

ac-cept (ăk-sept'), *v.t.* 1. to take or receive. 2. to receive with favor; approve. 3. to agree to, or acquiesce in. 4. to understand or receive in a particular sense. 5. to believe in. 6. to agree or promise to pay.

ac-cept-a-ble (ăk-sep'tá-bl), *adj.* 1. satisfactory. 2. adequate. —ac-cept-a-bil'i-ty (-bil'í-ti), ac-cept'a-ble-ness, *n.*

---

a in cap, ä in cane, ä in father, á in abet, e in met ē in be, ē in baker, ê in regent, i in pit, ī in fine, i in manifest, o in hot, ō in horse, ō in bone,

ac·cept·ance (ăk-sep'tăns), *n.* 1. the act of accepting. 2. the fact of being accepted, or received with approval. 3. the act of accepting an obligation, offer, etc.

ac·cept·ant ('tănt), *adj.* inclined to accept approvingly or with favor.

ac·cep·ta·tion (-tā'shŭn), *n.* 1. [Archaic], the act of accepting or state of being accepted. 2. the accepted meaning or sense of a word or statement.

ac·cept·ed ('tid), *adj.* regarded as right or proper; traditional.

ac·cep·tor, ac·cept·er ('tēr), *n.* one who accepts; especially, one who accepts a bill of exchange.

ac·cess (ăk'ses), *n.* 1. admittance. 2. the act of approaching or a means of approach or admission. 3. addition or increase. a fit or attack, as of a disease.

ac·ces·sa·ry (ăk-ses'ēr-i), *adj. & n., pl.* -ries, same as accessory.

ac·ces·si·ble (-ses'i-bl), *adj.* 1. capable of being approached. 2. easy to approach. 3. obtainable. 4. receptive. —ac·ces·si·bil'i·ty (-bil'i-ti), **ac·ces'si·ble·ness,** *n.* —ac·ces'si·bly, *adv.*

ac·ces·sion (-sesh'ŭn), *n.* 1. a coming to, as by succession or right; attainment. 2. the act of acceding by assent or agreement. 3. increase or augmentation. 4. something added, as to a library. 5. an attack, as of a disease. 6. in *Law,* the addition of property by improvement, growth, or labor expended.

ac·ces·sion·al ('ŭn-l), *adj.* 1. of or pertaining to an accession. 2. additional.

ac·ces·so·ri·al (ăk-sĕ-sôr'i-ăl), *adj.* of or pertaining to an accessory.

ac·ces·so·ry (ăk-ses'ēr-i), *adj.* aiding; contributing to result or effect: *n., pl.* -ries, 1. something additional. 2. in *Law,* one who aids in the commission of an unlawful act; accomplice. 3. a nonessential piece of equipment, clothing, etc.

access time, the time between requesting and receiving information from a computer.

ac·ci·dence (ăk'si-dĕns), *n.* 1. the portion of grammar which deals with the inflections of words. 2. the rudimentary elements of any subject.

ac·ci·dent (ăk'si-dĕnt), *n.* 1. an event which is unexpected, or the cause of which was unforeseen. 2. a casualty or mishap. 3. something happening by chance; contingency. 4. a property of a thing which is not essential to it.

ac·ci·den·tal (ăk-si-den'tl), *adj.* 1. happening by chance or unexpectedly. 2. nonessential; connected with, but not necessary to: *n.* 1. an adjunct, or nonessential part or quality. 2. a sharp, flat, or natural introduced into a piece of music to lower or raise the note before which it is placed. —ac·ci·den'tal·ly, *adv.*

accident insurance, a type of insurance which indemnifies the policyholder in case of injury due to accident.

ac·ci·dent-prone (ăk'si-dĕnt-prōn), *adj.* having an apparent tendency to have accidents. — **ac'ci·dent-prone·ness,** *n.*

ac·cip·i·ter (ăk-sip'i-tēr), *n.* 1. a small hawk

with short wings and a long tail. 2. any similar bird of prey.

ac·cip·i·trine (-trin), *adj.* resembling a hawk or similar bird of prey; hawklike.

ac·claim (ă-klām'), *v.t.* to greet or announce with praise or applause: *n.* shouts of joy or praise; acclamation.

ac·cla·ma·tion (ăk-lă-mā'shŭn), *n.* 1. applause or other demonstration of strong approval. 2. the adoption of a resolution by voice vote:

ac·clam·a·tor·y (ă-klam'ă-tôr-i), *adj.* expressing approval or praise.

ac·cli·mate (ăk'li-māt), *v.t. & v.i.* -mat·ed, -mat·ing, to accustom or become accustomed to a foreign climate or new surroundings.

ac·cli·ma·tion (ăk-li-mā'shŭn), *n.* 1. the process of acclimating. 2. the state of becoming inured to a foreign environment.

ac·cli·ma·tize (ă-kli'mă-tīz), *v.t. & v.i.* -tized, -tiz·ing, same as acclimate. —ac·cli·ma·ti·za'tion (-ti-zā'shŭn), *n.*

ac·cliv·i·ty (ă-kliv'i-ti), *n., pl.* -ties, an ascent or upward slope of the earth's surface.

ac·cli·vous (ă-kli'vŭs), *adj.* rising or sloping, as a hillside; gradually ascending.

ac·co·lade (ăk'ō-lād), *n.* 1. formerly, an embrace on the conferring of knighthood. 2. a gentle blow with the flat side of a sword, on the conferring of knighthood. 3. a showing of respect or approval; praise. 4. a brace in music joining two or more staffs.

ac·com·mo·date (ă-kom'ō-dāt), *v.t.* 1. to adapt or make fit or suitable; adjust. 2. to settle. 3. to supply or furnish. 4. to do a favor for. 5. to have or provide room for: *v.i.* to become adjusted; adapt. —ac·com'mo·da·tor, *n.*

ac·com·mo·dat·ing (-dāt·ing), *adj.* obliging; of a yielding disposition; adapting oneself to the desires of others. —ac·com'mo·dat·ing·ly, *adv.*

ac·com·mo·da·tion (ă-kom-ō-dā'shŭn), *n.* 1. the act of accommodating or the state of being accommodated. 2. settlement of a quarrel. 3. that which supplies a want or desire. 4. a being favorably disposed to the helping of others. 5. *pl.* lodgings. 6. a seat or other space on a train, airplane, etc.

accommodation ladder, a ladder or stairway suspended at the gangway of a ship.

accommodation paper, a bill or note cosigned by one party to enable the drawer to raise money on it, using the credit reputation of the cosigner: also **accommodation bill, accommodation note.**

accommodation train, a train which stops at all stations.

ac·com·mo·dat·ive (ă-kom'ō-dāt-iv), *adj.* disposed or tending to accommodate.

ac·com·pa·ni·ment (ă-kump'ni-mĕnt), *n.* 1. something which is added to the original or principal thing to provide ornament or symmetry. 2. instrumental music played to support the voice or another instrument.

ac·com·pa·nist (ă-kum'pă-nist), *n.* one who performs a musical accompaniment: also **ac·com'pa·ny·ist** (-ni-ist).

ac·com·pa·ny (ă-kum'pă-ni), *v.t.* -nied, -ny·ing, 1. to keep company with; escort. 2. to join in movement or action; supplement. 3. to perform the musical accompaniment for: *v.i.* to provide a musical accompaniment.

ac-com-plice (à-kom'plis), *n.* an associate or companion in crime.

ac-com-plish (à-kom'plish), *v.t.* to bring to completion; fulfill. —ac-com'plish-a-ble, *adj.*

ac-com-plished ('plisht), *adj.* 1. finished; perfected. 2. skilled. 3. socially polished.

ac-com-plish-ment ('plish-mènt), *n.* 1. the completion of an act or undertaking; fulfillment. 2. the thing completed; achievement. 3. *usu-ally pl.* a social art or skill obtained through training.

ac-cord (à-kôrd'), *v.t.* 1. to reconcile; make agree. 2. to give; grant; concede: *v.i.* to be in agreement or harmony (followed by *with*): *n.* agreement; concurrence of opinion; harmony.

ac-cord-ance ('ns), *n.* 1. the state of being in harmony or accord. 2. a giving or granting.

ac-cord-ant ('nt), *adj.* in agreement; harmonious. —ac-cord'ant-ly, *adv.*

ac-cord-ing ('ing), *adj.* agreeing; harmonious: *adv.* in accordance.

ac-cord-ing-ly (-li), *adv.* 1. in agreement with what has gone before. 2. therefore.

ac-cor-di-on (à-kôr'di-ôn), *n.* a musical instrument with keys and metal reeds, worked by means of a bellows. —ac-cor'di-on-ist, *n.*

ac-cost (à-kôst'), *v.t.* to come near and speak to.

ac-couche-ment (à-kōōsh'mènt), *n.* the act of bringing forth a child; parturition.

ac-cou-cheur (a-kōō-shūr'), *n.* a doctor who attends childbirth cases.

ac-cou-cheuse (-shooz'), *n.* a midwife.

ac-count (à-kount'), *v.t.* to reckon or hold to be; count: *v.i.* 1. to provide an explanation (followed by *for*). 2. to take into consideration. 3. to supply with a financial record (followed by *to*): *n.* 1. a reckoning. 2. a financial statement or memorandum. 3. a customer or client. 4. same as bank account. 5. same as charge account. 6. a narrative; anything in the form of a statement, written or verbal. 7. a reason. 8. importance or value.

ac-count-a-ble (à-kount'à-bl), *adj.* 1. answerable; responsible; liable to be called to account. 2. that can be accounted for; explainable. —ac-count-a-bil'i-ty (-bil'i-ti), ac-count'a-ble-ness, *n.*

ac-count-a-bly (-bli), *adv.* in a manner that can be accounted for, or explained.

ac-count-an-cy (à-kount'n-si), *n.* the skill or practice of an accountant.

ac-count-ant (à-kount'nt), *n.* one skilled in the keeping or examination of financial accounts.

account book, a book in which the financial accounts of a business are recorded.

account current, a statement of a business account showing the amount of money owed as of a specific date.

ac-count-ing (à-koun'ting), *n.* 1. the figuring and recording of financial accounts. 2. a statement of a financial account showing debits and credits. 3. an explanation.

ac-cou-ter (à-kōōt'ēr), *v.t.* to dress; equip; furnish with accouterments.

ac-cou-ter-ments (-mènts), *n.pl.* 1. dress; clothing. 2. the equipment of a soldier.

ac-cred-it (à-kred'it), *v.t.* 1. to have confidence in; believe and accept as true. 2. to authorize; stamp with authority. 3. to credit or assign. —ac-cred-it-a'tion (-i-tā'shùn), *n.*

ac-crete (à-krēt'), *v.i.* -cret-ed, -cret'ing, 1. to adhere. 2. to be added to: *v.t.* to cause to grow or unite (followed by *to*).

ac-cre-tion (à-krē'shùn), *n.* 1. growth, especially by the addition of parts. 2. matter that has accumulated. 3. the growing together of parts or members naturally separate. 4. a whole resulting from increase or growth.

ac-cre-tive ('tiv), *adj.* adding to or increasing by growth.

ac-cru-al (à-krōō'àl), ac-crue-ment (à-krōō'-mènt), *n.* 1. an accruing. 2. the amount that accrues.

ac-crue (à-krōō'), *v.i.* -crued', -cru'ing, to happen or to result as natural growth, as an increment on bonds.

ac-cul-tu-rate (à-kul'chù-rāt), *v.i. & v.t.* -rat-ed, -rat-ing, to change or cause to change by acculturation.

ac-cul-tu-ra-tion (à-kul-chù-rā'shùn), *n.* 1. the process of becoming adapted to a culture, especially a different culture. 2. the blending of different cultures.

ac-cum-bent (à-kum'bènt), *adj.* reclining or recumbent.

ac-cu-mu-late (à-kūm'yù-lāt), *v.t.* -lat-ed, -lat-ing, to collect or bring together; amass; heap up: *v.i.* to increase in size, number, or quantity. —ac-cu'mu-la-ble (-là-bl), *adj.*

ac-cu-mu-la-tion (à-kūm-yù-lā'shùn), *n.* 1. the act of accumulating or amassing. 2. the mass accumulated.

ac-cu-mu-la-tive (-lāt-iv), *adj.* 1. produced by accumulation. 2. tending to accumulate.

ac-cu-mu-la-tor (-ēr), *n.* 1. one who or that which accumulates. 2. [British], a storage battery.

ac-cu-ra-cy (ak'yoo-rà-si), *n.* the quality of being accurate; exactness or correctness.

ac-cu-rate (ak'yoo-rit), *adj.* 1. in exact conformity with the truth or a certain standard. 2. free from error; precise. —ac'cu-rate-ly, *adv.* —ac'cu-rate-ness, *n.*

ac-curs-ed (à-kūr'sid), ac-curst (à-kūrst'), *adj.* 1. under or subject to a curse; doomed to destruction. 2. detestable; execrable.

ac-cus-al (à-kū'zl), *n.* same as accusation.

ac-cu-sa-tion (ak-yù-zā'shùn), *n.* 1. the act of accusing or imputing. 2. the wrongdoing of which one is accused.

ac-cu-sa-ti-val (à-kū-zà-tī'vl), *adj.* of or pertaining to the accusative case.

ac-cu-sa-tive (à-kū'zà-tiv), *adj.* accusing: *n.* the grammatical case, as of Latin nouns, denoting the object of a transitive verb or of a preposition. —ac-cu'sa-tive-ly, *adv.*

ac-cu-sa-to-ri-al (à-kū-zà-tôr'i-àl), *adj.* of or pertaining to an accuser. —ac-cu-sa-to'ri-al-ly, *adv.*

ac·cu·sa·to·ry (á-kū′zá-tôr-i), *adj.* accusing, or containing an accusation.

ac·cuse (á-kūz′), *v.t.* -cused′, -cus′ing, 1. to charge with guilt or blame. 2. to bring an imputation against; charge with wrongdoing (followed by *of*). —**ac·cus′ing·ly,** *adv.*

ac·cus·er (′ēr), *n.* one who accuses or formally charges an offense against another.

ac·cus·tom (á-kus′tŏm), *v.t.* to habituate or familiarize by custom or use.

ac·cus·tomed (′tŏmd), *adj.* 1. usual; often practiced. 2. in the habit of.

ace (ās), *n.* 1. a unit; the number "one" in certain games. 2. a playing card or die marked with a single spot. 3. a military pilot who has destroyed a certain number of enemy airplanes. 4. a tennis serve that one's opponent cannot return. 5. in *Golf,* the act of getting the ball in the hole on the drive from the tee. 6. a person skilled at a particular activity: *v.t.* **aced** (āst), **ac′ing,** to make an ace in tennis or in golf: *adj.* [Informal], expert.

a·ce·di·a (á-sē′di-á), *n.* lassitude, listlessness, and general indifference.

a·cen·tric (ā-sen′trik), *adj.* away from the center; having no center.

a·ceph·a·lous (á-sef′á-lŭs), *adj.* 1. headless. 2. without a leader.

a·cerb (á-sûrb′), **a·cer·bic** (á-sûr′bik), *adj.* 1. sour to the taste. 2. acid in tone or language.

ac·er·bate (as′ēr-bāt), *v.t.* -bat·ed, -bat·ing, 1. to make sour or bitter. 2. to annoy or irritate.

a·cer·bi·ty (á-sûr′bi-ti), *n., pl.* -ties, 1. sourness. 2. sharpness; harshness or severity of temper or expression.

a·cer·vate (á-sûr′vāt), *adj.* in *Botany,* formed in heaps; growing in clusters.

a·ces·cence (á-ses′ns), *n.* a state of sourness or acidity.

a·ces·cent (′nt), *adj.* turning sour.

ac·e·tab·u·lum (as-ē-tab′yoo-lŭm), *n., pl.* -la (-lá), -lums, the socket in the hipbone into which the thighbone enters.

ac·e·tal (as′ē-tal), *n.* a colorless liquid used in medicine as a hypnotic agent.

ac·et·an·i·lide (as-ē-tan′i-lid), *n.* a white powder formed by the action of acetic acid on aniline: used in medicine to reduce fever.

ac·e·tate (as′ē-tāt), *n.* 1. a salt or ester of acetic acid. 2. same as **cellulose acetate** 3, something made with acetate or cellulose acetate.

ac·e·tat·ed (-id), *adj.* combined with acetic acid.

a·ce·tic (á-sēt′ik, -set′-), *adj.* of or pertaining to vinegar or acetic acid; sour.

acetic acid, a clear liquid with a strong acid taste and sharp smell: present in a dilute form in vinegar.

a·cet·i·fy (á-set′i-fī), *v.t. & v.i.* -fied, -fy·ing, to turn into vinegar or acetic acid. —**a·cet·i·fi·ca′tion** (-fi-kā′shŭn), *n.*

ac·e·tin (as′ē-tn), *n.* a thick liquid consisting of acetic acid combined with glycerol, used in making dynamite.

ac·e·tom·e·ter (as-ē-tom′ē-tēr), **ac·e·tim·e·ter** (-tim′-), *n.* an instrument for gauging the strength or purity of vinegar or acetic acid.

ac·e·tone (as′ē-tŏn), *n.* a clear, volatile liquid, composed of carbon, hydrogen, and oxygen: used as a solvent. —**ac·e·ton′ic** (-ton′ik), *adj.*

ac·e·to·phe·net·i·din (á-sēt-ō-fē-net′i-din), *n.* a white powder used to reduce fever and lessen pain.

ac·e·tous (as′ē-tŭs), **ac·e·tose** (-tōs), *adj.* of the quality of acid; sour; producing vinegar.

a·ce·tum (á-sēt′ŭm), *n.* vinegar or a drug prepared in acetic acid.

a·cet·y·lene (á-set′l-ēn), *n.* a clear, brilliant flammable gas, produced by subjecting calcium carbide to the action of water: used as a fuel in blowtorches.

ache (āk), *n.* a dull pain, more or less continuous: *v.i.* **ached, ach′ing,** 1. to suffer, or have pain. 2. to have sympathy (*for*). 3. [Informal], to desire or yearn.

a·chieve (á-chēv′), *v.t.* -a·chieved′, a·chiev′ing, 1. to perform; carry out; accomplish. 2. to gain or bring to success by effort: *v.i.* to bring about a desired result. —**a·chiev′a·ble,** *adj.*

a·chieve·ment (′mēnt), *n.* 1. the act of achieving. 2. accomplishment; that which is achieved or accomplished.

A·chil·les′ heel (á-kil′iz), a vulnerable spot: after Achilles, a Greek hero who was killed when an arrow pierced his heel, his only vulnerable spot.

Achilles′ tendon, the tendon which joins the heel and the muscles of the calf.

ach·ing (āk′ing), *adj.* enduring or causing pain; painful. —**ach′ing·ly,** *adv.*

ach·ro·mat·ic (ak-rō-mat′ik), *adj.* 1. free from coloration. 2. refracting light, as sunlight, without decomposing it into its constituent colors. 3. in *Music,* diatonic. —**ach·ro·mat′i·cal·ly,** *adv.*

achromatic lens, a lens forming images free from prismatic colors.

a·chro·ma·tize (á-krō′má-tīz), *v.t.* -tized, -tiz·ing, to deprive of color; render achromatic.

a·chro·ma·tous (-tŭs), *adj.* without color.

a·chro·mic (ā-krō′mik), **a·chro·mous** (′mŭs), *adj.* without color.

ach·y (āk′i), *adj.* ach′i·er, ach′i·est, having an ache.

a·cic·u·lum (á-sik′yoo-lŭm), *n., pl.* -lums, -la (-lá), a bristle; needlelike spine.

ac·id (as′id), *adj.* 1. sour and sharp or biting to the taste, as vinegar. 2. sharp or biting in manner or expression. 3. of an acid: *n.* 1. anything sour. 2. any compound that can produce a salt when combined with a base. 3. [Slang], same as LSD. —**ac′id·ly,** *adv.* —**ac′id·ness,** *n.*

a·cid·ic (á-sid′ik), *adj.* 1. containing a large proportion of any substance that forms an acid: opposed to *basic.* 2. same as **acid.**

a·cid·i·fi·er (á-sid′i-fī-ēr), *n.* a substance that acidifies.

a·cid·i·fy (-fī), *v.t. & v.i.* -fied, -fy·ing, 1. to make or become acid. 2. to convert into an acid. —**a·cid·i·fi·ca′tion** (-fi-kā′shŭn), *n.*

a·cid·i·ty (-ti), *n., pl.* -ties, the quality or degree of being acid or sour.

ac·i·do·sis (as-i-dō′sis), *n.* a condition in which the alkali content of the body is below normal.

---

acid rain, rain with a high concentration of acids produced by the gases from burning fossil fuels.

acid test, a thorough test to determine true value, originally applied to gold.

a·cid·u·late (ă-sij'oo-lāt), *v.t.* -lat·ed, -lat·ing, to make slightly acid. —**a·cid·u·la'tion**, *n.*

a·cid·u·lous (-lŭs), **a·cid·u·lent** (-lĕnt), *adj.* 1. somewhat acid; slightly sour. 2. sarcastic.

ac·i·er·ate (as'ĭ-ē-rāt), *v.t.* -at·ed, -at·ing, to convert into steel.

ac·i·form (as'ĭ-fôrm), *adj.* needle-shaped.

a·cin·i·form (ă-sin'ĭ-fôrm), *adj.* shaped like a cluster of grapes.

ac·knowl·edge (ăk-nol'ij), *v.t.* -edged, -edg·ing, 1. to admit or own to be true; confess. 2. to recognize. 3. to answer, as a greeting. 4. to show gratitude for. 5. to admit the receipt of. —**ac·knowl'edge·a·ble**, *adj.*

ac·knowl·edged ('ijd), *adj.* generally recognized or admitted.

ac·knowl·edge·ment, **ac·knowl·edg·ment** ('ij-mĕnt), *n.* 1. the act of acknowledging; admission or recognition of a truth. 2. that which is done in acknowledging, as an expression of appreciation. 3. recognition, as of another's authority. 4. a receipt.

a·clin·ic line (ā-klin'ik), the imaginary line near the equator where the magnetic needle has no dip.

ac·me (ăk'mē), *n.* the highest point; culmination.

ac·ne (ăk'nē), *n.* a chronic skin disease characterized by the eruption of pimples on the face, shoulders, chest, and back.

a·cock (ă-kok'), *adv. & adj.* in a cocked or turned-up manner.

ac·o·lyte (ak'ŏ-līt), *n.* 1. same as altar boy. 2. any person who acts as an attendant.

ac·o·nite (ak'ŏ-nīt), *n.* 1. any of a group of flowering plants, often poisonous, belonging to the buttercup family, especially monkshood or wolfsbane. 2. a drug made from monkshood.

a·co·ni·tum (ak-ŏ-nīt'ŭm), *n.* same as aconite.

a·corn (ā'kôrn), *n.* the fruit of the oak.

acorn duck, same as wood duck.

acorn squash, an acorn-shaped squash with a dark-green skin having deep ridges.

a·cous·tic (ă-kōōs'tik), *adj.* of or pertaining to the science of sound.

a·cous·ti·cal ('ti-kl), *adj.* same as acoustic. —**a·cous'ti·cal·ly**, *adv.*

ac·ous·ti·cian (a-kōōs-ti'shŭn), *n.* one whose work or field of study is acoustics.

a·cous·tics (ă-kōōs'tiks), *n.* 1. the qualities of an enclosed space pertaining to the transmission of sound in it. 2. the science of sound and its transmission.

ac·quaint (ă-kwānt'), *v.t.* 1. to make oneself familiar or conversant with. 2. to furnish information about.

ac·quaint·ance ('ns), *n.* 1. the state of being acquainted with a person or subject. 2. a person with whom one is acquainted, but only slightly. —**ac·quaint'ance·ship**, *n.*

ac·quaint·ed ('ĕd), *adj.* having personal knowledge; familiar.

ac·qui·esce (ak-wi·es'), *v.i.* -esced, -esc'ing, to agree; comply passively; assent (often with *in*).

ac·qui·es·cence ('ns), *n.* the act of acquiescing; passive compliance.

ac·qui·es·cent ('nt), *adj.* agreeing or complying tacitly. —**ac·qui·es'cent·ly**, *adv.*

ac·quire (ă-kwir'), *v.t.* -quired', -quir'ing, 1. to gain or obtain possession of by one's own physical or intellectual exertions. 2. to get for oneself. —**ac·quir'a·ble**, *adj.*

acquired character, **acquired characteristic**, in *Biology*, a change of form or function brought about by environmental conditions.

ac·quire·ment (mĕnt), *n.* 1. the act of acquiring. 2. that which is acquired.

ac·qui·si·tion (ak-wi·zish'ŭn), *n.* 1. the act of acquiring. 2. that which has been acquired.

ac·quis·i·tive (ă-kwiz'ĭ-tiv), *adj.* having a natural tendency to acquire; greedy. —**ac·quis'i·tive·ly**, *adv.* —**ac·quis'i·tive·ness**, *n.*

ac·quit (ă-kwit'), *v.t.* -quit'ted, -quit'ting, 1. to release; set free; discharge. 2. to pronounce not guilty. 3. to behave in a particular way.

ac·quit·tal ('l), *n.* 1. the act of releasing or acquitting. 2. the state of being acquitted; judicial pronouncement of "not guilty."

ac·quit·tance ('ns), *n.* 1. a discharge or release from debt or other liability. 2. a receipt showing this, barring further demand.

a·cre (āk'ĕr), *n.* a measure of land containing 4,840 square yards.

a·cre·age (-ij), *n.* the number of acres in a tract of land.

a·cre·foot (āk-ĕr-foot'), *n.* the amount of water necessary to cover one acre to the depth of one foot: equivalent to 43,560 cubic feet.

ac·rid (ak'rid), *adj.* 1. sharp or biting to the taste or smell; irritating. 2. stinging or caustic in speech. —**a·crid·i·ty** (ā-krid'ĭ-ti), **ac'·rid·ness**, *n.* —**ac'rid·ly**, *adv.*

ac·ri·mo·ni·ous (ak-rĭ-mō'nĭ-ŭs), *adj.* bitter, caustic, or stinging in temper or expression. —**ac·ri·mo'ni·ous·ly**, *adv.* —**ac·ri·mo'ni·ous·ness**, *n.*

ac·ri·mo·ny (ak'rĭ-mō-ni), *n., pl.* -nies, sharpness of temper; bitterness of expression.

a·crit·i·cal (ā-krit'ĭ-kl), *adj.* not critical.

ac·ro·bat (ak'rŏ-bat), *n.* a performer on the tightrope or trapeze, or one who practices tumbling, vaulting, etc. —**ac·ro·bat'ic**, *adj.* —**ac·ro·bat'i·cal·ly**, *adv.*

ac·ro·bat·ics ('iks), *n.pl.* 1. the work, skill, or intricate maneuvers of an acrobat. 2. any intricate maneuvers.

ac·ro·lith (ak'rŏ-lith), *n.* a sculptured figure, the head and extremities of which are of stone and the rest of wood.

ac·ro·meg·a·ly (ak-rŏ-meg'ă-li), *n.* a disease characterized by excessive growth of the head, hands, and feet. —**ac·ro·me·gal'ic** (-mĕ-gal'ik), *adj.*

ac·ro·nym (ak'rŏ-nim), *n.* a word composed of the first letters (or parts) of other words: *sonar* is derived from *sound navigation and ranging*.

ac·ro·pho·bi·a (ak-rŏ-fō'bi-ă), *n.* an abnormal fear of being in high places, as at the top of a building.

a·crop·o·lis (ă-krŏp'ŏ-lŭs), *n.* the highest part or citadel of an ancient Greek city, as [A-], that of Athens.

a·cross (ă-krŏs'), *adv.* 1. from side to side. 2.

---

a in *cap*, ā in *cane*, ä in *father*, å in *abet*, e in *met* ē in *be*, ĕ in *baker*, ė in *regent*, i in *pit*, ī in *fine*, i in *manifest*, o in *hot*, ô in *horse*, ō in *bone*,

from side to side at an angle; athwart: *prep.* 1. from side to side of. 2. over. 3. in contact with.

a-cros-tic (å-krôs'tik), *n.* a composition, usually in verse, in which certain letters in each line, such as the first or last letters, taken in order form a motto, phrase, name, or word.

a-cryl-ic (å-kril'ik), *n.* 1. same as **acrylic fiber.** 2. same as **acrylic paint.** 3. a painting, design, etc. done with acrylic paint.

acrylic fiber, a synthetic fiber manufactured from acetylene and hydrogen cyanide, and used for making fabrics.

acrylic paint, a fast-drying paint made from acrylic resin.

acrylic resin, a clear thermoplastic resin.

act (akt), *n.* 1. an action; process of doing. 2. an act or thing done. 3. a decree, edict, or enactment. 4. the judgment of a court. 5. one of the principal divisions of a drama. 6. insincere behavior, meant to deceive: *v.t.* to perform; play, as on the stage: *v.i.* 1. to perform. 2. to do something. 3. to serve as. 4. to behave. 5. to look or seem to be.

act-a-ble (ak'tå-bl), *adj.* that can be performed. —**act-a-bil'i-ty** (-bil'ĭ-ti), *n.*

ACTH, a hormone secreted by the pituitary gland: it stimulates the cortex of the adrenal gland, bringing about an increase in its hormone production.

act-ing (ak'ting), *adj.* 1. that which acts. 2. performing services, particularly official services, on a temporary basis: *n.* the art or profession of performing in plays or motion pictures.

ac-tin-ic (ak-tin'ik), *adj.* having the qualities of actinism. —**ac-tin'i-cal-ly,** *adv.*

ac-ti-nide series (ak'ti-nid), a group of radioactive chemical elements, including actinium, uranium, and lawrencium.

ac-tin-ism (ak'tin-izm), *n.* that property of the sun's rays, X-rays, etc. which produces chemical changes.

ac-tin-i-um (ak-tin'i-ŭm), *n.* a radioactive chemical element found in pitchblende and other minerals.

ac-tin-o-graph (ak-tin'ŏ-graf), *n.* same as **actinometer.**

ac-ti-noid (ak'ti-noid), *adj.* having rays; radial.

ac-ti-nol-o-gy (ak-ti-nol'ŏ-ji), *n.* the science dealing with the chemical action of light.

ac-ti-nom-e-ter (ak-ti-nom'ĕ-tēr), *n.* an instrument for measuring the intensity of, or chemical changes produced by, light rays.

ac-tion (ak'shŭn), *n.* 1. the state of being active, as opposed to rest. 2. the effect of one thing upon another. 3. an act or thing done. 4. *pl.* conduct. 5. a suit instituted by one party against another in a court of law. 6. the performance of a function. 7. effective motion, as of machinery. 8. the moving mechanism of something, as a firearm. 9. a military engagement. 10. the happenings in a story or play. 11. the appearance of animation given to figures, as in a painting. 12. [Slang], activity.

ac-tion-a-ble (-å-bl), *adj.* giving grounds for an action at law.

ac-ti-vate (ak'ti-vāt), *v.t.* -vat-ed, -vat-ing, 1. to cause to be active. 2. to make radioactive. 3. to put a (military unit) into a condition of being ready for action. 4. to aerate sewage, thus purifying it. —**ac-ti-va'tion,** *n.* —**ac'ti-va-tor,** *n.*

ac-tive (ak'tiv), *adj.* 1. endowed with or exercising the power or quality of action. 2. having much action; lively. 3. causing change or action. 4. signifying the voice of a verb whose subject performs the action. —**ac'tive-ly,** *adv.*

ac-tiv-ism (ak'ti-vizm), *n.* the policy or practice of taking action to achieve social or political goals. —**ac'tiv-ist,** *adj. & n.*

ac-tiv-i-ty (ak-tiv'i-ti), *n.* 1. the state of being active. 2. brisk action; liveliness. 3. *pl.* -ties, any particular action or area of interest.

ac-tor (ak'tēr), *n.* 1. one who does something. 2. one who acts in a play or motion picture. —**ac'tress,** *n.fem.*

Acts (akts), *n.* a book of the New Testament: in full, **The Acts of the Apostles.**

ac-tu-al (ak'choo-wål), *adj.* 1. real; existing. 2. present. —**ac'tu-al-ly,** *adv.*

ac-tu-al-i-ty (ak-choo-wal'i-ti), *n.* 1. the state of being real or actual. 2. *pl.* -ties, that which is real; thing or fact.

ac-tu-al-ize (ak'choo-wå-līz), *v.t.* -ized, -iz-ing, to make actual. —**ac-tu-al-i-za'tion,** *n.*

ac-tu-ar-y (ak'choo-wer-i), *n., pl.* -ar-ies, one who is skilled in computing insurance premiums and risks. —**ac-tu-ar'i-al,** *adj.*

ac-tu-ate (ak'choo-wāt), *v.t.* -at-ed, -at-ing, 1. to put into action; cause to be activated. 2. to move or incite to action. —**ac-tu-a'tion,** *n.*

a-cu-i-ty (å-kū'i-ti), *n.* sharpness; keenness of vision or thought.

a-cu-le-ate (å-kū'li-it), *adj.* having an aculeus or aculei.

a-cu-le-us (å-kū'li-ŭs), *n., pl.* -le-i (-ī), 1. a prickle, as on a blackberry bush. 2. a sting, as on an insect.

a-cu-men (å-kū'měn), *n.* quickness of perception; penetration; insight.

a-cu-mi-nate (å-kū'mi-nit), *adj.* ending in a point, as a leaf.

ac-u-punc-ture (ak'yoo-pungk-chēr), *n.* the practice of treating disease or relieving pain by inserting needles into various parts of the body: used by the Chinese since ancient times.

a-cute (å-kūt'), *adj.* 1. sharp-pointed. 2. intellectually sharp. 3. quick of perception. 4. severe, as pain or symptoms attending a disease. 5. high in pitch; shrill. 6. critical; dangerous. 7. denoting an angle smaller than a right angle. —**a-cute'ly,** *adv.* .

acute accent, a mark (´) showing vowel quality, stress, etc.

ad (ad), *n.* [Informal], an advertisement.

ad-age (ad'ij), *n.* an old proverb, or pithy saying.

a-da-gio (å-dä'jō), *adv.* in *Music,* slowly: *adj.* in *Music,* slow: *n., pl.* -gios, 1. a slow movement in music. 2. a slow ballet dance.

ad-a-mant (ad'å-månt), *n.* a substance of ex-

---

treme hardness: *adj.* 1. very hard. 2. unyielding; relentless. —**ad´a·mant·ly**, *adv.*

ad·a·man·tine (ad-à-man´tin), *adj.* 1. of or like adamant; unbreakable. 2. adamant; unyielding.

A·dam's apple (a´dămz), the prominence of cartilage in front of the throat, especially conspicuous in men.

a·dapt (à-dapt´), *v.t.* 1. to make to correspond; fit by alteration. 2. to adjust (oneself) to changed conditions. —**ad·ap·ta·tion** (ăd-ăp-tā´shŭn), *n.*

a·dapt·a·ble (´à-bl), *adj.* that can be adapted or adjusted. —**a·dapt·a·bil´i·ty** (-bil´à-ti), *n.*

A·dar (ä-där´), *n.* the sixth month of the Jewish year.

add (ad), *v.t.* 1. to join; unite. 2. to figure the total of. 3. to say further: *v.i.* 1. to bring about an increase. 2. to find a total by figuring.

ad·dax (ad´aks), *n.* an African antelope with long, twisted horns.

ad·dend (ad´end), *n.* a number or quantity to be added to another.

ad·den·dum (à-den´dŭm), *n., pl.* **-den´da** (´dä), an appendix or supplement.

ad·der (ad´ẽr), *n.* 1. the common viper of Europe. 2. a harmless snake of North America.

ad·dict (à-dikt´), *v.t.* to devote or give (oneself) up to (a habit): *n.* (ad´ikt), one who is addicted to a habit, esp. to the use of drugs. —**ad·dic´tion**, *n.* —**ad·dic´tive**, *adj.*

ad·di·tion (à-dish´ŭn), *n.* 1. the act or process of adding one thing to another. 2. something added. 3. the adding or uniting of two or more numbers to get one sum.

ad·di·tion·al (-ăl), *adj.* added; supplementary. —**ad·di´tion·al·ly**, *adv.*

ad·di·tive (ad´ĭ-tiv), *adj.* that may be, or is to be, added: *n.* a substance to be added to another for some purpose.

ad·dle (ad´l), *adj.* 1. rotten: said of eggs. 2. muddled: *v.t. & v.i.* **-dled, -dling,** 1. to make or become rotten. 2. to make or become muddled.

ad·dle·head·ed (-hed´id), *adj.* stupid; muddled: also **ad´dle-brained, ad´dle-pat·ed** (-păt-id).

ad·dress (à-dres´), *v.t.* 1. to speak or write to. 2. to direct (words) to. 3. to direct (energy). 4. to inscribe the destination on a letter or package: *n.* (also ad´res), 1. a speech delivered or written. 2. tact; adroitness. 3. the destination imprinted on a letter or package. 4. the place where one lives or works.

ad·dress·ee (ad-res-ē´), *n.* one to whom a letter or package is addressed.

ad·duce (à-dōōs´, à-dūs´), *v.t.* **-duced´, -duc´ing,** to bring forward or cite as proof or substantiation. —**ad·duc´i·ble**, *adj.*

ad·duc·tor (à-duk´tẽr), *n.* a muscle that pulls (a body part) toward the median axis.

ad·e·noids (ad´ē-noidz), *n.* growths of lymphoid tissue in the upper part of the throat.

ad·e·no·ma (ad-ē-nō´mà), *n.* a tumor of glandular origin.

ad·ept (à-dept´), *adj.* expert; skilled: *n.* (ad´ept), one who is highly proficient or skilled. —**a·dept´ly**, *adv.* —**a·dept´ness**, *n.*

ad·e·qua·cy (ad´ē-kwà-si), *n.* sufficiency for a particular purpose.

ad·e·quate (ad´ē-kwàt), *adj.* equal to the requirement or the occasion; fully sufficient. —**ad´e·quate·ly**, *adv.* —**ad´e·quate·ness**, *n.*

ad·here (ad-hir´), *v.i.* **-hered´, -her´ing,** 1. to stick fast; become firmly attached to. 2. to support; remain loyal to. —**ad·her´ence**, *n.*

ad·her·ent (´ĕnt), *adj.* adhering; sticking: *n.* one who adheres; a follower of a party, leader, or cause.

ad·he·sion (ăd-hē´zhŭn), *n.* 1. the state or act of adhering. 2. a molecular force compelling bodies of unlike substances to stick together. 3. an abnormal union of bodily parts or tissues.

ad·he·sive (´siv), *adj.* 1. holding fast. 2. gummed for use; sticky: *n.* an adhesive substance. —**ad·he´sive·ly**, *adv.* —**ad·he´sive·ness**, *n.*

ad·hib·it (ad-hib´it), *v.t.* 1. to admit; let in. 2. to affix. 3. to apply, as a remedy.

ad hoc (ad hok´), [Latin], for this special case or instance.

ad·i·aph·o·rous (ad-i-af´ō-rŭs), *adj.* 1. neutral; indifferent as to morals. 2. in *Medicine*, doing neither harm nor good.

a·dieu (à-dū´, à-dōō´), *n.* [French], farewell; good wishes at parting: *interj.* goodbye; farewell.

ad in·fi·ni·tum (ad in-fĭ-nīt´ŭm), [Latin], forever; without end.

a·di·os (a-di-ōs´), *interj.* [Spanish], goodbye; farewell.

ad·i·po·cere (ad´ĭ-pō-sir), *n.* fat produced in the decomposition of animal tissues.

ad·i·pose (-pōs), *adj.* fatty; of or pertaining to animal fat. —**ad·i·pos´i·ty** (-pos´ĭ-ti), *n.*

ad·it (ad´it), *n.* 1. an entrance or passage. 2. a horizontal entrance to a mine.

ad·ja·cent (à-jā´sĕnt), *adj.* near; close to. —**ad·ja´cen·cy**, *n.*

ad·jec·tive (aj´ik-tiv), *n.* a word used with a substantive or noun to express the quality or attribute of the thing named, or to limit and define a thing as distinct from something else. —**ad·jec·ti´val** (-tī´văl), *adj.*

ad·join (à-join´), *v.t.* 1. to be next to. 2. to unite or join: *v.i.* to lie next to. —**ad·join´ing**, *adj.*

ad·journ (à-jŭrn´), *v.t.* to put off to another time: *v.i.* 1. to suspend a meeting or session. 2. to withdraw to another place (followed by *to*). —**ad·journ´ment**, *n.*

ad·judge (à-juj´), *v.t.* **-judged´, -judg´ing,** 1. to determine judicially. 2. to award judicially.

ad·ju·di·cate (à-jōō´dĭ-kāt), *v.t.* **-cat·ed, -cat·ing,** to hear and determine (a case) in a court: *v.i.* to act as a judge. —**ad·ju·di·ca´tion**, *n.* —**ad·ju´di·ca·tor**, *n.*

ad·junct (aj´ungkt), *n.* something added to another thing, but not an essential part of it. —**ad·junc´tive**, *adj.* —**ad·junct´ly**, *adv.*

ad·jure (à-joor´), *v.t.* **-jured´, -jur´ing,** 1. to command on oath; charge solemnly. 2. to entreat. —**ad·ju·ra´tion**, *n.*

ad·just (à-just´), *v.t.* 1. to fit, or make exact. 2. to make accurate. 3. to settle in a just or correct way. 4. to determine the amount to be paid on (an insurance claim). —**ad·just´a-**

---

a in c*a*p, ā in c*a*ne, ä in f*a*ther, å in *a*bet, e in m*e*t, ē in b*e*, ê in bak*e*r, ê in reg*e*nt, i in p*i*t, ī in f*i*ne, ĭ in man*i*fest, o in h*o*t, ô in h*o*rse, ō in b*o*ne,

ble, *adj.* —ad·just'er, ad·jus'tor, *n.* —ad·just'ment, *n.*

ad·ju·tant (aj'ŭ-tănt), *n.* 1. a regimental staff officer who assists the commanding officer. 2. an assistant. 3. a very large stork of Africa and India. —ad'ju·tan·cy, *n.*

adjutant general, *pl.* adjutants general, a staff officer in the army, through whom all orders, etc. are received and issued by the commanding general.

ad·ju·vant (aj'ŭ-vănt), *adj.* helping; auxiliary; assistant: *n.* a substance added to a drug to strengthen its action.

ad-lib (ad-lib'), *v.t. & v.i.* -libbed', -lib'bing, [Informal], to improvise (speech not in a script): *n.* [Informal], an ad-libbed statement or comment: *adv.* [Informal], at one's pleasure.

ad-man (ad'man), *n., pl.* -men, one who works in the field of advertising: also ad man.

ad·meas·ure (ad-mezh'ĕr), *v.t.* -ured, -ur·ing, to measure out in shares; apportion. —admeas'ure·ment, *n.*

ad·min·is·ter (ad-min'is-tĕr), *v.t.* 1. to manage as chief agent or minister, as a king, president, or judge. 2. to dispense, as punishment. 3. to cause to be taken, as medicine. 4. to give, as an oath or a sacrament. 5. to act as administrator of (an estate). —admin'is·tra·ble, *adj.*

ad·min·is·trate (-trāt), *v.t.* -trat·ed, -trat·ing, to administer.

ad·min·is·tra·tion (ăd-min-ĭ-strā'shŭn), *n.* 1. the act of administering, as government, justice, medicine, a sacrament, or an estate. 2. administrators as a group; specifically, [A-], the chief officers of a government. 3. their term of office. —ad·min'is·tra·tive, *adj.*

ad·min·is·tra·tor (ăd-min'ĭ-strāt-ĕr), *n.* 1. one who administers affairs. 2. in *Law*, one appointed to settle an estate. —ad·min·is·tra'trix ('triks), *n.fem., pl.* -tri·ces ('tri-sēz), -trix·es.

ad·mi·ra·ble (ad'mir-ă-bl), *adj.* worthy of admiration; excellent. —ad'mi·ra·bly, *adv.*

ad·mi·ral (ad'mir-ăl), *n.* 1. the chief commander of a navy or fleet. 2. a naval officer of the highest rank.

ad·mi·ral·ty (-ti), *n., pl.* -ties, 1. [often A-], *a)* the department of government having authority over naval affairs, as in England. *b)* the building in which the affairs of this department are conducted. 2. the office of an admiral: *adj.* of maritime courts or law.

ad·mi·ra·tion (ad-mi-rā'shŭn), *n.* 1. the act of admiring. 2. wonder or approval brought about by beauty, excellence, etc.

ad·mire (ăd-mīr'), *v.t.* -mired', -mir'ing, 1. to regard with warm approval. 2. to have great respect for. —ad·mir'er, *n.* —ad·mir'ing·ly, *adv.*

ad·mis·si·ble (ăd-mis'ĭ-bl), *adj.* worthy of being admitted; allowable.

ad·mis·sion (ăd-mish'ŭn), *n.* 1. the act of admitting or the state of being admitted. 2. permission to enter. 3. a fee paid for this. 4. the granting of the truth of something, as an argument. 5. a confession. 6. a thing confessed or conceded.

ad·mit (ăd-mit'), *v.t.* -mit'ted, -mit'ting 1. to permit to enter. 2. to allow. 3. to confess. —ad·mit'tance, *n.* —ad·mit'ted·ly, *adv.*

ad·mix (ăd-miks'), *v.t. & v.i.* to mix with something else. —ad·mix'ture ('chĕr), *n.*

ad·mon·ish (ăd-mon'ish), *v.t.* 1. to reprove gently. 2. to warn. 3. to urge earnestly. — ad·mo·ni·tion (ad-mŏ-nish'ŭn), *n.* —ad·mon'ito·ry ('ĭ-tôr-i), *adj.*

ad·nate (ad'nāt), *adj.* in *Botany & Zoology*, congenitally joined: said of unlike parts. —ad·na'tion, *n.*

ad nau·se·am (ad nô'zē-ăm), [Latin], to a sickening or disgusting degree.

a·do (ă-dōō'), *n.* bustle; trouble.

a·do·be (ă-dō'bi), *n.* unburnt brick dried in the sun, used for building in the southwestern U.S., Mexico, and Central America.

ad·o·les·cence (ad-ŏ-les'ĕns), *n.* the period of life between puberty and maturity; youth.

ad·o·les·cent ('ĕnt), *adj.* of or in the period of life between puberty and maturity: *n.* a person in adolescence.

A·don·is (ă-dăn'is), *n.* 1. in *Greek Mythology*, a handsome young man loved by Aphrodite. 2. any handsome young man.

a·dopt (ă-dopt'), *v.t.* 1. to take (a child) into one's family. 2. to take and use (an opinion or practice) as one's own. 3. to choose and follow (a course of action). —a·dopt'a·ble, *adj.* —a·dop'tion, *n.*

a·dop·tive (ă-dop'tiv), *adj.* 1. pertaining to adoption. 2. by adoption.

a·dor·a·ble (ă-dôr'ă-bl), *adj.* 1. [Archaic], worthy of worship. 2. [Informal], charming; attractive. —a·dor'a·bly, *adv.*

ad·o·ra·tion (ad-ŏ-rā'shŭn), *n.* 1. an act of worship. 2. deep love or devotion.

a·dore (ă-dôr'), *v.t.* a·dored', a·dor'ing, 1. to venerate; honor highly. 2. to love intensely. 3. [Informal], to be very fond of. —a·dor'er, *n.* —a·dor'ing·ly, *adv.*

a·dorn (ă-dôrn'), *v.t.* 1. to beautify; dignify. 2. to ornament; embellish.

a·dorn·ment ('mĕnt), *n.* an ornament; decoration.

a·down (ă-doun'), *adv. & prep.* [Poetic], downward; down.

ad·re·nal (ă-drē'năl), *adj.* of either of two small, ductless glands (adrenal glands) above the kidneys, that secrete certain hormones.

Ad·ren·al·in (ă-dren'ăl-in), *n.* 1. a hormone secreted by the adrenal gland or produced synthetically, used as a heart stimulant: a trademark. 2. [a-], this substance: also adrenaline.

a·drift (ă-drift'), *adj. & adv.* floating freely.

a·droit (ă-droit'), *adj.* exhibiting skill; dexterous. —a·droit'ly, *adv.* —a·droit'ness, *n.*

ad·sorb (ad-sôrb'), *v.t.* to collect (molecules of gas or liquid) on a surface. —ad·sorb'a·ble, *adj.* —ad·sor'bent, *adj. & n.*

ad·sorp·tion (-sôrp'shŭn), *n.* the adherence of molecules of gas or liquid to a surface. —ad·sorp'tive, *adj.*

ad·u·late (aj'ŭ-lāt), *v.t.* -lat·ed, -lat·ing, to flatter extravagantly. —ad·u·la'tion, *n.*

a·dult (ă-dult'), *adj.* grown up to full age, size, and strength: *n.* a full-grown person, animal, or plant. —a·dult'hood, *n.* —a·dult'ness, *n.*

a-dul·ter·ant (á-dul'tér-ánt), adj. adulterating: n. something that adulterates.

a-dul·ter·ate (á-dul'tér-āt), v.t. -at·ed, -at·ing, to make less pure by admixture of a baser or unnecessary substance. —a·dul·ter·a'tion, n. —a·dul'ter·a·tor, n.

a-dul·ter·er (á-dul'tér-ér), n. a man who commits adultery. —a·dul'ter·ess, n.fem.

a-dul·ter·ous (-ús), adj. guilty of adultery. —a·dul'ter·ous·ly, adv.

a-dul·ter·y (á-dul'tér-i), n., pl. -ter·ies, sexual intercourse between two people not married to each other.

ad·um·brate (ad-um'brāt), v.t. -brat·ed, -brat·ing, 1. to sketch lightly; give a faint resemblance of. 2. to foreshadow vaguely. 3. to obscure. —ad·um·bra'tion, n.

a-dun·cous (á-dung'kús), adj. hooked, as a parrot's bill: also a·dunc'.

ad·vance (ád-vans'), v.i. -vanced', -vanc'ing, 1. to go forward. 2. to progress. 3. to rise: v.t. 1. to move forward. 2. to hasten the success of; further. 3. to propose. 4. to promote. 5. to raise the rate of. 6. to lend. 7. to make a payment of beforehand: n. 1. the act of moving forward. 2. an improvement. 3. an addition to or rise in value. 4. pl. overtures (to someone). 5. a loan. 6. payment beforehand: adj. 1. in front. 2. ahead of time.

ad·vanced (-vanst'), adj. 1. in front. 2. old; aged. 3. higher, as in price, or beyond, as in progress.

advance guard, a body of troops sent out to reconnoiter and protect the march.

ad·vance·ment (-vans'mént), n. 1. an act of advancing or the state of being advanced. 2. furtherance; progress. 3. promotion.

ad·van·tage (ád-van'tij), n. 1. a state of advance or forwardness; favorable position. 2. a beneficial situation or event. 3. a benefit. 4. the first point gained after deuce in tennis.

ad·van·ta·geous (ad-ván-tā'jús), adj. of advantage; beneficial. —ad·van·ta'geous·ly, adv.

Ad·vent (ad'vent), n. 1. the period including the four Sundays before Christmas. 2. [a-], an arrival; approach.

Ad·vent·ist (-ist), n. one of a religious sect which stresses that Christ's second coming is near.

ad·ven·ti·tious (ad-vén-tish'ús), adj. happening by chance; casual; fortuitous; accidental. —ad·ven·ti'tious·ly, adv.

ad·ven·ture (ád-ven'chér), n. 1. a risky or dangerous enterprise. 2. a stirring experience: v.t. & v.i. -ured, -ur·ing, to hazard or risk.

ad·ven·tur·er (-ér), n. 1. one who undertakes adventures. 2. a financial speculator. 3. one who seeks distinction or wealth by questionable schemes. —ad·ven'tur·ess, n.fem.

ad·ven·ture·some (-sóm), adj. adventurous; daring.

ad·ven·tur·ous (-ús), adj. 1. willing to incur risk; daring. 2. risky; dangerous. —ad·ven'tur·ous·ly, adv. —ad·ven'tur·ous·ness, n.

ad·verb (ad'vérb), n. a word used to modify a verb, adjective, or another adverb.

ad·ver·bi·al (ad-vúr'bi-ál), adj. of the nature of an adverb. —ad·ver'bi·al·ly, adv.

ad·ver·sar·y (ad'vér-ser-i), n., pl. -sar·ies, an opponent.

ad·ver·sa·tive (ad-vúr'sá-tiv), adj. expressing opposition.

ad·verse (ád-vúrs', ad'vérs), adj. 1. opposed to; contrary. 2. unfortunate; inimical. —ad·verse'ly, adv.

ad·ver·si·ty (ad-vúr'si-ti), n. 1. a state of distress, misfortune, or calamity. 2. pl. -ties, an instance of misfortune or distress.

ad·vert (ad-vúrt'), v.i. to turn one's attention to: refer.

ad·vert·ent (ént), adj. attentive. —ad·vert'ence, n. —ad·vert'ent·ly, adv.

ad·ver·tise (ad'vér-tīz), v.t. -tised, -tis·ing, to call attention to and praise, especially in order to sell: v.i. 1. to call attention to things for sale. 2. to ask for by public notice, as in print. Also sp. advertize. —ad'ver·tis·er, n.

ad·ver·tise·ment (ad-vér-tīz'mént, ád-vúr'tiz-mént), n. a paid public notice or announcement, as for goods or services for sale, or for something needed.

ad·ver·tis·ing (ad'vér-tīz-ing), n. 1. the business of preparing and selling advertisements. 2. advertisements in general.

ad·vice (ád-vīs'), n. 1. opinion given as recommendation for action; counsel. 2. formal notice or report (usually used in pl.).

ad·vis·a·ble (ád-vī'zá-bl), adj. prudent; expedient; sensible. —ad·vis·a·bil'i·ty (-bil'i-ti), n.

ad·vise (ád-vīz'), v.t. -vised', -vis'ing, 1. to offer an opinion; counsel. 2. to recommend. 3. to inform. —ad·vis'er, ad·vi'sor, n.

ad·vis·ed·ly (-vī'zid-li), adv. with advice; with intention; deliberately.

ad·vise·ment (-vīz'mént), n. careful thought; deliberation.

ad·vi·so·ry (-vī'zér-i), adj. 1. having power to advise. 2. containing advice: n., pl. -ries, a warning or report, especially one about weather conditions.

ad·vo·cate (ad'vó-kāt), v.t. -cat·ed, -cat·ing, to speak in favor of: n. 1. (also -kit), one who pleads the cause of another. 2. one who supports something, as a cause. —ad'vo·ca·cy (-ká-si), n. —ad'vo·ca·tor, n.

ad·vow·son (ad-vou'zón), n. in English Law, the right to present a church benefice.

ad·y·na·mi·a (ad-i-nā'mi-á), n. great debility; physical weakness.

adz, adze (adz), n. a cutting tool having a curved blade at right angles to the handle, used for dressing and trimming wood.

ae·dile (ē'dil), n. in ancient Rome, a magistrate who exercised supervision over temples, buildings, markets, public games, sanitation, roads, etc.

ae·gis (ē'jis), n. 1. a shield or protection. 2. sponsorship; support.

a·e·ne·ous (á-ē'ni-ús), adj. having the color of bronze.

a·e·o·li·an harp (ē-ō'li-án), n. a stringed instrument: it is a box with wires that produce musical sounds when they are set in motion by air currents.

ae·on (ē'ón, ē'on), n. same as eon.

aer·ate (er'āt), v.t. -at·ed, -at·ing, 1. to expose

to air or the circulation of air. 2. to oxy-genate (the blood) by respiration. 3. to charge (liquid) with gas. —aer·a'tion, n. —aer'a·tor, n.

aer·i·al (er'i-ăl), adj. 1. by, from, or in air. 2. imaginary. 3. of or relating to aircraft or flying: n. a radio or television antenna. —aer'i·al·ly, adv.

aer·i·al·ist (er'i-ăl-ist), n. a performer on a tightrope, trapeze, etc.

aer·ie (er'i), n. 1. the high nest of an eagle or other predatory bird. 2. the young of such a bird.

aer·i·form (er'i-fôrm), adj. having the form of air; gaseous; hence, not substantial.

aer·i·fy (er'i-fī), v.t. ·fied, ·fy·ing, 1. to change into air. 2. to put air into.

aer·o-, a combining form meaning air, of air, of gases, of aircraft or flying.

aer·o·bat·ics (er-ŏ-băt'iks), n.pl. stunt flying; rolls, loops, and other stunts done with an airplane.

aer·o·bic (er-ŏ'bik), adj. 1. able to live or grow only when free oxygen is present. 2. of exercise, as running, that conditions the heart and lungs by increasing efficient intake of oxygen by the body.

aer·o·bics (er'ŏ-biks), n.pl. aerobic exercises.

aer·o·dy·nam·ics (er-ŏ-dī-nam'iks), n. the science which deals with air in motion.

aer·o·lite (er'ŏ-līt), n. a kind of meteorite.

aer·o·med·i·cine (er-ŏ-med'I-sin), n. the study and treatment of diseases and disorders brought about by flight within the earth's atmosphere.

aer·om·e·ter (er-om'ĕ-tēr), n. an instrument for weighing the air or other gases.

aer·o·naut (er'ŏ-nôt), n. a balloonist: an old term.

aer·o·nau·tics (er-ŏ-nôt'iks), n. the science or business of making and flying aircraft. —aer·o·nau'ti·cal, aer·o·nau'tic, adj.

aer·o·pause (er'ŏ-pôz), n. the upper limits of the earth's atmosphere, before outer space.

aer·o·plane (er'ŏ-plān), n. British form for air-plane.

aer·o·scope (er'ŏ-skōp), n. a device for gathering bacteria, dust, etc. from the air. —aer·o·scop'ic (-skop'ik), adj.

aer·o·sol (er'ŏ-sŏl), n. a suspension of liquid or solid particles in a gas: adj. of or denoting a container in which gas under pressure is used to eject a liquid in the form of a spray or foam.

aer·o·space (er'ŏ-spās), n. the earth's atmosphere and the space beyond it.

aer·o·stat (er'ŏ-stat), n. a balloon, dirigible, or other aircraft that is lifted and kept up by gas lighter than air carried in containers.

aer·o·stat·ics (er-ŏ-stat'iks), n. the science that deals with the equilibrium of bodies floating in air. —aer·o·stat'ic, adj.

aer·y (er'i), n. same as aerie.

aes·thete (es'thēt), n. 1. one who appreciates beauty, especially in art. 2. one who pretends to have an appreciation of beauty and art. —aes·thet'i·cism (es-thet'ĭ-sizm), n.

aes·thet·ic (es-thet'ik), adj. 1. of or pertaining to aesthetics. 2. of or pertaining to beauty. 3. artistic. Also aes·thet'i·cal. —aes·thet'i·cal·ly, adv.

aes·thet·ics ('iks), n. the study or theory of the beautiful, in taste or art.

a·far (ă-fär'), adv. [Poetic] at, to, or from a distance.

af·fa·ble (af'ă-bl), adj. 1. easy to talk to; courteous and friendly. 2. kindly; pleasant. —af·fa·bil'i·ty (-bil'ĭ-ti), n. —af'fa·bly, adv.

af·fair (ă-fer'), n. 1. that which is done or is to be done; business. 2. pl. matters, as of business, to be dealt with. 3. any matter or event. 4. a romantic relationship, especially one regarded as improper.

af·fect (ă-fekt'), v.t. 1. to produce an effect upon. 2. to stir the emotions of. 3. to prefer to use or wear. 4. to assume the appearance of; pretend.

af·fec·ta·tion (af-ek-tā'shŭn), n. 1. a pretense. 2. the assumption of a manner or behavior not one's own in order to impress others.

af·fect·ed (ă-fek'tid), adj. 1. not natural; false. 2. having an effect on. 3. stirred emotionally. 4. afflicted by disease. —af·fect'ed·ly, adv. —af·fect'ed·ness, n.

af·fect·ing ('ting), adj. arousing the emotions; moving.

af·fec·tion (ă-fek'shŭn), n. 1. an emotional state; feeling. 2. fondness or attachment. 3. a disease. —af·fec'tion·al, adj.

af·fec·tion·ate (-ăt), adj. feeling affection; fond and loving. —af·fec'tion·ate·ly, adv.

af·fer·ent (af'ēr-ĕnt), adj. in Physiology, conducting inward toward a central part.

af·fi·ance (ă-fī'ăns), v.t. ·anced, ·anc·ing, to betroth; promise to marry: n. a promise of marriage.

af·fi·da·vit (af-ĭ-dā'vit), n. a sworn statement in writing.

af·fil·i·ate (ă-fil'ĭ-āt), v.t. ·at·ed, ·at·ing, 1. to connect with a society or group. 2. to take in as a branch or member: v.i. to join: n. (-ăt), a member. —af·fil·i·a'tion, n.

af·fin·i·ty (ă-fin'ĭ-ti), n., pl. ·ties, 1. close relationship. 2. relationship by marriage. 3. similarity of structure, as of species or groups, implying a common source. 4. a mutual attraction, as between a man and a woman.

af·firm (ă-fûrm'), v.t. 1. to assert strongly. 2. to confirm; ratify (a judgment, decree, or order): v.i. in Law, to declare solemnly, but not under oath. —af·firm'er, af·fir'mant ('nt), n.

af·firm·ance ('ns), n. 1. an affirming. 2. a confirming. 3. in Law, an upholding by a higher court of a lower court's judgment.

af·fir·ma·tion (af-ēr-mā'shŭn), n. 1. an assertion. 2. in Law, a solemn declaration, but not under oath: permitted to those having conscientious objections to taking oaths.

af·firm·a·tive (ă-fûr'mă-tiv), n. 1. that which affirms; expression of affirmation, assent, etc. 2. the side upholding the positive argument in a debate: adj. affirming that a statement is true; positive. —af·firm'a·tive·ly, adv.

affirmative action, a plan to offset past discrimination in employing or educating women, blacks, etc.

af·fix (ă-fiks'), v.t. 1. to fix to; attach. 2. to add at the end: n. (a'fiks). 1. something af-

fixed. 2. a letter or syllable added to a word; suffix or prefix.

af·fla·tus (ă-flāt'ŭs), *n.* inspiration, as of a poet.

af·flict (ă-flikt'), *v.t.* to cause pain to body or mind; distress.

af·flic·tion (ă-flik'shŭn), *n.* 1. an afflicted condition; pain of body or mind; distress. 2. anything that causes such distress, as calamity or an ailment.

af·flic·tive ('tiv), *adj.* causing pain.

af·flu·ence (af'loo-wĕns), *n.* 1. an abundant supply; abundance. 2. riches; wealth.

af·flu·ent (-wĕnt), *n.* a tributary stream: *adj.* 1. abundant; profuse. 2. wealthy; prosperous. —af'flu·ent·ly, *adv.*

af·ford (ă-fôrd'), *v.t.* 1. to supply; yield. 2. to be able to bear the expense of.

af·for·est (ă-fôr'ĕst), *v.t.* to convert a tract of land into forest. —af·for·es·ta·tion (-ĕs-tā'-shŭn), *n.*

af·fran·chise (ă-fran'chĭz), *v.t.* -chised, -chis·ing, to make free; enfranchise.

af·fray (ă-frā'), *n.* a brawl or noisy quarrel; public fight or riot.

af·fright (ă-frīt'), *v.t.* [Archaic], to frighten; terrify: *n.* [Archaic], fear; terror.

af·front (ă-frŭnt'), *v.t.* 1. to confront openly. 2. to insult intentionally: *n.* an intentional insult.

af·fu·sion (ă-fū'zhŭn), *n.* the act of pouring upon, as of water in baptism.

Af·ghan (af'gan), *adj.* of or pertaining to Afghanistan, a country in southwestern Asia: *n.* a native of Afghanistan.

af·ghan (af'gan), *n.* a crocheted or knitted soft wool blanket or robe.

a·fi·cio·na·do (ă-fish-ō-nä'dō), *n., pl.* -dos, [Spanish], an enthusiastic follower or devotee of some sport, art, or other activity.

a·field (ă-fēld'), *adv.* 1. in, to, or on the field. 2. astray.

a·fire (ă-fīr'), *adv. & adj.* burning; on fire.

a·flame (ă-flām'), *adv. & adj.* 1. in flames; ablaze. 2. excited.

a·float (ă-flōt'), *adv. & adj.* 1. floating. 2. on board ship. 3. in circulation. 4. adrift. 5. awash; flooded.

a·flut·ter (ă-flut'ēr), *adv. & adj.* fluttering; in a state of excitement or confusion.

a·foot (ă-foot'), *adv.* 1. on foot. 2. astir; in motion.

a·fore·men·tioned (ă-fôr-men'shŭnd), *adj.* mentioned at an earlier time.

a·fore·said (ă-fôr'sed), *adj.* spoken of previously.

a·fore·thought (ă-fôr'thôt), *adj.* thought out ahead of time; premeditated.

a·foul (ă-foul'), *adj. & adv.* enmeshed; entangled.

a·fraid (ă-frād'), *adj.* 1. frightened. 2. [Informal], regretful.

A·frame (ā'frām), *n.* a building, as a house, that has steep sides coming to a point at the top thereby giving the framework the appearance of the letter A.

a·fresh (ă-fresh'), *adv.* again; anew.

Af·ri·can (af'ri·kăn), *adj.* of or pertaining to Africa, a continent of the Eastern Hemi-

sphere, south of Europe: *n.* a native or inhabitant of Africa.

Af·ri·kaans (af-ri-känz'), *n.* an official language of South Africa, developed from Dutch.

Af·ri·ka·ner (af-ri-kän'ēr), *n.* a native of South Africa, of European, especially Dutch, ancestry; Boer.

Af·ro (af'rō), *adj.* denoting a full, puffed-out hair style worn by some Negroes: *n.* this hair style.

Af·ro-, a combining form meaning *Africa, African.*

aft (aft), *adj. & adv.* toward the stern.

af·ter (af'tēr), *adj.* 1. next; later. 2. nearer the rear: *prep.* 1. behind in place. 2. later in time. 3. in imitation of. 4. next in rank or excellence. 5. in pursuit of. 6. as a result of. 7. in honor of. 8. regardless of: *adv.* behind; subsequent in time or place: *conj.* later than.

af·ter·birth (-bĕrth), *n.* the placenta and membranes expelled from the uterus after parturition.

af·ter·burn·er (-bĕr-nĕr), *n.* a device on some engines for burning or making use of exhaust gases.

af·ter·clap (-klap), *n.* an unexpected happening coming after something is supposed to be at an end.

af·ter·damp (-damp), *n.* a suffocating gas found in coal mines after an explosion of firedamp.

af·ter·deck (-dek), *n.* the part of the deck of a ship toward the stern.

af·ter·ef·fect (-ĕ-fekt), *n.* 1. an effect coming at a later time. 2. a secondary effect.

af·ter·glow (-glō), *n.* a glow or radiance still seen after a light has gone, as in the sky after sunset.

af·ter·life (-līf), *n.* a life after death.

af·ter·math (-math), *n.* 1. a second mowing in a season. 2. a consequence, often an unpleasant one.

af·ter·noon (af-tēr-nōōn'), *n.* the part of the day between noon and evening: *adj.* of, pertaining to, or occurring in the afternoon.

af·ter·taste (af'tĕr-tāst), *n.* a taste remaining in the mouth after eating, drinking, or smoking.

af·ter·thought (-thôt), *n.* 1. thought, reflection, or explanation that comes later. 2. a thought that comes too late.

af·ter·ward (-wârd), **af·ter·wards** (-wârdz), *adv.* at a later time; subsequently.

a·gain (ă-gen'), *adv.* 1. as before. 2. anew; once more. 3. further. 4. on the other hand.

a·gainst (ă-genst'), *prep.* 1. opposite to. 2. in opposition to; contrary to. 3. so as to touch. 4. adjoining. 5. for the possibility of.

ag·a·ma (ag'ă-mă), *n.* an Old World lizard that can change color rapidly.

a·gape (ă-gāp'), *adj. & adv.* gaping; with the mouth wide open in a state of expectation or astonishment.

ag·a·pe (äg'ă-pā), *n.* in *Theology,* God's unselfish love for man.

a·gar (ā'gär, ag'ēr), *n.* a gelatinous substance made from seaweed, used in preserved foods, as a laxative, etc.: also agar-agar.

ag·ate (ag'ăt), *n.* 1. a semiprecious stone, a

---

a in cap, ā in cane, ä in father, å in abet, e in met ē in be, ē in baker, ē in regent, i in pit, ī in fine, i in manifest, o in hot, ô in horse, ō in bone,

variety of chalcedony. 2. a small ball of this or of glass, used in playing marbles.

a·ga·ve (ă-gā'vi), *n.* any of several related desert plants, as the century plant, of tropical and semitropical America.

age (āj), *n.* 1. the time that a person or thing has existed. 2. a certain time of life. 3. old age. 4. a period in history or geologic time. 5. [Informal], a long time: *v.i. & v.t.* **aged, ag'ing** or **age'ing,** 1. to grow or become old. 2. to become or cause to become mature. 3. to look or cause to look older.

a·ged (ā'jid), *adj.* 1. old. 2. (ājd), having reached the age of.

age·less (āj'lis), *adj.* 1. showing no signs of growing older. 2. everlasting; timeless.

a·gen·cy (ā'jĕn-si), *n.* 1. operation; action. 2. the means of getting something done. 3. an establishment for the purpose of doing business for another. 4. an administrative division of government.

a·gen·da (ă-jen'dă), *n., pl.* -das, 1. a program of business to be carried out. 2. a list of subjects to be discussed. Also **a·gen'dum** ('dŭm), *pl.* -da, -dums.

a·gent (ā'jĕnt), *n.* 1. one who is authorized to act or do business for another. 2. an active means for bringing something about. 3. a substance producing an effect. 4. one who represents a government agency.

a·gent pro·vo·ca·teur (a-zhän' prō-vŏk-ă-toor'), *pl.* **a·gents pro·vo·ca·teurs** (a-zhän' prō-vŏk-ă-toor'), [French], one who associates with members of a group in order to provoke them into committing illegal acts.

age-old (āj'ōld), *adj.* very old; ancient.

ag·er·a·tum (aj-ēr-ā'tŭm), *n.* a low, annual plant with clusters of small, dense, bluish flowers.

ag·glom·er·ate (ă-glăm'ēr-āt), *v.t. & v.i.* -at·ed, -at·ing, to gather into a heap or mass: *n.* (-it), a heap or mass. —**ag·glom·er·a'tion,** *n.* —**ag·glom'er·a·tive,** *adj.*

ag·glu·ti·nant (ă-glōōt'ĭ-nănt), *adj.* uniting; sticking: *n.* a substance that makes things stick together.

ag·glu·ti·nate (ă-glōōt'ĭ-nāt), *v.t. & v.i.* -nat·ed, -nat·ing, to stick together; unite, as with glue: *adj.* (-nit), stuck together, as with glue. —**ag·glu·ti·na'tion,** *n.* —**ag·glu'ti·na·tive,** *adj.*

ag·gran·dize (ă-gran'dīz, ag'răn-), *v.t.* -dized, -diz·ing, to make great or greater in power, rank, or riches. —**ag·gran'dize·ment** ('diz·mĕnt), *n.*

ag·gra·vate (ag'ră-vāt), *v.t.* -vat·ed, -vat·ing, 1. to add to (a burden); make more troublesome; intensify. 2. [Informal], to irritate; annoy. —**ag·gra·va'tion,** *n.*

ag·gre·gate (ag'rĕ-gāt), *v.t.* -gat·ed, -gat·ing, 1. to collect or bring together; gather into a mass. 2. to amount to: *n.* (-găt), a mass formed by the union of distinct but similar things: *adj.* (-găt), formed or gathered into a mass or total. —**ag·gre·ga'tion,** *n.* —**ag'gre·ga·tive,** *adj.*

ag·gress (ă-gres'), *v.i.* to attack; begin a quarrel or controversy.

ag·gres·sion (ă-gresh'ŭn), *n.* 1. an unprovoked attack. 2. a tendency to be hostile or quarrelsome.

ag·gres·sive (ă-gres'iv), *adj.* 1. quarrelsome; hostile. 2. willing to take the offensive; militant. 3. bold and enterprising. —**ag·gres'sive·ly,** *adv.* —**ag·gres'sive·ness,** *n.*

ag·gres·sor ('ēr), *n.* one who attacks, especially, one who makes an unprovoked attack.

ag·grieve (ă-grēv'), *v.t.* -grieved', -griev'ing, to cause grief or injury to.

a·ghast (ă-gast'), *adj.* struck with sudden horror or dismay; shocked.

ag·ile (aj'l), *adj.* 1. moving in a quick, easy way; active; nimble. 2. quick and sharp. — **ag'ile·ly,** *adv.* —**a·gil·i·ty** (ă-jil'ĭ-ti), *n.*

ag·i·o (aj'i-ō), *n., pl.* -os, the fee or charge for exchanging one kind of money for another. —**ag'i·o·tage** (-ō-tij), *n.*

ag·i·tate (aj'ĭ-tāt), *v.t.* -tat·ed, -tat·ing, 1. to stir violently. 2. to excite or disturb. 3. to keep discussing in order to win support for: *v.i.* to stir up interest so as to bring about changes. —**ag·i·ta'tion,** *n.*

ag·i·ta·tor (aj'ĭ-tā-tēr), *n.* 1. one who tries to stir up interest in support of some proposed political or social change. 2. an implement for stirring.

a·gleam (ă-glēm'), *adv. & adj.* gleaming.

ag·let (ag'lit), *n.* the metal tip on a lace, cord, or braid.

a·glow (ă-glō'), *adv. & adj.* in a glow; glowing.

ag·nail (ag'nāl), *n.* a sore under or near the nail; whitlow.

ag·nate (ag'nāt), *n.* a relative through male descent or on the father's side.

ag·no·men (ag-nō'měn), *n.* an epithet, usually in honor of some achievement.

ag·nos·tic (ag-năs'tik), *n.* one who denies that man possesses any knowledge of the ultimate nature of things; one who neither affirms nor denies the existence of God: *adj.* of or pertaining to agnostics or the beliefs and doctrines of agnostics. —**ag·nos'ti·cal·ly,** *adv.* —**ag·nos'ti·cism** ('ti-sizm), *n.*

Ag·nus De·i (āg'noos dā'i, ag'nŭs dē'ī), [Latin], 1. an image of a lamb, representing Christ, bearing a banner with a cross. 2. a piece of wax stamped with the figure of a lamb, blessed by the Pope. 3. a prayer in the Roman Catholic Mass, beginning with the words "Agnus Dei."

a·go (ă-gō'), *adj.* gone by; past: used after the noun: *adv.* in past time: used in the phrase long ago.

a·gog (ă-gäg'), *adj. & adv.* in expectation or excitement; eager.

ag·o·nize (ag'ō-nīz), *v.i.* -nized, -niz·ing, 1. to suffer anguish; be in agony. 2. to make convulsive efforts; struggle: *v.t.* to torture.

ag·o·ny (ag'ō-ni), *n., pl.* -nies, 1. extreme suffering; anguish. 2. death pains.

a·go·ra (ag'ō-ră), *n., pl.* -rae (-rē), -ras, in ancient Greece, a marketplace.

ag·o·ra·pho·bi·a (ag-ēr-ă-fō'bi-ă), *n.* an abnormal fear of being in large open spaces or public places.

a·gou·ti, a·gou·ty (ă-gōō'ti), *n., pl.* -tis, -ties, a rodent about the size of a rabbit, found in the West Indies and Central and South America.

a·grar·i·an (ă-grer'i-ăn), *adj.* 1. relating to land, or to land tenure. 2. of farmers or agriculture: *n*. one who is in favor of redistribution of land on a more equitable basis.

a·grar·i·an·ism (-izm), *n*. 1. the principle of a uniform division of land. 2. political agitation for land reform.

a·gree (á-grē'), *v.i.* -greed', -gree'ing, 1. to consent (*to*). 2. to be in harmony or accord. 3. to concur. 4. to suit the health of (followed by *with*). 5. to reach an understanding: *v.t.* to acknowledge.

a·gree·a·ble ('á-bl), *adj*. 1. pleasing to the mind or senses. 2. ready to accept or approve. 3. in accord. —**a·gree·a·bil'i·ty** (-bil'i-ti), **a·gree'a·ble·ness**, *n*. —**a·gree'a·bly**, *adv*.

a·gree·ment ('mĕnt), *n*. 1. harmony of opinions or feelings. 2. a mutual understanding; compact. 3. a contract. 4. concord of one word with another in gender, number, case, or person.

ag·ri·busi·ness (ag'ri-biz-nis), *n*. agriculture and businesses connected with agriculture.

ag·ri·cul·ture (ag'ri-kul-chĕr), *n*. the science and art of cultivating crops and raising livestock; farming. —**ag·ri·cul'tur·al**, *adj*. —**ag·ri·cul'tur·al·ly**, *adv*.

ag·ri·cul·tur·ist (ag·ri-kul'chĕr-ist), *n*. 1. an expert in agriculture. 2. a farmer. Also **ag·ri·cul'tur·al·ist**.

a·gron·o·my (á-gron'ō-mi), *n*. the scientific management of farm land, especially in relation to crop production. —**a·gron'o·mist**, *n*.

a·ground (á-ground'), *adj. & adv*. on or onto the ground, the shore, a reef, etc.: said of a ship.

a·gue (á'gū), *n*. 1. a fever, usually malarial, with intermittent chills. 2. these chills. 3. a fit of shivering. —**a'gu·ish**, *adj*.

ah (ä), *interj*. an expression of surprise, pleasure, longing, admiration, etc.

a·ha (ä-hä'), *interj*. an expression of satisfaction, often with irony.

a·head (á-hed'), *adv. & adj*. 1. in or toward the front. 2. forward. 3. in advance. 4. leading; winning.

a·hem (á-hem'), *interj*. a sound like a cough, made intentionally, as to get someone's attention.

a·hoy (á-hoi'), *interj*. a nautical call used in hailing.

aid (ād), *v.t. & v.i.* to assist; help: *n*. 1. help; assistance. 2. one who helps; assistant. 3. a device or thing that helps or supports.

aide (ād), *n*. 1. a helper. 2. an aide-de-camp.

aide-de-camp (ād'dĕ-kamp'), *n., pl.* **aides'-de-camp'**, a military officer who assists a superior.

AIDS (ādz), *n*. a condition of deficiency of certain leukocytes, resulting in infections, cancer, etc.: it stands for *acquired immune deficiency syndrome*.

ai·grette, ai·gret (ā'gret, ā-gret'), *n*. 1. a plume of white egret feathers, formerly used as decoration as on a woman's hat. 2. a decoration in imitation of this.

ail (āl), *v.t.* to give or cause pain to: *v.i.* to be in ill health.

ai·lan·thus (á-lan'thŭs), *n*. a tree or shrub having small, pointed leaves and tiny, greenish flowers with an offensive odor.

ai·le·ron (ā'lĕ-ron), *n*. a movable hinged section at the rear edge of an airplane wing.

ail·ing (āl'ing), *adj*. in ill health.

ail·ment (āl'mĕnt), *n*. a slight illness, often chronic.

aim (ām), *v.i. & v.t.* 1. to point or direct (a weapon, blow, missile, etc.) toward something to be struck. 2. to direct (one's efforts or course of action). 3. to intend: *n*. 1. the act of aiming. 2. a purpose or intention.

aim·less (ām'lĕs), *adj*. without aim or purpose. —**aim'less·ly**, *adv*.

ain't (ānt), [Informal], am not.

air (er), *n*. 1. the gaseous mixture surrounding the earth; atmosphere. 2. the space above the earth. 3. a wind or breeze. 4. external manner, appearance, or bearing. 5. publicity. 6. travel by aircraft. 7. a melody; tune: *v.t.* 1. to expose to the air, as to dry or freshen. 2. to expose to public knowledge; publicize: *v.i.* to be exposed to air.

air bag, a bag that inflates instantly within an automobile in a collision, to protect riders from being thrown forward.

air base, an installation for the maintenance and operation of military aircraft.

air·borne (er'bŏrn), *adj*. 1. borne by air, as tiny, light particles. 2. transported by aircraft. 3. flying.

air brake, an automatic brake operated by the action of air pressure on a piston.

air·brush (er'brush), *n*. a device for spraying ink, paint, etc. on a surface by the action of compressed air: also **air brush**: *v.t.* to spray, cover, or decorate by using an airbrush.

air·bus ('bus), *n*. a very large airliner.

air conditioner, an apparatus for controlling the temperature and humidity of air in an automobile, building, etc. —**air'-con·di·tion**, *v.t.* —**air'-con·di·tioned**, *adj*. —**air conditioning**.

air-cooled (er'kōōld), *adj*. cooled by air passing around, into, or through it.

air·craft ('kraft), *n*. any machine designed to be used for air transportation.

aircraft carrier, a very large warship that carries airplanes, with a flat deck for takeoff and landing.

air curtain, a curtain of air forced downward at an open entrance: also **air door**.

air cushion, 1. a cushion inflated with air. 2. a shock-absorbing device utilizing the elasticity of compressed air. 3. compressed air released underneath a vehicle for its own support as it travels just above land or water.

air-drop ('drop), *v.t.* -dropped, -drop·ping, to drop (supplies or personnel) by parachute from aircraft in flight: *n*. 1. the act of doing this. 2. supplies or personnel so dropped.

Aire·dale (er'dāl), *n*. a dog of the terrier family, characterized by wiry hair.

air·field (er'fēld), *n*. a level field for takeoff and landing of aircraft.

air·foil ('foil), *n*. a wing, rudder, etc. of an aircraft designed to keep it in the air and help control its movements.

air·head ('hed), *n*. [Slang], a frivolous, silly, and ignorant person.

---

a in *cap*, ā in *cane*, ä in *father*, â in *abet*, e in met　ē in be, ê in *baker*, ê in *regent*, I in *pit*, ī in *fine*, i in *manifest*, o in *hot*, ō in *horse*, ō in *bone*,

air force, the aviation branch of the armed forces of a country.

air gas, an illuminating or heating gas consisting of air charged with vapor from petroleum or some other hydrocarbon.

air gun, 1. a gun discharged by the release of compressed air. 2. a gunlike device operated by compressed air, for spraying insecticide, paint, etc.

air·i·ly (er′i-li), *adv.* in an airy manner; gaily.

air·i·ness (er′i-nis), *n.* 1. the state of being airy, or full of fresh air. 2. gaiety.

air·ing (′ing), *n.* 1. a walk, ride, or drive in the open air. 2. exposure to the air, as for drying or freshening. 3. exposure to public knowledge.

air·less (′lis), *adj.* 1. without air. 2. lacking fresh air. 3. without a breeze.

air·lift (′lift), *n.* the transporting of supplies by aircraft: *v.t.* to transport by airlift.

air·line (′lin), *n.* 1. a company for transporting passengers, freight, mail, etc. by aircraft. 2. the system set up by such a company. Also **air line:** *adj.* on, of, or pertaining to an airline.

air·lin·er (′li-nĕr), *n.* a large passenger airplane operated by an airline.

air lock, a compartment where air pressure can be adjusted, used as a transition chamber for persons going from one concentration of air pressure to another.

air·mail (′mäl), *n.* mail carried by aircraft: *adj.* denoting mail carried by aircraft: *v.t.* to send by airmail.

air·man (′măn), *n., pl.* **-men,** 1. an aviator. 2. an enlisted person in the U.S. Air Force.

air·plane (′plän), *n.* an aircraft, heavier than air, that is moved forward by jet propulsion or a propeller and kept aloft by the forces of air upon its wings.

air plant, same as epiphyte.

air·port (′pôrt), *n.* a place where aircraft can land and take off, usually with hangars, maintenance facilities, and provisions for handling passengers and freight.

air pressure, 1. the pressure of the atmosphere. 2. the pressure of compressed air.

air pump, an apparatus for pumping or compressing air.

air raid, an attack by aircraft on a ground location, especially with bombs.

air rifle, a rifle that shoots BB's or other pellets by means of compressed air.

air·ship (′ship), *n.* an aircraft that is lighter than air, is self-propelled, and can be steered.

air·sick (′sik), *adj.* nauseated or sick from the motion of an aircraft in flight. –**air′sick·ness,** *n.*

air·space (′spās), *n.* the space above an area of the earth's surface; especially, the space above a nation over which it maintains control.

air·speed (′spēd), *n.* the speed of an aircraft relative to the air rather than to the ground.

air·strip (′strip), *n.* a temporary airplane runway.

air·tight (′tīt), *adj.* 1. too tight for air to escape or penetrate. 2. unassailable.

air·waves (′wāvz), *n.* the medium through which radio signals travel.

air·way (′wā), *n.* 1. a regular route traveled by aircraft. 2. *pl.* airwaves. 3. a breathing passage to the lungs.

air·wor·thy (′wûr-thi), *adj.* fit to fly: said of an aircraft. –**air′wor·thi·ness,** *n.*

air·y (er′i), *adj.* **air′i·er, air′i·est,** 1. exposed to the air. 2. unsubstantial. 3. lighthearted; gay. 4. flippant. 5. [Informal], affected.

aisle (īl), *n.* a passageway between rows of seats.

aitch·bone (āch′bōn), *n.* 1. the rump bone. 2. a cut of beef around this bone.

a·jar (á-jär′), *adj. & adv.* 1. slightly open, as a door. 2. not in harmony.

a·kim·bo (á-kim′bō), *adj. & adv.* with the hands on the hips and the elbows turned outward.

a·kin (á-kin′), *adj.* 1. of one kin; related by blood. 2. of the same kind; similar.

-al (ál, l), a suffix meaning *relating to, like, suitable for* or *the action of, the process of.*

a·la (ā′lá), *n., pl.* **a′lae** (′lē), a wing or a part like a wing.

à la (ä′lä, ′lä), [French], 1. in the style of. 2. after or according to.

al·a·bas·ter (al′á-bas-tĕr), *n.* a white, smooth, translucent variety of gypsum, used for statues, vases, and the like: *adj.* made of or resembling alabaster.

à la carte (ä-lä-kärt′), [French], with a separate price for each item on the menu.

a·lack (á-lak′), *interj.* [Archaic], an expression of blame, sorrow, or surprise.

a·lac·ri·ty (á-lak′ri-ti), *n.* eager readiness, often with quick action; briskness.

à la king (ä lä king′), in a cream sauce containing mushrooms, green peppers, etc.

al·a·me·da (al-á-mē′dá, -mä′), *n.* [Spanish], a shaded walk.

al·a·mo (al′á-mō, ä′lá-), *n., pl.* **-mos,** [Spanish], a poplar tree.

à la mode (al-á-mōd′, ä-lä-), [French], 1. in the fashion. 2. served in a particular style, as pie with ice cream.

a·lar (ā′lár), *adj.* 1. of, pertaining to, or having wings. 2. shaped like a wing.

a·larm (á-lärm′), *v.t.* 1. to arouse to a sense of danger. 2. to strike with the apprehension of danger; frighten: *n.* 1. [Archaic], a call to arms. 2. a warning of danger. 3. the apprehension of danger; fear. 4. *a*) the bell or buzzer of an alarm clock. *b*) a siren or clanging device that warns of danger, of intruders, etc.

alarm clock, a clock that can be set to ring or signal in some other way at a certain time, as to awaken a sleeper.

a·larm·ing (′ing), *adj.* making one apprehensive or fearful; frightening. –**a·larm′ing·ly,** *adv.*

a·larm·ist (′ist), *n.* 1. one who spreads frightening rumors. 2. one who is easily frightened and expects the worst to happen: *adj.* of or like an alarmist.

a·lar·y (ā′lăr-ĭ), *adj.* of, pertaining to, or shaped like a wing.

a·las (ă-lăs′), *interj.* an expression of sorrow, disappointment, or pity.

a·late (ā′lāt), *adj.* having wings; winged: also **a′lat·ed**.

alb (alb), *n.* a long, white vestment worn by a priest at Mass.

al·ba·core (al′bă-kôr), *n., pl.* -cores, -core, a saltwater fish of the mackerel family, as the tuna or bonito.

al·ba·tross (al′bă-trôs, -tros), *n., pl.* -tross·es, -tross, a large sea bird related to the petrel.

al·be·it (ôl-bē′ĭt), *conj.* although; even though; notwithstanding.

al·bi·no (al-bī′nō), *n., pl.* -nos, 1. a person lacking normal coloration, having pink eyes, white skin, and whitish hair. 2. an animal or plant lacking normal coloration.

al·bu·gin·e·ous (al-byoo-jĭn′ĭ-ŭs), *adj.* of or pertaining to the white of the eye.

al·bum (al′bŭm), *n.* 1. a book with blank pages, in which to insert autographs, photographs, stamps, etc. 2. a booklike holder for phonograph records. 3. a long-playing record or tape recording.

al·bu·men (al-bū′mĕn), *n.* 1. the white of an egg. 2. the nutritious substance stored up with the embryo in the germinating cells of an animal or plant. 3. same as **albumin**.

al·bu·men·ize (al-bū′mĕn-īz), *v.t.* -ized, -iz·ing, to coat or mix with albumen or an albuminous substance.

al·bu·min (al-bū′mĭn), *n.* any of a class of proteins which form an important element of blood, muscle, milk, and egg, and of many vegetable fluids and tissues.

al·bu·mi·noid (′mĭ-noid), *adj.* like albumin: *n.* a protein.

al·bu·mi·nous (′mĭ-nŭs), *adj.* like or containing albumin or albumen.

al·bu·mi·nu·ri·a (al-bū-mĭ-noor′ĭ-ă), *n.* the abnormal presence of albumin in the urine.

al·bur·num (al-būr′nŭm), *n.* same as sapwood.

al·cal·de (al-kal′dĭ), *n.* the mayor and judicial officer of a Spanish or Spanish-American town.

al·caz·ar (al′kă-zär), *n.* a castle or fortress of the Moors in Spain.

al·chem·ist (al′kĕ-mist), *n.* one who studies or practices alchemy.

al·che·my (al′kĕ-mĭ), *n.* the chemistry of the Middle Ages: its chief aim was to transmute the baser metals into gold. —**al·chem′ic**, **al·chem′i·cal**, *adj.*

al·co·hol (al′kŏ-hôl, -hol), *n.* 1. a colorless, spirituous liquid used as a fuel, used in medicine, and that is the intoxicating element in fermented or distilled liquors. 2. any intoxicating liquor containing this liquid. 3. any of a class of compounds of a similar type, as wood alcohol.

al·co·hol·ic (al′kŏ-hôl′ĭk, -hol′-), *adj.* 1. containing or pertaining to alcohol. 2. afflicted with alcoholism: *n.* one who drinks alcoholic liquors to excess or is afflicted with alcoholism.

al·co·hol·ism (al′kŏ-hôl-izm, -hol-), *n.* 1. the continued excessive drinking of alcoholic liquor. 2. a diseased condition caused by this.

al·co·hol·ize (-īz), *v.t.* -ized, -iz·ing, 1. to treat with alcohol. 2 to convert into alcohol. —**al·co·hol·i·za′tion** (-ĭ-zā′shŭn), *n.*

Al·co·ran (al-kō-ran′), *n.* [Archaic], the Koran.

al·cove (al′kōv), *n.* 1. a recess in a room; nook. 2. a bower in a garden.

al·de·hyde (al′dĕ-hid), *n.* a volatile fluid obtained from alcohol by oxidation.

al·der (ôl′dĕr), *n.* a small tree or shrub of the birch family, growing in moist regions.

al·der·man (ôl′dĕr-măn), *n., pl.* -men, 1. in the U.S., a member of the municipal council in some cities. 2. in England and Ireland, a senior member of a county or borough council. —**al·der·man′ic** (-man′ĭk), *adj.*

ale (āl), *n.* an alcoholic drink made from malt and hops by fermentation, similar to beer.

a·lee (ă-lē′), *adv. & adj.* on or toward the lee or sheltered side of a ship.

a·lem·bic (ă-lem′bik), *n.* 1. an apparatus formerly used for distilling. 2. anything that purifies or refines.

a·leph (ä′lif), *n.* the first letter of the Hebrew alphabet.

a·lert (ă-lûrt′), *adj.* 1. watchful; ready for action. 2. quick; active: *n.* 1. an alarm or warning. 2. the period during which such an alarm should be observed: *v.t.* to warn to be ready. —**a·lert′ly**, *adv.* —**a·lert′ness**, *n.*

ale·wife (āl′wīf), *n., pl.* -wives, an edible North American fish resembling the herring.

al·ex·an·drine (al-ig-zan′drĕn, ′drin), *n.* a line of poetry having six iambic feet, or twelve syllables.

a·lex·i·a (ă-lek′sĭ-ă), *n.* loss of the ability to read, caused by injury to the brain.

al·fal·fa (al-fal′fă), *n.* a plant of the legume family with purple flowers, widely cultivated as a forage crop.

al·fres·co (al-fres′kō), *adv.* in the open air: *adj.* outdoor. Also **al fresco**.

al·gae (al′jē), *n., sing.* **al′ga** (′gă), a group of simple plants, including seaweed, containing chlorophyll, found in water and damp places. —**al′gal** (′găl), *adj.*

al·gar·ro·ba, **al·ga·ro·ba** (al-gă-rō′bă), *n.* 1. the carob tree or its pods. 2. the mesquite tree or its pods.

al·ge·bra (al′jĕ-bră), *n.* a system of mathematical calculation in which certain arithmetic operations are generalized by the use of letters and other symbols to stand for numbers. —**al′ge·bra·ist** (-bră-ist), *n.*

al·ge·bra·ic (al-jĕ-brā′ĭk), **al·ge·bra·i·cal** (′ĭ-kăl), *adj.* occurring in, or dealing with, algebra. —**al·ge·bra′i·cal·ly**, *adv.*

al·gid (al′jid), *adj.* cold; chilly. —**al·gid′i·ty** (′ĭ-tĭ), *n.*

al·gin (al′jĭn), *n.* a gelatinous substance obtained from seaweed, used in plastics, medicines, etc.: also **al·gin′ic acid** (-jin′ik).

a·li·as (ā′lĭ-ăs, ăl′yăs), *adv.* otherwise named: *n., pl.* -as·es, another name; assumed name.

al·i·bi (al′ĭ-bī), *n., pl.* -bis, 1. the plea by an accused person of having been elsewhere than at the scene when an illegal act was committed. 2. [Informal], an excuse: *v.i.* -bied, -bi·ing, [Informal], to offer an excuse.

---

a in *cap*, ā in *cane*, ä in *father*, ă in *abet*, e in *met*, ē in *be*, ê in *baker*, ê in *regent*, ĭ in *pit*, ī in *fine*, ĩ in *manifest*, o in *hot*, ô in *horse*, ō in *bone*,

al·ien (āl'yĕn, 'i-ĕn), *adj.* 1. belonging to another country; foreign. 2. strange. 3. opposed: *n.* 1. a foreigner. 2. a foreign-born resident of a country in which he is not naturalized.

al·ien·a·ble (-ä-bl), *adj.* that can be transferred to a new owner. —**al·ien·a·bil'i·ty** (-bil'ĭ-ti), *n.*

al·ien·age (-ij), *n.* the legal status of an alien.

al·ien·ate (-āt), *v.t.* **-at·ed, -at·ing,** 1. to estrange, as the affections. 2. to transfer to another, as property. 3. to cause to be aloof or withdrawn. —**al'ien·a·tor,** *n.*

al·ien·a·tion (āl-yĕ-nā'shŭn), *n.* 1. an estrangement. 2. transference. 3. mental derangement.

al·ien·ist (āl'yĕ-nist), *n.* a psychiatrist, especially one who testifies in legal proceedings.

al·i·form (al'ĭ-fôrm), *adj.* wing-shaped.

a·light (ä-līt'), *v.i.* **a·light'ed** or **a·lit** (ä-lit'), **a·light'ing,** 1. to dismount. 2. to descend and settle: *adj.* 1. lighted; aflame. 2. lighted up.

a·lign (ä-līn'), *v.t.* 1. to lay out or adjust by line. 2. to adjust (parts, as wheels of an automobile) so as to make work properly together. 3. to bring into alliance: *v.i.* to form or fall into line.

a·lign·ment (-mĕnt), *n.* 1. the act of aligning or adjusting by a line. 2. the state of being aligned or arranged in a straight line. 3. a being in alliance or agreement. 4. a ground plan, as of a railroad or road.

a·like (ä-līk'), *adj.* like one another: *adv.* 1. in a like manner; similarly. 2. equally. —**a·like'ness,** *n.*

al·i·ment (al'ĭ-mĕnt), *n.* 1. nourishment; food. 2. means of support: *v.t.* (al'ĭ-ment), to nourish. —**al·i·men'tal** (-men'tl), *adj.*

al·i·men·ta·ry (al-ĭ-men'tä-ri), *adj.* 1. of or pertaining to food. 2. nourishing. 3. furnishing support.

alimentary canal, the system of tubes and organs in the body, through which food passes and is assimilated: also **alimentary tract.**

al·i·men·ta·tion (-men-tā'shŭn), *n.* 1. the act of giving nourishment. 2. nourishment. 3. support. —**al·i·men'ta·tive** ('tä-tiv), *adj.*

al·i·mo·ny (al-ĭ-mō'ni), *n.* 1. originally, supply of the means of living. 2. an allowance that a court orders to be paid by a man to a woman (or by a woman to a man) following their divorce or separation.

a·line (ä-līn'), *v.t. & v.i.* **a·lined',** **a·lin'ing,** same as **align.** —**a·line'ment,** *n.*

al·i·quant (al'ĭ-kwänt), *adj.* being a part of a number that does not divide it without a remainder, as 8 is an aliquant part of 25.

al·i·quot (al'ĭ-kwŏt), *adj.* being a part of a number that will divide it without remainder, as 8 is an aliquot part of 24.

a·live (ä-līv'), *adj.* 1. having life. 2. in force. 3. in a state of action; lively. 4. sensitive; aware of (followed by *to*). 5. thronged; full of (followed by *with*).

a·liz·a·rin, a·liz·a·rine (ä-liz'ä-rin), *n.* a dyestuff formerly obtained from madder, but now made from anthracene.

al·ka·hest (al'kä-hest), *n.* the hypothetical universal solvent sought by the alchemists.

al·ka·les·cent (al-kä-les'ĕnt), *adj.* becoming alkaline.

al·ka·li (al'kä-lī), *n., pl.* **-lies, -lis,** 1. any base, as soda, potash, etc., that is soluble in water, combines with fats to form soap, neutralizes acids and forms salts with them, and turns red litmus blue. 2. any mineral salt or mixture of salts found in desert soils, that can neutralize acids.

al·ka·line (-lin, -līn), *adj.* 1. of, pertaining to, or having the properties of an alkali. 2. containing an alkali. —**al·ka·lin'i·ty** (-lin'ĭ-ti), *n.*

al·ka·lize (-līz), *v.t.* **-lized, -liz·ing,** to make alkaline. —**al·ka·li·za'tion** (-li-zä'shŭn), *n.*

al·ka·loid (-loid), *n.* any of several bitter organic substances, such as caffeine, morphine, or quinine, having alkaline properties, found in plants and, sometimes, animals: *adj.* resembling an alkali in its properties. also **al·ka·loid'al.**

al·ka·net (al'kä-net), *n.* 1. a plant with roots that yield a red dye. 2. the root of this plant. 3. the red dye.

al·kyd (al'kid), *n.* a synthetic resin used in varnishes, paints, or other protective coatings.

all (ôl), *adj.* 1. the whole quantity, duration, extent, or degree of. 2. the whole number of, as individuals or parts. 3. every one of. 4. any. 5. only: *n.* 1. the whole; total quantity or amount. 2. everything that one has: *pron.* 1. every bit. 2. every one: *adv.* 1. wholly; entirely; completely. 2. for each one.

Al·lah (al'ä, ä'lä), *n.* the Moslem name for God.

all-A·mer·i·can (ôl-ä-mer'ĭ-kän), *adj.* 1. made up completely of Americans. 2. chosen as the best in the U.S.

all-a·round (ôl'ä-round'), *adj.* able to do, or be used for, many things; versatile.

al·lay (ä-lā'), *v.t.* **-layed', -lay'ing,** 1. to quiet or calm; assuage. 2. to relieve or lessen, as pain or grief.

all-clear (ôl'klir'), *n.* a signal that an air raid or an alert is over.

al·le·ga·tion (al-ĕ-gä'shŭn), *n.* 1. the act of alleging. 2. an assertion; declaration. 3. an assertion made without proof. 4. in *Law,* a statement made in a case, that the person making the statement intends to prove.

al·lege (ä-lej'), *v.t.* **-leged', -leg'ing,** 1. to produce or adduce as argument, plea, or excuse. 2. to affirm; declare; assert.

al·leged (ä-lejd'), *adj.* so stated, but in doubt or without proof. —**al·leg·ed·ly** (ä-lej'id-li), *adv.*

al·le·giance (ä-lē'jäns), *n.* 1. the tie or obligation of a subject to his sovereign or government; fealty. 2. fidelity to a cause or person.

al·le·gor·i·cal (al-ĕ-gôr'ĭ-kl), **al·le·gor·ic** ('ik), *adj.* 1. of, pertaining to, or in the nature of allegory; figurative. 2. consisting of allegory. —**al·le·gor'i·cal·ly,** *adv.*

al·le·go·rist (al'ĕ-gô-rist), *n.* one who writes allegories. —**al·le·go·ris·tic** (al-ĕ-gô-ris'tik), *adj.*

ŏ in drag*o*n, ōō in cr*u*de, oo in w*oo*l, u in c*u*p, ū in c*u*re, û in t*u*rn, û in f*o*cus, oi in b*o*y, ou in h*ou*se, th in *th*in, *th* in shea*th*e, g in *g*et, j in *j*oy, y in *y*et.

al·le·go·rize (-gô·rīz), *v.t.* 1. to turn into allegory; treat allegorically. 2. to interpret in an allegorical sense: *v.i.* to make use of, or indulge in, allegory. —**al·le·go·ri·za'tion**, *n.*

al·le·go·ry (al'ê·gôr·i), *n., pl.* **-ries**, 1. a figurative way of treating a subject, as in a story, with the use of symbolic people, circumstances, etc. 2. a story in which the meaning is conveyed symbolically.

al·le·gret·to (al·ê·gret'ō), *adj. & adv.* in *Music*, moderately fast.

al·le·gro (â·leg'rō), *adj. & adv.* in *Music*, fast.

al·ler·gen (al'êr·jên), *n.* a substance which brings about an allergic reaction. —**al·ler·gen'ic** (-jen'ik), *adj.*

al·ler·gic (â·lûr'jik), *adj.* 1. having, pertaining to, or caused by an allergy. 2. unwilling or reluctant (*to*).

al·ler·gist (al'êr·jist), *n.* a doctor specializing in the treatment of allergies.

al·ler·gy (al'êr·ji), *n., pl.* **-gies**, 1. the state or condition of being abnormally sensitive to a substance or condition which, in similar amounts, does not affect others. 2. a great aversion; distaste.

al·le·vi·ate (â·lē'vi·āt), *v.t.* **-at·ed**, **-at·ing**, 1. to lighten; lessen; mitigate. 2. to reduce; decrease. —**al·le'vi·a·tor**, *n.* —**al·le'vi·a·to·ry** (-â·tôr·i). *adj.*

al·le·vi·a·tion (â·li·vi·ā'shùn), *n.* 1. the act of alleviating. 2. that which alleviates.

al·le·vi·a·tive (â·lē'vi·āt·ɪv), *adj.* tending to alleviate: *n.* that which alleviates.

al·ley (al'i), *n., pl.* **-leys**, 1. a narrow lane or passage, especially one between or behind buildings. 2. in *Bowling*, the long, narrow lane along which the balls are rolled.

al·ley·way (-wā), *n.* a narrow passage, as between buildings.

All Fools' Day, same as April Fools' Day.

all fours, 1. the hands and knees of a human being or all four limbs of an animal. 2. a card game based on four points or chances for scoring.

All·hal·lows (ôl·hal'ōz), *n.* [Archaic], same as All Saints' Day.

al·li·a·ceous (al·i·ā'shùs), *adj.* of or pertaining to the onion, garlic, or other strong-smelling plants of the lily family.

al·li·ance (â·lī'áns), *n.* 1. the state of being allied, as of families by marriage. 2. a union of nations or groups. 3. the agreement establishing this union. 4. the nations or groups constituting such a union.

al·lied (â·līd'), *adj.* 1. united; attached. 2. related or similar.

al·li·ga·tor (al'i·gāt·êr), *n.* 1. a large reptile similar to the crocodile, found in the United States and China. 2. a leather made from its hide.

alligator pear, same as avocado.

all-im·por·tant (ôl'im·pôr'tänt), *adj.* vital; necessary.

al·lit·er·ate (â·lit'ê·rāt), *v.i.* **-at·ed**, **-at·ing**, to use alliteration: *v.t.* to make alliterative.

al·lit·er·a·tion (â·lit·ê·rā'shùn), *n.* the repetition of the same initial letter in closely following words, or in words directly following each other.

al·lit·er·a·tive (â·lit'ê·rā·tiv), *adj.* of, pertaining to, or characterized by alliteration.

al·li·um (al'i·ûm), *n.* any of a number of bulb plants of the lily family, having a strong odor, as the garlic or onion.

al·lo·cate (al'ō·kāt), *v.t.* **-cat·ed**, **-cat·ing**, 1. to set aside for a specified use. 2. to assign or allot; distribute, as in equal or proportionate parts.

al·lo·ca·tion (al·ō·kā'shûn), *n.* 1. the act of allocating or assigning. 2. a thing or amount allocated; allotment or assignment.

al·lo·cu·tion (al·ō·kū'shûn), *n.* an address of a formal nature.

al·lo·di·al (â·lō'di·âl), *adj.* freehold; not feudal.

al·lo·di·um (-ûm), *n.* a freehold estate.

al·log·a·my (â·log'â·mi), *n.* fertilization of a flower by the pollen of another plant, another variety of plant, or another species; cross-fertilization. —**al·log'a·mous** (-mùs), *adj.*

al·lo·nym (al'ō·nim), *n.* a historical name adopted by a writer.

al·lo·path (al'ō·path), **al·lop·a·thist** (â·lop'â·thist), *n.* one who favors or practices allopathy.

al·lop·a·thy (â·lop'â·thi), *n.* treatment of disease by inducing effects opposite to those produced by the disease. —**al·lo·path·ic** (al·ō·path'ik), *adj.*

al·lot (â·lot'), *v.t.* **-lot'ted**, **-lot'ting**, 1. to distribute or divide, as by lot; apportion, as shares. 2. to assign or grant for a specific purpose.

al·lot·ment ('mênt), *n.* 1. the act of allotting. 2. that which is allotted.

al·lo·trope (al'ō·trōp), *n.* a form that is allotropic.

al·lo·trop·ic (al·ō·trop'ik), **al·lo·trop·i·cal** ('i·kl), *adj.* of, pertaining to, or characterized by allotropy. —**al·lo·trop'i·cal·ly**, *adv.*

al·lot·ro·py (al·lot'rō·pi), *n.* the property that certain chemical elements have of existing in different forms, each characterized by peculiar qualities, as the occurrence of carbon in the form of the diamond, charcoal, and graphite: also **al·lot'ro·pism** (-pizm).

al-out (ôl'out'), *adj.* total; complete.

al·low (â·lou'), *v.t.* 1. to admit; acknowledge. 2. to permit; let. 3. to let have. 4. to provide for: *v.i.* to make concession or provision (followed by *for*).

al·low·a·ble ('â·bl), *adj.* 1. that may be allowed; permissible. 2. lawful.

al·low·ance ('áns), *n.* 1. the act of allowing; admission; concession. 2. a definite sum granted, especially on a regular basis. 3. an abatement or deduction: *v.t.* **-anced**, **-anc·ing**, to put on an allowance; limit to a fixed expenditure or consumption.

al·low·ed·ly (â·lou'id·li), *adv.* by allowance or acknowledgment; admittedly.

al·loy (â·loi', al'oi), *v.t.* 1. to form a substance, as by fusion, of two or more metals. 2. to reduce in standard or quality by mixture, as with a metal of baser value: *n.* (usually al'oi). 1. a substance that is a compound of two or more metals. 2. something that lowers the quality of another thing when mixed with it. 3. formerly, a mixture of two metals of differing value.

---

a in *cap,* ā in *cane,* ä in *father,* â in *abet,* e in *met* ē in *be,* ê in *baker,* ê in *regent,* i in *pit,* ī in *fine,* ɪ in *manifest,* o in *hot,* ô in *horse,* ō in *bone,*

all right, 1. adequate; good enough. 2. not injured; safe. 3. correct.

all-round (ôl'round'), *adj.* same as **all-around.**

All Saints' Day, the church celebration on November 1 in honor of all the saints.

All Souls' Day, in some Christian churches, the day, usually November 2, of services in honor of the dead.

all-spice (ôl'spis), *n.* 1. the berry of a West Indian tree. 2. a spice with a flavor resembling a combination of other spices, made from this berry.

all-star ('stär), *adj.* composed of the very best performers.

all-time ('tīm), *adj.* not surpassed until the present day.

al-lude (ả-lōōd'), *v.i.* -lud'ed, -lud'ing, to refer indirectly or make an allusion (with *to*).

al-lure (ả-loor'), *v.t. & v.i.* -lured', -lur'ing, to tempt by the offer of something good; entice; attract: *n.* the ability to attract or charm.

al-lure-ment ('mẻnt), *n.* 1. the act of alluring. 2. that which allures.

al-lur-ing ('ing), *adj.* tempting; fascinating; tantalizing. —**al-lur'ing-ly,** *adv.*

al-lu-sion (ả-lōō'zhŭn), *n.* 1. an alluding. 2. a casual reference.

al-lu-sive (ả-lōōs'iv), *adj.* 1. having allusions, or indirect references, to something not definitely expressed. 2. having many allusions. —**al-lu'sive-ly,** *adv.* —**al-lu'sive-ness,** *n.*

al-lu-vi-al (ả-lōō'vĩ-ȧl), *adj.* of, pertaining to, or composed of alluvium.

al-lu-vi-on (-ȧn), *n.* same as **alluvium.**

al-lu-vi-um (-ŭm), *n., pl.* -vi-ums, -vi-a ('vi-ȧ), sand, clay, etc. deposited by the action of moving water, as along a river or shore.

al-ly (ả-lī', al'ī), *v.t.* -lied', -ly'ing, 1. to unite by marriage, treaty, league, or confederacy. 2. to bind, connect, or relate by resemblance: *v.i.* to become allied: *n., pl.* -lies (usually al'ī), one united, related, or associated with another.

al-ma ma-ter (al'mȧ mät'ẽr), 1. the school or college in which one has been educated. 2. the official song of a school or college.

al-ma-nac (ôl'mȧ-nak), *n.* 1. a calendar giving astronomical data, tide tables, etc. 2. a reference book, published yearly, containing varied information.

al-might-y (ôl-mīt'ĩ), *adj.* possessing all power; omnipotent: *n.* [A-], God (used with *the*).

al-mond (ä'mŏnd, am'ŏnd), *n.* 1. the edible, nutlike kernel of a fruit like the peach. 2. the small tree which yields this fruit. 3. anything resembling the almond in shape: *adj.* resembling the almond in shape; oval, with pointed ends.

al-mon-er (al'mŏn-ẽr), *n.* one who dispenses or distributes alms or charity.

al-most (ôl'mōst), *adv.* nearly; very nearly; all but.

alms (ämz), *n., pl.* alms, a gift or gifts to relieve the poor; charity; assistance. —**alms'-giv-er** ('giv'ẽr), *n.*

alms-house ('hous), *n.* 1. formerly, a poorhouse. 2. in England, a house endowed by private charity for the use of the aged and disabled poor.

al-oe (al'ō), *n., pl.* -oes, 1. any of a large group of plants of the lily family, native to southern Africa, with clusters of red or yellow flowers. 2. *pl.* a laxative drug obtained from the juice of the leaves of several species of aloe.

a-loft (ả-lôft'), *adv.* 1. on high; far above the earth. 2. at the masthead of a ship. 3. moving through the air; flying.

a-lo-ha (ả-lō'ȧ), *n. & interj.* greetings or farewell.

a-lone (ả-lōn'), *adj. & adv.* 1. apart from another; single or singly. 2. only; solely. 3. without any other person. 4. without equal.

a-long (ả-lông'), *prep.* 1. by the length; in a line parallel with the length. 2. in agreement with: *adv.* 1. lengthwise. 2. onward. 3. as a companion. 4. with one.

a-long-shore ('shôr'), *adv.* along the shore.

a-long-side ('sīd'), *adv.* at or by the side; side by side: *prep.* by the side of; side by side with.

a-loof (ả-lōōf'), *adv.* at a moderate distance but within sight: *adj.* 1. at a distance. 2. purposely withdrawn in sympathy, feelings, etc.; removed in manner. —**a-loof'ly,** *adv.* —**a-loof'ness,** *n.*

a-lo-pe-ci-a (al-ō-pēsh'i-ȧ), *n.* baldness; loss of hair.

a-loud (ả-loud'), *adv.* 1. with raised voice; loudly. 2. audibly.

alp (alp), *n.* a high mountain.

al-pac-a (al-pak'ȧ), *n., pl.* -pac'as, -pac'a, 1. a mammal of South America, closely allied to the llama. 2. the wool of this animal. 3. cloth woven from this wool.

al-pen-glow (al'pẻn-glō), *n.* a reddish glow on mountains, seen just before sunrise and after sunset.

al-pen-horn (-hôrn), *n.* a long, curved horn emitting a loud sound, used by the herdsmen of the Swiss Alps.

al-pen-stock (-stok), *n.* a staff with an iron spike, used by mountain climbers.

al-pha (al'fȧ), *n.* 1. the first letter of the Greek alphabet. 2. the beginning.

al-pha-bet (al'fȧ-bet), *n.* 1. the letters of a language arranged in the customary order. 2. the rudiments of any branch of knowledge: *v.t.* -bet-ed, -bet-ing, to arrange in alphabetical order.

al-pha-bet-i-cal (al-fȧ-bet'ĩ-kl), **al-pha-bet-ic** ('ik), *adj.* 1. of or pertaining to an alphabet. 2. in the order of the alphabet. —**al-pha-bet'i-cal-ly,** *adv.*

al-pha-bet-ize (al'fȧ-bẻ-tīz), *v.t.* -ized, -iz-ing, to arrange in alphabetical order.

alpha particle, a positively charged particle emitted by some radioactive materials.

alpha ray, 1. same as **alpha particle.** 2. a stream of alpha particles.

alp-horn (alp'hôrn), *n.* same as **alpenhorn.**

al-read-y (ôl-red'ĩ), *adv.* by, at, or before a specified time.

al-so (ôl'sō), *adv.* likewise; in addition.

al-tar (ôl'tẽr), *n.* 1. a raised structure for offering sacrifices to a god, burning incense, etc. 2. a table or stand used for sacred purposes during religious service.

altar boy, an acolyte: attendant who helps a

clergyman, especially a priest, at a religious service.

al·tar·piece (-pēs), *n.* a decorative screen, carving, etc. behind an altar.

alt·az·i·muth (alt-az'l-mûth), *n.* an instrument for determining the altitude and azimuth of a heavenly body.

al·ter (ôl'tēr), *v.t.* 1. to effect some change in; modify or vary. 2. to castrate or spay: *v.i.* to become different.

al·ter·a·ble (-à-bl), *adj.* capable of being changed.

al·ter·ant (-ânt), *adj.* producing or effecting change: *n.* 1. that which produces change. 2. a substance used in dyeing to change or modify a color.

al·ter·a·tion (ôl-tē-rā'shûn), *n.* 1. the act of altering or changing. 2. the change or modification effected.

al·ter·a·tive (ôl'tē-rāt-iv), *adj.* producing alteration or having the tendency to alter: *n.* a medicine which restores health.

al·ter·cate (ôl'tēr-kāt), *v.i.* -cat·ed, -cat·ing. to contend verbally; wrangle; dispute angrily.

al·ter·ca·tion (ôl-tēr-kā'shûn), *n.* the act of wrangling; angry verbal contention; dispute.

al·ter e·go (ôl'tēr ē'gō), 1. a second self. 2. a very close friend.

al·ter·nant (ôl'tēr-nânt), *adj.* alternating.

al·ter·nate (ôl'tēr-nāt), *v.i.* -nat·ed, -nat·ing. 1. to perform by turns. 2. to cause to succeed by turns: *v.i.* 1. to take place by turns (followed by *with*). 2. to take turns. 3. in *Electricity*, to periodically flow in the opposite direction: *n.* (-nit), a substitute: *adj.* (-nit), 1. following each other in succession. 2. every other. 3. in *Botany*, succeeding each other by turns on opposite sides of a stem. —**al'ter·nate·ly,** *adv.*

alternate angles, the internal angles on opposite sides and at opposite ends of a line crossing two other lines.

alternating current, an electric current that periodically reverses its direction.

al·ter·na·tion (ôl-tēr-nā'shûn), *n.* 1. the act of alternating; reciprocal succession. 2. the state of being alternate.

al·ter·na·tive (ôl-tûr'nà-tiv), *adj.* giving or being a choice of two things: *n.* 1. the option or choice of two possibilities, so that if one is rejected the other must be accepted. 2. either of the possibilities. 3. another option. —**al'ter'na·tive·ly,** *adv.*

al·ter·nat·or (ôl'tēr-nāt-ēr), *n.* an electric dynamo or generator that produces alternating current.

al·the·a, al·thae·a (al-thē'à), *n.* 1. any of a number of plants with tall spikes of showy flowers, as the hollyhock. 2. same as rose of Sharon.

alt·horn (alt'hôrn), *n.* an alto saxhorn, often used in military bands: also alto horn.

al·though (ôl-thō'), *conj.* granting that; though; even if; notwithstanding.

al·tim·e·ter (al-tim'ē-tēr), *n.* an instrument for measuring altitudes.

al·tim·e·try (-tri), *n.* the measuring of altitudes by the use of the altimeter.

al·ti·tude (al'ti-tōōd), *n.* 1. height of a thing,

especially above the earth's surface. 2. a high place, point, or degree. 3. the elevation of a celestial body above the horizon. 4. the perpendicular distance from the base of a figure to its highest point or to the side parallel to the base.

al·ti·tu·di·nal (al-ti-tōōd'n-âl), *adj.* of or pertaining to altitude.

al·to (al'tō), *n., pl.* -tos, 1. the lowest female singing voice. 2. the range of such a voice. 3. an instrument with the second highest range within a family of instruments: *adj.* having or for the range of an alto.

al·to·geth·er (ôl-tō-geth'ēr), *adv.* 1. wholly; completely; without exception. 2. all being counted. 3. everything being considered.

al·to·re·lie·vo (al'tō-ri-lē'vō), *n., pl.* -vos, high relief; relief in which the figures or forms stand out boldly from the background.

al·tru·ism (al'trŏŏ-izm), *n.* 1. the ethical doctrine which advocates the sacrifice of self in the interests of others or society: opposed to *egoism.* 2. unselfish behavior and concerns.

al·tru·ist (-ist), *n.* one who advocates or practices altruism.

al·tru·is·tic (al-trŏŏ-is'tik), *adj.* of, pertaining to, or following the principle of altruism. —**al·tru·is'ti·cal·ly,** *adv.*

al·um (al'ûm), *n.* a hydrated double sulfate of a trivalent metal, as aluminum, and a univalent metal, as potassium.

a·lu·mi·na (a-lōō'mi-nà), *n.* an oxide of aluminum: constituent of common clay and bauxite.

a·lu·mi·nate (-nāt), *n.* a salt of aluminum reacting as an acid in an alkaline solution.

al·u·min·i·um (al-yoo-min'yûm), *n.* British form for aluminum.

a·lu·mi·nous (à-lōō'mī-nûs), *adj.* of, pertaining to, or containing alum, alumina, or aluminum.

a·lu·mi·num (à-lōō'mi-nûm), *n.* a bluish-white, lightweight, ductile, malleable metal: one of the chemical elements.

a·lum·na (à-lum'nà), *n., pl.* -nae ('nē), a woman who is a graduate or a former pupil of a school, college, or university.

a·lum·nus ('nûs), *n., pl.* -ni ('nī), a person, especially a man, who is a graduate or a former pupil of a school, college, or university.

al·um·root (al'ûm-rŏŏt), *n.* a North American plant of the saxifrage family, with an astringent root.

al·ve·o·lar (al-vē'ō-lēr), *adj.* 1. relating to that part of the jaw that contains the sockets of the teeth. 2. like a socket or cavity.

al·ve·o·late (-lit), **al·ve·o·lat·ed** (-lāt-id), *adj.* full of small hollows or depressions.

al·vine (al'vin), *adj.* of or pertaining to the abdomen.

al·ways (ôl'wiz, 'wāz), *adv.* 1. constantly; ever. 2. continually. 3. at any time. 4. with no exception.

a·lys·sum (à-lis'ûm), *n.* 1. a plant of the mustard family,' with white or yellow flowers. 2. same as sweet alyssum.

Alz·hei·mer's disease (älts'hī-mērz), a degenerative brain disease.

am (am), first person singular, present indicative, of be.

am·a·da·vat (am-à-dà-vat'), *n.* a singing bird of India.

a·mah (ä'mà), *n.* in the Far East, a woman servant, particularly one who works as a baby's nurse.

a·main (à-mān'), *adv.* [Poetic], 1. with force or violence. 2. suddenly.

a·mal·gam (à-mal'gàm), *n.* 1. any metallic alloy of which mercury is a constituent. 2. a mixture or compound.

a·mal·gam·a·ble ('gàm-à-bl), *adj.* capable of being amalgamated.

a·mal·gam·ate ('gà-māt), *v.t. & v.i.* -mat·ed, -mat·ing, 1. to alloy mercury with another metal. 2. to combine; unite; join together.

a·mal·gam·a·tion (à-mal-gà-mā'shŭn), *n.* 1. the act or process of compounding mercury with another metal. 2. the separation of a precious metal from its ore by means of alloying it with mercury. 3. the blending or mixing of different elements or things. 4. the union or consolidation of two or more companies or businesses into one concern.

a·mal·gam·a·tor (à-mal'gà-māt-ēr), *n.* 1. one who or that which amalgamates. 2. a machine for the amalgamation of a precious metal.

a·man·u·en·sis (à-man-yoo-wen'sis), *n., pl.* -ses ('sēz), one who is employed to take dictation or perform other writing tasks at the direction of another; secretary.

am·a·ranth (am'à-ranth), *n.* 1. any of a number of plants with brightly colored leaves and, sometimes, showy flowers. 2. [Poetic], an imaginary, unfading flower. 3. magenta; purplish red.

am·a·ran·thine (am-à-ran'thin), *adj.* 1. of or pertaining to the amaranth. 2. unfading. 3. purplish red.

am·a·ryl·lis (am-à-ril'is), *n.* any of a number of bulbous plants with lilylike flowers of white, pink, red, or purple.

a·mass (à-mas'), *v.t.* 1. to collect into a heap. 2. to gather together in great quantity or amount; accumulate. —a·mass'er, *n.*

a·mass·ment ('mĕnt), *n.* 1. the act of amassing. 2. a heap or accumulation. 3. a great quantity or number.

am·a·teur (am'à-chēr, -tēr), *n.* 1. one who cultivates an art, engages in a sport, or studies a subject for interest or pleasure and without reference to money. 2. one who lacks the skill of a professional: *adj.* of or performed by amateurs. —a·mateur·ism, *n.*

am·a·teur·ish (am-à-choor'ish, -toor'ish), *adj.* like the work of an amateur; shallow; unskilled; clumsy. —am·a·teur'ish·ly, *adv.* —am·a·teur'ish·ness, *n.*

A·ma·ti (à-mät'i), *n.* a violin constructed by one of the Amati family of Cremona, Italy.

am·a·tive (am'à-tiv), *adj.* amorous; of love or sexual desire. —am'a·tive·ly, *adv.* —am'a·tive·ness, *n.*

am·a·to·ry (-tôr-i), *adj.* relating to or showing sexual love.

am·au·ro·sis (am-ô-rō'sis), *n.* partial or complete loss of sight.

am·au·rot·ic (-rät'ik), *adj.* relating to, or affected with, amaurosis.

a·maze (à-māz'), *v.t.* a·mazed', a·maz'ing, to confound or stun with surprise or wonder; astonish: *n.* [Poetic], astonishment. —a·maz'ed·ly ('id-li), *adv.* —a·maz'ing, *adj.* —a·maz'ing·ly, *adv.*

a·maze·ment ('mĕnt), *n.* the state of being amazed; astonishment.

Am·a·zon (am'à-zon), *n.* 1. any of a fabled race of female warriors of ancient Scythia, near the Black Sea. 2. [a-], a strong, masculine woman. 3. a kind of parrot.

Am·a·zo·ni·an (am-à-zō'ni-àn), *adj.* 1. of, like, or pertaining to an Amazon. 2. [often a-], masculine and warlike: said of a woman. 3. of the Amazon River of northern South America.

am·bage (am'bij), *n.* [Archaic], a winding path.

am·ba·ry (am-bä'ri), *n.* same as kenaf.

am·bas·sa·dor (am-bas'à-dēr), *n.* 1. the highest-ranking diplomatic official of a government or state representing it in another country. 2. a representative or agent of another charged with a special mission. —am·bas'sa·dor·ship, *n.*

ambassador extraordinary, an ambassador sent on a special mission.

am·bas·sa·do·ri·al (am-bas-à-dôr'i-àl), *adj.* of or belonging to an ambassador or to his office.

ambassador plenipotentiary, an ambassador with power to make a treaty.

am·bas·sa·dress (am-bas'à-dris), *n.* [Rare], 1. the wife of an ambassador. 2. a woman ambassador.

am·ber (am'bēr), *n.* 1. a yellowish or brownish-yellow fossil resin found on or near some seashores: used especially in jewelry. 2. the color of amber: *adj.* 1. made of amber. 2. with the color of amber.

am·ber·gris (-grēs, -gris), *n.* a waxy material from the intestines of the sperm whale, usually found floating in tropical seas: used in perfumery.

am·bi·ance, am·bi·ence (am'bi-àns), *n.* social or cultural surroundings; milieu.

am·bi·dex·ter (am-bi-dek'stēr), *adj.* [Archaic], same as ambidextrous: *n.* [Archaic], a person who is ambidextrous.

am·bi·dex·trous (-'strŭs), *adj.* 1. able to use both hands equally well. 2. very expert or having many talents. 3. double-dealing. —am·bi·dex·ter'i·ty (-dek·ster'i-ti), *n.*

am·bi·ent (am'bi-ĕnt), *adj.* surrounding; encompassing.

am·bi·gu·i·ty (am-bi-gū'i-ti), *n.* 1. the state of being ambiguous. 2. *pl.* -ties, that which is ambiguous, as a statement or expression.

am·big·u·ous (am-big'yoo-wŭs), *adj.* 1. having a double meaning. 2. vague; dubious; uncertain. —am·big'u·ous·ly, *adv.*

am·bit (am'bit), *n.* 1. a circuit or compass. 2. the line or lines by which a figure is bounded; perimeter.

am·bi·tion (am-bi'shŭn), *n.* 1. a strong desire to achieve some object or purpose, as to gain power, wealth, or fame. 2. the desired object or purpose.

ô in dragon, ōō in crude, oo in wool, u in cup, ū in cure, ū in turn, ů in focus, oi in boy, ou in house, th in thin, th in sheathe, g in get, j in joy, y in yet.

am-bi-tious ('shŭs), *adj.* 1. of or having ambition. 2. making great demands in terms of work, initiative, etc. —**am-bi'tious-ly**, *adv.*

am-biv-a-lence (am-biv'ă-lĕns), *n.* a mixture of feelings, as love and hate, for a person or thing. —**am-biv'a-lent**, *adj.*

am-ble (am'bl), *v.i.* -bled, -bling, 1. to move along easily by lifting the two feet on one side together and then the two feet on the other side, as a horse. 2. to walk leisurely: *n.* an easy pace or gait. —**am'bler**, *n.*

am-bly-o-pi-a (am-bli-ōp'i-ă), *n.* dimness of vision.

Am-boi-na, or **Am-boy-na wood** (am-boi'nă), the mottled and curled wood of a tree of the Orient: used in furniture.

am-bro-sia (am-brō'zhă), *n.* 1. the fabled food of the gods. 2. anything exquisitely pleasing to taste or smell. 3. any of a genus of plants of the ragweed family.

am-bro-sial ('zhal), **am-bro-sian** ('shăn), *adj.* 1. fit for the gods; divine. 2. like ambrosia; delicious or fragrant.

am-bro-type (am'brō-tīp), *n.* an early type of photograph taken on glass, with the dark parts showing as a background through the glass.

am-bry (am'bri), *n., pl.* -bries, [Archaic], a cupboard or pantry.

am-bu-lance (am'byŭ-lăns), *n.* 1. originally, a field hospital. 2. an automobile or other vehicle for transporting the sick and wounded.

am-bu-lant (-lănt), *adj.* walking; moving about.

am-bu-late (-lāt), *v.i.* -lat-ed, -lat-ing, to walk; move about.

am-bu-la-tion (am-byŭ-lā'shŭn), *n.* the act of walking about.

am-bu-la-to-ry (am'byŭ-lă-tôr-i), *adj.* 1. of or pertaining to walking. 2. able to walk. 3. movable. 4. in *Law*, changeable; temporary: *n., pl.* -ries, a covered place for walking.

am-bus-cade (am'bŭs-kād', am'bŭs-kād), *n.* & *v.i.* -cad'ed, -cad'ing, same as ambush.

am-bush (am'boosh), *n.* 1. a lying in wait to attack by surprise. 2. the persons lying in wait. 3. the hidden place of waiting: *v.t.* & *v.i.* 1. to hide in ambush. 2. to attack from ambush.

a-meer (ă-mēr'), *n.* same as amir.

a-mel-io-ra-ble (ă-mēl'yŏr-ă-bl), *adj.* capable of amelioration, or improvement.

a-mel-io-rate (ă-mēl'yŏ-rāt), *v.t.* & *v.i.* -rat-ed, -rat-ing, to grow or make better; improve. —**a-mel'io-ra-tor**, *n.*

a-mel-io-ra-tion (ă-mil-yŏ-rā'shŭn), *n.* a making or growing better; improvement.

a-mel-io-ra-tive (ă-mēl'yŏ-rāt-iv), *adj.* tending to ameliorate, or make better.

a-men (ā'men, ä'-), *adv.* [Archaic], verily: *interj.* may it be so!

a-me-na-ble (ă-mē'nă-bl), *adj.* 1. liable; responsible. 2. able to be controlled or led; submissive. —**a-me-na-bil'i-ty** (-bil'i-ti), **a** —**a-me'na-bly**, *adv.*

a-mend (ă-mend'), *v.t.* 1. to free from fault; correct. 2. to improve. 3. to change (a law, bill, etc.). —**a-mend'a-ble**, *adj.*

a-mend-a-to-ry (ă-men'dă-tôr-i), *adj.* tending to amend.

a-mend-ment (ă-mend'mĕnt), *n.* 1. a removal of faults; correction. 2. an improvement. 3. an alteration made or proposed in a bill, law, etc. 4. the process of making such an alteration.

a-mends (ă-mendz'), *n.* compensation for loss or injury; reparation.

a-men-i-ty (ă-men'i-ti), *n., pl.* -ties, 1. pleasantness, as of climate or demeanor. 2. something providing comfort; convenience. 3. *pl.* polite social acts; courtesies.

a-men-or-rhe-a, **a-men-or-rhoe-a** (ă-men-ô-rē'ă), *n.* abnormal absence or partial absence of menstruation.

a-merce (ă-mûrs'), *v.t.* **a-merced'**, **a-merc'ing**, to punish, especially by requiring the payment of an arbitrary fine. —**a-merce'ment**, *n.*

A-mer-i-can (ă-mer'i-kăn), *adj.* 1. of or in North America or South America. 2. in, belonging to, or characteristic of the U.S. or its people: *n.* 1. a native or citizen of the U.S. 2. the English language spoken in the U.S.

A-mer-i-ca-na (ă-mer-i-kan'ă), *n.* a collection of things American, as literary, scientific, and historical papers, pieces of information, art, etc.

American Indian, 1. any of the aboriginal peoples of North America and South America. 2. any of the languages of these peoples.

A-mer-i-can-ism (ă-mer'i-kăn-izm), *n.* 1. a form of expression or a custom or belief peculiar to the U.S. 2. devotion to the U.S.

A-mer-i-can-ize (-kă-nīz), *v.t.* & *v.i.* -ized, -iz-ing, to render or become American; assimilate to the customs and institutions of the U.S. —**A-mer-i-can-i-za'tion**, *n.*

am-er-ic-i-um (ă-mē-rish'i-ŭm), *n.* a chemical element produced by the nuclear bombardment of plutonium.

am-e-thyst (ă-mē'thist), *n.* 1. a violet or purple variety of quartz or corundum. 2. violet or purple.

am-e-thys-tine (am-ē-this'tin), *adj.* containing, composed of, or colored like amethyst.

am-e-tro-pi-a (am-ē-trōp'i-ă), *n.* any condition of the eye which causes distorted or imperfect refraction. —**am-e-tro'pic** (-trō'pik), *adj.*

a-mi-a-ble (ā'mi-ă-bl), *adj.* 1. friendly; genial; good-natured. 2. [Obs.], lovable. —**a-mi-a-bil'i-ty** (-bil'i-ti), *n.* —**a'mi-a-bly**, *adv.*

am-i-an-thus (am-i-an'thŭs), *n.* a fine kind of asbestos.

am-i-ca-ble (am'i-kă-bl), *adj.* friendly; peaceable. —**am-i-ca-bil'i-ty** (-bil'i-ti), *n.* —**am'i-ca-bly**, *adv.*

am-ice (am'is), *n.* a white linen cloth worn around the neck and shoulders by a priest at Mass.

a-mid (ă-mid'), *prep.* in the middle of; among.

am-ide (am'id), *n.* an organic compound derived from ammonia. —**a-mid-ic** (ă-mid'ik), *adj.*

am-i-din (am'i-din), *n.* the soluble substance made by heating starch in water.

am-i-dol (am'i-dōl), *n.* a colorless crystalline compound used as a photographic developer.

---

a in cap, ā in cane, ä in father, å in abet, e in met ē in be, ĕ in baker, ĕ in regent, i in pit, ī in fine, í in manifest, o in hot, ô in horse, ō in bone,

a-mid-ships (ă-mid'ships). *adv.* in the middle of a ship: also **a-mid'ship**.

a-midst (ă-midst'). *prep.* same as amid.

a-mi-go (ă-mē'gō), *n.*, *pl.* -gos ('gōz), [Spanish], a friend.

a-mine (ă-mēn'), *n.* a compound derived from ammonia. —**a-mi'nic** (-mē'nik), *adj.*

a-mi-no acid (ă-mē'nō), any of a group of organic compounds containing nitrogen, found in the proteins.

a-mir (ă-mēr'), *n.* a prince, governor, or commander in some Moslem countries.

Am-ish (ä'mish), *n.* members of a sect of Mennonites.

a-miss (ă-mis'), *adj.* wrong; faulty: *adv.* wrongly; faultily.

am-i-ty (am'ĭ-ti), *n.*, *pl.* -ties, friendly relations; friendship.

am-mo-nia (ă-mōn'yă), *n.* 1. a transparent, pungent, volatile gas, composed of hydrogen and nitrogen: used in medicine, in fertilizers, etc. 2. this gas in a water solution.

am-mo-ni-ac (ă-mō'ni-ak), *n.* a gum resin obtained from an Asian plant.

am-mo-nite (am'ō-nīt), *n.* the fossil shell of an extinct mollusk, shaped like a ram's horn.

am-mo-ni-um (ă-mō'ni-ŭm), *n.* a radical the compounds of which resemble those of the alkali metals, found in salts produced by the reaction of ammonia with an acid.

ammonium chloride, a white, crystalline compound of ammonia and hydrochloric acid: also **sal ammoniac**.

ammonium hydroxide, an alkali created by dissolving ammonia in water.

ammonium nitrate, a crystalline salt formed by the combination of ammonia with nitric acid, used in explosives and as a fertilizer.

ammonium sulfate, an ammonium salt, used in making fertilizers and in treating water.

am-mo-no (am'ō-nō), *adj.* of, containing, or derived from, ammonia.

am-mu-ni-tion (am-yŭ-nish'ŭn), *n.* 1. anything ejected from or detonated by a weapon, as bullets, bombs, torpedoes, etc. 2. any material used in attack or defense.

am-ne-sia (am-nē'zhă), *n.* loss of memory from shock, brain injury, etc. —**am-ne'si-ac** ('zē-ak), **am-ne'sic** ('sik, 'zik), *adj.* & *n.*

am-nes-ty (am'nĕs-ti), *n.*, *pl.* -ties, 1. a general pardon. 2. a pardon for political offenses: *v.t.* -tied, -ty-ing, to grant pardon to.

am-ni-on (am'ni-ŏn), *n.*, *pl.* -ni-ons, -ni-a (-ă), the thin, innermost membrane surrounding the embryo of a mammal, bird, or reptile.

a-moe-ba (ă-mē'bă), *n.*, *pl.* -bas, -bae ('bē), a microscopic, one-celled animal found in stagnant water. —**a-moe'bic** ('bik), *adj.*

a-mok (ă-muk'), *adj.* & *adv.* in a frenzy or violent rage.

a-mong (ă-mung'), *prep.* 1. in the middle of; surrounded by. 2. in the class or group of. 3. with a number of. 4. with something for each of. 5. with one another. Also **a-mongst** (ă-mungst').

a-mor-al (ā-môr'ăl), *adj.* 1. neither moral nor immoral. 2. not able to tell right from wrong. —**a-mor-al-i-ty** (ā-mō-ral'ĭ-ti), *n.* —**a-mor'al-ly**, *adv.*

am-o-rist (am'ĕr-ist), *n.* a lover; one inclined to be involved in love affairs.

am-o-rous (am'ĕr-ŭs), *adj.* 1. loving. 2. inclined to make love. 3. of or pertaining to sexual love. —**am'o-rous-ly**, *adv.* —**am'o-rous-ness**, *n.*

a-mor-phism (ă-môr'fizm), *n.* 1. a lack of regular or definite form. 2. in *Chemistry*, a lack of crystalline structure.

a-mor-phous ('fŭs), *adj.* 1. formless: irregularly shaped. 2. anomalous. 3. unorganized. 4. without a crystalline form. —**a-mor'phous-ly**, *adv.* —**a-mor'phous-ness**, *n.*

am-or-tize (am'ĕr-tīz, ă-môr'-), *v.t.* -tized, -tiz-ing, 1. to put money aside, as in a sinking fund, for a future payment, as a debt. 2. to prorate (expenditures) over a period of time. —**am-or-ti'za'tion** (-ti-zā'shŭn), *n.*

A-mos (ā'mŏs), *n.* a book of the Bible.

a-mount (ă-mount'), *v.i.* 1. to mount up; total. 2. to be equivalent or equal to: *n.* 1. a sum. 2. the whole of something; totality. 3. a quantity.

a-mour (ă-moor'), *n.* a love affair.

am-pe-lop-sis (am-pĕ-lop'sis), *n.* an ornamental vine or shrub of the grape family.

am-per-age (am'pĕr-ij), *n.* the strength of an electric current.

am-pere (am'pir), *n.* a unit for measuring the strength of an electric current.

am-per-sand (am'pĕr-sand), *n.* a sign (&) that stands for the word *and*.

am-phet-a-mine (am-fet'ă-mēn, -min), *n.* a drug used to suppress the appetite and as an antidepressant.

am-phib-i-an (am-fib'i-ăn), *n.* 1. any of a class of coldblooded vertebrates, as frogs and salamanders, which breathe by gills in their early state and later develop lungs. 2. a plant or animal that is amphibious. 3. an aircraft that can take off from or descend on either land or water. 4. any vehicle that can travel on either land or water.

am-phib-i-ous (-ŭs), *adj.* 1. being able to live both on land and in water. 2. that can function or move on both land and water. —**am-phib'i-ous-ly**, *adv.*

am-phi-bol-o-gy (am-fi-bol'ō-ji), *n.*, *pl.* -gies, 1. an expression or grammatical construction with more than one possible interpretation; ambiguity. 2. an ambiguous phrase or sentence. Also **am-phib'o-ly** (-fib'ō-li), *pl.* -lies.

am-phi-go-ry (am'fi-gôr-i), *n.*, *pl.* -ries, a nonsense composition; burlesque.

am-phi-ox-is (am-fi-ok'sŭs), *n.* the lancelet.

am-phi-the-a-ter, **am-phi-the-a-tre** (am'fi-thē-ă-tĕr), *n.* 1. a theater with seats all around a central, open space. 2. an arena. 3. a flat area encompassed by rising land. —**am-phi-the-at-ric** (am-fi-thi-at'rik), *adj.*

am-pho-ra (am'fĕr-ă), *n.*, *pl.* -rae (-ē), -ras, among the ancient Greeks and Romans, an oblong jar with two handles.

am-ple (am'pl), *adj.* 1. large. 2. abundant. 3. adequate. —**am'ple-ness**, *n.*

am-pli-a-tion (am-pli-ā'shŭn), *n.* [Archaic], an enlargement.

am-pli-fi-ca-tion (am-pli-fi-kā'shŭn), *n.* 1. the act of amplifying or expanding; enlargement. 2. particulars, examples, etc. added to amplify something, as a statement.

ŏ in dragon, ōō in crude, ǒǒ in wool, u in cup, ū in cure. û in turn, ů in focus, oi in boy, ou in house, th in thin, th in sheathe, g in get, j in joy. y in yet.

am·pli·fi·er (am'pli-fī-ēr), *n.* 1. that which amplifies. 2. in *Electronics*, a device for increasing the strength of electrical signals.

am·pli·fy (am'pli-fī), *v.t.* -fied, -fy·ing, 1. to make large or larger; expand. 2. to explain more fully, as a report or statement, by adding particulars, examples, etc. 3. to use an electronic device to increase the strength of (an electrical signal): *v.i.* to speak or write with elaboration or diffuseness.

am·pli·tude (am'pli-tōōd), *n.* 1. largeness. 2. fullness. 3. scope. 4. the angular distance of a celestial body at rising or setting from the eastern or western points of the horizon. 5. the range of something that fluctuates, as an alternating current or a vibration, measured from its average or mean to its extreme.

amplitude modulation, the changing of the amplitude of a radio wave being transmitted in relationship to the signal being broadcast.

am·ply (am'pli), *adv.* in an ample manner; liberally.

am·pul (am'pool), *n.* a glass container for a single dose of a medicine for hypodermic injection: also **am'pule** ('pyool), **am'poule** ('pōōl).

am·pul·la (am-pul'ä), *n.*, *pl.* -**pul'lae** ('ē), 1. a round, two-handled jar of the ancient Greeks and Romans. 2. a vessel for consecrated oil or wine used in church rites.

am·pu·tate (am'pyū-tāt), *v.t.* -tat·ed, -tat·ing, to cut off (an arm, leg, etc.). —**am'pu·ta·tor,** *n.*

am·pu·ta·tion (am-pyū-tā'shun), *n.* a cutting off; especially, the surgical operation of cutting off an arm or a leg.

am·pu·tee (-tē'), *n.* one who has had a limb or limbs amputated.

a·muck (ä-muk'), *adj. & adv.* same as **amok**.

am·u·let (am'yū-lit), *n.* a charm worn to protect against evil; talisman.

a·muse (ä-mūz'), *v.t.* **a·mused', a·mus'ing,** 1. to occupy pleasantly; entertain. 2. to make laugh or smile. 3. [Obs.], to divert. —**a·mus'a·ble,** *adj.*

a·muse·ment ('mènt), *n.* 1. a being amused. 2. that which amuses; pastime.

amusement park, an outdoor recreation area with devices for entertainment, as merry-go-rounds, and places for refreshment.

a·myg·da·la (ä-mig'dä-lä), *n., pl.* -**lae** (-lē), in *Anatomy,* an almond-shaped formation, as a tonsil.

a·myg·da·lin (ä-mig'dä-lin), *n.* a white crystalline substance obtained from bitter almonds.

am·yl·ase (am'i-lās), *n.* an enzyme contained in saliva and pancreatic juice, which helps to convert starch into sugar.

an (än, an), *adj. & indef. art.* 1. one. 2. any. 3. to, in, or for each.

a·nab·a·sis (ä-nab'ä-sis), *n., pl.* -**ses** (-sēz), a large military advance.

a·nab·o·lism (ä-nab'o-lizm), *n.* the process by which food is converted into living tissue within an organism. —**an·a·bol·ic** (an-ä-bol'-ik), *adj.*

a·nach·ro·nism (ä-nak'rö-nizm), *n.* any person or event existing or occurring at a point in time not consistent with history.

a·nach·ro·nis·tic (ä-nak-rö-nis'tik), *adj.* containing or involving an anachronism.

an·a·con·da (an-ä-kon'dä), *n.* 1. a large South American boa. 2. any large snake which crushes its prey.

a·nad·ro·mous (ä-nad'rö-mus), *adj.* ascending from sea to rivers to spawn, as the salmon.

a·nae·mi·a (ä-nē'mi-ä), *n.* same as **anemia**. —**a·nae'mic,** *adj.*

an·aer·o·bic (an-er-ō'bik), *adj.* able to live on oxygen from decomposing compounds, rather than on air or free oxygen, as some bacteria.

an·aes·the·sia (an-ès-thē'zhä), *n.* same as **anesthesia**. —**an·aes·thet'ic** (-thet'ik), *adj. & n.* —**an·aes·the·tist** (ä-nes'thē-tist), *n.* —**an·aes'the·tize** (-tīz), *v.t.* -**tized, -tiz·ing.**

an·a·glyph (an'ä-glif), *n.* an ornament carved in relief.

an·a·gram (an'ä-gram), *n.* 1. a word, or a sentence, constructed from another by the transposition of its letters. 2. *pl.* a game in which words are constructed by rearranging the letters of other words.

an·a·gram·mat·ic (an-ä-grä-mat'ik), **an·a·gram·mat·i·cal** ('i-kl), *adj.* relating to or forming an anagram. —**an·a·gram·mat'i·cal·ly,** *adv.*

an·a·gram·ma·tize (-gram'ä-tīz), *v.t.* -**tized, -tiz·ing,** to make into an anagram.

a·nal (ä'nl), *adj.* of or near the anus. —**a'nal·ly,** *adv.*

an·a·lects (an'ä-lekts), *n.* a collection of passages or extracts from published works.

an·al·ge·si·a (an-l-jē'zi-ä), *n.* insensibility to pain while conscious.

an·al·ge·sic ('zik), *adj.* of, pertaining to, or bringing about analgesia: *n.* a drug causing analgesia.

an·a·log computer (an'ä-lòg), an electronic computer which substitutes voltages for numbers which represent pieces of information.

an·a·log·i·cal (an-ä-loj'i-kl), **an·a·log·ic** ('ik), *adj.* of, pertaining to, or based upon analogy. —**an·a·log'i·cal·ly,** *adv.*

a·nal·o·gist (ä-nal'ö-jist), *n.* one who reasons from the standpoint of analogy.

a·nal·o·gize (-jīz), *v.t.* -**gized, -giz·ing,** to reason by, or expound by reference to, analogy: *v.i.* to treat or reason by using analogy.

a·nal·o·gous (-gús), *adj.* having similarities; linked by resemblance. —**a·nal'o·gous·ly,** *adv.*

an·a·logue, an·a·log (an'ä-lòg), *n.* an object which bears analogy to something else; part which corresponds to another in structure, function, etc.

a·nal·o·gy (ä-nal'ö-ji), *n., pl.* -**gies,** 1. agreement, resemblance, or correspondence between different objects. 2. an explanation based on the similarities of two things. 3. in *Linguistics,* the process by which new words and constructions conform to others already in the language.

an·al·y·sand (ä-nal'i-sand), *n.* one who is undergoing treatment by psychoanalysis.

an·a·lyse (an'ä-līz), *v.t.* -**lysed, -lys·ing,** British form for **analyze**.

a·nal·y·sis (ä-nal'i-sis), *n., pl.* -**ses** (-sēz), 1. the separation of a whole into its constituent parts. 2. the method of determining the na-

---

a in *cap*, ā in *cane*, ä in *father*, å in *abet*, e in *met*, ē in *be*, ē in *baker*, ė in *regent*, i in *pit*, ī in *fine*, i in *manifest*, o in *hot*, ô in *horse*, ō in *bone*,

ture of something, as a chemical compound, by separating it into its constituent parts. 3. a report of the findings of an analysis. 4. same as **psychoanalysis**. 5. in *Mathematics*, the solving of problems by reducing the conditions that are in them to equations.

an·a·lyst (an'ȧ-list), *n.* 1. one who is skilled in analysis. 2. a psychoanalyst.

an·a·lyt·ic (an-ȧ-lit'ik), **an·a·lyt·i·cal** ('i-kl), *adj.* relating to or characterized by analysis. — **an·a·lyt'i·cal·ly**, *adv.*

an·a·lyt·ics ('iks), *n.* logic that deals with analyzing.

an·a·lyz·a·ble (an'ȧ-līz-ȧ-bl), *adj.* capable of being analyzed or resolved by analysis.

an·a·lyze (-līz), *v.t.* -lyzed, -lyz·ing, 1. to separate a whole into its constituent parts. 2. to determine the nature of something, as a chemical compound, by separating it into its constituent parts. 3. to study carefully so as to understand. 4. to psychoanalyze. — **an'a·lyz·er,** *n.*

an·a·pest, an·a·paest (an'ȧ-pest), *n.* a metrical foot of two unaccented syllables followed by one accented syllable.

an·aph·ro·dis·i·ac (an-af-rō-diz'i-ak), *n.* a drug or treatment that lessens sexual desire: *adj.* that lessens sexual desire.

an·arch (an'ärk), *n.* same as **anarchist**.

an·ar·chic (an-är'kik), **an·ar·chi·cal** ('ki-kl), *adj.* 1. of or pertaining to anarchy. 2. favoring anarchy. 3. likely to bring about anarchy. —**an·ar'chi·cal·ly,** *adv.*

an·ar·chism (an'ér-kizm), *n.* 1. the doctrine advocating the nonexistence of governmental rule, stressing the belief that government imposes on individual liberty. 2. violent opposition to government.

an·ar·chist (-kist), *n.* 1. one who supports anarchism. 2. one who promotes a scheme for anarchy.

an·ar·chy (-ki), *n., pl.* -chies, 1. the state of having no government. 2. a lawless condition of society. 3. confusion or chaos generally.

an·as·tig·mat (an-as'tig-mat), *n.* a lens that is made to correct astigmatism.

an·as·tig·mat·ic (an-as-tig-mat'ik), *adj.* 1. free from astigmatism. 2. having a correction for astigmatism.

a·nas·to·mo·sis (ȧ-nas-tō-mō'sis), *n., pl.* -ses ('sēz), a running or joining together, as of two streams of water, two blood vessels, etc.

a·nas·tro·phe (ȧ-nas'trō-fi), *n.* an inversion of the usual sequence of words in a sentence as "echoed the hills" for "the hills echoed."

a·nath·e·ma (ȧ-nath'ē-mȧ), *n., pl.* -mas, 1. the curse accompanying excommunication. 2. any curse or imprecation. 3. a thing or person accursed. 4. any abhorred person or thing.

a·nath·e·ma·tize (-mȧ-tīz), *v.t. & v.i.* -tized, -tiz·ing, to pronounce an anathema (against); curse. —**a·nath·e·ma·ti·za'tion,** *n.*

an·a·tom·i·cal (an-ȧ-tom'i-kl), **an·a·tom·ic** ('ik), *adj.* relating to or connected with anatomy. —**an·a·tom'i·cal·ly,** *adv.*

a·nat·o·mist (ȧ-nat'ō-mist), *n.* 1. one possessing

a knowledge of anatomy. 2. one who anatomizes, or analyzes with great care.

a·nat·o·mize (-mīz), *v.t. & v.i.* -mized, -miz·ing, 1. to separate, as an animal, by dissection, in order to examine. 2. to analyze with great care. —**a·nat·o·mi·za'tion,** *n.*

a·nat·o·my (ȧ-nat'ō-mi), *n., pl.* -mies, 1. a separation by dissection of a plant or animal in order to examine its structure and study the relationship of its parts. 2. the scientific study of the structure of plants or animals. 3. the structure of a plant or animal. 4. a thorough study or examination.

an·ces·tor (an'ses-tēr), *n.* 1. a forefather or progenitor; person from whom one is descended. 2. anything that is held to be the precursor of a later or more developed thing.

an·ces·tral (an-ses'trȧl), *adj.* belonging to, or inherited from, one's ancestors. —**an·ces'tral·ly,** *adv.*

an·ces·tress (an'ses-très), *n.* a woman ancestor.

an·ces·try (-tri), *n., pl.* -tries, 1. a family line of descent traced from a period more or less remote; lineage. 2. the persons comprising such lineage.

an·chor (ang'kēr), *n.* 1. a heavy object, as an iron weight with flukes, attached to a cable and used for holding ships in place on water. 2. anything steady or secure: *v.t.* to fasten by an anchor: *v.i.* 1. to lower an anchor. 2. to become fixed or firm.

an·chor·age (-ij), *n.* 1. the act of anchoring or the state of being anchored. 2. a place for the anchoring of vessels. 3. the hold attained by an anchor. 4. charges for anchorage in a port.

anchor ice, ice formed at the bottom of a body of water that is otherwise unfrozen.

an·cho·rite (ang'kō-rīt), **an·cho·ret** (-rit), *n.* one who voluntarily secludes himself from society and lives a solitary life devoted to religious or philosophic meditation; recluse; hermit. —**an'cho·ress** (-ris), *n.fem.*

anchor man, one who broadcasts news on radio or television and coordinates incoming reports from various sources.

an·cho·vy (an'chō-vi), *n., pl.* -vies, -vy, a diminutive herringlike fish of warm seas, frequently canned or made into a paste.

an·cient (ān'shènt), *adj.* 1. of or pertaining to the early history of the world; of past times or remote ages. 2. of great age or antiquity: *n.* 1. an aged person. 2. one who lived long ago. 3. one of the classical authors. 4. *pl.* the people of antiquity. —**an'cient·ness,** *n.*

an·cient·ly (-li), *adv.* in ancient times.

an·cil·lar·y (an'si-ler-i), *adj.* 1. inferior or subservient (often with *to*). 2. attendant upon; accessory.

an·cip·i·tal (an-sip'ĭ-tl), *adj.* in *Botany*, doublefaced; two-edged, as some grasses.

an·con (ang'kon), *n., pl.* an·co·nes (ang-kō'nēz), in *Architecture*, a bracket or projection for the support of a cornice.

and (and), *conj.* 1. also; as well as: used to join words and sentences. 2. plus. 3. in consequence. 4. in contrast to. 5. [Informal], to.

ō in dragon, ōō in crude, oo in wool, u in cup, ū in cure, û in turn, u in focus, oi in boy, ou in house, th in thin, th in sheathe, g in get, j in joy, y in yet.

an-dan-te (än-dän'tä), *adj. & adv.* in *Music,* moderate in tempo.

an-des-ite (an'dé-zit), *n.* a granitelike feldspar containing iron and magnesium.

and-i-ron (an'di-ĕrn), *n.* either of a pair of metal standards used in a fireplace to support the logs.

an-dra-dite (an'drā-dit), *n.* a green garnet.

an-dro-gen (an'drŏ-jĕn), *n.* a male sex hormone. —**an-dro-gen'ic** (-jen'ik), *adj.*

an-drog-e-nous (an-droj'ĕ-nŭs), *adj.* producing males.

an-drog-y-nous (an-droj'i-nŭs), *adj.* combining both sexes, or bearing both male and female organs; hermaphroditic.

an-drog-y-ny ('i-ni), *n.* hermaphroditism.

an-droid (an'droid), *n.* an automaton resembling a man.

an-dro-sphinx (an'drŏ-sfingks), *n.* a sphinx with the body of a lion and the head of a man.

an-ec-dot-al (an'ik-dŏt-l), *adj.* relating to or consisting of anecdotes: also **an-ec-dot'ic** (-dŏt'ik).

an-ec-dote (an'ik-dŏt), *n.* a brief, entertaining narrative; pithy account of an incident, chiefly personal or biographical.

a-ne-mi-a (á-nē'mi-á), *n.* 1. a condition in which the blood has a deficiency in red corpuscles or hemoglobin or both. 2. listlessness; lack of energy. —**a-ne'mic** ('mik), *adj.* —**a-ne'mi-cal-ly,** *adv.*

an-em-o-graph (á-nem'ŏ-graf), *n.* an instrument for registering the force or direction of the wind. —**a-nem-o-graph'ic,** *adj.*

an-e-mom-e-ter (an-ē-mom'ē-tēr), *n.* a wind gauge; instrument which indicates the speed or force of the wind.

an-e-mom-e-try (-tri), *n.* the process of determining the force of the wind.

a-nem-o-ne (á-nem'ŏ-nē), *n.* 1 a plant with brightly colored, cup-shaped flowers. 2. same as **sea anemone.**

a-nem-o-scope (a-nem'ŏ-skōp), *n.* an instrument for indicating or registering the direction of the wind.

an-er-oid (an'ēr-oid), *adj.* having no liquid: *n.* same as **aneroid barometer.**

aneroid barometer, a barometer with action depending on the varying pressure of the atmosphere on the top of a metal box surrounding a partial vacuum.

an-es-the-sia (an-ĕs-thē'zhá), *n.* 1. a condition of insensibility to pain. 2. a temporary inability to feel pain, either in a localized area of the body or through loss of consciousness.

an-es-the-si-ol-o-gist (-thē-zi-ol'ŏ-jist), *n.* a physician specializing in anesthesiology.

an-es-the-si-ol-o-gy (-ji), *n.* the branch of medicine having to do with anesthesia and anesthetics.

an-es-thet-ic (an-ĕs-thet'ik), *adj.* of, pertaining to, or producing anesthesia: *n.* a drug or gas which produces anesthesia. —**an-es-thet'-i-cal-ly,** *adv.*

an-es-the-tist (á-nes'thē-tist), *n.* one trained in the use of anesthetics.

an-es-the-tize (-tiz), *v.t.* **-tized, -tiz-ing,** to bring under the influence of an anesthetic; render insensible to pain.

an-eu-rysm, an-eu-rism (an'yĕr-izm), *n.* a sac formed by a local swelling of an artery at a point where the wall is thinned or weakened by disease or injury.

a-new (á-nōō'), *adv.* 1. afresh; over again. 2. in a new manner or style.

an-gel (ān'jl), *n.* 1. in *Theology,* a messenger of God:. also, a spiritual being, either beneficent or evil. 2. a guardian spirit. 3. a person of angelic qualities or disposition. 4. a figure or pictured representation of a human form with wings and a halo. 5. [Informal], one who aids, as the financial backer of a play.

an-gel-fish (-fish), *n., pl.* **-fish, -fish-es,** 1. a shark with large pectoral fins, which give it a winged appearance. 2. any of various tropical fishes.

angel food cake, angel cake, a light-textured, white cake made with egg whites.

an-gel-ic (an-jel'ik), **an-gel-i-cal** ('i-kl), *adj.* 1. of an angel. 2. resembling an angel in nature, goodness, etc. —**an-gel'i-cal-ly,** *adv.*

an-gel-i-ca (an-jel'i-ká), *n.* a plant of the parsley family, with roots and seeds used for flavoring and in medicines.

An-ge-lus, an-ge-lus (an'jē-lŭs), *n.* 1. a Roman Catholic devotional exercise in commemoration of the Incarnation, said morning, noon, and night. 2. the bell which is rung to announce the time of such devotions.

an-ger (ang'gĕr), *n.* strong displeasure or wrath aroused by a sense of injury or wrong: *v.t.* to provoke to resentment; arouse to wrath; enrage *v.i.* to become greatly displeased or enraged.

an-gi-na (an-ji'ná), *n.* 1. an inflamed condition of the throat. 2. same as **angina pectoris.**

angina pec-to-ris (pek'tēr-is), a condition characterized by a painful muscle spasm of the chest, caused by sudden inadequate flow of blood to the heart.

an-gi-ol-o-gy (an-ji-ol'ŏ-ji), *n.* the branch of anatomy that deals with the study of blood vessels and lymph vessels.

an-gi-o-ma (an-ji-ō'má), *n., pl.* **-ma-ta** ('má-tá), a tumor composed largely of blood vessels and lymph vessels.

an-gle (ang'gl), *n.* 1. the shape made by two straight lines or two plane surfaces that meet. 2. the enclosed space formed by the two lines or surfaces. 3. the amount of difference in direction between the lines or surfaces, measured in degrees. 4. a sharp or projecting corner. 5. a perspective; point of view. 6. [Informal], a deceitful scheme: *v.t. & v.i.* **-gled, -gling,** to turn, go, bend, etc. at an angle.

an-gle (ang'gl), *v.i.* **-gled, -gling,** 1. to fish with a hook and line. 2. to use subterfuge or trickery to obtain something.

angle iron, a piece of iron or steel in the form of a right angle, used to join or strengthen two beams or girders.

an-gler (ang'glĕr), *n.* 1. one who fishes with hook and line. 2. one who angles to obtain something. 3. a saltwater fish which, by means of a filamentary appendage, attracts smaller fish on which it feeds.

---

a in cap, ā in cane, ä in father, á in abet, e in met ē in be, ĕ in baker, ė in regent, i in pit, ī in fine, i in manifest, o in hot, ŏ in horse, ō in bone,

an·gle·worm (ang'gl-wûrm), *n.* an earthworm; worm used for fishing bait.

An·gli·can (ang'gli-kǎn), *adj.* 1. of or pertaining to England or its people. 2. of or pertaining to the Church of England and churches in other countries in accord with it, as the Protestant Episcopal Church in the U.S.: *n.* a member of the Church of England or of a related church.

An·gli·can·ism (-izm), *n.* 1. the principles and ritual of the Anglican Church. 2. belief in these principles.

An·gli·ce (ang'gli-si), *adv.* according to the English language or manner.

An·gli·cism (ang'gli-sizm), *n.* 1. a word, principle, mannerism, etc. peculiar to the English. 2. a being English.

An·gli·cize (-sīz), *v.t.* & *v.i.* -cized, -ciz·ing, to make or render into English speech, manners, or customs.

an·gling (ang'gling), *n.* the act or art of fishing with hook and line.

An·glo-A·mer·i·can (ang'glō-à-mer'i-kǎn), *adj.* 1. of or pertaining to England and the U.S. 2. of or pertaining to Anglo-Americans: *n.* an American citizen of English birth or descent.

An·glo-Cath·o·lic (-kath'ō-lik), *n.* a member of the Church of England who follows ritualistic practices derived from the Church's historical connection with the Catholic Church: *adj.* of or pertaining to Anglo-Catholics or their beliefs.

An·glo·ma·ni·a (ang-glō-mā'ni-à), *n.* an excessive enthusiasm for English practices, manners, etc.

An·glo·phile (ang'glō-fil), *n.* [also a-]. one who greatly admires England, its people, etc.

An·glo·phil·i·a (ang-glō-fil'i-à), *n.* [also a-], great admiration for England, its people, etc.

An·glo·phobe (ang'glō-fōb), *n.* [also a-]. one who dislikes or fears England, its people, etc.

An·glo·pho·bi·a (ang-glō-fō'bi-à), *n.* [also a-], dislike or fear of England, its people, etc. —**An·glo·pho'bic** (-fō'bik), *adj.*

An·glo-Sax·on (ang'glō-sak'sn), *n.* 1. one of the Germanic invaders who settled in England prior to the twelfth century. 2. the language of the Anglo-Saxons. 3. a plain form of modern English derived from the language of the Anglo-Saxons. 4. an Englishman or the descendant of one: *adj.* of or pertaining to the Anglo-Saxons, their language or descendants, etc.

An·go·ra (ang-gôr'à), *n.* 1. a type of domestic cat with long fur: also **Angora cat.** 2. a type of goat with long, silky hair: also **Angora goat.** 3. [also a-], the hair of the Angora goat. 4. [also a-], fabric made from this hair. 5. a type of rabbit with long, silky hair: also **Angora rabbit.** 6. [also a-], yarn or fabric made from this hair.

an·gos·tu·ra (an-gôs-toor'à), a bitter aromatic bark used as a tonic and flavoring: also **angostura bark.**

an·gry (ang'gri), *adj.* -gri·er, -gri·est, 1. filled with anger; provoked; feeling resentment. 2.

turbulent. 3. inflamed. —**an'gri·ly**, *adv.* —**an'gri·ness**, *n.*

ang·strom (ang'strôm), *n.* one hundred-millionth of a centimeter: used in measuring the length of light waves.

an·guish (ang'gwish), *n.* intense pain or grief; acute suffering: *v.t.* & *v.i.* to feel or make feel anguish.

an·gu·lar (ang'gyū-lēr), *adj.* 1. having an angle or angles; sharp, bent, or cornered. 2. very thin; bony. —**an'gu·lar·ly**, *adv.* —**an'gu·lar·ness**, *n.*

an·gu·lar·i·ty (ang-gyū-ler'i-ti), *n., pl.* -ties, 1. the quality of being angular. 2. *pl.* things or shapes which are angular.

an·gu·late (ang'gyū-lǎt), *adj.* having angles: *v.i.* & *v.t.* (-lǎt), -lat·ed, -lat·ing, to become or cause to become angular.

an·hy·dride (an-hī'drid), *n.* a compound created by removing the elements of water from another compound.

an·hy·drite ('drit), *n.* anhydrous calcium sulfate.

an·hy·drous ('drǔs), *adj.* 1. without water. 2. not hydrated.

an·il (an'il), *n.* 1. a shrub of the West Indies that yields indigo. 2. same as **indigo.**

an·ile (an'il), *adj.* of or resembling an old woman; weak.

an·i·line (an'i-lin), *n.* 1. a poisonous, colorless liquid derived from benzene and used in making plastics, explosives, resins, and dyes. 2. any of several dyes produced from this or synthetically from coal tar: also called **aniline dye.**

an·i·mad·ver·sion (an-i-mad-vûr'zhǔn), *n.* 1. the act of making critical observations. 2. such an observation; censure; blame.

an·i·mad·vert (-vûrt'), *v.i.* to make critical observations; censure; blame.

an·i·mal (an'i-mǎl), *n.* 1. an organized, living being, sentient and capable of moving from place to place. 2. any nonhuman being of this kind, especially one with four feet. 3. a person who is brutish or debased: *adj.* 1. characteristic of animals. 2. physical, sensual; bestial, gross, etc. —**an'i·mal·ly**, *adv.*

an·i·mal·cule (an-i-mal'kyool), *n.* one of a class of minute or microscopic organisms. —**an·i·mal'cu·lar** (-kyū-lēr), *adj.*

an·i·mal·ism (an'i-mǎl-izm), *n.* 1. the state of being animal, or actuated by animal instincts or appetites. 2. the theory that regards man as a mere animal with no soul. —**an'i·mal·ist**, *n.* —**an·i·mal·is'tic**, *adj.*

an·i·mal·i·ty (an-i-mal'i-ti), *n.* 1. behavior or nature typical of animals. 2. animals collectively. 3. man's animal instincts.

an·i·mal·ize (an'i-mǎl-īz), *v.t.* -ized, -iz·ing, 1. to convert into animal substance by assimilation. 2. to make (a person) like a beast; sensualize or bestialize. —**an·i·mal·i·za'tion** (-i-zā'shǔn), *n.*

animal magnetism, 1. an earlier name for hypnotism. 2. physical attraction of one person for another.

an·i·mate (an'i-mǎt), *v.t.* -mat·ed, -mat·ing, 1. to impart life to. 2. to inspire to energy or action. 3. to make gay; enliven. 4. to make move or appear to move: *adj.* (-mit), 1. en-

---

dowed with animal life. 2. full of spirit and vigor.

animated cartoon, a motion picture made from successive photographs of cartoons projected rapidly so that figures appear to move.

an·i·ma·tion (an-i-mā'shŭn), *n.* 1. the act of giving life or spirit. 2. the state or condition of being animated; life. 3. vivacity; liveliness. 4. the process of drawing or preparing animated cartoons.

an·i·ma·tism (an'ĭ-mă-tizm), *n.* the belief that inanimate things are endowed with reason and intelligence.

an·i·mism (an'ĭ-mizm), *n.* 1. the theory of the existence of an immaterial principle or force separate from matter to which all life and action are attributable. 2. the belief that all natural things have a soul which is separate from their physical existence. 3. a belief in spirits, demons, etc. —an'i·mist, *n.* —an·i·mis'tic, *adj.*

an·i·mos·i·ty (an-ĭ-mos'ĭ-ti), *n., pl.* -ties, hostility: hatred; enmity.

an·i·mus (an'ĭ-mŭs), *n.* 1. a basic purpose or intention. 2. hostility; deep hatred or resentment.

an·i·on (an'ĭ-ŏn), *n.* an ion with a negative charge: opposed to *cation.* —an·i·on'ic (-on'-ik), *adj.*

an·ise (an'is), *n.* 1. a plant of the parsley family, with white or yellow flowers and aromatic seeds. 2. the seed of this plant, used for flavoring and as a carminative: also an'i·seed (an'ĭ-sēd).

an·i·sette (an-ĭ-set', -zet'), *n.* a sweet liqueur flavored with anise.

ankh (angk), *n.* a cross having a loop for its top, used in ancient Egypt as an emblem of life.

an·kle (ang'kl), *n.* 1. the joint connecting the foot with the leg. 2. the part of the leg below the calf.

an·klet (ang'klĕt), *n.* 1. an ornament worn around the ankle. 2. a fetter. 3. a short sock, worn especially by girls.

an·ky·lose (ang'ki-lōs), *v.t. & v.i.* -losed, -losing, to join together or stiffen by ankylosis.

an·ky·los·is (ang-ki-lō'sis), *n.* the stiffening of a joint by an abnormal growing together of bones or fibrous tissue.

an·nal·ist (an'ăl-ist), *n.* a writer of annals. —an·nal·is'tic, *adj.*

an·nals (an'ălz), *n.* 1. a description, history, or chronicle issued from time to time, and comprising the events of each year in order of sequence. 2. historical records; chronicles.

an·neal (ă-nēl'), *v.t.* 1. to temper (metal or glass) by heating and then very slow, regulated cooling to prevent brittleness. 2. to temper (the mind). —an·neal'er, *n.*

an·ne·lid (an'ĕl-id), *n.* a segmented worm, such as the earthworm: *adj.* of or pertaining to such worms.

an·nex (ă-neks'), *v.t.* 1. to add or affix, especially a smaller thing to a larger. 2. to incorporate into a country the territory of (another country). 3. to take without asking: *n.* (an'eks), that which is added; addition; especially, *a)* a wing added to a building. *b)*

an addition to a document. —an·nex·a'tion (an-ek-sā'shŭn), *n.*

an·ni·hi·late (ă-nī'ĭ-lāt), *v.t.* -lat·ed, -lat·ing, 1. to reduce to nothing; wipe out of existence; destroy. 2. to kill. 3. to conquer completely. —an·ni·hi·la'tion, *n.*

an·ni·ver·sa·ry (an-ĭ-vŭr'sĕr-i), *n., pl.* -ries, 1. the recurrence in each year of the date of an event. 2. the annual commemoration of an event: *adj.* of or pertaining to an anniversary.

an·no Do·mi·ni (ăn-ō dō'mĭ-nī), [Latin, in the year of the Lord], in a given year within the Christian era: abbreviated A.D.

an·no·tate (an'ō-tāt), *v.t. & v.i.* -tat·ed, -tat·ing, to mark or note by way of explanation or criticism, as a book or other literary work. —an'no·ta·tive, *adj.* —an'no·ta·tor, *n.*

an·no·ta·tion (an-ō-tā'shŭn), *n.* 1. the act of annotating. 2. an explanatory or critical note or series of notes in a literary work.

an·nounce (ă-nouns'), *v.t.* -nounced', -nounc'ing, 1. to make known formally or in a public manner; proclaim. 2. to give notice of the arrival of. 3. to be an announcer for: *v.i.* to serve as an announcer.

an·nounce·ment (ă'mĕnt), *n.* 1. the act of announcing. 2. that which is announced; proclamation. 3. a notice, usually printed.

an·nounc·er ('ēr), *n.* one who announces; especially, in radio or television, one who introduces the programs, gives news reports, etc.

an·noy (ă-noi'), *v.t.* 1. to vex or trouble by repeated acts, noise, etc.; irritate. 2. to harm by repeated petty injuries or hostile actions; harass: *v.i.* to be troubling or vexing. —an·noy'ing, *adj.* —an·noy'ing·ly, *adv.*

an·noy·ance ('ăns), *n.* 1. the act of annoying or causing vexation. 2. the state of being annoyed. 3. the thing or person that annoys.

an·nu·al (an'yoo-wăl), *adj.* 1. happening or coming once in twelve months; yearly. 2. of, belonging to, or measured by a year. 3. for a year's work, time, etc. 4. lasting or living only for a year or season: *n.* 1. a plant that completes its growth in a year or one season. 2. a publication appearing once a year, especially one issued by a school's senior class; yearbook. —an'nu·al·ly, *adv.*

an·nu·i·tant (ă-nōō'ĭ-tănt, ă-nū'ĭ-), *n.* one who receives, or is entitled to receive, an annuity.

an·nu·i·ty (ă-nōō'ĭ-ti, ă-nū'ĭ-), *n., pl.* -ties, 1. the payment of a sum of money by fixed, especially yearly, installments. 2. an investment that will return fixed payments for a given number of years, or for the remainder of a lifetime.

an·nul (ă-nul'), *v.t.* -nulled', -nul'ling, 1. to abolish or obliterate. 2. to make void, as a law, decree, or compact; invalidate.

an·nu·lar (an'yoo-lăr), *adj.* ringlike; in the form of a ring. —an'nu·lar·ly, *adv.*

an·nu·late (-lit, -lāt), *adj.* ringed; having ringlike bands or circles: also an'nu·lat·ed (-lā-tid).

an·nu·let (an'yoo-lĕt), *n.* a little ring.

an·nul·ment (ă-nul'mĕnt), *n.* 1. the act of annulling. 2. the dissolution or invalidation of a marriage by a court decree.

an·nu·lus (an'yoo-lŭs), *n., pl.* **-li** (-lī), **-lus·es,** any ring or ringlike part; specifically, *a)* the space between two concentric circles. *b)* any of various ringlike parts in animals, or plants.

an·nun·ci·ate (ă-nun'si-āt, 'shi-). *v.t.* **-at·ed, -at·ing,** to make known officially or publicly; announce.

an·nun·ci·a·tion (ă-nun-si-ā'shŭn, -shi-), *n.* 1. the act of annunciating. 2. an announcement. 3. [A-], *a)* the announcement of the coming birth of Jesus, made by the angel Gabriel to the Virgin Mary. *b)* a church festival commemorating this (March 25): also called, in England, *Lady Day.*

an·nun·ci·a·tor (ă-nun'si-āt-ēr, 'shi-), *n.* 1. one who announces. 2. an electric signaling apparatus used in hotels and offices to show from which room a call was made.

an·ode (an'ōd), *n.* 1. the positively charged electrode in an electrolytic cell or in an electron tube. 2. the negative terminal of a battery that supplies electric current.

an·o·dize (an'ō-dīz), *v.t.* **-dized, -diz·ing,** to put an oxide film on (a metal) by electrolysis.

an·o·dyne (an'ō-dīn), *adj.* relieving pain: *n.* anything that relieves pain or has a soothing effect, as a drug.

a·noint (ă-noint'), *v.t.* to apply oil to, especially in a religious ceremony of consecration. — **a·noint'ment,** *n.*

a·nom·a·lis·tic (a-nom-ă-lis'tik), *adj.* of or pertaining to an anomaly.

a·nom·a·lous (ă-nom'ă-lŭs), *adj.* 1. deviating from the natural order or usual method; abnormal. 2. odd, irregular, or inconsistent. — **a·nom'a·lous·ly,** *adv.* —**a·nom'a·lous·ness,** *n.*

a·nom·a·ly (ă-nom'ă-li), *n., pl.* **-lies,** 1. a deviation from the natural order or usual method; abnormality. 2. anything that is anomalous. 3. the angular distance of a planet from its perihelion.

an·o·mie, an·o·my (an'ō-mi), *n.* lack of purpose or values; instability; aimlessness.

a·non (ă-non'), *adv.* 1. soon; presently. 2. again.

an·o·nym (an'ō-nim), *n.* 1. a person who is anonymous. 2. a pseudonym.

an·o·nym·i·ty (an-ō-nim'i-ti), *n.* the state of being anonymous.

a·non·y·mous (ă-nän'i-mŭs), *adj.* 1. not having or bearing a name; nameless. 2. written, spoken, etc. by one whose name is kept secret. 3. without individuality or a clearly definable character. —**a·non'y·mous·ly,** *adv.*

a·noph·e·les (ă-nof'ĕ-lēz), *n.* the kind of mosquito that transmits malaria.

an·o·rex·i·a (an-ō-rek'si-ă), *n.* chronic lack of appetite for food.

an·os·mi·a (an-oz'mi-ă, -os'), *n.* loss of the sense of smell.

an·oth·er (ă-nuth'ēr), *adj.* 1. one more. 2. not the same. 3. some other of the same kind: *pron.* 1. an additional one. 2. one that is different. 3. one of the same kind.

an·ox·i·a (an-ok'si-ă), *n.* the condition resulting

from the lack of an adequate supply of oxygen in body tissues.

an·ser·ine (an'sēr-īn, -in), *adj.* 1. relating to or resembling a goose. 2. stupid.

an·swer (an'sēr), *v.t.* 1. to reply to a charge; defend oneself against. 2. to speak or write in reply; respond to. 3. to be sufficient or adequate for. 4. to agree with; conform to: *v.i.* 1. to reply. 2. to react (*to*). 3. to be adequate. 4. to be liable (*to*). 5. to correspond (*to*): *n.* 1. a reply to a charge. 2. a response or rejoinder. 3. a solution, as of a mathematical problem.

an·swer·a·ble (-ă-bl), *adj.* 1. liable to be called to account; responsible. 2. that can be refuted.

ant (ant), *n.* a small, black, red, or brown social insect, usually living in wood or in the ground.

-ant (-ănt, -nt), a suffix meaning *a person or thing that* or *that shows, does,* or *has.*

ant·ac·id (ant-as'id), *adj.* counteracting acidity: *n.* a substance which counteracts acidity, especially in the stomach.

an·tag·o·nism (an-tag'ō-nizm), *n.* 1. the active opposition of two opponents or opposing forces; hostility. 2. any opposing action or force.

an·tag·o·nist (-nist), *n.* 1. a competitor in any sphere of action; opponent. 2. something that acts against something else physiologically, as a muscle or drug.

an·tag·o·nis·tic (an-tag-ō-nis'tik), *adj.* acting in opposition; opposed. —**an·tag·o·nis'ti·cal·ly,** *adv.*

an·tag·o·nize (an-tag'ō-nīz), *v.t.* **-nized, -niz·ing,** 1. to oppose; hinder; counteract. 2. to make hostile; provoke.

ant·al·ka·li (ant-al'kă-lī), *n., pl.* **-lies, -lis,** a substance that neutralizes an alkali or counteracts an alkaline condition.

ant·arc·tic (ant-ärk'tik), *adj.* of or pertaining to the South Pole or the regions surrounding it.

Antarctic Circle, [also a- c-], an imaginary circle parallel to the equator and 23° 27' from the South Pole.

ant bear, a large anteater of tropical South America, with shaggy, gray fur and a bushy tail.

an·te (an'ti), *n.* 1. in the game of poker, a stake that each player puts into the pot before he receives his cards. 2. [Informal], an amount to be paid as one's share: *v.t. & v.i.* **-ted** or **-teed, -te·ing,** 1. in the game of poker, to put in (one's stake). 2. [Informal], to pay (one's share).

ante-, a prefix meaning *before.*

ant·eat·er (ant'ēt-ēr), *n.* one of a group of quadrupeds which feed upon ants, as the aardvark and ant bear: most have long, narrow snouts and very long, protrusile tongues.

an·te·bel·lum (an-ti-bel'ŭm), *adj.* before the war; especially, before the American Civil War.

an·te·cede (an-tĕ-sēd'), *v.t. & v.i.* **-ced'ed, -ced'ing,** to precede or go before in time or place.

an·te·ced·ence (-sē'dĕns), *n.* precedence; the act or state of going before; priority.

an·te·ced·ent ('dĕnt), *adj.* preceding: *n.* 1. something that comes or occurs before. 2. *pl. a)* the previous events of a person's life. *b)* one's ancestors. 3. the substantive or noun to which a pronoun refers. 4. the part of a conditional proposition on which the other part of the proposition depends. 5. the first term of a mathematical ratio. —**an·te·ced'ent·ly,** *adv.*

an·te·cham·ber (an'ti-chăm-bẽr), *n.* an outer room leading to a larger or principal room.

an·te·choir (-kwir), *n.* an enclosed or reserved space in a chapel in front of the choir.

an·te·date (-dāt), *v.t.* -dat·ed, -dat·ing, 1. to precede in time; happen earlier than. 2. to date earlier than the actual date: *n.* a date earlier than the actual date.

an·te·di·lu·vi·an (an-ti-di-lōō'vi-ăn), *adj.* 1. of or pertaining to the world, or time, before the Biblical Flood. 2. belonging to very ancient times. 3. antiquated or old-fashioned: *n.* 1. a person or thing of very ancient times. 2. one who is old-fashioned, or behind the times.

an·te·lope (an'tĕ-lōp), *n.* 1. *a)* any of various deerlike ruminants related to the ox and goat, with cylindrical, ringed horns. *b)* same as **pronghorn.** 2. leather made from an antelope's hide.

an·te·me·rid·i·an (an-ti-mĕ-rid'i-ăn), *adj.* before noon.

an·te·na·tal (-nāt'l), *adj.* before birth.

an·ten·na (an-ten'ä), *n.* 1. *pl.* -nae ('ē), -nas, either of a pair of jointed feelers on the head of an insect or crustacean. 2. *pl.* -nas, an upraised rod or system of rods and wires for transmitting and receiving the electromagnetic waves for radio or television.

an·te·pen·di·um (an-ti-pen'di-ŭm), *n., pl.* -di·a (-ä), -di·ums, the screen in front of an altar.

an·te·pe·nult (-pe'nŭlt), *n.* the syllable that is third from the end.

an·te·pe·nul·ti·mate (-pē-nul'ti-măt), *adj.* of or pertaining to the third from the end: *n.* 1. that which is third from the end. 2. an antepenult.

an·te·ri·or (an-tir'i-ẽr), *adj.* 1. at or near the front; forward. 2. former; previous; earlier. —**an·te'ri·or·ly,** *adv.*

an·te·room (an'ti-rōōm, -room), *n.* a room before, or forming an entrance to, a larger or more important room; antechamber.

an·te·type (-tīp), *n.* same as **prototype.**

ant·he·li·on (ant-hēl'yŏn, 'i-ŏn, an-thĕl'-), *n., pl.* -li·a ('yä, 'i-ä), -li·ons, a halo or colored ring formed around the shadow of an object projected by the sun on a cloud or on a rise of mist.

an·them (an'thĕm), *n.* 1. a religious song, often based on a Biblical passage, sung in church by a choir. 2. a song of praise or triumph.

an·ther (an'thẽr), *n.* the part of the stamen of a flower containing the pollen.

an·the·sis (an-thē'sis), *n.* full bloom; state of complete expansion of a flower.

ant·hill (ant'hil), *n.* a mound of soil heaped up by ants around the entrance to their underground nest.

an·tho·car·pous (an-thō-kär'pŭs), *adj.* having a fruit, as the pineapple, formed from the ovaries of several flowers.

an·thol·o·gist (an-thol'ō-jist), *n.* one who compiles an anthology.

an·thol·o·gize (-jīz), *v.i.* -gized, -giz·ing, to make anthologies: *v.t.* 1. to include in an anthology. 2. to make an anthology of.

an·thol·o·gy (-ji), *n., pl.* -gies, a collection of poems, stories, etc. by various authors. —**an·tho·log·i·cal** (an-thō-loj'i-kăl), *adj.*

an·thra·cene (an'thrä-sēn), *n.* a complex hydrocarbon obtained from coal tar, used in making dyes.

an·thra·cite (-sit), *n.* nonbituminous coal which burns with little smoke; hard coal. —**an·thra·cit'ic** (-sit'ik), *adj.*

an·thrax (an'thraks), *n.* 1. an infectious disease of sheep and cattle that can be transmitted to man. 2. a black pustule or boil characteristic of this disease.

an·thro·po·cen·tric (an-thrō-pō-sen'trik), *adj.* 1. regarding man as the most important element of the universe. 2. looking at the world and the universe according to human values.

an·thro·po·gen·e·sis (-pō-jen'ĕ-sis), *n.* that branch of knowledge which deals with the origin and development of man: also **an·thro·pog'e·my** (-pāj'ĕ-ni). —**an·thro·po·ge·net'ic** (-pō-jĕ-net'ik), *adj.*

an·thro·pog·ra·phy (-pŏg'rä-fi), *n.* the branch of anthropology that deals with the geographical distribution of man according to his different varieties as characterized by physical characteristics, languages, customs, etc.

an·thro·poid (an'thrō-poid), *adj.* 1. resembling man; manlike: said of any of the most highly developed apes, as the chimpanzee and gorilla. 2. resembling an ape; apelike: *n.* any of the most highly developed apes. —**an·thro·poi'dal,** *adj.*

an·thro·pol·o·gist (an-thrō-pol'ō-jist), *n.* a student of or an expert in anthropology.

an·thro·pol·o·gy (an-thrō-pol'ō-ji), *n.* the branch of science that deals with the study of mankind, especially of man's origin, social and cultural development, physical characteristics, and customs. —**an·thro·po·log'i·cal** (-pō-loj'i-kl), **an·thro·po·log'ic,** *adj.*

an·thro·pom·e·try (-pom'ĕ-tri), *n.* the branch of science dealing with the measurement or proportions of the human body according to age, sex, etc. —**an·thro·po·met'ric** (-pō-met'-rik), **an·thro·po·met'ri·cal,** *adj.*

an·thro·po·mor·phic (-pō-môr'fik), *adj.* of or pertaining to anthropomorphism. —**an·thro·po·mor'phi·cal·ly,** *adv.*

an·thro·po·mor·phism ('fizm), *n.* the ascription of a human form and attributes to a god, thing, or animal. —**an·thro·po·mor'phist,** *n.*

an·thro·po·mor·phize ('fiz), *v.t. & v.i.* -phized, -phiz·ing, to ascribe human characteristics to (a god, thing, or animal).

an·thro·po·mor·phous ('fŭs), *adj.* having or resembling human form.

an·thro·pop·a·thy (-pop'ä-thi), *n.* the ascription of human passions and emotions to a god, animal, or thing.

an-thro-poph-a-gi (-pof'ǎ-jī), *n.*, *sing.* **-a-gus** ('ǎ-gǔs), cannibals.

an-thro-poph-a-gy (-pof'ǎ-ji), *n.* cannibalism. — **an-thro-poph'a-gous** (-gǔs), *adj.*

an-thu-ri-um (an-thoor'i-ǔm), *n.* a tall, tropical American plant with a heart-shaped spathe at the base of its long flower spike.

an-ti-, a prefix meaning *opposite, against, reverse, neutralizing, curative, preventative, rivaling.*

an-ti-air-craft (an-ti-er'kraft, -tī-), *adj.* used for defense against enemy aircraft.

an-ti-bac-te-ri-al (an-ti-bǎk-tir'i-ǎl, -tī-), *adj.* that halts the growth or counteracts the effect of bacteria.

an-ti-bal-lis-tic missile (-bǎ-lis'tik), a ballistic missile designed to search out and demolish another ballistic missile in flight.

an-ti-bi-o-sis (an-ti-bī-ō'sis), *n.* in *Biology*, a relationship in which one organism is destroyed or harmed by another.

an-ti-bi-ot-ic (-bī-ot'ik, -bi-), *adj.* 1. of or pertaining to antibiosis. 2. destroying or checking the growth of bacteria: *n.* a chemical substance produced by living microorganisms, used in dilute solutions to destroy or check the growth of bacteria: antibiotics, such as penicillin, streptomycin, and tetracycline, are used to treat some infectious diseases.

an-ti-bod-y (an'ti-bod-i), *n.*, *pl.* **-bod-ies**, a protein produced in the body to destroy or counteract toxic or other harmful substances.

an-tic (an'tik), *adj.* 1. [Archaic], grotesque: also **an'tick**. 2. absurd; silly: *n.* 1. [Archaic], a clown. 2. a trick, prank, or caper: *v.i.* -ticked, -tick-ing, to perform antics; caper.

an-ti-cat-a-lyst (an-ti-kat'ǎ-list, -tī-), *n.* a substance that retards a chemical reaction.

an-ti-christ (an'ti-krist, 'tī-), *n.* 1. an opponent of Christ. 2. [A-], in the *Bible*, the great opponent of Christ expected to appear before the end of the world: see *I John* ii, 18. 3. a false Christ.

an-tic-i-pant (an-tis'i-pǎnt), *adj.* expecting; awaiting: *n.* one who anticipates.

an-tic-i-pate (an-tis'i-pǎt), *v.t.* -pat-ed, -pat-ing, 1. to look forward to. 2. to foresee and be prepared for. 3. to prevent by acting beforehand. 4. to be ahead of in doing something: *v.i.* to attempt to deal with a matter too soon. —**an-tic'i-pa-tor**, *n.* —**an-tic'i-pa-to-ry** (-pǎ-tōr-i), *adj.*

an-tic-i-pa-tion (an-tis-i-pā'shǔn), *n.* 1. the act of anticipating. 2. something that is anticipated; expectation. 3. a preconception or presentiment.

an-tic-i-pa-tive (an-tis'i-pā-tiv), *adj.* 1. tending to anticipate. 2. expectant; full of anticipation. —**an-tic'i-pa-tive-ly**, *adv.*

an-ti-cler-i-cal (an-ti-kler'i-kǎl, -tī-), *adj.* opposed to the clergy or church, especially to its influence on public affairs. —**an-ti-cler'i-cal-ism**, *n.*

an-ti-cli-mac-tic (-klī-mak'tik), *adj.* of, like, or pertaining to an anticlimax. —**an-ti-cli-mac'ti-cal-ly**, *adv.*

an-ti-cli-max (-klī'maks), *n.* 1. a sudden descent in thought or expression from the important

to the trivial. 2. an event at the end of a series that is disappointing or ludicrous in comparison to what has preceded it.

an-ti-cline (an'ti-klīn), *n.* a bent or curved fold of stratified rock with the convex side up: opposed to *syncline*. —**an-ti-cli'nal**, *adj.*

an-ti-co-ag-u-lant (an-ti-kō-ag'yǔ-lǎnt, -tī-), *adj.* a substance, as a drug, that delays or prevents the clotting of blood.

an-ti-de-pres-sant (-dē-pres'ǎnt), *n.* a drug used to treat depression: *adj.* of or acting as an antidepressant drug.

an-ti-dote (an'ti-dōt), *n.* 1. a remedy that counteracts the effect of poison. 2. anything that annuls or tends to prevent the unwanted effects of something else. —**an'ti-dot-al**, *adj.*

an-ti-fe-brile (an-ti-fē'bril, -feb'ril; -tī-), *adj.* capable of allaying fever: *n.* a medicine or drug that can allay fever.

an-ti-fed-er-al-ist (-fed'ēr-ǎ-list, -fed'rǎ-), *n.* one who is opposed to federalism: *adj.* [A-], denoting or of an early political party of the U.S., which opposed the Federalists.

an-ti-freeze (an'ti-frēz, 'tī-), *n.* a substance added to a liquid, as to the water in the radiator of an automobile, to prevent freezing.

an-ti-fric-tion (an-ti-frik'shǔn, -tī-), *n.* a substance or contrivance for reducing friction: *adj.* that reduces friction.

an-ti-gen (an'ti-jěn), *n.* a toxin, enzyme, etc. that stimulates the formation of antibodies.

an-ti-he-ro (an'ti-hir-ō, 'tī-), *n.*, *pl.* -roes, the central character of a drama, story, etc. who does not have the attributes of a conventional hero, such as nobility of character, purposefulness, etc.

an-ti-his-ta-mine (an-ti-his'tǎ-mēn, -tī-; -min), *n.* any of several drugs used to treat allergic conditions, such as hay fever and asthma. —**an-ti-his-ta-min'ic** (-his-tǎ-min'ik), *adj.*

an-ti-knock (an'ti-nok, 'tī-), *n.* a substance added to the fuel of an internal-combustion engine to help prevent knocking.

an-ti-la-bor (an-ti-lā'bēr, -tī-), *adj.* opposed to labor unions; unsympathetic to the interests of labor forces.

an-ti-log-a-rithm (-lôg'ǎ-rithm, -log'), *n.* the number corresponding to a specific logarithm, as the antilogarithm of 1 is 10.

an-ti-ma-cas-sar (an-ti-mǎ-kas'ēr), *n.* a cover for a piece of upholstered furniture, especially a small cover to protect the back or arms from becoming soiled.

an-ti-mag-net-ic (an-ti-mag-net'ik, -tī-), *adj.* made of metals that resist magnetism.

an-ti-ma-lar-i-al (-mǎ-ler'i-ǎl), *adj.* used to prevent or treat malaria: *n.* an antimalarial drug.

an-ti-mat-ter (an'ti-mat-ēr, 'tī-), *n.* matter whose particles have properties that are the reverse of those of ordinary matter.

an-ti-mis-sile (-mis-il), *adj.* designed to provide defense against ballistic missiles.

an-ti-mo-ni-al (an-ti-mō'ni-ǎl), *adj.* of, pertaining to, or containing antimony: *n.* a medicine containing antimony.

an-ti-mo-ny (an'ti-mō-ni), *n.* a white, lustrous, metallic chemical element: used in alloys with other metals, and in compounds for

---

ō in dragon, ōō in crude, ∞ in wool, u in cup, ū in cure, ū in turn, ů in focus, ci in boy, ou in house, th in thin, th in sheathe, g in get, j in joy, y in yet.

medicines, matches, etc. —an·ti·mon·ic (an-tĭ-măn'ik), an'ti·mo·nous (-mō-nŭs), adj.

an·ti·no·mi·an (an-tĭ-nō'mi-ăn), n. one who believes in antinomianism.

an·ti·no·mi·an·ism (-izm), n. in Christian Theology, the doctrine that faith alone, not adherence to the moral law, is sufficient for salvation.

an·tin·o·my (an-tin'ō-mi), n., pl. -mies, the opposition of one law, or part of a law, to another.

an·ti·par·al·lel (an-tĭ-par'ă-lel), n. either of two lines or planes which, when joined by two other lines or planes, form equal but opposite angles: adj. of or pertaining to such lines or planes.

an·ti·par·ti·cle (an'tĭ-pär-tĭ-kl, -'tĭ-), n. any of the particles that constitute antimatter.

an·ti·pas·to (an-tĭ-pas'tō), n. [Italian], an appetizer of salami, anchovies, ripe or green olives, etc.

an·ti·pa·thet·ic (an-tĭ-pă-thet'ik), an·ti·pa·thet·i·cal ('ĭ-kl), adj. having a natural antipathy or aversion (to). —an·ti·pa·thet'i·cal·ly, adv.

an·tip·a·thy (an-tip'ă-thi), n., pl. -thies, 1. natural aversion; instinctive dislike. 2. the object of such aversion or dislike.

an·ti·pe·ri·od·ic (an-tĭ-pir-i-ŏd'ik, -tĭ-), adj. preventing the return of periods, or spells, of disease, as fevers: n. a medicine for preventing the periodic attack of disease.

an·ti·per·son·nel (-pĕr-sŏ-nel'), adj. used against, or intended for use against, enemy military personnel rather than against buildings, vehicles, etc.

an·ti·per·spir·ant (-pŭr'spĭr-ănt), n. a preparation applied to the skin to retard perspiration.

an·ti·phlo·gis·tic (-flŏ-jis'tik), adj. efficacious in counteracting inflammation: n. any remedy which serves to check inflammation.

an·ti·phon (an'tĭ-fon), n. 1. a chant or hymn sung in alternating parts by two groups, or choirs. 2. a short piece of plainsong sung, or verses chanted, before or after some part of a church service.

an·tiph·o·nal (an-tif'ō-nǎl), adj. of or like antiphony or responsive singing: also an·tiph·on·ic (an-tĭ-fon'ik): n. same as antiphonary.

an·tiph·o·nar·y (an-tif'ō-ner-i), n., pl. -nar·ies, a book of antiphons or responses used in church services.

an·tiph·o·ny (-ni), n., pl. -nies, 1. the alternate or responsive rendering of psalms or chants by two groups, or choirs. 2. harmony resulting from the opposition of sounds. 3. an antiphon.

an·tiph·ra·sis (an-tif'ră-sis), n. the employment of a word or phrase in a sense contrary to its common meaning, as to express irony.

an·ti·pode (an'ti-pōd), n. anything that is a direct opposite of another.

an·tip·o·des (an-tip'ō-dēz), n., pl. 1. any two portions of the earth's surface which are exactly opposite to each other. 2. two things that are directly opposite. —an·tip'o·dal, an·tip·o·de'an, adj.

an·ti·py·ret·ic (an-tĭ-pī-ret'ik, -tĭ-), adj. prevent-

ing or reducing fever: n. a remedy that prevents or reduces fever.

an·ti·py·rine (-pī'rēn, 'rin), n. a white powder used as an antipyretic and for the relief of pain.

an·ti·quar·i·an (an-tĭ-kwer'i-ăn), adj. 1. of antiques or antiquities. 2. dealing in old or rare books: n. same as antiquary. —an·ti·quar'i·an·ism, n.

an·ti·quar·y (an'tĭ-kwer-i), n., pl. -quar·ies, one who studies ancient things or collects relics for the purpose of study.

an·ti·quate (an'ti-kwāt), v.t. -quat·ed, -quat·ing, to make old, old-fashioned, or obsolete. —an·ti·qua'tion, n.

an·ti·quat·ed (-kwāt-ĕd), adj. grown old; old-fashioned; obsolete.

an·tique (an-tēk'), adj. 1. of or belonging to a former age; ancient. 2. not modern; old-fashioned. 3. in the style of an earlier period. 4. dealing in antiques: n. 1. something of great age; relic of antiquity. 2. a piece of furniture, a vase, etc. produced in a former period: v.t. -tiqued', -tiqu'ing, to make look antique. —an·tique'ly, adv. —an·tique'ness, n.

an·tiq·ui·ty (an-tik'wi-ti), n., pl. -ties, 1. great age: ancientness. 2. the ancient period of history. 3. the people of ancient times. 4. pl. that which belonged to or survives from ancient times; relics, old customs, etc.

an·ti·scor·bu·tic (an-tĭ-skôr-bū'tik, -tĭ-), adj. that cures or prevents scurvy: n. a food, vitamin, etc. that cures or prevents scurvy.

an·ti·Sem·ite (-sem'ĭt), n. one who is anti-Semitic.

an·ti·Se·mit·ic (-sĕ-mit'ik), adj. 1. feeling or showing hostility toward Jews. 2. persecuting Jews. 3. of or caused by such hostility or persecution. —an·ti·Se·mit'i·cal·ly, adv. —an·ti·Sem'i·tism (-sem'ĭ-tizm), n.

an·ti·sep·sis (-sep'sis), n. 1. the process of preventing sepsis or the growth of microorganisms. 2. the use of antiseptics to check the growth of microorganisms.

an·ti·sep·tic (-sep'tik), adj. 1. preventing infection, decay, etc. by checking the growth of microorganisms. 2. free from microorganisms; sterile. 3. using antiseptics: n. any substance that checks the growth of microorganisms. —an·ti·sep'ti·cal·ly, adv.

an·ti·slav·er·y (-slā'vēr-i, 'vri), adj. opposed to slavery.

an·ti·so·cial (-sō'shǎl), adj. 1. not liking to be associated with others; unsocial. 2. detrimental to the welfare of society in general. —an·ti·so'cial·ly, adv.

an·ti·spas·mod·ic (-spaz-mod'ik), adj. counteracting or preventing spasms: n. a medicine having such an effect.

an·ti·stat·ic (-stat'ik), adj. reducing charges of static electricity, as in fabrics.

an·ti·stro·phe (an-tis'trŏ-fē), n. 1. in the ancient Greek chorus, the return movement from left to right following the previous strophe. 2. the part of the song, drama, etc. performed by the chorus during this movement. 3. the second of two contrasting metrical systems in a poem. —an·ti·stroph·ic (an-tĭ-strof'ik), adj.

---

a in cap, ā in cane, ä in father, ȧ in abet, e in met ē in be, ē in baker, ė in regent, i in pit, ī in fine, i in manifest, o in hot, ô in horse, ō in bone,

an·ti·tank (an-ti-tank', -ti-). *adj.* for use against armored combat vehicles, especially tanks.

an·tith·e·sis (an-tith'ĕ-sis). *n., pl.* **-ses** (-sēz). 1. opposition; contrast. 2. the expression of contrast or opposition, often in two phrases or sentences, as "to promise bread and give a stone." 3. the exact opposite.

an·ti·thet·i·cal (an-ti-thet'i-kăl). **an·ti·thet·ic** ('ik). *adj.* 1. of, pertaining to, or containing antithesis. 2. exactly opposite. **—an·ti·thet'i·cal·ly**, *adv.*

an·ti·tox·in (an-ti-tok'sin. -ti-). *n.* 1. an antibody formed in the body to act against a certain toxin. 2. a serum containing an antitoxin, taken from the blood of an immunized animal and used to treat or prevent diseases such as tetanus and diphtheria. **—an·ti·tox'ic** ('sik). *adj.*

an·ti·trades (an-ti-trādz', 'ti-). *n.* winds blowing steadily above and in an opposite direction to the trade winds.

an·ti·trust (an-ti-trust', -ti-). *adj.* in opposition to or regulating trusts, or business monopolies, national industrial organizations, etc.

an·ti·type (an'ti-tip, 'ti-). *n.* 1. that which preceded the type, and of which the type is the representation. 2. an opposite type. **— an·ti·typ'i·cal** (-tip'i-kăl). **an·ti·typ'ic**, *adj.*

an·ti·ven·in (an-ti-ven'in, -ti-). *n.* a serum containing an antitoxin against venom, as of snakes.

an·ti·viv·i·sec·tion (-viv-i-sek'shŭn). *n.* opposition to the use of live animals in medical research. **—an·ti·viv·i·sec'tion·ist**, *adj. & n.*

ant·ler (ant'lĕr). *n.* 1. the branched horn of a deer. 2. any of the individual branches of a deer's horn. **—ant'lered**, *adj.*

ant lion *n.* an insect larva that constructs a pit for trapping ants and other insects on which it feeds. 2. the adult form of this larva: also **ant lion fly.**

an·to·no·ma·sia (an-tŏ-nŏ-mā'zhả). *n.* 1. the use of a title or epithet for a name, as *His Honor* for a mayor. 2. the use of the name of an individual instead of a common noun, as *Romeo* for a lover.

an·to·nym (an'tŏ-nim). *n.* a word meaning the opposite of some other word, as *unhappy* is the antonym of *happy.* **—an·ton·y·mous** (an-ton'i-mŭs), *adj.*

an·trum (an'trŭm), *n., pl.* **-tra** ('trả), **-trums**, a cavity in a bone, especially a sinus in the upper jawbone.

an·u·re·sis (an-yoo-rē'sis). *n.* 1. partial or complete inability to discharge urine. 2. same as **anuria.** **—an·u·ret'ic** (-ret'ik), *adj.*

an·u·ri·a (an-yoor'i-å). *n.* inability of the kidneys to secrete urine. **—an·u'ric,** *adj.*

an·u·rous (an-yoor'ŭs). *adj.* tailless, as an adult frog or toad.

a·nus (ā'nŭs), *n., pl.* **a'nus·es, a·ni** (ā'nī). the opening at the lower end of the rectum for the passage of excrement from the alimentary canal.

an·vil (an'vil). *n.* 1. an iron or steel block on which metal objects are hammered and shaped. 2. the incus, one of the three bones of the inner ear.

anx·i·e·ty (ang-zī'ĕ-ti). *n., pl.* **-ties**, 1. a condi-

tion of mental uneasiness or worry about the future; concern about what may happen. 2. a highly emotional state characterized by exaggerated or unfounded worry or fear. 3. eagerness.

anx·ious (ang'shŭs), *adj.* 1. apprehensive; worried. 2. full of anxiety. 3. eager. **—anx'ious·ly,** *adv.* **—anx'ious·ness,** *n.*

an·y (en'i), *adj.* 1. one indefinitely. 2. some. 3. all; every. 4. even the smallest amount of: *pron.* any person; anyone: *adv.* to any degree or extent.

an·y·bod·y (-bud-i, -bod-i), *pron.* 1. any person. 2. someone of importance.

an·y·how (-hou), *adv.* 1. in any way or manner. 2. in any case; at any rate. 3. carelessly.

an·y·more (en-i-môr'), *adv.* at the present time; now: also **any more.**

an·y·one (en'i-wun), *pron.* anybody; any person.

an·y·place (-plăs), *adv.* [Informal]. anywhere.

an·y·thing (-thing), *pron.* any object or thing whatever: *n.* a thing of any kind: *adv.* to any degree; at all.

an·y·way (-wā), *adv.* 1. in any manner. 2. nevertheless. 3. carelessly.

an·y·where (-hwer), *adv.* 1. in or to any place. 2. [Informal], to any extent.

an·y·wise (-wiz), *adv.* in any manner; at all.

An·zac (an'zak), *n.* a member of the Australian and New Zealand Army Corps: *adj.* of or pertaining to the Anzacs.

A one (ā' wun'), [Informal], superior; first-class; very good: also **A number one, A 1.**

a·o·rist (ā'ō-rist), *n.* one of the tenses of Greek verbs denoting past indefinite time: *adj.* of this tense. **—a·o·ris'tic,** *adj.*

a·or·ta (ā-ôr'tả), *n., pl.* **-tas, -tae** ('tē), the chief artery or main trunk of the arterial system, carrying blood from the left ventricle of the heart to arteries in all organs and parts of the body. **—a·or'tic, a·or'tal,** *adj.*

a·ou·dad (ā'oo-dad, ou'dad), *n.* a kind of wild sheep of North Africa, with curved horns and a growth of long hair down the front of the body.

a·pace (á-pās'), *adv.* quickly; at a quick pace; speedily.

A·pach·e (á-pach'i), *n., pl.* **A·pach'es, A·pach'e,** a member of a North American Indian tribe of the southwestern U.S.

a·pache (á-pash'), *n.* a Parisian ruffian or gangster: *adj.* denoting an exhibition dance portraying an apache treating his girlfriend roughly.

a·part (á-pärt'), *adv.* 1. separately; away in time or place. 2. aside. 3. into parts or pieces; asunder.

a·part·heid (-hāt, 'hit), *n.* the policy and practice of racial segregation and discrimination in South Africa.

a·part·ment ('mĕnt), *n.* 1. a room or set of rooms used as a dwelling, especially one set of rooms in a building divided into dwelling units. 2. such a building: also **apartment house, apartment building.**

ap·a·thet·ic (ap-å-thet'ik), *adj.* 1. devoid of, or insensible to, emotion or feeling. 2. indifferent; not interested. **—ap·a·thet'i·cal·ly,** *adv.*

ap·a·thy (ap'å-thi), *n., pl.* **-thies,** 1. lack of feeling: want of passion or emotion. 2. indifference: lack of interest.

ap·a·tite (ap'á-tīt), *n.* a crystalline phosphate of lime.

APC, a compound of aspirin, phenacetin, and caffeine, usually in the form of a white tablet (*APC tablet*) used to reduce fever or relieve pain.

ape (āp), *n.* l. any of several tailless monkeys that can stand nearly erect and walk like man, such as the chimpanzee and gorilla. 2. one who imitates: mimic. 3. one who is clumsy or uncouth: *v.t.* **aped, ap'ing,** to imitate: mimic. —**ape'like,** *adj.*

a·peak (á-pēk'), *adv.* nearly vertical in position: a nautical term.

ape-man (āp'man), *n., pl.* **-men,** an extinct primate considered to be intermediate between the apes and man.

a·pe·ri·ent (á-pir'i-ěnt), *adj.* having a laxative effect: *n.* a laxative medicine.

a·pe·ri·tif (ä-pä-ri-tēf'), *n.* an alcoholic drink taken before a meal as an appetizer.

ap·er·ture (ap'ēr-chēr), *n.* l. an opening: gap, slit, hole, etc. 2. *a)* the opening in a camera or optical instrument through which the light passes to the lens. *b)* the diameter of this opening.

a·pet·a·lous (á-pet'á-lŭs), *adj.* without petals, or corolla.

a·pex (ā'peks), *n., pl.* **a'pex·es, ap·i·ces** (ap'í-sēz, ā'pi-), l. the highest point: summit. 2. a pointed extremity: tip. 3. a culmination: climax.

a·pha·si·a (á-fā'zhá), *n.* loss of the ability to use or understand language, due to disease or injury of the brain. —**a·pha'sic** ('zik), **a·pha'si·ac** ('zi-ak), *n. & adj.*

a·phe·li·on (á-fē'li-ŏn), *n., pl.* **-li·ons, -li·a** (-á), that point farthest from the sun, comet, etc. in the orbit of a planet: opposed to *perihelion.*

a·pher·e·sis, a·phaer·e·sis (á-fer'ē-sis), *n.* the dropping of a letter or syllable at the beginning of a word. —**aph·e·ret·ic, aph·ae·ret·ic** (af-ē-ret'ik), *adj.*

aph·e·sis (af'ē-sis), *n.* the dropping of a short, unaccented vowel at the beginning of a word. —**a·phet·ic** (á-fet'ik), *adj.* —**a·phet'i·cal·ly,** *adv.*

a·phid (ā'fid, af'id), *n.* a small, winged insect that sucks the juice from plants: plant louse. —**a·phid'i·an,** *adj. & n.*

a·phis (ā'fis, af'is), *n., pl.* **aph·i·des** (af'i-dēz), same as **aphid.**

a·pho·ni·a (á-fō'ni-á), *n.* loss of voice because of a disorder of the vocal chords.

a·phon·ic (á-fän'ik), *adj.* l. of or pertaining to aphonia. 2. in *Phonetics,* not pronounced.

aph·o·rism (af'ō-rizm), *n.* l. a concise statement of a rule or principle. 2. a short, pithy saying stating a general truth: maxim. —**aph'o·rist,** *n.* —**aph·o·ris'tic,** *adj.* —**aph·o·ris'ti·cal·ly,** *adv.*

a·pho·tic (ā-fōt'ik), *adj.* without light: dark: said especially of the depths of the ocean.

aph·ro·dis·i·ac (af-rō-diz'i-ak), *adj.* exciting or increasing sexual desire: *n.* a drug or other agent that increases sexual desire.

Aph·ro·di·te (af'rō-dīt-i), *n.* in *Greek Mythology,* the goddess of beauty and love.

a·phyl·lous (ā-fil'ŭs), *adj.* without leaves, as most cactuses: leafless.

a·pi·an (ā'pi-án), *adj.* of or pertaining to bees.

a·pi·ar·y (ā'pi-er-i), *n., pl.* **-ar·ies,** a place where bees are kept. —**a·pi·ar'i·an,** *adj.* —**a'pi·a·rist,** *n.*

a·pic·u·late (á-pik'yoo-lit), *adj.* with a pointed end: said of some leaves.

a·pi·cul·ture (ā'pi-kul-chēr), *n.* beekeeping. —**a·pi·cul'tur·al,** *adj.* —**a·pi·cul'tur·ist,** *n.*

a·piece (á-pēs'), *adv.* to or for each one: each.

A·pis (ā'pis), *n.* the sacred bull of ancient Egypt.

ap·ish (āp'ish), *adj.* l. resembling an ape. 2. foolish as an ape: silly. 3. ignorantly imitative. —**ap'ish·ly,** *adv.* —**ap'ish·ness,** *n.*

a·plen·ty (á-plen'ti), *adj. & adv.* [Informal], in plenty: in abundance.

a·plomb (á-pläm', á-plum'), *n.* self-possession: assurance: composure.

a·poc·a·lypse (á-pok'á-lips), *n.* l. [A-], the last book of the New Testament: book of Revelation. 2. any similar prophecy of a great final struggle. —**a·poc·a·lyp'tic** (-lip'tik), **a·poc·a·lyp'ti·cal,** *adj.* —**a·poc·a·lyp'ti·cal·ly,** *adv.*

a·po·car·pous (ap-ō-kär'pŭs), *adj.* having the seed-bearing organs (carpels) separate, or, sometimes, partially joined, as some flowers.

a·poc·o·pate (á-pok'ō-pāt), *v.t.* **-pat·ed, -pat·ing,** to shorten by apocope. —**a·poc·o·pa'tion,** *n.*

a·poc·o·pe ('ō-pi), *n.* the cutting off or deletion of the last letter or syllable of a word.

a·poc·ry·pha (á-pok'kri-fá), *n.* l. a writing or story of doubtful authenticity. 2. [A-], certain books of the Septuagint version of the Old Testament, some accepted as canonical by the Roman Catholic Church, but rejected by Protestants and Jews.

a·poc·ry·phal (-fál), *adj.* l. of doubtful authority. 2. not genuine: false. 3. [A-], of or pertaining to the Apocrypha.

ap·od (ap'ŏd), *adj.* same as **apodal:** *n.* an animal that has no feet or legs, such as a snake or certain legless lizards.

ap·o·dal (ap'ō-dál), *adj.* l. having no feet or legs, as snakes. 2. having no fins, as eels. Also **ap'o·dous** (-dŭs).

ap·o·dic·tic (ap-ō-dik'tik), *adj.* certain beyond all doubt: clearly demonstrable or necessarily true: also **ap·o·deic'tic** (-dīk'tik). —**ap·o·dic'ti·cal·ly,** *adv.*

a·pod·o·sis (á-päd'ō-sis), *n., pl.* **-ses** (-sēz), the latter portion, or consequent clause, of a conditional sentence.

a·pog·a·my (á-pog'á-mi), *n.* nonsexual development of certain plants. —**ap·o·gam·ic** (ap-ō-gam'ik), **a·pog'a·mous,** *adj.*

ap·o·gee (ap'ō-jē), *n.* l. the point at which an orbiting body or object is farthest from the body around which it is orbiting: opposed to *perigee.* 2. the farthest or highest point. —**ap·o·ge'an** (-jē'án), **ap·o·ge'al,** *adj.*

a·po·lit·i·cal (ā-pō-lit'í-kál), *adj.* unrelated to politics: not political. —**a·po·lit'i·cal·ly,** *adv.*

A·pol·lo (á-pol'ō), *n.* l. in *Greek & Roman Mythology,* the god of music, poetry, etc., represented as a handsome young man. 2.

---

a in cap, ā in cane, ä in father, á in abet, e in met, ē in be, ě in baker, ě in regent, i in pit, ī in fine, i in manifest, o in hot, ō in horse, ō in bone,

any handsome young man. —A·pol·lo·ni·an (ap-ȯ-lō'ni-ȧn), *adj.*

a·pol·o·get·ic (ȧ-pol-ȯ-jet'ik), —a·pol·o·get·i·cal ('i-kl), *adj.* 1. defending or vindicating something done or said. 2. expressing regret for something; apologizing. —a·pol·o·get'i·cal·ly, *adv.*

a·pol·o·get·ics ('iks), *n.* the branch of theology that defends Christian doctrine on the grounds of reason.

ap·o·lo·gi·a (ap-ȯ-lō'ji-ȧ), *n.* a formal argument in justification or defense.

a·pol·o·gist (ȧ-pol'ȯ-jist), *n.* one who apologizes; one who pleads in justification or defense of an action, idea, doctrine, etc.

a·pol·o·gize (-jīz), *v.i.* -gized, -giz·ing, 1. to make an apology or excuse; express regret for something done or said. 2. to present a formal defense, either in writing or speech. —a·pol'o·giz·er, *n.*

ap·o·logue (ap'ȯ-lŏg), *n.* a moral fable; a short fiction or allegory embodying a moral application.

a·pol·o·gy (ȧ-pol'ȯ-ji), *n., pl.* -gies, 1. the expressing of regret for something done or said; offering of explanation or excuse by way of amends. 2. a formal defense of an action, idea, doctrine, etc. 3. a poor substitute.

a·poph·y·sis (ȧ-pof'i-sis), *n., pl.* -ses (-sēz), an outgrowth, swelling, etc., as on a bone.

a·po·plec·tic (ap-ȯ-plek'tik), ap·o·plec·ti·cal ('ti·kȧl), *adj.* 1. of, pertaining to, or of the nature of apoplexy. 2. afflicted with apoplexy. 3. looking or acting as though about to be seized with apoplexy: *n.* one who has or is likely to have apoplexy.

ap·o·plex·y (ap'ȯ-plek-si), *n.* sudden paralysis, usually with loss of consciousness, resulting from the rupture or obstruction of a blood vessel in the brain; stroke.

a·port (ȧ-pōrt'), *adv.* on or to the port, or left, side of a ship.

ap·o·si·o·pe·sis (ap-ō-sī-ȯ-pē'sis), *n.* a sudden break in speech, as if the speaker were unwilling to go on. —ap·o·si·o·pet'ic (-pet'ik), *adj.*

a·pos·ta·sy (ȧ-pos'tȧ-si), *n., pl.* -sies, the forsaking or abandonment of what one has professed or adhered to, as faith, principles, or party.

a·pos·tate ('tāt, 'tit), *n.* one who has forsaken his faith, principles, etc.; renegade: *adj.* guilty of apostasy; traitorous; renegade.

a·pos·ta·tize ('tȧ-tīz), *v.i.* -tized, -tiz·ing, to abandon one's faith, principles, etc.

a pos·te·ri·o·ri (ȧ pos-tir-i-ōr'ī, -ôr'ī), [Latin], 1. that reasons from effect to cause or from facts to a general principle. 2. based on actual experience or observation. Opposed to *a priori.*

a·pos·tle (ȧ-päs'l), *n.* 1. one charged with a special mission; specifically, [usually A-], one of the twelve disciples selected by Christ to propagate the gospel. 2. the first Christian missionary in a region. 3. an initiator or early promoter of some movement, idea, etc. —a·pos'tle·ship, *n.*

Apostles' Creed, an ancient profession of belief in the basic Christian teachings.

a·pos·to·late (ȧ-pos'tȯl-it, 'tȯ-lāt), *n.* an apostle's office, dignity, authority, etc.

ap·os·tol·ic (ap-ȯs-tol'ik), ap·os·tol·i·cal ('i-kl), *adj.* 1. of or pertaining to an apostle. 2. of or pertaining to the Apostles, their times or work, etc. 3. [often A-], of the Pope; papal. —a·pos·to·lic·i·ty (ȧ-pos-tȯ-lis'i-ti), *n.*

apostolic see, 1. a see founded by an apostle. 2. [A- S-], the Pope's see at Rome.

apostolic succession, the succession of ecclesiastical authority in an unbroken line from the Apostle Peter.

a·pos·tro·phe (ȧ-pos'trȯ-fi), *n.* 1. a breaking off in a speech to address directly a person or thing that may or may not be present. 2. a sign (') used in writing and printing: *a)* to indicate the omission from a word of one or more letters. *b)* to signify the possessive case of some pronouns and nouns. *c)* to form the plural of some letters and figures.

a·pos·tro·phize (-fīz), *v.t. & v.i.* -phized, -phiz·ing, to address (a person or thing) by apostrophe.

a·poth·e·car·ies' measure (ȧ-poth'ē-ker-iz), the system of liquid measure used in pharmacy, 60 minims being equal to one dram in this measure, 8 drams to one ounce, and 16 ounces to one pint.

apothecaries' weight, the system of weight used in pharmacy: see **Weights & Measures** in Supplements.

a·poth·e·car·y (ȧ-poth'ē-ker-i), *n., pl.* -car·ies, a pharmacist; druggist.

ap·o·thegm (ap'ȯ-them), *n.* a short, pithy saying; maxim; aphorism. —ap·o·theg·mat'ic (-theg-mat'ik), ap·o·theg·mat'i·cal, *adj.*

a·poth·e·o·sis (ȧ-poth-i-ō'sis), *n., pl.* -ses ('sēz), 1. deification. 2. glorification. 3. a glorified person or thing.

a·poth·e·o·size (ȧ-poth'i-ȯ-sīz), *v.t.* -sized, -siz·ing, 1. to exalt to the rank of a god; deify. 2. to glorify.

ap·pall, ap·pal (ȧ-pôl'), *v.t.* -palled', -pal'ling, to horrify; dismay; shock. —ap·pal'ling, *adj.* —ap·pal'ling·ly, *adv.*

ap·pa·loo·sa (ap-ȧ-lōō'sȧ), *n.* one of a sturdy breed of riding horses, bred in the western U.S., having black and white markings.

ap·pa·nage (ap'ȧ-nij), *n.* something that belongs to one by custom or right; a usual or rightful adjunct or endowment.

ap·pa·ra·tus (ap-ȧ-rat'ús, -rāt'-), *n., pl.* -ra'tus, -ra'tus·es, 1. a set or outfit of tools, instruments, etc. for doing some specified work, experiment, or other operation. 2. any complex device, organization, system, etc. 3. a set of bodily organs with a single function.

ap·par·el (ȧ-per'ĕl), *n.* clothing; garb; dress: *v.t.* -eled or -elled, -el·ing or -el·ling, 1. to clothe; attire. 2. to adorn.

ap·par·ent (ȧ-per'ent), *adj.* 1. open to view. 2. capable of being readily understood; evident. 3. seeming, but not real. —ap·par'ent·ly, *adv.* —ap·par'ent·ness, *n.*

ap·pa·ri·tion (ap-ȧ-rish'ȧn), *n.* 1. an appearance that is sudden or unexpected, especially of something thought to be a ghost. 2. an appearing; manifestation.

ȯ in dragon, ōō in crude, oo in wool, u in cup, ū in cure, ů in turn, ů in focus, oi in boy, ou in house, th in thin, *th* in sheathe, g in get, j in joy, y in yet.

ap·peal (å-pēl′), *v.t.* to refer (a case) to a higher court: *v.i.* 1. to ask that a law case be reheard in a higher court. 2. to entreat, or call for, aid, sympathy, or mercy. 3. to refer or resort (*to*) for support, a decision, etc. 4. to be attractive, amusing, interesting, etc.: *n.* 1. a call for aid, sympathy, mercy, support, etc. 2. the power to attract, amuse, interest, etc. 3. a request that a case be reheard in a higher court. 4. the right to make this request. —ap·peal′a·ble, *adj.* —ap·peal′ing, *adj.* —ap·peal′ing·ly, *adv.*

ap·pear (å-pir′), *v.i.* 1. to become visible. 2. to seem. 3. to come formally before a court. 4. to perform publicly. 5. to be published.

ap·pear·ance (′åns), *n.* 1. the act of appearing. 2. a thing seen. 3. the way a person or thing looks; outward characteristics. 4. a pretense; semblance. 5. *pl.* outer indications or signs supporting some kind of judgment or conclusion.

ap·pease (å-pēz′), *v.t.* -peased′, -peas′ing, 1. to quiet; pacify; soothe, especially by yielding to demands. 2. to allay or assuage. —ap·peas′a·ble, *adj.* —ap·peas′er, *n.*

ap·pease·ment (′mēnt), *n.* 1. the act of appeasing. 2. the state of being appeased. 3. to give in to the demands of a belligerent nation in order to keep peace.

ap·pel·lant (å-pel′ånt), *n.* one who appeals, especially to a higher court: *adj.* of or pertaining to legal appeals.

ap·pel·late (′åt), *adj.* 1. of or pertaining to legal appeals. 2. denoting a court that hears appeals.

ap·pel·la·tion (ap-è-lā′shůn), *n.* the name, title, or designation by which a person or thing is called or known.

ap·pel·la·tive (å-pel′å-tiv), *adj.* of appellation: *n.* a name or descriptive title.

ap·pel·lee (ap-è-lē′), *n.* the person appealed against; the defendant in an appeal.

ap·pend (å-pend′), *v.t.* to attach or add, as an accessory part; subjoin.

ap·pend·age (å-pen′dij), *n.* 1. something appended. 2. in *Biology*, an external or lesser part, as a tail.

ap·pend·ant, ap·pend·ent (′dånt), *adj.* 1. attached or added. 2. that goes along with; associated with: *n.* same as appendage.

ap·pen·dec·to·my (ap-ėn-dek′tō-mi), *n.*, *pl.* -mies, a surgical operation for removing the vermiform appendix.

ap·pen·di·ci·tis (å-pen-di-sīt′is), *n.* inflammation of the vermiform appendix.

ap·pen·dix (å-pen′diks), *n.*, *pl.* -dix·es, -di·ces (′di-sēz), 1. supplementary material at the end of a book. 2. a small saclike extension of the cecum of the large intestine.

ap·per·cep·tion (ap-ėr-sep′shůn), *n.* 1. perception involving self-consciousness. 2. the relating of new ideas to old ideas.

ap·per·tain (ap-ėr-tān′), *v.i.* to belong or pertain to, as by relation or custom.

ap·pe·tite (ap′è-tīt), *n.* the desire for gratification of some want, craving, or passion, especially for food. —ap·pe·ti·tive (-tīt-iv) *adj.*

ap·pe·tiz·er (-tī-zèr), *n.* a drink or a small amount of flavorful food served before a meal to whet the appetite.

ap·pe·tiz·ing (-tī-zing), *adj.* 1. flavorful; zestful. 2. tempting the appetite. —ap′pe·tiz·ing·ly, *adv.*

ap·plaud (å-plôd′), *v.t. & v.i.* 1. to praise; express approval (of). 2. to clap the hands or cheer in order to show approval (of). —ap·plaud′er, *n.*

ap·plause (å-plôz′), *n.* the expression of approval, especially by clapping the hands or cheering.

ap·ple (ap′l), *n.* 1. a round, edible fruit with a red, yellow, or green skin, growing on trees in temperate climates. 2. any of the trees bearing this fruit. 3. any of several plants bearing applelike fruit.

apple butter, a smooth, sweet, thick spread made from apples stewed with spices.

ap·ple·jack (-jak), *n.* brandy distilled from fermented apple cider.

apple of one's eye, 1. the pupil of one's eye. 2. a person regarded with special affection.

ap·ple·sauce (-sôs), *n.* 1. apples stewed to a pulp, sweetened, and eaten as a relish or dessert. 2. [Slang], bosh; nonsense.

ap·pli·ance (å-plī′åns), *n.* an apparatus or piece of equipment devised to perform a specific function, especially in the home: a refrigerator, toaster, and washer are household appliances.

ap·pli·ca·ble (ap′li-kå-bl), *adj.* capable of being, or fit to be, applied. —ap·pli·ca·bil′i·ty, *n.*

ap·pli·cant (ap′li-kånt), *n.* one who applies, as for a position or for aid.

ap·pli·ca·tion (ap-li-kå′shůn), *n.* 1. the act of applying or requesting. 2. a thing applied, especially a remedy. 3. a putting into practice; a practical demonstration of a principle. 4. a request, or form used in making a request. 5. persistent effort. 6. practical use or relevance.

ap·pli·ca·tor (ap′li-kåt-ėr), *n.* a device or instrument used to apply a medication, paint, or the like.

ap·plied (å-plīd′), *adj.* actually put to practical use: said of a given science, field of study, etc.

ap·pli·qué (ap-li-kā′), *n.* a piece of one material applied to another, as by sewing, for a decoration: *v.t.* -quéd′, -qué′ing, to apply as ornamentation.

ap·ply (å-plī′), *v.t.* -plied′, -ply′ing, 1. to place, fasten, or spread on. 2. to put into practice or devote to a particular purpose. 3. to refer or ascribe as fitting to a person or thing. 4. to devote (oneself, one's mind, etc.) diligently: *v.i.* 1. to suit; be appropriate. 2. to make application (*to*). —ap·pli′er, *n.*

ap·point (å-point′), *v.t.* 1. to fix (a time, place, etc.); settle; decree. 2. to assign or designate officially. 3. to furnish or equip.

ap·point·ee (å-poin-tē′), *n.* one appointed to a certain office, job, etc.

ap·point·ive (å-poin′tiv), *adj.* of, pertaining to, or filled by appointment.

ap·point·ment (å-point′mēnt), *n.* 1. the act of appointing or state of being appointed. 2. the position or office assigned or held. 3. an arrangement or agreement to meet or be somewhere. 4. *pl.* furniture or equipment.

ap·por·tion (á-pôr'shún), *v.t.* to assign and distribute proportionately. —**ap·por'tion·ment**, *n.*

ap·pose (á-pōz'), *v.t.* **-posed'**, **-pos'ing**, to place side by side, opposite, or next to. —**ap·pos'·a·ble**, *adj.*

ap·po·site (ap'ō-zit), *adj.* proper; fit; pertinent; well-adapted. —**ap'po·site·ly**, *adv.* —**ap'po·site·ness**, *n.*

ap·po·si·tion (ap-ō-zish'ún), *n.* 1. the act of apposing or state of being apposed. 2. the position of something apposed. 3. the placing of a word or phrase next to another to explain the other, as in "Bill, my oldest son." —**ap·po·si'tion·al**, *adj.* —**ap·po·si'tion·al·ly**, *adv.*

ap·pos·i·tive (á-poz'ĭ-tiv), *n.* a word or phrase in apposition: *adj.* of, pertaining to, or in apposition. —**ap·pos'i·tive·ly**, *adv.*

ap·prais·al (á-prā'zl), *n.* 1. the act of appraising or state of being appraised. 2. the estimated worth of something. Also **ap·praise'ment**.

ap·praise (á-prāz'), *v.t.* **-praised'**, **-prais'ing**, 1. to set a value upon. 2. to judge the worth of. —**ap·prais'a·ble**, *adj.* —**ap·prais'er**, *n.* —**ap·prais'ing·ly**, *adv.*

ap·pre·ci·a·ble (á-prē'shá-bl, 'shi-á-bl), *adj.* capable of being perceived or noticed; not insignificant. —**ap·pre'ci·a·bly**, *adv.*

ap·pre·ci·ate (á-prē'shi-āt), *v.t.* **-at·ed**, **-at·ing**, 1. to value; esteem highly; prize. 2. to be sensible of; notice. 3. to be grateful for. 4. to raise in value: *v.i.* to rise in value. —**ap·pre'ci·a·tor**, *n.* —**ap·pre'ci·a·to·ry**, *adj.*

ap·pre·ci·a·tion (á-prē-shi-ā'shŭn), *n.* 1. the just valuation, or proper estimation, of worth or merit. 2. gratitude. 3. enjoyment. 4. a rise in value.

ap·pre·ci·a·tive (á-prē'shi-tiv, 'shi-ā-), *adj.* exhibiting or feeling appreciation. —**ap·pre'ci·a·tive·ly**, *adv.* —**ap·pre'ci·a·tive·ness**, *n.*

ap·pre·hend (ap-rē-hend'), *v.t.* 1. to seize; arrest. 2. to perceive; understand. 3. to anticipate or expect with dread: *v.i.* to understand.

ap·pre·hen·si·ble (-hen'si-bl), *adj.* capable of being apprehended, or perceived. —**ap·pre·hen·si·bil'i·ty**, *n.*

ap·pre·hen·sion ('shŭn), *n.* 1. the act of seizure; arrest. 2. perception; understanding. 3. dread, fear, or distrust of the future.

ap·pre·hen·sive ('siv), *adj.* 1. quick to learn, or grasp. 2. fearful of evil; anxious about the future. —**ap·pre·hen'sive·ly**, *adv.* —**ap·pre·hen'sive·ness**, *n.*

ap·pren·tice (á-pren'tis), *n.* 1. a person legally bound to a master craftsman to learn a trade. 2. a person learning a craft under a specified agreement. 3. a beginner; novice: *v.t.* **-ticed**, **-tic·ing**, to accept or set to work under the care of a master for instruction in some trade or craft.

ap·prise, **ap·prize** (á-priz'), *v.t.* **-prised'** or **-prized'**, **-pris'ing** or **-priz'ing**, 1. to give notice to; inform. 2. same as **appraise**.

ap·proach (á-prōch'), *v.i.* to draw or grow near: *v.t.* 1. to come near to. 2. to be the close or rough equivalent of; be like. 3. to suggest something to or ask something of. 4. to set

about; take steps toward: *n.* 1. the act of drawing near. 2. a close or rough equivalent. 3. *pl.* steps taken to suggest or ask something. 4. an access; passage; road. 5. a golf stroke intended to get the ball on the green. —**ap·proach·a·bil'i·ty**, *n.* —**ap·proach'a·ble**, *adj.*

ap·pro·ba·tion (ap-rō-bā'shŭn), *n.* 1. commendation. 2. official sanction or permission.

ap·pro·ba·tive (ap'rō-bāt-iv), *adj.* approving; expressing approbation: also **ap·pro·ba·to·ry** (á-prō'bá-tōr-i).

ap·pro·pri·a·ble (á-prō'pri-á-bl), *adj.* capable of being appropriated.

ap·pro·pri·ate (á-prō'pri-āt), *v.t.* **-at·ed**, **-at·ing**, 1. to take for oneself, to the exclusion of others. 2. to take improperly. 3. to set apart or assign to a particular use: *adj.* (-it), fit; apt; suitable. —**ap·pro'pri·ate·ly**, *adv.* —**ap·pro'pri·ate·ness**, *n.* —**ap·pro'pri·a·tive** (-āt-iv), *adj.* —**ap·pro'pri·a·tor**, *n.*

ap·pro·pri·a·tion (á-prō-pri-ā'shŭn), *n.* 1. the act of appropriating or being appropriated. 2. money set aside for a particular use.

ap·prov·al (a-prōōv'al), *n.* 1. the act of approving. 2. favorable reception or response. 3. formal sanction.

ap·prove (á-prōōv'), *v.t.* **proved'**, **-prov'ing**, 1. to consent to; sanction; ratify. 2. to regard with favor; express approval of: *v.i.* to feel or show approval (*of*). —**ap·prov'a·ble**, *adj.* —**ap·prov'er**, *n.* —**ap·prov'ing·ly**, *adv.*

ap·prox·i·mate (á-prok'si-māt), *v.t.* **-mat·ed**, **-mat·ing**, to come near to; be the close or rough equivalent of: *adj.* (-mit), 1. closely or roughly resembling. 2. fairly exact or correct. —**ap·prox'i·mate·ly**, *adv.*

ap·prox·i·ma·tion (á-prok-si-mā'shŭn), *n.* 1. the act of approximating. 2. a fairly close likeness or estimate.

ap·pur·te·nance (á-pûr'tĕ-nâns), *n.* 1. something added to a more important thing; adjunct; accessory. 2. *pl.* equipment for some activity, etc.

ap·pur·te·nant (-nânt), *adj.* belonging or pertaining to; accessory: *n.* an appurtenance.

ap·ri·cot (ap'ri-kot, ā'pri-), *n.* 1. a small yellowish-orange fruit, related to the peach and plum. 2. the tree it grows on.

A·pril (ā'pril), *n.* the fourth month of the year, having 30 days.

April fool, one who is deceived by a trick played on him on April 1, called *All Fools' Day* or *April Fools' Day*.

a pri·o·ri (ā prī-ôr'ī, ā prī-ōr'ī), [Latin], 1. that reasons from cause to effect or from a general principle to individual instances. 2. based on theory rather than on actual experience or observation. 3. not based on prior examination or study. Opposed to *a posteriori*.

a·pron (ā'prŏn, 'pĕrn), *n.* 1. a garment worn over the front part of the body and usually tied at the waist, to protect the clothes. 2. any protective covering or extension. 3. the projecting part of a stage. 4. a paved area for airplanes near a hangar: *v.t.* to put an apron on. —**a'pron·like**, *adj.*

ap·ro·pos (ap-rō-pō'), *adv.* 1. opportunely; to

ŏ in dragon, ōō in crude, oo in wool, u in cup, ū in cure, ŭ in turn, û in focus, oi in boy, ou in house, th in thin, *th* in sheathe, g in get, j in joy, y in yet.

the point. 2. with regard to (followed by *of*): *adj.* relevant; apt.

apse (aps), *n.* 1. a polygonal or semicircular recess terminating the choir or other portion of a church. 2. same as **apsis** (sense 1).

ap·si·dal (ap′sid-l), *adj.* of or pertaining to an apse or apsis.

ap·sis (ap′sis), *n., pl.* **-si·des** (′si-dēz), 1. either of the two points in the orbit of a planet or satellite at the time it is farthest (**higher apsis**) or nearest (**lower apsis**) to the body around which it is orbiting. 2. same as **apse** (sense 1).

apt (apt), *adj.* 1. suitable; pertinent; appropriate. 2. liable; likely; inclined. 3. quick to apprehend or learn. —**apt′ly**, *adv.* —**apt′ness**, *n.*

ap·ter·al (ap′tēr-ål), *adj.* 1. having columns at either end or both ends but not along the sides, as certain buildings of the Greek classical style. 2. same as **apterous**.

ap·ter·ous (-ŭs), *adj.* without wings or winglike parts; wingless.

ap·ter·yx (ap′tēr-iks), *n.* same as **kiwi**.

ap·ti·tude (ap′ti-tōōd, -tūd), *n.* 1. a natural capacity or talent for something. 2. a natural tendency; leaning; bent. 3. fitness or appropriateness. 4. quickness in learning.

a·py·ret·ic (â-pī-ret′ik), *adj.* free from fever.

aq·ua (ak′wå-′), *n., pl.* **aq′uas**, **aq′uae** (′wē), water; especially, in *Pharmacy,* a water solution: *adj.* bluish-green.

aqua am·mo·ni·ae (å-mō′ni-ē), water containing an infusion of ammonia gas; ammonia water.

aq·ua·cade (ak′wå-kåd, åk′-), *n.* a theatrical exhibition on and in water, as of spectacular swimming and diving performances, often set to music.

aq·ua·cul·ture (-kul-chēr), *n.* the growing of sea animals or plants for human consumption or use. —**aq·ua·cul′tur·al**, *adj.*

aqua for·tis (fôr′tis), [Latin, strong water], same as **nitric acid**.

Aq·ua·lung (åk′wå-lung, åk′-), a certain kind of scuba equipment: a trademark: *n.* such a piece of equipment: usually **aq′ua·lung**.

aq·ua·ma·rine (ak-wå-må-rēn′, åk-), *adj.* bluish-green: *n.* a pale, bluish-green variety of beryl. 2. its color.

aq·ua·naut (ak′wå-nôt), *n.* 1. same as **skindiver**. 2. one doing undersea research and study while working in and from a submersed chamber.

aq·ua·plane (ak′wå-plān, åk′-), *n.* a board towed by a speeding motorboat, which a person rides standing up: *v.i.* **-planed**, **-planing**, to ride on an aquaplane.

aqua pu·ra (pūr′å), [Latin], pure water; especially, water that has been distilled.

aqua re·gi·a (rē′ji-å), [Latin, kingly water], a powerfully corrosive yellow liquid made by mixing nitric and hydrochloric acids.

a·quar·ist (å-kwer′ist), *n.* 1. a person who has an aquarium as a hobby. 2. a person who has charge of an aquarium (sense 2).

a·quar·i·um (å-kwer′i-ùm), *n., pl.* **-i·ums**, **-i·a** (-å), 1. a tank or bowl for the keeping of aquatic plants and animals. 2. a building in

which a number of such tanks are on display.

A·quar·i·us (å-kwer′i-ùs), *n.* 1. a large southern constellation. 2. the eleventh sign of the zodiac.

a·quat·ic (å-kwät′ik), *adj.* 1. of or pertaining to water. 2. growing or living in or upon water. 3. performed in or upon water, as sports: *n.* 1. an aquatic plant or animal. 2. *pl.* sports performed in or upon water. —**a·quat′i·cal·ly**, *adv.*

aq·ua·tint (ak′wå-tint), *n.* 1. a type of etching resembling a watercolor. 2. the process used in creating such an etching: *v.t.* to etch in aquatint.

aq·ua·vit (ak′wå-vēt), *n.* an alcoholic liquor of Scandinavia, distilled from grain or potatoes.

aqua vi·tae (vīt′ē), 1. brandy or other alcoholic liquor. 2. in *Alchemy,* alcohol.

aq·ue·duct (ak′wē-dukt), *n.* 1. a large conduit for bringing water from its source, as to a large city. 2. a structure resembling a bridge, for carrying such a conduit over a valley or river.

a·que·ous (å′kwi-ùs), *adj.* of the nature of or containing water; watery.

aqueous humor, the fluid in the eye, between the cornea and the lens.

aq·ui·line (ak′wi-līn), *adj.* 1. of or resembling an eagle. 2. curved, as the beak of an eagle.

Ar·ab (er′åb), *n.* 1. a native of Arabia, a peninsula in southwestern Asia. 2. one of a Semitic people of Arabia and surrounding areas, including northern Africa. 3. a Bedouin. 4. a homeless child or outcast: *adj.* same as **Arabian**.

ar·a·besque (er-å-besk′), *n.* 1. an intricate design of flowers, leaves, and geometrical figures, either painted or carved. 2. in *Ballet,* the extension of one leg directly backward with one arm extended forward and the other backward: *adj.* of, having, or resembling an arabesque design.

A·ra·bi·an (å-rā′bi-ån), *adj.* of or pertaining to Arabia or the Arabs.

Ar·a·bic (er′å-bik), *adj.* 1. of or pertaining to Arabia. 2. of or pertaining to the Arabs, their language, customs, etc.: *n.* the language of the Arabs.

Arabic numerals, the figures 0, 1, 2, 3, 4, 5, 6, 7, 8, and 9, of Indian origin.

ar·a·ble (er′å-bl), *adj.* fit for the plow; suitable for cultivation. —**ar·a·bil′i·ty** (-bil′i-ti), *n.*

a·rach·nid (å-rak′nid), *n.* any of a class of arthropods, including spiders and scorpions.

Ar·a·ma·ic (er-å-mā′ik), *n.* a group of Semitic languages spoken in Biblical times.

ar·bi·ter (är′bi-tēr), *n.* an umpire or judge; arbitrator.

ar·bi·tra·ble (-trå-bl), *adj.* that can be arbitrated.

ar·bi·tra·ment (är-bit′rå-mėnt), *n.* 1. same as **arbitration**. 2. the decision of an arbitrator. 3. the right to judge.

ar·bi·trar·y (är′bi-trer-i), *adj.* 1. depending on will; discretionary. 2. capricious. 3. despotic. —**ar·bi·trar′i·ly**, *adv.* —**ar′bi·trar·i·ness**, *n.*

ar·bi·trate (är′bi-trāt), *v.t.* **-trat·ed**, **-trat·ing**, 1. to settle (a dispute). 2. to turn over to an

arbitrator: *v.i.* 1. to act as an arbitrator. 2. to turn over an issue to arbitration.

ar-bi-tra-tion (är-bi-trā'shŭn), *n.* the settlement of a dispute by an arbitrator. —**ar-bi-tra'-tion-al**, *adj.*

ar-bi-tra-tor (är'bi-trāt-ẽr), *n.* one chosen by the parties in a dispute to settle it; umpire.

ar-bor (är'bẽr), *n.* a bower; shaded nook or walk.

ar-bo-ra-ceous (är-bō-rā'shŭs), *adj.* 1. of, pertaining to, or like a tree. 2. living in trees.

Arbor Day, a day set apart in certain States for planting trees.

ar-bo-re-al (är-bôr'i-ăl), *adj.* 1. of, pertaining to, or like a tree. 2. living in trees.

ar-bo-re-ous (-ŭs), *adj.* 1. same as arboreal. 2. containing many trees.

ar-bo-res-cent (är-bô-res'nt), *adj.* treelike; shaped like a tree. —**ar-bo-res'cence,** *n.*

ar-bo-re-tum (-rēt'ŭm), *n., pl.* **-re'tums, -re'ta** (-rēt'ă), a place in which a great variety of trees are cultivated and exhibited.

ar-bo-ri-cul-ture (är'bẽr-i-kul-chẽr), *n.* the scientific cultivation of trees. —**ar-bo-ri-cul'tur-ist,** *n.*

ar-bor-ist (-ist), *n.* an expert in the cultivation of trees.

ar-bor-ous (-ŭs), *adj.* of, pertaining to, or consisting of trees.

ar-bor-vi-tae (-vit'ē), *n.* an evergreen tree with scalelike leaves.

ar-bu-tus (ar-būt'ŭs), *n.* 1. a trailing plant with white or pink flowers. 2. a tree of the heath family, with white or pink flowers and red berries.

arc (ärk), *n.* 1. originally, the portion of a circle described by the sun or any heavenly body in its apparent passage through the heavens. 2. a curved line or any part of a curve, especially one forming a segment of a circle. 3. in *Electricity,* a line of sparks or light produced by the movement of an electrical discharge across a gap from one electrode to another: also **electric arc:** *v.i.* **arced** or **arcked, arc'ing** or **arck'ing,** to move in or form an arc.

ar-cade (är-kād'), *n.* 1. a series of arches supported by pillars. 2. an enclosed passageway or promenade, lined with shops.

Ar-ca-di-a (är-kā'di-ă), *n.* a place or region of rural peace and simplicity.

Ar-ca-di-an (-ăn), *adj.* rurally peaceful and simple.

ar-cane (är-kān'), *adj.* 1. secret. 2. esoteric; not generally understood.

ar-ca-num (-kā'nŭm), *n., pl.* **-na** (-nă), **-nums,** 1. a secret; mystery. 2. a valuable elixir, or remedy.

arch (ärch), *n.* 1. a structure, as of brick or masonry, which follows a curved line over an open space. 2. the form of this structure. 3. any curvature having the form of an arch: *v.t.* 1. to supply with an arch. 2. to bend or curve in the form of an arch: *v.i.* 1. to form an arch. 2. to curve as an arch over an open space.

arch (ärch), *adj.* 1. chief; of the first rank. 2. crafty; shrewd. 3. mischievous; playful.

arch-, a prefix meaning *chief, principal.*

-arch (ärk), a suffix meaning *ruler.*

ar-chae-ol-o-gist (är-ki-ol'ô-jist), *n.* one who specializes in archaeology.

ar-chae-ol-o-gy (är-ki-ol'ô-ji), *n.* the study of the life and relics of ancient peoples. —**ar-chae-o-log'i-cal** (-ô-loj'i-kl), *adj.* —**ar-chae-o-log'i-cal-ly,** *adv.*

ar-cha-ic (är-kā'ik), *adj.* 1. of or pertaining to an earlier period of history; characterized by antiquity. 2. old-fashioned; antiquated. 3. that is now used only in certain contexts, as in poetry. —**ar-cha'i-cal-ly,** *adv.*

ar-cha-ism (är'ki-izm), *n.* 1. an archaic style or use. 2. an antiquated, old-fashioned, or obsolete word, expression, or idiom.

arch-an-gel (ärk'ān-jl), *n.* an angel of the highest order.

arch-bish-op (ärch'bish'ôp), *n.* a chief bishop; bishop of the highest rank.

arch-bish-op-ric (-ô'prik), *n.* the jurisdiction, office, or see of an archbishop.

arch-dea-con ('dēk'n), *n.* a church official ranking next below a bishop.

arch-dea-con-ry (-ri), *n., pl.* **-ries,** the office, rank, jurisdiction, or residence of an archdeacon.

arch-di-o-cese ('dī'ô-sis), *n.* the jurisdiction of an archbishop.

arch-du-cal ('dook'l), *adj.* of or pertaining to an archduke or an archduchy.

arch-duch-ess ('duch'is), *n.* 1. the wife of an archduke. 2. a princess of the former imperial family of Austria.

arch-duch-y ('duch'i), *n., pl.* **-duch'ies,** the territory or rank of an archduke or archduchess.

arch-duke ('dook'), *n.* a chief duke, especially a prince of the former imperial house of Austria.

arched (ärcht), *adj.* 1. having an arch. 2. curved like an arch.

arch-en-e-my (ärch'en'ê-mi), *n.* 1. *pl.* **-mies,** a principal enemy. 2. Satan.

ar-che-ol-o-gy (är-ki-ol'ô-ji), *n.* same as archaeology.

arch-er (är'chẽr), *n.* a bowman; one skilled in the use of the bow and arrow.

arch-er-fish (-fish), *n., pl.* **-fish, -fish-es,** a small freshwater fish of southern Asia, which catches insects by knocking them into the water with a spurting of water from its mouth.

arch-er-y (är'chẽr-i), *n.* the art, practice, or skill of one who uses the bow and arrow.

ar-che-type (är'kê-tip), *n.* 1. the original type or pattern upon which a thing is made; model. 2. an excellent specimen of a group or type. —**ar-che-typ'al** (-tip'ăl), —**ar-che-typ'i-cal** (-tip'i-kl), *adj.*

arch-fiend (ärch'fēnd'), *n.* 1. a principal fiend. 2. Satan.

ar-chi-e-pis-co-pal (är-ki-ê-pis'kô-pl), *adj.* pertaining to an archbishop or to his office. —**ar-chi-e-pis'co-pate** (-pāt), *n.*

ar-chi-man-drite (är-ki-man'drit), *n.* in the *Orthodox Eastern Church,* the head or superior of a monastery or monasteries.

arch-ing (är'ching), *adj.* curving like an arch: *n.* an arched part.

ar-chi-pel-a-go (är-ki-pel'ă-gō), *n.* 1. any sea or body of salt water interspersed with numer-

---

ô in dragon, ōō in crude, oo in wool, u in cup, ū in cure, ū in turn, ŭ in focus, oi in boy, ou in house, th in thin, th in sheathe, g in get, j in joy, y in yet.

ous islands. 2. a group of many islands. —
ar·chi·pe·lag'ic (-pe-laj'ik), *adj.*

ar·chi·tect (är'ki-tekt), *n.* 1. one who plans or
designs buildings and superintends their
construction; one versed in the art of building and in various styles of architecture. 2.
one who forms or designs.

ar·chi·tec·ton·ic (är-ki-tek-ton'ik), *adj.* 1. pertaining to architecture, its techniques, etc. 2.
based on forms regarded as architectural. —
ar·chi·tec·ton'i·cal·ly, *adv.*

ar·chi·tec·ton·ics (-iks), *n.* 1. the science of architecture. 2. a structure or design regarded
as architectural.

ar·chi·tec·tur·al (-tek'chēr-ăl), *adj.* 1. of or pertaining to architecture. 2. in accordance
with the rules of architecture. —**ar·chi·tec'-
tur·al·ly,** *adv.*

ar·chi·tec·ture (är'ki-tek-chēr), *n.* 1. the science,
art, or work of designing and building vari-
ous structures. 2. the method or style of
building. 3. construction; workmanship.

ar·chi·trave (är'ki-trāv), *n.* the lowest division
of an entablature, or that part which rests
immediately on the column.

ar·chi·val (är'ki-vl), *adj.* of, pertaining to, or included in public records.

ar·chives (är'kivz), *n.* 1. public or state documents, or records of historical value. 2. the
place where such records are kept.

ar·chi·vist (är'ki-vist), *n.* one in charge of ar-
chives.

arch·ly (ärch'li), *adv.* roguishly; waggishly;
coyly.

arch·ness ('nis), *n.* mischievousness; coyness.

ar·chon (är'kon), *n.* one of the nine chief magistrates of ancient Athens, who superintended civil and religious matters.

arch·priest (ärch'prēst'), *n.* a chief priest.

arch·way (ärch'wā), *n.* 1. an opening or passage beneath an arch. 2. the arch itself.

-ar·chy (är-ki), a suffix meaning *ruling.*

arc lamp, a lamp in which light is produced
by an arc of electricity passing between two
electrodes: also **arc light.**

arc·tic (ärk'tik, är'-), *adj.* 1. of or pertaining to
the North Pole or the regions surrounding
it. 2. frigid; extremely cold.

Arctic Circle, [also **a- c-**], an imaginary circle
parallel to the equator and 23°27' from the
North Pole.

ar·cu·ate (är'kyoo-wāt), *adj.* arched; shaped
like an arch. —**ar'cu·ate·ly,** *adv.*

ar·dent (är'dent), *adj.* 1. passionate; warm. 2.
eager; zealous. 3. glowing. 4. hot; burning;
fiery. —**ar'den·cy** ('dēn-si), *n.* —**ar'dent·ly,**
adv.

ardent spirits, alcoholic beverages, as brandy,
whiskey, etc.

ar·dor (är'dēr), *n.* 1. warmth of affection; passion. 2. zeal. 3. extreme heat.

ar·dour (är'dēr), *n.* British form for ardor.

ar·du·ous (är'joo-wŭs), *adj.* 1. steep; hard to
climb. 2. requiring great labor or exertion.
3. difficult. —**ar'du·ous·ly,** *adv.*

are (är), plural and second person singular,
present indicative, of **be.**

are (er), *n.* a unit of metric surface measure
containing 100 square meters or 1076.4
square feet.

ar·e·a (er'i-ā), *n.* 1. any plane surface having
bounds, whether natural or artificial. 2. any
extent of the earth's surface. 3. a part of a
building or land surface having a particular
function or attribute. 4. extent; range;
scope. 5. a section of any surface. 6. the
size of a surface. —**ar'e·al,** *adj.*

ar·e·ca (er'ē-kā), *n.* 1. any of various palms
with a smooth trunk and compound leaves.
2. the betel palm.

a·re·na (ā-rē'nā), *n.* 1. the central enclosed
space of a Roman amphitheater, in which
the gladiatorial combats took place. 2. any
scene or place of combat or struggle.

ar·e·na·ceous (er-ē-nā'shŭs), *adj.* 1. sandy;
abounding in, or having the properties of,
sand. 2. growing in sand.

arena theater, a theater with a stage surrounded by seats.

aren't (ärnt), are not.

Ar·e·op·a·gus (ar-i-op'ā-gŭs), *n.* 1. the tribunal,
or highest court, of ancient Athens. 2. any
high court or tribunal.

ar·ga·li (är'gā-li), *n., pl.* **-lis,** **-li,** a wild Asiatic
sheep with large horns.

Ar·gand burner (är'gänd), an oil or gas burner
having a hollow circular wick to permit the
passage of air inside and outside the flame.

ar·gent (är'jênt), *n.* 1. [Archaic or Poetic], silver:
adj. [Poetic], made of or resembling silver;
silvery white: also **ar·gen·tal** (är-jen'tl).

Ar·gen·tine (är'jēn-tēn), *adj.* of or pertaining to
Argentina, a country in southern South
America: *n.* a native of Argentina.

ar·gen·tine (är'jēn-tin), *adj.* of or resembling
silver: *n.* silver or something silvery.

ar·gen·tite (-tīt), *n.* silver sulfide of a dark-gray
color.

ar·gil·la·ceous (är-ji-lā'shŭs), *adj.* of the nature
of, or containing, clay; clayey.

ar·gil·lite (är'ji-līt), *n.* a mudstone without
laminated layers.

ar·gol (är'gl), *n.* crude tartar from which cream
of tartar is prepared.

ar·gon (är'gon), *n.* a gaseous chemical element,
one of the constituents of air.

Ar·go·naut (är'gō-nôt), *n.* 1. in *Greek Mythology,* one who sailed with Jason for the
Golden Fleece. 2. [also **a-**], one of the gold
seekers who went to California in 1848 or
1849. 3. [**a-**], same as **paper nautilus.**

ar·go·sy (är'gō-si), *n., pl.* **-sies,** [Poetic], 1. a
large merchant ship. 2. a fleet of such ships.

ar·got (är'gō), *n.* vocabulary peculiar to a type
of work or style of life, as the jargon of
criminals.

ar·gu·a·ble (är'gyoo-wā-bl), *adj.* capable of being disputed or discussed.

ar·gu·a·bly (-bli), *adv.* in a way that can be
backed by argument.

ar·gue (är'gyōō), *v.i.* **-gued,** **-gu·ing.** 1. to show
or offer reasons in support of, or in opposi-
tion to, a proposition, opinion, or measure.
2. to quarrel; dispute: *v.t.* 1. to debate or
discuss. 2. to contend or evince. 3. to convince by giving reasons. —**ar'gu·er,** *n.*

ar·gu·ment (är'gyŭ-mênt), *n.* 1. a reason or
reasons presented as support for or opposition to a proposition, with a view to persuade or convince. 2. a discussion, contro-

versy, or debate. 3. a short statement setting forth the subject of a discourse or writing; abstract or summary of a book.

ar-gu-men-ta-tion (är-gyŭ-men-tā'shŭn), n. 1. the act of arguing. 2. discussion of a contentious kind.

ar-gu-men-ta-tive (-men'tà-tiv), adj. 1. of or consisting of argument, or a process of reasoning. 2. liking to take part in argument; contentious.

Ar-gus-eyed (är'gŭs-īd), adj. watchful; vigilant; extremely observant.

ar-gyle (är'gīl), adj. knitted or woven in a pattern having diamond-shaped figures: n. pl. socks with such a pattern.

a-ri-a (är'i-à), n. an air or melody for a single voice with accompaniment; solo part in a cantata, oratorio, etc.

Ar-i-an (er'i-ân), adj. of or pertaining to Arianism.

Ar-i-an-ism (-à-nizm), n. 1. the doctrines of Arius of Alexandria in the 4th century, who proclaimed Christ the greatest of all created beings, but not the Son of God. 2. the beliefs based on the teachings of Arius.

ar-id (ar'id), adj. 1. dry; parched; barren. 2. uninteresting; monotonous. —ar'id-ly, adv.

a-rid-i-ty (à-rid'ĭ-ti), ar-id-ness (ar'id-nis), n. 1. the state of being dry; dryness. 2. lack of life or interest.

Ar-i-es (er'ēz, -ĭ-ēz), n. 1. a northern constellation between Pisces and Taurus. 2. the first sign of the zodiac.

ar-i-et-ta (ar-i-et'à), n. a short song or aria.

a-right (à-rīt'), adv. rightly; in a right way or form; without error.

a-rise (à-rīz'), v.i. a-rose (à-rōz'), a-ris-en (à-riz'n), a-ris-ing, 1. to ascend; come into view. 2. to rise or get up. 3. to spring or result (from). 4. to come into existence or action; originate.

a-ris-tate (à-ris'tāt), adj. bearded, as wheat.

ar-is-toc-ra-cy (ar-ĭ-sto'krà-si), n., pl. -cies, 1. government by persons of the upper class. 2. a state with such a government. 3. the nobility or ruling persons in a state. 4. an aristocratic manner. 5. those regarded as superior.

a-ris-to-crat (à-ris'tò-krat), n. 1. a person of rank and noble birth. 2. one who upholds the aristocracy or favors government by the nobility. 3. a person who possesses traits supposed to characterize the nobility.

a-ris-to-crat-ic (à-ris-tò-krat'ik), adj. 1. of, pertaining to, or favoring aristocracy as a government. 2. of, pertaining to, or characteristic of the upper class or nobility. —a-ris-to-crat'i-cal-ly, adv.

a-rith-me-tic (à-rith'mĕ-tik), n. 1. the science or art of computation by numbers. 2. skill in working with numbers: adj. (ar-ith-met'ik), of, pertaining to, or applying arithmetic: also ar-ith-met'i-cal. —ar-ith-met'i-cal-ly, adv.

a-rith-me-ti-cian (ar-ith-mĕ-tish'ân), n. one skilled in the science of arithmetic.

ark (ärk), n. 1. in the Bible, the boat in which Noah, his family, and two of every kind of animal were preserved during the Flood. 2. a place of safety; refuge. 3. same as ark of

the covenant. 4. a large boat once used to transport produce on American rivers.

ark of the covenant, the repository of the stone tablets inscribed with the Ten Commandments, in the ancient Jewish Tabernacle, subsequently placed in the Temple of Solomon.

arm (ärm), n. 1. the limb of the human body which extends from the shoulder to the hand. 2. the anterior or forelimb of any vertebrate animal. 3. any part projecting or diverging from a main body or trunk, as the tentacle of a starfish, the branch of a tree, an inlet of the sea, etc. 4. something which covers or touches the human arm, as the sleeve of a garment, the part of a chair on which the arm rests, etc. 5. might; power. —arm'less, adj. —arm'like, adj.

arm (ärm), n. 1. usually pl. a weapon. 2. a branch of the military service. 3. pl. heraldic or other insignia. 4. pl. battle; fighting: v.t. 1. to furnish or equip with weapons, tools, etc. 2. to fortify or provide against attack: v.i. 1. to provide oneself with arms. 2. to ready for conflict.

ar-ma-da (är-mä'dà), n. 1. a fleet of warships. 2. [A-]. the Spanish fleet sent against England in 1588.

ar-ma-dil-lo (är-mà-dil'ō), n., pl. -los, a small mammal of the hot regions of the Americas, covered with a bony shell consisting of numerous small plates and resembling mail armor.

Ar-ma-ged-don (är-mà-ged'n), n. 1. in the Bible, the place of a great battle against evil, to be fought before Judgment Day. 2. any conclusive battle.

ar-ma-ment (är'mà-mĕnt), n. 1. often pl. forces, either military or naval, equipped for war. 2. the weapons collectively of a warship, fortification, etc. 3. an equipping or being equipped for military conflict. 4. something used to protect or defend.

ar-ma-ture (är'mà-chēr), n. 1. same as armor (n. 1 & 2). 2. that which serves as a means of defense. 3. a piece of soft iron connecting the poles of a magnet to preserve the magnetic force. 4. the part of a generator or motor in which electromotive force is produced: it consists of an iron core wound with wire. 5. in Sculpture, a framework over which other materials are applied.

arm-chair (ärm'cher), n. a chair having supports for the elbows or arms.

armed (ärmd), adj. 1. having weapons. 2. having arms, or limbs: used in compounds, as long-armed.

armed forces, military, air, and naval forces.

arm-ful (ärm'fool), n., pl. -fuls, as much as can be held in one arm or both arms.

Ar-min-i-an-ism (är-min'i-ân-izm), n. the doctrines taught by Jacob Arminius (1560-1609), a Dutch Protestant theologian, placing emphasis on the free will of man.

ar-mi-stice (är'mĭ-stis), n. a temporary cessation of hostilities agreed upon by opposing forces; truce.

Armistice Day, November 11, the anniversary of the day in 1918 on which the hostilities of World War I ceased: see Veterans Day.

ô in dragon, ōō in crude, oo in wool, u in cup, ū in cure, û in turn, û in focus, oi in boy, ou in house, th in thin, th in sheathe, g in get, j in joy, y in yet.

arm·let (ärm′lit), *n.* 1. a small arm of the sea. 2. an ornamental band for the arm.

arm·lock (′lok), *n.* in *Wrestling,* a hold in which one wrestler's arm is tightly gripped by the other's hand and arm.

ar·moire (är-mwär′), *n.* a heavily decorated, movable cupboard.

ar·mor (är′mēr), *n.* 1. protective covering for the body in battle. 2. any protective covering, as the steel plating on a warship: *v.t. & v.i.* to put armor on.

ar·mor-clad (-klad), *adj.* protected by a covering of armor.

ar·mor·er (är′mēr-ēr), *n.* 1. formerly, a maker of arms or armor, or one who had charge of the armor of another. 2. one who makes firearms.

ar·mo·ri·al (är-môr′i-ăl), *adj.* of or pertaining to coats of arms or escutcheons.

armor plate, a covering of plates of steel, used for protection, as on a tank or ship. —**ar′·mor-plat·ed,** *adj.*

ar·mor·y (är′mēr-i), *n., pl.* -mor·ies, 1. a place for storing arms; arsenal. 2. a place for the assembly and drill of soldiers. 3. a place for manufacturing firearms.

ar·mour (är′mēr), *n. & v.i. & v.t.* British form for armor.

arm·pit (ärm′pit), *n.* the cavity beneath the shoulder; axilla.

arm·rest (′rest), *n.* a place to rest the arm or elbow, as in a car.

ar·my (är′mi), *n., pl.* -mies, 1. a large body of men trained and equipped for war. 2. a military unit. 3. a great number; multitude. 4. [often A-], an organized body of persons working for a common cause.

army ant, any of various ants that move in hordes, devouring animals in their path.

army worm, any of various moth larvae that move in hordes, destroying grain and other crops.

ar·ni·ca (är′ni-kă), *n.* 1. any of various plants with long stalks and yellow flowers. 2. an external medication made from some of these plants, formerly used for treating bruises and sprains.

a·ro·ma (ă-rō′mă), *n.* 1. the odor of plants, foods, etc., of an agreeable or spicy nature; perfume; fragrance. 2. any odor.

ar·o·mat·ic (er-ō-mat′ik), *adj.* of or having an aroma; fragrant; spicy; odoriferous: *n.* a plant, herb, or drug having a pleasant or spicy odor.

a·round (ă-round′), *adv.* 1. in a circle. 2. on every side; roundabout. 3. in circumference. 4. in a number of places. 5. in order or sequence. 6. to the opposite direction. 7. in every part of; through. 8. [Informal], close by. 9. [Informal], to a stated place: *prep.* 1. on all sides of; about. 2. encircling or surrounding. 3. on the border or outer part of. 4. in a number of places in.

a·rouse (ă-rouz′), *v.t.* a·roused′, a·rous′ing. 1. to excite or stir to action. 2. to bring about (an emotion or strong feeling). 3. to waken from sleep or a state of inactivity. —a·rous′al, *n.*

ar·peg·gio (är-pej′ō, -pej′i-ō), *n., pl.* -gios, 1. the playing of musical notes in quick succession to form a chord. 2. a chord formed in this way.

ar·rack (er′ăk), *n.* a strong alcoholic liquor of the Far East, usually made from rice or coconut milk.

ar·raign (ă-rān′), *v.t.* 1. to summon or bring before a law court to answer to a charge. 2. to censure publicly; accuse. —ar·raign′ment, *n.*

ar·range (ă-rānj′), *v.t.* -ranged′, -rang′ing, 1. to put in proper order or sequence. 2. to classify. 3. to adjust or settle. 4. to prepare or plan. 5. in *Music,* to make an arrangement of: *v.i.* 1. to reach an agreement (*with* or *about*). 2. to prepare or plan. 3. in *Music,* to write an arrangement. —ar·rang′er, *n.*

ar·range·ment (′mĕnt), *n.* 1. the act of putting in proper form or order. 2. that which is ordered or disposed. 3. the method of arranging. 4. *usually pl.* a preparatory measure; preparation. 5. settlement. 6. in *Music, a)* a composition that has been changed from the original to suit other instruments, different voices, etc. *b)* the production of such a composition.

ar·rant (ar′ănt), *adj.* notorious; unmitigated; shameless. —ar′rant·ly, *adv.*

ar·ras (er′ăs), *n.* 1. a tapestry of rich figured fabric. 2. a wall hanging of tapestry.

ar·ray (ă-rā′), *n.* 1. the grouping or arrangement of a body of men as drawn up for battle. 2. a collection or series of things imposingly displayed. 3. fine dress or apparel: *v.t.* 1. to place or dispose in order. 2. to deck or dress in finery.

ar·ray·al (′ăl), *n.* 1. the process of arraying. 2. the thing arrayed.

ar·rear·age (ă-rir′ij), *n.* 1. the state of being behind, as in paying a debt. 2. that which remains unpaid or overdue.

ar·rears (ă-rirz′), *n.* 1. debts that are overdue. 2. that which is not done on time or is outstanding.

ar·rest (ă-rest′), *v.t.* 1. to stop or stay; check or hinder the action or motion of. 2. to seize, take, or apprehend by legal authority. 3. to seize and fix, as the eye or attention: *n.* 1. the act of seizing; holding back by force or restraint. 2. the state of being seized or detained by legal authority.

ar·rest·ing (′ing), *adj.* catching the attention; interesting.

ar·rhyth·mi·a (ă-rith′mi-ă), *n.* irregularity of the heart's beating.

ar·ris (ar′is), *n.* in *Architecture,* the line or edge formed when two curved or straight surfaces meet each other, forming an angle.

ar·riv·al (ă-rī′văl), *n.* 1. the act of arriving. 2. the person or thing arriving, or that has arrived.

ar·rive (ă-rīv′), *v.i.* -rived′, -riv′ing, 1. to come to or reach, as a destination. 2. to reach a point or stage. 3. to attain a state or result. 4. to reach, as by traveling or working (followed by *at*).

ar·ri·ve·der·ci (ä-rē-ve-der′chi), *interj.* [Italian], goodbye.

ar-ro-gance (er'ŏ-gǎns), *n.* an undue degree of self-importance: also **ar'ro-gan-cy.**

ar-ro-gant (-gǎnt), *adj.* having or resulting from much pride or self-importance; overbearing; haughty. **—ar'ro-gant-ly,** *adv.*

ar-ro-gate (-gāt), *v.t.* **-gat-ed, -gat-ing,** to assume or lay claim to unduly. **—ar'ro-ga'tion,** *n.*

ar-row (er'ŏ), *n.* 1. a pointed weapon in the form of a thin shaft, usually feathered, made to be shot from a bow. 2. something resembling an arrow.

ar-row-head (-hed), *n.* 1. the detachable metal or stone head of an arrow. 2. something resembling an arrowhead. 3. an aquatic plant with leaves shaped like an arrow.

ar-row-root (-rōōt), *n.* 1. a starch obtained from the roots of a West Indian plant. 2. the plant yielding this starch.

ar-row-wood (-wood), *n.* any of a number of trees with straight stems used by North American Indians for arrows.

ar-roy-o (ā-roi'ŏ), *n., pl.* **-roy'os,** in the south-western U.S., 1. a watercourse or rivulet. 2. the dry bed of a stream.

ar-se-nal (är'sĕn-ǎl), *n.* 1. a place for the stor-age of arms and military supplies, or for their manufacture. 2. a collection or supply.

ar-se-nic (är'sĕn-ik), *n.* 1. a very poisonous, brittle chemical element of steel-gray color. 2. a compound of arsenic in the form of a poisonous white powder.

ar-sen-ic (är-sen'ik), **ar-sen-i-cal** ('ĭ-kl), *adj.* of, pertaining to, or containing arsenic: also **ar-se'ni-ous** (-sē'ni-ŭs), *adj.*

ar-se-nite (är'sĕ-nīt), *n.* a salt containing an acid of arsenic.

ar-son (är'sŏn), *n.* the malicious setting fire to any building or property belonging to another, or to one's own property, as with the intent to defraud an insurance company. **—ar'son-ist,** *n.*

art (ärt), *n.* 1. the ability of man to create things apart from nature. 2. the skillful adaptation and application of knowledge to some purpose. 3. a craft or profession, or its system of rules and established methods. 4. one of the fine arts. 5. the fine arts col-lectively. 6. the power or quality of perceiv-ing and transcribing the beautiful or aes-thetic, as in painting or sculpture. 7. the re-sults of creative production; pictures, sculp-tures, etc. 8. *pl.* the liberal arts. 9. *usually pl.* deceitful artifice.

art (ärt), archaic second person singular, pres-ent indicative, of be.

ar-te-ri-al (är-tir'i-ǎl), *adj.* 1. of or pertaining to an artery or arteries. 2. contained in an ar-tery.

ar-te-ri-al-ize (-īz), *v.t.* **-ized, -iz-ing,** to convert (venous blood) into arterial blood by the addition of oxygen in the lungs. **—ar-te-ri-al-i-za'tion,** *n.*

ar-te-ri-o-scle-ro-sis (är-tir-i-ŏ-sklē-rō'sis), *n.* a thickening of the walls of the arteries, with more or less hardening.

ar-te-ri-tis (är'tē-rīt'is), *n.* inflammation of the arteries.

ar-ter-y (är'tĕr-i), *n., pl.* **-ter-ies,** 1. any one of a system of tubes which convey the blood

from the heart to all parts of the body. 2. a thoroughfare.

ar-te-sian well (är-tē'zhǎn), a well formed by boring, often -to great depth, to a water source which is draining from higher ground and is under pressure which forces it to the surface.

art-ful (ärt'fŭl), *adj.* 1. cunning; crafty. 2. based on or exhibiting much skill. **—art'ful-ly,** *adv.* **—art'ful-ness,** *n.*

ar-thral-gia (är-thral'jǎ), *n.* neuralgic pain in a joint.

ar-thri-tis (är-thrīt'is), *n.* inflammation of a joint or joints. **—ar-thrit'ic** (-thrit'ik), *adj.*

ar-thro-pod (är'thrŏ-pod), *n.* any member of a group of invertebrate animals which have articulated bodies and jointed legs, as spi-ders, crabs, insects, etc.

Ar-thur (är'thĕr), *n.* a legendary British king of the sixth century, leader of the knights of the Round Table. **—Ar-thu-ri-an** (är-thoor'i-ǎn), *adj.*

ar-ti-choke (är'tĭ-chōk), *n.* 1. a plant with this-tlelike foliage and large flower heads. 2. the lower portion of the flower head consisting of a fleshy receptacle covered with thick scales, used as a vegetable. 3. same as Jerusalem artichoke.

ar-ti-cle (är'ti-kl), *n.* 1. a single clause, item, or particular, as in a formal agreement or treaty. 2. a prose composition, complete in itself, in a newspaper, magazine, or work of reference. 3. a material thing, as one of a class; item. 4. a commodity. 5. in *Grammar,* any one of the words *a, an,* or *the,* placed before nouns to limit their application or to show indefiniteness: *v.t.* **-cled, -cling,** to bind by articles of an agreement.

ar-tic-u-lar (är-tik'yū-lǎr), *adj.* of or pertaining to the joints or to a joint.

ar-tic-u-late (är-tik'yū-lāt), *v.t.* **-lat-ed, -lat-ing,** 1. to joint; unite by means of a joint. 2. to form words; utter in distinct syllables. 3. to state lucidly: *v.i.* 1. to unite or form an ar-ticulation (*with*). 2. to utter articulate sounds; speak with distinctness: *adj.* (-lit), 1. jointed; formed with joints: usually **ar-tic'u-lat-ed.** 2. uttered with distinctness. 3. capa-ble of human speech. 4. able to verbalize well; capable of expressing one's thoughts. 5. clearly expressed. **—ar-tic'u-late-ly,** *adv.* **—ar-tic'u-late-ness,** *n.*

ar-tic-u-la-tion (är-tik-yū-lā'shŭn), *n.* 1. the act of jointing or the state of being jointed. 2. a joint or juncture between bones. 3. a way of speaking. 4. a distinct utterance. 5. in *Botany,* a joint in a stem; also, a space be-tween two nodes.

ar-tic-u-la-tor (är-tik'yū-lāt-ēr), *n.* 1. something or someone that articulates. 2. any organ in the mouth or throat which, in its movement, assists in the production of speech.

ar-ti-fact (är'tĭ-fakt), *n.* a material thing made by man, particularly something basic or primitive.

ar-ti-fice (är'tĭ-fis), *n.* 1. trickery or deception. 2. an ingenious expedient. 3. a deceitful trick or stratagem. 4. skill or cleverness.

ar-tif-i-cer (är-tif'i-sēr), *n.* 1. a skilled worker.

2. a mechanic in the armed forces. 3. an inventor.

ar·ti·fi·cial (är-ti-fish'ǎl), *adj.* 1. made or contrived by art; produced by human skill or labor. 2. not genuine; imitation. 3. affected; unnatural. —*ar·ti·fi'cial·ly, adv.*

artificial intelligence, in *Computer Science,* the development of machines or programs capable of reasoning, learning, etc.

ar·ti·fi·ci·al·i·ty (-fish-i-al'ĭ-ti), *n.* 1. the quality of being artificial. 2. *pl.* -ties, that which is artificial.

artificial respiration, the continuation or resumption of the breathing process by artificial means, as by forcing breath into the mouth of one who has stopped breathing.

ar·til·ler·y (är-til'ěr-i), *n.* 1. large guns; cannon, missile launchers, etc. 2. the officers and men forming the division of an army that handles large guns. 3. the science of ordnance. —*ar·til'ler·ist, n.*

ar·til·ler·y·man (-mǎn), *n., pl.* -men (-měn), a member of the artillery.

ar·ti·san (är'tĭ-zn), *n.* one skilled in any art or trade; handicraftsman.

art·ist (är'tist), *n.* 1. one skilled in or practicing any one of the fine arts. 2. one skilled in painting, sculpture, graphics, etc. 3. one who does anything with great skill.

ar·tis·tic (är-tis'tik), *adj.* 1. of or pertaining to art or to artists. 2. characterized by aesthetic feelings. 3. performed with skill. —*ar·tis'ti·cal·ly, adv.*

art·ist·ry (är'tis-tri), *n.* the qualities peculiar to an artist, or to his ability, or work.

art·less (ärt'lis), *adj.* 1. lacking art; unskillful. 2. devoid of cunning; undesigning. 3. simple; natural; unaffected. —*art'less·ly, adv.* — *art'less·ness, n.*

art nou·veau (är nōō-vō'), [French], a style popular in the arts and crafts of the late 19th and early 20th centuries, noted for curving lines and motifs based on organic forms.

art·sy-craft·sy (ärt-si-kraft'si), *adj.* [Informal], pertaining to arts and crafts, especially those regarded as faddish or superficial.

art·y (ärt'i), *adj.* **art'i·er, art'i·est,** [Informal], pertaining to or exhibiting a superficial but flamboyant interest in the arts.

ar·um (er'ŭm), *n.* any of a family of plants with small flowers enclosed in a large, sheltering leaf, as the jack-in-the-pulpit.

Ar·y·an (er'i-ǎn), *n.* 1. originally, the hypothetical prehistoric language from which the Indo-European languages were thought to have derived. 2. one who is said to be descended from speakers of this language; one of a theoretically superior Caucasoid race.

as (az), *adv.* 1. comparable or proportionate to. 2. for example. 3. when regarded in a stated way: *conj.* 1. in the same manner that. 2. to the same degree that. 3. while. 4. because. 5. that the result is. 6. notwithstanding that. 7. [Informal], that: *pron.* 1. that. 2. a fact that: *prep.* 1. in the sense or capacity of. 2. like.

as·a·fet·i·da, as·a·foet·i·da (as-ǎ-fet'ĭ-dǎ), *n.* a

fetid gum resin obtained from several Asiatic plants.

as·bes·tos, as·bes·tus (as-bes'tôs), *n.* any of several fibrous minerals that separate into long, flexible filaments: some varieties do not burn or conduct heat and are used in insulation, roofing, fireproofing, etc.

as·cend (ǎ-send'), *v.i.* 1. to take an upward direction. 2. to mount; go up; rise. 3. to proceed from an inferior to a superior; rise from a lower to a higher level, as in pitch or tone: *v.t.* 1. to go or move upward upon or along; climb. 2. to attain (a throne). — **as·cend'a·ble, as·cend'i·ble,** *adj.*

as·cend·an·cy, as·cend·en·cy ('ĕn-si), *n.* a governing or controlling power or influence; domination: also **as·cend'ance, as·cend'ence.**

as·cend·ant, as·cend·ent ('ǎnt), *adj.* 1. rising. 2. superior; dominant: *n.* 1. superiority or commanding influence. 2. an ancestor; one who precedes in genealogy: opposed to *descendant.* 3. in *Astrology,* the particular zodiacal sign appearing above the horizon at a stated time.

as·cend·ing ('ing), *adj.* 1. rising upward. 2. in *Botany,* curving upward.

as·cen·sion (ǎ-sen'shǔn), *n.* 1. the act of moving upward; rising. 2. [A-], the ascent of Jesus into heaven. —*as·cen'sion·al, adj.*

Ascension Day, the commemoration of Jesus' ascension into heaven, celebrated on the fortieth day after Easter.

as·cent (ǎ-sent'), *n.* 1. the act of rising or climbing; upward movement. 2. an acclivity; upward slope.

as·cer·tain (as-ĕr-tān'), *v.t.* 1. [Archaic], to make certain. 2. to find out or determine definitely. —*as·cer·tain'a·ble, adj.* —*as·cer·tain'ment, n.*

as·cet·ic (ǎ-set'ik), *adj.* austere; severe; rigorous: also **as·cet'i·cal:** *n.* 1. one who renounces the world and devotes himself to religious meditation. 2. one who subjects himself to severe disciplinary methods of living. —*as·cet'i·cal·ly, adv.*

as·cet·i·cism ('i-sizm), *n.* the conditions or mode of life adopted by an ascetic.

as·cid·i·an (ǎ-sid'i-ǎn), *n.* any one of a group of marine animals, as the sea squirt, shaped like a sac, with a tough covering.

as·ci·tes (ǎ-sit'iz), *n.* an abnormal condition in which the peritoneum is filled with fluid.

a·scor·bic acid (ǎ-skôr'bik), same as **vitamin C.**

as·cot (as'kŏt), *n.* a scarf worn around the neck, with broad ends hanging from the knot.

as·cribe (ǎ-skrīb'), *v.t.* -cribed', -crib'ing, 1. to attribute (*to*); assign. 2. to think of as belonging (*to*) or coming from.

as·crip·tion (ǎ-skrip'shǔn), *n.* 1. the act of ascribing. 2. that which ascribes.

a·sep·sis (ā-sep'sis, ǎ-), *n.* the state of being aseptic.

a·sep·tic ('tik), *adj.* free from the germs of disease or putrefaction. —*a·sep'ti·cal·ly, adv.*

a·sex·u·al (ā-sek'shoo-wǎl), *adj.* 1. not sexual; having no sex. 2. of or denoting a process of reproduction in which there is no union of male and female germ cells. —*a·sex·u·al'i·ty* (-wal'ĭ-ti), *n.* —*a·sex'u·al·ly, adv.*

---

ash (ash), *n.* the powdery residue remaining after a substance has been burned.

ash (ash), *n.* 1. a timber and shade tree of the olive family. 2. the wood of this tree.

a·shamed (á-shāmd'), *adj.* 1. affected or touched by shame; downcast or dejected by a feeling of guilt, inferiority, etc. 2. reluctant through fear or shame. —a·sham·ed·ly (á-shā'mid-li), *adv.*

ash blond, 1. a very light, silvery blond. 2. someone with hair of this color. —**ash'-blond'**, *adj.*

ash·en (ash'ĕn), *adj.* 1. of or pertaining to ashes. 2. of the color of ashes; pale.

ash·es (ash'iz), *n.* 1. the particles and powdery residue remaining after a substance has been burned. 2. the remains of a human body when cremated. 3. a corpse.

a·shore (á-shôr'), *adv. & adj.* 1. on the shore or to the shore. 2. on land.

ash·ram (ash'rǎm), *n.* a commune for Hindu meditation.

ash·tray (ash'trā), *n.* a dish or other receptacle for the ashes from cigarettes, cigars, etc.; also **ash tray**.

Ash Wednesday, the first day of Lent.

ash·y (ash'i), *adj.* **ash'i·er**, **ash'i·est**, 1. of or pertaining to ashes or like ashes. 2. pale gray in color.

A·sian (ā'zhǎn), *adj.* of or pertaining to Asia, a continent of the Eastern Hemisphere, east of Europe: *n.* a native or inhabitant of Asia.

a·side (á-sīd'), *adv.* 1. on or to one side. 2. so as not to hinder or interfere. 3. away. 4. apart; notwithstanding: *n.* 1. a piece of writing that digresses from the topic under discussion. 2. a remark made by an actor on the stage, and assumed to be heard only by the audience and not by the other actors.

as·i·nine (as'i-nīn), *adj.* of or pertaining to an ass; especially, having characteristics thought of as like those of an ass; stupid; silly. —**as'i·nine·ly**, *adv.*

as·i·nin·i·ty (as-i-nin'i-ti), *n.* 1. the quality of being asinine. 2. *pl.* **-ties**, an instance of being asinine.

ask (ask), *v.t.* 1. to request. 2. to use words in seeking to obtain an answer. 3. to expect or require. 4. to inquire of; interrogate. 5. to invite: *v.i.* 1. to inquire (*for, after,* or *about*). 2. to make a request (*for*). —**ask'er**, *n.* —**ask'ing**, *n.*

a·skance (á-skans'), *adv.* 1. sideways; obliquely. 2. disdainfully.

a·skant (á-skant'), *adv.* [Archaic or Poetic], same as **askance**.

a·skew (á-skyoō'), *adv.* obliquely; awry; out of position or arrangement: *adj.* on one side; awry.

a·slant (á-slant'), *adv.* not at right angles: in a sloping or slanting way: *prep.* on a slope across: *adj.* sloping.

a·sleep (á-slēp'), *adj.* 1. sleeping. 2. dormant. 3. in a prickly, numb state. 4. dead: *adv.* in a state of slumber or dormancy.

a·so·cial (á-sō'shǎl), *adj.* 1. not social; preferring not to mix with others. 2. showing no interest in the welfare of others; selfish.

asp (asp), *n.* any one of several small, venomous snakes of Africa, Asia, and Europe, as the Egyptian cobra or the common European viper.

as·par·a·gus (á-spar'á-gús), *n.* 1. a plant with scalelike leaves and tender shoots. 2. these shoots, cooked and eaten as a vegetable.

as·pect (as'pekt), *n.* 1. looks; mien; air. 2. the appearance of a thing from a particular place or point. 3. the appearance of something, as an idea, as modified by a particular mental set or point of view. 4. the side facing a given direction. 5. in *Astrology*, the relative position of stars as viewed from the earth.

as·pen (as'pĕn), *n.* a kind of poplar whose leaves tremble in the slightest breeze: *adj.* 1. of or pertaining to the aspen. 2. [Poetic], quivering like an aspen leaf.

As·per·ges (á-spẽr'jez), *n.* in the *Roman Catholic Church*, 1. [also **a-**], a short service before a High Mass, during which holy water is sprinkled. 2. the hymn accompanying this service.

as·per·gil·lum (as-pẽr-jil'úm), *n., pl.* **-gil'la** ('á), **-gil'lums**, in the *Roman Catholic Church*, a brush or container for sprinkling holy water: also **as'per·gill**.

as·per·i·ty (as-per'i-ti), *n., pl.* **-ties**, 1. roughness or harshness, as of surface or sound. 2. bitterness or harshness of temper.

as·perse (á-spūrs'), *v.t.* **-persed**, **-pers'ing**, to injure the reputation of; slander.

as·per·sion (á-spūr'zhǔn), *n.* 1. a sprinkling of water. 2. a false and calumnious charge or report; slander.

as·per·so·ri·um (as-pẽr-sôr'i-úm), *n., pl.* **-ri·a** (-á), **-ri·ums**, in the *Roman Catholic Church*, 1. a font for holy water. 2. same as **aspergillum**.

as·phalt (as'fôlt), *n.* 1. a tarlike variety of bitumen. 2. a blend of this with sand or gravel, used for paving, roofing, and cementing: *v.t.* to lay down or cover with asphalt. —**as·phal'tic**, *adj.*

as·pho·del (as'fô-del), *n.* a plant of the lily family, with white or yellow flowers.

as·phyx·i·a (as-fik'si-á), *n.* loss of consciousness caused by insufficient oxygen.

as·phyx·i·ate (-āt), *v.t.* **-at·ed**, **-at·ing**, 1. to suffocate. 2. to deprive of oxygen and as a result cause asphyxia. —**as·phyx·i·a'tion**, *n.*

as·pic (as'pik), *n.* 1. [Archaic], an asp. 2. a molded jelly, as of meat juice or tomato juice, often containing meat or fish.

as·pi·dis·tra (as-pi-dis'trá), *n.* a plant with glossy evergreen leaves, grown as a house plant.

as·pir·ant (as'pẽr-ánt), *adj.* aspiring; ambitious: *n.* one who seeks honor or a high position.

as·pi·rate (as'pi-rāt), *v.t.* **-rat·ed**, **-rat·ing**, 1. to prefix the sound of the letter *h.* 2. to follow (a consonant) with a puff of breath. 3. to suck or draw in or up: *n.* ('pẽr-it), an aspirated sound: *adj.* ('pẽr-it), pronounced with audible breath: also **as'pi·rat·ed** ('pi-rāt-id).

as·pi·ra·tion (as-pi-rā'shǔn), *n.* 1. the act of aspirating. 2. an aspirated sound. 3. strong desire for something higher or better than

---

that already possessed or achieved; ambition. 4. the object of such desire.

as·pi·ra·tor (as'pĭ-rāt-ēr), *n.* a device for drawing off liquids or gases by suction.

as·pir·a·to·ry (ă-spīr'ă-tôr-ĭ), *adj.* of, pertaining to, or suited for suction or the inhaling of air.

as·pire (ă-spīr'), *v.i.* -pired', -pir'ing, to seek or desire (*after*); to be ambitious (*to* attain or achieve something).

as·pi·rin (as'pĭ-rin), *n.* 1. a white, crystalline powder used to treat fever, headaches, etc. 2. a tablet made of this powder.

a·squint (ă-skwint'), *adv. & adj.* with a squint; out of the corner of the eye.

ass (as), *n.* 1. a quadruped related to the horse, with longer ears and a shorter mane, used as a beast of burden. 2. a stupid or silly person.

as·sa·fet·i·da, as·sa·foet·i·da (as-ă-fet'ĭ-dă), *n.* same as asafetida.

as·sa·gai, as·se·gai (as'ă-gī), *n.* 1. a tree of the dogwood family, indigenous to southern Africa. 2. a light spear made from this wood, with an iron tip.

as·sail (ă-sāl'), *v.t.* 1. to assault physically in a violent way; attack. 2. to attack with argument or abuse. 3. to start vigorously working on. —as·sail'a·ble, *adj.* —as·sail'er, *n.*

as·sail·ant ('ănt), *n.* a person or thing that assaults or attacks.

as·sas·sin (ă-sas'n), *n.* 1. [A-], formerly, one of a sect of Moslems who killed Crusade leaders. 2. a person who murders a politically important person suddenly and unexpectedly.

as·sas·si·nate (-āt), *v.t.* -nat·ed, -nat·ing, 1. to kill (a politically important person) suddenly and unexpectedly; murder. 2. to hurt or ruin (a reputation), as by lies. —as·sas·si·na'tion, *n.*

as·sault (ă-sôlt'), *n.* 1. a violent attack of any sort. 2. rape. 3. in *Law*, an attempt or threat to do bodily violence to another: *v.t. & v.i.* 1. to attack violently. 2. to rape. —as·sault'ive, *adj.*

assault and battery, in *Law*, the carrying out of threatened physical violence.

as·say (as'ā, a-sā'), *n.* 1. a testing. 2. the chemical analysis of an ore, drug, etc. to determine the ingredients, the proportion of these, etc. 3. the substance to be tested. 4. the result of the test: *v.t.* (a-sā', ă-), 1. to subject to analysis; test. 2. to try; attempt: *v.i.* to be shown by analysis to be of a certain composition. —as·say'er, *n.*

as·sem·blage (ă-sem'blij), *n.* 1. the act of assembling or the state of being assembled. 2. a group of persons or things. 3. an art form in which a number of objects and materials are assembled and arranged.

as·sem·ble (ă-sem'bl), *v.t. & v.i.* -bled, -bling, 1. to gather together in one place or body; congregate. 2. to put together the parts of (a vehicle, device, etc.). —as·sem'bler, *n.*

as·sem·bly ('bli), *n., pl.* -blies, 1. the act of assembling or the state of being assembled. 2. a group of persons brought together in one place and for a common object; meeting. 3.

[A-], in some States, the lower house of the legislature. 4. a putting together of parts to produce a whole. 5. the separate parts.

assembly line, in many factories, a procedure of assembling things gradually by a line of workers, each worker doing one special operation.

as·sem·bly·man (-măn), *n., pl.* -men, 1. a member of a legislative assembly. 2. [A-], in some States, a member of the lower house of the legislature.

as·sent (ă-sent'), *v.i.* to admit as true; agree (*to*); consent: *n.* the act of agreeing to; consent; concurrence. —as·sent'er, *n.*

as·sen·ta·tion (as-en-tā'shŭn), *n.* an agreeing with the opinion of another, in a flattering or obsequious way.

as·sert (ă-sûrt'), *v.t.* 1. to aver; affirm; declare. 2. to maintain; defend or vindicate. —as·sert'er, as·ser·tor, *n.*

as·ser·tion (ă-sûr'shŭn), *n.* 1. the act of asserting. 2. that which is asserted; positive declaration.

as·ser·tive ('tiv), *adj.* showing assertion; positive; confident. —as·ser'tive·ly, *adv.* —as·ser'tive·ness, *n.*

as·sess (ă-ses'), *v.t.* 1. to estimate the taxable value of (a house, lands, etc.). 2. to fix or determine (a tax, fine, extent of damages, etc.). 3. to tax, fine, etc. 4. to evaluate; appraise. —as·sess'ment, *n.* —as·ses'sor, *n.*

as·set (as'et), *n.* 1. anything marketable or otherwise desirable. 2. *pl.* in *Accounting*, the entries on a balance sheet which show the resources of a person or business. 3. *pl.* in *Law*, property available to settle debts.

as·sev·er·ate (ă-sev'ĕ-rāt), *v.t.* -at·ed, -at·ing, to affirm or aver positively or with solemnity. —as·sev·er·a'tion, *n.*

as·sib·i·late (ă-sib'ĭ-lāt), *v.t.* -lat·ed, -lat·ing, to pronounce with a hissing sound; alter to a sibilant.

as·si·du·i·ty (as-ĭ-dū'ĭ-tĭ, -dōō'-), *n., pl.* -ties, 1. close application; diligence. 2. *pl.* great solicitude; attentions.

as·sid·u·ous (ă-sij'oo-wŭs), *adj.* 1. constant in application; devotedly attentive. 2. persevering; diligent. —as·sid'u·ous·ly, *adv.* —as·sid'u·ous·ness, *n.*

as·sign (ă-sīn'), *v.t.* 1. to appoint, as to a task. 2. to give as a task; allot. 3. to determine for some purpose; designate. 4. to attribute; ascribe. 5. in *Law*, to transfer or make over to another: *n.* same as assignee. —as·sign'er, in *Law*, as·sign'or, *n.* —as·sign'ment, *n.*

as·sig·na·tion (as-ig-nā'shŭn), *n.* 1. the act of assigning or the state of being assigned. 2. the thing assigned. 3. an agreement, as by lovers, to meet together, especially secretly; rendezvous; tryst.

as·sign·ee (ă-sī-nē'), *n.* in *Law*, 1. one to whom a claim, right, etc. is transferred. 2. one appointed to act for another.

as·sim·i·late (ă-sim'ĭ-lāt), *v.t.* -lat·ed, -lat·ing, 1. to bring into conformity or agreement with something else. 2. to absorb into the body; convert or incorporate into organic substance. 3. to absorb (ideas, outside elements, etc.); incorporate: *v.i.* 1. to become absorbed or incorporated. 2. to become like;

conform. —as·sim'i·la·ble ('i-lǎ-bl), adj. —as·sim·i·la'tion, n. —as·sim'i·la·tive, adj.

as·sist (ǎ-sist'), v.t. & v.i. 1. to give help or support (to); aid. 2. to work (with) as an assistant: n. the act of helping.

as·sis·tance (ǎ-sis'tǎns), n. help; aid.

as·sis·tant ('tǎnt), adj. helping; lending aid; auxiliary: n. one who, or that which, assists; helper.

as·siz·es (ǎ-sīz'iz), n. 1. court sessions for the trial by jury of civil and criminal cases, held periodically in each county of England. 2. the time or place of these.

as·so·ci·ate (ǎ-sō'shi-āt, 'si-), v.t. 1. to unite; join; connect. 2. to bring into relationship as a friend, partner, etc. 3. to join or connect mentally: v.i. 1. to go about or have dealings (with another) as a friend, partner, etc. 2. to unite; connect: adj. (usually -it), 1: joined or connected in some way with something else. 2. having some but not all rights, privileges, etc., as in an organization: n. (usually -it), 1. a person with whom one is associated. 2. one belonging to or connected with a society, institution, etc., but not having regular membership, privileges, etc. 3. anything connected in some way with something else. 4. a degree given by a junior college for two years of study.

as·so·ci·a·tion (ǎ-sō-si-ā'shǔn, -shi-ā'shǔn), n. 1. the act of associating or the state of being associated. 2. an organization formed for a common object; society. 3. a mental connection, as of thoughts or memories. —as·so·ci·a'tion·al, adj.

as·so·ci·a·tive (ǎ-sō'shi-āt-iv, 'si-; 'shā-tiv), adj. of, pertaining to, showing, or causing association, as of thoughts.

as·so·nance (as'ō-nǎns), n. 1. resemblance of sound. 2. rhyme in which stressed vowels are the same but the consonants are not. —as'so·nant, adj.

as·sort (ǎ-sôrt'), v.t. to divide or separate into groups according to type or size; classify; arrange. —as·sort'er, n.

as·sort·ed ('id), adj. 1. various; different. 2. classified according to type or size.

as·sort·ment ('mĕnt), n. 1. the act of assorting; classification. 2. a varied collection or group.

as·suage (ǎ-swāj'), v.t. -suaged', -suag'ing, 1. to lessen; mitigate; allay. 2. to appease; pacify. 3. to satisfy. —as·suage'ment, n.

as·sume (ǎ-sōōm', ǎ-sūm'), v.t. -sumed', -sum'ing, 1. to adopt (a form, role, etc.). 2. to seize or appropriate. 3. to take upon oneself. 4. to take for granted. 5. to pretend to possess. —as·sum'a·ble, adj. —as·sum'er, n.

as·sum·ing (ǎ-sōō'ming), adj. arrogant; presumptuous.

as·sump·tion (ǎ-sump'shǔn), n. 1. the act of assuming. 2. a supposition; hypothesis. 3. the taking up of a person to heaven. 4. [A-], the festival in honor of the ascent of the Virgin Mary into heaven, celebrated by the Roman Catholic Church on August 15. —as·sump'tive, adj.

as·sur·ance (ǎ-shoor'ǎns), n. 1. the act of assuring. 2. certain expectation; confidence. 3.

testimony or action intended to inspire confidence. 4. self-reliance; self-confidence. 5. impudence. 6. [Chiefly British], insurance.

as·sure (ǎ-shoor'), v.t. -sured', -sur'ing, 1. to make sure or certain. 2. to convey a feeling of confidence to. 3. to declare or promise. 4. to guarantee. 5. [British], to insure for indemnity. —as·sur'er, n.

as·sured (ǎ-shoord'), adj. 1. made certain; guaranteed. 2. self-possessed; confident. 3. insured: n. 1. a person insured. 2. a person to whom insurance is payable. —as·sur'ed·ly (ǎ-shoor'id-li), adv. —as·sur'ed·ness, n.

As·syr·i·an (ǎ-sir'i-ǎn), adj. of or pertaining to Assyria, an ancient empire in southwest Asia, or its inhabitants: n. a native or inhabitant of Assyria.

As·syr·i·ol·o·gy (ǎ-sir-i-ol'ō-ji), n. the study or scientific investigation of the antiquities of Assyria, its language, culture, etc.

a·stat·ic (ǎ-stat'ik), adj. lacking a tendency to take a definite position or direction; not affected by the earth's magnetism. —a·stat'i·cal·ly, adv. —a·stat'i·cism ('i-sizm), n.

as·ta·tine (as'tǎ-tēn), n. a radioactive chemical element formed from bismuth.

as·ter (as'tẽr), n. 1. any of a large genus of plants with purple, pink, blue, or white flowers similar to daisies. 2. in Biology, a star-shaped structure formed in an animal cell during mitosis.

-as·ter (as'tẽr), a suffix signifying inferiority, worthlessness.

as·te·ri·a·ted (as·tir'i-āt-ĕd), adj. 1. star-shaped. 2. in Mineralogy, having asterism.

as·ter·isk (as'tẽr-isk), n. the mark (*) used in printing as a reference to a marginal passage or footnote appended to the text, or to indicate letters or words omitted: v.t. to mark with an asterisk.

as·ter·ism (as'tẽr-izm), n. 1. in Astronomy, a group or cluster of stars. 2. three asterisks placed in the form of a triangle (⁎⁎ or *⁎*) to direct attention to a particular printed passage. 3. in Mineralogy, a starlike figure of light in certain crystals.

a·stern (ǎ-stũrn'), adv. 1. at or toward the back part of a ship or aircraft. 2. behind a ship or aircraft. 3. with the stern foremost.

a·ster·nal (ǎ-stũr'nǎl), adj. not joined to the sternum or breastbone.

as·ter·oid (as'tẽ-roid), adj. 1. starlike; shaped like a star. 2. resembling a starfish: n. 1. any of the many small planets whose orbits lie between those of Mars and Jupiter; planetoid. 2. same as starfish.

as·the·ni·a (as-thē'ni-ǎ), n. debility; weakness.

as·then·ic (as-then'ik), adj. 1. characterized by asthenia; feeble. 2. having a slight build.

asth·ma (az'mǎ), n. a chronic respiratory disease marked by difficulty of breathing, a wheezing cough, and a sense of constriction in the chest. —asth·mat'ic (-mat'ik), adj. & n. —asth·mat'i·cal, adj. —asth·mat'i·cal·ly, adv.

as·tig·mat·ic (as-stig-mat'ik), adj. 1. of or affected by astigmatism. 2. counteracting astigmatism. —as·tig·mat'i·cal·ly, adv.

a·stig·ma·tism (ǎ-stig'mǎ-tizm), n. 1. a defect in the curvature of a lens, as of the eye, resulting in an improper focus of the image. 2. distorted vision because of this.

a-stir (ă-stŭr'), adv. & adj. 1. on the move; in motion. 2. out of bed.

a-stom-a-tous (ā-stŏm'ă-tŭs, ā-stō'mă-), adj. having no stoma or stomata.

as-ton-ish (ă-stŏn'ish), v.t. to strike with sudden wonder; surprise; amaze. —**as-ton'ish-ing**, adj. —**as-ton'ish-ment**, n.

as-tound (ă-stound'), v.t. to stun with amazement. —**as-tound'ing**, adj.

a-strad-dle (ă-strad'l), adv. with one leg on each side of something; astride.

as-tra-gal (as'tră-gl), n. a small, convex molding or beading of semicircular form.

as-trag-a-lus (as-trag'ă-lŭs), n., pl. **-li** (-lī), [Rare], the anklebone, or talus, of man.

as-tra-khan (as'tră-kăn), n. 1. curly fur from very young lambs originally raised near Astrakhan, a city in Russia. 2. a wool fabric made to look like this.

as-tral (as'trăl), adj. 1. of, pertaining to, or like a star or stars. 2. in *Theosophy*, of or pertaining to a universal substance pervading space and forming part of all bodies.

astral lamp, an oil lamp with a tubelike wick and a ring-shaped reservoir: it casts no downward shadow.

a-stray (ă-strā'), adv. 1. out of the right way or in a wandering condition. 2. in or into error.

a-stride (ă-strīd'), adv. 1. with the legs wide apart. 2. astraddle: prep. 1. with a leg on either side of. 2. from one part, side, or member of to the other; in extension sense.

as-trin-gent (ă-strin'jĕnt), adj. 1. that produces contraction of the tissues and checks discharges, as of blood. 2. harsh: n. an astringent substance. —**as-trin'gen-cy** ('jĕn-si), n. —**as-trin'gent-ly**, adv.

as-tro-, a combining form meaning *of a star or stars.*

as-tro-bi-ol-o-gy (as-trō-bī-ŏl'ŏ-ji), n. the branch of biology investigating the existence of living organisms other than those found on the planet earth.

as-tro-dome (as'trŏ-dōm), n. a transparent dome on top of the fuselage of an aircraft, for the navigator and various instruments.

as-tro-dy-nam-ics (as-trō-dī-nam'iks), n. dynamics concerned with the study of movement and travel in outer space.

as-tro-labe (as'trŏ-lāb), n. an instrument anciently used in astronomical calculations.

as-trol-o-gy (ă-strol'ŏ-ji), n. 1. anciently, astronomy. 2. study of the relative positions of the stars, moon, and sun and the supposed influence of these on human affairs, in an attempt to predict the future. —**as-trol'o-ger**, n. —**as-tro-log-i-cal** (as-trŏ-loj'i-kl), adj. —**as-tro-log'i-cal-ly**, adv.

as-trom-e-try (ă-strom'ĕ-tri), n. the part of astronomy that treats of the measurement of the relative positions of heavenly bodies. —**as-tro-met-ric** (as-trŏ-met'rik), adj.

as-tro-naut (as'trŏ-nôt), n. one who travels in a spacecraft in outer space.

as-tro-nau-tics (as-trŏ-nôt'iks), n. the science of

travel in outer space, as to the moon or to other planets. —**as-tro-nau'ti-cal**, adj. —**as-tro-nau'ti-cal-ly**, adv.

as-tro-nav-i-ga-tion (as-trō-nav-i-gā'shŭn), n. same as celestial navigation. —**as-tro-nav'i-ga-tor**, n.

as-tro-nom-i-cal (as-trŏ-nom'i-kl), adj. 1. of or pertaining to astronomy. 2. exceedingly or bewilderingly large, as a number. Also **as-tro-nom'ic**. —**as-tro-nom'i-cal-ly**, adv.

astronomical unit, a unit of length equal to the mean radius of the orbit of the earth.

as-tron-o-my (ă-stron'ŏ-mi), n. the science that treats of the magnitude, motion, relative position, etc. of the stars, planets, and all other heavenly bodies. —**as-tron'o-mer**, n.

as-tro-pho-tog-ra-phy (as-trō-fŏ-tog'ră-fi), n. photography of heavenly bodies and of celestial phenomena.

as-tro-phys-ics (-fiz'iks), n. the part of astronomy that treats of the physical properties and phenomena of heavenly bodies. —**as-tro-phys'i-cal**, adj. —**as-tro-phys'i-cist**, n.

as-tute (ă-stōōt', ă-stūt'), adj. shrewd; keenly penetrating; sagacious; cunning; crafty. —**as-tute'ly**, adv. —**as-tute'ness**, n.

a-sun-der (ă-sun'dĕr), adv. 1. into separate parts. 2. in or into a position apart.

a-swarm (ă-swôrm'), adj. swarming.

a-sy-lum (ă-sī'lŭm), n. 1. a place of refuge. 2. refuge given; especially refuge granted by a country to political offenders from another country. 3. an institution for the care of the aged, destitute, mentally ill, etc.: an older term.

a-sym-me-try (ā-sim'ĕ-tri), n. lack of symmetry. —**a-sym-met-ri-cal** (ā-si-met'ri-kl), **a-sym-met'ric**, adj. —**a-sym-met'ri-cal-ly**, adv.

a-syn-de-ton (ă-sin'dĕ-ton), n. rhetorical omission of connectives, as in "I came, I saw, I conquered." —**as-yn-det-ic** (as-in-det'ik), adj. —**as-yn-det'i-cal-ly**, adv.

at (at), prep. 1. near; on; by; in. 2. up to; to the extent of. 3. according to; with reference to. 4. to; toward; through. 5. in response to. 6. engaged in; dependent on. 7. upon arrival or completion of. 8. during; within. 9. in, for, or by the rate, price, etc. of.

At-a-brine (at'ă-brin, -brĕn), n. a synthetic drug used in treating malaria and other diseases: a trademark.

at-a-rac-tic (at-ă-rak'tik), n. a drug used as a tranquilizer: adj. of or pertaining to tranquilizing drugs. Also **at-a-rax'ic** (-raks'ik).

at-a-rax-i-a (at-ă-rak'si-ă), n. complete peace of mind; tranquillity; calmness: also **at-a-rax'y** ('si).

at-a-vism (at'ă-vizm), n. the reversion, or tendency to revert, to the ancestral type of a species; resemblance to a remote ancestor. —**at-a-vis'tic**, adj. —**at-a-vis'ti-cal-ly**, adv.

a-tax-i-a (ă-tak'si-ă), n. loss of control over voluntary muscular movements. —**a-tax'ic**, n. & adj.

ate (āt), past tense of eat.

-ate (āt), a suffix meaning *to become, cause to become, form, treat with.*

a in cap, ā in cane, ä in father, å in abet, e in met, ē in be, ē in baker, ĕ in regent, I in pit, ī in fine, i in manifest, o in hot, ō in horse, ō in bone,

-ate (it, āt), a suffix meaning *of, having, characteristic of.*

-ate (āt, it), a suffix meaning *office, official, agent, function, thing done,* etc.

at·el·ier (at'ĕl-yā), n. [French], a workshop or studio, as of a painter or sculptor.

ath·a·na·si·a (ath-à-nā'zhä, 'zhi-à), **a·than·a·sy** (à-than'á-si), n. immortality; deathlessness.

a·the·ism (ā'thi-izm), n. disbelief in the existence of God or gods. —**a'the·ist**, n. —**a·the·is'tic**, **a·the·is'ti·cal**, adj. —**a·the·is'ti·cal·ly**, adv.

A·the·na (à-thē'nà), n. the Greek goddess of wisdom, warfare, and the useful arts: also **A·the·ne** (à-thē'nē).

ath·e·nae·um, **ath·e·ne·um** (ath-ē-nē'úm), n. an institution, club, building, or room devoted to literature, science, art, etc.

a·ther·man·cy (à-thûr'mán-si), n. incapacity to transmit heat rays. —**a·ther'ma·nous** ('mà-nûs), adj.

ath·er·o·ma (ath-ē-rō'má), n., pl. -**mas**, -**ma·ta** ('má-tá), 1. a small nodule of fatty substance on an inner arterial wall. 2. the condition marked by formation of such nodules. —**ath·er·o'ma·tous** ('má-tûs), adj.

ath·er·o·scle·ro·sis (ath-ēr-ō-sklē-rō'sis), n. arteriosclerosis accompanied by the formation of atheromas. —**ath·er·o·scle·rot'ic** (-rot'ik), adj.

a·thirst (à-thûrst'), adj. 1. eager (*for*). 2. [Poetic], thirsty.

ath·lete (ath'lēt), n. one trained and skilled in games, exercises, etc. that demand a combination of physical agility and endurance.

athlete's foot, ringworm of the feet.

ath·let·ic (ath-let'ik), adj. 1. of, pertaining to, or characteristic of athletes or athletics. 2. physically strong and agile. —**ath·let'i·cal·ly**, adv.

ath·let·i·cism ('i-sizm), n. 1. a special liking for athletics. 2. an athletic attribute.

ath·let·ics ('iks), n. gymnastic exercises, sports, or any system of physical training.

at-home (ăt-hōm'), n. an informal reception held at one's home, often in the afternoon: also **at home**.

a·thwart (à-thwôrt'), adv. across; crosswise; obliquely: prep. 1. from side to side of. 2. in opposition to. 3. in nautical usage, across the course or direction of.

a·tilt (à-tilt'), adv. & adj. 1. tilting, as with a lance. 2. tilted, tipped, inclined, etc.

a·tin·gle (à-ting'gl), adj. tingling, as from excitement.

-a·tion (ā-shún), a suffix meaning *the act of, the condition of, the result of.*

-a·tive (à-tiv, āt'iv), a suffix meaning *of or pertaining to, inclined to, serving to.*

at·lan·tes (ăt-lan'tēz, at-), n., sing. **at·las** (at'làs), figures or half-figures of men, used as columns or pilasters to support an entablature.

at·las (at'làs), n. 1. a collection of maps in a volume. 2. a work in tabulated form, usually with charts and illustrations. 3. [A-]. a giant Greek god who supported the heavens on his shoulders.

at·mom·e·ter (at-mom'ē-tēr), n. an instrument

for measuring the rate and amount of water evaporation.

at·mos·phere (at'mŏs-fir), n. 1. the entire mass of air, made up of oxygen, nitrogen, and other gases, surrounding the earth. 2. the gaseous envelope surrounding any heavenly body. 3. the air in any locality. 4. any pervading influence; general mood or tone. 5. in Physics, a unit of pressure equal to 14.69 lbs. per square inch.

at·mos·pher·ic (at-mŏs-fir'ik), **at·mos·pher'i·cal**, adj. 1. of or existing in the atmosphere. 2. caused or created by the atmosphere. 3. giving or suggestive of an atmosphere, or mood. —**at·mos·pher'i·cal·ly**, adv.

atmospheric pressure, the pressure exerted in every direction upon a body by the weight of the atmosphere, at sea level equal to 14.69 lbs. per square inch.

at·mos·pher·ics ('iks), n. 1. disturbances in radio reception; static. 2. conditions causing such disturbances, as electrical discharges during a storm.

at·oll (a'tŏl, ä'-), n. a coral island in the form of a ring surrounding a lagoon.

at·om (at'ŏm), n. 1. a tiny particle; bit; dot. 2. any one of the smallest particles of an element, that combine with similar particles of other elements to form compounds. 3. atomic energy (preceded by *the*).

atom bomb, same as **atomic bomb**.

a·tom·ic (à-tom'ik), adj. 1. extremely minute. 2. of an atom or atoms. 3. of, pertaining to, or using atomic bombs or atomic energy. —**a·tom'i·cal·ly**, adv.

atomic bomb, a bomb the power of which results from the immense quantity of energy suddenly released when a chain reaction of nuclear fission is set off by neutron bombardment in the atoms of a charge of plutonium or of the uranium isotope known as U 235.

atomic energy, energy released from an atom in nuclear fusion or nuclear fission.

at·o·mic·i·ty (at-ō-mis'i-ti), n. 1. the number of atoms in a molecule. 2. same as **valence**.

atomic number, the number representing the number of protons in the nucleus of the atom of a given element.

atomic weight, a number representing the weight of one atom of a given element as compared with that of one atom of another element taken as a standard, now usually carbon at 12.

at·om·ism (at'ō-mizm), n. the philosophical theory that the universe is composed of minute, indestructible, indivisible particles. —**at'om·ist**, n.

at·om·ize (at'ō-mīz), v.t. -**ized**, -**iz·ing**, 1. to reduce (a liquid) to fine spray. 2. to wipe out by use of an atomic bomb or other atomic weapons. 3. to reduce to tiny particles; disintegrate. —**at·om·i·za'tion** (-mi-zā'-shún), n.

at·om·iz·er (at'ō-mī-zēr), n. a device that reduces a liquid to spray; sprayer.

at·o·my (at'ō-mi), n., pl. -**mies**, [Archaic], 1. an atom. 2. a pygmy; tiny person.

a·ton·al (ā-tōn'ăl), adj. lacking tonality through conscious disregard of any conventional

---

musical key or scale. —a·to·nal·i·ty (ā-tō-nal'ĭ-tĭ), n.

a·tone (å-tōn'), v.i. a·toned', a·ton'ing, to make reparation or amends (for injury done, wrong committed, etc.).

a·tone·ment ('mĕnt), n. 1. reparation or satisfaction offered or made in return for an injury or wrong; expiation. 2. [A-]. in Theology, a) the recompense for sin brought about by the suffering and death of Christ. b) the reconciliation of God and man resulting from this.

a·ton·ic (å-tŏn'ĭk, å-), adj. 1. lacking muscle tone. 2. unaccented: n. an unaccented word or syllable. —a·to·nic·i·ty (ā-tō-nĭs'ĭ-tĭ), n.

at·o·ny (ăt'ŏn-ĭ), n. lack of tone in an organism, organ, or part.

a·top (å-tŏp'), prep. on top of: adv. at the top; on the top.

-a·to·ry (å-tôr'ĭ), a suffix meaning of, having the nature of, caused by.

at·ra·bil·ious (å-trå-bĭl'yŭs), adj. melancholy, morose, gloomy, etc.: also at·ra·bil·iar ('yĕr), adj.

a·tri·um (ā'trĭ-ŭm), n., pl. a'tri·a (-å), a'tri·ums, 1. the square, central court, lighted from above, of an ancient Roman house. 2. a hall or entrance court. 3. an anatomical cavity: especially, either of the upper chambers of the heart, that receive blood from the veins; auricle. —a'tri·al (-ål), adj.

a·tro·cious (å-trō'shŭs), adj. 1. extremely cruel, evil, brutal, etc. 2. outrageous; appalling. 3. [Informal], in poor taste; offensive; bad. — a·tro'cious·ly, adv. —a·tro'cious·ness, n.

a·troc·i·ty (å-trŏs'ĭ-tĭ), n., pl. -ties, 1. enormous wickedness; abominable cruelty. 2. an atrocious deed.

at·ro·phy (ăt'rō-fĭ), n. a wasting, or diminution in bulk, of the body, or any part of the body, from lack of nourishment; degeneration of an organ or part: v.i. -phied, -phy·ing, to waste away: v.t. to cause atrophy in. —a·troph·ic (å-trŏf'ĭk), adj.

at·ro·pine (ăt'rō-pēn, -pĭn). n. a poisonous, crystalline alkaloid extracted from belladonna, used to dilate the pupil of the eye and to relieve spasms: also at'ro·pin.

at·tach (å-tăch'), v.t. 1. to fasten or fix to or on; bind. 2. to connect; join. 3. to connect by ties of affection. 4. to appoint to. 5. to take or seize by legal authority. 6. to add (a signature, an amendment to a legal document, etc.). 7. to attribute. 8. to place (troops, a unit, etc.) temporarily with another military unit: v.i. to adhere; belong. —at·tach'a·ble, adj.

at·ta·ché (ăt-à-shā'), n. one who is attached to the diplomatic corps of a minister or ambassador, usually with special duties.

attaché case, a flat, rectangular case with stiff sides, for carrying documents and papers.

at·tach·ment (a-tăch'mĕnt), n. 1. the act of attaching. 2. fidelity or affectionate regard. 3. that which attaches; fastening. 4. something that is attached. 5. a device or piece of equipment attached to a machine or instrument. 6. the taking into custody of a person, goods, or an estate by legal process.

at·tack (å-tăk'), v.t. 1. to assault; fall upon with force; assail. 2. to talk or write

against; ridicule, discredit, etc. 3. to begin working on with vigor. 4. to begin to affect or act upon, as disease: v.i. to make an onset or assault: n. 1. the act of attacking. 2. a beginning of any work or enterprise. 3. the beginning or recurrence of a disease. — at·tack'er, n.

at·tain (a-tān'), v.t. 1. to achieve; accomplish; compass. 2. to reach; arrive at. —at·tain·a·bil'i·ty, n. —at·tain'a·ble, adj.

at·tain·der (å-tān'dēr), n. the deprivation of civil rights and forfeiture of the estate of one under sentence of death or outlawed for treason or a felony.

at·tain·ment (å-tān'mĕnt), n. 1. the act of attaining; act of arriving at or reaching as the result of effort and exertion. 2. that which is attained; accomplishment.

at·taint (å-tānt'), v.t. -taint'ed, -taint'ing, archaic past participle -taint', 1. to punish by attainder. 2. [Archaic], to disgrace: n. 1. an attainder. 2. [Archaic], disgrace.

at·tar (ăt'är), n. an essential oil expressed from the petals of roses: commonly called attar of roses.

at·tem·per (å-tem'pēr), v.t. 1. to reduce or modify by mixture. 2. to regulate the temperature of. 3. to moderate; temper; modify. 4. to fit or adapt.

at·tempt (å-tempt'), v.t. to make an effort to accomplish, perform, obtain, etc.; try; endeavor; essay: n. 1. a try; essay; effort; endeavor. 2. an attack or assault.

at·tend (å-tend'), v.t. 1. to wait upon; serve. 2. to accompany or be present with. 3. to be present at. 4. to go along with or follow as a result: v.i. 1. to pay heed; listen. 2. to be ready; wait (upon). 3. to devote oneself (to). 4. to look after; tend (to).

at·tend·ance (å-ten'dåns), n. 1. the act of attending. 2. the number of persons attending.

at·tend·ant ('dånt), n. 1. one who attends, serves, or accompanies. 2. one who is present. 3. that which is concomitant with anything else: adj. 1. waiting on; giving service to. 2. being present. 3. connected; consequent upon.

at·ten·tion (å-ten'shŭn), n. 1. the act of applying the mind to anything. 2. the act of noticing or observing. 3. consideration or regard. 4. an act of civility or courtesy. 5. a military command to assume an erect position with eyes ahead and arms to the sides, in readiness for another command: also, this position.

at·ten·tive ('tĭv), adj. 1. heedful; full of attention: intent. 2. considerate of the wishes of another or others. —at·ten'tive·ly, adv. —at·ten'tive·ness, n.

at·ten·u·ate (å-ten'yoo-wāt), v.t. -at·ed, -at·ing, 1. to make thin or slender. 2. to weaken or reduce. 3. to thin out by dilution; rarefy: v.i. to become thin, slender, weak, etc.; lessen: adj. (-wĭt), 1. made thin; dilute; rarefied. 2. in Botany, tapering to a point. —at·ten·u·a'tion, n.

at·test (å-test'), v.t. 1. to bear witness to. 2. to certify as being true or genuine. 3. to manifest; serve as proof of: v.i. to testify (to). — at·test'er, at·tes'tor, n.

ạ in cap, ā in cane, ä in father, å in abet, e in met, ē in be, ē in baker, ẽ in regent, ĭ in pit, ī in fine, ĭ in manifest, o in hot, ō in horse, ō in bone,

at·tes·ta·tion (ă-tes-tā'shŭn), *n.* 1. the act of attesting. 2. testimony, or evidence given under oath.

At·tic (at'ik), *adj.* 1. of or pertaining to Attica, either as a province of modern Greece or as an ancient region dominated by Athens. 2. classical; elegant.

at·tic (at'ik), *n.* an uppermost room or space in a house immediately beneath the roof; garret.

At·ti·cism (at'i-sizm), *n.* [also a-], 1. a style, idiom, etc. characteristic of Attic Greeks. 2. an elegant manner of expression.

at·tire (ă-tīr'), *v.t.* -tired', -tir'ing, to dress; clothe; array; adorn: *n.* 1. dress; garb; clothes; especially, splendid clothing. 2. in *Heraldry,* the horns of a stag.

at·ti·tude (at'i-tōōd), *n.* 1. bodily position or posture. 2. a bearing or manner assumed indicative of one's feeling, opinion, etc. 3. the orientation of an aircraft or spacecraft relative to something else, as the ground or horizon. —**at·ti·tu'di·nal,** *adj.*

at·ti·tu·di·nize (at-i-tōōd'n-īz), *v.i.* -nized, -nizing, to pose for effect.

at·tor·ney (ă-tûr'ni), *n., pl.* -neys, one legally qualified to act for another in the transaction of private business or in the management, prosecution, or defense of actions at law.

attorney at law, a lawyer.

attorney general, *pl.* attorneys general, attorney generals, 1. the chief law officer of a State or national government. 2. [A- G-], the head of the U.S. Department of Justice.

at·tract (ă-trakt'), *v.t.* 1. to draw to or toward; cause to approach. 2. to inspire the admiration of; allure; entice: *v.i.* to have the power of attraction. —**at·tract'er, at·trac'tor,** *n.*

at·trac·tion (ă-trak'shŭn), *n.* 1. the act of attracting. 2. the power of attracting; charm; appeal. 3. a person or thing that attracts. 4. the physical force that tends to draw bodies or particles of matter together so that they cohere: opposed to *repulsion.*

at·trac·tive ('tiv), *adj.* having the power or tendency to attract; alluring; inviting. —**at·trac'tive·ly,** *adv.* —**at·trac'tive·ness,** *n.*

at·trib·ute (ă-trib'yoot), *v.t.* -ut·ed, -ut·ing, to ascribe; impute; assign: *n.* (a'tri-būt). 1. that which is attributed, as a quality, trait, property, or characteristic. 2. a word or phrase ascribing a quality, characteristic, etc. to something or someone; adjective or adjectival phrase. —**at·trib'ut·a·ble,** *adj.* —**at·tri·bu'tion,** *n.*

at·trib·u·tive (ă-trib'yoo-tiv), *adj.* of, pertaining to, of the nature of, or expressing an attribute: *n.* a word or phrase denoting an attribute, joined to the substantive it describes or modifies; attributive adjective or adjectival phrase. —**at·trib'u·tive·ly,** *adv.*

at·trit·ed (ă-trīt'id), *adj.* worn down by attrition or friction.

at·tri·tion (ă-trish'ŭn), *n.* 1. the act of wearing away by rubbing or friction; abrasion. 2. a slow weakening or wearing down, as by harassment. 3. the loss of personnel from natural causes, as retirement or death. 4. in *Theology,* repentance of sin arising only from fear of punishment.

at·tune (ă-tōōn'), *v.t.* -tuned', -tun'ing, 1. to tune. 2. to bring into accordance or harmony.

a·typ·i·cal (ā-tip'i-kl), **a·typ·ic,** *adj.* not typical; deviating from the type, or norm. —**a·typ'i·cal·ly,** *adv.*

au·burn (ô'bĕrn), *adj. & n.* reddish brown.

au cou·rant (ō kōō-rän'), [French], up-to-date; informed.

auc·tion (ôk'shŭn), *n.* 1. a public sale at which the highest bidder becomes the purchaser of articles or pieces of property put up for sale, one at a time. 2. auction bridge. 3. the bidding at bridge or certain other card games: *v.t.* to sell by auction (often followed by *off*).

auction bridge, a game like contract bridge except that tricks taken beyond the winning bid count toward game.

auc·tion·eer (ôk-shŭ-nir'), *n.* one who conducts sales by auction: *v.t.* to sell by auction.

auc·to·ri·al (ôk-tôr'i-ăl), *adj.* 1. of or pertaining to an author. 2. by an author.

au·da·cious (ô-dā'shŭs), *adj.* 1. bold; daring; spirited. 2. insolent; impudent; characterized by shameless effrontery. —**au·da'cious·ly,** *adv.* —**au·da'cious·ness,** *n.*

au·dac·i·ty (ô-das'i-ti), *n.* 1. boldness; daring; courageous spirit. 2. impudence; effrontery. 3. *pl.* -ties, an audacious act or an audacious comment or assertion.

au·di·ble (ô'di-bl), *adj.* that can be heard. —**au·di·bil'i·ty,** *n.* —**au'di·bly,** *adv.*

au·di·ence (ô'di-ĕns), *n.* 1. the act of hearing. 2. a hearing or formal interview with one in a high position. 3. an assembly of persons to hear and see a play, lecture, concert, etc. 4. the persons reached by a radio or television program, book, etc.

au·di·ent (-ĕnt), *adj.* hearing; listening.

au·di·o (ô'di-ō), *adj.* 1. of frequencies corresponding to sound waves that can normally be heard by the human ear. 2. of or pertaining to the reproduction of sound, especially the sound portion of a telecast: distinguished from *video.*

audio frequency, a frequency within the range of audible sounds, or a corresponding frequency of electric current, from about 20 to about 20,000 hertz.

au·di·ol·o·gy (ô-di-ol'ô-ji), *n.* the science of hearing, especially the diagnosis of hearing defects and the habilitation of those with such defects. —**au·di·o·log'i·cal** (-ô-loj'i-kl), *adj.* —**au·di·ol'o·gist,** *n.*

au·di·om·e·ter (ô-di-om'ĕ-tĕr), *n.* an instrument for measuring the power of hearing. —**au·di·o·met'ric** (-ô-met'rik), *adj.*

au·di·o·phile (ô'di-ô-fīl), *n.* one who is especially interested in high-fidelity sound reproduction.

au·di·o·vis·u·al (ô-di-ō-vizh'oo-wăl), *adj.* of or pertaining to materials, especially educational materials, that involve the use of both sight and hearing, as motion pictures, recordings, etc.

au·di·phone (ô'di-fōn), *n.* an instrument that

conveys the vibrations of sound to the auditory nerves through the bones of the head.

au·dit (ô'dit), *n.* 1. a formal examination and verification of claims, financial accounts; etc. 2. a settlement of accounts. 3. a final statement by an auditor: *v.t. & v.i.* 1. to examine (claims, financial accounts, etc.). 2. to attend (college lectures, classes, etc.) only to listen and not for credit.

au·di·tion (ô-dish'ŭn), *v.i.* to perform when applying for a job as an actor, musician, etc.: *v.i.* to listen to or watch the performance of (an actor, musician, etc.) to determine fitness for a job: *n.* 1. such a performance or test. 2. the act of hearing. 3. the power of hearing.

au·dit·or (ô'di-tēr), *n.* 1. a hearer or listener. 2. one who is authorized to examine and verify financial accounts and claims. 3. one who audits classes.

au·di·to·ri·um (ô-di-tôr'i-ŭm), *n.* 1. the space in a theater or other public building assigned to the audience. 2. a hall or building for public gatherings.

au·di·to·ry (ô'di-tôr-i), *adj.* of or pertaining to hearing, or to the sense or organs of hearing: *n.* [Archaic], 1. an audience. 2. an auditorium. —au·di·to'ri·ly, *adv.*

auf Wie·der·se·hen (ouf vē'dēr-zā'ĕn), [German], until we see each other again; goodbye.

Au·ge·an (ô-jē'ăn), *adj.* extremely filthy, as the stables of Augeas, a legendary Greek king, that were cleaned after 30 years by Hercules.

au·ger (ô'gēr), *n.* a spiral boring tool.

aught (ôt), *n.* 1. anything whatever. 2. a zero: *adv.* [Archaic], in any way; at all.

au·gite (ô'jīt), *n.* a black, lustrous aluminous pyroxene found in igneous rock.

aug·ment (ôg-ment'), *v.t. & v.i.* 1. to increase; enlarge in size or extent. 2. in *Grammar*, to add an augment to: *v.i.* to grow larger; increase: *n.* (ôg'ment), in *Grammar*, a prefixed vowel, or a lengthening of the initial vowel, in Greek and Sanskrit verbs. —aug·ment'a·ble, *adj.* —aug·ment'er, *n.*

aug·men·ta·tion (ôg-men-tā'shŭn), *n.* 1. the act of augmenting. 2. something that augments; increase. 3. in *Music*, a lengthening of the time value of the notes of a theme, done to provide a variation of the theme.

aug·men·ta·tive (ôg-men'tă-tiv), *adj.* having the quality or power of augmenting: *n.* a word or affix that increases the force of the idea conveyed by the word to which it is affixed or added; intensifier.

aug·ment·ed (ôg-men'tid), *adj.* in *Music*, greater by a half step.

au gra·tin (ō grät'n), [French], prepared with a browned topping of cheese and bread crumbs.

au·gur (ô'gēr), *n.* 1. in ancient Rome, one who officially interpreted omens as being favorable or unfavorable for the outcome of a particular event. 2. a soothsayer; prophet: *v.t. & v.i.* 1. to conjecture or predict from signs or omens. 2. to be an omen (of).

au·gu·ry (ô'gyēr-i), *n., pl.* -ries, 1. the art or

practice of interpreting omens in connection with the outcome of upcoming events. 2. an omen; presage.

Au·gust (ô'gŭst), *n.* the eighth month of the year, having 31 days.

au·gust (ô-gust'), *adj.* 1. venerable; respected because of age, high position, etc. 2. grand; majestic; of a nature to inspire awe and reverence. —au·gust'ly, *adv.* —au·gust'ness, *n.*

au jus (ō zhōō', ō jōōs'), [French], served with its cooking juices: said of meat.

auk (ôk), *n.* a web-footed diving bird of Arctic seas.

auld (ôld), *adj.* [Scottish & Dial.], old.

auld lang syne (ôld' lang' zīn'), [Scottish], old times, especially times remembered with fondness.

au·lic (ô'lik), *adj.* of or pertaining to a royal court.

au na·tu·rel (ō na-too-rel'), [French], 1. as it would be naturally. 2. in the nude.

aunt (ant, änt), *n.* 1. a sister of one's father or mother. 2. the wife of one's uncle.

aunt·ie, aunt·y (an'ti, än'), *n., pl.* -ies, [Informal], aunt.

au·ra (ôr'ă), *n., pl.* -ras, -rae ('ē), 1. an effluvium or subtle essence, as the aroma of a flower. 2. an atmosphere diffused by and seeming to surround an individual or thing. 3. in *Medicine*, a sensation that is a forewarning of a seizure or the like. —au'ral, *adj.*

au·ral (ôr'ăl), *adj.* of or pertaining to the ear or to the sense of hearing.

au·re·ate (ôr'i-āt), *adj.* 1. golden; gilded. 2. ornate; brilliant. —au're·ate·ly, *adv.*

au·re·ole (ôr'i-ōl), **au·re·o·la** (ô-rē'ō-lă), *n.* 1. a halo or radiance encircling the head, as in religious paintings. 2. the sun's corona, as seen during an eclipse.

Au·re·o·my·cin (ôr-i-ō-mīs'n), *n.* an antibiotic used against various bacterial infections and some viruses; a trademark.

au re·voir (ō rĕ-vwär'), [French], until we meet again; goodbye.

au·ric (ôr'ik), *adj.* of, pertaining to, or containing gold.

au·ri·cle (ôr'i-kl), *n.* 1. the external part of the ear. 2. either of the chambers of the heart which receive blood from the veins and transmit it to the ventricles; atrium. 3. an earlike part.

au·ric·u·la (ô-rik'yoo-lă), *n., pl.* -las, -lae (-lē), 1. a variety of primrose native to Alpine regions. 2. same as **auricle.**

au·ric·u·lar (-lēr), *adj.* 1. of or pertaining to the ear or to the sense of hearing. 2. privately addressed, as to the priest in the confessional. 3. shaped like an ear. 4. of or pertaining to an auricle of the heart: *n.* any of the feathers overlying the ear of a bird: usually used in the plural. —au·ric'u·lar·ly, *adv.*

au·ric·u·late (-lit, -lāt), *adj.* 1. having ears or earlike parts. 2. shaped like an ear.

au·rif·er·ous (ô-rif'ēr-ŭs), *adj.* bearing, yielding, or containing gold.

au·ri·form (ôr'i-fôrm), *adj.* ear-shaped; having the form of the human ear.

---

a in cap, ā in cane, ä in father, ȧ in abet, e in met ē in be, ē in baker, ĕ in regent, i in pit, ī in fine, i in manifest, o in hot, ô in horse, ō in bone,

au·rochs (ô'roks), *n., pl.* **au'rochs,** a European bison, now nearly extinct.

au·ro·ra (ô-rôr'å), *n., pl.* **-ras, -rae** ('ē), 1. dawn. 2. same as **aurora australis** or **aurora borealis.** —au·ro'ral, au·ro're·an ('i-ǎn), *adj.*

aurora aus·tra·lis (ô-strā'lis), luminous lights in the sky of the Southern Hemisphere, corresponding to the aurora borealis; southern lights.

aurora bo·re·a·lis (bôr-i-al'is), luminous streams of light that shimmer between the northern horizon and the zenith or sometimes appear as an arc, thought to be electrical discharges; northern lights.

au·rous (ôr'ŭs), *adj.* of, pertaining to, or containing gold.

au·rum (ôr'ŭm), *n.* [Latin], gold.

aus·cul·tate (ôs'kŭl-tāt), *v.t. & v.i.* **-tat·ed, -tat·ing,** to examine by auscultation. —aus'cul·ta·tor, *n.* —aus·cul·ta·to·ry (ôs-kŭl'tá-tôr-i), *adj.*

aus·cul·ta·tion (ôs-kŭl-tā'shŭn), *n.* the act of listening, often with a stethoscope, to sounds within the body, as within the chest, so as to test or diagnose various conditions.

aus·pice (ôs'pis), *n., pl.* **-pi·ces** ('pi-sēz), 1. a divination from the flight of birds. 2. an indication of what is to happen; omen or augury, especially when favorable. 3. *pl.* support; sponsorship; patronage.

aus·pi·cious (ôs-pish'ŭs), *adj.* 1. having promise of success or happiness; propitious. 2. prosperous; fortunate. —aus·pi'cious·ly, *adv.* —aus·pi'cious·ness, *n.*

aus·tere (ô-stir'), *adj.* 1. severe, as in appearance or manner; forbidding; stern. 2. rigid in character or way of living; self-disciplined. 3. severely simple; plain. —aus·tere'ly, *adv.*

aus·ter·i·ty (ô-ster'ĭ-ti), *n., pl.* **-ties,** 1. severity, as of manner or life. 2. rigorous simplicity. 3. an austere practice, manner, look, etc. 4. a procedure or practice of maintaining strict economy.

aus·tral (ôs'trǎl), *adj.* southern; southerly.

Aus·tral·ian (ô-strāl'yǎn), *adj.* of or pertaining to Australia, a continent of the Southern Hemisphere, between the Indian and Pacific oceans: *n.* a native or inhabitant of Australia.

Aus·tri·an (ôs'tri-ǎn), *adj.* of or pertaining to Austria, a country in central Europe: *n.* a native or inhabitant of Austria.

au·tar·chy (ô'tär-ki), *n., pl.* **-chies,** 1. despotism; absolute rule or sovereignty. 2. a country ruled in this way. 3. same as **autarky.** —au·tar'chic, au·tar'chi·cal, *adj.*

au·tar·ky (ô'tär-ki), *n.* the condition, especially of a nation, of being economically independent; national self-sufficiency. —au·tar'kic, au·tar'ki·cal, *adj.*

au·then·tic (ô-then'tik), *adj.* 1. genuine; original; real. 2. true; trustworthy; reliable. 3. in *Law,* executed with all due formalities; legally attested. —au·then'ti·cal·ly, *adv.*

au·then·ti·cate ('ti-kāt), *v.t.* **-cat·ed, -cat·ing,** 1. to make authentic. 2. to give authority to by accordance with legal formalities. 3. to establish as true or genuine. —au·then·ti·ca'tion, *n.* —au·then'ti·ca·tor, *n.*

au·then·tic·i·ty (ô-thĕn-tis'ĭ-ti), *n.* the quality of being authentic; genuineness; validity.

au·thor (ô'thĕr), *n.* 1. the beginner of anything; creator; originator. 2. one who writes a book, article, etc.: *v.t.* to be the author of. —au'thor·ess [Now Rare], *n.fem.* —au·tho·ri·al (ô-thôr'i-ǎl), *adj.*

au·thor·i·tar·i·an (â-thôr-ĭ-ter'i-ǎn), *adj.* of, pertaining to, or characterized by blind obedience to authority, with suppression of independent thought or action: *n.* one who practices or supports such obedience. —au·thor·i·tar'i·an·ism, *n.*

au·thor·i·ta·tive (á-thôr'ĭ-tā-tiv), *adj.* 1. having due authority; official. 2. substantiated; trustworthy because coming from an expert or some other trusted source. 3. dictatorial. —au·thor'i·ta·tive·ly, *adv.* —au·thor'i·ta·tive·ness, *n.*

au·thor·i·ty (á-thôr'ĭ-ti), *n., pl.* **-ties,** 1. the power or right to act or command; dominion, jurisdiction; also, a position giving this power or right. 2. power, influence, or reliability derived from expertise, reputation, etc. 3. a person, writing, etc. referred to for justification or support for a statement or action, also, the citation of one or more of these. 4. one who is knowledgeable in a subject; expert. 5. *pl.* officials with power to enforce laws or rules. 6. a government agency for a project.

au·thor·i·za·tion (ô-thĕr-i-zā'shŭn), *n.* 1. the act of authorizing or the state of being authorized. 2. formal or legal permission, right, or sanction.

au·thor·ize (ô'thó-rīz), *v.t.* **-ized, -iz·ing,** 1. to give official sanction or approval for; legalize. 2. to give (someone) a right to act or command; empower. 3. to confirm; justify; warrant. —au'thor·iz·er, *n.*

au·thor·ized (-rīzd), *adj.* 1. vested with authority. 2. sanctioned or done by authority.

Authorized Version, the version of the English Bible authorized by King James I of England and published in 1611: also called *King James Version.*

au·thor·ship (ô'thĕr-ship), *n.* 1. the origin of a book, article, etc. 2. the craft or occupation of writing.

au·tism (ô'tizm), *n.* a psychological state marked by self-absorption and lack of contact with reality. —au·tis'tic, *adj.*

au·to (ôt'ō), *n., pl.* **-tos,** an automobile.

au·to-, a combining form meaning *self, by* or *of oneself* or *itself:* also, before a vowel, **aut-.**

Au·to·bahn (ôt'ō-bän), *n.* [German], in Germany, a superhighway.

au·to·bi·og·ra·phy (ôt-ō-bī-og'rä-fi), *n., pl.* **-phies,** the story or account of a person's life written by himself. —au·to·bi·og'ra·pher, *n.* —au·to·bi·o·graph'i·cal (-bī-ō-graf'i-kl), au·to·bi·o·graph'ic, *adj.*

au·to·ceph·a·lous (ôt-ō-sef'å-lŭs), *adj.* self-governing: said of certain branches within the communion of the Orthodox Eastern Church.

au·toch·tho·nous (ô-tok'thō-nŭs), *adj.* being in a place or locality from the very beginning; native; indigenous; aboriginal.

ô in drag*o*n, ōō in cr*u*de, oo in w*oo*l, u in c*u*p, ū in c*u*re, ü in t*u*rn, ŭ in f*o*cus, oi in b*oy*, ou in h*ou*se, th in *th*in, t͟h in shea*th*e, g in *g*et, j in *j*oy, y in *y*et.

au·to·clave (ôt'ō-klāv), *n.* a pressurized-steam device for sterilizing, cooking, etc.: *v.t.* **-claved, -clav·ing,** to sterilize, cook, etc. in this.

au·toc·ra·cy (ô-tok'rå-si), *n., pl.* **-cies,** 1. absolute, uncontrolled authority; supremacy. 2. government by a person having absolute authority. 3. a country having this kind of government.

au·to·crat (ôt'ō-krat), *n.* 1. an absolute ruler; despot; dictator. 2. one who has unrestricted power over others. 3. any dictatorial, overbearing person. **—au·to·crat'ic, au·to·crat'i·cal,** *adj.*

au·to·da·fé (ôt-ō-då-fā'), *n., pl.* **au·tos·da·fé,** [Portuguese, literally, act of the faith], 1. the public ecclesiastical sentencing of a heretic during the Inquisition. 2. the secular execution of the sentence passed; especially, the public burning of a heretic.

au·tog·a·my (ô-tog'å-mi), *n.* in *Botany*, self-fertilization, as in a flower pollinated by its own stamens. **—au·tog'a·mous,** *adj.*

au·to·gen·e·sis (ô-tō-jen'ê-sis), *n.* same as spontaneous generation. **—au·to·ge·net'ic** (-jê-net'ik), *adj.* **—au·to·ge·net'i·cal·ly,** *adv.*

au·tog·e·nous (ô-toj'ê-nŭs), *adj.* 1. self-generated. 2. produced within the same organism or body. Also **au·to·gen·ic** (ôt-ō-jen'ik). **—au·tog'e·nous·ly,** *adv.*

au·to·gi·ro, au·to·gy·ro (ôt-ō-jī'rō), *n., pl.* **-ros,** an aircraft with a propeller and with a horizontal rotor turned by air pressure.

au·to·graph (ôt'ō-graf), *n.* 1. a person's own handwriting, especially a signature. 2. an author's original manuscript, or a handwritten letter, document, etc.: *v.t.* 1. to write one's signature in or on. 2. to write with one's own hand.

au·to·graph·ic (ôt-ō-graf'ik), *adj.* 1. of or pertaining to an autograph. 2. written by one's own hand. 3. recording automatically, as some devices. **—au·to·graph'i·cal·ly,** *adv.*

au·tog·ra·phy (ô-tog'rå-fi), *n.* 1. one's own handwriting. 2. autographs.

au·to·harp (ôt'ō-härp), *n.* a kind of zither with dampers, used for simple chordal accompaniment.

au·to·hyp·not·ic (ôt-ō-hip-not'ik), *adj.* of or pertaining to the hypnotizing of oneself. **—au·to·hyp·no'sis** (-nō'sis), *n.*

au·to·in·fec·tion (-in-fek'shŭn), *n.* infection from within the body itself.

au·to·in·tox·i·ca·tion (-in-tok-si-kā'shŭn), *n.* poisoning by toxic substances formed within the body.

au·to·ist (ôt'ō-ist), *n.* a motorist.

au·to·ki·net·ic (ôt-ō-ki-net'ik), *adj.* self-moving.

au·to·mat (ôt'ō-mat), *n.* a restaurant with individual servings of food displayed in rows of little compartments to be opened by inserting a coin or coins.

au·to·mate (ôt'ō-māt), *v.t.* **-mat·ed, -mat·ing,** to adapt to, or operate by, automation: *v.i.* to utilize automation.

au·to·mat·ic (ôt-ō-mat'ik), *adj.* 1. self-moving, as a machine; self-operating. 2. done or controlled by self-operating equipment. 3. done in a mechanical way, without being directly thought about or willed. 4. function-

ing apart from the will, as certain muscles; involuntary in action: *n.* 1. an automatic (or, popularly, semiautomatic) firearm. 2. any automatic device. **—au·to·mat'i·cal·ly,** *adv.*

automatic firearm, a pistol or gun designed to keep on firing until the trigger is released.

au·to·ma·tion (ôt-ō-mā'shŭn), *n.* 1. use of highly refined automatic equipment, as electronic devices, for the production, control, inspection, etc. of work, as in a factory. 2. conversion to this.

au·tom·a·tism (ô-tom'å-tizm), *n.* 1. the quality or state of being automatic. 2. automatic action; also, an automatic piece of behavior. 3. a philosophical theory holding that all behavior is wholly mechanical. **—au·tom'a·tist,** *n.*

au·tom·a·tize (-tīz), *v.t.* **-tized, -tiz·ing,** 1. same as automate. 2. to cause to be automatic. **—au·tom·a·ti·za'tion,** *n.*

au·tom·a·ton (ô-tom'å-ton), *n., pl.* **-tons, -ta** (-tå), 1. a machine or device, often computerized, that operates automatically, as in response to preset controls or coded data. 2. a mechanical figure made to look like a man, animal, etc. and apparently moving by itself; robot. 3. anything acting merely mechanically; especially, a person acting mindlessly, as in blindly following instructions.

au·to·mo·bile (ôt-ō-mō-bēl', -mō'bēl), *n.* a self-propelling passenger vehicle, usually powered by an internal-combustion engine, for use on streets and highways.

au·to·mo·tive (-mōt'iv), *adj.* 1. of or pertaining to motor vehicles. 2. self-propelling.

au·to·nom·ic (-nom'ik), *adj.* 1. of or controlled by the autonomic nervous system. 2. in *Biology*, coming about from internal causes. **—au·to·nom'i·cal·ly,** *adv.*

autonomic nervous system, the part of the nervous system controlling involuntary functions, as of the heart or glands.

au·ton·o·mist (ô-ton'ō-mist), *n.* a supporter of autonomy.

au·ton·o·mous (-mŭs), *adj.* 1. of or pertaining to autonomy; self-governing. 2. not controlled from the outside; functioning independently. **—au·ton'o·mous·ly,** *adv.*

au·ton·o·my (-mi), *n.* 1. self-government; independence. 2. *pl.* **-mies,** a community, country, etc. that has self-government.

au·to·plas·ty (ôt'ō-plas-ti), *n.* the process of repairing injuries by the grafting of skin or other tissue from another part of the patient's body. **—au·to·plas'tic,** *adj.*

au·top·sy (ô'top-si), *n., pl.* **-sies,** a post-mortem examination and dissection of a body, as by a coroner, to determine the cause of death, the effects of disease, etc.

au·to·sug·ges·tion (ôt-ō-sŭg-jes'chŭn), *n.* suggestion to oneself, affecting one's mental outlook, habits, and bodily functions.

au·to·tox·in (ôt'ō-tok-sin), *n.* a toxin or poison formed within the body and doing it harm. **—au·to·tox'ic,** *adj.*

au·tumn (ôt'ŭm), *n.* 1. the season between summer and winter; in the astronomical year, the period beginning in the Northern Hemisphere at the autumnal equinox, about

September 22, and ending at the winter solstice, about December 22. 2. a period or condition resembling autumn, as in being a time of full maturity and a subsequent diminishing of strength: *adj.* of or like autumn. —au·tum·nal (ô-tum'n'l), *adj.* —au·tum'nal·ly, *adv.*

autumnal equinox, see equinox.

aux·e·sis (ôg-zē'sis), *n.* in *Biology*, growth of existing cells and absence of cell division.

aux·il·ia·ry (ôg-zil'yēr-i, -zil'ēr-i), *n., pl.* -ries, 1. a person or thing that helps; aid. 2. *pl.* foreign troops in the service of a country at war. 3. a supplementary organization. 4. a verb that helps form tenses, moods, or voices of other verbs, as *have, be, can, do, will*: also **auxiliary ver'**: *adj.* 1. helping; assisting. 2. subsidiary. 3. supplementary; reserve.

aux·in (ôk'sin), *n.* an organic compound, a kind of plant hormone, that promotes and controls plant growth.

a·vail (ā-vāl'), *v.i. & v.t.* to be of use, value, service, or advantage (to): *n.* 1. use; advantage; means toward an end. 2. *pl.* in *Law*, profits.

a·vail·a·ble (ā-vā'lā bl), *adj.* 1. ready for use or service. 2. easily obtainable; accessible. —a·vail·a·bil'i·ty, *n., pl.* -ties. —a·vail'a·bly, *adv.*

av·a·lanche (av'ā-lanch), *n.* 1. a sudden slide or rush of a great mass of snow, rocks, etc. down a mountain. 2. anything that overwhelms by suddenness and large quantity: *v.i. & v.t.* -lanched, -lanch·ing, to descend (on) as an avalanche.

a·vant-garde (ä-vänt-gärd'), *n.* individuals, especially in the arts, who initiate and experiment with bold, new ideas or procedures: *adj.* of such individuals, ideas, etc. —a·vant-gard'ism, *n.* —a·vant-gard'ist, *n.*

av·a·rice (av'ēr-is), *n.* inordinate or insatiable desire for gain; cupidity; greediness.

av·a·ri·cious (av-ā-rish'ús), *adj.* impelled by avarice; greedy for riches; grasping. —av·a·ri'cious·ly, *adv.* —av·a·ri'cious·ness, *n.*

a·vast (ā-vast'), *interj.* in *nautical usage,* stop! cease!

av·a·tar (av-ā-tär'), *n.* 1. in *Hinduism,* a descent of a diety to earth in an incarnate form. 2. a manifestation or embodiment.

a·vaunt (ā-vônt', ā-vänt'), *interj.* [Archaic], begone! depart!

a·ve (ä'vä, ä'vē), *interj.* [Latin], 1. hail! 2. farewell!: *n.* [A-], short for Ave Maria.

A·ve Ma·ri·a (ä-vä mä-rē'ä), 1. "Hail, Mary," the first words of the Latin form of a Roman Catholic prayer to the Virgin Mary. 2. this prayer.

a·venge (ā-venj'), *v.t.* a·venged', a·veng'ing, 1. to exact punishment or satisfaction for (a wrong or injury). 2. to take or get vengeance on behalf of (a person or oneself). —a·veng'er, *n.*

av·e·nue (av'ē-nōō), *n.* 1. a roadway or drive, often bordered with trees; especially. [British], such a drive leading to a house or estate. 2. a street, especially a broad one; often, one at right angles to others called

"streets." 3. a means of approach to something.

a·ver (ā-vūr'), *v.t.* a·verred', a·ver'ring, 1. to state positively; affirm. 2. in *Law*, to declare formally; assert; allege. —a·ver'ment, *n.*

av·er·age (av'rij, 'ēr-ij), *n.* 1. the numerical result obtained by adding two or more quantities and dividing by the number of quantities; also, any similar value. 2. same as **batting average**. 3. the common, usual, or normal amount, standard, kind, etc. 4. in *Marine Law*, loss incurred by a ship or its cargo from a voyage; also, the apportioned charge for this: *v.t.* -aged, -ag·ing, 1. to figure out the average of. 2. to do, get, etc. on an average. 3. to divide or assign proportionately: *v.i.* 1. to be or amount to as an average. 2. to deal in more shares, goods, etc. so as to get a better average price: *adj.* 1. of, pertaining to, or being an average. 2. of the usual, common, or expected kind; not exceptional; ordinary.

a·verse (ā-vūrs'), *adj.* unwilling; disinclined; loath (*to*). —a·verse'ly, *adv.* —a·verse'ness, *n.*

a·ver·sion (ā-vūr'zhūn), *n.* 1. antipathy; fixed dislike; hatred. 2. the object or cause of dislike or repugnance.

a·vert (ā-vūrt'), *v.t.* 1. to turn aside or away. 2. to turn or ward off; prevent.

A·ves·ta (ā-ves'tā), *n.* [Persian], the sacred writings of Zoroastrianism, written in an ancient Iranian language. —A·ves'tan, *adj.*

a·vi·an (ā'vi-ān), *adj.* of or pertaining to birds.

a·vi·ar·y (ā'vi-er-i), *n., pl.* -ar·ies, a big cage, enclosure, or building for keeping a large number of birds.

a·vi·a·tion (ā-vi-ā'shūn), *n.* 1. the art of flying aircraft heavier than air. 2. the development, design, and production of such aircraft.

a·vi·a·tor (ā'vi-āt-ēr), *n.* the pilot of an airplane; flier. —a·vi·a·trix (ā-vi-ā'triks), *n.fem.*

a·vi·cul·ture (ā'vi-kul-chēr), *n.* the raising and care of birds. —a·vi·cul'tur·ist, *n.*

av·id (av'id), *adj.* 1. craving intensely; greedy. 2. enthusiastic. —a·vid·i·ty (ā-vid'i-ti), *n.* —av'id·ly, *adv.*

a·vi·fau·na (ā-vi-fô'nā), *n.* the birds of any given region or period. —a·vi·fau'nal, *adj.*

a·vi·on·ics (ā-vi-on'iks), *n.* the science of electronics as applied in aviation and astronautics. —a·vi·on'ic, *adj.*

av·o·ca·do (av-ō-kä'dō, äv-), *n., pl.* -dos, 1. the buttery, edible, pear-shaped fruit of a tropical tree, having a thick skin that is greenish to black; alligator pear. 2. the tree on which this fruit grows.

av·o·ca·tion (av-ō-kä'shūn), *n.* an occasional occupation for pleasure; hobby. —av·o·ca'tion·al, *adj.*

av·o·cet (av'ō-set), *n.* a wading bird with long legs, webbed feet, and a slender bill.

a·void (ā-void'), *v.t.* 1. to shun; keep away from. 2. to prevent from happening. 3. in *Law*, to annul; void. —a·void'a·ble, *adj.* —a·void'a·bly, *adv.* —a·void'ance, *n.*

av·oir·du·pois (av-ēr-dū-poiz'), *n.* 1. same as **avoirdupois weight**. 2. [Informal], weight, especially from obesity.

avoirdupois weight, a system of weight in

ô in *dragon*, ōō in *crude*, oo in *wool*, u in *cup*, ū in *cure*, ū in *turn*, ū in *focus*, oi in *boy*, ou in *house*, th in *thin*, th in *sheathe*, g in *get*, j in *joy*, y in *yet*.

which 16 ounces equal one pound: see *Weights & Measures* in Supplements.

a·vouch (á-vouch'), *v.t.* 1. to affirm openly; declare positively; avow. 2. to guarantee; vouch for. —a·vouch'ment, *n.*

a·vow (á-vou'), *v.t.* 1. to declare openly; claim. 2. to acknowledge frankly; admit. —a·vow'al, *n.* —a·vowed', *adj.* —a·vow·ed·ly (á-vou'id-li), *adv.* —a·vow'er, *n.*

a·vul·sion (á-vul'shŭn), *n.* 1. a separation or tearing away. 2. the cutting off, as by water, of part of an estate, which part remains the property of the original owner, although joined to the land of another.

a·vun·cu·lar (á-vung'kyū-lēr), *adj.* of, pertaining to, or like an uncle.

aw (ô), *interj.* an expression of dislike, sympathy, etc.

a·wait (á-wāt'), *v.t.* 1. to wait for; look for or expect. 2. to lie ahead for; wait in readiness for: *v.i.* to be awaiting someone or something.

a·wake (á-wāk'), *v.t.* **a·woke'** or **a·waked'**, **a·waked'** (or, sometimes, British **a·woke'** or **a·wok'en**), **a·wak'ing**, 1. to rouse from sleep. 2. to put into action; stir up. 3. to make alert: *v.i.* 1. to cease to sleep; bestir oneself. 2. to become alert: *adj.* 1. not sleeping. 2. roused from inactivity. 3. vigilant; alert.

a·wak·en (á-wāk'n), *v.t. & v.i.* to awake; wake up. —a·wak'en·er, *n.*

a·wak·en·ing (-ing), *n.* 1. the act of awaking; a becoming awake, alert, etc. 2. a stirring up, reviving, or rebirth, as of ideas, desires, or ideals: *adj.* undergoing an awakening.

a·ward (á-wôrd'), *v.t.* 1. to adjudge; assign by judicial decision or by arbitration. 2. to bestow in consideration of merit; grant: *n.* 1. a judgment or decision, as by a judge or arbitrator. 2. that which is awarded or assigned. 3. a prize. —a·ward'a·ble, *adj.* —a·ward'er, *n.*

a·ware (á-wer'), *adj.* 1. originally, on guard; vigilant. 2. knowing; cognizant; conscious. 3. alert. —a·ware'ness, *n.*

a·wash (á-wôsh', -wäsh'), *adj. & adv.* 1. at such a level that water washes, or can wash, over. 2. floating on water. 3. covered with water.

a·way (á-wā'), *adv.* 1. from a specified place; off. 2. in another place or direction. 3. at quite some time or distance. 4. aside. 5. from oneself. 6. continuously. 7. into movement. 8. at once: *adj.* 1. absent. 2. at a distance. 3. farther or farthest off: said of a golf ball or its player. 4. in *Baseball*, out: *interj.* 1. begone! depart! 2. let's go!

awe (ô), *n.* reverence and fear: the emotion inspired by the contemplation of something sublime; profound admiration and respect: *v.t.* awed, aw'ing, to strike or inspire with reverential fear and respect. —awe'less, aw'less, *adj.*

a·weigh (á-wā'), *adj.* denoting an anchor that is just clearing the bottom.

awe·some (ô'sŏm), *adj.* 1. inspiring awe. 2. expressing awe. —awe'some·ly, *adv.* —awe'some·ness, *n.*

awe-struck (ô'struk), **awe-strick·en** (ô'strik-n), *adj.* filled with awe.

aw·ful (ô'fŭl), *adj.* 1. of, filled with, or inspiring awe. 2. fearful; dreadful; appalling. 3. [Informal], very bad, disagreeable, etc. 4. [Informal], very great in size, intensity, etc.: *adv.* [Informal], very; extremely. —aw'ful·ness, *n.*

aw·ful·ly (ô'fŭ-li, ô'fli), *adv.* 1. in such a way as to fill with awe. 2. [Informal], very badly, disagreeably, etc. 3. [Informal], very much; extremely.

a·while (á-hwīl'), *adv.* for a short period of time.

awk·ward (ôk'wård), *adj.* 1. lacking dexterity or gracefulness; not skillful; clumsy. 2. not easily used or handled; unwieldy. 3. lacking comfort or convenience. 4. not easily managed or dealt with. 5. embarrassed or embarrassing. —awk'ward·ly, *adv.* —awk'ward·ness, *n.*

awl (ôl), *n.* a small, pointed instrument for piercing holes.

awn (ôn), *n.* the bristlelike growth on a head of oats, barley, or numerous other grasses. —awn'less, *adj.*

awn·ing (ô'ning), *n.* a movable covering, typically of canvas stretched on a frame, projecting out above a window, over an entrance, etc. as a shelter from sun or rain.

A·WOL (ā'wôl), *adj.* absent without leave: *n.* one who is absent without leave.

a·wry (á-rī'), *adj. & adv.* 1. with a turning or twisting to one side; not straight. 2. amiss; wrong.

ax, axe (aks), *n., pl.* **ax'es**, 1. a tool consisting of a heavy head sharpened along a side and set on a long handle, used for hewing timber and chopping wood. 2. a battle-ax, hatchet, etc.: *v.t.* 1. to chop, strike, etc. with an ax. 2. to cut off, get rid of, destroy, dismiss, etc.

ax·i·al (ak'si-ăl), *adj.* 1. of, like, or forming an axis. 2. along, around, on, or in the direction of an axis. —ax'i·al·ly, *adv.*

ax·il (ak'sil), *n.* the angle between a branch, twig, leaf, etc. and the stem or trunk to which it is attached. —ax·ile ('sil, 'sīl), *adj.*

ax·il·la (ak-sil'á), *n., pl.* **-il'lae** ('ē), **-il'las**, 1. the armpit. 2. an axil.

ax·il·lar (ak'si-lēr), *adj.* same as **axillary**: *n.* any of the stiff feathers under a bird's wing where the wing is joined to the body.

ax·il·la·ry (ak'si-ler-i), *adj.* 1. of or pertaining to the axilla. 2. of or pertaining to the axil of a twig, leaf, etc.: *n.* same as **axillar**.

ax·i·om (ak'si-ŏm), *n.* 1. an assertion accepted by all as true; maxim. 2. a self-evident proposition, or one the truth of which is clear at once and beyond dispute. 3. an established principle in an art or science.

ax·i·o·mat·ic (ak-si-ô-mat'ik), *adj.* of, pertaining to, or like an axiom; self-evident. —ax·i·o·mat'i·cal·ly, *adv.*

ax·is (ak'sis), *n., pl.* **ax·es** ('sēz), 1. a straight line, real or imaginary, passing through a body, upon or around which such body revolves, or is regarded as revolving. 2. a straight line between the two parts of a bilaterally symmetrical figure; also, any

---

a in *cap*, ā in *cane*, ä in *father*, å in *abet*, e in *met*, ē in *be*, ẽ in *baker*, ẽ in *regent*, i in *pit*, ī in *fine*, i in *manifest*, o in *hot*, ô in *horse*, ō in *bone*,

straight line used for measurement or reference, as in a graph. 3. the central line or part of any symmetrical body, system, etc. 4. an axial body part, as the spinal column. 5. the main stem of a plant. 6. *a)* a state of diplomatic accord between two or more nations to further mutual aims. *b)* [A-], in World War II, the alliance of Nazi Germany, Fascist Italy, Japan, etc.

ax·le (ak′sl), *n.* 1. a rod that a wheel turns on. 2. a bar connecting opposite wheels, as of a car; also, the part at either end that fits into the hub of a wheel.

ax·le·tree (-trē), *n.* the axle of a wagon, carriage, or similar vehicle.

ax·on (ak′son), *n.* the process of a neuron that transmits impulses away from the cell body.

ay·ah (ā′yä), *n.* in India, a native nurse to care for children.

aye, ay (ā), *adv.* 1. always; forever. 2. (ī), yea; yes: *n.* (ī), an affirmative vote: *interj.* (ī), I will obey: a reply to a nautical command: usually doubled to aye, aye.

aye-aye (ī′ī), *n.* a nocturnal lemur, native to Madagascar, having long fingers with pointed claws, and a long tail.

a·yin (ä′yin), *n.* the sixteenth letter of the Hebrew alphabet.

Ayr·shire (er′shir), *n.* any of a breed of dairy cattle that originated in the county of Ayr, Scotland.

a·za·le·a (å-zāl′yå), *n.* 1. any of various shrubs of the heath family, with showy flowers of various colors. 2. the flower of this plant.

a·zan (ä-zän′), *n.* the Moslem call to prayer, proclaimed five times daily by the muezzin from the minaret of a mosque.

az·i·muth (az′ĭ-mǔth), *n.* an arc of the horizon intercepted between the meridian at a given point and the vertical circle passing through the center of a heavenly body. —**az·i·muth′- al,** *adj.*

ax·lon (az′lon), *n.* a kind of textile fiber.

a·zo·ic (å-zō′ik), *adj.* [Now Rare], without life; antedating life on the earth.

a·zon·al (ā-zōn′ål), *adj.* of or denoting zones, or layers, of earth without sharply defined characteristics.

az·o·te·mi·a (az-ō-tē′mi-å), *n.* an excess of nitrogen in the blood as a result of impaired kidney function. —**az·o·te′mic,** *adj.*

Az·ra·el (az′ri-ĕl), *n.* in ancient Jewish and Moslem belief, the angel of death.

Az·tec (az′tek), *n.* a member of the dominant people of Mexico, with an advanced civilization, when Cortes, a Spanish conqueror, invaded that country in 1519: *adj.* of or pertaining to the Aztecs: also Az′tec·an.

az·ure (azh′ẽr), *adj.* like the blue of the clear sky: *n.* 1. the clear blue of the sky. 2. any pigment of this color. 3. the blue sky: a poetic term.

az·u·rite (azh′ů-rīt), *n.* 1. a bright blue mineral, a carbonate of copper. 2. a semiprecious gemstone cut from this mineral.

az·y·gous (az′i-gŭs), *adj.* single; odd; not paired.

ȯ in dragon, ōō in crude, oo in wool, u in cup, ū in cure, ŭ in turn, ů in focus, oi in boy, ou in house, th in thin, *th* in sheathe, g in get, j in joy, y in yet.

B

B, b (bē), *n., pl.* **B's, b's,** 1. the second letter of the English alphabet. 2. the sound of this letter, as in *boy.* 3. a type or impression of *B* or *b.*

B (bē), *adj.* 1. shaped like *B.* 2. second-class; not the very best: *n.* 1. an object shaped like *B.* 2. a school mark or rating signifying better than average. 3. in *Music, a)* the seventh tone in the scale of C major. *b)* the key having this tone for a basic note.

ba (bä), *n.* in *Egyptian Mythology,* the soul, symbolized by a bird with a human head.

baa (bä), *v.i.* to cry, as a sheep; bleat: *n.* the cry or bleating of a sheep.

Ba·al (bā'ǎl, bäl), *n., pl.* **Ba·al·im** (-im), **Ba'als,** 1. the chief god of some ancient Semitic peoples; earlier, any of several fertility gods. 2. a false god; idol.

Ba·al·ism (bā'ǎl·izm), *n.* 1. the worship of Baal. 2. idolatry.

Ba·al·ist (bā'ǎl·ist), **Ba·al·i·te** (bā'ǎl·īt), *n.* 1. a worshiper of Baal. 2. an idolater.

Bab·bitt metal (bab'it), an antifriction alloy of copper, tin, and antimony, used in bearings, etc.

bab·ble (bab'l), *v.i.* **-bled, -bling,** 1. to utter indistinct or imperfect sounds; prattle. 2. to talk incessantly or foolishly. 3. to let out secrets; blab. 4. to murmur or bubble, as a brook: *v.t.* 1. to utter indistinctly; prate. 2. to repeat unintelligently; tell (secrets): *n.* 1. meaningless or indistinct vocal sounds. 2. foolish talk. 3. a murmuring or bubbling sound. —**bab'bler,** *n.*

babe (bāb), *n.* 1. an infant; baby. 2. an inexperienced person. 3. [Slang], a girl or young woman, especially a pretty one.

Bab·el (bā'bl, bab'l), *n.* 1. in the *Bible,* a city whose people tried to build a tower to reach heaven but were prevented from doing so by God who caused them to speak different languages so that they could not understand one another. 2. [also b-], a great confusion of speech or sounds; also, the place where this occurs.

bab·i·ru·sa, **bab·i·rous·sa, bab·i·rus·sa** (bab·i·rōōs'ä), *n.* a wild hog of southeastern Asia.

Bab·ism (bäb'izm), *n.* a Persian religion founded by Mirza Ali Muhammed c. 1844. —**Bab'ist, Bab'ite** ('īt), *n. & adj.*

bab·ka (bäb'kä), *n.* [Polish], a light, sweet yeast cake with raisins, often rum-flavored.

ba·boon (ba·bōōn'), *n.* any one of a large division of monkeys of Africa and Arabia, with a doglike snout, large canine teeth, a short tail, bare calluses on the rump, and a large head with cheek pouches.

ba·bush·ka (ba·boosh'ka, ba-), *n.* a kerchief or scarf worn on the head by a woman or girl.

ba·by (bā'bi), *n.* 1. an infant; young child. 2. one who behaves like an infant. 3. a young animal. 4. the youngest of a group. 5.

[Slang], a girl or young woman: *adj.* 1. of or pertaining to an infant or young child. 2. very young. 3. small. 4. childish: *v.t.* **-bied, -by·ing,** 1. to treat like a baby; coddle. 2. [Informal], to treat with care. —**ba'by·hood,** *n.* —**ba'by·ish,** *adj.*

baby beef, meat from a one- to two-year-old heifer or steer fattened for butchering.

baby boom·er (bōō'mēr), one born during the birthrate increase (the baby boom) after 1945.

baby carriage, a light, wheeled carriage, pushed by hand, used for a baby to ride in: also **baby buggy.**

baby grand, a small grand piano.

ba·by's breath (bā'biz breth), a plant of the pink family, having small, white or pink flowers: also **babies' breath.**

ba·by·sit (bā'bi·sit), *v.i. & v.t.* **-sat, -sit·ting,** to care for (a child or children) in the absence of the parents. —**baby sitter.**

bac·ca·lau·re·ate (bak·a·lôr'i·at), *n.* 1. the degree of bachelor of arts, science, etc. 2. a sermon or speech delivered to a graduating class at commencement: also **baccalaureate sermon, baccalaureate address.**

bac·ca·rat, bac·ca·ra (bak·a·rä', bak'a·rä), *n.* [French], a gambling game played with one or more packs of cards, by an unlimited number of players.

bac·cate (bak'āt), *adj.* 1. like a berry. 2. bearing berries.

bac·cha·nal (bak'a·nal, -nal), *adj.* 1. indulging in or characterized by drunken revelry. 2. drunken: *n.* 1. a worshiper of Bacchus, ancient Roman and Greek god of wine and revelry. 2. a drunken reveler. 3. a drunken feast; orgy: also **bac·cha·na·li·a** (-nā'li·ä).

bac·cha·na·li·an (bak·a·nā'li·an), *adj.* same as **bacchanal.**

bac·chant (bak'ant, ba·kant'), *n., pl.* **bac'chants, bac·chan·tes** (ba·kan'tēz), 1. a worshiper of Bacchus. 2. a drunken reveler: *adj.* 1. worshiping Bacchus. 2. fond of carousing.

bac·chan·te (ba·kan'ti, -kän'-), *n.* a woman votary of Bacchus.

bac·chan·tic (ba·kan'tik, -kän'-), *adj.* of or resembling bacchants or bacchantes.

Bac·chic (bak'ik), *adj.* 1. of or pertaining to Bacchus or to feasts in his honor. 2. [also b-], riotous; drunken.

bach·e·lor (bach'e·lēr, bach'lēr), *n.* 1. a man who has never been married. 2. one who has taken the degree of Bachelor of Arts (or Science): *adj.* of, for, or pertaining to a bachelor. —**bach'e·lor·hood, bach'e·lor·ship,** *n.*

bachelor girl, [Informal], an independent young woman who is unmarried.

Bachelor of Arts (or Science), 1. a degree granted by a university or college to a person who has taken a four-year course of studies in the arts (or science). 2. one who has this degree.

---

a in *cap,* ā in *cane,* ä in *father,* á in *abet,* e in *met,* ē in *be,* ē in *baker,* ė in *regent,* i in *pit,* ī in *fine,* i in *manifest,* o in *hot,* ô in *horse,* ō in *bone,*

bachelor's button, any one of a genus of flowering plants whose blossoms somewhat resemble buttons, including the cornflower.

bac-il-lar-y (bas'i-ler-i, bă-sil'ĕr-i), *adj.* 1. rod-shaped. 2. consisting of rodlike forms. 3. of, pertaining to, or caused by bacilli. Also **ba-cil-lar** (bă-sil'ĕr).

ba-cil-li-form (bă-sil'i-fôrm), *adj.* rod-shaped; shaped like a bacillus.

ba-cil-lus (bă-sil'ŭs), *n.*, *pl.* **-cil-li** ('ī), 1. any of a genus of rod-shaped, aerobic bacteria that produce spores. 2. any rod-shaped bacterium. 3. any disease-producing bacterium: a loose usage.

back (bak), *n.* 1. the hinder part of the body in man, or, in many other animals, the upper portion; region of the spine, extending from the base of the neck to the buttocks. 2. the dorsal region of a fish. 3. the spine; backbone. 4. the upright part of a chair, sofa, etc. against which the back rests. 5. that which is opposed to the front; rear or hinder part of anything. 6. the part of a tool or weapon opposed to the edge. 7. a player in football behind the front line: *adj.* 1. behind; in the rear. 2. in a backward direction. 3. overdue. 4. of or for a time earlier than now: *adv.* 1. into or toward the rear. 2. to or toward a former or original place, state, or condition. 3. to or toward times past. 4. in reply or return. 5. in reserve: *v.t.* 1. to provide with a back or backing. 2. to get upon the back of; mount. 3. to second or support. 4. to bet on. 5. to sign or endorse. 6. to cause to move backward (often followed by *up*): *v.i.* 1. to move or go backward. 2. to have the back situated in a given place.

back (bak), *n.* a large tub or vat used for brewing, dyeing, and other industrial processes.

back-ache (bak'āk), *n.* a pain in the back.

back-bench-er (-bench-ĕr), *n.* a member of a legislature who is not a leader or officer, especially such a member of the British House of Commons.

back-bite ('bit), *v.t. & v.i.* **-bit**, **-bit-ten** or **-bit**, **-bit-ing**, to slander or speak evil (of an absent person). —**back'bit-er,** *n.*

back-board ('bôrd), *n.* 1. a board or the like at or forming the back of something. 2. in *Basketball,* the surface behind the basket.

back-bone ('bōn), *n.* 1. the vertebral column in man and in many animals; spine. 2. that which serves as a main support. 3. firmness or resolution of character. —**back'boned,** *adj.*

back-break-ing ('brāk-ing), *adj.* entailing great effort and hard work; tiring.

back-date (-dāt'), *v.t.* **-dat'ed**, **-dat'ing**, to put a date on that is earlier than the actual date.

back-door (bak'dôr), *adj.* 1. of or pertaining to the back door of a building. 2. acting secretly or deceitfully.

back-down ('doun), *n.* [Informal], a retraction of an assertion, withdrawal from a position, etc.

back-drop ('drop), *n.* 1. a curtain at the rear of a stage. 2. any background.

back-er ('ĕr), *n.* 1. one who sustains or aids

another; sponsor. 2. one who bets in favor of a person or an animal in a contest.

back-field ('fēld), *n.* the football players behind the line of scrimmage.

back-fill ('fil), *v.t.* to fill (a hole in the ground) usually with the material removed in making the hole: *n.* this material.

back-fire ('fir), *v.i.* **-fired**, **-fir-ing**, 1. to fight a forest or prairie fire by starting a fire in its path, producing a burnt area that the original fire cannot cross. 2. to ignite as a backfire in an internal-combustion engine. 3. to have an unpleasant and unwanted effect: *n.* 1. a fire set to create a burnt area in fighting a forest or prairie fire. 2. a premature ignition of the gas and air mixture in the cylinder of an internal-combustion engine. 3. a backward explosion toward the breech of a gun.

back-for-ma-tion ('fôr-mā-shŭn), *n.* a word formed from another word, although it looks as if it were its base, as *administrate* is a back-formation from *administration.*

back-gam-mon ('gam-ŏn), *n.* a game played by two persons on a table or board made for the purpose; each player has fifteen pieces which he moves according to the roll of dice.

back-ground ('ground), *n.* 1. the portion of a picture, scene, landscape, etc. that seems farthest from the observer. 2. a surrounding area providing contrast or harmony with something prominent. 3. a subordinate or unobtrusive position or place. 4. a person's prior experience, education, etc. 5. conditions or happenings that explain or set the scene for something else.

background music, music played to set the mood or heighten the emotional effects of scenes in motion pictures, television dramas, etc.

back-hand ('hand), *n.* 1. writing which slopes backward, to the left. 2. a stroke, as in tennis, made with the back of the hand to the front and the arm across the body: *adj.* done backhand, as for a tennis stroke, or with the back of the hand turned inward, as for catching a ball: *adv.* in a backhand way: *v.t.* to catch, hit, or swing in a backhand way.

back-hand-ed ('han-did), *adj.* 1. same as **backhand.** 2. indirect; ambiguous; equivocal: *adv.* with a backhand.

back-ing ('ing), *n.* 1. something placed behind to support or strengthen. 2. aid or support given to a person or cause. 3. those providing such aid or support.

back-lash ('lash), *n.* 1. a quick recoil. 2. any sudden, sharp reaction, especially in the form of resistance, as to a social movement. 3. excessive play between parts in machinery. 4. a snarl in a fishing line on a reel, caused by a faulty cast.

back-less ('lis), *adj.* cut low in the back, as an evening gown, bathing suit, etc.

back-log ('lôg, 'läg), *n.* 1. a reserve for future use. 2. an accumulation of work to be done, orders to be filled, etc.: *v.t. & v.i.* **-logged**, **-log-ging**, to accumulate.

back order, an order not yet filled.

---

back·ped·al ('ped-ăl), *v.i.* **-ped·aled** or **-ped·alled, -ped·al·ing** or **-ped·al·ling,** 1. to reverse the action on the pedals of a bicycle in order to slow down or stop. 2. to move backward quickly, as in boxing. 3. to retreat; withdraw.

back·rest ('rest), *n.* 1. a support at the back of a machine, as a lathe. 2. a support for a person's back.

back seat, an inferior position.

back-seat driver ('sēt), a passenger in a car who persists in offering unasked-for advice on driving.

back·set ('set), *n.* 1. an obstacle to progress; relapse. 2. a reverse current; eddy.

back·side ('sīd), *n.* 1. the hind part of anything or that which is opposed to the front. 2. the buttocks; rump.

back·slap·per ('slap-ēr), *n.* [Informal], one who is friendly in an overly demonstrative way.

back·slide ('slīd), *v.i.* **-slid** ('slīd), **-slid** or **-slid·den, -slid·ing,** to slide backward in moral or religious matters; apostatize. —**back·slid·er,** *n.*

back·space ('spās), *v.i.* **-spaced, -spac·ing,** to move a typewriter carriage back a space at a time by the use of a specific key (**back space key** or **backspacer**).

back·spin ('spin), *n.* a reverse spin imparted to a ball when it is set into motion, causing it to stop, or bounce or roll backward.

back·stage ('stāj), *n.* the area of a theater or stage behind the proscenium, including the wings, dressing rooms, etc.; *adv. & adj.* off and behind the stage.

back·stairs ('sterz), **back·stair,** *adj.* secret; full of intrigue.

back·stay ('stā), *n.* a long rope or stay extending from the masthead to the side or stern of the ship, slanting aft.

back·stop ('stop), *n.* 1. a wall, screen, etc. to keep balls from going too far, as behind a baseball catch. 2. anything that supports.

back·stretch ('strech), *n.* the side of a race track opposite to the homestretch.

back·stroke ('strōk), *n.* 1. a swimming stroke performed by a swimmer while on his back, stretching the arms alternately over the head. 2. a stroke backward, or a backhanded stroke: *v.t.* **-stroked, -strok·ing,** to hit with a backhand motion: *v.i.* to perform a backstroke.

back·swept ('swept), *adj.* slanting away from the front; sweptback.

back·sword ('sôrd), *n.* 1. a sword with one sharp edge. 2. a hilted stick used in fencing practice or in the game of singlestick.

back talk, [Informal], saucy, impudent rejoinders.

back-to-back ('tǒ-bak'), *adj. & adv.* [Informal], consecutive(ly).

back·track ('trak), *v.i.* 1. to go back on the same course or route on which one came. 2. to reverse one's opinion; change one's attitude.

back·up, back-up ('up), *adj.* 1. supportive. 2. acting as an auxiliary or alternate: *n.* 1. support; aid. 2. someone or something serving as an alternate. 3. an increase in amount created by a stoppage.

back·ward ('wērd), *adv.* 1. with the back foremost. 2. toward the back. 3. toward past times or events. 4. from a better to a worse state. 5. in a way opposite to the usual way. 6. in reverse: *adj.* 1. directed to the back or rear. 2. reluctant; hesitant; shy. 3. slow or behind in learning or progress. —**back'ward·ly,** *adv.* —**back'ward·ness,** *n.*

back·wards ('wērdz), *adv.* same as **backward.**

back·wash ('wôsh, 'wäsh), *n.* 1. water thrown backward from a paddle wheel, oar, etc. 2. a backward current of air from an airplane propeller. 3. a turbulent reaction.

back·wa·ter ('wŏt-ēr, 'wät-ēr), *n.* 1. water caused to flow backward by obstruction of its course. 2. water held back by a dam or weir. 3. stagnant water in a small stream or pool beside a river. 4. a place considered to be intellectually or culturally stagnant.

back·woods ('woodz'), *n.* 1. forests or partially cleared land situated far from the centers of population. 2. any remote area with a small population: *adj.* of or pertaining to backwoods: also **back'wood.** —**back'woods'man,** *n., pl.* **-men.**

ba·con (bāk'ǒn), *n.* meat from the back or sides of a hog, cured by salting and smoking.

bac·te·ri·a (bak-tir'i-ă), *n., sing.* **-ri·um** (-ŭm), microscopic, single-celled organisms, some of which cause disease while others are important for fermentation. —**bac·te'ri·al,** *adj.*

bac·te·ri·cide ('i-sīd), *n.* a substance that destroys bacteria. —**bac·te·ri·ci'dal,** *adj.*

bac·te·ri·ol·o·gy (bak-tir-i-ol'ǒ-ji), *n.* the scientific investigation or study of bacteria. —**bac·te·ri·o·log'ic** (-ǒ-loj'ik), **bac·te·ri·o·log'i·cal,** *adj.* —**bac·te·ri·ol'o·gist,** *n.*

bac·te·ri·ol·y·sis ('i-sis), *n.* the destruction or dissolution of bacteria. —**bac·te·ri·o·lyt'ic** (-ǒ-lit'ik), *adj.*

bac·te·ri·o·phage (bak-tir'i-ǒ-fāj), *n.* any virus that is parasitic upon some bacteria, causing their disintegration. —**bac·te·ri·o·phag·ic** (bak-tir-i-ǒ-faj'ik), *adj.*

bac·te·ri·os·co·py (bak-tir-i-os'kǒ-pī), *n.* the examination or study of bacteria by use of the microscope.

bac·te·ri·um (bak-tir'i-ŭm), *n.* singular of **bacteria.**

Bac·tri·an camel (bak'tri-ăn), a camel of central Asia, having two humps on the back.

ba·cu·li·form (bă-ku'li-fôrm), *adj.* shaped like a rod.

bac·u·line (bak'yŭ-lin, -līn), *adj.* of or pertaining to a rod, or to punishment inflicted with a rod.

bad (bad), *adj.* **worse, worst,** 1. the opposite of good. 2. evil; wicked. 3. ill; not well. 4. offensive; disgusting. 5. harmful; hurtful. 6. decayed; rotten. 7. inferior; defective. 8. not skilled. 9. severe; harsh. 10. unpleasant; disagreeable. 11. distressed; wretched. 12. in *Law,* invalid: *adv.* [Informal], badly. —**bad'·ness,** *n.*

bad blood, bitterness; hostility; reciprocal hatred.

bad·der·locks (bad'ēr-loks), *n.* a large, dark-brown, edible seaweed.

bade (bad, bād), alternate past tense of **bid.**

badge (baj), *n.* 1. a mark, sign, or token to

denote the occupation, allegiance, association, or achievements of the person wearing it. 2. the mark or token of anything.

badg·er (baj'ẽr), *n., pl.* **-ers, -er,** 1. a carnivorous, burrowing mammal of North America, Asia, and Europe, with long claws on the forefeet. 2. the fur of this animal. 3. [B-], a person who lives in Wisconsin: a nickname: *v.t.* to harass; bedevil.

bad·i·nage (bad-i-näzh', bad'i-nij), *n.* light or playful raillery or banter: *v.t.* **-naged', -nag'ing,** to tease with light banter.

bad·lands (bad'landz), *n.* a barren region where the horizontal strata have been eroded into strange shapes; especially [B-], a region like this in South Dakota.

bad·ly (bad'li), *adv.* 1. in a bad manner; offensively, harmfully, defectively, disagreeably, etc. 2. [Informal], greatly; notably.

bad·man ('man), *n., pl.* **-men,** a desperado in the early American West.

bad·min·ton (bad'min-tón), *n.* a game similar to tennis, but played with lighter rackets and a shuttlecock.

bad·mouth (bad'mouth), *v.t. & v.i.* [Slang], to find fault (with); disparage.

bad·tem·pered (–'tem-pẽrd), *adj.* having a bad disposition; irritable.

baf·fle (baf'l), *v.t.* **-fled, -fling,** 1. to confuse; puzzle; perplex. 2. to foil or check; thwart: *n.* a device, as a screen or wall, for obstructing or deflecting sound, gases, etc. — **baf'fle·ment,** *n.* **–baf'fler,** *n.*

bag (bag), *n.* 1. a container of flexible material which may be closed at the top; sack; pouch. 2. that which is contained in a bag. 3. a suitcase or other piece of luggage. 4. a purse. 5. game caught or killed in hunting. 6. a thing or part of a thing shaped like a bag. 7. [Slang], one's special talent, interest, etc. 8. [Slang], a repulsive woman. 9. in *Baseball,* a base: *v.t.* **bagged, bag'ging,** 1. to enclose in a bag. 2 to distend; swell. 3. to kill or capture, as game. 4. [Slang], to get: *v.i.* 1. to bulge like a full bag. 2. to hang loosely.

ba·gasse (bá-gas'), *n.* crushed sugar-cane stalks, after the extraction of the juice, used as fuel, in making fiberboard, etc.

bag·a·telle (bag-á-tel'), *n.* 1. a trifle. 2. a game somewhat like billiards, played with nine balls on a table with nine holes. 3. a short, light piece of music for the piano.

ba·gel (bā'gl), *n.* a hard, doughnut-shaped bread roll.

bag·ful (bag'fool), *n., pl.* **-fuls,** as much as a bag will contain.

bag·gage (bag'ij), *n.* 1. the trunks, bags, and other articles of a traveler. 2. the portable gear and supplies of an army. 3. formerly, a prostitute or loose woman. 4. a pert, saucy girl.

bag·gy ('i), *adj.* **-gi·er, -gi·est,** 1. puffy or swelled so as to resemble a bag. 2. hanging loosely; sagging. **–bag'gi·ly,** *adv.* **–bag'gi·ness,** *n.*

bag lady, [Slang], a homeless, poor woman who wanders city streets carrying her belongings in shopping bags.

bag·man (bag'man), *n., pl.* **-men,** 1. [British], a traveling salesman. 2. [Slang], an intermediary who handles the money in illegal enterprises, as in paying bribes.

bag·nio (ban'yō), *n., pl.* **-ios.** 1. a brothel. 2. [Obs.], *a)* an Italian bathhouse. *b)* an Oriental prison.

bag·pipe (bag'pip), *n. often pl.* a shrill-toned musical instrument with a leather bag, kept filled by the breath, from which air is forced by pressure from the performer's elbow through reed pipes: chiefly a Scottish instrument. **–bag'pip·er,** *n.*

ba·guette, ba·guet (ba-get'), *n.* 1. a gem cut in a narrow, rectangular shape. 2. such a shape.

bah (bä), *interj.* an expression of contempt, disgust, annoyance, etc.

ba·ha·dur (bá-hä'door), *n.* a Hindu title of honor.

Ba·hai (bä-hī', bä-hä'i), *adj.* of or pertaining to Bahaism: *n.* 1. same as **Bahaism.** 2. a believer in Bahaism.

Ba·ha·ism (bä-hä'izm, -hī'-), *n.* a religion developed in Iran from Babism, teaching the brotherhood of man, social equality, etc. **–Ba·ha'ist,** *n. & adj.*

baht (bät), *n., pl.* **bahts, baht,** the monetary unit of Thailand.

bail (bāl), *v.t.* 1. to set free or liberate from arrest on security for reappearance. 2. to deliver (goods) in trust for a given purpose. 3. to help out of trouble: *n.* 1. security deposited with the court for the temporary release of an arrested person. 2. the person or persons who provide this security. — **bail'a·ble,** *adj.*

bail (bāl), *v.t.* to dip out (water) from (a boat): *v.i.* 1. to remove water from a boat by dipping. 2. to jump from an airplane with a parachute (followed by *out*): *n.* 1. a container for dipping water out of a boat. 2. a hoop-shaped handle of a pail or kettle. 3. a hoop-shaped support, as for a canopy. 4. a bar or framework for separating animals in a barn. 5. in *Cricket,* a crosspiece for a wicket. **–bail'er,** *n.*

bai·lie (bā'li), *n.* in Scotland, a municipal officer.

bai·liff (bā'lif), *n.* 1. a sheriff's deputy. 2. an officer in a court of law who keeps order in a courtroom, guards the jurors, etc. 3. in England, a manager of an estate or a local administrative officer.

bai·li·wick (bā'li-wik), *n.* 1. the district within which a bailiff has jurisdiction. 2. one's own special interest or particular area of authority, activity, etc.

bail·ment (bāl'mẽnt), *n.* 1. a delivery of goods held in trust for another. 2. the action of providing bail for one in custody.

bails·man (bālz'man), *n., pl.* **-men,** one who gives bail or acts as surety for another.

bairn (bern), *n.* [Scottish], a child.

bait (bāt), *v.t.* 1. to set dogs against. 2. to torment or annoy persistently. 3. to goad, tease, exasperate, etc. 4. to put food or some other enticement on (a hook, trap, or snare) in order to lure fish or game. 5. to entice: *v.i.* [Archaic], to stop for food during a journey: *n.* 1. food or some other entice-

---

ŏ in drag*o*n, ōō in cr*u*de, oo in w*oo*l, u in c*u*p, ū in c*u*re, ũ in t*u*rn, ù in f*o*cus, oi in b*oy*, ou in h*ou*se, th in *th*in, *th* in shea*th*e, g in g*e*t, j in *j*oy, y in *y*et.

ment used to lure fish or game. 2. an allurement; temptation. 3. [Archaic], a stop for refreshments during a journey. —bait'er, n.

baize (bāz), n. a coarse woolen cloth resembling felt, often used to cover billiard tables.

bake (bāk), v.t. baked, bak'ing, 1. to cook or prepare (food) by subjection to dry heat, as in an oven. 2. to dry and harden by heat; fire: v.i. 1. to do the work of baking. 2. to become baked. 3. to become dry and hard by exposure to heat: said of soil: n. 1. the act of baking. 2. a social event at which a baked food is served, as a clambake.

bake-house (bāk'hous), n. building where bread, pastries, etc. are baked.

Ba·ke·lite (bā'kĕ-līt), a substance of resin and plastic made from phenol and formaldehyde: a trademark: n. [b-], this substance.

bak·er (bāk'ẽr), n. one whose business is to bake bread, pastries, etc.

baker's dozen, thirteen.

bak·er·y (-i), n. 1. pl. -er·ies, a baker's shop; place where baked goods are made or sold. 2. baked goods.

bake-shop (bāk'shop), n. a place where baked goods are sold.

bak·ing ('ing), n. the quantity of anything baked at one time; batch.

baking powder, a leavening agent that contains baking soda and an acid substance, as cream of tartar, that causes dough to rise.

baking soda, same as sodium bicarbonate.

bak·la·va (bäk-lä-vä'), n. a Turkish or Greek pastry made with honey and nuts.

bak·sheesh, bak·shish (bak'shĕsh), n. in India, Turkey, Egypt, etc., alms, a tip, or gratuity.

bal·a·lai·ka (bal-ä-līk'ä), n. a Russian stringed instrument similar to a guitar, usually with three strings.

bal·ance (bal'áns), n. 1. an instrument for determining weight; pair of scales. 2. equilibrium or equipoise; equality. 3. an equality between the two sides of an account. 4. the sum or weight necessary to make two unequal sums or weights equal. 5. a remainder. 6. stability. 7. harmony, especially of elements in a design, composition, etc. 8. the act of balancing: v.t. -anced, -anc·ing, 1. to weigh. 2. to compare. 3. to bring to a state of equipoise. 4. to counterpoise or counterbalance. 5. to equal or make equal. 6. to adjust or settle. 7. to examine and compare accounts: v.i. 1. to be in equipoise. 2. to be equal, as in value or weight. 3. to have the credits and debits equal. —bal'ance·a·ble, adj. —bal'anc·er, n.

balance of payments, a balance for a certain period showing an excess or deficit in payments between countries for all business transactions, private and public.

balance of power, 1. a condition in which there is a relatively even distribution of military and economic power among nations, thereby keeping any one nation from becoming overwhelmingly dominant. 2. the power of a small country or a minority group to give control to a larger one by allying with it.

balance of trade, the difference between the imports and exports of a country.

balance sheet, a statement of the assets and liabilities of a business.

balance wheel, a wheel in a watch, chronometer, etc. that regulates the movement.

bal·a·ta (bal'á-tá), n. 1. any one of a number of trees of tropical America. 2. the dried sap of these trees, a gum similar to rubber and used in making golf ball covers, insulation for electric wires, etc.

bal·bo·a (bal-bō'á), n. a silver coin, the monetary unit of Panama.

bal·brig·gan (bal-brig'án), n. a cotton fabric used for underwear and hosiery. 2. pl. garments made of balbriggan.

bal·co·ny (bal'kō-ni), n. pl. -nies, 1. a platform or gallery projecting from the wall of a building, enclosed by a balustrade or railing. 2. an upper section of seats in a theater, often extending out over the main floor. —bal'co·nied, adj.

bald (bôld), adj. 1. having no hair on the head. 2. without a usual natural covering. 3. unadorned; bare. 4. having white feathers or fur on the head: said of some birds and animals. —bald'ly, adv. —bald'ness, n.

bal·da·chin, bal·da·quin (bal'dä-kin, bôl'-), n. a canopy of stone, wood, or cloth over an altar or throne.

bald·cy·press (bôld'sī'pris), n. a cone-bearing tree that grows in the swamps of the southeastern U.S.

bald eagle, a large, white-headed eagle of North America.

bal·der·dash (bôl'dẽr-dash), n. a nonsensical jumble of words; silly talk or writing.

bald-faced (bôld'fāst), adj. insolent; brash; shameless.

bald-head·ed ('hed-ĕd), adj. 1. having a bald head. 2. having white feathers on the head, as some birds.

bald·ing ('ing), adj. losing one's hair.

bal·dric, bal·drick (bôl'drik), n. a broad belt, often richly ornamented, worn over one shoulder and across the chest to support a sword, bugle, etc.

bale (bāl), n. a large bundle or package of goods, often bound: v.t. baled, bal'ing, to make up into a bale or bales. —bal'er, n.

bale (bāl), n. [Poetic], 1. calamity. 2. sorrow.

ba·leen (bá-lēn'), n. same as whalebone.

bale-fire (bāl'fir), n. 1. a beacon or signaling fire. 2. a bonfire. 3. formerly, a funeral pyre.

bale·ful (bāl'fûl), adj. malignant; ominous; harmful; deadly. —bale'ful·ly, adv. —bale'ful·ness, n.

Ba·li·nese (bä-li-nēz'), adj. of or pertaining to Bali, an island of Indonesia, or to its inhabitants: n. pl. -nese, a native or inhabitant of Bali.

balk (bôk), n. 1. a strip or ridge of land left unplowed. 2. a thick, heavy piece of timber. 3. something that thwarts; barrier, check, frustration, etc. 4. in Baseball, an illegal motion by the pitcher: v.t. 1. to let slip by. 2. to thwart or check: v.i. 1. to stop suddenly and refuse to go on again. 2. to recoil (at). —balk'er, n.

Bal·kan (bôl′kän), *adj.* of the Balkans, a group of countries in southeastern Europe, their people, etc.

balk-line (bôk′līn), *n.* a straight line across the end of a billiard table, from behind which the first shots are taken.

balk·y (′i), *adj.* **balk′i-er, balk′i-est**, stubbornly refusing or resisting.

ball (bôl), *n.* 1. any round object; sphere. 2. a planet or star, especially the earth. 3. a round or somewhat round object used in various games; also, any one of these games. 4. any roundish part of the body. 5. a solid projectile for a firearm or for a cannon. 6. in *Baseball*, a pitch that is not hit and is not a strike: *v.t. & v.i.* to form into a ball.

ball (bôl), *n.* 1. a large formal dance. 2. [Slang], a good time; enjoyable experience.

bal·lad (bal′ăd), *n.* 1. a narrative song or poem, with short stanzas, repetition, etc. 2. a sentimental song with the same melody for each stanza. 3. a slow, romantic popular song. **—bal·lad-eer′**, *n.* **—bal′lad-ry**, *n.*

bal·lade (bă-lād′, ba-), *n.* 1. a verse form of three stanzas and an envoy. 2. a romantic musical composition for piano.

bal·last (bal′ăst), *n.* 1. weighty material carried by a ship, aircraft, etc. to ensure stability. 2. gravel or rubble beneath, and filling the spaces between, the ties of a railroad. 3. that which imparts stability to the character: *v.t.* 1. to place ballast in or on. 2. to impart steadiness to.

ball bearing, 1. a bearing in which the moving parts turn or slide upon loose steel balls which roll freely, reducing friction. 2. any of these balls.

bal·le·ri·na (bal-ĕ-rē′nä), *n.* a woman ballet dancer.

bal·let (ba-lā′), *n.* 1. a theatrical representation of a story told by dancing, with conventionalized steps and movements, and usually with costumes. 2. dancing of this kind, or the music for it. 3. a company of persons who perform ballet. **—bal·let-ic** (ba-let′ik), *adj.*

bal·let-o-mane (bă-let′ô-mān), *n.* one who is especially fond of ballet. **—bal·let-o-ma′ni-a** (-mā′ni-ă), *n.*

bal·lis·ta (bă-lis′tä), *n., pl.* **-tae** (′tē), an ancient military device used to hurl heavy stones and similar objects.

bal·lis·tic (bă-lis′tik), *adj.* 1. of or pertaining to the scientific construction and use of projectiles. 2. of or pertaining to ballistics.

ballistic missile, a missile that is guided only during the initial part of its flight, after which it follows the same type of trajectory of any propelled object.

bal·lis·tics (′tiks), *n.* 1. the science that deals with the motion and impact of projectiles. 2. the study of the effects of firing on a cartridge, gun, etc. **—bal·lis·ti·cian** (bal-is-tish′ùn), *n.*

bal·loon (bă-lōōn′), *n.* 1. a large bag which, when inflated with hydrogen, helium, or heated air, ascends and floats in the atmosphere. 2. a bag like this with a gondola attached for holding instruments or passengers. 3. a small rubber bag, to be blown up and used as a plaything. 4. the line enclosing dialogue in comic strips: *v.t.* to distend; cause to swell like a balloon: *v.i.* 1. to swell out or expand like a balloon. 2. to ascend in a balloon: *adj.* resembling a balloon. **—bal·loon′ist**, *n.*

balloon sail, a large, light sail used on a yacht in a slight breeze.

bal·lot (bal′ŏt), *n.* 1. a ticket, paper, etc. by which a vote is registered. 2. the system of secret voting by use of tickets, papers, or voting machines. 3. the right to vote. 4. the total number of votes cast or recorded. 5. the list of candidates; ticket: *v.i.* to vote or decide by secret vote. **—bal′lot-er**, *n.*

ballot box, a receptacle for the deposit of ballots.

ball-park (bôl′pärk), *n.* a place where baseball games are played, with seats for spectators.

ball-play-er (′plā-ĕr), *n.* one who plays baseball.

ball-point pen (′point), a fountain pen with a small ball bearing instead of a point: also **ball point**.

ball-room (′rōōm), *n.* a large hall for balls and dancing.

bal·lute (ba-lōōt′), *n.* a balloonlike device used to decelerate a spacecraft reentering the atmosphere.

bal·ly·hoo (bal′i-hōō), *n.* 1. clamor; uproar; loud talking. 2. noisy, exaggerated advertising or propaganda: *v.t. & v.i.* **-hooed, -hooing,** [Informal], to advertise or present by blatant or showy methods. **—bal′ly-hoo-er**, *n.*

balm (bäm), *n.* 1. the oily, aromatic gum resin of certain trees or shrubs, used for healing or soothing; balsam. 2. anything that heals or soothes. 3. an odoriferous plant of the mint family. 4. any fragrance or fragrant ointment.

balm of Gil-e-ad (gil′i-ăd), 1. an Asian and African evergreen tree with a resinous juice used as an emollient in ancient times. 2. anything that heals or soothes. 3. same as **balsam fir**.

Bal·mor·al (bal-môr′ăl, -mär′-), *n.* 1. a woolen petticoat. 2. [also b-]. a high-top laced boot. 3. [also B-], a kind of Scottish cap.

balm·y (bäm′i, bälm′i), *adj.* **balm′i-er, balm′i-est**, 1. having the qualities of balm; soft, fragrant, refreshing, etc. 2. [Slang], foolish; daft. **—balm′i-ly**, *adv.* **—balm′i-ness**, *n.*

ba·lo·ney (bă-lō′ni), *n.* 1. bologna. 2. [Slang], silly talk; nonsense: *interj.* [Slang], nonsense!

bal·sa (bôl′să), *n.* 1. a tree of Central and South America having an extremely light, buoyant wood. 2. the wood of this tree. 3. a raft.

bal·sam (bôl′săm), *n.* 1. an oily, aromatic, resinous substance obtained from certain trees. 2. any one of these trees or certain other plants that yield balsam. 3. any of various aromatic, resinous oils or other preparations, as one used for medical dressings. 4. anything soothing or healing. 5. a variety of impatiens, a garden flower. **—bal·sam′ic** (-sam′ik), *adj.*

balsam fir, an evergreen tree of the pine family, that grows in the northern U.S. and Canada: it yields Canada balsam, and is

---

ŏ in drag*on*, ōō in cr*u*de, oo in w*oo*l, u in c*u*p, ū in c*u*re, ū in t*u*rn, ŭ in f*o*cus, oi in b*oy*, ou in h*ou*se, th in *th*in, th in shea*th*e, g in *g*et, j in *j*oy, y in *y*et.

much used for pulpwood and Christmas trees.

Bal·ti·more oriole (bôl'tĭ-môr), an American oriole with black and orange plumage.

bal·us·ter (băl'ŭs-tēr), n. any one of the small, upright columns, or posts, that support a railing, as of a staircase.

bal·us·trade (băl'ŭ-strād), n. a series of small columns, or posts, surmounted by a railing, as on a staircase.

bam·bi·no (bam-bē'nō), n., pl. -nos, -ni ('nē), [Italian], 1. a child or baby. 2. a figure of the infant Jesus.

bam·boo (bam-bōō'), n. a tropical grass, often resembling a tree, having thick-jointed, often hollow stems used for canes, furniture, etc.: it may grow to a height of 120 feet: adj. 1. of or pertaining to bamboo. 2. made of bamboo.

bam·boo·zle (bam-bōō'z'l), v.t. -zled, -zling, 1. to deceive by trickery. 2. to mystify or confuse. —**bam·boo'zle·ment**, n. —**bam·boo'zler**, n.

ban (ban), n. 1. in feudal times, a proclamation or summons to arms. 2. an excommunication. 3. a curse. 4. an edict or order prohibiting something. 5. strong public condemnation meant to prevent something: v.t. **banned, ban'ning**, 1. to forbid or prohibit by official order. 2. [Archaic], to curse.

ba·nal (bā'năl, bă-năl'), adj. commonplace; trite; dull. —**ba·nal·i·ty** (bă-năl'ĭ-tĭ), n., pl. -ties. —**ba'nal·ly**, adv.

ba·nan·a (bă-năn'ă), n. 1. a treelike tropical plant with long, frondlike leaves, and large clusters of fruit. 2. this fruit, finger-shaped and with a creamy, edible pulp and a thick, yellow or reddish skin.

band (band), n. 1. that which binds together, connects, encircles, supports, or restrains. 2. a strap, tie, or ring fastened around something. 3. a strip or stripe acting as a contrast or decoration. 4. a driving belt in machinery. 5. a range of wavelengths or frequencies, as in sound transmission. 6. a group of persons united by a common purpose. 7. a company of musicians playing together; especially, a group using wind and percussion instruments: v.t. 1. to tie with a band. 2. to put a band on (a bird's leg, etc.) for identification. 3. to gather together for a common purpose: v.i. to gather together; unite.

band·age (ban'dij), n. a strip of cotton cloth, as gauze, or other dressing used in binding up or covering wounds or other injuries: v.t. **-aged, -ag·ing**, to dress or bind with a bandage.

Band-Aid (ban'dād), n. 1. a small gauze bandage with adhesive tape, for application to small wounds: a trademark. 2. [also b- a-], a bandage of this kind: also **band'aid**.

ban·dan·na, ban·dan·a (ban-dan'ă), n. a large, colored handkerchief, usually with a pattern.

band·box (band'boks) n. a light pasteboard box for holding hats, collars, etc.

ban·deau (ban-dō'), n., pl. -deaux' (-dōz'), 1. a ribbon worn over the forehead to hold the hair in place. 2. a narrow brassiere.

band·ed rattlesnake (ban'dĕd), a rattlesnake with V-shaped bands on the back.

ban·de·ril·la (băn-de-rēl'yă), n. [Spanish], any of several barbed darts which the banderillero tries to stick into · the shoulders and neck of the bull.

ban·de·ril·le·ro (-ri-lye'rō), n., pl. -ros, [Spanish], the person in a bullfight who sticks the banderillas in the shoulders and neck of the bull.

ban·de·role, ban·de·rol (ban'dĕ-rōl), n. a narrow streamer or pennant, as one flown at the masthead of a ship, or one attached to a lance.

ban·di·coot (ban'di-kōōt), n. 1. a large rat, native to India and Ceylon, which is very destructive to rice fields and gardens. 2. a rat-like marsupial of several species found in Australia and nearby islands.

ban·dit (ban'dit), n., pl. -dits, ban·dit·ti (ban-dit'ĭ), a robber; highwayman; brigand.

band·mas·ter (band'mas·tēr), n. the conductor of a band, as a military band.

ban·dog (ban'dôg), n. 1. originally, a large, fierce dog kept chained. 2. a mastiff.

ban·do·leer, ban·do·lier (ban-dō-lir'), n. a broad belt worn over the shoulder and across the chest, for holding ammunition.

ban·dore (ban'dōr), n. an ancient stringed instrument resembling a guitar.

band saw, a power saw consisting of an endless steel band running on pulleys.

band·stand (band'stand), n. a platform for a band, often outdoors.

band·wag·on ('wag·ŏn), n. 1. a wagon to carry a band in a parade. 2. [Informal], the winning or popular side or cause: used in the phrase on the bandwagon.

ban·dy (ban'di), v.t. -died, -dy·ing, 1. to toss or hit to and fro, as a ball in play. 2. to pass (gossip or idle talk) about carelessly. 3. to give and take; exchange (words) in an angry way: n. 1. a club bent at one end for striking a ball. 2. an old game played with such a club, much like field hockey: adj. bent; having a bend or crook outward.

ban·dy-leg·ged (-leg-id, -legd), adj. having bandy legs; bowlegged.

bane (bān), n. 1. that which causes death, ruin, or distress. 2. a deadly poison: now obsolete except in ratsbane, henbane, etc.

bane·ful ('fŭl), adj. poisonous; destructive; pernicious; distressing. —**bane'ful·ly**, adv.

bang (bang), v.t. 1. to strike or thump hard and noisily. 2. to shut (a door, window, etc.) noisily. 3. to handle roughly: v.i. 1. to make a loud, explosive noise. 2. to bump or strike sharply (against): n. 1. a heavy blow. 2. a loud, sudden noise. 3. [Informal], excitement: adv. 1. noisily. 2. abruptly.

bang (bang), n. usually pl. hair cut straight across the forehead: v.t. to cut (hair) straight across the forehead.

ban·gle (bang'g'l), n. 1. a decorative bracelet or anklet. 2. a shiny ornament.

bang-tail (bang'tāl), n. [Slang], a racehorse.

ban·ian (ban'yăn), n. 1. same as **banyan**. 2. a Hindu merchant.

ban·ish (ban'ish), v.t. 1. to condemn to exile; expel from the country as punishment. 2. to

---

a ın *cap*, ā in *cane*, ä in *father*, ȧ in *abet*, e in *met*, ē in *be*, ẽ ın *baker*, ê in *regent*, i in *pit*, ī in *fine*, ĭ in *manifest*, o in *hot*, ô in *horse*, ō in *bone*,

drive away; get rid of; dismiss. **—ban'ish-ment,** *n.*

ban-is-ter (ban'is-tĕr), *n.* 1. a railing, as on a staircase. 2. *often pl.* a railing and the balusters supporting it.

ban-jo (ban-jō), *n., pl.* **-jos, -joes,** a musical instrument with from five to nine strings, a long neck like a guitar, and a circular body covered in front with tightly stretched parchment. **—ban'jo-ist,** *n.*

bank (bangk), *n.* 1. an establishment for the custody, loan, exchange, and, sometimes, issue of money. 2. the building or offices of a banking company. 3. in certain games of chance, the pool set aside for the winner or winners. 4. a place where blood or body parts are kept in reserve: *v.t.* to deposit (money) in a bank: *v.i.* to have an account in a bank.

bank (bangk), *n.* 1. a heap, mound, or ridge of earth. 2. a steep slope. 3. an elevation or rising ground along a stream, river, etc. 4. a shoal or shallow, as in the sea or at the mouth of a river. 5. the lateral inclination of an airplane on a turn. 6. the slant of a road on a curve. 7. a bench for rowers in a galley. 8. a tier or row, as of oars, lights, keys on a console, etc.: *v.t.* 1. to pile or heap up. 2. to cover (a fire) with ashes, coals, etc. to make it burn longer. 3. to incline (an airplane) laterally on a turn. 4. to slant (a road) on a curve. 5. to cause (a billiard ball) to recoil from a cushion.

bank account, money deposited in a bank and held for the depositor.

bank bill, 1. a bank note. 2. a bill of exchange.

bank-book (bangk'book), *n.* the book kept by a depositor, in which his bank account is recorded.

bank-er ('ĕr), *n.* 1. one who owns or manages a bank for the handling of money. 2. the holder of the bank in some gambling games. 3. a boat or person employed in cod fishing on the banks of Newfoundland. 4. the bench on which a mason, sculptor, etc. does his work.

bank holiday, 1. a weekday on which the banks are closed. 2. a period during which banks are ordered to close by the government, as because of a financial emergency. 3. [British], any one of several legal holidays.

bank-ing ('ing), *n.* 1. the work or business of operating a bank. 2. fishing on the banks of Newfoundland.

bank note, a promissory note issued by a legally authorized bank, payable on demand.

bank-roll ('rōl), *n.* a supply of available money; funds: *v.t.* [Informal], to finance.

bank-rupt (bangk'rupt), *n.* a person legally declared to be unable to discharge his liabilities; insolvent debtor: *adj.* 1. unable to meet one's obligations; insolvent. 2. deficient in some attribute: *v.t.* to cause to become bankrupt.

bank-rupt-cy ('rupt-si, 'rŭp-si), *n., pl.* **-cies,** 1. the state of being legally insolvent, or bankrupt. 2. failure; ruin.

ban-ner (ban'ĕr), *n.* 1. a piece of cloth sometimes attached to a staff and usually bearing a motto, design, emblem, etc., used as a battle standard. 2. a flag. 3. a newspaper headline that runs across the page: *adj.* important; successful.

ban-nis-ter (ban'is-tĕr), *n.* alternate spelling of banister.

ban-nock (ban'ŏk), *n.* a thick cake made of oatmeal or barley meal baked on a griddle.

banns (banz), *n.* the proclamation in church of an intended marriage, usually made on three successive Sundays.

ban-quet (bang'kwit), *n.* 1. a sumptuous entertainment and feast. 2. a large ceremonial dinner, usually with speeches: *v.t.* to treat or honor with a banquet: *v.i.* to participate in a banquet. **—ban'quet-er,** *n.*

ban-quette (bang-ket'), *n.* 1. a platform along the inside of a parapet or trench, on which soldiers stand to fire on the enemy. 2. a raised path; sidewalk. 3. an upholstered bench along a wall in a restaurant.

ban-shee, ban-shie (ban'shi), *n.* in *Irish & Scottish Folklore,* a female spirit who foretells a death in a family by wailing outside the house.

ban-tam (ban'tăm), *n.* 1. [sometimes **B-**], a diminutive breed of domestic fowl. 2. a small but pugnacious person. 3. a bantamweight: *adj.* 1. of or pertaining to a bantam. 2. small but pugnacious.

ban-tam-weight (-wāt), *n.* a boxer, wrestler, etc. between a flyweight and a featherweight.

ban-ter (ban'tĕr), *v.t.* to poke fun at good-humoredly; attack jestingly; tease: *v.i.* to exchange banter (*with* another person): *n.* good-natured joking or teasing.

Ban-tu (ban'tōō), *n., pl.* **-tus, -tu,** any of a great family of Negroid tribes of central and south Africa.

ban-yan (ban'yăn), *n.* an East Indian fig tree, which spreads over a large area by sending down shoots from its branches that take root and become new trunks.

ban-zai (bän'zī'), *interj.* a Japanese battle cry or cheer that means "May you live ten thousand years!"

ba-o-bab (bā'ō-bab, bä'-), *n.* a huge African or Indian tree with an edible, gourdlike fruit (*monkey bread*) and with bark whose fiber is used for making cord and paper.

bap-tism (bap'tizm), *n.* 1. the sacrament or rite of receiving a person into a Christian church with the application of water by pouring, sprinkling, or immersion, usually done by a clergyman. 2. an ordeal or initiation. **—bap-tis'mal** (-tiz'măl), *adj.* **—bap-tis'-mal-ly,** *adv.*

Bap-tist (bap'tist), *n.* one of a Christian denomination who baptize professed believers only and who maintain the necessity for immersion.

bap-tis-ter-y (bap'tis-trī, 'tis-tĕr-ĭ), *n., pl.* **-teries,** 1. a building or portion of a building in which the rite of baptism is administered. 2. a font or receptacle holding water for baptism. Also **bap'tis-try** (-tri), *pl.* **-tries.**

bap-tize (bap'tīz, bap-tīz'), *v.t.* **-tized, -tiz-ing,** 1. to administer the rite of baptism to; receive into the Christian Church by the ceremonial

---

ŏ in drag*o*n, ōō in crude, oo in wool, u in cup, ū in cure, ū in turn, ŭ in focus, oi in boy, ou in house, th in thin, th in sheathe, g in get, j in joy, y in yet.

application of water. 2. to christen. 3. to subject to an ordeal or initiation: *v.i.* to administer baptism. —bap′tiz•er, *n.*

bar (bär), *n.* 1. a piece of wood, metal, or other solid matter, long in proportion to its thickness. 2. anything that impedes or obstructs. 3. a bank of sand, gravel, etc. obstructing navigation at the entrance to a harbor or mouth of a river. 4. a band or stripe; also, a small metal strip worn to show military rank, etc. 5. the railing enclosing the space occupied by counsel in courts of law or where prisoners are brought to trial. 6. the members of the legal profession collectively. 7. any tribunal or place of judgment. 8. a counter (or room containing it) where alcoholic liquors are served. 9. a line drawn vertically through the staff of a piece of music, dividing it into measures; also, the space and notes enclosed by two such lines. 10. a horizontal stripe on a heraldic shield or bearing. 11. a joining thread or loop in needlework lace. 12. the space in a horse's mouth where the bit is placed, or the mouthpiece of the bit. 13. a part of a horse's hoof which bends inward toward the sole: *v.t.* barred, bar′ring, 1. to fasten with a bar. 2. to obstruct. 3. to exclude: *prep.* save; excepting.

barb (bärb), *n.* 1. a slender, beardlike growth, as at the mouth of some fish. 2. a sharp point or hook, especially one projecting backward from the point of a fishhook, arrow, etc. 3. any of the hairlike projections growing out from the shaft of a feather. 4. in *Botany*, a hooked hair or bristle, or an awn. 5. a sharp, cutting remark; jibe. 6. sharpness, as of a jibe: *v.t.* to provide with barbs. —barbed, *adj.*

barb (bärb), *n.* 1. a horse of a breed from Barbary, a region in northern Africa, remarkable for speed, endurance, and docility. 2. a breed of short-beaked pigeon originally brought from Barbary.

bar•bar•i•an (bär•ber′i•ǎn), *n.* 1. originally, a foreigner. 2. a person in a savage, primitive state. 3. an uncivilized person. 4. an unmannerly person, or one who lacks culture. 5. a cruel, brutal person: *adj.* of or like a barbarian; rude, uncivilized, cruel, etc. —bar•bar′i•an•ism, *n.*

bar•bar•ic ('ik), *adj.* 1. of, pertaining to, or characteristic of savage or uncivilized people. 2. coarse, unruly, and unrestrained. —bar•bar′i•cal•ly, *adv.*

bar•ba•rism (bär′ber•izm), *n.* 1. a word or expression not considered standard in the language. 2. the use of words or expressions of this kind. 3. an uncivilized state or condition. 4. a cruel or barbarous action. 5. an outrage.

bar•bar•i•ty (bär•ber′i•ti), *n., pl.* •ties, 1. cruelty; inhumanity. 2. an act of savage cruelty. 3. crudity.

bar•ba•rize (bär′bá•rīz), *v.t. & v.i.* •rized, •rizing, to make or become barbarous. —bar•ba•ri•za′tion, *n.*

bar•ba•rous (bär′bá•rŭs), *adj.* 1. originally, foreign. 2. uncivilized; rude and ignorant;

wild; barbaric. 3. using substandard words or expressions. 4. savage; cruel; ferocious. —bar′ba•rous•ly, *adv.* —bar′ba•rous•ness, *n.*

Bar•ba•ry ape (bär′ber•i), a tailless monkey of North Africa and Gibraltar.

bar•bate (bär′bāt), *adj.* 1. bearded. 2. having long, stiff hairs or tufts, as oats.

bar•be•cue (bär′bĕ•kū), *n.* 1. originally, a frame for roasting or smoke-drying meat or fish. 2. an ox, hog, etc. roasted whole. 3. any meat cooked on a spit. 4. a social affair, usually outdoors, at which such meat is prepared and eaten. 5. an outdoor grill: *v.t.* •cued, •cu•ing, 1. to roast (meat) outdoors over an open fire. 2. to cook (meat) with a sauce (barbecue sauce) made with tomatoes, vinegar, and spices.

barbed wire, strong wire with barbs at close intervals, used for fencing in animals or in warfare.

bar•bel (bär′běl), *n.* 1. a slender vermiform process growing from the lips or jaws of certain fishes. 2. a European freshwater fish with such growths.

bar•bell, bar•bell (bär′bel), *n.* a heavy rod with weights at each end, used for exercise and weight-lifting contests: also bar bell.

bar•ber (bär′ber), *n.* one whose occupation is cutting hair, shaving beards, shampooing, etc.: *v.i.* to work as a barber: *v.t.* to cut the hair of, shave, etc.

barber pole, a pole with spiraling parallel stripes of red and white, a symbol of the barber's trade.

bar•ber•ry (bär′ber•i), *n., pl.* •ries, 1. a spiny shrub with yellow flowers and red berries. 2. the berry.

bar•ber•shop (bär′ber•shop), *n.* the place where a barber works.

bar•bet (bär′bit), *n.* any of many brilliantly colored tropical birds with a broad bill having bristles at its base.

bar•bette (bär•bet′), *n.* 1. a platform or breastwork of a fortification, high enough for firing to be done over the walls. 2. a protective cylinder around a gun turret on a warship.

bar•bi•can (bär′bi•kǎn), *n.* a tower or fortification defending the entrance to a castle or city.

bar•bi•cel (bär′bi•sel), *n.* any of the minute, hairlike outgrowths of the barbules of a feather.

bar•bi•tal (bär′bi•tôl), *n.* a drug used for inducing sleep.

bar•bi•tu•rate (bär•bich′ēr•it, bär•bi•tūr′it), *n.* any salt or ester derived from barbituric acid and used to produce sedation or induce sleep.

bar•bi•tu•ric acid (-bi•tūr′ik), a white, crystalline, odorless acid used in making sedatives and hypnotics, in dyes, etc.

bar•bule (bär′būl), *n.* 1. a very tiny barb. 2. any of the tiny growths along the sides of the barb of a feather.

barb-wire (bärb′wir), *n.* same as barbed wire.

bar•ca•role, bar•ca•rolle (bär′ká•rōl), *n.* 1. a simple song or melody sung by Venetian gondoliers. 2. a piece of music imitating this.

---

a in *cap*, ā in *cane*, ä in *father*, å in *abet*, e in *met*, ē in *be*, ē in *baker*, ė in *regent*, i in *pit*, ī in *fine*, i in *manifest*, o in *hot*, ô in *horse*, ō in *bone*,

bar code, same as **Universal Product Code.**

bard (bärd), *n.* 1. an ancient Celtic poet and singer. 2. a poet. —**bard´ic,** *adj.*

bard, barde (bärd), *n.* one of the pieces of armor for a medieval war horse.

bare (ber), *adj.* 1. naked; without clothing. 2. without the usual covering. 3. unfurnished or empty. 4. simple. 5. threadbare. 6. mere: *v.t.* bared, bar´ing, to divest of covering; strip; expose. —**bare´ness,** *n.*

bare-back (ber´bak), *adv.* & *adj.* on a horse without a saddle: also **bare´backed.**

bare-faced (´fāst), *adj.* 1. with the face uncovered or undisguised. 2. beardless. 3. not hidden; open. 4. shameless; impudent. —**bare-fac´ed-ly** (-fās´id-li), *adv.* —**bare-fac´ed-ness,** *n.*

bare-foot (´foot), *adj.* & *adv.* not wearing shoes or stockings; having bare feet. —**bare´foot-ed,** *adj.*

bare-hand-ed (ber´han´did), *adj.* & *adv.* with nothing in or on the hands.

bare-head-ed (´hed-id), *adj.* & *adv.* without a hat or other head covering.

bare-leg-ged (´leg-id), *adj.* & *adv.* without stockings or other covering on the legs.

bare-ly (ber´li), *adv.* 1. openly. 2. scantily; sparsely. 3. hardly; scarcely.

barf (bärf), *v.t.* & *v.i.* [Slang], to vomit.

bar-fly (bär´flī), *n., pl.* -flies, [Slang], a barroom frequenter.

bar-gain (bär´gn), *n.* 1. an agreement or contract between parties in reference to a sale, service, exchange, etc. 2. the thing purchased or stipulated for. 3. that which is acquired or sold at a low price. 4. an advantageous purchase: *v.i.* to discuss or work out the terms of a bargain: *v.t.* to barter. —**bar´gain-er,** *n.*

bargain counter, a store counter for displaying goods at reduced prices.

barge (bärj), *n.* 1. a flat-bottomed boat for the conveyance of goods on rivers, canals, etc. 2. a large boat for pageants or ceremonial occasions: *v.t.* barged, barg´ing, to convey by barge: *v.i.* 1. to move clumsily. 2. to intrude rashly (*in* or *into*). —barge´man, *n., pl.* -men.

ba-ril-la (bä-ril´ä), *n.* an alkali obtained by burning certain Mediterranean plants, made up of sodium carbonate and sulfate and formerly used in making soap, glass, etc.

bar-ite (ber´īt), *n.* a white, very heavy mineral composed chiefly of barium sulfate.

bar-i-tone (ber´i-tōn), *n.* 1. a male singing voice between bass and tenor. 2. the range of such a voice. 3. any wind instrument with this range: *adj.* having or for the range of a baritone.

bar-i-um (ber´i-üm), *n.* a silver-white, metallic chemical element.

bark (bärk), *n.* 1. the exterior layer of woody stems or trunks. 2. short for **Peruvian bark** (cinchona): *v.t.* 1. to strip bark from (a tree, woody stem, etc.) 2. [Informal], to scrape some skin off.

bark (bärk), *v.i.* 1. to make the characteristic sharp, short sound of a dog. 2. [Informal], to cough. 3. [Slang], to tout a sideshow, sale, etc. by shouting: *v.t.* 1. to utter in a barking way. 2. to advertise as by shouting: *n.* 1. the sharp vocal sound made by a dog. 2. a sound resembling this.

bark (bärk), *n.* 1. a three-masted vessel with the two forward masts square-rigged and the rear mast fore-and-aft rigged. 2. any little sailing boat: a poetic term.

bark beetle, any of a number of beetles that nest and feed under the bark of trees.

bar-keep-er (bär´kēp-ēr), *n.* one who keeps or tends a bar for the sale of alcoholic liquors: also **bar´keep.**

bark-en-tine (bär´kēn-tēn), *n.* a three-masted vessel with a square-rigged foremast and the other masts rigged fore-and-aft.

bark-er (bär´kēr), *n.* 1. one who strips trees of their bark. 2. a machine used in pulp mills to remove the bark from logs.

bark-er (bär´kēr), *n.* one who stands outside a sideshow, sale, etc. and shouts about it to entice passers-by to enter.

bar-ley (bär´li), *n.* 1. a grain used in making malts, in soup, and as feed for livestock. 2. the plant on which it grows, a cereal grass with bearded spikes.

bar-ley-corn (-kôrn), *n.* 1. a grain of barley. 2. formerly, a measure of length equal to a third of an inch.

Barleycorn, John, a name sometimes jocularly given to malt liquor, corn liquor, etc.

barley sugar, a brittle, transparent candy made by melting sugar: it was formerly flavored with barley.

barm (bärm), *n.* the foamy yeast forming on beer or other malt liquors in fermentation.

bar-maid (bär´mād), *n.* a waitress who works in a bar.

bar-man (´män), *n., pl.* -men, a bartender.

bar mitz-vah, bar miz-vah (bär mits´vä), [Hebrew], [also B- M-], 1. a Jewish ceremony celebrating the assuming of religious responsibility by a boy at age thirteen. 2. the boy himself.

barm-y (bär´mi), *adj.* barm´i-er, barm´i-est, 1. containing or consisting of yeast; frothy. 2. [British Slang], silly; crazy. —barm´i-ness, *n.*

barn (bärn), *n.* 1. a covered building for the storage of farm products, livestock, farm machinery, etc. 2. a large building for buses, streetcars, etc.

bar-na-cle (bär´nä-kl), *n.* 1. a saltwater shellfish that attaches itself to rocks, ship bottoms, wharves, etc. 2. a hanger-on; something or someone hard to shake off. 3. a European wild goose: also **barnacle goose.** 4. *pl.* nose pincers for restraining a horse. —bar´na-cled, *adj.*

barn dance, a party, originally in a barn, featuring square dances.

barn owl, a brown and gray owl spotted with white, often found in barns.

barn-storm (bärn´stôrm), *v.i.* & *v.t.* to tour (the country) giving campaign speeches, competing in athletic games, or performing, etc. —barn´storm-er, *n.*

barn swallow, a common swallow, usually nesting in barns, with a deeply forked tail.

barn-yard (´yärd), *n.* the land adjoining a barn, often fenced in.

bar·o·gram (ber′ō̆-gram), *n.* the record traced by a barograph.

bar·o·graph (-graf), *n.* an instrument that automatically records variations in atmospheric pressure. —**bar·o·graph′ic**, *adj.*

ba·rom·e·ter (bả-rom′ĕ-tēr), *n.* 1. an instrument for measuring pressure of the atmosphere: used for indicating the various changes of weather or to determine altitude above sea level. 2. anything indicating change. —**bar·o·met·ic** (bar-ō̆-met′rik), **bar·o·met′ri·cal**, *adj.*

barometric pressure, the pressure of the atmosphere at a given point in terms of the height of a column of mercury.

bar·on (ber′ŏn), *n.* 1. an English peer of the lowest rank. 2. this title. 3. a nobleman of similar rank in other countries. 4. a capitalist who controls an industry or the sale of a commodity.

bar·on·age (′ō̆-nij), *n.* 1. barons collectively. 2. the peerage. 3. the rank, title, lands, etc. of a baron.

bar·on·ess (-nis), *n.* 1. a baron's wife or, in some countries, daughter. 2. a lady holding a baronial title in her own right.

bar·on·et (-nit, -net), *n.* 1. one who has the hereditary title next below a baron. 2. this title.

bar·on·et·age (-ij), *n.* 1. baronets collectively. 2. same as **baronetcy.**

bar·on·et·cy (-si), *n., pl.* -cies, the title, rank, and status of a baronet.

ba·ro·ni·al (bả-rō′ni-ȧl), *adj.* 1. of or pertaining to a baron. 2. suitable for a baron; magnificent, imposing, etc.

bar·on·y (ber′ō̆-ni), *n., pl.* -on·ies, 1. the title, rank, or status of a baron. 2. the domain of a baron.

ba·roque (bả-rōk′), *adj.* 1. of, pertaining to, or like a style of art and architecture distinguished by curving lines and elaborate forms. 2. of, pertaining to, or like a style of music distinguished by complex melodies and the use of fugue or counterpoint. 3. the period from about 1550 to 1750, characterized by these styles. 4. same as **rococo.** 5. fantastic in design or style; grotesque: *n.* something baroque.

bar·o·scope (ber′ō̆-skōp), *n.* an instrument for indicating variations in the pressure of the atmosphere. —**bar·o·scop′ic** (-skăp′ik), *adj.*

ba·rouche (bả-rōōsh′), *n.* a four-wheeled carriage with a folding top.

barque (bärk), *n.* same as **bark** (the boat).

bar·rack (ber′ik), *n.* 1. *pl.* a large building or set of buildings to lodge soldiers and officers. 2. *pl.* a large, often temporary building to lodge workmen: *v.t. & v.i.* to lodge in barracks.

bar·ra·cu·da (bar-ȧ-kōō′dȧ), *n., pl.* -da, -das, a voracious, pikelike fish found in tropical waters.

bar·rage (bả-räzh′), *n.* 1. a barrier; specifically, a dam. 2. an artillery-fire attack, often prior to a drive against the enemy. 3. a long, hard, physical or verbal attack: *v.i. & v.t.* -raged′, -rag′ing, to subject to a barrage.

bar·ran·ca (bả-rang′kȧ), *n.* a deep hole, steep bluff, or precipice, as in the southwestern U.S.: also **bar·ran′co** (′kō), *pl.* -cos.

bar·ra·tor, bar·ra·ter (ber′ȧ-tēr), *n.* one guilty of barratry.

bar·ra·try (-tri), *n.* 1. the offense of habitually inciting and encouraging lawsuits. 2. an act of fraud committed by a ship's officers or crew against the ship's owners. —**bar′ra·trous,** *adj.*

barred (bärd), *adj.* 1. provided with bars, as to prevent escape. 2. forbidden; not allowed. 3. striped with bars.

bar·rel (ber′ĕl), *n.* 1. a vessel or cask, cylindrical in form, bulging in the middle, typically made of wooden staves bound with hoops, and having flat ends. 2. the amount a barrel contains, usually 31.5 gallons in the U.S. 3. anything barrellike in shape or function; drum, cylinder, etc. 4. in a gun, the tube through which the projectile passes. 5. [Informal], a great deal: *v.t.* -reled or -relled, -rel·ing or -rel·ling, to place in a barrel or barrels: *v.i.* [Slang], to move very rapidly.

bar·rel-chest·ed (-ches-tid), *adj.* having a large, deep, rounded thorax.

barrel organ, a mechanical musical device producing tunes through the action of a studded cylinder turned to open pipe valves or strike metal tabs.

barrel roll, a maneuver in which an airplane makes a complete revolution about its longitudinal axis.

bar·ren (ber′ĕn), *adj.* 1. incapable of producing offspring; sterile. 2. unfruitful; not producing vegetation. 3. unproductive; profitless. 4. lacking interest or meaning; dull. 5. devoid; empty: *n.* an unproductive tract of land. —**bar′ren·ly,** *adv.* —**bar′ren·ness,** *n.*

bar·rette (bả-ret′), *n.* a small clasp used to keep a girl's or woman's hair in place.

bar·ri·cade (ber′i-kād), *n.* 1. a rapidly constructed fortification used to obstruct the attack of an enemy or as a shield. 2. any bar or obstruction: *v.t.* (also ber-i-kād′), -cad·ed, -cad·ing, 1. to obstruct or stop up. 2. to fortify or enclose by a barricade.

bar·ri·er (ber′i-ēr), *n.* 1. anything which hinders or obstructs; an obstacle to progress, approach, or attack. 2. an enclosing fence or boundary wall. 3. a limit or boundary.

barrier reef, a reef of coral parallel to the shore of an island, with a lagoon separating the two.

bar·ring (bär′ing), *prep.* excepting; leaving out of account.

bar·ri·o (bär′i-ō), *n., pl.* -ri·os, [Spanish], a city district or suburb.

bar·ris·ter (ber′is-tēr), *n.* in England, a legal counselor authorized to plead cases in superior courts.

bar·room (bär′rōōm), *n.* a room with a counter or bar at which alcoholic drinks are served.

bar·row (ber′ō), *n.* a wheelbarrow or a handbarrow; also, a pushcart.

bar·row (ber′ō), *n.* 1. a mountain; hill. 2. a heap of earth or stones marking an ancient grave.

bar·row (ber′ō), *n.* a castrated pig.

bar sinister, same as **bend sinister.**

a in c*a*p, ā in c*a*ne, ä in f*a*ther, ȧ in *a*bet, e in m*e*t, ē in b*e*, ē in b*a*ker, ĕ in r*e*gent, i in p*i*t, ī in f*i*ne, i in man*i*fest, o in h*o*t, ô in h*o*rse, ō in b*o*ne,

bar·tend·er (bär'ten-dēr), *n.* a dispenser of alcoholic drinks; barkeeper.

bar·ter (bär'tēr), *v.i.* to trade by exchanging one commodity or service for another: *v.t.* to give in exchange; trade: *n.* 1. trading by exchange of commodities or services. 2. the thing given in exchange. —**bar'ter·er**, *n.*

bar·ti·zan (bär'ti-zǎn), *n.* a small, overhanging turret projecting from the top of a tower or wall.

Bart·lett pear (bärt'lêt), a kind of large, juicy pear.

bar·y·on (ber'i-ǎn), *n.* a kind of heavy atomic particle.

ba·ry·ta (bâ-rīt'ǎ), *n.* 1. barium oxide. 2. barium hydroxide.

bas·al (bā's'l), *adj.* 1. of, pertaining to, or situated at the base. 2. fundamental; primary. —**bas'al·ly**, *adv.*

ba·salt (bâ-sôlt', bǎs'ôlt), *n.* a dark igneous rock. —**ba·sal'tic**, *adj.*

bas·cule (bas'kūl), *n.* a mechanical arrangement on the seesaw principle by which the lowering of one end raises the other.

base (bās), *n., pl.* **bas·es** ('ez), 1. the bottom part of a thing, or the part on which it rests or moves; foundation. 2. fundamental part; basis or groundwork. 3. the chief substance, especially a liquid, holding ingredients together; medium; also, the main ingredient. 4. the place or thing to which a part is attached. 5. a starting point, goal, etc.; specifically, in *Baseball,* any of the four goals which must be touched in order to score a run. 6. a headquarters, as of a military operation. 7. an undercoat, as of paint or makeup. 8. in *Chemistry,* a substance that combines with an acid to form a salt: *adj.* making a base: *v.t.* based, bas'·ing, 1. to make a base or foundation for. 2. to place or rest (*on*) as a base or basis. 3. to station (*in* or *at* a base).

base (bās), *adj.* bas'er, bas'est, 1. low, foul, mean, etc. 2. menial; degrading. 3. of inferior quality. 4. worthless; spurious. 5. not precious, as iron. —**base'ly**, *adv.* —**base'ness**, *n.*

base·ball (bās'bôl), *n.* 1. a game of ball using a hard, leather-covered ball, wood bat, four bases in a diamond figure, and two opposing teams of nine each. 2. the ball.

base·board ('bôrd), *n.* a board or molding along a wall where it meets the floor.

base·born ('bôrn), *adj.* 1. born out of wedlock. 2. of low or humble parentage. 3. mean or ignoble in character.

base hit, in *Baseball,* a hit getting a batter on base without an opponent's error and without forcing an out.

base·less ('lis), *adj.* without foundation in fact. —**base'less·ness**, *n.*

base line, 1. a line used as a base. 2. in *Baseball,* the lane between successive bases. 3. in *Tennis,* the back line at each end of the court.

base·man ('mǎn), *n., pl.* -**men** ('mēn), in *Baseball,* a player placed at first, second, or third base.

base·ment (bās'mênt), *n.* 1. the lower part of a

wall or structure. 2. the lowest story of a building, completely or partly below ground.

ba·sen·ji (bâ-sen'ji), *n.* a small, reddish-brown dog bred originally in Africa: its vocal sound is not a true bark.

base on balls, in *Baseball.* same as walk.

base pay, the basic rate of pay not counting overtime pay, etc.

base runner, in *Baseball,* a player who is on base or is trying to reach a base.

bash (bash), *v.t.* [Informal], to strike violently: *n.* 1. [Informal], a smashing blow. 2. [Slang], a festive party or happening.

ba·shaw (bâ-shô'), *n.* 1. same as pasha. 2. a magnate; important person.

bash·ful (bash'fǔl), *adj.* excessively shy or modest. —**bash'ful·ly**, *adv.* —**bash'ful·ness**, *n.*

bas·ic (bā'sik), *adj.* 1. fundamental; essential. 2. in *Chemistry,* alkaline: *n.* a basic principle, factor, etc.

bas·il (baz'l, bā'zl), *n.* a fragrant mint herb used for flavoring in cooking.

bas·i·lar (bas'i-lêr), *adj.* of or at the base, as of the skull: also bas'i·lar·y (-ler-i).

ba·sil·i·ca (i-kâ), *n., pl.* -**cas**, 1. in ancient Rome, a public hall or courtroom of rectangular shape. 2. a Christian church built on such a plan. 3. a Roman Catholic church with certain ceremonial rights.

bas·i·lisk (bas'i-lisk), *n.* 1. a mythical, lizardlike creature with a deadly glance and breath. 2. a lizard of the American tropics, with an inflatable pouch on its head.

ba·sin (bā's'n), *n.* 1. a circular, shallow container for holding water to wash in; also, any similar container. 2. its contents. 3. a washbowl or sink. 4. a large hollow or depression suggestive of a basin. 5. a pond, bay, harbor, etc. 6. the area drained by a river.

ba·sis (bā'sis), *n., pl.* **ba·ses** ('sēz), 1. a foundational part; base. 2. the underlying support of something, as a belief; also, the basic principle, as of a plan, system, etc. 3. the main thing of which something is made up.

bask (bask), *v.i.* 1. to luxuriate in pleasant warmth or surroundings, as in a sunny place. 2. to expand, thrive, or rejoice in gratified response to favors shown to one, kind things said or done, etc.

bas·ket (bas'kit), *n.* 1. a container made of plaited or interwoven wooden strips, cane, straw, or other flexible material; also, anything suggestive of this. 2. its contents. 3. the enclosure suspended beneath a balloon, for passengers and equipment. 4. in *Basketball,* the goal, an open net hanging from a raised, projecting metal ring; also, the toss of the ball through this net to score.

bas·ket·ball (-bôl), *n.* 1. a ball game for two teams of five players each, the object being to score by tossing the ball through an elevated goal (basket) at the opponents' end of the playing area. 2. the large, round, inflated ball used.

bas·ket·ry (bas'kě-tri), *n.* 1. the making of baskets. 2. baskets collectively.

basket weave, a kind of weave used to make fabrics, similar to the weave used in basketry.

ô in dragon, ōō in crude, oo in wool, u in cup, ū in cure, ū in turn, û in focus, oi in boy, ou in house, th in thin, th in sheathe, g·in get, j in joy, y in yet.

bas·ket·work (-würk), *n.* work that is woven or plaited like a basket.

basking shark, a large shark that inhabits northern seas: it lives on plankton and often basks on the surface.

Basque (bask), *adj.* of or pertaining to a people of northern Spain, or their language: *n.* a native or inhabitant of this region, consisting of three provinces (called the *Basque Provinces*).

basque (bask), *n.* a woman's closefitting tunic.

bas·re·lief (bä-rē-lēf'), *n.* low relief; form of sculpture in which the figures stand out very slightly from the background.

bass (bās), *n.* 1. a male singing voice of the lowest range, below baritone. 2. the range of such a voice. 3. any instrument with this range. 4. a low, deep sound: *adj.* of, for, or having the range of a bass.

bass (bas), *n.*, *pl.* bass, bass'es, any one of various edible fishes, found in salt and fresh water.

bass clef (bās), in *Music,* 1. the sign placed at the beginning of a staff on which the bass part of a harmonized composition is written. 2. the range of notes on such a staff.

bass drum, the largest kind of drum, emitting a deep bass sound.

bas·set (bas'it), *n.* a small hound with a long body, short legs, and long, hanging ears: also **basset hound.**

bas·set (bas'it), *v.i.* to crop out at the surface: *n.* the exposure of a rock stratum at the surface of the earth; outcrop.

basset horn, a clarinet pitched between the B-flat and the bass clarinets.

bass horn, same as tuba.

bas·si·net (bas-i-net'), *n.* a basketlike bed for an infant, often hooded at one end.

bas·so (bas'ō), *n.*, *pl.* -sos, 1. a bass voice. 2. a bass singer.

bas·soon (bā-sōōn'), *n.* a double-reed woodwind instrument with a bass range. —**bas·soon'ist,** *n.*

basso pro·fun·do (prō-fun'dō), 1. the lowest bass voice. 2. a singer having such a voice.

bass viol, same as double bass.

bass·wood (bas'wood), *n.* 1. the linden tree. 2. its wood. 3. the tulip tree. 4. its wood.

bast (bast), *n.* 1. a kind of plant tissue; phloem. 2. a tough fiber obtained from phloem, used for rope and matting.

bas·tard (bas'tẽrd), *n.* 1. a child born out of wedlock; illegitimate child. 2. something spurious, adulterated, nonstandard, etc.: *adj.* 1. born out of wedlock. 2. not standard in size or shape. 3. spurious; inferior. —**bas'tard·ly,** *adv.*

bas·tard·ize (bas'tẽr-dīz), *v.t.* -ized, -iz·ing, 1. to make or prove to be a bastard; declare to be illegitimate. 2. to make inferior; debase. —**bas·tard·i·za'tion,** *n.*

bas·tard·y (bas'tẽr-di), *n.*, *pl.* -ies, the state of being illegitimate, or born out of wedlock.

baste (bāst), *v.t.* bast'ed, bast'ing, to fasten temporarily by sewing with long, loose stitches.

baste (bāst), *v.t.* bast'ed, bast'ing, to drip or pour melted fat or butter over (meat, fish, etc.) while roasting, baking, etc. —**bast'er,** *n.*

baste (bāst), *v.t.* bast'ed, bast'ing, 1. to beat physically. 2. to abuse verbally.

bas·tille, bas·tile (bas-tēl'), *n.* 1. a tower used for the defense or siege of a fortified place. 2. a prison. 3. [B-], an old fortress in Paris used as a state prison, destroyed during the French Revolution.

bas·ti·na·do (bas-tĩ-näd'ō), *n.,* *pl.* -does, a method of punishment consisting in beating a person on the soles of the feet with a stick: *v.t.* -doed, -do·ing, to beat the soles of the feet with a stick.

bast·ing (bās'ting), *n.* 1. a sewing with loose temporary stitches. 2. these stitches.

bas·tion (bas'chŭn), *n.* 1. a projection from a fortification, designed to increase the firing range. 2. anything strong and fortified; bulwark.

bat (bat), *n.* 1. a heavy stick or club. 2. a club used to hit the ball in cricket, and baseball. 3. a turn at batting, as in baseball. 4. [Informal], a hit or blow: *v.t.* bat'ted, bat'ting, 1. to hit or strike. 2. to have a batting average of: *v.i.* to use or wield a bat, as in baseball.

bat (bat), *n.* a flying, insectivorous mammal resembling a mouse, usually active at night.

bat (bat), *v.t.* bat'ted, bat'ting, [Informal], to blink; flutter.

batch (bach), *n.* 1. the quantity, as of bread, baked at one time. 2. a quantity of anything produced at one operation. 3. a group or collection of similar persons or things.

bate (bāt), *v.t.* bat'ed, bat'ing, to lessen or reduce.

bate (bāt), *v.t. & v.i.* in *Tanning,* to soften in an alkaline solution: *n.* an alkaline solution used to soften hides.

ba·teau (ba-tō'), *n.,* *pl.* -teaux' (-tōz'), a light, flat-bottomed boat used on rivers in Canada and Louisiana.

bat·fish (bat'fish), *n.,* *pl.* -fish, -fish·es, 1. any one of several varieties of saltwater fishes resembling a bat. 2. a stingray. 3. same as flying gurnard.

bath (bath), *n.,* *pl.* baths (ba*th*z, baths), 1. the act of washing or immersing an object or body in water or exposing it to any other fluid or vapor. 2. the liquid for bathing, soaking, etc. 3. a container holding liquid for bathing. 4. a bathtub. 5. a bathroom. 6. a building with a room or rooms for bathing.

Bath brick, earth containing carbonate of lime or calcium, in the shape of a brick, used for scouring polished metal: first made at Bath, city in southwestern England.

Bath chair, a kind of hooded wheelchair.

bathe (bā*th*), *v.t.* bathed, bath'ing, 1. to subject to a bath; immerse in water or other liquid. 2. to wash. 3. to suffuse or moisten with a liquid. 4. to immerse or surround with anything analogous to water, as vapor or light: *v.i.* 1. to take a bath. 2. to immerse oneself in something. —**bath'er,** *n.*

ba·thet·ie (bá-thet'ik), *adj.* showing bathos. —**ba·thet'i·cal·ly,** *adv.*

bath·house (bath'hous), *n.* 1. a public building with facilities for bathing. 2. a building in which swimmers change clothes.

Bath-i-nette (bath-ĭ-nĕt'), *n.* a folding bathtub for babies: a trademark.

bathing cap, a closefitting rubber or plastic cap for covering the hair while swimming.

bathing suit, same as **swimsuit.**

ba-thos (bā'thos), *n.* 1. a sudden change from the elevated to the commonplace in writing or speech. 2. extreme sentimentality. 3. triteness.

bath-room (bath'rŏŏm), *n.* a room containing a bathtub, toilet, sink, etc.

bath-tub ('tŭb), *n.* a tub to take a bath in.

ba-tik (bā-tēk'), *n.* a process of dyeing designs in color on fabrics: the parts not to be colored are coated with wax which is later removed.

ba-tiste (ba-tēst'), *n.* a sheer, fine fabric of cotton, linen, wool, etc., used for clothing.

ba-ton (bā-tŏn'), *n.* 1. a staff used as a badge of office. 2. a heraldic mark indicating illegitimacy. 3. a small stick used by a music conductor in directing. 4. a metal rod, capped by a knob at one end, twirled by a drum major or drum majorette. 5. a small rod passed from one runner to the next in a relay race.

ba-tra-chi-an (bā-trā'ki-ăn), *adj.* of or pertaining to amphibians without tails: *n.* such an amphibian; frog or toad.

bats-man (bats'măn), *n., pl.* -men (-mĕn), the man wielding the bat in cricket.

bat-tal-ion (bā-tǎl'yǔn), *n.* 1. a large group of soldiers. 2. a tactical army unit, part of a division, made up of three or more companies or similar troop units.

bat-ten (bat'n), *n.* 1. a strip of wood, flooring, etc. 2. a strip of wood used as a fastening or covering over a seam between boards. 3. a strip for fastening a tarpaulin over a hatchway: *v.t.* to fasten with battens.

bat-ten (bat'n), *v.t.* to make fat: *v.i.* 1. to grow or become fat. 2. to thrive at the expense of others.

bat-ter (bat'ẽr), *v.t.* 1. to strike with heavy, repeated blows, so as to bruise, shatter, or demolish. 2. to injure or impair by or as by striking with heavy, repeated blows: *v.i.* to strike repeatedly.

bat-ter (bat'ẽr), *n.* the player whose turn it is to bat in baseball or cricket.

bat-ter (bat'ẽr), *n.* a semifluid mixture of flour, eggs, milk, etc. used for cakes, pancakes, etc.

battering ram, 1. a military machine used in ancient times to beat down walls, gates, etc., consisting of a large beam with a head of iron somewhat resembling the head of a ram. 2. any beam, bar, etc. used for forceable entry.

bat-ter-y (bat'ẽr-i), *n., pl.* -ter-ies, 1. the act of battering or beating. 2. an artillery unit consisting of equipment, men, and heavy guns. 3. an array or set of things used together. 4. in *Baseball,* the pitcher and the catcher. 5. in *Electricity,* a cell or group of cells storing an electrical charge and capable of furnishing an electric current. 6. in *Law,* an illegal beating or touching of another person.

bat-ting average (bat'ing), the number obtained by dividing the number of safe hits a base-

ball player has made by the number of times at bat.

bat-tle (bat'l), *n.* 1. a fight or encounter between opposing forces; armed conflict. 2. any conflict: *v.t.* -tled, -tling, to fight; oppose: *v.i.* 1. to fight; participate in a battle. 2. to struggle.

bat-tle-ax, bat-tle-axe (-aks), *n.* 1. a broad, flat ax, formerly used in battle as a weapon. 2. [Slang], an aggressive, domineering woman.

battle cruiser, a large warship with longer range and greater maneuverability than a battleship, but less heavily armed.

bat-tle-dore (bat'l-dôr), *n.* 1. a kind of light racket used for hitting shuttlecocks in a game similar to badminton. 2. this game (called **battledore and shuttlecock**).

bat-tle-field (bat'l-fēld), *n.* the place where a battle occurs or has occurred.

bat-tle-ment (-mĕnt), *n.* an indented parapet with open sections used as shooting posts.

battle royal, *pl.* battles royal, 1. a fight involving many people; melee. 2. a lengthy hard-fought conflict.

bat-tle-ship (-ship), *n.* a large warship with the greatest firepower and heaviest armor.

bat-tue (ba-tōō'), *n.* 1. a beating of woods and underbrush by beaters, driving game toward hunters. 2. a wanton slaughter.

bat-ty (bat'i), *adj.* -ti-er, -ti-est, 1. pertaining to or like a bat. 2. [Slang], insane. 3. [Slang], eccentric.

bau-ble (bô'bl), *n.* 1. a cheap trinket; showy trifle. 2. [Archaic], the club or staff carried by *e.* court jester or king's fool.

baux-ite (bôk'sīt), *n.* the claylike ore which yields aluminum.

bawd (bôd), *n.* 1. [Literary], a person who keeps a house of prostitution. 2. [Rare], a prostitute.

bawd-ry (bô'dri), *n.* 1. obscene or filthy language. 2. [Archaic], the business or practice of a bawd.

bawd-y (bô'di), *adj.* bawd'i-er, bawd'i-est, obscene; indecent; morally offensive. —bawd'i-ly, *adv.* —bawd'i-ness, *n.*

bawl (bôl), *v.i. & v.t.* 1. to cry out with a loud, full, and sustained sound. 2. to weep loudly: *n.* 1. a loud, prolonged shout; yell. 2. a loud weeping. —bawl'er, *n.*

bay (bā), *n.* 1. a recess in the shoreline of a sea or lake. 2. a recess or opening in a wall. 3. same as **bay window.** 4. a place or receptacle for storage. 5. same as **laurel.** 6. *pl.* an honorary garland or crown of woven laurel leaves, bestowed as a prize upon successful poets and conquerors. 7. *pl.* fame.

bay (bā), *v.i.* to bark with a deep sound, as a dog: *v.t.* 1. to bark at. 2. to pursue with barking. 3. to bring to a situation from which there is no escape; corner: *n.* 1. the deep, prolonged bark of a dog. 2. the situation of or as of a cornered animal.

bay (bā), *adj.* reddish-brown, close to chestnut: applied to horses: *n.* 1. a reddish-brown color. 2. a horse of such color.

bay-ber-ry (bā'ber-i), *n., pl.* -ries, 1. any one of a group of shrubs with a waxy, berrylike fruit. 2. the fruit. 3. a tree of the myrtle family, indigenous to the American tropics.

ŏ in dragon, ŏŏ in crude, oo in wool, u in cup, ū in cure, û in turn, ǎ in focus, oi in boy, ou in house, th in thin, t͟h in sheathe, g in get, j in joy, y in yet.

bay leaf, the aromatic leaf of the laurel, used in cooking.

bay·o·net (bā'ō-nit), *n.* a short daggerlike blade constructed to fasten on the barrel of a rifle: *v.t. & v.i.* -net·ed or -net·ted, -net·ing or -net·ting, to stab or drive with a bayonet.

bay·ou (bī'ōō), *n.* in the southern U.S., the outlet of a lake or one of the delta streams of a river, usually sluggish and marshy.

bay rum, a fragrant liquid formerly made from bayberry leaves, but now prepared from other oils, alcohol, and water: used in cosmetics.

bay window, 1. a window or windows forming a bay or recess in a room and extending outward from the wall, usually of a rectangular, semicircular, or polygonal shape. 2. [Slang], a large, bulging stomach.

ba·zaar (bā-zär'), *n.* i. in the East, a marketplace or street of shops and stalls. 2. a sale of articles to raise money in order to aid some charity or club.

ba·zoo·ka (bā-zōōk'ā), *n.* a portable weapon made of metal tubing, used for launching rockets.

BB (shot), a size of shot with a diameter of .18 inch, used in an air rifle (**BB gun**) or shotgun.

bdel·li·um (del'i-ŭm), *n.* an aromatic gum resin, used medicinally and as a perfume.

be (bē), *v.i.* was or were, been, being, 1. to exist; have existence in fact, physical or mental. 2. to happen or occur. 3. to remain. 4. to come to. 5. to become. 6. to have a place or position. 7. to signify. 8. to answer to. *Be* is also used as an auxiliary to form the passive voice, to show continuation, to express futurity, obligation, etc.

be-, a prefix meaning *around, thoroughly, away, about* and *to make, to furnish with.*

beach (bēch), *n.* 1. the sandy portion of the shore of a sea or lake, often washed by waves. 2. a part of a shore used for swimming, sunbathing, etc.: *v.t. & v.i.* to run aground or land (a boat) on a beach.

beach-comb·er ('kō-mĕr), *n.* 1. a long, curling wave rolling in from the ocean. 2. one who frequents the shore, living on what he can salvage or beg.

beach-head ('hed), *n.* 1. a position on a beach secured by an invading force. 2. any position gained as a foothold.

bea·con (bēk'n), *n.* 1. formerly, a fire lighted on a hill or high tower, as to signal danger. 2. any signal of warning or guidance, on sea or land. 3. a lighthouse. 4. a radio transmitter that emits guiding signals for aircraft: *v.t.* 1. to light up, as a beacon. 2. to furnish with beacons: *v.i.* to serve as a beacon.

bead (bēd), *n.* 1. a little perforated ball, as of glass or wood, intended to be strung with others and worn as an ornament. 2. *pl.* a rosary. 3. *pl.* an ornamental string of beads. 4. any small, globular body, as the knob of metal at the end of a gun barrel, used as a sight. 5. a drop or bubble. 6. a narrow, rounded molding. 7. bubbles or foam, as on beer. 8. the inner edge of a pneumatic tire where it fits on the rim: *v.t.* 1. to ornament

with beads or beading. 2. to string like beads: *v.i.* to form a bead or beads.

bead·ing ('ing), *n.* 1. beads or a decoration consisting of beads. 2. a molding, pattern, etc. resembling a row of beads. 3. a narrow, rounded molding.

bea·dle (bē'dl), *n.* formerly, a parish officer in the Church of England, with various minor duties.

bead·roll (bēd'rōl), *n.* [Archaic], in the *Roman Catholic Church,* a list of the dead for whose souls a certain number of prayers are to be said.

bead·work ('wŭrk), *n.* 1. ornamental work in beads. 2. same as **beading** (sense 3).

bead·y (bē'di), *adj.* bead'i·er, bead'i·est, covered with or resembling beads.

bea·gle (bē'gl), *n.* a small hound with short legs and hanging ears.

beak (bēk), *n.* 1. the bill of a bird. 2. anything pointed or shaped like a beak, as the jaws or mandibles of some insects and fishes. 3. the metal-sheathed prow of an ancient warship, intended to pierce enemy warships. 4. [Slang], a large, hooked nose. —**beaked** (bēkt), *adj.* —**beak'like,** *adj.*

beak·er (bēk'ēr), *n.* 1. a large drinking cup; goblet. 2. a wide-mouthed jarlike glass container with a projecting lip. 3. the amount a beaker will hold.

beam (bēm), *n.* 1. a long piece of timber or metal used in construction. 2. one of the principal horizontal timbers of a building or ship. 3. the breadth of a ship at its widest point. 4. an oscillating lever moved by a piston rod, transmitting its motion to a crank or other part. 5. a cylinder of wood around which the warp is wound before weaving. 6. the crossbar of a plow to which the handles and share are secured. 7. the bar of a balance which suspends the scales. 8. the principal stem of a deer's antlers. 9. a ray of light or other radiation. 10. a glowing look or smile. 11. a stream of radio or radar signals used to guide aircraft or ships: *v.t.* 1. to send forth (rays of light). 2. to direct (a radio signal): *v.i.* 1. to shine. 2. to smile.

beam·ing ('ing), *adj.* 1. emitting beams; shining. 2. very happy; joyful. —**beam'ing·ly,** *adv.*

beam·y ('i), *adj.* beam'i·er, beam'i·est, 1. emitting rays of light. 2. having much breadth of beam: said of a ship.

bean (bēn), *n.* 1. any one of a group of leguminous plants including the string bean, kidney bean, and lima bean. 2. the edible, smooth, kidney-shaped seed of any of these plants. 3. the seed and its pod, eaten as a vegetable. 4. any one of various other seeds or fruits resembling beans. 5. [Slang], the head or mind: *v.t.* [Slang], to hit on the head, as with a pitched ball in baseball. —**bean'like,** *adj.*

bean·er·y (bē'nēr-i), *n., pl.* -er·ies, [Informal], a cheap restaurant.

bear (ber), *v.t.* bore, borne or (sometimes for *v.t.* 10) born, bear'ing, 1. to support; hold up. 2. to carry; convey. 3. to suffer or endure. 4. to be answerable for; take on. 5. to possess; show or exhibit. 6.· to have in or on; contain. 7. to carry in the mind. 8. to admit or be capable of. 9. to bring forth or produce. 10. to give birth to. 11. to require; need. 12. to carry or conduct (oneself): *v.i.* 1. to be fruitful or productive. 2. to be, point, or go in a certain direction. 3. to relate to (followed by *on*). 4. to endure or tolerate. —bear'er, *n.*

bear (ber), *n.,·pl.* bears, bear, 1. a large, heavy, omnivorous mammal having shaggy fur and a short tail, found in temperate and arctic regions. 2. [B-], either of two constellations in the northern heavens, called the Great Bear and the Little Bear. 3. a rude, gruff, or clumsy person. 4. one who sells shares of stock with the expectation of buying them later at a lower price: opposed to *bull*: *adj.* of, pertaining to, or favorable to stockmarket bears. —bear'like, *adj.*

bear·a·ble (ber'ä-bl), *adj.* that can be tolerated or endured. —bear'a·bly, *adv.*

bear-bait·ing (ber'bāt-ing), *n.* formerly, the setting of dogs against a chained bear.

beard (bird), *n.* 1. the hair that grows on the chin, cheeks, and upper lip of a man's face. 2. anything which resembles a beard. 3. the awn of barley and other grains and grasses. 4. the barb of an arrow, fishhook, etc.: *v.t.* 1. to take as by the beard; oppose in a bold manner; defy. 2. to provide with a beard. —beard'ed, *adj.*

beard·less ('lis), *adj.* 1. without a beard. 2. not old enough to have a beard. 3. young, inexperienced, etc.

bear garden, 1. a place for bearbaiting. 2. any scene or place of tumult or disorder.

bear·ing (ber'ing), *n.* 1. the act of enduring with patience. 2. something that supports. 3. carriage; behavior. 4. relation of the parts of a whole; meaning or application. 5. the act or power of producing. 6. a part of a machine which bears friction from another part sliding, revolving, etc. on it. 7. the position of one object with respect to another. 8. *pl.* awareness of one's situation or position. 9. any of the heraldic figures which fill the field.

bearing rein, same as checkrein.

bear·ish ('ish), *adj.* 1. resembling a bear in qualities; rude, surly, etc. 2. of, pertaining to, or bringing about a lowering of prices in the stock market. —bear'ish·ly, *adv.*

bear·skin ('skin), *n.* 1. the skin or fur of a bear. 2. something made from this, as a rug, coat, or cap.

beast (bēst), *n.* 1. any four-footed animal, as distinguished from birds, insects, fishes, and man. 2. a domesticated animal. 3. a rude or coarse person.

beast·ie (bēs'ti), *n.* [Chiefly Scottish], a little animal.

beast·ly (bēst'li), *adj.* -li·er, -li·est, 1. like a beast. 2. [Informal], nasty; disagreeable: *adv.* [British Informal], very. —beast'li·ness, *n.*

beat (bēt), *v.t.* beat, beat'en, beat'ing, 1. to strike with repeated blows. 2. to thrash; knock; whip. 3. to pound or break. 4. to scour; search. 5. to dash or strike against,

as water or wind. 6. to tread, as a path. 7. to overcome or vanquish. 8. to excel or surpass. 9. to flutter, as wings. 10. to mix; whip (cream, eggs, etc.). 11. [Informal], to trick. 12. [Informal], to baffle; be too difficult for. 13. [Slang], to escape (a punishment): *v.i.* 1. to strike repeatedly. 2. to throb; pulse. 3. to search and strike underbrush and woods for game. 4. to take whipping or stirring. 5. to signal or summon by the beat of a drum. 6. to sound, as a drum, when struck: *n.* 1. a beating, as of the heart. 2. a recurring stroke or blow. 3. a pulsation; throb. 4. a round or course which is frequently gone over. 5. the rise or fall of a hand, foot, baton, etc. marking divisions of time, as in music. 6. the divisions of the measure so marked: *adj.* [Slang], exhausted, mentally or physically. —beat'er, *n.*

beat·en ('n), *adj.* 1. whipped; flogged. 2. pounded thin. 3. worn by use, as by the tread of feet. 4. conquered; defeated. 5. exhausted. 6. searched through for game.

be·a·tif·ic (bi-ä-tif'ik), *adj.* 1. having power to bless or render perfectly happy. 2. blissful. —be·a·tif'i·cal·ly, *adv.*

be·at·i·fi·ca·tion (bi-at-i-fi-kā'shŭn), *n.* 1. the act of blessing or the state of being blessed. 2. in the *Roman Catholic Church*, the act of declaring a deceased person to have attained the rank of the blessed in heaven: usually a step that leads to canonization.

be·at·i·fy (bi-at'i-fi), *v.t.* -fied, -fy·ing, 1. to make happy; bless. 2. in t.e *Roman Catholic Church*, to declare by papal decree that a deceased person has attained the rank of the blessed.

beat·ing (bēt'ing), *n.* 1. the act of striking. 2. a flogging; whipping. 3. a pulsation; throbbing. 4. a defeat.

be·at·i·tude (bi-at'i-tōōd), *n.* 1. consummate bliss. 2. one of the declarations made in the Sermon on the Mount: called *the Beatitudes.*

beat-up (bēt'up'), *adj.* [Slang], worn out; dilapidated.

beau (bō), *n., pl.* beaus, beaux (bōz), 1. [Now Rare], a fop; fashionably dressed young man. 2. a suitor; girl's or woman's sweetheart.

beau ideal, 1. ideal beauty. 2. ideal type, standard, or model.

beau monde (bō' mond'), the fashionable world.

beau·te·ous (būt'i-ŭs), *adj.* beautiful. —beau'te·ous·ly, *adv.*

beau·ti·cian (bū-tish'ăn), *n.* one who cuts and sets hair, gives manicures, etc. in a beauty shop.

beau·ti·ful (būt'i-fŭl), *adj.* possessing qualities which please the senses; having beauty; lovely. —beau'ti·ful·ly, *adv.*

beau·ti·fy (būt'i-fi), *v.t.* -fied, -fy·ing, to make beautiful: *v.i.* to grow or become beautiful. —beau·ti·fi·ca'tion, *n.* —beau'ti·fi·er, *n.*

beau·ty (būt'i), *n., pl.* -ties, 1. those qualities which are most pleasing to the senses or the mind. 2. something with such qualities. 3. physical attractiveness. 4. a beautiful woman.

beauty shop, a place of business that special-

ô in drag*o*n, ōō in cr*u*de, oo in w*oo*l, u in c*u*p, ū in c*u*re, û in t*u*rn, ŭ in foc*u*s, oi in b*o*y, ou in h*ou*se, th in *th*in, th in shea*th*e, g in *g*et, j in *j*oy, y in *y*et.

izes in hair styling, manicures, etc. for women: also beauty salon, beauty parlor.

beauty sleep, [Informal], 1. sleep taken before midnight, popularly thought to be more restorative than that taken later. 2. extra sleep.

beauty spot, 1. a dark patch or spot placed on the face with intent to heighten beauty by contrast with the whiteness of the skin. 2. a mole or natural mark on the skin. 3. a scenic place.

bea·ver (bē'vēr), *n.* 1. a large, amphibious rodent with soft, brown fur and a broad, flat tail. 2. the fur of the beaver. 3. a man's high silk hat, formerly made of this fur. 4. [Informal], an industrious person.

bea·ver (bē'vēr), *n.* 1. a movable piece of armor for protecting the lower part of the face. 2. a helmet visor.

Bea·ver·board (bē'vēr-bôrd), *n.* a kind of artificial board used as for making walls: a trademark. 2. [b-], artificial board of this kind.

be·calm (bi-käm'), *v.t.* 1. to make calm or still. 2. to keep (a sailing ship) from moving because of the absence of wind.

be·cause (bi-kôz'), *conj.* 1. by reason of; on account of the fact that. 2. that; the reason that.

bé·cha·mel (bāsh-ā-mel'), *n.* a fine white sauce made with cream.

bêche·de·mer (besh-dē-mer'), *n., pl.* **bêches-de-mer'** (besh-), [French], same as **trepang.**

beck (bek), *n.* a nod or other gesture used to summon.

beck (bek), *n.* [Chiefly British Dialectal], a small brook.

beck·et (bek'ēt), *n.* a contrivance in ships to fasten small spars, loose ropes, etc.

beck·on (bek'n), *v.i. & v.t.* 1. to summon or signal by gestures. 2. to attract; draw: *n.* a gesture that summons.

be·cloud (bi-kloud'), *v.t.* 1. to cloud over. 2. to obscure; confuse.

be·come (bi-kum'), *v.i.* -**came'** (-kām'), -**come'**, -**com'ing,** to pass from one state to another; come or grow to be: *v.t.* 1. to suit; befit. 2. to be suitable to; accord with.

be·com·ing (-ing), *adj.* 1. fit; proper; appropriate. 2. suitable in appearance.

bed (bed), *n.* 1. an article of furniture upon which one rests or sleeps. 2. a bedstead. 3. anything which serves as a resting place or in which something lies or is embedded. 4. a portion of land where plants are grown. 5. the bottom of a river, ocean, or other body of water. 6. a place on the bottom of an ocean where something grows. 7. a layer or stratum, as of rock. 8. any flat surface used as a base or support. 9. a mass or heap of anything resembling a bed: *v.t.* **bed'ded, bed'ding,** 1. to furnish with a bed. 2. to put to bed. 3. to embed. 4. to plant, as flowers. 5. to lay in a stratum; lay flat: *v.i.* 1. to go to bed. 2. to form in layers.

be·daz·zle (be-daz'l), *v.t.* -**daz'zled, -daz'zling,** to dazzle completely; confuse.

bed·bug (bed'bug), *n.* a small, bloodsucking, reddish-brown insect infesting furniture, especially beds.

bed·clothes ('klōz), *n.* sheets, blankets, etc. used on a bed.

bed·ding ('ing), *n.* 1. mattresses and bedclothes. 2. the materials of a bed for animals, as straw, hay, etc. 3. a foundation or bottom layer. 4. in *Geology,* stratification.

be·deck (bi-dek'), *v.t.* to adorn; ornament.

be·dev·il (bi-dev'l), *v.t.* -**iled** or -**illed,** -**il·ing** or -**il·ling,** 1. to torment; plague. 2. to throw into disorder or confusion. 3. to spoil or corrupt. —**be·dev'il·ment,** *n.*

be·dew (bi-dōō'), *v.t.* to moisten with or as with dew.

bed·fel·low (bed'fel-ō), *n.* 1. a person who shares one's bed. 2. an associate.

be·diz·en (bi-dī'zn), *v.t.* [Now Rare], to adorn in a showy way or with vulgar finery.

bed·lam (bed'lăm), *n.* 1. [Archaic], an insane asylum. 2. any scene of uproar and confusion.

bed·lam·ite (-īt), *n.* [Archaic], a madman; insane person.

bed molding, in *Architecture,* a molding below the corona and above the frieze.

Bed·ou·in (bed'oo-win), *n., pl.* -**ins,** -**in,** [also b-], 1. a nomadic Arab. 2. any nomad: *adj.* 1. of or pertaining to Bedouins. 2. nomadic.

bed·pan (bed'pan), *n.* a pan used as a toilet by a person confined to bed.

be·drag·gle (bi-drag'l), *v.t.* -**gled,** -**gling,** to make wet, limp, and dirty.

bed·rid·den (bed'rid-n), *adj.* confined to bed by illness, infirmity, etc.: also **bed'rid.**

bed·rock ('rok), *n.* 1. solid rock underneath the soil. 2. a firm foundation. 3. the bottom.

bed·roll ('rōl), *n.* a portable roll of bedding, used for sleeping outdoors.

bed·room ('rōōm), *n.* a room for sleeping, with a bed or beds.

bed·side ('sīd), *n.* the area beside a bed: *adj.* near a bed.

bed·sore ('sôr), *n.* a sore on the body of a person confined to bed, usually caused by the rubbing of the bedclothes.

bed·spread ('spred), *n.* a decorative cover spread over the bedclothes.

bed·spring ('spring), *n.* a framework of springs that supports the mattress of a bed.

bed·stead ('sted), *n.* an article of furniture consisting of a framework which supports a bedspring and mattress.

bed·straw ('strô), *n.* a small plant of the madder family, with white or colored flowers.

bed·time ('tīm), *n.* the time when one customarily goes to bed.

bee (bē), *n.* 1. a four-winged, hairy insect that gathers pollen and nectar. 2. a group of people gathered together for working on something or for competition.

bee·bread ('bred), *n.* a yellowish-brown substance consisting of pollen and honey, collected and stored by bees for food.

beech (bēch), *n.* 1. any one of a group of trees having gray bark, hard wood, and an edible nut. 2. the wood of any of these trees.

beech·nut ('nut), *n.* the small, edible nut of the beech tree.

beef (bēf), *n., pl.* **beeves, beefs,** 1. a full-grown ox, bull, cow, or steer, raised for meat. 2. the flesh of one of these, when killed for

---

a in *cap,* ä in *cane,* ä in *father,* á in *abet,* e in *met,* ē in *be,* ē in *baker,* é in *regent,* i in *pit,* ī in *fine,* i in *manifest,* o in *hot,* ô in *horse,* ō in *bone,*

use as food. 3. these animals, collectively. 4. [Slang], muscular strength. 5. [Slang], a complaint: *v.i.* [Slang], to complain.

beef·eat·er ('ēt·ēr), *n.* 1. one who eats beef. 2. same as yeoman of the guard. 3. [Slang], an Englishman.

beef·steak ('stāk), *n.* a thick slice of beef, as from the loin.

beef·y (bēf'i), *adj.* beef'i·er, beef'i·est, brawny; muscular and solid. —beef'i·ness, *n.*

bee·hive (bē'hiv), *n.* 1. a box or other covering for a swarm of bees, and serving as the place in which they make and store honey. 2. a place of much activity.

bee·keep·er ('kēp·ēr), *n.* one who keeps bees that produce honey. —bee'keep·ing, *n.*

bee·line ('līn), *n.* 1. the straight course believed to be followed by a bee returning, laden with nectar, to the hive. 2. the most direct way from one point to another.

Be·el·ze·bub (bi·el'zē·bub), *n.* in the *Bible*, the chief devil; Satan.

bee moth, a moth which lays its eggs in beehives, and whose larvae feed upon the wax of the honeycomb.

been (bin), past participle of be.

beep (bēp), *n.* the brief, high-pitched sound of a horn, electronic signal, etc.: *v.i. & v.t.* to make or cause to make this sound.

beer (bir), *n.* 1. a fermented, alcoholic beverage made from grain, usually malted barley, with hops added for flavor. 2. a soft drink made from an extract of the roots and other parts of any one of various plants, as ginger and spruce.

beer·y (bir'i), *adj.* beer'i·er, beer'i·est, 1. of or pertaining to beer. 2. affected by beer; maudlin, drunken, etc. —beer'i·ness, *n.*

beest·ings (bēs'tingz), *n.* the first milk given by a cow after having a calf.

bees·wax (bēz'waks), *n.* the wax secreted by bees to build their honeycombs: used in candles and polishes.

bees·wing ('wing), *n.* a gauzy film that forms in port and some other wines, indicative of age.

beet (bēt), *n.* 1. a biennial plant with edible leaves and a succulent, white or red root. 2. the root, some varieties of which are cooked as a vegetable, while others are used as a source of sugar.

bee·tle (bēt'l), *n.* any one of a group of insects having four wings, the anterior or outer pair being hardened and folding as a sheath over the inner membranous pair.

bee·tle (bēt'l), *n.* 1. a heavy wooden mallet used for driving wedges, packing down earth, etc. 2. a club for beating linen in washing. 3. a household mallet or pestle: *v.t.* -tled, -tling, to use a beetle on.

bee·tle (bēt'l), *v.i.* -tled, -tling, to be prominent; jut out; overhang: *adj.* jutting; overhanging: also bee'tling.

bee·tle-browed (-broud), *adj.* 1. having overhanging eyebrows. 2. sullen, lowering, morose, etc.

be·fall (bi·fôl'), *v.i.* -fell', -fall'en, -fall'ing, to come to pass: *v.t.* to happen or occur to.

be·fit (bi·fit'), *v.t.* -fit'ted, -fit'ting, to suit or be becoming to.

be·fit·ting ('ing), *adj.* appropriate; right; suitable. —be·fit'ting·ly, *adv.*

be·fog (bi·fôg'), *v.t.* -fogged', -fog'ging, 1. to surround with fog; make foggy. 2. to confuse; becloud; obscure.

be·fore (bi·fôr'), *prep.* 1. in front of. 2. preceding in space, time, or rank. 3. in the presence or sight of. 4. under jurisdiction of. 5. rather than. 6. earlier than: *adv.* 1. in front; in advance. 2. previously; formerly. 3. sooner: *conj.* 1. earlier than the time that. 2. rather than.

be·fore·hand ('hand), *adv. & adj.* 1. in advance. 2. in anticipation.

be·foul (bi·foul'), *v.t.* 1. to soil; make foul. 2. to slander.

be·friend (bi·frend'), *v.t.* to act as a friend to; aid or shield; assist.

be·fud·dle (bi·fud'l), *v.t.* -fud'dled, -fud'dling, 1. to confuse; mix up. 2. to stupefy, as with alcoholic drink. —be·fud'dle·ment, *n.*

beg (beg), *v.t. & v.i.* begged, beg'ging, 1. to ask for (charity or alms). 2. to beseech or entreat humbly.

be·gan (bi·gan'), past tense of begin.

be·get (bi·get'), *v.t.* be·got' or archaic be·gat' (-gat'), be·got'ten or be·got', be·get'ting, 1. to procreate; father or sire. 2. to generate; produce; cause to exist. —be·get'ter, *n.*

beg·gar (beg'ēr), *n.* 1. one who begs, or lives by begging or asking for alms. 2. one who lives in extreme poverty; pauper: *v.t.* 1. to exhaust the resources of; make poor. 2. to make seem inadequate.

beg·gar·ly (-li), *adj.* like or in the condition of a beggar; poor, worthless, etc. —beg'gar·li·ness, *n.*

beg·gar·y (beg'ēr·i), *n., pl.* -gar·ies, 1. the state of a beggar. 2. extreme poverty. 3. beggars collectively.

be·gin (bi·gin'), *v.i.* be·gan', be·gun', be·gin'ning, 1. to originate; arise. 2. to take the initiatory step; make a start: *v.t.* 1. to commence; cause to start. 2. to originate; make exist.

be·gin·ner ('ēr), *n.* 1. one who begins something. 2. one who enters upon anything for the first time; novice.

be·gin·ning ('ing), *n.* 1. a commencing. 2. the origin; source. 3. *usually pl.* the initial stage of anything. 4. the initial part.

be·gone (bi·gôn'), *interj. & v.i.* (to) go away; depart.

be·gon·ia (bi·gōn·yà), *n.* any one of a group of tropical plants, cultivated for their ornamental leaves and showy flowers.

be·got (bi·got'), past tense and alternate past participle of beget.

be·got·ten ('n), alternate past participle of beget.

be·grime (bi·grīm'), *v.t.* -grimed', -grim'ing, to soil; cover with dirt or grime.

be·grudge (bi·gruj'), *v.t.* -grudged', -grudg'ing, 1. to regard with envy or discontent. 2. to give with reluctance. 3. to regard disapprovingly. —be·grudg'ing·ly, *adv.*

be·guile (bi·gīl'), *v.t.* -guiled', -guil'ing, 1. to delude by guile; deceive. 2. to cheat. 3. to cause to pass pleasantly. 4. to divert or entertain. —be·guile'ment, n. —be·guil'er, n.

be·gum (bē'gŭm), n. in India, a Moslem princess or lady of high rank.

be·gun (bi-gŭn'), past participle of begin.

be·half (bi-haf'), n. favor; support; interest (preceded by in, on, or upon).

be·have (bi-hāv'), v.t. & v.i. -haved', -hav'ing, 1. to conduct (oneself) in a certain manner; act. 2. to conduct (oneself) in a proper manner.

be·hav·ior ('yĕr), n. 1. a person's manner of behaving; conduct. 2. the observable muscular or glandular responses of an organism to stimulation. 3. the way in which something functions. —be·hav'ior·al, adj.

behavioral science, any one of the sciences, as anthropology or psychology, that study human activities.

be·hav·ior·ism (-izm), n. in Psychology, the doctrine that only observed behavior is valid, rejecting theories of mind and consciousness. —be·hav'ior·ist, n. & adj. —be·hav·ior·is'tic, adj.

be·head (bi-hed'), v.t. to cut off the head of.

be·he·moth (bi-hē'mŏth), n. 1. a huge animal described in the Bible in Job xl,15–24, probably the hippopotamus. 2. anything huge or very powerful.

be·hest (bi-hest'), n. a command; order.

be·hind (bi-hīnd'), prep. 1. at the back of; in the rear of. 2. remaining after. 3. inferior to. 4. later than. 5. beyond. 6. finished for. 7. supporting. 8. hidden by: adv. 1. at the back; in or toward the rear. 2. past in point of time. 3. in a former place, state, etc. 4. in or into arrears. 5. late: n. [Informal], the buttocks.

be·hind·hand ('hand), adv. & adj. 1. in arrears. 2. late; slow. 3. behind in progress; in a state of backwardness.

be·hold (bi-hōld'), v.t. -held' (-held'), -held' or archaic -hold'en, -hold'ing, to fix the eyes upon; look at; observe: interj. look! see! —be·hold'er, n.

be·hold·en ('ĕn), adj. indebted; obliged; grateful.

be·hoof (bi-hōōf'), n. advantage; interest; behalf.

be·hoove (-hōōv'), v.t. -hooved', -hoov'ing, to be necessary or appropriate for: also [Chiefly British], be·hove (-hōv').

beige (bāzh), adj. 1. having its natural color, as an undyed and unbleached wool fabric. 2. of a light grayish-tan color: n. light grayish tan.

be·ing (bē'ing), n. 1. existence, as opposed to nonexistence. 2. essential nature. 3. one that lives or exists. 4. that which exists in any form, whether actual or ideal.

be·jew·el (bi-jōō'ĕl), v.t. -eled or -elled, -el·ing or -el·ling, to ornament or cover with jewels.

be·la·bor (bi-lā'bĕr), v.t. 1. to beat severely. 2. to scold or criticize. 3. same as labor (v.t.).

be·lat·ed (bi-lāt'id), adj. delayed; late or too late. —be·lat'ed·ly, adv. —be·lat'ed·ness, n.

be·lay (bi-lā'), v.t. & v.i. -layed', -lay'ing, 1. to make fast, as a rope, by winding around a

pin, cleat, etc. 2. to secure (a person or thing) by a rope.

belaying pin, a pin of wood or metal on a ship, around which a rope can be fastened.

belch (belch), v.i. & v.t. 1. to eject (gas) from the stomach through the mouth. 2. to eject with force or violence: n. the act of belching.

bel·dam, bel·dame (bel'dăm), n. 1. an old woman. 2. an ugly old woman; hag. 3. [Obs.], a grandmother.

be·lea·guer (bi-lē'gĕr), v.t. 1. to besiege; surround with an army so as to preclude escape. 2. to harass; trouble.

bel·em·nite (bel'ĕm-nīt), n. the fossil shell of a cuttlefish of an extinct group.

bel·fry (bel'fri), n., pl. -fries, 1. a bell tower. 2. that part of a steeple or tower which holds the bell or bells.

Bel·gian (bel'jăn), adj. of or pertaining to Belgium, a country in western Europe, or to its inhabitants: n. a native or inhabitant of Belgium.

Belgian hare, a domestic rabbit of a reddish-brown color.

Be·li·al (bē'li-ăl), n. 1. in the Old Testament, a personification of wickedness and evil. 2. in the New Testament, Satan.

be·lie (bi-lī'), v.t. -lied', -ly'ing, 1. [Archaic], to calumniate; slander. 2. to obscure the nature of; misrepresent. 3. to disappoint. 4. to show to be false. —be·li'er, n.

be·lief (bē-lēf'), n. 1. the acceptance of something as fact; conviction. 2. religious faith. 3. confidence; reliance. 4. the thing believed. 5. the whole body of tenets held by the professors of any faith; creed. 6. an opinion; expectation.

be·lieve (bē-lēv'), v.t. -lieved', -liev'ing, 1. to place credence in and accept as true. 2. to place confidence in. 3. to expect or think: v.i. 1. to have religious faith. 2. to be persuaded of the truth of anything. 3. to think or suppose. —be·liev'a·ble, adj. —be·liev'er, n. —be·liev'ing·ly, adv.

be·like (bē-līk'), adv. [Archaic], probably.

be·lit·tle (bi-lit'l), v.t. -tled, -tling, to lower or depreciate; run down by speaking slightingly of. —be·lit'tle·ment, n. —be·lit'tler, n.

bell (bel), n. 1. a hollow object, usually cup-shaped and made of metal, which gives forth a clear, ringing sound when struck. 2. the sound made by a bell. 3. anything in the form of a bell. 4. in nautical usage, any one of the half-hour divisions of the day, marked at the beginning of each by the ringing of a bell: v.t. 1. to put a bell on. 2. to shape like a bell: v.i. to flare out like a bell.

bell (bel), n. & v.i. & v.t. same as bellow.

bel·la·don·na (bel-ă-don'ă), n. 1. the deadly nightshade, a poisonous European plant with purplish flowers and black berries. 2. same as atropine.

bell·bird (bel'bŭrd), n. any of several birds whose sounds are like those of a bell, as the wood thrush.

bell·bot·tom ('bot-ŏm), adj. denoting trousers that flare at the bottom: also bell'-bot-tomed.

---

a in cap, ā in cane, ä in father, ă in abet, e in met, ē in be, ĕ in baker, ė in regent, i in pit, ī in fine, ĭ in manifest, o in hot, ô in horse, ō in bone,

bell·boy ('boi), n. a boy or man employed by a hotel to carry luggage and run errands.

belle (bel), n. a beautiful or extremely popular woman or girl.

Bel·leek ware (bĕ-lēk'), a very fine kind of pottery with a high gloss, resembling porcelain: made at Belleek, a town in Northern Ireland.

belles-let·tres (bel-let'rĕ), n. fiction, poetry, and other nontechnical literature, as opposed to technical or scientific writings.

bell·hop (bel'hop), n. same as bellboy.

bel·li·cose (bel'i-kōs), adj. pugnacious; contentious; warlike. —bel'li·cose·ly, adv.

bel·lied (bel'id), adj. having a belly: used in compounds, as yellow-bellied.

bel·lig·er·ence (bĕ-lij'ĕr-ĕns), n. hostility; pugnacity; warlike nature.

bel·lig·er·en·cy (-ĕn-si), n. 1. the state of warfare. 2. same as belligerence.

bel·lig·er·ent (bĕ-lij'ĕr-ĕnt), adj. 1. waging war. 2. of or pertaining to war or warfare. 3. warlike. 4. willing to fight or quarrel: n. 1. a belligerent person or group. 2. a nation recognized as carrying on war. —bel'lig'er·ent·ly, adv.

bell·man (bel'mǎn), n., pl. -men (-mĕn), 1. a town crier. 2. same as bellboy.

bell metal, an alloy of copper and tin, used for the manufacture of bells.

bel·low (bel'ō), v.i. 1. to utter a full, resonant sound, as a bull; roar. 2. to cry out loudly, as in pain: v.t. to utter with a loud, full voice: n. a roar, as of a bull. 2. a loud, resounding cry.

bel·lows (bel'ōz), n. sing. & pl. 1. an instrument that produces a current of air when its sides are pressed together: used for blowing fires, filling the pipes of an organ, etc. 2. anything like a bellows.

bell·weth·er (bel'weth-ĕr), n. 1. a male sheep, usually with a bell on his neck, that leads the flock. 2. a leader.

bel·ly (bel'i), n., pl. -lies, 1. the front part of the human body that extends from the chest to the thighs; abdomen. 2. the corresponding part in animals. 3. the stomach. 4. the deep interior of something. 5. the part of anything that swells out: v.t. & v.i. -lied, -ly·ing, to swell out; bulge.

bel·ly·ache (-āk), n. pain in the bowels or abdomen: v.i. -ached, -ach·ing, [Slang], to complain.

bel·ly·band (-band), n. a band that encircles the belly of an animal, as for holding a saddle in place.

bel·ly·but·ton (-but-n), n. [Informal], the navel: also belly button.

be·long (bi-lông'), v.i. 1. to be the property of. 2. to be connected with; pertain to. 3. to be a member of. 4. to have a fixed or suitable place. (Senses 1, 2, and 3 are followed by to.)

be·long·ing ('ing), n. 1. that which belongs to one. 2. pl. property; possessions. 3. affinity; rapport.

be·lov·ed (bi-luv'id), adj. greatly loved: n. one who is greatly loved.

be·low (bi-lō'), prep. 1. unworthy of; beneath.

2. inferior to in rank, excellence, or value; lower than: adv. & adj. 1. in or to a lower place. 2. on the earth. 3. in or to hell. 4. in a lower rank, amount, etc. 5. later (in a book, article, etc.).

belt (belt), n. 1. a band used to encircle the waist, as to hold clothing in place. 2. anything resembling a belt, or which encircles, restrains, or supports as a belt. 3. a band connecting two wheels or pulleys and transmitting motion or transporting objects from one to the other. 4. a region or zone with a certain distinguishing feature. 5. [Slang], a hard blow, as with the fist. 6. [Slang], a drink of liquor: v.t. 1. to encircle as with a belt; surround. 2. to fasten with or as with a belt. 3. to hit with a belt. 4. [Informal], to sing loudly and heartily. 5. [Slang], to hit forcefully. 6. [Slang], to drink (liquor).

Bel·tane (bel'tān), n. formerly, May 1 or May Day.

belt·ing (bel'ting), n. 1. belts collectively. 2. the material of which belts are made. 3. [Slang], a whipping.

be·lu·ga (bĕ-lōō'gä), n., pl. -ga, -gas, 1. a large, white sturgeon found in the Black and Caspian seas. 2. a large white dolphin of northern seas.

bel·ve·dere (bel'vĕ-dir), n. 1. a pavilion or open structure built on the top of a house. 2. a summerhouse built on an elevation.

be·mire (bi-mir'), v.t. -mired', -mir'ing, 1. to soil by or as by passing through mire. 2. to cause to bog down in mire.

be·moan (bi-mōn'), v.t. & v.i. to lament; bewail; deplore.

be·muse (bi-mūz'), v.t. -mused', -mus'ing, 1. to stupefy, as with liquor. 2. to preoccupy: usually in the passive voice.

bench (bench), n. 1. a long, hard seat. 2. a strong table on which machinists, mechanics, etc. do their work. 3. the seat where judges sit in court. 4. the persons, considered as a group, who sit as judges. 5. the office or status of a judge. 6. a law court: v.t. 1. to furnish with benches. 2. in Sports, to take or keep (a player) out of a game.

bench·er (ben'chĕr), n. 1. a judge. 2. a member of the British Parliament.

bench show, a competitive exhibition of small animals, especially dogs.

bench warrant, a warrant issued by a court or judge for the arrest of someone.

bend (bend), v.t. bent, bend'ing, 1. to curve or make crooked. 2. to move or deflect out of a straight line. 3. to direct to a certain point. 4. to incline (followed by to or toward). 5. to cause to yield. 6. to fasten (sails or ropes): v.i. 1. to be or become curved or crooked. 2. to yield by curving, as from pressure. 3. to curve the body; stoop (followed by over or down). 4. to bow or be submissive: n. 1. an act of bending or the condition of being bent. 2. something that bends or curves. 3. a stripe on a coat of arms, from the upper left to the lower right corner. 4. any one of several knots by which one rope is fastened to another or to something else. —bend'a·ble, adj.

bend·er (ben′dēr), *n.* 1. one that bends. 2. [Slang], a period of drunkenness.

bends (bendz), *n.* [Informal], same as decompression sickness.

bend sinister, in *Heraldry*, a band signifying illegitimacy, running from the upper right to the lower left corner of a coat of arms.

be·neath (bi-nēth′), *prep.* 1. lower than. 2. under. 3. lower than in rank, dignity, or excellence. 4. unworthy of: *adv. & adj.* 1. in a lower place; below. 2. underneath.

ben·e·dict (ben′ē-dikt), *n.* a newly married man.

Ben·e·dic·tine (ben-ē-dik′tin, -tēn), *n.* any one of the members of a religious order founded in the sixth century by St. Benedict of Nursia.

ben·e·dic·tion (ben-ē-dik′shun), *n.* 1. the act of blessing. 2. the blessing pronounced at the close of a religious service. 3. [B-], a service of the Roman Catholic Church, during which a consecrated Host is exposed and a blessing given.

ben·e·dic·to·ry (-dik′tōr-i), *adj.* of, pertaining to, or expressing a blessing.

ben·e·fac·tion (ben-ē-fak′shun), *n.* 1. the act of being helpful or doing good. 2. a giving of money for charitable purposes. 3. the good done or money given.

ben·e·fac·tor (ben′ē-fak-tēr), *n.* one who has given help, especially money. —**ben′e·fac·tress,** *n.fem.*

ben·e·fice (ben′ē-fis), *n.* 1. a fief held by a feudal tenant. 2. a church endowed with revenue, providing a living for the rector, vicar, etc. 3. this revenue or living.

be·nef·i·cence (bē-nef′i-sēns), *n.* 1. active goodness; kindness. 2. a benefaction.

be·nef·i·cent (-sēnt), *adj.* 1. characterized by beneficence. 2. having a beneficial result. Also **be·nef′ic** (bē-nef′ik). —**be·nef′i·cent·ly,** *adv.*

ben·e·fi·cial (ben-ē-fish′ǎl), *adj.* profitable; propitious; helpful; favorable. —**ben·e·fi′cial·ly,** *adv.*

ben·e·fi·ci·ar·y (ben-ē-fish′i-ēr-i, -fish′ēr-i), *n., pl.* -ar·ies, 1. one who holds a benefice. 2. one who receives benefits, advantages, etc. 3. the person to whom an insurance policy, trust, etc. is payable: *adj.* of or pertaining to a benefice.

ben·e·fit (ben′ē-fit), *n.* 1. [Archaic], an act of kindness. 2. whatever promotes the happiness or well-being of a person or thing or adds to the value of property. 3. a theatrical performance, social gathering, etc., the proceeds of which go to some cause or person. 4. *often pl.* an allowance, pension, etc. paid by a government, company, insurance company, etc. to someone who is retired, ill, etc.: *v.t.* -fit·ed, -fit·ing, to do good to; be of service to: *v.i.* to gain advantage; profit.

be·nev·o·lence (bē-nev′ō-lēns), *n.* 1. the disposition to do good; good will. 2. an act of kindness or generosity; charity.

be·nev·o·lent (-lēnt), *adj.* kind; charitable; philanthropic. —**be·nev′o·lent·ly,** *adv.*

ben·ga·line (beng′gǎ-lēn), *n.* a soft, corded fabric of silk or rayon, resembling poplin.

Ben·gal light (ben-gôl′), a firework, used also formerly for signaling at sea, giving a steady, bright blue light.

be·night·ed (bi-nīt′id), *adj.* 1. enshrouded in darkness; overtaken by night. 2. backward; unenlightened. —**be·night′ed·ness,** *n.*

be·nign (bi-nin′), *adj.* 1. of a kind or gentle disposition; genial. 2. favorable; salutary. 3. in *Medicine*, not malignant. —**be·nign′ly,** *adv.*

be·nig·nant (bi-nig′nǎnt), *adj.* 1. kind; gracious. 2. favorable. —**be·nig′nan·cy,** *n., adj.* **-cies.**

be·nig·ni·ty (′ni-ti), *n., pl.* -ties, 1. kindness; graciousness. 2. a kind act.

ben·i·son (ben′i-zn, -sn), *n.* a blessing.

ben·ne, **ben·e** (ben′i), *n.* same as **sesame.**

ben·ny (ben′i), *n., pl.* -nies, [Slang], an amphetamine pill.

bent (bent), *adj.* 1. curved; crooked. 2. strongly inclined; determined (followed by *on*): *n.* 1. an inclination; tendency. 2. a mental leaning; disposition; propensity. 3. a stiff, wiry, low-growing grass: also called **bent′grass.**

ben·thos (ben′thos), *n.* the fauna and flora at the bottom of the sea. —**ben′thic** ('thik), **ben·thon·ic** (ben-thon′ik), *adj.*

bent·wood (bent′wood), *n.* wood that is bent permanently into various shapes and used to make furniture.

be·numb (bi-num′), *v.t.* to deprive of sensation; stupefy; deaden.

Ben·ze·drine (ben′zē-drēn), *n.* amphetamine: a trademark.

ben·zene (ben′zēn, ben-zēn′), *n.* a flammable, poisonous liquid, obtained from coal gas or coal tar and used as a solvent, in varnishes, etc.

ben·zine (ben′zēn, ben-zēn′), *n.* a flammable liquid obtained from petroleum and used as a motor fuel and as a solvent.

ben·zo·ate (ben′zō-āt), *n.* a salt or ester of benzoic acid.

ben·zo·caine (ben′zō-kān), *n.* a white, crystalline powder used in an unguent to prevent sunburn and as a local anesthetic.

ben·zo·ic (ben-zō′ik), *adj.* of, pertaining to, or obtained from benzoin.

benzoic acid, a white, crystalline acid obtained from toluene, used in dyes and as a preservative and antiseptic.

ben·zo·in (ben′zō-in, ′zoin), *n.* 1. the resinous juice of certain tropical Asiatic trees, used as incense, in perfumes, and in medicine. 2. any one of certain aromatic plants of the laurel family, especially the spicebush of eastern North America. 3. a white, crystalline substance used in antiseptic ointments.

ben·zol (ben′zōl, ′zôl), *n.* same as **benzene.**

be·queath (bi-kwēth′, -kwēth′), *v.t.* 1. to leave by will. 2. to hand down; transmit. —**be·queath′al,** *n.*

be·quest (-kwest′), *n.* 1. the act of leaving by will. 2. something left by will; a legacy.

be·rate (bi-rāt′), *v.t.* -rat′ed, -rat′ing, to scold or rebuke severely.

Ber·ber (bûr′bēr), *n.* any member of a Moslem people of northern Africa: *adj.* of this people or their culture or language.

ber·ber·ine (bûr′bē-rēn, -bēr-in), *n.* a bitter,

yellow alkaloid obtained from the barberry and other plants, used in dyeing and as a drug.

ber-ceuse (ber-sooz'), n. 1. a lullaby. 2. a soothing, lullabylike musical composition.

be-reave (bi-rēv'), v.t. -reaved' or -reft' (-reft'), -reav'ing, 1. to deprive; rob (of). 2. to leave desolate and lonely, as by death. —be-reave'ment, n.

be-ret (bĕ-rā'), n. a flat, round cap of felt, wool, etc.

berg (bŭrg), n. same as iceberg.

ber-ga-mot (bŭr'gá-mot), n. 1. a kind of citrus fruit grown in southern Europe: it is pear-shaped and yields an oil used in perfumery. 2. the oil. 3. any of several kinds of mint that grow in North America.

ber-i-ber-i (ber'i-ber-i), n. a deficiency disease characterized by nerve damage, emaciation, weakness, etc. and caused by lack of vita-min B1, thiamine.

berke-li-um (bŭr'kli-ŭm), n. a radioactive chemical element produced artificially.

ber-lin (bĕr-lin'), n. 1. a four-wheeled closed carriage with a separate platform at the back. 2. [sometimes B-], a fine, soft wool yarn: also called Berlin wool.

berm, berme (bŭrm), n. the shoulder of a paved road.

Ber-mu-da onion (bĕr-mū'dá), a large, mild on-ion grown in California, Texas, etc.

ber-ry (ber'i), n., pl. -ries, 1. any small, pulpy or succulent fruit, as the strawberry, goose-berry, blackberry, etc. 2. in Botany, any pulpy fruit with a thin skin, as a tomato or grape. 3. the dry kernel of several plants, as a coffee bean or wheat seed. 4. an egg of a crayfish, lobster, etc.: v.i. -ried, -ry-ing, 1. to bear or produce berries. 2. to hunt for and gather berries. —ber'ry-like, adj.

ber-serk (bĕr-sŭrk'), adj. & adv. in or into a wild frenzy or destructive rage: n. same as berserker.

ber-serk-er ('ẽr), n. 1. any one of the warriors of Norse legend who became wrought up into a state of mad rage or fury before a battle. 2. one who acts like a berserker.

berth (bŭrth), n. 1. enough space at sea for a ship to stay clear of another ship, the shore, etc. 2. the space a ship occupies at anchor-age or in port. 3. a position, job, etc. 4. a sleeping place, especially a built-in bed, as for a passenger in a ship or train: v.t. 1. to allot a berth to. 2. to put into a berth: v.i. to come into a berth.

ber-tha (bŭr'thá), n. a woman's broad collar, often of lace.

Ber-til-lon system (bŭr'ti-lon), a system of identifying persons through records of body measurements and other physical character-istics.

ber-yl (ber'il), n. a hard, lustrous mineral of varying colors, commonly green or green-ish-blue: emerald and aquamarine are kinds of beryl.

be-ryl-li-um (bĕ-ril'i-ŭm), n. a rare, silver-white, metallic chemical element.

be-seech (bi-sēch'), v.t. -sought' or -seeched', -seech'ing, 1. to entreat; implore. 2. to beg eagerly for. —be-seech'ing-ly, adj.

be-seem (bi-sēm'), v.i. to be suitable (to).

be-set (bi-set'), v.t. -set', -set'ting, 1. to set or stud; distribute thickly over. 2. to assail from all sides. 3. to surround. —be-set'ment, n.

be-set-ting ('ing), adj. habitually attacking or coming upon.

be-shrew (bi-shrōō'), v.t. [Archaic], to wish a curse upon; wish evil to.

be-side (bi-sid'), prep. 1. at the side of; near. 2. apart from. 3. not relevant to. 4. com-pared with. 5. in addition to.

be-sides (-sidz'), adv. 1. more than that; in ad-dition. 2. else. 3. furthermore: prep. 1. over and above; in addition to. 2. separate or distinct from; aside from.

be-siege (bi-sēj'), v.t. -sieged', -sieg'ing, 1. to encompass with armed forces; lay siege to. 2. to advance upon. 3. to beset or harass. —be-sieg'er, n.

be-smear (bi-smir'), v.t. to smear over.

be-smirch (bi-smŭrch'), v.t. 1. to soil; dirty. 2. to sully or dishonor.

be-som (bē'zŏm), n. a broom; specifically, one made of twigs tied around a stick.

be-sot (bi-sot'), v.t. -sot'ted, -sot'ting, 1. to stupefy, as with alcoholic drink. 2. to in-fatuate. —be-sot'ted, adj.

be-span-gle (bi-spang'gl), v.t. -gled, -gling, 1. to adorn with spangles. 2. to dot or sprinkle with something that glitters.

be-spat-ter (bi-spat'ẽr), v.t. 1. to soil by spatter-ing. 2. to asperse with calumny.

be-speak (bi-spēk'), v.t. -spoke', -spo'ken or -spoke', -speak'ing, 1. to speak for before-hand; order or arrange in advance. 2. to in-dicate in advance; presage. 3. to be a reve-lation of; show forth.

be-spec-ta-cled (bi-spek'tá-kld), adj. wearing spectacles.

be-spread (bi-spred'), v.t. -spread', -spread'ing, to spread over.

be-sprin-kle (bi-spring'kl), v.t. -kled, -kling, to sprinkle over.

Bessemer converter, the container holding the molten pig iron in the Bessemer process.

Bes-se-mer process (bes'ĕ-mẽr), a process of making steel by forcing air through molten pig iron in a large container to burn out impurities.

best (best), adj. superlative of good, 1. having the highest degree of goodness or excel-lence; of the first quality or standing. 2. most desirable, suitable, advantageous, etc. 3. largest: adv. superlative of well. 1. in the highest degree; most. 2. in the most excel-lent manner: n. 1. the finest, most excellent, most suitable person, thing, situation, etc. 2. the utmost endeavor; all one can do or show. 3. superiority, or advantage over (with of): v.t. to get the better of; surpass; outwit.

bes-tial (bes'chál, 'tyál; bēs'chál), adj. 1. of an animal or animals. 2. typical or suggestive of a beast; brutal, vile, coarse, etc. —bes-ti-al-i-ty (bes-chi-al'i-ti, bēs-ti-), n., pl. -ties. —bes'tial-ly, adv.

bes-tial-ize (bes'chá-liz, 'tyá-; bēs'chá-), v.t. -ized, -iz-ing, to make like a beast; degrade to the level of a brute.

bes-ti-ar-y (bes'chi-er-i, 'ti-; bēs'chi-), n. a medieval book combining descriptions of real or mythical animals with fables about them designed to teach a lesson.

be-stir (bi-stür'), *v.t.* -stirred', -stir'ring, to rouse (oneself) to brisk or vigorous action.

best man, the principal attendant of the bridegroom at a wedding ceremony.

be-stow (bi-stō'), *v.t.* 1. to give or confer (often followed by *on* or *upon*). 2. to use or apply, as time, effort, etc. —be-stow'al, *n.*

be-strew (bi-strō̄'), *v.t.* -strewed', -strewed' or -strewn', -strew'ing, to strew or scatter over or about.

be-stride (bi-strīd'), *v.t.* -strode', -strid'den, -strid'ing, to stand or sit on with legs astride; straddle.

bet (bet), *v.t.* bet or bet'ted, bet'ting, 1. to stake or pledge (money, etc.) on the event of a future contingency. 2. to assert as in a bet. 3. to wager with (someone): *v.i.* to lay a wager: *n.* 1. the act of wagering. 2. that which is laid, staked, or pledged on any event or contest the issue of which is uncertain. 3. the terms on which a bet is arranged.

be-ta (bāt'ä), *n.* the second letter of the Greek alphabet.

be-take (bi-tāk'), *v.t.* -took', -tak'en, -tak'ing, to take or cause (oneself) to go somewhere.

beta particle, a radioactive particle ejected at high velocity from a disintegrating radioactive nucleus.

beta ray, 1. same as beta particle. 2. a stream of beta particles.

be-ta-tron (bāt'ä-tron), *n.* an apparatus used to accelerate electrons and keep them in a focused circular path.

be-tel (bēt'l), *n.* a tropical Asian plant of the pepper family: its leaves, along with betel nut and lime, are used for chewing by some Asian peoples.

betel nut, the fruit of the betel palm.

betel palm, a palm tree of southeastern Asia.

bête noire (bāt nwär'), *pl.* bêtes noires (bāt nwärz'), [French, black beast], a bugbear; something one fears or dreads.

beth (bāth, beth), *n.* the second letter of the Hebrew alphabet: also bet (bāt, bet).

beth-el (beth'él), *n.* 1. a hallowed spot. 2. a seamen's chapel or church.

be-think (bi-think'), *v.t.* -thought', -think'ing, to cause (oneself) to think (*of* something), reflect, etc.

be-tide (bi-tīd'), *v.t. & v.i.* -tid'ed, -tid'ing, to happen (to); befall.

be-times (bi-tīmz'), *adv.* in good season or time; sufficiently early.

be-to-ken (bi-tō'k'n), *v.t.* 1. to indicate by signs; serve as a sign or token of. 2. to foreshadow; show ahead of time.

bet-o-ny (bet'n-i), *n.* a plant of the mint family, with white, yellow, or lavender flowers.

be-tray (bi-trā'), *v.t.* 1. to deliver into the hands of an enemy by treachery. 2. to be a traitor to (one's country), especially by helping an enemy. 3. to violate by fraud or unfaithfulness. 4. to reveal (a secret, etc.) in a breach of confidence. 5. to disclose inadver-

tently. 6. to lead astray; especially, to seduce and desert (a woman). 7. to indicate or show. —be-tray'al, *n.* —be-tray'er, *n.*

be-troth (bi-trōth', -trôth'), *v.t.* to promise in marriage; affiance.

be-troth-al (-'ál), *n.* 1. the act of engaging to marry. 2. the state of being engaged. 3. an engagement to marry by mutual promise. Also **be-troth'ment** ('mént).

be-trothed (-trōthd', -trôtht'), *n.* the person one is engaged to marry: *adj.* engaged to be married.

bet-ta (bet'ä), *n.* a brightly colored tropical fish often kept in aquariums.

bet-ter (bet'ẽr), *adj.* comparative of good. 1. having good qualities in a greater degree than another. 2. preferable or more suitable. 3. improved in health. 4. larger; more than half: *adv.* comparative of well. 1. in a superior or more excellent manner. 2. more correctly or thoroughly. 3. in a higher degree. 4. more in extent: *v.t.* 1. to improve; increase the good qualities of. 2. to surpass; excel; outdo: *v.i.* to become better: *n.* 1. a superior; one who has a claim to precedence. 2. superiority, or advantage over (with *of*). 3. a thing, circumstance, etc. that is superior.

better half, [Slang], one's spouse.

bet-ter-ment (-mént), *n.* 1. a being made better or a becoming better; improvement. 2. the improvement of land or property.

bet-tor (bet'ẽr), *n.* one who places bets: also, less frequently, spelled bet'ter.

be-tween (bi-twēn'), *prep.* 1. in, of, or through the space, interval, etc. separating (two). 2. in intermediate relation to (two). 3. from one to the other of. 4. by the common action or effect of. 5. in the united possession of. 6. involving or connecting. 7. excluding all except the two of. 8. excluding all except one or the other of (two): *adv.* in an intervening space, time, position, etc.

be-tween-times ('tīmz'), *adv.* between periods involving some activity, condition, etc.: also **be-tween'whiles** ('hwīlz).

be-twixt (bi-twikst'), *prep. & adv.* between: now only in betwixt and between, in an undecided or middle position or situation.

bev, Bev (bev), *n., pl.* bev, Bev, a billion electron-volts.

bev-el (bev'l), *v.t.* bev'eled or bev'elled, bev'eling or bev'el-ling, to cut at a slant: *v.i.* to incline; slant: *n.* 1. an angle other than a right angle. 2. the inclination which one surface makes with another when not at right angles; also, a surface or part so angled. 3. a rule with a movable arm, for drawing or measuring angles and for adjusting surfaces to a given slant: also called **bevel square**: *adj.* sloped; beveled.

bevel gear, a gear in which the shaft of the driving wheel forms an angle with the shaft of the wheel that is driven.

bev-er-age (bev'rij, -'ẽr-ij), *n.* any drinkable liquid, especially other than ordinary water.

bev-y (bev'i), *n., pl.* bev'ies, 1. a company or assembly of persons, especially of girls or women. 2. a flock of quails, larks, etc.

be-wail (bi-wāl'), *v.t.* to mourn or weep aloud

for; lament: *v.i.* to wail. —be·wail'er, *n.* —be·wail'ment, *n.*

be·ware (bi-wer'), *v.i.* & *v.t.* -wared', -war'ing, to be on one's guard (against); be wary or cautious (of).

be·wil·der (bi-wil'dĕr), *v.t.* to lead into perplexity or confusion; puzzle. —be·wil'der·ing, *adj.*

be·wil·der·ment (-mĕnt), *n.* 1. the state of being greatly puzzled or perplexed. 2. a tangle; confusion; muddle.

be·witch (bi-wich'), *v.t.* 1. to cast a spell over; subject to witchcraft. 2. to charm beyond the power of resistance; fascinate. —be·witch'ing, *adj.*

be·witch·ment ('mĕnt), *n.* 1. fascination; charm. 2. power of bewitching. 3. a spell that bewitches. Also be·witch'er·y ('ĕr-i), *pl.* -er·ies.

be·wray (bi-rā'), *v.t.* [Archaic], to expose; reveal; betray.

bey (bā), *n.* formerly, 1. a governor of a province or district of the Turkish Empire. 2. the native ruler of Tunis (a former native state).

be·yond (bi-yond'), *prep.* 1. on or to the far side of; past. 2. outside the reach of. 3. later than. 4. above; exceeding or surpassing. 5. in addition to: *adv.* 1. farther out or away. 2. in addition: *n.* the state of existence that follows death (with *the*): often the great beyond.

bez antler (bez, bāz), the second branch of a stag's horn, next to the base.

bez·el (bez'l), *n.* 1. a sloped edge, as of a cutting tool. 2. the faceted part of a cut jewel. 3. the grooved rim holding a gem, watch crystal, etc. in place.

be·zique (bi-zēk'), *n.* a card game somewhat like pinochle, played with 64 cards.

be·zoar (bē'zôr), *n.* a concretion found in the intestines of certain animals, formerly supposed to be an antidote for poisons.

bhang, bang (bang), *n.* 1. the hemp plant, or its fiber, leaves, etc. 2. a drug, such as hashish, prepared from the dried leaves and flowers of this plant, which have narcotic and intoxicating properties.

bhees·ty, bhees·tie (bēs'ti), *n., pl.* bhees'ties, in India, a water carrier, as for military troops.

bi-, a prefix meaning *two, twice, doubly.*

bi·an·nu·al (bī-an'yoo-wăl), *adj.* occurring twice in a year; semiannual. —bi·an'nu·al·ly, *adv.*

bi·as (bī'ăs), *n., pl.* bi'as·es, 1. a line that is diagonal or oblique to the weave of cloth, as in making a seam. 2. in *Bowls,* the bulge in the ball, allowing the ball to roll in a curve. 3. propensity; inclination. 4. preconceived judgment or opinion; prejudice: *v.t.* bi'ased or bi'assed, bi'as·ing or bi'as·sing, to influence or prejudice: *adj.* slanting; diagonal: *adv.* in a slanting manner; obliquely.

bi·ath·lon (bī-ath'lŏn), *n.* a winter athletic game in the Olympics, combining marksmanship with a skiing competition.

bi·au·ric·u·late (bī-ô-rik'yoo-lit), *adj.* having two auricles: also bi·au·ric'u·lar (-lēr).

bi·ax·i·al (bī-ak'si-ăl), *adj.* having two axes, as some crystals. —bi·ax'i·al·ly, *adv.*

bib (bĭb), *n.* 1. a protective covering tied under an infant's chin at meals. 2. the top of an apron.

bib·ber (bib'ēr), *n.* a drinker; tippler.

bibb lettuce (bib), a kind of lettuce with dark-green leaves in loose heads.

bib·cock (bib'kok), *n.* a faucet with a nozzle turned downward.

bi·be·lot (bē-blō', bib'lō), *n.* [French], a small, artistic object or decorative trinket.

Bi·ble (bī'bl), *n.* 1. the writings of the Old and New Testament, which together constitute the sacred book of Christianity. 2. the writings of the Old Testament, the Holy Scriptures of Judaism. 3. the sacred writings of any religion, as the Koran. 4. a copy or edition of the Christian or Jewish Bible or of the sacred writings of any religion. 5. [b.] any book or publication viewed as authoritative in some field.

Bib·li·cal (bib'li-kl), *adj.* [also b-], 1. of, pertaining to, or in the Bible; scriptural. 2. in harmony with or like that in the Bible. —Bib'li·cal·ly, *adv.*

bib·li·og·ra·pher (bib·li-og'ră-fĕr), *n.* 1. a specialist in bibliography. 2. a compiler of a bibliography.

bib·li·og·ra·phy (bib·li-og'ră-fi), *n., pl.* -phies, 1. the study of the authorship, editions, etc. of books and other writings. 2. a list of writings classified by subject, author, period, etc. 3. a list of source or reference materials used for or related to a book, article, etc. —bib·li·o·graph'ic (-ô-graf'ik), bib·li·o·graph'i·cal, *adj.*

bib·li·ol·a·try (bib·li-ol'ă-tri), *n.* 1. exaggerated reverence for the literal meaning of sayings and stories in the Bible. 2. excessive love of books. —bib·li·ol'a·ter, *n.* —bib·li·ol'a·trous, *adj.*

bib·li·o·ma·ni·a (bib·li-ô-mā'ni-ă), *n.* a mania for collecting books, especially rare and curious ones. —bib·li·o·ma'ni·ac (-ak), *n.* & *adj.* —bib·li·o·ma·ni'a·cal (-ni'ă-kl), *adj.*

bib·li·op·e·gy (bib·li-op'ē-ji), *n.* the art of bookbinding. —bib·li·op'e·gist, *n.*

bib·li·o·phile (bib'li-ô-fīl), *n.* 1. a lover of books. 2. a collector of books. —bib·li·o·phil'ic (-fil'ik), *adj.*

bib·li·oph·i·lism (bib·li-of'i-lizm), *n.* love of books.

bib·li·o·pole (bib'li-ô-pōl), *n.* a bookseller, especially one who deals in rare works.

bib·li·o·the·ca (bib·li-ô-thē'kă), *n.* 1. a library. 2. a bookseller's catalog.

bib·u·lous (bib'yoo-lŭs), *adj.* 1. very absorbent. 2. given, especially excessively, to alcoholic liquor. —bib'u·lous·ness, *n.*

bi·cam·er·al (bi-kam'ēr-ăl), *adj.* of, pertaining to, or consisting of two legislative chambers. —bi·cam'er·al·ism, *n.*

bi·car·bon·ate (bī-kär'bŏ-nit), *n.* an acid salt of carbonic acid.

bicarbonate of soda, same as sodium bicarbonate.

bice (bīs), *n.* 1. a blue or green pigment obtained from an ore of copper. 2. a shade of blue duller than azure.

---

bi·cen·te·nar·y (bī-sen-ten'ēr-i), *adj. & n., pl.* **-nar·ies,** same as **bicentennial.**

bi·cen·ten·ni·al (-ten'i-âl), *adj.* marking a period or duration of two hundred years: *n.* a bicentennial anniversary or its celebration. —**bi·cen·ten'ni·al·ly,** *adv.*

bi·ceph·a·lous (bī-sef'à-lùs), *adj.* having two heads: also **bi·ce·phal·ic** (bī-sē-fal'ik).

bi·ceps (bī'seps), *n., pl.* **bi'ceps** or **bi'ceps·es,** a muscle with two points of origin, as the large flexor muscle of the upper part of the arm.

bi·chlo·ride (bī-klôr'īd), *n.* a compound having two atoms of chlorine for each atom of another element.

bi·chro·mate (bī-krō'māt), same as **dichromate.**

bi·cip·i·tal (bī-sip'ī-tâl), *adj.* 1. having two points of origin, as a biceps muscle. 2. of or pertaining to a biceps.

bick·er (bik'ēr), *v.i.* 1. to engage in a petty altercation; squabble. 2. to quiver, flicker, patter, etc.: *n.* a petty altercation; squabble. —**bick'er·er,** *n.*

bi·col·or (bī'kul-ēr), *adj.* of two colors: also **bi'col·ored.**

bi·con·cave (bī-kon-kāv'), *adj.* concave on both sides.

bi·con·vex (bī-kon-veks'), *adj.* convex on both sides.

bi·corn (bī'kôrn), *adj.* having two horns or hornlike projections: also **bi·cor·nu·ate** (bī-kôr'nyoo-wit).

bi·cor·po·ral (bī-kôr'pēr-âl), *adj.* having two bodies: also **bi·cor·po·re·al** (bī-kôr-pôr'i-âl).

bi·cus·pid (-kus'pid), *adj.* **bi·cus·pi·date** ('pi-dāt), *adj.* having two points: *n.* one of the two double-pointed teeth forming the first pair of molars on either side of the jaw, above and below.

bi·cy·cle (bī'si-kl), *n.* a vehicle consisting of two wire-spoked wheels placed in line and connected by a tubular frame that supports a saddle for the rider: it is propelled by pedals and has handlebars for steering: *v.i.* -cled, -cling, to ride a bicycle. —**bi'cy·clist,** **bi'cy·cler,** *n.*

bid (bid), *v.t.* **bade** or **bid, bid'den** or **bid, bid'ding,** 1. to command; ask; order or direct. 2. to offer or express (greetings, farewell, etc.): *v.i.* to seem: in **bid fair,** to seem likely (to be or do something): *n.* [Informal], an invitation. —**bid'der,** *n.*

bid (bid), *n.* 1. the offer of a price, as at an auction or sale; also, the price offered. 2. in *card games,* the proposal to get a specified number of tricks, points, etc.; also, the number specified. 3. a turn or chance to offer a price or, in cards, to propose a goal. 4. a try for something: *v.t. & v.i.* **bid, bid, bid'ding,** 1. to offer (a price). 2. in *card games,* to propose (a goal). —**bid'der,** *n.*

bid (bid), *n.* a try for something, as victory over competitors, the winning of support or sympathy, etc.: *v.i.* **bid, bid, bid'ding,** to make such a try.

bid·da·ble (bid'à-bl), *adj.* 1. docile; obedient. 2. denoting a hand or suit in cards that is acceptable for bidding.

bid·ding ('ing), *n.* 1. an order; command. 2. a summons. 3. the act of making a bid or bids, as at an auction.

bid·dy (bid'i), *n., pl.* **bid'dies,** 1. a fowl or chicken. 2. [Slang], an older woman, especially when gossipy, sharp-tongued, etc.

bide (bīd), *v.i.* **bode** or **bid'ed, bid'ed, bid'ing,** [Archaic or Dialectal], 1. to reside. 2. to continue. 3. to wait: *v.i.* 1. [Archaic or Dialectal], to endure. 2. to await: standard in **bide one's time,** to wait patiently for the right moment.

bi·den·tate (bī-den'tāt), *adj.* having two teeth or toothlike processes.

bi·det (bi-dā'), *n.* a low, basinlike fixture used in bathing the crotch.

bi·en·ni·al (bī-en'i-âl), *adj.* 1. occurring every two years. 2. continuing or existing for two years, as some plants: *n.* 1. a biennial occurrence, celebration, etc. 2. a plant that lives two years, producing roots and leaves the first year and flowers, fruit, and seed the second year. —**bi·en'ni·al·ly,** *adv.*

bier (bir), *n.* a frame or stand on which a coffin or corpse is placed.

bi·fa·cial (bī-fā'shâl), *adj.* 1. having two faces or principal surfaces. 2. having its opposite faces alike. 3. in *Botany,* having its opposite surfaces different.

bi·far·i·ous (bī-fer'i-ûs), *adj.* in *Botany,* arranged in two rows.

biff (bif), *n.* [Slang], a hit or blow: *v.t.* [Slang], to hit.

bi·fid (bi'fid), *adj.* partially divided into two by a cleft; forked. —**bi·fid'i·ty** ('i-ti), *n.* —**bi·fid·ly,** *adv.*

bi·fi·lar (bī-fī'lēr), *adj.* two-threaded; fitted with two threads or filaments.

bi·fo·cal (bī-fō'kl), *adj.* denoting a lens with two parts, one ground for near focus and one for distant focus: *n.* 1. a lens made like this. 2. *pl.* (bī'fō-klz), eyeglasses fitted with bifocal lenses.

bi·fo·li·ate (bī-fō'li-it, -āt), *adj.* in *Botany,* having two leaves.

bi·fur·cate (bī'fēr-kāt, bī-fûr'-; -kit), *adj.* divided into two branches; forked: *v.i. & v.t.* (bī'fēr-kāt, bī-fûr'-), -cat·ed, -cat·ing, to divide into two branches; fork. —**bi·fur·ca'tion,** *n.*

big (big), *adj.* **big'ger, big'gest,** 1. of great bulk, magnitude, capacity, force, etc. 2. grown up. 3. visibly pregnant. 4. important. 5. full; inflated. 6. pompous. 7. noble: *adv.* [Informal], 1. pompously. 2. importantly. 3. in a big way. —**big'ness,** *n.*

big·a·my (big'à-mi), *n., pl.* **-mies,** the crime of contracting a second marriage while a first marriage is still legally in effect. —**big'a·mist,** *n.* —**big'a·mous,** *adj.*

Big Dipper, a group of stars in dipperlike formation in the constellation Ursa Major (Great Bear).

big game, large wild animals hunted for sport, as lions.

big·gish (big'ish), *adj.* somewhat big.

big·head·ed (big'hed-id), *adj.* [Informal], conceited. —**big'head·ed·ness,** *n.*

big·heart·ed ('här-tid), *adj.* quick to give or forgive; generous. —**big'heart·ed·ly,** *adv.* —**big'heart·ed·ness,** *n.*

big·horn ('hôrn), *n.*, *pl.* **big'horns, big'horn,** a wild sheep of the Rocky Mountains, having shaggy hair and large, curved horns.

bight (bīt), *n.* 1. a loop or bend of a rope, in distinction from the ends. 2. a bend or curve in a coastline, forming a bay. 3. a bay so formed: *v.t.* to fasten with a bight.

big-league (big'lēg'), *adj.* 1. denoting a team, player, etc. of one of the major leagues in baseball. 2. [Informal], at a top level; important.

big-mouthed ('mouthd), *adj.* [Slang], talking too much or too loudly, especially in a self-important manner.

big·no·ni·a (big-nō'ni-â), *n.* any one of a genus of American tropical climbing plants with showy, trumpet-shaped flowers.

big·ot (big'ôt), *n.* 1. one who is unreasonably and blindly attached to a particular creed, church, party, or opinion. 2. one who is bitterly intolerant of the opinions or beliefs of others. 3. one who is odiously hostile toward people of a different race, religion, etc. —**big'ot·ed,** *adj.*

big·ot·ry (big'ô-tri), *n.*, *pl.* **-ries,** the state or condition of being a bigot; bitter intolerance; prejudice.

big shot, [Slang], an important person.

big time, 1. originally, vaudeville performed only in the large cities, with good pay. 2. the level regarded as the highest or best in any profession, occupation, etc. 3. a very enjoyable time. —**big'-time',** *adj.*

big top, [Informal], 1. the principal tent of a circus. 2. a circus, or circus life.

big·wig (big'wig), *n.* [Informal], a person of importance: usually used ironically.

bi·jou (bē'zhōō), *n.*, *pl.* **bi·joux** ('zhōōz), 1. a jewel. 2. any small and elegantly finished article.

bi·jou·te·rie (bi-zhōōt'ēr-i), *n.* jewelry or trinkets in general.

bike (bīk), *n.* [Informal], 1. a bicycle. 2. a motorcycle: *v.i.* **biked, bik'ing,** to ride on a bicycle or motorcycle.

bi·ki·ni (bi-kē'ni), *n.* a woman's scanty two-piece bathing suit.

bi·la·bi·al (bī-lā'bi-âl), *adj.* 1. of or having two lips. 2. in *Phonetics,* denoting a sound, as of *p* or *b,* made by bringing the lips together: *n.* a bilabial sound.

bi·la·bi·ate (bī-lā'bi-it), *adj.* in *Botany,* having two lips.

bil·an·der (bil'ân-dēr), *n.* a small, two-masted Dutch ship, used on canals and along the coast.

bi·lat·er·al (bī-lat'ēr-âl), *adj.* 1. of, having, or implicating two sides. 2. having an equal influence on both sides; reciprocal. 3. symmetrically arranged on both sides of a central line. —**bi·lat'er·al·ism,** *n.* —**bi·lat'er·al·ly,** *adv.*

bil·ber·ry (bil'ber-i), *n.*, *pl.* **-ries,** 1. a kind of North American blueberry. 2. its fruit.

bil·bo (bil'bō), *n.*, *pl.* **-boes,** 1. [Archaic], a rapier or sword. 2. *pl.* a long iron bar with sliding shackles for the feet, and a lock at the end, formerly used as fetters.

bile (bīl), *n.* 1. the yellow, bitter fluid secreted by the liver and found in the gallbladder: it helps in the digestion of fats. 2. anger; bitterness; choler.

bile-stone (bīl'stōn), *n.* same as **gallstone.**

bilge (bilj), *n.* 1. the bulging, rounded part of a ship's bottom. 2. the dirty water that accumulates there: also **bilge water.** 3. [Slang], nonsense: *v.t. & v.i.* **bilged, bilg'ing,** to break open in the bilge area.

bilge keel, a piece of timber secured lengthwise on either side of a ship's bilge to prevent heavy rolling: also **bilge piece.**

bil·i·ar·y (bil'i-er-i), *adj.* 1. of, pertaining to, or conveying the bile. 2. bilious.

bi·lin·e·ar (bī-lin'i-ēr), *adj.* of or having to do with two lines.

bi·lin·gual (bī-ling'gwâl), *adj.* 1. of or in two languages. 2. able to speak two languages equally well. —**bi·lin'gual·ism,** *n.* —**bi·lin'gual·ly,** *adv.*

bil·ious (bil'yûs), *adj.* 1. of or pertaining to the bile. 2. having or arising from a liver disorder. 3. looking or feeling as though one were suffering from such a disorder. 4. choleric; cross; peevish. —**bil'ious·ly,** *adv.* —**bil'ious·ness,** *n.*

bil·i·ru·bin (bil-i-rōō'bin), *n.* a reddish substance found in the bile and, in jaundiced persons, in the blood and urine.

bi·lit·er·al (bī-lit'ēr-âl), *adj.* consisting of two letters: *n.* a word, syllable, etc. made up of two letters.

bilk (bilk), *v.t.* 1. to thwart. 2. to defraud; cheat. 3. to evade payment of. 4. to elude. —**bilk'er,** *n.*

bill (bil), *n.* 1. an account for goods sold, services rendered, or work done. 2. a bill of exchange, or any promissory note. 3. a bank note or piece of paper money. 4. a draft of a proposed statute presented to a legislature. 5. a list of items, as on a menu or playbill. 6. a poster or handbill: *v.t.* 1. to present a bill of charges to. 2. to make out a bill of (items). 3. to advertise by bills. 4. to book (an actor, play, etc.). —**bill'a·ble,** *adj.* —**bill'er,** *n.*

bill (bil), *n.* 1. the beak of a bird. 2. a mouth part like this, as that of a turtle: *v.i.* 1. to touch bills together, as doves. 2. to give caresses: now especially in **bill and coo.**

bill (bil), *n.* 1. same as **billhook.** 2. a battle-ax with a long staff, used by infantry in ancient times. 3. the extremity of the fluke of an anchor.

bill·a·bong (bil'â-bong), *n.* in Australia, 1. a channel branching off from a river to form a pool or lagoon. 2. a branch or channel that returns to join a river.

bill-board (bil'bôrd), *n.* 1. a flat, vertical surface on which advertisements are posted. 2. a ledge at the bow of a ship.

bil·let (bil'it), *n.* 1. an order, as to a householder, to provide lodging for military personnel. 2. the lodging assigned. 3. a sleeping place for a seaman on a ship. 4. a job; position: *v.t.* 1. to assign lodging to by billet. 2. to assign a position to: *v.i.* to be billeted; lodge.

bil·let (bil'it), *n.* 1. a small stick or log, as for fuel. 2. a loglike ornamentation in a Norman molding. 3. a small, unfinished metal bar.

bil·let-doux (bil-i-dōō′), *n., pl.* **bil·lets-doux** (bil-i-dōōz′), [French], a love letter.

bill-fish (bil′fish), *n., pl.* **-fish, -fish·es**, any of various fishes having long, sharp heads, as many gars.

bill-fold (bil′fōld), *n.* a flat case for carrying paper money, credit cards, etc. in the pocket; wallet.

bill-head (′hed), *n.* a form for billing charges, with the biller's name, address, etc. printed on it.

bill-hook (bil′hook), *n.* a cutting tool with a blade that is hook-shaped at the point, used especially in pruning.

bil·liard (bil′yērd), *adj.* of or for billiards.

bil·liards (bil′yērdz), *n.* 1. a game played with three balls driven by cues on a rectangular, cloth-covered table that has raised, cushioned edges. 2. any of several similar games: compare **pool**.

bill-ing (bil′ing), *n.* 1. a list of actors' names, as on a playbill. 2. the order in which the names are listed.

bil·lings·gate (bil′ingz-gāt), *n.* coarse, vulgar speech filled with gross insults and foul vituperation: after *Billingsgate*, a fish market in London.

bil·lion (bil′yun), *n.* 1. in the U.S. and France, a thousand millions. 2. in Great Britain and Germany, a million millions: *adj.* consisting of a billion. —**bil·lionth**, *adj. & n.*

bil·lion·aire (bil-yu-ner′), *n.* one whose assets are worth a billion or more dollars, pounds, etc.

bill of exchange, a written order from one person or house to another to pay to the person designated a certain sum of money; draft.

bill of fare, a menu, or list of foods served.

bill of health, a certificate testifying to the presence or absence of infectious disease aboard a ship or in the port from which it is departing, to be shown by the captain at the ship's next port.

bill of lading, a document specifying goods shipped, acknowledging their receipt, and promising safe delivery to the consignee.

bill of rights, 1. a list of people's rights viewed as fundamental. 2. [B- R-], the first ten amendments of the U.S. Constitution, guaranteeing to the people certain rights, as freedom of speech and the right to assemble.

bill of sale, an instrument for the conveyance or transfer of goods, property, etc.

bil·lon (bil′ŏn), *n.* an alloy of gold or silver with a large proportion of copper or other base metal, used in coinage.

bil·low (bil′ō), *n.* 1. a great wave; large swell of water. 2. any great, swelling surge, as of sound, fog, etc.: *v.i.* to rise and roll in large waves or surges: *v.t.* to make billow.

bil·low·y (′ō-wi), *adj.* **-low·i·er, -low·i·est**, swelling or rolling like a billow or billows. — **bil′low·i·ness**, *n.*

bill-post·er (bil′pōs-tēr), *n.* one whose work is posting advertisements: also **bill′stick·er**. — **bill′post·ing**, *n.*

bil·ly (bil′i), *n., pl.* **-lies**, 1. a policeman's club. 2. a can or teapot used in outdoor cooking in Australia.

bil·ly-cock (bil′i-kok), *n.* [British Informal], a low-crowned felt hat.

billy goat, [Informal], a male goat.

bi·lo·bate (bī-lō′bāt), *adj.* divided into two lobes: also **bi·lo′bat·ed, bi-lobed′**.

bil·tong (bil′tông), *n.* in South Africa, dried strips of meat.

bi·ma·nous (bī-mā′nŭs, bim′ā-), *adj.* having two hands.

bi·man·u·al (bī-man′yoo-wăl), *adj.* done with two hands; requiring the use of both hands. —**bi·man′u·al·ly**, *adv.*

bi·me·tal·lic (bī-mē-tal′ik), *adj.* 1. of, consisting of, or pertaining to two metals. 2. of or pertaining to bimetallism.

bi·met·al·lism (bī-met′ăl-izm), *n.* 1. the legalized adoption of two metals (as gold and silver) as the monetary standard, at a fixed ratio. 2. the principles or theories advocating or supporting this. —**bi·met′al·list**, *n.*

bi·month·ly (bī-munth′li), *adj. & adv.* 1. once every two months. 2. twice a month: in this usage, *semimonthly* is preferred: *n., pl.* **-lies**, a publication that comes out once every two months.

bin (bin), *n.* a receptacle or enclosure for storing coal, corn, etc.

bi·na·ry (bī′nēr-i), *adj.* 1. consisting of two things or parts; twofold. 2. denoting or of a system of numbers having two as the base: *n., pl.* **-ries**, 1. something consisting of two parts. 2. same as **binary star**.

binary star, a double star; two stars that revolve around a common center of gravity.

bi·nate (bī′nāt), *adj.* arranged or growing in pairs, as leaves. —**bi′nate·ly**, *adv.*

bin·au·ral (bī-nôr′ăl), *adj.* 1. of or pertaining to the use of both ears. 2. denoting or of sound reproduction with two sources of sound, giving a stereophonic effect. —**bin·au′ral·ly**, *adv.*

bind (bīnd), *v.t.* **bound, bind′ing,** 1. to confine or make fast with a cord, band, etc. 2. to confine, restrain, or make firm by any physical, moral, or contractual force. 3. to compel or unite by bonds of affection, loyalty, duty, etc. 4. to hinder or restrain. 5. to protect, strengthen, wrap, or gird, as with a band, bandage, border, or covering. 6. to fasten together and enclose the printed pages of (a book, magazine, etc.). 7. to cause to cohere. 8. to constipate. 9. to place under legal obligation. 10. to bind by indenture (often with *out* or *over*): *v.i.* 1. to bind something. 2. to be obligatory. 3. to be tight, stiff, constricting, etc. 4. to stick together: — *n.* 1. anything that binds. 2. a musical tie or slur grouping notes together. 3. [Informal], an awkward situation; predicament; jam.

bind·er (bīn′dēr), *n.* 1. anything that binds. 2. a device on reaping machines for tying bundles of cut grain. 3. a cover for holding papers. 4. a substance that binds things together. 5. a person who binds; specifically, a bookbinder.

---

a in cap, ā in cane, ä in father, ȧ in abet, e in met, ē in be, ē in baker, ė in regent, i in pit, ī in fine, i in manifest, o in hot, ô in horse, ō in bone, .

bind·er·y (bīn'dēr-i), *n.*, *pl.* **-er·ies;** a place where books are bound.

bind·ing (bīn'ding), *n.* 1. the act of one that binds. 2. anything that binds. 3. a bandage, band, etc. 4. the cover of a book. 5. tape, braid, etc. to secure or ornament the edges of cloth. 6. a substance joining ingredients together: *adj.* that binds or obligates.

bind·weed (bīnd'wēd), *n.* any of several twining vines of the morning-glory family.

bine (bīn), *n.* 1. the slender stem of a twining plant. 2. a plant having this kind of stem.

Bi·net-Si·mon test (bi-nā'si'mòn), a test using graded questions, problems, etc. to determine the degree of intelligence, especially of children: also **Binet test**.

binge (binj), *n.* [Informal], 1. a drunken spree. 2. any spree.

bin·go (bing'gō), *n.* a lottolike gambling game, usually with many players.

bin·na·cle (bin'å-kl), *n.* the housing case of a ship's compass.

bin·oc·u·lar (bī-nok'yŭ-lēr, bi-), *adj.* of, for the use of, or using both eyes at once; twoeyed: *n. usually pl.* an optical instrument, as field glasses, designed for use by both eyes at once. **—bin·oc·u·lar'i·ty** (-ler'i-ti), *n.*

bi·no·mi·al (bī-nō'mi-ål), *n.* 1. a mathematical expression consisting of two terms connected by a plus or minus sign. 2. a scientific two-word name for a particular plant or animal, the name of the genus being followed by that of the species: *adj.* 1. of or pertaining to binomials. 2. having or consisting of two terms or two names. **—bi·no'mi·al·ly,** *adv.*

binomial theorem, a formula for showing the expansion of a binomial to a given power without actually doing the multiplications.

bi·o-, a combining form meaning *life, living thing* or *things, biological.*

bi·o·as·say (bī-ō-as'ā, -a-sā'), *n.* a method of determining the potency of a chemical, drug, etc. by comparing its effects to the effects of a standard.

bi·o·as·tro·nau·tics (-as-trô-nôt'iks), *n.* the study of the effects on living things of traveling in outer space or of living there.

bi·o·chem·i·cal (bī-ō-kem'i-kl, bī-ō-), *adj.* of, pertaining to, or involving biochemistry: *n.* a biochemical substance. **—bi·o·chem'i·cal·ly,** *adv.*

bi·o·chem·is·try (-kem'is-tri), *n.* the branch of chemistry having to do with living matter. **—bi·o·chem'ist,** *n.*

bi·o·cide (bī'ō-sīd), *n.* a chemical poison that kills living things. **—bi·o·ci'dal,** *adj.*

bi·o·de·grad·a·ble (bī-ī-di-grā'då-bl), *adj.* easily decomposing through the action of bacteria or by other biological means. **—bi·o·de·grad·a·bil'i·ty,** *n.*

bi·o·en·gi·neer·ing (-en-ji-nir'ing), *n.* the study or application of engineering principles or techniques to medical or biological problems.

bi·o·gen·e·sis (bī-ō-jen'ê-sis, bī-ō-), **bi·o·ge·ny** (bī-oj'ê-ni), *n.* 1. the postulate that living organisms can originate only from other living organisms that are closely akin: opposed to *abiogenesis.* 2. the generation of living organisms from others closely akin. **—bi·o·ge·net·ic** (-jê-net'ik), **bi·o·ge·net'i·cal,** *adj.*

bi·o·ge·og·ra·phy (-ji-og'rå-fi), *n.* the science treating of the distribution of animals and plants. **—bi·o·ge·o·graph'ic,** (-ō-graf'ik), **bi·o·ge·o·graph'i·cal,** *adj.*

bi·og·ra·pher (bī-og'rå-fēr), *n.* a person who writes a biography or biographies.

bi·o·graph·i·cal (bī-ō-graf'i-kl), **bi·o·graph·ic,** *adj.* 1. giving a biography. 2. of, pertaining to, or characteristic of biography. **—bi·o·graph'i·cal·ly,** *adv.*

bi·og·ra·phy (bī-og'rå-fi), *n.* 1. *pl.* **-phies,** the history of the life of a particular person as told by someone else. 2. biographical writings in general.

bi·o·log·i·cal (bī-ō-loj'i-kl), **bi·o·log·ic,** *adj.* 1. of or pertaining to biology. 2. of or having to do with plants and animals. 3. of, involving, or derived from physical life or life processes: *n.* a biological product or preparation. **—bi·o·log'i·cal·ly,** *adv.*

biological clock, a natural rhythmic cycle of the human body or lower organisms in response to such natural phenomena as the seasons or night and day.

biological warfare, warfare involving the deliberate production and dissemination of disease germs, toxins, etc. as a weapon against the enemy.

bi·ol·o·gy (bī-ol'ô-ji), *n.* 1. the science dealing with the origin, life history, physical characteristics, etc. of plants and animals. 2. the flora and fauna of a given area. **—bi·ol·o'gist,** *n.*

bi·o·mass (bī'ō-mas), *n.* the total mass or amount of living things in a given area.

bi·o·med·i·cine (bī-ō-med'i-sn), *n.* medical science combined with and assisted by biological research. **—bi·o·med'i·cal,** *adj.*

bi·o·met·rics (-met'riks), *n.* a branch of biology using statistical data. **—bi·o·met'ric, bi·o·met'ri·cal,** *adj.*

bi·on·ics (bī-on'iks), *n.* the science of designing instruments or systems patterned after living things.

bi·o·nom·ics (bī-ō-nom'iks, bī-ō-), *n.* same as ecology.

bi·o·phys·ics (-fiz'iks), *n.* a science combining biology and physics. **—bi·o·phys'i·cal,** *adj* — **bi·o·phys'i·cist,** *n.*

bi·o·plasm (bī'ō-plazm), *n.* living matter; protoplasm.

bi·op·sy (bī'op-si), *n.*, *pl.* **-sies,** the taking of bits of tissue, fluids, etc. from the living body for diagnostic study.

bi·o·sat·el·lite (bī-ō-sat'l-īt), *n.* a satellite put into orbit and later recovered to study the effects of space travel on living organisms contained within.

bi·o·sci·ence (bī'ō-si-êns), *n.* any science having to do with living organisms.

bi·o·sphere (bī'ō-sfir), *n.* 1. the total range of regions on earth or within the earth's atmosphere that support life. 2. all of the living things on earth and within its atmosphere.

bi·o·sta·tis·tics (bī-ō-stå-tis'tiks), *n.* the use of statistical methods in dealing with biological

---

ŏ in dragon, ōō in crude, oo in wool, u in cup, ū in cure, ü in turn, ů in focus, oi in boy, ou in house, th in thin, th in sheathe, g in get, j in joy, y in yet.

ínformation. —bi·o·sta·tis'ti·cal, _adj._ **—bi·o·stat·is·ti'cian** (-stat-is-tish'ǎn), _n._

bi·o·syn·the·sis (-sin'thē·sis), _n._ the formation of chemical compounds by living organisms. **—bi·o·syn·thet'ic** (-sin-thet'ik), _adj._ **—bi·o·syn·thet'i·cal·ly,** _adv._

bi·ot·ic (bī·ot'ik), **bi·ot·i·cal,** _adj._ of, pertaining to, or involving biological life.

bi·o·tin (bī·ō'tin), _n._ a growth factor of the vitamin B group, found in egg yolk, yeast, and liver.

bip·a·rous (bip'ĕr·ŭs), _adj._ bringing forth two at a birth.

bi·par·ti·san (bī·pär'ti·zn), _adj._ of, representing, or backed by two political parties or other groups. **—bi·par'ti·san·ship,** _n._

bi·par·tite (bī·pär'tīt), _adj._ 1. having two corresponding parts. 2. shared by or involving two. **—bi·par'tite·ly,** _adv._

bi·ped (bī'ped), _adj._ having two feet: also **biped'al:** _n._ a two-footed animal.

bi·pin·nate (bī·pin'āt), _adj._ having pinnate leaflets growing opposite each other on a main stem. **—bi·pin'nate·ly,** _adv._

bi·plane (bī'plān), _n._ an early type of airplane with double wings, one wing above the other.

bi·po·lar (bī·pō'lĕr), _adj._ 1. of, having, or involving two poles. 2. of or involving a pair of directly opposed opinions, tendencies, etc. **—bi·po·lar'i·ty** (bī·pō·lĕr'i·ti), **bi·po·lar·i·za'-tion,** _n._

bi·quad·rate (bī·kwäd'rit), _n._ in _Mathematics,_ the fourth power; square of the square. **—bi·quad·rat'ic** (-rat'ik), _adj. & n._

bi·ra·cial (bī·rā'shǎl), _adj._ of, pertaining to, or consisting of people from two races, especially black and white. **—bi·ra'cial·ism,** _n._ **—bi·ra'cial·ly,** _adv._

bi·ra·mous (bī·rā'mŭs), _adj._ having two branches.

birch (bûrch), _n._ 1. any one of a genus of northern trees or shrubs with a smooth bark and hard wood. 2. the wood. 3. a rod or bunch of twigs of birch, for whipping: _v.t._ to whip with a birch: _adj._ of birch: also **birch'en.**

bird (bûrd), _n._ 1. any one of a class of warm-blooded, feathered, egg-laying, bipedal vertebrates. 2. a clay pigeon. 3. a shuttlecock. 4. [Slang], a peculiar person. 5. [Slang], a derisive sound made by the lips. 6. [British Slang], a girl: _v.i._ 1. to shoot or catch birds. 2. to do bird watching.

bird·bath ('bath), _n._ a very shallow container, typically ornamental and set on a stand, to hold a little water for birds to bathe in.

bird·brain ('brān), _n._ [Informal], a flighty or silly person; scatterbrain. **—bird'brained,** _adj._

bird·call ('kôl), _n._ 1. the cry or song of a bird, or an imitation of this sound. 2. a device to imitate the cry or song of a bird. Also **bird call.**

bird dog, 1. a dog bred or trained for bird hunting. 2. [Informal], a person who is hired to search for or pursue something or someone. **—bird'-dog,** _v.t._ **bird'-dogged, bird'-dog·ging.**

bird·house ('hous), _n._ a small, often houselike,

structure set on a pole or hung, put in trees, etc., for birds to build nests in.

bird·ie (bûr'di), _n._ a golf score of one stroke less than par for a hole.

bird·lime (bûrd'līm), _n._ a viscous substance spread on surfaces to catch birds.

bird·man ('man), _n., pl._ **-men,** one whose work concerns birds, as an ornithologist.

bird of paradise, 1. a brightly colored bird of New Guinea. 2. a tropical African plant with bright blue and orange flowers.

bird of prey, any of many birds that catch and feed on other birds or small mammals.

bird's-eye (bûrdz'ī), _adj._ seen from above or at a glance, as by a flying bird; hence, general; not minute or detailed: _n._ 1. any one of several flowers with bright petals and contrasting centers. 2. a woven fabric pattern of a small diamond shape with a dot in the center.

bird's-eye maple, the wood of a variety of sugar maple with markings resembling the eyes of birds.

bird-watch·er (bûrd'wäch·ĕr), _n._ one who studies birds in their natural habitats. **—bird'watch·ing,** _n._

bi·ret·ta (bi·ret'ǎ), _n._ a square cap worn by Roman Catholic clergy.

birl (bûrl), _v.t. & v.i._ to revolve (a floating log) underfoot while trying to keep one's balance. **—birl'ing,** _n._

birth (bûrth), _n._ 1. the act of coming into life; a being born. 2. the act of bringing forth offspring. 3. lineage, especially noble lineage; extraction; descent. 4. the origin or beginning of anything. 5. natural talent.

birth control, regulation of childbearing, especially by the control of conception.

birth·day (bûrth'dā), _n._ the day of one's birth, or an anniversary of this day.

birth·mark ('märk), _n._ a mark on the body, present at birth.

birth·place ('plās), _n._ 1. one's place of birth. 2. a place where something originates.

birth·rate ('rāt), _n._ the proportion of births to the population of a given area, country, etc.: also **birth rate.**

birth·right ('rīt), _n._ 1. any right or privilege to which a person is entitled by birth. 2. the rights of the first-born son.

birth·stone ('stōn), _n._ a precious or semiprecious stone traditionally associated with a given month of the year and hence with the date of one's birth.

bis·cuit (bis'kit), _n., pl._ **-cuits, -cuit,** 1. in Britain, a cracker or cookie. 2. a small flaky, unsweetened cake of quick bread, usually leavened with baking powder or soda. 3. pottery or porcelain after the first baking and previous to glazing. 4. light tan.

bi·sect (bī·sekt', bī'sekt), _v.t. & v.i._ to cut or divide into two equal parts or branches. **—bi·sec'tion,** _n._ **—bi·sec'tion·al,** _adj._

bi·sec·tor (bī·sek'tĕr), _n._ 1. something that bisects. 2. a straight line bisecting an angle or line.

bi·sex·u·al (bī·sek'shoo·wǎl), _adj._ 1. of both sexes. 2. combining the organs of both sexes in one individual; hermaphroditic. 3. sexually attracted by both sexes: _n._ one that is

bisexual. **—bi·sex·u·al'i·ty, bi·sex'u·al·ism,** *n.* **—bi·sex'u·al·ly,** *adv.*

bish·op (bish'ŏp), *n.* 1. a high-ranking Christian clergyman usually overseeing a diocese. 2. a chess piece moving only diagonally over one or more squares. 3. a mulled beverage composed of port wine flavored with orange and cloves.

bish·op·ric (bish'ŏ-prik) *n.* 1. the office, rank, or authority of a bishop. 2. the jurisdiction of a bishop; diocese.

bis·muth (biz'mŭth), *n.* a hard, brittle, light-red metallic element used chiefly in alloys.

bi·son (bis'n, bi'zn), *n., pl.* **bi'son,** any one of several large, four-legged, bovine mammals with a shaggy mane and humped back, as the American buffalo or the European wisent.

bisque (bisk) *n.* 1. a thick cream soup, often made with seafood or vegetables. 2. a kind of ice cream containing finely ground nuts or crumbled macaroons. 3. biscuit porcelain or pottery left unglazed. 4. a handicap allowed in tennis, croquet, or golf. 5. a red-yellow color.

bis·sex·tile (bi-seks'tl, bī-), *n.* a leap year; *adj.* 1. denoting or of a leap year. 2. denoting the extra day (February 29) of a leap year.

bis·ter, bis·tre (bis'tĕr), *n.* a brown pigment, ranging from light to dark in shade, made from wood soot.

bis·tou·ry (bis'too-ri), *n., pl.* **-ries,** a narrow-bladed, knifelike instrument used in surgery.

bis·tro (bis'trō), *n., pl.* **-tros,** [French], a small tavern, café, nightclub, etc.

bi·sul·fate (bī-sul'fāt), *n.* an acid sulfate.

bi·sul·fite (bī-sul'fīt), *n.* an acid sulfite.

bit (bit), *n.* 1. a tool for boring. 2. the metal mouthpiece of a bridle; also, anything that curbs or checks behavior. 3. the part of a pipestem, cigarette holder, etc. inserted into one's mouth. 4. the part of a key that enters the lock and acts on the bolts and tumblers. 5. the cutting blade of a plane, or the cutting part of any tool. 6. a small piece or fragment of anything. 7. a short time or limited degree. 8. [Informal], an amount equal to a former small coin worth 12 1/2 cents. 9. a small part in a play, etc. 10. [Informal], a particular way of behaving, especially when characteristic or repeated. 11. a unit of information, as used in a computer utilizing a binary number system: *v.t.* **bit'ted, bit'ting,** 1. to put a bit into the mouth (of a horse). 2. to curb or check: *adj.* very small.

bitch (bich), *n.* 1. the female of the dog, wolf, etc. 2. a girl or woman: a vulgar, hostile term. 3. [Slang], a very difficult problem, situation, etc.: *v.i.* [Slang], to complain.

bitch·y (bich'i), *adj.* **bitch'i·er, bitch'i·est,** [Slang], ill-tempered, unpleasant, complaining, malicious, etc. **—bitch'i·ness,** *n.*

bite (bīt), *v.t.* **bit, bit'ten** or **bit, bit'ing,** 1. to cut or penetrate into; grip, crush, wound, etc. with or as with teeth, sharp jaws, etc. 2. to sting, as an insect. 3. to cause smarting pain to. 4. to pierce, bore into, etc., as a drill. 5. to take fast hold on, as a vise. 6. to corrode or eat into. 7. to cheat or trick:

v.i. 1. to have the habit or exercise the power of biting. 2. to cause to sting or smart. 3. to take a bait. 4. to take a firm hold on. 5. to be caught, as by a trick: *n.* 1. the act of biting. 2. a biting or stinging quality or effect. 3. a cut, wound, etc. made by biting. 4. a part bitten or to be bitten off; mouthful. 5. a quick or light meal; also, a snack. 6. a tight hold or grip. 7. [Informal], an amount deducted. 8. in *Etching,* the corrosion of the metal by an acid. **—bit'er,** *n.*

bit·ing (bīt'ing), *adj.* 1. sharp. 2. sarcastic. **—bit'ing·ly,** *adv.*

bitt (bit), *n.* a post to which cables are made fast, usually in pairs on a ship's deck: *v.t.* to put (a cable) around a bitt or bitts.

bit·ter (bit'ĕr), *adj.* 1. having a sharp or harsh taste; acrid. 2. painful; grievous. 3. piercing; severe. 4. showing or feeling resentment; sarcastic; caustic: *adv.* in a bitter manner: *n.* a bitter quality or substance. **—bit'ter·ly,** *adv.* **—bit'ter·ness,** *n.*

bitter end, 1. the end of a cable wound around a bitt. 2. the last extremity.

bit·ter-end·er (-en'dĕr), *n.* [Informal], one who holds out to the bitter end, even for a hopeless cause.

bit·tern (bit'ĕrn), *n., pl.* **bit'terns, bit'tern,** 1. a bird of the heron family, found in bogs, marshes, and swamps: the male utters a peculiar, thumping call. 2. a bitter liquid left after the common salt has crystallized from brine or sea water, and from which various other commercial salts are obtained.

bit·ter·nut (bit'ĕr-nut), *n.* a species of hickory of the eastern U.S.

bit·ter·root (-rōōt), *n.* a plant with a fleshy, edible root and pink flowers, which grows in the western U.S.

bit·ters (bit'ĕrz), *n.* liquor in which herbs or roots are steeped, used as a tonic or in some cocktails.

bit·ter·sweet (bit'ĕr-swēt), *n.* 1. a poisonous European climbing vine of the nightshade family, with purple flowers, now found commonly in the U.S. 2. a twining vine of North America with small orange fruits containing bright red seeds. 3. a flavor that has bitterness and sweetness combined. 4. happiness with an element of sadness: *adj.* bitter and sweet.

bit·ter·weed (-wēd), *n.* any of several plants having a bitter taste, as ragweed.

bit·ty (bit'i), *adj.* **-ti·er, -ti·est,** small; tiny; a child's term.

bi·tu·men (bi-tōō'mĕn, bī-; -tū'-), *n.* 1. originally, natural asphalt; mineral pitch. 2. any of various products resulting from the distillation of petroleum, coal tar, etc. **—bi·tu'mi·nous,** *adj.*

bituminous coal, coal producing much smoke and ashes when burned and yielding pitch or tar.

bi·va·lent (bī-vā'lĕnt), *adj.* 1. having two valences. 2. having a valence of two.

bi·valve (bī'valv), *adj.* having two valves or shells united by a ligament: also **bi'valved:** *n.* a mollusk whose shell is composed of two parts or valves which are opened or

ŏ in dragon, ōō in crude, oo in wool, u in cup, ū in cure, ū in turn, ŭ in focus, oi in boy, ou in house, th in thin, th in sheathe, g in get, j in joy, y in yet.

closed by muscles, as the oyster, mussel, or clam.

biv·ou·ac (biv'wak, biv'oo-wak), *n.* a temporary encampment, especially of soldiers, in the open air, with or without tents: *v.i.* -acked, -ack·ing, to pitch camp out in the open.

bi·week·ly (bī-wēk'lǐ), *adj.* & *adv.* 1. once every two weeks. 2. semiweekly: *n., pl.* -lies, a magazine, newspaper, etc. appearing once every two weeks.

bi·year·ly (bī-yir'li), *adj.* & *adv.* 1. once every two years; biennial(ly). 2. semiyearly.

bi·zarre (bi-zär'), *adj.* 1. odd, as in manner or appearance; fanciful; grotesque. 2. unusual; freakish; astonishing. **—bi·zarre'ly,** *adv.* **—bi·zarre'ness,** *n.*

blab (blab), *v.t.* & *v.i.* **blabbed, blab'bing,** 1. to tell (a secret or confidence) thoughtlessly. 2. to chatter idly; talk much: *n.* 1. idle chatter. 2. one who blabs.

blab·ber (blab'ēr), *v.t.* & *v.i.* to blab or babble: *n.* one who blabs.

blab·ber·mouth (blab'ēr-mouth), *n.* [Informal], one who talks indiscreetly or chatters endlessly and idly.

black (blak), *adj.* 1. devoid of light; completely dark. 2. of the darkest hue; of the color of coal. 3. having dark-colored skin and hair; especially, Negro. 4. without cream or milk: said of coffee. 5. dirty or soiled. 6. dismal; gloomy or forbidding. 7. atrocious; evil. 8. calamitous. 9. threatening. 10. clouded with anger; sullen. 11. cynically or morbidly humorous: *n.* 1. a black color. 2. something black, as a pigment or dye. 3. black clothes, especially when worn in mourning. 4. a Negro or other person with dark-colored skin: *black* is now generally preferred to *Negro.* 5. total darkness: *v.t.* & *v.i.* 1. to make black; blacken. 2. to apply blacking to. **—black'ly,** *adv.* **—black'ness,** *n.*

black alder, a shrub of eastern North America, with bright-red berries and with leaves that are dark in the fall.

black·a·moor (blak'ȧ-moor), *n.* [Archaic], an African Negro or other dark-skinned person.

black-and-blue (blak'ȧn-blōō'), *adj.* showing the bluish-black surface discoloration produced by congested blood under a bruised area of the skin.

Black and Tan, any one of the British troops sent to Ireland in 1919-1921 to counter the Sinn Fein rebellion.

black-and-tan terrier (blak-ȧn-tan'), same as Manchester terrier.

black arts, the various systems or procedures used in the practice of black magic.

black·ball (blak'bôl), *v.t.* 1. to reject or exclude (a candidate) by a negative vote, originally by placing black balls in the ballot box. 2. to ostracize: *n.* a negative vote.

black belt, a black sash or belt awarded to a top expert in karate or judo.

black·ber·ry (blak'ber-i), *n., pl.* -ries, 1. the fruit of several species of bramble, purple or black in color, and edible. 2. the bush or vine bearing this fruit.

black·bird (blak'bûrd), *n.* any of various birds the male of which has almost entirely black plumage, as the crow.

black·board (blak'bôrd), *n.* a smooth, dark surface, as of slate, on which to write or draw with chalk.

black·cap (blak'kap), *n.* 1. any one of several birds, as the chickadee, with a caplike black marking covering the top of the head. 2. same as black raspberry.

black·cock (blak'kok), *n., pl.* -cocks, -cock, the male of the black grouse.

black·damp (blak'damp), *n.* a noxious gas, a mixture of carbon dioxide and nitrogen, that may occur in mines.

Black Death, a virulent plague which ravaged Europe and Asia in the 14th century.

black·en (blak'n), *v.i.* to grow black or dark: *v.t.* 1. to make black or dark. 2. to defame; vilify. **—black'en·er,** *n.*

black eye, a darkened skin area about the eye, resulting from a contusion or blow.

black-eyed Su·san (blak'īd sōō'zn), a yellow flower with a dark center, a common wildflower in the U.S.

black·fish (blak'fish), *n., pl.* -fish, -fish·es, 1. any one of a genus of small, black whales that have teeth. 2. any one of several dark fishes, as the sea bass or tautog. 3. an edible, minnowlike freshwater fish of Alaska and Siberia.

black flag, a flag showing a skull and crossbones against a black background: a pirate's emblem.

black fly, any of several small, black North American flies found in forests.

Black·foot (blak'foot), *n., pl.* -feet, -foot, a member of a North American Indian tribe of Canada and Montana.

Black Friar, a Dominican friar.

black frost, a severe frost that turns plants black.

black grouse, a large grouse of Europe and Asia.

black·guard (blag'ērd, 'ärd), *n.* 1. a man of low character; scoundrel. 2. one who uses foul or abusive language: *adj.* 1. vicious; low; vile. 2. scurrilous; abusive: *v.t.* to revile scurrilously. **—black'guard·ly,** *adj.* & *adv.*

black·head (blak'hed), *n.* a dark-tipped bit of dried fatty matter in a skin pore.

black-heart·ed (blak'här-tid), *adj.* villainous; evil; bad. **—black'heart·ed·ness,** *n.*

black hole, a dark prison cell; dungeon: after the 18th-century *Black Hole* of Calcutta, a cramped prison cell where 123 European prisoners were said to have suffocated overnight.

black·ing (blak'ing), *n.* a preparation for shining black shoes.

black·ish (blak'ish), *adj.* somewhat black.

black·jack (blak'jak), *n.* 1. a large drinking mug, once made of leather. 2. same as black flag. 3. a small U.S. oak. 4. a small, leather-covered club with a flexible handle. 5. the card game twenty-one: *v.t.* to beat with a blackjack.

black·leg (blak'leg), *n.* 1. [Informal], a cheater at gambling. 2. a certain usually fatal bacterial disease affecting cattle and sheep; also, a certain disease of cabbages, or one affecting potatoes. 3. [British], a strikebreaker.

black letter, a heavy-faced type patterned after

a style of lettering used in early manuscripts.

black-list ('list), *n.* a list of persons who are to be ostracized, excluded from employment, etc.: *v.t.* to put on a blacklist.

black lung disease, a lung disease caused by prolonged breathing in of coal dust: also called **black lung.**

black magic, evil magic; sorcery.

black-mail ('māl), *n.* 1. a tax once paid in money, crops, or cattle, in the north of England and in Scotland, to robbers to get protection from pillage. 2. extortion by threatening to reveal embarrassing secrets. 3. the payment extorted: *v.t.* 1. to extort or try to extort money or goods from by threats of revealing something kept secret. 2. to force (*into* an action) as by threatening exposure. —**black'mail-er,** *n.*

Black Ma-ri-a (mä-rī'ä), [Old Slang], the small truck used for transporting prisoners to and from jail.

black mark, a mark signifying something bad in a person's record.

black market, an illegal system for selling things, especially in contravening rationing regulations. —**black marketeer.**

Black Mass, black mass, 1. a Requiem Mass, at which the priest wears black vestments. 2. a ceremony said to be practiced by worshipers of Satan, in which the Christian Mass is parodied and mocked.

Black Muslim, a member of an aggressive Islamic sect of American blacks supporting the separation of races.

black-out (blak'out), *n.* 1. the putting out of all stage lights in ending the scene of a play. 2. the putting out or concealing of all lights in a city or district as a protection during air raids. 3. a brief loss of consciousness.

black power, economic and political power sought by American blacks in striving for civil rights.

black raspberry, 1. a prickly shrub of the rose family, bearing juicy, dark-purple fruit. 2. the fruit.

black sheep, a member of a family or group who disgraces or embarrasses the other members by lack of success or respectability.

black-smith (blak'smith), *n.* a smith who works in iron, specializing in making horseshoes.

black-thorn ('thôrn), *n.* 1. a thorny shrub with black or purple fruit like plums. 2. a cane made from the shrub stem.

black-top ('top), *n.* asphalt or some other bituminous mixture used for surfacing roads, driveways, etc.: *v.t.* -topped, -top-ping, to cover with this.

black widow, an American black spider, the female of which is marked with red underneath, has a very poisonous bite, and sometimes eats its mate.

blad-der (blad'ẽr), *n.* 1. a thin, elastic, membranous bag in animals, in which a fluid, as urine from the kidneys, is collected. 2. any bladderlike thing.

blade (blād), *n.* 1. the leaf of a grass. 2. the broad, expanded part of a leaf. 3. the cutting part of a tool, instrument, etc. 4. the broad part of an oar, vane, etc. 5. the shoulder blade. 6. anything like a blade. 7. a sword, or one who uses a sword. 8. a dashing young fellow.

blain (blān), *n.* a pustule or blister.

blam-a-ble, blame-a-ble (blām'ä-bl), *adj.* deserving censure. —**blam'a-bly,** *adv.*

blame (blām), *v.t.* blamed, blam'ing, 1. to condemn or accuse; censure (*for*). 2. to reproach. 3. to place responsibility (*on*): *n.* 1. an act of blaming; censure. 2. responsibility for a wrong. —**blame'less,** *adj.*

blame-ful ('fl), *adj.* 1. imputing blame; blaming. 2. deserving censure. —**blame'ful-ly,** *adv.* —**blame'ful-ness,** *n.*

blame-wor-thy ('wûr-thi), *adj.* meriting blame.

blanch (blanch), *v.t.* 1. to take the color out; make white. 2. to make pale. 3. to scald (vegetables or almonds) in order to remove the outer covering or as a preparation for freezing: *v.i.* to become white; turn pale.

blanc-mange (blä-mänzh', -mänj'), *n.* a dessert made with starch or gelatin and milk, sweetened and flavored, and shaped in a mold.

bland (bland), *adj.* 1. affable; agreeable. 2. mild; soft; gentle; soothing. 3. without flavor; dull. —**bland'ly,** *adv.* —**bland'ness,** *n.*

blan-dish (blan'dish), *v.t. & v.i.* to flatter; cajole. —**blan'dish-ing-ly,** *adv.*

blan-dish-ment (-mĕnt), *n.* a winning or flattering expression or action.

blank (blangk), *adj.* 1. confounded; confused. 2. free from writing or printing; empty. 3. having an empty or dull expression. 4. without result. 5. having no ideas. 6. utter. 7. lacking characteristics: *n.* 1. an empty space. 2. a void in time. 3. an unfilled space in something written or printed; also, a paper, form, etc. with such spaces. 4. a lottery ticket that doesn't win. 5. a piece, as of metal, prior to being shaped, marked, etc. 6. the white spot in the center of a target. 7. a cartridge filled with powder but without a bullet. 8. a mark, as a dash, used to replace an oath, curse, etc.: *v.t.* to keep (an opponent) from scoring. —**blank'ly,** *adv.* —**blank'ness,** *n.*

blan-ket (blang'kit), *n.* 1. a soft, loosely woven cloth, as of wool, for a bed or as a covering for an animal. 2. any covering like a blanket: *adj.* covering all or many parts: *v.t.* 1. to cover with or as with a blanket. 2. to conceal or overshadow.

blank verse, poetry without rhyme.

blare (bler), *v.t. & v.i.* blared, blar'ing, 1. to sound loudly. 2. to trumpet forth; proclaim loudly: *n.* a noise like the blast of a trumpet.

blar-ney (blär'ni), *n.* soft, wheedling speech; flattery: *v.t. & v.i.* -neyed, -ney-ing, to influence or try to influence by sof', wheedling speeches.

Blarney stone, a stone in the wall of Blarney Castle, Cork County, Ireland: on kissing it a person is said to become adept in flattery.

bla-sé (blä-zā'), *adj.* bored by an excess of pleasure.

blas-pheme (blas-fēm'), *v.t.* -phemed', -phem'ing, 1. to speak irreverently of (that which is sacred). 2. to mock; revile: *v.i.* to utter blasphemy; use profane language. —**blas-phem'er,** *n.*

blas-phe-mous (blas'fē-mûs), *adj.* uttering, containing, or exhibiting blasphemy; profane. —**blas'phe-mous-ly,** *adv.*

blas-phe-my (-mi), *n., pl.* -**mies,** 1 impious, profane, or mocking speech, writing, or action concerning God or sacred things. 2. any extreme irreverence.

blast (blast), *n.* 1. a violent or sudden gust of wind. 2. a forced stream of air 3. the sound as produced by blowing a wind instrument. 4. any sudden, injurious influence, as a withering disease of plants; blight. 5. *a)* the explosion of dynamite, gunpowder, etc. *b)* the charge used for this. 6. a harsh burst of criticism. 7. [Slang], a wild good time; party: *v.i.* 1. to sound harshly. 2. to set off explosives: *v.t.* 1. to injure; cause to fade or wither; blight; ruin. 2. to break up or shatter by an explosive. 3. to criticize harshly.

blas-te-ma (blas-tē'mā), *n., pl.* -**mas,** -**ma-ta** ('mä-tä), embryonic tissue from which organs, tissues, or cells develop.

blast furnace, a furnace for the smelting of ores, the heat being intensified by a pressurized blast of air.

blas-to-derm (blas'tō-dûrm), *n.* the germinal spot in a fertilized ovum, from which the embryo is developed.

blas-to-gen-e-sis (blas-tō-jen'ē-sis), *n.* reproduction by asexual processes.

blas-tu-la (blas'choo-lä), *n., pl.* -**las,** -**lae** (-lē), an embryo that has developed to one or more layers of cells around a central hollow space.

bla-tant (blāt'nt), *adj.* 1. unpleasantly noisy. 2. very obvious. —**bla'tan-cy,** *n.*

blath-er (blath'ēr), *n.* foolish chatter: *v.i. & v.t.* to talk foolishly.

blaze (blāz), *n.* 1. a body of flame. 2. a brilliant light. 3. a sudden outburst. 4. a bright display. 5. a white spot on the face of an animal. 6. a mark cut on a tree, to serve as a guide: *v.i.* **blazed, blaz'ing,** 1. to burn or shine brightly. 2. to be stirred with excitement or anger: *v.t.* 1. to mark, as trees, by removing a portion of the bark. 2. to indicate (a path or trail) by blazing trees. 3. to announce widely.

blaz-er (blā'zēr), *n.* a sports jacket of a solid, bright color with stripes.

bla-zon (blā'zn), *n.* 1. a coat of arms. 2. a description of heraldic designs on armor. 3. ostentatious display: *v.t.* 1. to analyze technically or show (coats of arms). 2. to embellish; display. 3. to proclaim.

bla-zon-ry (-ri), *n., pl.* -**ries,** 1. a heraldic device. 2. a describing or showing of coats of arms. 3. decoration; display.

bleach (blēch), *v.t. & v.i.* to make or become white or colorless, specifically by the action of the sun's rays or by a chemical process: *n.* a material used to bleach.

bleach-ers ('ērz), *n.* cheaper seats, usually tiers of benches not under a roof, at sports events.

bleak (blēk), *adj.* 1. exposed to wind and cold;

desolate; unsheltered. 2. cheerless; gloomy. 3. piercing; harsh. 4. lacking promise or hope. —**bleak'ly,** *adv.* —**bleak'ness,** *n.*

bleak (blēk), *n., pl.* **bleak, bleaks,** a small river fish with brilliant silvery scales used to make artificial pearls.

blear (blir), *adj.* 1. dim from a watery discharge: said of the eyes. 2. blurred: *v.t.* 1. to dim (the eyes). 2. to blur.

blear-y ('i), *adj.* **blear'i-er, blear'i-est,** hazy or dim, as the eyes. —**blear'i-ly,** *adv.* —**blear'i-ness,** *n.*

bleat (blēt), *v.i. & v.t.* to cry as, or like, a sheep, goat, etc. *n.* such a cry.

bleb (bleb), *n.* 1. a blister; pustule. 2. an air bubble, as in water

bleed (blēd), *v.i.* **bled** (bled), **bleed'ing,** 1 to emit or lose blood. 2. to shed one's blood. 3. to grieve or sympathize. 4. to lose sap or juice: *v.t.* 1. to take blood from. 2. to lose (sap or juice). 3. to empty of liquid or gas. 4. to draw off (a liquid or gas) slowly. 5. [Informal], to take money from by extortion.

bleed-er ('ēr), *n.* same as **hemophiliac.**

bleeding heart, 1. a garden plant with pink-colored flowers. 2. a person viewed as overly concerned about social problems.

bleep (blēp), *n. & v.i.* same as **beep:** *v.t.* to censor (a word, phrase, etc.), as in a television broadcast, by using a beep instead.

blem-ish (blem'ish), *v.t.* to mar the perfection, appearance, quality, etc. of; flaw: *n.* any flaw, imperfection, defect, etc.

blench (blench), *v.t. & v.i.* to turn white or pale; blanch; bleach.

blench (blench), *v.i.* to flinch; quail.

blend (blend), *v.t.* **blend'ed** or **blent, blend'ing,** 1. to mix (kinds of tea, tobacco, etc.). 2. to mix together so that the things mixed cannot be separated or individually distinguished: *v.i.* 1. to mix or unite. 2. to shade imperceptibly into each other. 3. to go well together: *n.* 1. the act of blending. 2. a blended mixture.

blende (blend), *n.* any one of certain sulfides, as of zinc.

blend-er ('ēr), *n.* 1. a person or thing that blends. 2. an electrical appliance that can chop, whip, mix, or liquefy foods.

blen-ny (blen'i), *n., pl.* -**nies,** -**ny,** a small ocean fish with long dorsal fins and a narrow, slimy body.

bleph-a-ri-tis (blef-ä-rīt'is), *n.* inflammation of the eyelids.

bless (bles), *v.t.* **blessed** or **blest, bless'ing,** 1. to declare holy; consecrate. 2. to ask a blessing for. 3. to favor or provide (*with*). 4. to bestow happiness upon. 5. to praise or extol. 6. to congratulate (oneself). 7. to make the sign of the cross on or over.

bless-ed (bles'id, blest), *adj.* 1. consecrated. 2. very happy; blissful. 3. in eternal bliss. 4. bringing joy. —**bless'ed-ness,** *n.*

bless-ing (bles'ing), *n.* 1. a benediction or invocation. 2. a grace said in connection with eating. 3. a divine benefit or gift. 4. that which promotes happiness or prosperity; special favor. 5. approval.

blight (blīt), *n.* 1. a condition, disease, insect,

etc. causing plants to wither partly or wholly. 2. any one of certain plant diseases, as smut or mildew. 3. anything that checks, destroys, etc.: *v.t.* 1. to cause blight in; wither. 2. to check, destroy, etc.

blimp (blimp), *n.* a small, nonrigid or semirigid airship.

blind (blind), *adj.* 1. not having the sense of sight. 2. of or provided for sightless persons. 3. unable or unwilling to understand. 4. lacking sufficient knowledge, guidance, etc. 5. doing without logic, evidence, etc. 6. unseen or hard to see. 7. open at only one end, or not open at all. 8. not guided by intelligence, perception, etc. 9. in *Aeronautics,* done without being able to see out: *n.* 1. anything hindering or obstructing vision. 2. anything blocking the passage of light, as a window shade. 3. a place, as for a hunter, to lie hidden. 4. something designed to mislead; decoy: *adv.* in a blind way: *v.t.* 1. to deprive of sight. 2. to deprive of understanding or judgment. 3. to dazzle. 4. to obscure. 5. to conceal. —**blind′ly**, *adv.* —**blind′-ness**, *n.*

blind date, [Informal], 1. a social engagement for two strangers, arranged by a third person. 2. either stranger.

blind-er (blīn′dēr), *n.* either of two leather flaps on a horse's bridle to keep the horse from seeing any object except in front.

blind-fish (blīnd′fish), *n., pl.* -fish, -fish-es, a small fish with rudimentary eyes, that inhabits underground waters.

blind-fold (′fōld), *adj.* 1. having the eyes covered so as to be unable to see. 2. rash; heedless: *v.t.* to cover the eyes of, as with a bandage; hinder from seeing: *n.* a cloth used for covering the eyes.

blind-man's-buff (blind′manz buf′), a game in which one of the players is blindfolded and tries to catch another player.

blind spot, a sightless point in the retina where the optic nerve enters the eye.

blind staggers, a disease of horses or cattle characterized by staggering, falling, etc.

blind tiger, [Old Slang], same as **speak-easy**: also called **blind pig**.

blind-worm (′wûrm), *n.* a small, slender, limbless lizard having very small eyes.

blink (blingk), *v.i.* 1. to close and open the eyelids quickly. 2. to twinkle or glimmer. 3. to pretend not to see; disregard (followed by *at*): *v.t.* 1. to make (the eyes, a light, etc.) blink or wink. 2. to evade or shut one's eyes to: *n.* 1. the act of blinking. 2. a twinkle or glimmer. 3. [Chiefly Scottish], a glimpse or glance. 4. the gleam reflected from an ice field or iceberg at sea.

blink-er (′ēr), *n.* 1. a flashing light that signals or warns. 2. *pl. a)* a horse's blinders. *b)* goggles.

blintz (blints), *n.* a thin, rolled pancake filled with fruit, cottage cheese, etc.

blip (blip), *n.* a spot of light on an oscilloscope.

bliss (blis), *n.* 1. a very high degree of happiness. 2. heavenly joy. —**bliss′ful**, *adj.* —**bliss′ful-ly**, *adv.* —**bliss′ful-ness**, *n.*

blis-ter (blis′tēr), *n.* 1. a vesicle or pustule on the skin containing watery matter, as from a burn. 2. an application to cause this. 3. any elevation like a blister: *v.t.* 1. to raise a blister or blisters on. 2. to attack witheringly: *v.i.* to rise in blisters or become covered with blisters.

blithe (blīth, blīth), *adj.* gay; joyous; glad. —**blithe′ly**, *adv.* —**blithe′ness**, *n.*

blithe-some (′sŭm), *adj.* gay; merry.

blitz (blits), *n.* a sudden, crushing attack: *v.t.* to crush; destroy.

blitz-krieg (′krēg), *n.* a quick, large-scale war offensive to crush resistance.

bliz-zard (bliz′ērd), *n.* a storm of blinding snow and bitterly cold wind.

bloat (blōt), *v.t.* 1. to preserve or cure (mackerel, herring, etc.) in salt water and smoke. 2. to cause to swell; make turgid or swollen, as with water or air. 3. to make vain: *v.i.* to grow turgid.

bloat-er (′ēr), *n.* 1. a herring or mackerel cured by bloating. 2. a small fish of the Great Lakes.

blob (blob), *n.* a small or shapeless lump, drop, spot, etc.

bloc (blok), *n.* a group of nations, persons, etc. united to accomplish a common end.

block (blok), *n.* 1. any unshaped solid mass of matter, as of wood, stone, etc. 2. a table or stand like a block on which things are chopped, hammered, etc. 3. the platform used by an auctioneer. 4. a piece of engraved wood, linoleum, etc., for use in printing. 5. a wooden mold, as for shaping hats. 6. a pulley or groups of pulleys in a frame with a hook for attaching to something. 7. a large building or row of buildings in a unit. 8. a square of a city. 9. a number of things considered as a unit. 10. an obstruction; hindrance. 11. [Slang], a person's head. 12. in *Railroading,* a section of track in the block system: *v.t.* 1. to obstruct so as to hinder the passage of (persons or things). 2. to shape on a block. 3. to secure, support, control, etc. by a block or blocks. 4. to make a sketch of in rough detail (often followed by *out*). —**block′er**, *n.*

block-ade (blo-kād′), *n.* 1. the shutting up of a port or area by hostile ships or troops in order to force a surrender by preventing passage in or out. 2. any similar barrier: *v.t.* -ad′ed, -ad′ing, to surround and shut up; obstruct; block.

block-age (blok′ij), *n.* an obstruction.

block and tackle, a set of pulley blocks and cables, for pulling up heavy objects.

block-bust-ing (′bus-ting), *n.* [Informal], the persuading of residents in an area to sell their homes by making them fear that a minority group is moving in and that sale values will fall.

block-head (′hed), *n.* a stupid person.

block-house (′hous), *n.* 1. a wooden fort with holes for shooting out of. 2. a small, heavily constructed building for observing explosions, missile launchings, etc.

block letter, an alphabet character printed, often by hand, in simple form.

block signal, an automatic signal on railroads

to guide the movements of trains in the block system.

block system, a system of regulating railway traffic by which the track is divided into short sections so that no train is allowed to leave a section until the next section is signaled clear.

bloke (blōk), *n.* [Chiefly British Slang], a fellow; chap; man.

blond (blond), *adj.* 1. having light-colored hair and skin. 2. light-colored, as hair or wood: *n.* a blond person.

blonde (blond), *adj.* same as **blond**: *n.* 1. a blond girl or woman. 2. a silk bobbin lace.

blood (blud), *n.* 1. the fluid which circulates in the arteries and veins of an animal; also, any similar fluid. 2. the juice or sap of a plant. 3. blood spilling; murder. 4. the essential part of life; life. 5. frame of mind; mood. 6. family line; lineage. 7. race: not a scientific use. 8. blood relationship; kinship. 9. high birth. 10. a dandy. 11. people, especially youth: *v.t.* to give a taste of blood to (a hunting dog).

blood bank, 1. a place where blood is stored for later transfusions. 2. the supply.

blood count, a measure of the number of white and red corpuscles in an amount of blood.

blood-cur-dling ('kūrd'ling), *adj.* causing terror or great fright.

blood-ed ('id), *adj.* of the best stock or breed.

blood heat, the normal temperature of human blood, about 98.6°F.

blood-hound ('hound), *n.* 1. one of a breed of large dogs with a keen sense of smell, used to track fugitives, escaped criminals, etc. 2. a sleuth.

blood-less ('lĕs), *adj.* 1. without killing. 2. pale or anemic. 3. not having much energy. —**blood'less-ly,** *adv.* —**blood'less-ness,** *n.*

blood-mo-bile ('mō-bēl), *n.* a motor vehicle that carries equipment for collecting blood from donors for blood banks.

blood money, 1. atonement money received by the family of a murder victim. 2. money obtained at the cost of another's life.

blood poisoning, a disease in which the blood contains poison-producing microorganisms.

blood pressure, the pressure of the blood on the walls of the blood vessels, which varies according to age and condition.

blood relation, a person related by birth: also called **blood relative.**

blood-shed ('shed), *n.* the shedding of blood; slaughter; killing.

blood-shot ('shot), *adj.* having traces of red because small blood vessels are broken: said of the eyes.

blood-stone ('stōn), *n.* a dark-green variety of quartz spotted with red jasper, used for gems.

blood-suck-er ('suk-ẽr), *n.* 1. an animal that sucks blood; leech. 2. one who extorts.

blood-thirst-y ('thūr-sti), *adj.* eager to shed blood; extremely cruel.

blood vessel, a vein, artery, or capillary.

bloody (blud'i), *adj.* **blood'i-er, blood'i-est,** 1. of, pertaining to, containing, or resembling blood. 2. stained with, covered by, or dripping blood. 3. cruel; murderous. 4. marked by bloodshed. 5. [British Slang], damned: *adv.* [British Slang], very: *v.t.* **blood'ied, blood'y-ing,** to cover with blood or get blood on. —**blood'i-ly,** *adv.* —**blood'i-ness,** *n.*

Bloody Mary (mer'i), a mixed drink of vodka and tomato juice.

bloom (blōōm), *n.* 1. a flower; blossom. 2. the blossoming time or condition of flowers. 3. the state or period of highest health, freshness, or beauty. 4. a healthy glow or flush (of skin, cheeks, etc.). 5. the powdery, grayish covering on some fruits, as the grape. 6. a coating like this, as on new coins. 7. a rough mass of iron ready for working. 8. an iron or steel bar made by hammering or rolling an ingot: *v.i.* 1. to produce blossoms; flower. 2. to flourish with health, beauty, etc. 3. to glow with color, health, etc.

bloom-er (blōō'mẽr), *n.* 1. a 19th-century costume for women, advocated by Mrs. Amelia J. Bloomer of New York, consisting of a short skirt and loose trousers fastened around the ankle. 2. *pl.* loose trousers fastened at the knee, formerly worn by women and girls in athletic activities; also, a similar undergarment.

bloom-ing ('ming), *adj.* 1. flowering. 2. prospering. 3. [Informal], complete.

bloop-er (blōōp'ẽr), *n.* [Slang], 1. a foolish error. 2. in *Baseball*, a pitched or batted ball thrown or hit in an arc.

blos-som (blos'ŏm), *n.* 1. the flower of a plant that bears fruit. 2. the state of flowering; bloom: *v.i.* 1. to put forth blossoms; flower. 2. to flourish; develop.

blot (blot), *n.* 1. a spot or stain, as of ink. 2. a blemish. 3. a disgrace: *v.t.* **blot'ted, blot'ting,** 1. to spot or stain; mar. 2. to disgrace. 3. to erase, get rid of, or cover up (usually followed by *out*). 4. to dry, as with blotting paper: *v.i.* 1. to make blots. 2. to become blotted. 3. to absorb.

blotch (bloch), *n.* 1. a large spot or blot. 2. an eruption or pustule: *v.t.* to mark or cover with blots or spots. —**blotch'y,** *adj.* **blotch'i-er, blotch'i-est.**

blot-ter (blot'ẽr), *n.* 1. a blotting paper. 2. a book used for keeping records of events as they happen.

blotting paper, a soft paper used to dry an inked surface by absorbing excess ink.

blouse (blous, blouz), *n.* 1. a light, loose overgarment. 2. a kind of shirtwaist. 3. a military jacket.

blow (blō), *v.i.* **blew, blown, blow'ing,** 1. to form or make a current of air. 2. to pant; breathe quickly. 3. to sound by being blown. 4. to spout water and air, as whales. 5. to be carried away by an air current. 6. to be stormy. 7. to burst, break, or melt suddenly (often followed by *out*). 8. to deposit eggs: said of flies. 9. [Informal], to boast. 10. [Slang], to depart; leave: *v.t.* 1. to drive a current of air upon or through. 2. to propel by a current of air. 3. to sound (a wind instrument, whistle, etc.) by forcing air through. 4. to clear by forcing air through. 5. to form by blowing air or gas. 6. to shatter or scatter by explosives. 7. to spread (news). 8. to put (a horse) out of breath. 9.

to melt (a fuse, etc.). 10. to deposit eggs in: said of flies. 11. [Informal], to squander (money). 12. [Informal], to treat (*to* a meal, drink, etc.). 13. [Slang], to go away from. 14. [Slang], to botch: *n.* 1. the act of blowing. 2. a blast of air. 3. a gale of wind. 4. [Slang], one who brags. —blow'er, *n.*

blow (blō), *n.* 1. a hard stroke with the hand or with a weapon. 2. a sudden attack. 3. a sudden shock or calamity.

blow (blō), *n.* 1. a mass of blossoms. 2. the state or condition of flowering: *v.i.* [Poetical], to blossom; flower.

blow-by-blow ('bī-blō), *adj.* in full detail.

blow-fly (blō'flī), *n., pl.* -flies, a fly with two wings that deposits its eggs upon meat, open wounds, etc.

blow-gun ('gun), *n.* a tube or hollow reed through which darts, projectiles, etc. are forced by the breath.

blow-hole ('hōl), *n.* 1. a hole for air or gas to escape. 2. the nostril at the top of a whale's head. 3. a defect in a casting of metal, caused by a bubble of air or gas.

blown (blōn), *adj.* 1. swollen; inflated. 2. out of breath; exhausted. 3. covered with the eggs and larvae of flies.

blow-out ('out), *n.* 1. the act or consequence of blowing out. 2. the bursting of a tire. 3. the melting of an electric fuse. 4. [Slang], a big party, celebration, etc.

blow-pipe ('pīp), *n.* 1. a blowgun. 2. a tube through which air or gas is forced, as on a flame to increase its heat.

blow-torch ('tôrch), *n.* a hand-held device that shoots out an intensely hot jet of flame and air, used especially to melt metals.

blow-up ('up), *n.* 1. an explosion. 2. a photograph that has been enlarged. 3. [Informal], an outburst of anger or hysterics.

blow-y ('i), *adj.* blow'i-er, blow'i-est, windy.

blowz-y (blou'zi), *adj.* blowz'i-er, blowz'i-est, 1. ruddy, fat, and coarse-complexioned. 2. untidy; shabby. Also blows'y.

blub-ber (blub'ēr), *v.i.* to weep violently: *v.t.* to disfigure with weeping: *n.* the fat of whales and other sea mammals, used to make an oil. —blub'ber-er, *n.*

blu-cher (blōō'chēr, 'kēr), *n.* a shoe with vamp and tongue in one piece.

bludg-eon (bluj'n), *n.* a short club with a heavy end: *v.t. & v.i.* to hit or drive as with a bludgeon.

blue (blōō), *adj.* 1. of the color of the clear sky. 2. livid: said of the skin. 3. low-spirited; depressed. 4. puritanical; severe. 5. [Informal], suggestive; racy: *n.* 1. the color of the clear sky. 2. a dye or pigment of this color. 3. *pl.* [Informal], low spirits (preceded by *the*). 4. *pl.* Negro folk music usually slow in tempo and having sad lyrics (often preceded by *the*).

blue baby, a baby born with a heart defect or lungs not fully expanded which causes the skin to have a bluish tinge.

blue-bell (blōō'bel), *n.* a plant with blue, bell-shaped flowers, as the harebell.

blue-ber-ry ('ber-i), *n., pl.* -ries, 1. a shrub that has small, blue-black berries that can be eaten. 2. one of the berries.

blue-bird ('būrd), *n.* a small North American songbird: the male usually has a bluish back and reddish breast.

blue blood, 1. aristocratic lineage. 2. an aristocrat: also blue'blood, *n.* —blue'-blood-ed, *adj.*

blue-bon-net ('bon-it), *n.* 1. a former Scottish cap of blue wool. 2. a Scot. 3. a wildflower with blue blossoms, found in the southwestern U.S.

blue book, 1. [also B- B-], a governmental official report. 2. a listing of high society. 3. a booklet with blank pages and a blue paper cover, to write examination answers in: also blue'book, *n.*

blue-bot-tle ('bot-l), *n.* 1. a plant with blue, bottlelike flowers. 2. a blue blowfly.

blue cheese, a cheese resembling Roquefort.

blue-coat ('kōt), *n.* 1. a 19th-century U.S. soldier. 2. a policeman.

blue-col-lar ('kol'ēr), *adj.* of or denoting workers in industry.

blue devils, 1. mental depression. 2. delirium tremens or its hallucinations.

blue-fish ('fish), *n., pl.* -fish, -fish-es, a common, bluish food fish caught commercially along the Atlantic coast of North America.

blue-gill ('gil), *n.* a bluish sunfish found in fresh waters.

blue-grass ('gras), *n.* a pasture grass of temperate and arctic regions.

blue gum, a large Australian tree with smooth bark and sweet-smelling leaves.

blue-jack-et ('jak-it), *n.* an enlisted man in the navy of the U.S. or Great Britain.

blue jay, a bluish, often crested, American bird: also blue'jay, *n.*

blue law, 1. one of the very strict laws governing moral behavior or religious activity as originated by the Puritans in colonial New England. 2. any law viewed as puritanical, as one forbidding liquor sales on Sunday.

blue mold, a fungus that produces a quantity of bluish spores: some types are used in making penicillin and some to ripen cheeses.

blue-nose ('nōz), *n.* [Informal], a puritanical person.

blue-pen-cil ('pen-sl), *v.t.* -ciled or -cilled, -ciling or -cil-ling, to edit with a blue pencil.

blue peter, a small, blue flag with a white square in the center, used as a signal.

blue-point ('point), *n.* a small oyster from near Blue Point, Long Island.

blue-print ('print), *n.* 1. a white photographic print on a blue background, as of architectural plans. 2. a plan or outline in great detail: *v.t.* to make a blueprint of.

blue ribbon, the highest prize in a contest.

blue-sky law, [Informal], a law to prevent the issue of fraudulent stocks, bonds, etc.

blue-stock-ing ('stok-ing), *n.* a woman of literary tastes or occupation.

blue-stone ('stōn), *n.* same as copper sulfate.

blu-et (blōō'it), *n.* a small plant having tiny, light-blue flowers.

blue vitriol, same as copper sulfate.

bluff (bluf), *adj.* 1. having a broad, flattened front; rising steeply or boldly; broad and full. 2. rough and hearty: *n.* 1. a high, steep bank; a cliff with a broad steep face. 2. the act of bluffing. 3. someone who bluffs: *v.t.*

1. to try to deceive (an opponent in the game of poker) by inducing the other players to suppose one's hand is more valuable than it is in reality. **2.** to deceive or frighten (someone) by an assumed possession of strength or knowledge. —**bluff'er**, *n.*

blu-ing (blōō'ing), *n.* a bluish substance used to wash white fabrics to keep them from turning yellow: also **blue'ing**.

blun-der (blun'dẽr), *v.i.* **1.** to make a gross mistake; err stupidly. **2.** to move or act clumsily: *v.t.* to bungle: *n.* a gross or stupid mistake. —**blun'der-er**, —**blun'der-ing-ly**, *adv.*

blun-der-buss (blun'dẽr-bus), *n.* an obsolete short gun with a large bore.

blunt (blunt), *adj.* **1.** slow in understanding; dull. **2.** having a thick or rounded edge or point; not sharp. **3.** plain-spoken; abrupt: *v.t.* **1.** to make (a point or edge) dull. **2.** to lessen the force, keenness, or sensitivity of: *v.i.* to become dull. —**blunt'ly**, *adv.* —**blunt'ness**, *n.*

blur (blur), *v.t. & v.i.* blurred, blur'ring, **1.** to dim. **2.** to sully; stain; blemish. **3.** to make or become unclear or hazy: *n.* **1.** a smudge. **2.** a dim, confused appearance. —**blur'ri-ness**, *n.* —**blur'ry**, *adj.*

blurb (blûrb), *n.* [Informal], a usually exaggerated statement or advertisement about the contents, as on a book jacket.

blurt (blûrt), *v.t.* to speak inadvertently; divulge without thinking (followed by *out*).

blush (blush), *v.i.* **1.** to become red in the face, as from shame or confusion. **2.** to become rosy. **3.** to feel shame (usually followed by *at* or *for*): *n.* **1.** the suffusion of the cheeks or face with a red color through shame, confusion, modesty, etc. **2.** a rosy tint: *adj.* rosy. —**blush'ful**, *adj.*

blus-ter (blus'tẽr), *v.i.* **1.** to blow violently: said of the wind. **2.** to talk or behave in a noisy, swaggering manner: *v.t.* to say noisily or with a bullying manner: *n.* **1.** noise and violence, as of a storm. **2.** noisy talk or swagger. —**blus'ter-er**, —**blus'ter-ing-ly**, *adv.* —**blus'ter-y**, **blus'ter-ous**, *adj.*

bo-a (bō'ä), *n.* **1.** a tropical snake that destroys its prey by crushing with its coils. **2.** a long fur or feather scarf worn by a woman.

boa constrictor, a type of boa that reaches up to 15 feet long.

boar (bôr), *n.*, *pl.* **boars**, **boar**, **1.** a male hog or pig that has not been castrated. **2.** a wild hog.

board (bôrd), *n.* **1.** a piece of timber sawed thin, of considerable length and width compared with its thickness. **2.** *a)* a table for food. *b)* the food served; especially, regular meals provided for pay. **3.** a number of persons elected to the management of a business, school, etc.; council. **4.** a table or frame for some special use, as for games or ironing. **5.** a thick, stiff kind of construction material. **6.** pasteboard, as for book covers. **7.** *pl.* the stage (of a theater). **8.** the side of a ship. **9.** in *nautical usage*, a course taken against the wind; tack: *v.t.* **1.** to cover with boards (followed by *up*). **2.** to furnish with

food, or food and lodging, for a compensation. **3.** to place (someone) where board is furnished. **4.** to go on the deck of (a ship). **5.** to go beside (a ship), especially threateningly. **6.** to get on (a bus, aircraft, etc.): *v.i.* to be supplied with meals, or obtain food and lodging, at a fixed charge. —**board'er**, *n.*

board foot, *pl.* **board feet**, the volume of a board one foot square and one inch thick: a unit of measure.

board-ing (bôr'ding), *n.* **1.** light timber collectively. **2.** a covering of boards.

board-ing-house (-hous), *n.* a house where food, or food and lodging, is furnished for a fixed charge: also **boarding house**.

board of trade, same as **chamber of commerce**.

board-walk ('wôk), *n.* a walk of planking, often raised, especially at beaches and recreation grounds.

boar-hound (bôr'hound), *n.* a Great Dane or other large dog for hunting wild boars.

boar-ish ('ish), *adj.* swinish, brutal, etc.

boast (bōst), *v.i.* **1.** to speak too proudly of oneself or the accomplishments of someone close; brag. **2.** to exult: *v.t.* to brag of or be proud of: *n.* **1.** the act of boasting. **2.** the cause of boasting. —**boast'er**, *n.* —**boast'ing-ly**, *adv.*

boast-ful (bōst'fŭl), *adj.* given to boasting. —**boast'ful-ly**, *adv.* —**boast'ful-ness**, *n.*

boat (bōt), *n.* **1.** a small open vessel moved by oars, sails, or an engine. **2.** a ship. **3.** an open dish resembling a boat in shape: *v.t.* to transport in a boat: *v.i.* to go in a boat; row or sail.

boat-er (bōt'ẽr), *n.* a hat of stiff straw with a flat crown and brim.

boat-man ('măn), *n.*, *pl.* **-men**, a man who works on or deals in boats.

boat-swain (bō'sn), *n.* a ship's warrant officer or petty officer having any of various duties, as supervising the deck crew, taking charge of rigging, etc.

bob (bob), *v.t.* **1.** to give a short, jerking motion. **2.** to cut (hair, a tail, etc.) short: *v.i.* **1.** to make a short, jerking motion; move up and down. **2.** to fish with a bob: *n.* **1.** any small round object, as the weight at the end of a plumb line, hanging loosely at the end of a cord, chain, etc.; pendant. **3.** a float or knot of bait on the end of a fishing line. **4.** a short haircut on a woman or girl. **5.** a bobbing movement. **6.** [British Slang], a shilling.

bob-bin (bob'in), *n.* **1.** one of the small pins, as of wood, used to make bobbin lace. **2.** a spool or reel to hold yarn or thread for spinning, weaving, sewing, etc.

bob-bi-net (bob-i-net'), *n.* a machine-made netting of fabric, with a hexagonal mesh.

bobbin lace, a lace made on a pad like a pillow, with bobbins drawing the thread around pins.

bob-ble (bob'l), *n.* **1.** a bobbing movement. **2.** [Informal], a blunder; specifically, in *Sports*, a clumsy manipulating of the ball: *v.i.* **-bled**, **-bling**, **1.** to make a bobbing movement. **2.** [Informal], to blunder: *v.t.* [Informal], to handle clumsily.

---

a in cap, ā in cane, ä in father, ȧ in abet, e in met, ē in be, ê in baker, ê in regent, i in pit, ī in fine, i in manifest, o in hot, ō in horse, ō in bone,

bob·by (bob'i), *n., pl.* **-bies**, [British Informal], a policeman.

bobby pin, a small, metal hairpin with tightly pressed sides.

bobby socks, [Informal], socks reaching just over the ankle, worn by girls: also **bobby sox**.

bob·by·sox·er (bob'i-sok-sēr), *n.* [Informal], a teen-age girl: also **bob'by·sox·er**.

bob·cat (bob'kat), *n., pl.* **-cats**, **-cat**, a North American wildcat.

bob·o·link (bob'ō-lingk), *n.* a songbird of North America.

bob·sled (bob'sled), *n.* a long sled with a steering apparatus and brakes, often ridden by a team of two or four persons in races: *v.i.* **-sled·ded**, **-sled·ding**, to race or ride on a bobsled.

bob·stay ('stā), *n.* a rope or chain for holding down the bowsprit to keep a boat from moving up and down.

bob·tail ('tāl), *n.* a tail cut short.

bob·white (bob-hwit'), *n., pl.* **-whites**, **-white**, a small quail of North America.

boc·cie (boch'i), *n.* an Italian game played like bowls: also **boc'ce**, **boc'ci**.

bock (bok), *n.* a dark beer: also **bock beer**.

bode (bōd), *v.t.* **bod'ed**, **bod'ing**, to portend.

bode (bōd), alternate past tense of **bide**.

bod·ice (bod'is), *n.* the part of a woman's dress above the waist.

bod·i·ly (bod'l-i), *adj.* 1. not mental; physical. 2. of or pertaining to the body: *adv.* 1. physically. 2. entirely. 3. as one group.

bod·ing (hō'ding), *n.* an omen; presentiment: *adj.* foreboding; ominous.

bod·kin (bod'kn), *n.* 1. a pointed instrument for piercing holes in cloth. 2. a long pin to fasten up the hair. 3. a thick, blunt needle for drawing tape, ribbon, etc. through openwork. 4. an awllike printer's tool.

bod·y (bod'i), *n., pl.* **-ies**, 1. the material, organized substance of a physical being, as distinguished from the soul, spirit, etc. 2. the structure of an animal, plant, or human being. 3. the trunk, or main portion, of an animal or human being. 4. a dead person. 5. [Informal], a person. 6. the main part of anything. 7. an aircraft's fuselage. 8. a ship's hull. 9. a number of individuals united by some common tie. 10. anything having mass or form. 11. a separate mass, as of water. 12. a certain consistency or density, as of a liquid. 13. substance. 14. richness or flavor: *v.t.* **bod'ied**, **bod'y·ing**, 1. to furnish with a body. 2. to embody.

bod·y·guard (-gärd), *n.* one or more persons whose duty it is to guard someone.

body politic, all the people under a particular government.

body snatcher, one who steals bodies from graves, as formerly for dissection.

body stocking, a garment fitting tightly over the torso and, sometimes, the legs.

Boe·o·tian (bē-ō'shun), *adj.* of Boeotia, in central Greece, or its inhabitants: *n.* a native or inhabitant of Boeotia.

Boer (bôr, boor), *n.* a South African descendant of Dutch colonists.

bog (bog), *v.t. & v.i.* **bogged**, **bog'ging**, to sink or stick in or as in a bog (often followed by *down*); mire: *n.* an area of wet, spongy ground; marsh.

bo·gey (bō'gi), *n., pl.* **-geys**, 1. same as **bogy** (senses 1 & 2). 2. in *Golf*, one stroke more than par on a single hole.

bog·gle (bog'l), *v.i.* **-gled**, **-gling**, 1. to be shocked or frightened (followed by *at*). 2. to hesitate (followed by *at*). 3. to waver; equivocate (followed by *at*). 4. to bungle: *v.i.* to bungle: *n.* an act of boggling.

bog·gy (bog'i, bôg'i), *adj.* **-gi·er**, **-gi·est**, 1. full of bogs. 2. marshy.

bo·gie (bō'gi), *n., pl.* **-gies**, 1. same as **bogy** (senses 1 & 2). 2. same as **bogey** (sense 2). 3. a low, swiveling section under either end of a railroad car for rounding curves.

bog·trot·ter (bog'trot-ēr), *n.* someone who inhabits a bog.

bo·gus (bō'gûs), *adj.* counterfeit; spurious.

bo·gy (bō'gi), *n., pl.* **-gies**, 1. an imaginary frightful being. 2. a bugbear. 3. same as **bo·gie** (sense 3).

bo·gy·man, **bo·gey·man** (bō'gi-man, boog'i-), *n., pl.* **-men**, a frightening creature of the imagination, especially one used as a threat in trying to make children behave.

Bo·he·mi·an (bō-hē'mi-ăn), *n.* 1. a native or inhabitant of Bohemia, a region of western Czechoslovakia. 2. a gypsy. 3. [often b-], a person, as an artist or poet, who disregards social conventions: *adj.* 1. of or pertaining to Bohemia or its inhabitants. 2. [often b-], like a Bohemian (*n.* 3). —**Bo·he'mi·an·ism**, *n.*

boil (boil), *v.i.* 1. to bubble and turn into vapor through the action of heat. 2. to seethe. 3. to be agitated or excited by passion or anger. 4. to be subjected to the action of boiling water: *v.t.* 1. to heat to the boiling point. 2. to collect from, process, or separate, by boiling; subject to the action of heat in a boiling liquid: *n.* the act or condition of boiling.

boil (boil), *n.* an inflamed and painful pustule.

boil·er (boi'lēr), *n.* 1. a vessel in which anything is boiled. 2. a tank in which steam is generated, as for driving engines. 3. a tank for the storage of water after heating.

boiling point, the temperature at which a liquid boils: water boils at 212°F or 100°C at sea level.

bois·ter·ous (bois'tēr-ùs), *adj.* 1. rough and stormy; turbulent. 2. noisy or lively. —**bois'ter·ous·ly**, *adv.*

bo·la (bō'lä), *n.* a hunting device consisting of a long cord with heavy balls at the ends, thrown to entangle an animal: also **bo'las** ('läs).

bold (bōld), *adj.* 1. courageous; venturesome. 2. overstepping conventional rules. 3. forward; rude; impudent. 4. striking to the eye; prominent. 5. steep, as a cliff. —**bold'ly**, *adv.* —**bold'ness**, *n.*

bold-faced (bōld'fāst), *adj.* forward; rude.

ô in dragon, o͞o in crude, oo in wool, u in cup, ū in cure, ū in turn, ŭ in focus, oi in boy, ou in house, th in thin, th in sheathe, g in get, j in joy, y in yet.

bole (bōl), *n.* 1. a tree trunk. 2. a kind of reddish clay that can be easily crushed.

bo·le·ro (bō-ler'ō), *n., pl.* -ros, 1. a lively Spanish dance. 2. the music accompanying such a dance. 3. a short jacket with or without sleeves, that opens at the front.

bo·lide (bō'līd), *n.* a large meteor, especially one that explodes.

Bo·liv·i·an (bō-liv'i-ăn), *adj.* of or pertaining to Bolivia, a country of South America, or its inhabitants: *n.* a native or inhabitant of Bolivia.

boll (bōl), *n.* the seed pod of a plant, as of flax or cotton.

bol·lard (bol'ărd), *n.* a strong post for securing hawsers.

boll weevil, a small weevil which infests the cotton plant, laying its eggs in the bolls, on which the larvae afterward feed, destroying the bolls.

bo·lo (bō'lō), *n., pl.* -los, a large knife with a single edge, used in the Philippines as a cutting tool or weapon.

bo·lo·gna (bō-lō'ni), *n.* a smoked sausage of pork, beef, or veal, or of these meats mixed: also **bologna sausage.**

bo·lom·e·ter (bō-lom'ě-tĕr), *n.* a sensitive instrument for measuring minute amounts of radiant energy.

bolo tie, a string tie clasped with a slide piece, worn by men.

Bol·she·vik (bōl'shĕ-vik, bol'), *n., pl.* -viks, -vi'ki (-vē'ki), [also b-], 1. a member of the majority section of the Social Democratic Party which came to power in Russia in 1917 and formed the Communist Party. 2. a Communist, especially from the Soviet Union. —**bol'she·vism,** *n.*

bol·ster (bōl'stĕr), *n.* 1. a long pillow or cushion. 2. a pad to ease pressure on some part of the body. 3. anything like a bolster used as for support: *v.t.* to support as with a bolster; prop (often with *up*).

bolt (bōlt), *n.* 1. a short, thick arrow with a blunt head. 2. a lightning flash; thunderbolt. 3. a sudden movement; dash. 4. a metallic rod or pin, usually with threads, used with a nut to hold objects together. 5. the portion of a lock shot or withdrawn by the key. 6. a metal bar slid in and out, as in securing a door. 7. a roll of fabric, paper, etc. of a specified length. 8. a withdrawing from one's party or group: *adv.* 1. straight. 2. [Archaic]; suddenly: *v.i.* 1. to blurt (*out*). 2. to fasten or secure as with a bolt. 3. to swallow (food) hurriedly or without chewing. 4. to withdraw support from (a party, group, etc.). 5. [Archaic], to shoot (an arrow, etc.): *v.i.* 1. to spring out suddenly. 2. to start and run off, as a horse. 3. to withdraw support from one's party, group, etc.

bolt (bōlt), *v.t.* 1. to sift or separate the coarser from the finer particles of (grain, flour, etc.). 2. to examine with care; inspect and separate.

bolt·rope (bōlt'rōp), *n.* a rope sewn into the edges of a sail for strengthening.

bo·lus (bō'lŭs), *n., pl.* **bo'lus·es,** 1. a small round mass or lump. 2. a large pill.

bomb (bom), *n.* 1. an object filled with explosive, incendiary, or otherwise destructive material, for throwing, dropping, etc. 2. a small device holding compressed gas. 3. [Slang], a total failure: *v.t.* to damage or attack with bombs: *v.i.* [Slang], to fail.

bom·bard (bom-bärd'), *v.t.* 1. to attack with artillery or bombs. 2. to fire questions at. 3. to send particles, as neutrons, against the atomic nuclei of (an element). —**bom·bard'-ment,** *n.*

bom·bar·dier (bom-bă-dir', bom-bĕr-), *n.* the crew member releasing bombs from a bomber.

bom·bar·don (bom'bĕr-dŏn), *n.* a bass or contrabass tube.

bom·bast (bom'bast), *n.* 1. originally, soft material used for stuffing. 2. high-sounding words; pompous language or style.

bom·bas·tic (bom-bas'tik), *adj.* using high-sounding or pompous language; pompous. —**bom·bas'ti·cal·ly,** *adv.*

bom·ba·zine (bom-bă-zēn'), *n.* a twilled fabric of rayon or silk with worsted.

bomb·er (bom'ĕr), *n.* 1. an airplane designed for dropping bombs. 2. a person who bombs.

bomb·proof (bom'prōōf), *adj.* able to withstand bombs or shells.

bomb·shell ('shel), *n.* 1. a bomb. 2. an abrupt surprise.

bo·na fi·de (bō'nă fīd, fi'di), [Latin], in good faith; honest.

bo·nan·za (bō-nan'ză), *n.* 1. a rich vein of ore. 2. any source of profit.

bon·bon (bon'bon), *n.* a piece of candy, as a chocolate drop.

bond (bond), *n.* 1. anything that binds, fastens, or confines. 2. *pl.* fetters; also, [Archaic], bondage. 3. a binding substance, as glue. 4. a uniting force or agreement. 5. a duty or obligation resulting from a promise or contractual agreement. 6. the state of goods warehoused until taxes are met. 7. a certificate bearing interest, issued by a government or business to raise money. 8. a hard, strong, high-quality paper: also **bond paper.** 9. in *Chemistry*, a unit of combining power equivalent to one atom of hydrogen. 10. in *Law, a)* an instrument specifying certain payments or the doing or not doing of something specified. *b)* an amount paid as bail or security: *v.t.* 1. to bind with or as with a bond. 2. to supply a bond, or bail, for (a person). 3. to put (goods) under bond: *v.i.* to connect, hold together, etc. by or as by a bond.

bond·age (bon'dij), *n.* 1. slavery or serfdom. 2. subjection.

bond·ed (bon'did), *adj.* 1. placed under bond. 2. secured by bonds.

bonded warehouse, a warehouse for the storage of bonded goods.

bond·man (bond'măn), *n., pl.* -men, 1. a feudal serf. 2. a male bondservant. —**bond'wom·an,** *n.fem., pl.* -wom·en.

bond·ser·vant ('sŭr-vănt), *n.* 1. one obliged to serve without pay. 2. a slave.

bonds·man (bondz'măn), *n., pl.* -men, 1. same as **boudman**. 2. one going surety for another by bond.

bone (bōn), *n.* 1. the hard tissue forming the skeleton of most vertebrate animals. 2. one of the parts or pieces of an animal skeleton. 3. *pl.* the skeleton. 4. something made of bone. 5. a substance like bone. 6. *pl.* flat pieces used to make a clapping sound in minstrel shows: *v.t.* **boned, bon'ing,** 1. to remove the bones from. 2. to put whalebone into in order to stiffen: *v.i.* [Slang], to study intensely (usually followed by *up*). —**bone·less,** *adj.*

bone-black (bōn'blak), *n.* charcoal produced from burned animal bones, used as a coloring matter: also **bone black.**

bone china, china that is partially transparent, made from the ash of burned animal bones and white clay.

bone-dry (bōn'drī'), *adj.* very dry.

bone meal, bones that have been ground or crushed for use as animal feed or fertilizer.

bon·er (bōn'ẽr), *n.* [Slang], a stupid error.

bon·fire (hon'fīr), *n.* any large fire made in the open air, as to burn rubbish.

bong (bông, bong), *n.* a low, ringing sound, as of a large bell: *v.i.* to ring so.

bon·go (bong'gō), *n., pl.* -gos, either of two small drums joined together that are played by striking with the fingers: also **bongo drum.**

bon·ho·mie (bon-ô-mē'), *n.* a frank, friendly manner; good-heartedness: also **bon·hom·mie'.**

bo·ni·to (bô-nēt'ō), *n., pl.* -tos, -toes, a saltwater fish related to the tuna.

bon·jour (bôn-zhōōr'), *interj.* [French], good day.

bon mot (bôn' mō'), *pl.* **bons mots** (bôn' mōz'), [French], a witty saying; clever remark.

bonne (bôn), *n.* [French], 1. a nursemaid. 2. a female servant.

bon·net (bon'ĭt), *n.* 1. a flat cap without a brim, worn by men and boys in Scotland. 2. a women's or children's hat with a chin ribbon. 3. anything bonnetlike: *v.t.* to put a bonnet on.

bon·ny (bon'i), *adj.* -ni·er, -ni·est, 1. pretty or handsome, and glowing. 2. pleasant: also **bonnie.**

bon·sai (bon-sī'), *n., pl.* **bon·sai'**, [Japanese], a shrub or tree grown in a pot and kept dwarfed by special culture.

bon·soir (bôn-swär'), [French], good evening.

bon·spiel (bon'spēl), *n.* a curling match between players of different clubs.

bon ton (bôn tōn'), [French], 1. the fine manners associated with high society. 2. fashionable society. 3. the height of fashion.

bo·nus (bō'nŭs), *n., pl.* **bo'nus·es,** amount given, or paid, over and above what is required or customary; specifically, an amount paid in addition to regular pay or wages, especially as a reward.

bon voy·age (bon voi-äzh'), [French], pleasant trip.

bon·y (bō'ni), *adj.* **bon'i·er, bon'i·est,** 1. of, pertaining to, or resembling bone. 2. having many or prominent bones. 3. very thin. —**bon'i·ness,** *n.*

beo (bōō), *interj. & n., pl.* **boos,** a sound made to express contempt or to surprise or scare: *v.i. & v.t.* to cry "boo" (at).

boo-boo (bōō'bōō), *n., pl.* -boos, [Slang], a blunder: also **booboo.**

boo-by (bōō'bi), *n., pl.* -bies, 1. a stupid person: also **boob** (bōōb). 2. a diving bird like the gannet.

booby prize, a prize given in fun to the worst contestant in a game or competition.

booby trap, 1. a plan or device for deceiving someone unprepared. 2. a mine with its detonator attached to an innocent-looking object.

boo·dle (bōō'dl), *n.* [Slang], 1. bribe money; graft. 2. stolen money, valuables, etc.

boo-hoo (bōō-hōō'), *v.i.* -hooed', -hoo'ing, to cry noisily: *n., pl.* -hoos', noisy crying.

book (book), *n.* 1. a collection of sheets of paper or other material, blank, written, or printed, and bound together. 2. a long division, section, or part of a literary work. 3. a register or record. 4. a list of bets made, as on horses in a race. 5. the words of a musical play or opera. 6. a package, as of matches, opening like a book. 7. [B-], the Bible (preceded by *the*): *v.t.* 1. to enter or register in a book; record. 2. to engage (lodgings, performers, etc.) in advance. —**book'er,** *n.*

book·bind·ing (book'bīn-ding), *n.* the skill or business of binding books. —**book'bind·er,** *n.* —**book'bind·er·y,** *n., pl.* -er·ies.

book·case ('kās), *n.* a cabinet for books.

book·end ('end), *n.* a movable upright support at either end of a row of books.

book·ie ('i), *n.* [Slang], a bookmaker.

book·ing ('ing), *n.* a period or occasion of employment for a performance.

book·ish ('ish), *adj.* 1. given to reading; fond of study. 2. pedantic.

book·keep·ing ('kēp-ing), *n.* the work of recording financial or business transactions in a regular or systematic manner. —**book'keep·er,** *n.*

book·let ('lit), *n.* a little book.

book·mak·er ('māk-ẽr), *n.* 1. one who compiles or publishes books. 2. one whose occupation is taking bets, as on racehorses.

book·man ('măn), *n., pl.* -men, a scholarly person.

book·mark ('märk), *n.* a card or the like that a reader puts between book pages, as to indicate the last page read.

book·mo·bile ('mō-bēl), *n.* a traveling library in a vehicle for lending books to persons in areas without permanent libraries.

book·worm ('wŭrm), *n.* 1. any insect or its larva infesting and injuring books. 2. a person who studies or reads very much.

boom (bōōm), *n.* 1. a long pole or spar run out to extend the foot of certain sails from the mast. 2. an obstruction laid across an area of water, as to keep logs from floating away. 3. a long pole reaching out from a vertical part, used to raise or guide something. 4. a deep hollow sound. 5. a strong, fast development. 6. a sudden burst of popular favor. 7. a time of prosperous business conditions: *v.i.* 1. to make a deep, hollow, reverberating sound. 2. to go along with a rush. 3. to flourish rapidly: *v.t.* 1. to utter with a deep, hollow sound. 2. to make flourish rapidly. 3. to promote with energy.

boom·box ('boks), *n.* [Slang], a large, portable radio or tape player.

boom·er·ang (bōōm'ē-rang), *n.* 1. a weapon used by Australian aborigines, which consists of a flat, curved piece of wood that when thrown returns to a point near the thrower. 2. any action which goes wrong and results in damage to the doer: *v.i.* to act as a boomerang.

boon (bōōn), *n.* 1. a benefit; gift. 2. [Archaic], a request: *adj.* convivial: now only in **boon companion**.

boon·docks (bōōn'doks), *n.* [Informal], a wilderness or any remote area.

boon·dog·gle (bōōn'dog-l), *v.i.* -gled, -gling, [Informal], to do unimportant, meaningless work: *n.* unimportant, meaningless work. —**boon'dog·gler,** *n.*

boor (boor), *n.* 1. originally, a peasant. 2. [B-], same as **Boer.** 3. a rude or clumsy person. —**boor'ish,** *adj.*

boost (bōōst), *v.t.* 1. to lift by pushing from behind or below. 2. to promote; urge support for. 3. to make greater: *n.* 1. a push from behind or below. 2. an increase. —**boost'er,** *n.*

booster shot, an amount of vaccine injected at a time after the main portion to maintain immunity: also **booster injection.**

boot (bōōt), *n.* 1. a covering of leather, rubber, etc. for the foot and part of the leg. 2. a patch for the inside surface of a tire casing. 3. a kick: *v.t.* 1. to put boots on. 2. to kick. 3. [Slang], to discharge from a job or cause to leave a place. 4. to load, as from a disk (a program, etc.) into the memory of (a computer).

boot (bōōt), *n.* & *v.t.* & *v.i.* [Poetic], profit.

boot·black (bōōt'blak), *n.* a person who shines shoes and boots for a living.

boot·ee (bōō-tē'), *n.* 1. a short boot for women and children. 2. (bōōt'i), a soft shoe of cloth or knitting for a baby. Also **bootie.**

booth (bōōth), *n., pl.* **booths** (bōōthz), 1. a temporary structure. 2. a stall for selling goods, as at a market. 3. a small enclosed structure for voting. 4. a small permanent structure, as for housing a telephone. 5. a partial enclosure, with table and seats, usually one of several, as in a restaurant.

boot·jack (bōōt'jak), *n.* a device to grip the heel of a boot being pulled off.

boot·leg ('leg), *v.t.* & *v.i.* to make or sell (especially intoxicating liquor) unlawfully: *adj.* illegal: *n.* something bootlegged, especially intoxicating liquor. —**boot'leg·ger,** *n.*

boot·less ('lis), *adj.* profitless.

boot tree, same as **shoe tree.**

boo·ty (bōōt'i), *n., pl.* -ties, 1. spoils taken in war. 2. plunder.

booze (bōōz), *v.i.* **boozed, booz'ing,** [Informal], to drink alcoholic liquor immoderately: *n.* [Informal], 1. alcoholic liquor. 2. a drinking spree.

bop (bop), *n.* a style of jazz (c. 1945-55) marked by complex rhythms, experimental harmonic structures, etc.: *v.i.* **bopped, bop'ping,** [Slang], to walk, esp. in an easy but strutting way.

bo·rac·ic (bô-ras'ik), *adj.* same as **boric.**

bo·rax (bôr'aks), *n.* a white, crystalline salt, with an alkaline taste, used as a flux in soldering metals and in the manufacture of glass, enamel, soap, etc.

bor·der (bôr'dēr), *n.* 1. the outer part or edge of anything; margin. 2. a boundary frontier. 3. a narrow flower bed along the edge of a garden: *v.t.* 1. to make a border about. 2. to be along the edge of: adjoin: *v.i.* to touch at the edge or boundary (with *on* or *upon*).

bor·der·land (-land), *n.* 1. land forming a border or frontier. 2. an uncertain or vague state.

bor·der·line (-līn), *n.* a line that separates; boundary: *adj.* 1. on a boundary. 2. having a debatable or vague position.

bore (bôr), *v.t.* **bored, bor'ing,** 1. to pierce or drill a hole in. 2. to form (a hole) by piercing or drilling. 3. to force (a passage), as through a crowd. 4. to weary by tedious repetition or by dullness: *v.i.* 1. to pierce or penetrate by boring or drilling. 2. to push forward slowly: *n.* 1. a hole made as by boring. 2. *a)* the hollow part inside a tube, as of the barrel of a gun. *b)* the internal diameter of this hole; caliber. 3. a person or thing that wearies by being repetitious, dull, etc. —**bor'er,** *n.*

bore (bôr), *n.* a high tidal wave coursing furiously through a narrow channel.

bo·re·al (bôr'i-ăl), *adj.* 1. northern. 2. of or pertaining to the north wind.

Bo·re·as (bôr'i-ăs), *n.* the north wind viewed as a being.

bore·dom (bôr'dôm), *n.* the state of being bored or uninterested; ennui.

bo·ric (bôr'ik), *adj.* of or containing boron.

boric acid, a white, crystalline compound, like a weak acid in nature, used as an antiseptic.

born (bôrn), alternate past participle of **bear:** *adj.* 1. brought to birth. 2. from or by birth. 3. innate; inherited.

born·a·gain (bôrn'ă-gen'), *adj.* professing a new or renewed faith or enthusiasm.

borne (bôrn), alternate past participle of **bear.**

bo·ron (bôr'on), *n.* a nonmetallic chemical element occurring abundantly in borax.

bor·ough (bûr'ō), *n.* 1. in some U.S. States, a town that is self-governing and incorporated. 2. one of the five administrative units of New York City.

bor·row (bor'ō), *v.t.* & *v.i.* 1. to obtain on loan. 2. to adopt, appropriate, or copy.

borsch (bôrsh), *n.* a hot or cold beet soup, usually served with sour cream: also **borsht** (bôrsht).

---

a in cap, ā in cane, ä in father, à in abet, e in met, ē in be, ē in baker, è in regent, i in pit, ī in fine, i in manifest, o in hot, ô in horse, ō in bone,

bort (bôrt), *n.* a variety of imperfect diamond used for polishing, grinding, etc.

bos·cage (bos'kij), *n.* an area covered with trees and shrubs; woods; thickets.

bosh (bosh), *n. & interj.* [Informal], utter non-sense.

bos·om (booz'ŏm), *n.* 1. the human breast. 2. the part of clothing covering the breast. 3. something bosomlike. 4. the breast thought of as the place from which feelings come. 5. an inside part; midst: *adj.* intimate; cherished; beloved: *v.t.* 1. to place or hide in the bosom. 2. to cherish.

boss (bôs), *n.* 1. one who superintends or directs the work of others; an employer, foreman, etc. 2. a politician who controls the party organization, as in a district: *v.t.* 1. to direct; manage. 2. [Informal], to act domineering toward: *adj.* 1. [Informal], principal. 2. [Slang], fine.

boss (bôs), *n.* 1. a protuberant part; ornamental stud or knob. 2. an ornamental projection, as on a roof: *v.t.* to ornament with studs or knobs.

boss·ism (bôs'izm), *n.* rule or domination by a political boss or bosses.

boss·y (bôs'i), *adj.* **boss'i·er, boss'i·est,** [Informal], overbearing; domineering. —**boss'i·ly,** *adv.* —**boss'i·ness,** *n.*

bo·sun (bos'n), *n.* same as **boatswain.**

bot (bot), *n.* the larva of a botfly.

bo·tan·i·cal (bō-tan'i-kl), *adj.* 1. of or pertaining to botany. 2. of, or made from, plants. Also **bo·tan'ic**: *n.* a drug made from herbs, bark, etc. —**bo·tan'i·cal·ly,** *adv.*

bot·a·nist (bot'n-ist), *n.* a student of or expert in botany.

bot·a·nize (bot'n-īz), *v.i.* **-nized, -niz·ing,** 1. to collect plants for study. 2. to study plants. —**bot'a·niz·er,** *n.*

bot·a·ny (bot'n-i), *n.* the science which treats of plants, their structure, growth, classification, distribution, etc.

botch (boch), *v.t.* 1. to mend or patch in a clumsy manner. 2. to put together poorly; spoil by poor workmanship: *n.* 1. a clumsy patch. 2. a poor piece of work.

bot·fly (bot'flī), *n., pl.* **-flies,** any one of a number of related, bumblebeelike flies, with larvae parasitic in horses, sheep, etc.

both (bōth), *adj. & pron.* the one and the other; the two; the pair without excepting either: *adv. & conj.* as well; equally.

both·er (both'ēr), *v.t.* to annoy; tease; worry; give trouble to: *v.i.* to trouble or concern oneself: *n.* 1. worry; annoyance. 2. one who gives trouble.

both·er·a·tion (both-ēr-ā'shŭn), *n.* [Informal], bother.

both·er·some (both'ēr-sŭm), *adj.* causing bother; troublesome.

bo tree (bō), the sacred fig tree of Buddhism.

bot·tle (bot'l), *n.* 1. a hollow container, usually with a narrow neck, made of glass, plastic, etc., used especially for liquids. 2. the contents of a bottle. 3. milk or formula from a baby's bottle. 4. alcoholic liquor: *v.t.* **-tled, -tling,** to put into bottles, cylinders, etc. — **bot'tle·ful,** *n., pl.* **-fuls.** —**bot'tler,** *n.*

bot·tle·neck (-nek), *n.* 1. a place, road, etc.

slowing or halting movement. 2. a condition that impedes progress.

bot·tle-nose (-nōz), *n.* any one of several kinds of dolphins with a bottle-shaped nose.

bot·tom (bot'ŏm), *n.* 1. the lowest or deepest part of anything; also, the underside, lower part, etc. 2. the base; foundation. 3. the ground under a body of water. 4. the seat of a chair. 5. low land formed by alluvial deposits: also **bottom land.** 6. the part of a ship under water. 7. stamina. 8. the basic cause, import, explanation, etc. of something. 9. [Informal], the buttocks. 10. in *Baseball,* the second half (of an inning): *adj.* lowest; undermost: *v.t.* 1. to found (*on* or *upon*); base. 2. to furnish with a bottom. 3. to fathom; get to the bottom of: *v.i.* 1. to descend to or settle on the bottom. 2. to be based or grounded.

bot·tom·less (-lis), *adj.* 1. without a bottom. 2. unlimited, boundless, too deep to measure, etc.

bot·tom·ry (-ri), *n.* a contract wherein a shipowner borrows money for his ship, with the ship as security.

bot·u·lism (boch'ù-lizm), *n.* poisoning from eating foods in which a certain bacillus has developed because of improper canning or preserving.

bou·clé, bou·cle (boo-klā'), *n.* a fabric having a knotty or tufted texture.

bou·doir (bood'wär), *n.* a room for a lady's private use; bedroom, dressing room, etc.

bouf·fant (boo-fänt'), *adj.* puffed out, as a hairdo.

bouffe (boof), *n.* [French], same as **opéra bouffe.**

bou·gain·vil·le·a, bou·gain·vil·lae·a (boo-gân-vil'i-å), *n.* a tropical shrub or vine having small flowers with large purple or red bracts.

bough (bou), *n.* an arm or branch of a tree.

bought (bôt), past tense and past participle of **buy:** *adj.* [Dialectal], not made at home; bought at a store: also **bough't'en** ('n).

bou·gie (boo-zhē', boo'jē), *n.* 1. a wax taper or candle. 2. a slender instrument for insertion in the urethra, rectum, etc., as for dilation.

bouil·la·baisse (bool-yâ-bäs'), *n.* a thick soup made with several kinds of fish and shellfish.

bouil·lon (bool'yon), *n.* a clear broth made usually from beef.

boul·der (bōl'dēr), *n.* a large stone worn or rounded by the action of water and weather.

bou·le (bool'lē), *n.* a Greek legislative assembly.

boule (bool), *n.* 1. *pl.* a French game somewhat like bowls. 2. a lump of fused alumina to be used for a synthetic gemstone.

boul·e·vard (bool'é-värd), *n.* a broad street, often lined with trees and plantings.

bounce (bouns), *v.t.* **bounced, bounc'ing,** 1. to cause to bound. 2. [Slang], to eject summarily; also, to discharge from employment: *v.i.* 1. to strike against anything so as to rebound. 2. to leap or spring suddenly or unceremoniously. 3. [Slang], to be returned as worthless: said of a check for which there is insufficient funds: *n.* 1. the act of bounc-

---

ŏ in drag*on*, ōō in cr*u*de, oo in w*oo*l, u in c*u*p, ū in c*u*re, ŭ in t*u*rn, u in foc*u*s, oi in b*oy*, ou in h*ou*se, th in *th*in, *th* in shea*th*e, g in ge*t*, j in *j*oy, y in *y*et.

ing; a rebound. 2. a sudden bound or spring. 3. the ability to bounce. 4. [Informal], vitality. —bounc′y, *adj.*

bounc·er (boun′sēr), *n.* [Slang], a man employed, as at a bar, to eject undesirable persons.

bounc·ing (′sing), *adj.* strong, healthy, etc.

bound (bound), *v.i.* 1. to jump or leap suddenly or repeatedly. 2. to bounce; rebound: *v.t.* to cause to bound: *n.* 1. a leap; jump. 2. a springing back; rebound.

bound (bound), past tense and past participle of **bind**: *adj.* 1. made fast; confined. 2. obliged. 3. having a cover or binding. 4. constipated. 5. sure; certain. 6. [Informal], determined.

bound (bound), *adj.* headed (*for*); going.

bound (bound), *n.* 1. a limit; boundary. 2. *pl.* a place near or inside a boundary: *v.t.* 1. to confine. 2. to serve as a limit to; circumscribe. 3. to name the boundaries of: *v.i.* to border (*on* another state, etc.).

bound·a·ry (boun′dri, ′dăr·i), *n., pl.* -ries, a line or mark that fixes the limits, as of territory; border.

bound·en (boun′dĕn), *adj.* 1. obliged; indebted. 2. obligatory, as a duty.

bound·er (boun′dĕr), *n.* [British Informal], an ill-bred man; cad.

bound·less (bound′lis), *adj.* unlimited.

boun·te·ous (boun′ti·ŭs), *adj.* 1. giving freely; liberal in gifts; munificent. 2. plentiful. —**boun′te·ous·ly**, *adv.* —**boun′te·ous·ness**, *n.*

boun·ti·ful (′ti·ful), *adj.* 1. liberal in bestowing gifts; generous. 2. plentiful. —**boun′ti·ful·ly**, *adv.* —**boun′ti·ful·ness**, *n.*

boun·ty (boun′ti), *n., pl.* -ties, 1. liberality in giving; generosity. 2. a generous gift. 3. a premium or reward.

bou·quet (bō·kā′, bōō-), *n.* 1. a nosegay or bunch of flowers. 2. aroma characteristic of a wine.

bour·bon (bûr′bŏn), *n.* [sometimes B-], whiskey distilled from corn mash.

bour·geois (boor-zhwä′), *n., pl.* -geois′, [French], 1. a shopkeeper. 2. a member of the middle class: *adj.* 1. middle-class. 2. smug, narrow-minded, unrefined, etc.

bour·geoi·sie (boor-zhwä-zē′), *n.* the middle class.

bourn, bourne (bôrn, boorn), *n.* 1. a rivulet. 2. [Archaic], a boundary; also, a goal.

bour·rée (bōō-rā′), *n.* a lively 17th-century French dance in duple time; also, the music for it.

bourse (boors), *n.* a stock exchange for the transaction of business; especially [B-], the stock exchange of Paris.

bouse (bous), *v.t. & v.i.* **boused, bous′ing**, in *nautical usage,* to lift with a block and tackle.

bout (bout), *n.* 1. [Dialectal], a turn; a going and returning, as in plowing a field. 2. a session; spell of activity. 3. a trial or contest; match.

bou·tique (bōō-tēk′), *n.* a small store, or small department in a store, where fashionable articles are sold, especially for women.

bou·ton·niere, bou·ton·nière (bōōt-n-ir′), *n.* a flower worn in the buttonhole.

bou·zou·ki (bōō-zōō′ki), *n.* a Greek stringed instrument, used for folk music.

bo·vine (bō′vīn), *adj.* 1. of or pertaining to the ox or cow. 2. resembling or having the characteristics of an ox or cow; stolid, dull, slow, etc.: *n.* an ox, cow, etc.

bow (bou), *v.t.* 1. to bend or incline (the head or body) in respect, greeting, etc. 2. to subdue; crush (with *down*): *v.i.* 1. to bend the head or body in respect, agreement, etc. 2. to yield: *n.* an inclination of the head or bending of the body as a salute, or in respect, assent, etc.

bow (bō), *n.* 1. a flexible stick with its ends connected by a cord, used for discharging arrows. 2. something curved. 3. a rod strung with horsehairs, with which musical instruments of the violin family are played. 4. a looped ornamental knot of ribbon or similar material: also **bow′knot**: *v.t. & v.i.* 1. to bend or curve like a bow. 2. to play with a bow.

bow (bou), *n.* the forepart or prow of a ship: *adj.* of or near the bow.

bowd·ler·ize (boud′lēr-īz), *v.t.* -ized, -iz·ing, to expurgate from (a book, etc.) material considered to be offensive or indelicate. —**bowd′ler·ism**, *n.* —**bowd·ler·i·za′tion**, *n.*

bow·el (bou′el), *n.* 1. an intestine, especially of a human being; gut: usually used in the plural. 2. *pl.* the interior part of anything. 3. *pl.* [Archaic], tenderness; pity.

bow·er (bou′ēr), *n.* a shelter constructed of boughs or twining plants; arbor: *v.t.* to shelter in a bower. —**bow′er·y**, *adj.*

bow·er (bou′ēr), *n.* 1. the heaviest anchor carried at the bow of a ship. 2. either of the two highest cards in some card games.

bow·er·y (bou′ēr-i), *n., pl.* -er·ies, a country retreat or farm of an early Dutch settler of New York.

bow·ie knife (bōō′i, bō′i), a long knife with a single edge, used as a hunting knife or weapon.

bowl (bōl), *n.* 1. a circular, hollow dish or similar container. 2. a large drinking cup. 3. the hollow or concave part of anything. 4. an amphitheater. 5. the contents of a bowl.

bowl (bōl), *n.* 1. a heavy ball used in the game of bowls. 2. a single roll of the ball in bowling or bowls: *v.i. & v.t.* 1. to take part in (bowling). 2. to roll (a ball). 3. to move smoothly and swiftly. 4. [Informal], to astonish (followed by *over*). —**bowl′er**, *n.*

bowl·der (bōl′dĕr), *n.* same as **boulder**.

bow·leg (bō′leg), *n.* a leg that curves outward. —**bow′leg·ged** (′leg-id, ′legd), *adj.*

bow·line (bō′lin), *n.* a rope fastened near the middle of a square sail, to keep the sail taut.

bowl·ing (bōl′ing), *n.* 1. a game in which a heavy ball is rolled at ten wooden pins. 2. same as **bowls**.

bowling alley, the long wooden lane used in the game of bowling.

bowling green, the close-cropped lawn area used in the game of bowls.

bowls (bōlz), *n.* 1. a game in which wooden balls are rolled on a close-cropped lawn in a try to stop close to a target ball: also called **lawn bowling**. 2. any of certain other games, as skittles.

bow·man (bō'mán), *n., pl.* -**men**, an archer.

bow·sprit (bou'sprit, bō'-), *n.* a large boom or spar extending out from the bow of a ship to carry its sails forward.

bow·string (bō'string), *n.* the string, or cord, of an archer's bow.

bow tie (bō), a necktie made up of material tied to form a bow, or bowknot.

box (boks), *n.* 1. a case or receptacle, usually rectangular and with a lid. 2. the quantity a box contains. 3. the driver's seat on a carriage. 4. a seating compartment, as in a theater. 5. a booth, as for a man on outdoor duty. 6. a small country house used by sportsmen. 7. a case to protect a mechanism. 8. in *Baseball*, a designated area for the batter, catcher, etc.: *v.t.* 1. to put into a box. 2. to boxhaul: *adj.* 1. in a box. 2. like a box. —**box'like**, *adj.*

box (boks), *n.* a blow on the head with the fist or on the ear with the open hand: *v.t.* 1. to strike with such a blow. 2. to engage in boxing with: *v.i.* to fight with the fists.

box (boks), *n.* any one of a family of evergreen shrubs or small trees with small, leathery leaves: also **box'wood**.

box·car (boks'kär), *n.* a railroad freight car that is enclosed.

box·er (boks'ér), *n.* 1. one who fights with his fists; pugilist. 2. a medium-sized, short-haired dog related to the bulldog. 3. [B-], one of a Chinese society who led an unsuccessful uprising against foreigners in China in 1900.

box·haul (boks'hôl), *v.t.* to veer (a ship) round instead of tacking.

box·ing (boks'ing), *n.* the act or sport of fighting with the fists.

box·ing (boks'ing), *n.* 1. the act of enclosing in a box. 2. material used for boxes. 3. a boxlike covering or mold.

Boxing Day, in England, Canada, etc., the first weekday after Christmas, when Christmas boxes are given to postmen, employees, etc.

boxing glove, a padded leather glove or mitten worn in the sport of boxing.

box kite, a kite constructed of a boxlike framework, open at both ends.

box office, 1. an office at a theater or other public place where tickets may be bought or reservations made. 2. [Informal], the ability of a play, performance, etc. to attract an audience.

boy (boi), *n.* 1. a male child. 2. a young lad; youth. 3. a man; fellow: in familiar usage. 4. a male servant: a patronizing term: *interj.* an expression of surprise, pleasure, etc. —**boy'ish**, *adj.*

bo·yar (bō-yär'), *n.* 1. a Russian aristocrat just below the rank of prince, before the time of Peter the Great. 2. formerly, an aristocrat in Romania. Also **bo·yard'** ('-yärd').

boy·cott (boi'kot), *v.t.* to combine to prevent or hinder the conduct of a business by refusing to buy, deal with, etc., so as to punish or intimidate: *n.* the act or an instance of boycotting.

boy·friend (boi'frend), *n.* [Informal], an escort, close male companion, or sweetheart of a girl or woman.

boy·hood ('hood), *n.* the state of being a boy.

boy scout, a member of a worldwide organization, the *Boy Scouts*, founded in England: it emphasizes outdoor living and service to others.

boy·sen·ber·ry (boi'zn-ber-i), *n., pl.* -**ries**, a large, hybrid berry, dark red or almost black when ripe.

bra (brä), *n.* a brassiere.

brace (brās), *n.* 1. that which holds anything tightly, or supports it firmly; a prop, clamp, tie, etc. 2. a pair; couple. 3. either of a set of signs used to connect words or lines. 4. an instrument for holding and turning boring tools. 5. *pl.* [British], suspenders. 6. *often pl.* a device worn for straightening the teeth. 7. a rope passed through a block at the end of a yard, by which the yard is swung from the deck: *v.t.* braced, brac'ing, 1. to bind, tighten, etc. 2. to strengthen; support. 3. to prepare for a shock, etc. 4. to invigorate.

brace and bit, a boring tool with a rotating handle holding a removable drill.

brace·let (brās'lit), *n.* an ornamental band for the wrist or arm.

brac·er (brā'sér), *n.* 1. a band or support. 2. [Slang], an alcoholic drink.

bra·ce·ro (brä-ser'ō), *n., pl.* -**ros**, a Mexican migrant farm laborer in the U.S.

bra·chi·al (brāk'i-ál), *adj.* of or pertaining to an arm or armlike part.

bra·chi·ate (brāk'i-āt), *adj.* having wide branches in alternate pairs: *v.i.* -**at·ed**, -**at·ing**, to swing by the arms from one hold to the next. —**bra·chi·a'tion**, *n.*

brac·ing (brās'ing), *adj.* invigorating.

brack·en (brak'n), *n.* 1. any one of several coarse, weedy ferns. 2. a thicket of these.

brack·et (brak'it), *n.* 1. a supporting piece projecting from a wall, as a corbel. 2. an angle-shaped support, as for shelves. 3. either of a set of signs [ ] used to enclose words, symbols, etc. 4. a grouping; classification: *v.t.* 1. to furnish with brackets. 2. to enclose within brackets. 3. to couple or join together.

brack·ish (brak'ish), *adj.* 1. somewhat salty. 2. tasting unpleasant; nauseating.

bract (brakt), *n.* a modified leaf growing on a flower stalk or at the base of a flower. —**brac·te·al** (brak'ti-ál), *adj.*

brac·te·ate (brak'ti-it), *adj.* having bracts.

brad (brad), *n.* a slender nail with a small head: *v.t.* brad'ded, brad'ding, to fasten with brads.

brae (brā), *n.* [Scottish], a hillside, or sloping ground.

brag (brag), *v.t. & v.i.* bragged, brag'ging, to boast: *n.* 1. boastful talk or manner. 2. something boasted about. 3. one who brags: also **brag'ger**.

---

brag-ga-do-ci-o (brag-á-dō'shi-ō), *n.*, *pl.* -os, 1. a braggart. 2. empty or arrogant boasting.

brag-gart (brag'ért), *n.* a boaster; vain person: *adj.* boastful.

Brah-ma (brä'mä), *n.* the chief god of the Hindu trinity, thought of as the supreme creator, represented between Vishnu and Siva.

Brah-ma (brä'mä), *n.* [also b-], one of a variety of large domestic fowl.

Brah-man (brä'mán), *n.*, *pl.* -mans, 1. a member of the Hindu priestly caste. 2. (brä'-män), one of a breed of cattle developed from the zebu of India.

Brah-man-ism (-izm), *n.* the religion or doctrines of the Brahmans.

Brah-min (brä'min), *n.* 1. same as Brahman (sense 1). 2. an upper-class person, especially one viewed as being haughty.

braid (brād), *v.t.* 1. to weave or intertwine three or more strands of (straw, hair, etc.). 2. to form by such intertwining. 3. to trim or bind with braid: *n.* 1. a braided band or similar strip. 2. a length of braided hair. 3. a cordlike or ribbonlike trimming or binding, as on a jacket. —**braid'er**, *n.*

brail (brāl), *n.* any one of the small ropes that gather the leeches of a sail: *v.t.* to haul (*up* or *in*) with brails.

Braille (brāl), *n.* [also b-], 1. a system of printing for the blind, producing patterns of raised dots to be felt with the fingers. 2. the patterns produced: *v.t.* **Brailled, Brail'ling** to print or transcribe in such raised dots.

brain (brān), *n.* 1. the soft, convoluted mass of nerve tissue in the cranium of vertebrates, constituting the center of the nervous system and the seat of consciousness and volition. 2. *often pl.* intellectual power. 3. [Informal], a very intelligent person. 4. [Informal], the organizer or controller of an enterprise: *v.t.* 1. to dash out the brains of. 2. [Slang], to hit on the head.

brain-child (brān'child), *n.* [Informal], one's own idea, writing, or other product that has come from an effort of thought.

brain fever, inflammation of the brain or its membranes; meningitis.

brain-less ('lis), *adj.* very stupid. —**brain'less-ly**, *adv.* —**brain'less-ness**, *n.*

brain-pow-er ('pou-er), *n.* intellectual capacity.

brain-storm ('stôrm), *n.* [Informal], a sudden idea or inspiration.

brain-wash (wôsh), *v.t.* [Informal], to indoctrinate so thoroughly as to alter radically the beliefs or views of.

brain wave, 1. an electrical impulse given off by brain tissue, detectable by an electroencephalograph. 2. [Informal], a brainstorm.

brain-y (brān'i), *adj.* **brain'i-er, brain'i-est**, [Informal], very intelligent.

braise (brāz), *v.t.* **braised, brais'ing** to brown and then simmer (meat) slowly in a small amount of liquid in a covered pan.

brake (brāk), *n.* 1. a place overgrown with bracken, brushwood, etc. 2. a bracken fern.

brake (brāk), *n.* 1. an instrument or machine for beating flax or hemp. 2. the handle of a pump. 3. a heavy harrow for breaking clods. 4. a mechanical device for checking the motion of a vehicle or machine, as by pressure of a band or block against a moving part. 5. anything that slows or stops progress: *v.t. & v.i.* **braked, brak'ing** to slow down or stop with or as with a brake or brakes. —**brake'less**, *adj.*

brake (brāk), *n.* an old kind of large, four-wheeled carriage; break.

brake-man (brāk'mán), *n.*, *pl.* -men, a train crewman who assists the conductor and performs other operational duties.

brake shoe, the part of a brake that presses against the wheel.

bram-ble (bram'b'l), *n.* 1. a prickly shrub of the rose family, as the blackberry, raspberry, etc. 2. any prickly bush or shrub. —**bram'-bly**, *adj.*

bran (bran), *n.* husks of wheat, rye, etc., separated from the flour by bolting.

branch (branch), *n.* 1. a woody shoot or limb from a main trunk of a tree or bush. 2. a stream running out of or into a river. 3. any member or part of a body or system. 4. a department; section or subdivision. 5. any part of a family descending in a collateral line: *v.i.* 1. to ramify. 2. to diverge. 3. to spread diffusely (followed by *out*): *v.t.* to separate into branches.

bran-chi-ae (brang'ki-ē), *n.*, *sing.* **-chi-a** (-á), the respiratory organs of fishes; gills. —**bran'chi-al**, *adj.* —**bran'chi-ate** ('ki-it), *adj.*

brand (brand), *n.* 1. a burning piece of wood, or one partly burned. 2. a mark burned on the skin with a hot iron; also, the iron used. 3. a mark of infamy; stigma. 4. an identifying mark; trademark. 5. a line of trademarked goods. 6. any distinctive kind: *v.t.* 1. to mark with or as with a hot iron. 2. to stigmatize. —**brand'er**, *n.*

bran-dish (bran'dish), *v.t.* to move, wave, or shake, as a raised weapon: *n.* such a waving or flourishing.

brand-ling (brand'ling), *n.* 1. a salmon of the first year. 2. a small, red worm used for bait by fishermen.

brand name, the name by which a given brand of goods is known.

brand-new (brand'nōō'), *adj.* completely new.

bran-dy (bran'di), *n.*, *pl.* -dies, an alcoholic liquor distilled from wine or from fermented fruit juice: *v.t.* **died, -dy-ing** to flavor with or steep in brandy.

bran-ni-gan (bran'i-gán), *n.* [Slang], a noisy brawl.

bran-ny (bran'i), *adj.* **-ni-er, -ni-est**, of, like, or consisting of bran.

brant (brant), *n.*, *pl.* **brants, brant**, a small, dark species of wild goose of Europe and North America: also **brant goose**.

brash (brash), *adj.* 1. brittle, as wood. 2. quick-tempered; saucy. 3. rash; reckless: *n.* 1. acidity of the stomach; pyrosis. 2. [Scottish], a short shower of rain. —**brash'ly**, *adv.* —**brash'ness**, *n.*

brash (brash), *n.* broken, loose, and angular pieces, as of rock or ice.

brass (bras), *n.* 1. an alloy of copper and zinc. 2. articles or parts of brass; specifically, *often pl.*, brass-wind musical instruments. 3. [Informal], impudence. 4. [Slang], high-ranking officers or officials: *v.t.* to cover with brass: *adj.* of brass.

bras-sard (brä-särd', bras'ärd), *n.* 1. an identifying arm band. 2. armor for the upper arm: also **bras-sart** (bras'ärt).

brass hat, [Slang], a high-ranking military officer.

brass-ie (bras'i), *n.* a golf club with a wooden head that originally had a brass plate underneath, used for long shots on the fairway: now usually called number 2 wood.

bras-siere, bras-sière (brä-zir'), *n.* a woman's undergarment to support the breasts.

brass tacks, [Informal], what is essential; basic points: usually in **get (or come) down to brass tacks.**

brass winds (windz), musical instruments with coiled metal tubes and cup-shaped mouthpieces. —**brass'-wind,** *adj.*

brass-y (bras'i), *adj.* **brass'i-er, brass'i-est.** 1. of, pertaining to, or resembling brass. 2. gaudy, showy. 3. impudent; brazen. 4. blaring. — **brass'i-ly,** *adv.* —**brass'i-ness,** *n.*

brat (brat), *n.* a child, especially a naughty or spoiled child: a contemptuous or playful term. —**brat'tish,** *adj.* —**brat'ty, -ti-er, -ti-est,** *adj.*

brat-tice (brat'is), *n.* a partition in a mine shaft to form an air passage: *v.t.* **-ticed, -tic-ing,** to divide by a brattice.

brat-tle (brat'l), *v.i.* **-tled, -tling,** [Scottish], to make a rattling noise: *n.* [Scottish], a rattling, loud noise.

brat-wurst (brat'wẽrst), *n.* [German], a highly seasoned sausage of pork and veal.

braun-schwei-ger (broun'shwī-gẽr), *n.* [German], smoked liver sausage.

bra-va-do (brä-vä'dō), *n., pl.* **-dos, -does,** a pretended or arrogant display of courage.

brave (brāv), *adj.* **brav'er, brav'est,** 1. bold, courageous; intrepid. 2. making a fine appearance: *n.* 1. a North American Indian warrior. 2. any brave man: *v.t.* **braved, brav'ing,** 1. to encounter with courage and fortitude. 2. to defy. —**brave'ly,** *adv.* —**brav'er-y,** *n.*

bra-vo (brä'vō), *interj.* [Italian], well done! good!: *n., pl.* **-vos,** a cheer of "bravo."

bra-vo (brä'vō), *n., pl.* **-voes, -vos,** a bandit or assassin.

bra-vu-ra (brä-vyoor'ä), *n.* 1. brilliant musical technique; also, a passage or composition to display this. 2. a show of daring: *adj.* displaying bravura.

brawl (brôl), *v.i.* 1. to quarrel or fight noisily. 2. to make a noise as of water rushing over a rocky bed: *n.* 1. a noisy quarrel. 2. an uproar. —**brawl'er,** *n.*

brawn (brôn), *n.* 1. muscular strength. 2. strong muscles. 3. [British], cooked boar's flesh. — **brawn'y,** *adj.* **brawn'i-er, brawn'i-est.** — **brawn'i-ness,** *n.*

brax-y (brak'si), *n.* a disease in sheep, resembling anthrax: *adj.* having braxy.

bray (brā), *v.t.* to pound or beat fine or small: *v.i.* to utter a loud, harsh cry, as a donkey: *n.* such a cry.

braze (brāz), *v.t.* **brazed, braz'ing,** 1. to solder with brass or the like. 2. to make of or

cover with brass or similar metal. 3. to make hard like brass. —**braz'er,** *n.*

bra-zen (brä'zn), *adj.* 1. of or like brass. 2. harsh in sound. 3. impudent; shameless: *v.t.* to treat or do impudently. —**bra'zen-ly,** *adv.* —**bra'zen-ness,** *n.*

bra-zen-faced (-fāst), *adj.* impudent.

bra-zier (brä'zhẽr), *n.* an open pan for burning charcoal.

bra-zier (brä'zhẽr), *n.* a worker in brass.

Bra-zil-ian (brä-zil'yän), *adj.* of or pertaining to Brazil, the largest country in South America, or its inhabitants: *n.* a native or inhabitant of Brazil.

braz-i-lin (braz'l-in), *n.* a bright-yellow coloring substance extracted from brazilwood.

Bra-zil nut (brä-zil'), the three-sided, edible, oily nut of a huge tree of South America.

bra-zil-wood (brä-zil'wood), *n.* a heavy, reddish wood from any one of several related tropical American trees.

breach (brēch), *n.* 1. the violation of a law, contract, promise, etc. 2. a gap or opening made by breaking through. 3. a difference or quarrel between friends: *v.t.* to make a breach in: *v.i.* to leap out of the water: said of a whale.

bread (bred), *n.* 1. a food made from flour or meal, leavening, water, etc., mixed and baked. 2. food in general. 3. one's livelihood. 4. [Slang], money: *v.t.* to coat with bread crumbs before cooking.

bread-fruit (bred'frōōt), *n.* 1. a large, round fruit which, when baked, looks and tastes like bread. 2. the tropical tree on which it grows.

bread line, a line of people waiting for free food from an agency or charity.

bread-root (bred'rōōt), *n.* 1. a North American prairie plant. 2. its starchy root.

bread-stuff (stuf), *n.* 1. flour or meal from which bread is made. 2. bread.

breadth (bredth), *n.* 1. the measure of any surface from side to side; width. 2. freedom from narrowness. 3. extent.

bread-win-ner (bred'win-ẽr), *n.* the person earning money to support others.

break (brāk), *v.t.* **broke, bro'ken, break'ing,** 1. to crack, divide, or smash into pieces. 2. to burst, pierce, or cut open. 3. to weaken or destroy; disrupt 4. to interrupt or terminate (an action). 5. to tame or subdue. 6. to make bankrupt. 7. to make a first disclosure of. 8. to dismiss or reduce to the ranks. 9. to violate (a promise, law, etc.). 10. to decipher: *v.i.* 1. to become broken or shattered. 2. to begin, move, change, etc. suddenly. 3. to force one's way. 4. to fail, as in health or spirits. 5. to crack. 6. to become ineffective or unusable. 7. to have a sudden fall, as prices. 8. to stop associating (*with*). 9. to come into being: *n.* 1. a breach; rupture. 2. an interruption. 3. a change of direction. 4. a first appearance. 5. a pause, gap, or rest. 6. an escape. 7. the opening shot in a game of pool. 8. the number of points scored successively, as in billiards. 9. a sudden fall, as of prices. 10. [Informal], an out-of-place remark or action. 11. [Slang], a piece of luck. —**break'a-ble,** *adj.*

ô in dragon, ōō in crude, oo in wool, u in cup, ū in cure, û in turn, ů in focus, oi in boy, ou in house, th in thin, ŧh in sheathe, g in get, j in joy, y in yet.

break (brǎk), *n.* an old kind of large, four-wheeled carriage designed for at least six passengers.

break·age (brǎk'ij), *n.* 1. the act of breaking. 2. the quantity broken. 3. the damage from breaking. 4. the allowance made for accidental fracture.

break-a-way ('ǝ-wā), *n.* a breaking away from a certain group, position, etc.

break-bone fever ('bōn), same as dengue.

break-down ('doun), *n.* 1. a collapse. 2. a classification or analysis. 3. a lively, noisy dance.

break-er ('ẽr), *n.* 1. one who or that which breaks. 2. a machine to crush rocks, coal, etc. 3. a wave breaking against a shore. 4. a small water keg.

break-fast (brek'fǎst), *n.* the first meal of the day: *v.i.* to provide with breakfast: *v.i.* to eat breakfast. —**break'fast-er**, *n.*

break-front (brǎk'frunt), *n.* a cabinet with a projecting center section.

break-neck ('nek), *adj.* excessively speedy.

break-through ('thrōō), *n.* 1. the act of breaking through against resistance, as in warfare. 2. the place where this takes place. 3. a sudden advance of knowledge or social action, especially after protracted study or preparation.

break-up ('up), *n.* 1. a dispersion. 2. a collapse or disintegration. 3. a disruption.

break-wa-ter (wŏt-ẽr), *n.* any structure to break the force of waves.

bream (brēm), *n.* 1. a European minnowlike fish. 2. any one of certain freshwater sunfishes. 3. any one of certain saltwater fishes: *v.i.* to clear (a ship's bottom) of shells, seaweed, etc., by scorching and then scraping.

breast (brest), *n.* 1. the front part of the body between the neck and abdomen. 2. either of two milk-secreting glands on this part of a woman's body. 3. a gland similar to this in some female mammals. 4. the part of a garment, etc. that covers the breast. 5. the breast regarded as the seat of one's affections, conscience, etc.: *v.t.* 1. to present the front to. 2. to meet or oppose bravely or openly; stem.

breast-bone (brest'bōn), *n.* same as sternum.

breast-feed ('fēd), *v.t.* -fed, -feed-ing, to suckle (a baby) at the breast; nurse.

breast-plate ('plāt), *n.* 1. a piece of armor covering the breast. 2. anciently, a part of the Jewish high priest's vestment, worn over the chest: also **breast'piece**.

breast stroke a swimming stroke in which the swimmer drops the arms down to a position close to the chest.

breast-work ('wûrk), *n.* a hastily constructed work thrown up breast-high for defense, especially for gunners.

breath (breth), *n.* 1. air inhaled and exhaled in respiration. 2. respiration. 3. the power or capacity to breathe freely. 4. life or vitality. 5. a respite; pause. 6. an instant. 7. air in gentle motion. 8. air carrying fragrance. 9. a mere word. 10. a trifle; hint.

breathe (brēth), *v.i. & v.t.* breathed, breath'ing, 1. to inhale and expel (air) from the lungs.

2. to exhale. 3. to rest. 4. to blow or whisper softly. 5. to insinuate.

breath-er (brē'thẽr), *n.* 1. one that breathes. 2. [Informal], a rest period.

breath-ing (brē'thing), *n.* 1. respiration. 2. a rest period. 3. an aspirate.

breath-less (breth'lis), *adj.* 1. out of breath; panting. 2. lifeless. 3. breathing with difficulty, as from excitement. —**breath'less-ly**, *adv.* —**breath'less-ness**, *n.*

breath-tak-ing ('tāk-ing), *adj.* 1. checking one's breathing. 2. thrilling.

breath-y (breth'i), *adj.* breath'i-er, breath'i-est, marked by an audible letting out of the breath. —**breath'i-ness**, *n.*

brec-ci-a (brech'i-ä), *n.* angular rock fragments united by clay, lime, etc.

breech (brēch), *n.* 1. the buttocks. 2. the hinder part of anything, as the part of a firearm behind the barrel: *v.t.* 1. to clothe with breeches. 2. to fit (a gun) with a breech.

breech-cloth (brēch'klôth), *n.* a loincloth.

breech-es (brich'iz), *n.* 1. men's or boys' trousers reaching to the knees. 2. [Informal], any trousers.

breech-es buoy (brēch'iz, brich'iz), a rescue device made up of short canvas breeches attached to a life preserver hanging from and pulled along a taut rope.

breech-ing (brēch'ing), *n.* the harness that passes around a horse's hindquarters.

breech-load-er (brēch'lō-dẽr), *n.* a firearm loaded at the breech.

breed (brēd), *v.t.* bred, breed'ing, 1. to bring forth or hatch (young). 2. to train or rear. 3. to produce. 4. to raise (animals): *v.i.* 1. to bear young. 2. to be produced: *n.* 1. a stock or strain from the same parents or ancestors. 2. a type or sort. —**breed'er**, *n.*

breed-ing (brēd'ing), *n.* 1. the training of the young. 2. manners, especially good manners. 3. the production of animals or plants.

breeze (brēz), *n.* 1. a gentle, soft wind. 2. [Informal], an easy thing to do. 3. [British Informal], a commotion. 4. ashes and cinders left from burned coal, coke, etc.: *v.i.* breezed, breez'ing, [Slang], to progress quickly or in a carefree manner.

breeze-way (brēz'wā), *n.* a passageway with a roof but often without sides, connecting a house and garage.

breez-y (brēz'i), *adj.* breez'i-er, breez'i-est, 1. with a light wind blowing. 2. carefree; jaunty. —**breez'i-ly**, *adv.* —**breez'i-ness**, *n.*

breth-ren (breth'rēn), *n.* brothers: chiefly in religious usage.

breve (brēv), *n.* a mark (˘) used to indicate a short vowel or an unstressed syllable.

bre-vet (brē-vet'), *n.* a commission to a military officer conferring a higher rank, but without increase of pay or authority: *adj.* conferred by brevet: *v.t.* -vet'ed or -vet'ted, -vet'ing or -vet'ting, to promote by brevet.

bre-vi-ar-y (brē'vi-er-i), *n., pl.* -ar-ies, a book containing the daily offices and prayers for the canonical hours.

bre-vier (brē-vir'), *n.* a size of type, 8 point.

brev-i-ty (brev'i-ti), *n.* shortness; conciseness.

brew (brōō), *v.t.* 1. to make (beer, ale, etc.) from malt and hops by steeping and fer-

---

menting. 2. to steep (tea). 3. to contrive or scheme: *v.i.* to take form: *n.* that which is brewed. —brew'er, *n.*

brew·er·y (brōō'ĕr-i), *n.*, *pl.* -er·ies, a place where beer, ale, etc. is brewed.

bri·ar (brī'ĕr), *n.* 1. same as brier. 2. a tobacco pipe made of brierroot.

bri·ar·root (-rōōt), *n.* same as brierroot.

bribe (brīb), *n.* a gift or consideration given or promised to induce or persuade, especially to do something wrong or illegal: *v.t.* bribed, brib'ing, 1. to gain or influence by a bribe. 2. to give a bribe to: *v.i.* to give bribes. —brib'er, *n.*

brib·er·y (brī'bĕr-i), *n.*, *pl.* -er·ies, the act or practice of giving or taking bribes.

bric-a-brac (brik'ȧ-brak), *n.* small, decorative articles placed about a room; knickknacks.

brick (brik), *n.* 1. an oblong block of clay dried in the sun or burned in a kiln, used for building; also, these collectively. 2. anything shaped like a brick. 3. [Informal], a fine person: *v.t.* to cover or build with bricks: *adj.* made of bricks.

brick·bat (brik'bat), *n.* 1. a brick missile or the like. 2. a hostile criticism.

brick·lay·ing ('lā-ing), *n.* the act or occupation of laying bricks. —brick'lay·er, *n.*

brick·yard ('yärd), *n.* a place where bricks are made or sold.

bri·cole (bri-kōl'), *n.* an indirect shot, as in billiards.

brid·al (brīd'l), *n.* a wedding: *adj.* of or pertaining to a bride or wedding.

bride (brīd), *n.* a woman newly married or about to be married.

bride·groom (brīd'grōōm), *n.* a man newly married or about to be married.

brides·maid (brīdz'mād), *n.* a young woman who attends a bride during the wedding.

bridge (brij), *n.* 1. a structure of steel, stone, wood, etc. spanning a river, road, valley, etc. to permit passage across. 2. anything that resembles a bridge, or that makes a connection, etc. 3. an observation platform above the deck of a ship. 4. an arch over which the strings of a musical instrument are stretched. 5. a frame or mounting for false teeth, affixed to a real tooth. 6. the arch of the nose; also, the part of a pair of eyeglasses that rests on the nose. 7. a device for measuring electrical resistance. 8. a card game developed from whist, for two pairs of players: see auction bridge, contract bridge: *v.t.* bridged, bridg'ing, 1. to build a bridge over. 2. to find or provide a way across or between. —bridge'a·ble, *adj.*

bridge·board (brij'bôrd), *n.* a notched board into which the ends of the steps of a staircase are fastened; string.

bridge·head ('hed), *n.* a fortified place erected by attackers on the enemy's side of a bridge, defile, etc.

bridge·work ('wĕrk), *n.* a dental bridge or bridges.

bridg·ing (brij'ing), *n.* reinforcing pieces between timbers, as between floor joists.

bri·dle (brīd'l), *n.* 1. the headstall, bit, and reins by which a horse is controlled. 2. any restraint: *v.t.* 1. to put a bridle on. 2. to

control or guide: *v.i.* to hold the head up, with chin in, as an indication of scorn, anger, etc.

bridle path, a path for riding horses.

bri·doon (bri-dōōn'), *n.* the light snaffle and reins of a military bridle.

brief (brēf), *adj.* short or concise: *n.* 1. a summary; especially, a statement of the facts of a case to be argued in court. 2. a papal letter. 3. *pl.* legless underpants: *v.t.* 1. to summarize. 2. to give relevant data to in concise form. 3. [British], to retain as a lawyer. —brief'ly, *adv.*

brief-case (brēf'kās), *n.* a flat, flexible case for carrying papers.

bri·er (brī'ĕr), *n.* 1. any prickly bush or bushes, as the bramble, wild rose, etc. 2. a heath of southern Europe, with a root used for making tobacco pipes; also, the root itself, or a pipe made from it: in the latter senses, usually spelled briar.

bri·er·root (brī'ĕr-rōōt), *n.* 1. the root wood of the brier. 2. a tobacco pipe of brierroot.

brig (brig), *n.* 1. a two-masted, square-rigged ship. 2. a place of confinement on a U.S. warship; also, [Military Slang], the guardhouse; prison.

bri·gade (bri-gād'), *n.* 1. a subdivision of an army: in the U.S. Army, it consists of two or more battalions with service and administrative units. 2. an organized body acting together for a purpose, as to fight fires: *v.t.* -gad'ed, -gad'ing, to form into a brigade.

brig·a·dier (brig-ȧ-dir'), *n.* a general officer commanding a brigade.

brigadier general, *pl.* brigadier generals, a U.S. military officer ranking above a colonel.

brig·and (brig'ȧnd), *n.* a bandit or highwayman, usually a member of a gang.

brig·and·age ('ȧn-dij), *n.* 1. robbery done by brigands. 2. brigands collectively.

brig·an·tine (brig'ȧn-tēn), *n.* a small, two-masted ship with a square-rigged foremast and a fore-and-aft mainsail.

bright (brīt), *adj.* 1. luminous; sparkling; shining. 2. brilliant; vivid. 3. illustrious; glorious. 4. witty; clever. 5. lively; alert. 6. auspicious: *adv.* in a bright manner. —bright'ly, *adv.* —bright'ness, *n.*

bright·en (brīt'n), *v.t. & v.i.* 1. to make or grow bright or brighter. 2. to make or grow cheerful or gay.

Bright's disease (brīts), a kidney disease characterized by the presence of albumin in the urine; nephritis.

brill (bril), *n.* an edible flatfish related to the turbot.

bril·liant (bril'yȧnt), *adj.* 1. sparkling; lustrous; glittering. 2. distinguished; splendid. 3. very smart or intelligent. 4. vivid; bright: *n.* 1. a gem, especially a diamond, cut to exhibit its refracting qualities to the best advantage. 2. the smallest size of type ordinarily used in printing, 3 1/2 point. —bril'liance, bril'liancy, *n.* —bril'liant·ly, *adv.*

bril·lian·tine (bril'yȧn-tēn), *n.* an oily dressing for the hair to make it glossy.

Brill's disease (brilz), a kind of epidemic typhus fever in which the disease comes back years after the original infection.

ŏ in dragon, ōō in crude, oo in wool, u in cup, ū in cure, ū in turn, ŭ in focus, oi in boy, ou in house, th in thin, th in sheathe, g in get, j in joy, y in yet.

brim (brim), *n.* 1. the top edge of a glass, bowl, etc. 2. a projecting edge, as of a hat: *v.t. & v.i.* **brimmed, brim'ming,** to fill or be full to the brim.

brim-ful (brim'fool'), *adj.* full to the brim.

brim-stone (brim'stōn), *n.* same as *sulfur.*

brin-dle (brin'dl), *n.* a brindled animal or color: *adj.* brindled.

brin-dled ('dld), *adj.* tawny, with streaks or spots.

brine (brīn), *n.* 1. water saturated with salt. 2. the ocean. 3. ocean water: *v.t.* **brined, brin'ing,** to steep in brine.

bring (bring), *v.t.* **brought, bring'ing,** 1. to convey, or cause to come, to the place of the one speaking. 2. to sell for; fetch. 3. to cause to happen, be, etc. 4. to act upon or influence in such a way as to effect a specified way of thinking or acting. 5. in *Law,* to present or produce, as charges or evidence.

brink (bringk), *n.* the edge; verge.

brink-man-ship (bringk'măn-ship), *n.* the following of a risky course of action to the brink of calamity: also **brinks'man-ship.**

brin-y (brīn'ĭ), *adj.* **brin'i-er, brin'i-est,** very salty. —**brin'i-ness,** *n.*

bri-oche (bri-ōsh'), *n.* [French], a sweet yeast roll made with eggs and butter.

bri-quette, bri-quet (bri-ket'), *n.* coal dust compressed and molded in the shape of bricks.

brisk (brisk), *adj.* 1. live'ly; active; quick and energetic. 2. cool and invigorating; bracing. 3. pungent, keen, etc. —**brisk'ly,** *adv.* —**brisk'ness,** *n.*

bris-ket (bris'kit), *n.* 1. an animal's breast, or the part where the ribs join the breastbone. 2. meat cut from this part.

Brit-ish (brit'ish), *adj.* of or pertaining to Great Britain or its people: *n.* the people of Great Britain (with *the*).

British thermal unit, a unit of heat equal to about 252 calories.

bris-tle (bris'l), *n.* 1. a short, stiff, coarse hair. 2. such a hair from a hog, used for brushes. 3. a synthetic imitation of a bristle: *v.i.* **-tled, -tling,** 1. to stand stiffly, as a bristle. 2. to have the bristles become erect. 3. to become stiff with irritation, anger, etc. 4. to be thickly covered with.

bris-tly (bris'li), *adj.* **-tli-er, -tli-est,** 1. covered with bristles. 2. like a bristle or bristles. —**bris'tli-ness,** *n.*

Bris-tol board (bris'tl), a thick, smooth pasteboard, as for art use.

brit (brit), *n.,* *sing.* **brit,** 1. the young of certain fish, as of the herring. 2. small sea animals that certain whales eat.

bri-tan-ni-a metal (bri-tan'i-å), [also B-], an alloy of tin, copper, and antimony.

britch-es (brich'iz), *n.* [Informal], same as **breeches** (sense 2).

Brit-on (brit'n), *n.* a native or inhabitant of Great Britain.

brit-tle (brit'l), *adj.* 1. apt to break or shatter. 2. hard and sharp, as a tone of voice: *n.* brusque or stiffly formal, as in behavior: *n.* thin, crunchy candy, with nuts in it.

broach (brōch), *n.* 1. a spit for roasting meat. 2. a boring tool for making, enlarging, or

shaping holes; also, the hole made. 3. same as **brooch:** *v.t.* 1. to bore a hole in; pierce or tap, as to let out liquid. 2. to bring up or initiate (a certain subject for discussion). —**broach'er,** *n.*

broad (brôd), *adj.* 1. wide in extent or range; spacious; open. 2. not limited; comprehensive. 3. not overly detailed; generalized. 4. unmixed with shadow: said of daylight. 5. unmistakably clear, as a hint; not subtle. 6. easily distinguishable, as a foreign accent; marked. 7. indelicate; coarse; ribald. 8. tolerant; liberal. 9. in *Phonetics,* enunciated with the tongue low and flat, as the (ä) of *father:* *adv.* in a broad manner: *n.* [Slang], a woman: a vulgar term. —**broad'ly,** *adv.* —**broad'ness,** *n.*

broad arrow, a mark used by the British government to distinguish its property.

broad-cast (brôd'kast), *v.t.* **-cast** or, in radio, occasionally **-cast-ed, -cast-ing,** 1. to cast or scatter (seeds) over a broad area. 2. to tell (news, gossip, etc.) widely. 3. to transmit by radio or television: *v.i.* to broadcast radio or television programs: *adj.* 1. cast widely. 2. of, for, or by radio or television broadcasting: *n.* 1. the act of broadcasting. 2. a radio or television program: *adv.* so as to be scattered widely. —**broad'cast-er,** *n.*

Broad Church, a party of the Anglican Church with views midway between the High Church and Low Church. —**Broad'-Church,** *adj.* —**Broad'-Church-man,** *n.,* *pl.* **-men.**

broad-cloth (brôd'klôth), *n.* 1. a fine woolen cloth with a smooth-finished surface. 2. a fine, smooth silk or cotton cloth.

broad-en (brôd'n), *v.i. & v.t.* to become or make broad or broader; widen.

broad jump, same as *long jump.*

broad-loom (brôd'lōōm), *adj.* woven on a broad loom, as some carpeting.

broad-mind-ed (-'mīn'did), *adj.* tolerant of views differing from one's own. —**broad'mind'ed-ly,** *adv.* —**broad'mind'ed-ness,** *n.*

broad seal, the public seal of a country.

broad-side ('sīd), *n.* 1. the entire side of a ship above the waterline; also, any broad surface. 2. a simultaneous volley from one side of a warship. 3. a sheet of paper printed on one or both sides, as with advertising. 4. a critical attack, as against a person: *adj.* of or like a broadside: *adv.* 1. with the entire side turned toward something. 2. directly into the side. 3. in a way that suggests a broadside volley.

broad-spec-trum ('spek'trŭm), *adj.* denoting an antibiotic that is effective against a wide range of microorganisms.

broad-sword ('sôrd), *n.* a sword with a broad, flat blade.

broad-tail ('tāl), *n.* 1. a thick-tailed sheep of central Asia; karakul. 2. the pelt, wavy and glossy, of its lamb, especially of a prematurely born lamb; astrakhan.

bro-cade (brō-kād'), *n.* a fine fabric with a raised pattern woven throughout: *v.t.* **-cad'-ed, -cad'ing,** to weave with such a pattern.

broc-a-telle, broc-a-tel (brok-å-tel'), *n.* 1. a variegated marble. 2. a figured fabric like brocade, used in upholstery.

broc·co·li (brok'ō-li), *n.* a plant related to the cauliflower, with branching stalks and small green buds, used as a vegetable.

bro·chette (brō-shet'), *n.* a skewer used in broiling small pieces of meat and vegetables.

bro·chure (brō-shoor'), *n.* a pamphlet.

bro·gan (brō'gn), *n.* a sturdy, ankle-high work shoe.

brogue (brōg), *n.* 1. a heavy shoe for a man, often with decorative perforations. 2. a dialectal pronunciation, especially of English as spoken by the Irish.

broil (broil), *v.t.* to cook by, or expose to, direct heat, as that under or over a flame: *n.* 1. the act of broiling. 2. something broiled. 3. a noisy quarrel.

broil·er (broil'ēr), *n.* 1. a grill, section of a stove, etc. for broiling. 2. a young chicken suitable for broiling.

broke (brōk), past tense of **break**: *adj.* [Informal], without cash; penniless.

bro·ken (brō'kn), past participle of **break**: *adj.* 1. fractured, split into pieces, burst, etc. 2. not kept, as a promise. 3. rough; not even. 4. crushed, infirm, sick, etc. 5. not in operating condition. 6. imperfectly spoken. 7. not entire; incomplete. 8. interrupted or disrupted. 9. subdued; tamed. 10. [Informal], demoted, as in military rank. —**bro'ken·ly,** *adv.* —**bro'ken·ness,** *n.*

bro·ken-down (-doun'), *adj.* 1. not in operating condition. 2. old or sick.

bro·ken-heart·ed (-här'tid), *adj.* overwhelmed by grief or bitter disappointment.

bro·ker (brō'kēr), *n.* 1. one who acts as an agent for another in selling or making contracts. 2. same as **stockbroker**.

bro·ker·age (brō'kēr-ij), *n.* 1. the business of a broker. 2. a broker's fee.

bro·mal (brō'mal), *n.* a colorless, oily fluid obtained by the action of bromine on alcohol and used in medicine.

bro·mate (brō'māt), *n.* a salt of bromic acid: *v.t.* **-mat·ed, -mat·ing,** to treat or combine with bromine or a bromate.

bro·me·li·ad (brō-mē'li-ad), *n.* a pineapple or other plant of the pineapple family, as Spanish moss.

bro·mic acid (brō'mik), a compound of hydrogen, bromine, and oxygen, found only in aqueous solutions.

bro·mide (brō'mīd), *n.* 1. a compound of bromine with another element or with a radical. 2. potassium bromide, used as a sedative. 3. a trite saying; cliché.

bro·mid·ic (brō-mid'ik), *adj.* trite; dull; platitudinous.

bro·mine (brō'mēn), *n.* a chemical element; a reddish-brown, corrosive liquid, used in photography, in making dyes, etc.

bro·mize (miz), *v.t.* **-mized, -miz·ing,** to prepare or treat with a bromine or bromide.

bron·chi (brong'kī), *n.* plural of **bronchus.**

bron·chi·al (brong'ki-al), *adj.* of or having to do with the bronchi.

bronchial tubes, the bronchi and the tubes that branch off from them.

bron·chi·tis (brong-kīt'is), *n.* inflammation of the mucous lining of the bronchial tubes. —**bron·chit'ic** (-kit'ik), *adj.*

bron·cho·pneu·mo·nia (brong-kō-nōō-mō'nyȧ), *n.* inflammation of the lungs and bronchi.

bron·cho·scope (brong'kō-skōp), *n.* an instrument for viewing and treating the interior of the windpipe or bronchi. —**bron·cho·scop'ic** (-skop'ik), *adj.* —**bron·chos'co·py** (-kos'kō-pi), *n.*

bron·chus (brong'kus), *n.,* *pl.* **-chi** ('kī), one of the two principal branches of the windpipe, or trachea.

bron·co (brong'kō), *n.,* *pl.* **-cos,** a small, unbroken horse of the western U.S.: also spelled **bron'cho,** *pl.* **-chos.**

bron·co-bust·er (-bus·tēr), *n.* [Informal], a cowboy who tames broncos to the saddle. —**bron'co-bust·ing,** *n.*

bron·to·sau·rus (bron-tō-sôr'us), *n.,* *pl.* **-sau'rus·es, -sau'ri** ('ī), a huge, prehistoric, herbivorous dinosaur of North America: also **bron'to·saur.**

bronze (bronz), *n.* 1. an alloy of copper and tin. 2. a work of art cast or wrought in bronze. 3. a reddish-brown color like that of bronze: *adj.* made of or resembling bronze: *v.t.* **bronzed, bronz'ing,** to give the color of bronze to. —**bronz'y,** *adj.*

Bronze Age, the age of human development when tools and implements of bronze were used: it followed the Stone Age.

brooch (brōch, brōōch), *n.* a large ornamental clasp or pin.

brood (brōōd), *n.* 1. the young birds hatched at one time. 2. the children of a family: *adj.* kept for breeding, as a mare: *v.i.* 1. to sit on eggs, as a hen. 2. to ponder in a gloomy, resentful, or worried way: *v.t.* 1. to sit on (eggs) to hatch. 2. to hover over or protect. 3. to ponder gloomily, resentfully, etc.

brood·er (brōōd'ēr), *n.* 1. one that broods. 2. a heated room or enclosure used for raising fowl.

brook (brook), *n.* a small stream.

brook (brook), *v.t.* to bear; put up with.

brook·let (brook'lit), *n.* a small brook.

brook trout, a mottled trout native to the streams of northeastern North America.

broom (brōōm), *n.* 1. a shrub of the legume family bearing yellow flowers. 2. a bundle of fibers or straws fastened to a long handle and used for sweeping.

broom·stick ('stik), *n.* a broom handle.

brose (brōz), *n.* a porridge made by pouring boiling water or milk into oatmeal.

broth (brôth), *n.* a clear, thin soup made as by boiling meat in water.

broth·el (brôth'ĕl), *n.* a house of prostitution.

broth·er (bruth'ēr), *n.,* *pl.* **-ers** or, chiefly religious, **breth'ren,** 1. a man or boy having the same parents as another; male sibling. 2. a fellow member of the same society, profession, race, club, etc. 3. a lay member of a men's religious order. 4. a fellow man.

broth·er·hood (-hood), *n.* 1. the state of being a brother or brothers. 2. the bond between fellow human beings; brotherliness. 3. an organization or group of men united by common interests, beliefs, etc.

broth·er-in-law (-in-lô), *n.,* *pl.* **broth'ers-in-law,** 1. the brother of one's husband or wife. 2.

one's sister's husband. 3. the husband of the sister of one's husband or wife.

Brother Jon-a-than (jon'ă-thăn), an early name used to personify the United States or its people.

broth-er-ly (-li), *adj.* 1. of a brother. 2. as becomes a brother; affectionate, kindly, helpful, etc. —**broth'er-li-ness,** *n.*

brougham (brōōm, brōō'ăm), *n.* a closed, four-wheeled carriage, or a limousine, with the driver's seat outside.

brought (brôt), past tense and past participle of **bring.**

brou-ha-ha (brōō'hä-hä), *n.* a noisy wrangle or confusion; furor; fuss.

brow (brou), *n.* 1. the arch of the hair over the eye; eyebrow. 2. the forehead. 3. the general aspect of the countenance. 4. the edge of a steep hill or cliff.

brow-beat (brou'bēt), *v.t.* -**beat,** -**beat-en,** -**beat-ing,** to intimidate; bully.

brown (broun), *adj.* 1. of a dusky or dark color, a mixture of red and yellow with black. 2. dark-skinned; tanned: *n.* brown color: *v.t. & v.i.* to make or become brown. —**brown'ish,** *adj.*

brown-ie (broun'i), *n.* 1. in folk stories, a helpful elf. 2. [B-], a Girl Scout of the youngest group. 3. a small cookie cut in a bar or square from a rich chocolate cake.

brown-out ('out), *n.* a dimming or partial turning out of lights in a city, as to save electricity during a shortage.

brown-stone ('stōn), *n.* 1. a reddish-brown sandstone, used for building. 2. a house with a front of this: also **brownstone front.**

brown study, rumination; musing.

brown sugar, sugar not completely refined, retaining a thin coating of brown syrup.

browse (brouz), *n.* tender shoots or twigs that animals feed on: *v.t. & v.i.* **browsed, brows'-ing,** 1. to graze or nibble (leaves, twigs, etc.). 2. to look over (a book, items for sale, etc.) casually. —**brows'er,** *n.*

bru-cel-lo-sis (brōō-sĕ-lō'sis), *n.* undulant fever or some other disease caused by certain bacteria.

bru-in (brōō'in), *n.* a bear: name used in folklore.

bruise (brōōz), *n.* 1. an injury to surface tissue of an animal or plant, caused from a contusion that does not break the skin. 2. a discolored, spoiled, or dented spot resulting from or as if from such an injury: *v.t.* **bruised, bruis'ing,** 1. to cause such an injury to. 2. to hurt (one's feelings, ideals, etc.): *v.i.* to become bruised.

bruis-er (brōōz'ĕr), *n.* 1. a big, muscular man. 2. [Informal], a prizefighter.

bruit (brōōt), *n.* [Archaic], report; rumor: *v.t.* to spread a report of; rumor.

bru-mal (brōō'măl), *adj.* [Archaic], of, pertaining to, or like winter; wintry.

brum-ma-gem (brum'ă-jĕm), *adj.* [Informal], showy but worthless; sham: *n.* [Informal], cheap imitation jewelry.

brunch (brunch), *n.* [Informal], a late morning meal combining breakfast and lunch.

bru-net (brōō-net'), *n.* a person with dark or dark-brown hair and, often, dark eyes: *adj.* 1. denoting or of such a person. 2. dark or dark-brown.

bru-nette (brōō-net'), *n.* a girl or woman with dark or dark-brown hair and, often, dark eyes: *adj.* same as **brunet.**

brunt (brunt), *n.* the greatest impact or shock, as of a blow, attack, etc.

brush (brush), *n.* 1. a thicket of small trees. 2. the small trees and shrubs of a wood; also, small pieces of wood from these; brushwood. 3. a wooded, sparsely settled area. 4. an instrument with bristles or bristlelike wires projecting from a hard back that often has a handle, used for cleaning, applying paint, smoothing the hair, etc.; also, a stroking with or as with this. 5. the tail of a fox. 6. a slight encounter. 7. a brief fight. 8. a thin metallic plate, bundle of flexible wires, etc., used to conduct an electrical current to or from a moving part, as in a motor: *v.t.* 1. to sweep, clean, paint, apply, etc. with or as with a brush. 2. to touch lightly in passing: *v.i.* 1. to brush something. 2. to move with haste.

brush-off (brush'ôf), *n.* [Slang], quick, imperious rejection.

brush-wood ('wood), *n.* 1. rough, close bushes; underbrush. 2. small pieces of wood, broken or cut off from trees or bushes.

brusque (brusk), *adj.* abrupt in manner. —**brusque'ly,** *adv.* —**brusque'ness,** *n.*

Brus-sels carpet (brus'lz), [after *Brussels,* Belgium, where it was made], a kind of patterned carpet made from woolen yarn.

Brussels lace, 1. originally, a handmade lace with a raised design. 2. a lace with an appliquéd design, made by machine.

Brussels sprouts, 1. tiny, green, cabbagelike heads that grow on a single stem of a plant of the mustard family, eaten as a vegetable. 2. this plant.

brut (brōōt), *adj.* [French], very dry: said of wine, especially champagne.

bru-tal (brōōt'l), *adj.* 1. of, pertaining to, or like a brute; savage, cruel, etc. 2. harsh.— **bru'tal-ly,** *adv.*

bru-tal-i-ty (brōō-tal'i-ti), *n.* 1. the quality of being brutal. 2. *pl.* -**ties,** a brutal act.

bru-tal-ize (brōōt'l-iz), *v.t.* -**ized,** -**iz-ing,** 1. to make brutal. 2. to treat with brutality. — **bru-tal-i-za'tion,** *n.*

brute (brōōt), *adj.* 1. without reason or intelligence. 2. rough; brutal; uncivilized; like an animal. 3. having no feelings: *n.* 1. an animal. 2. a brutal person. —**brut'ish,** *adj.* — **brut'ish-ness,** *n.*

bub (bub), *n.* [Informal], little boy; brother.

bub-ble (bub'l), *n.* 1. a fragile, thin-walled, spherical formation, as of soap film, enveloping air or other gas. 2. a tiny ball of gas or air in a solid or liquid. 3. anything as transitory or insubstantial as a bubble. 4. a plastic or glass dome: *v.i.* -**bled,** -**bling,** 1. to make bubbles. 2. to be full of rising bubbles. 3. to make the sound of popping bubbles: *v.t.* to cause to bubble. —**bub'bly,** *adj.*

bubble gum, a special chewing gum that the chewer can blow into big bubbles.

bub·bler ('lẽr), *n.* a drinking fountain.

bu·bo (bū'bō, bōō'bō), *n., pl.* **-boes,** an inflamed swelling of a lymph gland, as in the groin or armpit. —**bu·bon'ic** (-bon'ik), *adj.*

bubonic plague, an epidemic, contagious disease caused by a bacterium carried by fleas from infected rats: it is marked by high fever, buboes, and delirium.

bu·bon·o·cele (bū-bon'ō-sēl, bōō-), *n.* an incomplete hernia in the groin.

buc·cal (buk'l), *adj.* 1. of the cheek or cheeks. 2. of the mouth.

buc·ca·neer (buk-ǎ-nir'), *n.* a pirate, or sea robber, especially one of the 17th century who raided the Spaniards in America.

buc·ci·na·tor (buk'si-nāt-ēr), *n.* the flat muscle on the cheek that acts as compressor.

buck (buk), *n.* 1. the male of the goat, antelope, rabbit, etc. 2. the act of bucking. 3. [Informal], a dashing, bold young man. 4. a signaling counter in the game of poker. 5. [Slang], a dollar: *v.i.* 1. to rear and plunge, with back arched, as a bronco. 2. to rush so as to butt, as a goat. 3. [Informal], to resist something. 4. [Informal], to move in jerks, as a car: *v.t.* 1. to throw by bucking. 2. to charge against, as in football. 3. [Informal], to work stubbornly against: *adj.* 1. male. 2. of the lowest military rating. — **buck'er,** *n.*

buck (buk), *n.* 1. a frame on which to saw wood; sawbuck. 2. a vaulting block in a gymnasium.

buck·a·roo (buk-ǎ-rōō'), *n., pl.* **-roos',** a cowboy.

buck·board (buk'bōrd), *n.* an open, four-wheeled carriage with the seat fastened to flooring laid on the axles.

buck·et (buk'it), *n.* 1. a round container with a hoop-shaped handle, for drawing or holding water, coal, etc.; pail. 2. the amount a bucket will hold: also **buck'et·ful,** *pl.* **-fuls.** 3. the scoop of a dredging machine or steam shovel. 4. any one of the receptacles of a water wheel.

bucket seat, a contoured seat for one person, as in some sports cars: it has a movable back.

bucket shop, a brokerage firm secretly gambling on market prices, speculating with customers' funds, etc.

buck·eye (buk'ī), *n.* 1. a tall tree of the horse-chestnut family, with large, shiny brown seeds enclosed in prickly seedcases. 2. any one of these seeds. 3. [B-], a person who lives in Ohio: a nickname.

buck·hound ('hound), *n.* a large hound used in hunting deer.

buck·le (buk'l), *n.* 1. a metal clasp consisting of a frame with a movable tongue or catch used for securing straps, bands, etc. 2. a bend or kink: *v.t. & v.i.* **-led, -ling,** 1. to fasten with a buckle. 2. to bend, warp, etc. 3. to apply (oneself) with vigor (with *down*).

buck·ler ('lēr), *n.* in ancient times, a kind of small, round shield.

buck·o (buk'ō), *n., pl.* **buck'oes,** 1. a bully. 2.

[Irish Informal], a young man: a term of address.

buck-pass·ing (buk'pas-ing), *n.* [Informal], the shifting of blame or accountability to someone else. —**buck'-pass·er,** *n.*

buck·ram (buk'rǎm), *n.* a coarse cloth stiffened with size: *adj.* of or like buckram.

buck·saw (buk'sô), *n.* a saw with a blade set in a frame to be grasped by both hands, used for cutting wood on a sawbuck.

buck·shot (buk'shot), *n.* lead shot of a large size, used for shooting deer, etc.

buck·skin ('skin), *n.* 1. the skin of a buck. 2. a soft, suedelike, yellowish or grayish leather made from deerskin or sheepskin. 3. *pl.* clothes made from this leather: *adj.* made of buckskin.

buck·thorn ('thôrn), *n.* 1. a thorny shrub or tree with small greenish flowers. 2. a tree of the sapodilla family, found in the southern U.S.

buck·tooth ('tōōth), *n., pl.* **-teeth,** a protruding upper front tooth. —**buck'toothed',** *adj.*

buck·wheat ('hwēt), *n.* 1. a plant cultivated for its triangular grains. 2. the grains, or the dark flour into which they are ground.

bu·col·ic (bū-kol'ik), *adj.* 1. pastoral. 2. of rural life; rustic: *n.* 1. a pastoral poem. 2. a rustic. —**bu·col'i·cal·ly,** *adv.*

bud (bud), *v.t.* **bud'ded, bud'ding,** to graft, using a bud: *v.i.* 1. to put forth or produce buds. 2. to begin to grow or develop: *n.* 1. the rudimentary, undeveloped stage of a branch, leaf, or flower; also, a gemma or gemmule. 2. someone or something undeveloped.

Bud·dha (bood'a, bōō'dã), *n.* 1. a statue or image of Siddhartha Gautama (563?–483? B. C.) of India, the founder of Buddhism. 2. a person viewed by Buddhists as embodying divine wisdom and virtue.

Bud·dhism (bood'izm, bōō'dizm), *n.* the religion and system of philosophy based on the teachings of Buddha: it teaches that right thinking and denial of self will bring the soul to Nirvana. —**Bud'dhist,** *n. & adj.*

bud·dy (bud'i), *n., pl.* **-dies,** [Informal], a friend; companion.

budge (buj), *v.t. & v.i.* **budged, budg'ing,** to manage to move, however slightly.

budge (buj), *n.* lambskin dressed with the wool outwards.

budg·er·i·gar (buj'ē-ri-gãr), *n.* an Australian parakeet with a greenish-yellow body: also [Informal], **budg·ie** (buj'i).

budg·et (buj'it), *n.* 1. originally, a bag or purse, or its contents. 2. a stock or store of things. 3. a plan that fits money spent to the amount of income. 4. the cost or estimated cost of doing anything: *v.t.* 1. to place on a budget. 2. to plan with detail. — **budg'et·ar·y,** *adj.* —**budg'et·er,** *n.*

buff (buf), *n.* 1. a thick, brownish-yellow leather prepared from the skin of the buffalo, ox, etc. 2. a military coat made of this. 3. same as **buffing wheel.** 4. a stick covered with cloth or leather, used in polishing and cleaning. 5. a brownish yellow. 6. the bare skin. 7. [Informal], a fan or enthusiast: *adj.* 1. made of buff. 2. buff-colored: *v.t.* 1. to polish with a buff. 2. to make smooth like buff.

buf·fa·lo (buf'å-lō), *n., pl.* -loes, -los, -lo, 1. a kind of wild ox, as the water buffalo. 2. popularly, the American bison: *v.t.* -loed, -lo·ing, [Slang], to confuse or impress.

buffalo robe, the skin of the bison, prepared with hair intact.

buff·er (buf'ẽr), *n.* 1. one who polishes or buffs. 2. a buffing stick or wheel.

buff·er (buf'ẽr), *n.* any intermediary thing lessening impact.

buffer state, a small country between two larger, usually unfriendly, countries.

buf·fet (buf'it), *n.* a blow, specifically with the hand: *v.t.* 1. to strike or beat, specifically with the hand. 2. to contend against: *v.i.* to struggle or contend with blows.

buf·fet (bŭ-fā', boo-), *n.* 1. a cupboard or sideboard. 2. a counter for refreshments at which guests serve themselves. 3. a meal served at such a counter.

buffing wheel, a wheel covered as with leather or cloth, used in polishing metal.

buf·foon (bŭ-fōōn'), *n.* a person who is always trying to amuse, as by clowning. —**buffoon'er·y,** *n.*

bug (bug), *n.* 1. an insect with sucking mouth parts. 2. any insect or small animal like an insect. 3. [Informal], a virus or germ. 4. [Slang], a small microphone hidden as in a room. 5. [Slang], an imperfection, as in a machine. 6. [Slang], an enthusiast: *v.t.* bugged, bug'ging, [Slang], 1. to conceal a microphone in (a room, telephone, etc.). 2. to bother, irritate, etc.

bug·a·boo (bug'å-bōō), *n., pl.* -boos, a bugbear.

bug·bear (bug'ber), *n.* 1. an imaginary cause of terror. 2. anything that causes unnecessary fear or worry.

bug-eyed ('īd), *adj.* [Slang], with the eyes protruding.

bug·ger (bug'ẽr), *n.* a dirty, low fellow.

bug·ger·y (-i), *n.* same as sodomy.

bug·gy (bug'i), *n., pl.* -gies, 1. a light, one-horse carriage. 2. a baby carriage. 3. [Slang], an auto.

bug·house (bug'hous), *n.* [Slang], an insane asylum: *adj.* [Slang], insane.

bu·gle (bū'gl), *n.* 1. a brass-wind instrument like a small, valveless trumpet. 2. a long glass bead used in dress trimming: *v.i. & v.t.* to sound (a bugle, bugle signal, etc.); also, to signal with or as with a bugle call.

buhl (bōōl), *n.* 1. inlaid decoration for furniture consisting of brass, tortoise shell, etc., worked into designs. 2. the furniture so ornamented. Also **buhl'work.**

build (bild), *v.t.* built, build'ing, 1. to construct; erect (a house, etc.). 2. to establish. 3. to create or develop (often followed by *up*): *v.i.* 1. to construct a building. 2. to depend or be based (followed by *on* or *upon*). 3. to increase; grow (often followed by *up*): *n.* mode or style of construction; form; figure. —**build'er,** *n.*

build·ing (bil'ding), *n.* 1. the act or work of constructing houses, ships, etc. 2. a structure; edifice.

build-up, build-up (bild'up), *n.* [Informal], 1. laudatory publicity. 2. a slow increase.

built-in (bilt'in'), *adj.* 1. constructed so as not to be removed. 2. existing as a natural part.

bulb (bulb), *n.* 1. an onion-shaped bud that extends roots and has a short, scaly stem. 2. a tuber or tuberous root that looks like such a bulb. 3. anything bulblike in shape.

bul·bif·er·ous (bul-bif'ẽr-ŭs), *adj.* producing bulbs.

bul·bous (bul'bŭs), *adj.* of, resembling, or having a bulb or bulbs.

bul·bul (bool'bool), *n.* a small songbird of Asia and Africa.

bulge (bulj), *n.* a swelling outward; protrusion or protuberance: *v.i. & v.t.* bulged, bulg'ing, to swell outward; protrude. —**bulg'y,** *adj.*

bulk (bulk), *n.* 1. magnitude or size; volume. 2. the main mass or body. 3. the cargo of a ship: *v.i.* to have, or increase in, size, importance, etc.: *adj.* 1. whole; total. 2. not in separate packages.

bulk·head (bulk'hed), *n.* 1. an upright partition in a ship, airplane, etc., separating one part from another for safety. 2. an embankment to hold back earth, fire, etc. 3. a frame covering an opening, as at a stairhead.

bulk·y (bul'ki), *adj.* bulk'i·er, bulk'i·est, of great size or bulk. —**bulk'i·ness,** *n.*

bull (bool), *n.* 1. the adult male of any bovine animal, as the ox. 2. the adult male of various other large animals, as the whale, elephant, etc. 3. one who buys shares of stock, expecting to sell them later at a profit: opposed to *bear.* 4. [Slang], a policeman. 5. [Slang], foolish talk; nonsense: *adj.* 1. male. 2. of large size. 3. rising in price: *v.t.* 1. to try to raise the market value of. 2. to push (one's way), as by bluster. 3. to mislead or fool with pretentious talk, falsehoods, etc.; bluff.

bull (bool), *n.* 1. same as bulla (sense 1). 2. an official document, edict, etc., as one with a bulla affixed.

bull (bool), *n.* a ludicrous inconsistency in language; blunder in speech or writing.

bul·la (bool'å, bul'å), *n., pl.* -lae ('ē), 1. a round lead seal affixed to an official Papal document. 2. in *Medicine,* a large vesicle.

bull-bait·ing (bool'bāt·ing), *n.* the sport, formerly popular in England, of having dogs attack bulls that are tied up or restricted.

bull-dog ('dôg), *n.* 1. a variety of short-haired dog with a square jaw, strong build, and stubborn grip. 2. a revolver of large caliber and short barrel: *adj.* characterized by the stubbornness of a bulldog: *v.t.* -dogged, -dog·ging, to throw (a steer) by gripping its horns and twisting its neck.

bull-doze ('dōz), *v.t.* -dozed, -doz·ing, 1. [Informal], to attempt to intimidate; bully. 2. to dig, level out, etc. with a bulldozer.

bull-doz·er ('dō-zẽr), *n.* a tractor with a large curved blade on the front, for moving earth, rubble, etc.

bul·let (bool'it), *n.* a small projectile to be fired, as from a pistol.

bul·le·tin (bool'ĕt-n), *n.* 1. an official report regarding some matter or event of public interest. 2. a short news statement. 3. a periodical publication: *v.t.* to publish or announce by bulletin.

bul·let·proof (bool'it-prōōf'), *adj.* that bullets cannot enter: *v.t.* to make bulletproof.

bull·fight (bool'fīt), *n.* a sport in which a matador maneuvers a bull into position for being killed. —**bull'fight·er**, *n.* —**bull'fight·ing**, *n.*

bull·finch ('finch), *n.* any one of various small songbirds.

bull·frog ('frôg), *n.* a large North American frog with a loud, bellowing croak.

bull·head ('hed), *n.* a broad-headed, scaleless, spiny fish of North America.

bull·head·ed ('hed-id), *adj.* very stubborn; determined. —**bull'head·ed·ness**, *n.*

bull·horn ('hôrn), *n.* a portable electronic device for amplifying the voice.

bul·lion (bool'yun), *n.* 1. gold or silver ingots. 2. a heavy twisted fringe of gold or silver thread.

bull·ish (bool'ish), *adj.* 1. of or like a bull. 2. rising, or bringing about a rise, in stock market price. 3. optimistic. —**bull'ish·ly**, *adv.* —**bull'ish·ness**, *n.*

bull·ock (bool'ŏk), *n.* a castrated bull; full-grown steer.

bull·pen ('pen), *n.* 1. [Informal], a barred room in a jail where prisoners are temporarily kept. 2. in *Baseball*, an area for relief pitchers to practice in.

bull's-eye (boolz'ī), *n.* 1. a circular piece of glass for letting in light. 2. any circular opening for light or air. 3. a lantern with a convex lens. 4. a convex lens for concentrating light. 5. a hard, round piece of candy. 6. *a)* the center of a target. *b)* a shot that hits this.

bull terrier, a strong, agile dog with a smooth, white coat, developed by crossing the bulldog and terrier.

bul·ly (bool'i), *n., pl.* -lies, one who domineers or frightens those not as strong: *v.t.* -lied, -ly·ing, to frighten or domineer like a bully: *v.i.* to act like a bully: *adj. & interj.* [Informal], good; fine.

bul·ly·rag (-rag), *v.t.* -ragged, -rag·ging, [Dialectal or Informal], to bully.

bully tree (bool'i), a tropical American tree that produces balata.

bul·rush (bool'rush), *n.* 1. a rushlike marsh plant. 2. [British], the cattail.

bul·wark (bool'wērk), *n.* 1. a rampart; fortification. 2. *usually pl.* the section around the sides of a ship, above the level of the deck. 3. any strong means of protection or defense: *v.t.* to fortify with a bulwark.

bum (bum), *n.* [Informal], 1. a hobo or tramp. 2. an idler; loafer. 3. an extreme enthusiast, as of skiing. 4. an idle life: (preceded by *the*): *v.i.* [Informal], to live idly or by begging: *v.t.* [Slang], to obtain by begging: *adj.* **bum'mer, bum'mest**, [Slang], 1. of bad quality. 2. incorrect. 3. disabled.

bum·ble·bee (bum'bl-bī), *n.* a large, hairy black-and-yellow bee.

bum·bling (bum'bling), *adj.* blundering; clumsy and stupid.

bum·boat (bum'bōt), *n.* a boat for selling provisions, fruit, etc. to offshore ships.

bum·mer (bum'ēr), *n.* [Slang], a disagreeable experience, especially from using drugs.

bump (bump), *n.* 1. a thump, knock, or jolt. 2. a swelling protuberance: *v.t. & v.i.* to hit or move joltingly.

bump·er (bum'pēr), *n.* 1. a buffer against shocks; specifically, a metal bar at the front or rear of a car. 2. a filled cup or glass: *adj.* very large, as a crop.

bump·kin (bump'kn), *n.* an awkward or simple person from a rural area.

bump·tious (bump'shus), *adj.* too self-assertive; forward. —**bump'tious·ly**, *adv.*

bun (bun), *n.* 1. a small roll, often sweet. 2. hair tied in a knot or roll.

bunch (bunch), *n.* 1. a cluster or tuft of things growing together. 2. a collection of things of the same kind grouped or fastened together. 3. [Informal], a group of similar people: *v.t. & v.i.* to form or gather into a bunch. —**bunch'y**, *adj.*

bun·co (bung'kō), *n., pl.* -cos, [Informal], a swindle; confidence game: *v.t.* -coed, -co·ing, [Informal], to cheat or swindle.

bun·combe (bung'kom), *n.* [Informal], idle or showy talk; anything said or done merely for effect; humbug: also **bunkum**.

bun·dle (bun'dl), *n.* 1. a number of things bound together. 2. a package or roll. 3. a group or collection: *v.t.* 1. to tie or bind in a bundle. 2. to dismiss unceremoniously (with *away, off,* etc.).

bung (bung), *n.* 1. a large cork or the like for stopping a hole in a cask or barrel. 2. a bunghole: *v.t.* 1. to stop with or as with a bung. 2. [Slang], to bruise or treat roughly.

bun·ga·low (bung'gǎ-lō), *n.* a low, one-story house.

bung·hole (bung'hōl), *n.* a hole in a barrel, cask, etc. through which liquid can be poured in or drawn out.

bun·gle (bung'gl), *v.i.* -gled, -gling, to botch; manage awkwardly: *v.t.* to perform clumsily: *n.* a clumsy performance; bungling. —**bun'gler**, *n.*

bun·ion (bun'yon), *n.* an inflamed swelling at the base of the big toe.

bunk (bungk), *n.* 1. a box or recess serving as a berth for sleeping, as in a ship. 2. [Informal], any place for sleeping, as a cot: *v.i.* to sleep in a bunk: *v.t.* to furnish a place to sleep for (someone).

bunk (bungk), *n.* [Slang], nonsense; humbug.

bunk·er (bung'kēr), *n.* 1. a large bin or receptacle, as for fuel. 2. a fortified position underground. 3. a sand trap on a golf course.

bunk·house ('hous), *n.* a separate building, as at a ranch, where workers sleep.

bun·ny (bun'i), *n., pl.* -nies, a rabbit: a child's word.

Bun·sen burner (bun'sn), a gas tube with holes at the bottom to admit air: when lighted, the mixture of air and gas gives an intensely hot, blue flame.

bunt (bunt), *v.t. & v.i.* in *Baseball*, to hit (a pitched ball) lightly to keep it in the infield: *n.* in *Baseball*, 1. the act of bunting. 2. a bunted ball.

ŏ in dragon, ōō in crude, oo in wool, u in cup, ü in cure, û in turn, u in focus, oi in boy, ou in house, th in thin, th in sheathe, g in get, j in joy, y in yet.

bunt (bunt), *n.* a fungus disease that destroys the grain of wheat, rye, etc.

bunt (bunt), *n.* the belly of a square sail.

bunt·ing (bun′ting), *n.* 1. a thin cloth used for making flags. 2. flags used for decoration.

bunt·ing (bun′ting), *n.* a small, brightly colored bird with a stout bill.

bunt·line (bunt′lin, ′lin), *n.* one of the ropes attached to the foot of a square sail to keep the sail from bellying when drawn up.

buoy (boo′i, boi), *n.* 1. a moored, floating body, used to indicate rocks, shoals, etc. 2. same as **life preserver:** *v.t.* 1. to keep afloat. 2. to mark with a buoy. 3. to raise the spirits of.

buoy·an·cy (boi′ǎn-si, boo′yǎn-), *n.* 1. floating ability; lightness. 2. lightness of spirits. — **buoy′ant,** *adj.*

bur (bûr), *n.* 1. the rough, prickly seedcase of certain plants. 2. a plant having burs. 3. same as **burr:** *v.t.* **burred, bur′ring,** to remove burs from.

bu·ran (boo-rän′), *n.* in Siberia, a windstorm or blizzard in winter, a dust storm in summer.

bur·bot (bûr′bŏt), *n., pl.* **-bot, -bots,** a flat-headed freshwater fish of the cod family.

bur·den (bûrd′n), *n.* 1. that which is borne or carried; a load. 2. something grievous, wearisome, or oppressive. 3. a ship's capacity for carrying a cargo. 4. a chorus or refrain of a song. 5. a topic on which one dwells: *v.t.* to load; lay a weight upon. — **bur′den·some,** *adj.*

bur·dock (bûr′dok), *n.* a large weed with burs and broad leaves.

bu·reau (bûr′ō), *n., pl.* **-reaus, -reaux** (′ōz), 1. [British], a writing desk or table. 2. a chest of drawers, as for clothing. 3. a service agency. 4. a government department or department section.

bu·reau·cra·cy (bū-rä′krǎ-si), *n., pl.* **-cies,** 1. a system of government using rigidly controlled bureaus. 2. the bureau officials. 3. any such rigid system.

bu·reau·crat (bûr′á-krat), *n.* an official in a bureaucracy. — **bu·reau·crat′ic,** *adj.*

bu·reau·cra·tize (bū-rä′krä-tīz), *v.t.* **-tized, -tiz·ing,** to make into a bureaucracy or bureaucrat. — **bu·reau·cra·ti·za′tion,** *n.*

burg (bûrg), *n.* [Informal], a town or city, especially one lacking excitement.

bur·gee (bûr′ji), *n.* a triangular or swallow-tailed signal flag used on ships.

bur·geon (bûr′jŭn), *v.i.* 1. to put forth buds, shoots, etc. 2. to flourish; expand.

-burg·er (bûr′gĕr), a suffix signifying *sandwich of ground meat, fish,* etc.

burgh (bûrg), *n.* 1. [British], a borough. 2. (bu′rá), in Scotland, a chartered town.

burgh·er (bûr′gĕr), *n.* a citizen of a borough or town.

bur·glar (bûr′glēr), *n.* one who breaks into a building in order to commit a felony.

bur·glar·i·ous (bêr-gler′i-ŭs), *adj.* of, pertaining to, or constituting burglary.

bur·gla·rize (bûr′glä-rīz), *v.t.* **-rized, -riz·ing,** [Informal], to commit burglary in or upon.

bur·gla·ry (bûr′glēr-i), *n., pl.* **-ries,** the act of breaking into a building to commit a felony, as larceny, or a misdemeanor.

bur·gle (bûr′gl), *v.t. & v.i.* **-gled, -gling,** [Informal], to burglarize.

bur·go·mas·ter (bûr′gŏ-mas-tĕr), *n.* the chief magistrate or mayor of a town in the Netherlands, Flanders, Austria, or Germany.

Bur·gun·dy (bûr′gŭn-di), *n.* [occasionally b-], *pl.* **-dies,** a wine, red or white, originally made in the Burgundy region of France. — **Bur·gun·di·an** (bẽr-gun′di-ǎn), *adj. & n.*

bur·i·al (ber′i-ǎl), *n.* the act of burying.

burke (bûrk), *v.t.* **burked, burk′ing,** 1. originally, to murder by suffocation. 2. to suppress or quietly dispose of (a proposed law, investigation, etc.).

burl (bûrl), *n.* 1. a small knot or lump in thread or cloth. 2. a knot in wood: *v.t.* to pick knots, loose threads, etc. from, in finishing cloth.

bur·lap (bûr′lap), *n.* a coarse fabric made of jute, hemp, etc., used in making bags.

bur·lesque (bûr-lesk′), *adj.* imitating comically or ridiculously: *n.* 1. a ludicrous, grotesque caricature; parody. 2. a kind of vaudeville featuring crude comedy, striptease, etc.: *v.t. & v.i.* **-lesqued′, -lesqu′ing,** to ridicule or make ridiculous by caricature; parody.

bur·ley (bûr′li), *n.* [also B-], a thin-bodied, light-colored tobacco.

bur·ly (bûr′li), *adj.* **-li·er, -li·est,** 1. heavy and muscular. 2. bluff; hearty. — **bur′li·ness,** *n.*

burn (bûrn), *v.t.* **burned** or **burnt, burn′ing,** 1. to subject to fire or combustion, as for the production of heat, light, etc. 2. to consume by fire. 3. to damage or injure by fire, acid, etc.; scorch. 4. to use as fuel. 5. to affect with a burning sensation. 6. to sunburn. 7. to cauterize. 8. to produce (a hole, mark, etc.) by means of fire: *v.i.* 1. to be on fire. 2. to suffer from or be injured by an excess of heat. 3. to glow; shine. 4. to be inflamed with passion, desire, etc.: *n.* 1. an injury or damage caused by fire, heat, etc. 2. the product or process of burning.

burn (bûrn), *n.* [Scottish], a brook.

burn·out (bûrn′out), *n.* 1. the point at which a rocket's fuel is burned up and the rocket enters free flight or is jettisoned. 2. emotional exhaustion from mental stress.

burn·er (bûr′nĕr), *n.* the part of a stove, furnace, etc. from which the flame comes.

burn·ing (bûr′ning), *adj.* 1. that burns. 2. of great importance.

burning glass, a convex lens used for concentrating the sun's rays upon an object, as to cause it to burn.

bur·nish (bûr′nish), *v.t. & v.i.* to polish by friction; make or become lustrous: *n.* polish; gloss; brightness.

bur·noose (bĕr-nōōs′), *n.* a long cloak with a hood, worn by Arabs: also **bur·nous′.**

burn·sides (bûrn′sīdz), *n.* a beard style with the chin shaven clean and full side whiskers: after Gen. A. E. Burnside.

burnt offering, something offered and burnt upon an altar as a sacrifice to a god.

---

burp (bûrp), *n. & v.i.* [Informal], belch: *v.t.* to make (a baby) expel stomach gas.

burp gun, [Military Slang], a type of automatic pistol or submachine gun.

burr (bûr), *n.* 1. a rough ridge left as on metal by cutting or drilling. 2. a bur. 3. the trilling of *r*, as in Scotland. 4. a whir: *v.t.* to form a rough ridge on.

bur·ro (bûr'ō), *n. pl.* -ros, in the southwestern U.S., a small donkey.

bur·row (bûr'ō), *n.* a hole in the ground, excavated as by a rabbit for habitation: *v.i.* 1. to dig a burrow. 2. to live or hide as in a burrow. 3. to work through or under something as by digging: *v.t.* to dig, as a burrow.

bur·sa (bûr'să), *n.*, *pl.* -sae ('sē), -sas, in Anatomy, a fluid-filled sac or saclike cavity diminishing friction.

bur·sar (bûr'sẽr), *n.* 1. a treasurer, as of a college. 2. in Scotland, a university student getting a support allowance.

bur·sa·ry (bûr'sẽr-i), *n.*, *pl.* -ries, 1. a treasury, as of a college. 2. in Scotland, a support allowance.

bur·si·tis (bẽr-sīt'is), *n.* inflammation of a bursa, as near the shoulder.

burst (bûrst), *v.i.* burst, burst'ing, 1. to rend or break open with violence; yield to internal force or pressure; explode. 2. to give way from grief, pain, pride, etc. 3. to move, appear, etc. suddenly. 4. to be as closely packed or filled as possible: *v.t.* to make explode or break violently: *n.* 1. a violent or sudden break or explosion. 2. a forceful effort; spurt. 3. a volley of shots.

bur·y (ber'i), *v.t.* bur'ied, bur'y·ing, 1. to deposit and cover up (a corpse, bone, box, etc.) in or as in ground. 2. to hide. 3. to put away, eliminate, etc. 4. to plunge (oneself) into.

bus (bus), *n.*, *pl.* bus'es, bus'ses, a large motor vehicle for carrying a number of passengers along a scheduled route: *v.t.* bused or bussed, bus'ing or bus'sing, to convey by bus: *v.i.* 1. to travel by bus. 2. to work as a busboy.

bus·boy (bus'boi), *n.* a waiter's assistant.

bush (boosh), *n.* 1. a thick shrub. 2. anything bushlike. 3. wild, uncleared country: *v.i.* to grow thick or bushy.

bush (boosh), *n.* same as bushing: *v.t.* to furnish with a bushing.

bushed (boosht), *adj.* [Informal], tired.

bush·el (boosh'l), *n.* 1. a dry measure containing eight gallons or four pecks. 2. a vessel of such a capacity.

bush·ing (boosh'ing), *n.* a lining or tube of metal inserted in a hole or machine part to reduce the size of the hole or to lessen friction.

bush league, [Slang], in *Baseball*, a small or inferior minor league. —bush'-league', *adj.* — bush leagu'er.

bush·man (boosh'măn), *n.*, *pl.* -men, 1. a person who inhabits the Australian bush. 2. a backwoodsman. 3. [B-], a member of a nomadic people of southwestern Africa.

bush·mas·ter ('mas-tẽr), *n.* a large, poisonous snake of Central and South America.

bush·whack (boosh'hwak), *v.i.* 1. to cut through bushes. 2. to attack from ambush in guerilla fighting: *v.t.* to ambush. —bush'whack·er, *n.*

bush·y (boosh'i), *adj.* bush'i·er, bush'i·est, 1. thick and spreading like a bush. 2. overgrown with shrubs. —bush'i·ness, *n.*

bus·i·ly (biz'i-li), *adv.* in a busy way.

busi·ness (biz'nis), *n.* 1. one's employment, trade, or profession. 2. something to be transacted or required to be done. 3. right of action. 4. affair; matter. 5. the buying and selling of goods and services. 6. a place where business is carried on: *adj.* of or pertaining to business.

business college, a school offering courses in typing, business practices, etc.: also business school.

busi·ness·like (-līk), *adj.* efficient, orderly, systematic, etc.

busi·ness·man (-man), *n.*, *pl.* -men (-men), a man engaged in business; executive. —busi'ness·wom·an, *n.fem., pl.* -wom·en.

bus·ing (bus'ing), *n.* the act of transporting children by bus to a school outside of their neighborhood, esp. in order to desegregate the school: also bus·sing.

bus·kin (bus'kin), *n.* 1. a kind of laced half boot or high shoe reaching to the middle of the calf, as worn in ancient tragedy. 2. tragic drama.

buss (bus), *n. & v.t. & v.i.* [Archaic or Dialectal], kiss.

bust (bust), *n.* 1. the head and shoulders of a person, as represented in sculpture. 2. the breasts of a woman.

bust (bust), *v.t. & v.i.* [Slang], 1. to break open or come apart. 2. to make or become penniless or reduced in rank. 3. to strike. 4. to take into custody; arrest: *n.* [Slang], 1. a complete failure. 2. an economic collapse. 3. a blow. 4. a spree. 5. an arrest.

bus·tard (bus'tẽrd), *n.* a large game bird of Africa, Asia, and Europe, related to the crane.

bus·tle (bus'l), *v.i. & v.t.* -tled, -tling, to move quickly or busily with a certain amount of noise and fuss: *n.* 1. noisy activity; tumult. 2. a pad or cushion worn by women to fill the back of the skirt.

bus·y (biz'i), *adj.* bus'i·er, bus'i·est, 1. earnestly or closely employed. 2. bustling. 3. being used, as a telephone. 4. officious; meddlesome. 5. so detailed as to be unpleasant: *v.t.* to keep constantly engaged; occupy (oneself) actively. —bus'y·ness, *n.*

bus·y·bod·y (-bod-i), *n.*, *pl.* -bod·ies, a meddling, officious person.

but (but), *prep.* except; excluding: *conj.* 1. on the contrary. 2. nevertheless; however. 3. unless. 4. that. 5. that...not: *adv.* 1. only. 2. merely. 3. just: *pron.* who...not; which...not.

bu·tane (bū'tān), *n.* a hydrocarbon used for fuel, in organic synthesis, etc.

butch·er (booch'ẽr), *n.* 1. one whose work is slaughtering animals for food. 2. one who cuts meat to be sold. 3. a savage killer: *v.t.* 1. to slaughter (animals) for food. 2. to kill savagely. 3. to bungle.

butch·er·bird (-bûrd), *n.* any of various shrikes

ô in dragon, ōō in crude, oo in wool, u in cup, ũ in cure, û in turn, ŭ in focus, oi in boy, ou in house, th in thin, ŧh in sheaŧhe, g in get, j in joy, y in yet.

that suspend their slaughtered prey upon thorns.

butch·er·y (booch´ĕr-i), *n.*, *pl.* **-er·ies**, 1. the business of slaughtering animals. 2. savage slaughter. 3. a bungling.

but·ler (but´lĕr), *n.* a manservant, usually the chief servant in a large household, in charge of the wines, plates, etc.

butt (but), *n.* 1. the thicker end of anything. 2. the remaining end, as the stub of a cigarette. 3. a target; also, a rifle or gunnery range. 4. a rear extremity, specifically of an animal's hide. 5. an object of ridicule. 6. [Slang], a cigarette: *v.t.* & *v.i.* to join so as to be touching.

butt (but), *n.* 1. a push or thrust delivered by the head of an animal. 2. a thrust in fencing: *v.t.* to strike by thrusting the head against: *v.i.* to stick out.

butt (but), *n.* 1. a large cask for wine or beer. 2. a liquid measure equal to 126 gallons.

butte (būt), *n.* a steep, isolated hill.

but·ter (but´ĕr), *n.* 1. a thick, yellowish substance obtained from cream or milk by churning. 2. any substance of butterlike consistency. 3. [Informal], flattery: *v.t.* 1. to spread or smear with butter. 2. [Informal], to flatter (often followed by *up*).

butter bean, same as: 1. lima bean. 2. wax bean.

but·ter·cup (-kup), *n.* a common plant with yellow, cup-shaped flowers.

but·ter·fat (-fat), *n.* the fatty part of milk: butter is churned from it.

but·ter·fin·gers (-fing-gĕrz), *n.* a person who is always dropping things.

but·ter·fly (-flī), *n.*, *pl.* **-flies**, 1. any one of a group of diurnal insects with narrow bodies and two pairs of brightly colored wings. 2. a frivolous person.

but·ter·milk (-milk), *n.* the sour liquid that remains after churning butter from milk.

but·ter·nut (-nut), *n.* 1. the oily nut of a walnut tree of eastern North America, which can be eaten. 2. this tree.

but·ter·scotch (-skoch), *n.* 1. a hard candy made of brown sugar and butter. 2. a syrup with the flavor of butterscotch.

but·ter·y (but´ĕr-i), *n.* 1. a storeroom for provisions, wine, etc. 2. a room in some colleges in England where liquors and provisions are kept for sale.

but·ter·y (but´ĕr-i), *adj.* 1. of, like, or spread with butter. 2. using flattery.

but·tock (but´ŏk), *n.* 1. one of the two rounded hind parts behind the hips; either part of the rump. 2. *pl.* the rump.

but·ton (but´n), *n.* 1. any small, usually rounded object used to fasten different parts of a garment, or attached for ornament. 2. something buttonlike. 3. a small sign worn, as on the lapel of the coat, to indicate membership, military service, etc. 4. the knob at the end of a fencing foil: *v.t.* & *v.i.* to fasten or furnish with buttons.

but·ton-down (-doun´), *adj.* 1. designating a collar, as on a shirt, fastened down by small buttons. 2. conservative, dull, etc.

but·ton·hole (-hōl), *n.* a slit or loop to receive

and hold a button: *v.t.* **-holed**, **-hol·ing**, 1. to make buttonholes in. 2. to stop and detain in conversation.

but·ton·wood (-wood), *n.* the plane tree.

but·tress (but´ris), *n.* 1. a stone or brick structure built on to an outside wall to provide support. 2. a support or prop: *v.t.* 1. to support by a buttress. 2. to prop up.

bu·tyr·ic (bū-tir´ik), *adj.* of, pertaining to, or derived from butter.

bux·om (buk´sŏm), *adj.* plump and comely; specifically, full-bosomed.

buy (bī), *v.t.* bought, buy´ing, 1. to acquire by paying an agreed price; purchase. 2. to bribe. 3. to obtain as by exchange. 4. [Slang], to believe valid, right, etc.: *n.* 1. something bought. 2. [Informal], a bargain.

buy·er (-ĕr), *n.* 1. one that buys. 2. one whose job is buying for a retail store.

buzz (buz), *n.* 1. a continous humming noise, as of bees. 2. a confused or blended murmur, as of many voices: *v.i.* 1. to make a low humming sound. 2. to move or speak thus. 3. to gossip. 4. to be full of noise and activity: *v.t.* 1. to tell (gossip). 2. to signal with a buzzer. 3. to fly an airplane low over.

buz·zard (buz´ĕrd), *n.* 1. any one of various hawks slow in flight. 2. same as turkey buzzard.

buzz·er (buz´ĕr), *n.* an electric signal making a buzzing sound.

buzz saw, a circular saw turned by a motor.

by (bī), *prep.* 1. beside or near; close to. 2. during. 3. for (an established time). 4. no later than. 5. through. 6. past. 7. toward. 8. in the interest of; for. 9. through the agency of. 10. according to. 11. in. 12. in series with. 13. with the sanction of. 14. in or to the amount of. 15. along with a measurement of. 16. using (the number given) to divide or multiply: *adv.* 1. near at hand. 2. aside; away. 3. past; beyond. 4. at the place understood: *n.* & *adj.* same as bye.

by-, a prefix signifying *near, on the side.*

by-and-by (bī´n-bī´), *n.* a future time.

by-blow (bī´blō), *n.* an illegitimate child.

bye (bī), *n.* 1. a run scored at cricket on a passed ball. 2. in *Sports*, the advancement of the unpaired contestant to the next level of rounds without playing: *adj.* incidental.

bye-bye (bī´bī), *n.* & *interj.* goodbye.

by·gone (bī´gôn), *adj.* past; former: *n.* anything past or gone.

by·law (bī´lô), *n.* a private law or statute framed by a corporate body.

by·line (´līn), *n.* a line at the top of a news story; etc., indicating the author.

by·name (´nām), *n.* a nickname.

by·pass (´pas), *n.* 1. a path, channel, etc. connecting two points and going around or being additional to the main route. 2. a surgical operation to allow fluid to pass around a diseased or blocked part or organ: in full bypass operation: *v.t.* 1. to avoid by a bypass. 2. to supply with a bypass. 3. to ignore, fail to consult, etc.; disregard.

by·play (´plā), *n.* action, gestures, etc. going on aside from the main action or conversation, as in a play.

by·prod·uct ('prod-ŭct), *n.* a secondary product resulting from the manufacture of the main product: also **by-product**.

byre (bīr), *n.* [British], a cow house.

by·road (bī'rōd), *n.* a side road.

By·ron·ic (bī-ron'ik), *adj.* having the style of Lord Byron (1788–1824) or his writings; romantic, cynical, ironic, etc.

by·stand·er (bī'stan-dẽr), *n.* one present but not taking part; onlooker.

byte (bīt), *n.* a string of binary digits *(bits)*, usually eight, operated on as a basic unit by a digital computer.

by·word ('wŭrd), *n.* 1. a familiar saying; proverb. 2. an object of derision. 3. [Rare], a nickname.

By·zan·tine (biz'n-tēn), *adj.* of or pertaining to Byzantium (Constantinople, now Istanbul) or the Byzantine Empire (eastern part of the Roman Empire, 395–1453 A.D.).

C

C, c (sē), _n._, _pl._ **C's, c's.** 1. the third letter of the English alphabet. 2. either of the two sounds of this letter, as in _ceiling_ and _card._ 3. a type or impression of _C_ or _c._

C (sē), _adj._ 1. shaped like _C._ 2. of average quality: _n._ 1. an object shaped like _C._ 2. a Roman numeral denoting 100. 3. a school mark or rating signifying average. 4. in _Music, a)_ the first tone in the scale of C major. _b)_ the key having this tone for a basic note. _c)_ common time.

Caa·ba (kä'bä), _n._ same as **Kaaba.**

cab (kab), _n._ 1. a horse-drawn public carriage. 2. same as **taxicab.** 3. the covered place for the driver or operator of a locomotive, crane, truck, etc.

ca·bal (kä-bal'), _n._ 1. an intrigue or plot, often political. 2. a small, secret group of persons engaged in such an intrigue: _v.i._ **-balled', -bal'ling,** to plot or intrigue; form a cabal.

cab·a·la (kab'ä-lä), _n._ 1. the occult theosophy of a group of medieval Jewish rabbis, built upon a mystical interpretation of the Scriptures. 2. any esoteric doctrine.

cab·a·lism (-lizm), _n._ occult doctrine. —**cab'a·list,** _n._ —**cab·a·lis'tic,** _adj._

ca·bal·le·ro (kab-â-ler'ō, -âl-yer'ō), _n._, _pl._ **-ros,** 1. a Spanish knight or gentleman. 2. in the southwestern U.S., _a)_ a lady's attendant; gallant. _b)_ a horseman.

ca·ba·na (kä-bän'â, -ban'yä), _n._ [Spanish], 1. a cabin. 2. a small shelter on a beach, sometimes used as a bathhouse.

cab·a·ret (kab-â-rā', kab'â-rä), _n._ 1. a café or restaurant serving alcoholic liquor and having a floor show. 2. the floor show presented in a cabaret.

cab·bage (kab'ij), _n._ a vegetable with closely packed, thick leaves formed into a head.

cabbage tree, a kind of palm tree with edible buds at the ends of the branches: also **cabbage palm.**

cab·driv·er (kab'drīv-ēr), _n._ a driver of a cab: also [Informal], **cab·by, cab·bie** (kab'i), _pl._ **-bies.**

cab·in (kab'n), _n._ 1. a small, crude, one-story building. 2. a room on a ship or boat. 3. the compartment in an airplane for passengers, crew, or cargo.

cabin boy, an errand boy on a ship.

cab·i·net (kab'i-nit), _n._ 1. a piece of furniture or a boxlike container with drawers or shelves for storing or holding things. 2. a case for a radio, record player, television set, etc. 3. [often C-], a body of advisers to the executive of a nation.

cab·i·net-mak·er (-mā-kēr), _n._ an artisan who turns out fine furniture and woodwork. — **cab'i·net-mak·ing,** _n._

cab·i·net·work (-würk), _n._ the finished products of a cabinetmaker.

ca·ble (kā'b'l), _n._ 1. a large, strong rope of hemp, wire, etc. 2. a heavy chain to which a ship's anchor is attached. 3. a unit of nautical measure equal to 100 (or sometimes 120) fathoms: also called **cable length.** 4. strands of insulated wire for carrying electric current, twisted together into a thick bunch and often laid underground or under the sea. 5. same as **cablegram:** _v.t._ **-bled, -bling,** 1. to fasten with a cable. 2. to transmit by undersea cable. 3. to send a cablegram to.

cable car, a car pulled on rails by a moving cable, or suspended from a moving cable attached to raised supports.

ca·ble·cast (-kast), _v.t._ **-cast, -cast·ing,** to transmit to receivers by coaxial cable: _n._ a television program that is cablecast.

ca·ble·gram (-gram), _n._ a message sent by submarine cable.

cable TV, a television system in which various antennas receive local and distant signals and transmit them by coaxial cable to subscribers' receivers.

ca·bo·chon (kab'ô-shon), _n._ a precious stone cut with a rounded face, polished but not faceted.

ca·boo·dle (kä-bōō'd'l), _n._ [Informal], lot: chiefly in _the whole caboodle._

ca·boose (kä-bōōs'), _n._ the trainmen's car attached to the rear of a freight train.

cab·ri·o·let (kab-ri-ô-lā', -let'), _n._ a covered carriage with two wheels, drawn by one horse.

ca·ca·o (kä-kā'ō, -kā'ō), _n._, _pl._ **-ca'os,** 1. a small evergreen tree of tropical America, from the seeds of which cocoa and chocolate are prepared. 2. the seed of this tree.

cac·ci·a·to·re (kach-â-tôr'i), _adj._ [Italian], cooked with tomatoes, onions, spices, etc., in a casserole.

cache (kash), _n._ 1. a place of concealment for provisions for future use. 2. provisions hidden in such a place: _v.t._ & _v.i._ **cached, cach'ing,** to hide in a cache.

cache·pot (kash'pot, -pō), _n._ a decorative jar for holding potted plants: also **cache pot.**

ca·chet (ka-shā', kash'ā), _n._ 1. a seal or stamp on an official document or letter. 2. a sign or mark of superiority, official approval, authenticity, etc. 3. a design, slogan, advertisement, etc. printed or stamped on mail.

ca·chex·i·a (kä-kek'si-â), _n._ ill health and a wasting of the body during a chronic illness: also **ca·chex'y** ('si).

cach·in·na·tion (kak-i-nā'shûn), _n._ loud or unrestrained laughter.

cack·le (kak'l), _v.i._ **-led, -ling,** 1. to make the cry of a hen. 2. to talk or laugh with sounds like those of a hen. _n._ 1. the cry of

---

a in _cap_, ā in _cane_, ä in _father_, â in _abet_, e in _met_, ē in _be_, ē in _baker_, ê in _regent_, i in _pit_, ī in _fine_, i in _manifest_, o in _hot_, ô in _horse_, ō in _bone_,

118

a hen. 2. laughter or talk with a cackling sound.

ca·co·ë·thes (kak-ō-ē'thēz), *n.* a mania; compulsion: also ca·co·e'thes.

cac·o·gen·e·sis (kak-ō-jen'ē-sis), *n.* the inability to produce hybrids that can both live and reproduce.

ca·cog·ra·phy (kā-kog'rā-fi), *n.* 1. erroneous spelling. 2. cramped, indistinct writing.

cac·o·mis·tle (kak'ō-mis-l), *n.* 1. a slender, flesh-eating animal of the southwestern U.S. and Mexico, related to the raccoon. 2. its fur Also cac'o·mix·le (-mis-l, -mik-sl).

ca·coph·o·ny (kā-kof'ō-ni), *n., pl.* -nies, a harsh, grating sound; dissonance. —ca·coph'o·nous (-nùs), *adj.*

cac·tus (kak'tùs), *n., pl.* -tus·es, -ti ('tī), a spiny, fleshy plant with showy flowers.

cad (kad), *n.* a vulgar, ill-bred man or boy.

ca·dav·er (kā-dav'ēr), *n.* a dead body, as for dissection.

ca·dav·er·ous (-ùs), *adj.* resembling a corpse; pale, ghastly, etc.

cad·die (kad'i), *n.* 1. a person who carries the golf clubs and assists a golf player. 2. a small cart for conveying golf bags, packages, etc.: *v.i.* -died, -dy·ing, to work as a caddie.

cad·dis (kad'is), *n.* a kind of coarse woolen material: also cad'dice.

caddis fly, a small insect resembling a moth.

cad·dish (kad'ish), *adj.* characteristic of a cad; coarse, vulgar, etc. —cad'dish·ly, *adv.* —cad'dish·ness, *n.*

caddis worm, the larva of the caddis fly, used as bait in fishing: also cad'dis, cad'dice.

cad·dy (kad'i), *n., pl.* -dies, 1. a small container for keeping tea. 2. a device for keeping various articles.

cad·dy (kad'i), *n. & v.i.* same as caddie.

-cade (kād), a suffix signifying *parade, procession.*

ca·dence (kād'ēns), *n.* 1. a lowering of pitch or volume in speaking. 2. inflection or modulation in tone. 3. rhythmic flow of sound. 4. timed movement, as in dancing or marching. Also ca'den·cy ('ēn-si). —ca'denced, *adj.*

ca·den·za (kā-den'zā), *n.* a vocal or instrumental flourish, often done solo.

ca·det (kā-det'), *n.* 1. a younger son or brother. 2. a student at an armed forces academy. 3. [Old Slang] a pimp.

cadge (kaj), *v.t. & v.i.* cadged, cadg'ing, to beg or sponge, or get by begging or sponging. —cadg'er, *n.*

ca·di (kä'di), *n.* a minor Moslem judge.

Cad·me·an victory (kad-mē'ān), a victory as destructive to those who win as to those who lose.

cad·mi·um (kad'mi-ùm), *n.* a bluish-white, ductile, metallic chemical element.

ca·dre (kad'ri), *n.* 1. a framework; skeleton. 2. a small unit or group around which a larger organization can be formed, as of military personnel.

ca·du·ce·us (kā-dōō'si-ùs), *n., pl.* -ce·i ('si-ī), the winged staff of Mercury with two serpents twined around it, used as a symbol of the medical profession. —ca·du'ce·an, *adj.*

cae·cum (sē'kùm), *n., pl.* -ca ('kā), same as cecum. —cae'cal, *adj.*

Cae·sar·e·an section (si-zer'i-ān), [also c- s-]. a delivery of a baby by cutting through the walls of the abdomen and uterus of the mother.

Cae·sar·ism (sē'zār-izm), *n.* [also c-], absolute rule of government; autocracy

cae·si·um (sē'zi-ùm), *n.* same as cesium.

cae·su·ra (si-zhoor'ā), *n., pl.* -ras, -rae ('ē), a pause in a line of verse.

ca·fé, ca·fe (ka-fā', kā-), *n.* 1. coffee. 2. a small restaurant, coffeehouse, or barroom.

caf·e·te·ri·a (kaf-ē-tir'i-ā), *n.* a restaurant in which customers serve themselves from counters.

caf·feine (kaf'in; ka-fēn'), *n.* a bitter alkaloid, contained in coffee, tea, and cola extract, that acts as a stimulant: also caf'fein.

caf·tan (kaf'tān), *n.* a robe with long sleeves, worn in the region of the eastern Mediterranean.

cage (kāj), *n.* 1. a box or enclosure furnished with bars, wire, etc. for confining birds or other animals. 2. any openwork structure or frame. 3. an elevator device: *v.t.* caged, cag'ing, to confine, as in a cage; shut up.

ca·gey (kā'ji), *adj.* ca·gi·er, ca·gi·est, [Informal], 1 cunning; sly. 2. wary; cautious. Also ca'gy —ca'gi·ly, *adv.* —ca'gi·ness, *n.*

ca·hoots (kā-hōōts'), *n.* [Slang], association of a questionable nature; league: now chiefly in *in cahoots.*

cai·man (kā'mān), *n., pl.* -mans, a tropical American reptile similar to the alligator in structure and habits.

cairn (kern), *n.* a conical heap of stones erected as a monument.

cairn·gorm (kern'gôrm), *n.* a yellow or brown variety of quartz, used as a gem.

cais·son (kā'son), *n.* 1. formerly, a box filled with explosives for firing as a mine. 2. an ammunition wagon or chest. 3. a watertight box or casing used for building structures under water. 4. a watertight box for raising and floating sunken vessels.

caisson disease, same as decompression sickness.

cai·tiff (kāt'if), *n.* a cruel or cowardly person: *adj.* cruel or cowardly.

ca·jole (kā-jōl'), *v.t. & v.i.* -joled', -jol'ing, to coax or deceive by flattery, wheedle. —ca·jol'er, *n.* —ca·jol'er·y, *n.*

cake (kāk), *n.* 1. a small mass of dough, hashed food, etc. that is fried or baked. 2. flour, milk, eggs, sugar, etc. mixed and baked, as in a loaf and often covered with icing. 3. a solidified or molded mass, as of soap or ice: *v.t. & v.i.* caked, cak'ing, to form into a compact mass; solidify. —cak'y, *adj.*

cake·walk ('wôk), *n.* 1. an exaggerated walk formerly performed by Negroes in the South in competition for a cake. 2. a dance that developed from this walk: *v.i.* to do a cakewalk. —cake'walk·er, *n.*

cal·a·bash (kal'ā-bash), *n.* 1. a tropical American tree bearing large, round fruit. 2. an Old World tropical vine bearing hard-rinded fruit. 3. the fruit of either of these plants. 4.

ō in dragon, ōō in crude, oo in wool, u in cup, ū in cure, ù in turn, ù in focus, oi in boy, ou in house, th in thin, th in sheathe, g in get, j in joy, y in yet.

the dried shell of a calabash, used as a bowl, bottle, pipe, etc.

cal-a-boose (kal'ă-bōōs), *n.* [Slang], a jail; prison.

cal-a-mine (kal'ă-min), *n.* 1. a hydrous silicate of zinc. 2. a powder of zinc and ferric oxides, used in skin lotions.

ca-lam-i-tous (kă-lam'i-tŭs), *adj.* producing, or resulting from, calamity. —ca-lam'i-tous-ly, *adv.* —ca-lam'i-tous-ness, *n.*

ca-lam-i-ty (-ti), *n., pl.* -ties, 1. any cause that produces evil, disaster, or extreme misfortune. 2. heavy affliction.

cal-a-mus (kal'ă-mŭs), *n., pl.* -mi (-mī), 1. same as sweetflag. 2. a climbing palm of the Old World, yielding rattan. 3. the quill of a feather.

ca-lash (kă-lash'), *n.* 1. a light carriage with low wheels and a folding top. 2. a folding hood formerly worn by women.

cal-car-e-ous (kal-ker'i-ŭs), *adj.* of, resembling, or containing calcium carbonate, lime, or calcium.

cal-cif-er-ous (kal-sif'ĕr-ŭs), *adj.* yielding calcium carbonate.

cal-ci-fi-ca-tion (kal-si-fi-kā'shŭn), *n.* 1. the process of calcifying. 2. the deposition of lime salts in tissues, normally in bone.

cal-ci-fy (kal'si-fī), *v.t.* to convert into lime: *v.i.* to become stony by conversion into lime.

cal-ci-mine (-min), *n.* a white or tinted wash for walls or ceilings: *v.t.* -mined, -min-ing, to wash or cover with calcimine.

cal-cine (kal'sin), *v.t. & v.i.* -cined, -cin-ing, 1. to reduce to powder by heat. 2. to burn to ashes. 3. to oxidize. —cal-ci-na-tion (kal-si-nā'shŭn), *n.*

cal-cite (kal'sīt), *n.* crystallized calcium carbonate, the main constituent of limestone, chalk, and marble.

cal-ci-um (kal'si-ŭm), *n.* a soft, silver-white metallic chemical element existing in combination in limestone, marble, chalk, etc.

calcium carbide, a crystalline compound of limestone and carbon from which acetylene is generated.

calcium carbonate, a white powder or crystalline compound found in limestone, marble, and chalk, and in bones, teeth, shells, and the ashes of plants.

calcium light, same as limelight (sense 1).

cal-cu-late (kal'kyū-lāt), *v.t.* -lat-ed, -lat-ing, 1. to find by mathematical operations; compute. 2. to ascertain or determine by any process of reasoning; estimate. 3. to devise for some purpose. 4. [Informal], to suppose or think: *v.i.* 1. to make a computation. 2. to depend (with *on*). —cal'cu-la-ble (-lă-bl), *adj.*

cal-cu-lat-ed (-lāt-id), *adj.* 1. computed. 2. taken on after estimating the results. 3. planned purposefully. 4. likely.

cal-cu-lat-ing (-ing), *adj.* 1. scheming; cunning. 2. computing.

cal-cu-la-tion (kal-kyū-lā'shŭn), *n.* 1. the act of calculating; computation. 2. an estimate based on study. 3. careful planning beforehand. —cal'cu-la-tive, *adj.*

cal-cu-la-tor (kal'kyū-lāt-ĕr), *n.* 1. one who

computes. 2. a machine for doing arithmetic rapidly: also calculating machine.

cal-cu-lous (kal'kyū-lŭs), *adj.* having or caused by a calculus (sense 1).

cal-cu-lus (kal'kyū-lŭs), *n., pl.* -li (-lī), -lus-es, 1. an abnormal stony mass in the body. 2. a method of computation using symbols. 3. a method of mathematical analysis.

cal-de-ra (kal-dir'ă), *n.* a large, caldronlike cavity on the summit of a volcano.

cal-dron (kôl'drŏn), *n.* a large boiler or kettle.

cal-en-dar (kal'ĕn-dĕr), *n.* 1. a system for fixing the length and sections of a year. 2. a chart showing the days, weeks, and months of at least one year. 3. a list, as of court cases arranged for trial: *v.t.* to place on a calendar or list.

cal-en-der (kal'ĕn-dĕr), *n.* a machine with rollers for smoothing or glossing paper, cloth, etc.: *v.t.* to put (paper, cloth, etc.) through a calender.

cal-ends (kal'ĕndz), *n.* in the ancient Roman calendar, the first day of a month.

calf (kaf), *n., pl.* calves; especially for 4, calfs, 1. a young cow or bull. 2. the young of certain other animals, as the whale, elephant, etc. 3. a large, floating piece of ice separated from an iceberg or glacier. 4. leather made from the skin of a calf. 5. [Informal], a clumsy or silly young person.

calf (kaf), *n., pl.* calves, the fleshy back part of the leg under the knee.

calf-skin (kaf'skin), *n.* 1. the skin of a calf. 2. a soft leather produced from this.

cal-i-ber (kal'i-bĕr), *n.* 1. the diameter of a cylindrical body, especially of a bullet or shell. 2. the diameter of a gun bore. 3. ability or quality of a person or thing.

cal-i-brate (kal'i-brāt), *v.t.* -brat-ed, -brat-ing, 1. to find the caliber of. 2. to determine or correct the graduations of (a thermometer, scale, etc.).

cal-i-co (kal'i-kō), *n., pl.* -coes, -cos, in the U.S., a kind of rough, printed cotton cloth: *adj.* 1. made of calico. 2. having spots like calico.

cal-i-for-ni-um (kal-i-fôr'ni-ŭm), *n.* a synthetic radioactive chemical element.

cal-i-pash (kal'i-pash), *n.* a dull, greenish gelatinous substance enclosed beneath the upper shell of a turtle: it can be eaten.

cal-i-pee (kal'i-pē), *n.* a light-yellow gelatinous substance enclosed by the lower shell of a turtle: it can be eaten.

cal-i-per (kal'i-pĕr), *n. usually pl.* a device with two movable legs on a hinge, for measuring the length, diameter, etc. of something: *v.t. & v.i.* to measure with calipers.

ca-liph (kā'lif), *n.* supreme ruler: a title of successors of Mohammed as heads of Moslem states: also calif.

cal-iph-ate (kal'i-fāt), *n.* the office, reign, or land of a caliph: also cal'if-ate.

cal-is-then-ics (kal-is-then'iks), *n.* 1. the art of promoting health and muscle tone by physical exercise. 2. simple gymnastics. Also cal-lis-then'ics. —cal-is-then'ic, *adj.*

calk (kôk), *v.t.* same as caulk.

calk (kôk), *n.* 1. that part of a horseshoe which projects downward to prevent slipping. 2. a spurred metal plate nailed to the sole of a shoe to stop slipping: *v.t.* to furnish with a calk.

call (kôl), *v.t.* 1. to announce in a loud voice; shout. 2. to summon· from or invite to any place. 3. to convoke judicially or officially. 4. to give a name to. 5. to think of as specified. 6. to rouse from sleep; awaken. 7. to contact by telephone. 8. to give orders for. 9. to halt (a game, contest, etc.). 10. to require payment of (a loan, bond, etc.). 11. in *Poker*, to force (a player) to display his hand by matching his bet: *v.i.* 1. to utter in a loud voice; shout. 2. to visit briefly (often followed by *on*). 3. to telephone: *n.* 1. an act of calling. 2. a shout. 3. the cry or sound of certain animals. 4. a summons or invitation. 5. a short visit. 6. an economic demand, as for some commodity. 7. need. 8. a demand for payment. 9. an option to buy certain stock for a limited time at a stipulated price. —**call'er,** *n.*

cal·la (kal'ä), *n.* a plant with a yellowish spadix and a white, yellow, or pink spathe surrounding it: also **calla lily.**

call girl, a prostitute who makes appointments over the telephone.

cal·lig·ra·phy (kā·lig'rä·fi), *n.* 1. elegant or beautiful handwriting. 2. penmanship. —**cal·lig'ra·pher, cal·lig'ra·phist,** *n.*

call·ing (kôl'ing), *n.* 1. the act of summoning. 2. one's occupation, trade, or profession. 3. an internal force driving one toward some occupation or activity; vocation.

cal·li·o·pe (kā·li'ō·pē, kal'i·ōp), *n.* an organlike musical instrument having a group of steam whistles.

cal·los·i·ty (ka·los'i·ti), *n.* 1. the state or quality of being hardened or unfeeling. 2. *pl.* -ties, a callus.

cal·lous (kal'ûs), *adj.* 1. hardened. 2. unfeeling; insensitive. —**cal'lous·ly,** *adv.* —**cal'lous·ness,** *n.*

cal·low (kal'ō), *adj.* 1. unfledged. 2. inexperienced. —**cal'low·ness,** *n.*

cal·lus (kal'ûs), *n., pl.* -lus·es, 1. a thickened or hardened place on the skin. 2. bony matter which unites the ends of fractured bones: *v.i.* & *v.t.* to form or cause to form a callus.

calm (käm), *adj.* tranquil; still; undisturbed: *n.* stillness; serenity: *v.t.* & *v.i.* to make or become calm (often followed by *down*). —**calm'ly,** *adv.* —**calm'ness,** *n.*

cal·o·mel (kal'ō·mel), *n.* mercurous chloride, formerly used as a purgative medicine, for intestinal worms, etc.

ca·lor·ic (kā·lôr'ik), *adj.* 1. of heat. 2. of or pertaining to calories.

cal·o·rie (kal'ō·ri), *n.* 1. the quantity of heat necessary to raise one degree centigrade the temperature of one kilogram of water (**large calorie**) or one gram of water (**small calorie**). 2. a unit equal to the large calorie, used to express the heat or energy value of food as used in the body. 3. an amount of food capable of producing one large calorie. Also **cal'o·ry,** *pl.* -ries.

cal·o·rif·ic (kal·ō·rif'ik), *adj.* generating heat.

cal·o·rim·e·ter (kal·ō·rim'ē·tēr), *n.* an apparatus for measuring amounts of heat.

cal·o·rim·e·try (kal·ō·rim'ē·tri), *n.* measurement of amounts of heat. —**cal·o·ri·met·ric** (kal·ō·ri·met'rik), cal·o·ri·met'ri·cal,** *adj.*

ca·lotte (kā·lot'), *n.* a skullcap, especially one worn by Roman Catholic clergymen.

cal·pac, cal·pack (kal'pak), *n.* a large felt or sheepskin hat, worn in the Near East.

cal·trop, cal·trap (kal'trŏp), *n.* 1. an iron device with four spikes, placed on the ground to hinder the advance of troops. 2. any of a number of plants with prickly flowers or fruit.

cal·u·met (kal'yû·met), *n.* a long-stemmed tobacco pipe, smoked as a symbol of peace by North American Indians.

ca·lum·ni·ate (kā·lum'ni·āt), *v.t.* & *v.i.* -at·ed, -at·ing, to accuse falsely and maliciously. —**ca·lum·ni·a'tion,** *n.* —**ca·lum'ni·a·tor,** *n.*

ca·lum·ni·ous (-ni·ûs), *adj.* slanderous; defamatory. —**ca·lum'ni·ous·ly,** *adv.*

cal·um·ny (kal'ûm·ni), *n., pl.* -nies, 1. a false and malicious accusation; slander. 2. the utterance of such an accusation.

Cal·va·ry (kal'vēr·i), *n.* 1. the place near Jerusalem where Jesus Christ was crucified. 2. [c-], *pl.* -ries, an outdoor representation of the Crucifixion.

calve (kav), *v.i.* & *v.t.* calved, calv'ing, 1. to give birth to (a calf). 2. to cast off (a mass of ice): said of an iceberg or a glacier.

calves (kavz), *n.* plural of calf.

Cal·vin·ism (kal'vin·izm), *n.* the doctrines of John Calvin (1509-64), French theologian and reformer, emphasizing predestination and salvation through faith rather than good works. —**Cal'vin·ist,** *n.* & *adj.* —**Cal·vin·is'tic,** *adj.*

cal·vi·ti·es (kal·vish'i·ēz), *n.* baldness.

calx (kalks), *n., pl.* calx'es, cal'ces (kal'sēz), the ash of a metal left after calcination.

ca·lyp·so (kā·lip'sō), *adj.* of or pertaining to topical folk songs, originally of Trinidad, with a lively rhythm: *n., pl.* -sos, music or a song with calypso rhythm.

ca·lyx (kā'liks, kal'iks), *n., pl.* ca'lyx·es, ca'ly·ces ('li·sēz), the outside whorl of a flower, usually green.

cam (kam), *n.* a moving piece of machinery, as a projecting part on a wheel, for imparting or transmitting an eccentric or alternating motion.

ca·ma·ra·de·rie (käm·ä·räd'ēr·i), *n.* [French], good fellowship; the spirit of loyalty among comrades.

cam·a·ril·la (kam·ä·ril'ä), *n.* a cabal; secret, unofficial advisers to someone in authority.

cam·ber (kam'bēr), *n.* 1. a convexity on an upper surface, as of a road, ship's deck, etc. 2. a piece of timber thus bent. 3. a setting given to each of a pair of motor vehicle wheels so that they are closer together at the bottoms than the tops: *v.t.* & *v.i.* to curve or bend; arch.

cam·bist (kam'bist), *n.* 1. one who deals in foreign notes or bills of exchange. 2. a book that lists the rates of exchange of different currencies.

cam·bi·um (kam'bi·ûm), *n.* the formative layer

of tissue lying between the young wood and the bark of trees and treelike plants.

Cam·bri·an (kăm′brĭ-ăn), *n.* the first period of the Paleozoic Era, marked by an abundance of marine life.

cam·bric (kām′brĭk), *n.* 1. a very fine, thin linen. 2. a cotton cloth like this.

cambric tea, a very weak infusion of tea, with sugar and milk.

cam·cord·er (kam′kôrd-ēr), *n.* a small, portable videotape recorder and TV camera.

came (kăm), past tense of come.

cam·el (kam′l), *n.* a large, domesticated, ruminant quadruped, with a long neck, a humped back, and the ability to store large quantities of water in its body tissues: it is used as a beast of burden in the deserts of Africa and Asia; *adj.* of the tan color of a camel.

ca·mel·lia (kă-mēl′yă), *n.* 1. an Asiatic evergreen shrub, cultivated for its roselike flowers and shining foliage. 2. the flower.

cam·el·o·pard (kă-mel′ō-pärd), *n.* early name for the giraffe.

camel's hair, 1. the hair of the camel. 2. a soft, tan fabric made from this. —**camel's-hair,** **camel-hair,** *adj.*

Cam·em·bert (kăm′ĕm-bēr), *n.* [French], a soft, white, creamy cheese: also **Camembert** **cheese.**

cam·e·o (kam′ĭ-ō), *n., pl.* **-e·os,** 1. a precious stone or shell on which figures are carved in relief. 2. a minor part in a play, movie, etc. played distinctively by a well-known player. 3. a small piece of fine writing.

cam·er·a (kam′ēr-ă), *n.* 1. a box in which the image of an object is thrown upon a sensitized plate or film by light entering through a lens. 2. the television transmitting device that receives the image to be transmitted and changes it into electrical impulses. 3. the private chamber of a judge.

camera lu·ci·da (loo′sĭ-dă), an optical instrument, often used with a microscope, having a prism or mirrors for reflecting an object onto paper for tracing.

cam·er·a·man (-man), *n., pl.* **-men,** a person who operates a camera, especially for television or motion pictures.

camera ob·scu·ra (ob-skyoor′ă), a darkened chamber in which the images of external objects are received through a lens and exhibited on the facing surface.

cam gear, a gear not centered on the shaft, used where discontinuous action is needed.

cam·i·on (kam′ĭ-ŏn), *n.* 1. a heavy wagon. 2. a motor truck.

cam·i·sole (kam′ĭ-sōl), *n.* 1. a woman's sleeveless underwaist, worn under a sheer blouse. 2. a woman's short negligee.

cam·let (kam′lĭt), *n.* 1. formerly, an Asian fabric of camel's hair or Angora wool. 2. a shiny fabric of silk and goat's hair or wool.

cam·o·mile (kam′ō-mīl, -mĕl), *n.* same as chamomile.

Ca·mor·ra (kă-mor′ă), *n.* a secret society of Naples, Italy, organized about 1820.

cam·ou·flage (kam′ŏo-flăzh, -fläj), *n.* a covering of any kind to hide or deceive, especially

nets, paint, etc. used to conceal military troops or guns, ships, etc. from the enemy: *v.t. & v.i.* **-flaged, -flag·ing,** to disguise (a person or thing) in order to conceal. — **cam′ou·flag·er,** *n.*

camp (kamp), *n.* 1. a place where an army lodges temporarily in tents, huts, etc. 2. such tents collectively. 3. a group that supports a particular cause, set of doctrines, etc. 4. an outdoor recreation area in the country for vacationers, especially children, often with organized activities. 5. those who live in a camp. 6. [Slang], commonplace, contrived, or trivial actions presented so seriously as to be amusing; *v.i.* 1. to make or establish a camp. 2. to live in a camp (often followed by out).

cam·paign (kam-pān′), *n.* 1. a series of military operations with a set objective. 2. a planned course of action for achieving an objective, as the election of a candidate: *v.i.* to serve in a campaign. —**cam·paign′er,** *n.*

cam·pa·ni·le (kam-pă-nē′li), *n., pl.* **-les, -li** (′lē), a bell tower, especially one that is separate from any other building.

cam·pea·chy wood (kam-pē′chi), same as logwood.

camp·er (kamp′ēr), *n.* 1. one who camps out. 2. any of several kinds of trailers or motor vehicles fitted for camping out.

camp·fire (kamp′fīr), *n.* 1. a bonfire at a camp. 2. a group gathered around such a fire.

camp·ground (′ground), *n.* a place for a camp or camp meeting.

cam·phor (kam′fēr), *n.* a volatile, aromatic substance obtained from the wood of the camphor tree: used to make plastics, in medicine, and as a moth repellent. —**cam·phor′ic** (-fôr′ik), *adj.*

cam·phor·ate (kam′fō-rāt), *v.t.* **-rat·ed, -rat·ing,** to saturate or treat with camphor.

camphor tree, an evergreen tree native to Japan and China: it is the source of camphor.

camp meeting, an outdoor religious meeting, usually lasting several days.

camp·site (kamp′sīt), *n.* 1. any site for a camp. 2. an area set aside for camping.

camp·stool (kamp′stōōl), *n.* a light folding stool.

cam·pus (kam′pŭs), *n., pl.* **-pus·es,** the grounds of a school or college.

camp·y (kam′pē), *adj.* **camp′i·er, camp′i·est,** [Slang], characterized by camp (sense 6).

cam·shaft (kam′shaft), *n.* a shaft having a cam, or to which a cam is fastened.

can (kan), *v.i., past tense* could, 1. to know how to. 2. to be able to. 3. to be likely to. 4. to be morally or legally able to. 5. [Informal], to be permitted to; may.

can (kan), *n.* 1. an airtight metal container in which foods, beverages, etc. are preserved. 2. a container, usually of metal, with a separate cover. 3. the contents of a can: *v.t.* **canned, can′ning,** to put up in cans for preservation.

Can·a·da balsam (kan′ă-dă), a yellowish, viscid resin from the balsam fir, used as a transparent cement.

Ca·na·di·an (kă-nā′dĭ-ăn), *adj.* of or pertaining to Canada, the country in northern North

America, or its inhabitants: *n.* a native or inhabitant of Canada.

ca·naille (kă-nāl'), *n.* the rabble; riffraff.

ca·nal (kă-nal'), *n.* 1. a man-made waterway for shipping or irrigation. 2. in *Anatomy*, any of various tubes or ducts.

ca·na·pé (kan'ă-pi), *n.* a small piece of bread, toast, or a cracker spread with cheese, meat, etc., served as an appetizer.

ca·nard (kă-närd'), *n.* a false or fabricated report.

ca·nar·y (kă-ner'i), *n., pl.* **-nar'ies,** a small singing bird with yellow plumage, native to the Canary Islands, off the northwest coast of Africa.

canary yellow, a bright yellow.

ca·nas·ta (kă-nas'tă), *n.* a card game for two to six players, using a double deck of cards.

can·can (kan'kan), *n.* a lively dance with much high kicking, performed by women.

can·cel (kan'sl), *v.t.* **-celed** or **-celled, -cel·ing** or **-cel·ling,** 1. to cross out by drawing lines across or marking over. 2. to void; annul. 3. to strike out (common factors). 4. to remove, abolish, etc.; wipe out: *v.i.* to offset each other (with *out*). **—can'cel·er, can'cel·ler,** *n.*

can·cel·la·tion (kan-sĕ-lā'shŭn), *n.* 1. the act of canceling. 2. something canceled. 3. marks indicating a canceling.

Can·cer (kan'sĕr), *n.* 1. a northern constellation between Gemini and Leo. 2. the fourth sign of the zodiac. 3. [c-], a malignant tumor or growth. 4. [c-], anything evil or destructive that spreads. **—can'cer·ous,** *adj.*

can·croid (kang'kroid), *adj.* 1. resembling a crab. 2. resembling cancer.

can·de·la·brum (kan-dĕ-lä'brŭm), *n., pl.* **-bra** ('brä), **-brums,** an ornamented branched candlestick: also **can·de·la'bra,** *pl.* **-bras.**

can·dent (kan'dĕnt), *adj.* [Archaic], glowing with heat.

can·des·cent (kan-des'nt), *adj.* glowing with great heat. **—can·des'cence,** *n.*

can·did (kan'did), *adj.* 1. honest; outspoken; sincere. 2. free from bias; fair. 3. unposed and relaxed.

can·di·da·cy (kan'di-dă-si), *n., pl.* **-cies,** the fact or state of being a candidate.

can·di·date (kan'di-dāt), *n.* one who offers himself, or is proposed by others, to fill some office.

can·died (kan'did), *adj.* 1. preserved or encrusted with sugar. 2. like sugar.

can·dle (kan'dl), *n.* a mass of tallow or wax, usually cylindrical in shape, enclosing a wick and burned to give light: *v.t.* **-dled, -dling,** to test (eggs) for freshness by examining in front of a light. **—can'dler,** *n.*

can·dle·fish (-fish), *n., pl.* **-fish, -fish·es,** a food fish of the northern Pacific, resembling the smelt.

Can·dle·mas (kan'dl-măs), *n.* a church feast on February 2, commemorating the purification of the Virgin Mary.

candle power, the illuminating power of a candle taken as a unit in determining the luminosity of a light source.

can·dle·stick (-stik), *n.* a holder for a candle, either cupped or spiked.

can·dle·wood (-wood), *n.* 1. any of a group of desert shrubs and trees. 2. the wood of any of these. 3. any resinous wood used for kindling, torches, etc.

can·dor (kan'dĕr), *n.* 1. impartiality; fairness. 2. frankness; openness.

can·dour (kan'dĕr), *n.* British form for **candor.**

can·dy (kan'di), *n., pl.* **-dies,** 1. a solid confection of sugar combined with flavoring. 2. a piece of this: *v.t.* **-died, -dy·ing,** 1. to cook with sugar or syrup. 2. to crystallize into sugar. 3. to sweeten.

can·dy·tuft (-tuft), *n.* a garden plant with clusters of white, pink, or purplish flowers.

cane (kān), *n.* 1. the stem of certain trees, grasses, and other plants, as bamboo, sugar, rattan, etc. 2. a stick or rod used for flogging. 3. a walking stick. 4. split rattan: *v.t.* **caned, can'ing,** 1. to beat with a cane. 2. to make or furnish with cane. **—can'er,** *n.*

cane-brake ('brāk), *n.* a thicket of canes.

ca·nel·la (kă-nel'ă), *n.* the aromatic and tonic bark of a tropical American tree.

cane sugar, sugar obtained from sugar cane.

cangue (kang), *n.* a square wooden collar formerly placed around the neck of a criminal in China.

Ca·nic·u·la (kă-nik'yoo-lă), *n.* the Dog Star.

ca·nic·u·lar (-lĕr), *adj.* of or pertaining to the dog days in July and August.

ca·nine (kā'nīn), *adj.* of or pertaining to dogs; having the nature or qualities of a dog: *n.* 1. a dog, wolf, fox, etc. 2. a sharp-pointed tooth on each side of the upper and lower jaws: also **canine tooth.**

can·is·ter (kan'is-tĕr), *n.* 1. a box or can, as of metal, for coffee, flour, etc. 2. a boxlike vacuum cleaner.

canister shot, formerly, a case that was fired from a gun and exploded to scatter the shot packed in it.

can·ker (kang'kĕr), *n.* 1. an ulcerous sore, as in the mouth. 2. diseased woody tissue in a plant. 3. anything that corrodes or corrupts: *v.t.* 1. to infect with canker. 2. to corrupt or corrode: *v.i.* 1. to become infected with canker. **—can'ker·ous,** *adj.*

can·ker·worm (-wŭrm), *n.* any of the larvae of certain moths, destructive to the leaves and fruit of trees.

can·na (kan'ă), *n.* a broad-leaved tropical plant with brilliant flowers.

can·na·bin (kan'ă-bin), *n.* a poisonous white resin extracted from cannabis.

can·na·bis (-bis), *n.* 1. same as **hemp.** 2. the flowering tops of hemp.

canned (kand), *adj.* 1. preserved in jars or cans. 2. [Slang], recorded or taped.

can·nel (kan'ĕl), *n.* an oily bituminous coal that burns with a clear, bright flame: also **cannel coal.**

can·ner·y (kan'ĕr-i), *n., pl.* **-ner·ies,** a place where foods are canned.

can·ni·bal (kan'i-bl), *n.* 1. a human being who eats human flesh. 2. any animal that eats the flesh of its own kind: *adj.* of, pertaining to, or characteristic of cannibals. **—can'ni·bal·ism,** *n.* **—can·ni·bal·is'tic,** *adj.*

can·ni·bal·ize (-īz), *v.t.* & *v.i.* **-ized, -iz·ing,** to take (parts) from old or damaged equipment or machinery in order to repair other units. —**can·ni·bal·i·za'tion,** *n.*

can·non (kan'ŏn), *n., pl.* **-nons, -non,** 1. a large, mounted piece of artillery. 2. an automatic gun mounted on an aircraft.

can·non·ade (kan-ŏ-nād'), *n.* 1. an artillery attack against a town, fort, etc. 2. a continuous firing of artillery: *v.t.* & *v.i.* **-ad'ed, -ad'ing,** to fire cannon (at).

can·non·ball (kan'ŏn-bôl), *n.* a heavy iron ball, formerly fired from a cannon.

cannon bone, the bone extending from the knee or hock to the fetlock in a hoofed animal.

can·non·eer (kan-ŏ-nir'), *n.* a man who fires a cannon; artilleryman.

can·not (kan'ŏt, kă-not'), can not.

can·nu·la (kan'yoo-lă), *n., pl.* **-lae** (-lē), **-las,** a small tube for insertion into a body cavity, as for drainage.

can·nu·lar (-lêr), *adj.* tubular: also **can'nu·late** (-lĭt, -lāt).

can·ny (kan'ĭ), *adj.* **-ni·er, -ni·est,** 1. shrewd; clever; cautious. 2. knowing; well-informed. 3. [Scottish], *a)* quiet; easy. *b)* artful: *adv.* [Scottish], in a canny manner. —**can'ni·ly,** *adv.* —**can'ni·ness,** *n.*

ca·noe (kă-nōō'), *n.* a narrow, light boat with curved sides and pointed ends, propelled by paddles: *v.t.* **-noed', -noe'ing,** to carry by canoe: *v.i.* 1. to travel by canoe. 2. to paddle a canoe. —**ca·noe'ist,** *n.*

can·on (kan'ŏn), *n.* 1. a law or set of laws of a church. 2. a rule or principle. 3. a criterion; standard. 4. the books of the Bible accepted as genuine by a church. 5. [often C-], *a)* a catalog of saints as of the Roman Catholic Church. *b)* the essential and unvarying part of the Mass. 6. a clergyman serving in a cathedral. 7. a member of a religious group living under a canon, or rule.

ca·ñon (kan'yŏn), *n.* same as **canyon.**

ca·non·i·cal (kă-non'ĭ-kl), *adj.* 1. of or pertaining to a rule or canon. 2. according to, or established by, church law. 3. belonging to the canon of the Bible. Also **ca·non'ic.** —**ca·non'i·cal·ly,** *adv.*

canonical hour, any of the seven times of the day set aside for specified prayers.

ca·non·i·cals (-kălz), *n.* the clothes prescribed by the canons to be worn by a clergyman when officiating at a service.

can·on·ist (kan'ŏn·ist), *n.* a student of or expert in canon law. —**can·on·is'tic,** *adj.*

can·on·ize (kan'ŏn-īz), *v.t.* **-ized, -iz·ing,** 1. to declare (a dead person) to be a saint by church procedure. 2. to exalt. —**can·on·i·za'tion,** *n.*

canon law, the ecclesiastical laws of a Christian church.

can·on·ry (kan'ŏn-ri), *n., pl.* **-ries,** 1. the benefice of a canon. 2. canons collectively.

can·o·py (kan'ŏ-pi), *n., pl.* **-pies,** 1. a decorative covering fixed above a bed, throne, etc. or held over a person. 2. a shelter of canvas over an area or leading to an entrance. 3. a transparent covering over the cockpit of an airplane. 4. a rooflike projection: *v.t.* **-pied, -py·ing,** to cover or shelter with a canopy.

ca·no·rous (kă-nōr'ŭs), *adj.* tuneful; melodious; musical. —**ca·no'rous·ly,** *adv.*

cant (kant), *n.* 1. the secret slang spoken by thieves, beggars, etc. 2. the special jargon of those in a certain occupation, profession, sect, etc. 3. insincere speech, especially when sanctimonious or hypocritical: *v.i.* to use cant: *adj.* of, or having the nature of, cant. —**cant'er,** *n.*

cant (kant), *n.* 1. an external angle: 2. a slanting surface. 3. a sudden jerk that causes a tilt, overturn, etc. 4. the tilt or slant so caused: *v.t.* 1. to incline or tilt. 2. to bevel. 3. to throw with a jerk: *v.i.* to slant or tilt.

can't (kant), cannot.

can·ta·loupe, can·ta·loup (kan'tă-lōp), *n.* a variety of small muskmelon with orange-colored, juicy, sweet flesh.

can·tan·ker·ous (kan-tang'kêr-ŭs), *adj.* ill-tempered; cross; contentious. —**can·tan'ker·ous·ness,** *n.*

can·ta·ta (kăn-tät'ă), *n.* a short choral composition, a setting for a story to be sung but not acted.

can·ta·tri·ce (kän-tă-trē'che), *n., pl.* **-tri'ci** ('chē), [Italian], a female singer, especially one who sings in operas.

can·teen (kan-tēn'), *n.* 1. same as post exchange. 2. a place where entertainment and refreshments are provided for servicemen, young people, etc. 3. a flask for carrying water.

can·ter (kan'tēr), *n.* an easy gallop: *v.i.* to move at an easy gallop: *v.t.* to make canter.

can·thar·i·des (kan-thar'ĭ-dēz), *n.* a preparation of Spanish flies formerly used as a diuretic, genitourinary stimulant, and skin irritant.

cant hook, a pole with a movable iron hook, used in logging.

can·thus (kan'thŭs), *n., pl.* **-thi** ('thī), the angle made by the meeting of the eyelids.

can·ti·cle (kan'tĭ-kl), *n.* 1. a song or chant. 2. a hymn with words taken from the Bible, arranged for chanting in church services. 3. *pl.* [C-], same as Song of Solomon: also, in the Douay Bible, called Canticle of Canticles.

can·ti·le·ver (kan'tĭ-lē'vêr), *n.* 1. a bracket or block projecting from a wall to support a balcony, cornice, etc. 2. a projecting structural member or beam that is supported at only one end. 3. one of two arms projecting from opposite banks serving to form a bridge: *v.t.* to construct as a cantilever. —**can'ti·le·vered,** *adj.*

can·til·late (kan'tĭ-lāt), *v.t.* & *v.i.* **-lat·ed, -lat·ing,** to intone (a Jewish liturgical chant). —**can·til·la'tion,** *n.*

can·tle (kan'tl), *n.* the part of a saddle that curves upward at the rear.

can·to (kan'tō), *n., pl.* **-tos,** one of the major divisions of some long poems.

can·ton (kan'tŏn, 'ton), *n.* 1. a district or division of a territory. 2. one of the Swiss federal states. 3. in France, a subdivision of a department. 4. a division of an heraldic escutcheon or of a flag: *v.t.* 1. to divide into districts or parts. 2. to allot separate quarters to (troops). —**can'ton·al,** *adj.*

can·ton·ment (kan-ton'mĕnt), *n.* military quarters, or assignment to these.

can·tor (kan'tĕr), *n.* 1. a choir leader or leader of singing. 2. an official in a synagogue who intones liturgical solos and leads the congregation in prayer. —**can·to'ri·al** (-tôr'ĭ-ăl), *adj.*

can·vas (kan'văs), *n.* 1. a coarse, heavy cloth of hemp, linen, or cotton, used for tents, sails, etc. 2. a sail, or sails in general. 3. a tent or tents, especially as used for a circus. 4. an oil painting on canvas.

can·vas·back (-bak), *n., pl.* **-backs, -back,** a large wild duck of North America, with a red head and dark-gray back.

can·vass (kan'văs), *v.t. & v.i.* 1. to examine; sift; discuss. 2. to go through (a district, group, etc.) and solicit (votes, opinions, orders for sales, etc.): *n.* 1. a close inspection; scrutiny. 2. a solicitation of votes, opinions, orders for sales, etc. —**can'vass·er,** *n.*

can·yon (kan'yŏn), *n.* a valley between high, steep hills; gorge.

can·zo·ne (kän-tsō'ne), *n., pl.* **-ni** ('nē), [Italian], a song or air resembling the madrigal. Also **can·zo'na** ('nä).

can·zo·net, can·zo·nette (kan-zŏ-net'), *n.* a short song, especially a cheerful one.

caou·tchouc (kou-chŏŏk'), *n.* rubber, especially its crude, natural state.

cap (kap), *n.* 1. a covering for the head, close-fitting and brimless or with a small visor. 2. anything caplike, as a bottle lid. 3. a size of writing paper. 4. same as percussion cap: *v.t.* **capped, cap'ping,** 1. to put a cap on. 2. to cover an end of. 3. to present with a special cap, as at a graduation. 4. to equal or surpass.

ca·pa·bil·i·ty (kā-pâ-bil'ĭ-ti), *n., pl.* **-ties,** 1. the quality of being capable. 2. the potentiality of being affected, developed, etc. 3. *pl.* qualities, abilities, etc. that can be used or developed.

ca·pa·ble (kā'pâ-bl), *adj.* having power, skill, or ability; competent. —**ca'pa·bly,** *adv.*

ca·pa·cious (kâ-pā'shŭs), *adj.* roomy; spacious. —**ca·pa'cious·ly,** *adv.* —**ca·pa'cious·ness,** *n.*

ca·pac·i·tance (kâ-pas'ĭ-tâns), *n.* the amount of electric charge that can be stored in a capacitor. —**ca·pac'i·tive,** *adj.*

ca·pac·i·tor (-tĕr), *n.* a device for gathering and holding an electric charge; condenser.

ca·pac·i·ty (kâ-pas'ĭ-ti), *n., pl.* **-ties,** 1. the ability to receive and hold. 2. the volume or amount that can be contained. 3. intellectual ability. 4. function; position. 5. maximum producing ability. 6. legal qualification.

cap·a·pie, cap·à·pie (kap-â-pē'), *adv.* from head to foot.

ca·par·i·son (kâ-per'ĭ-sn), *n.* 1. an ornamental covering for a horse; trappings. 2. rich clothing and equipment: *v.t.* 1. to cover a horse with ornamental trappings. 2. to adorn with rich clothing, ornaments, etc.

cape (kāp), *n.* 1. a covering for the shoulders, worn separately or attached to a dress, coat, etc. 2. a headland; promontory.

ca·per (kā'pĕr), *v.i.* to skip or jump; gambol: *n.* 1. a frolicsome leap or spring. 2. a prank or escapade.

ca·per (kā'pĕr), *n.* 1. the green flower bud of a Mediterranean shrub that is pickled and used as a condiment. 2. the plant.

cap·er·cail·lie (kap-ĕr-kāl'yi), *n.* a large, black, European grouse.

cap·ful (kap'fool), *n., pl.* **-fuls,** as much as fills the cap of a bottle.

ca·pi·as (kā'pĭ-âs), *n.* a writ authorizing the arrest of the person named in it.

cap·il·lar·i·ty (kap-ĭ-ler'ĭ-ti), *n.* 1. the state of being capillary. 2. same as capillary attraction.

cap·il·lar·y (kap'ĭ-ler-i), *adj.* 1. of or resembling a hair; minute; slender. 2. having a very small bore. 3. of or in a capillary or capillaries: *n., pl.* **-lar·ies,** 1. a tube with a small bore: also **capillary tube.** 2. one of the minute blood vessels connecting the arteries with the veins.

capillary attraction, the molecular force that causes a liquid to rise or fall when it is in contact with a solid, as in a capillary tube: also **capillary action.**

cap·i·tal (kap'ĭ-tl), *adj.* 1. punishable by death. 2. first in importance; chief; principal. 3. of or pertaining to the seat of government. 4. of or pertaining to capital, or wealth. 5. excellent; first-rate: *n.* 1. a city or town that is the seat of a government. 2. same as **capital letter.** 3. wealth in money or property owned, invested, or used in business. 4. wealth that is used or available for use to produce more wealth. 5. [often C-], capitalists as a group. 6. the top of a column, pillar, etc.

cap·i·tal·ism (-izm), *n.* the economic system based on the private ownership of the means of production and distribution, as land, factories, mines, railroads, etc., and their operation for profit, under more or less competitive conditions.

cap·i·tal·ist (-ist), *n.* 1. a person, especially a rich person, who invests or uses his wealth in business. 2. a supporter of capitalism: *adj.* same as **capitalistic.**

cap·i·tal·is·tic (kap-ĭ-tl-is'tik), *adj.* 1. of or characteristic of capitalism or capitalists. 2. favoring or practicing capitalism. —**cap·i·tal·is'ti·cal·ly,** *adv*

cap·i·tal·ize (kap'ĭ-tl-īz), *v.t.* **-ized, -iz·ing,** 1. to convert into capital. 2. to compute or realize the present value of in money, as a periodical payment. 3. to supply with capital. 4. to start (a word) with a capital letter. —**cap·i·tal·i·za'tion,** *n.*

capital letter, the form of a letter used to start a proper name or a sentence.

capital levy, a levy on capital, as distinguished from a levy on income.

cap·i·tal·ly (kap'ĭ-tl-i), *adv.* very well.

capital punishment, punishment by death for a crime; the death penalty.

capital ship, formerly, a large, armored warship.

capital stock, the total stock of a corporation, divided into shares.

ŏ in dragon, ōō in crude, oo in wool, u in cup, ū in cure, ŭ in turn, ů in focus, oi in boy, ou in house, th in thin, *th* in sheathe, g in get, j in joy, y in yet.

cap·i·tate (kap'ĭ-tāt), *adj.* growing in a head; head-shaped.

cap·i·ta·tion (kap-ĭ-tā'shŭn), *n.* a tax or fee of so much per head; see also **poll tax**.

Cap·i·tol (kap'ĭ-tl), *n.* 1. the temple of Jupiter at Rome, on the summit of the Capitoline Hill. 2. the building occupied by the U.S. Congress at Washington, D.C. 3. [c-], the legislative building of a State.

ca·pit·u·lar (kă-pich'ū-lēr), *adj.* of or pertaining to a religious chapter.

ca·pit·u·lar·y (-ler-ĭ), *n., pl.* **-lar·ies**, an ordinance or a collection of ordinances.

ca·pit·u·late (kă-pich'ū-lāt), *v.i.* **-lat·ed, -lat·ing,** 1. to surrender (*to* an enemy) on conditions agreed upon. 2. to give up. **—ca·pit·u·la'tion,** *n.*

ca·pon (kā'pon), *n.* a castrated male chicken, fattened for eating. **—ca·pon·ize** ('pō-nīz), *v.t.* **-ized, -iz·ing.**

ca·pote (kă-pōt'), *n.* a kind of long cloak or mantle, usually with a hood.

cap·per (kap'ēr), *n.* a person or device that makes caps or that caps bottles, jars, etc.

cap·ric acid (kap'rik), a fatty acid with a goat-like smell, occurring in natural fats and oils.

ca·price (kă-prēs'), *n.* 1. a sudden impulse of mind or action; whim. 2. a tendency to be capricious; changeableness.

ca·pri·cious (kă-prish'ŭs), *adj.* of or characterized by caprice; whimsical; erratic. **—ca·pri'cious·ly,** *adv.* **—ca·pri'cious·ness,** *n.*

Cap·ri·corn (kap'rĭ-kôrn), *n.* 1. a southern constellation between Sagittarius and Aquarius. 2. the tenth sign of the zodiac.

cap·ri·ole (kap'rĭ-ōl), *n.* a leap of a horse made without advancing: *v.i.* **-oled, -ol·ing,** to execute a capriole.

cap·sa·i·cin (kap-să'ĭ-sn), *n.* a bitter, white crystalline alkaloid extracted from capsicum.

cap·si·cum (kap'sĭ-kŭm), *n.* 1. any one of several red peppers, the pods of which are used as condiments, as chili peppers and cayenne peppers. 2. these pods used as condiments.

cap·size (kap'sīz), *v.t. & v.i.* **-sized, -siz·ing,** to overturn or upset, as a boat.

cap·stan (kap'stăn), *n.* an upright drum or cylinder revolving upon a shaft and worked by bars or levers: used mainly on ships to wind cables, lift weights, etc.

cap·su·lar (kap'sū-lēr), *adj.* of, pertaining to, or like a capsule.

cap·sule (kap'sl), *n.* 1. a small envelope of gelatin enclosing a dose of medicine. 2. an ejectable airplane cockpit. 3. a closed compartment for men, instruments, etc. designed to detach from a rocket: also **space capsule.** 4. a seed vessel or pod that bursts open at maturity. 5. a sac or membrane enclosing some part or organ. 6. in *Chemistry,* a small shallow dish.

cap·sul·ize (-īz), *v.t.* **-ized, -iz·ing,** 1. to put in a capsule. 2. to express concisely.

cap·tain (kap'tăn), *n.* 1. one who has command of, or authority over, others; chief; commander. 2. in the *U.S. Military,* an officer ranking above a lieutenant and below a major. 3. in the *U.S. Navy,* an officer ranking above a commander and below a rear ad-

miral. 4. the commander of a ship. 5. the head of a team or side. **—cap'tain·cy (-si),** *pl.* **-cies,** *n.*

cap·tion (kap'shŭn), *n.* 1. the title of, or introduction to, a legal document. 2. a heading or title, as for a chapter or illustration. 3. in *Motion Pictures,* a subtitle: *v.t.* to provide a caption for.

cap·tious ('shŭs), *adj.* 1. ready to catch others at fault; quibbling. 2. sophistical: presented only for argument. **—cap'tious·ly,** *adv.* **—cap'tious·ness,** *n.*

cap·ti·vate (kap'tĭ-vāt), *v.t.* **-vat·ed, -vat·ing,** to hold captive by beauty or excellence; charm; fascinate. **—cap'ti·vat·ing·ly,** *adv.* **—cap·ti·va'tion,** *n.*

cap·tive (kap'tiv), *adj.* 1. made prisoner. 2. held in bondage. 3. of or pertaining to bondage. 4. fascinated: *n.* 1. one who is taken prisoner, especially in war. 2. one who is fascinated.

cap·tiv·i·ty (kap-tiv'ĭ-tĭ), *n., pl.* **-ties,** the state of being held in bondage or confinement; imprisonment.

cap·tor (kap'tēr), *n.* one who captures.

cap·ture ('chēr), *n.* 1. the act of seizing or taking, as a prisoner or prize. 2. the thing taken: *v.t.* **-tured, -tur·ing,** 1. to take or seize by force, surprise, or stratagem. 2. to recognize and express (an innate, intangible quality) in a painting or other art form.

Cap·u·chin (kap'yoo-shin), *n.* 1. a member of a branch of the Franciscan order. 2. [c-], a woman's cloak and hood. 3. [c-], a new-world monkey with a nearly bare face and a hoodlike crown of hair.

cap·y·ba·ra (kap-ĭ-bär'ă), *n.* a large rodent of South America, about four feet long, with webbed feet.

car (kär), *n.* 1. any wheeled vehicle, especially an automobile. 2. a vehicle running on rails. 3. the basket or gondola of a balloon or airship. 4. an elevator cage.

ca·ra·bao (kär-ă-bou'), *n., pl.* **-baos', -bao',** same as **water buffalo.**

car·a·bi·neer, car·a·bi·nier (ker-ă-bi-nir'), *n.* a soldier armed with a carbine.

car·a·cal (kăr'ă-kal), *n.* 1. a reddish-brown lynx of Asia and Africa. 2. its fur.

ca·ra·ca·ra (kär-ă-kär'ă), *n.* a large, vulturelike hawk of South America.

car·a·cole (ker'ă-kōl), *n.* a half turn which a horseman makes, either to the right or left: *v.i.* **-coled, -col·ing,** to move in a caracole.

car·a·cul (ker'ă-kŭl), *n.* same as **karakul.**

ca·rafe (kă-raf'), *n.* a bottle of glass or metal for water, coffee, etc.

car·a·mel (ker'ă-ml), *n.* 1. burnt sugar, used for coloring and flavoring food and beverages. 2. a chewy candy.

car·a·mel·ize (ker'ă-mĕ-līz), *v.t. & v.i.* **-ized, -iz·ing,** to turn into caramel.

car·a·pace (ker'ă-pās), *n.* the horny upper shell of the turtle, crab, etc.

car·at (ker'ăt), *n.* 1. the weight of 200 milligrams, used for weighing precious stones and pearls. 2. same as **karat.**

car·a·van (ker'ă-van), *n.* 1. a company of travelers, as merchants or pilgrims, gathered together for mutual security, especially when

---

a in cap, ā in cane, ä in father, ȧ in abet, e in met, ē in be, ē in baker, ê in regent, i in pit, ī in fine, ĭ in manifest, o in hot, ô in horse, ō in bone,

traveling through deserts or dangerous areas.
2. a large covered wagon for conveying exhibitions or passengers. 3. a number of vehicles traveling together.

car·a·van·sa·ry (ker-å-van'så-ri), *n., pl.* **-ries,** in the Orient, a kind of inn consisting of a large building enclosing a spacious court where caravans rest at night.

car·a·vel (ker'å-vel), *n.* any one of several kinds of small sailing ships, as a 16th-century ship with a narrow, high poop and lateen sails.

car·a·way (ker'å-wå), *n.* 1. a biennial herb with pungently aromatic seeds. 2. the seeds, used medicinally and as a flavoring.

car·bide (kär'bīd), *n.* a compound of carbon with a metal.

car·bine (kär'bīn), *n.* 1. a short rifle. 2. a light, semiautomatic or automatic .30-caliber rifle.

car·bi·neer (kär-bi-nir'), *n.* same as **carabineer.**

car·bi·nol (kär'bi-nôl), *n.* methanol, or any alcohol homologously related to it.

car·bo·hy·drate (kär-bō-hī'drāt), *n.* any one of a group of organic compounds of carbon, hydrogen, and oxygen, including sugars, starches, and celluloses.

car·bo·lat·ed (kär'bō-lāt-id), *adj.* containing or treated with carbolic acid.

car·bol·ic acid (kär-bäl'ik), same as **phenol.**

car·bo·lize (kär'bō-līz), *v.t.* **-lized, -liz·ing,** to treat or sterilize with phenol.

car·bon (kär'bŏn), *n.* 1. a nonmetallic chemical element present in all organic compounds, occurring in nature in pure form as diamond and graphite. 2. a sheet of carbon paper. 3. same as **carbon copy:** *adj.* of, like, or treated with carbon.

car·bo·na·ceous (kär-bō-nā'shŭs), *adj.* of or containing carbon.

car·bon·ate (kär'bō-nit), *n.* a salt or ester of carbonic acid: *v.t.* (-nāt), **-at·ed, -at·ing,** 1. to charge with carbon dioxide. 2. to make a carbonate of. —**car·bo·na'tion,** *n.*

carbon black, a powdery, nearly pure form of carbon, as soot.

carbon copy, a copy, as of a letter, made with carbon paper.

car·bon-date (-dāt'), *v.t.* **-dat'ed, -dat'ing,** to determine the age of (a fossil, skull, etc.) by measuring the carbon 14 content.

carbon dioxide, a heavy, colorless, nonburning gas, a compound of oxygen and carbon, produced commercially and as a natural product of breathing.

carbon 14, a radioactive isotope of carbon.

car·bon·ic (kär-bän'ik), *adj.* of or from carbon or carbon dioxide.

carbonic acid, a weak acid produced by solution of carbon dioxide in water.

car·bon·if·er·ous (kär-bō-nif'ēr-ŭs), *adj.* containing or yielding carbon or coal: *n.* [C-], a period of the Paleozoic Era, in which immense coal beds began to form.

car·bon·ize (kär'bō-nīz), *v.t.* **-ized, -iz·ing,** 1. to convert into carbon, as by combustion. 2. to treat or combine with carbon: *v.i.* to become carbonized. —**car·bon·i·za'tion,** *n.*

carbon monoxide, a gas that is colorless, odorless, and very poisonous: it is a product of the incomplete combustion of carbon.

carbon paper, paper with a dark, transferable coating on one side, to make a copy of something being written or typed.

carbon tet·ra·chlo·ride (tet-rå-klôr'īd), a nonflammable, poisonous chlorine compound in liquid form, used in fire extinguishers, cleaning mixtures, etc.

car·bon·yl chloride (kär'bō-nil), same as **phosgene.**

Car·bo·run·dum (kär-bō-run'dŭm), *n.* 1. an exceedingly hard abrasive compound, as of silicon and carbon: a trademark. 2. [c-], such a substance.

car·boy (kär'boi), *n.* a large bottle of glass, protected as by basketwork, to hold corrosive liquids.

car·bun·cle (kär'bung-kl), *n.* 1. a deep-red garnet. 2. a painful, pus-filled, subcutaneous inflammation. —**car·bun'cu·lar** ('kyoo-lēr), *adj.*

car·bu·ret (kär'bŭ-rāt), *v.t.* **-ret·ed or -ret·ted, -ret·ing or -ret·ting,** 1. to combine chemically with carbon. 2. to charge with carbon compounds.

car·bu·ret·or (-ēr), *n.* a device that mixes vaporized gasoline with air in an internal-combustion engine.

car·cass (kär'kås), *n.* 1. the lifeless body of an animal, often of one slaughtered for meat. 2. the human body, living or dead: a scornful or humorous term. 3. a framework, as of a ship.

car·cin·o·gen (kär-sin'ō-jĕn), *n.* any cancer-causing substance. —**car·ci·no·gen·ic** (kär-si-nō-jen'ik), *adj.*

car·ci·no·ma (kär-si-nō'må), *n., pl.* **-mas, -ma·ta** ('må-tå), an epithelial cancerous growth.

card (kärd), *n.* 1. a piece of stiff paper or pasteboard, usually rectangular, often printed for various social or business purposes. 2. any one of a pack of small cards printed with figures, numbers, etc., used in various games. 3. same as **post card.** 4. [Informal], a joking or clever person.

card (kärd), *n.* a device, as a metal comb or special machine, for combing and cleaning fibers of wool, cotton, etc.: *v.t.* to use a card on, preparatory to spinning.

car·da·mom (kär'dä-mŏm), *n.* 1. the seed capsule or seed of an Asiatic plant of the ginger family, used medicinally and as a spice. 2. the plant. Also **car'da·mon** (-mŏn).

card·board (kärd'bôrd), *n.* a thick, stiff, paper-pulp product, thicker and stiffer than ordinary paper, used as for boxes.

car·di·ac (kär'di-ak), *adj.* of, near, involving, or acting on the heart: *n.* a medicinal stimulant for the heart.

car·di·al·gi·a (kär-di-al'ji-å), *n.* 1. a feeling of distress in or about the heart. 2. same as **heartburn.**

car·di·gan (kär'di-gän), *n.* a sweater, usually knitted, opening in front like a coat.

car·di·nal (kärd'n-ål), *adj.* 1. main; principal. 2. bright-red: *n.* 1. a member of the Pope's council, or Sacred College. 2. bright red. 3. a red American songbird.

cardinal number, a number used in counting, as *one, two,* etc., in distinction from *first, second,* etc., which are called *ordinal numbers.*

ŏ in drag*o*n, ōō in cr*u*de, oo in w*oo*l, u in c*u*p, ū in c*u*re, ü in t*u*rn, ů in foc*u*s, oi in b*oy,* ou in h*ou*se, th in *th*in, th in shea*th*e, g in *g*et, j in *j*oy, y in *y*et.

cardinal points, the four principal points of the compass.

cardinal virtues, virtues of primary importance: justice, prudence, temperance, and fortitude.

car-di-o-, a combining form signifying *of the heart.*

car-di-o-gram (kär'di-ō-gram), *n.* same as electrocardiogram. —**car'di-o-graph** (-graf), *n.*

car-di-ol-o-gy (kär-di-ol'ō-ji), *n.* study of the heart and its diseases. —**car-di-ol'o-gist,** *n.*

car-di-tis (kär-dīt'is), *n.* inflammation of the muscular tissue of the heart.

cards (kärdz), *n.* 1. a game or games using playing cards, as bridge, poker, etc. 2. card playing.

card shark, [Informal], 1. an expert at cards. 2. same as cardsharp.

card-sharp (kärd'shärp), *n.* [Informal], one who makes a living cheating at cards: also **card'sharp-er.**

care (ker), *n.* 1. concern, solicitude, or anxiety; also, its cause. 2. attention, watchfulness, or caution; also, the object of this; responsibility. 3. protective keeping; custody. 4. sympathetic or interested direction of attention; regard: *v.i.* **cared, car'ing,** 1. to be concerned, attentive, interested, etc. 2. to show regard. 3. to provide watchfulness, service, custody, etc. (with *for*). 4. to have desire or volition; wish (with *for*): *v.t.* 1. to have concern about. 2. to desire.

ca-reen (ka-rēn'), *v.i.* to make incline; tip; specifically, to incline (a ship) to one side, as for repairs: *v.i.* 1. to incline to one side, as a sailing ship in the wind. 2. to move fast, tipping to one side or the other.

ca-reer (ka-rir'), *n.* 1. a rapid course or run. 2. a general course of action. 3. an occupation or calling: *v.i.* to move or run rapidly.

care-free (ker'frē), *adj.* without solicitude, concern, worry, etc.

care-ful (fŭl), *adj.* 1. full of care, attentiveness, etc.; watchful. 2. not hasty or thoughtless; detailed and thorough. —**care'ful-ly,** *adv.*

care-less (-lis), *adj.* not careful; inattentive, hasty, etc. —**care'less-ly,** *adv.*

ca-ress (ka-res'), *n.* 1. any act or expression of affection. 2. a loving touch: *v.t.* 1. to treat with affection. 2. to touch lovingly. —**ca-ress'ing-ly,** *adv.*

car-et (ker'it), *n.* a mark (^) used in writing or in correcting proof, to indicate the place where something is to be added.

care-tak-er (ker'tāk-ēr), *n.* one engaged to look after a building, estate, etc.

care-worn ('wôrn), *adj.* showing the effects of worry; haggard.

car-fare (kär'fer), *n.* the amount charged to ride a streetcar, bus, etc.

car-go (kär'gō), *n., pl.* **-goes, -gos,** freight, as of a ship.

car-hop (kär'hop), *n.* a person who waits on customers in cars at a drive-in restaurant.

car-i-bou (ker'i-bōō), *n., pl.* **-bous, -bou,** a large deer of North America.

car-i-ca-ture (ker'i-kà-chēr), *n.* 1. a pictorial or descriptive representation of a person or thing, with defects or peculiarities exaggerated. 2. a distorted likeness: *v.t.* **-tured,**

-tur-ing, to represent by caricature. —**car'i-ca-tur-ist,** *n.*

car-ies (ker'ēz), *n.* 1. dental decay. 2. bone decay.

car-il-lon (ker'i-lon), *n.* 1. a set of tuned, stationary bells, usually played by keyboard. 2. a melody for these bells.

car-i-ole (ker'i-ōl), *n.* 1. a small, horse-drawn carriage. 2. a light, covered cart.

car-i-ous (ker'i-ûs), *adj.* affected with caries; decayed. —**car-i-os'i-ty** (-os'i-ti), *n.*

cark (kärk), *v.i. & v.i.* [Archaic], to concern or be concerned; worry.

carl, carle (kärl), *n.* 1. [Archaic], a rustic. 2. [Scottish], a churl. 3. [Scottish], a strong, sturdy fellow.

car-ling (kär'ling), *n.* a ship's timber running fore and aft from one transverse deck beam to another, serving as a foundation for the planks of the deck.

car-load (kär'lōd), *n.* the amount that a car, especially a freight car, will hold.

Car-mel-ite (kär'mê-līt), *n.* any one of the members of the order of Our Lady of Mount Carmel, founded in Syria about 1160.

car-min-a-tive (kär-min'à-tiv), *n.* a medicine which expels gas from the stomach and intestines: *adj.* expelling gas.

car-mine (kär'min), *n.* a rich crimson pigment obtained from cochineal: *adj.* crimson.

car-nage (kär'nij), *n.* slaughter; great destruction of life by violence; massacre.

car-nal (kär'nl), *adj.* 1. of or pertaining to the body, its passions and appetites; sensual. 2. fleshly; not spiritual; secular. —**car'nal-ly,** *adv.*

car-na-tion (kär-nā'shun), *n.* 1. a deep red. 2. a plant of the pink family, with pink, red, or white flowers. 3. its flower.

car-nel-ian (kär-nēl'yàn), *n.* a red chalcedony, made into gems.

car-ni-val (kär'ni-vàl), *n.* 1. a season of rejoicing before Lent. 2. feasting or revelry. 3. a traveling enterprise with rides, sideshows, etc. 4. a festive presentation, as at sports contests.

car-ni-vore (kär'ni-vôr), *n.* any flesh- or insect-eating animal or plant.

car-niv-o-rous (kär-niv'ō-rús), *adj.* eating flesh or insects. —**car-niv'o-rous-ness,** *n.*

car-ob (ker'ōb), *n.* 1. a leguminous tree of the eastern Mediterranean region: it has edible, sweet pods. 2. a carob pod.

car-ol (ker'ōl), *n.* 1. a song of joy or praise. 2. a Christmas song: *v.i.* **-oled** or **-olled, -ol-ing** or **-ol-ling,** 1. to sing in joy; warble. 2. to sing Christmas carols: *v.t.* 1. to sing (a song). 2. to praise or celebrate in song. —**car'ol-er, car'ol-ler,** *n.*

car-om (ker'ōm), *n.* 1. a billiards shot in which the cue ball strikes two other balls. 2. a rebound after striking: *v.i.* to make a carom.

ca-rot-id (ka-rät'id), *n.* one of the two principal arteries, one on either side of the neck, which convey the blood from the aorta to the head: *adj.* of or pertaining to these arteries.

ca-rouse (ka-rouz'), *v.i.* **-roused', -rous'ing,** to drink heavily and happily; revel: *n.* a happy, boisterous drinking party: also **ca·rous'al**.

car·ou·sel (ker-ŏ-sel'), n. same as **carrousel**.

carp (kärp), n., pl. **carp, carps**, any of a group of edible freshwater fishes living in quiet waters.

carp (kärp), v.i. to cavil; find fault. —**carp'er**, n.

car·pal (kär'pâl), adj. of or pertaining to the carpus or wrist: n. a carpal bone.

car·pel (kär'pĕl), n. 1. a simple pistil. 2. one of the parts of a compound pistil.

car·pen·ter (kär'pĕn-tĕr), n. an artificer who works in timber or woodwork, as for houses: v.i. to perform carpenter's work: v.t. to build or repair by such work.

car·pen·try (-tri), n. a carpenter's work.

car·pet (kär'pit), n. 1. a thick woven or felted fabric for covering floors, stairs, etc. 2. a piece of this. 3. any similar soft covering: v.t. to cover with a carpet.

car·pet·bag (-bag), n. an old kind of traveling bag, made of carpeting: v.i. -**bagged, -bagging**, to be a carpetbagger.

car·pet·bag·ger (-bag-ĕr), n. a Northern political adventurer who settled in the Southern States at the close of the Civil War: a contemptuous term.

car·pet·ing (-ing), n. 1. carpet material. 2. carpets in general.

car·pol·o·gy (kär-päl'ŏ-ji), n. the science having to do with the structure of fruits and seeds.

car·port (kär'pôrt), n. a roof extension for sheltering an automobile.

car·pus (kär'pûs), n., pl. -**pi** ('pī), the wrist, or the wrist bones.

car·ra·geen, car·ra·gheen (ker'á-gēn), n. a purplish, edible seaweed.

car·rel, car·rell (ker'ĕl), n. a secluded area in a library for undisturbed reading.

car·ri·age (ker'ij), n. 1. the act of carrying or transporting; also, the cost of this. 2. deportment; bearing. 3. a buggy or similar vehicle. 4. a moving or wheeled support, as for a gun.

car·ri·er (ker'i-ĕr), n. 1. one that carries; specifically, one in the business of transporting goods or people. 2. one that harbors and transmits a disease. 3. an aircraft carrier.

carrier pigeon, a pigeon trained to carry messages over great distances.

car·ri·ole (ker'i-ōl), n. same as **cariole**.

car·ri·on (ker'i-ŏn), n. dead, putrefying flesh: adj. of or feeding on carrion.

carrion crow, the common crow of Europe.

car·ron·ade (ker-á-nād'), n. an old kind of short, large-bored cannon.

car·rot (ker'ŏt), n. 1. a biennial plant of the parsley family. 2. its orange root, eaten as a vegetable.

car·rou·sel (ker-ŏ-sel'), n. a merry-go-round.

car·ry (ker'i), v.t. -**ried, -ry·ing**, 1. to hold while moving; bear. 2. to convey or transmit, as from one point to another. 3. to have on one's person. 4. to lead, direct, or impel. 5. to include. 6. to extend; move or bring along or over. 7. to bear the weight of. 8. to be pregnant with. 9. to involve; imply. 10. to hold or conduct (oneself) in a certain

way. 11. to sustain; support. 12. to win support for. 13. to win (an election, argument, etc.); also, to gain or capture. 14. to deal in; have regularly in stock. 15. to keep on one's account books. 16. in *Music*, to sing the notes of (a tune) accurately: v.i. 1. to act as a bearer. 2. to convey something, or be conveyed, to a distance. 3. to gain acceptance, as a proposal: n., pl. **car'ries**, 1. range, as of a projectile. 2. the act or way of carrying.

car·ry·all (-ôl), n. 1. a covered, four-wheeled vehicle drawn by one horse. 2. an enclosed trucklike vehicle for carrying passengers or merchandise. 3. a large bag, basket, etc.

carrying charge, in installment buying, a charge, as interest, on the balance owed.

car·ry·o·ver (-ō-vĕr), n. an amount or quantity remaining, transferred, etc.

car·sick (kär'sik), adj. queasy from the motion of a car, bus, etc. —**car'sick·ness**, n.

cart (kärt), n. 1. a small, two-wheeled vehicle. 2. a small wagon: v.t. & v.i. to transport by cart. —**cart'er**, n.

cart·age (kär'tij), n. conveyance by cart; also, the charge for this.

carte (kärt), n. same as **bill of fare**.

carte blanche (kärt'blänsh'), pl. **cartes blanches** (kärts'blänsh'), unconditional freedom or authority.

car·tel (kär-tel'), n. 1. an agreement between hostile states, as for exchanging prisoners. 2. a monopolistic association, as of industrialists.

Car·thu·sian (kär-thōō'zhân, -thū'zhán), n. any one of the members of a religious order founded in 1084 by St. Bruno.

car·ti·lage (kärt'l-ij), n. elastic animal tissue; gristle. —**car·ti·lag·i·nous** (kärt-l-aj'i-nûs), adj.

car·tog·ra·pher (kär-tog'rá-fĕr), n. one who makes maps or charts.

car·tog·ra·phy (-fi), n. the art or business of making maps or charts.

car·ton (kärt'n), n. 1. a cardboard box. 2. a small container, as for milk, of light, waxed cardboard. 3. such a box or container when filled; also, the contents.

car·toon (kär-tōōn'), n. 1. a study or design executed on paper and of the size to be reproduced in fresco, tapestry, etc. 2. a pictorial sketch, as in a newspaper, dealing with, and often caricaturing, some subject. 3. a humorous drawing. 4. a comic strip or animated cartoon: v.t. & v.i. to make cartoons (of).

car·touche, car·touch (kär-tōōsh'), n. 1. an ornament in the form of an unrolled scroll. 2. on Egyptian monuments, an oval figure containing the name of a sovereign or deity.

car·tridge (kär'trij), n. 1. a cylindrical case, as of cardboard or metal, containing the charge and primer of a firearm. 2. a small container for insertion into a larger device. 3. a replaceable stylus unit for a record player.

cart·wheel (kärt'hwēl), n. 1. a kind of handspring performed sideways. 2. [Slang], a large-sized coin.

carve (kärv), v.t. carved, carv'ing, 1. to shape, as wood, by cutting. 2. to cut into slices:

v.i. 1. to work as a sculptor or carver. 2. to cut up meat. —carv'er, *n.* —carv'ing, *n.*

car·vel (kär'vel), *n.* same as caravel.

car·wash (kär'wŏsh), *n.* a building or other place where automobiles are washed.

car·y·at·id (ker-i-at'id), *n., pl.* -ids, -id·es ('i-dez), the sculptured figure of a woman, used as a supporting column for an entablature.

ca·sa·ba (kå-sä'bä), *n.* a melon with thick, yellow rind and white, sweet flesh.

cas·cade (kas-kād'), *n.* 1. a small, steep fall of water, especially one of a series. 2. anything suggestive of a waterfall: *v.i. & v.t.* -cad'ed, -cad'ing, to fall or make fall in a cascade.

cas·car·a (kas-ker'å), *n.* 1. a small U.S. tree of the buckthorn family. 2. a laxative made from its bark.

cas·ca·ril·la (kas-kå-ril'å), *n.* 1. a West Indian shrub of the spurge family. 2. the bark: it has tonic properties.

case (kās), *n.* 1. an example or instance of something. 2. anything involved in, or requiring, discussion, investigation, etc. 3. a person being attended by a doctor, social worker, etc. 4. a suit or action at law; also, the details involved. 5. arguments or evidence. 6. one of the syntactic forms or inflections of a pronoun or noun: *v.t.* cased, cas'ing, [Slang], to study (a building, area, etc.), as in planning a robbery.

case (kās), *n.* 1. a covering, as for a book or watch. 2. a receptacle, as a crate or chest; also, the contents of such a receptacle. 3. the frame of a window, door, etc. 4. in *Printing*, a divided tray for type: *v.t.* -cased, -cas'ing, to put in, or cover with, a case.

case·har·den (kās'här-dn), *v.t.* 1. to harden the surface of (iron). 2. to harden the feelings of.

ca·se·in (kā'si-in), *n.* the protein that is a major constituent of milk.

case·mate (kās'māt), *n.* a shellproof chamber with embrasures as for cannon.

case·ment (kās'mĕnt), *n.* a hinged window frame made to open outward.

ca·sern, ca·serne (kā-zürn'), *n.* a barracks for soldiers, in a garrison.

case·work (kās'wûrk), *n.* the work done by a social worker in investigating individual cases. —case'work·er, *n.*

cash (kash), *n.* money; especially, ready money, or money on hand: *v.t.* to turn into, or exchange for, money: *adj.* of, in, or for money.

cash-and-car·ry (-ân-ker'i), *n.* a store system of cash payments, without deliveries.

cash·book (kash'book), *n.* a book in which a register is kept of money received or paid out.

cash·ew (kash'ōō), *n.* 1. a tropical evergreen tree. 2. its edible, kidney-shaped nut.

cash·ier (ka-shir'), *n.* one who has charge of the money and superintends the payments and receipts of a bank or business: *v.t.* 1. to dismiss from service or place of trust. 2. to discard.

cash·mere (kazh'mir), *n.* 1. soft wool from goats of south-central Asia. 2. a fabric of this or similar wool. 3. a garment of this.

cash register, a machine visibly registering each sale.

cas·ing (kās'ing), *n.* 1. the act of covering with or placing in a case. 2. a protective covering. 3. a frame, as for a window.

ca·si·no (kå-sē'nō), *n., pl.* -nos, 1. a small country house. 2. a public room or building for dancing, gambling, etc. 3. same as cassino.

cask (kask), *n.* 1. a hooped wooden barrel, for liquids. 2. its contents.

cas·ket (kas'kit), *n.* 1. a small chest or box, as for jewels. 2. a coffin: *v.t.* to place in a casket.

casque (kask), *n.* a helmet.

cas·sa·va (kå-sä'vå), *n.* 1. a tropical American plant of the spurge family, with edible, starchy roots. 2. the root or a starch derived from it, used in making a bread and tapioca.

cas·se·role (kas'ē-rōl), *n.* 1. a baking dish of glass or earthenware, for cooking and serving food. 2. the food.

cas·sette (ka-set', kå-), *n.* 1. a case containing roll film, for quickly loading a camera. 2. a case enclosing very thin magnetic tape on reels, inserted as a unit in a special recorder.

cas·sia (kash'å), *n.* 1. a tree of the laurel family, native to southeastern Asia. 2. its bark, a source of a coarse cinnamon. 3. any one of a genus of tropical plants yielding senna.

cas·si·mere (kas'i-mir), *n.* a twilled or plain woolen cloth, used for men's suits.

cas·si·no (kå-sē'nō), *n.* a card game for two to four players.

cas·sock (kas'ŏk), *n.* a long, closefitting vestment worn by clergymen, choristers, etc.

cas·so·war·y (kas'ŏ-wer-i), *n., pl.* -war·ies, a large bird of Australia and New Guinea, similar to but smaller than an ostrich.

cast (kast), *v.t.* cast, cast'ing, 1. to throw; hurl. 2. to shed. 3. to direct or turn. 4. to throw down or out. 5. to calculate. 6. to form into a certain shape. 7. to assign to various actors. 8. to select (an actor) for (a role). 9. to deposit (a ballot or vote): *v.i.* 1. to throw; hurl. 2. to throw the line in angling. 3. to ponder. 4. to be formed in a mold: *n.* 1. the act of casting. 2. a distance thrown. 3. a motion or turn of the eye; glance. 4. something formed in or as in a mold. 5. a mold or impression taken. 6. a plaster form, as to keep a broken limb in place. 7. the company of actors in a play or movie. 8. direction. 9. form, shape, or manner. 10. appearance. 11. tinge.

cas·ta·nets (kas-tå-nets'), *n.* a pair of small, shell-shaped pieces of hard wood, ivory, etc., fastened loosely at the top, held in the hand and clicked together to beat time.

cast·a·way (kas'tå-wā), *n.* 1. one who is cast out or off; outcast. 2. one who is shipwrecked: *adj.* 1. rejected; discarded. 2. shipwrecked; stranded.

caste (kast), *n.* 1. any of the hereditary Hindu social classes traditionally excluded from social contact with each other. 2. any similar system or class.

---

a in *cap*, ā in *cane*, ä in *father*, å in *abet*, e in *met*, ē in *be*, ê in *baker*, ê in *regent*, i in *pit*, ī in *fine*, ĭ in *manifest*, o in *hot*, ō in *horse*, ō in *bone*,

cas·tel·lan (kas'tĕ-lăn), *n.* the warden or keeper of a castle.

cas·tel·lat·ed (kas'tĕ-lāt-id), *adj.* having turrets and battlements, as a castle.

cast·er (kas'tĕr), *n.* 1. one that casts. 2. a condiment cruet. 3. a small wheel or ball in a swiveling frame.

cas·ti·gate (kas'ti-gāt), *v.t.* -gat·ed, -gat·ing, to chastise; punish; subject to severe criticism. —cas·ti·ga'tion, *n.* —cas'ti·ga·tor, *n.*

Cas·tile soap (kas-tēl'), [also c-], a fine soap made from olive oil and sodium hydroxide: originally made in Castile, Spain.

cast·ing (kas'ting), *n.* 1. the action of one that casts. 2. anything cast in a mold.

casting vote, the deciding vote of a chairman when the votes on both sides are equal: also **casting voice.**

cast iron, a hard, rigid alloy of iron made by casting.

cas·tle (kas'l), *n.* 1. a fortified large building, as of a medieval nobleman. 2. a mansion. 3. in *Chess,* same as rook: *v.t.* -tled, -tling, in *Chess,* to move the king two squares to the right or left and bring the castle to the square the king has passed over.

cast·off (kast'ôf), *adj.* thrown out: discarded: *n.* any person or thing that has been thrown out, rejected, etc.

cas·tor (kas'tĕr), *n.* 1. a hat made of the fur of the beaver or rabbit. 2. same as caster (senses 2 & 3).

castor-oil plant, a tropical plant of the spurge family, with beanlike seeds from which an oil (castor oil) used as a cathartic, is pressed.

cas·trate (kas'trāt), *v.t.* -trat·ed, -trat·ing, to emasculate; geld. —cas·tra'tion, *n.*

cast steel, steel formed by casting.

cas·u·al (kazh' oo-wăl), *adj.* 1. happening by chance; random. 2. occasional. 3. slight or superficial. 4. careless. 5. nonchalant. 6. informal. —cas'u·al·ly, *adv.*

cas·u·al·ty (kazh'ăl-ti, kazh'ŭ-wăl-ti), *n., pl.* -ties, 1. an accident, especially if resulting in death. 2. a person killed, wounded, captured, etc. 3. a thing lost, destroyed, etc.

cas·u·ist (kazh'oo-wist), *n.* one skilled in casuistry.

cas·u·ist·ry (-wis-tri), *n., pl.* -ries, 1. the solving of matters of conscience by ethical rules. 2. sophistical reasoning.

cat (kat), *n., pl.* **cats, cat,** 1. any of a family of carnivorous mammals, as the lion or tiger. 2. a small mammal of this family, long domesticated as a household pet and for catching mice. 3. a gossiping or spiteful woman. 4. a catfish. 5. a catboat. 6. a cat-o'-nine-tails. 7. the game of tipcat. 8. a strong tackle used at the cathead: *v.t.* **cat'ted, cat'ting,** to draw up (an anchor) to the cathead.

ca·tab·o·lism (kă-tab'ŏ-lizm), *n.* destructive metabolism; a series of changes by which complex bodies are broken down into simpler forms. —**cat·a·bol·ic** (kat-ă-bol'ik), *adj.* —**cat·a·bol'i·cal·ly,** *adv.*

cat·a·clysm (kat'ă-klizm), *n.* 1. a deluge; flood. 2. a violent or sudden upheaval producing great changes; an earthquake, war, etc. — **cat·a·clys'mic,** *adj.*

cat·a·comb (kat'ă-kōm), *n.* a subterranean burial place with niches hollowed out for the dead.

cat·a·falque (kat'ă-falk), *n.* a temporary structure erected to support the coffin of a distinguished person on the occasion of a ceremonious funeral.

cat·a·lep·sy (kat'l-ep-si), *n.* a sudden suspension of consciousness and feeling, with the muscles becoming rigid. —**cat·a·lep'tic,** *adj.* & *n.*

cat·a·log, cat·a·logue (kat'l-ôg), *n.* 1. an itemized list or file, generally in alphabetical order, as of books, things for sale, etc. 2. a book, brochure, etc. giving such a list: *v.t.* & *v.i.* -loged or -logued, -log·ing or -logu·ing, to put in or work at (a catalog). —**cat'a·log·er, cat'a·logu·er,** *n.*

ca·tal·pa (kă-tal'pă), *n.* any one of a group of trees of Asia and America, with large, heart-shaped leaves and thin, beanlike pods.

ca·tal·y·sis (kă-tal'ĭ-sis), *n., pl.* -ses (-sēz), acceleration or deceleration of a chemical reaction by a substance added and remaining chemically unchanged.

cat·a·lyst (kat'l-ist), *n.* 1. the substance effecting catalysis. 2. a person or thing acting as the stimulus in bringing about something.

cat·a·ma·ran (kat-ă-mă-ran'), *n.* 1. a narrow log raft using paddles or sails. 2. a boat made of twin hulls.

cat·a·me·ni·a (kat-ă-mē'ni-ă), *n.* the monthly period of women; menstruation.

cat·a·mount (kat'ă-mount), *n.* any one of a number of wildcats, as the puma or lynx.

cat·a·plasm (kat'ă-plazm), *n.* a poultice.

cat·a·pult (kat'ă-pult), *n.* 1. an ancient military engine for hurling darts, stones, etc. 2. a slingshot. 3. a device for launching airplanes, rockets, etc. at high speeds. 4. an ejection device, as for an airplane pilot: *v.t.* & *v.i.* to hurl or be hurled from or as from a catapult.

cat·a·ract (kat'ă-rakt), *n.* 1. a large waterfall. 2. a flood; rush of water. 3. an eye disease in which the crystalline lens becomes opaque and vision is impaired; also, the opaque area.

ca·tarrh (kă-tär'), *n.* inflammation of a mucous membrane, with increased flow of mucus: an old term.

ca·tas·tro·phe (kă-tas'trŏ-fi), *n.* 1. a great calamity or disaster. 2. the culminating event of a drama, as in ancient tragedy. —**cat·a·stroph·ic** (kat-ă-strof'ik), *adj.* —**cat·a·stroph'i·cal·ly,** *adv.*

Ca·taw·ba (kă-tô'bă), *n.* 1. a light-red variety of native American grape. 2. wine from it. Also **catawba.**

cat·bird (kat'bŭrd), *n.* a dark-gray North American songbird.

cat·boat ('bōt), *n.* a small boat with one sail on a mast near the bow.

cat·call (' kôl), *n.* a shrill noise to express disapproval: *v.t.* & *v.i.* to make catcalls (at).

catch (kach), *v.t.* **caught, catch'ing,** 1. to seize or grasp. 2. to lay hold of suddenly; intercept; grab. 3. to trap or snare. 4. to capture or captivate. 5. to apprehend by the intel-

lect or senses. 6. to be in time for; also, [Informal], to get to see, hear, etc. 7. to hit; strike. 8. to get by contagion or infection. 9. to surprise in some act. 10. to entangle or snag. 11. to trick or deceive: *v.i.* 1. to become entangled or snagged. 2. to take hold, as fire; burn. 3. to hold, as a lock. 4. to act as a catcher: *n.* 1. the act of catching; also, the throwing back and forth of a ball, for amusement. 2. that which is caught. 3. a thing that catches. 4. a person worth getting, hiring, etc. 5. a scrap or fragment. 6. a break in the voice. 7. [Informal], a tricky condition. 8. in *Music*, a kind of round.

catch-all (kat'ôl), *n.* a receptacle for all kinds of things.

catch-er (kach'ẽr), *n.* one that catches; specifically, in *Baseball*, the player behind the batter, catching unhit balls.

catch-ing ('ing), *adj.* 1. catchy. 2. infectious; contagious.

catch-pen-ny ('pen-i), *adj.* meretricious; tawdry: *n., pl.* -nies, such an article.

catch-up (kech'ûp, kach'ûp), *n.* same as ketchup.

catch-weight (kach'wāt), *adj. & adv.* with no weight restrictions, as a boxing match.

catch-word ('wûrd), *n.* 1. a word guiding a reader, as one printed at the top of a dictionary page. 2. a frequently used word or phrase epitomizing something.

catch-y ('i), *adj.* catch'i-er, catch'i-est, 1. catching attention. 2. easily noticed and remembered, as a tune. 3. tricky.

cat-e-chet-i-cal (kat-ê-ket'i-kl), *adj.* consisting of questions and answers.

cat-e-chin (kat'ê-chin), *n.* a yellow, powdery, acid compound, used in tanning, textile printing, etc.

cat-e-chism (kat'ê-kizm), *n.* 1. a manual of instruction, as in a religion, in the form of questions and answers. 2. any similar, searching set of questions. —cat'e-chist, *n.*

cat-e-chize (-kīz), *v.t.* -chized, -chiz-ing, 1. to instruct, as in religion, by means of questions and answers. 2. to examine closely by interrogation. Also **cat'e-chise**. —cat'e-chiz-er, *n.*

cat-e-chu (kat'ê-chōō), *n.* a brown astringent extract obtained from an Oriental acacia, used in dyeing, tanning, and as a medicine.

cat-e-chu-men (kat-ê-kū'men), *n.* 1. one taking religious instruction prior to baptism. 2. any new learner.

cat-e-gor-i-cal (kat-ê-gôr'i-kl), *adj.* 1. of or pertaining to a category. 2. unconditional. — cat-e-gor'i-cal-ly, *adv.*

cat-e-go-rize (kat'ê-gô-rīz), *v.t.* -rized, -riz-ing, to put in a category; class. —cat-e-go-ri-za'tion (-ri-zā'shŭn), *n.*

cat-e-go-ry (kat'ê-gôr-i), *n., pl.* -ries, 1. a class or division. 2. in *Logic*, one of the highest classes to which knowledge or thought can be reduced.

cat-e-nar-y (kat'n-er-i), *n.* the curve formed by a fine, flexible cord when suspended from its ends.

cat-e-nate (kat'n-āt), *v.t.* -nat-ed, -nat-ing, to connect the links of a chain; link.

ca-ter (kā'tẽr), *v.i.* 1. to supply food; be a caterer. 2. to try to meet another's needs or wishes (with *to*): *v.t.* to be the caterer for (a banquet, etc.).

cat-er-cor-nered (kat'i-kôr-nẽrd), *adj.* diagonal: *adv.* diagonally; cornerwise. Also **cat'er-cor-ner.**

ca-ter-er (kāt'ẽr-ẽr), *n.* 1. one who caters. 2. one whose work is to supply and serve food as at a wedding.

cat-er-pil-lar (kat'ẽr-pil-ẽr), *n.* 1. the wormlike larva of various insects, as the butterfly or moth. 2. [C-], a tractor moving by means of two endless belts, one at each side, that are driven by cogged wheels: a trademark.

cat-er-waul (kat'ẽr-wôl), *n.* the cry of a cat when rutting: *v.i.* to cry thus: *n.* such a cry.

cat-fish (kat'fish), *n., pl.* -fish, -fish-es, any one of various scaleless fishes with long barbels resembling a cat's whiskers.

cat-gut ('gut), *n.* a kind of cord made from the intestines of animals, as sheep or horses, and used for sutures, stringing musical instruments, etc.

ca-thar-sis (kâ-thär'sis), *n.* 1. purgation, especially of the bowels. 2. salutary outpouring or relief of the emotions.

ca-thar-tic ('tik), *adj.* purgative: *n.* a purgative medicine.

cat-head (kat'hed), *n.* a beam near a ship's bow, to which the anchor is secured.

ca-the-dral (kâ-thê'drâl), *n.* 1. the chief church in a see, containing the bishop's throne. 2. a large, impressive church.

cath-e-ter (kath'ê-tẽr), *n.* a tubular instrument to withdraw urine from the bladder.

cath-e-ter-ize (-īz), *v.t.* -ized, -iz-ing, to put a catheter into.

cath-ode (kath'ōd), *n.* 1. a negative electrode. 2. a positive battery terminal.

cathode rays, electron streams from a cathode, producing X-rays.

cath-o-lic (kath'ô-lik), *adj.* 1. universal; general; embracing all. 2. liberal; free from prejudice. 3. [C-], of any orthodox Christian church; especially, of the church headed by the Pope: *n.* [C-], a member of a Catholic church; especially, a Roman Catholic.

Ca-thol-i-cism (kâ-thol'I-sizm), *n.* the belief of, adherence to, or practices, etc. of a Catholic faith or church, especially the Roman Catholic.

cath-o-lic-i-ty (kath-ô-lis'i-ti), *n.* 1. the quality or state of being catholic. 2. [C-], Catholicism.

Ca-thol-i-cize (kâ-thol'I-sīz), *v.t. & v.i.* -cized, -ciz-ing, to convert to or be converted to Catholicism.

ca-thol-i-con ('I-kon), *n.* a panacea.

cat-i-on (kat'I-ôn), *n.* an ion with a positive charge: opposed to anion. —cat-i-on'ic (-on'-ik), *adj.*

cat-kin (kat'kin), *n.* a pendulous inflorescence, as on poplars.

cat-mint ('mint), *n.* [British], catnip.

a in *cap*, ā in *cane*, ä in *father*, å in *abet*, e in *met*, ē in *be*, ê in *baker*, ê in *regent*, i in *pit*, ī in *fine*, i in *manifest*, o in *hot*, ô in *horse*, ō in *bone*,

cat·nap ('nap), n. a brief doze: v.i. -napped, -nap·ping, to take a catnap.

cat·nip ('nip), n. a plant of the mint family, much liked by cats.

cat-o'-nine-tails (kat-ô-nīn'tālz), n., pl. -tails, a whip with nine lashes of knotted cords.

ca·top·trics (kă-top'triks), n. that branch of optics which treats of the principles of reflected light. —ca·top'tric, adj.

cat's-eye (kats'ī), n. a gem, glass, etc. reflecting light somewhat the way the eye of a cat does.

cat's-paw (kats'pô), n. 1. a dupe; one used as a tool to accomplish a purpose, usually sinister. 2. a light breeze ruffling water. 3. a hitch in a rope bight.

cat·sup (kech'ŭp, kat'sŭp), n. ketchup.

cat·tail (kat'tāl), n. a marsh plant with brown, fuzzy spikes.

cat·tle (kat'l), n. domesticated bovine animals collectively.

cat·tle·man (-măn), n., pl. -men, a man whose work is the tending or raising of cattle.

cat·ty (kat'i), adj. -ti·er, -ti·est, 1. of or suggestive of a cat. 2. malicious, spiteful, etc. — cat'ti·ness, n.

cat·ty-cor·nered (kat'i-kôr-nêrd), adj. & adv. cater-cornered: also cat'ty-cor'ner.

cat·walk (kat'wôk), n. a narrow, raised walk or platform, as above an engine room.

Cau·ca·sian (kô-kā'zhăn), adj. & n. same as Caucasoid.

Cau·ca·soid (kôk'ă-soid), adj. denoting or of those peoples that together make up what is loosely called the *white race*: n. a Caucasoid person.

cau·cus (kôk'ŭs), n. a private meeting of a political party or faction to decide on a line of policy, choose candidates, etc.: v.i. -cused or -cussed, -cus·ing or -cus·sing, to hold, or meet in, a caucus.

cau·dal (kôd'l), adj. 1. of, pertaining to, or like a tail. 2. at or near the tail.

cau·date (kô'dāt), adj. having a tail or taillike appendage: also cau'dat·ed.

cau·dle (kôd'l), n. a warm, spiced or sugared drink made of gruel with wine or ale added, for invalids.

caught (kôt), past tense and past participle of catch.

CAT scan (kat), 1. a diagnostic X-raying of soft tissues, using many single-plane X-rays (*tomograms*) to form the image. 2. such an image. —CAT scan'ner.

caul·dron (kôl'drŏn), n. same as caldron.

cau·li·flow·er (kôl'i-flou-ěr), n. 1. a garden variety of cabbage with an edible flowering head. 2. this head.

caulk (kôk), v.t. to put tar, oakum, or other filler into the seams or cracks of (a boat, window frame, pipe, etc.) as to make watertight.

caus·al (kôz'l), adj. 1. of, relating to, or expressing cause. 2. of or pertaining to a cause or causes. 3. being or involving a cause: n. a word, as *since*, indicating a cause or reason.

cau·sal·i·ty (kô-zal'i-ti), n., pl. -ties, 1. the relation of cause to effect. 2. causal quality or origin.

cau·sa·tion (-zā'shŭn), n. 1. the act of causing. 2. causality.

caus·a·tive (kôz'ă-tiv), adj. 1. that causes. 2. expressing causation.

cause (kôz), n. 1. that which produces or contributes to a result. 2. a reason or motive. 3. a side or party, as one espousing social reform. 4. in *Law*, a suit or action: v.t. caused, caus'ing, to act as the agent that brings about; be the source or origin of; effect. —cause'less, adj. —caus'er, n.

cause·way (kôz'wā), n. 1. a raised pathway or road. 2. a highway.

caus·tic (kôs'tik), adj. 1. burning; corrosive. 2. sarcastic; cutting: n. a corrosive substance. —caus'ti·cal·ly, adv. —caus·tic'i·ty (-tis'i-ti), n.

caustic potash, same as potassium hydroxide.

caustic soda, same as sodium hydroxide.

cau·ter·ant (kôt'ēr-ănt), n. a cauterizing substance: adj. that cauterizes.

cau·ter·ize (kôt'ēr-īz), v.t. -ized, -iz·ing, to burn or sear with a hot iron or needle or with a caustic, as to prevent the spread of infection. —cau·ter·i·za'tion, n.

cau·ter·y (kôt'ēr-i), n., pl. -ter·ies, 1. the act of cauterizing. 2. an instrument or drug to do this.

cau·tion (kô'shŭn), n. 1. heedfulness; prudence in regard to danger or difficulty. 2. an admonition; warning. 3. [Informal], a cause or occasion of wonderment, dismay, talk, etc.: v.t. to warn.

cau·tion·ar·y (-er-i), adj. alerting to danger or difficulty; warning.

cau·tious (kô'shŭs), adj. exercising caution; heedful; wary; circumspect. —cau'tious·ly, adv. —cau'tious·ness, n.

cav·al·cade (kav'l-kād), n. a procession, as of horsemen or carriages.

cav·a·lier (kav-ă-lîr'), n. 1. an armed horseman; knight. 2. a gallant gentleman. 3. a lady's escort: adj. 1. gay; sprightly. 2. careless or indifferent. 3. haughty; supercilious. —cav·a·lier'ly, adv. & adj.

ca·val·la (kă-val'ă), n. either of two fish, the cero or the crevalle.

cav·al·ry (kav'l-ri), n., pl. -ries, 1. horse soldiers. 2. soldiers in motorized armored vehicles. —cav'al·ry·man (-măn), n., pl. -men.

cav·a·ti·na (kav-ă-tē'nă), n. a short, simple melody.

cave (kāv), n. a hollow place or large natural cavity within the earth; cavern: v.t. caved, cav'ing, to hollow out: v.i. to yield or collapse (with *in*).

ca·ve·at (kā'vi-at), n. 1. in *Law*, a notice filed to stop procedure until the party giving such notice is heard. 2. a warning.

caveat emp·tor (emp'tôr), [Latin], let the buyer beware.

cave man, a human being belonging to a prehistoric race who inhabited caves: also cave dweller.

cav·ern (kav'ērn), n. a large, natural hollow under the earth; cave.

cav·ern·ous (kav'ēr-nŭs), adj. 1. having many caverns. 2. filled with cavities. 3. of, like, or suggestive of a cavern.

cav·i·ar, cav·i·are (kav'i-är), n. the salted roe of

certain large fish, as the sturgeon and salmon, eaten as an appetizer.

cav-il (kav'l), *v.i.* -iled *or* -illed, -il-ing *or* -il-ling, to raise captious or frivolous objections; carp (*at*): *n.* a captious or frivolous objection. —cav'il-er, cav'il-ler, *n.*

cav-i-ty (kav'i-ti), *n., pl.* -ties, 1. a hollow place or part. 2. a hollow place in a tooth, from decay.

ca-vort (kā-vôrt'), *v.i.* 1. to prance or leap about. 2. to frolic.

ca-vy (kā'vi), *n., pl.* -vies, any one of several short-tailed rodents of South America, as the guinea pig.

caw (kô), *v.i.* to cry like a crow: *n.* the cry of a crow.

cay-enne (kī-en'), *n.* 1. a hot red pepper made from the fruit of a pepper plant: also **cayenne pepper.** 2. the fruit itself.

cay-man (kā'mån), *n., pl.* -mans, same as cai-man.

cay-use (kī'ōōs), *n., pl.* -us-es, a small horse of the western U.S.

CD (sē'dē'), *n., pl.* CDs, CD's, a compact disc.

cease (sēs), *v.t. & v.i.* ceased, ceas'ing, to put or come to an end; stop.

cease-fire ('fir'), *n.* a truce in warfare.

cease-less ('lis), *adj.* never stopping; unending; constant. —cease'less-ly, *adv.*

ce-cum (sē'kům), *n., pl.* -ca (sē'kå), a blind pouch beginning the large intestine.

ce-dar (sē'dēr), *n.* 1. any one of a group of trees with needlelike leaves, cones, and wood of great duration and fragrance; also, a tree similar to this. 2. the wood: *adj.* of or pertaining to cedar.

cedar waxwing (waks'wing), a brown American bird with waxy, red feather tips.

cede (sēd), *v.t.* ced'ed, ced'ing, 1. to give up or surrender. 2. to transfer the ownership of.

ce-dil-la (si-dil'å), *n.* a mark placed under *c* to indicate the sound of *s*, as in French *leçon.*

ceil-ing (sēl'ing), *n.* 1. the inside, uppermost part of a room. 2. an uppermost limit.

cel-an-dine (sel'ån-dīn, -dēn), *n.* a yellow-flowered plant of the poppy family or buttercup family.

cel-e-brant (sel'ē-brånt), *n.* 1. one who celebrates. 2. the principal officiant at a religious rite.

cel-e-brate (sel'ē-brāt), *v.t.* -brat-ed, -brat-ing, 1. to perform (a ritual, ceremony, etc.) formally or solemnly in public. 2. to commemorate in a ceremonious or festive way. 3. to give public praise or honor to: *v.i.* 1. to celebrate something. 2. [Informal], to have a joyous time. —cel'e-bra-tor, *n.* —ce-leb-ra-to-ry (sė-leb'rå-tôr'i), *adj.*

cel-e-brat-ed (-id), *adj.* distinguished; famous; renowned.

cel-e-bra-tion (sel-ē-brā'shůn), *n.* 1. the act of celebrating. 2. an observance or ceremony to celebrate anything.

ce-leb-ri-ty (sė-leb'ri-ti), *n.* 1. fame; renown; distinction. 2. *pl.* -ties, a renowned person.

ce-ler-i-ty (sė-ler'i-ti), *n.* rapidity; swiftness.

cel-er-y (sel'ēr-i), *n.* a herbaceous plant with long, edible stalks eaten raw or cooked.

ce-les-tial (sė-les'chål), *adj.* 1. of or pertaining to the sky or heavens. 2. heavenly; divine. 3. supremely excellent; perfect: *n.* an inhabitant of heaven. —ce-les'tial-ly, *adv.*

celestial navigation, navigation that fixes position and course by observation of the position of heavenly bodies.

cel-i-ba-cy (sel'i-bå-si), *n.* 1. the state of being unmarried. 2. the single life of one bound by vows to remain unmarried. 3. total abstinence from sexual indulgence.

cel-i-bate (sel'i-båt), *n.* one who is unmarried or practices celibacy: *adj.* of or characterized by celibacy.

cell (sel), *n.* 1. a small room in a monastery, convent, or prison. 2. a small cavity or enclosed space. 3. a minute mass of protoplasm forming the structural unit of all plants and animals. 4. a single element of a storage battery. 5. a receptacle for generating electricity. 6. a small religious house attached to a monastery or convent. 7. the smallest organizational unit of a group or movement.

cel-lar (sel'ēr), *n.* 1. an underground room or group of rooms, as below a building. 2. a stock of wines.

cel-lar-age (-ij), *n.* cellar space.

cel-list (chel'ist), *n.* a cello player: also 'cel'list.

cel-lo (chel'ō), *n., pl.* -los, -li ('ē), a large instrument of the violin family, tuned an octave lower than a viola; violoncello: also 'cel'lo.

cel-lo-phane (sel'ō-fān), *n.* a thin, transparent wrapping made from cellulose.

cel-lu-lar (sel'yoo-lēr), *adj.* 1. of or like a cell. 2. having cells; porous.

Cel-lu-loid (sel'yoo-loid), *n.* 1. an ivorylike, flammable material made from pyroxylin and camphor, used for toilet articles, novelties, etc.: a trademark. 2. [c-], this material. 3. [c-], motion pictures.

cel-lu-lose (-lōs), *n.* the main material of cellular plant tissue: it is used in making paper, textiles, explosives, etc.

cellulose acetate, an acetic compound of cellulose used in plastics, textiles, etc.

Cel-si-us (sel'si-ůs), *adj.* denoting or of a thermometer with 0° the freezing point and 100° the boiling point of water; centigrade.

Celt (selt, kelt), *n.* any person belonging to or descended from speakers of the original native languages of Ireland, the Scottish Highlands, Wales, Brittany, etc. —Cel'tic, *adj.*

celt (selt), *n.* a prehistoric instrument or weapon of stone or metal, resembling a chisel or blade of an ax.

ce-ment (si-ment'), *n.* 1. any adhesive substance which makes two things cohere. 2. a powder of lime and clay, used to make mortar and concrete. 3. a bond; anything that joins together: *v.t.* 1. to unite or cover with cement. 2. to unite firmly: *v.i.* to become cemented. —ce-ment'er, *n.*

ce-men-ta-tion (sē-men-tā'shůn), *n.* 1. the act of cementing or the state of being cemented. 2. the chemical combining of a solid and a metallurgic cement by heat.

ce-ment-ite (si-men'tīt), *n.* iron combined with carbon.

cem·e·ter·y (sem'ĕ-ter-i), *n.*, *pl.* **-ter·ies**, a place for burying the dead.

Cen·a·cle (sen'ă-kl), *n.* the room in which Christ ate the Last Supper.

cen·o·bite (sen'ŏ-bit), *n.* one of a religious order living in a monastery or convent.

cen·o·taph (sen'ŏ-taf), *n.* an empty tomb or monument erected in honor of a person buried elsewhere.

Ce·no·zo·ic (sē-nŏ-zō'ik), *n.* the geological era from after the Mesozoic Era to now, marked by the appearance of mammals.

cen·ser (sen'sĕr), *n.* a covered, cup-shaped vessel pierced with holes, in which incense is burned, especially in religious rites.

cen·sor (sen'sĕr), *n.* 1. one of two magistrates of ancient Rome who took the census and regulated morals and manners. 2. an official appointed to examine books, manuscripts, plays, etc. to determine if there is anything immoral or offensive in them: *v.t.* to subject (a book, letter, writer, etc.) to the action of a censor. **—cen·so·ri·al** (sen-sôr'i-ăl), *adj.*

cen·so·ri·ous (sen-sôr'i-ŭs), *adj.* expressing censure; carping; critical. **—cen·so'ri·ous·ly,** *adv.* **—cen·so'ri·ous·ness,** *n.*

cen·sor·ship (sen'sĕr-ship), *n.* 1. the act or method of censoring. 2. the work or office of a censor.

cen·sur·a·ble (sen'shĕr-ă-bl), *adj.* blamable; deserving censure. **—cen'sur·a·bly,** *adv.*

cen·sure (sen'shĕr), *n.* blame; reproof; act of condemning as wrong: *v.t.* **-sured,** **-sur·ing,** to find fault with or condemn; criticize adversely. **—cen'sur·er,** *n.*

cen·sus (sen'sŭs), *n.* 1. in ancient Rome, the act of registering the people and their property for taxation. 2. an official enumeration of the inhabitants of a country, often including sex, age, occupation, etc.: taken in the U.S. at ten-year intervals.

cent (sent), *n.* 1. a 100th part of a dollar. 2. a coin of this value; penny.

cen·tal (sen'tl), *n.* [British], a unit of weight equal to 100 pounds avoirdupois, used for grain.

cen·tare (sen'tēr), *n.* same as **centiare.**

cen·taur (sen'tôr), *n.* in *Greek Mythology,* a monster with the head, trunk, and arms of a man and the body and legs of a horse.

cen·te·nar·i·an (sen-tĕ-ner'i-ăn), *adj.* 1. of or pertaining to a centenary. 2. of or pertaining to a person 100 years old: *n.* a person of such an age or older.

cen·te·nar·y (sen-ten'ĕr-i), *adj.* 1. relating to or consisting of 100 years. 2. of a centennial: *n., pl.* **-nar·ies,** 1. a century. 2. a centennial.

cen·ten·ni·al (sen-ten'i-ăl), *adj.* 1. of or pertaining to 100 years. 2. occurring once in 100 years. 3. of a 100th anniversary: *n.* the commemoration of a 100th anniversary. **—cen·ten'ni·al·ly,** *adv.*

cen·ter (sen'tĕr), *n.* 1. the middle point of anything. 2. a nucleus around which things revolve; pivot. 3. a place at which ideas or activities are originated and from which they spread. 4. [often C-], in *Politics,* members of a party or legislative assembly who hold moderate views between the Conservatives (right) and the Liberals (left). 5. in *Sports,* a player holding a middle position in the line or playing area. 6. a conical pin, as on a lathe, by which work is secured and around which it revolves. 7. troops positioned between the flanks. 8. a point equally distant from all points on the circumference of a circle or on the surface of a sphere: *v.t.* 1. to place on a center. 2. to collect to a point. 3. to provide with a center: *v.i.* to be concentrated or focused.

cen·ter·board (-bôrd), *n.* a movable board like a keel, used to keep a shallow sailboat from drifting.

cen·ter·ing (-ing), *n.* the woodwork by which vaulted work is supported during construction.

center of gravity, that point in a body or system around which the whole mass is concentrated and may be assumed to act.

cen·ter·piece (-pēs), *n.* an ornament, bowl of flowers, etc. for the center of a table.

cen·tes·i·mal (sen-tes'i-măl), *adj.* 1. hundredth. 2. pertaining to or divided into hundredths.

centi-, a combining form meaning *hundred, a 100th part of.*

cen·ti·are (sen'ti-er), *n.* a unit of land measure, equal to one square meter.

cen·ti·grade (sen'ti-grād), *adj.* 1. graduated or divided into 100 degrees. 2. same as Celsius.

cen·ti·gram (-gram), *n.* a measure of weight, equal to 1/100 gram: also **cen'ti·gramme.**

cen·ti·li·ter (-lēt-ĕr), *n.* a measure of capacity, equal to 1/100 liter: also **cen'ti·li·tre.**

cen·time (sän'tēm), *n.* the 1/100 part of a franc.

cen·ti·me·ter (sen'ti-mēt-ĕr), *n.* a measure of length, equal to 1/100 meter (.3937 inch): also **cen'ti·me·tre.**

cen·ti·pede (sen'ti-pēd), *n.* a wormlike arthropod with two legs to each body segment.

cen·tral (sen'trăl), *adj.* 1. relating to, situated in, or being the center. 2. chief; dominant. 3. constituting or pertaining to a source that directs operations in a system. **—cen'tral·ly,** *adv.*

cen·tral·i·ty (sen-tral'i-ti), *n.* 1. the quality or fact of being central. 2. the tendency to be or stay at the center.

cen·tral·ize (sen'tră-liz), *v.t.* **-ized,** **-iz·ing,** 1. to draw or bring to a center. 2. to bring under the control of a single authority. **—cen·tral·i·za'tion,** *n.*

Central Powers, in World War I, Germany and Austria-Hungary, and their allies, Turkey and Bulgaria.

cen·tre (sen'tĕr), *n. & v.t. & v.i.* **-tred,** **-tring,** British form for **center.**

centri-, same as **centro-.**

cen·tric (sen'trik), *adj.* 1. placed in or near the center; central. 2. pertaining to or having a center. **—cen·tric'i·ty** (-tris'i-ti), *n.*

cen·trif·u·gal (sen-trif'yŭ-găl), *adj.* 1. tending, or causing, to fly off from a center. 2. radiating from a central focus. 3. using or operated by centrifugal force. **—cen·trif'u·gal·ly,** *adv.*

centrifugal force, the force tending to pull a thing outward when it is rotating rapidly around a center.

cen·tri·fuge (sen'tri-fūj), *n.* an apparatus using

centrifugal force to separate substances of different density, or to remove moisture: *v.t.* **-fuged, -fug·ing,** to separate by the action of a centrifuge.

cen·trip·e·tal (sen-trip'ĕt-l), *adj.* 1. tending, or causing, to approach a center. 2. using or operated by centripetal force. —**cen·trip'e·tal·ly,** *adv.*

centripetal force, the force tending to pull a thing inward when it is rotating rapidly around a center.

cen·trist (sen'trist), *n.* one who belongs to a political party of the center.

centro-, a combining form meaning *center.*

cen·tu·ple (sen'too-pl), *adj.* hundredfold: *v.t.* **-pled, -pling,** to multiply or increase a hundredfold.

cen·tu·ri·on (sen-tyoor'i-ŏn), *n.* in ancient Rome, a military officer commanding 100 men.

cen·tu·ry (sen'chĕr-i), *n., pl.* **-ries,** 1. a period of 100 years, especially of the Christian Era. 2. in ancient Rome, *a)* a division of the people for voting. *b)* a military unit, originally of 100 men. 3. [Slang], 100 dollars.

century plant, an American agave that blooms once, after 10 to 30 years, then dies.

ce·phal·ic (sĕ-fal'ik), *adj.* 1. of or pertaining to the head or skull. 2. near, on, or toward the head.

ceph·a·lo·pod (sef'å-lŏ-pod), *n.* any one of various mollusks having a distinct head with tentacles, as the nautilus and octopus.

ce·ra·ceous (si-rā'shŭs), *adj.* like wax.

ce·ram·ic (sĕ-ram'ik), *adj.* of or pertaining to pottery, earthenware, porcelain, etc.: *n.* an object made of such materials.

ce·ram·ics ('iks), *n.* the art or occupation of making objects of baked clay.

ce·ram·ist ('ist), *n.* one who works in ceramics: also **ce·ram'i·cist** ('i-sist).

ce·rate (sir'āt), *n.* a thick ointment of wax, fat, etc., sometimes medicated.

cer·a·toid (ser'å-toid), *adj.* horny.

cere (sir), *n.* the waxy skin at the base of the bill of some birds, as the parrot.

cere (sir), *v.t.* **cered, cer'ing,** to wrap in or as in a cerecloth.

ce·re·al (sir'i-ăl), *adj.* of or pertaining to grain: *n.* 1. any edible grain, as wheat, oats, or rice. 2. any grass on which such grain grows. 3. breakfast food made from grain.

cer·e·bel·lum (ser-ĕ-bel'ŭm), *n., pl.* **-lums, -la** ('å), the hinder and lower part of the brain in vertebrate animals, where muscular movements are coordinated.

cer·e·bral (ser'ĕ-brål, sĕ-rē'brål), *adj.* 1. of or pertaining to the brain. 2. intellectual rather than emotional. —**cer·e'bral·ly,** *adv.*

cerebral hemisphere, one of the two lateral halves of the cerebrum.

cerebral palsy, a disorder of the central nervous system marked by impaired control of muscular movements.

cer·e·brate (ser'ĕ-brāt), *v.i.* **-brat·ed, -brat·ing,** to think. —**cer·e·bra'tion,** *n.*

cer·e·brum (ser'ĕ-brŭm, sĕ-rē'brŭm), *n., pl.* **-brums, -bra** (-brå), the upper and chief part

of the brain of vertebrates, thought to control conscious mental processes.

cere-cloth (sir'klôth), *n.* a cloth saturated with wax or some gummy substance, used formerly to wrap the dead.

cer·e·ment (ser'ĕ-mĕnt), *n.* 1. a cerecloth, shroud, etc. 2. *pl.* clothes for the dead.

cer·e·mo·ni·al (ser-ĭ-mō'ni-ål), *adj.* of, relating to, or performed with rites or ceremonies: *n.* a prescribed order for a ceremony or function; ritual. —**cer·e·mo'ni·al·ism,** *n.* —**cer·e·mo'ni·al·ly,** *adv.*

cer·e·mo·ni·ous ('ni-ŭs), *adj.* 1. full of ceremony. 2. careful to observe ceremony; very formal. —**cer·e·mo'ni·ous·ly,** *adv.* —**cer·e·mo'ni·ous·ness,** *n.*

cer·e·mo·ny (ser'ĕ-mō-ni), *n., pl.* **-nies,** 1. a prescribed rite for a special occasion, especially a religious rite. 2. behavior regulated by strict etiquette. 3. formality. 4. meaningless or conventional formality.

ce·rise (sĕ-rēs'), *n.* the color of a bright red cherry: *adj.* bright-red.

ce·ri·um (sir'i-ŭm), *n.* a malleable, gray, metallic chemical element.

cer·nu·ous (sŭr'nyoo-wŭs), *adj.* drooping, as a flower or bud.

ce·ro (sir'ō), *n., pl.* **-ro, -ros,** a large food and game fish of the South Atlantic, related to the mackerel.

ce·rog·ra·phy (si-rog'rå-fi), *n.* engraving on wax covering a metal plate.

ce·ro·plas·tic (sir-ō-plas'tik), *adj.* modeled in wax.

ce·ro·plas·tics ('tiks), *n.* the art of modeling in wax.

ce·rot·ic (sĕ-rot'ik), *adj.* of or denoting a fatty acid in beeswax and other waxes.

cer·tain (sŭrt'n), *adj.* 1. sure. 2. beyond a doubt. 3. fixed or stated. 4. definite. 5. dependable.

cer·tain·ly (-li), *adv.* surely; assuredly.

cer·tain·ty (-ti), *n.* 1. the state or fact of being certain. 2. *pl.* **-ties,** something that is certain.

cer·tes (sŭr'tēz), *adv.* [Archaic], certainly; assuredly.

cer·tif·i·cate (sĕr-tif'ĭ-kåt), *n.* written or printed testimony to a fact, ownership, qualifications, completion of an educational course, etc.: *v.t.* **(-kåt) -cat·ed, -cat·ing,** to give a certificate to; attest or vouch for by certificate.

cer·ti·fi·ca·tion (sŭr-ti-fi-kā'shŭn), *n.* 1. the act of certifying or state of being certified. 2. a certified statement.

cer·ti·fy (sŭr'ti-fi), *v.t.* **-fied, -fy·ing,** 1. to testify to the truth of (something) by formal statement. 2. to guarantee in writing or by an official stamp or seal the worth of (a check, etc.). 3. to issue a certificate to. —**cer'ti·fi·a·ble,** *adj.*

cer·ti·o·ra·ri (sŭr-shi-ŏ-rer'i, -rär'i), *n.* a writ issued from a superior court calling for the records of a case from a lower court for review.

cer·ti·tude (sŭr'ti-tōōd), *n.* 1. certainty. 2. freedom from doubt; assurance.

ce·ru·le·an (sĕ-rōō'li-ån), *adj.* azure; sky-blue.

ce·ru·men (sĕ-rōō'mĕn), *n.* same as **earwax.**

ce·ruse (sir'ōōs), *n.* same as **white lead.**

---

a in cap, ā in cane, ä in father, å in abet, e in met, ē in be, ĕ in baker, ê in regent, i in pit, ī in fine, i in manifest, o in hot, ô in horse, ō in bone,

cer·vi·cal (sûr'vi·kăl), *adj.* of or pertaining to a cervix or to the neck.

cer·vine (sûr'vīn), *adj.* of, pertaining to, or characteristic of a deer.

cer·vix (sûr'viks), *n., pl.* **-vi·ces** ('vi·sēz), **-vix·es**, 1. the neck. 2. any necklike part, as of the uterus.

ce·si·um (sē'zi·ŭm), *n.* a soft, silver-white, metallic chemical element: it is used in photoelectric cells.

cess (ses), *n.* in Ireland, 1. originally, an assessment; tax. 2. luck: in the phrase *bad cess to.*

ces·sa·tion (se·sā'shŭn), *n.* a temporary or complete ceasing, or stopping.

ces·sion (sesh'ŭn), *n.* a yielding, or ceding, as of territory, property, or rights.

ces·sion·ar·y (-er-i), *n., pl.* **-ar·ies**, same as assignee.

cess·pool (ses'pōōl), *n.* a deep hole in the ground to receive waste and sewage from a house, industry, etc.

ces·ta (ses'tä), *n.* [Spanish], the curved basket used as a racket in jai alai.

ces·tus (ses'tŭs), *n.* a kind of glove worn by ancient Roman boxers, often loaded with lead or iron and fastened by leather thongs to the hands and arms.

ce·su·ra (si·zhoor'ä, -zyoor'ä), *n., pl.* **-ras, -rae** ('ē), same as **caesura.**

ce·ta·cean (si·tā'shŭn), *n.* any one of a group of fishlike water mammals, including the dolphins, porpoises, and whales: *adj.* of or pertaining to these mammals: also **ce·ta'·ceous** ('shŭs).

ce·tol·o·gy (si·tol'ŏ·ji), *n.* the scientific study of whales. —**ce·to·log·i·cal** (sēt·ŏ·loj'i·kl), *adj.* — **ce·tol'o·gist,** *n.*

ce·vi·tam·ic acid (sē·vī·tam'ik), same as **vitamin C.**

Cha·blis (shab'lē), *n.* a dry, white wine.

chac·ma (chak'mä), *n.* a very large South African baboon.

chafe (chāf), *v.t.* **chafed, chaf'ing,** 1. to make warm by friction. 2. to wear away or make sore by rubbing. 3. to annoy; irritate: *v.i.* 1. to rub (*against* or *on*). 2. to be annoyed or irritated: *n.* irritation.

chaf·er (chāf'ẽr), *n.* any of various beetles.

chaff (chaf), *n.* 1. husks of grain, separated by threshing or winnowing. 2. straw or hay, cut fine for cattle feed. 3. anything worthless. 4. banter; teasing: *v.t. & v.i.* to tease.

chaf·fer (chaf'ẽr), *n.* [Archaic], the act of bargaining: *v.i.* 1. [Rare], to haggle about a purchase. 2. to talk idly. —**chaf'fer·er,** *n.*

chaf·finch (chaf'finch), *n.* a small European songbird, often kept in a cage as a pet.

chaff·y (chaf'i), *adj.* **chaff'i·er, chaff'i·est,** 1. full of chaff. 2. light; worthless.

chaf·ing dish (chāf'ing), a dish or pan with a heating element beneath it, for cooking at table or for keeping foods hot.

cha·grin (shȧ·grin'), *n.* vexation due to disappointment; ill-humor; mortification: *v.t.* **-grined', -grin'ing,** to cause to feel chagrin; mortify.

chain (chān), *n.* 1. a connected series of links

or rings fitted into one another. 2. a bond or tie. 3. *pl. a)* shackles; fetters. *b)* bondage; slavery. 4. a measuring device having 100 links: the surveyor's chain is 66 feet in length; the engineer's chain is 100 feet in length. 5. a series of related or connected things or happenings. 6. a number of stores, restaurants, etc. with the same ownership. 7. two or more connected atoms: *v.t.* 1. to fasten or connect with a chain. 2. to bind or confine.

chain gang, a gang of convicts working together in chains.

chain mail, flexible armor formed of metal links interwoven.

chain reaction, 1. a series of events in which each is the result of a foregoing event and the cause of a following event. 2. a nuclear or chemical reaction yielding products that result in continuing reactions of the same kind.

chain saw, a portable power saw with teeth set in an endless chain.

chain-smok·ing (chān'smō·king), *n.* the smoking of cigarettes one right after the other. — **chain'smoke,** *v.t. & v.i.* **-smoked, -smok·ing.** —**chain'smok·er,** *n.*

chain stitch, a fancy stitch resembling a chain, with each loop connected to the next.

chair (cher), *n.* 1. a seat for one person, usually with four legs and a back, and sometimes with armrests. 2. an official seat or a seat of authority, dignity, etc. 3. the position or office of a person holding authority. 4. a chairman: *v.t.* 1. to install. 2. to preside over as chairman.

chair car, a railroad passenger car having adjustable chairs.

chair-lift ('lift), *n.* an assemblage of chairs hung from a power-driven endless cable, used to transport people up or down a slope.

chair-man ('măn), *n., pl.* **-men** ('měn), one who presides over an assembly, meeting, board, committee, etc.: *v.t.* **-maned** or **-manned, -man·ing** or **-man·ning,** to preside over as chairman. —**chair'man·ship,** *n.*

chaise (shāz), *n.* a light, open carriage with two or four wheels.

chaise longue (shāz lông'), *pl.* **chaise** (or **chaises) longues** (shāz lôngz'), a chair with the seat lengthened to provide a leg rest.

chaise lounge (lounj), *pl.* **chaise lounges,** same as **chaise longue.**

chal·ced·o·ny (kal·sed'n·i, kal'sĕ·dō·ni), *n., pl.* **-nies,** a variety of quartz with a waxlike luster and found in many colors: it includes agate, jasper, onyx, carnelian, etc.

chal·co·cite (kal'kŏ·sīt), *n.* a native copper sulfide, black and lustrous.

chal·cog·ra·phy (kal·kog'rȧ·fi), *n.* the art of engraving on copper or brass. —**chal·co·graph'·ic** (-kŏ·graf'ik), *adj.*

Chal·de·an, Chal·dae·an (kal·dē'ăn), *adj.* 1. of or pertaining to Chaldea, an ancient province of Babylonia. 2. of or pertaining to astrology or occultism: *n.* 1. any one of the Semitic people who inhabited Chaldea. 2. an astrologer or soothsayer.

ŏ in drag*on,* ōō in cr*ude,* oo in w*ool,* u in c*u*p, ū in c*u*re, ũ in t*u*rn, ŭ in f*o*cus, oi in b*oy,* ou in h*ou*se, th in *thin,* *th* in shea*th*e, g in g*et,* j in *j*oy, y in *y*et.

chal·dron (chôl'drŏn), *n.* in England, a measure for coal or coke, equal to 36 bushels.

cha·let (sha-lā'), *n.* 1. a Swiss cottage or herdsman's dwelling. 2. a Swiss house with overhanging eaves. 3. a house or other building in this style.

chal·ice (chal'is), *n.* 1. a cup. 2. a cup used in the sacrament of Holy Communion.

chalk (chôk), *n.* 1. a soft limestone rock consisting chiefly of minute seashells. 2. prepared chalk for drawing, as on a blackboard: *adj.* pertaining to, made of, or drawn with chalk: *v.t.* 1. to rub, smear, or whiten with chalk. 2. to write or draw with chalk: *v.i.* to become powdery, as a painted surface from weathering.

chalk·board (chôk'bôrd), *n.* same as **blackboard**.

chalk·stone ('stōn), *n.* same as **tophus.**

chalk·y ('i), *adj.* **chalk'i·er, chalk'i·est,** 1. of, containing, or smeared with chalk. 2. of the consistency of chalk. 3. pasty white. — **chalk'i·ness,** *n.*

chal·lenge (chal'ẽnj), *n.* 1. a summons or invitation to a contest, duel, etc. 2. an objection taken to a voter or juror. 3. the demand of a sentry on duty for identification. 4. a calling for an explanation. 5. anything that demands special ambition or enterprise: *v.t.* **-lenged, -leng·ing,** 1. to summon to a contest, duel, etc. 2. to make special demands on; stimulate. 3. to stop and demand identification (of). 4. to take exception to: *v.i.* to put forth a challenge. **—chal'leng·er,** *n.*

chal·lis, chal·lie (shal'i), *n.* a light, soft fabric of wool, cotton, etc.

cha·lyb·e·ate (kâ-lib'i-ât), *adj.* impregnated with salts of iron, or tasting like iron.

cham·ber (chām'bẽr), *n.* 1. a private room in a house or apartment, especially a bedroom. 2. pl. a judge's private room near a courtroom. 3. a meeting hall. 4. a judicial or legislative body. 5. a business council. 6. a cavity; enclosed space. 7. the part of a gun that contains the charge or of a revolver that holds a cartridge. **—cham'bered,** *adj.*

cham·ber·lain (chām'bẽr-lin), *n.* 1. an officer who has charge of the living quarters of a sovereign or nobleman. 2. a high official of various royal courts. 3. in England, a treasurer, as of a city or corporation.

cham·ber·maid (-mād), *n.* a maid who takes care of bedrooms, as in a hotel.

chamber music, music to be performed by a small number of musicians, as a trio.

chamber of commerce, an organization of local businessmen to promote the commercial interests of a community.

chamber pot, a portable receptacle for use in a bedroom as a toilet.

cham·bray (sham'brā), *n.* a smooth, cotton fabric, made with white threads woven through a colored warp.

cha·me·le·on (kâ-mēl'yŏn, -mē'li-ŏn), *n.* 1. any one of various insect-eating lizards that can change the color of their skin. 2. a fickle or changeable person.

cham·fer (cham'fẽr), *n.* a beveled edge: *v.t.* 1. to cut a chamfer on. 2. to cut a groove or flute in.

cham·ois (sham'i), *n., pl.* **cham'ois,** 1. a small, goatlike antelope of the mountainous regions of Europe and Asia. 2. a soft, pliant leather made from the skin of the chamois, or from sheepskin, deerskin, etc. 3. a piece of this used as a polishing cloth: also **cham'my,** *pl.* **-mies.**

cham·o·mile (kam'ŏ-mīl, -mēl), *n.* a plant with strong-smelling leaves: its dried flowers are used to make a medicinal tea.

champ (champ), *v.t. & v.i.* 1. to bite upon repeatedly or impatiently. 2. to chew hard and noisily.

champ (champ), *n.* [Slang], a champion.

cham·pagne (sham-pān'), *n.* a light, sparkling, effervescent wine.

cham·paign (sham-pān'), *n.* flat, open country: *adj.* level; open.

cham·per·ty (cham'pẽr-ti), *n., pl.* **-ties,** a sharing in the proceeds of a lawsuit by an outsider who has financed it: illegal in most States.

cham·pi·on (cham'pi-ŏn), *n.* 1. one who defends the cause of another, by combat or other means. 2. a successful competitor against all rivals: *v.t.* to defend or support (a person or cause): *adj.* first among all competitors. **—cham'pi·on·ship,** *n.*

chance (chans), *n.* 1. an unforeseen event. 2. fortune; luck. 3. a possibility or probability. 4. an opportunity. 5. a hazard; risk. 6. a ticket in a lottery: *adj.* occurring by chance: *v.i.* **chanced, chanc'ing,** to have the luck (*to*): *v.t.* to risk.

chan·cel (chan'sl), *n.* the part of a church where the altar stands, sometimes set off by a railing or screen.

chan·cel·ler·y (chan'sě-lě-ri), *n., pl.* **-ler·ies,** 1. the office or position of a chancellor. 2. the room in which he presides. 3. the office of an embassy or consulate.

chan·cel·lor ('sě-lẽr), *n.* 1. a judge of a court of equity or chancery in some States. 2. the president or highest official of some universities. 3. in some countries, the chief minister of state or prime minister. 4. any of various church officials. **—chan'cel·lor·ship,** *n.*

Chancellor of the Exchequer, the minister of finance in the British government.

chance-med·ley (chans'med·li), *n.* justifiable homicide in self-defense.

chan·cer·y (chan'sẽr-i), *n., pl.* **-cer·ies,** 1. in England, a division of the High Court of Justice. 2. a court of equity. 3. the diocesan office that conducts the affairs of a diocese. 4. a court of public record. 5. a chancellery.

chan·cre (shang'kẽr), *n.* the primary or initial sore or ulcer of syphilis. **—chan'crous** ('krŭs), *adj.*

chan·croid ('kroid), *n.* a soft, venereal ulcer caused by a certain bacterium.

chanc·y (chan'si), *adj.* **chanc'i·er, chanc'i·est,** uncertain; risky.

chan·de·lier (shan-dě-lir'), *n.* a hanging fixture with branches for light bulbs, candles, etc.

chan·dler (chan'dlẽr), *n.* 1. a maker or vendor of candles. 2. a dealer or merchant, as of ship supplies. **—chan'dler·y,** *n., pl.* **-dler·ies.**

change (chānj), *v.t.* **changed, chang'ing,** 1. to alter. 2. to substitute. 3. to exchange or give an equivalent for: *v.i.* 1. to undergo change;

alter. 2. to pass from one place, vehicle, phase, etc. to another. 3. to put on other clothes. 4. to make an exchange: *n.* 1. an alteration or variation. 2. a substitution. 3. the balance of money returned when the amount paid is greater than the cost. 4. small coins. 5. variety; novelty. 6. a different set of clothes. —change'a·ble, *adj.* —change'a·bly, *adv.* —change'less, *adj.*

change·ling (chānj'ling), *n.* 1. a child left in place of another. 2. [Archaic], an idiot.

change of life, same as **menopause.**

change-o·ver (chānj'ō·vẽr), *n.* a complete change or conversion from one thing to another.

chan·nel (chan'l), *n.* 1. the bed of a stream. 2. the deepest part of a strait, bay, harbor, etc. 3. a passage of water connecting two large bodies of water. 4. any means of access, transmission, conveyance, etc. 5. *pl.* the official course for communications. 6. a groove. 7. a band of frequencies used by a radio or television station: *v.t.* -neled *or* -nelled, -nel·ing *or* -nel·ling, 1. to cut into a channel; groove. 2. to direct into a channel.

chan·nel·ize (chan'l-īz), *v.t.* -ized, -iz·ing, 1. to direct into a channel. 2. to furnish a channel for. —chan·nel·i·za'tion, *n.*

chan·son (shän-sōn'), *n., pl.* -sons' (-sōn'), [French], a song.

chant (chant), *n.* 1. a song. 2. any of many simple, solemn songs used in church services, in which many words are sung to a single tone. 3. a monotonous way of speaking: *v.t.* 1. to sing. 2. to intone. 3. to celebrate in song. 4. to say in a monotone: *v.i.* 1. to sing a chant. 2. to speak in a monotone. —chant'er, *n.*

chan·teuse (shän-tooz'), *n.* [French], a woman singer of popular ballads.

chan·tey (shan'ti, chan'ti), *n., pl.* -teys, a song sung by sailors at work, in rhythm with their motions: also **chan'ty,** *pl.* -ties.

chan·ti·cleer (chan'ti-klir), *n.* a rooster or cock: name used in folklore.

chan·try (chan'tri), *n., pl.* -tries, 1. an endowment for the saying of Masses for a deceased person's soul. 2. a chapel endowed for this purpose.

cha·os (kā'os), *n.* 1. the confused matter out of which, as in legend, the universe was formed. 2. total confusion or disorder. —cha·ot'ic (-ot'ik), *adj.* —cha·ot'i·cal·ly, *adv.*

chap (chap), *v.t. & v.i.* chapped *or* chapt, chap'ping, to crack or split open, as the skin from exposure to cold: *n.* 1. a chapped spot on the skin. 2. *pl.* the mouth and lower jaw; chops. 3. [Informal], a young fellow.

chap·ar·ral (chap-ä-ral', shap-), *n.* [Southwestern U.S.], a dense thicket.

chaparral cock (or bird), same as **roadrunner.**

chap·book (chap'book), *n.* a small book, usually of fairy tales, romances, etc., formerly sold by chapmen.

chape (chāp), *n.* a metal mounting or tip on a scabbard or sheathe.

cha·peau (sha·pō'), *n., pl.* -peaus', -peaux' (-pōz'), [French], a hat.

chap·el (chap'l), *n.* 1. a small place of Christian worship, subordinate to a church. 2. a place of worship in a palace, school, etc. 3.

in Great Britain, a place of worship of those not in the established church. 4. an association of workers in a printing house.

chap·er·on, chap·er·one (shap'ẽ-rōn), *n.* a person, usually an older woman, who supervises young unmarried people in public: *v.t. & v.i.* -oned, -on·ing, to act as chaperon (to). —chap'er·on·age, *n.*

chap·fall·en (chap'fô·lẽn, chap'-), *adj.* dejected; chagrined; dispirited.

chap·i·ter (chap'i-tẽr), *n.* the upper part, or capital, of a pillar.

chap·lain (chap'lĭn),' *n.* 1. a clergyman who conducts services in a chapel. 2. a clergyman who serves in the armed forces or in a hospital, prison, etc.

chap·lain·cy (-si), *n., pl.* -cies, the office or status of a chaplain: also **chap'lain·ship.**

chap·let (chap'lit), *n.* 1. a wreath or garland encircling the head. 2. a string of prayer beads. 3. any string of beads. 4. a round molding carved with small, beadlike decorations.

chap·man (chap'mǎn), *n., pl.* -men, [British], formerly, an itinerant merchant or peddler; hawker of wares.

chaps (chaps, shaps), *n.* seatless leather trousers worn over regular trousers by cowboys.

chap·ter (chap'tẽr), *n.* 1. a division of a book. 2. a meeting of certain clergy or of the members of a religious order. 3. a local branch of an organization, society, etc.: *v.t.* to divide into chapters.

char (chär), *v.t. & v.i.* charred, char'ring, 1. to burn or reduce to charcoal. 2. to burn partially: *n.* something charred.

char (chär), *n.* 1. same as **chore:** also **chare.** 2. [British], a charwoman: *v.i.* charred, char'ring, 1. to do chores. 2. [Chiefly British], to work as a charwoman.

char (chär), *n., pl.* chars, char, a kind of trout with small scales and a reddish belly.

char·a·banc, char·à·banc (sher'a-bangk), *n.* [British], a large, open sightseeing bus with long seats facing forward.

char·ac·ter (ker'ik-tẽr), *n.* 1. a letter, symbol, or figure used in printing or writing. 2. a distinctive quality or trait. 3. the essential nature of something or someone. 4. the moral quality of a person or group. 5. moral excellence. 6. reputation. 7. a person in a novel, movie, etc. 8. a reference as to conduct or ability. 9. [Informal], one who is eccentric.

char·ac·ter·is·tic (ker-ik-tẽr-is'tik), *adj.* of or indicating the character; distinctive: *n.* a distinctive feature, trait, etc. —char·ac·ter·is'ti·cal·ly, *adv.*

char·ac·ter·ize (ker'ik-tẽr-īz), *v.t.* -ized, -iz·ing, 1. to describe by particular qualities. 2. to mark or distinguish. —char·ac·ter·i·za'tion, *n.*

cha·rade (shā·rād'), *n. often pl.* a game in which a saying, phrase, or word to be guessed is visually portrayed.

char·coal (chär'kōl), *n.* 1. a black, porous substance resulting from the incomplete combustion of organic matter, as wood, in kilns from which air is excluded. 2. a pencil of this, or a drawing made with it. 3. an almost black color.

chard (chärd), *n.* a variety of beet with large leaves and succulent stalks, used as a vegetable.

charge (chärj), *v.t.* charged, charg'ing, 1. to rush on or attack. 2. to load or fill; also, to give an electrical charge to (a battery). 3. to impose or command as a duty, injunction, etc. 4. to instruct. 5. to accuse. 6. to make responsible for. 7. to ask as a price. 8. to place on the debit side: *v.i.* 1. to make an attack. 2. to demand a price: *n.* 1. an onset. 2. the quantity with which a firearm or device is charged; also, the quantity of chemical energy in a battery. 3. an obligation, or a person or thing entrusted to one's care. 4. an order or command. 5. authoritative instructions. 6. an entry on the debit side. 7. an accusation. 8. cost or price. 9. [Slang], a thrill. —charge'a-ble, *adj.*

charge account, an agreement between a customer and a business establishment by which goods may be bought on credit and billed at a later time.

char·gé d'af·faires (shär-zhä' dá-fer'), *pl.* **chargés d'affaires** (shär-zhäz' dá-fer', shär-zhä'), [French], 1. a government official who acts for an ambassador or minister in his absence. 2. a diplomatic official sent to a foreign country but ranking below an ambassador or minister.

charge plate, a plastic or metal plate bearing a customer's name and charge-account number and used in making credit purchases: also **charge-a-plate** (chärj'á-plāt), *n.*

charg·er (chärj'ēr), *n.* 1. a person or thing that charges. 2. a spirited cavalry horse. 3. a device for charging storage batteries.

char·i·ly (cher'i-li), *adv.* in a chary way.

char·i·ness ('i-nès), *n.* 1. the quality of being chary or cautious. 2. frugality.

char·i·ot (cher'i-ôt), *n.* an ancient, horse-drawn, two-wheeled cart for war, processions, racing, etc.

char·i·ot·eer (cher-i-ô-tir'), *n.* one who drives a chariot.

cha·ris·ma (ká-riz'má), *n., pl.* **-ma·ta** ('má-tá), 1. a divinely inspired quality. 2. a special quality of leadership. Also **char·ism** (ker'izm). —**char·is·mat·ic** (ker-iz-mat'ik), *adj.*

char·i·ta·ble (cher'i-tá-bl), *adj.* 1. benevolent; liberal; generous. 2. forgiving; merciful. 3. of, pertaining to, or for charity. —**char'i·ta·ble·ness,** *n.* —**char'i·ta·bly,** *adv.*

char·i·ty (cher'i-ti), *n., pl.* **-ties,** 1. in *Christian Theology,* spiritual love for mankind. 2. mercy or leniency in judging others. 3. liberality in giving to those in need; also, alms or gifts given. 4. an act of charity. 5. a charitable fund, institution, etc.

cha·ri·va·ri (shá-riv-á-rē', shiv'á-ri), *n.* 1. same as shivaree. 2. din; noise.

char·la·tan (shär'lá-tn), *n.* a quack; fraud. —**char'la·tan·ism, char'la·tan·ry,** *pl.* **-ries,** *n.*

Charles·ton (chärl'stŏn), *n.* a lively dance popular in the 1920's.

char·ley horse (chär'li), [Informal], a painful cramp in the arm or leg muscles, resulting from strain.

char·lotte (shär'lŏt), *n.* a dessert in which a

mold is lined with cake or bread and filled with fruit, custard, etc.

charlotte russe (rōōs), a charlotte of sponge-cake, whipped cream, custard, etc.

charm (chärm), *n.* 1. a spell or enchantment; also, an action, object, or utterance supposedly casting a spell or enchantment. 2. a quality of allurement or attraction. 3. a trinket worn on a bracelet, watch chain, etc.: *v.t. & v.i.* 1. to influence as if by magic. 2. to fascinate; delight.

charm·er ('ēr), *n.* 1. one who seems to cast a charm, or spell. 2. one who attracts or delights; a fascinating person.

char·meuse (shär-mōōz'), *n.* a soft, clinging silk cloth with a satin finish.

charm·ing (chärm'ing), *adj.* fascinating; alluring. —**charm'ing·ly,** *adv.*

char·nel (chär'nl), *n.* a building where dead bodies or bones are deposited: in full, **charnel house:** *adj.* sepulchral; deathlike; of or like a charnel.

charr (chär), *n., pl.* **charrs, charr,** same as char (the fish).

char·ry (chär'i), *adj.* **-ri·er, -ri·est,** like charcoal.

chart (chärt), *n.* 1. a map, especially one for use of a navigator. 2. an outline map showing special information, as about the weather. 3. a sheet with information in tabular form. 4. tables, diagrams, etc. on such a sheet: *v.t.* 1. to delineate on a chart. 2. to map out (a plan, route, etc.). —**chart'·less,** *adj.*

char·ter (chär'tēr), *n.* 1. a document setting forth certain rights or privileges to a person, corporation, etc., granted by a government or ruler. 2. a document stating basic principles; constitution. 3. a written permit for the establishment of a local chapter of a society. 4. an agreement or contract, as for the lease of a bus, airplane, etc.: *v.t.* 1. to bestow a charter on, or set up by charter. 2. to hire or lease (a bus, airplane, etc.).

charter member, an original member of an organization, club, etc.

charter party, an agreement between the owner of a ship and a carrier, merchant, etc. for the lease of the ship or certain space aboard her for a voyage or period of time.

char·treuse (shär-trōōz'), *n.* 1. a liqueur originally made in a certain monastery in France. 2. a clear, yellowish green.

char·wom·an (chär'woom-án), *n., pl.* **-wom·en,** a woman hired to do heavy cleaning, as in an office.

char·y (cher'i), *adj.* **char'i·er, char'i·est,** 1. careful; cautious. 2. sparing.

chase (chās), *v.t.* chased, chas'ing, 1. to pursue in order to capture or hurt. 2. to run after; follow. 3. to hunt. 4. to drive away: *v.i.* 1. to follow in pursuit. 2. [Informal], to rush: *n.* 1. the act of chasing; pursuit. 2. the sport of hunting game. 3. something hunted or chased. 4. [British], open ground for preserving game.

chase (chās), *n.* 1. a groove. 2. a metal frame in which columns or pages of type are secured for printing. 3. the bore of a gun barrel: *v.t.* chased, chas'ing, 1. to work or emboss (metal). 2. to cut a groove in.

---

a in cap, ā in cane, ä in father, à in abet, e in met, ē in be, ê in baker, ê in regent, i in pit, ī in fine, i in manifest, o in hot, ô in horse, ō in bone,

chas-er (chā'sĕr), *n.* 1. one who chases. 2. a gun at the stern or bow of a ship. 3. [Informal], a mild drink, as water, beer, etc., taken after a stronger one, as whiskey.

chas-er (chā'sĕr), *n.* 1. an engraver. 2. a tool for cutting screw threads.

chasm (kazm), *n.* 1. a deep gap or opening in the earth. 2. any breach or gap; rift.

chasse-pot (shas-pō'), *n.* a French breech-loading rifle used in the 19th century.

chas-seur (sha-sûr'), *n.* 1. a French cavalry or light-infantry soldier. 2. a uniformed attendant.

chas-sis (chas'i, shas'i), *n., pl.* **-sis** ('iz), 1. the framework and parts, as of a television or radio set. 2. the frame, wheels, etc. of an automobile, but not the engine or body. 3. the frame of the body of an aircraft.

chaste (chāst), *adj.* 1. characterized by abstinence from unlawful sexual activity. 2. characterized by abstinence from all sexual activity. 3. modest; decent. 4. simple in style; refined. —**chaste'ly**, *adv.* —**chaste'ness**, *n.*

chas-ten (chās'n), *v.t.* 1. to punish so as to reform. 2. to temper; restrain. 3. to purify or refine. —**chas'ten-er**, *n.*

chas-tise (chas-tīz'), *v.t.* **-tised'**, **-tis'ing**, 1. to punish or discipline, as by whipping. 2. to reprimand severely. —**chas-tise'ment**, *n.* —**chas-tis'er**, *n.*

chas-ti-ty (chas'ti-ti), *n.* the quality or state of being chaste; chasteness; purity.

chas-u-ble (chaz'yoo-bl, chas'-), *n.* a sleeveless outer vestment worn over the alb by a priest celebrating Mass.

chat (chat), *v.i.* **chat'ted**, **chat'ting**, to talk in an easy, familiar manner: *n.* informal or familiar talk.

châ-teau, **cha-teau** (sha-tō'), *n., pl.* **-teaux** (-tōz', -tō'), **-teaus**, 1. a French castle. 2. a French manor house and estate.

chat-e-laine (shat'l-ān), *n.* 1. the mistress of a château. 2. a woman's decorative chain or clasp worn at the waist, sometimes with a purse, keys, etc. suspended from it.

chat-tel (chat'l), *n.* a movable article of personal property.

chat-ter (chat'ĕr), *v.i.* 1. to utter short sounds rapidly, as monkeys do. 2. to click the teeth together, as in shivering or from fright. 3. to talk idly, rapidly, and mindlessly; jabber: *v.t.* to utter rapidly, idly, or indistinctly: *n.* 1. the sound or act of chattering. 2. idle, rapid talk. —**chat'ter-er**, *n.*

chat-ter-box (-boks), *n.* an incessant talker.

chat-ty (chat'i), *adj.* **-ti-er**, **-ti-est**, 1. talkative. 2. having a conversational tone or style. —**chat'ti-ly**, *adv.* —**chat'ti-ness**, *n.*

chauf-feur (shō'fĕr, shō-fûr'), *n.* one employed to drive a private automobile: *v.t.* to drive as a chauffeur.

chau-vin-ism (shō'vĭ-nizm), *n.* 1. blind, unreasoning, and militant patriotism; jingoism. 2. blind attachment to one's own party, sex, race, etc., with contempt for others not of it. —**chau'vin-ist**, *n. & adj.* —**chau-vin-is'tic**, *adj.* —**chau-vin-is'ti-cal-ly**, *adv.*

cheap (chēp), *adj.* 1. inexpensive. 2. worth more than the cost. 3. requiring little work or effort. 4. of small value. 5. petty. 6. [Informal], stingy: *adv.* at low cost. —**cheap'ly**, *adv.* —**cheap'ness**, *n.*

cheap-en ('n), *v.t. & v.i.* to make or become cheap or cheaper.

cheap-skate ('skāt), *n.* [Slang], one who is stingy.

cheat (chēt), *n.* 1. a fraud or deception. 2. one who practices fraud or deception: *v.t.* 1. to deceive or defraud. 2. to elude or escape: *v.i.* 1. to act as a cheat. 2. to violate rules. 3. [Slang], to be sexually unfaithful. —**cheat'er**, *n.*

check (chek), *n.* 1. a sudden stop or break. 2. a restraint. 3. something or someone that stops or restrains. 4. a test, scrutiny, etc. to see if something is as it should be. 5. a mark to indicate something has been given attention: also called **check mark**. 6. a ticket, token, etc. 7. a bill, as at a restaurant. 8. a vulnerable position of the king in the game of chess. 9. a small square that is one of a pattern, or this pattern. 10. an order or draft on a bank for money: *interj.* [Informal], that's right!: *v.t.* 1. to stop suddenly. 2. to restrain. 3. to examine by comparison. 4. to mark as having been examined. 5. to place (the opponent's king) in danger at chess. 6. to mark in small squares. 7. to leave (something) temporarily, as in a checkroom. 8. to turn over luggage for shipment: *v.i.* 1. to correspond. 2. to investigate. —**check'er**, *n.*

check-book ('book), *n.* a book of blank checks for use in writing checks on a bank.

check-er ('ĕr), *n.* 1. one of the squares of a checkered pattern. 2. a flat, round piece with which to play checkers. 3. *pl.* a game played on a checkerboard by two people with twelve playing pieces each: *v.t.* 1. to mark off in squares. 2. to diversify in color, pattern, character, etc.

check-er-board (-bōrd), *n.* a board for playing checkers or chess, marked off in 64 squares of two alternating colors.

check-ered (chek'ĕrd), *adj.* 1. having a pattern of squares. 2. diversified in color, pattern, character, etc.

checking account, an account that a depositor has in a bank, against which the depositor can draw checks without presenting the bankbook.

check-list ('list), *n.* a list of things to be checked, referred to, etc.: also **check list**.

check-mate ('māt), *n.* 1. the winning move at chess when the opponent's king cannot move out of check; also, the king's position entailing this move. 2. any blocking play making escape or victory impossible: *v.t.* **-mat-ed**, **-mat-ing**, to subject to a checkmate.

check-off ('ôf), *n.* the deduction of union dues from wages by an employer.

check-out ('out), *n.* 1. the itemization and totaling of purchases, as at a supermarket; also, the place for doing this. 2. the time a person is due to settle a bill, as in a hotel, and leave the premises. 3. inspection, as for accuracy or proper performance. Also **check-out**.

ŏ in drag*on*, ōō in cr*u*de, oo in w*oo*l, u in c*u*p, ū in c*u*re, ū in t*u*rn, u in f*o*cus, oi in b*oy*, ou in h*ou*se, th in *th*in, *th* in shea*th*e, g in *g*et, j in *j*oy, y in *y*et.

check·point ('point), *n.* a place, as on a border, where travelers, cars, etc. are inspected.

check·rein ('rān), *n.* a short rein from bridle to saddle to keep up a horse's head.

check·room ('rōōm), *n.* a room in which baggage, coats, etc. may be kept temporarily, under an attendant's care.

check·up ('up), *n.* a checkout or inspection, especially with regard to health.

Ched·dar (ched'ēr), *n.* [often c-], a kind of smooth, hard cheese: also **Cheddar cheese.**

che·der (kä'dēr), *n.* same as **heder.**

cheek (chēk), *n.* 1. the side of the face beneath either eye. 2. either of two corresponding sides. 3. [Informal], cool impudence.

cheek·bone ('bōn), *n.* the bony prominence just below either eye.

cheek·y ('i), *adj.* **cheek'i·er, cheek'i·est,** [Informal], impudent; brazen. **—cheek'i·ly,** *adv.* **—cheek'i·ness,** *n.*

cheep (chēp), *n.* the short, shrill noise made by a young chicken; peep: *v.i. & v.t.* to make, or express by, cheeps. **—cheep'er,** *n.*

cheer (chir), *n.* 1. temper or state of mind. 2. gladness; joy. 3. a shout of approval, joy, encouragement, etc. 4. anything that gives one happiness or comfort. 5. provisions for a feast: *v.t.* 1. to gladden. 2. to encourage or inspire. 3. to show approval of, joy over, etc. by shouting cheers: *v.i.* 1. to become cheerful or more cheerful (with *up*). 2. to shout cheers.

cheer·ful ('ful), *adj.* 1. full of good spirits. 2. pleasant and bright. 3. helpful and hearty. **—cheer'ful·ly,** *adv.* **—cheer'ful·ness,** *n.*

cheer·i·o ('i-ō), *interj. & n.,* pl. **-i·os,** [Chiefly British], goodbye.

cheer·lead·er ('lē-dēr), *n.* a person who leads others in cheering, as for a football team.

cheer·less ('lis), *adj.* devoid of cheer; dreary; gloomy; dismal. **—cheer'less·ly,** *adv.* **—cheer'less·ness,** *n.*

cheer·y ('i), *adj.* **cheer'i·er, cheer'i·est,** cheerful; gay. **—cheer'i·ly,** *adv.* **—cheer'i·ness,** *n.*

cheese (chēz), *n.* a dairy food made of pressed or molded milk curds.

cheese (chēz), *n.* [Slang], a person or thing that is important.

cheese·burg·er (chēz'būr-gēr), *n.* a hamburger with melted cheese on the patty.

cheese·cake ('kāk), *n.* 1. a cake made with sugar, eggs, etc. and cottage cheese or cream cheese. 2. [Slang], photographs of pretty girls, especially pictures that show off the legs.

cheese·cloth ('klôth), *n.* a flimsy, thin, loosely woven cotton cloth.

cheese·par·ing ('per-ing), *adj.* miserly: *n.* 1. something of little value, as a paring of cheese rind. 2. miserliness.

chees·y ('i), *adj.* **chees'i·er, chees'i·est,** 1. having the taste, smell, etc. of cheese. 2. [Slang], inferior. **—chees'i·ness,** *n.*

chee·tah (chēt'ā), *n.* a swift, leopardlike animal of Africa and southern Asia.

chef (shef), *n.* 1. a head cook. 2. any cook.

chef-d'oeu·vre (shā-dūv'rē), [French], a masterpiece.

chem·i·cal (kem'i-kl), *adj.* 1. of or pertaining to chemistry. 2. used in chemistry. 3. operated or produced by chemicals: *n.* a substance used in or produced by chemistry. **—chem'i·cal·ly,** *adv.*

chemical abuse, the habitual use of a mood-altering drug, alcoholic beverage, etc. **—chemical a·bus·er** (ā-bū'zēr).

chemical engineering, scientific application of chemistry to use in industry.

chemical warfare, warfare using poisonous gases or other chemicals.

che·mise (shē-mēz'), *n.* 1. a woman's short, loose undergarment. 2. a loose dress that hangs straight.

chem·ist (kem'ist), *n.* 1. one skilled in chemistry. 2. [British], a pharmacist.

chem·is·try (kem'is-tri), *n.* the science treating of the properties, composition, and transformations of substances.

chem·o·ther·a·py (kem-ō-ther'ā-pi), *n.* the treatment of disease or infection by the use of chemical drugs: also **chem·o·ther·a·peu'tics** (-ther-ā-pūt'iks). **—chem·o·ther·a·peu'tic,** *adj.* **—chem·o·ther'a·pist,** *n.*

che·nille (shi-nēl'), *n.* 1. a fluffy, velvety cord or yarn. 2. a fabric made from this.

cheque (chek), *n.* British form for **check** (sense 10).

cher·ish (cher'ish), *v.t.* 1. to hold dear. 2. to treat with tenderness; protect and aid. 3. to cling to in the mind.

Cher·o·kee (cher'ō-kē), *n.,* pl. **-kees, -kee,** a member of a tribe of American Indians originally of the southeastern U.S.

che·root (shē-rōōt'), *n.* a cigar with both ends cut square.

cher·ry (cher'i), *n.,* pl. **-ries,** 1. a small, pulpy, red or yellow fruit with a hard stone. 2. the tree it grows on, or the tree wood. 3. bright red: *adj.* 1. of or flavored like cherries. 2. bright-red. 3. of cherry wood.

cher·ub (cher'ūb), *n.,* 1. pl. **-u·bim** ('ū-bim, 'yoo-bim) or **-u·bims,** in the Bible, any of certain angels of heaven. 2. pl. **-ubs,** an especially beautiful baby or small child. **—che·ru·bic** (chē-rōō'bik), *adj.*

chess (ches), *n.* a game played by two with 16 shaped pieces each on a board like a checkerboard.

chess·man ('man, 'mån), *n.,* pl. **-men,** any piece used in chess.

chest (chest), *n.* 1. a box with a lid. 2. a cabinet with shelves, as for medicines, or drawers, as for clothes. 3. the part of the body enclosed by the breastbone and ribs.

ches·ter·field (ches'tēr-fēld), *n.* a topcoat with a velvet collar.

chest·nut (ches'nut), *n.* 1. the edible nut of certain trees of the beech family. 2. such a tree, or its wood. 3. a reddish-brown color. 4. a horse of such color. 5. [Informal], an old or stale joke, phrase, story, etc.: *adj.* reddish-brown.

che·val-de-frise (shē-val-dē-frēz'), *n.,* pl. **che·vaux-de-frise'** (shē-vō-), [French], 1. a timber or bar with long iron spikes to hinder cavalry. 2. projections of sharp stones, iron spikes, pieces of glass, etc. at the top of a wall.

---

a in cap, ā in cane, ä in father, à in abet, e in met, ē in be, ē in baker, è in regent, i in pit, ī in fine, i in manifest, o in hot, ô in horse, ō in bone,

che·val glass (shĕ-val′), a full-length mirror that may be tilted in its frame.

chev·a·lier (shev-å-lir′), *n.* 1. formerly, a knight. 2. a member of a French military society. 3. a gallant; cavalier.

Chev·i·ot (chev′i-ŏt), *n.* 1. one of a breed of sheep with short, heavy fleece. 2. (shev′i-ŏt), [usually c-], a rough fabric of, or suggestive of, such fleece.

chev·ron (shev′rŏn), *n.* an insignia in the shape of a V or inverted V, worn on the sleeve to show rank or service.

chev·ro·tain (shev′rŏ-tān), *n.* a small, deerlike, hornless ruminant of western Africa and southwestern Asia.

chev·y (chev′i), *n.*, *pl.* **chev′ies**, [British], a hunt; pursuit: *v.t.* & *v.i.* **chev′ied, chev′y·ing,** [British], 1. to hunt; pursue. 2. to worry, fret, or nag.

chew (chōō), *v.t.* 1. to crush and grind with the teeth; masticate. 2. to meditate upon. 3. to scold severely (often followed by *out*): *v.i.* 1. to chew something. 2. [Informal], to chew tobacco: *n.* 1. the act of chewing. 2. something to be chewed; specifically, a quid of chewing tobacco. **—chew′er,** *n.*

chew·ing gum (chōō′ing), a preparation for chewing, as chicle, flavored and sweetened.

chew·y (′i), *adj.* **chew′i·er, chew′i·est,** 1. requiring much chewing. 2. inviting pleasurable chewing, as some candies.

chi (kī), *n.* the 22d letter of the Greek alphabet.

Chi·an·ti (ki-än′ti), *n.* [Italian], a certain kind of dry, red wine.

chi·a·ro·scu·ro (ki-är-ŏ-skyoor′ō), *n.*, *pl.* **-ros,** 1. treatment of light and shade, as in a drawing or engraving. 2. a work of art emphasizing this.

chi·bouk, chi·bouque (chi-bōōk′), *n.* a long tobacco pipe with a clay bowl.

chic (shēk), *adj.* **chic·quer** (shēk′ēr), **chic′quest** (′ist), stylish; smart: *n.* elegance of style or dress.

chi·cane (shi-kān′), *n.* same as **chicanery:** *v.t.* **-caned′, -can′ing,** 1. to trick. 2. to quibble over: *v.i.* to use chicanery.

chi·can·er·y (′ēr-i), *n.*, *pl.* **-er·ies,** 1. a trick or artifice used to deceive or cheat. 2. the practice of using such tricks.

Chi·ca·no (chē-kä′nō), *n.*, *pl.* **-nos,** [also c-], a U.S. citizen or resident of Mexican descent.

chi·chi, chi·chi (shē′shē, chē′chē), *adj.* very chic, stylish, elegant, etc. in an affected way: *n.* a chichi quality.

chick (chik), *n.* 1. the young of a bird, especially of a domestic fowl. 2. a child. 3. [Slang], a young woman.

chick·a·dee (chik′å-dē), *n.* any one of certain small birds related to titmice.

chick·a·ree (chik′å-rē), *n.* a red squirrel of the western U.S.

chick·en (chik′ĕn), *n.* 1. the common domestic fowl, especially when young, raised for its eggs and meat. 2. the meat. 3. [Slang], a fearful person: *adj.* 1. made of chicken meat. 2. [Slang], fearful: *v.i.* [Slang], to quit because of fear (often with *out*).

chicken feed, [Slang], a very small amount of money.

chick·en-heart·ed (-här′tid), *adj.* timid; fearful: also **chick′en-liv·ered.**

chicken pox, an acute, contagious virus disease of children, marked by skin eruptions.

chick·pea (chik′pē), *n.* 1. an annual plant of the legume family, bearing hairy pods. 2. the edible seeds.

chick·weed (′wēd), *n.* a low-growing plant of the pink family, often found as a weed in lawns.

chic·le (chik′l), *n.* a gumlike substance from the sapodilla tree, used to make chewing gum.

chic·o·ry (chik′ō-ri), *n.*, *pl.* **-ries,** 1. a perennial plant with blue flowers and with leaves that are used for salad. 2. its root, roasted, ground, and added to or substituted for coffee.

chide (chīd), *v.t.* & *v.i.* **chid′ed** or **chid, chid′ed** or **chid** or **chid′den, chid′ing,** to reprove, usually mildly.

chief (chēf), *n.* a commander or leader; head or principal person: *adj.* 1. of the first order or rank; foremost. 2. principal; main.

chief·ly (′li), *adj.* of or like a chief: *adv.* 1. above all; principally. 2. mostly.

chief·tain (′tin), *n.* a chief, specifically of a clan or tribe.

chif·fon (shi-fon′), *n.* a sheer, filmy fabric of silk, nylon, etc.: *adj.* 1. of chiffon. 2. made light and spongy as by adding beaten egg whites.

chif·fo·nier, chif·fon·nier (shif-ŏ-nir′), *n.* a high chest of drawers.

chig·ger (chig′ēr), *n.* 1. the tiny, red larva of some mites: its bite causes severe itching. 2. same as **chigoe.**

chi·gnon (shēn′yon), *n.* a roll or coil of hair worn at the back of the neck by women.

chig·oe (chig′ō), *n.*, *pl.* **-oes** (′ōz), 1. a species of South American and African flea: the female chigoe burrows into the skin, causing sores. 2. same as **chigger.**

Chi·hua·hua (chi-wä′wä), *n.* a Mexican breed of very small dog.

chil·blain (chil′blān), *n.* a sore or swelling, as on the hands, from frost or cold.

child (chīld), *n.*, *pl.* **chil′dren,** 1. a son or daughter. 2. a young person or baby. 3. a person thought of as the product of a given place, time, influence, etc. 4. a descendant. 5. a person immature in judgment.

child·birth (′bûrth), *n.* the act of bringing forth a child; parturition.

childe (chīld), *n.* [Archaic], a youth of noble birth.

child·hood (chīld′hood), *n.* the time from infancy to puberty.

child·ish (′ish), *adj.* 1. of or like a child. 2. puerile; immature. **—child′ish·ly,** *adv.* **—child′ish·ness,** *n.*

child·less (′lis), *adj.* without children. **—child′less·ness,** *n.*

child·like (′līk), *adj.* of or like a child, as in innocence or simplicity.

chil·i (chil′i), *n.*, *pl.* **chil′ies,** 1. a tropical American plant bearing a very hot red pepper. 2. the dried pod, often ground for use

as a seasoning. 3. same as **chill con carne.**
Also spelled **chil'e** ('i), **chil'li.**

chil·i·ad (kil'i·ad), *n.* 1. a thousand. 2. a thousand years.

chil·i·asm (kil'i·azm), *n.* belief that the millennium will come.

chili con car·ne (kòn kär'ni), an originally Mexican dish of chopped meat, chilies or chili powder, onions, beans, and often tomatoes.

chili sauce, a sauce used as a condiment, made of chopped tomatoes, spices, green and red sweet peppers, and onions.

chill (chil), *n.* 1. a shivery coldness. 2. a moderate coolness. 3. a sudden onset of fear or apprehension. 4. a depressing, discouraging, or hostile manner or influence: *adj.* same as cool. **chilly:** *v.i. & v.t.* to make or become cold or cool.

chill·y ('i), *adj.* **chill'i·er, chill'i·est,** feeling, causing, or marked by coldness or a chill; cold. —**chill'i·ness,** *n.*

chime (chim), *n.* 1. *usually pl.* a set of bells or metal tubes tuned to a musical scale and struck with a hammer. 2. a single bell, as in a clock. 3. *usually pl.* the musical harmony of chimes: *v.i.* **chimed, chim'ing,** 1. to ring with the sound of a chime or chimes. 2. to harmonize; agree: *v.t.* to ring or signal as with a chime or chimes.

Chi·me·ra, Chi·mae·ra (ki·mir'ā, kī-), *n.* 1. in Greek Mythology, a fire-breathing monster with a lion's head, a goat's body, and a serpent's tail. 2. [c-], an impossible conception of the imagination.

chi·mer·i·cal (ki·mir'i·kl, -mer'i-), *adj.* 1. merely imaginary; fantastic; unreal. 2. inclined to make fanciful plans. Also **chi·mer'ic.** —**chi·mer'i·cal·ly,** *adv.*

chim·ney (chim'ni), *n., pl.* **-neys,** 1. the vent or passage through which smoke escapes from a fire, often extending above the roof. 2. a glass tube around a lamp flame.

chim·pan·zee (chim·pan·zē', -pan'zē), *n.* a medium-sized anthropoid ape of the forests of Africa, noted for its intelligence: also [Informal], **chimp** (chimp).

chin (chin), *n.* the part of the face below the lower lip: *v.t.* **chinned, chin'ning,** to pull (oneself) up, having grasped a horizontal bar above the head so that the body hangs free, until the chin is just above the bar: *v.i.* [Slang], to chat idly.

chi·na (chi'nā), *n.* 1. porcelain, originally from China. 2. vitrified ceramic ware like porcelain. 3. any earthenware. 4. dishes, figurines, etc. made of china. Also **chi'na·ware.**

chinch (chinch), *n.* 1. same as **bedbug.** 2. a small, black bug destructive to grain plants: also **chinch bug.**

chin·chil·la (chin·chil'ā), *n.* 1. a small South American rodent with a soft, fine, gray fur. 2. this valuable fur. 3. a heavy woolen material used for coats.

chine (chin), *n.* 1. the backbone or spine of an animal. 2. a piece of the backbone of an animal with adjacent parts, cut for cooking. 3. [British Dialectal], a rocky ravine or large fissure in a cliff.

Chi·nese (chī·nēz'), *adj.* of or pertaining to China, a large country of eastern Asia, or its people: *n.* 1. *pl.* **-nese'**, a native or inhabitant of China. 2. the languages of China, or any one of these.

Chinese checkers, a game in which marbles are moved as checkers, on a board with holes in a star-shaped pattern.

chink (chingk), *n.* a small fissure opening lengthwise; slit; crack: *v.t.* to fill up the chinks in.

chink (chingk), *n.* a sharp metallic or jingling sound, as of coins: *v.t. & v.i.* to make or cause to make this sound; jingle.

chi·no (chē'nō, shē'nō), *n., pl.* **-nos,** 1. a tough cotton cloth used in garments. 2. *pl.* trousers made of this.

chintz (chints), *n.* a cotton cloth, usually glazed, printed in various colors.

chintz·y ('i), *adj.* **chintz'i·er, chintz'i·est,** 1. decorated with chintz. 2. like chintz. 3. [Informal], cheap, gaudy, etc. 4. [Informal], stingy. —**chintz'i·ness,** *n.*

chip (chip), *v.t.* **chipped, chip'ping,** to break, hack, or knock small pieces off from: *v.i.* to break or fly off into small pieces: *n.* 1. a small piece of stone, wood, etc., chipped off. 2. a nick or spot where a piece has been chipped off. 3. a very thin slice of food. 4. a small counter used in gambling games. 5. same as **integrated circuit.**

chipped beef, dried or smoked beef sliced into shavings, often served in a cream sauce.

chip·munk (chip'mungk), *n.* a small squirrel of North America, having dark and light stripes on its back and head.

Chip·pen·dale (chip'n·dāl), *adj.* of or denoting a style of 18th-century furniture with slender, graceful lines and delicately carved rococo work, designed or made by Thomas Chippendale (1718?-79), an English cabinetmaker.

chip·per (chip'ēr), *adj.* [Informal], active; pert; cheerful.

Chip·pe·wa (chip'ē·wô, -wä, -wä), *n., pl.* **-was, -wa,** same as **Ojibwa:** also **Chip'pe·way** (-wā).

chi·rog·ra·phy (kī·rog'rà·fi), *n.* handwriting; penmanship. —**chi·rog'ra·pher,** *n.* —**chi·rograph·ic** (kī·rō·graf'ik), **chi·ro·graph'i·cal,** *adj.*

chi·ro·man·cy (ki'rō·man·si), *n.* same as **palmistry.** —**chi'ro·man·cer,** *n.*

chi·rop·o·dist (ki·rop'ō·dist, kī-), *n.* same as **podiatrist.** —**chi·rop'o·dy,** *n.*

chi·ro·prac·tic (kī·rō·prak'tik), *n.* a method of treatment to cure disease by manipulation of the spine. —**chi'ro·prac·tor,** *n.*

chirp (chûrp), *n.* a short, shrill sound, as made by some birds: *v.i. & v.t.* to make, or utter in, short, shrill notes.

chir·rup (chûr'up, chir'up), *v.i.* to chirp repeatedly: *n.* this sound.

chis·el (chiz'ĕl), *n.* an edged instrument for cutting wood, stone, or metal: *v.i. & v.t.* **-eled or -elled, -el·ing or -el·ling,** 1. to cut, gouge, or engrave with a chisel. 2. [Informal], to cheat, swindle, etc. or obtain thus. —**chis'el·er, chis'el·ler,** *n.*

chit (chit), *n.* 1. a child. 2. a pert, forward girl.

---

chit (chit), *n.* a voucher for a small sum owed for food, drinks, etc.

chit-chat (chit'chat), *n.* informal talk.

chi-tin (kīt'īn), *n.* the outer, hard, horny covering of arthropods. —chi'tin-ous, *adj.*

chit-ter-lings (chit'līnz), *n.* the small intestines of pigs, used for food, usually fried: also [Dialectal], chit'lins, chit'lings.

chiv-al-rous (shiv'l-rŭs), *adj.* 1. of or having to do with chivalry. 2. characterized by courtesy, gallantry, honor, etc. —chiv'al-rous-ly, *adv.* —chiv'al-rous-ness, *n.*

chiv-al-ry (shiv'l-rī), *n.* 1. the medieval system of knighthood. 2. knights collectively. 3. the qualifications of a knight, as gallantry toward women, bravery, nobility, and courtesy. —chiv-al-ric (shi-val'rīk), *adj.*

chives (chīvz), *n.* a hardy plant with a mild onion flavor, the hollow leaves being used for flavoring.

chiv-y, chiv-vy (chiv'ī), *n., pl.* chiv'ies or chiv'vies, [British], same as chevy: *v.t. & v.i.* chiv'ied or chiv'vied, chiv'y-ing or chiv'vy-ing, [British], same as chevy.

chlo-ral (klôr'ăl), *n.* 1. an oily, colorless compound obtained from the action of chlorine on alcohol. 2. a white, crystalline compound used as a sedative: also chloral hydrate.

chlor-am-phen-i-col (klôr-am-fen'ī-kōl), *n.* an antibiotic drug used against many bacterial diseases and some viruses.

chlo-rate (klôr'āt), *n.* a salt of chloric acid.

chlor-dane (klôr'dān), *n.* a toxic oil used as an insecticide: also chlor'dan ('dan).

chlo-ric (klôr'īk), *adj.* of, pertaining to, or containing chlorine.

chloric acid, an acid containing hydrogen, oxygen, and chlorine.

chlo-ride (klôr'īd), *n.* a compound of chlorine with another element or radical.

chloride of lime, a white powder obtained by treating slaked lime with chlorine, used for disinfecting and bleaching.

chlo-ri-nate (klôr'ī-nāt), *v.t.* -nat-ed, -nat-ing, to combine or treat with chlorine. —chlo-ri-na'-tion, *n.*

chlo-rine (klôr'ēn, -īn), *n.* a greenish-yellow, poisonous, gaseous chemical element with an unpleasant odor, used as a disinfectant, bleach, etc.

chlo-ro-form (klôr'ō-fôrm), *n.* a sweetish, colorless liquid compound used as an anesthetic and solvent: *v.t.* to administer chloroform to.

chlo-ro-phyll, chlo-ro-phyl (klôr'ō-fīl), *n.* the green coloring matter in plants.

chlo-ro-sis (klō-rō'sis), *n.* 1. an anemia sometimes affecting adolescent girls that causes the skin to turn a greenish hue. 2. a sickly condition of plants in which some of the green coloring is lost. —chlo-rot'ic (-rot'ik), *adj.*

chlor-prom-a-zine (klôr-prom'ă-zēn), *n.* a synthetic drug used as a tranquilizer.

chock (chok), *n.* a block or wedge that is used to fill a space or that is placed, as under a wheel, to prevent motion: *v.t.* to secure tightly as with chocks: *adv.* as tight or close as possible.

chock-full ('fool'), *adj.* as full as possible.

choc-o-late (chôk'lăt, chok'-), *n.* 1. a powder, syrup, etc. made from roasted and ground cacao seeds. 2. a candy or beverage made from this. 3. a reddish-brown color: *adj.* 1. made, covered, or flavored with chocolate. 2. reddish-brown.

Choc-taw (chok'tô), *n., pl.* -taws, -taw, a member of a tribe of North American Indians now centered in Oklahoma.

choice (chois), *n.* 1. the act of choosing. 2. a thing or person chosen. 3. the right or power to choose; option. 4. the best or preferable part. 5. an assortment from which to choose. 6. an alternative: *adj.* choic'er, choic'est select; carefully chosen. —choice'ly, *adv.* —choice'ness, *n.*

choir (kwīr), *n.* 1. a group of singers organized to sing together, especially in a church. 2. the part of a church for the choir.

choke (chōk), *v.t.* choked, chok'ing, 1. to hinder the breathing of by blocking or compressing the windpipe; suffocate. 2. to block up; clog. 3. to suppress. 4. to cut down air intake in the carburetor of (a gasoline engine) so as to enrich the fuel mixture: *v.i.* 1. to be suffocated. 2. to become clogged, blocked, etc.: *n.* 1. the act or sound of choking. 2. the device controlling the air intake of a carburetor.

choke-damp ('damp), *n.* same as blackdamp.

chok-er (chōk'ēr), *n.* 1. one that chokes. 2. a tight-fitting necklace.

chol-er (kol'ēr), *n.* anger.

chol-er-a (kol'ēr-ă), *n.* a severe infectious disease marked by vomiting and diarrhea.

chol-er-ic (kol'ēr-ik, kō-ler'ik), *adj.* quick-tempered; prone to anger.

cho-les-ter-ol (kō-les'tē-rōl, -rôl), *n.* a sterol found in animal fats and oils and in blood, bile, etc.

chomp (chomp), *v.t. & v.i.* to chew or chew on; munch; champ: *n.* the act of chomping.

choose (chōōz), *v.t.* chose, cho'sen, choos'ing, to take by preference; select: *v.i.* 1. to make a choice. 2. to see fit; desire.

choos-y, choos-ey (chōō'zi), *adj.* choos'i-er, choos'i-est, [Informal], very particular in making a choice; picky.

chop (chop), *v.t.* chopped, chop'ping, to cut, cut up, or cut apart or off with repeated blows; hack or hew: *v.i.* to make a quick, sharp stroke or movement or a series of these: *n.* 1. the act of chopping. 2. a cut of meat from the loin, rib, or shoulder. 3. a short, irregular motion of waves.

chop (chop), *n.* 1. a jaw or cheek. 2. *pl.* the mouth and lower cheeks.

chop (chop), *n.* a mark or brand denoting kind or quality.

chop-house ('hous), *n.* a restaurant specializing in chops, steaks, etc.

chop-per ('ēr), *n.* 1. one that chops. 2. a tool for chopping. 3. *pl.* [Slang], a set of teeth, especially false teeth. 4. [Informal], a helicopter.

chop-py ('ī), *adj.* -pi-er, -pi-est, 1. having the surface broken with short, irregular waves, as a lake. 2. jerky. —chop'pi-ness, *n.*

chop-sticks ('stiks), *n.* two small sticks held in

one hand and used as eating utensils in some countries of Asia.

chop su·ey (chop sōō'ī), a Chinese-American dish of meat, bean sprouts, mushrooms, etc. in a sauce, served over rice.

cho·ral (kôr'ål), adj. of, recited, or sung by a choir or chorus. —cho'ral·ly, adv.

cho·rale, cho·ral (kô·ral'), n. 1. a hymn or other song to be sung by a chorus. 2. a chorus or choir.

chord (kôrd), n. 1. [Poetic], the string of a musical instrument. 2. three or more notes in harmony. 3. a straight line joining two points of an arc of a circle. —chord'al, adj.

chore (chôr), n. a task, especially a recurring or laborious one.

cho·re·a (kô·rē'å), n. a nervous disorder characterized by convulsive twitchings; Saint Vitus' dance.

chor·e·o·graph (kôr'ī·ō·graf), v.t. & v.i. to work out and arrange the steps and movements of (a dance). —chor·e·og'ra·pher (-og'rå·fẽr), n.

chor·e·og·ra·phy (kôr·ī·og'rå·fī), n. 1. the art of dancing. 2. the art of working out and arranging the steps and movements of a dance, especially for the stage, as ballet. —chor·e·o·graph'ic (-ō·graf'ik), adj. —chor·e·o·graph'i·cal·ly, adv.

cho·rine (kôr'ēn), n. [Informal], same as chorus girl.

chor·is·ter (kôr'is·tẽr), n. a choir member.

chor·tle (chôr'tl), v.i. & v.t. -tled, -tling, to chuckle with great glee; a gleeful chuckle. —chor'tler, n.

cho·rus (kôr'ùs), n. 1. a number of people trained to sing or recite together. 2. a group of singers and dancers performing together. 3. the part of a song, show, etc. performed by the chorus. 4. a composition written for a chorus. 5. a part of a song repeated after each verse: v.t. & v.i. to sing or utter as a group.

cho·sen (chō'zn), past participle of choose: adj. selected; preferred.

chow (chou), n. 1. one of a breed of dogs with close, soft, brown or black hair, originally from China. 2. [Slang], food.

chow-chow (chou'chou), n. 1. chopped, mixed pickles in a mustard sauce. 2. an originally Chinese fruit preserve with ginger.

chow·der (chou'dẽr), n. a thick soup, usually with a base of potatoes and onions.

chow mein (chou mān'), a Chinese-American dish of meat, bean sprouts, celery, etc., served with noodles.

chrism (krizm), n. consecrated oil.

Christ (krīst), n. Jesus of Nazareth, considered to be the Messiah by Christians.

chris·ten (kris'n), v.t. 1. to baptize. 2. to give a name to at baptism. 3. to give a name to, as a ship at launching.

Chris·ten·dom (kris'n·dōm), n. Christians or Christian countries.

Chris·tian (kris'chån), n. one who professes belief in Jesus Christ as the Messiah or accepts the teachings of Jesus: adj. 1. of, professing belief in, or accepting Jesus Christ, the teachings of Jesus, or the religion based on these teachings. 2. of or typical of Christians or Christianity.

Christian Era, the era reckoned from the birth of Jesus Christ.

Chris·ti·an·i·ty (kris·chi·an'ī·tī), n. 1. the Christian religion. 2. Christians collectively. 3. the state of being a Christian.

Chris·tian·ize (kris'chå·nīz), v.t. -ized, -iz·ing, 1. to make Christian, as in characteristics. 2. to convert to Christianity. —Chris·tian·i·za'tion, n.

Christian name, a name given at Christian baptism, as distinguished from the family name; Christian first name.

Christian Science, a religion and system of maintaining health, founded by Mary Baker Eddy about 1866: official name, Church of Christ, Scientist. —Christian Scientist.

chris·tie, chris·ty (kris'tī), n., pl. -ties, a high-speed turn in skiing, as for changing direction or slowing down.

Christ·mas (kris'mås), n. the legal holiday and church festival on December 25 celebrating the birth of Jesus Christ.

Christ·mas·tide (-tīd), n. the Christmas season, from Christmas Eve through New Year's Day or to Epiphany (January 6).

Christmas tree, an evergreen or artificial tree decorated at Christmas time with lights and ornaments.

chro·mate (krō'māt), n. a salt or ester of chromic acid.

chro·mat·ic (krō·mat'ik), adj. 1. of or relating to color. 2. highly colored. 3. in Music, a) progressing by half tones. b) including tones not belonging to the diatonic scale: n. 1. a note affected by an accidental. 2. pl. the science or study of colors. —chro·mat'i·cal·ly, adv.

chro·ma·tin (krō'må·tin), n. protoplasmic matter in the nucleus of living cells that contains the genes.

chro·ma·tism (-tizm), n. variant coloring in parts of plants ordinarily green.

chrome (krōm), n. 1. chromium or chromium alloy. 2. chromium plating: v.t. chromed, chrom'ing, to plate with chromium: adj. of or denoting any of various pigments made with chromium.

chro·mi·um (krō'mi·ùm), n. a lustrous, very hard, metallic chemical element with a high resistance to corrosion.

chro·mo·gen (krō'mō·jẽn), n. any substance capable of conversion into a pigment or dye.

chro·mo·some (krō'mō·sōm), n. any of the microscopic bodies in the nucleus of living cells that carry the genes. —chro'mo·so·mal, adj.

chro·mo·sphere (-sfir), n. the atmospheric region between the surface and the corona of the sun or other star.

chron·ic (kron'ik), adj. 1. continuing a long time or recurring: said of a disease. 2. having had a fault, habit, disease, etc. for a long time or repeatedly. 3. ceaseless; perpetual. —chron'i·cal·ly, adv.

chron·i·cle (kron'i·kl), n. a historical record according to date; a register of facts or events chronologically arranged: v.t. -cled, -cling, to record in or as in a chronicle. —chron'i·cler, n.

Chron·i·cles (-klz), n. either of two books of the Bible, I Chronicles and II Chronicles.

chron·o·gram (kron'ō-gram), n. 1. an inscription having words of which certain letters are designed to express a date in Roman numerals. 2. a record made by a chronograph.

chron·o·graph (-graf), n. a device, as a stopwatch, for recording the exact time of an event.

chron·o·log·i·cal (kron-ō-loj'i-kl), adj. 1. of chronology; especially, relating to or containing an account of past events in the order of time. 2. arranged in order of time. Also chron·o·log'ic. —chron·o·log'i·cal·ly, adv.

chro·nol·o·gy (krō-nol'ō-ji), n., pl. -gies, 1. the science of measuring time and dating events. 2. a list or arrangement of events in the order in which they occurred. —chronol'o·gist, chro·nol'o·ger, n.

chro·nom·e·ter (krō-nom'ē·tēr), n. an instrument for measuring time with extreme accuracy.

chron·o·scope (kron'ō-skōp), n. an instrument for measuring minute intervals of time.

chrys·a·lis (kris'l·is), n., pl. chry·sal·i·des (kri·sal'i-dēz), chrys'a·lis·es, 1. the pupa of a butterfly, in a cocoon. 2. the cocoon.

chrys·an·the·mum (kri·san'thē-mŭm), n. 1. any of a genus of plants that bloom in the fall and that have showy flowers in many shades of yellow, red, purple, and white. 2. a flower of such a plant.

chrys·o·lite (kris'ō-līt), n. same as olivine.

chrys·o·prase (-prāz), n. a variety of chalcedony of a light-green color.

chtho·ni·an (thō'ni-ăn), adj. of or pertaining to the underworld of the dead of Greek mythology.

chub (chub), n., pl. chubs, chub, any of a number of small freshwater fishes related to the carp.

chub·by (chub'i), adj. -bi·er, -bi·est, plump. — chub'bi·ness, n.

chuck (chuk), v.t. 1. to tap or pat in a playful manner, especially under the chin. 2. to throw (something) a short distance, with a quick motion; toss. 3. [Slang], to discard or eject: n. 1. a light tap or pat under the chin. 2. a short toss. 3. a device on a lathe to secure the work to be turned. 4. the part of a carcass of beef around the neck and shoulder blade. 5. same as chock. 6. [Chiefly Western], food.

chuck (chuk), v.i. & n. same as cluck.

chuck-full (chuk'fool'), adj. same as chock-full.

chuck-hole (chuk'hōl), n. a hole in a roadway or pavement.

chuck·le (chuk'l), n. a quiet, suppressed laugh: v.i. -led, -ling, to laugh in such a manner. —chuck'ler, n.

chuck wagon, a wagon or truck equipped to prepare meals for a group of outdoor workers, as cowboys.

chug (chug), v.i. chugged, chug'ging, 1. to move with or as with a series of short, puffy sounds, as a locomotive. 2. to make these sounds: n. such a sound.

chuk·ka boot (chuk'ă), an ankle-high shoe for a man, often lined with fleece.

chuk·ker, chuk·kar (chuk'ēr), n. one of the playing periods of a polo game.

chum (chum), n. [Informal], 1. a roommate, as at college. 2. a close friend; buddy: v.i. chummed, chum'ming, [Informal], to be, or go about together as, close friends. —chum'mi·ness, n. —chum'my, adj. -mi·er, -mi·est.

chump (chump), n. 1. a short, thick, heavy piece of wood. 2. [Slang], a fool.

chunk (chunk), n. a short, thick piece.

chunk·y ('i), adj. chunk'i·er, chunk'i·est, 1. short and thick. 2. stocky. 3. containing chunks. —chunk'i·ness, n.

church (chûrch), n. 1. a building set apart for consecrated for divine worship, especially Christian worship. 2. religious service. 3. [usually C-], the collective body of Christians; also, a particular Christian denomination. 4. the clergy. 5. ecclesiastical, as opposed to secular, government: v.t. to say prayers of blessing over (a woman after childbirth): adj. of or pertaining to a church.

church·go·er ('gō-ēr), n. one who goes to church, especially habitually. —church'go·ing, n. & adj.

church·man ('măn), n., pl. -men, 1. a church member. 2. an ecclesiastic.

Church of England, the episcopal church of England: it is an established church with the sovereign as head.

church·ward·en ('wôr-dn), n. 1. either of two lay officers chosen annually in every parish of the Anglican or the Protestant Episcopal Church to attend to certain secular affairs. 2. [British], a long-stemmed clay pipe.

church·wom·an ('woom-ăn), n., pl. -wom-en, a woman member of a church.

church·yard ('yärd), n. the yard or enclosure around a church, often used as a burial ground.

churl (chûrl), n. 1. a peasant. 2. a surly, ill-bred person. 3. a miserly person. —churl'ish, adj. —churl'ish·ness, n.

churn (chûrn), n. a container in which milk or cream is agitated to form butter: v.t. & v.i. 1. to make (butter) by agitating (milk or cream). 2. to agitate or undergo agitation.

chute (shōōt), n. 1. an inclined trough or passage down which something can glide or flow. 2. a rapids or waterfall in a river.

chute (shōōt), n. [Informal], a parachute. — chut'ist, n.

chut·ney (chut'ni), n., pl. -neys, a relish of East Indian origin, made of fruit, spices, and herbs: also chut'nee.

chyle (kīl), n. a milklike fluid separated from digested matter in the small intestine, absorbed by the lacteal vessels, and assimilated into the blood.

chyme (kīm), n. the mass of digested food that passes from the stomach to the small intestine. —chy·mous (kī'mŭs), adj.

ci·bo·ri·um (si-bôr'i-ŭm), n., pl. -ri·a (-ă), 1. a canopy over an altar. 2. a receptacle for the consecrated wafers of the Eucharist.

ci·ca·da (si-kā'dă, -kā'dă), n., pl. -das, -dae ('dē), a large insect with transparent wings, the male of which makes a loud, penetrating sound by vibrating membranes of its abdomen.

cic·a·trix (sik'ă-triks), *n., pl.* **ci·cat·ri·ces** (si-kat'ri-sēz), 1. the scar remaining after a wound has healed. 2. the scar left on a stem where a branch was attached or on a seed where the seed stalk was attached.

cic·a·trize (-trīz), *v.t. & v.i.* **-trized, -triz·ing,** to heal, forming a cicatrix. –cic·a·tri·za'tion, *n.*

ci·ce·ro·ne (sis-ē-rō'nē), *n., pl.* **-nes, -ni** ('nē), [Italian], a guide who explains the antiquities and chief features of a place to sightseers.

ci·cis·be·o (si-sis'bi-ō), *n., pl.* **-be·os, -be·i** (-ē), [Italian], the lover of a married woman.

ci·der (sī'dẽr), *n.* the juice of apples expressed for drinking, often fermented.

ci·de·vant (sē-dă-vän'), *adj.* [French], former.

ci·gar (si-gär'), *n.* a small roll of tobacco leaves for smoking.

cig·a·rette, cig·a·ret (sig-ă-ret'), *n.* a small roll of cut tobacco in paper for smoking.

cig·a·ril·lo (-ril'ō), *n., pl.* **-los,** [Spanish], a small, thin cigar.

cil·i·a (sil'i-ă), *n., sing.* **-i·um** ('i-ŭm), 1. eyelashes. 2. long, minute, hairlike appendages, as at a leaf edge. 3. minute, vibratile filaments, as in protozoans.

cil·ice (sil'is), *n.* 1. a very coarse cloth made of hair. 2. a hair shirt.

ci·mex (sī'meks), *n., pl.* **cim·i·ces** (sim'ă-sēz), any of a genus of bloodsucking bugs, including the bedbug.

Cim·me·ri·an (si-mir'i-ăn), *adj.* 1. of or pertaining to the Cimmerians, a mythical people who lived in perpetual darkness. 2. intensely dark; gloomy.

cinch (sinch), *n.* 1. a saddle or pack girth firmly fastened in place by loop and knots. 2. [Informal], a sure grip or hold. 3. [Slang], a sure thing; something easy: *v.t.* 1. to tighten a saddle girth on. 2. [Slang], to get a hold upon or make sure of.

cin·cho·na (sin-kō'nă), *n.* 1. a tropical South American tree, now cultivated in the East Indies and Asia, the bark of which yields quinine. 2. the bark.

cin·cho·nism (sin'kă-nizm), *n.* a physical disorder characterized by headache, ringing in the ears, and deafness: it is caused by the excessive use of quinine.

cinc·ture (singk'chẽr), *n.* 1. a belt or girdle worn around the waist. 2. anything that encircles: *v.t.* **-tured, -tur·ing,** to encircle.

cin·der (sin'dẽr), *n.* 1. any piece, as of coal or wood, thoroughly burned but not reduced to ashes. 2. a piece of solid volcanic lava. 3. *pl.* ashes from wood or coal.

cin·e·ma (sin'ē-mă), *n.* [Chiefly British], 1. a motion picture. 2. a theater where motion pictures are shown. –cin·e·mat'ic (-mat'ik), *adj.* –cin·e·mat'i·cal·ly, *adv.*

cin·e·mat·o·graph (sin-ē-mat'ō-graf), *n.* [Chiefly British], a motion-picture camera, projector, theater, etc.

cin·e·ma·tog·ra·phy (sin-ē-mă-tog'ră-fi), *n.* the art or profession of making motion pictures. –cin·e·ma·tog'ra·pher, *n.* –cin·e·mat·o·graph'ic (-mat-ō-graf'ik), *adj.*

cin·e·rar·i·a (sin-ē-rer'i-ă), *n.* any one of certain plants with clusters of small, brightly colored flowers.

cin·e·rar·i·um (sin-ē-rer'i-ŭm), *n., pl.* **-i·a** ('i-a), an urn or place to deposit ashes of a cremated body or bodies. –cin'e·rar·y, *adj.*

cin·na·bar (sin'ă-bär), *n.* 1. a red sulfide of mercury. 2. a bright-red color.

cin·na·mon (sin'ă-mŏn), *n.* 1. the inner aromatic bark of an East Indian tree. 2. the yellowish-brown spice made from this dried bark: *adj.* 1. flavored or made with cinnamon. 2. yellowish-brown.

cinque (singk), *n.* a five, as on a playing card or at dice.

cinque-foil (singk'foil), *n.* 1. a plant of the rose family, with white, yellow, or red flowers. 2. in *Architecture*, a circular design made up of five cusps.

ci·pher (sī'fẽr), *n.* 1. the symbol 0; zero. 2. a person or anything without value or power. 3. a monogram. 4. a secret manner of writing, or the key to it; code. 5. an Arabic numeral: *v.i.* 1. [Now Rare], to do arithmetic. 2. to use secret writing: *v.t.* 1. [Now Rare], to solve by arithmetic. 2. to express in secret writing.

cir·ca (sûr'kă), *prep.* about: used before an approximate date, figure, etc.

cir·cle (sûr'k'l), *n.* 1. a plane figure consisting of a closed curved line of which each point is equally distant from the center of the area enclosed; also, the area enclosed. 2. anything shaped like a circle. 3. a theater balcony or seating tier. 4. a cycle; period. 5. a group; coterie. 6. in *Logic*, invalid argumentation confusing premise and conclusion: *v.t.* **-cled, -cling,** 1. to encompass. 2. to move around, as in a circle: *v.i.* to revolve. –cir'cler, *n.*

cir·clet (sûr'klit), *n.* 1. a small circle. 2. an ornamental ring or band.

cir·cuit (sûr'kit), *n.* 1. the act of going around anything. 2. the line forming the boundaries of an area. 3. the space enclosed. 4. a course or journey around. 5. journeying within an assigned area to fulfill duties, as by a judge; also, the area itself. 6. the judicial district of a U.S. Court of Appeals. 7. a number of associated theaters, nightclubs, athletic teams, etc. 8. the path of an electric current: *v.i.* to move in a circuit: *v.t.* to make a circuit about. –cir'cuit·al, *adj.*

circuit breaker, a device designed to interrupt an electric current automatically when necessary.

cir·cu·i·tous (sẽr-kū'i-tŭs), *adj.* roundabout; devious. –cir·cu'i·tous·ly, *adv.* –cir·cu'i·tous·ness, *n.*

cir·cuit·ry (sûr'kŭ-tri), *n.* 1. the layout of an electric circuit. 2. the parts constituting such a layout.

cir·cu·lar (sûr'kyŭ-lẽr), *adj.* 1. of, shaped like, or moving in a circle. 2. intended for wide circulation, as a notice. 3. roundabout; devious: *n.* a letter, notice, etc. intended for circulation. –cir·cu·lar'i·ty (-ler'i-ti), *n.* –cir'cu·lar·ly, *adv.*

cir·cu·lar·ize (-lă-rīz), *v.t.* **-ized, -iz·ing,** 1. to make circular. 2. to send circulars to. 3. to canvass for suggestions, help, etc. —cir·cu·lar·i·za'tion, *n.*

cir·cu·late (sûr'kyü-lāt), *v.t.* -lat·ed, -lat·ing, to cause to pass from point to point or from one person to another: *v.i.* 1. to move around and return to the same point. 2. to pass from hand to hand or place to place. 3. to be diffused or distributed. 4. to move about within a group, area, etc. —cir'cu·la·to·ry (-lâ-tôr-ì), *adj.* —cir'cu·la·tor, *n.*

cir·cu·la·tion (sûr-kyü-lā'shùn), *n.* 1. the act of circulating, or the extent of this. 2. the act of completing a circuit; specifically, the movement of blood through arteries and veins. 3. distribution or readership, as of a periodical.

cir·cum-, a prefix signifying *around*, *about*, *on all sides.*

cir·cum·am·bi·ent (sûr-kùm-am'bi-ěnt), *adj.* enclosing, or being surrounded, on all sides.

cir·cum·cise (sûr'kùm-sīz), *v.t.* -cised, -cis·ing, to cut off the foreskin of. —cir·cum·ci'sion, *n.*

cir·cum·fer·ence (sêr-kum'fēr-ĕns), *n.* 1. the line forming a circle. 2. its length. —cir·cum·fer·en'tial (-fê-ren'shàl), *adj.*

cir·cum·flex (sûr'kùm-flěks), *n.* a mark (~ ^ ˘) used over certain vowels to show how the vowels are to be pronounced: *adj.* 1. of or having a circumflex. 2. curving around: *v.t.* 1. to curve around. 2. to mark with a circumflex.

cir·cum·fuse (sûr·kùm-fūz'), *v.t.* -fused', -fus'-ing, to pour or spread around.

cir·cum·lo·cu·tion (-lō-kü'shùn), *n.* a roundabout way of speaking; an indirect mode of statement.

cir·cum·nav·i·gate (-nav'ì-gāt), *v.t.* -gat·ed, -gat·ing, to sail or fly around (the globe, an island, etc.). —cir·cum·nav·i·ga'tion, *n.* —cir·cum·nav'i·ga·tor, *n.*

cir·cum·scribe (sûr'kùm-skrīb), *v.t.* -scribed, -scrib·ing, 1. to enclose within certain lines or boundaries; restrict. 2. to encircle; encompass. —cir·cum·scrib'a·ble, *adj.*

cir·cum·scrip·tion (sûr-kùm-skrip'shùn), *n.* 1. the act of circumscribing. 2. the space or district circumscribed. 3. a boundary. 4. a limitation. 5. something written around. —cir·cum·scrip'tive, *adj.*

cir·cum·spect (sûr'kùm-spekt), *adj.* cautious; prudent; watchful. —cir·cum·spec'tion, *n.* —cir'cum·spect·ly, *adv.*

cir·cum·stance (sûr'kùm-stans), *n.* 1. something relevant to or accompanying a fact. 2. an event; happening. 3. *pl.* financial conditions affecting a person. 4. chance; luck. 5. display; ceremony: *v.t.* -stanced, -stanc·ing, to place in a particular situation.

cir·cum·stan·tial (sûr'kùm-stan'shàl), *adj.* 1. of, pertaining to, or depending on circumstances. 2. merely incidental. 3. full in detail. 4. ceremonial. —cir·cum·stan'tial·ly, *adv.*

circumstantial evidence, evidence of attendant circumstances, used in indirectly establishing another fact; indirect evidence.

cir·cum·stan·ti·ate ('shi-āt), *v.t.* -at·ed, -at·ing, to verify in every particular.

cir·cum·val·late (-val'āt), *v.t.* -lat·ed, -lat·ing, to surround with a wall or trench. —cir·cum·val·la'tion, *n.*

cir·cum·vent (sûr-kùm-vent'), *v.t.* 1. to circle around. 2. to entrap. 3. to gain an advantage over or prevent from happening by stratagem or deception. —cir·cum·ven'tion, *n.* —cir·cum·ven'tive, *adj.*

cir·cum·vo·lu·tion (-vô-lōō'shùn), *n.* 1. the act of rolling around a center. 2. a twist, spiral, etc. 3. a roundabout way of doing something.

cir·cus (sûr'kùs), *n.* 1. in ancient Rome, an oval or oblong arena for games, feats, races, etc., with tiered seats for spectators. 2. a show, as in a huge tent, with acrobats, trained animals, clowns, etc. 3. [British], a circular open intersection.

cir·rho·sis (sì-rō'sis), *n.* a degenerative disease of an organ, as the liver, characterized by abnormal formation of connective tissue.

cir·rus (sir'ùs), *n.*, *pl.* cir'ri ('ī), 1. a tendril. 2. a flexible appendage. 3. a wispy cloud formation.

cis·al·pine (sis-al'pīn), *adj.* on this side of the Alps with regard to Rome; south of the Alps.

cis·at·lan·tic (-ǎt-lan'tik), *adj.* on this side of the Atlantic Ocean.

Cis·ter·cian (sis-tûr'shàn), *n.* any one of the members of a religious order founded in 1098 for strict observance of the rule of St. Benedict of Nursia.

cis·tern (sis'têrn), *n.* a natural or artificial receptacle, especially one underground, for storing water; reservoir.

cit·a·del (sit'ā-dl, -del), *n.* a fortress; castle.

ci·ta·tion (sì-tā'shùn), *n.* 1. an official summons to appear before a court. 2. a quotation. 3. the act of quoting. 4. an official laudatory statement recognizing an individual's bravery or accomplishments. —ci'ta·tor, *n.*

cite (sīt), *v.t.* cit'ed, cit'ing, 1. to summon officially to appear in court. 2. to quote. 3. to give as a source, precedent, example, etc. 4. to favor with a citation (sense 4).

cith·a·ra (sith'ā-rā), *n.* a sort of ancient lyre.

cit·i·fied (sit'ì-fīd), *adj.* suggestive of city people, as certain behavior.

cit·i·zen (sit'ì-zěn), *n.* 1. formerly, a native or inhabitant of a town or city. 2. any native or inhabitant. 3. a member of a state or nation, owing service to it and having attendant political rights. 4. a civilian.

cit·i·zen·ry (-ri), *n.* citizens collectively.

cit·rate (si'trāt), *n.* a salt or ester of citric acid.

cit·ric (si'trik), *adj.* 1. of or from lemons, oranges, etc. 2. denoting or of an acid from these.

cit·rine (si'trin), *adj.* lemon-colored: *n.* 1. lemon yellow. 2. a variety of quartz of a yellow color.

cit·ron (si'trŏn), *n.* 1. a large, yellow, lemonlike fruit. 2. the tree it grows on. 3. the candied rind of this fruit.

cit·ron·el·la (si·trō-nel'ā), *n.* 1. an Asiatic grass, source of a volatile oil with a pungent odor. 2. this oil, used in perfume, insect repellents, etc: also **citronella oil.**

cit·rus (si'trùs), *n.* 1. any one of a genus of trees and shrubs of the rue family, including the orange, lemon, etc. 2. the fruit of any

---

ô in dragon, ōō in crude, oo in wool, u in cup, ū in cure, û in turn, û in focus, oi in boy, ou in house, th in thin, th in sheathe, g in get, j in joy, y in yet.

of these: *adj.* of or pertaining to these trees, shrubs, or fruits: also **cit'rous** ('trŭs).

cit·y (sit'ĭ), *n., pl.* **cit'ies,** 1. a large and important town. 2. in the U.S., an incorporated municipality with powers and boundaries defined by State charter. 3. all the people of a city.

city hall, 1. a building used for the offices of a municipal government. 2. a municipal government.

civ·et (siv'ĭt), *n.* 1. a fatty substance with a musklike scent, secreted by the civet cat. 2. the civet cat, or its fur.

civet cat, a catlike carnivore of Africa and southern Asia.

civ·ic (siv'ĭk), *adj.* of or pertaining to a city, citizens, or citizenship. —**civ'i·cal·ly,** *adv.*

civ·ics (siv'ĭks), *n.* political science concerning civic affairs and citizenship.

civ·il (siv'l), *adj.* 1. of or pertaining to a citizen or citizens. 2. of or relating to the affairs of a city or government. 3. cultured; urbane. 4. well-bred; complaisant. 5. of or pertaining to citizens in nonmilitary or nonreligious matters. 6. in *Law,* of or relating to the private rights of individuals and pertinent legal actions. —**civ'il·ly,** *adv.*

civil disobedience, nonviolent refusal to obey a government, on the grounds of conscience.

ci·vil·ian (si-vil'yăn), *n.* a person unconnected with the military or police: *adj.* of, pertaining to, or for civilians.

ci·vil·i·ty (si-vil'ĭ-tĭ), *n., pl.* **-ties,** courtesy, or an instance of it.

civ·i·li·za·tion (siv-ĭ-lĭ-zā'shŭn), *n.* 1. the act or state of being civilized. 2. highly developed social organization. 3. a particular culture, as of a nation. 4. civilized countries and peoples, or the characteristics of these.

civ·i·lize (siv'ĭ-līz), *v.t. & v.i.* **-lized, -liz·ing,** 1. to reclaim or emerge from a savage state. 2. to instruct in the arts and refinements of civilized life.

civil law, law relating to individuals' rights.

civil liberties, liberties an individual has by law.

civil service, governmental service other than military, legislative, or judicial.

civil war, war within a nation.

civ·vies (siv'ĭz), *n.* [Informal], civilian clothes.

clack (klak), *v.i.* 1. to make a sudden, sharp sound. 2. to chatter rapidly and continuously: *v.t.* to cause to make a sudden, sharp sound: *n.* 1. a sudden, sharp sound. 2. continual prattle. 3. a type of valve.

clad (klad), alternate past tense and past participle of **clothe:** *adj.* 1. clothed. 2. bonded to another metal or alloy.

claim (klām), *v.t.* 1. to demand as a right. 2. to make necessary; require. 3. to assert: *n.* 1. a demand for something that is rightfully due or held to be rightfully due. 2. a right or title to anything. 3. the thing claimed. 4. an assertion. —**claim'a·ble,** *adj.* —**claim'er,** *n.*

claim·ant (klā'mănt), *n.* one who demands anything as a right.

clair·voy·ance (kler-voi'ăns), *n.* 1. the power attributed to some people of seeing objects not usually perceptible. 2. keen perception; intuition.

clair·voy·ant ('ănt), *adj.* 1. of, pertaining to, or characterized by clairvoyance. 2. keenly perceptive: *n.* a clairvoyant person.

clam (klam), *n., pl.* **clams, clam,** 1. any one of various edible, bivalve mollusks with a hard shell. 2. [Informal], a taciturn person: *v.i.* **clammed, clam'ming,** to dig up clams.

cla·mant (klā'mănt), *adj.* 1. crying out; noisy. 2. urgent. —**cla'mant·ly,** *adv.*

clam·bake (klam'bāk), *n.* 1. the steaming or baking of clams, as at a picnic. 2. any party featuring this.

clam·ber (klam'bēr), *v.i. & v.t.* to ascend or climb with difficulty. —**clam'ber·er,** *n.*

clam·my (klam'ĭ), *adj.* **-mi·er, -mi·est,** disagreeably moist, cool, and sticky. —**clam'mi·ly,** *adv.* —**clam'mi·ness,** *n.*

clam·or (klam'ēr), *n.* 1. a loud and continued noise. 2. popular outcry; uproar: *v.i.* to indicate or effect by clamor; *v.i.* to make importunate demands; raise a clamor. —**clam'or·er,** *n.*

clam·or·ous (-ŭs), *adj.* 1. full of clamor; noisy. 2. vociferous. —**clam'or·ous·ly,** *adv.*

clam·our (klam'ēr), *n. & v.t. & v.i.* British form for **clamor.**

clamp (klamp), *n.* a device, typically of two parts moved together or apart by a screw arrangement, for gripping something or holding it rigid: *v.t.* to grip with or as with a clamp.

clamp·down ('doun), *n.* a repression or suppression.

clan (klan), *n.* 1. a tribe or association of families united under one chieftain, having one common ancestor. 2. a clique; set. 3. [Informal], family.

clan·des·tine (klan-des'tĭn), *adj.* secret; furtive. —**clan·des'tine·ly,** *adv.*

clang (klang), *n.* a loud, sharp, ringing metallic sound: *v.t.* to cause to resound with a clang: *v.i.* to give out or move with a clang.

clan·gor (klang'ēr), *n.* a clanging sound.

clank (klangk), *n.* a sharp, hard, brief metallic sound: *v.t.* to cause to resound with a clank: *v.i.* to give out or move with a clank.

clan·nish (klan'ish), *adj.* 1. of or pertaining to a clan. 2. avoiding others and adherent to one's own group. —**clan'nish·ly,** *adv.* —**clan'nish·ness,** *n.*

clans·man (klanz'măn), *n., pl.* **-men,** a member of a clan. —**clans'wom·an,** *n.fem., pl.* **-wom·en.**

clap (klap), *v.i.* **clapped, clap'ping,** 1. to strike one thing against another with a quick, sharp sound. 2. to strike the hands together, as to indicate approval: *v.t.* 1. to strike, or strike together, loudly. 2. to move, do, make, put, etc. suddenly: *n.* 1. a sudden, loud noise. 2. the act of clapping, or an instance of this.

clap·board (klab'ērd), *n.* a thin, narrow board, used for covering the sides of frame buildings: *v.t.* to cover with such boards.

clap·per (klap'ēr), *n.* 1. one who claps. 2. that which claps, as the tongue of a bell.

clap·trap ('trap), *n.* showy, empty talk or writing intended only to get notice: *adj.* flashy and cheap.

claque (klak), *n.* 1. a group paid to attend a

performance and applaud. 2. any group of fawning admirers.

clar·et (kler'it), *n.* 1. a dry red wine. 2. purplish red: *adj.* purplish-red.

claret cup, a mixture of brandy, claret, lemon juice, carbonated water, and sugar.

clar·i·fy (kler'ĭ-fī), *v.t. & v.i.* -**fied**, -**fy·ing**, 1. to make or become clear of impurities. 2. to make or become more comprehensible. — **clar·i·fi·ca·tion**, *n.* —**clar'i·fi·er**, *n.*

clar·i·net (kler-ĭ-net'), *n.* a long, single-reed woodwind instrument producing notes by means of keys and holes. —**clar·i·net'ist, clar·i·net'tist**, *n.*

clar·i·on (kler'ĭ-ŏn), *n.* a kind of medieval trumpet producing loud, clear tones: *adj.* clear and ringing, like the sound of a clarion.

clar·i·ty (kler'ĭ-tǐ), *n.* clearness.

cla·ro (klär'ō), *adj.* light-colored: said of certain cigars, usually mild.

clash (klash), *v.i.* 1. to hit together or contend with or as if with a loud, harsh noise, as of metal against metal. 2. to disagree sharply. 3. to conflict unpleasantly, as colors; not harmonize: *v.t.* to strike violently together: *n.* a clashing noise, situation, or effect.

clasp (klasp), *n.* 1. a hook, buckle, etc. to hold two things close or fast. 2. a close embrace. 3. a tight grip with the hand: *v.t.* 1. to hold close or fast with or as with a clasp. 2. to grasp firmly; embrace. 3. to take tight hold of with the hand. —**clasp'er**, *n.*

clasp knife, a large pocketknife with blade or blades folding into the handle.

class (klas), *n.* 1. a particular category of people or things; specifically, a group of animals or plants next in rank above an order. 2. a social or economic rank or caste. 3. high social position. 4. a number of students of the same status. 5. a grouping on the basis of grade or quality. 6. [Slang], high quality; excellence: *v.t. & v.i.* to classify or be classified. —**class'less**, *adj.*

clas·sic (klas'ik), *adj.* 1. of or relating to the highest class or rank in literature, art, technique, etc. 2. of, pertaining to, or like ancient Greek or Roman literature and art. 3. refined, pure, balanced, objective, etc., as a literary style. 4. epitomizing the best or most typical features of something: *n.* 1. a time-tested literary or artistic work of distinction, or the originator of it. 2. anything viewed as classic (sense 4).

clas·si·cal (klas'i-kl), *adj.* 1. same as classic (senses 1-3). 2. knowledgeable in or devoted to Greek and Roman literature, art, etc. 3. denoting or pertaining to music that meets traditional standards of form, complexity, etc. 4. denoting or pertaining to a course of study that is standard and traditionally authoritative. —**clas'si·cal·ly**, *adv.*

clas·si·cal·ism (-izm), *n.* same as classicism.

clas·si·cism (klas'ĭ-sizm), *n.* 1. the aesthetics viewed as typical of those of ancient Greece and Rome. 2. knowledge of or conformity to classical literature, art, principles, etc. 3. a classic expression or idiom. —**clas'si·cist**, *n.*

clas·si·fi·ca·tion (klas-ĭ-fĭ-kā'shŭn), *n.* 1. the act

of classifying or state of being classified. 2. a particular system of classifying. 3. a group of persons or things classified as alike in some way.

classified advertising, advertising, as in newspapers, arranged by subject, as jobs available or rentals offered, and typically set in columns.

clas·si·fy (klas'ĭ-fī), *v.t.* -**fied**, -**fy·ing**, 1. to arrange in classes; systematize. 2. to designate (government papers or data) as being highly confidential and hence restricted to the use of authorized personnel. —**clas'si·fi·a·ble**, *adj.* —**clas'si·fi·er**, *n.*

class·mate (klas'māt), *n.* a member of the same class at school or college.

class·room ('rōōm), *n.* a room for teaching classes in a school or college.

class·y ('ĭ), *adj.* **class'i·er, class'i·est**, [Slang], of very high quality.

clat·ter (klat'ēr), *v.i.* 1. to make a noise by knocking two or more things together continually. 2. to talk idly and noisily: *v.t.* to strike anything to make a clatter: *n.* 1. a continual, confused noise. 2. noisy chatter.

clause (klôz), *n.* 1. a group of words with a subject and finite verb. 2. a specific provision in a document.

claus·tral (klôs'trâl), *adj.* same as cloistral.

claus·tro·pho·bi·a (klôs-trô-fō'bi-â), *n.* abnormal fear of being in a room or other enclosed place. —**claus·tro·pho'bic**, *adj.*

cla·vate (klā'vāt), *adj.* club-shaped.

clav·i·chord (klav'ĭ-kôrd), *n.* an early keyboard instrument with strings struck by metal wedges.

clav·i·cle (klav'ĭ-kl), *n.* the bone joining breastbone and shoulder blade; collarbone.

cla·vier (klā-vir'), *n.* the keyboard of an organ, piano, etc.

claw (klô), *n.* 1. a sharp, hooked nail on the foot of a mammal, bird, or reptile; also, the foot itself. 2. anything clawlike: *v.t. & v.i.* to tear, scratch, etc. with or as if with claws.

claw hammer, a hammer with a forked, curved part for drawing nails.

clay (klā), *n.* 1. earth; specifically, a fine-grained kind that is plastic when wet. 2. anything easily molded. 3. the bodily or earthly nature of man.

clay·ey ('ĭ), *adj.* **clay'i·er, clay'i·est**, of, like, or full of clay.

clay·more (klā'môr), *n.* a Highland broadsword.

clay pigeon, a target in trapshooting, consisting of a disk, often of baked clay, thrown from a trap.

clean (klēn), *adj.* 1. free from dirt or extraneous matter. 2. morally or ceremonially pure. 3. aboveboard; not cheating. 4. orderly; tidy. 5. deft. 6. having no obstructions; clear. 7. entire; complete: *adv.* 1. in a clean manner. 2. entirely: *v.t. & v.i* to render or beome clean. —**clean'ness**, *n.*

clean-cut ('kut'), *adj.* 1. sharp and clear, as in outline. 2. not vague or ambiguous; plain. 3. good-looking, neat, etc.

clean·er ('ēr), *n.* 1. something used for cleaning. 2. a person doing cleaning, especially dry-cleaning.

clean·ly (klen'li), *adj.* -**li·er**, -**li·est**, keeping or kept free of dirt, grime, etc.: *adv.* (klēn'li), in a clean manner. —clean'li·ness, *n.*

cleanse (klenz), *v.t.* cleansed, cleans'ing, to make clean; purify. —cleans'er, *n.*

clean-up (klēn'up), *n.* 1. the act of cleaning thoroughly. 2. a getting rid of crime, vice, etc. as in a city; purge. 3. [Slang], profit.

clear (klir), *adj.* 1. bright; undimmed. 2. not obscured, fogged, etc.; transparent. 3. flawless. 4. sharply defined; distinct. 5. perceiving or perceived easily or unmistakably. 6. manifest to the understanding; easily understood. 7. certain; positive. 8. free, as from guilt, suspicion, etc. 9. not obstructed, weighted down, held back, restricted, etc. 10. net. 11. free from debt: *adv.* 1. in a clear manner. 2. completely: *v.t.* 1. to make clear. 2. to render evident. 3. to free from obstructions, flaws, etc. 4. to remove. 5. to prove or declare innocent. 6. to pass over, by, through, etc., as without difficulty, unwanted contact, etc. 7. to approve. 8. to make as profit. 9. to pay (a debt). 10. to get clearance for, as a check: *v.i.* 1. to become clear. 2. to go away. 3. to get authorization to leave a port. 4. to give or get clearance (sense 3). —clear'ly, *adv.* —clear'-ness, *n.*

clear·ance ('ǝns), *n.* 1. the act of clearing. 2. clear space, as between a moving object and what it is going by, over, etc. 3. the adjustment of debts and credits, exchange of checks, etc. in a clearinghouse.

clear-cut (klir'kut'), *adj.* 1. having a sharp, clearly defined outline, as if chiseled. 2. definite; not doubtful.

clear·ing (klir'ing), *n.* 1. the act of making clear. 2. land cleared of timber.

clear·ing·house ('hous), *n.* 1. an institution banks use to adjust balances, exchange checks, etc. 2. a central office, as for information.

cleat (klēt), *n.* 1. a piece of metal or wood fastened as to a shoe for better footing or to a ramp, shelf, etc. for added strength. 2. a piece of metal or wood to which a rope can be secured on board a ship: *v.t.* to secure or strengthen with a cleat.

cleav·age (klē'vij), *n.* 1. the act of cleaving, or splitting. 2. the property of some minerals and rocks to break in certain directions, making smooth surfaces. 3. a cleft or division; fissure. 4. in *Biology*, cell division.

cleave (klēv), *v.t.* cleaved or cleft or clove, cleaved or cleft or clo'ven, cleav'ing, 1. to divide with violence. 2. to part; sever. 3. to penetrate: *v.i.* to become divided or split.

cleave (klēv), *v.i.* cleaved, cleav'ing, 1. to adhere (*to*); be attached strongly (*to*). 2. to be faithful (*to*).

cleav·er ('ẽr), *n.* a butcher's heavy chopping or cutting tool.

cleav·ers (klēv'ẽrz), *n., pl.* -ers, a weedy plant with a prickly stem and small flowers.

clef (klef), *n.* a symbol at the beginning of each staff in music to indicate the pitch of the notes on the lines and spaces.

cleft (kleft), *n.* a crack; crevice: *adj.* divided; split.

clem·a·tis (klem'ā-tis), *n.* a perennial vine of the buttercup family, with bright flowers.

clem·en·cy (klem'ẽn-si), *n.* 1. compassion; leniency. 2. mildness, as of weather.

clem·ent ('ẽnt), *adj.* 1. compassionate; forgiving; forbearing. 2. mild, as weather. —clem'ent·ly, *adv.*

clench (klench), *v.t.* 1. to grip tightly. 2. to close (the jaws, hands, etc.) tightly: *n.* a firm grip. —clench'er, *n.*

cler·gy (klûr'ji), *n.* persons ordained for religious service; ministers, priests, rabbis, etc. collectively.

cler·gy·man (-mǎn), *n., pl.* -men, one ordained to the service of a religion; minister, priest, rabbi, etc.

cler·ic (kler'ik), *n.* a clergyman: *adj.* same as clerical.

cler·i·cal (kler'i-kl), *adj.* 1. of or pertaining to the clergy. 2. of or pertaining to office clerks.

clerk (klûrk; British klärk), *n.* 1. a layman with church duties. 2. one who works in an office keeping records, filing, typing letters, etc. 3. an official in charge of records, etc. for a town, school, etc. 4. a salesperson in a store: *v.i.* to act as a clerk or salesperson. —clerk'ship, *n.*

clev·er (klev'ẽr), *adj.* 1. skillful; dexterous. 2. witty, quick-minded, ingenious, etc. 3. superficially smart; facile. —clev'er·ly, *adv.* —clev'er·ness, *n.*

clew (klōō), *n.* 1. a ball of thread or yarn. 2. something that leads to a solution of perplexity: usually spelled clue. 3. one of the corners of a sail: *v.t.* 1. to wind (*up*) into a ball. 2. same as clue.

cli·ché (klī-shā'), *n.* a trite or commonplace expression or idea.

click (klik), *v.i.* 1. to make a short, sharp sound. 2. [Informal], to fit together well. 3. [Informal], to be suddenly understandable: *v.t.* to cause to click: *n.* 1. a short, sharp sound. 2. a catch or pawl that snaps into place.

cli·ent (klī'ẽnt), *n.* 1. one who engages the services of a lawyer, accountant, etc. 2. a customer.

cli·en·tele (klī-ẽn-tel'), *n.* clients or customers collectively.

cliff (klif), *n.* a high, steep face of rock; precipice.

cliff dweller, one of a race of ancient American Indians who lived in the hollows of cliffs. —cliff'-dwell·ing, *adj.*

cli·mac·ter·ic (klī-mak'tẽr-ik), *n.* 1. a time of important physiological change, as the menopause, in human life. 2. any crucial period: *adj.* crucial.

cli·mac·tic (klī-mak'tik), *adj.* of, being, or like a climax: also cli·mac'ti·cal. —cli·mac'ti·cal·ly, *adv.*

cli·mate (klī'mǎt), *n.* 1. the temperature and meteorological conditions of a country or region. 2. a region where certain weather conditions prevail. —cli·mat·ic (klī-mat'ik), *adj.* —cli·mat'i·cal·ly, *adv.*

cli·ma·tol·o·gy (klī-mǎ-tol'ō-ji), *n.* the study or

science of climate and climatic conditions. —cli-ma-to-log'i-cal (-tô-loj'i-kl), *adj.* —cli-ma-tol'o-gist, *n.*

cli-max (klī'maks), *n.* 1. the culmination or highest point in a progression. 2. the decisive point of action in a drama, etc.: *v.t. & v.i.* to bring to or reach a climax.

climb (klīm), *v.i. & v.t.* **climbed, climb'ing,** 1. to ascend by using the hands and feet. 2. to move (*down, along,* etc.) by using the hands and feet. 3. to ascend little by little. 4. to grow upward: *n.* 1. an ascent by climbing. 2. a place to be climbed. —climb'a-ble, *adj.* —climb'er, *n.*

clime (klīm), *n.* 1. a country, region, or tract. 2. climate. A poetic term.

clinch (klinch), *v.t.* 1. to fasten firmly by bending over the end, as of a nail. 2. to settle (a matter) decisively: *v.i.* 1. in *Boxing,* to hold the opponent firmly and tightly so that he is unable to punch. 2. [Slang], to embrace tightly: *n.* 1. a fastening or holding, or that which is held. 2. a tight grip in boxing. 3. [Slang], a tight embrace.

clinch-er ('ĕr), *n.* 1. that which clinches. 2. a conclusive statement, argument, etc.

cling (kling), *v.i.* **clung, cling-ing,** 1. to adhere closely; hold fast by embracing or entwining. 2. to be unwilling to part with (a person, idea, etc.). —cling'er, *n.*

cling-stone ('stōn), *adj.* denoting a peach whose flesh clings to the stone: *n.* such a peach.

clin-ic (klin'ik), *n.* 1. medical instruction at the bedside or in the presence of patients. 2. a place for dispensing medical services to out-patients. 3. an institution or facility where medical specialists practice as a group.

clin-i-cal ('i-kl), *adj.* 1. of or pertaining to a clinic. 2. denoting treatment and observation of patients as opposed to laboratory experiments or theory. 3. impersonal. 4. rigidly clean and undecorated, like a medical clinic. —clin'i-cal-ly, *adv.*

clin-i-cian (kli-nish'ån), *n.* a practitioner or advocate of clinical methods.

clink (klingk), *v.t. & v.i.* to strike with or make a slight, sharp sound, as coins or glass do: *n.* 1. this sound. 2. [Informal], a jail.

clink-er ('ĕr), *n.* 1. a chunk of hard, stony matter formed from impurities in coal as it burns. 2. [Slang], an error.

clip (klip), *v.t.* **clipped, clip'ping,** 1. to cut with shears or scissors; cut off. 2. to trim or cut the fleece or hair of. 3. to cut short. 4. to grip tightly. 5. [Informal], to hit with a sharp blow. 6. [Slang], to cheat: *v.i.* 1. to clip something. 2. to move quickly: *n.* 1. the act of clipping. 2. the wool of a season's shearing. 3. a fast pace. 4. something that clips or fastens, as a paper clip. 5. [Informal], a sharp blow.

clip-board ('bôrd), *n.* a writing board with a spring clip at one end to hold paper, etc.

clipped form (or **word**), a shortened form of a word, as *plane* for *airplane.*

clip-per ('ĕr), *n.* 1. *usually pl.* an instrument for clipping or trimming. 2. a type of fast sailing ship.

clip-ping ('ing), *n.* something cut off or out, as a piece clipped from a newspaper.

clique (klēk, klik), *n.* a small, exclusive coterie. —cliqu'ish, cliqu'ey, *adj.* —cliqu'ish-ly, *adv.* —cliqu'ish-ness, *n.*

cli-to-ris (klit'ĕr-is), *n.* a small, erectile organ of the vulva. —cli'to-ral, *adj.*

clo-a-ca (klō-ā'kả), *n., pl.* **-cae** ('sē, 'kē). 1. the cavity into which the digestive and reproductive systems empty in reptiles, birds, etc. 2. a cesspool or sewer. —clo-a'cal ('kål), *adj.*

cloak (klōk), *n.* 1. a sleeveless, loose outer garment. 2. that which conceals or covers; pretext; disguise: *v.t.* 1. to cover with a cloak. 2. to conceal.

clob-ber (klob'ĕr), *v.t.* [Slang], 1. to hit; batter. 2. to trounce; defeat.

cloche (klōsh), *n.* a woman's bell-shaped, closely fitting hat.

clock (klok), *n.* a device for measuring and indicating the divisions of time, usually by means of hands moving over a dial: *v.t.* to time (something or someone) with a timing device.

clock (klok), *n.* a woven or embroidered ornament on a stocking or sock.

clock-wise ('wīz), *adv. & adj.* in the direction of the hands of a clock.

clock-work ('wĕrk), *n.* a well-ordered mechanism, as or like that of a clock.

clod (klod), *n.* 1. a lump of earth or clay. 2. a dull, stupid fellow. 3. the part nearest the shoulder in the neck of a beef. —clod'dish, *adj.* —clod'dish-ly, *adv.*

clod-hop-per ('hop-ĕr), *n.* a rustic; lout.

clog (klog), *v.t.* **clogged, clog'ging,** 1. to fill or choke with anything that may impede motion. 2. to hinder: *v.i.* to become choked or clogged up: *n.* 1. a hindrance or obstruction. 2. a shoe with a thick sole of wood, cork, etc.

clog dance, a stamping, rhythmic dance in which clogs are worn. —clog dancer

cloi-son-né (kloi-zô-nā'), *n.* enamel work with decoration set in sections divided by metal strips: *adj.* denoting this work.

clois-ter (klois'tĕr), *n.* 1. a place of religious retirement; a monastery or convent. 2. life in such a place. 3. an arched way or covered walk on the side of a courtyard: *v.t.* to confine in or as in a cloister; seclude. —clois'tered, *adj.*

clois-tral ('trål), *adj.* pertaining to or confined in a cloister; secluded.

clomp (klomp), *v.i.* to clump; walk noisily.

clop (klop), *v.i.* **clopped, clop'ping,** to move with a clattering sound like hoofbeats: *n.* this sound.

close (klōz), *v.t.* **closed, clos'ing,** 1. to shut. 2. to obstruct (an opening). 3. to unite. 4. to finish; end: *v.i.* 1. to become shut. 2. to come together. 3. to come to an end: *n.* 1. a conclusion; end; finish. 2. (klōs), [British], enclosed grounds near a building: *adj.* (klōs), 1. confined. 2. without ventilation. 3. oppressive. 4. dense. 5. niggardly. 6. secluded. 7. reticent. 8. near together. 9. intimate. 10. careful; minute. 11. similar. 12. nearly even: *adv.* (klōs), in a close manner. —close'ly, *adv.* —close'ness, *n.*

close corporation, an incorporated business whose stock is owned by a few people: also **closed corporation.**

closed circuit, a system for transmitting television by wire only to connected sets.

closed season, certain months in the year when it is illegal to kill or capture certain game, wild birds, fish, etc.

closed shop, a factory employing only union members.

close-fist-ed (klōs'fis'tid), adj. miserly.

close-fit-ting ('fit'ing), adj. fitting tightly or snugly.

close-hauled ('hôld'), adj. heading as nearly into the wind as possible.

clos-et (kloz'it), n. 1. a small room for privacy. 2. a place for storing clothes, household supplies, etc.: v.t. to shut up in a private room for confidential conversation.

close-up (klōs'up), n. a motion-picture or television shot or a photograph taken at very close range.

clo-sure (klō'zhĕr), n. 1. the act of shutting up. 2. that which closes. 3. the end. 4. same as **cloture.**

clot (klot), v.i. & v.t. clot'ted, clot'ting, to coagulate: n. a coagulated mass or lump of soft or fluid matter, as blood.

cloth (klôth), n., pl. cloths (klôthz, kloths), 1. a woven, felted, or knitted fabric of some fibrous material, as wool, cotton, synthetic fibers, etc. 2. a piece of this for some special use, as a washcloth, tablecloth, etc. 3. the distinctive dress of the clergy: adj. made of cloth.

clothe (klōth), v.t. clothed or clad, cloth'ing, 1. to put raiment on. 2. to cover with, or as with, a garment.

clothes (klōz, klōthz), n. 1. clothing; raiment; apparel. 2. bedclothes.

clothes-horse ('hôrs), n. 1. a frame on which to hang clothes. 2. [Slang] one whose chief interest is his or her clothes.

clothes-line ('lin), n. a rope or wire upon which wet clothes are placed to dry.

clothes-pin ('pin), n. a fastener of wood or plastic, used to hold clothes, etc. on a clothesline.

cloth-ier (klōth'yĕr, klō'thi-ĕr), n. one who manufactures or sells clothes or cloth.

cloth-ing (klōth'ing), n. garments in general; wearing apparel.

clo-ture (klō'chĕr), n. the closing of a debate in a legislative assembly by calling for an immediate vote: v.t. -tured, -tur-ing, to apply cloture to (a speaker, debate, etc.).

cloud (kloud), n. 1. a mass of visible vapor in the atmosphere. 2. a volume of smoke or dust. 3. a multitude; swarm. 4. dark markings, as in marble. 5. something that obscures or darkens, or causes gloom: v.t. 1. to overspread as with a cloud. 2. to make gloomy. 3. to sully: v.i. to grow cloudy. — **cloud'less,** adj.

cloud-burst ('bĕrst), n. a violent rainstorm.

cloud-y ('i), adj. cloud'i-er, cloud'i-est, 1. overcast. 2. obscure; vague. 3. dark; opaque. 4. gloomy. —**cloud'i-ly,** adv. —**cloud'i-ness,** n.

clout (klout), n. 1. originally, a patch or rag. 2. an archery target. 3. an archery shot that strikes the target. 4. a blow with the hand. 5. [Informal], a long hit in baseball. 6. [Informal], political power: v.t. 1. [Informal], to strike with the hand. 2. [Slang], to hit (a ball) a long distance.

clove (klōv), n. a pungent, aromatic dried bud of an evergreen tree, used as a spice.

clove (klōv), alternate past tense of cleave: n. a section of a garlic bulb.

clo-ven (klō'vĕn), alternate past participle of cleave: adj. divided; split; cleft.

clo-ver (klō'vĕr), n. any of several leguminous herbs with dense flower heads and trifoliolate leaves.

clo-ver-leaf (-lēf), n., pl. -leafs, an interchange between two highways, shaped like a four-leaf clover.

clown (kloun), n. 1. originally, a rustic. 2. an ill-bred person; boor. 3. a professional performer of antics, as at a circus. 4. a buffoon. —**clown'ish,** adj.

cloy (kloi), v.t. & v.i. to surfeit with too much that is rich, sweet, etc.

club (klub), n. 1. a heavy stick. 2. a stick used in various games. 3. one of a suit of cards marked with black trefoils. 4. pl. this suit of cards. 5. a group of persons associated for a common purpose. 6. a building, etc. housing such a club: v.t. clubbed, club'bing, to beat with a club: v.i. to join together for a common purpose.

club-foot ('foot), n., pl. -feet, a congenitally deformed foot. —**club'foot-ed,** adj.

club-haul ('hôl), v.t. to tack (a ship) by dropping the lee anchor as soon as the wind is out of the sails.

club-house ('hous), n. a building or room occupied or used by a club or team.

club moss, any of a genus of low, flowerless plants, much like moss.

cluck (kluk), v.i. to make a low, clicking sound, as a hen calling to her chickens or brooding: v.t. to utter (an expression of concern, disapproval, etc.) with such a sound: n. 1. a hen's call to her chickens or a sound resembling this. 2. [Slang], a stupid person.

clue (kloo), n. a clew; especially, a hint or piece of evidence that helps to solve a mystery: v.t. clued, clu'ing, 1. to point out by a clue. 2. [Informal], to give necessary facts to (often followed by in).

clump (klump), n. 1. a thick cluster, as of shrubs. 2. a dull sound. 3. a lump or mass: v.t. to gather in a clump: v.i. 1. to tread heavily. 2. to form clumps. —**clump'y,** adj.

clum-sy (klum'si), adj. -si-er, -si-est, 1. awkward; without grace. 2. unwieldy. —**clum'si-ly,** adv. —**clum'si-ness,** n.

clung (klung), past tense and past participle of cling.

clunk (klungk), v.i. & v.t. to make or cause to make a nonresonant, metallic sound: n. such a sound.

clunk-er ('ĕr), n. [Slang], an old, dilapidated vehicle, device, machine, etc.

clus-ter (klus'tĕr), n. a number of things growing or collected together; bunch: v.i. & v.t. to grow or gather in clusters; congregate. —**clus'ter-y,** adj.

clutch (kluch), *v.t.* to grasp, seize, or grip firmly: *v.i.* to snatch or seize (*at*): *n.* 1. a grasp; grip. 2. a coupling for engaging and disengaging an engine, etc. 3. *usually pl. a)* the hands. *b)* control.

clutch (kluch), *n.* 1. the eggs in a nest at one time. 2. a brood of chickens.

clut·ter (klut'ẽr), *n.* a disorderly jumble of things: *v.t.* to jumble (*up*).

Clydes·dale (klīdz'dāl), *n.* one of a breed of heavy draft horses, originating in the Clyde valley in Scotland.

clys·ter (klis'tẽr), *n.* an enema.

co-, a prefix signifying *joint, equally, together with*.

coach (kōch), *n.* 1. a large, covered, four-wheeled carriage. 2. a bus. 3. a passenger car on a train. 4. the aft section of seats in most airliners. 5. one who gives instruction to a student, athletic team, etc.: *v.t. & v.i.* to instruct (a student, athletes, etc.).

coach dog, same as Dalmatian.

co·ad·ju·tor (kō-aj'ŭ-tẽr), *n.* a bishop's assistant.

co·ag·u·lant (kō-ag'yū-lǎnt), *n.* a substance that produces coagulation.

co·ag·u·late (kō-ag'yoo-lāt), *v.t.* -lat·ed, -lat·ing, to make (a liquid) become a clotted mass; curdle; congeal: *v.i.* to clot; congeal. —**co·ag·u·la'tion**, *n.* —**co·ag'u·la·tive,** *adj.* —**co·ag'-u·la·tor,** *n.*

co·ag·u·lum (-lŭm), *n., pl.* -la (-lă), a clot; curdled mass.

coal (kōl), *n.* 1. hardened, black, mineralized vegetable matter used as fuel. 2. a piece of this, or such pieces collectively. 3. a charred or glowing ember: *v.t. & v.i.* to provide or be provided with coal.

co·a·lesce (kō-à-les'), *v.i.* -lesced', -lesc'ing, to grow together; combine; unite. —**co·a·les'-cence,** *n.* —**co·a·les'cent,** *adj.*

co·a·li·tion (-lish'ŭn), *n.* 1. a union into one body or mass. 2. a temporary alliance.

coal oil, 1. kerosene. 2. petroleum. 3. unrefined oil from coal, used in lamps.

coal tar, a thick, black liquid distilled from bituminous coal: it is used to make dyes, drugs, synthetic fabrics, etc.

coam·ing (kō'ming), *n.* the raised border around the hatch of a ship.

co·ap·ta·tion (kō-ap-tā'shŭn), *n.* the adjustment or adaptation of parts to one another, as ends of a broken bone.

coarse (kōrs), *adj.* coars'er, coars'est, 1. large in texture or size. 2. of inferior quality. 3. rough. 4. not refined. —**coarse'ly,** *adv.* —**coarse'ness,** *n.*

coarse-grained ('grānd), *adj.* 1. having a coarse texture. 2. crude; not refined.

coars·en ('ẽn), *v.i. & v.t.* to become or make coarse.

coast (kōst), *n.* 1. the land next to the sea; seashore. 2. a slide on a sled down an incline: *v.i.* 1. to sail near or along the coast. 2. to descend an incline on a sled. 3. to continue to move on momentum: *v.t.* to sail close or near to.

coast·al ('l), *adj.* having to do with, near, or along a coast. —**coast'al·ly,** *adv.*

coast·er ('ẽr), *n.* 1. a ship that travels along a coast. 2. a sled. 3. a small mat, etc. placed under a glass.

coast guard, [also C- G-], 1. a member of the armed service that guards a country's coasts, prevents smuggling, aids ships in distress, etc. 2. this branch of the armed forces. —**coast guards'man, coast guard'man,** *pl.* -men.

coast-line ('līn), *n.* the outline of a coast.

coast·wise ('wīz), *adv. & adj.* by or along the coast.

coat (kōt), *n.* 1. an outer garment with sleeves, covering at least the upper part of the body. 2. an external covering of an animal, as fur, hair, etc. 3. the outer covering of a plant. 4. a layer, as of paint: *v.t.* to cover or spread over. —**coat'ed,** *adj.*

co·a·ti (kō-ät'ī), *n., pl.* -tis, a tropical American mammal similar to the raccoon: also called **co·a'ti·mun'di** (-mun'dī).

coat·ing (kōt'ing), *n.* a layer or coat of something.

coat of arms, the insignia of a family, institution, etc., consisting of a design of figures and emblems (heraldic bearings) emblazoned on an escutcheon.

coat of mail, *pl.* **coats of mail,** a suit of armor made of chain mail or overlapping plates.

coat-tail (kōt'tāl), *n.* one of the two lower back parts of a man's coat.

co·au·thor (kō-ô'thẽr), *n.* a collaborator, as in writing a book: *v.t.* to write (a book, etc.) together.

coax (kōks), *v.t. & v.i.* to wheedle or cajole. —**coax'er,** *n.* —**coax'ing·ly,** *adv.*

co·ax·i·al (kō-ak'si-ǎl), *adj.* 1. having an axis in common. 2. denoting a high-frequency transmission cable, as for television signals.

cob (kob), *n.* 1. a corncob. 2. a short-legged, thickset horse. 3. a male swan. 4. a large, black seagull of the northern Atlantic: also spelled **cobb.**

co·balt (kō'bôlt), *n.* a hard, steel-gray, ductile metallic chemical element.

cob·ber (kob'ẽr), *n.* [Slang], in Australia, a boon companion.

cob·ble (kob'l), *n.* 1. a cobblestone. 2. clumsy work: *v.t.* -bled, -bling, 1. to mend or patch (shoes, boots, etc.). 2. to mend or construct clumsily. 3. to pave with cobblestones.

cob·bler ('lẽr), *n.* 1. one who mends boots and shoes. 2. [Archaic], a clumsy workman. 3. an iced drink of wine, rum, citrus fruit, etc. 4. a deep-dish fruit pie with a biscuit crust on top.

cob·ble·stone ('l-stōn), *n.* a naturally rounded stone formerly much used for paving.

co·bra (kō'brà), *n.* a very venomous, hooded snake of Africa and Asia.

cob·web (kob'web), *n.* 1. a spider's web. 2. anything like this in being flimsy or sticky. —**cob'web·by,** *adj.*

co·ca (kō'kà), *n.* 1. the dried leaf of a small South American shrub, from which cocaine is obtained. 2. this shrub.

co·caine, co·cain (kō-kān'), *n.* a powerful alkaloid obtained from dried coca leaves, used as a narcotic and local anesthetic.

co-cain-ism ('izin), n. an unhealthy condition caused by excessive use of cocaine.

co-cain-ize ('īz), v.t. -ized, -iz-ing, to treat with or anesthetize with cocaine. —co-cain-i-za'-tion, n.

coc-cif-er-ous (kok-sif'ër-ùs), adj. producing berries.

coc-cyx (kok'siks), n., pl. coc-cy-ges (kok-sī'jēz), a small, triangular bone at the end of the spine. —coc-cyg'e-al (-sij'i-âl), adj.

coch-i-neal (koch'ī-nēl), n. a scarlet dye made from the dried body of an insect.

coch-le-a (koch'li-ä), n., pl. -ae (-ē), the spiral-shaped cavity of the inner ear.

coch-le-ate (-it, -āt), adj. shaped like a snail's shell: also coch'le-at-ed.

cock (kok), n. 1. the male of some birds, especially the domestic fowl. 2. a weathervane in the shape of a cock. 3. a leader or chief. 4. a valve that turns, for regulating the flow of a liquid or gas. 5. a) the hammer of a firearm. b) its position for firing. 6. a jaunty, tilted position. 7. a small, conical heap of hay: v.t. 1. to turn up or set (a hat, etc.) jauntily on one side. 2. to draw back (the hammer of a firearm).

cock-ade (ko-kād'), n. a badge or ribbon worn on the hat. —cock'ad'ed, adj.

cock-a-ma-mie (kok'ä-mä-mi), adj. [Slang], cheap; inferior; poor.

cock-a-too (kok'ä-tōō), n. a crested parrot of Australia, usually white.

cock-a-trice (kok'ä-tris), n. a fabulous serpent said to have been hatched from a cock's egg, and having the power to kill by a glance.

cock-boat (kok'bōt), n. a small boat, especially one used as a ship's tender.

cock-chaf-er ('chāf-ēr), n. a very destructive European beetle.

cock-crow (kok'krō), n. early morning; dawn: also called cock'crow-ing.

cocked hat, a wide-brimmed, three-cornered hat, formerly worn by men.

cock-er (kok'ēr), n. a small spaniel with long hair and drooping ears: also cocker spaniel.

cock-er-el (kok'ēr-èl), n. a young cock.

cock-eyed ('īd), adj. 1. cross-eyed. 2. [Slang], a) awry. b) silly. c) drunk.

cock-fight ('fīt), n. a fight between gamecocks with metal spurs on the legs: illegal in the U.S. —cock'fight-ing, n.

cock-le (kok'l), v.i. & v.t. -led, -ling, to pucker; wrinkle: n. 1. an edible shellfish with two heart-shaped, wrinkled shells. 2. a pucker; wrinkle. 3. any of several weeds found in grainfields.

cock-le-bur (-bŭr), n. a common weed that bears burs.

cock-ney (kok'ni), n. [often C-], 1. a native of the East End of London, England. 2. the characteristic dialect of this district: also cock-ney-ese' (-ēz'): adj. [often C-], of or pertaining to cockneys or their dialect. —cock'ney-ish, adj.

cock-pit (kok'pit), n. 1. an enclosed space for cockfighting. 2. the place in an airplane for the pilot.

cock-roach ('rōch), n. an insect with long feelers and a flat body.

cocks-comb (koks'kōm), n. 1. the red, fleshy crest on a rooster's head. 2. a plant with a flower somewhat resembling this.

cock-sure (kok'shoor), adj. 1. perfectly sure. 2. overconfident. —cock'sure-ness, n.

cock-tail ('tāl), n. 1. a mixed, iced alcoholic drink. 2. an appetizer, as fruit juice, shrimp, etc. 3. a horse with a docked tail.

cock-y ('i), adj. cock'i-er, cock'i-est, [Informal], conceited. —cock'i-ly, adv. —cock'i-ness, n.

co-co (kō'kō), n., pl. -cos, 1. the coconut palm tree. 2. the coconut: adj. made of coconut husk fiber.

co-coa (kō'kō), n. 1. the ground, roasted seeds of the cacao tree. 2. a beverage made from this, hot water or milk, etc. 3. reddish brown.

cocoa butter, a whitish fat obtained from cacao seeds, used in cosmetics, etc.

co-co-nut, co-coa-nut (kō'kä-nut), n. a large, oval nut with a fibrous, brown husk enclosing an edible white meat that is often shredded or chopped and used in desserts or candies.

coconut palm, a tall palm tree that bears coconuts: also coconut tree or coco palm.

co-coon (kō-kōōn'), n. the silky, oblong case covering the larvae of many spinning insects while in the chrysalis stage.

co-cotte (kō-kot'), n. [French], a sexually promiscuous woman.

cod (kod), n., pl. cod, cods, a large, edible fish found in northern seas, especially off the coasts of Newfoundland and Norway.

co-da (kō'dä), n. a final passage in music.

cod-dle (kod'l), v.t. -dled, -dling, 1. to pamper (a baby, invalid, etc.); treat tenderly. 2. to cook (eggs) in water just below boiling.

code (kōd), n. 1. a body of classified laws or regulations. 2. a set of principles, as of ethics. 3. a system of signals or symbols for communication: v.t. cod'ed, cod'ing, to translate into a code. —cod'er, n.

co-deine (kō'dēn), n. an alkaloid derived from opium, similar to morphine but milder, used as an anodyne and in cough medicines: also co'dein, co-de-ia (kō-dē'ä).

co-dex (kō'deks), n., pl. co-di-ces (kō'dī-sēz, kod'i-), 1. originally, a body of laws. 2. a manuscript volume, especially of the Scriptures or of an ancient classic.

cod-fish (kod'fish), n., pl. -fish, -fish-es, same as cod.

codg-er (koj'ēr), n. [Informal], an eccentric old fellow.

cod-i-cil (kod'i-sl), n. an appendix to a will, modifying it.

cod-i-fy (kod'i-fī, kō'dī-), v.t. -fied, -fy-ing, to arrange or systematize (laws, rules, etc.). —cod-i-fi-ca'tion, n. —cod'i-fi-er, n.

cod-ling (kod'ling), n. 1. a young cod. 2. a kind of apple used for cooking: also cod'lin.

codling moth, a small moth whose larvae feed on apples, pears, etc.: also codlin moth.

co-ed, co-ed (kō'ed), n. [Informal], a girl student at a coeducational college or university: adj. [Informal], 1. of or pertaining to a coed. 2. coeducational.

a in cap, ā in cane, ä in father, à in abet, e in met, ē in be, ē in baker, in regent, i in pit, ī in fine, i in manifest, o in hot, ô in horse, ō in bone,

co·ed·u·ca·tion·al (kō-ej-ú-kā'shún-ál), *adj.* of or pertaining to a system of education in which both sexes attend the same classes. —**co·ed·u·ca'tion,** *n.* —**co·ed·u·ca'tion·al·ly,** *adv.*

co·ef·fi·cient (kō-ê-fish'ênt), *n.* 1. a multiplier of a variable or of an unknown quantity. 2. a factor contributing to a result or measuring a property.

coe·len·ter·ate (si·len'tê-rāt), *n.* any of a number of sea animals with a large internal cavity, as the jellyfish, coral, etc.

co·erce (kō-ûrs'), *v.i.* -erced', -erc'ing, 1. to restrain or constrain by force. 2. to compel to do something. 3. to enforce. —**co·er'ci·ble,** *adj.* —**co·er'cion,** *n.*

co·er·cive (kō-ûr'siv), *adj.* having the power to coerce. —**co·er'cive·ly,** *adv.* —**co·er'cive·ness,** *n.*

co·e·val (kō-ê'vl), *adj.* contemporary: *n.* a contemporary. —**co·e'val·ly,** *adv.*

co·ex·ist (-ig-zist'), *v.i.* 1. to live during the same period or in the same place. 2. to exist together peacefully, in spite of differences. —**co·ex·ist'ence,** *n.* —**co·ex·ist'ent,** *adj.*

co·ex·ten·sive (-ik-sten'siv), *adj.* equally extensive in space or time. —**co·ex·ten'sive·ly,** *adv.*

cof·fee (kôf'i), *n.* 1. the seeds of a tall tropical shrub, roasted and ground and used to brew a hot beverage. 2. this drink. 3. the shrub. 4. the brown color of coffee.

cof·fee-cake (-kāk), *n.* a kind of sweet bread, often with nuts or raisins.

cof·fee-house (-hous), *n.* a place where coffee and other light refreshments are served, and where people gather to talk.

cof·fee-pot (-pot), *n.* a pot with a lid, handle, and spout, for brewing and serving coffee.

cof·fer (kôf'ēr), *n.* 1. a chest or strongbox. 2. a cofferdam. 3. a sunken panel, as on a ceiling. 4. *pl.* a treasury; funds: *v.t.* to enclose in a coffer.

cof·fer·dam (-dam), *n.* 1. a temporary enclosure of piles built in water and pumped dry to enable workmen to lay foundations for piers, etc. 2. a watertight enclosure used in making underwater ship repairs.

cof·fin (kof'in), *n.* 1. a case or box for the dead. 2. the horny part of a horse's hoof.

coffin bone, the foot bone of a horse, that is enclosed in the hoof.

cog (kog), *n.* 1. a tooth of a cogwheel. 2. a cogwheel. —**cogged,** *adj.*

co·gent (kō'jênt), *adj.* forcible; to the point; convincing. —**co'gen·cy,** *n.*

cog·i·tate (koj'i-tāt), *v.t. & v.i.* -tat·ed, -tat·ing, to meditate; ponder; think hard (about). —**cog·i·ta'tion,** *n.* —**cog'i·ta'tor,** *n.*

co·gnac (kōn'yak, kon'-), *n.* a kind of French brandy.

cog·nate (kog'nāt), *adj.* 1. related by blood. 2. of the same stock, nature, or quality. 3. from a common earlier form, as words: *n.* 1. a related person. 2. a related language, word, thing, etc. —**cog·na'tion,** *n.*

cog·ni·tion (kog-nish'ún), *n.* 1. the process of perceiving, or knowing. 2. a perception, idea, etc. —**cog'ni·tive,** *adj.*

cog·ni·za·ble (kog'ni·zá-bl), *adj.* 1. that may be

known. 2. within the jurisdiction of a given law court.

cog·ni·zance (kog'ni-záns), *n.* 1. perception. 2. judicial power or right; jurisdiction. 3. notice or heed. —**cog'ni·zant** (-zánt), *adj.*

cog·no·men (kog-nō'mên), *n.*, *pl.* **-no'mens,** **-nom'i·na** (-nom'i-nà), a surname; last name. —**cog·nom'i·nal,** *adj.*

cog·wheel (kog'hwēl, 'wēl), *n.* a wheel with teeth on the rim that mesh with those of another wheel, etc.

co·hab·it (kō-hab'it), *v.i.* to live together as husband and wife. —**co·hab·i·ta'tion,** *n.*

co·here (kō-hir'), *v.i.* -hered', -her'ing, 1. to stick together. 2. to be logically or naturally connected.

co·her·ence (kō-hir'êns), *n.* 1. the act or state of cohering. 2. consistency; logical connection. 3. intelligibility. Also **co·her'en·cy.** —**co·her'ent,** *adj.* —**co·her'ent·ly,** *adv.*

co·he·sion (kō-hē'zhún), *n.* 1. the force that unites together molecules of the same material. 2. a sticking together; coherence. —**co·he'sive,** *adj.* —**co·he'sive·ly,** *adv.* —**co·he'sive·ness,** *n.*

co·ho (kō'hō), *n.*, *pl.* **-hos,** **-ho,** a small salmon of the northern U.S.

co·hort (kō'hôrt), *n.* 1. a tenth of a legion in ancient Rome, from 300 to 600 soldiers. 2. any band or group. 3. an associate.

coif (koif), *n.* 1. a cap that fits closely. 2. (kwof), a hair style.

coif·feur (kwo-fûr'), *n.* a hairdresser.

coif·fure (kwo-fyoor'), *n.* 1. a headdress. 2. a style of arranging the hair: *v.t.* -fured', -fur'ing, to style (the hair).

coil (koil), *n.* 1. a series of connected rings or a spiral into which something has been wound. 2. a single ring from such a series. 3. a spiral of electrical wire.

coin (koin), *n.* 1. a piece of metal stamped with a legal impression and used as money. 2. such pieces collectively. 3. earlier spelling of **quoin:** *v.t.* 1. to make (coins) by stamping (metal). 2. to invent (a new word or phrase). —**coin'er,** *n.*

coin·age ('ij), *n.* 1. the process of coining. 2. coins collectively. 3. a system of metal currency. 4. an invented word or phrase.

co·in·cide (kō-in-sīd'), *v.i.* -cid'ed, -cid'ing, 1. to correspond exactly. 2. to occur at the same time. 3. to fall upon, or meet, in the same point.

co·in·ci·dence (kō-in'si-dêns), *n.* 1. the act or fact of coinciding. 2. a remarkable occurrence of events at the same time, with no apparent relationship. —**co·in'ci·dent,** *adj.* —**co·in'ci·dent·ly,** *adv.*

co·in·ci·den·tal (kō-in-si-den'tl), *adj.* happening by coincidence. —**co·in·ci·den'tal·ly,** *adv.*

coir (koir), *n.* the prepared fiber of coconut husks, ready for making rope, matting, etc.

co·i·tus (kō'it-ús), *n.* sexual intercourse: also **co·i·tion** (kō-ish'ún). —**co'i·tal,** *adj.*

coke (kōk), *n.* fuel prepared by heating coal until most of the gases have been removed: *v.t. & v.i.* **coked, cok'ing,** to convert into coke.

co·la (kō'lá), *n.* 1. an extract obtained from the nut of an African tree and used as flavoring and in medicines. 2. a carbonated soft drink flavored with this extract.

col·an·der (kul'ăn-dẽr, kol'-), n. a perforated container for draining liquids from foods.

col·chi·cum (kol'chi-kŭm), n. 1. a plant of the lily family with flowers like crocus that bloom in the fall. 2. the dried seeds or corms of this plant, used in making medicine.

cold (kōld), adj. 1. without heat or warmth. 2. of a subnormal temperature. 3. too cool; chilly. 4. indifferent; not friendly. 5. without passion or zeal. 6. not fresh, as a hunting track that is old. 7. [Informal], without preparation. 8. [Slang], unconscious. 9. [Slang], completely learned: n. 1. the opposite of heat. 2. the sensation produced by the loss of heat. 3. cold weather. 4. an inflammation of the respiratory tract that causes coughing, sore throat, etc. —cold'ly, adv. — cold'ness, n.

cold-blood·ed (kōld'blud'id), adj. 1. denoting animals, as fishes and reptiles, with body temperatures about that of the surrounding air or water. 2. heartless; brutal. —cold'blood'ed·ly, adv. —cold'blood'ed·ness, n.

cold·ish, ('ish), adj. somewhat cold.

cold shoulder, [Informal], a rebuff or snub.

cold turkey, [Slang], an abrupt withdrawal from drugs by an addict.

cold war, hostility between nations without armed conflict.

cole (kōl), n. any of several plants related to the cabbage; especially, rape.

co·le·op·ter·ous (kō'li-op'těr-ŭs), adj. denoting an order of insects with horny front wings covering the hind wings: the order includes the beetles.

cole·slaw (kōl'slô), n. cabbage salad: also cole slaw.

co·le·us (kō'li-ŭs), n. a plant of the mint family, with large, brightly colored leaves.

col·ic (kol'ik), n. acute spasmodic pain in the abdomen or bowels: adj. 1. of colic. 2. of the colon. —col'ick·y, adj.

col·i·se·um (kol-i-sē'ŭm), n. 1. [C-], the Colosseum. 2. a large stadium, building, or theater, for exhibitions, shows, etc.

co·li·tis (kō-lī'tis), n. inflammation of the colon.

col·lab·o·rate (kŏ-lab'ô-rāt), v.i. -rat·ed, -rat·ing, 1. to work jointly, especially in literary, scientific, or artistic work. 2. to cooperate with the enemy, especially enemy forces occupying one's own country. —col·lab·o·ra'tion, n. —col·lab'o·ra·tive, adj. —col·lab'o·ra·tor, n.

col·lab·o·ra·tion·ist (kŏ-lab-ô-rā'shŭn-ist), n. one who cooperates with enemy forces who have invaded his own country.

col·lage (kŏ-läzh'), n. 1. the composition of a work of art by pasting flowers, bits of paper, cloth, etc. on a surface. 2. such a work of art.

col·lapse (kŏ-laps'), n. 1. a falling in or together. 2. a sudden and complete failure or breakdown: v.i. -lapsed', -laps'ing, 1. to fall in or together. 2. to break down suddenly. 3. to fail suddenly in health; especially, to fall unconscious. 4. to fold

together neatly: v.t. to cause to collapse. — col·laps'i·ble, adj.

col·lar (kol'ẽr), n. 1. anything encircling the neck, as a part of a garment, a necklace, etc. 2. a leather band for the neck of a dog, cat, etc. 3. a ring or flange on a metal pipe, etc.: v.t. 1. to put a collar on. 2. to seize by the collar.

col·lar·bone (-bōn), n. same as clavicle.

col·lard (kol'ẽrd), n. a kind of kale with coarse leaves, eaten as cooked greens.

col·late (ko-lāt'), v.t. -lat'ed, -lat'ing, 1. to compare (texts, manuscripts, etc.) critically in order to determine points of agreement or disagreement. 2. to put (pages) in the proper order. 3. to place (a clergyman) in a benefice. —col·la'tor, n.

col·lat·er·al (kŏ-lat'ẽr-ăl), adj. 1. side by side. 2. corresponding. 3. corroborating. 4. descended from the same stock, but in a different line. 5. denoting money or property pledged as security for repayment of a loan, etc.: n. 1. a kinsman. 2. collateral security. —col·lat'er·al·ly, adv.

col·la·tion (ko-lā'shŭn), n. 1. the act of collating. 2. a conference or gathering. 3. a light repast.

col·league (kol'ēg), n. an associate in the same office, employment, or profession.

col·lect (kŏ-lekt'), v.t. 1. to gather together; assemble. 2. to accumulate (stamps, etc.) as a hobby. 3. to receive payment for. 4. to regain control of (one's thoughts, etc.): v.i. to meet together or accumulate: adj. & adv. to be paid for by the recipient. —col·lect'a·ble, col·lect'i·ble, adj. —col·lec'tor, n.

col·lect (kol'ekt), n. [also C-], a brief prayer used in certain church services.

col·lect·ed (kŏ-lek'tid), adj. 1. calm; composed. 2. brought together.

col·lec·tion ('shŭn), n. 1. the act of gathering together. 2. a mass; accumulation. 3. things collected, especially an assemblage of works of art, etc. 4. money collected.

col·lec·tive ('tiv), adj. 1. of or by a group. 2. formed by collection. 3. denoting a noun that stands for a group of individuals, as flock, team, or audience: n. 1. those working together in a collective enterprise. 2. such an enterprise, especially a collective farm. 3. a collective noun. —col·lec'tive·ly, adv.

collective bargaining, negotiations between an employer and workers collectively, as a union, to determine wages, hours, fringe benefits, etc.

col·lec·tiv·ism (-izm), n. collective control and ownership of the means of production and distribution. —col·lec'tiv·ist, adj. & n. —col·lec'tiv·ize, v.t. -ized, -iz·ing.

col·leen (kol'ēn), n. [Irish], a girl.

col·lege (kol'ij), n. 1. a group of persons with certain powers and rights. 2. an institution of higher learning that grants degrees. 3. one of the schools of a university. 4. an institution giving training in vocational or technical fields. 5. a building housing a college.

College of Cardinals, the council of cardinals of the Roman Catholic Church, who advise the Pope and elect his successor.

ă in cap, ā in cane, ä in father, å in abet, e in met, ē in be, ē in baker, ĭn regent, i in pit, ī in fine, i in manifest, o in hot, ô in horse, ō in bone,

col·le·gian (kŏ-lē'jăn), *n.* a college student.

col·le·giate ('jăt, 'jē-ăt), *adj.* of, pertaining to, or like a college or college students.

col·let (kol'it), *n.* the part of a ring in which the stone is set.

col·lide (kŏ-līd'), *v.i.* -lid'ed, -lid'ing, 1. to crash together violently. 2. to clash or disagree.

col·lie (kol'i), *n.* a large, long-haired dog of a breed originally raised in Scotland for herding sheep.

col·lier (kol'yĕr), *n.* [Chiefly British], 1. a coal miner. 2. a ship that transports coal.

col·lier·y (-ĭ), *n., pl.* -lier·ies, [Chiefly British], a coal mine and all its buildings, equipment, etc.

col·li·gate (kol'ĭ-gāt), *v.t.* -gat·ed, -gat·ing, to bind together. —**col·li·ga'tion,** *n.*

col·lin·e·ar (kŏ-lĭn'i-ĕr), *adj.* lying in the same straight line.

col·li·sion (kŏ-lĭzh'ŭn), *n.* 1. the act of colliding. 2. a clash or disagreement.

col·lo·cate (kol'ŏ-kāt), *v.t.* -cat·ed, -cat·ing, to arrange or place side by side. —**col·lo·ca'tion,** *n.*

col·lo·di·on (kŏ-lō'di-ŏn), *n.* a preparation of nitrocellulose with alcohol and ether, used in making photographic film and as a coating for wounds.

col·loid (kol'oid), *n.* a substance consisting of very finely divided particles suspended in a medium of different matter. —**col·loid'al,** *adj.*

col·lop (kol'ŏp), *n.* a small slice of meat.

col·lo·qui·al (kŏ-lō'kwi-ăl), *adj.* used in ordinary, informal conversation. —**col·lo'qui·al·ism,** *n.* —**col·lo'qui·al·ly,** *adv.*

col·lo·qui·um (kŏ-lō'kwi-ŭm), *n., pl.* -qui·a (-ă), -qui·ums, a conference or seminar on some subject.

col·lo·quy (kol'ŏ-kwi), *n., pl.* -quies, 1. a conversation; dialogue. 2. a conference.

col·lu·sion (kŏ-lōō'zhŭn), *n.* a secret agreement for fraudulent or illegal purposes. —**col·lu'sive,** *adj.* —**col·lu'sive·ly,** *adv.*

co·logne (kŏ-lōn'), *n.* a fragrant liquid used to freshen and perfume the skin.

co·lon (kō'lŏn), *n.* 1. a mark of punctuation (:) used before a series, example, etc. 2. *pl.* -lons, -la ('lă), the lower part of the large intestine.

colo·nel (kûr'nĕl), *n.* 1. a military officer ranking above a lieutenant colonel. 2. an honorary title in some southern and western States. —**colo'nel·cy,** *n., pl.* -cies.

co·lo·ni·al (kŏ-lō'ni-ăl), *adj.* 1. of or pertaining to a colony. 2. [often C-], of or pertaining to the 13 British colonies that became the U.S.: *n.* an inhabitant of a colony. —**co·lo'ni·al·ly,** *adv.*

co·lo·ni·al·ism (-ĭzm), *n.* the policy or practice of keeping foreign colonies, especially for economic exploitation. —**co·lo'ni·al·ist,** *adj. & n.*

col·o·nist (kol'ŏ-nist), *n.* 1. one who helps to found a colony. 2. an inhabitant of a colony.

col·o·nize (-nīz), *v.t. & v.i.* -nized, -niz·ing, 1. to settle in a colony. 2. to establish a colony in. —**col·o·ni·za'tion,** *n.* —**col'o·niz·er,** *n.*

col·on·nade (kol-ŏ-nād'), *n.* a series of columns. —**col·on·nad'ed,** *adj.*

col·o·ny (kol'ŏ-ni), *n., pl.* -nies, 1. a group of people who settle in another land, but are under the jurisdiction of their native land. 2. the country thus settled. 3. a section of a city inhabited by a particular nationality group. 4. a number of animals or plants living or growing together.

col·o·phon (kol'ŏ-fon), *n.* the distinctive emblem of a publisher.

col·or (kul'ĕr), *n.* 1. the appearance or hue of an object in regard to the wavelength of light reflected from it. 2. a pigment, paint, dye, or other coloring matter. 3. color of the face or skin. 4. *pl.* a flag. 5. *pl.* a uniform, badge, etc. of a distinctive color. 6. vividness. 7. a pretense; false show: *v.t.* 1. to impart color to; tint, dye, paint, etc. 2. to change the color of. 3. to distort: *v.i.* 1. to become colored. 2. to change color. 3. to blush.

col·o·rad·o (kol-ŏ-rad'ō), *adj.* reddish; medium in color and strength: said of cigars.

Colorado beetle, a yellow-and-black beetle that is very destructive to potato crops.

col·or·ant (kul'ĕr-ănt), *n.* a coloring agent, as a dye, pigment, etc.

col·or·a·tion (-ā'shŭn), *n.* 1. a method of using color. 2. appearance as to color.

col·o·ra·tu·ra (kul-ĕr-ă-tyoor'ă), *n.* a lyric soprano proficient in singing elaborate trills, runs, etc.: also **coloratura soprano.**

col·or·blind (-blīnd), *adj.* unable to perceive color or to distinguish certain colors. —**col'or·blind·ness,** *n.*

col·or·cast (-kast), *n.* a telecast in color: *v.t. & v.i.* -cast or -cast·ed, -cast·ing, to telecast in color.

col·ored (kul'ĕrd), *adj.* 1. having color. 2. of a race other than Caucasoid; specifically, Negro.

col·or·ful (kul'ĕr-fŭl), *adj.* 1. brightly colored. 2. picturesque. —**col'or·ful·ly,** *adv.*

col·or·im·e·ter (kul-ŏ-rim'ĕ-tĕr), *n.* an instrument for measuring the hue and intensity of color.

col·or·ing (kul'ĕr-ing), *n.* 1. the act or art of giving a color to. 2. the color so applied. 3. specious appearance.

col·or·ist (-ist), *n.* an artist whose works are characterized by beauty of color.

col·or·less (-lis), *adj.* 1. dull; pallid. 2. uninteresting. —**col'or·less·ness,** *n.*

color line, any set of political, social, or economic restrictions imposed on Negroes or other nonwhites: also **color bar.**

co·los·sal (kŏ-los'ăl), *adj.* 1. like a colossus in size; gigantic. 2. [Informal], noteworthy. —**co·los'sal·ly,** *adv.*

Col·os·se·um (kol-ŏ-sē'ŭm), *n.* 1. an amphitheater in Rome. 2. [c-], same as coliseum.

Co·los·sians (kŏ-losh'ănz), *n.* a book of the New Testament.

co·los·sus (kŏ-los'ŭs), *n., pl.* -los'si (-ī), -los'sus·es, 1. a statue of gigantic size. 2. anything huge or impressive.

col·our (kul'ĕr), *n. & v.t. & v.i.* British form for color.

col·por·tage (kol'pôr·tij), *n.* the distribution or sale of Bibles and religious tracts by colporteurs.

col·por·teur (-tĕr), *n.* one who travels from place to place distributing or selling Bibles and religious tracts.

colt (kōlt), *n.* 1. a young male horse, donkey, etc. 2. a young, inexperienced fellow. 3. a knotted end of a rope, formerly used for flogging, as aboard ship. —**colt'ish**, *adj.* —**colt'ish·ly**, *adv.*

col·ter (kōl'tĕr), *n.* a cutting blade on a plow that makes vertical cuts in the soil.

colts·foot (kōlts'foot), *n., pl.* -**foots**, a plant with small, yellow flower heads and large leaves shaped like a colt's foot.

col·u·brine (kol'yoo·brīn), *adj.* 1. of or like a snake. 2. denoting a large family of nonpoisonous snakes.

Co·lum·bi·an (kō·lum'bi·ăn), *adj.* 1. pertaining to Christopher Columbus (1451?-1506), discoverer of America. 2. of the U.S., poetically personified as a woman (*Columbia*).

col·um·bine (kol'ŭm·bīn), *n.* a plant of the buttercup family, having spurred flowers of various colors.

Co·lum·bus Day (kō·lum'bŭs), the second Monday in October, a legal holiday in most States, marking the discovery of America by Columbus in 1492.

col·umn (kol'ŭm), *n.* 1. a round pillar to support or adorn a building. 2. anything like a column in formation or function. 3. a vertical division of printed matter on a page. 4. a formation of troops, ships, etc. in a file. 5. a regular feature or department in a newspaper, etc. —**col'um·nar** (kō·lum'nĕr), *adj.*

col·um·nist (kol'ŭm·nist), *n.* a writer of a column in a newspaper, etc.

col·za (kol'zä), *n.* any of several plants of the mustard family; especially, rape.

colza oil, an oil from the seeds of the colza plant, used as a lubricant, etc.

co·ma (kō'mä), *n.* 1. a state of prolonged unconsciousness caused by disease, injury, poison, etc. 2. stupor.

co·ma (kō'mä), *n., pl.* -**mae** ('mē), 1. a nebulous envelope surrounding the nucleus of a comet. 2. a cluster of branches forming the leafy head of a tree. 3. a haze or blur caused by oblique rays of light passing through a lens. —**co'mate** ('māt), *adj.*

Co·man·che (kō·man'chi), *n., pl.* -**ches**, -**che**, a member of a North American Indian tribe of the southwestern U.S.

co·ma·tose (kō'mä·tōs, kom'ä-), *adj.* 1. in a coma. 2. lethargic.

comb (kōm), *n.* 1. a toothed instrument of hard rubber, plastic, metal, etc. for arranging the hair or holding it in place. 2. a tool for straightening wool, etc. 3. a currycomb. 4. a red, fleshy crest on the head of a rooster. 5. a honeycomb: *v.t.* 1. to dress (the hair) with a comb. 2. to search thoroughly: *v.i.* to roll over; break: said of waves.

com·bat (kom'bat), *n.* 1. armed fighting between enemy forces. 2. a struggle or controversy: *adj.* of or for active combat: *v.i.* (kōm-bat', kom'bat), -**bat'ed** or -**bat'ted**, -**bat'ing** or -**bat'ting**, to fight; contend; *v.t.* to fight with; oppose by force. —**com·bat·ant** (kom'bä·tănt, kŏm-bat'nt), *n. & adj.*

com·bat·ive (kōm-bat'iv, kom'bä-tiv), *adj.* pugnacious; fond of fighting. —**com·bat'ive·ly**, *adv.* —**com·bat'ive·ness**, *n.*

comb·er (kō'mĕr), *n.* a large wave that curls at the top as it nears the beach.

com·bi·na·tion (kom·bi·nā'shŭn), *n.* 1. the act of combining. 2. the state of being combined. 3. an association of persons for a common purpose. 4. something formed by combining. 5. the series of numbers to which a dial must be turned to open a combination lock.

combination lock, a keyless lock opened by turning a dial to a preset series of numbers.

com·bine (kŏm-bīn'), *v.t. & v.i.* to unite or join; link closely together: *n.* 1. a combination for business or political purposes, often a fraudulent combination. 2. a machine used to harvest and thresh grain.

comb·ings (kō'mingz), *n.* loose hair, fibers, etc. collected as a result of combing.

combining form, a word form that cannot exist alone, but can combine with affixes or other word forms to make compounds.

com·bo (kom'bō), *n., pl.* -**bos**, [Informal], a combination, as a small group playing jazz or popular music.

com·bus·ti·ble (kŏm-bus'ti-bl), *adj.* that catches fire; flammable: *n.* a flammable substance. —**com·bus·ti·bil'i·ty**, *n.* —**com·bus'ti·bly**, *adv.*

com·bus·tion ('chŭn), *n.* the act of burning, as the union of a flammable substance with oxygen.

come (kum), *v.i.* came, come, com'ing, 1. to move toward. 2. to draw near. 3. to reach. 4. to happen. 5. to take place in a certain order. 6. to be derived or descended. 7. to result. 8. to get to be. 9. to arrive at some state or condition. 10. to be obtainable. 11. to add up (*to*): *interj.* look! stop!

come·back (kum'bak), *n.* 1. a going back to a former condition, as of success. 2. a clever reply.

co·me·di·an (kō·mē'di·ăn), *n.* 1. an actor in comedies. 2. an entertainer who tells jokes.

co·me·di·enne (kō·mē·di·en'), *n.* a woman comedian.

come·down (kum'doun), *n.* a change for the worse in condition or circumstances.

com·e·dy (kom'ĕ·di), *n., pl.* -**dies**, 1. a dramatic representation of the humorous side of life with a happy ending. 2. a comic event.

come·ly (kum'li), *adj.* -**li·er**, -**li·est**, attractive; handsome. —**come'li·ness**, *n.*

co·mes·ti·ble (kō·mes'ti·bl), *adj.* [Rare], suitable for eating: *n. usually pl.* food.

com·et (kom'ĕt), *n.* a luminous celestial body, with an eccentric orbit, consisting, when perfect, of a nucleus, coma, and tail. —**com'et·ar·y** ('ĕ·ter·i), *adj.*

come·up·pance (kum·up'ns), *n.* [Informal], retribution.

com·fit (kum'fit), *n.* a sweetmeat, as a candied nut or fruit.

com·fort (kum'fŏrt), *v.t.* to soothe, ease, or console: *n.* 1. consolation. 2. a person or thing that comforts. 3. a state of quiet enjoyment. 4. a quilted bed covering.

com·fort·a·ble (kumf'tēr-bl, kum'fēr-tă-bl), *adj.* 1. imparting or enjoying comfort. 2. [Informal], adequate: *n.* a bed quilt. —**com'fort·a·bly**, *adv.*

com·fort·er (kum'fēr-tēr), *n.* 1. one who comforts. 2. a long woolen scarf. 3. a bed quilt. 4. [C-], the Holy Spirit (preceded by *the*).

comfort station, a public toilet.

com·frey (kum'fri), *n., pl.* -freys, a plant with rough, hairy leaves and small flowers.

com·fy (kum'fi), *adj.* -fi·er, -fi·est, [Informal], comfortable.

com·ic (kom'ik), *adj.* 1. of or pertaining to comedy. 2. humorous: *n.* 1. a comedian. 2. the funny part of life. 3. *a)* same as **comic strip.** *b) pl.* a newspaper section of comic strips.

com·i·cal (kom'i-kl), *adj.* causing laughter; humorous. —**com·i·cal'i·ty** (-kal'i-ti), *n.* —**com'i·cal·ly,** *adv.*

comic book, a thin paper book consisting of a series of long comic strips.

comic strip, a sequence of cartoons, as in a newspaper, telling a story.

com·ing (kum'ing), *adj.* 1. next. 2. likely to be popular, successful, etc: *n.* arrival.

com·i·ty (kom'i-ti), *n., pl.* -ties, 1. civility; politeness. 2. acts of international courtesy: also **comity of nations.**

com·ma (kom'ă), *n.* a punctuation mark (,), used to show a small separation between parts of a sentence.

com·mand (kŏ-mand'), *v.t.* 1. to order; direct with authority. 2. to have authority over; control. 3. to possess for use. 4. to require as deserved or proper. 5. to control (a location); look over: *v.i.* to act as a commander; exercise power or authority: *n.* 1. an order or direction. 2. authority. 3. a dominating power. 4. ability to use. 5. a naval or military force under the command of a particular authority.

com·man·dant (kom'ăn-dant), *n.* an officer in command of a fort, military school, etc.

com·man·deer (kom-an-dir'), *v.t.* to seize (property) for military or governmental needs.

com·man·der (kŏ-man'dēr), *n.* 1. one who commands. 2. a U.S. naval officer next below a captain.

commander in chief, *pl.* **commanders in chief,** the highest commander of a nation's armed forces.

com·mand·ment (kŏ-mand'mĕnt), *n.* 1. a command; precept; especially, one of the Ten Commandments.

com·man·do (kŏ-man'dō), *n., pl.* -dos, -does, 1. originally, a raid made by Boer troops in South Africa. 2. a member of a small raiding force that works inside enemy territory.

com·mem·o·rate (kŏ-mem'ō-rāt), *v.t.* -rat·ed, -rat·ing, to call to memory by a solemn act. 2. to be a memorial to. —**com·mem·o·ra'tion,** *n.* —**com·mem'o·ra·tive,** *adj.*

com·mence (kŏ-mens'), *v.i.* & *v.t.* -menced', -menc'ing, to begin; start.

com·mence·ment (-mĕnt), *n.* 1. a beginning; origin. 2. the periodic ceremony when degrees, diplomas, etc. are conferred at colleges or schools.

com·mend (kŏ-mend'), *v.t.* 1. to turn over to another's care; entrust. 2. to recommend as worthy of notice. 3. to praise. —**com·mend'a·ble,** *adj.* —**com·mend'a·bly,** *c.tv.*

com·men·da·tion (kom-en-dā'shŭn), *n.* the act of commending; especially, praise.

com·men·da·to·ry (kŏ-men'dă-tôr-i), *adj.* 1. serving to commend; containing praise. 2. recommending.

com·men·su·ra·ble (kŏ-men'shēr-ă-bl), *adj.* having, or reducible to, a common measure. —**com·men·su·ra·bil'i·ty,** *n.*

com·men·su·rate (-it), *adj.* 1. reducible to a common measure. 2. equal in measure or size. 3. corresponding in degree; proportionate.

com·ment (kom'ent), *n.* 1. a spoken or written remark. 2. a written note containing criticism, explanation, etc. 3. chatter; gossip: *v.t.* to make remarks or comments (followed by *on* or *upon*).

com·men·tar·y (kom'ĕn-ter-i), *n., pl.* -tar·ies, 1. a series of explanatory notes or annotations. 2. a series of remarks.

com·men·tate (-tāt), *v.i.* -tat·ed, -tat·ing, to act as a commentator.

com·men·ta·tor (-ĕr), *n.* 1. one who writes or gives a commentary. 2. a person who analyzes and reports news, developments, etc., as on television.

com·merce (kom'ērs), *n.* 1. the interchange of goods on a large scale between nations or individuals. 2. social intercourse.

com·mer·cial (kŏ-mŭr'shăl), *adj.* 1. of or pertaining to trade or commerce. 2. operating for profit: *n.* in *Radio & Television,* an advertisement. —**com·mer'cial·ly,** *adv.*

com·mer·cial·ism (-izm), *n.* commercial habits, methods, or principles, often as indicating too high a concern for profit.

com·mer·cial·ize (-īz), *v.t.* -ized, -iz·ing, to operate with business methods, often so as to make profit the main purpose.

com·mi·na·tion (kom-i-na'shŭn), *n.* a threat; denunciation.

com·min·gle (kŏ-ming'gl), *v.t.* & *v.i.* -gled, -gling, to mix; blend.

com·mi·nute (kom'i-nŏŏt), *v.t.* -nut·ed, -nut·ing, to make small or fine by grinding.

com·mis·er·ate (kŏ-miz'ē-rāt), *v.t.* -at·ed, -at·ing, to feel or show pity for: *v.i.* to sympathize (*with*). —**com·mis·er·a'tion,** *n.*

com·mis·sar (kom'i-sär), *n.* one of the heads of the former commissariats in the U.S.S.R.: now called *minister.*

com·mis·sar·i·at (kom-i-ser'i-ăt), *n.* 1. the department of an army concerned with the supply of provisions. 2. formerly, any of the government departments in the U.S.S.R.: now called *ministry.*

com·mis·sar·y (kom'i-ser-i), *n., pl.* -sar·ies, 1. one to whom some charge is given by a superior; delegate. 2. formerly, an army officer in the commissariat department. 3. a store, as in an army camp, which sells food and supplies. 4. a restaurant in a film or TV studio.

com·mis·sion (kŏ-mish'ŭn), *n.* 1. a delegation of business to anyone. 2. a warrant by which this is done. 3. a trust or charge. 4. the act of doing or committing. 5. one or more persons appointed to perform certain specified duties. 6. a brokerage or allowance based on sales. 7. in the *Military*, *a*) an official document giving rank. *b*) the rank given: *v.t.* 1. to give a commission to. 2. to empower; send with authority. 3. *in nautical usage*, to enter (a vessel) into service.

commissioned officer, an officer in the armed forces holding a commission.

com·mis·sion·er (kŏ-mish'ŭ-nêr), *n.* 1. a person empowered by a commission or warrant. 2. a commission member. 3. an officer in charge of certain departments of the government. 4. a person chosen to exercise control of a professional sport.

com·mis·sure (kom'i-shoor), *n.* a joint or seam; the point of union between two parts.

com·mit (kŏ-mit'), *v.t.* -mit·ted, -mit·ting, 1. to give in charge or trust; consign. 2. to send for trial, or to prison. 3. to perpetrate (a crime). 4. to engage; pledge. 5. to learn by heart. —**com·mit'ment, com·mit'tal,** *n.*

com·mit·tee (kŏ-mit'i), *n.* persons appointed to consider or manage a certain matter.

com·mode (kŏ-mōd'), *n.* 1. a high headdress worn by women around 1700. 2. a chest of drawers. 3. a portable washstand. 4. a toilet.

com·mo·di·ous (kŏ-mō'di-ŭs), *adj.* roomy; having plenty of space.

com·mod·i·ty (kŏ-mod'i-ti), *n., pl.* -ties, 1. that which is useful. 2. an article of commerce. 3. *pl.* goods; merchandise.

com·mo·dore (kom'ŏ-dôr), *n.* 1. in *U.S. Navy*, an officer ranking below a rear admiral: a former rank. 2. in *British Navy*, an unofficial title for a captain temporarily commanding a squadron. 3. a title of courtesy given as to the senior captain of a line of vessels.

com·mon (kom'ŏn), *adj.* 1. belonging equally to more than one. 2. public. 3. prevalent. 4. usual; frequent. 5. of low birth or origin. 6. inferior. 7. low; vulgar. 8. *a*) denoting a noun that refers to any of a class, as a book. *b*) designating nouns that are either masculine or feminine, as child: *n. sometimes pl.* a tract of open public land. —**com'mon·ly,** *adv.*

com·mon·age (-ij), *n.* the right of pasturing on public land.

com·mon·al·ty (kom'ŏn-ăl-ti), *n., pl.* -ties, the common people.

common carrier, a business or person that transports goods or passengers for a uniform rate.

common denominator, 1. a common multiple of the denominators of two or more fractions. 2. a characteristic, etc. held in common.

common divisor, a factor common to two or more numbers: also **common factor**

com·mon·er (-êr), *n.* 1. one of the ordinary people, not of the nobility. 2. at Oxford University, a student not receiving a schol-

arship or fellowship.

common law, the law of a country founded on usage, custom, and court decisions.

common market, an association of countries for closer economic union.

common multiple, a multiple of each of two or more quantities.

com·mon·place (-plās), *n.* 1. originally, a part of a written work noted for reference. 2. an obvious remark. 3. anything ordinary: *adj.* uninteresting; trite; common.

common pleas, in *Law*, in some States, a court that has jurisdiction over criminal and civil matters.

com·mons (kom'ŏnz), *n.* 1. the common people, as distinguished from the nobility. 2. [C-], same as **House of Commons.** 3. a room where food is served, as at a college.

common sense, sound practical judgment. —**com'mon-sense',** *adj.*

common time, in *Music,* a meter of four beats to the measure; 4/4 time.

com·mon·weal (-wēl), *n.* the public good.

com·mon·wealth (-welth), *n.* 1. the whole body of people in a state. 2. a republic or democracy. 3. a federation of states.

com·mo·tion (kŏ-mō'shŭn), *n.* 1. violent agitation. 2. a noisy confusion; bustle.

com·mu·nal (kom'yoon-l, kŏ-mūn'l), *adj.* 1. of or pertaining to a commune. 2. public. 3. designating shared ownership of property. —**com·mu'nal·ly,** *adv.*

com·mu·nal·ize (-īz), *v.t.* -ized, -iz·ing, to make communal. —**com·mu·nal·i·za'tion,** *n.*

com·mune (kŏ-mūn'), *v.i.* -muned', -mun'ing, 1. to converse together. 2. to receive Holy Communion.

com·mune (kom'ūn), *n.* 1. formerly, the common people. 2. a local self-governing body. 3. the smallest district of local government administration in France and some other European countries. 4. a small number of people living together in a communal fashion.

com·mu·ni·ca·ble (kŏ-mū'ni-kă-bl), *adj.* that can be passed along, as an idea or disease. —**com·mu·ni·ca·bil'i·ty,** *n.*

com·mu·ni·cant (-kănt), *n.* 1. one who receives Holy Communion. 2. [Rare], an informant: *adj.* [Rare], communicating.

com·mu·ni·cate (kŏ-mū'ni-kāt), *v.t.* -cat·ed, -cat·ing, 1. to pass along; impart. 2. to reveal: *v.i.* 1. to receive Holy Communion. 2. to share information. 3. to have a sympathetic relationship. 4. to be connected. —**com·mu'ni·ca·tor,** *n.*

com·mu·ni·ca·tion (kŏ-mū-ni-kā'shŭn), *n.* 1. the act of communicating. 2. a sharing of information. 3. a means of communicating, as a way of passing from one place to another. 4. news; a message. —**com·mu'ni·ca·tive,** *adj.*

com·mun·ion (kŏ-mūn'yŭn), *n.* 1. common possession. 2. a communing. 3. good fellowship. 4. a denomination of Christians. 5. [C-], same as **Holy Communion.**

com·mu·ni·qué (kŏ-mū-ni-kā'), *n.* any communication issued officially.

com·mu·nism (kom'yŭ-nizm), *n.* 1. the doctrine or system of having all property in common. 2. [often C-], *a*) the socialism of Len-in, Marx, etc. b) a government or political group advocating this.

com·mu·nist (-nist), n. 1. a supporter of communism. 2. [C-], a member of a Communist Party: adj. of or pertaining to communism or communists, or [C-], to a Communist Party. **—com·mu·nis·tic**, adj.

com·mu·ni·tar·i·an (kŏ-mū-nĭ-ter'ĭ-ăn), n. a member or supporter of a communistic community.

com·mu·ni·ty (kŏ-mū'nĭ-tĭ), n., pl. -ties, 1. a body of persons living in the same place or having common rights, interests, and privileges. 2. the area where such persons live. 3. society generally. 4. ownership in common. 5. common character.

community college, a junior college supported by a particular community for its students.

com·mut·a·ble (kŏ-mūt'ă-bl), adj. interchangeable. **—com·mut·a·bil'i·ty**, n.

com·mu·ta·tion (kom-yū-tā'shŭn), n. substitution of a lesser for a greater.

com·mu·ta·tive (kom'yū-tāt-ĭv), adj. of or pertaining to exchange.

com·mu·ta·tor (kom'yū-tāt-ēr), n. an electrical device that changes alternating current to direct current.

com·mute (kŏ-mūt'), v.t. -mut'ed, -mut'ing, 1. to exchange; substitute. 2. to reduce the severity of: v.i. 1. to pay in a gross amount. 2. to serve as a substitute. 3. to travel regularly as a commuter.

com·mut·er ('ēr), n. a person who travels regularly, esp. by train, bus, etc., between two points at some distance.

com·pact (kŏm-pakt', kom'pakt), adj. 1. dense; solid. 2. tightly arranged. 3. not wordy: n. (kom'pakt), 1. a small container for facial cosmetics. 2. a smaller car model. 3. an agreement or covenant: v.t. (kom-pakt'), 1. to press or pack closely. 2. to consolidate. **—com·pact'ly**, adv. **—com·pact'ness**, n.

compact disc, a disc on which a program, music, etc. have been encoded electronically for playing on a device using a laser beam to read the encoded matter.

com·pac·tor (-pak'tĕr), n. a device that compresses trash into small bundles.

com·pan·ion (kŏm-pan'yŭn), n. 1. a comrade; associate or partner. 2. a person whose job is to accompany another. 3. a thing that is part of a set or pair. 4. the covering of a companionway. **—com·pan'ion·a·ble**, adj.

com·pan·ion·ship (-ship), n. fellowship.

com·pan·ion·way (-wā), n. the stairs leading from the deck of a ship to the area below.

com·pa·ny (kum'pă-ni), n., pl. -nies, 1. fellowship; society. 2. a body of persons associated together. 3. a business firm. 4. one or a number of guests. 5. associates. 6. a ship's crew. 7. a small unit of troops: v.i. to associate (followed by with).

com·pa·ra·ble (kom'păr-ă-bl), adj. 1. capable of being compared. 2. of equal regard. **—com'pa·ra·bly**, adv.

com·par·a·tive (kŏm-par'ă-tĭv), adj. 1. that compares. 2. estimated by comparison. 3. in Grammar, pertaining to the next degree of comparison greater than the positive: n. the comparative degree.

com·pare (kŏm-per'), v.t. -pared', -par'ing, 1. to

make one thing the measure of another. 2. to analyze for likeness or difference. 3. in Grammar, to form the degrees of comparison: v.i. 1. to bear a comparison (followed by with). 2. to make comparisons.

com·par·i·son (kŏm-per'ĭ-sn), n. 1. the act of comparing. 2. similarity. 3. in Grammar, the alteration of an adjective or adverb to indicate the positive, comparative, and superlative degrees.

com·part·ment (kŏm-pärt'mĕnt), n. 1. a division by a partition. 2. a separate section or part.

com·part·men·tal·ize (kŏm-pärt-men'tă-līz), v.t. -ized, iz·ing, to put into separate divisions. **—com·part·men·tal·i·za'tion**, n.

com·pass (kum'păs), v.t. 1. to encircle. 2. to go around. 3. to comprehend. 4. to accomplish: n. 1. often pl. an instrument with two pointed legs on a pivot, for drawing circles and measuring. 2. a circumference. 3. a closed area. 4. an extent; scope. 5. an instrument indicating the magnetic north by means of a needle on a pivot.

com·pas·sion (kŏm-pash'ŭn), n. sorrow for the sufferings of others; sympathy; pity.

com·pas·sion·ate (-ĭt), adj. sympathetic; merciful: v.t. (-āt), -at·ed, -at·ing, to have compassion for. **—com·pas'sion·ate·ly**, adv.

com·pat·i·ble (kŏm-pat'ĭ-bl), adj. 1. congruous; in agreement. **—com·pat·i·bil'i·ty**, n. **—com·pat'i·bly**, adv.

com·pa·tri·ot (kŏm-pā'trĭ-ŏt), n. a fellow countryman: adj. belonging to the same country. **—com·peer** (kom'pir), n. 1. an equal. 2. a companion.

com·pel (kŏm-pel'), v.t. -pelled', -pel'ling, 1. to urge by force. 2. to get by force. **—com·pel'ling·ly**, adv.

com·pen·di·ous (kŏm-pen'di·ŭs), adj. concise but including all the necessary parts.

com·pen·di·um (-ŭm), n., pl. -di·ums, -di·a (-ă), a concise summary containing all the necessary parts: also **com·pend** (kom'pend).

com·pen·sate (kom'pĕn-sāt), v.t. -sat·ed, -sat·ing, 1. to be a counterbalance to. 2. to recompense; pay: v.i. to make compensation; make amends (followed by for). **—com·pen·sa'tion**, n. **—com·pen·sa·to·ry** (kom-pen'să-tōr-i), adj.

com·pete (kom-pēt'), v.i. -pet'ed, -pet'ing, to enter into competition with; rival.

com·pe·tence (kom'pē-tĕns), n. 1. the state of being competent. 2. sufficiency.

com·pe·tent (-tĕnt), adj. 1. fit; able; qualified. 2. sufficient. 3. in Law, legally fit or qualified. **—com·pe·tent·ly**, adv.

com·pe·ti·tion (kom-pē-tish'ŭn), n. 1. a competing; rivalry. 2. a contest. 3. rivalry in business. **—com·pet·i·tive** (kŏm-pet'ĭ-tĭv), adj.

com·pet·i·tor (kŏm-pet'ĭ-tĕr), n. a rival, as in business.

com·pi·la·tion (kom-pĭ-lā'shŭn), n. 1. the act of compiling. 2. the thing compiled.

com·pile (kŏm-pīl'), v.t. -piled', -pil'ing, 1. to put together (existing materials) in a fresh, orderly form. 2. to arrange and edit material for (a book, etc.).

com·pla·cen·cy (kŏm-plās'n-si), n. inward satisfaction or smugness: also **com·pla'cence** (plās'ns).

com-pla-cent ('nt), *adj.* 1. satisfied or smug. 2. affable. —**com-pla'cent-ly**, *adv.*

com-plain (kŏm-plān'), *v.i.* 1. to express grief, pain, or resentment. 2. to charge formally. —**com-plain'er**, *n.*

com-plain-ant ('ant), *n.* in *Law*, a plaintiff.

com-plaint (kŏm-plānt'), *n.* 1. an expression of pain, resentment, etc. 2. a cause for this. 3. an ailment. 4. in *Law*, a formal accusation.

com-plai-sance (kŏm-plā'zns), *n.* courtesy; affability. —**com-plai'sant**, *adj.*

com-plect (kŏm-plekt'), *v.t.* [Archaic], to interweave; twine together.

com-plect-ed (-plek'tid), *adj.* [Informal], same as complexioned.

com-ple-ment (kom'plĕ-mĕnt), *n.* 1. that which completes. 2. the amount necessary for completeness. 3. a complete set: *v.t.* (-ment), to supply a deficiency in.

com-ple-men-ta-ry (kom-plĕ-men'tĕr-i), *adj.* 1. completing; entire. 2. absolute. 3. finished: mutually making up what is lacking.

com-plete (kŏm-plēt'), *adj.* 1. free from deficiency; entire. 2. absolute. 3. finished: -plet'ed, -plet'ing, 1. to supply what is lacking. 2. to finish. —**com-plete'ly**, *adv.* —**com-plete'ness**, *n.* —**com-ple'tion** (-plē'shŭn), *n.*

com-plex (kŏm-pleks', kom'pleks), *adj.* 1. composed of related parts or things. 2. intricate; complicated: *n.* (kom'pleks), 1. a group of related things forming a whole. 2. a grouped assemblage, as of buildings. 3. in *Psychoanalysis*, *a*) unconscious, related impulses affecting behavior. *b*) popularly, an obsession. —**com-plex'ly**, *adv.*

com-plex-ion (kŏm-plek'shŭn), *n.* 1. the color, texture, etc. of the skin, especially of the face. 2. aspect.

com-plex-ioned (-shŭnd), *adj.* having a (specified) complexion.

com-plex-i-ty (kŏm-plek'sĭ-ti), *n.* 1. the state of being complex. 2. *pl.* -ties, anything complex.

complex sentence, a sentence composed of a main clause and one or a number of subordinate clauses.

com-pli-a-ble (kŏm-plī'ä-bl), *adj.* [Archaic], same as compliant.

com-pli-ance ('ăns), *n.* 1. acquiescence. 2. a submissive tendency.

com-pli-ant ('ănt), *adj.* yielding; submissive.

com-pli-cate (kom'plĭ-kāt), *v.t.* & *v.i.* -cat-ed, -cat-ing, to make or become intricate or involved: *adj.* 1. [Archaic], intricate. 2. in *Biology*, folded lengthwise.

com-pli-cat-ed (-kāt-id), *adj.* 1. intricately composed. 2. difficult to understand.

com-pli-ca-tion (kom-plĭ-kā'shŭn), *n.* 1. the act of complicating. 2. the state of being complicated.

com-plic-i-ty (kŏm-plis'ĭ-ti), *n.*, *pl.* -ties, 1. partnership in crime. 2. [Rare], complexity.

com-pli-ment (kom'plĭ-mĕnt), *n.* 1. a formal act or expression of courtesy. 2. something expressed in praise or flattery. 3. *pl.* courteous greetings: *v.t.* (-ment), to congratulate or flatter.

com-pli-men-ta-ry (kom-plĭ-men'tĕr-i), *adj.* 1. conveying a compliment. 2. extended freely as a courtesy.

com-ply (kŏm-plī'), *v.i.* -plied', -ply'ing, to act in agreement (followed by *with*).

com-po (kom'pō), *n.*, *pl.* -pos, a composite material, as plaster.

com-po-nent (kŏm-pō'nĕnt), *adj.* constituent: *n.* an elementary part.

com-port (kŏm-pōrt'), *v.i.* to agree; harmonize (followed by *with*): *v.t.* to behave (oneself) in a specified way.

com-port-ment ('mĕnt), *n.* bearing; behavior.

com-pose (kŏm-pōz'), *v.t.* -posed', -pos'ing, 1. to form in combination; constitute. 2. to put together; arrange in proper order. 3. to adjust. 4. to calm. 5. to create (a work of music or literature). 6. to arrange (type): *v.i.* to create works of literature, music, etc.

com-posed (-pōzd'), *adj.* tranquil; quiet.

com-pos-er (-pōz'ẽr), *n.* one who composes; especially, a musical author.

com-pos-ite (kŏm-poz'it), *adj.* 1. made up of separate elements; compound. 2. [C-], in *Architecture*, of or pertaining to an order that combines the Ionic and Corinthian orders. 3. in *Botany*, of or pertaining to a family of plants having flower heads massed together: *n.* 1. a compound. 2. in *Botany*, a plant of the composite family.

com-po-si-tion (kom-pō-zish'ŭn), *n.* 1. the act of composing. 2. the constitution of a person or thing. 3. the thing composed. 4. a mass formed by mingling various ingredients. 5. a musical or literary work. 6. mutual settlement or agreement. 7. the work of typesetting.

com-pos-i-tor (kŏm-poz'ĭ-tẽr), *n.* one who sets type.

com-post (kom'pōst), *n.* a mixture of rotting vegetable materials, manure, etc. for fertilizing the ground: *v.t.* to change (vegetable materials) into compost.

com-po-sure (kŏm-pō'zhẽr), *n.* tranquillity.

com-pote (kom'pōt), *n.* 1. a dish of stewed fruit. 2. a dish with a long stem for serving candy, fruit, etc.

com-pound (kom-pound'), *v.t.* 1. to mix or combine together. 2. to produce by combining parts. 3. to settle by mutual agreement. 4. to discharge (a debt) by paying a part. 5. to figure out (compound interest). 6. to increase by the addition of other elements: *adj.* (kom'pound), composed of two or more elements or ingredients: *n.* (kom'pound), 1. a mixture of two or more elements or ingredients. 2. a material containing two or more elements in chemical combination.

com-pound (kom'pound), *n.* an enclosed area of buildings, as in the Orient.

compound fracture, a bone fracture in which the bone ends cut through the skin.

compound interest, interest that accrues from the addition of principal and unpaid interest.

compound sentence, a sentence made up of two or more independent, coordinate clauses.

com-pre-hend (kom-prĕ-hend'), *v.t.* 1. to grasp with the mind; conceive. 2. to include or comprise. —**com-pre-hen'si-ble** (-hen'sĭ-bl), *adj.* —**com-pre-hen'sion**, *n.*

com·pre·hen·sive (-hen'siv), *adj.* including much; full. —**com·pre·hen'sive·ly**, *adv.*

com·press (kŏm-pres'), *v.t.* to press together; condense: *n.* (kom'pres), 1. a soft pad, often moistened, applied to the body. 2. a device for pressing bales of cotton. —**com·pres'sion**, *n.*

com·pressed air (-prest'), air under pressure in a container.

com·pres·sor (-pres'ēr), *n.* a device for compressing gas, air, etc.

com·prise (kŏm-prīz'), *v.t.* -**prised'**, -**pris'ing**, 1. to include. 2. to be composed of. 3. to constitute: not a formal usage. —**com·pris'al**, *n.*

com·pro·mise (kom'prō-mīz), *n.* 1. a settlement by mutual concession. 2. something between two other things: *v.t. & v.i.* -**mised**, -**mis·ing**, 1. to settle by compromise. 2. to expose to risk, disgrace, etc.

comp·trol·ler (kŏn-trō'lēr), *n.* same as **controller** (sense 1).

com·pul·sion (kŏm-pul'shŭn), *n.* the act of compelling; force; constraint. —**com·pul'sive** ('siv), *adj.*

com·pul·so·ry ('sēr-i), *adj.* 1. obligatory. 2. exercising compulsion.

com·punc·tion (kŏm-pungk'shŭn), *n.* 1. an uneasy, guilty feeling. 2. a regretful feeling.

com·pu·ta·tion (kom-pyoo-tā'shŭn), *n.* 1. the act or process of computing. 2. the amount computed.

com·pute (kŏm-pyōōt'), *v.t. & v.i.* to find (an amount) by calculating; reckon. —**com·put'a·ble**, *adj.*

com·put·er (-pyōōt'ēr), *n.* an electronic device for collecting and organizing data, or doing fast calculation. —**com·put'er·ize** (-īz), *v.t.* -**ized**, -**iz·ing**.

com·rade (kom'rad), *n.* 1. a companion; friend. 2. a partner. —**com'rade·ship**, *n.*

Com·sat (kom'sat), *n.* any of various communications satellites for relaying microwave transmissions, as of telephone and television signals: a trademark.

con (kon), *adv.* in opposition: *n.* a vote, position, etc. in opposition.

con (kon), *v.t.* to peruse carefully; fix in the mind. 2. same as **conn**.

con (kon), *adj.* [Slang], confidence: *v.t.* **conned**, **con'ning**, [Slang], to cheat or fool.

con (kon), *n.* [Slang], a convict.

co·na·tion (kō-nā'shŭn), *n.* in *Psychology*, the faculty of endeavoring or trying. —**con·a·tive** (kon'ă-tiv), *adj.*

con·cat·e·nate (kon'kat'n-āt), *v.t.* -**nat·ed**, -**nat·ing**, to join or link together.

con·cat·e·na·tion (kon-kat-n-ā'shŭn), *n.* a series of things united like links.

con·cave (kon-kāv', kon'kāv), *adj.* hollow and curved like the inner surface of a rounded, hollow body.

con·cav·i·ty (kon-kav'ĭ-ti), *n.* 1. the state of being concave. 2. *pl.* -**ties**, a concave surface.

con·ca·vo·con·cave (-kā'vō-kon-kāv'), *adj.* concave on both sides, as some lenses.

con·ca·vo·con·vex (-kon-veks'), *adj.* concave on one side, convex on the other.

con·ceal (kon-sēl'), *v.t.* 1. to hide. 2. to keep secret.

con·ceal·ment (-mĕnt), *n.* 1. the act of hiding or keeping secret. 2. a place of hiding; shelter.

con·cede (kŏn-sēd'), *v.t.* -**ced'ed**, -**ced'ing**, 1. to admit as valid. 2. to give as a right.

con·ceit (kŏn-sēt'), *n.* 1. originally, an idea. 2. an overestimate of one's own abilities. 3. a fanciful expression. 4. a fancy.

con·ceit·ed ('id), *adj.* vain.

con·ceiv·a·ble (kŏn-sē'vā-bl), *adj.* imaginable or understandable. —**con·ceiv·a·bil'i·ty**, *n.* —**con·ceiv'a·bly**, *adv.*

con·ceive (kŏn-sēv'), *v.t.* -**ceived'**, -**ceiv'ing**, 1. to imagine. 2. to understand. 3. to develop in the womb: *v.i.* 1. to think (followed by *of*). 2. to become pregnant.

con·cen·trate (kon'sĕn-trāt), *v.t.* -**trat·ed**, -**trat·ing**, 1. to bring to a common center. 2. to collect (one's thoughts, actions, etc.). 3. to intensify the strength or density of: *v.i.* to direct one's actions or thoughts (followed by *on* or *upon*): *n.* a material that has been concentrated: *adj.* concentrated. —**con·cen·tra'tion**, *n.* —**con'cen·tra·tor**, *n.*

concentration camp, a prison camp for political offenders, minority ethnic groups, etc.

con·cen·tric (kŏn-sen'trik), *adj.* having a common center.

con·cept (kon'sept), *n.* an abstract general notion or conception.

con·cep·tion (kŏn-sep'shŭn), *n.* 1. the impregnation of the ovum. 2. the act or power of conceiving in the mind. 3. the start of a process. 4. an idea or notion. 5. an original design or plan.

con·cep·tive (-tiv), *adj.* capable of conceiving mentally.

con·cep·tu·al (kon-sep'choo-wăl), *adj.* of or pertaining to conception or concepts. —**con·cep'tu·al·ly**, *adv.*

con·cep·tu·al·ism (-izm), *n.* a theory that universals exist in the mind as concepts. —**con·cep'tu·al·ist**, *n.*

con·cep·tu·al·ize (-īz), *v.t.* -**ized**, -**iz·ing**, to conceive; form an idea of. —**con·cep·tu·al·i·za'tion**, *n.*

con·cern (kŏn-sŭrn), *v.t.* 1. to relate or belong to. 2. to interest or engage. 3. to make uneasy: *n.* 1. business; affair. 2. interest. 3. anxiety; worry. 4. a business firm. 5. relation.

con·cerned (-sŭrnd'), *adj.* 1. engaged or interested (followed by *in*). 2. worried or uneasy.

con·cern·ing (-sŭr'ning), *prep.* about; in regard to.

con·cern·ment (-sŭrn'mĕnt), *n.* [Rare], 1. concern. 2. an affair. 3. worry.

con·cert (kŏn-sŭrt'), *v.t. & v.i.* to contrive or devise together: *n.* (kon'sĕrt), 1. a musical performance. 2. cooperation, harmony, or mutual agreement.

con·cert·ed (-sŭr'tid), *adj.* 1. mutually planned or agreed upon. 2. in *Music*, arranged in parts. —**con·cert'ed·ly**, *adv.*

con·cer·ti·na (kon-sēr-tē'nà), *n.* a musical instrument of the accordion class.

con·cer·ti·no (kon-cher-tē′nō), *n.* a short concerto.

con·cert·ize (kon′sĕr-tīz), *v.i.* -ized, -iz·ing, to take part in concerts as a soloist, as on a concert tour.

con·cer·to (kŏn-cher′tō), *n., pl.* -tos, -ti (′tē), a musical composition for one or a number of solo instruments, with an orchestral accompaniment.

con·ces·sion (kŏn-sesh′ŭn), *n.* 1. the act of conceding. 2. the thing conceded. 3. land, privileges, etc. granted by a government or company, for some specific purpose.

con·ces·sion·aire (-sesh-ŏ-ner′), *n.* the one holding a concession (sense 3).

con·ces·sive (-ses′iv), *adj.* suggesting concession.

conch (kongk, konch), *n., pl.* conchs (kongks), conch·es (kon′chĕz), 1. the large spiral shell of some sea mollusks. 2. the mollusk.

con·cha (kong′kä), *n., pl.* -chae (′kē), 1. the external ear; auricle. 2. the half dome of an apse.

con·choi·dal (kong′koi′dl), *adj.* having elevations or depressions like a clamshell.

con·chol·o·gy (-kol′ō-ji), *n.* the branch of zoology which treats of mollusks and shells.

con·ci·erge (kon-si-ûrzh′), *n.* in France, a doorman or custodian.

con·cil·i·ar (kŏn-sil′i-ĕr), *adj.* of, pertaining to, or by way of a council.

con·cil·i·ate (kŏn-sil′i-āt), *v.t.* -at·ed, -at·ing, 1. to win or gain the affections of. 2. [Archaic], to reconcile. —**con·cil·i·a′tion**, *n.* —**con·cil′i·a·tor**, *n.* —**con·cil′i·a·to·ry** (-â-tôr′i), *adj.*

con·cise (kŏn-sīs′), *adj.* condensed; terse; brief. —**con·cise′ly**, *adv.* —**con·cise′ness**, —**con·ci′sion** (-sizh′ŭn), *n.*

con·clave (kon′klāv), *n.* a private meeting, as of cardinals for the election of a Pope.

con·clude (kŏn-klōōd′), *v.t.* -clud′ed, -clud′ing, 1. to infer. 2. to determine. 3. to settle. 4. to end: *v.i.* 1. to arrive at agreement. 2. to end.

con·clu·sion (-klōō′zhŭn), *n.* 1. the end. 2. a final determination. 3. the result. 4. a final settling (followed by *of*).

con·clu·sive (′siv), *adj.* decisive; final. —**con·clu′sive·ly**, *adv.* —**con·clu′sive·ness**, *n.*

con·coct (-kokt′), *v.t.* 1. to compound. 2. to contrive or plan. —**con·coc′tion**, *n.*

con·com·i·tant (-kom′i-tănt), *adj.* accompanying; attendant: *n.* an attendant circumstance or thing. —**con·com′i·tance**, *n.*

con·cord (kon′kôrd), *n.* 1. harmony; agreement. 2. friendly relations.

con·cord·ance (kŏn-kôr′dns), *n.* 1. agreement. 2. a dictionary of important words, as in a book, with references to the places where they occur.

con·cord·ant (′dnt), *adj.* harmonious.

con·cor·dat (-kôr′dat), *n.* a compact or agreement, as between Church and State.

con·course (kon′kôrs, kông′-), *n.* 1. arriving together. 2. an assembly or crowd. 3. a large space for assembly. 4. a wide street.

con·cres·cence (kon-kres′ns), *n.* in *Biology*, a growing together of separate parts.

con·crete (kon-krēt′), *adj.* 1. real. 2. not abstract. 3. coalesced. 4. formed of concrete: *n.* 1. a concrete thing. 2. a compact mass of sand, gravel, cement, etc. used for building: *v.t.* -cret′ed, -cret′ing, 1. to make solid. 2. to cover with concrete: *v.i.* to solidify. —**con·crete′ly**, *adv.* —**con·crete′ness**, *n.*

con·cre·tion (-krē′shŭn), *n.* 1. the act of making something concrete. 2. a mass formed by the union of separate particles.

con·cu·bi·nage (kon-kū′bĭ-nij), *n.* the act of living as man and wife without being legally married.

con·cu·bine (kong′kyŭ-bīn), *n.* 1. a woman who lives with a man without being legally married. 2. in some cultures, a wife with lower status.

con·cu·pis·cence (kon-kū′pĭ-sns), *n.* strong appetite, especially for sex; lust. —**con·cu′pis·cent**, *adj.*

con·cur (kŏn-kūr′), *v.i.* -curred′, -cur′ring, 1. to agree or unite in action or opinion. 2. to coincide. —**con·cur′rence**, *n.*

con·cur·rent (′ĕnt), *adj.* 1. acting in union or conjunction. 2. existing together. 3. in *Law*, joint and equal in authority: *n.* that which concurs; a concurrent cause. —**con·cur′rent·ly**, *adv.*

con·cus·sion (kŏn-kush′ŭn), *n.* 1. the shock caused by two bodies coming violently together; agitation. 2. damaged activity of some organ, especially the brain, resulting from impact.

con·demn (kŏn-dem′), *v.t.* 1. to pronounce or judge guilty. 2. to censure; blame. 3. to declare to be forfeited. 4. to doom. 5. to declare unsuitable for use. —**con·dem·na·tion** (kon-dem-nä′shŭn), *n.* —**con·dem′na·to·ry** (′nä-tôr·i), *adj.* —**con·demn′er**, *n.*

con·dense (kŏn-dens′), *v.t.* -densed′, -dens′ing, 1. to make more compact; compress. 2. to abridge. 3. to make thicker or denser, as in changing a gas to a liquid: *v.i.* to grow dense. —**con·dens′a·ble**, **con·dens′i·ble**, *adj.* —**con·dens·a·bil′i·ty**, **con·dens·i·bil′i·ty**, *n.* —**con·den·sa·tion** (kon-dĕn-sā′shŭn), *n.*

condensed milk, a thick, sweet milk produced by boiling off a portion of the water from cow's milk and introducing more sugar.

con·dens·er (-den′sĕr), *n.* 1. an apparatus for reducing gases or vapors to a liquid form. 2. a device for storing electricity. 3. a lens for concentrating light.

con·de·scend (kon-dĕ-send′), *v.i.* 1. to descend graciously; deign. 2. to deal with in a superior way. —**con·de·scen′sion**, *n.*

con·dign (kŏn-dīn′), *adj.* well-deserved; suitable: used especially in reference to punishment.

con·di·ment (kon′dĭ-mĕnt), *n.* a seasoning or relish, as mustard, pepper, etc.

con·di·tion (kŏn-dish′ŭn), *n.* 1. a stipulation or terms of a contract. 2. external circumstance. 3. state; quality. 4. rank or station. 5. a healthy constitution. 6. [Informal], an ailment: *v.t.* 1. to contract or stipulate. 2. to bring into and keep in bodily health. 3. to cause to be used (followed by *to*). —**con·di′tion·er**, *n.*

con·di·tion·al (-l), *adj.* not absolute; qualified. —**con·di′tion·al·ly**, *adv.*

con·dole (kŏn·dōl′), *v.i.* -**doled′**, -**dol′ing**, to express sympathy for another: *v.t.* [Archaic], to lament.

con·do·lence (-dō′lĕns), *n. often pl.* sympathy.

con·do (kon′dō), *n., pl.* -**dos**, -**does**, same as **con·dominium** (sense 3).

con·dom (kon′dŏm), *n.* a thin, protective sheath for the penis, generally of rubber, used as a prophylactic or contraceptive.

con·do·min·i·um (kon·dō·min′i·ŭm), *n.* 1. political control held together by two or more states. 2. the area controlled. 3. an individually owned unit in a larger building or group of buildings.

con·done (kŏn·dōn′), *v.t.* -**doned′**, -**don′ing**, to forgive or pardon (a wrongdoing). —**con·don′a·ble**, *adj.* —**con·do·na·tion** (kon·dō·nā′shŭn), *n.*

con·dor (kon′dĕr), *n.* 1. a very large South American vulture, or a like one of southern California. 2. *pl.* **con·do·res** (kŏn·dō′res), a gold coin of South America.

con·duce (kŏn·dōōs′), *v.i.* -**duced′**, -**duc′ing**, to tend (followed by *to*); contribute. —**con·du′cive**, *adj.*

con·duct (kŏn·dukt′), *v.t.* 1. to guide. 2. to direct; manage. 3. to behave. 4. to carry or convey: *v.i.* 1. to lead. 2. to conduct: *n.* (kon′dukt), 1. personal behavior or practice. 2. management. —**con·duct′i·ble**, *adj.* —**con·duct·i·bil′i·ty**, *n.*

con·duct·ance (kŏn·duk′tăns), *n.* capacity for conducting electricity.

con·duc·tion (-shŭn), *n.* 1. the transmission of electricity, heat, or sound through a body. 2. same as **conductivity**.

con·duc·tive (′tiv), *adj.* having the quality or power of conducting. —**con·duc·tiv·i·ty** (kon·duk·tiv′i·ti), *n.*

con·duc·tor (kŏn·duk′tĕr), *n.* 1. one who conducts; leader or guide. 2. an orchestra or choir director. 3. one who has charge of train or bus passengers. 4. a substance which conducts or transmits electricity, heat, etc.

con·duit (kon′dit, ′doo·wit), *n.* a canal, pipe, etc. for the conveyance of water, electrical cables, etc.

cone (kōn), *n.* 1. a solid figure consisting of a circle at the bottom, lessening in circumference toward the tip. 2. anything coneshaped. 3. the fruit of the fir, pine, etc.: *v.t.* **coned, con′ing**, to shape like the segment of a cone.

co·ney (kō′ni), *n., pl.* -**neys**, -**nies**, 1. the European rabbit. 2. rabbit fur. 3. a small animal of the Bible.

con·fab (kon′fab), *n. & v.i.* -**fabbed′**, -**fab′bing**, [Informal], chat.

con·fec·tion (kŏn·fek′shŭn), *n.* anything preserved or prepared with sugar, as candy.

con·fec·tion·er (-ĕr), *n.* one who prepares and sells candy.

con·fec·tion·er·y (-er·i), *n., pl.* -**er·ies**, 1. confections. 2. a store where confections are sold.

con·fed·er·a·cy (kŏn·fed′ĕr·ă·si), *n., pl.* -**cies**, 1. persons, states, or nations united in a league. 2. an unlawful combination of people. 3. [C-], the alliance of eleven Southern States that seceded from the U.S. in 1860 & 1861 (preceded by *the*).

con·fed·er·ate (kŏn·fed′ĕ·rāt), *v.t. & v.i.* -**at·ed**, -**at·ing**, to unite in a league: *adj.* (′ĕr·it), 1. united by a league. 2. [C-], pertaining to the Confederacy: *n.* 1. a member of a confederation; ally. 2. an accomplice. 3. [C-], any supporter of the Confederacy.

con·fed·er·a·tion (kŏn·fed·ĕ·rā′shŭn), *n.* 1. the act of confederating. 2. an alliance, as of states previously independent. 3. [C-], the U.S. (1781-1789): preceded by *the*.

con·fed·er·a·tive (-fed′ĕ·rā·tiv), *adj.* of or pertaining to confederates or a confederation.

con·fer (kŏn·fur′), *v.t.* -**ferred′**, -**fer′ring**, to give or bestow: *v.i.* to consult together; converse. —**con·fer·ee** (kon·fĕ·rē′), *n.* —**con·fer′ment**, *n.*

con·fer·ence (kon′fĕr·ĕns), *n.* 1. the act of consulting together formally. 2. an appointed meeting for discussing some topic or business. 3. [often C-], an ecclesiastical assembly.

con·fess (kŏn·fes′), *v.t. & v.i.* 1. to admit or acknowledge; avow. 2. to relate (sins) to a priest. 3. to hear the confession (of): used of a priest.

con·fes·sion (-fesh′ŭn), *n.* 1. the act of confessing. 2. anything disclosed or acknowledged. 3. a code of religious beliefs. 4. a communion; sect.

con·fes·sion·al (-l), *n.* 1. an enclosed cabinet in which a priest sits to hear confessions. 2. the practice of confession.

con·fes·sor (kŏn·fes′ĕr), *n.* 1. one who confesses. 2. a Christian suffering persecution for his faith. 3. a priest who hears confession.

con·fet·ti (kŏn·fet′i), *n.* 1. confections. 2. minute pieces of colored paper thrown about at weddings, carnivals, etc.

con·fi·dant (kon′fi·dant), *n.* a close friend to whom one can tell confidences. —**con′fi·dante**, *n. fem.*

con·fide (kŏn·fīd′), *v.i.* -**fid′ed**, -**fid′ing**, to have trust (followed by *in*): *v.t.* 1. to talk of secretly. 2. to trust (followed by *to*).

con·fi·dence (kon′fi·dĕns), *n.* 1. trust; reliance. 2. certainty. 3. trust in oneself. 4. trust in secrecy. 5. information given as a secret: *adj.* swindling.

confidence game, the securing of money under pretenses of friendship by a person (**confidence man**) who makes false promises of gain.

con·fi·dent (-dĕnt), *adj.* full of confidence; positive; bold. —**con′fi·dent·ly**, *adv.*

con·fi·den·tial (kon·fi·den·shăl), *adj.* 1. spoken or written in confidence. 2. confiding. 3. trusted with secrets. —**con·fi·den′tial·ly**, *adv.*

con·fig·u·ra·tion (kŏn·fig·yŭ·rā′shŭn), *n.* external form.

con·fine (kon′fīn), *n. usually pl.* a boundary, border, or limit; frontier: *v.t.* (kŏn·fīn′) -**fined′**, -**fin′ing**, 1. to restrict within limits. 2. to enclose; imprison.

con·fine·ment (kŏn·fīn′mĕnt), *n.* 1. the act of confining. 2. childbirth.

con·firm (kŏn·fŭrm′), *v.t.* 1. to strengthen. 2. to ratify. 3. to verify. 4. to administer the ceremony of confirmation. —con-firm'a-to-ry (-fûr'mȧ-tôr-i), adj.

con-fir-ma-tion (kon-fẽr-mā'shŭn), n. 1. the act of confirming; verification. 2. evidence. 3. a ceremony bringing full membership in a church.

con-firmed (-fûrmd'), adj. 1..steady; habitual. 2. proven.

con-fis-cate (kon'fĭ-skāt), v.t. -cat-ed, -cat-ing, 1. to seize (property) as forfeited to the public treasury. 2. to seize under order; appropriate. —con-fis-ca'tion, n. —con'fis-ca-tor, n. — con-fis-ca-to-ry (kŏn-fĭs'kȧ-tôr-i), adj.

con-fla-gra-tion (kon-flȧ-grā'shŭn), n. a great fire.

con-flict (kŏn-flĭkt'), v.i. 1. originally, to contend; fight. 2. to clash or contradict: n. (kon'flĭkt), 1. a fight or struggle. 2. antagonism, as of purposes. 3. upset of emotions.

con-flu-ence (kon'flōō-ĕns), n. 1. the junction of two or more streams. 2. an assembly; crowd. Also con-flux (kon'fluks).

con-flu-ent (-ĕnt), adj. flowing or running together: n. a tributary river or stream.

con-form (kŏn-fôrm'), v.i. 1. to make like. 2. to bring into harmony: v.i. 1. to be like. 2. to be in harmony with. 3. to comply with conventions. 4. to follow the practices of the Established Church of England. —con-form'-ist, n.

con-form-a-ble (-fôr'mȧ-bl), adj. 1. like. 2. corresponding. 3. compliant. 4. harmonious. — con-form-a-bil'i-ty, n.

con-for-ma-tion (kon-fôr-mā'shŭn), n. 1. arrangement. 2. structure or shape.

con-form-i-ty (kŏn-fôr'mĭ-ti), n., pl. -ties, 1. compliance with established forms. 2. resemblance or agreement.

con-found (kŏn-found'), v.t. 1. to mingle; confuse. 2. to perplex or astonish. 3. to damn: an oath. 4. [Archaic]. to overthrow. —con-found'ed, adv.

con-fra-ter-ni-ty (kon-frȧ-tûr'nĭ-ti), n., pl. -ties, 1. a brotherhood or society of men associated for a common purpose. 2. a religious society of laymen.

con-frere (kon'frer), n. an associate.

con-front (kŏn-frunt'), v.t. 1. to stand face to face. 2. to oppose. 3. to cause to be face to face (followed by with). 4. to compare. — con-fron-ta-tion (kon-frŏn-tā'shŭn), n.

con-fuse (kŏn-fyōōz'), v.t. -fused', -fus'ing, 1. to mingle; jumble up. 2. to disconcert. 3. to perplex. 4. to be unable to separate. —con-fus'ed-ly, adv.

con-fu-sion (-fū'zhŭn), n. 1. the act of confusing. 2. perplexity. 3. disorder; tumult. 4. loss of self-possession.

con-fute (kŏn-fyōōt'), v.t. -fut'ed, -fut'ing, to prove to be false, invalid, or in error. — con-fu-ta-tion (kon-fyoo-tā'shŭn), n.

con-ge (kon'zhā), n. 1. leave-taking. 2. a dismissal. 3. a formal bow.

con-geal (kŏn-jēl'), v.t. & v.i. 1. to make or become rigid by cold; freeze. 2. to thicken. —con-geal'a-ble, adj. —con-ge-la-tion (kon-jē-lā'shŭn), n.

con-gen-er (kŏn'jē-nẽr), n. a person, animal,

plant, etc. of the same type, species, genus, etc.

con-gen-ial (kŏn-jēn'yȧl), adj. 1. kindred; cognate. 2. pleasant and sympathetic. 3. satisfying. —con-ge-ni-al'i-ty (-jēn-i-al'ĭ-ti), n. —con-gen'ial-ly, adv.

con-gen-i-tal (kŏn-jen'ĭ-tl), adj. 1. existing or produced at birth. 2. constitutional. —con-gen'i-tal-ly, adv.

con-ger (kong'gẽr), n. a large sea eel: also con-ger eel.

con-ge-ries (kon'jē-rēz), n., pl. con'ge-ries, a collection of parts into one mass.

con-gest (kŏn-jest'), v.t. 1. to accumulate an excess of blood in. 2. to crowd together: to become congested. —con-ges'tion (-jes'chŭn), n. —con-ges'tive, adj.

con-glom-er-ate (kŏn-glom'ē-rāt), v.t. & v.i. -at-ed, -at-ing, to gather into a round ball or mass: adj. ('ẽr-it), 1. collected or clustered together. 2. composed of conglomerated parts, as of fragments of rocks held together by clay: n. 1. a clustered mass. 2. one large corporation made up of several smaller corporations in different fields, merged together. 3. a conglomerate rock.

con-glom-er-a-tion (kŏn-glom-ē-rā'shŭn), n. 1. the act of conglomerating. 2. a miscellaneous collection.

con-glu-ti-nate (kŏn-glōōt'n-āt), v.t. & v.i. -nat-ed, -nat-ing, to unite: adj. glued together; united. —con-glu-ti-na'tion, n. —con-glu'ti-na-tive, adj.

congo eel (kong'gō), an eellike animal found in the muddy streams of the southeastern U.S.: also congo snake.

con-grat-u-late (kŏn-grach'ū-lāt), v.t. -lat-ed, -lat-ing, to felicitate on account of some happy event. —con-grat'u-la-to-ry (-lȧ-tôr-i), adj.

con-grat-u-la-tion (-grach-ū-lā'shŭn), n. 1. the act of congratulating. 2. pl. felicitations.

con-gre-gate (kong'grē-gāt), v.t. & v.i. -gat-ed, -gat-ing, to assemble; gather together.

con-gre-ga-tion (kong-grē-gā'shŭn), n. an assembly, especially of persons for religious worship. —con'gre-gant, n.

con-gre-ga-tion-al (-l), adj. 1. of or pertaining to a congregation. 2. [C-], of or pertaining to Congregationalism or Congregationalists.

Con-gre-ga-tion-al-ism (-izm), n. a form of Protestant church government, each church congregation being self-governing. —Con-gre-ga'tion-al-ist, n. & adj.

con-gress (kong'grĕs), n. 1. an association. 2. a conference or assembly, as of ambassadors, representatives, etc. 3. a legislature. 4. [C-] the U.S. legislature, made up of the Hou of Representatives and Senate. —con-gres-sion-al (kŏn-gresh'ŭn-l), adj.

con-gress-man (-măn), n., pl. -men (-mĕn), a member of Congress, especially of the House of Representatives.

con-gru-ent (kong'groo-wĕnt), adj. agreeing; harmonious. —con'gru-ence, n.

con-gru-ous (-wŭs), adj. 1. congruent. 2. fit; appropriate. —con-gru-i-ty (kŏn-grōō'ĭ-ti), n., pl. -ties.

con-ic (kon'ik), adj. same as conical: n. same as conic section.

---

con·i·cal ('ĭ-kĭl), *adj.* of, pertaining to, or shaped like a cone. —**con'i·cal·ly,** *adv.*

conic section, 1. an ellipse, parabola, hyperbola, or circle. 2. *pl.* the branch of geometry which treats of the parabola, ellipse, hyperbola, and circle: also **con'ics,** *n.*

con·i·fer (kon'ĭ-fẽr), *n.* a tree or shrub, as an evergreen, that bears cones. —**co·nif·er·ous** (kō-nĭf'ẽr-ŭs), *adj.*

con·jec·ture (kŏn-jek'chẽr), *n.* 1. a probable inference. 2. a guess: *v.t.* -tured, -tur·ing, to surmise; guess: *v.i.* to form conjectures. —**con·jec'tur·al,** *adj.*

con·join (-join'), *v.t. & v.i.* to join together; connect; unite. —**con·joint',** *adj.*

con·ju·gal (kon'jŭ-gǎl), *adj.* of or pertaining to marriage; connubial. —**con·ju·gal'i·ty** (-jŭ-gal'ĭ-tĭ), *n.* —**con'ju·gal·ly,** *adv.*

con·ju·gate (kon'jŭ-gāt), *v.t.* -gat·ed, -gat·ing, 1. [Archaic], to couple; unite. 2. in *Grammar,* to inflect (a verb), giving its different forms: *v.i.* to unite in conjugation: *adj.* (-gǎt), 1. combined in pairs. 2. kindred in meaning and origin: used of words: *n.* (-gǎt), a word agreeing in derivation with another word.

con·ju·ga·tion (kon'jŭ-gā'shŭn), *n.* 1. the act of conjugating. 2. the inflection of a verb, systematically arranged. 3. a kind of union or coupling of organisms.

con·junct (kŏn-jungkt'), *adj.* conjoined.

con·junc·tion (-jungk'shŭn), *n.* 1. union; association; connection. 2. the apparent meeting of two or more stars or planets. 3. in *Grammar,* a word used to connect sentences or words.

con·junc·ti·va (kon-jŭngk-tī'vȧ), *n., pl.* -vas, -vae ('vē), the mucous membrane lining the inner surface of the eyelids.

con·junc·tive (kŏn-jungk'tĭv), *adj.* 1. serving to unite. 2. closely connected: *n.* in *Grammar,* a conjunction. —**con·junc'tive·ly,** *adv.*

con·junc·ture ('chẽr), *n.* 1. a combination of many circumstances or causes. 2. a critical time.

con·ju·ra·tion (kon-jŭ-rā'shŭn), *n.* 1. the act of conjuring or invoking. 2. an incantation; enchantment. 3. magic. 4. [Archaic], a solemn entreaty.

con·jure (kŏn-joor'), *v.t.* 1. to summon in a sacred name; enjoin with the highest solemnity. 2. (kon'jẽr), to influence by, or as if by, magic: *v.i.* 1. to call by magic. 2. (kon'jẽr), to practice the arts of sorcery or magic. —**con'jur·er,** **con'jur·or,** *n.*

conk (kongk), *n.* [Slang], a blow to the head: *v.t.* [Slang], to strike the head.

con man, [Slang], same as **confidence man.**

conn (kon), *v.t.* **conned,** **con'ning,** to control the course of (a ship). —**con'ner,** *n.*

con·nate (kon'āt), *adj.* 1. innate. 2. congenital. 3. related.

con·nect (kŏ-nekt'), *v.t.* 1. to bind or fasten together. 2. to associate (followed by *with*): *v.i.* to be joined; cohere. —**con·nec'tor,** **con·nect'er,** *n.*

con·nec·tion (-nek'shŭn), *n.* 1. the state of being connected. 2. a thing uniting two parts. 3. cohesion. 4. association. 5. relation by marriage or blood. 6. *usually pl.* a business associate or acquaintance. 7. *usually pl.* a change to another bus, airplane, etc. in traveling. 8. a religious body. Also British spelling, **con·nex'ion.**

con·nec·tive (-nek'tĭv), *adj.* able to connect: *n.* that which connects, especially a word, as a conjunction, that connects.

con·ning tower (kon'ing), 1. a protected pilot-house on a warship. 2. a low tower for observation on a submarine.

con·nip·tion (kŏ-nip'shŭn), *n.* [Informal], *often pl.* a tantrum or hysterical outburst.

con·niv·ance (kŏ-nī'vǎns), *n.* the act of conniving; especially, passive cooperation in a crime; collusion.

con·nive (kŏ-nīv'), *v.i.* -nived', -niv'ing, 1. to close the eyes upon a wrongdoing (followed by *at*). 2. to be in secret complicity (followed by *with*). —**con·niv'er,** *n.*

con·nois·seur (kon-ĭ-sûr'), *n.* a critical judge or expert, as in determining taste.

con·note (kŏ-nōt'), *v.t.* -not'ed, -not'ing, 1. to designate by implication. 2. to imply as an attribute. —**con·no·ta·tion** (kon'ō-tā'shŭn), *n.* —**con'no·ta·tive,** *adj.*

con·nu·bi·al (kŏ-nōō'bi-ǎl), *adj.* of or pertaining to the marriage state.

co·noid (kō'noid), *adj.* cone-shaped: also **co·noi'dal.**

con·quer (kong'kẽr), *v.t.* 1. to gain by conquest. 2. to overcome; subdue: *v.i.* to get the victory. —**con'quer·or,** *n.*

con·quest ('kwest), *n.* 1. the act of conquering; subjugation; victory. 2. what is conquered. 3. a gaining of friendliness or good will.

con·quis·ta·dor (kon-kwis'tä-dôr, -kēs'-), *n., pl.* -dors, -dores, a Spanish conqueror of Latin America in the 1500's.

con·san·guin·e·ous (kon-sang-gwin'ĭ-ŭs), *adj.* related by blood; of the same ancestry. —**con'san·guin'i·ty,** *n.*

con·science (kon'shĕns), *n.* the moral sense which determines right and wrong, leading one to do right.

con·sci·en·tious (kon-shi-en'shŭs), *adj.* 1. influenced or regulated by conscience; scrupulous. 2. precise and careful. —**con·sci·en'-tious·ly,** *adv.* —**con·sci·en'tious·ness,** *n.*

conscientious objector, one who refuses to do military service because of objections to killing.

con·scious (kon'shŭs), *adj.* 1. aware of one's thoughts or actions; sensible. 2. mentally alert. 3. same as **self-conscious.** 4. with knowledge and purpose. —**con'scious·ly,** *adv.*

con·scious·ness (-nĭs), *n.* 1. the knowledge of that which passes in one's own mind. 2. all the feelings and thoughts that belong to a person.

con·script (kŏn-skript'), *v.t.* to enroll for compulsory military service: *adj.* (kon'skript), conscripted: *n.* (kon'skript), one thus conscripted. —**con·scrip'tion,** *n.*

con·se·crate (kon'sĕ-krāt), *v.t.* -crat·ed, -crat·ing, 1. to set apart as sacred. 2. to set apart to a sacred use or office. 3. to devote: *adj.* [Archaic], consecrated. —**con·se·cra'tion,** *n.* —**con'se·cra·tor,** *n.*

ŏ in dragon, ōō in crude, oo in wool, u in cup, ū in cure, u̇ in turn, u in focus, oi in boy, ou in house, th in thin, th in sheathe, g in get, j in joy, y in yet.

con·sec·u·tive (kŏn-sek'yŭ-tiv), adj. successive. —con·sec'u·tive·ly, adv.

con·sen·sus (kŏn-sen'sŭs), n. 1. general agreement; accord. 2. an opinion held in general.

con·sent (kŏn-sent'), n. 1. a yielding of the mind or will; acquiescence. 2. agreement. v.i. to comply; yield; accede; concur.

con·sen·ta·ne·ous (kon-sen-tā'ni-ŭs), adj. [Rare], accordant; suitable; harmonious.

con·sen·tient (kŏn-sen'shĕnt), adj. agreeing.

con·se·quence (kon'sē-kwens), n. 1. that which naturally follows; effect. 2. an inference. 3. importance; significance.

con·se·quent (-kwent), adj. following as a natural result or effect: n. a result or effect. —con'se·quent·ly, adv.

con·se·quen·tial (-kwen'shăl), adj. 1. following as an effect. 2. important.

con·ser·van·cy (kŏn-sûr'văn-si), n. preservation of natural resources.

con·ser·va·tion (kon-sēr-vā'shŭn), n. 1. the act of preserving from loss or injury. 2. the governmental protection of natural resources. —con·ser·va'tion·ist, n.

con·ser·va·tive (kŏn-sûr'vă-tiv), adj. 1. having the tendency or power to preserve. 2. careful; safe: n. 1. [Rare], that which preserves. 2. one opposed to hasty changes in the political, religious, or civil institutions of the country. —con·ser'va·tism, n. —con·ser'va·tive·ly, adv.

con·ser·va·tor (kon'sēr-vāt-ēr), n. one who protects or guards.

con·ser·va·to·ry (kŏn-sûr'vă-tôr-i), adj. [Rare], tending to preserve: n., pl. -ries, 1. a private greenhouse. 2. an institution for instruction in art, music, etc.: also con·ser·va·toire (kŏn-sûr-vä-twär').

con·serve (kŏn-sûrv'), v.t. -served', -serv'ing, 1. to preserve from injury or destruction. 2. to preserve (fruit) with sugar: n. (kon'sērv), often pl. preserved or candied fruit. —con·serv'a·ble, adj.

con·sid·er (kŏn-sid'ēr), v.t. 1. to fix the mind upon; contemplate. 2. to bear in mind. 3. to be considerate of. 4. to think or believe to be: v.i. to deliberate; reflect.

con·sid·er·a·ble (-ă-bl), adj. 1. worthy of notice; important. 2. more than a little. —con·sid'er·a·bly, adv.

con·sid·er·ate (-it), adj. 1. having regard for others; thoughtful. 2. [Obsolete], prudent; careful.

con·sid·er·a·tion (kŏn-sid-ē-rā'shŭn), n. 1. the act of considering. 2. mature thought. 3. regard for others. 4. that which is considered. 5. something given in return as a fee.

con·sid·ered (kŏn-sid'ērd), adj. thought out.

con·sid·er·ing (-ēr-ing), prep. taking into consideration; allowing for.

con·sign (kŏn-sin'), v.t. 1. to deliver in a formal manner to another. 2. to give in trust. 3. to relegate. 4. to send (goods).

con·sign·ee (kon-si-nē'), n. a person to whom goods are sent; agent.

con·sign·ment (kŏn-sin'mĕnt), n. 1. the act of consigning. 2. the thing consigned.

con·sign·or (kŏn-si'nēr), n. the person or company that consigns goods to another: also con·sign'er.

con·sist (kŏn-sist'), v.i. 1. to be composed (followed by of). 2. to subsist (followed by in). 3. to coexist (followed by with).

con·sis·ten·cy ('ĕn-si), n., pl. -cies, 1. density or firmness, or the degree of this. 2. harmony. 3. accordance with past situations. Also con·sis'tence.

con·sis·tent ('ĕnt), adj. 1. [Rare], solid. 2. not contradictory. 3. in conformity. —con·sis'tent·ly, adv.

con·sis·to·ry (kŏn-sis'tēr-i), n., pl. -ries, a church tribunal or council, as the papal senate, or a meeting of this group.

con·so·la·tion (kon-sō-lā'shŭn), n. 1. alleviation of mental distress; solace. 2. a person or thing consoling.

con·sole (kŏn-sōl'), v.t. -soled', -sol'ing, to give comfort to; cheer in sorrow; solace. —con·sol'a·ble, adj. —con·sol'a·to·ry ('ă-tôr-i), adj.

con·sole (kon'sōl), n. 1. an ornamental bracket supporting a cornice, shelf, etc. 2. same as console table. 3. the frame containing the keyboards and stops of an organ. 4. a phonograph or television container for floor placement. 5. a panel for controlling computers, airplanes, etc.

console table, 1. formerly, a table resting on consoles. 2. a small table with curved legs set against a wall.

con·sol·i·date (kŏn-sol'i-dāt), v.t. & v.i. -dat·ed, -dat·ing, 1. to merge; unite. 2. to make solid; condense. 3. to harden; make or become fixed. —con·sol·i·da'tion, n. —con·sol'i·da·tor, n.

con·sols (kŏn-solz'), n. the principal British government stock of consolidated government securities.

con·som·mé (kon-sō-mā'), n. a strong, clear soup or bouillon.

con·so·nance (kon'sō-năns), n. agreement of sounds, as in music; harmony; concord.

con·so·nant (-nănt), adj. harmonious; accordant: n. a letter other than a vowel.

con·sort (kon'sôrt), n. 1. originally, a companion; partner. 2. a husband or wife, as of the king or queen. 3. a ship accompanying another: v.i. & v.i. (kŏn-sôrt'), to associate.

con·sor·ti·um (kŏn-sôr'shi-ŭm), n., pl. -ti·a (-ă), an agreement between parties, as banks or businesses, for a specific purpose.

con·spec·tus (kŏn-spek'tŭs), n. a digest of a subject.

con·spic·u·ous (kŏn-spik'yoo-wŭs), adj. 1. mentally or physically visible; manifest. 2. distinguished; unusual. —con·spic'u·ous·ly, adv.

con·spir·a·cy (kŏn-spir'ă-si), n., pl. -cies, 1. a plot. 2. two or more persons engaged together for an unlawful or evil purpose. 3. the planning of this group.

con·spire (kŏn-spir'), v.i. -spired', -spir'ing, 1. to arrange in secret for a crime. 2. to combine for a common purpose. —con·spir'a·tor (-spir'ă-tēr), n.

con·sta·ble (kon'stă-bl), n. 1. a high officer of the state in medieval times. 2. [Chiefly British], a policeman.

con·stab·u·lar·y (kŏn-stab'yŭ-ler-i), n., pl. -ar·ies, 1. constables as a group. 2. a police force with a military system: adj. of or pertaining to constables.

---

a in cap, ā in cane, ä in father, à in abet, e in met, ē in be, ĕ in baker, ê in regent, i in pit, ī in fine, i in manifest, o in hot, ô in horse, ō in bone,

con·stant (kon'stånt), *adj.* 1. steadfast; firm. 2. continuous: *n.* anything that is not subject to change. —**con'stan·cy,** *n.* —**con'stant·ly,** *adv.*

con·stel·la·tion (kon-stě-lā'shŭn), *n.* 1. a group or cluster of fixed stars. 2. an assemblage of splendors.

con·ster·na·tion (kon-stĕr-nā'shŭn), *n.* excessive terror, wonder, or surprise.

con·sti·pate (kon'stĭ-pāt), *v.t.* -pat·ed, -pat·ing, to make the feces hard and difficult to pass from the bowels of.

con·sti·pa·tion (kon-stĭ-pā'shŭn), *n.* the condition of being constipated; costiveness.

con·stit·u·en·cy (kŏn-stich'oo-wĕn-si), *n., pl.* -cies, 1. the body of electors voting in a district for a representative. 2. the district represented.

con·stit·u·ent ('oo-wĕnt) *adj.* 1. necessary or essential. 2. that elects. 3. authorized to create or change a constitution: *n.* 1. an essential or component part. 2. an elector.

con·sti·tute (kon'stĭ-tōōt), *v.t.* -tut·ed, -tut·ing, 1. to compose or make up. 2. to appoint. 3. to enact. 4. to establish.

con·sti·tu·tion (kon-stĭ-tōō'shŭn), *n.* 1. the act of constituting. 2. the way a thing is constituted. 3. physical, or sometimes mental, makeup of a person. 4. the system of fundamental laws of a nation, state, society, etc. 5. a document containing this system; specifically, [C], the U.S. Constitution.

con·sti·tu·tion·al (-l), *adj.* 1. inherent in the constitution; fundamental. 2. harmonious with or contained in the constitution of a nation, state, etc.: *n.* a walk taken for the benefit of one's health. —**con·sti·tu·tion·al'i·ty** (-al'ĭ-ti), *n.* —**con·sti·tu'tion·al·ly,** *adv.*

con·sti·tu·tion·al·ist (-ăl-ist), *n.* an adherent of constitutional government.

con·sti·tu·tive (kon'stĭ-tōōt-iv), *adj.* 1. elemental. 2. essential. 3. productive.

con·strain (kŏn-strān'), *v.t.* 1. to hold in. 2. to hold down or keep back by force; restrain. 3. to force.

con·straint (-strānt'), *n.* 1. restriction. 2. compulsion. 3. an awkward manner.

con·strict (kŏn-strikt'), *v.t.* to bind; compress; contract. —**con·stric'tion,** *n.* —**con·stric'tive,** *adj.*

con·stric·tor (-strik'tēr), *n.* 1. that which contracts or compresses, as a muscle. 2. a large snake that squeezes its victims to death.

con·strin·gent (-strin'jĕnt), *adj.* [Rare], contracting or binding.

con·struct (kŏn-strukt'), *v.t.* to build; form; put together. —**con·struc'tor,** *n.*

con·struc·tion (-struk'shŭn), *n.* 1. the act or manner of building. 2. that which is constructed; edifice. 3. interpretation. 4. the arrangement of words in a sentence.

con·struc·tive ('tiv), *adj.* 1. having the character of construction; improving. 2. inferred.

con·strue (kŏn-strōō'), *v.t.* -strued', -stru'ing, 1. to put (a sentence) into proper order by syntactical rules. 2. to translate. 3. to interpret.

con·sub·stan·tial (kon-sŭb-stan'shăl), *adj.* having the same substance, essence, or nature. —**con·sub·stan·ti·al'i·ty** (-shi-al'ĭ-ti), *n.*

con·sub·stan·ti·a·tion (-stan-shi-ā'shŭn), *n.* the doctrine that the body and blood of Christ are substantially present in the Eucharistic elements after consecration.

con·sul (kon'sl), *n.* 1. in ancient Rome, a chief magistrate. 2. a person commissioned by a government to reside in a foreign country to protect and promote the interests of his country and its citizens. —**con'su·lar,** *adj.*

con·su·late (-it), *n.* the office, residence, or position of a consul.

consul general, *pl.* **consuls general, consul generals,** a chief consul (sense 2).

con·sult (kŏn-sult'), *v.t.* 1. to ask advice of; go to for information. 2. to regard: *v.i.* to take counsel together.

con·sult·ant (-sul'tnt), *n.* 1. one who consults with another. 2. an expert asked for advice.

con·sul·ta·tion (kon-sl-tā'shŭn), *n.* 1. the act of consulting. 2. a conference or deliberation on some special matter. —**con·sul·ta·tive** (kŏn-sul'tá-tiv), **con·sul'ta·to·ry** (-tôr-i), *adj.*

con·sume (kŏn-sōōm'), *v.t.* -sumed', -sum'ing, 1. to destroy, as by burning. 2. to waste; spend. 3. to devour or absorb: *v.i.* [Now Rare], to waste away.

con·sum·er (-sōō'mēr), *n.* one that consumes, especially using products or services for personal needs.

con·sum·er·ism (-izm), *n.* organized activity promoting the welfare of consumers.

con·sum·mate (kon'sŭ-māt), *v.t.* -mat·ed, -mat·ing, 1. to complete; finish. 2. to actualize (marriage) by sexual intercourse: *adj.* (kŏn-sum'it), perfect; total. —**con·sum·ma'tion,** *n.* —**con·sum'mate·ly,** *adv.*

con·sump·tion (kŏn-sump'shŭn), *n.* 1. the act of consuming. 2. the number consumed. 3. a bodily wasting away. 4. lung tuberculosis.

con·sump·tive ('tiv), *adj.* 1. of or pertaining to consumption. 2. affected with lung tuberculosis: *n.* one affected with lung tuberculosis.

con·tact (kon'takt), *n.* 1. a touch. 2. close union (followed by *with*). 3. a coupling.: *v.t.* 1. to put in contact. 2. to get in communication with: *v.i.* to be in contact.

contact lens, a small, very thin, glass or plastic lens laid in the fluid over the cornea.

con·ta·gion (kŏn-tā'jŭn), *n.* 1. transmission of disease by direct or indirect contact. 2. a disease transmitted this way. 3. the transmission of ideas, feelings, etc.

con·ta·gious ('jŭs), *adj.* 1. transmitted by contact: used of diseases. 2. able to transmit the cause of such diseases. 3. transmitted among people.

con·tain (kŏn-tān'), *v.t.* 1. to hold; enclose. 2. to be able to hold. 3. to keep within bounds: *v.i.* [Obsolete], to live in continence. —**con·tain'er,** *n.* —**con·tain'ment,** *n.*

con·tain·er·ize ('ēr-īz), *v.t.* -ized, -iz·ing, to load things in large, standard holders for transporting, as by ship.

con·tam·i·nant (kŏn-tam'ĭ-nănt), *n.* something which contaminates.

con·tam·i·nate (-nāt), *v.t.* -nat·ed, -nat·ing, to pollute. —**con·tam·i·na'tion,** *n.* —**con·tam'i·na·tive,** *adj.*

con·temn (kŏn-tem'), *v.t.* to despise.

---

con·tem·plate (kon'tĕm-plāt), v.t. -plat·ed, -plat-ing, 1. to consider with continued attention; meditate on; study. 2. to intend: v.i. to meditate. —con·tem·pla'tion, n. —con·tem-pla·tive (kŏn-tem'plā-tiv, kon'tem-plāt-iv), adj. & n. —con'tem·pla·tor, n.

con·tem·po·rar·y (kŏn-tem'pō-rer-i), adj. 1. existing or occurring at the same time. 2. having the same age. 3. in a present style. Also **con·tem·po·ra'ne·ous** (-rā'ni-ŭs): n., pl. -rar-ies, one living at the same time as another. —con·tem·po·ra'ne·ous·ly, adv.

con·tempt (kŏn-tempt'), n. 1. disdain; scorn. 2. the state of being scorned. 3. in Law, disobedience to the orders or offense to the honor of a court or legislature.

con·tempt·i·ble (-choo'wŭs), adj. meriting scorn. —con·tempt'i·bly, adv.

con·temp·tu·ous ('choo-wŭs), adj. disdainful. —con·temp'tu·ous·ly, adv.

con·tend (kŏn-tend'), v.i. 1. to strive in opposition. 2. to vie. 3. to dispute or debate: v.t. to assert. —con·tend'er, n.

con·tent (kŏn-tent'), adj. 1. satisfied. 2. willing; affirming: v.t. to satisfy; appease: n. contentment.

con·tent (kon'tent), n. 1. usually pl. that which is comprised in anything. 2. basic meaning. 3. the amount comprising.

con·tent·ed (kŏn-ten'tid), adj. gratified; satisfied. —con·tent'ed·ly, adv.

con·ten·tion (-ten'shŭn), n. 1. contest; debate. 2. a statement debated.

con·ten·tious ('shŭs), adj. 1. causing contention. 2. quarrelsome; litigious. —con·ten'tious·ly, adv. —con·ten'tious·ness, n.

con·tent·ment (-tent'mĕnt), n. satisfaction.

con·ter·mi·nous (-tûr'mi-nŭs), adj. 1. contiguous. 2. having the same bounds or limits.

con·test (kŏn-test'), v.t. 1. to dispute; litigate. 2. to struggle for; oppose: v.i. to strive; contend; vie: n. (kon'test), 1. a struggle for superiority. 2. a dispute, race, etc. —con·test'a·ble, adj.

con·test·ant (-tes'tant), n. 1. one who competes, as in a race. 2. one who contests an election, will, etc.

con·text (kon'tekst), n. the parts in a book, discourse, etc. immediately adjoining a word, phrase, or sentence under consideration and affecting its meaning. —con·tex·tu·al (kŏn-teks'choo-wăl), adj.

con·tex·ture (kŏn-teks'chĕr), n. 1. structure. 2. something interwoven.

con·tig·u·ous (kŏn-tig'yoo-wŭs), adj. 1. having contact. 2. adjacent. —con·ti·gu·i·ty (kon-ti-gū'i-ti), n., pl. -ties.

con·ti·nence (kont'n-ĕns), n. 1. chastity. 2. self-restraint; moderation.

con·ti·nent (-ĕnt), adj. 1. chaste. 2. exercising self-restraint: n. 1. a large extent of land forming a geographical division. 2. [C-], the European mainland (preceded by the).

con·ti·nen·tal (kont-n-en'tl), adj. 1. of or pertaining to a continent. 2. [sometimes C-], pertaining to Europe. 3. [C-], of or pertaining to the American colonies during and just after the American Revolution: n. 1. [usually C-], an inhabitant of Europe. 2. [C-], a soldier of the American Revolution.

3. a piece of the depreciated paper currency of the American Revolutionary government.

con·tin·gen·cy (kŏn-tin'jĕn-si), n., pl. -cies, 1. a chance or possible occurrence. 2. reliance on this. Also **con·tin'gence**.

con·tin·gent ('jĕnt), adj. 1. that can be. 2. accidental. 3. conditional (followed by on or upon): n. 1. something that happens accidentally. 2. a quota of troops, representatives, etc. 3. a section of a group.

con·tin·u·al (kŏn-tin'yoo-wăl), adj. 1. incessant; constant. 2. proceeding without interruption. —con·tin'u·al·ly, adv.

con·tin·u·ance (-wăns), n. 1. permanence. 2. uninterrupted succession. 3. duration. 4. in Law, the continuing of matters until some later time.

con·tin·u·a·tion (kŏn-tin-yoo-wā'shŭn), n. 1. the act of continuing. 2. a beginning again. 3. a supplement.

con·tin·ue (kŏn-tin'ū), v.t. -ued, -u·ing, 1. to carry on without interruption; persist in. 2. to take further. 3. to keep or retain. 4. in Law, to put off; postpone: v.i. 1. to remain; abide; endure. 2. to persevere. 3. to stretch. 4. to keep in a place. 5. to resume.

con·ti·nu·i·ty (kon-ti-nōō'i-ti), n., pl. -ties, 1. coherence. 2. uninterrupted succession or connection. 3. a motion picture or television scenario.

con·tin·u·ous (kŏn-tin'yoo-wŭs), adj. uninterrupted. —con·tin'u·ous·ly, adv.

con·tin·u·um ('yoo-wŭm), n., pl. -u·a (-wă), -u·ums, an uninterrupted thing.

con·tort (kŏn-tôrt'), v.t. & v.i. to twist violently. —con·tor'tion, n.

con·tor·tion·ist, n. one who can contort his body, as in performing gymnastics.

con·tour (kon'toor), n. an outline, profile, etc.: v.t. to make an outline of: adj. fitting the outline of something.

con·tra-, a prefix meaning contrary, against.

con·tra·band (kon'trä-band), adj. prohibited from importation; illegal: n. contraband goods.

con·tra·band·ist (-ist), n. a smuggler.

con·tra·bass (kon'trä-bās), adj. sounding an octave lower in pitch than bass: n. same as double bass.

con·tra·cep·tion (kon-trä-cep'shŭn), n. a prevention of conception or impregnation. —con·tra·cep'tive, adj. & n.

con·tract (kŏn-trakt'), v.t. 1. (usually kon'trakt), to do by written agreement. 2. to take on or get (a disease, debt, etc.). 3. to draw closer together; condense. 4. to shorten (a phrase or word): v.i. 1. (usually kon'trakt), to agree upon formally. 2. to shrink: n. (kon'trakt), 1. a compact; written agreement, as a legal document. 2. a formal betrothal. —con·tract·i·bil'i·ty, n. —con·tract'i·ble, adj.

contract bridge, a form of auction bridge in which only the tricks named may be counted toward game.

con·trac·tile (kŏn-trak'til), adj. having the power of shortening itself. —con·trac·til·i·ty (kon-trak-til'i-ti), n.

con·trac·tion (kŏn-trak'shŭn), n. 1. the act of contracting; state of being contracted. 2. in

Grammar. the reduction of two vowels or syllables into one, producing a new word.

con·trac·tor (kon'trak-tēr, kŏn-trak'tēr), *n.* 1. one of the parties to a contract. 2. one who contracts to supply or construct for a stipulated sum.

con·trac·tu·al (kŏn-trak'choo-wǎl), *adj.* of, pertaining to, or according to a contract.

con·tra·dance (kon'trǎ-dans), *n.* same as **contredanse.**

con·tra·dict (kon-trǎ-dikt'), *v.t.* 1. to assert the contrary or opposite of: gainsay; deny. 2. to go opposite to. **—con·tra·dic'to·ry,** *adj.*

con·tra·dic·tion (-dik'shŭn), *n.* 1. the act of contradicting. 2. a denial. 3. incongruity.

con·tra·dis·tinc·tion (-dĭs-tĭngk'shŭn), *n.* a distinction by opposite qualities. **—con·tra·dis·tinc'tive,** *adj.*

con·tra·dis·tin·guish (-dĭs-tĭng'gwĭsh), *v.t.* to distinguish by opposite qualities.

con·trail (kon'trāl), *n.* water vapor left in a trail behind an airplane.

con·tral·to (kŏn-tral'tō), *n., pl.* **-tos, -ti** ('tē), 1. the part sung by the lowest female voice. 2. the lowest female singing voice. 3. a woman who sings contralto: *adj.* having or for the range of a contralto.

con·trap·tion (kŏn-trap'shŭn), *n.* [Informal]. a device.

con·tra·pun·tal (kon-trǎ-pun'tl), *adj.* of, pertaining to, or having counterpoint.

con·tra·ri·e·ty (kon-trǎ-rī'ě-tĭ), *n.* 1. opposition. 2. *pl.* **-ties,** an inconsistency.

con·tra·ri·wise (kon'trer-i-wīz), *adv.* 1. from an opposite view. 2. conversely.

con·tra·ry (kon'trer-i), *adj.* 1. opposite. 2. opposed in direction, manner, etc. 3. not beneficial. 4. perverse: *n., pl.* **-ries,** a thing of opposite qualities. **—con'trar·i·ly,** *adv.* **—con'trar·i·ness,** *n.*

con·trast (kŏn-trast'), *v.t.* to place in contrast; compare: *v.i.* to exhibit contrast: *n.* (kon'trast), 1. the act of contrasting. 2. opposition or difference of qualities made manifest by comparison. 3. something exhibiting this difference.

con·tra·val·la·tion (kon-trǎ-vǎ-lā'shŭn), *n.* a fortification thrown up around a place by a besieging force for its own security.

con·tra·vene (kon-trǎ-vēn'), *v.t.* **-vened', -ven'ing,** 1. to obstruct; violate. 2. to dispute. **—con·tra·ven'tion** (-ven'shŭn), *n.*

con·tre·danse (kon'trě-dans), *n.* a dance in which the partners are arranged in opposite lines.

con·tre·temps (kon'trě-tŏn), *n., pl.* **-temps** (-tŏn'), [French], an unexpected event causing confusion.

con·trib·ute (kŏn-trib'ūt), *v.t. & v.i.* **-ut·ed, -ut·ing,** 1. to give to some common stock; furnish as a share. 2. to give (an article), as to a periodical. 3. to give (an idea). **—con·trib'u·tive,** *adj.* **—con·trib'u·tor,** *n.*

con·tri·bu·tion (kon-trĭ-bū'shŭn), *n.* 1. the act of contributing. 2. a charity subscription. 3. a writing furnished to a periodical. 4. [Archaic], a tax.

con·trite (kŏn-trīt'), *adj.* penitent. **—con·trite'ly,** *adv.* **—con·trite'ness,** *n.* **—con·tri'tion** (-trĭsh'ŭn), *n.*

con·triv·ance (kŏn-trī'vǎns), *n.* 1. the act or manner of contriving. 2. a device, scheme, plan, etc.

con·trive (kŏn-trīv'), *v.t.* **-trived', -triv'ing,** 1. to devise; scheme; plan. 2. to invent. 3. to manage. **—con·triv'er,** *n.*

con·trol (kŏn-trōl'), *v.t.* **-trolled', -trol'ling,** 1. to restrain. 2. to govern. 3. to regulate. 4. to check by contrast: *n.* 1. the act of controlling; authority. 2. a check. 3. a restraint. 4. *usually pl.* an instrument to regulate the mechanism of a machine. **—con·trol'la·ble,** *adj.*

controlled substance, a drug whose sale is regulated by law.

con·trol·ler ('ēr), *n.* 1. one who has charge of the expenditures of a government, corporation, etc. 2. that which controls.

con·tro·ver·sial (kon-trŏ-vûr'shǎl), *adj.* polemic. **—con·tro·ver'sial·ly,** *adv.*

con·tro·ver·sial·ist (-ist), *n.* a disputant.

con·tro·ver·sy (kon'trŏ-vûr-si), *n., pl.* **-sies,** agitation of contrary opinions; debate; disputation.

con·tro·vert (-vûrt), *v.t.* 1. to contend against; refute. 2. to discuss or debate. **—con·tro·vert'i·ble,** *adj.* **—con·tro·vert'i·bly,** *adv.*

con·tu·ma·cy (kon'too-mǎ-si), *n., pl.* **-cies,** obstinate opposition to authority, especially legal authority. **—con·tu·ma·cious** (kon-too-mā'-shǔs), *adj.*

con·tu·me·ly (-mē-li), *n., pl.* **-lies,** 1. haughty and contemptuous rudeness. 2. scornful and insolent abuse. **—con·tu·me·li·ous** (kon-too-mē'li-ǔs), *adj.*

con·tuse (kŏn-tōōz'), *v.t.* **-tused', -tus'ing,** to wound or bruise without breaking the skin.

con·tu·sion (-tōō'zhŭn), *n.* 1. the act of contusing. 2. state of being contused. 3. a bruise.

co·nun·drum (kŏ-nun'drŭm), *n.* 1. a riddle solved by a pun. 2. a confusing problem.

con·ur·ba·tion (kon-êr-bā'shŭn), *n.* a metropolitan area and its surroundings.

con·va·lesce (kon-vǎ-les'), *v.i.* **-lesced', -lesc'ing,** to recover strength and health after illness. **—con·va·les'cence,** *n.* **—con·va·les'cent,** *adj. & n.*

con·vec·tion (kŏn-vek'shŭn), *n.* 1. the act of conveying. 2. the action of parts in a fluid caused by heat differentials. 3. the conveyance of heat from this movement.

con·vene (kŏn-vēn'), *v.i.* **-vened', -ven'ing,** to meet together: *v.t.* 1. to cause to assemble. 2. to summon judicially.

con·ven·ience (kŏn-vēn'yěns), *n.* 1. fitness. 2. freedom from discomfort. 3. a useful or helpful accommodation.

con·ven·ient (-yěnt), *adj.* 1. affording accommodation; handy. 2. [Obsolete], suitable; appropriate. **—con·ven'ient·ly,** *adv.*

con·vent (kon'věnt), *n.* 1. a community of nuns, or, sometimes, monks. 2. the buildings they occupy.

con·ven·ti·cle (kŏn-ven'ti-kl), *n.* an assembly for worship, as of a schism.

con·ven·tion (kŏn-ven'shŭn), *n.* 1. an assembly, as of political or religious groups. 2. an agreement, as in diplomacy. 3. usual practice.

con·ven·tion·al (-l), *adj.* 1. of or pertaining to

a convention. 2. sanctioned by, or growing out of, custom or tacit agreement. 3. based on accepted models or artistic rules. —con·ven·tion·al·i·ty (-al'i-ti), n., pl. -ties. —con·ven'tion·al·ly, adv.

con·ven·tion·al·ize (kŏn-ven'shŭn-l-īz), v.t. -ized, -iz·ing, to harmonize with ordinary usage or custom.

con·ven·tu·al (kŏn-ven'choo-wăl), adj. of or pertaining to a convent: n. a member of a convent.

con·verge (kŏn-vûrj'), v.i. & v.t. -verged', -verg'ing, to tend or direct to one point. —con·ver'gence, n. —con·ver'gent, adj.

con·vers·a·ble (kŏn-vûr'sá-bl), adj. 1. sociable. 2. inclined to converse.

con·ver·sant (kŏn-vûr'snt), adj. acquainted or familiar (followed by with): proficient.

con·ver·sa·tion (kon'vēr-sā'shŭn), n. 1. informal or familiar talk. 2. colloquy. 3. [Obsolete], association or social intercourse. —con·ver·sa'tion·al, adj. —con·ver·sa'tion·al·ly, adv.

con·ver·sa·tion·al·ist (-l-ist), n. one who excels in conversation: also con·ver·sa'tion·ist.

conversation piece, a thing that causes remarks, as because it is unusual.

con·ver·sa·zi·o·ne (kon-vēr-sät-si-ō'ni), n., pl. -o'ni ('ni), -o'nes ('niz), [Italian], a meeting for conversation, especially on literary or artistic topics.

con·verse (kŏn-vērs'), v.i. -versed', -vers'ing, to interchange thoughts; talk familiarly: adj. (kŏn'vērs), reversed in order or relation; opposite: n. (kŏn'vērs), 1. the opposite thing. 2. informal talk. —con·verse'ly, adv.

con·ver·sion (kŏn-vûr'zhŭn), n. 1. the act of converting. 2. a change from one opinion, religion, etc. to another.

con·vert (kŏn-vûrt'), v.t. 1. to transmute. 2. to change from one religion, opinion, etc. to another. 3. to interchange equally. 4. to use illegally: v.i. to be converted: n. (kŏn'vērt), one who changes, as from one religion to another.

con·vert·er (kŏn-vûr'tēr), n. 1. one who converts. 2. a furnace used for converting pig iron into steel in the Bessemer process. 3. a device that changes radio frequencies.

con·vert·i·ble (kŏn-vûr'ti-bl), adj. transmutable; interchangeable: n. an auto with a removable top.

con·vex (kon-veks'), adj. curved on the exterior surface: n. (kon'veks), a convex body. —con·vex'i·ty, n., pl. -ties.

con·vex·o·con·cave (kŏn-vek-sō-kon-kāv'), adj. convex on one side, concave on the other.

con·vey (kŏn-vā'), v.t. 1. to carry or transport. 2. to transmit. 3. to communicate. 4. to transfer (title, property, etc.). —con·vey'a·ble, adj. —con·vey'or, con·vey'er, n.

con·vey·ance ('áns), n. 1. the act of conveying. 2. a vehicle. 3. a document transferring title to real estate.

con·vey·anc·ing ('án-sing), n. the business of drawing up property transfers. —con·vey'anc·er, n.

con·vict (kŏn-vikt'), v.t. to prove or pronounce guilty of a crime charged: n. (kon'vikt), a criminal in prison.

con·vic·tion (kŏn-vik'shŭn), n. 1. the act of be-

ing convicted. 2. the state of being convinced. 3. a strong belief.

con·vince (kŏn-vins'), v.t. -vinced', -vinc'ing, to satisfy by evidence or argument; persuade; cause to believe. —con·vinc'er, n. —con·vinc'ing·ly, adv.

con·viv·i·al (-viv'i-ăl), adj. 1. festive. 2. jovial. —con·viv·i·al'i·ty (-al'i-ti), n.

con·vo·ca·tion (kon-vō-kā'shŭn), n. 1. the act of convoking. 2. an assembly, especially of clergy. —con·vo·ca'tion·al, adj.

con·voke (kŏn-vōk'), v.t. -voked', -vok'ing, to call or summon together; convene.

con·vo·lute (kon'vō-loot), adj. rolled upon itself; coiled. —con·vo·lute·ly, adv.

con·vo·lut·ed (-id), adj. 1. spiraled. 2. intricate; complex.

con·vo·lu·tion (kon-vō-loo'shŭn), n. 1. a rolling together. 2. something rolled together; coil; twist.

con·volve (kŏn-volv'), v.t. & v.i. -volved', -volv'ing, to roll together.

con·vol·vu·lus (kon-vol'vyŭ-lŭs), n., pl. -lus·es, -li (-lī), any of a genus of trailing plants related to the morning glory.

con·voy (kon'voi, kŏn-voi'), v.t. to accompany on the way for protection, by land or sea: n. (kon'voi), 1. the act of convoying. 2. a protecting force accompanying ships, goods, persons, etc.; escort. 3. the group of things traveling together for protection.

con·vulse (kŏn-vuls'), v.t. -vulsed', -vuls'ing, 1. to agitate violently; shake. 2. to affect with convulsions. 3. to affect with laughter, anger, etc.

con·vul·sion (-vul'shŭn), n. 1. an agitation; tumult. 2. a violent and unnatural contraction of the muscles. 3. a spasm of laughter. —con·vul'sive, adj. —con·vul'sive·ly, adv.

co·ny (kō'ni), n., pl. -nies, same as coney.

coo (kōō), v.i. 1. to murmur like a dove or pigeon. 2. to converse in a loving manner: n. the sound of doves and pigeons.

cook (kook), v.t. to prepare for eating by boiling, baking, roasting, etc.: v.i. 1. to act as a cook. 2. to go through cooking: n. one who prepares food for the table. —cook'er, n.

cook·book ('book), n. a book telling how to prepare meals and dishes.

cook·er·y ('ēr-i), n. [Chiefly British], the art or practice of cooking.

cook·ie (kook'i), n. a small, flat, sweet cake: also cook'y, pl. cook'ies.

cool (kōōl), adj. 1. slightly or moderately cold. 2. lessening discomfort from heat. 3. calm. 4. indifferent or mildly hostile. 5. impudent. 6. [Informal], without overstatement. 7. [Slang], excellent: n. 1. a cool thing. 2. [Slang], cool, unemotional behavior: v.t. to make cool: v.i. to become cool. —cool'ly, adv. —cool'ness, n.

cool·ant ('ánt), n. a liquid for taking heat from engines.

cool·er ('ēr), n. 1. that which cools. 2. a vessel for cooling liquids, food, etc. 3. [Slang], a prison.

coo·lie (kōō'li), n. an unskilled laborer, especially in Asia at one time.

coon (kōōn), n. a shortened form of raccoon.

coop (kōōp), n. 1. a cage; pen. 2. [Slang],

prison: *v.t.* to confine in, or as in, a coop (usually followed by *up* or *in*).

co-op (kō′op), *n.* same as cooperative.

coop-er (kōō′ẽr), *n.* a maker of barrels, casks, etc.: *v.t.* to make (barrels or casks): *v.i.* to work as a barrel maker.

coop-er-age (-ij), *n.* 1. the workshop of a cooper. 2. the business of a cooper. 3. the price for a cooper's work.

co-op-er-ate (kō-op′ẽ-rāt), *v.i.* -at-ed, -at-ing, 1. to act or work jointly. 2. to concur to produce the same effect. Also **co-op′er-ate**, **co-öp′er-ate**. —**co-op-er-a′tion**, *n.* —**co-op′er-a-tor**, *n.*

co-op-er-a-tive (′ẽr-ā-tiv), *adj.* 1. promoting jointly the same end. 2. denoting something owned jointly by persons who profit from it mutually: *n.* a cooperative business, dwelling, etc. Also **co-op′er-a-tive**, **co-öp′er-a-tive**.

co-opt (kō-opt′), *v.t.* 1. to choose jointly. 2. to select as a partner. 3. to take into a group or system. Also **co-öpt′**. —**co-op-ta′tion**, **co-op′tion**, *n.*

co-or-di-nate (kō-ôr′di-nāt), *v.t.* 1. to place in the same order, class, etc. 2. to harmonize: *adj.* (′dn-it), 1. of the same rank or authority as another. 2. of or pertaining to coordinates or coordination: *n.* (′dn-it), 1. something coordinate. 2. in *Mathematics*, a line or other element by which the position of any point is determined by a fixed figure or lines. Also **co-or′di-nate**, **co-ör′di-nate**. —**co-or′di-nate-ly**, *adv.* —**co-or′di-na-tor**, *n.*

coordinating conjunction, a conjunction that joins coordinate words or phrases.

co-or-di-na-tion (-ôr-dn-ā′shún), *n.* 1. the act of coordinating. 2. the state of being coordinated, as in muscle movement. Also **co-or-di-na′tion**, **co-ör-di-na′tion**.

coot (kōōt), *n.* 1. a freshwater bird with webbed toes. 2. [Informal], a stupid person.

coot-ie (kōōt′i), *n.* [Slang], a louse.

cop (kop), *v.t.* copped, cop′ping, [Slang], to grab; steal: *n.* 1. a conical roll of thread or yarn coiled around a spindle. 2. [Slang], a policeman.

co-pai-ba (kō-pī′bä), *n.* a resin from various South American trees, formerly used as a medicine.

co-pal (kō′pâl), *n.* a resin used in varnishes.

co-par-ce-nar-y (kō-pär′sĕ-ner-i), *n., pl.* -nar-ies, in *Law*, heirship; partnership in inheritance. —**co-par′ce-ner**, *n.*

co-part-ner (kō-pärt′nẽr), *n.* one joined with another in any enterprise; associate.

cope (kōp), *v.i.* coped, cop′ing, to strive or contend (followed by *with*).

cope (kōp), *n.* 1. a large vestment worn by priests. 2. a canopy; vault.

Copernican system (kō-pûr′ni-kân), the system of Nicolaus Copernicus, a Polish astronomer (1473-1543), who asserted that the sun is the center of planetary space and that the diurnal turning of the earth on its axis accounts for the apparent revolution of the stars.

cop-i-er (kop′i-ẽr), *n.* 1. a transcriber. 2. an imitator. 3. a machine that duplicates.

co-pi-lot (kō′pī-lŏt), *n.* a pilot that aids the main pilot.

cop-ing (kō′ping), *n.* the top masonry of a wall.

co-pi-ous (kō′pi-ús), *adj.* 1. abundant. 2. diffusive. —**co′pi-ous-ly**, *adv.*

cop-out (kop′out), *n.* [Slang], a surrendering, going back, confessing, etc.

cop-per (kop′ẽr), *n.* 1. a reddish-brown, ductile, metal. 2. [Chiefly British], *a)* a penny. *b)* a boiler. 3. copper color; reddish-brown. 4. [Slang], a policeman: *adj.* 1. made of copper. 2. copper-colored: *v.t.* to cover with copper. —**cop′per-y**, *adj.*

cop-per-as (kop′ẽr-ás), *n.* a green, crystalline material, ferrous sulfate: used in dyeing and ink-making.

cop-per-head (kop′ẽr-hed), *n.* 1. a poisonous snake of North America. 2. [C-], a Northerner who sympathized with the South at the time of the Civil War.

cop-per-plate (-plāt), *n.* 1. a polished copper plate on which something is engraved for printing. 2. the art of engraving on copper plate.

copper sulfate, a blue crystalline material used in coloring matter, batteries, etc.

cop-pice (kop′is), *n.* same as copse.

co-pra (kō′prä), *n.* the dried meat of the coconut used for making coconut oil.

copse (kops), *n.* a thicket of brushwood.

cop-u-la (kop′yū-lä), *n., pl.* -las, in *Grammar & Logic*, a word which joins the subject and predicate in a sentence or proposition.

cop-u-late (-lāt), *v.i.* -lat-ed, -lat-ing, to have sexual intercourse. —**cop-u-la′tion**, *n.*

cop-u-la-tive (-lāt-iv), *adj.* uniting: *n.* a connecting conjunction.

cop-y (kop′i), *n., pl.* cop′ies, 1. an imitation; transcript. 2. one of many books or periodicals containing the same material. 3. manuscript to be set in type. 4. advertising contents: *v.t. & v.i.* cop′ied, cop′ying, 1. to transcribe; reproduce. 2. to imitate. —**cop′y-ist**, *n.*

cop-y-right (-rīt), *n.* the exclusive right of an author, artist, etc. in his literary or artistic work for a prescribed number of years: *v.t.* to guard by copyright.

co-quet (kō-ket′), *v.i.* -quet′ted, -quet-ting, 1. to flirt. 2. to trifle (followed by *with*). —**co-quet-ry** (kōk′ĕ-tri), *n., pl.* -ries.

co-quette (kō-ket′), *n.* a vain woman who seeks to gain men's attention and admiration: *v.i.* -quet′ted, -quet′ting, to act like a coquette. —**co-quet′tish**, *adj.*

cor-, same as com-.

cor-a-cle (kôr′ä-kl), *n.* a small boat made of a waterproof substance stretched over a wicker frame.

cor-a-coid (kôr′ä-koid), *adj.* denoting a bony process that extends from the scapula toward the sternum in mammals and some other vertebrates: *n.* the bony process.

cor-al (kôr′âl), *n.* 1. the hard, calcareous skeleton of certain marine polyps. 2. the ovaries of the lobster. 3. a yellowish pink: *adj.* of or pertaining to coral.

cor-al-line (kôr′ä-lin), *adj.* 1. consisting of, or

ô in dragon, ōō in crude, oo in wool, u in cup, ū in cure, û in turn, ù in focus, oi in boy, ou in house, th in thin, th in sheathe, g in get, j in joy, y in yet.

like, coral. 2. of a color like coral: *n.* a red algae.

coral reef, a reef made up mostly of coral fragments.

cor·beil (kôr′bel), *n.* a sculptured basket, as of flowers.

cor·bel (kôr′bĕl), *n.* a projection of stone, wood, or metal, to support some mass, as a cornice.

cord (kôrd), *n.* 1. a string. 2. a measure of wood. 3. a rib on the surface of a fabric. 4. corduroy. 5. a body part like a cord. 6. a thin electrical cable: *v.t.* to fasten or connect with a cord.

cord·age (′ij), *n.* ropes and rigging collectively.

cor·date (kôr′dāt), *adj.* heart-shaped.

cor·dial (kôr′jăl), *adj.* warm; hearty; sincere: *n.* an aromatic drink; liqueur. —**cor·di·al′i·ty**, (-ji-al′i-ti), *n., pl.* **-ties.**

cord·i·form (kôr′di-fôrm), *adj.* heart-shaped.

cor·dil·le·ra (kôr-dil-yer′ä), *n.* a continuous ridge or chain of mountains.

cord·ing (kôr′ding), *n.* the ribbed surface of a twilled fabric.

cord·ite (′dīt), *n.* an explosive composed of nitroglycerine, guncotton, and mineral jelly.

cord·less (kôrd′lis), *adj.* that can be used without batteries.

cor·don (kôr′dn), *n.* 1. a ribbon worn as a badge. 2. a course of projecting stones along a wall. 3. a line of troops, military posts, etc.: *v.t.* to surround with a cordon.

cor·don bleu (kôr-dôn-blŏŏ′), [French], 1. the ribbon of the Holy Ghost, a former decoration of French knights. 2. an eminent person. 3. a first-class cook.

cor·do·van (kôr′dō-văn), *n.* a soft leather made of goatskin or split horsehide.

cor·du·roy (kôr′dŭ-roi), *n.* a heavy, ribbed, piled cotton: *adj.* constructed with logs laid side by side: used of a roadway.

core (kôr), *n.* 1. the heart or innermost part of anything, especially of fruit. 2. the essence of anything. 3. the inner wires of an electrical cable: *v.t.* to remove the core from.

co·re·spond·ent (kō-ri-spon′dĕnt), *n.* a man or woman charged with having adulterous relations with the defendant in a divorce suit.

co·ri·a·ceous (kôr-i-ā′shŭs), *adj.* like leather.

co·ri·an·der (kôr-i-an′dĕr), *n.* 1. an herb related to parsley. 2. a fruit used for flavoring.

Co·rin·thi·an (kō-rin′thi-ăn), *adj.* 1. of or pertaining to Corinth, a city of ancient Greece, noted for its luxury and licentiousness. 2. luxurious. 3. denoting the Corinthian order, the most ornate and the lightest of the classic orders, with a bell-shaped capital, and ornamentation of acanthus leaves: *n.* 1. a native or inhabitant of Corinth. 2. a man-about-town. 3. a yachtsman.

Co·rin·thi·ans (-ănz), *n.* either of two books of the New Testament, I Corinthians and II Corinthians.

co·ri·um (kôr′i-ŭm), *n., pl.* **-ri·a** (-ä), the layer of skin just under the epidermis.

cork (kôrk), *n.* 1. the outer layer of the bark of an oak tree. 2. a stopper for a bottle: *adj.* made of cork: *v.t.* 1. to stop with a cork. 2. to blacken with cork.

cork·er (kôr′kĕr), *n.* 1. one or that which

corks. 2. [Slang], *a*) a clever fellow. *b*) a ridiculous story. *c*) an argument that vanquishes an opponent.

cork·screw (kôrk′skrōō), *n.* a device in the shape of a spiral for removing corks from bottles: *adj.* spiral-shaped: *v.t. & v.i.* to wind or spiral.

corm (kôrm), *n.* the thick stem of some plants, that runs underground, as of the gladiolus.

cor·mo·rant (kôr′mō-rănt), *n.* 1. a diving bird that preys voraciously on fish. 2. a glutton.

corn (kôrn), *n.* 1. a hard seed of cereal grass. 2. maize; Indian corn. 3. [British], *a*) plants that yield grain. *b*) grain, as of wheat, barley, etc. 4. [Slang], sentimental or trite humor, music, etc.

corn (kôrn), *n.* a horny growth on the foot, causing pain.

corn (kôrn), *v.t.* to preserve with salt or brine.

corn-cob (′kob), *n.* 1. the hard core of an ear of Indian corn. 2. a tobacco pipe made from this core.

corn-crake (′krāk), *n.* a short-billed, brown wading bird which inhabits the grainfields of northern Europe.

cor·ne·a (kôr′ni-ä), *n.* the transparent membrane which forms the outer portion of the eyeball. —**cor′ne·al**, *adj.*

corned (kôrnd), *adj.* preserved by steeping in brine.

cor·nel·ian (kôr-nēl′yăn), *n.* same as **carnelian.**

cor·ner (kôr′nĕr), *n.* 1. an angle. 2. an angle forming part of a street intersection. 3. a remote place. 4. a section or area. 5. a difficult situation. 6. a mercantile ring to monopolize some product: *v.t.* 1. to drive or force into some position from which it is difficult to escape. 2. to obtain a monopoly with: *adj.* on, at, or used in a corner.

cor·ner-stone (kôr′nĕr-stōn), *n.* 1. the principal part. 2. a stone in a building corner, especially an inscribed foundation stone laid at a formal ceremony.

cor·net (kôr-net′), *n.* a kind of trumpet.

corn-flow·er (kôrn′flou-ĕr), *n.* an annual plant with bright flowers.

cor·nice (kôr′nis), *n.* the highest projection or border on a wall or column.

corn-meal (kôrn′mēl), *n.* 1. meal made from Indian corn. 2. meal from other grains.

corn smut, a smut fungus very injurious to corn, causing black growths to form.

corn-stalk (′stok), *n.* a stalk of Indian corn.

corn-starch (′stärch), *n.* starch made from the meal of Indian corn, used in cooking, making syrups, etc.

cor·nu·co·pi·a (kôr-nŭ-kō′pi-ä), *n.* 1. the horn of plenty, represented in sculpture, as overflowing with fruit, flowers, etc. 2. a great supply; overflow.

corn·ut·ed (kôr-nūt′id), *adj.* horned.

corn·y (kôr′ni), *adj.* **corn′i·er, corn′i·est,** [Informal], sentimental, trite, etc.

co·rol·la (kō-rol′ä), *n.* flower petals. —**cor·ol·la·ceous** (kôr-ō-lā′shŭs), *adj.*

cor·ol·lar·y (kôr′ō-ler-i), *n., pl.* **-lar·ies,** 1. an additional deduction or inference drawn from a demonstrated proposition. 2. the usual consequence.

co·ro·na (kō-rō′nä), *n., pl.* **-nas, -nae** (′nē), 1. a crown. 2. the flat projecting part of a cornice. 3. the upper surface of a tooth. 4. a halo or colored ring surrounding the sun or moon. 5. a glow from an electric conductor. 6. a crownlike whorl of a flower, such as a daffodil.

cor·o·nach (kôr'ŏ-nàk), n. 1. [Scottish], a wild lamentation for the dead, usually played on the bagpipes. 2. [Irish], a wailing lamentation for the dead.

cor·o·nal (kôr'ŏ-nl), n. 1. a crown, coronet, or the like. 2. a garland: adj. (kŏ-rō'nl), of or pertaining to a crown, coronet, etc.

cor·o·nar·y (kôr'ŏ-ner-i), adj. 1. of or like a crown. 2. of or pertaining to the arteries that supply blood to the heart muscle: n., pl. -nar·ies, the obstruction of a coronary artery by a blood clot: also called coronary thrombosis or coronary occlusion.

cor·o·na·tion (kôr-ŏ-nā'shŭn), n. the act or ceremony of crowning a sovereign.

cor·o·ner (kôr'ŏ-nêr), n. a public officer who inquires into cases of sudden or accidental death.

cor·o·net (kôr'ŏ-net), n. 1. a small crown worn by one of lower rank than a sovereign. 2. an ornamental headdress. 3. the lowest part of the pastern of a horse. —cor'o·net·ed, cor'o·net·ted, adj.

cor·po·ral (kôr'pêr-ål), adj. relating to the body· n. 1. a cloth used on the altar during Communion. 2. a noncommissioned officer of the lowest rank. —cor'po·ral·ly, adv.

cor·po·rate (kôr'pêr-it), adj. 1. shared by all members of a group. 2. of a corporation. 3. incorporated. —cor'po·rate·ly, adv.

cor·po·ra·tion (kôr-pô-rā'shŭn), n. 1. a body politic legally authorized to act as an individual. 2. a group of people who, by charter, have certain legal rights and liabilities of an individual, as a business corporation. 3. [Informal], a protuberant belly. —cor'po·ra·ting, adj. —cor'po·ra·tor, n.

cor·po·re·al (kôr-pôr'i-ål), adj. 1. of a material nature. 2. of the body rather than the spirit. —cor·po·re·al'i·ty (al'i-ti), n. —cor·po're·al·ly, adv.

corps (kôr), n., pl. corps (kôrz), 1. a division or subdivision of armed forces. 2. a group of people working together.

corpse (kôrps), n. a dead body.

corps·man (kôr'mån), n., pl. -men, same as aid-man.

cor·pu·lent (kôr'pyoo-lênt), adj. obese; stout; fleshy. —cor'pu·lence, cor'pu·len·cy, n.

cor·pus (kôr'pŭs), n., pl. cor'po·ra ('pêr-å), 1. a body, especially a dead one. 2. a collection, as of writings, laws, etc. 3. the main body of anything.

Cor·pus Christ·i (kôr'pŭs kris'ti), [Latin, Body of Christ], a festival of the Roman Catholic Church, celebrated on the first Sunday after Trinity Sunday in honor of the institution of the Eucharist.

cor·pus·cle (kôr'pŭs-l), n. 1. a minute particle. 2. a specialized particle in the blood of vertebrates. Also cor·pus·cule (kôr'pŭs'kŭl). —cor·pus·cu·lar (kôr-pŭs'kyoo-lêr), adj.

corpus de·lic·ti (di-lik'ti), 1. the facts indicating that a crime has been committed. 2. loosely, the body of a murder victim.

corpus ju·ris (joor'is, yoor'is), a body of laws.

cor·ral (kŏ-ral'), n. 1. a pen or enclosure for capturing and holding livestock. 2. an enclosure made by drawing covered wagons into a circle: v.t. -ralled', -ral'ling, 1. to drive into or secure in a corral. 2. to round up; capture. 3. [Slang], to take possession of.

cor·rect (kŏ-rekt'), v.t. 1. to make right; rectify. 2. to punish or reprove so that faults will be mended. 3. to mark the mistakes of. 4. to remove or offset (a fault, etc.): adj. 1. exact; accurate; free from error. 2. conforming to a fixed rule or standard. 3. equal to a given amount. —cor·rect'a·ble, adj. —cor·rect'ly, adv. —cor·rect'ness, n. —cor·rec'tor, n.

cor·rec·tion (kŏ-rek'shŭn), n. 1. the act of correcting. 2. an alteration to correct a fault, error, etc. 3. punishment. —cor·rec'tion·al, adj.

cor·rec·tive ('tiv), adj. able to correct: n. that which corrects; antidote. —cor·rec'tive·ly, adv.

cor·re·late (kôr'ê-lāt), v.t. -lat·ed, -lat·ing, to put in relation with (another): v.i. to be reciprocally related: adj. reciprocally related: n. either of two reciprocally related things.

cor·re·la·tion (kôr-ê-lā'shŭn), n. 1. a reciprocal relationship or connection. 2. the act or fact of correlating. 3. the relative correspondence between things.

cor·rel·a·tive (kŏ-rel'å-tiv), adj. 1. having a reciprocal or mutual relationship. 2. related and used together, as either and or: n. 1. something closely related to another 2. a correlative word. —cor·rel'a·tive·ly, adv. —cor·rel·a·tiv'i·ty, n.

cor·re·spond (kôr-ê-spond'), v.i. 1. to be similar or equal (to). 2. to agree; suit, conform. 3. to communicate (with) by letters. —cor·re·spond'ing·ly, adv.

cor·re·spond·ence (-spon'dêns), n. 1 communication by letters. 2. mutual agreement, conformity 3. similarity.

cor·re·spond·ent (-spon'dênt), adj. agreeing with, similar: n. 1 a person with whom one communicates by letter 2. a journalist who sends news, articles, etc. to a newspaper or magazine as from a distant place

cor·ri·dor (kôr'i-dêr, -dôr), n. 1 a long hall in a building. 2 a narrow strip of land, as leading from a country to its seaport through foreign-held land.

cor·ri·gen·da (kôr-i-jen'då), n., sing. -dum ('dŭm), a list of errors in a printed work, with their corrections, inserted in the published work.

cor·ri·gi·ble (kôr'i-ji-bl), adj. capable of being corrected or improved. —cor·ri·gi·bil'i·ty, n. —cor'ri·gi·bly, adv.

cor·rob·o·rant (kŏ-rob'ŏ-rånt), adj. corroborating; confirming.

cor·rob·o·rate (-rāt), v.t. -rat·ed, -rat·ing, 1. originally, to strengthen. 2. to confirm; verify. —cor·rob·o·ra'tion, n. —cor·rob'o·ra·tor, n.

cor·rob·o·ra·tive (-rāt·iv), adj. corroborating; verifying; confirmatory: also cor·rob'o·ra·to·ry. —cor·rob'o·ra·tive·ly, adv.

ó in dragon, ōō in crude, oo in wool, u in cup, ū in cure, û in turn, ù in focus, oi in boy, ou in house, th in thin, th in sheathe, g in get, j in joy, y in yet.

cor·rob·o·ree (kô-rob′ēr-i), *n.* 1. a dance revel held at night by Australian aborigines. 2. in Australia, any festivity or tumult.

cor·rode (kô-rōd′), *v.t.* -rod′ed, -rod′ing, to eat away gradually, as by rust or chemical action. —cor·rod′i·ble, *adj.*

cor·ro·sion (kô-rō′zhŭn), *n.* 1. the act or process of corroding. 2. a substance resulting from the process of corroding.

cor·ro·sive (kô-rōs′iv), *adj.* capable of producing corrosion: *n.* a substance producing corrosion. —cor′ro′sive·ly, *adv.* —cor·ro′sive·ness, *n.*

cor·ru·gate (kôr′ŭ-gāt), *v.t. & v.i.* -gat·ed, -gat·ing, to draw or shape into parallel wrinkles or folds; furrow. —cor·ru·ga′tion, *n.*

corrugated iron, sheet iron pressed into alternate parallel ridges and grooves and usually galvanized.

cor·rupt (kô-rupt′), *adj.* 1. originally, spoiled, putrid, etc. 2. depraved; evil. 3. containing errors, alterations, etc. 4. open to bribery: *v.i. & v.t.* to become or cause to become corrupt. —cor·rupt′er, cor·rup′tor, *n.* —cor·rup′tive, *adj.* —cor·rupt′ly, *adv.* —cor·rupt′ness, *n.*

cor·rupt·i·ble (kô-rupt′ti-bl), *adj.* capable of being corrupted. —cor·rupt·i·bil′i·ty, *n.* —cor·rupt′i·bly, *adv.*

cor·rup·tion (kô-rup′shŭn), *n.* 1. the act of corrupting. 2. the state of being corrupted. 3. bribery or other dishonest practices. 4. depravity; evil.

cor·rup·tion·ist (-ist), *n.* a person in public life who takes part in, or condones, corrupt practices.

cor·sage (kôr-sāzh′), *n.* 1. a bodice or waist. 2. a small bouquet worn by women on the shoulder, wrist, etc.

cor·sair (kôr′ser), *n.* 1. a pirate. 2. a pirate ship.

corse·let (kôrs′lĕt), *n.* 1. light body armor: also **cors′let**. 2. (kôr-sĕ-let′), a lightweight corset: also **cor·se·lette**′.

cor·set (kôr′sit), *n.* a closefitting undergarment worn by women to support the body: *v.t.* to fit with a corset.

cor·tege, cor·tège (kôr-tezh′, -tāzh′), *n.* 1. a train of attendants; retinue. 2. a procession, as at a funeral.

Cor·tes (kôr′tiz), *n.* the legislative assembly of Spain.

cor·tex (kôr′teks), *n., pl.* -ti·ces (′ti-sēz), 1. the outer bark or covering of a plant. 2. the gray outer layer over most of the brain. 3. the surface of the kidneys, adrenal glands, etc. —cor′ti·cal (′ti-kl), *adj.* —cor′ti·cal·ly, *adv.*

cor·ti·sone (kôrt′i-sōn, -zōn), *n.* an adrenal hormone used in the treatment of various allergies and inflammatory diseases.

co·run·dum (kô-run′dŭm), *n.* a very hard mineral, aluminum oxide: dark varieties are used as abrasives and transparent varieties as gems.

co·rus·cant (kô-rus′kănt), *adj.* glittering.

cor·us·cate (kôr′ŭs-kāt), *v.i.* -cat·ed, -cat·ing, to sparkle, glitter —cor·us·ca′tion, *n.*

cor·vette (kôr-vet′), *n.* 1. formerly, a small sail-

ing warship. 2. [British], a small, lightly armed warship used for escort, etc.

cor·vine (kôr′vin), *adj.* of, pertaining to, or like a crow.

co·ry·za (kô-rī′zǎ), *n.* nasal congestion; a cold in the head.

co·se·cant (kô-sē′kant), *n.* in *Trigonometry*, the ratio of the hypotenuse in a right triangle to the side opposite a given acute angle.

co·sey, co·sie (kō′zi), *adj. & n.* same as cozy.

cosh·er (kosh′ēr), *v.t.* to pet; pamper.

co·sign (kō′sin′), *v.t. & v.i.* to sign jointly, thus becoming equally responsible. —co′sign·er, *n.*

co·sig·na·to·ry (kô-sig′nǎ-tôr-i), *n., pl.* -ries, a joint signer, as of a treaty: *adj.* signing jointly.

co·sine (kō′sin), *n.* in *Trigonometry*, the ratio between the side adjacent to an angle and the hypotenuse.

cos·met·ic (koz-met′ik), *adj.* 1. imparting or improving beauty, as of the face. 2. correcting or removing defects that mar the appearance, as by surgery: *n.* a preparation intended to beautify the skin, hair, nails, etc. —cos·met′i·cal·ly, *adv.*

cos·me·ti·cian (-mĕ-tish′ǎn), *n.* 1. a maker of cosmetics. 2. an expert in the application of cosmetics.

cos·me·tol·o·gy (-tol′ō-ji), *n.* the art or occupation of giving beauty treatments. —cos·me·tol′o·gist, *n.*

cos·mic (koz′mik), *adj.* 1. of or pertaining to the universe as an orderly system. 2. of the universe apart from the earth. 3. vast. —cos′mi·cal·ly, *adv.*

cosmic ray, a stream of radiation from outer space, consisting of atomic nuclei and other particles.

cos·mog·o·ny (koz-mog′ō-ni), *n.* 1. the origin or creation of the world or universe. 2. *pl.* -nies, a theory of how this occurred. —cos·mo·gon′ic (-mō-gon′ik), *adj.* —cos·mog′o·nist, *n.*

cos·mog·ra·phy (′rǎ-fi), *n.* 1. the science of the constitution of the universe, including astronomy, geography, and geology. 2. a description of the world or universe. —cos·mog′ra·pher, *n.* —cos·mo·graph·ic (koz-mō-graf′ik), *adj.* —cos·mo·graph′i·cal·ly, *adv.*

cos·mol·o·gy (-mol′ō-ji), *n.* the study of the nature and structure of the universe. —cos·mo·log′i·cal (-mō-loj′i-kl), *adj.* —cos·mo·log′i·cal·ly, *adv.* —cos·mol′o·gist, *n.*

cos·mo·naut (koz′mô-nôt), *n.* [Russian], an astronaut, especially one from Russia.

cos·mo·pol·i·tan (koz-mô-pol′i-tǎn), *n.* a citizen of the world: *adj.* 1. at home in any part of the world. 2. representative of many parts of the world. 3. found in many parts of the world. —cos·mo·pol′i·tan·ism, *n.*

cos·mop·o·lite (koz-mop′ō-līt), *n.* 1. one who is cosmopolitan. 2. an animal or plant common in many parts of the world. —cos·mop′o·lit·ism, *n.*

cos·mos (koz′môs), *n.* 1. the world or universe regarded as an orderly system. 2. *pl.* **cos′·mos**, a tall garden plant with pink, white, or purple flowers.

co·spon·sor (kō-spon′sēr), *n.* a joint sponsor:

v.t. to act as cosponsor of. —**co·spon'sor·ship**, *n.*

Cos·sack (kos'ăk), *n.* one of a people of southern Russia, skilled as horsemen: *adj.* of or like Cossacks.

cos·set (kos'it), *n.* a pet lamb: *v.t.* to make a pet of; pamper.

cost (kôst), *v.t.* cost, cost'ing, 1. to require or cause the expenditure or loss of. 2. to be obtainable for (a given price): *n.* 1. a charge; price; expense. 2. a sacrifice or loss. 3. *pl.* the court expenses of a lawsuit.

cos·ta (kos'tȧ), *n., pl.* -tae ('tē), a rib. —**cos'tal**, *adj.*

cos·ter·mon·ger (kôs'tẽr-mung-gẽr), *n.* [British], a street hawker of fruits, vegetables, etc.

cos·tive (kos'tiv), *adj.* constipating or constipated. —**cos'tive·ly**, *adv.* —**cos'tive·ness**, *n.*

cost·ly (kôst'li), *adj.* -li·er, -li·est, 1. expensive; dear. 2. requiring much labor, sacrifice, etc. 3. luxurious. —**cost'li·ness**, *n.*

cos·tume (kos'tōōm), *n.* 1. a style of dress characteristic of a period, country, etc. 2. a set of clothes worn in a play, etc. 3. a set of outer clothes: *v.t.* -tumed, -tum·ing, to dress in or provide with costumes.

cos·tum·er (kos'tōōm-ẽr), *n.* one who makes or rents costumes for balls, theaters, etc: also **cos·tum·ier** (kos-tōōm'yẽr).

co·sy (kō'zi), *adj.* -si·er, -si·est, & *n., pl.* -sies, same as cozy. —**co'si·ly**, *adv.* —**co'si·ness**, *n.*

cot (kot), *n.* 1. a shelter; cottage. 2. a sheath, as for an injured finger. 3. a small, collapsible bed.

co·tan·gent (kō-tan'jĕnt), *n.* the tangent of the complement of an arc or angle.

cote (kōt), *n.* 1. a small shelter for sheep, doves, etc. 2. a cottage.

co·tem·po·rar·y (kō-tem'pō-rer-i) *adj.* & *n.* archaic variant of contemporary.

co·te·rie (kōt'ẽr-i), *n.* a group of people associated closely for social purposes; clique.

co·ter·mi·nous (kō-tûr'mi-nŭs), *adj.* same as conterminous. —**co·ter'mi·nous·ly**, *adv.*

co·til·lion, co·til·lon (kō-til'yŭn), *n.* 1. a brisk, lively dance for many couples. 2. music for such a dance. 3. a formal ball, especially for presenting debutantes.

cot·tage (kot'ij), *n.* 1. a small dwelling. 2. a simple house used for vacations. —**cot'tag·er**, *n.*

cottage cheese, a soft, mild, white cheese, made from curds of sour milk.

cot·ter, cot·tar (kot'ẽr), *n.* 1. one who dwells in a cottage. 2. in Scotland, a tenant farmer.

cot·ter pin (kot'ẽr), a two-pronged metal fastener that is secured in place by ends that are spread apart after insertion.

cot·ton (kot'n), *n.* 1. a white, soft, downy substance enveloping the seeds in pods of a shrubby plant. 2. such a plant. 3. thread or cloth made from these fibers: *adj.* of cotton: *v.t.* [Informal]. to take a liking to (followed by to). —**cot'ton·y**, *adj.*

cotton gin, a machine for separating the seeds from cotton fibers.

cot·ton·mouth (-mouth), *n.* same as water moccasin.

cot·ton·seed (-sēd), *n.* the seed of the cotton plant, pressed for an oil used for cooking,

etc., with the hulls then ground for use as fertilizer, etc.

cot·ton·tail (-tāl), *n.* a common North American rabbit with a fluffy, white tail.

cot·ton·wood (-wood), *n.* a kind of poplar tree that has cottony fibers on the seeds.

cot·y·le·don (kot-i-lē'dŏn), *n.* the first leaf of an embryo.

couch (kouch), *v.t.* & *v.i.* 1. to lie down as on a couch. 2. to express in words: *n.* 1. a piece of furniture on which one may sit or lie down; sofa. 2. a layer of grain, as barley, spread out to germinate in brewing.

couch·ant ('ȧnt), *adj.* in *Heraldry*, crouching or lying down, but with the head up.

cou·gar (kōō'gẽr), *n.* a large, tawny wildcat of North and South America.

cough (kôf) *v.i.* to expel air from the lungs suddenly and noisily *v.t.* to expel by coughing: *n.* 1. the act of coughing. 2. the sound of coughing. 3. a disorder of the lungs, bronchial tubes, etc. that causes frequent coughing. —**cough'er**, *n.*

could (kood), 1. past tense of can. 2. an auxiliary generally equivalent to can.

could·n't ('nt), could not.

cou·lomb (kōō-lom'), *n.* the quantity of electricity transferred by a current of one ampere per second.

coul·ter (kōl'tẽr), *n.* same as colter.

coun·cil (koun'sl), *n.* 1. an assembly of persons met for consultation, or to give advice. 2. a legislative or administrative body. —**coun'cil·man**, *n., pl.* -men.

coun·ci·lor, coun·cil·lor (-ẽr), *n.* a member of a council.

coun·sel (koun'sl), *n.* 1. an interchange of opinion or ideas; consultation. 2. advice. 3. a lawyer or group of lawyers. 4. any consultant: *v.t.* -seled or -selled, -sel·ing or -sel·ling, 1. to give advice to. 2. to suggest or strongly urge (a plan, etc.): *v.i.* to give counsel or advice.

coun·se·lor, coun·sel·lor (-ẽr), *n.* 1. a lawyer. 2. an adviser.

count (kount), *v.t.* 1. to enumerate, one by one, in order to sum up. 2. to include; take into account. 3. to consider; esteem: *v.i.* 1. to tell off numbers or items in order 2. to be taken into account. 3. to have a certain value. 4. to rely (on): *n.* 1. the act of numbering or reckoning. 2. the total ascertained. 3. an accounting. 4. a separate charge in an indictment. —**count'a·ble**, *adj.*

count (kount), *n.* a European nobleman equal in rank to an English earl.

count·down (kount'doun), *n.* 1. a counting backward in fixed units of time from the commencement of an operation to zero. 2. the procedure followed during this period, as for the launching of a rocket.

coun·te·nance (koun'tė-nȧns), *n.* 1. the visage; face. 2. the expression on the face 3. support: *v.t.* -nanced, -nanc·ing, to tolerate.

count·er (koun'tẽr), *n.* 1. one who or that which counts. 2. a long table or board on which to display goods for sale, prepare or serve food, etc. 3. an imitation coin. 4. a disk used for keeping score in some games.

coun·ter (koun'tẽr), *adv.* contrary; in opposi-

tion: *adj.* opposite; contrary: *n.* the opposite or contrary: *v.t.* & *v.i.* 1. to oppose or check. 2. to do (something) in retaliation.

coun·ter·act (koun-tĕr-akt'), *v.t.* 1. to act in opposition to. 2. to neutralize. —**coun·ter·ac'·tion,** *n.* —**coun·ter·ac'tive,** *adj.*

coun·ter·at·tack (koun'tĕr-ă-tak'), *n.* an attack made as a reply to another attack: *v.t.* & *v.i.* to attack in reply.

coun·ter·bal·ance (koun'tĕr-bal-ăns), *n.* a weight or force equally balancing another: *v.t.* & *v.i.* (koun-tĕr-bal'ăns), -anced, -anc·ing, to balance (something) equally; offset.

coun·ter·charge (koun'tĕr-chärj), *n.* 1. an attack in return. 2. a charge against the accuser by one who has been accused: *v.t.* (koun-tĕr-chärj'), -charged', -charg'ing, to attack or accuse in return.

coun·ter·claim (koun'tĕr-clām), *n.* an opposing claim, especially in law: *v.t.* & *v.i.* (koun-tĕr-clām'), to make an opposing claim (of).

coun·ter·clock·wise (koun-tĕr-klok'wīz), *adj.* & *adv.* in a direction opposite to that in which the hands of a clock move.

coun·ter·es·pi·on·age (-es'pi-ŏ-näzh), *n.* measures taken against enemy espionage.

coun·ter·feit (koun'tĕr-fit), *v.t.* & *v.i.* 1. to make a copy of (money, etc.) without authority, for fraudulent purposes; forge. 2. to feign: *adj.* 1. imitation; forged. 2. feigned; spurious: *n.* an imitation intended to deceive. —**coun'ter·feit·er,** *n.* —**coun'ter·feit·ing,** *n.*

coun·ter·foil (-foil), *n.* that part of a check, receipt, money order, etc. that is kept by the issuer.

coun·ter·mand (koun-tĕr-mand'), *v.t.* 1. to cancel or annul, as an order or command. 2. to call back by contradictory orders: *n.* (koun'tĕr-mand), a revocation of a former order or command.

coun·ter·pane (koun'tĕr-pān), *n.* a coverlet for a bed; bedspread.

coun·ter·part (-pärt), *n.* 1. a duplicate. 2. something that closely resembles another.

coun·ter·plot (-plot), *n.* a plot or plan opposed to another in operation: *v.t.* & *v.i.* -plot·ted, -plot·ting, to plot against or frustrate (a plot).

coun·ter·point (-point), *n.* 1. the art of combining independent melodies into a harmonious whole. 2. a composition in which this is done.

coun·ter·poise (-poiz), *n.* 1. a counterbalance. 2. a state of equilibrium: *v.t.* -poised, -pois·ing, to counterbalance.

coun·ter·rev·o·lu·tion (-rev-ŏ-lōō'shŭn), *n.* 1. a revolution against a power recently invested by another revolution. 2. a movement to resist revolutionary trends. —**coun·ter·rev·o·lu'·tion·ar·y,** *n.* & *adj.* —**coun·ter·rev·o·lu'tion·ist,** *n.*

coun·ter·scarp (koun'tĕr-skärp), *n.* the exterior slope of a ditch, moat, etc. in a fort.

coun·ter·sign (-sīn), *v.t.* to confirm by adding one's own signature: *n.* 1. an additional signature to a document to confirm it. 2. a military password or secret signal to a sentry.

coun·ter·sink (-singk), *v.t.* -sunk, -sink·ing, 1. to drill (a conical depression) in wood or metal to receive a screw or bolt so that the head is flush with the surface. 2. to sink (a screw or bolt) into such a surface.

coun·ter·ten·or (-ten-ĕr), *n.* 1. the highest mature male singing voice, above tenor. 2. the range of such a voice: *adj.* having or for the range of a countertenor.

coun·ter·vail (koun-tĕr-vāl'), *v.t.* 1. to compensate. 2. to counteract.

count·ess (koun'tis), *n.* 1. the wife or widow of a count or earl. 2. a noblewoman whose rank is equal to a count or earl.

count·ing·house (koun'ting-hous), *n.* [Now Rare], a building or room where accounts are kept or business is transacted.

count·less (kount'lis), *adj.* innumerable.

coun·tri·fied (kun'tri-fīd), *adj.* rustic in behavior or appearance; not polished: also **coun'try·fied.**

coun·try (kun'tri), *n., pl.* -tries, 1. a tract of land; region. 2. the territory of a nation. 3. its people. 4. the land of one's birth or citizenship. 5. rural regions: *adj.* of or having to do with a rural district; rustic.

coun·try·man (-măn), *n., pl.* -men, 1. a man who lives in a rural district. 2. a compatriot. —**coun'try·wom·an,** *n.fem., pl.* -wom·en.

coun·try·side (-sīd), *n.* a rural district.

coun·ty (koun'ti), *n., pl.* -ties, 1. the largest administrative division of most States. 2. the people of a county.

coup (kōō), *n.* [French], 1. a blow. 2. a very successful stroke or action; master move. 3. same as **coup d'état.**

coup de grâce (kōō dĕ gräs'), [French], the death blow, delivered to end suffering.

coup d'état (dā tä'), [French], a sudden, violent overthrow of a government.

coupe (kōōp, kōō-pā'), *n.* 1. a closed carriage with two seats inside and an outside seat in front for the driver. 2. a closed, two-door automobile. Also **coupé.**

cou·ple (kup'l), *n.* 1. two of the same kind that are associated; pair. 2. a man and a woman who are partners in a dance, engaged, or married. 3. a bond or link. 4. [Informal], a few: *v.t.* -pled, -pling, to connect; link.

coup·let (kup'lit), *n.* two successive lines of verse that rhyme together.

cou·pling (kup'ling), *n.* a device for joining two things or parts. —**cou'pler,** *n.*

cou·pon (kōō'pon, kū'-), *n.* 1. a certificate attached to a bond, to be cut off and presented for payment of dividends. 2. a certificate entitling the holder to a discount, gift, etc., or for use in entering a contest, ordering something, etc.

cour·age (kûr'ij), *n.* fortitude; valor.

cou·ra·geous (kŭ-rā'jŭs), *adj.* brave; bold. —**cou·ra'geous·ly,** *adv.*

cou·ri·er (koor'i-ĕr), *n.* 1. a messenger. 2. a person who makes travel arrangements for another.

cour·lan (koor'lăn), *n.* an American bird of the marshes in the South, with a raucous cry.

course (kōrs), *n.* 1. a path or track. 2. direction or line of motion. 3. a regular sequence or manner of procedure. 4. the portion of a meal served at one time. 5. conduct. 6. an

---

a in cap, ā in cane, ä in father, å in abet, e in met, ē in be, ē in baker, ĕ in regent, i in pit, ī in fine, i in manifest, o in hot, ô in horse, ō in bone,

ordered series of things, as a layer of bricks. 7. a program of studies. 8. a series of classes in a subject of study: *v.i.* coursed, cours'ing, 1. to run, race, etc. 2. to hunt with hounds.

cours·er (kôr'sĕr), *n.* 1. a swift and spirited horse. 2. a war horse. 3. a running bird of Africa and Asia.

court (kôrt), *n.* 1. a small, uncovered, paved space surrounded by buildings. 2. a short street. 3. a marked playing space as for tennis. 4. a royal palace. 5. the attendants or councilors of a sovereign. 6. an assembly held by a sovereign. 7. a place where trials, etc. are held. 8. the judges, etc. engaged there. 9. courtship: *v.t.* 1. to pay attention to. 2. to woo. 3. to solicit.

cour·te·ous (kûr'ti·ŭs), *adj.* polite; obliging. —cour'te·ous·ly, *adv.*

cour·te·san, cour·te·zan (kôr'tĕ·zn), *n.* a prostitute.

cour·te·sy (kur'tĕ·si), *n.* 1. polite behavior. 2. *pl.* -sies, a polite, considerate action or comment.

court·house (kôrt'hous), *n.* 1. a building for holding courts of law. 2. a building of county government offices.

cour·ti·er (kôr'ti·ĕr), *n.* one in attendance at a royal court.

court·ly (kôrt'li), *adj.* -li·er, -li·est, refined; elegant. —court'li·ness, *n.*

court-mar·tial ('mär-shăl), *n., pl.* courts'-martial, 1. a naval or military court to try offenses against military law. 2. a trial by such a court: *v.t.* -tialed or -tialled, -tial·ing or -tial·ling, to try by such a court.

court·ship ('ship), *n.* the act or period of wooing.

court tennis, a kind of tennis played indoors, in which the ball is played against the walls as well as over the net.

court·yard ('yärd), *n.* an enclosed space adjoining or within a building.

cous·in (kuz'n), *n.* 1. the son or daughter of one's aunt or uncle. 2. a kinsman.

cous·in·ger·man (kuz-n-jûr'măn), *n., pl.* cous·ins·ger'man, a first cousin.

cou·tu·rier (kōō-toor'i-ā), *n.* one who designs and makes fashionable women's clothes. —cou'tu·rière (-i-er), *n.fem.*

cove (kōv), *n.* 1. a small, sheltered inlet or bay. 2. a concave molding.

cov·en (kuv'ĕn), *n.* a meeting of witches.

cov·e·nant (kuv'ĕ-nănt), *n.* 1. a solemn agreement; compact. 2. the promises made by God to man, as set forth in Scriptures. —cov'e·nant·er, *n.*

cov·er (kuv'ĕr), *v.t.* 1. to put something over or on. 2. to overspread. 3. to hide; conceal. 4. to shield or protect. 5. to clothe. 6. to aim at, as with a gun. 7. to include. 8. to gather news of: *v.i.* 1. to spread over in a thin layer. 2. to provide an alibi (*for*): *n.* 1. that which covers something else. 2. a shelter or hiding place. 3. a covert. 4. a tablecloth and setting for one person. 5. an envelope or wrapping for mail. 6. a pretense; front. —cov'er·ing, *n.*

cov·er·age (-ij), *n.* the range or amount covered by something.

cov·er·all (-ôl), *n.* a one-piece, protective work garment.

covered wagon, a large wagon with a high, arched canvas cover, as used by pioneers.

cov·er·let (kuv'ĕr-lit), *n.* a bedspread.

cov·ert (kuv'ĕrt), *adj.* 1. concealed, disguised, secret, or sheltered. 2. in *Law,* under the protection of her husband: said of a woman: *n.* 1. a place that protects or shelters. 2. a place of concealment for game, as a thicket. —cov'ert·ly, *adv.*

covert cloth, a very fine, twilled woolen fabric used for coats and suits.

cov·er·up (kuv'ĕr-up), *n.* something intended to conceal one's actual intentions, etc.

cov·et (kuv'it), *v.t. & v.i.* to desire inordinately; lust after. —cov'et·er, *n.*

cov·et·ous (-ŭs), *adj.* avaricious; desirous. —cov'et·ous·ly, *adv.*

cov·ey (kuv'i), *n.* a hatch or brood of birds, especially partridges.

cow (kou), *n.* the mature female of domestic cattle, or of the whale, elephant, etc.: *v.t.* to intimidate.

cow·ard (kou'ĕrd), *n.* one who is shamefully lacking in courage. —cow'ard·ly, *adj. & adv.* —cow'ard·li·ness, *n.*

cow·ard·ice (-is), *n.* a dishonorable lack of courage.

cow·bird ('bûrd), *n.* an American blackbird that accompanies herds of cattle.

cow·boy ('boi), *n.* 1. one who works on a ranch, often on horseback, as when tending cattle: also cow'hand. 2. a rodeo rider. —cow'girl, *n.fem.*

cow·catch·er ('kach-ēr), *n.* a wedge-shaped iron frame on the front of a locomotive to remove obstructions on the rails.

cow·er (kou'ĕr), *v.i.* 1. to crouch or huddle, as from cold or fear. 2. to cringe; quail.

cow·herd (kou'hûrd), *n.* a tender of cattle.

cow·hide ('hid), *n.* 1. the hide of a cow, especially when tanned and dressed into leather. 2. a whip of this or of rawhide: *v.t.* -hid·ed, -hid·ing, to whip with a cowhide.

cowl (koul), *n.* 1. a monk's hood. 2. a monk's cloak with a hood. 3. a revolving cover for a chimney top. 4. the top part of the front of an automobile body, to which the windshield is attached.

cow·lick (kou'lik), *n.* a tuft of hair that will not lie flat.

cowl·ing (kou'ling), *n.* a metal housing for an aircraft engine.

co-work·er (kō'wûr-kĕr), *n.* a fellow worker.

cow·pox (kou'poks), *n.* a contagious disease of cows causing pustules on the udders: vaccine made from cowpox virus is used to inoculate people against smallpox.

cow·rie, cow·ry (kou'ri), *n., pl.* -ries, a brightly colored marine gastropod shell, formerly used as money in parts of Africa.

cow·slip (kou'slip), *n.* a species of primrose with yellow or purple flowers.

cox·comb (koks'kŏm), *n.* 1. a cap with a top like a cock's comb, formerly worn by jesters. 2. a vain, conceited fellow; fop.

ŏ in drag*o*n, ōō in cr*u*de, oo in w*oo*l, u in c*u*p, ū in c*u*re, ü in t*u*rn, ŭ in f*o*cus, oi in b*o*y, ou in h*ou*se, th in *th*in, *th* in shea*th*e, g in get, j in joy, y in yet.

cox·swain (kok'sn, 'swān), *n.* the steersman of a boat, especially in a race.

coy (koi), *adj.* 1. shy; demure. 2. pretending to be shy. —**coy'ly**, *adv.* —**coy'ness**, *n.*

coy·o·te (kī-ōt'i, kī'ōt-), *n.*, *pl.* **-tes**, **-te**, the small prairie wolf of North America.

coy·pu (koi'pōō), *n.*, *pl.* **-pus**, **-pu**, same as **nutria**.

coz·en (kuz'n), *v.t. & v.i.* to cheat; deceive.

co·zy (kō'zi), *adj.* **-zi·er**, **-zi·est**, warm and comfortable; snug: *n.*, *pl.* **-zies**, a padded cover to keep a teapot warm. —**coz'i·ly**, *adv.* —**coz'i·ness**, *n.*

crab (krab), *n.* 1. an eight-legged crustacean with a pair of pincers. 2. [C-], same as **Cancer** 3. any of various mechanical devices for hoisting. 4. an ill-tempered person: *v.i.* **crabbed**, **crab'bing**, 1. to fish for crabs. 2. [Informal], to complain.

crab apple, 1. a small, sour apple. 2. the tree on which it grows.

crab·bed (krab'id), *adj.* 1. crabby; cross. 2. hard to decipher, as poor writing.

crab·by ('i), *adj.* **-bi·er**, **-bi·est**, ill-tempered; grouchy. —**crab'bi·ness**, *n.*

crab grass, an annual grass that is a weedy pest in lawns.

crab louse, a small body louse that infests the pubic area.

crack (krak), *n.* 1. a chink; fissure. 2. a partial fracture. 3. a sudden, sharp sound. 4. a changing tone of voice. 5. [Informal], a sharp, resonant blow. 6. [Informal], an attempt: *v.i.* 1. to make a sudden, sharp sound; snap. 2. to break, usually without coming apart. 3. to change abruptly: said of the voice. 4. [Informal], to give way; fail: *v.t.* 1. to cause to make a sudden, sharp noise. 2. to cause to break. 3. to break down (petroleum hydrocarbons) into simpler ones. 3. to solve. 4. [Informal], to break open or hit hard: *adj.* [Informal], first-rate.

crack·down (krak'doun), *n.* a strict or stricter enforcement of laws or rules.

cracked (krakt), *adj.* 1. fissured; split. 2. strident. 3. [Informal], crazy

crack·er (krak'ēr), *n.* 1. a thin, crisp biscuit. 2. a firecracker.

crack·er·jack (-jak), *n.* [Slang], a very fine person or thing: *adj.* [Slang], very fine; first-rate.

crack·le (krak'l), *v.i.* **-led**, **-ling**, to make a series of slight, sharp, explosive noises: *n.* 1. the noise of crackling. 2. a network of fine cracks, as on some ceramics or paintings.

crack·ling ('ling), *n.* 1. a series of slight, sharp, explosive noises. 2. (also 'lin), *pl.* the small, crisp pieces left when hog fat is rendered.

crack·nel ('nl), *n.* 1. a hard biscuit. 2. *pl.* cracklings or fat pork fried crisp.

crack·pot ('pot), *n.* [Informal], one who is eccentric: *adj.* [Informal], eccentric.

cra·dle (krā'dl), *n.* 1 a baby's little bed, often on rockers. 2. infancy. 3. a place of origin. 4. a frame to keep bedclothes from an injured limb. 5. a framework to support or lift a ship, aircraft, etc. 6. a box on rockers for separating gravel or sand from gold particles by washing. 7. a frame of wood with long teeth, fastened to a scythe: *v.t.* **-dled**,

-dling, 1. to rock or place in or as in a cradle. 2. to nurse or train in infancy.

craft (kraft), *n.* 1. manual skill. 2. an occupation requiring manual skill. 3. the members of a skilled trade. 4. cunning; guile. 5. *pl.* craft, a ship, boat, or aircraft.

crafts·man (krafts'mān), *n.*, *pl.* **-men**, a skilled artisan. —**crafts'man·ship**, *n.*

craft union, a labor union for only those of a specified trade or craft.

craft·y (kraft'i), *adj.* **craft'i·er**, **craft'i·est**, cunning; deceitful; sly. —**craft'i·ly**, *adv.* —**craft'i·ness**, *n.*

crag (krag), *n.* a steep, rugged rock. —**crag'gy**, *adj.* **-gi·er**, **-gi·est**.

cram (kram), *v.t.* **crammed**, **cram'ming**, 1. to stuff full or too full. 2. to feed past satiety: *v.i.* 1. to eat greedily. 2. [Informal], to study intensively for an examination.

cramp (kramp), *n.* 1. a spasmodic muscular contraction. 2. *usually pl.* abdominal spasms. 3. a piece of iron bent at both ends for holding: *v.t.* 1. to cause cramps in. 2. to secure with a cramp. 3. to hamper. 4. to turn (wheels) sharply.

cramped (krampt), *adj.* 1. crowded. 2. small and badly formed, as some writing.

cram·pon (kram'pon), *n.* 1. one of a pair of grappling hooks for raising heavy weights. 2. a spiked iron plate fastened to a shoe, etc. to prevent slipping on ice or for climbing. Also **cram-poon** (kram-pōōn').

cran·ber·ry (kran'ber-i), *n.*, *pl.* **-ries**, 1. a small, sour, red berry used in making sauce, jelly, etc. 2. the evergreen shrub on which it grows.

crane (krān), *n.* 1. a large wading bird with long legs and neck. 2. a machine for lifting and moving heavy weights: *v.t. & v.i.* **craned**, **cran'ing**, to stretch (the neck).

cra·ni·ol·o·gy (krā-ni-ol'ō-ji), *n.* the scientific study of skulls.

cra·ni·um (krā'ni-ŭm), *n.*, *pl.* **-ni·ums**, **-ni·a** (-à), the skull. —**cra'ni·al**, *adj.*

crank (krangk), *n.* 1. a bent handle connected to a shaft, used to transmit motion or to convert rotary into reciprocal motion, or vice versa. 2. [Informal], *a)* a crotchety person. *b)* an irritable person: *v.t.* to start by turning a crank.

crank·case ('kās), *n.* the metal casing enclosing a crankshaft.

crank·shaft ('shaft), *n.* a shaft or rod with one or more cranks.

crank·y ('i), *adj.* **crank'i·er**, **crank'i·est**, 1. shaky or loose. 2. irritable. 3. eccentric. —**crank'i·ness**, *n.*

cran·ny (kran'i), *n.*, *pl.* **-nies**, a chink; fissure.

crap (krap), *n.* [Vulgar Slang], 1. nonsense. 2. rubbish; trash. —**crap'py**, *adj.*

crape (krāp), *n.* crepe, especially black crepe worn for mourning.

crape-hang·er ('hang-ēr), *n.* [Slang], a glum person; killjoy.

craps (kraps), *n.* a gambling game played with two dice.

crash (krash), *v.t.* 1. to cause (an airplane, car, etc.) to fall, collide, etc. noisily. 2. to force or drive violently and noisily (*through, in, out,* etc.). 3. [Informal], to get into (a place)

a in cap, ā in cane, ä in father, à in abet, e in met, ē in be, ē in baker, ĕ in regent, i in pit, ī in fine, i in manifest, o in hot, ô in horse, ō in bone,

although uninvited: *v.i.* 1. to break, fall, collide, etc. noisily. 2. to break down; fail: *n.* 1. a loud, sudden noise. 2. the act of crashing. 3. a collapse, as of business. 4. a coarse linen fabric: *adj.* [Informal], marked by speed and great effort.

crash-land ('land), *v.i.* & *v.i.* to land (an aircraft) in an emergency, usually with some damage. —**crash landing.**

crass (kras), *adj.* grossly dense or obtuse.

-crat (krat), a suffix meaning *one who advocates a specific form of government.*

crate (krāt), *n.* a box or shipping container made of wooden slats: *v.t.* crat'ed, crat'ing, to put into a crate.

cra·ter (krāt'ẽr), *n.* 1. the cup-shaped cavity of a volcano. 2. a pit or hole where a bomb, shell, etc. has exploded.

cra·vat (krā-vat'), *n.* a necktie.

crave (krāv), *v.t.* craved, crav'ing, 1. to beg for. 2. to long for eagerly.

cra·ven (krā'vẽn), *adj.* shamefully fearful: *n.* a coward. —**cra'ven·ly,** *adv.*

crav·ing (krā'ving), *n.* a strong desire.

craw (krô), *n.* 1. a bird's crop. 2. the stomach.

craw·fish (krô'fish), *n.* same as crayfish.

crawl (krôl), *v.i.* 1. to move slowly with the body along the ground, or on hands and knees. 2. to progress slowly. 3. to teem (*with* things that crawl). 4. to feel as if insects were crawling on the skin: *n.* 1. the act of crawling. 2. a swimming stroke in which the prone swimmer uses overarm movements. —**crawl'er,** *n.* —**crawl'y,** *adj.*

cray·fish (krā'fish), *n.* a freshwater crustacean like a small lobster.

cray·on (krā'ôn, 'on), *n.* 1. a small stick of colored wax, chalk, etc. for writing or drawing. 2. a drawing made with crayons: *v.t.* to draw or color with crayons.

craze (krāz), *v.i.* & *v.t.* crazed, craz'ing, 1. to become or cause to become mentally ill. 2. to crackle, as some pottery, etc.: *n.* 1. a mania or fad. 2. a crackle.

cra·zy (krā'zi), *adj.* -zi·er, -zi·est, 1. mentally deranged; insane. 2. [Informal], not sensible; impractical. 3. [Informal], very enthusiastic. —**cra'zi·ly,** *adv.* —**cra'zi·ness,** *n.*

crazy quilt, a quilt made of irregular pieces of various sizes and colors.

creak (krēk), *v.i.* to make a sharp, harsh, grating sound: *n.* such a sound. —**creak'y,** *adj.* —**creak'i·ly,** *adv.* —**creak'i·ness,** *n.*

cream (krēm), *n.* 1. the rich, oily part of milk. 2. the choicest part of anything. 3. a soft, unctuous cosmetic. 4. yellowish white: *v.t.* 1. to add cream to. 2. to mix to a creamy consistency. —**cream'y,** *adj.* —**cream'i·ness,** *n.*

cream cheese, a soft, white cheese made of sweet milk and cream.

cream·er ('ẽr), *n.* a cream pitcher.

cream·er·y ('ẽr-i), *n., pl.* -er·ies, a place where milk or milk products are processed or sold.

cream of tartar, a white, acid powder used chiefly in baking powder.

crease (krēs), *n.* 1. a mark made by folding and pressing. 2. a wrinkle or fold: *v.t.* creased, creas'ing, 1. to make a crease in. 2. to wound slightly by shooting: *v.i.* to become creased. —**creas'er,** *n.*

cre·ate (krē-āt'), *v.t.* -at'ed, -at'ing, 1. to cause to come into existence; originate. 2. to cause; bring about. 3. to invest with a new rank, etc.

cre·a·tine (krē'ä-tēn), *n.* a white crystalline substance in muscular tissue.

cre·a·tion (krē-ā'shŭn), *n.* 1. the act of creating. 2. the thing created. 3. [C-], God's creating of the universe. 4. the universe.

cre·a·tion·ism (-izm), *n.* the doctrine that the soul of every human being is a distinct creation.

cre·a·tive (-āt'iv), *adj.* 1. having the power to create. 2. imaginative; original. 3. productive. —**cre·a·tiv'i·ty,** *n.*

cre·a·tor (-āt'ẽr), *n.* one who creates. 2. [C-], God; the Supreme Being.

crea·ture (krē'chẽr), *n.* 1. anything created, especially a living being. 2. a domestic animal. 3. one dependent on another.

crèche (kresh), *n.* a representation of the stable scene at the birth of Jesus.

cre·dence (krēd'ns), *n.* belief or trust in the statements of others.

cre·den·tials (kri-den'shälz), *n.* letters or certificates showing that one has a right to a position, authority, etc.

cre·den·za (kri-den'zä), *n.* a kind of sideboard or buffet.

cred·i·ble (kred'i-bl), *adj.* believable; reliable. —**cred·i·bil'i·ty,** *n.*

cred·it (kred'it), *v.t.* 1. to believe; trust. 2. to give acknowledgment or honor to. 3. to enter (a sum) in a bank account, etc.: *n.* 1. belief; trust reposed. 2. honor or praise. 3. a person or thing bringing honor. 4. money available, as in a bank account. 5. confidence in one's ability to pay. 6. the time allowed for payment. 7. a unit of academic study.

cred·it·a·ble (-a-bl), *adj.* bringing or deserving credit or honor. —**cred'it·a·bly,** *adv.*

credit card, a card allowing one to charge goods or services.

cred·i·tor (kred'it-ẽr), *n.* one to whom money is due.

credit union, a cooperative financial association in which members may take loans at low interest rates and deposit savings.

cre·do (krē'dō, krā'-), *n., pl.* -dos, [Latin], a creed.

cred·u·lous (krej'oo-lŭs), *adj.* easily convinced; gullible. —**cre·du·li·ty** (krē-dōō'li-ti), *n.* —**cred'u·lous·ly,** *adv.*

creed (krēd), *n.* a brief statement of belief.

creek (krēk, krik), *n.* a stream smaller than a river and larger than a brook.

creel (krēl), *n.* a wicker basket used by fishermen for carrying fish.

creep (krēp), *v.i.* crept, creep'ing, 1. to move slowly along the ground, as on hands and knees. 2. to move stealthily. 3. to grow along the ground or a wall, as a plant: *n.* [Slang], a boring or disgusting person. —**creep'er,** *n.*

creep·y (krēp'i), *adj.* creep'i·er, creep'i·est, causing or having a feeling of disgust, horror, etc. —**creep'i·ness,** *n.*

cre·mate (krē'māt), *v.t.* -mat'ed, -mat'ing, to

ō in drag*o*n, ōō in cr*u*de, oo in w*oo*l, u in c*u*p, ū in c*u*re, û in t*u*rn, ŭ in foc*u*s, oi in b*o*y, ou in h*ou*se, th in *th*in, *th* in shea*th*e, g in *g*et, j in *j*oy, y in *y*et.

reduce (a dead body) to ashes by heat. —cre·ma'tion, n.

cre·ma·to·ry (krē'mä·tôr·i), adj. of or pertaining to cremation: n., pl. -ries, a furnace for cremating: also cre·ma·to'ri·um ('i·ŭm), pl. -ri·ums, -ri·a (-ä).

crème de menthe (krēm dè menth'), a green, mint-flavored liqueur.

Cre·mo·na (kri·mō'nä), n. any of the famous violins made in Cremona, Italy, in the 17th and 18th centuries.

cre·nate (krē'nāt), adj. notched.

cren·el·ate, cren·el·late (kren'l·āt), v.t. -el·at·ed or -el·lat·ed, -el·at·ing or -el·lat·ing, to furnish with battlements, or squared notches, as a wall. —cren·el·a'tion, cren·el·la'tion, n.

Cre·ole, cre·ole (krē'ōl), n. 1. a person descended from the original French settlers of Louisiana. 2. a person of mixed Creole and Negro ancestry. 3. French as spoken by Creoles: adj. denoting a spicy tomato sauce with green peppers.

cre·o·sote (krē'ō·sōt), n. a pungent, oily liquid used as an antiseptic and as a preservative for wood: v.t. -sot·ed, -sot·ing, to impregnate (wood) with creosote.

crepe, crêpe (krāp), n. 1. a light, crinkled fabric of silk, wool, rayon, etc. 2. same as crape. 3. thin, crinkly paper: also crepe paper. 4. a kind of crinkled rubber: also crepe rubber. 5. (also krep), a thin, delicate pancake.

crep·i·tate (krep'i·tāt), v.i. -tat·ed, -tat·ing, to make slight, sharp, crackling noises. —crep·i·ta'tion, n.

crept (krept), past tense and past participle of creep.

cre·pus·cule (kri·pus'kūl), n. twilight: also cre·pus'cle ('l). —cre·pus'cu·lar ('kyoo·lēr), adj.

cre·scen·do (krē·shen'dō), n., pl. -dos, a gradual increase in volume, as in music: adv. & adj. gradually increasing in volume.

cres·cent (kres'nt), n. 1. the shape of the moon in its first or last quarter, with a convex and a concave edge. 2. anything shaped like this. 3. [also C-], a) a symbol shaped like this, used as the emblem of Turkey. b) Turkish or Moslem power: adj. shaped like a crescent.

cress (kres), n. a leafy plant of the mustard family, as watercress, used in salads.

cres·set (kres'it), n. an open frame of iron in which oil or wood is burned, used as a torch or lantern.

crest (krest), n. 1. a plume of feathers on a helmet, the head of a bird, etc. 2. a heraldic device, as on a coat of arms. 3. the top of a ridge; summit. 4. the highest point: v.i. to reach or form a crest. —crest'ed, adj.

crest·fall·en ('fôl·ĕn), adj. dejected.

cre·ta·ceous (kri·tā'shŭs), adj. composed of or like chalk; chalky. n. [C-], a period of the Mesozoic Era, during which chalk was formed and the dinosaurs died out.

cre·tin (krēt'n), n. a person afflicted with cretinism.

cre·tin·ism (-izm), n. a deficiency of thyroid secretion, resulting in deformity and idiocy.

cre·tonne (krē'ton), n. a heavy, unglazed,

printed cotton fabric used for curtains, upholstery, etc.

cre·val·le (krē·val'i), n. a powerful, voracious game fish.

cre·vasse (kri·vas'), n. 1. a deep fissure in a glacier. 2. a break in a levee.

crev·ice (krev'is), n. a crack; narrow fissure.

crew (krōō), n. 1. a ship or aircraft's company. 2. a rowing team. 3. a group working together. —crew'man, n., pl. -men.

crew (krōō), alternate past tense of crow.

crew·el (krōō'ĕl), n. a fine worsted yarn used for embroidery. —crew'el·work, n.

crib (krib), n. 1. a rack or manger. 2. a stall for horses or cattle. 3. a baby's bed, with high sides. 4. a framework for grain storage. 5. a structure in a lake, etc., as for water intake. 6. [Informal], a translation or notes used dishonestly in doing schoolwork: v.t. cribbed, crib'bing, 1. to confine. 2. [Informal], to plagiarize: v.i. [Informal], to use cribs in schoolwork. —crib'ber, n.

crib·bage (krib'ij), n. a card game for which the score is kept on a small pegboard.

crick (krik), n. a painful muscle spasm in the neck or back.

crick·et (krik'it), n. 1. an outdoor game played with wickets, bats, and a ball, by eleven players on each side. 2. a leaping insect having long antennae: the male makes a chirping sound.

cried (krīd), past tense and past participle of cry.

cri·er (krī'ēr), n. one who shouts out announcements.

crime (krīm), n. 1. a violation of the law. 2. an offense against morality; sin. 3. criminal activity.

crim·i·nal (krim'i·nl), adj. 1. being a crime. 2. of or pertaining to crime. 3. guilty of crime: n. one guilty of a crime. —crim·i·nal'i·ty (-nal'i·ti), n. —crim'i·nal·ly, adv.

crim·i·nate (krim'i·nāt), v.t. -nat·ed, -nat·ing, 1. to accuse, or declare guilty, of crime. 2. to involve in a crime. —crim'i·na·tive, crim'i·na·to·ry, adj.

crim·i·nol·o·gy (krim·i·nol'ō·ji), n. the scientific investigation of crimes and criminals. —crim·i·nol'o·gist, n.

crimp (krimp), v.t. 1. to bend or press into small folds. 2. to curl (hair). 3. to hinder. 4. to decoy (men) into service as soldiers or sailors: n. 1. the act of crimping. 2. something that is crimped. 3. one who decoys men into service as soldiers or sailors.

crim·son (krim'zn), n. a deep, purplish red: adj. deep-red: v.t. to color crimson: v.i. 1. to become crimson. 2. to blush.

cringe (krinj), v.i. cringed, cring'ing, 1. to crouch or cower, as from fear. 2. to act servilely; fawn: n. a cringing action.

crin·kle (kring'kl), v.t. & v.i. -kled, -kling, 1. to wrinkle; ripple. 2. to rustle: n. 1. a wrinkle. 2. a rustling sound. —crin·kly, adj. -kli·er, -kli·est.

crin·o·line (krin'l·in), n. 1. a hoop skirt. 2. a stiff fabric for stiffening garments.

crip·ple (krip'l), v.t. -pled, -pling, 1. to lame. 2. to disable: n. one who is lame or disabled. —crip'pler, n.

cri·sis (krī'sis), *n., pl.* **-ses** ('sēz), 1. the turning point in a disease, when a change for better or worse occurs. 2. any turning point. 3. a crucial condition.

crisp (krisp), *adj.* 1. easily broken; brittle; friable. 2. terse; sharp. 3. fresh; not wilted. 4. invigorating. 5. curly and wiry. Also **crisp'y.** —**crisp'ly,** *adv.* —**crisp'ness,** *n.*

cris·pate (kris'pāt), *adj.* curled or crisped: also **cris'pat·ed.**

criss·cross (kris'krôs), *n.* 1. a mark like a cross made as a signature by one unable to write. 2. a pattern of crossed lines: *adj.* moving in or marked by a crisscross: *adv.* 1. crosswise. 2. awry: *v.t. & v.i.* to move back and forth across.

cri·ter·i·on (krī-tir'i-ŏn), *n., pl.* **-i·a** (-ā), **-i·ons,** a standard, law, or rule by which a correct judgment can be formed.

crit·ic (krit'ik), *n.* 1. one who criticizes music, plays, etc. professionally. 2. one who points out faults or shortcomings.

crit·i·cal ('i-kl), *adj.* 1. of or pertaining to a crisis; decisive. 2. inclined to find fault. 3. relating to critics or criticism. 4. showing or requiring careful judgment. —**crit'i·cal·ly,** *adv.*

crit·i·cism ('i-sizm), *n.* 1. the art, process, or principles of judging literary or artistic works. 2. an article or review giving such judgment; critique. 3. faultfinding; censure.

crit·i·cize ('i-sīz), *v.i. & v.t.* **-cized, -ciz·ing,** 1. to censure. 2. to examine or judge as a critic. British form **crit'i·cise.** —**crit'i·ciz·er,** *n.*

cri·tique (kri-tēk'), *n.* a careful analysis of a literary or artistic work.

crit·ter, crit·tur (krit'ēr), *n.* dialectal form of creature.

croak (krōk), *v.i.* 1. to make a low, hoarse sound like a frog. 2. to grumble. 3. [Slang], to die: *v.t.* to utter by croaking: *n.* a croaking sound.

cro·chet (krō-shā'), *n.* a kind of needlework done with a single hooked needle: *v.t. & v.i.* **-cheted' (-shād'), -chet'ing,** to work in or make by crochet. —**cro·chet'er,** *n.*

crock (krok), *n.* 1. an earthenware pot or jar. 2. coloring matter from dyed cloth. 3. [Slang], something worthless or nonsensical: *v.i.* to give off coloring matter: said of dyed cloth.

crock·er·y ('er-i), *n.* earthenware

crock·et (krok'it), *n.* a carved ornament used to decorate the angles of gables, spires, etc. on Gothic buildings.

croc·o·dile (krok'ŏ-dīl), *n.* a large, lizardlike reptile of the tropics, having a pointed snout and thick, horny scales.

crocodile tears, hypocritical grief.

cro·cus (krō'kŭs), *n.* 1. a plant of the iris family with grasslike leaves and spring flowers of white, yellow, or purple. 2. powdered iron oxide, used for polishing.

croft (kroft), *n.* 1. a field. 2. a small farm worked by a renter. —**croft'er,** *n.*

crois·sant (krŏ-sänt', krwä-sän'), *n.* [French], a rich, crescent-shaped roll.

croix de guerre (krwä dĕ ger'), a French military decoration for bravery in action.

Cro-Ma·gnon (krō-mag'nŏn), *adj.* of a type of man living in Europe in the Stone Age.

crom·lech (krom'lek),·*n.* 1. same as dolmen. 2. a circle of huge, upright stones.

crone (krōn), *n.* an old woman; hag.

cro·ny (krō'ni), *n., pl.* **-nies,** a familiar companion; old friend.

crook (krook), *n.* 1. a bend. 2. a shepherd's hooked staff. 3. a bishop's staff; crosier. 4. [Informal], a swindler: *v.t. & v.i.* to curve or bend.

crook·ed (krook'id), *adj.* 1. not straight; bent. 2. dishonest; swindling. 3. (krookt), having a crook or hook. —**crook'ed·ly,** *adv.* —**crook'ed·ness,** *n.*

croon (krōōn), *v.i. & v.t.* to sing or hum in a low, soft voice: *n.* the sound of crooning. —**croon'er,** *n.*

crop (krop), *n.* 1. the produce of the ground, growing or harvested. 2. the yield in one place or time. 3. a pouch in a bird's gullet, in which food is stored before digestion; craw. 4. a riding whip. 5. the handle of a whip. 6. hair cut close or short: *v.t.* **cropped, crop'ping,** 1. to bite or cut off the ends or tops of. 2. to cut short. 3. to reap: *v.i.* to appear unexpectedly (followed by *out* or *up*).

crop·per ('ēr), *n.* 1. a sharecropper. 2. [Informal], *a*) a heavy fall. *b*) failure.

cro·quet (krō-kā'), *n.* a lawn game played with mallets, balls, and hoops.

cro·quette (krō-ket'), *n.* a fried ball or cone of chopped meat, fish, or vegetables.

cro·sier (krō'zhēr), *n.* a bishop's staff.

cross (krôs), *n.* 1. a wood structure formed of an upright and a cross piece, used by the ancient Romans for crucifixion. 2. [often C-], a representation of the cross on which Jesus died, used as an emblem of Christianity. 3. any trial or burden. 4. any mark made by crossing lines. 5. a hybridizing of breeds or varieties: *v.t. & v.i.* 1. to put or lie across. 2. to pass (each other). 3. to thwart; obstruct. 4. to make the sign of the cross upon. 5. to draw a line or lines across. 6. to interbreed (plants or animals): *adj.* 1. lying across. 2. opposite; contrary. 3. ill-tempered. 4. hybrid. —**cross'ly,** *adv.* —**cross'ness,** *n.*

cross·bill ('bil), *n.* any of several finches with curved mandibles that cross at the tip.

cross·bow ('bō), *n.* a medieval shooting weapon having a bow across the stock.

cross·breed ('brēd), *v.t. & v.i.* **-bred, -breed·ing,** same as hybridize: *n.* same as hybrid (*n.* 1).

cross·ex·am·i·na·tion (krôs-ig-zam-i-nā'shŭn), *n.* the questioning of a witness after he has been questioned by the opposing side. —**cross·ex·am'ine,** *v.t. & v.i.* **-ined, -in·ing.**

cross·eyed (krôs'id), *adj.* having eyes that are turned toward each other.

cross·fer·ti·li·za·tion (krôs-fŭr-tl-i-zā'shŭn), *n.* 1. the fertilization of a plant by pollen from a plant of another variety or species. 2. the fusion of a male and female gamete from different varieties or species. —**cross·fer'ti·lize,** *v.t. & v.i.* **-lized, -liz·ing.**

---

cross-grained (krôs'grānd), *adj.* with an irregular grain or fiber: said of wood.

cross-hatch ('hach), *v.t. & v.i.* to mark or shade (a drawing) with intersecting lines.

cross·ing ('ing), *n.* 1. a place where a river, street, etc. may be crossed. 2. an intersection. 3. opposition.

cross-pol·li·nate (krôs-pol'ĭ-nāt), *v.t. & v.i.* -nat·ed, -nat·ing, to transfer the pollen from the anther of (one flower) to the stigma of (another).

cross-pur·pose (krôs'pûr'pŏs), *n.* a contrary or conflicting purpose.

cross-ref·er·ence ('ref'ẽr-ĕns), *n.* a reference from one part of a book, index, etc. to another.

cross·road ('rōd), *n.* 1. a road that crosses another. 2. a road that runs between two main roads. 3. *usually pl.* a place where roads intersect.

cross section, 1. a section cut through something. 2. a representation of this. 3. a selection or sample chosen to show the characteristics of the whole.

cross·walk ('wôk), *n.* a lane marked for the use of pedestrians crossing a street.

cross·wise ('wīz), *adv.* across: also **cross'ways**.

crotch (kroch), *n.* the place where two limbs branch off from a tree, or the legs branch off from the body.

crotch·et (kroch'ĭt), *n.* 1. a peculiar whim or fancy. 2. [British], a musical quarter note.

crotch·et·y ('ĭt-ĭ), *adj.* whimsical; odd.

cro·ton (krōt'n), *n.* 1. any one of a large genus of trees, shrubs, and herbs: some are used medicinally, others are poisonous weeds. 2. a related shrub grown for its large, showy leaves.

crouch (krouch), *v.i.* 1. to stoop low. 2. to cringe: *n.* a stooping posture.

croup (krōōp), *n.* 1. the rump of a horse. 2. an inflammation of the trachea and larynx, with a hoarse cough and difficult breathing. —**croup'y**, *adj.*

crou·pi·er (krōō'pi-ā), *n.* one who presides at a gambling table, collecting and paying out the money.

crou·ton (krōō'ton), *n.* a small, crisp piece of toasted bread, served in soup.

crow (krō), *v.i.* 1. to make the shrill sound of a cock. 2. to boast in triumph. 3. to utter a cry of pleasure, as a baby does: *n.* 1. a crowing sound. 2. any of several large blackbirds with a harsh cry.

crow·bar (krō'bär), *n.* a heavy, steel bar, flattened at one end and used for prying.

crowd (kroud), *n.* a number of persons or things collected closely together: *v.t.* 1. to press closely together. 2. to fill to excess; cram: *v.i.* 1. to throng. 2. to push or press forward.

crow·foot (krō'foot), *n., pl.* -foots, a plant with divided leaves that resemble a crow's foot, especially the buttercup.

crown (kroun), *n.* 1. a royal headdress worn as the insignia of sovereignty. 2. [often C-], *a*) a monarch. *b*) a monarch's power. 3. a wreath worn on the head. 4. the top. 5. a British coin equal to five shillings. 6. the highest point, quality, etc. of something. 7.

the visible part of a tooth: *v.t.* 1. to invest with a crown. 2. to make (a person) a monarch. 3. to complete. 4. to be the highest part of. 5. to honor.

crown prince, the male heir to a throne.

crow's-foot (krōz'foot), *n., pl.* -feet, one of the small wrinkles at the outer corner of the eye.

crow's-nest ('nest), *n.* a lookout's platform near the top of a ship's mast.

cro·zier (krō'zhẽr), *n.* same as **crosier**.

cru·cial (krōō'shål), *adj.* 1. severe; difficult. 2. extremely critical; decisive. —**cru'cial·ly**, *adv.*

cru·ci·ble (krōō'si·bl), *n.* 1. a container for melting ores, metal, etc. 2. a severe trial.

cru·ci·fix (krōō'si-fiks), *n.* a figure of a cross with Jesus crucified on it.

cru·ci·fix·ion (krōō-si-fik'shŭn), *n.* 1. the act of crucifying. 2. [C-], the crucifying of Jesus, or a representation of this. 3. great suffering.

cru·ci·form (krōō'si-fôrm), *adj.* cross-shaped. —**cru'ci·form·ly**, *adv.*

cru·ci·fy (krōō'si-fī), *v.t.* -fied, -fy·ing, 1. to put to death by nailing to a cross and leaving to die. 2. to treat cruelly; torture. —**cru'ci·fi·er**, *n.*

crude (krōōd), *adj.* 1. in a natural state; not refined. 2. lacking polish; uncultured. 3. not carefully made. —**crude'ly**, *adv.* —**crude'ness**, *n.*

cru·el (krōō'ĕl), *adj.* causing pain and suffering; merciless; pitiless. —**cru'el·ly**, *adv.* —**cru'el·ty**, *n., pl.* -ties.

cru·et (krōō'ĭt), *n.* a small glass bottle.

cruise (krōōz), *v.i.* cruised, cruis'ing, 1. to sail or drive around from one place to another, as in looking for something or for pleasure. 2. to travel at the most efficient speed: *n.* a voyage made by cruising, especially by ship.

cruise control, a device for keeping the speed of a motor vehicle constant for a period of time, as when driving on a turnpike.

cruise missile, a long-range, jet-propelled winged missile that can be launched from an airplane, submarine, ship, etc. and guided by remote control.

cruis·er ('ẽr), *n.* 1. something that cruises, as a police car. 2. a fast warship.

crul·ler (krul'ẽr), *n.* dough cut in a strip, or ring-shaped, fried in deep fat.

crumb (krum), *n.* 1. the soft, inner part of bread. 2. a fragment of bread. 3. a little piece: *v.t.* 1. to break into crumbs. 2. to cover with crumbs for cooking. —**crumb'y**, *adj.* **crumb'i·er**, **crumb'i·est**.

crum·ble (krum'bl), *v.t.* -bled, -bling, to break into crumbs: *v.i.* to fall to pieces. —**crum'bly**, *adj.* -bli·er, -bli·est.

crum·my (krum'ĭ), *adj.* -mi·er, -mi·est, [Slang], inferior, seedy, measly, etc.

crum·pet (krum'pĭt), *n.* a small, round cake baked on a griddle.

crum·ple (krum'pl), *v.t. & v.i.* -pled, -pling, 1. to press into wrinkles; rumple. 2. to collapse. —**crum'ply**, *adj.*

crunch (krunch), *v.t. & v.i.* to chew, crush, or grind audibly with the teeth: *n.* 1. the act or sound of crunching. 2. [Slang], a crisis or showdown. —**crunch'y**, *adj.* —**crunch'i·ness**, *n.*

crup·per (krup′ẽr), *n.* 1. a horse's rump. 2. a leather strap from the back of a saddle, passed under a horse's tail.

cru·ral (kroor′ăl), *adj.* of or pertaining to the leg or thigh.

cru·sade (krōō-sād′), *n.* 1. [often C-], any of several medieval Christian military expeditions to recover the Holy Land from the Moslems. 2. vigorous, concerted action for some cause: *v.i.* -**sad**′ed, -**sad**′ing, to engage in a crusade. —**cru·sad**′er, *n.*

cruse (krōōz), *n.* a small jar for liquids.

crush (krush), *v.t.* 1. to press between opposing forces so as to break or deform. 2. to extract by squeezing. 3. to pound into small particles. 4. to defeat; quell: *v.i.* to become crushed: *n.* 1. a violent compression. 2. a crowding, as of people. 3. [Informal], an infatuation. —**crush**′er, *n.*

crust (krust), *n.* 1. the hard, outside part of bread. 2. a piece of hard, stale bread. 3. the pastry shell or cover of a pie. 4. the solid part of the earth's surface. 5. any shell or hard covering. 6. [Slang], effrontery: *v.t. & v.i.* to cover with or form a crust.

crus·ta·cean (krus-tā′shŭn), *n.* any of a large group of arthropods that have a hard shell, as shrimps, lobsters, crabs, etc. —**crus·ta**′**ceous,** *adj.*

crust·y (krus′ti), *adj.* crust′i·er, crust′i·est, 1. like a crust. 2. rough in manner; surly. —**crust**′i·**ness,** *n.*

crutch (kruch), *n.* a support for the use of a lame person: it has a piece across the top that fits under the armpit.

crux (kruks), *n.* 1. a perplexing problem. 2. the basic or decisive point.

cry (krī), *v.i.* cried, cry′ing, 1. to make a loud vocal sound, as in grief or pain. 2. to shed tears. 3. to plead (*for*). 4. to give forth a characteristic sound: said of an animal: *v.t.* 1. to utter loudly; shout. 2. to call out publicly as for sale: *n., pl.* cries, 1. a loud utterance; shout. 2. a spell of weeping. 3. an outcry; clamor. 4. popular report. 5. a slogan. 6. the characteristic sound of an animal.

cry·ba·by (′bā-bi), *n., pl.* -bies, 1. one who cries readily. 2. a complainer.

cry·ing (′ing), *adj.* urgently requiring attention; pressing.

cry·o·gen·ics (krī-ò-jen′iks), *n.* the study of very low temperatures, their creation, and their effects.

cry·o·lite (krī′ò-līt), *n.* a fluoride of sodium and aluminum, from which aluminum is obtained.

cry·om·e·ter (krī-om′ê-tẽr), *n.* a thermometer, usually filled with alcohol, for measuring a lower temperature than mercury will register.

cry·o·sur·ger·y (krī-ò-sûr′jê-ri), *n.* surgery involving the selective destruction of tissues by freezing them.

crypt (kript), *n.* a subterranean vault or cell, usually under a church.

cryp·tic (krip′tik), *adj.* 1. hidden; secret. 2. mysterious; obscure. —**cryp**′ti·cal·ly, *adv.*

cryp·to·crys·tal·line (krip-tō-kris′tl-in), *adj.* denoting rocks with a crystalline structure so fine that the particles cannot be distinguished even with a microscope.

cryp·to·gam (krip′tô-gam), *n.* a plant that has no true flowers or seeds, being propagated from spores. —**cryp·to·gam**′**ic, cryp·tog·a·mous** (krip-tog′à-mŭs), *adj.*

cryp·to·gram (-gram), *n.* a writing in cipher or code. —**cryp·to·gram**′**mic,** *adj.*

cryp·tog·ra·phy (krip-tŏg′rà-fi), *n.* 1. the art of writing in cipher or secret characters. 2. the particular system used. —**cryp·tog**′ra·pher, *n.*

crys·tal (kris′tl), *n.* 1. a transparent quartz. 2. a glass of superior clearness. 3. products made from such glass. 4. the glass covering the face of a watch. 5. anything as clear as crystal. 6. a solidified substance having a definite geometric form that is repeated regularly in three dimensions: *adj.* 1. of or consisting of crystal. 2. like crystal; clear; transparent.

crys·tal·line (kris′tà-lin), *adj.* 1. of, pertaining to, or having the form of, a crystal. 2. clear; transparent.

crys·tal·lite (-līt), *n.* 1. a tiny, incipient, nonidentifiable crystal. 2. a rock made up chiefly of such crystals.

crys·tal·lize (kris′tà-līz), *v.t.* -lized, -liz·ing, 1. to cause to form crystals or a crystalline structure. 2. to make distinct in form. 3. to coat with sugar: *v.i.* 1. to be converted into crystals. 2. to assume a definite shape. —**crys·tal·li·za**′**tion,** *n.*

crys·tal·log·ra·phy (kris-tà-log′rà-fi), *n.* the science of the forms, structure, and properties of crystals.

cub (kub), *n.* 1. the young of certain mammals, as the bear. 2. a clumsy youth. 3. a beginner.

cub·age (kū′bij), *n.* cubic content.

Cu·ban (kū′băn), *adj.* of or pertaining to Cuba, an island in the West Indies, or its inhabitants: *n.* a native or inhabitant of Cuba.

cub·by·hole (kub′i-hōl), *n.* 1. a snug place. 2. a pigeonhole.

cube (kūb), *n.* 1. a solid body with six equal square sides or faces. 2. anything cubelike in shape. 3. the product obtained by multiplying the square of a quantity by the quantity itself: *v.t.* cubed, cub′ing, 1. to raise to the third power, or cube. 2. to cut into cubes; dice. —**cub**′er, *n.*

cu·beb (kū′beb), *n.* the small, spicy berry of a kind of pepper.

cube root, the first power of a cube; a number or quantity the cube of which is the given number or quantity.

cu·bic (kū′bik), *adj.* 1. having the form or properties of a cube. 2. having three dimensions: used of certain units of measurement. 3. in *Mathematics,* of the third power or degree.

cu·bi·cle (′bi-kl), *n.* a small compartment, as for sleeping or studying.

cub·ism (kū′bizm), *n.* an art movement of the early 20th century, based on the use of geometric forms. —**cub**′**ist** (′bist), *n. & adj.* —**cu·bis**′**tic** (-bis′tik), *adj.*

cu·bit (kū'bit), *n.* an ancient measure of length, roughly 18-22 inches.

cuck·ing stool (kuk'ing), a chair in which disorderly females, scolds, etc. were placed and exposed to public ridicule.

cuck·old (kuk'ld), *n.* the husband of an adulterous woman: *v.t.* to make a cuckold of. — **cuck'old·ry** (-ri), *n.*

cuck·oo (kŏŏ'kŏŏ), *n.* 1. any one of a group of birds with a long, slender body, grayish-brown on top and white below. 2. the cry of the cuckoo: *adj.* [Slang], crazy; silly.

cuckoo spit (or **spittle**), a frothy substance found on plant leaves, exuded by certain insects.

cu·cum·ber (kū'kum-bĕr), *n.* 1. a trailing annual vine, grown for its edible fruit. 2. the long fruit: it has a green rind and white flesh and is used in salads or pickled.

cucumber tree, an American magnolia tree.

cud (kud), *n.* a portion of food brought from the first stomach of a ruminating animal back into the mouth and chewed again.

cud·dle (kud'l), *v.t.* **-dled, -dling,** to embrace closely: *v.i.* to lie close or snug: *n.* 1. a cuddling. 2. a hug.

cud·dle·some (-sŏm), *adj.* so sweet or lovable as to invite cuddling.

cud·dly ('li), *adj.* **-dli·er, -dli·est,** 1. cuddlesome. 2. liking to cuddle.

cud·dy (kud'i), *n., pl.* **-dies,** [Chiefly Scottish], 1. a donkey. 2. a fool.

cudg·el (kuj'ĕl), *n.* a short, thick stick: *v.t.* **-eled** or **-elled, -el·ing** or **-el·ling,** to beat with a cudgel.

cue (kū), *n.* 1. a piece of dialogue, music, etc. signaling something, as that an actor should begin his lines. 2. anything serving as a signal. 3. the tapering rod used in billiards and pool.

cuff (kuf), *n.* 1. the fold of the sleeve of a garment at the wrist. 2. the fold at the bottom of a pants leg. 3. a blow: *v.t.* to strike with the hand.

cuff link, one of a pair of small devices for closing a shirt cuff.

cui·rass (kwi-ras'), *n.* a breastplate.

cui·ras·sier (kwi-rà-sir'), *n.* a cavalry soldier armed with a cuirass.

cui·sine (kwi-zēn'), *n.* 1. the kitchen. 2. the style or way of cooking.

cul-de-sac (kul-dĕ-sak'), *n., pl.* **cul-de-sacs',** a passage open only at one end.

cu·li·nar·y (kū'li-ner'i), *adj.* of or pertaining to the kitchen or cooking.

cull (kul), *v.t.* to pick out; select; gather: *n.* 1. something picked out. 2. anything that has been cast aside or rejected.

cul·mi·nate (kul'mi-nāt), *v.i.* **-nat·ed, -nat·ing,** to reach the highest point of altitude, rank, power, etc. —**cul·mi·na'tion,** *n.*

cu·lotte (koo-lät'), *n.* often pl. trousers cut to resemble a skirt: worn by women.

cul·pa·ble (kul'pà-bl), *adj.* deserving censure; blameworthy. —**cul·pa·bil'i·ty,** *n.* —**cul'pa·bly,** *adv.*

cul·prit (kul'prit), *n.* 1. one arraigned before a judge; one accused of a crime or fault. 2. one guilty of a crime or fault.

cult (kult), *n.* 1. a particular ritual or system of worship. 2. devoted or extravagant homage or adoration. 3. a group devoted to some person or idea. —**cult'ist,** *n.*

cultch (kulch), *n.* materials forming a spawning bed for oysters.

cul·ti·vate (kul'ti-vāt), *v.t.* **-vat·ed, -vat·ing,** 1. to till. 2. to grow. 3. to improve by care, labor, or study. 4. to seek familiarity with. — **cul'ti·va·tor,** *n.*

cul·ti·va·tion (kul-ti-vā'shŭn), *n.* 1. the act of cultivating. 2. culture.

cul·trate (kul'trāt), *adj.* sharp-edged and pointed.

cul·ture (kul'chĕr), *n.* 1. tillage. 2. the training or refining of the intellectual or behavioral faculties. 3. care given to the growth and development of animals and plants. 4. the propagation of bacteria, as for scientific use. 5. civilization: *v.t.* **-tured, -tur·ing,** to till. — **cul'tur·al,** *adj.*

culture medium, a substance in which bacteria or other microorganisms are developed.

cul·ver·in (kul'vĕr·in), *n.* a long cannon of the 16th century.

cul·vert (kul'vĕrt), *n.* a drain or waterway of brick, concrete, or stone, as under a road.

cum·ber (kum'bĕr), *v.t.* 1. to hinder. 2. to oppress. 3. [Obsolete], to perplex.

cum·ber·some (kum'bĕr-sŏm), *adj.* burdensome; unwieldy: also **cum'brous** ('brŭs).

cum·in (kum'in), *n.* 1. a plant with aromatic fruits, used to add taste. 2. this fruit.

cum·mer·bund (kum'ĕr-bund), *n.* a wide piece of cloth worn around the waist, as in formal dress by men.

cu·mu·la·tive (kūm'yū-lāt-iv), *adj.* augmenting or giving force; increasing by successive additions.

cu·mu·lus (kūm'yū-lŭs), *n., pl.* **-li** (-lī), 1. a thick cloud in round masses. 2. a heap, mass, or pile.

cu·ne·ate (kū'ni-it), *adj.* wedge-shaped: also **cu'ne·at·ed** (-āt-id).

cu·ne·i·form (kū-nē'i-fôrm), *adj.* having the form of a wedge: said of the wedge-shaped characters of the Assyrian and ancient Persian inscriptions: *n.* cuneiform inscriptions.

cun·ner (kun'ĕr), *n.* a small food fish of the Atlantic coast of North America.

cun·ning (kun'ing), *adj.* 1. crafty; sly; designing. 2. expertly produced. 3. subtly attractive: *n.* deceit; craftiness. —**cun'ning·ly,** *adv.*

cup (kup), *n.* 1. a small, bowl-shaped drinking vessel. 2. what a cup holds. 3. the amount in a cup. 4. something shaped like a cup. 5. a decorative cup offered as a prize. 6. a chalice. 7. a beverage or dish served in a cup. 8. *pl.* repeated potations. 9. a device for drawing blood to the surface: *v.t.* **cupped, cup'ping,** 1. to make resemble a cup. 2. to bleed by means of a cup device.

cup·board (kub'ård), *n.* a closet fitted with shelves for holding cups, plates, etc.

cup·cake (kup'kāk), *n.* a little cake.

cu·pel (kū'pĕl), *n.* 1. a shallow, porous vessel in which gold or silver is assayed. 2. a hearth for metal refining: *v.t.* **-peled** or **-pelled, -pel·ing** or **-pel·ling,** to refine or assay with a cupel. —**cu·pel·la'tion** (-pē-lā'-shŭn), *n.*

cup·ful (kup'fool), *n., pl.* **-fuls,** as much as a cup will contain; a half pint in standard measure.

cu·pid (kū'pid), *n.* an image of the Roman god of love as a boy with wings, carrying a bow and arrow.

cu·pid·i·ty (kū-pid'i-ti), *n.* covetousness.

cu·po·la (kū'pō-là), *n.* 1. a spherical, cup-shaped roof. 2. a small dome structure on a roof.

cu·pre·ous (kū'pri-ùs), *adj.* of, containing, or colored like copper; coppery.

cu·pric (kū'prik), *adj.* of or pertaining to copper with a valence of two.

cu·prif·er·ous (kū-prif'ēr-ùs), *adj.* containing copper.

cu·prite (kū'prīt), *n.* red oxide of copper.

cu·pro·nick·el (kū'prō-nik'l), *n.* a copper and nickel alloy.

cu·pule (kū'pyool), *n.* a little cup, as of the acorn.

cur (kūr), *n.* 1. a mongrel dog. 2. a surly, ill-bred person.

cu·ra·çao (kyoor-à-sō'), *n.* a liqueur made by distilling spirits with dried peel of oranges.

cu·ra·re (kyoo-rä'ri), *n.* a black, resinous substance prepared from the juices of some plants of South America: it is used by the Indians for poisoning their arrows, and in medicine as a muscle relaxant: also **cu·ra'ri.**

cu·ra·rine ('rin), *n.* an alkaloid extract of curare used to relax muscles.

cu·ras·sow (kūr'à-sō), *n.* a large bird of South America that resembles a turkey.

cu·rate (kūr'it), *n.* a clergyman who is assistant to a vicar or rector. —**cu'ra·cy** ('à-ci), *n., pl.* **-cies.**

cur·a·tive (kūr'à-tiv), *adj.* 1. of or pertaining to the cure of disease. 2. promoting cure: *n.* that which cures; remedy.

cu·ra·tor (kū-rāt'ēr), *n.* the superintendent of a museum, art gallery, etc. —**cu·ra·to·ri·al** (kūr-à-tōr'i-àl), *adj.*

curb (kūrb), *v.t.* 1. to restrain; keep in subjection. 2. to furnish with a curb: *n.* 1. that which checks, restrains, or subdues. 2. a part of a horse's bridle. 3. a curbstone.

curb·ing (kūrb'ing), *n.* 1. curbstones collectively. 2. material for curbing.

curb·stone ('stōn), *n.* the stone edge of a street.

curd (kūrd), *n.* the coagulated part of milk, containing casein: *v.t.* to cause to curdle.

cur·dle (kūr'dl), *v.t. & v.i.* **-dled, -dling,** to thicken into curd; coagulate.

cure (kūr), *n.* 1. restoration to health: act of healing. 2. system of medical treatment. 3. spiritual charge of an area. 4. a medical remedy: *v.t.* **cured, cur'ing,** 1. to heal; restore to health. 2. to set free from. 3. to preserve, as by salting, or process, as by drying. —**cur'a·ble,** *adj.*

cu·ré (kū-rā'), *n.* in France, a parish priest.

cure·all (kūr'ôl), *n.* a panacea.

cur·few (kūr'fū), *n.* 1. a bell originally rung in the evening as a signal that fires and lights were to be extinguished. 2. a time at night after which persons may not be on the streets.

Cu·ri·a (kūr'i-à), *n., pl.* **-ri·ae** (-ē), the Pope's department of administration.

cu·rie (kūr'i), *n.* a unit used in measuring radioactivity.

cu·ri·o (kūr'i-ō), *n., pl.* **-ri·os,** an uncommon thing.

cu·ri·os·i·ty (kyoor-i-os'i-ti), *n., pl.* **-ties,** 1. the quality of being curious. 2. inquisitiveness. 3. something strange or rare.

cu·ri·ous (kyoor'i-ùs), *adj.* 1. eager to see or know. 2. inquisitive. 3. strange; rare. —**cu'ri·ous·ly,** *adv.*

cu·ri·um (kūr'i-ùm), *n.* a radioactive element produced by neutron bombardment.

curl (kūrl), *n.* 1. a ringlet of hair. 2. an undulation or bend. 3. a plant disease: *v.t.* 1. to twist into ringlets. 2. to raise in undulations. 3. to curve: *v.i.* 1. to contract or bend into ringlets; become curled. 2. to move in spirals or undulations. 3. to play at the game of curling. —**curl'er,** *n.* —**curl'y,** *adj.* **curl'i·er, curl'i·est.**

cur·lew (kūr'loō), *n., pl.* **-lews, -lew,** a short-tailed wading bird with a long, curved bill.

curl·i·cue (kūr'li-kū), *n.* something curled or spiral, as a flourish made with pen on paper.

curl·ing (kūr'ling), *n.* a game played on ice with smooth, flat stones fitted with handles.

cur·mudg·eon (kūr-muj'ôn), *n.* a grasping, churlish person.

cur·rant (kūr'ànt), *n.* 1. a small variety of seedless raisin used in cooking. 2. the small, round acid berry of certain shrubs, used for jellies and jams. 3. this shrub.

cur·ren·cy (kūr'ên-si), *n., pl.* **-cies,** 1. a continual passing from hand to hand. 2. the circulating money of a nation. 3. prevalence.

cur·rent (kūr'ênt), *adj.* 1. widely circulated; passing from hand to hand. 2. now passing, as time. 3. generally accepted or credited; prevalent; common: *n.* 1. a flow or passing: said of fluids. 2. a body of air or water flowing in a certain direction. 3. flow of electricity. 4. a general tendency. —**cur'rent·ly,** *adv.*

cur·ri·cle (kūr'i-kl), *n.* a two-wheeled carriage drawn by two horses abreast.

cur·ric·u·lum (kū-rik'yù-lùm), *n., pl.* **-u·la** (-là), **-u·lums,** 1. a course. 2. a prescribed course of study in a university, school, etc. —**cur·ric'u·lar,** *adj.*

cur·ri·er (kūr'i-ēr), *n.* one who curries leather or horses.

cur·rish (kūr'ish), *adj.* snappish; quarrelsome.

cur·ry (kūr'i), *v.t.* **-ried, -ry·ing,** 1. to dress (leather) after tanning. 2. to beat. 3. to flatter. 4. to dress or clean (a horse).

cur·ry (kūr'i), *n., pl.* **-ries,** 1. curry powder. 2. a sauce made with curry powder. 3. a stew flavored with curry: *v.t.* **-ried, -ry·ing,** to cook or flavor with curry.

cur·ry·comb (kūr'i-kōm), *n.* a comb used in grooming horses: *v.t.* to groom with a currycomb.

curry powder, a powder composed of crushed spices and aromatic seeds, used for flavoring.

curse (kūrs), *n.* 1. an asking God to bring evil upon. 2. a profane oath or imprecation. 3.

ŏ in drag*o*n, o͞o in cr*u*de, oo in w*oo*l, u in c*u*p, ū in c*u*re, û in t*u*rn, ù in f*o*cus, oi in b*oy*, ou in h*ou*se, th in *th*in, t͟h in shea*th*e, g in *g*et, j in *j*oy, y in *y*et.

that which brings or causes evil or trouble. 4. the evil or trouble: *v.t.* cursed or curst, curs'ing, 1. to imprecate evil upon. 2. to anathematize. 3. to cause evil to: *v.i.* to swear.

curs·ed (kûr'sid, kûrst), *adj.* 1. under a curse. 2. hateful.

cur·sive (kûr'siv), *adj.* flowing: said of writing in which the letters are joined in each word.

cur·sor (kûr'sŏr), *n.* a movable indicator light, sometimes blinking, on a computer video screen marking the current position at which a character may be entered.

cur·so·ry (kûr'sĕr-i), *adj.* hasty or superficial. —cur'so·ri·ly, *adv.*

curt (kûrt), *adj.* abrupt; short. —curt'ly, *adv.* — curt'ness, *n.*

cur·tail (kĕr-tāl'), *v.t.* to cut short; reduce. — cur·tail'ment, *n.*

cur·tain (kûr'tn), *n.* 1. a cloth hanging screen which can be drawn up or set aside. 2. the part of a rampart and parapet between two bastions or gates. 3. a wall not holding up part of a roof: *v.t.* to enclose in, or as with, curtains.

curtain call, 1. a direction, by audience applause, to the performers to come back to the stage. 2. this return.

curt·sy (kûrt'si), *n., pl.* -sies, a woman's salutation made by bending the knees and lowering the body: *v.i.* -sied, -sy·ing, to make a curtsy. Also curt'sey.

cur·va·ceous (kĕr-vā'shŭs), *adj.* [Informal], shapely in a feminine way.

cur·va·ture (kûr'vå-chēr), *n.* 1. a bending. 2. a curved section.

curve (kûrv), *n.* 1. a bending without angles. 2. something formed like a curve: *v.t. & v.i.* curved, curv'ing, to bend or move in a curve. —curv'y, *adj.* curv'i·er, curv'i·est.

cur·vet (kûr'vit), *n.* a particular leap of a horse: *v.i.* (kĕr-vet'), -vet'ted or -vet'ed, -vet'ting or -vet'ing, 1. to leap as a horse. 2. to frisk or bound.

cur·vi·lin·e·ar (kûr-vi·lin'i-ĕr), *adj.* consisting of or bound by curved lines: also cur·vi·lin'e·al.

cush·ion (koosh'ŭn), *n.* 1. a pillow or soft pad for sitting or reclining upon. 2. a pillow used in lacemaking. 3. anything to deaden an impact, as the elastic rim of a billiard table: *v.t.* 1. to seat upon a cushion. 2. to furnish with a cushion.

cush·y (koosh'ē), *adj.* -i·er, -i·est, [Slang], easy; comfortable.

cusp (kusp), *n.* 1. a sharp point. 2. the point on a tooth. 3. the horn of a crescent, as of the moon. 4. a point at the intersection of two arcs.

cus·pi·dor (kus'pi-dŏr), *n.* a spittoon.

cuss (kus), *n.* [Informal]. 1. a worthless or irritating person or animal. 2. a curse: *v.t. & v.i.* [Informal], to curse.

cus·tard (kus'tård), *n.* 1. a composition of milk and eggs, sugar, etc., baked or boiled. 2. a frozen combination like this: also frozen custard.

cus·to·di·an (kûs-tō'di-ån), *n.* 1. one who has

the care of anything. 2. one who maintains a building.

cus·to·dy (kus-tō'di), *n.* 1. guardianship. 2. imprisonment. —cus·to·di·al (kûs-tō'di-ål), *adj.*

cus·tom (kus'tŏm), *n.* 1. frequent or habitual repetition of the same act. 2. established usage. 3. regular business support. 4. unwritten law. 5. *pl.* duties on imported and, sometimes, exported goods: *adj.* 1. made as specified. 2. making things as specified.

cus·tom·ar·y ('tŏ-mer-i), *adj.* habitual; conventional; common. —cus·tom·ar'i·ly, *adv.*

cus·tom-built (kus'tŏm-bilt), *adj.* built to order, to the customer's specifications.

cus·tom·er (kus'tō-mēr), *n.* a purchaser.

cus·tom·house (kus'tŏm-hous), *n.* a place where duties are paid on goods, and vessels are cleared.

cut (kut), *v.t.* cut, cut'ting, 1. to cleave or separate with a sharp instrument. 2. to make an incision in. 3. to wound deeply. 4. to trim. 5. to divide; intersect. 6. to castrate. 7. to abridge; diminish. 8. to form (a tooth). 9. to excavate. 10. to fell. 11. to produce by cutting. 12. to divide (a pack of cards) at random. 13. to strike (a ball), so as to send it to the side. 14. [Informal], to pass deliberately without recognition. 15. [Informal], to be away from (class). 16. [Slang], to discontinue: *v.i.* 1. to make an incision. 2. to be separated. 3. to permit cutting. 4. to work with an edged instrument. 5. to grow through the gum. 6. to move a bat (at a ball). 7. to have a sudden change in direction. 8. [Slang], to run away; skip out: *n.* 1. the act of cutting. 2. an incision or wound made by a sharp instrument; gash. 3. a sharp stroke. 4. a sarcastic remark. 5. a part removed; slice. 6. a trench, channel, etc. made by digging. 7. a short passage. 8. the shape of a garment. 9. a block on which an engraving is cut. 10. a diminution, as in price. 11. a stroke at a ball. 12. [Informal], the deliberate ignoring of an acquaintance. 13. [Informal], a being away from school without permission. 14. [Slang], a share: *adj.* 1. divided or separated. 2. gashed. 3. having the surface ornamented or fashioned.

cu·ta·ne·ous (kū-tā'ni-ŭs), *adj.* of or pertaining to the skin.

cut·a·way (kut'å-wā), *n.* a coat, the skirts of which slope from the waist.

cute (kūt), *adj.* cut'er, cut'est, [Informal], 1. sharp; clever. 2. delicately pretty. —cute'ly, *adv.* —cute'ness, *n.*

cut glass, flint glass cut into facets or figures.

cut·i·cle (kūt'i-kl), *n.* 1. the epidermis. 2. the tougher skin beside a fingernail. 3. the thin, exterior skin of a plant.

cut·lass (kut'lås), *n.* a broad, curved cutting sword.

cut·ler·y (-i), *n.* edged or cutting instruments.

cut·let (kut'lit), *n.* 1. a slice of meat from the leg or ribs. 2. a flat piece of chopped meat or fish.

cut·off (kut'ôf), *n.* 1. a shorter road. 2. a new, shorter channel cut by a river across a bend. 3. a device for stopping a stream of liquid.

a in cap, ā in cane, ä in father, å in abet, e in met, ē in be, ē in baker, ê in regent, i in pit, ī in fine, i in manifest, o in hot, ô in horse, ō in bone,

cut-out ('out), *n.* a switch used to cut off an electric circuit.

cut-ter (kut'ēr), *n.* 1. one or that which cuts. 2. one who cuts out and shapes garments. 3. a light sleigh. 4. a small, fast vessel.

cut-throat (kut'thrōt), *n.* a murderer: *adj.* 1. brutal. 2. ruthless.

cut-ting (kut'ing), *adj.* 1. edged; sharp. 2. chilling. 3. sarcastic: *n.* 1. an incision. 2. a piece cut off. 3. a slip for grafting.

cut-tle-fish (kut'l-fish), *n., pl.* -fish, -fish-es, a cephalopod with an internal shell, the arms furnished with suckers, two large eyes, and an inkbag containing a dark fluid.

cut-wa-ter (kut'wôt-ēr), *n.* 1. the fore part of a ship's prow. 2. the angular edge of a pier of a bridge.

cut-worm (kut'wûrm), *n.* a destructive caterpillar.

-cy (si), a suffix meaning *condition, rank.*

cy-a-nate (sī'ā-nāt), *n.* a cyanic acid salt.

cy-an-ic (sī-an'ik), *adj.* of or containing cyanogen.

cyanic acid, a strong, poisonous acid.

cy-a-nide (sī'ā-nīd), *n.* a very poisonous, white, crystalline compound used as a reagent, as potassium cyanide.

cyanide process, a method of extracting gold or silver from ore by treating with potassium cyanide solution.

cy-a-nite (-nīt), *n.* a silicate of aluminum.

cy-a-no-, a combining form meaning *having present the cyanogen group, dark-blue.*

cy-an-o-gen (sī-an'ō-jēn), *n.* a colorless, poisonous gas that burns.

cy-a-no-sis (sī-ā-nō'sis), *n.* a condition of the skin in which it becomes blue from insufficient oxygen in the blood.

cy-ber-net-ics (sī-bēr-net'iks), *n.* a science studying the human nervous system in comparison with electronic computers.

cy-cla-mate (sik'lā-māt, sī'klā-), *n.* a salt of an organic acid, especially a calcium or sodium salt that tastes sweet.

cy-cla-men (sik'klā-mēn), *n.* a plant related to the primrose, with heart-shaped leaves.

cy-cla-zo-cine (sī-klā-zō'sin), *n.* an analgesic drug that nullifies heroin or morphine.

cy-cle (sī'kl), *n.* 1. a revolution of a certain period of time which recurs again in the same order. 2. the events in this period. 3. the aggregate of traditional or legendary material connected with a mythological person or event. 4. a group of songs or poems. 5. a bicycle, motorcycle, etc.: *v.i.* -cled, **-cling,** 1. to occur, or recur, in cycles. 2. to ride a bicycle or motorcycle. **—cy-clic** (sī'-klik, sik'lik), *adj.*

cy-clist (sī'klist), *n.* a cycle rider.

cy-clo-, a combining form meaning *circular.*

cy-cloid (sī'kloid), *n.* a geometrical curve traced out by any point of a circle rolling along a straight line until it has completed a revolution.

cy-clom-e-ter (sī-klom'ē-tēr), *n.* an instrument for registering the revolutions of a wheel.

cy-clone (sī'klōn), *n.* 1. a violent storm. 2. a storm in which the wind blows around a moving center.

cyclone cellar, a cellar or underground room built as a refuge from violent storms.

Cy-clo-pe-an (sī-klō-pē'ān), *adj.* 1. of or pertaining to the Cyclops. 2. [c-], huge; vast; massive.

cy-clo-pe-di-a (sī'klō-pē'di-ā), *n.* same as encyclopedia: also cy-clo-pae'di-a.

Cy-clops (sī'klops), *n., pl.* Cy-clo-pes (sī-klō'-pēz), *in Greek Mythology,* any one of a race of giants, with one eye.

cy-clo-ra-ma (sī-klō-ram'ā), *n.* a series of related pictures extended circularly so as to appear in natural perspective to the spectator standing in the center.

cy-clo-tron (sī'klō-tron), *n.* a device used to impart particles, as protons, with high energy, in order to cause nuclear changes.

cyg-net (sig'nēt), *n.* a young swan.

cyl-in-der (sil'in-dēr), *n.* 1. a long, circular body, solid or hollow, of uniform diameter. 2. a chamber in which force is exerted on the piston of an engine. 3. the barrel of a pump. 4. the rotating part of a revolver. 5. a roller for printing. 6. a roller-shaped stone with cuneiform inscriptions. **—cy-lin-dri-cal** (si-lin'dri-kl), **cy-lin'dric,** *adj.*

cyl-in-droid (sil'in-droid), *n.* a solid body resembling a cylinder, but with the ends elliptical.

cym-bal (sim'bl), *n.* a circular, dish-shaped brass plate which, when struck, produces a ringing sound. **—cym'bal-ist,** *n.*

cyme (sīm), *n.* a flattened flower cluster.

cy-mo-gene (sī'mō-jēn), *n.* a flammable distillate of petroleum which, when condensed, is used as a freezing mixture.

cyn-ic (sin'ik), *n.* 1. a person who is cynical. 2. [C-], one of a school of ancient Greek philosophers.

cyn-i-cal (sin'i-kl), *adj.* 1. thinking that people do things only because they are selfish. 2. sarcastic, morose, etc. **—cyn'i-cal-ly,** *adv.*

cyn-i-cism (sin'i-sizm), *n.* 1. the temper and practices of a cynic. 2. [C-], the system of the Cynics.

cy-no-sure (sī'nō-shoor, sin'ō-), *n.* an object of general attraction.

cy-press (sī'prēs), *adj.* 1. a coniferous evergreen tree whose branches are used as a symbol of mourning. 2. its wood: *n.* belonging to, or made of, cypress.

Cyp-ri-ot (sip'ri-ōt), *adj.* of or pertaining to Cyprus, an island country in the eastern Mediterranean, or to its inhabitants: *n.* a native or inhabitant of Cyprus.

cyst (sist), *n.* a bladder or pouch containing unhealthy matter.

cyst-ic (sis'tik), *adj.* of, pertaining to, or contained in a cyst.

cys-ti-tis (sis-tīt'is), *n.* an inflammation of the urinary bladder.

cys-to-cele (sis'tō-sēl), *n.* a hernia occasioned by protrusion of the bladder into the vagina.

cyst-oid (sis'toid), *adj.* resembling a cyst; bladderlike.

cys-tos-co-py (sis-tos'kō-pi), *n., pl.* -pies, the examination of the urinary bladder with an electric light device.

---

cys·tot·o·my (sis-tot'ŏ-mi), *n., pl.* **-mies,** surgical opening of the urinary bladder.

cy·tol·o·gy (si-tol'ŏ-ji), *n.* the branch of biology which treats of cells.

cy·tol·y·sis ('ĭ-sis), *n.* the degeneration of cells.

czar (zär), *n.* 1. a despot. 2. the title of the former emperors of Russia. **—czar'dom,** *n.* **— cza·ri·na** (zä-rē'nä), *n.fem.*

Czech (chek), *adj.* of or pertaining to Czechoslovakia, a country in central Europe, or to its inhabitants: *n.* any of certain Slavic people living in Czechoslovakia.

D

D, d (dē), *n.*, *pl.* **D's, d's, 1.** the fourth letter of the English alphabet. **2.** the sound of this letter, as in *dab.* **3.** a type or impression of *D* or *d.*

D (dē), *adj.* **1.** shaped like *D.* **2.** below average quality: *n.* **1.** an object shaped like *D.* **2.** a Roman numeral denoting 500. **3.** a school mark or rating signifying below average, or just passing. **4.** in *Music, a)* the second tone in the scale of C major. *b)* the key having this tone for a basic note.

dab (dab), *v.t. & v.i.* **dabbed, dab'bing, 1.** to touch gently; *pat.* **2.** to apply with a light touch: *n.* **1.** a gentle tap; *pat.* **2.** a small amount of something, especially a substance that is moist or soft. **3.** a saltwater flounder.

dab-ber ('ẽr), *n.* an inking pad used by printers and engravers.

dab-ble (dab'l), *v.t.* **-bled, -bling, 1.** to dip in a liquid slightly and often. **2.** to moisten in this way; *spatter: v.i.* **1.** to play in water. **2.** to do anything in a superficial manner. — **dab'bler,** *n.*

dab-chick ('chik), *n.* either of two varieties of grebe, a small, freshwater swimming and diving bird.

dab-ster ('stẽr), *n.* **1.** [British Informal], an expert. **2.** [Informal], an amateur; trifler.

dace (dās), *n.*, *pl.* **dace, dac'es,** any of a number of small, freshwater fish.

da-cha (dä'chä, 'shä), *n.* [Russian], a country house used in the summer.

dachs-hund (däks'hoond, dash'hund), *n.* a small breed of dog, originally from Germany, with a long body and short legs.

da-coit (də-koit'), *n.* a bandit of India or Burma. — **da-coit'y** ('ē), *n.*

dac-tyl (dak'tl), *n.* **1.** a poetical foot of three syllables, the first accented and the others unaccented. **2.** a finger or toe.

dac-tyl-o-gram (dak-til'ō-gram), *n.* a fingerprint.

dac-ty-log-ra-phy (dak-ti-läg'rä-fi), *n.* the scientific study of fingerprints.

dac-ty-lol-o-gy (-läl'ō-ji), *n.* the art of communication by a manual sign language.

dad (dad), *n.* [Informal], father.

dad-dy ('i), *n.*, *pl.* **-dies,** [Informal], father.

dad-dy-long-legs (dad-i-lông'legz), *n.*, *pl.* **-legs,** a kind of small, spiderlike animal with long, thin legs and a round body.

da-do (dä'dō), *n.*, *pl.* **-does, 1.** the solid block forming the body of a pedestal. **2.** an ornamental border around the lower part of the wall of a room: *v.t.* **-doed, -do-ing,** to ornament with a dado.

dae-mon (dē'mŏn), *n.* same as **demon.**

daff (daf), *v.i.* [Scottish], to act foolishly.

daf-fo-dil (ō-dil), *n.* a kind of narcissus that blooms in the spring, having a yellow flower with a trumpetlike center.

daf-fy (daf'i), *adj.*, **-fi-er, -fi-est,** [Informal], **1.** crazy; daft. **2.** giddy. — **daf'fi-ness,** *n.*

daft (daft), *adj.* foolish; idiotic. — **daft'ly,** *adv.* — **daft'ness,** *n.*

dag-ger (dag'ẽr), *n.* **1.** a short, knifelike weapon with a sharp point, used for stabbing. **2.** a reference mark in printing (†).

dag-gle (dag'l), *v.t. & v.i.* **-gled, -gling,** [Archaic or Dial.], to trail or drag through the mud.

da-guerre-o-type (dä-ger'ō-tip), *n.* **1.** an early photograph produced on a silvered plate. **2.** this method of photography: *v.t.* **-typed, -typ-ing,** to photograph by this method. — **da-guerre'o-typ-y,** *n.*

dahl-ia (dal'yä, däl'-, däl'-), *n.* a garden plant with tuberous roots and large, bright-colored flowers.

Dail Eir-eann (dôl er'än), the lower house of the Irish legislature.

dai-ly (dā'li), *n.*, *pl.* **-lies,** a newspaper published each day or every weekday: *adj.* occurring or published each day or every weekday: *adv.* day by day.

dain-ty (dān'ti), *n.*, *pl.* **-ties,** a choice or delicious food: *adj.* **1.** delicious; choice. **2.** refined as regards taste; fastidious. **3.** overly sensitive. — **dain'ti-ly,** *adv.* — **dain'ti-ness,** *n.*

dai-qui-ri (dak'ẽr-i), *n.* a cocktail of combined rum, sugar, and lemon or lime juice.

dair-y (der'i), *n.*, *pl.* **dair'ies, 1.** a place where milk is kept and converted into butter, cheese, etc. **2.** a farm that produces milk and milk products. **3.** a store that sells these products. — **dair'y-man** (-män), *n.*, *pl.* **-men.**

dair-y-ing (-ing), *n.* the business or occupation of making and selling dairy products.

da-is (dā'is), *n.*, *pl.* **da'is-es,** a raised platform.

dai-sy (dā'zi), *n.*, *pl.* **-sies,** a composite plant with a yellow disk and white rays.

Da-lai La-ma (dä-li lä'mä), the high priest of Lamaism.

dale (dāl), *n.* a valley or glen.

dal-eth (däl'et), *n.* the fourth letter of the Hebrew alphabet ( ): also **da'ledh** ('ĕd).

dal-ly (dal'i), *v.i.* **-lied, -ly-ing,** **1.** to flirt with casually. **2.** to trifle away time; loiter; procrastinate. **3.** to toy (*with*). — **dal'li-ance** ('i-äns), *n.*

Dal-ma-tian (dal-mā'shŭn), *n.* a large dog with short hair and dark spots on a white coat.

dam (dam), *n.* **1.** a barrier that stops the flow of water. **2.** a female parent: said of four-legged animals: *v.t.* **dammed, dam'ming, 1.** to construct a dam in. **2.** to confine or restrain (usually with *up*).

dam-age (dam'ij), *n.* **1.** injury or harm done to a person's character, person, or estate. **2.** *pl.* in *Law,* money recovered for loss suffered: *v.t.* **-aged, -ag-ing,** to injure: *v.i.* to receive injury. — **dam'age-a-ble,** *adj.*

da-man (dam'än), *n.* same as **hyrax.**

dam-a-scene (dam'ä-sēn), *v.t.* **-scened, -scen-ing,**

ō in drag*o*n, ōō in cr*u*de, oo in w*oo*l, u in c*u*p, ū in c*u*re, ū in t*u*rn, u in f*o*cus, oi in b*o*y, ou in h*ou*se, th in *th*in, th in sh*ea*the, g in *g*et, j in *j*oy, y in *y*et.

to ornament (iron, steel, etc.) with wavy markings or inlaid designs of silver or gold: *n.* metal ornamented by damascening: *adj.* of or pertaining to damascening or damask.

Damascus steel, a steel noted for hardness and elasticity, originally manufactured at Damascus, the capital of Syria.

dam·ask (dam'ǎsk), *n.* 1. a rich silk or linen fabric used for table linen, coverings, etc. and having a design. 2. same as Damascus steel. 3. deep pink: *adj.* pertaining to or made of damask: *v.t.* to ornament with a wavy or flowered design.

damask rose, a very fragrant, large rose from which the perfume attar of roses is derived.

dame (dām), *n.* 1. [D-], a title formerly given to a mistress (sense 1). 2. an elderly woman. 3. [D-], in Great Britain, the title of the wife of a knight, or a woman who has been knighted. 4. a lady. 5. [Slang], a woman.

damn (dam), *v.t.* damned, damn'ing, 1. to condemn to punishment. 2. to consign to a certain fate. 3. to condemn as bad or as a failure. 4. to invoke a curse upon: *v.i.* to curse: *adj. & adv.* [Informal], same as damned: *interj.* a statement of anger or irritation.

dam·na·ble (dam'nà-bl), *adj.* 1. meriting damnation. 2. execrable; detestable.

dam·na·tion (dam-nā'shǔn), *n.* 1. the state of being damned. 2. the act of damning: *interj.* a statement of anger or irritation.

dam·na·to·ry (dam'nà-tôr-i), *adj.* assigning to; or containing a threat of, damnation.

damned (damd), *adj.* 1. condemned, as to perdition. 2. [Informal], execrably bad: used as an intensive: *adv.* [Informal], very.

damp (damp), *n.* 1. moisture. 2. a dangerous gas in mines, as firedamp: *adj.* moist; humid: *v.t.* 1. to slow (a fire). 2. to moisten. 3. to diminish or check. 4. to deaden the vibrations of. —damp'ness, *n.*

damp-dry ('drī'), *v.t.* -dried', -dry'ing, to dry (clothes) with a little moisture remaining: *adj.* of or pertaining to clothes so laundered.

damp·en (dam'pĕn), *v.t.* 1. to moisten. 2. to diminish or lessen: *v.i.* to become moistened. —damp'en·er, *n.*

damp·er ('pĕr), *n.* 1. something which depresses or deadens. 2. a valve in a flue to regulate the draft. 3. a device for diminishing the oscillations of a magnetic needle. 4. a contrivance for deadening the vibrations of a musical instrument.

dam·sel (dam'zl), *n.* [Archaic], a maiden; girl.

dam·son (dam'zn), *n.* a small, purple plum.

dance (dans), *v.i.* danced, danc'ing, 1. to move with measured steps or to a musical accompaniment. 2. to move nimbly, or merrily: *v.t.* 1. to give a dancing motion to. 2. to perform as a dancer: *n.* 1. a regulated movement of the feet to a rhythmical musical accompaniment. 2. a specific dance. 3. the skill of dancing. 4. a dancing party. 5. a piece of dance music. 6. lively movement. —danc'er, *n.*

dan·de·li·on (dan'dĕ-lī-ǔn), *n.* a composite plant

with large yellow flowers and deeply notched leaves.

dan·der (dan'dĕr), *n.* 1. dandruff. 2. [Informal], anger.

dan·dle (dan'dl), *v.t.* -dled, -dling, 1. to move up and down on the knee or in the arms affectionately. 2. to fondle.

dan·druff (dan'drǔf), *n.* white, flaky scales on the scalp.

dan·dy (dan'di), *n., pl.* -dies, 1. a fop; coxcomb. 2. [Informal], something excellent: *adj.* -di·er, -di·est, [Informal], excellent. —dan'dy·ism, *n.*

dan·ger (dān'jĕr), *n.* 1. a hazard; peril. 2. that which may injure or harm.

dan·ger·ous (-ǔs), *adj.* involving or beset with danger; perilous; hazardous. —dan'ger·ous·ly, *adv.*

dan·gle (dang'gl), *v.i.* -gled, -gling, 1. to hang or swing loosely. 2. to follow (after): *v.t.* to cause to dangle.

Dan·iel (dan'yĕl), *n.* a book of the Bible.

Dan·ish (dā'nish), *adj.* of or pertaining to Denmark, a country in northern Europe, or its inhabitants: *n.* [also d-], a rich pastry containing cheese, fruit, etc.: also Danish pastry.

dank (dangk), *adj.* unpleasantly damp; humid.

dan·seuse (dan-sooz'), *n., pl.* -seus'es (-sooz'ěz), a female dancer or ballet dancer.

dap·per (dap'ĕr), *adj.* 1. small and active. 2. trim and neat in appearance.

dap·ple (dap'l), *adj.* spotted; variegated: also dap'pled: *v.t.* -pled, -pling, to cover with spots.

dare (der), *v.i.* dared, dar'ing, to have courage; venture: *v.t.* 1. to have courage for. 2. to defy. 3. to challenge: *n.* a challenge.

dare·dev·il ('dev-l), *adj.* reckless: *n.* a reckless person.

dar·ing (der'ing), *adj.* fearless; bold; intrepid: *n.* intrepidity.

dark (därk), *adj.* 1. not having or reflecting light. 2. wholly black or gray. 3. producing gloom. 4. unenlightened mentally. 5. secret. 6. hidden. 7. sinister. 8. of a brunet complexion: *n.* 1. the condition of being dark. 2. nightfall. —dark'ly, *adv.* —dark'ness, *n.*

Dark Ages, the Middle Ages, especially the part from 476 A.D. to about 1000 A.D.

dark·en (därk'kĕn), *v.t.* to make dark; obscure: *v.i.* to become dark.

dark horse, [Informal], an obscure person considered unlikely as a winner in some contest.

dark·ling (där'kling), *adj.* dimly seen; characterized by darkness.

dark·room (därk'room), *n.* a room for developing photographs, from which light has been excluded.

dar·ling (där'ling), *n.* 1. a loved one. 2. a favorite: *adj.* 1. tenderly beloved; very dear. 2. [Informal], attractive.

darn (därn), *v.t. & v.i.* & *adj.* to mend (a tear) by filling in the hole with yarn or thread by means of a needle: *n.* a patch made by darning.

darn (därn), *v.t. & v.i.* & *adj.* & *adv.* & *interj.* [Informal], same as damn: used as a euphemism. —darned, *adj. & adv.*

dar·nel (där′nl), *n.* a rye grass which grows in grainfields.

dart (därt), *n.* 1. a small lance or spear. 2. anything resembling a dart. 3. a tapered seam to make a garment closefitting. 4. a swift, sudden movement: *v.t. & v.i.* to send forth or move swiftly.

Dar·von (där′von), *n.* an analgesic drug: a trademark.

Dar·win·i·an (där′win′i·ăn), *adj.* of or pertaining to Charles Darwin, the naturalist (1809-82): *n.* an evolutionist.

Darwinian theory, Darwin's theory of evolution by natural selection.

Dar·win·ism (där′win-izm), *n.* the Darwinian theory. —Dar′win·ist, *adj. & n.*

dash (dash), *v.t.* 1. to throw violently (*against*). 2. to break by collision; shatter. 3. to hurl (*down, away,* etc.). 4. to splatter. 5. to mingle. 6. to depress. 7. to sketch, write, etc. rapidly (with *off*): *v.i.* 1. to rush with violence. 2. to throw violently against: *n.* 1. collision. 2. violent motion. 3. a slight addition. 4. a quick race. 5. vigor and exuberance. 6. ostentatious display. 7. a mark (—) in writing or printing that shows a pause or that something is left out.

dash·board (dash′bôrd), *n.* 1. a protection against splashing on a boat, carriage, etc. 2. an instrument panel in an automobile.

das·tard (das′tărd), *n.* an evil coward.

das·tard·ly (-li), *adj.* cowardly. —das′tard·li·ness, *n.*

das·y·ure (das′i-yoor), *n.* an arboreal marsupial of Australia.

da·ta (dat′ă, dāt′ă), *n.* facts; information.

data processing, the recording and handling of information by means of mechanical or electronic equipment.

date (dāt), *n.* 1. the time of an event. 2. the inscription which specifies when a writing or inscription was executed. 3. duration. 4. the day of the month. 5. a social appointment, as with a person of the opposite sex. 6. that person. 7. the edible fruit of the date palm: *v.t.* dat′ed, dat′ing, 1. to mark with a date. 2. to set the date of. 3. to cause to appear out of date. 4. to go on social dates with: *v.i.* 1. to have a date. 2. to have social dates.

date-line (′lin), *n.* the time and location when written or issued, as in a newspaper story.

date palm, a type of palm.

da·tive (dāt′iv), *adj.* denoting the case of a noun, pronoun, or adjective which expresses the indirect object: *n.* the dative case: usually indicated in English by *to* or *for* or the order of the words.

da·tum (dāt′ŭm, dat′ŭm), *n., pl.* da·ta (′ă), something assumed, known, or conceded for the basis of argument or inference.

daub (dôb), *v.t. & v.i.* 1. to cover or smear with adhesive matter. 2. to paint coarsely or unskillfully: *n.* 1. a smear. 2. something daubed on. 3. a crudely executed painting. —daub′er, *n.*

daugh·ter (dôt′ĕr), *n.* 1. a female child or descendant. 2. something conceived of as a daughter in relationship to its origin. 3. a

daughter-in-law. 4. a stepdaughter. —daugh°-ter·ly, *adj.*

daugh·ter-in-law (-in-lô), *n., pl.* daugh′ters-in-law, a son's wife.

daunt (dônt), *v.t.* to intimidate; dishearten.

daunt·less (′lis), *adj.* fearless.

dau·phin (dô′fin), *n.* in France, the king's oldest son.

dav·en·port (dav′ĕn-pôrt), *n.* 1. a large couch or sofa which sometimes can be converted into a bed. 2. [British], a writing desk with the lid on a hinge.

Da·vid (dā′vid), *n.* in the *Bible,* the second king of Israel.

dav·it (dav′it), *n.* either of a pair of f-shaped uprights projecting over the side of a vessel, for suspending or lowering a boat.

Da·vy Jones (dā′vi jōnz′), the humorous name for the spirit of the sea.

Davy Jones's locker, 1. the bottom of the sea. 2. the burial place of those drowned at sea.

daw (dô), *n.* same as jackdaw.

daw·dle (dôd′l), *v.i. & v.t.* -dled, -dling, to waste (time) in a trifling manner; loiter. —daw′dler, *n.*

dawn (dôn), *v.i.* 1. to begin to grow light; break as the day. 2. to start appearing. 3. to start being known or sensed: *n.* 1. the first appearance of light in the morning. 2. the beginning (with *of*).

day (dā), *n.* 1. the period of light between sunrise and sunset. 2. daylight. 3. sunshine. 4. the space of 24 hours, reckoning from midnight to midnight in the civil day or from noon to noon in the astronomical day. 5. a specified day, time, or period. 6. a successful or glorious period. 7. the duration of a workday.

day·bed (dā′bed), *n.* a couch convertible into a bed.

day·book (′book), *n.* a book in which the transactions of the day are entered in the order of their occurrence.

day·break (′brāk), *n.* the dawn.

day·dream (′drēm), *n.* 1. reverie. 2. visionary fancy: *v.i.* to have daydreams.

day·light (′lit), *n.* 1. sunlight. 2. daybreak. 3. daytime. 4. comprehension.

day·light-sav·ing time (-sā′ving), time which is an hour later than the standard time.

day nursery, a place where mothers can leave their children for care and training during the day: also day-care center (′ker).

days of grace, a period of time allowed for payment of certains debts or premiums after they are due.

day-time (′tim), *n.* the daylight time.

day-to-day (dā′tŏ-dā′), *adj.* daily.

daze (dāz), *v.t.* dazed, daz′ing, 1. to stupefy, stun, or confuse. 2. to dazzle: *n.* the state of being dazed.

daz·zle (daz′l), *v.t.* daz′zled, daz′zling, 1. to overpower or dim one's vision by a glare or excess of light. 2. to overpower by splendor: *v.i.* to be overpowered by light or splendor: *n.* 1. the act of dazzling. 2. a dazzling thing. —daz′zler, *n.*

de-, a prefix meaning *off, down, completely.*

dea·con (dēk′n), *n.* 1. the order of clergy ranking just below a priest in the Roman Catholic and Anglican churches. 2. in some other Christian churches, a layman who helps the minister and manages some church business.

dea·con·ess (dēk'n-is), *n.* a woman who acts as a church assistant, as in helping the sick and poor of a parish.

de·ac·ti·vate (di-ak'ti-vāt), *v.t.* -vat·ed, -vat·ing, 1. to discontinue the possible activity or operation of (an explosive material). 2. to put (a military group) on a reserved basis.

dead (ded), *adj.* 1. destitute of life. 2. inanimate. 3. resembling death. 4. without vitality. 5. powerless or motionless. 6. extinct. 7. inactive. 8. insignificant. 9. unerring. 10. absolute. 11. exact. 12. not transmitting an electrical current. 13. [Informal], exhausted. 14. in *Sports,* out of the game or play: *n.* 1. the time of greatest intensity. 2. dead persons (preceded by *the*): *adv.* 1. absolutely. 2. exactly.

dead·beat (ded'bēt), *adj.* making succesive movements with no recoil: *n.* [Slang], 1. a sponger. 2. a loafer.

dead center, that position of a crank and connecting rod in which they are in a straight line.

dead·en (ded'n), *v.t.* 1. to diminish the acuteness, intensity, or vigor of. 2. to blunt. 3. to render nonconductive of sound.

dead end, an alley, street, etc. that has only one exit. —**dead'-end',** *adj.*

dead·eye (ded'ī), *n.* a round, flat block of wood pierced with three holes to receive lanyards, used for tying down the shrouds.

dead·head (*'*hed), *n.* 1. a person who has a free pass. 2. a bollard. 3. [Slang], a stupid person: *v.i.* to use free passes.

dead heat, a tie in a race.

dead letter, 1. an unclaimed letter. 2. that which has lost its authority.

dead·light (*'*līt), *n.* a strong shutter placed over a cabin window of a ship in stormy weather.

dead·line (*'*līn), *n.* the final time at which completion is permitted.

dead·lock (*'*lok), *n.* a situation in which progress is impossible: *v.t. & v.i.* to cause or become a deadlock.

dead·ly (*'*lī), *adj.* -li·er, -li·est, 1. causing death. 2. destructive. 3. implacable. 4. resembling death. 5. to an excess. 6. tiresome. 7. precise: *adv.* very. —**dead'li·ness,** *n.*

dead march, solemn funeral music.

dead·pan (*'*pan), *adj. & adv.* [Slang], expressionless(ly).

dead reckoning, the calculation of a ship's place at sea by the log and the compass courses.

dead set, 1. the fixed position of a dog in pointing game. 2. a determined effort or attack.

dead weight, 1. the weight of an inactive person or thing. 2. freight charged for by weight.

dead·wood (*'*wood), *n.* 1. timbers above the keel of a vessel at the stern. 2. worthless material or a useless person. 3. wood or branches dead on a tree.

deaf (def), *adj.* 1. deprived of hearing. 2. unwilling to hear or pay regard to. —**deaf'ly,** *adv.* —**deaf'ness,** *n.*

deaf·en (def'n), *v.t.* 1. to make deaf. 2. to overpower with noise. 3. to render impervious to noise. —**deaf'en·ing,** *adj. & n.*

deaf-mute (*'*mūt'), *n.* a deaf person not having the knowledge of speech.

deal (dēl), *n.* 1. an indefinite quantity or degree. 2. a division of cards to the players. 3. a mercantile agreement. 4. a secret bargain. 5. the wood of the fir or pine tree cut into boards. 6. [Informal], manner of treating: *v.t.* dealt (delt), **deal'ing,** 1. to distribute or apportion. 2. to dispense: *v.i.* 1. to have concern (*with*). 2. to act (*with*). 3. to have business (*with* or *in*). —**deal'er,** *n.*

deal·er·ship (*-*ship), *n.* the exclusive right to sell a product in a location.

deal·ing (dēl'ing), *n.* 1. conduct toward others. 2. distribution. 3. *usually pl.* business agreements.

dean (dēn), *n.* 1. the presiding ecclesiastical dignitary in cathedral and collegiate churches. 2. the administrator of a faculty, body of students, etc. in a college. 3. the oldest or most experienced member of a group.

dean·er·y (dēn'ēr-i), *n., pl.* -er·ies, the office, jurisdiction, or residence of a dean.

dear (dir), *adj.* 1. expensive; costly. 2. beloved. 3. highly esteemed. 4. intensely felt: *n.* a darling; favorite: *adv.* at a high price or rate: *interj.* an expression of surprise, pity, etc. —**dear'ly,** *adv.* —**dear'ness,** *n.*

dearth (dûrth), *n.* 1. want; scarcity. 2. famine.

dear·y (dir'i), *n., pl.* dear'ies, [Informal], darling: also **dear'ie.**

death (deth), *n.* 1. extinction of life. 2. the state of the dead. 3. general mortality. 4. destruction. 5. that which causes death. —**death'like,** *adj.*

death-bed (deth'bed), *n.* 1. the bed of a dying person. 2. the final hours of a dying person.

death-blow (*'*blō), *n.* 1. a blow that leads to death. 2. an event fatal (*to*).

death-less (*'*lis), *adj.* immortal.

death-ly (*'*li), *adj.* 1. mortal; fatal. 2. resembling death: *adv.* very.

death mask, a cast of the face taken after death.

death rate, the percentage of deaths, usually per thousand, among the population of a country, city, etc., as for a year.

death's-head (deths'hed), *n.* a human skull, or representation of a skull, emblematic of death.

death-trap (deth'trap), *n.* a dangerous place, thing, situation, etc.

death-watch (*'*wäch), *n.* 1. a vigil beside a dying person. 2. a guard set over a person prior to execution. 3. a beetle which makes a ticking sound: superstitiously supposed to forbode death.

deb (deb), *n.* [Informal], same as **debutante.**

de-ba-cle (di-bäk'l, -bak'l), *n.* 1. the breaking up of ice on a river. 2. a violent flood carrying great masses of debris. 3. a dispersion; rout.

de-bar (di-bär'), *v.t.* -barred', -bar'ring, 1. to

shut out; exclude (*from*). 2. to hinder; preclude. —de·bar'ment, *n*.

de·bark (di-bärk'), *v.t. & v.i.* to disembark. —de·bar·ka·tion (dē-bär-kā'shŭn), *n*.

de·base (di-bās'), *v.t.* -based', -bas'ing, to lower in character, value, quality, etc. —de·base'ment, *n*.

de·bate (di-bāt'), *v.t.* -bat'ed, -bat'ing, 1. to contend for in words or arguments. 2. to meditate upon. 3. to deliberate together: *v.i.* 1. to argue or discuss a point. 2. to reflect: *n.* 1. contention in words or argument. 2. discussion. —de·bat'a·ble, *adj.* —de·bat'er, *n*.

de·bauch (di-bôch'), *v.t.* to corrupt in morals or principles: *v.i.* to engage in debauchery: *n.* 1. excessive intemperance. 2. an orgy.

deb·au·chee (di-bôch-ē'), *n.* one who engages in debauchery.

de·bauch·er·y (di-bôch'ēr-i), *n., pl.* -er·ies, 1. excessive intemperance. 2. seduction from purity or virtue. 3. *pl.* orgies.

de·bil·i·tate (di-bil'i-tāt), *v.t.* -tat·ed, -tat·ing, to enfeeble; enervate. —de·bil·i·ta'tion, *n*.

de·bil·i·ty (-ti), *n., pl.* -ties, weakness, as of the body.

deb·it (deb'it), *n.* that which is owing, entered on the left-hand side of a ledger: *v.t.* to enter on the left-hand side of an account.

deb·o·nair (deb-ō-ner'), *adj.* 1. cheerfully friendly. 2. easy; carefree. Also deb·o·naire'.

de·bouch (di-bōōsh'), *v.i.* to come out of a confined space into open ground.

dé·bou·ché (dā-bōō-shā'), *n.* [French], an opening, as for military troops to emerge.

de·bouch·ment (di-bōōsh'mĕnt), *n.* 1. an outlet, as of a river. 2. the act of debouching.

de·bris (dē-brē'), *n.* 1. fragments; rubble. 2. broken rubbish. 3. loose pieces of rock. Also débris.

debt (det), *n.* 1. that which is due from one person to another. 2. an obligation. 3. the state of owing.

debt·or (det'ēr), *n.* one who owes something to another.

de·bug (dē-bug'), *v.t.* 1. to correct defects in. 2. [Informal], to find and remove hidden electronic listening devices from.

de·but (di-bū', dā'bū), *n.* 1. a first appearance in public. 2. the first formal appearance of a girl in society. Also début.

deb·u·tant (deb'yoo-tänt), *n.* one who makes a debut.

deb·u·tante (-tänt'), *n.* a young girl making a first formal appearance in society.

dec·a-, a combining form meaning *ten*.

dec·ade (dek'ād), *n.* 1. a group of ten. 2. a ten-year period.

dec·a·dence (dek'ā-děns), *n.* a state of decay; deterioration; retrogression. —dec'a·dent, *adj. & n*.

de·caf·fein·at·ed (dē-kaf'ē-nāt-id), *adj.* having all or most of its caffeine removed.

dec·a·gon (dek'ā-gon), *n.* a plane figure having ten sides and ten angles. —de·cag·o·nal (di-kag'ō-năl), *adj*.

dec·a·gram (dek'ā-gram), *n.* a weight of ten grams.

dec·a·he·dron (dek-ā-hē'drŏn), *n., pl.* -drons, -dra ('drā), a solid figure bounded by ten plane faces.

de·cal·ci·fy (di-kal'si-fī), *v.t.* -fied, -fy·ing, to free (bones) of lime or calcium.

de·cal·co·ma·ni·a (di-kal-kō-mā'ni-ā), *n.* 1. the process of transferring pictures, designs, etc. from prepared paper to china, glass, etc. 2. such a picture, design, etc. Also de·cal (di-kal').

Dec·a·logue (dek'ā-lôg), *n.* [sometimes d-], same as Ten Commandments: also Dec'a·log.

dec·a·me·ter (dek'ā-mēt-ēr), *n.* a measure of length, equal to 10 meters (32.8 feet).

de·camp (di-kamp'), *v.i.* 1. to depart camp. 2. to go away secretly or speedily.

de·cant (di-kant'), *v.t.* to pour off (liquid) gently.

de·cant·er ('ēr), *n.* an ornamental glass bottle for holding wines, etc.

de·cap·i·tate (di-kap'i-tāt), *v.i.* -tat·ed, -tat·ing, to behead. —de·cap·i·ta'tion, *n*.

dec·a·pod (dek'ā-pod), *adj.* having ten feet or arms: *n.* a ten-footed crustacean, or ten-armed cephalopod.

de·car·bon·ate (di-kär'bō-nāt), *v.t.* -at·ed, -at·ing, to deprive of carbon dioxide or carbonic acid.

de·car·bon·ize (-nīz), *v.t.* -ized, -iz·ing, to deprive (steel, etc.) of carbon.

dec·are (dek'er), *n.* a surface measure, equal to 1,000 square meters (0.247 acre).

dec·a·stere (dek'ā-stir), *n.* a measure of volume, equal to 10 cubic meters (13.08 cubic yards).

de·cath·lon (di-kath'lon), *n.* an athletic contest consisting of ten different sports in each of which the contestants take part.

de·cay (di-kā'), *v.i.* 1. to waste away; decline. 2. to rot. 3. to disintegrate radioactively: *n.* 1. deterioration. 2. decline. 3. rottenness.

de·cease (di-sēs'), *v.i.* -ceased', -ceas'ing, to die: *n.* death.

de·ceased (-sēst'), *adj.* dead: *n.* a dead person or dead persons (preceded by *the*).

de·ce·dent (di-sēd'nt), *n.* in *Law*, a deceased person.

de·ceit (di-sēt'), *n.* 1. deception. 2. a falsehood. 3. the quality of being false.

de·ceit·ful ('fŭl), *adj.* 1. full of deceit. 2. false. —de·ceit'ful·ly, *adv.* —de·ceit'ful·ness, *n*.

de·ceive (di-sēv'), *v.t. & v.i.* -ceived', -ceiv'ing, to mislead; delude. —de·ceiv'a·ble, *adj.* —de·ceiv'er, *n*.

de·cel·er·ate (di-sel'ē-rāt), *v.i. & v.t.* -at·ed, -at·ing, to go or make go more slowly. —de·cel·er·a'tion, *n*.

De·cem·ber (di-sem'bēr), *n.* the twelfth and last month of the year, having 31 days.

de·cem·vir (di-sem'vēr), *n., pl.* -virs, -vir·i ('vi-ri), one of ten Roman magistrates who possessed authority in ancient Rome.

de·cem·vi·rate ('vi-rit), *n.* 1. a body of ten men in authority. 2. their office, or term of office.

de·cen·cy (dē'sn-si), *n., pl.* -cies, the state of being decent or modest.

de·cen·na·ry (di-sen'ēr-i), *n., pl.* -ries, a period of ten years.

de·cen·ni·al (di-sen'i-ăl), *adj.* 1. lasting for ten years. 2. occurring every ten years: *n.* a decennial occurrence, celebration, etc.

de·cent (dē'snt), *adj.* 1. decorous. 2. modest. 3.

respectable. 4. passable. 5. sympathetically fair. —de'cent·ly, adv.

de·cen·tral·ize (dī-sen'trȧ-līz), v.t. -ized, -iz·ing, to distribute what has been concentrated: said of the administration of public affairs, industry, etc.

de·cep·tion (dī-sep'shŭn), n. 1. the act of deceiving. 2. the state of being deceived. 3. fraud. —de·cep'tive, adj.

dec·i·are (des'i-er), n. a measure of surface, equal to 1/10 are (11.96 square yards).

dec·i·bel (des'i-bel), n. a measure of sound loudness.

de·cide (dī-sīd'), v.t. -cid'ed, -cid'ing, 1. to bring to an issue or conclusion; fix the end of. 2. to resolve: v.i. to give a judgment or decision.

de·cid·ed (dī-sīd'id), adj. 1. free from ambiguity; unquestionable. 2. determined; resolute. —de·cid'ed·ly, adv.

de·cid·u·ous (dī-sij'oo-wŭs), adj. 1. falling off at maturity, or in season. 2. dropping leaves each year.

dec·i·gram (des'i-gram), n. a measure of weight, equal to 1/10 gram: also, chiefly British, decigramme.

dec·i·li·ter (des'i-lēt-ẽr), n. a measure of capacity, equal to 1/10 liter.

dec·il·lion (dī-sil'yŭn), n. 1. in France and the U.S., 1 followed by 33 zeros. 2. in England, 1 followed by 60 zeros.

dec·i·mal (des'i-ml), adj. of, pertaining to, or based on the number 10: n. same as **decimal fraction**.

decimal fraction, a fraction having 10 or some power of 10 as an unwritten denominator.

decimal point, a point placed before the numerator of a decimal fraction.

decimal system, a system of reckoning or measuring by 10 or powers of 10.

dec·i·mate (des'i-māt), v.t. -mat·ed, -mat·ing, to destroy a large proportion of. —dec·i·ma'tion, n.

dec·i·me·ter (des'i-mēt-ẽr), n. a measure of length, equal to 1/10 meter (3.937 inches).

de·ci·pher (dī-sī'fẽr), v.t. 1. to decode (secret writing). 2. to discover or make out the meaning of; solve; unravel.

de·ci·sion (dī-sizh'ŭn), n. 1. the act of deciding; settlement. 2. determination. 3. judgment.

de·ci·sive (dī-sī'siv), adj. 1. conclusive. 2. firm; determined. —de·ci'sive·ly, adv.

dec·i·stere (des'i-stir), n. a measure of volume, equal to 1/10 stere (3.53 cubic feet).

deck (dek), v.t. 1. to array in finery or ornaments; adorn. 2. to furnish with a deck: n. 1. the flooring of a ship. 2. anything like this. 3. a pack of playing cards.

deck·le (dek'l), n. in paper making, a wooden frame to confine the pulp to a desired shape.

deck·le-edged (dek'l-ejd), adj. having the edges rough and uncut: said of paper.

de·claim (dī-klām'), v.t. & v.i. 1. to speak in a pompous, passionate, or dramatic manner. 2. to harangue.

dec·la·ma·tion (dek-lȧ-mā'shŭn), n. 1. the art of declaiming. 2. impassioned oratory.

de·clam·a·to·ry (dī-klam'ȧ-tôr-i), adj. 1. of, pertaining to, or characterized by declaiming. 2. noisy in style; appealing to the passions.

dec·la·ra·tion (dek-lȧ-rā'shŭn), n. 1. the act of declaring or proclaiming. 2. that which is declared. 3. a formal assertion; a statement reduced to writing.

Declaration of Independence, the public act, passed July 4, 1776, by which the Second Continental Congress declared the 13 original North American colonies free states independent of Great Britain.

de·clar·a·tive (dī-kler'ȧ-tiv), adj. explanatory: also de·clar·a·to·ry ('ȧ-tôr-i).

de·clare (dī-kler'), v.t. -clared', -clar'ing, 1. to make known; tell openly, publicly, or formally. 2. to disclose or display. 3. to make a solemn affirmation. 4. to make a full statement as to goods, etc. 5. in card games, to control a suit by bidding successfully: v.i. to make a declaration.

de·clas·si·fy (dē-klas'i-fī), v.t. -fied, -fy·ing, to remove (government documents) from secret classifications. —de·clas·si·fi·ca'tion, n.

de·clen·sion (dī-klen'shŭn), n. 1. a slope. 2. a decline; falling off or away; deterioration. 3. in *Grammar*, the inflection of nouns, pronouns, and adjectives.

dec·li·na·tion (dek-lī-nā'shŭn), n. 1. the act or state of bending or moving downward. 2. an oblique variation from some definite direction. 3. the angular distance of a heavenly body north or south of the celestial equator. 4. the angle made by the magnetic needle with the geographical meridian.

de·cline (dī-klīn'), v.i. -clined', -clin'ing, 1. to bend or lean downward. 2. to draw to a close. 3. to become weak. 4. to deviate from rectitude. 5. to refuse something politely: v.t. 1. to refuse. 2. to make bend downward. 3. in *Grammar*, to inflect: n. 1. diminution; decay; deterioration. 2. a period of this. 3. tuberculosis. 4. a depressed slope.

de·cliv·i·tous (dī-kliv'i-tŭs), adj. moderately steep.

de·cliv·i·ty (-ti), n., pl. -ties, a descent; deviation from a horizontal line.

de·coct (dī-kokt'), v.t. to extract the essence of by boiling. —de·coc'tion, n.

de·code (dī-kōd'), v.t. -cod'ed, -cod'ing, to translate (a message) into ordinary language from a cipher or code.

de·col·late (dī-kol'āt), v.t. -lat·ed, -lat·ing, to behead. —de·col·la'tion (dē-ko-lā'shŭn), n.

dé·col·le·té (dā-kol-ê-tā'), adj. cut low in the neck so as to expose the neck and shoulders: said of a dress.

de·col·o·ni·za·tion (dē-kol-ô-nī-zā'shŭn), n. the removal of colonial administration and ending of colonial government. —de·col'o·nize (-ô-nīz), v.t. & v.i. -nized, -niz·ing.

de·com·pose (dē-kŏm-pōz'), v.t. & v.i. -posed', -pos'ing, 1. to divide into constituent elements or parts. 2. to decay or rot; putrefy. —de·com·pos'a·ble, adj. —de·com·po·si'tion (-kom-pō-zish'ŭn), n.

de·com·pound (dē-kŏm-pound'), v.t. to reduce

---

a in cap, ā in cane, ä in father, ȧ in abet, e in met, ē in be, ê in baker, ê in regent, i in pit, ī in fine, i in manifest, o in hot, ô in horse, ō in bone,

(a compound) to the constitutive parts: *adj.* compounded more than once.

de·com·press (dē-kŏm-pres'), *v.t.* to remove pressure or compression from (a person in an air lock, a deep-sea diver, etc.). —de·com·pres'sion, *n.*

decompression sickness, a painful, sometimes convulsive disorder afflicting deep-sea divers surfacing too quickly.

de·con·gest·ant (dē-kŏn-jes'tănt), *n.* something to get rid of congestion, as in the nose.

de·con·tam·i·nate (dē-kŏn-tam'ĭ-nāt), *v.t.* -nat·ed, -nat·ing, to rid of contamination.

dé·cor, de·cor (dā-kôr'), *n.* the way a place is furnished or decorated.

dec·o·rate (dek'ô-rāt), *v.t.* -rat·ed, -rat·ing, 1. to ornament or beautify. 2. to confer a badge of honor upon. —dec·o·ra'tion, *n.* —dec'o·ra·tive, *adj.*

Decoration Day, same as **Memorial Day**.

dec·o·ra·tor (-ēr), *n.* a person who specializes in the decoration of rooms, etc.

dec·o·rous (dek'ēr-ŭs, di-kôr'ŭs), *adj.* marked by propriety; proper; decent; fit.

de·cor·ti·cate (di-kôr'ti-kāt), *v.t.* -cat·ed, -cat·ing, to remove the bark, husk, or peel from. — de·cor·ti·ca'tion, *n.*

de·co·rum (di-kôr'ŭm), *n.* propriety; decency; fitness.

dé·cou·page, de·cou·page (dā-kōō-pāzh'), *n.* the art of decorating a surface with paper cutouts.

de·coy (di-koi'), *v.t.* & *v.i.* to lead by artifice, as into danger, or to be so drawn: *n.* (also dē'koi), 1. a deceptive stratagem; lure. 2. one leading another into danger or self-betrayal; often, specifically, a person employed to trap suspects. 3. a real or imitation bird or animal used to lure game to a spot where it can be killed or taken; also, this spot.

de·crease (di-krēs'), *v.i.* & *v.t.* to become or make gradually less in size, number, etc.; diminish: *n.* (usually dē'krēs), 1. the act of decreasing; diminution. 2. the amount of diminution.

de·cree (di-krē'), *n.* 1. an ordinance, law, or edict. 2. a judicial decision: *v.t.* to determine, settle, command, or establish by decree; ordain: *v.i.* to make or publish a decree.

dec·re·ment (dek'rē-měnt), *n.* a diminution.

de·crep·it (di-krep'it), *adj.* enfeebled or deteriorated by age, infirmity, or extensive use; worn-out.

de·crep·i·tude (di-krep'ĭ-tōōd), *n.* the condition or state of being decrepit.

de·cre·scen·do (dē-krē-shen'dō, dā-), *n., pl.* -dos, a gradual decrease in volume, as of music: *adv.* & *adj.* decreasing thus.

de·cre·tal (di-krēt'l), *n.* a decree.

dec·re·to·ry (dek'rē-tôr-i), *adj.* of, pertaining to, being, or fixed by a decree: also **de·cre·tive** (di-krēt'iv).

de·crim·i·nal·ize (dē-krim-ĭ-năl-īz'), *v.t.* -ized, -iz'ing, to eliminate or reduce the penalties for (a crime).

de·cry (di-krī'), *v.t.* -cried', -cry'ing, to blame clamorously; cry down; censure; disparage. —de·cri'al, *n.*

de·cum·bent (di-kum'běnt), *adj.* lying down; prostrate; reclining.

dec·u·ple (dek'yoo-pl), *adj.* tenfold: *n.* a number taken ten times: *v.t.* -pled, -pling, to increase tenfold.

de·cu·ri·on (di-kūr'i-ŏn), *n.* in old Rome, an officer in charge of 10 men.

de·cur·rent (di-kūr'ěnt), *adj.* in *Botany*, running or extending downward.

de·cus·sate (di-kus'āt, dek'ŭ-sāt), *v.t.* & *v.i.* -sat·ed, -sat·ing, to intersect or cross at an acute angle: *adj.* (di-kus'it), intersected; decussated.

ded·i·cate (ded'ĭ-kāt), *v.t.* -cat·ed, -cat·ing, 1. to set apart for or by religious ceremony; set apart solemnly. 2. to devote or set apart to some work, duty, use, etc. 3. to inscribe, as a literary work. —ded·i·ca'tion, *n.* —ded'i·ca·tor, *n.*

ded·i·ca·to·ry (ded'i-kă-tôr-i), *adj.* of or constituting a dedication.

de·duce (di-dōōs', -dūs'), *v.t.* -duced', -duc'ing, 1. to gather by reasoning; infer. 2. to determine the source or development of; derive. —de·duc'i·ble, *adj.*

de·duct (di-dukt'), *v.t.* to take away; subtract. —de·duct'i·ble, *adj.*

de·duc·tion (di-duk'shŭn), *n.* 1. the act or process of deducting; subtraction. 2. what is deducted. 3. the act or process of deducing; a proceeding from what is known to what is unknown or from general propositions to particular cases. 4. what is so deduced. — de·duc'tive, *adj.*

deed (dēd), *n.* 1. something done; act. 2. an illustrious achievement. 3. a written instrument for the transfer of real estate: *v.t.* to convey by deed.

deem (dēm), *v.t.* & *v.i.* to think; judge.

de·em·pha·size (dē-em'fá-sīz), *v.t.* -sized, -siz·ing, to reduce or avoid emphasis on; make less prominent.

deep (dēp), *adj.* 1. extending, penetrating, or being far down, in, back, etc. 2. not easily understood; complex or abstruse. 3. not superficial; not light or shallow; profound. 4. not trivial or passing; serious; grave. 5. wholly occupied, as in thinking; absorbed. 6. deep-seated; intense. 7. not aboveboard; tricky; devious. 8. not pale or faint; full and rich: said of colors. 9. not easily known or plumbed; hidden, as a secret. 10. low in pitch or range: *n.* 1. a deep body of water; specifically, the sea. 2. a deep part, place, expanse, etc.: *adv.* to great or considerable depth. —deep'ly, *adv.* —deep'ness, *n.*

deep·en (dēp'n), *v.t.* & *v.i.* to make or become deep or deeper.

Deep-freeze (dēp'frēz'), a deep freezer: a trademark: *n.* [d-], 1. a deep freezer. 2. storage in, or as in, such a device: *v.t.* [d-], -froze' or -freezed', -fro'zen or -freezed', -freez'ing, 1. same as **quick-freeze**. 2. to store in a deep freezer.

deep freezer, a freezer designed to quick-freeze and store food.

deep-fry (dēp'frī'), *v.t.* -fried', -fry'ing, to fry, using much fat or oil so as to completely cover the food being fried.

ŏ in dragon, ōō in crude, oo in wool, u in cup, ū in cure, ū in turn, ú in focus, oi in boy, ou in house, th in thin, th in sheathe, g in get, j in joy, y in yet.

deep-laid ('lād'), *adj.* elaborated with great care and typically with secrecy.

deep-root·ed ('rōōt'id), *adj.* 1. having deep roots. 2. so deeply embedded as not to be easily changed or removed.

deep-sea ('sē'), *adj.* of or pertaining to the open sea or its deeper parts.

deer (dir), *n.*, *pl.* **deer**, occasionally **deers**, any one of a family of hoofed ruminants, as a reindeer or moose, the males of which are usually distinguished by antlers that are shed annually: in popular usage, the term is restricted to smaller animals of this family.

deer·hound ('hound), *n.* a Scottish breed of large dog, once trained to hunt deer.

deer·skin ('skin), *n.* 1. the hide of a deer. 2. leather made from this; also, an article of apparel made of this leather.

deer·stalk·er ('stôk-ēr), *n.* 1. a hunter stalking deer. 2. a low-crowned cap with a visor in front and back, for hunters.

de·es·ca·late (dē-es'kă-lāt), *v.i.* & *v.t.* **-lat·ed**, **-lat·ing**, to lessen the escalation of (something); restrain or slow down.

de·face (di-fās'), *v.t.* **-faced'**, **-fac'ing**, 1. to mar or disfigure the surface of; spoil. 2. to impair thus the legibility of. **—de·face'ment**, *n.* **—de·fac'er**, *n.*

de fac·to (di-fak'tō, dā), being such in reality, though not so set up officially.

de·fal·cate (di-fal'kāt), *v.i.* **-cat·ed**, **-cat·ing**, to steal or misappropriate funds by breach of trust; embezzle. **—de·fal·ca'tion** (dē-), *n.* **—de·fal'ca·tor**, *n.*

de·fame (di-fām'), *v.t.* **-famed'**, **-fam'ing**, to injure the good reputation of by malicious false statements either oral or written; asperse; vilify; calumniate. **—def·a·ma·tion** (def-ă-mā'shŭn), *n.* **—de·fam·a·to·ry** (di-fam'ă-tôr-i), *adj.*

de·fault (di-fôlt'), *n.* failure to do something required or expected; specifically, failure to pay, failure to satisfy the acts required in a lawsuit, or failure to enter or complete a contest: *v.i.* 1. to omit or neglect to pay; be delinquent in. 2. to forfeit by default: *v.i.* to make a default. **—de·fault'er**, *n.*

de·fea·sance (di-fē'zns), *n.* annulment, specifically of a contract or deed.

de·fea·si·ble (di-fē'zi-bl), *adj.* subject to defeasance.

de·feat (di-fēt'), *v.t.* 1. to overcome or vanquish. 2. to frustrate. 3. to nullify: *n.* the act of defeating or the state or condition of being defeated.

de·feat·ist ('ist), *n.* a person too much inclined to expect defeat: *adj.* of or typical of a defeatist. **—de·feat'ism**, *n.*

def·e·cate (def'ē-kāt), *v.t.* **-cat·ed**, **-cat·ing**, to free from impurities: *v.i.* to discharge excrement from the bowels. **—def·e·ca'tion**, *n.*

de·fect (dē'fekt, di-fekt'), *n.* 1. an imperfection; fault; flaw. 2. lack of what should be present; insufficiency: *v.i.* (di-fekt') to abandon a cause, group, etc. without its sanction and, typically, go over to the opposition. **—de·fec'tion**, *n.* **—de·fec'tor**, *n.*

de·fec·tive (di-fek'tiv), *adj.* 1. having one or more defects. 2. in *Grammar*, lacking certain forms: *n.* one that is defective, especially mentally.

de·fence (di-fens'), *n.* British form for **defense**.

de·fend (di-fend'), *v.t.* 1. to guard or protect. 2. to advance arguments or support for, so as to justify. 3. in *Law*, *a)* to oppose a suit, charge, etc.). *b)* to act as lawyer for (someone accused): *v.i.* to make a defense. **—de·fend'er**, *n.*

de·fend·ant (-fen'dănt), *n.* a person sued or accused in a civil or criminal court.

de·fense (di-fens', dē'fens), *n.* 1. the act of defending or state of being defended. 2. protection. 3. vindication by force or argument. 4. the defending side in a contest. 5. a defendant's plea or answer; also, the defendant or his lawyer. **—de·fense'less**, *adj.* **—de·fen'si·ble**, *adj.*

de·fen·sive (di-fen'siv), *adj.* of, marked by, or serving to defend: *n.* a defending position. **—de·fen'sive·ly**, *adv.*

de·fer (di-fūr'), *v.t.* & *v.i.* **-ferred'**, **-fer'ring**, 1. to put off to a future time; delay. 2. to hold off inducting (someone) into the military. **—de·fer'ment**, *n.* **—de·fer'ral**, *n.*

de·fer (di-fūr'), *v.i.* **-ferred'**, **-fer'ring**, to yield respectfully or politely (*to*).

def·er·ence (def'ēr-ĕns), *n.* respectful yielding, or readiness to do so. **—def·er·en'tial**, *adj.* **—def·er·en'tial·ly**, *adv.*

def·er·ent (def'ēr-ĕnt), *adj.* that carries down or out.

de·fi·ance (di-fī'ăns), *n.* 1. the act of defying; bold opposition. 2. a challenge.

de·fi·ant ('ănt), *adj.* marked by defiance; boldly opposing or challenging.

de·fi·cien·cy (di-fish'ĕn-si), *n.* 1. the state of being deficient. 2. *pl.* **-cies**, a specified insufficiency; shortage.

deficiency disease, a disease, as rickets, resulting from faulty nutrition.

de·fi·cient (di-fish'ĕnt), *adj.* marked by lack of something needed for wholeness, completeness, perfection, etc.; falling short, often in a specified way.

def·i·cit (def'i-sit), *n.* a deficiency or shortage, specifically in money received.

def·i·lade (def'i-lād), *v.t.* **-lad·ed**, **-lad·ing**, to lay out, as a fort, for maximum protection from gunfire or other fire coming from various angles.

de·file (di-fīl'), *v.t.* **-filed'**, **-fil'ing**, 1. to make foul, impure, or corrupt. 2. to blacken or tarnish, as a reputation. 3. to dishonor or profane. **—de·file'ment**, *n.*

de·file (di-fīl', dē'fīl), *v.i.* **-filed'**, **-fil'ing**, to march along or off in a file or files: *n.* a long, narrow pass or passage, as in a mountainous region. 2. a marching in file.

de·fine (di-fīn'), *v.t.* **-fined'**, **-fin'ing**, 1. to indicate clearly the limits or outlines of. 2. to determine, show forth, or describe the nature or properties of. 3. to give the meaning or meanings of (a word, phrase, concept, etc.): *v.i.* to define words, phrases, etc. **—de·fin'a·ble**, *adj.* **—de·fin'er**, *n.*

def·i·nite (def'i-nit), *adj.* 1. having fixed or distinct limits. 2. not vague or uncertain; clear; precise; positive. 3. in *Grammar*, pointing out, as the definite article. —def′I-nite-ly, adv.

def·i·ni·tion (def-i-nish′ùn), n. 1. the act of defining or state of being defined. 2. a defining statement or formulation, especially one giving the meaning of a word, phrase, etc. 3. sharpness or clarity, as of a photographic image or of sound reproduction. —def·i·ni′tion·al, adj.

de·fin·i·tive (di-fin′i-tiv), adj. 1. determining or determined with finality; conclusive. 2. indisputably complete, exact, and reliable, as a text. 3. indicating the nature, extent, meaning, etc. of something.

de·la·grate (def′là-grāt), v.i. & v.t. -grat·ed, -grat·ing, to undergo, or cause to undergo, sudden and rapid combustion.

de·flate (di-flāt′), v.t. & v.i. -flat·ed, -flat·ing, 1. to bring or return to an undistended or less distended condition by release of the distending air or gas. 2. to reduce from any inflated condition.

de·fla·tion (-flā′shùn), n. 1. the act of deflating or state of being deflated. 2. reduction in the amount of money being circulated. 3. in Geology, wind erosion.

de·flect (di-flekt′), v.t. & v.i. to turn aside or bend from a straight line; swerve. —de·flec′tion, n. —de·flec′tive, adj. —de·flec′tor, n.

def·lo·ra·tion (def-lō-rā′shùn), n. the act of deflowering.

de·flow·er (di-flou′ẽr), v.t. 1. to deprive of virginity. 2. to despoil of pristine grace or beauty. 3. to deprive of flowers or bloom.

de·fo·li·ant (dē-fō′li-ánt), n. a chemical spray that destroys foliage.

de·fo·li·ate (′li-āt), v.t. -at·ed, -at·ing, 1. to destroy the foliage of. 2. to spray a defoliant on.

de·for·est (dē-fôr′ist), v.t. to clear of forest or trees.

de·form (di-fôrm′), v.t. 1. to spoil or distort the form of. 2. to render ugly.

de·for·ma·tion (dē-fôr-mā′shùn, def-ẽr-), n. a deforming or disfigurement.

de·form·i·ty (di-fôr′mi-ti), n., pl. -ties, 1. the state of being deformed. 2. something deformed, as a physically malformed part. 3. any disfigurement. 4. want of beauty or harmony.

de·fraud (di-frôd′), v.t. to deprive of property, rights, etc. by fraud; cheat.

de·fray (di-frā′), v.t. to provide the money for payment of (expenses, charges, etc.); pay; settle. —de·fray′al, n.

de·frost (di-frôst′), v.t. 1. to remove ice or frost from by thawing. 2. to subject (frozen foods) to thawing: v.i. to become defrosted. —de·frost′er, n.

deft (deft), adj. dexterous; handy; clever. —deft′ly, adv. —deft′ness, n.

de·funct (di-fungkt′), adj. dead; extinct.

de·fuse, de·fuze (dē-fūz′), v.t. -fused′, -fus′ing, to remove the fuse from (a bomb or similar explosive device).

de·fy (di-fī′), v.t. -fied′, -fy′ing, 1. to set at defiance; resist boldly. 2. to challenge (someone) to do something.

de·gen·er·a·cy (di-jen′ẽr-á-si), n. degenerate condition or action.

de·gen·er·ate (′ẽr-it), adj. deteriorated; degraded; depraved: n. one that is degenerate: v.i. -at·ed, -at·ing, 1. to pass to a worse, inferior, or impaired condition. 2. to sink below a previous condition of goodness, normality, etc. —de·gen·er·a′tion, n. —de·gen′er·a·tive, adj.

de·grade (di-grād′), v.t. -grad′ed, -grad′ing, 1. to reduce in grade or rank. 2. to lower physically, morally, etc.; debase. 3. to deprive of honors, dignity, etc. —deg·ra·da·tion (deg-rá-dā′shùn), n.

de·gree (di-grē′), n. 1. a step, grade, or interval. 2. rank or station. 3. relationship between a person and the next in line of descent. 4. rank conferred by a college or university. 5. one of the three degrees in the comparison of an adjective or adverb. 6. a unit of measure equal to the 360th part of the circumference of a circle. 7. a unit of measure on a thermometer or other instrument or scale. 8. the power to which a number is raised. Symbol for senses 6 and 7 (°).

de·gres·sion (di-gresh′ùn), n. a going down; decrease by steps, as in tax rate.

de·hisce (di-his′), v.i. -hisced′, -hisc′ing, to open up, as a seedpod. —de·his′cence, n. —de·his′cent, adj.

de·hu·man·ize (dē-hū′má-nīz), v.t. -ized, -iz·ing, to deprive of human qualities; deprive of pity, tenderness, etc; make inhuman. —de·hu·man·i·za′tion, n.

de·hu·mid·i·fy (dē-hū-mid′i-fī), v.t. -fied, -fy·ing, to rid (air or other gas) of moisture. —de·hu·mid·i·fi·ca′tion, n. —de·hu·mid′i·fi·er, n.

de·hy·drate (dē-hī′drāt), v.t. -drat·ed, -drat·ing, to dry out; remove the water content from (foods, bodily tissues, etc.): v.i. to become dehydrated.

de·i·cide (dē′i-sid), n. 1. the slaying of a god. 2. the slayer of a god.

de·i·fy (dē′i-fī), v.t. -fied, -fy·ing, to make into, or exalt to the rank of, a deity; idolize. —de·i·fi·ca′tion, n.

deign (dān), v.i. & v.t. to condescend or vouchsafe.

de·ism (dē′izm), n. a variety of rationalistic belief holding that God exists but that he remains and has always remained wholly apart from any supernatural intervention in the universe after its creation by him. —de′ist, n.

de·i·ty (dē′i-ti), n., pl. -ties, 1. godhood; divinity. 2. a god or goddess. 3. [D-], God (preceded by the).

de·ject (di-jekt′), v.t. to depress the spirits of; dishearten; sadden. —de·ject′ed, adj. —de·ject′ed·ly, adv.

de·jec·tion (-jek′shùn), 1. lowness of spirits. 2. in Medicine, evacuation.

de ju·re (di joor′i, dā), by legal right or by legal determination.

de·laine (dē-lān′), n. a light textile fabric of wool or of wool and cotton.

de·lay (di-lā′), 1. to postpone. 2. to hinder for a time: v.i. to linger or proceed slowly for a time: n. a delaying.

ô in dragon, ōō in crude, oo in wool, u in cup, ū in cure, ū in turn, ù in focus, oi in boy, ou in house, th in thin, th in sheathe, g in get, j in joy, y in yet.

de·le (dē'lē), *v.t.* -led, -le·ing, to take out (a letter, word, etc.) in proofreading: *n.* a mark to show this.

de·lec·ta·ble (di·lek'tá-bl), *adj.* enjoyable; delightful. —**de·lec·ta·bil'i·ty,** *n.* —**de·lec'ta·bly,** *adv.*

de·lec·ta·tion (dē-lek-tā'shŭn), *n.* delight; pleasure.

del·e·gate (del'ē-gāt), *v.t.* -gat·ed, -gat·ing, 1. to send or appoint as a representative with authority to act. 2. to entrust or commit (authority, power, etc.) to one being thus sent or appointed: *n.* (-gāt, -git), a person delegated.

del·e·ga·tion (del-ē-gā'shŭn), *n.* 1. the act of delegating or condition of being delegated. 2. a delegated person or group.

de·lete (di-lēt), *v.t.* -let'ed, -let'ing, to strike out or remove (a letter, word, etc.) in or as if in proofreading; expunge. —**de·le'tion,** *n.*

del·e·te·ri·ous (del-ē-tir'i-ŭs), *adj.* harmful, morally or physically.

delft·ware (delft'wer), *n.* a glazed earthenware: also **delft, delf** (delf).

de·lib·er·ate (di-lib'ēr-āt), *v.t.* -at·ed, -at·ing, to think upon or consider; weigh in the mind; ponder: *v.i.* to take counsel with oneself or others: *adj.* ('ēr-it), 1. well-considered. 2. circumspect. 3. done or determined with care or leisurely forethought. —**de·lib'er·ate·ly,** *adv.* —**de·lib'er·ate·ness,** *n.*

de·lib·er·a·tion (di-lib-ē-rā'shŭn), *n.* 1. calm and careful consideration. 2. slow, deliberate action, procedure, etc.

de·lib·er·a·tive (-lib'ē-rāt-iv, 'ēr-ā-tiv), *adj.* of or marked by deliberation.

del·i·ca·cy (del'i-kā-si), *n., pl.* -cies, 1. the quality of being delicate; fineness, lightness, daintiness, sensitivity, etc. 2. an especially fine food or dish.

del·i·cate (del'i-kit), *adj.* 1. subtly agreeable or pleasant to the taste or other senses. 2. exquisitely fine, light, dainty, graceful, deft, etc. 3. extremely sensitive or responsive. 4. highly perceptive. 5. most refined. 6. fastidious. 7. not obvious or gross; slight and subtle. 8. highly critical and needing great care. 9. easily disturbed, upset, shocked, etc. 10. ·more than ordinarily susceptible to ailments or disease. 11. easily damaged or hurt; frail; weak. —**del'i·cate·ly,** *adv.*

del·i·ca·tes·sen (del-i-kā-tes'n), *n.* a shop specializing in serving or packing hot and cold meats ready for eating, cheeses, salads, sandwiches, etc.

de·li·cious (di-lish'ŭs), *adj.* highly pleasing to the senses, especially of taste or smell; also, greatly delighting the mind, sensibilities, aesthetic sense, etc.

de·light (di-lit'), *v.t.* to gratify or please greatly: *v.i.* 1. to give great gratification or pleasure. 2. to be greatly gratified or pleased (with *in* or an infinitive): *n.* great gratification or pleasure; joy. —**de·light'ed,** *adj.*

de·light·ful ('fŭl), *adj.* affording delight. —**de·light'ful·ly,** *adv.*

de·lim·it (di-lim'it), *v.t.* to mark out or fix the limits of, as a territory; bound. —**de·lim·i·ta'tion,** *n.*

de·lin·e·ate (di-lin'i-āt), *v.t.* -at·ed, -at·ing, 1. to mark out with lines; outline. 2. to sketch or portray. 3. to describe in words. —**de·lin·e·a'tion,** *n.* —**de·lin'e·a·tor,** *n.*

de·lin·quen·cy (di-ling'kwĕn-si), *n., pl.* -cies, 1. neglect of or failure in duty or observance of law. 2. a debt, tax, etc. that is overdue. 3. a misdeed; fault. 4. behavior violating social codes or the law.

de·lin·quent ('kwĕnt), *adj.* 1. neglecting, or failing in, duty or observance of law. 2. being overdue, as taxes: *n.* one that is delinquent.

del·i·quesce (del-i-kwes'), *v.i.* -quesced', -quesc'ing, 1. to melt away. 2. to liquefy by absorbing moisture from the air. —**del·i·ques'cence,** *n.* —**del·i·ques'cent,** *adj.*

de·lir·i·ous (di-lir'i-ŭs), *adj.* 1. of or typical of delirium. 2. raving; mad. 3. frenzied; frantic. —**de·lir'i·ous·ly,** *adv.*

de·lir·i·um (-ŭm), *n.* wild excitement, mental aberration, and confused babbling, as from fever.

delirium tre·mens (trē'mĕnz), extreme delirium marked especially by terrifying hallucinations and caused chiefly by excessive and long use of alcoholic liquor.

de·liv·er (di-liv'ēr), *v.t.* 1. to set free; save. 2. to yield possession or control of. 3. to send forth; discharge. 4. to express verbally; utter; speak. 5. to distribute. 6. to strike (a blow). 7. to bring to or through birth.

de·liv·er·ance (-ēns), *n.* 1. the act of delivering or state of being delivered; especially, liberation. 2. a formal or public utterance, as by an official.

de·liv·er·y (-i), *n., pl.* -er·ies, 1. the act of delivering or state of being delivered; especially, transfer, surrender, discharge, or distribution. 2. the manner of delivering something, as a speech. 3. something delivered, as goods. 4. a passing through birth or the labor of birth.

dell (del), *n.* a small, secluded valley.

Del·phic (del'fik), *adj.* of the city of Delphi in ancient Greece or its oracle of Apollo: also **Del'phi·an** ('fi-ăn).

del·phin·i·um (del-fin'i-ŭm), *n.* a tall plant with spikes of usually blue flowers.

del·ta (del'tá), *n.* 1. the fourth letter, triangle-shaped, of the Greek alphabet. 2. an alluvial deposit, usually triangular, formed at the mouth of some rivers. —**del·ta'ic** (-tā'ik), *adj.*

del·toid ('toid), *adj.* 1. triangular. 2. denoting or of a large, triangular muscle, in the shoulder joint, serving to raise the arm laterally: *n.* the deltoid muscle.

de·lude (di-lōōd'), *v.t.* -lud'ed, -lud'ing, to impose upon the mind or judgment of; beguile; deceive; trick; fool.

del·uge (del'ūj), *n.* 1. a flood over a large area; inundation; specifically, [D-], in the *Bible,* a great flood in the time of Noah: see *Genesis vii.* 2. an extremely heavy downpour. 3. a delugelike rush of something, as of mail: *v.t.* -uged, -ug·ing, to flood or pour down on heavily.

de·lu·sion (di-lōō'zhŭn), *n.* 1. the act of deluding or state of being deluded. 2. an erroneous, persistent, misleading idea or conviction, often a beguiling one. —de·lu'sion·al, *adj.* —de·lu'sive, *adj.*

de·luxe (di-luks', -looks'), *adj.* fine or finest in quality, style, etc.; altogether elegant; luxurious: *adv.* in a deluxe way.

delve (delv), *v.i.* delved, delv'ing, 1. [Archaic], to dig with a spade. 2. to go deep (*into* books, memories, etc.) in searching out information, ideas, etc.

de·mag·net·ize (dē-mag'nĕ-tīz), *v.t.* -ized, -iz·ing, to make nonmagnetic.

dem·a·gog·ic (dem-ȧ-goj'ik, -gog'ik), *adj.* of or like a demagogue or demagogy: also dem·a·gog'i·cal. —dem·a·gog'i·cal·ly, *adv.*

dem·a·gog·ism (dem'a-gog·izm), *n.* the principles or practices of a demagogue: also dem'a·gogu·ism.

dem·a·gogue (dem'a-gog), *n.* an orator who keeps trying to influence people by playing on their prejudices, possible lack of knowledge, etc.: also dem'a·gog.

dem·a·gog·y (dem'ȧ-gō-ji, -gog-i), *n.* demagogism: also dem'a·gogu·er·y (-gog-ēr-i).

de·mand (di-mand'), *v.t.* 1. to ask for in a peremptory manner. 2. to summon thus. 3. to claim as by right or authority. 4. to necessitate: *v.i.* to demand something: *n.* 1. the act of demanding, or a thing demanded. 2. a peremptory or authoritative claim or request. 3. the state of being much sought after. 4. in *Economics,* desire for and ability to buy something; also, the amount thus effectively desired.

de·mand·ing (ing), *adj.* requiring much time, energy, patience, attention, etc.

de·mar·cate (di-mär'kāt, dē'mär-), *v.t.* -cat·ed, -cat·ing, 1. to define the bounds of. 2. to distinguish. Also de·mark'. —de·mar·ca'tion, de·mar·ka'tion, *n.*

dé·marche (dā-märsh'), *n.* a maneuver.

de·mean (di-mēn'), *v.t.* to debase, lower, or degrade.

de·mean (di-mēn'), *v.t.* to conduct or comport (oneself).

de·mean·or (-ēr), *n.* behavior; deportment.

de·mean·our (di-mēn'ēr), *n.* British form for demeanor.

de·ment·ed (di-men'tid), *adj.* insane.

de·men·tia ('shä), *n.* 1. originally, insanity. 2. in *Psychiatry,* an organically caused loss or impairment of mental powers.

dementia prae·cox (prē'koks), [Obs.], same as schizophrenia.

de·mer·it (di-mer'it), *n.* 1. want of merit; blameworthiness. 2. a mark denoting remissness in proficiency or conduct.

de·mesne (di-mān', -mēn'), *n.* 1. landed estate, often attached to a manor. 2. a region or domain.

De·me·ter (di-mēt'ēr), in *Greek Mythology,* the goddess of agriculture and fertility.

dem·i-, a prefix signifying *half, less than usual* in *size, extent, power,* etc.

dem·i·god (dem'i-god), *n.* 1. an inferior deity. 2. the offspring of a god or goddess and a human being.

dem·i·john (-jon), *n.* a large-bodied, small-necked bottle of glass or earthenware, encased in wicker.

de·mil·i·ta·rize (dē-mil'i-tȧ-rīz), *v.t.* -rized, -riz-ing, 1. to prohibit use of (an area) for military purposes. 2. to rid of military installations. 3. to make nonmilitary, as a government.

dem·i·mon·daine (dem-i-mon-dān'), *n.* a woman of the demimonde.

dem·i·monde (dem'i-mond), *n.* a group or world on the fringes of society, as that of mistresses, prostitutes, etc.

de·mise (di-mīz'), *n.* 1. death. 2. transfer of an estate or title: *v.t.* -mised', -mis'ing, to transfer (an estate or title).

de·mis·sion (di-mish'ŭn), *n.* a demitting.

de·mit (-mit'), *v.t. & v.i.* -mit'ted, -mit'ting, to resign (a position or office).

dem·i·tasse (dem'i-tas, -tās), *n.* a small cup of, or for, black coffee.

dem·i·volt (dem'i-vōlt), *n.* a half turn made by a horse, the forelegs raised.

de·mo·bi·lize (dē-mō'bĭ-līz), *v.t.* -lized, -liz·ing, 1. to disband (troops). 2. to discharge from military service.

de·moc·ra·cy (di-mok'rȧ-si), *n., pl.* -cies, 1. government of themselves by the people collectively, either directly or by elected representatives. 2. a country, state, etc. so governed. 3. rule by the majority. 4. the principle or practice of equality of rights, opportunity, etc.

dem·o·crat (dem'ȯ-krat), *n.* 1. a believer in or practicer of democracy. 2. [D-], a member of the Democratic Party.

dem·o·crat·ic (dem-ȯ-krat'ik), *adj.* 1. of, supporting, or practicing democracy. 2. of or for people in general. 3. [D-], of or characteristic of the Democratic Party. —dem·o·crat'i·cal·ly, *adv.*

Democratic Party, one of the two largest political parties in the U.S.

de·moc·ra·tize (di-mok'rȧ-tīz), *v.t. & v.i.* -tized, -tiz·ing, to make or become democratic.

de·mod·u·late (dē-moj'oo-lāt), *v.t.* -lat·ed, -lat·ing, to subject to demodulation.

de·mod·u·la·tion (-moj-oo-lā'shŭn), *n.* in *Radio,* recovery at the receiver of a modulated signal.

de·mod·u·la·tor (-moj'oo-lāt-ēr), *n.* in *Radio,* a device for demodulating a signal.

de·mog·ra·phy (di-mog'rȧ-fi), *n.* a science dealing with the vital and social conditions of people. —de·mog'ra·pher, *n.* —de·mo·graph·ic (dē-mȯ-graf'ik, dem ȏ), *adj.*

dem·oi·selle (dem-wȧ-zel'), *n.* 1. a young lady. 2. a certain small crane of Africa, Asia, and Europe. 3. any one of a large group of brightly colored dragonflies.

de·mol·ish (di-mol'ish), *v.t.* 1. to pull down, smash apart, or wreck, as a building. 2. to destroy utterly; ruin.

dem·o·li·tion (dem-ȯ-lish'ŭn, dē-mȯ-), *n.* the act of demolishing or condition of being demolished.

de·mon (dē'mȯn), *n.* 1. an evil spirit; devil. 2. a guardian spirit. —de·mon'ic (-mon'ik), *adj.* —de·mon'i·cal·ly, *adv.*

de·mon·e·tize (dē-mon'ĕ-tīz), *v.t.* -tized, -tiz·ing, 1. to deprive (currency) of standard value. 2. to give up use of (silver or gold) as a monetary standard.

de·mo·ni·ac (di-mō'ni-ak), *adj.* of or typical of

ŏ in drag*o*n, ōō in cr*u*de, oo in w*oo*l, u in c*u*p, ū in c*u*re, ŭ in t*u*rn, ů in f*o*cus, oi in b*oy,* ou in h*ou*se, th in *th*in, *th* in shea*th*e, g in get, j in *j*oy, y in *y*et.

a demon; fiendish: also **de·mo·ni·a·cal** (dē-mō-nī'ä-kl): *n.* one possessed by a devil. —**de·mo·ni'a·cal·ly,** *adv.*

de·mon·ism (dē'mŏn-izm), *n.* 1. belief in demons. 2. demonolatry. —**de'mon·ist,** *n.*

de·mon·ol·a·try (dē-mŏ-nŏl'ä-tri), *n.* devil worship. —**de·mon·ol'a·ter,** *n.*

de·mon·ol·o·gy (-ji), *n.* the study of demons or demonism. —**de·mon·ol'o·gist,** *n.*

de·mon·stra·ble (di-mon'strä-bl), *adj.* provable. —**de·mon'stra·bly,** *adv.*

dem·on·strate (dem'ŏn-strāt), *v.t.* -**strat·ed,** -**strat·ing,** 1. to give outward indication or evidence of; show outwardly. 2. to make convincing or plain to the mind or understanding; show as true, incontrovertible, etc., as by reasoning, documentation, or experiment; establish clearly or prove. 3. to make clear the working or nature of by direct presentation or operation: *v.i.* 1. to engage in public display of one's convictions or attitudes, as by picketing. 2. to engage in a show of power or military strength. —**dem·on·stra'tion,** *n.* —**dem'on·stra·tor,** *n.*

de·mon·stra·tive (di-mon'strä-tiv), *adj.* 1. that demonstrates; illustrative, convincing, conclusive, etc. 2. involving demonstration. 3. given to or marked by open display as of feelings. 4. effusive. 5. in *Grammar,* that points out, as *this* is a demonstrative pronoun: *n.* a demonstrative pronoun or adjective.

de·mor·al·ize (di-môr'ä-līz), *v.t.* -**ized,** -**iz·ing,** 1. to affect the morale of adversely; weaken the spirit, energy, etc. of. 2. to throw into confusion.

de·mos (dē'mos), *n.* 1. the people or commonalty of an ancient Greek state. 2. the common people.

de·mote (di-mōt'), *v.t.* -**mot·ed,** -**mot·ing,** to lower in rank. —**de·mo'tion,** *n.*

de·mot·ic (di-mot'ik), *adj.* of or typical of the common people, as colloquialisms.

de·mul·cent (di-mul'snt), *adj.* softening; lenitive: *n.* a demulcent medication.

de·mur (di-mûr'), *v.i.* -**murred,** -**mur'ring,** 1. to refuse assent or agreement because of doubts, uneasiness, etc. felt and indicated. 2. in *Law,* to enter a demurrer: *n.* 1. the act of demurring, or an instance of this. 2. an objection, misgiving, etc. indicated in demurring. Also **de·mur'ral,** *n.*

de·mure (di-mûr'), *adj.* modest, reserved, or decorous, sometimes affectedly so.

de·mur·rage (di-mûr'ij), *n.* 1. delay, as of a ship, occasioned as by a freighter's failure to load, unload, etc. within the time stipulated. 2. the compensation paid.

de·mur·rer ('ẽr), *n.* 1. one that demurs. 2. same as *demur* (sense 2). 3. in *Law,* a plea that even if the facts of the opposition are true they do not constitute a good cause of action or defense.

de·my (di-mī'), *n., pl.* -**mies',** any one of certain sizes of writing or printing paper, about 15 by 20 to 18 by 23 inches.

den (den), *n.* 1. a cave or other lair, as of a wild beast; hidden, often squalid place. 2. a secluded place, as for study.

de·nar·i·us (di-ner'i-ŭs), *n., pl.* -**i·i** (-i-ī), an ancient Roman silver or gold coin.

den·a·ry (den'ẽr-i, dē'nẽr-i), *adj.* decimal; containing 10; tenfold.

de·na·tion·al·ize (dē-nash'ä-nl-īz), *v.t.* -**ized,** -**iz·ing,** 1. to deprive of national rights or character. 2. to make private, rather than governmental, in ownership.

de·nat·u·ral·ize (dē-nach'ẽr-ä-līz), *v.t.* -**ized,** -**iz·ing,** 1. to make unnatural. 2. to deprive of citizenship.

de·na·ture (dē-nā'chẽr), *v.t.* -**tured,** -**tur·ing,** to deprive of natural qualities; change; alter; specifically, to render unfit for eating or drinking without taking away usefulness for other purposes.

den·drite (den'drīt), *n.* 1. a stone or mineral with a treelike marking; also, the marking. 2. a nerve-cell part carrying impulses toward the cell body. —**den·drit·ic** (den-drit'ik), *adj.*

den·droid ('droid), *adj.* looking treelike.

den·drol·o·gy (den-drol'ō-ji), *n.* the scientific study of trees.

den·gue (deng'gē, 'gä), *n.* an infectious tropical disease marked by fever, bone pain, and rash: mosquitoes transmit it.

de·ni·al (di-nī'äl), *n.* 1. the act of denying; refusal; contradiction. 2. a disowning; repudiation.

de·nier (den'yẽr), *n.* a unit of weight for measuring thread fineness, as of silk.

de·ni·er (di-nī'ẽr), *n.* one that denies.

den·i·grate (den'i-grāt), *v.t.* -**grat·ed,** -**grat·ing,** to sully or defame.

den·im (den'im), *n.* a strong, twilled, coarse cotton fabric used as for overalls.

den·i·zen (den'i-zĕn), *n.* 1. an inhabitant. 2. one that frequents a certain place. 3. one that is naturalized.

de·nom·i·nate (di-nom'i-nāt), *v.t.* -**nat·ed,** -**nat·ing,** to name; call: *adj.* (-nit), designating a number qualifying specified units.

de·nom·i·na·tion (di-nom-i-nā'shŭn), *n.* 1. the act of denominating. 2. a name. 3. a class or kind with a particular name or value. 4. a religious body or sect with its own particular name.

de·nom·i·na·tion·al (-l), *adj.* of or controlled by a religious denomination.

de·nom·i·na·tion·al·ism (-izm), *n.* 1. denominational policy or practice. 2. adherence to or support of these. 3. division into religious denominations.

de·nom·i·na·tive (di-nom'i-nä-tiv, -nāt-iv), *adj.* 1. that denominates. 2. in *Grammar,* formed from a noun or adjective: *n.* a denominative word.

de·nom·i·na·tor (-nāt-ẽr), *n.* 1. a characteristic of the members of a group. 2. in *Mathematics,* the term below or right of the line in a fraction.

de·no·ta·tion (dē-nō-tā'shŭn), *n.* 1. the act of denoting. 2. the exact meaning of a term, as opposed to what the term connotes. 3. an indication; sign. —**de·no·ta·tive** (dē'nō-tāt-iv, di-nōt'ä-tiv), *adj.*

de·note (di-nōt'), *v.t.* -**not·ed,** -**not·ing,** 1. to indicate; betoken. 2. to express by way of exact meaning rather than by connotation; mean strictly.

---

de·noue·ment, dé·noue·ment (dā-nōō′mŏn, -nōō-môn′), n. [French], 1. the unraveling or outcome of the plot in a play, novel, etc. 2. any final outcome.

de·nounce (di-nouns′), v.t. -nounced′, -nounc′-ing, 1. to accuse publicly or to one or more authorities; also, to inform against or stigmatize thus as being a criminal, culprit, etc. 2. to censure strongly as being evil, vicious, corrupt, etc. 3. to make formally known the termination of (a treaty or similar agreement). —de·nounce′ment, n. —de·nounc′er, n.

dense (dens), adj. dens′er, dens′est, 1. crowded or packed tight; compact. 2. so thick, heavy, etc. as to be hard to penetrate as by light rays or sight. 3. slow-witted; dull or stupid. 4. in Photography, marked by an opacity giving good contrast in light and shade. —dense′ly, adv. —dense′ness, n.

den·si·ty (den′si-ti), n., pl. -ties, 1. the quality or condition of being dense. 2. mass or number per unit as of area.

dent (dent), n. a slight depression caused by a blow or pressure: v.t. to make a dent in: v.i. to become dented.

den·tal (den′tl), adj. 1. of or pertaining to the teeth or dentistry. 2. in Phonetics, articulated with the tongue tip at or close to the upper front teeth: n. in Phonetics, a dental consonant. —den′tal·ly, adv.

den·tate (den′tāt), adj. having teeth or projections suggestive of these.

den·tic·u·late (den-tik′yoo-lit, -lāt), adj. 1. having small teeth or toothlike projections. 2. having dentils.

den·ti·form (den′ti-fôrm), adj. tooth-shaped.

den·ti·frice (-fris), n. any preparation designed for cleaning the teeth.

den·til (den′til), n. in Architecture, a small, rectangular, projecting block in a series of these, as along cornices.

den·tin (den′tin), n. hard, dense, calcareous tissue, under the enamel, forming the body of a tooth: also den′tine (-tēn, -tin).

den·tist (den′tist), n. a professional specialist in the care and treatment of the teeth and surrounding tissues.

den·tist·ry (-tri), n. a dentist's work.

den·ti·tion (den-tish′ŭn), n. 1. the process or period of cutting the teeth. 2. arrangement, kind, and number of teeth.

den·toid (den′toid), adj. tooth-shaped.

den·ture (den′chĕr), n. a set of teeth, especially artificial.

de·nu·cle·ar·ize (dē-nōō′kli-â-rīz), v.t. -ized, -iz-ing, to keep (an area or nation) from having nuclear weapons.

de·nu·date (di-nōō′dāt, den′yoo-dāt), v.t. -dat-ed, -dat-ing, to denude. —de·nu·da·tion (dē-nōō-dā′shŭn, den-yoo-), n.

de·nude (di-nōōd′), v.t. -nud′ed, -nud′ing, 1. to make bare or naked. 2. to destroy all life in (an area). 3. in Geology, to lay bare as by erosion.

de·nun·ci·ate (di-nun′si-āt), v.t. -at-ed, -at-ing, same as denounce. —de·nun·ci·a′tion, n. —de·nun′ci·a·tor, n.

de·ny (di-nī′), v.t. -nied′, -ny′ing, 1. to declare

(a statement) to be false; reject as untrue, invalid, etc.; contradict. 2. to refuse acceptance or acknowledgment of; repudiate. 3. to refuse to yield to, to refuse to answer favorably, etc. 4. to refuse to grant.

de·o·dar (dē′ō-där), n. 1. a cedar of the Himalayas, with durable, light-red wood. 2. the wood of this cedar.

de·o·dor·ant (dē-ō′dĕr-ânt), adj. masking, checking, or obliterating unwanted odors: n. a deodorant agent, as a spray.

de·o·dor·ize ('dō-rīz), v.t. -ized, -iz-ing, to counteract unwanted odors in or on. —de·o′dor·iz-er, n.

de·on·tol·o·gy (dē-on-tol′ō-ji), n. the theory or study of moral obligation; ethics of duty.

de·ox·i·dize (di-ok′si-dīz), v.t. -dized, -diz-ing, to remove oxygen from.

de·ox·y·ri·bo·nu·cle·ic acid (di-ok′si-rī-bō-nōō-klē′ik), an essential chromosomal material that transmits the hereditary pattern.

de·part (di-pärt′), v.i. 1. to go or move away. 2. to start out, as on a journey; leave. 3. to go aside or deviate (from a practice, custom, etc.). 4. to die.

de·part·ed (-id), adj. 1. gone; past. 2. dead.

de·part·ment (di-pärt′mĕnt), n. 1. a branch or division, as of a government or school. 2. a section, especially in a department store, featuring a particular line of goods or services. 3. a particular area of knowledge or activity. 4. an administrative district, as in France.

de·part·men·tal (di-pärt-men′tl, dē-), adj. of, pertaining to, or divided into departments. —de·part·men′tal·ly, adv.

de·part·men·tal·ize ('tâ-līz), v.t. -ized, -iz-ing, to organize or divide into departments. —de·part·men·tal·i·za′tion, n.

department store, a large retail store offering many kinds of goods and services and divided into departments.

de·par·ture (di-pär′chĕr), n. 1. the act of departing. 2. [Archaic], death.

de·pend (di-pend′), v.i. 1. to be controlled, as to happening, existing, being achieved, changing, etc., by circumstances, developments, or other conditions; be contingent. 2. to have firm confidence in the quality, performance, etc. of someone or something specified (with on). 3. to rely for help, support, needs, etc.

de·pend·a·ble (di-pen′dâ-bl), adj. deserving firm confidence; capable of being trusted; reliable. —de·pend·a·bil′i·ty, n.

de·pend·ence ('dĕns), n. the state or fact of being dependent: also de·pend·ance.

de·pend·en·cy ('dĕn-si), n., pl. -cies, 1. same as dependence. 2. a thing dependent or subordinate. 3. a trust territory or other area similarly controlled by a country.

de·pend·ent ('dĕnt), adj. 1. hanging down. 2. contingent; conditional. 3. depending for help, support, etc. 4. subordinate: n. one dependent upon another. Also, especially for n., de·pend′ant.

de·pict (di-pikt′), v.t. to make a pictorial or verbal representation of; portray or describe. —de·pic′tion, n.

dep·i·late (dep'î-lāt), v.t. -lat·ed, -lat·ing, to rid (a bodily part) of hair.

de·pil·a·to·ry (di-pil'ā-tôr-i), adj. that removes hair: n., pl. -ries, a depilatory agent, as a cream.

de·plane (dē-plān'), v.i. -planed', -plan'ing, to disembark from a plane.

de·plete (di-plēt'), v.t. -plet'ed, -plet'ing, to lessen, exhaust, or empty by using up the supply. —de·ple'tion, n.

de·plor·a·ble (di-plôr'ā-bl), adj. that is to be deplored; regrettable; sad.

de·plore (di-plôr'), v.t. -plored', -plor'ing, 1. to view with sorrow, unhappiness, or regret. 2. to grieve over; lament.

de·ploy (di-ploi'), v.t. & v.i. in military strategy, to extend or position, as troops, or be extended or positioned, so as to achieve a planned objective, as of presenting a wider front. —de·ploy'ment, n.

de·po·lar·ize (dē-pō'lā-rīz), v.t. -ized, -iz·ing, to deprive of polarity or polarization. —de·po·lar·i·za'tion, n.

de·po·nent (di-pō'nênt), adj. denoting a Latin or Greek verb with a passive form but an active meaning: n. 1. a deponent verb. 2. in Law, one making an affidavit.

de·pop·u·late (dē-pop'yŭ-lāt), v.t. -lat·ed, -lat·ing, to lessen the number of inhabitants in, as through devastation.

de·port (di-pôrt'), v.t. 1. to comport (oneself). 2. to expel (an alien). —de·por·ta'tion (dē-pôr·tā'shŭn), n.

de·port·ment ('mênt), n. comportment.

de·pose (di-pōz'), v.t. -posed', -pos'ing, 1. to remove from a throne or other high station; deprive of office. 2. in Law, to state under oath but not in open court: v.i. in Law, to make such a statement.

de·pos·it (di-poz'it), v.t. 1. to put or set down; place. 2. to form a layer of, as sediment. 3. to entrust to another for security; specifically, to put (money) in a bank. 4. to hand over, as in making the first of several payments: n. 1. the act of depositing. 2. anything deposited.

de·pos·i·tar·y ('i-ter-i), n., pl. -tar·ies, 1. one entrusted with something for security. 2. same as depository.

dep·o·si·tion (dep·ō-zish'ŭn, dē-pō-), n. 1. the act of deposing or condition of being deposed. 2. the act of depositing or condition of being deposited. 3. anything deposed or deposited.

de·pos·i·tor (di-poz'î-tēr), n. one that deposits, especially money in a bank.

de·pos·i·to·ry ('i-tôr-i), n., pl. -ries, 1. a place where something is deposited for security. 2. same as depositary.

de·pot (dē'pō, dep'ō), n. 1. a warehouse. 2. a railroad station or bus terminal. 3. a place where military supplies are stored. 4. a military station for assembling recruits or assigning combat replacements.

dep·ra·va·tion (dep·rā-vā'shŭn), n. 1. the act of depraving or becoming depraved. 2. depraved condition; depravity.

de·prave (di-prāv'), v.t. -praved', -prav'ing, to cause to be morally corrupt, vicious, or perverted. —de·praved', adj.

de·prav·i·ty (-prav'î-ti), n. 1. moral corruption. 2. pl. -ties, a depraved act.

dep·re·cate (dep'rē-kāt), v.t. -cat·ed, -cat·ing, 1. to express disapproval of. 2. to disparage. —dep·re·ca'tion, n.

dep·re·cat·ing (-ing), adj. deprecatory.

dep·re·ca·to·ry (dep'rē-kā-tôr-i), adj. 1. that deprecates. 2. apologetic.

de·pre·ci·ate (di-prē'shi-āt), v.t. -at·ed, -at·ing, 1. to lower the value or price of. 2. to disparage: v.i. to fall in value or price. —de·pre·ci·a'tion, n.

dep·re·da·tion (dep·rē-dā'shŭn), n. the act of plundering or laying waste.

de·press (di-pres'), v.t. 1. to press or push down. 2. to lower the spirits of; dispirit; sadden. 3. to make less active, energetic, etc. 4. to make go down in value, amount, etc. —de·press'ing, adj.

de·press·ant (-ănt), adj. that depresses; specifically, lowering functional activity or vital force: n. something depressant.

de·pressed (di-prest'), adj. 1. undergoing or having undergone the act of depressing; pressed down, lowered, dejected, etc. 2. flattened, dented, etc., or appearing so. 3. marked by economic depression.

de·pres·sion (-presh'ŭn), n. 1. the act of depressing or condition of being depressed. 2. a hollow, dent, etc.; depressed area or spot. 3. low spirits; dejection. 4. a period of grave economic stagnation.

de·pres·sive (-pres'iv), adj. of, producing, or marked by depression.

de·pres·sor (-pres'ēr), n. 1. one that depresses. 2. a muscle drawing down a bodily part.

de·prive (di-prīv'), v.t. -prived', -priv'ing, 1. to take something away from. 2. to debar from having, using, or enjoying something. 3. to depose from office. —dep·ri·va·tion (dep·rî-vā'shŭn), n.

depth (depth), n. 1. the state or degree of being deep. 2. usually pl. the part or parts that are deep or deepest.

dep·u·ta·tion (dep-yoo-tā'shŭn), n. 1. the act of deputing. 2. a delegation.

de·pute (di-pūt'), v.t. -put'ed, -put'ing, to delegate.

dep·u·tize (dep'yŭ-tīz), v.t. & v.i. -tized, -tiz·ing, to delegate or act as delegate.

dep·u·ty (dep'yŭ-ti), n. -ties, a delegate.

de·rail (di-rāl'), v.i. & v.t. to go, or make go, off the rails, as a train.

de·rail·leur (di-rā'lēr), n. a gearshifting mechanism on a bicycle for controlling its speed.

de·range (di-rānj'), v.t. -ranged', -rang'ing, 1. to throw into confusion or disorder, or upset the normal functioning of. 2. to drive insane. —de·range'ment, n.

Der·by (dûr'bi; British, där'bi), n., pl. -bies, 1. a race for three-year-old horses, run annually at Epsom Downs in Surrey, near London; also, any similar horse race. 2. [d-], a kind of stiff felt hat with round crown and curved brim.

der·e·lict (der'ē-likt), adj. 1. abandoned; deserted. 2. neglectful; remiss: n. 1. something abandoned, especially a ship deserted at sea. 2. a homeless, jobless, totally impoverished social outcast.

der·e·lic·tion (der-ĕ-lik'shŭn), *n.* 1. the state of being derelict, or an instance of this. 2. the act of abandoning or forsaking.

de·ride (di-rīd'), *v.t.* -rid'ed, -rid'ing, to make contemptuous fun of; mock. —**de·ri'sion** (-rizh'ŭn), *n.* —**de·ri'sive** (-rī'siv), *adj.*

der·i·va·tion (der-i-vā'shŭn), *n.* 1. the act of deriving or condition of being derived. 2. something derived. 3. a source, as of a word.

de·riv·a·tive (dĕ-riv'ă-tiv), *adj.* 1. derived. 2. taken from elsewhere instead of being original; borrowed or secondary: *n.* 1. something derived, as a word. 2. in *Mathematics*, the instantaneous rate of change of one variable with respect to another.

de·rive (di-rīv'), *v.t.* -rived', -riv'ing, 1. to get from a source. 2. to deduce or infer. 3. to trace, as a word, back to or from the source: *v.i.* to be derived.

der·ma (dûr'mă), *n.* same as **dermis.** —**der'mal,** **der'mic,** *adj.*

der·ma (dûr'mă), *n.* beef casing stuffed with seasoned bread crumbs, onion, etc. and roasted.

der·ma·bra·sion (dûr-mă-brā'zhŭn), *n.* the surgical procedure of scraping off the upper layers of the skin in order to remove scars.

der·ma·ti·tis (dûr-mă-tīt'is), *n.* inflammation of the skin.

der·ma·tol·o·gy (-tol'ŏ-ji), *n.* the science treating of the skin and its diseases. —**der·ma·tol'o·gist,** *n.*

der·mis (dûr'mis), *n.* the layer of skin beneath the epidermis.

der·o·gate (der'ŏ-gāt), *v.i.* -gat·ed, -gat·ing, to take something away; detract. —**der·o·ga'·tion,** *n.*

de·rog·a·to·ry (di-rog'ă-tôr-i), *adj.* 1. that detracts. 2. disparaging.

der·rick (der'ik), *n.* 1. a large, pivoted apparatus for hoisting heavy weights. 2. a towerlike supportive structure for machinery, tackle, etc., as over an oil well.

der·ri·ère (der-i-er'), *n.* the buttocks.

der·ring-do (der'ing-dōō'), *n.* recklessly courageous deeds or boldness.

der·rin·ger (der'in-jĕr), *n.* a pocket pistol with a short barrel of large caliber.

der·vish (dûr'vish), *n.* a member of any one of various Moslem orders of ascetics.

de·sal·i·nate (dē·sal'i-nāt), *v.t.* -nat·ed, -nat·ing, to remove salt from, as in making sea water drinkable: also **de·sal'i·nize.** —**de·sal·i·na'tion,** *n.*

des·cant (des'kant), *n.* 1. two-part singing combining a main melodic line and a subordinate upper one. 2. the subordinate melody. 3. in *Polyphony,* the highest voice. 4. a varied song or melody. 5. a commentary or disquisition: *v.i.* (also des-kant'), 1. to sing; sing or play a descant. 2. to engage in commentary or disquisition.

de·scend (di-send'), *v.i.* 1. to pass from a higher to a lower position. 2. to pass from more to less, from the general to the specific, etc. 3. to derive. 4. to come as an inheritance. 5. to demean oneself (with *to*). 6. to attack or invade (with *on, upon*). 7. in

Astronomy, to move toward the south or horizon: *v.t.* to go down or down along.

de·scend·ant ('ănt), *n.* one in any degree related to or connected with some indicated ancestor, group, etc.: *adj.* that descends: also **de·scend'ent.**

de·scent (di-sent'), *n.* 1. the act of descending. 2. derivation from an ancestor, group, etc.; lineage. 3. a downward slope, way, or passage.

de·scribe (di-skrīb'), *v.t.* -scribed', -scrib'ing, 1. to set forth verbally; narrate. 2. to delineate.

de·scrip·tion (di-skrip'shŭn), *n.* 1. the act of describing; narration or delineation. 2. a descriptive phrase, paragraph, etc. 3. a given set of characteristics; variety.

de·scrip·tive ('tiv), *adj.* describing.

de·scry (di-skrī'), *v.t.* -scried', -scry'ing, 1. to discover visually, as a distant object. 2. to manage to detect.

des·e·crate (des'ĕ-krāt), *v.t.* -crat·ed, -crat·ing, to violate the sacredness or venerability of. —**des'e·crat·er,** **des'e·cra·tor,** *n.* —**des·e·cra'·tion,** *n.*

de·seg·re·gate (dē-seg'rĕ-gāt), *v.i.* & *v.t.* -gat·ed, -gat·ing, to end racial segregation (in).

de·sen·si·tize (dē-sen'si-tīz), *v.t.* -tized, -tiz·ing, to remove or lessen the sensitivity of.

de·sert (di-zûrt'), *v.t.* 1. to forsake or abandon. 2. to depart from (one's post, military service, etc.) without permission: *v.i.* to depart from one's post, military duty, etc. without intending to return or seeking to avoid danger.

des·ert (dez'ĕrt), *n.* 1. a barren tract incapable of supporting most life or vegetation. 2. a wilderness: *adj.* of, pertaining to, or like a desert.

de·sert (di-zûrt'), *n., often pl.* a reward or punishment deserved; merit.

de·serve (di-zûrv'), *v.t.* & *v.i.* -served', -serv'ing, to be entitled (to) or worthy (of); merit (something).

de·served (-zûrvd'), *adj.* merited; earned; just. —**de·serv'ed·ly** (-zûr'vid-li), *adv.*

de·serv·ing (-zûr'ving), *adj.* meritorious; worthy: *n.* desert; merit.

des·ic·cant (des'i-kănt), *adj.* that desiccates: *n.* a desiccating agent.

des·ic·cate (-kāt), *v.t.* & *v.i.* -cat·ed, -cat·ing, to dry through and through. —**des·ic·ca'tion,** *n.* —**des'ic·ca·tive,** *adj.* & *n.*

des·ic·ca·tor (-ĕr), *n.* a device for desiccating, as in preserving foods.

de·sid·er·ate (di-sid'ĕ-rāt), *v.t.* -at·ed, -at·ing, to feel need of and desire to have. —**de·sid'er·a·tive,** *adj.*

de·sid·er·a·tum (-sid-ĕ-rāt'ŭm), *n., pl.* -ta (-'ă), something desiderated.

de·sign (di-zīn'), *v.t.* 1. to originate and sketch out the plan, pattern, etc. of. 2. to plan out; project. 3. to plan and produce or effect accordingly. 4. to work up or contrive, as plans. 5. to have in mind or intention; purpose. 6. to produce or effect toward a given objective: *v.i.* 1. to design things. 2. to work as a designer: *n.* 1. something designed; plan, pattern, etc.; also, the art of designing things. 2. purpose; intention. 3. *pl.* an underhanded scheme.

des·ig·nate (dez'ig-nāt), *v.t.* **-nat·ed, -nat·ing,** 1. to point out; indicate; specify. 2. to distinguish or characterize as by a certain name or title. 3. to name as being chosen for a particular office or responsibility: *adj.* (also -nit), appointed to, but not yet functioning in, a given office or responsibility. **—des'ig·na·tor,** *n.*

des·ig·na·tion (dez-ig-nā'shŭn), *n.* 1. the act of designating or condition of being designated. 2. appointment, as to an office. 3. a name, title, etc. used to specify someone or something.

de·sign·ed·ly (di-zīn'id-li), *adv.* by intention; on purpose; purposely.

de·sign·er (di-zīn'ẽr), *n.* one that designs; specifically, a person whose work is the designing of patterns, models, etc.

de·sign·ing ('ing), *adj.* scheming; artful.

de·sir·a·ble (di-zīr'á-bl), *adj.* pleasing; agreeable. **—de·sir·a·bil'i·ty,** *n.*

de·sire (di-zīr'), *v.t.* 1. to wish earnestly for; crave. 2. to request: *v.i.* to wish or crave something: *n.* 1. a longing to have something. 2. sexual craving. 3. a request. 4. the object desired.

de·sir·ous ('ŭs), *adj.* that desires.

de·sist (di-zist'), *v.i.* to cease; abstain.

desk (desk), *n.* a tablelike piece of furniture, used for writing on, paper work, etc.

des·o·late (des'ō-lit), *adj.* 1. solitary. 2. deserted. 3. laid waste. 4. miserable: *v.t.* (-lāt), **-lat·ed, -lat·ing,** to make desolate.

des·o·la·tion (des-ō-lā'shŭn), *n.* 1. the act of desolating or condition of being desolated. 2. a desolate place.

de·spair (di-sper'), *v.i.* to abandon all hope or expectation: *n.* 1. loss of hope or expectation. 2. a cause of despair.

des·patch (di-spach'), *v.t. & n.* same as dispatch.

des·per·a·do (des-pē-rä'dō, -rā'dō), *n., pl.* **-does, -dos,** a dangerous, lawless person; recklessly bold criminal.

des·per·ate (des'pēr-it), *adj.* 1. dangerously rash or violent and disregarding consequences. 2. extreme, drastic, frantic, etc., as from despair. 3. so serious, critical, or overwhelming as to lead to despair. 4. marked by extreme need.

des·per·a·tion (des-pē-rā'shŭn), *n.* 1. desperate condition. 2. reckless despair.

des·pi·ca·ble (des'pik-á-bl, di-spik'á-), *adj.* contemptible. **—des'pi·ca·bly,** *adv.*

de·spise (di-spiz'), *v.t.* **-spised·, -spis·ing,** 1. to look down upon with scorn or contempt. 2. to dislike greatly.

de·spite (di-spit'), *n.* 1. an act of contempt; insult. 2. malice; spite: *prep.* notwithstanding.

de·spite·ful ('fŭl), *adj.* malicious.

de·spoil (di-spoil'), *v.t.* to rob; deprive.

de·spo·li·a·tion (di-spō-li-ā'shŭn), *n.* a despoiling or being despoiled.

de·spond (di-spond'), *v.i.* to be cast down in spirits: *n.* despondency.

de·spond·en·cy (di-spon'dĕn-si), *n.* absence of hope or courage; great mental depression: also **de·spond'ence.**

de·spond·ent ('dĕnt), *adj.* dejected.

des·pot (des'pŏt), *n.* an absolute ruler; autocrat; tyrant. **—des'pot·ism,** *n.*

des·pot·ic (de-spot'ik), *adj.* of or like a despot; tyrannical: also **des·pot'i·cal. —des·pot'i·cal·ly,** *adv.*

des·sert (di-zûrt'), *n.* a sweet course, as cake, to top off lunch or dinner.

des·ti·na·tion (des-ti-nā'shŭn), *n.* 1. the final end set for a person or thing. 2. the place, specifically the final one, someone or something is going to or being sent to.

des·tine (des'tin), *v.t.* **-tined, -tin·ing,** 1. to predetermine; fix inalterably. 2. to appoint to a specific use or purpose.

des·tin·y (des'ti·ni), *n., pl.* **-tin·ies,** 1. predetermined lot; fate; inevitable necessity. 2. the cause of this.

des·ti·tute (des'ti-tōōt), *adj.* 1. devoid. 2. lacking means of existence; totally impoverished; penniless.

des·ti·tu·tion (des-ti-tōō'shŭn), *n.* destitute condition; great poverty; want.

de·stroy (di-stroi'), *v.t.* 1. to pull, break, or smash into pieces; wreck; ruin. 2. to defeat completely; crush. 3. to put an end to; put out of existence; annihilate. 4. to kill. 5. to counteract or check decisively; make totally useless.

de·stroy·er ('ẽr), *n.* 1. one that destroys. 2. a small, high-speed warship.

de·struct (di-strukt', dē'strukt), *n.* intentional destruction, after launch, of a poorly functioning rocket, missile, etc.: *v.i.* to be automatically destroyed.

de·struct·i·ble (di-struk'ti-bl), *adj.* that can be destroyed.

de·struc·tion ('shŭn), *n.* 1. the act of destroying or condition of being destroyed. 2. a cause or means of this.

de·struc·tive ('tiv), *adj.* 1. tending to or causing destruction. 2. completely negative and unhelpful, as some criticism; not constructive. **—de·struc'tive·ly,** *adv.*

des·ue·tude (des'wi-tōōd), *n.* disuse.

des·ul·to·ry (des'l-tōr-i), *adj.* 1. passing from one thing to another without order or method; cursory; erratic. 2. random.

de·tach (di-tach'), *v.t.* 1. to separate and remove; disconnect. 2. to put, as troops, on a special mission. **—de·tach'a·ble,** *adj.*

de·tached (-tacht'), *adj.* indifferent and emotionally uninvolved; objective.

de·tach·ment (-tach'mĕnt), *n.* 1. separation; disconnection. 2. a detaching, as of troops, for a mission; also, a unit so detached. 3. detached condition, attitude, or quality.

de·tail (di-tāl', dē'tāl), *v.t.* 1. to give the particulars of. 2. to select for a particular task: *n.* 1. a point or item forming part of the totality of something; particular; often, a less obvious or minute particular, or one of little or no importance. 2. any such points, items, or particulars collectively; also, enumeration of or attention to these. 3. a small section or part of a painting, statue, building, etc., specifically as reproduced from the whole. 4. such sections or parts collectively. 5. one or more soldiers, sailors, etc. selected for a particular task; also, the task itself.

---

a in cap, ā in cane, ä in father, á in abet, e in met, ē in be, ẽ in baker, ế in regent, i in pit, ī in fine, i in manifest, o in hot, ô in horse, ō in bone,

de-tailed (di-tāld', dē'tāld), *adj.* full of detail; presenting much detail; thorough.

de-tain (di-tān'), *v.t.* 1. to hold in custody. 2. to keep from proceeding; hold back; delay. —de-tain'ment, *n.*

de-tect (di-tekt'), *v.t.* 1. to succeed in discovering, finding out, or noticing (something elusive, obscure, etc.). 2. in *Radio*, to demodulate. —de-tect'a-ble, de-tect'i-ble, *adj.* —de-tec'tion, *n.*

de-tec-tive (-tek'tiv), *n.* a person whose work is the investigation of crimes or of other unlawful or illicit acts or activities, tracing suspects, etc.

de-tec-tor ('tēr), *n.* 1. one that detects. 2. in *Radio*, a demodulating device.

de-tent (di-tent', dē'tent), *n.* a pin, stud, etc. that releases or stops a movement, as in a clock.

de-tente, de-tente (dā-tänt'), *n.* a relaxation of strained or difficult relations, especially between nations.

de-ten-tion (di-ten'shŭn), *n.* the act of detaining or condition of being detained.

detention home, a place where juvenile offenders are confined.

de-ter (di-tûr'), *v.t.* -terred', -ter'ring, to keep from doing something by arousing fear, doubt, etc. in. —de-ter'ment, *n.*

de-terge (-tûrj'), *v.t.* -terged', -terg'ing, to cleanse, as a wound.

de-ter-gent (-tûr'jĕnt), *adj.* cleansing: *n.* a cleansing chemical preparation that is soaplike but not made from fats and lye.

de-te-ri-o-rate (di-tir'i-ō-rāt), *v.t. & v.i.* -rat-ed, -rat-ing, to make or become worse. —de-te-ri-o-ra'tion, *n.*

de-ter-mi-na-ble (di-tûr'mi-nȧ-bl), *adj.* 1. capable of being determined. 2. terminable. —de-ter'mi-na-bly, *adv.*

de-ter-mi-nant (-nȧnt), *adj.* that determines: *n.* that which determines.

de-ter-mi-nate (-nit), *adj.* 1. having fixed limits; clearly defined. 2. conclusive.

de-ter-mi-na-tion (di-tûr-mi-nā'shŭn), *n.* 1. the act of determining or state of being determined. 2. firm resolution.

de-ter-mi-na-tive (-tûr'mi-nȧt-iv, -nȧ-tiv), *adj. & n.* same as **determinant**.

de-ter-mine (di-tûr'min), *v.t.* -mined, -min-ing, 1. to fix the bounds of. 2. to settle decisively. 3. to decide or decide upon. 4. to fix the nature or kind of. 5. to calculate exactly. 6. to give a particular shape or direction to: *v.i.* to decide.

de-ter-mined (-mīnd), *adj.* resolute; fixed.

de-ter-min-ism ('mi-nizm), *n.* the doctrine that choice and all else is predetermined.

de-ter-rent (di-tûr'ĕnt), *adj.* deterring: *n.* that which deters. —de-ter'rence, *n.*

de-test (di-test'), *v.t.* to dislike intensely; loathe; hate. —de-test'a-ble, *adj.* —de-tes-ta-tion** (dē-tes-tā'shŭn), *n.*

de-throne (dē-thrōn'), *v.t.* -throned', -thron'ing, to remove from or as from a throne. —de-throne'ment, *n.*

det-o-nate (det'n-āt), *v.i. & v.t.* -nat-ed, -nat-ing, to explode, as dynamite. —det-o-na'tion, *n.* —det'o-na-tor, *n.*

de-tour (dē'toor, di-toor'), *n.* 1. a circuitous

way. 2. a road, way, etc. used instead of the usual one: *v.i. & v.t.* to use or make use a detour.

de-tox (dē-toks', dē'toks), [Informal]. *v.t.* same as **detoxify**: *n.* same as **detoxification**.

de-tox-i-fy (dē-tok'si-fī), *v.t.* -fied, -fy-ing, to remove a poison or poisonous effect from. —de-tox-i-fi-ca'tion, *n.*

de-tract (di-trakt'), *v.t. & v.i.* to draw or take (something) away.

de-trac-tion (-trak'shŭn), *n.* a malicious discrediting of someone; defamation.

de-trac-tor (-tēr), *n.* one practicing or given to detraction.

de-train (dē-trān'), *v.t. & v.i.* to remove or alight from a railroad train.

det-ri-ment (det'ri-mĕnt), *n.* damage; harm. —det-ri-men'tal** (-men'tl), *adj.*

de-tri-tus (di-trīt'ŭs), *n.* 1. rock fragments, as from friction. 2. any debris. —de-tri'tal (-l), *adj.*

de trop (de trō), [French], superfluous.

de-trun-cate (-trung'kāt), *v.t.* -cat-ed, -cat-ing, to lop off a part of.

deuce (dōōs, dūs), *n.* 1. a playing card with two spots; also, a two-spot die, or a throw equalling two. 2. in *Tennis*, a score of 40 each or of 5 games each.

deuce (dōōs, dūs), *n. & interj.* the devil: a mild oath or exclamation.

deu-ced (dū'sid, dū'sid; dōōst), *adj.* 1. devilish; confounded. 2. extreme. Used in mild oaths and exclamations: *adv.* extremely: also **deu'ced-ly.**

deu-te-ri-um (dōō-tir'i-ŭm), *n.* the hydrogen isotope with an atomic weight of 2.0141 and boiling point of -249.7°C.

Deu-ter-on-o-my (dōōt-ē-ron'ō-mi), *n.* the fifth book of the Pentateuch.

deut-sche mark (doi'chĕ märk), *pl.* **mark**; English **marks**, the monetary unit of West Germany.

de-va (dā'vȧ), *n.* in *Hindu Mythology*, a god or good spirit.

de-val-ue (dē-val'ū), *v.t.* -ued, -u-ing, 1. to lessen the value of. 2. to lower the exchange value of (a currency). Also **de-val'u-ate** ('ū-wāt), -at-ed, -at-ing. —de-val-u-a'tion, *n.*

dev-as-tate (dev'ȧ-stāt), *v.t.* -tat-ed, -tat-ing, 1. to lay waste; make desolate; ravage. 2. to overwhelm or confound, as with a cutting remark. —dev-as-ta'tion, *n.* —dev'as-ta-tor, *n.*

de-vel-op (di-vel'ŏp), *v.t.* 1. to make get gradually bigger, better, stronger, etc. 2. to unfold gradually. 3. to make known in detail. 4. to complete. 5. in *Photography*, to treat (an exposed film, plate, etc.) to bring the picture out: *v.i.* 1. to become developed. 2. to become gradually apparent. 3. to happen. —de-vel'op-ment, *n.*

de-vi-ant (dē'vi-ȧnt), *adj.* deviating, especially from the normal: *n.* a deviant individual. —de'vi-an-cy, de'vi-ance, *n.*

de-vi-ate (dē'vi-āt), *v.i.* -at-ed, -at-ing, to turn aside from a certain course; diverge: *v.t.* to cause to deviate: *adj.* ('vi-it); deviant: *n.* ('vi-it), a deviant, especially in sexual behavior. —de-vi-a'tion, *n.* —de'vi-a-tor, *n.*

de-vice (di-vīs'), *n.* 1. something devised; contrivance. 2. a plan, especially a wily one;

stratagem or trick. 3. a fanciful design or pattern. 4. an emblem, specifically a heraldic one.

dev·il (dev'l), *n.* 1. [often D-], in *Theology*, the chief evil spirit of hell and foe of God; Satan (with *the*); also, [d-], any lesser evil spirit of hell. 2. a very wicked person. 3. a person who is bold and dashing, or mischievous, reckless, full of drive, etc. 4. an unfortunate person. 5. something extremely difficult to deal with. 6. a printer's apprentice. 7. a machine to tear rags, paper, etc. to bits: *v.t.* -iled or -illed, -il·ing or -il·ling, 1. to season (food) highly. 2. to tear up in a machine. 3. to vex or annoy greatly; plague.

dev·il·fish (-fish), *n.* 1. a large species of ray, of warm seas. 2. an octopus.

dev·il·ish (-ish), *adj.* 1. of or like a devil. 2. [Informal], excessive: *adv.* [Informal], extremely.

dev·il-may-care (-mā-ker'), *adj.* 1. reckless. 2. jauntily carefree.

dev·il·ment (-mėnt), *n.* roguishness.

devil's advocate, 1. in the *Roman Catholic Church*, an official chosen to argue against the beatification or canonization of a candidate. 2. a wrongheaded disputant.

dev·il's-food cake (dev'lz-fōōd), a rich cake made with chocolate or cocoa.

dev·il·try (dev'l-tri), *n., pl.* -tries, 1. roguishness. 2. witchcraft. 3. very evil behavior. Also **dev'il·ry,** *pl.* -ries.

de·vi·ous (dē'vi-ŭs), *adj.* 1. rambling; circuitous. 2. deviating. 3. not aboveboard; deceiving.

de·vise (di-vīz'), *v.t. & v.i.* -vised', -vis'ing, 1. to imagine; scheme; contrive or concoct. 2. in *Law*, to bequeath (real property) by will: *n.* in *Law*, a gift of property devised, or the will devising this. —**de·vis'a·ble,** *adj.*

dev·i·see (dev·i-zē', di-vī-zē'), *n.* in *Law*, a person devised property.

de·vis·er (di-vīz'ėr), *n.* one who devises.

dev·i·sor (dev·i-zôr', di-vī'zôr), *n.* in *Law*, one who devises property.

de·vi·tal·ize (dē-vīt'l-īz), *v.t.* -ized, -iz·ing, to deprive of vitality.

de·void (di-void'), *adj.* destitute (*of*).

de·voir (dē-vwär', dev'wär), *n.* 1. a service or duty owed. 2. *pl.* courtesies; respects.

dev·o·lu·tion (dev-ō-lōō'shŭn), *n.* transference from one to another, as of property, duties, or power.

de·volve (di-volv'), *v.t. & v.i.* -volved', -volv'ing, to pass from one to another: pass by devolution. —**de·volve'ment,** *n.*

De·vo·ni·an (di-vō'ni-ăn), *n.* the fourth period of the Paleozoic Era, in which there were many fishes and in which the first authentic land plants and amphibians appeared.

de·vote (di-vōt'), *v.t.* -vot'ed, -vot'ing, 1. to set apart as for some special use; dedicate. 2. to apply (oneself, one's time, etc.) to some object.

de·vot·ed ('id), *adj.* loyal, wholly attentive, ardent, etc. —**de·vot'ed·ly,** *adv.*

dev·o·tee (dev-ō-tē', -tā'), *n.* a votary; enthusiast.

de·vo·tion (di-vō'shŭn), *n.* 1. the act of devoting or state of being devoted. 2. the quality

of being very religious; piety. 3. religious worship. 4. *pl.* prayers. 5. loyalty or strong affection.

de·vo·tion·al (-l), *adj.* of or marked by devotion: *n.* a short worship service.

de·vour (di-vour'), *v.t.* 1. to eat greedily or ravenously. 2. to consume or destroy rapidly. 3. to take in or enjoy with avidity. 4. to occupy wholly; engross. 5. to engulf.

de·vout (-vout'), *adj.* 1. devoted to religious thoughts and exercises. 2. reverential. 3. sincere; heartfelt.

dew (dōō, dū), *n.* 1. aqueous vapor condensed on cool bodies. 2. any moisture in little drops. 3. that which falls lightly and refreshingly.

dew·claw ('klò), *n.* a rudimentary digit in some quadrupeds and ungulates, or the claw or hoof terminating it.

dew-drop ('drop), *n.* a drop of dew.

dew·lap ('lap), *n.* a loose fold of skin under the neck of some animals, as cattle.

dew·y ('i), *adj.* dew'i·er, dew'i·est, 1. of or like dew. 2. moist with dew.

dex·ter (deks'tėr), *adj.* of or on the right-hand side.

dex·ter·i·ty (dek-ster'i-ti), *n.* 1. manual skill; adroitness. 2. cleverness.

dex·ter·ous (dek'strŭs, -ster-ŭs), *adj.* marked by dexterity; adroit or clever: also **dex'trous.** — dex'ter·ous·ly, *adv.*

dex·trin ('strin), *n.* any one of certain complex, gummy carbohydrates: also **dex'trine** (-strēn, -strin).

dex·trose ('strōs), *n.* a certain crystalline glucose found in plants and animals.

dey (dā), *n.* 1. the former title of the governor of Algiers. 2. a pasha in certain former native states of northern Africa.

dhar·ma (dŭr'mä, där'mä), *n.* [Sanskrit], cosmic law, or conformity to this.

dhole (dōl), *n., pl.* **dholes, dhole,** a wild dog of central and eastern Asia.

dhow (dou), *n.* a ship with a lateen sail and raised rear deck, common along coasts of the Indian Ocean.

di-, a prefix meaning *twice, double, twofold.*

di-, same as **dis-.**

di·a·base (dī'ā-bās), *n.* a certain dark, fine-grained igneous rock.

di·a·be·tes (dī-ā-bēt'is, -ēz), *n.* a disease in which there is excessive discharge of urine; especially, diabetes mellitus.

diabetes mel·li·tus (mė-lit'ŭs), a chronic diabetes in which there is excess sugar in the blood and urine.

di·a·bet·ic (dī-ā-bet'ik), *adj.* of or having diabetes: *n.* a diabetic person.

di·a·ble·rie (di-ä'blė-ri), *n.* deviltry.

di·a·bol·ic (dī-ā-bol'ik), *adj.* 1. of or like a devil or the devil. 2. outrageously wicked or cruel. Also **di·a·bol'i·cal.** —**di·a·bol'i·cal·ly,** *adv.*

di·ab·o·lism (dī-ab'ō-lizm), *n.* 1. invocation, worship, etc. of devils or the devil. 2. diabolical behavior or characteristics.

di·ab·o·lo (di-ab'ō-lō), *n.* a toy consisting of a spool to be whirled and balanced on a cord attached to two sticks, one held by each hand.

---

a in cap, ā in cane, ä in father, å in abet, e in met, ē in be, ê in baker, ė in regent, i in pit, ī in fine, i in manifest, o in hot, ô in horse, ō in bone,

di·ac·o·nal (dī-ak'ŏ-nl), *adj.* of a deacon.

di·ac·o·nate (-nit), *n.* 1. the office or dignity of a deacon. 2. a group or board of deacons.

di·a·crit·ic (dī-ă-krit'ik), *adj.* same as diacritical: *n.* a diacritical mark.

di·a·crit·i·cal ('i-kl), *adj.* serving to separate or distinguish.

diacritical mark, a mark, as a macron, added to a letter or symbol to distinguish it in some way, as to show pronunciation.

di·a·dem (dī'ă-dem, -dĕm), *n.* a crown, tiara, or crownlike headband.

di·aer·e·sis (dī-er'ĕ-sis), *n.* alternate spelling of dieresis.

di·ag·nose (dī'ăg-nōs, -nōz), *v.t. & v.i.* -nosed, -nos·ing, to make a diagnosis of (a disease, difficulty, etc.).

di·ag·no·sis (dī-ăg-nō'sis), *n., pl.* -ses ('sēz), 1. analysis and determination of the nature of something, as a disease, by examination, tests, etc. 2. the decision arrived at.

di·ag·nos·tic (-nos'tik), *adj.* of or aiding diagnosis: *n.* 1. *usually pl.* scientific diagnosis, or a method used. 2. a distinctive indication aiding diagnosis. —di·ag·nos'ti·cal·ly, *adv.*

di·ag·nos·ti·cian (-nos-tish'ăn), *n.* one making, or specializing in, diagnosis.

di·ag·o·nal (dī-ag'ŏ-nl), *adj.* extending slantingly, as from a top corner of a rectangle to the farther bottom corner: *n.* a diagonal line, row, part, etc. —di·ag'o·nal·ly, *adv.*

di·a·gram (dī'ă-gram), *n.* 1. a geometrical figure. 2. an outline, drawing, or figure; specifically, a mechanical figure. 3. a chart or graph: *v.t.* -gramed or -grammed, -gram·ing or gram·ming, to show, explain, etc. by a diagram; make a diagram of. —di·a·gram·mat'ic (-gră-mat'ik), *adj.* —di·a·gram·mat'i·cal·ly, *adv.*

di·al (dī'ăl), *n.* 1. a sundial. 2. the face of a timepiece. 3. the face of a tuner, compass, gauge, etc. showing frequencies, directions, pressure, revolutions, etc. as by means of a pointer. 4. a revolving indicator or selector, as of radio frequencies, oven temperatures, or telephone numbers: *v.t. & v.i.* -aled or -alled, -al·ing or -al·ling, 1. to get, set, or indicate (a specified reading, number, etc.) with or as with a dial. 2. to call on a telephone by means of a telephone dial.

di·a·lect (dī'ă-lekt), *n.* 1. the distinctive way a language is spoken or written in a given locality or by a given group or individual. 2. a form of language viewed as deviating from a standard. 3. a language viewed in relationship to its parent language or languages: *adj.* of or in dialect. —di·a·lec'tal, *adj.*

di·a·lec·tic (dī-ă-lek'tik), *n.* 1. *often pl.* logical examination of opinions or ideas to determine their validity. 2. reasoning, or argumentation based on reasoned principles: *adj.* dialectical.

di·a·lec·ti·cal ('ti-kl), *adj.* 1. of or using dialectic. 2. of or typical of dialect.

di·a·lec·ti·cian (dī-ă-lek-tish'ăn), *n.* a specialist in dialectic or dialect.

di·a·logue, di·a·log (dī'ă-lôg), *n.* 1. conversation. 2. exchange of ideas. 3. passages of talk, as in a novel.

di·al·y·sis (dī-al'ĭ-sis), *n., pl.* -ses (-sēz), separation of certain substances in solution by diffusion through a membrane that restricts or blocks diffusion of larger molecules and colloidal particles. —di·a·lyt·ic (dī-ă-lit'ik), *adj.*

di·a·lyze (dī'ă-līz), *v.t.* -lyzed, -lyz·ing, to subject to dialysis: *v.i.* to undergo dialysis. — di'a·lyz·er, *n.*

di·a·mag·net·ism (dī-ă-mag'nĕ-tizm), *n.* the property of certain substances of being repelled by both poles of a magnet.

di·am·e·ter (dī-am'ĕt-ĕr), *n.* 1. a straight line passing through the center of a figure or body, especially a circle or sphere, from one side or surface to the other. 2. the length of such a line.

di·a·met·ri·cal (dī-ă-met'ri-kl), *adj.* 1. of or pertaining to a diameter. 2. being (opposite or something opposite, contrary, etc.) utterly or wholly: also di·a·met'ric. —di·a·met'ri·cal·ly, *adv.*

di·a·mond (dī'mŏnd, dī'ă-mŏnd), *n.* 1. a mineral that is nearly pure carbon, crystalline and usually colorless, the hardest mineral known. 2. a gem or other piece cut from this. 3. a lozenge-shaped figure. 4. one of a suit of cards marked with red diamonds. 5. *pl.* this suit. 6. in *Baseball*, the infield or the entire field: *adj.* of, like, or set with one or more diamonds.

diamond anniversary, a sixtieth, or sometimes seventy-fifth, anniversary: also diamond jubilee.

di·a·mond·back (-bak), *n.* 1. a large, poisonous rattlesnake of the southeastern U.S., with diamond-shaped markings on its back. 2. an edible turtle similarly marked, found from Cape Cod to Mexico: also diamondback terrapin.

diamond wedding, a sixtieth, or sometimes seventy-fifth, wedding anniversary.

Di·an·a (dī-an'ă), *n.* the virgin goddess of the moon and of hunting.

di·a·pa·son (dī-ă-pāz'n), *n.* 1. the entire compass of a voice or instrument. 2. one of the foundation stops of an organ. 3. a recognized musical standard of pitch.

di·a·per (dī'pĕr, dī'ă-pĕr), *n.* 1. originally, cloth in geometric patterns; later, any similar pattern. 2. a soft, absorbent cloth arranged between the legs and about the buttocks of a baby: *v.t.* to put a diaper on (a baby).

di·aph·a·nous (dī-af'ă-nŭs), *adj.* denoting gauze or other material that lets light through wholly or partially.

di·a·pho·re·sis (dī-ă-fŏ-rē'sis), *n.* perspiration, especially when profuse.

di·a·pho·ret·ic (-ret'ik), *adj.* producing perspiration: *n.* a diaphoretic agent.

di·a·phragm (dī'ă-fram), *n.* 1. a partition of muscles and tendons separating the chest cavity from the abdominal cavity. 2. any dividing partition or membrane. 3. a device, as in a camera, regulating the flow of light. 4. a kind of contraceptive pessary. 5. a thin disk or cone vibrated by sound waves or electrical signals and used as in a microphone or loudspeaker. —di·a·phrag·mat'ic (-frag-mat'ik), *adj.*

di·a·rist (dī'ă-rist), *n.* a diary keeper.

di·ar·rhe·a, di·ar·rhoe·a (dī-â-rē'â), n. excessive frequency and looseness of bowel movements. —**di·ar·rhe'al, di·ar·rhe'ic,** adj.

di·a·ry (dī'â-ri), n., pl. -ries, a register of or for daily occurrences.

Di·as·po·ra (dī-as'pô-râ), n. 1. the scattering of the Jews after their 6th-century B.C. forced sojourn in Babylonia; also, the Jews thus scattered, or the places they settled in. 2. [d-], any similar scattering of a people or group.

di·a·stase (dī'â-stās), n. an enzyme in seeds of grains and malt: it can convert starch to maltose and then dextrose.

di·as·to·le (dī-as'tô-lē), n. 1. the rhythmical expansion of the heart in beating. 2. the lengthening of a short syllable, as in Latin. —**di·a·stol'ic** (-â-stol'ik), adj.

di·a·ther·my (dī'â-thûr-mi), n. production of medicinal heat in subcutaneous tissues by using a high-frequency electric current.

di·ath·e·sis (dī-ath'ē-sis), n. predisposition to certain diseases.

di·a·tom (dī'â-tom, 'ât-ôm), n. any one of various related microscopic algae.

di·a·ton·ic (dī-â-ton'ik), adj. designating the regular tones of a key or scale.

di·a·tribe (dī'â-trīb), n. a piece of bitter criticism; violent denunciation.

dib·ble (dib'l), n. a gardening tool for making holes in the earth: also **dib'ber**: v.t. -**bled**, -**bling**, 1. to perforate (earth) with a dibble. 2. to plant with a dibble: v.i. to dip bait gently.

dib·buk (dib'ûk), n. same as dybbuk.

dibs (dibz), n. [Informal], rights to share something good, as candy: interj. an exclamation asserting such rights: chiefly a child's term.

dice (dīs), n.pl., sing. die or dice, 1. small cubes marked on each side with from one to six spots and used in games of chance. 2. a gambling game using these. 3. any small cubes: v.i. diced, dic'ing, to play dice or use dice: v.t. 1. to cut into cubes. 2. to decorate with a pattern suggestive of cubes or squares. —dic'er, n.

di·ceph·a·lous (dī-sef'l-ûs), adj. having two heads.

di·chlo·ride (dī-klôr'īd, 'id), n. a chemical compound having two atoms of chlorine combined with an element or radical.

di·chot·o·mize (dī-kot'ô-mīz), v.t. & v.i. -mized, -miz·ing, to divide or separate into two parts.

di·chot·o·my (-ô-mi), n., pl. -mies, division into two parts.

di·chro·ism (dī'krō-izm), n. the property of showing contrasting colors in transmission of light, as in doubly refracting crystals, or in transmission and reflection of light.

di·chro·mate (dī-krō'māt), n. any salt of dichromic acid.

di·chro·mat·ic (dī-krō-mat'ik), adj. 1. having two colors. 2. of or showing dichromatism.

di·chro·ma·tism (-krō'mâ-tizm), n. 1. the quality or condition of being dichromatic. 2. color blindness in which only two of the primary colors (red, green, blue) can be seen. 3. same as dichroism.

di·chro·mic (dī-krō'mik), adj. 1. dichromatic. 2.

in Chemistry, a) having two atoms of chromium per molecule. b) designating a hypothetical acid containing chromium and oxygen, from which dichromates are formed.

dick (dik), n. [Slang], a detective.

dick·cis·sel (dik-sis'l), n. a black-throated, yellow-breasted American bunting.

dick·ens (dik'nz), n. & interj. [Informal], devil; deuce: used in mild oaths.

dick·er (dik'ēr), v.i. & v.t. to barter or trade on a small scale: n. a dickering.

dick·ey (dik'i), n. 1. a detachable shirt front or blouse front. 2. a child's bib or pinafore. 3. a small bird. Also **dick'y**, pl. **dick'ies**.

di·cot·y·le·don (dī-kot-l-ēd'n, dī-), n. a flowering plant with two seed leaves. —**di·cot·y·le'don·ous**, adj.

di·crot·ic (dī-krot'ik), adj. of or having a double pulse beat at each beat of the heart. —**di'cro·tism** (-krô-tizm), n.

dic·ta (dik'tâ), n. alternate plural of dictum.

Dic·ta·phone (dik'tâ-fōn), n. a machine recording spoken words to be played back, as for typed transcripts: a trademark.

dic·tate (dik'tāt, dik-tāt'), v.t. & v.i. -tat·ed, -tat·ing, 1. to express (words) orally so that another may take the words down in writing. 2. to command expressly. 3. to impose or set forth (orders, terms, etc.) with or as with authority and finality, or arbitrarily. 4. to make (something) necessary or inescapable; require: n. (dik'tāt), 1. an injunction; command. 2. a controlling principle; requirement.

dic·ta·tion (dik-tā'shûn), n. 1. the dictating of words for transcription. 2. words so dictated. 3. the dictating of orders, terms, etc.

dic·ta·tor (dik'tāt-ēr, dik-tāt'ēr), n. 1. an ancient Roman magistrate with supreme authority, appointed in times of emergency. 2. one having absolute powers of government, often one exercising these tyrannically. 3. one ordering others about tyrannically or forcing his views on others. 4. one dictating words for transcription.

dic·ta·to·ri·al (dik-tâ-tôr'i-âl), adj. of or like a dictator; tyrannical, domineering, etc. —**dic·ta·to'ri·al·ly**, adv.

dic·ta·tor·ship (dik-tāt'ēr-ship), n. 1. the office, position, or tenure of a dictator. 2. a state or government ruled by a dictator. 3. dictatorial power or authority.

dic·tion (dik'shûn), n. 1. manner of verbal expression; choice of words; wording. 2. articulation; enunciation.

dic·tion·ar·y (dik'shûn-ner-i), n., pl. -ar·ies, 1. a book listing words of a language alphabetically, defining the words, indicating pronunciation, etc. 2. a similar book listing words of one language and giving the equivalents of these in another language.

Dic·to·graph (dik'tô-graf), n. a telephonic instrument used for secretly hearing or recording conversations: a trademark.

dic·tum (dik'tûm), n., pl. -tums, -ta (-tâ), a statement, especially a formal one, often intended as authoritative or taken to be so, making an observation or expressing a reasoned judgment, a principle or opinion, etc.

did (did), past tense of do.

di-dact (dī'dakt), *n.* a didactic person.
di-dac-tic (dī-dak'tik), *adj.* 1. teaching; instructive. 2. pedantic. Also **di-dac'ti-cal.** —**di-dac'ti-cal-ly,** *adv.*
di-dac-tics ('tiks), *n.* pedagogy.
did-dle (did'l), *v.i. & v.t.* -dled, -dling, 1. to move with quick, slight jerks; jiggle. 2. to waste (time), as in puttering. 3. to cheat or swindle. —**did'dler,** *n.*
did-n't (did'nt), did not.
di-do (dī'dō), *n., pl.* -does, -dos, a trick; prank; caper.
di-dy (dī'di), *n., pl.* -dies, [Informal], a diaper (sense 2).
die (dī), *v.i.* died, dy'ing, 1. to cease to live; expire; perish. 2. to cease functioning; come to an end. 3. to pass out of existence, especially gradually; become extinct. 4. to wither away. 5. to lose energy, strength, intensity, etc.; weaken or fade; languish. 6. to lose importance, relevance, etc. 7. to become indifferent or uncaring (with *to*). 8. [Informal], to desire intensely; yearn.
die (dī), *n.* 1. alternate singular of **dice.** 2. a tool or device for stamping, cutting, shaping, etc., as a piece of engraved metal used in stamping money, medals, etc. or a tool used in cutting threads of screws, bolts, etc.: *v.t.* died, die'ing, to stamp, cut, etc. with a die.
die-hard, die-hard (dī'härd), *adj.* not yielding easily; stubbornly resistant, as to change: *n.* a die-hard person.
di-e-lec-tric (dī-ē-lek'trik), *adj.* nonconducting: *n.* a material or medium, as glass or a vacuum, that does not conduct electricity and that can sustain an electric field.
di-er-e-sis (dī-er'ē-sis), *n., pl.* -ses (-sēz), a mark (¨) over a vowel, as over the second of two adjacent ones, to indicate it is to be sounded separately or with some modification of sound.
die-sel (dē'zl, 'sl), *n.* 1. an internal-combustion engine using petroleum distillate as fuel, ignition being effected by the heat of air compression: also **diesel engine** (or **motor**). 2. a locomotive, truck, etc. having such an engine.
di-e-sis (dī'ē-sis), *n., pl.* -ses (-sēz), a mark (‡) used in printing, typically to refer a reader to a footnote.
di-et (dī'ět), *n.* 1. what an individual usually eats or drinks; fare. 2. a special selection or limitation of food or drink, as for a patient or in controlling weight. 3. what an individual usually reads, does, etc. 4. a deliberative convention or legislative assembly: *v.i. & v.t.* to follow or cause to follow a special or limited diet of food or drink. —**di'et-er,** *n.*
di-e-tar-y (dī'ē-ter-i), *adj.* of or pertaining to a diet of food or drink: *n.* a particular dietary system, regimen, etc.
di-e-tet-ic (dī-ē-tet'ik), *adj.* of, pertaining to, or designed for a diet of food or drink: also **di-e-tet'i-cal.**
di-e-tet-ics ('iks), *n.* the science or study of proper nutrition.

di-e-ti-tian, di-e-ti-cian (dī-ē-tish'ån), *n.* a specialist in dietetics or in providing meals as for patients.
dif-, same as **dis-:** used before *f.*
dif-fer (dif'ēr), *v.i.* 1. to be different. 2. to judge or think differently; disagree.
dif-fer-ence (dif'ēr-ēns, dif'rēns), *n.* 1. the act or state of being different or of differing. 2. a particular way in which individuals or groups are different from each other. 3. an individual disagreement or point of disagreement. 4. a controversy or quarrel. 5. a discrimination or distinction. 6. the amount by which one quantity is greater or less than another.
dif-fer-ent (dif'ēr-ėnt, dif'rėnt), *adj.* 1. unlike; dissimilar. 2. not the same; distinct. 3. various. 4. unlike most others; unusual. —**dif'fer-ent-ly,** *adv.*
dif-fer-en-ti-a (dif-ē-ren'shi-å, 'shå), *n., pl.* -ti-ae ('shi-ē), a distinguishing characteristic; especially, that which distinguishes one species from another of the same genus.
dif-fer-en-ti-a-ble ('shi-å-bl, 'shå-bl), *adj.* capable of being differentiated.
dif-fer-en-tial ('shål), *adj.* 1. of, indicating, or depending on a difference. 2. being or creating a specific difference; distinguishing. 3. effecting or working in accordance with various differences: *n.* 1. a differentiating amount, quantity, or other factor. 2. same as **differential gear.** 3. in *Mathematics, a)* an infinitesimal difference between two consecutive values of a variable quantity. *b)* the derivative of a function multiplied by the increment of the independent variable. 4. in *Railroading,* a difference in rates, as between different routes.
differential calculus, the branch of higher mathematics dealing with derivatives and their applications.
differential gear, an arrangement of gears so connecting two axles driving equally in the same line that when necessary one axle can revolve faster than the other: also **differential gearing.**
dif-fer-en-ti-ate (dif-ē-ren'shi-āt), *v.t.* -at-ed, -at-ing, 1. to constitute a difference in or between. 2. to make different; specialize as in structure or function. 3. to distinguish between; discriminate. 4. in *Mathematics,* to work out the differential or derivative of: *v.i.* 1. to become differentiated. 2. to note a difference or distinction. —**dif-fer-en-ti-a'tion,** *n.*
dif-fi-cult (dif'i-kůlt, -kult), *adj.* 1. not easy to do, make, deal with, understand, etc.; giving trouble or making extra effort, thought, skill, etc. necessary. 2. not easily satisfied, persuaded, etc.
dif-fi-cul-ty (dif'i-kul-ti, -kůl-), *n., pl.* -ties, 1. the condition or fact of being difficult. 2. something difficult; a difficult problem, situation, etc. 3. an objection raised, as to a line of argumentation. 4. a disagreement; controversy.
dif-fi-dence (dif'i-dėns), *n.* lack of self-confidence; timidity.

dif·fi·dent (-dĕnt), *adj.* lacking self-confidence; timid.

dif·fract (di-frakt′), *v.t.* to break into parts; specifically, to subject to diffraction: *v.i.* to undergo diffraction.

dif·frac·tion (di-frak′shŭn), *n.* 1. the breaking up of a ray of light into dark and light bands or the colors of the spectrum. 2. deflection of the wave motion of sound, electricity, etc. —**dif·frac′tive,** *adj.*

dif·fuse (di-fūz′), *v.t. & v.i.* -fused′, -fus′ing, 1. to pour, spread out, or disperse widely or all around; scatter. 2. in *Physics,* to mix as gases, by diffusion: *adj.* (-fūs′), 1. diffused. 2. wordy; verbose; prolix. —**dif·fuse′ly,** *adv.* —**dif·fuse′ness,** *n.*

dif·fus·er, dif·fu·sor (di-fū′zĕr), *n.* one that diffuses, as a device to distribute light evenly.

dif·fus·i·ble (′zĭ-hl), *adj.* capable of being diffused. —**dif·fus·i·bil′i·ty,** *n.*

dif·fu·sion (′zhŭn), *n.* 1. the act of diffusing or condition of being diffused; dissemination, dispersion, etc. 2. intermingling, as of molecules. 3. wordiness.

dif·fu·sive (′sĭv), *adj.* 1. that diffuses or is marked by diffusion. 2. diffuse.

dig (dig), *v.t.* dug, dig′ging, 1. to break and turn up (ground) with or as with a spade. 2. to make (a hole, one's way, etc.) by or as by digging ground. 3. to get from the ground by digging. 4. to search out and find as if by digging. 5. to thrust or jab. 6. [Slang] to understand; also, to like: *v.i.* 1. to dig something; undertake digging. 2. [Informal] to study hard: *n.* 1. the act of digging. 2. [Informal] a thrust, jab, etc.; also, a gibe. 3. an archaeological excavation. 4. *pl.* [Informal] living quarters.

di·gest (dī′jest), *n.* an abridgment, summary, or synopsis, or a compilation of these. 2. [D-], often *pl.* the Pandects of the 6th-century A.D. Roman Emperor Justinian: *v.t.* (di-jest′, dī-), 1. to put into digest form. 2. to subject (food) to digestion. 3. to think over and arrange in the mind. 4. to soften and prepare by heat: *v.i.* to undergo digestion.

di·gest·er (di-jes′tĕr, dī-), *n.* 1. one that makes a digest. 2. a container to soften things or extract soluble elements by heat.

di·gest·i·ble (′tĭ-bl), *adj.* capable of being digested. —**di·gest·i·bil′i·ty,** *n.*

di·ges·tion (′chŭn), *n.* 1. the act of digesting or condition of being digested. 2. conversion of food by gastric and intestinal juices and bacteria into soluble products that can be absorbed by the body. 3. ability to digest food.

di·ges·tive (′tĭv), *adj.* of, for, or promoting digestion: *n.* something promoting digestion, as a food, drink, or medication.

dig·ger (dig′ĕr), *n.* 1. one that digs. 2. [D-], a member of any one of several western U.S. Indian tribes who dug roots for food. 3. [D-], [Slang], an Australian or New Zealander.

dig·gings (′ingz), *n.pl.* 1. materials dug up. 2. a site of digging or mining, especially gold mining. 3. [Slang] living quarters; digs.

dight (dīt), *v.t.* dight or dight′ed, dight′ing, [Archaic], to adorn or equip.

dig·it (dij′it), *n.* 1. a finger or toe. 2. a measure of length, equal to 3/4 inch. 3. any one of the Arabic numerals (0-9).

dig·i·tal (-l), *adj.* 1. of or like a digit or digits. 2. having, using, or done with a digit or digits: *n.* 1. a finger. 2. a key, as on a piano, to be played with a finger. —**dig′i·tal·ly,** *adv.*

digital clock, a clock that shows the time in digits rather than by hands on a dial.

digital computer, a computer using numbers in calculating.

dig·i·tal·in (dij-ĭ-tal′in; chiefly British, -tā′lin), *n.* a poisonous crystalline glucoside from digitalis seed.

dig·i·tal·is (-tal′is; chiefly British, -tā′lis), *n.* 1. any one of a genus of plants of the figwort family, having thimblelike flowers in long spikes. 2. a medicine made from the dried leaves of the purple foxglove, used as a heart stimulant.

dig·i·tate (dij′i-tāt), *adj.* 1. having separate fingers or toes. 2. fingerlike.

dig·i·ti·grade (-ti-grād), *adj.* walking on the toes, as cats, dogs, etc.: *n.* a digitigrade animal.

di·glot (dī′glot), *adj.* bilingual.

dig·ni·fied (dig′ni-fīd), *adj.* marked by dignity; commanding respect; stately.

dig·ni·fy (dig′ni-fī), *v.t.* -fied, -fy·ing, to invest with, or exalt in, dignity or rank; confer honor upon; elevate; ennoble.

dig·ni·tar·y (-ter-i), *n., pl.* -tar·ies, one holding a position of dignity or honor: *adj.* of or like a dignitary.

dig·ni·ty (dig′ni-ti), *n., pl.* -ties, 1. the quality of being such as to command respect or honor; impressive inner excellence; stateliness; nobility; majesty. 2. any high rank, position, or title; also, the honor or respect due or accorded such. 3. any rank or position entitled to at least some respect. 4. proper regard for oneself as an individual entitled to at least some respect. 5. composure or reserve of manner or bearing that elicits respect.

di·graph (dī′graf), *n.* a combination of two characters indicating just one sound, as the *ea* in *read.*

di·gress (di-gres′, dī-), *v.i.* to turn away from the main subject being talked or written about and consider something else, especially for just a short time. —**di·gres′sion,** *n.* —**di·gres′sive,** *adj.*

di·he·dral (dī-hē′drăl), *adj.* 1. having or formed by two intersecting plane faces. 2. inclined to each other at a dihedral angle, as some airplane wings; also, having wings so inclined: *n.* a dihedral angle.

dike (dīk), *n.* 1. an embankment thrown up as a protection against the sea, floods, etc. 2. [Slang], same as dyke: *v.t.* diked, dik′ing, 1. to provide, protect, or enclose with a dike. 2. to drain with a ditch.

di·lac·er·ate (di-las′ĕ-rāt), *v.t.* -at·ed, -at·ing, to tear to pieces; rend asunder.

di·lap·i·date (di-lap′i-dāt), *v.i. & v.t.* -dat·ed, dat·ing, to become partially ruined, as through misuse or neglect, or bring into such a condition. —di·lap'i·dat·ed, adj. —di·lap·i·da'tion, n.

di·lat·ant (dī-lāt'nt, dī-), adj. dilating: n. something that can dilate.

dil·a·ta·tion (dil·ā·tā'shŭn, dī-lā-), n. a dilating, especially of a bodily part.

di·late (dī-lāt', dī-), v.t. -lat'ed, -lat'ing, to enlarge, expand, or stretch: v.i. 1. to become dilated. 2. to speak or write copiously. —di·lat'a·ble, adj. —di·la'tion, n.

di·la·tor (dī-lāt'ēr, dī-), n. one that dilates; specifically, a surgical instrument for dilating a bodily part.

dil·a·to·ry (dil'ā-tôr-i), adj. causing or inclining toward delay.

di·lem·ma (di-lem'ä), n. 1. an argument forcing a choice between equally undesirable alternatives. 2. any situation involving such alternatives; quandary.

dil·et·tante (dil·ē·tänt', -tän'ti, -tan'ti), n., pl. -tantes', -tan'ti (-tän'ti), one who merely dabbles in an art or science, chiefly for diversion: adj. of or like a dilettante. —dil·et·tant'ish, adj. —dil·et·tant'ism, n.

dil·i·gence (dil'i-jēns), n. a stagecoach.

dil·i·gent (dil'i-jēnt), adj. earnest, steady, and hard-working. —dil'i·gence, n. —dil'i·gent·ly, adv.

dill (dil), n. an herb of the parsley family, with aromatic leaves and seeds used in pickling.

dil·ly·dal·ly (dil'i-dal-i), v.i. -lied, -ly·ing, to waste time in dawdling.

di·lute (di-lōōt', dī-), v.t. -lut'ed, -lut'ing, to thin or weaken by mixing with another fluid, especially water: v.i. to become thinner: adj. diluted. —di·lut'er, di·lu'tor, n.

di·lu·tion (-lōō'shŭn), n. the act of diluting. 2. a weak liquid.

di·lu·vi·al (di-lōō'vi-äl), adj. 1. of or pertaining to a flood, especially the Biblical Deluge. 2. denoting debris left by a flood or glacier.

dim (dim), adj. dim'mer, dim'mest, 1. somewhat dark. 2. hazy; ill-defined. 3. faint. 4. not clearly perceiving: v.t. & v.i. dimmed, dim'ming, to make or grow dim. —dim'ly, adv. —dim'ness, n.

dime (dīm), n. a coin of the U.S. and Canada equal to ten cents.

dime novel, a cheap, sensational novel, originally costing a dime.

di·men·sion (di-men'shŭn), n. 1. magnitude that can be measured, as length, width, etc. 2. pl. measurements in length, width, and thickness. 3. often pl. a) extent or size. b) scope or importance. —di·men'sion·al, adj.

di·min·ish (di-min'ish), v.t. & v.i. to decrease in size, importance, degree, etc.; lessen; reduce.

di·min·u·en·do (di-min-yoo-wen'dō), adj. & adv. in Music, gradually reducing in volume.

dim·i·nu·tion (dim-i-nū'shŭn, -nōō'shŭn), n. a reduction or lessening.

di·min·u·tive (di-min'yoo-tiv), adj. little; tiny: n. a word formed from another with a suffix that denotes smallness or endearment. —di·min'u·tive·ly, adv.

dim·i·ty (dim'i-ti), n., pl. -ties, a thin cotton fabric used for curtains, etc.

dim·mer (dim'ēr), n. a device, as a rheostat, for dimming electric lights.

di·mor·phism (di-môr'fizm), n. the property of growing, crystallizing, or existing in two forms. —di·mor'phic, di·mor'phous, adj.

dim·ple (dim'pl), n. a small depression or hollow, as in the cheek or chin: v.t. -pled, -pling, to make dimples in: v.i. to form or show dimples. —dim'ply, adj.

din (din), n. a loud, confused, continued noise; uproar: v.t. dinned, din'ning, 1. to stun with noise. 2. to press with persistent repetition: v.i. to make a din.

dine (dīn), v.i. dined, din'ing, to eat dinner: v.t. to provide dinner for; feed.

din·er (dī'nēr), n. 1. a person dining. 2. a railroad dining car, where meals are served. 3. a small restaurant built to look like a railroad dining car.

din·ette (dī-net'), n. a small space or alcove used as a dining room.

ding (ding), v.i. to sound, as a bell, with a continuous, insistent tone: n. the sound of a bell: also ding'-dong ('dông).

din·ghy (ding'gi), n., pl. -ghies, 1. originally, a boat in India. 2. a ship's tender. 3. a small rowboat or sailboat. 4. a rubber life raft.

din·gle (ding'gl), n. a wooded valley.

din·go (ding'go), n., pl. -goes, the Australian wild dog.

din·gy (din'ji), adj. -gi·er, -gi·est, 1. dirty; grimy. 2. shabby. —din'gi·ness, n.

din·kum (ding'kŭm), adj. [Australian Slang], 1. fair; honest. 2. genuine; true: n. [Australian Slang], truth.

din·ky (ding'ki), adj. -ki·er, -ki·est, [Informal], tiny and unimportant.

din·ner (din'ēr), n. 1. the chief meal of the day. 2. a public banquet.

di·no·saur (di'nō-sôr), n. a huge, four-limbed, prehistoric reptile, now extinct.

di·no·there (di'nō-thir), n. a huge, elephantlike, extinct mammal of the Miocene Epoch.

dint (dint), n. 1. a dent. 2. force or power: now chiefly in by dint of.

di·o·cese (di'ō-sis, -sēs), n. the district under the jurisdiction of a bishop. —di·oc'e·san (-os'ē-sn), adj.

di·ode (di'ōd), n. an electron tube or a semiconductor used as a rectifier.

di·op·tase (di-op'tās), n. a vitreous, emerald-green ore of copper.

di·op·tric (dī-op'trik), adj. assisting vision by lenses with refractive correction.

di·o·ra·ma (di-ō-ram'ä), n. a three-dimensional scene of figures against a painted background.

di·o·rite (di'ō-rīt), n. an igneous rock consisting of feldspar and hornblende.

di·ox·ide (di-ok'sid), n. an oxide that has two atoms of oxygen per molecule.

dip (dip), v.t. dipped, dip'ping, 1. to immerse briefly in a liquid. 2. to scoop up or out. 3. to lower and raise quickly: v.i. 1. to plunge briefly into a liquid. 2. to sink. 3. to incline downward. 4. to put the hand, a container, etc. as into a liquid. 5. to delve slightly into something: n. 1. the act of dipping. 2. a brief plunge. 3. a liquid, etc. in which something is dipped. 4. the angle of inclination

---

ô in dragon, ōō in crude, oo in wool, u in cup, û in cure, ū in turn, ů in focus, oi in boy, ou in house, th in thin, th in sheathe, g in get, j in joy, y in yet.

of strata to the horizon. 5. a downward slope.

diph-the-ri-a (dif-thir'i-ă, dip-), n. an acute contagious disease characterized by a high fever and formation in the throat of a membrane that hinders breathing.

diph-thong (dif'thŏng, dip'thŏng), n. the union of two vowel sounds pronounced in one syllable.

di-ple-gi-a (dī-plē'ji-ă), n. paralysis of corresponding parts on both sides, as of the legs.

di-plo-ma (di-plō'mă), n. a document issued by a school, college, etc. conferring a degree or certifying graduation.

di-plo-ma-cy (di-plō'mă-si), n. 1. the art of conducting negotiations between nations, or of transacting international business. 2. skill in doing this. 3. tact.

dip-lo-mat (dip'lŏ-mat), n. 1. one skilled in diplomacy. 2. one who represents his government in negotiations with another nation. Also **di-plo-ma-tist** (di-plō'mă-tist).

dip-lo-mat-ic (dip-lŏ-mat'ik), adj. 1. of or pertaining to diplomacy. 2. tactful. **—dip-lo-mat'i-cal-ly,** adv.

di-pole antenna (dī'pōl), a radio or television antenna with two equal rods extending horizontally.

dip-per (dip'ĕr), n. 1. a long-handled, cuplike container for dipping. 2. any of a group of diving birds, as the water ouzel. 3. [D-], either of two groups of stars: see **Big Dipper, Little Dipper.**

dip-so-ma-ni-a (dip-sŏ-mā'ni-ă), n. an abnormal craving for alcoholic drink. **—dip-so-ma'ni-ac** (-ak), n.

dip-stick (dip'stik), n. a graduated rod for measuring the quantity of a liquid in its container, as of oil in a crankcase.

dip-ter-al (dip'tĕr-ăl), adj. having a double row of columns, as a temple.

dip-ter-an (dip'tĕr-ăn), n. any of a large order of insects, including the housefly, mosquito, and gnat, having one pair of wings. **—dip'ter-ous,** adj.

dire (dīr), adj. dir'er, dir'est, 1. dreadful; awful. 2. urgent. **—dire'ly,** adv. **—dire'ness,** n.

di-rect (di-rekt'), adj. 1. straight; not circuitous. 2. open; straightforward. 3. of lineal descent. 4. immediate; close. 5. complete. 6. in the exact words: v.t. 1. to aim, turn, or point. 2. to guide or show. 3. to point out or determine with authority. 4. to address (a letter, etc.). 5. to supervise the action of (a play, motion picture, etc.): v.i. 1. to act as a guide. 2. to be a director: adv. directly. **—di-rect'ness,** n.

direct current, electric current that flows in one direction.

di-rec-tion (di-rek'shŭn), n. 1. the act of directing. 2. a command; order. 3. usually pl. guidance or instructions for making, doing, etc. 4. the course or line along which something is directed in facing or moving toward a given point. **—di-rec'tion-al,** adj.

di-rec-tive ('tiv), adj. directing: n. a general instruction or order.

di-rect-ly (-rekt'li), adv. 1. in a direct or straight line. 2. immediately. 3. exactly.

direct object, the word or words denoting the receiver of the action of a verb.

di-rec-tor (di-rek'tĕr), n. one who directs a company, school, government bureau, etc., or an orchestra, motion picture, etc. **—di-rec'tor-ship,** n.

di-rec-to-rate ('tĕr-it), n. 1. the position of a director. 2. a board of directors.

di-rec-to-ry ('tĕr-i), n., pl. -ries, a book containing the names, addresses, etc. of some group: adj. advising.

direct primary election, an election in which the people choose candidates who are to run for political office, rather than having them chosen by delegates at a convention.

dire-ful (dīr'fŭl), adj. dreadful; dismal. **—dire'-ful-ly,** adv.

dirge (dŭrj), n. 1. a funeral hymn. 2. a song or tune expressive of grief.

dir-i-gi-ble (dir'i-ji-bl), adj. that may be guided or steered: n. same as **airship.**

dirk (dŭrk), n. a dagger.

dirn-dl (dŭrn'dl), n. a full skirt.

dirt (dŭrt), n. 1. any unclean substance; filth. 2. earth; soil. 3. vileness; corruption. 4. obscenity. 5. gossip. 6. the gravel or soil from which gold is washed: adj. having a dirt surface, as a road.

dirt-y ('i), adj. dirt'i-er, dirt'i-est, 1. unclean; soiled. 2. obscene. 3. disgusting; nasty. 4. unfair. 5. unpleasant, as weather: v.t. & v.i. dirt'ied, dirt'y-ing, to make or become dirty. **—dirt'i-ness,** n.

dis-, a prefix signifying separation, deprivation, negation.

dis-a-bil-i-ty (dis-ă-bil'i-ti), n., pl. -ties, 1. the condition of being disabled. 2. that which disables, as a physical handicap. 3. legal incapacity.

dis-a-ble (-ā'bl), v.t. -bled, -bling, 1. to incapacitate; cripple. 2. to disqualify legally. **—dis-a'ble-ment,** n.

dis-a-buse (-ă-būz'), v.t. -bused', -bus'ing, to rid of false conceptions.

dis-ad-van-tage (-ad-van'tij), n. 1. an unfavorable condition. 2. detriment; loss. **—dis-ad-van-ta'geous** (-ad-văn-tā'jŭs), adj.

dis-ad-van-taged (-tijd), adj. underprivileged.

dis-af-fect (dis-ă-fekt'), v.t. to alienate the affection of; make discontented or disloyal. **—dis-af-fec'tion,** n.

dis-af-fil-i-ate (-ă-fil'i-āt), v.t. & v.i. -at-ed, -at-ing, to break off an affiliation (with). **—dis-af-fil-i-a'tion,** n.

dis-a-gree (-ă-grē'), v.i. -greed', -gree'ing, 1. to fail to agree. 2. to quarrel. 3. to give discomfort (followed by with). **—dis-a-gree'ment,** n.

dis-a-gree-a-ble ('ă-bl), adj. 1. offensive; repugnant. 2. unpleasant; quarrelsome. **—dis-a-gree'a-bly,** adv.

dis-ap-pear (dis-ă-pir'), v.i. 1. to vanish. 2. to pass away; end. **—dis-ap-pear'ance,** n.

dis-ap-point (-ă-point'), v.t. to thwart or frustrate the hopes or expectations of. **—dis-ap-point'ment,** n.

a in cap, ā in cane, ä in father, ă in abet, e in met, ē in be, ė in baker, ĕ in regent, i in pit, ī in fine, ĭ in manifest, o in hot, ō in horse, ō in bone,

dis·ap·pro·ba·tion (-ap-rò-bā'shŭn), *n.* disapproval.

dis·ap·prove (-å-prōōv'), *v.t. & v.i.* -proved', -prov'ing, 1. to think unfavorably (of); censure. 2. to refuse to sanction. **-dis·ap·prov'al,** *n.*

dis·arm (-ärm'), *v.t.* 1. to deprive of arms. 2. to render harmless. 3. to make friendly: *v.i.* to reduce armed forces or armaments. **-dis·ar·ma·ment** (-är'mà-mènt), *n.*

dis·ar·range (-å-rānj'), *v.t.* -ranged', -rang'ing, to disorder; unsettle. **-dis·ar·range'ment,** *n.*

dis·ar·ray (-å-rā'), *v.t.* to throw into disorder: *n.* 1. disorder; confusion. 2. disorderly or insufficient dress.

dis·as·sem·ble (-å-sem'bl), *v.t.* -bled, -bling, to take apart.

dis·as·so·ci·ate (-å-sō'shi-āt), *v.t.* -at-ed, -at-ing, to stop associating with.

dis·as·ter (di-zas'tēr), *n.* a serious misfortune that causes much damage; calamity. **-dis·as'trous** ('trŭs), *adj.*

dis·a·vow (dis-å-vou'), *v.t.* to deny; repudiate. **-dis·a·vow'al,** *n.*

dis·band (-band'), *v.t. & v.i.* to break up, as a military organization.

dis·bar (-bär'), *v.t.* -barred', -bar'ring, to deprive (a lawyer) of his right to practice law. **-dis·bar'ment,** *n.*

dis·be·lief (-bê-lēf'), *n.* a refusal to believe.

dis·be·lieve (-lēv'), *v.t.* -lieved', -liev'ing, to refuse to believe. **-dis·be·liev'er,** *n.*

dis·bur·den (-bûr'dn), *v.t.* to remove a burden from: *v.i.* to get rid of a burden. **-dis·bur'den·ment,** *n.*

dis·burse (-bûrs'), *v.t.* -bursed', -burs'ing, to expend; pay out. **-dis·burse'ment,** *n.* **-dis·burs'er,** *n.*

disc (disk), *n.* 1. same as disk. 2. a phonograph record.

dis·card (dis-kärd'), *v.t.* 1. to cast off as useless. 2. in *card games,* to play (an undesired card) from one's hand: *n.* (dis'kärd), 1. the act of discarding. 2. something discarded.

dis·cern (di-sûrn', -zûrn'), *v.t.* to distinguish or perceive clearly: *v.i.* to distinguish. **-dis·cern'i·ble,** *adj.* **-dis·cern'ment,** *n.*

dis·cern·ing ('ing), *adj.* showing good judgment. **-dis·cern'ing·ly,** *adv.*

dis·charge (dis-chärj'), *v.t.* -charged', -charg'ing, 1. to unload. 2. to dismiss. 3. to free from restraint. 4. to perform (a trust or duty). 5. to fire (a gun or missile): *v.i.* 1. to emit liquid matter, as a wound. 2. to go off, as a gun. 3. to get rid of something: *n.* (dis'chärj), 1. the act of discharging. 2. that which is discharged.

disc harrow, a harrow with thin, flat, circular blades, used to break up the soil.

dis·ci·ple (di-sī'pl), *n.* 1. a pupil or follower of a teacher. 2. an early follower of Jesus.

Disciples of Christ, a Christian denomination, organized in 1809, that rejects creeds and accepts only the Bible as the basis of faith.

dis·ci·pli·nar·i·an (dis-i-pli-ner'i-ån), *n.* one who advocates or enforces strict discipline.

dis·ci·pline (dis'i-plin), *n.* 1. a field of learning; subject. 2. training to develop self-control,

right conduct, etc. 3. orderly conduct. 4. subjection to control or regulation. 5. a set of rules. 6. punishment: *v.t.* -plined, -plin-ing, 1. to train to obedience or efficiency. 2. to punish. **-dis'ci·plin·a·ble,** *adj.* **-dis'ci·pli·nar·y** (-pli-ner-i), *adj.*

disc jockey, one who conducts a radio program of recorded music.

dis·claim (dis-klām'), *v.t.* 1. to relinquish any claim to. 2. to repudiate: *v.i.* to make a disclaimer. **-dis·cla·ma'tion** (-klå-mā'shŭn), *n.*

dis·claim·er ('ẽr), *n.* 1. a denial of responsibility. 2. a renunciation of a title, claim, etc.

dis·close (dis-klōz'), *v.t.* -closed', -clos'ing, to uncover; reveal. **-dis·clo'sure** (-klō'zhẽr), *n.*

dis·coid (dis'koid), *adj.* disk-shaped.

dis·col·or (dis-kul'ẽr), *v.t. & v.i.* to change or alter in color by fading, staining, etc.: British form **dis·col'our.** **-dis·col·or·a'tion,** *n.*

dis·com·fit (-kum'fit), *v.t.* 1. to frustrate; thwart. 2. to upset; confuse. **-dis·com'fi·ture** ('fi·chẽr), *n.*

dis·com·fort (-kum'fẽrt), *n.* 1. lack of comfort; distress. 2. anything that causes discomfort: *v.t.* to cause discomfort to.

dis·com·mode (-kŏ-mōd'), *v.t.* -mod'ed, -mod'ing, to inconvenience.

dis·com·pose (-kŏm-pōz'), *v.t.* -posed', -pos'ing, 1. [Now Rare], to disarrange. 2. to perturb; agitate. **-dis·com·po'sure,** *n.*

dis·con·cert (-kŏn-sûrt'), *v.t.* 1. to disturb the composure of. 2. to frustrate.

dis·con·nect (-kŏ-nekt'), *v.t.* to sever the connection of; unplug, detach, etc. **-dis·con·nec'tion,** *n.*

dis·con·nect·ed ('id), *adj.* 1. not connected. 2. incoherent.

dis·con·so·late (dis-kon'sŏ-lit), *adj.* 1. sad; inconsolable. 2. cheerless. **-dis·con'so·late·ly,** *adv.*

dis·con·tent (-kŏn-tent'), *n.* a restless dissatisfaction. **-dis·con·tent'ed,** *adj.*

dis·con·tin·ue (-kŏn-tin'ū), *v.t. & v.i.* -ued, -u·ing, to stop; cease; break off. **-dis·con·tin'u·ance,** *dis·con·tin·u·a'tion* (-å'shŭn), *n.*

dis·cord (dis'kôrd), *n.* 1. disagreement. 2. a confused noise. 3. a combination of inharmonious musical tones. **-dis·cord'ant,** *adj.*

dis·co·theque (dis'kô-tek), *n.* a public place for dancing to recorded music.

dis·count (dis'kount), *n.* 1. an amount below the usual or list price. 2. interest deducted in advance on a loan of money: *v.t.* (dis-kount'), 1. to pay or receive money for (a note, bill, etc.) less the interest. 2. to deduct an amount from (a bill, charge, etc.). 3. to sell at a reduced price. 4. to make an allowance for (exaggeration, etc.). 5. to disregard. 6. to anticipate.

dis·coun·te·nance (dis-koun'tê-nåns), *v.t.* -nanced, -nanc·ing, 1. to disconcert or embarrass. 2. to show disfavor of.

dis·cour·age (dis-kûr'ij), *v.t.* -aged, -ag·ing, 1. to deprive of courage or confidence. 2. to deter. 3. to try to dissuade. **-dis·cour'age·ment,** *n.*

dis·course (dis'kôrs), *n.* 1. conversation. 2. a treatise or dissertation: *v.i.* (dis-kôrs'), -coursed', -cours'ing, to talk.

---

dis·cour·te·ous (dis-kûr'ti-ûs), *adj.* impolite; rude. —**dis·cour'te·sy**, *n., pl.* -sies.

dis·cov·er (dis-kuv'ēr), *v.t.* to find, see, or learn about (something previously unknown). — **dis·cov'er·er**, *n.*

dis·cov·er·y (-i), *n., pl.* -er·ies, 1. the act of discovering. 2. something discovered.

Discovery Day, same as **Columbus Day.**

dis·cred·it (dis-kred'it), *v.t.* 1. to disbelieve. 2. to injure the credit or reputation of. 3. to disgrace: *n.* 1. distrust; loss or lack of belief. 2. disgrace. —**dis·cred'it·a·ble,** *adj.*

dis·creet (dis-krēt'), *adj.* prudent; circumspect. —**dis·creet'ly,** *adv.*

dis·crep·an·cy (dis-krep'ån-si), *n., pl.* -cies, inconsistency; difference.

dis·crep·ant ('ånt), *adj.* disagreeing; different. —**dis·crep'ant·ly,** *adv.*

dis·crete (dis-krēt'), *adj.* separate from others; distinct; unrelated. —**dis·crete'ly,** *adv.* —**dis·crete'ness,** *n.*

dis·cre·tion (dis-kresh'ûn), *n.* 1. the freedom or power to make choices. 2. the quality of being discreet; prudence. —**dis·cre'tion·ar·y** (-er-i), *adj.*

dis·crim·i·nate (dis-krim'i-nāt), *v.i.* -nat·ed, -nat·ing, 1. to observe or mark accurately the differences between. 2. to show preference for or prejudice against. —**dis·crim'i·nat·ing,** **dis·crim'i·na·tive,** *adj.* —**dis·crim·i·na'tion,** *n.*

dis·crim·i·na·to·ry (-nå-tôr-i), *adj.* showing prejudice or bias.

dis·cur·sive (dis-kûr'siv), *adj.* desultory; rambling. —**dis·cur'sive·ly,** *adv.*

dis·cus (dis'kûs), *n.* 1. a disk of metal and wood thrown as a test of strength and skill. 2. the throwing of the discus as a contest: also **discus throw.**

dis·cuss (dis-kus'), *v.t.* to talk or write about in detail; consider the various aspects of. — **dis·cus'sion** (-kush'ûn), *n.*

dis·dain (dis-dān'), *v.t.* to think unworthy; look upon with contempt or scorn: *n.* contempt; haughty scorn. —**dis·dain'ful,** *adj.* —**dis·dain'ful·ly,** *adv.*

dis·ease (di-zēz'), *n.* 1. sickness in general. 2. a particular destructive process in an organism, with a cause and certain symptoms. 3. any deranged or harmful state of affairs, as in society: *v.t.* -eased', -eas'ing, to cause disease in.

dis·em·bark (dis-im-bärk'), *v.t. & v.i.* to remove from or leave a ship, aircraft, etc. —**dis·em·bark·a'tion,** *n.*

dis·em·bod·y (-im-bod'i), *v.t.* -bod'ied, -bod'y·ing, to divest of bodily existence. —**dis·em·bod'i·ment,** *n.*

dis·em·bogue (-im-bōg'), *v.t. & v.i.* -bogued', -bogu'ing, to pour out or discharge at the mouth: said of a river.

dis·em·bow·el (-im-bou'ėl), *v.t.* -eled or -elled, -el·ing or -el·ling, to take out the entrails of; eviscerate. —**dis·em·bow'el·ment,** *n.*

dis·en·chant (-in-chant'), *v.t.* 1. to set free from an enchantment. 2. to disillusion. —**dis·en·chant'ment,** *n.*

dis·en·cum·ber (-in-kum'bēr), *v.t.* to free from a burden.

dis·en·gage (-in-gāj'), *v.t. & v.i.* -gaged', -gag'-ing, 1. to release. 2. to disentangle; detach. —**dis·en·gage'ment,** *n.*

dis·en·tan·gle (-in-tang'gl), *v.t.* -gled, -gling, 1. to free from something that entangles; extricate. 2. to straighten out; untangle. —**dis·en·tan'gle·ment,** *n.*

dis·fa·vor (-fā'vēr), *n.* 1. disapproval. 2. a state of being disliked.

dis·fig·ure (-fig'yēr), *v.t.* -ured, -ur·ing, to injure the shape, form, or beauty of; deform. — **dis·fig'ure·ment, dis·fig·ur·a'tion** (-fig·yēr-ā'-shûn), *n.*

dis·fran·chise (-fran'chīz), *v.t.* -chised, -chis·ing, to deprive of rights or privileges, especially the right to vote. —**dis·fran'chise·ment,** *n.*

dis·gorge (-gôrj'), *v.t. & v.i.* -gorged', -gorg'ing, 1. to vomit. 2. to discharge (its contents). 3. to give up (something).

dis·grace (-grās'), *n.* 1. the state of being out of favor; ignominy; shame. 2. a person, thing, or act that brings shame: *v.t.* -graced', -grac'ing, to bring shame, reproval, or dishonor upon. —**dis·grace'ful,** *adj.* —**dis·grace'-ful·ly,** *adv.*

dis·grun·tled (-grun'tld), *adj.* sulky; bad-humored; peevish.

dis·guise (-gīz'), *v.t.* -guised', -guis'ing, 1. to change the looks or sound of so as to hide the identity or to seem to be someone else. 2. to conceal the real nature of: *n.* 1. clothing or makeup designed to conceal the identity of the wearer. 2. false pretense.

dis·gust (-gust'), *v.t.* to cause aversion in or repugnance to; offend: *n.* a strong aversion or repugnance. —**dis·gust'ing,** *adj.*

dish (dish), *n.* 1. a shallow, concave container for serving food. 2. as much as a dish will hold. 3. a kind of food: *v.t.* to put into a dish (with *up* or *out*).

dis·ha·bille (dis-â-bēl'), *n.* the state of being partly dressed or in night clothes.

dis·har·mo·ny (dis-här'mō-ni), *n.* discord. —**dis·har·mo'ni·ous** (-mō'ni·ûs), *adj.*

dis·heart·en (dis-här'tn), *v.t.* to depress; discourage. —**dis·heart'en·ing,** *adj.*

di·shev·el (di-shev'l), *v.t.* -eled or -elled, -el·ing or -el·ling, to muss up (hair, clothes, etc.); rumple; tousle. —**di·shev'el·ment,** *n.*

dis·hon·est (dis-on'ist), *adj.* not honest; lacking in integrity; inclined to cheat, etc. —**dis·hon'est·ly,** *adv.*

dis·hon·es·ty (-i), *n.* 1. lack of honesty or integrity; inclination to lie, cheat, steal, etc. 2. *pl.* -ties, a dishonest act.

dis·hon·or (dis-on'ēr), *v.t.* 1. to bring shame upon; disgrace. 2. to insult. 3. to refuse, or fail, to pay (a bill, etc.): *n.* 1. loss of honor; disgrace; ignominy. 2. a cause of disgrace. 3. a refusal or failure to pay a bill, etc. — **dis·hon'or·a·ble,** *adj.* —**dis·hon'or·a·bly,** *adv.*

dish·wash·er (dish'wôsh·ēr, 'wäsh·ēr), *n.* a person or machine that washes dishes.

dis·il·lu·sion (dis-i-lōō'zhûn), *v.t.* 1. to free from illusion. 2. to deprive of ideals, etc. —**dis·il·lu'sion·ment,** *n.*

dis·in·cline (-in-klīn'), *v.t.* -clined', -clin'ing, to cause to be reluctant. —dis·in·cli·na'tion (-in-kli-nā'shŭn), n.

dis·in·fect (-in-fekt'), v.t. to purify; destroy disease germs, harmful bacteria, etc.; sterilize. —dis·in·fect'ant, n.

dis·in·for·ma·tion (-in-fĕr-mā'shŭn), n. deliberately false information leaked so as to confuse another nation's intelligence operations.

dis·in·gen·u·ous (-in-jen'yoo-wŭs), adj. lacking in sincerity or frankness. —dis·in·gen'u·ous·ly, adv.

dis·in·her·it (-in-her'it), v.t. to deprive of an inheritance. —dis·in·her'i·tance, n.

dis·in·te·grate (-in'tĕ-grāt), v.t. & v.i. -grat·ed, -grat·ing, to break up into parts or fragments. —dis·in·te·gra'tion, n.

dis·in·ter (-in-tŭr'), v.t. -terred', -ter'ring, to take out of the grave; exhume. —dis·in·ter'-

dis·in·ter·est·ed (-in'trist-id), adj. 1. unbiased. 2. indifferent.

dis·in·ter·me·di·a·tion (-in-tĕr-mē-dē-ā'shŭn), n. the withdrawal of funds from banks to invest them at higher rates of interest, as in government securities.

dis·joint·ed (-joint'id), adj. 1. out of joint. 2. dismembered. 3. incoherent; disconnected. —dis·joint'ed·ly, adv.

disk (disk), n. 1. a thin, flat, circular plate, or anything resembling it. 2. same as disc. 3. a thin, flat, circular plate coated with magnetic particles, for storing computer data.

disk·ette (di-sket'), n. same as floppy disk.

dis·like (dis-līk'), n. a feeling of aversion or distaste: v.t. -liked', -lik'ing, to regard with aversion or displeasure.

dis·lo·cate (dis'lō-kāt), v.t. -lo·cat·ed, -lo·cat·ing, 1. to put (a joint) out of position. 2. to upset; disrupt. —dis·lo·ca'tion, n.

dis·lodge (dis-loj'), v.t. & v.i. -lodged', -lodg'ing, to drive from or leave a place of lodgment or hiding.

dis·loy·al (-loi'ăl), adj. not loyal; faithless. — dis·loy'al·ty, n., pl. -ties.

dis·mal (diz'ml), adj. 1. gloomy; dark. 2. causing gloom; depressing. 3. miserable. —dis'·mal·ly, adv.

dis·man·tle (dis-man'tl), v.t. -tled, -tling, 1. to strip or divest of furniture, equipment, or means of defense. 2. to take apart.

dis·may (-mā'), v.t. to dispirit; discourage; intimidate: n. loss of courage through fear.

dis·mem·ber (-mem'bĕr), v.t. 1. to cut or tear limb from limb. 2. to divide up or mutilate. —dis·mem'ber·ment, n.

dis·miss (-mis'), v.t. 1. to send away. 2. to permit to depart. 3. to discharge from office or employment. 4. to put out of the mind. — dis·miss'al, n.

dis·mount (-mount'), v.i. to get down, as from a horse; v.t. 1. to take apart. 2. to remove (something) from its mounting.

dis·o·be·di·ence (-ō-bē'di-ĕns), n. a refusal to obey authority. —dis·o·be'di·ent, adj.

dis·o·bey (-ō-bā'), v.t. & v.i. to refuse or fail to obey.

dis·o·blige (-ō-blīj', -ō-), v.t. 1. to refuse to oblige. 2. to offend.

dis·or·der (-ôr'dĕr), n. 1. a lack of order or arrangement. 2. a breach of public order; riot.

3. an ailment; disfunction: v.t. 1. to throw into confusion. 2. to disturb the normal mental or physical function of.

dis·or·der·ly (-li), adj. 1. not orderly; confused; unmethodical. 2. turbulent; unruly. 3. in Law, violating public peace, safety, or order. —dis·or'der·li·ness, n.

dis·or·gan·ize (-ôr'gă-nīz), v.t. -ized, -iz·ing, to disarrange; throw into confusion. —dis·or·gan·i·za'tion, n.

dis·o·ri·ent (-ôr'i-ĕnt), v.t. 1. to cause to lose one's bearings. 2. to confuse mentally. Also dis·o'ri·en·tate, -tat·ed, -tat·ing. —dis·o·ri·en·ta'tion, n.

dis·own (-ōn'), v.t. to deny relationship with or ownership of; repudiate.

dis·par·age (-per'ij), v.t. -aged, -ag·ing, 1. to treat with contempt. 2. to belittle. —dis·par'age·ment, n.

dis·pa·rate (dis'pĕr-it), adj. that cannot be compared; distinctly different in kind. —dis·par'i·ty (-per'i-ti), n., pl. -ties.

dis·pas·sion·ate (-pash'ŭn-it), adj. free from passion or bias; calm; unprejudiced; impartial. —dis·pas'sion·ate·ly, adv.

dis·patch (dis-pach'), v.t. 1. to send off or away swiftly. 2. to kill. 3. to attend to quickly: n. 1. the act of sending off. 2. speedy action. 3. a message. 4. a news story sent to a newspaper, etc. —dis·patch'er, n.

dis·pel (-pel'), v.t. -pelled', -pel'ling, to drive away by scattering; disperse.

dis·pen·sa·ble (-dis·pen'sà-bl), adj. that can be dispensed with or done without.

dis·pen·sa·ry (-sà-ri), n., pl. -ries, a place where medicines are dispensed and first-aid treatment is given.

dis·pen·sa·tion (dis-pĕn-sā'shŭn), n. 1. the act of dispensing. 2. something distributed. 3. a system of management. 4. an exemption from a rule or release from an obligation. 5. in Theology, a) the divine ordering of events on earth. b) any religious system.

dis·pense (dis-pens'), v.t. -pensed', -pens'ing, 1. to distribute. 2. to prepare and distribute (medicines). 3. to administer (justice or the law).

dis·perse (dis-pŭrs'), v.t. -persed', -pers'ing, 1. to scatter in different directions or parts; diffuse. 2. to break up (light) into colored rays. 3. to dispel; cause to vanish: v.i. to scatter. —dis·per'sal, n. —dis·per'sion, n.

dis·pir·it (dis-spir'it), v.t. to depress; dishearten. —dis·pir'it·ed, adj.

dis·place (dis-plās'), v.t. -placed', -plac'ing, 1. to put out of place. 2. to supplant. 3. to depose from office.

dis·place·ment (-plās'mĕnt), n. 1. the act of displacing. 2. the weight of water or other fluid displaced by a floating object.

dis·play (-plā'), v.t. 1. to spread out; unfold. 2. to exhibit.

dis·please (-plēz'), v.t. & v.i. -pleased', -pleas'-ing, to be offensive or annoying to.

dis·pleas·ure (-plezh'ĕr), n. annoyance; vexation; pique.

dis·port (-pōrt'), v.t. to amuse (oneself): v.i. to frolic; indulge in amusement.

dis·pos·a·ble (-pō'zǎ-bl), *adj.* 1. available; not restricted. 2. that can be thrown away.

dis·pose (-pōz'), *v.t.* -posed', -pos'ing, 1. to place; arrange. 2. to settle (affairs). 3. to incline. —**dis·pos'al,** *n.*

dis·pos·er (-pō'zēr), *n.* a kitchen device installed in a sink drain to grind garbage which is then washed down the drain.

dis·po·si·tion (-pō·zish'ŭn), *n.* 1. order; arrangement. 2. settlement of affairs. 3. a transfer of something, as by sale or gift. 4. a tendency. 5. one's natural temperament.

dis·pos·sess (-pŏ-zes'), *v.t.* to deprive of possession; eject; oust.

dis·pro·por·tion·ate (-prō-pōr'shŭn-it), *adj.* out of proportion, as in number, size, etc. —**dis·pro·por'tion·ate·ly,** *adv.*

dis·prove (-prōōv'), *v.t.* -proved', -prov'ing, to prove to be false; refute. —**dis·proof',** *n.*

dis·pu·ta·tion (-pū·tā'shŭn), *n.* 1. the act of disputing. 2. a formal debate.

dis·pu·ta·tious (-pū·tā'shŭs), *adj.* quarrelsome; contentious.

dis·pute (dis·pūt'), *v.i.* -put'ed, -put'ing, 1. to debate; argue. 2. to quarrel: *v.t.* 1. to argue about. 2. to question; doubt. 3. to oppose: *n.* 1. a debate or argument. 2. a quarrel.— **dis·pu'ta·ble,** *adj.* —**dis·pu'tant,** *n. & adj.*

dis·qual·i·fy (-kwǎl'ī-fī), *v.t.* -fied, -fy·ing, to make or declare to be ineligible or unfit. — **dis·qual·i·fi·ca'tion,** *n.*

dis·qui·et (-kwī'ĕt), *v.t.* to make anxious; disturb. —**dis·qui'e·tude** ('ē·tōōd), *n.*

dis·qui·si·tion (-kwi·zish'ŭn), *n.* a formal discourse; treatise; essay.

dis·rate (-rāt'), *v.t.* -rat'ed, -rat'ing, to demote or lower in rating or rank.

dis·re·gard (-ri·gärd'), *n.* 1. lack of due regard. 2. lack of attention: *v.t.* 1. to fail to treat with due regard or respect. 2. to ignore; slight; neglect.

dis·re·pair (-ri·per'), *n.* a state of needing repairs; dilapidation.

dis·rep·u·ta·ble (-rep'yoo-tā-bl), *adj.* 1. having a bad reputation. 2. shoddy; shabby. —**dis·rep'u·ta·bly,** *adv.*

dis·re·pute (-ri·pūt'), *n.* loss of reputation; dishonor; disgrace; ill favor.

dis·re·spect (-ri·spekt'), *v.t.* to show lack of respect for. *n.* lack of respect; discourtesy; incivility. —**dis·re·spect'ful,** *adj.* —**dis·re·spect'·ful·ly,** *adv.*

dis·robe (-rōb'), *v.t. & v.i.* -robed', -rob'ing, to undress.

dis·rupt (-rupt'), *v.t. & v.i.* 1. to break asunder; rend. 2. to interrupt; break up. —**dis·rup'·tion,** *n.* —**dis·rup'tive,** *adj.*

dis·sat·is·fy (-sat'is-fī), *v.t.* -fied, -fy·ing, to fail to satisfy; displease. —**dis·sat·is·fac'tion,** *n.*

dis·sect (di·sekt'), *v.t.* 1. to cut up in order to study, as a body. 2. to analyze minutely. — **dis·sec'tion,** *n.*

dis·seize (dis·sēz'), *v.t.* -seized', -seiz'ing, to dispossess unlawfully. —**dis·sei'zor,** *n.*

dis·sem·ble (di·sem'bl), *v.t. & v.i.* -bled, -bling, to conceal (one's motives, the truth, etc.) under a false appearance. —**dis·sem'blance,** *n.* —**dis·sem'bler,** *n.*

dis·sem·i·nate (di·sem'ī·nāt), *v.t.* -nat·ed, -nat·ing, to scatter abroad, like seed; spread widely. —**dis·sem·i·na'tion,** *n.* —**dis·sem'i·na·tor,** *n.*

dis·sen·sion (di·sen'shŭn), *n.* a strong disagreement; argument or wrangling.

dis·sent (di·sent'), *v.i.* 1. to disagree. 2. to refuse to adhere to an established church: *n.* the act of dissenting. —**dis·sent'er,** *n.* —**dis·sent'ing,** *adj.*

dis·sen·tient (-sen'shĕnt), *n.* one who dissents; dissenter: *adj.* dissenting.

dis·ser·ta·tion (dis·ēr·tā'shŭn), *n.* a formal argumentative discourse; thesis; essay; treatise.

dis·ser·vice (dis·sûr'vis), *n.* harm.

dis·sev·er (di·sev'ēr), *v.t.* 1. to cut in two. 2. to divide into parts: *v.i.* to separate. —**dis·sev'·er·ance,** *n.*

dis·si·dent (dis'ī·dĕnt), *adj.* not agreeing or conforming: *n.* one who disagrees; dissenter. —**dis'si·dence,** *n.*

dis·sil·i·ent (di·sil'ī·ĕnt), *adj.* springing or bursting open with force, as some seedpods.

dis·sim·i·lar (di·sim'ī·lēr), *adj.* not similar; unlike. —**dis·sim·i·lar'i·ty** (-lēr'ī·ti), *n., pl.* -ties.

dis·si·mil·i·tude (dis·si·mil'ī·tōōd), *n.* a state of being dissimilar; variance.

dis·sim·u·late (di·sim'yŭ·lāt), *v.t. & v.i.* -lat·ed, -lat·ing, to dissemble. —**dis·sim·u·la'tion,** *n.* —**dis·sim'u·la·tor,** *n.*

dis·si·pate (dis'ī·pāt), *v.t.* -pat·ed, -pat·ing, 1. to scatter completely; disperse. 2. to make disappear; dissolve. 3. to squander: *v.i.* 1. to disappear. 2. to indulge oneself excessively in pleasures. —**dis·si·pa'tion,** *n.*

dis·so·ci·ate (di·sō'shi·āt), *v.t.* -at·ed, -at·ing, to separate; disconnect. —**dis·so·ci·a'tion,** *n.*

dis·sol·u·ble (di·sol'yoo·bl), *adj.* capable of being dissolved. —**dis·sol·u·bil'i·ty,** *n.*

dis·so·lute (dis'ô·lōōt), *adj.* given to dissipation; loose in morals or conduct.

dis·so·lu·tion (dis·ô·lōō'shŭn), *n.* 1. the act of dissolving or liquefying. 2. a separation into component parts. 3. a breaking up of an association, business, etc. 4. death.

dis·solve (di·zolv'), *v.t. & v.i.* -solved', -solv'ing, 1. to liquefy; melt. 2. to pass or cause to pass into solution. 3. to break up. 4. to terminate. 5. to waste or fade away. — **dis·solv'a·ble,** *adj.*

dis·so·nance (dis'ô·nǎns), *n.* discord; lack of harmony. —**dis'so·nant,** *adj.*

dis·suade (di·swād'), *v.t.* -suad'ed, -suad'ing, to advise or counsel against; divert by argument or persuasion. —**dis·sua'sion** (-swā'zhŭn), *n.* —**dis·sua'sive,** *adj.*

dis·taff (dis'taf), *n.* the staff from which flax, wool, etc. is drawn in spinning: *adj.* 1. female. 2. of or pertaining to the maternal side of a family.

dis·tance (dis'tǎns), *n.* 1. the space or interval between two objects or points in space or time. 2. remoteness of time, rank, relationship, or place. 3. reserve of manner. 4. a distant place.

dis·tant ('tǎnt), *adj.* 1. remote. 2. not closely related. 3. reserved; aloof. 4. from or to a distance. —**dis'tant·ly,** *adv.*

dis·taste (dis·tāst'), *n.* dislike; disinclination. — **dis·taste'ful,** *adj.*

dis·tem·per (dis·tem'pēr), *v.t.* 1. to disorder or derange the functions of. 2. to mix (colors or pigments) with water and a binding medium: *n.* 1. a disease. 2. an infectious disease of young dogs. 3. a method of painting with distempered paint, as in murals. 4. distempered paint.

dis-tend (-tend'), *v.t. & v.i.* 1. to stretch out in all directions. 2. to make or become swollen. —dis-ten'tion, *n.*

dis-tich (dis'tik), *n.* a couplet.

dis-till, dis-til (dis-til'), *v.i. & v.t.* -tilled', -till'-ing, 1. to fall or let fall in drops. 2. to obtain by or undergo distillation. —dis-till'er, *n.*

dis-til-late (dis'ti-lāt, 'tl-it), *n.* the product obtained in distillation.

dis-til-la-tion (dis-ti-lā'shŭn), *n.* 1. the act or process of evaporating a substance by heat and condensing the vapors in order to produce a more concentrated or purer substance. 2. a product of distillation.

dis-till-er-y (-til'ẽr-i), *n., pl.* -er-ies, a building with equipment for the distillation of alcoholic liquors.

dis-tinct (dis-tingkt'), *adj.* 1. different. 2. separate. 3. clear; plain. 4. well-defined. —dis-tinct'ly, *adv.*

dis-tinc-tion (-tingk'shŭn), *n.* 1. difference. 2. discrimination. 3. a mark of difference or superiority. 4. eminence; fame. 5. a mark of honor.

dis-tinc-tive (-tingk'tiv), *adj.* marking a difference or distinction; characteristic. —dis-tinc'tive-ly, *adv.* —dis-tinc'tive-ness, *n.*

dis-tin-gué (dis-tang-gā'), *adj.* [French], distinguished; having a distinguished bearing. —dis-tin-guée' (-gā'), *adj.fem.*

dis-tin-guish (dis-ting'gwish), *v.t.* 1. to differentiate; separate from others. 2. to designate by special characteristics. 3. to make famous. 4. to divide into classes. 5. to discern clearly: *v.i.* to make a distinction (*between* or *among*). —dis-tin'guish-a-ble, *adj.*

dis-tin-guished ('gwisht), *adj.* eminent; celebrated; noted.

dis-tort (dis-tôrt'), *v.t.* 1. to twist or turn from the natural shape or figure. 2. to misrepresent (truth, facts, etc.). —dis-tor'tion, *n.*

dis-tract (-trakt'), *v.t.* 1. to divert, as the mind or attention. 2. to confuse; bewilder.

dis-trac-tion (-trak'shŭn), *n.* 1. the act of distracting. 2. an amusing diversion. 3. something that confuses or bewilders. 4. perturbation or mental distress. —dis-trac'tive, *adj.*

dis-train (-trān'), *v.t. & v.i.* to seize and hold (goods or chattels) as security for payment of a debt.

dis-traint (-trānt'), *n.* the act of distraining for debt; seizure.

dis-trait (-trā'), *adj.* [French], absent-minded; distracted.

dis-traught (-trôt'), *adj.* 1. bewildered; confused. 2. harassed; crazed.

dis-tress (-tres'), *v.t.* to inflict pain or suffering upon; harass: *n.* 1. physical or mental anguish. 2. affliction; trouble. 3. a state of misfortune or trouble. —dis-tress'ful, *adj.* —dis-tress'ful-ly, *adv.*

dis-tressed (-trest'), *adj.* 1. full of distress; upset. 2. made to look old, as wood with a marred finish. 3. denoting a poverty-stricken area.

dis-trib-ute (-trib'yoot), *v.t.* -ut-ed, -ut-ing, 1. to deal out or divide; allot. 2. to arrange according to classification. 3. to disperse; scatter. 4. to separate and place (things) in their respective places. —dis-tri-bu'tion (-trî-bū'-shŭn), *n.* —dis-trib'u-tive, *adj.*

dis-trib-u-tor ('yoo-tẽr), *n.* 1. a person or firm that distributes merchandise to the consumer. 2. a device in an internal-combustion engine that distributes electricity to the spark plugs in a proper sequence.

dis-trict (dis'trikt), *n.* 1. a division of a county, city, etc. for a specific purpose. 2. any area, locality, etc.

district attorney, the public prosecutor of criminal cases in a given State or Federal district.

dis-trust (dis-trust'), *n.* lack of trust; suspicion; doubt: *v.t.* to have no trust in; suspect; doubt. —dis-trust'ful, *adj.*

dis-turb (-tûrb'), *v.t.* 1. to agitate; throw into confusion. 2. to trouble; upset. 3. to interrupt. —dis-turb'ance, *n.*

di-sul-fate (dī-sul'fāt), *n.* a sulfate containing one atom of hydrogen, replaceable by a basic element.

di-sul-fide ('fīd), *n.* a sulfide containing two atoms of sulfur.

dis-u-nite (dis-yoo-nīt'), *v.t.* -nit'ed, -nit'ing, to take away the unity of; separate; alienate: *v.i.* to become separated. —dis-u'ni-ty (-ū'ni-ti), *n.*

dis-use (-ūs'), *n.* the state or condition of not being used: *v.t.* (-ūz'), -used', -us'ing, to stop using.

di-syl-la-ble (dī-sil'ă-bl), *n.* a word of two syllables. —di-syl-lab-ic (-si-lab'ik), *adj.*

ditch (dich), *n.* a trench dug in the earth, as for drainage: *v.t.* 1. to dig a ditch in or around. 2. to set (a damaged aircraft) down on water and abandon it. 3. [Slang], to get rid of.

di-the-ism (dī'thi-izm), *n.* belief in two equally powerful supreme gods.

dith-er (di*th*'ẽr), *n.* a flustered, excited, or confused state.

dith-y-ramb (dith'i-ram), *n.* 1. an ancient Greek choral hymn in honor of the god of wine and revelry. 2. any similar work.

dit-to (dit'ō), *n., pl.* -tos, 1. the same as the above or what was said before. 2. same as ditto mark: *adv.* as before; likewise: *v.t.* -toed, -to-ing, 1. to make copies of. 2. to repeat.

ditto mark, a mark (") used to indicate that the preceding item is to be repeated.

dit-ty (dit'i), *n., pl.* -ties, a simple song.

di-u-re-sis (dī-yoo-rē'sis), *n.* an excessive excretion of urine.

di-u-ret-ic (-ret'ik), *adj.* increasing the secretion and flow of urine: *n.* a diuretic medicine or substance.

di-ur-nal (dī-ûr'nl), *adj.* 1. daily. 2. in or of the daytime. —di-ur'nal-ly, *adv.*

di-va (dē'vä), *n.* a prima donna.

di-va-lent (dī-vā'lĕnt), *adj.* same as bivalent.

di-van (dī'van), *n.* a large sofa or couch.

dive (dīv), *v.i.* dived or dove, dived, div'ing, 1.

to plunge headfirst into water. 2. to submerge. 3. to penetrate suddenly into something. 4. to descend through the air at a steep angle: *n.* 1. a plunge or descent. 2. [Informal], a cheap, dingy bar, etc. —div'er, *n.*

dive bomber, an airplane that releases its bombs as it dives toward its target.

di·verge (di-vūrj'), *v.i.* -verged', -verg'ing, 1. to lie, go, or spread out from a common point; branch off. 2. to differ, as in form, opinion, etc. —di·ver'gence, *n.* —di·ver'gent, *adj.*

di·vers (dī'vērz), *adj.* various; sundry.

di·verse (di-vūrs'), *adj.* 1. different; dissimilar. 2. varied. —di·verse'ly, *adv.*

di·ver·si·fy (di-vūr'si-fī), *v.t.* -fied, -fy·ing, 1. to make different; vary. 2. to divide up (investments) among different companies. 3. to expand (a business) by offering more products or services. —di·ver·si·fi·ca'tion, *n.*

di·ver·sion (di-vūr'zhŭn), *n.* 1. the act of diverting or turning aside. 2. a distraction of attention. 3. a pastime. —di·ver'sion·ar·y (-er-i), *adj.*

di·ver·si·ty (di-vūr'si-ti), *n., pl.* -ties, 1. the state of being different. 2. variety.

di·vert (di-vūrt'), *v.t.* 1. to turn aside (*from* a direction or course). 2. to entertain; amuse.

di·ver·tic·u·li·tis (dī-vēr-tik-yoo-līt'is), *n.* inflammation of a diverticulum.

di·ver·tic·u·lum (-lŭm), *n., pl.* -la (-lä), a small sac opening out from a tubular organ.

di·ver·ti·men·to (di-vēr-ti-men'tō), *n., pl.* -ti ('ti), -tos, a light, melodic instrumental composition.

di·ver·tisse·ment (di-vūrt'is-mĕnt), *n.* [French], 1. amusement; recreation. 2. an entr'acte, as a ballet, etc. 3. same as *divertimento*.

di·vest (di-vest'), *v.t.* 1. to strip (of ornament, clothing, etc.). 2. to deprive (of rank, etc.). 3. to rid (of something). —di·vest'i·ture ('i-chēr), *n.*

di·vide (di-vīd'), *v.t.* -vid'ed, -vid'ing, 1. to separate into parts, sections, etc. 2. to keep apart. 3. to disunite by discord. 4. to apportion; distribute. 5. in *Mathematics*, to separate into equal parts by a divisor: *v.i.* 1. to be separated. 2. to diverge. 3. to share. 4. in *Mathematics*, to do division: *n.* a watershed.

div·i·dend (div'i-dend), *n.* 1. a number or quantity to be divided. 2. a sum to be divided among stockholders, creditors, etc. 3. one person's share of this. 4. a bonus.

di·vid·er (di-vid'ēr), *n.* 1. a screen, bookcase, etc. that divides one section of a room from another. 2. *pl.* a pair of compasses for dividing lines, etc.

div·i·di·vi (div'i-div'i), *n.* 1. astringent husks of a South American tropical plant, used for dyeing and tanning. 2. this plant.

div·i·na·tion (div-i-nā'shŭn), *n.* 1. the practice of attempting to foretell the future or reveal the unknown by occult means. 2. a prophecy.

di·vine (di-vīn'), *adj.* 1. of or having the nature of God or a god. 2. excellent in the highest degree. 3. holy; sacred. 4. religious: *n.* 1. a theologian. 2. a clergyman: *v.t.* -vined',

-vin'ing, 1. to foretell. 2. to conjecture. 3. to perceive by intuition. —di·vine'ly, *adv.*

diving bell, a hollow apparatus filled with air, in which divers can work under water.

divining rod, a forked stick, as of hazel, that is said to bend downward toward an underground supply of water, minerals, etc.

di·vin·i·ty (di-vin'i-ti), *n., pl.* -ties, 1. the state or quality of being divine. 2. a god. 3. [D-], God. 4. theology.

di·vis·i·ble (di-viz'i-bl), *adj.* capable of being divided, especially without leaving a remainder. —di·vis·i·bil'i·ty, *n.*

di·vi·sion (di-vizh'ŭn), *n.* 1. the act of dividing. 2. the state of being divided. 3. something that divides. 4. a section, class, etc. 5. a disagreement. 6. a unit of one of the armed forces. 7. the process of finding how many times one number (the *divisor*) is contained in another (the *dividend*). —di·vi'sion·al, *adj.*

di·vi·sive (di-vī'siv), *adj.* causing discord or dissension. —di·vi'sive·ly, *adv.*

di·vi·sor (di-vī'zēr), *n.* the number by which the dividend is divided.

di·vorce (di-vôrs'), *n.* 1. the dissolution of a marriage by legal authority. 2. complete separation: *v.t.* -vorced', -vorc'ing, 1. to dissolve the marriage between. 2. to obtain a divorce from (one's spouse). 3. to separate. —di·vorce'ment, *n.*

di·vor·cée, di·vor·cee (di·vôr-sā', -sē'), *n.* a divorced woman.

div·ot (div'ŏt), *n.* a clump of turf dug up by a golf club when hitting a ball.

di·vulge (di-vulj'), *v.t.* -vulged', -vulg'ing, to make known, as something previously kept secret; disclose. —di·vulg'ence, *n.*

di·vul·sion (di-vul'shŭn), *n.* the act of pulling or tearing apart.

div·vy (div'i), *v.t. & v.i.* -vied, -vy·ing, [Slang], to divide (*up*); share.

dix·it (dik'sit), *n.* an arbitrary statement.

diz·zy (diz'i), *adj.* -zi·er, -zi·est, 1. having a confused, whirling sensation in the head; giddy. 2. causing such a feeling. 3. [Informal], foolish. —diz'zi·ly, *adv.* —diz'zi·ness, *n.*

DNA, a basic component of all living cells, that builds proteins and transmits hereditary characteristics.

do (dōō), *v.t.* did, done, do'ing, 1. to perform (an action, etc.). 2. to cause. 3. to make an effort to. 4. to work at. 5. to finish. 6. [Informal], to swindle. 7. [Informal], to serve (time in prison): *v.i.* 1. to behave. 2. to suffice. 3. to fare. 4. to occur: Used as an auxiliary, 1. as a substitute verb. 2. for emphasis. 3. in an interrogative construction: *n., pl.* do's, dos, 1. something to be done. 2. [Informal], a party.

do (dō), *n.* the first and eighth tone in any major or minor musical scale of eight tones.

doc·ile (dos'il), *adj.* easy to teach or manage; tractable. —doc'ile·ly, *adv.* —do·cil·i·ty (do-sil'i-ti), *n.*

dock (dok), *n.* 1. a basin with floodgates, for ships between voyages. 2. the water between two piers. 3. a pier or wharf. 4. a platform for loading or unloading trucks, etc. 5. the place in a court where a prisoner stands or sits during trial. 6. a coarse weed with broad leaves. 7. an animal's bobbed tail: *v.t.* 1. to bring (a ship) to dock. 2. to join (vehicles) in outer space. 3. to cut off the end of (a tail, etc.); bob. 4. to deduct from (wages, etc.): *v.i.* to come into a dock, as a ship.

dock·age ('ij), *n.* 1. a curtailment or deduction. 2. provision for the docking of ships. 3. the fee charged for the use of a dock.

dock·et (dok'it), *n.* 1. a summary, as of legal proceedings. 2. a list of law cases to be tried in a court. 3. an agenda: *v.t.* to list or enter in a docket.

dock·yard (dok'yärd), *n.* a place where ships are built or repaired.

doc·tor (dok'tĕr), *n.* 1. one who holds one of the highest academic degrees. 2. a physician or surgeon. 3. one who is licensed to practice any of the healing arts, as a dentist, veterinarian, etc.: *v.t.* [Informal], 1. to apply medicine to. 2. to repair. 3. to tamper with: *v.i.* [Informal], 1. to undergo medical treatment. —**doc'tor·al,** *adj.*

doc·tor·ate (-it), *n.* the degree of doctor.

doc·tri·naire (dok-tri-nĕr'), *adj.* dogmatic.

doc·trine (dok'trin), *n.* that which is taught, as the principles and beliefs of a church, sect, or party; dogma. —**doc'tri·nal,** *adj.*

doc·u·ment (dok'yŭ-mĕnt), *n.* a printed or written paper relied upon to establish some fact: *v.t.* to prove or support by the use of documents. —**doc·u·men·ta'tion,** *n.*

doc·u·men·ta·ry (-men'tä-ri), *adj.* 1. of, supported by, or serving as a document or documents. 2. denoting a film or television program that depicts events, conditions, etc. factually but artistically: *n., pl.* -ries, a documentary film, television program, etc.

dod·der (dod'ĕr), *n.* a parasitic plant: *v.i.* 1. to totter. 2. to shake; tremble.

do·dec·a·gon (dō-dek'ā-gon), *n.* a plane figure with twelve sides and twelve angles.

do·dec·a·he·dron (dō-dek-ā-he'drŏn), *n., pl.* -drons, -dra ('drā), a solid figure with twelve faces.

dodge (doj), *v.i.* dodged, dodg'ing, 1. to shift suddenly aside. 2. to use tricky devices or evasions: *v.t.* 1. to avoid by a sudden shift aside. 2. to evade by tricky devices: *n.* 1. the act of dodging. 2. a trick. 3. a clever contrivance or ruse.

do·do (dō'dō), *n., pl.* -dos, -does, a large, extinct bird with a hooked bill, short legs, and rudimentary wings.

doe (dō), *n.* the female of the deer, hare, rabbit, antelope, etc.

do·er (dōō'ĕr), *n.* one who is efficient and energetic.

doe·skin (dō'skin), *n.* 1. the skin of a female deer. 2. leather made from this, or from lambskin. 3. a fine woolen cloth.

does·n't (duz'nt), does not.

doff (dôf), *v.t.* 1. to take off (clothes). 2. to remove (the hat) in greeting. 3. to get rid of.

dog (dôg), *n.* 1. a domesticated, carnivorous animal related to the wolf, fox, and jackal. 2. the male of any of these animals. 3. a mean, despicable fellow. 4. a dogfish, prairie dog, etc. 5. a mechanical device for holding

or gripping. 6. *pl.* [Slang], feet. 7. [Slang], a person or thing that is unsatisfactory: *v.t.* **dogged, dog'ging,** to hunt or follow like a dog.

dog·bane ('bān), *n.* any of several, sometimes poisonous, plants with an acrid, milky juice and small pink or white flowers.

dog·ber·ry ('bĕr-i), *n., pl.* -ries, 1. the fruit of any of various plants, as the mountain ash. 2. any of these plants.

dog·cart ('kärt), *n.* a light carriage with two transverse seats back to back.

dog·catch·er ('kach-ĕr), *n.* a municipal official who catches and impounds stray animals.

dog days, the sultry, hot days of July and August when the Dog Star rises and sets with the sun.

doge (dōj), *n.* the chief magistrate in the ancient republics of Venice and Genoa.

dog·ear (dôg'ir), *v.t.* to turn down a corner of (a page): *n.* a corner of a page that has been turned down. —**dog'eared,** *adj.*

dog·fish ('fish), *n., pl.* -fish, -fish·es, a species of small shark.

dog·ged (dôg'id), *adj.* stubborn; persistent.

dog·ger (dôg'ĕr), *n.* a two-masted fishing boat with a broad beam, used in the North Sea.

dog·ger·el (dôg'ĕr-ĕl), *n.* inferior verse, often irregular in form or rhythm, usually comic in nature: *adj.* of or pertaining to such verse. Also **dog'grel** ('rĕl).

dog·house (dôg'hous), *n.* 1. a dog's kennel. 2. disfavor: in the phrase *in the doghouse.*

do·gie, do·gy (dō'gi), *n., pl.* -gies, in the western U.S., a motherless calf.

dog·ma (dôg'mä), *n.* -mas, -ma·ta ('mä-tä), a principle, tenet, or doctrine, especially a formal, authoritative doctrine of a church.

dog·mat·ic (dôg-mat'ik), *adj.* 1. of or pertaining to dogma. 2. stating opinions arrogantly or without proof. —**dog·mat'i·cal·ly,** *adv.*

dog·ma·tism (dôg'mä-tizm), *n.* dogmatic assertion of opinion. —**dog'ma·tist,** *n.*

dog·ma·tize (-tīz), *v.i.* -tized, -tiz·ing, to make dogmatic assertions in writing or speech: *v.t.* to express as dogma.

do·good·er (dōō'good-ĕr), *n.* [Informal], one who tries to remedy social ills in a well-intentioned but impractical way.

Dog Star, same as Sirius.

dog·trot (dôg'trot), *n.* a gentle trot.

dog·watch ('wäch, 'wŏch), *n.* one of two watches on board ship of two hours each, from 4 to 6 P.M. or 6 to 8 P.M.

dog·wood ('wood), *n.* 1. a flowering tree of the eastern U.S. with large white or pink blossoms. 2. its hard wood.

doi·ly (doi'li), *n., pl.* -lies, a small mat, as of lace, put under a plate, etc.

do·ings (dōō'ingz), *n.* actions, happenings, events, etc.

dol·drums (dŏl'drŭmz, dōl'-), *n.* 1. tropical ocean zones known for dead calms. 2. depression; low spirits. 3. dullness, listlessness, etc.

dole (dōl), *n.* 1. that which is given out sparingly. 2. a charitable gift of food or money. 3. government funds to the unemployed: *v.t.* **doled, dol'ing,** to deal out sparingly or as a dole.

ŏ in drag*o*n, ōō in cr*u*de, oo in w*oo*l, u in c*u*p, ū in c*u*re, ū in t*u*rn, ŭ in foc*u*s, oi in b*o*y, ou in h*ou*se, th in *th*in, th in shea*th*e, g in *g*et, j in *j*oy, y in *y*et.

dole·ful ('fŭl), *adj.* sorrowful; mournful. — **dole'ful·ly,** *adv.*

dol·er·ite (dŏl'ẽ-rīt), *n.* a dark, crystalline igneous rock.

dol·i·cho·ce·phal·ic (dŏl-i-kō-sĕ-fal'ĭk), **dol·i·cho·ceph·a·lous** (-sĕf'ȧ-lŭs), *adj.* having a long head. —**dol·i·cho·ceph'a·ly,** *n.*

doll (dŏl), *n.* 1. a child's toy made to resemble a human being. 2. [Slang], one who is pleasant, helpful, pretty, etc.: *v.t. & v.i.* [Informal], to dress smartly (followed by *up*).

dol·lar (dŏl'ẽr), *n.* the monetary unit of the U.S. and some other countries, as Canada, equal to 100 cents.

dollar diplomacy, a policy of a government by which it promotes its citizens' business interests in foreign countries.

dol·lop (dŏl'ŏp), *n.* a small quantity, as of food or liquid; dash.

dol·ly (dŏl'i), *n., pl.* **-lies,** 1. a doll. 2. a low platform with small wheels for moving heavy loads: *v.t. & v.i.* **-lied, -ly·ing,** to move (a television or motion-picture camera) on a dolly.

Dolly Var·den (vär'dn), 1. a dress of sheer, flowered muslin over a bright-colored petticoat. 2. a woman's flower-trimmed hat with a broad brim.

dol·man (dŏl'măn, dōl'-), *n., pl.* **-mans,** 1. a long Turkish outer garment. 2. a hussar's uniform jacket worn like a cape.

dolman sleeve, a woman's dress or coat sleeve that tapers from a very large armhole to a tight wrist.

dol·men (dŏl'mĕn, dōl'-), *n.* a prehistoric monument consisting of a large, unhewn stone resting on upright stones; cromlech.

do·lor (dō'lẽr), *n.* [Poetic], sorrow; grief: British form **do'lour.**

do·lor·ous (dō'lẽr-ŭs, dŏl'ẽr-), *adj.* sorrowful. — **do'lor·ous·ly,** *adv.*

dol·phin (dŏl'fĭn), *n.* a cetaceous mammal, often with a snout like a beak, found in warm seas.

dolt (dōlt), *n.* a slow, stupid fellow. —**dolt'ish,** *adj.* —**dolt'ish·ly,** *adv.*

Dom (dŏm), *n.* a title of respect formerly given to gentlemen of Portugal and Brazil.

do·main (dō-mān'), *n.* 1. land or dominion under one rule or government. 2. a field of action, knowledge, etc.

dome (dōm), *n.* 1. a hemispherical roof. 2. anything that is dome-shaped.

do·mes·tic (dō-mes'tĭk), *adj.* 1. of or pertaining to the home or household affairs. 2. devoted to the home. 3. of or made in the home country. 4. domesticated: said of animals: *n.* 1. a household servant. 2. *pl.* products made in the home country. —**do·mes'ti·cal·ly,** *adv.*

do·mes·ti·cate ('tĭ-kāt), *v.t.* **-cat·ed, -cat·ing,** 1. to make domestic; accustom to home life. 2. to tame (a wild animal): *v.i.* to become domestic. —**do·mes·ti·ca'tion,** *n.*

do·mes·tic·i·ty (dō-mes-tis'ĭ-ti), *n.* 1. home life. 2. devotion to home.

dom·i·cile (dŏm'ĭ-sĭl, dŏ'mĭ-sĭl), *n.* a permanent residence or place of abode; home: *v.t.* **-ciled, -cil·ing,** to establish in a fixed residence. —**dom·i·cil'i·ar·y** (-sĭl'ĭ-er-i), *adj.*

dom·i·nant (dŏm'ĭ-nänt), *adj.* ruling; predomi-

nant; dominating. —**dom'i·nance,** *n.* —**dom'i·nant·ly,** *adv.*

dom·i·nate (-nāt), *v.t. & v.i.* **-nat·ed, -nat·ing,** 1. to govern or rule by superior strength. 2. to tower above.

dom·i·na·tion (dom-i-nā'shŭn), *n.* the act of dominating; control; power.

dom·i·neer (dom-i-nēr'), *v.t. & v.i.* to rule over arrogantly or tyrannically; tyrannize.

dom·i·neer·ing ('ing), *adj.* tyrannical.

do·min·i·cal (dō-min'ĭ-kl), *adj.* 1. of or pertaining to Christ, as Lord. 2. of or pertaining to Sunday, as the Lord's day.

dominical letter, one of the first seven letters of the alphabet, used in the church calendar to denote Sundays throughout a given year and corresponding with the letter assigned to Sunday when the first seven days of January are lettered consecutively.

Do·min·i·can (dō-min'ĭ-kȧn), *n.* 1. any one of the members of an order of mendicant friars or nuns founded in 1215. 2. a native or inhabitant of the Dominican Republic, a country in the West Indies.

dom·i·nie (dom'ĭ-ni), *n.* 1. in Scotland, a schoolmaster. 2. [Informal], any clergyman.

do·min·ion (dō-min'yŭn), *n.* 1. control or rule; sovereignty. 2. a governed territory, or, sometimes, a self-governing country. 3. in *Law,* ownership of property and the right to its control.

dom·i·no (dom'ĭ-nō), *n., pl.* **-noes, -nos,** 1. a large, loose cape or cloak with wide sleeves and a hood, used as a masquerade garment. 2. a mask for the eyes. 3. an oblong piece of bone, wood, etc. divided into halves that are left blank or marked with one to six dots. 4. *pl.* a game played with a set of these pieces.

don (don), *n.* 1. [D-], Sir; Mister: a Spanish title of respect, used with the Christian name. 2. a Spanish gentleman. 3. [Informal], the head of a college of Oxford or Cambridge, or any one of the fellows or tutors.

don (don), *v.t.* **donned, don'ning,** to put on; dress in.

Do·ña (dō'nyä), *n.* 1. Lady; Madam: a Spanish title of respect. 2. [d-], a Spanish lady.

do·nate (dō'nāt, dō-nāt'), *v.t. & v.i.* to contribute, especially to some religious or philanthropic organization. —**do·na'tion,** *n.*

do·na·tive ('nä-tiv), *n.* a charitable gift; donation.

do·na·tor ('nā-tẽr), *n.* a giver.

done (dun), past participle of **do:** *adj.* 1. completed; finished. 2. cooked sufficiently. 3. socially acceptable: *interj.* agreed.

do·nee (dō-nē'), *n.* a person to whom a gift, property, etc. is given.

don·jon (dun'jŏn, don'-), *n.* the massive, heavily fortified, principal tower or keep of a medieval castle.

Don Ju·an (don jōō'ȧn, don wän'), *n.* 1. in *Spanish Legend,* a profligate nobleman and libertine. 2. any man who seduces women; philanderer.

don·key (dong'ki, dung'ki), *n., pl.* **-keys,** 1. a domesticated ass. 2. a stupid or obstinate individual.

Don·na (don'ä), *n.* 1. Lady; Madam: an Italian title of respect, used with the Christian name. 2. [d-], an Italian lady.

don·ny·brook (don'i-brook), *n.* a rowdy brawl or free-for-all.

do·nor (dō'nēr), *n.* 1. a giver, especially to a charity. 2. a person who donates blood for a transfusion or tissue for a transplant.

Don Qui·xo·te (don ki-hōt'i, don kwik'sèt), *n.* 1. the idealistic, ineffectual hero of a satirical romance of the 17th century. 2. any impractical idealist.

don't (dōnt), do not.

doo·dle (dōō'd'l), *v.i.* -dled, -dling, to scribble without purpose: *n.* a scribble made in doodling. —doo'dler, *n.*

doom (dōōm), *n.* 1. a judicial sentence or decision. 2. fate; destiny. 3. ruin; extinction: *v.t.* 1. to pronounce condemnation upon; sentence. 2. to destine to an unhappy fate.

dooms·day (dōōmz'dā), *n.* 1. same as **Judgment Day.** 2. any day of accounting.

door (dôr), *n.* 1. a movable frame of wood or other material, usually on hinges and giving ingress to, or egress from, a room, apartment, vehicle, etc. 2. an entrance; portal. 3. a means of access.

door·bell ('bel), *n.* a bell or buzzer rung by someone desiring admission to a room or building.

door·man ('man, 'mån), *n., pl.* -men ('men, 'mén), a man who opens the door of a building, hails taxicabs, etc.

door·mat ('mat), *n.* a mat laid before a door to wipe the shoes on.

door·step ('step), *n.* a step leading to an outside door.

door·way ('wā), *n.* 1. an opening that can be closed by a door. 2. a means of access.

door·yard ('yärd), *n.* a yard to which the door of a house leads.

dope (dōp), *n.* 1. a thick liquid or viscid substance, used as a lubricant, absorbent, filler, etc. 2. [Slang], a drug or narcotic. 3. a stupid person. 4. [Slang], information: *v.t.* doped, dop'ing, to give a narcotic to; drug.

dop·ey, dop·y (dō'pi), *adj.* dop'i·er, dop'i·est, [Slang], 1. drugged by a narcotic: 2. dull or stupid.

Do·ri·an (dôr'i-ån), *adj.* same as **Doric**: *n.* any member of the Doric race, one of the four chief divisions of the ancient Greeks.

Dor·ic (dôr'ik), *adj.* 1. of or pertaining to Doris, an ancient mountainous region in Greece. 2. denoting the Doric order, a classic order of architecture with heavy, fluted columns and simple capitals.

Dor·king (dôr'king), *n.* any one of a breed of five-toed domestic fowl, raised chiefly for the table.

dorm (dôrm), *n.* [Informal], a dormitory.

dor·mant (dôr'månt), *adj.* 1. sleeping; not active. 2. in a quiescent or resting condition. —dor'man·cy, *n.*

dor·mer (dôr'mēr), *n.* a window set vertically in a gable projecting from a sloping roof.

dor·mi·to·ry (dôr'mi-tôr-i), *n.* 1. a large room with sleeping facilities for a number of persons. 2. a building, as at a college, with many rooms for housing a number of persons.

dor·mouse (dôr'mous), *n., pl.* -mice ('mīs), a small, squirrellike, European rodent.

dor·sal (dôr'sl), *adj.* of, on, or near the back.

do·ry (dôr'i), *n., pl.* -ries, a small, flat-bottomed fishing boat with a sharp prow.

do·ry (dôr'i), *n., pl.* -ries, an edible saltwater fish with spiny fins and a flat body.

dos·age (dōs'ij), *n.* 1. the administration of medicine in prescribed amounts. 2. the amount prescribed. 3. the adding of an ingredient to wine to give it a distinctive flavor.

dose (dōs), *n.* 1. the quantity of medicine to be taken at one time or at stated times. 2. an amount of something disagreeable experienced at one time: *v.t.* dosed, dos'ing, to give a dose to.

dos·si·er (dos'i-ā, dôs'-), *n.* a bundle or file of papers dealing with a particular person or subject.

dost (dust), [Archaic], second person singular, present indicative of **do**.

dot (dot), *n.* a small point or speck. 2. a tiny round spot: *v.t.* dot'ted, dot'ting, to mark with a dot or dots.

dot·age (dōt'ij), *n.* 1. a childish state of mind caused by old age; senility. 2. foolish or excessive affection.

dot·ard ('ērd), *n.* a person whose intellect is impaired by old age.

dote (dōt), *v.i.* dot'ed, dot'ing, 1. to be foolish or feebleminded because of old age. 2. to bestow excessive affection (with *on* or *upon*). —dot'ing, *adj.*

doth (duth), [Archaic], third person singular, present indicative of **do**.

dot·ter·el (dot'ēr-èl), *n.* a small plover of Europe and Asia.

Dou·ay Bible (dōō-ā'), an English translation of the Bible for the use of Roman Catholics.

dou·ble (dub'l), *adj.* 1. twofold. 2. having two layers. 3. composed of two of the same kind. 4. composed of two different kinds. 5. twice as much. 6. designed for two: *adv.* 1. twofold. 2. in a pair: *n.* 1. twice the quantity. 2. a duplicate. 3. a fold. 4. *pl.* a game, as tennis, having two players on each side. 5. in *Baseball*, a hit on which the batter reaches second base. 6. in *Bridge*, a bid doubling an opponent's bid: *v.t.* -bled, -bling, 1. to make twice as much or as great. 2. to fold. 3. to duplicate or repeat. 4. in *Bridge*, to increase the penalty or point value of an opponent's bid: *v.i.* 1. to increase twofold. 2. to turn sharply backward. 3. to serve an additional purpose. 4. in *Baseball*, to hit a double.

double agent, a person who engages in espionage against a country while pretending to be spying for it.

dou·ble-bar·reled (-bar'ēld), *adj.* 1. having two barrels, as a kind of shotgun. 2. having two purposes.

double bass, the largest and deepest-toned instrument of the violin family.

double boiler, a utensil designed for cooking food in an upper pan that fits into a lower pan containing boiling water.

ô in dragon, ōō in crude, oo in wool, u in cup, û in cure, ü in turn, ù in focus, oi in boy, ou in house, th in thin, th in sheathe, g in get, j in joy, y in yet.

dou·ble-breast·ed (-bres'tid), *adj.* overlapping across the front, as some suit coats.

dou·ble-cross (-krôs'), *v.t.* [Informal], to betray by acting contrary to a course of action that has been agreed upon: *n.* [Informal], such an act of betrayal; treachery. —**dou'ble-cross'er,** *n.*

double dagger, same as diesis.

double date, a social function that two couples participate in. —**dou'ble-date',** *v.t.* & *v.i.* **-dat'ed, -dat'ing.**

dou·ble-deal·ing (-dēl'ing), *n.* duplicity.

dou·ble-en·ten·dre (dōō-blän-tän'drě), *n.* [French], a word or phrase with two meanings, especially when one is risqué.

dou·ble-head·er (-hed'ēr), *n.* two games played one after the other on the same day.

dou·ble-joint·ed (-join'tid), *adj.* having extremely flexible joints that allow fingers, limbs, etc. to bend at unusual angles.

double play, in *Baseball,* a play in which two players are put out.

dou·ble-reed (-rēd'), *adj.* denoting or of a woodwind instrument, as the oboe, that has two reeds that vibrate against each other.

double standard, a system or code less strict for one than another; especially, a moral code granting men greater freedom than women.

dou·blet (dub'lit), *n.* 1. a closefitting jacket, worn by men chiefly from the 14th to 16th centuries. 2. a pair. 3. one of a pair.

double take, a delayed reaction to an unexpected remark, circumstance, etc.

double talk, 1. evasive or misleading talk. 2. meaningless speech that pretends to be meaningful.

dou·bloon (du-blōōn'), *n.* an obsolete Spanish gold coin.

doubt (dout), *v.i.* to be uncertain or wavering in opinion: *v.t.* 1. to be uncertain about. 2. to tend to disbelieve: *n.* 1. a state of uncertainty of mind. 2. lack of conviction or confidence. 3. a condition of uncertainty. —**doubt'er,** *n.*

doubt·ful ('fŭl), *adj.* 1. uncertain. 2. arousing suspicion. 3. insecure.

doubt·less ('les), *adv.* 1. certainly. 2. probably. —**doubt'less·ly,** *adv.*

douche (dōōsh), *n.* 1. a jet or current of liquid directed upon some part of the body. 2. a device for douching: *v.t.* & *v.i.* **douched, douch'ing,** to apply a douche (to).

dough (dō), *n.* 1. a soft mass of moistened flour for baking. 2. [Slang], money.

dough·boy ('boi), *n.* [Informal], a U.S. infantryman, especially of World War I.

dough·nut ('nut), *n.* a small roll or cake of sweetened dough, cooked in boiling fat.

dough·ty (dout'i), *adj.* **-ti·er, -ti·est,** valiant; strong. —**dough'ti·ness,** *n.*

dough·y (dō'i), *adj.* **dough'i·er, dough'i·est,** soft and pasty like dough.

dour (door, dōōr, dour), *adj.* 1. in Scotland, stern; harsh. 2. sullen; threatening.

douse (dous), *v.t.* 1. to **doused, dous'ing,** 1. to plunge suddenly into a liquid. 2. to drench. 3. [Informal], to extinguish.

dove (duv), *n.* 1. a pigeon with a cooing cry.

2. a person who advocates peaceful solutions to international problems.

dove (dōv), alternate past tense of *dive.*

dove·cote (duv'kōt), *n.* a small house or box with compartments for nesting doves.

dove·tail (duv'tāl), *n.* a projecting part shaped like a dove's tail that fits into a similar indentation to make a joint: *v.t.* & *v.i.* to fit closely and exactly.

dow·a·ger (dou'ă-jēr), *n.* 1. the widow of a king, prince, or person of rank. 2. a wealthy elderly woman.

dow·dy (dou'di), *adj.* **-di·er, -di·est,** slovenly or ill-dressed; shabby. —**dow'di·ness,** *n.*

dow·el (dou'ĕl), *n.* a wooden pin inserted into corresponding holes in two pieces to join the pieces.

dow·er (dou'ēr), *n.* 1. that part of a man's property that his widow enjoys during her life. 2. a dowry: *v.t.* to endow (with).

dow·itch·er (dou'i-chēr), *n.* a long-legged North American shore bird.

down (doun), *adv.* 1. in or to a lower place or position. 2. from a higher to a lower degree or position. 3. from earlier to later times. 4. from one's hands. 5. in an earnest way. 6. entirely. 7. in cash. 8. in writing: *adj.* 1. leading to or into a lower place. 2. brought down. 3. dejected. 4. ill. 5. completed. 6. in cash: *prep.* along, toward, through, or upon: *v.t.* to put or toss down: *n.* 1. a mishap. 2. in *Football,* one of the plays in which the offense tries to advance the ball.

down (doun), *n.* soft feathers or hair.

down (doun), *n.* hilly, grassy land: *usually used in plural.*

down·beat (doun'bēt), *n.* in *Music,* a conductor's downward stroke indicating the first beat of a measure.

down·cast ('kast), *adj.* 1. directed downwards. 2. sad.

Down East, [Informal], the northeastern part of the United States, especially Maine.

down·er ('ēr), *n.* [Slang], any depressant.

down·fall ('fôl), *n.* 1. a sudden fall, as from a high position. 2. the cause of this.

down·fall·en ('fôl-n), *adj.* fallen; ruined.

down·grade ('grād), *n.* a descending slope: *v.t.* **-grad·ed, -grad·ing,** 1. to demote. 2. to disparage.

down·heart·ed ('här'tid), *adj.* discouraged.

down·hill ('hil'), *adv.* & *adj.* downward.

Down·ing Street (doun'ing), a street in London containing British government offices.

down·pour ('pōr), *n.* a heavy rain.

down·right ('rit), *adv.* completely: *adj.* 1. absolute. 2. candid.

down·stage ('stāj'), *adj.* & *adv.* of or toward the front of the stage.

down·stairs ('sterz'), *adv.* 1. down the stairs. 2. on or to a lower floor: *adj.* on a lower floor: *n.* a lower floor.

down·state ('stāt'), *adj.* & *adv.* of, to, or from the southern part of a State.

down·stream ('strēm'), *adj.* & *adv.* in the direction of a stream's current.

down·swing ('swing), *n.* 1. a downward swing. 2. a downward trend.

down-to-earth ('tō-ūrth'), *adj.* realistic.

---

a in cap, ā in cane, ä in father, å in abet, e in met, ē in be, ē in baker, ě in regent, i in pit, ī in fine, i in manifest, o in hot, ô in horse, ō in bone,

down-town ('toun'), *adj. & adv.* in or toward the business center of a city: *n.* this center.

down-trod-den ('trod-n), *adj.* oppressed.

down-ward ('wērd), *adj. & adv.* 1. from a higher to a lower place, grade, condition, etc. 2. from an earlier to a later time: also **down'wards,** *adv.*

down-y ('i), *adj.* **down'i-er, down'i-est,** 1. of or covered with down. 2. soft.

dow-ry (dou'ri), *n., pl.* **-ries,** the property brought to her husband by a bride at marriage.

dowse (douz), *v.i.* dowsed, **dows'ing,** to search for water or ores with a divining rod.

dox-ol-o-gy (dok-sol'ŏ-ji), *n., pl.* **-gies,** a hymn of praise to God.

dox-y (dok'si), *n., pl.* **dox'ies,** [Old British Slang], 1. a prostitute. 2. a mistress.

doy-en (doi'ĕn), *n.* [French], the senior member of a group. —**doy'enne** ('en), *n.fem.*

doze (dōz), *v.i.* dozed, **doz'ing,** to sleep lightly; nap: *n.* a light sleep.

doz-en (duz'n), *n., pl.* **-ens** or, especially after a number, **-en,** a set of 12. —**doz'enth,** *adj.*

doz-y (dō'zi), *adj.* **doz'i-er, doz'i-est,** sleepy.

drab (drab), *n.* a kind of dull brown or yellowish-gray cloth of wool or cotton: *adj.* **drab'ber, drab'hest,** 1. of a drab color. 2. dull; dreary. —**drab'ness,** *n.*

drab-bet (drab'it), *n.* a coarse linen.

drab-ble (drab'l), *v.t.* -bled, **-bling,** to make wet and dirty by dragging through mud and water.

drach-ma (drak'mä), *n., pl.* **-mas, -mae** (-mē), **-mai** (-mī), 1. an ancient Greek silver coin. 2. the monetary unit of modern Greece.

draff (draf), *n.* refuse or dregs.

draft (draft), *n.* 1. the act of pulling a load. 2. a drawing in of a fish net. 3. the fish caught in one draw. 4. the act of drinking or the amount drunk in a single act. 5. [Informal], the portion of liquid, as beer, drawn from a cask. 6. an inhalation. 7. a preliminary outline of a document, piece of writing, etc. 8. a sketch of something to be done. 9. a current of air. 10. a device in a heating system for controlling the current of air. 11. a written instruction for payment of money. 12. the choosing of persons for a particular duty, especially for compulsory military service. 13. those so chosen. 14. the depth of water to which the keel of a vessel sinks: *v.t.* 1. to select from a group, as for military service. 2. to make a sketch or outline for: *adj.* 1. used for drawing loads. 2. drawn from a cask.

draft-ee (draf-tē'), *n.* a person drafted for military service.

drafts-man (drafts'măn), *n., pl.* **-men** (-měn), one who draws plans of buildings or machinery. —**drafts'man-ship,** *n.*

draft-y (draf'ti), *adj.* **draft'i-er, draft'i-est,** full of or open to drafts of air.

drag (drag), *v.t. & v.i.* dragged, **drag'ging,** 1. to pull or be pulled along the ground by force. 2. to search a body of water with a grapnel, net, etc. 3. to prolong something tiresomely over a period of time: *n.* 1. something pulled along the ground, as a harrow. 2. a

dragnet, grapnel, etc. 3. anything that brakes or retards. 4. a dragging. 5. [Slang], influence. 6. [Slang], a puff, as on a pipe. 7. [Slang], street. 8. [Slang], same as drag race. 9. [Slang], a tiresome person, activity, etc.

drag-gle (drag'l), *v.t. & v.i.* -gled, **-gling,** to make or become wet or soiled by dragging in mud or water.

drag-gy (drag'i), *adj.* **-gi-er, -gi-est,** dragging; dull, lethargic, etc.

drag-net (drag'net), *n.* 1. a net dragged along the bottom of a river, lake, etc., as for catching fish. 2. a systematized procedure used by police to capture suspects.

drag-o-man (drag'ō-măn), *n., pl.* **-mans, -men** (-měn), in the Near East, a professional guide.

drag-on (drag'ŏn), *n.* a fabulous animal, usually represented as a winged, fire-breathing reptile.

drag-on-fly (-flī), *n., pl.* **-flies,** a large, long-bodied insect with two pairs of transparent wings.

dragon's blood, a red resin from various tropical trees.

dra-goon (drā-gōōn'), *n.* a heavily armed cavalryman: *v.t.* to force or coerce.

drag race, [Slang], a race between cars to find out which has the quickest acceleration from a full stop.

drain (drān), *v.t.* 1. to draw off (a liquid) gradually. 2. to empty or dry. 3. to use up (energy, reserves, etc.) gradually: *v.i.* 1. to flow off or go from gradually. 2. to become empty by draining: *n.* 1. a draining. 2. a duct or pipe for draining.

drain-age ('ij), *n.* 1. the act or means of draining. 2. that which is drained off. 3. an area drained.

drain-pipe (drān'pīp), *n.* a large pipe for carrying off water, sewage, etc.

drake (drāk), *n.* a male duck.

dram (dram), *n.* 1. a measure of weight, equal to 1/8 ounce troy or 1/16 ounce avoirdupois. 2. a small quantity of spirituous liquor.

dra-ma (drä'mä, dram'ä), *n.* 1. a prose or poetical composition presenting a story of human life through the performance of actors; play. 2. dramatic art, including writing, acting, etc. 3. a series of real-life events similar to those of a play.

Dram-a-mine (dram'ä-mēn), *n.* a drug to relieve motion sickness: a trademark.

dra-mat-ic (drä-mat'ik), *adj.* 1. of or like drama. 2. vivid, striking, etc. —**dra-mat'l-cal-ly,** *adv.*

dra-mat-ics ('iks), *n.* 1. the performance or staging of plays. 2. dramatic behavior.

dram-a-tis per-so-nae (dram'ä-tis pĕr-sō'nē), [Latin], the characters in a play.

dram-a-tist (dram'ä-tist), *n.* a playwright.

dram-a-tize (-tīz), *v.t.* -tized, **-tiz-ing,** 1. to adapt for stage presentation. 2. to present in a dramatic way. —**dram-a-ti-za'tion,** *n.*

dram-a-tur-gy (-tūr-ji), *n.* the art of writing or producing plays. —**dram'a-tur-gist,** *n.*

drank (drangk), past tense of **drink.**

drape (drāp), *v.t.* draped, **drap'ing,** 1. to cover or hang as with cloth in loose folds. 2. to arrange (curtains, cloth, etc.) in folds: *n.* a drapery; curtain: *usually pl.*

drap-er (drā′pēr), *n.* [British], a dealer in cloth and dry goods.

dra-per-y (-i), *n., pl.* -per-ies, 1. [British], same as dry goods. 2. hangings, clothing, etc. arranged in loose folds. 3. *pl.* curtains of heavy fabric.

dras-tic (dras′tik), *adj.* 1. having a violent effect. 2. severe; extreme. —dras′ti-cal-ly, *adv.*

draught (draft), *n.* & *v.t.* & *adj.* British form for draft.

draughts (drafts), *n.* [British], the game of checkers.

draw (drô), *v.t.* drew, drawn, draw′ing, 1. to pull along or haul. 2. to pull up, in, out, down, or across. 3. to require (a certain depth of water) in floating. 4. to attract. 5. to inhale. 6. to evoke. 7. to receive. 8. to withdraw. 9. to write (a check). 10. to deduce. 11. to get (cards) 12. to elongate. 13. to sketch: *v.i.* 1. to draw something. 2. to produce motion. 3. to shrink. 4. to take in, as a draft of air. 5. to make a demand (*on*): *n.* 1. the act of drawing. 2. a thing drawn. 3. a contest ending in a tie. 4. something that attracts.

draw-back (′bak), *n.* 1. a shortcoming; disadvantage. 2. a refund.

draw-bridge (′brij), *n.* a bridge that can be raised or drawn aside.

draw-ee (drô-ē′), *n.* one on whom an order for a payment in money is drawn.

draw-er (drô′ēr), *n.* 1. one who draws. 2. (drôr), a sliding boxlike compartment in a table, bureau, etc.

draw-ers (drôrz), *n.* an undergarment for the lower body.

draw-ing (drô′ing), *n.* 1. the act of drawing. 2. the art of delineating something, as with a pencil. 3. a representation so made. 4. a lottery.

drawing card, an attraction drawing a large audience.

drawing room, a room for the reception and entertainment of guests.

drawl (drôl), *v.t.* & *v.i.* to lengthen the vowels while speaking slowly: *n.* a manner of speaking this way.

drawn (drôn), past participle of draw: *adj.* 1. disemboweled. 2. haggard.

drawn butter, melted butter.

draw-string (drô′string), *n.* a string drawn through a hem, as for closing a bag.

dray (drā), *n.* a sturdy wagon for hauling heavy loads.

dread (dred), *v.t.* to anticipate with great anxiety or fear: *n.* 1. intense fear. 2. fear combined with awe: *adj.* terrifying.

dread-ful (′fûl), *adj.* 1. inspiring dread. 2. [Informal], extremely bad, distasteful, etc. — dread′ful-ly, *adv.*

dread-nought, dread-naught (′nôt), *n.* a large, heavily armed battleship.

dream (drēm), *n.* 1. a train of thoughts, images, etc. passing through a sleeping person's mind. 2. a daydream; fantasy. 3. an idle hope. 4. anything dreamlike: *v.i.* & *v.t.* dreamed or dreamt (dremt), dream′ing,

to have a dream or indistinct conception (*of*). —dream′er, *n.*

dream-y (′i), *adj.* dream′i-er, dream′i-est, 1. of or resembling a dream. 2. full of dreams. 3. visionary. 4. restful. 5. [Slang], wonderful.

drear-y (drir′i), *adj.* drear′i-er, drear′i-est, cheerless; gloomy: also [Poetical], drear.

dredge (drej), *n.* an apparatus for scooping up mud, debris, etc., as in deepening waterways: *v.t.* & *v.i.* dredged, dredg′ing, 1. to clear out and deepen by a dredge. 2. to gather with a dredge.

dredge (drej), *v.t.* dredged, dredg′ing, to coat (food) with flour, sugar, etc.

dregs (dregz), *n.* 1. the sediment in a liquid. 2. worthless matter.

drench (drench), *v.t.* to soak thoroughly.

Dres-den (drez′dĕn), *n.* a fine decorated porcelain.

dress (dres), *v.t.* dressed or drest, dress′ing, 1. to clothe. 2. to adorn. 3. to do up (the hair). 4. to align (troops). 5. to put medication and bandages on (a wound). 6. to clean and eviscerate (an animal) for cooking. 7. to put a finish on: *v.i.* 1. to put on clothes. 2. to wear formal clothes. 3. to get into a straight line: *n.* 1. clothing. 2. the outer garment usually worn by women, generally of one piece with a skirt: *adj.* 1. of or pertaining to dresses. 2. for formal wear.

dres-sage (drĕ-säzh′), *n.* [French, training], horsemanship in which barely perceptible movements of the rider control the horse.

dress circle, a section of seats in a theater, originally reserved for persons in formal dress.

dress-er (dres′ēr), *n.* 1. one who dresses someone or something. 2. a chest of drawers with a mirror.

dress-ing (′ing), *n.* 1. the act of dressing. 2. protection or medicine applied to a wound. 3. a sauce for certain dishes, as salads. 4. a stuffing, as for poultry.

dressing gown, a loose robe worn before dressing or when lounging.

dress-mak-er (′māk-ēr), *n.* one who makes clothes for women. —dress′mak-ing, *n.*

dress rehearsal, a final rehearsal, as of a play, performed as it is to be presented.

dress-y (dres′i), *adj.* dress′i-er, dress′i-est, 1. showy or elaborate in attire. 2. stylish.

drew (drōō), past tense of draw.

drib-ble (drib′l), *v.t.* & *v.i.* -bled, -bling, 1. to flow or fall in drops. 2. to drool. 3. in *Sports*, to move (a ball) by a succession of light bounces, kicks, etc.: *n.* the act of dribbling. 2. a small amount: also drib′let (′lit).

dried (drīd), past tense and past participle of dry.

dri-er (drī′ēr), *n.* 1. a substance added to paint, ink, etc. to make it dry quickly. 2. same as dryer: *adj.* comparative of dry.

dri-est (′ist), *adj.* superlative of dry.

drift (drift), *n.* 1. the act or condition of drifting. 2. the direction of this. 3. a trend. 4. general meaning. 5. an accumulation, as of snow, heaped up by the wind. 6. rocks, gravel, etc. deposited by a glacier: *v.i.* 1. to be carried along, as by a current. 2. to

---

proceed without purpose. 3. to accumulate in heaps. —**drift'er**, *n*.

drift·wood ('wood), *n*. wood drifting or washed ashore.

drill (dril), *n*. 1. a tool for boring holes. 2. disciplined and repeated training as a means for developing a skill, as by military, physical, or mental exercises: *v.t. & v.i.* 1. to pierce with a drill. 2. to instruct by drill (sense 2).

drill (dril), *n*. a machine for planting seeds in holes or furrows made by it.

drill (dril), *n*. coarse cotton twill.

drill·mas·ter ('mas-tēr), *n*. one who instructs by drilling.

drill press, a power-driven machine for drilling holes, as in metal.

dri·ly (drī'li), *adv*. same as dryly.

drink (dringk), *v.t.* **drank**, **drunk**, **drink'ing**, 1. to swallow or absorb (liquid). 2. to swallow the contents of: *v.i.* 1. to swallow liquid. 2. to imbibe alcoholic liquor, especially in excess: *n*. 1. any liquid for drinking. 2. alcoholic liquor. —**drink'er**, *n*.

drip (drip), *v.i. & v.t.* **dripped** or **dript**, **drip'ping**, to fall or let fall in drops: *n*. 1. the process of falling in drops. 2. [Slang], a tiresome or dull person.

drip-dry ('drī), *adj*. denoting fabrics that dry quickly and need little ironing when hung wet.

drive (drīv), *v.t.* **drove**, **driv'en**, **driv'ing**, 1. to impel or force forward. 2. to thrust into or from a state or act. 3. to compel to work, often to excess. 4. to hit (a ball, nail, etc.) hard. 5. to force to penetrate. 6. to control (a vehicle). 7. to carry in a vehicle: *v.i.* 1. to push forward violently. 2. to strive hard to attain an objective. 3. to drive a ball, blow, etc. 4. to be driven: said of a vehicle. 5. to go or be carried in a vehicle: *n*. 1 the act of driving. 2. a trip in a vehicle. 3. a road or driveway for vehicles. 4. a rounding up of animals. 5. a campaign. 6. aggressiveness and initiative. 7. a strong compulsion or tendency. 8. the mechanism for propelling and controlling a machine.

drive-in (drīv'in), *n*. a restaurant, bank, etc. designed to provide service to customers remaining in their cars.

driv·el (driv'l), *v.t. & v.i.* **-eled** or **-elled**, **-el-ing** or **-el-ling**, 1. to let (saliva) flow from the mouth. 2. to talk in a silly or stupid way: *n*. senseless talk.

driv·er (drī'vēr), *n*. 1. a person or thing that drives. 2. one who drives a car. 3. one who herds cattle. 4. a golf club for hitting long shots from the tee.

drive-train (drīv'trān), *n*. the system that transmits an engine's power to wheels, a propeller, etc.

drive-way (drīv'wā'), *n*. a private road leading from the street to a garage, shelter, etc.

driz·zle (driz'l), *v.i. & v.t.* **-zled**, **-zling**, to rain in fine, mistlike drops: *n*. such a rain. — **driz'zly**, *adj*.

drogue (drōg), *n*. a funnel-shaped device towed behind an aircraft as a target or for drag effect.

droll (drōl), *adj*. comical in an odd way. — **droll'er·y** ('ēr-i), *n.*, *pl.* **-er·ies**.

drom·e·dar·y (drom'ē-der-i), *n.*, *pl.* **-dar·ies**, the one-humped or Arabian camel.

drone (drōn), *n*. 1. the male of the honeybee, that does no work. 2. a loafer.

drone (drōn), *v.i.* **droned**, **dron'ing**, 1. to make a continuous humming sound. 2. to talk in a monotonous tone or way: *n*. a droning sound.

drool (drōōl), *v.i.* 1. to let saliva run from the mouth. 2. to drip from the mouth, as saliva.

droop (drōōp), *v.i.* 1. to sink or hang down. 2. to become listless. 3. to become depressed: *v.t.* to let droop: *n*. the act of drooping. — **droop'y**, *adj*. **droop'i-er**, **droop'i-est**.

drop (drop), *n*. 1. a small amount of liquid that falls in a spherical or pear-shaped mass. 2. anything shaped like this. 3. a minute quantity of anything. 4. the act of falling; a sudden descent. 5. something designed to fall, as a curtain, trapdoor, etc. 6. the distance between an upper and lower level: *v.i.* **dropped**, **drop'ping**, 1. to fall in drops. 2. to fall suddenly down. 3. to fall wounded, dead, etc. 4. to pass into a specified condition. 5. to come to an end: *v.t.* 1. to let or cause to fall. 2. to say casually. 3. to send (a note). 4. to terminate or dismiss. 5. to lower. 6. [Informal], to leave at a particular place.

drop kick, in *Football*, a kick of a dropped ball just as it hits the ground. —**drop'-kick** (-kik), *v.t. & v.i.* —**drop'-kick·er**, *n*.

drop-off ('ôf), *n*. 1. a steep declivity. 2. a decrease, as in sales.

drop-out ('out), *n*. a student who leaves school before graduating.

drop·per ('ēr), *n*. a small tube with a bulb for suction at one end, used to draw up and release liquid in drops.

drop·sy (drop'si), *n*. an earlier term for edema. —**drop'si·cal** ('si-kl), *adj*.

dross (drôs), *n*. 1. the scum on melted metal. 2. rubbish.

drought (drout), *n*. a continued absence of rain: also **drouth** (drouth).

drove (drōv), *n*. 1. a herd of cattle, sheep, etc. driven in a body. 2. a moving mass of people.

drove (drōv), past tense of **drive**.

dro·ver (drō'vēr), *n*. a driver of cattle or sheep.

drown (droun), *v.i.* to perish by suffocation in water: *v.t.* 1. to suffocate by immersion in water. 2. to inundate. 3. to overwhelm and lesser ('a sound) by a stronger sound: often with *out*.

drowse (drouz), *v.i.* **drowsed**, **drows'ing**, to be half asleep; doze: *n*. a light sleep.

drow·sy ('zi), *adj*. **-si·er**, **-si-est**, 1. sleepy; lethargic. 2. making sleepy. —**drow'si·ly**, *adv*. —**drow'si·ness**, *n*.

drub (drub), *v.t.* **drubbed**, **drub'bing**, 1. to cudgel. 2. to defeat badly. —**drub'bing**, *n*.

drudge (druj), *n*. a person who does tedious, unremunerative work: *v.i.* **drudged**, **drudg'ing**, to perform such labor. —**drudg'er·y**, *n.*, *pl.* **-er·ies**.

drug (drug), *n*. 1. any substance used as medicine. 2. a narcotic, hallucinogen, etc.: *v.t.* **drugged**, **drug'ging**, 1. to mix (drugs) in food or drink. 2. to render stupid, as with a drug.

drug·get (drug'it), *n.* a coarse fabric used in floor coverings.

drug·gist (drug'ist), *n.* 1. a pharmacist. 2. one who deals in drugs.

drug·store ('stôr), *n.* a store where drugs and other items are sold and prescriptions are filled.

dru·id (drōō'id), *n.* [often D-], any member of an order of priests, soothsayers, etc. in ancient Ireland, Britain, and France.

drum (drum), *n.* 1. a percussion instrument made up of a hollow cylinder with a membrane stretched tautly over the end or ends. 2. the sound produced by beating this instrument. 3. any object resembling a drum. 4. the eardrum: *v.i.* **drummed, drum'ming,** 1. to play a drum. 2. to tap repeatedly: *v.t.* 1. to play (a tune) as on a drum. 2. to drill (facts, ideas, etc. *into*) by constant repetition.

drum·fire ('fīr), *n.* heavy and continuous gunfire.

drum·head ('hed), *n.* 1. the membrane over a drum. 2. the top of a capstan.

drum major, a person who leads a marching band, often twirling a baton. —**drum ma·jor·ette** (mā·jô·ret'), *fem.*

drum·mer ('ēr), *n.* 1. a drum player. 2. [Informal], a traveling salesman.

drum·stick ('stik), *n.* 1. a stick for beating a drum. 2. the lower half of the leg of a cooked fowl.

drunk (drungk), past participle of **drink:** *adj.* 1. overwhelmed by alcoholic liquor. 2. [Informal], same as **drunken** (sense 2): *n.* [Slang], 1. a drunken person. 2. a drinking bout.

drunk·ard (drung'kērd), *n.* one who is often drunk.

drunk·en ('ken), *adj.* 1. intoxicated. 2. pertaining to, caused by, or happening during intoxication. —**drunk'en·ly,** *adv.* —**drunk'en·ness,** *n.*

drupe (drōōp), *n.* any fleshy fruit, as a peach, having an inner stone containing a seed.

dry (drī), *adj.* **dri'er, dri'est,** 1. not under water. 2. free from moisture. 3. deficient in rain or water; arid. 4. thirsty. 5. not giving milk. 6. solid; not liquid. 7. not sweet. 8. prohibiting alcoholic beverages. 9. humorous in a sharp but restrained way. 10. not productive. 11. tedious; dull: *n., pl.* **drys,** [Informal], a prohibitionist: *v.t. & v.i.* **dried, dry'ing,** to make or become dry. —**dry'ly,** *adv.* —**dry'ness,** *n.*

dry·ad (drī'ăd), *n.* in *Classical Mythology*, [also D-], a wood nymph.

dry battery, an electric battery made up of two or more dry cells.

dry cell, a voltaic cell in which the electrolyte is a paste that cannot spill.

dry-clean (drī'klēn), *v.t.* to clean (clothing, drapes, etc.) with chemical solvents. —**dry cleaner.**

dry dock, a dock from which the water can be drained, used in building and repairing ships.

dry·er ('ēr), *n.* 1. a person or apparatus that dries. 2. same as **drier.**

dry farming, farming in an arid region without irrigation by retaining the soil moisture and planting drought resistant crops.

dry goods, clothing, textiles, etc.

dry ice, a solid cake of carbon dioxide, used as a refrigerant.

dry nurse, a nurse who cares for a baby but does not breast-feed it.

dry point, 1. a fine, hard needle for incising lines on copper plate without using acid. 2. this method of engraving. 3. a work thus engraved.

dry run, [Slang], a practice test; rehearsal.

dry-salt (drī'sôlt), *v.t.* to preserve (meat, skins, etc.) by drying and salting.

dry wall, a wall made of fibrous material.

du·al (dōō'ǎl), *adj.* 1. of or pertaining to two. 2. double; twofold. —**du'al·ism,** *n.* —**du·al'i·ty** (-al'i·ti), *n.*

dub (dub), *v.t.* **dubbed, dub'bing,** 1. to confer a title or rank upon. 2. to name in jest; nickname. 3. to rub, dress, or smooth. 4. [Slang], to execute badly, as a golf stroke.

dub (dub), *v.t.* **dubbed, dub'bing,** to insert (words, music, sounds, etc.) into a sound track, tape, etc.

du·bi·e·ty (dōō·bī'ĕ·ti), *n.* 1. the state of being dubious. 2. *pl.* **-ties,** an uncertain thing.

du·bi·ous (dōō'bi·ŭs), *adj.* 1. causing or feeling doubts. 2. undecided. —**du'bi·ous·ly,** *adv.*

du·cal (dōō'kl), *adj.* of or pertaining to a duke or dukedom.

duc·at (duk'ăt), *n.* any of several former European coins.

duch·ess (duch'is), *n.* 1. a duke's wife or widow. 2. a woman who rules a duchy.

duch·y ('i), *n., pl.* **duch'ies,** the territory or jurisdiction of a duke or duchess.

duck (duk), *n.* 1. a web-footed water bird with short legs and a flat bill. 2. the female of this bird. 3. the flesh of a duck used as food.

duck (duk), *v.t. & v.i.* 1. to submerge under water momentarily. 2. to lower or twist (the head, body, etc.) quickly, as to avoid a blow. 3. [Informal], to evade (a person, issue, etc.): *n.* the act of ducking.

duck (duk), *n.* a cotton fabric like canvas but lighter in weight.

duck·bill (duk'bil), *n.* same as **platypus.**

duck·board ('bôrd), *n.* a board or planking across a wet or muddy place.

ducking stool, a chair at the end of a plank in which offenders were formerly tied and ducked into water.

duck·ling ('ling), *n.* a young duck.

duck·pins ('pinz), *n.* a game like bowling, played with smaller pins and balls.

duck·weed ('wēd), *n.* a small, flowering plant that floats on ponds and sluggish waters.

duck·y (duk'i), *adj.* **duck'i·er, duck'i·est,** [Slang], excellent, pleasing, etc.

duct (dukt), *n.* a passage, tube, or canal, as for conveying a fluid. —**duct'less,** *adj.*

duc·tile (duk'tl), *adj.* 1. capable of being drawn out into threads, as some metals. 2. tractable. —**duc·til·i·ty** (duk·til'i·ti), *n.*

ductless gland, an endocrine gland.

dud (dud), *n.* [Informal], 1. a bomb or shell that fails to explode. 2. a failure.

dude (dōōd), *n.* 1. a dandy; fop. 2. [Western Slang], a person from the city.

dudg·eon (duj'ŭn), *n.* anger: now chiefly in *in high dudgeon*.

duds (dudz), *n.* [Informal], 1. clothing. 2. trappings.

due (dōō, dū), *adj.* 1. owed or owing; payable. 2. suitable; appropriate. 3. sufficient. 4. scheduled to arrive: *adv.* directly: *n.* 1. anything owed or deserved. 2. *pl.* fees or other charges.

du·el (dōō'ĕl, dū'-), *n.* 1. a prearranged combat between two persons with deadly weapons. 2. any contest resembling this: *v.i. & v.i.* -eled or -elled, -el·ing or -el·ling, to fight a duel with (a person).

du·en·na (dōō-en'ä), *n.* 1. an elderly woman who acts as governess to the unmarried girls in a Spanish or Portuguese family. 2. a chaperon.

due process of law, legal proceedings following established rules that protect individual rights.

du·et (dōō-et'), *n.* 1. a vocal or instrumental composition for two performers. 2. the two performers.

duff (duf), *n.* 1. a pudding of flour boiled in a bag. 2. decaying leaves, twigs, etc. on forest ground.

duf·fel (duf'l), *n.* 1. a coarse woolen cloth with a thick nap. 2. essential supplies carried by a camper, soldier, etc.

duffel bag, a large cloth bag for carrying personal effects.

duf·fer (duf'ēr), *n.* [Slang], 1. formerly, a peddler of merchandise. 2. something worthless or spurious. 3. an incompetent or dull-witted person; specifically, an unskillful golfer.

dug (dug), past tense and past participle of dig.

dug (dug), *n.* a teat or udder.

du·gong (dōō'gông), *n.* an aquatic, herbivorous mammal inhabiting tropical coastal regions of the Old World.

dug·out (dug'out), *n.* 1. a canoe hollowed out from a log. 2. a shelter excavated in a hillside or in the ground. 3. in *Baseball*, a covered shelter for the use of players not in the field.

duke (dōōk, dūk), *n.* 1. a prince ruling an independent duchy. 2. a nobleman ranking next to a prince. —**duke'dom,** *n.*

Du·kho·bors (dōō'kô-bôrz), *n.* a Christian sect of Russia, many of whom settled in Western Canada in the 1890's to avoid persecution.

dul·cet (dul'sit), *adj.* pleasant-sounding; harmonious.

dul·ci·an·a (dul-si-an'ä), *n.* a soft-toned organ stop.

dul·ci·mer (dul'si-mēr), *n.* a musical instrument with wire strings that are struck by two padded hammers.

dull (dul), *adj.* 1. slow in apprehension. 2. sluggish. 3. not bright or clear. 4. not sharp; blunt. 5. tedious. 6. not felt acutely: *v.t. &*

v.i. to make or become dull. —**dull'ness,** *n.* —**dul'ly,** *adv.*

dull·ard ('ērd), *n.* a stupid person.

du·ly (dōō'li, dū'li), *adv.* in the proper manner, way, time, etc.

dumb (dum), *adj.* 1. incapable of speech; mute. 2. silent. 3. [Informal], stupid. —**dumb'ly,** *adv.* —**dumb'ness,** *n.*

dumb·bell ('bel), *n.* 1. a weight made up of two metal balls connected by a short bar, lifted for muscular exercise. 2. [Slang], a stupid person.

dumb·found, dum·found (dum-found'), *v.t.* to make speechless with amazement.

dumb show, gestures without speech.

dumb·wait·er ('wāt-ēr), *n.* 1. a small elevator for conveying food, goods, etc. from floor to floor. 2. a portable serving table.

dum-dum bullet (dum'dum), a soft-nosed bullet that expands on contact, causing a gaping wound.

dum·my (dum'i), *n., pl.* -mies, 1. a figure shaped like a human, as for showing clothing. 2. an imitation; substitute for something real. 3. a person secretly representing another. 4. [Slang], a stupid person. 5. in *Bridge*, the partner whose hand is exposed and played by the declarer: *adj.* sham; artificial.

dump (dump), *v.t.* 1. to empty out in a large mass. 2. to dispose of (rubbish, garbage, etc.): *n.* 1. a place for dumping refuse. 2. in *military usage*, a place for storing supplies, vehicles, etc. 3. [Slang], an unpleasant, dilapidated place.

dump·ling (dump'ling), *n.* 1. a small ball of dough cooked with meat or soup. 2. fruit covered with dough and baked for a dessert.

dump·y (dum'pi), *adj.* **dump'i·er, dump'i·est,** 1. short and thick; squat. 2. [Slang], dilapidated.

dump·y (dum'pi), *adj.* **dump'i·er, dump'i·est,** discontented; depressed.

dun (dun), *adj. & n.* dull grayish-brown.

dun (dun), *v.t. & v.i.* dunned, dun'ning, to entreat (a debtor) persistently for payment: *n.* an urgent demand for payment.

dunce (duns), *n.* a dull, ignorant person.

dun·der·head (dun'dēr-hed), *n.* a dunce.

dune (dōōn, dūn), *n.* a ridge or heap of wind-blown sand.

dune buggy, an automobile with oversized tires, designed for driving on sand.

dung (dung), *n.* 1. the excrement of animals; manure. 2. filth: *v.t.* to manure with dung.

dun·ga·ree (dun-gä-rē'), *n.* 1. a sturdy cotton cloth. 2. *pl.* overalls or work pants made of this.

dun·geon (dun'jŭn), *n.* 1. same as donjon. 2. a dark chamber or prison, often underground.

dung·hill (dung'hil), *n.* a heap of dung.

Dunk·ers (dung'kērz), *n.* a sect of German-American Baptists opposed to military service and the taking of oaths: also called **Dunk'ards** ('kērdz).

dun·lin (dun'lin), *n.* a small sandpiper.

dun·nage (dun'ij), *n.* 1. loose, bulky packing for the protection of cargo during shipment. 2. baggage or personal effects.

ô in dragon, ōō in crude, oo in wool, u in cup, ū in cure, û in turn, ů in focus, oi in boy, ou in house, th in thin, th in sheathe, g in get, j in joy, y in yet.

dun·nite (dun′īt), *n.* a high explosive used especially in armor-piercing shells.

du·o (dōō′ō), *n.*, *pl.* du′os, same as duet.

du·o-, a combining form signifying *two, double.*

du·o·dec·i·mal (dōō-ō-des′ĭ-ml), *adj.* 1. of or pertaining to twelve or twelfths. 2. consisting of or counting by twelves or powers of twelve: *n.* one twelfth.

du·o·dec·i·mo (-mō), *n.*, *pl.* -mos, 1. the page size (5 by 7 1/2 inches) of a book made by folding printer's sheets into twelve leaves. 2. a book with such pages.

du·o·de·num (dōō-ō-dē′nŭm), *n.*, *pl.* -de′na (′nå), -de′nums, the upper section of the small intestine, leading from the stomach. —du·o·de′nal, *adj.*

du·o·logue (dōō′ō-lôg), *n.* a conversation between two people.

dupe (dōōp, dŭp), *n.* a person who is easily deceived or fooled: *v.t.* duped, dup′ing, to deceive by trickery; cheat.

du·ple (dōō′pl), *adj.* 1. double. 2. in *Music,* having two (or a multiple of two) beats to the measure.

du·plex (dōō′pleks, dū′-), *adj.* 1. double; twofold. 2. in *Machinery,* having two parts operating in the same way. 3. in *Electronics,* able to send two messages over a single wire at the same time in the opposite or same directions: *n.* 1. an apartment having rooms on two floors. 2. a house separated into two living units.

du·pli·cate (dōō′plĭ-kĭt, dū′-), *adj.* 1. double. 2. identical: *n.* a facsimile: *v.t.* (-kāt), -cat·ed, -cat·ing, 1. to make an exact copy or copies of. 2. to cause to occur again. —du·pli·ca′tion, *n.*

duplicating machine, a machine for making exact reproductions of written or printed material.

du·plic·i·ty (dōō-plĭs′ĭ-tĭ), *n.* deceit; hyprocrisy.

du·ra·ble (door′ȧ-bl), *adj.* 1. enduring despite use. 2. not perishing; stable. —du·ra·bil′i·ty, *n.*

du·ra ma·ter (door′ȧ māt′ẽr), the tough outer covering of the brain and spinal cord.

du·ra·men (doo-rā′mĕn), *n.* same as heartwood.

dur·ance (door′ȧns), *n.* imprisonment: chiefly in *in durance vile.*

du·ra·tion (doo-rā′shŭn), *n.* 1. continuance in time. 2. the time a thing lasts.

du·ress (doo-res′), *n.* 1. compulsion or constraint. 2. imprisonment.

du·ri·an, du·ri·on (door′i-ȧn), *n.* 1. the edible fruit of an East Indian tree, having a thick, spiny rind and a soft pulp. 2. the tree.

dur·ing (door′ing), *prep.* 1. throughout the duration of. 2. within the course of.

dur·mast (dŭr′mȧst), *n.* any of several European oaks with tough, valuable wood.

durst (dŭrst), archaic past tense of dare.

du·rum (door′ŭm), *n.* the hard wheat yielding flour used in macaroni, spaghetti, etc.

dusk (dŭsk), *n.* 1. the darker part of twilight. 2. gloom. —dusk′y, *adj.* dusk′i·er, dusk′i·est.

dust (dŭst), *n.* 1. powdered earth or any fine particles easily carried in the air. 2. earth. 3. disintegrated matter, as mortal remains reduced to earth. 4. something worthless: *v.t.*

1. to sprinkle with dust. 2. to free of dust, as by wiping: *v.i.* 1. to remove dust. —dust′y, *adj.* dust′i·er, dust′i·est. —dust′i·ness, *n.*

dust bowl, a region that receives little moisture and whose dry topsoil is easily blown away by the winds.

dust·er (′ẽr), *n.* 1. a person or thing that dusts. 2. a loose, light housecoat.

dust·pan (′pan), *n.* a shovellike, short-handled pan for floor sweepings.

Dutch (dŭch), *adj.* 1. of or pertaining to the Netherlands, a country in western Europe, or its people, language, etc. 2. [Slang], German: *n.* the language of the Netherlands.

Dutch door, a door divided across the middle so that either half opens separately.

Dutch·man (′mȧn), *n.*, *pl.* -men (′mĕn), a native or inhabitant of the Netherlands.

Dutch metal, same as tombac.

Dutch oven, a heavy pot with a tightfitting, domelike lid, used for stewing, braising, etc.

Dutch treat, [Informal], a dinner, dance, etc. for which each person pays his own way.

Dutch uncle, [Informal], one who criticizes another sternly and candidly.

du·te·ous (dōō′tĭ-ŭs), *adj.* obedient.

du·ti·a·ble (dōō′tĭ-ȧ-bl), *adj.* subject to import duty.

du·ti·ful (dōō′tĭ-fŭl), *adj.* 1. showing or proceeding from a sense of duty. 2. obedient.

du·ty (dōō′tĭ), *n.*, *pl.* -ties, 1. respect due one's parents, elders, etc. 2. any action necessitated by one's social or occupational status, by moral or legal requirements, etc. 3. obligatory service, especially military service. 4. a tax or impost, as on imports.

du·um·vir (dōō-ŭm′vẽr), *n.* either of two ancient Roman magistrates holding office jointly.

du·ve·tyne, du·ve·tyn (dōō′vĕ-tēn), *n.* a soft velvetlike fabric.

dwarf (dwôrf), *n.*, *pl.* dwarfs, dwarves (dwôrvz), an unnaturally small person, animal, or plant: *v.t.* 1. to thwart the growth of; stunt. 2. to make appear small by comparison: *v.i.* to become stunted: *adj.* atypically small. —dwarf′ish, *adj.*

dwarf chestnut, same as chinquapin.

dwell (dwel), *v.i.* dwelt or dwelled, dwell′ing, to make one's abode; reside. —dwell′er, *n.*

dwell·ing (′ing), *n.* a house or place of abode: also dwelling place.

dwin·dle (dwin′dl), *v.i. & v.t.* -dled, -dling, to become or make gradually less; diminish; shrink.

dyb·buk (dĭb′ŭk), *n.* in *Jewish Folklore,* the spirit of a dead person that possesses the body of a living person.

dye (dī), *n.* 1. a substance or liquid for coloring cloth, hair, etc. 2. the color produced: *v.t. & v.i.* dyed, dye′ing, to color with dye. —dy′er, *n.*

dyed-in-the-wool (dīd′n-*t*hē-wool′), *adj.* unchanging; uncompromising.

dye-stuff (dī′stuf), *n.* any substance used for or yielding a dye.

dy·ing (dī′ing), present participle of die: *adj.* 1. about to die or come to a close. 2. at death.

dyke (dīk), *n.* 1. same as **dike**. 2. [Slang], a lesbian: *v.t.* **dyked, dyk'ing,** same as **dike**.

dy·nam·e·ter (dī-nam'ê-tēr), *n.* an instrument for determining the magnifying power of telescopes.

dy·nam·ic (dī-nam'ik), *adj.* 1. of or pertaining to energy or force in motion. 2. vigorous; productive.

dy·nam·ics ('iks), *n.* 1. the branch of mechanics treating of the effects of force in producing motion. 2. the forces operating in any area.

dy·na·mism (dī'nå-mizm), *n.* forcefulness.

dy·na·mite (dī'nå-mīt), *n.* a highly explosive mixture of nitroglycerin and an absorbent: *v.t.* **-mit·ed, -mit·ing,** to blow up with dynamite. —**dy'na·mit·er,** *n.*

dy·na·mo (dī'nå-mō), *n., pl.* **-mos,** 1. earlier term for generator. 2. a very energetic person.

dy·na·mom·e·ter (dī-nå-mom'ê-tēr), *n.* an apparatus for measuring force or power.

dy·nas·ty (dī'nås-ti), *n., pl.* **-ties,** 1. a line or succession of sovereigns from the same family. 2. the period of time during which a particular family rules. —**dy'nas·tic** (dī-nas'-tik), *adj.*

dyne (dīn), *n.* the force that imparts to a mass of one gram an acceleration of one centimeter per second per second.

dys-, a prefix signifying *bad, ill, impaired, difficult.*

dys·en·ter·y (dis'ên-ter-i), *n.* an intestinal disease attended by pain, fever, and severe diarrhea.

dys·func·tion (dis-fungk'shŭn), *n.* abnormal or impaired functioning.

dys·gen·ic (dis-jen'ik), *adj.* pertaining to or causing deterioration of hereditary qualities.

dys·lex·i·a (dis-lek'sē-å), *n.* impairment of the ability to read, often as the result of genetic defect or brain injury. —**dys·lex'ic** or **dis·lec'tic,** *adj. & n.*

dys·men·or·rhe·a (dis-men-ô-rē'å), *n.* painful menstruation.

dys·pep·si·a (dis-pep'shå, 'si-å), *n.* indigestion. —**dys·pep'tic,** *adj. & n.*

dys·pha·gi·a (-fā'ji-å), *n.* difficulty in swallowing.

dys·pha·si·a (-fā'zhå, -fā'zhi-å), *n.* difficulty in speaking, as from brain injury.

dys·pho·ni·a (-fō'ni-å), *n.* any difficulty in making speech sounds.

dys·pho·ri·a (-fôr'i-å), *n.* a state of feeling ill, unhappy, anxious, restless, etc.

dysp·ne·a (disp'ni-å, disp-nē'å), *n.* difficult breathing.

dys·u·ri·a (dis-yoor'i-å), *n.* difficult or painful urination.

ô in dra*g*on, ōō in cr*u*de, oo in w*oo*l, u in c*u*p, ū in c*u*re, û in t*u*rn, ů in foc*u*s, oi in b*o*y, ou in h*ou*se, th in *th*in, *th* in shea*th*e, g in *g*et, j in *j*oy, y in *y*et.

E

E, e (ē), *n., pl.* **E's, e's,** 1. the fifth letter of the English alphabet. 2. any of the various sounds of this letter, as in *met, be, baker,* and *agent.* 3. a type or impression of *E* or *e.*

E (ē), *adj.* shaped like *E*: *n.* 1. an object shaped like *E.* 2. a school mark or rating signifying below average, or, sometimes, excellent. 3. in *Music, a)* the third tone in the scale of C major. *b)* the key having this tone for a basic note.

e- (ē; unstressed ĕ), a prefix signifying *out of, from, without:* the *e-* becomes *ex-* before vowels.

each (ēch), *adj. & pron.* 1. one of two. 2. every one of two or more: *adv.* apiece.

ea·ger (ē'gĕr), *adj.* impetuous; vehement; earnest; anxious; enthusiastic. **—ea'ger·ly,** *adv.* **—ea'ger·ness,** *n.*

ea·gle (ē'gl), *n.* 1. a bird of prey of the falcon family, noted for its strength, size, and keenness of vision. 2. a likeness of the eagle, used as a symbol or emblem, as the national symbol of the U.S. 3. a former gold coin worth $10. 4. a golf score of two under par on any hole.

ea·gle-eyed (-īd), *adj.* having keen sight.

ea·glet (ē'glit), *n.* a young eagle.

ear (ir), *n.* 1. the organ of hearing, especially the external part of it. 2. a delicate perception of sounds, especially in differences of musical tones. 3. attention. 4. a spike of corn. 5. anything that resembles an ear. **—ear'like,** *adj.*

ear·ache ('āk), *n.* an ache or pain in the ear.

ear·drop ('dräp), *n.* 1. a pendant earring. 2. medication to be put in the ear by drops.

ear·drum ('drum), *n.* the thin membrane through which sound is transmitted from the external ear to the inner ear.

ear·ful ('fool), *n., pl.* **-fuls,** something that is heard, especially gossip or exciting news.

ear·ing ('ing), *n.* a small rope for fastening the upper corner of a sail to the yard or gaff.

earl (ürl), *n.* a British nobleman next in rank below a marquess. **—earl'dom,** *n.*

ear·ly (ür'li), *adj. & adv.* **-li·er, -li·est,** 1. before the usual time. 2. soon. 3. at or near the beginning. 4. in ancient times. **—ear'li·ness,** *n.*

ear·mark (ir'märk), *n.* a mark for identification, as on the ear of an animal: *v.t.* 1. to set a distinctive mark upon. 2. to reserve for a special use.

ear·muff ('muf), *n.* a covering to protect the ear: usually used in the plural.

earn (ürn), *v.t.* 1. to receive as a return for work or service. 2. to deserve; merit. **—earn'er,** *n.*

ear·nest (ür'nist), *adj.* 1. in serious reality; serious in speech or action; zealous; determined. 2. not trivial; important: *n.* 1. a portion of something given or done in advance as a pledge. 2. money given in this way: also called **earnest money.** 3. seriousness. **—ear'nest·ly,** *adv.* **—ear'nest·ness,** *n.*

earn·ings (ür'ningz), *n.* 1. wages or other remuneration. 2. profits.

ear·plug (ir'plug), *n.* a small plug to be inserted in the ear to keep out water or noise.

ear·ring ('ring), *n.* an ear ornament.

ear·shot ('shät), *n.* hearing distance, especially the range within which the human voice may be heard.

ear·split·ting ('split-ing), *adj.* deafening; overpoweringly noisy.

earth (ürth), *n.* 1. the inhabited terraqueous globe: it is the third planet in distance from the sun and the fifth largest in the solar system. 2. the solid surface of this planet; dry land. 3. ground; soil. 4. worldly things or interests. 5. the inhabitants of the globe. 6. the lair of a burrowing animal. 7. a metallic oxide: *v.t.* 1. to cover with earth. 2. to pursue (an animal) to its burrow.

earth-bound ('bound), *adj.* 1. unable to escape from earthly things; worldly. 2. moving toward the earth.

earth-en (ür'thĕn), *adj.* made of earth or clay.

earth-en-ware (-wer), *n.* containers, dishes, etc. made of baked clay.

earth·ly (ürth'li), *adj.* 1. of or pertaining to the earth; sensual, worldly, temporal, etc. 2. possible.

earth·quake ('kwāk), *n.* a shaking or trembling of the earth caused by subterranean volcanic sources or by rock shifting below the surface.

earth·shak·ing ('shā·king), *adj.* significant; important; decisive.

earth·work ('wĕrk), *n.* 1. the digging and piling up of earth for embankments. 2. an offensive or defensive fortification constructed chiefly of earth, as an embankment or rampart.

earth·worm ('wĕrm), *n.* a long, round, segmented worm that burrows in damp soil.

earth·y (ür'thi), *adj.* **earth'i·er, earth'i·est,** 1. composed of or resembling earth. 2. coarse.

ear·wax (ir'waks), *n.* the yellowish, waxy matter in the ear; cerumen.

ear·wig (ir'wig), *n.* an insect with a pair of forceps at its tail.

ease (ēz), *n.* 1. freedom from pain, disturbance, etc. 2. freedom from affectation or awkwardness. 3. facility. 4. quiet; repose. 5. financial security: *v.t.* **eased, eas'ing,** 1. to free from pain, anxiety, or trouble. 2. to give rest or relief. 3. to make less difficult. 4. to make looser. 5. to move carefully: *v.i.* to become reduced in pain, anxiety, etc.

---

a in *cap,* ā in *cane,* ä in *father,* â in *abet,* e in *met,* ē in *be,* ē in *baker,* ĕ in *regent,* i in *pit,* ī in *fine,* ĭ in *manifest,* o in *hot,* ô in *horse,* ō in *bone,*

ea·sel (ē′zl), *n.* a frame or tripod for supporting a canvas, blackboard, etc.

ease·ment (ēz′mĕnt), *n.* 1. the act of easing or state of being eased. 2. that which gives ease or relief. 3. in *Law*, a right, as of passage, in another's land.

eas·i·ly (ē′zl-i), *adv.* 1. without difficulty, anxiety, etc. 2. certainly. 3. with great likelihood.

east (ēst), *n.* 1. that part of the sky where the sun rises. 2. a region or area toward this part. 3. [E-], the eastern part of the earth; Orient: *adj.* 1. of, in, or coming from the east. 2. designating the position of the altar of a church: *adv.* in an easterly direction.

East·er (ēs′tēr), *n.* a festival of the Christian Church to commemorate the resurrection of Jesus Christ: it is observed on the first Sunday after the full moon that occurs on or after March 21.

east·er·ly (ēs′tēr-li), *adj.* 1. situated in, or moving toward, the east. 2. coming from the east: *adv.* in the direction of the east.

east·ern (′tērn), *adj.* 1. situated toward, or lying in, the east. 2. from the east. 3. [E-], of or pertaining to the East.

Eastern Church, same as **Orthodox Eastern Church.**

east·ern·er (-ēr), *n.* a person who resides in the eastern part of any country.

East·er·tide (ēs′tēr-tīd), *n.* the period after Easter until various other church days.

east·ing (ēs′ting), *n.* the distance traversed by a vessel sailing eastward.

east·ward (ēst′wărd), *adj. & adv.* toward the east: also **east′wards**, *adv.*

eas·y (ē′zi), *adj.* **eas′i·er, eas′i·est**, 1. free from pain, disturbance, etc. 2. not burdensome. 3. affording comfort. 4. credulous. 5. natural; not formal. 6. slow; gentle. 7. yielding: *adv.* [Informal], in an easy manner. —**eas′i·ness,** *n.*

easy chair, an armchair with padding.

eas·y-go·ing (-gō′ing), *adj.* unhurried; relaxed.

eat (ēt), *v.t.* **ate, eat′en, eat′ing**, 1. to chew and swallow (food). 2. to devour; consume; waste or wear away. 3. to produce by eating. 4. [Slang], to cause anxiety in: *v.i.* to take food. —**eat′er,** *n.*

eat·a·ble (ēt′ā-bl), *adj.* edible: *n. usually pl.* food.

eat·er·y (′ēr-i), *n., pl.* **-er·ies**, [Informal], a restaurant.

eats (ēts), *n.* [Informal], meals.

eau (ō), *n., pl.* **eaux** (ō), [French], water.

eau de Co·logne (dĕ kô-lōn′), a perfumed toilet liquid made up of alcohol and aromatic oils that was originally made at Cologne, Germany.

eau de vie (ōd-vē′), [French], brandy.

eaves (ēvz), *n.* the edges of the roof which overhang a building.

eaves·drop (ēvz′drop), *v.i.* **-dropped, -drop·ping,** to listen to the private conversation of others. —**eaves′drop·per,** *n.*

ebb (eb), *n.* 1. the flowing back of the tide. 2. decline: *v.i.* 1. to flow back or return, as the tide to the sea; recede. 2. to decline.

eb·on·ite (eb′ŏn-īt), *n.* same as **vulcanite.**

eb·on·ize (-īz), *v.t.* **-ized, -iz·ing,** to make black by staining like ebony.

eb·on·y (-i), *n., pl.* **-on·ies,** a hard, heavy, durable, black wood: *adj.* 1. made of ebony. 2. like ebony; black.

e·bul·lient (i-bool′yĕnt), *adj.* 1. boiling up. 2. manifesting excitement; showing feeling. — **e·bul′lience,** *n.*

e·bul·li·tion (eb-ŭ-lish′ŭn), *n.* 1. the act of boiling; effervescence. 2. a sudden outburst of feeling.

e·bur·na·tion (ē-bēr-nā′shŭn), *n.* ossification of cartilage or bone.

é·car·té (ā-kär-tā′), *n.* a game of cards for two persons in which five cards are dealt to each and the eleventh turned up as trump.

ecce homo (ek′ā), [Latin, behold the man], a representation of Christ crowned with thorns.

ec·cen·tric (ik-sen′trik), *adj.* 1. not situated in, or deviating from, the center. 2. peculiar in manner or character. 3. not having the same center. 4. not circular: *n.* 1. a mechanical device for converting continuous circular motion into reciprocating rectilinear motion. 2. a peculiar person. —**ec·cen′tri·cal·ly,** *adv.*

ec·cen·tric·i·ty (ek-sen-tris′l-ti), *n., pl.* **-ties,** 1. deviation from a center. 2. peculiarity of manner or character.

ec·chy·mo·sis (ek-i-mō′sis), *n.* a livid spot on the skin, caused by extravasated blood.

Ec·cle·si·as·tes (i-klē-zi-as′tiz), *n.* a book of the Bible.

ec·cle·si·as·tic (i-klē-zi-as′tik), *adj.* same as **ecclesiastical:** *n.* a clergyman.

ec·cle·si·as·ti·cal (-ti-kl), *adj.* of or pertaining to the church, its organization, or the clergy.

ec·cle·si·as·ti·cism (′ti-sizm), *n.* strong attachment to the forms, usages, organization, and privileges of the church.

ec·cle·si·ol·o·gy (i-klē-zi-ol′ŏ-ji), *n.* the science which treats of church art and architecture.

ec·dy·sis (ek′di-sis), *n.* moulting; shedding of integument or outer skin layer, as in snakes.

ech·e·lon (esh′ĕ-lon), *n.* 1. an arrangement of a body of troops in the form of steps. 2. an arrangement of ships or planes in a similar form. 3. a section of a military group. 4. an organizational level of importance: *v.t. & v.i.* to form in echelon.

e·chid·na (i-kid′nà), *n.* an egg-laying, ant-eating mammal of Australia, covered with spines.

ech·i·nate (ek′i-nāt), *adj.* covered with spines; prickly; bristling: also **ech′i·nat·ed.**

e·chi·no·derm (i-kī′nŏ-dūrm), *n.* any of a large division of marine animals including starfishes, sea urchins, etc.

e·chi·nus (i-kī′nŭs), *n., pl.* **e·chi′ni** (′nī), 1. same as **sea urchin.** 2. the molding of the capital of a Doric column.

ech·o (ek′ō), *n., pl.* **-oes,** 1. the repetition of a sound caused by reflection. 2. such a sound. 3. the repetition of the words or opinions of others: *v.i.* **-oed, -o·ing,** to emit an echo; give, or reflect back, a sound: *v.t.* 1. to repeat (sound). 2. to repeat closely (the words, etc. of others).

ŏ in dragon, ōō in crude, oo in wool, u in cup, ū in cure, ŭ in turn, û in focus, oi in boy, ou in house, th in thin, *th* in sheathe, g in get, j in joy, y in yet.

e·cho·ic (e·kō´ĭk), *adj.* approximating the sound of something.

é·clair (ā·kler´), *n.* a small, oblong cake containing flavored cream, custard, etc., covered on the top with sugar or chocolate.

é·clair·cisse·ment (ā·kler·sēs·män´), *n.* [French], an explanation or clearing up of something previously obscure or misunderstood.

é·clat (ā·klä´), *n.* 1. applause or admiration. 2. renown. 3. striking effect; splendor. 4. great accomplishment.

ec·lec·tic (i·klek´tik), *adj.* selecting from or made up of different systems, doctrines, or sources: *n.* a person who operates in an eclectic manner. —ec·lec´ti·cal·ly, *adv.*

ec·lec·ti·cism (´ti·sizm), *n.* an eclectic system or philosophy, or its use.

e·clipse (i·klips´), *n.* 1. the total or partial obscuring of the light of the sun or moon when it enters the shadow of the other. 2. the blotting out of light, glory, etc.: *v.t.* e·clipsed´, e·clips´ing, 1. to cover or obscure by an eclipse. 2. to darken or conceal. 3. to overshadow.

e·clip·tic (i·klip´tik), *n.* the apparent path of the sun, or real path of the earth, during a year.

ec·logue (ek´lôg), *n.* a pastoral poem.

e·col·o·gy (i·kol´ō·ji), *n.* the science that deals with the relationship between living things and their surroundings. —e·col´o·gist, *n.*

e·co·nom·ic (ē·kō·nom´ik), *adj.* 1. of or pertaining to economy or economics. 2. of material satisfactions.

e·co·nom·i·cal (´i·kl), *adj.* 1. frugal; thrifty. 2. same as economic. —e·co·nom´i·cal·ly, *adv.*

e·co·nom·ics (´iks), *n.* the science that treats of wealth, its nature, production, distribution, and consumption and accompanying relationships. 2. the elements of an economy.

e·con·o·mist (i·kon´ō·mist), *n.* a student of or expert in economics.

e·con·o·mize (·mīz), *v.i.* ·mized, ·miz·ing, to be thrifty in spending: *v.t.* to manage with thrift. —e·con´o·miz·er, *n.*

e·con·o·my (·mi), *n., pl.* ·mies, 1. the regulation of household or government affairs. 2. frugality in expenditures. 3. an act of frugality. 4. a system of producing, distributing, and consuming wealth.

e·co·sys·tem (ē´kō·sis·tĕm), *n.* a system of relationships between animals, plants, and their surroundings.

ec·ru (ek´rōō), *adj. & n.* beige.

ec·sta·sy (ek´stā·si), *n., pl.* ·sies, 1. the state of being very joyful. 2. great joy. 3. a trance. —ec·stat·ic (ik·stat´ik), *adj.* —ec·stat´i·cal·ly, *adv.*

ec·to·derm (ek´tō·dûrm), *n.* the outer layer of cells, or skin, of an organism.

-ec·to·my (ek´tō·mi), a combining form meaning *a removing of* in surgery.

ec·to·pi·a (ek·tō´pi·ā), *n.* an irregular displacement of organs or parts of the body. —ec·top·ic (ek·top´ik), *adj.*

ec·to·plasm (ek´tō·plazm), *n.* 1. the exterior cytoplasm of a cell. 2. a substance which spiritualists claim surrounds the body of a medium in a trance.

ec·type (ek´tīp), *n.* a reproduction or imitation of an original.

ec·u·men·i·cal (ek·ū·men´i·kl), *adj.* 1. general; universal. 2. of or pertaining to the Christian Church throughout the world. 3. advancing or advocating Christian unification. Also ec·u·men´ic. —ec·u·men´i·cal·ism, *n.* — ec·u·men´i·cal·ly, *adv.*

ec·u·men·ism (ek´ū·mē·nizm, e·kū´mē·nizm), *n.* ecumenical activity among Christian churches: also ec·u·men·i·cism (ek·u·men´i·sizm).

ec·ze·ma (ek´sē·mā, eg´sē·mā, ig·zē´mā), *n.* an inflammatory disease of the skin, characterized by itching and the formation of scales.

e·da·cious (i·dā´shŭs), *adj.* given to excessive eating; voracious. —e·dac´i·ty (i·das´i·ti), *n.*

ed·dy (ed´i), *n., pl.* ·dies, a contrary current of air or water causing a circular motion; a small whirlpool: *v.i.* ·died, ·dy·ing, to move with a circular motion; whirl.

e·del·weiss (ā´dl·vīs), *n.* a small, white, wooly composite plant.

e·de·ma (i·dē´mā), *n., pl.* ·mas, ·ma·ta (´mā·tā), a swelling caused by too much fluid in tissues or spaces in the body.

E·den (ē´dn), *n.* 1. in the *Bible,* the garden where Adam and Eve were placed; Paradise. 2. any particularly delightful region or condition.

e·den·tate (i·den´tāt), *adj.* destitute of teeth: *n.* one of the group of mammals that have no teeth, as the sloths, anteaters, etc.

edge (ej), *n.* 1. the thin, sharp part of a cutting instrument. 2. the extreme border; margin. 3. the brink. 4. keenness. 5. [Informal], a better position: *v.t.* edged, edg´ing, 1. to furnish with an edge or border. 2. to move (something) little by little. 3. to advance (one's way) sideways through a crowd: *v.i.* 1. to advance sideways. 2. to move little by little. —edg´er, *n.*

edge tool, a sharp tool, as a chisel.

edge·ways (ej´wāz), *adv.* with the edge first: also edge´wise (´wīz).

edg·ing (ej´ing), *n.* that which forms an edge or border, as lace or embroidery for a garment.

edg·y (ej´i), *adj.* edg´i·er, edg´i·est, nervous; tense so as to be upset. —edg´i·ly, *adv.* — edg´i·ness, *n.*

ed·i·ble (ed´i·bl), *adj.* fit to be eaten as food: *n. usually pl.* something fit to be eaten. — ed·i·bil´i·ty (·bil´i·ti), *n.*

e·dict (ē´dikt), *n.* a public proclamation or decree issued by authority.

ed·i·fice (ed´i·fis), *n.* a building, especially a large, imposing structure.

ed·i·fy (ed´i·fī), *v.t.* ·fied, ·fy·ing, 1. to build up or strengthen in faith or morals. 2. to instruct. —ed·i·fi·ca´tion, *n.* —ed´i·fi·er, *n.*

ed·it (ed´it), *v.t.* 1. to revise and prepare (a manuscript) for publication. 2. to direct, select, and adapt literary matter for (the press). 3. to put together (a tape, film, etc.) by dubbing, splicing, etc.

e·di·tion (i·dish´ŭn), *n.* 1. the published form of a literary work. 2. the number of copies of a book, magazine, or newspaper published at one time. 3. one of the regular issues of a newspaper.

ed·i·tor (ed'i-tẽr), *n.* 1. one who superintends, revises, or prepares a literary work for publication. 2. one who conducts a newspaper, magazine, etc. 3. one who writes editorials.

ed·i·to·ri·al (ed-i-tôr'i-ǎl), *adj.* of or pertaining to an editor or his duties: *n.* an article in a newspaper, etc. that clearly puts forth opinions. —**ed·i·to'ri·al·ly,** *adv.*

ed·u·cate (ej'ū-kāt), *v.t.* -cat·ed, -cat·ing, 1. to cultivate the moral or intellectual faculties of; impart knowledge to; train. 2. to pay for the education of.

ed·u·ca·tion (ej-ū-kā'shŭn), *n.* 1. the act or process of educating. 2. the result of this. —**ed·u·ca'tion·al,** *adj.*

ed·u·ca·tion·ist (-ist), *n.* one versed in the art, theory, and methods of education: often used to condemn those who are either overly rigid or are opposed to standard methods.

ed·u·ca·tor (ej'ū-kāt-ẽr), *n.* 1. one who educates; teacher. 2. one who specializes in educational theory and methods.

e·duce (i-dōōs'), *v.t.* -duced', -duc'ing, 1. to draw out. 2. to infer; deduce. —**e·duc·tion** (i-duk'shŭn), *n.*

eel (ēl), *n., pl.* eels, eel, an elongated fish without ventral fins, having a slippery skin.

eel·pout (ēl'pout), *n., pl.* -pout, -pouts, 1. same as burbot. 2. a marine fish resembling the blenny.

-eer (ir), a suffix designating *a person concerned with.*

ee·rie, ee·ry (ir'i), *adj.* -ri·er, -ri·est, weird; mysterious. —**ee'ri·ly,** *adv.*

ef-, same as ex-.

ef·face (i-fās'), *v.t.* -faced', -fac'ing, 1. to obliterate; destroy. 2. to render unnoticeable. —**ef·face'ment,** *n.*

ef·fect (ē-fekt'), *v.t.* to produce as a cause, consequence, or result; accomplish: *n.* 1. a result. 2. realization. 3. efficiency. 4. purport. 5. a mental impression, or that which produces it. 6. *pl.* personal property.

ef·fec·tive (ē-fek'tiv), *adj.* 1. having the power to effect. 2. operative. 3. efficient. 4. powerful: *n. usually pl.* a soldier, division, etc. fit for duty. —**ef·fec'tive·ly,** *adv.* —**ef·fec'tiveness,** *n.*

ef·fec·tu·al (ē-fek'choo-wǎl), *adj.* 1. producing or having effect. 2. valid. —**ef·fec'tu·al·ly,** *adv.*

ef·fem·i·nate (i-fem'i-nit), *adj.* having the qualities or characteristics thought to be those of a woman; delicate or unmanly. —**ef·fem'i·na·cy** (-nǎ-si), *n.*

ef·fer·ent (ef'ẽr-ĕnt), *adj.* in *Physiology,* conveying outward.

ef·fer·vesce (ef-ẽr-ves'), *v.i.* -vesced', -vesc'ing, 1. to bubble or hiss. 2. to give way to excitement or high feeling.

ef·fer·ves·cent (-ves'nt), *adj.* 1. bubbling and hissing from the giving off of gas. 2. irrepressibly excited; displaying feeling. —**ef·ferves'cence,** *n.*

ef·fete (e-fēt'), *adj.* 1. worn out; barren; exhausted. 2. too refined; morally decadent. —**ef·fete'ly,** *adv.* —**ef·fete'ness,** *n.*

ef·fi·ca·cious (ef-i-kā'shŭs), *adj.* producing or capable of producing a desired effect. —**ef·fi·ca'cious·ly,** *adv.*

ef·fi·ca·cy (ef'i-kǎ-ci), *n., pl.* -cies, power to produce results or effects.

ef·fi·cient (ē-fish'ĕnt), *adj.* 1. producing or causing effects or results. 2. producing products, results, etc. with the least amount of money or work. —**ef·fi'cien·cy** ('ĕn-si), *n.* —**ef·fi'cient·ly,** *adv.*

ef·fi·gy (ef'i-ji), *n., pl.* -gies, an image, likeness, or figure in sculpture, painting, etc., especially a rough figure of someone who is hated.

ef·flo·resce (ef-lô-res'), *v.i.* -resced', -resc'ing, 1. to blossom. 2. in *Chemistry,* to become covered with a whitish crust or fine, white crystals.

ef·flo·res·cence (-res'ns), *n.* 1. the time or state of flowering. 2. the production of flowers. 3. redness of the skin. 4. in *Chemistry,* the formation of fine, white crystals on the surface of efflorescing substances. —**ef·flo·res'cent,** *adj.*

ef·flu·ent (ef'loo-wĕnt), *adj.* flowing or issuing forth: *n.* 1. a stream which flows out of another water source. 2. that which flows out of a sewer. —**ef'flu·ence,** *n.*

ef·flu·vi·um (e-flōō'vi-ŭm), *n., pl.* -vi·a (-ǎ), -viums, 1. an unseen invisible, subtle emanation. 2. disagreeable exhalation arising from decaying matter. —**ef·flu'vi·al,** *adj.*

ef·flux (ef'luks), *n.* 1. the act of flowing out; effluence. 2. an emanation. 3. a passing away.

ef·fort (ef'ẽrt), *n.* 1. a strenuous exertion, mental or physical. 2. a struggle; attempt. 3. that which is achieved through exertion or struggle. —**ef'fort·less,** *adj.* —**ef'fort·less·ly,** *adv.*

ef·fron·ter·y (e-frun'tẽr-i), *n., pl.* -ter·ies, impudence; presumption; boldness.

ef·ful·gence (e-ful'jĕns), *n.* a great luster, brightness, or splendor. —**ef·ful'gent,** *adj.*

ef·fuse (e-fūz'), *v.i. & v.i.* -fused', -fus'ing, 1. to pour forth. 2. to spread; radiate.

ef·fu·sion (e-fū'zhŭn), *n.* 1. the act of pouring out. 2. an outpouring of thought or sentiment. 3. the escape of various fluids into the tissues or passages of the body.

ef·fu·sive ('siv), *adj.* overflowing with emotion.

eft (eft), *n.* same as newt.

e·gad (i-gad'), *interj.* a mild curse.

e·gal·i·tar·i·an (i-gal-i-ter'i-ǎn), *adj.* of or supporting equal economic and social rights for everyone: *n.* a person supporting this.

e·gest (i-jest'), *v.t.* to void (excrement, etc.). —**e·ges'tion,** *n.*

egg (eg), *n.* 1. the oval or roundish body laid by female birds, insects, fish, etc., from which their young are produced. 2. an ovum. 3. something shaped like a egg. 4. the egg of a hen: *v.t.* to urge or incite (with on).

egg·beat·er (eg'bēt-ẽr), *n.* a kitchen tool for beating eggs, cream, etc.

ŏ in dragon, ōō in crude, oo in wool, u in cup, ū in cure, ū in turn, ŭ in focus, oi in boy, ou in house, th in thin, th in sheathe, g in get, j in joy, y in yet.

egg coal, anthracite coal about two to four inches thick.

egg foo yong (eg fōō yung'), a Chinese-American dish of eggs, bean sprouts, shrimp, etc.

egg·head (eg'hed), *n.* [Slang], an intellectual person: a term of contempt.

egg·nog ('nog), *n.* a beverage of eggs, sugar, milk, and often alcoholic liquor.

egg·plant ('plant), *n.* a plant producing large, ovoid fruit of a dark purple color, eaten as a vegetable.

e·gis (ē'jis), *n.* same as aegis.

eg·lan·tine (eg'lǎn-tīn, -tēn), *n.* a European rose with pink flowers and fragrant leaves.

e·go (ē'gō), *n., pl.* -gos, 1. the self. 2. same as egotism. 3. in *Psychoanalysis,* that part of the mind that controls action in a logical manner.

e·go·cen·tric (ē-gō-sen'trik), *adj.* self-centered; selfish: *n.* one who is egocentric.

e·go·ism (ē'gō-izm), *n.* 1. the habit of regarding oneself as the center of everything. 2. same as egotism. 3. the doctrine that all human actions should be directed toward one's own interest. —**e'go·ist,** *n.* —**e·go·is'tic, e·go·is'ti·cal,** *adj.*

e·go·ma·ni·ac (ē-gō-mā'ni-ak), *n.* one whose self-love is abnormally excessive.

e·go·tism (ē'gō-tizm), *n.* 1. constant self-exaltation in thought, speech, or writing. 2. vanity. —**e'go·tist,** *n.* —**e·go·tis'tic, e·go·tis'ti·cal,** *adj.*

e·gre·gious (i-grē'jŭs), *adj.* prominent in a bad sense; flagrant. —**e·gre'gious·ly,** *adv.*

e·gress (ē'gres), *n.* 1. a departure; going out. 2. a place of exit.

e·gret (ē'grit, eg'rit), *n.* 1. *pl.* -grets, -gret, a bird like a heron. 2. its white plume.

E·gyp·tian (i-jip'shŭn), *adj.* of or pertaining to Egypt, a country in northeastern Africa, or to its inhabitants: *n.* a native or inhabitant of Egypt.

E·gyp·tol·o·gy (ē-jip·tol'ō-ji), *n.* the study or scientific investigation of the antiquities of Egypt, its language, culture, etc.

eh (ā, e), *interj.* an expression of wonder or disbelief.

ei·der (ī'dēr), *n.* 1. *pl.* -ders, -der, a large marine duck. 2. same as eiderdown.

ei·der·down (-doun), *n.* the soft down of the eider duck used to stuff pillows, quilts, etc.

eight (āt), *adj.* one more than seven: *n.* the cardinal numeral that is the sum of seven and one; 8; VIII.

eight·een (ā'tēn'), *adj.* one more than 17: *n.* the cardinal numeral that is the sum of 17 and one; 18; XVIII.

eight·een·mo ('mō), *n., pl.* -mos, a book whose sheets are folded into 18 leaves.

eight·eenth (ā'tēnth'), *adj.* next after 17th: *n.* 1. the one after the 17th. 2. one of 18 equal parts.

eighth (ātth, āth), *adj.* next after seventh; 8th: *n.* 1. the one after the seventh. 2. one of eight equal parts. 3. in *Music,* an interval of an octave.

eight·i·eth (āt'i-ith), *adj.* next after 79th: *n.* the one after the 79th.

eight·y (āt'i), *adj.* eight times 10: *n., pl.* **eight'-ies,** 1. the cardinal numeral that is the sum of 79 and one; 80; LXXX. 2. *pl.* years or numbers from 80 through 89 (preceded by *the*).

ei·kon (ī'kon), *n.* same as icon.

ein·stein·i·um (īn-sti'ni-ŭm), *n.* a radioactive element produced by the bombardment of plutonium with neutrons.

eis·tedd·fod (ī-steth'vôd), *n.* an annual congress of Welsh poets, minstrels, musicians, etc. during which contests are held and prizes awarded.

ei·ther (ē'thēr, ī'thēr), *adj.* 1. one or the other of two. 2. one and the other: *pron.* one of two: *conj.* the correlative to *or,* indicating a choice: *adv.* also.

e·jac·u·late (i-jak'yŭ-lāt), *v.t. & v.i.* -lat·ed, -lat·ing, 1. to utter suddenly. 2. to discharge. —**e·jac·u·la'tion,** *n.* —**e·jac'u·la·to·ry,** *adj.*

e·ject (i-jekt'), *v.t.* 1. to cast out; emit; expel. 2. to evict. —**e·jec'tion,** *n.* —**e·jec'tive,** *adj.* —**e·jec'tor,** *n.*

e·jec·ta (i-jek'tà), *n.* refuse.

e·ject·ment (i-jekt'mĕnt), *n.* 1. the act of ejecting. 2. in *Law,* an action for the recovery of lands.

eke (ēk), *v.t.* eked, ek'ing, to succeed in earning (a livelihood) with difficulty (with *out*).

e·lab·o·rate (i-lab'ō-rāt), *v.t.* -rat·ed, -rat·ing, 1. to produce with labor. 2. to develop carefully: *v.i.* to increase detail (usually with *on* or *upon*): *adj.* highly finished; complicated. —**e·lab'o·rate·ly,** *adv.* —**e·lab'o·rate·ness,** *n.* —**e·lab·o·ra'tion,** *n.* —**e·lab'o·ra·tor,** *n.*

e·lan (ā-län'), *n.* dash; spirit.

e·land (ē'lǎnd), *n., pl.* **e'land, e'lands,** a large African antelope.

e·lapse (i-laps'), *v.i.* **e·lapsed', e·laps'ing,** to slip away: said of time.

e·las·tic (i-las'tik), *adj.* 1. springing back; having the power of returning to its original form; springy. 2. having a resilient spirit. 3. easily changing with the circumstances: *n.* an elastic woven fabric or band. —**e·las·tic·i·ty** (i-las-tis'i-ti), *n.*

e·las·ti·cize ('ti-sīz), *v.t.* -cized, -ciz·ing, to cause to become elastic, as by weaving rubber strands into fabric.

elastic tissue, elastic yellow fibers in the connective tissue of the body.

e·late (i-lāt'), *v.t.* -lat·ed, -lat·ing, to raise the spirits of; cause to feel exultant. —**e·la'tion,** *n.*

el·a·te·ri·um (el-à-tir'i-ŭm), *n.* the dried residue of the juice of the wild cucumber, used as a diuretic and cathartic.

el·bow (el'bō), *n.* 1. the joint or bend of the arm. 2. anything bent or curved like an elbow: *v.t.* to thrust or jostle: *v.i.* 1. to jut into an angle. 2. to push or jostle.

elbow grease, [Informal], great labor or effort.

el·bow·room (-rōōm), *n.* enough space for the desired activity.

eld·er (el'dēr), *adj.* 1. older; exceeding another in age. 2. prior in time, origin, or appointment. 3. ancient: *n.* 1. one older in age, rank, or station. 2. one of a body of lay-

---

a in *cap,* ā in *cane,* ä in *father,* ȧ in *abet,* e in *met,* ē in *be,* ē in *baker,* ĕ in *regent,* i in *pit,* ī in *fine,* ĭ in *manifest,* o in *hot,* ō in *horse,* ō in *bone,*

men, in certain churches, authorized to assist the minister. 3. a shrub or small tree with purple berries.

el·der·ber·ry (-ber-i), *n., pl.* **-ries,** 1. same as **elder** (n. 3). 2. the berry of the elder used in jelly, wines, etc.

eld·er·ly (-li), *adj.* somewhat old.

eld·est (el'dist), *adj.* oldest; first-born.

El Do·ra·do, El·do·ra·do (el-dô-rä'dō), *n., pl.* **-dos,** 1. an imaginary country in South America, fabled to be very rich in gold and precious stones. 2. any area said to have treasure, the chance to succeed, etc.

el·dritch (el'drich), *adj.* weird; mysterious.

el·e·cam·pane (el-i-kam-pān'), *n.* a coarse plant of the composite family with yellow flowers.

e·lect (i-lekt'), *v.t. & v.i.* 1. to choose for any office by ballot. 2. to select: *adj.* 1. taken in preference. 2. chosen for an office but not yet invested officially: *n. pl.* in *Theology,* those chosen for eternal life by God (preceded by *the*).

e·lec·tion (i-lek'shŭn), *n.* 1. the act of electing. 2. the act of choosing a person for some office by ballot. 3. in *Theology,* the selection by God of certain individuals for eternal life.

e·lec·tion·eer (i-lek-shŭ-nir'), *v.i.* to canvass or employ other means to secure or influence votes at an election.

e·lec·tive (i-lek'tiv), *adj.* 1. regulated by choice. 2. exerting the power of choice. 3. left to one's choice: *n.* an optional course of study in a school curriculum.

e·lec·tor (-tēr), *n.* 1. one legally qualified to vote. 2. a member of the United States electoral college. **—e·lec'tor·al,** *adj.*

electoral college, a body of representatives elected by the voters to choose a president of the United States, according to the popular vote of their individual States.

e·lec·tor·ate ('tēr-it), *n.* the whole body of persons entitled to vote.

e·lec·tric (i-lek'trik), *adj.* 1. of, pertaining to, containing, generated by, or produced by electricity. 2. thrilling or exciting. Also **e·lec'tri·cal. —e·lec'tri·cal·ly,** *adv.*

electric chair, a chair used in legal executions by electricity.

electric guitar, a guitar in which musical sounds are electrically carried to an amplifier from a microphone device on the instrument.

e·lec·tri·cian (i-lek-trish'ăn), *n.* a maker or fixer of electric devices.

e·lec·tric·i·ty (-tris'i-ti), *n.* 1. a physical property of electrons, protons, etc. used for producing light, heat, chemical decomposition, etc. 2. the science that treats of electricity. 3. an electric charge or current. 4. electric current supplied to the public.

e·lec·tri·fy (i-lek'tri-fī), *v.t.* **-fied, -fy·ing,** 1. to charge with electricity. 2. to pass an electric current through. 3. to arouse or excite suddenly. 4. to supply with electric power. **—e·lec·tri·fi'a·ble,** *adj.* **—e·lec·tri·fi·ca'tion,** *n.*

e·lec·tro-, a combining form meaning *electric, electricity.*

e·lec·tro·car·di·o·gram (i-lek-trō-kär'di-ō-gram), *n.* a sheet of paper with lines indicating electrical changes caused by heart movement.

e·lec·tro·car·di·o·graph (-graf), *n.* a device used to produce electrocardiograms.

e·lec·tro·chem·is·try (i-lek-trō-kem'is-tri), *n.* the science that treats of the use and production of electrical energy for and by chemical reactions.

e·lec·tro·cute (i-lek'trō-kūt), *v.t.* **-cut·ed, -cut·ing,** to put to death by an electric current. **—e·lec·tro·cu'tion,** *n.*

e·lec·trode (i-lek'trōd), *n.* either of the terminals of an electric source, as the anode or cathode.

e·lec·tro·dy·nam·ics (i-lek-trō-dī-nam'iks), *n.* that branch of physics which treats of electric currents.

e·lec·tro·dy·na·mom·e·ter (-dī-nō-mom'ě-tēr), *n.* an instrument for measuring the strength of an electric current.

e·lec·tro·en·ceph·a·lo·gram (-en-sef'ă-lō-gram), *n.* a sheet of paper with lines indicating electric fluctuations in the brain.

e·lec·tro·en·ceph·a·lo·graph (-graf), *n.* a device used to produce electroencephalograms.

e·lec·tro·graph (i-lek'trō-graf), *n.* an apparatus for electrically engraving plates.

e·lec·tro·ki·net·ics (i-lek-trō-ki-net'iks), *n.* that branch of electrodynamics which treats of electric currents or electricity in motion.

e·lec·trol·y·sis (i-lek-trol'i-sis), *n.* 1. the decomposition of a chemical compound by electricity. 2. the destruction of hair roots with an electric needle, resulting in the removal of undesired hair.

e·lec·tro·lyte (i-lek'trō-līt), *n.* a dissolved substance which can carry electric current by means of its ions in motion. **—e·lec·tro·lyt'ic** (-lit'ik), *adj.*

e·lec·tro·lyze (i-lek'trō-līz), *v.t.* **-lyzed, -lyz·ing,** to decompose by electrolysis.

e·lec·tro·mag·net (i-lek-trō-mag'nit), *n.* a core of soft iron rendered magnetic by the passage of an electric current through a coil of wire around it. **—e·lec·tro·mag·net'ic,** *adj.*

electromagnetic wave, a wave sent by the oscillation of an electric charge.

e·lec·tro·mag·net·ism (-mag'ně-tizm), *n.* 1. magnetism from an electric current. 2. the science which deals with the relations between electricity and magnetism.

e·lec·tro·met·al·lur·gy (-mét'l-ûr-ji), *n.* the branch of metallurgy which deals with precipitating certain metals from their solutions, or separating metals from their ores, etc. by electric current.

e·lec·trom·e·ter (i-lek-trom'ě-tēr), *n.* an instrument for measuring potential differences by static electrical forces.

e·lec·tro·mo·tive (i-lek-trō-mōt'iv), *adj.* causing electric current by means of potential differences.

electromotive force, the electric force that produces a flow of current, measured in volts.

e·lec·tron (i-lek'tron), *n.* a particle that is a component of all atoms, having a negative charge and a mass of about 1/1836 of a proton.

e·lec·tro·neg·a·tive (i-lek-trō-neg'ă-tiv), *adj.* having a tendency to pass to the positive pole in electrolysis.

e·lec·tron·ic (i-lek-tron'ik), *adj.* of or pertaining to electrons or that depending on the effect of electrons. —**e·lec·tron'i·cal·ly,** *adv.*

electronic music, music that is produced and manipulated by electronic apparatus and recorded on tape.

e·lec·tron·ics ('iks), *n.* the branch of physics that deals with the action and effects of electrons, as in electron tubes.

electron microscope, a powerful microscope that uses a beam of electrons to make an image larger.

electron tube, a metal or glass tube that completely encloses a gas or vacuum, used to direct an electron flow.

e·lec·tron-volt (-võlt), *n.* an energy unit of one electron moving through a one-volt difference of potential.

e·lec·tro·phys·i·ol·o·gy (i-lik-trõ-fiz-i-ol'õ-ji), *n.* that science which investigates the electrical phenomena of living cells and organisms.

e·lec·tro·plate (i-lek'trõ-plāt), *v.t.* **-plat·ed, -plat·ing,** to give a coating of metal to by means of a current of electricity: *n.* an article thus coated.

e·lec·tro·pos·i·tive (i-lek-trõ-poz'i-tiv), *adj.* tending to pass to the negative pole in electrolysis.

e·lec·tro·scope (i-lek'trõ-skõp), *n.* a kind of electrometer.

e·lec·tro·shock therapy (-shok), shock therapy using electricity.

e·lec·tro·stat·ics (i-lek-trõ-stat'iks), *n.* the science which treats of the phenomena of electricity at rest. —**e·lec·tro·stat'ic,** *adj.*

e·lec·tro·ther·a·py (-ther'ã-pi), *n.* medical care using electricity, as in diathermy.

e·lec·tro·ther·mal (-thûr'ml), *adj.* of or pertaining to the generation of heat by electricity.

e·lec·tro·type (i-lek'trõ-tīp), *n.* in *Printing,* a facsimile of a surface made by covering a mold, plate, etc. with a coating of copper using electroplating processes, and then removing the copper layer.

e·lec·trum (i-lek'trûm), *n.* an alloy of silver and gold of a light-yellow color.

el·ee·mos·y·nar·y (el-i-mos'i-ner-i), *adj.* 1. of or pertaining to alms; devoted to charitable purposes. 2. dependent upon charity.

el·e·gant (el'ê-gãnt), *adj.* 1. characterized by refinement and good taste. 2. graceful in form, color, or design. 3. [Informal], first-rate. —**el'e·gance,** *n.* —**el'e·gant·ly,** *adv.*

el·e·gi·ac (el-ê-jī'ãk, i-lē'ji-ak), *adj.* 1. of, pertaining to, or of the nature of an elegy. 2. plaintive; mournful.

el·e·gy (el'ê-ji), *n., pl.* **-gies,** 1. a funeral song; dirge; requiem. 2. a song or poem in a mournful style.

el·e·ment (el'ê-mênt), *n.* 1. of, first or constituent principles (preceded by *the*). 2. a component or essential part; ingredient. 3. the natural environment of something. 4. *pl.* the Eucharistic bread and wine. 5. in *Chemistry,* a substance which cannot be decomposed by chemical methods.

el·e·men·tal (el-ê-men'tl), *adj.* 1. of, pertaining to, or characteristic of nature; unrefined. 2.

fundamental. 3. of or pertaining to a constituent part or parts.

el·e·men·ta·ry (el-ê-men'tër-i), *adj.* 1. same as **elemental.** 2. simple.

elementary particle, any of the indivisible particles smaller than an atom.

elementary school, a school of the first six or eight grades with a basic curriculum.

el·e·phant (el'ê-fãnt), *n., pl.* **-phants, -phant,** a large mammal of Asia and Africa, the largest four-footed animal, distinguished by a long, flexible proboscis and two tusks of ivory.

el·e·phan·ti·a·sis (el-ê-fãn-tī'ã-sis), *n.* a cutaneous disease characterized by great enlargement of the affected parts of the body.

el·e·phan·tine (el-ê-fan'tēn, -fan'tīn), *adj.* 1. of or pertaining to an elephant. 2. resembling an elephant; huge; unwieldy.

el·e·vate (el'ê-vãt), *v.t.* **-vat·ed, -vat·ing,** 1. to raise from a lower to a higher position. 2. to raise in position; ennoble. 3. to animate; inspire; intoxicate. 4. to raise by training or education.

el·e·va·tion (el-ê-vã'shûn), *n.* 1. the act of elevating. 2. the state of being elevated. 3. a sketch plan of a side of a building. 4. the altitude of a heavenly body above the horizon. 5. a high location or position. 6. height above sea level or the earth's surface.

el·e·va·tor (el-ê-vãt-êr), *n.* 1. that which raises up. 2. a hoisting machine or lift. 3. a warehouse for the storage of grain. 4. a car or cage for moving people or things up and down. 5. a part on an airplane for controlling upward and downward flight.

el·ev·en (i-lev'ên), *adj.* one more than 10: *n.* the cardinal numeral that is the sum of 10 and one; 11; XI.

el·ev·enth ('ênth), *adj.* next after 10th; 11th: *n.* 1. the one after the 10th. 2. one of eleven equal parts.

elf (elf), *n., pl.* **elves** (elvz), a diminutive, mischievous sprite supposed to haunt hills and wild places. —**elf'ish,** *adj.*

elf-in (el'fin), *n.* same as **elf:** *adj.* 1. of or pertaining to elves. 2. like a fairy.

elf-lock (elf'lok), *n.* a knot of hair twisted in an intricate manner.

e·lic·it (i-lis'it), *v.t.* to draw out.

e·lide (i-līd'), *v.t.* **e·lid'ed, e·lid'ing,** to slur over or omit (a vowel) in pronouncing. —**e·li·sion** (i-lizh'ûn), *n.*

el·i·gi·ble (el'i-ji-bl), *adj.* capable of being, or fit to be, chosen; legally qualified: *n.* one who is eligible. —**el·i·gi·bil'i·ty,** *n.*

e·lim·i·nate (i-lim'i-nãt), *v.t.* **-nat·ed, -nat·ing,** 1. to cast aside. 2. to leave out of consideration. 3. to excrete. —**e·lim·i·na'tion,** *n.* —**e·lim'i·na·tor,** *n.*

e·lite, é·lite (i-lēt', ã-), *n.* the choicest or most influential part, as of society, a profession, an army, etc.

e·lit·ism (i-lēt'izm, ã-), *n.* government or control by an elite. —**e·lit'ist,** *adj. & n.*

e·lix·ir (i-lik'sêr), *n.* 1. an imaginary material thought by alchemists to be capable of prolonging life indefinitely, or of changing base metals into gold. 2. a medicinal tincture.

E·liz·a·be·than (i-liz-å-bē'thån), *adj.* of the age of Elizabeth I of England (1558-1603).

elk (elk), *n., pl.* **elk, elks,** 1. a large deer of northern Europe that resembles the moose. 2. same as **wapiti.** 3. a light, flexible leather made from cowhide.

ell (el), *n.* 1. a measure formerly used for cloth, varying in different countries, an English ell being 45 inches. 2. anything shaped like the letter L, as a pipe joint, a building wing, etc.

el·lipse (i-lips'), *n., pl.* **-lip'ses** ('siz), one of the sections of a cone; an oval-shaped curve.

el·lip·sis (i-lip'sis), *n., pl.* **-ses** ('siz), 1. the omission of a word or words in a sentence, the sense of which is obvious. 2. a mark in printing denoting the omission of words, a pause, etc.

el·lip·soid ('soid), *n.* an elliptical spheroid.

el·lip·ti·cal (i-lip'ti-kl), *adj.* 1. of, pertaining to, or formed like an ellipse. 2. having a part omitted. Also **el·lip'tic.** —**el·lip'ti·cal·ly,** *adv.*

el·lip·tic·i·ty (i-lip-tis'î-ti), *n.* 1. the quality of being elliptical. 2. the extent of any divergence of an ellipse from the circle, or a spheroid from the sphere.

elm (elm), *n.* 1. a large, leafy tree with spreading top branches affording much shade. 2. the strong wood of this tree.

el·o·cu·tion (el-ō-kū'shún), *n.* the art, manner, or style of speaking in public; delivery. —**el·o·cu'tion·ar·y,** *adj.* —**el·o·cu'tion·ist,** *n.*

E·lo·him (e-lō'him), *n.* one of the Old Testament names of God.

E·lo·hist ('hist), *n.* the assumed author of those portions of the Old Testament in which Elohim is used for God.

e·lon·gate (i-lŏng'gāt), *v.t. & v.i.* **-gat·ed, -gat·ing,** to stretch out; extend; lengthen. —**e·lon·ga'tion,** *n.*

e·lope (i-lōp'), *v.i.* **e·loped', e·lop'ing,** 1. to escape privately. 2. to run away with a lover, as to get married. —**e·lope'ment,** *n.*

el·o·quence (el'ō-kwêns), *n.* the art of speaking with fluency and elegance.

el·o·quent (-kwênt), *adj.* having the power of fluent and elegant oratory. —**el'o·quent·ly,** *adv.*

else (els), *adv.* otherwise: *adj.* 1. other. 2. more.

else·where (els'hwer), *adv.* in another place.

e·lu·ci·date (i-lū'si-dāt), *v.t. & v.i.* **-dat·ed, -dat·ing,** to make clear; render intelligible. —**e·lu·ci·da'tion,** *n.* —**e·lu'ci·da·tor,** *n.*

e·lude (i-lood'), *v.t.* **e·lud'ed, e·lud'ing,** 1. to avoid by artifice or dexterity. 2. to escape comprehension by. —**e·lu'sion,** *n.*

e·lu·sive ('siv), *adj.* having a tendency to elude; confusing. —**e·lu'sive·ness,** *n.*

el·ver (el'vêr), *n.* a young eel.

elves (elvz), *n.* plural of **elf.**

E·ly·sian (i-lizh'ån), *adj.* 1. of or pertaining to Elysium. 2. yielding the highest enjoyment.

E·ly·si·um ('î-úm), *n.* 1. in *Greek Mythology,* the paradise or residence of the blessed after death. 2. a condition or place of perfect happiness.

em (em), *n.* the square body of any size of type, serving as a unit of measurement.

'em (êm), *pron.* [Informal], them.

em-, same as en-.

e·ma·ci·ate (i-mā'shi-āt, -mā'si-), *v.t.* **-at·ed, -at·ing,** to cause to lose flesh; make thin. —**e·ma·ci·a'tion,** *n.*

em·a·nate (em'å-nāt), *v.i.* **-nat·ed, -nat·ing,** to flow out, issue, or proceed, as from a source. —**em·a·na'tion,** *n.*

e·man·ci·pate (i-man'si-pāt), *v.t.* **-pat·ed, -pat·ing,** 1. to liberate from servitude or bondage. 2. to set free from controls. —**e·man·ci·pa'tion,** *n.* —**e·man'ci·pa·tor,** *n.*

Emancipation Proclamation, a proclamation issued by President Lincoln declaring that as of January 1, 1863, all slaves in States then in rebellion were henceforth to be free.

e·mar·gi·nate (i-mär'ji-nit), *adj.* indented at the edges; having the apex notched.

e·mas·cu·late (i-mas'kyû-lāt), *v.t.* **-lat·ed, -lat·ing,** 1. to castrate; deprive of virility. 2. to weaken, as by expurgation: *adj.* (-lît), castrated; deprived of vigor. —**e·mas·cu·la'tion,** *n.*

em·balm (im-bäm'), *v.t.* to preserve (a corpse) from decay by various chemical substances. —**em·balm'er,** *n.*

em·bank (im-bangk'), *v.t.* to enclose or protect with a bank of earth, stones, etc. —**em·bank'ment,** *n.*

em·bar·go (im-bär'gō), *n., pl.* **-goes,** 1. an order by government authority prohibiting the departure of vessels from a port. 2. any check or impediment, as a stoppage of the foreign trade of a country by official order: *v.t.* **-goed, -go·ing,** to place an embargo on.

em·bark (im-bärk'), *v.t.* 1. to put on board ship. 2. to venture or invest: *v.i.* 1. to go on board a vessel, aircraft, etc. 2. to engage in any affairs. 3. to enter upon travel. —**em·bar·ka·tion** (em-bär-kā'shún), *n.*

em·bar·rass (im-bar'ås), *v.t.* 1. to hinder. 2. to perplex. 3. to involve in pecuniary difficulties. 4. to distress. —**em·bar'rass·ment,** *n.*

em·bas·sy (em'bå-si), *n., pl.* **-sies,** 1. the function, mission, or official residence of an ambassador. 2. the ambassador together with his staff. 3. an official delegation.

em·bat·tle (im-bat'l), *v.t.* **-tled, -tling,** to furnish with battlements.

em·bat·tled ('ld), *adj.* arrayed or prepared for battle.

em·bed (im-bed'), *v.t.* **-bed'ded, -bed'ding,** to set in surrounding matter. —**em·bed'ment,** *n.*

em·bel·lish (im-bel'ish), *v.t.* 1. to set off by adding ornamentation. 2. to touch up with additional details. —**em·bel'lish·ment,** *n.*

em·ber (em'bêr), *n.* 1. a small live coal, piece of wood, etc. 2. *pl.* unextinguished smoldering ashes.

em·ber (em'bêr), *adj.* [often E-], denoting the Wednesday, Friday, and Saturday of a particular week during each of the four seasons in the year, which are set aside as a period of fasting and prayer by the Roman Catholic Church and some other churches.

em·bez·zle (im-bez'l), *v.t.* **-zled, -zling,** to appropriate fraudulently (property entrusted to one's care). —**em·bez'zle·ment,** *n.* —**em·bez'-zler,** *n.*

ò in dragon, ōō in crude, oo in wool, u in cup, ū in cure, û in turn, ù in focus, oi in boy, ou in house, th in thin, th in sheathe, g in get, j in joy, y in yet.

em·bit·ter (-bit'ẽr), *v.t.* to make bitter or more bitter.

em·bla·zon (im-blā'zn), *v.t.* 1. to adorn (*with* heraldic figures). 2. to blazon; decorate. 3. to celebrate the praises of. —**em·bla'zon·ment**, *n.*

em·bla·zon·ry (-ri), *n., pl.* -ries, heraldic decoration.

em·blem (em'blĕm), *n.* 1. a symbolical figure or design. 2. a visible sign of an idea, group, etc. 3. a device, badge, etc. —**em·blem·at·ic** (em'blĕ-mat'ik), *adj.*

em·ble·ments (em'blĕ-mĕnts), *n.pl.* in *Law*, annual crops produced by the labor of the cultivator.

em·bod·y (im-bod'i), *v.t.* -bod'ied, -bod'y·ing, 1. to collect into one mass or united whole; incorporate. 2. to invest with, or as with, a material body. —**em·bod'i·ment**, *n.*

em·bold·en (-bōl'dn), *v.t.* to encourage; make bolder.

em·bo·lism (em'bō-lizm), *n.* 1. an intercalation; insertion of days, months, or years into the calendar to produce regularity of time. 2. the presence of obstructing clots in the blood vessels.

em·bo·lus (-lŭs), *n., pl.* -li (-lī), a clot or obstruction in a blood vessel.

em·bon·point (än-bôn-pwan'), *n.* [French], plumpness of figure.

em·bos·om (im-booz'ŏm), *v.t.* 1. to hold in the bosom; hug. 2. to enclose; shelter.

em·boss (-bôs'), *v.t.* 1. to cover with designs, patterns, etc. raised above the surface. 2. to raise, as a design, in relief.

em·bou·chure (äm-boo-shoor'), *n.* 1. the mouth of a river. 2. the mouthpiece of a musical wind instrument.

em·bow·er (im-bou'ẽr), *v.t.* to cover with, or as with, a bower.

em·brace (im-brās'), *v.t.* -braced', -brac'ing, 1. to take in close, or press to the bosom with affection; hug. 2. to receive with willingness. 3. to adopt enthusiastically. 4. to enclose. 5. to comprise. 6. in *Law*, to attempt to influence (a jury) by threats or bribes: *v.i.* to join in an embrace: *n.* the act of embracing; clasping in the arms; hug. —**em·brace'a·ble**, *adj.*

em·brac·er·y (-brā'sẽr-i), *n.* in *Law*, the act of attempting to corrupt or influence a jury.

em·bra·sure (im-brā'zhẽr), *n.* 1. an opening in a wall or parapet from which to fire guns. 2. a window or door having its sides slanted so as to be wider on the inside.

em·bro·cate (em'brō-kāt), *v.t.* -cat·ed, -cat·ing, to moisten and rub (a body part) with a lotion, oil, etc.

em·bro·ca·tion (em-brō-kā'shŭn), *n.* 1. the act of embrocating. 2. a liniment for applying to, or rubbing, a part of the body.

em·broi·der (im-broi'dẽr), *v.t. & v.i.* 1. to decorate with needlework. 2. to embellish with additions.

em·broi·der·y (-i), *n., pl.* -der·ies, 1. the work of embroidering. 2. fabric that has been embroidered. 3. embellishment.

em·broil (im-broil'), *v.t.* 1. to throw into confusion; mix up. 2. to involve in contention; entangle. —**em·broil'ment**, *n.*

em·bry·o (em'bri-ō), *n., pl.* -bry·os, 1. the first germ or rudiment of an organism, as in the uterus, a seed, etc. 2. the first or undeveloped state of anything.

em·bry·og·e·ny (em-bri-oj'ē-ni), *n.* the development of the embryo.

em·bry·ol·o·gy (-ol'ō-ji), *n.* the branch of biology which treats of the development of embryos. —**em·bry·ol'o·gist**, *n.*

em·bry·on·ic (-on'ik), *adj.* 1. of, pertaining to, or resembling an embryo. 2. rudimentary.

em·cee (em'sē'), *v.t. & v.i.* -ceed', -cee'ing, [Informal], to serve as a master of ceremonies (for): *n.* [Informal], a master of ceremonies.

e·mend (i-mend'), *v.t.* to make corrections; alter the form of words, as in a literary composition to improve it: also **e·men·date** (ē'mĕn-dāt), -dat·ed, -dat·ing. —**e'men·da·tor**, *n.*

e·men·da·tion (ē-mĕn-dā'shŭn, em-ĕn-), *n.* the alteration or correction of a text, so as to give an improved reading.

em·er·ald (em'ẽr-ăld), *n.* 1. a precious stone of a rich, deep-green color; variety of beryl. 2. bright green. 3. a size of printing type: *adj.* bright-green.

e·merge (i-mŭrj'), *v.i.* e·merged', e·merg'ing, 1. to rise up or come forth from anything which conceals, as a liquid. 2. to become apparent. 3. to develop. —**e·mer'gence**, *n.* —**e·mer'gent**, *adj.*

e·mer·gen·cy (i-mŭr'jĕn-si), *n., pl.* -cies, a sudden occasion, pressing necessity, etc. which requires fast response: *adj.* of, pertaining to, or used in, an emergency.

e·mer·i·tus (i-mer'i-tŭs), *adj.* retired from service, though retaining one's title: said of college professors, clergymen, etc.: *n., pl.* -ti (-tī), a person who has been retired with such a title.

e·mer·sion (i-mŭr'zhŭn), *n.* the act of emerging; emergence.

em·er·y (em'ẽr-i), *n., pl.* -er·ies, a very hard variety of corundum used for grinding or polishing.

em·e·sis (em'ē-sis), *n.* vomiting.

e·met·ic (i-met'ik), *adj.* inducing vomiting: *n.* a medicine possessing emetic properties.

e·meute (ā-mut'), *n.* [French], an outbreak; riot.

-e·mi·a (ēm'i-à), a suffix meaning *a state or disease of.*

em·i·grant (em'i-grănt), *n.* one that emigrates: *adj.* 1. emigrating. 2. of or pertaining to emigrants or emigration.

em·i·grate (em'i-grāt), *v.i.* -grat·ed, -grat·ing, to leave a country or region to settle in another. —**em·i·gra'tion**, *n.*

em·i·nence (em'i-nĕns), *n.* 1. that which is lofty; elevation; height. 2. exalted rank, station, celebrity, or repute. 3. [E-], a title given to cardinals in the Roman Catholic Church.

em·i·nent (-nĕnt), *adj.* 1. high in office, rank, or reputation; distinguished. 2. lofty; exalted. 3. conspicuous. 4. worthy of notice. —**em'i·nent·ly**, *adv.*

e·mir (i-mir′), n. a prince or ruler in some Moslem countries. —e·mir′ate (′it, ′āt), n.

em·is·sar·y (em′i-ser-i), n., pl. -sar·ies, a person, or agent, sent on a mission, especially of a secret nature.

e·mis·sion (i-mish′ŭn), n. 1. the act of sending out. 2. that which is sent out.

e·mis·sive (i-mis′iv), adj. sending out.

e·mit (i-mit′), v.t. e·mit′ted, e·mit′ting, 1. to send or give forth. 2. to speak (sounds). 3. to issue (bank notes).

em·men·a·gogue (i-men′ă-gog), n. something that stimulates the menstrual flow.

em·mer (em′ĕr), n. a kind of wheat.

em·me·tro·pi·a (em-ĕ-trō′pi-ă), n. a normal refractive condition of the eye, denoting perfect vision.

e·mol·li·ent (i-mol′yĕnt), adj. softening: n. a medicine that has a softening effect on body surface tissues.

e·mol·u·ment (i-mol′ū-mĕnt), n. profit; remuneration; income; pecuniary gain.

e·mote (i-mōt′), v.i. e·mot′ed, e·mot′ing, [Informal], to behave emotionally or dramatically.

e·mo·tion (i-mō′shŭn), n. 1. excited feeling; passion. 2. a particular reaction, as love, hate, etc.

e·mo·tion·al (′shŭn-l), adj. 1. of, pertaining to, or characterized by emotion. 2. quickly brought to a state of emotion. 3. causing emotion. —e·mo′tion·al·ly, adv. —e·mo·tion·al′i·ty, n.

e·mo·tion·al·ism (-izm), n. 1. the inclination to display emotion. 2. such a display.

e·mo·tive (i-mōt′iv), adj. producing or displaying emotion.

em·pa·thize (em′pă-thīz), v.i. -thized, -thiz·ing, to experience empathy (with).

em·pa·thy (-thi), n. participation or sharing in another′s feelings or emotions. —em·path·ic (im·path′ik), em·pa·thet·ic (em-pă-thet′ik), adj.

em·pen·nage (em-pĕ-näzh′), n. the tail section of an aircraft that comprises the stabilizers, rudder, etc.

em·per·or (em′pĕr-ĕr), n. the highest ruler or sovereign of an empire.

em·pha·sis (em′fă-sis), n., pl. -ses (-sēz), 1. a particular stress of the voice on a word, syllable, phrase, etc. 2. special force of expression, thought, action, etc. 3. attention; importance.

em·pha·size (-sīz), v.t. -sized, -siz·ing, to give emphasis to; stress.

em·phat·ic (im-fat′ik), adj. 1. uttered with emphasis. 2. forcible; significant. 3. full of emphasis. —em·phat′i·cal·ly, adv.

em·phy·se·ma (em-fi-sē′mă), n. a disease of the lungs in which the air cells are abnormally distended.

em·pire (em′pīr), n. 1. supreme power or dominion. 2. rule or sovereignty by an emperor or empress. 3. a group of states under one ruler.

em·pir·ic (em-pir′ik), adj. same as empirical: n. one who relies on practical experience rather than science or theory.

em·pir·i·cal (em-pir′i-kl), adj. founded upon or derived from experiment or experience. —

em·pir′i·cal·ly, adv. —em·pir′i·cism (′i-sizm), n.

em·place·ment (im-plās′mĕnt), n. the position, platform, etc. from which a heavy gun or guns are fired.

em·ploy (im-ploi′), v.t. 1. to make use of. 2. to keep busy. 3. to provide work for; engage; hire: n. occupation; employment.

em·ploy·ee, em·ploy·e (im-ploi′ē, em-ploi-ē′), n. one who is hired to work for another for wages or salary.

em·ploy·er (im-ploi′ĕr), n. one who employs others to work for wages or salary.

em·ploy·ment (′mĕnt), n. business; occupation; work; job.

em·po·ri·um (em-pôr′i-ŭm), n., pl. -ri·ums, -ri·a (-ă), 1. a commercial center or place of trade. 2. a large store.

em·pow·er (im-pou′ĕr), v.t. 1. to authorize. 2. to enable.

em·press (em′pris), n. 1. the wife of an emperor. 2. a woman with sovereign rule over an empire.

em·presse·ment (än-pres-män′), n. [French], an effusive display of cordiality.

emp·ty (emp′ti), adj. -ti·er, -ti·est, 1. containing nothing. 2. vacant. 3. meaningless: v.t. -tied, -ty·ing, 1. to make empty. 2. to discharge (the contents): v.i. 1. to become empty. 2. to discharge: n., pl. -ties, an empty bottle, can, etc. —emp′ti·ly, adv. —emp′ti·ness, n.

emp·ty·hand·ed (-han′did), adj. bringing nothing or carrying nothing away.

em·py·re·an (em-pi-rē′ăn), n. 1. the highest and purest region of heaven or the region of pure fire or light. 2. the sky; firmament. —em·pyr·e·al (em-pir′i-ăl), adj.

e·mu (ē′mū), n. a large bird of Australia, like an ostrich but smaller.

em·u·late (em′yŭ-lāt), v.t. -lat·ed, -lat·ing, 1. to strive to equal or excel, especially by imitating. 2. to rival. —em·u·la·tion, n. —em·u·la·tor, n. —em′u·lous, adj.

e·mul·si·fy (i-mul′si-fī), v.t. & v.i. -fied, -fy·ing, to make into an emulsion. —e·mul·si·fi·ca·tion, n.

e·mul·sion (i-mul′shŭn), n. 1. a liquid, as milk, in which minute particles remain in suspension. 2. a pharmaceutical preparation of an oily substance held in suspension in a watery liquid. 3. a suspension of a salt of silver in gelatin or collodion, used in photography. —e·mul′sive, adj.

e·munc·to·ry (i-mungk′tĕr-i), n., pl. -ries, any organ or part of the body which serves to carry off wastes, as the kidneys or skin: adj. carrying off waste products; excretory.

en (en), n. in Printing, half an em.

en-, a prefix meaning to put or get into, wrap, cause to be; in, into: also used as an intensifier.

en·a·ble (in-ā′bl), v.t. -bled, -bling, to make able; furnish with adequate means and power.

en·act (in-akt′), v.t. 1. to decree; pass into law. 2. to act the part of.

en·act·ment (′mĕnt), n. 1. the act of enacting. 2. something enacted; a statute, law, etc.

en·am·el (i-nam′l), n. 1. an opaque, colored, glassy substance used in coating the surface

---

ō in dragon, ōō in crude, oo in wool, u in cup, ū in cure, û in turn, ù in focus, oi in boy, ou in house, th in thin, th in sheathe, g in get, j in joy, y in yet.

of metals or porcelain, and afterward fired. 2. anything enameled. 3. any smooth, hard, glossy coating, especially the white substance of the crown of a tooth. 4. paint or varnish that dries to a smooth, hard surface: *v.t.* -eled or -elled, -el·ing or -el·ling, to lay on, cover, or decorate with enamel.

en·am·or (in-am'ẽr), *v.t.* to captivate; charm: British form en·am'our.

en·camp (in-kamp'), *v.i.* to form a camp: *v.t.* 1. to form into a camp. 2. to put in a camp. —en·camp'ment, *n.*

en·cap·su·late (in-kap'sù-lāt), *v.t.* -lat·ed, -lat·ing, 1. to encase in a capsule. 2. to condense. Also en·cap'sule ('sl), -suled, -sul·ing. —en·cap·su·la'tion, *n.*

en·case (in-kās'), *v.t.* -cased', -cas'ing, 1. to enclose; cover. 2. to put into a case. —en·case'ment, *n.*

en·caus·tic (en-kôs'tik), *adj.* burned in or done by burning in: *n.* the art of painting by which colors in wax are burned into a surface with hot irons.

-ence (ẽns), a suffix meaning *act, process, state.*

en·ceinte (än-sänt'), *n.* [French], 1. the line of works that forms the main enclosure of a fortified place. 2. the enclosure: *adj.* with child; pregnant.

en·ce·phal·ic (en-sẽ-fal'ik), *adj.* of, pertaining to, or near the brain.

en·ceph·a·li·tis (en-sef'å-lī'tis), *n.* inflammation of the brain.

en·chain (en-chān'), *v.t.* to hold fast with or as with chains; fetter.

en·chant (in-chant'), *v.t.* 1. to bewitch, as by spells or sorcery. 2. to charm; fill with delight. —en·chant'ment, *n.*

en·chase (in-chās'), *v.t.* -chased', -chas'ing, 1. to enclose in a setting or border, as a jewel. 2. to ornament by inlaying.

en·chi·la·da (en-chi-lä'dä), *n.* a rolled tortilla filled with meat, served with a chili-flavored sauce and cheese.

en·ci·na (en-sē'nä), *n.* the California live oak.

en·cir·cle (in-sūr'kl), *v.t.* -cled, -cling, 1. to enclose in a circle; surround. 2. to circle around. —en·cir'cle·ment, *n.*

en·clave (en'klāv), *n.* 1. a tract or territory enclosed within foreign territory. 2. a specific group of people living as a unit within a larger group, especially in a city.

en·clit·ic (en-klit'ik), *adj.* denoting a word that is unstressed after being combined with another, as *man* in *fisherman*: *n.* any such word or particle.

en·close (in-klōz'), *v.t.* -closed', -clos'ing, 1. to shut in; encompass; surround. 2. to put into an envelope, etc. with something else. 3. to contain; hold.

en·clo·sure (-klō'zhẽr), *n.* 1. the act or state of being enclosed. 2. that which encloses, as a fence or wall. 3. that which is enclosed; especially, a check, brochure, etc. enclosed with a letter in an envelope.

en·code (in-kōd'), *v.t.* -cod'ed, -cod'ing, to convert (a message, etc.) into code.

en·co·mi·as·tic (en-kō-mi-as'tik), *adj.* expressing praise; eulogistic.

en·co·mi·um (en-kō'mi-ûm), *n., pl.* -mi·ums, -mi·a (-å), a formal expression of praise; tribute; eulogy.

en·com·pass (in-kum'pås), *v.t.* 1. to surround. 2. to include. —en·com'pass·ment, *n.*

en·core (ong'kôr), *interj.* [French], once more; again: *n.* a repetition or further performance in response to a call or applause by an audience: *v.t.* -cored, -cor·ing, to call for an encore.

en·coun·ter (in-koun'tẽr), *v.t. & v.i.* 1. to come upon suddenly; meet face to face. 2. to meet in combat: *n.* 1. a sudden or accidental meeting. 2. a conflict; battle: *adj.* of or denoting a small group that meets for a kind of intimate psychological therapy.

en·cour·age (in-kũr'ij), *v.t.* -aged, -ag·ing, 1. to give courage to; inspire; stimulate. 2. to support; help. —en·cour'age·ment, *n.*

en·cri·nite (en'kri-nīt), *n.* a fossil sea invertebrate covered with spines.

en·croach (in-krōch'), *v.i.* to invade gradually or by stealth; infringe; intrude (*on* or *upon*). —en·croach'ment, *n.*

en·crust (in-krust'), *v.t. & v.i.* same as incrust. —en·crus·ta'tion, *n.*

en·cum·ber (in-kum'bẽr), *v.t.* 1. to impede; retard; hinder. 2. to obstruct. 3. to burden; load down, as with claims or debts. —en·cum'brance ('bråns), *n.*

-en·cy (en-si), a suffix meaning *act, process, state.*

en·cyc·li·cal (in-sik'li-kl), *adj.* intended for general circulation: also en·cyc'lic: *n.* a letter from the Pope to the bishops, usually concerning doctrine.

en·cy·clo·pe·di·a, en·cy·clo·pae·di·a (in-sī-klō-pē'di-å), *n.* a book or set of books with articles on all or many branches of knowledge; also, a similar work dealing with one branch of knowledge. —en·cy·clo·pe'dic, *adj.* —en·cy·clo·pe'dist, *n.*

en·cyst (en-sist'), *v.t. & v.i.* to enclose or become enclosed in a cyst or sac.

end (end), *n.* 1. the extreme limit or terminal point of anything. 2. the last part; conclusion. 3. a purpose in view; aim. 4. a logical outcome; consequence. 5. death or ruin; termination of existence. 6. a football player at either end of the line: *v.t. & v.i.* to bring or come to an end; cease; terminate: *adj.* 1. at or on the end. 2. final.

en·dan·ger (in-dān'jẽr), *v.t.* to expose to or bring into harm; hazard; imperil.

en·dear (in-dir'), *v.t.* to make dear or beloved. —en·dear'ing, *adj.*

en·dear·ment ('mẽnt), *n.* 1. affection. 2. a word that expresses affection.

en·deav·or (in-dev'ẽr), *v.i.* to strive for the attainment of some object; try: *n.* an effort or attempt. British form en·deav'our.

en·dem·ic (en-dem'ik), *adj.* 1. peculiar to a particular country or region. 2. restricted to but common in a certain nation or locality, as a disease.

en·der·mic (en-dūr'mik), *adj.* acting through the skin: said of remedies applied to the skin. —en·der'mi·cal·ly, *adv.*

a in cap, ā in cane, ä in father, å in abet, e in met, ē in be, ẽ in baker, ẽ in regent, i in pit, ī in fine, ı in manifest, o in hot, ô in horse, ō in bone,

end·ing (en'ding), *n.* 1. result; end; finish. 2. death. 3. a suffix.

en·dive (en'div, on'dēv), *n.* a cultivated herb with curly leaves used in salads.

end·less (end'lis), *adj.* 1. without end; infinite; eternal. 2. going on too long; interminable. 3. having the ends joined to form a closed ring that can move continuously, as an endless chain. —**end'less·ly,** *adv.* —**end'less·ness,** *n.*

end man, the performer at either end of the line at a minstrel show.

en·do-, a combining form meaning *inner, within.*

en·do·carp (en'dō-kärp), *n.* the inner shell of a fruit, as the pit around the seed of a peach.

en·do·crine (en'dō-krin, -krīn), *n.* an internal secretion or the gland that produces it, as the thyroid, pituitary, and adrenal glands: *adj.* of or denoting a gland that produces one or more internal secretions that are carried in the bloodstream to regulate functions in other parts of the body.

en·dog·e·nous (en·doj'ē-nŭs), *adj.* 1. originating or growing within. 2. developing from within.

end organ, a specialized structure at the end of sensory or motor nerve fibers.

en·dorse (in·dôrs'), *v.t.* **-dorsed', -dors'ing,** 1. to write on the back of, as a check, etc. 2. to express approval of; sanction. 3. to tell of one's satisfaction with (a product, etc.) in an advertisement, often for money. —**en·dors'a·ble,** *adj.* —**en·dorse'ment,** *n.*

en·do·scope (en'dō-skōp), *n.* an instrument for examining some internal part of the body, as the urethra or rectum.

en·dos·mo·sis (en-dos-mō'sis), *n.* in osmosis, the more rapid mixing of the less concentrated substance with the more concentrated. —**en·dos·mot'ic** (-mot'ik), *adj.*

en·do·sperm (en'dō-spŭrm), *n.* the albumen of a seed.

en·dos·to·sis (en-dos-tō'sis), *n.* an ossification within cartilage.

en·do·the·li·um (en-dō-thē'li-ŭm), *n., pl.* **-li·a** (-ǎ), the layer of thin cells lining the inside of the heart, the lymph and blood vessels, and some other closed cavities.

en·dow (in·dou'), *v.t.* 1. to bestow a fund or income upon. 2. to furnish, as with some quality, talent, etc.

en·dow·ment ('mĕnt), *n.* 1. the act of endowing. 2. property, funds, etc. bestowed upon an institution or person to provide a permanent income. 3. a natural gift; talent, ability, etc.

en·due (in·dōō'), *v.t.* **-dued', -du'ing,** to provide or endow (*with* a quality, power, etc.).

en·dur·ance (in-door'ǎns), *n.* the capacity to endure; power to withstand stress or suffering; fortitude.

en·dure (in·door'), *v.t.* **-dured', -dur'ing,** 1. to stand (stress, suffering, etc.). 2. to put up with: *v.i.* 1. to remain in the same state; last. 2. to suffer patiently. —**en·dur'a·ble,** *adj.*

en·dur·ing ('ing), *adj.* permanent.

end·ways (end'wāz), *adv.* 1. on end. 2. with the end forward. 3. lengthwise. Also **end'wise** ('wiz).

en·e·ma (en'ē-må), *n.* the injection of a liquid into the rectum through the anus.

en·e·my (en'ē-mi), *n., pl.* **-mies,** 1. one who is hostile to another or tries to harm him. 2. an armed foe, as a soldier or nation at war. 3. one who opposes a cause, idea, etc.: *adj.* of an enemy; hostile.

en·er·get·ic (en-ēr·jet'ik), *adj.* having or displaying energy; vigorous; forceful. —**en·er·get'i·cal·ly,** *adv.*

en·er·gize (en'ēr-jīz), *v.t.* **-gized, -giz·ing,** to fill with energy; stimulate; rouse. —**en'er·giz·er,** *n.*

en·er·gu·men (en-ēr-gū'mĕn), *n.* 1. a fanatic. 2. one supposedly possessed by an evil spirit.

en·er·gy (en'ēr-ji), *n., pl.* **-gies,** 1. inherent power; capacity for vigorous activity. 2. such activity. 3. power efficiently or forcibly exerted. 4. emphasis. 5. in *Physics,* the capacity for performing work.

en·er·vate (en'ēr-vāt), *v.t.* **-vat·ed, -vat·ing,** to deprive of energy, force, or vigor; to make feeble; debilitate. —**en·er·va'tion,** *n.*

en fa·mille (än fâ-mē'), [French], 1. with one's family; at home. 2. informally.

en·fee·ble (in-fē'bl), *v.t.* **-bled, -bling,** to make feeble. —**en·fee'ble·ment,** *n.*

en·feoff (en-fef', -fēf'), *v.t.* to invest with a freehold in land or a fief.

en·fi·lade (en'fi-lād), *n.* 1. a placement of troops making them subject to sweeping gunfire along the entire length of the column or line. 2. gunfire directed at such troops: *v.t.* **-lad·ed, -lad·ing,** to direct such gunfire at (a column, etc.).

en·fold (in-fōld'), *v.t.* 1. to wrap up; envelop. 2. to embrace.

en·force (in-fôrs'), *v.t.* **-forced', -forc'ing,** 1. to bring about by force. 2. to compel obedience to. —**en·force'a·ble,** *adj.* —**en·force'ment,** *n.*

en·fran·chise (in-fran'chīz), *v.t.* **-chised, -chis·ing,** 1. to liberate from slavery. 2. to grant the right to vote. —**en·fran'chise·ment** ('chiz-mĕnt, 'chīz-), *n.*

en·gage (in-gāj'), *v.t.* **-gaged', -gag'ing,** 1. to pledge by oath or contract. 2. to betroth. 3. to secure for employment; hire. 4. to encounter in battle. 5. to occupy the time or attention of. 6. to interlock: *v.i.* 1. to pledge oneself. 2. to occupy oneself. 3. to enter into conflict. 4. to mesh; interlock.

en·gage·ment ('mĕnt), *n.* 1. the act of engaging. 2. the state of being engaged. 3. betrothal. 4. occupation. 5. a conflict between armed forces. 6. an appointment.

en·gag·ing ('ing), *adj.* endearing; attractive. —**en·gag'ing·ly,** *adv.*

en·gen·der (in-jen'dēr), *v.t.* to bring into existence; cause; give rise to.

en·gine (en'jin), *n.* 1. any machine that converts energy to mechanical power for producing motion or force. 2. a railroad locomotive. 3. any apparatus or machine.

en·gi·neer (en-ji-nir'), *n.* 1. one skilled in some branch of engineering. 2. the operator of an engine. 3. one who supervises work done with engines, etc. 4. a member of the armed forces who is trained in engineering: *v.t.* 1.

to plan, lay out, or direct engineering work. 2. to manage proficiently.

en·gi·neer·ing ('ing), n. 1. the planning and construction of machinery, bridges, roads, and the like. 2. the practical application of scientific knowledge.

Eng·lish (ing'glish), adj. of or pertaining to England, its inhabitants, or its language: n. 1. the people of England. 2. the official language of England, the U.S., Canada, etc. 3. [sometimes e-], a spinning motion given to a ball: v.t. 1. to translate into English. 2. [sometimes e-], to give a spinning motion to a ball. —Eng'lish·man (-mán), n.

en·gorge (in-gôrj'), v.t. -gorged', -gorg'ing, 1. to gorge; swallow greedily. 2. to congest (bodily tissue, a blood vessel, etc.) with blood or other fluid: v.i. to eat ravenously. —en·gorge'ment, n.

en·grail (-grāl'), v.t. to indent or curve (an ornamental border). —en·grail'ment, n.

en·grave (in-grāv'), -graved', -grav'ing, v.t. 1. to cut or etch in sunken patterns. 2. to incise (metal or wood) with letters or pictures for printing. 3. to print from such a surface. 4. to impress deeply. —en·grav'er, n.

en·grav·ing ('ing), n. 1. the act, process, or art of incising designs, etc. on metal, stone, wood, etc. 2. an engraved design, printing plate, etc. 3. an impression or print from this.

en·gross (in-grōs'), v.t. 1. to write out in large, round letters. 2. to absorb; occupy fully the attention of. —en·gross'ing, adj. —en·gross'-ment, n.

en·gulf (in-gulf'), v.t. to swallow up.

en·hance (-hans'), v.t. -hanced', -hanc'ing, to make greater, finer, more attractive or valuable, etc. —en·hance'ment, n.

e·nig·ma (ē-nig'má), n. 1. a riddle. 2. a puzzling situation, person, etc. —e·nig·mat·ic (en-ig-mat'ik, ē-nig-), adj. —e·nig·mat'i·cal·ly, adv.

en·join (in-join'), v.t. 1. to direct with authority; order. 2. to prohibit or restrain by injunction.

en·joy (-joi'), v.t. 1. to feel or perceive with pleasure. 2. to have the use or benefit of. —en·joy'a·ble, adj. —en·joy'ment, n.

en·large (-lärj'), v.t. -larged', -larg'ing, to make larger; expand or extend; broaden: v.i. 1. to become larger. 2. to expatiate (on or upon). —en·large'ment, n.

en·light·en (-līt'n), v.t. 1. to instruct; make clear to the mind. 2. to give insight to; set free from prejudice, etc. —en·light'en·ment, n.

en·list (-list'), v.t. & v.i. 1. to enroll for military service. 2. to involve or become involved in serving a cause, enterprise, etc. —en·list·ee', n. —en·list'ment, n.

enlisted man, any man in the armed forces who is not a commissioned officer or a warrant officer.

en·liv·en (-lī'vn), v.t. 1. to make active or lively. 2. to make cheerful; brighten.

en masse (en mas'), in a group; collectively; all together.

en·mesh (en-mesh'), v.t. to trap or entangle as in a net.

en·mi·ty (en'mi-ti), n., pl. -ties, animosity; hatred; hostility; ill will.

en·no·ble (i-nō'bl), v.t. -bled, -bling, to make noble; dignify; exalt. —en·no'ble·ment, n.

en·nui (än'wi), n. listlessness; boredom; discontentment.

e·nol·o·gy (ē-nol'ō-ji), n. the science or study of wines. —e·nol'o·gist, n.

e·nor·mi·ty (i-nôr'mi-ti), n., pl. -ties, 1. something outrageous; a heinous crime. 2. extreme wickedness. 3. loosely, great size or extent.

e·nor·mous (i-nôr'mús), adj. very great; immense; huge. —e·nor'mous·ly, adv. —e·nor'mous·ness, n.

e·nough (i-nuf'), adj. sufficient: n. a sufficient amount: adv. 1. so as to be sufficient. 2. quite. 3. passably.

e·now (i-nou'), adj. & n. & adv. [Archaic], enough.

en pas·sant (än pa-sän'), [French], in passing; by the way.

en·plane (en-plān'), v.i. -planed', -plan'ing, to board an airplane.

en·quire (in-kwīr'), v.t. & v.i. -quired', -quir'ing, same as inquire. —en·quir'y ('i), n., pl. -quir'ies.

en·rage (-rāj'), v.t. -raged', -rag'ing, to throw into a rage; infuriate.

en rap·port (än ra-pôr'), [French], in sympathy; in accord.

en·rapt (in-rapt'), adj. enraptured.

en·rap·ture (-rap'chĕr), v.t. -tured, -tur·ing, to entrance; delight; please intensely.

en rè·gle (än reg'l), [French], in due order.

en·rich (in-rich'), v.t. 1. to make rich or richer. 2. to adorn. 3. to fertilize (soil). 4. to add vitamins, minerals, etc. to (flour, bread, etc.). —en·rich'ment, n.

en·robe (-rōb'), v.t. -robed', -rob'ing, to clothe; attire in or as in a robe.

en·roll, en·rol (-rōl'), v.t. & v.i. -rolled', -roll'-ing, 1. to record or be recorded in a register. 2. to enlist. 3. to include as or become a member. —en·roll'ment, en·rol'ment, n.

en route (än rōōt'), on the way.

ens (enz), n. in Philosophy, an entity or abstract being.

en·san·guine (in-sang'gwin), v.t. -guined, -guining, to cover or smear with blood.

en·sconce (-skons'), v.t. -sconced', -sconc'ing, to settle securely or comfortably.

en·sem·ble (än-säm'bl), n. 1. the whole. 2. a complete costume. 3. the united performance of a group of musicians or singers. 4. a small group of musicians or singers.

en·sheathe (in-shēth'), v.t. -sheathed', -sheath'-ing, to enclose in a sheath.

en·shrine (-shrīn'), v.t. -shrined', -shrin'ing, 1. to place in a shrine. 2. to keep sacred.

en·shroud (-shroud'), v.t. to cover as with a shroud; conceal; obscure.

en·si·form (en'si-fôrm), adj. sword-shaped.

en·sign (en'sin), n. 1. a flag or banner, especially a national flag. 2. ('sn), in the U.S. Navy, a commissioned officer of the lowest rank.

a in cap, ā in cane, ä in father, å in abet, e in met, ē in be, ē in baker, ē in regent, i in pit, ī in fine, i in manifest, o in hot, ô in horse, ō in bone,

en·si·lage (en'sl-ij), *n.* green fodder stored in a silo.

en·slave (in-slāv'), *v.t.* -**slaved'**, -**slav'ing**, 1. to bring into or reduce to slavery. 2. to subjugate. —**en·slave'ment**, *n.*

en·snare (-sner'), *v.t.* -**snared'**, -**snar'ing**, to take in or as in a snare; trap. —**en·snare'ment**, *n.*

en·sue (-sōō'), *v.i.* -**sued'**, -**su'ing**, 1. to follow as a consequence. 2. to come afterward.

en suite (än swēt'), [French], in a series.

en·sure (in-shoor'), *v.t.* -**sured'**, -**sur'ing**, 1. to make sure. 2. to secure.

-ent (ĕnt), a suffix meaning *that has, acts, or indicates*; also, *one who or that which.*

en·tab·la·ture (en-tab'lá-chēr), *n.* the horizontal structure supported by a column or pillar, composed of architrave, frieze, and cornice.

en·ta·ble·ment (en-tā'bl-mĕnt), *n.* the series of platforms supporting a statue.

en·tail (in-tāl'), *n.* an estate of property limited to a specific line of heirs: *v.t.* 1. to limit the inheritance of (a landed estate) to a specific line of heirs. 2. to necessitate; require. —**en·tail'ment**, *n.*

en·tan·gle (-tang'gl), *v.t.* -**gled**, -**gling**, 1. to tangle. 2. to involve in something like a tangle; enmesh. 3. to perplex; bewilder. 4. to complicate. —**en·tan'gle·ment**, *n.*

en·tente (än-tänt'), *n.* 1. an understanding between nations. 2. the nations involved in this.

en·ter (en'tēr), *v.t.* 1. to go or come into. 2. to begin. 3. to penetrate. 4. to set down on a list. 5. to join or become a member of. 6. to insert. 7. to cause to be admitted. 8. to place on the records of a court: *v.i.* 1. to effect an entrance. 2. to penetrate.

en·ter·ic (en-ter'ik), *adj.* intestinal.

en·ter·i·tis (en-tē-rīt'is), *n.* inflammation of the small intestines.

en·ter·prise (en'tēr-prīz), *n.* 1. an undertaking, especially one of importance or risk. 2. boldness and initiative.

en·ter·pris·ing (-prī-zing), *adj.* adventurous, energetic, and progressive.

en·ter·tain (en-tēr-tān'), *v.t.* 1. to receive as a guest and treat hospitably. 2. to divert; amuse. 3. to keep in the mind. 4. to take into consideration: *v.i.* to receive guests hospitably.

en·ter·tain·er ('ēr), *n.* a well-known comedian, singer, or other performer.

en·ter·tain·ing ('ing), *adj.* amusing; diverting; interesting.

en·ter·tain·ment ('mĕnt), *n.* 1. the act of entertaining. 2. hospitality. 3. a show or performance; amusement.

en·thrall, en·thral (in-thrôl'), *v.t.* -**thralled'**, -**thrall'ing**, to captivate; bring or hold under some overpowering influence.

en·throne (-thrōn'), *v.t.* -**throned'**, -**thron'ing**, 1. to place on a throne. 2. to exalt. —**en·throne'ment**, *n.*

en·thuse (-thōōz'), *v.t.* -**thused'**, -**thus'ing**, [Informal], to make enthusiastic: *v.i.* [Informal], to show enthusiasm.

en·thu·si·asm (-thōō'zi-azm), *n.* fervent zeal; excited or eager interest. —**en·thu'si·ast** (-ast),

n. —**en·thu·si·as'tic**, *adj.* —**en·thu·si·as'ti·cal·ly**, *adv.*

en·tice (-tīs'), *v.t.* -**ticed'**, -**tic'ing**, to attract or allure; tempt. —**en·tice'ment**, *n.*

en·tire (in-tīr'), *adj.* 1. complete in all parts; whole. 2. undivided or unbroken. —**en·tire'ly**, *adv.*

en·tire·ty ('ti), *n., pl.* -**ties**, 1. wholeness; completeness. 2. a whole thing.

en·ti·tle (in-tīt'l), *v.t.* -**tled**, -**tling**, 1. to give a title, name, or designation to. 2. to give a right to. —**en·ti·tle'ment**, *n.*

en·ti·ty (en'ti-ti), *n., pl.* -**ties**, 1. anything that exists; being. 2. existence.

en·to-, a combining form meaning *within.*

en·tomb (in-tōōm'), *v.t.* to place in a tomb; bury. —**en·tomb'ment**, *n.*

en·to·mol·o·gy (en-tô-mol'ô-ji), *n.* the branch of zoology that treats of insects. —**en·to·mo·log'i·cal** (-mô-loj'i-kl), *adj.* —**en·to·mol'o·gist**, *n.*

en·to·moph·a·gous (-mof'á-gŭs), *adj.* feeding on insects.

en·tou·rage (än-too-räzh'), *n.* a retinue; associates or attendants.

en·to·zo·on (en-tô-zō'on), *n., pl.* -**zo'a** (-ä), a parasite living in the intestines of another animal; especially, a parasitic worm. —**en·to·zo'al**, *adj.* —**en·to·zo'ic**, *adj.*

en·tr'acte (än-trakt'), *n.* 1. the interval between the acts of a play or opera. 2. a musical piece, or dance, etc. performed during this period.

en·trails (en'trālz), *n.pl.* the intestines; viscera.

en·train (-trān'), *v.t. & v.i.* to put or go aboard a railroad train.

en·trance (en'trăns), *n.* 1. the act of entering. 2. a door, gate, or other place for going in. 3. permission to enter.

en·trance (in-trans'), *v.t.* -**tranced'**, -**tranc'ing**, to enrapture; charm; delight.

en·trant (en'trănt), *n.* one who enters; especially, one who enters a competition.

en·trap (in-trap'), *v.t.* -**trapped'**, -**trap'ping**, to ensnare; trap.

en·treat (in-trēt'), *v.t.* to ask earnestly; implore; beseech.

en·treat·y ('i), *n., pl.* -**treat'ies**, an earnest petition or request; prayer.

en·tree, en·trée (än'trā), *n.* 1. right of entry; access. 2. the main course of a meal.

en·trench (in-trench'), *v.t.* 1. to surround with trenches. 2. to place in a strong defensive position. —**en·trench'ment**, *n.*

en·tre nous (än-trä nōō'), [French], confidentially; between ourselves.

en·tre·pôt (än'trē-pō'), *n.* a warehouse or distribution center for goods.

en·tre·pre·neur (än-trē-prē-nûr'), *n.* one who organizes and takes responsibility for a business enterprise in order to make profits. —**en·tre·pre·neur'i·al**, *adj.* —**en·tre·pre·neur'ship**, *n.*

en·tre·sol (en'tēr-sol), *n.* a low story just above the main floor; mezzanine.

en·tro·py (en'trô-pi), *n.* 1. a measure of the amount of energy unavailable for work in a system. 2. a tendency to run down and eventually become inert.

ô in drag*o*n, ōō in cr*u*de, oo in w*oo*l, u in c*u*p, ū in c*u*re, û in t*u*rn, ŭ in f*o*cus, oi in b*oy*, ou in h*ou*se, th in *th*in, th in shea*th*e, g in *g*et, j in *j*oy, y in *y*et.

en·trust (in-trust'), *v.t.* 1. to charge with. 2. to give into someone's care.

en·try (en'tri), *n., pl.* **-tries,** 1. an entrance. 2. a place to enter. 3. an item entered in a book, list, etc. 4. one entered in a competition, as a race. 5. in *Law,* the act of taking possession by entering.

en·twine (in-twin'), *v.t. & v.i.* **-twined', -twin'-ing,** to twine around; twist together.

e·nu·cle·ate (i-nōō'kli-āt), *v.t.* **-at·ed, -at·ing,** 1. to remove the nucleus from. 2. to remove (an organ, tumor, etc.) whole. **—e·nu·cle·a'tion,** *n.*

e·nu·mer·ate (i-nōō'mēr-āt), *v.t.* **-at·ed, -at·ing,** 1. to name singly. 2. to count. **—e·nu·mer·a'tion,** *n.*

e·nun·ci·ate (i-nun'si-āt), *v.t.* **-at·ed, -at·ing,** 1. to proclaim. 2. to declare positively. 3. to pronounce (words). **—e·nun·ci·a'tion,** *n.* **—e·nun'ci·a·tor,** *n.*

en·u·re·sis (en-yoo-rē'sis), *n.* involuntary discharge of urine, especially during sleep. **—en·u·ret'ic** (-ret'ik), *adj.*

en·vel·op (in-vel'ŏp), *v.t.* to surround with or as with a wrapper; hide; cover. **—en·vel'op·ment,** *n.*

en·vel·ope (en'vĕ-lōp, än'-), *n.* 1. a folded paper cover, usually with a gummed flap, for letters sent by mail. 2. a wrapper or covering. 3. the outer covering or bag that holds the gas of a balloon or dirigible.

en·ven·om (in-ven'ŏm), *v.t.* 1. to infuse with venom. 2. to embitter.

en·vi·a·ble (en'vi-ȧ-bl), *adj.* exciting envy; desirable. **—en'vi·a·bly,** *adv.*

en·vi·ous (en'vi-ŭs), *adj.* feeling or characterized by envy; jealous. **—en'vi·ous·ly,** *adv.* **—en'vi·ous·ness,** *n.*

en·vi·ron (in-vī'rŏn), *v.t.* to surround or enclose; encompass; encircle.

en·vi·ron·ment (in-vī'rŏn-mĕnt), *n.* 1. surroundings. 2. the external conditions around an organism, affecting its development. **—en·vi·ron·men·tal** (-men'tl), *adj.* **—en·vi·ron·men'tal·ly,** *adv.*

en·vi·ron·men·tal·ist (in-vī-rŏn-men'tl-ist), *n.* one whose work involves the study and alleviation of environmental problems, as water pollution.

en·vi·rons ('rŏnz, 'ērnz), *n.pl.* 1. places near a town or city; suburbs. 2. vicinity.

en·vis·age (en-viz'ij), *v.t.* **-aged, -ag·ing,** to form a mental picture of; visualize.

en·vi·sion (en-vizh'ŭn), *v.t.* to imagine; form a mental picture of.

en·voy (en'voi, än'-), *n.* 1. a diplomatic representative second in rank to an ambassador. 2. an agent or messenger.

en·voy (en'voi, än'-), *n.* a short stanza that summarizes, as at the end of a ballade.

en·vy (en'vi), *v.t.* **-vied, -vy·ing,** to begrudge; feel discontent over the prosperity, success, etc. of: *n., pl.* **-vies,** 1. ill will or discontent felt at another's prosperity or success. 2. an object of envy. **—en'vy·ing·ly,** *adv.*

en·wrap (en-rap'), *v.t.* **-wrapped', -wrap'ping,** to wrap up.

en·zo·ot·ic (en-zō-ot'ik), *adj.* pertaining to a disease that affects animals of a particular area, or in a certain season.

en·zyme (en'zīm), *n.* a chemical compound of animal or vegetable origin which acts as an organic catalyst in chemical changes. **—en·zy·mat'ic** (-zī-mat'ik, -zi-), *adj.*

E·o·cene (ē'ō-sēn), *n.* an epoch of the Cenozoic Era, in which mammals became the dominant animals and the major mountain ranges were formed.

e·on (ē'ŏn, ē'on), *n.* a very long, indefinite period of time.

-e·ous (i-ŭs), a suffix meaning *having or characterized by.*

e·pact (ē'pakt), *n.* 1. the excess of the solar over the lunar year, about 11 days. 2. the age of the moon at the beginning of the calendar year.

ep·au·let, ep·au·lette (ep'ȧ-let), *n.* a shoulder ornament worn on uniforms.

e·pee, é·pée (e-pā', ā-), *n.* a kind of fencing sword.

ep·en·the·sis (e-pen'thē-sis), *n., pl.* **-ses** (-sēz), the insertion of a letter or syllable in the middle of a word.

e·pergne (i-pûrn', ā-pern'), *n.* an ornamental stand with branches for holding fruit, flowers, etc.

e·phed·rine (i-fed'rin), *n.* a crystalline alkaloid used in medication for allergies, respiratory ailments, etc.

e·phem·er·a (i-fem'ēr-ȧ), *n., pl.* **-er·as, -er·ae** (-ē), 1. something that is ephemeral. 2. same as mayfly.

e·phem·er·al (-ȧl), *adj.* 1. existing only for a day. 2. short-lived. **—e·phem'er·al·ly,** *adv.*

E·phe·sians (i-fē'zhŭnz), *n.* a book of the New Testament.

epi-, a prefix meaning *on the outside.*

ep·ic (ep'ik), *n.* a narrative poem of some length telling of heroic deeds or events: *adj.* 1. of or like such a poem. 2. heroic; grand. Also **ep'i·cal. —ep'i·cal·ly,** *adv.*

ep·i·can·thus (ep-i-kan'thŭs), *n.* a fold of the skin of the upper eyelid over the inner angle of the eye, as in many Asian peoples. **—ep·i·can'thic,** *adj.*

ep·i·cen·ter (ep'i-sen-tēr), *n.* a point on the surface of the earth directly above the place of origin of an earthquake.

ep·i·cra·ni·um (ep-i-krā'ni·ŭm), *n., pl.* **-ni·a** (-ȧ), the scalp.

ep·i·cure (ep'i-kyoor), *n.* one who has a refined taste in food and drink.

ep·i·cu·re·an (ep-i-kyoo-rē'ȧn), *adj.* 1. fond of luxury and sensuous pleasures. 2. of or pertaining to an epicure: *n.* same as epicure. **—ep·i·cu·re'an·ism,** *n.*

ep·i·cy·cle (ep'i-sī-kl), *n.* a small circle whose center is situated on the circumference of a larger circle.

ep·i·cy·cloid (ep-i-sī'kloid), *n.* the curve described by a point on the circumference of a circle that rolls around the outside of a fixed circle.

ep·i·dem·ic (ep-i-dem'ik), *adj.* affecting many people in a community at the same time: said of a contagious disease: *n.* 1. an outbreak of such a disease. 2. a disease causing such an outbreak. **—ep·i·dem'i·cal·ly,** *adv.*

ep·i·der·mis (ep-i-dûr'mis), *n.* 1. the outermost

---

a in c*a*p, ā in c*a*ne, ä in f*a*ther, ȧ in *a*bet, e in m*e*t ē in b*e*, ē in bak*e*r, ê in reg*e*nt, i in p*i*t, ī in f*i*ne, ı̆ in man*i*fest, o in h*o*t, ô in h*o*rse, ō in b*o*ne,

layer of the skin. 2. the outer covering or bark of a plant. —ep·i·der′mal, *adj.*

ep·i·gas·tric (ep·i·gas′trik), *adj.* 1. of or in the epigastrium. 2. of or having to do with the front walls of the abdomen.

ep·i·gas·tri·um (-gas′tri·ùm), *n., pl.* -tri·a (-ă), the upper middle part of the abdomen.

ep·i·gen·e·sis (ep·i·jen′ě·sis), *n.* the theory that the embryo develops as a new organism from a structureless germ cell.

ep·i·glot·tis (ep·i·glot′is), *n.* the leaf-shaped cartilage which covers the upper part of the larynx during swallowing, to prevent food, etc. from entering the lungs. —ep·i·glot′tal, ep·i·glot′tic, *adj.*

ep·i·gram (ep′i·gram), *n.* a short poem or a saying that is witty, ingeniously expressed, pithy, etc. —ep·i·gram·mat′ic (-grā·mat′ik), *adj.* —ep·i·gram·mat′i·cal·ly, *adv.*

ep·i·graph (-graf), *n.* 1. an inscription on a building, monument, etc. 2. a motto or quotation prefixed to a literary work.

e·pig·ra·phy (ē·pig′rā·fē, i-), *n.* the study of inscriptions, esp. ancient ones.

ep·i·lep·sy (ep′i·lep·si), *n.* a chronic nervous disease characterized by convulsions, and, sometimes, loss of consciousness.

ep·i·lep·tic (′tik), *adj.* of, pertaining to, or having epilepsy: *n.* one who has epilepsy.

ep·i·logue (ep′i·lôg), *n.* 1. a poem or speech given by one of the actors at the conclusion of a play. 2. a concluding part added to a play or novel giving more information.

ep·i·neph·rine (ep·i·nef′rin), *n.* 1. a hormone produced by the adrenal glands. 2. this substance produced synthetically or taken from the adrenal glands of animals, used as a heart stimulant, etc.

E·piph·a·ny (i·pif′ă·ni), *n.* a Christian festival (January 6) held to commemorate the revealing of Jesus as Christ to the Gentiles.

ep·i·phyte (ep′i·fīt), *n.* a plant that grows on another but is not a parasite and derives its own nutrients from the air, rain, etc.; air plant. —ep·i·phyt′ic (-fit′ik), *adj.*

e·pis·co·pa·cy (i·pis′kŏ·pá·si), *n., pl.* -cies, 1. church government by bishops. 2. same as episcopate.

e·pis·co·pal (-pl), *adj.* 1. of or pertaining to a bishop. 2. governed by bishops. 3. [E-], denoting various churches governed by bishops. —e·pis′co·pal·ly, *adv.*

E·pis·co·pa·li·an (i·pis·kŏ·pāl′yùn), *adj.* same as Episcopal: *n.* a member of the Protestant Episcopal Church.

e·pis·co·pate (i·pis′kŏ·pit, -pāt), *n.* 1. the office, rank, etc. of a bishop. 2. a bishop's see. 3. bishops collectively.

ep·i·sode (ep′i·sōd), *n.* 1. an incident, event, or series of events. 2. a part of a poem, novel, etc. that is complete in itself, sometimes presented as a digression. —ep·i·sod′ic (-sod′ik), *adj.*

e·pis·tle (i·pis′l), *n.* 1. a letter. 2. [E-], any of the letters in the New Testament. —e·pis′to·lar·y (′tŏ·ler·i), *adj.*

ep·i·taph (ep′i·taf), *n.* a memorial inscription on a tomb or monument.

ep·i·tha·la·mi·um (ep·i·thă·lā′mi·ùm), *n., pl.*

-mi·ums, -mi·a (-ă), a nuptial song or poem in honor of a bride and bridegroom.

ep·i·the·li·um (ep·i·thē′li·ùm), *n., pl.* -li·ums, -li·a (-ă), a cellular tissue that forms a lining for body cavities and covers body surfaces. —ep·i·the′li·al, *adj.*

ep·i·thet (ep′i·thet), *n.* a word or phrase that characterizes a person or thing.

e·pit·o·me (i·pit′ŏ·mi), *n., pl.* -mes, 1. a summary; abstract. 2. a person or thing that is typical of a whole class.

e·pit·o·mize (-mīz), *v.t.* -mized, -miz·ing, to make or be an epitome of.

ep·i·zo·on (ep·i·zō′on), *n., pl.* -zo′a (′ă), a parasite living on the outside of the body of an animal.

ep·i·zo·ot·ic (-zō·ot′ik), *adj.* epidemic among animals: *n.* an epizootic disease.

e plu·ri·bus u·num (ē ploor′i·bùs ū′nùm), [Latin], out of many, one: a motto of the U.S.

ep·och (ep′ŏk), *n.* 1. the beginning of a new period in the history of anything. 2. a period of time considered in reference to distinctive events or conditions. 3. a subdivision of a geologic period. 4. the time when a star or planet reaches a known position. —ep′och·al, *adj.*

ep·o·nym (ep′ŏ·nim), *n.* 1. the presumed ancestor or founder of a race, tribe, city, nation, etc., and from whom its name is derived. 2. one whose name is associated with some movement, theory, etc.

ep·ox·y (e·pok′si), *adj.* denoting a resin used in coatings, strong adhesives, etc.: *n., pl.* -ox′-ies, an epoxy resin.

ep·si·lon (ep′sī·lon), *n.* the fifth letter of the Greek alphabet.

Ep·som salts (ep′sòm), sulfate of magnesium, a white, crystalline salt used as a cathartic: also Epsom salt.

Ep·stein-Barr virus (ep′stēn-bär′), a herpes-like virus that causes mononucleosis and may cause various forms of cancer.

eq·ua·ble (ek′wă·bl), *adj.* uniform; consistently steady; tranquil. —eq·ua·bil′i·ty, *n.* —eq′ua·bly, *adv.*

e·qual (ē′kwàl), *adj.* 1. of the same extent, magnitude, value, etc. 2. uniformly proportioned. 3. of the same rank, abilities, rights, etc. 4. adequate in power, etc. (with *to*): *n.* a person or thing that is equal: *v.t.* e′qualed or e′qualled, e′qual·ing or e′qual·ling, 1. to be equal to; match. 2. to make or do something equal to. —e·qual·i·ty (i·kwäl′i·ti), *n., pl.* -ties. —e′qual·ly, *adv.*

e·qual·ize (ē′kwả·līz), *v.t.* -ized, -iz·ing, to make equal; render uniform. —e·qual·i·za′tion, *n.* —e′qual·iz·er, *n.*

equal sign, the symbol (=) used in mathematics to indicate that the terms on either side of it are equal: also equal mark.

e·qua·nim·i·ty (ek·wả·nim′i·ti, ē·kwả-), *n.* evenness of temper or mind; calmness; composure.

e·quate (i·kwāt′), *v.t.* e·quat′ed, e·quat′ing, 1. to make equal. 2. to reduce to an average. 3. to put in the form of an equation. —e·quat′a·ble, *adj.*

e·qua·tion (i·kwā′zhùn), *n.* 1. the act of equating. 2. equality, equilibrium, etc. 3. an expression of equality between two quantities, indicated by the equal sign (=). 4. a representation of a chemical reaction expressed by symbols and formulas.

e·qua·tor (i-kwāt'ẽr), *n.* an imaginary circle around the earth, midway between the North Pole and the South Pole.

e·qua·to·ri·al (ē-kwä-tôr'i-ǎl, ek-wǎ-), *adj.* 1. of, pertaining to, or near the equator. 2. typical of the regions around the equator: *n.* a telescope mounted on two axes, one of which is parallel to the earth's axis, the other at right angles to it: by rotating as the earth does, it can follow the apparent motion of a heavenly body. —**e·qua·to·ri·al·ly**, *adv.*

eq·uer·ry (ek'wẽr-i), *n., pl.* -ries, 1. formerly, an officer in a royal or noble household in charge of horses. 2. a personal attendant on some member of a royal family.

e·ques·tri·an (i-kwes'tri-ǎn), *adj.* 1. of or pertaining to horses or horsemanship. 2. mounted on horseback: *n.* 1. one who rides horses. 2. a skilled horseman, especially a performer in a circus. —**e·ques·tri·enne** (-tri-en'), *n.fem.*

e·qui-, a combining form meaning *equal, equally.*

e·qui·an·gu·lar (ē-kwi-ang'gyǔ-lẽr), *adj.* having all the angles equal.

e·qui·dis·tant (-dis'tǎnt), *adj.* equally distant. — **e·qui·dis'tance**, *n.*

e·qui·lat·er·al (-lat'ẽr-ǎl), *adj.* having all sides equal: *n.* a figure with equal sides.

e·qui·lib·ri·um (-lib'ri-ǔm), *n., pl.* -ri·ums, -ri·a (-ǎ), 1. equality of weight, power, force, etc. 2. the ability of a body to keep its balance. 3. emotional stability.

e·quine (ē'kwin, ek'win), *adj.* of, pertaining to, or resembling a horse: *n.* a horse.

e·qui·noc·tial (ē-kwi-nok'shǔl), *adj.* of or happening at about the time of the equinoxes: *n.* a storm occurring at or near the time of the equinoxes.

e·qui·nox (ē'kwi-noks), *n.* the time when the sun crosses the equator, when the days and nights are of equal length in all parts of the earth: the *vernal equinox* occurs about March 21 and the *autumnal equinox* about September 22.

e·quip (i-kwip'), *v.t.* **e·quipped'**, **e·quip'ping**, to furnish or provide with whatever is needed; outfit.

e·qui·page (ek'wi-pij), *n.* 1. the outfit or equipment of a ship, army, expedition, etc. 2. a carriage with its horses and liveried servants.

e·quip·ment (i-kwip'mẽnt), *n.* 1. the act of equipping or state of being equipped. 2. the articles or supplies necessary for any particular purpose. 3. the rolling stock of a railroad.

e·qui·poise (ek'wi-poiz), *n.* 1. equilibrium. 2. a counterbalance.

e·qui·pon·der·ant (ē-kwi-pon'dẽr-ǎnt), *adj.* of the same weight.

eq·ui·ta·ble (ek'wit-ǎ-bl), *adj.* impartial; just; fair. —**eq'ui·ta·bly**, *adv.*

eq·ui·ty (ek'wit-i), *n., pl.* -ties, 1. justice; impartiality. 2. the administration of law accord-

ing to principles of natural fairness when existing statutes are not adequate. 3. the value of property over what is owed on it; net worth.

e·quiv·a·lence (ĭ-kwiv'ǎ-lĕns), *n.* 1. equality of value, power, meaning, etc. 2. in *Chemistry,* the quality of having equal valence. Also **e·quiv'a·len·cy.**

e·quiv·a·lent (-lĕnt), *adj.* equal in value, power, meaning, etc.: *n.* something that is equivalent.

e·quiv·o·cal (i-kwiv'ō-kl), *adj.* 1. doubtful; uncertain. 2. suspicious. 3. having a double meaning; ambiguous. —**e·quiv'o·cal·ly**, *adv.*

e·quiv·o·cate (-kāt), *v.i.* -cat·ed, -cat·ing, to use words of double meaning in an attempt to mislead or deceive. —**e·quiv·o·ca'tion**, *n.* —**e·quiv'o·ca·tor**, *n.*

-er (ẽr), a suffix meaning *one connected* or *associated with, an inhabitant of, a person or thing that.*

-er (ẽr), a suffix forming the comparative degree.

e·ra (ir'ǎ, er'ǎ), *n.* 1. a period of time reckoned from some important happening 2. a period of history marked by some distinctive characteristic. 3. one of the main divisions of geologic time.

e·rad·i·cate (i-rad'i-kāt), *v.t.* -cat·ed, -cat·ing, to destroy utterly; exterminate; wipe out. —**e·rad·i·ca'tion**, *n.* —**e·rad'i·ca·tor**, *n.*

e·rase (i-rās'), *v.t.* **e·rased'**, **e·ras'ing** to obliterate (as writing) by scratching or rubbing out; expunge. —**e·ras'a·ble**, *adj.*

e·ras·er (i-rā'sẽr), *n.* 1. a piece of rubber for erasing pencil marks, etc. 2. a pad for erasing chalk from a blackboard.

E·ras·ti·an·ism (i-ras'chǎn-izm), *n.* advocacy of supreme authority of the state in church matters: advanced by Thomas Erastus (1524-83), German theologian.

e·ra·sure (i-rā'shẽr), *n.* 1. the act of erasing. 2. a mark left after erasing.

er·bi·um (ũr'bi-ǔm), *n.* a metallic chemical element of the rare-earth group.

ere (er), *prep. & conj.* [Archaic], before.

Er·e·bus (er'ē-bǔs), *n.* in *Greek Mythology,* a dark place under the earth where the dead were sent.

e·rect (i-rekt'), *v.t.* 1. to raise upright. 2. to construct; build (a house, etc.). 3. to assemble; set up: *adj.* upright. —**e·rec'tion**, *n.* —**e·rec'tor**, *n.*

e·rec·tile (i-rek'tl), *adj.* of or denoting tissue that becomes distended and stiff when filled with blood. —**e·rec·til'i·ty**, *n.*

er·e·mite (er'ē-mīt), *n.* a recluse; hermit.

erg (ũrg), *n.* a unit of work or energy.

er·go (ũr'gō, er'gō), *conj. & adv.* [Latin], therefore; consequently.

er·gom·e·ter (ẽr-gom'ĕ-tẽr), *n.* an instrument for measuring the amount of work done by muscles. —**er·gom'e·try**, *n.*

er·gos·ter·ol (ẽr-gos'tĕ-rōl), *n.* a crystalline sterol found in ergot and yeast, and from which vitamin D is obtained.

er·got (ũr'gŏt), *n.* 1. a fungus that grows on kernels of rye and other cereal grains. 2. the disease in which this occurs. 3. an extract of the dried rye fungus, used medici-

---

a in cap, ā in cane, ä in father, ȧ in abet, e in met ē in be, ē in baker, ė in regent, i in pit, ī in fine, i in manifest, o in hot, ô in horse, ō in bone,

nally to check hemorrhaging and to contract smooth muscle tissue.

er·mine (ûr'min), *n.* 1. a weasel whose fur becomes white in the winter, except for the tip of its tail. 2. this valuable fur. 3. the emblem, rank, or office of some judges in Europe.

er·mined ('mind), *adj.* 1. wearing ermine. 2. trimmed with ermine, as a robe.

erne, *n* (ûrn), *n.* the white-tailed sea eagle of Europe.

e·rode (i-rōd'), *v.t.* e·rod'ed, e·rod'ing, 1. to wear away; eat into. 2. to form (a channel, gully, etc.) by wearing away gradually, as natural forces: *v.i.* to become eroded.

e·rog·e·nous (ē-roj'ē-nŭs), *adj.* sensitive to sexual stimulation.

E·ros (er'os, ir'os), *n.* 1. in *Greek Mythology,* the god of love. 2. [e-], sexual love or desire.

e·ro·sion (i-rō'zhŭn), *n.* 1. the act of eroding. 2. a gradual destruction or wearing away. 3. an eroded part or area.

e·ro·sive (i-rō'siv), *adj.* wearing away; causing erosion.

e·rot·ic (i-rot'ik), *adj.* 1. of, pertaining to, or having to do with sexual love; amatory. 2. arousing sexual desires.—**e·rot'i·cal·ly,** *adv.*

e·rot·i·ca ('i·kä), *n.* erotic pictures, literature, films, etc.

e·rot·i·cism (-sizm), *n.* 1. erotic quality. 2. sexual drive. 3. an abnormal emphasis on sex. Also **er·o·tism** (er'ō-tizm).

e·ro·to·gen·ic (i-rot-ō-jen'ik), *adj.* of or denoting areas of the body, as the genital, oral, and anal areas, that are sexually sensitive.

err (ûr, er), *v.i.* 1. to make a mistake; be wrong. 2. to go astray morally.

er·rand (er'ănd), *n.* 1. a trip to convey a message or do something, often for someone else. 2. the message conveyed or the thing done; purpose or commission.

er·rant (er'ănt), *adj.* 1. roving; wandering, as a knight in search of adventure. 2. in error. 3. moving about lightly, as a breeze. —**er'rant·ly,** *adv.*

er·rant·ry (-ri), *n.* the conduct or condition of a knight-errant; chivalry.

er·rat·ic (i-rat'ik), *adj.* 1. wandering; irregular; random. 2. peculiar; eccentric. 3. transported, as a boulder, from its original site, as by a glacier. —**er·rat'i·cal·ly,** *adv.*

er·ra·tum (e-rāt'ŭm, -rāt'ŭm), *n., pl.* -ta ('ä), an error in printing or writing.

er·ro·ne·ous (ĕ-rō'ni-ŭs), *adj.* characterized by error; incorrect; mistaken; wrong. —**er·ro'·ne·ous·ly,** *adv.*

er·ror (er'ĕr), *n.* 1. belief in something untrue. 2. deviation from the truth. 3. a mistake; blunder. 4. a transgression; wrongdoing. 5. a misplay in fielding a baseball. —**er'ror·less,** *adj.*

er·satz (ûr'zats, er'-), *adj.* substitute; artificial and inferior.

Erse (ûrs), *adj. & n.* same as Gaelic.

erst (ûrst), *adv.* [Archaic], formerly.

erst·while ('hwīl), *adv.* [Archaic], formerly: *adj.* former.

e·ruct (i-rukt'), *v.t. & v.i.* to belch. —**e·ruc·ta'·tion,** *n.*

er·u·dite (er'yoo-dīt), *adj.* learned. —**er'u·dite·ly,** *adv.*

er·u·di·tion (-dish'ŭn), *n.* knowledge obtained by the study of books; learning.

e·rupt (i-rupt'), *v.i.* 1. to burst forth. 2. to eject water, lava, etc. 3. to break out in a skin rash: *v.t.* to eject. —**e·rup'tion,** *n.* —**e·rup'tive,** *adj.*

-er·y (ēr-i), a suffix meaning *the act of, a place, goods of, a collection of.*

er·y·sip·e·las (er-i-sip'l-ăs), *n.* an acute, infectious disease of the skin or mucous membranes, with inflammation and fever.

er·y·the·ma (er-i-thē'mä), an abnormal redness of the skin resulting from capillary congestion.

e·ryth·ro·cyte (i-rith'rō-sīt), *n.* a red blood corpuscle.

-es (iz, ĕz), a suffix used to form: 1. the third person singular, present indicative, of certain verbs, as *catches.* 2. certain plurals, as *wishes.*

es·ca·drille (es'kä-dril), *n.* a squadron of warplanes of France in World War I.

es·ca·lade (es'kä-lād), *n.* the act of scaling the wall of a fortified place by ladders: *v.t.* -lad·ed, -lad·ing, to scale (a wall) by ladders.

es·ca·late (es'kä-lāt), *v.i.* -lat·ed, -lat·ing, 1. to rise as on an escalator. 2. to rise or increase rapidly. —**es·ca·la'tion,** *n.*

es·ca·la·tor (es'kä-lāt-ĕr), *n.* a moving stairway on an endless belt.

es·cal·lop, **es·cal·op** (e-skal'ŏp), *n. & v.t.* same as scallop.

es·ca·pade (es'kä-pād), *n.* a reckless adventure or wild prank, especially one that is contrary to the rules of propriety.

es·cape (ĕ-skāp', e-), *v.i.* -caped', -cap'ing, 1. to flee from. 2. to avoid. 3. to slip from unintentionally. 4. to be forgotten by: *v.i.* 1. to get out of danger. 2. to avoid injury or harm. 3. to elude, slip away, leak away, etc.: *n.* 1. the act of escaping. 2. a means of escape. 3. a leakage. 4. a temporary mental evasion of reality: *adj.* providing escape.

es·cap·ee (ĕ-skā-pē', e-), *n.* one who has escaped, as from imprisonment.

es·cape·ment (ĕ-skāp'mĕnt, e-), *n.* 1. a mechanism that controls the movement of a clock or watch by means of a notched wheel with a pawl that moves regularly, one notch at a time. 2. a ratchet mechanism in a typewriter that controls the horizontal movement of the carriage.

escape velocity, the minimum speed required for a particle, satellite, space vehicle, etc. to escape permanently from the gravitational field of a planet, star, etc.

es·cap·ism (ĕ-skāp'izm, e-), *n.* the avoidance of reality by seeking entertainment, or by reading, daydreaming, etc. —**es·cap'ist,** *adj. & n.*

es·car·got (es-kär-gō'), *n.* [French], an edible snail.

es·ca·role (es'kä-rōl), *n.* a broad-leaved endive used for salads.

es·carp·ment ('mĕnt), n. a long, precipitous ridge of land or rock; cliff; steep slope.

-es·cent (es'nt), a suffix meaning *becoming* or *starting to be, giving off light.*

esch·a·lot (esh'ă-lot), n. same as shallot.

es·char (es'kär), n. a dry scab that forms on the skin from a burn.

es·cha·tol·o·gy (es-kă-tol'ŏ-ji), n. the theological doctrines in regard to death, judgment, immortality, etc. —es·cha·to·log'i·cal (-tŏ-loj'i-kl), adj.

es·cheat (es-chēt'), v.t. to confiscate (property, etc.) because there are no legal heirs: v.i. to forfeit by escheat: n. 1. the reverting of property to the state (or, in England, to the crown) when there are no legal heirs or claimants. 2. the right to take property by escheat.

es·chew (es-chōō'), v.t. to shun; avoid.

es·co·lar (es'kŏ-lär), n. a large food fish, somewhat like the mackerel.

es·cort (es'kôrt), n. 1. one or more persons (or cars, ships, planes, etc.) accompanying another for honor or protection. 2. a man accompanying a woman: v.t. (i-skôrt'), 1. to accompany as an escort.

es·cri·toire (es-kri-twär'), n. a writing desk or table.

es·crow (es'krō), n. in *Law*, a deed or bond in the care of a third person and not turned over or put in effect until certain conditions are fulfilled.

es·cu·do (es-kōō'dō), n., pl. -dos, the monetary unit of Chile and Portugal.

es·cu·lent (es'kyoo-lĕnt), adj. edible.

es·cutch·eon (i-skuch'ŭn), n. a shield or shield-like surface upon which a heraldic coat of arms is displayed.

-ese (ēz, ēs), a suffix meaning: 1. *of a country or place* or *in the language of.* 2. *a person who lives in* or *the language of.*

Es·ki·mo (es'ki-mō), n., pl. -mos, -mo, a member of a people inhabiting Greenland and arctic regions of North America: adj. of or pertaining to Eskimos.

Eskimo dog, a strong breed of dog with shaggy hair, used by Eskimos to pull sleds.

e·soph·a·gus (i-sof'ă-gŭs), n., pl. -gi (-jī), the tube through which food and drink pass from the pharynx to the stomach; gullet.

es·o·ter·ic (es-ŏ-ter'ik), adj. 1. intended for or understood by only a select few. 2. abstruse. 3. confidential. —es·o·ter'i·cal·ly, adv.

ESP, extrasensory perception.

es·pa·drille (es'pă-dril), n. a shoe for casual wear, with a canvas upper.

es·pal·ier (es-pal'yēr), v.t. 1. to train (trees or bushes) to grow flat on trellis work. 2. to provide with an espalier: n. 1. a trellis frame on which small trees and bushes are trained to grow flat. 2. a tree or bush trained in this way.

es·par·to (es-pär'tō), n. either of two species of coarse Spanish grass used for making paper, rope, etc.

es·pe·cial (ĕ-spesh'ăl), adj. special; particular. —es·pe'cial·ly, adv.

Es·pe·ran·to (es-pĕ-rän'tō), n. an artifical language for international (chiefly European)

use, based on words from the important European languages.

es·pi·o·nage (es'pi-ŏ-näzh), n. 1. the act or practice of spying. 2. the use of spies by a government to learn military or political secrets of a foreign country.

es·pla·nade (es-plă-nād', -näd'), n. a level walk or drive, especially a public one; promenade.

es·pous·al (i-spou'zl), n. 1. a wedding. 2. the espousing or advocacy of a cause, etc.

es·pouse (i-spouz'), v.t. -poused, -pous'ing, 1. to marry. 2. to advocate (some cause, etc.). —es·pous'er, n.

es·pres·so (es-pres'ō), n., pl. -sos, [Italian,] coffee prepared by forcing steam through finely ground coffee beans.

es·prit de corps (es-prē' dĕ kôr'), a spirit of common devotion, honor, pride, etc. binding together people in the same work, profession, etc.

es·py (ĕ-spī'), v.t. -pied', -py'ing, to see as at a distance; catch sight of.

-esque (esk), a suffix meaning *like, in the style of.*

Es·qui·mau (es'ki-mō), n., pl. -maux (-mō, -mōz), -mau, same as Eskimo.

es·quire (es'kwir, ĕ-skwir'), n. 1. formerly, an attendant on a knight. 2. in England, a man of the gentry ranking just below a knight. 3. [E-], a title of courtesy, usually abbreviated *Esq.*, *Esqr.* and placed after a man's surname.

es·say (es'ā), n. 1. an attempt; experiment. 2. a short written composition, dealing with a single subject: v.t. (e-sā'), to try.

es·sence (es'ns), n. 1. a concentrated preparation of a substance, that keeps the basic flavor, etc. 2. perfume. 3. the basic, true, or real nature of anything.

Es·sene (es'ēn, ĕ-sēn'), n. a member of a strict, ascetic order of Jews which existed from the 2d century B.C. to the 2d century A.D.

es·sen·tial (ĕ-sen'shŭl), adj. 1. necessary to the existence of a thing; most important; indispensable. 2. constituting the essence of something; basic: n. that which is essential or fundamental. —es·sen'tial·ly, adv.

-est (ist, ĕst), a suffix forming the superlative degree.

es·tab·lish (ĕ-stab'lish), v.t. 1. to fix firmly; settle. 2. to appoint or ordain permanently. 3. to found (a business, nation, etc.). 4. to prove. 5. to bring about.

es·tab·lish·ment (-mĕnt), n. 1. the act of establishing. 2. a place of residence or business. 3. [E-], those holding authority in a nation, business, etc.

es·tate (ĕ-stāt'), n. 1. condition of life; rank or position. 2. property or possessions. 3. the property of a deceased person. 4. a large piece of land containing a large residence, privately owned.

es·teem (ĕ-stēm'), v.t. 1. to set a high value upon; respect. 2. to consider: n. favorable opinion; respect.

es·ter (es'tēr), n. an organic compound formed by the reaction of an acid and an alcohol.

Es·ther (es'tēr), n. a book of the Bible.

es·thet·ics (es-thet'iks), n. same as aesthetics.

es·ti·ma·ble (es'tĭ-mȧ-bl), *adj.* worthy of regard, esteem, or honor.

es·ti·mate (es'tĭ-mȧt), *v.t.* -mat·ed, -mat·ing, 1. to calculate or determine approximately (cost, value, weight, etc.). 2. to form a judgment about: *n.* (-mit), 1. an approximate calculation of probable cost. 2. a judgment or opinion. —es'ti·ma·tor, *n.*

es·ti·ma·tion (es-tĭ-mā'shŭn), *n.* 1. an appraisal; approximate calculation. 2. honor, respect, or esteem. 3. conjecture.

es·ti·val (es'tĭ-vl), *adj.* of or pertaining to summer.

es·ti·vate (-vāt), *v.i.* -vat·ed, -vat·ing, 1. to spend the summer. 2. to pass the summer in a dormant state: opposed to hibernate. —es·ti·va'tion, *n.*

es·top (e-stŏp'), *v.t.* -topped', -top'ping, to place under estoppel; bar.

es·top·pel ('l), *n.* in *Law,* a bar to prevent a person from making a statement or claim that contradicts a previous statement or claim made by him.

es·to·vers (e-stō'vẽrz), *n.pl.* in *Law,* necessities allowed by law, as alimony to a divorced wife, wood that a tenant may take for fuel or repairs, etc.

es·trange (ĕ-strānj'), *v.t.* -tranged', -trang'ing, to alienate; turn from kindness to indifference or enmity. —es·trange'ment, *n.*

es·tray (e-strā'), *n.* a domestic animal found wandering.

es·tro·gen (es'trŏ-jĕn), *n.* any of several female sex hormones.

es·trus (-trŭs), *n.* the period of sexual excitement in most female mammals, corresponding to *rut* in males; heat. —es·trous, *adj.*

es·tu·ar·y (es'choo-wer-i), *n., pl.* -ar·ies, the wide mouth of a river, where the tide meets the current. —es·tu·ar'i·al, *adj.*

e·ta·gère (ā-tä-zher'), *n.* [French], a whatnot with open shelves for ornamental objects.

et cet·er·a (et set'ẽr-ȧ), and others; and so forth: abbreviated *etc.*

etch (ech), *v.t.* to engrave by biting out with an acid a design, picture, etc. previously drawn with an etching needle: *v.i.* to make etchings. —etch'er, *n.*

etch·ing ('ing), *n.* 1. the art or process of etching on metal, glass, etc. with acid. 2. a plate, drawing, design, etc. that has been etched.

e·ter·nal (i-tũr'nl), *adj.* 1. without beginning or end; everlasting. 2. unchanging. 3. perpetual; incessant: *n.* [E-], God. —e·ter'nal·ly, *adv.*

e·ter·ni·ty (i-tũr'ni-ti), *n., pl.* -ties, 1. infinite duration; unending existence. 2. time without limits. 3. a seemingly endless length of time. 4. the time after death.

e·te·sian (i-tē'zhŭn), *adj.* annual: said of the winds from the northwest Mediterranean that blow in the summer.

e·ther (ē'thẽr), *n.* 1. a material that was supposed fill all space beyond the moon. 2. the sky. 3. in *Chemistry, a)* a volatile, flammable liquid produced from alcohol and sulfuric acid. *b)* any similar oxide of hydrocarbon radicals.

e·the·re·al (i-thir'i-ȧl), *adj.* 1. of, pertaining to,

or like ether. 2. airy; exquisite. 3. heavenly. —e·the're·al·ly, *adv.*

eth·i·cal (eth'i-kl), *adj.* 1. of or pertaining to ethics; moral. 2. following the standards of a profession. —eth'i·cal·ly, *adv.*

eth·ics (eth'iks), *n.* 1. the science that treats of the principles of human morality and duty; moral philosophy. 2. the moral system of an individual, group, etc.

E·thi·o·pi·an (ē-thi-ō'pi-ăn), *adj.* of or pertaining to Ethiopia, a country in eastern Africa, or to its inhabitants: *n.* a native or inhabitant of Ethiopia.

eth·moid (eth'moid), *adj.* of or pertaining to the nasal cavity or the ethmoid bone: *n.* a bone in the skull behind the root of the nose that is part of the nasal septum.

eth·nic (eth'nik), *adj.* of, pertaining to, or characteristic of the basic groups of people with a common history, language, etc. —eth'ni·cal·ly, *adv.*

eth·nog·ra·phy (eth-nog'rȧ-fi), *n.* the science that treats of the description of primitive cultures.

eth·nol·o·gy (eth-nol'ŏ-ji), *n.* the science that treats of the various cultures of man and their distribution, characteristics, customs, etc. —eth·no·log'i·cal (-nŏ-log'i-kl), *adj.* —eth·nol'o·gist, *n.*

e·thol·o·gy (e-thol'ŏ-ji), *n.* in *Biology,* the science that treats of animal behavior.

e·thos (ē'thos), *n.* the characteristic spirit, customs, etc. of a group, individual, institution, system, etc.

eth·yl (eth'l), *n.* the hydrocarbon contained in alcohol, ether, etc.

ethyl alcohol, same as alcohol (sense 1).

eth·yl·ene (eth'i-lēn), *n.* a flammable, gaseous hydrocarbon that smells bad.

ethylene glycol, a colorless, viscid liquid, a kind of alcohol, used as an antifreeze, etc.

e·ti·o·late (ēt'i-ō-lāt), *v.t.* -lat·ed, -lat·ing, in *Botany,* to blanch or whiten by exclusion from sunlight.

e·ti·ol·o·gy (ēt-i-ol'ŏ-ji), *n., pl.* -gies, 1. the reason given. 2. the study of origins. 3. the branch of science which treats of the origin of disease. —e·ti·o·log'ic (-ŏ-loj'ik), *adj.*

et·i·quette (et'i-kĕt), *n.* the conventional rules or ceremony observed in polite society, a profession, etc.

E·trus·can (i-trus'kăn), *adj.* of or pertaining to Etruria, an ancient country in Italy, or to its inhabitants: *n.* a native or inhabitant of Etruria.

e·tude (ā'tōōd), *n.* a musical piece for a solo instrument, intended for the study of a technique.

et·y·mol·o·gist (et-i-mol'ŏ-jist), *n.* one who is an expert in etymology.

et·y·mol·o·gize (-jīz), *v.t. & v.i.* -gized, -giz·ing, to investigate and submit the origin of a word or words.

et·y·mol·o·gy (-ji), *n., pl.* -gies, 1. that branch of linguistics which treats of the origin and development of words. 2. the origin and development of a word or words. —et·y·mo·log'i·cal (-mŏ-loj'i-kl), *adj.* —et·y·mo·log'i·cal·ly, *adv.*

ŏ in drag*o*n, ōō in cr*u*de, oo in w*oo*l, u in c*u*p, ū in c*u*re, ũ in t*u*rn, ủ in foc*u*s, oi in b*o*y, ou in h*ou*se, th in *th*in, th in shea*th*e, g in g*e*t, j in *j*oy, y in *y*et.

et·y·mon (et'ĭ-mon), *n., pl.* **-mons, -ma** (-mä), the root of a word.

eu-, a prefix meaning *well, good.*

eu·ca·lyp·tol, eu·ca·lyp·tole (ū-kă-lip'tōl), *n.* a liquid that smells like camphor, used in perfumes, medicines, etc.

eu·ca·lyp·tus ('tŭs), *n., pl.* **-tus·es, -ti** (-tī), a tall Australian evergreen tree which furnishes gum, oil, etc.: also **eu'ca·lypt.**

Eu·cha·rist (ū'kă-rist), *n.* 1. same as Holy Communion. 2. the bread and wine for Holy Communion. —**Eu·cha·ris'tic,** *adj.*

eu·chre (ū'kĕr), *n.* a game of cards, all those between seven and ace being discarded: *v.t.* **-chred, -chring,** 1. to prevent (an opponent at euchre) from taking three of the five tricks. 2. [Informal], to outwit (often followed by *out*).

eu·di·om·e·ter (ū-di-om'ĕ-tēr), *n.* a graduated instrument for measuring the volume of a gas.

eu·gen·ics (ū-jen'iks), *n.* the science relating to the betterment of the human species by improving the conditions of heredity. —**eu·gen'ic,** *adj.* —**eu·gen'i·cal·ly,** *adv.* —**eu·gen'i·cist** ('i-sist), *n.*

eu·lo·gis·tic (ū-lō-jis'tik), *adj.* laudatory. —**eu·lo·gis'ti·cal·ly,** *adv.*

eu·lo·gize (ū'lō-jīz), *v.t.* **-gized, -giz·ing,** to praise highly; commend. —**eu'lo·gist, eu'lo·giz·er,** *n.*

eu·lo·gy (-ji), *n., pl.* **-gies,** 1. spoken or written praise of a person, especially a panegyric for the recently deceased. 2. commendation.

eu·nuch (ū'nŭk), *n.* a castrated man, especially an attendant in an Oriental harem.

eu·pep·si·a (ū-pep'shä), *n.* healthy digestion.

eu·phe·mism (ū'fĕ-mizm), *n.* 1. the substitution of a delicate or pleasing expression in place of that which is offensive or indelicate. 2. such an expression. —**eu·phe·mis'tic,** *adj.* —**eu·phe·mis'tic·al·ly,** *adv.*

eu·phon·ic (ū-fon'ik), *adj.* 1. of or pertaining to euphony. 2. same as **euphonious.**

eu·pho·ni·ous (ū-fō'ni-ŭs), *adj.* sounding pleasant to the ear.

eu·pho·ni·um (ū-fō'ni-ŭm), *n.* a brass-wind instrument related to the baritone.

eu·pho·ny (ū'fō-ni), *n., pl.* **-nies,** an agreeable sound or pronunciation.

eu·pho·ri·a (ū-fōr'i-ä), *n.* a condition of feeling well or in good spirits, especially in an exaggerated way. —**eu·phor'ic,** *adj.*

eu·phu·ism (ū'fyoo-wizm), *n.* the pedantic or affected use of words or language.

Eur·a·sian (yoo-rā'zhŭn), *adj.* of or pertaining to a person whose parentage is partly European and partly Asian: *n.* the offspring of a European and an Asian.

eu·re·ka (yoo-rē'kä), *interj.* an exclamation of triumph, meaning "I have found it."

Eu·ro·pe·an (yoor-ō-pē'ăn), *adj.* of or pertaining to Europe, the continent between Asia and the Atlantic Ocean: *n.* a native or inhabitant of Europe.

European plan, in hotel keeping, the system of furnishing room accommodations and service to guests, leaving the taking of meals optional.

eu·ro·pi·um (yoo-rō'pi-ŭm), *n.* a metallic chemical element of the rare-earth group.

eu·ryth·mics (yoo-rith'miks), *n.* rhythmic movements of the body done to musical accompaniment.

Eu·sta·chi·an tube (yoo-stā'shŭn), a tube which leads from the middle ear to the pharynx.

eu·tec·tic (yoo-tek'tik), *adj.* melting at the lowest temperature possible.

eu·tha·na·si·a (ū-thă-nā'zhä), *n.* 1. the practice of putting to death in a painless manner one suffering from fatal disease or disability. 2. a painless death.

eu·then·ics (ū-then'iks), *n.* the study of environmental conditions that tend to improve species, breeds, etc.

e·vac·u·ate (i-vak'yoo-wāt), *v.t.* **-at·ed, -at·ing,** 1. to make void or empty. 2. to discharge through the excretory passages. 3. to withdraw from: *v.i.* to withdraw. —**e·vac·u·ee'** (-wē'), *n.*

e·vac·u·a·tion (i-vak-yoo-wā'shŭn), *n.* 1. the act of evacuating. 2. withdrawal of troops. 3. the voiding of excreta.

e·vade (i-vād'), *v.i. & v.t.* **e·vad'ed, e·vad'ing,** 1. to elude; escape by artifice, stratagem, etc. 2. to get out of. —**e·vad'a·ble,** *adj.* —**e·vad'er,** *n.*

e·val·u·ate (i-val'yoo-wāt), *v.t.* **-at·ed, -at·ing,** 1. to find the value or amount of. 2. to appraise. 3. in *Mathematics*, to find the numerical value of. —**e·val·u·a'tion,** *n.*

ev·a·nes·cent (ev-ă-nes'nt), *adj.* disappearing gradually from sight; vanishing. —**ev·a·nes'cence,** *n.*

e·van·gel (i-van'jĕl), *n.* the gospel.

e·van·gel·i·cal (ē-van-jel'i-kl, ev-ăn-), *adj.* 1. of or pertaining to the Gospels. 2. maintaining the fundamental doctrines of the Protestant faith: *n.* one who holds evangelical doctrines. —**e·van·gel'i·cal·ly,** *adv.*

e·van·gel·ism (i-van'jĕ-lizm), *n.* the doctrine or preaching of evangelical principles.

e·van·gel·ist (-list), *n.* 1. [E-], one of the four writers of the Gospels. 2. an itinerant preacher. —**e·van·gel·is'tic,** *adj.*

e·van·gel·ize (-līz), *v.t.* **-ized, -iz·ing,** 1. to instruct in the gospel. 2. to convert to Christianity.

e·vap·o·rate (i-vap'ō-rāt), *v.i.* **-rat·ed, -rat·ing,** 1. to disperse in vapor. 2. to emit vapor. 3. to pass away without effect: *v.t.* 1. to convert into vapor. 2. to reduce to a concentrate by taking out the moisture. —**e·vap·o·ra'tion,** *n.* —**e·vap'o·ra·tor,** *n.*

e·va·sion (i-vā'zhŭn), *n.* 1. the act of evading. 2. an excuse; equivocation. 3. subterfuge.

e·va·sive (i-vā'siv), *adj.* 1. tending or seeking to evade. 2. elusive. —**e·va'sive·ly,** *adv.* —**e·va'sive·ness,** *n.*

Eve (ēv), *n.* the first woman, according to the Bible.

eve (ēv), *n.* 1. [often E-], the day preceding a holiday. 2. the period immediately preceding some important event. 3. [Poetic], evening.

e·ven (ē'vĕn), *adj.* 1. level; smooth. 2. uniform. 3. parallel. 4. divisible by two without a remainder. 5. balanced. 6. equal. 7. calm. 8. whole. 9. with no debts: *v.t. & v.i.* to level; make or become even (with *off*): *adv.* 1. in-

---

a in *cap,* ā in *cane,* ä in *father,* ȧ in *abet,* e in *met,* ē in *be,* ẽ in *baker,* ĕ in *regent,* i in *pit,* ī in *fine,* ĭ in *manifest,* o in *hot,* ō in *horse,* ō in *bone,*

deed. 2. exactly. 3. yet. —**e′ven·ly**, *adv.*
—**e′ven·ness**, *n.*

e·ven-hand·ed (ē′vĕn-han′dĭd), *adj.* just.

eve·ning (ēv′nĭng), *n.* 1. the close of the day and beginning of the night. 2. the latter end of life: *adj.* of, for, or during the evening.

evening star, a bright planet, as Venus, that is visible in the western sky in the early evening.

e·ven·song (ē′vĕn-sŏng), *n.* 1. vespers in the Roman Catholic Church. 2. the prayers recited during the evening in the Anglican Church.

e·vent (i-vĕnt′), *n.* 1. an occurrence; incident. 2. a consequence of an action. 3. any single item in a program of sports or games.

e·vent·ful (i-vĕnt′fŭl), *adj.* 1. full of important incidents or events. 2. momentous. —**e·vent′ful·ly**, *adv.* —**e·vent′ful·ness**, *n.*

e·ven·tide (ē′vĕn-tīd), *n.* [Poetic] evening.

e·ven·tu·al (i-ven′choo-wăl), *adj.* happening as a result; ultimate; contingent. —**e·ven′tu·al·ly**, *adv.*

e·ven·tu·al·i·ty (i-ven-choo-wal′ĭ-ti), *n.*, *pl.* -ties, a possible occurrence; contingency.

e·ven·tu·ate (i-ven′choo-wāt), *v.i.* -at·ed, -at·ing, to happen; result (often with *in*).

ev·er (ev′ẽr), *adv.* 1. at any time. 2. always. 3. in any way.

ev·er·glade (ev′ẽr-glād), *n.* a low, swampy tract of land, with patches of tall grass.

ev·er·green (ev′ẽr-grēn), *n.* a tree or plant which retains its foliage throughout the year: *adj.* always green.

ev·er·last·ing (ev·ẽr-las′tĭng), *adj.* perpetual: *n.* 1. eternity. 2. a plant whose flowers retain their color when dried. 3. [E-], God (preceded by *the*).

ev·er·more (-môr′), *adv.* eternally; always.

e·vert (i-vũrt′), *v.t.* to turn outward.

ev·er·y (ev′ri), *adj.* 1. the whole, taken one at a time; each. 2. all that could be. 3. each group of.

ev·er·y·bod·y (ev′ri-bod·i), *pron.* every person.

ev·er·y·day (-dā), *adj.* 1. each day. 2. for ordinary days. 3. familiar.

ev·er·y·one (-wŏn), *pron.* everybody.

ev·er·y·thing (-thing), *pron.* all things.

ev·er·y·where (-hwer), *adv.* in or to all places.

e·vict (i-vikt′), *v.t.* to expel or dispossess by legal process. —**e·vic′tion**, *n.*

ev·i·dence (ev′i-dĕns), *n.* 1. the condition of being evident. 2. proof. 3. indication. 4. a legal statement submitted in court: *v.t.* -denced, -denc·ing, 1. to indicate. 2. to make evident or plain.

ev·i·dent (-dĕnt), *adj.* plain; obvious. —**ev′i·dent·ly**, *adv.*

ev·i·den·tial (ev-i-den′shăl), *adj.* proving clearly. —**ev·i·den′tial·ly**, *adv.*

e·vil (ē′vl), *adj.* 1. morally bad; wicked; sinful. 2. unfortunate; disastrous. 3. bringing trouble or pain: *adv.* wickedly: *n.* 1. moral depravity. 2. injury; affliction. —**e′vil·ly**, *adv.* —**e′vil·ness**, *n.*

e·vil-do·er (e′vl-dōō-ẽr), *n.* one who is always doing evil. —**e′vil·do·ing**, *n.*

evil eye, a glance or look which is supposed to injure persons on whom it falls (preceded by *the*).

e·vil-mind·ed (-mīn′did), *adj.* having an evil disposition; disposed to harm or mischief; malicious.

e·vince (i-vins′), *v.t.* e·vinced′, e·vinc′ing, to make manifest or make evident; demonstrate. —**e·vin′ci·ble**, *adj.*

e·vis·cer·ate (i-vis′ĕ-rāt), *v.t.* -at·ed, -at·ing, 1. to disembowel. 2. to remove a fundamental section of. —**e·vis·cer·a′tion**, *n.*

e·voke (i-vōk′), *v.t.* e·voked′, e·vok′ing, 1. to call forth. 2. to draw forth (a response, etc.). —**ev·o·ca·tion** (ev-ō-kā′shŭn), *n.*

ev·o·lu·tion (ev-ō-lōō′shŭn), *n.* 1. a development or growth process. 2. the thing developed from this process. 3. a movement or pattern. 4. the extraction of roots of any arithmetical or algebraic power. 5. the gradual development of forms of life from simple types, as those consisting of one cell. 6. the theory that all plants and animals developed from previous forms. —**ev·o·lu′tion·al**, *adj.* —**ev·o·lu′tion·ar·y**, *adj.*

ev·o·lu·tion·ist (-ist), *adj.* of or pertaining to evolution: *n.* one who maintains the doctrine of evolution.

e·volve (i-volv′), *v.t. & v.i.* e·volved′, e·volv′ing, 1. to develop; unfold. 2. to produce from within.

ewe (ū), *n.* a female sheep.

ew·er (ū′ẽr), *n.* a large, wide-mouthed water jug.

ex (eks), *prep.* 1. out of. 2. without.

ex-, a prefix meaning *from, out, out of, away from, beyond, completely, going up, previous.*

ex·ac·er·bate (ig-zas′ẽr-bāt), *v.t.* -bat·ed, -bat·ing, 1. to irritate; exasperate. 2. to intensify (pain, irritation, etc.). —**ex·ac·er·ba′tion**, *n.*

ex·act (ig-zakt′), *adj.* 1. very correct or accurate; methodical. 2. precise. 3. strict. 4. particular: *v.t.* 1. to require or claim authoritatively. 2. to compel to be paid. 3. to insist upon as a right. —**ex·act′ly**, *adv.* —**ex·act′ness**, *n.*

ex·act·ing (′ing), *adj.* 1. making very great demands; severe. 2. arduous. —**ex·act′ing·ly**, *adv.*

ex·ac·tion (ig-zak′shŭn), *n.* 1. the act of exacting. 2. extortion. 3. that which is exacted.

ex·ac·ti·tude (ig-zak′ti-tōōd), *n.* precision.

ex·ag·ger·ate (ig-zaj′ĕ-rāt), *v.t. & v.i.* -at·ed, -at·ing, to enlarge or heighten by overstatement; color highly. —**ex·ag·ger·a′tion**, *n.* —**ex·ag′ger·a·tor**, *n.*

ex·alt (ig-zôlt′), *v.t.* 1. to elevate in rank, station, or dignity. 2. to raise on high. 3. to glorify or extol. 4. to make joyful, proud, etc.

ex·al·ta·tion (eg-zôl-tā′shŭn), *n.* 1. the state of being exalted. 2. elevation. 3. a high sense of personal power or well-being.

ex·am·i·na·tion (ig-zam-i-nā′shŭn), *n.* 1. the act of examining; testing. 2. a test: also [Informal], **ex·am** (ig-zam′).

ex·am·ine (ig-zam′in), *v.t.* -ined, -in·ing, 1. to scrutinize or investigate carefully; search or inquire into. 2. to test orally or by writing the knowledge, qualifications, etc. of, as a candidate for degree, office, job, etc. —**ex·am′in·er**, *n.*

ex·am·i·nee (ig-zam-i-nē'), *n.* one who is examined.

ex·am·ple (ig-zam'pl), *n.* 1. a pattern; model. 2. an illustration of a rule or precept. 3. a sample; specimen. 4. one punished as an admonition to others.

ex·an·them (ek-san'thĕm), *n.* 1. an eruption of the skin caused by some diseases. 2. a disease characterized by rash. Also **ex·an·the·ma** (ek-san-thē'mà), *pl.* **-mas, -ma·tas** (-them'à-tăz, -thē'mà-tăz).

ex·as·per·ate (ig-zas'pĕ-rāt), *v.t.* **-at·ed, -at·ing,** to irritate exceedingly; enrage greatly. —**ex·as·per·a'tion,** *n.*

ex ca·the·dra (eks kà-thē'drà), 1. with official authority. 2. dogmatically.

ex·ca·vate (eks'kà-vāt), *v.t.* **-vat·ed, -vat·ing,** 1. to dig or hollow out. 2. to form by digging. 3. to reveal by digging. 4. to scoop out (soil). —**ex·ca·va'tion,** *n.*

ex·ca·va·tor (-vāt-ĕr), *n.* 1. one who or that which excavates. 2. a digging machine, as a steam shovel.

ex·ceed (ik-sēd'), *v.i.* 1. to go beyond (a limit, measure, etc.). 2. to surpass; excel: *v.i.* to be greater; go beyond bounds.

ex·ceed·ing ('ing), *adj.* very great; going beyond. —**ex·ceed'ing·ly,** *adv.*

ex·cel (ik-sel'), *v.i.* **-celled', -cel'ling,** to possess good qualities in a great degree: *v.t.* to surpass; outdo in comparison; be superior to.

ex·cel·lence (ek'sl-ĕns), *n.* 1. the state of excelling in anything; superior merit or goodness. 2. something specific in which someone excels.

ex·cel·len·cy (-ĕn-si), *n., pl.* **-cies,** 1. [E-], a title of honor of various high officials, as an ambassador, governor, etc. 2. same as excellence.

ex·cel·lent (-ĕnt), *adj.* eminently distinguished for goodness or ability; of great value, merit, or virtue. —**ex'cel·lent·ly,** *adv.*

ex·cel·si·or (ek-sel'si-ôr), *adj. & interj.* yet higher: *n.* (ik-sel'si-ĕr), long wood shavings used for packing or stuffing.

ex·cept (ik-sept'), *v.t.* to omit or leave out; exclude: *v.i.* to object (with *to* or *against*): *prep.* omitting; without inclusion of; besides: *conj.* [Informal], but.

ex·cept·ing ('ing), *prep. & conj.* same as except.

ex·cep·tion (ik-sep'shŭn), *n.* 1. the state of being excepted; omission; exclusion. 2. an objection. 3. offense taken. 4. an example of something or someone that does not fit into a general rule or category. 5. in *Law*, a formal objection to a decision of a court during trial.

ex·cep·tion·a·ble (-à-bl), *adj.* objectionable.

ex·cep·tion·al (-ăl), *adj.* 1. unusual; superior. 2. in need of special education because of handicaps or superior abilities. —**ex·cep'tion·al·ly,** *adv.*

ex·cerpt (ik-sŭrpt'), *v.t.* to take out or select from (a book): *n.* (ek'sŭrpt), a selection or extract from a book or writing.

ex·cess (ik-ses'), *n.* 1. that which exceeds the ordinary limit, measure, or experience. 2. surplus. 3. superfluity. 4. intemperance: *adj.* (ek'ses), surplus.

ex·ces·sive (ik-ses'iv), *adj.* extreme; unreasonable. —**ex·ces'sive·ly,** *adv.* —**ex·ces'sive·ness,** *n.*

ex·change (iks-chānj'), *v.t.* **-changed', -chang'ing,** 1. to give in return for an equivalent; barter. 2. to receive and give (equivalents): *n.* 1. the act of exchanging; barter. 2. reciprocity. 3. the act of putting one thing in place of another. 4. something exchanged. 5. a place where merchants, brokers, etc. meet. 6. a central telephone office. 7. the rate of exchange for money. —**ex·change'a·ble,** *adj.* —**ex·chang'er,** *n.*

ex·cheq·uer (iks-chek'ĕr, eks'chek-ĕr), *n.* 1. a treasury. 2. cash or funds. 3. [often E-], the department of state in Great Britain which has charge of the public revenues.

ex·cise (ik-sīz'), *v.t.* **-cised', -cis'ing,** to levy an excise duty upon: *n.* (ek'sīz, 'sis), an inland tax levied on commodities of home production and consumption: also **excise tax.**

ex·cise (ik-sīz'), *v.t.* **-cised', -cis'ing,** to cut out (a tumor, etc.). —**ex·ci'sion** (-sizh'ŭn), *n.*

ex·cit·a·ble (ik-sīt'à-bl), *adj.* that can be excited readily. —**ex·cit·a·bil'i·ty,** *n.*

ex·cit·ant (ik-sīt'ănt), *adj.* tending to excite: *n.* something that arouses organic activity; stimulant.

ex·cite (ik-sīt'), *v.t.* **-cit'ed, -cit'ing,** 1. to animate; put into motion or action. 2. to rouse up; provoke. 3. to arouse; stimulate. —**ex·ci·ta·tion** (ek-si-tā'shŭn), *n.* —**ex·cit'ed·ly,** *adv.*

ex·cite·ment ('mĕnt), *n.* 1. the state of being excited; stimulation. 2. something exciting.

ex·cit·er ('ĕr), *n.* 1. one who or that which excites. 2. a small generator supplying current. 3. an oscillator supplying voltage in a radio transmitter.

ex·cit·ing ('ing), *adj.* tending to excite; stirring; lively. —**ex·cit'ing·ly,** *adv.*

ex·claim (iks-klām'), *v.i. & v.t.* to cry out abruptly and passionately.

ex·cla·ma·tion (eks-klà-mā'shŭn), *n.* 1. an abrupt or clamorous outcry. 2. that which is exclaimed. —**ex·clam·a·to·ry** (iks-klam'à-tôr-i), *adj.*

exclamation mark, a mark (!) in writing or printing to denote emotion, surprise, etc.: also **exclamation point.**

ex·clave (eks'klāv), *n.* a small part of a country lying within the territory of another power.

ex·clude (iks-klōōd'), *v.t.* **-clud'ed, -clud'ing,** 1. to shut out; hinder from entrance or admission. 2. to eject; expel. —**ex·clu'sion** (-klōō'zhŭn), *n.*

ex·clu·sion·ist (-klōō'zhŭn-ist), *n.* one who would debar another from any privilege or right.

ex·clu·sive (iks-klōō'siv), *adj.* 1. tending to exclude or shut out others. 2. with no joint participation. 3. keeping out specified groups, as because of prejudice: *n.* an exclusive thing. —**ex·clu'sive·ly,** *adv.* —**ex·clu'sive·ness,** *n.*

ex·cog·i·tate (eks-koj'ĭ-tāt), *v.t.* **-tat·ed, -tat·ing,** to invent or discover by thinking.

ex·com·mu·ni·cate (eks-kŏ-mū'ni-kāt), *v.t.* **-cat·ed, -cat·ing,** to punish by cutting off from the membership of, and communion with, a church. —**ex·com·mu·ni·ca'tion,** *n.*

---

a in c*a*p, ā in c*a*ne, ä in f*a*ther, å in *a*bet, e in m*e*t, ē in b*e*, ē in b*a*ker, ĕ in r*e*gent, i in p*i*t, ī in f*i*ne, i in man*i*fest, o in h*o*t, ô in h*o*rse, ō in b*o*ne,

ex·co·ri·ate (ik-skôr′i-āt), *v.t.* -at·ed, -at·ing, 1. to strip off the skin of; rub; abrade. 2. to criticize severely. —**ex·co·ri·a′tion,** *n.*

ex·cre·ment (eks′krē-mĕnt), *n.* matter discharged from the body of an animal after digestion; feces. —**ex·cre·men′tal** (-men′tl), **ex·cre·men·ti′tious** (-men-tish′ŭs), *adj.*

ex·cres·cence (iks-kres′ns), *n.* an unnatural or disfiguring outgrowth.

ex·cres·cent (′nt), *adj.* of or pertaining to an excrescence; superfluous.

ex·cre·ta (eks-krēt′ă), *n.pl.* useless matter eliminated from the body, as perspiration, urine, etc. —**ex·cre′tal,** *adj.*

ex·crete (iks-krēt′), *v.t. & v.i.* -cret′ed, -cret′ing, to throw off or eject (waste matter) from the body.

ex·cre·tion (-krē′shŭn), *n.* 1. the excreting of waste matter from the body. 2. the matter ejected or thrown off.

ex·cre·to·ry (eks′krē-tôr-i),' *adj.* of or pertaining to excretion: *n., pl.* -ries, a duct or vessel that transmits excreted matter.

ex·cru·ci·ate (iks-krōō′shi-āt), *v.t.* -at·ed, -at·ing, 1. to inflict severe pains upon; torture. 2. to torment. —**ex·cru·ci·a′tion,** *n.*

ex·cru·ci·at·ing (-āt-ing), *adj.* 1. agonizing. 2. very strong; sharp.

ex·cul·pate (eks′kŭl-pāt), *v.t.* -pat·ed, -pat·ing, to clear from the imputation of a fault; exonerate. —**ex·cul·pa·ble** (ik-skul′pă-bl), —**ex·cul·pa′tion,** *n.*

ex·cur·rent (ek-skūr′ĕnt), *adj.* running out or beyond the edge: said of trees or leaves.

ex·cur·sion (ik-skūr′zhŭn), *n.* 1. a pleasure trip; short or rapid tour. 2. a round trip at a lower rate. 3. a digression: *adj.* of or pertaining to an excursion. —**ex·cur′sion·ist,** *n.*

ex·cur·sive (ik-skūr′siv), *adj.* rambling. —**ex·cur′sive·ly,** *adv.* —**ex·cur′sive·ness,** *n.*

ex·cur·sus (ik-skūr′sŭs), *n., pl.* -sus·es or -sus, 1. a dissertation supplemental to a work, giving additional information on certain points. 2. a digression.

ex·cus·a·ble (ik-skū′ză-bl), *adj.* pardonable. —**ex·cus′a·bly,** *adv.*

ex·cuse (ik-skūz′), *v.t.* -cused′, -cus′ing, 1. to extenuate by apology. 2. to pardon; remit. 3. to free from obligation or duty. 4. to allow to depart. 5. to justify: *n.* 1. a plea offered in apology for some fault or neglect of duty. 2. something that justifies. 3. a pretext.

ex·e·cra·ble (ek′sē-krá-bl), *adj.* 1. disgusting. 2. of low quality. —**ex′e·cra·bly,** *adv.*

ex·e·crate (-krāt), *v.t.* -crat·ed, -crat·ing, 1. to revile harshly. 2. to detest; abhor.

ex·e·cra·tion (ek-sē-krā′shŭn), *n.* 1. the act of execrating. 2. an imprecation. 3. a detestation.

ex·e·cute (ek′sē-kūt), *v.t.* -cut·ed, -cut·ing, 1. to perform. 2. to carry into effect. 3. to put to death. 4. to make in conformity to a design. 5. to make valid or legal by signing or sealing. 6. to perform (some piece of music).

ex·e·cu·tion (ek-sē-kū′shŭn), *n.* 1. the act of executing; performance. 2. the manner of carrying anything into effect. 3. a legal warrant or order. 4. the act of giving validity to a legal instrument. 5. capital punishment.

ex·e·cu·tion·er (-ĕr), *n.* one who legally executes others.

ex·ec·u·tive (ig-zek′yŭ-tiv), *adj.* 1. of or pertaining to the management of business. 2. administrative. 3. of or pertaining to executing functions: *n.* 1. an administrator or manager. 2. the administrative branch of government.

ex·ec·u·tor (ig-zek′yoo-tĕr), *n.* a person appointed by a testator to see that the terms of his will are carried out. —**ex·ec·u·trix** (ig-zek′yoo-triks), *n.fem., pl.* -trix·es, **ex·ec·u·tri·ces** (ig-zek-yoo-trī′sēz).

ex·ec·u·to·ry (ig-zek′yoo-tôr-i), *adj.* 1. of or pertaining to the execution of laws; carrying out official duties. 2. in *Law,* to be performed at a future time.

ex·e·ge·sis (ek-sē-jē′sis), *n., pl.* -ge′ses (′sēz), explanation or interpretation of a text or passage, especially of the Bible. —**ex·e·get′ic** (-jet′ik), **ex·e·get′i·cal,** *adj.*

ex·em·plar (ig-zem′plär), *n.* 1. something to be copied or serve as a model. 2. an example.

ex·em·pla·ry (′plă-ri), *adj.* serving as a copy or model; commendable.

ex·em·pli·fi·ca·tion (ig-zem-pli-fi-kā′shŭn), *n.* 1. illustration by example. 2. a legally certified copy.

ex·em·pli·fy (ig-zem′pli-fī), *v.t.* -fied, -fy·ing, 1. to illustrate by example. 2. to transcribe for legal purposes.

ex·empt (ig-zempt′), *v.t.* to free from some duty or obligation; grant immunity to: *adj.* free from some duty or obligation: *n.* one thus set free. —**ex·emp′tion,** *n.*

ex·e·qua·tur (ek′sē-kwät-ĕr), *n.* a written recognition of a consul or commercial agent given by a foreign government to which he is accredited, authorizing him to exercise his authority in the place where he is stationed.

ex·er·cise (ek′sĕr-sīz), *v.t.* -cised, -cis·ing, 1. to train by use. 2. to exert. 3. to employ actively. 4. to make anxious; harass: *v.i.* to undergo training or exercise: *n.* 1. bodily exertion. 2. mental or physical development. 3. labor. 4. a lesson or example for practice. 5. *pl.* a scheduled group of formal acts.

ex·ergue (ig-zūrg′), *n.* the small space beneath the principal design on a coin or medal for the insertion of a date, etc.

ex·ert (ig-zūrt′), *v.t.* 1. to put forth or use with an effort. 2. to employ (oneself) strenuously.

ex·er·tion (-zūr′shŭn), *n.* 1. exercise. 2. effort.

ex·e·unt (ek′si-ŭnt), they go out: a word used in plays to denote that the actors leave the stage.

ex·fo·li·ate (eks-fō′li-āt), *v.t. & v.i.* -at·ed, -at·ing, to scale or peel off. —**ex·fo·li·a′tion,** *n.*

ex·ha·la·tion (eks-hă-lā′shŭn), *n.* 1. the act of exhaling. 2. an emanation.

ex·hale (eks-hāl′), *v.t.* -haled′, -hal′ing, 1. to breathe forth. 2. to emit or send out; cause to evaporate: *v.i.* 1. to rise in vapor. 2. to breathe forth air.

ex·haust (ig-zôst′), *v.t.* 1. to empty by drawing off the contents; drain. 2. to weaken; wear out by exertion. 3. to discuss or treat thoroughly. 4. to consume completely: *n.* 1. emission of gas, steam, etc. from the cylinder of an engine after accomplishing the

---

work. 2. the pipe through which such emission takes place. 3. something emitted. —**exhaust'i-ble,** adj.

ex·haus·tion (ig-zôs'chŭn), n. 1. the state of being exhausted. 2. the condition of being consumed. 3. lack of strength or energy.

ex·haus·tive ('tiv), adj. 1. exhausting. 2. complete. —**ex·haus'tive-ly,** adv.

ex·hib·it (ig-zib'it), v.t. 1. to present to view; display; show. 2. to manifest publicly. 3. to reveal: v.i. to place objects on display for the public: n. 1. a public show or display. 2. an object offered for public view. 3. in Law, a legal document presented in proof of facts. —**ex·hib'i-tor,** n.

ex·hi·bi·tion (ek-si-bish'ŭn), n. 1. the act of exhibiting. 2. an object exhibited. 3. a public show. 4. [British], an amount of money for the support of a scholar at a university.

ex·hil·a·rate (ig-zil'ā-rāt), v.t. -rat·ed, -rat·ing, 1. to make joyous or cheerful. 2. to enliven. —**ex·hil·a·ra'tion,** n.

ex·hort (ig-zôrt'), v.t. & v.i. to incite by appeal or argument; caution; admonish.

ex·hor·ta·tion (eg-zôr-tā'shŭn), n. 1. the act of exhorting. 2. language designed to arouse to laudable effort; admonition.

ex·hor·ta·to·ry (ig-zôr'tå-tôr-i), adj. containing exhortation; tending to exhort: also **ex·hor'ta·tive** (-tiv).

ex·hume (ig-zūm', iks-hūm'), v.t. -humed', -hum'ing, to disinter; dig up (what has been buried). —**ex·hu·ma·tion** (eks-hyoo-mā'shŭn), n.

ex·i·gen·cy (ek'si-jĕn-si), n., pl. -cies, 1. pl. pressing necessities or demands. 2. urgency. 3. an urgent situation.

ex·i·gent (-jĕnt), adj. 1. urgent; pressing. 2. demanding. —**ex'i·gent-ly,** adv.

ex·ig·u·ous (eg-zig'yoo-wŭs), adj. small; diminutive; insufficient.

ex·ile (eg'zīl, ek'sīl), v.t. -iled, -il·ing, to banish from one's native country: n. 1. the state of being banished from one's native country; condition of living away from one's home or friends. 2. one who is exiled.

ex·ist (ig-zist'), v.i. 1. to have existence. 2. to be found. 3. to live.

ex·ist·ence ('ĕns), n. 1. the state of being. 2. life; duration. 3. occurrence. —**ex·ist'ent,** adj.

ex·is·ten·tial (eg-zis-ten'shăl), adj. of or pertaining to existence or existentialism.

ex·is·ten·tial·ism ('shăl-izm), n. a philosophical movement of the 20th century which emphasizes immediate individual existence as the focus of reality and meaning. —**ex·is·ten'tial·ist,** adj. & n.

ex·it (eg'zit, ek'sit), n. 1. the act of going out. 2. an egress. 3. the departure of an actor from the stage: v.i. to go out.

ex·o-, a prefix meaning outer, outside.

ex·o·dus (ek'sŏ-dŭs), n. a going out or forth, as of a multitude from a country. 2. [E-], the departure of the Israelites from Egypt, under the guidance of Moses. 3. [E-], the second book of the Pentateuch.

ex of·fi·ci·o (eks ŏ-fish'i-ō), by virtue of office.

ex·og·a·my (eks-sog'å-mi), n. a custom forbid-

ding marriage within one's own tribe or clan.

ex·og·e·nous (ek-soj'ĕ-nŭs), adj. affecting externally.

ex·on·er·ate (ig-zon'ĕ-rāt), v.t. -at·ed, -at·ing, to free from the imputation of guilt; acquit. —**ex·on·er·a'tion,** n. —**ex·on'er·a·tive,** adj.

ex·oph·thal·mos (ek-sof-thal'mŏs), n. unnatural prominence of the eyeball: also **ex·oph·thal'mus** ('mŭs), **ex·oph·thal'mi·a** ('mi-å).

ex·o·ra·ble (ek'sĕr-å-bl), adj. capable of being moved or persuaded.

ex·or·bi·tant (ig-zôr'bi-tănt), adj. going beyond due limits; excessive. —**ex·or'bi·tance,** n.

ex·or·cise, ex·or·cize (ek'sôr-siz), v.t. -cised or -cized, -cis·ing or -ciz·ing, 1. to expel (an evil spirit) by prayers or incantations. 2. to pronounce incantations over in order to exorcise. —**ex'or·cism** (-sizm), n. —**ex'or·cist,** n.

ex·or·di·um (ig-zôr'di-ŭm), n., pl. -di·ums, -di·a (-å), 1. the opening part of a speech or composition. 2. a prelude.

ex·os·mo·sis (ek-sos-mō'sis), n. the less rapid mixing of the more concentrated substance with a less concentrated substance. —**ex·os·mot'ic** (-mot'ik), adj.

ex·os·to·sis (ek-sos-tō'sis), n., pl. -ses (-sēz), an unnatural enlargement of, or protuberance on, a bone or tooth.

ex·o·ter·ic (ek-sō-ter'ik), adj. 1. external. 2. capable of being understood by the public; opposed to esoteric.

ex·ot·ic (ig-zot'ik), adj. 1. foreign. 2. fascinating or beautiful in an unusual way. —**ex·ot'i·cism** ('i-sizm), n.

ex·pand (ik-spand'), v.t. 1. to distend. 2. to dilate; extend. 3. to enlarge: v.i. to increase in size.

ex·panse (ik-spans'), n. a continuous area; large extent.

ex·pan·si·ble (ik-span'si-bl), adj. capable of, or permitting, expansion: also **ex·pand'a·ble.**

ex·pan·sion (ik-span'shŭn), n. 1. the state of being expanded. 2. the act of expanding. 3. that which has been expanded. 4. the amount of expansion.

ex·pan·sive (ik-span'siv), adj. 1. capable of being expanded. 2. widely extended; large. 3. frank and generous. —**ex·pan'sive-ly,** adv.

ex par·te (eks-pärt'i), one-sided.

ex·pa·ti·ate (ik-spā'shi-āt), v.i. -at·ed, -at·ing, to be copious in detail in statement or language. —**ex·pa·ti·a'tion,** n.

ex·pa·tri·ate (eks-pā'tri-āt), v.t. & v.i. -at·ed, -at·ing, to drive or remove from one's native country: adj. (-it), an exile.

ex·pect (ik-spekt'), v.t. 1. to look for with apprehension. 2. to anticipate as suitable. 3. [Informal], to assume: v.i. [Informal], to be pregnant.

ex·pect·an·cy (ik-spek'tăn-si), n., pl. -cies, 1. the act or state of expecting. 2. the thing expected. Also **ex·pect'ance** ('tăns).

ex·pect·ant ('tănt), adj. waiting in expectation. —**ex·pect'ant-ly,** adv.

ex·pec·ta·tion (ek-spek-tā'shŭn), n. 1. the act of looking forward to; anticipation. 2. that which is expected. 3. also pl. a contingent prospect, as of wealth.

a in cap, ā in cane, ä in father, å in abet, e in met, ē in be, ē in baker, ė in regent, i in pit, ī in fine, ĭ in manifest, o in hot, ô in horse, ō in bone,

ex·pec·to·rant (ik-spek′tĕr-ănt), *adj.* a medicine that promotes expectoration.

ex·pec·to·rate (′tŏ-rāt), *v.t. & v.i.* -rat·ed, -rat·ing, 1. to eject from the lungs by spitting. 2. to spit. —**ex·pec·to·ra′tion,** *n.*

ex·pe·di·en·cy (ik-spē′di-ĕn-si), *n., pl.* -cies, 1. suitability to an end or purpose. 2. interest only in one's own needs. 3. that which is expedient. Also **ex·pe′di·ence.**

ex·pe·di·ent (-ĕnt), *adj.* 1. convenient; suitable. 2. giving gain only to oneself: *n.* that which aids as a means to an end. 2. an emergency device.

ex·pe·dite (ek′spĕ-dīt), *v.t.* -dit·ed, -dit·ing, 1. to hasten; facilitate. 2. to perform promptly.

ex·pe·dit·er (-ēr), *n.* a person whose work is expediting projects, as in business and industry.

ex·pe·di·tion (ek-spĕ-dish′ŭn), *n.* 1. haste; dispatch; promptness. 2. a march, voyage, etc. by an army or several persons for some particular purpose. —**ex·pe·di′tion·ar·y,** *adj.*

ex·pe·di·tious (ek-spĕ-dish′ŭs), *adj.* quick; speedy. —**ex·pe·di′tious·ly,** *adv.*

ex·pel (ik-spel′), *v.t.* -pelled′, -pel′ling, 1. to drive away; force out. 2. to send away by authority; exclude. —**ex·pel′la·ble,** *adj.* —**ex·pel′ler,** *n.*

ex·pend (ik-spend′), *v.t.* 1. to lay out; spend. 2. to consume.

ex·pend·a·ble (ik-spen′dă-bl), *adj.* 1. that can be spent. 2. denoting military equipment or personnel that can be used or destroyed to accomplish some purpose.

ex·pend·i·ture (′dĭ-chēr), *n.* 1. a laying out of money, time, labor, etc. 2. the disbursement made.

ex·pense (ik-spens′), *n.* 1. drain on resources; source of expenditure. 2. cost. 3. *pl.* costs in doing business.

ex·pen·sive (ik-spen′siv), *adj.* causing expense; high-priced.

ex·pe·ri·ence (ik-spir′i-ĕns), *n.* 1. knowledge gained by trial and practice. 2. test; practice. 3. participation and observation of situations. 4. what is seen or participated in.

ex·pe·ri·enced (-ĕnst), *adj.* possessing knowledge gained from experience.

ex·per·i·ment (ik-sper′ĭ-mĕnt), *n.* 1. a trial or operation to discover something or to verify something; proof. 2. trial: *v.i.* to search out by trial. —**ex·per·i·men·ta′tion** (-mĕn-tā′shŭn), *n.* —**ex·per′i·ment·er,** *n.*

ex·per·i·men·tal (ik-sper-ĭ-men′tl), *adj.* 1. of, pertaining to, or founded on experiment. 2. for the purpose of testing. —**ex·per·i·men′tal·ly,** *adv.*

ex·pert (ek′spĕrt), *adj.* skillful through practice or experience: *n.* one who has special skill in some branch of knowledge; specialist. —**ex′pert·ly,** *adv.* —**ex′pert·ness,** *n.*

ex·per·tise (ek-spĕr-tēz′), *n.* the skill, knowledge, or judgment of an expert.

ex·pi·ate (ek′spi-āt), *v.t.* -at·ed, -at·ing, 1. to atone for. 2. to suffer punishment for. —**ex·pi·a′tion,** *n.* —**ex′pi·a·to·ry** (-ả-tôr-i), *adj.*

ex·pire (ik-spīr′), *v.t.* -pired′, -pir′ing, to breathe out from the lungs: *v.i.* 1. to

breathe out air. 2. to die. 3. to terminate. —**ex·pi·ra′tion** (ek-spĭ-rā′shŭn), *n.*

ex·plain (ik-splān′), *v.t.* 1. to make intelligible or clear. 2. to expound or interpret. 3. to give causes for: *v.i.* to offer causes.

ex·pla·na·tion (eks-plă-nā′shŭn), *n.* 1. the act of explaining. 2. elucidation; interpretation. 3. a mutual clearing up of a misunderstanding.

ex·plan·a·to·ry (ik-splan′ả-tôr-i), *adj.* serving to explain.

ex·ple·tive (eks′plĕ-tiv), *n.* 1. a word not necessary for the sense, inserted in a sentence or line of verse. 2. a curse; interjection: *adj.* filling up; added or inserted for emphasis, etc.

ex·pli·ca·ble (eks′pli-kả-bl), *adj.* that may be explained or interpreted.

ex·pli·cate (eks′pli-kăt), *v.t.* -cat·ed, -cat·ing, to explain clearly. —**ex′pli·ca·tive** (-kăt-iv), *adj.*

ex·plic·it (ik-splis′it), *adj.* 1. definite. 2. stating directly. 3. plain. —**ex·plic′it·ly,** *adv.*

ex·plode (ik-splōd′), *v.i.* -plod′ed, -plod′ing, to burst forth with sudden noise and violence: *v.t.* 1. to cause to pass from a solid to a gaseous state. 2. to refute. 3. to cause to burst noisily; demolish.

ex·ploit (ik-sploit′), *v.t.* 1. to make improper use of for one's own profit. 2. to put to use: *n.* (eks′ploit), a remarkable deed or heroic act. —**ex·ploi·ta′tion,** *n.* —**ex·ploit′er,** *n.*

ex·plore (ik-splôr′), *v.t.* -plored′, -plor′ing, 1. to search into or examine thoroughly. 2. to travel in or over (a country) to discover its characteristic features, etc. —**ex·plo·ra·tion** (eks-plô-rā′shŭn), *n.* —**ex·plor′a·to·ry** (-ả-tôr-i), *adj.* —**ex·plor′er,** *n.*

ex·plo·sion (ik-splō′zhŭn), *n.* 1. the act of exploding; sudden bursting forth with a loud noise. 2. the loud noise so made. 3. a loud outbreak. 4. a quick growth.

ex·plo·sive (′siv), *adj.* 1. of, pertaining to, or causing explosion. 2. likely to burst forth noisily: *n.* 1. any substance that causes an explosion. 2. same as plosive.

ex·po·nent (ik-spō′nĕnt), *n.* 1. one who explains or interprets (principles, etc.). 2. a representative symbol. 3. (ek′spō-nĕnt), the index of an algebraic power indicating the number of factors involved. —**ex·po·nen·tial** (eks-pō-nen′shăl), *adj.*

ex·port (ik-spôrt′, eks′pôrt), *v.t.* to send or carry out (merchandise) from a country: *n.* (eks′pôrt), 1. a commodity carried to a foreign country. 2. the act of exporting. Also **ex·por·ta′tion.** —**ex·port′er,** *n.*

ex·pose (ik-spōz′), *v.t.* -posed′, -pos′ing, 1. to lay open (*to* peril, censure, or ridicule). 2. to leave to the action of any force or circumstance. 3. to disclose. 4. to place (sensitized photographic film or plates) before actinic rays.

ex·po·sé (eks-pō-zā′), *n.* an exposure of something discreditable.

ex·po·si·tion (eks-pō-zish′ŭn), *n.* 1. an explanation or interpretation, as in writing or speech. 2. an exhibition, especially a large international show.

ex·pos·i·tor (ik-spoz′ĭ-tēr), *n.* one who expounds or interprets.

ŏ in drag*o*n, ōō in cr*u*de, oo in w*oo*l, u in c*u*p, ū in c*u*re, ŭ in t*u*rn, ŭ in foc*u*s, oi in b*o*y, ou in h*ou*se, th in *th*in, th in shea*th*e, g in *g*et, j in *j*oy, y in *y*et.

ex·pos·i·to·ry ('ĭ-tôr-ĭ), *adj.* of, pertaining to, or conveying exposition.

ex post fac·to (eks pôst fak'tō), [Latin, from an act done afterward], by virtue of something done afterward, as of a law enacted with retroactive effect.

ex·pos·tu·late (ik-spos'chŭ-lāt), *v.i.* -lat·ed, -lat·ing, to reason earnestly or remonstrate (followed by *with*). —**ex·pos·tu·la'tion,** *n.* —**ex·pos'tu·la·to·ry** (-lȧ-tôr-ĭ), *adj.*

ex·po·sure (ik-spō'zhĕr), *n.* 1. the act of exposing. 2. situation; aspect. 3. a coming before the public often. 4. the period in which film is exposed to light. 5. one section of film for this.

ex·pound (ik-spound'), *v.t.* 1. to set forth. 2. to explain or interpret; make clear.

ex·press (ik-spres'), *v.t.* 1. to exhibit by language; utter. 2. to show. 3. to represent. 4. to squeeze out. 5. to dispatch by express: *adj.* 1. plainly stated; not implied. 2. exact; resembling precisely. 3. specially prepared. 4. of or pertaining to quick or direct conveyance: *n.* 1. a person or vehicle that carries letters or small packages expeditiously. 2. an express train, bus, etc. 3. a message or dispatch sent by express. 4. a regular and systematic method of conveyance for passengers, mails, goods of small bulk, etc.: *adv.* by express. —**ex·press'i·ble,** *adj.*

ex·pres·sion (ik-spresh'ŭn), *n.* 1. the act or power of representing anything. 2. a saying. 3. mode of speech. 4. change of the countenance indicating emotion. 5. modulation of the voice. 6. mathematical symbols. —**ex·pres'sion·less,** *adj.*

ex·pres·sion·ism (-izm), *n.* an artistic movement of the early 20th century that used alteration of reality and symbols to show thoughts and feelings from within.

ex·pres·sive (ik-spres'ĭv), *adj.* 1. serving to express. 2. full of significance or emotion. —**ex·pres'sive·ly,** *adv.*

ex·press·ly (ik-spres'lĭ), *adv.* 1. plainly. 2. especially.

ex·press·man (ik-spres'măn), *n., pl.* -men ('mĕn), the person who takes charge of express matter and attends to its delivery, as the driver of an express truck.

ex·press·way (ik-spres'wā), *n.* a highway for high-speed traffic with divided lanes and overpasses and underpasses at most intersections.

ex·pro·pri·ate (eks-prō'prĭ-āt), *v.t.* -at·ed, -at·ing, to take from a private owner for public use. —**ex·pro·pri·a'tion,** *n.*

ex·pul·sion (ik-spul'shŭn), *n.* forcible ejection. —**ex·pul'sive** (-sĭv), *adj.*

ex·punge (ik-spunj'), *v.t.* -punged', -pung'ing, to blot out; erase; destroy.

ex·pur·gate (eks'pēr-gāt), *v.t.* -gat·ed, -gat·ing, to remove whatever is offensive to good taste or morality from (books, etc.). —**ex·pur·ga'tion,** *n.* —**ex'pur·ga·tor,** *n.*

ex·qui·site (eks'kwi-zit, ik-skwiz'it), *adj.* 1. refined; delicate. 2. highly finished. 3. excellent. 4. felt with great sensitivity. 5. extreme: *n.* a person too obviously refined in taste.

ex·tant (ek'stănt, ik-stant'), *adj.* still existing.

ex·tem·po·ra·ne·ous (ik-stem-pô-rā'nĭ-ŭs), *adj.* unpremeditated; without previous notes or study; offhand. —**ex·tem·po·ra'ne·ous,** *adv.*

ex·tem·po·re (ik-stem'pô-rĭ), *adv. & adj.* without study or premeditation; offhand.

ex·tem·po·rize (-rĭz), *v.i. & v.t.* -rized, -riz·ing, to compose, discourse, do, etc. on the spur of the moment.

ex·tend (ik-stend'), *v.t.* 1. to stretch out. 2. to enlarge. 3. to continue; prolong. 4. to diffuse; disseminate. 5. to force effort from (oneself): *v.i.* 1. to reach to any distance. 2. to be prolonged. —**ex·tend'ed,** *adj.* —**ex·tend'er,** *n.* —**ex·ten'si·ble** (sten'sĭ-bl), **ex·tend'i·ble,** *adj.*

extended care, nursing care in a facility for convalescents, the disabled, etc.

extended family, a group of parents, their children, and various other relatives living in close proximity or together, esp. if three generations are involved.

ex·ten·sion (ik-sten'shŭn), *n.* 1. the act of extending. 2. the state of being extended. 3. the amount of this. 4. a supplemental part; addition. 5. in *Physics,* space regarded as having dimensions.

ex·ten·sive ('sĭv), *adj.* 1. having great extent; wide. 2. comprehensive. —**ex·ten'sive·ly,** *adv.* —**ex·ten'sive·ness,** *n.*

ex·ten·sor (ik-sten'sĕr), *n.* a muscle that extends or straightens a limb.

ex·tent (ik-stent'), *n.* 1. the space or degree to which a thing is extended; size. 2. compass; reach. 3. a large area.

ex·ten·u·ate (ik-sten'yoo-wāt), *v.t.* -at·ed, -at·ing, to offer excuses for; palliate; mitigate. —**ex·ten'u·a·tor,** *n.* —**ex·ten'u·a·to·ry** (-wȧ-tôr-ĭ), *adj.*

ex·te·ri·or (ik-stir'ĭ-ĕr), *adj.* 1. outward; external. 2. acting externally: *n.* that which is outside; outer surface.

ex·ter·mi·nate (ik-stür'mĭ-nāt), *v.t.* -nat·ed, -nat·ing, to destroy utterly; annihilate. —**ex·ter·mi·na'tion,** *n.* —**ex·ter'mi·na·tor,** *n.*

ex·ter·nal (ik-stür'nl), *adj.* 1. outside; exterior. 2. objective. 3. superficial. 4. foreign. 5. acting from the exterior: *n.* 1. an exterior or outward part. 2. *pl.* outward form; superficialities. —**ex·ter'nal·ly,** *adv.*

ex·tinct (ik-stingkt'), *adj.* 1. extinguished; put out. 2. worn out; inactive. 3. no longer existing.

ex·tinc·tion (ik-stingk'shŭn), *n.* 1. the act of putting out. 2. annihilation. 3. the state of being extinct.

ex·tin·guish (ik-sting'gwish), *v.t.* 1. to put out; quench. 2. to put an end to. 3. to eclipse. 3. in *Law,* to void. —**ex·tin'guish·er,** *n.*

ex·tir·pate (ek'stēr-pāt), *v.t.* -pat·ed, -pat·ing, to eradicate. 2. to destroy; exterminate. —**ex·tir·pa'tion,** *n.*

ex·tol, ex·toll (ik-stōl'), *v.t.* -tolled', -tol'ling, to praise highly; laud.

ex·tort (ik-stôrt'), *v.t.* to obtain by threats, violence, or injustice (followed by *from*).

ex·tor·tion (ik-stôr'shŭn), *n.* 1. the act or practice of extorting; oppressive or unjust exaction. 2. that which is extorted. —**ex·tor'tion·ate** (-ĭt), *adj.* —**ex·tor'tion·er,** *n.*

ex·tra (eks'trȧ), *adj.* additional: *n.* 1. something

not included in the usual fee or charge. 2. an edition of a newspaper once issued for some particular reason. 3. an additional aspect. 4. an actor paid daily for a small role: *adv.* in addition to normal.

ex·tra-, a prefix meaning *over and above, beyond, besides.*

ex·tract (ik-strakt'), *v.t.* 1. to draw out of; pull out. 2. to get by distillation, solution, etc. 3. to select from a larger literary work. 4. to conclude or infer: *n.* (eks'trakt), 1. a substance extracted by distillation, solution, etc. 2. an abstract or excerpt from a book; quotation. —**ex·tract'a·ble, ex·tract'i·ble,** *adj.*

ex·trac·tion (ik-strak'shŭn), *n.* 1. the act of extracting. 2. lineage, birth, or descent.

ex·trac·tor ('tēr), *n.* 1. one who or that which extracts. 2. a device for removing cartridges or shells from a breechloader.

ex·tra·cur·ric·u·lar (eks-trä-kŭ-rik'yŭ-lēr), *adj.* outside regular academic studies.

ex·tra·dite (eks'trä-dīt), *v.t.* -dit·ed, -dit·ing, to surrender (a person accused of a crime) to another government under the terms of an agreement. —**ex'tra·dit·a·ble,** *adj.* —**ex·tra·di'tion** (-dish'ŭn), *n.*

ex·tra·dos (eks'trä-dōs), *n.* the exterior curve of an arch.

ex·tra·mu·ral (eks-trä-myoor'ăl), *adj.* outside of the walls, as of a school.

ex·tra·ne·ous (ik-strä'ni-ŭs), *adj.* 1. external; foreign. 2. not essential or relevant. —**ex·tra'ne·ous·ly,** *adv.*

ex·traor·di·nar·y (ik-strôr'dn-er-i), *adj.* 1. out of the usual course. 2. beyond the usual; uncommon; unusual; remarkable.

ex·trap·o·late (ik-strap'ō-lāt), *v.t. & v.i.* -lat·ed, -lat·ing, to infer (unknown information) from the information given. —**ex·trap·o·la'tion,** *n.*

ex·tra·sen·so·ry (eks-trä-sen'sēr-i), *adj.* of or denoting that which is not within the usual area that the senses register.

ex·tra·ter·ri·to·ri·al·i·ty (-ter-i-tōr-i-al'i-ti), *n.* the right possessed by ambassadors to live under the laws of their own country.

ex·trav·a·gant (ik-strav'ă-gănt), *adj.* 1. exceeding reasonable limits. 2. needlessly lavish in expenditure; wasteful; prodigal. —**ex·trav'a·gance,** *n.*

ex·trav·a·gan·za (ik-strav-ă-gǎn'zǎ), *n.* 1. a loosely organized stage or musical piece involving burlesque. 2. a mammoth presentation for the stage.

ex·trav·a·sate (ik-strav'ă-sāt), *v.t.* -sat·ed, -sat·ing, to force out (blood, etc.) from a duct or vessel into tissues: *v.i.* to escape from a blood vessel into the tissues.

ex·treme (ik-strēm'), *adj.* 1. of the highest degree. 2. last; utmost; furthest. 3. most severe or strict. 4. uncompromising, as in beliefs: *n.* 1. the utmost degree of anything. 2. excess. 3. a complete opposite in nature or distance. 4. an expediency. —**ex·treme'ly,** *adv.*

ex·trem·ism ('izm), *n.* the support of extreme views or practice, as in politics. —**ex·trem'ist,** *adj. & n.*

ex·trem·i·ty (ik-strem'ĭ-ti), *n., pl.* -ties, 1. the utmost point or part; end. 2. the utmost degree. 3. utmost violence, vigor, or necessity. 4. *usually pl.* a severe action. 5. *pl.* the limbs.

ex·tri·cate (eks'trĭ-kāt), *v.t.* -cat·ed, -cat·ing, to free from difficulties, complications, or perplexities. —**ex·tri·ca'tion,** *n.*

ex·trin·sic (ek-strin'sik), *adj.* 1. not inherent or essential; foreign. 2. external. —**ex·trin'si·cal·ly,** *adv.*

ex·tro·vert (eks'trō-vŭrt), *n.* in *Psychology,* one whose interests lie mainly in external objects rather than in introspection. —**ex·tro·ver'sion** (-vŭr'zhŭn), *n.*

ex·trude (ik-strōōd'), *v.t. & v.i.* -trud·ed, -trud'ing, to thrust out. —**ex·tru'sion** (-strōō'zhŭn), *n.*

ex·u·ber·ant (ig-zōō'bēr-ănt), *adj.* 1. copious. 2. spirited; uninhibited. —**ex·u'ber·ance,** *n.* —**ex·u'ber·ant·ly,** *adv.*

ex·ude (ig-zōōd'), *v.t. & v.i.* -ud·ed, -ud'ing, 1. to discharge gradually through the pores. 2. to flow out; radiate. —**ex·u·da·tion** (eks-yŭdā'shŭn), *n.*

ex·ult (ig-zult'), *v.i.* to rejoice in triumph; be joyous. —**ex·ult'ant,** *adj.* —**ex·ul·ta·tion** (egzŭl-tā'shŭn, ek-sŭl-), *n.*

ex·ur·bi·a (eks-ŭr'bi-ă), *n.* the outer city areas of a partly rural character that are mainly populated by wealthy persons. —**ex·ur'ban,** *adj.* —**ex·ur'ban·ite,** *n. & adj.*

ex·u·vi·ae (ig-zōō'vi-ē, ik-sōō'vi-ē), *n.pl., sing.* -vi·a (-ă), the castoff skins, shells, etc. of animals.

ex·u·vi·ate ('vi-āt), *v.t. & v.i.* -vi·at·ed, -vi·at·ing, to shed (skins, shells, etc.); molt. —**ex·u·vi·a'tion,** *n.*

eye (ī), *n.* 1. the organ of sight. 2. the eyeball or iris. 3. the part surrounding the eye. 4. *often pl.* sight. 5. a look or expression. 6. observation; regard. 7. mental estimation by looking. 8. that which resembles an eye. 9. a small perforation. 10. a bud. 11. *often pl.* view; opinion: *v.t.* eyed, eye'ing or ey'ing, to watch closely; keep in view.

eye-ball (ī'bôl), *n.* the globe of the eye.

eye-bright ('brīt), *n.* a plant of the figwort family.

eye-brow ('brou), *n.* the hairy arch above the eye.

eye-catch·er ('kach-ēr), *n.* an attention getter. —**eye'-catch·ing,** *adj.*

eye·ful ('fool), *n.* [Slang], someone or something unusual.

eye-glass ('glas), *n.* 1. a corrective lens for the eye. 2. *pl.* two lenses coupled together; glasses.

eye-lash ('lash), *n.* the ridge of hair that edges the eyelid.

eye·let ('lit), *n.* 1. a small hole to receive a lace or cord. 2. a circular metal piece lining this hole. 3. a small hole the edge of which is embroidered.

eye·lid ('lid), *n.* the movable skin which covers over and closes the eye.

eye-o·pen·er ('ō-pen-ēr), *n.* 1. something incredible or surprising, as news. 2. [Slang], an early drink of alcohol.

ŏ in dragon, ōō in crude, oo in wool, u in cup, ū in cure, û in turn, ŭ in focus, oi in boy, ou in house, th in thin, th in sheathe, g in get, j in joy, y in yet.

eye·piece ('pēs), *n.* the lens or lenses in an optical instrument, as a telescope, nearest the user's eye.

eye·sight ('sīt), *n.* 1. the sight of the eye. 2. the range of vision.

eye·sore ('sôr), *n.* anything that offends the sight.

eye·spot ('spot), *n.* 1. a rudimentary visual organ. 2. an eyelike marking.

eye·strain ('strān), *n.* a fatigued condition of the eye muscles.

eye·tooth ('tōōth), *n., pl.* **-teeth,** one of the upper canine teeth in the human jaw.

eye·wit·ness ('wit-nis), *n.* 1. one who has seen something take place. 2. one who testifies to what he has seen.

eyre (er), *n.* a circuit of traveling judges.

ey·rie, ey·ry (er'i, ir'i), *n., pl.* **-ries,** same as **aerie.**

E·zek·i·el (i-zē'ki-ǎl, 'kyèl), *n.* a book of the Bible.

Ez·ra (ez'rǎ), *n.* a book of the Bible.

F

F, f (ef), *n., pl.* **F's, f's,** 1. the sixth letter of the English alphabet. 2. the sound of this letter, as in *father*. 3. a type or impression of *F* or *f*.

F (ef), *adj.* shaped like *F*: *n.* 1. an object shaped like *F*. 2. a school mark or rating signifying failing work, or, sometimes, fair. 3. in *Music, a)* the fourth tone in the scale of C major. *b)* the key having this tone as a basic note.

fa (fä), *n.* the fourth tone in any major or minor musical scale of eight tones.

fa·ba·ceous (fȧ-bā'shŭs), *adj.* pertaining to or belonging to the legume family of plants.

fa·ble (fā'bl), *n.* 1. a short, fictitious narrative intended to convey some moral, especially one whose characters are animals or objects. 2. a legend or myth. 3. a fabrication; falsehood: *v.i. & v.t.* **-bled, -bling,** to invent or tell (fables).

fa·bled ('bld), *adj.* 1. made famous in fables, legends, stories, etc. 2. not true; invented.

fab·ric (fab'rik), *n.* 1. an edifice or building. 2. a framework or structure. 3. a woven, felted, or knitted material.

fab·ri·cate (fab'rĭ-kāt), *v.t.* **-cat·ed, -cat·ing,** 1. to construct; form by manufacture or art. 2. to invent (a story, excuse, etc.) falsely. — **fab·ri·ca'tion,** *n.* **fab'ri·ca·tor,** *n.*

fab·u·list (fab'yoo-list), *n.* 1. a writer of fables. 2. a liar.

fab·u·lous (fab'yoo-lŭs), *adj.* 1. like a fable; fictitious. 2. incredible. 3. [Informal], wonderful. **—fab'u·lous·ly,** *adv.* **—fab'u·lous·ness,** *n.*

fa·cade, fa·çade (fȧ-säd'), *n.* 1. the front of a building. 2. a false appearance.

face (fās), *n.* 1. the countenance; visage. 2. *a)* expression; look. *b)* an expressive grimace. 3. outward appearance. 4. *a)* the front surface of a clock, playing card, etc. *b)* a facet, as of a gem. 5. confidence; dignity; prestige: *v.t.* **faced, fac'ing,** 1. to turn the face toward. 2. to oppose with boldness or confidence. 3. to cover with an additional surface: *v.i.* to turn the face.

face lifting, 1. plastic surgery for removing wrinkles, etc. from the face. 2. a renovation of the front of a building.

fac·er (fās'ẽr), *n.* 1. something that faces. 2. [British Informal], *a)* a hit in the face. *b)* a problem or defeat.

face-sav·ing (sā'ving), *adj.* for the purpose of safeguarding or maintaining self-respect.

fac·et (fas'it), *n.* 1. a small surface or face, as one of the planes into which the surface of a diamond is cut. 2. an aspect or single part: *v.t.* **-et·ed** or **-et·ted, -et·ing** or **-et·ting,** to cut facets on.

fa·ce·ti·ae (fȧ-sē'shĭ-ē), *n.pl.* 1. witty sayings. 2. books characterized by coarse wit.

fa·ce·tious (fȧ-sē'shŭs), *adj.* humorous; jocular. **—fa·ce'tious·ly,** *adv.* **—fa·ce'tious·ness,** *n.*

face value, the value printed or written on a bill, bond, etc.

fa·cial (fā'shǎl), *adj.* of or pertaining to the face: *n.* a beauty treatment of the face, as by massage, the application of lotions, etc. **—fa'cial·ly,** *adv.*

facial angle, the angle formed by the two lines drawn respectively from the nostrils to the ear, and from the nose to the forehead.

fa·ci·es (fā'shĭ-ēz, -sēz), *n., pl.* **fa'ci·es,** 1. the appearance of the face. 2. the general aspect of any group of organisms or of rock.

fac·ile (fas'il), *adj.* 1. easily done. 2. fluent. 3. superficial; hasty. **—fac'ile·ly,** *adv.* **—fac'ile·ness,** *n.*

fa·cil·i·tate (fȧ-sil'ĭ-tāt), *v.t.* **-tat·ed, -tat·ing,** to make easy or less difficult; lessen the labor of. **—fa·cil·i·ta'tion,** *n.* **—fa·cil'i·ta·tive,** *adj.*

fa·cil·i·ty ('ĭ-ti), *n., pl.* **-ties,** 1. freedom from difficulty. 2. dexterity; ease. 3. *pl.* the means by which something can be accomplished. 4. a building or some kind of installation for some activity.

fac·ing (fās'ing), *n.* 1. a lining at the edge of a garment. 2. a covering in front, as for decoration of a building. 3. *pl.* collars, cuffs, etc. of a different color on a military uniform.

fac·sim·i·le (fak-sim'ĭ-lĭ), *n.* (an) exact reproduction, counterpart, or likeness of an original.

fact (fakt), *n.* 1. anything that is done; event. 2. reality; truth. 3. something that may be a reality. 4. an illegal act: now chiefly in *before the fact, after the fact.*

fac·tion (fak'shŭn), *n.* 1. a group working in opposition within a larger group. 2. dissension. **—fac'tion·al,** *adj.* **—fac'tion·al·ism,** *n.*

fac·tious (fak'shŭs), *adj.* given to or characterized by faction.

fac·ti·tious (fak-tish'ŭs), *adj.* artificial; sham.

fac·tor (fak'tẽr), *n.* 1. an agent who transacts business for another. 2. any circumstance, condition, etc. which produces a result. 3. same as gene. 4. in *Mathematics,* one of two or more quantities which, multiplied together, give a product: *v.t.* in *Mathematics,* to resolve into factors.

fac·tor·age (-ij), *n.* a factor's commission.

fac·to·ry (fak'tō-ri), *n., pl.* **-ries,** 1. a place for manufacturing. 2. a trading settlement.

fac·to·tum (fak-tōt'ŭm), *n.* a person who does all kinds of work.

fac·tu·al (fak'choo-wǎl), *adj.* of or pertaining to facts; real.

fac·u·lae (fak'yoo-lē), *n.pl., sing.* **-la** (-lȧ), luminous spots on the sun's surface.

ŏ in drag*o*n, ōō in cr*u*de, oo in w*oo*l, u in c*u*p, ū in c*u*re, ū in t*u*rn, ŭ in f*o*cus, oi in b*oy*, ou in h*ou*se, th in *th*in, *th* in shea*th*e, g in g*e*t, j in *j*oy, y in *y*et.

fac·ul·ta·tive (fak'l-tāt-iv), *adj.* enabling; permissive.

fac·ul·ty (fak'l-ti), *n., pl.* **-ties,** 1. any mental or physical power. 2. skill obtained by practice; ability. 3. the members collectively of any one of the learned professions. 4. the teachers of a department in a school or college or of the school or college as a whole.

fad (fad), *n.* a passing fashion. **—fad'dish,** *adj.*

fad·dist (fad'ist), *n.* one given to fads.

fade (fād), *v.i.* **fad'ed, fad'ing,** 1. to lose color or distinctness. 2. to languish; wither; droop. 3. to die away: *v.t.* to make fade.

fae·ces (fē'siz), *n.* same as feces. **—fae·cal (fē'kăl),** *adj.*

faer·ie, faer·y (fer'i), *n., pl.* **-ies,** same as fairy.

fag (fag), *v.i.* **fagged, fag'ging,** to work hard and grow weary: *v.t.* to tire out or exhaust: *n.* [Slang], a homosexual male.

fag end, 1. the last or end part of anything. 2. the frayed end of a piece of cloth, rope, etc.

fag·ot (fag'ŏt), *n.* 1. a bundle of sticks, twigs, or branches. 2. a pile of scrap iron or steel to be worked into bars: *v.t.* to form into fagots.

fag·ot·ing, fag·ot·ting (-ing), *n.* a method of ornamenting textile fabrics.

Fahr·en·heit (fer'ĕn-hīt), *n.* a thermometer scale having 32° as the freezing point and 212° as the boiling point of water: devised by Gabriel Daniel Fahrenheit (1686-1736), German physicist: *adj.* of or relating to the Fahrenheit scale.

fa·ience (fī-äns'), *n.* a variety of glazed earthenware.

fail (fāl), *v.i.* 1. to fall short; be deficient. 2. to waste away; decline. 3. to cease functioning. 4. to turn out badly. 5. to become bankrupt: *v.t.* 1. to be wanting or insufficient for. 2. to omit. 3. to forsake. 4. in *Education,* to give or receive a failing grade (in).

fail·ing (fāl'ing), *n.* 1. a fault; weakness; imperfection. 2. a failure: *prep.* not having.

faille (fīl, fāl), *n.* a soft rayon or silk fabric with ribbing.

fail-safe (fāl'sāf), *adj.* of or pertaining to a method of forestalling the setting off of nuclear explosives by accident.

fail·ure (fāl'yĕr), *n.* 1. the act of failing. 2. omission. 3. neglect. 4. nonperformance. 5. want of success. 6. a lapse. 7. the act of becoming bankrupt. 8. a person that fails. 9. in *Education,* a mark showing that one has failed.

fain (fān), *adj. & adv.* [Archaic], glad(ly); willing(ly).

faint (fānt), *v.i.* to lose consciousness; swoon: *adj.* 1. feeble; languid. 2. without confidence; shy. 3. spiritless. 4. not clear. 5. swooning: *n.* a sudden and temporary loss of consciousness. **—faint'ly,** *adv.* **—faint'ness,** *n.*

fair (fer), *adj.* 1. beautiful; handsome; pleasing to the eye or mind. 2. free from any dark hue. 3. spotless. 4. not cloudy. 5. clear; legible. 6. just; equitable; honest; impartial. 7. within established procedures. 8. promising; propitious. 9. favorable. 10. above mediocrity. 11. of somewhat large size. 12. legally

hunted. 13. in *Baseball,* within the limits of the base line: *adv.* 1. distinctly. 2. openly; honestly. 3. on good terms. 4. legibly. 5. directly: *n.* 1. a market held at particular times. 2. a charity bazaar. 3. a display of various products along with entertainment. **—fair'ness,** *n.*

fair-haired (fer'herd'), *adj.* 1. characterized by blond hair. 2. [Informal], preferred.

fair·ly (fer'li), *adv.* 1. honorably; openly. 2. to some degree. 3. truly.

fair-trade (fer'trād'), *adj.* of or denoting a contract situation in which the manufacturer sets the price below which the seller may not charge for the product.

fair·y (fer'i), *n., pl.* **fair'ies,** 1. an imaginary being of graceful and diminutive human form, supposed to interfere in human affairs. 2. [Slang], a male homosexual: *adj.* of, pertaining to, or resembling fairies.

fair·y·land (-land), *n.* 1. supposed abode of fairies. 2. an enchanting and pleasant abode.

fairy ring, a circle of mushrooms with grass of a different color than the turf surrounding it.

fairy tale, 1. an account or narration concerning fairies. 2. a lie.

fait ac·com·pli (fe-tä-kŏn-plē'), [French], something already done.

faith (fāth), *n.* 1. belief not based on proof or evidence. 2. belief in God, religious doctrines, etc. 3. a system of religion. 4. complete trust or confidence. 5. fidelity; loyalty.

faith cure, 1. a method of treating illness by prayer, etc. 2. a cure allegedly effected by this method. Also **faith healing.**

faith·ful ('fŭl), *adj.* 1. trustworthy; reliable. 2. honest; conscientious. 3. loyal. **—faith'ful·ly,** *adv.* **—faith'ful·ness,** *n.*

faith·less ('lis), *adj.* disloyal, unreliable, etc. **—faith'less·ly,** *adv.* **—faith'less·ness,** *n.*

fake (fāk), *v.t. & v.i.* **faked, fak'ing,** 1. to make (something) seem genuine or fine by deception. 2. to feign (illness, etc.). 3. to coil (a rope, etc.): *n.* 1. a fraud or hoax; counterfeit. 2. a coil of rope: *adj.* false; not genuine. **—fak'er,** *n.* **—fak'er·y,** *n.*

fa·kir (fā-kir'), *n.* a Hindu or Moslem religious ascetic or wandering beggar.

fal·cate (fal'kāt), *adj.* sickle-shaped.

fal·chion (fôl'chŭn), *n.* a medieval sword having a short, broad, slightly curved blade.

fal·con (fal'kŏn, fôl'-, fô'-), *n.* 1. a hawklike bird with a curved, notched beak. 2. any hawk trained to hunt and kill small game. **—fal'con·er,** *n.*

fal·con·ry (-ri), *n.* 1. the art of training falcons to hunt small game. 2. the sport of hunting with falcons.

fal·de·ral (fŏl'dĕ-rŏl, fal'dĕ-ral), *n.* 1. a trinket. 2. a trifle. 3. mere nonsense.

fald·stool (fôld'stōōl), *n.* 1. a desk at which the litany is read. 2. a bishop's chair for use when he is away from his throne or in a church not his own.

fall (fôl), *v.i.* **fell, fall'en, fall'ing,** 1. to drop from a higher to a lower place. 2. to drop from an erect posture; collapse. 3. to go downward; sink. 4. to perish or be wounded in battle. 5. to decline; become weaker, lower, less, etc. 6. to be degraded or disgraced. 7. to do wrong; sin. 8. to happen. 9. to become the property of. 10. to pass into some condition. 11. to come by chance: *adj.* of or pertaining to the autumn: *n.* 1. the act of falling or descending. 2. the distance anything falls. 3. overthrow or capture. 4. wrongdoing; lapse into sin. 5. autumn. 6. a cascade. 7. something that falls, or the amount of this. 8. a decrease in value, status, etc.

fal·la·cious (fā-lā'shŭs), *adj.* 1. deceptive. 2. containing a fallacy; mistaken.

fal·la·cy (fal'ā-si), *n., pl.* -cies, 1. a deceptive or false notion; mistake. 2. reasoning that is logically unsound; sophism.

fall-fish (fôl'fish), *n., pl.* -fish, -fish·es, a freshwater fish of the carp family, often found near falls in streams of the northeastern U.S.

fal·li·ble (fal'i-bl), *adj.* 1. liable to be deceived or misled. 2. prone to error. **—fal·li·bil'i·ty, fal'li·ble·ness,** *n.* **—fal'li·bly,** *adv.*

fall·ing-out (fôl'ing-out'), *n.* an estrangement or disagreement.

falling star, same as meteor.

Fal·lo·pi·an tube (fā-lō'pi-ăn), either of two tubes that carry ova to the uterus.

fall·out (fôl'out), *n.* 1. the settling to earth of radioactive particles that result from a nuclear explosion. 2. the particles.

fal·low (fal'ō), *v.t.* to leave (land) unplanted after plowing: *adj.* 1. left unplanted or uncultivated. 2. of a pale-yellow or brownish-yellow color. 3. inactive: said of the mind: *n.* land plowed but not seeded.

fallow deer, a small European deer having branched antlers and a yellowish-brown coat with white spots in summer.

false (fôls), *adj.* **fals'er, fals'est,** 1. untrue; wrong. 2. lying; dishonest. 3. not faithful. 4. unreliable. 5. not real; counterfeit. 6. pitched inaccurately, as a musical note: *adv.* in a false manner. **—false'ly,** *adv.* **—false'ness,** *n.*

false·hood ('hood), *n.* 1. a lie. 2. lack or absence of truth or accuracy.

fal·set·to (fôl-set'ō), *n., pl.* -tos, an artificial singing tone higher in key than the natural compass of the voice.

fal·si·fy (fôl'si-fī), *v.t.* -fied, -fy·ing, 1. to make false, especially so as to deceive. 2. to alter (accounts, etc.) fraudulently. 3. to misrepresent. 4. to prove to be false: *v.i.* to lie. **—fal·si·fi·ca'tion,** *n.* **—fal'si·fi·er,** *n.*

fal·si·ty (-ti), *n., pl.* -ties, 1. the quality of being false. 2. a lie.

Fal·staff·i·an (fôl-staf'i-ăn), *adj.* like Sir John Falstaff, a character in Shakespeare's plays; jovial, witty, boastful but cowardly.

fal·ter (fôl'tĕr), *v.t.* to utter haltingly: *v.i.* 1. to hesitate; waver. 2. to move unsteadily; stumble; totter. 3. to speak with hesitation; stammer.

fame (fām), *n.* 1. reputation, especially good reputation. 2. celebrity; renown.

famed (fāmd), *adj.* renowned; celebrated.

fa·mil·ial (fā-mil'yăl), *adj.* of or having to do with a family.

fa·mil·iar (fā-mil'yĕr), *adj.* 1. well acquainted (*with*). 2. friendly; intimate. 3. too friendly; taking liberties. 4. unconstrained; unceremonious: *n.* 1. a close friend. 2. a spirit, often in animal form, supposed to act as a servant, as to a witch. **—fa·mil'iar·ly,** *adv.*

fa·mil·i·ar·i·ty (fā-mil-yer'i-ti), *n., pl.* -ties, 1. intimacy. 2. freedom from ceremony; informality. 3. undue intimacy; behavior that is too bold. 4. close acquaintance (*with* something).

fa·mil·iar·ize ('yă-rīz), *v.t.* -ized, -iz·ing, 1. to bring (something) into common knowledge. 2. to accustom (another or oneself) to something. **—fa·mil·iar·i·za'tion,** *n.*

fam·i·ly (fam'i-li, fam'li), *n., pl.* -lies, 1. a household. 2. parents and their children. 3. a group of people related by blood or marriage. 4. the descendants of a common ancestor; tribe or clan. 5. a group of animals, plants, etc. having common characteristics or coming from the same source.

fam·ine (fam'in), *n.* an extreme and widespread shortage of food.

fam·ish ('ish), *v.t. & v.i.* to suffer or cause to suffer great hunger.

fa·mous (fā'mŭs), *adj.* 1. renowned; noted; celebrated. 2. [Informal], fine; first-rate. **—fa'mous·ly,** *adv.*

fam·u·lus (fam'yoo-lŭs), *n., pl.* -li (-lī), an attendant or assistant of a medieval sorcerer.

fan (fan), *v.t. & v.i.* **fanned, fan'ning,** 1. to agitate or cool (the air) as with a fan. 2. to cause air to blow upon, as with a fan. 3. to winnow (grain). 4. to stir up to activity. 5. to strike out in baseball: *n.* 1. originally, an implement for winnowing grain. 2. any device used to agitate the air in order to ventilate or cool, as *a*) a folding device of paper, cloth, feathers, etc. that opens to the shape of a semicircle. *b*) an electric device with vanes that revolve around a hub.

fan (fan), *n.* [Informal], one who is enthusiastic about a particular sport, performer, form of entertainment, etc.

fa·nat·ic (fā-nat'ik), *n.* one who is overly zealous or excessively enthusiastic: *adj.* characterized by excessive enthusiasm or zeal: also **fa·nat'i·cal. —fa·nat'i·cal·ly,** *adv.* **—fa·nat'i·cism,** *n.*

fan·cied (fan'sid), *adj.* imaginary.

fan·ci·er (fan'si-ĕr), *n.* one who has a special interest, as in plant or animal breeding.

fan·ci·ful (fan'si-fŭl), *adj.* 1. indulging in fancies; imaginative. 2. unreal; imaginary. **—fan'ci·ful·ly,** *adv.*

fan·cy (fan'si), *v.t.* -cied, -cy·ing, 1. to imagine. 2. to like. 3. to suppose: *adj.* -ci·er, -ci·est, 1. ornamental; elegant. 2. fanciful. 3. of exceptional quality or skill: *n., pl.* -cies, 1. creative or whimsical imagination. 2. a notion; whim. 3. a liking or fondness. 4. a mental image. **—fan'ci·ly,** *adv.* **—fan'ci·ness,** *n.*

fan·cy-free (-frē), *adj.* 1. not engaged or married. 2. carefree.

fan·cy·work (-wûrk), *n.* ornamental needlework.

ŏ in dragon, ōō in crude, oo in wool, u in cup, ū in cure, ŭ in turn, ŭ in focus, oi in boy, ou in house, th in thin, th in sheathe, g in get, j in joy, y in yet.

fan-dan-go (fan-dang′gō), *n.*, *pl.* -gos, a lively Spanish dance or music for this.

fane (fān), *n.* [Archaic or Poetic], a temple or church.

fan-fare (fan′fer), *n.* 1. a loud flourish of trumpets. 2. a noisy or ostentatious display.

fan-fa-ron-ade (fan-fēr-ŏ-nād′), *n.* blustering talk or swaggering.

fang (fang), *n.* 1. a long, hollow, pointed tooth through which a poisonous snake injects its venom. 2. one of the long, pointed teeth of carnivorous animals; canine tooth. —**fanged,** *adj.*

fan-light (fan′līt), *n.* a semicircular window over a door.

fan-tail (fan′tāl), *n.* 1. a variety of pigeon. 2. the stern part of the main deck of a ship.

fan-tan (fan′tan), *n.* a Chinese gambling game.

fan-ta-sia (fan-tā′zhà), *n.* 1. a musical composition fanciful in form. 2. a medley of familiar tunes.

fan-ta-size (fan′tà-sīz), *v.t.* & *v.i.* -sized, -siz-ing, to conceive fantasies; daydream.

fan-tas-tic (fan-tas′tik), *adj.* 1. odd; grotesque. 2. unreal; imaginary. 3. incredible. —**fan-tas′ti-cal-ly,** *adv.*

fan-ta-sy (fan′tà-si), *n.*, *pl.* -sies, 1. a fancied image; illusion. 2. imagination. 3. a reverie; spell of daydreaming. 4. an imaginative literary creation.

fan-tods (fan′todz), *n.* a highly nervous condition or state.

far (fär), *adj.* **far′ther, far′thest,** 1. distant in time or space; remote. 2. more distant: *adv.* 1. to or from a great distance. 2. very much. 3. to a certain point or degree: *n.* a distant place.

far-ad (fer′ad, ′ăd), *n.* a unit of electric capacity.

far-an-dole (fer′ăn-dōl), *n.* a lively dance of southern France in which many dancers join hands to form a chain.

far-a-way (fär′à-wā), *adj.* 1. distant; remote. 2. abstracted; dreamy.

farce (färs), *n.* 1. a comedy in which qualities and actions are much exaggerated. 2. broad humor. 3. a ridiculous display or pretense.

far-ci-cal (fär′si-kl), *adj.* of, or having the nature of, a farce; ludicrous; absurd. —**far′ci-cal-ly,** *adv.*

far-cy (fär′si), *n.* a disease of horses that is a form of glanders.

fare (fer), *v.i.* **fared, far′ing,** 1. to be in any state, good or ill. 2. to result; happen. 3. to eat: *n.* 1. the charge for transportation. 2. a passenger paying a fare. 3. food; diet.

fare-well (fer′wel′), *n.* good wishes at parting: *interj.* goodbye: *adj.* final; parting.

far-fetched (fär′fecht′), *adj.* 1. strained. 2. not likely.

fa-ri-na (fà-rē′nà), *n.* flour or meal obtained by grinding cereal grains, potatoes, etc., eaten as a cooked cereal.

far-i-na-ceous (fer-i-nā′shŭs), *adj.* 1. consisting of or made from farina. 2. like meal.

far-i-nose (fer′i-nōs), *adj.* 1. producing farina. 2. mealy. 3. covered with a mealy powder.

farm (färm), *n.* 1. a piece of land with a house, barns, etc., on which crops or domestic animals are raised; originally, land like this rented to a tenant: *v.t.* 1. to cultivate (land). 2. to assign to another for a fee: *v.i.* to carry on the operations of farming.

farm-er (′ēr), *n.* one who manages or cultivates the land on a farm.

farm-hand (′hand), *n.* a hired worker on a farm.

farm-house (′hous), *n.* a house on a farm.

farm-ing (′ing), *n.* the business or work of operating a farm; agriculture.

far-o (fer′ō), *n.* a gambling game played with cards.

far-out (fär′out′), *adj.* [Informal], very advanced or extreme; avant-garde.

far-ra-go (fà-rā′gō), *n.*, *pl.* -goes, a medley; hodgepodge; jumble.

far-reach-ing (fär′rēch′ing), *adj.* having a widespread effect or influence.

far-ri-er (fer′i-ēr), *n.* [British], a blacksmith. —**far′ri-er-y,** *n.*, *pl.* -er-ies.

far-row (fer′ō), *v.t.* & *v.i.* to give birth (to a litter of pigs): *n.* a litter of pigs.

far-sight-ed (fär′sīt′id), *adj.* 1. seeing distant objects more clearly than those that are close. 2. able to plan or foresee the future well: also **far′see′ing.**

far-ther (fär′thēr), comparative of **far:** *adj.* 1. more distant or remote. 2. additional: *adv.* 1. at or to a greater distance or degree. 2. in addition.

far-thest (′thist), superlative of **far:** *adj.* most distant: *adv.* at or to the greatest distance or degree.

far-thing (fär′thing), *n.* a former British coin, equal to one fourth of a penny.

far-thin-gale (fär′thing-gāl), *n.* a kind of hoop skirt worn by women in the 16th and 17th centuries.

fas-ces (fas′ēz), *n.pl.* a bundle of rods containing an ax with projecting blade, carried before the ancient Roman magistrates as a symbol of authority: later the symbol of Italian fascism.

fas-ci-a (fash′i-à), *n.*, *pl.* -ci-ae (-ē), -ci-as, 1. a flat strip or band; fillet. 2. a layer of connective tissue binding or supporting the muscles or internal organs of the body. —**fas′ci-al,** *adj.*

fas-ci-nate (fas′i-nāt), *v.t.* -nat-ed, -nat-ing, 1. originally, to bewitch. 2. to transfix, as though with terror. 3. to captivate; charm. —**fas-ci-na′tion,** *n.*

fas-cine (fa-sēn′), *n.* a bundle of sticks bound together, formerly used to strengthen the sides of ramparts, etc.

fas-cism (fash′izm), *n.* 1. [F-], the doctrines of a political organization of Italy (*Fascisti*), in power 1922-43. 2. [sometimes F-], a system of government based on these doctrines, characterized by strong nationalist, racist, and military policies, and by dictatorship, regulation of news, suppression of opposition, and centralized governmental control over industry. 3. fascist behavior.

fas-cist (′ist), *n.* one who advocates or practices fascism: *adj.* of, advocating, or practicing fascism. —**fa-scis′ti-cal-ly,** *adv.*

fash-ion (fash′ŭn), *n.* 1. the shape or form of anything. 2. manner; way. 3. the current custom, mode, or style, especially in dress: *v.t.* 1. to form; shape. 2. to adapt; fit.

fash·ion·a·ble (-å-bl), *adj.* 1. conforming to the fashion of the day; stylish. 2. of or used by fashionable people. —**fash'ion·a·bly,** *adv.*

fashion plate, 1. a picture showing a new fashion in clothes. 2. a person who is fashionably dressed.

fast (fast), *adj.* 1. quick; speedy in motion. 2. ahead of time, as a timepiece. 3. firm; immovable. 4. faithful. 5. nonfading, as some colors. 6. wild, dissipated, or promiscuous: *adv.* 1. rapidly. 2. firmly. 3. soundly.

fast (fast), *v.i.* to abstain from all or certain foods: *n.* 1. abstinence from food. 2. a day or period of fasting.

fast day, a day set aside for fasting, especially as a religious observance.

fas·ten (fas'n), *v.t.* 1. to join; attach. 2. to fix securely, as with a lock, bolt, button, etc. 3. to direct (the gaze, attention, etc. *on*): *v.i.* to become fastened. —**fas'ten·er,** *n.*

fas·ten·ing (-ing), *n.* something that is used to fasten, as a lock, hook, clasp, zipper, etc.

fast-food (fast'fōōd'), *adj.* denoting a business that sells food which is prepared and served quickly.

fas·tid·i·ous (fas-tid'i-ŭs), *adj.* 1. squeamish; oversensitive. 2. hard to please. —**fas·tid'i·ous·ly,** *adv.* —**fas·tid'i·ous·ness,** *n.*

fat (fat), *adj.* fat'ter, fat'test, 1. full of fat; oily or greasy. 2. fleshy; chubby. 3. too fleshy; corpulent; obese. 4. broad; thick. 5. fertile, as land. 6. lucrative. 7. ample: *n.* 1. a solid or semisolid oily substance forming part of the tissue of animals and plant seeds. 2. the best or richest part of anything. 3. excess. —**fat'ly,** *adv.* —**fat'ness,** *n.*

fa·tal (fāt'l), *adj.* 1. causing death or destruction. 2. fateful. —**fa'tal·ly,** *adv.*

fa·tal·ism (-izm), *n.* 1. the doctrine that all things happen by fate and are hence inevitable. 2. acceptance of fate. —**fa'tal·ist,** *n.* —**fa·tal·is'tic,** *adj.* —**fa·tal·is'ti·cal·ly,** *adv.*

fa·tal·i·ty (fā-tal'i-ti, fā-), *n., pl.* -ties, 1. a fatal quality; deadly effect. 2. a death resulting from a calamity or accident.

fa·ta mor·ga·na (fät'å môr-gän'ä), a mirage sometimes seen off the coast of Sicily.

fat·back (fat'bak), *n.* fat from the back of a hog, cured by salting.

fate (fāt), *n.* 1. destiny; inevitable necessity. 2. one's predestined lot. 3. ultimate outcome. 4. death or destruction. 5. *pl.* [F-], the three mythological goddesses who preside over the destinies of mankind.

fat·ed (fāt'id), *adj.* 1. destined; decreed by fate. 2. doomed.

fate·ful (-fŭl), *adj.* 1. prophetic or ominous. 2. determining what is to be; significant. 3. controlled by destiny. 4. fatal. —**fate'ful·ly,** *adv.*

fa·ther (fä'thēr), *n.* 1. a male parent or ancestor. 2. [F-], God. 3. one who stands in the relation of a father. 4. an originator, founder, or inventor. 5. a Christian priest: used especially as a title. 6. an ancient Roman senator. 7. *pl.* the leaders of a city, community, etc.: *v.t.* 1. to beget. 2. to care

for or take responsibility for. —**fa'ther·hood,** *n.* —**fa'ther·less,** *adj.*

fa·ther-in-law (-in-lô), *n., pl.* **fa'thers-in-law,** the father of one's husband or wife.

fa·ther·land (-land), *n.* one's native country.

fa·ther·ly (-li), *adj.* 1. befitting a father. 2. like a father; kindly and protective. —**fa'ther·li·ness,** *n.*

Father Time, time personified as an elderly man with a long beard and carrying a scythe.

fath·om (fath'ŏm), *n.* a nautical measure of length or depth equal to six feet: *v.t.* 1. to measure the depth of. 2. to understand. —**fath'om·a·ble,** *adj.* —**fath'om·less,** *adj.*

fa·tigue (fā-tēg'), *n.* 1. weariness; bodily or mental exhaustion. 2. *pl.* work clothes worn by soldiers: *v.t. & v.i.* -tigued', -tigu'ing, to make or become weary; tire. —**fat·i·ga·bil·i·ty** (fat·i-gā-bil'i-ti), *n.* —**fat'i·ga·ble,** *adj.*

fat·ling (fat'ling), *n.* a young animal fattened for slaughter.

fat·ten (*n), *v.t. & v.i.* 1. to make or become fat, as by feeding. 2. to become or cause to become fertile, as land. 3. to make or become richer, etc. —**fat'ten·er,** *n.*

fat·ty ('i), *adj.* -ti·er, -ti·est, containing or resembling fat; oily or greasy: *n., pl.* -ties, [Informal], a fat person. —**fat'ti·ness,** *n.*

fatty acid, any of several saturated or unsaturated organic acids occurring naturally in animal and vegetable fats and oils.

fat·u·ous (fach'oo-wŭs), *adj.* smugly foolish or stupid; inane. —**fa·tu·i·ty** (fā-tōō'i-ti), *n., pl.* -ties. —**fat'u·ous·ly,** *adv.*

fau·bourg (fō'boorg), *n.* [French], a suburb.

fau·ces (fō'sēz), *n.* the upper part of the throat, leading into the pharynx.

fau·cet (fô'sit), *n.* a device with a valve, used for drawing off liquid from a pipe.

faugh (fô), *interj.* an exclamation of disgust.

fault (fôlt), *n.* 1. a misdeed; transgression. 2. a blemish or defect. 3. blame or responsibility for something wrong. 4. a fracture of rock strata. 5. a defect in an electric circuit that prevents the correct flow of current. 6. an error in service in tennis, squash, etc.: *v.t.* to find fault with.

fault·find·er (-'fin-dēr), *n.* one given to finding fault; constant complainer. —**fault'find·ing,** *n. & adj.*

fault·less (-'lis), *adj.* without fault; perfect. —**fault'less·ly,** *adv.* —**fault'less·ness,** *n.*

fault·y ('i), *adj.* fault'i·er, fault'i·est, imperfect, defective, or erroneous. —**fault'i·ly,** *adv.* —**fault'i·ness,** *n.*

faun (fôn), *n.* a mythological Roman deity represented as part man and part goat.

fau·na (fô'nâ), *n., pl.* -nas, -nae ('nē), the animals of a particular region or time.

Faust (foust), *n.* in medieval legends, a man who sells his soul to the devil in exchange for knowledge and power: also **Faus·tus** (fôs'tŭs, fous'-). —**Faust'i·an,** *adj.*

fau·teuil (fō-tü'yē), *n.* [French], an upholstered armchair.

faux pas (fō' pä'), *pl.* **faux pas** (fō' päz'), a social blunder; tactless behavior.

fa·vo·ni·an (fā-vō'ni-ân), *adj.* 1. of or pertain-

ŏ in dragon, ōō in crude, oo in wool, u in cup, ū in cure, û in turn, ŭ in focus, oi in boy, ou in house, th in thin, th in sheathe, g in get, j in joy, y in yet.

ing to the west wind. 2. like the west wind; gentle and mild.

fa·vor (fā'vĕr), *n.* 1. kind regard; good will. 2. support; partiality. 3. a kind act. 4. a small gift or token: *v.t.* 1. to regard with favor. 2. to advocate. 3. to aid or support. 4. to be partial to. 5. to resemble. 6. to spare.

fa·vor·a·ble (-ā-bl), *adj.* 1. advantageous. 2. approving. 3. winning favor; pleasing. —**fa'vor·a·bly,** *adv.*

fa·vored (fā'vĕrd), *adj.* 1. having certain features, as *ill-favored.* 2. treated with partiality. 3. talented.

fa·vor·ite (fā'vĕr-it), *n.* 1. a person or thing that is particularly esteemed. 2. one treated with undue preference. 3. one considered to have the best chance of winning in a contest: *adj.* preferred; esteemed.

fa·vor·it·ism (-izm), *n.* an unfair favoring of one over another; partiality; bias.

fa·vour (fā'vĕr), *n. & v.t.* British form for favor.

fa·vus (fā'vŭs), *n.* an infectious disease of the scalp, caused by a fungus.

fawn (fôn), *n.* 1. a young deer. 2. a light yellowish brown: *adj.* a light yellowish-brown: *v.i.* 1. to exhibit affection by licking hands, wagging the tail, etc.: said of a dog. 2. to act servilely; flatter and cringe. —**fawn'er,** *n.*

fay (fā), *n.* a fairy: *v.t. & v.i.* to fit (timbers) closely or exactly together.

faze (fāz), *v.t.* fazed, faz'ing, [Informal], to bother; disturb.

fe·al·ty (fē'ăl-ti), *n., pl.* -ties, the duty of a vassal or tenant to his feudal superior; loyalty; fidelity.

fear (fir), *n.* 1. dread or anxiety caused by impending pain, danger, etc. or the possibility of these. 2. reverence; awe. 3. apprehension. 4. a cause of fear: *v.t. & v.i.* 1. to be afraid (of). 2. to be apprehensive (of). —**fear'less,** *adj.* —**fear'less·ly,** *adv.*

fear·ful ('fŭl), *adj.* 1. afraid. 2. causing fear. 3. showing fear. 4. [Informal], very bad. —**fear'ful·ly,** *adv.* —**fear'ful·ness,** *n.*

fear·some ('sŏm), *adj.* 1. causing fear; dreadful. 2. frightened; timid. —**fear'some·ly,** *adv.* —**fear'some·ness,** *n.*

fea·si·ble (fē'zi-bl), *adj.* 1. capable of being done; practicable. 2. probable. 3. suitable. —**fea·si·bil'i·ty,** *n.*

feast (fēst), *n.* 1. a sumptuous meal. 2. a religious festival: *v.t.* 1. to entertain sumptuously. 2. to delight: *v.i.* to have a feast. —**feast'er,** *n.*

feat (fēt), *n.* a notable achievement, deed, or performance.

feath·er (feth'ĕr), *n.* 1. one of the light, soft growths that cover the body of a bird; plume. 2. *pl. a)* plumage. *b)* clothes. 3. something resembling a feather. 4. kind or class: *v.t.* 1. to ornament or cover with feathers. 2. to turn (an oar or propeller blade) so that the edge is foremost. —**feath'er·less,** *adj.* —**feath'er·y,** *adj.*

feath·er·bed·ding (-bed'ing), *n.* the practice of requiring employment of extra workers in order to prevent unemployment.

feath·er·brained (-brānd), *adj.* foolish; frivolous.

feath·er·weight (-wāt), *n.* a boxer, wrestler, etc. between a bantamweight and a lightweight.

fea·ture (fē'chĕr), *n.* 1. *pl.* the form or appearance of the face. 2. any of the parts of the face; lineament. 3. a leading point or characteristic. 4. a special attraction, newspaper article, etc. 5. the main motion picture presented on a program: *v.t. & v.t.* -tured, -tur·ing, to make or be a feature of.

feb·ri·fuge (feb'ri-fūj), *n.* a medicine that lessens or dispels fever.

fe·brile (fē'bril, feb'ril), *adj.* feverish.

Feb·ru·ar·y (feb'rū-wer-i, -yoo-), *n.* the second and shortest month of the year, having 28 days in a regular year and 29 days in a leap year.

fe·ces (fē'sēz), *n.* excrement. —**fe'cal** ('kăl), *adj.*

feck·less (fek'lis), *adj.* 1. feeble; ineffective. 2. shiftless. —**feck'less·ly,** *adv.*

fec·u·lence (fek'yoo-lĕns), *n.* 1. muddiness, contamination, filthiness, etc. 2. dregs or sediment. 3. filth. 4. feces. —**fec'u·lent,** *adj.*

fe·cund (fē'kŭnd, fek'ŭnd), *adj.* fruitful; prolific. —**fe·cun·di·ty** (fi-kun'di-ti), *n.*

fe·cun·date (fē'kŭn-dāt, fek'ŭn-), *v.t.* -dat·ed, -dat·ing, to make fruitful or prolific; fertilize; impregnate. —**fe·cun·da'tion,** *n.*

fed (fed), past tense and past participle of feed.

fed·er·al (fed'ĕr-ăl, fed'răl), *adj.* 1. pertaining to or consisting of a union of states, etc. under a central government that regulates certain common affairs, while each state remains in control of its own internal affairs. 2. of or pertaining to a central government like this; specifically, [usually F-], the central government of the U.S. 3. [F-], of or supporting an early U.S. political party (**Federalist Party**) that advocated a strong central government. 4. [F-], of or supporting the cause of the Union in the Civil War: *n.* [F-], a supporter of the Union during the Civil War, especially a soldier in the Union army. —**fed'er·al·ism,** *n.* —**fed'er·al·ly,** *adv.*

fed·er·al·ist (-ist), *n.* 1. one who believes in federalism. 2. [F-], a member or supporter of the Federalist Party: *adj.* 1. of or supporting federalism. 2. [F-], of or supporting the Federalist Party.

fed·er·al·ize (-ā-līz), *v.t.* -ized, -iz·ing, 1. to bring together in a federal union. 2. to put under the authority of a federal government. —**fed·er·al·i·za'tion,** *n.*

Federal Land Bank, any of twelve regional banks established in 1916 to enable farmers to get long-term mortgage loans.

Federal Reserve System, a centralized banking system in the U.S., consisting of twelve banks (**Federal Reserve Banks**) in various districts, and about 6,000 member banks: it was established in 1913 to provide a fluctuating currency to meet business demands.

fed·er·ate (fed'ĕr-it), *adj.* united by common agreement under a centralized government: *v.i. & v.i.* ('ĕ-rāt), -at·ed, -at·ing, to unite in a federation.

fed·er·a·tion (fed-ĕ-rā'shŭn), *n.* 1. a union of states, etc. under a central, federal government. 2. a federated government, organization, etc.

---

a in cap, ā in cane, ä in father, à in abet, e in met ē in be, ē in baker, ĕ in regent, ĭ in pit, ī in fine, ĭ in manifest, o in hot, ô in horse, ō in bone,

fed·er·a·tive (fed'ĕ-rāt-iv), *adj.* forming a league or federation. —**fed'er·a·tive·ly,** *adv.*

fe·do·ra (fĕ-dôr'ȧ), *n.* a soft felt hat with a somewhat curved brim, worn by men.

fee (fē), *n.* 1. a charge or payment for services, especially professional services. 2. a charge for admission, tuition, a license, etc. 3. in *Law,* an inheritance in land.

fee·ble (fē'bl), *adj.* **-bler, -blest,** 1. weak; lacking in vigor; infirm. 2. having little force. —**fee'ble·ness,** *n.* —**fee'bly,** *adv.*

fee·ble-mind·ed (-mīn'did), *adj.* mentally retarded.

feed (fēd), *v.t.* **fed, feed'ing,** 1. to give food to. 2. to provide with something necessary; sustain. 3. to provide (material) to be used. 4. to satisfy: *v.i.* to eat: said especially of animals: *n.* 1. food for animals; fodder. 2. an amount of fodder given at one time. 3. material fed into a machine. 4. the part of a machine feeding this material. 5. [Informal], a meal.

feed·back ('bak), *n.* 1. the transfer of part of the output back into the input, as of electricity. 2. the manner in which a process may be modified, corrected, etc. by its own results during a continuing operation.

feed·er ('ēr), *n.* 1. a person or thing that feeds. 2. an animal being fattened for market. 3. a tributary or branch, especially a branch transportation line (feeder line). 4. an electric wire supplying current to a main conductor.

feel (fēl), *v.t.* **felt, feel'ing,** 1. to perceive through physical sensation. 2. to be conscious of. 3. to understand or believe. 4. to be affected by; experience. 5. to examine by touching or handling: *v.i.* 1. to seem to the touch. 2. to be moved emotionally. 3. to grope: *n.* 1. the act of feeling. 2. the sense of touch. 3. the quality of something perceived by feeling.

feel·er ('ēr), *n.* 1. an organ of touch in an animal or insect, as an antenna. 2. a subtle proposal or remark made to find out opinions or information.

feel·ing ('ing), *adj.* sensitive; sympathetic: *n.* 1. the sense of touch. 2. an awareness; sensation. 3. *pl.* sensibilities. 4. an emotion or sentiment.

fee simple, absolute ownership of land, with no restrictions.

feet (fēt), *n.* plural of foot.

fee tail, ownership of land with inheritance restricted to a given class of heirs.

feh (fā), *n.* a variant of peh, the 17th letter of the Hebrew alphabet.

feign (fān), *v.t.* & *v.i.* 1. to fabricate (a story, excuse, etc.). 2. to pretend.

feigned (fānd), *adj.* pretended; sham.

feint (fānt), *n.* a mock attack intended to distract an opponent from the real point of attack: *v.i.* & *v.t.* to direct (a mock attack) toward someone.

feld·spar (feld'spär), *n.* any of several crystalline minerals, usually glassy and hard, occurring in igneous rocks and composed principally of silicate of alumina.

fe·lic·i·tate (fĕ-lis'ĭ-tāt), *v.t.* **-tat·ed, -tat·ing,** to congratulate. —**fe·lic·i·ta'tion,** *n.*

fe·lic·i·tous (-tŭs), *adj.* suitable; apt; appropriate. —**fe·lic'i·tous·ly,** *adv.*

fe·lic·i·ty (-ti), *n., pl.* **-ties,** 1. great happiness; bliss. 2. something that causes happiness. 3. an apt or well-chosen expression in writing, etc.

fe·line (fē'līn), *adj.* 1. of or pertaining to a cat or the cat family. 2. catlike. 3. sly; treacherous. 4. sleek; graceful: *n.* any animal of the cat family.

fell (fel), past tense of fall: *v.t.* 1. to hew, cut, or knock down. 2. to turn down (a seam): *adj.* cruel; savage; fierce: *n.* 1. the skin of an animal. 2. a felled seam. 3. a rocky or barren hill.

fel·lah (fel'ȧ), *n.* a peasant or farm laborer in Egypt or other Arabic countries.

fel·low (fel'ō), *n.* 1. a companion or associate. 2. one of the same kind or rank; equal. 3. mate; one of a pair. 4. a graduate member of a college who holds a fellowship. 5. a member of a learned society. 6. [Informal], a man or boy: *adj.* associated; doing the same work, etc.

fel·low·ship (-ship), *n.* 1. companionship; close association. 2. an association of people having the same interests. 3. a college endowment for the support of a student doing advanced study.

fellow traveler, one who advocates the cause of a party, especially the Communist Party, without being a member.

fel·ly (fel'i), *n., pl.* **-lies,** one of the curved pieces that form the rim of a wheel; the rim: also **fel'loe** ('ō).

fe·lo-de-se (fel'ō-dē-sā'), *n.* in *Law,* suicide.

fel·on (fel'ŏn), *n.* 1. one guilty of a felony; criminal. 2. a painful infection near a fingernail or toenail; whitlow: *adj.* [Poetic], evil; wicked.

fel·o·ny (fel'ō-ni), *n., pl.* **-nies,** a major crime, punishable by death or imprisonment in a penitentiary. —**fe·lo·ni·ous** (fĕ-lō'ni-ŭs), *adj.*

fel·site (fel'sīt), *n.* a fine-grained igneous rock consisting of feldspar and quartz.

fel·spar (fel'spär), *n.* same as feldspar.

felt (felt), *n.* an unwoven fabric of wool or wool and hair, compacted together by pressure or heat: *adj.* made of felt: *v.t.* to make into felt; mat.

felt (felt), past tense and past participle of feel.

felt·ing ('ing), *n.* the material of which felt is made, or the process of making it.

fe·luc·ca (fĕ-lŭk'ȧ, -lōō'kȧ), *n.* a small ship propelled by lateen sails and oars, used in the Mediterranean.

fe·male (fē'māl), *n.* 1. a member of the sex that conceives and produces young. 2. the plant or flower that bears the pistil and receives the pollen of the male flower. 3. something having a hollow part, as a pipe fitting, into which a corresponding part is inserted: *adj.* 1. of or pertaining to a female person, animal, plant, etc. 2. like or suited to a woman or girl; feminine.

feme covert (fem kuv'ẽrt), a married woman.

feme sole, an unmarried woman.

---

fem·i·nine (fem'ĭ-nĭn), *adj.* 1. of or pertaining to women or girls. 2. characteristic of women; delicate, gentle, etc. 3. effeminate. 4. in *Grammar*, denoting the gender of words referring to females or to things originally thought of as female. —**fem·i·nin'i·ty,** *n.*

fem·i·nism (-nĭzm), *n.* 1. the belief that women should have the same legal, economic, political, and social rights as men. 2. the movement to achieve these rights for women. —**fem'i·nist,** *n. & adj.*

femme (fem), *n.* [Slang], a woman or wife.

femme de cham·bre (fäm dĕ shän'br), [French], a chambermaid.

femme fa·tale (fä-täl'), *pl.* **femmes fa·tales** (fäm fä-täl'), [French], an irresistible woman who leads men to ruin; siren.

fe·mur (fē'mẽr), *n., pl.* **fe'murs; fem·o·ra** (fem'-ẽr-å), the thighbone. —**fem'o·ral,** *adj.*

fen (fen), *n.* low, flat, marshy land; bog; swamp.

fence (fens), *v.i.* **fenced, fenc'ing,** 1. to practice the art of fencing. 2. to be evasive (*with*). 3. to buy or sell stolen property: *v.t.* 1. to enclose or surround with a fence. 2. to keep (*out*) with a fence: *n.* 1. the art of fencing. 2. a boundary or barrier of posts, wire mesh, etc., used to protect or enclose. 3. one who deals in stolen goods. —**fenc'er,** *n.*

fenc·ing ('ing), *n.* 1. the art of skillfully using a foil, saber, etc. for attack or defense. 2. material used for constructing fences. 3. a system of fences.

fend (fend), *v.i.* to resist: *v.t.* to repel (followed by *off*).

fend·er (ẽr), *n.* 1. the part of the body of a motor vehicle over a wheel. 2. a cushion of rope or wood hung over a ship's side to prevent injury in docking. 3. a metal guard in front of a fireplace.

fen·es·tra·tion (fen-ĕ-strā'shŭn), *n.* 1. the arrangement of doors and windows in a building. 2. a surgical operation of making an opening between the middle and inner ear.

Fe·ni·an (fē'nĭ-ăn), *n.* one of a secret Irish revolutionary brotherhood formed in New York (1858) to free Ireland from English rule: *adj.* of the Fenians.

fen·nec (fen'ek), *n.* a small desert fox of Arabia and northern Africa.

fen·nel (fen'l), *n.* an aromatic biennial herb of the parsley family, with yellow flowers, and seeds used in cooking.

fe·rae na·tu·rae (fir'ē nå-toor'ē), [Latin], in *Law*, wild animals as distinguished from those that are domesticated.

fe·ral (fir'ăl), *adj.* 1. wild; undomesticated. 2. savage; ferocious.

fer·de·lance (fer-dĕ-läns'), *n.* a large, poisonous pit viper of tropical America.

fe·ri·al (fir'ĭ-ăl), *adj.* 1. pertaining to week days, especially those not designated as festivals or fast days. 2. in ancient Rome, pertaining to holidays.

fer·ment (fũr'ment), *n.* 1. an organism or substance producing fermentation. 2. tumult; agitation: *v.t.* (fẽr-ment'), 1. to produce fermentation in. 2. to excite: *v.i.* 1. to be in the process of fermentation. 2. to be excited or agitated.

fer·men·ta·tion (fũr-mĕn-tā'shŭn, -men-), *n.* 1. the chemical decomposition in organic compounds exposed to a ferment, as bacteria, yeast, enzymes, etc. 2. excitement.

fer·ment·a·tive (fẽr-men'tā-tĭv), *adj.* causing or characteristic of fermentation.

fer·mi·um (fer'mi-ŭm), *n.* a radioactive chemical element produced by neutron irradiation of plutonium.

fern (fũrn), *n.* any of a large group of flowerless green plants having feathery fronds and reproducing by spores. —**fern'y,** *adj.*

fern·er·y (fũr'nẽr-ĭ), *n., pl.* **-er·ies,** a place where ferns are cultivated.

fe·ro·cious (fê-rō'shŭs), *adj.* 1. savage; fierce. 2. extreme; intense. —**fe·ro'cious·ly,** *adv.* —**fe·roc·i·ty** (fê-ros'ĭ-tĭ), *n.*

fer·rate (fer'āt), *n.* a salt of ferric acid.

fer·re·ous (fer'ĭ-ŭs), *adj.* pertaining to, like, or made of iron.

fer·ret (fer'ĭt), *n.* a small, weasellike animal, trained to hunt rats, rabbits, etc.: *v.t.* 1. to drive out of hiding with a ferret. 2. to search (*out*). —**fer'ret·er,** *n.*

fer·ri·age (fer'ĭ-ĭj), *n.* 1. transportation by ferry. 2. the fare for this.

fer·ric (fer'ĭk), *adj.* of, pertaining to, containing, or obtained from iron.

ferric oxide, a reddish oxide of iron, occurring naturally as hematite or rust.

Fer·ris wheel (fer'ĭs), a large, upright wheel with suspended seats, used as an amusement ride.

fer·ro-, a combining form meaning *iron, containing iron, iron and.*

fer·ro·chro·mi·um (fer-ō-krō'mĭ-ŭm), *n.* an alloy of iron and chromium: also **fer'ro-chrome.**

fer·ro·cy·an·ic (-sī-an'ĭk), *adj.* of or pertaining to an acid formed by the interaction of iron and cyanogen.

fer·ro·cy·a·nide (-sī'å-nĭd), *n.* a salt of ferrocyanic acid.

fer·ro·man·ga·nese (-mang'gå-nēs, -nēz), *n.* an alloy of iron and manganese, used in making hard steel.

fer·ro·type (fer'ō-tīp), *n.* a positive photograph taken directly on a sensitized iron plate; tintype.

fer·rous (fer'ŭs), *adj.* of, pertaining to, containing, or obtained from iron.

ferrous oxide, monoxide of iron.

fer·ru·gi·nous (fê-rōō'ji-nŭs), *adj.* 1. containing or having the nature of iron. 2. rust-colored.

fer·rule (fer'ŭl, 'ool), *n.* a metal ring or cap placed at the end of a cane, tool handle, etc. to strengthen it: *v.t.* **-ruled, -rul·ing,** to furnish with a ferrule.

fer·ry (fer'ĭ), *n., pl.* **-ries,** 1. a passage across a river, bay, or the like. 2. a boat for the transportation of passengers, vehicles, etc. across water: also **fer'ry-boat:** *v.t. & v.i.* **-ried, -ry·ing,** 1. to cross or take across (a river, etc.) by boat. 2. to deliver (aircraft) by flying them. 3. to transport by aircraft. —**fer'ry·man,** *n., pl.* **-men.**

fer·tile (fũr'tl), *adj.* 1. producing abundantly; fruitful. 2. capable of producing offspring, seeds, pollen, spores, fruit, etc. 3. fertilized.

---

a in cap, ā in cane, ä in father, å in abet, e in met ē in be, ē in baker, ê in regent, i in pit, ī in fine, i in manifest, o in hot, ô in horse, ō in bone,

4. rich in resources or invention. —**fer′tile-ly,** *adv.* —**fer′til′i-ty,** *n.*

fer-til-ize (-īz), *v.t.* -ized, -iz-ing, 1. to make fertile. 2. to impregnate or pollinate; to render (the female or female cell) fruitful by union with the male. 3. to spread fertilizer on. — **fer-til-i-za′tion,** *n.*

fer-til-iz-er (-ēr), *n.* any substance used to enrich the soil, as manure or chemicals.

fer-ule (fer′ŭl, ′ool), *n.* a flat stick used to chastise a child.

fer-vent (fûr′věnt), *adj.* 1. burning or glowing. 2. showing great intensity of emotion; enthused; ardent. —**fer′ven-cy,** *n.* —**fer′vent-ly,** *adv.*

fer-vid (′vid), *adj.* intense; eager; fervent; — **fer′vid-ly,** *adv.*

fer-vor (′vēr), *n.* intensity of emotion; zeal; warmth; ardor.

fes-cue (fes′kū), *n.* a grass used for lawns or pasture.

fes-tal (fes′tl), *adj.* pertaining to a feast or festival; joyous.

fes-ter (fes′tēr), *v.i.* 1. to form pus. 2. to cause ulceration. 3. to rankle: *n.* a small sore containing pus.

fes-ti-val (fes′ti-vl), *n.* 1. a day or time of feasting or celebration. 2. a religious celebration. 3. a series of performances or entertainment. 4. merrymaking.

fes-tive (fes′tiv), *adj.* 1. of, pertaining to, or used for a feast or festival. 2. joyous; gay. —**fes′tive-ly,** *adv.* —**fes′tive-ness,** *n.*

fes-tiv-i-ty (fes-tiv′i-ti), *n., pl.* -ties, 1. social gaiety; merrymaking. 2. a festival. 3. *pl.* festive activities.

fes-toon (fes-tōōn′), *n.* 1. a garland of flowers, leaves, etc. suspended in a curve between two points where it is fastened. 2. a carving or molding in this form: *v.t.* to decorate with or form into festoons.

fet-a (fet′ä), *n.* a soft, white cheese made from goat's milk or ewe's milk: also **feta cheese.**

fe-tal (fēt′l), *adj.* of a fetus.

fetch (fech), *v.i.* 1. to go after and bring back. 2. to elicit; cause to come. 3. to bring as a price. 4. to heave (a sigh, groan, etc.). 5. [Informal], to fascinate; attract: *n.* a wraith.

fetch-ing (′ing), *adj.* fascinating; charming.

fete (fāt), *n.* a festival or holiday; entertainment, especially outdoors: *v.t.* fet′ed, fet′ing, to entertain or honor with festivities. Also written **fête.**

fête cham-pê-tre (fet shän-pe′tr), [French], an outdoor festival or entertainment.

fe-ti-cide (fēt′i-sīd), *n.* an abortion of a fetus. —**fe-ti-ci′dal,** *adj.*

fet-id (fet′id, fēt′-), *adj.* having an offensive smell; stinking; putrid. —**fet′id-ness,** *n.*

fet-ish (fet′ish, fēt′-), *n.* 1. any object regarded as having magical powers. 2. anything receiving unreasonable devotion. 3. a nonsexual thing or part of the body, as a shoe or foot, that arouses erotic feelings. Also **fet′ich.** —**fet′ish-ism,** *n.* —**fet′ish-ist,** *n.*

fet-lock (fet′lok), *n.* 1. a tuft of hair above the hoof on the back of a horse's leg. 2. the joint where this tuft grows.

fe-tor (fēt′ēr, fē′tôr), *n.* a strong, disgusting smell; stench.

fet-ter (fet′ēr), *n.* 1. a chain or shackle for the feet. 2. a restraint; hindrance: *v.t.* 1. to place fetters upon; chain; bind. 2. to hinder; restrain.

fet-tle (fet′l), *v.t.* -tled, -tling, to cover with ore or cinders, as the hearth of a puddling furnace: *n.* condition of mind and body, as in fine *fettle.*

fe-tus (fēt′ŭs), *n., pl.* -tus-es, 1. the young of an animal while still in the egg or uterus, especially in the later stages. 2. the human offspring in the uterus from the end of the third month until birth.

feud (fūd), *n.* a continuing, bitter quarrel between clans or families: *v.i.* to engage in a feud, especially over a period of years.

feud (fūd), *n.* formerly, land held from a feudal lord in return for service; fief. —**feu′dal,** *adj.*

feu-dal-ism (-izm), *n.* the European medieval social and economic system, in which land was worked by serfs and held by vassals in exchange for military and other services to an overlord. —**feu′dal-ist,** *n.* —**feu-dal-is′tic,** *adj.*

feu-dal-i-ty (fū-dal′i-ti), *n.* 1. the state of being feudal. 2. a feudal holding in land; fief.

feu-dal-ize (fūd′l-īz), *v.t.* -ized, -iz-ing, to make conform to feudalism. —**feu-dal-i-za′tion,** *n.*

feudal system, same as **feudalism.**

feu-da-to-ry (fū′dä-tôr-i), *n., pl.* -ries, 1. one holding land by feudal tenure. 2. the land held; fief: *adj.* pertaining to or held by feudal tenure.

feuil-le-ton (fū-yĕ-tôn′), *n.* 1. the part of a French newspaper containing fiction, critical reviews, etc. 2. an article, story, etc. printed in this section.

fe-ver (fē′vēr), *n.* 1. a condition of increased body temperature. 2. any of several diseases marked by this, often with a fast pulse, thirst, etc. 3. nervous excitement: *v.t.* to put into a fever. —**fe′ver-ish,** *adj.* —**fe′ver-ish-ly,** *adv.*

fe-ver-few (-fū), *n.* a bushy plant with small, white flowers.

few (fū), *adj.* not many: *n. & pron.* a small number. —**few′ness,** *n.*

fey (fā), *adj.* 1. [Archaic or Scottish], doomed. 2. strange, whimsical, etc.

fez (fez), *n., pl.* fez′zes, a brimless, closefitting felt hat, usually red with a black tassel, worn, especially formerly, by men in Turkey.

fi-a-cre (fē-ä′kēr), *n.* in France, a small, horse-drawn carriage for hire.

fi-an-cé (fē-än-sā′), *n.* a man engaged to be married.

fi-an-cée (fē-än-sā′), *n.* a woman engaged to be married.

fi-as-co (fi-as′kō), *n., pl.* -coes, -cos, a complete or ludicrous failure, especially of an ambitious enterprise.

fi-at (fī′at, ′ät), *n.* 1. a legal order or decree. 2. a sanction.

fiat money, paper currency made legal tender by law or fiat, but not necessarily redeemable in coin.

ô in drag*o*n, ōō in cr*u*de, oo in w*oo*l, u in c*u*p, ū in c*u*re, û in t*u*rn, ŭ in f*o*cus, oi in b*o*y, ou in h*ou*se, th in *th*in, th in shea*th*e, g in *g*et, j in *j*oy, y in *y*et.

fib (fĭb), n. a falsehood or lie about something trivial: v.i. **fibbed, fib'bing,** to tell a fib. — **fib'ber,** n.

fi·ber, fi·bre (fī'bĕr), n. 1. a slender, threadlike element that joins with others to form animal or vegetable tissue. 2. any material that can be separated into threads for weaving, etc. 3. quality or character. 4. texture.

fi·ber·board (-bôrd), n. a flexible building material made from pressed fibers of wood, sugar cane, etc.

Fi·ber·glas (-glas), finely spun glass pressed and molded into a plastic material, used as yarn to make textiles, or used in a fibrous mass as insulation: a trademark: n. [f-], this substance: also **fiberglass.**

fiber optics, 1. the science of transmitting light and images, as around curves, through transparent fibers. 2. the fibers thus used. — **fi'ber·op'tic** (-op'tik), adj.

fi·bril (fī'brĭl), n. a small fiber.

fi·bril·la·tion (fib-rĭ-lā'shŭn), n. a series of contractions of the cardiac muscles, causing irregular, weak heartbeats.

fi·brin (fī'brĭn), n. a white, threadlike protein that forms the network of a blood clot. — **fi'brin·ous,** adj.

fi·brin·o·gen (fī-brĭn'ō-jĕn), n. a protein in the blood from which fibrin is formed.

fi·broid (fī'broid), adj. composed of or like fibrous tissue: n. a benign, fibrous tumor of the uterus.

fi·bro·ma (fī-brō'mä), n., pl. -mas, -ma·ta ('mä·tä), a fibrous tumor.

fi·bro·sis (fī-brō'sĭs), n. an excessive growth of fibrous connective tissue in an organ or part. — **fi·brot'ic** (-brot'ik), adj.

fi·brous (fī'brŭs), adj. 1. composed of or containing fibers. 2. resembling fibers.

fib·ster (fib'stĕr), n. [Informal], one who tells fibs.

fib·u·la (fib'yoo-lä), n., pl. -lae (-lē), -las, 1. the outer and smaller of the two bones of the lower leg. 2. an ornamental brooch in ancient Rome or Greece. — **fib'u·lar,** adj.

fich·u (fish'ōō), n. a light, three-cornered cape for women, worn with the ends crossed in front.

fick·le (fik'l), adj. capricious; changeable; not loyal. — **fick'le·ness,** n.

fic·tion (fik'shŭn), n. 1. a literary work of the imagination, as a story, novel, or play. 2. works of this kind collectively. 3. a made-up story. 4. in Law, something accepted as fact for the sake of convenience. — **fic'tion·al,** adj. — **fic'tion·al·ly,** adv.

fic·tion·al·ize (-l-īz), v.t. -ized, -iz·ing, to tell an imaginary version of (a true story, as in history or biography): also **fic'tion·ize.** — **fic·tion·al·i·za'tion,** n.

fic·tion·ist (-ist), n. one who writes fiction.

fic·tive (fik'tiv), adj. 1. of fiction. 2. imaginary. — **fic'tive·ly,** adv.

fic·ti·tious (fik-tish'ŭs), adj. 1. of or like fiction; made up by the imagination. 2. unreal; false. 3. assumed for disguise. — **fic·ti'tious·ly,** adv.

fid·dle (fid'l), n. 1. [Informal], a violin. 2. a frame used on a ship's table to keep dishes, etc. from sliding off in rough weather: v.i.

-**dled, -dling,** 1. [Informal], to play on the fiddle. 2. to tinker (with) in a nervous manner. — **fid·dler,** n.

fid·dle-dee-dee (fid-l-dē-dē'), n. & interj. nonsense.

fid·dle-fad·dle (fid'l-fad-l), n. & interj. nonsense: v.i. -dled, -dling, [Informal], to fuss about trifles.

fid·dle-sticks (-stiks), interj. nonsense!

fi·del·i·ty (fi-del'i-ti, fī-), n., pl. -ties, 1. loyalty; faithful adherence to obligation or duty. 2. accuracy.

fidg·et (fij'it), n. 1. one who is restless and nervous. 2. a condition of restless nervousness, especially in the phrase the fidgets: v.i. to make restless or nervous movements. — **fidg'et·y,** adj. — **fidg'et·i·ness,** n.

fi·du·cial (fi-dōō'shúl), adj. 1. based on trust. 2. accepted as a standard for measurement or comparison.

fi·du·ci·ar·y (fi-dōō'shi·er-i), n., pl. -ar·ies, a trustee: adj. holding or held in trust.

fie (fī), interj. for shame!

fief (fēf), n. in feudalism, land held from a feudal lord in return for service; feud.

field (fēld), n. 1. open country. 2. a piece of land cleared for pasture or crops. 3. a piece of land used for a specified purpose. 4. a region yielding some natural product. 5. the site of a battle. 6. a battle. 7. a sphere of action or learning. 8. a wide expanse. 9. the area visible through a microscope, etc. 10. an area for games or athletic events. 11. the competitors in a contest. 12. the background, as of a flag. 13. a space of active magnetic or electrical force: v.t. 1. to catch or stop and return (a baseball, etc.). 2. to place (a player or team) into the field to play. — **field'er,** n.

field artillery, mobile artillery for use in the field.

field day, 1. a day for military review. 2. a day of outdoor scientific research. 3. a day for athletic contests and events. 4. a day of enjoyable excitement.

field·fare ('fer), n. the brown European thrush.

field glasses, a small, portable, binocular telescope: also field glass.

field goal, 1. in Basketball, a goal made while the ball is in active play. 2. in Football, a goal kicked from the field while the ball is in active play.

field hand, a hired farm laborer.

field hockey, a team game played outdoors, in which the players try to drive a ball into the opponents' goal, using a curved stick with a flat blade.

field hospital, a temporary military hospital near the scene of combat, for emergency treatment.

field marshal, an officer of the highest rank in the British and some other armies.

field officer, a colonel, lieutenant colonel, or major in the army.

field-test (fēld'test), v.t. to test (a device, method, etc.) under operating conditions.

field·work (fēld'wĕrk), n. outdoor observations and collecting of material, as by a geologist, archaeologist, etc.

fiend (fēnd), n. 1. an evil spirit; demon. 2. one

who is inhumanly malicious or wicked. 3. [Informal], an addict.

fiend-ish ('ish), *adj.* 1. like a fiend; inhumanly wicked or cruel. 2. vexatious. —**fiend'ish-ly**, *adv.*

fierce (firs), *adj.* fierc'er, fierc'est, 1. savage; ferocious. 2. violent. 3. eager; intense. 4. [Informal], very bad. —**fierce'ly**, *adv.* — **fierce'ness**, *n.*

fi-er-y (fi'ēr-i), *adj.* -er-i-er, -er-i-est, 1. consisting of or like fire; hot; flaming. 2. easily roused. 3. fervent; ardent. 4. inflamed. —**fi'er-i-ness**, *n.*

fiery cross, 1. a wooden cross, blazing at the ends, used by ancient Scottish clans as a signal call to battle. 2. a burning cross, used as an emblem by the Ku Klux Klan.

fi-es-ta (fi-es'tä), *n.* 1. a religious festival. 2. any festive celebration.

fife (fif), *n.* a shrill-toned musical instrument like a flute: *v.t. & v.i.* fifed, fif'ing, to play on a fife. —**fif'er**, *n.*

fif-teen (fif'tēn'), *adj.* five more than ten: *n.* the cardinal numeral that is the sum of five and ten; 15; XV.

fif-teenth ('tēnth'), *adj.* next after 14th: *n.* the one after the 14th.

fifth (fifth), *adj.* next in order after fourth: *n.* 1. the one after the fourth. 2. one of five equal parts. 3. a fifth of a gallon. —**fifth'ly**, *adv.*

Fifth Amendment, an amendment to the Constitution of the U.S. that includes a provision that no person be required to testify against himself in a criminal case.

fifth column, a group of traitors within a country who, by subversive activity, give aid to an enemy.

fif-ti-eth (fif'ti-ith), *adj.* next after 49th; 50th: *n.* 1. the one after the 49th. 2. one of 50 equal parts.

fif-ty (fif'ti), *adj.* five times 10: *n.*, *pl.* -ties, 1. the cardinal numeral that is the sum of 49 and one; 50; L. 2. *pl.* years or numbers from 50 through 59 (preceded by *the*).

fif-ty-fif-ty (-fif'ti), *adj.* [Informal], equal; half and half: *adv.* [Informal], equally.

fig (fig), *n.* 1. a small, edible, pear-shaped fruit grown on a tree of the mulberry family. 2. this tree. 3. anything insignificant; trifle. 4. [Informal], dress; appearance.

fight (fit), *v.i.* fought, fight'ing, to contend; take part in a battle, bout, contest, etc., especially against an enemy or for some purpose: *v.t.* 1. to war against. 2. to oppose physically. 3. to strive for the mastery of. 4. to box with in a contest: *n.* 1. a combat, bout, struggle, etc. 2. a quarrel. 3. ability or disposition to fight.

fight-er ('ēr), *n.* 1. one that fights. 2. a boxer. 3. a small, swift, combat airplane.

fig leaf, 1. the leaf of a fig tree. 2. a representation of this used to conceal the sexual organs on a nude statue.

fig marigold, a fleshy plant with showy flowers, that grows in warm climates.

fig-ment ('mĕnt), *n.* a mere product of the imagination; something imagined.

fig-u-line (fig'yoo-lin, -lin), *n.* a clay pot or statue.

fig-u-rant (fig'yŭ-rant), *n.* a ballet dancer who performs as one of a group. —**fig'u-rante** (-rant), *n.fem.*

fig-u-ra-tion (fig-yŭ-rā'shŭn), *n.* 1. the act of giving form or shape to. 2. form; appearance.

fig-u-ra-tive (fig'yēr-à-tiv), *adj.* 1. representing by figure or symbol. 2. not literal; metaphorical. 3. using or full of figures of speech. —**fig'u-ra-tive-ly**, *adv.*

fig-ure (fig'yēr), *n.* 1. the outline or shape of an object. 2. the human form. 3. an image or statue. 4. a diagram or picture; illustration. 5. a pattern; design. 6. a sign or character denoting a number. 7. *pl.* arithmetic. 8. an amount of money. 9. a movement in a dance. 10. a motif in music. 11. in *Geometry*, a space bounded on all sides by planes or lines: *v.t.* -ured, -ur-ing, 1. to depict in definite form. 2. to imagine. 3. to cover with figures. 4. to calculate or compute. 5. [Informal], to consider: *v.i.* 1. to do arithmetic. 2. to be conspicuous.

fig-ured ('yērd), *adj.* 1. covered or adorned with figures. 2. pictured.

fig-ure-head ('yēr-hed), *n.* 1. a carved figure on the prow of a ship. 2. one who is in a position of authority, but who has no real power.

figure of speech, a nonliteral expression, as a metaphor or simile.

figure skating, ice skating in which the skater traces various elaborate prescribed patterns on the ice.

fig-u-rine (fig-yŭ-rēn'), *n.* a small, ornamental molded or sculptured figure; statuette.

fig-wort (fig'wērt), *n.* a small plant with square stems and small, brownish flowers.

fil-a-ment (fil'à-mĕnt), *n.* 1. a very fine thread or threadlike process. 2. the stalk of an anther. 3. the fine wire in a light bulb or electron tube. —**fil-a-men'ta-ry** (-men'tēr-i), *adj.*

fi-lar (fi'lēr), *adj.* 1. of or pertaining to threads. 2. having fine threads stretched across the field of view, as a microscope, etc.

fi-lar-i-a (fi-ler'i-à), *n.*, *pl.* -i-ae (-ē), any of a number of parasitic worms that live in the blood or tissues of vertebrates. —**fi-lar'i-al**, *adj.*

fil-a-ri-a-sis (fil-à-rī'à-sis), *n.* a disease caused by filarial worms in the lymphatic vessels, causing chronic swelling of the legs.

fil-bert (fil'bērt), *n.* same as **hazelnut**.

filch (filch), *v.t.* to pilfer; steal (something petty).

file (fil), *n.* 1. a folder or cabinet for keeping papers, letters, etc. in order. 2. a collection of records, cards, etc. in an orderly arrangement. 3. a line of persons one behind the other. 4. a steel tool with a rough surface for grinding and smoothing: *v.t.* filed, fil'ing, 1. to grind or smooth with a file. 2. to put (papers, etc.) in a file for future reference. 2. to dispatch (a news story). 3. to submit (an application, etc.). 4. to place on public record: *v.i.* 1. to march in a file or line. 2. to apply (*for* divorce, etc.).

ô in drag*on*, ōō in cr*u*de, oo in w*oo*l, u in c*u*p, ū in c*u*re, ŭ in t*u*rn, û in f*o*cus, oi in b*oy*, ou in h*ou*se, th in *th*in, *th* in shea*th*e, g in *g*et, j in *j*oy, y in *y*et.

file-fish (fīl'fish), *n., pl.* -fish, -fish-es, a fish with very small, rough scales.

fi-let mi-gnon (fi-lā' min-yōn', -yon'), a thick, round tenderloin steak.

fil-i-al (fil'i-ál, 'yál), *adj.* suitable to, or expected from, a son or daughter.

fil-i-bus-ter (fil'i-bus-tēr), *n.* 1. a freebooter; lawless military adventurer who invades a foreign country. 2. a member of a legislature, especially the Senate, who obstructs the passage of a bill by making long speeches, etc.: also fil'i-bus-ter-er. 3. the use of this tactic: *v.i. & v.t.* to obstruct (a bill) by filibuster.

fil-i-form (fil'i-fôrm, fī'li-), *adj.* threadlike.

fil-i-gree (fil'i-grē), *n.* ornamental work resembling delicate lace, made of intertwined gold, silver, etc. wire: *v.t.* -greed, -gree-ing, to decorate with filigree.

fil-ing (fīl'ing), *n.* a small particle, as of metal, removed by a file: *usually used in pl.*

Fil-i-pi-no (fil-i-pē'nō), *n., pl.* -nos, a native or inhabitant of the Philippines, a group of islands off the southeast coast of Asia.

fill (fil), *v.t.* 1. to put as much as can be contained into. 2. to put a person into or to hold (an office, position, etc.). 3. to occupy completely. 4. to supply the things required for (an order, need, etc.). 5. to stop or plug (an opening, hole, etc.): *n.* 1. as much as is needed to make full or completely satisfy. 2. anything that fills.

fill-er ('ēr), *n.* 1. one who or that which, fills. 2. something added to increase size, consistency, etc. 3. a pasty substance used to fill crevices or holes in wood, plaster, etc. before finishing. 4. the body of a cigar. 5. a short item used to fill space in a publication.

fil-let (fil'it), *n.* 1. a narrow strip or band, as of ribbon. 2. a boneless piece of meat or fish: *v.t.* (fil'ā, fi-lā'), to cut into fillets.

fill-in (fil'in), *n.* 1. a person or thing that fills a vacancy or need. 2. [Informal], a short summary of relevant facts.

fill-ing (fil'ing), *n.* something serving to fill an empty space, cavity, etc.

fil-lip (fil'ip), *n.* 1. an outward snap made by the flick of a finger from the thumb. 2. something exciting: *v.t.* to hit or propel with a fillip.

fil-lis-ter (fil'is-tēr), *n.* 1. a rabbet plane. 2. a groove, as at the edge of a window sash, to receive glass.

fil-ly (fil'i), *n., pl.* -lies, 1. a young mare. 2. [Informal], a lively, spirited girl.

film (film), *n.* 1. a thin skin or filament. 2. a pliant cellulose material with a coating of a light-sensitive emulsion, used in photography. 3. a blur or mist. 4. a motion picture: *v.t. & v.i.* 1. to cover or become covered with a film. 2. to make a motion picture (of).

film-strip ('strip), *n.* a length of film for still projection, containing photographs, charts, graphic matter, etc.

film-y (fil'mi), *adj.* film'i-er, film'i-est, 1. gauzy; transparent. 2. hazy; blurred.

fi-lose (fī'lōs), *adj.* threadlike.

fil-ter (fil'tēr), *n.* 1. an apparatus or substance for removing suspended matter, impurities, etc. from a liquid or a gas. 2. any of various devices that pass radiations, signals, etc. of certain frequencies while rejecting others: *v.t. & v.i.* 1. to pass through or as through a filter. 2. to remove by means of a filter. — fil'ter-a-ble, fil'tra-ble, *adj.*

filth (filth), *n.* 1. foul matter; refuse. 2. obscenity. —filth'i-ness, *n.* —filth'y, *adj.* filth'i-er, filth'i-est.

fil-trate (fil'trāt), *v.t.* -trat-ed, -trat-ing, to filter: *n.* a filtered liquid. —fil-tra'tion, *n.*

fin (fin), *n.* 1. a winglike appendage on the body of a fish or other aquatic animal, used for locomotion, balance, etc. 2. something like this in appearance or function.

fin-a-ble (fīn'nā-bl), *adj.* liable to a fine.

fi-na-gle (fi-nā'gl), *v.i.* -gled, -gling, to secure or achieve by crafty arguments or clever tricks: *v.i.* to use such arguments, tricks, etc. —fi-na'gler, *n.*

fi-nal (fī'nl), *adj.* 1. of or occurring at the end; last. 2. decisive; terminating: *n.* 1. anything final. 2. *pl.* the deciding heat in an athletic contest. 3. a final examination. —fi-nal'i-ty (-nal'i-ti), *n.* —fi'nal-ly, *adv.*

fi-na-le (fi-nā'li, 'lā), *n.* 1. the last passage of a musical composition. 2. the final act, scene, part, etc.

fi-nal-ist (fī'nl-ist), *n.* a contestant in the final competition of a series.

fi-nal-ize (fī'nl-iz), *v.t.* -ized, -iz-ing, to put in finished form; complete. —fi-nal-i-za'tion, *n.*

fi-nance (fi-nans', fī'nans), *n.* 1. *pl.* the monetary resources, investments, etc. of a state, corporation, person, etc. 2. the science of managing money, loans, etc.: *v.t.* -nanced', -nanc'ing, to obtain or supply funds for. — fi-nan'cial (-nan'shúl), *adj.*

fin-an-cier (fin-an-sir', fi-nan-), *n.* one who is trained in, or expert in, financial affairs.

fin-back (fin'bak), *n.* a whale with a prominent dorsal fin.

finch (finch), *n.* any one of various songbirds, as the canary, cardinal, etc.

find (find), *v.t.* 1. to discover accidentally. 2. to obtain by searching. 3. to learn; ascertain. 4. to regain (something lost). 5. to arrive at; attain. 6. to determine and state to be: *v.i.* to arrive at a legal verdict: *n.* 1. an act of finding. 2. the discovery of something.

find-er ('ēr), *n.* 1. one that finds. 2. a device on a camera that shows the field of view.

fin de siè-cle (fant sye'kl), [French], of or distinguishing the end of the 19th century, especially its sterility.

find-ing (fīn'ding), *n.* 1. a discovery. 2. *often pl.* the verdict of a jury, examiner, etc.

fine (fīn), *adj.* fin'er, fin'est, 1. excellent; superior. 2. having no impurities. 3. free from clouds or rain. 4. made up of very small particles. 5. very thin or small. 6. sharp; keen. 7. precise; subtle. 8. refined; elegant: *adv.* 1. in a fine manner. 2. [Informal], very well. —fine'ly, *adv.* —fine'ness, *n.*

fine (fīn), *n.* money paid as a punishment for an offense: *v.t.* fined, fin'ing to impose a fine on.

fine arts, any one of certain art forms, including painting, sculpture, etc.

fine-cut (fin'kut'), *adj.* cut into small, equal strips, as tobacco.

fine-drawn ('drôn'), *adj.* 1. spun out very fine, as wire. 2. extremely subtle, as an argument.

fine-grained ('grānd'), *adj.* having a fine, even grain, as some wood.

fin·er·y (fin'ēr-i), *n., pl.* **-er·ies,** personal adornment, as showy clothes, jewelry, etc.

fi·nesse (fi-nes'), *n.* 1. skill; dexterity. 2. the ability to resolve difficult situations diplomatically. 3. artifice. 4. in *Bridge,* the act of finessing: *v.t.* **-nessed, -ness'ing,** 1. to accomplish by artifice or skill. 2. in *Bridge,* to play (a card) lower than one's highest card in the belief this card will win the trick because an intervening card is held by an opponent who has already played.

fin·ger (fing'gēr), *n.* 1. any one of the five projecting divisions of the hand. 2. any one of these excluding the thumb. 3. anything resembling a finger: *v.t.* 1. to handle with the fingers. 2. in *Music,* to employ the fingers in a particular way in playing.

fin·ger-board (-bôrd), *n.* 1. the part of a stringed instrument against which the strings are pressed to obtain the wanted tones. 2. the keyboard of a piano, organ, etc.

finger bowl, a bowl containing water for washing the fingers at table.

fin·ger·ing (-ing), *n.* 1. the act of touching with the fingers. 2. the act or technique of manipulating the fingers on certain musical instruments.

fin·ger-nail (-nāl), *n.* the horny material covering the upper surface at the tip of a finger.

finger painting, the art or process of painting by using the fingers, hand, or arm to spread on wet paper, paints (**finger paints**) made of starch, glycerin, and pigments. **—fin'ger-paint** (-pānt), *v.i. & v.t.*

fin·ger-print (-print), *n.* an impression of the lines and whorls on the fleshy tip of a finger, used for identification.

fin·ger-stall (-stôl), *n.* a protective covering for an injured finger.

finger tip, the tip of a finger.

fin·i·al (fin'i-ăl), *n.* a pointed ornament at the top of a spire, lamp shade, etc.

fin·ick·y (fin'i-ki), *adj.* overly fastidious or particular: also **fin'i·cal** (-kl), **fin'ick·ing.**

fin·ing (fi'ning), *n.* the act or process of purifying liquids.

fi·nis (fin'is), *n., pl.* **-nis·es,** the end; conclusion.

fin·ish (fin'ish), *v.t.* 1. to bring to an end; complete. 2. to arrive at the end of. 3. to use up. 4. to put the final touches on; perfect. 5. to kill or destroy: *v.i.* to come to an end: *n.* 1. the final part; end. 2. something used in finishing a surface. 3. the finished texture. 4. something that completes or perfects. 5. refinement in manners, speech, etc. **—fin'ished,** *adj.* **—fin'ish·er,** *n.*

fi·nite (fi'nīt), *adj.* having limits.

fink (fink), *n.* [*Slang*], an informer or strike breaker.

fin·nan had·die (fin'ăn had'i), smoked haddock.

finned (find), *adj.* having a fin or fins.

fin·ny (fin'i), *adj.* 1. having fins. 2. resembling a fin. 3. of, pertaining to, or being fish.

fiord (fyôrd), *n.* a long, narrow arm of the sea between high cliffs.

fir (fûr), *n.* any one of various cone-bearing, evergreen trees of the pine family.

fire (fir), *n.* 1. heat and light produced by ignition and combustion. 2. such a combustion. 3. a destructive conflagration. 4. intense feeling. 5. a discharge of firearms. 6. a severe trial or affliction: *v.t. & v.i.* **fired, fir'ing,** 1. to set on fire; ignite. 2. to supply with fuel. 3. to bake in a kiln. 4. to excite or become stimulated. 5. to discharge (a gun, mine, etc.). 6. to project or direct suddenly and forcefully. 7. to discharge from a position; dismiss.

fire alarm, 1. a signal given at the outbreak of a fire. 2. a bell, siren, etc. for giving this signal.

fire-arm ('ärm), *n.* a hand weapon, as a revolver or rifle, from which a bullet is fired by an explosive charge.

fire-ball ('bôl), *n.* 1. something resembling a ball of fire, as a meteor. 2. [*Informal*], a very energetic person.

fire-base ('bās), *n.* a military base in a combat zone, from which artillery, rockets, etc. are fired in support of advancing troops, etc.

fire-bomb ('bom), *n.* an incendiary bomb: *v.t.* to attack or damage with a firebomb.

fire-box ('boks), *n.* the chamber containing the fire, as in a steam engine.

fire-brand ('brand), *n.* 1. a piece of burning wood. 2. an incendiary who inflames others to strife, rebellion, etc.

fire-brick ('brik), *n.* a brick resistant to great heat, used to line furnaces, chimneys, etc.

fire brigade, chiefly British form for **fire department.**

fire-bug ('bug), *n.* [*Informal*], a pyromaniac.

fire-crack·er ('krak-ēr), *n.* a paper cylinder enclosing an explosive, used to make noise, as at celebrations.

fire-damp ('damp), *n.* a gas formed in coal mines, explosive when mixed with air.

fire department, a municipal service, consisting of buildings, apparatus, and men, for preventing and extinguishing fires.

fire-dog ('dôg), *n.* same as **andiron.**

fire drill, a drill for teaching proper procedures, as orderly exit, in case of a fire.

fire-eat·er ('ēt-ēr), *n.* 1. a performer who pretends to swallow fire. 2. a hot-tempered, pugnacious person.

fire engine, a large motor vehicle for carrying men and equipment to fight fires.

fire escape, an outside stairway, ladder, etc. for quick escape in case of fire.

fire-fight·er ('fīt-ēr), *n.* a person whose work is fighting fires. **—fire'fight·ing,** *n.*

fire-fly ('flī), *n.* a winged beetle whose abdominal organs emit a luminescent light.

fire irons, the shovel, poker, and tongs used to tend a fireplace.

fire-man ('măn), *n., pl.* **-men** ('mĕn), 1. same as **firefighter.** 2. a stoker.

ô in drag*o*n, o͞o in cr*u*de, oo in w*oo*l, u in c*u*p, ū in c*u*re, ū in t*u*rn, ŭ in foc*u*s, oi in b*o*y, ou in h*ou*se, th in *th*in, th in shea*th*e, g in *g*et, j in *j*oy, y in *y*et.

fire-place ('plās), *n.* a recess, as in a wall, for a fire; hearth.

fire-plug ('plug), *n.* a street hydrant used as a source of water in case of fire.

fire-proof ('prŏŏf), *adj.* not easily combustible: *v.t.* to make fireproof.

fire ship, a ship loaded with explosives, set on fire, and drifted among enemy vessels to destroy them.

fire-side ('sīd), *n.* 1. the space near a hearth. 2. home or domestic life.

fire-trap ('trap), *n.* a building unsafe in the event of fire because it is readily combustible or hard to escape from.

fire-wa-ter ('wôt-ẽr), *n.* [Informal], hard liquor.

fire-wood ('wood), *n.* wood used as fuel.

fire-works ('wûrks), *n.pl.* 1. combustible and explosive materials packed in containers and ignited to produce brilliant colors and loud noises, as at celebrations. 2. a display of or as of fireworks.

fir-ing ('ing), *n.* 1. the act of discharging firearms, cannon, etc. 2. the use of intense heat, as in glazing or hardening ceramics. 3. fuel.

firing line, 1. the line from which gunfire is aimed at a target or troops. 2. the forward position in any activity.

firing squad, 1. a group of soldiers detailed to execute by shooting someone condemned to death. 2. a group selected to fire volleys at a military funeral.

fir-kin (fûr'kin), *n.* 1. a small wooden vessel for butter, lard, etc. 2. a measure of capacity, equal to 1/4 barrel or nine gallons.

firm (fûrm), *adj.* 1. hard; solid. 2. securely fixed; stable. 3. staunch; steadfast. 4. determined; resolute. 5. unfluctuating: *v.t. & v.i.* to make or become firm. —**firm'ly,** *adv.* —**firm'ness,** *n.*

firm (fûrm), *n.* a business partnership.

fir-ma-ment (fûr'mȧ-mĕnt), *n.* the sky.

fir-man (fûr'mȧn), *n., pl. -mans,* a decree or license of an Oriental potentate.

first (fûrst), *adj.* 1. coming before all others in a series; 1st. 2. foremost in rank, dignity, excellence, etc.; chief. 3. earliest: *adv.* 1. before all others. 2. for the first time. 3. sooner; preferably: *n.* 1. the one that is first. 2. the start. 3. the winning place in a competition. 4. low gear.

first aid, emergency treatment given to an injured or ill person before professional medical help can be provided. —**first'-aid',** *adj.*

first-born ('bôrn), *adj.* born first; oldest: *n.* the firstborn offspring.

first-class ('klas), *adj.* 1. of the highest rank, quality, etc. 2. denoting or of a class of sealed mail requiring the highest regular postage rates: *adv.* 1. in first-class accommodations. 2. by first-class mail.

first fruits, 1. the first produce of the season. 2. the first products or profits of any undertaking.

first-hand ('hand'), *adj. & adv.* obtained from the original source; direct.

first lady, [often F- L-], the wife of the U.S. president.

first lieutenant, a military officer ranking above a second lieutenant.

first-ling ('ling), *n.* the first of a category, as the firstborn offspring.

first-ly ('lī), *adv.* in the first place.

first mate, the officer ranking next below the captain on a merchant ship.

first person, the form of a pronoun or verb that denotes the speaker.

first-rate ('rāt'), *adj.* of the highest rank, quality, etc.: *adv.* [Informal], excellently.

first-string ('string'), *adj.* [Informal], in *Sports,* being the first choice to play regularly at a particular position.

firth (fûrth), *n.* a narrow inlet of the sea.

fis-cal (fis'kȧl), *adj.* 1. of or pertaining to the public treasury or revenues. 2. financial. —**fis'cal-ly,** *adv.*

fish (fish), *n.* a piece of wood, metal, plastic, etc. fastened to another or to a joint to strengthen it.

fish (fish), *n., pl.* **fish** or **fish'es,** 1. any one of a large group of coldblooded aquatic vertebrates, typically having fins, permanent gills, and scales. 2. the flesh of fish used as food. 3. [F-], same as Pisces: *v.i.* 1. to catch or try to catch fish. 2. to seek something by indirection or craftiness (often with *for*): *v.t.* to seek and bring forth, as in fishing.

fish-bowl ('bōl), *n.* 1. a transparent bowl for keeping fish, snails, etc. 2. any exposed place where one's activities are on public display.

fish-er ('ẽr), *n.* 1. a fisherman. 2. *pl.* **fish'ers, fish'er,** a carnivorous mammal resembling a weasel but larger.

fish-er-man (-mȧn), *n., pl. -men* (-mĕn), 1. one who fishes for a living or sport. 2. a commercial fishing vessel.

fish-er-y (-i), *n., pl. -er-ies,* 1. the business of catching fish. 2. a fishing ground. 3. a fish hatchery.

fish hawk, same as osprey.

fish-hook ('hook), *n.* a usually barbed metal hook for fishing.

fish-ing ('ing), *n.* the art, sport, or business of catching fish.

fish joint, a joint, as of two rails, beams, etc., formed by fastening fishes along each side.

fish-mon-ger ('mung-gẽr, 'măng-), *n.* one who sells fish.

fish story, [Informal], an incredible narrative.

fish-wife ('wīf), *n., pl. -wives* ('wīvz), a scolding, abrasive woman.

fish-y ('i), *adj.* **fish'i-er, fish'i-est,** 1. resembling fish in odor, taste, etc. 2. dull; vacant. 3. [Informal], questionable; unlikely.

fis-sile (fis'l), *adj.* capable of being split.

fis-sion (fis'ŭn), *n.* 1. the act of splitting into parts. 2. same as nuclear fission. 3. the division of a simple organism into two or more parts, each of which is a complete individual. —**fis'sion-a-ble,** *adj.*

fis-sip-a-rous (fi-sip'ẽr-ŭs), *adj.* reproducing by fission.

fis-si-ped (fis'i-ped), *adj.* having the toes separated: *n.* a carnivorous mammal, as the dog, cat, etc., having such toes.

fis-sure (fish'ēr), *n.* 1. a cleft or crack. 2. a furrow dividing an organ into parts or lobes, as in the brain: *v.t. & v.i.* -sured, -sur-ing, to split into parts.

fist (fist), *n.* a hand with the fingers closed tightly or clenched.

fist-ic (fis'tik), *adj.* of or pertaining to pugilism.

fis-ti-cuffs (fis'ti-kufs), *n.* 1. a fist fight. 2. same as boxing.

fis-tu-la (fis'choo-lá), *n., pl.* -las, -lae (-lē), an abnormal passage, as from an abscess to the skin surface.

fit (fit), *v.t.* fit'ted or fit, fit'ted, fit'ting, 1. to be appropriate to. 2. to be the proper size, shape, etc. for. 3. to adjust; adapt. 4. to equip; outfit: *v.i.* 1. to be suitable or proper. 2. to correspond in size or shape: *adj.* fit'ter, fit'test, 1. suitable, prepared, or qualified for some end, function, etc. 2. appropriate; right. 3. healthy. 4. [Informal], inclined: *n.* the manner in which something fits. —fit'ness, *n.* —fit'ter, *n.*

fit (fit), *n.* 1. any sudden attack, as of sneezing. 2. a sudden display of emotion, as of laughter. 3. an attack attended with convulsions or loss of consciousness.

fitch (fich), *n.* the old-world polecat: also **fitch'et** ('it), **fitch'ew** ('ōō).

fit-ful (fit'fül), *adj.* irregular; spasmodic. —fit'ful-ly, *adv.* —fit'ful-ness, *n.*

fit-ting (fit'ing), *adj.* suitable; appropriate: *n.* 1. the act of trying on, as of clothes, for a fit or alteration. 2. a part used for linking or adapting other units. 3. *pl.* fixtures or accessories.

five (fīv), *adj.* one more than four: *n.* the cardinal numeral that is the sum of four and one; 5; V.

five-and-ten-cent store ('n-ten'sent'), a variety store selling a large selection of mostly inexpensive articles: also **five'-and-ten'**, *n.*

five-fold (fīv'fōld), *adj.* 1. consisting of five parts. 2. five times as much or as many: *adv.* multiplied by five.

fix (fiks), *v.t.* fixed, fix'ing, 1. to make fast; secure. 2. to lodge firmly in the mind. 3. to direct or concentrate steadily. 4. to make solid, rigid, or permanent. 5. to specify (a date, time, etc.) definitely. 6. to adjust. 7. to restore; repair. 8. to make ready; prepare. 9. [Informal], to affect the outcome of (a contest, trial, etc.), as by threat or bribery. 10. [Informal], to get even with: *v.i.* to become fixed: *n.* 1. [Informal], an awkward or difficult position; quandary. 2. the position, as of a ship or aircraft, determined by observations, bearings, or radio. 3. [Slang], a position that has been fixed (sense 9). 4. [Slang], an intravenous injection of a drug by an addict.

fix-a-tion (fik-sā'shŭn), *n.* 1. the act of fixing or state of being fixed. 2. an obsession. 3. in *Psychology*, a persistence of early childhood attachments.

fix-a-tive (fik'sä-tiv), *n.* something that serves to make permanent, unfading, etc., as a mordant.

fixed (fikst), *adj.* 1. firmly in position. 2. definitely established. 3. unwavering; constant. 4. continued; enduring. —fix-ed-ly (fik'sid-li), *adv.*

fixed star, a star so distant that it seems to maintain the same position in the heavens.

fix-ings (fik'singz), *n.pl.* [Informal], accessories; trimmings.

fix-i-ty ('si-ti), *n.* 1. stability; permanence. 2. *pl.* -ties, something fixed.

fix-ture (fiks'chēr), *n.* 1. that which is firmly in place. 2. a fitting or article of furniture so attached to realty that it is legally regarded as part of it. 3. a person or thing that has long remained in a particular position or place.

fizz (fiz), *n.* 1. a hissing sound. 2. an effervescent drink: *v.i.* fizzed, fiz'zing, 1. to make a hissing sound. 2. to effervesce.

fiz-zle (fiz'l), *v.i.* -zled, -zling, 1. to make a hissing or bubbling sound. 2. [Informal], to fail after an auspicious start: *n.* 1. a hissing sound. 2. [Informal], a failure.

fjeld (fyeld), *n.* a lofty, barren plateau in Scandinavian countries.

fjord (fyôrd), *n.* same as fiord.

flab (flab), *n.* [Informal], flaccid flesh.

flab-ber-gast (flab'ēr-gast), *v.t.* to astonish; astound; confound.

flab-by (flab'i), *adj.* -bi-er, -bi-est, 1. lacking firmness; flaccid. 2. lacking strength; feeble. —flab'bi-ly, *adv.* —flab'bi-ness, *n.*

fla-bel-late (flá-bel'āt), *adj.* fan-shaped.

fla-bel-lum ('ŭm), *n., pl.* -bel'la, 1. a large fan carried by the Pope's attendants on certain occasions. 2. a body organ or structure shaped like a fan.

flac-cid (flak'sid, flas'id), *adj.* 1. soft and limp; flabby. 2. feeble. —flac-cid'i-ty, *n.*

flack (flak), *n.* [Slang], same as press agent.

fla-con (flä-kôn'), *n.* [French], a small, stoppered flask, as for perfume.

flag (flag), *n.* a piece of cloth or bunting distinctive in design, color, and shape, used as a symbol, standard, signal, etc.: *v.t.* flagged, flag'ging, to signal, as with a flag; especially, to signal to stop (often with *down*).

flag (flag), *n.* a flagstone: *v.t.* flagged, flag'ging, to pave with flagstones.

flag (flag), *n.* any one of various irises or the flower of any of these.

flag (flag), *v.i.* flagged, flag'ging, 1. to hang limp; droop. 2. to lose vigor; become weak or spiritless.

Flag Day, June 14, the anniversary of the adoption in 1777 of the U.S. flag.

flag-el-lant (flaj'ē-lánt), *adj.* using a whip: *n.* one who whips; especially, one who scourges himself for religious discipline.

flag-el-late ('ē-lāt), *v.t.* -lat-ed, -lat-ing, to whip: *adj.* having whiplike processes. —flag-el-la'tion, *n.*

fla-gel-lum (flä-jel'ŭm), *n., pl.* -la a whiplike part in protozoans, etc., used for locomotion.

flag-eo-let (flaj-ē-let'), *n.* a small musical instrument of the flute class.

flag-ging (flag'ing), *adj.* drooping or weakening.

flag-ging (flag'ing), *n.* flagstones or a pavement of these.

---

fla·gi·tious (flȧ-jish′ŭs), *adj.* shockingly wicked; vicious.

flag officer, in the *U.S. Navy,* any officer holding or above the rank of rear admiral.

flag·on (flag′ŏn), *n.* a vessel for liquids, having a handle and spout.

flag·pole (flag′pōl), *n.* a pole on which a flag is raised: also **flag′staff.**

fla·grant (flā′grȧnt), *adj.* conspicuously wrong; notorious. —**fla′grant·ly,** *adv.*

fla·gran·te de·lic·to (flȧ-gran′tĭ dĕ-lik′tō), in the very act of committing the offense.

flag·ship (flag′ship), *n.* the ship that carries the commander of a fleet or squadron.

flag·stone (flag′stōn), *n.* a flat stone for paving.

flail (flāl), *n.* a wooden instrument for threshing grain by hand: *v.t. & v.i.* 1. to thresh with a flail. 2. to strike. 3. to wave (one's arms) like flails.

flair (fler), *n.* 1. a natural aptitude; knack. 2. [Informal], a sense of what is fashionable; verve.

flak (flak), *n.* the exploding shells from antiaircraft guns.

flake (flāk), *n.* 1. a flat, thin mass. 2. a thin piece or layer; chip: *v.t. & v.i.* **flaked, flak′ing,** 1. to form into flakes. 2. to scale or peel off in flakes. —**flak·y** (′ĭ), *adj.* **flak′i·er, flak′i·est.**

flake white, a pigment of flakes of white lead.

flam (flam), *n.* 1. a false pretense; lie. 2. blarney; nonsense.

flam·beau (flam′bō), *n., pl.* **-beaux** (′bōz), **-beaus,** 1. a lighted torch. 2. a large, ornamental candlestick.

flam·boy·ant (flam-boi′ȧnt), *adj.* 1. flamelike; resplendent. 2. overly ornate; showy. —**flam·boy′ance,** *n.* —**flam·boy′ant·ly,** *adv.*

flame (flām), *n.* 1. the hot, luminous, gaseous part of a fire. 2. the state of active combustion with a blaze. 3. a thing resembling a flame in appearance, brilliance, etc. 4. an ardent passion. 5. [Informal], sweetheart: *v.i.* **flamed, flam′ing,** 1. to burst into flame. 2. to become red; glow. 3. to become agitated.

fla·men (flā′men), *n., pl.* **fla′mens, flam·i·nes** (flam′ĭ-nēz), a priest in the service of a Roman god.

fla·men·co (flȧ-meng′kō), *n., pl.* **-cos,** a dance or music style of Spanish gypsies.

flame·out (flām′out), *n.* the failure of a jet engine in flight.

flame thrower, a military weapon that projects a burning stream of fuel.

flame tree, a shrublike tree of Australia, with showy scarlet flowers.

flam·ing (flā′ming), *adj.* 1. on fire; blazing. 2. flamelike; brilliant. 3. intensely emotional; ardent.

fla·min·go (flȧ-ming′gō), *n.* a large wading bird of the tropics, with long legs, a long neck, and red or pinkish plumage.

flam·ma·ble (flam′ȧ-bl), *adj.* highly combustible and able to burn very rapidly.

flan (flan), *n.* 1. a blank metal disk prepared to be stamped into a coin. 2. a tart with a filling of custard, fruit, cheese, etc.

flange (flanj), *n.* a raised or protruding rim, as on a wheel, used to keep it in place, or for

strength, guidance, or attachment to another object.

flank (flangk), *n.* 1. the fleshy part of an animal between the ribs and hip. 2. a side of anything. 3. in *military usage,* the right or left side of a formation, army, etc.: *v.t.* 1. to be located at the side of. 2. to attack, threaten, or turn the flank of (enemy forces).

flank·er (′ẽr), *n.* 1. any one of several soldiers stationed as a guard for the flanks of a marching column. 2. in *Football,* an offensive back stationed closer to the sideline than any of his teammates.

flan·nel (flan′l), *n.* 1. a soft woolen or cotton cloth loosely woven with a light nap. 2. *pl.* underwear, trousers, etc. made of this.

flan·nel·ette, flan·nel·et (flan-ĕ-let′), *n.* a soft, lightweight cotton cloth.

flap (flap), *n.* 1. anything broad and flexible that hangs loosely and is fastened at one end. 2. the motion or noise of anything flapping. 3. a slap. 4. [Slang], a state of agitation; turmoil: *v.t. & v.i.* **flapped, flap′ping,** 1. to slap. 2. to move rapidly up and down or back and forth.

flap·doo·dle (flap′dood-l), *n.* silly or nonsensical talk.

flap·jack (flap′jak), *n.* a pancake.

flap·per (flap′ẽr), *n.* 1. one that flaps. 2. [Informal], in the 1920's, a saucy, free-spirited young woman.

flare (fler), *n.* 1. a brief, unsteady, intense light. 2. a very bright light, used for signaling, illumination, etc. 3. a sudden, short-lived outbreak, as of emotion. 4. a curved contour: *v.i.* **flared, flar′ing,** 1. to burn brightly or unsteadily. 2. to erupt suddenly, as in anger. 3. to curve outward, as the lip of a jar.

flare-up (′up), *n.* a sudden outburst of flame, emotion, etc.

flash (flash), *n.* 1. a sudden transitory blaze of light. 2. a moment. 3. a sudden brief display, as of wit. 4. a brief news report sent by radio, cable, etc.: *v.i.* 1. to emit a sudden, transient light. 2. to scintillate. 3. to move or pass suddenly: *v.t.* 1. to cause to flash. 2. to transmit (information) quickly: *adj.* occurring rapidly or suddenly.

flash·back (′bak), *n.* an interruption of the sequence of a story, film, etc. by the interposition of an earlier event.

flash·bulb (′bulb), *n.* an electric light bulb producing a brief, brilliant light for taking photographs.

flash·cube (′kūb), *n.* a revolving cube having flashbulbs in four sides.

flash·ing (′ing), *n.* sheet metal used in weatherproofing joints, edges, etc. of a roof.

flash·light (′līt), *n.* 1. a portable electric lamp. 2. a momentarily brilliant light for taking photographs.

flash point, the lowest temperature at which the vapors of a volatile, combustible liquid will ignite in air.

flash·y (′ĭ), *adj.* **flash′i·er, flash′i·est,** 1. dazzling for the moment. 2. showy; gaudy.

flask (flask), *n.* 1. any one of various containers used in laboratories. 2. a broad, flat tened container for liquor, carried in the pocket.

flat (flat), *n.* an apartment on one floor.

flat (flat), *adj.* 1. having a level, smooth surface. 2. lying at full length. 3. having little depth; shallow and thin. 4. downright. 5. unvarying. 6. uninteresting; insipid. 7. deflated. 8. not glossy. 9. in *Music*, lower than true pitch: *adv.* 1. in a flat manner or position. 2. directly. 3. in *Music*, lower than the true pitch: *n.* 1. a flat surface, part, or area. 2. a deflated tire. 3. in *Music*, a note one half step lower than another or the symbol for this: *v.t. & v.i.* **flat'ted, flat'ting,** to make or become flat. —**flat'ly,** *adv.* —**flat'ness,** *n.*

flat-boat ('bōt), *n.* a flat-bottomed boat for transporting freight.

flat-car ('kär), *n.* a railroad freight car without sides or a roof.

flat-fish ('fish), *n., pl.* **-fish, -fish-es,** any one of numerous fishes, as the flounders, with a flattened body and both eyes on the upper side.

flat-foot ('foot), *n.* 1. a condition of the foot in which the arch is flattened. 2. *pl.* **-foots,** [Slang], a policeman. —**flat'-foot-ed** ('foot-id), *adj.*

flat-i-ron ('ī-ẽrn), *n.* same as **iron** (sense 2).

flat-ten ('n), *v.t. & v.i.* to make or become flat or flatter.

flat-ter (flat'ẽr), *v.t.* 1. to compliment hypocritically. 2. to attempt to win over, as by praise. 3. to portray attractively. 4. to feed the vanity of: *v.i.* to employ flattery. —**flat'-ter-er,** *n.*

flat-ter (flat'ẽr), *n.* 1. one that flattens. 2. a plate for flattening strips of metal, as for watch springs.

flat-ter-y (flat'ẽr-i), *n.* 1. the act of flattering. 2. hypocritical, untrue, or adulatory praise.

flat-top ('top), *n.* [Slang], an aircraft carrier.

flat-u-lent (flach'ŭ-lĕnt), *adj.* 1. afflicted with or making gas in the intestinal tract. 2. pretentious; high-flown. —**flat'u-lence,** *n.*

flat-ware (flat'wer), *n.* tableware that is comparatively flat.

flat-wise ('wīz), *adv.* with the flat side downwards: also **flat'ways** ('wāz).

flaunt (flônt), *v.i. & v.i.* to display ostentatiously or impudently.

fla-vin (flā'vin), *n.* any of a group of water-soluble yellow pigments; specifically, riboflavin.

fla-vor (flā'vẽr), *n.* 1. the distinctive smell and taste of a substance. 2. seasoning. 3. a distinguishing quality: *v.t.* to impart flavor to. —**fla'vor-ful,** *adj.*

fla-vor-ing (-ing), *n.* an essence or extract for giving a flavor to something.

fla-vour (flā'vẽr), *n. & v.t.* British form for **flavor.**

flaw (flô), *n.* 1. a fault; inherent defect. 2. a crack; blemish: *v.t. & v.i.* to make or become defective. —**flaw'less,** *adj.* —**flaw'-less-ness,** *n.*

flax (flaks), *n.* 1. a plant with blue flowers, seeds that yield linseed oil, and stems whose fibers are spun into linen cloth. 2. the threadlike fibers of this plant.

flax-en ('n), *adj.* 1. resembling or made of flax. 2. pale-yellow.

flax-seed ('sēd), *n.* the seed of the flax; linseed.

flay (flā), *v.t.* 1. to strip off the skin of. 2. to criticize severely.

flea (flē), *n.* a small, wingless, jumping insect that is a parasitic bloodsucker as an adult.

flea-bane ('bān), *n.* a plant having asterlike flowers.

flea-bite ('bīt), *n.* 1. the bite of a flea. 2. the red spot it causes. 3. a minor inconvenience or trifling annoyance.

fleam (flēm), *n.* a lancet formerly used in phlebotomy.

flea market, an outdoor market selling used goods, cheap articles, etc.

fleck (flek), *n.* a streak, spot, or particle: *v.t.* to speckle.

flec-tion (flek'shŭn), *n.* 1. the act of bending. 2. a bent part. 3. in *Grammar,* inflection.

fled (fled), past tense and past participle of **flee.**

sledge (flej), *v.i.* **fledged, fledg'ing,** to grow the full plumage necessary for flight: *v.t.* to rear (a young bird) until ready for flight.

fledg-ling ('ling), *n.* 1. a young bird just fledged. 2. a young or inexperienced person.

flee (flē), *v.i. & v.t.* **fled, flee'ing,** 1. to hasten away from, as danger, trouble, etc. 2. to disappear.

fleece (flēs), *n.* 1. the coat of wool of a sheep or like animal. 2. all the wool shorn from a sheep at one time. 3. a soft fabric with a nap: *v.t.* **fleeced, fleec'ing,** 1. to shear the wool from. 2. to defraud.

fleec-y ('i), *adj.* **fleec'i-er, fleec'i-est,** 1. made of fleece. 2. resembling fleece. —**fleec'i-ly,** *adv.* —**fleec'i-ness,** *n.*

fleer (flir), *v.i.* 1. to laugh scornfully (at); sneer (at): *n.* a taunting grimace; gibe.

fleet (flēt), *n.* 1. an assemblage of warships under one command. 2. any group of ships, trucks, airplanes, etc. owned or operated as a unit.

fleet (flēt), *adj.* swift; rapid; nimble. —**fleet'-ness,** *n.*

fleet-ing ('ing), *adj.* passing quickly.

Flem-ish (flem'ish), *adj.* of or pertaining to Flanders, a region in northwestern Europe, its people, or their language: *n.* the Germanic language of Flanders.

flense (flens), *v.t.* **flensed, flens'ing,** to strip the blubber or skin from (a whale, seal, etc.).

flesh (flesh), *n.* 1. the soft part of the body underlying the skin; especially, the skeletal muscle. 2. meat. 3. the pulp of fruit and vegetables. 4. the body as separate from the soul or mind. 5. man's sensual nature. 6. mankind. 7. yellowish pink: *v.t.* 1. to inure or harden. 2. to fatten. —**flesh'y,** *adj.* **flesh'-i-er, flesh'i-est.**

flesh-ings ('ingz), *n.pl.* 1. flesh-colored tights. 2. scrapings from hides.

flesh-ly ('lĭ), *adj.* **-li-er, -li-est,** 1. of or pertaining to the body. 2. carnal. 3. corpulent.

fleur-de-lis (flûr-dĕ-lē'), *n., pl.* **fleurs-de-lis'** (-lēz'), an irislike, heraldic emblem of the French kings.

flew (flōō), past tense of **fly.**

ō in drag**o**n, ōō in cr**u**de, oo in w**oo**l, u in c**u**p, ū in c**u**re, ū in t**u**rn, ŭ in f**o**cus, oi in b**oy,** ou in h**ou**se, th in **th**in, th in shea**th**e, g in **g**et, j in **j**oy, y in **y**et.

flex (fleks), *v.t.* & *v.i.* 1. to bend (a joint, finger, etc.). 2. to contract (a muscle).

flex·i·ble (flek'si-bl), *adj.* 1. easily bent without breaking; pliant. 2. yielding easily to persuasion. 3. adaptable to change. —**flex·i·bil'i·ty**, *n.*

flex·or (flek'sēr), *n.* a muscle that acts in bending the joints.

flex·u·ous (flek'shoo-wŭs), *adj.* sinuous.

flex·ure ('shēr), *n.* 1. the act of bending. 2. a curve or fold.

flib·ber·ti·gib·bet (flib'ēr-ti-jib'it), *n.* a silly, restless person.

flick (flik), *n.* a light, quick blow: *v.t.* to hit, toss, touch, etc. lightly.

flick (flik), *n.* [Slang], a movie.

flick·er ('ēr), *v.i.* 1. to move with an unsteady, quick motion. 2. to burn or shine unsteadily: *n.* 1. an act of flickering. 2. a flash or gleam of light.

flick·er ('ēr), *n.* a North American woodpecker with golden wings.

fli·er (flī'ēr), *n.* 1. one that flies. 2. an aviator. 3. a train, bus, etc. scheduled for fast runs. 4. a widely circulated handbill. 5. [Informal], a wild speculation.

flight (flīt), *n.* 1. the act, process, manner, or power of flying. 2. a group flying together. 3. the distance traveled. 4. an airplane scheduled to fly a certain route. 5. an airplane trip. 6. a soaring above the usual. 7. a series of steps, as between stair landings.

flight (flīt), *n.* the act of running away.

flight·less ('lis), *adj.* unable to fly.

flight·y ('i), *adj.* **flight'i·er, flight'i·est,** 1. given to sudden caprice. 2. silly; irresponsible. —**flight'i·ness,** *n.*

flim·flam (flim'flam), *n.* 1. nonsense. 2. trickery: *v.t.* -**flammed, -flam·ming,** [Informal], to swindle.

flim·sy (flim'zi), *adj.* -**si·er, -si·est,** 1. thin and insubstantial. 2. unconvincing. —**flim'si·ness,** *n.*

flinch (flinch), *v.i.* to draw back, as from a blow, pain, danger, etc.: *n.* an act of flinching.

flin·ders (flin'dērz), *n.pl.* splinters; fragments.

fling (fling), *v.t.* **flung, fling'ing,** 1. to throw or hurl. 2. to send suddenly or violently. 3. to move (the arms, legs, etc.) unexpectedly: *n.* 1. an act of flinging. 2. a short period of unrestrained pleasure. 3. a lively dance. 4. [Informal], an attempt.

flint (flint), *n.* 1. a very hard variety of quartz that sparks when struck with steel. 2. a flint implement. 3. anything flintlike in hardness. —**flint·y,** *adj.* **flint'i·er, flint'i·est.**

flip (flip), *v.t.* **flipped, flip'ping,** 1. to throw with a quick jerk. 2. to propel (a coin) into the air so that it spins. 3. to turn or overturn: *v.i.* 1. to move jerkily. 2. [Slang], to be overwhelmed, as with emotion: *n.* an act of flipping.

flip (flip), *n.* a sweetened drink, often mixed with beaten eggs and spices.

flip (flip), *adj.* **flip'per, flip'pest,** [Informal], flippant.

flip-flop (flip'flop), *n.* 1. a noise caused by flapping. 2. a backward handspring. 3. a sudden change in direction or point of view.

flip·pant (flip'ănt), *adj.* not serious; disrespectful; saucy. —**flip'pan·cy,** *n., pl.* -**cies.** —**flip'pant·ly,** *adv.*

flip·per ('ēr), *n.* 1. a wide, flat appendage developed for swimming, as in seals. 2. a flexible, paddlelike device worn on the feet by swimmers.

flirt (flŭrt), *v.t.* to move to and fro briskly: *v.i.* 1. to play at love. 2. to toy with fleetingly: *n.* 1. an abrupt, jerky motion. 2. one who flirts.

flir·ta·tion (flēr-tā'shŭn), *n.* a casual love affair. —**flir·ta'tious,** *adj.*

flit (flit), *v.i.* **flitted, flit'ting,** to move about lightly and quickly.

flitch (flich), *n.* the side of a hog salted and cured.

fliv·ver (fliv'ēr), *n.* [Old Slang], a cheap car.

float (flōt), *v.i.* 1. to be buoyed up on the surface of a liquid. 2. to remain suspended in space without falling. 3. to drift randomly. 4. to fluctuate in relationship to other currencies: said of a currency: *v.t.* 1. to cause to float. 2. to place (securities) on the market. 3. to negotiate (a loan): *n.* 1. anything that floats, as a raft, fishing bob, etc. 2. a low vehicle with a platform for carrying an exhibit in a parade.

float·er ('ēr), *n.* 1. one that floats. 2. a person who votes illegally at several polling places. 3. a person who drifts from place to place or job to job.

float valve, a valve operated by a float.

floc·cose (flok'ōs), *adj.* covered with thick, woolly tufts.

floc·cu·lent (flok'yoo-lĕnt), *adj.* 1. like wool; fluffy. 2. made up of woolly masses. —**floc'·cu·lence,** *n.*

floc·cu·lus ('yoo-lŭs), *n., pl.* -**li** (-lī), 1. a small woolly or fluffy mass or tuft. 2. in *Anatomy,* a small lobe on the lower side of each hemisphere of the cerebellum.

floc·cus (flok'ŭs), *n., pl.* **floc'ci** ('sī), a woolly or hairy mass or tuft.

flock (flok), *n.* 1. an assemblage of animals, as sheep or birds, that live, feed, etc. together. 2. any group of people or things: *v.i.* to assemble or move in a flock.

flock (flok), *n.* 1. a small tuft, as of wool or cotton. 2. waste wool or cotton used to stuff furniture, mattresses, etc. 3. fibers of wool, felt, etc. put on cloth, paper, etc. to make a patterned or textured surface.

flock·ing ('ing), *n.* a pattern in flock.

floe (flō), *n.* same as **ice floe.**

flog (flog), *v.t.* **flogged, flog'ging,** to whip or chastise by lashing with a strap, rod, etc.

flood (flud), *n.* 1. a flow of water inundating land usually dry; deluge. 2. high tide. 3. an abundant supply or outpouring, as of goods. 4. [F-], the Deluge: *v.t.* 1. to inundate. 2. to deluge: *v.i.* 1. to pour forth in a flood. 2. to become flooded.

flood·gate ('gāt), *n.* 1. a gate in a waterway, for control of the flow of water. 2. anything checking a flood or outpouring.

flood·light ('līt), *n.* 1. a lamp with a very bright, wide beam. 2. such a beam: *v.t.* -**light·ed** or -**lit, -light·ing,** to illuminate with a floodlight.

flood tide, the incoming tide.

floor (flôr), *n.* 1. the bottom surface of a room, on which one treads. 2. the lowermost surface of anything. 3. a story of a building. 4. the right to address an assembly· *v.t.* 1. to provide with a floor. 2. to knock down. 3. [Informal], to daze, bewilder, overpower, etc.

floor-board ('bôrd), *n.* 1. a board in a floor. 2. the floor of an automobile.

floor exercise, any gymnastic exercise done without apparatus.

floor-ing ('ing), *n.* 1. a floor or floors. 2. material for floors.

floor show, a succession of acts performed in a nightclub.

flop (flop), *v.t.* **flopped, flop'ping,** to move, drop, etc. noisily and heavily: *v.i.* 1. to plump down or flap loosely and flatly. 2. [Informal], to fall: *n.* 1. the act or sound of flopping. 2. [Informal], a total failure. — **flop'py,** *adj.* **-pi-er, -pi-est.**

flop-house ('hous), *n.* [Informal], a cheap hotel.

floppy disk, a small, flexible computer disk for storing data.

flo-ra (flôr'ä), *n.* 1. the plants of a particular region or period. 2. a systematic listing of such plants.

flo-ral ('äl), *adj.* of, pertaining to, or representative of flowers.

floral envelope, same as perianth.

flo-res-cence (flô-res'ěns), *n.* the act or condition of blooming. —**flo-res'cent,** *adj.*

flo-ret (flôr'it), *n.* a little flower.

flo-ri-cul-ture (flôr'i-kul-chěr), *n.* the cultivation of flowering plants. —**flo-ri-cul'tur-al,** *adj.* — **flo-ri-cul'tur-ist,** *n.*

flor-id (flôr'id), *adj.* 1. ruddy in complexion. 2. overly embellished; ornate.

flo-rif-er-ous (flô-rif'ēr-ŭs), *adj.* bearing flowers.

flor-in (flôr'in), *n.* any of various gold or silver coins of Europe or South Africa.

flo-rist (flôr'ist), *n.* a person who grows or sells flowers.

floss (flôs), *n.* 1. the short waste fibers of silk. 2. a soft, loosely twisted thread, as of cotton, for embroidery. 3. a similar substance, as in certain plants. —**floss'y,** *adj.* **floss'i-er, floss'i-est.**

flo-ta-tion (flô-tā'shŭn), *n.* the act or condition of floating; specifically, the act of financing a commercial enterprise by selling an issue of securities.

flo-til-la (flô-til'ä), *n.* 1. a small fleet. 2. a fleet of small vessels.

flot-sam (flot'săm), *n.* the goods or wreckage of a ship, found floating on the sea: chiefly in *flotsam and jetsam.*

flounce (flouns), *v.i.* **flounced, flounc'ing,** 1. to move with jerky motions of the body and limbs, as from displeasure. 2. to twist or turn suddenly: *n.* the act of flouncing.

flounce (flouns), *n.* an ornamental ruffle sewed on a skirt, curtain, etc.

flounc-ing ('sing), *n.* material for flounces.

floun-der (floun'dēr), *v.i.* 1. to struggle or proceed with difficulty, as in deep mire. 2. to speak or move clumsily or in confusion.

floun-der (floun'dēr), *n.* any of various flatfishes, as the sole, valued as food fishes.

flour (flour), *n.* 1. a fine, powdery meal from ground cereal grains, especially wheat, or from certain roots, nuts, etc. 2. any fine, soft powder: *v.t.* to sprinkle or coat with flour. —**flour'y,** *adj.*

flour-ish (flûr'ish), *v.i.* 1. to grow profusely; thrive. 2. to be at a height of development, production, etc.: *v.t.* to swing or wave (a sword, baton, etc.) in the air; brandish: *n.* 1. an act or instance of brandishing. 2. anything done in an ostentatious manner. 3. an ornamental line or lines in writing. 4. a musical fanfare.

flout (flout), *v.t. & v.i.* to treat contemptuously; scorn: *n.* a scornful action or remark.

flow (flô), *v.i.* 1. to run or spread, as water. 2. to circulate. 3. to pour forth. 4. to glide. 5. to arise. 6. to abound. 7. to hang loosely: *n.* 1. the act of flowing. 2. the amount that flows. 3. a stream or current. 4. the incoming of the tide.

flow-chart ('chärt), *n.* a diagram showing steps in a sequence of operations, as in manufacturing.

flow-er (flou'ēr), *n.* 1. that part of a flowering plant that contains the reproductive organs. 2. a blossom. 3. a plant grown for its blossoms. 4. the best, or choicest, part of anything: *v.i.* 1. to put forth flowers; blossom. 2. to develop completely.

flow-er-et ('ēr-it), *n.* same as floret.

flow-er-ing (-ing), *adj.* 1. in bloom. 2. bearing striking flowers.

flow-er-pot (-pot), *n.* a container for growing flowers.

flow-er-y (-i), *adj.* **-er-i-er, -er-i-est,** 1. adorned with flowers. 2. full of highly embellished and ornate expressions. —**flow'er-i-ness,** *n.*

flown (flôn), past participle of **fly.**

flu (flōō), *n.* 1. short for **influenza.** 2. popularly, a viral infection of the lungs or intestines.

flub (flub), *v.t. & v.i.* **flubbed, flub'bing,** [Informal], to make a mess of (an opportunity, shot, etc.).

fluc-tu-ate (fluk'choo-wāt), *v.i.* **-at-ed, -at-ing,** 1. to undulate. 2. to waver or vary irregularly. —**fluc-tu-a'tion,** *n.*

flue (flōō), *n.* a pipe or passage for the escape of smoke, hot air, etc.

flu-ent (flōō'ěnt), *adj.* 1. flowing smoothly. 2. ready and expressive in the use of language. —**flu'en-cy,** *n.* —**flu'ent-ly,** *adv.*

fluff (fluf), *n.* 1. light down. 2. a light, soft mass, as of cotton: *v.t.* 1. to make fluffy. 2. to botch or forget (one's lines), as in acting.

fluff-y ('i), *adj.* **fluff'i-er, fluff'i-est,** resembling fluff; feathery. —**fluff'i-ness,** *n.*

flu-id (flōō'id), *adj.* 1. that can flow; liquid or gaseous. 2. that can change readily or quickly. 3. accessible in cash or for investment: *n.* a liquid or gas. —**flu-id'i-ty,** *n.*

fluid dram, a liquid measure, equal to 1/8 fluid ounce.

fluid ounce, a liquid measure, equal to 8 fluid drams or 1/16 pint.

fluke (flōōk), *n.* 1. a flatfish; especially, a flounder. 2. a flatworm parasitic in vertebrates.

---

fluke (flŏŏk), *n.* 1. the pointed end of an anchor that digs into the ground. 2. a barbed head, as on an arrow. 3. one of the two lobes of a whale's tail. 4. [Informal], a stroke of good luck.

fluk-y ('i), *adj.* **fluk'i-er, fluk'i-est,** [Informal], 1. happening from mere chance. 2. continually changing; uncertain.

flume (flŏŏm), *n.* an inclined channel for conveying water, as for power.

flum-mer-y (flum'ẽr-i), *n., pl.* **-mer-ies,** 1. any of several soft, easily swallowed foods. 2. nonsensical flattery or talk.

flung (flung), past tense and past participle of **fling.**

flunk (flungk), *v.t. & v.i.* [Informal], to fail, as an examination: *n.* [Informal], a failing grade.

flun-ky (flung'ki), *n., pl.* **-kies,** 1. a liveried servant. 2. a toady. 3. one who performs menial work. Also **flunkey.**

flu-o-resce (flŏŏ-ô-res'), *v.i.* **-resced', -res'ing,** to undergo or exhibit fluorescence.

flu-o-res-cence ('ẽns), *n.* 1. the property of giving off light during the absorption of radiant energy. 2. the light so emitted. —**flu-o-res'cent,** *adj.*

fluorescent lamp, a tubular glass lamp having a fluorescent coating on its inside surface that fluoresces when struck by ultraviolet light given off by mercury vapor acted upon in the tube by a stream of electrons.

fluor-i-date (flŏr'i-dāt), *v.t.* **-dat-ed, -dat-ing,** to add fluorides to (a water supply) to lessen tooth decay. —**fluor-i-da'tion,** *n.*

flu-o-ride (floor'īd, flŏŏ'ô-rīd), *n.* any of various compounds of fluorine.

flu-o-rine (floor'ēn, flŏŏ'ô-rēn), *n.* a yellowish-green gaseous chemical element, forming compounds with most elements.

flu-o-rite (floor'īt, flŏŏ'ô-rīt), *n.* a transparent, crystalline mineral composed of calcium fluoride.

fluor-o-scope (floor'ô-skōp), *n.* an instrument for viewing internal structures of an opaque object, as a human body, by studying the intensity of shadows cast on a fluorescent screen by X-rays sent through the object.

flu-or-spar (flŏŏ'ẽr-spär), *n.* same as **fluorite.**

flur-ry (flûr'i), *v.t.* **-ried, -ry-ing,** to agitate; bewilder: *n., pl.* **-ries,** 1. a sudden gust of wind. 2. a brief snowfall. 3. a sudden commotion or excitement.

flush (flush), *v.t.* 1. to cause to blush. 2. to excite. 3. to clean out with a rush of water. 4. to drive (game) from cover: *v.i.* 1. to flow quickly. 2. to blush or glow. 3. to be cleaned out by a rush of water: *n.* 1. a sudden rush, as of water. 2. sudden excitement. 3. a blush or glow. 4. a sudden growth or maturation. 5. a fleeting sensation of heat, as from a fever: *adj.* 1. plentifully supplied, as with money. 2. abundant. 3. level. 4. direct, as a blow: *adv.* 1. so as to be level. 2. directly.

flush (flush), *n.* a hand of cards all of the same suit.

flus-ter (flus'tẽr), *v.t. & v.i.* to make or become bewildered: *n.* a state of agitation.

flute (flŏŏt), *n.* 1. a high-pitched, tubular wind instrument with finger holes and keys. 2. a long groove in the shaft of a column, in cloth, etc. —**flut'ed,** *adj.* —**flut'ing,** *n.* —**flut'ist,** *n.*

flut-ter (flut'ẽr), *v.i.* 1. to move or flap the wings rapidly, without flying. 2. to beat, move, or vibrate quickly and irregularly. 3. to be in a state of agitation or uncertainty: *v.t.* to cause to flutter: *n.* 1. a quick and irregular movement or pulsation. 2. a state of excitement, anxiety, bewilderment, etc.

flut-y (flŏŏt'i), *adj.* **flut'i-er, flut'i-est,** flutelike in tone.

flu-vi-al (flŏŏ'vi-ål), *adj.* of, pertaining to, found in, or caused by a river.

flux (fluks), *n.* 1. a flow. 2. any abnormal discharge of fluid from the body. 3. a continual fluctuation. 4. a substance used to induce fusion, as of metals and minerals.

fly (flī), *v.i.* **flew, flown, fly'ing,** 1. to move through, or rise in, the air by using wings. 2. to float or flutter in the air. 3. to move or pass by quickly. 4. to flee. 5. **flied, fly'ing,** in *Baseball,* to hit a fly: *v.t.* 1. to cause to float in the air. 2. to pilot (an aircraft). 3. to run away from; shun: *n., pl.* **flies,** 1. a flap of cloth on a garment that hides a zipper, buttons, etc. 2. a flap that covers a tent entrance. 3. in *Baseball,* a ball batted into the air. 4. *pl.* the space over the stage of a theater.

fly (flī), *n., pl.* **flies,** 1. any one of a large number of two-winged insects; especially, the housefly. 2. an artificial fly used in angling.

fly-a-ble ('ă-bl), *adj.* suitable for flying.

fly-a-way ('ă-wā), *adj.* 1. giddy. 2. streaming in the wind. 3. ready to fly.

fly-blow ('blō), *n.* the larva or egg of a blowfly: *v.t. & v.i.* **-blew, -blown, -blow-ing,** 1. to deposit flyblows in (meat, wounds, etc.). 2. to contaminate; taint.

fly-blown ('blōn), *adj.* 1. full of flyblows. 2. tainted; spoiled. 3. seedy, shabby, corrupt, etc.

fly-boat ('bōt), *n.* any of various fast vessels; especially, a flat-bottomed Dutch boat.

fly-by-night ('bi-nīt), *adj.* financially unreliable: *n.* an absconding debtor.

fly-cast ('kast), *v.i.* **-cast, -cast-ing,** to fish by casting and retrieving artificial flies.

fly-catch-er ('kach-ẽr), *n.* any one of numerous passerine birds that catch insects on the wing.

fly-er ('ẽr), *n.* same as **flier.**

flying buttress, an arched brace connected to a wall, pier, etc. and abutting against a part of a building to receive the thrust.

flying colors, 1. flags waving in the air. 2. a notable triumph.

Flying Dutchman, 1. a fabled Dutch mariner condemned to sail the seas until Judgment Day. 2. his spectral ship, held by sailors to be a bad portent.

flying fish, a warm-water sea fish with long pectoral fins enabling it to sustain itself in the air for a short time.

---

a in cap, ā in cane, ä in father, å in abet, e in met　ē in be, ē in baker, ẽ in regent, i in pit, ī in fine, ǐ in manifest, o in hot, ō in horse, ō in bone,

flying gurnard, a kind of flying fish.

flying jib, a sail beyond the jib.

flying saucer, same as UFO.

flying squirrel, a North American squirrel with elastic folds of skin along the legs and body: it makes long, flying leaps.

fly-leaf (flī'lēf), *n.,* *pl.* -leaves ('lēvz), an unprinted leaf at the beginning or end of a book.

fly-pa-per ('pā-pēr), *n.* a sticky or poisonous paper to catch flies.

fly-speck ('spek), *n.* 1. the tiny excremental deposit of a fly. 2. a tiny spot or flaw.

fly-weight ('wāt), *n.* a boxer, wrestler, etc. whose weight is 112 pounds or less.

fly-wheel ('hwēl), *n.* a heavy wheel regulating the motion of a machine.

f-num-ber (ef'num-bēr), *n.* in *Photography,* the ratio of a lens diameter to its focal length: the lower the number, the shorter the exposure required.

foal (fōl), *n.* a young horse, donkey, etc.: *v.t. & v.i.* to give birth to (a foal).

foam (fōm), *n.* 1. the frothy white substance formed on a liquid by agitation, fermentation, etc. 2. something foamlike, as frothy saliva. 3. a cellular mass as of rubber: *v.i.* to cause to foam: *v.i.* to form foam. — **foam'y,** *adj.* **foam'i-er, foam'i-est.**

fob (fob), *n.* 1. a small pocket at the front of pants or vests, especially for a watch. 2. a short ribbon or chain for a watch there. 3. an ornament attached to the end of such a ribbon or chain.

fob (fob), *v.t.* **fobbed, fob'bing,** 1. to dispose of or pass off by fraud or trickery (with *off*). 2. to deceive, trick, or fend off (with *off*).

fo-cal (fō'kl), *adj.* of, pertaining to, or placed at a focus. — **fo'cal-ly,** *adv.*

focal length, the distance between the optical center of a lens and the point where the rays converge: also **focal distance.**

fo'c's'le (fōk'sl), *n.* phonetic spelling of **forecastle.**

fo-cus (fō'kŭs), *n., pl.* -cus-es, -ci ('sī), 1. the meeting point of rays of light, heat, etc. or of waves of sound, or the point from which they spread; specifically, the point where light rays meet after being reflected or refracted. 2. same as **focal length.** 3. adjustment of focal length to get a clear image. 4. any central point: *v.t.* -cused or -cussed, -cus-ing or -cus-sing, 1. to adjust for clarity of image or proper focal length. 2. to center or concentrate: *v.i.* 1. to meet, as light rays. 2. to become focused.

fod-der (fod'ēr), *n.* food for horses, cattle, sheep, etc.: *v.t.* to feed with fodder.

foe (fō), *n.* same as **enemy.**

foehn (fān), *n.* a warm, dry wind blowing down into valleys, as in the Alps.

foe-man (fō'mǎn), *n., pl.* -men, [Archaic], an adversary in war.

foe-tus (fēt'ŭs), *n.* alternate spelling of **fetus.** — **foe'tal,** *adj.*

fog (fŏg, fog), *n.* 1. condensed watery vapor near the surface of land or of a body of water. 2. a state of bewilderment. 3. a cloud or haze obscuring a photograph or film: *v.t.*

& v.i. **fogged, fog'ging,** to make or become foggy.

fog bank, a dense mass of fog.

fog-gy (fŏg'i, fog'i). *adj.* -gi-er, -gi-est, 1. abounding in, covered with, or obscured by fog. 2. bewildered, confused, or uncertain. — **fog'gi-ly,** *adv.* **fog'gi-ness,** *n.*

fog-horn ('hòrn), *n.* a loud horn used in fog by ships as a warning device.

fo-gy (fō'gi), *n., pl.* -gies, a hidebound, old-fashioned person: also **fo'gey,** *pl.* -geys.

foi-ble (foi'bl), *n.* 1. a minor imperfection of character; failing. 2. the weaker part of the blade in a sword.

foil (foil), *v.t.* to baffle, frustrate, or thwart: *n.* 1. a long, thin fencing sword with a button on the point. 2. a thin sheet or leaf of metal. 3. something giving prominence to another by contrast, especially to the advantage of the other. 4. a small, ornamental arc, as in the tracery of a Gothic window.

foist (foist), *v.t.* 1. to place in wrongfully or surreptitiously. 2. to impose deceitfully or fraudulently, often by force (with *on* or *upon*); fob off.

fold (fōld), *v.t.* 1. to bring one part of over and against another. 2. to bring together and join with parts crossing each other. 3. to put (wings) close to the body. 4. to draw into a close embrace. 5. to wrap up; enclose. 6. to shut up in a pen or fold: *v.i.* 1. to undergo folding or become folded. 2. [Informal], to collapse or fail: *n.* 1. a folded part. 2. a crease, indentation, etc. made by folding. 3. a pen, as for sheep; also, a flock of sheep. 4. a united group or organization, as a church.

-fold (fōld), a suffix meaning (*an indicated number of*) times as many, as much, as large or having (*an indicated number of*) parts.

fold-er (fōl'dēr), *n.* 1. one that folds. 2. a stiff or thick folded sheet, as of Manila paper, to hold loose papers. 3. any flat, folding container or holder, as a small one of thin, light cardboard to hold paper safety matches. 4. a folding circular, timetable, etc.

fol-de-rol (fol'dē-rol, fôl'dē-rôl), *n.* same as **falderal.**

folding door, a door made up of hinged sections that fold together or of a heavy pleated material folding compactly like the bellows of an accordion.

fo-li-a-ceous (fō-li-ā'shŭs), *adj.* 1. of or like a plant leaf. 2. having leaves. 3. consisting of thin plates or laminae.

fo-li-age (fō'li-ij), *n.* 1. leaves collectively. 2. an artistic representation of leaves, flowers, branches, etc.

fo-li-ate ('li-āt), *v.t.* -at-ed, -at-ing, 1. to split up into thin layers. 2. to beat into foil. 3. to decorate with leaflike ornamentation. 4. to number the leaves of (a book or manuscript): *v.i.* 1. to separate into thin layers. 2. to put forth leaves: *adj.* ('li-it), 1. having leaves. 2. leaflike.

fo-li-a-tion (fō-li-ā'shŭn), *n.* 1. production of, or development into, leaves. 2. the state of having leaves. 3. arrangement of leaves in a leaf bud. 4. the act or process of beating into foil. 5. layer formation, as of certain

---

ŏ in drag*o*n, ōō in cr*u*de, oo in w*oo*l, u in c*u*p, ū in c*u*re, ū in t*u*rn, ŭ in f*o*cus, oi in b*oy,* ou in h*ou*se, th in *th*in, th in shea*th*e, g in *g*et, j in *j*oy, y in *y*et.

minerals; lamination. 6. the consecutive numbering of leaves, rather than pages, of a book. 7. foliate decoration.

fo·lic acid (fō'lik), a certain crystalline substance, a common source of which is green leaves, exhibiting vitamin B activity.

fo·li·o (fō'li-ō), n., pl. -os, 1. a large sheet of paper folded once, thus forming two leaves, or four pages, as of a book. 2. a book of the largest regular size, now often 12 by 15 inches. 3. a leaf, as of a manuscript, numbered on only one side. 4. the number of a page as of a book. 5. a number of words (100 in the U.S.) taken as a unit to measure the length of a legal or official document. 6. in *Bookkeeping,* a ledger page, or facing pages numbered the same: *adj.* having sheets folded once; of folio size: *v.t.* -oed, -o·ing, to number the pages of, as a book.

folk (fōk), n., pl. folk, folks, 1. a particular people, nation, etc. 2. pl. the ordinary individuals belonging to and representative of any such grouping. 3. pl. people in general. 4. pl. individuals of an indicated locality, economic or social level, etc.: *adj.* of, typical of, or originating among folk (sense 2). See also folks.

folk·lore ('lōr), n. popular traditions, customs, beliefs, etc.

folks (fōks), n.pl. [Informal], one's family or relatives, especially one's parents.

folk song, 1. a traditional, usually anonymous song originating among the common people. 2. a song imitative of this. —**folk singer.**

folk·sy (fōk'si), adj. -si·er, -si·est, [Informal], friendly, direct, or simple in a manner suggestive of, or meant to be suggestive of, plain, neighborly people: often derogatory. —**folk'si·ness,** n.

folk·way (fōk'wā), n. a way of living, thinking, etc. common to members of a given social group.

fol·li·cle (fol'i-kl), n. 1. in *Anatomy,* a small sac, cavity, or gland. 2. in *Botany,* a dry, one-celled seed capsule or pod, as of a milkweed, opening along only one side to release its seeds. —**fol·li·cu·lar** (fō-lik'yoo-lēr), adj.

fol·lies (fol'iz), n. revue: in titles.

fol·low (fol'ō), v.t. 1. to go or come after. 2. to accompany; attend. 3. to chase after; pursue. 4. to proceed along or over. 5. to succeed in time, series, order, etc. 6. to cause to be succeeded by another specified thing (with *with*). 7. to engage in; practice. 8. to conform to or imitate. 9. to see (something) through; carry out fully (with *through, out, up*). 10. to espouse the cause, opinions, etc. of. 11. to watch or attend to closely. 12. to see or understand the thought, logic, or interconnection of: *v.i.* 1. to go, come, or happen next or afterward. 2. take place in consequence; occur as a result. 3. to continue and complete an action (with *through*).

fol·low·er (-ēr), n. one that follows; specifically, a supporter, disciple, attendant, or servant.

fol·low·ing (-ing), adj. 1. that follows; next. 2. (to be) mentioned, listed, etc. next: n. a group of disciples, adherents, etc.: *prep.* after.

fol·low-through (-ō-thrōō), n. the act of following through; continuation or completion of an action.

fol·low-up (-up), adj. designating or of that which follows something else as by way of continuation or completion: n. 1. anything so following. 2. the act of following up.

fol·ly (fol'i), n., pl. -lies, 1. lack of understanding. 2. foolishness. 3. any procedure leading or likely to lead to disaster.

fo·ment (fō-ment'), v.t. 1. to treat with warm or medicated liquids, compresses, etc. 2. to stir up or instigate; incite.

fo·men·ta·tion (fō-mĕn-tā'shŭn), n. 1. the act of fomenting. 2. a warm liquid, medication, etc. used in fomenting.

fond (fond), adj. 1. affectionate; loving. 2. ardently attached or devoted. 3. ardently cherished, as hope. 4. too indulgent; doting. 5. partial to something specified (with *of*). —**fond'ness,** n.

fon·dant (fon'dănt), n. 1. a sweet, soft, creamy preparation made from sugar, often a filling in bonbons. 2. such a candy.

fon·dle (fon'dl), v.t. -dled, -dling, to handle or stroke with affection; caress.

fond·ly (fond'li), adv. 1. in a fond way. 2. in an overly confident or credulous way.

fon·due, fon·du (fon-dōō', fon'dōō), n. any one of various dishes, especially seasoned melted cheese or a cheese soufflé.

font (font), n. 1. a basinlike receptacle for water used in baptizing. 2. a basinlike receptacle, as inside a church entrance, in which holy water is kept. 3. a source; origin. 4. in *Printing,* a complete assortment of a particular kind of type.

fon·ta·nel, fon·ta·nelle (fon-tă-nel'), n. any one of the soft, boneless areas in the skull of an infant or young animal.

food (fōōd), n. 1. nourishment; nutriment, especially in solid form. 2. anything that sustains life.

food poisoning, illness from eating contaminated food or apparently edible things, as poisonous varieties of mushrooms, that are in fact inedible.

food-stuff ('stuf), n. any material converted into or used as food.

fool (fōōl), n. 1. a person greatly deficient in good judgment, common sense, etc; total idiot. 2. a medieval jester. 3. the butt of a joke or trick; dupe: adj. [Informal], foolish: *v.i.* 1. to act like a fool. 2. to say or do things only as a joke or in mere pretense of being serious. 3. [Informal], to putter, toy, or involve oneself; dawdle, trifle, or meddle (often with *around*): *v.t.* to mislead or trick; dupe.

fool·er·y (-ēr-i), n., pl. -er·ies, foolish behavior or an instance of this.

fool·har·dy ('här-di), adj. -di·er, -di·est, foolishly bold; rash; reckless. —**fool'har·di·ly,** adv. —**fool'har·di·ness,** n.

fool·ish (fōōl'ish), adj. 1. greatly deficient in good judgment, common sense, real wisdom, etc.; idiotic. 2. contrary to all good sense; absurd. 3. inviting mockery, scorn, or derision; ridiculous. 4. disconcerted; abashed;

embarrassed. —**fool′ish·ly**, *adv.* —**fool′ish·ness**, *n.*

fool·proof (fōōl′prōōf), *adj.* incapable of being misused, botched, damaged, etc. even by a fool.

fools·cap (fōōlz′kap), *n.* a size of writing paper, especially (in the U.S.) one measuring 13 by 16 inches.

foot (foot), *n., pl.* **feet.** 1. the terminal part of the leg of a person or animal, contacting the surface on which the individual stands, walks, etc. 2. the lower part, base, foundation, or end of anything. 3. the part, as of a stocking, that covers the foot. 4. *pl. often* **foot,** a measure of length, equal to 12 inches: symbol (′). 5. [British], infantry. 6. a group of syllables constituting a unit of meter in verse: *v.i.* to walk, run, or dance (often with *it*): *v.t.* 1. to walk, run, or dance on, over, or through. 2. to make or restore the foot of, as a stocking. 3. to total *up* (a column of figures). 4. [Informal], to pay, as a bill.

foot·age (′ij), *n.* length in feet.

foot·ball (′bôl), *n.* 1. a field game in which each of two contesting teams tries to get an inflated leather ball across the opponents′ goal. 2. the ball used.

foot·bridge (′brij), *n.* a narrow bridge for pedestrains.

foot·fall (′fôl), *n.* the sound of a footstep.

foot·hill (′hil), *n.* a low hill at or near the foot of a mountain or mountain range.

foot·hold (′hōld), *n.* 1. a place where the foot can be set securely, without slipping, as in climbing. 2. any initial or subsequent secure position in progressing.

foot·ing (′ing), *n.* 1. a secure placing of the feet. 2. condition of a given surface for this. 3. same as **foothold.** 4. condition allowing establishment or development of some relationship. 5. the totaling or total of a column of figures. 6. in *Architecture,* a supporting base or enlarged foundation as for a wall.

foot·lights (′lits), *n.pl.* a row of lights along the front of a stage, at foot level.

foot·lock·er (′lok·ĕr), *n.* a small trunk kept at the foot of a bed, as in a barracks.

foot·loose (′lōōs), *adj.* free to go anywhere or do anything.

foot·man (′mán), *n., pl.* **-men,** a male servant to assist a butler.

foot·note (′nōt), *n.* a note put at the bottom of a page as to indicate a source.

foot·pad (′pad), *n.* one going on foot who forcibly stops and robs people.

foot·path (′path), *n.* a narrow path for use by pedestrians.

foot·pound (′pound′), *n.* a unit of energy, equal to the energy needed to raise one pound a distance of one foot.

foot·print (′print), *n.* an impression or mark from a foot or shoe, as on wet sand.

foot·race (′ras), *n.* a race run by persons on foot.

foot·rest (′rest), *n.* a support, as a rail or stool, on which the feet can rest.

foot soldier, an infantryman.

foot·sore (′sôr), *adj.* having tired, tender, or aching feet, as from walking too long.

foot·step (′step), *n.* 1. a stepping; tread. 2. the distance covered by stepping. 3. a footfall. 4. a footprint. 5. a step, as of a staircase.

foot·stool (′stōōl), *n.* a portable support, as a hassock, on which the feet of a seated person can rest.

foot·wear (′wer), *n.* things worn on the feet, as shoes, boots, or slippers.

foot·work (′wŭrk), *n.* use of the feet, as in dancing or boxing.

fop (fop), *n.* a vain man obsessed with wearing ultramodish clothes. —**fop′pish,** *adj.*

fop·per·y (′er·i), *n., pl.* **-per·ies,** 1. the clothes, behavior, etc. of a fop. 2. something foppish.

for (fôr, fēr), *prep.* 1. instead of. 2. as representative or advocate of. 3. in honor of. 4. with the goal of. 5. directed toward. 6. with regard to. 7. because of. 8. in spite of. 9. to or at the amount of: *conj.* inasmuch as; since.

fo·ra (fôr′ä), *n.* alternate plural of forum.

for·age (fôr′ij, for′ij), *n.* 1. fodder. 2. a search for provisions or other things wanted: *v.i.* **-aged, -ag·ing,** 1. to search about for provisions or other things wanted. 2. to make a raid for these: *v.t.* 1. to get by foraging. 2. to supply with fodder.

fo·ra·men (fō-rä′mĕn, fô-), *n., pl.* **-ram′i·na** (-ram′i-nä), **-ra′mens,** a short passage or opening, as in a bone or plant ovule.

for·as·much (fôr-áz-much′), *conj.* inasmuch.

for·ay (fôr′ä), *n.* a sudden, predatory attack or raid: *v.t. & v.i.* to attack thus.

for·bear (fôr-ber′, fēr-), **-bore′, -borne′, -bear′ing,** to abstain from (doing, saying, etc.): *v.i.* 1. to abstain. 2. to restrain oneself; be patient: *n.* same as forebear. —**for·bear′ance,** *n.*

for·bid (fēr-bid′, fôr-), *v.t.* **-bade′** or **-bad′, -bid′den, -bid′ding,** 1. to prohibit. 2. to command avoidance of or exclusion from; bar. 3. to prevent; preclude.

for·bid·ding (′ing), *adj.* 1. threatening. 2. disagreeable; repellent.

force (fôrs), *n.* 1. power; vigor; strength; energy. 2. coercion; violence. 3. ability to convince, move, persuade, etc.; also, something embodying this. 4. exact meaning; point. 5. military power. 6. *pl.* collective armed strength. 7. a body of troops, sailors, etc. 8. any organized body. 9. in *Law,* validity; legality. 10. in *Physics,* a cause of motion or change of motion in a body: *v.t.* **forced, forc′ing,** 1. to compel. 2. to overpower. 3. to break open, into, or through by force. 4. to wrest; extort. 5. to push; press; strain; impel. 6. to cause to grow or ripen by artificial means.

forced (fôrst), *adj.* strained; affected.

force-feed (fôrs′fēd′), *v.t.* **-fed′, -feed′ing,** to feed by force.

force·ful (′fŭl), *adj.* full of force; strong, energetic, effective, etc. —**force′ful·ly,** *adv.* —**force′ful·ness,** *n.*

force-meat (fôrs'mĕt), *n.* meat chopped fine and seasoned.

for-ceps (fôr'sĕps), *n., pl.* **-ceps,** small tongs or pincers, especially surgical ones.

force pump, a pump with a valveless plunger to force liquid through a pipe.

for-ci-ble (fôr'si-bl), *adj.* 1. done by or involving force. 2. same as **forceful.** **—for'ci-bly,** *adv.*

ford (fôrd), *n.* a shallow part, as of a stream, that can be waded through: *v.t.* to traverse a ford of.

fore (fôr), *n.* the foremost or leading place: *adv.* toward the bow; forward: *adj.* situated in front: *interj.* in *Golf,* a warning shout before a drive.

fore-, a prefix meaning *before, in front.*

fore-and-aft (fôr'n-aft'), *adj.* from the bow to the stern; lengthwise.

fore-arm (fôr'ärm), *n.* the part of the arm between wrist and elbow: *v.t.* to prepare in advance, as against attack or trouble.

fore-bear ('ber), *n.* an ancestor.

fore-bode (fôr-bōd'), *v.t.* **-bod'ed, -bod'ing,** 1. to presage, especially evil. 2. to have a presentiment of. **—fore-bod'ing,** *n.*

fore-brain (fôr'brān), *n.* the front part of the three primary divisions of the brain of a vertebrate embryo.

fore-cast (fôr'kast), *n.* a prediction, as of weather conditions: *v.t. & v.i.* **-cast** or **-cast-ed, -cast-ing,** to predict.

fore-cas-tle (fōk'sl, fôr'kas-l), 1. the upper deck of a ship, before the foremast. 2. the front part of a merchant ship, where the sailors' quarters are located.

fore-close (fôr-klōz'), *v.t. & v.i.* **-closed, -clos'-ing,** to take away the right to redeem, as a mortgage. **—fore-clo'sure,** *n.*

fore-doom (-dōōm'), *v.t.* to doom in advance.

fore-fa-ther (fôr'fä-thẽr), *n.* a forebear.

fore-fin-ger (f'fing-gẽr), *n.* the finger nearest the thumb.

fore-foot ('foot), *n., pl.* **-feet,** either of the front feet of a quadruped, etc.

fore-front ('frunt), *n.* 1. the extreme front. 2. the most prominent position.

fore-gath-er (fôr-gath'ẽr), *v.i.* same as **forgather.**

fore-go (-gō'), *v.t. & v.i.* **-went', -gone', -go'ing,** to precede.

fore-go (-gō'), *v.t.* same as **forgo.**

fore-go-ing (fôr'gō-ing), *adj.* preceding.

fore-gone (-gôn'), *adj.* 1. previous. 2. inevitable: said of a conclusion.

fore-ground (fôr'ground), *n.* 1. the part of a scene, picture, etc. nearest or represented as nearest the viewer. 2. the most prominent position.

fore-hand ('hand), *n.* a stroke, as in tennis, with arm extended and palm turned forward: *adj.* 1. foremost; front. 2. done as or with a forehand: *adv.* with a forehand.

fore-hand-ed (fôr-han'did), *adj.* 1. provident; prudent. 2. prosperous. 3. same as **forehand** (*adj.* 2). **—fore-hand'ed-ness,** *n.*

fore-head (fôr'id, fär'id; 'hed), *n.* the part of the face from eyebrows to hairline.

for-eign (fôr'in, fär'in), *adj.* 1. lying outside one's own country, locality, etc. 2. of or typical of another country. 3. of or involv-

ing the relations of one country with another. 4. not subject to the laws or jurisdiction of the specified country. 5. not natural to the thing specified; alien. 6. not pertinent; irrelevant.

for-eign-born (-bôrn), *adj.* born in another country; not native.

for-eign-er (-ẽr), *n.* 1. one from another country. 2. any outsider or stranger.

fore-know (fôr-nō'), *v.t.* **-knew', -known', -know'ing,** to know beforehand.

fore-knowl-edge (fôr'nol-ij), *n.* knowledge of something in advance.

fore-leg ('leg), *n.* either of the front legs of a quadruped, etc.

fore-lock ('lok), *n.* 1. a lock of hair just above the forehead. 2. a linchpin.

fore-man ('măn), *n., pl.* **-men,** 1. the spokesman of a jury. 2. an overseer.

fore-mast ('mast, 'måst), *n.* the mast nearest the bow of a ship.

fore-most (fôr'mōst), *adj.* first, as in place, rank, or importance: *adv.* first.

fore-noon (fôr'nōōn), *n.* the time from sunrise to noon; morning.

fo-ren-sic (fô-ren'sik), *adj.* of, pertaining to, or used in courts of justice or public debate: *n., pl.* debate or formal argumentation. **—fo-ren'si-cal-ly,** *adv.*

forensic medicine, medical jurisprudence.

fore-or-dain (fôr-ôr-dān'), *v.t.* to ordain or determine in advance; predestine.

fore-part (fôr'pärt), *n.* 1. the first or early part. 2. the front part.

fore-paw ('pô), *n.* an animal's front paw.

fore-play ('plā), *n.* mutual sexual stimulation before intercourse.

fore-quar-ter ('kwôr-tẽr), *n.* 1. the front half, as of a side of beef. 2. *pl.* the front quarters and forelegs, as of a horse.

fore-run-ner (fôr'run-ẽr, fôr-run'ẽr), *n.* 1. a messenger sent before; herald. 2. an omen; prognostic. 3. a predecessor.

fore-sail (fôr'sāl, -săl), *n.* the lowest or principal sail on a foremast.

fore-see (fôr-sē'), *v.t.* **-saw', -seen', -see'ing,** to see or know in advance.

fore-shad-ow (-shad'ō), *v.t.* to indicate or suggest in advance; point to; prefigure.

fore-short-en (-shôr'tn), *v.t.* to make some lines of (something being sketched, painted, etc.) shorter so as to give the illusion of proper relative size.

fore-sight (fôr'sīt), *n.* 1. the act or power of foreseeing. 2. wise anticipation.

fore-skin ('skin), *n.* the terminal fold of skin of the penis.

for-est (fôr'ist, for'ist), *n.* a large, thick growth of trees: *v.t.* to cover with trees.

fore-stall (fôr-stôl'), *v.t.* 1. to be beforehand with; anticipate. 2. to buy up in advance. **—fore-stall'ment,** *n.*

for-est-a-tion (fôr-is-tā'shun, for-), *n.* the planting or care of forests.

fore-stay (fôr'stā), *n.* a rope or cable from a foremast head to the ship bow, to support the foremast.

for-est-er (fôr'is-tẽr, for'is-), *n.* 1. one skilled in forestry. 2. one in charge of a forest or trees.

for·est·ry (-tṛi), *n.* the art of cultivating forests or managing growing timber.

fore·taste (fôr'tāst), *n.* an advance small sampling of something to be enjoyed later.

fore·tell (fôr-tel'), *v.t.* -told', -tell'ing, to predict or prophesy.

fore·thought (fôr'thôt), *n.* 1. advance thinking or planning. 2. wise anticipation.

fore·top ('top), *n.* a platform at the top of a foremast.

fore·top·mast (fôr-top'mast, 'mast), *n.* the section of mast above the foremast.

for·ev·er (fēr-ev'ẽr, fôr-), *adv.* 1. for eternity: also **for·ev·er·more'.** 2. always.

fore·warn (fôr-wôrn'), *v.t.* to warn ahead of time.

fore·word (fôr'wẽrd), *n.* an introductory remark, preface, or prefatory note.

for·feit (fôr'fit), *n.* 1. a fine, penalty, or the like. 2. the act of forfeiting: *adj.* lost by way of forfeit: *v.t.* to lose by way of forfeit. —**for'fei·ture,** *n.*

for·fend (fôr-fend'), *v.t.* [Archaic], 1. to forbid. 2. to ward off.

for·gath·er (fôr-gath'ẽr), *v.i.* to come together; assemble.

forge (fôrj), *v.t.* **forged, forg'ing,** 1. to shape (metal), usually by heating and by hammering or pressure. 2. to fashion (something) in or as if in this way. 3. to counterfeit with intent to deceive or defraud: *v.i.* 1. to work at a forge. 2. to commit forgery: *n.* 1. a furnace for metal to be wrought. 2. a place in which metal is forged or wrought; smithy. 3. a place where wrought iron is made.

forge (fôrj), *v.t. & v.i.* **forged, forg'ing,** 1. to move ahead steadily, though with effort. 2. to move ahead suddenly and swiftly in a burst of energy.

forg·er (fôr'jẽr), *n.* 1. one that forges metals, moves ahead, etc. 2. one that commits forgery. 3. a fabricator.

for·ger·y (fōr'jẽr-i), *n., pl.* -ger·ies, 1. the act of counterfeiting documents, signatures, works of art, etc. with intent to deceive or defraud. 2. anything so counterfeited.

for·get (fẽr-get', fôr-), *v.t.* -got', -got'ten or -got', -get'ting, 1. to lose remembrance of. 2. to overlook or neglect: *v.i.* 1. to be forgetful. 2. to forget one or more things, — **for·get'ta·ble,** *adj.*

for·get·ful ('fl), *adj.* 1. apt to lose remembrance. 2. careless; negligent. —**for·get'ful·ly,** *adv.* —**for·get'ful·ness,** *n.*

for·get-me-not ('mē-not), *n.* a marsh plant with blue, white, or pink flowers.

for·give (fẽr-giv', fôr-), *v.t.* -gave', -giv'en, -giv'ing, to pardon or remit, as a sin, offense, debt, etc.: *v.i.* to exhibit forgiveness. —**for·giv'a·ble,** *adj.*

for·give·ness ('nis), *n.* pardon; remission.

for·giv·ing ('ing), *adj.* that forgives or is so disposed. —**for·giv'ing·ly,** *adv.*

for·go (fôr-gō'), *v.t.* -went', -gone', -go'ing, to do without; give up.

fork (fôrk), *n.* 1. an instrument with two or more prongs. 2. anything forklike. 3. a division into branches, as of a road or river; also, any such branch: *v.i.* to divide into branches: *v.t.* 1. to make forklike. 2. to spear, raise, throw, or dig with a fork. — **fork'ful,** *n., pl.* -fuls.

forked (fôrkt), *adj.* 1. divided into a fork or forks. 2. having forklike prongs.

fork-lift ('lift), *n.* a mechanism with heavy prongs slid under loads to be raised, lowered, stacked, etc.

for·lorn (fēr-lôrn', fôr-), *adj.* 1. abandoned; deserted. 2. miserable. 3. desperate; hopeless. 4. bereft.

forlorn hope, 1. a body of soldiers detached for a mission of extreme risk. 2. a desperate enterprise. 3. a wan hope.

form (fôrm), *n.* 1. external appearance or shape. 2. arrangement, especially an orderly or conventional one; determinate structure; organization. 3. established or customary practice. 4. a fixed or official formula. 5. a mold, pattern, or model. 6. the body of a person or animal; figure. 7. a particular mode of existence or being. 8. a particular procedure, style, or technique. 9. a printed paper or document with blanks to be filled in. 10. a type, kind, class, etc. 11. mental or physical condition, with regard to fitness for performing as in a game or race. 12. a long, wooden, backless bench, as formerly in a schoolroom; also, in some schools, a grade or class. 13. in *Grammar,* a particular spelling, inflection, etc. of a term. 14. in *Linguistics,* any meaningful unit of speech. 15. in *Philosophy,* essence as distinguished from matter. 16. in *Printing,* an assemblage of type, engravings, etc. locked for printing or plating: *v.t.* 1. to give form to; fashion; shape; mold. 2. to develop (habits). 3. to frame mentally; conceive or imagine. 4. to put together; create or organize. 5. to compose; constitute: *v.i.* 1. to become formed. 2. to come into existence. 3. to take a particular form.

-form (fôrm), a suffix meaning *having the form of, having (a specified number of) forms.*

for·mal (fôr'mál), *adj.* 1. of or in accordance with form or a form. 2. of or following fixed rules, procedures, etc. 3. conventionalized or ceremonious. 4. apparent or external, rather than actual or essential. 5. reserved or stiff in manner. 6. designed for, or requiring the kind of clothes worn at, highly ceremonious receptions, dinners, dances, etc.: *n.* 1. a formal dance. 2. a woman's evening dress. —**for'mal·ly,** *adv.*

form·al·de·hyde (fôr-mal'dē-hid), *n.* a gas used in solution to disinfect or preserve and in making resins, dyes, etc.

for·mal·ism (fôr'mál-izm), *n.* strict observance of outward forms and conventional usages, often to an excessive degree, as in art or religion. —**for'mal·ist,** *n. & adj.* —**for·mal·is'·tic,** *adj.*

for·mal·i·ty (fôr-mal'ĭ-ti), *n., pl.* -ties, 1. strict adherence to fixed rules, procedures, ceremonies, etc. 2. formalism. 3. rigid conventionality; stiffness. 4. an instance or act of formality.

for·mal·ize (fôr'mă-liz), *v.t.* -ized, -iz·ing, 1. to make formal. 2. to give form to; fashion; shape.

for·mat (fôr′mat), *n.* 1. the physical form of a book, magazine, etc., including shape, size, binding, paper, typeface, and general arrangement. 2. the overall arrangement or scheme of a presentation.

for·ma·tion (fôr-mā′shŭn), *n.* 1. the act of forming or condition of being formed. 2. something formed. 3. arrangement.

form·a·tive (fôr′mä-tiv), *adj.* of, involved in, or contributing to formation.

for·mer (fôr′mēr), *adj.* 1. preceding in time; earlier; past. 2. first mentioned.

for·mer·ly (-lĭ), *adv.* in the past.

for·mic (fôr′mik), *adj.* 1. of ants. 2. designating or of an acid found in ants, spiders, etc. and also prepared commercially as a dye and a food preservative.

For·mi·ca (fôr-mĭk′ä), *n.* a laminated, heat-resistant plastic used as for table and sink tops: a trademark.

for·mi·car·y (fôr′mĭ-ker-ĭ), *n., pl.* **-car·ies**, an anthill or ants' nest.

for·mi·da·ble (fôr′mĭ-dä-bl), *adj.* 1. exciting dread; fearful. 2. hard to deal with or surmount. 3. awesomely impressive.

form·less (fôrm′lĭs), *adj.* shapeless.

for·mu·la (fôr′myŭ-lä), *n., pl.* **-las, -lae** (-lē), 1. a fixed phrase; conventional expression. 2. a set, unoriginal way of doing something. 3. a fixed, formal statement, as of doctrine. 4. a set prescription or recipe, as for baby food; also, the thing prepared. 5. a fixed algebraic expression. 6. a set of symbols expressing chemical composition.

for·mu·lar·y (-ler-ĭ), *n., pl.* **-lar·ies**, a formula or set of formulas.

for·mu·late (-lāt), *v.t.* **-lat·ed, -lat·ing,** 1. to express by formula. 2. to express systematically. **—for·mu·la′tion,** *n.*

for·ni·cate (fôr′nĭ-kāt), *v.i.* **-cat·ed, -cat·ing,** to engage in sexual intercourse outside of marriage. **—for·ni·ca′tion,** *n.*

for·nix (fôr′nĭks), *n., pl.* **-ni·ces** (′nĭ-sēz), an anatomical arch or fold.

for·sake (fĕr-sāk′, fôr-), *v.t.* **-sook′, -sak′en, -sak′ing,** to renounce or abandon.

for·sooth (fĕr-sōōth′, fôr-), *adv.* [Archaic], in truth; verily.

for·swear (fôr-swer′), *v.t.* **-swore** (-swôr′), **-sworn′, -swear′ing,** to renounce or deny, often on oath: *v.i.* to commit perjury.

for·syth·i·a (fĕr-sĭth′ĭ-ä, fôr-), *n.* a yellow-flowered shrub of the olive family.

fort (fôrt), *n.* an enclosed fortified place.

forte (fôrt), *n.* 1. one's strong point. 2. the strongest part of a sword blade.

for·te (fôr′tā, -tĭ), *adj. & adv.* in *Music,* loud: *n.* a forte note or passage.

forth (fôrth), *adv.* onward or outward.

forth·com·ing (′kum′ing), *adj.* 1. about to appear. 2. readily available, as funds.

forth·right (fôrth′rīt), *adj.* direct; frank.

forth·with (fôrth-with′, -with′), *adv.* without delay; immediately; at once.

for·ti·eth (fôr′tĭ-ith), *adj.* next after 39th; 40th: *n.* 1. the one after the 39th. 2. one of 40 equal parts.

for·ti·fi·ca·tion (fôr-tĭ-fĭ-kā′shŭn), *n.* 1. the act or science of fortifying. 2. a military defensive work. 3. a fort.

for·ti·fy (fôr′tĭ-fī), *v.t.* **-fied, -fy·ing,** 1. to make strong. 2. to strengthen as by military works against attack. 3. to support or confirm. 4. to increase the alcoholic content of (liquor). 5. to add vitamins, minerals, etc. to.

for·tis·si·mo (fôr-tĭs′ĭ-mō), *adj. & adv.* very loud: *n., pl.* **-mos, -mi** (-mē), a fortissimo note or passage.

for·ti·tude (fôr′tĭ-tōōd), *n.* strength to bear suffering or difficulty patiently.

fort·night (fôrt′nīt), *n.* two weeks.

fort·night·ly (-lĭ), *adv. & adj.* at two-week intervals: *n., pl.* **-lies,** a publication appearing every two weeks.

for·tress (fôr′trĕs), *n.* a fort.

for·tu·i·tous (fôr-tōō′ĭ-tŭs, -tū′-), *adj.* 1. happening by chance. 2. fortunate.

for·tu·i·ty (-tĭ), *n., pl.* **-ties,** 1. fortuitous quality. 2. chance occurrence.

for·tu·nate (fôr′chŭ-nit), *adj.* lucky.

for·tune (fôr′chŭn), *n.* 1. fate; destiny. 2. luck. 3. a store of wealth.

for·tune-tell·er (-tel-ēr), *n.* one claiming to foretell future events in others' lives.

for·ty (fôr′tĭ), *adj.* one more than 39: *n.* the cardinal number that is the sum of 39 and one; 40; XL.

fo·rum (fôr′ŭm), *n., pl.* **-rums, -ra** (′ä), 1. in ancient Roman times, a public square or marketplace. 2. a law court. 3. a place or chance to discuss public matters.

for·ward (fôr′wērd), *adj.* 1. of, near, or toward the front. 2. advanced. 3. moving onward. 4. ready or prompt. 5. presumptuous or impertinent. 6. of or for the future: *adv.* in a forward direction or location: also **for′wards:** *n.* a front player, as in hockey: *v.t.* 1. to help advance. 2. to send; transmit. 3. to send on to one's new address, as a letter. **—for′ward·ness,** *n.*

for·ward·er (-ēr), *n.* 1. one that forwards. 2. a receiver and expediter of shipments.

for·went (fôr-went′), past tense of forgo.

fos·sa (fos′ä), *n., pl.* **-sae** (′ē), in *Anatomy,* a cavity, small pit, or hollow.

fosse, foss (fos), *n.* a ditch or moat.

fos·sil (fos′l, fôs′l), *n.* 1. a hardened remnant or trace of animal or plant life of a past geological age, preserved in rock formations. 2. anything fossilized or fossillike. 3. a person with antiquated ideas: *adj.* 1. of, like, or derived from a fossil or fossils. 2. antiquated.

fos·sil·ize (-īz), *v.t.* **-ized, -iz·ing,** to make into or like a fossil: *v.i.* to become fossilized. **—fos·sil·i·za′tion,** *n.*

fos·ter (fôs′tēr, fos′tēr), *v.t.* 1. to rear; nurture. 2. to bring about; stimulate; promote. 3. to harbor; cherish: *adj.* having a specified familial status but not by birth or adoption.

fought (fôt), past tense and past participle of fight.

foul (foul), *adj.* 1. extremely offensive; disgusting; loathsome. 2. extremely dirty or impure; filthy. 3. clogged with dirt or debris. 4. extremely vicious or evil; heinous. 5. stormy, cloudy, etc. 6. snarled, tangled, etc. 7. not fair as played, hit, done, etc. 8. treacherous; dishonest. 9. [Informal], very unpleasant: *adv.* in a foul way: *n.* 1. an entanglement, clogging, etc. 2. a blow, move, hit, etc. other than fair: *v.t.* 1. to make foul. 2. to make a foul against. 3. in *Baseball*, to hit (the ball) outside the fair area: *v.i.* 1. to be, get, or go foul. 2. to foul someone or something. —foul'ly, *adv.*

fou-lard (fōō-lārd'), *n.* 1. a light silk, rayon, etc. 2. a scarf, tie, etc. of this.

foul-up (foul'up), *n.* [Informal], a mix-up.

found (found), past tense and past participle of find.

found (found), *v.t.* 1. to support, ground, or establish; base. 2. to bring into being, originate, or set up. 3. to melt and pour, as metal, into a mold; also, to make thus; cast. —found'er, *n.*

foun-da-tion (foun-dā'shŭn), *n.* 1. a founding; establishment. 2. an endowment or endowed institution. 3. a base or basis. 4. the supporting underground part of a structure.

foun-der (foun'dẽr), *v.i.* 1. to become disabled or go lame, as a horse. 2. to give way; break down; collapse. 3. to fill and sink, as a ship. 4. to stumble about or get stuck, as in soft ground: *v.t.* to cause to founder: *n.* same as laminitis.

found-ling (found'ling), *n.* a child of unknown parentage, found abandoned.

found-ry (foun'dri), *n., pl.* -ries, a place where metal casting is carried on.

fount (fount), *n.* 1. a fountain or spring. 2. a source.

foun-tain (foun'tin), *n.* 1. a spring of water. 2. a source; fount. 3. an artificial jet or flow of water, or the assemblage of pipes, basin, etc. used for it. 4. a reservoir, as for ink.

foun-tain-head (-hed), *n.* 1. the spring from which a stream flows. 2. a main source.

fountain pen, a pen having a reservoir feeding ink to the nib.

four (fōr), *adj.* one more than three: *n.* the cardinal number that is the sum of three and one; 4; IV.

four-chette (foor-shet'), *n.* 1. a piece constituting the side of a finger of a glove. 2. a small fold of connective vulval skin, at the posterior end.

four-flush-er (fôr'flush-ẽr), *n.* [Informal], a blustering braggart; bluffer; fake.

four-fold ('fōld), *adj.* 1. having four parts. 2. having four times as much or as many: *adv.* four times as much or as many.

four-in-hand (fôr'in-hand), *n.* 1. a coach with four horses and one driver. 2. the horses. 3. a necktie tied in a slipknot, the lengths overlapping and vertical.

four-post-er ('pōs'tẽr), *n.* a bedstead with tall posts, often with canopy or curtains.

four-score ('skôr'), *adj.* eighty.

four-some ('sŭm), *n.* 1. a group of four persons. 2. a game of golf for four.

four-square ('skwer'), *adj.* 1. perfectly square. 2. resolute. 3. direct and frank: *adv.* in a foursquare way.

four-teen ('tēn'), *adj.* one more than 13: *n.* the cardinal number that is the sum of 13 and one; 14; XIV.

four-teenth ('tēnth'), *adj.* next after 13; 14th:

n. 1. the one after the 13th. 2. one of 14 equal parts.

fourth (fôrth), *adj.* next after third; 4th: *n.* 1. the one after the third. 2. one of four equal parts. 3. the fourth forward gear ratio of an automotive vehicle. 4. in *Music, a)* same as subdominant. *b)* any tone three degrees above or below a tone of a diatonic scale. *c)* the interval between, or a combination of, such tones.

fourth-class ('klas), *adj. & adv.* of or in a class of mail that includes packages, as of books, weighing over a pound.

fourth dimension, time viewed as a dimension along with length, width, and depth.

fourth estate, [often F- E-], journalism or journalists.

Fourth of July, see Independence Day.

fowl (foul), *n., pl.* fowls, fowl, a bird; specifically, a chicken, duck, goose, etc., or the flesh of any of these used as food: *v.i.* to hunt wild fowl. —fowl'er, *n.*

fowling piece, a shotgun for fowling.

fox (foks), *n., pl.* fox'es, fox, 1. a small, wild, bushy-tailed, carnivorous mammal of the dog family: conventionally viewed as crafty. 2. its fur. 3. a sly person: *v.t.* 1. to stain reddish-brown. 2. to trick.

fox-glove ('gluv), *n.* a certain plant with long spikes of thimblelike flowers.

fox-hole ('hōl), *n.* a shallow hole scooped out in the earth, used by soldiers as a temporary shelter from enemy fire.

fox-hound ('hound), *n.* any one of a breed of dogs bred to hunt foxes and other game.

fox squirrel, any one of several tree squirrels of eastern North America.

fox-tail ('tāl), *n.* any one of various grasses with bristly spikes.

fox terrier, any one of a breed of small, active terriers.

fox trot, 1. a dance in 4/4 time for couples. 2. a piece of music for this.

fox-y (fok'si), *adj.* fox'i-er, fox'i-est, 1. crafty; sly. 2. colored or stained reddish-brown. —fox'i-ness, *n.*

foy-er (foi'ā, foi'yā), *n.* an entrance hall or lobby, as in a theater, hotel, etc.

fra-cas (frā'kăs, frak'ăs), *n.* a noisy fight.

frac-tion (frak'shŭn), *n.* 1. a breaking: now only of the Eucharistic bread. 2. a part of a whole. 3. a small portion, degree, etc. 4. in *Chemistry,* a part separated, as by distillation. 5. in *Mathematics,* a notation, as 3/10 or .3, indicating by a separating line or a decimal point the division of one quantity by another.

frac-tion-al (-l), *adj.* 1. of or pertaining to a fraction. 2. very small.

frac-tious (frak'shŭs), *adj.* 1. unruly; refractory. 2. peevish; cross.

frac-ture (frak'chẽr), *n.* 1. a breaking or being broken. 2. a break, crack, or split. 3. a break in a bone; also, a tear in a cartilage. 4. the texture of the broken surface of a mineral as distinct from its cleavage: *v.t. & v.i.* -tured, -tur-ing, to break, crack, break up, etc.

frag-ile (fraj'l), *adj.* easily broken, damaged, etc.; frail.

ŏ in dragon, ōō in crude, oo in wool, u in cup, ū in cure, u in turn, u in focus, oi in boy, ou in house, th in thin, th in sheathe, g in get, j in joy, y in yet.

fra·gil·i·ty (frȧ-jil′ĭ-tĭ), *n.* the condition or quality of being fragile.

frag·ment (frag′mĕnt), *n.* 1. a part broken off from a whole. 2. a detached or incomplete part: *v.t. & v.i.* (also **frag·ment'**), to break into fragments.

frag·men·tal (frag-mĕn′t'l), *adj.* 1. fragmentary. 2. in *Geology,* designating or made up of fragments of older rocks.

frag·men·tar·y (frag′mĕn-ter-ĭ), *adj.* made up of fragments; incomplete; disconnected.

frag·men·tate (-tāt), *v.t. & v.i.* -tat·ed, -tat·ing, to break into fragments. —**frag·men·ta′tion,** *n.*

fra·grance (frā′grȧns), *n.* 1. the quality of being fragrant. 2. a pleasant odor.

fra·grant (′grȧnt), *adj.* pleasant in odor.

frail (frāl), *adj.* 1. easily broken, damaged, or destroyed; delicate; fragile. 2. weak, physically or morally: *n.* [Slang], a woman or girl. —**frail′ty,** *n., pl.* -ties.

fram·be·si·a, **fram·boe·si·a** (fram-bē′zhȧ, -zhĭ-ȧ), *n.* same as yaws.

frame (frām), *n.* 1. body structure; build. 2. a basic supporting or shaping structure. 3. a case, casing, or enclosure, as about a window or picture. 4. the way something is put together or organized; shape; form. 5. a particular humor; temper. 6. one exposure in a movie film or a filmstrip. 7. in *Bowling, etc.,* a division of a game: *v.t.* framed, fram′ing, 1. to put together; fashion; shape; construct. 2. to devise; contrive; invent. 3. to adapt, regulate, or adjust. 4. to put into words. 5. to put in a frame, as a picture. 6. [Informal], to subject to a frame-up: *adj.* having a wooden framework.

frame-up (′up), *n.* [Informal], 1. a scheme to incriminate falsely, as by contrived evidence. 2. any underhanded scheme.

frame·work (′wûrk), *n.* 1. a supporting or shaping structure. 2. a basic structure, arrangement, or system.

franc (frank), *n.* the monetary unit and a coin of France, Belgium, Switzerland, etc.

fran·chise (fran′chĭz), *n.* 1. a right or privilege granted by a government, as to vote, be a corporation, etc. 2. an authorization as by a manufacturer or company, as to market a product. 3. the limits assigned to a franchise granted: *v.t.* -chised, -chis·ing, to grant a franchise to.

Fran·cis·can (fran-sis′kȧn), *n.* any one of the members of a religious order founded by St. Francis of Assisi in 1209.

fran·ci·um (fran′si-ûm), *n.* a radioactive metallic chemical element of the alkali group.

Franco-, a combining form meaning *French, France.*

fran·gi·ble (fran′ji-b'l), *adj.* easily broken. — **fran·gi·bil′i·ty,** *n.*

fran·gi·pan·i (fran-ji-pan′i), *n., pl.* -pan′-is, 1. any one of certain tropical American shrubs and trees with large fragrant flowers. 2. a perfume derived from the flowers. 3. a pastry made with ground almonds. Also **fran′gi·pane** (′pān).

Frank (frangk), *n.* any one of certain German tribesmen (3d-9th century A.D.) who estab-

lished an empire eventually extending over modern France, Italy, and Germany.

frank (frangk), *adj.* 1. open; candid; outspoken. 2. undisguised; evident; plain: *v.t.* 1. to send (mail) post-free, as by official privilege. 2. to mark officially for this: *n.* 1. the privilege of sending mail post-free. 2. a mark showing this. 3. a piece of franked mail.

frank (frangk), *n.* [Informal], a frankfurter.

Frank·en·stein (frang′kĕn-stīn), *n.* 1. the title character, a medical student, of M. W. Shelley's 19th-century novel: he constructs a monster from cadavers and is destroyed by the monster. 2. the monster.

frank·furt·er (frangk′fẽr-tẽr), *n.* a reddish smoked sausage, as of beef, to be served individually as in a roll: also **frank′furt, frank′fort·er** (′fẽr-), **frank′fort.**

frank·in·cense (frang′kin-sens), *n.* a gum resin from certain Arabian and African trees, often burned as incense.

frank·ly (frangk′li), *adv.* in a frank way.

fran·tic (fran′tik), *adj.* frenzied, as with worry or pain. —**fran′ti·cal·ly,** *adv.*

frap·pé (fra-pā′), *adj.* partly frozen; iced: *n.* 1. a sherbetlike dessert. 2. a liqueur poured over shaved ice. 3. a milkshake. Also **frappe** (frap).

frat (frat), *n.* [Informal], a fraternity.

fra·ter·nal (frȧ-tûr′n'l), *adj.* 1. brotherly. 2. of a fraternity.

fra·ter·ni·ty (frȧ-tûr′ni-tĭ), *n., pl.* -ties, 1. brotherly relationship. 2. a group of men joined by common interests. 3. a group of the same profession or class.

frat·er·nize (frat′ẽr-nīz), *v.i.* -nized, -niz·ing, to associate with in a fraternal or friendly way.

frat·ri·cide (frat′ri-sĭd), *n.* 1. the act of killing one's brother or, sometimes, one's sister. 2. one doing this.

Frau (frou), *n., pl.* **Frau'en** (′ĕn), [German], a married woman; wife: used like *Mrs.*

fraud (frôd), *n.* 1. deceit; artifice; trick. 2. a deceiver or impostor; cheat.

frau·du·lent (frô′jṳ-lĕnt), *adj.* marked by fraud. —**frau′du·lence, frau′du·len·cy,** *n.*

fraught (frôt), *adj.* laden; charged.

Fräu·lein (froi′lin), *n., pl.* -lein, an unmarried woman: used like *Miss.*

fray (frā), *n.* a fight: *v.t. & v.i.* to wear down, unravel, etc. as by rubbing.

fraz·zle (fraz′'l), *v.t. & v.i.* -zled, -zling, [Informal], to fray: *n.* a being frayed.

freak (frēk), *n.* 1. a whim; caprice. 2. an odd turn or happening. 3. a monstrosity. 4. [Slang], a drug user; also, a devotee. — **freak′ish, freak′y,** *adj.*

freck·le (frek′'l), *n.* a small, brownish spot on the skin, from sunlight: *v.t. & v.i.* -led, -ling, to spot with these.

free (frē), *adj.* fre′er, fre′est, 1. not restricted, controlled, or compelled by another; independent. 2. able to move without restraint. 3. not kept in custody. 4. not hindered or weighted down as by obligations or debts. 5. having full option; at liberty. 6. not word-by-word; not literal. 7. not occupied; available. 8. not stingy; liberal. 9. not holding back or held back. 10. not costing anything. 11. unobstructed; open; clear:

adv. 1. without cost. 2. in a free way: *v.t.* freed, free'ing, to cause to be free. —free'ly, *adv.*

free-boot-er ('bōōt-ēr), *n.* a plunderer.

freed-man (frēd'măn), *n.*, *pl.* -men, a freed slave.

free-dom (frē'dŏm), *n.* 1. the quality or state of being free; liberty. 2. a right or privilege.

free fall, an unchecked fall or plunge.

free flight, continued flight of a rocket after termination of fuel powering.

free-for-all (fre'fēr-ôl), *n.* an uncontrolled fight, as a fist fight, with one combatant after another joining in; melee.

free-hand (frē'hand), *adj.* done by hand, as a drawing, without mechanical guides.

free-hold ('hōld), *n.* 1. an estate in land held for life or with the right to pass it on through inheritance. 2. the holding of an estate, office, etc. thus: *adj.* of or held by freehold. —free'hold-er, *n.*

free lance, a writer, actor, etc. available to do short-term work for various publishers, companies, etc. simultaneously or in sequence: also **free lanc'er**. —free'-lance', *adj.* & *v.i.* -lanced', -lanc'ing.

free-load-er ('lō-dēr), *n.* [Informal], one always trying to get food, lodging, etc. at others' expense; sponger. —free'load, *v.i.* —free'load-ing, *adj.*

free-man (-măn), *n.*, *pl.* -men, 1. one not in slavery or bondage. 2. one with full civil and political rights in a city or state; citizen.

Free-ma-son (frē'mās'n), *n.* a member of an international secret society having as its principles brotherly love and mutual aid: also **Free and Accepted Mason, Mason.** —Free'ma'son-ry, *n.*

free on board, transferred by the seller to a ship, train, or other carrier without charge to the purchaser.

free port, 1. a port where merchandise can be transferred from one ship to another without payment of duties, as long as it is not imported. 2. a port available equally to ships from all countries.

free-si-a (frē'zhi-ā, 'zhā), *n.* a plant of the iris family, with white or yellow flowers.

Free-Soil (frē'soil), *adj.* [also f- s-], 1. opposed to the extension of slavery. 2. denoting a former (1848-1854) U.S. political party (**Free-Soil Party**) that opposed the extension of slavery beyond State borders into the Territories. —Free'-Soil'er, *n.*

free-stone (frē'stōn), *n.* 1. a sandstone or limestone that cuts easily without splitting. 2. a peach, plum, etc. in which the pulp does not cling to the pit.

free-think-er ('thingk'ēr), *n.* one who forms his opinions about religion independently.

free trade, trade with other countries unrestricted by tariffs or customs duties.

free verse, poetry that does not conform to conventional metrical forms, with little or no rhyming.

free-way ('wā), *n.* a divided highway with interchanges for fully controlled access.

free-will ('wil), *adj.* 1. voluntary. 2. holding the doctrine (**free will**) that man is not subject to physical or divine forces when choosing a course of action.

freeze (frēz), *v.t.* froze, fro'zen, freez'ing, 1. to harden into, or cover with, ice. 2. to kill or damage by frost. 3. to preserve (food) by rapid refrigeration. 4. to make motionless. 5. to fix (rents, prices, etc.) at a certain stage. 6. to make (assets) unavailable: *v.i.* 1. to be hardened into, or become covered with, ice. 2. to be killed or damaged by frost. 3. to have the temperature lowered rapidly. 4. to become motionless. 5. to act unfriendly: *n.* 1. the act or state of being frozen. 2. a spell of freezing weather.

freeze-dry (frēz'drī), *v.t.* -dried, -dry-ing, to freeze (food, etc.) quickly, then dry under high vacuum at low temperature.

freez-er ('ēr), *n.* 1. a refrigerator, compartment, etc. for food storage at low temperatures. 2. a machine or device for making ice cream.

freezing point, the temperature at which a liquid freezes: water freezes at 32°F or 0°C at sea level.

freight (frāt), *n.* 1. goods transported by land, water, or air, especially bulky goods. 2. the transportation of such goods. 3. payment for this. 4. a railroad train for carrying goods: also **freight train**: *v.t.* 1. to load (with goods). 2. to send by freight.

freight-age ('ij), *n.* 1. the charge for carrying freight. 2. cargo.

freight car, a railroad car for carrying freight.

freight-er ('ēr), *n.* 1. one who loads freight. 2. one who ships by freight. 3. a ship or aircraft for carrying freight.

French (french), *adj.* of or pertaining to France, its inhabitants, or its language: *n.* 1. the language of France. 2. the people of France. —French'man (-măn), *n.*, *pl.* -men.

French cuff, a sleeve cuff folded back and fastened with a cuff link.

French doors, a pair of doors with glass panes full length, hinged on the sides and opening in the middle.

French dressing, a salad dressing made of oil, vinegar, and seasonings.

French fry, [often f- f-], to fry in deep, hot fat.

French horn, a brass-wind instrument with a long, coiled tube and a mellow tone.

French-i-fy (french'i-fī), *v.t.* & *v.i.* -fied, -fy-ing, to make or become French. —French-i-fi-ca'tion, *n.*

French toast, bread dipped in an egg batter and fried.

fre-net-ic (fre-net'ik), *adj.* frantic; frenzied: also **fre-net'i-cal**. —fre-net'i-cal-ly, *adv.*

fren-zy (fren'zi), *n.*, *pl.* -zies, a frantic outburst; delirium: *v.t.* -zied, -zy-ing, to agitate violently; drive mad. —fren'zied, *adj.*

fre-quen-cy (frē'kwen-si), *n.*, *pl.* -cies, 1. repeated occurrence at short intervals. 2. the number of times an event recurs in a given time. 3. the number of cycles, oscillations, waves, etc. per unit of time. Also **fre'-quence**.

frequency modulation, the modulation of the frequency of a transmitting radio wave in accordance with the signal transmitted.

fre-quent ('kwĕnt), *adj.* 1. recurring often. 2.

ŏ in dragon, ōō in crude, oo in wool, u in cup, ū in cure, û in turn, ů in focus, oi in boy, ou in house, th in thin, th in sheathe, g in get, j in joy, y in yet.

constant: *v.t.* to visit (a place) often. —**fre'-quent-ly,** *adv.*

fre-quen-ta-tive (fri-kwen'tā-tiv), *adj.* in *Grammar,* expressing repetition of an action, as certain verbs.

fres-co (fres'kō), *n., pl.* **-coes, -cos,** a method of painting on wet plaster with watercolors: *v.t.* to decorate or paint in fresco.

fresh (fresh), *adj.* 1. new; recent. 2. not injured by time; unfaded, unsoiled, etc. 3. strong and active; not wearied. 4. refreshing and cool. 5. not salt: said of water. 6. inexperienced. 7. not salted, pickled, canned, etc. 8. brisk: said of wind. 9. [Slang] bold; impudent: *adv.* in a fresh manner. —**fresh'ly,** *adv.* —**fresh'ness,** *n.*

fresh-en ('ĕn), *v.t.* to make fresh: *v.i.* 1. to become fresh. 2. to blow harder: said of wind. 3. to start to give milk, as a cow. 4. to wash, change clothes, etc. (followed by *up*). —**fresh'en-er,** *n.*

fresh-et ('it), *n.* the flooding of a stream caused by melting snow or heavy rain.

fresh-man ('măn), *n., pl.* **-men,** 1. a novice. 2. a person in the first year of college or the ninth grade in high school: *adj.* of or for students in the first year.

fresh-wa-ter ('wot-ēr, 'wăt-ēr), *adj.* 1. of or living in water that is fresh rather than salty. 2. pertaining to navigation only on inland waters.

fret (fret), *v.t.* **fret'ted, fret'ting,** 1. to wear away by rubbing, gnawing, etc. 2. to ripple or ruffle. 3. to vex or irritate; worry. 4. to ornament with a joined or interlaced pattern. 5. to furnish (a stringed instrument) with frets: *v.i.* 1. to become worn away, eaten, etc. 2. to become rippled or ruffled. 3. to be vexed; worry: *n.* 1. the act or process of fretting. 2. worry; irritation. 3. a running ornamentation of joined or interlaced bars. 4. a ridge on the fingerboard of some stringed instruments. —**fret'ter,** *n.*

fret-ful (-fŭl), *adj.* peevish; irritable. —**fret'fully,** *adv.* —**fret'ful-ness,** *n.*

fret saw, a long, thin, narrow saw with fine teeth, used for cutting scrolls, etc.

fret-work ('wŭrk), *n.* carved, raised, or open ornamental work.

Freud-i-an (froi'di-ăn), *adj.* of or according to Sigmund Freud (1856-1939), or his theories or practices in regard to psychoanalysis: *n.* a follower of Freud; one who believes in or practices his methods. —**Freud'i-an-ism,** *n.*

fri-a-ble (frī'ă-bl), *adj.* easily crumbled. —**fri-a-bil'i-ty,** **fri'a-ble-ness,** *n.*

fri-ar (frī'ēr), *n.* a member of any of several mendicant orders of the Roman Catholic Church.

fri-ar-bird (-bûrd), *n.* a kind of honey eater of Australia, that has a featherless head.

fri-ar-y (-i), *n., pl.* **-ar-ies,** 1. a monastery. 2. a brotherhood of friars.

fric-as-see (frik-ă-sē'), *n.* meat cut into pieces, stewed or fried, and served in its gravy: *v.t.* **-seed', -see'ing,** to prepare (meat) in this way.

fric-a-tive (frik'ă-tiv), *adj.* pronounced by passing the breath through a narrow opening in the mouth, as *v, f, z.*

fric-tion (frik'shŭn), *n.* 1. the rubbing of one surface against another. 2. the resistance to motion of surfaces in contact. 3. irritation or conflict because of differing opinions. —**fric'tion-al,** *adj.*

Fri-day (frī'di, 'dā), *n.* 1. the sixth day of the week. 2. a loyal assistant: often *man Friday* or *girl Friday.*

fried (frīd), past tense and past participle of **fry.**

fried-cake ('kāk), *n.* a small cake fried in deep fat.

friend (frend), *n.* 1. a person attached to another by affection, regard, or esteem. 2. a supporter or sympathizer. 3. a person who is not an enemy; ally. 4. [F-], a member of the Society of Friends; Quaker. —**friend'less,** *adj.* —**friend'less-ness,** *n.*

friend-ly ('li), *adj.* **-li-er, -li-est,** 1. of or having the characteristics of a friend; kindly, affable, etc. 2. not hostile; showing good will. 3. supportive. —**friend'li-ness,** *n.*

friend-ship ('ship), *n.* 1. an association as friends. 2. intimacy. 3. a friendly attitude; friendliness.

frieze (frēz), *n.* 1. a horizontal band between the architrave and cornice of a building, often ornamented with sculpture. 2. a horizontal band with decorations or carving around a wall or room.

frig-ate (frig'it), *n.* a fast sailing ship of the 18th and 19th centuries, carrying from 24 to 60 guns and of a medium size.

frigate bird, a large, predatory, tropical sea bird with very long wings.

fright (frīt), *n.* 1. a sudden and violent fear; alarm. 2. a person or thing with an appearance that is ugly, ridiculous, or shocking.

fright-en ('n), *v.t.* 1. to terrify; scare. 2. to drive (*away* or *off*) by scaring. —**fright'en-ing-ly,** *adv.*

fright-ful ('fŭl), *adj.* 1. terrible; shocking. 2. alarming. 3. [Informal], disagreeable. 4. [Informal], very great. —**fright'ful-ly,** *adv.*

frig-id (frij'id), *adj.* 1. without warmth; very cold. 2. stiff and formal in manner. 3. lacking a normal interest in, or response to, sexual activity: said of a woman. —**fri-gid'i-ty,** *n.*

Frigid Zone, either of the two zones between the poles and the Arctic or Antarctic Circles.

fri-jol (frē'hōl), *n., pl.* **fri-jo'les** (frē'hōlz, frē-hō'lĕz), a bean much cultivated for food in Mexico and the southwestern U.S.: also **fri-jo-le** (frē-hō'lē).

frill (fril), *n.* 1. a pleated edging or ruffle. 2. an unnecessary ornament. 3. something added for show: *v.t.* to make into, or decorate with, a frill. —**frill'y,** *adj.*

fringe (frinj), *n.* 1. an ornamental border of cords or threads, hanging loose or tied in bunches. 2. a border; edge. 3. a minor or marginal part: *v.t.* **fringed, fring'ing,** to border with, or as with, a fringe: *adj.* 1. at the margin or edge. 2. additional. 3. less important.

fringe benefit, a benefit to an employee, as insurance, pension, etc., in addition to wages or salary.

---

a in *cap,* ā in *cane,* ä in *father,* ȧ in *abet,* e in *met* ē in *be,* ē in *baker,* ē in *regent,* i in *pit,* ī in *fine,* ï in *manifest,* o in *hot,* ō in *horse,* ŏ in *bone,*

fringed gentian, a plant of the northern U.S. and Canada, having blue flowers with fringed petals.

frip·per·y (frip'ēr-i), *n., pl.* **-per·ies,** 1. cheap, tawdry finery. 2. showy ostentation in dress or manner.

Fris·bee (friz'bi), *n.* a plastic disk that is tossed back and forth in play: a trademark.

fri·sé (fri-zā'), *n.* an upholstery fabric with a pile of cut or uncut loops.

frisk (frisk), *v.i.* to gambol or dance in frolic: *v.t.* [Slang], to search (a person) for concealed weapons by feeling his clothing lightly: *n.* 1. a frolic; gambol. 2. [Slang], the act of frisking a person.

fris·ket (fris'kit), *n.* a mask laid over certain areas in printing or in using an airbrush to prevent color or ink on the area.

frisk·y (frisk'i), *adj.* **frisk'i·er, frisk'i·est,** lively in action; gay; frolicsome. —**frisk'i·ly,** *adv.* —**frisk'i·ness,** *n.*

frit (frit), *n.* 1. the partly fused mixture of sand and fluxes from which glass is made. 2. a partly fused, ground, vitreous base for enamels and glazes: *v.t. & v.i.* **frit'ted, frit'ting,** to make into frit.

frit fly, a small, shiny, black European fly injurious to grain.

frith (frith), *n.* same as **firth.**

frit·ter (frit'ēr), *v.t.* to waste or squander little by little (usually with *away*): *n.* a small cake of batter, usually containing apples, corn, etc. and fried.

friv·o·lous (friv'ō-lūs), *adj.* 1. of little worth or importance; trivial. 2. silly; inclined to undue levity. —**friv·ol·i·ty** (fri-vol'i-ti), *n., pl.* **-ties.** —**friv'o·lous·ly,** *adv.*

frizz, friz (friz), *v.t. & v.i.* **frizzed, friz'zing,** to form into tight, little curls: *n.* hair that is frizzed. —**friz'zy,** *adj.* **-zi·er, -zi·est.** —**friz'zi·ness,** *n.*

friz·zle (friz'l), *v.t. & v.i.* **-zled, -zling,** 1. to curl up or crisp by frying or broiling. 2. to make or cause to make a sizzling noise, as in frying. 3. to form into tight, little curls; frizz: *n.* a tight, little curl. —**friz'zly,** *adj.* **-zli·er, -zli·est.**

fro (frō), *adv.* away; backward; back: now only in *to and fro,* back and forth.

frock (frok), *n.* 1. a dress. 2. an outer garment worn by monks, friars, etc. 3. a coarse outer garment worn by workmen; smock.

frock coat, a double-breasted coat worn by men, chiefly in the 19th century, reaching to the knees and of equal length all around.

frog (frog), *n.* 1. a small, tailless, web-footed, leaping amphibian. 2. a tender, horny pad on the sole of a horse's foot. 3. a decorative loop used as a fastener on clothes. 4. a section of railroad track at an intersection or switch. 5. a holder to keep flowers upright in a vase or bowl. 6. hoarseness.

frog·man ('man), *n., pl.* **-men,** a swimmer who is trained and equipped for underwater work, as scientific observation, demolition, etc.

frol·ic (frol'ik), *n.* 1. a party; merrymaking. 2. a prank or trick. 3. fun; gaiety: *v.i.* **-icked, -ick·ing,** 1. to play merrily; have fun. 2. to gambol or romp. —**frol'ick·er,** *n.*

frol·ic·some (-sŏm), *adj.* merrily playful.

from (frum, from), *prep.* 1. out of. 2. starting with; beginning. 3. by reason of. 4. sent by. 5. as being unlike. 6. at a distance.

frond (frond), *n.* the leaf of a fern, palm, seaweed, or the like.

frons (fronz), *n.* the upper portion of the head of an insect.

front (frunt), *n.* 1. formerly, the forehead. 2. the foremost part of anything. 3. the beginning. 4. the land bordering a lake, street, etc. 5. the facade of a building. 6. a combat area in warfare. 7. a sphere of activity. 8. a person or group that serves to cover the activities of another. 9. outward behavior or appearance. 10. [Informal], an appearance of wealth, high status, etc. 11. in *Meteorology,* the line between two different air masses: *v.t. & v.i.* 1. to face. 2. to serve as a front (*for*): *adj.* 1. of or pertaining to the front. 2. situated in or at the front.

front·age ('ij), *n.* 1. the front part of a building. 2. the extent of the front line of a lot. 3. land bordering a lake, street, river, etc.

fron·tal ('l), *adj.* of or pertaining to the front or forehead: *n.* 1. the broad bone in the front of the skull, forming the forehead in man: also **frontal bone.** 2. an ornamental hanging for the front of an altar. 3. a small pediment over a window or door.

fron·tier (frun-tir'), *n.* 1. a border between two countries. 2. the region of a country that borders on unexplored land. 3. the limits of achievement or learning in a specified field: *adj.* of or on a frontier. —**fron·tiers'man** (-tirz'mǎn), *n., pl.* **-men.**

fron·tis·piece (frun'tis-pēs), *n.* an illustration facing the title page in a book.

front·run·ner (frunt'run-ēr), *n.* one who is leading in a race or competition.

front-wheel drive ('hwēl), an automotive design in which only the front wheels receive driving power.

frost (frost), *n.* 1. minute, frozen particles of moisture, forming a white, crystalline coating. 2. freezing temperature. 3. [Informal], an enterprise that is a failure: *v.t.* 1. to cover with frost. 2. to put frosting on. 3. to impart a frostlike, opaque surface to (glass).

frost-bite ('bit), *v.t.* **-bit, -bit·ten, -bit·ing,** to nip or numb with frost; injure by exposure to extreme cold: *n.* injury caused to body tissues by frost.

frost·ing ('ing), *n.* 1. a mixture of sugar, butter, flavoring, etc. for covering cakes; icing. 2. a frostlike finish on glass or metal. 3. rough, powdered glass mixed with varnish and used in decorative work.

frost·y ('i), *adj.* **frost'i·er, frost'i·est,** 1. producing frost; freezing. 2. covered with or as with frost. 3. cold or distant in manner. —**frost'i·ly,** *adv.* —**frost'i·ness,** *n.*

froth (frôth), *n.* 1. a mass of bubbles formed on the surface of a liquid; foam. 2. foaming saliva. 3. superficial ideas, frivolous talk, etc.: *v.i.* to foam.

froth·y ('i), *adj.* **froth'i·er, froth'i·est,** 1. full of, like, or covered with froth. 2. frivolous; unsubstantial. —**froth'i·ly,** *adv.* —**froth'i·ness,** *n.*

frou-frou (frōō'frōō), *n.* [French], 1. a rustling,

as of silk. 2. [Informal], elaborate decoration.

fro·ward (frō'ērd, 'wērd), *adj.* perverse; wayward; contrary. —**fro'ward·ness**, *n.*

frown (froun), *n.* a contraction of the brow to indicate displeasure, etc.: *v.i.* 1. to contract the brows to indicate displeasure. 2. to look with disapproval (*on* or *upon*).

frow·zy (frou'zi), *adj.* -zi·er, -zi·est, untidy; slovenly; unkempt: also spelled **frow'sy.** —**frow'zi·ly**, *adv.* —**frow'zi·ness**, *n.*

froze (frōz), past tense of freeze.

fro·zen (rō'z'n), past participle of freeze: *adj.* 1. injured or killed by freezing. 2. covered with ice. 3. turned into ice. 4. fixed; incapable of being moved or changed. 5. that cannot be turned into cash. 6. unfeeling.

fruc·ti·fy (fruk'ti-fī), *v.t.* -fied, -fy·ing, to make productive; fertilize: *v.i.* to bear fruit. —**fruc·ti·fi·ca'tion**, *n.*

fruc·tose (fruk'tōs, frook'-), *n.* a sugar found in ripe fruits, honey, etc.; levulose.

fru·gal (frōō'g'l), *adj.* 1. thrifty; economical. 2. scanty; meager, —**fru·gal'i·ty** (-gal'i-ti), *n.* —**fru'gal·ly**, *adv.*

fru·giv·o·rous (frōō-jiv'ēr-ŭs), *adj.* fruit-eating.

fruit (frōōt), *n.* 1. the product of a tree or plant bearing the seed. 2. an edible, sweet plant structure with a juicy pulp enclosing the seeds. 3. result, product, or profit: *v.i.* & *v.t.* to produce or cause to produce fruit.

fruit·age ('ij), *n.* 1. fruits collectively. 2. a product; result.

fruit·cake (kāk), *n.* a rich cake containing nuts, preserved fruit, etc.

fruit·ful ('fŭl), *adj.* 1. yielding much fruit. 2. prolific. 3. profitable. —**fruit'ful·ly**, *adv.* —**fruit'ful·ness**, *n.*

fruit·ing ('ing), *adj.* bearing fruit.

fru·i·tion (frōō-ish'ŭn), *n.* 1. the bearing of fruit. 2. realization; fulfillment. 3. enjoyment derived from use or possession.

fruit·less (frōōt'lis), *adj.* 1. without success or results; vain. 2. sterile; barren.—**fruit'less·ly**, *adv.* —**fruit'less·ness**, *n.*

fruit sugar, same as fructose.

fruit·y ('i), *adj.* fruit'i·er, fruit'i·est, 1. resembling fruit in flavor or odor. 2. rich or mellow. 3. full of interest; juicy. 4. [Slang], eccentric. —**fruit'i·ly**, *adv.* —**fruit'i·ness**, *n.*

fru·men·ta·ceous (frōō-men-tā'shŭs), *adj.* of, like, or having the nature of wheat or other grain.

fru·men·ty (frōō'mĕn-ti), *n.* [British], a dish of hulled wheat boiled in milk, with sugar and cinnamon.

frump (frump), *n.* a dowdy, slovenly woman. —**frump'ish, frump'y,** *adj.*

frus·trate (frus'trāt), *v.t.* -trat·ed, -trat·ing, 1. to bring to nothing; nullify. 2. to thwart; prevent from attaining satisfaction or achievement. —**frus·tra'tion**, *n.*

frus·tum (frus'tŭm), *n., pl.* -tums, -ta ('tà), the part of a solid figure, as of a cone or pyramid, left after cutting off the top with a plane parallel to the base.

fry (frī), *v.t.* & *v.i.* fried, fry'ing, to cook in a pan over direct heat, usually in fat: *n.* 1. a social gathering, often outdoors, where food is fried and eaten. 3. *pl.* fry, *a*) young or small fish, especially in a swarm. *b*) children: often small fry.

fry·er ('ēr), *n.* 1. a pan or utensil for frying food. 2. a young, tender chicken, suitable for frying.

fuch·sia (fū'shà), *n.* 1. a shrubby plant with pendulous pink, red, or purple flowers. 2. purplish red: *adj.* purplish-red.

fud·dle (fud'l), *v.t.* -dled, -dling, to stupefy with alcoholic liquor; intoxicate: *n.* a fuddled state.

fud·dy-dud·dy (fud'i-dud-i), *n., pl.* -dies, [Slang], one who is fussy, stuffy, or old-fashioned.

fudge (fuj), *n.* a candy made with sugar, butter, and often chocolate: *v.i.* fudged, fudg'ing, 1. to hedge; equivocate. 2. to cheat.

fu·el (fū'ĕl), *n.* 1. combustible material burned to supply heat or power; coal, wood, gas, oil, etc. 2. material used to produce atomic energy. 3. anything that maintains intense emotion, etc.: *v.t.* & *v.i.* -eled or -elled, -el·ing or -el·ling, to supply with or obtain fuel.

fuel cell, a device that produces electric current directly from chemical energy.

fuel injection, a system for forcing fuel into combustion chambers of a diesel, gasoline, jet, or rocket engine.

fu·gi·tive (fū'ji-tiv), *adj.* 1. fleeting; not permanent. 2. fleeing, as from danger, pursuit, or justice: *n.* one who is fleeing from danger, pursuit, or justice. —**fu'gi·tive·ly**, *adv.*

fugue (fūg), *n.* a musical composition in which the different instruments or voices take up the theme successively.

-ful (fŭl, fl) a suffix meaning *full of, able to, apt to.*

-ful (fool), *pl.* **-fuls**, a suffix meaning *the amount that would fill.*

ful·crum (fool'krŭm, ful'-), *n., pl.* -crums, -cra ('krà), the support on which a lever rests or turns in moving something.

ful·fill, ful·fil (fool-fil'), *v.t.* -filled', -fill'ing, 1. to complete. 2. to perform or carry out, as that which is promised, foretold, anticipated, etc. 3. to execute (a duty, etc.). 4. to satisfy (requirements, etc.). —**ful·fill'ment, ful·fil'ment**, *n.*

ful·gent (ful'jĕnt), *adj.* [Rare], extremely bright; radiant. —**ful'gent·ly**, *adv.*

full (fool), *adj.* 1. filled; having no empty space. 2. well supplied. 3. satiated. 4. rounded out; plump. 5. having reached the greatest extent, size, etc. 6. complete. 7. clear; sonorous. 8. having ample folds of cloth: *n.* the greatest extent, size, etc.: *adv.* 1. to the greatest degree. 2. directly: *v.i.* 1. to become full: said of the moon: *v.t.* 1. to gather (cloth) with ample folds. 2. to shrink and thicken (cloth, especially of wool) with heat, moisture, and pressure. —**full'ness, ful'ness**, *n.*

full·back ('bak), *n.* a football player who is a member of the offensive backfield.

full-blood·ed ('blud'id), *adj.* 1. of unmixed breed or race: also **full'-blood'.** 2. vigorous.

full-blown ('blōn'), *adj.* 1. in full bloom. 2. matured.

full dress, clothes worn for formal or

ceremonial occasions, especially formal evening clothes.

full-er (fool'ẽr), *n.* one whose work is to full cloth.

full-er's earth (fool'ẽrz), an absorbent, powdery clay, used in fulling to remove grease from woolen cloth, and in clarifying fats and oils.

full-fledged (fool'flejd'), *adj.* 1. having all its feathers: said of a young bird. 2. of full rank.

full house, in *Poker*, a hand containing three of a kind and a pair.

full moon, the phase of the moon when the whole disk is illuminated.

full-scale ('skāl'), *adj.* 1. of the same size as the original. 2. complete.

full-y ('i), *adv.* 1. completely. 2. abundantly. 3. at least.

ful-mar (fool'mẽr, 'mãr), *n.* a large sea bird of arctic regions, of the petrel family.

ful-mi-nant (ful'mi-nǎnt, fool'-), *adj.* 1. fulminating. 2. progressing suddenly, as a disease.

ful-mi-nate (ful'mi-nāt), *v.i. & v.t.* -nat-ed, -nat-ing, 1. to explode; detonate. 2. to shout forth. —**ful-mi-na'tion,** *n.*

fulminating powder, an explosive substance used to detonate dynamite, etc.

ful-min-ic acid (ful-min'ik), an unstable acid, known in the form of its explosive salts, used to detonate dynamite, etc.

ful-some (fool'sǒm, ful'-), *adj.* offensive or gross, expecially as being excessive. —**ful'-some-ly,** *adv.* —**ful'some-ness,** *n.*

ful-vous (ful'vǔs), *adj.* tawny; dull yellow.

fu-ma-role (fū'mǎ-rōl), *n.* a small vent from which volcanic smoke and gases issue.

fum-ble (fum'bl), *v.i. & v.t.* -bled, -bling, 1. to feel about or grope *(for)* clumsily. 2. to bungle (something). 3. to lose one's hold on (a ball, etc.): *n.* an act of fumbling. —**fum'-bler,** *n.*

fume (fūm), *n.* a vapor, gas, or smoke, especially of a harmful or offensive nature: *v.i.* fumed, fum'ing, 1. to emit fumes. 2. to express anger or agitation. —**fum'ing-ly,** *adv.* —**fum'y,** *adj.*

fu-mi-gate (fū'mi-gāt), *v.t.* -gat-ed, -gat-ing, to expose to the action of fumes, especially to exterminate the vermin in. —**fu-mi-ga'tion,** *n.* —**fu'mi-ga-tor,** *n.*

fu-mi-to-ry (fū'mi-tôr-i), *n., pl.* -ries, an herb formerly used in medicine.

fun (fun), *n.* 1. a source of amusement, mirth, enjoyment, etc. 2. gay activity; sport, recreation, etc. 3. amusement; enjoyment.

fun-nam-bu-list (fyoo-nam'byoo-list), *n.* a tightrope walker.

func-tion (fungk'shǔn), *n.* 1. the action or activity normal to anything. 2. the specialized action of a plant or animal organ. 3. a special duty required of someone. 4. a formal or official ceremony. 5. a thing whose value depends on and changes according to another thing. 6. in *Mathematics*, a quantity whose value depends on another quantity or quantities: *v.i.* to perform a function; act.

func-tion-al (-ǎl), *adj.* 1. of or pertaining to a function. 2. performing a function. 3. in

Medicine, affecting the function of an organ, but not its structure. —**func'tion-al-ly,** *adv.*

func-tion-ar-y (-er-i), *n., pl.* -ar-ies, one who performs a certain function; official.

fund (fund), *n.* 1. money set aside for a special purpose. 2. *pl.* money on hand; financial resources. 3. a stock in reserve; supply that can be drawn upon: *v.t.* to convert into, or place in, an interest-bearing debt to extend over a long period.

fun-da-ment (fun'dǎ-mĕnt), *n.* 1. the buttocks. 2. the anus.

fun-da-men-tal (fun-dǎ-men'tl), *adj.* of or serving as a foundation; essential; basic: *n.* 1. a primary or essential principle; basis. 2. the lowest, or root, tone of a musical chord. 3. the main tone of a musical harmonic series. —**fun-da-men'tal-ly,** *adv.*

fundamental bass, the part in musical harmony that consists of the lowest tones of the chords.

fun-da-men-tal-ism (-izm), *n.* [sometimes F-], 1. a Protestant movement of the 20th century based on beliefs in the literal interpretation of the Bible. 2. such beliefs. —**fun-da-men'-tal-ist,** *adj. & n.*

fun-dus (fun'dǔs), *n., pl.* -di ('dī), the base of a hollow organ, or the part farthest from its opening. —**fun'dic,** *adj.*

fu-ner-al (fū'nēr-ǎl), *n.* 1. the ceremonies held for a dead person, often directly preceding burial or cremation. 2. the procession accompanying a body to the place of burial or cremation: *adj.* of, used at, or having to do with a funeral.

funeral director, the manager of a funeral home.

funeral home, an establishment where dead bodies are prepared for burial and where funerals are held: also **funeral parlor.**

fu-ne-re-al (fū-nir'i-ǎl), *adj.* suitable for a funeral; solemn; sad.

fun-gi-cide (fun'ji-sid), *n.* a substance that kills fungi.

fun-gus (fung'gǔs), *n., pl.* -gi (fun'ji), -gus-es, any of various plants having no chlorophyll, stems, or leaves and reproducing by spores: the group includes mushrooms, mildews, molds, smuts, ringworms, etc.: *adj.* of, like, or caused by a fungus: also **fun-gous** (fung'gǔs).

fu-ni-cle (fū'ni-kl), *n.* a small cord, ligature, or fiber.

fu-nic-u-lar (fyoo-nik'yoo-lēr), *adj.* 1. of or resembling a funiculus. 2. pertaining to, operated by, or hanging from a rope or cable: *n.* a short, steep railway on a mountain, with counterbalanced cable cars: also **funicular railway.**

fu-nic-u-lus (fyoo-nik'yoo-lus), *n., pl.* -li (-lī), 1. a bundle of nerve fibers. 2. the stalk of an ovule or seed.

funk (fungk), *n.* [Informal], 1. a flinching because of fear. 2. a mood of depression.

funk-y (fung'ki), *adj.* -ki-er, -ki-est, denoting a style of jazz related to the early blues.

fun-nel (fun'l), *n.* 1. a wide-mouthed, conical device tapering to a hole at the small end, for pouring liquids into small-mouthed containers. 2. the smokestack of a steamship:

---

v.i. & *v.t.* -neled or -nelled, -nel·ing or -nel·ling, to pour through or as through a funnel.

fun·ny (fun'i), *adj.* -ni·er, -ni·est, 1. comical; droll; provoking laughter. 2. [Informal], *a)* queer; odd. *b)* deceitful: *n., pl.* -nies, [Informal], a comic strip: usually plural. —fun'ni·ly, *adv.* —fun'ni·ness, *n.*

funny bone, the part of the elbow where the ulnar nerve passes: a blow to this spot causes a strange, tingling sensation.

fur (fūr), *n.* 1. the soft, thick hair growing on the skin of certain animals. 2. the dressed pelt of such an animal. 3. a garment, neck-piece, etc. made of such pelts. 4. any fuzzy coating: *adj.* of fur: *v.t.* furred, fur'ring, 1. to cover, line, or trim with fur. 2. to coat with a furry substance. 3. to make (a floor, ceiling, etc.) level by using furring.

fur·be·low (fūr'bē·lō), *n.* 1. a flounce; ruffle. 2. *usually pl.* any showy ornamentation.

fur·bish (fūr'bish), *v.t.* 1. to make bright by rubbing, polishing, or burnishing. 2. to renovate.

fur·cate (fūr'kāt), *v.i.* -cat·ed, -cat·ing, to fork; branch: *adj.* (also 'kit), forked. —fur'cate·ly, *adv.* —fur·ca'tion, *n.*

fur·fur (fūr'fēr), *n., pl.* -fur·es (-ēz), 1. dandruff; scurf. 2. *pl.* dandruff scales.

fu·ri·ous (fyoor'i·us), *adj.* 1. full of fury or rage; wildly angry. 2. violent, uncontrolled, wild, etc. —fu'ri·ous·ly, *adv.*

furl (fūrl), *v.t.* to roll up tightly and secure to something, as a sail, flag, etc.: *v.i.* to become rolled up.

fur·long (fūr'long), *n.* a unit of distance equal to one eighth of a mile.

fur·lough (fūr'lō), *n.* a leave of absence, especially for military enlisted personnel: *v.t.* to grant leave of absence to.

fur·nace (fūr'nâs), *n.* 1. a chamber or apparatus for producing heat, as by burning fuel, for heating a building, or for reducing ores or metals. 2. a severe trial.

fur·nish (fūr'nish), *v.t.* to supply with what is requisite; equip; specifically, to supply furniture.

fur·nish·ings (-ings), *n.pl.* 1. the furniture, rugs, etc. for a room, house, etc. 2. things to wear.

fur·ni·ture (fūr'ni·chēr), *n.* 1. the articles, usually movable, in a room, home, etc., that are necessary for living, as chairs, beds, tables, etc. 2. necessary equipment.

fu·ror (fyoor'ôr), *n.* 1. fury; rage. 2. a great outburst of excitement, enthusiasm, or controversy: also spelled **fu'rore**.

fur·ri·er (fūr'i·ēr), *n.* one who processes or sells furs or fur garments.

fur·ring (fūr'ing), *n.* 1. the act of lining, trimming, etc. with fur. 2. a furry coating. 3. thin strips of wood, metal, etc. used to level a wall, ceiling, etc. before adding plaster, boards, or the like.

fur·row (fūr'ō), *n.* 1. a trench made in the ground by a plow. 2. something resembling this, as a groove or deep wrinkle: *v.t.* to make grooves or wrinkles in: *v.i.* to become wrinkled.

fur·ry (fūr'i), *adj.* -ri·er, -ri·est, 1. of or resem-

bling fur. 2. covered with fur. —fur'ri·ness, *n.*

fur·ther (fūr'thēr), *adj.* 1. more distant; farther. 2. additional: *adv.* 1. to a greater distance or degree. 2. in addition: *v.t.* to promote; help forward.

fur·ther·ance (-âns), *n.* advancement.

fur·ther·more (-môr), *adv.* moreover; besides.

fur·ther·most (-mōst), *adv.* most remote.

fur·thest (fūr'thist), *adj.* most distant in time or degree: *adv.* at or to the greatest distance or degree.

fur·tive (fūr'tiv), *adj.* sly; sneaky; stealthy. —fur'tive·ly, *adv.* —fur'tive·ness, *n.*

fu·ry (fyoor'i), *n., pl.* -ries, 1. violent or uncontrollable rage. 2. violence. 3. *pl.* [F-], any of the three vengeful, female deities of Greek mythology.

furze (fūrz), *n.* a hardy, spiny, evergreen shrub with yellow flowers, native to Europe; gorse. —fur'zy, *adj.*

fus·cous (fus'kus), *adj.* grayish-brown or grayish-black; dusky.

fuse (fūz), *v.t.* & *v.i.* fused, fus'ing, 1. to liquefy by heat; melt. 2. to blend or unite as if by melting together: *n.* 1. a small tube or wick filled with flammable material, used for exploding a charge. 2. a wire or strip of easily melted metal placed in an electric circuit: it melts and breaks the circuit if the current becomes excessively strong.

fu·see (fū·zē'), *n.* 1. formerly, a wooden match with a large head, that would burn in the wind. 2. a colored signal flare used by truck drivers, railwaymen, etc.

fu·se·lage (fū'sě·läzh), *n.* the body of an airplane, aside from the engines, wings, and tail.

fu·sel oil (fū'zl, 'sl), an oily, poisonous liquid, a mixture of several kinds of alcohol, formed in the distillation of some alcoholic products.

fu·si·ble (fū'zi·bl), *adj.* capable of being fused. —fu·si·bil'i·ty, *n.*

fu·si·form (fū'zi·fôrm), *adj.* shaped like a spindle.

fu·sil·ier (fū·zi·lir'), *n.* 1. formerly, a soldier armed with a light musket (**fusil**): also spelled **fu·sil·eer'**. 2. *pl.* [F-], any of certain British regiments.

fu·sil·lade (fū'si·lād, -läd), *n.* a continuous or simultaneous discharge of many firearms: *v.t.* -lad·ed, -lad·ing, to shoot down or attack by fusillade.

fu·sion (fū'zhun), *n.* 1. the act or process of fusing or melting together. 2. the state or fact of being fused. 3. union by or as by melting; coalition. 4. same as **nuclear fusion**.

fuss (fus), *n.* 1. a flurry of excited activity; bustle. 2. a state of agitation, nervousness, etc. 3. [Informal], a commotion or quarrel. 4. [Informal], an exaggerated show of concern, delight, etc.: *v.i.* 1. to be nervously concerned about trifles. 2. to whimper, as a baby.

fuss·budg·et ('buj·it), *n.* [Informal], a worrier; fussy person.

fuss·y ('i), *adj.* fuss'i·er, fuss'i·est, 1. nervously concerned or worried about trifles. 2. finicky. 3. whimpering, as a baby. 4. requiring close attention. 5. having too many, or too elaborate, details. —fuss′i·ly, *adv.* —fuss′i·ness, *n.*

fus·tian (fus′chǔn), *n.* 1. a kind of thick cotton cloth with a short nap, as velveteen or corduroy. 2. a pretentious or pompous style in writing or speaking; bombast: *adj.* 1. made of fustian. 2. bombastic.

fus·ty (fus′ti), *adj.* fus′ti·er, fus′ti·est, 1. stale-smelling; musty or moldy. 2. old-fashioned. —fus′ti·ly, *adv.* —fus′ti·ness, *n.*

fu·tile (fū′tl), *adj.* vain; useless. —fu·til′i·ty, *n., pl.* -ties.

fu·ton (foō′ton), *n.* a thin mattress like a quilt, placed on the floor for use as a bed.

fut·tock (fut′ŏk), *n.* an upright curved rib of a wooden ship.

futtock shroud, any of a number of short iron rods extending upward from the top of a ship's lower mast to brace the topmast where it joins the lower mast.

fu·ture (fū′chěr), *adj.* 1. that is to come after the present; of time ahead. 2. indicating time to come, as the form of a verb: *n.* 1. time that is to come. 2. what will happen. 3. later success, life, career, etc. 4. the future tense in grammar, or a verb form expressing this tense. 5. *usually pl.* a contract for a commodity bought or sold for delivery at a later date.

future shock, the inability to cope with the rapid changes of modern society, or the distress resulting from this.

fu·tur·ism (-izm), *n.* a movement in the arts of the early 20th century that disregarded conventional form and tried to express the mechanization, speed, violence, power, etc. of modern days. —fu′tur·ist, *n. & adj.* —fu·tur·is′tic, *adj.*

fu·tu·ri·ty (fū-toor′i-ti, -tyoor′-), *n., pl.* -ties, 1. the future. 2. a future event. 3. a future condition. 4. a horse race for two-year-olds in which the contestants are chosen long beforehand: also **futurity race.**

fu·tur·ol·o·gy (fū-chěr-ol′ô-ji), *n.* the study of probable or presumed future conditions, as by making assumptions based on known facts. — fu·tur·ol′o·gist, *n.*

fuze (fūz), *n. & v.t. & v.i.* fuzed, fuz′ing, same as fuse.

fuzz (fuz), *n.* 1. fine, minute particles of down, wool, etc.; loose hairs or fibers. 2. [Slang], a policeman or the police.

fuzz·y (′i), *adj.* fuzz′i·er, fuzz′i·est, 1. covered with or like fuzz. 2. not clear or precise. — fuzz′i·ly, *adv.* —fuzz′i·ness, *n.*

-fy (fi), a suffix meaning *to become, to imbue with, to cause to be or become.*

fyke (fik), *n.* a kind of fish trap made of net with hoops.

futz (futs), *v.i.* [Slang], to trifle or meddle; fool (*around*).

G

G, g (jē), *n., pl.* **G's, g's,** 1. the seventh letter of the English alphabet. 2. either of the two sounds of this letter, as in *get* or *gee.* 3. a type or impression of *G* or *g.*

G (jē), *adj.* shaped like *G: n.* 1. an object shaped like *G.* 2. a school mark or rating signifying good. 3. in *Music, a)* the fifth tone in the scale of C major. *b)* the key having this tone for a basic note. 4. in *Physics, a)* gravity. *b)* a unit of measurement for the gravitational force exerted on a body during acceleration.

gab (gab), *n.* [Informal], idle chatter; loquacity: *v.i.* gabbed, gab'bing, to chatter idly. —gab'ber, *n.*

gab·ar·dine (gab'ẽr-dēn), *n.* 1. a firm fabric of wool, cotton, etc. with diagonal ribs, used for coats, suits, etc. 2. an article of clothing made of this. 3. same as gaberdine.

gab·ble (gab'l), *v.t.* -bled, -bling, to utter rapidly without sense: *v.i.* to chatter incoherently: *n.* rapid, incoherent talk. —gab'bler, *n.*

gab·bro (gab'rō), *n.* an igneous, granular rock, composed essentially of feldspar and pyroxene.

gab·by (gab'ē), *adj.* -bi·er, -bi·est, [Informal], given to talk much; loquacious. —gab'bi·ness, *n.*

gab·er·dine (gab'ẽr-dēn), *n.* 1. a coarse cloak or mantle, worn in the Middle Ages by Jews. 2. [Chiefly British], same as gabardine.

gab·fest (gab'fest), *n.* [Informal], an informal gathering to talk.

ga·bi·on (gā'bi-ŏn), *n.* 1. a large, cylindrical basket filled with earth or stones, formerly used in fortifications. 2. a similar cylinder used underwater for breakwaters.

ga·ble (gā'bl), *n.* 1. the triangular upper end of a building. 2. the end wall of a building, of which the upper part is triangular: *v.t. & v.i.* -bled, -bling, to build with, or add, gables to a structure.

ga·by (gā'bi), *n., pl.* -bies, [British Dial.], a foolish fellow; dunce.

gad (gad), *v.i.* gad'ded, gad'ding, to roam about in a purposeless manner: *n.* 1. the act of roaming about idly. 2. an iron or steel pointed mining tool.

gad·a·bout (gad'ä-bout), *n.* [Informal], an idler; a person who gads about.

gad·fly (gad'flī), *n., pl.* -flies, 1. a fly that stings livestock; a horsefly. 2. one who harasses others or attempts to rouse them.

gadg·et (gaj'ĕt), *n.* a device or contrivance, especially one that is mechanical. —gadg'et·ry, *n.*

gad·o·lin·ite (gad'ō-lin-īt), *n.* a silicate mineral containing gadolinium or a similar metal, in combination with iron.

gad·o·lin·i·um (gad·ō-lin'i-ŭm), *n.* a metallic chemical element that is very magnetic at low temperatures.

gad·wall (gad'wôl), *n., pl.* -walls, -wall, a large freshwater duck of North America.

Gae·a (jē'ä), *n.* in *Greek Mythology,* the earth goddess.

Gael (gāl), *n.* a Celtic inhabitant of Ireland or Scotland, especially a Scottish Highlander.

Gael·ic ('ik), *adj.* 1. pertaining to the Gaels. 2. pertaining to the branch of the Celtic language spoken by the inhabitants of the Scottish Highlands or of Ireland: *n.* the Celtic language spoken in the Scottish Highlands and in Ireland.

gaff (gaf), *n.* 1. a large hook on a pole for landing salmon or other large fish. 2. a spar to extend the upper edge of a fore-and-aft sail. 3. the metal spur put on a gamecock: *v.t.* to seize or land with a gaff.

gaffe (gaf), *n.* [French], a blunder; error.

gaf·fer (gaf'ẽr), *n.* 1. an old man, especially an old man from the country. 2. in England, the foreman of a gang of laborers.

gaff-top·sail (gaf'top-sl, -sāl), *n.* a light sail set above a gaff.

gag (gag), *n.* 1. something placed in the mouth to hinder speech. 2. anything checking or restraining free speech. 3. a joke or funny story. 4. a hoax: *v.t.* gagged, gag'ging, 1. to stop the mouth with a gag. 2. to prevent from speaking. 3. to cause to retch: *v.i.* to retch.

gage (gāj), *n.* 1. something offered as a pledge or security for the fulfillment of an obligation. 2. a gauntlet or glove thrown down as a challenge to combat. 3. a kind of plum; greengage. 4. same as gauge: *v.t.* gaged, gag'ing, same as gauge.

gag·gle (gag'l), *n.* 1. a flock of geese. 2. any group.

gahn·ite (gän'īt), *n.* a zinc aluminate, found as black, brown, or green crystals.

gai·e·ty (gā'i-ti), *n., pl.* -ties, 1. the state or quality of being gay; merriment. 2. festivity; merrymaking. 3. finery.

gai·ly (gā'li), *adv.* 1. merrily; happily. 2. brightly; showily.

gain (gān), *n.* 1. an improvement; advantage. 2. *often pl.* an increase in earnings; profits. 3. an addition or acquisition: *v.t.* 1. to obtain as profit or advantage. 2. to earn. 3. to win. 4. to arrive at. 5. to make an increase in: *v.i.* 1. to improve or make progress. 2. to increase in weight. 3. to be fast, as a timepiece.

gain·er ('ẽr), *n.* a dive in which the diver faces forward, does a backward somersault in the air, and enters the water feet first.

gain·ful ('fl), *adj.* profitable. —gain'ful·ly, *adv.* —gain'ful·ness, *n.*

gain·say (gān-sā'), *v.t.* -said' (-sed', -sād'), -say'ing, 1. to contradict. 2. to speak against or oppose. —gain·say'er, *n.*

gait (gāt), *n.* 1. manner of walking or running.

---

a in cap, ā in cane, ä in father, à in abet, e in met, ē in be, ē in baker, ė in regent, ĭ in pit, ī in fine, i in manifest, o in hot, ô in horse, ō in bone,

2. any of the distinctive patterns of a horse's foot movements, as a trot, canter, pace, gallop, etc.

gai·ter (gāt′ẽr), *n.* 1. a covering of cloth or leather for the ankle, instep, and, sometimes, the calf. 2. an overshoe with a cloth top.

gal (gal), *n.* [Informal], a girl.

ga·la (gā′lā, gal′ā), *n.* a festive affair; celebration: *adj.* of or suitable for a festive occasion.

ga·lac·tic (gā-lak′tik), *adj.* 1. pertaining to milk. 2. of or pertaining to the Milky Way or to some other galaxy.

gal·an·tine (gal′ān-tēn), *n.* a dish of boned white meat, as of chicken or veal, seasoned and boiled and served chilled in its own jelly.

gal·a·te·a (gal-ā-tē′ā), *n.* a strong cotton cloth, often striped, used for play clothes, etc.

Ga·la·tians (gā-lā′shŭnz), *n.* a book of the New Testament.

ga·lax (gā′laks), *n.* an evergreen plant of the southeastern U.S. with small, white flowers and shiny leaves often used in wreaths.

gal·ax·y (gal′ăk-si), *n., pl.* -ax·ies, 1. any of many vast systems of stars. 2. an assemblage of splendid persons or things. 3. [often G-], same as Milky Way.

gale (gāl), *n.* 1. a strong wind. 2. an outburst, as of laughter. 3. a kind of myrtle that grows in bogs: also sweet gale.

ga·le·a (gā′li-ā), *n., pl.* ga′le·ae (-ē), 1. in ancient Rome, a helmet. 2. in *Botany*, a helmet-shaped part.

ga·le·ate (-āt), *adj.* 1. wearing or shaped like a helmet. 2. having a galea.

ga·le·na (gā-lē′nä), *n.* a sulfide of lead, a gray, somewhat lustrous mineral.

gal·i·ot (gal′i-ŏt), *n.* same as galliot.

gal·i·pot (gal′i-pot), *n.* a crude turpentine exuded from a pine tree of Europe.

gall (gôl), *n.* 1. bile, the bitter, greenish secretion of the liver. 2. something bitter. 3. rancor; bitter feeling. 4. a tumor or excrescence on plants, caused by various insects, fungi, viruses, etc. 5. a wound on the skin, caused by friction. 6. irritation. 7. [Slang], effrontery; impudence: *v.t.* 1. to make sore by friction; chafe. 2. to vex; harass; annoy.

gal·lant (gal′ănt), *adj.* 1. stately; grand. 2. high-spirited; brave; noble. 3. (gā-lant′), showing courtesy and respectful deference to women: *n.* (gā-lant′), a man who is polite and attentive to women: *v.t.* (gā-lant′), [Rare], to accompany or escort (a woman). —gal′lant·ly, *adv.*

gal·lant·ry (gal′ănt-ri), *n., pl.* -ries, 1. bravery; heroic courage. 2. gallant and deferential attention to women. 3. a gallant act, action, or remark.

gall·blad·der (gôl′blad-ẽr), *n.* a membranous sac attached to the liver, in which excess bile is stored.

gal·le·ass (gal′i-as), *n.* a large, three-masted, Mediterranean vessel propelled by sails and oars and carrying heavy guns, used in the 16th and 17th centuries.

gal·le·on (gal′i-ăn), *n.* a large Spanish ship of the 15th and 16th centuries, having three or four decks at the stern and used as a warship or as a merchantman.

gal·ler·y (gal′ẽ-ri), *n., pl.* -ler·ies, 1. a covered walk open at one side; veranda or porch. 2. a long, outside balcony. 3. the upper seats in a church, theater, etc.; balcony. 4. the people in these seats, especially in the very highest, cheapest seats of a theater. 5. a group of spectators, as at a golf match. 6. a building or room used for the exhibition of works of art, etc. 7. an underground passage. 8. a balcony at the stern of an early sailing ship.

gal·ley (gal′i), *n., pl.* -leys, 1. an ancient, low, flat vessel propelled by oars and sails. 2. a kitchen aboard a ship. 3. in *Printing, a)* a flat, oblong frame for holding composed type. *b)* proof printed from type in a galley: also galley proof.

galley slave, a person convicted of a crime and sentenced to work an oar on a galley.

Gal·lic (gal′ik), *adj.* of or pertaining to ancient Gaul or modern France.

gal·lic acid (gal′ik), an organic crystalline compound found in gallnuts, tannin, etc., used in photography and in making dyes, etc.

Gal·li·can·ism (gal′i-kăn-izm), *n.* the claim in 1682 of the French Roman Catholic Church to limited autonomy.

Gal·li·cism (gal′i-sizm), *n.* [also g-], a French custom, expression, idiom, etc.

gall·ing (gôl′ing), *adj.* chafing; irritating. —gall′ing·ly, *adv.*

gal·li·nip·per (gal′i-nip-ẽr), *n.* [Informal], a large mosquito.

gal·li·nule (gal′i-nūl, -nōōl), *n.* a large marsh bird of the rail family.

gal·li·pot (gal′i-pot), *n.* 1. a small, glazed earthenware pot used by druggists. 2. same as galipot.

gal·li·um (gal′i-ŭm), *n.* a bluish-white, soft, metallic chemical element, used in dentistry, etc.

gal·li·vant (gal′i-vant), *v.i.* 1. originally, to gad about with members of the opposite sex. 2. to roam about searching for amusement. —gal′li·vant·er, *n.*

gal·li·wasp (gal′i-wäsp, -wŏsp), *n.* 1. a large, harmless lizard of Central America and the West Indies. 2. a lizard fish of the Caribbean.

gall·nut (gôl′nut), *n.* a nutlike gall, especially those on oaks, used commercially.

gal·lon (gal′ŏn), *n.* 1. a liquid measure equal to four quarts. 2. a dry measure equal to one eighth of a bushel.

gal·loon (gā-lōōn′), *n.* a braid or tape of worsted, cotton, or silk or of silver or gold thread, used for trimming.

gal·lop (gal′ŏp), *n.* 1. the fastest gait of a horse or other quadruped, a springing leap in which all four feet leave the ground at one time. 2. the act of riding at a gallop: *v.i. & v.t.* 1. to go or cause to go at a gallop. 2. to move very fast. —gal′lop·er, *n.*

gal·lows (gal′ōz), *n., pl.* -lows·es, -lows, 1. a wooden structure consisting of two uprights with a cross bar on the top, used for hanging condemned persons. 2. execution by hanging.

ô in dragon, ōō in crude, oo in wool, u in cup, ū in cure, ū in turn, ů in focus, oi in boy, ou in house, th in thin, th in sheathe, g in get, j in joy, y in yet.

gall·stone (gôl′stōn), *n.* a calculus formed in the gallbladder or biliary duct.

gall wasp, a tiny insect whose larvae produce galls on roses, oaks, and other plants.

ga·loot (gá-lōōt′), *n.* [Slang], a clumsy, silly person.

ga·lore (gá-lôr′), *adv.* in great plenty.

ga·losh (gá-losh′), *n.* a high overshoe of fabric and rubber: also spelled ga·loshe′.

gal·van·ic (gal-van′ik), *adj.* 1. of, producing, or caused by an electric current, especially from a battery. 2. shocking.

gal·va·nism (gal′vá-nizm), *n.* electricity produced by chemical action.

gal·va·nize (gal′vá-nīz), *v.t.* -nized, -niz·ing, 1. to subject to the action of an electric current. 2. to stimulate; excite. 3. to plate (metal) with zinc. —gal·va·ni·za′tion, *n.*

gal·va·nom·e·ter (gal-vá-nom′ê-tēr), *n.* an instrument for detecting and measuring a small electric current. —gal·va·nom′e·try, *n.*

gam (gam), *n.* 1. a school of whales. 2. a social visit, as between crews of whaling ships at sea: *v.i.* gammed, gam′ming, 1. to assemble into a school: said of whales. 2. to meet socially, especially at sea: *v.t.* to call upon; visit, especially at sea.

gam (gam), *n.* [Slang], a woman's shapely leg.

gam·ba·do (gam-bā′dō), *n., pl.* -dos, -does, 1. a upward leap by a horse. 2. a prank. 3. a legging attached to a saddle, often serving as a stirrup.

gam·bit (gam′bit), *n.* 1. an opening in chess in which a pawn or other piece is sacrificed to obtain a favorable position for the action of the more important pieces. 2. a move by which an advantage may be gained.

gam·ble (gam′bl), *v.i.* -bled, -bling, 1. to play for money or other stakes at games of chance. 2. to take a chance or venture for some advantage: *v.t.* to bet; wager: *n.* any matter or venture involving risk or uncertainty. —gam′bler, *n.*

gam·boge (gam-bōj′, -bōōzh′), *n.* a yellow gum resin obtained from a tropical Asian tree, used as a pigment and as a cathartic.

gam·bol (gam′bl), *n.* a dancing or skipping about for play: *v.i.* -boled or -bolled, -bol·ing or -bol·ling, to dance and skip about; frolic.

gam·brel (gam′brĕl), *n.* 1. the hock of a horse. 2. a frame resembling a horse's hind leg used by butchers for suspending a slaughtered animal.

gambrel roof, a roof with two sides, each of which has two slopes, the lower steeper than the upper.

game (gām), *n.* 1. any amusement or diversion. 2. sport or play in the form of a contest lasting until a result is obtained or a time limit expires. 3. a single match at play. 4. the advantage or number of points required in order to win. 5. a scheme or strategy. 6. wild birds or animals hunted for food or sport: *adj.* 1. of or pertaining to wild birds or animals hunted for food or sport. 2. gam′er, gam′est, *a*) ready. *b*) plucky: *v.i.* gamed, gam′ing, to play for stakes, gamble. —game′ly, *adv.* —game′ness, *n.*

game (gām), *adj.* [Informal], lame or injured:

said especially of a leg.

game-cock (′kok), *n.* a cock bred and trained for fighting.

game fowl, any of a breed of fowl bred and kept for cockfighting.

game-keep·er (′kēp-ēr), *n.* a person employed to breed and preserve game on State farms or private estates.

game plan, 1. the strategy planned before a game. 2. any long-range strategy.

game point, 1. the situation when the next point scored could win a game. 2. the winning point.

games-man·ship (gāmz′mán-ship), *n.* the expert use of clever strategies or maneuvers to gain an advantage.

game·ster (gām′stēr), *n.* a person who makes a business of gambling.

gam·ete (gam′ēt, gá-mēt′), *n.* a reproductive cell that in conjunction with another forms a zygote that develops into a new individual. —gam·met′ic (gá-met′ik), *adj.*

gam·in (gam′in), *n.* 1. a neglected child left to roam the streets; street urchin. 2. a saucy, pert girl: also ga·mine (gá-mēn′).

gam·ing (gā′ming), *n.* the act or practice of playing games for stakes; gambling.

gam·ma (gam′á), *n.* the third letter of the Greek alphabet.

gamma glob·u·lin (glob′yŭ-lin), the part of blood plasma containing the most antibodies.

gamma rays, intense, penetrating rays emitted by radioactive substances.

gam·mer (gam′ēr), *n.* an old woman, especially an old woman from the country.

gam·mon (gam′ŏn), *v.t.* 1. to defeat at the game of backgammon. 2. to lash (the bowsprit) to the stem of a ship: *n.* 1. a victory at backgammon in which the winner disposes of all his pieces before his opponent disposes of any. 2. a smoked, cured side of bacon or ham. 3. the lower end of a side of bacon.

gam·o·gen·e·sis (gam-ô-jen′ê-sis), *n.* sexual reproduction. —gam·o·ge·net′ic, *adj.*

gamp (gamp), *n.* [British], a large umbrella.

gam·ut (gam′ŭt), *n.* 1. any complete musical scale, especially the major scale. 2. the entire range or extent.

gam·y (gā′mi), *adj.* gam′i·er, gam′i·est, 1. strong-flavored, like the meat of cooked game. 2. slightly tainted. 3. plucky; courageous. 4. daring; suggestive. —gam′i·ness, *n.*

gan·der (gan′dēr), *n.* 1. a male goose. 2. a stupid or silly fellow. [Slang], a look: chiefly in *take a gander.*

gang (gang), *n.* a number of people who go around together, work together, or are associated for some purpose: *v.i.* to form into a gang (with *up*).

gan·gling (gang′gling), *adj.* lanky; awkwardly tall and spindly: also gan′gly.

gan·gli·on (gang′gli-ŏn), *n., pl.* -gli·a (-á), -gli·ons, 1. a mass of nerve cells from which nerve impulses issue. 2. a cystic tumor on a tendon. —gan·gli·on′ic (-on′ik), *adj.*

gang-plank (gang′plangk), *n.* a plank or movable ramp for boarding or leaving a ship.

gan·grene (gang′grēn, gang-grēn′), *n.* death and decay of body tissues because of an ob-

---

a in *cap*, ā in *cane*, ä in *father*, å in *abet*, e in *met*, ē in *be*, ē in *baker*, ê in *regent*, I in *pit*, ī in *fine*, i in *manifest*, o in *hot*, ô in *horse*, ō in *bone*,

struction of the blood supply. —gan′gre-nous (′grē-nŭs), adj.

gang·ster (gang′stĕr), n. a member of a gang of criminals. —gang′ster-ism, n.

gangue (gang), n. the worthless stony or earthy matter often occurring with valuable mineral deposits in a vein of ore.

gang·way (gang′wā), n. 1. same as gangplank. 2. an opening on a ship for passengers or for loading and unloading cargo. 3. the main level in a mine. 4. [British], a passageway between rows of seats.

gan·net (gan′it), n. a large, white, web-footed sea bird resembling a goose, found along the northern coasts of the Atlantic.

gan·oid (gan′oid), adj. of a large division of primitive fishes with hard, glossy scales or plates, including the sturgeons, paddlefishes, and gars: n. a ganoid fish.

gant·let (gônt′lit, gant′-), n. 1. an old form of punishment in which the offender was compelled to run between two rows of men who struck him with clubs, etc. as he passed: also spelled gaunt′let. 2. a section of railroad track where two lines of track overlap.

gan·try (gan′tri), n., pl. -tries, 1. a framework over railroad tracks for displaying signals. 2. a framework, often on wheels, for a traveling crane. 3. a framework with platforms at various levels for constructing and preparing a rocket for vertical launching.

gaol (jāl), n. British form for jail.

gap (gap), n. 1. an opening made by breaking, splitting, etc.; breach. 2. a mountain passage or cleft. 3. a hiatus. 4. a disparity; divergence or lag: v.i. gapped, gap′ping, to come apart: v.t. to make an opening in.

gape (gāp), v.i. gaped, gap′ing, 1. to open the mouth wide, as from drowsiness; yawn. 2. to stare with the mouth open. 3. to open, as a fissure or chasm: n. 1. the act of gaping. 2. a wide gap or breach. 3. pl. a disease of poultry and birds.

gar (gär), n., pl. gar, gars, a voracious fish with a long body and a beaklike snout: also gar′fish.

ga·rage (gȧ-räzh′, -räj′), n. 1. a shelter for motor vehicles. 2. an establishment where motor vehicles are serviced or repaired: v.t. -raged′, -rag′ing, to put or store in a garage.

garb (gärb), n. 1. fashion or style of dress. 2. clothing; apparel. 3. external form: v.t. to clothe.

gar·bage (gär′bij), n. food waste; refuse.

gar·ban·zo (gär-ban′zō, -bän′-), n., pl. -zos, same as chickpea.

gar·ble (gär′b'l), v.t. -bled, -bling, 1. to distort (a story, etc.) so as to mislead. 2. to confuse (a quotation, etc.) unintentionally. —gar′bler, n.

gar·board (gär′bôrd), n. the first planks or plates attached to the keel in shipbuilding: also garboard strake.

gar·con (gär-sôn′), n. [French], 1. a boy or young man. 2. a waiter or servant.

gar·den (gär′dn), n. 1. a piece of ground set apart for the cultivation of flowers, vegetables, etc. 2. an especially delightful or fertile place: also garden spot. 3. a public place like a park, often with flower beds, etc.: v.i. to lay out or work in a garden: adj. of, for, or from a garden. —gar′den-er, n.

gar·de·ni·a (gär-dēn′yȧ), n. 1. a subtropical shrub with waxy leaves and a fragrant white flower. 2. this flower.

Gar·gan·tu·an (gär-gan′choo-wȧn), adj. [also g-], 1. huge; very large. 2. having an enormous appetite. Named after Gargantua, a giant king in a novel by Rabelais (1552).

gar·gle (gär′g'l), n. a liquid, often medicinal, for rinsing the throat and mouth: v.i. -gled, -gling, to rinse the throat and mouth with a gargle.

gar·goyle (gär′goil), n. a waterspout projecting from the gutter of a building, often in the form of a grotesquely shaped animal or fantastic creature.

gar·ish (ger′ish), adj. gaudy; dazzling. —gar′ish-ly, adv. —gar′ish-ness, n.

gar·land (gär′lånd), n. 1. a wreath of flowers, leaves, etc., often used as a symbol of victory or honor. 2. a collection of songs, poetry, etc.: v.t. to deck or adorn with a garland.

gar·lic (gär′lik), n. 1. a plant of the lily family with a strong-scented, pungent bulb used in cooking. 2. this bulb.

gar·ment (gär′mĕnt), n. 1. any article of clothing. 2. pl. clothes.

gar·ner (gär′nĕr), n. a granary: v.t. to gather up and store.

gar·net (gär′nit), n. a hard, translucent mineral, used as an abrasive, or, in a deep-red variety, as a gem.

gar·nish (gär′nish), v.t. 1. to adorn; embellish. 2. to decorate (food) with something that adds flavor and color. 3. in Law, to garnishee: n. 1. a decoration. 2. something put on or around food as an embellishment, as parsley.

gar·nish·ee (gär-ni-shē′), n. in Law, the person holding property of the defendant pending settlement of the claims of a third party: v.t. -eed′, -ee′ing, in Law, 1. to attach (property) by court order, so that it can be used to pay a debt. 2. to serve (a person) with a garnishment.

gar·nish·ment (gär′nish-mĕnt), n. 1. an embellishment. 2. in Law, a legal notice forbidding the disposal of a defendant's property until the settlement of a lawsuit.

gar·ni·ture (gär′ni-chĕr), n. embellishment.

gar·pike (gär′pik), n. same as gar.

gar·ret (gar′it), n. an attic.

gar·ri·son (gar′i-sn), n. 1. a body of troops stationed in a fort or fortified place. 2. a fortified place with troops, guns, etc.: v.t. to furnish (a fortified place) with (troops) for its defense.

gar·rote (gȧ-rot′, -rōt′), n. 1. a method of execution by strangulation, formerly used in Spain. 2. a cord or wire for strangling a robbery victim, enemy sentry, etc.: v.t. -rot′ed or -rot′ted, -rot′ing or -rot′ting, to execute or attack by strangling. Also spelled ga·rotte′, gar·rotte′. —gar·rot′er, n.

gar·ru·lous (ger′ŏo-lŭs, -yoo-), adj. talkative, especially about trivial matters; verbose;

loquacious. —**gar·ru·li·ty** (gà-rŏŏ'li-ti), **gar'- ru·lous·ness,** n. —**gar'ru·lous·ly,** adv.

gar·ter (gär'tĕr), n. an elastic band or strap by which a stocking is held up on the leg: v.t. to bind or fasten with a garter.

garter snake, a small, harmless, striped snake common in North America.

gas (gas), n. 1. a fluid and elastic form of matter tending to expand indefinitely. 2. a mixture of flammable fluids used for heating, cooking, or lighting. 3. a fluid, such as nitrous oxide, used as an anesthetic. 4. a highly poisonous fluid, such as phosgene, dispersed in the air in warfare. 5. a gaseous substance formed in the digestive tract. 6. [Informal], a) gasoline. b) the accelerator in a motor vehicle. 7. [Slang], something exciting, amusing, etc.: v.t. gassed, gas'sing, 1. to supply with gas. 2. to injure or kill by gas, as in war: v.i. [Slang], to talk idly.

gas chamber, a room in which people are put to be killed with poison gas.

gas·con·ade (gas-kŏ-nād'), n. boastful or blustering talk: v.i. -ad'ed, -ad'ing, to boast or bluster.

gas·e·ous (gas'i-ûs, gas'yûs), adj. having the nature or form of gas.

gash (gash), n. a deep or gaping wound or cut: v.t. to make a long, deep cut in.

gas·i·fy (gas'i-fī), v.t. -fied, -fy·ing, to change into gas. —**gas·i·fi·ca'tion,** n.

gas jet, a burner or nozzle at the end of a gas fixture.

gas·ket (gas'kit), n. 1. a rope or cord by which a sail is furled or tied to a yard. 2. a thin, round piece of metal, rubber, etc. used to pack a gasket or joint to make it leakproof.

gas·light (gas'līt), n. 1. light produced by the combustion of illuminating gas. 2. a gas jet.

gas log, an imitation log in a fireplace, made of hollow, perforated metal and lighted by illuminating gas.

gas mask, a breathing apparatus worn over the face to prevent the inhalation of poisonous gases, as in warfare or by firefighters, etc.

gas meter, an instrument for recording the quantity of gas consumed in a given period, especially gas used as fuel.

gas·o·hol (gas'ŏ-hôl, -hol), n. a motor fuel mixture of gasoline and alcohol.

gas·o·line, gas·o·lene (gas-ŏ-lēn'), n. a volatile, highly flammable, colorless liquid, a product of petroleum, used chiefly as fuel in internal-combustion engines.

gasp (gasp), n. a convulsive effort to catch the breath: v.i. to catch the breath with difficulty: v.t. to say with gasps.

gas station, a business establishment that sells gasoline and oil and provides services for motor vehicles.

gas·sy (gas'i), adj. -si·er, -si·est, 1. full of or producing gas. 2. flatulent. 3. resembling gas. 4. [Informal], given to boastful talk. — **gas'si·ness,** n.

gas·trec·to·my (gas-trek'tŏ-mi), n., pl. -mies, excision of a part of the stomach.

gas·tric (gas'trik), adj. of or pertaining to the stomach.

gastric juice, the thin, acid fluid secreted in the mucous membrane of the stomach, that is an agent in digestion.

gas·tri·tis (gas-trīt'is), n. inflammation of the stomach.

gas·tro-, a combining form meaning the stomach, the stomach and.

gas·tro·en·ter·i·tis (gas-trŏ-en-tĕ-rīt'is), n. inflammation of the stomach and intestines.

gas·tro·in·tes·ti·nal (-in-tes'ti-nl), adj. of or pertaining to the stomach and the intestines.

gas·tro·nome (gas'trŏ-nōm), n. a person who has a highly developed taste in foods: also **gas·tron·o·mist** (gas-tron'ŏ-mist).

gas·tron·o·my (gas-tron'ŏ-mi), n. the art of good eating. —**gas·tro·nom'ic** (-trŏ-nom'ik), **gas·tro·nom'i·cal,** adj.

gas·tro·pod (gas'trŏ-pod), n. one of a division of mollusks which move by means of a broad muscular foot under the belly, including the snails and slugs.

gat (gat), n. a channel inland between cliffs.

gate (gāt), n. 1. a frame of wood, iron, etc., closing an entrance or passage, usually moving on hinges. 2. a large entrance to a city, castle, etc. 3. an entrance. 4. the money received for entrance. 5. the total number admitted. 6. [Slang], dismissal; rejection.

gate·crash·er (gāt'krash-ĕr), n. [Informal], a person who obtains admission to an event without paying or being invited.

gate·fold (gāt'fōld), n. an oversize page, as in a magazine, bound so it can be unfolded.

gate·way ('wa), n. 1. a means of entry in an obstacle with a gate. 2. an entry point.

gath·er (gath'ĕr), v.t. 1. to bring into one place; assemble. 2. to collect; accumulate. 3. to pick up; pluck. 4. to infer. 5. to pucker or plait: v.i. 1. to congregate. 2. to generate pus. 3. to increase: n. a plait or pucker in cloth, made by drawing thread through the folds. —**gath'er·er,** n.

gath·er·ing (-ing), n. 1. the act of assembling together. 2. an assemblage. 3. pleats or puckers. 4. an abscess.

Gat·ling gun (gat'ling), a gun with numerous small barrels, which are discharged in succession by turning a handle: after R.J. Gatling (1818-1903), U.S. inventor.

gauche (gōsh), adj. not having skill in dealing with people; clumsy.

gau·che·rie (gō-shĕ-rē'), n. socially clumsy behavior or a clumsy act.

gau·cho (gou'chō), n., pl. -chos, a cowboy on the South American plains.

gaud (gôd), n. a flashy or ostentatious ornament.

gaud·y (gôd'i), adj. gaud'i·er, gaud'i·est, showy, but cheap and vulgar. —**gaud'i·ly,** adv. — **gaud'i·ness,** n.

gauge (gāj), n. 1. a standard of measure. 2. the position of one ship to another and the wind. 3. the distance between the rails of a railway. 4. the diameter of a shotgun bore. 5. a means of measuring. 6. the diameter of wire, etc.: v.t. gauged, gaug'ing, 1. to ascertain the size, capacity, etc. of. 2. to estimate.

gaug·er (gāj'ĕr), n. 1. one who gauges. 2. one

who ascertains the contents of casks for excise taxes.

gaunt (gônt), *adj.* 1. pinched and lean. 2. harsh, forlorn, etc. in appearance. —**gaunt′ness,** *n.*

gaunt·let (gônt′lit), *n.* 1. a protective glove worn by knights. 2. a long glove with a wide cuff. 3. same as **gantlet.**

gauze (gôz), *n.* 1. a very thin, light, transparent fabric, as of cotton or silk. 2. a light openwork material, as of wire. —**gauz′y,** *adj.*

gav·el (gav′l), *n.* a small mallet, as that used by a presiding officer at meetings.

ga·vi·al (gā′vi-ǎl), *n.* a crocodile of India with a long, narrow snout.

ga·votte, ga·vot (gȧ-vot′), *n.* 1. a lively dance like the minuet. 2. music for this dance in 4/4 time.

gawk (gôk), *n.* a simpleton: *v.i.* to gaze like a gawk.

gawk·y (gô′ki), *adj.* **gawk′i·er, gawk′i·est,** awkward; ungainly. —**gawk′i·ness,** *n.*

gay (gā), *adj.* 1. lively; merry; full of spirits. 2. bright and cheerful. 3. given to pleasure; licentious. 4. homosexual: *n.* a homosexual, esp. a male homosexual. —**gay′ness,** *n.*

gay·e·ty (gā′ē-ti), *n.,* pl. **-ties,** same as **gaiety.**

gay·ly (gā′li), *adv.* same as **gaily.**

gaze (gāz), *v.i.* **gazed, gaz′ing,** to look earnestly and fixedly: *n.* a steady, fixed look. —**gaz′er,** *n.*

ga·ze·bo (gȧ-zē′bō, -zā′bō), *n.,* pl. **-bos, -boes** a summerhouse, balcony, etc. with windows for viewing the surroundings.

ga·zelle (gȧ-zel′), *n., pl.* **-zelles′, -zelle′,** a small, graceful, swift antelope with large, shining eyes.

ga·zette (gȧ-zet′), *n.* 1. a newspaper: now largely appearing only in the names of newspapers. 2. an English newspaper containing official announcements, as of the government: *v.t.* **-zet′ted, -zet′ting,** [Chiefly British], to publish in a gazette.

gaz·et·teer (gaz-ĕ-tir′), *n.* a dictionary of geographical names.

gaz·pa·cho (gȧs-pä′chō, gäz-), *n.* a cold Spanish soup of tomatoes, chopped cucumbers, onions, peppers, oil, vinegar, etc.

gear (gir), *n.* 1. accouterments. 2. apparatus, as tackle, harness, etc. 3. a moving part with teeth in machinery. 4. *often pl.* a series of these parts that transmit motion. 5. one setting of this series. 6. a separate mechanical part: *v.t.* 1. to put gear on; harness. 2. to adjust to conformity.

gear·ing (′ing), *n.* a series of toothed wheels for transmitting motion.

gear·shift (′shift), *n.* a mechanical contrivance for joining the motor to transmission gears.

gear·wheel (′hwēl), *n.* a cogwheel.

geck·o (gek′ō), *n., pl.* **geck′os, geck′oes,** a lizard that has suction pads on its feet, eats insects, etc.

gee (jē), *interj.* an expression of amazement.

geese (gēs), *n.* plural of **goose.**

gee·zer (gē′zēr), *n.* [Slang], an odd old man.

ge·fil·te fish (gĕ-fil′tĕ), balls of boiled, chopped fish with seasoning.

Ge·hen·na (gi-hen′ȧ), *n.* 1. a valley near Jerusalem where garbage was burned. 2. hell or a place of suffering.

Gei·ger counter (gī′gēr), a device for measuring radioactivity.

gei·sha (gā′shä), *n., pl.* **-sha, -shas,** a Japanese woman who works as an entertainer of and companion to men.

gel (jel), *n.* a substance with a consistency like that of jelly, produced by the coagulation of a colloid: *v.i.* **gelled, gel′ling,** to produce a gel.

gel·a·tin, gel·a·tine (jel′ȧt-n), *n.* 1. a substance resembling jelly and having no taste or odor, that is found in bones, hoofs, connective tissue, etc. from which it is extracted by boiling: used in photography, food, etc. 2. a vegetable substance like this. —**ge·lat·i·nous** (jĕ-lat′n-ŭs), *adj.*

ge·lat·i·nize (jĕ-lat′n-īz), *v.t.* **-nized, -niz·ing,** to convert into gelatin or a jellylike substance: *v.i.* to be converted into gelatin.

geld (geld), *v.t.* **geld′ed** or **gelt, geld′ing,** 1. to castrate (horses, etc.). 2. to deprive of any essential part.

geld·ing (gel′ding), *n.* a horse which has been castrated.

gel·id (jel′id), *adj.* frozen. —**ge·lid·i·ty** (jĕ-lid′i-ti), *n.*

gel·ig·nite (jel′ig-nīt), *n.* a high-powered explosive made up of nitrocellulose, nitroglycerin, ammonium nitrate, etc.

gem (jem), *n.* 1. a precious stone; jewel. 2. any perfect, rare, or beautiful object: *v.t.* **gemmed, gem′ming,** to adorn with or as with gems.

gem·i·nate (jem′i-nāt), *adj.* growing or occurring in pairs: *v.t.* **-nat·ed, -nat·ing,** to double: *v.i.* to become doubled or paired. —**gem·i·na′tion,** *n.*

Gem·i·ni (jem′i-nī, -nē), *n.* 1. a northern constellation between Cancer and Taurus. 2. the third sign of the zodiac.

gem·ma (jem′ȧ), *n., pl.* **-mae** (′ē), a bud which can develop into a new structure.

gem·mate (jem′āt), *adj.* reproducing by buds: *v.i.* **-mat·ed, -mat·ing,** to propagate by buds.

gem·mule (jem′ūl), *n.* a bud or gemma.

gem·ol·o·gy, gem·mol·o·gy (jem-ol′ō-ji), *n.* the science or study of gems.

gems·bok (gemz′bok), *n., pl.* **-bok, -boks,** the South African antelope.

gem·stone (jem′stōn), *n.* any material that can be cut or polished for use as a gem.

ge·müt·lich (gĕ-mēt′lich), *adj.* [German], giving joy, comfort, etc.

-gen (jĕn, jen), a suffix meaning *that which produces* or *is produced.*

gen·darme (zhän′därm), *n., pl.* **-darmes** (′därmz), in France, Belgium, etc., an armed policeman.

gen·dar·me·rie (zhän-där′mĕ-ri), *n.* gendarmes collectively.

gen·der (jen′dēr), *n.* the grammatical distinction of sex, expressed by suffixes, prefixes, or by a different word.

gene (jēn), *n.* a part in the chromosome, transmitted from parent to child, determining the development of certain characteristics in the child.

ge·ne·al·o·gy (jē-ni-ol′ō-ji, -al′ō-ji), *n., pl.* **-gies,**

ô in dragon, ōō in crude, oo in wool, u in cup, ū in cure, û in turn, ů in focus, oi in boy, ou in house, th in thin, th in sheathe, g in get, j in joy, y in yet.

1. a family history tracing descent. **2.** lineage. **3.** a science that traces descent. —ge·ne·a·log′i·cal (-å-loj′i-kl), *adj.* —ge·ne·al′o·gist, *n.*

gen·er·a (jen′ēr-å), *n.* plural of genus.

gen·er·al (jen′ēr-ål), *adj.* **1.** relating to a whole kind, class, or race. **2.** not special or particular; of or pertaining to the majority. **3.** not restricted; common. **4.** usual; ordinary. **5.** indefinite. **6.** senior: *n.* **1.** a general principle, statement, etc. **2.** a high military officer ranking above a colonel. **3.** the chief of a religious order.

general assembly, **1.** a State legislature in some States of the U.S. **2.** [G- A-], the legislature of the United Nations. **3.** the highest ecclesiastical tribunal in the Presbyterian church.

general delivery, the sending of mail to the post office, where it is picked up by the person to whom it is addressed.

gen·er·al·is·si·mo (jen-ēr-å-lis′i-mō), *n., pl.* -mos, a commander in chief of the army, navy, and air force in some nations.

gen·er·al·i·ty (jen-ēr-al′i-ti), *n., pl.* -ties, **1.** the state of being general. **2.** a concept that is not specific. **3.** the bulk; majority.

gen·er·al·ize (jen′ēr-å-līz), *v.t.* -ized, -iz·ing, **1.** to express in a general way. **2.** to infer (a general principle) from (particular instances): *v.i.* **1.** to make general inferences. **2.** to speak in a general way. —gen·er·al·i·za′tion, *n.*

gen·er·al·ly (-li), *adv.* **1.** commonly. **2.** in the main. **3.** without exact limitation.

general practitioner, a doctor who deals with all kinds of medical problems.

gen·er·al·ship (-ship), *n.* **1.** the office, rank, or skill of a general. **2.** skillful leadership.

general staff, a group of officers who assist the commanding officer in directing military tactics.

gen·er·ate (jen′ē-rāt), *v.t.* -at·ed, -at·ing, **1.** to procreate. **2.** to produce; originate. **3.** in *Mathematics,* to trace out or form by motion.

gen·er·a·tion (jen-ēr-ā′shun), *n.* **1.** the act or process of generating. **2.** a single succession in natural descent. **3.** people of the same period. **4.** the time period separating generations: normally 30 years. **5.** in *Mathematics,* formation of a geometric figure by the motion of a point, line, or surface. —gen·er·a′tion·al, *adj.*

gen·er·a·tive (jen′ēr-å-tiv), *adj.* **1.** of or pertaining to generation. **2.** having the power to generate.

gen·er·a·tor (jen′ē-rāt-ēr), *n.* **1.** one who or that which generates. **2.** a machine in which steam or gas is produced. **3.** a machine for producing electrical energy from mechanical energy.

ge·ner·ic (jē-ner′ik), *adj.* **1.** of or pertaining to a genus, kind, or class; comprehensive. **2.** not being a trademark.

gen·er·ous (jen′ēr-ůs), *adj.* **1.** high-minded; honorable. **2.** characterized by liberality; munificent. **3.** bountiful. **4.** strong; stimulating: used of wine. —gen·er·os·i·ty (jen-ē-ros′i-ti), *n., pl.* -ties. —gen′er·ous·ly, *adv.*

gen·e·sis (jen′ē-sis), *n.* **1.** *pl.* -ses (-sēz), the act or process of producing or originating; beginning. **2.** [G-], the first book of the Pentateuch in the Old Testament.

gen·et (jen′ēt), *n.* **1.** an African animal allied to the civet. **2.** its fur.

ge·net·ic (jē-net′ik), *adj.* **1.** of or relating to genesis. **2.** of or pertaining to genetics. Also ge·net′i·cal. —ge·net′i·cal·ly, *adv.*

ge·net·ics (′iks), *n.* the branch of biology which treats of heredity and deviation in animals and plants. —ge·net′i·cist (′i-sist), *n.*

ge·nial (jēn′yål), *adj.* **1.** kindly and sympathetic in disposition; cordial. **2.** contributing to cheerfulness and life; agreeably warm and cheerful. —ge·ni·al·i·ty (jē-ni·al′i-ti), *n.* —ge′nial·ly, *adv.*

ge·nic·u·late (je-nik′yoo-lit), *adj.* having knee-like joints.

ge·nie (jē′ni), *n.* same as jinni.

gen·i·tal (jen′i-tl), *adj.* of or pertaining to generation or the reproductive organs.

gen·i·tals (jen′i-tlz), *n.pl.* the external organs of reproduction: also gen·i·ta′li·a (-tāl′yå).

gen·i·tive (jen′i-tiv), *n.* a grammatical case indicating origin, possession, or relation: *adj.* of, denoting, or in the genitive case: also gen·i·ti·val (jen-i-tī′vl).

gen·i·to·u·ri·nar·y (jen-i-tō-yoor′i-ner-i), *adj.* of or denoting the urinary and genital organs as a whole.

gen·ius (jēn′yůs), *n.* **1.** powerful bent of mind or disposition. **2.** remarkable aptitude or natural endowment (*for* some special pursuit). **3.** character or essential principle; embodiment. **4.** high mental powers or faculties. **5.** a person possessing these.

gen·o·cide (jen′ō-sid), *n.* a planned extermination of an entire people or country.

gen·re (zhän′rē), *n.* **1.** a style of painting representing some scene of common life: also genre painting. **2.** a particular kind or sort: often applied to works of literature or art.

gens (jenz), *n., pl.* gen·tes (jen′tiz), among the ancient Romans, a clan.

gent (jent), *n.* [Informal], a man: used in jest or in a common way.

gen·teel (jen-tēl′), *adj.* **1.** graceful or elegant in manners or dress; well-bred. **2.** elegant or polite in a forced manner.

gen·tian (jen′shůn), *n.* **1.** a plant noted for blue, white, or yellow flowers. **2.** the bitter root of the yellow gentian from which a tonic is produced.

gen·tile (jen′til), *n.* [also G-], one who is not a Jew: *adj.* [also G-], not belonging to the Jewish faith.

gen·til·i·ty (jen-til′i-ti), *n., pl.* -ties, **1.** high social status or refinement. **2.** those belonging to the upper classes.

gen·tle (jen′l), *adj.* -tler, -tlest, **1.** mild and refined in manner and disposition. **2.** kindly. **3.** moderate in action. **4.** peaceful; docile. **5.** easy. **6.** well born or descended. **7.** developing a little at a time. —gen′tle·ness, *n.* —gent′ly, *adv.*

gen·tle·folk (-fōk), *n.pl.* persons of high social status: also gen′tle·folks.

gen·tle·man (-mån), *n., pl.* -men (-mĕn), **1.** a well-bred man. **2.** a person of independent income. 3. an honorable or polite man. 4. any man: a term of politeness, used as in address. —gen'tle-man-ly, adj. —gen'tle-wom-an (-woom-ăn), n.fem., pl. -wom-en (-wim-in).

gen-try (jen'tri), n. 1. the upper class of society. 2. those of a specific group.

gen-u-flect (jen'yŭ-flĕkt), v.i. to bend the knee, especially in worship. —gen-u-flec'tion, chiefly British gen-u-flex'ion (-flek'shŭn), n.

gen-u-ine (jen'yoo-win), adj. 1. real; unadulterated. 2. belonging to, or derived from, the original or true stock. 3. not hypocritical; open. —gen'u-ine-ly, adv. —gen'u-ine-ness, n.

ge-nus (jē'nŭs), n., pl. gen-er-a (jen'ēr-ă), ge'nus-es, 1. an order; class. 2. in Biology, a classification of allied animals or plants; a group of related species of animals or plants. 3. in Logic, a class made up of two or more subordinate classes or species.

ge-o-, a combining form meaning earth, ground.

ge-o-cen-tric (jē-ō-sen'trik), adj. 1. having the earth as a center. 2. viewed as from the earth's center. Also ge-o-cen'tri-cal.

ge-ode (jē'ōd), n. a rounded stone that is hollow and lined with crystals.

ge-o-des-ic (jē-ō-des'ik), adj. 1. same as geodetic (sense 1). 2. denoting the shortest line between any two points on a surface. 3. of or relating to the geometry of such a line.

ge-od-e-sy (jē-od'ě-si), n. the science of measuring large portions of the earth's surface or determining the earth's figure and size.

ge-o-det-ic (jē-ō-det'ik), adj. 1. of, pertaining to, or determined by geodesy. 2. same as geodesic (sense 2).

ge-og-no-sy (ji-og'nō-si), n. the branch of geology that treats of the composition of the earth.

ge-og-ra-phy (ji-og'ră-fi), n., pl. -phies, 1. the science that describes the surface of the earth, its division into continents, nations, etc., and its natural and human features. 2. the surface features of an area. —ge-og'ra-pher, n. —ge-o-graph'i-cal (-ō-graf'i-kl), ge-o-graph'ic, adj. —ge-o-graph'i-cal-ly, adv.

ge-ol-o-gy (ji-ol'ō-ji), n., pl. -gies, the science that investigates the structure of the earth and the causes that have produced alterations in the earth's crust, as well as the makeup of its fossils, rocks, etc. —ge-o-log'ic (-ō-loj'ik), ge-o-log'i-cal, adj. —ge-o-log'i-cal-ly, adv. —ge-ol'o-gist, n.

ge-o-man-cy (jē'ō-man-si), n. divination by lines and figures taken at random.

ge-oph-a-gy (ji-of'ă-ji), n. the practice of eating earth.

ge-o-phys-ics (jē-ō-fiz'iks), n. the science that treats of the weather and other physical phenomena and their influences on the earth.

geor-gette (jôr-jet'), n. a thin, transparent crepe fabric of very fine texture: after Georgette de la Plante, Parisian dressmaker.

geor-gic (jôr'jik), adj. of or pertaining to husbandry or agriculture: n. a poem on agriculture.

ge-o-ther-mic (jē-ō-thûr'mik), adj. of or pertaining to the heat from the inside of the earth: also ge-o-ther'mal.

ge-ot-ro-pism (ji-ot'rō-pizm), n. a tendency in living things to turn, as the roots of plants, in the direction of the earth's center (called positive geotropism): when the tendency is to turn away from the center it is called negative geotropism.

ge-ra-ni-um (jě-rā'ni-ŭm), adj. any of a group of related plants having purple or pink flowers.

ger-bil, ger-bille (jûr'bl), n. a rodent of Asia and Africa with a long tail and long hind legs.

germ (jûrm), n. 1. the rudimentary form of an organism; cell, bud, etc. 2. a microscopic organism, especially a bacterium, apt to cause disease. 3. an origin.

Ger-man (jûr'măn), adj. 1. of or pertaining to Germany, a divided country in north central Europe, or to its inhabitants. 2. [g-], of the same parents or grandparents: n. 1. a native or inhabitant of Germany. 2. the language used in Germany, Austria, etc.

ger-mane (jěr-mān'), adj. 1. related; akin. 2. relevant; appropriate.

Ger-man-ic (jěr-man'ik), adj. 1. same as German. 2. of or pertaining to the earliest German language or its descendants: n. the language branch including German, English, Swedish, Dutch, etc.

ger-ma-ni-um (jěr-mā'ni-ŭm), n. a grayish-white metallic element from which transistors are manufactured.

German silver, same as nickel silver.

germ cell, a cell that is the source of a living thing; sperm or egg cell.

ger-mi-cide (jûr'mi-sīd), n. a substance used to destroy disease germs. —ger-mi-ci'dal, adj.

ger-mi-nal (jûr'mi-nl), adj. 1. of, pertaining to, or similar to a germ cell or germ. 2. in the initial period of development.

ger-mi-nate (-nāt), v.i. & v.t. -nat-ed, -nat-ing, 1. to sprout or bud. 2. to begin to develop into a higher form. —ger'mi-nant (-nănt), adj. —ger-mi-na'tion, n.

germ plasm, the substance in the reproductive cells through which the hereditary traits of the parents are transmitted.

ger-on-tol-o-gy (jer-ŏn-tol'ō-ji), n. the science that treats of growing old and the problems of persons who are elderly.

ger-ry-man-der (jer'i-man-dēr), v.t. to divide (a voting district) so as to give an unfair advantage to a particular political party.

ger-und (jer'ŭnd), n. a kind of verbal noun with an -ing termination.

Ge-sta-po (gě-stä'pō), n. the secret police of the Nazi regime in Germany noted for the use of force, threats, violence, etc.

ges-tate (jes'tāt), v.t. -tat-ed, -tat-ing, to be pregnant with.

ges-ta-tion (jes-tā'shŭn), n. pregnancy.

ges-tic-u-late (jes-tik'yŭ-lāt), v.i. -lat-ed, -lat-ing, to make gestures or motions, as in speaking. —ges-tic-u-la'tion, n. —ges-tic'u-la-tor, n.

ges-ture (jes'chēr), n. 1. a movement of the face, body, or limbs, to express ideas, emotions, etc. 2. anything done or said to communicate purpose or feeling, sometimes as a convention: v.i. -tured, -tur-ing, to employ gestures.

ŏ in dragon, ōō in crude, oo in wool, u in cup, ū in cure, û in turn, ů in focus, oi in boy, ou in house, th in thin, th in sheathe, g in get, j in joy, y in yet.

get (get), *v.t.* got, got or got'ten, get'ting, 1. to obtain; procure; win; gain; acquire. 2. to arrive at. 3. to capture. 4. to learn. 5. to prevail upon. 6. to realize. 7. to make ready. 8. to procreate. 9. [Informal], to feel required to (with *have* or *has*). 10. [Informal], to own. 11. [Informal], to hit, master, etc. 11. [Informal], to comprehend. 12. [Slang], to annoy, excite, satisfy, etc.: *v.i.* 1. to arrive. 2. to become. 3. to find time, opportunity, etc. 4. [Informal], to depart quickly (usually with *out*): *n.* an offspring of an animal. —get'ter, *n.*

get·a·way (get'ă-wā), *n.* the act of beginning or of breaking loose.

get-to·geth·er (get'tŏ-geth-ēr), *n.* a social meeting lacking in ceremony.

get-up (get'up), *n.* [Informal], style of dress.

gew·gaw (gū'gô), *n.* a showy trifle.

gey·ser (gī'zēr), *n.* a hot or boiling spring from which water or steam is ejected in streams into the air intermittently.

ghast·ly (gast'li), *adj.* -li·er, -li·est, 1. deathlike; pale; haggard. 2. horrible. 3. [Informal], extremely disagreeable. —ghast'li·ness, *n.*

ghat, **ghaut** (gôt), *n.* 1. in India, a mountain pass. 2. a chain of mountains. 3. in India, a flight of steps to a river.

gher·kin (gūr'kin), *n.* a small cucumber used for pickling.

ghet·to (get'ō), *n.*, *pl.* -tos, -toes, 1. a section of a European city where Jews were formerly required to dwell. 2. an area of a city in which a minority group predominates.

ghost (gōst), *n.* 1. the supposed spirit of a deceased person; apparition. 2. a shadow; remotest likelihood. 3. a second image in a lens. —ghost'ly, *adv.*

ghost·writ·er (rīt'ēr), *n.* a person who composes speeches, literary material, etc. for someone else who claims to have created the material. —ghost'write, *v.i.* & *v.t.*

ghoul (gōōl), *n.* a supposed demon who robs graves and feeds on the flesh of the dead. —ghoul'ish, *adj.*

GI (jē'ī'), *adj.* 1. government issue: denoting military uniforms, etc. 2. [Informal], of or typical of the armed forces of the U.S.: *n.*, *pl.* GI's, GIs, [Informal], an enlisted soldier in the U.S. armed forces.

gi·ant (jī'ănt), *n.* 1. a person of extraordinary bulk or stature, or of great physical or intellectual power. 2. in *Greek Mythology*, one of a race of monstrous size who assailed the gods: *adj.* like a giant; huge. —gi'ant·ess, *n.fem.*

gib·ber (jib'ēr, gib'-), *v.t.* & *v.i.* to speak incoherently.

gib·ber·ish (-ish), *n.* rapid, incoherent talk.

gib·bet (jib'it), *n.* 1. a gallows. 2. a construction on which dead criminals were exposed to public scorn: *v.t.* 1. to hang on a gibbet. 2. to expose to public scorn.

gib·bon (gib'ŏn), *n.* a long-armed anthropoid ape of southern Asia.

gib·bos·i·ty (gi-bos'ĭ-ti), *n.* 1. the condition of being gibbous. 2. *pl.* -ties, a swelling.

gib·bous (gib'ŭs), *adj.* 1. protuberant; swelling.

2. between full and half-full: said of the moon. 3. humpbacked.

gibe (jīb), *n.* a scoff; taunt; sneering or sarcastic expression: *v.t.* & *v.i.* gibed, gib'ing, to sneer (at); taunt; scoff.

gib·let (jib'lit), *n.* one of the edible internal parts of a fowl, as the gizzard.

gid (gid), *n.* a disease in sheep.

gid·dy (gid'i), *adj.* -di·er, -di·est, 1. having a confused, whirling sensation; lightheaded. 2. frivolous; fickle. —gid'di·ness, *n.*

gift (gift), *n.* 1. something given or bestowed; present. 2. the act of donation; offering. 3. a natural talent: *v.t.* 1. to present a gift to. 2. to present in the form of a gift.

gift·ed (gift'id), *adj.* 1. talented. 2. having very great intelligence.

gig (gig), *n.* 1. a two-wheeled open chaise drawn by one horse. 2. a rotary machine for raising nap on cloth. 3. a long ship's boat reserved for the commanding officer. 4. a pronged instrument for catching fish: *v.i.* & *v.t.* gigged, gig'ging, to stick with a gig in fishing.

gi·gan·tic (jī-gan'tik), *adj.* huge; colossal.

gig·gle (gig'l), *v.i.* -gled, -gling, to laugh in a nervous, foolish, tittering manner: *n.* a nervous, silly laugh. —gig'gler, *n.* —gig'gly, *adj.* -gli·er, -gli·est.

gig·o·lo (jig'ō-lō), *n.*, *pl.* -los, a man who receives money for acting as an escort to a woman.

gig·ot (jig'ŏt), *n.* a leg of mutton, lamb, veal, etc.

Gi·la monster (hē'lä), a large, poisonous lizard of rough skin and orange and black in color, found in the arid parts of the southwestern U.S.: so called from the *Gila* River, Arizona.

gild (gild), *v.t.* gild'ed or gilt, gild'ing, 1. to overlay or cover with gold or gold color. 2. to give a vivid appearance to; illuminate. 3. to give a semblance of worth or beauty to: *n.* same as guild.

gild·ing (gil'ding), *n.* 1. the art or process of overlaying or covering with gold. 2. gold leaf, powder, etc. applied to a surface. 3. a superficial covering to give a pleasant appearance.

gill (gil), *n.* 1. the respiratory organ of most aquatic animals, as fish. 2. the wattle of a fowl. 3. one of the thin plates under a cap of a mushroom. 4. [British], a glen or brook.

gill (gil), *n.* a measure of liquid, equal to 1/4 pint.

gil·li·flow·er (jil'i-flou-ēr), *n.* any of various plants of the mustard family, as the wallflower, stock, etc.: also gil'ly·flow·er.

gilt (gilt), alternate past tense or past participle of gild: *adj.* covered with gold or gold color: *n.* gilding.

gilt-edged (gilt'ejd'), *adj.* having the most worth or excellence.

gim·bals (gim'blz), *n.* two rings moving within each other at right angles: used for suspending a mariner's compass, etc.

gim·crack (jim'krak), *adj.* showy, but of no value: *n.* a showy, useless thing.

---

a in cap, ā in cane, ä in father, ă in abet, e in met, ē in be, ê in baker, ê in regent, i in pit, ī in fine, i in manifest, o in hot, ô in horse, ō in bone,

gim·el (gim'l), *n.* the third letter of the Hebrew alphabet.

gim·let (gim'lit), *n.* a small boring tool with a pointed screw at the end: *v.t.* to make a hole in with a gimlet.

gim·mick (gim'ik), *n.* 1. [Informal], a thing used to deceive. 2. [Slang], something used to attract interest, as in advertising, publicizing, etc.

gimp (gimp), *n.* a kind of interlaced material of silk, cotton, etc., sometimes interwoven with wire: used as trimming on furniture, dresses, etc.

gimp (gimp), *n.* [Informal], 1. a person who is disabled. 2. a lameness in walking.

gin (jin), *n.* 1. an aromatic alcoholic liquor obtained by distilling rye with juniper berries. 2. a trap or snare. 3. same as cotton gin. 4. a hoisting machine: *v.t.* ginned, gin'ning, 1. to catch in a trap. 2. to clear (cotton) of seeds by employing a gin.

gin·ger (jin'jẽr), *n.* 1. the aromatic rootstalk of an Asiatic plant, utilized as a spice. 2. this plant. 3. [Informal], spunk; courage: *v.t.* 1. to flavor with ginger. 2. to render lively or spunky.

ginger ale, a carbonated beverage flavored with ginger.

ginger beer, a beverage similar to ginger ale, but having a more pungent taste.

gin·ger·bread (-bred), *n.* 1. a cake made with ginger and molasses. 2. gaudy decoration.

gin·ger·ly (-li), *adj. & adv.* very cautious(ly).

gin·ger·snap (-snăp), *n.* a firm cookie with molasses and ginger added.

ging·ham (ging'ăm), *n.* a cotton material dyed in the yarn before weaving into striped or checked patterns.

gin·gi·val (jin-jī'vl), *adj.* of or relating to the gums.

gin·gi·vi·tis (jin-ji-vīt'is), *n.* inflammation of the gums.

gink·go (ging'kō), *n., pl.* gink'goes, an Asiatic tree with leaves that spread like a fan: also **ging'ko,** *pl.* ging'koes.

gin rummy, a kind of rummy: also gin.

gin·seng (jin'seng), *adj.* a plant with an aromatic root used in China as a medicine.

gip (jip), *n. & v.t. & v.i.* same as gyp.

Gip·sy (jip'sĭ), *n. & adj. & v.i.* same as Gypsy.

gi·raffe (ji-raf'), *n., pl.* -raffes', -raffe', a large ruminant mammal of Africa, the tallest of all animals, with long legs and a long neck: giraffes often grow to a height of 18 feet.

gir·an·dole (jir'ăn-dōl), *n.* 1. a branching candlestick. 2. revolving fireworks.

gir·a·sol (jir'ă-sôl), *n.* a reddish opal.

gird (gûrd), *v.t.* gird'ed or girt, gird'ing, 1. to surround with a belt, etc. 2. to bind; encircle. 3. to make (oneself) ready for.

gird·er (gûr'dẽr), *n.* a main beam that holds up joists in a floor, a building frame, etc.

gir·dle (gûr'dl), *n.* 1. a belt or sash for the waist. 2. anything that encompasses. 3. a piece of elastic underwear worn around the hips and waist, usually by women: *v.t.* -dled, -dling, 1. to bind with a girdle. 2. to enclose. 3. to cut around the bark of (a tree).

girl (gûrl), *n.* 1. a female child. 2. a young,

unmarried woman. 3. a female employee. 4. [Informal], a sweetheart. —**girl'hood,** *n.* — **girl'ish,** *adj.*

girl scout, a member of an organization of girls, the *Girl Scouts,* emphasizing healthful activities in a character-building program.

girt (gûrt), alternate past tense and past participle of gird: *v.t.* 1. same as gird. 2. to attach by a girth.

girth (gûrth), *n.* 1. the band by which the saddle is kept secured on a horse. 2. the circumference of a tree, waist, etc.

gist (jist), *n.* the substance of a matter; main point.

give (giv), *v.t.* gave, giv'en, giv'ing, 1. to bestow; confer without price or reward. 2. to yield. 3. to deliver; supply. 4. to emit. 5. to pass into keeping or in exchange. 6. to convey. 7. to impart. 8. to sponsor; host. 9. to proffer. 10. to enact or render. 11. to set or place (a penalty). 12. to sacrifice; dedicate: *v.i.* 1. to donate. 2. to yield to pressure; retreat; shrink: *n.* the act of giving or yielding. —**giv'er,** *n.*

give-and-take (giv'n-tăk'), *n.* 1. yielding on both sides. 2. a series of witty or joking replies.

give·a·way (giv'ă-wā), *n.* [Informal], 1. an unintentional betrayal or disclosure. 2. a thing dispensed with little or no charge. 3. a program on radio or television which offers prizes to participants.

giv·en (giv'n), past participle of give: *adj.* 1. bestowed. 2. disposed to. 3. executed. 4. granted. 5. declared.

given name, one's first name.

giz·mo (giz'mō), *n.* [Slang], a device.

giz·zard (giz'ãrd), *n.* the second stomach of birds, an organ with thick muscular walls.

gla·bel·la (glă-bel'ă), *n., pl.* -lae ('ē), the smooth prominence on the forehead just above the nose.

gla·brous (glā'brŭs), *adj.* bald.

gla·cé (gla-sā'), *adj.* 1. finished with a smooth surface; glossy: said of cloth, leather, etc. 2. coated with sugar, as fruit.

gla·cial (glā'shăl), *adj.* 1. of, pertaining to, consisting of, or caused by ice, glaciers, or a glacial epoch. 2. freezing. 3. cold and unfriendly. —**gla'cial·ly,** *adv.*

glacial epoch, a time span when glaciers extended over much of the earth's surface.

gla·ci·ate (glā'shi-āt), *v.t.* -at·ed, -at·ing, to cover over with or transform into ice.

gla·cier (glā'shẽr), *n.* a vast accumulation of ice and snow, found in valleys and on mountain slopes, which moves slowly until it melts or breaks away.

gla·cis (glā'sis), *n., pl.* -cis ('siz), -cis·es ('sis-ĕz), a sloping bank of earth directly in front of a fortification for defense.

glad (glad), *adj.* glad'der, glad'dest, 1. pleased; cheerful. 2. producing happiness. 3. favorably disposed. 4. radiant. —**glad'ly,** *adv.* — **glad'ness,** *n.*

glad·den (glad'n), *v.t. & v.i.* to make or come to be glad.

glade (glād), *n.* 1. an open space in a wood or forest. 2. same as everglade.

glad hand, [Slang], a hearty or overly emotional greeting. —**glad′hand′,** *v.t.* & *v.i.*

glad·i·ate (glad′i-āt), *adj.* in *Botany,* sword-shaped.

glad·i·a·tor (glad′i-āt-ēr), *n.* 1. in ancient Rome, a professional swordsman who fought in an arena with men or animals. 2. a combatant. —**glad·i·a·to′ri·al** (-ȧ-tòr′i-ȧl), *adj.*

glad·i·o·lus (glad-i-ō′lŭs), *n., pl.* **-lus·es, -li** (′lī), a plant related to the iris with sword-shaped leaves and flowers like cones: also **glad·i·o′la** (′lȧ).

glad·some (glad′sŏm), *adj.* joyous; pleased; cheerful. —**glad′some·ly,** *adv.*

Glad·stone (glad′stŏn), *n.* a traveling bag that opens into two equal sections: also **Gladstone bag.**

glair (gler), *n.* 1. the white of egg, used as a size or varnish. 2. any sticky white matter resembling this substance.

glam·or·ize (glam′ō-riz), *v.t.* **-ized, -iz·ing,** to produce glamor in. —**glam·or·i·za′tion,** *n.*

glam·our, glam·or (glam′ēr), *n.* an unexplainable fascination; charm. —**glam′or·ous, glam′-our·ous,** *adj.*

glance (glans), *n.* 1. a sudden burst of light. 2. a quick passing look of the eye. 3. a blow turned aside: *v.i.* **glanced, glanc′ing,** 1. to shoot a sudden ray of light. 2. to view with a quick movement of the eye. 3. to hit obliquely. 4. to allude in passing (with *at, over,* etc.): *v.t.* to cause to hit obliquely.

gland (gland), *n.* 1. a bodily organ by which secretion of substances from the blood is carried on. 2. a secreting organ in a plant. —**glan·du·lar** (glan′jŭ-lēr), *adj.*

glan·ders (glan′dērz), *n.* a contagious disease of horses in which the mucous membranes of the nostrils are inflamed.

glan·dule (glan′jool), *n.* a small gland.

glans (glanz), *n., pl.* **glan·des** (glan′dēz), the end part of the penis or clitoris.

glare (gler), *n.* 1. a bright, dazzling light. 2. a smooth, slippery surface. 3. a fierce, piercing look. 4. vulgar splendor: *v.i.* **glared, glar′ing,** 1. to shine with a dazzling light. 2. to look with fierce, piercing eyes. 3. to be excessively gaudy in ornamentation: *adj.* having a smooth, slippery surface, as ice.

glar·ing (gler′ing), *adj.* 1. emitting or reflecting a dazzling light. 2. gaudy. 3. looking with fierce eyes. 4. very evident. —**glar′ing·ly,** *adv.*

glas·nost (glas′nŏst), *n.* [Russian], Soviet official policy of candor in publicizing problems and weaknesses of Soviet society.

glass (glas), *n.* 1. a hard, brittle, transparent substance formed of silica, soda, lime, and certain metallic oxides. 2. an instrument or vessel made of glass, as a mirror, lens, telescope, or barometer. 3. a drinking glass, or the quantity contained in it. 4. *pl.* eyeglasses: *adj.* of, pertaining to, or made of glass: *v.t.* 1. to mirror or reflect. 2. to glaze (windows, etc.). —**glass′ful,** *n., pl.* **-fuls.**

glass·ware (glas′wer), *n.* things made of glass.

glass·y (′i), *adj.* **glass′i·er, glass′i·est,** 1. resembling glass. 2. lifeless. —**glass′i·ly,** *adv.*

glau·co·ma (glô-kō′mȧ), *n.* a diseased condition of the eye characterized by a hardening of the eyeball, sometimes resulting in blindness.

glau·cous (glô′kŭs), *adj.* 1. yellowish-green or bluish-green. 2. in *Botany,* covered with a bluish-white bloom.

glaze (glāz), *v.t.* **glazed, glaz′ing,** 1. to furnish with glass. 2. to overlay with a transparent substance resembling glass. 3. to coat (food) with a sugary substance: *v.i.* to become glassy or glazed: *n.* a glassy coating.

gla·zier (glā′zhēr), *n.* one who sets glass in windows, etc.

glaz·ing (glā′zing), *n.* 1. a glaze. 2. the operation of setting glass or applying a glaze. 3. windowpanes; glass.

gleam (glēm), *n.* 1. a stream of light. 2. a small amount of light. 3. a small trace, as of comprehension: *v.i.* 1. to emit brightness. 2. to be shown for a short time.

glean (glēn), *v.t.* & *v.i.* 1. to gather (grain, etc.). 2. to collect (information) little by little. —**glean′ings,** *n.pl.*

glebe (glēb), *n.* land belonging to an ecclesiastical benefice.

glee (glē), *n.* 1. gaiety; mirth; exhilaration. 2. a musical composition for three or more voices in harmony. —**glee′ful,** *adj.*

glee club, a group formed to sing songs in harmony.

glen (glen), *n.* a narrow valley; secluded hollow between hills.

Glen·gar·ry (glen-gar′i), *n., pl.* **-ries,** a cap, first worn by the natives of Glengarry in Scotland, with a hollow in the middle and ribbons hanging from the back.

glen plaid, a plaid pattern, in black and white with one or more muted colors, of thin stripes forming a crossing pattern of irregular checks: also **Glen plaid.**

glib (glib), *adj.* **glib′ber, glib′best,** done or expressed easily, often too easily to be persuasive. —**glib′ly,** *adv.* —**glib′ness,** *n.*

glide (glīd), *v.i.* **glid′ed, glid′ing,** 1. to flow or move along smoothly. 2. to fly an airplane with the power shut off: *n.* 1. the act of gliding; gliding movement. 2. a small spherical part underneath furniture legs for easy gliding.

glid·er (glīd′ēr), *n.* 1. that which glides. 2. an aircraft with no motor power. 3. a porch seat that swings in a frame.

glim·mer (glim′ēr), *v.i.* 1. to shine faintly and intermittently. 2. to be visible to only a small degree: *n.* 1. a faint, intermittent light. 2. something that is only slightly visible. —**glim′mer·ing,** *n.*

glimpse (glimps), *n.* 1. a flash of light. 2. a fleeting view. 3. a slight trace: *v.t.* **glimpsed, glimps′ing,** to catch a glimpse of: *v.i.* to glance (with *at*).

glint (glint), *n.* a gleam of light: *v.i.* to gleam or flash out.

gli·o·ma (gli-ō′mȧ), *n.* a tumor on the brain, spinal cord, etc.

glis·sade (gli-säd′), *n.* 1. a sliding down a snow slope. 2. a glide in ballet: *v.i.* **-sad′ed, -sad′ing,** to slide or glide.

glis·san·do (gli-sän′dō), *n., pl.* **-di** (′dē), **-dos,** in *Music,* a playing of neighboring tones in a quick sequence, as by sliding the fingers over the keys of a piano: *adj. & adv.* (executed) with this sound.

glis·ten (glis′n), *v.i.* to sparkle with light: *n.* a glitter.

glitch (glich), *n.* [Slang], a mishap, error, etc.

glit·ter (glit′ēr), *v.i.* 1. to sparkle with light; gleam. 2. to be showy, attractive, etc.: *n.* 1. a sparkling light. 2. a showy luster or brilliance. 3. pieces of a sparkling substance. — **glit′ter·y**, *adv.*

glitz (glits), *n.* [Informal], gaudy or glittery showiness or attractiveness. —**glitz′y**, *adj.* glitz′i·er, glitz′i·est.

globe (glōb), *n.* 1. a spherical body; ball. 2. the earth. 3. a sphere with representations of divisions of the earth or the heavenly bodies.

gloam·ing (glō′ming), *n.* twilight.

gloat (glōt), *v.i.* to stare or exult with feelings of lust or cruelty.

glob (glob), *n.* a spherical body, as of a dense liquid.

glob·al (glō′bl), *adj.* of or pertaining to the entire world. —**glob′al·ly**, *adv.*

glob·al·ism (-izm), *n.* a philosophy, plan, etc. that takes the whole world into account.

globe-flow·er (′flou′ēr), *n.* a plant related to the buttercup with globe-shaped yellow, white, or orange flowers.

globe-trot·ter (′trot·ēr), *n.* a person who travels extensively.

glo·bin (glō′bin), *n.* the protein constituent of hemoglobin.

glob·u·lar (glob′yū-lēr), *adj.* 1. globelike; spherical. 2. consisting of globules.

glob·ule (′ūl), *n.* a small spherical particle, especially of liquid.

glob·u·lin (′yū-lin), *n.* a protein substance forming one of the constituents of animal and plant tissue.

glock·en·spiel (glok′ĕn-spēl), *n.* a musical instrument made up of a set of flat metal bars which, when struck, give forth bell-like tones.

glom·er·ate (glom′ēr-it), *adj.* gathered into a rounded mass.

gloom (glōōm), *n.* 1. partial darkness; obscurity. 2. depression; sadness: *v.i.* 1. to become partially dark. 2. to present a gloomy aspect: *v.t.* to make gloomy; sadden.

gloom·y (′i), *adj.* gloom′i·er, gloom′i·est. 1. overspread with or enveloped in darkness. 2. dismal. 3. melancholy; cheerless; dispirited; morose. —**gloom′i·ness**, *n.*

glop (glop), *n.* [Slang], any thick, sticky material.

glo·ri·fy (glôr′i-fī), *v.t.* -fied, -fy·ing, 1. to praise highly. 2. to honor (God) as in worship. 3. to raise in honor or dignity. 4. to give the appearance of greater beauty, size, etc. — **glo·ri·fi·ca′tion**, *n.* —**glo′ri·fi·er**, *n.*

glo·ri·ole (glôr′i-ōl), *n.* a circle of light.

glo·ri·ous (glôr′i-ùs), *adj.* 1. full of glory; illustrious. 2. celebrated. 3. magnificent. —**glo′ri·ous·ly**, *adv.*

glo·ry (glôr′i), *n.*, *pl.* -ries, 1. splendor; magnificence. 2. praise ascribed in adoration. 3. distinction; renown or its cause. 4. the felicity of heaven. 5. a pictured emanation

of light around the head of a saint: *v.i.* -ried, -ry·ing, to rejoice; exult (with *in*).

gloss (glôs), *n.* 1. luster from a polished surface. 2. a specious show. 3. an explanation or comment to elucidate some difficulty in the text: *v.t.* 1. to explain by notes or comments. 2. to palliate by plausible representation. 3. to give a lustrous surface to: *v.i.* to annotate. —**gloss′y**, *adj.* -i·er, -i·est.

glos·sa (glos′ä), *n.*, *pl.* -sae (′ē), -sas, the tongue, especially of insects.

glos·sa·ry (glos′ä-ri), *n.*, *pl.* -ries, a short dictionary of obsolete, technical, or obscure words, as an explanatory vocabulary for a particular text.

glos·si·tis (glo-sīt′is), *n.* inflammation of the tongue.

glos·so-, a combining form meaning *tongue.*

glos·so·la·li·a (glos-ō-lä′lē-ä, glōs-), *n.* an uttering of incomprehensible speech, as in a religious ecstasy.

glot·tal (glot′l), *adj.* of, pertaining to, or produced by the glottis: also **glot′tic** (′ik).

glot·tis (glot′is), *n.* the opening separating the vocal cords in the larynx.

glove (gluv), *n.* 1. a hand covering with a separate sheath for each finger. 2. a boxing glove. 3. a mitt for baseball players: *v.t.* **gloved, glov′ing,** to cover with or as with a glove.

glov·er (gluv′ēr), *n.* a person who manufactures or sells gloves.

glow (glō), *v.i.* 1. to shine with intense heat; be incandescent. 2. to radiate heat or light. 3. to be red or flushed. 4. to be animated with passion. 5. to be bright and colorful: *n.* 1. intense or shining light; incandescence. 2. brightness of color. 3. passion; ardor; emotion.

glow·er (glou′ēr), *v.i.* to stare with a threatening or angry countenance; frown: *n.* a threatening, angry stare.

glow-worm (glō′wûrm), *n.* a wingless insect which emits a shining light; especially, the female firefly.

glox·in·i·a (glok-sin′i-ä), *n.* a tropical plant with bell-shaped flowers.

gloze (glōz), *v.t.* **glozed, gloz′ing,** to gloss (over).

glu·cose (glōō′kōs), *n.* a crystalline sugar existing naturally in fruits and honey: it is produced for commercial use by the action of dilute acid on starch.

glue (glōō), *n.* 1. a tenacious, viscous cement made by boiling some animal substance to a jelly. 2. a similar adhesive of a different origin: *v.t.* **glued, glu′ing,** to unite or cement with or as with glue. —**glue′y**, *adj.* glu′i·er, glu′i·est.

glum (glum), *adj.* **glum′mer, glum′mest,** gloomy; moody; sullen. —**glum′ly**, *adv.* — **glum′ness**, *n.*

glut (glut), *n.* 1. a superabundance; surfeit. 2. the act of glutting: *v.t.* glut′ted, glut′ting, 1. to fill to repletion. 2. to oversupply *v.i.* to eat gluttonously.

glu·ten (glōōt′n), *n.* a tough, gray protein substance obtained from wheat and other grains. —**glu′ten·ous**, *adj.*

glu·ti·nous (glōōt′n-ùs), *adj.* viscid; gluey.

ô in dragon, ōō in crude, oo in wool, u in cup, ū in cure, û in turn, ù in focus, oi in boy, ou in house, th in thin, th in sheathe, g in get, j in joy, y in yet.

glut·ton (glut'n), *n.* 1. one who eats to excess. 2. a person who has much capability for some activity. 3. an animal of northern lands with long shaggy fur, related to the weasel. —**glut'ton·ous,** *adj.*

glut·ton·y (-ĭ), *n., pl.* -ton·ies, the act or habit of eating to excess.

glyc·er·ide (glis'ĕr-īd), *n.* a compound of glycerol.

glyc·er·in, glyc·er·ine (glis'ĕr-in), *n.* a commercial term for glycerol.

glyc·er·ol (glis'ĕr-ôl), *n.* a colorless, viscid liquid obtained from oils, fat, etc.: used extensively in various manufactures and in medicine.

gly·co·gen (glī'kō-jĕn), *n.* an incompletely soluble, starchlike substance in the tissue of animals, that the body can convert into a sugar when necessary.

gly·col (glī'kôl), *n.* same as ethylene glycol.

glyph (glĭf), *n.* 1. a vertical fluting. 2. a carved figure in relief. —**glyph'ic,** *adj.*

glyph·og·ra·phy (glī-fŏg'rä-fĭ), *n.* a method of producing electrotypes for printing plates by etching the picture on a copperplate covered thinly with wax.

glyp·tic (glĭp'tĭk), *adj.* of or pertaining to engraving on gems.

glyp·tics ('tĭks), *n.* the art of engraving designs on precious stones, etc.

glyp·to·dont (glĭp'tō-dŏnt), *n.* a very large, extinct mammal of South America, of which the armadillo is a modern type.

glyp·to·graph (glĭp'tō-graf), *n.* a design cut or engraved on a gem. —**glyp·tog·ra·phy** (glĭp-tŏg'rä-fĭ), *n.*

gnarl (närl), *n.* a knot on the trunk or branch of a tree: *v.t.* to twist; distort: *v.i.* 1. to develop gnarls. 2. to snarl. —**gnarled,** *adj.*

gnash (nash), *v.t.* to strike together (the teeth): *v.i.* to grind the teeth in anger or agony: *n.* the act of gnashing.

gnat (nat), *n.* a small, stinging or biting, winged insect.

gnaw (nô), *v.t. & v.i.* 1. to bite off or eat away by degrees. 2. to corrode. 3. to cause pain or anguish (in).

gneiss (nīs), *n.* a rock similar to granite, composed of quartz, mica, feldspar, etc. in bands.

gnome (nōm), *n.* a small, deformed being supposed to dwell in the earth and protect its riches. —**gnom'ish,** *adj.*

gnome (nōm), *n.* a pithy saying. —**gno'mic,** *adj.*

gno·mon (nō'mon), *n.* 1. the pin of a sundial. 2. the part of a parallelogram left after a similar parallelogram has been taken from one of its corners.

gno·sis (nō'sĭs), *n.* higher knowledge or insights.

gnos·tic (nos'tĭk), *adj.* 1. of, pertaining to, or possessing knowledge. 2. [G-], of or pertaining to the Gnostics or Gnosticism: *n.* [G-], an advocate or supporter of Gnosticism.

Gnos·ti·cism (nos'tĭ-sĭzm), *n.* a system of religion based on a mixture of Greek and Oriental philosophy and Christianity, which taught that through knowledge alone could salvation be attained.

gnu (nōō), *n.* a large, ruminant, horned animal of the antelope type, with a head resembling an ox, inhabiting Africa.

go (gō), *v.i.* went, gone, go'ing, 1. to depart. 2. to proceed. 3. to move on. 4. to pass from one state or place to another. 5. to conduce; contribute. 6. to be habitually used or said. 7. to fall out or terminate. 8. to move by a mechanism; function. 9. to act in harmony; fit or suit. 10. to be expended. 11. to do as stated. 12. to happen as a consequence. 13. to pass. 14. to develop. 15. to be stated. 16. to be sound, or valid. 17. to stretch. 18. to be divisible. 19. to have a place in. 20. [Informal], to succeed (with *over*): *v.t.* 1. to proceed. 2. [Informal], to bear; tolerate: *n., pl.* goes, 1. a favorable outcome. 2. [Informal], enterprise or push. 3. [Informal], a state of affairs. 4. [Informal], an endeavor.

go-a (gō'ä), *n.* the Tibetan antelope.

goad (gōd), *n.* 1. a pointed stick used to drive on oxen. 2. a stimulus: *v.t.* to urge on with or as with a goad; stimulate.

go-a·head (gō'ä-hed), *n.* consent or a sign to begin (usually preceded by *the*).

goal (gōl), *n.* 1. the winning post, line, etc. in a race, game, etc. 2. the end aimed at. 3. a score achieved in a game.

goal-keep·er (gōl'kēp-ẽr), *n.* a player who guards against a ball or puck passing the goal: also goal'le ('ĭ), goal'tend·er.

goat (gōt), *n.* 1. a ruminating, horned quadruped. 2. a lustful man. 3. [Informal], same as scapegoat.

goat·ee (gō-tē'), *n.* a small, pointed tuft of hair on a man's chin.

goat·herd (gōt'hûrd), *n.* a person who herds goats.

goats-beard (gōts'bird), *n.* a plant with clusters of small, white flowers.

goat-skin (gōt'skin), *n.* a goat's hide or leather produced from it.

goat-suck·er (gōt'suk-ẽr), *n.* an insectivorous bird of nocturnal habits, as the whippoorwill.

gob (gob), *n.* 1. a lump, piece, or chunk. 2. *pl.* [Informal], a large amount. 3. refuse from coal mining. 4. [Slang], a sailor of the U.S. Navy.

gob·ble (gob'l), *v.t. & v.i.* -bled, -bling, 1. to swallow hastily or greedily. 2. to grab. 3. to utter a cry like a turkey: *n.* the noise of a turkey.

gob·ble·dy·gook (gob'l-di-gook'), *n.* [Slang], high-sounding nonsense in talk or writing.

gob·bler (gob'lẽr), *n.* a male turkey.

go-be·tween (gō'bi-twēn), *n.* one who deals with both sides in making preparations; intermediary.

gob·let (gob'lĭt), *n.* a drinking glass with a stem and base.

gob·lin (gob'lĭn), *n.* an evil, mischievous spirit; gnome; fairy.

go-by (gō'bĭ), *n., pl.* -bies, -by, a small fish with spiny fins.

go-by (gō'bĭ), *n.* [Informal], an avoidance; evasion; passing.

---

go-cart ('kärt), *n.* 1. a device for teaching children to walk. 2. a baby carriage.

God (god), *n.* 1. the Supreme Being and self-existent creator of the universe. 2. [g-], a supernatural being conceived of as possessing divine powers or attributes. 3. [g-], a person or thing deified or honored to excess.

god-child (god'chīld), *n., pl.* **-chil-dren** ('children), one for whom one is a sponsor at baptism.

god-daugh-ter ('dôt-ēr), *n.* a female godchild.

god-dess (god'is), *n.* 1. a female deity. 2. a woman of superior charm or excellence.

god-fa-ther (god'fä-thēr), *n.* a male godparent.

God-head ('hed), *n.* 1. the Supreme Being (usually preceded by *the*). 2. [g-], the divine essence, nature, attributes, etc.

god-hood ('hood), *n.* divinity.

god-less ('lis), *adj.* 1. atheistic. 2. bad or evil. —god'less-ness, *n.*

god-ly ('li), *adj.* **-li-er, -li-est**, devout; pious. —god'li-ness, *n.*

god-moth-er ('muth-ēr), *n.* a female godparent.

god-par-ent ('per-ĕnt), *n.* one who sponsors a child at baptism.

God's acre, a church graveyard.

god-send (god'send), *n.* unexpected assistance or acquisition, as if from God.

god-son ('sun), *n.* a male godchild.

God-speed (god'spēd'), *n.* success.

god-wit (god'wit), *n.* a wading bird related to the snipe.

go-er (gō'ēr), *n.* one who goes.

gof-fer (gof'ēr), *v.t.* to form flutes in; crimp: *n.* fluting, pleats, etc.: also **gof'fer-ing**.

go-get-ter (gō'get'ēr), *n.* [Informal], an ambitious and forceful person who usually accomplishes his aims.

gog-gle (gog'l), *v.i.* **-gled, -gling**, to protrude or roll the eyes: *adj.* staring; prominent: used of the eyes. *n.* 1. a protruding of the eyes. 2. *pl.* large spectacles for protecting the eyes from dust, excessive light, etc.

gog-gle-eyed (-īd), *adj.* having bulging or rolling eyes.

go-go (gō'gō), *adj.* of or pertaining to rock-and-roll dancing for pay, as carried on in some nightclubs.

go-ing (gō'ing), *n.* 1. the act of departing or moving. 2. the state of roads, etc.: *adj.* 1. operating; running. 2. prevalent.

go-ing-o-ver (-ō'vēr), *n.* [Informal], 1. a complete examination. 2. a harsh rebuke or thrashing.

go-ings-on (gō'ingz-on'), *n.pl.* [Informal], condemned activities.

goi-ter, goi-tre (goit'ēr), *n.* a swelling of the thyroid gland in the front part of the neck. —goi-trous (goi'trus), *adj.*

gold (gōld), *n.* 1. a heavy, yellow, highly ductile metallic element. 2. money; wealth. 3. bright yellow: *adj.* 1. made of gold. 2. having the color of gold.

gold-beat-er (gōld'bēt-ēr), *n.* one who beats gold into thin leaves for gilding.

gold-brick ('brik), *n.* 1. [Informal], a bar of spurious metal gilded and used by swindlers to deceive. 2. [Informal], a worthless substitute delivered for the genuine article. 3. [Military Slang], a loafer: also **gold'brick-er:** *v.i.* [Military Slang], to loaf.

gold-en (gōl'dn), *adj.* 1. formed of, consisting of, or resembling gold. 2. shining; lustrous like gold; bright-yellow. 3. most valuable; excellent. 4. conducive to success.

Golden Age, 1. in *Greek & Roman Mythology*, the fabled primeval age of perfect human happiness and innocence. 2. [g- a-], any period of progress, prosperity, and enlightenment.

golden ag-er (āj'ēr), [Informal], [also G- A-], one who is usually retired and 65 or older.

golden eagle, a large and powerful eagle of the Northern Hemisphere with brown feathers on its head and neck.

gold-en-eye (gōl'dn-ī), *n., pl.* **-eyes, -eye**, a wild duck with a dark-green back and white breast: noted as a diver and for its swift flight.

Golden Fleece, in *Greek Mythology*, the fleece of gold taken by Jason.

golden pheasant, a brightly colored Chinese and Tibetan pheasant.

gold-en-rod (gōl'dn-rod), *n.* any one of a genus of chiefly North American plants with long stalks and small, yellow flower heads.

golden rule, the rule of treating others in the same way one wants to be treated.

gold-filled (gōld'fild'), *adj.* made of a base metal overlaid with gold.

gold-finch ('finch), *n.* 1. a European songbird with yellow-streaked wings. 2. any one of several small American finches.

gold-fish ('fish), *n., pl.* **-fish, -fish-es**, a small, golden-yellow or orange fish of the carp family, often kept in fishbowls.

gold leaf, gold beaten into very thin sheets, used for gilding.

gold-smith ('smith), *n.* a maker of or dealer in articles of gold.

gold standard, a monetary standard based on gold alone as the unit of value.

go-lem (gō'lĕm), *n.* in *Jewish Legend*, an artificial manlike creature made by cabalistic rites; also, a robot or automaton.

golf (gôlf), *n.* an outdoor game in which a small, hard ball is hit with the fewest possible strokes into a series of holes, the ball being hit with various sticklike clubs: *v.i.* to play golf. —golf'er, *n.*

golf course, a tract of land with greens, fairways, etc, for golf: also **golf links**.

Gol-go-tha (gol'gä-thä), *n.* 1. the place where Jesus was crucified. 2. [g-], a burial place; also, a place of agony.

Go-li-ath (gō-lī'äth), *n.* in the *Bible*, a giant killed by David: see *I Sam. xvii.*

gol-ly (gol'i), *interj.* an exclamation as of surprise.

-gon (gon, gôn), a combining form meaning *figure with* (a specified number of) *angles*.

go-nad (gō'nad), *n.* an animal organ producing reproductive cells, as a testis.

gon-do-la (gon'dō-lä, gon-dō'lä), *n.* 1. a long, narrow Venetian pleasure boat propelled by a pole or one oar. 2. a kind of river barge. 3. a railroad car with low sides and no top, for freight. 4. the cabin of a dirigible or

---

ô in dragon, ōō in crude, oo in wool, u in cup, ū in cure, u in turn, ŭ in focus, oi in boy, ou in house, th in thin, th in sheathe, g in get, j in joy, y in yet.

balloon, for the motors, passengers, etc. 5. a car hung from a cable, for passengers.

gon·do·lier (gon-dō-lir'), *n.* one that poles or rows a gondola.

gone (gôn, gon), past partici'*e* of **go**: *adj.* 1. departed. 2. ruined. 3. lost. 4. deceased. 5. faint; weak. 6. used up. 7. ago; past. 8. [Slang], *a*) excellent. *b*) enthralled. *c*) pregnant.

gon·er ('ēr), *n.* [Informal], one sure to die soon, be hopelessly lost, ruined, etc.

gon·fa·lon (gon'fâ-lôn, -lon), *n.* a flag hung from a crosspiece.

gong (gông, gong), *n.* a metallic disk ringing resonantly when struck.

go·ni·om·e·ter (gō-ni-om'ê-têr), *n.* a device to measure or track angles.

gon·o·coc·cus (gon-ô-kok'ŭs), *n., pl.* -coc'ci (-kok'sī), the microorganism causing gonorrhea.

gon·or·rhe·a, gon·or·rhoe·a (gon-ô-rē'â), *n.* a venereal disease marked by a discharge of highly infectious mucus and pus.

goo (gōō), *n.* [Slang], something sticky and viscid, as glue or syrup.

goo·ber (gōō'bêr), *n.* [Chiefly Southern], a peanut.

good (good), *adj.* **bet'ter, best,** 1. altogether satisfactory; fine; pleasing. 2. proper, fit for, adapted to, or conducive to any particular object; effective, favorable, useful, etc. 3. fresh; unspoiled. 4. valid; genuine. 5. reliable. 6. respectable; unblemished. 7. thorough; complete. 8. not ordinary; superior. 9. morally acceptable or praiseworthy. 10. devout; pious. 11. dutiful. 12. kind, benevolent, sympathetic, etc. 13. skilled; accomplished. 14. loyal; wholehearted. 15. well-disposed. 16. well-informed. 17. being altogether what is specified; full: *n.* 1. that which is good, specifically from the standpoint of morals or merit; benefit, desirability, etc.: see also **goods.** 2. all time: only in *for good: interj.* an exclamation of assent, satisfaction, pleasure, etc.: *adv.* [Dialectal or Informal], well, completely, etc.

good-bye (good-bī'), *n., pl.* -byes', farewell; good wishes at parting: *interj.* farewell. Also **good-bye', good-by', good-by'.**

Good Friday, the Friday before Easter Sunday, commemorating the Crucifixion.

good-heart·ed (good'härt'id), *adj.* kind and generous; considerate.

good humor, a cheerful, pleasant mood. —**good'-hu'mored,** *adj.*

good-look·ing (look'ing), *adj.* attractive in appearance.

good·ly ('li), *adj.* -li·er, -li·est, 1. good-looking. 2. good in quality. 3. fairly large. —**good'li·ness,** *n.*

good·man ('mân), *n., pl.* -men, [Archaic], 1. a husband or master of a household. 2. a title like *Mr.*, used for a man of lower social status.

good-na·tured ('nā'chêrd), *adj.* affable.

good·ness ('nis), *n.* 1. the state or quality of being good; 2. the central or essential good part of something: *interj.* an exclamation of surprise or wonderment.

goods (goodz), *n.pl.* 1. movable personal property. 2. merchandise; wares. 3. fabric; cloth. 4. [British], freight.

good Samaritan, a compassionate bestower of unselfish assistance: see *Luke x,* 30-37.

good-sized (good'sīzd'), *adj.* quite large.

good-tem·pered ('tem'pêrd), *adj.* amiable.

good turn, a kindly, helpful deed; favor.

good·wife ('wīf), *n., pl.* -wives ('wīvz), [Archaic], 1. a wife or mistress of a household. 2. a title like *Mrs.*, used for a woman of lower social status.

good will, 1. friendly disposition; kindly feeling; benevolence. 2. willingness; readiness. 3. the value of a business, as in public attitudes toward it, beyond its tangible assets. Also **good·will** ('wil').

good·y ('i), *n., pl.* good'ies, 1. [Informal], something delicious, as a sweet. 2. [Informal], same as **goody-goody.** 3. [Archaic], same as **goodwife:** *adj.* [Informal], same as **goody-goody:** *interj.* a child's exclamation of joy.

good·y-good·y (good'i-good'i), *adj.* [Informal], affectedly moral or pious: *n.* [Informal], such a person.

goo·ey (gōō'i), *adj.* goo'i·er, goo'i·est, [Slang], of, full of, or covered with something sticky and viscid.

goof (gōōf), *n.* [Slang], 1. a stupid or foolish individual. 2. a stupid or foolish mistake or blunder: *v.i.* [Slang], 1. to make a stupid or foolish mistake or blunder. 2. to fail badly at something; bungle. 3. to waste time, shirk duty, etc. (usually with *around, off,* etc.).

goof·ball ('bôl), *n.* [Slang], a pill, capsule, etc. containing a barbiturate or, sometimes, a stimulant drug or a tranquilizer.

goof·y ('i), *adj.* goof'i·er, goof'i·est, [Slang], of or like a goof; stupid or foolish. —**goof'i·ly,** *adv.*

gook (gook, gōōk), *n.* [Slang], something clinging and heavily viscid or slimy.

goon (gōōn), *n.* [Slang], 1. a ruffian or thug. 2. a stupid or grotesque individual.

goo·ney bird (gōō'ni), a black or dusky albatross of the Pacific Ocean.

goop (gōōp), *n.* [Slang], goo or gook.

goose (gōōs), *n.* 1. *pl.* **geese** (gēs), a long-necked, web-footed wild or domestic bird, similar to a duck but larger; often, specifically, a female bird of this kind: cf. **gander.** 2. its flesh as food. 3. *pl.* **geese,** a silly person. 4. *pl.* **goos'es,** a tailor's smoothing iron. 5. *pl.* **goos'es,** [Slang], a sudden, playful prod in the backside: *v.t.* **goosed, goos'ing,** [Slang], to prod by or as by a goose (sense 5).

goose·ber·ry (gōōs'ber-i, -bē-ri, gōōz'ber-i), *n., pl.* -ries, 1. a small, sour, currantlike berry used as in preserves. 2. any one of a group of prickly shrubs producing it.

goose flesh, a temporary condition of the skin in which it feels rough like that of a plucked goose, caused as by fear or cold: also **goose bumps, goose pimples.**

goose-neck (gōōs'nek), *n.* something suggestive of the neck of a goose, as a flexible rod in a desk lamp.

goose step, a marching step in which the legs are kept straight and stiff. —**goose'-step** ('step), *v.i.* -stepped, -step·ping.

---

a in cap, ā in cane, ä in father, â in abet, e in met   ē in be, ē in baker, ê in regent, i in pit, ī in fine, i in manifest, o in hot, ô in horse, ō in bone,

go·pher (gō′fẽr), n. 1. a ratlike burrowing rodent with wide cheek pouches. 2. a striped squirrel of North American prairies.

Gor·di·an knot (gôr′di-ăn), in Greek Legend, an intricate knot tied by Gordius, a king in Asia Minor, and capable of being undone, according to an oracle, only by whoever would conquer Asia: Alexander the Great tried, failed, and then cut it apart.

gore (gôr), n. 1. blood from a wound, especially after clotting. 2. a triangular piece sewn into a dress, sail, etc.: v.t. gored, gor′ing, 1. to pierce with or as with a horn. 2. to provide, as a dress, with a gore.

gorge (gôrj), n. 1. the throat; gullet. 2. the contents of the stomach. 3. a deep, narrow passage as between mountains. 4. a blockage, as of ice: v.i. & v.t. gorged, gorg′ing, to feed full; glut.

gor·geous (gôr′jŭs), adj. 1. brilliant in color and display; rich and showy; full of splendor; magnificent. 2. [Informal], utterly beautiful, fine, good, etc.

gor·get (gôr′jit), n. 1. in armor, a protective throat covering. 2. a collar.

Gor·gon (gôr′gŏn), n. in Greek Mythology, any one of three terrifying sisters with snakes for hair and with eyes that turned anyone looking directly at them into stone.

Gor·gon·zo·la (gôr-gŏn-zō′lä), n. a white Italian cheese with a strong flavor.

go·ril·la (gó-ril′ä), n. 1. an African anthropoid ape: it is the largest and most powerful of apes. 2. [Slang], a thug.

gor·mand·ize (gôr′mǎn-diz), v.i. & v.t. -ized, -iz·ing, to eat greedily; devour.

gorse (gôrs), n. same as furze.

gor·y (gôr′i), adj. gor′i·er, gor′i·est, of, like, or full of gore. —gor′i·ness, n.

gosh (gosh), interj. an exclamation of surprise, wonderment, etc.

gos·hawk (gos′hôk), n. a large, swift hawk.

Go·shen (gō′shĕn), n. in the Bible, the fertile land assigned to the Israelites in Egypt: see Genesis xlv, 10.

gos·ling (goz′ling), n. 1. a young goose. 2. a young, foolish individual.

gos·pel (gos′pĕl), n. 1. [often G-], the teachings of Jesus and the Apostles; also, the narrative of the life of Jesus. 2. [G-], any one of the first four books of the New Testament, or a selection from one. 3. something viewed as absolute truth: also gospel truth. 4. any doctrine or principle ardently or widely maintained. 5. a kind of folk singing associated with evangelistic revival meetings.

gos·pel·er, gos·pel·ler (-ẽr), n. 1. a gospel preacher; evangelist. 2. in some church services, the Gospel reader.

gos·sa·mer (gos′ä-mẽr), n. 1. a very fine cobweb floating in the air or spread as on bushes. 2. a very thin, soft, filmy cloth: adj. of or like gossamer.

gos·sip (gos′ip), n. 1. idle talk, especially when revolving about often unsubstantiated rumors, hidden or supposed scandals, etc. 2. such rumors, scandals, etc. 3. a person given to idle talk or talebearing: v.i. to indulge in gossip. —gos′sip·y, adj.

gos·soon (gó-sōōn′), n. [Irish], a boy; lad.

got (got), past tense and alternate past participle of get.

Goth (goth, gôth), n. 1. any member of a Germanic people that overran the Roman Empire in the 3d-5th centuries A.D. 2. an uncouth individual; barbarian.

Goth·ic ('ik), adj. 1. of the Goths. 2. of or designating a medieval style of architecture using high and pointed arches, clustered columns, etc. 3. [sometimes g-], barbaric. 4. of or like a kind of literature using a medieval or macabre setting, atmosphere, etc. to suggest horror and mystery: n. 1. the language of the Goths. 2. Gothic style.

got·ten (got′n), alternate past participle of get.

Gou·da (gou′dä, gōō′dä), n. a mild cheese, usually coated with red wax.

gouge (gouj), n. 1. a rounded, hollow chisel for cutting grooves or holes in wood. 2. the groove or hole made with this. 3. the act of gouging; also, what is gouged out: v.t. gouged, goug′ing, 1. to make (a groove or hole) in with or as with a gouge. 2. to scoop or dig out as if with a gouge. 3. to force out the eye of with the thumb or other finger. 4. [Informal], to cheat, swindle, overcharge, etc.: v.i. to gouge someone or something. —goug′er, n.

gou·lash (gōō′läsh, 'lash), n. a Hungarian meat stew seasoned with paprika.

gou·ra·mi (goor′ä-mi, goo-rä′mi), n., pl. -mis, -mi, a food fish of southeastern Asia; also, a brightly colored related fish often kept in aquariums.

gourd (gôrd, goord), n. 1. any one of a group of trailing or climbing plants, as a melon or pumpkin. 2. a calabash.

gourde (goord), n. the monetary unit and a coin of Haiti.

gour·mand (goor′mǎnd; goor-mänd′), n. a hearty, somewhat overindulging, eater.

gour·met (goor′mā, goor-mā′), n. a connoisseur of fine food and drink.

gout (gout), n. 1. a disease marked by disturbed uric acid metabolism and by painful swelling of tissues and joints, as of the big toe. 2. a splash, spurt, glob, etc. —gout′y, adj. gout′i·er, gout′i·est.

gov·ern (guv′ẽrn), v.t. 1. to control by authority; direct, manage, etc. 2. to influence, steer, shape, etc., as public opinion. 3. to keep under control; restrain; curb. 4. to regulate the speed of (a vehicle, engine, etc.) with a governor. 5. to determine by way of being the principle, rule, or law of. 6. in Grammar, to require (an indicated case or mood) or be used with (a term in an indicated case or mood): v.i. to exercise government.

gov·ern·ance ('ẽr-nǎns), n. the act, function, or power of government.

gov·ern·ess ('ẽr-nĕs), n. a woman hired to train and give school lessons to a child or children in a private home.

gov·ern·ment (guv′ẽr-mĕnt, 'ẽrn-mĕnt), n. 1. the act of governing; specifically, of controlling, directing, etc. by authority. 2. the right, function, or power of this, or a particular system used. 3. the individuals or agencies exercising this; also, [often G-], a particular political administration. 4. a territory governed. —gov·ern·men'tal, *adj.*

gov·er·nor (guv'ě-něr, 'ěr-něr), *n.* 1. one that governs, as one elected or appointed to govern a state, province, etc. 2. a mechanical device regulating the speed of an engine or motor. —gov'er·nor·ship, *n.*

gown (goun), *n.* a long, loose outer garment; specifically, a dress especially when elegant, a flowing robe, a dressing gown, a nightgown, a kind of smock, etc.

grab (grab), *v.t.* grabbed, grab'bing, 1. to seize suddenly and forcibly; snatch. 2. to take unscrupulously; appropriate. 3. [Slang], to have an effect on; affect: *v.i.* to grab or try to grab something: *n.* 1. a grabbing. 2. something grabbed. 3. a mechanical device that grabs.

grab·ble (grab'l), *v.i.* -bled, -bling, 1. to feel about; grope. 2. to sprawl.

grab·by (grab'i), *adj.* -bi·er, -bi·est, greedily grabbing.

grace (grās), *n.* 1. beauty, charm, or elegance. 2. any excellence or attractive quality. 3. propriety, or a feeling for it. 4. considerateness. 5. good will; favor. 6. extra time granted to meet an obligation. 7. a prayer before or after meals. 8. [G-], a respectful title of address or reference, used to or of an archbishop, duke, or duchess. 9. in *Theology, a)* the unmerited love and favor of God toward man. *b)* divine sanctifying, regenerating, and preserving influence. *c)* condition of one so sanctified and preserved. *d)* a special virtue given an individual by God: *v.t.* graced, grac'ing, 1. to adorn; embellish. 2. to honor; dignify. 3. to favor.

grace·ful (fl), *adj.* having beauty, charm, elegance, etc. —grace'ful·ly, *adv.*

grace·less ('lis), *adj.* 1. lacking grace. 2. clumsy. 3. inept. 4. ungracious.

grace note, a merely ornamental musical note.

gra·cious (grā'shǔs), *adj.* 1. kind, courteous, charming, etc. 2. merciful. 3. affable; polite. 4. pleasant and comfortable: *interj.* an exclamation of surprise.

grack·le (grak'l), *n.* an American blackbird.

grad (grad), *n.* [Informal], a graduate.

gra·date (grā'dāt), *v.t. & v.i.* -dat·ed, -dat·ing, to blend or shade very gradually, as colors, from one degree to another.

gra·da·tion (grā-dā'shǔn), *n.* 1. formation or arrangement in grades, stages, or steps. 2. gradual change or advancement, step by step. 3. a gradating. 4. a given step, stage, or degree in a series.

grade (grād), *n.* 1. a step, stage, or degree in a progression. 2. a rating or rank in an ordered scale of classification. 3. a slope or the degree of it. 4. a level of progress at a school, by years; also, a class of pupils at a given level. 5. a mark or rating given as for a 'test taken: *v.t.* grad'ed, grad'ing, 1. to sort or rate by grade. 2. to give a grade (sense 5) to. 3. to level (ground) or slope evenly: *v.i.* to take or be of a given rank.

grade crossing, an intersection, on the same level, of one railroad with another or with a roadway.

grade school, same as elementary school.

gra·di·ent (grā'di-ěnt), *n.* a slope or gradation, or the degree of this.

gra·din (grā'd'n), *n.* 1. a step or seat of a tiered series. 2. a shelf behind an altar, as for candles or flowers.

grad·u·al (graj'oo-wǎl), *adj.* moving, happening, or developing by slight or nearly imperceptible steps or degrees: *n.* 1. a response sung at Mass, after the Epistle. 2. a book containing these and other sung parts of the Mass. —grad'u·al·ly, *adv.*

grad·u·al·ism (-izm), *n.* the principle of gradual social or political change.

grad·u·ate (graj'oo-wit), *n.* 1. one on whom an academic degree has been conferred for a course completed. 2. a marked container, as a flask, for measuring liquids or solids: *v.t.* (-wāt), -at·ed, -at·ing, 1. to confer an academic degree on for a course completed. 2. to mark (a flask, gauge, etc.) with degrees for measuring. 3. to arrange into grades according to amount, size, etc.: *v.i.* 1. to receive an academic degree for a course completed. 2. to change or progress gradually: *adj.* 1. having received an academic degree for a course completed. 2. of or engaged in studies leading to degrees above the bachelor's degree. —grad'u·a·tor, *n.*

grad·u·a·tion (graj-oo-wā'shǔn), *n.* 1. the conferring or reception of an academic degree for a course completed. 2. the marking of, or a marking on, a graduate (sense 2). 3. arrangement into grades by size, amount, etc.

gra·dus (grā'dǔs), *n.* a dictionary of Greek and Latin prosody.

graf·fi·to (grǎ-fēt'ō), *n., pl.* -ti ('ē), a drawing, slogan, remark, etc., usually crude, scrawled or scratched in a public place by passers-by, as on a wall.

graft (graft), *n.* 1. a shoot or bud of a plant or tree, inserted or for insertion into another plant or tree. 2. the insertion. 3. a similar transfer of skin, bone, etc. 4. bribery or the like; also, the unlawful or irregular perquisite involved: *v.t. & v.i.* 1. to insert or undergo (a graft). 2. to obtain by graft.

gra·ham (grā'ǎm), *adj.* designating or made of finely ground whole-wheat flour.

Grail (grāl), *n.* in *Medieval Legend,* the cup used by Jesus at the Last Supper and brought to Britain, where it was often sought.

grain (grān), *n.* 1. a small, hard seed, as of wheat or rice. 2. such seeds, or a plant or plants producing them. 3. a grainlike particle, as of sand. 4. a tiny bit of something. 5. a unit of weight, equal to 0.0648 gram. 6. the way that particles, fibers, etc., as of wood, lie. 7. in leather, the side stripped of hair: *v.t. & v.i.* to granulate.

grain·y (grā'ni), *adj.* grain'i·er, grain'i·est, 1. of or like grains; granular. 2. coarse in texture. 3. having its grain prominent or clearly visible, as wood.

gram (gram), *n.* the basic unit of weight in the metric system, equal to about 1/28 ounce: also gramme (gram).

---

a in cap, ā in cane, ä in father, å in abet, e in met, ē in be, ē in baker, ě in regent, I in pit, ī in fine, i in manifest, o in hot, ô in horse, ō in bone,

-gram (gram), a combining form meaning *thing written, grams, gram fraction.*

gra·ma (grä'mä, gram'ä), *n.* any one of a genus of range grasses of the western U.S.

gra·mer·cy (grä·mûr'si, gram'ẽr-si), *interj.* 1. thanks very much. 2. an exclamation of surprise.

gra·min·e·ous (grä-min'i-ŭs), *adj.* of, pertaining to, or like grass.

gram·i·niv·o·rous (gram-i-niv'ẽr-ŭs), *adj.* feeding on grass.

gram·mar (gram'ẽr), *n.* 1. the science of the principles governing the word forms and word arrangements of a language. 2. the body of rules based on this. 3. a book of or about such rules. 4. use or knowledge of such rules.

gram·mar·i·an (grä-mer'i-ân), *n.* a specialist in grammar.

grammar school, same as **elementary school.**

gram·mat·i·cal (grä-mat'i-kl), *adj.* 1. of grammar. 2. following established rules of grammar. —**gram·mat'i·cal·ly,** *adv.*

gram·o·phone (gram'ö-fōn), *n.* [Chiefly British], same as **phonograph.**

gram·pus (gram'pŭs), *n., pl.* -**pus·es,** a small, black, fierce whale.

gran·a·dil·la (gran-ä-dil'ä), *n.* the edible fruit of certain passionflowers.

gran·a·ry (gran'ẽr-i, grä'nẽr-i), *n., pl.* -**ries,** 1. a building or storehouse for threshed grain. 2. a region of much grain.

grand (grand), *adj.* 1. high in dignity. 2. illustrious. 3. principal; chief. 4. impressive. 5. sublime; noble. 6. magnificent; splendid. 7. pretentious; haughty. 8. comprehensive; complete. 9. [Informal], excellent; superb: *n.* 1. a grand piano. 2. [Slang], a thousand dollars.

grand-, a combining form meaning *of the generation older* (or *younger*) *than.*

gran·dam (gran'dam, 'dâm), *n.* [Archaic], 1. a grandmother. 2. an old woman.

grand·child (gran'chīld), *n., pl.* -**chil·dren,** a child of one's son or daughter.

grand·dad ('dad), *n.* [Informal], grandfather.

grand·daugh·ter ('dôt-ẽr), *n.* a daughter of one's son or daughter.

gran·dee (gran-dē'), *n.* 1. a Spanish or Portuguese nobleman of highest rank. 2. any man of great eminence.

gran·deur (gran'jẽr), *n.* splendor, magnificence, sublimity, nobility, etc.

grand·fa·ther (gran'fä-thẽr), *n.* the father of one's father or mother.

gran·dil·o·quent (gran'dil'ö-kwènt), *adj.* bombastic. —**gran·dil'o·quence,** *n.*

gran·di·ose (gran'di-ōs), *adj.* really or affectedly grand or impressive.

grand jury, a jury investigating accusations and indicting if evidence warrants.

grand·ma (gran'mä, grä'mä), *n.* [Informal], grandmother.

grand·moth·er ('muth-ẽr), *n.* the mother of one's father or mother.

grand opera, serious opera, all in music.

grand·pa (gran'pä, gram'pä), *n.* [Informal], grandfather.

grand·par·ent (gran'per-ênt), *n.* either parent of one's parent.

grand piano, a large piano, the case being horizontal and shaped like a harp.

grand slam, 1. in *Bridge,* the taking of all the tricks in a deal. 2. in *Baseball,* a home run with bases loaded.

grand·son (gran'sun), *n.* a son of one's son or daughter.

grand·stand ('stand), *n.* the main structure for seating spectators, as in a stadium.

grange (grānj), *n.* 1. a farm. 2. [G-], a farmers' association or a lodge of this.

gran·ite (gran'it), *n.* a very hard, crystalline rock of feldspar and quartz.

gran·ny, gran·nie (gran'i), *n., pl.* -**nies,** [Informal], a grandmother.

gran·o·la (grä-nō'lä), *n.* a prepared breakfast cereal of rolled oats, wheat germ, brown sugar or honey, and bits of dried fruit or nuts.

grant (grant), *v.t.* 1. to give or confer (a request, favor, etc.). 2. to convey by legal procedure. 3. to admit or concede (something unproved): *n.* 1. the act of granting. 2. a thing granted, as land. —**grant'er,** in *Law* **grant'or,** *n.*

grant·ee (grant-ē'), *n.* in *Law,* one to whom a grant, as of land, is made.

gran·u·lar (gran'yū-lẽr), *adj.* 1. of or like grains or granules. 2. grainy.

gran·u·late (-lāt), *v.t.* & *v.i.* -**lat·ed,** -**lat·ing,** 1. to form into grains or granules. 2. to roughen with granules formed.

gran·ule (gran'ūl), *n.* a small grain.

grape (grāp), *n.* 1. a round, smooth berry growing in bunches on woody vines. 2. the vine. 3. a dark red. 4. grapeshot.

grape·fruit ('frōōt), *n.* a sour citrus fruit, large, round, and yellow-skinned.

grape·shot ('shot), *n.* a former cannon charge of small, connected iron balls.

grape·vine ('vīn), *n.* 1. a grape-bearing vine. 2. a network of rumors.

graph (graf), *n.* a diagram showing successive changes in the value of a variable: *v.t.* to show thus.

-graph (graf), a combining form meaning *thing writing, thing written.*

graph·ic (graf'ik), *adj.* 1. realistically vivid. 2. designating or of visual arts, such as drawing or etching. 3. written. 4. of a graph. Also **graph'i·cal.**

graph·ite ('īt), *n.* a natural, pure carbon used as in pencils.

graph·ol·o·gy (gra-fol'ö-ji), *n.* the study of handwriting, specifically as a clue to character. —**graph·ol'o·gist,** *n.*

-graph·y (grä-fi), a combining form meaning *writing.*

grap·nel (grap'nl), *n.* 1. a small anchor with several flukes. 2. a kind of tongs.

grap·ple (grap'l), *v.t.* -**pled,** -**pling,** to lay fast hold of: *v.i.* 1. to use a grapnel (tongs). 2. to grab and struggle: *n.* 1. a grapnel (tongs). 2. a grappling.

grasp (grasp), *v.t.* & *v.i.* 1. to grab or grip. 2. to understand: *n.* a grasping.

grasp·ing (ing), *adj.* greedy; grabby.

grass (gras), *n.* 1. any one of various plants, as

wheat, with narrow leaves, jointed stems, and seedlike fruit. 2. any one of various narrow-leaved green plants growing densely as in lawns; also, land covered with these. 3. grass collectively. 4. [Slang], marijuana. —grass'y, adj. grass'i-er, grass'i-est.

grass-hop-per ('hop-ĕr), n. a large, winged, plant-eating insect with strong hind legs enabling it to make long leaps.

grass roots, [Informal], 1. ordinary people. 2. basic support.

grass widow, a divorced or separated wife.

grate (grāt), n. 1. a frame of metal bars to hold fuel. 2. a fireplace. 3. a grating: v.t. & v.i. grat'ed, grat'ing, 1. to grind or rub harshly. 2. to irritate. —grat'er, n.

grate-ful (grāt'fŭl), adj. 1. thankful. 2. pleasing. —grate'ful-ly, adv.

grat-i-fy (grat'i-fī), v.t. -fied, -fy-ing, 1. to please or satisfy. 2. to indulge or humor. —grat-i-fi-ca'tion, n.

grat-ing (grāt'ing), n. an open framework or lattice of bars: adj. irritating.

gra-tis (grat'is, grāt'), adv. & adj. free.

grat-i-tude (grat'i-tōōd), n. thankfulness.

gra-tu-i-tous (grā-tōō'i-tŭs, -tū'), adj. 1. freely bestowed or received. 2. unjustified; unwarranted; arbitrary.

gra-tu-i-ty (-ti), n., pl. -ties, a tip or other similar free gift.

gra-va-men (grā-vā'mĕn), n., pl. -va'mens, -vam'i-na (-vam'i-nä), 1. a grievance. 2. in Law, the essential part of a charge.

grave (grāv), adj. 1. serious; important; weighty. 2. not light; causing concern. 3. solemn; sedate. 4. dull; drab. 5. deep in pitch: n. 1. an excavation or other place of interment. 2. death; extinction: v.t. graved, grav'en or graved, grav'ing, 1. to cut, carve, or shape as with a chisel. 2. to impress deeply as if by engraving. —grave'ly, adv. — grav'er, n. —grave'ness, n.

grave accent, a mark (`) showing vowel quality, stress, etc.

grav-el (grav'l), n. 1. rock fragments coarser than sand. 2. a deposit of concretions as in the bladder: v.t. -eled or -elled, -el-ing or -el-ling, to put gravel on (a path, driveway, etc.).

grav-el-ly (-i), adj. 1. of, like, or full of gravel. 2. harsh; rasping.

grave-stone (grāv'stōn), n. a tombstone.

grave-yard ('yärd), n. a cemetery.

grav-id (grav'id), adj. pregnant.

gra-vim-e-ter (grā-vim'ĕ-tĕr), n. 1. a device to determine specific gravity. 2. an instrument to measure the earth's gravitational pull at different places on the earth.

grav-i-met-ric (grav-i-met'rik), adj. of gravitational or weight measurement.

gra-vim-e-try (grā-vim'ĕ-tri), n. measurement of weight or density.

grav-i-tate (grav'i-tāt), v.i. & v.t. -tat-ed, -tat-ing, to move with or as if with the force of gravity.

grav-i-ta-tion (grav-i-tā'shŭn), n. 1. a gravitating. 2. the attracting force between masses or particles of matter. —grav-i-ta'tion-al, adj.

grav-i-ty (grav'i-ti), n., pl. -ties, 1. a grave condition or quality; seriousness, solemnity, etc.

2. weight; heaviness. 3. gravitation; especially, the force drawing all bodies in the earth's sphere toward the center of the earth.

gra-vy (grā'vi), n., pl. -vies, 1. juice drawn from cooking meat. 2. such juice thickened, seasoned, etc. 3. [Slang], easy extra benefit or profit.

gray (grā), adj. 1. of a color that is a mixture of black and white. 2. having hair of this color. 3. rather dark, dull, or dreary. 4. old. 5. wearing gray clothes. 6. indeterminate: n. 1. gray color, a blend of black and white. 2. something of this color: v.t. & v.i. to make or turn gray.

gray-beard ('bird), n. an old man.

gray-ling ('ling), n., pl. -ling, -lings, a freshwater game fish of the salmon family.

gray matter, 1. grayish nerve tissue of the brain and spinal cord. 2. [Informal], brains; intellectual capacity.

graze (grāz), v.t. grazed, graz'ing, 1. to nibble (herbage, as in a pasture). 2. to put (livestock) out to do this. 3. to tend (livestock so feeding). 4. to furnish pasture for. 5. to touch lightly in passing. 6. to rub, scratch, or scrape thus: v.i. 1. to graze herbage. 2. to touch, rub, etc. something lightly in passing: n. 1. the act of grazing. 2. a scratch, scrape, etc. from getting grazed.

gra-zier (grā'zhĕr), n. [Chiefly British], one that grazes beef cattle for market.

grease (grēs), n. 1. melted animal fat. 2. oily, thick matter: v.t. (also grēz), greased, greas'ing, to rub, smear, or lubricate with or as if with grease.

grease-paint ('pānt), n. a greasy coloring preparation used as makeup by performers.

greas-y (grē'si, 'zi), adj. greas'i-er, greas'i-est, of, like, or full of grease.

great (grāt), adj. 1. very much larger, bigger, longer, etc. than the ordinary. 2. very much more intense, notable, etc. than the ordinary. 3. most important; chief; principal. 4. older or younger by one generation, as in great-grandparent, great-grandchild. 5. [Informal], skilled. 6. [Informal], superb; excellent. 7. [Archaic], pregnant: adv. [Informal], very well: n. a highly distinguished individual. —great'ly, adv. —great'ness, n.

Great Bear, same as Ursa Major.

great-coat ('kōt), n. a heavy overcoat.

Great Dane, any one of a breed of large, strong dogs with short, smooth hair.

great-grand-child (-gran'child), n., pl. -chil-dren, a child of a grandchild.

great-grand-par-ent (-gran'per-ĕnt), n. a parent of a grandparent.

great-heart-ed ('härt'id), adj. 1. brave. 2. magnanimous.

greaves (grēvz), n.pl. armor to protect the legs from the knee to the ankle.

grebe (grēb), n., pl. grebes, grebe, a diving and swimming bird related to the loons.

Gre-cian (grē'shän), adj. & n. Greek.

Gre-co- (grē'kō), a combining form meaning Greek, Greek and, Greece and

greed (grēd), n. avarice; greediness.

greed-y (grē'di), adj. greed'i-er, greed'i-est, 1. avaricious; covetous. 2. gluttonous; voracious. 3.

eagerly desirous. —**greed'i·ly**, adv. —**greed'i·ness**, n.

Greek (grēk), n. 1. a native or inhabitant of Greece. 2. the language of the Greeks: adj. 1. of or like Greece or the Greeks. 2. of the Orthodox Eastern Church.

Greek Church, 1. the established church of Greece, an autonomous part of the Orthodox Eastern Church. 2. popular name for **Orthodox Eastern Church**. Also **Greek Orthodox Church**.

Greek cross, a cross with four equal arms.

green (grēn), adj. 1. of the color of growing grass. 2. full of green plants or foliage. 3. bilious; sickly. 4. fresh; flourishing. 5. immature; unripe. 6. inexperienced; raw. 7. naive. 8. not dried, seasoned, or cured; unprocessed: n. 1. the color of growing grass, a color between blue and yellow. 2. something green; specifically, pl. green leafy vegetables such as spinach. 3. a smooth grass plot, bowling green, putting area around golf-course holes, etc.: v.t. & v.i. to turn green.

green·back ('bak), n. a piece of U.S. paper money printed green on the back.

green bean, the edible, immature pod of the kidney bean.

green·belt ('belt), n. a beltlike area around a city, reserved for park land or farms.

green·er·y ('ēr·i), n., pl. -er·ies. 1. green vegetation. 2. leafy green vegetables.

green-eyed ('īd), adj. jealous.

green·gage ('gāj), n. a large, greenish plum.

green·gro·cer ('grō·sēr), n. [British], a retail dealer in fresh vegetables and fruit.

green·horn ('hôrn), n. 1. an inexperienced individual. 2. one easily deceived; dupe.

green·house ('hous), n. a mainly glass building with temperature and humidity controlled for plant cultivation.

greenhouse effect, the warming of a planet, as the earth, and its lower atmosphere, caused by trapped solar radiation.

green·mail ('māl), n. the buying of a large amount of a company's stock so that the management, fearing a takeover, will buy it back at a premium. —**green'mail·er**, n.

green manure, a crop, as clover, plowed under to fertilize the soil.

green power, money, as the source of economic power and, hence, social and political power.

green onion, a long-stalked immature onion with green leaves, eaten raw.

green pepper, the green, immature fruit of the sweet red pepper, eaten as a vegetable.

green-room ('rōōm), n. an actors' waiting room in some theaters.

green·sward ('swôrd), n. green turf.

green thumb, an apparent talent for growing plants easily.

green·wood ('wood), n. a forest in leaf.

greet (grēt), v.t. 1. to speak to, write to, address, meet, etc. in a manner evidencing cordiality, pleasure, etc. 2. to meet, receive, address, etc. in any specified way.

greet·ing ('ing), n. 1. the act, manner, words, etc. of one that greets. 2. often pl. a saluta-tion from someone absent.

gre·gar·i·ous (grē·ger'i·ûs), adj. 1. associating in herds or flocks. 2. liking to be with others; sociable.

Gre·go·ri·an calendar (grē·gôr'i·ân), the calendar now generally in use, introduced in 1582 by Pope Gregory XIII.

Gregorian chant, the ritual plainsong introduced by Pope Gregory I and used in the Roman Catholic Church.

grem·lin (grem'lin), n. an imaginary little imp humorously blamed as the cause of mechanical troubles and other mischief.

gre·nade (grē·nād'), n. 1. a small bomb detonated by a fuse and thrown by hand or fired from a rifle. 2. a glass container holding chemicals as for extinguishing fires, designed to be thrown and to break upon impact so as to release the chemicals.

gren·a·dier (gren·â·dir'), n. 1. originally, a foot soldier who threw grenades. 2. a member of a special regiment or corps, as of the Grenadier Guards of the British Army.

gren·a·dine (gren'â·dēn, gren·â·dēn'), n. 1. a syrup from pomegranate juice, used for flavoring or coloring. 2. a thin, loosely woven fabric as of silk or rayon.

grew (grōō), past tense of grow.

grey (grā), adj. & n. & v.t. & v.i. British spelling of gray.

grey·hound (grā'hound), n. a slender, swift hound with a narrow head.

grid (grid), n. 1. a framework of parallel bars, as a gridiron or grating. 2. an arrangement of lines forming even squares. 3. a conducting metallic plate in a storage battery. 4. in an electronic tube, a wire mesh or spiral controlling the passage of electrons or ions: adj. [Informal], of or pertaining to football.

grid·dle (grid'l), n. a flat metal plate or pan as for cooking pancakes: v.t. -dled, -dling, to cook on this.

grid·dle·cake (-kāk), n. a pancake.

grid·i·ron (grid'ī-ērn), n. 1. a grill for broiling. 2. a football field.

grid·lock (grid'lok), n. a traffic jam in which no vehicle can move in any direction.

grief (grēf), n. deep sorrow or its cause.

griev·ance (grē'vâns), n. a ground for complaint or the complaint itself.

grieve (grēv), v.t. grieved, griev'ing, to subject to grief: v.i. to feel grief.

griev·ous (grē'vûs), adj. 1. causing or showing grief. 2. grave and most distressing, as a wound or illness. 3. intense or bitter, as sorrow or other suffering. 4. atrocious; heinous.

grif·fin (grif'in), n. a mythical monster, half eagle and half lion.

grif·fon (grif'ôn), n. 1. a griffin. 2. a small Belgian dog with a flat face. 3. a medium-sized Dutch dog with a wiry coat.

grill (gril), n. 1. a flat frame as of metal bars, on which steaks, chops, etc. are laid for broiling. 2. a large griddle. 3. grilled food. 4. a grillroom: v.t. 1. to cook on a grill. 2. to cross-examine.

grill (gril), n. same as grille.

gril·lage (gril'ij), n. a crosswise system of beams forming a foundation in soft soil.

ŏ in dragon, ōō in crude, oo in wool, u in cup, ū in cure, ū in turn, ů in focus, oi in boy, ou in house, th in thin, th in sheathe, g in get, j in joy, y in yet.

grille (gril), *n.* a grating as of iron, used as in a window or door opening.

grill-room (gril'rōōm), *n.* a place specializing in grilled foods.

grill-work ('wûrk), *n.* an arrangement of bars, strips, etc. forming a grille.

grilse (grils), *n., pl.* **grilse, grils'es,** a young salmon first returning to fresh water from the sea.

grim (grim), *adj.* **grim'mer, grim'mest,** 1. cruel; savage. 2. sternly resolute or relentless. 3. harsh and forbidding. 4. depressingly unpleasant or uninviting. 5. horrible; grisly; ghastly.

gri-mace (gri-mās', grim'ās), *n.* a distortion of the face, as from pain: *v.i.* **-maced', -mac'-ing,** to distort the face.

gri-mal-kin (gri-mal'kin, -môl'kin), *n.* a cat, especially an old female one.

grime (grim), *n.* heavy dirt on or embedded in a surface, as of the skin. **—grim'y,** *adj.* **grim'i-er, grim'i-est**

grin (grin), *v.i.* **grinned, grin'ning,** to draw the corners of the mouth wide apart in or as if in an extremely broad smile so that the teeth often show, so indicating great pleasure, pain, malice, stupidity, etc.: *n.* a grinning.

grind (grīnd), *v.t.* **ground, grind'ing,** 1. to reduce to bits by crushing; pulverize. 2. to afflict, oppress, or harass. 3. to sharpen, shape, or smooth by friction. 4. to rub or scrape harshly together; grate. 5. to operate by cranking. 6. to produce by grinding: *v.i.* 1. to grind something. 2. to undergo grinding. 3. [Informal], to work or study unremittingly: *n.* 1. a grinding. 2. the relative fineness of something ground. 3. [Informal], a student who studies unremittingly.

grind-er ('ẽr), *n.* 1. one that grinds. 2. *pl.* [Informal], the teeth. 3. same as hero sandwich.

grind-stone ('stōn), *n.* a revolving stone disk used as for sharpening tools.

grin-go (gring'gō), *n., pl.* **-gos,** in Latin America, a foreigner: hostile term.

grip (grip), *n.* 1. a firm grasp; tight hold. 2. the way something is grasped or held. 3. a device that grasps. 4. a handle, as of a tool. 5. a small traveling bag: *v.t.* **gripped** or **gript, grip'ping,** 1. to grasp or join tight. 2. to capture the attention or emotions of: *v.i.* to get a grip. **—grip'per,** *n.*

grip (grip), *n.* same as grippe.

gripe (grip), *v.t.* **griped, grip'ing,** 1. formerly, to grasp or to afflict. 2. to pain sharply the bowels of. 3. [Slang], to vex intensely: *v.i.* [Slang], to complain: *n.* 1. a sharp pain in the bowels. 2. [Slang], a complaint. **—grip'er,** *n.*

grippe (grip), *n.* influenza: earlier term.

gri-saille (gri-zā', -zāl'), *n.* a painting using only gray tints.

gri-sette (gri-zet'), *n.* a French working girl.

gris-ly (griz'li), *adj.* **-li-er, -li-est,** horrible; ghastly. **—gris'li-ness,** *n.*

grist (grist), *n.* grain that is to be ground or that has been ground.

gris-tle (gris'l), *n.* cartilage, especially in meat cuts. **—gris'tly,** *adj.*

grit (grit), *n.* 1. rough, hard particles, as of sand. 2. a coarse sandstone. 3. stubborn courage; pluck. 4. *pl.* coarsely ground wheat or corn: *v.t.* **grit'ted, grit'ting,** to clench or grind (the teeth), as in an ordeal: *v.i.* to make a grating sound.

grit-ty ('i), *adj.* **-ti-er, -ti-est,** 1. of, like, or full of grit. 2. stubbornly courageous; plucky. **—grit'ti-ness,** *n.*

griv-et (griv'it), *n.* a small, long-tailed monkey of Africa, with a greenish back.

griz-zled (griz'ld), *adj.* 1. gray or partly gray. 2. having gray hair.

griz-zly ('li), *adj.* **-zli-er, -zli-est,** grizzled; somewhat gray: *n., pl.* **-zlies,** a large, fierce, brown or grayish bear of western North America: also grizzly bear.

groan (grōn), *n.* 1. a low, deep sound uttered in pain, sorrow, disapproval, etc. 2. a harsh, creaking sound, as made by wood under great strain: *v.i.* to make a groan: *v.t.* to utter with a groan. **—groan'ing-ly,** *adv.*

groat (grōt), *n.* 1. an obsolete British coin equal to one third of a shilling. 2. a trifling sum. 3. *pl.* hulled grain, as buckwheat, oats, wheat, or barley.

gro-cer (grō'sẽr), *n.* one who sells groceries.

gro-cer-y (grō'sẽr-i), *n., pl.* **-cer-ies,** 1. *pl.* food and household supplies bought from a store. 2. a store selling these items.

grog (grog), *n.* 1. originally, rum diluted with water. 2. any alcoholic liquor.

grog-gy ('i), *adj.* **-gi-er, -gi-est,** 1. originally, drunk. 2. unsteady or shaky, as from lack of sleep or a blow to the head. **—grog'gi-ly,** *adv.* **—grog'gi-ness,** *n.*

gro-gram (grog'rām), *n.* a fabric of silk and mohair, formerly used for cloaks, etc.

grog-shop (grog'shop), *n.* [Chiefly British], a saloon.

groin (groin), *n.* 1. the fold of the human body where the thigh joins the abdomen. 2. the angular curve made by the intersection of two arches: *v.t.* to build or form into a groin or groins.

grom-met (grom'it, grum'-), *n.* 1. a ring formed of a strand of rope. 2. an eyelet of metal in cloth, leather, etc.

groom (grōōm), *n.* 1. a man or boy who has charge of horses. 2. a bridegroom: *v.t.* 1. to curry and brush (a horse, etc.). 2. to make neat and trim. 3. to prepare (a person) for a position, office, etc.

grooms-man (grōōmz'mān), *n., pl.* **-men,** a man who attends a bridegroom; best man.

groove (grōōv), *n.* 1. a long, narrow channel or furrow as cut with a tool. 2. a settled habit or routine: *v.t.* **grooved, groov'ing,** to form or cut a groove in: *v.i.* [Slang], to enjoy and understand (an experience, person, etc.).

groov-y ('i), *adj.* **groov'i-er, groov'i-est,** [Slang], very appealing, interesting, etc.

grope (grōp), *v.i.* **groped, grop'ing,** to feel one's way with the hands, as in the dark; seek blindly: *v.t.* to search out or find by groping. **—grop'er,** *n.*

gros·beak (grōs'bēk), *n.* any of various finch-like songbirds having a large, strong bill.

gro·schen (grō'shĕn), *n., pl.* -schen, 1. a coin of Austria equal to 1/100 schilling. 2. a small silver coin formerly used in Germany.

gros·grain (grō'grān), *n.* a ribbed silk or rayon fabric used for ribbons, etc.

gross (grōs), *adj.* 1. thick; dense. 2. very fat. 3. coarse; indelicate. 4. flagrant; bad. 5. unrefined. 6. total; with no deductions: *n.* 1. overall total. 2. *pl.* gross, twelve dozen: *v.t. & v.i.* [Informal], to earn (a specified total). —gross'ly, *adv.* —gross'ness, *n.*

gross national product, the total value of all the goods and services produced by a country in any one year.

gro·tesque (grō-tĕsk'), *adj.* 1. fantastic or odd in form, appearance, etc. 2. ridiculous; ludicrous. —gro·tesque'ly, *adv.*

grot·to (grŏt'ō), *n., pl.* -toes, -tos, 1. a cave. 2. a cavelike shrine or the like.

grouch (grouch), *n.* 1. a sulky mood. 2. one who grumbles or is sulky: *v.i.* to grumble or complain in a sulky manner. —grouch'y, *adj.* grouch'i·er, grouch'i·est. —grouch'i·ness, *n.*

ground (ground), *n.* 1. the earth or soil. 2. *often pl.* a piece of land, as the land of an estate. 3. the bottom of a body of water. 4. *often pl.* foundation; basis. 5. *often pl.* reason or cause. 6. the background, as of a work of art. 7. *pl.* dregs or sediment. 8. the connection of an electrical circuit with the ground: *v.t.* 1. to place on the ground. 2. to base; found. 3. to run aground. 4. to instruct in first principles. 5. to prevent (a pilot or aircraft) from flying. 6. to connect (an electric circuit) with the ground: *v.i.* 1. to run ashore. 2. in *Baseball,* to be put out on a grounder (usually with *out*): *adj.* of, near, growing from, or on the ground.

ground (ground), past tense and past participle of grind.

ground control, the people and electronic equipment that guide spacecraft or aircraft from the ground.

ground cover, any of various low-growing plants grown especially in areas where it is hard to grow grass.

ground·er (-ẽr), *n.* a baseball hit along the ground.

ground floor, the floor of a building that is approximately level with the ground.

ground·hog (-'hog), *n.* same as woodchuck: also **ground hog.**

ground ivy, a creeping plant with round leaves and blue flowers.

ground·less ('lis), *adj.* without reason; unjustified. —ground'less·ly, *adv.*

ground·sel (ground'sl, groun'-), *n.* a weed with yellow flowers.

ground·speed (ground'spēd), *n.* the speed of an aircraft relative to the ground rather than to the air.

ground·swell ('swel), *n.* 1. a broad, deep, heavy, rolling sea, caused by a distant storm or earthquake. 2. a fast-growing wave of public sentiment. Also **ground swell.**

ground·work ('wûrk), *n.* a foundation; basis.

group (grōōp), *n.* 1. a number of individuals gathered or classified together. 2. an assemblage of figures or objects forming an artistic whole: *v.t. & v.i.* to form into a group or groups.

group·er (-'ẽr), *n.* a food fish found in tropical and subtropical waters.

grouse (grous), *n., pl.* grouse, any of a number of game birds with a plump body and feathered legs, as the sage hen.

grouse (grous), *v.i.* groused, grous'ing, [Informal], to complain: *n.* [Informal], a complaint. —grous'er, *n.*

grout (grout), *n.* 1. a fine plaster for finishing surfaces. 2. a thin mortar used as between tiles. 3. coarse meal: *v.t.* to fill in or finish with grout. —grout'er, *n.*

grove (grōv), *n.* 1. a small wood, usually without undergrowth. 2. an orchard.

grov·el (gruv'l, grov'l), *v.i.* -eled or -elled, -el-ing or -el-ling, 1. to lie or move with the body prostrate on the ground. 2. to cringe; behave abjectly. —grov'el·er, grov'el·ler, *n.*

grow (grō), *v.i.* grew, grown, grow'ing, 1. to cultivate; raise: *v.i.* 1. to increase in stature or size by natural organic development. 2. to be produced naturally. 3. to increase; flourish; thrive. 4. to become. 5. to become fixed or attached. —grow'er, *n.*

growl (groul), *n.* a deep, angry snarl; threatening sound in the throat: *v.i. & v.t.* to make or utter with such a sound.

growl·er (-'ẽr), *n.* 1. a person or thing that growls. 2. a small iceberg. 3. [Slang], formerly, a pitcher or pail for carrying out beer bought in a saloon.

grown (grōn), past participle of grow: *adj.* 1. having arrived at full growth; mature. 2. raised in a specified way, as home-grown.

grown-up (grōn'up), *adj.* 1. mature. 2. of, for, or like an adult: *n.* (grōn'up), an adult.

growth (grōth), *n.* 1. a progressive increase in size, weight, etc. 2. the full extent of this. 3. something that has grown or developed. 4. an abnormal mass of tissue, as a tumor.

grub (grub), *v.t.* grubbed, grub'bing, 1. to dig up; root out of the ground. 2. to clear (ground) of roots: *v.i.* 1. to drudge or toil; especially, to perform dirty or menial work. 2. to dig in the ground: *n.* 1. the wormlike larva of a beetle, moth, or other insect. 2. a drudge. 3. [Slang], food.

grub·by ('ĭ), *adj.* -bi·er, -bi·est, 1. infested with grubs, especially with botfly larvae: said of cattle or sheep. 2. dirty; slovenly. —grub'bi·ness, *n.*

grub·stake ('stāk), *n.* [Informal], 1. money or an outfit advanced to a prospector on condition that he share his findings. 2. money advanced for any venture: *v.t.* -staked, -stak·ing, [Informal], to provide with a grubstake. —grub'stak·er, *n.*

grudge (gruj), *v.t.* grudged, grudg'ing, 1. to regard (someone) with envy and resentment because of (something). 2. to give with reluctance: *n.* malice or ill will toward someone over a grievance, extending for a long period.

gru·el (grōō'ĕl), *n.* a thin, light food made of meal cooked in water or milk, often fed to invalids.

gru·el·ing, gru·el·ling (-ing), *adj.* laborious; oppressive; burdensome.

grue·some (grōō′sŏm), *adj.* causing horror; loathsome; grisly. —**grue′some·ly,** *adv.*

gruff (gruf), *adj.* 1. rough or surly. 2. harsh in voice; hoarse. —**gruff′ly,** *adv.* —**gruff′ness,** *n.*

gru·gru (grōō′grōō), *n.* 1. a spiny palm of the West Indies. 2. the wormlike, edible larva of a weevil that infests this palm.

grum·ble (grum′bl), *v.i.* -**bled,** -**bling,** to murmur discontentedly; find fault: *v.t.* to utter by grumbling: *n.* something grumbled; complaint. —**grum′bler,** *n.*

grump·y (grum′pi), *adj.* **grump′i·er, grump′i·est,** surly; cross; grouchy. —**grump′i·ly,** *adv.* —**grump′i·ness,** *n.*

grunt (grunt), *n.* 1. the deep, short, guttural, vocal sound of a hog. 2. a sound like this. 3. any of various saltwater fishes that grunt when taken from the water: *v.i.* & *v.t.* to utter (with) a grunt. —**grunt′er,** *n.*

Gru·yère (grōō-yer′, grē-), *n.* a pale-yellow Swiss cheese that is rich in butterfat, or an American cheese like this: also **Gruyère cheese.**

G-string (jē′string), *n.* 1. a loincloth. 2. a similar band or strip of cloth, usually decorated, worn by striptease dancers.

gua·cha·ro (gwä′chä-rō), *n., pl.* -**ros,** a nocturnal bird of South America.

gua·co (gwä′kō), *n., pl.* -**cos,** a South American plant used in treating snake bites.

guai·a·cum (gwī′å-kům), *n.* 1. a tropical American tree with blue or purple flowers. 2. the hard wood of this tree. 3. a greenish-brown resin from two species of this tree, used commercially: now usually **guai′ac** ('ak).

guan (gwän), *n.* a chickenlike game bird of Central and South America.

gua·na·co (gwä-nä′kō), *n., pl.* -**cos,** -**co,** a brown, wild ruminant of the Andes, related to the llama and camel.

gua·nine (gwä′nēn), *n.* an organic base found in all plant and animal tissue.

gua·no (gwä′nō), *n., pl.* -**nos,** 1. the manure of sea birds found on islands off the Peruvian coast, used as fertilizer. 2. any fertilizer resembling this.

guar·an·tee (gar-ăn-tē′, gär-), *n.* 1. same as **guaranty** (sense 1). 2. a promise or assurance as to the quality, content, etc. of something or the length of time it may be expected to last. 3. a guarantor: *v.t.* -**teed′,** -**tee′ing,** 1. to promise. 2. to give a guarantee for.

guar·an·tor (gar′ăn-tôr, -tēr), *n.* one who gives a guarantee or guaranty.

guar·an·ty (-ti), *n., pl.* -**ties,** 1. an undertaking of responsibility for a debt or obligation of another. 2. a security for the maintenance or existence of something. 3. a guarantor.

guard (gärd), *v.t.* 1. to watch over or protect; shield or defend. 2. to prevent from escaping: *v.i.* 1. to be cautious (*against*). 2. to act as a guard: *n.* 1. security or defense against injury or attack. 2. a posture to meet attack, as in fencing. 3. any contrivance or device for security or protection. 4. any of various military units. 5. a railway brake-

man. 6. one who guards prisoners. 7. an offensive football lineman. 8. a defensive basketball player.

guard·ed ('id), *adj.* 1. protected; kept safe. 2. kept from escape. 3. cautious.

guard·house ('hous), *n.* 1. a building used by military personnel on guard duty. 2. a military jail for temporary detention of prisoners.

guard·i·an ('i-ån), *n.* 1. one who has the care of another person or of another's property; custodian. 2. one legally in charge of the affairs of a minor or someone unable to manage his own affairs: *adj.* protecting. — **guard′i·an·ship,** *n.*

guard·rail ('rāl), *n.* a protective railing, as along a roadway.

guards·man (gärdz′mån), *n., pl.* -**men,** 1. an officer or soldier of any military unit called a "guard." 2. a member of the National Guard.

gua·va (gwä′vä), *n.* 1. a tropical American tree of the myrtle family, that bears a pear-shaped, yellow fruit. 2. this fruit, used for jelly.

gu·ber·na·to·ri·al (gōō-běr-nå-tôr′i-ål), *adj.* of a governor or his office.

gudg·eon (guj′ŭn), *n.* 1. a small, freshwater fish easily caught and used for bait. 2. a person who is easily imposed upon. 3. a metal pin or shaft on which a wheel revolves.

gue·non (gē-nōn′), *n.* any of several long-tailed African monkeys, as the grivet.

guer·don (gûr′dn), *n.* [Archaic], a reward.

Guern·sey (gûrn′zi), *n., pl.* -**seys,** 1. any of a breed of dairy cattle, brown with white markings. 2. [g-], a knit shirt.

guer·ril·la, gue·ril·la (gě-ril′ä), *n.* any one of a small band of irregular soldiers, usually volunteer, that harass an enemy, especially an invading force: *adj.* of or pertaining to guerrillas or to irregular warfare.

guess (ges), *n.* a conjecture; estimate; surmise: *v.t.* & *v.i.* 1. to estimate or surmise without actual evidence or knowledge. 2. to judge accurately by doing this. 3. to suppose or think. —**guess′er,** *n.*

guess·work ('wûrk), *n.* 1. the act of guessing. 2. a conclusion arrived at by guessing.

guest (gest), *n.* 1. one who is entertained at the home, club, etc. of another. 2. a customer in a hotel, restaurant, etc.: *adj.* 1. for guests. 2. appearing by special invitation, as a *guest* conductor.

guff (guf), *n.* [Slang], 1. nonsense. 2. insolent talk.

guf·faw (gů-fô′), *n.* a loud, boisterous burst of laughter: *v.i.* to laugh in this way.

guid·ance (gīd′ns), *n.* 1. the act of guiding. 2. advice or counsel.

guide (gīd), *n.* 1. one who leads or serves as a model. 2. one whose work is directing strangers around an area, building, etc. 3. a device to direct or control the motion of something. 4. a book of instructions: *v.t.* **guid′ed, guid′ing,** 1. to lead or direct. 2. to regulate or control. —**guid′a·ble,** *adj.*

guide·book ('book), *n.* a handbook of information and directions for travelers.

guided missile, a military missile whose course

is controlled during flight by radar, radio signals, etc.

guide-line ('līn), *n.* a rule or principle to use in making a decision.

gui-don (gīd'n, gī'don), *n.* 1. formerly, a forked flag carried by the rider who set the pace for a troop of mounted cavalry. 2. the soldier carrying this flag.

guild (gild), *n.* 1. a medieval union of men in the same craft or of merchants. 2. an association of persons with common interests.

guil-der (gil'dēr), *n.* the monetary unit and a coin of the Netherlands.

guile (gīl), *n.* deceit; cunning; duplicity. —**guile'ful**, *adj.* —**guile'less**, *adj.*

guil-le-mot (gil'ē-mot), *n.* any of several northern diving birds.

guil-loche (gi-losh'), *n.* a series of interwoven or twisted ornaments.

guil-lo-tine (gil'ō-tēn, gē'ō-), *n.* an apparatus, used in France, for beheading a condemned person by means of a heavy knife sliding in two upright grooves: *v.t.* (gil-ō-tēn', gē-ō-), -**tined'**, -**tin'ing**, to behead with a guillotine.

guilt (gilt), *n.* 1. the state of one who has done a wrong or committed an offense. 2. a feeling of remorse from a belief that one has done wrong 3. conduct that deserves punishment; crime; sin. —**guilt'less**, *adj.*

guilt-y ('ī), *adj.* **guilt'i-er**, **guilt'i-est**, 1. having been legally judged an offender or criminal; not innocent. 2. having or showing a feeling of guilt. 3. deserving blame or punishment. —**guilt'i-ly**, *adv.* —**guilt'i-ness**, *n.*

guimpe (gimp, gamp), *n.* 1. a blouse worn under a jumper. 2. a wide cloth for covering the neck and shoulders in some nuns' habits.

guin-ea (gin'ī), *n.* a gold coin formerly used in England, equal to 21 shillings.

guinea fowl, a domestic fowl, originally from Africa, having a rounded body and grayish feathers dotted with white: also **guinea hen**.

guinea pig, 1. a small, fat, domesticated, South American rodent, sometimes used in biological experiments. 2. a person or thing used in an experiment.

gui-pure (gi-pyoor'), *n.* 1. a kind of gimp (fabric). 2. lace without any ground mesh, the pattern being held in place with threads.

guise (gīz), *n.* 1. external appearance. 2. dress or garb. 3. a deceiving appearance; pretense.

gui-tar (gi-tär'), *n.* a six-stringed musical instrument: the strings are strummed or plucked with the fingers or a plectrum. —**gui-tar'ist**, *n.*

gu-lar (gū'lēr, gōō'-), *adj.* of or on the throat.

gulch (gulch), *n.* a narrow, deep valley cut by a stream; ravine.

gul-den (gool'dēn), *n., pl.* -**dens**, -**den**, same as guilder.

gules (gūlz), *n.* the color red in heraldry: the color is indicated by parallel perpendicular lines in engravings without color.

gulf (gulf), *n.* 1. an arm of the sea extending into the land, larger than a bay. 2. a deep, wide place in the earth; chasm; abyss. 3. a whirlpool. 4. a separation nearly too wide to breach.

gull (gul), *n.* 1. *pl.* **gulls**, **gull**, a web-footed water bird with gray and white plumage and large wings. 2. one who is easily cheated: *v.t.* to cheat; dupe.

gul-let (gul'ēt), *n.* 1. the throat. 2. the esophagus.

gul-li-ble (gul'i-bl), *adj.* easily gulled or duped. —**gul-li-bil'i-ty**, *n.* —**gul'li-bly**, *adv.*

gul-ly (gul'ī), *n., pl.* -**lies**, a channel or hollow worn by water; narrow ravine.

gulp (gulp), *v.t. & v.i.* 1. to swallow down eagerly or in large amounts. 2. to choke back as if by swallowing: *n.* the act of gulping or swallowing.

gum (gum), *n.* 1. the firm flesh of the jaws surrounding the teeth. 2. a viscid substance that exudes from certain trees and shrubs and hardens into a brittle mass. 3. such a substance processed for use in industry or art. 4. an adhesive. 5. same as **chewing gum**: *v.t.* **gummed**, **gum'ming**, 1. to chew with toothless gums. 2. to coat, glue, smear, etc. with or as with gum. —**gum'mi-ness**, *n.* —**gum'my**, *adj.* -**mi-er**, -**mi-est**.

gum arabic, a gum obtained from several African acacias, used in pharmaceuticals, candy, adhesives, etc.

gum-bo (gum'bō), *n.* 1. a soup thickened with unripe okra pods. 2. [often G-], a Creole patois. 3. a silty prairie soil that becomes gummy when wet: also **gumbo soil**.

gum-drop (gum'drop), *n.* a small, firm, jellylike candy made of sweetened gum arabic, gelatin, etc. and coated with sugar.

gum-ma (gum'á), *n., pl.* -**mas**, -**ma-ta** ('á-tá), a soft, syphilitic tumor.

gump-tion (gump'shun), *n.* [Informal], 1. originally, common sense. 2. initiative; spunk.

gum resin, a mixture of gum and resin, given off by some trees and plants.

gun (gun), *n.* 1. a weapon with a metal tube from which a shot is discharged by the force of an explosive. 2. technically, a heavy, mounted gun; piece of ordnance, as a cannon. 3. a rifle. 4. in popular usage, any portable firearm. 5. a device like a gun, that discharges something under pressure. 6. [Slang], an engine's throttle: *v.i.* **gunned**, **gun'ning**, to hunt or shoot with a gun: *v.t.* 1. [Informal], to shoot (a person). 2. [Slang], to open up the throttle of (an engine) so as to increase speed.

gun-boat ('bōt), *n.* a small, armed ship of shallow draft, used to patrol harbors, rivers, etc.

gun-cot-ton ('kot-n), *n.* a highly explosive substance formed by the action of nitric acid on cotton.

gun-fight ('fīt), *n.* a fight between persons using handguns. —**gun'fight-er**, *n.*

gun-fire ('fīr), *n.* the firing of guns.

gung-ho (gung'hō'), *adj.* enthusiastic.

gunk (gungk), *n.* [Slang], a thick, gummy, messy substance.

gun-man (gun'mán), *n., pl.* -**men**, an armed gangster or killer.

gun-met-al ('met-l), *n.* 1. a tarnished bronze. 2. a dark-gray color.

gun-nel (gun'l), *n.* same as gunwale.

gun-ner (gun'ēr), *n.* 1. a military man who helps fire artillery; artilleryman. 2. a warrant officer in the navy who has charge of the ordnance of a warship. 3. a hunter who uses a gun.

gun·ner·y (-i), *n.* the science of constructing and using heavy guns.

gun·ny (gun'i), *n.*, *pl.* -nies, 1. a coarse, heavy cloth made of jute or hemp. 2. a sack or bag made of gunny: also **gun'ny-sack** or **gun'ny-bag**.

gun·play (gun'plā), *n.* gunfire exchanged between contending parties, as police and gunmen.

gun·pow·der ('pou-dẽr), *n.* 1. an explosive mixture of sulfur, saltpeter, and charcoal, used in guns and for blasting. 2. a fine, Chinese green tea: also **gunpowder tea**.

gun·shot ('shot), *n.* 1. shot fired from a gun. 2. the sound of a gun shooting. 3. the range of a gun.

gun·shy ('shī), *adj.* frightened by the shooting of a gun.

gun·smith ('smith), *n.* one who makes or repairs small guns.

Gun·ter's chain (gun'tẽrz), a surveyor's chain used in measuring land: it is 66 feet long, and is divided into 100 links of 7.92 inches each.

gun·wale (gun'l), *n.* the upper edge of the side of a ship or boat.

gup·py (gup'i), *n.*, *pl.* -pies, a tiny, freshwater, tropical fish often kept in aquariums.

gur·gi·ta·tion (gũr-ji-tā'shũn), *n.* [Rare], a state of boiling, or whirling around.

gur·gle (gũr'gl), *v.i.* -gled, -gling, to flow with, or make, a purling, bubbling sound: *n.* a purling, bubbling sound.

Gur·kha (goor'kä, gũr'-), *n.* a member of the warlike Rajput people living in Nepal, a mountainous country of south central Asia.

gur·nard (gũr'nẽrd), *n.*, *pl.* -nards, -nard, any of a number of marine fishes with enlarged pectoral fins and a large head covered with bony plates.

gur·ry (gũr'i), *n.* offal from fish, as from a fish cannery: *v.t.* -ried, -ry·ing, to foul (a lake, stream, etc.) with fish offal.

gu·ru (goor'ōō, goo-rōō'), *n.* 1. in *Hinduism*, one's personal spiritual adviser or leader. 2. [Informal], any highly regarded leader.

gush (gush), *n.* 1. a sudden, copious outflow. 2. an effusive display of sentiment or enthusiasm: *v.i.* 1. to flow out copiously. 2. to be extravagantly sentimental or enthusiastic: *v.t.* to cause to gush. —**gush'y**, *adj.* gush'i·er, gush'i·est.

gush·er ('ẽr), *n.* 1. one who gushes. 2. an oil well that discharges oil without the use of a pump.

gus·set (gus'it), *n.* a small, triangular or diamond-shaped piece of cloth inserted in a garment to strengthen or enlarge a part.

gus·sie, gus·sy (gus'i), *v.t. & v.i.* -sied, -sy·ing, [Slang], to dress (*up*) in a fashionable or dashing way.

gust (gust), *n.* 1. a sudden squall or strong blast of wind. 2. a sudden outburst of emotion. 3. [Archaic], *a)* taste; relish. *b)* enjoyment. —**gust'y**, *adj.* gust'i·er, gust'i·est.

gus·ta·to·ry (gus'tä-tôr-i), *adj.* of or pertaining to the taste.

gus·to (gus'tō), *n.* 1. zest; relish. 2. vigor; animation.

gut (gut), *n.* 1. the intestinal tract. 2. *pl.* the stomach or bowels. 3. a tough cord made from animal intestines. 4. a narrow channel or gully. 5. *pl.* [Informal], the inner, basic parts. 6. *pl.* [Slang], courage: *v.t.* gut'ted, gut'ting, 1. to remove the intestines from; eviscerate. 2. to destroy the interior of, as by fire: *adj.* [Slang], 1. easy. 2. fundamental.

gut·less ('lis), *adj.* [Slang], having no fortitude; not aggressive; weak.

guts·y (gut'si), *adj.* guts'i·er, guts'i·est, [Slang], daring, plucky, aggressive, etc.

gut·ta (gut'ä), *n.*, *pl.* -tae ('ē), 1. in *Pharmacy*, a drop. 2. a small, droplike ornament on a Doric entablature, occurring in series.

gut·ta-per·cha (gut'ä-pũr'chä), *n.* a gum extracted from the latex of various trees of southeastern Asia, used in golf balls, electric insulation, etc.

gut·ter (gut'ẽr), *n.* 1. a channel for carrying away water, as along a roadside. 2. a trough for carrying off rain water from eaves. 3. the groove on either side of a bowling alley: *v.i.* 1. to flow in a stream. 2. to melt and run down in channels: said of candle wax.

gut·ter·snipe (-snip), *n.* an urchin of the streets; gamin; street Arab.

gut·tur·al (gut'ẽr-äl), *adj.* 1. of or pertaining to the throat. 2. produced in the throat; harsh. —**gut'tur·al·ly**, *adv.*

guy (gī), *n.* 1. a rope, chain, etc. attached to something heavy to keep it steady. 2. in England, an effigy of Guy Fawkes, 16th-century conspirator. 3. [Slang], a fellow; man or boy: *v.t.* 1. to steady or guide with a guy. 2. to ridicule; tease.

guz·zle (guz'l), *v.i. & v.t.* -zled, -zling, to drink greedily or immoderately. —**guz'zler**, *n.*

gym (jim), *n.* [Informal], same as: 1. **gymnasium**. 2. **physical education**.

gym·kha·na (jim-kä'nä), *n.* 1. a place where athletic events are held. 2. an exhibition or contest of equestrian skill. 3. an automobile race, water-skiing competition, etc. that involves skill.

gym·na·si·um (jim-nā'zi-ũm), *n.*, *pl.* -si·ums, -si·a (-ä), a building or room for sports or physical training.

gym·nas·tics (jim-nas'tiks), *n.pl.* physical exercises that develop the muscles, especially those done in a gymnasium, such as calisthenics. —**gym'nast**, *n.* —**gym·nas'tic**, *adj.* —**gym·nas'ti·cal·ly**, *adv.*

gyn·arch·y (jin'är-ki, ji'när-), *n.*, *pl.* -arch·ies, government by a woman or women.

gyn·e·co-, a combining form meaning *woman, female:* also **gyn·ec-**.

gyn·e·col·o·gy (gī-nĕ-kol'ō-ji), *n.* the branch of medical science that deals with the bodily functions and diseases of women. —**gyn·e·co·log'ic** (-kô-loj'ik), **gyn·e·co·log'i·cal**, *adj.* —**gyn·e·col'o·gist**, *n.*

gyn·e·pho·bi·a (jin-ê-fō'bi-å, jī-nê-), *n.* an abnormal fear of women.

gyn·o-, a combining form meaning *female, female reproductive organ, ovary, pistil.*

gy·noe·ci·um (ji-nē'si-ùm, jī-), *n., pl.* -ci·a (-å), the carpels in the flower of a seed plant collectively; pistil or pistils.

gyn·o·phore (jin'ō-fôr, jī'nō-), *n.* a stalk bearing the gynoecium above the petals. —gyn·o·phor'ic, *adj.*

gyp (jip), *n.* [Informal], 1. a fraud; swindle. 2. a swindler; cheat: also gyp'per, gyp.'ster: *v.t. & v.i.* gypped, gyp'ping, [Informal], to cheat or swindle.

gyp·soph·i·la (jip-sof'ĭ-lå), *n.* a plant of the pink family, with tiny white or pink flowers.

gyp·sum (jip'sùm), *n.* a sulfate of calcium, used to make plaster of Paris, in fertilizer, etc.

Gyp·sy (jip'si), *n., pl.* -sies, 1. [also g-], a member of a wandering Caucasoid people, probably originating in India, with dark skin and dark eyes. 2. their language; Romany. 3. [g-], a person who likes to wander: *adj.* of or like the Gypsies.

gypsy moth, a European moth now common in the eastern U.S.: its larvae feed on leaves, doing much damage to forest and shade trees.

gy·ral (jī'rål), *adj.* rotatory; whirling.

gy·rate (jī'rāt), *v.i.* -rat·ed, -rat·ing, to revolve around a central point; rotate; whirl. —gy·ra'tion, *n.*

gyre (jīr), *n.* [Chiefly Poetic], 1. the circular motion of a moving body. 2. a circular or spiral form: *v.i. & v.t.* gyred, gyr'ing, [Chiefly Poetic], to gyrate.

gyr·fal·con (jūr'fal-kôn, 'fôl-, 'fô-), *n.* any of several large, strong falcons of the arctic regions.

gy·ro (yir'ō, jī'rō), *n., pl.* -ros, 1. layers of lamb and beef roasted and sliced. 2. a sandwich made of this: also gy·ros.

gy·ro (jī'rō), *n., pl.* -ros, short for: 1. gyrocompass. 2. gyroscope.

gy·ro·com·pass (jī'rō-kum-pås), *n.* a compass operated by a gyroscope whose axis points to the geographic north pole and is uninfluenced by the earth's magnetism.

gy·ro·scope (-skōp), *n.* a wheel or disk mounted in a ring, so that it can turn freely: when spun rapidly, the wheel keeps its original plane of rotation.

gy·ro·stat (-stat), *n.* a gyroscope set in a case, used for demonstrating the dynamics of rotating bodies.

gyve (jīv), *n.* [Archaic or Poetic], a fetter, especially for the leg: usually used in the plural: *v.t.* gyved, gyv'ing, [Archaic or Poetic], to fetter; shackle.

ŏ in drag*o*n, ōō in cr*u*de, oo in w*oo*l, u in c*u*p, ū in c*u*re, ū in t*u*rn, ŭ in foc*u*s, oi in b*o*y, ou in h*o*use, th in *th*in, *th* in shea*th*e, g in *g*et, j in *j*oy, y in *y*et.

H

H, h (āch), *n., pl.* **H's, h's,** 1. the eighth letter of the English alphabet. 2. the sound of this letter, as in *have*: an initial *h* is sometimes silent, as in *honor*. 3. a type or impression of *H* or *h*.

H (āch), *adj.* shaped like *H*: *n*. 1. an object shaped like *H*. 2. [Slang], heroin.

ha (hä), *interj.* an expression of wonder, joy, amusement, triumph, etc.

Ha·bak·kuk (hab'ā-kuk), *n.* a book of the Bible.

ha·be·as cor·pus (hā'bi-ás kôr'pŭs), [Latin, you have the body], a writ to produce a prisoner at a stated time and place to determine the legality of his detention.

hab·er·dash·er (hab'ēr-dash-ēr), *n.* 1. a dealer in men's furnishings, such as neckties, shirts, etc. 2. in England, a dealer in small wares, as ribbons, laces, tapes, needles, etc.

hab·er·dash·er·y (-i), *n., pl.* **-er·ies,** 1. the wares sold by a haberdasher. 2. a haberdasher's shop.

hab·er·geon (hab'ēr-jŏn), *n.* a coat of mail covering the neck and breast.

ha·bil·i·ments (hä-bil'ĭ-mĕnts), *n.pl.* 1. dress; attire. 2. equipment; furnishings.

ha·bil·i·tate (-tāt), *v.t.* **-tat·ed, -tat·ing,** 1. to clothe. 2. to train (the handicapped). —**ha·bil·i·ta'tion,** *n.* —**ha·bil'i·ta·tive,** *adj.*

hab·it (hab'ĭt), *n.* 1. originally, dress. 2. a woman's riding costume. 3. the distinctive dress worn by members of a religious order. 4. an ordinary course of conduct. 5. a general condition or tendency. 6. an established custom or pattern that has become automatic. 7. an addiction, as to narcotics.

hab·it·a·ble (-ă-bl), *adj.* fit to be dwelt in. —**hab·it·a·bil'i·ty,** *n.* —**hab'it·a·bly,** *adv.*

hab·it·ant (-ănt), *n.* 1. a dweller; permanent resident. 2. a farmer of French descent in Canada and Louisiana.

hab·i·tat (-tat), *n.* the natural locality of animals, plants, etc. in their wild state; the geographical range of any animal.

hab·i·ta·tion (hab-i-tā'shŭn), *n.* 1. the act of inhabiting. 2. a residence or place of abode. 3. a settlement.

hab·it-form·ing (hab'it-fôr'ming), *adj.* that brings about or causes an addiction: said especially of narcotic drugs.

ha·bit·u·al (hä-bich'oo-wăl), *adj.* 1. formed or acquired by habit; customary. 2. steady; inveterate. 3. usual. —**ha·bit'u·al·ly,** *adv.*

ha·bit·u·ate (-āt), *v.t.* **-at·ed, -at·ing,** to make familiar by use or custom; familiarize.

hab·i·tude (hab'ĭ-tōōd), *n.* habit; customary manner or mode.

ha·bit·u·e (hä-bich'oo-wā), *n.* one who frequents a place or places.

ha·ci·en·da (hä-si·en'dä, has·i-), *n.* in Spanish America, 1. a large plantation, estate, or ranch. 2. the main house on such an estate.

hack (hak), *v.t.* 1. to cut or chop (something) irregularly. 2. to notch or trim in this way. 3. to injure by cutting. 4. to break up (clods of earth). 5. to let out (a horse) for hire: *v.i.* 1. to cut or chop irregularly. 2. [Informal], to drive a taxicab. 3. to cough harshly: *n.* 1. a notch or irregular cut. 2. an implement for breaking up earth. 3. a harsh cough. 4. a horse let out for hire. 5. a carriage let out for hire; hackney. 6. [Informal], *a)* a taxicab. *b)* the driver of a taxicab. 7. a literary drudge; a writer hired to do routine work: *adj.* done by a hack.

hack·a·more (hak'ă-môr), *n.* a halter of rawhide or rope, used for breaking horses in the western U.S.

hack·ber·ry (hak'ber-i), *n., pl.* **-ries,** a large North American tree, with an edible fruit somewhat resembling a cherry.

hack·but (hak'but), *n.* an old type of hand firearm.

hack·ing (hak'ing), *adj.* irritating and wearing: said of a cough.

hack·le (hak'l), *v.t.* **-led, -ling,** 1. to dress or comb, as flax or hemp. 2. to mangle in cutting: *n.* 1. an implement with sharp spikes for separating fibers of flax or hemp. 2. a cock's feather, used in angling. 3. *pl.* the bristly hairs on the neck of a dog which become erect when the animal is excited or angry.

hack·man (hak'măn), *n., pl.* **-men,** the driver of a hack or carriage for hire.

hack·ma·tack (hak'mä-tak), *n.* 1. same as tamarack. 2. the balsam poplar of the willow family. 3. wood from either of these trees.

hack·ney (hak'ni), *n., pl.* **-neys,** 1. a horse used for ordinary riding or driving. 2. a carriage for hire.

hack·neyed ('nēd), *adj.* trite and commonplace because of overuse; banal.

hack·saw (hak'sô), *n.* a fine-toothed saw for cutting metal, with a narrow blade held in a frame: also **hack saw.**

had (had), past tense and past participle of **have.**

had·dock (had'ŏk), *n., pl.* **-dock, -docks,** a food fish of the Atlantic, related to the cod.

Ha·des (hā'dēz), *n.* 1. in *Greek Mythology,* the abode of the dead; the underworld. 2. [often **h-**], [Informal], hell.

hadj (haj), *n.* same as **hajj.**

hadj·i (ʹī), *n.* same as **haji.**

had·n't (had'nt), had not.

hae·mo-, same as **hemo-.**

haf·ni·um (haf'ni·ŭm), *n.* a metallic chemical element found in zirconium ores.

haft (haft), *n.* a handle or hilt of a knife or tool: *v.t.* to furnish with a haft or handle.

hag (hag), *n.* 1. a witch. 2. an ugly old woman, especially one that is malicious. 3. same as **hagfish.** —**hag'gish,** *adj.*

---

a in cap, ā in cane, ä in father, â in abet, e in met, ē in be, ẽ in baker, ẽ in regent, i in pit, ī in fine, i in manifest, o in hot, ô in horse, ō in bone,

hag·fish (hag'fĭsh), n., pl. **-fish, -fish·es**, a small, eellike, parasitic fish found in salt water, having a round, sucking mouth and horny teeth, with which it bores into other fish.

Hag·ga·i (hag'ē·ī, hag'ī), n. a book of the Bible.

hag·gard (hag'ērd), adj. worn and anxious in appearance; lean and hollow-eyed. —**hag'gard·ly**, adv. —**hag'gard·ness**, n.

hag·gis (hag'ĭs), n. a Scottish dish made of the heart, liver, etc. of a calf or sheep, minced and mixed with suet, oatmeal, seasonings, etc. and boiled in the stomach of the animal.

hag·gle (hag'l), v.t. **-gled, -gling**, to hack; cut crudely: v.i. to dispute or argue over prices, terms, etc.: n. the act of haggling. —**hag'gler**, n.

hag·i·oc·ra·cy (hag·i·ok'rǎ·si, hā·ji·), n., pl. **-cies**, government by ecclesiastics; theocracy.

Hag·i·og·ra·pha (-og'rǎ·fǎ), n.pl. the third division of the Jewish Scriptures, those books not in the Law or the Prophets.

hag·i·og·ra·phy (-og'rǎ·fi), n., pl. **-phies**, 1. a biography of a saint or other writing about the lives and works of saints. 2. the study of the lives of saints.

hag·i·ol·a·try (-ol'ǎ·tri), n. worship of or reverence for saints. —**hag·i·ol'a·ter**, n.

hah (hä), interj. same as ha.

haik (hīk, hāk), n. an outer woolen or cotton garment, often with colored stripes, worn by Arabs.

hail (hāl), n. 1. frozen raindrops; small, rounded pieces of ice that fall especially during thunderstorms. 2. a shower or falling of hail. 3. a shower of anything, as a hail of arrows. 4. a call or salutation. 5. the distance that a shout can be heard: v.t. 1. to shower, pour, throw, etc. hard, like hail. 2. to call to or salute. 3. to greet with cheers: v.i. to pour down hail: interj. an expression of approval, acclaim, tribute, etc. —**hail'er**, n.

hail·stone (hāl'stōn), n. a pellet of hail.

hail·storm (hāl'stôrm), n. a storm in which hail falls.

hair (her), n. 1. any of the fine, threadlike outgrowths from the skin of a mammal. 2. a covering or mass of these, as on the head of a human. 3. an extremely small margin, measure, etc. 4. a minute, hairlike filament on the surface of a plant. —**hair'less**, adj. —**hair'like**, adj.

hair·ball (her'bôl), n. a ball of hair often forming in the stomach of a cat or other animal that licks its coat.

hair·breadth (her'bredth), n. an extremely small space or distance: adj. very narrow. Also **hairs'breadth**, **hair's'-breadth**.

hair·cloth (her'clôth), n. cloth woven from horsehair, etc., used mainly for upholstery.

hair·cut (her'kut), n. 1. the act or process of cutting the hair. 2. the style in which the hair is cut.

hair·dress·ing (her'dres·ing), n. 1. the act, process, or vocation of cutting, curling, styling, etc. women's hair. 2. an ointment or other preparation for the hair. —**hair'dress·er**, n.

hair·line (her'lĭn), n. 1. a very thin line or stripe. 2. a very small distance or degree of difference. 3. the edge of hair above the forehead. 4. a very thin stroke on a printing type.

hair·piece (her'pēs), n. a wig or toupee.

hair·pin (her'pĭn), n. a U-shaped pin used to keep the hair in place: adj. shaped like a hairpin, as a hairpin curve.

hair-rais·ing (her'rā·zing), adj. [Informal], terrifying; thrilling; shocking. —**hair'-rais·er**, n.

hair shirt, a rough shirt of haircloth, worn by religious ascetics and penitents for self-punishment.

hair-split·ting (her'split·ing), adj. & n. making oversubtle or very minute distinctions; quibbling; niggling. —**hair'split·ter**, n.

hair·spring (her'spring), n. a very fine, hairlike spring to regulate the balance wheel of a watch.

hair-trig·ger (her'trig·ēr), adj. operated or started off by the slightest touch.

hair trigger, a trigger so delicately adjusted that the slightest touch fires the firearm.

hair·y (her'i), adj. **hair'i·er, hair'i·est**, 1. covered with hair. 2. resembling hair. 3. [Slang], vexing; harrowing. —**hair'i·ness**, n.

hajj (haj), n. the pilgrimage to Mecca that every Moslem is expected to make at least once in his lifetime.

haj·ji, haj·i (haj'i), n. a Moslem who has made a pilgrimage to Mecca.

hake (hāk), n., pl. **hake, hakes**, any of several edible sea fishes related to the cod.

ha·la·tion (hā·lā'shŭn, ha·-), n. an unwanted radiation or halo, as around a light, in a photograph.

hal·berd (hal'bērd), n. a weapon of the 15th and 16th centuries consisting of a long staff to which an ax was affixed with a spearlike point.

hal·cy·on (hal'si·ŏn), adj. peaceful, happy, calm, etc., especially in the phrase halcyon days, the peaceful days of an earlier time.

hale (hāl), adj. **hal'er, hal'est**, healthy and hearty: v.t. **haled, hal'ing**, to constrain (a person) to go. —**hal'er**, n.

half (haf), n., pl. **halves** (havz), 1. one of two equal parts. 2. either of the two equal periods of certain games: adj. 1. being a half. 2. partial: adv. 1. to the extent of a half. 2. [Informal], partly.

half-and-half (haf'n-haf'), n. 1. a mixture of equal parts milk and cream. 2. [British], a mixture of equal parts porter and ale, beer and stout, etc.

half·back (haf'bak), n. either of two players in football back of the line of scrimmage, with the quarterback and fullback.

half-blood (haf'blud), n. 1. one whose parents are of different races. 2. a person related to another through one parent only.

half boot, a boot extending about halfway to the knee.

half-breed (haf'brēd), n. a person whose parents are of different races, especially American Indian and white.

half brother, a brother through one parent only.

half-caste (haf'kast), n. a person whose parents

are of different races, especially as from Europe and Asia.

half dollar, a coin of the U.S. and Canada equal to fifty cents.

half-heart-ed ('har'tid), *adj.* spiritless; lacking determination, enthusiasm, etc. —**half'-heart'ed-ly**, *adv.*

half hitch, a knot made by passing the end of the rope around the rope and then through the loop thus made.

half-life ('lif), *n.* the length of time required for half of the atoms in a given radioactive substance to disintegrate: also **half life**.

half-mast ('mast), *n.* the position of a flag halfway down its staff, as a sign of mourning or as a signal of distress.

half moon, the phase of the moon when only half its disk is illuminated.

half nel-son (nel'sn), a hold in wrestling in which one arm is placed under the opponent's arm from behind with the hand pressed against the back of his neck.

half note, a musical note having half the duration of a whole note.

half-pen-ny (hā'pē-ni, hap'ni), *n., pl.* **-pence** (hā'pēns), **-pen-nies**, a British coin equal to half a penny: no longer coined.

half sister, a sister through one parent only.

half slip, a woman's slip without a top.

half sole, the part of the sole of a shoe or boot from the toe to the arch.

half-tone ('tōn), *n.* an illustration made by photographing an object through a fine screen, so that the lights and shadows appear as very minute dots.

half-track ('trak), *n.* an armored vehicle, truck, etc. with continuous treads at the rear, instead of wheels.

half-way ('wā), *adj.* 1. equally distant between two points. 2. incomplete: *adv.* 1. half the distance. 2. partially.

half-wit ('wit), *n.* a foolish person; blockhead; dolt. —**half'wit'ted**, *adj.*

hal-i-but (hal'i-bǔt), *n., pl.* **-but, -buts**, a large, edible flatfish of northern seas.

hal-i-to-sis (hal-i-tō'sis), *n.* bad breath.

hall (hôl), *n.* 1. a large room for entertainments, exhibits, etc. 2. [sometimes H-], a building with public offices or for transacting business, etc. 3. an entrance room; foyer, vestibule, or lobby. 4. a manor house. 5. a college dormitory, eating center, etc. 6. a passageway or corridor, onto which rooms open.

hal-le-lu-jah, hal-le-lu-iah (hal-ē-lōō'yä), *interj.* praise (ye) the Lord! *n.* a song or hymn of praise to God.

hall-mark (hôl'märk), *n.* 1. the official mark of the Goldsmiths' Hall in London and other British assay offices, attesting the genuineness of gold and silver articles. 2. any mark or proof of genuineness.

hal-loo (hā-lōō'), *interj. & n.* a loud call or shout to call attention or to urge on hounds in hunting: *v.i. & v.t.* **-looed', -loo'ing**, to call out or shout.

hal-low (hal'ō), *v.t.* 1. to consecrate; devote to sacred purposes. 2. to revere; regard as holy. —**hal'lowed**, *adj.*

Hal-low-een, Hal-low-e'en (hal-ō-wēn', häl-), *n.*

the evening of October 31, the eve of All Saints' Day, or Allhallows.

hal-lu-ci-nate (hā-lōō'si-nāt), *v.i. & v.t.* **-nat-ed, -nat-ing**, to have or cause to have hallucinations.

hal-lu-ci-na-tion (hā-lōō-si-nā'shǔn), *n.* 1. the perception of something that has no reality outside the mind: an occurrence in certain mental disorders. 2. the thing, sound, etc. that seems to have been perceived. —**hal-lu'ci-na-to-ry** (-nā-tôr-i), **hal-lu'ci-na-tive**, *adj.*

hal-lu-ci-no-gen (hā-lōō'si-nō-jen, hal-yoo-sin'ō-jen), *n.* a drug or other substance that produces hallucinations. —**hal-lu-ci-no-gen'ic**, *adj.*

hall-way (hôl'wä), *n.* a corridor; hall.

ha-lo (hā'lō), *n., pl.* **-los, -loes**, 1. a circle of light, as around the sun or moon, caused by refraction. 2. a circle of light around the head of a saint, etc. in pictures; aureole. 3. a quality of glory, majesty, etc. surrounding an idealized person or thing.

hal-o-gen (hal'ō-jēn), *n.* any of the very active chemical elements, fluorine, chlorine, bromine, astatine, and iodine.

halt (hôlt), *n.* 1. a stop, especially a temporary stop, as in marching. 2. those who are lame (with *the*): *adj.* crippled or lame: *v.i.* 1. [Archaic], to be lame; limp. 2. to be dubious. 3. to hesitate. 4. to stop, as in marching.

hal-ter (hôl'tēr), *n.* 1. a rope for hanging people. 2. a rope, strap, etc. for leading or holding a horse. 3. a woman's garment worn above the waist, tied behind the neck and across the back, leaving the back and arms bare.

halve (hav), *v.t.* **halved, halv'ing**, 1. to divide into two equal parts. 2. to share equally (*with* someone). 3. to reduce to half. 4. in *Golf*, to play (a hole or match) in the same number of strokes as an opponent.

halves (havz), *n.* plural of **half**.

hal-yard (hal'yērd), *n.* a rope or tackle for hoisting a sail, flag, etc.

ham (ham), *n.* 1. the back of the thigh. 2. the upper part of the hind leg of a hog, smoked, salted, etc. 3. [Informal], an amateur radio operator. 4. [Slang], an actor or performer who overacts. —**ham'my**, *adj.* **-mi-er, -mi-est**.

ham-a-dry-ad (ham-á-drī'ǎd), *n.* 1. [also H-], in *Greek Mythology*, a wood nymph who lived in a tree and died when the tree did. 2. same as **king cobra**. 3. a baboon of Arabia and northern Africa.

ha-mal (hä-mäl', -môl'), *n.* a porter in the Middle East: also **ha-maul** (-môl').

ham-burg-er (ham'bûr-gēr), *n.* 1. ground beef. 2. a sandwich made of a cooked patty of such meat, usually in a round bun. Also **ham'burg**.

hame (hām), *n.* either of the two curved bars on a horse's collar to which the traces are fastened.

ham-let (ham'lit), *n.* a very small village.

ham-mer (ham'ēr), *n.* 1. a tool with a handle and a metal head for driving nails, beating metals, etc. 2. something resembling this tool in use or form. 3. the part of a gun that strikes the firing pin. 4. a mallet or gavel. 5. a bone of the inner ear: *v.t. & v.i.* 1. to hit with, or as with, a hammer, especially repeatedly. 2. to shape, force, etc. as with a hammer.

ham·mer·head (-hed), *n.* 1. any one of several sharks with a head somewhat resembling a double-headed hammer. 2. an African bat. 3. a sea fish of the sucker family.

ham·mer·toe (-tō), *n.* a toe deformed so that its first joint bends downward.

ham·mock (ham'ŏk), *n.* 1. a swinging bed, usually of network or canvas. 2. in the southern U.S., a raised tract of fertile land with trees growing on it.

ham·per (ham'pẽr), *n.* 1. a large basket, originally of wickerwork, usually with a cover. 2. the rigging of a ship: *v.t.* to impede; hinder; hold back.

ham·ster (ham'stẽr), *n.* a ratlike animal from Europe or Asia, with cheek pouches.

ham·string (ham'string), *v.t.* -**strung**, -**string·ing**, 1. to cripple by cutting the tendon at the back of the knee. 2. to make more or less powerless: *n.* the tendon at the back of the knee.

han·a·per (han'ā-pẽr), *n.* a small wicker receptacle formerly used to hold official documents.

hand (hand), *n.* 1. the divided part of the arm below the wrist, used for grasping. 2. something resembling a hand in appearance or use, as a pointer on a clock. 3. a unit of measure equal to four inches, used in measuring horses. 4. dexterity in skill or performance. 5. a direction or side. 6. possession. 7. style of writing. 8. a worker who labors with his hands. 9. a sailor. 10. cards held in a player's hand at one time. 11. a round of play in a card game. 12. a promise to marry. 13. authority. 14. source. 15. agency. 16. manner of doing something. 17. help. 18. applause: *v.t.* 1. to give or transmit as with the hand. 2. to help or lead with the hand: *adj.* 1. of or used by the hand or hands. 2. made by hand.

hand-bag (bag), *n.* a woman's purse.

hand-ball (bŏl), *n.* a game in which two or more players bat a small rubber ball against the wall with the hand.

hand-bar·row (bar-ō), *n.* a flat frame with handles at each end, by which it is carried by two people.

hand-bill (bil), *n.* a small, printed notice for distribution by hand.

hand-book (book), *n.* 1. a small reference book; manual. 2. a bookmaker's betting list. 3. same as guidebook.

hand-car (kär), *n.* a small, four-wheeled car, originally propelled by hand, used by workers on a railroad.

hand-cart (kärt), *n.* a small cart, often with two wheels, pulled or pushed by hand.

hand-cuff (kuf), *n.* one of a pair of connected metal rings used to fetter a prisoner's wrists; shackle: usually used in the plural: *v.t.* to put handcuffs on; manacle.

hand-fast·ing (fas'ting), *n.* [Archaic], a betrothal or form of trial marriage signified by joining hands.

hand·ful (fool), *n., pl.* -**fuls**, 1. as much as or as many as a hand will hold. 2. a small amount or number. 3. [Informal], a person or thing hard to control.

hand grenade, a small grenade to be thrown by hand, exploded by impact or by a fuse.

hand-gun (gun), *n.* a firearm that is held and fired by one hand, as a revolver.

hand-i-cap (han'di-kap), *n.* 1. difficulties imposed upon or advantages granted to contestants in a race or other competition to equalize their chances of winning. 2. a hindrance; disability: *v.t.* -**capped**, -**cap·ping**, 1. to give a handicap to (contestants). 2. to hinder.

hand-i-cap·per (-ẽr), *n.* 1. an official who assigns handicaps in a competition. 2. one who tries to predict winners in horse races.

hand-i-craft (han'di-kraft), *n.* 1. skill in working with the hands. 2. an art or trade requiring manual dexterity. —**hand'i-crafts-man** (-krafts-mǎn), *n., pl.* -**men**.

hand-i-work (-wũrk), *n.* 1. work done by the hands; handwork. 2. work done personally.

hand-ker-chief (hang'kẽr-chif), *n.* a small cloth for wiping the face, nose, etc.

han·dle (han'dl), *n.* 1. that part of a tool, utensil, etc. that is held or grasped by the hand. 2. something resembling a handle in appearance or use: *v.t.* -**dled**, -**dling**, 1. to grasp, lift, operate, etc. with the hand. 2. to manage. 3. to act toward or treat. 4. to sell or deal in: *v.i.* to react in a specified way to being handled. —**han'dler**, *n.*

han·dle-bar (-bär), *n.* a metal bar, usually curved, with a handle on each end, for steering a bicycle, etc.: often used in the plural.

hand-made (hand'mād'), *adj.* made by hand rather than by machine.

hand-maid·en (mād-n), *n.* [Archaic], a female servant or attendant: also **hand'maid**.

hand-out (out), *n.* 1. food, money, etc. given as to a beggar. 2. a news release, as from a government agency. 3. a publicity or advertising leaflet.

hand-pick (pik), *v.t.* 1. to pick by hand, as fruits and vegetables. 2. to select with special care. —**hand'picked**, *adj.*

hand-rail (rāl), *n.* a rail serving as a support or guard along the side of a stairway, balcony, etc.

hand-sel (han'sl, hant'sl), *n.* 1. a gift for good luck, as at the new year or at the opening of a new business. 2. the first experience or use of something, taken as a foretaste of what will follow: *v.t.* -**seled** or -**selled**, -**sel·ing**, -**sel·ling**, 1. to give a handsel to. 2. to use or do for the first time.

hand-shake (shāk), *n.* a clasping of each other's hand, as in greeting or to signify an agreement, etc.

hand-some (han'sŏm), *adj.* 1. good-looking; pleasing to look at: said especially of personal appearance that is manly rather than delicate. 2. well-formed; attractive, as a *handsome* chair. 3. liberal; generous. 4. considerable; impressive. —**hand'some-ly**, *adv.* —**hand'some-ness**, *n.*

hand-spring (hand'spring), *n.* a feat of acrobatics in which the performer turns over completely in midair.

hand-to-hand (han'tŏ-hand'), *adj.* at close quarters: said of fighting.

hand-to-mouth (han'tŏ-mouth'), *adj.* spending or consuming all that is obtained.

hand-work ('wûrk), *n.* work done by hand rather than by machine.

hand-writ-ing ('rīt-ing), *n.* 1. writing done by hand, as with a pen or pencil. 2. a style of writing; penmanship. —**hand'writ-ten**, *adj.*

hand-y ('i), *adj.* **hand'i-er, hand'i-est,** 1. dexterous; skillful. 2. convenient; close at hand. 3. manageable. 4. useful; that saves time or work. —**hand'i-ly,** *adv.* —**hand'i-ness,** *n.*

hand-y-man (-man), *n., pl.* **-men,** a man hired to do odd jobs.

hang (hang), *v.t.* **hung, hang'ing,** 1. to suspend; fasten from above with no support from below. 2. to fasten (a door, etc.) to something so as to be movable. 3. *p.t.* **hanged,** *a)* to suspend by the neck from a rope, etc. until dead. *b)* to execute in this fashion. 4. to let (the head) droop. 5. to display, as works of art. 6. to attach or fasten. 7. to ornament or cover with (things that hang): *v.i.* 1. to be suspended. 2. *p.t.* **hanged,** to die by hanging. 3. to bend forward; droop. 4. to float or hover in the air. 5. to swing freely; dangle. 6. to be in a deadlock, as a jury. 7. to hesitate; be doubtful: *n.* the manner in which a thing hangs.

hang-ar (hang'ẽr), *n.* a shelter or repair shed for aircraft.

hang-dog (hang'dôg), *adj.* abject; guilty.

hang-er (hang'ẽr), *n.* 1. a frame of wire, wood, or plastic on which to hang clothes. 2. a part of a thing by which it is hung.

hang gliding, the sport of gliding through the air while hanging suspended by a harness from a large type of kite (**hang glider**).

hang-ing ('ing), *adj.* 1. suspended or dangling. 2. involving a death penalty 3. unsettled: *n.* 1. an execution by hanging. 2. something hung on a wall.

hang-man ('man), *n., pl.* **-men,** an executioner who hangs people condemned to death.

hang-nail ('nāl), *n.* a small piece of skin hanging next to a fingernail.

hang-o-ver ('ō-vẽr), *n.* a feeling of sickness, especially nausea and headache, from drinking much alcoholic liquor.

hang-up ('up), *n.* [Slang], a psychological problem, as an obsession, etc.

hank (hangk), *n.* a quantity of coiled thread or yarn.

hank-er (hangk'ẽr), *v.i.* to desire eagerly; yearn (*for*). —**hank'er-ing,** *n.*

han-ky-pan-ky (hang-ki-pang'ki), *n.* [Informal], unethical dealings or immoral behavior.

han-som (han'sŏm), *n.* a two-wheeled, covered carriage for two passengers, with the driver's seat behind: also **hansom cab.**

Ha-nu-ka (khä'noo-kä, -kä; hä'-), *n.* an eight-day Jewish festival commemorating the rededication of the Temple: also spelled **Ha'nuk-kah, Ha'nuk-ka.**

hap (hap), *v.i.* **happed, hap'ping,** to happen; befall casually: *n.* chance; luck.

hap-haz-ard (hap-haz'ẽrd), *n.* mere chance; accident: *adv.* by chance; casually: *adj.* not planned; casual.

hap-less (hap'lis), *adj.* unfortunate; unlucky. —**hap'less-ly,** *adv.* —**hap'less-ness,** *n.*

hap-ly ('li), *adv.* [Archaic], by chance; perhaps.

hap-pen (hap'n), *v.i.* 1. to occur. 2. to occur by chance. 3. to chance.

hap-pi coat (hap'i), a short, light Japanese coat worn with a sash over regular clothes.

hap-pen-ing (-ing), *n.* an event; occurrence.

hap-pen-stance (-stans), *n.* [Informal], something that happens by chance.

hap-py (hap'i), *adj.* **-pi-er, -pi-est,** 1. enjoying pleasure or good; joyous; glad. 2. lucky; fortunate. 3. living in concord. 4. felicitous; apt. —**hap'pi-ly,** *adv.* —**hap'pi-ness,** *n.*

ha-ra-ki-ri (ha'rä-kir'i), *n.* ritual suicide by ripping open the bowels: it was practiced by Japanese nobility and officers to escape the disgrace of public execution.

ha-rangue (hä-rang'), *n.* a tirade; long, vehement, scolding speech, especially one given in public: *v.i. & v.t.* **-rangued', -rangu'ing,** to deliver or address by a harangue. —**ha-rangu'er,** *n.*

har-ass (hä-ras', har'ăs), *v.t.* 1. to annoy or vex; torment. 2. to tire out and annoy (an enemy) by incessant petty attacks. —**har-ass'ment,** *n.*

har-bin-ger (här'bin-jẽr), *n.* a herald; forerunner; indication of what is to come.

har-bor (här'bẽr), *n.* 1. a port; protected inlet for the anchorage of ships. 2. any place of refuge or safety: *v.t.* 1. to shelter or protect. 2. to keep in the mind. British spelling **har'bour.**

hard (härd), *adj.* 1. compact and solid; firm; not easily pierced or broken. 2. difficult to do, manage, understand, explain, etc. 3. cruel. 4. severe; harsh; stern. 4. inclement; stormy. 5. settled; definite. 6. diligent. 7. containing salts that hinder the lathering of soap. 8. containing much alcohol. 9. addictive: *adv.* 1. forcibly. 2. diligently. 3. close; near. 4. to the fullest extent. 5. soundly. 6. firmly. —**hard'ness,** *n.*

hard-back ('bak), *n.* a hardcover book.

hard-ball ('bôl), *n.* same as **baseball.**

hard-boiled ('boild), *adj.* 1. boiled until hard: said of an egg. 2. [Informal], tough and unyielding.

hard copy, a computer printout, often supplied along with or instead of a video screen display.

hard-core ('kôr'), *adj.* 1. of or denoting the hard, unyielding, central core or part of something. 2. absolute.

hard-cov-er ('kuv'ẽr), *adj.* designating any book bound in a stiff cover.

hard-en (här'dn), *v.t. & v.i.* to make or become hard or harder. —**hard'en-er,** *n.*

hard hat, 1. a rigid helmet worn for protection by construction workers, etc. 2. a person wearing such a hat.

hard-head-ed (hard'hed'id), *adj.* 1. willful; stubborn. 2. realistic and unsentimental. —hard'-head'ed·ly, adv.

hard·heart·ed ('här'tid), adj. pitiless; mean. —hard'heart'ed·ly, adv.

har·di·hood (här'di·hood), n. effrontery; boldness.

hard labor, labor imposed on a prisoner as part of a prison sentence.

hard·ly (härd'li), adv. 1. scarcely; barely. 2. probably not.

hard·nosed ('nōzd), adj. [Slang], 1. practical. 2. stubborn.

hard·pan ('pan), n. 1. a compact layer of hard soil nearly impenetrable to roots. 2. a solid foundation.

hard·shell (hard'shel), adj. 1. with a hard shell, as a crab not recently molted; also hard'-shelled. 2. [Informal], strait-laced; uncompromising, especially on religious matters.

hard·ship ('ship), n. something that is difficult to endure; suffering, want, etc.

hard·tack ('tak), n. a large, hard cracker or biscuit, traditionally part of army or navy rations.

hard·ware ('wer), n. 1. manufactured articles of metal, as tools, nails, etc. 2. military weapons, vehicles, and equipment used in combat. 3. the mechanical and electronic components of a computer. 4. control apparatus for spacecraft.

hard·wood ('wood), n. 1. any hard, heavy, compact timber of close texture. 2. any of the broad-leaved trees bearing this kind of wood.

har·dy (här'di), adj. -di·er, -di·est, 1. robust; strong. 2. bold; daring. 3. able to survive cold: said of plants: n. a square chisel used by blacksmiths. —har'di·ly, adv. —har'di·ness, n.

hardy hole, a hole in a blacksmith's anvil for the hardy.

hare (her), n. a mammal with long ears and short tail, larger than and related to the rabbit.

hare·bell ('bel), n. a delicate perennial plant with blue flowers shaped like bells.

hare·brained ('brānd), adj. inclined to be flighty, rash, and reckless.

hare·lip ('lip), n. a malformation of the upper lip, which is divided in the middle.

ha·rem (her'ĕm), n. 1. the section of a Moslem house in which the women and children live. 2. the women in a harem.

har·i·cot (her'i·kō), n. [French], 1. a stew of lamb and vegetables, highly seasoned. 2. [Chiefly British], the kidney bean.

hark (härk), v.i. to listen carefully: used chiefly in the imperative.

hark·en (här'kn), v.i. & v.t. same as hearken.

Har·le·quin (här'lĕ·kwin, -kin), n. 1. a performer in a pantomime, who wears a bright, parti-colored costume and a mask. 2. [h-], a buffoon: adj. [h-], 1. comic. 2. of many colors.

har·le·quin·ade (här·lĕ·kwi·nād'), n. 1. the part of a pantomime in which the Harlequin appears. 2. buffoonery.

har·lot (här'lŏt), n. a prostitute. —har'lot·ry (-ri), n.

harm (härm), n. injury; hurt; damage: v.t. to inflict hurt, damage, or injury upon.

harm·ful ('ful), adj. hurtful; injurious. —harm'-ful·ly, adv. —harm'ful·ness, n.

harm·less ('lis), adj. not harmful; causing no harm; mild. —harm'less·ly, adv. —harm'less-ness, n.

har·mon·ic (här·mon'ik), adj. in Music, of, pertaining to, or in harmony: n. same as overtone. —har·mon'i·cal·ly, adv.

har·mon·i·ca ('i·kà), n. 1. a musical instrument, the tones of which are produced by rubbing the rims of a number of graduated glasses with a wet finger. 2. a small wind instrument played by exhaling or inhaling across a series of metal reeds; mouth organ.

har·mon·ics ('iks), n. the science of musical sounds.

har·mo·ni·ous (här·mō'ni·ŭs), adj. 1. agreeably put together or proportioned. 2. conforming; in agreement; having like interests. 3. melodious; having pleasing musical tone combinations. —har·mo'ni·ous·ly, adv.

har·mo·ni·um (-ŭm), n. an instrument like a small organ, with a keyboard and played by forcing air by a bellows through a series of metallic reeds.

har·mo·nize (här'mŏ·nīz), v.t. -nized, -niz·ing, to make harmonious; bring into agreement: v.i. 1. to agree; be in harmony. 2. to sing in harmony. —har·mo·ni·za'tion, n. —har'mo-niz·er, n.

har·mo·ny (här'mŏ·ni), n., pl. -nies, 1. a combination of tones making up a chord that is pleasing to the ear. 2. a pleasing adaptation of parts in proportion, color, etc. 3. friendly relations; accord. 4. a literary work showing agreement or differences between parallel or similar passages, as of the Scriptures.

har·ness (här'nis), n. 1. originally, armor and other equipment for a knight and horse. 2. the working gear of a horse, etc., made up of leather straps and bands and metal pieces. 3. any arrangement of straps, etc. similar to this, as on a parachute: v.t. 1. to put a harness on. 2. to utilize.

harp (härp), n. a stringed instrument of triangular shape, played by plucking with the fingers: v.i. 1. to play a harp. 2. to dwell tediously and persistently (on or upon some subject).

harp·ings ('ings), n.pl. 1. wales on the bow of a ship, thicker than elsewhere, to withstand the forward plunging. 2. timbers for supporting a vessel during construction. Also harp'ins ('pinz).

har·poon (här·pōōn'), n. a long, barbed spear having a line attached to the shaft, for striking whales, sharks, etc.: v.t. to strike, kill, etc. with a harpoon. —har·poon'er, n.

harp·si·chord (härp'si·kôrd), n. a stringed instrument with a keyboard, whose strings are plucked rather than sounded with hammers.

Har·py (här'pi), n., pl. -pies, 1. in Greek Mythology, a filthy, rapacious monster, having a woman's head and body and the wings and claws of a bird. 2. [h-], a rapacious person.

har·que·bus (här'kwi-bŭs), *n.* a heavy, portable, medieval firearm.

har·ri·dan (har'i-dn), *n.* an ugly, ill-tempered old woman.

har·ri·er (har'i-ēr), *n.* 1. a variety of dog used for hunting hares. 2. a cross-country runner.

har·ri·er (har'i-ēr), *n.* 1. one who harries. 2. any one of several hawks that prey on small animals.

har·row (har'ō), *n.* an agricultural implement with spikes, teeth, or disks, for breaking up clods and smoothing plowed ground: *v.t.* 1. to drag a harrow over (ground). 2. to torment. —**har'row·ing,** *adj.*

har·ry (har'i), *v.t.* -**ried,** -**ry·ing,** 1. to plunder; lay waste to. 2. to harass or annoy.

harsh (härsh), *adj.* 1. disagreeably rough to the ear, touch, etc. 2. jarring to the mind. 3. severe; stern. —**harsh'ly,** *adv.* —**harsh'ness,** *n.*

hart (härt), *n.* the male of the red deer.

har·te·beest (här'tĕ-bēst, härt'bēst), *n., pl.* -**beests,** -**beest,** a large South African antelope.

harts·horn (härts'hôrn), *n.* 1. the antler of a hart. 2. same as sal volatile.

hart's-tongue ('tung), *n.* a fern with narrow, undivided fronds.

har·um-scar·um (her'ŭm-sker'ŭm), *adj.* giddy; reckless; unthinking: *n.* an irresponsible person or act.

ha·rus·pex (hă-rus'peks), *n., pl.* -**rus'pi·ces** ('pĭ-sēz), an ancient Roman diviner.

har·vest (här'vist), *n.* 1. a crop, as of grain, gathered in or ready to be gathered. 2. the season of such gathering. 3. the act of gathering a crop. 4. the result of any effort: *v.t. & v.i.* to gather in (a crop). —**har'vest·er,** *n.*

harvest home, 1. the completion of the harvest. 2. an English festival to celebrate this. 3. a song sung by harvesters finishing the harvest.

harvest moon, the full moon near the time of the autumnal equinox.

harvest mouse, any one of several small field mice.

has (haz), third person singular, present indicative, of have.

has-been (haz'bin), *n.* [Informal], a person or thing whose popularity or usefulness has waned.

hash (hash), *n.* 1. a dish of meat chopped and cooked with vegetables. 2. a mixture of things, materials, etc. used previously. 3. a muddle; jumble: *v.t.* 1. to chop into little pieces. 2. [Informal], to bungle.

hash·ish (hash'ish), *n.* a narcotic drug made from Indian hemp.

has·let (has'lit, haz'-), *n.* the lungs, heart, etc. of an animal, as a hog, used as food.

has·n't (haz'nt), has not.

hasp (hasp), *n.* a clasp folded over a staple and secured with a padlock or bolt.

has·sle (has'l), *n.* [Informal], a heated dispute: *v.i.* -**sled,** -**sling,** [Informal], to have such a dispute.

has·sock (has'ŏk), *n.* 1. a padded cushion that serves as a seat or footstool. 2. a thick tuft of grass.

hast (hast), archaic second person singular, present indicative, of have: used with *thou.*

haste (hāst), *n.* 1. quickness of movement; celerity. 2. urgency: *v.t. & v.i.* [Rare], same as hasten.

has·ten (hās'n), *v.t.* to cause to move rapidly: *v.i.* to move rapidly.

hast·y (hāst'i), *adj.* hast'i·er, hast'i·est, 1. done with speed; quick. 2. done too quickly; rash; precipitate. —**hast'i·ly,** *adv.* —**hast'i·ness,** *n.*

hasty pudding, 1. cornmeal mush. 2. [British], a mush of oatmeal or flour cooked in boiling water.

hat (hat), *n.* 1. a covering for the head, especially one with a crown and brim. 2. a cardinal's hat or the rank of cardinal.

hat·band ('band), *n.* a band of cloth worn around a hat just above the brim.

hatch (hach), *v.t.* 1. to produce (young) from eggs. 2. to originate (a plan, plot, etc.): *v.i.* to come out of an egg: *n.* 1. the act of hatching. 2. the young produced at a hatching; brood.

hatch (hach), *n.* 1. same as hatchway. 2. a cover for a hatchway. 3. a small opening in a floor or roof.

hatch (hach), *v.t.* to shade by marking or engraving with fine, crossed or parallel lines: *n.* any one of these lines.

hatch·er·y ('ēr-i), *n., pl.* -**er·ies,** a place where eggs are hatched, especially those of fish or poultry.

hatch·et (hach'it), *n.* a small, short-handled ax.

hatchet job, an unconscionable, vicious assault on the reputation or conduct of a person, institution, etc.

hatch·ing ('ing), *n.* 1. the hatch lines used in marking or engraving. 2. the process of making such lines.

hatch·ment ('mĕnt), *n.* in *Heraldry,* a panel bearing the escutcheon of a recently deceased person, exhibited for a time before his house.

hatch·way ('wā), *n.* 1. an opening in the deck of a ship for access below. 2. any similar opening in a floor or roof.

hate (hāt), *v.t.* hat'ed, hat'ing, 1. to dislike intensely; detest. 2. to wish to shun: *v.i.* to feel hatred: *n.* 1. an intense feeling of dislike. 2. a person or thing detested.

hate·ful ('ful), *adj.* causing hate. —**hate'ful·ly,** *adv.* —**hate'ful·ness,** *n.*

hath (hath), archaic third person singular, present indicative, of have.

ha·tred (hā'trid), *n.* abhorrence; hate.

hat·ter (hat'ēr), *n.* one who makes or sells men's hats.

hau·berk (hô'bĕrk), *n.* a coat of armor formed of steel rings.

haugh·ty (hôt'i), *adj.* -**ti·er,** -**ti·est,** arrogantly proud; contemptuous. —**haugh'ti·ly,** *adj.* —**haugh'ti·ness,** *n.*

haul (hôl), *v.t.* 1. to pull or draw with force; drag. 2. to transport by truck, cart, etc.: *v.i.* to change the course of a ship: *n.* 1. the act of hauling. 2. everything obtained, seized, etc. at a single time. 3. the distance over which something is hauled. 4. the load hauled.

haul·age ('ij), *n*. 1. the act of hauling. 2. the charge made for hauling.

haulm (hôm), *n*. the stems of grain, beans, etc., often used as bedding or for thatching.

haunch (hônch), *n*. 1. the hip, buttock, and upper thigh. 2. the loin and leg of an animal; joint of venison, mutton, etc. 3. the shoulder of an arch.

haunt (hônt), *n*. a place of accustomed resort: *v.t.* 1. to visit frequently or habitually. 2. to recur to constantly.

haunt·ed ('id), *adj*. supposedly inhabited by ghosts.

haunt·ing ('ing), *adj*. constantly recurring to the mind; unforgettable.

haut·boy (hō'boi, ō'·), *n*. former name for oboe.

hau·teur (hō-tûr'), *n*. haughtiness.

Ha·van·a (há-van'á), *n*. a cigar made of Cuban tobacco.

have (hav), *v.t.* had, hav'ing, 1. to possess; own. 2. to bear or beget. 3. to experience. 4. to feel obliged. 5. to obtain, get, seize, or consume. 6. to hold in mind. 7. to state. 8. to participate in. 9. to cause or compel. 10. to permit. 11. [Informal], to cheat; trick. 12. [Informal], to obtain the advantage of: *n*. a rich person or nation.

ha·ven (hā'vén), *n*. 1. a sheltered anchorage; harbor. 2. a place of safety; sanctuary.

have-not (hav'not), *n*. a nation or person with little or no resources.

have-n't (hav'nt), have not.

ha·ver (hā'vêr), *v.i.* [British], to talk foolishly.

ha·vers ('vērz), *interj*. [British], nonsense.

hav·er·sack (hav'êr-sak), *n*. a one-strapped canvas bag for carrying supplies, as by soldiers or hikers.

Ha·ver·sian canals (há-vûr'shŭn), small canals in the bones through which blood vessels pass: after C. *Havers*, English physician (1650?-1702).

hav·oc (hav'ŏk), *n*. wide and general destruction; devastation.

haw (hô), *n*. the hawthorn or its berry.

haw (hô), *interj. & n*. a command to an animal to turn left: *v.t. & v.i.* to turn to the left.

haw (hô), *v.i.* to hesitate in speaking: usually in *hem* and *haw*: *n*. a sounded pause in speaking.

haw·finch (hô'finch), *n*. the common grosbeak of Europe.

hawk (hôk), *n*. 1. any one of a group of birds of prey with a hooked beak and strong claws. 2. an advocate of war: *v.i.* to hunt with hawks trained for the field. —**hawk'ish**, *adj*.

hawk (hôk), *v.t. & v.i.* to cry or peddle (goods) in the streets.

hawk (hôk), *v.i. & v.t.* to clear the throat (of) noisily.

hawk (hôk), *n*. a small board with a handle on the underside, for holding mortar.

hawk·er (hôk'êr), *n*. a peddler.

hawk·er ('êr), *n*. a falconer.

hawk-eyed ('īd), *adj*. having very keen vision.

hawk·moth (hôk'môth), *n*. any one of various moths with a stout body, narrow wings, and a long sucking tube.

hawks·bill (hôks'bil), *n*. a tropical sea turtle

with a hawklike beak and horny plates yielding tortoise shell.

hawk·weed (hôk'wēd), *n*. any one of various plants having yellow or scarlet ray flowers.

hawse (hôz), *n*. that part of a ship's bow where the hawseholes are situated.

hawse-hole ('hōl), *n*. an opening in the bow of a ship through which a hawser or cable is passed.

haw·ser (hô'zêr), *n*. a thick rope or cable for mooring or towing a ship.

haw·thorn (hô'thôrn), *n*. a prickly shrub or small tree of the rose family, with pink or white flowers and red fruits called *haws*.

hay (hā), *n*. grass, clover, etc. cut and dried for fodder.

hay·cock ('käk), *n*. a conical pile of hay.

hay fever, an acute inflammation of the eyes and upper respiratory tract, characterized by sneezing, itching, headaches, etc. and caused by an allergic reaction to certain pollens.

hay·loft ('lôft), *n*. a loft for storing hay.

hay·mow ('mou), *n*. 1. same as hayloft. 2. a heap of hay in a barn.

hay·stack ('stak), *n*. a large stack of hay stored in the open.

hay·wire ('wīr), *n*. wire for baling hay or straw: *adj*. [Slang], 1. out of order. 2. crazy.

haz·ard (haz'êrd), *n*. 1. chance. 2. risk; peril. 3. an obstacle on a golf course: *v.i.* 1. to chance; risk. 2. to dare; venture.

haz·ard·ous (-ŭs), *adj*. 1. risky; perilous. 2. depending on chance.

haze (hāz), *n*. 1. a light vapor, smoke, dust, etc. in the atmosphere that limits visibility. 2. a vague or confused mental state: *v.i. & v.t.* hazed, haz'ing, to make or become hazy (often with *over*).

haze (hāz), *v.t.* hazed, haz'ing, to force to perform humiliating or painful tasks, as in initiation.

ha·zel (hā'zl), *n*. 1. a shrub or tree of the birch family, with edible nuts. 2. a reddish brown: *adj*. light reddish-brown.

ha·zel·nut (-nut), *n*. the edible nut of the hazel; filbert.

ha·zy (hā'zi), *adj*. -zi·er, -zi·est, 1. slightly misty or smoky. 2. obscure; vague. —**ha'zi·ness**, *n*.

H-bomb (āch'bom), *n*. same as **hydrogen bomb**.

he (hē), *pron., pl.* **they**, 1. the male personified; any male person or animal: sometimes used in combination, as *he*-goat. 2. an object traditionally regarded as of masculine gender. 3. anyone; the one: used indefinitely. 4. the masculine third personal singular pronoun: *n., pl.* **hes**, a male person or animal.

he (hā), *n*. the fifth letter of the Hebrew alphabet.

head (hed), *n*. 1. the uppermost part of the body containing the brain and the eyes, ears, nose, jaws, and mouth. 2. the seat of reason; mind. 3. the highest part of a thing; top. 4. a leader or ruler. 5. a position of honor or authority. 6. the foremost part of a thing; front. 7. the principal topic of a chapter, speech, book, etc. 8. the origin or source, as of a river. 9. froth, as on beer. 10. pressure, as from steam. 11. *pl.* **head**, each person or animal in a group. 12. the obverse side of a coin. 13. the part made for hitting, holding, etc. 14. the membrane on the end of a drum: *adj.* 1. principal or chief. 2. at the front or top. 3. coming from the front: *v.t.* 1. to direct; command. 2. to take the first place in. 3. to lead; precede. 4. to direct in a specified course: *v.i.* to set out; proceed.

head·ache ('āk), *n.* 1. a pain in the head. 2. [Informal], something that causes worry, irritation, etc.

head·band ('band), *n.* a band worn around the head.

head·board ('bôrd), *n.* a board or panel that forms the head of a bed.

head·cheese ('chēz), *n.* a jellied loaf of meat from the head and feet of a hog, chopped fine, seasoned, and boiled.

head cold, a common cold with congestion of the nasal passages.

head·dress ('dres), *n.* 1. a covering for the head. 2. a hairdo; coiffure.

head·ed ('id), *adj.* having a head: used in compounds, as *clear-headed.*

head·er ('ēr), *n.* 1. one that puts heads on an object. 2. a machine that removes the heads of grain and sends them to a receptacle. 3. [Informal], a headlong plunge or fall. 4. in *Masonry*, a brick or stone laid so its short face is to be seen in a wall.

head·first ('fûrst'), *adv.* 1. with the head preceding; headlong. 2. recklessly; rashly.

head·gear ('gir), *n.* a hat, cap, helmet, etc.

head·hunt·er ('hunt-ēr), *n.* 1. any member of certain primitive peoples who decapitate their enemies and preserve the heads as trophies. 2. [Slang], an individual or agency that recruits personnel having special skills. —**head'hunt·ing**, *n.*

head·ing ('ing), *n.* 1. something serving as the head, front, etc. 2. a word or phrase giving the title, subject, etc. of a letter, chapter, paragraph, etc. 3. the direction a ship or aircraft is following.

head·land ('länd), *n.* a promontory.

head·light ('līt), *n.* a reflecting lamp on the front of a vehicle.

head·line ('līn), *n.* the caption displayed conspicuously at the top of a newspaper page or article: *v.t.* -lined, -lin·ing, 1. to supply (an article) with a headline. 2. to give prominent billing to.

head·long ('lông), *adv.* same as headfirst: *adj.* 1. with the head preceding. 2. uncontrollably fast. 3. rash; impetuous.

head·mas·ter (hed'mas'tēr), *n.* the principal in certain private schools. —**head'mis'tress**, *n. fem.*

head·on ('on'), *adj. & adv.* with the head in front.

head·phone ('fōn), *n.* a receiver, as for a telephone or radio, held to the ear by a band over the head.

head·quar·ters ('kwôr-tērz), *n.pl.* 1. the executive offices of a commander, as in an army, police force, etc. 2. the center of authority in any organization.

head·rest ('rest), *n.* a support for the head.

head·room ('rōōm), *n.* space overhead in a doorway, tunnel, etc.

heads·man (hedz'măn), *n., pl.* -men ('mĕn), an executioner.

head start, an early start or other similar advantage.

head·stone ('stōn), *n.* a stone set at the head of a grave.

head·strong ('strông), *adj.* willful.

head·wa·ters ('wôt-ērz), *n.pl.* the tributaries at the beginning of a river.

head·way ('wā), *n.* 1. movement forward. 2. progress or achievement.

head wind, a wind blowing opposite to the course of a ship or aircraft.

head·y ('i). *adj.* **head'i·er**, **head'i·est**, 1. willful. 2. intoxicating.

heal (hēl), *v.t. & v.i.* 1. to make or become sound or healthy again. 2. to cure, as a disease. —**heal'er**, *n.*

health (helth), *n.* 1. freedom from bodily or mental pain, disorder, or disease; physical and mental soundness. 2. state of body or mind at a given time. 3. a wish for someone's health and success, as in a toast. 4. soundness, as of an organization.

health food, food thought to be very healthful, as food grown with natural fertilizers and free of chemical additives.

health·ful ('fûl), *adj.* 1. promoting good health. 2. [Rare], healthy. —**health'ful·ness**, *n.*

health·y (hel'thi), *adj.* **health'i·er**, **health'i·est**, 1. possessing good health. 2. exhibiting good health. 3. same as healthful. —**health'i·ness**, *n.*

heap (hēp), *n.* 1. a pile or collection of things jumbled together. 2. [Informal], a large quantity: *v.t.* 1. to form into a heap. 2. to supply in abundance. 3. to fill (a container, plate, etc.) to overflowing.

hear (hir), *v.t.* heard (hûrd), **hear'ing**, 1. to perceive (sounds) by the ear. 2. to listen to. 3. to conduct a legal hearing of (a trial, testimony, etc.). 4. to learn of by hearing: *v.i.* 1. to have the ability to perceive sounds. 2. to learn (*of* or *about*). —**hear'er**, *n.*

hear·ing ('ing), *n.* 1. the act of perceiving sounds. 2. the ability to hear. 3. a chance to be heard. 4. an appearance before a judge, referee, arbiter, etc. 5. same as ear-shot.

heark·en (här'kĕn), *v.i.* to listen attentively; pay heed: *v.t.* [Archaic], to hear; heed.

hear·say (hir'sā), *n.* rumor; gossip.

hearse (hûrs), *n.* a conveyance for transporting a corpse to church or grave.

heart (härt), *n.* 1. the hollow organ in vertebrates by whose muscular contraction and dilation the blood is circulated through the arteries. 2. the vital, inner, or chief part of anything. 3. the human heart thought of as the seat of emotions, affections, feelings, courage, strength, endurance, etc. 4. something shaped like a heart. 5. one of a suit of cards marked with red hearts. 6. *pl.* this suit.

heart·ache ('āk), *n.* sorrow; grief.

a in *cap*, ā in *cane*, ä in *father*, á in *abet*, e in *met*, ē in *be*, ē in *baker*, ė in *regent*, i in *pit*, ī in *fine*, i in *manifest*, o in *hot*, ô in *horse*, ō in *bone*,

heart-beat ('bēt), *n.* one complete contraction and dilation of the heart.

heart-break ('brāk), *n.* overwhelming grief. — **heart'bro-ken,** *adj.*

heart-burn ('bŭrn), *n.* a burning sensation in the esophagus, caused by an acid backflow from the stomach.

heart-ed ('id), *adj.* having a heart: used in compounds, as *good-hearted.*

heart-en ('n), *v.t.* to give courage to.

heart-felt ('felt), *adj.* sincere; earnest.

hearth (härth), *n.* 1. the floor of a fireplace, usually made of brick or stone. 2. the fireside. 3. the family circle; home.

heart-less (härt'lis), *adj.* 1. lacking enthusiasm. 2. cruel; pitiless. —**heart'less-ness,** *n.*

heart-rend-ing ('rend-ing), *adj.* causing great grief or anguish.

hearts-ease (härts'ēz), *n.* 1. peace of mind. 2. the wild pansy.

heart-sick (härt'sik), *adj.* extremely grieved; despondent: also **heart'sore** ('sôr).

heart-strings ('stringz), *n.pl.* the deepest feelings or affections.

heart-to-heart ('tô-härt), *adj.* intimate and frank.

heart-warm-ing ('wôr-ming), *adj.* such as to kindle sympathetic feelings; cheering.

heart-whole ('hōl), *adj.* 1. not in love. 2. sincere.

heart-wood ('wood), *n.* the hard, inactive wood at the center of a tree.

heart-y ('i), *adj.* **heart'i-er, heart'i-est,** 1. warm and open; very cordial. 2. unrestrained. 3. strong and vigorous. 4. nourishing and abundant: *n., pl.* **heart'ies,** [Archaic], a comrade; especially, a fellow sailor. —**heart'i-ly,** *adv.* —**heart'i-ness,** *n.*

heat (hēt), *n.* 1. a form of energy produced by the chaotic movement of molecules. 2. hotness or its recognition by the senses. 3. excessive hotness. 4. the warming of a house, room, etc. 5. the state of being hot. 6. sudden or intense emotion; ardor, vehemence, etc. 7. a period of sexual excitement in animals, especially females. 8. hot weather. 9. in *Sports,* a single course, round, trial, etc. 10. [Slang], intense pressure; coercion: *v.t. & v.i.* 1. to make or become hot or warm. 2. to make or become animated, inflamed, etc.

heat-ed ('id), *adj.* 1. hot. 2. intense; fervent; angry. —**heat'ed-ly,** *adv.*

heat-er ('ēr), *n.* an apparatus providing heat; stove, radiator, etc.

heath (hēth), *n.* 1. any one of various small shrubs with evergreen leaves and pink or purplish flowers. 2. an extensive tract of wasteland covered with such shrubs or like plants; moor.

hea-then (hē'thěn), *n., pl.* **-thens, -then,** 1. anyone not a Jew, Christian, or Moslem. 2. an irreligious person; pagan: *adj.* 1. pagan. 2. irreligious, unenlightened, etc. —**hea'then-ish,** *adj.* —**hea'then-ism,** *n.*

hea-then-ize (-īz), *v.t. & v.i.* **-ized, -iz-ing,** to make or become heathen.

heath-er (heth'ēr), *n.* a plant related to the heaths, with overlapping, scalelike leaves and purplish-pink flowers. 2. same as **heath** (sense 1).

heath-y (hē'thi), *adj.* of, pertaining to, or abounding with heath.

heat lightning, flashes of light unaccompanied by thunder.

heat-stroke ('strōk), *n.* a condition of high fever, headache, etc., caused by exposure to extreme heat.

heave (hēv), *v.t.* **heaved** or **hove, heav'ing,** 1. to lift up by great effort; hoist. 2. to cast; hurl. 3. to force from the breast, as a sigh. 4. in *nautical usage,* to pull or haul (a rope, cable, etc.): *v.i.* 1. to swell up. 2. to rise and fall alternately. 3. to vomit. 4. to pant; gasp. 5. in *nautical usage,* to pull (*on* or *at* a rope, cable, etc.): *n.* the act or effort of heaving.

heav-en (hev'n), *n.* 1. *usually pl.* the firmament; visible sky. 2. in *Theology,* [H-], *a)* the abode of God, his angels, and those blessed who have attained salvation; *b)* God. 3. any place or condition of bliss. —**heav'en-ly,** *adj.* —**heav'en-li-ness,** *n.*

heav-en-ward (-wĕrd), *adv. & adj.* toward heaven: also **heav'en-wards,** *adv.*

heav-y (hev'i), *adj.* **heav'i-er, heav'i-est,** 1. difficult to lift; ponderous. 2. hard to bear; grievous; oppressive. 3. hard to do; laborious. 4. larger in number, intensity, force, extent, etc. than usual. 5. serious; grave. 6. sorrowful. 7. dense; thick. 8. pungent. 9. difficult to digest. 10. employing massive facilities or equipment to produce materials, machinery, etc. needed by other industries: *adv.* in a heavy manner: *n., pl.* **heav'ies,** a villain or scoundrel in a story or play. — **heav'i-ly,** *adv.* —**heav'i-ness,** *n.*

heav-y-du-ty (-dōōt'i, -dūt'i), *adj.* built for hard use, strain, etc.

heav-y-hand-ed (-han'did), *adj.* 1. clumsy or blunt. 2. tyrannical.

heav-y-heart-ed (-härt'id), *adj.* sorrowful; depressed.

heav-y-set (-set'), *adj.* having a stocky, compact build.

heav-y-weight (-wāt), *n.* 1. a boxer, wrestler, etc. whose weight is 176 pounds or more.

heb-dom-a-dal (heb-däm'ä-dál), *adj.* weekly.

heb-e-tate (heb'ě-tāt), *v.t. & v.i.* to make or become dull or stupid.

heb-e-tude (-tōōd), *n.* dullness; sluggishness.

He-bra-ic (hi-brā'ik), *adj.* of or pertaining to the Hebrews, their language, culture, etc.

He-bra-ism (hē'bri-izm), *n.* 1. a Hebrew idiom. 2. Hebrew customs, attitudes, etc. —**He'bra-ist,** *n.*

He-brew (hē'brōō), *n.* 1. *a)* any member of an ancient Semitic people; *b)* a Jew. 2. the Semitic language of the ancient Hebrews. 3. its modern form, the language of Israel, a country at the eastern end of the Mediterranean Sea.

He-brews ('brōōz), *n.* a book of the New Testament.

Hec-a-te (hek'ä-ti), *n.* in *Greek Mythology,* a goddess of the moon, earth, and underworld.

hec-a-tomb (hek'ä-tōm, -tōōm), *n.* 1. in ancient

Greece, a sacrifice of 100 oxen. 2. any large sacrifice or slaughter.

heck (hek), *interj.* [Informal], a euphemism for **hell**.

heck·le (hek'l), *v.t.* **-led, -ling,** to badger (a speaker) with questions or jeers. —**heck'ler,** *n.*

hec·tare (hek'ter), *n.* a surface measure, equal to 10,000 square meters (2.471 acres).

hec·tic (hek'tik), *adj.* 1. feverish. 2. flushed. 3. confused; reckless; hasty.

hec·to·gram (hek'tȯ-gram), *n.* a measure of weight, equal to 100 grams (3.527 ounces).

hec·to·graph (-graf), *n.* a duplicating apparatus using a gelatin pad coated with glycerin for making many copies of written or typed matter.

hec·to·li·ter (-lēt-ĕr), *n.* a measure of volume, equal to 100 liters (26.418 gallons or 2.838 bushels).

hec·to·me·ter (-mēt-ĕr), *n.* a measure of length, equal to 100 meters (109.36 yards).

Hec·tor (hek'tĕr), *n.* in Homer's *Iliad,* a Trojan hero killed by Achilles: *v.t. & v.i.* [h-], to bully or bluster.

he'd (hēd), 1. he had. 2. he would.

hed·dle (hed'l), *n.* any one of a series of parallel wires in a loom, used to guide the warp threads.

he·der (khä'dĕr), *n., pl.* **ha·dar·im** (khä-dä'rēm), a Hebrew school for young children.

hedge (hej), *n.* 1. a fence of dense bushes or shrubs. 2. any barrier or boundary. 3. an act of hedging: *v.t.* **hedged, hedg'ing,** 1. to enclose with a hedge. 2. to obstruct or protect, as with a hedge. 3. to diminish the risk of loss (in a bet, a stock, etc.) by making an offsetting bet: *v.i.* to avoid taking a position by resort to noncommittal or misleading statements. —**hedg'er,** *n.*

hedge·hog ('hȯg), *n.* 1. any one of several Old World mammals covered on the back with spines. 2. the American porcupine.

hedge sparrow, a small reddish-brown European warbler with white-tipped wings.

he·don·ic (hē-don'ik), *adj.* 1. of or pertaining to pleasure. 2. [Rare], hedonistic.

he·don·ics ('iks), *n.* the branch of psychology dealing with painful and pleasurable sensations.

he·don·ism (hēd'n-izm), *n.* 1. the doctrine that pleasure is the chief end of life. 2. the willful pursuit of pleasure. —**he'don·ist,** *n.* —**he·do·nis'tic,** *adj.*

-he·dron (hē'drȯn), a combining form meaning *a figure* or *crystal with a certain number of surfaces.*

heed (hēd), *v.t. & v.i.* to pay attention (to): *n.* careful attention. —**heed'ful,** *adj.* —**heed'less,** *adj.* —**heed'less·ness,** *n.*

hee·haw (hē'hȯ), *v.i.* 1. to bray. 2. to laugh loudly: *n.* 1. the braying sound of a donkey. 2. a guffaw.

heel (hēl), *n.* 1. the hind part of the foot below the ankle. 2. the hind part of a boot, shoe, or stocking. 3. anything suggesting a heel in shape, position, purpose, etc. 4. [Informal], an unfeeling, contemptible person: *v.t.* 1. to furnish with a heel. 2. to follow closely: *v.i.* to follow at someone's heels.

heel (hēl), *v.i.* to lean to one side; list: *v.t.* to make (a ship) list.

heel·er (hē'lĕr), *n.* 1. one that heels. 2. [Informal], same as **ward heeler.**

heel·tap ('tap), *n.* 1. a small thickness of material used as a lift in a shoe heel. 2. a small quantity of liquor left in a drinking glass or bottle.

heft (heft), *n.* [Informal], 1. weight; heaviness. 2. influence; authority: *v.t.* [Informal], 1. to estimate weight by lifting. 2. to lift.

heft·y (hef'ti), *adj.* **heft'i·er, heft'i·est,** [Informal], 1. weighty; heavy. 2. bulky and powerful. —**heft'i·ness,** *n.*

he·gem·o·ny (hi-jem'ȯ-ni), *n.* leadership or superiority; especially, predominance of one state over others.

he·gi·ra (hi-jī'rä), *n.* 1. [often H-], the flight of Mohammed from Mecca to Medina in 622 A.D. 2. any flight, as for refuge or escape.

heif·er (hef'ĕr), *n.* a young cow that has not had a calf.

heigh·ho (hī'hō), *interj.* an expression of languor, indifference, ennui, excitement, etc.

height (hīt), *n.* 1. the highest point. 2. the amount of elevation above a level; altitude. 3. the highest state or degree; culmination. 4. *often pl.* an eminence; hill. 5. stature.

height·en ('n), *v.t. & v.i.* 1. to make or become high or higher. 2. to make or become greater in quality, degree, amount, etc.; intensify.

Heim·lich maneuver (hīm'lik), an emergency technique for dislodging an object stuck in the windpipe, using air forced out from the victim's lungs: after H.J. *Heimlich* (1920-), U.S. surgeon.

hei·nous (hā'nŭs), *adj.* extremely wicked; odiously evil. —**hei'nous·ness,** *n.*

heir (er), *n.* one who succeeds another in the possession of property, title, office, mental qualities, etc.

heir apparent, *pl.* **heirs apparent,** the heir whose right to succeed is indefeasible at law if he survives his ancestor.

heir·ess ('is), *n.* a female heir, especially to great wealth.

heir·loom ('lōōm), *n.* 1. any movable or personal chattel that descends to the heir by its connection with the estate. 2. any cherished possession handed on through succeeding generations.

heir presumptive, *pl.* **heirs presumptive,** an heir whose right can be barred by the birth of a relative nearer in succession.

heist (hīst), *n.* [Slang], a robbery: *v.t.* [Slang], to rob; steal.

held (held), past tense and past participle of **hold.**

Helen of Troy, in *Greek Legend,* the beautiful wife of Menelaus, king of Sparta: her elopement to Troy with Paris brought about the Trojan War.

he·li·an·thus (hē-li-an'thŭs), *n.* same as **sunflower.**

hel·i·cal (hel'i-kăl), *adj.* spiral-shaped.

hel·i·coid ('i-koid), *adj.* shaped like a flat coil, as the shell of a snail.

hel·i·cop·ter (hel'i-kop-tĕr), *n.* an aircraft lifted into the air by the reaction created by rotary blades revolving around an essentially vertical central axis.

he·li·o-, a combining form signifying *the sun, bright, brilliant.*

he·li·o·cen·tric (hē-li-ō-sen'trik), *adj.* having the sun as the center.

he·li·o·chrome (hē'li-ō-krōm), *n.* a photograph in natural colors.

he·li·o·gram (-gram), *n.* a message transmitted by heliograph.

he·li·o·graph (-graf), *n.* an apparatus for transmitting signals or messages by reflecting the sun's rays from a movable mirror: *v.t.* & *v.i.* to signal by heliograph. —**he·li·og'ra·phy** (-og'rà-fi), *n.*

he·li·o·gra·vure (hē-li-ō-grà-vyoor'), *n.* earlier term for photogravure.

he·li·o·la·try (-ol'à-tri), *n.* sun worship.

he·li·om·e·ter (-om'ē-tēr), *n.* an instrument for measuring small distances between celestial objects.

he·li·o·stat (hē'li-ō-stat), *n.* an instrument having a mirror that is moved by clockwork so that the sun's rays are constantly reflected in one direction.

he·li·o·ther·a·py (hē-li-ō-ther'à-pi), *n.* treatment of disease by exposure of the body to the sun's rays.

he·li·o·trope (hē'li-ō-trōp), *n.* 1. any one of several plants or shrubs with small white or purple flowers. 2. a type of heliograph used in surveying. 3. same as **bloodstone**. 4. reddish purple: *adj.* reddish-purple.

he·li·ot·ro·pism (hē-li-ot'rō-pizm), *n.* the tendency of certain plants or other organisms to move toward or away from sunlight.

hel·i·port (hel'i-pôrt), *n.* a place, as a field or roof, where helicopters take off or land.

he·li·um (hē'li-ùm), *n.* a light, inert, gaseous chemical element, found in various natural gases and used to inflate balloons, in low-temperature research, etc.

he·lix (hē'liks), *n., pl.* -**lix·es**, -**li·ces** (hel'i-sēz, hē'li-), 1. anything spiral in shape or structure. 2. a curve that coils around a cylinder or cone at a constant angle. 3. the rim of cartilage curved in around the external ear. 4. in *Architecture*, a volute on a Corinthian or Ionic capital.

hell (hel), *n.* 1. in the *Bible*, the abode of the dead where departed souls live; Sheol. 2. same as **Hades**. 3. [often H-], in *Christianity*, the dwelling place of the devil and evil spirits in which the wicked suffer eternal punishment after death. 4. any place or condition of extreme misery, torment, evil, etc.

he'll (hel), he will. 2. he shall.

Hel·las (hel'às), *n.* 1. ancient Greece. 2. the modern Greek name for Greece.

hell·bend·er (hel'ben-dēr), *n.* 1. a large, edible, water salamander of the eastern and central U.S. 2. [Slang], a drinking spree; orgy.

hell·cat ('kat), *n.* 1. a spiteful, shrewish, vindictive woman. 2. a witch; hag.

hel·le·bore (hel'ē-bôr), *n.* 1. any one of various old-world, perennial plants that open their buttercuplike flowers in earliest spring, or sometimes in the winter, and whose poisonous roots have been used as a cathartic. 2.

any one of various plants of North America and Europe whose rhizomes yield poisonous alkaloids formerly used in medicine and as an insecticide.

Hel·lene (hel'ēn), *n.* a Greek.

Hel·len·ic (hē-len'ik), *adj.* of, pertaining to, or characteristic of the language, history, art, or literature of the ancient Greeks; specifically, from the 8th century B.C. to the 4th century B.C.

Hel·len·ism (hel'ēn-izm), *n.* 1. a Greek idiom, custom, etc. 2. the spirit, civilization, culture, thought, and ideals of ancient Greece.

Hel·len·ist (-ist), *n.* 1. a person, especially one of Jewish extraction, who adopted the Greek language, customs, etc. during classical times. 2. a specialist in the language, literature, culture, etc. of ancient Greece. 3. any one of the Byzantine scholars instrumental in reviving classical Greek learning and culture in Europe at the time of the Renaissance.

hell·gram·mite (hel'grà-mīt), *n.* the large, flesh-eating, aquatic larva of a North American fly, often used as a bait in fishing.

hel·lion (hel'yùn), *n.* [Informal], a person who delights in causing trouble; a mischievous rascal.

hell·ish (hel'lish), *adj.* 1. of, pertaining to, or resembling hell. 2. fiendish. 3. [Informal], extremely disagreeable. —**hell'ish·ly**, *adv.* —**hell'ish·ness**, *n.*

hel·lo (he-lō', hel'ō), *n., pl.* -**los**, the call or greeting "hello": *interj.* an exclamation of greeting, reply, surprise, etc.

helm (helm), *n.* 1. the whole apparatus for steering a ship. 2. the wheel or tiller of a ship. 3. a position of control or guidance.

hel·met (hel'mēt), *n.* 1. a covering of hard material, often metal, designed to protect the head in warfare, certain sports, deep-sea diving, etc. 2. in *Botany*, the hood-shaped upper sepal or corolla in certain flowers.

hel·minth (hel'minth), *n.* a worm; especially, a worm parasitic in the intestines.

hel·min·thic (hel-min'thik), *adj.* 1. of or pertaining to helminths. 2. expelling or killing helminths: *n.* same as **vermifuge**.

hel·min·thol·o·gy (hel-min-thol'ō-ji), *n.* the branch of zoology having to do with the study of helminths.

helms·man (helmz'màn), *n., pl.* -**men** ('mèn), the man who steers a ship.

He·lot (hel'ōt, hē'lōt), *n.* 1. a member of the lowest class of serfs in ancient Sparta. 2. [h-], a slave or serf.

hel·ot·ism (-izm), *n.* the state of being a helot; serfdom or slavery.

hel·ot·ry (-ri), *n.* 1. helots as a class; serfs or slaves. 2. serfdom or slavery.

help (help), *v.t.* 1. to give assistance to; aid. 2. to succor or relieve. 3. to refrain from; avoid. 4. to prevent or rectify. 5. to wait on or serve in a store or at table. 6. to bring about improvement in; remedy; cure: *v.i.* to lend aid; be useful: *n.* 1. assistance; aid; support. 2. a remedy; relief. 3. that which helps. 4. succor. 5. a person who assists another. 6. a person, as a servant or farm worker, hired to assist. —**help'er**, *n.*

ö in drag*o*n, ōō in cr*u*de, oo in w*oo*l, u in c*u*p, ū in c*u*re, u̇ in t*u*rn, u̇ in f*o*cus, oi in b*oy*, ou in h*ou*se, th in *th*in, *t*h in shea*th*e, g in *g*et, j in *j*oy, y in *y*et.

help·ful ('fool), *adj.* rendering assistance; useful. —**help'ful·ly**, *adv.* —**help'ful·ness**, *n.*

help·ing ('ing), *n.* 1. the act of giving aid. 2. a portion of food for one person.

help·less ('lis), *adj.* 1. unable to help oneself; feeble. 2. lacking support or protection. 3. lacking power; ineffective. —**help'less·ly**, *adv.* —**help'less·ness**, *n.*

help·mate ('māt), *n.* a helpful companion; specifically, a wife or husband.

help·meet ('mēt), *n.* same as **helpmate.**

hel·ter-skel·ter (hel'tēr-skel'tēr), *adv.* in haste and disorder: *adj.* hurried and haphazard.

helve (helv), *n.* a handle of an ax, hammer, etc.

hem (hem), *n.* the border of a garment, curtain, etc. folded under and sewn down: *v.t.* **hemmed, hem'ming,** to fold under the edge of and sew down.

hem (hem), *interj. & n.* an ejaculatory sound made in clearing the throat: *v.i.* **hemmed, hem'ming,** 1. to produce this sound, as in seeking attention, giving warning, expressing doubt, etc. 2. to hesitate and grope for the proper word while speaking: usually used in the phrase **hem and haw.**

he·mal (hē'mäl), *adj.* 1. of or pertaining to blood or blood vessels. 2. of or pertaining to the side of the body containing the heart and chief blood vessels.

he·mat·ic (hi·mat'ik), *adj.* of, pertaining to, full of, or having the color of blood: *n.* a medicine for a blood disorder.

hem·a·tin (hem'ä·tin), *n.* a dark-brown or black pigment containing iron, resulting from the decomposition of hemoglobin.

hem·a·tite (hem'ä·tīt, hē'mä·), *n.* native ferric oxide, a brownish-red or black mineral that is an important ore of iron.

hem·a·tog·e·nous (hem·ä·toj'ē·nŭs), *adj.* 1. producing blood. 2. spread by the blood.

he·ma·tol·o·gy (hē·mä·tol'ō·ji), *n.* the branch of medical science that treats of the making, composition, functions, diseases, etc. of blood. —**he·ma·tol'o·gist,** *n.*

heme (hēm), *n.* the nonprotein, iron-containing component of hemoglobin.

hem·el·y·tron (he·mel'i·tron), *n., pl.* **-tra** (-trä), either of the forewings, thickened at the base and membranous at the end, found in certain insects, as the true bugs.

hem·i-, a prefix signifying *half.*

he·mic (hē'mik, hem'ik), *adj.* of blood.

hem·i·cra·ni·a (hem·i·krā'ni·ä), *n.* pain in one side of the head only, as in migraine.

hem·i·he·dral (hem·i·hē'drăl), *adj.* having half the planes or faces for complete symmetry: said of crystals.

hem·i·ple·gi·a (·plē'ji·ä, ·jä), *n.* paralysis of one side of the body. —**hem·i·ple'gic,** *adj. & n.*

he·mip·ter·an (hi·mip'tēr·än), *n.* any of a large order of insects having piercing and sucking mouthparts, including lice, aphids, bedbugs, etc. —**he·mip'ter·oid,** *adj.* —**he·mip'ter·ous,** *adj.*

hem·i·sphere (hem'i·sfir), *n.* 1. half of a sphere. 2. any one of the halves into which the earth is divided by the equator or a meridian. 3. a map or projection of one of

these halves. —**hem·i·spher'i·cal** (·sfir'i·kăl), **hem·i·spher'ic,** *adj.*

hem·i·stich (him'i·stik), *n.* in *Poetry,* an incomplete line or the half of a line.

hem·line (hem'lin), *n.* the bottom edge, usually hemmed, of a skirt, coat, dress, etc.

hem·lock (hem'lok), *n.* 1. *a)* a wild, poisonous, European plant of the parsley family: also **poison hemlock;** *b)* a poison made from this plant. 2. *a)* an evergreen tree of the pine family, with fine, flat needles; *b)* its wood. 3. same as **water hemlock.**

hem·mer (hem'ēr), *n.* 1. a person that hems. 2. an attachment to a sewing machine for hemming.

he·mo-, a combining form meaning *blood.*

he·mo·glo·bin (hē'mō·glō·bin), *n.* the red coloring matter of the red corpuscles of the blood.

he·mo·ly·sin (hē·mō·lī'sn), *n.* a substance developed in the blood, as by bacteria, that destroys red corpuscles.

he·mo·phil·i·a (hē·mō·fil'i·ä, ·fil'yä), *n.* a hereditary condition in which the blood fails to clot properly, causing excessive bleeding from even minor cuts.

he·mo·phil·i·ac (·fil'i·ak, ·fil'yak), *n.* a person who has hemophilia.

he·mop·ty·sis (hi·mop'ti·sis), *n.* a spitting or coughing up of blood.

hem·or·rhage (hem'ēr·ij, hem'rij), *n.* profuse or heavy bleeding, as from a ruptured blood vessel: *v.i.* **-rhaged, -rhag·ing,** to bleed heavily. —**hem·or·rhag'ic** (·ō·raj'ik), *adj.*

hem·or·rhoid (hem'ō·roid, hem'roid), *n.* a painful swollen vein at the anus, often with bleeding: *usually used in the plural.*

hemp (hemp), *n.* 1. a tall plant, native to Asia, cultivated for its tough fiber. 2. this fiber, used for cordage, coarse fabric, etc. 3. a preparation, as hashish, marijuana, etc. made from the flowers and leaves of this plant.

hemp·en (hem'pĕn), *adj.* of, pertaining to, or made of hemp.

hem·stitch (hem'stich), *n.* an ornamental stitch made by drawing out several parallel threads and sewing the cross threads together in regular, small bunches: *v.i.* to sew hemstitches on (fabric, etc.).

hen (hen), *n.* the female of a bird, especially the domestic fowl.

hen·bane (hen'bān), *n.* a poisonous, coarse, hairy herb of the nightshade family, used in medicine.

hence (hens), *adv.* 1. from this place. 2. from this time. 3. from this life. 4. therefore; as a result: *interj.* [Archaic], away! begone!

hence·forth ('fôrth'), *adv.* 1. from this time forward: also **hence·for'ward** (-fôr'wĕrd). 2. subsequently.

hench·man (hench'măn), *n., pl.* **-men,** 1. originally, a male attendant or servant. 2. a trusted follower. 3. a political worker or supporter who seeks mainly to advance himself. 4. a follower of the leader of a criminal gang.

hen·dec·a·gon (hen·dek'ä·gon), *n.* a plane figure having eleven sides and eleven angles. —**hen·de·cag·o·nal** (hen·dē·kag'ō·năl), *adj.*

hen-dec-a-syl-la-ble (hen-dek-á-sil'á-bl), *n.* a metrical line or verse of eleven syllables.

hen-na (hen'á), *n.* 1. an old-world tropical shrub with tiny flowers. 2. a dye made from the powdered leaves of this plant, used to tint the hair reddish brown. 3. reddish brown: *adj.* reddish-brown: *v.t.* -naed, -na-ing, to tint with henna.

hen-ner-y (hen'ér-i), *n., pl.* -ner-ies, a place where hens are kept.

hen-o-the-ism (hen'ō-thē-izm), *n.* the worship of a particular god without denying the existence of others.

hen-peck (hen'pek), *v.t.* to nag, scold, or try to dominate (one's husband). —**hen'pecked,** *adj.*

hen-ry (hen'ri), *n., pl.* -rys, -ries, the unit of inductance in electricity: after Joseph *Henry* (1797-1878), U.S. physicist.

he-pat-ic (hi-pat'ik), *adj.* of, like, or having to do with the liver.

he-pat-i-ca (hi-pat'i-ká), *n.* a small, American plant that blooms in the spring, with three-lobed leaves and white, pink, blue, or purple flowers.

hep-a-ti-tis (hep-á-tīt'is), *n.* inflammation of the liver.

hept-a-, a combining form meaning *seven.*

hep-tad (hep'tad), *n.* a series or group of seven.

hep-ta-gon (hep'tá-gon), *n.* a plane figure having seven sides and seven angles. —**hep-tag'-o-nal** (-tag'ō-nl), *adj.*

hep-ta-he-dron (hep-tá-hē'drŏn), *n., pl.* -drons, -dra ('drá), a solid figure with seven sides.

hep-tam-e-ter (hep-tam'ě-těr), *n.* a line of verse of seven metrical feet.

hep-tane (hep'tān), *n.* any one of several isomeric hydrocarbons obtained from petroleum: the normal isomer is used as a standard to test octane ratings.

hep-tar-chy (hep'tär-ki), *n.* 1. government by seven rulers. 2. a group of seven confederated states; specifically, [the H-], the seven Anglo-Saxon kingdoms supposed to have been informally allied before the 9th century in England.

Hep-ta-teuch (hep'tá-tōōk), *n.* the first seven books of the Old Testament.

her (hūr), *pron.* the objective case of she: *adj.* of or belonging to her.

He-ra (hir'á), *n.* in *Greek Mythology,* the wife of Zeus and queen of the gods.

her-ald (her'áld), *n.* 1. formerly, any one of various officials who proclaimed news of importance, bore messages from sovereigns or commanders, superintended ceremonies, tournaments, or other public functions, etc. 2. in England, an official whose duty it is to trace genealogies, record or blazon heraldic arms, etc. 3. a precursor; harbinger: *v.t.* 1. to introduce, proclaim, etc.; usher in. 2. to publicize.

he-ral-dic (hě-ral'dik), *adj.* of or pertaining to heralds or heraldry.

her-ald-ry (her'ál-dri), *n.* 1. the art or science that treats of armorial bearings, genealogies, etc. 2. heraldic pomp and ceremony.

herb (ūrb, hūrb), *n.* 1. a seed-bearing plant with a soft, fleshy stem, as distinguished from the woody stem of trees and shrubs, that dies to the ground after each growing season. 2. any one of various plants used especially in medicines, seasoning, or flavoring.

her-ba-ceous (hēr-bā'shŭs), *adj.* 1. of, pertaining to, or characteristic of an herb or herbs. 2. like a green leaf in texture and appearance.

herb-age (ūr'bij, hūr'-), *n.* 1. herbs collectively; especially grass or like vegetation used for grazing. 2. the fleshy or juicy parts of plants. 3. in *Law,* the right of pasture on the lands of another.

herb-al (ūr'bál, hūr'-), *adj.* of or pertaining to herbs: *n.* formerly, a book about plants and herbs, especially those of value to man.

herb-al-ist (-ist), *n.* 1. originally, the author of a herbal. 2. a person who collects, grows, or provides herbs, especially medicinal herbs.

her-bar-i-um (hēr-ber'i-ŭm, ēr-), *n., pl.* -i-ums, -i-a (-á), 1. a systematic collection of dried plants prepared for botanical study. 2. a room, building, etc. that houses such a collection.

her-bi-cide (hūr'bi-sīd, ūr'-), *n.* a substance used to kill or retard plants, especially weeds. —**her-bi-ci'dal,** *adj.*

her-biv-o-rous (hēr-biv'ēr-ŭs), *adj.* feeding on plants; plant-eating.

her-cu-le-an (hūr-kyū-lē'án, hēr-kū'li-án), *adj.* [sometimes H-], 1. of Hercules. 2. resembling Hercules in size, power, or courage. 3. requiring great strength, size, or courage; extremely difficult.

Her-cu-les (hūr'kyū-lēz), *n.* 1. in *Greek and Roman Mythology,* a hero renowned for his superhuman strength. 2. [h-], any big, strong man.

herd (hūrd), *n.* 1. a collection of cattle or other animals living, feeding, or being driven together. 2. any large group likened to this; crowd. 3. the common people; masses: a scornful term: *v.t. & v.i.* to unite or move as a herd, crowd, etc.

herds-man (hūrdz'mán), *n., pl.* -men ('měn), a person who tends or drives a herd.

here (hir), *adv.* 1. at or in this place. 2. to, toward, or into this place. 3. at this point, issue, detail, etc.; now. 4. on earth; in the present life: *n.* this place.

here-a-bout (hir'á-bout'), *adv.* in this general vicinity: also **here'a-bouts'.**

here-af-ter (hir-af'tĕr), *n.* 1. the future. 2. the state or condition after death; world to come: *adv.* 1. after this; in the future. 2. in the world to come.

here-by (hir-bī'), *adv.* by virtue of this; by this means.

he-red-i-ta-ble (hě-red'i-tá-bl), *adj.* same as heritable.

her-e-dit-a-ment (her-ě-dit'á-měnt), *n.* any property that can be inherited.

he-red-i-tar-y (hě-red'i-ter-i), *adj.* 1. passing down by inheritance from an ancestor to a legal heir. 2. having title, possession, etc. by inheritance. 3. of or transmitted by heredity.

he-red-i-ty ('i-ti), *n., pl.* -ties, 1. the transmission of physical or mental characteristics from parent to offspring. 2. the whole of the characteristics and potentialities received genetically by an organism from its ancestors.

Her·e·ford (hŭr'fôrd, her'ê-fôrd), *n.* any one of a breed of beef cattle, having a red coat and white markings.

here·in (hir-in'), *adv.* in or into this.

here·in·af·ter (hir-in-af'tĕr), *adv.* in the subsequent part (of this book, deed, etc.).

here·of (hir-uv'), *adv.* of or pertaining to this.

her·e·sy (her'ê-si), *n., pl.* -**sies**, 1. an opinion or doctrine at variance with orthodox church teachings; especially, such nonconformity explicitly condemned by the church. 2. any belief or opinion in science, politics, etc. dissenting from official or commonly held convictions.

her·e·tic (her'ê-tik), *n.* one who holds or maintains heretical beliefs; especially, one who publicly rejects an official church doctrine.

he·ret·i·cal (hê-ret'i-kl), *adj.* 1. of or pertaining to heresy or heretics. 2. tending toward, exhibiting, or having the character of heresy. —**he·ret'i·cal·ly,** *adv.*

here·to·fore (hir-tô-fôr', hir'tô-fôr), *adv.* up to the present time; previously.

here·up·on (hir-ŭ-pon', hir'ŭ-pon), *adv.* 1. at this moment; immediately after this. 2. concerning this point.

here·with (hir-with', -with'), *adv.* 1. together with this. 2. by this means.

her·it·a·ble (her'it-â-bl), *adj.* 1. capable of being inherited. 2. capable of inheriting.

her·it·age (her'it-ij), *n.* 1. property that passes from an ancestor to a descendant. 2. something passed down from one's predecessors; legacy; birthright.

her·maph·ro·dite (hĕr-maf'rô-dīt), *n.* 1. a person or animal with both the male and female sexual organs. 2. a plant having stamens and pistils in the same floral envelope. 3. short for **hermaphrodite brig:** *adj.* same as **hermaphroditic.** —**her·maph'ro·dit·ism,** *n.*

hermaphrodite brig, a two-masted vessel square-rigged forward and schooner-rigged aft.

her·maph·ro·dit·ic (hĕr-maf-rô-dit'ik), *adj.* of, pertaining to, or having the nature of a hermaphrodite.

her·me·neu·tics (hŭr-mê-nōōt'iks, -nūt'-), *n.* the science and the principles of interpretation and explanation; especially, the theological study of the laws by which the meaning of the Scriptures can be elucidated. —**her·me·neu'tic,** *adj.*

Her·mes (hŭr'mēz), *n.* in *Greek Mythology,* a god who served as messenger for the other gods.

her·met·ic (hĕr-met'ik), *adj.* perfectly closed and sealed; airtight: also **her·met'i·cal.** —**her·met'i·cal·ly,** *adv.*

her·mit (hŭr'mit), *n.* a person who withdraws from society and lives in solitude, especially for devotional contemplation; anchorite; recluse.

her·mit·age (-ij), *n.* 1. the abode of a hermit. 2. a place where a person can reside in seclusion; hidden retreat.

Her·mit·age (er-mê-täzh'), *n.* a full-bodied, usually red, French wine.

hermit crab, any of various crustaceans with soft abdomens, that live in the empty shells of univalve mollusks.

her·mit·i·cal (hĕr-mit'i-kl), *adj.* of, pertaining to, or suited for a hermit; solitary.

hern (hŭrn), *n.* archaic or dialectal variant of **heron.**

her·ni·a (hŭr'ni-â), *n., pl.* -**ni·as,** -**ni·ae** (-ē), the protrusion of an organ or part of an organ through the wall of the structure that normally encloses it; especially, the protrusion of part of the intestine through the abdominal wall; rupture. —**her'ni·al,** *adj.*

her·ni·ate ('ni-āt), *v.i.* -**at·ed,** -**at·ing,** to protrude abnormally so as to produce a hernia. —**her·ni·a'tion,** *n.*

he·ro (hir'ō, hē'rō), *n., pl.* -**roes,** 1. in *Myth & Legend,* a demigod. 2. any man renowned for his courage or feats of valor. 3. any man admired for his character, ideals, or accomplishments. 4. the chief male character in a novel, play, etc.

he·ro·ic (hi-rō'ik), *adj.* 1. of, displaying, or distinguished by the qualities of a hero; strong, valorous, high-minded, etc. 2. of or concerning a hero or his exploits. 3. in *Art,* larger than life-size. 4. bold and risky: *n.* 1. *pl.* same as **heroic verse.** 2. *pl.* extravagant or melodramatic speech or conduct. —**he·ro'i·cal·ly,** *adv.*

heroic verse, any of several verse forms conventionally used for the writing of epic poetry, as dactylic hexameter in Latin and Greek and iambic pentameter in English.

her·o·in (her'ô-win), *n.* a white crystalline acetyl derivative of morphine that is a potent, addictive narcotic.

her·o·ine (her'ô-win), *n.* 1. a female hero. 2. the chief female character in a novel, play, etc.

her·o·ism (-wizm), *n.* the qualities and conduct of a hero or heroine.

her·on (her'ôn), *n.* a wading bird with a long neck, long legs, and a long bill.

her·on·ry (-ri), *n., pl.* -**ries,** a place where herons gather and breed.

hero sandwich, a large roll split lengthwise and filled with cold cuts, cheeses, etc.

hero worship, 1. profound reverence for heroes. 2. excessive adulation of popular idols.

her·pes (hŭr'pēz), *n.* any one of several viral diseases, characterized by clusters of small blisters on the skin or mucous membranes.

her·pe·tol·o·gy (hŭr-pê-tol'ô-ji), *n.* the branch of zoology that treats of reptiles and amphibians.

Herr (her), *n., pl.* **Her'ren** ('ĕn), [German], 1. a man; gentleman. 2. Mister; Sir.

her·ring (her'ing), *n.* an edible fish abundant in the temperate waters of the North Atlantic, smoked or salted when adult or canned as sardines when young.

her·ring·bone (-bōn), *n.* 1. a pattern consisting of rows of slanting parallel lines with contiguous rows slanted in opposite directions. 2. a fabric, stitch, etc. with such a pattern.

hers (hŭrz), *pron.* that or those belonging to her.

her·self (hĕr-self'), *pron.* 1. the emphatic or reflexive form of she. 2. her true self.

hertz (hŭrts), *n.,* *pl.* **hertz,** the international unit of frequency, equal to one cycle per second: after H. *Hertz* (1857-94), German physicist.

Hertz·i·an waves (hŭrt'si-ăn, hert'-), [sometimes h-], electromagnetic radiation resulting from the oscillations of electricity in a conductor.

he's (hēz), 1. he is. 2. he has.

hes·i·tan·cy (hez'i-tăn-si), *n.,* *pl.* **-cies,** 1. indecision. 2. an instance of hesitating. Also **hes'i·tance** (-tăns).

hes·i·tant (-tănt), *adj.* tending to hesitate; doubtful. **—hes'i·tant·ly,** *adv.*

hes·i·tate (-tāt), *v.i.* **-tat·ed, -tat·ing,** 1. to pause in uncertainty; vacillate. 2. to stop briefly. 3. to demur. 4. to stammer. **—hes·i·ta'tion,** *n.*

Hes·pe·ri·an (hes-pir'i-ăn), *adj.* 1. western; occidental. 2. [Poetic], of the Hesperides.

Hes·per·i·des (hes-per'i-dēz), *n.* in *Greek Mythology,* 1. the four sisters who, with the aid of a dragon, guarded the golden apples. 2. the garden in which the golden apples grew.

Hes·per·us (hes'pĕr-ŭs), *n.* the evening star, especially Venus.

Hes·sian (hesh'ŭn), *n.* 1. a native or inhabitant of Hesse, a former region in west central Germany. 2. any one of the Hessian mercenaries who served in the British army during the American Revolution.

Hessian boots, knee-high boots with tassels in front.

Hessian fly, a small, two-winged fly having larvae destructive to wheat.

hest (hest), *n.* [Archaic], behest; command.

het, heth (khet), *n.* the eighth letter of the Hebrew alphabet.

he·tae·rism (hi-tir'izm), *n.* 1. same as **concubinage.** 2. a system of communal marriage supposed to have characterized certain primitive tribes.

het·er·o-, a combining form meaning *other, another, different.*

het·er·o·cer·cal (het-ĕr-ō-sŭr'kl), *adj.* denoting, of, or possessing a tail fin with the upper lobe larger than the lower and with the upper lobe containing the extended and upturned end of the vertebral column.

het·er·o·clite (het'ĕr-ō-klīt), *n.* 1. any person or thing deviating from the normal or standard. 2. in *Grammar,* a word, especially a noun, irregular in inflection: *adj.* deviating from the ordinary; anomalous.

het·er·o·dox (-doks), *adj.* deviating from accepted doctrines or beliefs; heretical.

het·er·o·dox·y (-dok-si), *n., pl.* **-dox·ies,** 1. the quality or condition of being heterodox. 2. a heterodox doctrine or opinion.

het·er·o·dyne (-dīn), *adj.* denoting or of the mingling of two frequencies to generate two new frequencies equal to the sum and difference of the original frequencies.

het·er·o·ge·ne·ous (het-ĕr-ō-jē'ni-ŭs, -jēn'yŭs), *adj.* 1. opposite or dissimilar in character, quality, structure, etc. 2. consisting of miscellaneous parts. **—het·er·o·ge·ne'i·ty** (-jē-

nē'i-ti), *n.,* *pl.* **-ties. —het·er·o·ge'ne·ous·ly,** *adv.*

het·er·o·gen·e·sis (-jen'ē-sis), *n.* 1. the occurrence in certain organisms of forms that are reproduced differently in the life cycle, requiring in alternate order a generation that reproduces sexually followed by one that reproduces asexually. 2. same as **abiogenesis.**

het·er·ol·o·gous (-ol'ō-gŭs), *adj.* 1. not corresponding in structure, position, or growth, as certain seemingly analogous body parts, due to a difference in origin or composition. 2. derived from a different species. 3. abnormal in structure, type, etc. **—het·er·ol'o·gy,** *n.*

het·er·o·mor·phism (-môr'fizm), *n.* 1. deviation from the typical form or structure. 2. having different forms at various stages in the life cycle, as the diverse forms exhibited by insects in the larval and pupal stages during metamorphosis. **—het·er·o·mor'phic** ('fik), **het·er·o·mor'phous** (-fŭs), *adj.*

het·er·on·o·mous (-on'ō-mŭs), *adj.* 1. subject to external laws, controls, or domination. 2. dissimilar or specialized, as certain body segments in most insects. **—het·er·on'o·my** (-mi), *n.*

het·er·o·nym (het'ĕr-ō-nim), *n.* a word spelled like another but different in meaning and pronunciation.

het·er·on·y·mous (het-ĕr-on'i-mŭs), *adj.* 1. of, pertaining to, or characteristic of a heteronym. 2. having different names but interrelated.

het·er·oph·o·ny (-of'ō-ni), *n.* the playing of a melody by two or more performers who modify the rhythm or melody simultaneously.

het·er·o·plas·ty (het'ĕr-ō-plas-ti), *n.* plastic surgery by grafting tissue taken from another.

het·er·o·sex·u·al (het-ĕr-ō-sek'shoo-wăl), *adj.* 1. belonging to different sexes. 2. sexually attracted to the opposite sex: *n.* a heterosexual organism or person.

het·er·o·sis (het-ĕr-ō'sis), *n.* growth and development of hybrid plants and animals resulting in greater strength and size.

het·er·o·to·pi·a (-ō-tō'pi-ă), *n.* displacement from natural position, as of a body organ; also **het·er·ot'o·py** (-ot'ō-pi).

heu·land·ite (hū'lăn-dīt), *n.* a brittle, hydrous silicate of calcium and aluminum.

hew (hū), *v.t.* **hewed, hewed** or **hewn, hew'ing,** 1. to cut or shape with or as with an axe or other sharp instrument. 2. to hack; chop: *v.i.* to stick firmly (*to* a doctrine, etc.).

hex (heks), *n.* an incantation, charm, etc. supposed to cause misfortune: *v.t.* to bring misfortune to.

hexa-, a combining form meaning *six.*

hex·a·gon (hek'să-gon), *n.* a plane figure having six angles and six sides. **—hex·ag·o·nal** (hek-sag'ō-nl), *adj.*

hex·a·he·dron (hek-să-hē'drŏn), *n.,* *pl.* **-drons, -dra** ('dră), a solid bounded by six plane faces.

hex·am·e·ter (hek-sam'ē-tĕr), *n.* 1. a verse of six feet. 2. verse of hexameters.

ō in drag*on,* oo in cr*u*de, oo in w*oo*l, u in c*u*p, ū in c*u*re, ũ in t*u*rn, ũ in f*o*cus, oi in b*oy,* ou in h*ou*se, th in *th*in, th in shea*th*e, g in *g*et, j in *j*oy, y in *y*et.

hex·ang·u·lar (hek-sang'gyă-lẽr), *adj.* having six angles.

hex·a·pod (hek'să-pod), *n.* an insect with six legs: *adj.* six-legged.

Hex·a·teuch (hek'să-tōŏk), *n.* the first six books of the Old Testament.

hex·one (hek'sōn), *adj.* designating certain compounds having six atoms of carbon to the molecule.

hex·ose ('sōs), *n.* any of a group of sugars containing six atoms of carbon to the molecule.

hey (hā), *interj.* an exclamation of interrogation, surprise, etc.

hey-day (hā'dā), *n.* time of highest vigor, bloom, perfection, etc.

hi (hī), *interj.* an exclamation of salutation.

hi·a·tus (hī-āt'ŭs), *n., pl.* **-tus·es, -tus,** 1. a break, vacancy, or gap. 2. a pronunciation break between two vowels, words, or syllables.

hi·ba·chi (hi-bä'chi), *n., pl.* **-chis,** a Japanese grill that utilizes charcoal held in a brazier.

hi·ber·nal (hī-bŭr'năl), *adj.* wintry.

hi·ber·nate (hī'bẽr-nāt), *v.i.* **-nat·ed, -nat·ing,** to pass the winter in a state of torpor, as certain animals.

hi·bis·cus (hi-bis'kŭs), *n.* a plant, shrub, or tree of a group related to the mallow, having showy flowers.

hic·cup, hic·cough (hik'ŭp), *n.* a short, convulsive catching sound in the throat caused by a spasmodic contraction of the diaphragm: *v.i.* **-cuped** or **-cupped, -cup·ing** or **-cup·ping,** to utter a short, convulsive cough.

hic ja·cet (hik jā'sit), [Latin, here lies], an inscription on tombstones.

hick (hik), *n.* [Informal], a yokel; hayseed; naive person from the country.

hick·o·ry (hik'ẽr-i), *n., pl.* **-ries,** 1. a nut-bearing tree of North America, related to the walnut. 2. its very tough, heavy wood. 3. the nut of this tree, which can be eaten: also **hickory nut.**

hid (hid), past tense and alternate past participle of **hide.**

hi·dal·go (hi-dal'gō), *n., pl.* **-goes,** in Spain, a nobleman of lower rank.

hide (hīd), *v.t.* **hid, hid'den** or **hid, hid'ing,** 1. to conceal; secrete. 2. to maintain secrecy about. 3. to disguise; obscure: *v.i.* 1. to be concealed. 2. to secrete oneself.

hide (hīd), *v.t.* **hid'ed, hid'ing,** [Informal], to whip; beat: *n.* an animal skin, raw or dressed.

hide·a·way (hīd'ă-wā), *n.* [Informal], a place for concealment, seclusion, etc.

hide·bound (hīd'bound), *adj.* 1. having the skin close or contracted. 2. prejudiced; bigoted.

hid·e·ous (hīd'i-ŭs), *adj.* offensive to the sight, ear, or taste; shocking; dreadful; horrible. **—hid'e·ous·ly,** *adv.*

hide-out (hīd'out), *n.* [Informal], a place of concealment, as for criminals.

hid·ing (hīd'ing), *n.* 1. concealment. 2. a beating.

hi·dro·sis (hī-drō'sis), *n.* 1. excessive perspiration. 2. any skin disease characterized by profuse perspiration.

hi·drot·ic (-drot'ik), *adj.* causing perspiration: *n.* a drug causing perspiration.

hie (hī), *v.i. & v.t.* **hied, hie'ing** or **hy'ing,** to hasten.

hi·e·mal (hī'i-măl), *adj.* of winter.

hi·er·arch (hī'ẽ-rärk), *n.* the chief ruler of an ecclesiastical body.

hi·er·ar·chism (hī'ẽ-rär-kizm), *n.* the rule of a hierarchy.

hi·er·ar·chy (-ki), *n., pl.* **-chies,** 1. the ranks of clergy in a church. 2. the priesthood. 3. the ranks of angels. 4. a systematic grouping of persons or things in ranks, order, etc. **—hi·er·ar·chi·cal** (hī-ẽ-rär'ki-kl), **hi·er·ar'chic,** *adj.*

hi·er·at·ic (hī-ẽ-rat'ik), *adj.* of or pertaining to priests; sacred; consecrated.

hi·er·oc·ra·cy (hī-ẽ-rok'ră-si), *n., pl.* **-cies,** government by ecclesiastics.

hi·er·o·glyph·ic (hī-ẽr-ô-glif'ik), *n.* 1. a character in the picture writings of the ancient Egyptians and others. 2. *pl.* picture writing. 3. a character or symbol difficult to comprehend. 4. *pl.* illegible penmanship. Also **hi·er·o·glyph** (hī'ẽr-ô-glif): *adj.* 1. of or pertaining to hieroglyphics. 2. emblematic.

hi·er·ol·o·gy (hī-ẽ-rol'ô-ji), *n., pl.* **-gies,** the collective knowledge of sacred things.

hi-fi (hī'fī'), *n.* a high-fidelity phonograph: *adj.* of or exhibiting high fidelity in the reproduction of sound.

hig·gle (hig'l), *v.i.* **-gled, -gling,** to dispute about financial matters; haggle.

hig·gle·dy-pig·gle·dy (hig'l-di-pig'l-di), *adv.* in confusion; topsy-turvy.

high (hī), *adj.* 1. elevated; lofty. 2. placed at or performed from an elevation. 3. stretching to a (specified) elevation. 4. chief; head. 5. of an unusually large amount or quantity. 6. strong; powerful. 7. very intense. 8. serious. 9. full or complete. 10. tainted. 11. shrill; acute. 12. joyous. 13. [Slang], intoxicated: *n.* 1. an elevated place. 2. the fastest gear in a transmission. 3. [Slang], drug intoxication: *adv.* in a profound or luxurious manner.

high·ball (hī'bôl), *n.* a drink of whiskey or brandy served in a high glass with crushed ice and effervescent water, etc.

high·bind·er ('bin-dẽr), *n.* [Informal], a swindler.

high·born ('bôrn), *adj.* aristocratic.

high·boy ('boi), *n.* a tall chest of drawers mounted on legs.

high·brow ('brou), *n.* [Informal], one who assumes an attitude of intellectual superiority: *adj.* [Informal], of or for a highbrow. A derisive term.

High Church, that division of the Anglican Church which attaches much importance to ritual, ceremonies and symbols, the priesthood, etc.

high·er-up (hī'ẽr-up), *n.* [Informal], one who has a lofty position.

high·fa·lu·tin, high·fa·lu·ting (hī'fă-lōōt'n), *adj.* [Informal], pretentious; self-important.

high fidelity, a very high quality of sound reproduction, as in recording, radio, etc.

high-flown ('flōn), *adj.* 1. extravagantly enterprising. 2. elevated; inflated.

high-hand·ed ('han'did), *adj.* arrogant and arbitrary. —**high'hand'ed·ly**, adv. —**high'hand'ed·ness**, n.

high-hat ('hat), adj. [Slang], smugly aloof: v.t. -**hat'ted, -hat'ting**, [Slang], to treat in a smugly superior fashion.

high·land ('lànd), n. 1. a mountainous region. 2. pl. [H-], the mountainous districts of northern Scotland (preceded by the). —**High'land·er**, n.

high-lev·el ('lev'l), adj. 1. of or by persons of high office. 2. in a high office.

high life, the manner of living of fashionable society.

high-light ('līt), n. 1. the brightest area of light reflection, representation, etc.: also **high light**. 2. the most distinguished area, etc.: v.t. 1. to produce highlights in. 2. to make outstanding.

high·ly ('li), adv. 1. in a great degree. 2. with high esteem or opinion. 3. at an elevated position, salary, etc.

High Mass, a Mass with full ceremonials, music, and incense, at which a deacon and subdeacon assist the celebrant.

high-mind·ed ('mīn'did), adj. possessing elevated feelings, philosophy, etc.

high muck-a-muck (muk'à-muk'), [Slang], an arrogant boss in supreme command: also **high muckamuck.**

high·ness ('nis), n. 1. the state or quality of being high. 2. [H-], a title of honor applied to royal persons: used with a possessive pronoun.

high-pres·sure ('presh'ër), adj. 1. under or resisting high pressure. 2. utilizing aggressive ways to win over: v.t. -**sured, -sur·ing,** [Informal], to press or solicit with high-pressure means.

high priest, 1. a chief priest. 2. the principal priest of the ancient Jewish priestly hierarchy.

high-rise ('rīz), n. a building of more than a few stories.

high-road ('rōd), n. 1. [Chiefly British], a chief road; highway. 2. an easy course or method.

high school, a school after primary school, which usually consists of grades 10 through 12 and supplies instruction in both academic and vocational areas.

high seas, ocean water beyond national territorial limits.

high sign, a sign agreed upon beforehand or understood, as to indicate danger.

high-spir·it·ed ('spir'i-tid), adj. 1. brave. 2. animated.

high-strung ('strung'), adj. extremely sensitive.

high-tech ('tek), adj. 1. of specialized, complex technology: also **high'-tech'nol'o·gy**. 2. of or involving furnishings, fashions, etc. industrial in design or look.

high-ten·sion ('ten-shùn), adj. using or transmitting a high voltage.

high tide, the highest tide level.

high time, a time when it is almost too late.

high treason, a breach of allegiance to the sovereign power of a country.

high·way ('wā), n. 1. a public road. 2. a course. 3. a primary road.

high·way·man ('wā-màn), n., pl. -**men** (-mèn), one who robs on the public road.

high wire, a cable stretched high above the ground, on which aerialists perform.

hi·jack (hī'jak), v.t. [Informal], 1. to take illegally (property being freighted). 2. to force the pilot of (an airplane) to make an unplanned flight. —**hi'jack·er**, n.

hike (hīk), v.i. hiked, hik'ing, to tramp or march over a long course: v.t. [Informal], 1. to raise up. 2. to cause (prices, etc.) to rise: n. 1. a tramp or march. 2. [Informal], an upward move. —**hik'er**, n.

hi·lar·i·ous (hi-ler'i-ùs), adj. noisily merry; lively. —**hi·lar'i·ty** ('i-ti), n.

hill (hil), n. 1. an elevation less than a mountain. 2. a small mound or heap, as of earth around plants: v.t. to draw earth about (plants in mounds).

hill·bil·ly (hil'bil-i), n., pl. -**lies**, [Informal], one who inhabits the mountains or backwoods of the South: sometimes a derisive term.

hill·ock ('òk), n. a small hill.

hill·side ('sid), n. a hill slope.

hill·top ('top), n. the top of a hill.

hill·y ('i), adj. hill'i·er, hill'i·est, 1. abounding with or characterized by hills; rugged. 2. steep. —**hill'i·ness**, n.

hilt (hilt), n. the handle of a sword, etc.

him (him), pron. the objective case of he.

him·self (him-self'), pron. 1. the emphatic or reflexive form of he. 2. his true self.

hind (hīnd), n., pl. **hinds, hind**, the female of the red deer: adj. **hind'er**, **hind'most** or **hind'er·most**, back; hinder.

hin·der (hin'dêr), v.t. to obstruct or impede: v.i. to impose obstructions or impediments.

hind·er (hīn'dêr), adj. belonging to, or constituting, the back or rear of anything.

Hin·di (hin'di), n. the official language of India.

hind·most (hīnd'mōst), adj. farthest from the front; in the extreme rear: also **hind'er·most** (hīn'dêr-).

Hin·doo (hin'dōō), adj. & n., pl. -**doos**, same as Hindu.

hind·quar·ter (hīnd'kwôr-têr), n. the rear section of an animal carcass.

hin·drance (hin'drâns), n. 1. the act of hindering. 2. an obstruction.

hind·sight (hīnd'sīt), n. the ability of understanding later what was actually the best thing to do.

Hin·du (hin'dōō), n. 1. a member of various groups of people in India. 2. a believer in Hinduism: adj. of or pertaining to the Hindus, their language, or to Hinduism.

Hin·du·ism (hin'doo-wizm), n. the religion and society of the Hindus, developed from Brahmanism.

hinge (hinj), n. 1. the joint or hook on which a door, etc. turns or swings. 2. the joint of a bivalve shell. 3. that on which anything depends or turns: v.t. hinged, hing'ing, to furnish or attach with a hinge: v.i. to stand, turn, or depend, as on a hinge.

ō in dragon, ōō in crude, oo in wool, u in cup, ū in cure, û in turn, ù in focus, oi in boy, ou in house, th in thin, th in sheathe, g in get, j in joy, y in yet.

hint (hint), *v.t. & v.i.* to suggest; mention casually: *n.* a suggestion; distant allusion.

hin·ter·land (hin´tẽr-land), *n.* 1. the region lying behind coast districts. 2. the area far from the city.

hip (hip), *n.* 1. the upper fleshy part of the thigh; haunch. 2. the upper segment of an insect's leg. 3. the angle at the junction of two sloping roofs. 4. the fruit of the rose: *v.t.* **hipped, hip'ping,** to build (a roof) with a hip: *interj.* a cheer.

hip (hip), *adj.* **hip'per, hip'pest,** [Slang]. 1. urbane. 2. in fashion. 3. of or pertaining to hippies.

hip·bone (hip´bōn), *n.* the large bone on each side of the body to which the long bone of the upper leg is joined.

hip·pie (hip´i), *n.* [Slang], a young person who has turned away from the conventions of society, and who experiments with different life styles, philosophies, etc.

hip·po-, a combining form meaning horse.

Hip·po·crat·ic oath (hip-ō-krat´ik), an oath embodying a code of medical ethics, frequently taken by students entering the profession of medicine: from *Hippocrates* (460?-370? B.C.), Greek physician, known as "the Father of Medicine."

hip·po·drome (hip´ō-drōm), *n.* 1. an ancient Greek or Roman course for the racing of horses and chariots. 2. a circus, arena, etc.

hip·po·pot·a·mus (hip-ō-pot´ā-mŭs), *n., pl.* **-mus·es, -a·mi** (-mī), **-a·mus,** a large mammal with thick skin, that inhabits river areas in Africa: it lives on plants.

hire (hīr), *v.t.* **hired, hir'ing,** to engage for service at a certain price: *n.* 1. recompense or consideration paid for the use of anything. 2. the act of hiring.

hire·ling (hīr´ling), *n.* one who serves for payment: *adj.* mercenary.

hir·sute (hŭr´sōōt, hir´sōōt), *adj.* hairy; shaggy.

his (hiz), *adj.* of or belonging to him: *pron.* that or those belonging to him.

His·pan·ic (hi-span´ik), *adj.* 1. Spanish or Spanish-and-Portuguese. 2. of or relating to Hispanics: *n.* a Spanish-speaking person of Latin American origin living in the U.S.

hiss (his), *n.* a sound resembling that of a snake, made by forcing the breath between the teeth: *v.i.* to utter such a sound, especially as in expressing disapprobation or contempt: *v.t.* to utter by hissing.

hist (st, hist), *interj.* quiet!

his·ta·mine (his´tá-mēn), *n.* a substance in organic matter which is freed from the tissues during allergic reactions.

his·to·gen·e·sis (his-tō-jen´ē-sis), *n.* the formation and development of tissues.

his·toid (his´toid), *adj.* of, pertaining to, or resembling normal tissue.

his·tol·o·gy (his-tol´ō-ji), *n.* the biological science which studies tissues by the use of the microscope.

his·tol·y·sis (´i-sis), *n.* the degeneration and dissolution of organic tissue.

his·to·ri·an (his-tôr´i-án), *n.* a writer of or specialist in history.

his·tor·ic (his-tôr´ik), *adj.* 1. same as historical. 2. celebrated in history.

his·tor·i·cal (´i-kl), *adj.* 1. of or pertaining to history. 2. contained in history; related to the past. 3. real; factual. **—his·tor'i·cal·ly,** *adv.*

his·to·ric·i·ty (his-tō-ris´i-ti), *n.* historical authenticity.

his·to·ri·og·ra·phy (his-tôr-ē-og´rā-fi), *n.* the study of the techniques of historical research and historical writing.

his·to·ri·og·ra·pher (his-tôr-i-og´rā-fẽr), *n.* 1. a writer of history. 2. an official historian.

his·to·ry (his´tō-ri), *n., pl.* **-ries,** 1. a narration or description of facts and events arranged chronologically with their causes and effects. 2. a knowledge of facts. 3. all of the known past. 4. the scientific study of the past.

his·tri·on·ic (his-tri-on´ik), *adj.* 1. of or pertaining to actors or the stage. 2. affected; melodramatic.

his·tri·on·ics (´iks), *n.pl.* 1. the art of theatrical presentation. 2. affected behavior or an exaggerated emotional display.

hit (hit), *v.t.* **hit, hit'ting,** 1. to strike. 2. to give a blow to. 3. to touch (the mark). 4. to attain to. 5. to have a strong effect on. 6. to find. 7. in *Baseball,* to achieve (a hit): *v.i.* 1. to clash or collide. 2. to find (usually with *upon*): *n.* 1. a stroke or blow. 2. a collision. 3. a lucky event. 4. a smart remark. 5. a popular success. 6. in *Baseball,* a ball sent to a fair area resulting in a batter getting to a base.

hitch (hich), *n.* 1. a catch. 2. an impediment. 3. a pulling or jerking. 4. a lame walk. 5. a knot. 6. [Slang], a length of time passed or spent: *v.i.* 1. to become entangled or caught. 2. to move by jerks. 3. to strike the feet together, as horses: *v.t.* 1. to fasten or tie. 2. to pull or move with a jerk. 3. [Slang], to hitchhike.

hitch·hike (hich´hīk), *v.i.* **-hiked, -hik·ing,** to make a journey by soliciting automobile rides along the route: *v.t.* to obtain (rides) by hitchhiking. **—hitch'hik·er,** *n.*

hith·er (hith´ẽr), *adv.* to this place: *adj.* on the side nearest to the speaker.

hith·er·to (-tōō), *adv.* until now.

hit man, [Informal], a hired murderer.

hit-or-miss (hit´ẽr-mis´), *adj.* without method; unplanned.

hive (hīv), *n.* 1. an artificial receptacle for bees. 2. a swarm of bees. 3. a busy assemblage or location: *v.t.* **hived, hiv'ing,** 1. to gather or put into a hive. 2. to harbor: *v.i.* 1. to go into a hive. 2. to live or take shelter together.

hives (hīvz), *n.* same as **urticaria.**

HMO, *n., pl.* **HMO's,** a health care system in which an organization hires medical professionals to provide a wide range of services for its subscribers: it stands for *health maintenance organization.*

ho (hō), *interj.* stop! hold!

hoar (hôr), *adj.* same as **hoary:** *n.* same as: 1. hoarfrost. 2. hoariness.

hoard (hôrd), *n.* a store or accumulation of things laid up secretly: *v.t.* to collect and lay up secretly: *v.i.* to lay up and store secretly.

hoard-ing (hôr'ding), *n.* [British], a fence of rough boards enclosing a building site.

hoar-frost (hôr'frôst), *n.* white particles of frozen dew.

hoar-hound ('hound), *n.* same as horehound.

hoarse (hôrs), *adj.* 1. rough and harsh in sound. 2. with the voice rough and dry. —hoarse'ly, *adv.* —hoarse'ness, *n.*

hoar-y (hôr'i), *adj.* hoar'i-er, hoar'i-est, 1. white. 2. ancient. 3. covered with grayish-white hairs from age. —hoar'i-ness, *n.*

hoax (hōks), *n.* 1. a deceptive trick. 2. a practical joke: *v.t.* to take in or delude by a hoax.

hob (hob), *n.* 1. a projection at the side of a fireplace. 2. an apparatus for punching teeth in a cogwheel. 3. [English Dialectal], a hobgoblin or clumsy fellow.

hob-ble (hob'l), *v.i.* -bled, -bling, to walk with a limp or awkward step: *v.t.* 1. to make walk with a limp. 2. to shackle the legs of (a horse, etc.). 3. to impede: *n.* 1. a limping or awkward step. 2. a shackle for hobbling a horse.

hob-ble-de-hoy (hob'l-di-hoi), *n.* an awkward youth.

hob-by (hob'i), *n.,* *pl.* -bies, 1. a favorite pursuit or diversion. 2. a hobbyhorse. 3. a kind of falcon.

hob-by-horse (-hôrs), *n.* 1. a stick with a representation of a horse's head, with which children play. 2. same as rocking horse.

hob-gob-lin (hob'gob-lin), *n.* 1. a goblin, sprite, or elf. 2. an alarming apparition.

hob-nail (hob'nāl), *n.* a short nail with a large head, used for protecting the soles of heavy shoes: *v.t.* to equip with hobnails.

hob-nob (hob'nob), *v.i.* -nobbed, -nob-bing, to associate intimately (*with*).

ho-bo (hō'bō), *n.,* *pl.* -bos, -boes, 1. an itinerant worker. 2. a tramp.

hock (hok), *n.* 1. the joint between the knee and the fetlock, as of a horse. 2. [Chiefly British], any white Rhine wine. 3. [Slang], same as pawn (senses 1 & 2): *v.t.* 1. to hamstring; disable or render cattle useless by cutting the tendon of the hock. 2. [Slang], same as pawn.

hock-ey (hok'i), *n.* same as: 1. field hockey. 2. ice hockey.

hock-shop (hok'shop), *n.* [Slang], same as pawnshop.

ho-cus-po-cus (hō'kŭs-pō'kŭs), *n.* 1. deception. 2. chatter used to confuse during deception. 3. same as sleight of hand.

hod (hod), *n.* 1. a wooden trough affixed to a long handle, for carrying mortar or bricks. 2. a coal scuttle.

hod carrier, a person who carries a hod: also [British], hod-man (hod'măn), *n.,* *pl.* -men ('měn).

hodge-podge (hoj'poj), *n.* a medley of ingredients.

hoe (hō), *n.* an agricultural tool with a thin blade for breaking up soil around plants, cutting weeds, etc.: *v.t.* hoed, hoe'ing, to cut or till with a hoe.

hoe-cake (hō'kāk), *n.* a thin cornmeal bread.

hog (hog), *n.,* *pl.* hogs, hog, 1. the domestic pig, sow, or boar. 2. an animal like a pig. 3. [Informal], a grasping, gluttonous, or dirty person: *v.t.* hogged, hog'ging, 1. to cut (the hair of a horse's mane) short. 2. [Slang], to grasp with gluttony: *v.i.* to droop at both ends: said of a ship's bottom.

ho-gan (hō'gôn), *n.* an abode of Navaho Indians with a wooden roof and earthen walls.

hog-back (hog'bak), *n.* a sharp, rocky ridge.

hog-gish (hog'ish), *adj.* acting like a hog; rough, rude, boorish, unclean, etc.

hogs-head (hogz'hed), *n.* a measure of capacity, equal to 63 gallons.

hog-tie (hog'tī), *v.t.* -tied, -ty-ing or -tie-ing, 1. to tie the hands and feet of. 2. [Informal], to render ineffective.

hog-wash ('wosh), *n.* 1. refuse fed to pigs; swill. 2. anything of little or no value.

hoi-den (hoid'n), *n.* same as hoyden.

hoi pol-loi (hoi' pô-loi'), the common populace; the masses.

hoist (hoist), *v.t.* to lift or raise, as with tackle: *n.* 1. an apparatus for lifting things. 2. a lift.

hoke (hōk), *v.t.* hoked, hok'ing, [Slang], to deal with in an overly sentimental fashion (usually with *up*). —hok'ey, *adj.*

ho-kum (hō'kŭm), *n.* [Slang], 1. nonsense. 2. something said or done by an actor or writer to crudely amuse an audience.

hold (hōld), *v.t.* held, hold'ing, 1. to grasp and keep in the hands, etc.; clutch. 2. to retain. 3. to keep. 4. to possess. 5. to connect. 6. to judge or consider. 7. to contain. 8. to maintain. 9. to guard: *v.i.* 1. to cling; adhere. 2. to stand good for. 3. to continue. 4. to refrain. 5. to maintain soundness: *n.* 1. the act of holding. 2. a place to get a grasp or clutch. 3. a support. 4. a ruling power. 5. a jail. 6. that part of a vessel, aircraft, etc. where the cargo is stored.

hold-fast (hōld'fast), *n.* a hook or other means of attaching.

hold-ing ('ing), *n.* 1. land. 2. a rented farm. 3. *usually pl.* stocks and bonds.

hold-o-ver ('ō-vĕr), *n.* [Informal], someone or something carried over from a prior time.

hold-up ('up), *n.* 1. a detainment. 2. an assault on a person for the purpose of robbery.

hole (hōl), *n.* 1. a cavity; hollow place. 2. a pit. 3. a perforation. 4. the burrow of an animal. 5. a mean habitation. 6. [Informal], a difficulty or dilemma. 7. in *Golf*, a small hollow into which the ball is hit; also, the fairway, tee, etc. that precedes it: *v.t.* holed, hol'ing, 1. to dig or cut a hole in. 2. to drive into a hole.

hol-i-day (hol'i-dā), *n.* 1. a day for the celebration of some event. 2. a day of freedom from labor. 3. a religious festival. 4. *often pl.* [Chiefly British], a vacation period: *adj.* of or pertaining to a festival; joyous.

ho-li-er-than-thou (hō'li-ĕr-thăn-thou'), *adj.* smugly moral.

ho-li-ness (hō'li-nis), *n.* 1. the state or quality of being holy. 2. [H-], a title of the Pope (with *His* or *Your*).

ô in dragon, ōō in crude, oo in wool, u in cup, ū in cure, û in turn, ù in focus, oi in boy, ou in house, th in thin, *th* in sheathe, g in get, j in joy, y in yet.

hol·land (hol'ånd), *n.* a kind of linen, glazed or unglazed.

hol·lo (hol'ō), *interj. & n., pl.* **-los,** 1. a shout. 2. an exclamation of greeting, etc.: *v.i. & v.t.* **-loed, -lo·ing,** to shout to (one).

hol·low (hol'ō), *adj.* 1. having a void space within; not solid. 2. lowered below the surrounding area. 3. sunken. 4. superficial; unreal; insincere. 5. deep; low. 6. needing food: *n.* a cavity; pit; groove. 2. a space between hills or elevations: *v.t. & v.i.* to make or become hollow: *adv.* in a hollow way.

hol·lo·ware (hol'ō-wer), *n.* concave-shaped dishes and silverware: also **hol'low-ware.**

hol·ly (hol'i), *n., pl.* **-lies,** an evergreen tree or shrub with glossy, prickly leaves and red berries.

hol·ly·hock (hol'i-hok), *n.* a tall biennial plant related to the mallow, with large flowers.

holm (hōm), *n.* [British]. 1. low, flat land by the side of a river. 2. a small river island.

hol·mi·um (hōl'mi-ùm), *n.* a metallic element of the rare-earth group.

holm oak, 1. an evergreen tree of southern Europe with leaves like the holly. 2. its wood.

hol·o-, a combining form meaning *whole.*

hol·o·blas·tic (hol-ō-blas'tik), *adj.* wholly germinal.

hol·o·caust (hol'ō-kôst), *n.* 1. a sacrifice wholly consumed by fire. 2. massive destruction, especially by fire.

hol·o·graph (hol'ō-graf), *n.* a document entirely in the handwriting of the author. **—hol·o·graph'ic,** *adj.*

hol·o·zo·ic (hol-ō-zō'ik), *adj.* using organic material as food, as most animals.

Hol·stein (hōl'stīn), *n.* one of a breed of black-and-white cattle famous for both milk and beef.

hol·ster (hōl'stēr), *n.* a leather pistol case carried on a belt.

ho·ly (hō'li), *adj.* **-li·er, -li·est,** [often H-], 1. pure; morally and spiritually perfect; sinless. 2. very respected; awesome. 3. sacred; consecrated.

Holy Communion, the sacrament of the consecration of bread and wine.

holy day, a religious festival.

Holy Father, the Pope.

Holy Ghost, the third person of the Trinity.

Holy Grail, same as **Grail.**

holy of holies, the innermost and most sacred shrine of the Jewish tabernacle, containing the ark of the covenant.

holy orders, the state of being ordained into the ministry of the Christian Church: applied chiefly in the Roman Catholic and Anglican churches.

Holy Rood, [sometimes h- r-], 1. the cross of Christ's crucifixion. 2. a cross or crucifix, especially one over the entrance to the chancel.

Holy Saturday, the Saturday preceding Easter.

Holy Spirit, 1. God. 2. the third person of the Trinity.

ho·ly·stone (hō'li-stōn), *n.* a large, flat piece of sandstone used for scouring wooden ship decks: *v.t.* **-stoned, -ston·ing,** to scrub (a deck) with a holystone.

Holy Thursday, the Thursday preceeding Easter.

holy water, water blessed by a priest.

Holy Week, the week preceding Easter.

Holy Writ, the Bible.

hom·age (hom'ij, om'ij), *n.* respect paid to another; reverence.

home (hōm), *n.* 1. one's abode or residence. 2. one's country, city, etc. 3. a place one considers home. 4. a habitat. 5. a family unit. 6. a benevolent or charitable institution. 7. same as **home plate:** *adj.* 1. of or pertaining to one's abode or country; domestic. 2. at the center. 3. to the point; effective: *adv.* 1. to or at home. 2. to the point where directed. 3. closely. **—home'less,** *adj.* **—home'like,** *adj.*

home-brew (hōm'brōō'), *n.* beer or alcoholic liquor brewed or distilled in the home.

home economics, the science that deals with the administration of affairs in the home.

home·land ('land), *n.* one's country by birth or residence.

home·ly (hōm'li), *adj.* **-li·er, -li·est,** 1. plain-featured. 2. wanting polish. 3. unpretending; simple. **—home'li·ness,** *n.*

home·made ('mād'), *adj.* of or designating household manufacture.

home·mak·er ('māk-ēr), *n.* one who administers a home, especially a housewife.

ho·me·o-, a combining form meaning *like.*

ho·me·o·path (hō'mi-ō-path), *n.* one who practices or believes in homeopathy: also **ho·me·op·a·thist** (hō-mi-op'å-thist).

ho·me·op·a·thy (hō-mi-op'å-thi), *n.* the medical system which seeks to cure diseases by the administration of minute quantities of medicines which would produce symptoms similar to those of the disease in a healthy person if administered in large quantities. **—ho·me·o·path·ic** (-ō-path'ik), *adj.*

home plate, in *Baseball,* the base at which the batter stands, and which must be touched last in scoring a run.

hom·er (hō'mēr), *n.* [Informal]. 1. in *Baseball,* same as **home run.** 2. same as **homing pigeon.**

home run, in *Baseball,* a run scored by the batter in which he rounds all the bases without stopping at any on the way.

home·sick (hōm'sik), *adj.* sad or dejected because of absence from home. **—home'sick·ness,** *n.*

home·spun ('spun), *n.* a coarse woolen cloth, formerly spun at home: *adj.* 1. made at home. 2. produced from homespun. 3. simple; unpretentious.

home·stead ('sted), *n.* 1. a family's dwelling with the adjacent land. 2. a U.S. land grant of 160 acres for farming. **—home'stead·er,** *n.*

home·stretch ('strech'), *n.* 1. the section of a race track leading from the final turn to the finish. 2. the last section of anything.

home·ward ('wård), *adv. & adj.* in the direction of home.

home·work ('wūrk), *n.* 1. piecework completed in the home. 2. lessons or studies not completed in class.

---

a in *cap,* ā in *cane,* ä in *father,* å in *abet,* e in *met,* ē in *be,* ê in *baker,* è in *regent,* i in *pit,* ī in *fine,* ı in *manifest,* o in *hot,* ô in *horse,* ō in *bone,*

home·y ('ĭ), *adj.* **hom′i·er, hom′i·est**, characterized by the ease, intimacy, snugness, etc. of home. —**home′y·ness**, *n.*

hom·i·ci·dal (hom-ĭ-sīd′l), *adj.* of, pertaining to, or having a tendency to homicide.

hom·i·cide (hom′ĭ-sīd), *n.* 1. the killing of a human being. 2. one who kills another.

hom·i·let·ics (hom-ĭ-let′iks), *n.* that branch of theology which treats of sermons and their composition; art of preaching. —**hom·i·let′ic**, *adj.*

hom·i·list (hom′ĭ-list), *n.* a preacher or writer of homilies.

hom·i·ly (-lĭ), *n., pl.* **-lies**, 1. a long discourse on morals, virtue, etc. 2. a sermon.

hom·ing (hō′mĭng), *adj.* returning home.

homing pigeon, a pigeon trained to reach home from a far distance.

hom·i·ny (hom′ĭ-nĭ), *n.* Indian corn soaked so as to remove the hull and then coarsely ground.

hominy grits, ground hominy, boiled for eating.

ho·mo (hō′mō), *n., pl.* **hom·in·es** (hom′ĭ-nēz), any of a genus of mammals consisting of man.

ho·mo-, a combining form meaning *same*.

ho·mo·cen·tric (hō-mō-sen′trik), *adj.* same as concentric.

ho·mog·a·my (hō-mog′ā-mĭ), *n.* 1. interbreeding and inbreeding of an isolated group with the same characteristics. 2. the maturing of stamens and pistils in a flower at the same time. —**ho·mog′a·mous** (-mŭs), *adj.*

ho·mo·ge·ne·ous (hō-mō-jē′nĭ-ŭs), *adj.* 1. uniform; composed of similar parts or elements. 2. resembling nearly or exactly. —**ho·mo·ge·ne′i·ty** (-jē-nē′ĭ-tĭ), *n.*

ho·mog·e·nize (hō-moj′ē-nīz), *v.t.* **-nized, -niz·ing**, 1. to make uniform throughout. 2. to treat (milk), so as to prevent cream separation.

ho·mog·e·nous ('ē-nŭs), *adj.* resembling in structure because of the same origin. —**ho·mog′e·ny** (-nĭ), *n.*

hom·o·graph (hom′ō-graf), *n.* a word spelled the same way as another word, but having a different meaning and derived from a different root.

ho·mol·o·gous (hō-mol′ō-gŭs), *adj.* 1. identical; having the same structure. 2. corresponding in type. 3. characterized by homology.

hom·o·logue, hom·o·log (hom′ō-lôg), *n.* 1. the same organ or part in different animals, but varying in form and functions, as a hand, fin, etc. 2. something that corresponds structurally with something else.

ho·mol·o·gy (hō-mol′ō-jĭ), *n., pl.* **-gies**, 1. affinity of structure. 2. correspondence between the parts of different organisms owing to derivation from a common primitive origin.

ho·mo·mor·phism (hō-mō-môr′fizm), *n.* 1. similarity in form. 2. in *Biology*, superficial resemblance of organisms or organs of different types. 3. in *Botany*, the state of having the same length or shape, as of pistils and stamens. 4. in *Zoology*, likeness of an insect larva to the adult. Also **ho′mo·mor·phy.**

hom·o·nym (hom′ō-nim), *n.* 1. a word like another in sound but differing in meaning, as *pair, pare, pear.* 2. one of two persons of the same name.

ho·mo·pho·bi·a (hō-mō-fō′bĭ-à), *n.* hatred or fear of homosexuals or homosexuality. —**ho·mo·pho·bic** (-fō′bik), *adj.*

hom·o·phone (hom′ō-fōn), *n.* 1. a letter representing the same sound as another letter or group of letters. 2. same as **homonym** (sense 1). —**ho·moph·o·nous** (hō-mof′ō-nŭs), *adj.*

ho·moph·o·ny (hō-mof′ō-ni), *n., pl.* **-nies,** the quality of being alike in sound but dissimilar in meaning.

Ho·mo sa·pi·ens (hō′mō sā′pĭ-ĕnz), a human being.

ho·mo·sex·u·al (hō-mō-sek′shoo-wăl), *adj.* of or having sexual attraction to persons of the same sex: *n.* one who is homosexual. —**ho·mo·sex·u·al′i·ty** (-sek-shoo-wal′ĭ-tĭ), *n.*

hone (hōn), *n.* a kind of fine whetstone: *v.t.* **honed, hon′ing,** to sharpen on or as on a hone.

hon·est (on′ĕst), *adj.* 1. sincere; fair. 2. acquired equitably. 3. frank or open. 4. veracious; reliable. —**hon′est·ly,** *adv.* —**hon′es·ty,** *n.*

hon·ey (hun′ĭ), *n., pl.* **-eys,** 1. a sweet, viscid, syrupy substance produced by bees from the nectar they collect from flowers. 2. sweetness. 3. darling or sweet one: *adj.* resembling honey: *v.t.* **-eyed** or **-ied, -ey·ing,** to talk to in an endearing manner.

hon·ey·bee (-bē), *n.* the common hive bee.

hon·ey·comb (-kōm), *n.* 1. the waxen, hexagonal cells made by bees to contain their honey, eggs, etc. 2. any structure resembling a honeycomb: *v.t. & v.i.* to make or become full of holes like a honeycomb: *adj.* of, resembling, or patterned after a honeycomb.

hon·ey·dew (-dōō), *n.* 1. a saccharine secretion of certain plants. 2. a sweet substance secreted by aphids, a fungus, etc. 3. a variety of sweet melon with a whitish rind: also **honeydew melon.**

honey eater, one of a family of birds of Australia and Asia, having a long protruding tongue capable of extracting nectar from flowers: also **hon′ey·suck·er** (-suk-ēr).

honey locust, a thorny North American tree with beanlike pods.

hon·ey·moon (hun′ĭ-mōōn), *n.* the vacation spent by a newlywed couple before taking up married life: *v.i.* to take a honeymoon.

hon·ey·suck·le (-suk-l), *n.* a woody variety of plant with red, yellow, or white fragrant flowers.

honk (hôngk), *n.* 1. the cry of wild geese. 2. a like sound, as of an automobile horn: *v.i. & v.t.* to utter or cause to make these sounds.

hon·ky-tonk (hông′kĭ-tôngk), *n.* [Slang], a cheap, noisy nightclub: *adj.* designating music played on a piano with a tinkling sound.

hon·or (on′ēr), *n.* 1. respectful regard; esteem; worship. 2. reputation. 3. exalted rank. 4. fame; glory. 5. chastity. 6. an outward mark of high esteem. 7. [H-], a title used in addressing certain officials (preceded by *His, Her,* or *Your*). 8. moral soundness. 9. *pl.* recognition of superior accomplishment granted at graduation from a university. 10.

that which provides esteem and glory: *v.t.* 1. to treat with respect, deference, or civility. 2. to revere or worship. 3. to bestow marks of honor upon. 4. to accept and pay when due.

hon·or·a·ble (-å-bl), *adj.* 1. worthy of or conferring honor. 2. distinguished in rank. 3. high-minded; upright. 4. illustrious. 5. indicating honor. —**hon'or·a·bly,** *adv.*

hon·o·ra·ri·um (on'ö-rer'i-um), *n., pl.* **-ri·ums, -ri·a** (-å), a fee paid to a professional person when there is no prescribed fee.

hon·or·ar·y (on'ö-rer-i), *adj.* 1. conferred as an honor. 2. of, denoting, or occupying a position without actually working or being paid. —**hon·or·ar'i·ly,** *adv.*

hooch (hōōch), *n.* [Slang], alcoholic liquor surreptitiously obtained or manufactured.

hood (hood), *n.* 1. a covering for the head and neck, as that of a monk, falcon, etc. 2. something resembling a hood; a cowl. 3. a cover for the motor of an automobile. 4. an ornamental fold hanging down the back, denoting a university degree, etc.: *v.t.* to cover with or as with a hood.

-hood (hood), a suffix meaning *condition, the entire unit or aggregation.*

hood·ed (hood'id), *adj.* 1. covered with a hood. 2. hood-shaped. 3. in *Zoology,* having the head color differing from that of the body.

hooded crow, a European crow having a black head and wings, with gray back and underparts.

hood·lum (hōōd'lûm), *n.* a rowdy person, often part of a criminal group.

hoo·doo (hōō'dōō), *n., pl.* **-doos,** 1. same as voodoo. 2. [Informal], a person or thing that causes ill luck; also, the ill luck: *v.t.* [Informal], to bring ill luck upon.

hood·wink (hood'wingk), *v.t.* to deceive.

hoof (hoof, hōōf), *n., pl.* **hoofs,** rarely **hooves,** 1. the horny substance covering the feet of certain animals, as horses, cattle, etc. 2. the whole foot of these animals: *v.t. & v.i.* [Informal], to walk (often with *it*). —**hoofed,** *adj.*

hook (hook), *n.* 1. a curved piece of metal, wood, etc. for holding, catching, or pulling. 2. something resembling a hook. 3. a fishhook. 4. a curved instrument for cutting, as a sickle. 5. a trap. 6. a cape or headland. 7. in *Boxing,* a short blow swung with a bent elbow: *v.t.* 1. to catch, attach, strike, etc. with or as with a hook. 2. to gore or attack with the horns. 3. [Informal], to take unlawfully: *v.i.* 1. to bend or curve. 2. to be attached by a hook.

hook·ah, hook·a (hook'å), *n.* a pipe with a long flexible tube which draws the smoke through water, cooling it.

hooked (hookt), *adj.* 1. curved like a hook. 2. produced by a hook. 3. [Slang], *a)* addicted. *b)* engrossed. *c)* married.

hook·er (hook'ēr), *n.* 1. one who hooks. 2. an Irish or English fishing smack. 3. a small Dutch vessel. 4. any clumsy, ill-fitted, old craft. 5. [Slang], a big drink of whiskey. 6. [Slang], a prostitute.

hook-nose (hook'nōz), *n.* an aquiline nose.

hook-up ('up), *n.* a system of connected circuits, as in radio, television, etc.

hook·worm ('wûrm), *n.* a roundworm parasite which enters the body, often through the feet, and infests the small intestine of the human body.

hoo·li·gan (hōō'li·gån), *n.* [Slang], same as hoodlum.

hoop (hōōp), *n.* 1. a round band to hold together the staves of a cask, etc. 2. a circular ring used by children for trundling. 3. anything curved like a hoop: *v.t.* to bind or secure with or as with a hoop; encircle.

hoop·er (hōōp'ēr), *n.* same as cooper.

hoop·la (hōōp'lä), *n.* [Informal], 1. fuss and commotion. 2. exaggerated advertising.

hoo·poe (hōō'pōō), *n.* a bird of the Old World, having a curved bill and erectile crest.

hoop skirt, a skirt spread over a framework of hoops.

hoop snake, a variety of American snake: so called because at one time supposed to have rolled along the ground with its tail in its mouth.

hoo·ray (hoo-rā'), *interj. & n. & v.i. & v.t.* same as hurrah.

hoose·gow, hoos·gow (hōōs'gou), *n.* [Slang], a jail; guardhouse.

hoot (hōōt), *n.* 1. a contemptuous shout. 2. the cry of an owl: *v.i.* to make a hoot: *v.t.* to show (contempt) for (a person) by hooting. —**hoot'er,** *n.*

hootch (hōōch), *n.* [Slang], same as hooch.

hoot·en·an·ny (hōōt'n-an-i), *n., pl.* **-nies,** an assemblage of folk singers.

hooves (hoovz, hōōvz), rare plural of hoof.

hop (hop), *v.i.* 1. to proceed by short leaps on one leg. 2. to proceed by leaps on all legs simultaneously, as some animals. 3. [Informal], to proceed quickly: *v.t.* 1. to leap over. 2. to go on board: *n.* 1. a jump on one leg, etc. 2. a twining plant the ripened cones of which are dried and used in brewing to impart a taste to beer, etc. 3. *pl.* the dried ripened cones. 4. [Informal], a dance. 5. [Informal], a brief air flight. 6. [Slang], a narcotic drug; opium.

hope (hōp), *n.* 1. desire accompanied by expectation; anticipation. 2. the object desired. 3. that which may be the cause for hope: *v.t.* hoped, hop'ing, to expect with desire: *v.i.* to cherish a desire (*for*). —**hope'ful,** *adj.* —**hope'less,** *adj.*

hop·lit (hop'lit), *n.* a heavily armed foot solider of ancient Greece.

hop·per (hop'ēr), *n.* 1. one who or that which hops. 2. a leaping insect. 3. a holder or funnel which can be evacuated at a uniform rate.

hop·ple (hop'l), *n. & v.t.* **-pled, -pling,** same as hobble.

hop·sack·ing (hop'sak-ing), *n.* 1. a rough material used for making bags. 2. a strong material like it, used for clothing. Also **hop'sack.**

hop-scotch ('skoch), *n.* a children's game in which a player throws a stone from one numbered compartment to another of a geometric figure drawn on the ground, and then hops to pick up the stone.

a in cap, ā in cane, ä in father, å in abet, e in met, ē in be, ẽ in baker, ĕ in regent, i in pit, ī in fine, ĭ in manifest, o in hot, ô in horse, ō in bone,

ho·ral (hôr′ăl), *adj.* of or pertaining to an hour or hours.

horde (hôrd), *n.* 1. a nomadic tribe or clan. 2. a vast multitude; pack or swarm: *v.i.* hord′ed, hord′ing, to live or act together in hordes.

hore·hound (hôr′hound), *n.* 1. a white, bitter plant related to the mint. 2. a cough remedy or candy produced from a decoction of its leaves.

ho·ri·zon (hō-rī′zn), *n.* 1. the line where the sky and earth or sea appear to meet. 2. *usually pl.* the limit of one's mental vision, activities, etc.

hor·i·zon·tal (hôr-ĭ-zon′tl), *adj.* 1. parallel to the horizon; not vertical. 2. level. 3. situated near the horizon. —**hor·i·zon′tal·ly,** *adv.*

hor·mone (hôr′mōn), *n.* a chemical secretion of a body organ which is transmitted by a body fluid and stimulates the activities of other organs or tissues. —**hor·mo·nal** (hôr-mō′nl), *adj.*

horn (hôrn), *n.* 1. a hard, projecting, bony protuberance on the head of certain hoofed animals, as cattle, deer, etc. 2. anything made of horn or like a horn. 3. a brass-wind instrument. 4. either extremity of a crescent. 5. a powder flask. 6. a part that juts above the pommel of a saddle. 7. the substance that composes horn. 8. a contrivance that produces a noise indicating danger: *adj.* composed of horn. —**horned,** *adj.* —**horn′less,** *adj.*

horn·beam (hôrn′bēm), *n.* a small tree yielding a tough, white wood.

horn·bill (′bil), *n.* a tropical bird having a large bill often with a bony outgrowth.

horn·blende (′blend), *n.* a black mineral that forms rocks.

horned toad, a small, spiny lizard of the New World.

horned viper, a venomous snake of northern Africa with a horny protuberance over each eye.

hor·net (hôr′nit), *n.* a large wasp colored yellow and black.

horn of plenty, same as **cornucopia.**

horn·pipe (hôrn′pīp), *n.* 1. a lively dance formerly done by sailors. 2. an obsolete wind instrument partly made of horn.

horn·y (hôr′ni), *adj.* **horn′i·er, horn′i·est,** 1. composed of or like horn. 2. having horns. 3. hard; calloused. 4. [Slang] preoccupied with the desire for sexual intercourse.

ho·ro·loge (hôr′ō-lōj), *n.* a mechanism, as a clock, for marking the hours.

ho·rol·o·gy (hō-rol′ō-ji), *n.* the art of measuring time or of constructing timepieces.

hor·o·scope (hôr′ō-skōp), *n.* a representation of the heavens at any time, especially at one's birth.

ho·ros·co·py (hō-ros′kō-pi), *n.* the art of casting horoscopes and claiming to determine the destiny of persons from them.

hor·ren·dous (hō-ren′dŭs), *adj.* horrible; frightful.

hor·ri·ble (hôr′ĭ-bl), *adj.* 1. terrible; dreadful. 2. [Informal], very disagreeable, repulsive, etc.

hor·ri·bly (-bli), *adv.* 1. terribly; dreadfully. 2. [Informal], very.

hor·rid (hôr′id), *adj.* 1. dreadful; terrible. 2. hideous; very obnoxious.

hor·rif·ic (hô-rif′ik), *adj.* causing horror or repulsion.

hor·ri·fy (hôr′ĭ-fī), *v.t.* -fied, -fy·ing, 1. to fill or strike with horror. 2. [Informal], to distress or repulse.

hor·rip·i·la·tion (hô-rip-i-lā′shŭn), *n.* the standing up of the hair, as from cold.

hor·ror (hôr′ĕr), *n.* 1. excessive fear accompanied by shuddering; extreme dread. 2. great disgust. 3. *pl.* extreme depression. 4. that which induces the feeling of horror.

hors de com·bat (ôr dě kôn-bä′), [French], out of the fight; disabled.

hors d'oeu·vre (ôr-dûrv′), *pl.* **hors d'oeuvres** (-dûrvz′), light food served before a meal as an appetizer.

horse (hôrs), *n., pl.* **hors′es, horse,** 1. a solid-hoofed, four-legged animal used for riding on or drawing burdens. 2. the male horse; stallion. 3. a framework with legs for the support of anything. 4. rock found in a vein of ore. 5. a jocular name for a man. 6. in *military usage,* the cavalry: *v.t.* **horsed, hors′ing,** to furnish with a horse or horses; place astride a horse: *v.i.* to mount on a horse; get on horseback: *adj.* 1. of or mounted on horses. 2. denoting something coarse or large.

horse·back (hôrs′bak), *n.* a horse's back: *adv.* on a horse's back.

horse chestnut, 1. a tree related to the buckeye with large palmate leaves, clusters of white flowers, and shiny brown seeds. 2. its seed.

horse·fly (hôrs′flī), *n., pl.* -flies, a large fly that is annoying to horses and cattle.

horse·hair (′her), *n.* 1. hair from a horse's mane or tail. 2. a rigid material produced from this.

horse·laugh (′laf), *n.* a coarse, noisy laugh, often in ridicule.

horse·man (′măn), *n., pl.* -men (′měn), a skilled rider or trainer of horses. —**horse′man·ship,** *n.* —**horse′wom·an** (′woom-ăn), *n., pl.* -wom·en (′wim-in).

horse opera, [Slang], a film about cowboys.

horse pistol, a large pistol formerly carried by a man riding on horseback.

horse·play (′plā), *n.* loud, boisterous conduct.

horse·pow·er (′pou-ēr), *n.* the unit of power of an engine, equal to 33,000 pounds raised one foot in one minute.

horse·rad·ish (′rad-ish), *n.* 1. a plant related to the mustard with a root having a pungent taste. 2. a seasoning produced from the ground root.

horse sense, [Informal], practical common sense; shrewdness.

horse·shoe (hôr′shōō), *n.* 1. a U-shaped metal shoe to protect the hoof of a horse. 2. anything U-shaped. 3. *pl.* a game in which the object is to hook a horseshoe around a stake by throwing it from 40 feet.

horseshoe crab, a sea animal shaped like a horseshoe, having a long, thin tail.

horse·weed (′wēd), *n.* same as **wild lettuce.**

horse·whip (′hwip), *n.* a whip for beating or

managing a horse: *v.t.* -whipped, -whip·ping, to beat with a horsewhip.

hors·y (hôr'si), *adj.* hors'i·er, hors'i·est, 1. of, pertaining to, or characteristic of horses. 2. of or characteristic of those who have a liking for activities connected with horses.

hor·ta·to·ry (hôr'tə-tôr-i), *adj.* giving exhortation; inciting: also hor'ta·tive (-tiv).

hor·ti·cul·ture (hôr'ti-kul-chēr), *n.* the art of cultivating plants in gardens. —hor·ti·cul'tur·al, *adj.* —hor·ti·cul'tur·ist, *n.*

hose (hōz), *n.pl.* stockings, socks, etc.

hose (hōz), *n.*, *pl.* hos'es, a flexible tubing for conveying water, etc.: *v.t.* hosed, hos'ing, to apply water by means of a hose.

Ho·se·a (hō-zē'ə, -zā'ə), *n.* a book of the Bible.

ho·sier (hō'zhēr), *n.* [Chiefly British], one who deals in hosiery.

ho·sier·y (-i), *n.* stockings, socks, etc.

hos·pice (hos'pis), *n.* 1. a place for accommodating travelers. 2. a homelike facility for the care of terminally ill patients.

hos·pi·ta·ble (hos'pi-tə-bl), *adj.* receiving and entertaining friends or strangers.

hos·pi·tal (hos'pi-tl), *n.* an institution for the medical treatment and care of the sick or injured.

hos·pi·tal·i·ty (hos-pi-tal'i-ti), *n.*, *pl.* -ties, the practice or act of entertaining friends or strangers with kindness and generosity.

hos·pi·tal·ize (hos'pi-tl-īz), *v.t.* -ized, -iz·ing, to place in or allow to enter a hospital. —hos·pi·tal·i·za·tion (hos-pi-tl-i-zā'shun), *n.*

host (hōst), *n.* 1. a crowd; multitude. 2. an army. 3. one who entertains others in public or private. 4. a manager or owner of a hotel or inn. 5. an organism on which another is parasitic. 6. [H-], the consecrated wafer of the Eucharist: *v.t. & v.i.* to be a host (to).

hos·tage (hos'tij), *n.* a person who remains in the hands of another as a pledge for the fulfillment of certain conditions.

hos·tel (hos'tl), *n.* a place for temporary accommodation; inn: also hos'tel·ry (-ri), *pl.* -ries. —hos'tel·er, *n.*

host·ess (hōs'tis), *n.* 1. a female host. 2. a woman supervisor in a restaurant.

hos·tile (hos'tl), *adj.* 1. showing animosity. 2. inimical. 3. adverse: *n.* one who is hostile. —hos'tile·ly, *adv.*

hos·til·i·ty (hos-til'i-ti), *n.*, *pl.* -ties, 1. the state of being hostile; antagonism; enmity; animosity. 2. the act of expressing hostility. 3. *pl.* war actions.

hos·tler (hos'lēr), *n.* one who takes charge of horses at an inn.

hot (hot), *adj.* hot'ter, hot'test, 1. having much heat. 2. burning; pungent; acrid. 3. fiery; passionate. 4. lustful. 5. ardent. 6. furious. 7. near to the object being sought. 8. causing much debate. 9. having an electrical charge. 10. [Informal], current; new. 11. [Slang], newly stolen. 12. [Slang], outstanding; very good. —hot'ly, *adv.* —hot'ness, *n.*

hot air, [Slang], meaningless talk.

hot·bed (hot'bed), *n.* 1. a bed of earth covered with glass and made warm by the fermentation of manure, for growing plants more quickly. 2. a place that encourages action and expansion.

hot-blood·ed ('blud-id), *adj.* passionate.

hot·box ('boks), *n.* an axle or shaft bearing that has become too hot.

hot cake, a pancake.

hot dog, [Informal], a frankfurter, usually in a hot bun.

ho·tel (hō-tel'), *n.* a lodging place accommodating travelers with rooms, food, etc.

hot·head (hot'hed), *n.* 1. one easily aroused to anger. 2. one who acts rashly.

hot-head·ed ('hed'id), *adj.* 1. easily aroused to anger. 2. rash.

hot·house (hot'hous), *n.* a glass building artificially heated for cultivating plants.

hot line, a direct communications line, as by telephone, used in emergencies, as an international crisis.

hot plate, a small burner for cooking.

hot potato, [Informal], a troubling problem that no one wants to handle.

hot rod, [Slang], an old car altered to increase speed and acceleration. —hot rod'der.

hot seat, [Slang], 1. same as electric chair. 2. a distressing condition.

hot·shot ('shot), *n.* [Slang], one who is expert at something in an aggressive way.

Hot·ten·tot (hot'n-tot), *n.* one of a nomadic people of southwestern Africa.

hot tub, a large wooden tub in which several people can soak in hot water.

hound (hound), *n.* 1. a breed of hunting dog. 2. a dog. 3. a despicable person: *v.t.* 1. to chase with or as with hounds. 2. to incite.

hounds·tooth check (houndz'tööth), a pattern of irregular broken checks, used in woven material: also hound's-tooth check.

hour (our), *n.* 1. the 1/24th part of a day; 60 minutes. 2. a particular time. 3. an hour's journey. 4. *pl.* a set period for some activity. 5. the time of day. 6. in *Astronomy*, a sidereal hour. 7. *pl.* in *Ecclesiasticism*, certain specified prayers or the time for these. 8. in *Education*, an hour's time spent in class each week, equal to one credit unit.

hour·glass (our'glas), *n.* a device for measuring time by running sand through a narrow opening between two compartments of a glass vessel.

hou·ri (hoor'i, hou'ri), *n.*, *pl.* -ris, a nymph of the Moslem Paradise.

hour·ly (our'li), *adj. & adv.* of, by, or within the hour.

house (hous), *n.*, *pl.* hous·es (hou'ziz), 1. a building for residence; place of abode. 2. the persons there; household. 3. a family, including relatives and ancestors and descendants. 4. a building things are kept in. 5. a theater; also, an audience there. 6. a business place or company. 7. [often H-], a legislative assembly or governing body, or the place it meets in. 8. in *Astrology*, a 12th part of the heavens: *v.t.* (houz), housed, hous'ing, 1. to put, keep, or shelter in a house. 2. to provide a house for. 3. to put or keep, as a mechanism, into or within a housing: *v.i.* 1. to take shelter. 2. to reside; live.

house arrest, detention at home, rather than in prison, of one arrested.

house·boat ('bōt), *n.* a boat with a houselike superstructure for living in.

house·bro·ken ('brō-kn), *adj.* of an animal, trained to live in one's home, going outdoors to void or using a box, etc.

house·fly ('flī), *n., pl.* **-flies,** a two-winged fly common in and about houses.

house·hold ('hōld), *n.* 1. everyone living in a house. 2. contents of a home.

house·hold·er (-ẽr), *n.* 1. one owning or maintaining a house. 2. a household head.

household word, a common word, saying, etc.

house·keep·er (hous'kēp-ẽr), *n.* one doing or supervising regular daily home tasks.

house·maid ('mād), *n.* a maid for housework.

housemaid's knee, inflammation of the saclike covering of the kneecap, caused by much kneeling as in scrubbing floors.

House of Commons, the lower branch of the legislature of Great Britain or Canada.

House of Lords, the upper branch of the legislature of Great Britain.

House of Representatives, the lower branch of the legislature, as of the U.S.

house·warm·ing ('wôrm-ing), *n.* a celebration on moving into a new home.

house·wife ('wīf), *n., pl.* **-wives** ('wīvz), 1. a wife occupied chiefly or solely with home tasks. 2. (usually huz'if), a small sewing kit.

house·work ('wûrk), *n.* regular home tasks.

hous·ing (hou'zing), *n.* 1. provision of lodging or houses. 2. a lodging or shelter; also, a covering. 3. houses collectively. 4. an enclosure, as for a mechanism. 5. *often pl.* ornamental trappings as for a horse.

hove (hōv), alternate past tense and past participle of **heave.**

hov·el (huv'l, hov'l), *n.* a mean habitation; hut; also, a sheltering shed: *v.t.* **-eled** or **-elled, -el·ing** or **-el·ling,** to shelter in a hovel.

hov·er (huv'ẽr, hov'ẽr), *v.i.* 1. to stay in position above or near something as if suspended: said of a bird, helicopter, etc. 2. to stay near someone or something, with constant slight advances and retreats. 3. to keep moving back and forth slightly, as in indecision; waver; vacillate: *n.* the act of hovering.

how (hou), *adv.* 1. in what way or condition. 2. for what reason. 3. to what degree, extent, etc.: *n.* the way of doing something.

how·be·it (hou-bē'it), *adv.* [Archaic] however it may be; nevertheless.

how·dah (hou'dä), *n.* a canopied seat for riding on an elephant or camel.

how·ev·er (hou-ev'ẽr), *adv.* 1. in whatever manner, degree, or extent. 2. in spite of that; at all events: *conj.* [Archaic], although.

how·itz·er (hou'it-sẽr), *n.* a short cannon.

howl (houl), *n.* 1. a long, loud, wailing cry, as of a wolf or dog. 2. [Informal], a hilarious joke: *v.i.* 1. to make the wailing cry of a dog, wolf, etc. 2. to laugh or shout unrestrainedly: *v.t.* 1. to utter by howling. 2. to drive or effect by howling.

howl·er ('ẽr), *n.* 1. one that howls. 2. [Informal], an uproariously funny blunder.

howl·ing ('ing), *adj.* 1. that howls. 2. [Informal], great, as a *howling* success.

how·so·ev·er (hou-sō-ev'ẽr), *adv.* 1. to whatever degree or extent. 2. by whatever means; in whatever manner.

hoy·den (hoid'n), *n.* a tomboy.

Hoyle (hoil), *n.* a book of rules for indoor games, especially for card games, originally compiled by E. Hoyle (1672-1769).

hua·ra·ches (hû-rä'chĕz, wä-rä'ches), *n.pl.* flat sandals with uppers of straps or woven leather strips.

hub (hub), *n.* 1. the center part, as of a wheel, fastened to or turning on the axle. 2. a center of activity, importance, etc.

hub·bub (hub'ub), *n.* noisy confusion; uproar.

hub·by (hub'i), *n., pl.* **-bies,** [Informal], a husband.

hu·bris (hū'bris), *n.* extreme arrogance.

huck·a·back (huk'å-bak), *n.* a rough kind of linen or cotton cloth, used for toweling.

huck·le·ber·ry (huk'l-ber-i), *n., pl.* **-ries,** 1. a plant of the heath family with dark-blue berries. 2. the berry.

huck·ster (huk'stẽr), *n.* 1. a peddler or hawker of wares. 2. an aggressive or haggling merchant, especially one using questionable methods. 3. [Informal], a person engaged in advertising or promotion.

hud·dle (hud'l), *v.i.* **-dled, -dling,** 1. to crowd close together. 2. to hunch oneself up, as from cold. 3. [Informal], to confer privately and informally. 4. in *Football,* to gather in a huddle: *v.t.* 1. to crowd close together. 2. to hunch (oneself) up. 3. to perform, place, make, or thrust in a hurried or disorderly way: *n.* 1. a confused crowd or heap; jumble. 2. [Informal], a private, informal conference. 3. in *Football,* a grouping of a team to get signals before a play.

Hud·son seal (hud'sn), muskrat fur processed to imitate seal.

hue (hū), *n.* 1. originally, general aspect. 2. color; especially, the distinctive characteristics of a particular color. 3. a particular shade or tint of a color.

hue (hū), *n.* a shouting: now only in *hue and cry.*

huff (huf), *v.t.* 1. originally, to puff up. 2. to treat with insolence; bully. 3. to anger or offend: *v.i.* 1. to blow or puff. 2. to get angry or offended: *n.* a state of indignation or resentment; pique.

huff·y ('i), *adj.* **huff'i·er, huff'i·est,** 1. easily offended; touchy. 2. indignant or resentful. —**huff'i·ness,** *n.*

hug (hug), *v.t.* **hugged, hug'ging,** 1. to clasp or embrace, squeezing tightly; especially, to embrace fondly and closely. 2. to hold fast to (a belief, opinion, etc.). 3. to keep close to: *v.i.* to hug someone or something: *n.* a hugging.

huge (hūj), *adj.* **hug'er, hug'est,** extremely big or large; gigantic. —**huge'ness,** *n.*

hug·ger·mug·ger (hug'ẽr-mug-ẽr), *n.* 1. secrecy. 2. a confusion; jumble: *adj.* 1. secret. 2. confused; jumbled: *adv.* in a huggermugger way.

ô in dragon, ōō in crude, oo in wool, u in cup, ū in cure, û in turn, ů in focus, oi in boy, ou in house, th in thin, th in sheathe, g in get, j in joy, y in yet.

Hu·gue·not (hū′gù-not), *n.* a French Protestant of the 16th or 17th century.

huh (hu), *interj.* an exclamation of interrogation, surprise, etc.

hu·la (hōō′lä), *n.* an undulating native Hawaiian dance: also **hu′la-hu′la.**

hulk (hulk), *n.* 1. a big, cumbrous ship. 2. the body of a ship, especially if old and dismantled. 3. *usually pl.* a non-seagoing ship used as a prison. 4. an abandoned wreck; empty ruin. 5. an awkwardly large person or thing: *v.i.* to rise bulkily.

hulk·ing (′ing), *adj.* awkwardly large.

hull (hul), *n.* 1. an outer covering, specifically of a seed or fruit. 2. the frame or main body of a ship: *v.t.* to remove the hull from (a seed or fruit).

hul·la·ba·loo (hul′á-bá-lōō), *n.* hubbub.

hum (hum), *v.i.* **hummed, hum′ming,** 1. to make a steady, usually light, sound as of murmuring voices, buzzing bees, or whirring motors. 2. to sound a tone or tones, as of a melody, by vibrating the vocal cords but not articulating. 3. [Informal], to be in full and active operation: *v.t.* to sound (tones, a melody, etc.) by humming: *n.* a humming.

hu·man (hū′mán), *adj.* of, like, or typical of man or mankind; of, like, or typical of people or persons: *n.* an individual man, woman, or child: also **human being.**

hu·mane (hū-mān′), *adj.* 1. showing such nobler qualities of mankind as kindness, compassion, mercy, etc. 2. humanizing.

hu·man·ism (hū′má-nizm), *n.* 1. any system of thought or conduct, specifically a nontheistic one, aiming at the advance and betterment of mankind. 2. study of the humanities. 3. [H-], the intellectual and cultural movement, prompted by rediscovery of classic Greek and Roman culture, that produced the Renaissance. —**hu′man·ist,** *n. & adj.* —**hu·man·is′tic,** *adj.*

hu·man·i·tar·i·an (hū-man·i-ter′i-án), *n.* a philanthropist: *adj.* helping humanity. —**hu·man·i·tar′i·an·ism,** *n.*

hu·man·i·ty (hū-man′i-ti), *n., pl.* **-ties,** 1. the fact, state, or quality of being human or humane. 2. mankind; people. 3. *pl.* such studies as literature, art, or philosophy, as distinguished from the sciences (with *the*).

hu·man·ize (hū′mán-īz), *v.t. & v.i.* **-ized, -iz·ing,** to make or become human or humane.

hu·man·kind (-kīnd), *n.* mankind; people.

hu·man·ly (-li), *adv.* 1. in a human way. 2. by human means.

hu·man·oid (-oid), *adj.* nearly human: *n.* a humanoid individual.

hum·ble (hum′bl, um′bl), *adj.* **-bler, -blest,** 1. not proud; modest. 2. lowly; unpretentious: *v.t.* **-bled, -bling,** to make humble; bring down. —**hum′bly,** *adv.*

hum·bug (hum′bug), *n.* 1. deception; hoax. 2. nonsense. 3. an impostor: *v.t.* **-bugged, -bugging,** to dupe; deceive: *interj.* nonsense!

hum·ding·er (hum-ding′ēr), *n.* [Slang], something viewed as excelling.

hum·drum (hum′drum), *adj.* dull; unexciting.

hu·mer·us (hū′mēr-ús), *n., pl.* **-mer·i** (-ī), the bone from the shoulder to the elbow. —**hu·mer·al,** *adj.*

hu·mid (hū′mid), *adj.* damp; moist.

hu·mid·i·fy (hū-mid′i-fī), *v.t.* **-fied, -fy·ing,** to make humid. —**hu·mid′i·fi·er,** *n.*

hu·mid·i·ty (′i-ti), *n., pl.* **-ties,** 1. dampness. 2. degree of air moisture.

hu·mi·dor (hū′mi-dôr), *n.* a jar, chest, etc. to keep tobacco moist, as by means of an enclosed dampened sponge.

hu·mil·i·ate (hū-mil′i-āt), *v.t.* **-at·ed, -at·ing,** to humble the pride or dignity of; abase. —**hu·mil·i·a′tion,** *n.*

hu·mil·i·ty (hū-mil′i-ti), *n.* the state or quality of being humble.

hum·ming·bird (hum′ing-bûrd), *n.* a tiny, brightly colored new-world bird that feeds on nectar and has narrow wings which vibrate rapidly, allowing it to hover in flight.

hum·mock (hum′ôk), *n.* a hillock; mound.

hu·mor (hū′mēr), *n.* 1. any anatomical fluid or fluidlike substance. 2. disposition; mood. 3. whim; caprice. 4. what makes something seem to be funny or ludicrous; also, ability to see or express this, or the expression itself: *v.t.* to indulge or adapt oneself to a mood, whim, etc.

hu·mor·ist (-ist), *n.* 1. one quick to see and appreciate or express the funny side of things. 2. such a writer, raconteur, etc.

hu·mor·ous (-ús), *adj.* funny; amusing.

hu·mour (hū′mēr), *n. & v.t.* British form for humor.

hump (hump), *n.* 1. a rounded protuberance on the back. 2. a hummock: *v.t.* to hunch.

hump·back (′bak), *n.* 1. a humped, deformed back. 2. a person with such a back.

hu·mus (hū′mús), *n.* organic soil, dark in color and made up of decaying material.

Hun (hun), *n.* one of an Asiatic people invading Europe in the 4th-5th centuries A.D.

hunch (hunch), *n.* 1. a hump. 2. a chunk; lump. 3. [Informal], an impression or intuition of something imminent: *v.t.* to arch into a hump: *v.i.* to move jerkily.

hunch·back (′bak), *n.* same as **humpback.**

hun·dred (hun′drid), *adj.* one more than ninety-nine; ten times ten: *n.* the cardinal number that is ten times ten; 100; C. 2. a division of an English county.

hun·dred·fold (-fōld), *adj. & adv. & n.* a hundred times as much or as many.

hun·dredth (hun′dridth), *adj.* next after 99th; 100th: *n.* 1. the one after the 99th. 2. one of 100 equal parts.

hun·dred·weight (′drid-wāt), *n.* a unit of weight, equal to 100 pounds in the U.S. and 112 pounds in England.

hung (hung), past tense and past participle of hang.

Hun·gar·i·an (hung-ger′i-án), *adj.* of or pertaining to Hungary or its inhabitants: *n.* 1. a native or inhabitant of Hungary. 2. the language of the Hungarians.

hun·ger (hung′gēr), *n.* 1. desire for or need of food. 2. the distress brought about by lack of food. 3. famine. 4. craving: *v.i.* 1. to feel or undergo hunger. 2. to crave.

hunger strike, a refusal to eat, as in making a protest.

hun·gry (hung′gri), *adj.* **-gri·er, -gri·est,** 1. feeling or showing hunger. 2. infertile, as soil. —hun′gri‧ly, adv.

hunk (hungk), n. [Informal], a large piece; large lump; chunk.

hun‧ker (hung′kẽr), v.i. to squat: n.pl. haunches or buttocks.

hunt (hunt), v.t. 1. to go after (game) so as to kill or catch as for food or sport. 2. to try hard to find. 3. to search after; follow closely; pursue; chase. 4. to go through (a place or area) in hunting something: v.i. to hunt something: n. 1. a hunting. 2. a group hunting together. 3. the area covered in hunting.

hunt‧er (′ẽr), n. 1. one that hunts. 2. a watch with a hunting case: also **hunting watch.**

hunting case, a watchcase with a protective hinged cover over the crystal.

hunt‧ress (′ris), n. a female hunter.

hunts‧man (hunts′mǎn), n., pl. -men (′mĕn), 1. a hunter. 2. the manager of a hunt, in charge of the hounds.

hur‧dle (hûr′dl), n. 1. [Chiefly British], a movable fence as of branches. 2. a rude frame formerly used in England to carry prisoners to execution. 3. one of a series of framelike barriers to be leaped over in a special kind of race. 4. any barrier or obstacle: v.t. -dled, -dling, 1. to enclose with hurdles. 2. to leap over (a hurdle). —hur′dler, n.

hur‧dy-gur‧dy (hûr′di-gûr′di), n., pl. -gur′dies, same as **barrel organ.**

hurl (hûrl), v.t. 1. to throw with violence; drive forcibly. 2. to utter with vehemence. 3. [Informal], in Baseball, to pitch: v.i. 1. to hurl something. 2. to hurtle. 3. [Informal], in Baseball, to pitch: n. a hurling. —hurl′er, n.

hurl‧ing (′ing), n. an Irish game resembling field hockey.

hurl‧y-burl‧y (hûr′li-bûr′li), n., pl. -burl′ies, great commotion; tumult.

hur‧rah (hǔ-rô′, -rä′), interj. & n. a shout of joy, triumph, etc.: v.i. & v.t. to cheer with hurrahs. Also **hur′ray′** (-rā′).

hur‧ri‧cane (hûr′i-kǎn, -kǎn), n. a violent tropical cyclone with winds of 73 or more miles per hour.

hurricane deck, the upper deck of a passenger ship, especially of a river steamer.

hurricane lamp, an oil lamp or candlestick with a tall chimney to guard the flame.

hur‧ried (hûr′id), adj. rushed or rushing.

hur‧ry (hûr′i), v.t. -ried, -ry‧ing, to impel to great or greater speed; rush; accelerate: v.i. to move or act fast or faster: n. a hurrying; rush. —hur′ri‧er, n.

hur‧ry-scur‧ry, hur‧ry-skur‧ry (-skûr′i), n. confused bustling about; agitation: v.i. -ried, -ry‧ing, to hurry about in a confused, agitated way: adj. hurried and confused: adv. in a hurry-scurry way.

hurt (hûrt), v.t. **hurt, hurt′ing,** 1. to cause pain to; make suffer. 2. to wound; injure. 3. to grieve. 4. to impair or damage: v.i. 1. to hurt someone or something. 2. to produce or undergo pain or suffering: n. 1. the act of hurting; pain, wound, or injury. 2. damage; harm.

hurt‧ful (′fŭl), adj. injurious; harmful. —hurt′ful‧ly, adv. —hurt′ful‧ness, n.

hur‧tle (hûrt′l), v.i. -tled, -tling, to move fast and violently: v.t. to hurl.

hur‧tle‧ber‧ry (hûrt′l-ber-i), n., pl. -ries, a huckleberry or whortleberry.

hus‧band (huz′bǎnd), n. a married man: v.t. to manage or use with economy.

hus‧band‧man (-mǎn), n., pl. -men (-mĕn), [Archaic], a farmer.

hus‧band‧ry (huz′bǎn-dri), n. 1. thrifty management or use. 2. farming.

hush (hush), interj. be still! silence!: n. quiet; silence: v.t. 1. to make quiet or silent. 2. to soothe: v.i. to be or become quiet.

hush-hush (′hush′), adj. [Informal], very confidential; highly secret.

hush puppy, in the South, a cornmeal fritter.

husk (husk), n. 1. the dry outer covering of certain fruits or seeds. 2. any husklike outer covering: v.t. to remove the husk or husks from. —husk′er, n.

hus‧ky (hus′ki), n., pl. -kies, [sometimes H-], a dog used to pull sleds in the Arctic.

husk‧y (hus′ki), adj. husk′i‧er, husk′i‧est, 1. of, full of, or like husks. 2. of the voice, more or less rough and throaty; somewhat hoarse. 3. big and strong; muscular: n., pl. husk′ies, a husky person. —husk′i‧ly, adv. —husk′i‧ness, n.

hus‧sar (hoo-zär′, hŭ-), n. a light-armed European cavalryman, usually with a brilliant dress uniform.

hus‧sy (huz′i, hus′i), n., pl. -sies, a bold, impudent girl or woman.

hus‧tings (hus′tingz), n. political campaigning or the place of this.

hus‧tle (hus′l), v.t. -tled, -tling, 1. to push roughly; jostle. 2. [Informal], to get (something) done, moved, etc. hurriedly. 3. [Slang], to obtain, promote, sell, take advantage of, etc. aggressively: v.i. 1. to move hurriedly. 2. [Informal], to work or act fast or with energy. 3. [Slang], to get money in aggressive or dishonest ways. 4. [Slang], to work as a prostitute: n. 1. the act of hustling. 2. [Informal], energetic action; drive; push. —hus′tler, n.

hut (hut), n. a small, crude structure used as a place to live in or for shelter.

hutch (huch), n. 1. a bin, box, or chest. 2. a kind of china cabinet with open shelves at the top. 3. a coop or pen. 4. a hut. 5. a mining trough for washing ore; also, a truck to carry ore out of a mine.

huz‧zah, huz‧za (hŭ-zä′), interj. & n. & v.i. & v.t. same as **hurrah.**

hy‧a‧cinth (hī′ǎ-sinth), n. 1. anciently, a sapphire or the like. 2. a reddish variety of mineral, as of zircon, used as a semiprecious stone. 3. a plant of the lily family, with narrow leaves and spikes of bell-shaped flowers. 4. a bluish purple. —hy‧a‧cin′thine (-sin′thin), adj.

Hy‧a‧des (hī′ǎ-dēz), n.pl. a cluster of over 200 stars in Taurus, five making a V.

hy‧a‧line (hī′ǎ-lin, -lin), adj. glassy; transparent: also **hy′a‧loid** (-loid).

hy‧a‧lite (-līt), n. a glassy opal.

hy‧brid (hī′brid), n. 1. the offspring of two individuals genetically unalike. 2. anything of mixed origin, composition, etc. 3. a word with elements from different languages: *adj.* of, or having the nature of, a hybrid.

hy·brid·ize (hī′brī-dīz), *v.t. & v.i.* -ized, -iz·ing, to interbreed, cross, or join with another, producing a hybrid or hybrids.

Hy·dra (hī′drä), *n., pl.* -dras, -drae (′drē), 1. in Greek Mythology, a nine-headed serpent, two heads replacing any head cut off: Hercules killed it. 2. [h-], a many-rooted or multiplying evil. 3. [h-], a small freshwater polyp with tentacles.

hy·drac·id (hī-dras′id), *n.* an acid without oxygen.

hy·dran·ge·a (hī-drän′jä, -dran′-), *n.* a shrubby plant of the saxifrage family, with large, showy clusters of flowers.

hy·drant (hī′dränt), *n.* an outlet from a water main, typically a large pipe with one or more nozzles.

hy·drar·gy·rum (hī-drär′ji-rŭm), *n.* mercury.

hy·drate (hī′drāt), *n.* a chemical compound of water and something else in a definite molecular ratio: *v.t. & v.i.* -drat·ed, -drat·ing, 1. to make into or become a hydrate. 2. to combine with water.

hy·drau·lic (hī-drô′lik, -drä′lik), *adj.* 1. of hydraulics. 2. operated by the movement and force of liquid, as brakes. 3. setting or hardening under water, as such mortar. —**hy·drau′li·cal·ly,** *adv.*

hy·drau·lics (′liks), *n.* the study or application of the mechanical properties of liquids in motion.

hy·dric (hī′drik), *adj.* of or containing hydrogen.

hy·dride (′drīd), *n.* a compound of hydrogen with another element or radical.

hy·dro-, a combining form meaning *water, hydrogen.*

hy·dro·car·bon (hī-drö-kär′bŏn), *n.* a compound containing only hydrogen and carbon, as benzene or methane.

hy·dro·ceph·a·lus (-sef′ä-lŭs), *n.* abnormal increase in cranial fluid: also **hy·dro·ceph′a·ly** (-li). —**hy·dro·ce·phal′ic** (-sē-fal′ik), *adj. & n.*

hy·dro·chlo·ric acid (-klôr′ik), a highly corrosive acid, a solution of the gas hydrogen chloride in water, used as in ore processing.

hy·dro·cy·an·ic acid (-sī-an′ik), an exceedingly poisonous, colorless acid, a solution of hydrogen cyanide in water, used as in metallurgy.

hy·dro·dy·nam·ic (-dī-nam′ik), *adj.* 1. of hydrodynamics. 2. of, from, or operated by the action of liquid in motion. —**hy·dro·dy·nam′i·cal·ly,** *adv.*

hy·dro·dy·nam·ics (′iks), *n.* the study or principles of the dynamics involved in the motion and action of liquids.

hy·dro·e·lec·tric (-i-lek′trik), *adj.* 1. producing electricity by water power or by the friction of water or steam. 2. of or pertaining to such production. —**hy·dro·e·lec·tric′i·ty,** *n.*

hy·dro·fluor·ic acid (-flôr′ik,-floor′ik), a colorless, fuming, corrosive acid, a solution of hydrogen fluoride in water, used as in etching glass.

hy·dro·foil (hī′drô-foil), *n.* 1. any one of a set of bladelike structures attached to certain watercraft hulls to give upward thrust at a given speed so as to lift the hull for high-speed operation. 2. a watercraft so equipped.

hy·dro·gen (hī′drô-jĕn), *n.* a flammable, colorless, odorless, gaseous chemical element, the lightest substance known.

hydrogen bomb, an extremely destructive atom bomb using an exploding nuclear-fission unit to fuse hydrogen atoms.

hydrogen peroxide, a colorless, syrupy compound of hydrogen and oxygen, often used diluted to bleach or disinfect.

hy·drog·ra·phy (hī-drog′rä-fi), *n.* 1. the study and mapping of oceans, lakes, and rivers. 2. the oceans, lakes, etc. of a given region. —**hy·drog′ra·pher,** *n.*

hy·drol·y·sis (-drol′i-sis), *n., pl.* -ses (-sēz), a chemical reaction in which a compound reacts with the ions of water to produce a weak acid, weak base, or both.

hy·dro·met·al·lur·gy (hī-drô-met′l-ûr-ji), *n.* the recovery of metals from ores by a liquid process, as by leaching with acid.

hy·drom·e·ter (hī-drom′ē-tēr), *n.* an instrument for determining the specific gravity of liquids.

hy·dro·pa·thy (-drop′ä-thi), *n.* treatment of disease by the use of water.

hy·dro·pho·bi·a (hī-drô-fō′bi-ä), *n.* 1. abnormal fear of water. 2. rabies.

hy·dro·phyte (hī′drô-fīt), *n.* a plant growing only in water or very wet earth.

hy·dro·plane (-plän), *n.* 1. a seaplane. 2. a light motorboat with hydrofoils or with a stepped flat bottom enabling it to skim along at high speeds: *v.i.* -planed, -plan·ing, to skim along in or like a hydroplane.

hy·dro·pon·ics (hī-drô-pon′iks), *n.* the cultivation of plants in solutions or in moist inert material supplied with minerals, instead of in soil.

hy·dro·stat·ics (-stat′iks), *n.* the principles governing fluid pressure and equilibrium, or the study of these. —**hy·dro·stat′ic,** *adj.*

hy·dro·ther·a·py (-ther′ä-pi), *n.* treatment of disease by baths, compresses, etc.

hy·dro·ther·mal (-thûr′mäl), *adj.* of or pertaining to the action of hot water.

hy·drous (hī′drŭs), *adj.* containing water, as certain minerals or chemical compounds.

hy·drox·ide (hī-drok′sid), *n.* a compound consisting of an element or radical combined with the hydroxyl radical.

hy·drox·yl (′sil), *n.* a univalent radical that consists of one atom of oxygen and one atom of hydrogen and that is present in bases and alcohols.

hy·e·na (hī-ē′nä), *n.* a wolflike animal of Africa and Asia that feeds on carrion: it has a bristly mane and short hind legs.

hy·giene (hī′jēn), *n.* 1. the science of health and its preservation. 2. sanitary practices; cleanliness.

hy·gi·en·ic (hī-ji-en′ik, -jē′nik, -jen′ik), *adj.* 1. of or pertaining to hygiene. 2. sanitary. —**hy·gi·en′i·cal·ly,** *adv.*

---

a in cap, ā in cane, ä in father, â in abet, e in met, ē in be, ê in baker, ê in regent, I in pit, ī in fine, i in manifest, o in hot, ô in horse, ō in bone, hy·gi·en·ist (hī'ji·ĕ·nist, -ji·nist; hī·jē'nist), *n.* a specialist in hygiene.

hy·grom·e·ter (hī·grom'ĕ·tēr), *n.* an instrument for determining the amount of moisture in the air. —hy·grom'e·try, *n.*

hy·gro·scope (hī'grŏ·skōp), *n.* an instrument indicating but not actually measuring atmospheric humidity.

hy·ing (hī'ing), alternate present participle of hie.

hy·men (hī'mĕn), *n.* a thin mucous membrane partly closing the vaginal orifice in virgins.

hy·me·ne·al (hī·mĕ·nē'ăl), *adj.* nuptial.

hy·me·nop·ter·an (-nop'tēr·ăn), *n.* any one of a large order of biting or sucking insects, as a bee or ant, marked by complete metamorphosis and, when winged, having four membranous wings: *adj.* of the hymenopterans: also hy·me·nop'ter·ous.

hymn (him), *n.* 1. a song praising the Supreme Being or any god or gods. 2. any song of praise: *v.t.* to express or praise in a hymn: *v.i.* to sing a hymn.

hym·nal (him'năl), *n.* a book or collection of religious hymns: also hymn'book (him'book). —hym·na·ry (him'nă·ri), *n., pl.* -ries.

hym·no·dy ('nŏ·di), *n.* 1. hymn singing. 2. hymns. 3. hymnology. —hym'no·dist, *n.*

hym·nol·o·gy (him·nol'ŏ·ji), *n.* 1. the study or writing of hymns. 2. hymnody. —hym·nol'o·gist, *n.*

hy·oid (hī'oid), *n.* a bone or bones, U-shaped in man, at the base of and supporting the tongue: *adj.* designating or of the hyoid bone or bones.

hy·os·cy·a·mine (hī·ŏ·sī'ă·mēn, -min), *n.* a colorless, crystalline, very poisonous alkaloid from plants of the nightshade family, used medically as a sedative, etc.

hyper-, a prefix meaning *over, above.*

hy·per·bo·la (hī·pûr'bŏ·lă), *n., pl.* -las, -lae (-lē) a curve formed by cone section, the cutting plane being more steeply inclined to the base than the cone side is.

hy·per·bo·le (-li), *n.* rhetorical overstatement or understatement.

hy·per·bol·ic (hī·pēr·bol'ik), *adj.* 1. of hyperbole; exaggerated or exaggerating. 2. of or like a hyperbola. Also hy·per·bol'i·cal. —hy·per·bol'i·cal·ly, *adv.*

hy·per·bo·re·an (-bŏ·rē'ăn), *adj.* 1. of the far north. 2. very cold.

hy·per·crit·i·cal (-krit'i·kl), *adj.* excessively critical.

hy·per·du·li·a (-dōō·lī'ă), *n.* in the *Roman Catholic Church,* the special veneration given to the Virgin Mary.

hy·per·sen·si·tive (-sen'si·tiv), *adj.* excessively sensitive.

hy·per·ten·sion (-ten'shŭn), *n.* 1. excessive tension. 2. abnormally high blood pressure.

hy·per·tro·phy (hī·pûr'trŏ·fi), *n.* notable increase in the size of an organ or tissue: *v.i. & v.t.* -phied, -phy·ing, to undergo or cause to undergo hypertrophy.

hy·phen (hī'fn), *n.* a mark (-) joining the parts of a compound word or, as at the end of a line, the parts of a divided word: *v.t.* to hyphenate.

hy·phen·ate (-āt), *v.t.* -at·ed, -at·ing, to join or write with a hyphen. —hy·phen·a'tion, *n.*

hyp·noid (hip'noid), *adj.* resembling sleep or hypnosis: also hyp·noid'al.

hyp·no·sis (hip·nō'sis), *n., pl.* -ses ('sēz), 1. a sleeplike, suggestible condition psychically induced. 2. same as hypnotism.

hyp·not·ic (-not'ik), *adj.* 1. sleep-inducing. 2. of, like, or inducing hypnosis. 3. easily hypnotized: *n.* 1. something inducing sleep. 2. something inducing hypnosis. 3. one hypnotized or easily hypnotized. —hyp·not'i·cal·ly, *adv.*

hyp·no·tism (hip'nŏ·tizm), *n.* 1. the act or practice of inducing hypnosis. 2. the science of hypnosis. —hyp'no·tist, *n.*

hyp·no·tize (-tīz), *v.t.* -tized, -tiz·ing, 1. to put into a state of hypnosis. 2. to influence by or as if by hypnosis.

hy·po (hī'pō), *n., pl.* -pos (-pōz), short for hypodermic.

hypo-, a prefix meaning *under, beneath.*

hy·po·chon·dri·a (hī·pŏ·kon'dri·ă), *n.* too much concern with one's health, typically accompanied by a readiness to imagine one is constantly ill or diseased or in danger of becoming so.

hy·po·chon·dri·ac (-ak), *n.* one characterized by hypochondria: *adj.* of hypochondria: also hy·po·chon·dri'a·cal (-kŏn·dri'ă·kl).

hy·poc·ri·sy (hi·pok'ri·si), *n., pl.* -sies, 1. a feigning of something so as to gain respect, honor, etc.; pretense of being something one is not; especially, a mere show of being sincere, virtuous, etc. 2. an instance or display of this.

hyp·o·crite (hip'ŏ·krit), *n.* one practicing or given to hypocrisy. —hyp·o·crit·i·cal (hip·ŏ·krit'i·kl), *adj.*

hy·po·der·mal (hī·pŏ·dûr'măl), *adj.* 1. of the hypodermis. 2. lying under the epidermis.

hy·po·der·mic (-dûr'mik), *adj.* 1. of the parts under the skin. 2. injected under the skin. 3. of the hypodermis: *n.* same as hypodermic injection or hypodermic syringe.

hypodermic injection, injection of a medicine or drug under the skin.

hypodermic syringe, a piston syringe attached to a hollow metal needle, for giving hypodermic injections.

hy·po·der·mis (hī·pŏ·dûr'mis), *n.* 1. in *Botany,* a specialized layer of cells, as for water storage, beneath the outermost layer of cells of a plant organ. 2. in *Zoology,* a layer of cells lying beneath and secreting the tough, nonliving outer structure of arthropods, etc.

hy·po·gas·tri·um (hī·pŏ·gas'tri·úm), *n., pl.* -tri·a (-ă), the lower, middle part of the abdomen. —hy·po·gas'tric, *adj.*

hy·pos·ta·sis (hi·pos'tă·sis), *n., pl.* -ses (-sēz), 1. in *Philosophy,* substance; essence. 2. in *Theology,* any of the three persons of the Trinity.

hy·po·style (hī'pŏ·stīl, hip'ŏ-), *n.* a structure with a roof supported by rows of pillars or columns.

hy·pot·e·nuse (hī·pot'n·ōōs), *n.* the side of a right-angled triangle opposite the right angle.

hy·poth·e·cate (hī·poth'ĕ·kāt), *v.t.* -cat·ed, -cat-

---

ing, 1. to pledge (property) to another as security without transferring possession or title; mortgage. 2. same as **hypothesize**. —**hy·poth·e·ca'tion**, *n.*

hy·poth·e·sis (hī-poth'ē-sis, hi-), *n., pl.* **-ses** (-sēz), a supposition, assumption, unproved theory, etc. advanced to provide a tentative explanation of something or a basis for further discussion, investigation, action, etc.

hy·poth·e·size (-sīz), *v.t. & v.i.* **-sized, -siz·ing,** to advance (something) as a hypothesis.

hy·po·thet·i·cal (hī-pō-thet'i-kl), *adj.* 1. of or based on a hypothesis. 2. not certain; conjectural. Also **hy·po·thet'ic.** —**hy·po·thet'i·cal·ly,** *adv.*

hyp·sog·ra·phy (hip-sog'rā-fi), *n.* 1. study and measurement of elevations of land and underwater surfaces as in relation to sea level. 2. the configuration of these; also, their representation or description. 4. same as hypsometry.

hyp·som·e·ter (-som'ē-tēr), *n.* 1. a device for determining height above sea level by measuring atmospheric pressure as indicated by the boiling point of water. 2. an instrument for measuring heights of trees by triangulation.

hyp·som·e·try (-tri), *n.* scientific measurement of heights, as done in hypsography.

hy·rax (hī'raks), *n., pl.* **-rax·es, -ra·ces** ('rā-sēz), a small, herbivorous, hoofed mammal of Africa and southwestern Asia.

hy·son (hī'sn), *n.* a green tea of China.

hys·sop (his'ŏp), *n.* 1. a fragrant plant of the mint family, with blue flowers. 2. in the *Bible,* a plant used for sprinkling in certain rites of the ancient Hebrews.

hys·ter·ec·to·my (his-tē-rek'tō-mi), *n., pl.* **-mies,** surgical removal of all or part of the uterus.

hys·te·ri·a (his-tir'i-ā, -ter'-), *n.* 1. a neurotic condition marked by physical disturbances of nonorganic origin, great excitability, etc. 2. any outburst of uncontrolled feeling.

hys·ter·ic (-ter'ik), *adj.* hysterical: *n.* one affected by hysteria.

hys·ter·i·cal ('i-kl), *adj.* 1. of, like, or typical of hysteria. 2. affected by or given to hysteria. 3. eliciting wild laughter. —**hys·ter'i·cal·ly,** *adv.*

hys·ter·ics ('iks), *n.pl.* a fit of hysteria.

hys·ter·ot·o·my (his-tē-rot'ō-mi), *n., pl.* **-mies,** incision of the uterus, as in a Caesarean section.

---

a in cap, ā in cane, ä in father, á in abet, e in met, ē in be, ē in baker, ê in regent, i in pit, ī in fine, i in manifest, o in hot, ô in horse, ō in bone,

I

I, i (ī), *n., pl.* **I's, i's** (īz), 1. the ninth letter of the English alphabet. 2. any of the various sounds of this letter, as in *pit, fine,* and *manifest.* 3. a type or impression of *I* or *i.*

I (ī), *adj.* shaped like *I: n.* 1. an object shaped like *I.* 2. a Roman numeral denoting 1: when placed after another numeral, a unit is to be added; when placed before another numeral, a unit is to be taken away.

I (ī), *pron., pl.* **we,** 1. the one speaking or writing. 2. the first personal singular pronoun: *n., pl.* **I's,** the ego, or self.

i (ī), *n.* 1. a Roman numeral for 1, as page *iii.* 2. the mathematical symbol for the square root of minus one.

-i-al (i-ăl), same as **-al.**

i·amb (ī'amb, 'am), *n.* a metrical foot of two syllables, the first unaccented, the second accented: also **i·am'bus** ('bŭs), *pl.* **-bus·es, -bi** ('bĭ).

i·am·bic (ī-am'bĭk), *adj.* 1. consisting of iambs. 2. pertaining to iambs: *n.* 1. an iamb. 2. an iambic verse.

-i·at·rics (i-at'riks), a suffix meaning *treatment of disease.*

i·at·ro·gen·ic (ī-at-rŏ-jen'ik), *adj.* of or pertaining to a fancied ailment or medical problem brought on by a neurotic reaction to a doctor's statements or treatments.

-i·a·try (ī'ă-tri), a suffix meaning *medical treatment.*

I-beam (ī'bēm), *n.* a steel beam having the shape, in cross section, of a capital I.

i·bex (ī'beks), *n., pl.* **i'bex·es, i·bi·ces** (ib'ĭ-sēz, ī'bĭ-), any of a species of wild mountain goats of Asia, Africa, or Europe, with large, ridged horns that curve backward.

i·bis (ī'bis), *n., pl.* **i'bis·es, i'bis,** any of several large wading birds related to the heron, characterized by a long, thin, downward-curved bill and long legs: the sacred ibis of the Nile was venerated in ancient Egypt.

-i·ble (i-bl, ĭ-bl), same as **-able.**

-ic (ik), a suffix meaning *like, pertaining to, caused by, causing, containing, having or one that produces, supports, has the nature of,* etc.: also **-i·cal** (ĭ-kl).

ice (īs), *n.* 1. water that has been frozen solid. 2. a piece or sheet of this. 3. a frozen, sweet dessert, often containing fruit juice or fruit flavoring. 4. [*Slang*], diamonds. 5. [*Slang*], graft or bribes: *v.i.* **iced, ic'ing,** 1. to convert into ice; freeze. 2. to preserve or make cold with ice. 3. to put icing on: *v.i.* to freeze (often followed by *up* or *over*).

ice age, same as **glacial epoch.**

ice bag, a bag of waterproof material to hold ice for application to a bruise, swelling, etc. on the body.

ice·berg (īs'bŭrg), *n.* a large mass of ice de-

tached from a glacier and floating in the sea.

ice·boat ('bōt), *n.* 1. a boat used to break a channel through ice; icebreaker. 2. a light boat mounted on runners and propelled by sails on ice.

ice·bound ('bound), *adj.* obstructed or hemmed in by ice, as a port or ship.

ice·box ('bäks), *n.* 1. a box or cabinet with a compartment for ice, used to refrigerate food. 2. any refrigerator.

ice·break·er ('brā-kĕr), *n.* 1. a strong boat used to break a channel through ice. 2. a structure to safeguard a pier against floating ice. 3. anything that breaks down formality or tension in a social group.

ice cream, cream, milk, or custard in various proportions and mixtures that is sweetened, flavored, and frozen to make a rich dessert: it is stirred during the freezing process to keep the ice crystals small and impart a smooth texture.

ice field, an extensive sheet of floating sea ice.

ice floe, a piece of floating sea ice.

ice hockey, a team game played on ice, in which the players, wearing ice skates, try to drive a puck into the opponents' goal, using a curved stick with a flat blade.

ice·man ('man), *n., pl.* **-men** ('men), 1. one who delivers ice. 2. one who sells ice.

ice milk, a dessert resembling ice cream, but made with skim milk.

ice pack, 1. a field of drifting ice, consisting of great masses packed together. 2. an ice bag or cold compress enclosing ice, for application to the body.

ice pick, a small, sharply pointed tool for breaking ice into small pieces.

ice plant, a low-growing plant used as ground cover, having fleshy leaves that glisten on the surface.

ice shelf, a thick extension of glacial ice protruding out to sea from a polar shore.

ice skate, a shoe with a metal blade or blades, for skating on ice. —**ice skater.**

ice-skate ('skāt), *v.i.* **-skat·ed, -skat·ing,** to skate on ice.

ice water, water chilled for drinking as by ice.

ich·neu·mon (ik-nū'mŏn, -nōō'-), *n.* 1. the Egyptian mongoose. 2. same as **ichneumon fly.**

ichneumon fly, a winged insect that lays its eggs on the larvae of other insects: the larvae of the ichneumon fly proceed to become parasites in or on the host larvae: also **ichneumon wasp.**

ich·nite (ik'nīt), **ich·no·lite** ('nŏ-lit), *n.* a stone impressed with a fossil footprint.

ich·nog·ra·phy (ik-näg'rä-fi), *n.* 1. the ground plan of a building; floor plan. 2. the art of drawing ground plans.

ŏ in dragon, ōō in crude, oo in wool, u in cup, ü in cure, ū in turn, ŭ in focus, oi in boy, ou in house, th in thin, th in sheathe, g in get, j in joy, y in yet.

ich·nol·o·gy (ik-näl′ô-ji), *n.* the branch of science which treats of fossil footprints.

i·chor (ī′kôr, -kŏr), *n.* 1. in *classical mythology,* the ethereal fluid which ran, instead of blood, in the veins of the gods. 2. a thin, watery, acrid serum from an ulcer or wound.

ich·thy·ic (ik′thi-ik), *adj.* fishlike; pertaining to fishes.

ich·thy·o- (ik′thi-ō, -ô), a combining form meaning *fish.*

ich·thy·oid (-oid), *adj.* 1. like a fish. 2. shaped like a fish: *n.* any fishlike vertebrate.

ich·thy·o·lite (-ô-līt), *n.* a fossil fish (or part of a fish).

ich·thy·ol·o·gy (ik-thi-ol′ô-ji), *n.* the branch of zoology treating of fishes, their structure, classification, etc.

ich·thy·o·saur (ik′thi-ô-sôr), *n.* an extinct prehistoric marine reptile with a fishlike body, flippers, and a dolphinlike head.

ich·thy·o·sis (ik-thi-ō′sis), *n.* a hereditary skin disease in which the skin is thickened, rough, dry, and scaly.

i·ci·cle (ī′si-kl), *n.* a tapering piece of ice formed in a pointed, spikelike mass hanging as from eaves where water runs down and freezes.

i·ci·ly (ī′si-li), *adv.* in an icy way.

i·ci·ness (ī′si-nis), *n.* icy condition.

ic·ing (ī′sing), *n.* a flavored sugary covering for cakes and other pastries.

i·con (ī′kon), *n.* an image or representation; specifically, in the *Orthodox Eastern Church,* a sacred image or picture.

i·con·o·clasm (ī-kon′ô-klazm), *n.* the actions or beliefs of an iconoclast.

i·con·o·clast (-klast), *n.* 1. an image breaker; specifically, one destroying religious images or opposed to their use. 2. one attacking established ideas or institutions. —**i·con·o·clas′tic,** *adj.*

i·co·nog·ra·phy (ī-kô-nog′rá-fi), *n.* representation by images or pictures.

i·co·nol·o·gy (-nol′ô-ji), *n.* 1. the study of icons. 2. icons collectively.

i·co·nos·ta·sis (ī-kô-nos′tá-sis), *n., pl.* -ses (-sēz), in the *Orthodox Eastern Church,* a partition decorated with icons and dividing off the sanctuary: also **i·con·o·stas** (ī-kon′ô-stas).

i·co·sa·he·dron (ī-kô-sá-hē′drôn), *n., pl.* -dra (′drá), -drons, a solid figure with twenty plane surfaces.

-ics (iks), a suffix meaning *art, science, study.*

ic·ter·us (ik′tēr-ŭs), *n.* jaundice.

ic·tus (ik′tŭs), *n., pl.* -tus·es, -tus, 1. rhythmical stress. 2. in *Medicine,* a stroke or sudden attack.

i·cy (ī′si), *adj.* **i′ci·er, i′ci·est,** 1. of, full of, or like ice. 2. frigid; glacial.

id (id), *n.* in *Psychoanalysis,* the aggregate of instinctual drive and psychic energy, viewed as dominated by the desire to gain pleasure and avoid pain.

ID (ī′dē′), *n., pl.* **ID's,** a card or document used to identify a person, verify personal data, etc.: also written I.D.

I'd (īd), 1. I had. 2. I would. 3. I should.

i·de·a (ī-dē′á), *n.* 1. a mental image or conception. 2. an opinion or belief. 3. a plan or intention. 4. meaning or significance.

i·de·al (ī-dē′ál), *adj.* 1. existing as an idea, archetype, etc. 2. conforming to what is viewed as perfect. 3. of or exemplifying an idea or conception; conceptual. 4. existing only in the mind: *n.* 1. a conception of something in its most perfect form. 2. an individual or thing viewed as being the objective fulfillment of such a conception. 3. something existing in the mind only. 4. a goal or principle, especially when noble.

i·de·al·ism (-izm), *n.* 1. behavior or thought based on idealization. 2. a striving after ideals. 3. in art or literature, representation of what is viewed as perfect. 4. in *Philosophy,* a theory holding that objects of perception are actually ideational.

i·de·al·ist (-ist), *n.* 1. one who pursues the ideal. 2. one holding to idealism.

i·de·al·is·tic (ī-dē-á-lis′tik), *adj.* 1. of, pertaining to, or typical of an idealist or idealism. 2. of or based on idealism. —**i·de·al·is′ti·cal·ly,** *adv.*

i·de·al·i·ty (ī-di-al′ĭ-ti), *n.* 1. the state or quality of being ideal. 2. the faculty to form ideals.

i·de·al·ize (ī-dē′á-līz), *v.t.* -ized, -iz·ing, to make or represent as ideal: *v.i.* to form ideals. —**i·de·al·i·za′tion,** *n.*

i·de·al·ly (ī-dē′ál-i), *adv.* 1. in an ideal way; perfectly. 2. in theory.

i·de·ate (ī′di-āt, ī-dē′āt), *v.t. & v.i.* -at·ed, -at·ing, to form an idea (of); imagine or conceive.

i·de·a·tion (ī-di-ā′shŭn), *n.* the formation or conception of ideas by the mind. —**i·de·a′tion·al,** *adj.*

i·dée fixe (ē-dā′ fēks′), [French], a fixed idea; obsession.

i·dem (ī′dem, ē′dem), *pron.* [Latin], the same as that previously mentioned.

i·den·ti·cal (ī-den′ti-kl), *adj.* being exactly or essentially the same or alike.

i·den·ti·fi·ca′tion (ī-den-ti-fi-kā′shŭn, i-), *n.* 1. an identifying or being identified. 2. anything by which a person or thing can be identified.

i·den·ti·fy (ī-den′ti-fī, i-), *v.t.* -fied, -fy·ing, 1. to make, prove to be, or consider as the same, nearly the same, or closely associated. 2. to recognize or indicate the identity of: *v.i.* to put oneself sympathetically into another's place; empathize. —**i·den·ti·fi′a·ble,** *adj.*

i·den·ti·ty (ī-den′ti-ti, i-), *n., pl.* -ties, 1. exact or essential sameness. 2. the condition of being the same as a person or thing described or claimed. 3. the condition or fact of being a specific person or thing; individuality.

id·e·o·gram (id′i-ô-gram, ī′di-), *n.* a graphic symbol used to stand for, without actually naming, an object or idea: also **id′e·o·graph.**

id·e·o·graph·ic (id-i-ô-graf′ik, ī-di-), *adj.* of or like an ideogram or idiography: also **id·e·o·graph′i·cal.**

id·e·og·ra·phy (id-i-og′rá-fi, ī-di-), *n.* the use of idiograms.

i·de·o·log·i·cal (ī-di-ŏ-loj'i-kl, id-i-ŏ'-), *adj.* of or pertaining to ideology: also **i·de·o·log'ic.**

i·de·ol·o·gist (ī-di-ol'ŏ-jist, id-i-), *n.* a specialist in, or devotee of, a particular ideology or ideology in general.

i·de·ol·o·gy (-ji), *n., pl.* **-gies,** 1. the study of ideas. 2. a particular body of ideas, as that on which a certain political system is based. 3. abstract or fanciful speculation.

ides (īdz), *n. pl.* in the ancient Roman calendar, the 15th of March, May, July, or October, or the 13th of other months.

id·i·o·cy (id'i-ŏ-si), *n., pl.* **-cies,** 1. the state of being an idiot. 2. **idiotic** behavior. 3. an idiotic act or remark.

id·i·om (id'i-ŏm), *n.* 1. the language or dialect of a people, region, class, etc. 2. the way the words of a language are characteristically joined together to express thought. 3. any accepted locution having a construction peculiar to itself or a particular meaning not derivable from its elements. 4. any characteristic style, as in art or music. —**id·i·o·mat'ic** (-ŏ-mat'ik), *adj.* —**id·i·o·mat'i·cal·ly,** *adv.*

id·i·o·path·ic (id-i-ŏ-path'ik), *adj.* designating or of a disease whose cause is unknown or uncertain.

id·i·o·syn·cra·sy (-sing'krä-si, -sin'-), *n., pl.* **-sies,** 1. a peculiarity of constitution or temperament. 2. a mannerism or other such peculiarity. 3. an individualistic reaction, as to a drug, different from the expected reaction. —**id·i·o·syn·crat'ic** (-sin-krat'ik), *adj.*

id·i·ot (id'i-ŏt), *n.* 1. an adult with an intelligence quotient of less than 25: obsolescent term. 2. a very foolish person.

id·i·ot·ic (id-i-ot'ik), *adj.* of or like an idiot. —**id·i·ot'i·cal·ly,** *adv.*

i·dle (ī'dl), *adj.* **i'dler, i'dlest,** 1. unoccupied; unemployed; not active or busy. 2. averse to labor; lazy. 3. useless; worthless. 4. vain; futile. 5. baseless; unfounded: *v.i.* **i'dled, i'dling,** 1. to move slowly or aimlessly; loaf. 2. to be doing nothing; be inactive. 3. to run without transmitting power, as a motor with disengaged gears: *v.t.* 1. to waste; squander. 2. to make inactive or unemployed. 3. to cause to idle, as a motor. —**i'dle·ness,** *n.* —**i'dly,** *adv.*

i·dler (īd'lēr), *n.* 1. one that wastes time; loafer. 2. a gearwheel placed between two others to transfer motion from one to the other without changing their direction or speed: also **idle wheel.**

i·dol (ī'dl), *n.* 1. an image of a divinity, used as an object of worship. 2. a person or thing loved or admired to excess.

i·dol·a·ter (ī-dol'ă-tēr), *n.* 1. one that worships idols. 2. one that loves or admires another to excess.

i·dol·a·trous (-trŭs), *adj.* of an idolater or idolatry.

i·dol·a·try (-tri), *n., pl.* **-tries,** 1. worship of idols. 2. excessive love of or admiration for another.

i·dol·ize (ī'dl-īz), *v.t.* **-ized, -iz·ing,** to worship, love, or admire as or as if an idol. —**i·dol·i·za'tion,** *n.*

i·dyll, i·dyl (ī'dl), *n.* 1. a short writing describing a simple, pleasant, peaceful scene of rural, pastoral, or domestic life. 2. a scene or incident suitable for this. —**i·dyll'ic** (i-dil'ik), *adj.*

-ie (i), a suffix meaning *small, one that is as specified.*

-ier (ir, ēr, ē'ēr, yēr), a suffix meaning *one concerned with* (*a specified thing*).

if (if), *conj.* 1. on condition that; supposing that. 2. allowing that; granting that. 3. whether: *n.* a condition or supposition.

ig·loo (ig'lōō), *n., pl.* **-loos,** an Eskimo house or hut, usually dome-shaped and built of blocks of packed snow.

ig·ne·ous (ig'ni-ŭs), *adj.* 1. of or like fire; fiery. 2. produced by fire; specifically, formed by volcanic action or intense heat, as certain rocks.

ig·nes·cent (ig-nes'nt), *adj.* 1. bursting into flame. 2. emitting sparks when struck with steel: *n.* an ignescent substance.

ig·nis fat·u·us (ig'nis fach'oo-wŭs), *pl.* **ig·nes fat·u·i** (ig'nēz fach'oo-wī), 1. a shifting, elusive light seen at night moving over swamps and marshes, probably caused by combustion of gases from decaying organic matter: popularly called *will-o'-the-wisp, jack-o'-lantern.* 2. a misleading hope, goal, or influence; deception; delusion.

ig·nit·a·ble, ig·nit·i·ble (ig-nīt'ă-bl), *adj.* capable of being ignited.

ig·nite (ig-nīt'), *v.t.* **-nit'ed, -nit'ing,** 1. to set fire to; get burning. 2. to heat intensely; specifically, to make incandescent. 3. to excite or set aflame the feelings of: *v.i.* to become ignited; start burning. —**ig·nit'er, ig·ni'tor,** *n.*

ig·ni·tion (ig-nish'ŭn), *n.* 1. an igniting or being ignited. 2. a means of igniting. 3. the igniting of the explosive mixture in the cylinder of an internal-combustion engine; also, the igniting device or system.

ig·no·ble (ig-nō'bl), *adj.* not noble; base; mean. —**ig·no'bly,** *adv.*

ig·no·min·i·ous (ig-nŏ-min'i-ŭs), *adj.* 1. of or full of ignominy; shameful; disgraceful. 2. despicable. 3. humiliating.

ig·no·min·y (ig'nŏ-min-i), *n., pl.* **-min·ies,** 1. loss of one's good name; public disgrace or dishonor. 2. disgraceful, shameful, or contemptible quality, behavior, or act.

ig·no·ra·mus (ig-nŏ-rā'mŭs, -ram'ŭs), *n., pl.* **-mus·es,** an ignorant person.

ig·no·rance (ig'nēr-ăns), *n.* the state or quality of being ignorant; want of knowledge or awareness.

ig·no·rant (-ănt), *adj.* 1. lacking knowledge, education, or experience. 2. showing or resulting from such lack. 3. unaware.

ig·nore (ig-nōr'), *v.t.* **-nored', -nor'ing,** 1. to disregard deliberately; treat as if unseen, unrecognized, unknown, etc. 2. in *Law,* to reject (a bill of indictment) for lack of evidence.

i·gua·na (i-gwä'nă), *n.* a large, harmless, tropical American lizard.

i·kon (ī'kon), *n.* same as icon.

il·e·um (il'i-ŭm), *n., pl.* **-e·a** (-ā), the lower part of the small intestine.

i·lex (ī'leks), *n.* a holly or a holm oak.

Il·i·ad (il'i-ăd), *n.* a long Greek epic poem, ascribed to Homer, set in the tenth year of the Trojan War.

ilk (ilk), *n.* class; sort; kind: only in phrases like *of that ilk, of his ilk,* etc.

ill (il), *adj.* worse, worst, 1. harmful; evil; bad. 2. causing or attended by suffering, hardship, etc.; adverse. 3. not kind or friendly; harsh; cruel. 4. not favorable; unpropitious. 5. not proper; faulty; imperfect. 6. not healthy or well; indisposed, sick, or diseased: *adv.* worse, worst, 1. in an ill manner; badly, improperly, etc. 2. with difficulty; scarcely: *n.* anything bringing harm, trouble, suffering, etc.

I'll (īl), 1. I shall. 2. I will.

ill-ad·vised (il'ăd-vīzd'), *adj.* showing or resulting from faulty advice or lack of proper consideration; injudicious; unwise. —**ill'-ad·vis'ed·ly** (-vī'zid-li), *adv.*

il·la·tion (i-lā'shŭn), *n.* an inference, deduction, or conclusion.

il·la·tive (il'ă-tiv, i-lāt'iv), *adj.* of, like, introducing, or based on an illation: *n.* 1. an illative term, as *therefore.* 2. an illation.

ill-bred (il'bred'), *adj.* impolite; rude.

il·le·gal (i-lē'găl), *adj.* not legal.

il·leg·i·ble (i-lej'i-bl), *adj.* not easily legible or not legible at all. —**il·leg'i·bly,** *adv.*

il·le·git·i·mate (il-ē-jit-i-mit), *adj.* 1. born out of wedlock; bastard. 2. not correctly deduced; not logical. 3. not lawful; irregular. 4. unsanctioned.

ill-fat·ed (il'fāt'id), *adj.* unlucky.

ill-fa·vored ('fā'vĕrd), *adj.* 1. not pleasant or agreeable in appearance. 2. offensive.

ill-got·ten ('got'n), *adj.* obtained in an unjust or dishonest way.

ill humor, a disagreeable, cross, or sullen mood. —**ill'-hu'mored,** *adj.*

il·lib·er·al (i-lib'ĕr-ăl), *adj.* 1. not tolerant; narrow-minded. 2. stingy.

il·lic·it (i-lis'it), *adj.* not allowed by law, custom, rule, etc.; unlawful or unauthorized. —**il·lic'it·ly,** *adv.*

il·lim·it·a·ble (i-lim'it-ă-bl), *adj.* without limit; immeasurable.

il·lit·er·a·cy (i-lit'ĕr-ă-si), *n.* 1. the state or quality of being illiterate; especially, inability to read or write. 2. *pl.* **-cies,** a mistake in writing or speaking, as a grammatical blunder, that indicates a lack of education.

il·lit·er·ate (-it), *adj.* ignorant; uneducated; especially, not knowing how to read or write: *n.* an illiterate person.

ill-man·nered (il'man'ĕrd), *adj.* impolite.

ill-na·tured ('nā'chĕrd), *adj.* cross; surly.

ill-ness (il'nis), *n.* the condition of being ill; sickness or disease.

il·log·i·cal (i-loj'i-kl), *adj.* not logical; lacking sound reasoning.

ill-starred (il'stärd'), *adj.* unlucky.

ill-tem·pered ('tem'pĕrd), *adj.* easily angered; irritable; quarrelsome.

ill-timed ('tīmd'), *adj.* inopportune.

ill-treat ('trēt'), *v.t.* to treat badly.

il·lu·mi·nant (i-lōō'mi-nănt), *adj.* giving light; illuminating: *n.* something giving light.

il·lu·mi·nate (-nāt), *v.t.* **-nat·ed, -nat·ing,** 1. to give light to; make light or bright. 2. to throw light upon; make plain or clear; elucidate. 3. to inform; enlighten. 4. to decorate with lights. 5. to decorate (an initial letter, a manuscript, etc.) with gold, silver, bright colors, tiny pictures, etc. —**il·lu'mi·na·tor,** *n.*

il·lu·mi·na·tion (i-lōō-mi-nā'shŭn), *n.* 1. the act of illuminating or condition of being illuminated. 2. supply of light; specifically, the intensity of light per unit of area. 3. the decoration used in illuminating initial letters, manuscripts, etc.

il·lu·mine (i-lōō'min), *v.t.* **-mined, -min·ing,** to illuminate.

ill-us·age (il'ū'sij, 'zij), *n.* bad treatment; unkindness, abuse, etc.

ill-use (il'ūz'), *v.t.* **-used', -us'ing,** to treat badly; ill-treat: *n.* ('ūs'), ill-usage.

il·lu·sion (i-lōō'zhŭn), *n.* 1. a false idea, opinion, or belief. 2. a deceptive appearance. 3. a false perception, interpretation, etc.; also, the misleading image resulting in such a false impression. 4. a hallucination.

il·lu·sion·ist (-ist), *n.* 1. one subject to illusion. 2. a sleight-of-hand performer.

il·lu·sive (i-lōō'siv), *adj.* illusory.

il·lu·so·ry ('sĕr-i), *adj.* of, like, based on, or causing illusion; deceptive; unreal.

il·lus·trate (il'ŭs-trāt, i-lus'trāt), *v.t.* **-trat·ed, -trat·ing,** 1. to make clear or intelligible; elucidate or explain, as with examples. 2. to provide (books, magazines, etc.) with explanatory or decorative pictures, drawings, etc.: *v.i.* to provide an example or examples so as to make something clear.

il·lus·tra·tion (il-ŭs-trā'shŭn), *n.* 1. the act of illustrating or the state of being illustrated. 2. a picture, drawing, example, etc. used to illustrate something.

il·lus·tra·tive (i-lus'trā-tiv, il'ŭs-trāt-iv), *adj.* serving as an illustration.

il·lus·tra·tor (il'ŭs-trāt-ĕr, i-lus'trāt-ĕr), *n.* one that illustrates; specifically, an artist doing illustrations as for a book.

il·lus·tri·ous (i-lus'tri-ŭs), *adj.* distinguished; eminent; renowned.

ill will, unfriendly or hostile disposition.

I'm (īm), I am.

im·age (im'ij), *n.* 1. a likeness, especially a statue, of a person or thing. 2. an idol. 3. the visual semblance of something, formed by rays of light, as in a mirror. 4. a person or thing that is a close counterpart or a copy of another. 5. a mental picture; conception, idea, or impression. 6. a personification or embodiment of something. 7. a metaphor, simile, or other figure of speech: *v.t.* **-aged, -ag·ing,** 1. to represent or portray; delineate. 2. to reflect; mirror. 3. to picture mentally; imagine. 4. to personify or embody.

im·age·ry (im'ij-ri, -ĕr-i), *n., pl.* **-ries,** 1. mental images. 2. figurative language.

---

a in cap, ā in cane, ä in father, å in abet, e in met, ē in be, ē in baker, ê in regent, i in pit, ī in fine, ĭ in manifest, o in hot, ô in horse, ō in bone,

i·mag·i·na·ble (i-maj'i-nà-bl), *adj.* that can be imagined. —i·mag'i·na·bly, *adv.*

i·mag·i·nar·y (-ner-i), *adj.* existing only in the imagination; unreal; fanciful.

i·mag·i·na·tion (i-maj-i-nā'shŭn), *n.* 1. the act or power of forming mental images of what is not actually present. 2. the creative faculty. 3. anything imagined; mental picture or conception. 4. an irrational notion; mere fancy. 5. responsiveness to imaginative creations of others. 6. quick or creative resourcefulness, as in solving difficulties.

i·mag·i·na·tive (i-maj'i-nà-tiv, -nāt-iv), *adj.* of, from, or marked by imagination.

i·mag·ine (i-maj'in), *v.t.* -ined, -in·ing, 1. to form a mental picture of; conceive mentally; produce by the imagination. 2. to think; suppose; conjecture: *v.i.* 1. to use the imagination. 2. to think; suppose.

im·ag·ism (im'à-jizm), *n.* a movement in modern poetry (c. 1909-1917), marked by use of precise, concrete images, free verse, and suggestion. —im'ag·ist, *n.*

i·ma·go (i-mā'gō), *n., pl.* -goes, -gos, i·mag·i·nes (i-maj'i-nēz), a fully matured insect.

i·mam (i-mäm'), *n.* 1. the leader of prayer in a Moslem mosque. 2. [often I-], a title for any of various Moslem leaders and rulers.

i·ma·ret (i-mä'ret), *n.* in Turkey, an inn or hospice.

im·bal·ance (im-bal'ăns), *n.* lack of balance, as in proportion, functioning, etc.

im·be·cile (im'bē-sl), *n.* 1. an adult with an intelligence quotient of from 25 to 50: obsolescent term. 2. a very foolish person: *adj.* showing feeble intellect; foolish or stupid: also im·be·cil'ic (-sil'ik).

im·be·cil·i·ty (im-bē-sil'i-ti), *n., pl.* -ties, 1. the state of being an imbecile. 2. imbecile behavior. 3. an imbecile act or remark.

im·bibe (im-bīb'), *v.t. & v.i.* -bibed', -bib'ing, 1. to drink or drink in. 2. to absorb. 3. to inhale. —im·bib'er, *n.*

im·bi·bi·tion (im-bi-bish'ŭn), *n.* absorption or adsorption of water by certain colloids, as in seeds, wood, etc., with resultant swelling of tissues.

im·bri·cate (im'bri-kit, -kāt), *adj.* 1. overlapping evenly, as tiles or fish scales. 2. decorated or patterned thus: *v.t.* (-kāt), -cat·ed, -cat·ing, to place (tiles, shingles, etc.) in overlapping order: *v.i.* to overlap. —im·bri·ca'tion, *n.*

im·bro·glio (im-brōl'yō), *n., pl.* -glios, an intricate and perplexing state of affairs, often one involving misunderstanding or strife.

im·brue (im-brōō'), *v.t.* -brued', -bru'ing, to wet, soak, drench, or stain, especially with blood.

im·bue (im-bū'), *v.t.* -bued', -bu'ing, 1. to tinge deeply; dye. 2. to permeate, as with principles or aims; pervade.

im·i·ta·ble (im'i-tā-bl), *adj.* capable of being imitated.

im·i·tate (im'i-tāt), *v.t.* -tat·ed, -tat·ing, 1. to follow or use as a model or pattern; take example by. 2. to mimic; copy. 3. to produce a likeness or semblance of, as in qualities, form, color, or conduct. 4. to resemble closely; counterfeit.

im·i·ta·tion (im-i-tā'shŭn), *n.* 1. the act of imitating. 2. that which is produced by imitating: *adj.* that merely imitates or that is made in imitation; not genuine.

im·i·ta·tive (im'i-tāt-iv), *adj.* 1. that imitates or reproduces something original, genuine, or different. 2. given to imitating.

im·i·ta·tor (-ēr), *n.* one that imitates.

im·mac·u·late (i-mak'yŭ-lit), *adj.* 1. spotlessly clean. 2. flawless; without blemish. 3. pure; sinless.

Immaculate Conception, the Roman Catholic doctrine that the Virgin Mary, though conceived naturally, was kept free of all stain of original sin from the instant of her conception.

im·ma·nence (im'à-nĕns), *n.* the quality or state of being immanent: also im'ma·nen·cy.

im·ma·nent (-nĕnt), *adj.* 1. living, remaining, or operating within; inherent. 2. in *Theology,* present throughout the universe: said of God.

Im·man·u·el (i-man'yoo-wĕl), *n.* a name given by Isaiah to the Messiah of his prophecy (*Isa. vii,* 14), often applied to Jesus (*Matt. i,* 23).

im·ma·te·ri·al (im-à-tir'i-ăl), *adj.* 1. not consisting of matter; incorporeal. 2. not important or not pertinent.

im·ma·ture (im-à-toor'), *adj.* not mature; not ripe; not fully grown, developed, perfected, etc. —im·ma·tu'ri·ty, *n.*

im·meas·ur·a·ble (i-mezh'ēr-à-bl), *adj.* not measurable; limitless; vast. —im·meas·ur·a·bil'i·ty, *n.* —im·meas'ur·a·bly, *adv.*

im·me·di·a·cy (i-mē'di-à-si), *n.* the quality or state of being immediate; especially, direct relevance or direct presence.

im·me·di·ate (i-mē'di-it), *adj.* not having anything between; not separated by intervening space, time, etc.; not mediate, remote or secondary; direct, closest, nearest, next, or instant.

im·me·di·ate·ly (-li), *adv.* without anything intervening; directly; instantly.

im·me·mo·ri·al (im-è-môr'i-ăl), *adj.* extending beyond the reach of memory, record, or tradition.

im·mense (i-mens'), *adj.* 1. originally, immeasurable. 2. very large; huge. 3. [Informal], excellent.

im·mense·ly (-'li), *adv.* 1. to an immense degree. 2. very much, extremely, or excessively.

im·men·si·ty (i-men'si-ti), *n.* 1. the quality or state of being immense. 2. vastness. 3. infinity.

im·merge (i-mŭrj'), *v.i.* -merged', -merg'ing, to plunge or disappear, as into a liquid.

im·merse (i-mŭrs'), *v.t.* -mersed', -mers'ing, 1. to plunge or dip into or as if into a liquid. 2. to baptize by dipping under water. 3. to plunge into a given condition or state, as of thought or preoccupation.

im·mers·i·ble ('l-bl), *adj.* capable of being immersed in water without harm, as some electric appliances.

im·mer·sion (i-mŭr'shŭn, 'zhŭn), *n.* 1. the act of immersing or state of being immersed. 2. baptism in which the whole body is dipped under water.

immersion heater, an electric coil or rod to heat water while immersed in it.

im·mi·grant (im'i-gränt), *n.* one that immigrates: *adj.* 1. immigrating. 2. of or pertaining to immigrants or immigration.

im·mi·grate (im'i-grät), *v.i.* -grat·ed, -grat·ing, to come into a new country or region, especially so as to settle in it. —**im·mi·gra'tion,** *n.*

im·mi·nence (im'i-nèns), *n.* 1. the quality or condition of being imminent: also **im'mi·nen·cy.** 2. something imminent.

im·mi·nent (im'i-nènt), *adj.* about to take place or happen, as evil or catastrophe; threatening.

im·mo·bile (i-mō'bl), *adj.* 1. not movable; firmly in place; stable. 2. not moving; motionless. —**im·mo·bil'i·ty,** *n.*

im·mo·bi·lize ('bi-līz), *v.t.* -lized, -liz·ing, to make immobile; keep from moving. —**im·mo·bi·li·za'tion,** *n.*

im·mod·er·ate (i-mod'ēr-it), *adj.* not moderate; not kept within reasonable limits; intemperate; excessive.

im·mod·est (i-mod'ist), *adj.* not modest; not properly restrained; too bold; forward; showing a lack of decorum or decency. —**im·mod'es·ty,** *n.*

im·mo·late (im'ō-lāt), *v.t.* -lat·ed, -lat·ing, to make a sacrificial offering of by killing. —**im·mo·la'tion,** *n.*

im·mo·ral (i-môr'ál), *adj.* 1. contrary to accepted principles of right and wrong; bad; evil. 2. unchaste.

im·mo·ral·i·ty (im-ō-ral'i-ti), *n.* 1. the quality or state of being immoral. 2. immoral behavior. 3. *pl.* -ties, an immoral act or practice; vice.

im·mor·tal (i-môr'tl), *adj.* not mortal; not subject to death; imperishable: *n.* 1. an immortal being. 2. *pl.* the ancient Greek or Roman gods.

im·mor·tal·i·ty (i-môr-tal'i-ti), *n.* the quality or state of being immortal; exemption from death or oblivion.

im·mor·tal·ize (i-môr'tá-līz), *v.t.* -ized, -iz·ing, to render immortal; especially, to bestow lasting fame upon.

im·mor·telle (im-ôr-tel'), *n.* same as **everlasting** (noun 2).

im·mov·a·ble (i-mōōv'á-bl), *adj.* 1. incapable of being moved; fixed. 2. steadfast; unchanging: *n. pl.* in *Law,* land, trees, buildings, etc., that by their nature cannot be moved. —**im·mov·a·bil'i·ty,** *n.* —**im·mov'a·bly,** *adv.*

im·mune (i·mūn'), *adj.* 1. exempt. 2. not susceptible to a specific disease.

immune body, same as **antibody.**

im·mu·ni·ty (i-mūn'i-ti), *n., pl.* -ties, 1. exemption from a duty, office, tax, etc. 2. a condition by which one is able to resist a specified disease, as by the formation of antibodies.

im·mu·nize (im'yù-nīz), *v.t.* -nized, -niz·ing, to make immune, as by inoculation. —**im·mu·ni·za'tion,** *n.*

im·mu·nol·o·gy (im-yoo-nol'ō-ji), *n.* the branch of medicine dealing with immunity from disease, rejection of foreign tissue, etc. —**im·mu·nol'o·gist,** *n.*

im·mure (i-myoor'), *v.t.* -mured, -mur·ing, to enclose within walls; confine. —**im·mure'ment,** *n.*

im·mu·ta·ble (i-mūt'á-bl), *adj.* unchangeable; invariable; permanent. —**im·mu·ta·bil'i·ty,** *n.* —**im·mu'ta·bly,** *adv.*

imp (imp), *n.* 1. a young or small demon. 2. a mischievous child.

im·pact (im'pakt), *n.* 1. a collision; forcible contact. 2. the shock of a collision. 3. the power to move feelings, influence thinking, etc.: *v.t.* (im-pakt'), 1. to force tightly together. 2. [Informal], to affect: *v.i.* 1. to hit with force. 2. [Informal], to have an effect *(on).*

im·pact·ed (im-pak'tud), *adj.* 1. wedged in tightly. 2. unable to erupt because lodged in the jaw abnormally: said of a tooth. 3. densely crowded.

im·pair (im-per'), *v.t.* to make worse; lessen in value, strength, etc.; damage. —**im·pair'ment,** *n.*

im·pa·la (im-pä'lá), *n., pl.* -la, -las, an African antelope with a reddish coat, noted for its graceful leaping: the male has lyre-shaped horns.

im·pale (im-pāl'), *v.t.* -paled', -pal'ing, 1. to fix on a stake or pierce through with something pointed. 2. to transfix, as with a glance. 3. in *Heraldry,* to join (two coats of arms) side by side on one shield. —**im·pale'ment,** *n.*

im·pal·pa·ble (im-pal'pá-bl), *adj.* 1. that cannot be perceived by touch. 2. not readily grasped by the mind; subtle. —**im·pal'pa·bly,** *adv.*

im·pan·el (im-pan'l), *v.t.* -eled or -elled, -el·ing or -el·ling, 1. to enter the names of (jurors) on a jury list. 2. to choose (a jury) from such a list. —**im·pan'el·ment,** *n.*

im·par·i·ty (im-per'i-ti), *n., pl.* -ties, [Rare], inequality; disparity.

im·part (im-pärt'), *v.t.* 1. to bestow a share or portion of; give. 2. to make known; reveal.

im·par·tial (im-pär'shúl), *adj.* free from partiality; fair; unprejudiced. —**im·par·ti·al'i·ty** (-shi-al'i-ti), *n.* —**im·par'tial·ly,** *adv.*

im·part·i·ble (im-pär'ti-bl), *adj.* that cannot be divided: said of an estate.

im·pass·a·ble (im-pas'á-bl), *adj.* not passable; incapable of being passed over or traversed. —**im·pass·a·bil'i·ty,** *n.* —**im·pass'a·bly,** *adv.*

im·passe (im'pas, im-pas'), *n.* 1. a blind alley. 2. a position affording no escape; problem without a solution; deadlock.

im·pas·si·ble (im-pas'i-bl), *adj.* 1. incapable of suffering. 2. invulnerable. 3. unfeeling; unmoved. —**im·pas·si·bil'i·ty,** *n.* —**im·pas'si·bly,** *adv.*

im·pas·sioned (im-pash'únd), *adj.* moved to strong feeling; animated; excited.

im·pas·sive (im-pas'iv), *adj.* not showing or feeling emotion; calm; apathetic. —**im·pas·siv·i·ty** (im-pá-siv'i-ti), *n.* —**im·pass'ive·ly,** *adv.*

im·pas·to (im-päs'tō), *n.* 1. painting in which the paint is laid thickly on the canvas. 2. paint so laid on.

im·pa·ti·ens (im-pā'shi-ènz, -'shènz), *n.* any of a number of plants with small, colorful flowers and seedpods that scatter their seeds when ripe.

im·pa·tient (im-pā'shènt), *adj.* 1. having little

---

patience. 2. intolerant of delay, opposition, control, etc. 3. restlessly eager to do something. —im·pa'tience, n. —im·pa'tient·ly, adv.

im·peach (im·pēch'), v.t. 1. to accuse (a public official), before a tribunal, of misconduct in office. 2. to discredit or call in question (a person's honor, etc.). —im·peach'ment, n.

im·pec·ca·ble (im·pek'ä·bl), adj. 1. not liable to sin. 2. faultless; flawless; irreproachable. — im·pec·ca·bil'i·ty, n. —im·pec'ca·bly, adv.

im·pec·cant (ˈănt), adj. sinless; blameless. —im·pec'can·cy, n.

im·pe·cu·ni·ous (im·pi·kū'ni·ûs), adj. having little or no money; poor; penniless. —im·pe·cu·ni·os·i·ty (-os'ĭ·ti), im·pe·cu'ni·ous·ness, n. —im·pe·cu'ni·ous·ly, adv.

im·ped·ance (im·pēd'ns), n. 1. the total resistance to an alternating current of a single frequency in an electric circuit: it is measured in ohms. 2. a unit of measurement in sound transmission.

im·pede (im·pēd'), v.t. -ped'ed, -ped'ing, to obstruct; hinder. —im·ped'er, n.

im·ped·i·ment (im·ped'i·mĕnt), n. 1. that which impedes; hindrance. 2. a speech defect, as a stammer or lisp. 3. a bar to marriage, such as a blood relationship.

im·ped·i·men·ta (im·ped·i·men'tä), n. pl. encumbrances, especially the equipment, baggage, and supplies carried along with an army.

im·pel (im·pel'), v.t. -pelled', -pel'ling 1. to drive or push forward; propel. 2. to constrain, force, or urge. —im·pel'lent, adj. & n. —im·pel'ler, n.

im·pend (im·pend'), v.i. 1. to be about to happen; be imminent. 2. to be a threat. —im·pend'ence, im·pend'en·cy, n. —im·pend'ent, adj.

im·pend·ing ('ing), adj. about to happen; imminent; threatening.

im·pen·e·tra·ble (im·pen'i·trä·bl), adj. 1. not penetrable; unable to be penetrated, entered, perforated, etc. 2. incapable of being understood or solved; unfathomable. 3. in Physics, having the property of matter by which no two bodies can occupy the same space at the same time. —im·pen·e·tra·bil'i·ty, n. — im·pen'e·tra·bly, adv.

im·pen·i·tent (im·pen'i·tĕnt), adj. not penitent or contrite; feeling no regret; shameless. — im·pen'i·tence, im·pen'i·ten·cy, n.

im·per·a·tive (im·per'ä·tiv), adj. 1. expressing a command. 2. obligatory; urgent; necessary. 3. denoting the mood of a verb that expresses command, entreaty, or exhortation: n. a command; order. —im·per'a·tive·ly, adv. —im·per'a·tive·ness, n.

im·pe·ra·tor (im·pê·rāt'ĕr, -rāt'-; 'ôr), n. in ancient Rome, originally a general, later an emperor.

im·per·cep·ti·ble (im·pĕr·sep'ti·bl), adj. very slight, gradual, or subtle, so as to be not easily perceived by the mind or senses. — im·per·cep·ti·bil'i·ty, n. —im·per·cep'ti·bly, adv.

im·per·fect (im·pûr'fikt), adj. 1. not perfect; having a defect or fault, etc. 2. not complete. 3. of or pertaining to a verb tense indicating a past action or state that is continuous or incomplete. —im·per'fect·ly, adv.

im·per·fec·tion (im·pĕr·fek'shŭn), n. 1. the state of being imperfect. 2. a defect or blemish; fault.

im·per·fo·rate (im·pûr'fĕr·it, 'fō·rāt), adj. 1. having no holes or openings. 2. having a straight edge without perforations: said of some postage stamps. Also im·per'fo·rat·ed: n. a postage stamp without perforated edges. —im·per·fo·ra'tion, n.

im·pe·ri·al (im·pir'i·ăl), adj. 1. of or pertaining to an empire, emperor, or empress. 2. sovereign; having supreme authority. 3. of superior size or excellence. 4. regal; august: n. 1. the top of a carriage. 2. a size of paper 23 by 31 inches. 3. a pointed tuft of beard on the lower lip and chin: so called from the emperor Louis Napoleon, who set this fashion. —im·pe'ri·al·ly, adv.

im·pe·ri·al·ism (-izm), n. 1. imperial authority or government. 2. the policy of extending the authority or rule of a country by establishing colonies or conquering other nations; territorial expansion. 3. the policy of trying to dominate the affairs of weaker countries. —im·pe'ri·al·ist, n. & adj. —im·pe·ri·al·is'tic, adj.

im·per·il (im·per'il), v.t. -iled or -illed, -il·ing or -il·ling, to put in peril; endanger; jeopardize. —im·per'il·ment, n.

im·pe·ri·ous (im·pir'i·ûs), adj. 1. domineering; dictatorial; overbearing. 2. urgent; imperative. —im·pe'ri·ous·ly, adv. —im·pe'ri·ous·ness, n.

im·per·ish·a·ble (im·per'ish·ä·bl), adj. indestructible; not subject to decay; permanently enduring. —im·per·ish·a·bil'i·ty, n. —im·per'ish·a·bly, adv.

im·pe·ri·um (im·pir'i·ŭm), n., pl. -ri·a (-ä), 1. supreme power or dominion. 2. the right of a state to employ force to maintain the laws.

im·per·ma·nent (im·pûr'mä·nĕnt), adj. not permanent or lasting; temporary. —im·per'ma·nence, n. —im·per'ma·nent·ly, adv.

im·per·me·a·ble (im·pûr'mi·ä·bl), adj. not permeable; not permitting passage of a fluid through it; impenetrable. —im·per·me·a·bil'i·ty, n. —im·per'me·a·bly, adv.

im·per·son·al (im·pûr'sn·ăl), adj. 1. not referring to a particular person. 2. without personality. 3. denoting or of a verb having only third person singular forms, usually with it as a subject. —im·per·son·al'i·ty (-al'ĭ·ti), n. —im·per'son·al·ly, adv.

im·per·son·ate (im·pûr'sŏ·nāt), v.t. -at·ed, -at·ing, 1. to pretend to be (another person) for purposes of fraud. 2. to mimic (a person) for entertainment, as on the stage. —im·per·son·a'tion, n. —im·per'son·a·tor, n.

im·per·ti·nent (im·pûr'tn·ĕnt), adj. 1. not pertinent; of no relation to the matter at hand. 2. rude; uncivil; impudent. —im·per'ti·nence, n. —im·per'ti·nent·ly, adv.

im·per·turb·a·ble (im·pêr·tûr'bä·bl), adj. not easily disturbed, agitated, or disconcerted; cool; calm. —im·per·turb·a·bil'i·ty, n. —im·per·turb'a·bly, adv.

im·per·vi·ous (im·pûr'vi·ûs), adj. 1. impenetrable; that cannot be penetrated, as by moisture. 2. not influenced or affected by (with *to*). **—im·per'vi·ous·ly,** *adv.* **—im·per'vi·ous·ness,** *n.*

im·pe·ti·go (im-pē-tī'gō), *n.* a contagious, pustular eruption of the skin.

im·pe·trate (im'pē-trāt), *v.t.* **-trat·ed, -trat·ing.** 1. to gain by entreaty. 2. [Rare], to entreat. **—im·pe·tra'tion,** *n.*

im·pet·u·ous (im-pech'oo-wŭs), *adj.* 1. rushing with force and violence. 2. done impulsively and rashly. **—im·pet·u·os'i·ty** (-wos'i-ti), *n.* **—im·pet'u·ous·ly,** *adv.*

im·pe·tus (im'pē-tŭs), *n.* 1. the force with which a body moves against resistance. 2. any driving force; stimulus or impulse.

im·pi·e·ty (im-pī'ē-ti), *n.* 1. lack of piety; lack of reverence for God; ungodliness. 2. lack of respect, as for parents. 3. *pl.* **-ties,** an impious act.

im·pinge (im-pinj'), *v.i.* **-pinged', -ping'ing.** 1. to strike or dash (with *on, upon,* or *against*). 2. to infringe; encroach (with *on* or *upon*). **—im·ping'ment,** *n.* **—im·ping'er,** *n.*

im·pi·ous (im'pi-ŭs), *adj.* 1. not pious; irreligious; lacking reverence for God. 2. not showing proper respect, as for parents. **—im'pi·ous·ly,** *adv.* **—im'pi·ous·ness,** *n.*

imp·ish (im'pish), *adj.* mischievous, like an imp. **—imp'ish·ly,** *adv.* **—imp'ish·ness,** *n.*

im·plac·a·ble (im-plak'ā-bl, -plā'kā-), *adj.* not to be pacified or appeased; constant in anger or enmity; relentless. **—im·plac·a·bil'i·ty,** *n.* **—im·plac'a·bly,** *adv.*

im·plant (im-plant'), *v.t.* 1. to set or fix deeply or firmly; embed. 2. to fix for growth; insert, as for grafting. 3. to instill in the mind; imbue. **—im·plan·ta'tion,** *n.*

im·plau·si·ble (im-plô'zi-bl), *adj.* not plausible or credible; seeming not to be true. **—im·plau·si·bil'i·ty,** *n., pl.* **-ties. —im·plau'si·bly,** *adv.*

im·ple·ment (im'plē-mĕnt), *n.* 1. a useful article or device; tool, instrument, utensil, etc. 2. a means to an end: *v.t.* (-ment). 1. to accomplish. 2. to put into effect by providing means. **—im·ple·men'tal, —im·ple·men·ta'tion,** *n.*

im·pli·cate (im'pli-kāt), *v.t.* **-cat·ed, -cat·ing.** 1. to involve; show to be connected with a crime, wrongdoing, fault, etc. 2. to imply. **—im'pli·ca·tive,** *adj.*

im·pli·ca·tion (-kā'shŭn), *n.* 1. the act of implicating. 2. the act of implying. 3. something implied; especially, in *Logic,* a condition between two propositions such that if the first is true, the second is necessarily true.

im·plic·it (im-plis'it), *adj.* 1. implied; not expressly stated, but suggested. 2. inherent; essentially involved. 3. unquestioning; without reservation or doubt. **—im·plic'it·ly,** *adv.* **—im·plic'it·ness,** *n.*

im·plode (im-plōd'), *v.t. & v.i.* **-plod'ed, -plod'ing,** to burst inward. **—im·plo'sion** (-plō'zhŭn), *n.*

im·plore (im-plôr'), *v.t.* **-plored', -plor'ing.** 1. to entreat earnestly for. 2. to call upon or beg (a person) for something; supplicate. **—im·plor'ing·ly,** *adv.*

im·ply (im-plī'), *v.t.* **-plied', -ply'ing.** 1. to express indirectly; insinuate; hint. 2. to con-

tain or include as a necessary or inherent part or condition.

im·pol·i·cy (im-pol'i-si), *n., pl.* **-cies,** an inexpedient or unwise act or policy.

im·po·lite (im-pō-līt'), *adj.* not polite; lacking good manners; rude. **—im·po·lite'ly,** *adv.* **—im·po·lite'ness,** *n.*

im·pol·i·tic (im-pol'i-tik), *adj.* contrary to good policy; unwise; injudicious. **—im·pol'i·tic·ly,** *adv.*

im·pon·der·a·ble (im-pon'dēr-â-bl), *adj.* 1. not capable of being weighed or measured. 2. not capable of being thought out or explained: *n.* anything that is imponderable. **—im·pon·der·a·bil'i·ty,** *n.* **—im·pon'der·a·bly,** *adv.*

im·port (im-pôrt'), *v.t.* 1. to bring into a country from another. 2. to bring in from the outside. 3. to signify; mean: *v.i.* to be of moment; matter: *n.* (im'pôrt), 1. something, as merchandise, brought into a country from another. 2. meaning. 3. importance. **—im·por·ta'tion,** *n.* **—im·port'er,** *n.*

im·por·tant (im-pôr'tnt), *adj.* 1. of much significance or value; momentous. 2. of high standing or considerable influence or authority. 3. pompous. **—im·por'tance,** *n.* **—im·por'tant·ly,** *adv.*

im·por·tu·nate (im-pôr'chŭ-nit), *adj.* persistent; annoyingly demanding; insistent. **—im·por'tu·nate·ly,** *adv.* **—im·por'tu·nate·ness,** *n.*

im·por·tune (im-pôr-tōōn'), *v.t. & v.i.* **-tuned', -tun'ing,** to trouble with persistent, urgent demands or entreaties. **—im·por·tu'ni·ty,** *n.* **—im·por·tune'ly,** *adv.*

im·pose (im-pōz'), *v.t.* **-posed', -pos'ing.** 1. to place or lay upon, as a burden, tax, etc. 2. to thrust (oneself, one's will, etc.) upon others, especially without right. 3. to palm off; foist. 4. to arrange (pages of type or printing plates) in proper order for printing. **—im·pos'er,** *n.*

im·pos·ing (-pō'zing), *adj.* stately; grand; impressive. **—im·pos'ing·ly,** *adv.*

im·po·si·tion (im-pō·zish'ŭn), *n.* 1. a laying on of hands in ordination or confirmation. 2. the thrusting of oneself, one's ideas, etc. on others, especially without right. 3. a taking advantage of a person's good nature, etc. 4. a tax or fine. 5. an unfair burden or duty. 6. a fraud or deception. 7. the arrangement of type pages in proper order for printing.

im·pos·si·ble (im-pos'i-bl), *adj.* 1. that cannot be done; inconceivable. 2. not practicable. 3. hopelessly unsuitable or disagreeable. **—im·pos·si·bil'i·ty,** *n., pl.* **-ties. —im·pos'si·bly,** *adv.*

im·post (im'pōst), *n.* 1. a tax or duty levied by a government on imports. 2. the top part of a pillar or wall supporting an arch.

im·pos·tor (im-pos'tēr), *n.* one who pretends to be what he is not in order to deceive or cheat others.

im·pos·ture ('chēr), *n.* fraud or deception, as that practiced by an impostor.

im·po·tent (im'pō-tĕnt), *adj.* 1. not physically strong or vigorous. 2. weak; ineffective; lacking in power. 3. not able to engage in sexual intercourse: said of males. **—im'po·tence, im'po·ten·cy,** *n.*

---

a in cap, ā in cane, ä in father, â in abet, e in met, ē in be, ê in baker, ê in regent, i in pit, ī in fine, ı in manifest, o in hot, ō in horse, ō in bone,

im-pound (im-pound'), v.t. 1. to shut up in a pound or pen, as a stray animal. 2. to hold in the custody of a court. 3. to collect and hold (water) for irrigation, as in a reservoir. —im-pound'ment, n.

im-pov-er-ish (im-pov'ẽr-ish), v.t. 1. to make poor; reduce to poverty. 2. to cause to deteriorate in quality or productiveness. — im-pov'er-ish-ment, n.

im-prac-ti-ca-ble (im-prak'ti-ká-bl), adj. 1. not able to be put into practice, as a plan; not practicable. 2. not usable. —im-prac-ti-ca-bil'i-ty, im-prac'ti-ca-ble-ness, n. —im-prac'ti-ca-bly, adv.

im-prac-ti-cal (im-prak'ti-kl), adj. 1. not useful. 2. not able to deal with practical matters effectively. 3. dreamy; idealistic. —im-prac-ti-cal'i-ty, n.

im-pre-cate (im'prē-kāt), v.t. -cat-ed, -cat-ing, to invoke (an evil or curse) upon; curse; wish evil to. —im-pre-ca'tion, n. —im'pre-ca-to-ry, adj.

im-pre-cise (im-pri-sīs'), adj. not precise; vague or uncertain. —im-pre-cise'ly, adv. —im-pre-ci'sion (-sizh'ŭn), n.

im-preg-na-ble (im-preg'nȧ-bl), adj. 1. able to resist an attack; that cannot be entered, as a fortress. 2. firm; unshakable. 3. able to be impregnated. —im-preg-na-bil'i-ty, n. —im-preg'na-bly, adv.

im-preg-nate (im-preg'nāt), v.t. -nat-ed, -nat-ing, 1. to make pregnant. 2. to make fertile or fruitful. 3. to saturate; cause to be permeated (with some substance). 4. to inspire or imbue (with): adj. ('nit), impregnated. —im-preg-na'tion, n. —im-preg'na-tor, n.

im-pre-sa-ri-o (im-prē-sär'i-ō), n., pl. -ri-os, the manager of an opera or concert company.

im-pre-scrip-ti-ble (im-pri-skrip'ti-bl), adj. that cannot be rightfully lost or taken away; inalienable; inviolable. —im-pre-scrip'ti-bly, adv.

im-press (im-pres'), v.t. 1. to mark, stamp, or print by pressure; imprint. 2. to stamp deeply on the mind. 3. to affect the emotions of. 4. to influence favorably. 5. to compel to enter military service; especially, to carry off to serve in the navy. 6. to seize for public use, as land or money: n. (im'-pres), 1. the act of impressing. 2. a mark made by pressure; image; stamp. 3. a strongly fixed image or effect.

im-press-i-ble ('i-bl), adj. capable of being impressed. —im-press-i-bil'i-ty, n.

im-pres-sion (im-presh'ŭn), n. 1. the act of impressing. 2. a mark or figure made by impressing. 3. the effect produced on the mind by a sensation, emotion, etc. 4. an indistinct or vague notion or remembrance. 5. an impersonation, especially for amusement. 6. an imprint of teeth and gums in wax, etc., used in making dentures. 7. a copy of set type taken by pressure, usually on paper. 8. the number of copies printed at once. —im-pres'sion-al, adj.

im-pres-sion-a-ble (-á-bl), adj. easily impressed or influenced. —im-pres-sion-a-bil'i-ty, n. — im-pres'sion-a-bly, adv.

im-pres-sion-ism (-izm), n. a style of painting, music, or literature in which the artist, composer, or writer attempts to portray an immediate effect or impression, without elaboration of details.

im-pres-sion-ist (-ist), n. 1. a painter, composer, or writer who adheres to the style of impressionism. 2. a performer who does impressions, or impersonations, especially of well-known people: adj. of or pertaining to impressionism or impressionists.

im-pres-sion-is-tic (-is'tik), adj. 1. same as impressionist. 2. giving a momentary or general impression. —im-pres-sion-is'ti-cal-ly, adv.

im-pres-sive (im-pres'iv), adj. that may make a deep impression; stirring, imposing, etc. — im-pres'sive-ly, adv. —im-pres'sive-ness, n.

im-press-ment (im-pres'mĕnt), n. the act of seizing for public use, or compelling to enter the service of the public.

im-pri-ma-tur (im-pri-mät'ẽr, -māt'ẽr), n. 1. license or permission granted to print or publish books, papers, etc.; specifically, permission granted by a censor in the Roman Catholic Church. 2. any sanction from authorized sources.

im-pri-mis (im-prī'mis), adv. in the first place.

im-print (im-print'), v.t. 1. to mark or stamp by pressure. 2. to press or apply. 3. to impress deeply, as on the mind or memory: n. (im'print), 1. an impress or mark left by something. 2. a lasting effect. 3. a publisher's or printer's name, usually with time and place of publication, on the title page or at the end of a book.

im-print-ing (im-print'ing), n. in Psychology, a behavior pattern established very early in life in regard to a given stimulus.

im-pris-on (im-priz'n), v.t. 1. to put into a prison; detain in custody. 2. to confine or restrain in any way. —im-pris'on-ment, n.

im-prob-a-ble (im-prob'ȧ-bl), adj. unlikely; not to be expected. —im-prob-a-bil'i-ty, n., pl. -ties. —im-prob'a-bly, adv.

im-pro-bi-ty (im-prō'bi-ti), n., pl. -ties, lack of probity or rectitude; dishonesty.

im-promp-tu (im-promp'tōō), adv. & adj. without advance preparation; offhand: n. an impromptu speech or effort.

im-prop-er (im-prop'ẽr), adj. 1. not well adapted or suited to the purpose. 2. erroneous. 3. in poor taste; indecorous. —im-prop'er-ly, adv.

improper fraction, a fraction whose numerator is greater than the denominator.

im-pro-pri-ate (im-prō'pri-āt), v.t. -at-ed, -at-ing, to transfer (ecclesiastical property or money) to lay people: adj. (-it), impropriated. —im-pro-pri-a'tion, n.

im-pro-pri-e-ty (im-prō-prī'ē-ti), n., pl. -ties, 1. the quality of being improper. 2. an improper act or remark. 3. an improper usage, as of a word or phrase.

im-prove (im-prōōv'), v.t. -proved', -prov'ing, 1. to make better. 2. to use profitably. 3. to cause (land, buildings, etc.) to increase in value by cultivation, structural work, etc.: v.i. to become better. —im-prov'a-ble, adj. — im-prov'er, n.

im-prove-ment ('mĕnt), n. 1. the advancement of anything to a better condition or state; betterment. 2. an addition or change that increases the value or condition of something.

im·prov·i·dent (im-prov'i-dĕnt), *adj.* lacking foresight or thrift. —**im·prov'i·dence,** *n.* —**im·prov'i·dent·ly,** *adv.*

im·pro·vise (im'prŏ-vīz), *v.t. & v.i.* -vised, -vising, 1. to compose and perform extemporaneously, as music; create on the spur of the moment. 2. to devise (something) out of what is at hand, for immediate use. —**im·prov·i·sa'tion** (-prŏv-i-zā'shŭn), *n.* —**im·prov'i·sa'tion·al,** *adj.*

im·pro·vis·er, **im·pro·vi·sor** (im'prŏ-vī-zĕr), *n.* one who improvises, especially music: also **im·prov'i·sa·tor** (-prŏv'i-zāt-ĕr).

im·pru·dent (im-prood'nt), *adj.* not prudent; not using good judgment; rash; indiscreet. —**im·pru'dence,** *n.* —**im·pru'dent·ly,** *adv.*

im·pu·dent (im'pū-dĕnt), *adj.* 1. originally, shameless; immodest. 2. too forward or bold; saucy; insolent —**im'pu·dence,** *n.* —**im'pu·dent·ly,** *adv.*

im·pu·dic·i·ty (im-pyoo-dis'i-ti), *n.* shamelessness.

im·pugn (im-pūn'), *v.t.* to attack by argument or criticism; challenge as false or wrong. —**im·pugn'a·ble,** *adj.* —**im·pug·na·tion** (im-pŭg-nā'shŭn), *n.*

im·pu·is·sance (im-pū'i-sns, -pwis'ns), *n.* feebleness; lack of power. —**im·pu'is·sant,** *adj.*

im·pulse (im'puls), *n.* 1. a sudden thrust or force; impetus; push. 2. the motion induced by an impelling force. 3. a prompting to action. 4. a sudden inclination to act.

im·pul·sion (im-pul'shŭn), *n.* 1. the act of impelling. 2. a state of being impelled. 3. instigation; impetus.

im·pul·sive (im-pul'siv), *adj.* 1. thrusting forward; impelling. 2. likely to act on impulse. 3. resulting from sudden impulse. —**im·pul'sive·ly,** *adv.* —**im·pul'sive·ness,** *n.*

im·pu·ni·ty (im-pū'ni·ti), *n.* freedom from punishment, injury, or harmful consequences.

im·pure (im-pyoor'), *adj.* 1. mixed with foreign matter; contaminated. 2. unchaste; obscene. 3. unclean; dirty. 4. unclean according to religious ritual; defiled. 5. not accurate or idiomatic: said of language or speech. —**im·pure'ly,** *adv.* —**im·pure'ness,** *n.*

im·pu·ri·ty ('i-ti), *n.* 1. a quality or state of being impure. 2. *pl.* -ties, a thing or particle that is impure.

im·put·a·ble (im-pūt'á-bl), *adj.* that may be imputed, charged, or ascribed. —**im·put·a·bil'i·ty,** *n.* —**im·put'a·bly,** *adv.*

im·pute (im-pūt'), *v.t.* -put'ed, -put'ing, 1. to attribute or ascribe (a fault or wrong) to another. 2. in *Theology,* to ascribe (sin or righteousness) to a person as derived from another. —**im·pu·ta'tion,** *n.* —**im·put'a·tive,** *adj.*

in (in), *n.* 1. a person or group that is in office, power, etc.: *usually used in the plural.* 2. [Informal], special influence: *adj.* 1. internal; inner. 2. inward. 3. completed, done, etc. 4. that is in power. 5. [Informal], currently popular: *adv.* 1. from outside to inside. 2. at home. 3. within. 4. into or enclosed in a place: *prep.* 1. among; amidst. 2. into. 3. enclosed. 4. in reference to; con-

cerning. 5. by means of. 6. being a member of. 7. during the course of. 8. wearing. 9. influenced or affected by. 10. in possession of. 11. as a part of. 12. because of. 13. within the scope of.

in-, a prefix meaning *in, into, on, within, toward:* used also as an intensive in words from the Latin and assimilated to *il-* before *l, ir-* before *r,* and *im-* before *m, p,* and *b.*

in-, a prefix meaning *not, no, without, non-* and assimilated to *il-* before *l, ir-* before *r,* and *im-* before *m, p,* and *b.*

in·a·bil·i·ty (in-á-bil'i-ti), *n.* the state of being unable; lack of ability, power, strength, or resource.

in ab·sen·ti·a (in ăb-sen'shá, 'shi-á), [Latin], although not present.

in·ac·ces·si·ble (in-ăk-ses'i-bl), *adj.* denoting that which cannot be reached, obtained, seen, talked to, etc. —**in·ac·ces·si·bil'i·ty,** *n.* —**in·ac·ces'si·bly,** *adv.*

in·ac·cu·ra·cy (in-ak'yĕr-á-si), *n.* 1. the state of being inaccurate. 2. *pl.* -cies, an error; mistake.

in·ac·cu·rate ('yĕr-it), *adj.* not accurate; incorrect; wrong; erroneous. —**in·ac'cu·rate·ly,** *adv.*

in·ac·tion (in-ak'shŭn), *n.* lack of activity; suspension from labor; idleness.

in·ac·ti·vate (in-ak'ti-vāt), *v.t.* -vat·ed, -vat·ing, 1. to cause (a government agency or military unit) to be inactive; break up. 2. to stop the activity of (a biological substance) by heat. —**in·ac·ti·va'tion,** *n.*

in·ac·tive (in-ak'tiv), *adj.* 1. not active; inert. 2. idle; indolent; lazy. 3. not functioning. 4. not in active military service. 5. having no effect. —**in·ac'tive·ly,** *adv.* —**in·ac·tiv'i·ty,** *n.*

in·ad·e·qua·cy (in-ad'ĕ-kwá-si), *n.* 1. a state of being inadequate; insufficiency. 2. *pl.* -cies, an instance of being inadequate.

in·ad·e·quate (-kwát), *adj.* not adequate; deficient; insufficient. —**in·ad'e·quate·ly,** *adv.* —**in·ad'e·quate·ness,** *n.*

in·ad·mis·si·ble (in-ăd-mis'i-bl), *adj.* not admissible; not to be allowed, received, conceded, etc. —**in·ad·mis·si·bil'i·ty,** *n.* —**in·ad·mis'si·bly,** *adv.*

in·ad·vert·ence (in-ad-vûr'tĕns), *n.* 1. lack of attention. 2. an oversight; mistake. Also **in·ad·vert'en·cy,** *pl.* -cies.

in·ad·vert·ent (-tĕnt), *adj.* 1. inattentive; heedless. 2. unintentional. —**in·ad·vert'ent·ly,** *adv.*

in·ad·vis·a·ble (in-ăd-vī'zá-bl), *adj.* inexpedient; not advisable; unwise. —**in·ad·vis·a·bil'i·ty,** *n.*

in·al·ien·a·ble (in-āl'yĕn-á-bl), *adj.* that may not be alienated, taken away, or transferred to another. —**in·al·ien·a·bil'i·ty,** *n.* —**in·al'ien·a·bly,** *adv.*

in·al·ter·a·ble (in-ôl'tĕr-á-bl), *adj.* unchangeable; not alterable. —**in·al·ter·a·bil'i·ty,** *n.* —**in·al'ter·a·bly,** *adv.*

in·am·o·ra·ta (in-am-ô-rät'á), *n.* a woman with whom one is in love; sweetheart or mistress.

in·ane (in-ān'), *adj.* 1. empty; void. 2. senseless; silly; pointless: *n.* the infinite void of space. —**in·ane'ly,** *adv.*

in·an·i·mate (in-an'i-mit), *adj.* 1. not animate. 2. not animated; spiritless; dull. —**in·an'i·mate·ly,** *adv.* —**in·an'i·mate·ness,** *n.*

---

a in *cap*, ā in *cane*, ä in *father*, å in *abet*, e in *met*, ē in *be*, ĕ in *baker*, ė in *regent*, i in *pit*, ī in *fine*, i in *manifest*, o in *hot*, ô in *horse*, ō in *bone*,

in-a-ni-tion (in-á-nish'ún), *n.* 1. exhaustion from lack of nourishment. 2. weakness; lack of strength.

in-an-i-ty (in-an'í-ti), *n.* 1. emptiness. 2. mental vacuity; silliness; senselessness. 3. *pl.* -ties, an inane act, remark, etc.

in-ap-par-ent (in-á-per'ênt), *adj.* not apparent.

in-ap-pli-ca-ble (in-ap'li-ká-bl), *adj.* unsuitable; not adapted to; inappropriate. —in-ap-pli-ca-bil'i-ty, *n.* —in-ap'pli-ca-bly, *adv.*

in-ap-po-site (in-ap'ô-zit), *adj.* irrelevant. —in-ap'po-site-ly, *adv.* —in-ap'po-site-ness, *n.*

in-ap-pre-ci-a-ble (in-á-prē'shi-bl, 'shi-á-bl), *adj.* not perceptible; insignificant. —in-ap-pre'ci-a-bly, *adv.*

in-ap-pre-hen-sive (in-ap-ri-hen'siv), *adj.* 1. not able to apprehend, or understand. 2. without apprehension of danger; unconcerned. —in-ap-pre-hen'sive-ly, *adv.*

in-ap-proach-a-ble (in-á-prō'chá-bl), *adj.* 1. not approachable. 2. unrivaled. —in-ap-proach-a-bil'i-ty, *n.*

in-ap-pro-pri-ate (in-á-prō'pri-it), *adj.* not appropriate; unsuitable; improper. —in-ap-pro'pri-ate-ly, *adv.* —in-ap-pro'pri-ate-ness, *n.*

in-apt (in-apt'), *adj.* 1. unsuitable; inappropriate. 2. inept; unskillful. —in-apt'i-tude (-ap'-ti-tōōd, -tūd), *n.* —in-apt'ness, *n.*

in-arch (in-ärch'), *v.t.* to graft by uniting (a scion) to a stock without separating the scion from its parent plant.

in-ar-tic-u-late (in-är-tik'yù-lit), *adj.* 1. not uttered with intelligible distinctness. 2. incapable of speech; mute. 3. not able to speak coherently. 4. inexpressible. 5. in *Zoology,* not jointed, segmented, or valved. —in-ar-tic'u-late-ly, *adv.* —in-ar-tic'u-late-ness, *n.*

in-ar-tis-tic (in-är-tis'tik), *adj.* 1. not conforming to the principles of art. 2. without artistic taste. —in-ar-tis'ti-cal-ly, *adv.*

in-as-much as (in-áz-much' áz), 1. seeing that; because. 2. to the extent that.

in-at-ten-tion (in-á-ten'shún), *n.* heedlessness; lack of attention; neglect. —in-at-ten'tive, *adj.* —in-at-ten'tive-ly, *adv.*

in-au-di-ble (in-ô'di-bl), *adj.* not audible; that cannot be heard. —in-au-di-bil'i-ty, *n.* —in-au'di-bly, *adv.*

in-au-gu-ral (in-ô'gyù-rál), *adj.* 1. pertaining to an inauguration. 2. coming first in a succession: *n.* 1. an inauguration. 2. an inauguration speech.

in-au-gu-rate (-rāt), *v.t.* -rat-ed, -rat-ing, 1. to induct into office with appropriate ceremonies. 2. to make a formal beginning of; initiate, as a new policy. 3. to celebrate the first public use of by an opening ceremony; dedicate, as a new building. —in-au-gu-ra'-tion, *n.* —in-au'gu-ra-tor, *n.*

Inauguration Day, the day on which a president of the U.S. is inaugurated, which is January 20 (March 4 before 1934) of the year following his election.

in-aus-pi-cious (in-ô-spish'ús), *adj.* not auspicious; ill-omened; unlucky; unfavorable. —in-aus-pi'cious-ly, *adv.* —in-aus-pi'cious-ness, *n.*

in-be-ing (in'bē-ing), *n.* 1. inherent existence. 2. essence.

in-board (in'bôrd), *adv. & adj.* 1. inside the hull of a ship or boat. 2. toward or close to the fuselage of an aircraft: *n.* 1. a motor installed inboard and connected to a propeller below a boat. 2. a boat with an inboard motor.

in-born (in'bôrn), *adj.* present at birth; innate; inherent; not acquired.

in-bound (in'bound), *adj.* bound inward.

in-bred (in'bred'), *adj.* 1. resulting from or produced by inbreeding. 2. inborn; innate.

in-breed (in'brēd'), *v.t. & v.i.* -bred', -breed'ing, 1. to breed from animals closely related; especially, to do this over many generations so as to produce desired characteristics and eliminate undesired characteristics. 2. to make or become overrefined.

In-ca (ing'ká), *n.* 1. a member of the highly civilized tribe of South American Indians that dominated Peru until the Spanish conquest. 2. one of their rulers; specifically, the emperor. —In'can, *adj.*

in-cal-cu-la-ble (in-kal'kyù-lá-bl), *adj.* 1. beyond calculation; too many to be counted. 2. unforeseeable. —in-cal-cu-la-bil'i-ty, *n.* —in-cal'cu-la-bly, *adv.*

in cam-er-a (in kam'ēr-á), 1. in the private chamber of a judge. 2. meeting in a closed session, not open to the public.

in-can-desce (in-kán-des'), *v.i. & v.t.* -desced', -desc'ing, to glow or cause to glow with heat.

in-can-des-cent ('nt), *adj.* 1. glowing with heat. 2. brilliant; very bright. —in-can-des'cence, *n.* —in-can-des'cent-ly, *adv.*

incandescent lamp, a lamp in which the light is produced by a filament of conducting material contained in a vacuum and heated to incandescence by an electric current.

in-can-ta-tion (in-kan-tā'shún), *n.* 1. the use of spells or charms as part of a magical ritual. 2. a magical charm said or sung; also, the words used for this. 3. any sorcery or magic. —in-can-ta'tion-al, *adj.* —in-can'ta-to-ry (-kan'tá-tôr-i), *adj.*

in-ca-pa-ble (in-kā'pá-bl), *adj.* 1. not capable; lacking in power, capacity, ability, strength, etc. 2. not legally eligible or qualified. —in-ca-pa-bil'i-ty, in-ca'pa-ble-ness, *n.* —in-ca'pa-bly, *adv.*

in-ca-pac-i-tate (in-ká-pas'í-tāt), *v.t.* -tat-ed, -tat-ing, 1. to deprive of natural capacity; render incapable; disable. 2. in *Law,* to disqualify; make ineligible. —in-ca-pac-i-ta'tion, *n.*

in-ca-pac-i-ty (-ti), *n., pl.* -ties, 1. lack of capacity or power. 2. legal disqualification or ineligibility.

in-car-cer-ate (in-kär'sê-rāt), *v.t.* -at-ed, -at-ing, 1. to imprison. 2. to confine. —in-car-cer-a'-tion, *n.* —in-car'cer-a-tor, *n.*

in-car-na-dine (in-kär'ná-din, -dēn), *adj.* 1. flesh-colored; pink. 2. crimson; blood-red: *n.* the color of flesh red or of blood: *v.t.* -dined, -din-ing, to dye red or flesh-colored.

in-car-nate (in-kär'nát), *v.t.* -nat-ed, -nat-ing, 1. to embody in flesh; give bodily form to. 2. to make real. 3. to be the embodiment or personification of: adj. ('nit), 1. invested with a bodily form. 2. brought to life. 3. personified.

in-car-na-tion (in-kär-nā'shŭn), n. 1. the act of incarnating. 2. embodiment in human form. 3. any person or thing thought of as the embodiment of a quality. 4. [I-], the taking on of human form by Jesus conceived of as the Son of God.

in-case (in-kās'), v.t. -cased', -cas'ing, same as encase.

in-cau-tious (in-kô'shŭs), adj. not cautious or careful; careless. —in-cau'tious-ly, adv. —in-cau'tious-ness, n.

in-cen-di-ar-y (in-sen'di-er-i), adj. 1. pertaining to arson, or the malicious burning of property. 2. made to start fires, as some bombs. 3. tending to incite riots, violence, etc.: n., pl. -ar-ies, 1. one who incites violence; agitator. 2. an arsonist. 3. an incendiary bomb. —in-cen'di-a-rism, n.

in-cense (in'sens), n. 1. any aromatic material burned to produce a pleasant odor, as spices, balsam, frankincense, etc., sometimes used in religious rites. 2. the fragrance or smoke from such a substance. 3. any pleasant odor: v.t. -censed, -ceas-ing, 1. to perfume with incense. 2. to offer incense to: v.i. to burn incense.

in-cense (in-sens'), v.t. -censed', -cens'ing, to provoke; enrage; make angry.

in-cen-tive (in-sen'tiv), adj. inciting; encouraging: n. an incitement; encouragement; motive; spur; stimulus.

in-cep-tion (in-sep'shŭn), n. a start; beginning; commencement; initiation.

in-cep-tive ('tiv), adj. 1. beginning; initial. 2. in Grammar, expressing a beginning of action. —in-cep'tive-ly, adv.

in-cer-ti-tude (in-sûr'ti-tōōd), n. 1. a feeling of doubt; uncertainty. 2. an uncertain condition; insecurity.

in-ces-sant (in-ses'nt), adj. unceasing; ceaseless; continuous. —in-ces'san-cy, n. —in-ces'sant-ly, adv.

in-cest (in'sest), n. sexual intercourse between persons too closely related to marry legally.

in-ces-tu-ous (in-ses'choo-wŭs), adj. 1. of or having to do with incest. 2. guilty of incest. —in-ces'tu-ous-ly, adv. —in-ces'tu-ous-ness, n.

inch (inch), n. 1. a measure of length, equal to 1/12 of a foot: symbol ("). 2. an amount of snow or rain covering a surface to a depth of one inch. 3. a unit of pressure equal to the weight of a column of mercury one inch high. 4. a very small quantity or degree; bit: v.i. & v.t. to move by inches or degrees; move very slowly.

in-cho-ate (in-kō'it), adj. 1. just begun; incipient. 2. not yet clearly formed; incomplete. —in-cho'ate-ly, adv. —in-cho'ate-ness, n.

in-cho-a-tion (in-kō-ā'shŭn), n. a beginning; origin. —in-cho'a-tive, adj.

inch-worm (inch'wŭrm), n. same as measuring worm.

in-ci-dence (in'si-dĕns), n. the degree or range of occurrence or effect.

in-ci-dent (in'si-dĕnt), adj. 1. falling upon, as a ray of light on a reflecting surface. 2. apt to occur in connection with something else.

3. affecting; appertaining: n. 1. an occurrence; something that happens. 2. something that happens beside the main event; minor event or episode. 3. such a minor episode in a play or story. 4. a happening or conflict between people, nations, etc. that appears to be minor but that may have serious results.

in-ci-den-tal (in-si-den'tl), adj. 1. casual; happening in connection with something else. 2. subordinate: n. 1. something that is incidental. 2. pl. miscellaneous expenses or items.

in-ci-den-tal-ly (-dent'li, -den'tl-i), adv. 1. in an incidental manner. 2. by the way.

in-cin-er-ate (in-sin'ĕ-rāt), v.t. & v.i. -at-ed, -at-ing, to burn to ashes. —in-cin-er-a'tion, n.

in-cin-er-a-tor (-rāt-ĕr), n. a furnace for burning refuse.

in-cip-i-ent (in-sip'i-ĕnt), adj. beginning to be or to appear; initial. —in-cip'i-en-cy, n. —in-cip'i-ent-ly, adv.

in-cise (in-sīz'), v.t. -cised', -cis'ing, 1. to cut into. 2. to carve or engrave.

in-cised (-sīzd'), adj. 1. cut into. 2. caused by cutting. 3. carved or engraved. 4. deeply notched, as a leaf.

in-ci-sion (-sizh'ŭn), n. 1. the act of incising. 2. a cut or gash. 3. a deep notch, as on a leaf. 4. a cut made in surgery. 5. incisiveness; keenness.

in-ci-sive (in-sī'siv), adj. 1. having the quality of cutting into. 2. sharp; penetrating. —in-ci'sive-ly, adv. —in-ci'sive-ness, n.

in-ci-sor (in-sī'zēr), n. a cutting tooth; one of the teeth between the canines in both jaws: man has eight incisors.

in-cite (in-sīt'), v.t. -cit'ed, -cit'ing, to move to action; stir up; spur on; impel. —in-cite'-ment, in-ci-ta'tion, n.

in-ci-vil-i-ty (in-si-vil'i-ti), n., pl. -ties, 1. lack of civility or courtesy; impoliteness. 2. an uncivil remark or act.

in-clem-ent (in-klem'ĕnt), adj. 1. not clement; stormy; tempestuous. 2. unmerciful; harsh. —in-clem'en-cy, n., pl. -cies. —in-clem'ent-ly, adv.

in-cli-na-tion (in-kli-nā'shŭn), n. 1. an act of bending or leaning, especially a bowing or nodding. 2. a slope or declivity; slant; incline. 3. the extent or degree of deviation from a normal direction or position. 4. disposition or tendency. 5. a preference. 6. anything toward which one is inclined. —in-cli-na'tion-al, adj.

in-cline (in-klīn'), v.i. -clined', -clin'ing, 1. to deviate from the normal direction or position; lean. 2. to bow or nod. 3. to have a mental bent or tendency. 4. to have a preference: v.t. 1. to cause to lean, slope, etc.; bend. 2. to bend or bow (the body or head). 3. to give a tendency to; dispose: n. (in'klīn), a slope; inclined plane or surface; slant; grade. —in-clin'er, n.

in-clined (in-klīnd'), adj. 1. sloping. 2. disposed; tending. 3. forming an angle with another surface; line, etc.

inclined plane, a plane that makes an oblique angle with a horizontal plane.

in-cli-nom-e-ter (in-kli-nom'ĕ-tēr), n. 1. an apparatus for determining the direction of the earth's magnetism. 2. an instrument that measures the angle an aircraft or ship makes with the horizontal.

in·close (in-klōz'), *v.t.* -closed', -clos'ing, same as enclose. —in·clo'sure, *n.*

in·clude (in-klōōd'), *v.t.* -clud'ed, -clud'ing, 1. to enclose. 2. to comprise; have as part of; contain. 3. to put into a total or category. —in·clud'a·ble, *adj.* —in·clu'sion (-klōō'zhŭn), *n.*

in·clud·ed ('id), *adj.* 1. enclosed; contained. 2. not projecting beyond the mouth of the corolla of a flower: said of stamens and pistils.

in·clu·sive (in-klōō'siv), *adj.* 1. including everything concerned. 2. including the stated limits or extremes. —in·clu'sive·ly, *adv.* —in·clu'sive·ness, *n.*

in·co·er·ci·ble (in-kō-ûr'si-bl), *adj.* incapable of being forced or coerced.

in·cog·i·tant (in-koj'i-tănt), *adj.* thoughtless; unthinking.

in·cog·ni·to (in-kog-nēt'ō, in-kog'ni-tō), *adv. & adj.* unrevealed or disguised under an assumed name: *n., pl.* -tos, 1. one who is incognito. 2. the disguise of one who is incognito. 3. the state of being incognito. —in·cog'ni·ta (-nēt'â, -ni-tä), *n.fem., pl.* -tas.

in·cog·ni·zant (in-kog'ni-zănt), *adj.* unaware; not cognizant (with *of*). —in·cog'ni·zance, *n.*

in·co·her·ence (in-kō-hir'ăns), *n.* 1. lack of coherence. 2. looseness; lack of logical connection. 3. something that is incoherent, as a speech or piece of writing. Also **in·co·her'en·cy,** *pl.* -cies.

in·co·her·ent ('ĕnt), *adj.* 1. not sticking together; loose. 2. not logically connected. 3. characterized by incoherent speech or thought. —in·co·her'ent·ly, *adv.*

in·com·bus·ti·ble (in-kŏm-bus'ti-bl), *adj.* that cannot be burned. —in·com·bus·ti·bil'i·ty, *n.*

in·come (in'kum), *n.* the money or other gain received for labor or services or from property, investments, etc. by a person or business, as in a given year.

income tax, a tax levied on net income or on the part of income exceeding a given amount.

in·com·ing (in'kum-ing), *adj.* coming in: *n.* 1. the act of coming in. 2. *usually pl.* income.

in·com·men·su·ra·ble (in-kŏ-men'shĕr-â-bl), *adj.* 1. having no common standard of measurement or basis of comparison. 2. having no common divisors, as some numbers. 3. that cannot be compared. —in·com·men·su·ra·bil'i·ty, *n.* —in·com·men'su·ra·bly, *adv.*

in·com·men·su·rate (-it), *adj.* 1. not having a common measure; incommensurable. 2. inadequate. —in·com·men'su·rate·ly, *adv.*

in·com·mode (in-kŏ-mōd'), *v.t.* -mod'ed, -mod'ing, to inconvenience; give trouble to; disturb.

in·com·mo·di·ous (-mō'di-ŭs), *adj.* 1. tending to cause inconvenience; troublesome. 2. uncomfortably narrow, cramped, etc. —in·com·mo'di·ous·ly, *adv.* —in·com·mo'di·ous·ness, *n.*

in·com·mu·ni·ca·ble (in-kŏ-mū'ni-kà-bl), *adj.* that cannot be communicated or told. —in·com·mu·ni·ca·bil'i·ty, *n.* —in·com·mu'ni·ca·bly, *adv.*

in·com·mu·ni·ca·do (in-kŏ-mū-ni-kä'dō), *adj.* not allowed or able to communicate with others.

in·com·mu·ni·ca·tive (in-kŏ-mū'ni-kàt-ĭv), *adj.* not communicative; reserved; quiet.

in·com·mut·a·ble (in-kŏ-mūt'â-bl), *adj.* not changeable or exchangeable. —in·com·mut·a·bil'i·ty, *n.* —in·com·mut'a·bly, *adv.*

in·com·pa·ra·ble (in-kom'pĕr-à-bl), *adj.* 1. that cannot be compared. 2. beyond comparison; unequaled; peerless. —in·com·pa·ra·bil'i·ty, *n.* —in·com'pa·ra·bly, *adv.*

in·com·pat·i·ble (in-kŏm-pat'i-bl), *adj.* 1. not compatible; incapable of harmonious existence; incongruous, discordant, etc. 2. denoting medical or pharmaceutical substances that, when mixed together, have an undesirable action on each other or on the body. —in·com·pat·i·bil'i·ty, *n.* —in·com·pat'i·bly, *adv.*

in·com·pe·tent (in-kom'pĕ-tĕnt), *adj.* 1. not having sufficient ability; inadequate; not fit; unskillful. 2. not legally qualified: *n.* a person who is incompetent; especially, a mentally retarded person. —in·com'pe·tence, in·com'pe·ten·cy, *n.*

in·com·plete (in-kŏm-plēt'), *adj.* 1. not fully finished or developed. 2. not having all its parts; defective. 3. not perfect. —in·com·plete'ness, in·com·ple'tion, *n.*

in·com·pre·hen·si·ble (in-kom-pri-hen'si-bl), *adj.* not comprehensible; that cannot be understood or grasped by the mind. —in·com·pre·hen·si·bil'i·ty, *n.* —in·com·pre·hen'si·bly, *adv.*

in·com·press·i·ble (in-kŏm-pres'i-bl), *adj.* that cannot be reduced in volume by pressure; resisting pressure. —in·com·press·i·bil'i·ty, *n.*

in·con·ceiv·a·ble (in-kŏn-sē'vâ-bl), *adj.* incapable of being conceived or imagined; incredible. —in·con·ceiv·a·bil'i·ty, *n.* —in·con·ceiv'a·bly, *adv.*

in·con·clu·sive (in-kŏn-klōō'siv), *adj.* not leading to a conclusion or result; unconvincing; indefinite. —in·con·clu'sive·ly, *adv.* —in·con·clu'sive·ness, *n.*

in·con·den·sa·ble, in·con·den·si·ble (in-kŏn-den'sâ-bl), *adj.* incapable of being condensed. —in·con·den·sa·bil'i·ty, in·con·den·si·bil'i·ty, *n.*

in·con·gru·ous (in-kong'groo-wŭs), *adj.* 1. inappropriate; unsuitable. 2. inharmonious; not in agreement; incompatible. —in·con·gru'i·ty, *n., pl.* -ties. —in·con'gru·ous·ly, *adv.*

in·con·nu (in-kŏ-nōō'), *n., pl.* -nus', -nu', a large, freshwater food fish resembling the salmon, found in northwestern North America and northeastern Asia.

in·con·se·quent (in-kon'sĕ-kwent), *adj.* 1. not following from the premises. 2. illogical. 3. out of proper relation. 4. irrelevant. —in·con'se·quence, *n.* —in·con'se·quent·ly, *adv.*

in·con·se·quen·tial (in-kon-sĕ-kwen'shŭl), *adj.* 1. illogical. 2. of no consequence; trivial. —in·con·se·quen'tial·ly, *adv.*

in·con·sid·er·a·ble (in-kŏn-sid'ĕr-â-bl), *adj.* not deserving consideration; unimportant; small. —in·con·sid'er·a·bly, *adv.*

in·con·sid·er·ate (-it), *adj.* without consideration for others; thoughtless. —in·con·sid'er·ate·ly, *adv.* —in·con·sid'er·ate·ness, in·con·sid·er·a'tion, *n.*

ō in dragon, ōō in crude, oo in wool, u in cup, ū in cure, û in turn, ù in focus, oi in boy, ou in house, th in thin, th in sheathe, g in get, j in joy, y in yet.

in·con·sis·tent (in-kŏn-sis'tĕnt), *adj.* 1. lacking harmony or agreement; discrepant. 2. self-contradictory. 3. not consistent in action or principles; changeable. —**in·con·sis'ten·cy**, *n.*, *pl.* **-cies.** —**in·con·sis'tent·ly**, *adv.*

in·con·sol·a·ble (in-kŏn-sōl'ă-bl), *adj.* unable to be consoled or comforted; disconsolate. —**in·con·sol·a·bil'i·ty**, *n.* —**in·con·sol'a·bly**, *adv.*

in·con·spic·u·ous (in-kŏn-spik'yoo-wŭs), *adj.* not noticeable or conspicuous; hardly discernible. —**in·con·spic'u·ous·ly**, *adv.* —**in·con·spic'u·ous·ness**, *n.*

in·con·stant (in-kon'stănt), *adj.* subject to change; unstable; variable; fickle. —**in·con'stan·cy**, *n.* —**in·con'stant·ly**, *adv.*

in·con·test·a·ble (in-kŏn-tes'tă-bl), *adj.* unquestionable; that cannot be disputed. —**in·con·test·a·bil'i·ty**, *n.* —**in·con·test'a·bly**, *adv.*

in·con·ti·nent (in-kont'n-ĕnt), *adj.* 1. unrestrained. 2. lacking self-restraint, especially in regard to sexual activity. 3. unable to control a natural discharge, as of urine, from the body. —**in·con'ti·nence**, *n.* —**in·con'ti·nent·ly**, *adv.*

in·con·tro·vert·i·ble (in-kon-trŏ-vûr'tĭ-bl), *adj.* that cannot be disputed or denied. —**in·con·tro·vert·i·bil'i·ty**, *n.* —**in·con·tro·vert'i·bly**, *adv.*

in·con·ven·ience (in-kŏn-vēn'yĕns), *n.* 1. the state or quality of being inconvenient; trouble or bother. 2. something causing inconvenience or discomfort. Also **in·con·ven'ien·cy**, *pl.* **-cies**: *v.t.* **-ienced**, **-ienc·ing**, to put to inconvenience; incommode; trouble.

in·con·ven·ient (-yĕnt), *adj.* causing annoyance or trouble; not easy to deal with, use, get to, etc. —**in·con·ven'ient·ly**, *adv.*

in·con·vert·i·ble (in-kŏn-vûr'tĭ-bl), *adj.* incapable of being converted into or exchanged for something else. —**in·con·vert·i·bil'i·ty**, *n.*

in·co·or·di·na·tion (in-kō-ôr-dn-ā'shŭn), *n.* lack of coordination, especially in muscular movement.

in·cor·po·rate (in-kôr'pŏ-rāt), *v.t.* **-rat·ed**, **-rat·ing**, 1. to combine into one unit; merge. 2. to give physical form to; embody. 3. to assimilate; combine; include; join. 4. to form into a corporation recognized by law: *v.i.* 1. to unite or be combined into a single whole. 2. to form a corporation: *adj.* (-rĭt), 1. combined into one unit. 2. organized as a corporation. Also **in·cor'po·rat·ed** (-rāt-id). —**in·cor·po·ra'tion**, *n.*

in·cor·po·ra·tor (-ēr), *n.* 1. one who incorporates. 2. an original member of a corporation.

in·cor·po·re·al (in-kôr-pôr'i-ăl), *adj.* 1. not corporeal; immaterial; not having bodily form. 2. in *Law*, intangible; existing only as a right to a material thing, as a copyright, etc. —**in·cor·po're·al·ly**, *adv.*

in·cor·rect (in-kŏ-rekt'), *adj.* 1. not in accord with good manners or behavior; improper. 2. not according to fact; inaccurate; faulty; wrong. —**in·cor·rect'ly**, *adv.* —**in·cor·rect'ness**, *n.*

in·cor·ri·gi·ble (in-kôr'i-jĭ-bl), *adj.* bad beyond correction or reformation; that cannot be improved. —**in·cor·ri·gi·bil'i·ty**, *n.* —**in·cor'ri·gi·bly**, *adv.*

in·cor·rupt (in-kŏ-rupt'), *adj.* 1. not morally

corrupt; not evil. 2. upright and honest; not taking bribes. 3. denoting a language, literary passage, etc. with no alterations, errors, etc.

in·cor·rupt·i·ble ('l-bl), *adj.* 1. incapable of physical corruption or decay. 2. not liable to moral corruption; especially, incapable of being bribed. —**in·cor·rupt·i·bil'i·ty**, *n.* —**in·cor·rupt'i·bly**, *adv.*

in·cras·sate (in-kras'āt), *v.t. & v.i.* **-sat·ed**, **-sat·ing**, [Rare], to make or become thick or thicker in consistency: *adj.* in *Biology*, swollen; thickened. —**in·cras·sa'tion**, *n.*

in·crease (in-krēs'), *v.i.* **-creased'**, **-creas'ing**, to become greater in any respect; augment, multiply, grow, wax, etc.: *v.t.* to make greater in any respect; enhance, enlarge, etc.: *n.* (in'krēs), 1. a growing larger. 2. the amount by which something is increased; increment. 3. something that results from increase, as profit, offspring, produce, etc. —**in·creas'a·ble**, *adj.* —**in·creas'er**, *n.*

in·creas·ing·ly ('ing-li), *adv.* more and more.

in·cred·i·ble (in-krĕd'l-bl), *adj.* 1. hard to believe; not credible. 2. unimaginable; seeming to be not possible. —**in·cred·i·bil'i·ty**, *n.* —**in·cred'i·bly**, *adv.*

in·cred·u·lous (in-krej'oo-lŭs), *adj.* 1. skeptical, unbelieving; doubtful. 2. showing doubt or skepticism. —**in·cre·du·li·ty** (in-krĕ-dōō'li-ti), *n.* —**in·cred'u·lous·ly**, *adv.*

in·cre·ment (in'krĭ-mĕnt, ing'-), *n.* 1. an increase or augmentation. 2. amount of increase. 3. in *Mathematics*, the quantity by which a variable increases: a decrease is the result of a negative increment. —**in·cre·men'tal** (-men'tl), *adj.*

in·cres·cent (in-kres'nt), *adj.* increasing; waxing: said especially of the moon.

in·crim·i·nate (in-krim'ĭ-nāt), *v.t.* **-nat·ed**, **-nat·ing**, 1. to charge with a crime; accuse. 2. to implicate or involve in a criminal situation or lesser wrongdoing. —**in·crim·i·na'tion**, *n.* —**in·crim'i·na·to·ry** (-nă-tôr-i), *adj.*

in·crust (in-krust'), *v.t.* 1. to cover with or as with a crust. 2. to inlay or decorate with gems: *v.i.* to form a crust. —**in·crus·ta'tion**, *n.*

in·cu·bate (ing'kyŭ-bāt), *v.t. & v.i.* **-bat·ed**, **-bat·ing**, 1. to sit upon (eggs) and hatch them. 2. to keep (bacteria, embryos, eggs, etc.) in a favorable, especially warm, environment so that they can develop. 3. to develop, as by thought.

in·cu·ba·tion (in-kyŭ-bā'shŭn), *n.* 1. the process of incubating. 2. the period in the development of a disease between the time the organism is exposed to it and the sign of the first symptom. —**in·cu·ba'tion·al**, *adj.* —**in'cu·ba·tive**, *adj.*

in·cu·ba·tor (ing'kyŭ-bāt-ēr), *n.* 1. a heated apparatus for hatching eggs artificially. 2. a somewhat similar apparatus in which to keep premature babies for a time. 3. an apparatus, as in a laboratory, for developing microorganisms.

in·cu·bus (ing'kyŭ-bŭs), *n.*, *pl.* **-bus·es**, **-bi** (-bī), 1. a nightmare. 2. in medieval times, a demon thought to have sexual intercourse with sleeping women. 3. an oppressive burden.

---

a in cap, ā in cane, ä in father, á in abet, e in met, ē in be, ē in baker, è in regent, I in pit, ī in fine, i in manifest, o in hot, ô in horse, ō in bone,

in·cul·cate (in-kul'kāt), *v.t.* -cat·ed, -cat·ing, to impress upon the mind by frequent admonition or urging. —**in·cul·ca'tion,** *n.* —**in·cul'ca·tor,** *n.*

in·cul·pate (in-kul'pāt), *v.t.* -pat·ed, -pat·ing, to impute guilt to; blame; incriminate. —**in·cul·pa'tion,** *n.* —**in·cul'pa·to·ry,** *adj.*

in·cum·ben·cy (in-kum'bėn-si), *n.,* *pl.* -cies, 1. the condition or state of being incumbent. 2. an obligation that is incumbent. 3. the holding and exercise of an office. 4. the holding of a church benefice.

in·cum·bent ('bėnt), *adj.* 1. lying, inclining, or pressing on something. 2. imposed as a duty; obligatory. 3. now in office: *n.* the holder of an office or church benefice.

in·cum·ber (in-kum'bėr), *v.t.* same as encumber. —**in·cum'brance,** *n.*

in·cur (in-kūr'), *v.t.* -curred', -cur'ring, 1. to become liable to by one's own actions; bring upon oneself. 2. to contract, as a debt.

in·cur·a·ble (in-kyoor'ȧ-bl), *adj.* not capable of being cured; irremediable: *n.* a person afflicted with an incurable disease. —**in·cur·a·bil'i·ty,** *n.* —**in·cur'a·bly,** *adv.*

in·cur·sion (in-kūr'zhun), *n.* 1. the act of running or entering into; inroad. 2. a sudden, brief attack; raid.

in·cur·vate (in-kūr'vit, 'vāt), *adj.* bent or curved inward.

in·curve (in-kūrv'), *v.t. & v.i.* -curved', -curv'ing, to curve inward: *n.* (in'kūrv), 1. an act of curving inward. 2. in *Baseball,* same as screwball (sense 1).

in·cus (ing'kŭs), *n.,* *pl.* **in·cu·des** (in-kū'dēz), the central, small, anvil-shaped bone in the middle ear.

in·debt·ed (in-det'id), *adj.* 1. being in debt; obligated to repay something. 2. owing gratitude; beholden.

in·debt·ed·ness (-nis), *n.* 1. the state of being indebted. 2. the amount owed; the totality of one's debts.

in·de·cen·cy (in-dē'sėn-si), *n.* 1. the state or quality of being indecent; want of modesty, good manners, etc. 2. *pl.* -cies, an indecent word, gesture, etc.

in·de·cent ('snt), *adj.* 1. violating propriety in language, behavior, etc.; unseemly. 2. violating public moral values; obscene.

in·de·ci·pher·a·ble (in-di-sī'fėr-ȧ-bl), *adj.* that cannot be deciphered; illegible.

in·de·ci·sion (in-di-sizh'un), *n.* want of decision; wavering in decision; irresolution.

in·de·ci·sive (-sī'siv), *adj.* 1. not decisive; inconclusive. 2. characterized by indecision; irresolute; hesitant. —**in·de·ci'sive·ly,** *adv.* —**in·de·ci'sive·ness,** *n.*

in·de·clin·a·ble (in-di-klīn'ȧ-bl), *adj.* not declinable; having no grammatical inflections.

in·dec·o·rous (in-dek'ėr-ùs, in-di-kōr'ùs), *adj.* violating decorum, propriety, etc.; unseemly.

in·de·co·rum (in-di-kōr'ûm), *n.* 1. want of decorum or good taste. 2. a breach of propriety in speech, behavior, etc.

in·deed (in-dēd'), *adv.* 1. without doubt; certainly. 2. in fact; in reality: *interj.* an exclamation of surprise, irony, uncertainty, etc.

in·de·fat·i·ga·ble (in-di-fat'i-gȧ-bl), *adj.* that cannot be fatigued; not yielding to weariness; unremitting in effort. —**in·de·fat'i·ga·bly,** *adv.*

in·de·fea·si·ble (-fē'zi-bl), *adj.* that cannot be revoked or made void, as a title.

in·de·fect·i·ble (-fek'ti-bl), *adj.* 1. without defect or blemish; perfect. 2. not subject to failure, decay, etc.

in·de·fen·si·ble (-fen'si-bl), *adj.* 1. that cannot be defended or maintained. 2. that cannot be justified; inexcusable.

in·de·fin·a·ble (-fīn'ȧ-bl), *adj.* that cannot be defined.

in·def·i·nite (in-def'i-nit), *adj.* 1. not defined; having no prescribed limits. 2. not precise; vague. 3. uncertain. 4. in *Grammar,* not identified or restricted. —**in·def'i·nite·ly,** *adv.* —**in·def'i·nite·ness,** *n.*

in·de·his·cent (in-di-his'ėnt), *adj.* not splitting open at maturity to discharge seeds. —**in·de·his'cence,** *n.*

in·del·i·ble (in-del'i-bl), *adj.* 1. that cannot be blotted out, effaced, or obliterated. 2. leaving an ineradicable mark. —**in·del'i·bly,** *adv.*

in·del·i·ca·cy (in-del'i-kȧ-si), *n.* 1. the quality or condition of being indelicate. 2. *pl.* -cies, something indelicate.

in·del·i·cate ('i-kit), *adj.* 1. offensive to modesty or propriety; improper. 2. coarse; indecent. 3. tactless.

in·dem·ni·fi·ca·tion (in-dem-ni-fi-kā'shun), *n.* 1. the act of indemnifying or the state of being indemnified. 2. something that indemnifies; reimbursement.

in·dem·ni·fy (in-dem'ni-fī), *v.t.* -fied, -fy·ing, 1. to secure or insure against loss, damage, etc. 2. to reimburse for loss, damage, etc.

in·dem·ni·ty (-ti), *n.* 1. security or insurance against loss, damage, etc. 2. legal exemption from punishment or liability incurred. 3. compensation for loss, damage, etc.

in·dent (in-dent'), *v.t. & v.i.* 1. to notch or be formed by notches. 2. to begin (a line, paragraph, etc.) leaving a space between the first word and the regular margin: *n.* 1. a notch in an edge. 2. a space in from a margin. 3. an order or a contract for foreign merchandise.

in·dent (in-dent'), *v.t.* 1. to make a dent or shallow depression in. 2. to push down upon so as to form an impression; stamp in.

in·den·ta·tion (in-den-tā'shun), *n.* 1. the act of indenting or of being indented. 2. a notch, dent, recess, coastal inlet, etc. 3. a blank space to the left of an indented line.

in·den·tion (in-den'shun), *n.* 1. the act of indenting or the condition of being indented. 2. the blank space produced by this.

in·den·ture ('chėr), *n.* 1. a written contract or covenant, formerly in duplicate, with the edges notched so as to correspond. 2. *often pl.* a contract obligating one party to work for another for a designated period of time: *v.t.* -tured, -tur·ing, to bind by indenture, as an apprentice.

in·de·pen·dence (in-di-pen'dėns), *n.* 1. the state or quality of being independent; freedom from support, control, etc. by others. 2.

ô in drag*o*n, ōō in cr*u*de, oo in w*oo*l, u in c*u*p, ū in c*u*re, ŭ in t*u*rn, û in f*o*cus, oi in b*oy*, ou in h*ou*se, th in *th*in, th in shea*th*e, g in g*e*t, j in *j*oy, y in *y*et.

[Now Rare], an income sufficient for one's support.

Independence Day, the Fourth of July, the anniversary of the Declaration of Independence on July 4, 1776: a legal holiday in the U.S.

in-de-pend-en-cy ('děn-si), *n., pl.* **-cies,** 1. same as **independence.** 2. [I-], the church polity of the Independents. 3. an independent political entity.

in-de-pend-ent ('děnt), *adj.* 1. not under the influence, control, governance, etc. of another or others; self-reliant. 2. having an income large enough to allow one to live without working. 3. not subject to bias or influence; objective. 4. politically free; self-governing. 5. not affiliated with any political party. 6. not affiliated with a group, system, etc.; separate. 7. not resulting from something else; not contingent: *n.* 1. one who is independent in belief, thought, support, etc.; especially, a voter who is not allied to any political party. 2. [I-], *a)* one who believes that a local organized Christian church should be competent to govern itself without any external ecclesiastical authority. *b)* in England, a Congregationalist.

in-depth (in'depth'), *adj.* thoroughly researched and described; profound.

in-de-scrib-a-ble (in-di-skrī'bǎ-bl), *adj.* beyond description; not describable. **—in-de-scrib'a-bly,** *adv.*

in-de-struct-i-ble (-struk'tǐ-bl), *adj.* not capable of being destroyed; everlasting. **—in-de-struct-i-bil'i-ty,** *n.*

in-de-ter-mi-na-ble (-tūr'mǐ-nǎ-bl), *adj.* 1. incapable of being resolved or settled. 2. incapable of being bounded or ascertained.

in-de-ter-mi-nate (-nit), *adj.* 1. not determined exactly; vague; indefinite. 2. not yet settled; inconclusive.

in-de-ter-min-ism ('mi-nizm), *n.* 1. the doctrine that man in some acts is capable of choosing freely and that his choices are not dependent upon previous causes. 2. the quality or state of being indeterminate.

in-dex (in'deks), *n., pl.* **-dex-es, -di-ces** ('dī-sēz), 1. short for **index finger.** 2. something that points out or indicates; sign. 3. an alphabetical table of names, topics, etc. dealt with in a printed work, listing the pages where found. 4. a ratio or other number expressing a relation or relative change. 5. a figure or letter that shows the power or root of a quantity. 6. [I-], in the *Roman Catholic Church,* formerly, a list of books whose reading was restricted or prohibited: *v.t.* to provide with an index.

index finger, same as **forefinger.**

In-di-a ink (in'di-ǎ), a black liquid ink.

In-di-a-man (in'di-ǎ-mǎn), *n., pl.* **-men** (-měn), a large merchant vessel formerly used in trade with India.

In-di-an (in'di-ǎn), *adj.* 1. of or pertaining to India, a region in southern Asia, or its people. 2. of or pertaining to the aboriginal peoples of North America, South America, or the West Indies, or their cultures. 3. made from maize, or Indian corn: *n.* 1. a native or inhabitant of India or of the East

Indies. 2. any member of any of the aboriginal American Indian peoples. 3. loosely, any one of the native languages spoken by the American Indians.

Indian club, a wooden club shaped like a tenpin and swung in the hand for exercise.

Indian corn, 1. a cultivated American cereal plant of the grass family, with seeds growing from cobs that are covered by husks. 2. the ears or edible kernels of this cereal grass.

Indian file, same as **single file:** this was the way American Indians walked a trail, especially through forests.

Indian giver, [Informal], a person who gives another something as a gift and then requests or demands its return: from the belief that American Indians expected the recipient of a gift to reciprocate with one of equal value.

Indian hemp, 1. an American dogbane with a tough bark formerly used in making rope and a medicinal root formerly used in making an emetic. 2. same as **hemp** (sense 1).

Indian meal, ground Indian corn; cornmeal.

Indian Mutiny, a revolt by native troops against British authority in India (1857-58), caused by British aggressions, the introduction of British customs, and the suppression of certain native customs.

Indian paintbrush, any one of various plants having orange or red flowers and showy, brightly colored bracts.

Indian pipe, any one of several waxy-white, leafless plants that live on dead or decaying matter and bear a single, nodding, white or pink flower on a fleshy stem.

Indian red, a dark-red iron oxide, used as a paint pigment and in cosmetics and polishing compounds.

Indian sign, a spell or jinx: chiefly in *to put the Indian sign on.*

Indian summer, 1. a period of mild weather late in autumn, following the first frost and characterized by a cloudless sky and hazy atmosphere. 2. an undisturbed, serene, or productive stage coming late in a period, life, etc.

Indian tobacco, a poisonous North American lobelia, bearing small, blue flowers and swollen pods.

Indian wrestling, 1. a contest in which two persons lock hands, position their elbows on a flat surface, and attempt to gain a victory by forcing each other's arm flat on the surface. 2. a contest in which two persons stand with one foot alongside the corresponding foot of the other, clasp hands, and attempt to force each other off balance.

In-di-a paper (in'di-ǎ), 1. a thin, absorbent paper made from vegetable fiber in China and Japan: used for taking prints from engraved plates. 2. a very thin, tough, opaque paper, used in printing certain books, especially Bibles.

India rubber, crude, natural rubber prepared by drying the milky sap of various tropical plants; caoutchouc. **—In'di-a-rub'ber,** *adj.*

In-dic (in'dik), *adj.* 1. of India. 2. denoting or of a group of languages of the Indo-

European language family, many of which are spoken or were spoken in India, Pakistan, etc.

in·di·can (in'di-kan), *n.* a colorless substance obtained from various indigo-producing plants that is converted into natural indigo by water and oxygen.

in·di·cant ('di-cănt), *adj.* indicating: *n.* that which points out or indicates.

in·di·cate ('di-kăt), *v.t.* -cat·ed, cat·ing, 1. to point out; show. 2. to serve as a sign or indication of; signify. 3. to suggest or show the necessity or practicality of. 4. to express or disclose briefly.

in·di·ca·tion (in-di-kā'shŭn), *n.* 1. the act of indicating. 2. that which indicates; sign; symptom. 3. something pointed out as needed or advantageous. 4. the reading recorded on a measuring device.

in·dic·a·tive (in-dik'ă-tiv), *adj.* 1. serving to point out, suggest, or imply. 2. denoting or of that mood of a verb used to signify that an action, happening, or condition is a fact, or to ask a factual question: *n.* 1. the indicative mood. 2. a verb form in the indicative mood. —**in·dic'a·tive·ly**, *adv.*

in·di·ca·tor (in'di-kăt-ĕr), *n.* 1. one who or that which indicates, as an arrow, pointer, etc. 2. any one of various dials, meters, gauges, needles, or other devices that measure, display, etc. physical quantities, as pressure, voltage, time, height, amount, etc. 3. any one of various substances that indicate, as by change in color, the acidity, concentration, presence, absence, etc. of a substance. 4. in *Ecology,* an organism, species, etc. that indicates the existence of certain environmental conditions.

in·dict (in-dīt'), *v.t.* 1. to charge with a crime or other offense. 2. to accuse of a crime by the presentment of a jury, especially a grand jury. —**in·dict'er, in·dict'or,** *n.*

in·dict·a·ble ('ă-bl), *adj.* 1. that should be indicted, as a person. 2. that makes indictment possible, as a crime.

in·dict·ment ('mĕnt), *n.* 1. the act of indicting or the state of being indicted. 2. a charge; specifically, a formal, written statement drawn up by the prosecutor and presented to the court by a grand jury that has found the evidence sufficient for trial of the accused.

in·dif·fer·ence (in-dif'ĕr-ĕns), *n.* 1. the state, fact, or quality of being indifferent. 2. absence of concern, preference, or interest. 3. absence of value, importance, distinction, etc.

in·dif·fer·ent (-ĕnt), *adj.* 1. displaying impartiality; lacking bias. 2. showing no particular feeling or concern; apathetic. 3. having no importance; insignificant. 4. moderate; fair; mediocre. 5. neutral; inactive. —**in·dif'fer·ent·ly,** *adv.*

in·di·gene (in'di-jēn), *n.* an animal or plant that is native to an area.

in·dig·e·nous (in-dij'ĕ-nŭs), *adj.* 1. born, produced, or growing naturally in an area or country; native. 2. inborn; innate; intrinsic. —**in·dig'e·nous·ly,** *adv.*

in·di·gent (in'di-jĕnt), *adj.* impoverished; poor; needy: *n.* an indigent person. —**in'di·gence,** *n.*

in·di·gest·ed (in-di-jes'tid), *adj.* 1. not digested, as food. 2. not carefully thought out or reflected upon. 3. formless; confused.

in·di·gest·i·ble ('ti-bl), *adj.* difficult or impossible to digest.

in·di·ges·tion (in-di-jes'chŭn), *n.* 1. difficulty in digesting food. 2. discomfort resulting from this.

in·dig·nant (in-dig'nănt), *adj.* exhibiting or filled with indignation. —**in·dig'nant·ly,** *adv.*

in·dig·na·tion (in-dig-nā'shŭn), *n.* anger or disdain evoked by something unworthy, unjust, dishonorable, or base.

in·dig·ni·ty (in-dig'ni-ti), *n., pl.* -ties, an action that lowers, insults, or degrades the dignity of another; affront.

in·di·go (in'di-gō), *n., pl.* -gos, -goes, 1. a blue dye obtained from certain plants by changing the indican produced by these. 2. a blue dye made synthetically. 3. a deep violet-blue.

indigo bunting, a small bird of eastern North America, the male of which is indigo blue in color and the female brownish: also **indigo bird.**

indigo snake, a large, nonpoisonous, bluish-black snake of the southern U.S.

in·di·rect (in-di-rekt'), *adj.* 1. not direct; roundabout. 2. not proceeding straight to the point. 3. evasive; devious; deceitful. 4. not expected immediately; secondary. —**in·di·rect'ly,** *adv.* —**in·di·rect'ness,** *n.*

indirect object, the word or words denoting the indirect receiver of the action of a verb.

in·dis·creet (in-dis-krēt'), *adj.* wanting in discretion; imprudent.

in·dis·crete (in-dis-krēt'), *adj.* not divided or separated into distinct parts.

in·dis·cre·tion (in-dis-kresh'ŭn), *n.* 1. want of judicious judgment; imprudence. 2. an imprudent action or remark.

in·dis·crim·i·nate (-krim'i-nit), *adj.* 1. not marked by selectivity or discrimination. 2. haphazard; motley; promiscuous. —**in·dis·crim'i·nate·ly,** *adv.*

in·dis·crim·i·na·tion (-krim-i-nā'shŭn), *n.* the state or quality of being indiscriminate; want of discrimination. —**in·dis·crim'i·na·tive,** *adj.*

in·dis·pen·sa·ble (in-dis-pen'să-bl), *adj.* 1. that cannot be dispensed or set aside. 2. absolutely necessary; requisite.

in·dis·pose (in-dis-pōz'), *v.t.* -posed', -pos'ing, 1. to render unfit; disqualify. 2. to make unwilling or averse; disincline. 3. to make mildly ill.

in·dis·posed (-pōzd'), *adj.* 1. mildly ill. 2. averse; disinclined. —**in·dis·po·si'tion,** *n.*

in·dis·pu·ta·ble (in-dis-pūt'ă-bl, in-dis'pū-tă-bl), *adj.* unquestionable; undeniable. —**in·dis·pu'ta·bly,** *adv.*

in·dis·sol·u·ble (in-di-sol'yoo-bl), *adj.* 1. not capable of being broken, undone, or abrogated; permanent. 2. not capable of being dissolved, disintegrated, or decomposed; stable. —**in·dis·sol·u·bil'i·ty,** *n.*

in·dis·tinct (in-dis-tingkt'), *adj.* 1. not distinct to the senses or mind; obscure. 2. not clearly delimited; not sharply defined; blurred. —**in·dis·tinct'ly,** adv.

in·dis·tinc·tive (-tingk'tiv), adj. 1. wanting distinctive qualities. 2. not capable of distinguishing; undiscriminating.

in·dis·tin·guish·a·ble (-ting'gwish-ā-bl), adj. incapable of being distinguished, discriminated, or perceived. —**in·dis·tin'guish·a·bly,** adv.

in·dite (in-dīt'), v.t. -**dit'ed,** -**dit'ing,** 1. to compose; write. 2. to put down in writing.

in·di·um (in'dĭ-ŭm), n. a rare, soft, white, metallic chemical element, found chiefly in zinc ores and used in making transistors, in plating, etc.

in·di·vid·u·al (in-di-vij'oo-wăl, -vij'ăl), adj. 1. existing as a single, indivisible entity; separate; particular. 2. of, by, for, pertaining to, or distinguishing a single person or thing: n. 1. a particular thing or organism as distinguished from a group, species, etc. 2. a person. —**in·di·vid'u·al·ism** (-izm), n. 1. individuality. 2. an idiosyncrasy. 3. the doctrine that the individual should be allowed to pursue his own economic interests, unrestricted by the state or society. 4. the doctrine that the individual is preeminent over the state. 5. the living of one's life unfettered by societal conventions or restrictions. —**in·di·vid'u·al·ist,** n. —**in·di·vid·u·al·is'tic,** adj.

in·di·vid·u·al·i·ty (in-di-vij-oo-wal'ĭ-ti), n. 1. the condition of being a distinct individual; separate existence. 2. the totality of the attributes or characteristics that distinguish a particular individual from others. 3. personality.

in·di·vid·u·al·ize (-vij'oo-wă-līz, -vij'oo-līz), v.t. -**ized,** -**iz·ing,** 1. to invest with individuality; distinguish from others. 2. to tailor to the needs, interest, desires, etc. of a particular individual or group. —**in·di·vid·u·al·i·za'tion,** n.

in·di·vid·u·al·ly (-vij'oo-wăl-i, -vij'ăl-i), adv. 1. as an individual or individuals; singly. 2. as an individual with particular attributes; personally.

in·di·vid·u·ate (-vij'oo-wāt), v.t. -**at·ed,** -**at·ing,** 1. to make distinct; individualize. 2. to form into a unique entity or individual. —**in·di·vid·u·a'tion,** n.

in·di·vis·i·ble (in-di-viz'ĭ-bl), adj. 1. not separable into parts. 2. in *Mathematics,* incapable of being divided exactly so that no remainder is left. —**in·di·vis·i·bil'i·ty,** n. —**in·di·vis'i·bly,** adv.

Indo-, a combining form signifying *of India, of Indian origin, of India and.*

In·do-Ar·y·an (in-dō-er'ĭ-ăn), adj. 1. of the Indo-Aryans. 2. same as **Indic** (sense 2): n. any one of the natives of India who speaks an Indic language.

In·do-chi·nese, **In·do-Chi·nese** (in'dō-chī-nēz'), adj. of or pertaining to Indochina, a peninsula in southeast Asia, its peoples, their languages, or their cultures: n., pl. -**nese',** a native or inhabitant of Indochina.

in·doc·tri·nate (in-dok'tri-nāt), v.t. -**nat·ed,** -**nat·ing,** 1. to imbue with principles, doctrines, beliefs, etc. 2. to teach; instruct. —**in·doc·tri·na'tion,** n.

In·do-Eu·ro·pe·an (in-dō-yoor-ō-pē'ăn), adj. denoting, of, or constituting a family of languages that includes most of the languages of Europe and many of the languages of India and southwestern Asia: n. 1. the Indo-European family of languages. 2. the presumed parent language of this family.

in·do·lent (in'dō-lĕnt), adj. avoiding labor; indulging in ease; lazy. —**in'do·lence,** n. —**in'do·lent·ly,** adv.

in·dom·i·ta·ble (in-dom'it-ā-bl), adj. not capable of being overwhelmed, discouraged, or vanquished; invincible.

In·do·ne·sian (in-dō-nē'zhŭn), adj. of or pertaining to Indonesia, a country comprising many islands in the southeastern Pacific: n. a native or inhabitant of Indonesia.

in·door (in'dôr), adj. 1. of or pertaining to the interior of a house or building. 2. residing, occurring, or belonging within doors.

in·doors (in'dôrz'), adv. in or into a room, house, or building.

in·dorse (in-dôrs'), v.t. -**dorsed',** -**dors'ing,** same as **endorse.**

in·drawn (in'drôn'), adj. 1. drawn in. 2. reserved; introspective.

in·du·bi·ta·ble (in-dōō'bi-tā-bl, -dū'-), adj. too evident to be doubted; unquestionable. —**in·du'bi·ta·bly,** adv.

in·duce (in-dōōs', -dūs'), v.t. -**duced',** -**duc'ing,** 1. to lead on; influence; persuade. 2. to bring about; effect; cause. 3. to infer by induction. 4. in *Physics,* to produce (an electric or magnetic effect) by induction.

in·duce·ment ('mĕnt), n. 1. the act or process of inducing. 2. that which induces; motive; incentive. 3. in *Law,* an introductory statement of explanation in a proceeding.

in·duct (in-dukt'), v.t. 1. to install ceremoniously in an office or benefice. 2. to introduce as a member of; initiate. 3. to call into the armed forces.

in·duct·ance (-duk'tăns), n. that property of an electric circuit that opposes any change in the current flowing through it and which is present only when the current is varying.

in·duct·ee (in-duk-tē'), n. a person inducted, especially into the armed forces.

in·duc·tion (in-duk'shŭn), n. the act of inducting or state of being inducted.

induction coil, an apparatus for generating a high-voltage alternating current in a secondary coil by the interruption of the flow of low-voltage direct current in the primary coil.

in·duc·tive ('tiv), adj. 1. of, pertaining to, or using induction. 2. produced by induction. 3. of or pertaining to inductance or electrical induction.

in·duc·tor ('tĕr), n. 1. one who inducts. 2. that part of an electrical apparatus that operates by induction or produces induction in a circuit.

in·due (in-dōō', -dū'), v.t. -**dued',** -**du'ing,** same as **endue.**

in·dulge (in-dulj'), v.t. -**dulged',** -**dulg'ing,** 1. to yield to (a desire or whim); satisfy. 2. to give free course to; gratify; humor: v.i. 1. to yield to one's individual desires or pleasure; indulge oneself (in something).

---

a in cap, ā in cane, ä in father, å in abet, e in met, ē in be, ê in baker, ê in regent, i in pit, ī in fine, î in manifest, o in hot, ô in horse, ō in bone,

in-dul-gence (in-dul'jĕns), *n.* 1. the act of indulging or the state of being indulgent. 2. something indulged in. 3. a favor or privilege. 4. in *Commerce*, an extension of time for payment or performance, given as a favor. 5. in the *Roman Catholic Church*, full or partial remission of the temporal punishment due for sins that have been forgiven through the sacrament of penance.

in-dul-gent ('jĕnt), *adj.* disposed to indulge; kind; lenient. —**in-dul'gent-ly,** *adv.*

in-du-line (in'dyoo-lēn, -lin), *n.* any of numerous blue or black dyes.

in-dult (in-dult'), *n.* a privilege granted by the Pope to bishops and others to do something not allowed by the common law of the Church, as permitting a missionary priest to administer the sacrament of confirmation.

in-du-rate (in'doo-rāt), *v.t.* -rat-ed, -rat-ing. 1. to make hard; harden. 2. to render callous, unfeeling, or obdurate. 3. to establish firmly: *v.i.* to become indurated: *adj.* 1. hardened. 2. unfeeling; obdurate. —**in-du-ra'tion,** *n.*

in-dus-tri-al (in-dus'tri-ăl), *adj.* 1. of, pertaining to, or obtained from industry. 2. having or characterized by industries. 3. working in industries. 4. used or required by industries: *n.* a stock or bond issued by an industrial corporation or enterprise. —**in-dus'tri-al-ly,** *adv.*

industrial arts, a school subject designed to develop basic skills in using tools, machines, etc.

in-dus-tri-al-ism (-izm), *n.* a social system or mode of living marked by the predominance of industrial pursuits, mass production techniques, the crowding of workers into urban areas, etc.

in-dus-tri-al-ist (-ist), *n.* a person who owns or is responsible for the management of an industry.

in-dus-tri-al-ize (-ă-liz), *v.t.* -ized, -iz-ing. 1. to make industrial. 2. to organize as an industry.

industrial park, an area zoned, designed, and developed for industrial use, usually outside a city.

industrial union, a labor union that accepts all workmen for membership regardless of their individual trades or crafts.

in-dus-tri-ous ('tri-us), *adj.* characterized by diligence and assiduous application to work or study; hard-working.

in-dus-try (in'dus-tri), *n., pl.* -tries, 1. steady application or unremitting diligence in work. 2. systematic labor. 3. a specific branch of an art, craft, business, etc. 4. a particular group of productive enterprises. 5. manufacturing enterprises as a whole.

in-e-bri-ate (in-ē'bri-āt), *v.t.* -at-ed, -at-ing. 1. to make drunk; intoxicate. 2. to exhilarate; arouse: *adj.* (-it), drunk; intoxicated: *n.* (-it), an intoxicated person, especially a habitual drunkard. —**in-e-bri-a'tion,** *n.*

in-e-bri-at-ed (-āt-id), *adj.* drunk; intoxicated.

in-e-bri-e-ty (in-i-brī'ĕ-ti), *n.* drunkenness; intoxication.

in-ed-i-ble (in-ed'i-bl), *adj.* not fit for food.

in-ed-u-ca-ble (in-ej'ŭ-kă-bl), *adj.* not capable of being educated.

in-ef-fa-ble (in-ef'ă-bl), *adj.* 1. not capable of being expressed in words; inexpressible. 2. too sacred or awesome to be uttered; unspeakable.

in-ef-face-a-ble (in-i-fās'ă-bl), *adj.* that cannot be erased or obliterated; indelible.

in-ef-fec-tive (in-i-fek'tiv), *adj.* 1. not producing the desired effect; ineffectual. 2. incapable of performing efficiently; incompetent.

in-ef-fec-tu-al ('choo-wăl), *adj.* not producing or incapable of producing the desired or usual effect; unavailing.

in-ef-fi-ca-cious (in-ef-i-kā'shŭs), *adj.* ineffective; powerless; inadequate.

in-ef-fi-ca-cy (in-ef'i-kă-si), *n.* lack of efficacy.

in-ef-fi-cient (in-ē-fish'ĕnt), *adj.* 1. not efficient. 2. not producing the intended effect. 3. lacking the needed ability or skill; incompetent. —**in-ef-fi'cien-cy,** *n.* —**in-ef-fi'cient-ly,** *adv.*

in-e-las-tic (in-i-las'tik), *adj.* wanting in elasticity; unyielding; inflexible.

in-el-e-gance (in-el'ĕ-găns), *n.* 1. want of elegance. 2. something inelegant: also **in-el'e-gan-cy,** *n., pl.* -cies.

in-el-e-gant (-gĕnt), *adj.* offensive to good taste; unrefined; coarse; vulgar. —**in-el'e-gant-ly,** *adv.*

in-el-i-gi-ble (in-el'i-ji-bl), *adj.* not eligible; unsuitable; unworthy of being chosen for some office. —**in-el-i-gi-bil'i-ty,** *n.*

in-e-luc-ta-ble (in-i-luk'tă-bl), *adj.* irresistible; inevitable; not to be overcome or avoided. —**in-e-luc'ta-bly,** *adv.*

in-ept (in-ept'), *adj.* 1. unsuitable; unfit. 2. nonsensical; foolish. 3. clumsy; inefficient. —**in-ept'ly,** *adv.* —**in-ept'ness,** *n.*

in-ept-i-tude (in-ep'ti-tōōd), *n.* 1. the quality or state of being inept. 2. a foolish act, remark, etc.

in-e-qual-i-ty (in-i-kwäl'ĭ-ti), *n.* 1. the condition of being unequal. 2. difference in social position, rank, size, amount, etc. 3. unevenness; lack of smoothness. 4. variability; changeableness. 5. in *Mathematics*, an algebraic statement that a quantity is greater or less than another quantity.

in-eq-ui-ta-ble (in-ek'wit-ă-bl), *adj.* not equitable; unfair; unjust. —**in-eq'ui-ta-bly,** *adv.*

in-eq-ui-ty ('wit-i), *n.* 1. injustice; unfairness. 2. *pl.* -ties, an instance of injustice or unfairness.

in-e-rad-i-ca-ble (in-i-rad'i-kă-bl), *adj.* incapable of being rooted out. —**in-e-rad'i-ca-bly,** *adv.*

in-er-rant (in-er'ănt), *adj.* free from error; making no errors; infallible. —**in-er'ran-cy,** *n.*

in-ert (in-ürt'), *adj.* 1. having no power of motion or action. 2. slow; sluggish; listless. 3. exhibiting little or no chemical activity. —**in-ert'ly,** *adv.* —**in-ert'ness,** *n.*

in-er-tia (in-ür'shă), *n.* 1. disinclination for activity, change, etc.; inertness. 2. in *Physics,* that property of matter by virtue of which it tends to remain at rest, or, if in motion, to continue in the same direction unless acted upon by an outside force. —**in-er'tial,** *adj.*

in-es-cap-a-ble (in-ē-skăp'ă-bl), *adj.* that cannot

---

be escaped or avoided; inevitable. —**in·es·cap′a·bly**, *adv.*

in·es·sen·tial (in-ē-sen′shŭl), *adj.* 1. not essential or important; unessential. 2. [Rare], without essence or being; immaterial.

in·es·ti·ma·ble (in-es′tǐ-má-bl), *adj.* not to be estimated; beyond measure or price; incalculable; invaluable. —**in·es′ti·ma·bly**, *adv.*

in·ev·i·ta·ble (in-ev′ǐ-tá-bl), *adj.* not to be evaded or prevented; unavoidable. —**in·ev·i·ta·bil′i·ty**, *n.* —**in·ev′i·ta·bly**, *adv.*

in·ex·act (in-ig-zakt′), *adj.* not precise, correct, accurate, or punctual. —**in·ex·act′i·tude** (-zak′tǐ-tōōd), **in·ex·act′ness**, *n.* —**in·ex·act′ly**, *adv.*

in·ex·cus·a·ble (in-ik-skū′zá-bl), *adj.* incapable of being excused; unpardonable; unjustifiable. —**in·ex·cus′a·bly**, *adv.*

in·ex·haust·i·ble (in-ig-zôs′tǐ-bl), *adj.* 1. not to be exhausted or spent. 2. tireless; unwearied; indefatigable. —**in·ex·haust′i·bly**, *adv.*

in·ex·o·ra·ble (in-ek′sēr-á-bl), *adj.* 1. not to be moved or persuaded by prayers or entreaties; unyielding; unrelenting. 2. not to be changed, halted, resisted, etc. —**in·ex′o·ra·bly**, *adv.*

in·ex·pe·di·ent (in-ik-spē′di-ĕnt), *adj.* not expedient; unsuitable for the given circumstances; inadvisable. —**in·ex·pe′di·ence**, **in·ex·pe′di·en·cy**, *n.* —**in·ex·pe′di·ent·ly**, *adv.*

in·ex·pen·sive (in-ik-spen′siv), *adj.* not expensive; low in cost; cheap. —**in·ex·pen′sive·ly**, *adv.* —**in·ex·pen′sive·ness**, *n.*

in·ex·pe·ri·ence (in-ik-spir′i-ĕns), *n.* want of experience or of the knowledge or skill that comes from experience.

in·ex·pe·ri·enced (-ĕnst), *adj.* lacking experience; unpracticed; unskilled; unversed.

in·ex·pert (in-ek′spĕrt, in-ik-spûrt′), *adj.* unskilled; lacking the knowledge and dexterity derived from practice.

in·ex·pi·a·ble (in-ek′spi-á-bl), *adj.* that cannot be expiated or atoned for.

in·ex·pli·ca·ble (in-eks′pli-ká-bl), *adj.* not to be explained, comprehended, or accounted for; that cannot be interpreted. —**in·ex′pli·ca·bly**, *adv.*

in·ex·plic·it (in-ik-splis′it), *adj.* not clear; not fully expressed; vague; indefinite. —**in·ex·plic′it·ly**, *adv.* —**in·ex·plic′it·ness**, *n.*

in·ex·press·i·ble (in-ik-spres′ǐ-bl), *adj.* incapable of being expressed, uttered, or described. —**in·ex·press′i·bly**, *adv.*

in·ex·pres·sive (-′iv), *adj.* lacking expression or distinct significance; dull. —**in·ex·press′ive·ness**, *n.*

in·ex·ten·si·ble (in-ik-sten′sǐ-bl), *adj.* that cannot be extended or stretched; inelastic.

in·ex·tin·guish·a·ble (in-ik-sting′gwish-á-bl), *adj.* that cannot be extinguished; unquenchable.

in ex·tre·mis (in ik-strē′mis), [Latin, in the final bounds], at the point of death.

in·ex·tri·ca·ble (in-eks′tri-ká-bl), *adj.* 1. that one cannot escape from or remedy. 2. not able to be disentangled or untied. 3. too intricate or perplexing to resolve. —**in·ex′tri·ca·bly**, *adv.*

in·fal·li·ble (in-fal′ǐ-bl), *adj.* 1. incapable of err-

ing. 2. unlikely to err, fail, etc.; certain; unfailing. —**in·fal·li·bil′i·ty**, *n.* —**in·fal′li·bly**, *adv.*

in·fa·mous (in′fá-mŭs), *adj.* 1. having a notoriously bad reputation. 2. producing or deserving infamy; odious; scandalous; shocking. —**in′fa·mous·ly**, *adv.*

in·fa·my (-mi), *n., pl.* -**mies**, 1. a notoriously evil reputation; disrepute. 2. the condition of being infamous. 3. an infamous deed; ingnominious.

in·fan·cy (in′fán-si), *n., pl.* -**cies**, 1. the state of being an infant; very early childhood. 2. the first age or start of anything. 3. in *Law*, the state or period of being a minor.

in·fant (′fânt), *n.* 1. a very young child. 2. a person legally an infant; minor: *adj.* 1. of or pertaining to infants or infancy. 2. being in an early or youthful stage of growth.

in·fan·ta (in-fan′tä), *n.* 1. a daughter of a Spanish or Portuguese king. 2. the wife of an infante.

in·fan·te (′tä), *n.* any son of a Spanish or Portuguese king other than the heir to the throne.

in·fan·ti·cide (in-fan′tǐ-sīd), *n.* 1. the murder of a baby. 2. a person who kills a baby.

in·fan·tile (in′fán-tīl), *adj.* 1. of or pertaining to infants or infancy. 2. characteristic of an infant; immature; childish.

infantile paralysis, same as **poliomyelitis**.

in·fan·til·ism (in′fân-tǐl-izm, in-fan′-), *n.* childish acts or behavior; specifically, in *Psychology*, a condition of being abnormally childlike, with the retention of immature responses and behavior in adulthood and characterized by the failure of physical, mental, and sexual development.

in·fan·tine (in′fân-tĭn, -tīn). *adj.* infantile; babyish or childish.

in·fan·try (in′fân-tri), *n., pl.* -**tries**, 1. soldiers trained to fight on foot. 2. that branch of an army made up of units of foot soldiers. —**in′fan·try·man** (-mán), *n., pl.* -**men** (-mĕn).

in·farct (in-färkt′), *n.* an area of tissue in an organ or part that dies because the blood supply has been cut off by occlusion or stenosis in the local circulation: also **in·farc′tion** (-färk′shŭn).

in·fare (in′far, ′fer), *n.* [Dial.], a housewarming; especially, a feast or reception given for a newly married couple.

in·fat·u·ate (in-fach′oo-wāt), *v.t.* -**at·ed**, -**at·ing**, 1. to make extravagantly foolish. 2. to inspire with a foolish or mindless passion or love: *adj.* infatuated.

in·fat·u·at·ed (-id), *adj.* 1. completely possessed by foolish passion. 2. acting without reason or common sense; foolish.

in·fat·u·a·tion (in-fach-oo-wā′shŭn), *n.* 1. the state or condition of being infatuated. 2. an object that inspires foolish passion.

in·fect (in-fekt′), *v.t.* 1. to influence or imbue with ideas or attitudes, especially ones that are noxious or corrupting. 2. to contaminate with disease-producing germs, matter, etc. 3. to communicate a disease or pathogenic organism to (a person).

in·fec·tion (in-fek′shŭn), *n.* 1. the act of infecting or the condition of being infected. 2. that which infects. 3. a disease that results from an infecting agent. 4. an idea, emotion, quality, etc. communicated by persuasion or contact.

in-fec-tious ('shŭs), adj. 1. able to cause infection. 2. denoting a disease communicable by infection. 3. tending to spread easily. —in-fec'tious-ly, adv. —in-fec'tious-ness, n.

in-fe-cund (in-fē'kŭnd, -fek'ŭnd), adj. barren; infertile. —in-fe-cun-di-ty (in-fi-kun'di-ti), n.

in-fe-lic-i-tous (in-fĕ-lis'i-tŭs), adj. unfortunate; unhappy; inappropriate; inopportune. —in-fe-lic'i-tous-ly, adv.

in-fe-lic-i-ty (-ti), n. 1. the quality or condition of being infelicitous. 2. pl. -ties, something that is infelicitous; inappropriate act, expression, etc.

in-fer (in-fûr'), v.t. -ferred', -fer'ring, 1. to conclude or decide from evidence at hand or assumed; deduce. 2. to have as a logical conclusion; indicate. 3. to imply: sometimes not accepted as a standard usage. —in-fer'a-ble, adj.

in-fer-ence (in'fĕr-ĕns), n. 1. the act or process of inferring. 2. something inferred, as a conclusion derived logically.

in-fer-en-tial (in-fĕ-ren'shŭl), adj. derived from or pertaining to inference. —in-fer-en'tial-ly, adv.

in-fe-ri-or (in-fir'i-ẽr), adj. 1. situated lower in space; beneath. 2. low or lower in rank, status, order, etc.; subordinate. 3. lower in quality, merit, value, etc. 4. between the earth and the sun, as Venus. 5. in Biology, situated below another organ or part: n. an inferior person or thing. —in-fe-ri-or'i-ty, n.

in-fer-nal (in-fûr'nl), adj. 1. of or pertaining to the world of the dead in classical myth. 2. of or pertaining to hell. 3. hellish; fiendish; diabolical. 4. [Informal], outrageous. —in-fer'nal-ly, adv.

infernal machine, an earlier name for a booby trap or time bomb.

in-fer-no (in-fûr'nō), n., pl. -nos, 1. same as hell. 2. [I-], the first of the three parts of Dante's Divine Comedy that describes hell as a huge pit of nine circles in each of which the punishment meted out corresponds with the sins committed on earth.

in-fer-tile (in-fûr'tl), adj. 1. not fertile; barren. 2. not fertilized, as an egg. —in-fer-til'i-ty, n.

in-fest (in-fest'), v.t. 1. to dwell in or overrun in great multitudes so as to be noxious, irritating, or troublesome; to spread or swarm over. 2. to be a parasite in or on. —in-fes-ta'tion, n.

in-fi-del (in'fi-dl), n. 1. a person who does not believe in a particular religion, especially Christianity. 2. a person who holds no religious beliefs: adj. 1. manifesting unbelief. 2. of or characteristic of infidels.

in-fi-del-i-ty (in-fi-del'i-ti), n. 1. disbelief in all religion. 2. breach of trust; disloyalty. 3. a disloyal act. 4. same as adultery.

in-field (in'fēld), n. 1. a field near a farmhouse on a farm. 2. the area enclosed by the foul lines and the curve of grass just beyond the bases on a baseball field. 3. the infielders as a group. 4. the area enclosed by a race track or running track.

in-field-er (-ẽr), n. in Baseball, a player whose defensive position is in the infield; first baseman, second baseman, shortstop, or third baseman.

in-fight-ing (in'fīt-ing), n. 1. fighting at close range, especially in boxing. 2. heated rivalry or sharp disagreement between factions or individuals, as within a business or department or between prima donnas.

in-fil-trate (in-fil'trāt, in'fil-trāt), v.i. & v.t. -trat-ed, -trat-ing, 1. to pass, or cause (a liquid or gas) to pass, through small meshes or holes. 2. to pass through, as in filtering. 3. to pass, or cause (troops) to pass, gradually through enemy lines. 4. to enter, or cause to enter, (an area, political party, etc.) little by little or imperceptibly, in order to harass, gain control, etc.

in-fi-nite (in'fi-nit), adj. 1. without limit; immeasurable; endless. 2. extremely great; immense: n. something infinite. —in'fi-nite-ly, adv. —in'fi-nite-ness, n.

in-fin-i-tes-i-mal (in-fin-i-tes'i-măl), adj. immeasurably small; extremely minute: n. 1. an infinitesimal quantity. 2. in Mathematics, a function with values that arbitrarily approach zero.

in-fin-i-tive (in-fin'i-tiv), adj. in Grammar, of, pertaining to, or formed with an infinitive: n. in Grammar, the form of the verb that expresses action or existence, that is not inflected to show number, person, or tense, that can be used as a noun, and that in English is usually identical with the first person singular present preceded by to or by an auxiliary or other verb form.

in-fin-i-tude (-tōōd), n. 1. the state or quality of being infinite. 2. an unlimited number, quantity, or extent.

in-fin-i-ty (-ti), n., pl. -ties, 1. the quality of being infinite. 2. an unlimited extent of time, space, etc. 3. an indefinitely great number or amount.

in-firm (in-fûrm'), adj. 1. feeble in body or health; not strong. 2. irresolute in mind, purpose, or character; vacillating. 3. not structurally sound; unstable. —in-firm'ly, adv.

in-fir-ma-ry (in-fûr'mă-ri), n., pl. -ries, a place for the care and treatment of the sick, injured, or infirm; especially, a room or building serving as a hospital or dispensary.

in-fir-mi-ty ('mi-ti), n. 1. the quality or state of being infirm; debility; frailty. 2. pl. -ties, a physical or moral weakness or defect.

in-fix (in-fiks'), v.t. 1. to fix or fasten securely in, as by piercing. 2. to implant in the mind; instill; inculcate. 3. to insert (an infix) in a word: n. (in'fiks), in Linguistics, an element, equivalent to a prefix or suffix, inserted within a word to change its meaning or function.

in-flame (in-flām'), v.t. & v.i. -flamed', -flam'ing, 1. to set on fire. 2. to enkindle passion in. 3. to raise the intensity of (passion, desire, etc.). 4. to produce inflammation in (some organ or tissue).

in-flam-ma-bil-i-ty (in-flam-ă-bil'i-ti), n. the quality or state of being inflammable.

in-flam-ma-ble (in-flam'ă-bl), adj. 1. same as flammable. 2. easily aroused, excited, angered, etc.: *n*. anything flammable. —**in-flam'ma-bly**, *adv*.

in-flam-ma-tion (in-flă-mā'shŭn), *n*. 1. the act of inflaming or the state of being inflamed. 2. a reaction of the tissues of the body to injury, infection, etc., characterized by local heat, swelling, redness, and pain.

in-flam-ma-to-ry (in-flam'ă-tôr-i), *adj*. 1. tending to excite passion, violence, disorder, etc. 2. producing, accompanied by, or indicative of inflammation.

in-flate (in-flāt'), *v.t*. -**flat'ed**, -**flat'ing**, 1. to swell or distend with air or gas. 2. to puff up; elate. 3. to expand or raise abnormally, as prices, wages, etc.: *v.i*. to become inflated; swell. —**in-flat'a-ble**, *adj*.

in-flat-ed ('id), *adj*. 1. distended as with air; swollen; puffed out. 2. pompous; bombastic. 3. raised or expanded beyond normal levels. 4. characteristic of or resulting from inflation.

in-fla-tion (in-flā'shŭn), *n*. 1. the act of inflating or state of being inflated. 2. an abrupt increase in the supply of money and credit over available goods, resulting in a marked and persistent rise in prices. —**in-fla'tion-ar-y** (-er-i), *adj*.

in-fla-tion-ist (-ist), *n*. one who advocates an increased issue of paper money. —**in-fla'-tion-ism**, *n*.

in-flect (in-flekt'), *v.t*. 1. to bend; turn from a direct line. 2. to alter the tone or pitch of (the voice); modulate. 3. to alter the form of (a word), as by declining or conjugating: *v.i*. to be changed by inflection.

in-flec-tion (in-flek'shŭn), *n*. 1. the act of curving, bending, or turning. 2. a variation in pitch or tone of the voice; modulation. 3. in *Grammar*, a change in the form of a word to distinguish different grammatical relationships, as the declension of nouns and the conjugation of verbs. 4. an inflectional element, as the *s* in *plums* used for the plural form in English.

in-flec-tion-al (-l), *adj*. of, possessing, or exhibiting grammatical inflection, as Latin and Greek.

in-flex-i-ble (in-flek'si-bl), *adj*. 1. that cannot be bent; rigid; stiff. 2. that cannot be moved or changed; unalterable. 3. firm in will or intent; stubborn; obstinate. —**in-flex-i-bil'i-ty**, **in-flex'i-ble-ness**, *n*. —**in-flex'i-bly**, *adv*.

in-flict (in-flikt'), *v.t*. 1. to cause (pain, damage, etc.) by or as if by striking; cause to bear. 2. to impose (a punishment, restriction, etc. *on* or *upon*).

in-flic-tion (in-flik'shŭn), *n*. 1. the act of inflicting. 2. that which is inflicted, as punishment, suffering, etc.

in-flight (in'flīt'), *adj*. done, happening, etc. while an aircraft is in flight.

in-flo-res-cence (in-flô-res'ĕns, -flŏ-), *n*. in *Botany*, 1. a characteristic arrangement of flowers exhibited by a plant species. 2. a flowering; unfolding of blossoms. 3. a group of flowers on a common main axis.

in-flu-ence (in'floo-wĕns), *n*. 1. the power of producing effects indirectly and invisibly on persons, things, or events. 2. the power to sway or control the actions of others by virtue of wealth, station, prestige, etc. 3. an occult power supposed to flow from the stars and planets, believed by astrologers to exercise control over human destiny. 4. one that has influence. 5. electrical induction: *v.t*. -**enced**, -**enc-ing**, 1. to exercise or have physical or moral influence on. 2. to modify the character, actions, thought, etc. of.

in-flu-en-tial (in-floo-wen'shŭl), *adj*. having or exercising influence. —**in-flu-en'tial-ly**, *adv*.

in-flu-en-za (in-floo-wen'ză), *n*. 1. a contagious viral disease, characterized by fever, muscular pain, and inflammation of the respiratory tract. 2. any of various viral diseases of domestic animals, marked by inflammation of the mucous membranes.

in-flux (in'fluks), *n*. 1. an inflow; inpouring. 2. a continual streaming in of persons or things. 3. the point at which a stream flows into another or into the sea.

in-fold (in-fōld'), *v.t*. same as **enfold**.

in-form (in-fôrm'), *v.t*. 1. to impart information to; tell. 2. to give form or essence to. 3. to give or animate with some quality; imbue: *v.i*. 1. to give information. 2. to act as an informer.

in-for-mal (in-fôr'măl), *adj*. 1. not formal. 2. not according to form, custom, or rule. 3. unceremonious; casual. 4. same as **colloquial**. —**in-for'mal-ly**, *adv*.

in-for-mal-i-ty (in-fôr-mal'ĭ-ti), *n*. 1. the state or quality of being informal. 2. *pl*. -**ties**, an informal act.

in-form-ant (in-fôr'mănt), *n*. a person who gives or discloses information.

in-for-ma-tion (in-fĕr-mā'shŭn), *n*. 1. the act of informing or state of being informed. 2. communicated knowledge. 3. knowledge acquired by some means, as study, exploration, etc.; facts; data. 4. knowledge of some special event; news. 5. in *Law*, an accusation of a crime presented by a public officer instead of by indictment by a grand jury.

in-form-a-tive (in-fôr'mă-tiv), *adj*. instructive; imparting knowledge.

in-formed (in-fôrmd'), *adj*. having knowledge; educated.

in-form-er (in-fôr'mĕr), *n*. 1. same as **informant**. 2. a person who gives information about or evidence against others, often to escape punishment or for money.

in-fra-, a prefix meaning *below, beneath*.

in-frac-tion (in-frak'shŭn), *n*. a violation or breach, especially of law; infringement.

in-fra-hu-man (in-fră-hū'măn), *adj*. lower than human in taxonomic classification; especially, anthropoid.

in-fra-lap-sar-i-an (in-fră-lap-ser'i-ăn), *adj*. of or pertaining to infralapsarianism: *n*. a believer in infralapsarianism.

in-fra-lap-sar-i-an-ism (-izm), *n*. the doctrine held by some Calvinists that the divine decrees of election and predestination succeeded the fall of man from grace.

in-fran-gi-ble (in-fran'ji-bl), *adj*. 1. that cannot be broken or separated. 2. that cannot be violated; inviolable.

in-fra-red (in-fră-red'), *adj*. 1. of or pertaining

to the invisible radiation lying beyond the visible radiation of the spectrum at its red end, and having wavelengths greater than those of visible light but shorter than radio waves. 2. generating, employing, or sensitive to this thermal radiation.

in·fra·son·ic (-son'ik), *adj.* denoting or of vibrations having a frequency below that of sounds audible to the human ear.

in·fra·struc·ture (in'frá-struk-chér), *n.* the foundation serving as a base for the installations and developments that maintain an organization, community, etc. and support its expansion, diversification, etc.

in·fre·quent (in-frē'kwĕnt), *adj.* 1. seldom occurring; rare. 2. happening at long or irregular intervals; occasional. —**in·fre'quen·cy**, **in·fre'quence**, *n.* —**in·fre'quent·ly**, *adv.*

in·fringe (in-frinj'), *v.t.* -**fringed'**, -**fring'ing**. 1. to violate or break (a law, obligation, etc.); transgress. 2. to proceed beyond the boundaries of; trespass: used with *on* or *upon*.

in·fringe·ment ('mĕnt), *n.* 1. the act of infringing; violation or breach, as of a law, treaty, etc. 2. an encroachment or trespass, as of a trademark, patent, etc.

in·fu·ri·ate (in-fyoor'i-āt), *v.t.* -**at·ed**, -**at·ing**, to enrage; madden. —**in·fu'ri·at·ing·ly**, *adv.*

in·fuse (in-fūz'), *v.t.* -**fused'**, -**fus'ing**, 1. to introduce (courage, strength, etc.) into, as if by pouring; instill. 2. to imbue; inspire.

in·fu·si·ble (in-fū'zi-bl), *adj.* not capable of being fused or melted. —**in·fu·si·bil'i·ty**, *n.*

in·fu·sion (in-fū'zhŭn), *n.* 1. the act of pouring. 2. something poured in or mingled. 3. a liquid extract obtained by steeping or soaking a substance in water.

in·fu·so·ri·an (in-fyoo-sôr'i-ân, -zôr'-), *n.* 1. formerly, any one of a heterogenous group of very minute animals, and sometimes plants, found in stagnant water or in decomposing infusions of organic matter. 2. formerly, any one of a group of protozoans characterized by the possession of cilia for locomotion.

-ing (ing), a suffix used to form the present participle or verbal nouns.

in·gen·ious (in-jēn'yŭs), *adj.* 1. having ingenuity or inventive skill; clever. 2. conceived or executed in an original or resourceful manner. —**in·gen'ious·ly**, *adv.* —**in·gen'ious·ness**, *n.*

in·gé·nue (an-zhĕ-nōō', -jĕ-), *n.*, *pl.* -**nues'** (-nōōz'), 1. an artless, inexperienced girl or young woman. 2. an actress who plays such a character in the theater.

in·ge·nu·i·ty (in-jĕ-nōō'i-ti, -nū'-), *n.* cleverness in contriving or inventing; skill.

in·gen·u·ous (in-jen'yoo-wŭs), *adj.* 1. frank; candid; sincere. 2. artless; unsophisticated; naive. —**in·gen'u·ous·ly**, *adv.* —**in·gen'u·ous·ness**, *n.*

in·gest (in-jest'), *v.t.* to take (food, liquids, etc.) into the body by or as if by swallowing. —**in·ges'tion**, *n.*

in·glo·ri·ous (in-glôr'i-ŭs), *adj.* disgraceful; ignominious; shameful.

in·got (ing'gŏt), *n.* a cast mass of metal shaped into a bar or other convenient form for storage or transportation.

in·grain (in-grān'), *v.t.* 1. to dye or stain into the fiber of. 2. to establish firmly or

ineradicably in the mind or character of; implant deeply: *adj.* (in'grān), 1. dyed into the fiber prior to being manufactured. 2. made of fibers dyed before use: *n.* (in'grān), an article, as a carpet, made of ingrain fibers.

in·grained (in-grānd', in'grānd), *adj.* 1. solidly established; deep-seated. 2. utter; inveterate.

in·grate (in'grāt), *n.* an ungrateful person; one who does not appreciate kindness or favors.

in·gra·ti·ate (in-grā'shi-āt), *v.t.* -**at·ed**, -**at·ing**, to insinuate (oneself) into the favor of another by purposeful intent. —**in·gra'ti·at·ing**, *adj.* —**in·gra·ti·a'tion**, *n.*

in·grat·i·tude (in-grat'ĭ-tōōd), *n.* absence of gratitude; insensibility to kindness.

in·gre·di·ent (in-grē'di-ĕnt), *n.* 1. a component part, or element, in anything. 2. something that is added to or is a needed part of a mixture.

in·gress (in'gres), *n.* 1. a place of entrance; entrance. 2. permission or freedom to enter. 3. the act of entering.

in·grown (in'grōn), *adj.* 1. grown into; especially, grown into the flesh, as a hair or toenail. 2. innate; inborn.

in·gui·nal (ing'gwi-nl), *adj.* of, pertaining to, or located in the region of the groin.

in·gulf (in-gulf'), *v.t.* same as engulf.

in·gur·gi·tate (in-gûr'ji-tāt), *v.t. & v.i.* -**tat·ed**, -**tat·ing**, to eat or drink voraciously or in excessive amounts; guzzle; swill.

in·hab·it (in-hab'it), *v.t.* to dwell in or occupy (a house, area, etc.); reside in: *v.i.* [Archaic], to dwell; reside.

in·hab·it·a·ble (-á-bl), *adj.* that can be lived in; fit for habitation.

in·hab·it·an·cy (in-hab'i-tán-si), *n.*, *pl.* -**cies**, 1. the act of inhabiting or the state of being inhabited. 2. dwelling place; residence; home.

in·hab·it·ant (-tánt), *n.* one who, or that which, inhabits a particular area, house, etc.; permanent resident.

in·hab·i·ta·tion (in-hab-i-tā'shŭn), *n.* the act of inhabiting or the state of being inhabited.

in·hab·it·ed (in-hab'it-id), *adj.* having inhabitants; occupied; populated.

in·hal·ant (in-hāl'ánt), *n.* something, as a medicine, fumes, etc., that is inhaled.

in·ha·la·tion (in-há-lā'shŭn), *n.* 1. the act of inhaling. 2. same as inhalant.

in·ha·la·tor (in'há-lāt-ēr), *n.* a device that releases a vapor to assist breathing or that dispenses a medicinal inhalant. 2. same as respirator (sense 2).

in·hale (in-hāl'), *v.t.* -**haled'**, -**hal'ing**, to draw (air, fumes, etc.) into the lungs: *v.i.* 1. to breathe in. 2. to draw tobacco smoke into the lungs.

in·hal·er (-ēr), *n.* 1. one who inhales. 2. same as respirator (sense 1). 3. same as inhalator (sense 1).

in·har·mo·ni·ous (in-här-mō'ni-ŭs), *adj.* unmusical; discordant.

in·here (in-hir'), *v.i.* -**hered'**, -**her'ing**, to be inherent or innate; be an essential part of.

in·her·ence (in-hir'ĕns, -her'-), *n.* the quality, state, or fact of inhering or of being inherent.

ŏ in dra*g*on, ōō in cr*u*de, oo in w*oo*l, u in c*u*p, ū in c*u*re, ŭ in t*u*rn, ú in f*o*cus, oi in b*o*y, ou in h*o*use, th in *th*in, *th* in sh*ea*the, g in *g*et, j in *j*oy, y in *y*et.

in·her·ent ('ĕnt), *adj.* existing naturally and inseparably in something or someone as a right, essential quality, or intrinsic characteristic; innate. **—in·her'ent·ly,** *adv.*

in·her·it (in-her'it), *v.t.* 1. to come into possession of. 2. to receive (property, a title, etc.) from an ancestor at his death by right of succession. 3. to receive (something) by bequest. 4. to receive (a character) from ancestors by genetic transmission. 5. to receive as if from an ancestor: *v.i.* to come into possession of property by inheritance; to succeed as an heir. **—in·her'i·tor,** *n.*

in·her·it·a·ble (-ă-bl), *adj.* 1. capable of obtaining by inheritance; having the right to inherit. 2. capable of being inherited, as a character; transmissible.

in·her·it·ance (-ăns), *n.* 1. the act of inheriting. 2. that which is inherited or is to be inherited; legacy. 3. something received as a heritage from a predecessor or from the past. 4. a genetic character transmitted from ancestors to offspring.

in·hib·it (in-hib'it), *v.t.* 1. to restrain; repress. 2. to prohibit; forbid. **—in·hib'i·tive, in·hib'i·to·ry,** *adj.*

in·hi·bi·tion (in-hi-bish'ŭn), *n.* 1. an act of inhibiting or a condition of being inhibited. 2. interference with or restriction of some activity or function. 3. in *Psychology,* a condition in which an activity, mode of expression, etc. is suppressed by physical or mental impediments.

in·hib·i·tor, in·hib·it·er (in-hib'it-ẽr), *n.* 1. a person or thing that inhibits. 2. a substance used to retard or prevent an unwanted chemical reaction, as rust.

in·hos·pi·ta·ble (in-hos'pi-tă-bl), *adj.* 1. unfriendly; not showing hospitality. 2. affording no shelter, support, etc.; barren; cheerless.

in·hu·man (in-hū'măn), *adj.* 1. not human. 2. not exhibiting desirable human qualities; cruel, unfeeling, savage, heartless, etc. **—in·hu'man·ly,** *adv.*

in·hu·man·i·ty (in-hū-man'ĭ-ti), *n.* 1. the quality or condition of being inhuman or pitiless. 2. *pl.* -ties, an inhuman or barbarous act.

in·hume (in-hūm'), *v.t.* -humed', -hum'ing, to bury (a corpse); inter.

in·im·i·cal (in-im'i-kl), *adj.* 1. not friendly; hostile. 2. adverse; harmful.

in·im·i·ta·ble (in-im'i-tă-bl), *adj.* matchless; beyond imitation; unrivaled.

in·i·on (in'i-ŏn), *n.* the occipital protuberance on the external part of the skull.

in·iq·ui·tous (in-ik'wi-tŭs), *adj.* displaying iniquity; wicked; unjust. **—in·iq'ui·tous·ly,** *adv.*

in·iq·ui·ty ('wi-ti), *n.* 1. wickedness; injustice; unrighteousness. 2. *pl.* -ties, an immoral or unjust act; sin.

in·i·tial (i-nish'ăl), *adj.* of, pertaining to, or placed at the beginning; marking the commencement: *n.* 1. a capital, or upper-case, letter placed at the beginning of a printed verse, chapter, paragraph, etc. 2. the first letter of a person's name: *v.t.* -tialed or -tialled, -tial·ing or -tial·ling, to make or

sign with an initial or initials. **—in·i'tial·ly,** *adv.*

in·i·ti·ate (i-nish'i-āt), *v.t.* -at·ed, -at·ing, 1. to instruct in the first principles of anything; introduce. 2. to originate or bring into first use; begin. 3. to induct into membership of a fraternity, club, etc. by secret or ceremonial rites: *n.* (-it), a person who is undergoing or has recently undergone initiation. **—in·i'ti·a·tor,** *n.*

in·i·ti·a·tion (i-nish-i-ā'shŭn), *n.* 1. the act of initiating or the state of being initiated. 2. the rites, ceremonies, etc. observed in admitting a candidate into a lodge, society, or organization, especially a secret society.

in·i·ti·a·tive (i-nish'i-ā-tiv), *adj.* introductory; initial: *n.* 1. an introductory or first step. 2. the power or ability to commence and see a project, task, etc. through without external pressure; enterprise. 3. the power residing in a legislature to introduce new measures. 4. the right or the procedure by which a group of citizens can propose a law and secure its consideration by the electorate or by the legislature.

in·i·ti·a·to·ry (-tôr'i), *adj.* 1. initial; introductory. 2. of or serving in an initiation.

in·ject (in-jekt'), *v.t.* 1. to force or drive into. 2. to introduce (a fluid) into a vein, the skin, a body cavity, etc., as by a syringe. 3. to interpose (a factor, observation, etc.) into a discussion.

in·jec·tion (in-jek'shŭn), *n.* 1. an act or instance of injecting. 2. a fluid injected into the body. 3. a fuel pumped under pressure into a combustion chamber.

in·jec·tor ('tẽr), *n.* one who or that which injects, as an apparatus for forcing water into a steam boiler or fuel into a combustion chamber.

in·ju·di·cious (in-jōō-dish'ŭs), *adj.* not judicious; indiscreet; unwise. **—in·ju·di'cious·ly,** *adv.*

in·junc·tion (in-jungk'shŭn), *n.* 1. an act of enjoining. 2. that which is enjoined; command; directive. 3. a court order restraining or prohibiting a defendant from doing a certain thing or commanding that a certain thing be done. **—in·junc'tive,** *adj.*

in·jure (in'jẽr), *v.t.* -jured, -jur·ing, 1. to damage or harm physically; hurt. 2. to perpetrate an injustice or offense against; wound; wrong.

in·ju·ri·ous (in-joor'i-ŭs), *adj.* 1. harmful or causing hurt; detrimental. 2. abusive; slanderous; defamatory.

in·ju·ry (in'jẽr-i), *n., pl.* -ries, 1. damage or harm done to a person, property, good name, etc. 2. an act that hurts or damages a person's rights, feelings, business, etc.

in·jus·tice (in-jus'tis), *n.* 1. the quality of being unjust. 2. an unjust act; injury; wrong.

ink (ingk), *n.* 1. a colored liquid or a viscous material used for writing, drawing, printing, etc. 2. a black fluid secreted and ejected by cuttlefish, octopuses, etc.: *v.t.* 1. to spread ink upon. 2. to color, blacken, or draw with ink.

ink·ber·ry ('ber-i), *n., pl.* -ries, 1. a small evergreen holly of eastern North America, having glistening, black berries. 2. the fruit of an inkberry.

ink·ling ('ling), n. 1. a slight hint; intimation. 2. a vague idea.

ink·well ('wel), n. a container for ink, usually recessed in a desk top for ready accessibility.

ink·y (ing'ki), adj. **ink'i·er, ink'i·est,** 1. of or consisting of ink. 2. colored, smeared, or marked with ink. —**ink'i·ness,** n.

in·laid (in'lād, in-lād'), adj. decorated by the insertion of wood, ivory, metal, jewels, etc. into a surface.

in·land (in'lānd), adj. 1. of, pertaining to, or situated in the interior part of a country; remote from the sea. 2. [British], not foreign; domestic: adv. into or toward the interior.

in·law (in'lô), n. [Informal], any relative by marriage.

in·lay (in'lā), v.t. **-laid, -lay·ing,** 1. to ornament (a surface) by laying in pieces of ivory, wood, metal, etc. 2. to set (pieces of ivory, wood, etc.) into a surface to form a pattern usually at the same level as the surface: n., pl. **-lays,** 1. a decoration or design made by inlaying. 2. a filling of gold, porcelain, etc. molded to fit a tooth cavity and cemented in place.

in·let (in-let'), v.t. to inlay; insert: n. (in'let, 'lit), 1. a narrow channel or strip of water extending inland from a lake, ocean, etc. 2. a small bay or creek. 3. an entrance or opening.

in·ly (in'li), adv. [Poetic], 1. inwardly. 2. intimately.

in·mate (in'māt), n. one who inhabits a house or institution with others.

in·most (in'mōst), adj. 1. located deepest within. 2. most secret; innermost.

inn (in), n. 1. a public house for the reception and lodging of travelers, offering food and drink; hotel; motel. 2. a tavern or restaurant.

in·nards (in'ērdz), n. [Informal], 1. the inner bodily organs; entrails. 2. the internal parts of anything.

in·nate (i-nāt', in'āt), adj. 1. possessed by or residing at birth; inborn. 2. belonging to as an essential quality; inherent. —**in·nate'ly,** adv. —**in·nate'ness,** n.

in·ner (in'ēr), adj. 1. located deeper inside; internal; interior. 2. of or pertaining to the mind or spirit. 3. less obvious or perceivable; more central or secret.

inner circle, a small, restrictive group of people who direct or influence the actions, beliefs, etc. of others.

inner city, the central sectors of a city, often old, run-down, and heavily populated.

in·ner·most (in'ēr-mōst), adj. same as **inmost.**

in·ner·sole (-sōl), n. same as **insole.**

in·ner·vate (i-nûr'vāt, in'ēr-vāt), v.t. **-vat·ed, -vat·ing,** 1. to supply (a bodily part) with nerves. 2. to stimulate (a nerve, muscle, etc.) to respond. —**in·ner·va'tion,** n.

in·ning (in'ing), n. 1. [Now Rare], the reclamation of land, as from the sea. 2. pl. lands so reclaimed. 3. in Baseball, one of the divisions in a game in which each team bats

until it makes three outs. 4. often pl. any period affording the chance for action, accomplishment, redress, etc.

inn·keep·er (in'kē-pêr), n. the owner or operator of an inn.

in·no·cence (in'ō-sēns), n. 1. freedom from guilt or moral dereliction. 2. freedom from legal guilt for a specific crime or breach of law. 3. freedom from artifice or guile. 4. harmlessness.

in·no·cent (-sēnt), adj. 1. free from guilt, corruption, sin, wrongdoing, evil, etc. 2. free from legal guilt or fault. 3. not sophisticated; guileless; naive. 4. harmless; innocuous. 5. not exposed to or familiar with evil: n. 1. a person who is innocent, as a child. 2. a simple, naive, credulous person. —**in'no·cent·ly,** adv.

in·noc·u·ous (i-nok'yoo-wùs), adj. 1. harmless. 2. inoffensive; uninspiring; vapid. —**in·noc'-u·ous·ly,** adv. —**in·noc'u·ous·ness,** n.

in·no·vate (in'ō-vāt), v.i. **-vat·ed, -vat·ing,** to make alterations or changes in something already established; be creative: v.t. to introduce (new things). —**in·no·va'tive,** adj. —**in·no·va'tor,** n.

in·no·va·tion (in-ō-vā'shûn), n. 1. the act or procedure of innovating. 2. that which is freshly introduced; change; novelty.

in·nu·en·do (in-yoo-wen'dō), n., pl. **-does, -dos,** an oblique or indirect hint; a usually derogatory remark; insinuation.

in·nu·mer·a·ble (i-nōō'mēr-â-bl, -nū'-), adj. that cannot be counted; very numerous.

in·oc·u·late (i-nok'yoo-lāt), v.t. **-lat·ed, -lat·ing,** 1. to introduce a vaccine, attenuated virus, etc. into (an organism) in order to protect against or cure a disease. 2. to communicate (a disease) in this way. 3. to implant (ideas, fears, etc.) in the mind of; imbue; infect.

in·oc·u·la·tion (i-nok·yoo-lā'shûn), n. the act or procedure of inoculating; especially, the introduction of an infectious agent into an animal or plant in order to produce a mild form of the disease and thus stimulate the development of antibodies that will confer immunity to that disease.

in·o·dor·ous (in-ō'dēr-ûs), adj. lacking odor; having no smell.

in·of·fen·sive (in-ō-fen'siv), adj. harmless; not objectionable.

in·op·er·a·tive (in-op'ēr-â-tiv), adj. not in operation; without effect.

in·op·por·tune (in-op-ēr-tōōn'), adj. untimely; not appropriate.

in·or·di·nate (in-ōr'dn-it), adj. 1. immoderate; excessive. 2. disordered.

in·or·gan·ic (in-ōr-gan'ik), adj. 1. designating or composed of matter other than vegetable or animal. 2. of or pertaining to the branch of chemistry which treats of this matter.

in·pa·tient (in'pā-shēnt), n. a patient who is lodged and fed, as well as medically treated, in a hospital.

in·put (in'poot), n. 1. what is put in; specif., a) electric power put into a machine, circuit, etc. b) data or programs into a computer. 2. opinion; advice: v.t. **-put, -put·ting,** to feed (data) into a computer.

in·quest (in'kwest), n. 1. a coroner's inquiry

with a jury into the cause of a death. 2. a judicial inquiry.

in·qui·e·tude (in-kwī'ĕ-tōōd), *n.* an unrelaxed or disturbed condition.

in·quire (in-kwīr'), *v.i.* **-quired', -quir'ing,** 1. to seek knowledge by questions. 2. to make inquiry (usually with *into*): *v.t.* to ask for knowledge concerning.

in·quir·y (in'kwi-ri, in-kwīr'i), *n., pl.* **-quir·ies,** 1. the act of inquiring. 2. an investigation. 3. a question.

in·qui·si·tion (in-kwi-zish'ŭn), *n.* 1. inquiry; examination. 2. a judicial inquiry. 3. [I-], in the *Roman Catholic Church,* formerly, the general tribunal developed in the 13th century for the suppression of heresy. 4. any long and difficult questioning, or cruel crushing of opposition. **—in·quis'i·tor,** *n.*

in·quis·i·tive (in-kwiz'ĭ-tiv), *adj.* 1. given to asking questions. 2. prying; overly curious. **—in·quis'i·tive·ness,** *n.*

in·quis·i·to·ri·al (in-kwiz-ĭ-tôr'i-ăl), *adj.* 1. of or pertaining to an inquisitor or an inquisition. 2. prying.

in·res·i·dence (in-rez'i-dĕns), *adj.* appointed to work and usually residing at an institution, as a college, for a certain period.

in·road (in'rōd), *n.* 1. a hostile incursion. 2. *usually pl.* a harmful intrusion.

in·sa·lu·bri·ous (in-să-lōō'bri-ŭs), *adj.* unhealthful.

in·sane (in-sān'), *adj.* 1. mentally deranged; mad; irrational. 2. of or for people who are insane. 3. very foolish. **—in·sane'ly,** *adv.* **—in·san'i·ty** (-san'ĭ-ti), *n.*

in·sa·ti·a·ble (in-sā'shi-bl), *adj.* that cannot be satisfied or appeased. **—in·sa'ti·a·bly,** *adv.*

in·scribe (in-skrīb'), *v.t.* **-scribed', -scrib'ing,** 1. to write or engrave (designs, etc.) upon (a surface). 2. to enroll or register. 3. to write in (a book). 4. to dedicate to. 5. in *Geometry,* to draw (one figure within another).

in·scrip·tion (in-skrip'shŭn), *n.* 1. the act of inscribing. 2. that which is inscribed. 3. a dedication, as in a book.

in·scru·ta·ble (in-skrōōt'á-bl), *adj.* not to be penetrated by inquiry or reason; incomprehensible. **—in·scru·ta·bil'i·ty,** *n.* **—in·scru'ta·bly,** *adv.*

in·seam (in'sēm), *n.* an inner seam; specif., the seam from the crotch to the bottom of a trouser leg.

in·sect (in'sekt), *n.* 1. one of a numerous group of small arthropods having three pairs of legs, two pairs of wings, and a head, thorax, and abdomen. 2. a minute animal. 3. one who is contemptible.

in·sec·ti·cide (in-sek'tĭ-sīd), *n.* a compound for destroying insects. **—in·sec·ti·cid'al,** *adj.*

in·sec·ti·fuge (-fūj), *n.* any substance for killing or driving away insects.

in·sec·tile (in-sek'tl), *adj.* 1. composed of insects. 2. like or of the nature of an insect.

in·sec·ti·vore (in-sek'ti-vôr), *n.* any of a group of nocturnal, insectivorous mammals, which includes hedgehogs and moles.

in·sec·tiv·o·rous (in-sek-tiv'ĕr-ŭs), *adj.* feeding mostly on insects.

in·se·cure (in-si-kyoor'), *adj.* 1. unsafe; liable

to danger or injury. 2. uncertain; apprehensive. 3. unreliable. **—in·se·cure'ly,** *adv.* **—in·se·cu'ri·ty,** *n.*

in·sem·i·nate (in-sem'i-nāt), *v.t.* **-nat·ed, -nat·ing,** 1. to sow; impregnate. 2. to implant. **—in·sem·i·na'tion,** *n.*

in·sen·sate (in-sen'sāt, 'sit), *adj.* 1. destitute of sensation or mental perception. 2. insensitive to others.

in·sen·si·ble (in-sen'sĭ-bl), *adj.* 1. that cannot feel or perceive mentally or physically. 2. apathetic. 3. so small as not to be perceived. **—in·sen·si·bil'i·ty,** *n.*

in·sen·si·tive ('si·tiv), *adj.* without feeling; unimpressionable. **—in·sen·si·tiv'i·ty,** *n.*

in·sen·ti·ent (in-sen'shi-ĕnt), *adj.* not living; unconscious. **—in·sen'ti·ence,** *n.*

in·sep·a·ra·ble (in-sep'ĕr-á-bl), *adj.* incapable of being separated: *n.pl.* those that are inseparable.

in·sert (in-sûrt'), *v.t.* to place in or among; introduce into: *n.* (in'sĕrt), that which is inserted, as a supplement placed in a newspaper.

in·ser·tion (in-sûr'shŭn), *n.* 1. the act of inserting. 2. that which is inserted, as lace or embroidery in a garment.

in·set (in'set), *n.* 1. a piece of cloth let into a garment. 2. a smaller picture set on the ground of a larger one. 3. an insert: *v.t.* (in-set'), **-set', -set'ting,** to set in.

in·shore (in'shōr), *adv. & adj.* near or towards the shore.

in·side (in'sīd', 'sīd), *adj.* 1. interior; being within. 2. secret: *n.* 1. that which is within; inner part. 2. *pl.* [Informal], the entrails: *adv.* (in-sīd'), 1. within. 2. in or onto a building: *prep.* (in-sīd'), within.

in·sid·er (in-sī'dĕr), *n.* 1. one in an organization, location, etc. 2. one having or in a position to obtain firsthand information.

in·sid·i·ous (in-sid'i-ŭs), *adj.* 1. treacherous; deceitful. 2. not obviously dangerous.

in·sight (in'sīt), *n.* 1. penetration; intuition; discernment. 2. an example of insight.

in·sig·ni·a (in-sig'ni·á), *n.pl., sing.* **-sig'ni·a, -sig'ne** ('ni), badges of office; distinguishing marks or characteristics.

in·sig·nif·i·cant (in-sig-nif'ĭ-kănt), *adj.* 1. without importance, force, influence, or meaning; trivial. 2. contemptible. **—in·sig·nif'i·cance,** *n.*

in·sin·cere (in-sin-sir'), *adj.* hypocritical; untrustworthy; deceitful. **—in·sin·cer'i·ty** (-ser'i-ti), *n.*

in·sin·u·ate (in-sin'yoo-wāt), *v.t.* **-at·ed, -at·ing,** 1. to ingratiate, as into the confidence or affections of. 2. to suggest or hint indirectly: *v.i.* to work oneself into the confidence or affection of another.

in·sin·u·a·tion (in-sin-yoo-wā'shŭn), *n.* 1. the act of insinuating. 2. a sly hint.

in·sip·id (in-sip'id), *adj.* 1. without flavor; tasteless. 2. without interest; boring. **—in·si·pid'i·ty,** *n., pl.* **-ties.**

in·sist (in-sist'), *v.i.* to urge or press a wish, command, etc.; be persistent or peremptory: *v.t.* 1. to ask for forcefully. 2. to persist in saying (something).

in·sist·ent (in-sis'tĕnt), *adj.* 1. conspicuous. 2.

forcing forward; demanding; insisting. —in-sist'ence, n.

in-snare (in-sner'), v.t. -snared', -snar'ing, same as ensnare.

in-so-bri-e-ty (in-sŏ-brī'ĕ-ti), n. drunkenness.

in-so-far (in-sŏ-fär'), adv. to such a limit (usually with as).

in-so-late (in'sŏ-lāt), v.t. -lat-ed, -lat-ing, to expose to the rays of the sun in order to whiten, dry, etc.

in-sole (in'sōl), n. 1. the inner sole of a shoe. 2. a strip placed inside a shoe, as to improve the fit.

in-so-lent (in'sŏ-lĕnt), adj. insulting; grossly rude. —in'so-lence, n.

in-sol-u-ble (in-sol'yoo-bl), adj. 1. that cannot be dissolved; not soluble. 2. inexplicable. —in-sol-u-bil'i-ty, n.

in-solv-a-ble (in-sol'vă-bl), adj. not admitting of solution or explanation.

in-sol-ven-cy (in-sol'věn-si), n., pl. -cies, the state of being insolvent; bankruptcy.

in-sol-vent ('věnt), adj. 1. unable to pay all debts; bankrupt. 2. inadequate to satisfy claims, as an estate: n. one who cannot pay all his debts; bankrupt.

in-som-ni-a (in-som'ni-ä), n. abnormal sleeplessness. —in-som'ni-ac (-ak), n.

in-so-much (in-sŏ-much'), adv. 1. to such a limit (with that). 2. because (with as).

in-sou-ci-ant (in-sŏŏ'si-änt), adj. indifferent; without care or concern. —in-sou'ci-ance (-äns), n.

in-spect (in-spekt'), v.t. 1. to examine critically. 2. to review officially. —in-spec'tion, n.

in-spec-tor (-spek'tĕr), n. 1. one who inspects or oversees. 2. a police officer ranking next below a superintendent.

in-spi-ra-tion (in-spi-rā'shun), n. 1. the act of drawing air into the lungs. 2. a creative influence. 3. an influence on one's feelings. 4. in Theology, the influence of God on persons. —in-spir-a-to-ry (in-spīr'ă-tôr-i), adj.

in-spire (in-spīr'), v.t. -spired', -spir'ing, 1. to draw (air) into the lungs. 2. to imbue with ideas; infuse into the mind. 3. to convey, as by divine influence. 4. to excite by an emotion or idea. 5. to produce: v.i. 1. to inhale air. 2. to impart inspiration. —in-spir'er, n.

in-spir-it (in-spir'it), v.t. to infuse spirit into; animate; exhilarate; cheer.

in-spis-sate (in-spis'āt), v.t. to thicken by boiling or evaporation.

in-sta-bil-i-ty (in-stă-bil'i-ti), n. lack of stability or firmness.

in-sta-ble (in-stā'bl), adj. same as unstable.

in-stall, -stal (in-stôl'), v.t. -stalled', -stall'ing, 1. to place in an office or rank, with ceremony. 2. to set or settle in a location. 3. to fasten, attach, or put in.

in-stal-la-tion (in-stă-lā'shun), n. 1. the act of installing; induction into office, etc. 2. a system of machinery ready for operation.

in-stall-ment, -stal-ment (in-stôl'měnt), n. 1. the act of installing. 2. payment of part of a sum of money due. 3. one of a number of parts of anything produced.

installment plan, a system of selling and buy-

ing whereby what is sold is to be paid for in stated sums at regular intervals.

in-stance (in'stăns), v.t. -stanced, -stanc-ing, to refer to, or offer as an example: n. 1. something offered as an illustration or example. 2. an occurrence.

in-stant (in'stănt), adj. 1. urgent. 2. immediate. 3. of the present month. 4. without delay. 5. denoting a food which can be cooked and served quickly because of previous treatment: n. 1. a particular moment of time. 2. a point of duration.

in-stan-ta-ne-ous (in-stăn-tā'ni-ŭs), adj. 1. acting or occurring in a moment. 2. at a particular moment. —in-stan-ta'ne-ous-ly, adv.

in-stan-ter (in-stan'tĕr), adv. immediately.

in-stant-ly (in'stănt-li), adv. at once; without delay.

in-state (in-stāt'), v.t. -stat'ed, -stat'ing, to put in a specific office or rank; install.

in-stau-ra-tion (in-stô-rā'shŭn), n. renewal; renovation; repair.

in-stead (in-sted'), adv. in place of the stated person or thing.

in-step (in'step), n. 1. the arched upper side of the human foot. 2. the part of a shoe, or stocking, that covers this part of the foot. 3. that part of a horse's hind leg from the hock to the pastern joint.

in-sti-gate (in'sti-gāt), v.t. -gat-ed, -gat-ing, 1. to urge, incite, etc. to some evil deed. 2. to provoke by instigating. —in-sti-ga'tion, n. —in'sti-ga-tor, n.

in-still, in-stil (in-stil'), v.t. -stilled, -still'ing, 1. to insinuate gradually (with in or into). 2. to pour in by drops.

in-stinct (in-stingkt'), adj. stimulated from within; animated (with with): n. (in'stingkt), 1. a natural response. 2. an aptitude or bent that is natural or learned. 3. in Psychoanalysis, the inward, unconscious prompting that incites man and other animals to those actions which are necessary for their guidance, preservation, and development.

in-stinc-tive (in-stingk'tiv), adj. prompted or done by instinct; spontaneous.

in-sti-tute (in'sti-tōŏt), v.t. -tut-ed, -tut-ing, 1. to establish; set up; fix. 2. to originate; set in operation. 3. to invest with a spiritual office: n. 1. an established law. 2. a society for encouraging literature, science, etc. 3. pl. a summary of fundamental laws. 4. a center of learning for some subject. —in'sti-tut-er, in'sti-tu-tor, n.

in-sti-tu-tion (in-sti-tōŏ'shŭn), n. 1. the act of instituting. 2. that which is instituted or established. 3. a corporate body or society for promoting a particular object. 4. the building where such a society meets. 5. the investment of a clergyman in his office. 6. establishment of a sacrament. 7. [Informal], a long-established or well-known firm or organization. —in-sti-tu'tion-al, adj.

in-sti-tu-tion-al-ism ('shŭn-l-izm), n. the upholding of the authority or sanctity of the established forms and institutions.

in-sti-tu-tion-al-ize (-īz), v.t. -ized, -iz-ing, 1. to form into or make like an institution. 2. to put into an institution for care, custody, etc.

in-struct (in-strukt'), v.t. 1. to teach; educate.

2. to furnish with orders or directions. 3. to give explanation or guidance.

in·struc·tion (-struk'shŭn), *n.* 1. the act of instructing; education. 2. knowledge acquired by education. 3. a precept, rule, etc. 4. *pl.* orders as to duty or procedure; directions. 5. a command; order, etc. —**in·struc'tion·al,** *adj.*

in·struc·tive ('tiv), *adj.* tending to instruct; conveying instruction.

in·struc·tor ('tẽr), *n.* 1. one who instructs; teacher. 2. a college teacher of a rank inferior to that of assistant professor.

in·stru·ment (in'strŭ-mĕnt), *n.* 1. that by which anything is effected; agent. 2. a tool or implement. 3. a contrivance for producing musical sounds. 4. a means of estimating, controlling, etc. 5. in *Law,* a writing containing the terms of a contract, deed, etc.

in·stru·men·tal (in-strŭ-men'tl), *adj.* 1. of, pertaining to, or done by an instrument. 2. conducive to some end; helpful (with *in*).

in·stru·men·tal·ist (-ist), *n.* one who plays a musical instrument.

in·stru·men·tal·i·ty (-men·tal'l-ti), *n., pl.* -ties, an agency; means.

in·stru·men·ta·tion (-tā'shŭn), *n.* 1. the arrangement of music for a combination of instruments, as for an orchestra. 2. the providing or use of scientific instruments.

in·sub·or·di·nate (in-sŭ-bôr'dn-it), *adj.* not submitting to authority; mutinous. —**in·sub·or·di·na'tion,** *n.*

in·sub·stan·tial (in-sŭb-stan'shŭl), *adj.* 1. not genuine; fanciful. 2. unsteady; fragile. 3. not substantial.

in·suf·fer·a·ble (in-suf'fer·ā·bl), *adj.* intolerable; unendurable. —**in·suf'fer·a·bly,** *adv.*

in·suf·flate (in-suf'lāt), *v.t.* -flat·ed, -flat·ing, 1. to blow into or upon. 2. to breathe upon (a person at baptism) symbolizing exorcism. 3. in *Medicine,* to blow (a substance) into a body cavity. —**in·suf·fla'tion,** *n.*

in·su·lar (in'sŭ-lẽr), *adj.* 1. of, pertaining to, or like an island; isolated. 2. of, pertaining to, or like the inhabitants of an island, as when thought of as bigoted or intolerant. —**in·su·lar·i·ty** (in-sŭ-ler'ĭ-ti), *n.*

in·su·late (in'sŭ-lāt), *v.t.* -lat·ed, -lat·ing, 1. to place alone or in a detached situation. 2. to separate by a nonconductor from other conducting bodies.

in·su·la·tion (in-sŭ-lā'shŭn), *n.* 1. the act of insulating. 2. the state of being insulated. 3. material used in insulating.

in·su·la·tor (in'sŭ-lāt-ẽr), *n.* 1. that which insulates. 2. a nonconductor of electricity, heat, or sound.

in·su·lin (in'sŭ-lin), *n.* 1. a hormone secreted by the pancreas, which facilitates the assimilation of carbohydrates. 2. a diabetic remedy prepared from the pancreas of sheep, oxen, etc.

in·sult (in'sult), *n.* an affront or indignity; gross abuse in word or in action: *v.t.* (in-sult'), to treat with gross indignity, contempt, or abuse, by word or act.

in·su·per·a·ble (in-sōō'pēr-ā-bl), *adj.* not to be overcome; invincible.

in·sup·port·a·ble (in-sŭ-pôrt'ā-bl), *adj.* unendurable; intolerable; undemonstrable.

in·sup·press·i·ble (in-sŭ-pres'ĭ-bl), *adj.* denoting what cannot be suppressed.

in·sur·ance (in-shoor'ăns), *n.* 1. the act or system of insuring against loss or damage. 2. a contract entered into to secure against loss, damage, etc. by the payment of a specified sum: also **insurance** policy. 3. the amount insured. 4. the occupation of insuring against loss or damage.

in·sure (in-shoor'), *v.t.* -sured', -sur·ing, 1. to contract to pay or be paid under certain conditions, as loss by fire. 2. same as ensure. —**in·sur'a·ble,** *adj.*

in·sur·gent (in-sŭr'jĕnt), *adj.* rising against constituted authority: *n.* a rebel. —**in·sur'gence,** *n.*

in·sur·mount·a·ble (in-sŭr-moun'tā-bl), *adj.* incapable of being passed over; insuperable.

in·sur·rec·tion (in-sŭ-rek'shŭn), *n.* active or open hostility to constituted authority; rebellion. —**in·sur·rec'tion·ar·y,** *adj. & n., pl.* -ar·ies. —**in·sur·rec'tion·ist,** *n.*

in·tact (in-takt'), *adj.* entire; uninjured.

in·tagl·io (in-tal'yō), *n., pl.* -ios, 1. a gem or stone having a design cut in the surface. 2. an incised carving.

in·take (in'tāk), *n.* 1. that which is taken in. 2. the point in a channel where a liquid or gas enters. 3. the act of taking in.

in·tan·gi·ble (in-tan'ji-bl), *adj.* 1. incapable of being touched or perceived by touch. 2. imperceptible. 3. that which has a value not dependent on its physical makeup or inherent worth. —**in·tan'gi·bly,** *adv.*

in·te·ger (in'tĕ-jẽr), *n.* 1. the whole. 2. a whole number, as opposed to a fraction.

in·te·gral (in'tĕ-grăl), *adj.* 1. constituting a whole. 2. complete. 3. necessary to constitute an entire thing. 4. in *Mathematics,* of or pertaining to an integer: *n.* the whole made up of parts.

in·te·grant (-grănt), *adj.* same as integral.

in·te·grate (in'tĕ-grāt), *v.t.* -grat·ed, -grat·ing, 1. to bring together the parts of. 2. to give the sum total of. 3. to consolidate (parts). 4. to do away with societal or legal restrictions on (members of a racial group). 5. to eliminate segregation in: *v.i.* to become integrated. —**in·te·gra'tion,** *n.*

integrated circuit, an electronic circuit contained on a semiconductor substance, having several circuit elements that are connected to each other.

in·teg·ri·ty (in-teg'rĭ-ti), *n.* 1. the state of being complete or whole. 2. uprightness; virtue; honesty; soundness. 3. an unimpaired or unbroken state of anything.

in·teg·u·ment (in-teg'yoo-mĕnt), *n.* an external covering or skin.

in·tel·lect (in'tl-ekt), *n.* 1. the mind or understanding; reasoning. 2. high mental capability. 3. one who has great mental faculties.

in·tel·lec·tu·al (in-tl-ek'choo-wăl), *adj.* 1. of, pertaining to, or apprehended by the intellect. 2. demanding mental capability. 3. exhibiting mental capability: *n.* a person with an intellectual bent. —in·tel·lec·tu·al'i·ty (-ek-choo-wal'i-ti), n. —in·tel·lec'tu·al·ly, adv.

in·tel·lec·tu·al·ism (-izm), n. 1. an intellectual power or quality. 2. in *Philosophy*, the doctrine that all knowledge is derived from pure reason.

in·tel·lec·tu·al·ize (-īz), v.t. -ized, -iz·ing, to study or explain using reason, without taking feeling into proper account.

in·tel·li·gence (in-tel'i-jēns), n. 1. intellectual capacity; understanding; mind. 2. the power to comprehend and act speedily. 3. notification; news. 4. the department of a government, etc. charged with obtaining secret information, as in regard to foreign affairs.

intelligence quotient, a number derived by a test, that reflects a person's mental capacity.

in·tel·li·gent (-jēnt), adj. 1. endowed with intelligence or understanding. 2. exhibiting knowledge; clever; discerning. —in·tel'li·gent·ly, adv.

in·tel·li·gi·ble (in-tel'i-ji-bl), adj. capable of being understood; clear. —in·tel'li·gi·bly, adv.

in·tem·per·ance (in-tem'pēr-ăns), n. 1. want of moderation or self-restraint. 2. excess in the use of alcoholic liquor.

in·tem·per·ate (-it), adj. 1. characterized by want of moderation or self-restraint; excessive. 2. using too much alcoholic liquor.

in·tend (in-tend'), v.t. 1. to purpose. 2. to destine (with *for*). 3. to mean; indicate.

in·tend·ant (in-ten'dănt), n. a superintendent.

in·tend·ed (in-ten'did), n. [Informal], the person that one intends to marry.

in·tense (in-tens'), adj. 1. increased to a strong level; vehement. 2. strained; forced; ardent. 3. showing strong feelings or being very active. —in·tense'ly, adv.

in·ten·si·fy (in-ten'si-fī), v.t. -fied, -fy·ing, 1. to render more intense. 2. to increase the density of (a photographic film) so as to bring out the image more clearly by a contrast of light and shade, by treating with a solution: v.i. to increase in intensity. —in·ten·si·fi·ca'tion, n.

in·ten·sion (in-ten'shŭn), n. intentness; determination; strong exercise of the will.

in·ten·si·ty (in-ten'si-ti), n., pl. -ties, 1. the state or quality of being intense. 2. extreme energy or passion. 3. the quantity of force or energy of any physical agent, as heat, light, or sound.

in·ten·sive ('siv), adj. 1. serving to intensify. 2. designating a system of land cultivation, the object of which is to cause a given area to produce the utmost yield of crops. 3. denoting special care extended to hospital patients in a critical condition. 4. in *Grammar*, giving force or emphasis. —in·ten'sive·ly, adv.

in·tent (in-tent'), adj. 1. having the mind trained or closely fixed on a subject. 2. anxiously diligent. 3. constantly or assiduously directed (with *on*): n. 1. purpose; aim. 2. significance; import. 3. in *Law*, the state of mind in which one commits an act, and the character imputed to that state of mind. —in·tent'ly, adv.

in·ten·tion (in-ten'shŭn), n. 1. the act of intending. 2. fixed design; end or aim.

in·ten·tion·al ('shŭn-l), adj. of, pertaining to, or done by intention; designed; intended.

in·ter (in-tūr'), v.t. -terred', -ter'ring, to bury (a corpse).

in·ter-, a combining form meaning *among, between, amid, mutually*, as *intercultural, interact*, etc.: many words using *inter-* in combination may be understood if "between," "amid," etc. are used before the base word.

in·ter·breed (in-tēr-brēd'), v.t. & v.i. -bred', -breed'ing, same as **hybridize**.

in·ter·ca·lar·y (in-tūr'kă-ler-i), adj. inserted in the calendar, as February 29 in leap year.

in·ter·ca·late (-lāt), v.t. -lat·ed, -lat·ing, to insert (a day in a leap year, etc.) in a calendar.

in·ter·cede (in-tēr-sēd'), v.i. -ced'ed, -ced'ing, 1. to mediate as a friend between persons at variance; interpose. 2. to plead for another.

in·ter·cept (in-tēr-sept'), v.t. 1. to stop and seize in the way. 2. in *Mathematics*, to cut off or include between two points, lines, etc. —in·ter·cep'tion, n.

in·ter·ces·sion (in-tēr-sesh'ŭn), n. the act of interceding; mediation; prayer for other persons. —in·ter·ces'sor (-ses'ēr), n. —in·ter·ces'so·ry, adj.

in·ter·change (in-tēr-chānj'), v.t. -changed', -chang'ing, 1. to give and receive (equivalent things). 2. to transpose. 3. to make succeed in turns: n. (in'tēr-chānj), 1. the act of or interchanging. 2. an entrance or exit on a freeway. —in·ter·change'a·ble, adj.

in·ter·col·le·gi·ate (-kŏ-lē'jăt), adj. between or among colleges or universities, as *intercollegiate* contests, football, etc.

in·ter·com (in'tēr-kom), n. a means of communication using radio or telephone, as between parts of a building.

in·ter·com·mu·ni·cate (in-tēr-kŏ-mū'ni-kāt), v.t. & v.i. -cat·ed, -cat·ing, to communicate with or to. —in·ter·com·mu·ni·ca'tion, n.

in·ter·con·nect (-kŏ-nekt'), v.t. & v.i. to connect with mutually. —in·ter·con·nec'tion, n.

in·ter·con·ti·nen·tal (-kon-ti-nen'tl), adj. 1. between or amid continents. 2. having the capability of passing from one continent to another.

in·ter·cos·tal (-kos'tl), adj. being or occurring between the ribs: n. a rib muscle, etc.

in·ter·course (in'tēr-kōrs), n. 1. connection, correspondence, or communication between individuals, nations, etc.; mutual exchange. 2. sexual connection; coitus: also **sexual intercourse**.

in·ter·crop (in-tēr-krop'), v.t. & v.i. -cropped', -crop'ping, to raise (a crop) between rows of another: n. (in'tēr-krop), a crop raised between the rows of another.

in·ter·de·pend·ence (-di-pen'dēns), n. joint dependence on one another. —in·ter·de·pend'ent, adj.

in·ter·dict (in-tēr-dikt'), v.t. 1. to restrain or forbid. 2. to cut off from certain spiritual services of the Roman Catholic Church: n. (in'tēr-dikt), a restraint by authority. —in·ter·dic'tion, n.

in·ter·est (in'trist, in'tēr-ist), v.t. 1. to engage

ŏ in dragon, ōō in crude, oo in wool, u in cup, ū in cure, û in turn, û in focus, oi in boy, ou in house, th in thin, th in sheathe, g in get, j in joy, y in yet.

the attention of; awaken concern in. 2. to cause to take a share in: *n.* 1. *pl.* advantage; benefit. 2. personal concern. 3. the source of personal concern. 4. the ability to cause personal concern. 5. influence. 6. the premium paid for the use of money. 7. the rate of this premium. 8. *usually pl.* those sharing the same authority or involvement in something. 9. a claim. 10. something to which one has a claim in part.

in-ter-est-ed (-id), *adj.* 1. concerned or sharing in. 2. having prejudice. 3. exhibiting interest.

in-ter-est-ing (-ing), *adj.* engaging the attention; inviting curiosity.

in-ter-face (in'tẽr-fās), *n.* 1. a plane forming the common boundary between two parts of matter or space. 2. a point or means of interaction between two systems, disciplines, groups, etc: *v.t. & v.i.* -faced, -fac'ing, to interact with (another system, discipline, group, etc.).

in-ter-fere (in-tẽr-fir'), *v.i.* -fered', -fer'ing, 1. to interpose or meddle in the affairs of others; oppose. 2. to come into collision. 3. to strike one foot with the other: used of a horse. 4. in *Sports*, to improperly obstruct a player of the opposing side. —**in-ter-fer'ence,** *n.*

in-ter-fer-on (in-tẽr-fir'on), *n.* a cellular protein produced in response to infection by a virus and acting to inhibit viral growth.

in-ter-im (in'tẽr-im), *n.* the intervening time or period: *adj.* for the meantime.

in-te-ri-or (in-tir'i-ẽr), *adj.* 1. not exterior; internal; inner. 2. remote from the coast or frontier. 3. secret: *n.* 1. the inside. 2. the inland. 3. the domestic department of a government.

interior decoration, the act, art, or business of decorating and furnishing the interiors of houses, rooms, offices, or other structural spaces. —**interior decorator.**

in-te-ri-or-ize (-īz), *v.t.* -ized, -iz-ing, to include in one's character.

in-ter-ject (in-tẽr-jekt'), *v.t.* to throw between; interpose.

in-ter-jec-tion (-jek'shũn), *n.* 1. the act of interjecting. 2. a word or phrase thrown in. 3. in *Grammar,* an exclamation.

in-ter-lace (-lās'), *v.t. & v.i.* -laced', -lac'ing, to connect by lacing or weaving.

in-ter-lard (-lärd'), *v.t.* to insert or inject (matter in a discourse).

in-ter-leu-kin (in-tẽr-lōō'kin), *n.* any of several proteins derived from many cell types and having an effect on the activity of other cells: used experimentally in cancer therapy.

in-ter-line (in-tẽr-līn'), *v.t.* -lined', -lin'ing, to write or print between the lines of. —**in-ter-lin'e-ar** (-lin'i-ẽr), *adj.*

in-ter-line (in'tẽr-līn), *v.t.* -lined, -lin-ing, to have the main lining of supplemented by another lining inside.

in-ter-lock (in-tẽr-lok'), *v.t. & v.i.* to unite (with); interlace; connect so that one part bears a relation to another.

in-ter-loc-u-tor (-lok'yũ-tẽr), *n.* 1. a participant in a conversation. 2. (also often -lok'ū-tẽr), the person in a minstrel show who elicits funny replies from the end men.

in-ter-loc-u-to-ry (-lok'yũ-tôr-i), *adj.* 1. conversational. 2. in *Law,* not final.

in-ter-lop-er (in'tẽr-lō-pẽr), *n.* one who intrudes in the affairs of others.

in-ter-lude (in'tẽr-lōōd), *n.* 1. a short entertainment given between acts of a play, etc. 2. a short instrumental passage played between the stanzas of a hymn, etc. 3. that which takes place between two points in time.

in-ter-mar-ry (in-tẽr-mer'i), *v.i.* -ried, -ry-ing, 1. to contract matrimony: used in reference to those who are closely related. 2. to become related by marriage: used in reference to those of different races, religions, etc. —**in-ter-mar'riage** ('ij), *n.*

in-ter-me-di-ar-y (-mē'di-ẽr-i), *adj.* 1. intervening. 2. going between two persons: *n., pl.* -ar-ies, 1. a go-between. 2. an agent; medium.

in-ter-me-di-ate (-mē'di-it), *adj.* existing or lying in the middle; intervening: *v.i.* (-āt), -at-ed, -at-ing, to act as an intermediary: *n.* a mediator.

in-ter-ment (in-tũr'mẽnt), *n.* burial.

in-ter-mez-zo (in-tẽr-met'sō), *n., pl.* -zos, -zi ('si), 1. a chorus or short entertainment given between the acts of a play, etc. 2. any short piece of music to be played during the intervals of a longer composition.

in-ter-mi-na-ble (in-tũr'mi-nã-bl), *adj.* having no limit; continuing for a very long time.

in-ter-min-gle (in-tẽr-ming'gl), *v.t. & v.i.* -gled, -gling, to mix together or among.

in-ter-mis-sion (-mish'ũn), *n.* 1. an interruption. 2. a pause; recess, as between the acts of a play.

in-ter-mit (-mit'), *v.t. & v.i.* -mit'ted, -mit'ting, to cease for a time; interrupt; suspend.

in-ter-mit-tent (-mit'nt), *adj.* recurrent; coming and going at intervals.

in-tern (in-tũrn'), *v.t.* to place under arrest or confine within a town, the interior of a country, etc.: *v.i.* (in'tẽrn), to work as an intern: *n.* (in'tẽrn), 1. a resident, graduate physician who assists in a hospital to gain experience. 2. a person learning a profession by assisting one who is experienced.

in-ter-nal (in-tũr'nl), *adj.* 1. of or pertaining to the center; interior; inward. 2. not foreign; domestic. 3. intended for use within the body. 4. essential; inherent. —**in-ter'nal-ly,** *adv.*

in-ter-nal-com-bus-tion engine (-kŏm-bus'chũn), an engine that produces heat and energy when there is an explosion of oxygen combined with a flammable substance in its cylinders.

in-ter-nal-ize (in-tũr'nl-īz), *v.t.* -ized, -iz-ing, to take on (concepts, opinions, etc.) as one's own.

internal medicine, the branch of medicine that deals with the diagnosis and nonsurgical treatment of diseases.

internal revenue, the income of the government derived from taxes.

in-ter-na-tion-al (in-tẽr-nash'ũn-l), *adj.* 1. of or pertaining to two or more nations in common. 2. of or regarding the affairs between nations. 3. of or in the interests of all nations or their people. —in·ter·na'tion·al·ly, adv.

in·ter·na·tion·al·ize (-īz), v.t. -ized, -iz·ing, to bring under international control.

in·terne (in'têrn), n. same as intern.

in·ter·ne·cine (in-têr-nē'sin), adj. mutually destructive or deadly. —in·ter·po·la'tion, n.

in·tern·ee (in-têr-nē'), n. one who is interned as a prisoner of war or enemy alien.

in·ter·nist (in'têr-nist, in-tûr'nist), n. a physician who deals with the treatment of disease without using surgery.

in·ter·of·fice (in-têr-ôf'is), adj. between the offices within a business or organization.

in·ter·per·son·al (-pûr'sô-nl), adj. between persons.

in·ter·plan·e·tar·y (in-têr-plan'ê-ter-i), adj. between planets.

in·ter·play (in'têr-plā), n. reciprocal influence.

in·ter·po·late (in-tûr'pô-lāt), v.t. -lat·ed, -lat·ing, 1. to insert in (a book or writing) new matter; corrupt by insertions. 2. to place between or amid. —in·ter·po·la'tion, n.

in·ter·pose (in-têr-pōz'), v.t. -posed', -pos'ing, 1. to place between; thrust in. 2. to interfere with. 3. to interrupt with: v.i. 1. to intercede. 2. to come between. 3. to interrupt. —in·ter·po·si'tion (-pô-zish'ûn), n.

in·ter·pret (in-tûr'prit), v.t. 1. to explain the meaning of; expound. 2. to construe. 3. to show one's impression of: v.i. to be an interpreter; translate. —in·ter·pre·ta'tion, n.

in·ter·pret·er (-prê'têr), n. 1. one who interprets. 2. one whose occupation is translating foreign speech or writing.

in·ter·ra·cial (in-têr-rā'shûl), adj. between, among, or for persons belonging to different races: also in·ter·race'.

in·ter·reg·num (-reg'nûm), n., pl. -reg'nums, -reg'na (-nà), 1. the period between two reigns, governments, or ministries. 2. a time of abeyance.

in·ter·re·late (-ri-lāt'), v.t. & v.i. -lat'ed, -lat'ing, to make or be related jointly.

in·ter·ro·gate (in-ter'ô-gāt), v.t. & v.i. -gat·ed, -gat·ing, to ask questions (of) in an orderly fashion. —in·ter'ro·ga·tor, n.

in·ter·ro·ga·tion (in-ter-ô-gā'shûn), n. 1. the act of interrogating. 2. a question; inquiry. 3. a mark (?) denoting a question.

in·ter·rog·a·tive (in-tê-rog'à-tiv), adj. denoting or containing a question or inquiry: n. a word, construction, etc. used in asking a question. —in·ter·rog'a·tive·ly, adv.

in·ter·rog·a·to·ry (in-tê-rog'à-tôr-i), adj. of, pertaining to, or expressing, a question: n., pl. -ries, a question posed formally.

in·ter·rupt (in-tê-rupt'), v.t. 1. to stop or hinder by breaking in upon. 2. to break the continuity of. 3. to end suddenly: v.i. to break in or disrupt a speech, action, etc. —in·ter·rup'tion, n.

in·ter·rupt·er ('êr), n. 1. one who or that which interrupts. 2. a device for breaking an electric current, as automatically at recurring intervals.

in·ter·scho·las·tic (in-têr-skô-las'tik), adj. between or among schools.

in·ter·sect (in-têr-sekt'), v.t. to cut or divide in two: v.i. to cross each other.

in·ter·sec·tion (-sek'shûn), n. 1. the act of intersecting. 2. a place of crossing. 3. the point or line in which two lines or two planes cut each other.

in·ter·sperse (-spûrs'), v.t. -spersed', -spers'ing, 1. to scatter between or among. 2. to ornament with randomly scattered additions.

in·ter·state (in'têr-stāt), adj. between or among states.

in·ter·stel·lar (in-têr-stel'êr), adj. of, pertaining to, or situated in space between the stars.

in·ter·stice (in-tûr'stis), n., pl. -stic·es ('stis-iz, 'sti-sēz), a narrow place between things closely set; crevice.

in·ter·sti·tial (in-têr-stish'âl), adj. of, pertaining to, containing, or existing in interstices.

in·ter·tid·al (-tīd'l), adj. between the high-tide and low-tide marks.

in·ter·twine (-twīn'), v.t. & v.i. -twined', -twin'ing, to twist together.

in·ter·ur·ban (-ûr'bân), adj. between or uniting two or more towns or cities.

in·ter·val (in'têr-vl), n. 1. space between objects; distance between points. 2. time between events. 3. range between conditions. 4. difference in pitch between two musical tones.

in·ter·vene (in-têr vēn'), v.i. -vened', -ven'ing, 1. to come or be situated between. 2. to interpose. 3. to interfere.

in·ter·ven·tion (-ven'shûn), n. 1. the act of intervening; interposition; mediation. 2. the interference of one state or government in the affairs of another.

in·ter·view (in'têr-vū), n. 1. a personal conference or meeting for the purpose of obtaining information, views, etc., as for publication. 2. a publication of an interview: v.i. to obtain an interview with. —in'ter·view·er, n.

in·ter·weave (in-têr-wēv'), v.t. & v.i. -wove', -wov'en, -weav'ing, 1. to weave together; interlace; intertwine. 2. to intermingle.

in·tes·ta·cy (in-tes'tà-si), n. the state of dying without a will.

in·tes·tate (in-tes'tāt, 'tit), adj. dying without having made a valid will: n. one who dies without having made a will.

in·tes·tine (in-tes'tin), adj. internal; not foreign: n. usually pl. the lower section of the alimentary canal through which food passes, which is made up of two parts reaching from the stomach to the anus; entrails. —in·tes'tin·al, adj.

in·ti·ma·cy (in'ti-mà-si), n., pl. -cies, 1. close or confidential friendship. 2. usually pl. illicit sexual intercourse.

in·ti·mate (in'ti-mit), adj. 1. close in friendship. 2. well-acquainted; familiar. 3. confidential. 4. complete. 5. having illicit sexual intercourse: n. a very close friend or companion: v.t. (-māt), -mat·ed, -mat·ing, to indicate or make known indirectly. —in·ti·mate·ly, adv.

in·ti·ma·tion (in-ti-mā'shûn), n. 1. an indirect suggestion or hint. 2. a legal announcement.

in·tim·i·date (in-tim'i-dāt), v.t. -dat·ed, -dat·ing, 1. to make afraid. 2. to influence the actions of another by the use of threats or violence. —in·tim·i·da'tion, n.

in·to (in'tōō, 'too), prep. 1. to the inside of;

within. 2. from one state or condition to another. 3. with motion toward. 4. going to the center of. 5. with the result of hitting.

in-tol-er-a-ble (in-tol'ẽr-à-bl), *adj.* unbearable. —in-tol'er-a-bly, *adv.*

in-tol-er-ant (-ànt), *adj.* bigoted; unable to bear or endure the opinions, practices, etc. of others. —in-tol'er-ance, *n.*

in-to-na-tion (in-tõ-nã'shǔn), *n.* 1. the act of intoning. 2. the manner of sounding musical notes in regard to how correctly the pitch is achieved. 3. modulation of the voice.

in-tone (in-tõn'), *v.t.* -toned', -ton'ing, to recite in monotone or chanting.

in to-to (in tõ'tõ), [Latin], entirely; completely.

in-tox-i-cant (in-tok'si-kànt), *n.* that which intoxicates, as alcoholic liquor.

in-tox-i-cate (-kāt), *v.t.* -cat-ed, -cat-ing, 1. to make drunk. 2. to excite greatly.

in-tox-i-ca-tion (in-tok-si-kā'shǔn), *n.* 1. the act of intoxicating. 2. drunkenness. 3. extreme excitement.

in-tra-, a combining form meaning *within.*

in-tra-cel-lu-lar (in-trà-sel'yoo-lẽr), *adj.* within and around a cell.

in-trac-ta-ble (in-trak'tà-bl), *adj.* unmanageable. —in-trac-ta-bil'i-ty, *n.*

in-tra-dos (in'trà-dos), *n.* the interior curve or face of an arch.

in-tra-mu-ral (in-trà-myoor'ål), *adj.* 1. within the walls, as of a city or town. 2. between or among those belonging to the same school.

in-tran-si-gent (in-tran'si-jĕnt), *adj.* irreconcilable; uncompromising: *n.* a person intransigent in politics. —in-tran'si-gence, *n.*

in-tran-si-tive (in-tran'si-tiv), *adj.* denoting a verb that does not require a direct object. —in-tran'si-tive-ly, *adv.*

in-tra-state (in-trà-stāt'), *adj.* within a state.

in-tra-u-ter-ine device (in-trà-ūt'ẽr-in), a plastic coil or loop used as a contraceptive by placing in the uterus.

in-trav-a-sa-tion (in-trav-à-sā'shǔn), *n.* in *Medicine,* the entrance of foreign matter into a vessel, especially a blood vessel.

in-tra-ve-nous (in-trà-vē'nǔs), *adj.* into a vein. —in-tra-ve'nous-ly, *adv.*

in-trench (in-trench'), *v.t.* same as entrench.

in-trep-id (in-trep'id), *adj.* bold; fearless. —in-tre-pid'i-ty (-trē-pid'ĭ-ti), *n.* —in-trep'id-ly, *adv.*

in-tri-cate (in'tri-kit), *adj.* 1. entangled; involved; complex. 2. very detailed. —in'tri-ca-cy (-kà-si), *n.*

in-tri-gant (in'tri-gànt), *n.* one who intrigues or plots. —in-tri-gante' (-gant'), *n.fem.*

in-trigue (in-trēg'), *v.i.* -trigued', -trigu'ing, 1. to carry on a secret plot. 2. to engage in clandestine love affairs: *v.t.* to make curious; fascinate: *n.* 1. a secret plot or plotting. 2. a clandestine love affair. —in-trigu'er, *n.* —in-trigu'ing-ly, *adv.*

in-trin-sic (in-trin'sik), *adj.* of or pertaining to that which is inherent; real; genuine. —in-trin'si-cal-ly, *adv.*

in-tro-, a combining form meaning *within, into.*

in-tro-duce (in-trõ-dõõs'), *v.t.* -duced', -duc'ing, 1. to conduct or bring in. 2. to bring into

use or notice. 3. to bring into acquaintance. 4. to insert. 5. to commence. 6. to make an addition of.

in-tro-duc-tion (-duk'shǔn), *n.* 1. the act of introducing. 2. a presentation. 3. a preface. 4. an elementary treatise on a branch of study.

in-tro-duc-to-ry (-duk'tẽr-i), *adj.* serving to introduce.

in-tro-it (in-trõ'it), *n.* 1. an opening psalm in a Christian religious service. 2. [I-], in the *Roman Catholic Church,* the opening section of the Mass made up of psalm verses that are repeated.

in-tro-mit (in-trõ-mit'), *v.t.* -mit'ted, -mit'ting, 1. to insert. 2. to admit; allow to pass in. —in-tro-mis'sion (-mish'ǔn), *n.*

in-tro-spec-tion (-spek'shǔn), *n.* a looking inward; examination of one's own thoughts or motives. —in-tro-spec'tive, *adj.*

in-tro-vert (in'trõ-vũrt), *n.* in *Psychology,* a person inclined to introspection; one who is preoccupied with his own thoughts, emotions, and motives. —in-tro-ver-sion (in-trõ-vũr'zhǔn), *n.*

in-trude (in-trõõd'), *v.i.* -trud'ed, -trud'ing, to thrust oneself in without invitation or welcome: *v.t.* to force in. —in-trud'er, *n.*

in-tru-sion (in-trõõ'zhǔn), *n.* 1. the act of intruding. 2. unlawful entry into the land of another. —in-tru'sive (-siv), *adj.* —in-tru'sive-ly, *adv.* —in-tru'sive-ness, *n.*

in-trust (in-trust'), *v.t.* same as entrust.

in-tu-i-tion (in-too-wish'ǔn), *n.* instinctive knowledge or feeling; immediate perception. —in-tu-i'tion-al, *adj.*

in-tu-i-tive (in-tõõ'i-tiv), *adj.* perceived immediately by the mind. —in-tu'i-tive-ly, *adv.*

in-tu-mesce (in-too-mes'), *v.i.* -mesced', -mesc'-ing, to expand, as with heat; swell up.

in-tu-mes-cence (-mes'ns), *n.* 1. a swelling or bubbling up, as under the action of heat. 2. a tumid growth; tumor. —in-tu-mes'cent, *adj.*

in-tus-sus-cep-tion (in-tǔ-sǔ-sep'shǔn), *n.* 1. the reception of one part within another. 2. the slipping of one part of the intestine into another part.

in-un-date (in'ǔn-dāt), *v.t.* -dat-ed, -dat-ing, to fill with an overflowing abundance; flood. —in-un-da'tion, *n.*

in-ure (in-yoor'), *v.t.* -ured', -ur'ing, to habituate; accustom: *v.i.* to become operative.

in u-ter-o (in ūt'ẽr-õ), [Latin], in the womb.

in-u-tile (in-ūt'l), *adj.* useless.

in-vade (in-vād'), *v.t.* -vad'ed, -vad'ing, 1. to enter with hostility or force. 2. to infringe upon; violate. —in-vad'er, *n.*

in-vag-i-nate (in-vaj'ĭ-nāt), *v.t.* -nat-ed, -nat-ing, to enclose in a sheath.

in-vag-i-na-tion (in-vaj-ĭ-nā'shǔn), *n.* 1. the state of being invaginated. 2. same as intussusception.

in-va-lid (in'và-lid), *adj.* 1. feeble; sickly. 2. serving invalids: *n.* one who is weak or infirm in health: *v.t.* 1. to make infirm in health; affect with disease. 2. to remove from military service because of ill health.

in-val-id (in-val'id), *adj.* of no force or authority; null and void. —in-va-lid-i-ty (in-và-lid'-ĭ-ti), *n.*

in-val-i-date (in-val'ĭ-dāt), *v.t.* -dat-ed, -dat-ing,

a in cap, ã in cane, ä in father, å in abet, e in met, ē in be, ẽ in baker, ĕ in regent, i in pit, ī in fine, ĭ in manifest, o in hot, ô in horse, õ in bone,

to weaken or destroy the force or legal validity of.

in·val·u·a·ble (in-val′yoo-wå-bl), *adj.* priceless.

In·var (in-vär′), *n.* an alloy of steel and nickel that does not expand when exposed to heat: used for balances and instruments: a trademark.

in·var·i·a·ble (in-ver′i-å-bl), *adj.* constant. —**in·var′i·a·bly,** *adv.*

in·va·sion (in-vä′zhŭn), *n.* the act of invading; hostile incursion; encroachment. —**in·va′sive,** *adj.*

in·vec·tive (in-vek′tiv), *n.* 1. a violent utterance of censure, sarcasm, or abuse: *adj.* verbally abusive.

in·veigh (in-vä′), *v.i.* to rail (*against*) persons or things with vehemence; utter censure or reproach.

in·vei·gle (in-vē′gl, -vä′gl), *v.t.* -**gled,** -**gling,** to entice into some action; seduce. —**in·vei′gler,** *n.*

in·vent (in-vent′), *v.t.* 1. to devise or contrive mentally. 2. to produce by original study or contrivance. —**in·ven′tor,** *n.*

in·ven·tion (-ven′shŭn), *n.* 1. the act of inventing. 2. the thing invented. 3. discovery; creative faculty. 4. a concoction; fabrication.

in·ven·tive (′tiv), *adj.* 1. of or pertaining to invention. 2. able to invent. —**in·ven′tive·ly,** *adv.* —**in·ven′tive·ness,** *n.*

in·ven·to·ry (in′vĕn-tôr-i), *n., pl.* -**ries,** 1. a catalog or list of goods, possessions, etc. 2. the supply of goods, etc. so listed. 3. an account: *v.t.* -**ried,** -**ry·ing,** to draw up an inventory or catalog of.

in·ve·rac·i·ty (in-vĕ-ras′i-ti), *n.* untruthfulness.

in·verse (in-vûrs′), *adj.* 1. contrary in tendency, direction, or effect. 2. in *Mathematics,* opposite in nature and result: said of certain operations: *n.* (also in′vûrs), that which is inverse. —**in·verse′ly,** *adv.*

in·ver·sion (in-vûr′zhŭn), *n.* 1. the act of inverting. 2. the state of being inverted. 3. that which is inverted. 4. in *Grammar,* a contrary change in order or position. 5. in *Music,* the contrary change of tone positions, as by raising a lower tone or dropping an upper tone by an octave. —**in·ver′sive,** *adj.*

in·vert (in-vûrt′), *v.t.* 1. to turn upside down. 2. to change in order, position, etc. to the contrary way.

in·ver·te·brate (in-vûr′tĕ-brit, -brāt), *adj.* 1. having no backbone. 2. having no force of character; weak: *n.* any animal which has no vertebrae or spinal column.

in·vest (in-vest′), *v.t.* 1. to dress; deck out. 2. to place or lay out (money) in order to get a financial return. 3. to surround. 4. to supply with office, authority, or dignity. 5. to put into office with the appropriate ritual: *v.i.* to make an investment. —**in·ves′tor,** *n.*

in·ves·ti·gate (in-ves′ti-gāt), *v.t.* -**gat·ed,** -**gat·ing,** to ascertain by careful inquiry; search; examine: *v.i.* to perform an investigation. —**in·ves′ti·ga′tor,** *n.*

in·ves·ti·ga·tion (in-ves-ti-gā′shŭn), *n.* 1. the act of investigating. 2. a thorough search or inquiry.

in·ves·ti·ture (in-ves′ti-chĕr), *n.* the ceremony of inducting into office.

in·vest·ment (in-vest′mĕnt), *n.* 1. the act of investing. 2. money invested. 3. that in which money can be invested.

in·vet·er·ate (in-vet′ĕr-it), *adj.* 1. deep-rooted. 2. habitual. —**in·vet′er·a·cy,** *n.*

in·vid·i·ous (in-vid′i-ŭs), *adj.* 1. likely to provoke ill will or envy. 2. creating anger or insult by unjust treatment. —**in·vid′i·ous·ly,** *adv.* —**in·vid′i·ous·ness,** *n.*

in·vig·or·ate (in-vig′ŏ-rāt), *v.t.* -**at·ed,** -**at·ing,** to give vigor to; strengthen; animate. —**in·vig·or·a′tion,** *n.*

in·vin·ci·ble (in-vin′si-bl), *adj.* unconquerable. —**in·vin·ci·bil′i·ty,** *n.*

in·vi·o·la·ble (in-vī′ŏ-lå-bl), *adj.* 1. that cannot be profaned or injured. 2. unbreakable. —**in·vi·o·la·bil′i·ty,** *n.*

in·vi·o·late (in-vī′ŏ-lit, -lāt), *adj.* not violate; unhurt; unbroken.

in·vis·i·ble (in-viz′i-bl), *adj.* 1. that cannot be seen. 2. not in sight. 3. not distinct. —**in·vis·i·bil′i·ty,** *n.* —**in·vis′i·bly,** *adv.*

in·vi·ta·tion (in-vi-tā′shŭn), *n.* 1. the act of inviting. 2. polite solicitation. 3. the words or document by which one is invited.

in·vi·ta·tion·al (-l), *adj.* participated in only by those invited to take part.

in·vi·ta·to·ry (in-vīt′å-tôr-i), *adj.* containing or using an invitation: *n., pl.* -**ries,** an exhortation to worship.

in·vite (in-vīt′), *v.t.* -**vit·ed,** -**vit′ing,** 1. to summon; request the presence of. 2. to persuade; allure. 3. to solicit; ask for. 4. to cause to happen: *n.* (in′vīt), [*Informal*], an invitation.

in·vit·ing (-vīt′ing), *adj.* tempting; seductive.

in·vo·ca·tion (in-vō-kā′shŭn), *n.* 1. the act or form of invoking. 2. earnest entreaty. 3. a prayer calling upon divine assistance or guidance.

in·voice (in′vois), *n.* a document listing goods sent with their prices, quantity, etc.: *v.t.* -**voiced,** -**voic·ing,** to send or give an invoice to or for.

in·voke (in-vōk′), *v.t.* -**voked,** -**vok′ing,** 1. to address in prayer or supplication. 2. to solicit (aid or protection). 3. to make use of (a relevant law, punishment, etc.). 4. to call forth (a devil, etc.).

in·vol·un·tar·y (in-vol′ŭn-tĕr-i), *adj.* 1. without will or choice; spontaneous. 2. automatic. —**in·vol·un·tar′i·ly,** *adv.*

in·vo·lute (in′vō-lōōt), *adj.* 1. folded or rolled inward, as certain leaves and flowers. 2. coiled spirally: *n.* in *Mathematics,* a particular kind of curve turned inward at the margin.

in·vo·lu·tion (in-vō-lōō′shŭn), *n.* 1. the act of involving or enfolding. 2. a complication. 3. in *Mathematics,* the process of raising a quantity to a given power. 4. in *Medicine,* the return of an organ to its normal size after distention.

in·volve (in-volv′), *v.t.* -**volved,** -**volv′ing,** 1. to complicate; entangle. 2. to embroil. 3. to include or contain. 4. to have a connection to. 5. to necessitate. 6. to cause to be engaged, working, etc. —**in·volve′ment,** *n.*

in·vul·ner·a·ble (in-vul′nẽr-ȧ-bl), *adj.* 1. that cannot be wounded or injured. 2. without any weak point. **—in·vul·ner·a·bil′i·ty,** *n.*

in·ward (in′wãrd), *adj.* 1. situated within. 2. in the mind. 3. going to the interior: *adv.* 1. toward the interior, center, etc. 2. into the mind.

in·ward·ly (-li), *adv.* 1. in the interior; internally. 2. in the mind. 3. toward the interior or center.

in·ward·ness (-nis), *n.* 1. the internal state; inner consciousness. 2. the essential nature, spiritual and mental. 3. devotion; earnestness; intensity.

in·wards (in′wãrds), *adv.* same as **inward.**

in·wrought (in-rôt′), *adj.* worked in; adorned with figures or patterns.

i·od·ic (ī-ŏd′ik), *adj.* of, pertaining to, or containing iodine.

i·o·dide (ī′ō-dīd), *n.* a compound of iodine with another element.

i·o·dine (ī′ō-dīn, -din), *n.* 1. a nonmetallic grayish-black crystalline element of the halogen group, which when heated gives forth fumes of a violet color: it is an antiseptic. 2. tincture of iodine, used as an antiseptic.

i·o·dism (ī′ō-dizm), *n.* an illness caused by excessive use of iodine.

i·o·dize (-dīz), *v.t.* **-dized, -diz·ing,** to treat with iodine.

i·o·do·form (ī-ō′dō-fôrm), *n.* a crystalline compound of iodine, used as an antiseptic.

I·o·dol (ī′ō-dōl), *n.* a yellowish-brown crystalline compound of iodine, used as an antiseptic: a trademark.

i·on (ī′ŏn), *n.* an atom or atoms bearing an electric charge.

-ion (ī-ŭn, -on), a suffix meaning *the action, state, or consequence of.*

I·o·ni·an (ī-ō′ni-ȧn), *adj.* of or pertaining to Ionia, an ancient area in western Asia Minor, or to its inhabitants: *n.* a native or inhabitant of Ionia.

I·on·ic (ī-on′ik), *adj.* 1. of or pertaining to Ionia, an ancient area in western Asia Minor, or its inhabitants. 2. designating an order of Greek architecture characterized by the volute scroll of its capital: *n.* 1. in *Greek & Latin Prosody, a)* a foot consisting of four syllables, two long and two short or two short and two long. *b)* a verse composed of Ionic feet. 2. the Ionic dialect.

i·on·o·sphere (ī-on′ō-sfir), *n.* the outer section of the atmosphere, consisting of several layers with a noticeable level of ions and electrons.

i·o·ta (ī-ōt′ȧ, i-), *n.* 1. the ninth letter of the Greek alphabet. 2. a very small quantity; particle; jot.

IOU, I.O.U. (ī-ō-ū′), 1. I owe you. 2. a written note indicating that money is owed: it is signed by the debtor.

ip·e·cac (ip′ē-kak), *n.* the dried root of a South American plant, used in medicine as an emetic: also **ip·e·cac·u·an·ha** (ip-ē-kak-yoo-wan′ȧ).

ip·se dix·it (ip′si dik′sit), [Latin, he himself has said (it)], an assertion; dictum; dogma.

ip·so fac·to (ip′sō fak′tō), by the fact itself.

i·ra·cund (ī′rȧ-kund), *adj.* irascible; given to anger.

I·ra·ni·an (i-rä′ni-ȧn, ī-), *adj.* of or pertaining to Iran, a nation in southwestern Asia, or to its inhabitants: *n.* 1. a native or inhabitant of Iran; Persian. 2. a group of languages spoken in the area of Iran and the Caucasus.

i·ras·ci·ble (i-ras′i-bl), *adj.* easily excited to anger. **—i·ras·ci·bil′i·ty,** *n.*

i·rate (ī-rāt′), *adj.* angry; enraged. **—i·rate′ly,** *adv.* **—i·rate′ness,** *n.*

ire (īr), *n.* wrath; passion.

i·ren·ic (i-ren′ik), *adj.* designed to promote peace; conciliatory: also **i·ren′i·cal.**

i·ren·ics (i-ren′iks, i-rē′niks), *n.pl.* the principles of Christian unity; teaching that inculcates harmony among Christians and churches of the various sects and denominations.

ir·i·des·cent (ir-i-des′nt), *adj.* having an interaction of shifting colors as those of the rainbow. **—ir·i·des′cence,** *n.*

i·rid·i·um (i-rid′i-ŭm), *n.* a white, metallic chemical element found in the same ore with platinum.

i·ris (ī′ris), *n., pl.* **i′ris·es, ir·i·des** (ir′i-dēz, ī′ri-), 1. the colored, circular membrane around the pupil of the eye. 2. a rainbow or appearance of colors like a rainbow. 3. any of a group of plants with swordlike leaves and large, showy flowers of many colors.

I·rish (ī′rish), *adj.* of or pertaining to Ireland, a nation taking up most of an island west of Great Britain, or its inhabitants: *n.* 1. the people of Ireland. 2. the Celtic language of Ireland. 3. [Informal], temper. **—I′rish·man** (-mȧn), *n.*

Irish stew, a stew of meat, potatoes, onions, and other vegetables.

irk (ûrk), *v.t.* to weary, bother, etc.

irk·some (ûrk′sŏm), *adj.* irritating or wearisome.

i·ron (ī′ẽrn), *n.* 1. a metallic chemical element, the most common of the metals. 2. an instrument made of iron, as a flat, smooth implement heated and used to press cloth. 3. *pl.* fetters. 4. vigor or force. 5. a kind of golf club with the head set on an angle: *adj.* 1. of, pertaining to, resembling, or made of iron. 2. forceful; solid: *v.t.* 1. to smooth (cloth) with an iron implement. 2. to furnish with iron. 3. to fetter: *v.i.* to iron cloth.

Iron Age, 1. the last prehistoric age, characterized by the use of iron for weapons and tools: it followed the Bronze Age. 2. in *Greek & Roman Mythology,* the last and worst of the ages of the world, characterized by degeneracy, iniquity, etc.

i·ron·clad (-klad), *n.* formerly, a warship protected by thick iron plates: *adj.* 1. covered or protected with iron. 2. pertaining to a contract or agreement that is very difficult to break or change.

iron curtain, a barrier of censorship and secrecy between the Soviet Union or the other states within its sphere of influence and the rest of the countries of the world.

i·ron·i·cal (i-ron′i-kl), *adj.* 1. expressing one thing but meaning the contrary. 2. using or tending to use irony. 3. of or having the nature of irony. Also **i-ren'ic.** —**i-ron'i-cal-ly,** *adv.*

i-ron-ing (ī'ĕr-ning), *n.* 1. the process of pressing clothes and household linens with a hot flatiron. 2. the clothes, household linens, etc. thus ironed or to be ironed.

i-ron-mas-ter (ī'ĕrn-mas-tĕr), *n.* a manufacturer of iron.

i-ron-mon-ger (-mung-gĕr), *n.* [British], a hardware dealer. —**i'ron-mon-ger-y,** *n.*

i-ron-stone (-stōn), *n.* a hard, white ceramic ware.

i-ron-ware (-wer), *n.* articles made of iron.

i-ron-wood (-wood), *n.* 1. any of various trees that produce timber of exceptional hardness and durability. 2. this wood.

i-ron-work-er (-wûr-kĕr), *n.* 1. a person who makes iron or iron products. 2. one who works on structural steel, as the framework of a bridge.

i-ro-ny (ī'rŏn-i, ī'ĕr-ni), *n., pl.* **-nies,** 1. subtle sarcasm; a mode of expression in which the intended meaning of the words is the opposite of their usual sense. 2. an outcome or event that is the opposite from what might be expected.

Ir-o-quoi-an (ir-ō-kwoi'ăn), *adj.* of or pertaining to an extensive North American Indian family of languages: *n.* 1. a member of an Iroquoian tribe. 2. the Iroquoian languages collectively.

Ir-o-quois (ir'ō-kwoi), *n., pl.* **-quois** (-kwoi, -kwoiz), 1. a member of a confederation of North American Indian tribes that lived in western and northern New York and in Quebec and Ontario: their descendants also live in Oklahoma. 2. the Iroquoian language family: *adj.* of the Iroquois.

ir-ra-di-ance (i-rā'di-ăns), *n.* 1. radiance. 2. the amount of light or radiant energy per unit area. Also **ir-ra'di-an-cy.** —**ir-ra'di-ant,** *adj.*

ir-ra-di-ate (-āt), *v.t.* **-at-ed, -at-ing,** 1. to shed light upon; illuminate. 2. to make clear to the understanding. 3. to radiate; spread out. 4. to expose to X-rays, ultraviolet rays, or some other form of radiant energy: *v.i.* 1. to emit rays of light. 2. to become radiant: *adj.* (-it), lighted up. —**ir-ra'di-a-tor,** *n.*

ir-ra-di-a-tion (i-rā-di-ā'shŭn), *n.* 1. an exposure to radiation. 2. mental enlightenment. 3. the emission of radiant energy. 4. in *Optics,* the apparent enlargement of an object seen against a dark background.

ir-ra-tion-al (i-rash'ŭn-l), *adj.* 1. incapable of reasoning. 2. illogical; absurd; unreasonable. 3. in *Mathematics,* not capable of being expressed as an integer or as a quotient of two integers. —**ir-ra-tion-al'i-ty** (-ă-nal'i-tĭ), *n., pl.* **-ties.** —**ir-ra'tion-al-ly,** *adv.*

ir-re-claim-a-ble (ir-i-klā'mă-bl), *adj.* not reclaimable. —**ir-re-claim-a-bil'i-ty,** *n.* —**ir-re-claim'a-bly,** *adv.*

ir-rec-on-cil-a-ble (i-rek-ŏn-sīl'ă-bl), *adj.* not reconcilable; not able to be brought into harmony or agreement; implacable: *n.* 1. a person who refuses to compromise on anything to which he is opposed. 2. *pl.* ideas, doctrines, etc. that cannot be reconciled. —

ir-rec-on-cil-a-bil'i-ty, *n.* —**ir-rec-on-cil'a-bly,** *adv.*

ir-re-cov-er-a-ble (ir-i-kuv'ĕr-ă-bl), *adj.* 1. not able to be recovered or regained. 2. not able to be remedied. —**ir-re-cov'er-a-bly,** *adv.*

ir-re-deem-a-ble (-dēm'ă-bl), *adj.* 1. not redeemable; that cannot be bought back or paid off. 2. not convertible into coin, as some paper money. 3. beyond redemption or reformation; hopeless. —**ir-re-deem'a-bly,** *adv.*

ir-re-den-tist (ir-i-den'tist), *n.* 1. [I-], a member of an Italian political party organized in 1878, advocating the recovery of adjacent territory under foreign control but with mainly Italian population. 2. a person who advocates a policy of reclaiming territory formerly a part of his country. —**ir-re-den'tism,** *n.*

ir-ref-u-ta-ble (i-ref'yoo-tă-bl), *adj.* that cannot be disproved or disputed. —**ir-ref'u-ta-bly,** *adv.*

ir-reg-u-lar (i-reg'yŭ-lĕr), *adj.* 1. not conforming to rule. 2. not uniform, straight, etc. 3. not belonging to the regular army: said of some troops. 4. in *Grammar,* not conforming to the regular manner of inflection: *n.* 1. something that is irregular. 2. a soldier not belonging to a regular army. 3. a piece of merchandise that does not conform to a standard. —**ir-reg-u-lar'i-ty** (-ler'i-tĭ), *n., pl.* **-ties.** —**ir-reg'u-lar-ly,** *adv.*

ir-rel-e-vant (i-rel'e-vănt), *adj.* not relevant or pertinent; unrelated to the subject at hand. —**ir-rel'e-van-cy,** *n., pl.* **-cies.** —**ir-rel'e-vant-ly,** *adv.*

ir-re-li-gious (ir-i-lij'ŭs), *adj.* 1. having little or no interest in religion; not religious. 2. hostile toward religion. 3. impious. —**ir-re-li'gion** ('ŭn), *n.* —**ir-re-li'gion-ist,** *n.*

ir-re-me-di-a-ble (ir-i-mē'di-ă-bl), *adj.* not able to be remedied; past cure or repair. —**ir-re-me'di-a-ble-ness,** *n.* —**ir-re-me'di-a-bly,** *adv.*

ir-re-mov-a-ble (-mōō'vă-bl), *adj.* not movable; fixed. —**ir-re-mov-a-bil'i-ty,** *n.* —**ir-re-mov'a-bly,** *adv.*

ir-rep-a-ra-ble (i-rep'ĕr-ă-bl), *adj.* not able to be repaired, mended, etc. —**ir-rep-a-ra-bil'i-ty,** *n.* —**ir-rep'a-ra-bly,** *adv.*

ir-re-place-a-ble (ir-i-plās'ă-bl), *adj.* not able to be replaced.

ir-re-press-i-ble (-pres'ĭ-bl), *adj.* not able to be repressed or held back. —**ir-re-press-i-bil'i-ty,** *n.* —**ir-re-press'i-bly,** *adv.*

ir-re-proach-a-ble (-prō'chă-bl), *adj.* without blame or reproach; faultless. —**ir-re-proach-a-bil'i-ty,** *n.* —**ir-re-proach'a-bly,** *adv.*

ir-re-sist-i-ble (-zis'ti-bl), *adj.* not to be resisted; fascinating; enticing. —**ir-re-sist-i-bil'i-ty,** **ir-re-sist'i-ble-ness,** *n.* —**ir-re-sist'i-bly,** *adv.*

ir-res-o-lute (i-rez'ō-lōōt), *adj.* indecisive; vacillating in purpose or opinion. —**ir-res'o-lute-ly,** *adv.* —**ir-res-o-lu'tion,** *n.*

ir-re-spec-tive (ir-i-spek'tiv), *adj.* regardless (*of*). —**ir-re-spec'tive-ly,** *adv.*

ir-re-spon-si-ble (-spon'si-bl), *adj.* 1. not responsible or accountable for actions. 2. feeling or showing no sense of responsibility; unreliable. 3. done or said by one who is irresponsible. —**ir-re-spon-si-bil'i-ty,** *n.* —**ir-re-spon'si-bly,** *adv.*

ŏ in dragon, ōō in crude, oo in wool, u in cup, ū in cure, û in turn, ŭ in focus, oi in boy, ou in house, th in thin, th in sheathe, g in get, j in joy, y in yet.

ir·re·triev·a·ble (-trēv′ä-bl), adj. not retrievable. —**ir·re·triev·a·bil′i·ty**, n. —**ir·re·triev′a·bly**, adv.

ir·rev·er·ence (i-rev′ẽr-ẽns), n. 1. lack of reverence or respect. 2. a remark or action showing lack of reverence. —**ir·rev′er·ent**, adj. —**ir·rev′er·ent·ly**, adv.

ir·re·vers·i·ble (ir-i-vûr′si-bl), adj. not able to be reversed; especially, not able to be repealed, turned back, etc. —**ir·re·vers·i·bil′i·ty**, n. —**ir·re·vers′i·bly**, adv.

ir·rev·o·ca·ble (i-rev′ŏ-kä-bl), adj. not revocable; not able to be revoked or recalled. —**ir·rev·o·ca·bil′i·ty**, n. —**ir·rev′o·ca·bly**, adv.

ir·ri·ga·ble (ir′i-gä-bl), adj. capable of being irrigated.

ir·ri·gate (ir′i-gāt), v.t. -gat·ed, -gat·ing, 1. to supply (land) with water by ditches or by sprinklers. 2. in Medicine, to wash out (a body cavity, wound, etc.). —**ir·ri·ga′tion**, n. —**ir′ri·ga·tor**, n.

ir·ri·ta·ble (ir′i-tä-bl), adj. 1. easily provoked or irritated. 2. in Medicine, very sensitive; likely to become inflamed, etc. —**ir·ri·ta·bil′i·ty**, n. —**ir′ri·ta·bly**, adv.

ir·ri·tant (-tänt), adj. causing irritation: n. anything that causes irritation. —**ir′ri·tan·cy**, n.

ir·ri·tate (-tāt), v.t. -tat·ed, -tat·ing, 1. to provoke or make angry. 2. to cause soreness or inflammation in. —**ir·ri·ta′tion**, n.

ir·rupt (i-rupt′), v.i. 1. to burst in forcibly or violently. 2. in Ecology, to increase suddenly in size of population. —**ir·rup′tion**, n. —**ir·rup′tive**, adj.

is (iz), third person singular, present indicative, of be.

i·sa·gog·ics (ī-sä-goj′iks), n. the study of the literary history of the Bible.

I·sa·iah (ī-zā′ä), n. a book of the Bible.

is·che·mi·a (is-kē′mi-ä), n. insufficiency of blood supply to a part of the body. —**is·che′mic**, adj.

-ish (ish), a suffix meaning like, somewhat, of (a specified people), or [Informal], approximately.

Ish·ma·el·ite (ish′mē-ä-līt), n. 1. a descendant of Ishmael, the traditional progenitor of Arab peoples. 2. an outcast.

Ish·tar (ish′tär), n. the goddess of fertility of ancient Assyria and Babylonia.

i·sin·glass (ī′zn-glas), n. 1. a gelatin prepared from fish bladders. 2. mica in thin sheets.

I·sis (ī′sis), n. the Egyptian goddess of fertility.

Is·lam (is′läm, iz′-), n. 1. the Moslem religion, set forth in the Koran: it teaches that there is one deity, Allah, with Mohammed as the chief prophet and founder of the religion. 2. Moslems collectively. 3. the countries in which the Moslem religion predominates. —**Is·lam′ic**, **Is·lam·it′ic**, adj.

Is·lam·ism (-izm), n. the religion, doctrines, civilization, and customs of Mohammedans. —**Is′lam·ite**, n.

is·land (ī′länd), n. 1. a land area not as large as a continent and surrounded by water. 2. anything resembling an island, as in being isolated.

is·land·er (-ẽr), n. a native or inhabitant of an island.

isle (īl), n. an island, especially a small one.

is·let (ī′lit), n. a very small island.

ism (izm), n. a system, theory, doctrine, etc. with a name that ends in -ism.

-ism (izm), a suffix meaning an instance, act, or result of; theory of; adherence to; state, condition, or behavior of.

is·n't (iz′nt), is not.

iso-, a combining form meaning equal, the same, similar.

i·so·bar (ī′sŏ-bär), n. a line on a map connecting places on the earth's surface having the same barometric pressure. —**i·so·bar′ic** (-ber′ik), adj.

i·so·chro·mat·ic (ī-sŏ-krō-mat′ik), adj. having the same color.

i·soch·ro·nal (ī-sok′rŏ-nl), adj. 1. occurring at equal intervals of time. 2. equal in time. Also **i·soch′ro·nous**. —**i·soch′ro·nal·ly**, adv.

i·so·cli·nal (ī-sŏ-klī′nl), adj. 1. having the same inclination or dip. 2. connecting points on a map of the earth's surface having the same inclination or dip.

i·so·dy·nam·ic (-dī-nam′ik), adj. having equal force.

i·sog·e·nous (ī-soj′ē-nŭs), adj. having the same origin. —**i·sog′e·ny**, n.

i·so·geo·therm (ī-sŏ-jē′ŏ-thûrm), n. an imaginary line beneath the earth's surface through points having the same average temperature. —**i·so·geo·ther′mal**, adj.

i·so·hel (ī′sŏ-hel), n. a line on a map connecting places having equal hours of sunshine over a given period of time.

i·so·late (ī′sŏ-lāt), v.t. -lat·ed, -lat·ing, 1. to place alone; set apart from others. 2. to separate (a compound or element) so that it is in an uncombined form. 3. to put (a person with a contagious disease) apart from others to prevent the spread of the disease: n. a person or group that is isolated. —**i′so·la·ble** (-lä-bl), adj. —**i·so·la′tion**, n.

i·so·la·tion·ism (ī-sŏ-lā′shŭn-izm), n. a national policy by which a country does not become involved with other nations in agreements, alliances, or the like. —**i·so·la′tion·ist**, n. & adj.

i·so·mer (ī′sŏ-mẽr), n. any of two or more chemical compounds composed of the same number and kinds of atoms, but with different structural arrangement within the molecules. —**i·so·mer′ic** (-mer′ik), adj. —**i·som′er·i·cal·ly**, adv.

i·so·met·ric (ī-sŏ-met′rik), adj. 1. equal in measure. 2. denoting exercises in which muscles are tensed in resistance to other muscles or against a solid surface: n. 1. a line on a chart that indicates changes in temperature or pressure. 2. pl. isometric exercises. —**i·so·met′ri·cal·ly**, adv.

i·som·e·try (ī-som′ē-tri), n. 1. equality of measure. 2. equality of elevation above sea level.

i·so·mor·phism (ī-sŏ-môr′fizm), n. 1. in Biology, similarity of organisms of different species, etc. 2. in Chemistry, the property of having the same crystalline form, but of varied elements. —**i·so·mor′phic**, **i·so·mor′phous**, adj.

i·son·o·my (ī-son′ŏ-mi), n. equality of civil rights, privileges, and laws.

i·so·pod (ī′sŏ-pŏd), n. any of an order of small, mostly aquatic crustaceans, with a flat body and seven pairs of walking legs: adj. of the isopods.

i·sos·ce·les (ī-sos′ē-lēz), adj. denoting a triangle having two equal sides.

i·sos·ta·sy (ī-sos′tā-si), n. a state of equilibrium in large areas of the crust of the earth, preserved by gravitational forces. —i·so·stat·ic (ī-sō-stat′ik), adj.

i·so·there (ī′sō-thir), n. a line on a map connecting points which have the same mean summer temperature. —i·soth·er·al (ī-soth′ēr-ăl), adj.

i·so·therm (-thûrm), n. 1. a line on a map connecting places having the same mean temperature or the same temperature at a given time. 2. a line indicating changes of pressure at constant temperature. —i·so·ther′mal, adj.

i·so·tope (ī′sō-tōp), n. any of two or more forms of an element having the same atomic number but differing slightly in atomic weight. —i·so·top′ic (-top′ik, -tō′pik), adj. —i·so·top′i·cal·ly, adv.

Is·ra·el (iz′ri-ĕl, ′rā-), n. the Jewish people.

Is·rae·li (iz-rā′li), adj. of or pertaining to modern Israel, a Jewish state at the southeast end of the Mediterranean Sea, or its inhabitants: n., pl. -lis, -li, a native or inhabitant of modern Israel.

Is·ra·el·ite (iz′ri-ĕ-līt), n. any of the Hebrew people who lived in ancient Israel, or their descendants; Hebrew; Jew: adj. of ancient Israel or the Israelites; Jewish.

is·su·ance (ish′oo-wăns), n. 1. the act of issuing. 2. issue.

is·sue (ish′ōō), n. 1. the act of passing or flowing out. 2. an exit; place of going out. 3. all that is put forth at one time. 4. offspring. 5. an essential point in pleading or debate. 6. a consequence; result. 7. profits from lands, etc.; produce; proceeds. 8. a discharge of blood, pus, etc.: v.i. -sued, -suing, 1. to come or pass out; emerge. 2. to be descended. 3. to end or result. 4. to accrue. 5. to be published: v.t. 1. to send or give out, as supplies. 2. to discharge. 3. to publish; put into circulation. —is′su·er, n.

-ist (ist, ĭst), a suffix meaning an adherent of; one who is concerned with; one who does, makes, or practices (something).

isth·mus (is′mŭs), n., pl. -mus·es, -mi (′mī), a neck of land with water on each side and connecting two larger bodies of land. —isth′mi·an (′mi-ăn), adj. & n.

is·tle (ist′li), n. a coarse fiber obtained from some tropical American plants, as various agaves: used for cordage and basketry.

it (it), pron., pl. they, 1. the animal or thing previously mentioned. 2. the subject of an impersonal verb, as it is raining. 3. an indefinite subject or object: n. the player in children's games who must perform some task, catch the others, or the like.

I·tal·ian (i-tal′yŭn), adj. of or pertaining to Ital, a country in southern Europe, or its inhabitants or language: n. 1. a native or inhabitant of Italy. 2. the Romance language of Italy.

i·tal·ic (i-tal′ik), adj. denoting a slender kind of type in which the letters slope upward to the right (italic): n. pl. italic type.

i·tal·i·cize (′i-sīz), v.t. -cized, -ciz·ing, 1. to print in italics. 2. to underscore copy to indicate it is to be printed in italics. —i·tal·i·ci·za′tion, n.

itch (ich), n. 1. any of various skin disorders causing great irritation of the skin. 2. an irritation of the skin that makes one want to scratch. 3. a teasing desire for something: v.i. 1. to feel irritation of the skin so that one wants to scratch. 2. to have a teasing desire for something: v.t. 1. to make itch. 2. to irritate. —itch′y (′i), adj. itch′i·er, itch′i·est. —itch′i·ness, n.

-ite (īt), a suffix meaning a descendant from, a believer in, an inhabitant of, a salt or ester of an acid, a manufactured product.

i·tem (īt′ĕm), n. 1. a separate article or particular; unit. 2. a piece of news or information, as a paragraph in a newspaper: adv. also.

i·tem·ize (-īz), v.t. -ized, -iz·ing, to list the individual items of. —i·tem·i·za′tion, n.

it·er·ate (it′ē-rāt), v.t. -at·ed, -at·ing, to repeat in action or speech. —it·er·a′tion, n. —it′er·a·tive, adj.

i·tin·er·an·cy (i-tin′ĕr-ăn-si), n. 1. a traveling from place to place, especially in the performance of some official function, as by a judge or preacher on circuit. 2. a group of itinerant judges or preachers. Also i·tin′er·a·cy.

i·tin·er·ant (-ănt), adj. traveling from place to place: n. one who travels from place to place. —i·tin′er·ant·ly, adv.

i·tin·er·ar·y (ī-tin′ē-rer-i), n. 1. a route. 2. a record of a journey. 3. a detailed outline of a proposed journey.

i·tin·er·ate (i-tin′ē-rāt), v.i. -at·ed, -at·ing, to travel from place to place or on a circuit. —i·tin·er·a′tion, n.

-i·tion (ish′ŭn), a suffix meaning the act of, the condition of, the result of.

-i·tious (ish′ŭs), a suffix meaning of, like, characterized by.

-i·tis (īt′is), a suffix meaning inflammation of (an organ or part).

its (its), pron. that or those belonging to it: adj. of or belonging to it.

it's (its), 1. it is. 2. it has.

it·self (it-self′), pron. 1. the emphatic or reflexive form of it. 2. its true self.

I've (īv), I have.

-ive (iv), a suffix meaning that tends to, of or like.

i·vied (ī′vid), adj. overgrown with ivy.

i·vo·ry (ī′vēr-i, ī′vri), n., pl. -ries, 1. the hard, bony, white dentine which forms the tusks of the elephant, walrus, etc. 2. the creamy-white color of ivory. 3. any substance like ivory. 4. pl. things made of ivory or a substance resembling ivory, as piano keys, teeth, dice, etc.: adj. 1. of or made of ivory. 2. creamy-white.

i·vo·ry-billed woodpecker, (-bild′), a large, glossy black woodpecker, formerly of the southeastern U.S., now nearly extinct.

ŏ in dragon, ōō in crude, oo in wool, u in cup, ū in cure, û in turn, ů in focus, oi in boy, ou in house, th in thin, th in sheathe, g in get, j in joy, y in yet.

ivory black, a fine black pigment prepared from burnt ivory.

ivory nut, same as **vegetable ivory** (sense 1).

ivory palm, the palm from which ivory nuts are obtained.

ivory tower, a place, situation, or mental attitude of withdrawal or retreat from reality and practical affairs.

i·vy (ī'vi), *n., pl.* **i'vies,** 1. a climbing evergreen vine with a woody stem, grown as an ornamental plant on walls, buildings, etc. 2. any of various plants resembling the ivy.

ix·i·a (ik'si-ā), *n.* any one of a genus of South African plants of the iris family with grass-like leaves.

ix·tle (iks'tli, is'), *n.* same as **istle.**

-i·za·tion (i-zā'shŭn, ī-), a suffix meaning *a becoming like or changing into, a combination of, the practice of.*

-ize (īz), a suffix meaning *to make or cause to be, to become* (*like*), *to act in a specified way, to treat or combine with.*

iz·zard (iz'ẽrd), *n.* [Dialectal or Archaic], the letter Z.

J

J, J (jā), *n., pl.* **J's, J's, 1.** the tenth letter of the English alphabet. **2.** the customary sound of this letter, as in *jam.* **3.** a type or impression of *J* or *j.*

J (jā), *adj.* shaped like *J*: *n.* an object shaped like *J.*

jab (jab), *v.t. & v.i.* **jabbed, jab'bing, 1.** to thrust or poke sharply. **2.** to punch abruptly with force: *n.* a poke, punch, or sharp thrust.

jab·ber (jab'ẽr), *v.i. & v.t.* to talk or say rapidly and indistinctly; chatter: *n.* chatter; unintelligible talk. —**jab'ber·er,** *n.*

jab·ber·wock·y (-wäk-ĭ), *n.* nonsense syllables; gibberish.

jab·i·ru (jab'ĭ-rōō) *n.* either of two large, wading storks, one of Africa and one of tropical America.

ja·bot (zha-bō', ja-), *n.* a frill, as of lace, worn down the front of a blouse, shirt, or the bodice of a dress.

ja·cal (hä-käl'), *n., pl.* **-cal'es** (-kä'lās), **-cals'**, a native Mexican dwelling made of thin poles covered with mud.

jac·a·mar (jak'å-mär), *n.* any of several insectivorous birds of the Central and South American tropical forests.

ja·ca·na (zhä-sä-nä'), *n.* any of a family of tropical wading birds, with long, straight toes that enable them to walk on floating vegetation.

jac·a·ran·da (jak-å-ran'då), *n.* an American tropical tree with fragrant wood and lavender flowers.

ja·cinth (jā'sinth, jas'inth), *n.* **1.** a reddish-orange variety of zircon; hyacinth. **2.** a reddish-orange color.

jack (jak), *n.* **1.** any of various mechanical devices, as a spit that turns roasting meat (also called *smokejack*), a bootjack, a lever, etc.; especially, a machine for lifting or moving heavy objects a short distance. **2.** a playing card with a picture of a soldier or servant; knave. **3.** any of various fishes. **4.** a small ball used as a mark in the game of bowls. **5.** any of the small pieces used to play jacks. **6.** the male of certain animals, as the donkey or rabbit. **7.** a small flag flown at the bow of a ship. **8.** an electrical socket into which a plug is inserted. **9.** [J-], *a)* a man; fellow. *b)* a sailor: *v.t.* **1.** to lift (something) with a jack. **2.** [Informal], to raise (prices): followed by *up.*

jack·al (jak'ăl, 'ôl), *n., pl.* **-als, -al, 1.** a doglike, carnivorous wild animal of Asia and Africa, that acts as a scavenger and hunts in packs. **2.** one who does base work for another.

jack·a·napes (jak'å-nāps), *n.* a conceited or impudent fellow.

jack·ass (jak'as), *n.* **1.** the male ass; donkey. **2.** a fool; dolt.

jack·boot ('bōōt), *n.* a heavy boot reaching above the knee.

jack·daw ('dô), *n.* **1.** a European bird much like the crow, but smaller. **2.** same as grackle.

jack·et (jak'it), *n.* **1.** a short coat, usually with sleeves, and opening in front. **2.** a cover to prevent radiation of heat. **3.** a wrapper or envelope. **4.** a protective casing, as a paper over the cover of a book or a stiff envelope for a phonograph record. **5.** the skin of a cooked potato: *v.t.* **1.** to clothe with a jacket. **2.** to cover with a casing. —**jack'et·ed,** *adj.*

Jack Frost, frosty weather or frost personified.

jack·ham·mer (jak'ham-ẽr), *n.* a portable pneumatic hammer used for drilling pavements, rocks, etc.

jack·in·the·box (jak'in-*th*ĕ-bäks), *n., pl.* **-box·es,** a toy in the shape of a box: when the cover is lifted, a doll on a spring pops up: also **jack'-in-a-box.**

jack·in·the·pul·pit (-pool'pit), *n., pl.* **-pits,** a North American plant having a fleshy flower spike arched over by a spathe.

Jack Ketch, formerly, in Great Britain, a public hangman.

jack·knife (jak'nīf), *n., pl.* **-knives** ('nīvz), **1.** a large pocketknife. **2.** a dive in which the diver bends and touches his toes while he is in the air, then straightens before he enters the water: *v.t.* **-knifed, -knif·ing,** to cause to bend in the middle: *v.i.* **1.** to bend in the middle, as one doing a jackknife dive. **2.** to swing forward or back and form a sharp angle with each other: said of connected vehicles, cars, etc.

jack·of·all·trades (jak-ŏv-ôl'trādz), *n., pl.* **jacks-,** [sometimes J-], one who is adept at many kinds of work; handyman.

jack·o'·lan·tern (jak'ŏ-lan-tẽrn), *n., pl.* **-terns, 1.** a pumpkin hollowed out and with holes cut in the shell so that it resembles a face: the light of a candle or flashlight is allowed to show through. **2.** an artificial pumpkin like this. **3.** same as **ignis fatuus** (sense 1).

jack pine, a pine tree of the northern U.S. with short needles.

jack·pot (jak'pät), *n.* **1.** a pot that has accumulated over several plays or series of plays, then is won all at once, as in poker, bingo, or a slot machine. **2.** the highest success.

jacks (jaks), *n.* a children's game in which small stones or six-pointed metal pieces are tossed and picked up while bouncing a ball.

jack·snipe (jak'snip), *n., pl.* **-snipes, -snipe, 1.** a small, old-world snipe. **2.** any of various American sandpipers.

ŏ in dr*a*gon, ōō in cr*u*de, ꞷ in w*oo*l, u in c*u*p, ū in c*u*re, ū in t*u*rn, ꭒ in f*o*cus, oi in b*o*y, ou in h*ou*se, th in *th*in, th in shea*th*e, g in *g*et, j in *j*oy, y in *y*et,

jack-stay ('stā), *n.* a rope stretched along the yard of a ship, to which sails are fastened.

jack-stone ('stōn), *n.* 1. a small stone or metal piece used in playing jacks. 2. *pl.* the game of jacks.

jack-straws ('strôz), *n.* a children's game in which a number of straws, or similar narrow strips, are tossed into a confused heap, from which the players attempt to remove one at a time without disturbing the others.

Jac-o-bite (jak'ō-bīt), *n.* one of the adherents to the cause of James II of England, and his descendants. —**Jac-o-bit'ic** (-bit'ik), **Jac-o-bit-i-cal**, *adj.*

jac-o-net (jak'ō-net), *n.* 1. a fine, soft, white cotton material somewhat like cambric. 2. a glazed cotton cloth used in bookbinding.

Jac-quard (jā-kärd'), *n.* 1. a loom with a device used in weaving a figured pattern: also **Jacquard loom.** 2. the weave made on this loom: also **Jacquard weave.** 3. a fabric made with this weave.

jade (jād), *n.* 1. a tired or worn-out horse. 2. a disreputable woman; hussy. 3. a hard stone, usually green, used for ornaments and jewelry. 4. a soft, medium shade of green: *v.t. & v.i.* **jad'ed, jad'ing,** to become, or cause to become, tired or worn-out: *adj.* 1. made of the gemstone jade. 2. of the green color of jade.

jad-ed (jā'dĕd), *adj.* 1. tired; worn-out. 2. satiated, as by overindulgence. 3. bored; dissipated. —**jad'ed-ly,** *adv.* —**jad'ed-ness,** *n.*

jae-ger (yā'gẽr), *n.* 1. a rapacious sea bird that forces weaker birds to give up their prey. 2. a hunter. Also **ja'ger.**

jag (jag), *n.* 1. a projecting point. 2. [Dial.], a small load. 3. a condition of partial intoxication: *v.t.* **jagged, jag'ging,** to cut jags in or to tear raggedly.

jag-ged (jag'ĕd), *adj.* having sharp, toothlike projections. —**jag'ged-ly,** *adv.* —**jag'ged-ness,** *n.*

jag-uar (jag'wär, 'yoo-wär), *n., pl.* -**uars,** -**uar,** a large cat with black spots, somewhat like the leopard: it is found in the southwestern U.S. and in Central and South America.

jai a-lai (hī'lī), a game, popular in Latin America, somewhat like handball and played with a basketlike racket.

jail (jāl), *n.* a place of confinement for accused persons awaiting trial or for those convicted of minor offenses: *v.t.* to put or hold in jail.

jail-bird ('bûrd), *n.* [Informal], a person who has often been in jail.

jail-er, jail-or ('ẽr), *n.* a person in charge of a jail or of prisoners.

jal-ap (jal'ăp), *n.* the dried root of a Mexican plant, or a resin obtained from it.

ja-lop-y (jā-lop'i), *n., pl.* -**lop'ies,** [Slang], an old, ramshackle automobile.

jal-ou-sie (jal'ū-si), *n.* a kind of window, door, shutter, etc. made with horizontal wood, metal, or glass slats that can be adjusted.

jam (jam), *n.* 1. a sweet food made by boiling fruit with sugar to a thick mixture. 2. a squeezing or crushing together. 3. [Slang], the state of being in trouble: *v.t.* **jammed, jam'ming,** 1. to squeeze into a small space. 2. to crush. 3. to press in tightly; crowd. 4. to block up by crowding. 5. to cause to be stuck tight. 6. to garble (radio signals, etc.) by broadcasting on the same frequency: *v.i.* 1. to become blocked, stuck, wedged, etc. 2. to become unworkable because of the jamming of a part. 3. to become squeezed into a small space. 4. [Slang], in *Jazz,* to improvize.

jamb (jam), *n.* 1. one of the upright sides of a doorway, window, or fireplace. 2. a piece of leg armor: also **jambe.**

jum-ba-lay-a (jum-bá-lī'á), *n.* a Creole stew made of rice and shrimp, spices, etc.

jam-bo-ree (jam-bô-rē'), *n.* 1. [Informal], a noisy celebration or festivity. 2. a gathering of boy scouts from various areas.

James (jāmz), *n.* a book of the New Testament.

jan-gle (jang'gl), *v.i.* -**gled,** -**gling,** 1. to quarrel or wrangle noisily. 2. to make a discordant sound, as a bell out of tune: *v.t.* 1. to cause to make a discordant or harsh sound. 2. to irritate: *n.* 1. a discordant sound. 2. wrangle; altercation. —**jan'gler,** *n.*

jan-i-tor (jan'i-tẽr), *n.* one who is employed to care for a building, apartments, etc., as in doing general repairs, cleaning, etc. —**jan-i-to'ri-al** (-tôr'i-ál), *adj.*

jan-i-zar-y (jan'i-zer-i), *n., pl.* -**zar-ies,** [often J-], formerly, one of the guards of the Turkish sultan: also **jan'is-sar-y** (-ser-i).

Jan-sen-ism (jan'sn-izm), *n.* the strict beliefs of Cornelis Jansen (1585-1638), Dutch theologian, who taught predestination and that man is wicked by nature but unable to resist God's grace. —**Jan'sen-ist,** *n. & adj.*

Jan-u-ar-y (jan'yoo-wer-i), *n.* the first month of the year, having 31 days.

ja-pan (jā-pan'), *n.* 1. work varnished and lacquered in the Japanese style. 2. a lacquer or varnish giving a hard, glossy finish: *v.t.* -**panned',** -**pan'ning,** to varnish or lacquer with japan.

Jap-a-nese (jap-â-nēz'), *adj.* of or pertaining to Japan, an island country in the Pacific, off the eastern coast of Asia, or its inhabitants or language: *n.* 1. a native or inhabitant of Japan. 2. the language of Japan.

Japanese beetle, a glossy, green beetle that is damaging to crops and ornamental plants, originally from Japan.

jape (jāp), *v.i.* **japed, jap'ing,** 1. to joke; jest. 2. to play tricks: *n.* a joke or trick. —**jap'er-y,** *n., pl.* -**er-ies.**

jar (jär), *n.* 1. an earthenware or glass container with a wide mouth. 2. the amount a jar will hold: also **jar'ful.** 3. a vibration from sudden shock; jolt. 4. a harsh noise. 5. a conflict: *v.i.* **jarred, jar'ring,** 1. to quarrel or clash. 2. to emit a harsh sound. 3. to vibrate from a sudden shock. 4. to have an unpleasant, irritating effect (on one's nerves, etc.): *v.t.* to make vibrate; jolt.

jar-di-niere (jär-dn-ir'), *n.* 1. an ornamental flowerpot or stand for plants. 2. a vegetable garnish for meats.

jar-gon (jär'gŏn), *n.* 1. confused, unintelligible talk. 2. a mixture of two or more languages, especially pidgin. 3. a language or dialect unknown to one. 4. the special vocabulary

---

a in cap, ā in cane, ä in father, å in abet, e in met, ē in be, ê in baker, ê in regent, I in pit, ī in fine, i in manifest, o in hot, ô in horse, ō in bone,

of a group that works together or has a common interest.

jas·mine (jaz'min), *n.* any of several tropical plants with fragrant flowers of white, red, or yellow: also **jas'min.**

jas·per (jas'pēr), *n.* an opaque, colored variety of quartz, polished and made into ornamental articles.

jaun·dice (jôn'dis), *n.* 1. a disorder characterized by abnormal yellowness of the eyeballs, skin, and urine because of bile in the blood. 2. popularly, a disease causing this, as hepatitis. 3. a bitter state of mind caused by jealousy, envy, etc.: *v.t.* **-diced, -dic·ing,** to prejudice through jealousy, envy, etc.

jaunt (jônt), *n.* a short excursion or ramble for pleasure: *v.i.* to roam or ramble; take a short excursion.

jaun·ty (jônt'i), *adj.* **-ti·er, -ti·est,** airy; sprightly; easy and casual. **—jaun'ti·ly,** *adv.* **—jaun'ti·ness,** *n.*

jav·e·lin (jav'lin, 'ē-lin), *n.* a light spear, especially one thrown for distance and skill in a competition.

jaw (jô), *n.* 1. either of the two bony parts of the mouth that hold the teeth and act as frames for the mouth. 2. either of a pair of movable parts that crush or grip something. 3. [Slang], talk, especially idle or boring talk: *v.i.* [Slang], to talk, especially in an idle, boring, or scolding manner: *v.t.* [Slang], to scold.

jaw·bone ('bōn), *n.* a bone of a jaw, especially of a lower jaw: *v.t. & v.i.* **-boned, -bon·ing,** to try to convince or persuade by using the influence of one's high position.

jay (ja), *n.* 1. a brightly colored bird of the crow family. 2. same as **blue jay.**

jay-walk·er (jā'wôk-ēr), *n.* [Informal], one who crosses a street or highway carelessly without attention to traffic regulations. **—jay'walk,** *v.i.* **—jay'walk·ing,** *n.*

jazz (jaz), *n.* 1. a kind of strongly rhythmic, syncopated music, often with improvisation, originated by American Negro musicians. 2. [Slang], pretentious or empty talk: *v.t.* 1. to arrange or play as jazz. 2. [Slang], to enliven (with *up*).

jazz·y ('i), *adj.* **jazz'i·er, jazz'i·est,** 1. of or like jazz. 2. [Slang], showy, animated, exciting, etc. **—jazz'i·ly,** *adv.* **—jazz'i·ness,** *n.*

jeal·ous (jel'ùs), *adj.* 1. careful in guarding 2. anxiously suspicious, as of a rival. 3. envious and resentful. 4. showing envy and resentment. **—jeal'ous·ly,** *adv.*

jeal·ous·y (-i), *n., pl.* **-ous·ies,** 1. the condition of being jealous. 2. a jealous feeling.

jean (jēn), *n.* 1. a durable twilled cotton fabric. 2. *pl.* trousers made of this.

jeep (jēp), *n.* 1. a small, sturdy, military vehicle with a four-wheel drive, used by the U.S. armed forces in World War II. 2. [J-], a similar vehicle now manufactured for civilian use: a trademark.

jeer (jir), *v.i. & v.t.* to scoff (at); speak (to) in a derisive or sarcastic manner: *n.* a scoffing remark or cry; derisive gibe. **—jeer'ing·ly,** *adv.*

Je·ho·vah (ji-hō'và), *n.* God.

je·june (ji-jōōn'), *adj.* 1. not interesting; dull. 2. childish. **—je·june'ly,** *adv.* **—jc·june'ness,** *n.*

je·ju·num (ji-jōō'nùm), *n., pl.* **-na** ('nà), the portion of the small intestine between the duodenum and ileum. **—je·ju'nal,** *adj.*

jell (jel), *v.i.* 1. to come to have the consistency of jelly. 2. to solidify; become clear, as a plan.

jel·ly (jel'i), *n., pl.* **-lies,** 1. the stiffened, gelatinous juice of fruit, meat, etc. after boiling. 2. any semitransparent, soft, resilient substance: *v.t. & v.i.* **-lied, -ly·ing,** to make into or become jelly. **—jel'ly·like,** *adj.*

jel·ly·fish (-fish), *n., pl.* **-fish, -fish·es,** 1. any of several sea animals with tentacles and a body composed of a jellylike substance. 2. [Informal], a person who is irresolute.

jen·ny (jen'i), *n., pl.* **-nies,** 1. a machine for spinning; spinning jenny. 2. the female of some birds. 3. a female donkey.

jeop·ard·ize (jep'ēr-dīz), *v.t.* **-ized, -iz·ing,** to expose to loss or injury; risk failure of; endanger.

jeop·ard·y (-di), *n., pl.* **-ard·ies,** hazard; exposure to great danger, death, etc.

jer·e·mi·ad (jer-ē-mī'àd), *n.* a lamentation or long, woeful complaint.

Jer·e·mi·ah (jer-ē-mī'à), *n.* a book of the Bible.

jerk (jūrk), *v.t.* 1. to give a sudden pull, twist, or push to. 2. to throw with a sudden quick movement. 3. to cut into strips and dry in the sun, as beef. 4. to make and serve (ice cream sodas): *v.i.* 1. to move with a jerk. 2. to twitch: *n.* 1. a sudden quick pull, twist, or push. 2. a spasmodic muscular contraction, usually involuntary. 3. [Slang], a stupid or foolish person.

jer·kin (jūr'kin), *n.* a closefitting vest or jacket worn in the 16th and 17th centuries.

jerk·wa·ter (jūrk'wôt-ēr, 'wät-ēr), *adj.* [Informal], small and insignificant, as a *jerkwater* town.

jerk·y (jūrk'i), *adj.* **jerk'i·er, jerk'i·est,** 1. characterized by spasmodic movement. 2. [Slang], stupid or foolish. **—jerk'i·ly,** *adv.*

jer·ky (jūr'ki), *n.* meat preserved by slicing into strips and drying in the sun.

jer·ry-built (jer'i-bilt), *adj.* constructed hastily and of poor materials.

Jer·sey (jūr'zi), *n., pl.* **-seys,** 1. any one of a breed of dairy cattle of a reddish-brown color. 2. [j-], *a*) a soft, elastic, knitted cloth, *b*) a closefitting, pullover sweater or shirt.

Je·ru·sa·lem artichoke (jê-rōō'sà-lĕm), 1. a tall North American plant of the sunflower family. 2. its potatolike tuber, used as a vegetable.

jes·sa·mine (jes'â-min), *n.* same as **jasmine.**

jest (jest), *n.* 1. a joke; humorous pleasantry. 2. fun; joking. 3. a taunt. 4. a laughingstock: *v.i.* 1. to joke. 2. to jeer.

jest·er ('ēr), *n.* 1. a joker; buffoon. 2. a retainer kept by a medieval prince or noble to amuse him.

Jes·u·it (jezh'oo-wit, jez'-), *n.* a member of a Roman Catholic order, the Society of Jesus, founded in 1534. **—Jes·u·it'ic, Jes·u·it'i·cal,** *adj.* **—Jes'u·it·ism,** *n.*

Je·sus (jē'zùs, 'zùz), *n.* founder of the Chris-

---

tian religion: also called **Jesus Christ, Jesus of Nazareth.**

jet (jet), *n.* 1. a stream of liquid or gas suddenly emitted. 2. a spout or nozzle for emitting a jet. 3. a jet-propelled airplane. 4. a hard, black mineral polished and used in jewelry. 5. a deep, lustrous black: *adj.* 1. having to do with jet propulsion. 2. black: *v.t. & v.i.* **jet′ted, jet′ting,** 1. to shoot or gush out in a stream. 2. to travel by jet airplane.

jet lag, a disruption of the daily body rhythms, associated with high-speed travel by jet airplane to distant time zones.

jet·lin·er (′lin-ẽr), *n.* a commercial jet aircraft for carrying passengers.

jet·port (′pôrt), *n.* a large airport with long runways, for use by jetliners.

jet-pro·pelled (′prŏ-peld″), *adj.* driven by jet propulsion.

jet propulsion, a method of propelling projectiles, airplanes, etc. by causing gases under pressure to be emitted from a vent at the rear.

jet·sam (jet′săm), *n.* part of a ship's cargo thrown into the sea to lighten the ship in case of peril.

jet set, a social set of fashionable people who frequently travel, often by jet, as for pleasure or business.—**jet-set·ter** (′set′ẽr), *n.*

jet stream, high-velocity winds moving from west to east, high above the earth.

jet·ti·son (jet′i-sn), *v.t.* 1. to throw (goods) overboard to lighten a ship or airplane in case of peril. 2. to discard.

jet·ty (jet′i), *n., pl.* **-ties,** 1. a structure extending into the water, used as a pier or as a wall to restrain or direct currents. 2. a projection of a building.

Jew (jōō), *n.* 1. one who is descended or regarded as descended from the ancient Hebrews. 2. one whose religion is Judaism.

jew·el (jōō′ĕl), *n.* 1. a valuable ornament, especially one set with gems. 2. a gem; precious stone. 3. a thing or person very dear to one: *v.t.* **-eled** or **-elled, -el·ing** or **-el·ling,** to adorn or set with jewels.

jew·el·er (-ẽr), *n.* one who makes or deals in jewels: also spelled **jew′el·ler.**

jew·el·ry (jōō′ĕl-ri), *n.* jewels collectively.

Jew·ish (jōō′ish), *adj.* of or pertaining to Jews or Judaism: *n.* [Informal], same as **Yiddish.**—**Jew′ish·ness,** *n.*

Jewish calendar, a calendar used by the Jews in reckoning holidays and history, based on the lunar month: it reckons from the year 3761 B.C., the traditional date of the Creation.

Jew·ry (jōō′ri), *n.* the Jewish people.

jew's-harp (jōōz′härp), *n.* a small, lyre-shaped musical instrument with a thin metal piece held between the teeth and plucked to produce a twanging sound.

jib (jib), *n.* a triangular sail projecting in front of the foremast.

jibe (jib), *v.i.* **jibed, jib′ing,** 1. to shift from one side to the other, as a fore-and-aft sail. 2. to alter course so that a ship's sails jibe. 3. [Informal], to be in agreement.

jibe (jib), *n. & v.t. & v.i.* same as **gibe.**

jif·fy (jif′i), *n., pl.* **-fies,** [Informal], an instant; very short time: also **jiff.**

jig (jig), *n.* 1. a quick, lively dance in triple time, or music for this. 2. a kind of fishing lure. 3. a sieve for separating ores by jigging. 4. a device used to hold work or guide a tool: *v.i. & v.t.* **jigged, jig′ging,** 1. to dance (a jig). 2. to move rapidly back and forth or up and down.

jig·ger (′ẽr), *n.* 1. a small glass, usually holding 1.5 ounces, used to measure liquor. 2. the contents of a jigger. 3. a small sailboat.

jig·gle (jig′l), *v.t. & v.i.* **-gled, -gling,** to move with slight, rapid jerks: *n.* a slight, rapid jerk or a series of these.

jig·saw (jig′sô), *n.* a fine-toothed saw set vertically in a frame, used for cutting ornamental patterns, as in scroll work: also **jig saw:** *v.t.* to cut with a jigsaw.

jigsaw puzzle, a puzzle made by cutting a picture or design on heavy cardboard, wood, etc. into irregular pieces which are to be put back together.

jilt (jilt), *v.t.* to cast aside (a sweetheart or lover) after encouragement.

Jim Crow, [Informal], discrimination against Negroes.—**Jim Crow′ism.**

jim·my (jim′i), *n., pl.* **-mies,** a short, stout iron bar with a sharp, flattened end, used by burglars to pry open windows, etc.: *v.t.* **-mied, -my·ing,** to pry open with a jimmy or something like this.

jim·son weed (jim′sŏn), a poisonous, foul-smelling weed of the nightshade family.

jin·gle (jing′gl), *n.* 1. a sharp, tinkling, metallic sound, as of a little bell or rattle. 2. a verse or syllables, sometimes set to music, that has a simple, light rhythm and repetition of sounds: *v.i. & v.t.* **-gled, -gling,** to make or cause to make jingling sounds.—**jin′gly** (′gli), *adj.*

jin·go (jing′gŏ), *n., pl.* **-goes,** one who favors an aggressive, warlike foreign policy.—**jin′go·ism,** *n.*—**jin′go·ist,** *n.*—**jin·go·is′tic,** *adj.*

jin·ni (ji-nē′, jin′i), *n., pl.* **jinn,** any of a number of good or evil spirits in Moslem mythology who can influence human affairs.

jin·rik·i·sha (jin-rik′shô), *n.* a small, Oriental, two-wheeled carriage with a hood, pulled by one or two men, especially formerly: also spelled **jin·rick′sha.**

jinx (jingks), *n.* [Informal], 1. a person or thing supposed to bring bad luck. 2. a spell of bad luck: *v.t.* [Informal], to bring bad luck to.

jit·ney (jit′ni), *n., pl.* **-neys,** 1. [Old Slang], a nickel. 2. a car or bus carrying passengers for a low fare, originally five cents.

jit·ter·bug (jit′ẽr-bug), *n.* a fast, lively dance for couples in the 1940's: *v.i.* **-bugged, -bugging,** to do this dance.

jit·ters (jit′ẽrz), *n.pl.* [Informal], a highly nervous feeling.

jit·ter·y (′ri), *adj.* [Informal], highly nervous.—**jit′ter·i·ness,** *n.*

jive (jiv), *v.t.* **jived, jiv′ing,** [Slang], to use deceptive or foolish talk: *v.i.* to dance to, or play, jive music: *n.* 1. [Slang], deceptive or

---

a in cap, ā in cane, ä in father, ȧ in abet, e in met, ē in be, ẽ in baker, ê in regent, i in pit, ī in fine, i in manifest, o in hot, ô in horse, ō in bone,

foolish talk. 2. an earlier term for jazz or swing.

Job (jōb), *n.* a book of the Bible.

job (job), *n.* 1. a piece of work done for pay. 2. a chore; task. 3. something being worked on. 4. employment: *adj.* done by the job: *v.t. & v.i.* jobbed, job'bing, 1. to let out for hire. 2. to buy up (goods) and retail. —job'less, *adj.* —job'less·ness, *n.*

job action, refusal by a group of employees (esp. a group forbidden by law to strike) to perform all or part of their duties in an effort to win certain demands.

job·ber ('ẽr), *n.* 1. one who does work by the job. 2. a middleman; one who buys goods in quantity and sells to retailers.

job lot, a collection of various articles for sale as one lot.

jock (jok), *n.* 1. same as jockey. 2. same as jockstrap. 3. [Slang], a male athlete.

jock·ey (jok'i), *n., pl.* -eys, one who rides a horse in a race: *v.t. & v.i.* -eyed, -ey·ing, 1. to cheat; deceive. 2. to maneuver for an advantageous position.

jock·strap (jok'strap), *n.* an elastic belt with a pouch for supporting the genitals, worn by male athletes.

jo·cose (jō-kōs'), *adj.* humorous; joking in a playful manner. —jo·cose'ly, *adv.* —jo·cos'i·ty (-kos'ĭ-ti), *pl.* -ties, jo·cose'ness, *n.*

joc·u·lar (jok'yū-lẽr), *adj.* making jokes; jesting; jovial. —joc·u·lar'i·ty (-lẽr'ĭ-ti), *n., pl.* -ties. —joc'u·lar·ly, *adv.*

joc·und (jok'ŭnd, jō'kŭnd), *adj.* jovial; sportive; genial. —jo·cun·di·ty (jō-kun'dĭ-ti), *n., pl.* -ties. —joc'und·ly, *adv.*

jodh·purs (jod'pẽrz), *n.pl.* riding breeches that fit closely around the lower part of the leg.

Jo·el (jō'ĕl), *n.* a book of the Bible.

jog (jog), *v.t.* jogged, jog'ging, 1. to shake slightly; nudge. 2. to stimulate (the memory): *v.i.* to travel along with a slow trotting motion: *n.* 1. a slight shake or nudge. 2. a slow trotting motion. 3. a projecting or indented section of a line or surface. 4. a sharp change in direction, as of a road. —jog'ger, *n.*

jog·ging (jog'ing), *n.* trotting slowly and steadily as a form of exercise.

jog·gle (jog'l), *v.t. & v.i.* -gled, -gling, to jolt or shake slightly: *n.* a slight jolt.

John (jon), *n.* 1. a book of the New Testament, the fourth Gospel. 2. any one of three other books of the New Testament that were epistles written by the Apostle John, I John, II John, III John.

john (jon), *n.* [Slang], 1. a toilet. 2. [also J-], a prostitute's customer.

John Bull, the English nation or an Englishman personified.

John Doe (dō), a fictitious name used, especially in legal forms, for a person whose name is unknown.

john·ny·cake (jon'i-kāk), *n.* a flat griddlecake made of cornmeal.

join (join), *v.t. & v.i.* 1. to unite; connect; bring or come together (with). 2. to become a member of (a church or club). 3. to take part (*in* an activity, conversation, etc.).

join·er ('ẽr), *n.* 1. a carpenter who finishes interior woodwork. 2. [Informal], one who joins many clubs, associations, etc.

joint (joint), *n.* 1. the place where two or more things join. 2. a place where two bones are joined; articulation of limbs. 3. a large cut of meat with the bone in it. 4. a node where a leaf or branch grows out of a stem. 5. a fissure dividing a rock mass, but with no displacement. 6. [Slang], a cheap bar or restaurant, or an old house, etc. 7. [Slang], a marijuana cigarette: *adj.* 1. common to two or more. 2. united in or sharing: *v.t.* 1. to form with or unite by joints. 2. to cut into joints, as meat.

joint·ly, ('li), *adv.* together; in common.

joint-stock company (joint'stok'), a company with stock that is divided into transferable shares.

joist (joist), *n.* a horizontal timber to which the boards of a floor or laths of a ceiling are fastened: *v.t.* to provide with joists.

joke (jōk), *n.* 1. something said or done to arouse mirth or laughter, as a funny story or a trick played on someone. 2. a thing said or done merely in fun. 3. someone or something to be laughed at: *v.i.* joked, jok'ing, to make jokes. —jok'ing·ly, *adv.*

jok·er (jō'kẽr), *n.* 1. a jester; one who jokes. 2. an extra playing card, used as the highest trump card in some games. 3. a hidden or tricky provision, as in a law or agreement, that makes it different than what it appears to be. 4. [Slang], a fellow: used disparagingly.

jol·li·fi·ca·tion (jol-ĭ-fi-kā'shŭn), *n.* merrymaking; fun or frivolity.

jol·li·ty (jol'ĭ-ti), *n.* the state of being jolly; merriment; fun.

jol·ly (jol'i), *adj.* 1. full of life and mirth; merry. 2. [Informal], joyous; causing happiness: *adv.* [British Informal], very: *v.t. & v.i.* -lied, -ly·ing, [Informal], 1. to treat (a person) in a jocular manner to keep him in a good humor. 2. to make fun of (someone). —jol'li·ly, *adv.* —jol'li·ness, *n.*

jol·ly (jol'i), *n.* a ship's small boat: also jolly boat.

jolt (jōlt), *v.t.* 1. to shake up or jar, as by sudden jerks. 2. a sudden shock: *v.i.* to have a jerky motion: *n.* 1. a sudden jerk or bump. 2. a shock. —jolt'ing·ly, *adv.* —jolt'y, *adj.*

Jo·nah (jō'nă), *n.* 1. a book of the Bible. 2. a person supposed to bring bad luck.

jon·quil (jon'kwil, jong'-), *n.* a species of narcissus with small, yellow flowers.

jo·rum (jōr'ŭm), *n.* a large drinking bowl, or its contents.

josh (josh), *v.t. & v.i.* [Informal], to banter; tease. —josh'ing·ly, *adv.*

Josh·u·a (josh'oo-wă), *n.* a book of the Bible.

joss (jos), *n.* a Chinese idol.

joss house, a Chinese temple.

joss stick, a perfumed stick, burned by the Chinese as incense.

jos·tle (jos'l), *v.t. & v.i.* -tled, -tling, to push against; elbow or shove roughly: *n.* the act of shoving or jostling. —jos'tler, *n.*

jot (jot), *n.* a little bit; the least part: *v.t.* jot'ted, jot'ting, to make a memorandum of (with *down*). —jot'ter, *n.*

ô in dragon, ōō in crude, oo in wool, u in cup, ū in cure, ü in turn, ů in focus, oi in boy, ou in house, th in thin, th in sheathe, g in get, j in joy, y in yet.

joule (jōōl, joul), *n.* a unit of work or energy, equal to ten million ergs.

jounce (jouns), *v.t. & v.i.* **jounced, jounc'ing,** to jolt along with a bounce, as in riding over a rough road: *n.* a jolting bounce. —**jounc'y,** *adj.*

jour·nal (jûr'nl), *n.* **1.** a record of news or events. **2.** a daily newspaper. **3.** a diary. **4.** a bookkeeping record book for entering particular transactions. **5.** a ship's logbook. **6.** the part of the shaft of a machine that rotates against the bearing.

jour·nal·ism (jûr'nl-izm), *n.* **1.** the occupation of gathering news and preparing it for publication or broadcast. **2.** newspapers, magazines, etc. collectively. —**jour'nal·ist,** *n.* —**jour·nal·is'tic,** *adj.*

jour·ney (jûr'ni), *n., pl.* **-neys** passage or travel from one place to another: *v.i.* **-neyed, -ney·ing,** to travel from one place to another. —**jour'ney·er,** *n.*

jour·ney·man (-mǎn), *n., pl.* **-men, 1.** a worker who has learned his trade. **2.** a good, experienced worker, but one who is not outstanding.

joust (joust, just), *n.* a combat with lances between two mounted knights, especially as part of a tournament: *v.i.* to engage in a joust. —**joust'er,** *n.*

jo·vi·al (jō'vi-ǎl), *adj.* convivial; merry; genial and jolly. —**jo·vi·al'i·ty** (-al'i-ti), *n.* —**jo'vi·al·ly,** *adv.*

jowl (joul), *n.* **1.** the lower jaw. **2.** the cheek of a hog. **3.** the head of a fish. **4.** a fleshy part under the jaw, as the wattles of fowl or dewlap of cattle. —**jowl'y,** *adj.* **jowl'i·er, jowl'i·est.**

joy (joi), *n.* **1.** exhilaration of spirits; happiness; delight. **2.** anything causing this: *v.i.* to rejoice. —**joy'less,** *adj.*

joy·ful ('fǔl), *adj.* full of joy; happy. —**joy'ful·ly,** *adv.* —**joy'ful·ness,** *n.*

joy·ous ('ǔs), *adj.* full of joy; happy. —**joy'ous·ly,** *adv.* —**joy'ous·ness,** *n.*

joy ride [Informal], a short ride in a car, often reckless and without the owner's permission. —**joy rider.**

ju·bi·lant (jōō'bl-ǎnt), *adj.* expressing exultation; triumphant. —**ju'bi·lance,** *n.* —**ju'bi·lant·ly,** *adv.*

ju·bi·late (jōō'bi-lāt), *v.i.* **-lat·ed, -lat·ing,** to express exultation; rejoice; shout for joy. —**ju·bi·la'tion,** *n.*

ju·bi·lee (jōō'bi-lē), *n.* **1.** in Jewish history, a year-long celebration traditionally held every 50 years. **2.** a 50th or 25th anniversary. **3.** an occasion or the act of rejoicing; jubilation. **4.** in the *Roman Catholic Church,* a year of special indulgence occurring every 25 years.

Ju·da·ism (jōō'dā-izm), *n.* the Jewish religion. —**Ju·da'ic** (-dā'ik), *adj.*

Ju·da·ize (-īz), *v.i.* **-ized, -iz·ing,** to conform to Jewish rites and traditions: *v.t.* to bring into conformity with Judaism. —**Ju·da·i·za'tion,** *n.*

Ju·das (jōō'dǎs), *n.* a treacherous person; traitor; betrayer.

Jude (jōōd), *n.* a book of the New Testament.

judge (juj), *n.* **1.** the presiding official in a court of law, having authority to hear and determine cases. **2.** one chosen to make a decision about a controversy, determine a winner in a competition, etc. **3.** one who is qualified to decide the merit of something: *v.t. & v.i.* **judged, judg'ing, 1.** to examine and pass judgment (on) in a law court. **2.** to decide on the winner of (a competition) or settle (a controversy). **3.** to come to a conclusion about. **4.** to criticize or condemn. **5.** to think.

judge advocate, *pl.* **judge advocates,** a military officer who acts as prosecutor at a court-martial.

judge advocate general, *pl.* **judge advocates general,** the chief legal officer of the U.S. Army, Navy, or Air Force.

Judg·es (juj'iz), *n.* a book of the Bible.

judg·ment ('ment), *n.* **1.** the act of judging. **2.** a judicial decision; legal order. **3.** the mental faculty of coming to an opinion. **4.** a decision or conclusion. **5.** [J-], God's final trial of mankind; the Last Judgment. Also **judge'ment.** —**judg·men'tal** (-men'tl), *adj.*

Judgment Day, the time of God's final judgment on mankind.

ju·di·ca·to·ry (jōō'di·kǎ-tôr-i), *adj.* of or pertaining to the administration of justice: *n., pl.* **-ries,** a court of law or law courts collectively.

ju·di·ca·ture (-chēr), *n.* **1.** a court of law. **2.** the power, office, etc. of a judge. **3.** judges collectively. **4.** jurisdiction.

ju·di·cial (jōō-dish'ǎl), *adj.* **1.** of or pertaining to courts of law or the administration of justice. **2.** allowed, enforced by, or proceeding from a court. **3.** proper to or like a judge. **4.** unbiased; fair. —**ju·di'cial·ly,** *adv.*

ju·di·ci·ar·y (jōō-dish'i-er-i), *adj.* of judges or courts: *n., pl.* **-ar·ies, 1.** judges collectively. **2.** the branch of government concerned with the administration of civil and criminal justice.

ju·di·cious ('ǔs), *adj.* prudent; showing or using sound judgment. —**ju·di'cious·ly,** *adv.* —**ju·di'cious·ness,** *n.*

ju·do (jōō'dō), *n.* a form of jujitsu taught as a means of self-defense and as a sport.

jug (jug), *n.* **1.** a container for liquids, with a small opening and a handle. **2.** the contents of a jug: also **jug'ful. 3.** [Slang], a jail: *v.t.* **jugged, jug'ging, 1.** to put into a jug. **2.** [Slang], to put into jail.

ju·gate (jōō'gāt, 'git), *adj.* in *Biology,* connected or paired.

Jug·ger·naut (jug'ēr-nôt), *n.* **1.** an incarnation of the Hindu god Vishnu. **2.** [usually j-], any terrible, overpowering force.

jug·gle (jug'l), *v.t.* **-gled, -gling, 1.** to keep (several balls, etc.) in motion in the air at one time by skillful movements of the hands. **2.** to manipulate deceitfully: *v.i.* to toss up balls, etc. and skillfully keep them in motion in the air. —**jug'gler,** *n.* —**jug'gler·y,** *n.*

jug·u·lar (jug'yoo-lēr), *adj.* of the neck or throat: *n.* either of the two large veins in the neck which carry blood from the head: also **jugular vein.**

juice (jōōs), *n.* **1.** the liquid part of a fruit, vegetable, or plant. **2.** a natural liquid of animal tissues or organs. **3.** [Informal], energy. 4. [Slang], *a)* alcoholic liquor. *b)* electricity: *v.t.* juiced, juic'ing, to extract juice from.

juic·er (jōō'sêr), *n.* an appliance or device for extracting juice from fruit.

juic·y (jōō'si), *adj.* juic'i·er, juic'i·est, 1. full of juice. 2. [Informal], *a)* very profitable. *b)* intriguing; interesting, especially because slightly improper or scandalous. —juic'i·ness, *n.*

ju·jit·su (jōō-jit'sōō), *n.* a Japanese method of wrestling in which the opponent's own strength is used against him: also ju·jut'su (-jit'sōō, -jut'-).

ju·jube (jōō'jōōb), *n.* 1. the datelike, edible fruit of a subtropical tree. 2. (jōō'jōō-bi), a fruit-flavored lozenge.

juke·box (jōōk'boks), *n.* a coin-operated electric phonograph: also juke box.

ju·lep (jōō'lêp), *n.* same as mint julep.

ju·li·enne (jōō-li-en'), *n.* a clear meat soup with vegetables cut into strips, etc.: *adj.* cut into strips: said of vegetables, meat, etc.

Ju·ly (jōō-lī', jū-), *n.* the seventh month of the year, having 31 days.

jum·ble (jum'bl), *n.* 1. a confused heap or mass. 2. a ring-shaped cookie: *v.t. & v.i.* -bled, -bling, to throw or be thrown together in a confused heap or mass..

jum·bo (jum'bō), *n., pl.* -bos, a huge person, animal, or thing: *adj.* huge.

jump (jump), *n.* 1. a spring or bound. 2. a distance jumped. 3. a sudden increase, as in prices. 4. an abrupt transition. 5. a sudden, nervous start or twitch: *v.i.* 1. to leap or pass over. 2. to cause to spring or bound. 3. to seize (a mining claim) belonging to another. 4. [Informal], to attack suddenly: *v.i.* 1. to spring forward or upward; leap. 2. to bob; bounce. 3. to rise suddenly. 4. to leap from an aircraft with a parachute. 5. to act or move energetically. 6. [Slang], to be lively.

jump·er (jum'pêr), *n.* 1. a person, animal, or thing that jumps. 2. a wire used to close a break in an electric circuit. 3. a loose jacket or blouse worn by workmen or sailors. 4. a sleeveless dress worn over a blouse or sweater.

jump·y (jum'pi), *adj.* jump'i·er, jump'i·est, easily startled; nervous. —jump'i·ly, *adv.* — jump'i·ness, *n.*

jun·co (jung'kō), *n., pl.* -cos, a small bird with a gray or black head and white tail.

junc·tion (jungk'shün), *n.* 1. the act of being joined; union. 2. a point or place of union, as of railroad lines.

junc·ture ('chêr), *n.* 1. a junction. 2. a point of time. 3. a particular or critical occasion; crisis.

June (jōōn), *n.* the sixth month of the year, having 30 days.

jun·gle (jung'gl), *n.* 1. a dense tropical growth of trees, tall plants, vines, etc., inhabited by predatory animals. 2. [Slang], a place of ruthless struggle or competition. —jun'gly, *adj.*

jun·ior (jōōn'yêr), *adj.* 1. the younger: written

as *Jr.* after the name of a son who has the same name as his father. 2. of a lower or more recent standing: *n.* 1. one who is younger or of a lower standing. 2. a student in the next-to-last year, as of high school or college.

junior college, a college offering two years of studies beyond high school.

ju·ni·per (jōō'ni-pêr), *n.* an evergreen shrub or tree of the cypress family, with berrylike cones used for flavoring gin.

junk (jungk), *n.* 1. originally, old cable or rope used for making mats, oakum, etc. 2. hard, salted meat used by sailors on shipboard. 3. scraps of metal, glass, etc. or old paper or rags. 4. [Informal], rubbish. 5. a Chinese flat-bottomed ship. 6. [Slang], a narcotic drug; especially, heroin: *v.t.* [Informal], to throw away; discard. —junk'y, *adj.* junk'i·er, junk'i·est.

junk bond, [Informal], a speculative interest-bearing certificate, often issued to finance the takeover of a corporation.

jun·ket (jung'kit), *n.* 1. a preparation of milk, sweetened, flavored, and thickened with rennet. 2. a public feast or picnic. 3. an excursion, especially one by an official at public expense: *v.i.* to go on an excursion, especially at public expense. —jun·ket·eer' (-kê-tir'), jun'ket·er, *n.*

junk food, snack food with chemical additives and little food value.

junk·ie, junk·y (jung'ki), *n., pl.* junk'ies, [Slang], a drug addict, especially a heroin addict.

junk·man (jungk'man), *n., pl.* -men, ('men), a dealer in scrap metal, rags, paper, etc.: also junk dealer.

junk·yard ('yärd), *n.* a place for the collection, storage, processing, or sale of junk.

Ju·no (jōō'nō), *n.* the chief goddess in Roman mythology.

jun·ta (hoon'ta, jun'-), *n.* 1. a Spanish or Latin-American legislative assembly or council. 2. a group of military men in power after a coup d'état: also jun·to (jun'tō), *pl.* -tos.

Ju·pi·ter (jōō'pi-têr), *n.* 1. the chief god in Roman mythology. 2. the fifth planet in distance from the sun and the largest in the solar system.

ju·pon (jōō'pon), *n.* a tunic worn over armor.

Ju·ras·sic (joo-ras'ik), *n.* a period of the Mesozoic Era, in which the dinosaurs flourished.

ju·rat (joor'at), *n.* a certificate added to an affidavit stating by whom and when the affidavit was made.

ju·rid·i·cal (joo-rid'i-kl), *adj.* of or pertaining to law, judicial proceedings, or jurisprudence.

ju·ris·con·sult (joor-is-kon'sult', -kon'sült), *n.* one learned in law; jurist.

ju·ris·dic·tion (joor-is-dik'shün), *n.* 1. legal authority. 2. extent of power or authority. 3. the region over which any authority extends. —ju·ris·dic'tion·al, *adj.*

ju·ris·pru·dence (joor-is-prōō'dns), *n.* 1. the science or philosophy of law. 2. a division of law, as medical *jurisprudence.*

ju·rist (joor'ist), *n.* 1. one skilled in legal science. 2. a writer in the field of law. 3. a judge.

ju·ror (joor'ēr), *n.* a member of a jury: also **ju'ry·man**, *pl.* -men.

ju·ry (joor'i), *n., pl.* -ries, 1. a group of people chosen according to law and sworn to inquire into and decide on evidence in a given law case. 2. a committee of experts selected to award prizes, etc., as at a public exhibition.

ju·ry (joor'i), *adj.* for emergency or temporary use, as a *jury* mast.

jus (jus, yōōs), *n., pl.* **ju·ra** (joor'ā, yōō'rā), 1. the whole body of law. 2. a system of law. 3. a right.

just (just), *adj.* 1. conformable to law; lawful. 2. upright. 3. impartial; fair. 4. exact; accurate. 5. reasonable: *adv.* 1. exactly; precisely. 2. nearly; almost. 3. barely. 4. [Informal], really. —**just'ness,** *n.*

jus·tice (jus'tis), *n.* 1. the quality of being just; impartiality. 2. rectitude in dealing with others. 3. the administration of law, especially in assigning deserved reward or punishment. 4. a judge or magistrate.

justice of the peace, a local magistrate who may pass on minor cases, perform marriages, etc.

jus·ti·ci·ar·y (jus·tish'i-er-i), *n., pl.* -ar·ies, a judge.

jus·ti·fy (jus'ti-fī), *v.t.* -fied, -fy·ing, 1. to show or prove to be just or right. 2. in *Theology,* to vindicate or pardon. 3. to provide grounds for. 4. to adjust type by proper spacing. —**jus·ti·fi'a·ble,** *adj.* —**jus·ti·fi'a·bly,** *adv.* —**jus·ti·fi·ca'tion,** *n.*

just·ly (just'li), *adv.* 1. in a just manner. 2. accurately. 3. deservedly.

jut (jut), *v.i. & v.t.* jut'ted, jut'ting, to project beyond the main body: *n.* a projection.

jute (jōōt), *n.* 1. a strong fiber of an Indian plant used for making rope, burlap, mats, etc. 2. the plant.

ju·ve·nes·cent (jōō-vē-nes'nt), *adj.* becoming young; growing young. —**ju·ve·nes'cence,** *n.*

ju·ve·nile (jōō'vē-nīl, -nil), *adj.* 1. youthful; immature. 2. characteristic of or suitable to young people: *n.* 1. a young person. 2. an actor or actress who plays youthful roles. 3. a book for children. —**ju·ve·nil'i·ty** (-nil'i-ti), *n., pl.* -ties.

juvenile delinquency, antisocial or unlawful behavior by young people, usually 18 or younger. —**juvenile delinquent.**

jux·ta-, a combining form meaning *near, in close proximity.*

jux·ta·po·si·tion (juk-stă-pô-zi'shŭn), *n.* the placing of a person or thing close to, or side by side with, another person or thing; contiguity. —**jux·ta·pose'** (-pōz'), *v.t.* -posed', -pos'ing.

K

K, k (kā), **K's, k's, 1.** the eleventh letter of the English alphabet. **2.** the sound of this letter, as in *kite*. **3.** a type or impression of *K* or *k*.

K (kā), *adj.* shaped like *K*: *n.* an object shaped like *K*.

ka (kä), *n.* in ancient Egyptian religion, the spirit or soul, which resided in the body and survived after death.

Ka·a·ba (kä'bä, kä'ä-bä), *n.* the square building at Mecca containing a sacred black stone: Moslems turn toward it when praying.

ka·bob (kå-bäb'), *n.* same as kebab.

kad·dish (käd'ish), *n.* **1.** a hymn of praise recited as part of the Jewish daily service. **2.** a form of this hymn recited by mourners.

ka·di (kä'di, kä'-), *n.* same as cadi.

kaf (käf, kôf), *n.* the eleventh letter of the Hebrew alphabet, corresponding to English *K*, *k*.

kaf·fee·klatsch (kä'fä-kläch', kô'-fi-kläch), *n.* [German], a meeting of housewives during the day to drink coffee and talk.

Kaf·fir (kaf'ẽr), *n.* **1.** a member of any of several Bantu tribes of southeast Africa: often a term of contempt. **2.** [k-], same as kaffir.

kaf·ir (kaf'ẽr), *n.* **1.** a grain sorghum with juicy, leafy stalks: also **kafir corn**. **2.** [K-], same as Kaffir.

kaf·tan (kaf'tån, käf-tän'), *n.* same as caftan.

ka·go (kä'gō), *n.* a Japanese palanquin, carried on a pole by two bearers.

kai·ak (kī'ak), *n.* same as kayak.

Kai·ser (kī'zẽr), *n.* the title of the former emperors of Germany and Austria.

ka·ka (kä'kä), *n.* a New Zealand parrot, having greenish-brown feathers with red markings: it is easily taught to talk and mimic.

ka·ka·po (kä-kä-pō'), *n., pl.* -pos', a large, nocturnal parrot of New Zealand having green and yellow feathers: it is nearly flightless.

kale (kāl), *n.* a cabbage with open, curled leaves.

ka·lei·do·scope (kå-lī'dô-skōp), *n.* an optical instrument in which bits of colored glass in a small tube, by an arrangement of mirrors, appear in symmetrical patterns. —**ka·lei·do·scop'ic** (-skäp'ik), *adj.* —**ka·lei·do·scop'i·cal·ly**, *adv.*

kal·ends (kal'ĕndz), *n.pl.* same as calends.

Ka·li (kä'li), *n.* a Hindu goddess of life and death.

kal·mi·a (kal'mi-å), *n.* a group of North American evergreen shrubs with showy, pink or white flowers, as the mountain laurel.

Kal·muck, Kal·muk (kal'muk), *n.* any of a group of Mongol peoples living chiefly in a region north of the Caspian Sea: also **Kal'-myk** ('mik).

kal·so·mine (kal'sô-mīn), *n. & v.t.* -mined, -min·ing, same as calcimine.

Ka·ma (kä'mä), *n.* the Hindu god of love.

Ka·ma·su·tra (kä-mä-sōō'trä), *n.* an ancient Hindu love manual.

ka·mi (kä'mi), *n., pl.* -mi, [Japanese], in *Shintoism*, a sacred power from the spirits of the dead, or from deities.

kam·pong (käm'pông), *n.* a small Malay village.

Ka·nak·a (kå-nak'å, kan'å-kä), *n.* **1.** a Hawaiian. **2.** a Polynesian.

kan·ga·roo (kang-gå-rōō'), *n., pl.* -roos', -roo', a herbivorous, marsupial mammal peculiar to Australia, having short forelegs and long, powerful hind legs with which it leaps.

ka·o·lin (kä'ô-lin), *n.* a fine white clay used in making porcelain and in medicine for diarrhea.

kaph (käf, kôf), *n.* same as kaf.

ka·pok (kä'pok), *n.* the silky down from around the seeds of a tropical tree, used for stuffing cushions and life preservers, and for insulation.

kap·pa (kap'å), *n.* the tenth letter of the Greek alphabet, corresponding to the English *K*, *k*.

ka·put (kå-poot', -pŏŏt'), *adj.* [German], [Slang], lost, destroyed, ruined, etc.

kar·a·kul (kar'å-kŭl), *n.* **1.** the curly fur from the hides of newborn lambs of a broadtailed sheep of central Asia; caracul. **2.** the sheep itself.

kar·at (kar'åt), *n.* one 24th part (of pure gold).

ka·ra·te (kå-rät'i), *n.* a system of self-defense without the use of weapons, that originated in Japan: the defender smites the attacker with the edge of the open hand, the elbow, knee, or foot.

kar·ma (kär'må), *n.* **1.** in *Buddhism & Hinduism*, the inevitable result in a future reincarnation of the acts done in the present life. **2.** fate: considered to be a loose usage. —**kar'mic**, *adj.*

kart (kärt), *n.* a small, low, motor vehicle for one person, used for racing (**karting**) or recreation.

kat·i·on (kat'ī-ŏn), *n.* same as cation.

ka·ty·did (kāt'i-did), *n.* a green, arboreal insect with long antennae, related to the grasshopper: the male makes a shrill sound.

kau·ri (kou'ri), *n.* **1.** a tall, New Zealand pine tree. **2.** its fine wood. **3.** a resin from this tree, used in varnishes, etc.

ka·va (kä'vä), *n.* **1.** a plant of the pepper family. **2.** an intoxicating drink made from its roots.

kay·ak (kī'ak), *n.* an Eskimo canoe made by covering a framework completely with seal-skins, leaving only an opening in the middle for the paddler.

kay·o (kā'ō'), *v.t.* **kay'oed'**, **kay'o'ing**, [Slang],

ŏ in drag*o*n, ōō in cr*u*de, ๐๐ in w*oo*l, u in c*u*p, ū in c*u*re, ū in t*u*rn, u in f*o*cus, oi in b*o*y, ou in h*ou*se, th in *th*in, t*h* in hea*th*e, g in *g*et, j in *j*oy, y in *y*et.

to knock (someone) unconscious in boxing: *n.* [Slang], a knockout in boxing.

ka·zat·sky, ka·zat·ski (kä·zät'ski), *n., pl.* **-kies,** a Russian folk dance in which a man kicks out each of his legs alternately while in a squatting position.

ke·a (kā'ä, kē'ä), *n.* a green New Zealand parrot that attacks sheep.

ke·bab (kē·bäb'), *n.* small pieces of seasoned meat broiled on a skewer, usually along with vegetables.

kedge (kedj), *n.* a light anchor dropped at some distance from a ship: the ship is moved by hauling on a rope fastened to the anchor: also **kedge anchor:** *v.t. & v.i.* **kedged, kedg'ing,** to move (a ship) along in this fashion.

keel (kēl), *n.* 1. the chief and lowest timber of a ship, extending from stem to stern and supporting the whole frame. 2. [Poetic] a ship: *v.t.* 1. to furnish with a keel. 2. to turn (a ship) over so as to turn up its keel.

keel·boat ('bōt), *n.* a shallow, covered freight boat, formerly used on rivers.

keel·haul ('hôl), *v.t.* 1. to drag under water beneath the keel of a ship from one side to the other: formerly, a naval punishment or torture. 2. to reprimand sternly.

keel·son (kel'sn, kēl'-), *n.* a beam, set of timbers, or metal plates fastened on the floor timbers over the keel of a ship to strengthen its structure.

keen (kēn), *adj.* 1. sharp; able to cut easily. 2. piercing. 3. eager; much interested. 4. acute; shrewd. 5. intense: *n.* in Ireland, a wailing for the dead; dirge: *v.t. & v.i.* in Ireland, to wail for (the dead). —**keen'ly,** *adv.* —**keen'ness,** *n.*

keep (kēp), *v.t.* **kept, keep'ing,** 1. to have the care of; guard; preserve. 2. to provide for. 3. to maintain. 4. to employ; have in one's service. 5. to set down regularly in writing. 6. to observe; celebrate. 7. to conduct; manage. 8. to hold back. 9. to conceal. 10. to detain. 11. to confine: *v.i.* 1. to remain in any state or condition. 2. to last. 3. to persist. 4. to refrain: *n.* 1. subsistence; food and shelter. 2. the stronghold or donjon of a medieval castle. 3. a fort or stronghold.

keep·er ('ēr), *n.* 1. a guard, as of prisoners. 2. one who cares for animals. 3. a guardian. 4. a custodian.

keep·ing ('ing), *n.* 1. care; custody; charge. 2. subsistence. 3. observance. 4. harmony; congruity. 5. retention.

keep·sake ('sāk), *n.* something kept as a reminder of the giver; memento.

keg (keg), 1. a small barrel. 2. a unit of weight for nails, equal to 100 pounds.

keg·ler (keg'lēr), *n.* a bowler.

kel·ep (kel'ép), *n.* a Central American ant which feeds on insects.

kelp (kelp), *n.* 1. a large, coarse, brown seaweed. 2. the calcined ashes of this, from which iodine is obtained.

kel·pie, kel·py (kel'pi), *n., pl.* **-pies,** a malevolent water spirit of Gaelic folklore, supposed to take the form of a horse and drown people.

Kelt (kelt), *n.* same as Celt.

ken (ken), *n.* view; knowledge: *v.t.* **kenned, ken'ning,** [Scottish], to know.

ke·naf (kē·naf'), *n.* 1. a tropical plant of Asia. 2. its coarse fiber, much like jute.

Ken·dal (ken'dl), *n.* 1. a coarse, woolen, green cloth. 2. the color: also Kendal green.

ken·nel (ken'l), *n.* 1. a house for a dog; doghouse. 2. a place for breeding or keeping dogs. 3. a pack of dogs: *v.t.* **-neled** or **-nelled, -nel·ing** or **-nel·ling,** to put or keep in a kennel: *v.i.* to live or take shelter in a kennel.

ke·no (kē'nō), *n.* a gambling game resembling bingo.

ke·no·sis (ki·nō'sis), *n.* in *Theology,* the act of humility of Jesus, as Son of God, in taking on human form. —**ke·not'ic** (-not'ik), *adj.*

kep·i (kep'i, kā'pi), *n., pl.* **kep'is,** a French military cap with a stiff visor and round, flat top.

kept (kept), past tense and past participle of **keep:** *adj.* financially supported by a lover.

ker·a·tin (ker'ät·n), *n.* a tough, fibrous protein that goes to make up the principal substance of horn, nails, hair, etc. —**ke·rat·i·nous** (kē·rat'n·ŭs), *adj.*

ker·a·to·sis (ker·ä·tō'sis), *n., pl.* **-ses** ('sēz), 1. a skin disease marked by horny growths. 2. any horny growth on the skin, as a wart.

kerb (kûrb), *n.* British form of curb.

ker·chief (kûr'chif), *n.* 1. a square cloth worn over the head or around the neck. 2. a handkerchief. —**ker'chiefed** ('chift), *adj.*

ker·mes (kûr'mēz), *n.* 1. the purple-red dye made from the dried bodies of certain scale insects. 2. these insects. 3. an evergreen oak tree on which kermes insects are found: also kermes oak.

ker·mis, ker·mess (kûr'mis), *n.* 1. in the Netherlands, Belgium, etc., an outdoor festival or fair. 2. any somewhat similar entertainment, usually held for charity.

kern (kûrn), *n.* 1. a projecting part of a letter on a piece of type. 2. a medieval Irish or Scottish foot soldier: also kerne.

ker·nel (kûr'nl), *n.* 1. a grain or seed. 2. the inner, usually edible part of a nut, pit, etc. 3. essence.

ker·o·sene (ker'ō·sēn), *n.* a thin oil distilled from petroleum, used as a fuel, etc.: also spelled kerosine.

Ker·ry (ker'i), *n., pl.* **-ries,** any one of a breed of small, black dairy cattle.

ker·sey (kûr'zi), *n., pl.* **-seys,** a coarse, lightweight cloth of wool and cotton, often ribbed.

ker·sey·mere (-mir), *n.* same as cassimere.

kes·trel (kes'trēl), *n.* a small, old-world falcon that can hover in the air against the wind.

ketch (kech), *n.* a two-masted, fore-and-aft rigged sailing vessel.

ketch·up (kech'ŭp), *n.* a sauce prepared from tomatoes, onions, salt, etc.

ket·tle (ket'l), *n.* 1. a metallic vessel for boiling liquids. 2. a teakettle.

ket·tle·drum (-drum), *n.* a percussion instrument consisting of a hollow hemisphere of copper or brass and a parchment top stretched tight.

---

a in cap, ä in cane, ä in father, å in abet, e in met, ē in be, ē in baker, ĕ in regent, i in pit, ī in fine, i in manifest, o in hot, ô in horse, ō in bone,

kev, Kev (kev), *n., pl.* **kev, Kev,** a thousand electron-volts.

key (kē), *n., pl.* **keys,** 1. a portable instrument, usually of metal, for operating a lock. 2. any of certain instruments or devices by which something is turned, secured, or operated. 3. a set of answers, explanatory symbols, etc. used in connection with something else, as a quiz. 4. the pitch of the voice in singing or speaking; also, the tonality of a music scale. 5. any overall tone or style. 6. a reef or low island: *adj.* controlling; essential; important: *v.t.* **keyed, key′ing,** 1. to fasten or lock with a key. 2. to provide with a key. 3. to regulate the tone or pitch of.

key·board (′bôrd), *n.* 1. the row or rows of keys of a piano, typewriter, computer terminal, etc. 2. a musical instrument with a keyboard: *v.t. & v.i.* to write (text) or input (data) by means of a keyboard. —**key′board·er,** *n.*

key club, a private nightclub or the like, each member having his own key.

key·hole (′hōl), *n.* a hole into which a key is inserted to open or close a lock.

key·note (′nōt), *n.* 1. the basic note of a diatonic scale; tonic. 2. the basic idea or ruling principle, as of a policy: *v.t.* **-not′ed, -not′ing,** 1. to give the keynote of. 2. to give the keynote speech at. —**key′not·er,** *n.*

keynote speech, a speech, as at a political rally, giving the main line of policy: also **keynote address.**

key punch, a machine, operated by keyboard, that records data by punching holes into cards for use in data processing.

key·stone (kē′stōn), *n.* 1. the central stone of an arch. 2. a part or thing holding associated parts or things together.

key·stroke (′strōk), *n.* any of the strokes made in operating a keyboard.

kha·ki (kak′i, kä′ki), *n., pl.* **-kis,** 1. a dull yellowish-brown. 2. a cloth so colored, of strong, twilled wool or cotton. 3. *often pl.* a khaki uniform or trousers.

khan (kän, kan), *n.* 1. a title given Genghis Khan, medieval Mongol conqueror, and his successors. 2. a title given various officials in Iran, Afghanistan, etc. 3. in certain Eastern countries, a caravansary.

khaph (khäf, khôf), *n.* same as **kaf.**

khe·dive (kĕ-dēv′), *n.* the title of the Turkish viceroys of Egypt, 1867-1914.

khet, kheth (khet), *n.* same as **het.**

kib·butz (ki-bōōts′, -boots′), *n., pl.* **kib·but·zim** (kē-bōō-tsēm′), an Israeli collective settlement, especially a farm.

kib·itz (kib′its), *v.i.* [Informal], to act as a kibitzer.

kib·itz·er (-ēr), *n.* [Informal], an onlooker at a card game, especially when offering advice.

ki·bosh (kī′bosh, ki-bosh′), *n.* [Slang], originally, nonsense: now usually in **put the kibosh on,** to squelch; end; veto.

kick (kik), *n.* 1. a blow with the foot. 2. a movement or thrust of the foot, as in dancing or swimming. 3. a recoil or jolt, as of a gun being fired. 4. [Informal], a complaint:

objection. 5. [Informal], a pleasurably stimulating effect. 6. a kicked football: *v.i.* 1. to strike, thrust, or shove with or as with the foot. 2. to move, drive, force, etc. thus. 3. to score (a gcal or point in football) by kicking. 4. [Slang], to quit (a drug, habit, etc.): *v.i.* 1. to make a kick with or as with the foot or feet. 2. to recoil, as a gun being fired. 3. [Informal], to make an objection or objections; complain. 4. in *Football,* to kick the ball.

kick·back (′bak), *n.* 1. [Informal], a sharp reaction. 2. [Slang], a giving back of part of money received as payment, commission, etc., as through a previous understanding; also, the money returned.

kick·er (′ēr), *n.* 1. one that kicks. 2. [Slang], an odd twist, hidden difficulty, surprise, etc.

kick·off (′ôf), *n.* 1. in *Football,* a place kick putting the ball into play, as at the beginning of each half. 2. a launching of a political campaign, fund-raising drive, etc.

kick·stand (′stand), *n.* a pivoted metal bar that can be kicked down to support a bicycle, etc. in an upright position.

kick·y (kik′ē), *adj.* **-i·er, -i·est,** [Slang], 1. fashionable. 2. exciting.

kid (kid), *n.* 1. a young goat. 2. leather made from the skin of young goats. 3. [Informal], a child or young person: *adj.* 1. made of kid, as gloves. 2. [Informal], younger, as my *kid* sister: *v.t. & v.i.* **kid′ded, kid′ding,** [Informal], to deceive, fool, tease, etc. in a playful way.

kid·dy, kid·die (′i), *n., pl.* **-dies,** [Informal], a child.

kid·nap (kid′nap), *v.t.* **-napped** or **-naped, -napping** or **-nap·ing,** to seize and hold or carry off (a person) against his will, by force or fraud, often for ransom. —**kid′nap·per, kid′nap·er,** *n.*

kid·ney (kid′ni), *n., pl.* **-neys,** 1. either of a pair of glandular organs that separate waste products from the blood and excrete them as urine. 2. the kidney of an animal, used as food. 3. temperament; disposition. 4. sort; kind.

kidney bean, the kidney-shaped seed of the common garden bean.

kidney stone, a hard mineral concretion of varying size, sometimes formed in a kidney.

kiel·ba·sa (kēl-bä′sä), *n., pl.* **-si** (′sē), **-sas,** a kind of Polish sausage flavored with garlic and smoked.

kill (kil), *v.t.* 1. to deprive of life; slay; destroy. 2. to defeat or veto (legislation). 3. to pass (time) more or less aimlessly. 4. to stop the operation of; turn off. 5. to lessen, deaden, disguise, or muffle. 6. to halt the publication of. 7. [Informal], to amuse, surprise, etc. greatly; also, to pain greatly, weary, etc. 8. [Slang], to finish off (something drinkable, especially liquor): *n.* 1. a killing. 2. something killed. —**kill′er,** *n.*

kill·deer (kil′dir), *n., pl.* **-deers,** **deer,** a small North American bird of the plover family, with a high, piercing cry: also **kill′dee** (′dē).

killer whale, a large dolphin that hunts in packs and preys on large fish, seals, etc.

kill-joy (kil'joi), *n.* one that dampens or completely spoils others' fun.

kiln (kil, kiln), *n.* a heated chamber in which to dry or bake bricks, pottery, etc.

ki-lo (kē'lō, kil'ō), *n., pl.* -los, short for kilogram or kilometer.

kil-o-, a combining form meaning *a thousand*.

kil-o-cy-cle (kil'ō-si-kl), *n.* former name for kilohertz.

kil-o-gram (-gram), *n.* a unit of weight and mass, equal to 1,000 grams (2.2046 pounds).

kil-o-hertz (-hûrts), *n., pl.* -hertz, one thousand hertz.

kil-o-li-ter (-lēt-ēr), *n.* a unit of capacity, equal to 1,000 liters, or one cubic meter (264.18 gallons, or 1,308 cubic yards).

ki-lo-me-ter (ki-lom'ē-tēr, kil'ō-mēt-ēr), *n.* a unit of length or distance, equal to 1,000 meters (3,280.8 feet or about 5/8 mile).

kil-o-watt (kil'ō-wät), *n.* a unit of electrical power, equal to 1,000 watts.

kilt (kilt), *n.* a pleated tartan skirt reaching to the knees, sometimes worn by men of the Scottish Highlands.

kil-ter (kil'tēr), *n.* [Informal], good condition; proper order.

ki-mo-no (ki-mō'nō, -nō), *n., pl.* -nos, 1. the traditional loose outer robe of the Japanese. 2. a woman's dressing gown similar to this.

kin (kin), *n.* relatives; family: *adj.* related, as by blood.

-kin (kin), a suffix meaning *little*.

kind (kind), *adj.* 1. benevolent, sympathetic, gentle, indulgent, etc. 2. cordial: *n.* 1. a natural group or division. 2. essential character. 3. variety; sort.

kin-der-gar-ten (kin'dēr-gär-tn), *n.* a class preparatory to first grade, developing children's skills by games, music, etc. — **kin'der-gart-ner, kin'der-gar-ten-er** (-gärt-nēr), *n.*

kind-heart-ed (kind'här'tid), *adj.* kind.

kin-dle (kin'dl), *v.t. & v.i.* -dled, -dling, 1. to start burning. 2. to get aroused or excited. 3. to brighten.

kin-dling ('dling), *n.* easily ignitable material used to get a fire burning.

kind-ly (kind'li), *adj.* -li-er, -li-est, 1. kind; benevolent. 2. agreeable; pleasant: *adv.* 1. in a kind way. 2. favorably. 3. please. —**kind'li-ness,** *n.*

kind-ness (-nis), *n.* 1. the state, quality, or habit of being kind. 2. a kind act.

kin-dred (kin'drid), *n.* relatives; kin: *adj.* alike in nature or qualities.

kine (kin), *n.pl.* [Archaic], cows; cattle.

kin-e-mat-ics (kin-ē-mat'iks), *n.* the science of pure motion, without reference to force or mass. —**kin-e-mat'ic, kin-e-mat'i-cal,** *adj.*

ki-net-ic (ki-net'ik), *adj.* 1. of or from motion. 2. energetic or dynamic.

ki-net-ics ('iks), *n.* same as **dynamics** (sense 1).

king (king), *n.* 1. a male sovereign or ruler; monarch. 2. a man especially distinguished in some field. 3. something supreme in its class. 4. a piece or card representing a king in a game: *adj.* chief, as in size.

king cobra, a large, very poisonous snake of India.

king-dom ('dōm), *n.* 1. a territory ruled by a king or queen. 2. a sphere of action, influence, etc.; domain. 3. any one of the three primary classifications of natural objects (animal, vegetable, mineral).

king-fish-er ('fish-ēr), *n.* a bright-colored, short-tailed bird with a large, crested head and a large, strong beak.

King James Version, same as **Authorized Version.**

king-ly (king'li), *adj.* -li-er, -li-est, of or fit for a king. —**king'li-ness,** *n.*

Kings (kingz), *n.* 1. either of two books of the Bible, I Kings and II Kings. 2. any one of four books of the Douay Bible: I Samuel, II Samuel, I Kings, II Kings.

kink (kingk), *n.* 1. a twist, bend, etc., as in a wire. 2. a painful muscle spasm or cramp. 3. an eccentricity; quirk. 4. a difficulty or defect, as in a plan: *v.i. & v.t.* to form a kink or kinks.

kin-ka-jou (king'kā-jōō), *n.* a nocturnal, arboreal, raccoonlike mammal of Central and South America: it has a long, prehensile tail.

kink-y (king'ki), *adj.* kink'i-er, kink'i-est, 1. full of kinks. 2. [Slang], eccentric.

ki-no (kē'nō), *n.* an astringent gum obtained from certain tropical plants.

kin-ship (kin'ship), *n.* relationship.

kins-man (kinz'mán), *n., pl.* -men, a relative; especially, a male relative. —**kins'wom-an** ('woom-án), *n.fem., pl.* -wom-en ('wim-ĕn).

ki-osk (kē'osk, ki-osk'), *n.* 1. in Turkey and Persia, a summerhouse or open pavilion. 2. any of various similar structures, as a bandstand, newsstand, or subway entrance.

kip (kip), 1. the untanned skin of a calf, lamb, etc. 2. a unit of weight, equal to 1,000 pounds. 3. the monetary unit of Laos.

kip-per (kip'ēr), *n.* 1. any of certain male saltwater fishes, especially a salmon, at or just after spawning. 2. a salmon, herring, etc. that has been cleaned, salted, and dried or smoked: *v.t.* to cure (salmon, herring, etc.) by cleaning, salting, and drying or smoking.

kirk (kûrk, kirk), *n.* [Scottish & North English], a church.

kir-tle (kûr'tl), *n.* [Archaic], 1. a man's tunic or coat. 2. a woman's dress or skirt.

kis-met (kiz'met, kis'-), *n.* fate.

kiss (kis), *n.* 1. an indication or communication of love, affection, desire, salutation, etc. made by touching, pressing, or caressing with the lips. 2. any slight touch or contact. 3. any of various candies: *v.t.* 1. to touch, press, or caress with the lips; give a kiss or kisses to. 2. to touch lightly: *v.i.* to kiss someone or something.

kiss-er ('ēr), *n.* 1. one that kisses. 2. [Slang], the mouth or face.

kit (kit), *n.* 1. a set of equipment; outfit. 2. a container for this.

kitch-en (kich'ĕn), *n.* a room for preparing and cooking food.

---

a in cap, ā in cane, ä in father, à in abet, e in met, ē in be, ē in baker, ē in regent, i in pit, ī in fine, i in manifest, o in hot, ō in horse, ō in bone,

kitch·en·ette (kich-ĕ-net′), *n.* a little kitchen or a small area used as a kitchen.

kite (kit), *n.* 1. any of various long-winged, fork-tailed birds of the hawk family. 2. a very light framework, typically of thin wooden strips and paper, attached to a long string and designed to sail up into the air by wind pressure. 3. a commercial paper having no funds deposited for it but used to get money or credit: *v.t.* **kit′ed, kit′ing,** 1. to issue as a kite (sense 3). 2. to make soar like a kite: *v.i.* 1. to get money or credit by using a kite (sense 3). 2. to soar or move like a kite.

kith (kith), *n.* friends, acquaintances, or neighbors: now only in the phrase **kith and kin,** relatives.

kitsch (kich), *n.* pretentious but shallow popular art, writing, etc. —**kitsch′y,** *adj.*

kit·ten (kit′n), *n.* a young cat.

kit·ten·ish (-ish), *adj.* playful like a kitten; often, coy.

kit·ty (kit′i), *n., pl.* **-ties,** 1. a kitten or, as a pet name, a cat. 2. the stakes in a poker game. 3. any money pooled.

kit·ty-cor·nered (kit′i-kôr-nērd), *adj. & adv.* same as **cater-cornered:** also **kit′ty-cor·ner.**

ki·wi (kē′wi), *n., pl.* **-wis,** a flightless bird of New Zealand with undeveloped wings and hairlike feathers.

Klan (klan), *n.* 1. short for **Ku Klux Klan.** 2. a Ku Klux Klan chapter.

Klans·man (klanz′mǎn), *n., pl.* **-men,** a member of the Ku Klux Klan.

klatch, klatsch (klǎch, klach), *n.* [Informal], an informal gathering, as to chat.

Klax·on (klak′sn), *n.* 1. a kind of loud, shrill electric horn: a trademark. 2. [k-], such a horn.

Klee·nex (klē′neks), *n.* 1. soft tissue used as a handkerchief, facial tissue, etc.: a trademark. 2. [occasionally k-], a piece of such paper.

klep·to·ma·ni·a (klep-tō-mā′ni-ǎ), *n.* a persistent, strong tendency to steal, unprompted by need. —**klep·to·ma′ni·ac,** *n.*

klieg light (klēg), a very bright, hot arc light used to light motion-picture sets: also spelled **kleig.**

klutz (kluts), *n.* [Slang], 1. a clumsy, awkward person. 2. a stupid person.

knack (nak), *n.* a more or less instinctive ability or skill required to do something indicated; special dexterity.

knack·wurst (näk′wŭrst), *n.* a thick, highly seasoned sausage.

knap·sack (nap′sak), *n.* a leather or canvas traveling case carried on the back.

knap·weed (nap′wēd), *n.* any one of certain weedy plants, especially one having heads of rose-purple flowers.

knave (nāv), *n.* 1. [Archaic], a male servant; also, a lowly man. 2. a rogue; rascal. 3. in a pack of cards, the jack. —**knav′ish,** *adj.*

knav·er·y (′ēr-i), *n., pl.* **-er·ies,** roguery.

knead (nēd), *v.t.* 1. to mix and work (dough, clay, etc.) by folding, pressing, and squeezing. 2. to massage. 3. to make by kneading. —**knead·er,** *n.*

knee (nē), *n.* 1. the articulation of the leg and thigh bones. 2. any similar joint. 3. something kneelike. 4. the part of a trouser leg, stocking, etc. covering the knee: *v.t.* **kneed, knee′ing,** to hit or touch with the knee.

knee breeches, same as **breeches** (sense 1).

knee-cap (′kap), *n.* a movable bone on the forepart of the human knee; patella.

kneel (nēl), *v.i.* **knelt** or **kneeled, kneel′ing,** to bend, or fall upon, the knee or knees.

knee-jerk (′jŭrk), *adj.* [Informal], characterized by or reacting with an automatic, predictable response.

knee-pad (nē′pad), *n.* a protective pad worn over the knee, as by a basketball player.

knell (nel), *v.i. & v.t.* to sound or toll, as a funeral bell: *n.* 1. the sound of a bell so struck. 2. an omen, as of death.

knelt (nelt), alternate past tense and past participle of **kneel.**

knew (nōō, nyōō), past tense of **know.**

Knick·er·bock·er (nik′ēr-bok-ēr), *n.* 1. a descendant of the early Dutch settlers of New York. 2. a person from New York State. 3. [k-], *pl.* wide breeches gathered in at or just below the knee: also **knick′ers** (nik′ērz).

knick-knack (nik′nak), *n.* a gewgaw; trinket.

knife (nif), *n., pl.* **knives** (nivz), 1. a cutting instrument with a sharp-edged blade or blades set in a handle. 2. an edged blade, as of a machine: *v.t.* 1. to cut or stab with or as if with a knife: *v.i.* to move swiftly or smoothly like a knife cutting through.

knight (nit), *n.* 1. in Great Britain, a man holding nonhereditary rank next below a baronet and entitled to use *Sir* before his given name. 2. in the Middle Ages, a man raised to honorable military rank after serving as page and squire. 3. [Poetical], a lady's champion or attendant; also, any devoted follower as of a cause. 4. a chess piece shaped like a horse's head: *v.t.* to confer knighthood upon.

knight-er·rant (′er′ant), *n.* a medieval knight in search of adventure, especially of a chance to show his skill and redress wrongs. —**knight′-er′rant·ry,** *n.*

knight·hood (′hood), *n.* 1. the profession, rank, or dignity of a knight. 2. the conduct of a knight. 3. knights collectively.

knight·ly (′li), *adj.* 1. of, like, or befitting a knight. 2. made up of knights.

Knights of Columbus, an international fraternal, benevolent, and proselytizing society of Roman Catholic men, founded in 1882.

Knight Templar, 1. *pl.* **Knights Templars,** a member of a military and religious order established among the Crusaders early in the 12th century. 2. *pl.* **Knights Templar,** a member of a certain order of Masons.

knit (nit), *v.t. & v.i.* **knit′ted** or **knit, knit′ting,** 1. to make (a fabric or garment) by looping yarn together with special needles. 2. to join together very closely or into one; unite. 3. to draw together or contract in wrinkles, as the brows: *n.* a knitted fabric or garment. —**knit′ter,** *n.*

knit·ting (′ing), *n.* 1. the action of one that knits. 2. knitted work.

knit·wear (′wer), *n.* knitted clothing.

knob (nob), *n.* 1. a handle, usually rounded, as

---

of a door. 2. a round protuberance. 3. a rounded hill, knoll, etc.

knob·by ('ĭ), *adj.* -bi·er, -bi·est, like or full of knobs. —**knob'bi·ness,** *n.*

knock (nŏk), *v.i.* 1. to strike a surface with a quick, short blow, as in rapping on a door. 2. to bump; collide. 3. to rattle or thump, as an engine with poor combustion. 4. [Informal], to find fault: *v.t.* 1. to hit; strike. 2. [Informal], to find fault with: *n.* 1. a knocking. 2. a blow; rap. 3. a rattle or thump, as in an engine. 4. [Informal], an unfavorable remark, criticism, etc. 5. [Informal], a piece of adversity.

knock·a·bout ('ă-bout), *n.* 1. a small yacht with no bowsprit. 2. something for casual or rough use: *adj.* 1. noisy; boisterous. 2. of or for casual or rough use.

knock·er ('ĕr), *n.* 1. one that knocks. 2. a rapping contrivance attached to a door.

knock-knee ('nē), *n.* 1. a physical condition in which the knees touch together as the legs are moved. 2. *pl.* such knees. —**knock'-kneed,** *adj.*

knock·out ('out), *n.* 1. the act of making unconscious or incapacitated or the condition of having been made so, especially by a blow, as in boxing. 2. [Slang], a very attractive person or thing.

knock·wurst (nŏk'wŭrst), *n.* same as **knack·wurst.**

knoll (nōl), *n.* a hillock; mound.

knop (nŏp), *n.* a knob, especially when ornamental.

knot (nŏt), *n.* 1. an interweaving or tying of cord, string, thread, etc.; also, a lump made thus or by an entanglement. 2. something knotlike. 3. a small group or cluster. 4. a difficulty, problem, etc. 5. a hard lump on a tree, where a branch emerges; also, a cross section of this as in a board. 6. in *nautical usage,* a unit of speed of one nautical mile (6,076.12 feet) an hour. 7. a small sandpiper breeding in arctic regions and then migrating: *v.t.* **knot'ted, knot'ting,** 1. to tie or fasten in or with a knot or knots; make a knot or knots in. 2. to tie closely or intricately. 3. to entangle: *v.i.* to become knotted.

knot·hole ('hōl), *n.* a hole marking a missing knot, as in a plank.

knot·ty ('ĭ), *adj.* -ti·er, -ti·est, 1. full of knots. 2. perplexing; difficult.

knout (nout), *n.* a leather whip formerly used in Russia to flog criminals.

know (nō), *v.t.* **knew, known, know'ing,** 1. to have clearly and securely in the mind, memory, or understanding. 2. to have within the mental grasp or perception; be aware of. 3. to be acquainted or familiar with. 4. to understand or have skill in. 5. to recognize: *v.i.* to know something.

know-how ('hou), *n.* [Informal], the special knowledge and skill needed to get things done, made, built, etc.

know·ing ('ĭng), *adj.* 1. having knowledge; intelligent. 2. shrewd; cunning. 3. indicating that one has more than ordinary knowledge

of or information about something, as a *knowing* look. 4. deliberate; intentional. —**know'ing·ly,** *adv.*

know-it-all ('it-ôl), *adj.* [Informal], knowing or pretending to know just about everything: *n.* [Informal], such a person.

knowl·edge (nŏl'ĭj), *n.* 1. the act, fact, or condition of knowing; mental grasp, perception, familiarity, etc. 2. the specific extent of what is known about something, as by an individual. 3. all that is known or that can be known; learning, science, etc. in general.

knowl·edge·a·ble (-ă-bl), *adj.* well-informed in general or in some particular field, activity, etc. —**knowl·edge·a·bil'i·ty,** *n.* —**knowl'edge·a·bly,** *adv.*

knuck·le (nŭk'l), *n.* 1. a finger joint, especially where the finger joins the hand. 2. the knee or hock joint, as of a pig, used as food.

knuck·le·head ('l·hed), *n.* [Informal], a stupid or foolish person.

knur (nûr), *n.* a knot, as on a tree trunk.

knurl (nûrl), *n.* 1. a knot, knob, nodule, etc. 2. any one of a series of small ridges or beads, as about the edge of a coin: *v.t.* to make knurls on.

KO (kā'ō'), *v.t.* **KO'd, KO'ing,** [Slang], in *Boxing,* to deal a knockout blow to: *n., pl.* **KO's,** [Slang], in *Boxing,* a knockout. Also **K.O., k.o.**

ko·a (kō'ă), *n.* a Hawaiian acacia tree valued for its wood and bark.

ko·a·la (kō-ä'lä), *n.* an arboreal tailless Australian marsupial about two or three feet long: it has thick, gray fur and large tufted ears.

kob (kŏb), *n.* an orange-red antelope of southeastern Africa.

ko·bold (kō'bŏld, -bōld), *n.* in *German Folklore,* a household sprite; also, a gnome in mines, caves, etc.

ko·di·ak bear (kō'di-ak), a very large brown bear found on Kodiak Island and adjacent areas off the southwestern coast of Alaska.

Koh·i·noor, Koh·i·noor (kō'ĭ-noor), *n.* a famous large Indian diamond, now one of the British crown jewels.

kohl (kōl), *n.* a cosmetic preparation, as antimony sulfide, used especially in some Eastern countries as eye makeup.

kohl·ra·bi (kōl-rä'bĭ), *n., pl.* -bies, a garden vegetable related to the cabbage: the edible part is a bulbous portion of the stem just above the ground.

ko·la (kō'lä), *n.* same as **cola.**

ko·lin·sky (kō-lĭn'skĭ), *n., pl.* -skies, 1. any one of several weasels of Asia. 2. the golden-brown fur of these.

Kol Nid·re (kōl nē'drä, nĭd'rĕ), 1. the prayer of atonement recited in synagogues at the opening of the Yom Kippur eve services. 2. a traditional melody to which this is sung.

Ko·mo·do dragon (kō-mō'dō), a giant flesh-eating lizard of southeastern Asian jungles: it is the largest living lizard, reaching a length of 9 feet.

koo·doo (kōō'dōō), *n., pl.* -doos, -doo, same as **kudu.**

---

kook (kōōk), *n.* [Slang], one regarded as eccentric, foolish, etc. —**kook'y,** *adj.*

ko‑peck, ko‑pek (kō'pek), *n.* 1. a monetary unit, equal to 1/100 of a Russian ruble. 2. a coin of this unit.

koph (kôf), *n.* the nineteenth letter of the Hebrew alphabet.

kop‑je (kop'i), *n.* [Afrikaans], in South Africa, a small hill; hillock.

Ko‑ran (kō‑ran', ‑rän'; kō‑, kô‑), *n.* the sacred book of the Moslems.

Ko‑re‑an (kō‑rē'ån), *adj.* of Korea, a country in eastern Asia, or its people, their language, etc.: *n.* 1. a native of Korea. 2. the Korean language.

ko‑ru‑na (kô‑rōō'nä), *n., pl.* **ko‑ru'nas, ko‑run'**, 1. the monetary unit of Czechoslovakia. 2. a coin of this unit.

ko‑sher (kō'shĕr), *adj.* 1. in *Judaism, a)* fit to eat according to the dietary laws: see *Leviticus xi. b)* serving or dealing in such food. 2. loosely, prepared according to traditional Jewish recipes. 3. [Slang], all right, proper, correct, etc.: *n.* kosher food: *v.t.* (usually kosh'ĕr), to cause to be kosher.

ko‑to (kōt'ō), *n.* a Japanese musical instrument resembling the zither.

kow‑tow (kou'tou', kō'‑), *n.* an act of deference, homage, etc. made by kneeling down and touching the forehead to the ground, as formerly in China: *v.i.* 1. to make a kowtow. 2. to abase oneself.

kraal (kräl, krôl), *n.* 1. a South African native village, usually enclosed with a stockade. 2. a South African pen for cattle or sheep.

krait (krīt), *n.* any one of several very poisonous snakes, typically black or dark with yellow or tan bands, of central and eastern regions in southern Asia.

krem‑lin (krem'lin), *n.* 1. the citadel of a Russian city, specifically [K‑], of Moscow. 2. [K‑], the government of the Soviet Union.

krim‑mer (krim'ĕr), *n.* a grayish, tightly curled fur similar to astrakhan, made from the pelts of lambs raised in the region of the southern Ukraine.

kris (krēs), *n.* a Malayan dagger with a wavy blade.

Krish‑na (krish'nä), *n.* in *Hindu Theology,* one of the incarnations of Vishnu.

Kriss Krin‑gle (kris kring'gl), Santa Claus.

kro‑na (krō'nä, krōō'nä), *n., pl.* **kro'nor** ('nôr), the monetary unit and a coin of Sweden.

kro‑ne (krō'nĕ), *n., pl.* **kro'ner** ('nĕr), the monetary unit and a coin of Denmark or Norway.

kryp‑ton (krip'ton), *n.* a rare gaseous chemical element.

Kshat‑ri‑ya (kshat'ri‑ä), *n.* among the Hindus, a member of the military caste, next below the Brahmans.

ku‑chen (kōō'kĕn), *n.* a German coffeecake made of yeast dough.

ku‑dos (kōō'dos, 'dōs; kū'dos), *n.* glory; fame; renown.

ku‑du (kōō'dōō), *n., pl.* ‑**dus,** ‑**du,** a large, grayish‑brown antelope of Africa: it has white stripes on its back and its horns are long and twisted.

Ku Klux (kōō' kluks', kū'), 1. short for Ku Klux Klan. 2. a member of the Ku Klux Klan: also **Ku Klux'er.**

Ku Klux Klan (klan), a secret U.S. society promoting white Protestant supremacy.

küm‑mel (kim'l), *n.* a colorless liqueur flavored with caraway seeds, anise, etc.

kum‑quat (kum'kwät), *n.* 1. a small, oval, orange‑colored citrus fruit produced by a tree of the rue family and used in preserves and confections. 2. the tree.

kur‑ra‑jong (kŭr'å‑jŏng), *n.* any of several Australian trees and shrubs, especially a tree yielding fibers used by the natives for weaving nets, mats, etc.

kwa‑shi‑or‑kor (kwä‑shi‑ôr'kôr), *n.* a condition in young children that is produced by malnutrition and is characterized by potbelly, stunted growth, and other severe effects.

ky‑an‑ize (kī'å‑nīz), *v.t.* ‑**ized,** ‑**iz‑ing,** to impregnate (wood) for preservation with a solution of corrosive sublimate.

ky‑mo‑graph (kī'mô‑graf), *n.* an apparatus consisting of a rotating drum that traces wavelike motions, as of the pulse.

ky‑pho‑sis (kī‑fō'sis), *n.* abnormal backward curvature of the spine, producing a hump.

L

L, l (el), *n.*, *pl.* **L's, l's,** 1. the twelfth letter of the English alphabet. 2. the usual sound of this letter, as in *late* and *fail.*

L (el), *adj.* shaped like L: *n.* 1. an object shaped like L. 2. an extension at a right angle to a building, so that the two parts form an L; ell. 3. a Roman numeral denoting 50. 4. an elevated railroad; el.

la (lä), *n.* the sixth tone in any major or minor musical scale of eight tones.

laa·ger (lä'gẽr), *n.* [Afrikaans], in South Africa, an extemporized camp for defense, formed within a circle of wagons, etc.: *v.t. & v.i.* to form or encamp in a laager.

lab (lab), *n.* [Informal], a laboratory.

la·bel (lä'bl), *n.* 1. a small slip of paper, etc. attached to anything to indicate its destination, ownership, origin, etc. 2. a descriptive word or phrase; epithet. 3. a projecting molding: *v.t.* **-beled** or **-belled, -bel·ing** or **-bel·ling,** 1. to mark with or affix a label to. 2. to classify as. —**la'bel·er, la'bel·ler,** *n.*

la·bi·al (lä'bi-ǎl), *adj.* 1. of the labia, or lips. 2. formed by the lips: said of the letters *b, m,* and *p: n.* 1. a sound made by the lips. 2. a letter representing one of these sounds. — **la'bi·al·ly,** *adv.*

la·bi·ate (lä'bi-āt, -it), *adj.* 1. lipped. 2. like a lip. 3. in *Botany,* having the calyx in two unequal parts, one overlapping the other.

la·bile (lä'bl, 'bīl), *adj.* liable to change, especially chemical change; unstable. —**la·bil·i·ty** (lä-bil'ĭ-ti), *n.*

la·bi·o·den·tal (lä-bi-ō-den'tǎl), *adj.* articulated by the lips and teeth, as the sounds of *v* and *f: n.* 1. a labiodental sound. 2. a letter representing such a sound.

la·bi·um (lä'bi-ùm), *n.*, *pl.* **-bi·a** (-ǎ), 1. a lip or liplike organ. 2. *pl.* the folds of the vulva.

la·bor (lä'bẽr), *n.* 1. toil or exertion, physical or mental. 2. a task. 3. those who do manual work or work for wages. 4. labor unions as a group. 5. parturition; the work of childbirth: *v.t.* to work at too hard: *v.i.* 1. to exert muscular strength or mental effort. 2. to be hard pressed. 3. to move slowly. 4. to pitch and roll heavily. 5. to suffer the pains of childbirth.

lab·o·ra·to·ry (lab'rá-tôr-i, 'ẽr-á-tôr-i; British lä-bär'á-tôr-i, 'á-tri), *n.*, *pl.* **-ries,** a place where scientific experiments and research are carried on: *adj.* of or in a laboratory.

Labor Day, a legal holiday in the U.S. and Canada in honor of labor, observed the first Monday in September.

la·bored (lä'bẽrd), *adj.* strained; not easily done.

la·bor·er (lä'bẽr-ẽr), *n.* 1. one whose work involves manual labor. 2. an unskilled workman who acts as helper to a skilled tradesman.

la·bo·ri·ous (lá-bôr'i-ŭs), *adj.* 1. difficult; toilsome. 2. industrious. —**la·bo'ri·ous·ly,** *adv.* — **la·bo'ri·ous·ness,** *n.*

la·bor·ite (lä'bô-rīt), *n.* 1. a member of a group or political party concerned with the rights of workers. 2. [L-], a member of such a political party in Great Britain: British spelling, **Labourite.**

labor party, 1. a political party concerned with the rights of workers. 2. [L- P-], such a political party in Great Britain: British spelling, **Labour Party.**

la·bor·sav·ing (lä'bẽr-sā-ving), *adj.* intended to save or reduce manual work.

labor union, an organization of workers to promote their mutual welfare, especially by collective bargaining.

la·bour (lä'bẽr), *n. & v.t. & v.i.* British spelling of labor.

lab·ra·dor·ite (lab'rá-dôr-īt), *n.* a variety of feldspar displaying an iridescent play of colors.

la·brum (lä'brŭm, lab'rŭm), *n.*, *pl.* **-bra** ('brǎ, 'rǎ), 1. the liplike shield of an insect's mouth. 2. any liplike edge.

la·bur·num (lá-bûr'nŭm), *n.* an ornamental tree or shrub with pendent yellow flowers.

lab·y·rinth (lab'ĭ-rinth), *n.* 1. a series of intricate, winding passages; maze. 2. an inexplicable difficulty or puzzlement. 3. the winding tubes of the inner ear.

lab·y·rin·thine (lab-i-rin'thĕn, 'thin), *adj.* 1. resembling a labyrinth. 2. intricate; puzzling; involved. Also **lab·y·rin'thi·an** ('thi-ǎn), **lab·y·rin'thic.**

lac (lak), *n.* a resinous substance that is used to make shellac: it is formed on certain trees, especially in India, by various insects.

lace (lās), *n.* 1. an ornamental fabric or edging of fine linen, cotton, silk, etc., elaborately woven. 2. a cord used for binding or fastening. 3. an ornamental braid of silver or gold: *v.t.* **laced, lac'ing,** 1. to fasten with a lace. 2. to adorn with lace. 3. to intertwine. 4. to add a small amount of alcoholic liquor to (food or drink). 5. to beat; thrash: *v.i.* 1. to be fastened with a lace. 2. to attack (followed by *into*).

lac·er·ate (las'ẽ-rāt), *v.t.* **-at·ed, -at·ing,** 1. to rend; tear roughly; mangle. 2. to harrow or wound (one's feelings, etc.): *adj.* (also 'ẽr-it), in *Biology,* jagged. —**lac'er·a·ble** ('ẽr-á-bl), *adj.*

lac·er·a·tion (las-ẽr-ā'shŭn), *n.* 1. the act of lacerating. 2. a rough, jagged wound or tear.

lace·wing (lās'wing), *n.* an insect with gauzy wings resembling lace.

lach·es (lach'iz), *n.* in *Law,* neglect or failure to assert a right or claim a privilege at the proper time.

---

a in *cap,* *ā* in *cane,* *ä* in *father,* *å* in *abet,* e in *met,* *ē* in be, *ẽ* in baker, *ê* in regent, ĭ in *pit,* ī in *fine,* ĭ in *manifest,* o in *hot,* ô in *horse,* ō in *bone,*

lach·ry·mal (lak′ri-mál), *adj.* 1. of or pertaining to tears. 2. same as **lacrimal**.

lach·ry·mose (-mōs), *adj.* tearful; sad.

lac·ing (lās′ing), *n.* 1. the act of one that laces. 2. a cord, shoestring, etc. 3. braid, as of a uniform.

lack (lak), *v.t.* to be without; fall short of: *v.i.* to lack something; have a deficiency or be in need: *n.* a being without or falling short of something; partial or total deficiency; want; need.

lack·a·dai·si·cal (lak-á-dā′zi-kl), *adj.* lacking interest or enthusiasm; listless.

lack·ey (lak′i), *n., pl.* -eys, 1. a menial male attendant. 2. any servile follower.

lack·lus·ter (lak′lus-tēr), *adj.* not bright; dull.

la·con·ic (lá-kon′ik), *adj.* brief and to the point; succinct. —**la·con′i·cal·ly**, *adv.*

lac·quer (lak′ēr), *n.* 1. a quick-drying liquid application of resinous materials in a solvent, often colored: it leaves a tough, adherent film. 2. a resinous wood varnish, from certain trees of China and Japan; also, an article or articles coated with this: *v.t.* to apply lacquer to.

lac·ri·mal (lak′ri-mál), *adj.* 1. designating, of, or near the tear-secreting glands. 2. same as **lachrymal**.

la·crosse (lá-krôs′), *n.* a game in which a pair of opposing teams using long-handled, pouched rackets attempt to throw, catch, and carry a small rubber ball across a field so as to throw it into the opponents' goal.

lac·tate (lak′tāt), *v.i.* -tat·ed, -tat·ing, to secrete milk. —**lac·ta′tion**, *n.*

lac·te·al (lak′ti-ál), *adj.* 1. of or like milk. 2. containing or conveying chyle: *n.* any one of the lymphatic vessels conveying chyle to the thoracic duct.

lac·tes·cent (-tes′nt), *adj.* 1. milky in appearance or turning so. 2. secreting milk or a fluid that looks like milk.

lac·tic (lak′tik), *adj.* of or from milk.

lactic acid, a syrupy organic acid produced by souring milk and also from sucrose and certain other carbohydrates.

lac·tif·er·ous (lak-tif′ēr-ús), *adj.* 1. containing or conveying milk. 2. forming a milky fluid.

lac·tom·e·ter (-tom′é-tēr), *n.* an instrument to ascertain the specific gravity of milk.

lac·to·pro·te·in (lak-tō-prō′tēn), *n.* any of the proteins found in milk.

lac·tose (lak′tōs), *n.* a white, crystalline sugar present in milk.

la·cu·na (lá-kū′ná), *n., pl.* -nas, -nae (′nē), 1. a blank space, where something is missing; hiatus; gap. 2. in *Anatomy & Biology,* a space, pit, or hollow.

la·cus·trine (lá-kus′trin), *adj.* of or occurring within a lake or lakes.

lac·y (lā′si), *adj.* lac′i·er, lac′i·est, of or like lace. —**lac′i·ness,** *n.*

lad (lad), *n.* 1. a boy; youth. 2. [Informal], a man; fellow; comrade.

lad·der (lad′ēr), *n.* 1. a framework consisting of two parallel sidepieces connected by bars or other joining pieces spaced and parallel to each other so as to form a series of steps to go up or down on, as in mounting a wall. 2. anything ladderlike.

lad·die (lad′i), *n.* [Chiefly Scottish], lad.

lade (lād), *v.t. & v.i.* lad′ed, lad′ed or lad′en, lad′ing, 1. to load. 2. to ladle.

la·di·da (lä′di-dä′), *adj.* [Informal], affectedly refined or elegant.

lad·ing (lā′ding), *n.* 1. the act of one that lades. 2. a load; cargo; freight.

la·dle (lā′dl), *n.* a deep spoon with a long handle for dipping out liquids: *v.t.* -dled, -dling, to dip out with a ladle.

la·dy (lā′di), *n., pl.* -dies, 1. a refined, well-bred woman. 2. [L-], in Great Britain, a title of respect given to women of various ranks. 3. a woman of high social position. 4. the mistress of a household: now only in *the lady of the house.* 5. [L-], the Virgin Mary (usually with *Our*). 6. any woman: *adj.* female.

la·dy·bird (-būrd), *n.* a ladybug.

la·dy·bug (-bug), *n.* a small, more or less round, usually brightly colored beetle with a spotted back: it feeds chiefly on insect pests.

la·dy·fin·ger (-fing-gēr), *n.* a small spongecake with a fingerlike shape.

la·dy·in·wait·ing (-in-wāt′ing), *n., pl.* **la·dies·in·wait′ing,** a woman chosen to attend a queen or princess, as in court.

la·dy·like (-lik), *adj.* refined, courteous, decorous, etc. in a manner viewed as befitting a well-bred girl or woman.

la·dy·love (-luv), *n.* a girl or woman who is a sweetheart of someone specified.

la·dy·ship (-ship), *n.* the rank or title of a lady (with *her* or *your*).

la·e·trile (lā′é-tril), *n.* any of several organic compounds obtained from certain substances, as almond seeds, and claimed to be effective in treating cancer.

lag (lag), *v.i.* lagged, lag′ging, 1. to move slowly; loiter; stay behind. 2. to grow less intense, weaker, etc.; wane: *n.* 1. a lagging. 2. the degree of this. 3. an interval.

la·ger (lā′gēr), *n.* beer stored several months on completion of brewing: also **lager beer.**

lag·gard (lag′ērd), *n.* a slow person; loiterer: *adj.* lagging; dilatory.

la·gniappe, la·gnappe (lan-yap′), *n.* 1. [Chiefly South], a little present given someone buying something. 2. a gratuity.

la·goon (lá-gōōn′), *n.* 1. a shallow lake, especially near the sea. 2. an expanse of water within a circular coral reef.

la·ic (lā′ik), *adj.* of or pertaining to the laity: also **la′i·cal:** *n.* a layman.

la·i·cize (lā′i-siz), *v.t.* -cized, -ciz·ing, to make laic; secularize.

laid (lād), past tense and past participle of **lay.**

laid-back (′bak), *adj.* [Slang], relaxed, easygoing, etc.; not hurried.

laid paper, paper with fine parallel ribbed lines.

lain (lān), past participle of **lie** (recline).

lair (ler), *n.* the den of a wild animal.

lais·sez faire (les-ā fer′, lez-), noninterference, as by government in commerce.

la·i·ty (lā′it-i), *n., pl.* -ties, laymen.

lake (lāk), *n.* 1. a large inland body of usually fresh water. 2. a large pool. 3. a pigment of dark-red color, prepared from cochineal. 4. an insoluble metallic dye compound.

lal·ly·gag (lăl'ĭ-gag), v.i. -gagged, -gag·ging, [Informal], same as lollygag.

lam (lam), v.t. & v.i. lammed, lam'ming, [Slang], to hit, sock, or thrash.

lam (lam), n. [Slang], headlong flight: v.i. lammed, lam'ming, [Slang], to flee.

la·ma (lä'mä), n. a priest or monk in Lamaism.

La·ma·ism (lä'mä-ĭzm), n. a form of Buddhism centered in Tibet and Mongolia and characterized by elaborate ritual and strong hierarchical organization.

La·maze (lä-mäz'), n. a training program in natural childbirth, emphasizing breathing control and relaxation during labor together with the presence and encouraging assistance of the father: after F. Lamaze, 20th-century French physician.

lamb (lam), n. 1. a young sheep. 2. its flesh, used as food. 3. lambskin. 4. one who is gentle or innocent: v.i. to give birth: said of a ewe.

lam·baste (lam-bāst', -bast'), v.t. -bast'ed, -bast'ing, [Informal], 1. to beat soundly. 2. to scold severely. Also spelled lam·bast'.

lamb·da (lam'dä), n. the eleventh letter of the Greek alphabet.

lam·bent (lam'bĕnt), adj. 1. flickering, as a flame. 2. glowing softly, as a sky. 3. light and graceful, as wit.

lamb·kin (lam'kin), n. a little lamb.

lam·bre·quin (lam'bĕr-kin, -'brĕ-kin), n. a drapery hanging from a shelf, doorway, etc.

lamb·skin (lam'skin), n. 1. the skin of a lamb, especially with the fleece still on it. 2. leather or parchment made from the skin of a lamb.

lame (lām), adj. 1. crippled; disabled; especially, so disabled in the leg or foot as to have to limp. 2. not effective or efficient; faulty; unsound: v.t. lamed, lam'ing, to make lame.

la·mé (la-mā'), n. a fabric, as of silk, that is interwoven with metal threads, as of gold.

la·med (lä'mid), n. the twelfth letter of the Hebrew alphabet.

lame duck, 1. a disabled person or thing. 2. an official failing to get reelected but serving for a time after this defeat.

la·mel·la (lä-mĕl'ä), n., pl. -lae ('ē), -las, a thin scale or plate or platelike part, as on the underside of a mushroom cap.

la·ment (lä-ment'), v.t. & v.i. to mourn (for) or grieve (over): n. an expression of grief; lamentation.

lam·en·ta·ble (lam'ĕn-tä-bl, lä-men'tä-bl), adj. that is to be lamented; deplorable.

lam·en·ta·tion (lam-ĕn-tā'shŭn), n. a groan, wail, or other outward sign of lamenting.

Lam·en·ta·tions ('shŭnz), n. a book of the Bible: in full, The Lamentations of Jeremiah.

lam·i·na (lam'ĭ-nä), n., pl. -nae (-nē), -nas, 1. a thin scale, plate, layer, etc., as of metal or of animal tissue. 2. the blade of a leaf.

lam·i·nar (-nĕr), adj. of, like, or arranged in laminae: also lam'i·nal.

lam·i·nate (lam'ĭ-nāt), v.t. -nat·ed, -nat·ing, 1. to make into a thin sheet or layer. 2. to separate into laminae. 3. to cover with or bond to one or more thin layers. 4. to build up in layers: v.i. to split into laminae: adj. (-nit), same as laminated: n. (-nit), something laminated. —lam·i·na'tion, n. —lam'i·na·tor, n.

lam·i·nat·ed (-id), adj. of, made up of, or built into thin sheets or layers bonded or pressed together.

lam·mer·gei·er; lam·mer·gey·er (lam'ĕr-gī-ĕr), n. a large European and Asiatic bird of prey: it belongs to the vulture family and it has grayish-black plumage.

lamp (lamp), n. 1. a vessel with a wick for burning oil, alcohol, etc. to give light or heat. 2. any device for producing light; also, a device producing therapeutic rays. 3. something that enlightens morally or intellectually.

lamp·black ('blak), n. a finely divided soot produced by the incomplete combustion of oil, tar, etc.

lam·poon (lam-pōōn'), n. a piece of satire, especially of a strongly personal and abusive kind: v.t. to subject to a lampoon.

lamp·post (lam'pōst, lamp'pōst), n. a post supporting a street lamp.

lam·prey (lam'prĭ), n. a jawless parasitic fish with an eellike body and a funnel-shaped mouth with which it bores into the flesh of other fish and sucks their blood.

la·nai (lä-nī', la-), n. in Hawaii, a kind of veranda or open-sided living room.

lance (lans), n. 1. a long shaft of wood with a spearhead. 2. any similar device. 3. a surgical lancet: v.t. lanced, lanc'ing, to pierce with a lance or lancet.

lance·let ('lit), n. any one of a group of small, invertebrate, fishlike sea animals closely related to the vertebrates.

Lan·ce·lot (lan'sĕ-lot, -lŏt), n. in Arthurian Legend, the bravest of the knights of the Round Table.

lan·ce·o·late (lan'sĭ-ō-lāt, -lit), adj. narrow and tapering, as certain leaves.

lanc·er (lan'sĕr), n. 1. a cavalry soldier who is armed with a lance or who belongs to a regiment originally so armed. 2. pl. a certain quadrille of the 19th century.

lan·cet (lan'sit), n. 1. a small, pointed surgical knife used as for making incisions. 2. a narrow, sharply pointed arch: in full, lancet arch; also, a sharply pointed window set in such an arch: in full, lancet window.

lance·wood (lans'wood), n. 1. any of various tropical trees yielding a tough, elastic wood used as for making the cues employed in billiards. 2. this wood.

lan·ci·form (lan'sĭ-fôrm), adj. narrow and pointed like a lance.

lan·ci·nate (lan'sĭ-nāt), v.t. -nat·ed, -nat·ing, to stab or pierce, as pain.

land (land), n. 1. the solid portion of the surface of the globe; earth. 2. a country or district. 3. real estate. 4. rural regions: v.i. 1. to set on shore from a ship. 2. to bring to a certain place or condition. 3. to maneuver (as an aircraft) down to touch and rest upon earth or water. 4. to capture and draw (a fish, etc.) into a boat or onto land. 5. [Informal], to manage to get, as a job. 6. [Informal], to deliver (a blow): v.i. 1. to leave a ship and go on shore; disembark. 2. to come to port or shore: said of a ship. 3. to get to a specified place; end up. 4. to go or come down to a surface and stop or rest upon it, as after a flight or fall.

lan·dau (lan'dou, -'dô), *n.* a four-wheeled covered carriage with a two-part top, either part of the top being capable of being separately lowered.

land·ed (lan'did), *adj.* 1. owning land. 2. of land or real estate.

land·fall (land'fôl), *n.* 1. a sighting of land from a ship at sea. 2. the land sighted. 3. a landing by ship or airplane.

land·fill ('fil), *n.* disposal of garbage or rubbish by burying it.

land·form ('fôrm), *n.* any distinctive topographic feature of the earth's surface, as a hill or valley.

land·grab·ber ('grab-ēr), *n.* one that takes land unfairly or fraudulently.

land·grave ('grāv), *n.* a title of certain German princes, originally of a count with jurisdiction over a specified territory.

land·hold·er ('hōl-dēr), *n.* an owner or occupant of land. —**land'hold·ing,** *adj. & n.*

land·ing (lan'ding), *n.* 1. the act of one that lands. 2. the level part at the bottom of a flight of stairs. 3. the place where a ship is loaded or unloaded.

landing gear, the wheels, pontoons, etc. of an aircraft, for resting on a surface.

land·la·dy (land'lā-di), *n., pl.* -**dies,** a woman landlord.

land·locked ('lokt), *adj.* 1. enclosed wholly or nearly wholly by land, as a particular region. 2. blocked from returning to the sea, as salmon.

land·lord ('lôrd), *n.* 1. one, especially a man, renting or leasing land, houses, etc. to other persons. 2. a man who keeps a rooming house, inn, etc.

land·lub·ber ('lub-ēr), *n.* one not a sailor.

land·mark ('märk), *n.* 1. something used to mark the boundary of a piece of land. 2. a distinctive feature identifying a region or serving as a guide. 3. something viewed as marking a decisive development, high point, etc., as in history.

land·mass ('mas), *n.* a very large area of land, especially a continent.

land office, a government office handling sales of public lands.

land-of·fice business (land'of-is), [Informal], a booming business.

land rail, same as **corncrake.**

land reform, the breaking up of large landholdings so that these may be shared by small farmers, peasants, etc.

land·scape (lan'skāp, land'skāp), *n.* the general aspect of the natural scenery in a particular land region; also, a picture representing such scenery: *v.t.* -**scaped,** -**scap·ing,** to modify for greater beauty the natural features of (an area), as by trimming bushes, adding trees, etc. —**land'scap·er,** *n.*

land·scap·ist (-ist), *n.* a landscape painter.

land·slide (lan'slīd, land'slīd), *n.* 1. a sliding down of earth and rock, as along a mountainside; also, the earth and rock so sliding. 2. a huge victory, as by an overwhelming number of votes in an election.

land·ward (land'wērd), *adv.* toward the land: also **land'wards:** *adj.* situated or facing toward the land.

lane (lān), *n.* 1. a narrow way, as between walls or hedges. 2. a narrow road, as in the country. 3. a particular route or way to be followed, as by a ship or car. 4. in a bowling establishment, the long, narrow wooden strip along which the balls are rolled.

lan·guage (lang'gwij), *n.* 1. vocal expression and communication of ideas and feelings; human speech. 2. any means of expression or communication. 3. the speech of any one speech community, as of a particular nation, as contrasted with that of another. 4. the style of speech peculiar to or distinctive of an individual or group of individuals.

lan·guid (lang'gwid), *adj.* lacking vigor or spirit; listless; sluggish.

lan·guish (lang'gwish), *v.i.* 1. to lose energy or vitality; become spiritless or weak; droop. 2. to pine away. 3. to become suffused with a yearning tenderness or melancholy.

lan·guor (lang'gēr), *n.* a condition of languishing; listlessness, spiritlessness, pining away, yearning melancholy or tenderness, etc. — **lan'guor·ous,** *adj.*

lan·gur (lung·goor'), *n.* any one of a number of slender, long-tailed monkeys of southeastern Asia.

lank (langk), *adj.* 1. lean or slender. 2. lacking curl or springiness; hanging straight and limp: said of hair.

lank·y (lang'ki), *adj.* **lank'i·er, lank'i·est,** tall and lean. —**lank'i·ness,** *n.*

lan·ner (lan'ēr), *n.* a Mediterranean falcon.

lan·o·lin (lan'l-in), *n.* a fatty substance from sheep wool, used as in ointments.

lan·tern (lan'tērn), *n.* 1. a transparent case for holding or carrying a light. 2. in a lighthouse, the room where the lamp is, at the top. 3. an open or windowed structure, as on a rooftop, to let in light or air.

lan·tern-jawed (-jôd), *adj.* having long, thin jaws.

lan·tha·nide series (lan'thà-nīd), the rare-earth group of chemical elements, including lanthanum and lutetium.

lan·tha·num (-nūm), *n.* a silvery metallic chemical element of the rare-earth group.

lan·yard, lan·iard (lan'yērd), *n.* a piece of rope or cord used aboard a ship to hold or fasten something.

lap (lap), *n.* 1. the front part of the body, from the waist to the knees, of a person seated; also, the clothing over this. 2. a part extending over another; also, such extension. 3. a turn or loop, as of rope. 4. a disk for cutting gems. 5. a completed round of a race track, in a race made up of more than one such circuit. 6. the act of lapping: *v.t.* **lapped, lap'ping,** 1. to fold, wrap, or enfold. 2. to overlap. 3. to get a lap ahead of in a race. 4. to dip up (liquid) with the tongue, as a dog does; also, to move against or move gently as if so lapping, as water does, with light, splashing sounds: *v.i.* 1. to lap or

---

overlap something. 2. to be or become lapped. 3. to extend beyond (with *over*).

lap·board ('bôrd), *n.* a board placed on the lap for use as a table or desk.

lap dog, a pet dog small enough to be held in the lap.

la·pel (lả-pel'), *n.* a folded-back part, a continuation of the collar, at the upper front of a coat.

lap·i·dar·y (lap'ĭ-der-i), *n., pl.* **-dar·ies**, 1. an artificer who cuts, polishes, and engraves precious stones. 2. a collector of or dealer in gems: also **lap'i·dar·ist**.

lap·in (lap'in), *n.* rabbit fur, often dyed to resemble other skins.

lap·is la·zu·li (lap'is laz'yoo-lī), an opaque, azure, semiprecious stone.

Lapp (lap), *n.* 1. a member of a Mongoloid people of Lapland, a region in northernmost Europe along the Arctic coast: also **Lapp·land·er** (lap'lan-dẽr). 2. the language of the Lapps: also **Lap'pish**.

lap·pet (lap'it), *n.* 1. a small flap or fold of a garment. 2. a flap of flesh, as the dewlap of a cow.

lap robe, a heavy blanket, fur covering, etc. laid over the lap for warmth.

lapse (laps), *v.i.* **lapsed, laps'ing**, 1. to elapse. 2. to slip, slide, or fall by degrees, especially into a specified condition. 3. to slip down or away from a standard. 4. to slip down or back into error, fault, sin, etc. 5. to fail in duty. 6. to come to an end, as a subscription. 7. to become forfeit or void because of nonpayment of premium: said of an insurance policy. 8. in *Law*, to pass to another proprietor by negligence or death: *n.* 1. a slight fault or mistake. 2. a slip of the tongue, pen, or memory. 3. a falling away or slipping down or back into a lower or worse condition or into error, fault, sin, etc. 4. a going by or passing, as of time. 5. in *Law*, termination or forfeiture of a right or privilege as through disuse; also, failure of a bequest to take effect because of the death of the intended beneficiary.

lap·wing (lap'wing), *n.* an old-world crested plover with an irregular, wavering flight.

lar·board (lär'bẽrd, 'bôrd), *n.* the left-hand side of a ship, looking toward the bow; port: *adj.* of this side.

lar·ce·ny (lär'sẽ-ni), *n., pl.* **-nies**, the unlawful taking away of the goods of another; theft. —**lar'ce·nist**, *n.* —**lar'ce·nous**, *adj.*

larch (lärch), *n.* 1. a cone-bearing deciduous tree of the pine family. 2. its wood.

lard (lärd), *n.* the fat of swine, melted down: *v.t.* 1. to cover with lard. 2. to insert strips of pork or bacon into before cooking. 3. to mix in; add to; garnish.

lard·er (lär'dẽr), *n.* 1. a pantry. 2. a food supply; assemblage of provisions.

lar·es (ler'ēz), *n.pl.* in the belief of ancient Romans, deified ancestral spirits watching over households.

lares and penates, the household gods of the ancient Romans.

large (lärj), *adj.* **larg'er, larg'est**, 1. great as in size or amount; big, bulky, extensive, wide, etc. 2. not narrow or limited; comprehen-

sive: *adv.* in a large way: *n.* liberty: now only in *at large*, 1. not confined; not in jail. 2. in a full way; in detail. 3. representing a whole State or other entire unit having its own subdivisions. —**large'ness**, *n.*

large-heart·ed ('här'tid), *adj.* not petty, mean, or stingy; liberal and kindly.

large·ly ('li), *adv.* 1. to a large extent. 2. for the most part; on the whole.

large-scale ('skāl'), *adj.* 1. large in scale, as a map. 2. extensive, as a campaign.

lar·gess, lar·gesse (lär-jes', lär'jis), *n.* 1. liberal giving; bounty. 2. a gift or gifts bestowed in an unusually liberal way. 3. breadth of vision, sentiment, etc.

lar·go (lär'gō), *adj. & adv.* in *Music*, slow and stately: *n., pl.* **-gos**, such a movement or passage.

lar·i·at (ler'i-it), *n.* 1. a rope used for tethering. 2. a lasso: *v.t.* to catch or tie with a lariat.

lark (lärk), *n.* 1. any one of a large family of songbirds; especially, the skylark. 2. any one of various similar birds, as the meadowlark. 3. a merry time; frolic: *v.i.* to frolic.

lark·spur (lärk'spũr), *n.* a delphinium.

lar·rup (ler'ŭp), *v.t.* [Informal], to whip, beat, or flog.

lar·va (lär'vả), *n., pl.* **-vae** ('vē), **-vas**, an independent but immature animal form that undergoes basic structural changes in becoming adult, usually by a complex metamorphosis, as a caterpillar that changes into a butterfly. —**lar'val**, *adj.*

la·ryn·ge·al (lả-rin'ji-ål), *adj.* 1. of, near, or for the larynx. 2. produced in the larynx: said of a sound.

lar·yn·gi·tis (ler-in-jīt'is), *n.* inflammation of the larynx.

lar·yn·got·o·my (-got'ō-mi), *n., pl.* **-mies**, surgical incision of the larynx.

lar·ynx (ler'ingks), *n., pl.* **lar'ynx·es, la·ryn'ges** (lả-rin'jēz), the upper part of the trachea, or windpipe.

la·sa·gna (lả-zän'yả), *n.* a dish consisting of wide noodles baked in layers with tomato sauce, cheese, and ground meat.

las·civ·i·ous (lả-siv'i-ús), *adj.* lustful; lewd; wanton.

la·ser (lā'zẽr), *n.* a device emitting a narrow, very intense beam of light waves that have been amplified and concentrated by stimulated atoms.

laser disc, a videodisc for recording audio and video data to be read by a laser beam: also **laser disk**.

lash (lash), *v.t.* 1. to whip; scourge; flog. 2. to move with quick, sweeping swings or jerks; switch. 3. to dash against with whipping movements. 4. to censure or rebuke scathingly. 5. to arouse or incite by or as if by a series of stinging remarks. 6. to fasten or bind as with a rope: *v.i.* 1. to sweep or jerk quickly; switch. 2. to strike or as if with a whip: *n.* 1. a whip, especially the flexible striking part. 2. a stroke with or as if with a whip. 3. a scathing censure or rebuke. 4. an eyelash.

lash·ing ('ing), *n.* 1. the act of one that lashes. 2. a whipping, scourging, etc. 3. a scathing censure or rebuke. 4. a rope or cord, etc. used for fastening or binding.

---

a in *cap*, ā in *cane*, ä in *father*, ả in *abet*, e in *met*, ē in *be*, ẽ in *baker*, ẽ in *regent*, i in *pit*, ī in *fine*, ĭ in *manifest*, o in *hot*, ô in *horse*, ō in *bone*,

lass (las), n. a young woman; girl.

las·sie ('i), n. [Scottish], a lass.

las·si·tude (las'i-tōōd), n. weariness.

las·so (las'ō, 'ōō), n., pl. -sos, -soes, a long rope with a sliding noose, used for catching wild horses and cattle: v.t. -soed, -so·ing, to catch with a lasso.

last (last), adj. 1. coming after all others in time, place, or order. 2. just passed; most recent. 3. lowest. 4. utmost. 5. least likely: adv. 1. after all others. 2. on the last time or occasion. 3. finally: v.i. to remain in existence or operation; endure: v.t. 1. to endure throughout. 2. to be enough to supply throughout a given time: n. 1. the one that is last. 2. a block or form shaped like a human foot and used to hold a shoe being made or repaired.

Las·tex (las'teks), n. a fine, round rubber thread wound with cotton, rayon, etc. and woven or knitted into a fabric: a trademark.

last·ing (las'ting), adj. that lasts; durable: n. a strong, twilled cloth.

Last Judgment, in Theology, the final judgment at the end of the world.

last·ly (last'li), adv. in conclusion; finally.

Last Supper, the last supper eaten by Jesus with his disciples before the Crucifixion.

last word, 1. a final or conclusive word, remark, or authority. 2. [Informal], the very latest style.

latch (lach), n. a catch or fastening for a door, gate, window, etc.: v.t. & v.i. to fasten or close with a latch.

latch·et ('it), n. [Archaic], a shoestring or a sandal thong.

late (lāt), adj. lat·er or lat'ter, lat'est or last, 1. coming after the usual, proper, or expected time; tardy. 2. far on in the day, night, etc. 3. being toward the end; belonging to a far-advanced period, development, etc. 4. recent. 5. recently deceased: adv. lat'er, lat'est or last, 1. tardily. 2. at or until an advanced time. 3. toward the end of a certain period, development, etc. 4. recently; lately. —late'ness, n.

la·teen (la-tēn', lā-), adj. denoting or of a rig of vessels used chiefly on the Mediterranean, consisting of a triangular sail, short mast, and long yard: n. a vessel so rigged.

late·ly (lāt'li), adv. not long ago; recently.

la·tent (lāt'nt), adj. present, but inactive or invisible; hidden and undeveloped; dormant. —la'ten·cy, n.

lat·er·al (lat'ẽr-al), adj. of, pertaining to, proceeding from, or acting upon, the side. —lat'er·al·ly, adv.

Lat·er·an (lat'ẽr-ăn), n. 1. the church of St. John Lateran, cathedral of the Pope as bishop of Rome. 2. the palace, now a museum, adjoining this church.

la·tex (lā'teks), n., pl. lat·i·ces (lat'i-sēz), la'tex·es, 1. a milky liquid containing resins, proteins, etc. and found in certain trees and plants: it is used especially as the basis of rubber. 2. a suspension in water of particles of rubber or plastic: used in rubber goods, adhesives, paints, etc.

lath (lath), n., pl. laths (lathz, laths), 1. any one of the thin, narrow strips of wood that are

used as for lattices, groundwork for plastering, etc. 2. any framework for plaster, as of wire screening. 3. laths collectively.

lathe (lāth), n. a machine for shaping something of wood, metal, etc. by turning the article against a cutting or abrading tool: v.t. lathed, lath'ing, to shape so.

lath·er (lath'ẽr), n. 1. the foam or froth made as by soap in water. 2. profuse sweat, as on a racehorse: v.t. to cover with lather: v.i. to form, or become covered with, lather.

Lat·in (lat'n), adj. 1. of or pertaining to ancient Latium, a country southeast of ancient Rome; also, of or pertaining to ancient Rome. 2. of or pertaining to the people of ancient Latium or ancient Rome. 3. of or in the language of these people. 4. designating or of the languages derived from this language, the peoples speaking them, their countries and cultures, etc. 5. of or pertaining to the Roman Catholic Church: n. 1. a native or inhabitant of ancient Latium or ancient Rome. 2. the Indo-European language of the people of ancient Latium or ancient Rome. 3. a native of a country, such as Italy or Spain, in which the language spoken is derived from Latin. 4. a member of the Roman Catholic Church.

Latin cross, a plain, right-angle cross with the lower extension the longest.

Lat·in·ism (-izm), n. a Latin idiom.

Lat·in·ist (-ist), n. a Latin scholar.

La·tin·i·ty (la-tin'i-ti), n. use or knowledge of Latin.

Lat·in·ize (lat'n-īz), v.t. -ized, -iz·ing, 1. to translate into Latin. 2. to give Latin characteristics to.

lat·i·tude (lat'i-tōōd), n. 1. distance on the earth's surface as measured by degrees north or south from the equator; also, a place as determined by such measurement. 2. scope; extent; range. 3. freedom from restraint, restriction, etc.

lat·i·tu·di·nal (lat-i-tōōd'n-ăl), adj. of or in the direction of latitude.

lat·i·tu·di·nar·i·an (lat-i-tōōd-n-er'i-ăn), adj. given to, tolerating, or promoting freedom of thought and conduct, especially in religious matters: n. one that is latitudinarian.

la·tri·a (lā-trī'a), n. in the Roman Catholic Church, worship due to God only: the highest form of worship.

la·trine (la-trēn'), n. a camp privy.

lat·ten (lat'n), n. metal in thin sheets.

lat·ter (lat'ẽr), adj. 1. alternative comparative of late. 2. second of two things previously mentioned. 3. recent; modern. 4. closer to the final part. —lat'ter·ly, adv.

lat·tice (lat'is), n. crossed openwork of metal or wood: v.t. -ticed, -tic·ing, to furnish or cross with a lattice.

lat·tice·work (-wûrk), n. a lattice or a number of lattices.

laud (lôd), v.t. to praise highly; extol: n. 1. praise. 2. a hymn of praise.

laud·a·ble (lôd'a-bl), adj. commendable.

laud·a·num (lôd'n-ům), n. 1. formerly, a preparation of opium. 2. opium dissolved in alcohol.

laud·a·to·ry (lôd'a-tôr-i), adj. expressing praise.

laugh (laf), *n.* 1. a convulsive sound caused by merriment; expression of mirth, scorn, etc. 2. that which causes such a sound or expression: *v.i.* 1. to express merriment, scorn, etc. by a laugh. 2. to appear joyful, pleasant, etc. 3. to jeer (with *at*): *v.t.* to express or utter with laughter.

laugh·a·ble (laf'ā-bl), *adj.* tending to cause laughter; comic; ludicrous.

laugh·ing ('ing), *n.* the action of expressing merriment, scorn, etc. with a laugh.

laughing gas, nitrous oxide: this gas may cause laughter when breathed in as an anesthetic.

laughing jackass, a type of kingfisher found in Australia and characterized by its harsh, strident call.

laugh·ing·stock (laf'ing-stok), *n.* an object of laughter; person subject to ridicule or scorn.

laugh·ter (laf'tēr), *n.* a movement of the facial muscles and the eyes and a convulsive sound caused by a feeling of merriment, pleasure, scorn, etc.

launch (lônch), *v.t.* 1. to move or cause to slide (a vessel) into the water. 2. to hurl. 3. to send forth powerfully. 4. to begin, as on a new career: *v.i.* 1. to put to sea. 2. to enter on something new (often with *out* or *forth*). 3. to plunge (with *into*): *n.* 1. the act of launching a vessel. 2. a large, usually open, pleasure boat propelled by a motor: *adj.* of or pertaining to places, machinery, etc. for launching missiles, etc.

laun·der (lôn'dēr), *v.t. & v.i.* to wash, iron, etc. (clothes): *n.* a water gutter, as for mining. —**laun'der·er,** *n.* —**laun'dress** ('dris), *n.fem.*

laun·dry (lôn'dri), *n., pl.* **-dries,** 1. a place where clothes are washed and ironed. 2. the items that are laundered or are to be laundered.

laun·dry·man (-mån), *n., pl.* **-men** (-mėn), one who works in or delivers for a laundry.

lau·re·ate (lôr'i-it), *adj.* decked or invested with laurel: *n.* 1. an honored person. 2. same as poet laureate.

lau·rel (lôr'ĕl), *n.* 1. an evergreen shrub or tree with shiny, fragrant leaves. 2. a crown or wreath of laurel. 3. *pl.* honor; distinction. 4. a tree or shrub similar to the laurel. —**lau'reled** ('ĕld), *adj.*

lau·res·ti·nus, lau·rus·ti·nus (lô-rĕ-stī'nŭs, -stē'nŭs), *n.* a shrub of southern Europe with fragrant white flowers: also **lau'rus·tine** (-stin, -stēn).

la·va (lä'vä, lav'ä), *n.* 1. molten volcanic matter. 2. cooled and hardened volcanic matter.

lav·a·liere, lav·a·lier (lav-å-lir', lä-vä-), *n.* a pendant on a necklace.

lav·a·to·ry (lav'å-tôr-i), *n., pl.* **-ries,** 1. a bowl for washing. 2. a place equipped with a washbowl, toilet, etc.

lave (lāv), *v.t. & v.i.* **laved, lav'ing,** [Poetic], to wash or bathe.

lav·en·der (lav'ĕn-dēr), *n.* 1. an aromatic plant related to the mint, which produces an oil, known as *oil of lavender.* 2. a perfume made from the dried leaves, flowers, etc. of this plant. 3. a pale purple: *adj.* pale-purple.

la·ver (lā'vēr), *n.* an edible seaweed.

lav·ish (lav'ish), *adj.* 1. profuse. 2. extravagant:

v.t. to expend or bestow with profusion. —**lav'ish·ly,** *adv.*

law (lô), *n.* 1. the rules of action established by authority. 2. an edict, statute, or custom. 3. an act or enactment of a legislative body. 4. jurisprudence. 5. the judicial process. 6. the legal profession. 7. an axiom of science. 8. an established principle. 9. [L-], the Mosaic code (preceded by *the*).

law·a·bid·ing (lô'å-bid-ing), *adj.* submitting to the law.

law·break·er ('brā-kēr), *n.* a person who does not follow the law. —**law'break·ing,** *adj. & n.*

law·ful ('fŭl), *adj.* 1. agreeable or conformable to law. 2. just; legal. —**law'ful·ly,** *adv.*

law·less ('lis), *adj.* 1. not obedient to law; unruly. 2. not controlled by law; ungoverned. 3. not according to law. —**law'less·ness,** *n.*

law·mak·er ('mā-kēr), *n.* a person who brings law into being, as a legislator.

lawn (lôn), *n.* 1. a plot of grass kept closely mown. 2. fine cambric used for blouses, curtains, etc.

lawn mower, a machine with revolving blades, used to clip the grass of a lawn.

lawn tennis, see tennis.

law·ren·ci·um (lô-ren'si-ŭm), *n.* a radioactive chemical element.

law·suit (lô'sŏŏt), *n.* an action before a court.

law·yer (lô'yēr), *n.* a professional person skilled in legal knowledge who practices in the law courts.

lax (laks), *adj.* 1. loose. 2. not rigid. 3. vague.

lax·a·tive (lak'så-tiv), *adj.* loosening; purgative: *n.* a laxative medicine.

lax·i·ty ('si-ti), *n.* the state or quality of being lax.

lay (lā), *v.t.* **laid, lay'ing,** 1. to put or place. 2. to cause to lie down. 3. to settle; calm. 4. to wager. 5. to deposit. 6. to impose (with *upon*). 7. to impute. 8. to place and position. 9. to contrive. 10. to bring forward: *v.i.* to produce eggs: *n.* 1. relative arrangement. 2. a share of profits. 3. a poem telling a story. 4. [Archaic], a song: *adj.* 1. of or pertaining to the people, as distinguished from the clergy. 2. nonprofessional.

lay (lā), past tense of **lie** (recline).

lay·a·way plan (lā'å-wā), a system of purchase in which money is paid periodically until the full amount is reached and then the merchandise is turned over to the buyer.

lay·er (lā'ēr), *n.* 1. that which lays. 2. a single thickness of a stratum, row, or bed. 3. the runner of a plant covered with earth for propagation.

lay·ette (lā-et'), *n.* a full set of clothes, etc. for a new baby.

lay figure, 1. an artist's jointed model for hanging drapery upon. 2. a mere puppet.

lay·man (lā'mån), *n., pl.* **-men** ('mĕn), 1. one of the people, as distinguished from a clergyman. 2. a nonprofessional person.

lay·off (lā'ôf), *n.* the act of removing from employment for a limited time, or the duration of this.

lay·out ('out), *n.* 1. the act of arranging according to a plan. 2. that which is arranged.

---

a in *cap,* ā in *came,* ä in *father,* â in *abet,* e in *met,* ē in *be,* ē in *baker,* ĕ in *regent,* I in *pit,* ī in *fine,* i in *manifest,* o in *hot,* ô in *horse,* ō in *bone,*

3. the way of arranging. 4. an outfit, as of tools.

lay·o·ver ('ō-vĕr), *n.* a temporary cessation during travel.

laze (lāz), *v.i.* lazed, laz'ing, to be lazy: *v.t.* to idle (time, etc.) (often with *away*).

la·zy (lā'zi), *adj.* -zi·er, -zi·est, 1. idle; indolent; slothful. 2. slow-moving. —la'zi·ly, *adv.* —la'zi·ness, *n.*

la·zy·bones (-bōnz), *n.* [Informal], one who is lazy.

Lazy Su·san (sōō'zn), a food tray that revolves for selection.

lea (lē), *n.* [Poetic], a meadow; grassland.

leach (lēch), *v.t.* 1. to cause (a liquid) to filter through a mass. 2. to wash by filtering a liquid through. 3. to remove (a substance) by filtering water through and dissolving the substance in it: *v.i.* to have a dissolved substance be removed through filtering: *n.* the substance resulting from leaching.

lead (lēd), *v.t.* led, lead'ing, 1. to conduct with the hand, etc. 2. to guide; conduct. 3. to precede. 4. to allure (with *on*). 5. to induce. 6. to spend. 7. to direct or command. 8. to be first as compared with: *v.i.* 1. to take precedence. 2. to act as a leader. 3. to play the first card. 4. to be a guide. 5. to go (with *to, from,* etc.). 6. to develop as a consequence (with *to*): *n.* 1. guidance. 2. precedence. 3. the right to play first in cards. 4. the one who has the most important role in a play, etc. 5. something that provides a clue. 6. the distance in front. 7. the top place.

lead (led), *n.* 1. a soft, heavy, malleable, bluish-gray metallic element. 2. a plummet for sounding depths at sea. 3. a thin strip of type metal for separating lines in printing. 4. a stick of graphite in a pencil. 5. *pl.* [British], sheets of lead for roof covering: *adj.* consisting wholly or partially of lead: *v.t.* 1. to furnish, cover, or line with lead. 2. to place leads between lines of type.

lead·en (led'n), *adj.* 1. made of, or colored like, lead. 2. heavy. 3. sluggish. 4. dejected.

lead·er (lē'dĕr), *n.* 1. one who leads. 2. the chief article in a newspaper. 3. a musical conductor. 4. the player of the first instrument in a band. 5. a pipe to carry away liquid. 6. a tendon. 7. the foremost horse pulling a vehicle.

lead·ing (lē'ding), *n.* 1. the action of one who leads. 2. a guiding influence: *adj.* 1. chief. 2. guiding; controlling.

leading article, the most important article in a newspaper.

lead time (lēd), the period of time required from the decision to make a product to the beginning of actual production.

leaf (lēf), *n., pl.* leaves, 1. one of the thin, flat, usually green parts of a plant, growing laterally from a stem or branch. 2. a petal. 3. a part of a book; sheet of paper. 4. anything resembling a leaf. 5. a hinged part, as of a table. 6. a very thin, flat piece of metal: *v.i.* 1. to extend leaves. 2. to turn over the pages of (with *through*). —leaf'less, *adj.*

leaf·age (lēf'ij), *n.* leaves collectively.

leaf·let ('lit), *n.* 1. a small leaf. 2. a folding circular.

leaf·stalk ('stôk), *n.* the thin, long part of a leaf connecting the blade to the stem.

leaf·y (lē'fi), *adj.* leaf'i·er, leaf'i·est, full of leaves.

league (lēg), *n.* 1. an alliance for mutual interests. 2. a distance of three miles. 3. in *Sports,* a number of teams grouped to play against each other: *v.t. & v.i.* leagued, leagu'ing, to combine for mutual interests. —leagu'er, *n.*

leak (lēk), *n.* 1. an accidental hole that lets something in or out. 2. a way of escape that is not intended. 3. the condition of leaking: *v.i.* 1. to let a liquid or gas in or out through an accident. 2. to come in or get out through an accident. 3. to be perceived a little at a time: *v.t.* to permit an accidental escape or entry of. —leak'y, *adj.*

leak·age (lēk'ij), *n.* 1. the act of leaking. 2. a thing that leaks. 3. the amount of leaking. 4. a monetary allowance for loss by leaking.

lean (lēn), *v.i.* 1. to incline or deviate from an upright position. 2. to depend (with *on* or *upon*). 3. to have a tendency (with *to* or *toward*): *v.t.* to cause to lean: *adj.* 1. thin. 2. devoid of excess fat. 3. lacking in productivity, profit, etc.: *n.* meat having no excess fat. —lean'ness, *n.*

lean·ing (lēn'ing), *n.* a bent; predilection.

lean-to (lēn'tōō), *n., pl.* lean'-tos, a building whose rafters rest on another building or structure.

leap (lēp), *v.t.* leaped or leapt (lept, lēpt), leap'ing, 1. to pass over by leaping; jump or spring over. 2. to make leap: *v.i.* 1. to jump; vault. 2. to receive enthusiastically (with *at*): *n.* 1. the act of leaping; jump; spring. 2. the space passed in leaping. 3. an abrupt passing from one condition into another.

leap·frog (lēp'frôg), *n.* a game played by one leaping over the back of another, while the latter is in a stooping position: *v.t. & v.i.* -frogged, -frog·ging, to leap in this manner (with *over*).

leap year, a year of 366 days, when February has 29 days.

learn (lûrn), *v.t.* learned or learnt (lûrnt), learn'ing, 1. to acquire knowledge of. 2. to fix in the mind. 3. to get to be cognizant of: *v.i.* 1. to gain knowledge or skill. 2. to receive information (*of* or *about*). —learn'er, *n.*

learn·ed (lûr'nid), *adj.* 1. erudite; skilled. 2. (lûrnd), obtained by living, training, etc.

learn·ing (lûr'ning), *n.* 1. the obtaining of knowledge, skill, etc. 2. the knowledge or skill acquired; scholarship.

learning disability, any of several conditions, believed to involve the nervous system, which limit the ability to read, write, etc.

lease (lēs), *n.* 1. a written contract for the letting of land or dwellings for a specified period of time. 2. the period of time: *v.t.* leased, leas'ing, 1. to let by a written contract. 2. to take a lease of.

lease-hold (lēs′hōld), n. property held by lease: adj. held on lease.

leash (lēsh), n. 1. a thong, cord, or thin rope for holding in restraint, as a dog. 2. in Hunting, a brace and a half; three of a kind: v.t. to tie or bind by or as by a leash.

least (lēst), alternative superlative of little: adj. smallest in degree, size, value, importance, etc.: adv. in the lowest or smallest degree.

least-wise (lēst′wīz), adv. [Informal], at least; anyhow: also least′ways (′wāz).

leath-er (leth′ēr), n. 1. the tanned skin of an animal. 2. a piece of, or an article made from, a tanned hide. 3. anything made of leather: v.t. 1. to cover with leather. 2. [Informal], to thrash with or as with a leather strap.

leath-er-back (-bak), n. a large turtle of tropical seas with a leatherlike outer shell.

Leath-er-ette (leth-ê-ret′), n. imitation leather of cloth or paper: a trademark.

leath-ern (leth′ērn), adj. made of or resembling leather.

leath-er-neck (leth′ēr-nek), n. [Slang], a United States Marine.

leath-er-y (-i), adj. resembling leather in consistency; tough.

leave (lēv), n. 1. permission granted. 2. departure. 3. farewell. 4. a period of time during which one is allowed to be away: v.t. left, leav′ing, 1. to depart from. 2. to forsake; abandon. 3. to bequeath. 4. to desist from (with off). 5. to turn over to the care of (with to or up to). 6. to let stay. 7. to have left over. 8. [Slang], to permit: v.i. to go away.

leave (lēv), v.i. leaved, leav′ing, to bear leaves.

leav-en (lev′'n), v.t. 1. to produce fermentation in (dough) and thus make rise. 2. to spread through (something), bringing about a difference: n. 1. a fermenting substance used to make dough rise. 2. an influence that slowly causes changes in things or opinions.

leav-en-ing (-ing), n. 1. same as leaven. 2. a producing of the effect of being leavened.

leave of absence, an allowing to be away from employment, etc. for a long period of time; also, the length of this absence.

leaves (lēvz), n. plural of leaf.

leave-tak-ing (lēv′tāk-ing), n. the act of saying goodbye.

leav-ing (lēv′ing), n. 1. the act of going away; departure. 2. pl. remnants; refuse; scraps.

lech (lech), v.i. & n. [Slang], same as lust.

lech-er (lech′ēr), n. a lewd man.

lech-er-ous (-ŭs), adj. characterized by lust.

lech-er-y (-i), adj. lustfulness; lewdness.

lec-i-thin (les′i-thin), n. a phosphorous compound contained in the cell material of animals and vegetables: added to medicines, food, etc.

lec-tern (lek′tērn), n. 1. the reading desk of a church. 2. a lecturer's rack for holding notes, etc.

lec-tion (lek′shŭn), n. a portion of the Scriptures to be read in church service.

lec-tion-ar-y (-er-i), n., pl. -ar-ies, a table of Scripture readings for the year.

lec-tor (lek′tēr), n. 1. a reader in a church

service. 2. one ordained to minor orders of the Roman Catholic Church.

lec-ture (lek′chēr), n. 1. a formal discourse on any subject. 2. a long reprimand: v.i. to deliver a lecture: v.t. 1. to deliver a lecture to. 2. to reprimand. —lec′tur-er, n.

led (led), past tense and past participle of lead.

ledge (lej), n. 1. a shelf. 2. a ridge of rocks. 3. a layer of ore.

ledg-er (lej′ēr), n. 1. the principal account book in a business. 2. a flat stone over a tomb.

ledger line, same as leger line.

lee (lē), n. 1. the side opposite that from which the wind blows. 2. the calm or sheltered side on a ship: adj. of or on the sheltered side.

leech (lēch), n. 1. an aquatic worm with a sucker, formerly used in medicine for bleeding. 2. one who hangs on and takes away from another; parasite. 3. the outside edge of a sail: v.i. to behave as a leech (often with onto).

leek (lēk), n. a biennial plant resembling the green onion.

leer (lir), n. a sly, sidelong look indicative of malice, triumph, or insolence.

leer-y (lir′i), adj. leer′i-er, leer′i-est, on one's guard; feeling suspicion.

lees (lēz), n.pl. dregs of wine.

lee shore, the shore on the lee side of a ship.

lee-ward (lē′wārd), n. the lee side: adj. of or pertaining to the lee side.

lee-way (lē′wā), n. 1. the drift of a vessel to the leeward of its course. 2. [Informal], room or margin for action, etc.

left (left), adj. 1. of or pertaining to the side of the human body towards the west when one is facing the north. 2. nearer to this side when turned in the direction of a thing specified: n. 1. the left side. 2. the part or direction on the left side. 3. [often L-], in Politics, a stance or party favoring change (often preceded by the): adv. on or in the direction of the left side.

left (left), past tense and past participle of leave.

left-hand (left′hand′), adj. 1. on or toward the left. 2. of, designed for, or done by the left hand.

left-hand-ed (left′han′did), adj. 1. using the left hand with greater strength or dexterity than the right. 2. made for or done by the left hand. 3. awkward. 4. indirectly malicious: adv. by the left hand.

left-ist (′ist), n. a person who favors radical or liberal change in politics: adj. of or pertaining to a leftist or leftists.

left wing, the part of a political party or group favoring radical or liberal change. —left′-wing′, adj. —left′-wing′er, n.

leg (leg), n. 1. one of the limbs by which human beings and animals walk. 2. in human beings, often the part between the knee and the ankle. 3. anything resembling a leg. 4. a support. 5. a covering for the leg. 6. a part of a trip. 7. the run of a ship on one tack. 8. in Cricket, the field to the left and in back of the batsman: v.i. legged, leg′ging, [Informal], to run (usually with it).

---

leg-a-cy (leg'ã-si), n., pl. -cies, 1. a gift by will of money or property; bequest. 2. anything inherited from an ancestor, etc.

le-gal (lē'gâl), adj. 1. of or pertaining to law or lawyers. 2. authorized or permitted by law; legitimate. —le'gal-ly, adv.

legal holiday, a holiday authorized by statute.

le-gal-ism (lē'gâl-izm), n. 1. close adherence or conformity to law. 2. the observance of the strict letter of the law rather than its spirit. —le-gal-is'tic, adj.

le-gal-i-ty (li-gal'i-ti), n., pl. -ties, conformity to law.

le-gal-ize (lē'gâ-līz), v.t. -ized, -iz-ing, to make lawful.

legal tender, money that must be taken in payment according to the law.

leg-ate (leg'it), n. a Papal ambassador or envoy. —leg'a-tine (-tin, -tïn), adj.

leg-a-tee (leg-â-tē'), n. a person to whom a legacy is bequeathed.

le-ga-tion (li-gā'shǔn), n. 1. a diplomatic mission on a level below that of an embassy. 2. the persons composing such a mission. 3. the official residence of such persons.

le-ga-to (li-gät'ō), adj. & adv. in Music, smooth(ly); even(ly).

leg-end (lej'ĕnd), n. 1. a romantic or non-historical story; myth; fable. 2. an inscription, as on a coin, coat of arms, etc. 3. a famous person or that person's past history. 4. a short explanation that goes along with a picture or map.

leg-end-ar-y (lej'ĕn-der-i), adj. of or founded on legend; mythical.

leg-er-de-main (lej-ēr-di-mān'), n. 1. sleight of hand. 2. deception.

leg-er line (lej'ēr), in Music, a line either above or below the staff.

leg-ged (leg'id, legd), adj. having legs.

leg-ging (leg'ing), n. a protective covering for the leg below the knee.

Leg-horn (leg'hôrn), n. 1. [sometimes l-], a variety of small domestic chicken. 2. [l-], a plaiting for hats and bonnets made of a straw grown in Italy for the purpose and which is cut green and bleached when dry; also, a hat or bonnet of this straw.

leg-i-ble (lej'i-bl), adj. capable of being read; clear; distinct; easily apparent. —leg-i-bil'i-ty, n. —leg'i-bly, adv.

le-gion (lē'jǔn), n. 1. a division of the ancient Roman army. 2. a great number. 3. an army. —le-gion-naire (lē-ji-ner'), n.

le-gion-ar-y (-er-i), adj. of, pertaining to, or consisting of legions; n., pl. -ar-ies, a soldier of a legion.

Legion of Honor, an order of merit instituted by Napoleon in 1802 as a reward for civil and military service.

leg-is-late (lej'is-lāt), v.i. -lat-ed, -lat-ing, to make or enact a law: v.t. to effect by legislation.

leg-is-la-tion (lej-is-lā'shǔn), n. 1. the act of making a law or laws. 2. the law or laws so made.

leg-is-la-tive (lej'is-lāt-iv), adj. 1. of, pertaining to, or enacted by legislation. 2. having the power to legislate. 3. of or pertaining to a

legislature: n. the legislature; lawmaking power in government.

leg-is-la-tor (-lāt-ēr), n. a lawgiver; member of a legislative assembly.

leg-is-la-ture (-lā-chēr), n. that body in a state which is invested with the power of enacting and repealing laws; legislative body of a State or territory.

le-git-i-mate (lē-jit'i-mit), adj. 1. lawful. 2. born in wedlock. 3. logically correct. 4. according to the rules. 5. of or pertaining to the professional theater: v.t. (-māt), -mat-ed, -mat-ing, to make, or sanction as, lawful; render legitimate. —le-git'i-ma-cy (-mâ-si), n. —le-git'i-mate-ly, adv. —le-git-i-ma'tion, n.

le-git-i-mize (-miz), v.t. -mized, -miz-ing, to make legitimate; justify, authorize, etc.: also le-git'i-ma-tize.

leg-man (leg'man), n., pl. -men ('men), 1. a reporter who actually goes out and gathers the information. 2. one who gets information or does outside work for someone inside an office.

leg-room (leg'rōōm), n. enough space for the legs when in a sitting position.

leg-ume (leg'ūm, li-gūm'), n. 1. a two-valve seed vessel having its seeds attached to one side only, as a pea pod. 2. any of these seeds. 3. any of a family of plants including the peas, beans, etc. having these seed vessels. —le-gu-mi-nous (li-gū'min-ŭs), adj.

le-gu-min (li-gū'min), n. a legume globulin.

leg-work (leg'wûrk), n. [Informal], customary travel connected with a job.

lei (lā, lā'i), n., pl. leis, a wreath of flowers and leaves in Hawaii.

lei-sure (lē'zhēr, lezh'ēr), n. spare time for relaxation: adj. free from business; unoccupied. —lei'sured, adj.

lei-sure-ly (-li), adj. done at leisure; deliberate; slow: adv. in a deliberate way.

lem-ma (lem'â), n., pl. -mas, -ma-ta ('â-tâ), 1. in Logic, a secondary proposition accepted for use in a demonstration of a primary one. 2. the title of a gloss or annotation.

lem-ming (lem'ing), n., pl. -mings, -ming, a small, short-tailed Arctic rodent.

lem-on (lem'ǒn), n. 1. a small fruit like an orange with a light-yellow skin and very acid pulp and juice. 2. the tree bearing this fruit. 3. the pale-yellow color of a lemon. 4. [Slang], a faulty article: adj. of, pertaining to, or of the color of a lemon.

lem-on-ade (lem-ô-nād'), n. a beverage of sweetened water flavored with lemon.

le-mur (lē'mēr), n. a small, nocturnal animal related to the monkeys.

lend (lend), v.t. lent, lend'ing, 1. to grant to another for temporary use. 2. to loan (money) with interest. 3. to grant; give over: v.i. to make a loan.

lend-lease (lend'lēs'), n. in World War II, guns, food, etc. given to help other countries whose defense was related to that of the United States.

length (length), n. 1. the measure of anything from end to end. 2. extent. 3. duration. 4. a long reach. 5. a single piece of a standard length.

length·en (lengkth'n), *v.t. & v.i.* to make or grow longer.

length·wise ('wīz), *adv. & adj.* in the direction of the length: also **length'ways** ('wāz).

length·y ('i), *adj.* **length'i·er, length'i·est,** long and tiresome. —**length'i·ly,** *adv.*

le·ni·ent (lē'ni·ént, lēn'yènt), *adj.* mild; merciful. —**le'ni·en·cy,** *pl.* **-cies, le'ni·ence,** *n.*

len·i·tive (lēn'i-tiv), *adj.* assuaging; emollient.

len·i·ty (-ti), *n.* mildness; kindness.

le·no (lē'nō), *n.* a kind of gauzy material.

lens (lenz), *n.* 1. a convex or concave glass, etc. adapted for changing the direction of rays of light and thus magnifying or diminishing the apparent size of objects. 2. a contrivance for changing the direction of sound or electrical waves. 3. the transparent part of the eye that focuses light.

Lent (lent), *n.* an annual season of fasting consisting of 40 weekdays, in preparation for Easter Sunday. —**Lent'en, lent'en,** *adj.*

lent (lent), past tense and past participle of lend.

len·tic·u·lar (len-tik'yoo·lēr), *adj.* 1. doubly convex. 2. of or pertaining to a lens.

len·til (lent'l), *n.* 1. a leguminous plant. 2. its orbicular seed, used for food.

Le·o (lē'ō), *n.* 1. a northern constellation between Cancer and Virgo. 2. the fifth sign of the zodiac.

le·o·nine (lē'ō·nīn), *adj.* of or like a lion; powerful; kingly.

leop·ard (lep'ērd), *n., pl.* **-ards, -ard,** 1. a large, wild animal related to the cat, having a tan coat with black spots. 2. same as jaguar.

le·o·tard (lē'ō·tärd), *n.* a closely fitting garment of one piece that covers the torso.

lep·er (lep'ēr), *n.* one affected with leprosy.

lep·i·dop·ter·an (lep·i·dop'tēr·ăn), *n.* one of a large group of insects, including the butterflies and moths.

lep·re·chaun (lep'rē·kôn), *n.* in *Irish Folklore,* a fairy who can enrich anyone quick enough to catch him.

lep·ro·sy (lep'rō·si), *n.* a chronic skin disease characterized by ulcers and white scaly scabs.

lep·rous ('rŭs), *adj.* 1. infected with leprosy. 2. covered with white scales.

les·bi·an (lez'bi·ăn), *n.* a female homosexual. —**les'bi·an·ism,** *n.*

lese maj·es·ty (lēz maj'is-ti), a crime against royalty or the sovereign power; treason.

le·sion (lē'zhŭn), *n.* 1. an injury. 2. a morbid change in a function or organism.

less (les), alternative comparative of little: *adj.* not so much; smaller: *adv.* in a smaller or lower degree: *n.* a smaller quantity: *prep.* reduced by the subtraction of.

les·see (les-ē'), *n.* one to whom a lease is granted.

less·en (les'n), *v.t. & v.i.* to make or become less; reduce.

less·er (les'ēr), alternative comparative of little: *adj.* smaller or less significant.

les·son (les'n), *n.* 1. that which a pupil learns or is supposed to learn. 2. an instruction or lecture given at one time. 3. a precept. 4. *pl.* exercises for study. 5. a portion of Scrip-

ture read at a church service. 6. an admonition.

les·sor (les'ôr), *n.* one who grants a lease.

lest (lest), *conj.* for fear that.

let (let), *v.t.* **let, let'ting,** 1. to permit. 2. to lease. 3. to give out on contract. 4. to emit; discharge. 5. to enable. 6. to abandon or relinquish: now only in the phrases *let alone* or *let be.* 7. to allow to be done: *v.i.* to be hired or leased: *n.* 1. an obstacle; impediment. 2. in *Tennis, etc.* a stroke in which the course of the ball is interfered with.

-let (lit, let), a suffix meaning *small.*

let·down (let'doun), *n.* 1. a retarding or relaxing. 2. the downward flight of an aircraft. 3. a feeling of dissatisfaction after high hope.

le·thal (lē'thǎl), *adj.* deadly; fatal.

lethal chamber, an execution room where persons are put to death by poison gas.

leth·ar·gy (leth'ēr-ji), *n., pl.* **-gies,** 1. morbid drowsiness; unnatural, prolonged slumber. 2. apathy; dullness. —**le·thar·gic** (li-thär'jik), *adj.* —**le·thar'gi·cal·ly,** *adv.*

Le·the (lē'thē), *n.* 1. in *Greek & Roman Mythology,* the stream of forgetfulness of the underworld, whose waters, when drunk, produced loss of memory. 2. oblivion; forgetfulness.

let's (lets), let us.

let·ter (let'ēr), *n.* 1. a mark or character used to represent a sound. 2. a written or printed communication. 3. a printing type. 4. literal meaning. 5. a document certifying certain privileges. 6. *pl.* literary culture; literature in the aggregate. 7. *pl.* erudition; learning: *v.t.* to inscribe or mark with letters.

let·tered (let'ērd), *adj.* 1. learned. 2. literate. 3. inscribed or marked with letters.

let·ter·ing (-ing), *n.* the act or process of inscribing with letters.

letter of credit, a letter from a bank to other banks stating that the person mentioned in the letter is entitled to credit up to a stated amount.

let·ter·per·fect (-pūr'fikt), *adj.* completely accurate.

letters of administration, in *Law,* a document by which an administrator is authorized to administer the goods or property of a deceased person.

letters patent, a written document under government seal, authorizing a person to do some act or enjoy some privilege.

let·tuce (let'is), *n.* 1. a plant with succulent, green leaves. 2. the leaves of this plant used as a salad.

let·up (let'up), *n.* [Informal], 1. a decreasing. 2. a cessation.

leu·co-, a combining form meaning *white, colorless:* also, before a vowel, **leuc-:** many medical or biological words are spelled **leuko-** or **leuk-.**

leu·ke·mi·a (lōō-kē'mi·ǎ), *n.* a disease in which there is an excess of leukocytes: also **leu·kae'mi·a.**

leu·ko·cyte (lōō'kō-sīt), *n.* any one of the blood corpuscles which help protect the body against infection; white blood corpuscle.

---

a in c*a*p, ā in c*a*ne, ä in f*a*ther, á in *a*bet, e in m*e*t, ē in b*e*, ē ın bak*e*r, é in reg*e*nt, i in p*i*t, ī in f*i*ne, ı in man*i*fest, o in h*o*t, ô in h*o*rse, ō ın b*o*ne,

leu·ko·ma (lōō-kō′må), *n.* a white opacity of the cornea of the eye.

leu·ko·pe·ni·a (lōō-kō-pē′ni-å), *n.* a deficiency of white blood corpuscles in the blood.

leu·kor·rhe·a (lōō-kō-rē′å), *n.* a white discharge from the vagina due to inflammation of the membranes.

Lev·an·tine (lev′ån-tūn), *adj.* of or pertaining to the Levant, a region on the eastern Mediterranean, or its inhabitants: *n.* 1. a native or inhabitant of the Levant. 2. [l-], a strong, twilled silk fabric.

le·va·tor (lĕ-vāt′ẽr), *n.*, *pl.* lev·a·to·res (lev-å-tōr′iz). le·va′tors, a muscle that serves to raise some part.

lev·ee (lev′i), *n.* a river embankment to stop flooding: *v.t.* to embank with a levee.

lev·el (lev′l), *n.* 1. a horizontal area, line, or plane. 2. a surface without inequalities. 3. a state of equality. 4. a standard; normal state. 5. an instrument for indicating a horizontal line or plane. 6. a social distinction: *adj.* 1. even; smooth. 2. horizontal. 3. equal to something else in importance. 4. calm; well-balanced. 5. up to the same height (with *with*): *v.t.* & *v.i.* -eled or -elled, -el·ing or -el·ling, 1. to make or become even. 2. to free from inequalities. 3. to knock down. 4. to point (a gun) in taking aim. 5. in *Surveying*, to determine heights at different points.

lev·el·er, lev·el·ler (lev′l-ẽr), *n.* 1. one who or that which levels. 2. one who would abolish social inequalities.

lev·el·head·ed (-hed′id), *adj.* calm and sensible.

lev·er (lev′ẽr, lē′vẽr), *n.* 1. a bar used for raising or moving. 2. a way of accomplishing something. 3. a bar of metal, etc. turning on a fixed support, for raising a weight.

lev·er·age (-ij), *n.* 1. the mechanical power gained from using a lever. 2. lever action.

lev·er·et (lev′ẽr-it), *n.* a very young hare.

lev·i·a·ble (lev′i-å-bl), *adj.* that may be levied upon; assessable.

le·vi·a·than (lĕ-vī′å-thån), *n.* 1. in the *Bible*, a large unidentified aquatic animal. 2. anything huge, as a whale.

lev·i·gate (lev′i-gāt), *v.t.* -gat·ed, -gat·ing, to reduce to a fine, smooth powder.

Le·vi's (lē′vīz), *n.* tight denim trousers: a trademark.

lev·i·tate (lev′i-tāt), *v.t.* -tat·ed, -tat·ing, to make buoyant in the air: *v.i.* to rise by buoyancy or lightness.

lev·i·ta·tion (lev-i-tā′shŭn), *n.* 1. the act of levitating. 2. the illusion of a heavy body in air without support.

Le·vit·i·cus (lē-vit′i-kŭs), *n.* the third book of the Pentateuch.

lev·i·ty (lev′i-ti), *n.*, *pl.* -ties, 1. lightness of disposition, conduct, etc.; trifling gaiety. 2. inconsistency.

lev·u·lose (lev′yoo-lōs), *n.* a fruit sugar.

lev·y (lev′i), *v.t.* lev′ied, lev′y·ing, 1. to raise or collect (an army, tax, etc.). 2. to make (war): *v.i.* 1. to make a levy. 2. in *Law*, to seize property in execution of a judgment (often with *on*): *n.*, *pl.* lev′ies, 1. the act of raising money or troops. 2. the amount or number raised.

lewd (lōōd), *adj.* licentious; libidinous. —lewd′·ly, *adv.* —lewd′ness, *n.*

lex·i·cog·ra·phy (lek-si-kog′rå-fi), *n.* the art or occupation of compiling dictionaries. —lex·i·cog′ra·pher, *n.*

lex·i·col·o·gy (-kol′ō-ji), *n.* the science of the derivation and meaning of words.

lex·i·con (lek′si-kon), *n.* 1. the vocabulary of a particular area, writer, etc. 2. a dictionary of words.

Ley·den jar (līd′n), a glass jar coated outside and inside with tinfoil, for accumulating electricity.

li·a·bil·i·ty (lī-å-bil′i-ti), *n.*, *pl.* -ties, 1. the state of being liable. 2. *pl.* debts. 3. that which causes one to be liable. 4. that which is unfavorable or detrimental.

li·a·ble (lī′å-bl), *adj.* 1. exposed to damage, danger, expense, etc.; responsible. 2. being probable (with *to*).

li·ai·son (lē′å-zon, -zōn), *n.* 1. unlawful intimacy between a man and a woman. 2. the joining of two adjacent words in spoken French. 3. a relationship established between bodies of troops, etc., for communication, mutual function, etc.

li·a·na (li-än′å), *n.* any climbing vine: also li·ane′ (-än′).

li·ar (lī′ẽr), *n.* one inclined to lying.

lib (lib), *n.* short for liberation.

li·ba·tion (lī-bā′shŭn), *n.* 1. the act of pouring wine or oil on the ground, as a sacrifice to some deity. 2. the liquid so poured out. 3. a drink of alcoholic liquor.

li·bel (lī′bl), *n.* 1. defamation of character or reputation; slander. 2. any writing, print, publication, or picture calculated to injure reputation or character. 3. the act of publishing libel: *v.t.* -beled or -belled, -bel·ing or -bel·ling, 1. to publish a libel against. 2. to defame; asperse character. 3. to file a complaining suit against (a ship or goods). —li′·bel·er, li′bel·ler, *n.* —li′bel·ous, li′bel·lous, *adj.*

li·ber (lī′bẽr, lē′bẽr), *n.*, *pl.* li·bri (lī′brī, lē′brī), [Latin], a book.

lib·er·al (lib′ẽr-ål), *adj.* 1. generous; munificent. 2. plentiful. 3. free from narrowness in ideas or doctrines. 4. not literal. 5. advocating extension of individual freedom to all persons within a political institution: *n.* 1. an opponent of conservatism; one who advocates progress and an extension of personal freedom in institutions, as politics, religion, etc. 2. [L-], one who belongs to a liberal political party, as of England. —lib′er·al·ism, *n.* —lib′er·al·ly, *adv.* —lib′er·al·ness, *n.*

liberal arts, college subjects of a nontechnical nature, as literature, history, etc.

lib·er·al·i·ty (lib-ĕ-ral′i-ti), *n.*, *pl.* -ties, 1. the quality of being liberal. 2. generosity; magnanimity. 3. mental breadth; catholicity.

lib·er·al·ize (lib′ẽr-å-līz), *v.t.* & *v.i.* -ized, -iz·ing, to free or become free from narrowness or prejudice.

lib·er·ate (lib′ĕ-rāt), *v.t.* -at·ed, -at·ing, to set free, as from slavery. —lib·er·a′tion, *n.* —lib′er·a·tor, *n.*

lib·er·tar·i·an (lib-ẽr-ter′i-ån), *n.* 1. one who advocates, or upholds, the principles of per-

---

ŏ in drag*on*, ōō in cr*u*de, oo in w*oo*l, u in c*u*p, ū in c*u*re, ū in t*u*rn, ŭ in foc*u*s, oi in b*oy*, ou in h*ou*se, th in *th*in, *th* in shea*th*e, g in *g*et, j in *j*oy, y in *y*et.

sonal liberty in thought and action. 2. a believer in freedom of will: *adj.* of or pertaining to the doctrine upheld by libertarians.

lib·er·tine (lib′ẽr-tēn), *n.* one who leads a sexually unrestrained life: *adj.* morally or socially unrestrained; licentious.

lib·er·ty (lib′ẽr-ti), *n., pl.* -ties, 1. freedom from slavery, imprisonment, etc. 2. a special privilege or exemption. 3. permission for a sailor to go ashore. 4. an ungranted or undue freedom.

li·bid·i·nous (li-bid′n-ŭs), *adj.* lustful.

li·bi·do (li-bē′dō, -bī′-), *n.* 1. the instinct for sex. 2. in *Psychoanalysis*, the mental energy of love and positiveness.

Li·bra (lī′brä, lē′-), *n.* 1. a southern constellation between Virgo and Scorpio. 2. the seventh sign of the zodiac.

li·brar·i·an (lī-brer′i-ăn), *n.* 1. the custodian of a library. 2. one who is skilled in the science of library use.

li·brar·y (lī′brer-i), *n., pl.* -brar·ies, 1. an arranged collection of books, etc. 2. the building where such a collection is kept. 3. an institution in charge of the collection.

li·brate (lī′brāt), *v.i.* -brat·ed, -brat·ing, to vibrate, as a balance; oscillate. —li′bra·to·ry (′brā-tôr-i), *adj.*

li·bra·tion (li-brā′shŭn), *n.* 1. the act of balancing. 2. in *Astronomy*, an apparent or real irregularity in the moon's motion.

li·bret·to (li-bret′ō), *n., pl.* -tos, -ti (′ī), 1. a book containing the words of an opera, oratorio, etc. 2. the text itself. —li·bret′tist, *n.*

li·cense (līs′ns), *n.* 1. permission; legal permit to do something. 2. unrestrained liberty stretched to an excess. 3. a legal document authorizing leave. 4. freedom to turn from the prescribed path or precept. Also British spelling **licence**: *v.t.* -censed, -cens·ing, to authorize by a legal permit.

li·cen·see (līs-n-sē′), *n.* one who receives a license.

li·cen·ti·ate (lī-sen′shi-it, -āt), *n.* one licensed to practice a profession.

li·cen·tious (lī-sen′shŭs), *adj.* unrestrained morally or legally; lascivious; dissolute. —li·cen′tious·ness, *n.*

li·chen (lī′kĕn), *n.* 1. a plant made up of a particular fungus and alga, growing as on stones, etc. 2. an eruptive skin disease.

lic·it (lis′it), *adj.* lawful.

lick (lik), *v.t.* 1. to pass the tongue over. 2. to move over as with the tongue. 3. to lap (with *up*). 4. [Informal], to vanquish. 5. [Informal], to flog; beat: *v.i.* to make a licking movement: *n.* 1. the act of licking. 2. a minute amount. 3. short for **salt lick**. 4. [Informal], a sharp stroke. 5. [Informal], a quick or careless act.

lick·ing (lik′ing), *n.* 1. lapping with the tongue. 2. [Informal], a flogging; also, a vanquishing.

lick·spit·tle (lik′spit-l), *n.* a servile flatterer.

lic·o·rice (lik′ẽr-ish, -is), *n.* 1. the root or inspissated juice of a European perennial plant with blue flowers. 2. candy which contains this root or juice.

lic·tor (lik′tẽr), *n.* an ancient Roman official who attended the chief magistrates and bore the fasces.

lid (lid), *n.* 1. a movable cover closing an aperture; top. 2. short for **eyelid**. 3. [Informal], a check or control. 4. [Slang], a cap; hat. —lid′ded, *adj.*

lie (lī), *v.i.* lay, lain, ly′ing, 1. to rest in a recumbent position; recline. 2. to be situated or placed. 3. to rest or remain. 4. to be. 5. in *Law*, to be maintainable: *n.* 1. position; arrangement. 2. the lair of an animal.

lie (lī), *v.i.* lied, ly′ing, 1. to utter a falsehood. 2. to represent falsely: *v.t.* to do by lying: *n.* a falsehood; willful misstatement.

lie detector, same as **polygraph**.

lief (lēf), *adv.* willingly: only in the phrases *would as lief, had as lief*, etc.

liege (lēj), *adj.* 1. bound by feudal service or tenure. 2. maintaining allegiance; constant: *n.* a feudal vassal, lord, or sovereign.

li·en (lēn, lē′ĕn), *n.* a legal claim on property as security for payment.

lieu (lōō), *n.* place; stead: in the phrase *in lieu of.*

lieu·ten·ant (lōō-ten′ănt), *n.* an officer next below a captain in the U.S. military. 2. an officer next below a lieutenant commander in the U.S. Navy. 3. a deputy. —lieu·ten′an·cy (′ăn-si), *n., pl.* -cies.

lieutenant colonel, a U.S. military officer ranking next below a colonel.

lieutenant commander, in the *U.S. Navy*, an officer ranking below a commander and above a lieutenant.

lieutenant governor, an official authorized by election to perform the duties of a governor in the latter's absence or in case of death.

lieutenant junior grade, in the *U.S. Navy*, an officer ranking next above an ensign.

life (līf), *n., pl.* **lives**, 1. animate existence. 2. vitality, or the cause of it. 3. the soul's presence. 4. the period between birth and death. 5. an essential to the maintenance of something. 6. all living things. 7. the quality or state of growth and reproduction in animals and plants. 8. a human being. 9. a way of existence. 10. those persons and actions of a particular location or time. 11. a biography.

life belt, a kind of life preserver that resembles a belt.

life-blood (līf′blud′), *n.* 1. the blood essential for life. 2. an essential part.

life-boat (′bōt), *n.* a small emergency rescue boat taken on a larger ship.

life buoy, same as **life preserver**.

life-guard (′gärd), *n.* an expert swimmer employed at a bathing place for safety.

life insurance, insurance on a person's life for a specified amount to be paid when the person dies.

life jacket, a life preserver that resembles a jacket without sleeves: also **life vest**.

life-less (′lis), *adj.* 1. never having had life. 2. no longer with life. 3. languid.

---

a in cap, ā in cane, ä in father, ȧ in abet, e in met, ē in be, ẽ in baker, ĕ in regent, ĭ in pit, ī in fine, i in manifest, o in hot, ô in horse, ō in bone,

life·like ('līk), *adj.* 1. having the qualities of a real person or thing. 2. similar to real life.

life·line ('līn), *n.* 1. a rope connected to a diver. 2. a trade route of great significance.

life·long (līf-lông'), *adj.* continuing or unchanging throughout a lifetime.

life net, a net used by firemen to break the fall of persons jumping from a burning building.

life preserver, a device in the form of a ring or jacket, composed of cork or kapok covered with canvas, for keeping a person afloat.

lif·er (līf'ēr), *n.* [Slang] one imprisoned for life because of a crime.

life raft, a small boat or raft which can be inflated for use in an emergency at sea.

life·sav·er ('sā-vēr), *n.* 1. same as lifeguard. 2. [Informal], a help or aid during difficulty.

life-size ('sīz), *adj.* of the same height and proportions as that which is depicted: also **life'-sized.**

life style, the entire makeup of one's way of living.

life·time ('tīm), *n.* the extent of life or of function or effect.

life·work ('würk), *n.* the occupation that takes up one's entire life.

lift (lift), *v.t.* 1. to raise from the ground. 2. to elevate. 3. to support in the air. 4. to settle (a debt). 5. to discontinue (a siege, etc.). 6. [Slang], to steal: *v.i.* 1. to exert strength in raising. 2. to rise in the air: *n.* 1. the act of lifting. 2. the extent of this. 3. the total lifted. 4. promotional power. 5. elevation of placement, feeling, etc. 6. a means of journeying to one's destination. 7. aid. 8. a machine for raising or lifting. 9. [British], an elevator.

lift-off (lift'ôf), *n.* 1. the vertical thrust and rising of a spacecraft, missile, etc. at launching. 2. the time at which this takes place.

lig·a·ment (lig'â-mĕnt), *n.* 1. a bond or tie. 2. in *Anatomy*, a strong elastic tissue connecting the extremities of moving bones and keeping organs in place.

lig·a·ture (lig'â-chēr), *n.* 1. a tie or bond. 2. a tying or bonding. 3. two or more letters united and cast on one piece of type. 4. in *Music*, a slur or notes joined by a slur. 5. in *Surgery*, a narrow tie for closing arteries, etc.

light (līt), *n.* 1. the energy form by which objects are rendered visible by its action on the retina; also, infrared and ultraviolet energy. 2. day. 3. an illuminating or enlightening agent. 4. an aspect. 5. a window. 6. that which emits light. 7. the manner in which light falls on an object. 8. something to kindle or make a light. 9. a noteworthy person; one regarded as a model. 10. general awareness: *adj.* 1. bright. 2. pale. 3. not heavy or burdensome; unencumbered. 4. not difficult. 5. gay; joyful. 6. trifling; unimportant. 7. nimble. 8. short in weight, etc. 9. well-leavened and raised. 10. graceful. 11. undignified. 12. dizzy. 13. unchaste. 14. lacking seriousness. 15. denoting the

manufacture of small objects: *adv.* 1. without brightness. 2. same as lightly: *v.t.* light'-ed or lit, light'ing. 1. to set fire to; inflame. 2. to illuminate; furnish with light. 3. to guide by a light. 4. to make spirited: *v.i.* 1. to burn. 2. to become spirited (usually with *up*). 3. to rest or settle. 4. to happen (on or *upon*) by chance.

light·en (līt'n), *v.t.* 1. to make light; illuminate. 2. to make flash (*out*). 3. to render less heavy. 4. to make happier: *v.i.* 1. to brighten. 2. to shine out. 3. to become less heavy. 4. to become happier.

light·er (līt'ēr), *n.* 1. that which initiates burning. 2. a large, open barge for loading and unloading vessels in deep water.

light-fin·gered (līt'fing'gērd), *adj.* artful at stealing.

light-foot·ed ('foot'id), *adj.* stepping lightly or nimbly.

light-head·ed ('hed'id), *adj.* 1. confused; dizzy. 2. lacking seriousness.

light-heart·ed ('härt'id), *adj.* joyful. —**light'-heart'ed·ly,** *adv.* —**light'heart'ed·ness,** *n.*

light heavyweight, a boxer, wrestler, etc. between a middleweight and a heavyweight.

light·house ('hous), *n.* a structure furnished with a brilliant light to indicate points of danger to mariners at night.

light·ing ('ing), *n.* 1. the act of illuminating. 2. the way a thing is illuminated.

light·ly ('lī), *adv.* 1. without a heavy weight or force. 2. to a small degree. 3. with grace and ease. 4. joyfully. 5. neglectfully.

light-mind·ed ('mīn'did), *adj.* not serious.

light·ning ('ning), *n.* 1. a sudden flash of light in the sky. 2. a discharge of atmospheric electricity.

lightning bug, same as firefly.

lightning rod, a metal pole located on the top of a building, connected to the ground to conduct lightning away from the building.

light opera, same as operetta.

light·weight ('wāt), *n.* a boxer, wrestler, etc. between a featherweight and a welterweight: *adj.* not heavy.

light-year ('yir), *n.* the space traversed by a beam of light in a year.

lig·ne·ous (lig'ni-ûs), *adj.* woody.

lig·nin (lig'nin), *n.* an organic substance which binds woody fiber.

lig·nite (lig'nīt), *n.* wood converted into brownish-black coal.

lig·num vi·tae (lig'nûm vīt'ī), the very hard wood of a tropical American tree.

lik·a·ble (līk'â-bl), *adj.* pleasurable, tasteful, pleasing, etc.: also **like'a·ble.** —**lik'a·ble·ness,** *n.* —**lik'a·bil'i·ty,** *n.*

like (līk), *adj.* similar; resembling; equal: *adv.* [Informal], probably: *prep.* 1. having a resemblance to. 2. in a way nearly the same as. 3. harmonious with the character of. 4. in a state of mind as to be wanting. 5. indicative of. 6. as for instance: *conj.* [Informal], 1. as. 2. as if: *v.t.* liked, lik'ing. 1. to have a taste for; enjoy. 2. to want: *v.i.* to prefer: *n.* 1. a counterpart. 2. *pl.* predilections; partialities.

-like (līk), a suffix meaning *like, typical of.*

ô in *dragon*, ōō in *crude*, oo in *wool*, u in *cup*, ū in *cure*, û in *turn*, û in *focus*, oi in *boy*, ou in *house*, th in *thin*, th in *sheathe*, g in *get*, j in *joy*, y in *yet.*

like-li-hood (līk'li-hood), *n.* the quality or state of being likely, or probable; probability.

like-ly (līk'li), *adj.* -li-er, -li-est, 1. probable. 2. suitable. 3. evidently determined beforehand: *adv.* probably.

like-mind-ed (līk'mīn'did), *adj.* agreeing in thoughts, preferences, etc.

lik-en (līk'n), *v.t.* to compare.

like-ness ('nis), *n.* 1. similarity. 2. semblance. 3. a portrait, copy, etc.

like-wise ('wīz), *adv.* 1. in the same way. 2. besides; also.

lik-ing (lī'king), *n.* 1. preference. 2. fondness.

li-lac (lī'lak), *n.* 1. a shrub with small, sweet-smelling flowers of different shades of purple. 2. a pale purple color: *adj.* pale-purple.

Lil-li-pu-tian (lil-i-pū'shŭn), *n.* 1. a bigoted person. 2. a tiny person. 3. an inhabitant of Lilliput, the land of people six inches high, in Swift's "Gulliver's Travels": *adj.* 1. very small. 2. bigoted.

lilt (lilt), *n.* a song with rhythmic movement; merry and animated tune.

lil-y (lil'i), *n., pl.* -ies, 1. a plant with bulbous roots and white flowers that flare out like a trumpet bell. 2. the flower or bulb of this plant. 3. a plant resembling the lily: *adj.* unsullied; white.

lily of the valley, *pl.* lilies of the valley, a plant with two large oblong leaves and a raceme of fragrant, bell-like flowers.

li-ma bean (lī'mä), [also L- b-], 1. a variety of bean bearing large, flat seeds. 2. the seed of this bean.

limb (lim), *n.* 1. a jointed or articulated part of an animal body, as an arm or a leg. 2. a branch of a tree. 3. an edge or border.

lim-ber (lim'bĕr), *n.* the detachable forepart of a gun carriage: *adj.* 1. pliant. 2. lithe: *v.t.* 1. to make pliant or lithe. 2. to attach a limber to (a gun carriage): *v.i.* to become lithe.

lim-bo (lim'bō), *n., pl.* -bos, 1. [often L-], in some Christian theologies, an intermediate state between heaven and hell. 2. a state of being forgotten. 3. an uncertain state.

Lim-bur-ger cheese (lim'bĕr-gĕr), a semisoft cheese having a potent odor, originally made in Limburg, Belgium.

lime (līm), *n.* 1. a calcareous substance obtained by the action of heat upon limestone, etc. 2. a shortened form of birdlime. 3. a small tree yielding an edible, juicy, sour fruit shaped somewhat like a lemon. 4. the fruit of this tree. 5. same as linden: *v.t.* limed, lim'ing, to apply lime to.

lime-ade (līm'ād), *n.* a beverage consisting of lime juice, water, and usually sugar.

lime-light ('līt), *n.* 1. a brilliant light produced by incandescent lime, formerly cast upon a stage performer. 2. a position of conspicuousness.

li-men (lī'mĕn), *n., pl.* li'mens, lim-i-na (lim'i-nä), in *Psychology & Physiology,* same as threshold.

lim-er-ick (lim'ĕr-ik), *n.* a nonsense stanza of five lines, of which the first, second, and fifth are of three feet and rhyme, while the third and fourth have only two feet each and also rhyme.

lime-stone (līm'stōn), *n.* a rock having calcium carbonate as its base.

lim-it (lim'it), *n.* 1. a border or boundary; utmost extent. 2. *pl.* boundaries. 3. the maximum number permitted: *v.t.* to confine within bounds; restrict. —**lim-it-er,** *n.* —**lim'it-less,** *adj.*

lim-it-ed (lim'it-id), *adj.* 1. confined within limits. 2. accommodating a specified number of passengers, making only a few stops, etc.: said of a train, bus, etc. 3. of or pertaining to a government with constitutional restrictions. 4. [Chiefly British], of or pertaining to a company in which the liability of a shareholder is held to the amount of stock owned.

limn (lim), *v.t.* limned, limn'ing, 1. to paint or draw. 2. to represent verbally.

lim-nol-o-gy (lim-nol'ō-ji), *n.* the scientific study of lakes and ponds with respect to their geographical, physical, chemical, and biological nature.

lim-ou-sine (lim'ō-zēn), *n.* a large, comfortable automobile, usually driven by a chauffeur.

limp (limp), *adj.* 1. flexible. 2. flaccid. *n.* a halt in walking: *v.i.* to walk with a halt. —**limp'-ly,** *adv.* —**limp'ness,** *n.*

lim-pet (lim'pit), *n.* a small mollusk found adhering to rocks, etc.

lim-pid (lim'pid), *adj.* completely clear; unclouded. —**lim-pid'i-ty,** *n.* —**lim'pid-ly,** *adv.*

lim-y (lī'mi), *adj.* lim'i-er, lim'i-est, of, characteristic of, or consisting of lime.

lin-age (lī'nij), *n.* the total number of written or printed lines.

linch-pin (linch'pin), *n.* the pin which goes through the end of the axle of a wheel and keeps it in its place.

lin-den (lin'dĕn), *n.* a tree with heart-shaped leaves.

line (līn), *n.* 1. length without breadth. 2. a slender string or cord. 3. a cord for fishing. 4. an extended row. 5. a short letter. 6. one's occupation. 7. a thin, hairlike mark in the hand or face. 8. an outline. 9. a verse of poetry. 10. an extent. 11. a direction. 12. the equator or other geographical circle. 13. a particular class of goods. 14. descent. 15. a wire, pipe, etc. for conveying electricity, fluid, etc., or a group of such wires, pipes, etc. 16. an associated series of persons or things. 17. a system of transport. 18. a fact. 19. *pl.* dramatic speeches. 20. the first troops in combat. 21. in *Football,* the first group of players: *v.t.* lined, lin'ing, 1. to draw lines upon. 2. to place along side by side. 3. to come together into a line over the length of. 4. to cover on the inside.

lin-e-age (lin'i-ij), *n.* 1. ancestral line of descent from a common progenitor. 2. family.

lin-e-al (lin'i-äl), *adj.* 1. composed of lines. 2. in direct line from an ancestor. 3. transmitted genetically.

lin-e-a-ment (lin'i-å-mĕnt), *n. usually pl.* a feature; outline.

lin-e-ar (lin'i-ĕr), *adj.* 1. of, pertaining to, or composed of lines. 2. having a straight direction.

lin-e-ate ('i-it), *adj.* marked with lines.

line-back-er (līn′bak-ẽr), n. in *Football*, a player behind the line on the defense.

line drive, in *Baseball*, a ball hit along a line parallel with the ground.

line-man (līn′mán), n., pl. -men (′mén), 1. one who carries a surveying line, tape, or chain. 2. one who inspects and repairs telegraph and telephone wires. 3. in *Football*, a player on the line. Also **lines'man**.

lin-en (lĭn′én), n. 1. cloth made of flax. 2. *often pl.* articles made of linen: *adj.* made of linen.

lin-er (lī′nẽr), n. 1. a steamship, aircraft, etc. in scheduled service. 2. a cosmetic put in a thin line on the eyelid. 3. same as **lining**. 4. one who makes or attaches linings.

line-up (līn′up), n. a group of persons, things, etc. placed in a line.

lin-ey (lī′ni), adj. **lin′i-er**, **lin′i-est**, same as **liny**.

ling (ling), n. 1. *pl.* **ling**, **lings**, an edible fish related to the cod. 2. same as **heather**.

-ling (ling), a suffix meaning *tiny*, *insignificant*.

lin-ger (ling′gẽr), v.i. 1. to delay; loiter. 2. to remain long, because not wanting to go away. —**lin′ger-er**, n. —**lin′ger-ing**, adj.

lin-ge-rie (län-zhĕ-rā′, -rē′; län-jĕ-), n. a woman's underclothing.

lin-go (ling′gō), n., pl. -goes, 1. language. 2. a strange dialect, vocabulary, etc.

lin-gual (ling′gwál), adj. 1. of, pertaining to, or formed by the tongue. 2. of language: n. a sound articulated by the tongue, as *s*, *th*, etc.

lin-guist (ling′gwist), n. 1. one skilled in languages. 2. an expert in linguistics.

lin-guis-tics (ling-gwis′tiks), n.pl. 1. the science of languages. 2. the comparative study of languages. —**lin-guis′tic**, adj.

lin-gu-late (ling′gyá-lit, -lāt), adj. tongue-shaped.

lin-i-ment (lin′i-mént), n. a medicated liquid for rubbing into the skin.

lin-ing (lī′ning), n. an inside covering.

link (lingk), n. 1. a single ring or division of a chain. 2. anything joined, as two or more links. 3. a single part of a connected series. 4. a land measure of 7.92 inches. 5. a connection. 6. a torch made of pitch and tow. 7. *pl.* a golf course: *v.t.* & *v.i.* to connect by or as by a link.

link-age (ling′kij), n. 1. the act of linking. 2. links connected in succession.

link-up (lingk′up), n. a connection of two things.

lin-net (lin′it), n. a finch of Europe, Africa, and Asia.

li-no-le-um (li-nō′li-úm), n. a material for covering the floor, composed of ground cork, linseed oil, etc.

Lin-o-type (līn′ō-tīp), n. a machine for composing and casting an entire line of type at a time: a trademark.

lin-seed (lin′sēd), n. the seed of flax.

linseed oil, a yellowish oil from flaxseed, used in paints, printer's ink, etc.

lin-sey-wool-sey (lin′zi-wōōl′zi), n., pl. -wool′-seys, a rough cloth of mixed linen and wool or cotton and wool.

lint (lint), n. 1. scraped linen formerly used for dressing wounds. 2. small pieces of cloth or yarn. —**lint′y**, adj. **lint′i-er**, **lint′i-est**.

lin-tel (lin′tl), n. the horizontal top piece of a door or window.

lin-y (lī′ni), adj. **lin′i-er**, **lin′i-est**, 1. thin like a line. 2. having lines.

li-on (lī′ón), n., pl. **li′ons**, **li′on**, 1. a large powerful mammal of the cat family, found in Africa and southwestern Asia, and having a tawny body, tufted tail, and shaggy mane in the male. 2. a very strong or courageous person. 3. a person of interest; celebrity. —**li′on-ess**, n.fem.

li-on-ize (lī′ó-nīz), v.t. -ized, -iz-ing, to treat as an object of great interest.

lion's share, the major part.

lip (lip), n. 1. one of the two borders of the mouth. 2. the edge of anything. 3. a liplike organ. 4. [Slang], impudent speech: *v.t.* lipped, lip′ping, 1. to touch with the lips. 2. to utter quietly: adj. said, but not honestly.

lipped (lipt), adj. 1. having lips or rounded edges. 2. in *Botany*, same as **labiate**.

lip-py (lip′i), adj. -pi-er, -pi-est, [Slang], disrespectful; impertinent. —**lip′pi-ness**, n.

lip reading, the comprehension of spoken words by interpreting lip movements, as by the deaf. —**lip′-read** (′rēd), v.t. & v.i. -read (′red), -read-ing. —**lip read-er**.

lip-stick (′stik), n. a colored cosmetic paste for the lips.

li-quate (lī′kwāt), v.t. -quat-ed, -quat-ing, to melt out (a metal from an ore, etc.). —**li-qua′tion**, n.

liq-ue-fa-cient (lik-wē-fā′shént), adj. serving to liquefy.

liq-ue-fy (lik′wē-fī), v.t. & v.i. -fied, -fy-ing, to melt or become liquid. —**liq-ue-fac′tion** (-fak′shún), n.

li-ques-cent (li-kwes′nt), adj. melting.

li-queur (li-kûr′), n. an alcoholic liquor sweetened and given a flavoring.

liq-uid (lik′wid), adj. 1. clear. 2. readily flowing. 3. smoothly flowing. 4. that can be easily changed into cash: n. 1. a liquid substance. 2. a body, the particles of which move freely while remaining in one mass. 3. one of certain consonants, as *l*, *m*, *n*, *r*.

liquid air, air brought to a liquid condition by great pressure and cooled by its own expansion to a temperature below the boiling point of its chief constituents, nitrogen and oxygen.

liq-ui-date (lik′wi-dāt), v.t. -dat-ed, -dat-ing, 1. to pay off (a debt). 2. to arrange (the affairs of a bankrupt). 3. to change into cash. 4. to eliminate. —**liq-ui-da′tion**, n. —**liq′ui-da-tor**, n.

liq-uid-ize (lik′wi-dīz), v.t. -ized, -iz-ing, to melt or make liquid.

liq-uor (lik′ẽr), n. 1. an alcoholic beverage, especially one that has been distilled. 2. a liquid: v.t. & v.i. [Informal], to cause to take in or imbibe alcoholic liquor.

liq-uo-rice (lik′ẽr-ish, -is), n. same as **licorice**: chiefly British.

li-ra (lir′ä), n., pl. **li′re** (′ā), **li′ras**, the monetary unit of Italy.

lisle (līl), n. 1. a hard, fine thread of cotton. 2. a fabric or article of clothing formed from it.

lisp (lisp), v.i. 1. to pronounce *s* and *z* nearly

like *th.* 2. to speak in an imperfect manner: *v.t.* to utter imperfectly or with a lisp: *n.* an imperfect utterance.

lis·some, lis·som (lis'ŏm), *adj.* supple; lithe.

list (list), *n.* 1. a catalog, roll, or register. 2. the edge or selvage of cloth. 3. formerly, a strip of cloth. 4. an inclination to one side. 5. *pl.* an enclosing for a tournament: *v.t.* 1. to catalog, register, or enroll. 2. formerly, to cover with strips of cloth. 3. to tilt to one side: *v.i.* to become tilted.

lis·ten (lis'n), *v.i.* 1. to attend closely, so as to hear. 2. to accept advice. —**lis'ten·er,** *n.*

list·ing (lis'ting), *n.* the act of making a schedule, list, etc.

list·less (list'lis), *adj.* indifferent; languid. — **list'less·ly,** *adv.* —**list'less·ness,** *n.*

list price, the retail price as given in a catalog or list.

lit (lit), alternate past tense and past participle of light.

lit·a·ny (lit'n-i), *n., pl.* **-nies,** a solemn responsive form of prayer.

li·tchi (lē'chē), *n.* 1. an evergreen tree of China, producing a sweet, pulpy fruit. 2. this fruit, often eaten dried or preserved.

li·ter (lēt'ēr), *n.* the basic unit of capacity in the metric system, equal to 61.025 cubic inches or about a quart: also, British spelling, li'tre.

lit·er·a·cy (lit'ēr-ā-si), *n.* the state of being able to read or write.

lit·er·al (lit'ēr-ăl), *adj.* 1. consisting of or expressed by letters. 2. following the exact words of the original. 3. in the actual or fundamental meaning. 4. taking written or spoken assertions to mean exactly what they say. 5. accurate.

lit·er·al·ly (lit'ēr-ăl-i), *adv.* in a literal sense.

lit·er·ar·y (lit'ē-rer-i), *adj.* 1. of, pertaining to, or appropriate to literature. 2. versed in or engaged in literature.

lit·er·ate (lit'ēr-it), *adj.* 1. having the ability to read and write. 2. learned; having a good education: *n.* one who is literate.

lit·e·ra·ti (lit-ē-rät'i, -rä'ti), *n.pl.* the learned.

lit·e·ra·tim (-rät'im, -rät'im), *adv.* [Latin], literally.

lit·er·a·ture (lit'ēr·ā-chēr), *n.* 1. the written or printed literary productions of a country, period, subject area, etc. 2. writings or printed matter produced from the imagination. 3. those writings, etc. which are highly valued or have a lasting importance. 4. [Informal], any kind of printed matter.

lith·arge (lith'ärj, li-thärj'), *n.* monoxide of lead.

lithe (līth), *adj.* supple; pliant; nimble; lissome: also **lithe'some** ('sŏm).

lith·i·a (lith'i-ä), *n.* oxide of lithium.

lith·ic ('ik), *adj.* of or pertaining to stone.

lith·i·um (lith'i-ŭm), *n.* a silver-white, light metallic element.

litho-, a combining form meaning *stone:* also, before a vowel, lith-.

lith·o·graph (lith'ŏ-graf), *n.* a print produced from a drawing on stone or metal: *v.t. & v.i.* to draw on stone or metal and transfer to paper.

li·thog·ra·phy (li-thog'rā-fi), *n.* the art of making a design on stone or metal so that ink impressions can be taken from it. —**lith·o·graph·ic** (lith-ŏ-graf'ik), *adj.*

lith·oid (lith'oid), *adj.* like a stone; of the structure of stone.

li·thot·o·my (li-thot'ŏ-mi), *n., pl.* **-mies,** the surgical operation of cutting into the bladder to remove a stony mass.

li·thot·ri·ty (li-thot'ri-ti), *n., pl.* **-ties,** the surgical operation of crushing stone in the bladder for elimination in the urine.

lit·i·gant (lit'i-gănt), *n.* one who contends in a lawsuit.

lit·i·gate (-gāt), *v.t.* **-gat·ed, -gat·ing,** to contest in a court of law: *v.i.* to engage in a lawsuit. —**lit'i·ga·tor,** *n.*

lit·i·ga·tion (lit-i-gā'shŭn), *n.* 1. the act or process of carrying on a lawsuit. 2. a judicial contest.

li·ti·gious (li-tij'ŭs), *adj.* 1. given to carrying on lawsuits. 2. quarrelsome.

lit·mus (lit'mŭs), *n.* a purple dye, obtained from certain lichens, which turns blue when dipped in a base or red in an acid.

lit·ter (lit'ēr), *n.* 1. straw, hay, etc. used for animal bedding. 2. a framework with a bed, for carrying a person in a recumbent position. 3. a state of confusion or untidiness. 4. objects scattered about untidily. 5. a number of young produced at one birth, as by dogs, pigs, etc.: *v.t.* 1. to supply with litter; cover with straw, etc. 2. to scatter about carelessly. 3. to make untidy with litter: *v.i.* to bring forth a litter of young.

lit·te·ra·teur (lit-ēr-ā-tūr'), *n.* a literary man: also **litterateur.**

lit·ter·bug (lit'ēr-bug), *n.* one who makes public areas untidy with discarded waste items.

lit·tle (lit'l), *adj.* **lit'tler** or **less** or **less'er, lit'tlest** or **least,** 1. small in size, quantity, or duration. 2. small in importance. 3. insignificant. 4. young. 5. narrow; prejudiced: *adv.* **less, least,** 1. in a small degree; not much. 2. not at all: *n.* a small size, quantity, etc.

Little Dipper, a group of stars shaped like a dipper, in Ursa Minor.

little slam, in *Bridge,* the taking of all tricks but one in a single deal.

lit·to·ral (lit'ēr-ăl), *adj.* of, pertaining to, or on the shore.

lit·ur·gy (lit'ēr-ji), *n., pl.* **-gies,** 1. the prescribed forms of ritual for public worship. 2. the celebration of the Eucharist in the Orthodox Eastern Church. —**li·tur·gi·cal** (li-tūr'ji-kl), *adj.* —**li·tur'gi·cal·ly,** *adv.* —**lit'ur·gist,** *n.*

liv·a·ble (liv'ā-bl), *adj.* 1. suitable for habitation. 2. that can be undergone. Also **liveable.**

live (liv), *v.i.* 1. to exist or have life. 2. to pass or enjoy life. 3. to reside. 4. to endure. 5. to subsist. 6. to escape destruction: *v.t.* 1. to carry out in one's life. 2. to go through: *adj.* (līv), 1. having life. 2. ignited. 3. effective. 4. energetic, interesting, etc. 5. charged with electricity. 6. unexploded. 7. living. 8. in the flesh. 9. recorded or transmitted in the course of the performance. 10. in person. 11. in *Sports,* in play.

-lived (livd), a combining form meaning *having life*.

live·li·hood (līv'li-hood), *n.* a means of living.

live·long (liv'lông), *adj.* complete; entire.

live·ly (līv'li), *adj.* -li·er, -li·est, 1. active. 2. brisk. 3. animated. 4. sprightly. 5. vivid. 6. bright; joyful. 7. bouncy. —live'li·ness, *n.*

liv·en (lī'vén), *v.t. & v.i.* to make or become joyful or animated (often with *up*).

live oak, an American oak valuable for shipbuilding or construction.

liv·er (liv'ẽr), *n.* 1. one who lives. 2. a glandular organ secreting bile.

liv·er·ied (liv'ẽr-id), *adj.* clothed in a livery.

liver spot, a darkened skin area once thought to result from a defective liver.

liv·er·wort (liv'ẽr-würt), *n.* one of a group of mosslike plants, differing from true mosses in reproduction and development.

liv·er·wurst (-würst), *n.* a sausage of ground liver.

liv·er·y (liv'ẽr-i), *n., pl.* -er·ies, 1. a particular costume worn by servants. 2. the keeping and feeding of horses at a stipulated rate. 3. the renting out of horses, etc. at a stipulated rate.

liv·er·y·man (-mǎn), *n., pl.* -men (-měn), the keeper of a livery stable.

livery stable, a stable where horses, etc. are kept and let out for hire.

lives (līvz), *n.* plural of *life*.

live·stock (līv'stok), *n.* farm animals or those raised for profit.

liv·id (liv'id), *adj.* 1. black-and-blue; discolored by a blow. 2. ashy-pale.

liv·ing (liv'ing), *adj.* 1. having life. 2. flowing naturally. 3. vigorous; active. 4. of or pertaining to those alive. 5. of or pertaining to the continuance of life. 6. resembling real life: *n.* 1. a livelihood. 2. in England, a church benefice. 3. a mode of life. 4. the condition of life.

living room, a room in a house furnished for receiving guests and entertaining on social occasions.

living wage, compensation paid at a level that will provide a satisfactory living condition.

lix·iv·i·ate (lik-siv'i-āt), *v.t.* -at·ed, -at·ing, same as *leach*. —lix·iv·i·a'tion, *n.*

lix·iv·i·um (lik-siv'i-ŭm), *n., pl.* -i·ums, -i·a (-ấ), a substance produced by leaching, as lye.

liz·ard (liz'ãrd), *n.* a reptile having a narrow, scaly body, four limbs, and a tail.

lizard fish, a small, narrow-bodied marine fish with a head resembling that of a lizard.

lla·ma (lä'mä), *n., pl.* -mas, -ma, a domesticated, woolly-haired ruminant of South America, somewhat resembling a camel.

lla·no (lä'nō), *n., pl.* -nos, any one of the extensive, level, grassy plains of South America.

lo (lō), *interj.* behold! see!: now chiefly in *lo and behold!*

loach (lōch), *n.* any one of various small, edible, freshwater fishes of the Old World, having barbels around the mouth.

load (lōd), *v.t.* 1. to place something in or upon for carrying. 2. to fill with as much as can be conveyed. 3. to weigh down; burden; oppress. 4. to supply with an abundance or excess. 5. to insert (a charge, ammunition, etc.) into a firearm or gun: *v.i.* to take on a load: *n.* 1. a quantity transported at one time by a conveyance, ship, animal, etc. 2. something that weighs down or oppresses; burden. 3. *often pl.* [Informal], a large quantity or amount. 4. in *Computers*, to transfer (a program or data) into the memory from a disk, tape, etc. —load'er, *n.* —load'ing, *n.*

load·ed ('id), *adj.* 1. bearing a load. 2. [Slang], intoxicated or under the influence of drugs. 3. [Slang], having a large supply of money.

load line, any one of a series of lines on the side of a ship indicating the level to which it may be loaded under specified conditions.

load·star ('stär), *n.* same as *lodestar*.

load·stone ('stōn), *n.* same as *lodestone*.

loaf (lōf), *n., pl.* loaves (lōvz), 1. a cake of bread baked in one piece, often oblong. 2. a food shaped like a loaf and baked.

loaf (lōf), *v.i.* to idle away time; loiter; dawdle.

loaf·er ('ẽr), *n.* an idler; cadger.

loam (lōm), *n.* rich vegetable mold, with clay and sand, forming a soil: *v.t.* to fill or cover with loam. —loam'y, *adj.* loam'i·er, loam'i·est.

loan (lōn), *n.* 1. the act of lending, especially for temporary use. 2. something granted for temporary use. 3. a sum of money lent for a period and usually repayable with interest: *v.t. & v.i.* to lend.

loan-word ('würd), *n.* a word taken over by one language from another.

loath (lōth), *adj.* unwilling; reluctant.

loathe (lōth), *v.t.* loathed, loath'ing, to regard with abhorrence or disgust; detest.

loath·ing ('ing), *n.* disgust; hatred; abhorrence.

loath·some ('sôm), *adj.* producing loathing; repulsive.

loaves (lōvz), *n.* plural of *loaf*.

lob (lob), *v.t.* lobbed, lob'bing, to toss or hit (something) slowly and in a high arc: *v.i.* to go slowly and heavily: *n.* 1. in *Cricket*, a slow, underhand toss. 2. in *Tennis*, a ball stroked in a high arc. 3. [British Dial.], a lout; stupid fellow.

lo·bate (lō'bāt), *adj.* 1. having lobes. 2. lobelike.

lob·by (lob'i), *n., pl.* -bies, 1. a small hall or waiting room at the entrance of a hotel, apartment, theater, etc. 2. a large hall next to the assembly chamber of a legislative body to which the public has access. 3. a group of lobbyists acting to influence legislation: *v.i.* -bied, -by·ing, to act as a lobbyist: *v.t.* to solicit the votes of members of a legislature to pass or defeat (a particular measure).

lob·by·ist (-ist), *n.* a private person employed by a particular group for the purpose of getting legislators to favor measures advantageous to the special interests of the group.

lobe (lōb), *n.* 1. any rounded or projecting part, as the lower part of the human ear. 2. a subdivision of a bodily organ set apart by tissue, fissures, etc.

lo·be·li·a (lō-bēl'yǎ, -be'li-ǎ), *n.* any one of a group of plants having terminal clusters of white, blue, or red flowers.

lob·ster (lob'stẽr), *n.* an edible marine crustacean with five pairs of legs, the first pair of which are modified into large claws.

lobster tail, the tail of any one of various crustaceans, cooked as food.

lob-ule (lob'yool), *n.* 1. a small lobe. 2. a subdivision of a lobe. —**lob'u-lar** ('yoo-lēr), *adj.*

lo-cal (lō'kl), *adj.* 1. of or pertaining to place. 2. existing in or restricted to a particular place. 3. not extensive; confined. 4. of or affecting a particular part of the body: *n.* 1. a train that stops at all stations. 2. a regional branch of an organization, especially of a labor union. —**lo'cal-ly,** *adv.*

lo-cale (lō-kal'), *n.* 1. a place; locality. 2. the background, events, peculiarities, etc. of a certain place.

lo-cal-ism (lō'kǎl-izm), *n.* 1. a manner of behaving or talking peculiar to a locality. 2. a word, idiom, or custom restricted to a particular locality. 3. provincialism.

lo-cal-i-ty (lō-kal'ĭ-ti), *n., pl.* -ties. 1. the fact or condition of having a position in space or time. 2. a particular place; neighborhood.

lo-cal-ize (lō'kǎ-līz), *v.t.* -ized, -iz'ing. 1. to limit or restrict to a particular place or part. 2. to discover the place of origin or source of. 3. to collect in one area or part; concentrate. —**lo-cal-i-za'tion,** *n.*

local option, the right of the residents of a district, county, etc. to determine by vote whether the sale of intoxicating liquors will be allowed in their locality.

lo-cate (lō'kāt, lō-kāt'), *v.t.* -cat-ed, -cat-ing. 1. to place or establish. 2. to mark out and specify the position of. 3. to find the place of after searching. 4. to point out the position of. 5. to station, assign, or place: *v.i.* [Informal], to settle.

lo-ca-tion (lō-kā'shŭn), *n.* 1. the act of locating or the fact of being located. 2. a place or position where something is or may be located. 3. an area, plot of ground, etc. marked out by boundaries. 4. in *Motion Pictures,* a site away from the studios, where scenes are filmed.

loc-a-tive (lok'ā-tiv), *adj.* in *Linguistics,* of or denoting a noun case in some languages, as Latin, designating place in which or at which: *n.* the locative case.

loch (lok, lokh), *n.* [Scottish], 1. a lake. 2. an inlet of the sea.

lock (lok), *n.* 1. a mechanical device furnished with a spring and bolt for fastening a door, box, etc. by means of a key or combination. 2. anything that fastens or secures. 3. an enclosure, as in a canal, having gates so that the water within can be raised or lowered for the passage of ships. 4. the mechanism in a firearm for firing the charge. 5. any of several holds used in wrestling: *v.t.* 1. to fasten (a door, box, etc.) with a lock. 2. to prevent from leaving or entering; shut (*up, in,* or *out*); confine. 3. to fit; link; intertwine. 4. to force together so as to make immovable: *v.i.* 1. to become locked. 2. to entwine.

lock (lok), *n.* 1. a curl or ringlet of hair. 2. a tuft, as of wool or cotton.

lock-age (lok'ij), *n.* 1. the difference in water levels achieved in the locks of a canal. 2.

the act of passing a ship through a lock. 3. the charge for such passage.

lock-er ('ēr), *n.* 1. a chest, closet, trunk, etc. that can be locked. 2. a cabinet or room for storing frozen foods.

lock-et (lok'it), *n.* a small gold or silver case for holding a picture, keepsake, etc. and usually attached to a necklace or chain.

lock-jaw (lok'jô), *n.* same as tetanus (sense 1).

lock-out ('out), *n.* the exclusion of workers from a plant by an employer to compel them to accept his terms.

lock-smith ('smith), *n.* a person who makes or repairs locks and keys.

lock step, a form of marching in which the marchers follow each other closely, each moving the legs in corresponding time with the person before him.

lock stitch, the usual stitch of a sewing machine made by the interlocking of the upper and lower threads.

lock-up ('up), *n.* 1. the act of locking up or the state of being locked up. 2. a jail.

lo-co (lō'kō), *n.* [Western], 1. same as locoweed. 2. same as loco disease: *v.t.* -coed, -co-ing, 1. to poison with locoweed. 2. [Slang], to craze: *adj.* [Slang], crazy; insane.

loco disease, a nervous disease of livestock caused by locoweed poisoning.

lo-co-mo-bile (lō-kō-mō'bl), *adj.* [Rare], moving under its own power.

lo-co-mo-tion (-mō'shŭn), *n.* the act of moving or the power of moving from place to place.

lo-co-mo-tive (-mōt'iv), *adj.* 1. of or pertaining to locomotion. 2. moving or able to move from place to place. 3. of or denoting engines that move under their own power: *n.* an engine, as an electric or diesel engine on wheels, for pushing or pulling railway cars.

lo-co-mo-tor ('ēr), *adj.* of or pertaining to locomotion: *n.* one having the power of locomotion.

locomotor ataxia, same as tabes dorsalis.

lo-co-weed (lō'kō-wēd), *n.* any one of several plants found in western North America that cause loco disease.

lo-cust (lō'kŭst), *n.* 1. any one of various grasshoppers often migrating in vast swarms and destroying much vegetation in their travels. 2. same as seventeen-year locust. 3. a spiny tree of the legume family having hard, durable wood. 4. this wood. 5. same as carob (sense 1).

lo-cu-tion (lō-kū'shŭn), *n.* 1. a mode of speech; phraseology. 2. a particular word or expression.

lode (lōd), *n.* a vein containing a rich supply of metallic ore.

lode-star (lōd'stär), *n.* 1. a guiding star, especially the North Star. 2. a guiding principle.

lode-stone ('stōn), *n.* 1. magnetite that is strongly magnetic. 2. something that attracts strongly.

lodge (loj), *v.t.* lodged, lodg'ing, 1. to furnish with a temporary dwelling. 2. to deposit for safekeeping. 3. to fix, place, or implant. 4. to file (a formal charge) with the proper authorities. 5. to grant (powers) to (with *in*): *v.i.* 1. to reside for a time. 2. to be deposited or fixed: *n.* 1. a small house or cabin for a particular use. 2. a resort motel or hotel. 3. the den of certain wild animals, as the beaver. 4. the hut, wigwam, etc. of an American Indian. 5. the residents of one of these shelters. 6. the place where a local chapter of an association meets. 7. the members of such a chapter.

lodg-er ('ēr), *n.* a person who resides in lodgings.

lodg-ing ('ing), *n.* 1. a place of temporary residence. 2. *pl.* a room or rooms rented in the house of another.

lodg-ment ('mĕnt), *n.* 1. the act of lodging or the state of being lodged. 2. a lodging place. 3. an accumulation of something deposited. 4. in military usage, a foothold or salient secured in enemy territory.

loft (lôft), *n.* 1. a room or space directly below the roof; attic. 2. any one of the upper floors of a warehouse, commercial building, etc. 3. a gallery, as in a church. 4. height imparted to a hit or thrown ball: *v.t.* to propel (a ball) in a high arc.

loft-y (lôf'ti), *adj.* loft'i-er, loft'i-est, 1. very high. 2. stately; sublime. 3. haughty; arrogant. —loft'i-ly, *adv.* —loft'i-ness, *n.*

log (lôg), *n.* 1. an undressed length of timber cut from the trunk or from a large branch of a felled tree. 2. a daily record of a ship's position, speed, course, etc.; logbook. 3. a similar record of an aircraft's flight. 4. an instrument for determining the speed of a ship: *v.t.* logged, log'ging, 1. to saw (trees) into logs. 2. to enter in a log. 3. to sail, drive, fly, etc. (a specified distance or time): *v.i.* to hew down, trim, and transport timber. —log'ger, *n.*

log (lôg), *n.* same as logarithm.

-log, same as **-logue**.

lo-gan-ber-ry (lō'găn-ber-i), *n.*, *pl.* **-ries**, 1. a bramble similar to the blackberry, widely cultivated for its fruit. 2. the acid, red fruit of this plant.

log-a-rithm (lôg'ă-rithm, log'-), *n.* in *Mathematics*, the exponent expressing the power to which a fixed number (the *base*) must be raised in order to produce a given number (the *antilogarithm*). —log-a-rith'mic, *adj.*

log-book (lôg'book), *n.* same as log (senses 2 & 3).

loge (lōzh), *n.* 1. a box in a theater. 2. the front rows of a mezzanine or balcony of a theater.

log-ger-head (lôg'ēr-hed), *n.* 1. a marine turtle with a large, beaked head. 2. [Dial.], a stupid fellow; blockhead.

loggerhead shrike, a North American shrike with white and black plumage and a hooked beak.

log-gi-a (lo'ji-ă, lo'jă), *n.*, *pl.* **-gi-as**, a covered gallery or portico built into or extending from the side of a building, especially an upper story overlooking an open court.

log-ging (lôg'ing), *n.* the business of cutting down timber and transporting it.

log-ic (loj'ik), *n.* 1. the science of correct reasoning. 2. method of reasoning. 3. the inter-connection of elements or events producing an inevitable outcome. —lo-gi-cian (lō-jish'-ŭn), *n.*

log-i-cal ('i-kl), *adj.* 1. of, pertaining to, or used in the science of logic. 2. according to the rules of logic. 3. expected because of what has preceded. 4. having the ability to reason correctly. —log'i-cal-ly, *adv.*

lo-gis-tic (lō-jis'tik), *adj.* of calculation: *n.* [Rare], the art of calculation; ordinary arithmetic.

lo-gis-tics ('tiks), *n.* the branch of military science concerned with supplying and transporting men and material. —lo-gis'tic, lo-gis'ti-cal, *adj.* —lo-gis'ti-cal-ly, *adv.*

log-jam (lôg'jam), *n.* 1. a mass of floating logs jammed together in a stream. 2. a deadlock produced in organizing, negotiating, etc.

log-o-, a combining form meaning *word, speech.*

log-o-gram (lôg'ō-gram), *n.* a letter or sign standing for a whole word, as # for number: also log'o-graph (-graf).

lo-gog-ra-phy (lō-gog'ră-fi), *n.* a method of printing in which the type contains whole words or combinations of letters.

lo-gom-a-chy (lō-gom'ă-ki), *n.* a battle of words; furious argument or debate.

log-o-type (lôg'ō-tip), *n.* a single piece of type containing two or more letters usually cast separately.

log-roll (lôg'rōl), *v.i.* to engage in logrolling: *v.t.* to secure passage of (legislation) by logrolling. —log'roll-er, *n.*

log-roll-ing (-ing), *n.* 1. the act of rolling logs. 2. the exchange of favors among legislators, as by trading votes for the passage of certain legislation. 3. mutual exchange of assistance, praise, etc., as to promote sales.

-logue (lôg), a combining form meaning *speech, writing.*

log-wood (lôg'wood), *n.* 1. the dark wood of a tropical American tree, yielding a dye. 2. this tree. 3. this dye.

lo-gy (lō'gi), *adj.* -gi-er, -gi-est, [Informal], dull; lethargic. —lo'gi-ness, *n.*

-lo-gy (lō-ji), a combining form meaning *speech, discourse, science, theory.*

loin (loin), *n.* 1. the lower part of the back on either side between the lower rib and hipbone. 2. a cut of meat from this part of an animal carcass. 3. *pl.* the region of the lower abdomen and hips regarded as the seat of strength or procreation.

loin-cloth ('klôth), *n.* a cloth worn around the loins.

loi-ter (loit'ēr), *v.t.* to idle (with *away*): *v.i.* 1. to spend time idly. 2. to go slowly, pausing frequently. —loi'ter-er, *n.*

loll (lol), *v.i.* 1. to lounge at ease. 2. to hang loosely, as a dog's tongue: *v.t.* to let droop.

lol-li-pop, lol-ly-pop (lol'i-pop), *n.* a lump of candy on a stick; sucker.

lone (lōn), *adj.* 1. solitary; by oneself. 2. unmarried or widowed. 3. isolated; lonely.

lone-ly ('li), *adj.* -li-er, -li-est, 1. deserted; unfrequented. 2. solitary. 3. dejected at being alone. 4. causing such dejection. —lone'li-ness, *n.*

ŏ in dragon, ōō in crude, oo in wool, u in cup, ū in cure, û in turn, ù in focus, oi in boy, ou in house, th in thin, th in sheathe, g in get, j in joy, y in yet.

lon·er (lō'nĕr), *n.* [Informal], one who avoids other people, their advice, assistance, etc.

lone·some (lōn'sŏm), *adj.* 1. secluded from society; desolate. 2. sad from being alone.

long (lông), *adj.* 1. not short; extended in time or length. 2. having a specified length or duration. 3. greater than average or normal. 4. drawn out; slow; tedious. 5. pertaining to what is distant; far-reaching. 6. abundantly supplied: *adv.* 1. for a long period. 2. from start to finish. 3. far distant; remote.

long (lông), *v.i.* to desire eagerly; yearn.

long·boat ('bōt), *n.* the largest and strongest boat on a sailing ship.

long·bow ('bō), *n.* a long, powerful bow drawn by hand.

long·cloth ('klôth), *n.* a fine cotton fabric.

long distance, a telephone operator or exchange that handles communications between distant places. —**long'·dis'tance**, *adj. & adv.*

long dozen, thirteen.

long-drawn ('drôn), *adj.* protracted; tedious.

lon·gev·i·ty (lon-jev'i-ti), *n.* 1. long life. 2. duration of life. 3. amount of time spent in continued use, service, or employment.

long-faced (lông'fāst), *adj.* glum; perturbed; unhappy.

long·hair ('her), *adj.* [Informal], denoting or of intellectuals or intellectual interests, especially in the arts.

long·hand ('hand), *n.* ordinary handwriting, as distinguished from shorthand.

long·horn ('hôrn), *n.* any one of a breed of cattle with long horns, formerly numerous in the southwestern U.S.

long·ing ('ing), *n.* earnest desire; yearning: *adj.* feeling strong desire.

long·i·tude (lon'ji-tōōd), *n.* distance -east or west on the earth's surface from the prime meridian, expressed in degrees or in hours, minutes, and seconds.

lon·gi·tu·di·nal (lon-ji-tōōd'n-ǎl), *adj.* 1. of or pertaining to length. 2. placed or running lengthwise. 3. of or pertaining to longitude.

long jump, in *Sports*, a jump for distance from either a standing or running start.

long-lived ('līvd', -līvd'), *adj.* 1. having a long life. 2. enduring long.

long play, a long-playing record.

long-play·ing (lông'plā'ing), *adj.* denoting or of a microgroove phonograph record that turns at 33 1/3 revolutions per minute.

long prim·er (prim'ĕr), a size of type, 10 point.

long-range (lông'rānj'), *adj.* 1. able to cover a great distance. 2. taking the future into account.

long·shore·man (lông'shôr-mǎn), *n., pl.* -**men** (-mĕn), a person who works at a port loading and unloading ships.

long shot, [Informal], 1. a bet at great odds. 2. a very risky venture that, if successful, will return heavy profits.

long-stand·ing ('stan-ding), *adj.* having lasted for a long time.

long-suf·fer·ing (-suf'ĕr-ing), *adj.* enduring troubles, difficulties, tribulations, etc. patiently for a long time.

long-term ('tûrm'), *adj.* of, continuing, or growing over an extended period of time.

long ton, the British ton, equal to 2,240 pounds.

long-wind·ed (-win'did), *adj.* tediously verbose in speaking or writing.

loo (lōō), *n.* an old card game having a pool made up of stakes contributed by the players.

loo·by (lōō'bi), *n., pl.* -**bies**, [Now Rare or Dial.], an awkward fellow.

look (look), *v.i.* 1. to direct one's eyes in order to view something. 2. to direct the mind or attention to. 3. to attempt to find; search. 4. to seem; appear. 5. to be facing in a particular direction: *v.t.* 1. to turn one's eyes upon. 2. to express by one's appearance. 3. to have an appearance conforming to: *n.* 1. the act of looking. 2. external appearance; mien; aspect. 3. *usually pl.* [Informal], *a)* the way something appears to be. *b)* physical appearance: *interj.* 1. see! 2. pay heed!

look·er-on (look-ĕr-on'), *n., pl.* **look·ers-on'**, a spectator; onlooker.

looking glass, a mirror.

look·out ('out), *n.* 1. careful observation. 2. a high place for observation. 3. a person who keeps watch. 4. [Informal], a problem; worry.

look-see ('sē), *n.* [Slang], a quick look or survey.

loom (lōōm), *n.* 1. a frame or machine for weaving thread or yarn into cloth. 2. the art of weaving.

loom (lōōm), *v.i.* to come into view indistinctly, especially in an enlarged and misshapen form.

loon (lōōn), *n.* a diving bird of northern regions with a sharp bill and strange cry.

loon (lōōn), *n.* 1. a dull, awkward person. 2. a demented person.

loon·y ('i), *adj.* **loon'i·er**, **loon'i·est**, [Slang], crazy; insane: *n., pl.* **loon'ies**, [Slang], a loony person.

loop (lōōp), *n.* 1. a folding or doubling of string, rope, etc. 2. a noose. 3. anything resembling a loop. 4. an aerial maneuver with an airplane describing a curve or circle. 5. an intrauterine contraceptive device: *v.t.* 1. to form into a loop. 2. to secure with a loop: *v.i.* to form a loop or loops.

loop·hole ('hōl), *n.* 1. a narrow aperture for observation or defense. 2. a means of evasion.

loose (lōōs), *adj.* 1. not fast. 2. unbound; not fixed. 3. not tight or crowded together. 4. vague; unconnected. 5. lax in principles or sexual morals. 6. [Informal], relaxed: *v.t.* loosed, loos'ing, 1. to set free. 2. to unbind; disengage. 3. to relax. 4. to release (a barrage, missile, etc.).

loos·en (lōōs'n), *v.t. & v.i.* to free from tightness, restraint, or tension.

loot (lōōt), *v.t.* to pillage; plunder; despoil: *n.* 1. booty taken by force in time of war. 2. [Slang], money or valuable articles.

lop (lop), *v.t.* 1. lopped, lop'ping, 1. to cut off (a part). 2. to trim (a tree, bush, etc.) by cutting off twigs or branches.

---

a in cap, ā in cane, ä in father, ȧ in abet, e in met, ē in be, ê in baker, ĕ in regent, i in pit, ī in fine, I in manifest, o in hot, ô in horse, ō in bone,

lop (lop), *v.i.* lopped, lop'ping, to hang down loosely; droop.

lope (lōp), *v.i.* loped, lop'ing, to trot with a swinging motion: n. an easy canter.

lop-sid-ed (lop'sid-id), *adj.* 1. heavier on one side; unsymmetrical. 2. leaning to one side.

lo-qua-cious (lō-kwā'shŭs), *adj.* talkative. —**lo-qua'cious-ly**, *adv.* —**lo-quac'i-ty** (-kwas'ĭ-tĭ), *n.*

lord (lôrd), *n.* 1. a ruler or governor; master. 2. the owner of a feudal manor. 3. [L-], *a)* God. *b)* Jesus Christ. 4. in Great Britain, *a)* a man holding a title of nobility, as a baron, viscount, earl, or marquess. *b)* a man given the courtesy title of Lord, as the son of a duke, or because of his position, as a bishop or a Lord Mayor: *v.i.* to act like a lord; domineer: used in the phrase *lord it over.*

lord-ling ('ling), *n.* an unimportant or would-be lord.

lord-ly ('lĭ), *adj.* -li-er, -li-est, 1. of or pertaining to a lord. 2. noble; grand. 3. arrogant; haughty: *adv.* in the manner of a lord. —**lord'li-ness**, *n.*

lor-do-sis (lôr-dō'sis), *n.* a curvature of the spine in a forward direction.

Lord's Day, Sunday.

lord-ship (lôrd'ship), *n.* 1. the rank or position of a lord. 2. dominion; rule. 3. the territory of a lord. 4. a form of address used in speaking to or of a lord: with *his* or *your.*

Lord's Prayer, the prayer beginning *Our Father:* see *Matthew* vi, 9-13.

Lord's Supper, Holy Communion; Eucharist.

lore (lôr), *n.* 1. learning; acquired knowledge. 2. tradition accumulated and handed down about a particular subject.

lore (lôr), *n.* the space between the eye and bill of a bird.

Lor-e-lei (lôr'ĕ-lī), *n.* in German folklore, a siren of the Rhine River who lured boatmen to shipwreck by her singing.

lor-gnette (lôr-nyet'), *n.* opera glasses or eyeglasses attached to a handle.

lor-i-keet (lôr'ĭ-kēt), *n.* any one of several small, mostly Australian, parrots.

lo-ris (lôr'is), *n., pl.* lo'ris, either of two small, slow-moving, Asiatic lemurs active at night.

lorn (lôrn), *adj.* [Archaic], forsaken; forlorn.

lor-ry (lôr'ĭ), *n., pl.* -ries, 1. a low, four-wheeled wagon without sides. 2. [British], a motor truck.

lo-ry (lôr'ĭ), *n., pl.* -ries, any one of several small, brightly colored, Australian parrots.

lose (lōōz), *v.t.* lost, los'ing, 1. to be deprived of by accident, death, etc. 2. to cease to have in possession; mislay. 3. to fail to control. 4. to fail to see, hear, or understand. 5. to fail to keep, obtain, etc. 6. to fail to win. 7. to cause the loss of. 8. to stray from. 9. to squander: *v.i.* 1. to suffer loss. 2. to be defeated. —**los'er**, *n.*

loss (lôs), *n.* 1. the act of losing. 2. the injury, privation, etc. caused by losing. 3. a person, thing, or amount lost.

lost (lôst), past tense and past participle of **lose**: *adj.* 1. missing; misplaced. 2. no longer possessed, visible, etc. 3. ruined; destroyed. 4. perplexed or bewildered.

lot (lot), *n.* 1. fortune; destiny. 2. a plot or parcel of land. 3. anything used to determine an outcome by chance. 4. the result thus obtained. 5. a number of people or things. 6. *often pl.* [Informal], a large number or quantity. 7. [Informal], sort: *adv.* very much: also **lots**.

Lo-thar-i-o (lō-ther'ĭ-ō), *n., pl.* -i-os, a gay deceiver; libertine.

lo-tion (lō'shŭn), *n.* a medicated fluid for outward application.

lot-ter-y (lot'ẽr-i), *n.* a distribution of prizes by lot to the buyers of winning tickets.

lot-to (lot'ō), *n.* a game of chance played with numbered disks drawn by lot, in which the players put counters on the squares on their cards having corresponding numbers until one player wins by covering five squares in a row.

lo-tus (lōt'ŭs), *n.* 1. a leguminous plant having irregularly pinnate leaves and yellow, purple, or white, pealike flowers. 2. any of several waterlilies, especially the white lotus of Egypt. 3. a representation of this plant in ancient Egyptian sculpture. 4. in *Greek Legend,* a plant whose fruit was fabled to cause forgetfulness and induce a state of dreamy indolence.

lo-tus-eat-er (-ēt-ẽr), *n.* in the *Odyssey,* any one of a people who lived in a state of ease, indolence, and forgetfulness from eating the fruit of the lotus.

loud (loud), *adj.* 1. sounding strongly and with great intensity. 2. producing a sound of great intensity. 3. noisy; insistent. 4. [Informal], ostentatious in dress or manner; showy. 5. [Informal], vulgar: *adv.* in a loud manner. —**loud'ly**, *adv.* —**loud'ness**, *n.*

loud-mouthed ('moutht, 'mou/hd), *adj.* having a noisy, offensive, or indiscreet manner of speaking.

loud-speak-er ('spē-kẽr), *n.* a device that changes electrical energy to sound and amplifies the sound.

lough (lokh), *n.* [Irish], 1. a lake. 2. an inlet of the sea.

lou-is d'or (lōō-i dôr'), an old French gold coin of varying value.

lounge (lounj), *v.i.* lounged, loung'ing, 1. to saunter, sit, stand, etc. in a lazy manner; loll. 2. to live indolently: *n.* 1. a room with comfortable furniture for lounging. 2. a couch or sofa. —**loung'er**, *n.*

lounge lizard, [Slang], an idle fellow who loafs away his time in bars, hotels, etc., often as a gigolo.

louse (lous), *n., pl.* **lice**, 1. any one of several small, flat, wingless insects, parasitic on man and other animals or on plants. 2. *pl.* **lous'es**, [Slang], a low, despicable person.

lous-y (lou'zi), *adj.* lous'i-er, lous'i-est, 1. infested with lice. 2. [Slang], *a)* dirty; contemptible. *b)* poor; worthless. *c)* abundantly supplied.

lout (lout), *n.* an awkward, stupid fellow; boor. —**lout'ish**, *adj.*

lou-ver (lōō'vẽr), *n.* 1. an open turret or lantern on the roof of a medieval building. 2. a vent, window, etc. fitted with stationary or movable slats for ventilation or illumination. 3. one of these slats.

ō in dragon, ōō in crude, oo in wool, u in cup, ū in cure, û in turn, ŭ in focus, oi in boy, ou in house, th in thin, th in sheathe, g in get, j in joy, y in yet.

Lou·vre (lōō'vrĕ), *n.* an ancient royal palace in Paris, now converted into an art museum.

lov·a·ble (luv'å-bl), *adj.* inspiring love; adorable: also spelled **love'a·ble**. —**lov·a·bil'i·ty**, **lov'a·ble·ness**, *n.* —**lov'a·bly**, *adv.*

love (luv), *n.* 1. a strong feeling of affection for someone or something. 2. a passionate affection for another. 3. the person eliciting such affection; sweetheart. 4. in *Tennis*, a score of zero: *v.t. & v.i.* **loved**, **lov'ing**, 1. to feel devotion (toward). 2. to feel love (for).

love apple, [Archaic], the tomato.

love·bird ('bûrd), *n.* any of various small parrots, often kept as cage birds.

love feast, 1. a religious feast of commemoration and fellowship. 2. any banquet characterized by good feeling.

love-lies-bleeding ('līz-blēd'ing), *n.* a cultivated amaranth with red flowers.

love·lorn ('lôrn), *adj.* forsaken by or pining for one's love.

love·ly ('li), *adj.* **-li·er**, **-li·est**, 1. inspiring love or admiration. 2. beautiful; delightful. 3. amiable; gracious. 4. [Informal], very enjoyable. —**love'li·ly**, *adv.* —**love'li·ness**, *n.*

lov·er ('ĕr), *n.* 1. one who loves. 2. a paramour. 3. *pl.* two persons in love with each other. 4. a person who deeply enjoys something, as art.

lov·ing ('ing), *adj.* 1. devoted. 2. showing love; affectionate. —**lov'ing·ly**, *adv.*

loving cup, 1. a large wine cup with several handles and other ornaments, formerly passed around to guests at ceremonial banquets. 2. a similar cup presented as a trophy in modern sporting events.

low (lō), *adj.* 1. not high or elevated. 2. depressed below the surrounding area. 3. of small depth; shallow. 4. subdued and quiet. 5. near the horizon. 6. less in size, degree, value, etc. than normal. 7. feeble or weak. 8. not of high rank; humble. 9. vulgar; coarse. 10. inferior; poor. 11. of little intensity; not loud. 12. deep in pitch: *adv.* 1. in or to a low level, direction, etc. 2. in a low manner. 3. softly: *n.* 1. a low level, degree, etc. 2. the gear, as in a motor vehicle, producing the most power and least speed. 3. in *Meteorology*, an area of low barometric pressure. 4. the lowest trump card.

low (lō), *v.i.* to utter the characteristic sound of cattle; moo: *n.* this sound.

low-born (lō'bôrn), *adj.* of humble birth.

low-boy ('boi), *n.* a chest of drawers reaching table height.

low-brow ('brou), *n.* [Informal], one regarded as having uncultivated tastes.

Low Church, that section of the Anglican Church that is evangelical and has small interest in ritual, ceremony, tradition, etc. — **Low'-Church**, *adj.*

low-down (lō'doun), *n.* [Slang], the essential, basic facts (with *the*): *adj.* (also lō'doun'), [Informal], mean; despicable.

low·er (lō'ĕr), *adj.* comparative of **low**. 1. below in place, rank, etc. 2. below in quantity, value, etc.: *v.t.* 1. to lessen. 2. to bring down in position, respect, etc.; demean. 3. to reduce in price, value, etc. 4. to let or move down. 5. to change to a lower pitch: *v.i.* to become lower; sink; fall.

low·er (lou'ĕr), *v.i.* 1. to look angry; scowl. 2. to appear dark, gloomy, or threatening, as the weather.

lower-case (lō'ĕr-kās), *adj.* in *Printing*, of, pertaining to, or denoting lower case: *v.t.* **-cased**, **cas·ing**, to set (type) in lower case or change (type) to lower case.

lower case, small letters used in printing, as distinguished from capital letters.

low·er·ing (lou'ĕr-ing), *adj.* 1. scowling. 2. dark and threatening; overcast.

low·er·most (lō'ĕr-mōst), *adj.* same as **lowest**.

Low German, 1. the German dialects of northern Germany. 2. the branch of the Germanic languages that includes English, Dutch, etc.

low-grade (lō'grād), *adj.* 1. inferior in value, quality, etc. 2. weak in degree, intensity, etc.

low-key ('kē), *adj.* having low intensity; restrained: also **low'-keyed'**.

low·land (lō'lånd), *adj.* of or pertaining to land that is lower than the surrounding country: *n.* such land.

low·ly ('li), *adj.* **-li·er**, **-li·est**, 1. low in rank or size. 2. humble; modest: *adv.* humbly. — **low'li·ness**, *n.*

Low Mass, a Mass that is recited rather than sung.

low-mind·ed (-mīn'did), *adj.* exhibiting a coarse, vulgar disposition.

low profile, a scarcely observable presence or hidden action.

low-spir·it·ed (-spir'i-tid), *adj.* sad; melancholy.

Low Sunday, the Sunday after Easter.

low tide, 1. the lowest level reached by the ebbing tide. 2. the lowest point reached by anything.

lox (loks), *n.* a kind of smoked salmon.

lox (loks), *n.* liquid oxygen, used in rocket fuel mixtures.

lox·o·drom·ic (lok-sŏ-drom'ik), *adj.* of or denoting rhumb lines.

loy·al (loi'ål), *adj.* 1. faithful in allegiance to one's government, sovereign, or country. 2. true to a person, faith, duty, etc. 3. of or professing loyalty. —**loy'al·ly**, *adv.*

loy·al·ist (-ist), *n.* one who adheres to and supports the government, especially during a revolt.

loz·enge (loz'ĕnj), *n.* 1. a rhombus that is not a square. 2. a small candy in this shape, often medicated.

LP, a long-playing record: a trademark.

LSD, a chemical compound used in the study of mental aberrations and as a hallucinogen.

lu·au (lōō-ou', lōō'ou), *n.* a Hawaiian feast.

lub·ber (lub'ĕr), *n.* 1. an awkward, clumsy person. 2. an inexperienced, awkward sailor.

lu·bri·cant (lōō'bri-kånt), *n.* a substance for lubricating, as grease, oil, etc.: *adj.* reducing friction of contacting parts by covering with a thin film.

lu·bri·cate (-kāt), *v.t.* **-cat·ed**, **-cat·ing**, 1. to make smooth or slippery. 2. to supply with a lubricant. —**lu·bri·ca'tion**, *n.* —**lu'bri·ca·tor**, *n.*

lu·bric·i·ty (lōō-bris'i-ti), *n.* 1. slipperiness. 2.

shiftiness. 3. lewdness. —lu·bri'cious (-brish'-ŭs), adj.

lu·carne (lōō'kärn), n. a dormer window.

lu·cerne, lu·cern (lōō-sûrn'), n. [Chiefly British], same as alfalfa.

lu·cid (lōō'sid), adj. 1. clear; readily understood. 2. shining. 3. transparent. 4. sane. —lu·cid'i·ty, n. —lu'cid·ly, adv.

Lu·ci·fer (lōō'si-fêr), n. 1. the planet Venus as the morning star. 2. the archangel who led the revolt of the angels; Satan. 3. [l-], an early friction match.

luck (luk), n. 1. the accidental occurrence of events affecting an individual; fortune; fate. 2. good fortune, success, etc. —luck'less, adj.

luck·y ('i), adj. luck'i·er, luck'i·est, 1. having good luck or fortune. 2. occurring by chance. 3. assumed to bring good luck. —luck'i·ly, adv. —luck'i·ness, n.

lu·cra·tive (lōō'krā-tiv), adj. profitable. —lu'cra·tive·ly, adv.

lu·cre (lōō'kêr), n. money; riches; profit; gain.

lu·cu·brate (lōō'kyoo-brāt), v.i. -brat·ed, -brat·ing, to work, study, or write industriously, especially late at night. —lu·cu·bra'tion, n.

lu·cu·lent (lōō'kū-lênt), adj. easily understood; clear; lucid.

lu·di·crous (lōō'di-krùs), adj. exciting mirth; comical; droll. —lu'di·crous·ly, adv. —lu'di·crous·ness, n.

luff (luf), n. 1. the act of sailing closer into the wind. 2. the fullest part of a ship's bow: v.i. to steer nearer to the wind.

lug (lug), v.t. lugged, lug'ging, to pull or draw along; move laboriously: n. 1. [Archaic], the act of lugging. 2. a projecting part by which a thing is held or supported. 3. [Scottish], an ear. 4. same as lugsail. 5. a heavy nut for holding a wheel on an axle.

lug·gage (lug'ij), n. the effects of a traveler; baggage.

lug·ger (lug'êr), n. a small vessel with two or three masts, each mast having a lugsail.

lug·sail (lug'sâl), n. a square sail without a boom or lower yard, bent to an upper yard that hangs at nearly right angles to the mast.

lu·gu·bri·ous (loo-gōō'bri-ùs), adj. very mournful; especially, comically or ridiculously doleful. —lu·gu'bri·ous·ly, adv.

lug·worm (lug'wûrm), n. a segmented sand worm much used for bait.

Luke (lōōk), n. a book of the New Testament, the third Gospel.

luke·warm (lōōk'wôrm'), adj. 1. moderately warm; tepid. 2. lacking warmth or feeling.

lull (lul), v.t. 1. to soothe or quiet by soft sound or gentle motion. 2. to bring about a suspension of caution: v.i. to become calm: n. abatement of activity; temporary calm.

lull·a·by ('ă-bī), n. 1. a cradlesong for lulling a child to sleep. 2. music for this: v.t. -bied, -by·ing, to calm with or as with a lullaby.

lum·ba·go (lum-bā'gō), n. a painful rheumatism of the muscles of the lumbar region.

lum·bar (lum'bâr, -'bär), adj. of or denoting the lower part of the back between the ribs and the pelvis.

lum·ber (lum'bêr), n. 1. surplus of discarded articles of furniture or other goods stored away. 2. timber cut into boards, planks, etc.: v.t. to cut down (timber) and prepare it for market.

lum·ber (lum'bêr), v.i. to move or walk clumsily.

lum·ber·jack (lum'bêr-jak), n. a man who cuts down trees and makes them ready for the sawmill.

lum·ber·man (-mân), n., pl. -men (-mĕn), 1. same as lumberjack. 2. one who is engaged in the lumber trade.

lu·mi·nar·y (lōō'mi-ner-i), n. 1. a body that gives light, especially a heavenly body. 2. a person who enlightens or instructs. 3. a notable or famous person.

lu·mi·nes·cence (lōō-mi-nes'ĕns), n. the emission of light, as in fluorescence or phosphorescence, by certain bodies that undergo chemical or biochemical changes or that have been exposed to radiant energy.

lu·mi·nes·cent (-'ĕnt), adj. emitting or able to emit light without incandescence.

lu·mi·nif·er·ous (-nif'êr-ùs), adj. emitting or transmitting light.

lu·mi·nous (lōō'mi-nùs), adj. 1. emitting light; shining. 2. clear; easily understood. —lu·mi·nos'i·ty (-nos'i-ti), n.

lum·mox (lum'ŏks), n. [Informal], an awkward, stupid person.

lump (lump), n. 1. a small, shapeless mass of something. 2. a swelling. 3. a stupid, ungainly person. 4. pl. [Informal], heavy blows, sharp criticism, punishment, etc.: adj. in a lump or lumps: v.t. 1. to put together in a lump or lumps. 2. to unite in one group or mass: v.i. to become lumpy. —lump'y, adj. lump'i·er, lump'i·est.

lump (lump), v.i. to put up with (something unpleasant).

lump·er ('êr), n. a longshoreman.

lump·fish (lump'fish), n., pl. -fish, -fish·es, a fish of the Atlantic Ocean with bony knobs covering the body.

lump·ish ('ish), adj. 1. heavy; dull; spiritless. 2. like a lump.

lump sum, full payment made at one time.

lu·na·cy (lōō'nā·si), n., pl. -cies, 1. mental unsoundness. 2. insanity. 3. senseless conduct or a rash action.

lu·nar (lōō'nêr), adj. 1. of or pertaining to the moon. 2. resembling, measured by, or influenced by the moon. 3. of or containing silver.

lunar caustic, silver nitrate used for cauterizing.

lunar month, the period of a complete revolution of the moon, equal to approximately 29 1/2 days.

lunar year, a year of twelve lunar months, equal to approximately 354 1/2 days.

lu·nate (lōō'nāt), adj. crescent-shaped.

lu·na·tic (lōō'nā·tik), adj. 1. affected with or characteristic of lunacy. 2. completely foolish: n. an insane person.

lu·na·tion (lōō-nā'shùn), n. a complete revolution of the moon; lunar month.

lunch (lunch), n. a light meal between breakfast and dinner: v.i. to eat lunch.

lunch·eon (lun'chĕn), n. a lunch; especially, a formal lunch.

lunch·eon·ette (lun-chĕ-net'), n. a place where light lunches are served.

luncheon meat, meat prepared and packaged by a packing house and ready to eat.

lu·nette (lōō'net'), n. 1. anything shaped like a crescent. 2. a crescent-shaped or semicircular space over a door or window.

lung (lung), n. one of two organs of respiration in the thorax of vertebrates.

lunge (lunj), n. 1. a sudden thrust or pass with a sword. 2. a sudden lurch: v.i. & v.t. lunged, lung'ing, to move, or cause to move, with a lunge.

lung-wort (lung'wŭrt), n. a European plant having dark leaves spotted with white and clusters of blue or purple flowers.

lu·ni·so·lar (lōō-ni-sō'lẽr), adj. of or pertaining to the sun and moon conjointly or their combined attraction.

lunk·head (lungk'hed), n. [Informal], a stupid person. —lunk'head·ed, adj.

lu·nu·la (lōō'nyoo-lä), n., pl. -lae (-lē) any crescent-shaped part or marking, as the white half-moon at the base of a fingernail. —lu'nu·lar, adj.

lu·pine (lōō'pin), n. 1. any one of several leguminous plants bearing pods with bean-like seeds, used for fodder, forage, etc. 2. the edible seed of some of these plants.

lu·pine (lōō'pīn), adj. 1. of or pertaining to a wolf or wolves. 2. rapacious; wolfish.

Lu·pus (lōō'pŭs), n. a southern constellation near the Milky Way.

lu·pus (lōō'pŭs), n. any of several skin diseases often causing lesions, as on the face and nose, which tend to become incrusted and leave scars.

lurch (lŭrch), n. a sudden roll to one side: v.i. 1. to pitch or sway suddenly forward or to one side. 2. to stagger.

lurch (lŭrch), n. 1. a difficult or forlorn position: now only in the phrase to leave (someone) in the lurch. 2. the losing position in cribbage in which one has half or less than half the points of the winner.

lurch·er ('ẽr), n. 1. a person who lurks or lies in wait. 2. a poacher; thief. 3. [British], any one of a crossbreed of dogs that hunt silently by scent, used by poachers.

lure (loor), v.t. lured, lur'ing, to attract, tempt, or entice: n. 1. the power of attracting or enticing. 2. anything used as an enticement. 3. a decoy used in catching animals; especially, an artificial bait used in fishing.

lu·rid (loor'id), adj. 1. grayish-orange. 2. [Rare], wan; ghastly. 3. startling; shocking. 4. glowing through a haze.

lurk (lŭrk), v.i. 1. to lie in wait; be concealed. 2. to move stealthily.

lus·cious (lush'ŭs), adj. 1. pleasant to taste or smell; delicious. 2. having a strong appeal to the senses. 3. [Archaic], sweet to excess. —lus'cious·ly, adv. —lus'cious·ness, n.

lush (lush), adj. 1. tender and juicy. 2. growing luxuriantly. 3. excessively elaborate; rich; extravagant.

lush (lush), n. [Slang], an alcoholic: v.t. & v.i. [Slang], to drink (liquor).

lust (lust), n. 1. a strong desire to possess or enjoy. 2. concupiscence: v.i. to have a strong, inordinate desire, especially sexual desire (often with after or for).

lus·ter (lus'tẽr), n. 1. brightness; radiance. 2. splendor; renown. 3. shining by reflected light; sheen. 4. any one of the glass pendants on a chandelier. 5. a chandelier adorned with such pendants. 6. a glossy fabric. 7. the quality and intensity of the reflecting surface of a mineral.

lust·ful (lust'fool), adj. 1. filled with lust. 2. [Archaic], robust; vigorous. —lust'ful·ly, adv.

lus·tral (lus'trál), adj. of, pertaining to, or used in ceremonial purification.

lus·trate (lus'trāt), v.t. -trat·ed, -trat·ing, to purify by means of ceremony. —lus·tra'tion, n.

lus·tring (lus'tring), n. same as lutestring.

lus·trous (lus'trŭs), adj. having luster; shining; radiant.

lust·y (lus'ti), adj. lust'i·er, lust'i·est, robust and vigorous; healthy; strong. —lust'i·ly, adv. —lust'i·ness, n.

lu·ta·nist (lōōt'n-ist), n. a player on the lute.

lute (lōōt), n. a stringed musical instrument of the guitar family, having a body shaped like half a pear.

lute (lōōt), n. a composition of clay, cement, etc. used for sealing pipe joints, porous surfaces, etc. to make them airtight.

lute·string (lōōt'string), n. a strong, glossy silk, formerly used in women's wear.

Lu·ther·an (lōō'thẽr-án), adj. 1. of Martin Luther (1483-1546), German theologian and reformer. 2. of or pertaining to the Protestant denomination founded by Luther or its doctrines, especially that of justification by faith alone: n. a member of the Lutheran Church. —Lu'ther·an·ism, n.

lux (luks), n., pl. lux, lux'es, a unit of illumination, equal to one lumen per square meter.

lux·ate (luk'sāt), v.t. -at·ed, -at·ing, to put out of joint; dislocate. —lux·a'tion, n.

luxe (luks), n. elegance, richness, sumptuousness, etc.

lux·u·ri·ant (lug-zhoor'i-ánt), adj. 1. growing abundantly and vigorously; lush. 2. extravagantly ornate; florid. —lux·u'ri·ance, n. —lux·u'ri·ant·ly, adv.

lux·u·ri·ate (-āt), v.i. -at·ed, -at·ing, 1. to grow vigorously and profusely. 2. to live in solid luxury. 3. to indulge unrestrainedly (used with in).

lux·u·ri·ous (-ŭs), adj. 1. of or pertaining to luxury; elaborate; comfortable. 2. indulging in or administering to luxury. —lux·u'ri·ous·ly, adv. —lux·u'ri·ous·ness, n.

lux·u·ry (luk'shŭ-ri), n., pl. -ries, 1. extravagant indulgence in and enjoyment of physical comforts. 2. anything producing such enjoyment: adj. characterized by luxury.

ly·can·thro·py (li-kan'thrō-pi), n. 1. a form of insanity in which the patient imagines himself a wolf. 2. in Folklore, the magical ability to assume the form and nature of a wolf.

Ly·ce·um (li-sē'ŭm), n. 1. the grove in Athens

where Aristotle taught. 2. [l-], a hall where lectures, concerts, etc. are presented. 3. [l-], an organization sponsoring such events.

lydd·ite (lid'īt), *n.* a powerful explosive consisting chiefly of picric acid.

Lyd·i·an (lid'ĭ-ən), *adj.* 1. of or pertaining to Lydia, an ancient kingdom in western Asia Minor, noted for its luxury, music, etc. 2. effeminate. 3. voluptuous.

lye (lī), *n.* 1. originally, a strong, alkaline solution obtained by leaching wood ashes. 2. any strongly alkaline substance used in making soap, cleaning, etc.

ly·ing (lī'ing), present participle of lie.

ly·ing (lī'ing), *adj.* untruthful; false: *n.* the telling of lies.

ly·ing-in (lī'ing-in'), *adj.* of or pertaining to childbirth: *n.* the confinement of a woman at parturition.

lymph (limf), *n.* a colorless, watery fluid containing white blood cells, that travels through the lymphatic system in vertebrates.

lym·phat·ic (lim-fat'ik), *adj.* 1. of, pertaining to, or conveying lymph. 2. sluggish; phlegmatic: *n.* a lymphatic duct.

lymph node, any one of many small, round structures found in groups along the lymphatic vessels.

lymph·oid (lim'foid), *adj.* of or similar to lymph or lymphatic tissue.

lynch (linch), *v.t.* to murder (a suspect) by mob violence without due process of law, as by hanging.

lynch law, lawless punishment by private individuals of persons suspected of crime.

lynx (lingks), *n.* 1. any one of several wildcats having a short tail, pointed ears, and keen sight. 2. [L-], a northern constellation.

lynx-eyed ('īd), *adj.* having keen vision.

ly·on·naise (lī-ŏ-nāz'), *adj.* prepared with sliced, fried onions.

ly·rate (lī'rāt), *adj.* shaped like a lyre.

lyre (līr), *n.* a stringed instrument of the harp family, used by the ancient Greeks to accompany the voice.

lyre·bird ('bûrd), *n.* an Australian bird having a lyre-shaped tail when spread.

lyr·ic (lir'ik), *adj.* 1. of or pertaining to a lyre. 2. appropriate for accompaniment by a lyre. 3. of or denoting poetry that expresses the poet's inner emotions and thoughts. 4. of or possessing a singing voice that is high and flexible: *n.* 1. a lyric poem, as an ode, sonnet, etc. 2. *pl.* the words of a song.

lyr·i·cal ('i-kl), *adj.* 1. same as lyric. 2. expressing rapture or excitement.

lyr·i·cist ('i-sist), *n.* a writer of lyrics for popular songs.

lyr·ist (lir'ist), *n.* a lyric poet.

ly·ser·gic acid (lī-sûr'jik), see LSD.

-ly·sis (lī-sis), a combining form meaning *a loosing, dissolving, decomposition.*

-lyte (līt), a combining form meaning *a substance that can be decomposed by a particular process.*

M

M, m (em), *n., pl.* **M's, m's, 1.** the thirteenth letter of the English alphabet. **2.** the sound of this letter, as in *mother, hammer,* or *dam.* **3.** a type or impression of *M* or *m.* **4.** in *Printing,* an em.

M (em), *adj.* shaped like *M*: *n.* **1.** an object shaped like *M.* **2.** a Roman numeral denoting 1000.

ma (mä), *n.* [Informal], mamma; mother.

ma'am (mam), *n.* [Informal], madam.

ma·ca·bre (má·käb're, má·käb', -kä'ber), *adj.* suggestive of a dance of death; weird; gruesome.

ma·ca·co (má·kä'kō, -kä'-), *n.* any of several kinds of lemur found in Africa or Asia, especially the *black lemur.*

mac·ad·am (má·kad'ám), *n.* **1.** a road or pavement made with small, broken, hard stones, bound together with tar or a similar substance. **2.** the stones used for this.

mac·a·dam·i·a nut (mak·á·dā'mi·á), an edible nut grown in Hawaii.

mac·ad·am·ize (má·kad'á·mīz), *v.t.* -ized, -iz·ing, **1.** to cover or repair (a road) with macadam. **2.** to construct (a road) with layers of macadam on a hard roadbed. —**mac·ad·a·mi·za'tion,** *n.*

ma·caque (má·käk'), *n.* any of several monkeys of Africa, Asia, and the East Indies, with nonprehensile tails; especially, the rhesus monkey.

mac·a·ro·ni (mak·á·rō'ni), *n.* **1.** pasta in the form of tubes, often cooked with cheese. **2.** *pl.* -nies, a dandy or fop in 18th-century England.

mac·a·ron·ic (-ron'ik), *adj.* pertaining to a burlesque composition consisting of a jumble of words of various languages: *n.* a macaronic verse.

mac·a·roon (mak·á·rōōn'), *n.* a small cookie made of flour, egg white, sugar, and coconut or almond.

ma·caw (má·kô'), *n.* a large, handsome, brightly colored parrot with a long tail and hooked bill, native to Central and South America.

Mace (mās), *n.* a chemical that stuns its victims, packaged in aerosol containers, intended for use to ward off attackers or in riot control: a trademark: in full, Chemical Mace.

mace (mās), *n.* **1.** a heavy, medieval club with a spiked head, used as a weapon. **2.** an ornamented staff carried before a sovereign or official in some ceremonies. **3.** same as macebearer. **4.** the outer covering of nutmeg, ground and used as a spice.

mace·bear·er ('ber·êr), *n.* one who carries a mace in a procession.

ma·cé·doine (mas·i·dwon'), *n.* a mixture or medley.

mac·er·ate (mas'ē·rāt), *v.t.* -at·ed, -at·ing, **1.** to soften or separate the parts of by steeping in a fluid. **2.** loosely, to separate into bits. **3.** to cause to grow thin: *v.i.* to grow thin; waste away. —**mac·er·a'tion,** *n.* —**mac'er·a·tor,** *n.*

Mach (mäk), *n.* see Mach number.

ma·che·te (má·shet'i), *n.* a large, heavy knife used in Central and South America for cutting underbrush, sugar cane, etc.

Mach·i·a·vel·li·an (mak·i·á·vel'i·án, -vel'yán), *adj.* pertaining to Machiavelli, the Florentine statesman, or to his principles of political duplicity; crafty; double-dealing: *n.* a cunning, unprincipled politician. —**Mach·i·a·vel'li·an·ism,** *n.*

mach·i·na·tion (mak·i·nā'shún), *n.* a plot; artifice, especially a secret scheme to do harm.

ma·chine (má·shēn'), *n.* **1.** any contrivance to increase and regulate motive power. **2.** an apparatus for doing some kind of work; mechanism. **3.** a vehicle, especially an automobile: an old term. **4.** a person or group operating mechanically or automatically. **5.** the members of a political party who control its policy and confer patronage: *adj.* **1.** of or pertaining to machines. **2.** done by machinery: *v.t.* -**chined'**, -**chin'ing,** to shape, finish, etc. by machinery.

machine gun, an automatic gun that fires a rapid stream of bullets that are mechanically fed into it. —**ma·chine'-gun,** *v.t.* -**gunned, -gun·ning.**

ma·chin·er·y (má·shēn'êr·i, -shēn'ri), *n.* **1.** machines collectively. **2.** the parts of a machine. **3.** any combination by which something is kept in action or the desired result is obtained.

ma·chin·ist ('ist), *n.* **1.** a constructor of machines. **2.** one skilled in the principles or repair of machinery. **3.** one who operates a machine.

ma·chis·mo (mä·chēz'mō), *n.* [Spanish], masculinity; virility.

Mach number (mäk), [also m-], a number representing the ratio of the speed of an object to the speed of sound.

mack·er·el (mak'ér·êl, mak'rêl), *n., pl.* -el, -els, a food fish found in the North Atlantic: it is mottled with green and blue.

Mack·i·naw coat (mak'i·nô), a short, double-breasted, plaid woolen coat.

mack·in·tosh (mak'in·tosh), *n.* **1.** a waterproof overcoat; raincoat. **2.** the rubberized cloth used to make such a coat.

mack·le (mak'l), *v.t.* -led, -ling, to blot or blur in printing: *n.* a blot; blur.

ma·cle (mak'l), *n.* a twin crystal.

mac·ra·mé (mak'rá·mā), *n.* a coarse fringe

---

a in cap, ā in cane, ä in father, á in abet, e in met, ē in be, ê in baker, ê in regent, i in pit, ī in fine, i in manifest, o in hot, ô in horse, ō in bone,

knotted in designs, for decorating furniture, etc. and for making wall hangings.

mac-ro-, a combining form meaning *large, enlarged, long* (*in extent or duration*).

mac-ro-bi-ot-ics (mak-rō-bī-ot'iks), *n.* the practice of helping people to live longer, as through proper diet. —**mac-ro-bi-ot'ic**, *adj.*

mac-ro-ceph-a-lous (mak-rō-sef'ă-lŭs), *adj.* having an abnormally large head. —**mac-ro-ceph's-ly**, *n.*

mac-ro-cosm (mak'rō-kozm), *n.* 1. the universe. 2. any complex, large entity. —**mac-ro-cos-mic** (mak-rō-koz'mik), *adj.*

ma-cron (mā'kron), *n.* a mark (¯) over a vowel to indicate its pronunciation.

mac-u-la (mak'yoo-lă), *n., pl.* -**lae** (-lē), -**las,** 1. a spot or stain. 2. a dark spot on the sun. Also **mac'ule** (-ŭl).

mad (mad), *adj.* **mad'der, mad'dest,** 1. mentally ill; insane. 2. rash; foolish. 3. fond; infatuated. 4. frantic. 5. infected with rabies; rabid. 6. wildly gay. 7. very angry: *n.* a spell of ill temper. —**mad'ly,** *adv.* —**mad'ness,** *n.*

mad-am (mad'ăm), *n.* 1. *pl.* **mes-dames** (mā-däm'), a woman; lady: polite term of address. 2. a woman in charge of a house of prostitution.

mad-ame (mad'ăm, *Fr.* mä-däm'), *n., pl.* **mesdames** (mā-däm'), [French], a married woman: a title equivalent to *Mrs.*

mad-cap (mad'kap), *n.* a wild, thoughtless, impulsive person: *adj.* wild; impulsive.

mad-den (mad'n), *v.t. & v.i.* to make or become mad, furious, excited, angry, etc. —**mad'den-ing,** *adj.*

mad-der (′ĕr), *n.* 1. a red dye made from the root of a perennial vine with yellow flowers. 2. this vine.

mad-ding (′ing), *adj.* [Rare], frenzied.

made (mād), past tense and past participle of **make.**

Ma-deir-a (mă-dir'ă), *n.* [also **m-**], a white wine made on Madeira, a Portuguese island off the coast of Morocco.

ma-de-moi-selle (mad-ĕ-mō-zel', *Fr.* mäd-mwä-zel'), *n., French* **mesde-moi-selles** (mäd-mwä-zel'), [French], an unmarried woman or girl: title equivalent to *Miss.*

made-to-or-der (mād'tō-ōr'dĕr), *adj.* 1. made according to exact measurements or instructions. 2. well-suited to the occasion or use.

made-up (-up'), *adj.* 1. fabricated; invented, as a story. 2. arranged; ready for use. 3. wearing makeup.

mad-house (mad'hous), *n.* 1. an insane asylum. 2. a place of turmoil or uproar.

mad-man (′man), *n., pl.* -**men** (′men), one who is mentally ill; maniac. —**mad'wom-an,** *n. fem., pl.* -**wom-en.**

Ma-don-na (mă-don'ă), *n.* a picture or statue of Mary, the mother of Jesus, usually with the infant Jesus.

ma-dras (mad'răs, mă-dras'), *n.* a fine, light cotton fabric, often plaid.

mad-re-pore (mad'rĕ-pōr), *n.* a kind of branching coral that forms tropical reefs and islands. —**mad-re-por'ic,** *adj.*

mad-ri-gal (mad'ri-găl), *n.* 1. a light, amorous song. 2. a part song unaccompanied by music, popular from the 15th to the 17th centuries. —**mad'ri-gal-ist,** *n.*

ma-dri-lène (mad-ri-len'), *n.* a consommé made with tomatoes, sometimes served cold.

mael-strom (māl'strŏm), *n.* 1. a large, violent, destructive whirlpool. 2. any violent state of agitation that tends to absorb or destroy.

ma-es-tro (mis'trō), *n., pl.* -**tros,** a master in any art, especially that of music; especially, a great conductor or composer.

Ma-fi-a, Maf-fi-a (mä'fi-ă), *n.* [Italian], a secret society, allegedly of criminals.

mag-a-zine (mag-ă-zēn'), *n.* 1. a warehouse or supply depot for military supplies. 2. a room in a fort or section in a warship in which ammunition is stored. 3. the chamber in a gun from which cartridges are fed. 4. a periodical publication containing articles, stories, illustrations, etc.

mag-da-lene (mag'dă-lēn, -lin), *n.* 1. a reformed prostitute. 2. [British], a reformatory for prostitutes.

ma-gen-ta (mă-jen'tă), *n.* 1. a purplish-red aniline dye. 2. purplish red: *adj.* purplish-red.

mag-got (mag'ŏt), *n.* 1. the legless larva of a housefly. 2. a whim; fantastic notion. —**mag'got-y,** *adj.*

Ma-gi (mā'jī), *n.pl., sing.* **Ma'gus** (′gŭs), 1. the priestly and learned caste in ancient Persia and Media. 2. in the *Douay Bible,* the wise men from the East who came with gifts for the infant Jesus. —**Ma'gi-an** (′ji-ăn), *adj. & n.*

mag-ic (maj'ik), *n.* 1. the art or pretence of seeking to control events by the use of spells, charms, etc.; sorcery; witchcraft. 2. an unexplainable influence; enchantment. 3. the use of sleight of hand for entertainment: *adj.* 1. of, using, or produced by magic. 2. extraordinary, as if by magic. —**mag'i-cal,** *adj.* —**mag'i-cal-ly,** *adv.*

ma-gi-cian (mă-jish'ăn), *n.* an expert in magic, especially one who entertains by tricks, sleight of hand, etc.

magic lantern, an early type of projector for showing still pictures from transparent slides.

magic square, a series of numbers in equal rows so arranged that the vertical, horizontal, and diagonal rows add up to the same amount.

mag-is-te-ri-al (maj-is-tir'i-ăl), *adj.* 1. of or pertaining to a magistrate. 2. authoritative.

mag-is-tra-cy (maj'is-tră-si), *n., pl.* -**cies,** 1. the office or term of a magistrate. 2. magistrates collectively. 3. a magistrate's jurisdiction.

mag-is-trate (-trāt', -trit), *n.* 1. a civil officer who has the power to administer the law. 2. a minor official, as a justice of the peace. —**mag-is-trat'i-cal** (-trat'i-kăl), *adj.*

mag-ma (mag'mă), *n.* molten rock.

Mag-na Char-ta (mag'nă kär'tă), 1. the great charter granted to the English in 1215, providing them with certain civil and political liberties. 2. any constitution that guarantees personal liberty and civil rights. Also **Mag'na Car'ta.**

mag-nan-i-mous (mag-nan'ĭ-mŭs), *adj.* noble; able to rise above pettiness and meanness;

generous. —mag·na·nim'i·ty (-nâ-nim'ĭ-tĭ), n. —mag·nan'i·mous·ly, adv.

mag·nate (mag'nāt), n. a person of distinction and importance, especially in business.

mag·ne·sia (mag-nē'zhâ, 'shâ), n. a white, earthy powder, the oxide of magnesium, used as a laxative and antacid.

mag·ne·si·um (mag-nē'zi-ùm, 'zhi-ùm), n. a silvery, malleable, ductile metallic element that burns with a brilliant light.

mag·net (mag'nĕt), n. 1. lodestone. 2. any piece of iron or steel that has the property of attracting iron or steel, etc. 3. something or someone that attracts.

mag·net·ic (mag-net'ĭk), adj. 1. of, producing, or caused by magnetism. 2. having the properties of a magnet. 3. pertaining to the earth's magnetism. 4. that can be or is magnetized. 5. charming; attractive. —mag·net'i·cal·ly, adv.

magnetic field, an area in which a magnetic force is operative.

magnetic force, the attracting or repelling force between a magnet and electrical conductor or between a magnet and iron or steel.

magnetic needle, a magnetized piece of steel that points toward the magnetic poles, approximately north and south, when mounted to swing freely in a pivot, as within a compass.

magnetic poles, 1. the two points on the earth's surface toward which the ends of a magnetic needle point, north and south. 2. the two poles of a magnet, where the force is concentrated.

mag·net·ics (mag-net'ĭks), n.pl. the science that deals with magnets and magnetism.

magnetic tape, a thin plastic tape coated with a magnetized substance and used for recording sound, computer data, etc.

mag·net·ism (mag'nĕ-tizm), n. 1. the property or condition of being magnetic. 2. the force that causes this. 3. the science dealing with magnets or magnetic phenomena; magnetics. 4. personal appeal; charm.

mag·net·ite (-tīt), n. a black oxide of iron, an important iron ore.

mag·net·ize (-tīz), v.t. -ized, -iz·ing, 1. to give magnetic properties to (iron, steel, etc.). 2. to strongly attract (a person). —mag·net·i·za'tion, n. —mag'net·iz·er, n.

mag·ne·to (mag-nēt'ō), n., pl. -tos, a small electric generator, as used to provide the spark for the ignition in an internal-combustion engine.

mag·ne·to-, a combining form meaning magnetic force, magnetism.

mag·ne·to·e·lec·tric·i·ty (mag-nĕt-ō-i-lek-tris'i-tĭ), n. electricity produced by changing magnetic fields in the vicinity of electric conductors. —mag·ne·to·e·lec'tric, adj.

mag·ne·tom·e·ter (mag-nĕ-tom'ê-tēr), n. 1. an instrument for measuring the intensity of magnetic forces. 2. a device for detecting the presence of metal objects.

mag·nif·i·cence (mag-nif'i-sns), n. grandeur of appearance; splendor of dress, color, etc.; stately beauty. —mag·nif'i·cent, adj. —mag·nif'i·cent·ly, adv.

mag·ni·fy (mag'ni-fī), v.t. -fied, -fy·ing, 1. to exaggerate; attribute great importance to. 2. to make (an object) appear to be larger, as with a lens. 3. [Archaic], to glorify: v.i. to have the power of making objects appear larger, as a magnifying glass does. —mag·ni·fi·ca'tion, n. —mag'ni·fi·er, n.

magnifying glass, a lens, usually in a frame, that makes objects seen through it appear larger than they are.

mag·nil·o·quent (mag-nil'ô-kwĕnt), adj. pompous in style or speech; bombastic. —mag·nil'o·quence, n. —mag·nil'o·quent·ly, adv.

mag·ni·tude (mag-ni-tōōd), n. 1. comparative size or bulk. 2. importance. 3. size. 4. volume of sound. 5. the degree of brightness of a star.

mag·no·li·a (mag-nō'li-â), n. any of several trees with large white, pink, or purple flowers.

mag·num (mag'nŭm), n. a large wine bottle.

magnum o·pus (ō'pùs), [Latin], a great work; masterpiece.

mag·pie (mag'pī), n. 1. a chattering, black-and-white bird of the crow family. 2. one who chatters.

Mag·yar (mag'yär), n. 1. a member of the chief ethnic people in Hungary. 2. their language.

ma·ha·ra·jah, ma·ha·ra·ja (mä-hâ-rä'jâ), n. a prince in India; formerly, one of the ruling princes of the native states. —ma·ha·ra'ni, ma·ha·ra'nee ('ni), n.fem.

ma·hat·ma (mâ-hat'mâ, -hät'-), n. a Buddhist revered as one of a special class of wise and holy persons.

Mah·di (mä'di), n. the Moslem Messiah, expected by Moslems to appear as leader before the end of the world. —Mah'dism, n. —Mah'dist, n.

mah·jongg, mah·jong (mä'jông'), n. a game of Chinese origin, played with decorated tiles, usually by four persons.

ma·hog·a·ny (mâ-hog'â-ni, -hôg'-), n., pl. -nies, 1. a tree of tropical America yielding a dark, reddish-brown wood, used for furniture. 2. the wood. 3. reddish brown.

ma·hout (mâ-hout'), n. an elephant driver or keeper in India or the East Indies.

maid (mād), n. 1. a girl or young unmarried woman. 2. a virgin. 3. a female servant.

maid·en (mād'n), n. 1. a girl or young unmarried woman. 2. a virgin. 3. a race horse that has never won a race. 4. [M], a kind of guillotine, formerly used in Scotland: adj. 1. of or suitable to a maiden. 2. first; earliest. 3. new; inexperienced. —maid'en·hood, n.

maid·en·hair (-her), n. a kind of delicate fern with fine stalks and dark fronds.

maid·en·head (-hed), n. the hymen.

maid·en·ly (-li), adj. 1. of or pertaining to a maiden or maidenhood. 2. suitable to a maiden; modest, gentle, etc.

maiden name, the surname of a woman before marriage.

maid of honor, an unmarried woman who is chief attendant to a bride at her wedding.

maid·ser·vant (mād'sûr-vânt), n. a female servant.

---

a in cap, ā in cane, ä in father, å in abet, e in met, ē in be, ě in baker, ê in regent, ĭ in pit, ī in fine, i in manifest, o in hot, ô in horse, ō in bone,

mail (māl), *n.* 1. defensive body armor of metal plates, chains, rings, etc. that overlap. 2. a system for conveying letters, packages, etc.; postal system. 3. letters, packages, etc. conveyed and delivered by a postal system: *adj.* of, pertaining to, or used in the handling of mail: *v.t.* 1. to clothe with or as with mail. 2. to send by mail, as by putting in a mailbox. —**mail·a·bil'i·ty**, *n.* —**mail'a·ble**, *adj.*

mail·box ('boks), *n.* 1. a box into which mail is put when delivered, as at a home. 2. a box into which mail is deposited for collection. Also **mail box.**

mail·man (māl'man), *n., pl.* **-men**, a person whose work is delivering mail: also **mail carrier.**

mail·or·der ('ôr·dēr), *adj.* denoting an order for goods to be delivered by mail.

maim (mām), *v.t.* to deprive of the use of a limb; cripple or mutilate. —**maim'er**, *n.*

main (mān), *adj.* chief; principal; leading: *n.* 1. the principal part. 2. a chief conduit, pipe, etc. of a utility system. 3. [Poetic], the ocean.

main clause, a clause that can function alone as a complete sentence.

main·frame (mān'frām), *n.* 1. the central processing unit of a large computer. 2. a very large, relatively expensive computer, to which several terminals may be connected.

main·land ('land, 'lănd), *n.* the principal land of a country or continent, as distinguished from islands.

main·line ('līn), *n.* the principal road, course, etc.: *v.t.* **-lined, -lin·ing,** [Slang], to inject a narcotic drug directly into a vein.

main·ly ('lĭ), *adv.* principally; chiefly.

main·mast (mān'măst, 'mast), *n.* the principal mast of a vessel.

main·sail ('sl, 'sāl), *n.* the principal sail of a vessel, set from the mainmast.

main·spring ('spring), *n.* the chief spring in a watch, clock, or similar mechanism.

main·stay ('stā), *n.* 1. the stay extending from the mainmast forward, holding it in position. 2. a chief support.

main·stream ('strēm), *n.* 1. the most active part. 2. a main trend or line of thought or action.

main·stream·ing (mān'strēm'ing), *n.* the placement of disabled people into regular school classes, workplaces, etc.

main·tain (măn·tān'), *v.t.* 1. to carry on; continue. 2. to keep in a certain state, as of repair. 3. to defend, as by argument; affirm. 4. to support by providing means of existence. —**main·tain'a·ble**, *adj.*

main·te·nance (mān'tn·ăns), *n.* 1. the keeping of a building, etc. in good condition. 2. sustenance; support.

maî·tre d'hô·tel (me'tr dô·tel'), [French], a headwaiter: also [Informal], **maî·tre d'** (măt·ēr dē').

mai tai (mī'tī'), [*often* M- T-], a cocktail of rum, fruit juices, etc.

maize (māz), *n.* same as **Indian corn.**

ma·jes·tic (mă·jes'tĭk), *adj.* having dignity of person; stately; noble; grand: also **ma·jes'·ti·cal.** —**ma·jes'ti·cal·ly**, *adv.*

maj·es·ty (maj'is·tĭ), *n., pl.* **-ties**, 1. the dignity or stateliness of a sovereign. 2. sovereign power. 3. a sovereign. 4. [M-], a title used in speaking of or to a sovereign.

ma·jol·i·ca (mă·jol'i·kă), *n.* a fine, glazed pottery of Italy.

ma·jor (mā'jēr), *adj.* 1. greater in number, extent, size, importance, etc. 2. in *Music, a)* higher than the corresponding minor by a half tone. *b)* denoting one of the two standard diatonic scales: *v.i.* in *Education,* to specialize in a particular field of study: *n.* 1. a United States military officer ranking just above a captain. 2. in *Education,* a principal field of study. 3. in *Law,* a person of full legal age. 4. in *Logic,* the first proposition of a syllogism.

ma·jor·do·mo (-dō'mō), *n., pl.* **-mos**, the chief steward of a great household.

major general, *pl.* **major generals,** a United States military officer ranking just above a brigadier general.

ma·jor·i·ty (mă·jôr'i·tĭ), *n., pl.* **-ties,** 1. the greater number; more than half. 2. the excess of the greater number of votes cast for a winning candidate over all the rest of the votes. 3. full legal age.

make (māk), *v.t.* **made, mak'ing,** 1. to create, fashion, fabricate, produce, etc. 2. to prepare for use. 3. to cause to be or become. 4. to acquire. 5. to force. 6. to amount to. 7. to score. 8. to arrive at; reach. 9. to do or perform. 10. to understand. 11. [Informal], to acquire a position on: *v.i.* 1. to tend (*to* or *toward*). 2. to begin (to do something). 3. to have effect: *n.* product of manufacture; brand.

make-be·lieve ('bĕ·lēv'), *adj.* pretended; not real: *n.* pretense.

mak·er ('ēr), *n.* 1. a person or thing that makes. 2. [M-], God.

make-shift ('shift), *n.* a temporary expedient: *adj.* that will do temporarily.

make-up, make-up ('up), *n.* 1. the general composition of anything. 2. disposition. 3. cosmetics.

make-work ('wûrk), *adj.* that serves no other purpose than to give an idle or unemployed person something to do.

mal-, a prefix meaning *ill, evil, bad* or *badly.*

Mal·a·chi (mal'ă·kī), *n.* a book of the Bible.

mal·a·chite (mal'ă·kīt), *n.* a native carbonate of copper, a green mineral.

mal·ad·just·ed (mal·ă·jus'tĭd), *adj.* not well adjusted, especially to the environment. —**mal·ad·just'ment**, *n.*

mal·a·droit (mal·ă·droit'), *adj.* clumsy; awkward; inept. —**mal·a·droit'ness**, *n.*

mal·a·dy (mal'ă·di), *n., pl.* **-dies**, a disease; illness; ailment.

Mal·a·ga (mal'ă·gă), *n.* 1. a kind of large, white grape. 2. a white wine.

ma·laise (ma·lāz'), *n.* a vague feeling of uneasiness, as early in an illness.

mal·a·mute (mal'ă·mūt), *n.* an Eskimo sled dog: also **Alaskan malamute.**

mal·a·prop·ism (mal'ă·prop·izm), *n.* a ludicrous misuse of words that sound alike: from Mrs. *Malaprop*, in Sheridan's play (of the 18th century) "The Rivals."

ô in dragon, ōō in crude, oo in wool, u in cup, ū in cure, ū in turn, û in focus, oi in boy, ou in house, th in thin, th in sheathe, g in get, j in joy, y in yet.

mal·ap·ro·pos (mal-ap-rō-pō'), *adj.* inappropriate: *adv.* inappropriately.

ma·lar (mā'lẽr), *adj.* of or pertaining to the cheek or cheekbone: *n.* the cheekbone.

ma·lar·i·a (mä-ler'i-ȧ), *n.* an infectious disease transmitted by a mosquito, marked by recurrent chills and fever. —**ma·lar'i·al, ma·lar'i·ous,** *adj.*

ma·la·key, ma·lar·ky (mä-lär'ki), *n.* [Slang], insincere or misleading talk.

mal·a·thi·on (mal-ȧ-thī'on), *n.* an organic insecticide.

Ma·lay (mā'lā), *n.* any one of a group of brown-skinned, black-haired people of the Malay Peninsula of southeastern Asia, and nearby islands. —**Ma·lay'an,** *adj. & n.*

mal·con·tent (mal'kŏn-tent), *adj.* discontented or rebellious: *n.* a discontented or rebellious person, especially one who is critical of the government.

male (māl), *n.* 1. a member of the sex that begets young. 2. the plant or flower bearing stamens and producing pollen to fertilize the female. 3. something having a part that fits into a corresponding hollow part, as a pipe fitting, electrical plug, etc.: *adj.* 1. of or pertaining to a male person, animal, plant, etc. 2. like or suited to a man or boy; masculine. —**male'ness,** *n.*

mal·e·dic·tion (mal-ē-dik'shŭn), *n.* a curse.

mal·e·fac·tor (mal'ē-fak-tẽr), *n.* 1. an evildoer. 2. a criminal. —**mal·e·fac'tion,** *n.*

ma·lev·o·lent (mä-lev'ō-lĕnt), *adj.* wishing evil or harm; rejoicing at the misfortune of others. —**ma·lev'o·lence,** *n.*

mal·fea·sance (mal-fē'zns), *n.* an unlawful act or deed, especially by a public official. —**mal·fea'sant,** *adj.*

mal·for·ma·tion (mal-fŏr-mā'shŭn), *n.* faulty or abnormal structure of an organism or part. —**mal·formed',** *adj.*

mal·func·tion (mal-fŭngk'shŭn), *n.* a failure to function or work properly: *v.i.* to fail to function or work properly.

mal·ic acid (mal'ik, mā'lik), an acid occurring in apples and other fruits.

mal·ice (mal'is), *n.* 1. a desire to injure another; spite. 2. in *Law*, evil intent.

ma·li·cious (mä-lish'ŭs), *adj.* 1. bearing ill will or spite. 2. showing or caused by malice. —**ma·li'cious·ly,** *adv.* —**ma·li'cious·ness,** *n.*

ma·lign (mä-līn'), *v.t.* to speak evil of; slander: *adj.* 1. hurtful; malicious. 2. baleful; evil. 3. malignant.

ma·lig·nan·cy (mä-lig'năn-si), *n.* 1. the quality or condition of being malignant. 2. *pl.* -cies, a malignant tumor.

ma·lig·nant (mä-lig'nänt), *adj.* 1. intending or effecting evil. 2. very harmful. 3. virulent; capable of causing death; not benign. —**ma·lig'nant·ly,** *adv.*

ma·lig·ni·ty ('ni-ti), *n.* 1. the quality of being very harmful; malignancy. 2. persistent malice. 3. *pl.* -ties, something malignant.

ma·lin·ger (mä-ling'gẽr), *v.i.* to feign illness in order to evade duty. —**ma·lin'ger·er,** *n.*

mall (môl), *n.* 1. originally, *a)* a mallet used in the game of pall-mall. *b)* the game. *c)* an alley where the game was played. 2. a

shaded public walk. 3. a street lined with shops, for pedestrians only. 4. an enclosed shopping center.

mal·lard (mal'ẽrd), *n.* a common wild duck.

mal·le·a·ble (mal'i-ȧ-bl), *adj.* 1. capable of being extended or shaped by hammering or rolling, without breaking. 2. tractable. —**mal·le·a·bil'i·ty,** *n.*

mal·lee (mal'i), *n.* in Australia, a dense thicket formed by shrubby eucalyptuses.

mal·le·o·lus (mä-lē'ȧ-lŭs), *n., pl.* -li (-lī), the rounded bony protuberance on each side of the ankle joint. —**mal·le'o·lar,** *adj.*

mal·let (mal'it), *n.* 1. a wooden hammer with a short handle, used for driving a chisel, etc. 2. a long-handled hammer, as for use in polo or croquet.

mal·le·us (mal'i-ŭs), *n., pl.* -le·i (-ī), the outermost of the three small auditory bones of the ear.

mal·low (mal'ō), *n.* any one of a large family of plants with large, showy flowers, as the cotton plant, hollyhock, or okra.

malm (mäm), *n.* 1. [British], a soft, friable limestone or a rich loam formed from this. 2. chalk and clay mixed for making bricks.

malm·sey (mäm'zi), *n.* 1. a sweet, white grape. 2. a white wine made from this grape.

mal·nour·ished (mal-nũr'isht), *adj.* not properly nourished.

mal·nu·tri·tion (mal-nōō-trish'ŭn), *n.* faulty or inadequate nutrition.

mal·oc·clu·sion (-ŏ-klōō'zhŭn), *n.* faulty occlusion so that the teeth do not meet properly in biting.

mal·o·dor·ous (-ō'dẽr-ŭs), *adj.* smelling bad; stinking. —**mal·o'dor·ous·ly,** *adj.*

mal·prac·tice (-prak'tis), *n.* professional misconduct, improper treatment, or neglect, as by a physician.

malt (môlt), *n.* 1. barley or other grain steeped in water, fermented, and kiln-dried, used chiefly for brewing. 2. a beverage made from malt, as beer or ale. 3. [Informal], same as **malted milk:** *adj.* made with malt: *v.t. & v.i.* to change or be changed into malt. —**malt'y,** *adj.*

malted milk, dried milk and powdered malt, used with milk to make a drink.

Mal·tese (môl-tēz'), *n.* 1. *pl.* -tese', a native or inhabitant of Malta, an island country in the Mediterranean. 2. a cat with bluish-gray fur: also **Maltese cat.**

malt extract, a sweet, sticky substance obtained from malt soaked in water, used as a medicinal food.

Mal·thu·sian (mal-thōō'zhŭn, 'zi-ȧn), *adj.* of the theory of Thomas Malthus (1766-1834), English economist, holding that world population increases faster than the food supply and that disease, war, and famine serve to restrict the increase.

malt liquor, an alcoholic liquor made from malt, as beer, ale, stout, or the like.

malt·ose (môl'tōs), *n.* a white, crystalline sugar obtained from starch by action of the diastase of malt.

mal·treat (mal-trēt'), *v.t.* to treat roughly; abuse. —**mal·treat'ment,** *n.*

Mam·e·luke (mam'ē-lōōk), *n.* one of a military

caste, originally made up of slaves, that dominated Egypt for several centuries.

mam-ma, ma-ma (mä'mä, må-mä'), *n.* mother.

mam-ma (mam'å), *n., pl.* **-mae** ('ē), a gland for secreting milk, present in the female of mammals. —**mam'ma-ry,** *adj.*

mam-mal (mam'ål), *n.* any one of a large class of warm-blooded vertebrates whose young are fed by milk from the mammary glands of the female. —**mam-ma-li-an** (må-mä'li-ån, ma-), *adj. & n.*

mam-mal-o-gy (må-mal'ò-ji, ma-), *n.* the branch of zoology that treats of mammals.

mam-mil-la (ma-mil'å, må-), *n., pl.* **-lae** ('ē), a nipple. —**mam'mil-lar-y,** *adj.*

mam-mon (mam'ón), *n.* [often M-], riches or worldly gain regarded as an evil and sometimes as a demon.

mam-moth (mam'óth), *n.* one of an extinct species of huge elephant with long tusks: *adj.* gigantic; huge.

man (man), *n., pl.* **men,** 1. a human being. 2. an adult human male. 3. mankind. 4. an adult male servant, employee, etc. 5. a husband. 6. one of the pieces in chess, checkers, etc.: *v.t.* **manned, man'ning,** 1. to furnish with men. 2. to take one's place at. 3. to brace or fortify (oneself).

man-a-cle (man'å-kl), *n.* a handcuff: usually used in the plural: *v.t.* **-cled, -cling,** to place handcuffs on; shackle.

man-age (man'ij), *v.t.* **-aged, -ag-ing,** 1. to conduct or carry on; direct. 2. to make docile or submissive. 3. to handle, govern, or control. 4. to succeed in bringing about (something): *v.i.* 1. to conduct affairs. 2. to continue to function. —**man-age-a-bil'i-ty,** *n.* —**man'age-a-ble,** *adj.*

man-age-ment (-mént), *n.* 1. the act of managing; control or direction. 2. those managing an institution, business, etc.

man-ag-er (-ēr), *n.* one who directs or controls, especially a business.

man-a-ge-ri-al (man-å-jir'i-ål), *adj.* of a manager or management.

man-a-kin (man'å-kin), *n.* a small, brightly colored bird of Central and South America.

ma-ña-na (mä-nyä'nä), *n.* [Spanish], tomorrow: *adv.* 1. tomorrow. 2. in the indefinite future.

man-a-tee (man'å-ti), *n.* a large, plant-eating aquatic mammal of tropical waters.

Man-ches-ter terrier (man'ches-tēr, 'chi-stēr), any one of a breed of terrier with a black-and-tan coat.

man-chi-neel (man-chi-nēl'), *n.* a tree of tropical America with a milky, acid juice and poisonous fruit resembling plums.

Man-chu (man-chōō'), *n., pl.* **-chus', -chu',** any one of a Mongolian people who ruled China from 1643 to 1912.

man-da-mus (man-dā'mùs), *n.* a writ issued by a superior court directing an inferior court, corporation, official, government agency, etc. to perform some specified act.

man-da-rin (man'då-rin), *n.* 1. a high official of the former Chinese Empire. 2. [M-], the official and main dialect of China. 3. a sweet orange: also **mandarin orange.** 4. a crested

Asian duck: also **mandarin duck:** *adj.* denoting a Chinese dress style with a stand-up collar.

man-date (man'dāt), *n.* 1. an order; command. 2. a court decision. 3. formerly, *a)* a League of Nations' commission to a country to administer the affairs of some region. *b)* the region. 4. the directive expressed through voters to a legislature, administration, etc.

man-da-to-ry (man'då-tôr-i), *adj.* 1. of or containing a mandate. 2. obligatory. —**man'da-to-ri-ly,** *adv.*

man-di-ble (man'di-bl), *n.* the jaw: in vertebrates, the under jaw; in birds, either jaw; in insects and crustaceans, one of the anterior pair.

man-do-lin (man'dl-in), *n.* a stringed musical instrument with a rounded body, played with a plectrum.

man-drake (man'drāk), *n.* a poisonous plant of the nightshade family: its thick, forked root was formerly thought to have magical powers and was used in m. licine.

man-drel, man-dril (man'drél), *n.* 1. a metal spindle placed in a lathe center to support work while it is being machined or turned. 2. a metal rod used as a core around which metal, wire, glass, etc. is cast, molded, etc.

man-drill (man'dril), *n.* a large, ferocious baboon of western Africa.

mane (mān), *n.* the long hair on the neck of certain animals, as the horse and lion.

man-eat-er (man'ēt-ēr), *n.* an animal that eats human flesh, as certain sharks or tigers. —**man'-eat-ing,** *adj.*

ma-nège, ma-nege (ma-nezh', -näzh'), *n.* 1. the art of horsemanship. 2. the training of horses. 3. a school for horsemanship.

ma-nes (mä'nēz), *n.pl.* [often M-], in ancient Rome, the souls of the dead, sometimes deified.

ma-neu-ver (må-nōō'vēr), *n.* 1. a regulated and planned movement of military, naval, or air forces. 2. an adroit or shrewd step toward some objective; stratagem. 3. a movement or series of movements by an aircraft in a pattern: *v.i. & v.t.* 1. to perform or cause to perform maneuvers. 2. to manipulate; scheme shrewdly. —**ma-neu-ver-a-bil'i-ty,** *n.* —**ma-neu'ver-a-ble,** *adj.*

man-ful (man'fúl), *adj.* courageous; resolute. —**man'ful-ly,** *adv.* —**man'ful-ness,** *n.*

man-ga-nate (mang'gå-nāt), *n.* a salt of manganic acid.

man-ga-nese (mang'gå-nēs, -nēz), *n.* a hard, brittle, gray, metallic chemical element used in alloys.

man-gan-ic (man-gan'ik), *adj.* of certain chemical compounds containing manganese.

manganic acid, an acid known only in the form of its salts.

mange (mānj), *n.* a skin disease of dogs, cattle, etc. causing itching, loss of hair, and lesions.

man-gel-wur-zel (mang'gl-wūr-zl, -wûrt-), *n.* a coarse variety of beet, the fleshy roots of which are used for cattle feed, especially in Europe: also **mangel.**

ô in drag*o*n, ōō in cr*u*de, o͝o in w*oo*l, u in c*u*p, û in c*u*re, ŭ in t*u*rn, û in foc*u*s, oi in b*oy*, ou in h*ou*se, th in *th*in, *th* in shea*th*e, g in *g*et, j in *j*oy, y in *y*et.

man-ger (mān'jēr), *n.* a feeding trough for horses or cattle.

man-gle (mang'gl), *v.t.* -gled, -gling, 1. to lacerate; mutilate; hack. 2. to spoil; ruin. 3. to press in a mangle: *n.* a machine with heated rollers for pressing sheets, etc. — **man'gler,** *n.*

man-go (mang'gō), *n., pl.* -goes, -gos, 1. a yellowish-red fruit with an acid, juicy pulp. 2. the tropical tree on which it grows.

man-go-steen (mang'gō-stēn), *n.* 1. an East Indian fruit somewhat like an orange. 2. the tree on which it grows.

man-grove (mang'grōv), *n.* a tropical tree growing in swampy ground, with branches that send down roots, often causing a thick growth over a large area.

man-gy (mān'ji), *adj.* -gi-er, -gi-est, 1. infected with the mange. 2. unkempt; filthy. 3. mean-spirited; despicable. — **man'gi-ly,** *adv.* — **man'gi-ness,** *n.*

man-han-dle (man'han-dl), *v.t.* -dled, -dling, to handle roughly.

man-hat-tan (man-hat'n), *n.* a cocktail made of whiskey and sweet vermouth, usually with bitters and a maraschino cherry.

man-hole (man'hōl), *n.* a hole permitting entrance as to a sewer, underground pipes, etc.

man-hood ('hood), *n.* 1. the state of being a man. 2. courage, virility, etc.

man-hour ('our), *n.* a time unit equal to one hour of work done by one person.

ma-ni-a (mā'ni-å, mān'yå), *n.* 1. mental illness marked by violence or wildness. 2. an obsession; craze.

ma-ni-ac (mā'ni-ak), *adj.* wildly insane: *n.* one who is wildly insane. — **ma-ni-a-cal** (må-ni'å-kl), *adj.*

man-ic (man'ik), *adj.* having, like, or characterized by mania.

man-ic-de-pres-sive (-di-pres'iv), *adj.* of or pertaining to a condition of alternating spells of mania and depression: *n.* one who suffers from this condition.

Man-i-chae-ism, Man-i-che-ism (man'i-kē-izm), *n.* an early Persian religious philosophy teaching of two contending principles, the good (God, light, the soul), and evil (Satan, darkness, the body). — **Man-i-chae'an,** *n. & adj.* — **Man'i-chee,** *n.*

man-i-cure (man'i-kyoor), *v.t.* -cured, -cur-ing, to trim and polish (the fingernails): *n.* a trimming and polishing of the fingernails. — **man'i-cur-ist,** *n.*

man-i-fest (man'i-fest), *adj.* clear; plain; apparent: *v.t.* 1. to make clear; show plainly. 2. to prove: *n.* 1. the invoice of a cargo for customs officials. 2. a list of passengers and cargo on an airplane. — **man'i-fest-ly,** *adv.*

man-i-fes-ta-tion (man-i-fes-tā'shŭn), *n.* 1. an act of manifesting. 2. a display; indication. 3. a public demonstration.

man-i-fes-to (man-i-fes'tō), *n., pl.* -toes, a public declaration of objectives, intentions, etc. by someone important.

man-i-fold (man'i-fōld), *adj.* 1. many and various in kind. 2. having many different forms,

uses, elements, etc. 3. complicated: *n.* a pipe with several outlets for exhaust, as in an internal-combustion engine: *v.t.* to make copies of, as with carbon paper. — **man'i-fold-er,** *n.* — **man'i-fold-ly,** *adv.*

man-i-kin, man-ni-kin (man'i-kn), *n.* 1. a little man; dwarf. 2. same as **mannequin.**

Ma-nil-a hemp (må-nil'å), [often m—], a tough fiber from abacá stalks, used for making rope (*Manila rope*), cloth, etc.

Manila paper, [often m—], a light-brown paper used for wrappings, envelopes, etc.

man-i-oc (man'i-ok), *n.* same as **cassava.**

man-i-ple (man'i-pl), *n.* a band worn on the left arm by a priest at Mass.

ma-nip-u-late (må-nip'yŭ-lāt), *v.t.* -lat-ed, -lat-ing, 1. to operate or work by means of the hands. 2. to control or manage skillfully and often unfairly. 3. to falsify (figures, etc.) for one's own benefit. — **ma-nip-u-la'tion,** *n.* — **ma-nip'u-la-tive,** *adj.* — **ma-nip'u-la-tor,** *n.*

man-i-tou (man'i-tōō), *n.* a supernatural spirit or deity of the Algonquian Indians with control over nature: also **manitu.**

man-kind (man-kīnd'), *n.* 1. the human race. 2. all human males.

man-ly (man'li), *adj.* -li-er, -li-est, having characteristics suitable to a man; courageous, noble, etc. — **man'li-ness,** *n.*

man-made ('mād'), *adj.* synthetic; artificial.

man-na (man'å), *n.* in the *Bible,* food miraculously supplied to the Israelites in the wilderness.

man-ne-quin (man'i-kin), *n.* 1. a woman who models new clothes. 2. a model of the human body used by tailors, artists, etc.

man-ner (man'ēr), *n.* 1. a method; way or fashion of doing something. 2. a habit or custom. 3. *pl.* ways of social behavior. 4. *pl.* polite ways of social behavior. 5. sort; kind.

man-ner-ism (-izm), *n.* a peculiarity of style, action, or bearing, especially if constrained or affected.

man-ner-ly (-li), *adj.* courteous.

man-nish (man'ish), *adj.* of or denoting a woman with masculine characteristics. — **man'nish-ly,** *adv.*

ma-noeu-vre (må-nōō'vēr), *n. & v.i. & v.t.* -vred, -vring, chiefly British form of **maneuver.**

man of letters, a scholar, writer, etc., especially in the literary field.

man-of-war (man-ōv-wôr'), *n., pl.* **men-of-war,** a large warship.

ma-nom-e-ter (må-nom'ē-tēr), *n.* an instrument for measuring the pressure of gases.

man-or (man'ēr), *n.* 1. in England, the district over which a feudal lord held authority. 2. in England, a landed estate. 3. the main residence of an estate or plantation. 4. a mansion. — **ma-no-ri-al** (må-nōr'i-ål), *adj.*

manor house, the house of the lord of a manor.

man-pow-er (man'pou-ēr), *n.* 1. power supplied by human strength. 2. the number of people working or available for work; labor force.

man-sard roof (man'särd), a roof having two slopes on all four sides, the lower steeper than the upper slope.

manse (mans), *n.* the residence of a minister.

man·ser·vant (man'sûr-vànt), n., pl. men'ser·vants, a male servant: also man servant.

-man·ship (mǎn-ship), a combining form meaning ability or skill in.

man·sion (man'shǔn), n. a large, impressive house.

man·slaugh·ter ('slôt-ēr), n. the unlawful killing of a human being by another, but without malice or premeditation.

man·ta (man'tȧ), n. 1. a cheap shawl or cape of coarse cotton fabric, worn in Spanish America. 2. this fabric.

man·teau (man'tō), n., pl. -teaus, a woman's cape or cloak.

man·tel (man't'l), n. 1. an ornamental shelf above a fireplace: also man'tel-piece. 2. the entire framework around a fireplace.

man·til·la (man-til'ȧ, -tē'ȧ), n. a woman's scarf, often lace, worn over the shoulders and hair, as in Spanish America or Spain.

man·tis (man'tis), n., pl. -tis·es, -tes ('tēz), a long insect that holds its forelegs folded as though in prayer.

man·tle (man'tl), n. 1. a loose cloak or cape. 2. a covering or envelope. 3. the flap of the membrane of a mollusk. 4. an incandescent hood placed over a flame, as of a gas jet, to give off light. 5. the layer of the earth's interior below the crust: v.t. -tled, -tling, to cover as with a mantle: v.i. 1. to be or become covered. 2. to flush or blush.

man·tra (mun'trȧ, man'-), n. a Hindu hymn or chanted prayer.

man·u·al (man'yoo-wȧl), adj. 1. of the hands. 2. done or made by hand. 3. involving hard work done with the hands: n. 1. a handy reference or instruction book. 2. an organ keyboard. 3. prescribed drill in handling a rifle: also manual of arms. —man'u·al·ly, adv.

manual training, training in practical arts and crafts, as woodworking.

man·u·fac·ture (man-yū-fak'chēr), v.t. -tured, -tur·ing, 1. to make or fabricate, as by machinery, especially on a large scale and with division of labor. 2. to make up (excuses, evidence, etc.); concoct: n. 1. the conversion of raw materials into articles for use, as by machinery on a large scale. 2. the making of anything. —man-u-fac'tur-er, n.

man·u·mit (man-yū-mit'), v.t. -mit'ted, -mit'ting, to free from slavery; liberate. —man·u·mis·sion (-mish'ǔn), n.

ma·nure (mȧ-noor'), n. any fertilizing substance, as animal excrement, used for enriching the soil: v.t. -nured', -nur'ing, to fertilize (soil) by putting manure or other substance on or into.

ma·nus (mā'nǔs), n., pl. ma'nus, the human hand or the forefoot of an animal.

man·u·script (man'yū-skript), adj. written or typed, not printed: n. 1. a book, document, etc. written by hand. 2. an author's copy of a work, written or typewritten, as given to a publisher or printer. 3. writing as distinguished from print.

Manx (mangks), adj. of or pertaining to the Isle of Man, an island between Northern Ireland and England, or to its inhabitants or language: n. the language formerly spoken on the Isle of Man, now nearly extinct.

Manx cat [also ma-], a kind of domestic cat with only a vestigial tail.

man·y (men'i), adj. more, most, 1. numerous; consisting of a great, indefinite number. 2. relatively numerous: n. a great number (of persons or things): pron. a great number of persons or things.

Mao·ri (mou'ri), n., pl. -ris, -ri, any one of a brown-skinned people native to New Zealand.

map (map), n. 1. a representation of the earth or some portion of it, showing seas, countries, etc. 2. a representation of the sky, showing the stars, etc. 3. [Slang] the face: v.t. mapped, map'ping, 1. to delineate on a map. 2. to plan.

ma·ple (mā'pl), n. 1. any of a large group of deciduous trees of temperate regions grown for shade, wood, or sap. 2. its hard, light-colored wood, used for furniture. 3. the flavor of maple syrup or maple sugar.

maple sugar, sugar made by boiling down maple syrup.

maple syrup, syrup made by boiling down sap from maple trees.

mar (mär), v.t. marred, mar'ring, to disfigure; injure; damage: n. a blemish; mark of injury.

mar·a·bou (mer'ȧ-bōō), n. 1. a large stork of India or Africa. 2. its soft feathers, used for trimming hats, etc. 3. a fine raw silk that can be dyed with the natural gum still in it. 4. fabric made from this.

ma·ra·ca (mȧ-rä'kä), n. a gourd with pebbles in it, shaken as a percussion instrument.

mar·a·schi·no (mer-ȧ-skē'nō, -shē'-), n. a liqueur made from the juice of a small, black wild cherry.

maraschino cherry, a kind of cherry in a syrup flavored with maraschino.

ma·ras·mus (mȧ-raz'mǔs), n. a wasting away; gradual emaciation, especially of infants, as from inability to assimilate food.

mar·a·thon (mer'ȧ-thon), n. 1. a foot race of 26 miles, 385 yards. 2. any long-distance or endurance contest.

ma·raud (mȧ-rod'), v.i. & v.t. to raid for plunder; pillage. —ma·raud'er, n.

mar·ble (mär'bl), n. 1. a hard limestone of various colors, capable of taking a fine polish. 2. a sculptured piece of this stone. 3. anything resembling marble. 4. a small ball of marble or stone. 5. pl. a children's game, played with such balls: adj. 1. of marble. 2. like marble; cold, hard, etc.: v.t. 1. -bled, -bling, 1. to stain (book edges) so they are streaked like marble. 2. to cause (meat) to be streaked with fat.

mar·ble·ize (-īz), v.t. -ized, -iz·ing, to color, streak, etc. like marble.

mar·cel (mär-sel'), v.t. -celled', -cel'ling, to wave (the hair) with a curling iron: n. a style of hairdressing consisting of a series of even waves done with a curling iron: also marcel wave.

March (märch), *n.* the third month of the year, having 31 days.

march (märch), *n.* 1. a regular, measured walk, especially of soldiers. 2. steady onward movement. 3. a musical composition suitable for marching to. 4. the distance covered in marching for a given period. 5. a frontier or border. 6. borderland: *v.i.* to cause to march: *v.i.* 1. to walk with regular steps, as in military formation. 2. to progress steadily. —march'er, *n.*

mar-chion-ess (mär'shŭ-nis), *n.* 1. the wife or widow of a marquess. 2. a lady of the rank of a marquess.

Mar-di gras (mär'di grä'), Shrove Tuesday, the last day before Lent: a day of merrymaking and carnival.

mare (mer), *n.* the female of the horse, donkey, etc.

ma-re (mer'i), *n.,* *pl.* -ri-a ('i-ä), a large, dark area on the moon, as seen from the earth.

mare's-nest (merz'nest), *n.* 1. some fancied discovery which proves to be a hoax. 2. a confused jumble; mess.

mare's-tail ('tāl), *n.* 1. an aquatic plant. 2. a cirrus cloud resembling the tail of a horse.

mar-ga-rine (mär'jä-rin), *n.* a spread or cooking fat composed mostly of vegetable oils processed with skim milk to the consistency of butter: also **mar'ga-rin.**

mar-gin (mär'jin), *n.* 1. a border; edge. 2. the part of a page at the edge, not printed upon. 3. a spare or reserve amount. 4. the difference between the cost and selling price. —**mar'gin-al,** *adj.* —**mar'gin-al-ly,** *adv.*

mar-gi-na-li-a (mär-ji-nä'li-ä), *n.pl.* marginal notes, as in a book.

ma-ri-a-chi (mär-i-ä'chi), *n., pl.* -chis, in Mexico, 1. any of a band of strolling musicians. 2. the band. 3. its music.

mar-i-gold (mer'i-gōld), *n.* a common garden plant with yellow or orange flowers.

ma-ri-jua-na, ma-ri-hua-na (mer-i-wä'nä), *n.* 1. the hemp plant. 2. the dried leaves and flowers of the hemp plant, smoked, especially in cigarettes, for the psychological and euphoric effects.

ma-rim-ba (mä-rim'bä), *n.* a musical instrument resembling the xylophone.

ma-ri-na (mä-rē'nä), *n.* a docking area for small boats.

mar-i-nade (mer-i-nād'), *n.* 1. a brine or liquid mixture as of vinegar, wine, spices, etc. in which meat or fish are steeped, often before cooking. 2. the food thus steeped: *v.t.* -nad'ed, -nad'ing, same as marinate.

mar-i-nate (mer'i-nāt), *v.t.* -nat-ed, -nat-ing, to steep (meat, fish, etc.) in a marinade. —**mar-i-na'tion,** *n.*

ma-rine (mä-rēn'), *adj.* 1. of the sea. 2. living in or formed by the sea. 3. nautical. 4. naval: *n.* 1. a soldier who serves on a warship. 2. [often M-], a member of the Marine Corps. 3. the naval or merchant ships of a nation; fleet.

Marine Corps, a branch of the U.S. armed forces trained for sea, land, and aerial combat.

mar-i-ner (mer'i-nĕr), *n.* a sailor.

mar-i-o-nette (mer-i-ô-net'), *n.* a small, jointed doll worked by wires or strings.

Mar-ist (mer'ist), *n.* a member of a Roman Catholic group of priests, the Society of Mary.

mar-i-tal (mer'i-tl), *adj.* of marriage; matrimonial. —**mar'i-tal-ly,** *adv.*

mar-i-time (mer'i-tīm), *adj.* 1. on, bordering upon, or living near the sea. 2. of navigation, shipping, etc.

mar-jo-ram (mär'jĕr-ăm), *n.* a perennial herb of the mint family, used for flavoring.

Mark (märk), *n.* a book of the New Testament, the second Gospel.

mark (märk), *n.* 1. a visible impression on a surface. 2. evidence of some quality, etc. 3. a symbol, as in printing or writing. 4. a brand, seal, etc. on something to show the owner, maker, etc. 5. a target. 6. a standard of quality. 7. something serving as a guide or indicating position, etc. 8. a grade in school. 9. the monetary unit of East Germany: *v.t.* 1. to make a mark upon. 2. to distinguish as by a mark. 3. to take notice of. 4. to characterize. 5. to grade or rate: *v.i.* to observe; take note. —**mark'er,** *n.*

mark-down ('doun), *n.* 1. a lowering of price. 2. the amount by which a price is lowered.

marked (märkt), *adj.* 1. suspicious. 2. obvious. —**mark'ed-ly,** *adv.*

mar-ket (mär'kit), *n.* 1. a public place for the selling and buying of commodities: also **mar'ket-place.** 2. a gathering of people for buying and selling things. 3. trade. 4. a store for selling food, or a particular kind of food. 5. demand (for goods or services). 6. a region where trade may be carried on: *v.t.* to sell or offer for sale: *v.i.* to buy food. —**mar'ket-a-ble,** *adj.* —**mar'ket-er, mar-ket-eer'** (-kē-tir'), *n.*

mark-ing (mär'king), *n.* 1. a mark made. 2. an arrangement of marks or coloring, as on an animal or plant.

marks-man (märks'măn), *n., pl.* -men, one skilled in shooting. —**marks'man-ship,** *n.*

mark-up (märk'up), *n.* 1. an increase in price. 2. the amount by which a price is increased.

marl (märl), *n.* a soft, crumbly mixture of limestone, clay, and sand: *v.t.* 1. to fertilize or cover with marl. 2. to wind (rope, etc.) with marlines. —**marl'y,** *adj.*

mar-lin (mär'lin), *n., pl.* -lin, -lins, a large, slender ocean fish.

mar-line (mär'lin), *n.* a two-stranded cord used for winding around ropes, etc. to prevent fraying: also **mar'lin, mar'ling** ('ling).

mar-line-spike, mar-lin-spike (-spīk), *n.* a pointed piece of iron used for separating the strands of rope in splicing or marling: also **marlingspike.**

mar-ma-lade (mär'mä-lād), *n.* a preserve containing pieces of fruit and rind, as of orange.

mar-mo-set (mär'mō-zet), *n.* a small monkey of Central and South America.

mar-mot (mär'mŏt), *n.* a thick-bodied rodent with coarse hair and bushy tail, as the prairie dog or woodchuck.

ă in cap, ā in cane, ä in father, å in abet, e in met, ē in be, ê in baker, ĕ in regent, ĭ in pit, ī in fine, ĭ in manifest, o in hot, ô in horse, ō in bone,

ma·roon (mȧ-rōōn'), *v.t.* to abandon as on a desert island: *n.* a dark brownish red.

mar·plot (mär'plot), *n.* one who frustrates some plan by officious interference.

marque (märk), *n.* an identifying emblem or nameplate on an automobile.

mar·quee (mär-kē'), *n.* a rooflike projection, as over the doorway to a theater or hotel.

mar·quess (mär'kwis), *n.* 1. a British peer ranking above an earl. 2. same as marquis.

mar·que·try (mär'kè-tri), *n.* decorative inlaid work, as in furniture.

mar·quis (mär'kwis), *n.* a nobleman ranking above an earl or count.

mar·quise (-kēz'), *n.* 1. the wife or widow of a marquis. 2. a lady of the rank of a marquis.

mar·qui·sette (mär-ki-zet', -kwi-), *n.* a thin, mesh fabric used for curtains, etc.

mar·riage (mar'ij), *n.* 1. a wedding ceremony. 2. the state of being married. 3. a close union. —**mar'riage·a·ble**, *adj.*

mar·ried ('id), *adj.* 1. united in wedlock. 2. of marriage; conjugal.

mar·row (mer'ō), *n.* 1. the fatty tissue that fills the cavities of most bones. 2. the essence of anything.

mar·row·bone (-bōn), *n.* 1. a bone containing marrow. 2. *pl.* the knees.

mar·row·fat (-fat), *n.* a variety of large pea: also **marrowfat pea.**

mar·ry (mer'i), *v.t.* -ried, -ry·ing, 1. to unite as husband and wife. 2. to take as husband or wife. 3. to join closely: *v.i.* to get married: *interj.* [Archaic or Dialectal], an exclamation of surprise.

Mars (märz), *n.* 1. the Roman god of war. 2. a planet in the solar system, fourth in distance from the sun: it is conspicuous for its redness.

Mar·seil·laise (mär-sè-lāz'), *n.* the national anthem of France.

marsh (märsh), *n.* a tract of low, wet, soft land; swamp; bog. —**marsh'y**, *adj.* —**marsh'i·ness,** *n.*

mar·shal (mär'shȧl), *n.* 1. an official who superintends ceremonies, processions, etc. 2. in some foreign armies, a general officer of the highest rank. 3. a Federal officer of a U.S. judicial district, with duties like those of a sheriff. 4. the chief administrative officer of some fire and police departments in the U.S.: *v.t.* -shaled or -shalled, -shal·ing or -shal·ling, 1. to arrange or dispose in order. 2. to guide.

marsh·mal·low (märsh'mel-ō, 'mal-ō), *n.* a soft confection made of sugar, gelatin, corn syrup, etc., coated with powdered sugar.

marsh mallow, a perennial plant with pink flowers.

mar·su·pi·al (mär-sōō'pi-ȧl), *adj.* of or pertaining to a group of mammals that carry their incompletely developed young in an external pouch on the abdomen of the mother: *n.* any one of this kind of animal, as the kangaroo or opossum.

mart (märt), *n.* a market.

mar·ten (mär'tn), *n., pl.* -tens, -ten, 1. a small, carnivorous mammal like a weasel, with valuable fur. 2. the fur.

mar·tial (mär'shȧl), *adj.* 1. pertaining to or suitable for war. 2. military. 3. warlike. —**mar'tial·ly,** *adv.*

martial arts, systems of self-defense originating in the Orient, such as karate, etc.

martial law, temporary rule by military authorities over civilians, as during a war or insurrection.

Mar·tian (mär'shùn), *n.* a supposed inhabitant of the planet Mars, in science fiction.

mar·tin (mär'tn), *n.* any one of several birds related to or like the swallow.

mar·ti·net (mär-tn-et'), *n.* a very strict disciplinarian.

mar·tin·gale (mär'tn-gāl), *n.* a broad strap passing from the nose to the girth of a horse between its forelegs, to keep its head down.

mar·ti·ni (mär-tē'ni), *n., pl.* -nis, [also M-], a cocktail made of gin (or vodka) and dry vermouth, often with a green olive or twist of lemon peel.

mar·tyr (mär'tēr), *n.* 1. one who is willing to suffer or die for his principles or faith. 2. one who suffers acutely for a long time: *v.t.* 1. to put to death or torture for adherence to some belief. 2. to torture; persecute. —**mar'tyr·dom,** *n.*

mar·tyr·ol·o·gy (mär-ti-rol'ò-ji), *n., pl.* -gies, a list or history of martyrs, especially Christian martyrs. —**mar·tyr·ol'o·gist,** *n.*

mar·vel (mär'vl), *n.* something extraordinary and astonishing; miracle; prodigy: *v.i.* -veled or -velled, -vel·ing or -vel·ling, to feel wonder or astonishment.

mar·vel·ous (-ùs), *adj.* 1. exciting wonder; extraordinary. 2. incredible. 3. [Informal], superb; splendid. —**mar'vel·ous·ly,** *adv.*

Marx·ism (märk'sizm), *n.* the economic, political, and social theories and principles developed by Karl Marx and Friedrich Engels (19th-century German political theorists), used as a basis for communism and socialism. —**Marx'ist, Marx'i·an,** *adj. & n.*

mar·zi·pan (mär'zi-pan), *n.* a confection made of sugar, ground almonds, and egg whites.

mas·ca·ra (mas-ker'ȧ), *n.* a cosmetic for coloring the eyebrows and eyelashes.

mas·con (mäs'kon), *n.* a mass of very dense substance beneath the moon's surface.

mas·cot (mas'kot), *n.* a person, animal, or thing supposed to bring good luck.

mas·cu·line (mas'kyu-lin), *adj.* 1. of or pertaining to men or boys. 2. characteristic of men; manly, powerful, robust, etc. 3. mannish. 4. in *Grammar,* denoting the gender of words referring to males or to things originally thought of as male. —**mas·cu·lin'i·ty,** *n.*

ma·ser (mā'zèr), *n.* a device for the amplification of crystal or gas atoms by stimulated emission of radiation.

mash (mash), *n.* 1. a soft or pulpy mass. 2. a mixture of bran and water for horses. 3. crushed malt or meal steeped in hot water for making wort: *v.t.* 1. to mix with hot water (as malt), in brewing. 2. to change to a soft, pulpy state by beating, crushing, etc. 3. to damage.

mash·er ('ēr), *n.* 1. an implement for mashing vegetables, etc. 2. [Slang], a man who makes unwanted sexual advances to women he does not know.

ȯ in *dragon,* ōō in *crude,* oo in *wool,* u in *cup,* ū in *cure,* ū in *turn,* ȧ in *focus,* oi in *boy,* ou in *house,* th in *thin,* th in *sheathe,* g in *get,* j in *joy,* y in *yet.*

mask (mask), *n.* 1. a cover or partial cover to conceal or protect the face. 2. something that conceals or disguises. 3. a masquerade. 4. a likeness of a face as cast in a mold. 5. a comic, stylized, or grotesque representation of a face: *v.t.* to conceal or cover as with a mask: *v.i.* to put on a mask.

mas·och·ism (mas'ŏ-kizm), *n.* gratification or pleasure, often sexual, from being hurt or humiliated. —mas'o·chist, *n.* —mas·och·is'tic, *adj.*

ma·son (mā'sn), *n.* 1. a builder in stone, brick, etc. 2. [M-], same as Freemason.

Ma·son-Dix·on line (mā'sn-dik'sn), boundary line between Maryland and Pennsylvania, regarded as separating the South from the North.

Ma·son·ic (mă-son'ik), *adj.* [also m-], of or pertaining to Freemasons or Freemasonry.

ma·son·ry (mā'sn-ri), *n., pl.* -ries, 1. the art or occupation of a mason. 2. something constructed by a mason, as of stone or brick. 3. [also M-], same as Freemasonry.

masque (mask), *n.* 1. a masquerade; masked ball. 2. a former kind of dramatic performance with an allegorical theme.

mas·quer·ade (mas-kě-rād'), *n.* 1. a ball or festive gathering at which masks are worn. 2. a disguise. 3. a pretense; false show: *v.i.* -ad'ed, -ad'ing, 1. to take part in a masquerade. 2. to go about under false pretenses. —mas·quer·ad'er, *n.*

Mass (mas), *n.* [also m-], the service of the Eucharist in the Roman Catholic Church.

mass (mas), *n.* 1. a large quantity or number. 2. a body of matter; lump. 3. size; bulk. 4. the main part. 5. *pl.* the common people. 6. in *Physics,* the quantity of matter in a body in relation to inertia: *v.t.* & *v.i.* to gather together into a mass.

mas·sa·cre (mas'å-kĕr), *n.* indiscriminate slaughter with unnecessary cruelty: *v.t.* -cred, -cring, to slaughter indiscriminately in large numbers with unnecessary cruelty.

mas·sage (mă-säzh'), *n.* a rubbing or kneading of the body, as to stimulate circulation: *v.t.* -saged', -sag'ing, to give a massage to. —mas·sag'er, mas·sag'ist, *n.*

mas·se·ter (ma-sēt'ĕr), *n.* the short, thick muscle that raises the lower jaw.

mas·seur (ma-sûr', mă-), *n.* a man who gives massages. —mas·seuse' (-sooz', -sööz'), *n.fem.*

mas·si·cot (mas'i-kot), *n.* yellow monoxide of lead.

mas·sive (mas'iv), *adj.* 1. forming or consisting of a large mass; bulky. 2. large and impressive. —mas'sive·ly, *adv.* —mas'sive·ness, *n.*

mass media, those means of communication that reach large numbers of people, as newspapers, radio, television, etc.

mass production, the production of goods in large quantities by machinery. —mass-pro·duce', *v.t.* -duced', -duc'ing.

mast (mast), *n.* 1. a tall spar or metal tube, sometimes in sections, raised vertically on the keel of a ship to support the sails. 2. acorns, beechnuts, etc. as food for hogs.

mas·tec·to·my (mas-tek'tŏ-mi), *n., pl.* -mies, the surgical removal of a breast.

mas·ter (mas'tĕr), *n.* 1. one who rules or commands others, as a director, employer, owner of a slave or animal, head of a household, captain of a merchant ship, etc. 2. an expert. 3. a great artist. 4. [M-], *a)* a title given to boys too young to be called "Mister." *b)* one who holds an advanced academic degree, as *Master* of Arts: *adj.* 1. pertaining to a master. 2. chief: *v.t.* 1. to become master of; overcome. 2. to become an expert in.

mas·ter·ful (-ful), *adj.* 1. imperious; domineering. 2. expert. —mas'ter·ful·ly, *adv.*

master key, a key that can open every one of a set of locks.

mas·ter·ly (-li), *adj.* showing skill; expert: *adv.* in a masterly manner.

mas·ter·mind (-mīnd), *n.* one with the ability to plan and execute a complex project: *v.i.* to be the mastermind of (a project).

master of ceremonies, one who presides at a banquet, entertainment, etc.

mas·ter·piece (-pēs), *n.* 1. a piece of work done with great skill. 2. the greatest work of a person or group.

master sergeant, a noncommissioned military officer of high rank.

mas·ter·stroke (-strōk), *n.* a masterly achievement or action.

mas·ter·y (-i), *n., pl.* -ter·ies, 1. dominion or control. 2. victory; preeminence. 3. great skill or ability.

mast·head (mast'hed), *n.* 1. the top part of a ship's mast. 2. the section of a newspaper or magazine giving the name of the publisher, address, rates, etc.

mas·tic (mas'tik), *n.* 1. a resin obtained from an evergreen tree of Mediterranean regions, used in making varnish, etc. 2. a kind of cement used as for wall tiles.

mas·ti·cate (mas'ti-kāt), *v.t.* -cat·ed, -cat·ing, to grind with the teeth; chew up. —mas·ti·ca'tion, *n.* —mas'ti·ca·tor, *n.*

mas·tiff (mas'tif), *n.* a large, powerful, smooth-coated dog, often used as a watchdog.

mas·ti·tis (mas-tīt'is), *n.* inflammation of the breast or udder.

mas·to·don (mas'tŏ-don), *n.* an extinct mammal resembling the elephant but larger.

mas·toid (mas'toid), *adj.* designating or near a projection of the temporal bone behind the ear: *n.* the mastoid projection.

mas·toid·i·tis (mas-toi-dīt'is), *n.* inflammation of the mastoid.

mas·tur·bate (mas'tĕr-bāt), *v.i.* & *v.t.* -bat·ed, -bat·ing, to manipulate the genitals (of) for sexual gratification. —mas·tur·ba'tion, *n.*

mat (mat), *n.* 1. a flat piece of woven fibers, rubber, cloth, padding, etc. variously used for protection as on the floor, under dishes, etc. 2. anything growing thickly, or densely interwoven. 3. [Informal], a printing matrix. 4. a border around a picture. 5. same as **matte**: *v.t.* **mat'ted, mat'ting,** 1. to cover as with a mat. 2. to entangle or interweave. 3. to frame with a mat. 4. to put a dull finish on: *v.i.* to be tangled into a thick mass.

---

mat·a·dor (mat′ā-dôr), *n.* a bullfighter who kills the bull with a sword.

match (mach), *n.* 1. a short, slender piece of wood, cardboard, etc. with a combustible tip that readily ignites by friction. 2. either of two things or persons that go well together. 3. a person or thing similar or equal to another. 4. a game or contest. 5. a marriage or mating: *v.i.* 1. to set against or oppose. 2. to be similar or equal to. 3. to marry. 4. to procure a counterpart for. 5. to fit (one thing) to another: *v.i.* to be equal, suitable, etc.

match-book (′book), *n.* a folder of cardboard matches.

match·less (′lis), *adj.* having no equal.

match·mak·er (′mā-kĕr), *n.* 1. one who arranges marriages. 2. one who arranges boxing or wrestling matches.

mate (māt), *n.* 1. a companion or associate. 2. one of a matched pair. 3. a husband or wife. 4. the male or female of animals paired for breeding. 5. an officer of a merchant ship, ranking below the captain: *v.t.* **mat′ed**, **mat′ing**, 1. to fit together; couple. 2. to join together as mates.

ma·té (mā′tā, mat′ā), *n.* a tea made of the dried leaves of a South American tree.

mat·e·lote (mat′l-ōt), *n.* a dish of stewed fish, flavored with wine.

ma·ter (māt′ĕr), *n.* [Chiefly British Informal], mother.

ma·ter·fa·mil·i·as (-fā-mil′i-ăs), *n.* the mother of a family; woman head of a household.

ma·te·ri·al (mā-tir′i-ăl), *adj.* 1. of or consisting of matter; physical. 2. of the body rather than of the spirit; not spiritual; corporeal. 3. relevant, important, or essential: *n.* 1. the substance of which something is made. 2. the basic things used and combined to produce something else, as the ideas and data needed for a book. 3. *pl.* the things needed to do something, as the tools used to get a job done. 4. cloth; fabric.

ma·te·ri·al·ism (-izm), *n.* 1. the doctrine that everything in the world, including thought, is the result of organized matter. 2. devotion to material interests rather than to intellectual or spiritual things.

ma·te·ri·al·ist (-ist), *n.* one believing in or characterized by materialism: *adj.* of or like a materialist or materialism.

ma·te·ri·al·is·tic (mā-tir-i-ă-lis′tik), *adj.* 1. of or like a materialist. 2. of, believing in, or characterized by materialism. —**ma·te·ri·al·is′ti·cal·ly**, *adv.*

ma·te·ri·al·i·ty (mā-tir-i-al′i-ti), *n.* 1. the state or quality of being material, or physical. 2. matter; substance. 3. *pl.* -ties, something material.

ma·te·ri·al·ize (mā-tir′i-ă-līz), *v.t.* -**ized**, -**iz·ing**, 1. to cause to be material in form or characteristics; give material characteristics to. 2. to make (a spirit, etc.) appear in bodily form. 3. to make materialistic: *v.i.* 1. to become real or tangible. 2. to appear in bodily form, as a spirit. 3. to arrive or appear suddenly or unexpectedly. —**ma·te·ri·al·i·za′tion**, *n.*

ma·te·ri·al·ly (-li), *adv.* 1. so far as the matter

substance, or content, rather than the form, is concerned. 2. with regard to what is material; from the physical side. 3. to a large extent; considerably.

ma·te·ri·a med·i·ca (mā-tir′i-ă med′i-kā), 1. the science treating of substances used in medicine, investigating their nature, uses, and effects. 2. the substances.

ma·te·ri·el, **ma·té·ri·el** (mā-tir-i-el′), *n.* the materials needed for an enterprise, especially for a large-scale organized operation; specifically, weapons, equipment, etc. of armed forces.

ma·ter·nal (mā-tūr′nl), *adj.* 1. of, like, or from a mother. 2. being a specified relative or relatives through the mother's side of the family.

ma·ter·ni·ty (′ni-ti), *n.* 1. the state or character of being a mother; motherhood or motherliness. 2. a maternity ward in a hospital: *adj.* 1. designed for pregnant women. 2. devoted to the care of women giving birth and of newborn babies.

math (math), *n.* [Informal], mathematics.

math·e·mat·i·cal (math-ē-mat′i-kl), *adj.* 1. of, like, or involving mathematics. 2. rigorously exact.

math·e·ma·ti·cian (math-ē-mā-tish′ăn), *n.* one skilled or specializing in mathematics.

math·e·mat·ics (math-ē-mat′iks), *n.pl.* the group of sciences that includes arithmetic, geometry, algebra, etc. and, using numbers and symbols, deals with quantities, magnitudes, and forms and the relationships, attributes, etc. of these.

mat·i·nee, **mat·i·née** (mat-n-ā′), *n.* 1. a stage play, movie, etc. presented in the afternoon. 2. a daytime reception.

mat·ins (mat′nz), *n.pl.* [often M-], 1. in the *Roman Catholic Church*, the first and longest part of the daily canonical prayers. 2. in the *Anglican Church*, the order for, or the service of, public morning prayer.

ma·tri·arch (mā′tri-ärk), *n.* a woman ruling her family or tribe. —**ma·tri·ar′chal** (-är′kl), *adj.*

ma·tri·ar·chy (-i), *n.*, *pl.* -**chies**, 1. social organization recognizing the mother, rather than the father, as head of the family or tribe, with kinship and succession traced through her. 2. rule by women.

mat·ri·cide (mat′ri-sīd, mā′tri-), *n.* 1. murder of a mother by her son or daughter. 2. the murderer. —**mat·ri·ci′dal**, *adj.*

ma·tric·u·late (mā-trik′yoo-lāt), *v.t. & v.i.* -**lat·ed**, -**lat·ing**, to admit or become admitted to membership, especially in a college or university; enroll. —**ma·tric·u·la′tion**, *n.*

mat·ri·mo·ny (mat′ri-mō-ni), *n.*, *pl.* -**nies**, marriage. —**mat·ri·mo′ni·al**, *adj.*

ma·trix (mā′triks), *n.*, *pl.* -**tri·ces** (mā′tri-sēz, mat′ri-), -**trix·es**, 1. originally, the womb. 2. the cavity in which something is formed or cast; mold. 3. in *Geology*, the rock in which a fossil, mineral, etc. is embedded. 4. in *Printing*, a metal plate for molding the face of a type; also, any of various impressions of type, etc. from which a plate can be made.

ma·tron (mā′trŏn), *n.* 1. a married woman or a widow, especially one who has borne children. 2. a woman superintendent of, or attendant in, an institution.

ma·tron·ly (-li), *adj.* of, pertaining to, or typical of a matron.

mat·ro·nym·ic (mat-rō-nim'ik), *n.* a name derived from one's mother or from a female ancestor.

matte (mat), *n.* 1. a dull surface or finish. 2. a crude metallic product containing sulfur, resulting from the smelting of various metals: *adj.* not shiny; dull.

mat·ted (mat'id), *adj.* 1. covered with a mat. 2. closely tangled together.

mat·ter (mat'ēr), *n.* 1. that which occupies space and is perceptible by the senses. 2. any particular substance. 3. what is expressed in speech or writing, apart from style or form. 4. an indefinite amount. 5. a subject of discussion. 6. importance or a thing of importance. 7. a difficulty; trouble. 8. something sent by mail. 9. pus or other bodily discharge. 10. in *Printing*, material set or to be set: *v.i.* to have importance.

mat·ter-of-fact (-ŏv-fakt'), *adj.* soberly avoiding or ignoring what is not factual.

Mat·thew (math'ū), *n.* a book of the New Testament, the first Gospel.

mat·ting (mat'ing), *n.* 1. mats collectively. 2. material for mats.

mat·tock (mat'ŏk), *n.* a tool similar to a pickax but with an adzlike blade on one or both sides.

mat·tress (mat'ris), *n.* a casing of strong cloth with a filling of soft material, such as cotton, usually containing coiled springs, used on a bed.

mat·u·rate (mach'oo-rāt, mat'yoo-), *v.t. & v.i.* -rat·ed, -rat·ing, to mature; ripen. —**mat·u·ra'tion**, *n.*

ma·ture (mā-toor', -choor', -tyoor'), *adj.* 1. ripe. 2. fully grown. 3. fully developed. 4. due; payable: *v.t. & v.i.* -tured', -tur'ing, to make or become mature.

ma·tu·ri·ty ('i-ti), *n.* 1. the state or quality of being mature; ripeness; full growth or development. 2. a becoming due or payable, or the date of this.

ma·tu·ti·nal (mā-tōōt'n-ǎl, -tūt'-; mach-oo-tī'nl), *adj.* of or pertaining to the morning; early.

mat·zo (mät'sō, 'sô), *n., pl.* -zot, -zoth ('sôt), -zos, an unleavened bread eaten by Jews during the Passover: also **mat'zah**.

maud (môd), *n.* 1. a gray-striped Scotch plaid. 2. a wrap or rug of this plaid.

maud·lin (môd'lin), *adj.* easily moved to tears; weakly and foolishly sentimental.

mau·gre, mau·ger (mô'gēr), *prep.* [Archaic], in spite of.

maul (môl), *n.* a large, heavy hammer: *v.t.* to wound or bruise in a rough manner.

maun·der (môn'dēr), *v.i.* 1. to move aimlessly. 2. to mumble on and on.

Maun·dy Thursday (môn'di), Holy Thursday.

mau·so·le·um (mô-sô-lē'ŭm, mô-zô-), *n., pl.* -le'ums, -le'a (-lē'ä), a stately tomb.

mauve (mōv, môv), *n.* a soft lilac or purple color: *adj.* of this color.

mav·er·ick (mav'ēr-ik), *n.* 1. an unbranded ani-

mal, especially a lost calf. 2. a nonconformist, as in politics.

ma·vis (mā'vis), *n.* same as song thrush.

maw (mô), *n.* the mouth or stomach of an animal.

mawk·ish (mô'kish), *adj.* 1. insipid or nauseating. 2. weakly sentimental.

max-i-, a combining form meaning *very large, very long.*

max·il·la (mak-sil'ä), *n., pl.* -lae ('ē), in vertebrates, the upper jaw.

max·il·lar·y (mak'si-ler-i), *adj.* of or pertaining to the maxilla.

max·im (mak'sim), *n.* an established principle or truth; proverb; aphorism.

max·i·mal (mak'si-ml), *adj.* of or being maximum; largest or greatest possible.

max·i·mize (-mīz), *v.t.* -mized, -miz·ing, to cause to be maximum.

max·i·mum (mak'si-mŭm), *n., pl.* -mums, -ma (-mä), the highest or greatest number, quantity, or degree attained or attainable: *adj.* of, pertaining to, or being a maximum or the maximum.

May (mā), *n.* 1. the fifth month of the year, having 31 days. 2. springtime. 3. the heyday of life. 4. [m-], a European hawthorn. 5. the festivities of May Day: *v.i.* [also m-], to gather flowers in the springtime.

may (mā), *v., p.t.* might, an auxiliary expressing *a)* possibility or probability; *b)* permission; *c)* purpose, result, etc.; *d)* wish, hope, etc.

Ma·ya (mä'yä), *n., pl.* -yas, -ya, a member of a tribe of Indians of Central America and southeastern Mexico: they had a highly developed civilization. —**Ma'yan**, *adj. & n.*

May apple, 1. a woodland plant of the eastern U.S., with a white, cuplike flower and a yellow, edible fruit. 2. the fruit.

may·be (mā'bi), *adv.* perhaps.

May Day, May 1, date of a traditional spring festival or, more recently, an international labor holiday.

may·flow·er (mā'flou-ēr), *n.* any one of various plants flowering in May or earlier.

may·fly ('flī), *n., pl.* -flies, a slender, short-lived insect with gauzy wings.

may·hap (mā'hap, mā-hap'), *adv.* [Archaic], perhaps: also **may·hap'pen.**

may·hem (mā'hem, mā'ēm), *n.* an unlawful attack on a person which results in mutilation or maiming.

may·on·naise (mā-ô-nāz', mā'ô-nāz), *n.* a creamy salad dressing made of egg yolks, olive oil or other vegetable oil, lemon juice or vinegar, and seasoning.

may·or (mā'ēr, mer), *n.* the chief magistrate of a city, town, or other municipality. —**may'or·al,** *adj.*

may·or·al·ty (-ăl-ti), *n., pl.* -ties, the office or term of office of a mayor.

May·pole (mā'pōl), *n.* a pole around which May festivities are held.

maze (māz), *n.* 1. a labyrinth. 2. bewilderment: *v.t.* mazed, maz·ing, to bewilder.

maz·el tov (mä'zl tōv, tôf), [Hebrew], good luck: an expression of congratulation.

ma·zur·ka (mä-zûr'kä), *n.* a lively Polish dance in 3/4 or 3/8 time.

---

a in cap, ā in cane, ä in father, à in abet, e in met, ē in be, ê in baker, ê in regent, i in pit, ī in fine, î in manifest, o in hot, ô in horse, ō in bone,

ma·zy (mā'zĭ), adj. -zi·er, -zi·est, bewildering or intricately winding, like a maze.

me (mē), pron. the objective case of I.

mead (mĕd), n. 1. a liquor of fermented honey and water, often with spices, fruit, etc. added. 2. [Poetic], a meadow.

mead·ow (mĕd'ō), n. 1. a tract of rich pasture land. 2. an area of low, grassy land near a stream, lake, etc.

mead·ow·lark (-lärk), n., pl. -larks, -lark, either one of two North American songbirds streaked black and brown and having a bright-yellow breast.

mead·ow·sweet (-swēt), n. 1. any one of several spireas. 2. any one of a certain genus of plants of the rose family with fragrant, clustering flowers of white, pink, or purple.

mead·ow·y (-ĭ), adj. of, like, or consisting of a meadow or meadows.

mea·ger (mē'gēr), adj. 1. thin; lean. 2. small in amount; scanty. 3. weak, barren, or of poor quality. —mea'ger·ness, n.

mea·gre (mē'gēr), adj. British form for meager.

meal (mēl), n. 1. edible ground grain. 2. any similar material. 3. a repast.

meal·y ('ĭ), adj. meal'i·er, meal'i·est, consisting of, sprinkled with, or having the qualities of meal.

meal·y·mouthed (mēl'ĭ·mouthd', -mouth'), adj. using soft words; unwilling to tell the truth in plain words.

mean (mēn), adj. 1. wanting in dignity or honor. 2. inferior; insignificant. 3. stingy. 4. bad-tempered. 5. equally distant from extremes; middle. 6. average. 7. [Slang], not easily dealt with; difficult; also, highly skilled: n. 1. a point, quality, condition, etc. equally distant from extremes. 2. pl. the thing or way by which something is done or gained. 3. pl. resources or riches. 4. in Mathematics, a) a number between the smallest and the largest values of a set of quantities; b) the second or third term of a four-term proportion: v.t. meant, mean'ing, 1. to intend or have in mind. 2. to signify; denote. 3. to destine: v.i. 1. to have an intention. 2. to have a (specified) degree of importance, effect, etc.

me·an·der (mĭ-an'dēr), v.i. 1. to have a winding course: said of a stream. 2. to wander about aimlessly; ramble: n. a wandering about; rambling; meandering.

mean·ie (mē'nĭ), n. [Informal], one that is bad-tempered, hard to deal with, etc.

mean·ing (mē'nĭng), n. that which is meant; sense, intention, etc.

mean·ing·ful (-fŭl), adj. full of meaning.

mean·ing·less (-lĭs), adj. without meaning.

mean·time (mēn'tīm), adv. meanwhile: n. the intervening time.

mean·while ('hwīl), adv. 1. in the intervening time. 2. at the same time: n. same as meantime.

mean·y (mēn'ĭ), n., pl. mean'ies, [Informal], same as meanie.

mea·sles (mē'zlz), n. an infectious disease with fever and small, red spots on the skin.

mea·sly (mēz'lĭ), adj. -sli·er, -sli·est, 1. having measles. 2. [Informal], mean, contemptibly inferior, skimpy, etc.

meas·ur·a·ble (mezh'ēr-ȧ-bl), adj. capable of being measured. —meas'ur·a·bly, adv.

meas·ure (mezh'ēr), n. 1. a standard by which volume, extent, etc. is determined. 2. the extent, dimensions, etc. of a thing. 3. measurement. 4. an instrument for measuring. 5. a measured quantity. 6. proportion. 7. a particular procedure or step. 8. a law or statute. 9. metrical or musical time, or a division of this. 10. in Mathematics, a divisor leaving no remainder: v.t. -ured, -ur·ing, 1. to ascertain the extent, dimensions, etc. of. 2. to set apart, mark off, etc. by measuring. 3. to estimate, appraise, etc.: v.i. 1. to take measurements. 2. to be of specified measurements.

meas·ured ('ērd), adj. 1. determined by a standard. 2. steady; uniform. 3. moderated. 4. rhythmical or metrical.

meas·ure·less (mezh'ēr-lĭs), adj. too large or too great to be measured; immense; vast.

meas·ure·ment (-mĕnt), n. 1. the act of measuring or condition of being measured. 2. extent, size, etc. as determined by this. 3. a system of measuring.

measuring worm, the caterpillar larva of a certain family of moths.

meat (mēt), n. 1. food: archaic except in meat and drink. 2. animal flesh used as food. 3. the edible part of anything. 4. substance or gist.

meat·pack·ing ('pak-ing), n. the industry of slaughtering animals and preparing the meat for market.

me·a·tus (mĭ-āt'ŭs), n., pl. -tus·es, -tus, a natural opening or passage in the body.

meat·y (mēt'ĭ), adj. meat'i·er, meat'i·est, 1. of, like, or full of meat. 2. thickset; chunky. 3. pithy. —meat'i·ness, n.

Mec·ca (mek'ȧ), n. [often m-], 1. a place drawing many visitors, as does the Moslem pilgrimage city of Mecca in Saudi Arabia. 2. any place or goal ardently sought.

me·chan·ic (mĕ-kan'ĭk), n. 1. one skilled in using tools or in machine work. 2. pl. the science of the laws of matter and motion; also, the science of machinery. 3. pl. the mechanical or technical element involved in something, as in writing.

me·chan·i·cal ('ĭ-kl), adj. 1. of, pertaining to, or skilled in the use of machinery or tools. 2. produced or done by machinery or a mechanism. 3. of, in accordance with, or using the principles and terminology of the science of mechanics. 4. lacking spontaneity; automatic.

mech·a·ni·cian (mek-ȧ-nish'ȧn), n. one skilled in the theory, design, or operation of machinery.

mech·a·nism (mek'ȧ-nizm), n. 1. the parts or construction of a machine. 2. any machinelike system, means, or agent. 3. the mechanical or technical element; mechanics. —mech·a·nis'tic, adj.

mech·a·nize (mek'ȧ-nīz), v.t. -nized, -niz·ing, 1. to make mechanical. 2. to convert, as an industry, to the use of machinery. 3. to equip, as an army, with armored vehicles, self-propelled guns, etc. —mech·a·ni·za'tion, n.

mech·an·o·ther·a·py (mek-ȧ-nō-ther'ȧ-pĭ), n.

treatment of disease by mechanical means, as by massage. —mech·an·o·ther'a·pist, n.

med·al (med'l), n. 1. a small, flat piece of metal bearing a design or inscription, made to commemorate something or given as an award. 2. a similar piece of metal worn as a religious token.

med·al·ist (-ist), n. 1. a designer or maker of medals. 2. a medal recipient.

me·dal·lion (mĕ-dal'yŭn), n. 1. a large medal. 2. a medallike decorative panel, tablet, etc. used as in architecture.

med·al·list (med'l-ist), n. British form for medalist.

med·dle (med'l), v.i. -dled, -dling, to interpose or interfere officiously. —med'dler, n. — med'dle·some (-sŏm), adj.

me·di·a (mē'di-ă), n. 1. alternate plural of medium. 2. pl. -di·ae, a means of mass communication, as television: mediuh is preferred by most for this sense.

me·di·a·cy (mē'di-ă-si), n., pl. -cies, 1. the quality or state of being mediate. 2. mediation.

me·di·ae·val (mē-di-ē'vl, med-i-, mid-i-), adj. alternate spelling of medieval.

me·di·al (mē'di-ăl), adj. 1. of or in the middle; median. 2. average; mean.

me·di·an (-ăn), adj. 1. of, pertaining to, or connected with the middle of anything. 2. designating the middle number in a series: n. 1. a median point, number, etc. 2. same as median strip.

median strip, a strip of land dividing a highway into two parallel lanes.

me·di·ate (mē'di-āt), v.i. -at·ed, -at·ing, 1. to be intermediate. 2. to act as an intermediary: v.t. to settle, effect, convey, etc. by being intermediate or by functioning as an intermediary: adj. (-it), functioning or effective indirectly. —me·di·a'tion, n. —me'di·a·tor, n.

med·ic (med'ik), n. [Informal], 1. a physician or surgeon. 2. a medical trainee. 3. a member of a medical military corps.

Med·i·caid (med'i-kād), n. [also m-], a public health program financed by State and Federal funds to pay certain medical expenses of persons of low income or no income.

med·i·cal (med'i-kl), adj. of, pertaining to, or connected with medicine.

medical jurisprudence, use of medical knowledge to settle some questions of law, as to ascertain the cause of a death.

med·i·ca·ment (med'i-kă-mĕnt, mĕ-dik'ă-), n. a medical substance; medicine.

Med·i·care (med'i-ker), n. [also m-], a national health program financed by Federal funds to pay certain medical expenses of the aged.

med·i·cate (med'i-kāt), v.t. -cat·ed, -cat·ing, 1. to treat with medicine. 2. to impregnate or tincture with anything medicinal. —med·i·ca'tion, n.

me·dic·i·nal (mĕ-dis'n-ăl), adj. of or having the properties of medicine.

med·i·cine (med'i-sn), n. 1. the science of treating and preventing disease, relieving pain, and furthering health. 2. a drug or other substance used in this.

medicine ball, a large, heavy, stuffed ball tossed about for exercise.

medicine man, among certain peoples, as North American Indians, a conjurer who professes to drive away evil spirits or disease by magical rites.

me·di·e·val (mē-di-ē'vl, med-i-, mid-i-), adj. of or typical of the Middle Ages.

me·di·e·val·ism (-izm), n. 1. medieval spirit, customs, etc. 2. a belief, practice, etc. that is medieval or that is viewed as being medieval.

me·di·e·val·ist (-ist), n. 1. one specializing in the literature, art, etc. of the Middle Ages. 2. one given to medieval beliefs, practices, etc.

me·di·o·cre (mē-di-ō'kĕr), adj. 1. quite ordinary; not outstanding; run-of-the-mill. 2. not up to standard; inferior.

me·di·oc·ri·ty (mē-di-ok'ri-ti), n., pl. -ties, 1. the quality or state of being mediocre. 2. someone or something that is mediocre.

med·i·tate (med'i-tāt), v.i. -tat·ed, -tat·ing, to muse or ponder; think abstractedly: v.t. to plan or intend.

med·i·ta·tion (med-i-tā'shŭn), n. the act of meditating, often, specifically, on spiritual matters.

med·i·ta·tive (med'i-tāt-iv), adj. 1. engaged in or given to meditation. 2. showing meditation.

Med·i·ter·ra·ne·an (med-i-tĕ-rā'ni-ăn), adj. of the Mediterranean Sea or the region surrounding it.

me·di·um (mē'di-ŭm), n., pl. -di·ums, -di·a (-ă), 1. an intermediate thing, as in transmitting a force or effect; also, a middle state or degree; mean. 2. pl. usually -di·a, an agency or means; especially, a means of communication supported by advertising, as television or the press. 3. a substance or space in which bodies exist or move; environment. 4. a sterilized substance for cultivating bacteria, viruses, etc. 5. pl. -di·ums, one through whom the spirits of the dead are believed to communicate with the living. 6. an art material or technique. 7. a liquid vehicle for a pigment. 8. a size of printing paper (18 x 23 inches): adj. intermediate: adv. to an intermediate degree.

med·lar (med'lĕr), n. 1. a small tree of the rose family, of Europe and Asia. 2. its small, hard, brown, applelike fruit, edible when partly decayed.

med·ley (med'li), n., pl. -leys, 1. a jumble; hodgepodge. 2. a musical presentation made up of various selections connected together.

me·dul·la (mi-dul'ă), n., pl. -las, -lae (-ē), 1. the medulla oblongata. 2. the inner substance of an organ, as of the kidney. 3. the soft, spongy tissue in the center of certain plant stems; pith. —med·ul·lar·y (med'ŭ-ler-i, mej'-; mi-dul'ĕr-i), adj.

medulla ob·lon·ga·ta (ob-lŏng-gāt'ă, -gāt'ă), the posterior part of the brain, made up of a widened continuation of the spinal cord.

Me·du·sa (mĕ-dōō'să), n. 1. in Greek Mythology, one of the Gorgons. 2. [m-], pl. -sas, -sae ('sē), a jellyfish.

meed (mēd), n. [Archaic], a recompense.

meek (mēk), *adj.* mild of temper; gentle; yielding; submissive.

meer·schaum (mir'shŭm, 'shôm), *n.* 1. a white, claylike, mineral material used as for tobacco pipes. 2. a pipe so made.

meet (mēt), *v.t.* met, **meet'ing**, 1. to come up to; encounter; come upon. 2. to be on hand for the arrival of. 3. to come into contact with. 4. to make the acquaintance of. 5. to confront. 6. to deal with. 7. to comply with, as an obligation. 8. to satisfy, as an expectation or payment: *v.i.* 1. to come together, into contact, etc. 2. to make the acquaintance of someone or something: *n.* 1. a coming together, as for a sports event. 2. those assembled, or the place of this: *adj.* [Now Rare], appropriate.

meet·ing ('ing), *n.* 1. an assembling or coming together. 2. those assembled. 3. a point of intersection; junction.

meg·a-, a combining form meaning *large, great, million.*

meg·a·cy·cle (meg'ă-sī-kl), *n.* former name for megahertz.

meg·a·hertz (-hŭrts), *n., pl.* -**hertz**, one million hertz.

meg·a·lith (-lith), *n.* a huge stone or boulder, as in a prehistoric monument.

meg·a·lo·ma·ni·a (meg-ă-lō-mā'ni-ă), *n.* a mental disorder marked by delusions of grandeur, power, etc. —**meg·a·lo·ma'ni·ac** (-ak), *adj. & n.*

meg·a·lop·o·lis (meg-ă-lop'ō-lĭs), *n.* a very large urban area.

meg·a·phone (meg'ă-fōn), *n.* a funnel-shaped device to amplify the voice.

meg·a·ton ('ă-tun), *n.* the explosive force of a million tons of TNT.

me·grims (mē'grĭmz), *n.* 1. low spirits; the blues. 2. a nervous disease of horses, cattle, etc., marked by staggering.

mei·o·sis (mī-ō'sĭs), *n.* in the formation of reproductive cells, double division of the central mass of cells with consequent halving of the number of chromosomes that are found in ordinary cells.

mel·a·mine (mel'ă-mēn), *n.* 1. a white, crystalline compound used in making synthetic resins. 2. such a resin, or a plastic made from it.

mel·an·cho·li·a (mel-ăn-kō'li-ă), *n.* a mental disorder characterized by great depression of spirits.

mel·an·chol·y (mel'ăn-kol-i), *n.* 1. great depression of spirits. 2. sad pensiveness: *adj.* sad; gloomy; depressed. —**mel·an·chol'ic**, *adj.* —**mel·an·chol'i·cal·ly**, *adv.*

Mel·a·ne·sian (mel-ă-nē'zhăn, 'shăn), *n.* a member of a dark-skinned people native to the Pacific islands south of the equator and northeast of Australia: *adj.* of this people or region.

mé·lange (mā-länzh', -länj'), *n.* a confused mixture; hodgepodge.

me·lan·ic (mē-lan'ik), *adj.* of, typical of, or having melanism or melanosis.

mel·a·nin (mel'ă-nĭn), *n.* a brownish-black pigment in skin, hair, etc.

mel·a·no·ma (mel-ă-nō'mă), *n., pl.* -**mas**, -**ma·ta** ('mă-tă), a tumor the cells of which contain melanin.

mel·a·no·sis (mel-ă-nō'sĭs), *n.* excessive production of melanin.

Mel·ba toast (mel'bă), [also m-], thin, crisp slices of toasted bread.

meld (meld), *v.t. & v.i.* 1. in *card games*, to declare or show (a card or cards that score). 2. to blend or merge: *n.* 1. a melding. 2. a card or cards for melding.

me·lee, mê·lée (mā'lā, mā-lā'), *n.* a hand-to-hand conflict; scuffle; affray.

mel·i·lot (mel'i-lot), *n.* sweet clover.

mel·io·rate (mēl'yō-rāt), *v.t. & v.i.* -**rat·ed**, -**rat·ing**, to make or get better; improve. —**mel·io·ra'tion**, *n.*

mel·io·rism (-rĭzm), *n.* belief that human society keeps getting better by itself and that mankind can further the process by conscious effort.

mel·lif·lu·ent (mē-lif'loo-wĕnt), *adj.* mellifluous. —**mel·lif'lu·ence**, *n.*

mel·lif·lu·ous (-wŭs), *adj.* sweet and smooth in sound. —**mel·lif'lu·ous·ness**, *n.*

mel·low (mel'ō), *adj.* 1. fully ripe and pleasant-tasting. 2. not hard, harsh, or rigid; mild: *v.t. & v.i.* to make or become mellow.

me·lo·de·on (mē-lō'di-ŏn), *n.* a small reed organ.

me·lo·di·ous ('di-ŭs), *adj.* 1. full of or producing melody. 2. pleasant to the ear; tuneful. —**me·lo'di·ous·ly**, *adv.* —**me·lo'di·ous·ness**, *n.*

mel·o·dist (mel'ō-dist), *n.* a singer or composer of melodies.

mel·o·dize (-dīz), *v.t.* -**dized**, -**diz·ing**, to make melodious: *v.i.* to compose melodies or make melody.

mel·o·dra·ma (mel'ō-drä-mă), *n.* a play characterized by highly sensational or extravagantly emotional incidents.

mel·o·dra·mat·ic (mel-ō-dră-mat'ik), *adj.* of or pertaining to melodrama; highly sensational, sentimental, etc. —**mel·o·dra·mat'i·cal·ly**, *adv.*

mel·o·dra·mat·ics (-dră-mat'iks), *n.pl.* melodramatic behavior.

mel·o·dy (mel'ō-di), *n., pl.* -**dies**, 1. the arrangement of different musical sounds for a single voice or instrument. 2. a rhythmic succession of tones, usually in the same key. 3. a musical quality, as in a poem. —**me·lod·ic** (mē-lod'ik), *adj.* —**me·lod'i·cal·ly**, *adv.*

mel·on (mel'ŏn), *n.* 1. any one of several large, juicy fruits with a hard rind and many seeds, as the watermelon, muskmelon, etc. 2. any one of the plants bearing these fruits.

melt (melt), *v.t. & v.i.* 1. to change from a solid to a liquid state, usually by heat. 2. to dissolve. 3. to disappear or cause to vanish by degrees. 4. to soften by love, tenderness, etc.

melt·down (melt'doun), *n.* a dangerous situation in which a nuclear reactor begins to melt its fuel rods and releases radiation.

melting pot, an area, country, etc. comprised of people of various backgrounds and origins.

ŏ in dragon, ōō in crude, oo in wool, u in cup, ū in cure, û in turn, ŭ in focus, oi in boy, ou in house, th in thin, th in sheathe, g in get, j in joy, y in yet.

mel·ton (mel'tŏn), *n.* a kind of thick woolen cloth, used chiefly for jackets and overcoats.

mem (mem), *n.* the thirteenth letter of the Hebrew alphabet.

mem·ber (mem'bĕr), *n.* 1. an organ, limb, or part of a human or animal body. 2. a part of a plant. 3. an essential part of a whole. 4. a person who belongs to a community, association, church, etc.

mem·ber·ship (-ship), *n.* 1. the state of being a member. 2. the full number of members in a group. 3. the members considered as a single body.

mem·brane (mem'brān), *n.* a thin fold or layer of tissue forming a covering or lining of some organ or part in an animal or plant.

mem·bra·nous ('brá-nŭs), *adj.* of, pertaining to, consisting of, or resembling a membrane. —**mem'bra·nous·ly,** *adv.*

me·men·to (mi-men'tō, mě-), *n.* 1. a souvenir; reminder. 2. [M-], in the *Roman Catholic Church,* either of two prayers, one for the living and one for the dead, said in the Canon of the Mass.

mem·o (mem'ō), *n., pl.* **mem'os,** same as **memorandum.**

mem·oir (mem'wär), *n.* 1. a narrative written from personal experience and knowledge. 2. a biography. 3. a record of investigation, scientific examination, etc. 4. *pl.* the record of the proceedings of a learned society. 5. *pl.* an autobiography.

mem·o·ra·bil·i·a (mem-ĕr-á-bil'i-á, -bil'yá), *n.pl.* things worthy of remembrance or record.

mem·o·ra·ble (mem'ĕr-á-bl, mem'rá-), *adj.* worthy of remembrance; remarkable; notabie. —**mem'o·ra·bly,** *adv.*

mem·o·ran·dum (mem-ŏ-ran'dŭm), *n., pl.* **-dums, -da** ('dá), 1. a short note written to assist the memory. 2. a short record of events, activities, etc. to be remembered. 3. informal correspondence, as between departments in a business office. 4. in diplomacy, a summary or outline.

me·mo·ri·al (mě-môr'i-ăl), *adj.* 1. serving to perpetuate the memory of a person or event; commemorative. 2. of or pertaining to memory: *n.* 1. something, as a monument, that serves to keep the memory of a person or event alive. 2. a statement of facts presented to a government, often with a petition for action or redress.

Memorial Day, in the U.S., a legal holiday (the last Monday in May in most States) for honoring the dead servicemen of all wars.

me·mo·ri·al·ist (-ist), *n.* 1. a person who prepares, signs, or presents a memorial. 2. a person who writes memoirs.

me·mo·ri·al·ize (-īz), *v.t.* -ized, -iz·ing, 1. to commemorate. 2. to present a memorial to; petition.

mem·o·rize (mem'ŏ-rīz), *v.t.* -rized, -riz·ing, to commit to memory; learn by heart. —**mem·o·ri·za'tion,** *n.*

mem·o·ry (mem'ĕr-i), *n.* 1. that faculty of the mind by which it retains or recalls previous occurrences, facts, etc. 2. that which is remembered; a recollection. 3. everything that a person remembers. 4. the period of time covered by the faculty of remembrance. 5. commemoration or remembrance. 6. storage or storage capacity, as of a computer, disk, etc.

mem·sa·hib (mem-sä'ib), *n.* in India, lady: a former title of respect given to a European married woman by servants, salespeople, etc.

men (men), *n.* plural of **man.**

men·ace (men'is), *n.* 1. a threat. 2. the act of threatening: *v.t. & v.i.* -aced, -ac·ing, to threaten or be a threat (to). —**men'ac·ing·ly,** *adv.*

mé·nage, me·nage (mã-näzh', mě-), *n.* 1. a household. 2. household management.

me·nag·er·ie (mě-naj'ĕr-i, -nazh'-), *n.* 1. a place where wild animals are kept. 2. a collection of wild animals shut in for exhibition.

mend (mend), *v.t.* 1. to repair (something broken or worn). 2. to make better; reform; improve: *v.i.* 1. to grow better. 2. to heal: *n.* 1. the act of mending. 2. a part that has been mended. —**mend'er,** *n.*

men·da·cious (men-dā'shŭs), *adj.* given to falsehood; lying; false. —**men·da·cious·ly,** *adv.*

men·dac·i·ty (-das'ĭ-ti), *n., pl.* -ties, 1. the quality or state of being mendacious. 2. a lie; falsehood.

Men·de·li·an (men-dē'li-ăn), *adj.* of or pertaining to G. Mendel (1822-1884), Austrian monk and botanist or the theory of heredity formulated by him.

Men·del·ism (men'dĕl-izm), *n.* the Mendelian theory of heredity, which states that: 1) ancestral characters are transmitted as separate, independent units; 2) these genes are paired in the body cells, but a germ cell receives only one member of such a pair; 3) if one of a pair of genes is dominant, the recessive character can appear only if both genes of the pair are recessive; 4) every trait is inherited independently of every other trait.

men·di·can·cy (men'di-kăn-si), *n.* 1. the state of being a beggar. 2. the practice of begging.

men·di·cant (-kănt), *adj.* 1. practicing begging; dependent on alms. 2. of a beggar: *n.* 1. a beggar. 2. a mendicant friar.

mendicant order, any one of various religious orders, including Dominicans, Augustinians, Franciscans, and Carmelites, whose members renounce all personal and community property and who, formerly, depended upon alms for their maintenance.

men·dic·i·ty (měn-dis'ĭ-ti), *n.* same as **mendicancy.**

men·folk (men'fōk), *n.pl.* [Dial. or Informal], men.

men·ha·den (men-hād'n), *n., pl.* -den, -dens, an inedible marine fish related to the herring, that is abundant off the Atlantic coast of the U.S. and is used as a source of fish oil, fertilizer, etc.

me·ni·al (mē'ni-ăl, mēn'yăl), *adj.* 1. of or pertaining to servants. 2. mean; servile: *n.* 1. a domestic servant. 2. a servile, low person. —**me'ni·al·ly,** *adv.*

me·nin·ges (mě-nin'jēz), *n.pl.* the three membranes that envelop the brain and spinal cord.

---

a in c*a*p, ã in c*a*ne, ä in f*a*ther, á in *a*bet, e in m*e*t, ē in b*e*, ě in bak*e*r, ê in reg*e*nt, i in p*i*t, ī in f*i*ne, I in man*i*fest, o in h*o*t, ô in h*o*rse, ō in b*o*ne,

men-in-gi-tis (men-in-jīt'is), *n.* inflammation of the meninges.

me-nis-cus (mi-nis'kŭs), *n., pl.* **-nis'cus-es, -nis'-ci** (-nis'ī, 'kī), 1. a crescent or crescent-shaped body. 2. a lens convex on one side and concave on the other.

Men-non-ite (men'ō-nīt), *n.* any member of an evangelical Protestant denomination founded in Holland in the 16th century, opposed to infant baptism, military service, and the holding of public office.

men-o-pause (men'ō-pôz), *n.* the cessation of menstruation or the period marked by this.

men-o-rah (mē-nō'rä), *n.* in *Judaism,* a candelabrum with seven or nine branches.

men-or-rha-gi-a (men-ō-rā'ji-ä), *n.* excessive flow at menstruation.

men-ses (men'sēz), *n.pl.* the periodic flow of blood and tissue debris from the uterus, discharged by adult women approximately every four weeks from puberty to menopause.

men-stru-al (men'stroo-wăl), *adj.* 1. of or pertaining to menstruation. 2. occurring monthly.

men-stru-ate ('stroo-wāt, 'strāt), *v.i.* **-at-ed, -at-ing,** to have the menstrual flow.

men-stru-a-tion (men-stroo-wā'shŭn, -strā'shŭn), *n.* the discharge of the menses or the period of this flow.

men-stru-um ('stroo-wŭm), *n., pl.* **-stru-ums, -stru-a** (-wă), a solvent.

men-su-ra-ble (men'shĕr-ă-bl), *adj.* measurable.

men-su-ra-tion (men-shŭ-rā'shŭn), *n.* 1. the act or process of taking the measure or dimensions of anything. 2. the branch of mathematics that treats of the measurement of length, area, or volume.

-ment (mĕnt, mint), a suffix meaning *a result, a means, an act, a state.*

men-tal (men'tl), *adj.* 1. of, by, for, or pertaining to the mind. 2. mentally ill. 3. for the mentally ill. **—men'tal-ly,** *adv.*

men-tal (men'tl), *adj.* of the chin.

men-tal-ist (-ist), *n.* same as mind reader.

men-tal-i-ty (men-tal'ī-tis), *n., pl.* **-ties,** mental ability, capacity, or power.

mental retardation, subnormal intelligence from birth.

men-thol (men'thōl, 'thôl), *n.* a crystalline alcohol with a penetrating odor, used in medicine, cigarettes, etc. **—men'tho-lat-ed** ('thō-lāt-id), *adj.*

men-tion (men'shŭn), *n.* 1. a brief notice; casual remark. 2. a citation for an accomplishment: *v.t.* 1. to speak of briefly or in passing. 2. to cite for honor.

men-tor (men'tĕr), *n.* 1. a wise and faithful counselor. 2. a teacher or coach.

men-u (men'ū), *n., pl.* **men'us,** 1. a bill of fare. 2. the food served.

me-ow, me-ou (mē'ou), *n.* the characteristic cry of a cat: *v.i.* to make such a crying sound.

Me-phis-to-phe-le-an, Me-phis-to-phe-li-an (mef-is-tō-fē'li-ăn, -fēl'yăn), *adj.* 1. of or pertaining to Mephistopheles. 2. like Mephistopheles; crafty, diabolical, evil, cynical, etc.

Meph-i-stoph-e-les (mef-i-stof'ĕ-lēz), *n.* one of the principal devils in medieval legend, to whom Faust sold his soul.

me-phit-ic (mē-fit'ik), *adj.* 1. poisonous; noxious. 2. foul-smelling.

me-phi-tis (-fīt'is), *n.* 1. a foul or poisonous vapor emitted from the earth, as from decaying matter. 2. a disgusting smell; stench.

mer-can-tile (mŭr'kăn-til), *adj.* of or pertaining to merchants or trade.

Mer-ca-tor projection (mĕr-kāt'ĕr), a system of making maps invented by G. Mercator (1512-94), Flemish cartographer, in which the meridians are represented by parallel straight lines at equal intervals, and the parallels of latitude by lines perpendicular to the meridians at increasing intervals, so that areas appear larger further from the equator.

mer-ce-nar-y (mŭr'sĕ-ner-ī), *adj.* 1. working for pay or reward only; venal; greedy. 2. denoting or of a soldier hired by a foreign army: *n., pl.* **-nar-ies,** 1. a soldier hired for service in a foreign army. 2. a person who serves only for money; hireling. **—mer'ce-nar-i-ly,** *adv.*

mer-cer (mŭr'sĕr), *n.* [British], a dealer in textiles.

mer-cer-ize (mŭr'sĕr-īz), *v.t.* **-ized, -iz-ing,** to give (cotton thread or cloth) a silky luster and greater strength by treating it with a solution of potash.

mer-chan-dise (mŭr'chăn-dīz, -dīs), *n.* goods, wares, or commodities bought and sold: *v.t. & v.i.* **-dised, -dis-ing,** 1. to buy and sell. 2. to promote the sale of (a product), as by attractive displays.

mer-chant (mŭr'chănt), *n.* 1. a person who buys and sells commodities for a profit, especially one who deals with foreign countries. 2. a storekeeper; retail businessman: *adj.* of, pertaining to, or employed in trade; commercial; mercantile.

mer-chant-man (-măn), *n., pl.* **-men** (-mĕn), a ship used in commerce.

merchant marine, 1. all of a nation's ships that are engaged in commerce. 2. their personnel.

mer-ci (mer-sē'), *interj.* [French], thanks; thank you.

mer-ci-ful (mŭr'si-fŭl), *adj.* full of or showing mercy; tenderhearted; compassionate; lenient. **—mer'ci-ful-ly,** *adv.*

mer-ci-less (-lis), *adj.* destitute of mercy; unfeeling; cruel; implacable. **—mer'ci-less-ly,** *adv.*

mer-cu-ri-al (mĕr-kyoor'i-ăl), *adj.* 1. eloquent; cunning; thievish. 2. swift; volatile; fickle. 3. of, pertaining to, made of, or caused by mercury. **—mer-cu'ri-al-ly,** *adv.*

Mer-cu-ro-chrome (mĕr-kyoor'ō-krōm), *n.* a mild, antiseptic compound of mercury: a trademark.

Mer-cu-ry (mŭr'kyoo-ri), *n.* 1. in *Roman Mythology,* the messenger of the gods and god of commerce, travel, and thievery. 2. the planet in the solar system that is smallest in size and nearest the sun. 3. [m-], *pl.* **-ries,** a messenger; bearer of tidings. 4. [m-], a heavy, silver-white, metallic chemical element, liquid at room temperature and used in thermometers, dentistry, etc.; quicksilver. 5. [m-], the column of mercury in a thermometer or barometer.

ô in drag*o*n, ōō in cr*u*de, oo in w*oo*l, u in c*u*p, ŭ in c*u*re, ŭ in t*u*rn, ŭ in f*o*cus, oi in b*oy*, ou in h*ou*se, th in *th*in, *th* in s*th*ee, g in *g*et, j in *j*oy, y in *y*et.

mer·cy (mûr'sĭ), *n., pl.* **-cies,** 1. the disposition to be kindly and forgiving. 2. compassion and forbearance toward an enemy, offender, etc. 3. imprisonment in place of death for a capital crime. 4. clemency. 5. something to be thankful for; blessing.

mercy killing, same as euthanasia.

mere (mir), *adj.* superlative **mer'est,** such and no more; bare.

mere (mir), *n.* [Archaic or British Dial.], a boundary.

mere·ly (mir'lĭ), *adv.* simply; only.

mer·e·tri·cious (mer-ê-trish'ŭs), *adj.* 1. of, pertaining to, or resembling a prostitute. 2. alluring but vulgar; tawdry. 3. insincere; specious. —**mer·e·tri'cious·ly,** *adv.*

mer·gan·ser (mêr-gan'sêr), *n., pl.* **-sers, -ser,** any one of several fish-eating, diving ducks with a hooked bill.

merge (mûrj), *v.i. & v.t.* **merged, merg'ing,** 1. to lose or cause to lose identity by being absorbed or swallowed up. 2. to combine; unite.

merg·er (mûr'jêr), *n.* 1. in *Law,* the absorption of a lesser estate, interest, action, offense, etc. into a greater one. 2. the uniting of two or more businesses, companies, corporations, etc. into one or under the control of one.

me·rid·i·an (mê-rid'i-ân), *adj.* of, pertaining to, or at noon: *n.* 1. [Obs.], noon. 2. the highest point or culmination of power, prestige, etc.; zenith. 3. in *Astronomy,* an imaginary great circle passing through the poles of the celestial sphere and the zenith and nadir of any given place, and cutting the equator at right angles. 4. in *Geography, a)* a great circle on the earth's surface passing through the geographical poles and any given place on the surface; *b)* the half of such a circle between the poles; *c)* any one of the lines of longitude on a map or globe.

me·rid·i·o·nal ('i-ŏ-nl), *adj.* 1. of or pertaining to a meridian. 2. southern. 3. of, pertaining to, or characteristic of the south or people living in the south.

me·ringue (mê-rang'), *n.* whites of eggs mixed with sugar and beaten until stiff, often browned and used as icing on pies, cakes, etc.

me·ri·no (mê-rê'nō), *n., pl.* **-nos,** 1. any one of a hardy breed of sheep with fine wool. 2. the wool. 3. a soft yarn or fabric made from this wool.

mer·it (mer'ĭt), *n.* 1. excellence; value; worth. 2. something deserving reward or esteem. 3. *pl.* the intrinsic right or wrong of a matter: *v.t.* to earn; be entitled to; be deserving of.

mer·i·to·ri·ous (mer-ĭ-tôr'ĭ-ŭs), *adj.* having merit; deserving reward or praise.

merl, merle (mûrl), *n.* [Archaic or Poetic], the European blackbird.

Mer·lin (mûr'lĭn), *n.* in *Arthurian Legend,* a magician and prophet, adviser of King Arthur.

mer·lin (mûr'lĭn), *n.* a small European falcon.

mer·lon (mûr'lŏn), *n.* the solid part of a parapet, between two openings.

mer·maid (mûr'mād), *n.* a fabled marine creature having the upper body and head of a woman and the tail of a fish.

mer·man (mûr'man), *n., pl.* **-men** ('men), a fabled marine creature having the upper body and head of a man and the tail of a fish.

mer·ri·ment (mer'ĭ-mênt), *n.* mirth; fun; gaiety.

mer·ry (mer'ĭ), *adj.* **-ri·er, -ri·est,** 1. full of mirth and good humor; gay. 2. offering fun and joviality; festive. —**mer'ri·ly,** *adv.* —**mer'ri·ness,** *n.*

mer·ry-an·drew (mer'i-an'drōō), *n.* a buffoon.

mer·ry-go-round (mer'i-gō-round), *n.* 1. a circular platform with seats in the form of chariots, animals, etc., turned by machinery, often to music, and ridden at carnivals, amusement parks, etc.; carrousel. 2. any whirl or round, as of routine activities.

mer·ry·mak·ing (-mā-king), *n.* participation in a good time; festivity.

mer·ry·thought (-thôt), *n.* [Chiefly British], the wishbone.

me·sa (mā'sä), *n.* an elevated tableland with sheer slopes.

mé·sal·li·ance (mā-zal'i-âns), *n.* marriage with one of lower social position.

mes·cal (mes-kal'), *n.* 1. a Mexican alcoholic liquor distilled from the fermented juice of certain agaves. 2. any plant that is a source of this liquor. 3. a spineless cactus of Mexico and the southwestern U.S., having buttonlike tops that are chewed by certain Indians as a hallucinogen.

mes·ca·line (mes'kå-lēn, -lǐn), *n.* a crystalline alkaloid drug that produces hallucinogenic effects.

mes·dames (mā-dām'), *n.* plural of madame or madam (sense 1).

mes·de·moi·selles (mā-dê-mô-zel'), *n.* plural of mademoiselle.

mesh (mesh), *n.* 1. any one of the open spaces in a screen, net, etc. 2. a net or network. 3. a netlike material, as for stockings. 4. the engagement of gear teeth: *v.t. & v.i.* 1. to entangle or become entangled. 2. to engage or become engaged: said of gears. 3. to interlock.

me·si·al (mē'zi-âl), *adj.* middle; median.

mes·mer·ism (mez'mêr-izm), *n.* hypnotism as developed and practiced by F. Mesmer (1734-1815), German physician.

mes·mer·ize (-īz), *v.t.* **-ized, -iz·ing,** 1. to hypnotize. 2. to enthrall; fascinate. —**mes·mer'ic** (-mer'ik), *adj.* —**mes'mer·ist,** *n.*

mesne (mēn), *adj.* in *Law,* between two extremes; intermediate; middle.

mes·o-, a combining form meaning *middle, intermediate, central.*

mes·o·blast (mes'ō-blast), *n.* same as mesoderm.

mes·o·carp (-kärp), *n.* the middle, usually fleshy, layer of a pericarp.

mes·o·derm (-dûrm), *n.* the middle layer of embryonic germ cells from which develop connective, muscular, reproductive, etc. tissues.

mes·o·gas·tri·um (mes-ō-gas'tri-ŭm), *n.* 1. either mesentery of the embryonic stomach. 2. the region around the navel.

Mes·o·zo·ic (-zō'ik), *n.* the geologic era after the Paleozoic and before the Cenozoic, marked by the predominance of reptiles, especially the dinosaurs.

mes·quite, mes·quit (mes-kēt', mes'kēt), *n.* a

---

a in cap, ā in cane, ä in father, å in abet, e in met, ē in be, ê in baker, ê in regent, i in pit, ī in fine, ǐ in manifest, o in hot, ô in horse, ō in bone,

spiny, leguminous shrub or tree of the southwestern U.S. and Mexico.

mess (mes), *n.* 1. a quantity of food for a meal or a serving. 2. a group of persons who regularly sit at table together, especially soldiers or sailors. 3. the meal they eat. 4. a hodgepodge. 5. a state of dirtiness, confusion, untidiness, etc.: *v.i.* 1. to eat together in a mess (sense 2). 2. to make a mess. 3. to interfere; meddle (*in, with,* etc.): *v.t.* 1. to furnish meals to. 2. to soil; make untidy. 3. to mismanage; botch (*up*). —mess'y, *adj.* mess'i-er, mess'i-est. —mess'i-ly, *adv.* — mess'i-ness, *n.*

mes-sage (mes'ij), *n.* 1. a communication transmitted between persons by written or spoken words, signals, etc. 2. an official communication. 3. the basic idea or meaning of something, as of a literary work, painting, etc.

mes-sa-line (mes-å-lēn'), *n.* a thin, lustrous, twilled silk.

mes-sen-ger (mes'n-jēr), *n.* 1. a person who conveys messages or runs errands. 2. [Archaic], a herald or harbinger.

mess hall, a room or building where soldiers, sailors, etc. eat their regular meals.

Mes-si-ah (mě-sī'å), *n.* 1. in *Judaism*, the promised and anticipated deliverer of the Jews. 2. in *Christianity*, Jesus Christ. Also **Mes-si'as** ('ås). —Mes-si-an-ic (mes-i-an'ik), *adj.*

mes-sieurs (mes'ērz), *n.* plural of monsieur.

mes-suage (mes'wij), *n.* in *Law*, a dwelling house with its adjacent buildings and land for the use of the household.

mes-ti-zo (mes-tē'zō), *n., pl.* -zos, -zoes, a person of mixed ancestry; especially, a person of mixed European and American Indian parentage. —mes-ti'za ('zä), *n.fem.*

met (met), past tense and past participle of meet.

met-a-, a prefix meaning *change, after, behind, between, beyond*: also, before a vowel, **met-**.

met-a-bol-ic (met-å-bol'ik), *adj.* 1. of, pertaining to, resulting from, or undergoing metabolism. 2. of or undergoing metamorphosis.

me-tab-o-lism (mě-tab'ō-lizm), *n.* the continuous process by which living organisms and cells undergo chemical and physical changes necessary to life, involving the building up and breaking down of protoplasm, accompanied by the release of needed energy. — me-tab'o-lize (-līz), *v.t. & v.i.* -lized, -liz-ing.

met-a-car-pus (met-å-kär'pŭs), *n., pl.* -pi ('pī), that part of the hand between the wrist and fingers, composed of five bones. —met-a-car'pal ('pål), *adj.*

met-a-cen-ter (met'å-sen-tēr), *n.* that point in a floating body on the position of which its equilibrium or stability depends.

met-a-chro-ma-tism (met-å-krō'må-tizm), *n.* alteration in color caused by change in physical conditions, as by heating or cooling.

met-a-gen-e-sis (-jen'ē-sis), *n.* in *Biology*, the occurrence, as in many coelenterates, of a reproductive cycle in which there is an alternation of a sexual and an asexual generation. —met-a-ge-net'ic (-jě-net'ik), *adj.*

me-tag-na-thous (mě-tag'nå-thŭs), *adj.* having the tips of the mandibles crossed, as in the crossbills.

met-al (met'l), *n.* 1. any one of a group of chemical elements, as silver, iron, manganese, etc., having certain physical characteristics, as luster, ductility, malleability, fusibility, and conductivity of heat and electricity. 2. an alloy of two or more of these elements, as brass. 3. a substance or object composed of metal. 4. molten glass. 5. the material or substance from which a person or thing is made; stuff. 6. [British], broken stones, slag, etc. used in surfacing roads, making railroad beds, etc. 7. in *Printing*, type made of metal. 8. molten cast iron: *adj.* made of metal: *v.t.* -aled or -alled, -al-ing or -al-ling, to cover with metal.

me-tal-lic (mě-tal'ik), *adj.* 1. of, pertaining to, consisting of, or yielding metal. 2. like or resembling metal. —me-tal'li-cal-ly, *adv.*

met-al-lif-er-ous (met-l-if'ēr-ŭs), *adj.* containing or yielding metal or metallic ore.

met-al-log-ra-phy (-og'rä-fi), *n.* the study of the structure and properties of metals and their alloys, especially with a microscope and X-rays.

met-al-loid (met'l-oid), *n.* a nonmetallic element, as arsenic or carbon, that has some of the chemical properties of a metal or that can combine with a metal to form an alloy: *adj.* 1. of, or having the properties of, a metalloid. 2. having the appearance of a metal.

met-al-lur-gy (met'l-ūr-ji), *n.* the science or process of extracting metals from their ores, of readying them for use by smelting, purifying, etc., and of producing desired objects from such metals. —met-al-lur'gi-cal, met-al-lur'gic, *adj.* —met'al-lur-gist, *n.*

met-a-mor-phic (met-å-môr'fik), *adj.* of, pertaining to, or produced by metamorphism or metamorphosis.

met-a-mor-phism (-môr'fizm), *n.* 1. same as metamorphosis. 2. the process by which masses of rock under pressure, heat, chemical action, etc. are changed from their original structure, texture, etc., as limestone into marble.

met-a-mor-phose ('fōz, 'fōs), *v.t. & v.i.* -phosed, -phos-ing, to alter in form, structure, or nature; subject or be subjected to metamorphism or metamorphosis.

met-a-mor-pho-sis (-môr'fō-sis), *n., pl.* -ses (-sēz), 1. change in form, shape, or structure, as by magic or spell. 2. the transformation produced by such change. 3. in *Biology*, change in form, structure, or function of an animal during growth; specifically, a change from larva to pupa and pupa to adult, as in butterflies, or a change from tadpole to frog.

met-a-phor (met'å-fôr), *n.* a figure of speech in which a word or phrase, usually literally applied to one object, is transferred to another to suggest a similarity or analogy between the two. —met-a-phor'i-cal, met-a-phor'ic, *adj.* —met-a-phor'i-cal-ly, *adv.*

met-a-phrase (met'å-frāz), *n.* a literal, word-for-word translation from one language into another, as contrasted with a paraphrase:

ŏ in dragon, ōō in crude, oo in wool, u in cup, ū in cure, ŭ in turn, û in focus, oi in boy, ou in house, th in thin, th in sheathe, g in get, j in joy, y in yet.

v.t. -phrased, -phras·ing, 1. to translate literally. 2. to alter the wording of (a text). —met·a·phras′tic (-fras′tik), *adj.*

met·a·phrast (-frast), *n.* a person who turns a written text into a different literary form, as prose into verse.

met·a·phys·i·cal (met-ă-fiz′i-kl), *adj.* 1. of, pertaining to, or having the nature of metaphysics. 2. extremely abstract; very subtle. 3. immaterial; supernatural. —met·a·phys′i·cal·ly, *adv.*

met·a·phy·si·cian (-fĭ-rĭsh′ŭn), *n.* a person skilled in metaphysics.

met·a·phys·ics (met-ă-fiz′iks), *n.* 1. the branch of philosophy that examines the nature of first principles, the problems of being and reality, and the origin and structure of the universe. 2. speculative philosophy in general.

met·a·plasm (met′ă-plazm), *n.* 1. inert material in a cell, that is not part of the protoplasm and that consists chiefly of carbohydrates or fatty granules. 2. a change in a word by addition, deletion, or transposition of a letter or syllable.

me·tas·ta·sis (mĕ-tas′tă-sis), *n.* 1. in *Medicine*, the spread of disease from its place of origin in the body to another site or sites, as in the transfer of cancerous cells by the bloodstream. 2. a change in state, form, or function. —met·a·stat·ic (met-ă-stat′ik), *adj.*

me·tas·ta·size (-sīz), *v.i.* -sized, -siz·ing, in *Medicine*, to spread to other sites in the body by metastasis.

met·a·tar·sus (met-ă-tär′sŭs), *n.*, *pl.* -tar′si (′sī), that part of the foot between the ankle and toes, composed of five bones. —met·a·tar′sal (′sl), *adj.*

me·tath·e·sis (mĕ-tath′ĕ-sis), *n.*, *pl.* -ses (-sēz), 1. the transposition of letters or sounds in a word. 2. in *Chemistry*, the reaction of two substances to produce two new substances. —met·a·thet·ic (met-ă-thet′ik), met·a·thet′i·cal, *adj.*

mete (mēt), *v.t.* met′ed, met′ing, 1. to allot; distribute; apportion (usually with *out*). 2. [Archaic], to measure.

mete (mēt), *n.* 1. a boundary; limit. 2. a boundary line or mark.

met·em·psy·cho·sis (mi-temp-si-kō′sis, met-ĕm-sĭ-), *n., pl.* -ses (′sēz), the transmigration of the soul after death into another human body or into the body of an animal.

me·te·or (mēt′i-ĕr), *n.* 1. the flash of light and luminous trail that is seen in the sky when a meteoroid becomes heated by the friction of the earth's atmosphere. 2. a meteoroid or meteorite.

me·te·or·ic (mēt-i-ôr′ik), *adj.* 1. of, pertaining to, formed of, or like a meteor or meteors. 2. resembling a meteor in speed and transitory brilliance.

me·te·or·ite (mēt′i-ô-rīt), *n.* a stony or metallic body that has fallen on the earth after surviving passage through the earth's atmosphere.

me·te·or·o·graph (mēt-i-ôr′ô-graf), *n.* an instrument that automatically registers meteorological phenomena, as temperature, moisture, pressure, etc.

me·te·or·oid (mēt′i-ô-roid), *n.* any one of the numerous small, solid bodies traveling through space, that appear as meteors upon entering the earth's atmosphere.

me·te·or·o·log·i·cal (mēt-i-ĕr-ô-loj′i-kl), *adj.* 1. of or pertaining to the atmosphere or its phenomena. 2. of or pertaining to meteorology: also me·te·or·o·log′ic. —me·te·or·o·log′i·cal·ly, *adv.*

me·te·or·ol·o·gy (mēt-i-ô-rol′ô-ji), *n.* the science dealing with the atmosphere and atmospheric phenomena, especially with weather and climate. —me·te·or·ol′o·gist, *n.*

me·ter (mēt′ĕr), *n.* 1. a rhythmic arrangement of syllables in verse. 2. a rhythmic pattern in music. 3. the fundamental unit of length in the metric system, equal to 39.37 inches.

me·ter (mēt′ĕr), *n.* 1. any one of various instruments for measuring time, distance, amount, etc. or for regulating or recording the quantity or volume of something, as the flow of gas or electricity. 2. same as **parking meter**: *v.t.* 1. to measure, regulate, or record with a meter. 2. to imprint with postal markings in a meter for this purpose.

-me·ter (mēt′ĕr, mi-tĕr), a suffix meaning *a measuring device, meters in length, a fraction of a meter in length.*

me·ter·age (mēt′ĕr-ij), *n.* measurement, as by meter, or the cost for this.

meter maid, a woman hired by a police department to issue tickets for overtime parking, to collect parking fees, etc.

meth·a·done (meth′ă-dōn), *n.* a synthetic narcotic drug that is more potent than morphine but less habit-forming.

meth·ane (meth′ān), *n.* a colorless gas present in natural gas, formed by the decomposition of vegetable matter, as in marshes.

me·thinks (mi-thingks′), *v. impersonal, past tense* me·thought′, [Archaic], it seems to me.

meth·od (meth′ŏd), *n.* 1. a way or procedure for doing things; especially, an orderly manner of accomplishing something. 2. regular and systematic arrangement; orderliness; classification.

me·thod·i·cal (mĕ-thod′i-kl), *adj.* characterized by, or arranged with regard to, method; systematic; orderly. —me·thod′i·cal·ly, *adv.*

Meth·od·ism (meth′ô-dizm), *n.* the doctrines, manner of organization, and worship of Methodists.

Meth·o·dist (-dist), *n.* 1. any member of a sect of Protestant Christians having a theology developed from the teachings of John Wesley (1703-91), English evangelist. 2. [m-], a person who regulates his life and actions by an orderly system or arrangement: *adj.* of or pertaining to the Methodists.

meth·od·ize (-dīz), *v.t.* -ized, -iz·ing, to reduce to method; systematize.

meth·od·ol·o·gy (meth-ô-dol′ô-ji), *n.* a system of rules, methods, and procedures used in a particular discipline or science.

Me·thu·se·lah (mĕ-thōō′zĕ-lă), *n.* in the *Bible*, a patriarch who lived 969 years: see *Genesis v*, 27.

meth·yl (meth′l), *n.* the hydrocarbon radical derived from methane and present in many organic compounds.

methyl alcohol, same as **wood alcohol**.

meth·yl·ene (-lēn), *n.* an organic hydrocarbon radical, normally existing only in combination.

me·thyl·ic (me-thil'ik), *adj.* derived from or containing methyl.

me·tic·u·lous (mē-tik'yoo-lûs), *adj.* 1. extremely or unduly careful and exact. 2. very scrupulous about details. —**me·tic'u·lous·ly,** *adv.*

mé·tier (mā-tyā'), *n.* 1. a calling, profession, or trade. 2. a specialty; forte.

mé·tis (mā-tēs', -tē'), *n., pl.* **-tis,** a person of mixed blood; especially, a man of French-Canadian and American Indian ancestry.

me·ton·y·my (mē-ton'i-mi), *n., pl.* **-mies,** a figure of speech in which the name of one thing is used for that of another connected with it or suggested by it.

me·tre (mē'tēr), *n.* British spelling of meter.

met·ric (met'rik), *adj.* 1. same as metrical. 2. of or pertaining to the meter (unit of length) or the metric system.

met·ri·cal ('ri-kl), *adj.* 1. of or pertaining to poetic meter or rhythm. 2. of, pertaining to, or used in measurement; metric. —**met'ri·cal·ly,** *adv.*

metric system, a decimal system of weights and measures based on the meter, kilogram, and liter.

met·ri·cate (me'tri-kāt), *v.t.* **-cat·ed, -cat·ing,** to change over to the metric system. —**met·ri·ca·tion** (me-tri-kā'shûn), *n.*

met·ro-, a combining form meaning *measure.*

me·trol·o·gy (me-trol'ō-ji), *n.* 1. the science of weights and measures. 2. *pl.* **-gies,** a system of weights and measures. —**met·ro·log·i·cal** (met-rō-loj'i-kl), *adj.* —**me·trol'o·gist,** *n.*

met·ro·nome (met'rō-nōm), *n.* an instrument that beats musical time at a steady rate by means of an inverted pendulum having an adjustable weight attached to it.

me·tro·nym·ic (mē-trō-nim'ik, met-rō-), *adj. & n.* same as matronymic.

me·trop·o·lis (mē-trop'l-is), *n.* 1. the chief city, often the capital, of a kingdom, country, or region. 2. any large or influential city. 3. the seat, or see, of a metropolitan bishop.

met·ro·pol·i·tan (met-rō-pol'it-n), *adj.* 1. of or pertaining to a capital or a chief city. 2. denoting or of a metropolitan bishop or his see. 3. denoting or of a chief city together with the cities and areas surrounding or bordering it: *n.* an archbishop presiding over the bishops of a church province.

me·tror·rha·gi·a (mē-trō-rā'ji-ā), *n.* bleeding from the womb that is not of menstrual origin.

met·tle (met'l), *n.* inherent character or spirit; ardor; fortitude; temperament.

met·tle·some (-sôm), *adj.* high-spirited; brave, ardent, plucky, etc.

mev, Mev (mev), *n., pl.* mev, Mev, a million electron-volts.

mew (mū), *n.* 1. a cage for hawks. 2. a secret den or hiding place: *v.t.* to immure; confine.

mew (mū), *n.* the characteristic crying sound of a cat: *v.i.* to cry like a cat.

mew (mū), *n.* a sea gull of northern regions.

mewl (mūl), *v.i.* to cry weakly, like an infant;

n. a whimper or weak cry.

mews (mūz), *n.pl.* [Chiefly British], 1. stables for carriage horses, often clustered along an alley or around a court and now mostly converted into small apartments. 2. such an alley or court.

mez·za·nine (mez'ā-nēn, mez-ā-nēn'), *n.* 1. a low-ceilinged story intermediate between two main stories in a building. 2. the first rows of seats in the balcony of some theaters.

mez·zo (met'sō), *adj.* in *Music,* medium; moderate.

mez·zo·so·pra·no (-sō-pran'ō, -prä'nō), *n., pl.* **-nos, -ni** ('ē, 'nē), 1. the female singing voice or part between soprano and contralto. 2. a woman who sings mezzo-soprano: *adj.* having or for the range of a mezzo-soprano.

mez·zo·tint (-tint), *n.* 1. a method of engraving copper or steel by scraping and burnishing surface areas to produce light and shade. 2. an engraving or print made by mezzotint.

mi (mē), *n.* the third tone in any major or minor musical scale of eight tones.

mi·as·ma (mī-az'mā, mi-), *n., pl.* **-mas, -ma·ta** ('mā-tā), 1. noxious effluvium in the air; fetid exhalations as from decomposing matter, formerly believed to cause disease, as malaria. 2. any unwholesome atmosphere or influence.

mi·ca (mī'kā), *n.* any one of a group of minerals (complex silicates) divisible into thin transparent or colored plates that are used in insulation.

mi·ca·ceous (mī-kā'shûs), *adj.* of, pertaining to, consisting of, or like mica.

Mi·cah (mī'kā), *n.* a book of the Bible.

mice (mīs), *n.* plural of mouse.

Mich·ael·mas (mik'l-mâs), *n.* the feast of the archangel Michael, celebrated on September 29.

mi·cro-, a combining form meaning *small, enlarging, microscopic.*

mi·crobe (mī'krōb), *n.* a minute organism; especially, any one of the microorganisms that cause disease; germ. —**mi·cro'bic, mi·cro'bi·al,** *adj.*

mi·cro·bi·cide (mī-krō'bi-sīd), *n.* an agent for destroying microbes.

mi·cro·ceph·a·ly (mī-krō-sef'l-i), *n.* a condition of having an abnormally small head. —**mi·cro·ceph'a·lous, mi·cro·ce·phal'ic** (-si-fal'ik), *adj.*

mi·cro·chip (-chip), *n.* same as integrated circuit.

mi·cro·coc·cus (-kok'ûs), *n., pl.* **-coc'ci** (-kok'sī), any one of a group of spherical or oval bacteria occurring in irregular clusters.

mi·cro·com·put·er (-kôm-pyōōt'ēr), *n.* a small, relatively inexpensive computer having a microchip and used in the home, etc.

mi·cro·cosm (mī'krō-kozm), *n.* 1. a miniature universe or world. 2. man regarded as typifying the world. 3. a district, community, or institution regarded as a little world in itself.

mi·cro·cyte (mī'krō-sīt), *n.* an abnormally small red blood cell, found especially in certain anemias.

ō in dragon, ōō in crude, oo in wool, u in cup, ū in cure, û in turn, ù in focus, oi in boy, ou in house, th in thin, th in sheathe, g in get, j in joy, y in yet.

mi·cro·fiche (-fēsh), *n.* a sheet of microfilm on which many pages of greatly reduced copy can be recorded.

mi·cro·film (-film), *n.* a film on which photographic records of books, manuscripts, etc. are kept in reduced size: *v.t. & v.i.* to photograph (material) on microfilm.

mi·cro·groove (mī'krō-grōōv), *n.* a very narrow groove for the needle, used on long-playing phonograph records to increase the amount of material recorded.

mi·crom·e·ter (-krom'ē-tēr), *n.* an instrument for measuring minute distances, diameters, angles, etc., used on a microscope or telescope.

mi·cron (mī'kron), *n., pl.* **-crons, -cra** ('krä), a unit of length that is equal to one millionth of a meter.

Mi·cro·ne·sian (mī-krō-nē'zhăn, 'shăn), *n.* a member of a dark-skinned people native to the Pacific islands north of the equator and east of the Philippines: *adj.* of this people or region.

mi·cro·or·gan·ism (-ôr'gă-nizm), *n.* an animal or plant of microscopic size; especially, any one of the bacteria, protozoans, viruses, etc.

mi·cro·phone (mī'krō-fōn), *n.* an instrument that converts sound waves into an electric current, usually for amplifying, recording, etc.

mi·cro·pho·to·graph (mī-krō-fōt'ō-graf), *n.* 1. an extremely small photograph that is magnified for viewing. 2. same as **photomicrograph.** —**mi·cro·pho·tog'ra·phy,** *n.*

mi·cro·scope (mī'krō-skōp), *n.* an optical instrument for magnifying minute objects so as to render them visible for study.

mi·cro·scop·ic (mī-krō-skop'ik), *adj.* 1. of, pertaining to, or determined by the aid of a microscope. 2. very small; minute. —**mi·cro·scop'i·cal·ly,** *adv.*

mi·cros·co·py (mī-kros'kō-pi), *n.* the use of a microscope; microscopic investigation. —**mi·cros'co·pist,** *n.*

mi·cro·spore (mī'krō-spôr), *n.* the smaller of two kinds of spores produced by certain plants, as ferns.

mi·cro·wave (-wāv), *adj.* 1. of or designating equipment, etc. using microwaves for radar, communications, etc. 2. designating an oven that cooks quickly using microwaves: *v.t.* **-waved, -wav·ing,** to cook in a microwave oven: *n.* 1. a very short electromagnetic radiation lying between infrared and shortwave radio frequencies. 2. a microwave oven.

mid (mid), *adj.* middle.

mid (mid), *prep.* [Poetic], amid: also **'mid.**

mid-, a combining form meaning *middle, middle part of.*

mid-air (-er'), *n.* any point or region in space not in contact with any surface.

Mi·das (mī'dăs), *n.* in *Greek Mythology*, a mythical king granted the power to turn all he touched to gold.

mid·day (mid'dā), *n. & adj.* noon.

mid·dle (mid'l), *adj.* 1. equally distant from the extremes; mean; medial. 2. intermediate: *n.* 1. the point equally distant from the ex-

tremes; central part. 2. something intervening. 3. the waist.

middle age, the time in human life between youth and old age. —**mid'dle-aged',** *adj.*

Middle Ages, the period in European history between antiquity and modern times, often dated from 476 A.D. to about 1450 A.D.

Middle America, the American middle class, seen as being conventional or conservative.

mid·dle·brow (-brou), *n.* [Informal], a person who does not have a high degree of culture.

middle class, a class in society intermediate between the wealthy and the laboring class.

middle ear, the part of the ear containing the eardrum and a cavity with three small bones; tympanum.

Middle English, the English language from 1100 to 1500.

mid·dle·man (mid'l-man), *n., pl.* **-men,** 1. a trader who buys from producers and sells to wholesalers, retailers, or consumers. 2. a go-between.

mid·dle·most (-mōst), *adj.* same as **midmost.**

mid·dle-of-the-road (-ŏv-thē-rōd'), *adj.* following a course that is between extremes, especially political or economic ones.

middle school, a school with, usually, grades five through eight.

mid·dle·weight (-wāt), *n.* 1. a person of medium weight. 2. a boxer or wrestler between a welterweight and a light heavyweight (148-160 pounds).

mid·dling (mid'ling), *adj.* of middle rank, size, quality, etc.; mediocre: *adv.* [Informal], fairly; moderately: *n., pl.* the coarser part of flour.

mid·dy (mid'i), *n., pl.* **-dies,** 1. [Informal], a midshipman. 2. a loose blouse with a sailor collar, worn by women and children.

midge (mij), *n.* any one of various gnatlike flies.

midg·et (mij'it), *n.* 1. a very small person. 2. something smaller than the usual type: *adj.* miniature.

mid·land (mid'lănd), *n.* the interior part of a country: *adj.* of or pertaining to the middle part of a country; inland.

mid·most ('mōst), *adj.* precisely in the middle or closest to the middle.

mid·night ('nīt), *n.* 1. twelve o'clock at night. 2. a period of darkness or gloom: *adj.* 1. of or pertaining to midnight. 2. resembling or suggestive of midnight.

midnight sun, the sun visible at midnight during the summer in the arctic or antarctic regions.

mid·point ('point), *n.* the point at the center or near the middle.

mid·riff ('rif), *n.* 1. same as **diaphragm** (sense 1). 2. the middle portion of the human body from the chest to waist.

mid·ship·man ('ship-măn), *n., pl.* **-men** (-mĕn), 1. a student training to be commissioned an ensign. 2. formerly, in the British navy, a junior officer ranking next above a cadet.

mid-size, mid·size (mid'sīz), *adj.* of a size intermediate between large and small.

midst (midst), *n.* the middle.

midst (midst), *prep.* [Poetic], amidst: also **'midst.**

---

a in *cap,* ā in *cane,* ä in *father,* ậ in *abet,* e in *met,* ē in *be,* ê in *baker,* ê in *regent,* i in *pit,* ī in *fine,* ĭ in *manifest,* o in *hot,* ô in *horse,* ō in *bone,*

mid-stream (mid'strēm), *n.* the middle of a stream.

mid-sum-mer ('sum'ēr), *n.* 1. the middle of the summer. 2. the summer solstice, about June 21.

mid-term ('tūrm), *adj.* occurring in the middle of a term: *n.* [Informal], a midterm examination.

mid-way ('wā), *n.* that part of a fair, carnival, etc. where sideshows and amusements are located: *adj. & adv.* in the middle of the way or distance; halfway.

mid-wife ('wīf), *n.* a woman who assists at childbirth. —**mid'wife-ry** ('wĭ-fĕ-ri, 'wĭf-ri), *n.*

mid-win-ter (-win'tēr), *n.* 1. the middle of the winter. 2. the winter solstice, about December 22.

mid-year ('yir), *adj.* occurring in the middle of the year: *n.* [Informal], a midyear examination.

mien (mēn), *n.* 1. external appearance; look. 2. carriage.

miff (mif), *v.t. & v.i.* [Informal], to offend or take offense.

MIG (mig), *n.* a military jet aircraft of Russian design: also **MiG**.

might (mit), *v.* 1. past tense of may. 2. an auxiliary verb generally equivalent to may.

might (mit), *n.* power, strength, or force.

might-y ('i), *adj.* **might'i-er**, **might'i-est**, 1. powerful; strong; influential. 2. very large; monumental: *adv.* [Informal], very; extremely. —**might'i-ly**, *adv.* —**might'i-ness**, *n.*

mi-gnon (min'yon), *adj.* [French], small; pretty; delicate. —**mi-gnonne** (min'yon), *adj.fem.*

mi-gnon-ette (min-yŏ-net'), *n.* a fragrant annual with small greenish-white flowers.

mi-graine (mī'grān), *n.* a painful, recurrent headache, usually afflicting only one side of the head.

mi-grant (mī'grānt), *adj.* migratory: *n.* 1. a person, bird, or animal who migrates. 2. a farm worker who follows the seasonal crops.

mi-grate (mī'grāt), *v.i.* **-grat-ed**, **-grat-ing**, 1. to move to another country or region to settle. 2. to move from one place to another with the seasons, as many birds.

mi-gra-tion (mi-grā'shŭn), *n.* 1. the action or an act of migrating. 2. a group migrating together.

mi-gra-to-ry (mī'grā-tôr-i), *adj.* 1. migrating. 2. of migration. 3. roving; nomadic.

mi-ka-do (mi-kä'dō), *n., pl.* **-dos**, [Obs.], an emperor of Japan.

mike (mīk), *n.* [Informal], a microphone.

mil (mil), *n.* a unit of length that is equal to .001 of an inch.

mi-la-dy, **mi-la-di** (mi-lā'di), *n.* 1. a noblewoman. 2. a woman of fashion.

milch (milch), *adj.* yielding milk.

mild (mīld), *adj.* 1. gentle in temper and disposition. 2. soft; placid. 3. moderate. 4. not sharp, sour, or bitter. —**mild'ly**, *adv.* —**mild'ness**, *n.*

mil-dew (mil'dōō, 'dū), *n.* 1. a disease of plants in which a fungus growth is visible on the plant. 2. whitish spots of mold appearing on organic matter, as paper, cloth, etc., especially when exposed to dampness. 3. any fungus causing mildew: *v.t. & v.i.* to affect or become affected with mildew.

mile (mīl), *n.* a unit of linear measure that is equal to 5,280 feet: the nautical mile is 6,076.12 feet.

mile-age ('ij), *n.* 1. an allowance for traveling expenses at a particular rate per mile. 2. total distance in miles traveled. 3. the average number of miles that a vehicle can travel on a certain amount of fuel.

mile-post ('pōst), *n.* a sign showing the distance in miles to or from a place.

mil-er ('ēr), *n.* one who runs in mile races.

mile-stone ('stōn), *n.* 1. a stone showing the distance in miles to or from a place. 2. an important event in history or in a person's life.

mil-foil (mil'foil), *n.* same as yarrow.

mi-lieu (mēl-yoo'), *n.* environment; setting.

mil-i-tant (mil'i-tănt), *adj.* 1. fighting; engaged in war. 2. warlike; aggressive, especially in furthering some cause. —**mil'i-tan-cy**, *n.* — **mil'i-tant-ly**, *adv.*

mil-i-ta-rism (mil'i-tēr-izm), *n.* 1. military spirit or the glorification of the attitudes of professional soldiers. 2. a policy of continuously maintaining strong military forces. — **mil'i-ta-rist**, *n.* —**mil-i-ta-ris'tic**, *adj.*

mil-i-ta-rize (mil'i-ta-rīz), *v.t.* **-rized**, **-riz-ing**, to supply and make ready for war.

mil-i-tar-y (mil'i-ter-i), *adj.* 1. of or pertaining to soldiers or to armed forces. 2. of, for, or ready for war. 3. of the army.

military police, soldiers assigned to perform as police for the army.

mil-i-tate (mil'i-tāt), *v.i.* **-tat-ed**, **-tat-ing**, to operate or work (*against*).

mi-li-tia (mi-lish'ă), *n.* citizens trained for military service, as distinct from professional soldiers, and called to active duty in time of emergency.

milk (milk), *n.* 1. a white fluid secreted by the mammary glands of female mammals for the nourishment of their young. 2. cow's milk. 3. any fluid resembling this, as the juice of certain plants: *v.t.* 1. to draw milk from (a cow, goat, etc.). 2. to draw out or obtain (information, money, venom, etc.) from as if by milking. —**milk'er**, *n.*

milk-and-wa-ter (-ăn-wôt'ēr), *adj.* weak; insipid; flat; unreliable.

milk fever, 1. a mild fever formerly assumed to be caused by an accumulation of milk in the breasts but caused by infection. 2. a disease of dairy cows occurring shortly after calving.

milk-liv-ered ('liv-ērd), *adj.* cowardly.

milk-maid ('mād), *n.* a girl or woman who milks cows.

milk-man ('man), *n., pl.* **-men** ('men), a man who sells or delivers milk for a dairy.

milk of magnesia, a suspension in water of magnesium hydroxide, used as an antacid and laxative.

milk-shake, *n.* a drink made of milk, flavoring, and, usually, ice cream, shaken or whipped thoroughly.

milk-sop ('sop), *n.* a sissy.

milk tooth, any one of the temporary first set of teeth in the young of mammals.

milk-weed ('wēd), *n.* any one of various plants having a milky juice and pods that split open to release cottony seeds.

milk·y (mil'ki), *adj.* milk'l-er, milk'l-est, 1. like milk, especially in color. 2. of, containing, or giving milk.

Milky Way, a broad, luminous band across the heavens consisting of many billions of stars and clouds of gas.

mill (mil), *n.* 1. a machine for grinding grain into flour. 2. any one of various machines for grinding, crushing, cutting, etc. 3. a building containing such machines. 4. a factory. 5. a steel roller for making a die, printing plate, etc. by pressure: *v.t.* 1. to grind, polish, press, crush, etc. by or as in a mill. 2. to flute the edge of (a coin): *v.i.* to move in a circle, as cattle, or in confusion, as a crowd.

mill (mil), *n.* one tenth of a cent: unit used in calculating.

mill·age (mil'ij), *n.* taxation in mills per dollar of valuation.

mill-board ('bōrd), *n.* a kind of thick pasteboard, used in bookbinding, etc.

mil·le·nar·y (mil'ĕ-ner-i), *adj.* 1. of or pertaining to a thousand, especially a thousand years. 2. of or pertaining to the millennium: *n.*, *pl.* -nar·ies, 1. a thousand. 2. a thousand years. 3. a thousandth anniversary.

mil·len·ni·um (mi-len'i-ŭm), *n.*, *pl.* -ni·ums, -ni·a (-ä), 1. any span of a thousand years. 2. in *Theology*, the period of a thousand years during which Satan will be bound and Christ will reign on earth: see *Revelation xx*, 1-5. 3. any period of great happiness, peace, etc. —mil·len'ni·al, *adj.*

mil·le·pede (mil'ĕ-pēd), *n.* same as millipede.

mil·le·pore (-pōr), *n.* any one of a group of corallike animals that build calcareous reefs.

mill·er (mil'ĕr), *n.* 1. one who keeps or operates a flour mill. 2. any one of various moths with floury wings.

mil·let (mil'it), *n.* a cereal grass cultivated in the U.S. as forage and in the Old World for food.

milli-, a combining form meaning *a one-thousandth part of*.

mil·liard (mil'yĕrd), *n.* [British], 1,000 millions; billion.

mil·li·gram (mil'i-gram), *n.* the 1000th part of a gram.

mil·li·li·ter (-lēt-ĕr), *n.* the 1000th part of a liter.

mil·li·me·ter (-mēt-ĕr), *n.* the 1000th part of a meter.

mil·li·ner (mil'i-nĕr), *n.* one who makes or sells women's hats, headdresses, etc.

mil·li·ner·y (-ner-i), *n.* 1. the articles made and sold by a milliner. 2. the business or work of a milliner.

mill·ing (mil'ing), *n.* 1. the act or business of grinding grain into flour. 2. the process of cutting, shaping, etc. metal or other products in a mill. 3. the process of making a serrated edge on a coin.

mil·lion (mil'yŭn), *n.* 1. a thousand thousands. 2. a million units of money, as dollars,

pounds, etc. 3. an indefinitely large number. —mil'lionth, *adj. & n.*

mil·lion·aire (mil-yŭn-ner'), *n.* a person who is worth a million dollars, pounds, etc.

mil·li·pede (mil'i-pēd), *n.* any one of various insects with numerous feet.

mill·pond (mil'pond), *n.* a reservoir of water for driving a mill wheel.

mill·race ('rās), *n.* the current of water that drives a mill wheel.

mill·stone ('stōn), *n.* 1. either one of two flat, cylindrical stones for grinding grain. 2. a heavy burden.

mill·stream ('strēm), *n.* water flowing in a millrace.

mill wheel, the water wheel that drives the machinery of a mill.

mill·wright ('rīt), *n.* one skilled in, or who attends to, the machinery of a mill.

milt (milt), *n.* 1. the reproductive organ of male fishes. 2. the sperm and milky fluid produced in this organ: *v.t.* to impregnate (fish ova) with milt.

mime (mīm), *n.* 1. a kind of drama among the Greeks and Romans in which persons and events were represented in a satirical manner. 2. a performance in which action, speech, etc. is suggested by gestures. 3. a mimic; clown: *v.t.* mimed, mim'ing, to mimic.

mim·e·o·graph (mim'i-ō-graf), *n.* a machine for making copies of letters, drawings, etc. by an inked stencil: *v.t.* to make (copies) on such a machine.

mi·me·sis (mi-mē'sis), *n.* a mimicking of the speech, accent, style, etc. of another.

mi·met·ic (-met'ik), *adj.* 1. imitative. 2. characteristic of mimicry.

mim·ic (mim'ik), *adj.* 1. imitative. 2. pretended; false: *n.* one who mimics or imitates: *v.t.* mim'icked, mim'ick·ing, 1. to imitate or ridicule by imitation. 2. to imitate or resemble closely. —mim'ick·er, *n.*

mim·ic·ry (-ri), *n.*, *pl.* -ries, 1. imitation for sport or ridicule. 2. close external likeness.

mi·mo·sa (mi-mō'sä), *n.* any one of various trees, shrubs, and plants of warm regions, with clusters of small white or pink flowers.

min·a·ret (min-ä-ret'), *n.* a tall, slender turret attached to a mosque, with overhanging balconies from which a muezzin summons the people to prayer.

min·a·to·ry (min'ä-tōr-i), *adj.* threatening.

mince (mins), *v.t.* minced, minc'ing, 1. to cut or chop (meat, fruit, etc.) into minute pieces. 2. to pronounce or act affectedly. 3. to weaken or suppress, as for decorum: *v.i.* to talk, walk, or act with affected elegance.

mince·meat ('mēt), *n.* chopped fruit, suet, raisins, etc., and sometimes meat, mixed together and used as a pie filling.

minc·ing (min'sing), *adj.* affectedly elegant.

mind (mīnd), *n.* 1. the intellectual or rational faculty in man. 2. the seat of consciousness; intellect or intelligence. 3. same as psyche (sense 2). 4. memory or recollection. 5. intention or purpose. 6. opinion or state of feeling. 7. sanity: *v.t.* 1. to attend to. 2. to be cognizant of. 3. to have charge of. 4. to obey. 5. to watch out for. 6. to object to:

---

v.i. 1. to pay attention. 2. to be watchful. 3. to object. 4. to be obedient.

mind·ed (mīn'did), *adj.* 1. having a mind: used in compounds, as noble-*minded*. 2. disposed or inclined.

mind·ful (mīnd'fûl), *adj.* bearing in mind; observant; heedful; attentive. —**mind'ful·ly**, *adv.* —**mind'ful·ness**, *n.*

mind reader, one who professes to know the thoughts in the mind of another.

mine (mīn), *pron.* that or those belonging to me.

mine (mīn), *n.* 1. an excavation in the earth from which minerals, precious stones, etc. are extracted. 2. a deposit of coal, ore, etc. 3. a rich source of wealth. 4. in *military usage, a)* a tunnel in which explosives are placed to blow up an enemy's fortifications. *b)* an explosive device placed underground or undersea for destroying enemy troops, equipment, ships, etc. on contact: *v.t. & v.i.* **mined, min'ing,** 1. to extract (coal, ores, etc.) from (the earth). 2. to plant (military mines) in (the ground or sea). 3. to undermine.

min·er ('ēr), *n.* one who labors to extract coal, ores, etc. from the earth.

min·er·al (min'ēr-ǎl), *n.* 1. any inorganic substance having a definite physical and chemical composition, found on or in the earth. 2. a substance that is not vegetable or animal: *adj.* of, pertaining to, consisting of, or impregnated with a mineral.

min·er·al·o·gy (min-ê-rǎl'ô-ji), *n.* the science of minerals. —**min·er·a·log'i·cal** (-ēr-â-loj'i-kl), *adj.* —**min·er·al'o·gist**, *n.*

mineral oil, a clear, tasteless oil distilled from petroleum and used as a laxative.

mineral water, a natural or prepared water containing minerals or gases, often used medicinally.

Mi·ner·va (mi-nûr'vâ), *n.* the Roman goddess of wisdom.

mi·ne·stro·ne (min-ê-strō'ni), *n.* a soup containing vegetables, barley, etc. in a meat broth.

min·gle (ming'gl), *v.t.* -**gled, -gling,** 1. to intermix; join or combine. 2. to compound: *v.i.* to be mixed or united with.

min·i-, a combining form meaning *very small, very short.*

min·i·a·ture (min'i-â-chēr), *n.* 1. a very small painting, especially a portrait on ivory. 2. a copy or model reducing something to a very small size: *adj.* produced to a small scale; diminutive; minute.

min·i·a·tur·ize (-īz), *v.t.* -**ized, -iz·ing,** to make in a greatly reduced size. —**min·i·a·tur·i·za'tion**, *n.*

min·i·bus (min'i-bus), *n.* a very small bus.

min·i·cam (min'i·kam), *n.* a portable TV camera operated from the shoulder for telecasting or videotaping news events, sports, etc.

min·i·com·put·er (-kŏm-pyōōt'ēr), *n.* a computer intermediate in size, power, etc. between a mainframe and a microcomputer.

min·im (min'im), *n.* 1. the smallest liquid measure, equal to 1/60 fluid dram. 2. a single drop; tiny portion. 3. in *Music,* a half note.

min·i·mal·ism (min'i-mǎl-izm), *n.* a movement in art, music, etc. in which only the simplest design, forms, etc. are used, often repetitiously. —**min'i·mal·ist**, *adj. & n.*

min·i·mize (min'i-mīz), *v.t.* -**mized, -miz·ing,** 1. to decrease to the smallest amount, degree, etc. 2. to lessen in value, importance, etc.

min·i·mum (-mûm), *n., pl.* -**mums, -ma** (-mâ), the lowest or smallest value, degree, etc.: *adj.* consisting of or pertaining to the smallest amount or degree.

min·ion (min'yŭn), *n.* 1. in *Printing,* a size of type, 7 point. 2. a servile flatterer; sycophant.

min·i·se·ries (min'i-sir-ēz), *n., pl.* -**ries,** a TV drama broadcast serially in a limited number of episodes.

min·i·skirt (min'i·skûrt), *n.* a short skirt ending several inches above the knees.

min·i·ster (min'is-tēr), *n.* 1. a person serving for another by carrying out his orders or desires; agent. 2. a person appointed to head a department of government. 3. a person authorized to represent his government in diplomatic affairs. 4. a clergyman or pastor authorized by a church to preach, administer the sacraments, etc.: *v.t.* to dispense; administer: *v.i.* to attend to the wants of others; serve. —**min·is·te'ri·al** (-tir'i-âl), *adj.* —**min'is·trant** (-trânt), *adj. & n.*

min·is·tra·tion (min-is-trā'shŭn), *n.* the act of administering; service; care.

min·is·try (min'is-tri), *n., pl.* -**tries,** 1. the agency, service, etc. of a minister of religion. 2. the act of ministering, or serving. 3. a government department under a minister. 4. the term in office of such a minister. 5. the ministers of a state collectively.

min·i·ver (min'i-vēr), *n.* a white fur used for trimming ceremonial robes.

mink (mingk), *n.* any one of several carnivorous mammals yielding a valuable fur.

min·now (min'ō), *n.* any one of numerous, small, freshwater fishes, often used as bait.

mi·nor (mī'nēr), *adj.* 1. smaller or less in size, extent, quantity, etc. 2. lesser in importance or eminence. 3. in *Music, a)* lower by a half tone. *b)* denoting one of the two standard diatonic scales: *n.* 1. one who has not reached full legal age. 2. in *Education,* a secondary area of study. 3. in *Logic,* the second proposition of a syllogism: *v.i.* to have a secondary area of study.

mi·nor·i·ty (mi-nôr'i-ti), *n.* 1. the smaller number; less than half of a total. 2. a racial, religious, ethnic, etc. group different from the dominant group. 3. the state of being under legal age.

Min·o·taur (min'ô-tôr), *n.* in *Greek Mythology,* a monster with the head of a bull and the body of a man.

min·ster (min'stēr), *n.* 1. the church of a monastery. 2. a cathedral church.

min·strel (min'strĕl), *n.* 1. in medieval times, any one of a class of men who traveled about singing their compositions to the accompaniment of a harp or lute. 2. a performer in a minstrel show.

minstrel show, a variety show in which the

performers, usually in blackface, sing, dance, and tell jokes.

min·strel·sy (-si), *n., pl.* **-sies.** 1. the art or occupation of a minstrel. 2. minstrels collectively. 3. a collection of minstrel ballads.

mint (mint), *n.* 1. a place where money is coined by government authority. 2. a source of seemingly unlimited supply. 3. a place of invention or fabrication: *adj.* new, as if just minted: *v.t.* to coin (money). —**mint'age,** *n.*

mint (mint), *n.* 1. any one of various plants with aromatic leaves used in flavoring. 2. a candy flavored with mint.

mint julep, a drink of whiskey or brandy, sugar, and crushed ice, flavored with mint leaves.

min·u·end (min'yoo-wend), *n.* the number from which another is to be subtracted.

min·u·et (min-yoo-wet'), *n.* 1. a slow, graceful dance. 2. the music for this.

mi·nus (mī'nus), *prep.* 1. less. 2. [informal], lacking: *adj.* 1. indicating subtraction. 2. negative. 3. less than: *n.* the sign (-) indicating subtraction or a negative quantity.

mi·nus·cule (mi-nus'kūl, min'ŭ-skūl), *adj.* very small; minute.

min·ute (min'it), *n.* 1. the sixtieth part of an hour or of a degree of an arc: symbol ('). 2. an instant. 3. a particular point in time. 4. *pl.* an official record of proceedings of a meeting.

mi·nute (mī-noot'), *adj.* 1. very small. 2. insignificant. 3. precise; exact. —**mi·nute'ly,** *adv.*

min·ute·man (min'it-man), *n., pl.* **-men,** [also M-], any one of the armed citizens who pledged themselves to take the field at a minute's notice during the American Revolution.

min·ute steak (min'it), a small, thin steak that can be quickly cooked.

mi·nu·ti·ae (mi-nōō'shi-ē), *n.pl., sing.* **-ti·a** ('shē-ā), small or trifling details.

minx (mingks), *n.* a pert, saucy girl.

Mi·o·cene (mī'ō-sēn), *n.* the fourth epoch of the Tertiary Period, characterized by the development of many mammals having a modern form.

mir·a·cle (mir'ā-kl), *n.* 1. an occurrence or act that seems inexplicable and is thought to be a manifestation of the supernatural. 2. a wonder; marvel.

mi·rac·u·lous (mi-rak'yoo-lŭs), *adj.* 1. performed supernaturally. 2. wonderful. 3. capable of performing miracles. —**mi·rac'u·lous·ly,** *adv.*

mi·rage (mi-räzh'), *n.* an optical illusion, as of a ship in the air or an oasis in a desert, in which the image of a distant object appears nearby due to the refraction of light through layers of hot air and cool air.

mire (mīr), *n.* 1. deep mud. 2. an extent of wet, clayey earth: *v.t.* mired, mir'ing, 1. to soil with mire. 2. to cause to sink or stick in mire: *v.i.* to sink or stick in mire.

mir·i·ness ('i-nis), *n.* the state of being miry.

mir·ror (mir'ēr), *n.* 1. a looking glass; a surface, as of glass, that reflects the images of objects. 2. anything that gives a faithful representation: *v.t.* to reflect, as in a mirror.

mirth (mûrth), *n.* noisy gaiety, enjoyment, or merriment, especially when expressed by laughter. —**mirth'ful,** *adj.*

mir·y (mīr'i), *adj.* mir'i·er, mir'i·est, 1. abounding in mire; swampy. 2. covered with mire; dirty.

mir·za (mir'zā), *n.* a Persian title of honor given to a prince, hero, scholar, etc.

mis-, a prefix indicating *wrong, wrongly, bad, badly, no, not, hatred.*

mis·ad·ven·ture (mis-ăd-ven'chēr), *n.* an unlucky accident; misfortune.

mis·al·li·ance (-ā-lī'áns), *n.* an improper alliance, especially in marriage.

mis·an·thrope (mis'ăn-thrōp, miz'-), *n.* a person who hates mankind: also **mis·an·thro·pist** (mis-ăn'thrō·pist). —**mis·an·throp'ic** (-ăn-throp'ik), *adj.* —**mis·an'thro·py,** *n.*

mis·ap·ply (mis-ā-plī'), *v.t.* -plied', -ply'ing, to apply badly, wastefully, or dishonestly.

mis·ap·pre·hend (-ap-rē-hend'), *v.t.* to misunderstand. —**mis·ap·pre·hen'sion** (-hen'shŭn), *n.*

mis·ap·pro·pri·ate (mis-ā-prō'pri-āt), *v.t.* -at·ed, -at·ing, to apply to a wrong or dishonest use or purpose.

mis·be·got·ten (-bi-gāt'n), *n.* illegally or wrongly begotten; illegitimate.

mis·be·have (-bi-hāv'), *v.i. & v.i.* -haved', -hav'ing, to behave (oneself) wrongly. —**mis·be·hav'ior** ('yēr), *n.*

mis·cal·cu·late (mis-kal'kyu-lāt), *v.t. & v.i.* -lat·ed, -lat·ing, to calculate wrongly; misjudge. —**mis·cal·cu·la'tion,** *n.*

mis·call (-kôl'), *v.t.* to call by a wrong name.

mis·car·ry (-ker'i), *v.i.* -ried, -ry·ing, 1. to go wrong; be unsuccessful. 2. to fail to arrive: said of mail. 3. to give birth to a fetus before it can survive. —**mis·car'riage,** *n.*

mis·cast (-kast'), *v.t.* -cast', -cast'ing, to cast (an actor or play) inappropriately.

mis·ce·ge·na·tion (mis-i-jē-nā'shŭn, mi-sej-ē-), *n.* marriage or sexual relations between a man and woman different in race.

mis·cel·la·ne·a (mis-ē-lā'ni-ā, -lān'yā), *n.pl.* a collection of miscellaneous matters or things.

mis·cel·la·ne·ous (-ŭs, -yŭs), *adj.* consisting of several kinds mixed together.

mis·cel·la·ny (mis'ē-lā-ni), *n., pl.* -nies, 1. a mixture of various kinds. 2. a book containing a variety of literary compositions.

mis·chance (mis-chans'), *n.* misfortune.

mis·chief (mis'chif), *n.* 1. harm; injury; hurt. 2. a cause of damage or disturbance. 3. a prank. 4. playful teasing.

mis·chie·vous (mis'chi-vŭs), *adj.* 1. producing injury or damage. 2. hurtful. 3. inclined to mischief; naughty; prankish.

mis·ci·ble (mis'ĭ-bl), *adj.* capable of being mixed.

mis·con·ceive (mis-kŏn-sēv'), *v.t. & v.i.* to misapprehend. —**mis·con·cep'tion** (-sep'shŭn), *n.*

mis·con·duct (-kŏn-dukt'), *v.t.* 1. to mismanage. 2. to conduct (oneself) wrongly: *n.* (-kon'-dukt), 1. wrong or unlawful management. 2. bad behavior.

mis·con·strue (-kŏn-strōō'), *v.t.* -strued', -stru'-ing, to interpret wrongly. —**mis·con·struc'tion,** *n.*

mis·count (mis-kount'), *v.t.* & *v.i.* to count incorrectly: *n.* (mis'kount), an incorrect count.

mis·cre·ant (mis'kri-ânt), *n.* an unscrupulous person; villain: *adj.* villainous; wicked.

mis·deal (mis-dēl'), *v.t.* & *v.i.* -dealt', -deal'ing, to deal (playing cards) improperly: *n.* an improper deal.

mis·deed (-dēd'), *n.* an evil, criminal, or sinful act.

mis·de·mean·ant (-di-mēn'ânt), *n.* in *Law*, one guilty of a misdemeanor.

mis·de·mean·or ('ēr), *n.* in *Law*, any minor offense carrying lesser punishment than that for a felony.

mis·di·rect (mis-di-rekt', -dī-), *v.t.* to direct incorrectly or badly. —**mis·di·rec'tion,** *n.*

mis·do·ing (-dōō'ing), *n.* evil conduct.

mi·ser (mī'zēr), *n.* a covetous person who denies himself all comforts in order to hoard money. —**mi'ser·ly,** *adj.* —**mi'ser·li·ness,** *n.*

mis·er·a·ble (miz'ēr-â-bl, miz'râ-), *adj.* 1. wretched; unhappy. 2. producing misery or discomfort. 3. shameful; despicable. 4. very poor; inferior.

mis·er·y (miz'ēr-i), *n., pl.* -er·ies, 1. a state of extreme pain, suffering, distress, etc. 2. a cause or source of such wretchedness.

mis·fea·sance (mis-fē'zâns), *n.* in *Law*, wrongdoing; the doing of a lawful act in an unlawful manner.

mis·file (-fīl'), *v.t.* -filed', -fil'ing, to file (papers, reports, etc.) in the wrong place.

mis·fire (-fīr'), *v.i.* -fired', -fir'ing, 1. to fail to ignite or explode at the proper time. 2. to fail to accomplish the desired result: *n.* an act or occasion of misfiring.

mis·fit (-fit'), *v.t.* & *v.i.* -fit'ted, -fit'ting, to fit poorly: *n.* 1. anything that doesn't fit properly. 2. (mis'fit), a badly adjusted person.

mis·for·tune (mis-fôr'chûn), *n.* 1. bad luck; calamity. 2. an unfortunate accident; mishap.

mis·give (-giv'), *v.t.* -gave', -giv'en, -giv'ing, to impart doubt or fear to; make suspicious.

mis·giv·ing (-giv'ing), *n.* a premonition of evil; state of apprehension.

mis·gov·ern (-guv'ērn), *v.t.* to govern badly. —**mis·gov'ern·ment,** *n.*

mis·guide (-gīd'), *v.t.* -guid'ed, -guid'ing, to guide wrongly; lead astray. —**mis·guid'ance,** *n.*

mis·han·dle (mis-han'dl), *v.t.* -dled, -dling, to deal with roughly or inefficiently.

mis·hap (mis'hap), *n.* an unfortunate accident.

mish·mash (mish'mash), *n.* a jumble.

mis·in·form (mis-in-fôrm'), *v.t.* to give false information to. —**mis·in·for·ma'tion,** *n.*

mis·in·ter·pret (-in-tûr'prit), *v.t.* 1. to misunderstand. 2. to explain incorrectly. —**mis·in·ter·pre·ta'tion,** *n.*

mis·judge (-juj'), *v.t.* & *v.i.* -judged', -judg'ing, to judge incorrectly or harshly.

mis·la·bel (-lā'bl), *v.t.* & *v.i.* -beled or -belled, -bel·ing or -bel·ling, to label wrongly.

mis·lay (-lā'), *v.t.* -laid', -lay'ing, 1. to misplace. 2. to set in place improperly.

mis·lead (-lēd'), *v.t.* -led', -lead'ing, 1. to lead in the wrong direction. 2. to deceive. 3. to lead into error.

mis·man·age (-man'ij), *v.t.* & *v.i.* -aged, -ag·ing,

to manage wrongly or carelessly. —**mis·man'age·ment,** *n.*

mis·match (-mach'), *v.t.* to match unsuitably or inappropriately: *n.* a bad match.

mis·mate (-māt'), *v.t.* & *v.i.* -mat'ed, -mat'ing, to mate unsuitably.

mis·name (-nām'), *v.t.* -named', -nam'ing, to apply a wrong name to.

mis·no·mer (-nō'mēr), *n.* a wrong name.

mi·sog·a·my (mi-sog'â-mi), *n.* hatred of marriage. —**mi·sog'a·mist,** *n.*

mi·sog·y·ny (mi-soj'i-ni), *n.* hatred of women. —**mi·sog'y·nist,** *n.*

mis·place (mis-plās'), *v.t.* -placed', -plac'ing, 1. to put in a wrong place. 2. to place (trust, faith, etc.) in an unworthy person or thing. 3. to lose.

mis·play (-plā'), *v.t.* & *v.i.* to play badly, as in games or sports: *n.* a wrong play.

mis·print (-print'), *v.t.* to print incorrectly: *n.* a printing error.

mis·pri·sion (-prizh'ûn), *n.* in *Law*, 1. wrongful performance in public office. 2. contempt against a government or a court.

misprision of felony, the concealment of a felony by one who knows of it but did not assist in it.

mis·pro·nounce (mis-prô-nouns'), *v.t.* & *v.i.* -nounced', -nounc'ing, to pronounce incorrectly. —**mis·pro·nun·ci·a'tion** (-nun-si-ā'shûn), *n.*

mis·quote (-kwōt'), *v.t.* & *v.i.* -quot'ed, -quot'ing, to quote incorrectly.

mis·read (-rēd'), *v.t.* & *v.i.* -read' (-red'), -read'ing (-red'ing), 1. to read wrongly. 2. to misinterpret.

mis·rep·re·sent (-rep-ri-zent'), *v.t.* to represent improperly. —**mis·rep·re·sen·ta'tion,** *n.*

mis·rule (-rōōl'), *v.t.* -ruled', -rul'ing, to rule badly or unwisely; misgovern: *n.* bad government.

miss (mis), *v.t.* 1. to fail to hit, reach, obtain, catch, see, etc. 2. to omit or pass by. 3. to avoid. 4. to feel the want of: *v.i.* 1. to fail to hit. 2. to fail to reach a goal. 3. to misfire: *n.* a failure to hit, reach, etc.

Miss (mis), *n., pl.* miss'es, 1. [M-], a title used before the name of an unmarried woman. 2. a young unmarried girl or woman.

mis·sal (mis'l), *n.* the book containing the order of service for the Roman Catholic Mass throughout the year.

mis·shape (mis-shāp'), *v.t.* -shaped', -shap'ing, to shape wrongly; deform. —**mis·shap'en,** *adj.*

mis·sile (mis'l), *n.* a weapon or thing designed to be thrown or launched at a target.

mis·sile·ry, mis·sil·ry (-ri), *n.* 1. the science of constructing and launching guided missiles. 2. such missiles.

miss·ing (mis'ing), *adj.* lost; absent.

mis·sion (mish'ûn), *n.* 1. the act of sending or state of being sent for a particular purpose. 2. a diplomatic establishment in a foreign country. 3. a body of missionaries. 4. its headquarters. 5. a force of specialists, scientists, etc. sent to a foreign country. 6. the special duty of such a force. 7. one's calling in life.

mis·sion·ar·y (-er-i), *n., pl.* -ar·ies, a person

ŏ in drag**o**n, ōō in cr**u**de, oo in w**oo**l, u in c**u**p, ū in c**u**re, û in t**u**rn, ŭ in foc**u**s, oi in b**oy**, ou in h**ou**se, th in **th**in, *t*h in shea**th**e, g in **g**et, **j** in **j**oy, y in **y**et.

who is sent to propagate religion, especially in a foreign country: *adj.* of or pertaining to religious missions.

mis-sive (mis'iv), *n.* a letter or message.

mis-spell (mis-spel'), *v.t. & v.i.* -spelled' or -spelt', -spell'ing, to spell wrongly.

mis-spend (-spend'), *v.t.* -spent', -spend'ing, to spend unwisely.

mis-state (-stāt'), *v.t.* -stat'ed, -stat'ing, to state wrongly. —mis-state'ment, *n.*

mis-step (-step'), *n.* 1. a wrong step. 2. an error in conduct.

mist (mist), *n.* 1. visible watery vapor at or near the earth's surface, less dense than fog. 2. any fine spray or cloud. 3. anything that dims or obscures the vision: *v.i. & v.i.* to make or become misty.

mis-take (mi-stāk'), *v.t.* -took', -tak'en, -tak'ing, to misunderstand; misconceive: *v.i.* to err: *n.* an error; blunder; fault. —mis-tak'a-ble, *adj.*

mis-tak-en (-tāk'n), *adj.* 1. wrong. 2. erroneous.

mis-ter (mis'tēr), *n.* 1. [M-], a title of address prefixed to a man's name. 2. [Informal], sir.

mis-tle-toe (mis'l-tō), *n.* an evergreen parasitic shrub with white waxy berries and yellowish flowers.

mis-took (mi-stook'), past tense of mistake.

mis-treat (mis-trēt'), *v.t.* to treat badly. —mis-treat'ment, *n.*

mis-tress (mis'tris), *n.* 1. a woman who exercises authority or governs. 2. the female head of a family, school, etc. 3. a woman well skilled in anything. 4. a female paramour, engaging in sexual relations with a particular man over a long period. 5. [M-], formerly, a title of address prefixed to the name of a woman.

mis-tri-al (mis-trī'āl), *n.* in *Law,* an invalid trial resulting from error or disagreement by the jury.

mis-trust (mis-trust'), *n.* doubt: *v.t. & v.i.* to doubt. —mis-trust'ful, *adj.*

mist-y (mis'ti), *adj.* mist'i-er, mist'i-est, 1. of, characterized by, or obscured with mist. 2. dimmed; clouded. —mist'i-ly, *adv.*

mis-un-der-stand (mis-un-dēr-stand'), *v.t.* -stood', -stand'ing, to take in a wrong sense; misconceive.

mis-un-der-stand-ing (-stan'ding), *n.* 1. misconception. 2. a disagreement.

mis-use (mis-ūz'), *v.t.* -used', -us'ing, 1. to put to a wrong use. 2. to hurt; mistreat: *n.* (-ūs'), wrong use.

mite (mīt), *n.* 1. a minute arachnid, often living on animals and plants as a parasite. 2. a very small object or quantity of money.

mi-ter (mīt'ēr), *n.* 1. the headdress of the ancient high priest of the Jews. 2. a kind of ornamental headdress worn by bishops, abbots, and the pope as a sign of the office. 3. the office of a bishop. 4. the junction of moldings at an angle: also miter joint: *v.t.* 1. to adorn with a miter. 2. to match or join moldings in a miter.

miter box, a contrivance for cutting strips of wood to an angle forming a miter joint.

mit-i-gate (mit'l-gāt), *v.t. & v.i.* -gat-ed, -gat-ing, to render less severe, rigorous, or painful;

soften; alleviate. —mit-i-ga'tion, *n.* —mit'i-ga-tive, *adj.* —mit'i-ga-tor, *n.* —mit'i-ga-to-ry (-gā-tôr-i), *adj.*

mi-to-sis (mī-tō'sis), *n., pl.* -ses ('sēz), the complex process of multiplication of animal or vegetable cells.

mi-tral (mī'trǎl), *adj.* of, pertaining to, or shaped like a miter.

mi-tre (mīt'ēr), *n. & v.t.* -tred, -tring, British spelling of miter.

mitt (mit), *n.* 1. a heavily padded baseball glove. 2. a boxing glove. 3. a glove worn by a woman over a portion of the arm, hand, and sometimes a portion of the fingers. 4. [Slang], a hand.

mit-ten (mit'n), *n.* a glove with no separate divisions for the fingers.

mit-ti-mus (mit'i-mùs), *n.* in *Law,* a warrant of commitment to prison.

mix (miks), *v.t.* mixed or mixt, mix'ing, 1. to unite or blend into one mass or compound. 2. to produce by blending. 3. to join: *v.i.* 1. to become united in a compound. 2. to associate; mingle: *n.* 1. that which is produced by mixing. 2. a liquid combined with alcoholic liquor. —mix'er, *n.*

mixed (mikst), *adj.* 1. made up of different parts or elements. 2. blended; compounded. 3. confused; muddled.

mixed marriage, a union of persons of different race or religion.

mixed number, the sum of an integer and a fraction.

mix-ture (miks'chēr), *n.* 1. the state of being mixed. 2. a mass formed by mixing. 3. in *Chemistry,* a mass in which the particles of each ingredient retain their properties.

mix-up (miks'up), *n.* disorder; jumble.

miz-zen, miz-en (miz'n), *n.* the hindmost of the fore-and-aft sails of a vessel.

miz-zen-mast (-mâst, -mast), *n.* the hindmost mast on a vessel.

mne-mon-ic (ni-mon'ik), *adj.* assisting the memory.

mne-mon-ics ('iks), *n.* the art of developing and improving the memory.

mo-a (mō'ä), *n.* a huge, extinct, ostrichlike bird of New Zealand, that had wings not adapted to flight.

moan (mōn), *v.i. & v.t.* 1. to utter or say with a low sound as a result of pain or sorrow. 2. to complain (about): *n.* a low, prolonged expression of sorrow or pain.

moat (mōt), *n.* a deep ditch, often containing water, as around a fortress: *v.t.* to surround with a moat.

mob (mob), *n.* 1. the populace: a derisive term. 2. a rude, disorderly crowd; riotous assembly; rabble. 3. any crowd. 4. [Slang], a criminal group: *v.t.* mobbed, mob'bing, 1. to attack in a disorderly crowd. 2. to crowd about and annoy.

mo-bile (mō'bl, 'bil), *adj.* 1. easily moved. 2. that can be transported by a truck, car, etc. 3. quickly changeable; flexible. 4. denoting flexibility in change of social rank: *n.* a moving, suspended piece of abstract art. —mo-bil-i-ty (mō-bil'i-ti), *n.*

mobile home, a long trailer furnished like a home.

mo·bi·lize (mō'bi-līz), *v.t.* **-lized, -liz·ing,** to make (soldiers, etc.) ready for active service; prepare to take part in warfare, etc. **—mo·bi·li·za'tion,** *n.*

mob·oc·ra·cy (mob-ok'rǎ-si), *n., pl.* **-cies,** the rule or ascendancy of the mob.

mob·ster (mob'stēr), *n.* [Slang], same as **gang·ster.**

moc·ca·sin (mok'ǎ-sn), *n.* 1. a slipper without a heel, as that worn by the North American Indians. 2. same as **water moccasin.** 3. a slipper with a heel.

mo·cha (mō'kǎ), *n.* 1. a kind of coffee, first grown in Arabia. 2. a soft kind of leather: *adj.* having a coffee or coffee-and-chocolate flavor.

mock (mok), *v.t.* 1. to ridicule; deride. 2. to mimic in sport or derision. 3. to disappoint the hopes of; tantalize. 4. to frustrate: *v.i.* to be derisive (often with *at*): *n.* derision; ridicule: *adj.* false; counterfeit.

mock·er·y ('ēr-i), *n., pl.* **-er·ies,** 1. derision; ridicule. 2. the object of this. 3. an insulting imitation.

mock·ing·bird (mok'ing-bûrd), *n.* an American bird noted for mimicry of the notes of other birds.

mock-up (mok'up), *n.* a model constructed in the same relative dimensions or of the same size as a device, building, etc.

mod (mod), *adj.* [also M-], in a fashion or style characteristic of the 1960's.

mod·al (mōd'l), *adj.* of or pertaining to mode or form; indicating some mode of expression.

mo·dal·i·ty (mō-dal'i-ti), *n., pl.* **-ties,** in *Logic,* the qualification in a proposition which asserts or denies possibility; expression of a sequence of necessity or contingency.

mode (mōd), *n.* 1. form; manner. 2. custom; fashion; style. 3. in *Grammar,* same as **mood.** 4. in *Logic,* the connection between antecedent and consequent.

mod·el (mod'l), *n.* 1. a pattern of something to be made or reproduced. 2. an example for imitation. 3. a standard copy. 4. a person who poses as a subject for a painter, sculptor, etc. 5. a mannequin; person employed to demonstrate fashions: *adj.* 1. serving as a pattern or model. 2. typical of a class, style, etc.: *v.t.* **-eled** or **-elled, -el·ing** or **-el·ling,** 1. to form after a model (of). 2. to form in some plastic material. 3. to demonstrate by wearing for inspection: *v.i.* to make or be a model. **—mod'el·er, mod'el·ler,** *n.*

mod·er·ate (mod'ě-rāt), *v.t.* **-at·ed, -at·ing,** 1. to keep within bounds; lessen; qualify. 2. to preside over: *v.i.* 1. to become less violent or intense. 2. to preside as a moderator: *adj.* ('ēr-it), 1. kept within bounds; not extreme or excessive; restrained. 2. calm; reasonable; mild. 3. average; medium: *n.* a person of reasonable views or opinions in politics or religion. **—mod'er·ate·ly,** *adv.*

mod·er·a·tion (mod-ě-rā'shǔn), *n.* 1. the act of moderating. 2. the state of being moderate. 3. freedom from excess. 4. equanimity.

mod·er·a·tor (mod'ě-rāt-ēr), *n.* 1. one that moderates. 2. the presiding officer of a meeting, church assembly, etc.

mod·ern (mod'ērn), *adj.* 1. of or pertaining to the present time; recent. 2. [often M-], of or denoting the present language type: *n.* a person of modern times. **—mo·der·ni·ty** (mo-dûr'ni-ti), *n.*

mod·ern·ism (-izm), *n.* 1. the state of being characteristically modern, as distinguished from that of olden or classical times. 2. [often M-], a system of philosophy or theology which endeavors to reconcile the teachings of the Church with the discoveries of modern science. **—mod'ern·ist,** *n.* & *adj.* **—mod·ern·is'tic,** *adj.*

mod·ern·ize (mod'ēr-nīz), *v.t.* **-ized, -iz·ing,** to render or become modern in usage or taste. **—mod·ern·i·za'tion,** *n.*

mod·est (mod'ist), *adj.* 1. restrained by a due sense of propriety. 2. diffident. 3. decent. 4. reasonable. **—mod'est·ly,** *adv.* **—mod'es·ty,** *n.*

mod·i·cum (mod'i-kúm), *n.* a little bit.

mod·i·fy (mod'i-fī), *v.t.* **-fied, -fy·ing,** 1. to change slightly in form; vary. 2. to reduce slightly. 3. in *Grammar,* to qualify. **—mod·i·fi·ca'tion,** *n.* **—mod'i·fi·er,** *n.*

mod·ish (mōd'ish), *adj.* in the current fashion. **—mod'ish·ness,** *n.*

mod·u·lar (moj'ū·lēr), *adj.* of or pertaining to modules.

mod·u·late (-lāt), *v.t.* **-lat·ed, -lat·ing,** 1. to modify, adjust, etc. 2. to change the pitch of (the voice). 3. in *Radio,* to change the frequency of (oscillations): *v.i.* to pass from one musical key to another. **—mod·u·la'tion,** *n.* **—mod'u·la·tor,** *n.*

mod·ule (moj'ōōl), *n.* 1. a basic measuring unit. 2. one of a standard type that is designed to be combined with others. 3. a section having a specific use, that can be separated from a main unit.

mo·fette, mof·fette (mō-fet'), *n.* an emanation of noxious gases from an opening in the earth or from a fissure.

mo·gul (mō'gul), *n.* a person of great wealth or influence.

mo·hair (mō'her), *n.* 1. the hair of the Angora goat. 2. a fabric made from this.

Mo·ham·med (mō-ham'id), *n.* an Arabian prophet (570-632), founder of the Moslem religion.

Mo·ham·med·an (mō-ham'i-dn), *adj.* of or pertaining to Mohammed or to the Moslem religion: *n.* same as **Moslem. —Mo·ham'med·an·ism,** *n.*

moi·e·ty (moi'ě-ti), *n., pl.* **-ties,** 1. one of two equal parts or shares; half. 2. a part or share.

moil (moil), *v.i.* to toil; drudge.

moire (mwor, môr), *n.* any textile fabric to which a watered appearance has been given: also **moi·ré** (mwo-rā', mô-).

moist (moist), *adj.* containing water or other liquid; damp. **—moist'ly,** *adv.* **—moist'ness,** *n.*

mois·ten (mois'n), *v.t.* & *v.i.* to make or become moist.

mois·ture ('chēr), *n.* a moderate degree of dampness; slight wetness.

---

mois·tur·ize (-īz), *v.t.* & *v.i.* **-ized, -iz·ing,** to cause to be moist. —**mois'tur·iz·er,** *n.*

mo·lar (mō'lẽr), *n.* a tooth for grinding: *adj.* used for or capable of grinding.

mo·las·ses (mō-las'iz), *n.* a brown syrup drained from sugar in the process of refining.

mold (mōld), *n.* 1. fine, soft earth, rich in organic matter. 2. a minute growth on decaying or damp organic matter, caused by fungi. 3. the fungus causing the growth. 4. a matrix or hollow in which something is shaped. 5. that on which anything is modeled. 6. a model; pattern. 7. a particular character or nature: *v.t.* 1. to form into a particular shape. 2. to form on a mold. 3. to ornament with molding. 4. to cover with mold: *v.i.* to be covered with mold.

mold·board (mōld'bôrd), *n.* a curved section on a plowshare, for breaking up earth.

mold·er (mōl'dẽr), *v.i.* to crumble to dust; waste away.

mold·ing (mōl'ding), *n.* 1. the act of one that molds. 2. anything made in or by a mold. 3. an ornamental strip, as on a wall.

mold·y (mōl'di), *adj.* **-i·er, -i·est,** 1. covered with mold. 2. smelling from decay. —**mold'i·ness,** *n.*

mole (mōl), *n.* 1. a dark-colored mark or small protuberance on the skin. 2. a fleshy mass generated in the uterus. 3. a small, soft-furred, burrowing animal. 4. a breastwork of masonry, etc. serving to protect a harbor from the violence of the waves; breakwater.

mo·lec·u·lar (mō-lek'yū-lẽr), *adj.* of, pertaining to, consisting of, produced by, or existing between molecules. —**mo·lec·u·lar'i·ty** (-lẽr'ĭ-tī), *n.*

mol·e·cule (mol'ĕ-kūl), *n.* 1. the smallest quantity of an element or compound which can exist separately and still retain the properties and character of the mass from which it is separated. 2. any very minute particle.

mole·hill (mōl'hil), *n.* a little ridge thrown up by moles burrowing underground.

mole·skin ('skin), *n.* 1. a mole's skin. 2. a twilled, fustian cloth with a soft surface.

mo·lest (mō-lest'), *v.t.* 1. to annoy or interfere with; trouble; vex. 2. to approach unsuitably for sexual reasons. —**mo·les·ta·tion** (mō-les-tā'shǔn), *n.*

moll (mol), *n.* [Slang], a gang member's mistress.

mol·les·cent (mō-les'nt), *adj.* softening or having a tendency to soften. —**mol·les'cence,** *n.*

mol·li·fy (mol'ĭ-fī), *v.t.* **-fied, -fy·ing,** 1. to calm; assuage. 2. to soften. —**mol'li·fi·er,** *n.*

mol·lusc (mol'ǔsk), *n.* same as **mollusk.** —**mol·lus·can** (mō-lus'kǎn), *adj.* & *n.*

mol·lusk (mol'ǔsk), *n.* an invertebrate animal with a soft, fleshy body, covered completely or partly with a calcareous shell, as the snail, shellfish, etc. —**mol·lus·kan** (mō-lus'kǎn), *adj.* & *n.*

mol·ly·cod·dle (mol'ĭ-kod-l), *n.* a male accustomed to being indulged and protected: *v.t.* **-dled, -dling,** to indulge; pamper.

Mo·loch (mō'lok, mol'ǒk), *n.* 1. the god of the ancient Phoenicians and Ammonites to whom human sacrifices were offered. 2. [*m-*], a spiny Australian lizard.

molt (mōlt), *v.i.* to cast off feathers, hair, skin, etc., before the process of renewing them.

mol·ten (mōl'tn), *adj.* 1. melted. 2. made of material melted and then molded.

mo·lyb·de·num (mō-lib'dē-nǔm), *n.* a silver-white metallic element.

mom (mom), *n.* [Informal], mother.

mo·ment (mō'měnt), *n.* 1. a small portion of time; instant. 2. importance; value. 3. a particular time. 4. a short time of fame. 5. the product of a force and the perpendicular of its line of action from the point on which it acts.

mo·men·tar·i·ly (mō-měn-ter'ĭ-lī), *adv.* 1. for a moment. 2. from moment to moment. 3. in a moment.

mo·men·tar·y (mō'měn-ter-i), *adj.* lasting only for, or done in, a moment.

mo·men·tous (mō-men'tǔs), *adj.* very important.

mo·men·tum (mō-men'tǔm), *n.,* *pl.* **-tums, -ta** ('tă), the impetus of a moving body, equal to the product of its mass and its velocity.

mom·my (mom'ī), *n.,* *pl.* **-mies,** same as **mother:** used by a child.

mo·nad (mō'nad), *n.* 1. a simple, primary constituent. 2. an elementary organism or cell. 3. a simple flagellated protozoan. 4. in *Chemistry,* an atom or radical with a valence of one. 5. in *Philosophy,* an ultimate unit.

mo·nan·dry (mō-nan'dri), *n.* the practice of having only one husband at a time.

mon·arch (mon'ẽrk), *n.* 1. a supreme ruler; sovereign. 2. a hereditary ruler. 3. the chief of its class or kind.

mo·nar·chi·cal (mō-när'ki-kl), *adj.* 1. of or pertaining to a monarch or a monarchy. 2. vested in a monarch. Also **mo·nar'chic.**

mon·arch·ism (mon'ẽr-kizm), *n.* the principles of or preference for monarchy. —**mon'arch·ist,** *n.* & *adj.*

mon·arch·y (mon'ẽr-ki), *n.,* *pl.* **-arch·ies,** government in which the supreme power, either absolute or limited, is vested in a monarch.

mon·as·ter·y (mon'ǎ-stēr-i), *n.,* *pl.* **-ter·ies,** a residence for monks or nuns. —**mon·as·te'ri·al** (-stīr'i-ăl), *adj.*

mo·nas·tic (mō-nas'tik), *adj.* of, pertaining to, or like monasteries, monks, their rules, etc.: also **mo·nas'ti·cal.**

mo·nas·ti·cism ('ti-sizm), *n.* the way of life of a monk.

mon·au·ral (mon-ôr'ăl), *adj.* monophonic.

Mon·day (mun'di, 'dā), *n.* the second day of the week.

mon·e·tar·y (mon'ĕ-ter-i), *adj.* 1. of or pertaining to money. 2. of or pertaining to the currency of a nation.

mon·e·tize (-tīz), *v.t.* **-tized, -tiz·ing,** 1. to convert into money. 2. to give standard or current value to. —**mon·e·ti·za'tion,** *n.*

mon·ey (mun'i), *n.,* *pl.* **-eys, -ies,** 1. coin; specie; gold, silver, or other metal stamped by legal authority and used as currency. 2. any currency used as money. 3. wealth.

mon·ey·bag (-bag), *n.* 1. a bag for carrying money. 2. *pl.* [Informal], a person of great wealth.

money belt, a belt with a hiding place for money.

mon·eyed (mun'id), *adj.* wealthy.

mon·ey·mak·er (mun'i-mā-kēr), *n.* 1. a person who is accomplished at getting money. 2. that which produces profits. —**mon'ey·mak·ing**, *adj. & n.*

money order, an order for the payment of money, issued at a post office or bank and payable at another.

money market, the short-term system for lending and borrowing funds, especially for governments and large corporations.

Mon·gol (mong'gŏl, '-gōl), *adj. & n.* same as Mongolian.

Mon·go·li·an (mong-gō'li-ån), *adj.* 1. of or pertaining to Mongolia, a region in east central Asia, or its inhabitants. 2. same as **Mongoloid**. 3. same as **Mongolic**: *n.* 1. a native or inhabitant of Mongolia. 2. same as **Mongoloid**. 3. same as **Mongolic**.

Mon·gol·ic (mong-gol'ik), *adj.* of or denoting a group of languages spoken in Mongolia: *n.* one of these languages.

Mon·gol·oid (mong'gŏ-loid), *adj.* 1. of or pertaining to the Mongolians. 2. of or denoting one of the great divisions of mankind comprising most Asian peoples: *n.* a member of the Mongoloid division.

mon·goose (mong'gōōs), *n., pl.* -**goos·es**, an old-world mammal resembling a weasel, that can overcome snakes, rats, etc.

mon·grel (mung'grĕl, mong'grĕl), *adj.* of a mixed breed or kind: *n.* anything of a mixed breed or kind, as a dog.

mon·ied (mun'id), *adj.* same as moneyed.

mon·i·ker, mon·ick·er (mon'i-kēr), *n.* [Slang], a name.

mo·nism (mō'nizm, mon'izm), *n.* 1. a doctrine of the unity of substance, as one identifying matter and mind. 2. a theory that all phenomena are derived from a single ultimate agent. —**mo'nist**, *n.* —**mo·nis'tic**, *adj.*

mo·ni·tion (mō-nish'ŭn), *n.* 1. admonition; warning. 2. a notice. —**mon·i·to·ry** (mon'i-tōr-i), *adj.*

mon·i·tor (mon'i-tēr), *n.* 1. something that warns. 2. a pupil selected to assist the teacher. 3. a control for machines, missiles, etc. 4. a kind of lizard. 5. in *Radio & TV*, a receiver for verifying a broadcast level: *v.t. & v.i.* to regulate, observe, etc. —**mon·i·to·ri·al** (-tōr'i-ål), *adj.*

monk (mungk), *n.* a man who devotes himself exclusively to a religious life and lives together with others similarly bound by vows of chastity, obedience, and poverty. —**monk'ish**, *adj.*

mon·key (mung'ki), *n., pl.* -**keys**, 1. any primate except a man or lemur. 2. a person resembling a monkey: a term of ridicule. 3. any of various tools, implements, etc.: *v.i.* [Informal], to tamper, interfere, or toy (often with *around, with,* etc.).

monkey business, [Informal], silliness, tricks, or vexation.

monkey jacket, [Informal], a short, close-fitting jacket.

mon·key·shines (-shīnz), *n.pl.,* [Informal], tricks, jokes, etc.

monkey wrench, a wrench with a sliding jaw which can be regulated to fit various sizes of bolts and nuts.

monks·hood (mungks'hood), *n.* a poisonous plant with blue, purple, or yellow hoodlike flowers.

mon·o (mon'ō), *n.* a shortened form of mononucleosis.

mon·o-, a prefix meaning *one, single, alone.*

mon·o·bas·ic (mon-ō-bā'sik), *adj.* having but one hydrogen atom capable of replacement: said of certain acids.

mon·o·chrome (mon'ō-krōm), *n.* a painting, drawing, etc. in one color.

mon·o·cle (mon'ō-kl), *n.* an eyeglass for one eye.

mo·noc·u·lar (mō-nok'yŭ-lēr), *adj.* 1. adapted for use for one eye. 2. having only one eye.

mon·o·dra·ma (mon'ō-drä-må), *n.* a drama written to be acted by one person.

mon·o·dy (mon'ō-di), *n., pl.* -**dies**, a plaintive poem or song for one voice.

mo·nog·a·my (mō-nog'å-mi), *n.* 1. marriage to one person at a time. 2. in *Zoology*, pairing with a single mate. —**mo·nog'a·mist**, *n.* —**mo·nog'a·mous**, *adj.*

mon·o·gen·e·sis (mon-ō-jen'ē-sis), *n.* 1. in *Biology*, the theory that all life is developed from a single cell. 2. in *Zoology*, asexual reproduction.

mon·o·gram (mon'ō-gram), *n.* a character formed by the interweaving of two or more letters.

mon·o·graph (mon'ō-graf), *n.* a paper or treatise written on one particular subject or some branch of it.

mon·o·lith (mon'ō-lith), *n.* 1. a pillar or column formed of a single stone. 2. a large, strong, unbending thing. —**mon·o·lith'ic**, *adj.*

mon·o·logue, mon·o·log (mon'ō-lôg), *n.* 1. a lengthy tale. 2. a dramatic scene in which one person only speaks; soliloquy. 3. a drama written for one person.

mon·o·ma·ni·a (mon-ō-mā'ni-å), *n.* 1. zeal or fervor in a single area. 2. mental derangement in regard to one subject only. —**mon·o·ma'ni·ac** (-må'ni-ak), *n.* —**mon·o·ma·ni'a·cal** (-må-nī'å-kl), *adj.*

mon·o·met·al·lism (mon-ō-met'l-izm), *n.* the legalized use of one metal only as currency.

mon·o·nu·cle·o·sis (mon-ō-nōō-klī-ō'sis), *n.* a severe disease of youth causing fever, swollen lymph nodes, etc.

mo·noph·a·gous (mō-nof'å-gŭs), *adj.* in *Biology*, partaking of but one kind of food.

mon·o·pho·bi·a (mon-ō-fō'bi-å), *n.* a morbid dread of being alone.

mon·o·phon·ic (mon-ō-fon'ik), *adj.* of or pertaining to the duplication of sound by means of a single channel source.

mon·oph·thong (mon'ōf-thông), *n.* a simple vowel sound in which the vocal organs do not change position.

mon·o·phyl·lous (mon-ō-fil'ŭs), *adj.* in *Botany*, having but one leaf.

ŏ in drag*o*n, ōō in crude, ∞ in wool, u in cup, ū in cure, û in turn, ŭ in focus, · oi in boy, ou in house, th in thin, th in sheathe, g in get, j in joy, y in yet.

mon·o·plane (mon'ŏ-plān), *n.* an airplane with a single set of wings.

mon·o·ple·gi·a (mon-ŏ-plē'ji-á), *n.* paralysis affecting a single limb or part of the body.

mon·o·pode (mon'ŏ-pōd), *adj.* having one foot.

mo·nop·o·list (mŏ-nop'ŏ-list), *n.* one who has a monopoly, supports monopoly, or monopolizes. —**mo·nop·o·lis'tic,** *adj.*

mo·nop·o·lize (-līz), *v.t.* **-lized, -liz·ing,** 1. to acquire the possession of, so as to be the only seller. 2. to engross the whole of.

mo·nop·o·ly (-li), *n., pl.* **-lies,** 1. complete power over the sale of a product or service in a particular area, as that authority extended by a government. 2. that which is controlled as a monopoly. 3. a business concern which retains a monopoly.

mon·o·rail (mon'ŏ-rāl), *n.* a single rail serving as a track for vehicles.

mon·o·syl·la·ble (mon'ŏ-sil-à-bl), *n.* a word of one syllable. —**mon·o·syl·lab'ic** (-si-lab'ik), *adj.*

mon·o·the·ism (mon'ŏ-thē-izm), *n.* the doctrine of, or belief in, the existence of one God. —**mon·o·the·is'tic,** *adj.*

mon·o·tone (mon'ŏ-tōn), *n.* 1. speech in an unchanging pitch or key. 2. an unvarying tone, style, color, etc. 3. recitation on a single note or pitch.

mo·not·o·nous (mŏ-not'n-ŭs), *adj.* 1. continued in the same unvarying tone. 2. unvarying. 3. wearisome because of this. —**mo·not'o·ny,** *n.*

mon·o·treme (mon'ŏ-trēm), *n.* any of the lowest order of mammals, the only existing representatives of which are the duckbill and echidna.

Mon·o·type (mon'ŏ-tīp), *n.* a machine that sets type by casting single letters instead of lines of words: a trademark.

mon·o·va·lent (mon-ŏ-vā'lĕnt), *adj.* having one valence or having a valence of one.

mon·ox·ide (mŏ-nok'sīd), *n.* an oxide having one atom of oxygen in each molecule.

Mon·sei·gneur (môn-sen-yūr'), *n., pl.* **Mes·sei·gneurs** (mes-en-yūrz'), a title in France given to persons of high birth, as princes, or high church rank, as bishops.

mon·sieur (mô-syūr'), *n., pl.* **mes·sieurs** (mes'ĕrz), a man; gentleman: French title [M-], equivalent to *Sir* or *Mr.*

Mon·si·gnor (mon-sēn'yĕr), *n.* an ecclesiastical title conferred on distinguished clerics of the Roman Catholic Church.

mon·soon (mon-sōōn'), *n.* 1. a periodical wind in the Indian Ocean blowing from the southwest from April to October, and from the northeast during the other part of the year. 2. the season of heavy rains from April to October.

mon·ster (mon'stĕr), *n.* 1. anything out of the usual course of nature, as from the imagination. 2. something greatly deformed. 3. a person remarkable for extreme wickedness, cruelty, etc. 4. anything of unusual size: *adj.* of unusual size; very large.

mon·strance (mon'stráns), *n.* in the *Roman Catholic Church,* the receptacle in which the consecrated Host is exposed for the adoration of the faithful.

mon·stros·i·ty (mon-stros'ĭ-ti), *n.* 1. the state or quality of being monstrous. 2. *pl.* **-ties,** an unnatural production.

mon·strous (mon'strŭs), *adj.* 1. out of the common course of nature; deformed. 2. huge; enormous. 3. horrible. 4. dreadfully incorrect or depraved.

mon·tage (mon-tāzh'), *n.* 1. in *motion pictures,* a quick fading from one scene to another in which part of both are simultaneously visible, used for effect. 2. in *still photography,* the printing of several negatives on one sheet so that parts of one picture are visible through others.

mon·te (mon'ti), *n.* a Spanish card game in which players gamble on the colors of cards turned up.

month (munth), *n.* 1. one of the twelve divisions of the calendar year. 2. a revolution of the moon. 3. a duration of 30 days or 4 weeks. 4. one of the twelve parts of a solar year.

month·ly (munth'li), *adj.* 1. continued, performed, or happening in a month. 2. that can be paid every month: *adv.* once each month: *n., pl.* **-lies,** a magazine or periodical published each month.

mon·u·ment (mon'yŭ-mĕnt), *n.* 1. anything that perpetuates the memory of a person or event. 2. a structure erected as a memorial of some past occurrence. 3. something of continuing importance.

mon·u·men·tal (mon-yŭ-men'tl), *adj.* 1. of, pertaining to, or serving as a monument. 2. lasting; permanent.

moo (mōō), *v.i.* **mooed, moo'ing,** to make the sound of a cow; low: *n., pl.* **moos,** the lowing of a cow.

mooch (mōōch), *v.t. & v.i.* [Slang], to obtain by entreaty or sponging.

mood (mōōd), *n.* 1. style; manner. 2. temper of mind. 3. variation in the form of a verb to express the manner of action or being. 4. in *Logic,* same as mode.

mood·y (mōō'di), *adj.* **mood'i·er, mood'i·est,** abstracted and pensive; out of temper; sad; gloomy. —**mood'i·ly,** *adv.* —**mood'i·ness,** *n.*

moon (mōōn), *n.* 1. the satellite that revolves around the earth. 2. a satellite of a planet. 3. something in the form of a moon, as a crescent: *v.i.* to wander and look about in an abstracted and listless manner.

moon·beam (mōōn'bēm), *n.* a thin line of light from the moon.

moon blindness, inflammation of the eyes of a horse, usually resulting in blindness.

moon·calf ('kaf), *n.* a stupid person; dolt; idiot.

moon·fish ('fish), *n., pl.* **-fish, -fish·es,** a flat fish of silvery or yellow hue found in the waters along the coast of North and South America.

moon·light ('līt), *n.* light from the moon.

moon·light·ing ('līt-ing), *n.* working at another job in addition to one's regular job.

moon·lit ('lit), *adj.* illuminated by moonlight.

moon·quake ('kwāk), *n.* a shaking of the surface of the moon caused by the impact of meteorites or the movement of rock beneath the surface.

---

a in *cap,* ā in *cane,* ä in *father,* à in *abet,* e in *met,* ē in *be,* ē in *baker,* ĕ in *regent,* I in *pit,* ī in *fine,* i in *manifest,* o in *hot,* ô in *horse,* ō in *bone,*

moon-scape ('skăp), *n.* the moon's surface or a picture of it.

moon-shine ('shīn), *n.* 1. same as **moonlight**. 2. foolishness. 3. [Informal], whiskey that has been smuggled or illegally distilled.

moon-shin-er ('shī-nẽr), *n.* [Informal], a distiller and seller of illegal whiskey.

moon-shot ('shot), *n.* the sending of a rocket or spacecraft to the moon.

moon-stone ('stōn), *n.* a translucent stone of a whitish color, exhibiting pearly reflections.

moon-struck ('struk), *adj.* 1. lunatic; deranged. 2. in a romantic reverie.

moon-wort ('wũrt), *n.* a fern with crescent-shaped fronds.

moon-y ('i), *adj.* **moon'i-er**, **moon'i-est**, 1. crescent-shaped. 2. weakly sentimental; mooning.

Moor (moor), *n.* one of a group of Moslem people dwelling in northwestern Africa. — **Moor'ish**, *adj.*

moor (moor), *n.* an extensive tract of wasteland covered with heather, often marshy or peaty: *v.t.* 1. to secure (a ship) by a cable or anchor. 2. to make firm: *v.i.* to be secured by a cable or anchor.

moor-age ('moor'ij), *n.* a mooring place.

moor cock, [British], a male red grouse.

moor-ing ('ing), *n.* 1. the act of securing. 2. *often pl.* the cables, anchors, etc. laid at the bottom of a harbor, etc. to which a vessel is moored. 3. *pl.* the place where a vessel is moored.

moose (mōōs), *n., pl.* **moose**, a large animal of northern North America related to the deer.

moot (mōōt), *v.t.* to propose for discussion: *n.* a discussion on a supposed case: *adj.* 1. subject to or open for discussion or debate. 2. supposed; assumed.

moot court, a mock court in which law students try imaginary cases for practice.

mop (mop), *n.* 1. an instrument for washing floors, decks, etc., consisting of a bundle of cloth, rags, etc. fastened to the end of a long handle. 2. any loose bunch or tangle, as of hair: *v.t.* **mopped**, **mop'ping**, to rub or dry with a mop.

mope (mōp), *v.i.* **moped**, **mop'ing**, to be dull or dispirited. — **mop'ey**, **mop'y**, **mop'ish**, *adj.*

mop-pet (mop'it), *n.* [Informal], a small child.

mo-quette (mō-ket'), *n.* a kind of carpet or heavy upholstery fabric having the surface dotted with tufts of soft yarn.

mo-raine (mō-rān'), *n.* a line of rocks and gravel at the edges and base of glaciers.

mor-al (mōr'ăl), *adj.* 1. of or pertaining to morality or morals. 2. conforming to right; virtuous. 3. subject to or influenced by moral law. 4. serving to teach a moral. 5. practically sufficient. 6. extremely likely. 7. in accord but not with active support: *n.* 1. an inner meaning; the lesson or truth taught by or derived from a fable. 2. *pl.* moral philosophy or ethics; conduct of life. 3. *pl.* standards of sexual behavior. — **mor'al-ly**, *adv.*

mo-rale (mō-ral'), *n.* moral condition; mental state which renders one capable of endurance and of exhibiting courage in the presence of danger, hardship, etc.

mo-ral-i-ty (mō-ral'ĭ-tĭ), *n., pl.* **-ties**, 1. the doctrine or practice of ethics. 2. ethics. 3. virtue in sexual behavior. 4. moral conduct. 5. a kind of allegorical play.

mor-al-ize (mōr'ă-līz), *v.t.* **-ized**, **-iz-ing**, 1. to apply or explain in a moral sense. 2. to render moral: *v.i.* to make reflections on good and evil, often in a tiresome way. — **mor'al-ist**, *n.* — **mor-al-is'tic**, *adj.*

moral philosophy, same as **ethics**.

mo-rass (mō-ras'), *n.* a swamp; fen.

mor-a-to-ri-um (môr-ă-tōr'ĭ-ŭm), *n., pl.* **-ri-ums**, **-ri-a** (-ă), 1. a legalized right to postpone payment of a debt after it would otherwise fall due. 2. a legalized postponement of any pursuit.

mor-a-to-ry (môr'ă-tōr-ĭ), *adj.* in *Law*, of or pertaining to delay; also, denoting a law granting a moratorium.

Mo-ra-vi-an (mō-rā'vi-ăn), *adj.* 1. of or pertaining to Moravia, a region in Czechoslovakia, or its inhabitants. 2. of or pertaining to a Protestant religious sect, the Moravians: *n.* 1. a native or inhabitant of Moravia. 2. one of a Protestant religious sect founded by Moravians.

mo-ray (mō-rā'), *n.* a bright-colored eel found in warm seas.

mor-bid (môr'bid), *adj.* 1. of or pertaining to disease; sickly; unhealthy. 2. produced by a deranged mind. 3. horrible. — **mor-bid'i-ty**, *n.* — **mor'bid-ly**, *adv.*

mor-bif-ic (môr-bif'ik), *adj.* producing disease.

mor-ceau (môr-sō'), *n., pl.* **-ceaux** (-sō'), [French], a small piece; morsel.

mor-dant (môr'dnt), *adj.* 1. biting into surfaces or fixing colors. 2. sarcastic; caustic: *n.* 1. a substance that has a chemical affinity for coloring matter and serves to fix certain colors in dyeing. 2. a corroding substance used in etching.

more (môr), *adj.* superlative **most**, 1. greater in number, quality, extent, etc. 2. additional: *adv.* superlative **most**, 1. to a greater degree. 2. again; besides: *n.* 1. a greater quantity, number, etc. 2. something further or additional.

mo-reen (mō-rēn'), *n.* a stout woolen or cotton fabric.

mo-rel (mō-rel'), *n.* a small mushroom used for food.

mo-rel-lo (mō-rel'ō), *n., pl.* **-los**, a dark-red cherry.

more-o-ver (môr-ō'vẽr), *adv.* besides; further.

mo-res (môr'iz, 'āz), *n.pl.* common standards of conduct which have taken on the quality of law.

Mo-resque (mō-resk'), *adj.* of a Moorish design: *n.* architectural decoration of interlacing, gilt, etc.

mor-ga-nat-ic (môr-gă-nat'ik), *adj.* denoting the marriage of a man of royal rank with a woman of inferior degree, whose children are legitimate but cannot inherit their father's rank or possessions.

morgue (môrg), *n.* 1. a place where bodies of dead persons are kept temporarily for identification, autopsy, etc. 2. a library of materials including old issues, kept by a newspaper, magazine, etc.

ô in dragon, ōō in crude, oo in wool, u in cup, ū in cure, ũ in turn, ủ in focus, oi in boy, ou in house, th in thin, th in sheathe, g in get, j in joy, y in yet.

mor·i·bund (môr'i-bund), *adj.* dying; at the point of death.

mo·ri·on (môr'i-on), *n.* 1. an open helmet without beaver or visor. 2. a black variety of quartz.

Mor·mon (môr'mŭn), *n.* one of a sect organized in 1830 as the Church of Jesus Christ of Latter-day Saints, called the *Mormon Church.* —**Mor'mon·ism,** *n.*

morn (môrn), *n.* [Poetic], same as **morning.**

morn·ing (môr'ning), *n.* the early part of the day from dawn (or sometimes midnight) to noon: *adj.* of, pertaining to, occurring, or performed in the morning.

morning glory, a twining vine with large trumpet-shaped pink, purple, or white flowers.

Mo·ro (môr'ō), *n.* 1. a member of one of the Moslem tribes of the Philippines. 2. the language of these tribes.

mo·roc·co (mô·rŏ'kō), *n.* a fine kind of leather of goatskin or sharkskin.

mo·ron (môr'on), *n.* 1. a stupid person. 2. an adult whose mentality is that of a child between the ages of eight and 12: a term no longer used.

mo·rose (mô·rōs'), *adj.* sullen; gloomy. —**mo·rose'ness,** *n.*

mor·pheme (môr'fēm), *n.* the smallest meaningful unit in a language, as an affix.

mor·phine (môr'fēn), *n.* a white, crystalline alkaloid of opium used as an anodyne in medicine.

mor·phin·ism (môr'fin-izm), *n.* a morbid state occasioned by the excessive use of morphine.

mor·phol·o·gy (môr·fol'ō-ji), *n.* 1. a science that deals with form and structure, especially such a branch of biology. 2. the form and structure of something. —**mor·pho·log'i·cal** (-fô-loj'i-kl), *adj.*

mor·ris (môr'is), *n.* an old English folk dance.

Morris chair (môr'is), an easy chair with a back that can be inclined at any comfortable angle.

mor·ro (mor'ō), *n., pl.* **-ros** ('ōz), a hill having a round top.

mor·row (mor'ō), *n.* [Poetic], 1. the next day; day following the present. 2. morning.

Morse (môrs), *adj.* denoting a dot-and-dash system for telegraphing messages.

mor·sel (môr'sl), *n.* 1. a small piece. 2. a small bit of food.

mort (môrt), *n.* 1. a note sounded on a hunting horn to announce the death of game. 2. [Dial.], a great quantity or number.

mor·tal (môr'tl), *adj.* 1. subject to death. 2. causing death; fatal. 3. extreme. 4. tedious. 5. violent. 6. of or pertaining to human beings: *n.* a human being; a person, as subject to death. —**mor'tal·ly,** *adv.*

mor·tal·i·ty (môr·tal'i-ti), *n.* 1. the condition of being mortal. 2. mankind. 3. the frequency or number of deaths in ratio to population. 4. a large number of deaths, as from disease.

mor·tar (môr'tẽr), *n.* 1. a vessel in which substances are pounded with a pestle. 2. a short cannon used for throwing shells at high angles of elevation. 3. a building ce-

ment of lime, sand, and water: *v.t.* to plaster or secure with mortar.

mor·tar·board (-bôrd), *n.* 1. a small, square board with a short handle underneath, used for holding mortar by masons, bricklayers, plasterers, etc. 2. an academic cap having a broad, flat top in the form of a square.

mort·gage (môr'gij), *n.* 1. a conveying of property to a creditor as security for the payment of a debt. 2. the deed by which such a conveyance is made: *v.t.* **-gaged, -gag·ing,** 1. to convey or make over to a creditor as security; pledge. 2. to make liable ahead of time.

mort·ga·gee (môr·gȧ-jē'), *n.* the person to whom a mortgage is made or given.

mort·ga·gor, mort·gag·er (môr'gi-jẽr), *n.* the person who grants a mortgage.

mor·ti·cian (môr-tish'ȧn), *n.* a funeral director.

mor·ti·fi·ca·tion (môr-ti-fi-kā'shŭn), *n.* 1. the act of mortifying. 2. subjugation of the passions and appetites by abstinence. 3. a cause of humiliation, vexation, or chagrin.

mor·ti·fy (môr'ti-fī), *v.t.* **-fied, -fy·ing,** 1. to subdue by penance or austerities. 2. to humble; depress; chagrin: *v.i.* to be subdued; practice austerities.

mor·tise (môr'tis), *n.* a hole or space made in wood to receive a tenon: *v.t.* **-tised, -tis·ing,** to cut or make a mortise in.

mort·main (môrt'mān), *n.* 1. permanent transfer of lands or buildings to any corporate body. 2. inalienable tenure.

mor·tu·ar·y (môr'choo-wer-i), *n., pl.* **-ar·ies,** a building for the dead pending burial: *adj.* of or pertaining to the burial of the dead.

Mo·sa·ic (mō-zā'ik), *adj.* of or pertaining to Moses, the Law, institutions, etc. given through him, or his writings.

mo·sa·ic (mō-zā'ik), *adj.* of or pertaining to mosaic work: *n.* a design or type of artistic work formed by inlaying minute pieces of glass, stone, etc., of various colors, in a ground of mortar.

Mo·selle (mō-zel'), *n.* a white wine.

Mo·ses (mō'ziz), *n.* in the *Bible,* the giver of laws to the people he led out of Egypt and slavery.

Mos·lem (moz'lĕm), *adj.* of or pertaining to Islam or those believing in it: *n.* a believer in Islam.

mosque (mosk), *n.* a Moslem temple.

mos·qui·to (mŏ-skēt'ō), *n., pl.* **-toes, -to,** a two-winged insect, the female of which has a long proboscis with which it punctures the skin and extracts blood from animals.

moss (mos), *n.* 1. a green plant that grows in bunches on wet ground, rocks, etc. 2. a similar plant, as some lichens or algae: *v.t.* to cover with moss.

moss·bunk·er (môs'bung-kẽr), *n.* same as **menhaden.**

moss rose, a fragrant variety of rose with a mosslike calyx.

moss·y ('i), *adj.* **moss'i·er, moss'i·est,** covered with or abounding in moss.

most (mōst), *adj.* comparative **more,** 1. greatest in quantity or degree: superlative of **much.** 2. greatest in number: superlative of **many.** 3. in most cases: *n.* the greatest number, part, quantity, or value: *adv.* comparative more, in or to the greatest amount or intensity.

-most (mōst), a suffix that forms superlatives.

most-ly ('lĭ), *adv.* 1. for the greatest part. 2. principally. 3. generally.

mot (mō), *n.* a witty saying.

mote (mōt), *n.* a very small particle.

mo-tel (mō-tel'), *n.* a hotel for those journeying by automobile.

mo-tet (mō-tet'), *n.* a short vocal composition of a sacred character.

moth (môth), *n., pl.* **moths** (môthz, môths), a four-winged insect which is active at night and is related to the butterfly: one variety has a larva which feeds on cloth, fur, etc.

moth-ball (moth'bôl), *n.* a small lump of camphor or naphthalene which repels moths by its noxious odor.

moth-er (muth'ēr), *n.* 1. a female parent or ancestor. 2. one who has given birth to a child. 3. one who stands in the relation of a mother. 4. an elderly woman. 5. an origin or source. 6. the female superior of a religious house. 7. a thick, slimy substance that develops on liquids during fermentation: *adj.* 1. of or resembling a mother. 2. native. 3. producing others: *v.i.* 1. to give birth to. 2. to care for as a mother. —**moth'er-hood,** *n.* —**moth'er-less,** *adj.*

Mother Goose, the fictional originator of a group of nursery rhymes.

Mother Hub-bard (hub'ērd), 1. the subject of an old nursery rhyme. 2. a long, loose gown worn by women.

moth-er-in-law (-ĭn-lô), *n., pl.* **moth'ers-in-law,** the mother of one's husband or wife.

moth-er-land (-land), *n.* the land in which a person was born or from which his ancestors came.

moth-er-ly (-lĭ), *adj.* of or suited to a mother; maternal. —**moth'er-li-ness,** *n.*

Mother of God, the Virgin Mary.

moth-er-of-pearl (-ŏv-pûrl'), *n.* the hard, silvery internal layer of various kinds of shells, as of pearl oysters; nacre.

Mother's Day, in the U.S., the second Sunday in May, when mothers are honored.

mo-tif (mō-tēf'), *n.* a principal idea, theme, etc. worked out in a piece of music, literature, etc.

mo-tile (mōt'l), *adj.* in *Biology*, able to move naturally.

mo-tion (mō'shŭn), *n.* 1. the act, process, or state of moving; passage of a body from one place to another. 2. animal life and action. 3. impulse or desire. 4. bodily activity. 5. a proposition made in a deliberative assembly: *v.i.* to make a significant movement or gesture: *v.t.* to control by a bodily movement. —**mo'tion-less,** *adj.*

motion picture, 1. a connected series of pictures flashed on a screen in rapid succession by a projector, giving the effect of motion in the subject matter. 2. a story presented as a motion picture.

mo-ti-vate (mōt'ĭ-vāt), *v.t.* -vat-ed, -vat-ing, to urge or push on. —**mo-ti-va'tion,** *n.*

mo-tive (mōt'ĭv), *adj.* causing motion; able to move: *n.* 1. that which excites to action; inducement; stimulus. 2. same as motif.

-mo-tive (mōt'ĭv), a suffix meaning *moving.*

motive power, any agent, as wind, water, steam, electricity, etc. employed to produce motion, as in a machine.

mot-ley (mot'lĭ), *adj.* 1. covered with parts of various colors. 2. heterogeneous.

mot-mot (mot'mot), *n.* any of various groups of jaylike birds of tropical America.

mo-tor (mōt'ēr), *n.* 1. that which produces motion or power. 2. a machine which performs mechanical work, as an internal-combustion engine. 3. a machine for transmuting electrical energy into mechanical motion: *adj.* 1. giving motion. 2. of or given power by a motor. 3. of or used for motor vehicles. 4. of or utilizing motion by the muscles: *v.i.* to journey by motor vehicle.

mo-tor-boat (-bōt), *n.* a boat propelled by a gasoline or other marine motor.

mo-tor-cade (-kād), *n.* a parade of automobiles.

mo-tor-car (-kär), *n.* a vehicle propelled by means of petroleum, electricity, etc.

mo-tor-cy-cle (-sĭ-kl), *n.* a large, heavy bicycle propelled by a motor.

mo-tor-drome (-drōm), *n.* a course for automobile and motorcycle races or testing.

motor hotel, same as motel: also motor court, motor inn, motor lodge.

mo-tor-ist (-ĭst), *n.* one that drives an automobile or travels in an automobile.

mo-tor-ize (mōt'ō-rīz), *v.t.* -ized, -iz-ing, to supply with motor power.

mo-tor-man (mōt'ēr-mǎn), *n., pl.* -men (-mĕn), the operator of an electric passenger car.

motor vehicle, a vehicle propelled by an internal motor, as an automobile.

mot-tle (mot'l), *v.t.* -tled, -tling, to mark with spots of various colors; variegate. —**mot'tled,** *adj.*

mot-to (mot'ō), *n., pl.* -toes, -tos, a concise sentence or phrase suggesting some guiding principle, goal, etc.

mouf-lon, mouf-flon (mōōf'lon), *n., pl.* -lons, -lon, a wild, large-horned sheep of Corsica and Sardinia.

mould (mōld), *n. & v.t. & v.i.* chiefly British spelling of mold. —**mould'y,** *adj.* mould'i-er, mould'i-est.

mou-lin (mōō-lan'), *n.* a deep crack intersecting a glacier, into which water pours.

moult (mōlt), *v.i.* chiefly British spelling of molt.

mound (mound), *n.* 1. an artificial bank of earth or stone, as for defensive purposes. 2. a hillock. 3. a small globe surmounted by a cross, symbolic of empire: *v.t.* to gather in a mound.

Mound Builders, the early Indians who erected large earthen mounds in the Middle West and the Southeast.

mount (mount), *n.* 1. a hill or mountain. 2. the act of mounting. 3. a horse for mounting. 4. a backing or support on which something is fixed: *v.t.* 1. to raise on high. 2. to climb; ascend. 3. to bestride. 4. to furnish with horses. 5. to prepare for use by fixing on or in something else. 6. to prepare (a dead animal) for showing. 7. to arrange (a gun) for firing; v.i. 1. to rise up; tower; project. 2. to get on horseback. 3. to grow; multiply.

moun·tain (moun'tn), n. 1. a large mass of rock or earth rising above the level of the adjacent country. 2. anything very large: adj. of or pertaining to mountains.

mountain ash, a small tree or shrub related to the rose with bunches of white flowers and red berries.

moun·tain·eer (moun-tn-ir'), n. one who dwells among or climbs mountains: v.i. to climb mountains.

mountain goat, a thickset, white-haired antelope inhabiting the mountains of the northwestern U.S.

mountain laurel, an evergreen shrub with glossy, poisonous leaves and white or pink flowers.

mountain lion, same as cougar.

moun·tain·ous (moun'tn-ŭs), adj. full of or resembling mountains.

mountain sheep, same as bighorn.

mount·ed (moun'tid), adj. 1. seated or serving on horseback. 2. placed on a suitable support.

mount·ing (moun'ting), n. 1. the act of mounting, embellishing, or equipping. 2. that which provides a suitable support.

mourn (môrn), v.i. 1. to grieve; be sorrowful. 2. to wear mourning: v.t. 1. to grieve for. 2. to bewail.

mourn·er (môr'nēr), n. 1. one who mourns. 2. one who attends a funeral.

mourn·ful (môrn'fŭl), adj. causing or expressing sorrow; doleful; sad. —mourn'ful·ly, adv.

mourn·ing (môr'ning), n. 1. the expression of grief; lamenting. 2. the black clothes of a mourner.

mourning dove, a small, gray wild dove: so called from its plaintive note.

mouse (mous), n., pl. mice, 1. a small rodent that infests houses, granaries, etc. 2. a shy person. 3. [Slang], a dark swelling around the eye. 4. a hand-held device for controlling the video display of a computer: v.i. moused, mous'ing, 1. to watch for or catch mice. 2. to watch for something in a sly manner; pry curiously. 3. to search for something busily or stealthily.

mousse (mōōs), n. a light dessert made from whipped cream and white of eggs, flavored and frozen.

mousse·line (mōōs-lēn'), n. [French], 1. a muslin. 2. a fine glass.

mousse·line de laine (dĕ-len'), [French], a very light, woolen dress material.

mousse·line de soie (dĕ-swä'), [French], a soft, thin, rayon or silk fabric with a plain weave.

mous·tache (mŭ-stash', mus'tash), n. same as mustache.

mous·y, mous·ey (mou'si, 'zi), adj. mous'i·er, mous'i·est, of, pertaining to, or resembling a mouse; shy, dull in color, etc.

mouth (mouth), n., pl. mouths (mouthz), 1. the opening in the head of an animal by which it receives food and utters sounds. 2. an entrance ·or opening. 3. the instrument of speaking. 4. a grimace: v.t. (mouth), 1. to

utter with an affected manner or pompous voice. 2. to stroke with the mouth.

mouth·ful (mouth'fool), n., pl. -fuls, 1. as much as can be put into the mouth at one time. 2. the capacity of the mouth. 3. a small quantity. 4. [Slang], an appropriate remark or allusion.

mouth organ, same as harmonica.

mouth·piece ('pēs), n. 1. that part of an instrument which is held in or applied to the mouth. 2. a spokesman.

mouth·wash ('wŏsh), n. a liquid for flushing the mouth or for gargling.

mouth·wa·ter·ing (wŏt'ēr-ing), adj. sufficiently pleasing to the taste or smell as to cause juices to flow in the mouth.

mouth·y (mouth'ē), adj. -i·er, -i·est, talkative, esp. in a bombastic or rude way.

mou·ton (mōō'ton), n. the skin of a lamb altered to look like that of a seal or beaver.

mov·a·ble (mōō'vā-bl), adj. 1. capable of being moved or conveyed. 2. changing in date from one year to another: n. 1. that which can be moved. 2. pl. in Law, goods, wares, furniture, etc. —mov·a·bil'i·ty, n. —mov'a·bly, adv.

move (mōōv), v.t. moved, mov'ing, 1. to cause to change place or position. 2. to impel; set in motion. 3. to rouse to action. 4. to excite the emotions of. 5. to propose formally: v.i. 1. to change place or position; go from place to place. 2. to take action. 3. to change residence. 4. to go forward. 5. to stir. 6. to make a formal proposition (for). 7. to empty: used of the bowels. 8. to be sold: said of goods: n. 1. the act of moving; movement. 2. an act leading toward some end. 3. the act of moving or the right to move in a game.

move·ment (mōōv'mĕnt), n. 1. the act or manner of moving. 2. change of place or position. 3. a motion. 4. a sequence of related actions leading toward some end. 5. the parts of a mechanism, as of a watch or clock. 6. in Music, a) any single part in a musical composition; b) tempo.

mov·er ('ēr), n. 1. one that moves. 2. a person in the business of transporting household articles from one location to another.

mov·ie (mōō'vi), n. same as motion picture.

mov·ing (mōō'ving), adj. 1. causing motion or change of position. 2. stirring the passions or affections; pathetic.

moving staircase, same as escalator: also moving stairway.

mow (mō), v.t. & v.i. mowed, mowed or mown, mow'ing, 1. to cut down (grass, grain, etc.) with or as with a scythe. 2. to cut grass, grain, etc. from. —mow'er, n.

mow (mou), n. 1. a heap of hay, grain, etc. in a barn. 2. the compartment in a barn where hay, grain, etc. are stored.

moz·zet·ta, mo·zet·ta (mō·zet'ä), n. a cape with a small hood attached, which the Pope and other high ecclesiastics of the Roman Catholic Church wear over the rochet.

Mr. (mis'tēr), pl. Messers. (mes'ērz); mister: before a man's name or title.

---

a in cap,· ā in cane, ä in father, å in abet, e in met, ē in be, ē in baker, ē in regent, ĭ in pit, ī in fine, i in manifest, o in hot, ô in horse, ō in bone,

Mrs. (mis'iz), *pl.* **Mmes.** (mā-dām'), mistress: before a married woman's name.

Ms. (miz, mis), a title without reference to marital status, used in substitution for *Miss* or *Mrs.*

much (much), *adj.* more, most, great in quantity or amount: *adv.* 1. to a great degree or extent. 2. often. 3. nearly: *n.* 1. a great quantity. 2. something considerable or unusual.

mu·ci·lage (mū'sl-ij), *n.* a gummy or gelatinous substance, as that used for sticking things together.

mu·ci·lag·i·nous (mū-sĭ-laj'ĭ-nŭs), *adj.* of, pertaining to, resembling, or secreting mucilage or gum.

muck (muk), *n.* 1. moist dung. 2. anything filthy or vile. 3. black earth with decaying matter, used for fertilizing. 4. mire; mud: *v.t.* to fertilize with dung. —**muck'y**, *adj.* **muck'i·er, muck'i·est.**

muck·er (muk'ẽr), *n.* [Slang], a low, vulgar person.

muck·rake (muk'rāk), *v.i.* -raked, -rak·ing, to search for and publish material on which to base charges of corruption against public officials. —**muck'rak·er**, *n.*

muck·worm ('wûrm), *n.* 1. a grub or larva bred in muck, or manure. 2. a miser.

mu·cous (mū'kŭs), *adj.* 1. of, like, or secreting mucus. 2. slimy; viscous.

mucous membrane, a membrane that lines certain body cavities and canals and secretes mucus.

mu·cus (mū'kŭs), *n.* a viscid fluid secreted by mucous membranes: it moistens and protects them.

mud (mud), *n.* soft, wet earth.

mud·dle (mud'l), *v.t.* -dled, -dling, 1. to mix up; jumble; confuse. 2. to produce stupor in, as with strong drink; befuddle: *v.i.* to act or think ineptly or confusedly: *n.* a muddled condition; general confusion.

mud·dle·head·ed (-hed'id), *adj.* marked by stupid blundering and general confusion.

mud·dler (mud'lẽr), *n.* a stick for stirring mixed drinks.

mud·dy (mud'i), *adj.* -di·er, -di·est, 1. full of or covered with mud. 2. not clear; cloudy, dark, dull, or turbid. 3. mixed up; jumbled; generally confused.

mud·fish (mud'fish), *n.* any one of several fishes living in mud or muddy water.

mud·guard ('gärd), *n.* older name for fender (sense 1).

mud hen, any one of various birds, as the coot, that live in marshes.

mud·sling·ing ('sling-ing), *n.* the act of making malicious accusations, especially publicly, typically to promote one's own interests. —**mud'sling·er**, *n.*

mud·stone ('stòn), *n.* sedimentary rock that is shalelike but not distinctly laminated.

mu·ez·zin (mū-ez'in), *n.* in Moslem countries, a crier who summons the faithful to prayer.

muff (muf), *n.* 1. a warm, soft, cylindrical covering, as of fur, to keep the hands warm. 2. failure to hold a ball when catching it. 3.

any bungling action: *v.t. & v.i.* to bungle (something); specifically, to bungle catching (a ball).

muf·fin (muf'n), *n.* a small, soft, round quick bread.

muf·fle (muf'l), *v.t.* -fled, -fling, 1. to wrap up closely and warmly. 2. to cover or conceal, as the face. 3. to wrap or cover so as to deaden sound. 4. to prevent or stifle (sound, speaking, etc.) by or as if by wrapping or covering: *n.* 1. something used for muffling. 2. an oven to fire material by indirect flame.

muf·fler (muf'lẽr), *n.* 1. a scarf worn around the throat, as in cold weather. 2. a device to reduce or deaden sound, as in the exhaust pipe of an automobile.

muf·ti (muf'ti), *n., pl.* -tis, 1. among Moslems, an official expounder of religious law. 2. civilian dress, as of an off-duty military officer.

mug (mug), *n.* 1. an earthenware or metallic drinking vessel. 2. [Slang], the face or mouth; also, a grimace: *v.t.* **mugged, mug'ging,** to assault, usually with intent to rob: *v.i.* [Slang], to grimace.

mug·ger ('ẽr), *n.* 1. one that mugs. 2. a large crocodile of India and Malaysia.

mug·gy (mug'i), *adj.* -gi·er, -gi·est, warm, damp, and close: said of weather. —**mug'gi·ness**, *n.*

mug·wump (mug'wump), *n.* 1. a Republican who refused to support the party ticket in 1884. 2. any independent.

Mu·ham·mad·an (moo-ham'ă-dn), *adj. & n.* same as Mohammedan.

mu·jik (moo-zhĕk', moo'zhik), *n.* same as muzhik.

muk·luk (muk'luk), *n.* 1. an Eskimo boot of sealskin or reindeer skin. 2. a boot suggestive of this but of other material.

mu·lat·to (mū-lat'ō, mū-), *n., pl.* -toes, 1. an offspring of one Negro parent and one white parent. 2. in popular usage, a person of mixed Negro and Caucasoid ancestry.

mul·ber·ry (mul'ber-i, 'ber-i), *n., pl.* -ries, 1. any one of a large group of shrubs or trees with milky juice and fruit resembling a raspberry. 2. the fruit. 3. a purplish red.

mulch (mulch), *n.* straw, litter, etc. used to protect the roots of plants: *v.t.* to cover with mulch.

mulct (mulkt), *v.t.* 1. to punish by fine or deprivation. 2. to take (money, etc.) from, as by cheating: *n.* a fine or the like.

mule (mūl), *n.* 1. the offspring of a donkey and a horse. 2. a machine to spin cotton. 3. a lounging slipper not covering the heel. 4. [Informal], a stubborn person.

mu·le·teer (mū-lĕ-tir'), *n.* a mule driver.

mul·ey (mū'li, mool'i), *adj.* hornless: said of cattle: *n.* a hornless cow or any cow.

mu·li·eb·ri·ty (mū-li-eb'ri-ti), *n.* 1. womanhood. 2. womanliness.

mul·ish (mūl'ish), *adj.* like a mule; stubborn.

mull (mul), *v.t. & v.i.* [Informal], to ponder; cogitate; meditate; ponder (over).

mull (mul), *n.* a thin, soft kind of muslin: *v.t.* to warm, spice, and sweeten, as wine.

mul·lah, mul·la (mul'ă, mool'ă), *n.* a Moslem expounder of religious law: title of respect.

mul·lein (mul'in), *n.* any one of a genus of tall plants with spikes of flowers that are yellow, lavender, or white.

mull·er (mul'ēr), *n.* a kind of pestle or other grinding device.

mul·let (mul'it), *n., pl.* -lets, -let, any one of a family of edible fish with spiny fins.

mul·ley (mool'ĭ, mŏŏ'lĭ), *adj. & n.* same as muley.

mul·li·ga·taw·ny (mul·i-gă-tô'nĭ), *n.* a meat soup flavored with curry.

mul·lion (mul'yŭn), *n.* an upright bar or division between the lights of windows, panels, etc.: *v.t.* to divide with these.

mul·ti-, a combining form meaning *more than one or two, many, many times more.*

mul·ti·far·i·ous (mul-ti-fer'i-ŭs), *adj.* having great variety or diversity.

mul·ti·lat·er·al (-lat'ēr-ăl), *adj.* having several or many sides.

mul·ti·mil·lion·aire (-mil-yŭ-ner'), *n.* one having many millions of dollars, francs, etc.

mul·tip·a·ra (mul-tip'ēr-ă), *n., pl.* -ras, -rae (-ē), *n.* a woman who has borne two or more children.

mul·ti·ple (mul'ti-pl), *adj.* having or consisting of many parts: *n.* a number containing another an exact number of times.

multiple sclerosis, a chronic disease of the central nervous system, marked by speech defects, loss of coordination, etc.

mul·ti·plex (mul'ti-pleks), *adj.* 1. manifold. 2. designating or of a system, as in radio, for two or more simultaneous signals.

mul·ti·pli·cand (mul-ti-pli-kand'), *n.* a number to be multiplied.

mul·ti·pli·ca·tion (-kā'shŭn), *n.* the act of multiplying or condition of being multiplied; specifically, in *Mathematics,* the operation by which a given number or quantity is multiplied.

mul·ti·plic·i·ty (mul-ti-plis'i-ti), *n.* 1. manifold condition. 2. a great number.

mul·ti·pli·er (mul'ti-pli-ēr), *n.* one that multiplies; specifically, in *Mathematics,* a number multiplying anoher.

mul·ti·ply (-pli), *v.t. & v.i.* -plied, -ply·ing, to increase, as in number; specifically, in *Mathematics,* to repeat (a number or quantity) by the number of units in another number, the result being equal to adding the number or quantity that many times.

mul·ti·tude (-tōōd), *n.* 1. a great number. 2. a crowd or assembly. 3. populace; masses (with *the*).

mul·ti·tu·di·nous (mul-ti-tōōd'n-ŭs, -tūd'-), *adj.* of, pertaining to, or consisting of a multitude; numerous.

mum (mum), *n.* 1. a strong beer. 2. [Informal], a chrysanthemum: *adj.* remaining silent: *v.i.* mummed, mum'ming, to mask or disguise oneself for sport: also **mumm.**

mum·ble (mum'bl), *v.t. & v.i.* -bled, -bling, to speak or say indistinctly; mutter: *n.* something mumbled. —mum'bler, *n.*

mum·bo jum·bo ('bō jum'bō), *n.* 1. [M- J-], a West African idol or object of superstitious reverence or dread. 2. meaningless ritual. 3. gibberish.

mum·mer (mum'ēr), *n.* 1. one that mums. 2. an actor.

mum·mer·y (-i), *n., pl.* -mer·ies, 1. performance by mummers. 2. empty or hypocritical display.

mum·mi·fy (mum'i-fi), *v.t. & v.i.* -fied, -fy·ing, to make into or become a mummy.

mum·my ('i), *n., pl.* -mies, a preserved dead body, specifically one embalmed after the manner of the ancient Egyptians.

mumps (mumps), *n.* a viral disease, acute and communicable, marked by swelling of the salivary glands.

munch (munch), *v.t. & v.i.* to chew, often with an audible crunching sound.

mun·dane (mun-dān', mun'dān), *adj.* 1. of or pertaining to the world; worldly. 2. ordinary; commonplace.

mu·nic·i·pal (mū-nis'i-pl), *adj.* 1. of or pertaining to a city, town, etc. or its local self-government. 2. having local self-government.

mu·nic·i·pal·i·ty (mū-nis-i-pal'i-ti), *n., pl.* -ties, 1. a city, town, etc. having its own incorporated government for local affairs. 2. its governing officials.

mu·nif·i·cent (mū-nif'i-sĕnt), *adj.* very generous; lavish. —mu·nif'i·cence, *n.*

mu·ni·ment (mū'ni-mĕnt), *n.* 1. [Now Rare], a stronghold; fortification. 2. *pl.* in *Law,* a legal record defending a title.

mu·ni·tions (mū-nish'ŭnz), *n.pl.* war supplies; weapons, ammunition, etc.

munt·jac, munt·jak (munt'jak), *n.* any one of various small deer of the jungles of southeastern Asia and the East Indies.

mu·ral (mūr'ăl), *adj.* of, on, or resembling a wall: *n.* a picture painted directly on a wall or ceiling, or a similar decoration. —mu'ral·ist, *n.*

mur·der (mūr'dēr), *n.* 1. the unlawful, intentional killing of one human being by another. 2. [Informal], something extremely difficult, unpleasant, etc.: *v.t.* 1. to kill (a human being) unlawfully and intentionally. 2. to ruin utterly. —mur'der·er, *n.* —mur'der·ess, *n.fem.*

mur·der·ous (-ŭs), *adj.* 1. of, pertaining to, or like murder. 2. involving murder. 3. inclined toward, aiming at, or guilty of murder. 4. [Informal], extremely difficult, unpleasant, etc.

mu·ri·at·ic acid (mūr-i-at'ik), hydrochloric acid: a commercial term.

murk (mūrk), *n.* darkness; gloom.

murk·y ('i), *adj.* murk'i·er, murk'i·est, 1. dark; gloomy. 2. full of heavy fog, thick haze, etc. —murk'i·ness, *n.*

mur·mur (mūr'mēr), *n.* 1. a low, indistinct sound, as of a running stream. 2. a complaint in a low, muttering tone. 3. in *Medicine,* an abnormal sound heard by auscultation, as about the heart: *v.i.* 1. to make a low, indistinct sound. 2. to mutter in discontent; grumble; complain: *v.t.* to voice or express in a murmur.

Mur·phy bed (mûr'fi), a bed that swings up or folds into a closet when not in use.

mur·rain (mûr'in), *n.* any one of various infectious diseases of cattle.

mus·ca·dine (mus'kâ-din, -dīn), *n.* an American grape of the southeastern United States: the grapes are large and musky.

mus·cat (mus'kât, 'kat), *n.* 1. a sweet European grape from which muscatel and raisins are made. 2. muscatel.

mus·ca·tel (mus-kâ-tel'), *n.* 1. a rich, sweet wine made from the muscat. 2. muscat. Also **mus·ca·del** (-del').

mus·cle (mus'l), *n.* 1. a highly contractile organ of fibrous tissue effecting movement in the body. 2. the tissue of such an organ. 3. muscular strength: *v.i.* -cled, -cling, [Informal], to force one's way (*in*).

mus·cle-bound (-bound), *adj.* having some muscles so overly developed that free movement is more or less impeded.

Mus·co·vite (mus'kô-vīt), *n.* 1. an inhabitant of Moscow. 2. any Russian. 3. [m-], a common, light-colored mica.

Mus·co·vy duck (mus'kô-vi), *n.* any one of various tropical American ducks with a large crest and red wattles.

mus·cu·lar (mus'kyŭ-lêr), *adj.* 1. of, pertaining to, or effected by muscles. 2. strong; brawny; powerful; vigorous. —**mus·cu·lar'i·ty** (-lêr'i-ti), *n.*

muscular dys·tro·phy (dis'trô-fi), a chronic, noncontagious disease marked by a progressive wasting of the muscles.

mus·cu·la·ture (mus'kyŭ-lá-chêr), *n.* arrangement of muscles throughout the body or in a bodily part.

Muse (mūz), *n.* 1. in *Greek Mythology*, any one of nine goddesses presiding over poetry, history, music, etc. 2. such a goddess or guiding influence thought of as inspiring a poet, musician, etc.

muse (mūz), *v.i.* mused, mus'ing, to give oneself to quiet reflection; think abstractedly; meditate: *v.t.* to think or say meditatively: *n.* meditation.

mu·sette (mū-zet'), *n.* 1. a variety of small bagpipe. 2. a soft melody.

mu·se·um (mū-zē'ûm), *n.* a building, room, etc. for exhibiting works of art, historical or scientific objects, curiosities, etc.

mush (mush), *n.* 1. cornmeal or other meal boiled in water or milk. 2. any thick, soft mass suggestive of this. 3. [Informal], silly or maudlin talk.

mush (mush), *interj.* in Canada and Alaska, a shout to dogs trained to pull sleds to begin pulling or to speed up: *v.i.* to travel in a region of snow, specifically on a sled pulled by dogs: *n.* such a trip.

mush·room (mush'rŏŏm, 'room), *n.* 1. any one of various fleshy fungi remarkable for their quick growth, typically consisting of a stalk with an umbrellalike cap: some are edible and some are poisonous. 2. anything mushroomlike in appearance or quick growth: *adj.* of or like mushrooms: *v.i.* 1. to grow quickly, like a mushroom. 2. to spread out

at the end or top in the form of a mushroom.

mush·y (mush'i), *adj.* mush'i·er, mush'i·est, 1. thick and soft like mush; mushlike. 2. [Informal], foolishly sentimental; silly.

mu·sic (mū'zik), *n.* 1. the art and science of combining vocal or instrumental sounds in various patterns of melody, rhythm, etc. 2. the sounds or compositions so produced; also, the written or printed score of these. 3. any musiclike sequence of sounds.

mu·si·cal ('zi-kl), *adj.* 1. of, pertaining to, or like music. 2. responsive to or skilled in music. 3. set to music: *n.* a production geared to popular tastes and featuring a usually light story set to music, with spoken lines, songs, and often elaborate costumes, dancing, etc. —**mu·si·cal'i·ty** (-kal'i-ti), *n.*

mu·si·cale (mū-zi-kal'), *n.* a party or similar social gathering featuring music.

mu·si·cian (mū-zish'ûn), *n.* one skilled in music; especially, an instrumentalist, singer, composer, or conductor.

mu·si·col·o·gy (mū-zi-kol'ô-ji), *n.* systematized study of the history, forms, etc. of music. —**mu·si·col'o·gist,** *n.*

mus·ing (mū'zing), *n.* the act of one that muses: *adj.* marked by musing; meditative.

musk (musk), *n.* 1. a strong-scented secretion of the male musk deer, used in perfumery; also, a similar secretion of certain other animals. 2. the odor of this. 3. any of several plants with such an odor.

musk deer, a small, hornless Asian deer.

musk duck, 1. an Australian duck with a musky odor in the breeding season. 2. same as Muscovy duck.

mus·kel·lunge (mus'kê-lunj), *n., pl.* -lunge, a very large pike of the Great Lakes and of upper Mississippi drainages.

mus·ket (mus'kit), *n.* a long-barreled firearm fired from the shoulder: it predates the rifle.

mus·ket·eer (mus-kê-tir'), *n.* a soldier armed with a musket.

mus·ket·ry (mus'kê-tri), *n.* 1. the skill of firing muskets or other small arms. 2. muskets or musketeers, collectively.

mus·kie (mus'ki), *n.* same as muskellunge.

musk·mel·on (musk'mel·ôn), *n.* 1. any one of several round or oblong melons with a thick, ribbed rind, sweet, juicy flesh, and a musky odor. 2. a plant with such fruit. 3. popularly, a casaba or any one of various other melons.

musk ox, an ox of arctic America and Greenland: it has a shaggy coat and long horns.

musk·rat (musk'rat), *n., pl.* -rats, -rat, 1. a North American aquatic rodent with glossy brown fur and webbed hind feet. 2. the fur of this rodent.

musk·y (mus'ki), *adj.* musk'i·er, musk'i·est, of, like, or smelling of musk.

Mus·lim (muz'lim, mooz'lim), *n. & adj.* same as Moslem.

mus·lin (muz'lin), *n.* a strong cotton cloth of plain weave.

muss (mus), *n.* a mess; disorder: *v.t.* to make messy or disordered.

mus·sel (mus'l), *n.* any one of various saltwater or freshwater bivalve mollusks.

Mus-sul-man (mus'l-măn), *n.*, *pl.* -mans, same as Moslem.

muss-y (mus'ĭ), *adj.* muss'i-er, muss'i-est, [Informal], messy or disordered.

must (must), *v.aux.*, past tense must, an auxiliary verb expressing *a)* obligation or necessity; *b)* probability; *c)* certainty: *n.* [Informal], something that by all means is to be done, read, seen, acquired, etc.

must (must), *n.* 1. grape juice, etc. not yet fermented. 2. mustiness. 3. a frenzy in animals, especially the male elephant, associated with sexual excitement.

mus-tache (mŭ-stash', mus'tash), *n.* a growth of hair on a man's upper lip.

mus-tang (mus'tang), *n.* a small, wild horse of the southwestern U.S.

mus-tard (mus'tĕrd), *n.* 1. an annual plant with yellow flowers and round seeds. 2. a pungent powder made from the crushed seeds, or a condiment made from it.

mus-ter (mus'tĕr), *n.* 1. an assembly, as of troops for review or active service; assemblage. 2. a register of those in a military or naval unit: *v.i.* 1. to assemble, as troops for review. 2. to bring or gather together; collect. 3. to summon up, as courage: *v.i.* to assemble.

mus-ti-ness (mus'ti-nis), *n.* the quality or state of being musty.

must-n't (mus'nt), must not.

mus-ty (mus'ti), *adj.* -ti-er, -ti-est, 1. moldy, as in smell or taste. 2. stale; antiquated. 3. spiritless; apathetic.

mu-ta-ble (mūt'ă-b'l), *adj.* 1. susceptible to change. 2. fickle; unstable. —mu-ta-bil'i-ty, *n.* —mu'ta-bly, *adv.*

mu-tant (mūt'nt), *n.* an animal or plant differing from the parents in characteristics to be passed on to offspring.

mu-tate (mū'tāt), *v.i.* & *v.t.* -tat-ed, -tat-ing, to change; specifically, to undergo or cause to undergo mutation.

mu-ta-tion (mū-tā'shun), *n.* 1. change; modification; deviation. 2. in *Biology*, *a)* an abrupt shift in inheritable characteristics; *b)* an individual marked by such a shift; mutant. —mu-ta'tion-al, *adj.*

mute (mūt), *adj.* 1. silent; speechless. 2. not pronounced; not sounded: *n.* 1. one not speaking or unable to speak. 2. an unpronounced consonant or vowel. 3. a contrivance to deaden or soften the sound of a musical instrument: *v.t.* mut'ed, mut'ing, to deaden or soften the sound, intensity, etc. of. —mute'ly, *adv.*

mu-ti-late (mūt'l-āt), *v.t.* -lat-ed, -lat-ing, to cut off, remove, or badly injure or impair an essential or important part of; maim. —mu-ti-la'tion, *n.* —mu'ti-la-tor, *n.*

mu-ti-neer (mūt-n-ir'), *n.* one that mutinies.

mu-ti-nous (mūt'n-us), *adj.* of, tending toward, or typical of mutiny.

mu-ti-ny (mūt'n-i), *n.*, *pl.* -nies, insurrection against or forcible resistance to constituted authority, especially by soldiers or sailors against their officers: *v.i.* -nied, -ny-ing, to rise against constituted authority.

mutt (mut), *n.* [Slang], a mongrel dog; cur.

mut-ter (mut'ĕr), *v.i.* & *v.t.* to utter (words) in a low voice and indistinctly, with compressed lips; murmur: *n.* something muttered.

mut-ton (mut'n), *n.* the flesh of sheep as a food.

mutton chops, whiskers at each side of the face, narrow at top, broad and rounded at bottom, with the chin closely shaved.

mu-tu-al (mū'choo-wǎl), *adj.* 1. reciprocal. 2. shared in common. —mu'tu-al-ly, *adv.*

mutual fund, a corporation investing shareholders' funds in various securities.

mu-tu-al-i-ty (mū-choo-wal'i-ti), *n.*, *pl.* -ties, the quality or state of being mutual.

muu-muu (mōō'mōō), *n.* a long, loose garment for women, Hawaiian in style.

mu-zhik, **mu-zjik** (mōō-zhēk', mōō'zhik), *n.* [Russian], in czarist Russia, a peasant.

muz-zle (muz'l), *n.* 1. the projecting mouth, lips, and nose of an animal; snout. 2. a fastening or cover put over this to keep the animal from biting or eating. 3. the mouth of a firearm: *v.t.* -zled, -zling, to shut the mouth of as with a muzzle.

muz-zy (muz'i), *adj.* -zi-er, -zi-est, [Informal], 1. confused. 2. blurred.

my (mī), *adj.* of or belonging to me: *interj.* an exclamation of surprise, dismay, etc.

my-al-gi-a (mī-al'ji-ă), *n.* muscular pain.

my-as-the-ni-a (mī-ăs-thē'ni-ă), *n.* muscular weakness or fatigue.

my-ce-to-ma (mī-si-tō'mă), *n.* a chronic infection of the skin and underlying tissues, usually of the foot: it is characterized by a tumorous mass chiefly of fungi.

my-col-o-gy (mī-kol'ŏ-ji), *n.* the branch of botany dealing with fungi.

my-co-sis (mī-kō'sis), *n.*, *pl.* -ses, 1. growth of parasitic fungi in any bodily part. 2. a disease due to such growth.

my-dri-a-sis (mi-drī'ă-sis, mī-), *n.* excessive dilatation of the pupil of the eye.

my-e-li-tis (mī-ĕ-lit'is), *n.* inflammation of the spinal cord or the bone marrow.

My-lar (mī'lär), *n.* 1. a strong, very thin polyester used as in tapes for tape recorders: a trademark. 2. [m-], such a polyester.

my-na, **my-nah** (mī'nă), *n.* any one of a group of tropical birds related to the starling and found in southeastern Asia.

Myn-heer (mĭn-her', -hir'), *n.* Sir; Mr.: a Dutch title of address.

my-ol-o-gy (mī-ol'ŏ-ji), *n.* the branch of anatomy that treats of muscles.

my-o-pi-a (mī-ō'pi-ă), *n.* an eye condition in which distant objects are not seen distinctly, whereas nearby objects are seen well or fairly well; nearsightedness. —my-op'ic (-op'ik), *adj.*

myr-i-ad (mir'i-ăd), *n.* an indeterminate but very large number of persons or things; multitude: *adj.* multitudinous.

myr-i-a-pod (mir'i-ă-pod), *n.* a centipede or similar many-legged arthropod having a long body in many segments.

myr-mi-don (mur'mi-don, -dŏn), *n.* an unprotesting, devoted adherent or subordinate, especially one executing orders without pity or scruple.

myrrh (mur), *n.* an aromatic gummy resin exuded by several plants of Arabia and eastern Africa and used as in perfume.

myr·tle (mûr'tl), *n.* any one of various plants, specifically one having evergreen leaves and dark, fragrant berries.

my·self (mi-self'), *pron.* 1. the emphatic or reflexive form of I. 2. my true self.

mys·ta·gogue (mis'tǎ-gog, -gǒg), *n.* an initiator into, or interpreter of, religious mysteries.

mys·te·ri·ous (mis-tir'i-ùs), *adj.* full of mystery; not clear to the understanding; incomprehensible or obscure. —**mys·te'ri·ous·ly,** *adv.*

mys·ter·y (mis'tē-ri), *n., pl.* **-ter·ies,** 1. something beyond comprehension, hard to understand, or obscure. 2. something unknown or unknowable. 3. something kept secret. 4. a novel, play, etc. about a secret crime, typically a murder, with the criminal revealed only at the end. 5. *pl.* secret rites or teachings known only to the initiated, as in certain cults of ancient Greece. 6. any one of fifteen subjects of meditation used in reciting a section of the rosary.

mys·tic (mis'tik), *adj.* 1. same as **mystical.** 2. involving mysterious powers, secret rites or teachings, etc.; occult: *n.* in *Theology, Theosophy, etc.,* one elevated to an extraordinary, suprarational knowledge or experience of spiritual, especially divine, things.

mys·ti·cal ('ti-kl), *adj.* 1. spiritually significant or symbolic; allegorical; emblematic. 2. of, pertaining to, or involving mystics or mysticism. 3. occult; mystical. —**mys'ti·cal·ly,** *adv.*

mys·ti·cism (mis'ti-sizm), *n.* 1. the quality or condition of being mystic. 2. mystic character, knowledge, or experience. 3. obscure thought or belief.

mys·ti·fy ('ti-fī), *v.t.* **-fied, -fy·ing,** 1. to involve in mystery; obscure. 2. to puzzle or bewilder. —**mys·ti·fi·ca'tion,** *n.*

mys·tique (mis-tēk'), *n.* an agglomeration of quasi-mystical elements pervasive in or associated with something.

myth (mith), *n.* 1. a traditional story, as about gods or heroes, seemingly historical but actually created to explain such things as the origin of man or of a people, the causes of natural phenomena, the beginning of a religion, etc. 2. any similar fictitious story. 3. any account, theory, belief, etc. that is unscientific or otherwise invalid. 4. such stories, theories, etc. collectively. 5. a nonexistent person or thing viewed as though existent or factual.

myth·i·cal ('i-kl), *adj.* of, being, or involving a myth or myths: also **myth'ic.** —**myth'i·cal·ly,** *adv.*

myth·o·log·i·cal (mith-ō-loj'i-kl), *adj.* 1. of or pertaining to mythology. 2. mythical. Also **myth·o·log'ic.**

my·thol·o·gist (mi-thol'ō-jist), *n.* 1. one who specializes in mythology. 2. one who writes or compiles myths.

my·thol·o·gy (-ji), *n., pl.* **-gies,** 1. the science or study of myths. 2. a treatise on, or a book of, myths. 3. myths collectively or a particular set of myths.

myx·e·de·ma (mik-sē-dē'mǎ), *n.* a disease caused by failure of the thyroid gland: the skin dries and thickens and both physical and mental activity are impaired.

myx·o·my·cete (mik-sō-mi'sēt, -mī-sēt'), *n.* any one of a group of primitive organisms generally classified as plants (fungi) and usually found on decaying vegetation.

ō in dragon, ōō in crude, oo in wool, u in cup, ū in cure, ū in turn, ů in focus, oi in boy, ou in house, th in thin, th in sheathe, g in get, j in joy, y in yet.

N

N, n (en), *n., pl.* **N's, n's,** 1. the fourteenth letter of the English alphabet. 2. the usual sound of this letter, as in *nab* and *banner.* 3. a type or impression of *N* or *n.* 4. in *Printing,* an en (half an em).

N *adj.* shaped like *N*: *n.* an object shaped like *N*.

n (en), *n.* the symbol for an indefinite quantity: see **nth.**

nab (nab), *v.t.* **nabbed, nab'bing,** [Informal], 1. to snatch or steal. 2. to catch or arrest.

na-bob (nā'bob), *n.* 1. In India, a deputy or administrator under the Mogul Empire. 2. a European who amassed wealth in India. 3. a very wealthy man. —**na'bob-ish,** *adj.*

na-celle (nā-sel'), *n.* an outer, streamlined casing on certain aircraft, enclosing an engine.

na-cre (nā'kēr), *n.* same as **mother-of-pearl.**

na-cre-ous ('kri-ùs), *adj.* 1. having an iridescent luster. 2. resembling mother-of-pearl. 3. yielding nacre, as some shells.

na-dir (nā'dēr, 'dir), *n.* 1. the point opposite to the zenith in the celestial sphere, directly below the observer. 2. the lowest point.

nae-vus (nē'vùs), *n., pl.* **-vi** ('vī), British spelling of nevus. —**nae'void,** *adj.*

nag (nag), *n.* 1. originally, a small saddle horse. 2. an old, decrepit horse. 3. [Slang], a racehorse. 4. a person, especially a woman, who nags: also **nag'ger:** *v.t.* **nagged, nag'ging,** to scold or find fault with continually: *v.i.* 1. to find fault constantly. 2. to cause constant pain, annoyance, etc. —**nag'ging-ly,** *adv.* —**nag'gy,** *adj.* **-gi-er, -gi-est.**

na-ga-na (nä-gä'nä), *n.* an infectious disease of horses and cattle in tropical Africa, caused by the bite of infected tsetse flies.

Na-hum (nā'ùm, 'hùm), *n.* a book of the Bible.

nai-ad (nā'ad, nī'-; 'ād), *n., pl.* **-ads, -a-des** ('ā-dēz), 1. [also N-], in *Greek & Roman Mythology,* any of the nymphs living in lakes, rivers, springs, etc. 2. a kind of aquatic plant.

na-if, na-ïf (nä-ēf'), *n.* same as **naive.**

nail (nāl), *n.* 1. the horny substance at the ends of the human fingers and toes. 2. the claw of a bird or other animal. 3. an old cloth measure of 2 1/4 inches. 4. a pointed piece of metal with a flattened head for fastening woodwork, etc.: *v.t.* 1. to fasten or attach with nails. 2. to make certain (followed by *down*). 3. to expose (a lie, etc.). 4. [Informal], to catch. 5. [Informal], to hit.

nail polish, a glossy, quick-drying lacquer, usually colored, applied with a brush to the fingernails or toenails.

nail set, a short, blunted tool used to drive the head of a nail even with, or below the surface of, wood.

nain-sook (nān'sook), *n.* a fine, lightweight cotton fabric.

na-ive, na-ïve (nä-ēv'), *adj.* 1. artless; ingenuous; unaffectedly simple. 2. trusting; unsuspecting. —**na-ive'ly, na-ïve'ly,** *adv.* —**na-ive'-ness, na-ïve'ness,** *n.*

na-ive-té, na-ïve-té (nä-ēv-tā', -ēv'tā), *n.* 1. natural, unaffected simplicity. 2. a naive statement, action, etc. Also **na-ive'ty, na-ïve'ty** ('ti).

na-ked (nā'kěd), *adj.* 1. unclothed; bare; nude. 2. exposed to view. 3. unarmed; defenseless. 4. plain; without addition or ornament. 5. without a usual covering. 6. without the aid of an optical instrument. —**na'ked-ly,** *adv.* —**na'ked-ness,** *n.*

nam-by-pam-by (nam'bi-pam'bi), *n., pl.* **-bies,** one who is weak, indecisive, insipid, unspirited, etc.: *adj.* of or like a namby-pamby; weak, insipid, etc.

name (nām), *n.* 1. that by which a person or thing is called; title; designation; appellation. 2. a descriptive term; epithet. 3. character, reputation, or fame. 4. mere designation, not reflected by fact. 5. authority, as in the name of the law: *v.t.* **named, nam'ing,** 1. to give a name or appellation to. 2. to nominate. 3. to specify. 4. to mention by name. 5. to identify by the correct name: *adj.* well-known. —**name'a-ble, nam'a-ble,** *adj.* —**nam'er,** *n.*

name-drop-ping (nām'drop-ing), *n.* the frequent mentioning of well-known or prestigious people in an effort to impress others. —**name'drop-per,** *n.*

name-less (nām'lis), *adj.* 1. without a name. 2. unknown; anonymous. 3. obscure. 4. unspeakable; dreadful. 5. that cannot be described. —**name'less-ly,** *adv.* —**name'less-ness,** *n.*

name-ly ('li), *adv.* that is to say.

name-plate ('plāt), *n.* 1. a plaque bearing a name. 2. the name of a newspaper or magazine in its distinctive styling on the cover, front page, etc.

name-sake ('sāk), *n.* one having the same name.

nan-keen, nan-kin (nan-kēn'), *n.* a buff-colored cotton cloth, originally from China.

nan-ny (nan'i), *n., pl.* **-nies,** [British], a nursemaid for a child.

nanny goat, [Informal], a female goat.

nap (nap), *n.* 1. a short slumber; doze. 2. the woolly substance on the surface of some cloth; pile. 3. a downy coating on plants. 4. the card game napoleon: *v.i.* **napped, nap'ping,** to doze: *v.t.* to raise a nap on (cloth) by brushing. —**nap'less,** *adj.* —**napped,** *adj.*

na-palm (nā'päm), *n.* a flammable, jellylike substance used in bombs and flame throwers: *v.t.* to burn, bomb, or attack with napalm.

---

a in cap, ā in cane, ä in father, â in abet, e in met, ē in be, ê in baker, ê in regent, i in pit, ī in fine, ĭ in manifest, o in hot, ô in horse, ō in bone,

nape (nāp), *n.* the back of the neck.

na·per·y (nā′pēr-i), *n.* linens used in a household, especially tablecloths and napkins.

naph·tha (naf′thä, nap′-), *n.* 1. a clear, volatile, flammable liquid hydrocarbon distilled from coal tar, petroleum, wood, etc. and used in dry cleaning or as fuel. 2. same as petroleum.

naph·tha·lene (-lēn), *n.* a hydrocarbon from coal tar, forming a white solid crystal and used in moth repellents, dyestuffs, etc.

naph·thol (naf′thōl), *n.* either of two compounds from naphthalene, used in dyes, antiseptics, etc.

na·pi·form (nā′pi-fôrm), *adj.* turnip-shaped.

nap·kin (nap′kin), *n.* a small cloth or paper, used at table to wipe the hands, lips, etc.

na·po·le·on (nå-pō′li-ŏn), *n.* 1. a gold coin formerly current in France, worth 20 francs. 2. a card game similar to euchre.

nap·py (nap′i), *n.* -**pies**, an oval, flat-bottomed dish.

nap·py (nap′i), *adj.* -**pi·er**, -**pi·est**, covered with nap; downy.

nar·ce·ine (när′sē-ēn), *n.* a white crystalline narcotic obtained from opium.

nar·cis·sism (när′si-sizm), *n.* love of self.

nar·cis·sus (när-sis′ŭs), *n., pl.* -**sus**, -**sus·es**, -**si** (ī), a bulbous plant with fragrant flowers.

nar·co·sis (när-kō′sis), *n.* stupefaction from the effects of a narcotic.

nar·cot·ic (-kot′ik), *adj.* producing coma or torpor: *n.* a drug, as morphine, used to alleviate pain and induce sleep: narcotics are often habit-forming.

nar·co·tize (när′kō-tīz), *v.t.* -**tized**, -**tiz·ing**, to stupefy, as with a narcotic. —**nar·co·ti·za′tion,** *n.*

nard (närd), *n.* same as **spikenard**.

nar·es (ner′ēz), *n.pl., sing.* **nar′is** (′is), the nostrils. —**nar′i·al, nar′ine,** *adj.*

nar·ghi·le (när′gi-lē), *n.* same as **hookah.**

nark (närk), *n.* [British Slang], a police informer: *v.t. & v.i.* to inform on (a person).

nar·rate (ner′āt, na-rāt′), *v.t. & v.i.* -**rat·ed**, -**rat·ing**, 1. to tell or recite (a story). 2. to give an account of (events, doings, etc.).— **nar′ra·tor,** *n.*

nar·ra·tion (na-rā′shŭn), *n.* 1. the act of narrating. 2. a narrative.

nar·ra·tive (nar′ä-tiv), *adj.* of or pertaining to narration: *n.* a recital of a story or event.

nar·row (ner′ō), *adj.* 1. of little breadth. 2. limited in area, scope, extent, etc. 3. limited in viewpoint; bigoted. 4. meager; straightened. 5. barely enough: *v.t. & v.i.* to lessen in breadth, extent, scope, etc.: *n. usually pl.* a strait or narrow passage. —**nar′row·ly,** *adv.* —**nar′row·ness,** *n.*

nar·row·mind·ed (-mīn′did), *adj.* of little mental scope; bigoted; illiberal.

nar·whal (när′wäl, ′hwäl), *n.* an arctic cetacean the male of which has a large projecting tusk.

nar·y (ner′i), *adj.* [Dial.], not any.

na·sal (nā′zl), *adj.* 1. of the nose. 2. pronounced with most of the breath exhaled through the nose: *n.* a nasal sound.

na·sal·ize (′zå-līz), *v.t. & v.i.* -**ized**, -**iz·ing**, to pronounce or produce with a nasal sound. —**na·sal·i·za′tion,** *n.*

nas·cent (nas′ĕnt, nā′snt), *adj.* 1. beginning to exist. 2. starting to grow.

na·stur·tium (nå-stûr′shŭm), *n.* any of various plants with yellow, orange, or red flowers and pungent leaves and seeds.

nas·ty (nas′ti), *adj.* -**ti·er**, -**ti·est**, 1. dirty; filthy. 2. nauseous. 3. obscene. 4. foul; unpleasant. 5. spiteful. —**nas′ti·ly,** *adv.* —**nas′ti·ness,** *n.*

na·tal (nāt′l), *adj.* 1. of or pertaining to one's birth. 2. indigenous.

na·tant (nāt′nt), *adj.* floating or swimming.

na·ta·tion (nā-tā′shŭn), *n.* the act or art of swimming.

na·ta·to·ri·al (nāt-å-tôr′i-ål), *adj.* of, pertaining to, or adapted for swimming.

na·tes (nā′tiz), *n.pl.* the buttocks.

na·tion (nā′shŭn), *n.* 1. the inhabitants of a particular area having a history, culture, language, etc. in common. 2. a people under a common government; country.

na·tion·al (nash′ŭ-nl), *adj.* of or pertaining to a nation: *n.* a citizen or subject of a particular country.

National Guard, in the U.S., the organized militia ordinarily under the control of each state.

na·tion·al·ism (-izm), *n.* 1. devotion to an individual nation; patriotism or chauvinism. 2. hope or demand for national independence. —**na′tion·al·ist,** *n. & adj.*

na·tion·al·i·ty (nash-ŭ-nal′i-ti), *n., pl.* -**ties**, 1. the status of being a member of a nation by birth or naturalization. 2. a nation or national group.

na·tion·al·ize (nash′ŭ-nå-līz), *v.t.* -**ized**, -**iz·ing**, 1. to render national. 2. to convert ownership or control of (land, industries, etc.) to government control. —**na·tion·al·i·za′tion,** *n.*

na·tion·wide (nā′shŭn-wīd), *adj.* throughout a whole nation; national.

na·tive (nāt′iv), *adj.* 1. of or pertaining to the time and place of birth or growth; indigenous. 2. innate, not acquired. 3. produced by nature; natural. 4. of or pertaining to the original inhabitants of a place: *n.* 1. one who is born in a particular place. 2. an original inhabitant. 3. a plant or animal originating in a particular place.

na·tive-born (-bôrn), *adj.* born in a particular place or country.

na·tiv·ism (nāt′iv-izm), *n.* the advocacy of the claims of native-born citizens as opposed to those of immigrants.

na·tiv·i·ty (nå-tiv′i-ti), *n., pl.* -**ties**, 1. birth. 2. [N.], the birth of Jesus.

na·tro·lite (nat′rō-līt), *n.* a hydrated silicate of aluminum and sodium.

na·tron (nā′tron), *n.* hydrated sodium carbonate.

nat·ty (nat′i), *adj.* -**ti·er**, -**ti·est**, tidy; neat; smart. —**nat′ti·ly,** *adv.*

nat·u·ral (nach′ēr-ål), *adj.* 1. of or pertaining to nature. 2. produced by or present in nature; not artificial. 3. inborn. 4. expected; normal. 5. true to life. 6. free from affectation; spontaneous. 7. of the real or material world. 8. illegitimate. 9. in *Music*, without

sharps or **flats**: n. [Informal], a person or thing certain to succeed. —**nat'u·ral·ness**, n.

natural childbirth, childbirth prepared for by training and requiring no anesthesia.

natural history, the study of natural objects and organisms, especially in a popular way.

nat·u·ral·ism (-izm), n. 1. behavior or thought conforming to the state of nature. 2. the theory that literature and art should conform to nature.

nat·u·ral·ist (-ist), n. 1. one skilled in the study of animals and plants. 2. a believer in naturalism. —**nat·u·ral·is'tic**, adj.

nat·u·ral·ize (-å-līz), v.t. -ized, -iz·ing, 1. to make natural. 2. to grant citizenship to (an alien). —**nat·u·ral·i·za'tion**, n.

nat·u·ral·ly (-i), adv. 1. by nature; inherently. 2. spontaneously. 3. as expected.

natural resources, natural sources of wealth, as coal, timber, etc.

natural science, a science, as physics, biology, etc., dealing mostly with measurable relationships.

natural selection, in evolution, the process whereby certain individuals best adapted to their particular environment leave more descendants.

natural theology, theology based on nature, independent of revelation.

na·ture (nå'chēr), n. 1. the physical universe. 2. the essential qualities of a thing. 3. sort; type. 4. the innate character of a person. 5. [often N-], the source, principle, etc. that seems to maintain the universe and life. 6. the primitive state of life.

na·tur·op·a·thy (nā-chēr-op'å-thi), n. a drugless system of treating disease, using natural agencies, as sunshine, diet, etc.

naught (nôt), n. 1. nothing. 2. a zero (0).

naugh·ty (nôt'i), adj. -ti·er, -ti·est, 1. disobedient; mischievous. 2. indecorous. —**naugh'ti·ly**, adv. —**naugh'ti·ness**, n.

nau·se·a (nô'shå, 'si·å), n. 1. a strong sensation of sickness in the stomach. 2. loathing; disgust.

nau·se·ate ('shē·āt, 'sē-, 'zē-), v.t. -at·ed, -at·ing, to affect with nausea: v.i. to feel nausea.

nau·seous (nô'shŭs), adj. producing nausea; loathsome; abhorrent.

nautch (nôch), n. in India, an entertainment by dancing girls.

nau·ti·cal (nôt'i-kl), adj. of or pertaining to ships, sailors, or navigation. —**nau'ti·cal·ly**, adv.

nau·ti·lus (nôt'l-ŭs), n., pl. -lus·es, -li (-ī), a tropical cephalopod mollusk with a chambered spiral shell.

Nav·a·ho, Nav·a·jo (nav'å-hō), n., pl. -hos, -ho, -hoes, any member of an Indian tribe of the southwestern U.S.

na·val (nā'vl), adj. of or pertaining to a navy, its ships, etc.

nave (nåv), n. the main body of a church, from the chancel to the principal entrance.

nave (nāv), n. the hub of a wheel.

na·vel (nā'vl), n. the depression in the center of the abdomen, indicating where the umbilical cord was attached to the fetus.

navel orange, a seedless orange with a depression at the apex.

nav·i·ga·ble (nav'i-gå-bl), adj. 1. deep and wide enough to allow passage of ships. 2. capable of being steered. —**nav·i·ga·bil'i·ty**, n.

nav·i·gate (nav'i-gāt), v.t. & v.i. -gat·ed, -gat·ing, 1. to steer or guide (a ship or aircraft). 2. to pass through or over (water, air, etc.) in a ship or aircraft. 3. [Informal], to walk.

nav·i·ga·tion (nav·i-gā'shŭn), n. 1. the act of navigating. 2. the science of determining the position and charting the course of ships or aircraft.

nav·i·ga·tor (nav'i-gāt-ēr), n. one skilled in the science of navigation.

nav·vy (nav'i), n., pl. -vies, [British], an unskilled laborer on rail beds, canals, etc.

na·vy (nā'vi), n., pl. -vies, 1. the ships of war of a nation. 2. [often N-], a nation's whole sea strength, including ships, men, supplies, etc. 3. very dark blue.

navy bean, a white variety of bean.

nay (nā), adv. not only so, but more than that: n. 1. a denial. 2. a negative vote.

Naz·a·rene (naz-å-rēn'), n. 1. a native or inhabitant of Nazareth, a town in northern Israel where Jesus lived as a child. 2. any member of a sect of early Christians of Jewish origin.

Na·zi (nät'si, nat'-), adj. denoting or of the German fascist party that ruled Germany from 1933-1945 under Hitler: n. a member of this party.

Ne·an·der·thal (ni-an'dēr-thôl, -tāl), adj. denoting or of an early type of man who lived in the Old World during the Pleistocene Epoch.

neap (nēp), adj. denoting or of a high tide of lowest range, occurring at the first and third quarters of the moon.

Ne·a·pol·i·tan ice cream (ni-å-pol'i-tăn), brick ice cream with layers of different colors and flavors.

near (nir), adj. 1. not far distant in time, place, or degree. 2. close; intimate. 3. close in relationship. 4. narrow. 5. parsimonious. 6. on the left side: adv. 1. at little distance in space or time. 2. almost. 3. intimately: prep. close to: v.t. & v.i. to approach.

near·by (nir'bī'), adj. & adv. near.

near·ly ('li), adv. almost; not quite.

near miss, a result that is almost successful.

near·sight·ed (-sīt'id), adj. myopic. —**near'sight'ed·ness**, n.

neat (nēt), adj. 1. tidy; trim and clean. 2. simple and elegant. 3. well-proportioned. 4. skillful; adroit. 5. not diluted with other things. 6. [Slang], stylish, pleasing, etc. —**neat'ly**, adv. —**neat'ness**, n.

neat (nēt), n., pl. neat, [Now Rare], a domestic bovine animal.

'neath, neath (nēth), prep. poetic variant of beneath.

neb (neb), n. [British Dial.], 1. a bird's beak. 2. an animal's snout. 3. a person's nose or mouth. 4. a tip; point.

neb·u·la (neb'yŭ·lå), n., pl. -lae (-lē), -las, 1. a faint misty patch of light in the sky formed by far distant stars, diffused gaseous matter, or external galaxies. 2. a white spot on the cornea. —neb'u·lar, adj.

neb·u·los·i·ty (neb·yŭ-los'ĭ-tǐ), n. 1. the state or quality of being nebulous. 2. pl. -ties, same as nebula (sense 1).

neb·u·lous (neb'yŭ-lŭs), adj. 1. of or resembling a nebula. 2. [Rare], cloudy; misty. 3. vague; unclear.

nec·es·sar·i·ly (nes·ĕ-ser'ĭ-li), adv. 1. by necessity. 2. inevitably.

nec·es·sar·y (nes'ĕ-ser-ǐ), adj. 1. that cannot be otherwise. 2. essential; indispensable. 3. obligatory; n. pl. -ies, 1. that which is essential, as food, shelter, etc. 2. [Dial.], a privy. 3. pl. in Law, things requisite to the welfare of a dependent.

ne·ces·si·tar·i·an·ism (nē-ses-ĭ-ter'ĭ-ăn-izm), n. the theory that every event is predetermined by some antecedent cause. —ne·ces·si·tar'i·an, n. & adj.

ne·ces·si·tate (nē-ses'ĭ-tāt), v.t. -tat·ed, -tat·ing, 1. to make (something) necessary or unavoidable. 2. [Now Rare], to constrain; compel.

ne·ces·si·tous (-tŭs), adj. 1. very poor; destitute. 2. required; essential.

ne·ces·si·ty (-ti), n., pl. -ties, 1. the state of being required or indispensable. 2. that which is unavoidable. 3. natural compulsion. 4. pressing or urgent need. 5. extreme poverty.

neck (nek), n. 1. that part of the body between the head and trunk. 2. the constricted part of a bodily organ. 3. something shaped like a neck. 4. the part of a garment that covers or is close to the neck: v.t. & v.i. [Slang], to kiss and caress in making love.

neck·er·chief (nek'ĕr-chif, -chēf), n. a handkerchief worn around the neck.

neck·lace ('lis), n. an ornamental chain or string of beads, jewels, etc. worn around the neck.

neck·tie ('tī), n. a band worn under a collar and around the neck and tied in front.

necktie party, [Slang], a lynching.

neck·wear ('wer), n. articles worn around the neck, as ties, scarfs, etc.

nec·ro- (nek'rō, 'rō), a combining form meaning death, corpse, dead tissue.

ne·crol·o·gy (ne-krol'ō-ji), n., pl. -gies, 1. a list of people who have died during a certain period. 2. an obituary. —nec·ro·log·i·cal (nek-rō-loj'ĭ-kl), adj.

nec·ro·man·cy (nek'rō-man-si), n. 1. the pretended art of predicting the future by communication with the dead. 2. sorcery. —nec'ro·man·cer, n.

ne·croph·a·gous (ne-krof'ă-gŭs), adj. subsisting on carrion.

nec·ro·pho·bi·a (nek-rō-fō'bi-ă), n. an abnormal fear of death or dead bodies.

ne·crop·o·lis (nē-krop'ō-lis), n., pl. -lis·es, -leis (-līs), a cemetery, especially of an ancient city.

nec·rop·sy (nek'rop-si), n., pl. -sies, an autopsy.

ne·cro·sis (ne-krō'sis), n., pl. -ses (-sēz), 1. the decay and death of tissue in an organ or part, as from disease, injury, etc. 2. in Botany, the death of plant tissue as from frost. —ne·crot'ic (-krot'ik), adj.

ne·crot·o·my (ne-krot'ō-mi), n., pl. -mies, 1. the

dissection of dead bodies. 2. the excision of dead bone.

nec·tar (nek'tĕr), n. 1. in Greek Mythology, the drink of the gods. 2. any delicious beverage. 3. in Botany, a sweet liquid from many flowers, gathered by bees to make honey.

nec·tar·ine (nek-tă-rēn'), n. a variety of peach with a smooth skin.

nec·ta·ry (nek'tĕr-i), n., pl. -ries, that part of a flower that secretes nectar.

nee, née (nā, nē), adj. born: used to indicate the maiden name of a married woman.

need (nēd), n. 1. necessity. 2. a want of something required or wished for. 3. something desired or lacking. 4. something that is requisite. 5. a condition of poverty or exigency: v.t. 1. to have need of; require. 2. to be obliged.

need·ful ('fŭl), adj. necessary; required.

nee·dle (nēd'l), n. 1. a small, sharp-pointed steel instrument with an eye for thread. 2. a slender, pointed rod used in knitting. 3. a small rod, usually steel, with a hook for crocheting. 4. a small, sharp stylus that runs in the grooves of phonograph records to transmit vibrations. 5. the indicator on a compass, dial, etc. 6. a sharp pointed leaf, as on the conifers. 7. a sharp-pointed, hollow metal tube fitted to the end of a hypodermic syringe: v.t. [Informal], 1. to goad; incite. 2. to tease.

nee·dle·point (-point), n. 1. decorative embroidery upon canvas. 2. lace worked with a needle over a paper pattern.

need·less (nēd'lis), adj. not needed; unnecessary. —need'less·ly, adv.

needle valve, a valve having a needlelike point that fits into a conical opening to control the flow of a fluid.

nee·dle·work (nēd'l-wûrk), n. work done with a needle, as embroidery.

need·n't (nēd'nt), need not.

needs (nēdz), adv. necessarily.

need·y (nēd'i), adj. need'i·er, need'i·est, very poor; necessitous; indigent.

ne'er (ner), adv. [Poetic], never.

ne'er-do-well ('doo-wel), n. an idle, irresponsible person.

ne·far·i·ous (ni-fer'ĭ-ŭs), adj. extremely wicked; vile; infamous.

ne·gate (ni-gāt'), v.t. -gat·ed, -gat·ing, 1. to rule out. 2. to nullify.

ne·ga·tion (-gā'shŭn), n. 1. a denial. 2. the absence or lack of some positive quality.

neg·a·tive (neg'ă-tiv), adj. 1. expressing or implying negation. 2. lacking or opposite to that which is positive. 3. in Mathematics, denoting a quantity less than zero, or one to be subtracted. 4. in Electricity, denoting or of any body having an excess of electrons: n. 1. a proposition by which something is denied. 2. a word, phrase, etc. expressing denial. 3. a photographic image on film in which the lights and shades are the opposite of those in the positive printed from this. 4. the plate in a voltaic battery at the lower potential.

neg·lect (ni-glekt'), n. 1. the act of neglecting. 2. negligence; disregard. 3. the state of being neglected: v.t. 1. to omit by carelessness or design. 2. to disregard. 3. to slight. — **neg·lect'ful**, *adj.*

neg·li·gee (neg·li-zhā'), *n.* a woman's loose dressing gown.

neg·li·gent (neg'li-jěnt), *adj.* 1. continually neglectful. 2. very careless. —**neg'li·gence**, *n.*

neg·li·gi·ble (neg'li-ji-bl), *adj.* that may be neglected; trifling.

ne·go·ti·ate (ni-gō'shi-āt), *v.i.* -at·ed, -at·ing, to treat with others in an attempt to reach agreement: *v.t.* 1. to conclude (a treaty, bargain, etc.). 2. to sell or transfer (stocks, funds, etc.) to another for value received. 3. to succeed in traveling over, surmounting, etc. —**ne·go'ti·a·ble** ('shi-á-bl, 'shá-bl), *adj.* —**ne·go·ti·a'tion**, *n.* —**ne·go'ti·a·tor**, *n.*

Ne·gress (nē'grìs), *n.* a Negro woman or girl: now sometimes regarded as a patronizing or hostile term.

Ne·gri·to (nē-grēt'ō), *n., pl.* -tos, -toes, any member of various groups of Negroid people of small stature living in Asia and Africa.

ne·gri·tude (neg'ri-tōōd, nē'gri-), *n.* an affirmation by blacks of the intrinsic value of their culture and heritage.

Ne·gro (nē'grō), *n., pl.* -groes, 1. any member of the division of mankind dominant in Africa, characterized by a dark skin. 2. a person with Negro ancestry: *adj.* of or pertaining to Negroes.

Ne·groid ('groid), *adj.* denoting or of one of the major divisions of mankind, including most of the peoples of Africa.

Ne·gro·phile (nē'grò-fīl), *n.* one friendly to Negroes, their culture, etc.

Ne·gro·phobe (-fōb), *n.* one who hates or fears Negroes.

ne·gus (nē'gûs), *n.* a beverage of hot water, wine, and lemon juice, sweetened and spiced.

Ne·he·mi·ah (nē-ĕ-mī'å), *n.* a book of the Bible.

neigh (nā), *v.i.* to utter the cry, or whinny, of a horse: *n.* this cry.

neigh·bor (nā'bēr), *n.* 1. one who dwells near another. 2. a fellow man: *adj.* nearby; adjacent: *v.t. & v.i.* to live or be situated close by.

neigh·bor·hood (-hood), *n.* 1. a particular district, area, etc. 2. the state of being neighbors. 3. the people living near one another.

neigh·bor·ing (-ing), *adj.* nearby.

neigh·bor·ly (-li), *adj.* like or becoming to neighbors; social, friendly, etc. —**neigh'bor·li·ness**, *n.*

nei·ther (nē'thēr, nī'), *adj. & pron.* not the one or the other: *conj.* 1. not either. 2. nor yet.

nek·ton (nek'ton), *n.* all the larger, free-swimming animals in the waters of lakes, seas, etc.

nem·a·tode (nem'å-tōd), *n.* any one of a group of worms, with long, unsegmented bodies, including many, as the hookworm, that are parasitic.

nem·e·sis (nem'ĕ-sis), *n., pl.* -ses, 1. retributive justice. 2. one who exacts retribution. 3. anyone or anything that defeats or frustrates one regularly.

ne·o-, [often N-], a combining form meaning *new, in a different way.*

ne·o·clas·sic (nē-ō-klas'ik), *adj.* denoting or of a revival of classic ideals and forms in literature, art, etc.

Ne·o·Dar·win·ism (-där'win-izm), *n.* a theory of evolution that adjusts the original Darwinian concepts to modern genetics.

ne·o·dym·i·um (-ō-dim'i-ùm), *n.* a metallic chemical element of the rare-earth group.

Ne·o·La·marck·ism (-ō-lá-märk'izm), *n.* a theory of evolution claiming that acquired characteristics can be inherited and that environment can influence genetic changes.

ne·o·lith (nē'ō-lith), *n.* a neolithic stone tool.

ne·o·lith·ic (-lith'ik), *adj.* denoting or of a period in man's history late in the Stone Age, characterized by the beginnings of agriculture and domestication of animals.

ne·ol·o·gism (ni-ol'ō-jizm), *n.* 1. a newly coined word or a new meaning for an old word. 2. the use of new words or of new meanings for old words.

ne·ol·o·gize (-jīz), *v.i.* -gized, -giz·ing, to introduce or frequently use neologisms. —**ne·ol'o·gist**, *n.*

ne·ol·o·gy (-ji), *n., pl.* -gies, same as neologism.

ne·on (nē'on), *n.* an inert gaseous chemical element existing in small amounts in the atmosphere.

neon lamp, a glass tube containing neon which glows with a red light when a current is passed through it.

ne·o·phyte (nē'ō-fīt), *n.* 1. a new convert. 2. a newly ordained priest or new member of a convent. 3. a beginner in anything; novice.

ne·o·plasm (-plazm), *n.* an abnormal growth of tissue, as a tumor. —**ne·o·plas'tic**, *adj.*

ne·o·prene (-prēn), *n.* a synthetic rubber resistant to light, heat, etc.

ne·o·ter·ic (nē-ō-ter'ik), *adj.* recent; new.

ne·pen·the (ni-pen'thi), *n.* 1. a drug supposed by the ancient Greeks to have the power of causing forgetfulness of sorrow. 2. anything causing this phenomenon.

neph·ew (nef'ū), *n.* 1. the son of a brother or sister. 2. the son of a brother-in-law or sister-in-law.

ne·phrit·ic (ni-frit'ik), *adj.* 1. of or pertaining to the kidneys; renal. 2. having disease of the kidneys.

ne·phri·tis (ni-frīt'is), *n.* a disease of the kidneys resulting in inflammation, etc.

ne·phrot·o·my (ni-frot'ō-mi), *n., pl.* -mies, incision into the kidney.

ne plus ul·tra (ni plus ul'trá), the furthest point; summit of achievement; highest degree.

nep·o·tism (nep'ō-tizm), *n.* favoritism shown to relatives by patronage, disbursements, conferring of favors, etc. —**nep'o·tist**, *n.*

Nep·tune (nep'tōōn), *n.* 1. the Roman god of the sea. 2. a planet in the solar system, eighth in distance from the sun.

nep·tu·ni·um (nep-tōō'ni-ùm), *n.* a radioactive element produced by bombarding uranium atoms with neutrons.

nerd (nûrd), *n.* [Slang], a person regarded as dull, ineffective, etc.

ne·re·is (nir'i-is), *n., pl.* **ne·re·i·des** (nē-rē'i-dēz), any of a large group of marine worms with segmented bodies.

ner·o·li (ner'ô-li), n. the essential oil of orange flowers, used in perfume.

ner·va·tion (ner-vā'shŭn), n. an arrangement of veins.

nerve (nŭrv), n. 1. one of the fibers which convey sensation from all parts of the body to the nervous system and convey impulses from the brain to other parts of the body. 2. strength. 3. bravery. 4. pl. the quality of being nervous. 5. [Informal], shameless boldness. 6. a vein of a leaf: v.t. **nerved, nerv'-ing,** to invigorate or strengthen.

nerve center, a control center; headquarters.

nerve gas, a poison gas which paralyzes a person's breathing organs.

nerve·less (nŭrv'lis), adj. 1. weak. 2. showing no emotion, upset, etc. —**nerve'less·ly,** adv.

nerve-rack·ing, nerve-wrack·ing ('rak·ing), adj. exasperating or annoying.

nerv·ous (nŭr'vŭs), adj. 1. of, pertaining to, or composed of nerves. 2. easily agitated or highly emotional. 3. vigorous in style. 4. anxious; uneasy. —**ner'vous·ly,** adv. —**ner'vous·ness,** n.

nervous system, the nerves considered collectively as the coordinating agency which regulates the muscles and organs and enables them to carry on their functions; aggregate of all the tissues stimulated by nerve force.

nerv·y (nŭr'vi), adj. **nerv'i·er, nerv'i·est,** 1. courageous. 2. [Informal], showing assurance; cheeky.

nes·ci·ence (nesh'ĕns), n. 1. the state of not knowing; ignorance. 2. the theory that God is unknowable.

-ness (nis, nĕs), a suffix meaning quality, state, case.

nest (nest), n. 1. the bed or dwelling prepared by a bird for incubation and the rearing of its young. 2. the place where eggs are laid and hatched. 3. a cozy residence. 4. a number of things, one fitting inside another. 5. a place often visited, as by thieves: v.i. & v.t. 1. to build and occupy (a nest). 2. to place (something) tightly inside another.

n'est-ce pas? (nĕs pä'), [French], is that not true?

nest egg, 1. an egg in a nest, left to encourage a hen to lay other eggs. 2. money forming a nucleus or reserve.

nes·tle (nes'l), v.i. **-tled, -tling,** 1. to lie close and snug. 2. to take shelter: v.t. to lay snugly.

nest·ling (nest'ling), n. a bird too young to leave the nest.

net (net), n. 1. a fabric of twine or rope knotted into meshes for catching birds, fish, etc. 2. anything resembling or made like a net. 3. a snare. 4. that which is left after all charges, deductions, etc. have been made: adj. remaining after charges, deductions, etc. have been made: v.t. **net'ted, net'ting,** 1. to make into a net. 2. to take with a net; snare. 3. to earn as clear profit: v.i. to form a network.

neth·er (neth'ĕr), adj. 1. lying beneath; belonging to the regions below. 2. lower.

neth·er·most (-mōst), adj. lowest; farthest down.

net·su·ke (net'soo-kā, -kē), n. a small bob of carved ivory or wood which the Japanese formerly attached to a belt, fob, etc.

net·ting (net'ing), n. material in the form of a net.

net·tle (net'l), n. a weed covered with hairs that sting: v.t. **-tled, -tling,** to provoke or irritate.

nettle rash, same as urticaria.

net·tle·some (-sŭm), adj. that provokes or irritates.

net·work (net'wŭrk), n. 1. an openwork of crossed, parallel threads, wires, etc.; netting. 2. a similar arrangement of crossing streets, tracks, etc. 3. a group of persons connected in some way. 4. in Radio & TV, a connected group of broadcasting stations.

net·work·ing ('wŭrk·ing), n. 1. the developing of contacts or exchanging of information, as to further a career. 2. the interconnection of computer systems.

neu·ral (noor'ăl), adj. of or pertaining to the nerves or the nervous system.

neu·ral·gia (noo-ral'jă), n. acute pain in a nerve. —**neu·ral'gic** ('jik), adj.

neu·ras·the·ni·a (noor-ăs-thē'ni-ă), n. a neurotic condition with exhaustion, uneasiness, etc. —**neu·ras·then'ic** (-then'ik), adj. & n.

neu·ri·tis (noo-rīt'is), n. inflammation of a nerve. —**neu·rit'ic** (-rit'ik), adj.

neu·ro-, a combining form meaning of nerves, of the nervous system.

neu·rog·li·a (noo-rog'li-ă), n. the delicate connective tissue between the nerve fibers of the brain and spinal cord.

neu·rol·o·gy (noo-rol'ô-ji), n. the science that deals with the nervous system. —**neu·ro·log·i·cal** (noor-ô-loj'i-kl), adj. —**neu·rol'o·gist,** n.

neu·ro·ma (noo-rō'mă), n., pl. **-mas, -ma·ta,** ('mă-tă), a fibrous tumor occurring in a nerve trunk.

neu·ron (noor'on), n. the body of a nerve cell and its projecting filaments.

neu·ro·path·ic (noor-ô-path'ik), adj. of, pertaining to, or suffering from a disease of the nervous system.

neu·ro·pa·thol·o·gy (noor-ô-pă-thol'ô-ji), n. the pathology of diseases of the nervous system.

neu·ro·sis (noo-rō'sis), n., pl. **-ses** ('sēz), a mental ailment with uneasiness, dejection, excessive fears or concerns, etc.

neu·rot·ic (-rot'ik), adj. of, pertaining to, or having a neurosis: n. a person who has a neurosis. —**neu·rot'i·cal·ly,** adv.

neu·rot·o·my ('ô-mi), n., pl. **-mies,** the severing of a nerve to relieve pain.

neu·ter (nōōt'ĕr), adj. 1. in Biology, of neither sex; sexless. 2. in Grammar, not masculine or feminine; also, intransitive: n. 1. a sexless animal or plant. 2. a castrated animal.

neu·tral (nōō'trăl), adj. 1. unbiased; taking no part on either side in a contest. 2. neither very good nor very bad; indifferent. 3. not brightly colored. 4. in Chemistry, neither acid nor alkaline: n. 1. one who or that which is neutral. 2. a nation which takes no

ŏ in dragon, ōō in crude, oo in wool, u in cup, ū in cure, ŭ in turn, ů in focus, oi in boy, ou in house, th in thin, th in sheathe, g in get, j in joy, y in yet.

side in time of war between other nations. 3. in *Mechanics,* a position of gears in which they are disengaged and no motion is conveyed. —neu′tral·ly, *adv.*

neu·tral·ism (-izm), *n.* a neutral course of action during international war.

neu·tral·i·ty (noo-tral′i-ti), *n.* 1. the state of being neutral. 2. a neutral principle followed by a nation.

neu·tral·ize (nōō′trə-līz), *v.t.* -ized, iz·ing, 1. to make (a nation) neutral in war. 2. to render inactive. —neu·tral·i·za′tion, *n.*

neu·tri·no (nōō-trē′nō), *n., pl.* -nos, in *Physics,* a neutral particle with barely any mass and no charge.

neu·tron (nōō′tron), *n.* an uncharged particle having nearly the mass of a proton.

né·vé (nā-vā′), *n.* the granular, compressed snow which forms glacier ice.

nev·er (nev′ēr), *adv.* 1. not at any time. 2. in no degree or condition.

nev·er·more (nev-ēr-môr′), *adv.* at no time ever again.

never-never land (nev-ēr-nev′ēr), a place of fantasy.

nev·er·the·less (-thē-les′), *adv.* notwithstanding; in spite of that.

ne·vus (nē′vŭs), *n., pl.* ne′vi (′vī), a spot of color on the skin.

new (nōō), *adj.* 1. recent in origin; modern; novel. 2. lately made, produced, invented, or discovered. 3. recently entered upon or commenced. 4. not previously used. 5. fresh. 6. foreign. 7. added: *adv.* 1. again. 2. recently.

new blood, recently arrived people that may bring fresh ideas, force, etc.

new·born (′bôrn′), *adj.* 1. recently born. 2. born again.

new·com·er (′kum-ēr), *n.* one who has come recently.

New Deal, the plans and actions formulated and followed by President F. D. Roosevelt in the United States in the 1930′s to further social and economic growth and development.

new·el (nōō′ĕl), *n.* 1. in a winding staircase, the central upright pillar around which the steps turn. 2. the post holding the handrail on a stairway

new·fan·gled (nōō′fang′gld), *adj.* done or made in a new way: a humorous or belittling term.

new·fash·ioned (′fash′ŭnd), *adj.* 1. having come recently into fashion. 2. having a new style or structure.

New·found·land dog (nōō′fŭnd-land), a large variety of North American dog with shaggy hair.

New Jerusalem, in the *Bible,* the heavenly city.

New Jerusalem, Church of the, the church which holds to the doctrine taught by Emanuel Swedenborg: the members usually are called *Swedenborgians.*

new·ly (nōō′li), *adv.* recently.

new·ly·wed (-wed), *n.* a person who has been married only a short time.

new moon, the moon phase in which the dark side faces the earth.

news (nōōz), *n.pl.* 1. recent information. 2. ti-

dings; recent occurrences. 3. shortened form of newscast.

news·boy (nōōz′boi), *n.* a boy who peddles or delivers newspapers.

news·cast (′kast), *n.* a news broadcast over radio or television.

news·deal·er (′dĕl-ēr), *n.* one who sells newspapers at retail.

news·let·ter (′let-ēr), *n.* a regular, specialized news bulletin.

news·man (′man, ′măn), *n., pl.* -men (′men, ′mĕn), 1. same as newsdealer. 2. a reporter for radio, newspapers, etc.

news·mon·ger (′mŭng-gēr), *n.* one who deals in news; gossip.

news·pa·per (nōōz′pā-pēr), *n.* a paper published periodically, usually daily or weekly, containing the most recent happenings, advertisements, etc.

news·pa·per·man (-man), *n., pl.* -men (-men), 1. a person employed by a newspaper, as a reporter. 2. the owner or publisher of a newspaper. —news′pa·per·wom·an, *n.fem., pl.* -wom·en.

new·speak (nōō′spēk), *n.* [sometimes N-], utilization of confusing and tricky language.

news·print (nōōz′print), *n.* paper of low quality used in making newspapers.

news·stand (′stand), *n.* a booth or stall where newspapers, magazines, etc. are sold.

New Style, the Gregorian or present style of computing the calendar.

news·wor·thy (nōōz′wŭr-thi), *adj.* significant or worthy of attention as news.

news·y (′i), *adj.* news′i·er, news′i·est, [Informal], including a great deal of news.

newt (nōōt), *n.* a small salamander which inhabits both land and water.

New Testament, that portion of the Bible that contains the covenant of God with man as it is embodied in the teaching of Jesus Christ and his disciples.

New World, the Western Hemisphere. —new′-world′, New′-World′, *adj.*

next (nekst), *adj.* nearest in time, place, degree, or rank: *prep.* nearest to: *adv.* 1. at the first succeeding instance. 2. immediately succeeding or preceding.

nex·us (nek′sŭs), *n., pl.* -us·es, nex′us, a connection or tie between the members of a group or series.

ni·a·cin (nī′ă-sin), *n.* same as nicotinic acid.

nib (nib), *n.* 1. a bird′s beak. 2. the point of anything. 3. the point of a pen: *v.t.* nibbed, nib′bing, to fix (a pen point).

nib·ble (nib′l), *v.t. & v.i.* -bled, -bling, 1. to bite (*at*) a little at a time. 2. to continue to bite gently and quickly: *n.* 1. a small bite. 2. a seizing at to bite.

nib·lick (nib′lik), *n.* a heavy, sloped golf club, now usually called a *number nine iron.*

nibs (nibz), *n.* [Informal], an important or pompous person (preceded by *his*).

nice (nis), *adj.* nic′er, nic′est, 1. fastidious; refined. 2. precise; delicate. 3. minutely discriminative. 4. socially agreeable. 5. pleasing as to the palate. 6. scrupulously exact. 7. requiring skill in handling. —nice′ly, *adv.* —nice′ness, *n.*

ni·ce·ty (nī′sĕ-ti), *n., pl.* -ties, 1. precision. 2.

minute accuracy. 3. fastidious delicacy. 4. the requirement of delicate management. 5. a fine detail or difference. 6. something graceful or of high quality.

niche (nich), *n.* 1. a recess in a wall, as for a statue. 2. a suitable place: *v.t.* niched, nich'-ing, to place in a niche.

nicht wahr? (nikht vär'), [German], is that not true?

nick (nik), *n.* 1. a small cut or indentation in wood, china, or other material, on the edge or surface. 2. the critical moment: in the phrase in the **nick** of time: *v.t.* 1. to cut nicks or notches in. 2. to injure on the surface. 3. [Slang], to cheat. 4. [British Slang], to steal.

nick-el (nik'l), *n.* 1. a silver-white, malleable metallic element, used in forming alloys. 2. a five-cent coin, made of nickel and copper alloy.

nick-el-o-de-on (nik-ĕ-lō'di-ŭn), *n.* a musical machine, as a player piano or jukebox, operated by putting a nickel in a slot.

nickel silver an alloy of nickel, copper, and zinc; German silver.

nick-er (nik'ĕr), *v.i. & n.* same as neigh.

nick-name (nik'nām), *n.* another name, given in derision or familiarity: *v.t.* -named, -nam-ing, to give a nickname to.

nic-o-tine (nik'ō-tēn), *n.* an acrid, poisonous alkaloid, in the form of an oily, colorless liquid, extracted from tobacco leaves.

nic-o-tin-ic acid (nik-ō-tin'ik, -tē'nik), a white, crystalline substance that is part of the complex of vitamin B.

nic-tate (nik'tāt), *v.i.* -tat-ed, -tat-ing, to wink quickly: also **nic'ti-tate** ('ti-tāt), -tat-ed, -tat-ing.

nid-i-fy (nid'I-fī), *v.i.* -fied, -fy-ing, to build a nest. —**nid-i-fi-ca'tion**, *n.*

ni-dus (nī'dŭs), *n., pl.* -di ('dī), -dus-es, a nest or breeding place.

niece (nēs), *n.* 1. the daughter of a brother or sister. 2. the daughter of a brother-in-law or sister-in-law.

ni-el-lo (nĭ-el'ō), *n., pl.* -li ('ē), -los, 1. a metallic alloy of sulfur with copper, lead, etc. 2. the process of decorating metal in carved grooves filled with this alloy.

nif-ty (nif'tĭ), *adj.* -ti-er, -ti-est, [Slang], pleasing, fashionable, etc.

nig-gard (nig'ĕrd), *adj.* parsimonious; miserly: *n.* a miser. —nig'gard-ly, *adj. & adv.* —nig'gard-li-ness, *n.*

nig-gle (nig'l), *v.i.* -gled, -gling, to fuss over trifling matters or petty details. —nig'gling, *adj. & n.*

nigh (nī), *adj. & adv. & prep.* [Chiefly Archaic], near.

night (nīt), *n.* 1. the time from sunset to sunrise. 2. a period of darkness. 3. death. 4. intellectual or moral darkness: *adj.* of, pertaining to, occurring, or performed in the night.

night-bloom-ing ce-re-us (nīt'blōō-ming sir'ĭ-ŭs), a cactus with large, fragrant, white flowers which open at night.

night-cap ('kap), *n.* 1. a cap worn in bed at night. 2. [Informal], a drink of alcoholic liquor taken before going to bed.

night clothes, clothes for wearing in bed, as a nightgown.

night-club ('klub), *n.* a place of entertainment open at night for drinking, dancing, etc.

night-dress ('dres), *n.* same as nightgown.

night-fall ('fôl), *n.* the close of the day; early evening; dusk.

night-gown ('goun), *n.* a loose gown worn in bed by women or girls.

night-hawk ('hôk), *n.* 1. a new-world bird related to the goatsucker and whippoorwill. 2. same as nightjar. 3. same as night owl (sense 2).

night heron, a type of heron most active at night.

night-ie (nīt'ĭ), *n.* [Informal], same as nightgown.

night-in-gale (nīt'n-gāl), *n.* a small thrush of Europe, noted for the melodious song of the male at night.

night-jar ('jär), *n.* the European goatsucker.

night-ly ('lĭ), *adj.* 1. of or having the nature of night. 2. happening or performed at night: *adv.* 1. night after night. 2. during the night.

night-mare ('mer), *n.* 1. a frightening dream accompanied by a feeling of oppression and helplessness. 2. an experience like such a dream.

night owl, 1. a nocturnal owl. 2. one who keeps late hours or is employed at night.

night-shade ('shād), *n.* 1. a poisonous weed with white flowers and black berries. 2. same as belladonna (sense 1).

night-shirt ('shŭrt), *n.* a loose nightgown formerly worn by men and boys in bed.

night-spot ('spot), *n.* [Informal], same as nightclub.

night stand, a small table or cabinet placed adjacent to a bed.

night stick, a long club carried by a policeman.

night-time ('tīm), *n.* the period of darkness from sunset to sunrise.

night-wear ('wer), *n.* same as night clothes.

ni-gres-cent (nī-gres'nt), *adj.* blackish; becoming black. —ni-gres'cence, *n.*

nig-ri-fy (nig'rĭ-fī), *v.t.* -fied, -fy-ing, to blacken.

ni-hil (nī'hil), *n.* nothing; a thing of no value.

ni-hil-ism (nī'ĭ-lizm), *n.* 1. skepticism which denies that anything, even existence, can be known. 2. the dismissal of any moral or religious standards. —ni'hil-ist, *n.* —ni-hil-is'tic, *adj.*

nil (nil), *n.* nothing.

nil-gai (nil'gī), *n., pl.* -gais, -gai, a large Indian antelope.

nim-ble (nim'bl), *adj.* -bler, -blest, 1. quick and active; lively; brisk. 2. alert.

nim-bus (nim'bŭs), *n., pl.* -bi ('bī), -bus-es, 1. a rain cloud. 2. in *Art*, the halo or cloud of light surrounding the heads of divinities, saints, or sovereigns.

Nim-rod (nim'rod), *n.* in the *Bible*, a very successful hunter, the son of Cush: see *Genesis x*, 8.

nin-com-poop (nin'kŏm-pōōp), *n.* a stupid person; fool.

nine (nīn), *adj.* one more than eight: *n.* the cardinal numeral that is the sum of eight and one; 9; IX.

ô in dragon, ōō in crude, oo in wool, u in cup, ū in cure, ŭ in turn, ŭ in focus, oi in boy, ou in house, th in thin, th in sheathe, g in get, j in joy, y in yet.

nine-pins (nīn′pinz), *n.* a game in which nine pins or pegs of wood are set up to be bowled at with wooden bowls or balls.

nine-teen ('tēn'), *adj.* one more than 18: *n.* the cardinal numeral that is the sum of 18 and one; 19; XIX.

nine-teenth ('tēnth'), *adj.* next after 18th; 19th: *n.* 1. the one after the 18th. 2. one of 19 equal parts.

nine-ti-eth (nīn′ti-ith), *adj.* next after 89th; 90th: *n.* 1. the one after the 89th. 2. one of 90 equal parts.

nine-ty (nīn′ti), *adj.* nine times ten: *n., pl.* -ties, 1. the cardinal numeral that is the sum of 89 and one; 90; XC (or LXXXX). 2. *pl.* years or numbers from 90 through 99 (preceded by *the*).

nin-ny (nin′i), *n., pl.* -nies, a simpleton; fool.

ninth (ninth), *adj.* next after eighth; 9th: *n.* 1. the one after the eighth. 2. one of nine equal parts. 3. in *Music*, an interval of an octave and a second.

ni-o-bi-um (nī-ō′bi-ùm), *n.* a metallic element of steel-gray color.

nip (nip), *n.* 1. a pinch as with the nails or teeth. 2. a blast as by cold. 3. frost. 4. a small drink of alcoholic liquor: *v.t.* **nipped, nip′ping,** 1. to pinch. 2. to cut off the end of. 3. to check the growth or vigor of. 4. to blast or injure, as by frost.

nip-per (nip′ēr), *n.* 1. one who or that which nips. 2. *pl.* small pincers. 3. a lobster or crab claw.

nip-ple (nip′l), *n.* 1. the part of the breast of a woman from which milk is drawn by a child; teat. 2. a rubber part like a teat that fits over the mouth of a baby's bottle.

nip-py (nip′i), *adj.* **-pi-er, -pi-est,** 1. pinching or nipping. 2. bitingly cold.

nir-va-na (nir-vä′nä), *n.* [also N-], 1. in *Buddhism,* the highest religious state, in which all desire is extinguished and the soul is absorbed into the Deity. 2. a very peaceful or happy condition.

ni-sei (nē′sā), *n., pl.* **ni′sei, ni′seis,** a person born of immigrant Japanese parents in the United States.

nit (nit), *n.* 1. the egg of a louse or other parasitic insect. 2. a young louse, etc.

ni-ter (nīt′ēr), *n.* potassium nitrate or sodium nitrate used in the production of fertilizer, explosives, etc.: also, British spelling, ni′tre.

nit-pick-ing (nit′pik-ing), *adj. & n.* fussing over trifling matters.

ni-trate (nī′trāt), *n.* a salt of nitric acid: *v.t.* **-trat-ed, -trat-ing,** to combine with nitric acid.

ni-tric (nī′trik), *adj.* 1. of or having nitrogen. 2. containing nitrogen in the highest valence.

nitric acid, a powerful, colorless acid composed of hydrogen, nitrogen, and oxygen obtained by the action of sulfuric acid on nitrates.

ni-tride (nī′trīd), *n.* a compound of nitrogen with another chemical element, as boron.

ni-tri-fy (nī′tri-fī), *v.t.* **-fied, -fy-ing,** 1. to combine with nitrogen or its compounds. 2. to oxidize (ammonium salts, nitrogen in the atmosphere, etc.) into nitrites and nitrates, as by the action of bacteria in the soil. **—ni-tri-fi-ca′tion,** *n.* **—ni′tri-fi-er,** *n.*

ni-trite (nī′trīt), *n.* a salt or ester of nitrous acid.

ni-tro-, a combining form denoting *the presence of nitrogen in some form.*

ni-tro-cel-lu-lose (nī-trō-sel′yoo-lōs), *n.* a combination of cellulose and nitric acid, used in producing explosives, plastics, etc.

ni-tro-gen (nī′trō-jēn), *n.* a gaseous, colorless, odorless, tasteless chemical element constituting about 4/5 of the atmosphere by volume and also found in minerals and in all living tissues.

ni-tro-gen-fix-ing (-fik′sing), *adj.* of or pertaining to bacteria that grow in the nodules of certain leguminous plants and change atmospheric nitrogen into nitrates which are then made available to the plant. **—nitrogen fixation.**

ni-trog-e-nize (nī-troj′ĕ-nīz), *v.t.* **-nized, -niz-ing,** to impregnate with nitrogen.

ni-trog-e-nous (nī-troj′ĕ-nŭs), *adj.* of, pertaining to, or containing nitrogen.

ni-tro-glyc-er-in, ni-tro-glyc-er-ine (nī-trō-glis′ĕr-in), *n.* a light-yellow, oily, heavy liquid of a highly explosive quality, obtained by mixing nitric and sulfuric acids and using that mixture to treat glycerine: used to form dynamite.

ni-trous (nī′trŭs), *adj.* resembling, obtained from, or impregnated with niter.

nitrous acid, an acid composed of nitrogen and oxygen, found only in solution or in its salts.

nitrous oxide, a colorless gas composed of nitrogen and oxygen and used as an anesthetic; laughing gas.

nit-ty-grit-ty (nit′i-grit′i), *n.* [Slang], the essence or fundamental nature.

nit-wit (nit′wit), *n.* a fool or idiot.

ni-val (nī′vl), *adj.* of, pertaining to, or growing under snow.

niv-e-ous (niv′i-ŭs), *adj.* snowlike.

nix (niks), *n.* 1. in *Germanic Mythology,* a water sprite. 2. nothing: *adv.* [Slang], 1. no. 2. not at all: *interj.* [Slang], 1. cease! 2. I decline, prohibit, etc.: *v.t.* [Slang], to condemn or stop.

no (nō), *adv.* 1. not so: used for denial or refusal. 2. not to any degree: *adj.* not any: *n., pl.* **noes, nos,** 1. a negative reply. 2. one who votes in the negative.

No-ah (nō′ä), *n.* in the *Bible,* the one who built the ark under God's order.

nob (nob), *n.* [Slang], the head.

nob-by (nob′i), *adj.* **-bi-er, -bi-est,** [Chiefly British Slang], stylish.

No-bel prize (nō-bel′), one of the annual prizes given by the Nobel Foundation for distinction in various departments of science, in literature, or in the promotion of peace: after Alfred Bernhard Nobel (1833-96), Swedish chemist and inventor of dynamite, who left a large sum to keep up the prizes.

no-bil-i-ty (nō-bil′i-ti), *n., pl.* **-ties,** 1. the state or quality of being noble; grandeur; dignity. 2. noble birth. 3. nobles collectively.

no-ble (nō′bl), *adj.* **-bler, -blest,** 1. high in excellence or worth. 2. illustrious. 3. magnificent. 4. exalted in rank. 5. of ancient lineage: *n.* a peer or nobleman. —**no'ble·ness,** *n.* —**no'bly,** *adv.*

no·ble·man (-măn), *n., pl.* -men (-měn), a peer; man of noble rank.

no·blesse o·blige (nō·bles' ō·blēzh'), the assumed duty of the nobility to be civil and generous in behavior toward others.

no·bod·y (nō'bud-i), *pron.* no one: *n., pl.* -bod·ies, a person of no influence or importance.

noc·tur·nal (nok-tûr'nl), *adj.* of, pertaining to, done, or happening at night. —**noc·tur'nal·ly,** *adv.*

noc·turne (nok'tĕrn), *n.* 1. a picture of a night scene. 2. a romantic musical composition considered appropriate to the night.

nod (nod), *n.* 1. a quick inclination of the head. 2. an indication of assent, approval, etc.: *v.i.* nod·ded, nod·ding, 1. to incline or bend (the head) quickly. 2. to signify by a nod: *v.i.* 1. to give a quick forward motion of the head, in an indication of assent, command, etc. 2. to let the head fall forward in drowsiness. —**nod'der,** *n.*

nod·dy (nod'i), *n., pl.* -dies, 1. a simpleton. 2. a sea fowl.

node (nōd), *n.* 1. a knot; knob. 2. one of the two points at which the orbit of a planet intersects the ecliptic. 3. any one of the points on the stem of a plant from which a leaf springs. 4. the problematic point of a play, etc. 5. a protuberance on the body.

nod·ule (noj'ōōl), *n.* a little knot or irregular, rounded lump. —**nod'u·lar,** *adj.*

No·el (nō-el'), *n.* same as Christmas.

no-fault (nō'fôlt'), *adj.* 1. designating a form of automobile insurance in which those insured collect damages without blame being fixed. 2. designating a form of divorce granted without blame being charged.

nog·gin (nog'in), *n.* 1. a small cup or mug. 2. one fourth of a pint of liquor. 3. [Informal], the head.

nog·ging (nog'ing), *n.* a brick partition between timbers.

no-good (nō'good), *adj.* [Slang], worthless.

noise (noiz), *n.* 1. outcry; clamor. 2. any sound. 3. a grating, loud, or discordant sound: *v.t.* noised, nois'ing, to spread (a rumor, story, etc.): used with *about, around,* etc.

noise·less (noiz'lis), *adj.* with no sound. —**noise'less·ly,** *adv.*

noi·some (noi'sŭm), *adj.* 1. injurious to health; noxious. 2. smelling of an unpleasant odor; disgusting.

nois·y (noi'zi), *adj.* nois'i·er, nois'i·est, 1. producing noise. 2. full of noise; turbulent. —**nois'i·ly,** *adv.* —**nois'i·ness,** *n.*

no-load (nō'lōd'), *adj.* designating mutual funds charging no commission on sales.

no·mad (nō'mad), *n.* 1. one of a tribe that wanders about. 2. a rover. —**no·mad'ic,** *adj.*

no man's land, an unoccupied area lying between opposing sides on a field of battle.

nom de plume (nom dĕ plōōm'), *pl.* noms de plume', same as pseudonym.

no·men·cla·ture (nō'měn-klā-chĕr), *n.* the group of names used in any science or art, or in describing the parts of a machine, etc.

nom·i·nal (nom'i-nl), *adj.* 1. of, pertaining to, or containing names. 2. existing only in name. 3. slight in comparison. —**nom'i·nal·ly,** *adv.*

nom·i·nate (nom'i-nāt), *v.t.* -nat·ed, -nat·ing, 1. to propose for an office. 2. to appoint, as to an office. —**nom·i·na'tion,** *n.* —**nom'i·na·tor,** *n.*

nom·i·na·tive (nom'i-nā-tiv), *adj.* in *Grammar,* denoting the case of the subject: *n.* 1. the case of the subject. 2. a word in this case.

nom·i·nee (nom-i-nē'), *n.* one who is proposed for an office.

non-, a prefix meaning *not*: it denotes simple negation, and, as many words to which it is affixed are self-explanatory, such words are omitted from the list of definitions.

non·age (non'ij), *n.* the legal state of minority.

non·a·ge·nar·i·an (non-ă-jĕ-ner'i-ăn), *n.* one who is ninety years old, or between ninety and one hundred: *adj.* of or denoting a nonagenarian.

non·a·gon (non'ă-gon), *n.* a plane figure with nine sides and nine angles.

non·a·ligned (non-ă-līnd'), *adj.* not taking sides in political power struggles. —**non·a·lign'ment,** *n.*

nonce (nons), *n.* the present time: chiefly in for the nonce.

non·cha·lant (non-shă-länt'), *adj.* 1. indicating a lack of sympathy or zeal. 2. cool; indifferent. —**non·cha·lance',** *n.* —**non·cha·lant'ly,** *adv.*

non·com (non'kom), *n.* [Informal], a shortened form of noncommissioned officer.

non·com·bat·ant (non-kom'bă-tănt, -kŏm-bat'ănt), *n.* 1. one who is part of the armed forces, but does not actually fight. 2. a civilian during wartime.

non·com·mis·sioned officer (non-kŏ-mish'ŭnd), an enlisted person in the armed forces, as in the U.S. Army, one in a grade from corporal through sergeant major.

non·com·mit·tal (non-kŏ-mit'l), *adj.* not indicating one's opinion or intentions.

non·con·duc·tor (non-kŏn-duk'tĕr), *n.* a substance that does not readily transmit heat, electricity, sound, or the like.

non·con·form·ist (-kŏn-fôr'mist), *n.* 1. one who does not conform to the established laws, rules, or customs. 2. [N-], one who does not conform to the established church of England. —**non·con·form'i·ty,** *n.*

non·de·script (non-di-skript'), *n.* a person or thing so lacking in distinctive qualities as not to be easily described or classed: *adj.* lacking distinctive qualities.

none (nun), *pron.* 1. no one. 2. not any: *adv.* not at all: *n.* nothing.

non·en·ti·ty (non-en'ti-ti), *n., pl.* -ties, 1. a thing not existing. 2. a person or thing of no importance or influence.

nones (nōnz), *n.pl.* in the ancient Roman calendar, the ninth day before the ides.

none-such (nun'such), *n.* one that has no equal.

none·the·less (nun-*th*e-les'), *adv.* however.

ŏ in drag*o*n, ōō in cr*u*de, oo in w*oo*l, u in c*u*p, ŭ in c*u*re, ŭ in t*u*rn, ŭ in foc*u*s, oi in b*oy,* ou in h*ou*se, th in *th*in, *th* in shea*th*e, g in *g*et, j in *j*oy, y in *y*et.

non·ex·ist·ence (non-ig-zis'tĕns), *n.* the state of not existing. —**non·ex·ist'ent**, *adj. & n.*

non·fea·sance (non-fē'zns), *n.* in *Law*, neglect in doing what should have been done.

no·nil·lion (nō-nil'yŭn), *n.* 1. in the U.S. and France, the number indicated by 1 followed by 30 zeros. 2. in Great Britain and Germany, the number indicated by 1 followed by 54 zeros. —**no·nil'lionth**, *adj. & n.*

non·in·ter·ven·tion (non-in-tĕr-ven'shŭn), *n.* the policy of one country not interfering in the activities of another.

non·met·al (-met'l), *n.* an element that does not have the qualities associated with metals, as oxygen, sulfur, etc. —**non·me·tal'lic**, *adj.*

non·pa·reil (non-pă-rel'), *adj.* without an equal: *n.* 1. someone or something unequaled. 2. in *Printing*, a size of type.

non·par·ti·san (non-pär'tĭ-zn), *adj.* not connected with a particular political party: also **non·par'ti·zan**.

non·plus (non-plus'), *v.t.* -**plused'** or -**plussed'**, -**plus'ing** or -**plus'sing**, to throw into complete perplexity; puzzle: *n.* an insuperable difficulty; puzzle.

non·prof·it (non-prof'it), *adj.* not achieving a profit by purpose or design.

non·res·i·dent (-rez'ĭ-dĕnt), *adj.* not living where one works, attends school, etc.: *n.* one who is nonresident.

non·re·stric·tive (-ri-strik'tiv), *adj.* in *Grammar*, denoting a word or phrase set off by commas because it is not fundamental to the meaning of the sentence.

non·sched·uled (-skej'oold), *adj.* of or denoting airlines or flights which operate only when needed, and not on a regular schedule.

non·sec·tar·i·an (-sek-ter'i-ăn), *adj.* not connected to a particular religion.

non·sense (non'sens), *n.* language without meaning; anything absurd.

non·sen·si·cal (non-sen'si-kl), *adj.* absurd; unmeaning; foolish. —**non·sen'si·cal·ly**, *adv.*

non se·qui·tur (non sek'wi-tĕr), 1. in *Logic*, a conclusion or inference which does not follow from the premises. 2. something uttered which has no connection with previous statements.

non·stop (non'stop'), *adj. & adv.* without stopping; straight through to a destination.

non·suit (non'sōōt'), *n.* in *Law*, the withdrawal of a suit during trial either voluntarily or by judgment of the court for various reasons: *v.t.* to subject to a nonsuit.

non·sup·port (non-sŭ-pôrt'), *n.* negligence in supplying financial support for a dependent.

non·un·ion (non-ūn'yŭn), *adj.* 1. not a member of a labor union. 2. not manufactured or repaired in a union shop. 3. not contracting with a labor union.

non·vi·o·lence (-vī'ō-lĕns), *n.* a refusing to participate in violence, as in political protest. —**non·vi'o·lent**, *adj.*

noo·dle (nōō'dl), *n.* 1. a simpleton. 2. [Slang], the head. 3. a strip of dried dough, served in soup, baked in casseroles, etc.

nook (nook), *n.* 1. a small recess or secluded retreat. 2. a corner.

noon (nōōn), *n.* the middle of the day; 12 o'clock: *adj.* of, pertaining to, or happening at noon. Also **noon'day**, **noon'time**.

no one, nobody.

noose (nōōs), *n.* a circle of rope, etc. with a slipknot that binds closer the more tightly it is drawn: *v.t.* **noosed**, **noos'ing**, to secure by a noose.

nor (nôr), *conj.* and not; likewise not: a negative correlative to *neither* or *not*.

Nor·dic (nôr'dik), *adj.* of or pertaining to the Caucasoid physical category of which tall, blond Scandinavians are typical.

norm (nôrm), *n.* 1. a model or type. 2. the standard of a group.

nor·mal (nôr'ml), *adj.* 1. according to a rule or a standard pattern; regular; usual. 2. having an average intelligence. 3. in *Mathematics*, perpendicular: *n.* 1. that which is normal. 2. the average. —**nor'mal·cy**, **nor·mal'i·ty** (-mal'ĭ-ti), *n.*

nor·mal·ize ('mă-līz), *v.t. & v.i.* -**ized**, -**iz·ing**, to make or become normal. —**nor·mal·i·za'tion**, *n.*

nor·mal·ly (-lĭ), *adv.* 1. in a normal way. 2. with normal conditions.

normal school, formerly, a school for the training of teachers for elementary schools.

Nor·man (nôr'măn), *adj.* of or pertaining to the Normans, Normandy, a region of northwestern France, or to a style of architecture introduced into England by the Normans, characterized by the rounded arch and massive square towers: *n.* a native or inhabitant of Normandy.

nor·ma·tive (nôr'mă-tiv), *adj.* of, pertaining to, or forming a norm.

Norse (nôrs), *adj.* same as *Scandinavian*: *n.* the Scandinavian language group.

Norse·man (nôrs'măn), *n., pl.* -**men** ('mĕn), one of the ancient Scandinavian people.

north (nôrth), *n.* 1. the part of the sky to the left of where the sun rises. 2. a region or area toward this part. 3. [often N-], the northern part of the earth; arctic areas: *adj.* of, in, or coming from the north: *adv.* in a northerly direction.

north·east (nôrth-ēst'), *n.* 1. the direction or point halfway between north and east; 45° east of due north. 2. a region or area toward this direction: *adj.* of, in, or coming from the northeast: *adv.* in, to, or from the northeast. —**north·east'er·ly**, *adj. & adv.* — **north·east'ern**, *adj.*

north·east·ward (-wĕrd), *adv. & adj.* toward the northeast: also **north·east·wards**, *adv.*

north·er (nôr'thĕr), *n.* a gale from the north, as one which at periods sweeps over the Gulf States.

north·er·ly (-lĭ), *adj. & adv.* to or from the north.

north·ern (nôr'thĕrn), *adj.* 1. in, from, or toward the north. 2. [N-], of or pertaining to the North.

north·ern·er ('thĕr-nĕr), *n.* 1. one born or living in the north. 2. [N-], a native or inhabitant of the northern U.S.

northern lights, same as *aurora borealis*.

north·ing (nôr'thing), *n.* the distance traversed by a vessel sailing northward.

North Star, Polaris, the star situated almost exactly above the northern pole; polestar.

north·ward (nôrth'wĕrd), *adv. & adj.* toward the north: also **north'wards,** *adv.*

north·west (nôrth-west'), *n.* 1. the direction or point halfway between north and west; 45° west of due north. 2. a region or area toward this direction: *adj.* of, in, or coming from the northwest: *adv.* in, to, or from the northwest. —**north·west'er·ly,** *adj. & adv.* — **north·west'ern,** *adj.*

north·west·ward (nôrth'west'wĕrd), *adv. & adj.* toward the northwest: also **north·west·wards,** *adv.*

Nor·we·gian (nôr-wē'jăn), *adj.* of or pertaining to Norway, a nation in northern Europe, or to its inhabitants: *n.* a native or inhabitant of Norway.

nose (nōz), *n.* 1. the part of the face over the mouth, used for smelling and respiration. 2. scent. 3. anything resembling a nose, as a nozzle, prow, etc. 4. a snout; muzzle: *v.t.* **nosed, nos'ing,** 1. to trace by smell. 2. to discover by prying. 3. to touch or push with or as with the nose: *v.i.* 1. to smell; snuff. 2. to look around suspiciously. 3. to go ahead.

nose bag, a canvas bag for holding feed for a horse, etc., suspended from the animal's head.

nose·bleed (nōz'blēd), *n.* a nose hemorrhage.

nose cone, the frontal tip of a rocket or missile, in the shape of a cone.

nose dive, 1. the downward plunge of an aircraft with the nose in front. 2. an abrupt lowering, as in profits.

nose drops, medicine introduced by a dropper into the nose.

nose·gay (nōz'gā), *n.* a small bouquet.

nose·piece ('pēs), *n.* 1. the nozzle of a pipe, hose, or other tubing. 2. a part fitting over the nose.

nos·ing (nō'zing), *n.* 1. the projecting part on the tread of a stair. 2. a projecting edge, as of a molding.

no·sog·ra·phy (nō-sog'rä-fi), *n.* a description of diseases.

no·sol·o·gy (nō-sol'ō-ji), *n.* a systematic classification of diseases.

nos·tal·gia (nos-tal'jä), *n.* 1. homesickness. 2. a desire for something in the past or a long distance away. —**nos·tal'gic** ('jik), *adj.*

nos·tril (nos'tril), *n.* one of the two openings in the nose.

nos·trum (nos'trŭm), *n.* 1. a quack medicine. 2. a supposed cure for social ills.

nos·y, nos·ey (nō'zi), *adj.* **nos'i·er, nos'i·est,** [Informal], unnecessarily curious.

not (not), *adv.* in no way; to no extent: a word expressive of denial or refusal.

no·ta·bil·i·a (nō-tä-bil'i-ä), *n.pl.* things worthy of note.

no·ta·bil·i·ty (nōt-ä-bil'ĭ-ti), *n.* 1. *pl.* **-ties,** a person of note. 2. the quality of being notable.

no·ta·ble (nōt'ä-bl), *adj.* worthy of notice; memorable; remarkable: *n.* a person of distinction. —**no'ta·bly,** *adv.*

no·tar·i·al (nō-ter'i-ăl), *adj.* of, pertaining to, or done by a notary.

no·ta·rize (nōt'ä-rīz), *v.t.* **-rized, -riz·ing,** to attest (documents) as a notary.

no·ta·ry (nōt'ĕr-i), *n., pl.* **-ries,** an official authorized to attest documents, certify affidavits, etc.: in full **notary public.**

no·ta·tion (nō-tā'shŭn), *n.* 1. the act or practice of recording by marks or symbols. 2. a system of signs or symbols. 3. a short written reminder. 4. the act of making a note.

notch (noch), *n.* 1. a small hollow cut; indentation. 2. a gap. 3. [Informal], a grade; level: *v.t.* to cut small hollows into.

note (nōt), *n.* 1. a memorandum. 2. reputation; fame. 3. a brief explanation. 4. a short letter. 5. a diplomatic communication. 6. a paper acknowledging a debt and promising payment. 7. a piece of paper currency. 8. *pl.* a summary of a speech, experience, etc. 9. a bird call. 10. a sign of something. 11. attention or examination. 12. in *Music,* a mark or sign representing a tone; also, the tone itself: *v.t.* **not'ed, not'ing,** 1. to make a note of; record in writing. 2. to show attention to. 3. to remark on specifically.

note·book (nōt'book), *n.* a book in which things are noted.

not·ed (nōt'id), *adj.* well-known; celebrated; remarkable.

note paper, writing paper.

note·wor·thy (nōt'wŭr-*th*i), *adj.* worthy of note; remarkable.

noth·ing (nuth'ing), *n.* 1. not anything. 2. a thing of no value, use, or importance. 3. a cipher. 4. a person of little consequence or value. 5. nonexistence. 6. an imaginary thing: *adv.* in no degree.

noth·ing·ness (-nis), *n.* 1. nonexistence. 2. worthlessness. 3. lack of consciousness.

no·tice (nōt'is), *n.* 1. mental or visual observation; attention. 2. information; warning. 3. a printed and posted public warning. 4. press criticism of art, literature, etc. 5. a legal announcement of the termination of a contract, etc.: *v.t.* **-ticed, -tic·ing,** 1. to see or observe; regard. 2. to make remarks upon.

no·tice·a·ble (-ä-bl), *adj.* 1. conspicuous. 2. worthy of observation; remarkable. —**no'tice·a·bly,** *adv.*

no·ti·fi·ca·tion (nōt-ĭ-fi-kä'shŭn), *n.* 1. the act of giving notice. 2. the notice given. 3. the document by which information is communicated.

no·ti·fy (nōt'ĭ-fī), *v.t.* **-fied, -fy·ing,** 1. to inform. 2. [Chiefly British], to make known.

no·tion (nō'shŭn), *n.* 1. a general idea. 2. an opinion; belief. 3. an inclination. 4. *pl.* small, useful articles, as needles, etc. sold in a store.

no·tion·al (-l), *adj.* 1. of, pertaining to, or conveying a notion. 2. ideal; imaginary.

no·to·ri·e·ty (nōt-ō-rī'ĕ-ti), *n.* the state of being notorious.

no·to·ri·ous (nō-tôr'i-ŭs), *adj.* publicly known, usually unfavorably.

no-trump (nō'trŭmp'), *n.* in *Bridge,* 1. a bid to play with no trump suit. 2. the hand played.

not·with·stand·ing (not-with-stan'ding), *prep.* in spite of: *conj.* although: *adv.* however; yet.

nou·gat (nōō'gät), *n.* a confection of almonds, other nuts, and sugar paste.

nought (nôt), *n.* 1. nothing. 2. zero.

noun (noun), *n.* in *Grammar*, 1. the name of any person, place, or thing. 2. a substantive.

nour·ish (nûr'ish), *v.t.* 1. to feed; maintain; support. 2. to bring up; educate. 3. to promote growth in.

nour·ish·ing (-ing), *adj.* nutritious; contributing to health or growth.

nour·ish·ment (-ment), *n.* 1. the act of nourishing. 2. the state of being nourished. 3. that which nourishes.

nou·veau riche (nōō-vō rēsh'), *pl.* **nou·veaux riches** (nōō-vō rēsh'), a person who has only recently become rich, esp. one lacking cultural taste, or social grace.

no·va (nō'vä), *n., pi.* **-vas, -vae** ('vē), a star that abruptly increases in brightness and then decreases slowly.

nov·el (nov'l), *adj.* of recent origin or introduction; new; strange or unusual: *n.* a long fictitious tale, as printed in a book.

nov·el·ette (nov-ĕ-let'), *n.* a short novel.

nov·el·ist (nov'l-ist), *n.* a writer of novels. .

nov·el·ty (nov'l-ti), *n., pl.* **-ties,** 1. newness. 2. something new. 3. *usually pl.* a small inexpensive thing, as for amusement.

No·vem·ber (nō-vem'bĕr), *n.* the eleventh month of the year, having 30 days.

no·ve·na (nō-vē'nä), *n.* in the *Roman Catholic Church,* the recitation of prayers and practicing of devotions during a period of nine days for some particular intention.

nov·ice (nov'is), *n.* 1. a beginner. 2. one who has entered a religious house or group but has not yet taken the final vows.

no·vi·ti·ate (nō-vish'i-it), *n.* 1. the state of a novice. 2. the time of probation as a novice.

now (nou), *adv.* 1. at the present time. 2. immediately. 3. then. 4. quite recently. 5. under the circumstances: *conj.* since: *n.* the current period: *adj.* of the current period.

now·a·days (nou'ä-dāz), *n.* the present time: *adv.* in these days; at the present time.

no·where (nō'hwer), *adv.* not anywhere.

no-win (nō'win'), *adj.* designating or of a situation, policy, etc. that cannot lead to success no matter what measures are taken.

no·wise ('wiz), *adv.* not in any manner or degree: also **no'way, no'ways.**

nox·ious (nok'shŭs), *adj.* harmful or pernicious, as to health or morals.

noz·zle (noz'l), *n.* a tube forming the vent of a hose or pipe.

nth (enth), *adj.* of an amount or degree too large to be measured.

nu (nōō), *n.* the 13th letter of the Greek alphabet.

nu·ance (nōō'äns), *n.* a shade of difference; slight variation in expression, feeling, tone, color, etc.

nub (nub), *n.* 1. a knob, lump, protuberance, etc. 2. [Informal], the gist or central point.

nub·bin (nub'in), *n.* 1. a small or imperfect ear of corn. 2. a small thing.

nub·by (nub'i), *adj.* **-bi·er, -bi·est,** having lumps on the surface.

nu·bile (nōō'bl, 'bil), *adj.* marriageable; fit for marriage: said of a young woman.

nu·cle·ar (nōō'kli-ĕr), *adj.* 1. of, pertaining to, constituting, or resembling a nucleus. 2. of, pertaining to, or utilizing atomic power or atomic nuclei.

nuclear energy, the energy released from an atom in nuclear reactions, esp. in nuclear fission or nuclear fusion.

nuclear family, a basic social unit consisting of parents and their children living in one household.

nuclear fission, the division of atomic nuclei into two parts, resulting in a conversion of part of the mass into energy: utilized in atomic bombs.

nuclear fusion, the union of atomic nuclei resulting in a loss of mass that is changed into energy: utilized in the hydrogen bomb.

nuclear physics, the part of physics that deals with atomic energy, radioactive materials, etc.

nuclear reactor, a device for producing a nuclear fission reaction with more fuel or energy as the result.

nuclear winter, a hypothetical scenario following a major nuclear war in which the atmosphere will be clouded with radioactive smoke, dust, etc. for a long time causing loss of sunlight, frigid temperatures, destruction of life forms, etc.

nu·cle·ate (nōō'kli-it), *adj.* having a nucleus.

nu·cle·o·lus (nōō-klē'ō-lŭs), *n., pl.* **-li** (-lī), a minute body inside a nucleus.

nu·cle·us (nōō'kli-ŭs), *n., pl.* **-cle·i** (-ī), **-cle·us·es,** 1. the central mass around which matter accretes or grows. 2. a center part. 3. the center of an atom. 4. the central protoplasm in a cell. 5. the bright part of the head of a comet.

nude (nōōd), *adj.* 1. bare; naked. 2. in *Law,* made without consideration; void: *n.* 1. a nude person. 2. an unclothed body, as in art. 3. nakedness. **—nude'ly,** *adv.* **—nude'ness,** *n.*

nudge (nuj), *v.t.* **nudged, nudg'ing,** to touch gently, as with the elbow: *n.* a gentle touch, as with the elbow.

nu·dism (nōō'dizm), *n.* the custom of appearing nude. **—nud'ist,** *n. & adj.*

nu·di·ty (nōō'di-ti), *n.* 1. nakedness. 2. *pl.* **-ties,** an undraped figure, as in art.

nu·ga·to·ry (nōō'gä-tôr-i), *adj.* 1. trifling; useless. 2. not functioning.

nug·get (nug'it), *n.* a lump or mass, especially of gold.

nui·sance (nōō'sns), *n.* anything offensive, injurious, vexatious, or annoying.

null (nul), *adj.* 1. of no legal force: usually in the phrase **null and void.** 2. adding up to nothing. 3. valueless. **—null'i·ty** ('i-ti), *n.*

nul·lah (nul'ä), *n.* in India, the dry bed of a stream.

nul·li·fy (nul'i-fī), *v.t.* **-fied, -fy·ing,** 1. to annul or render void. 2. to make useless. 3. to cross out or abolish. **—nul·li·fi·ca'tion,** *n.* **—nul'li·fi·er,** *n.*

---

a in cap, ä in cane, ä in father, å in abet, e in met, ē in be, ĕ in baker, ė in regent, i in pit, ī in fine, i in manifest, o in hot, ô in horse, ō in bone,

numb (num), *adj.* deprived of sensation or motion; torpid: *v.t.* to benumb.

num·ber (num'bĕr), *n.* 1. a unit; one or more than one. 2. one of a series, as a magazine, song, etc. 3. *pl.* a multitude. 4. a collection of things or persons. 5. *pl.* arithmetic. 6. *pl.* a greater total. 7. amount. 8. [Informal], a person or thing singled out. 9. in *Grammar,* a form showing singular or plural. 10. *pl.* in *Poetry,* meter or verses: *v.t.* 1. to count. 2. to mark with a number. 3. to consider as part. 4. to restrict. 5. to constitute: *v.i.* 1. to make an enumeration. 2. to be considered as part.

num·ber·less (-lis), *adj.* that cannot be counted because there are too many.

Num·bers (num'bĕrz), *n.* the fourth book of the Pentateuch.

nu·mer·al (nōō'mĕr-ăl), *adj.* of, pertaining to, consisting of, or denoting a number: *n.* a symbol, figure, or word expressing a number.

nu·mer·ar·y (nōō'mĕ-rer-i), *adj.* of or pertaining to a number or numbers.

nu·mer·ate (-rāt), *v.t.* -at·ed, -at·ing, 1. to reckon or enumerate. 2. to read (figures).

nu·mer·a·tion (nōō-mĕ-rā'shŭn), *n.* the act or art of numbering or of reading and writing numbers.

nu·mer·a·tor (nōō'mĕ-rāt-ĕr), *n.* 1. one who or that which numbers. 2. the figure above the line in fractions, which indicates how many parts of a unit are taken.

nu·mer·i·cal (nōō-mer'i-kl), *adj.* 1. of or relating to numbers. 2. represented by numbers. —**nu·mer'i·cal·ly**, *adv.*

nu·mer·ous (nōō'mĕr-ŭs), *adj.* 1. consisting of a great number. 2. very many.

nu·mis·mat·ic (nōō-miz-mat'ik), *adj.* of or pertaining to coins or medals.

nu·mis·mat·ics ('iks), *n.* the science or collection of coins, medals, etc. —**nu·mis'ma·tist** (-miz'mā-tist), *n.*

num·mu·lar (num'yoo-lĕr), *adj.* shaped like a coin.

num·skull, numb·skull (num'skul), *n.* a stupid person.

nun (nun), *n.* 1. a woman devoted to a religious life under vows. 2. a variety of pigeon.

nun (nōōn, noon), *n.* the fourteenth letter of the Hebrew alphabet.

nun·ci·a·ture (nun'shi-ă-chĕr), *n.* the office or term of a nuncio.

nun·ci·o (nun'shi-ō), *n., pl.* -ci·os, a papal ambassador.

nun·cu·pa·tive (nung'kyoo-pāt-iv), *adj.* verbal, not written: said of wills.

nun·ner·y (nun'ĕr-i), *n., pl.* -ner·ies, same as convent.

nup·tial (nup'shŭl), *adj.* of, pertaining to, or constituting marriage: *n. usually pl.* a marriage ceremony.

nurse (nûrs), *n.* 1. a woman who has the care of infants or of the child of another person. 2. one who tends the sick or infirm. 3. one who or that which protects or fosters: *v.t.* nursed, nurs'ing, 1. to suckle (an infant). 2. to tend (a child). 3. to bring up. 4. to tend

in sickness. 5. to promote; develop. 6. to treat. 7. to economize in the use of: *v.i.* 1. to be suckled. 2. to tend the sick or infirm.

nurse·maid (nûrs'mād), *n.* a female employed to tend to children.

nurs·er·y (nûr'sĕ-ri), *n., pl.* -er·ies, 1. a room for young children. 2. a school for young children temporarily left there by their parents. 3. a place for rearing or selling young plants.

nurs·er·y·man (-măn), *n., pl.* -men (-mĕn), a person who owns or is employed by a plant nursery.

nursery rhyme, a child's poem.

nursery school, a school before kindergarten, for young children.

nursing home, a place where those injured or infirm may live and receive extended care.

nurs·ling (nûrs'ling), *n.* a suckling infant.

nur·ture (nûr'chĕr), *n.* 1. that which nourishes; food. 2. education; upbringing: *v.t.* -tured, -tur·ing, 1. to bring up; educate. 2. to nourish.

nut (nut), *n.* 1. the fruit of certain trees, containing a kernel enclosed in a hard shell. 2. the kernel. 3. a long-lasting fruit with a hard shell, as a peanut. 4. a piece of metal with a grooved center hole for screwing onto the end of a bolt. 5. a difficult problem or matter. 6. [Slang], the head. 7. [Slang], a person of strange or peculiar ideas; also, a devotee: *v.i.* nut'ted, nut'ting, to gather nuts.

nu·tant (nōōt'nt), *adj.* having the top bent downward; nodding; drooping.

nu·ta·tion (nōō-tā'shŭn), *n.* 1. the periodic vibratory movement of the axis of the earth. 2. a nodding of the head.

nut·crack·er (nut'krak-ĕr), *n.* 1. a device or instrument for breaking hard shells of nuts. 2. a dark-brown bird related to the crow, spotted with whi,e.

nut·hatch (nut'hach), *n.* a small bird with a short tail and sharp beak, related to the titmouse.

nut·meat ('mēt), *n.* a nut kernel.

nut·meg (nut'meg), *n.* the aromatic kernel of the fruit of an East Indian tree, used as a spice.

nu·tri·a (nōō'tri-ă), *n.* the brown fur of a South American aquatic rodent.

nu·tri·ent (nōō'tri-ĕnt), *adj.* promoting growth: *n.* anything promoting growth.

nu·tri·ment ('tri mĕnt), *n.* nourishment.

nu·tri·tion (nōō-trish'ŭn), *n.* 1. that which nourishes; food. 2. the action of promoting growth or repairing tissues in organic bodies. 3. the science of health and diet. —**nu·tri'tion·al,** *adj.* —**nu·tri·tive** ('tri-tiv), *adj.*

nu·tri·tious ('ŭs), *adj.* affording nutrition.

nuts (nuts), *adj.* [Slang], crazy; silly: *interj.* [Slang], an exclamation of disdain, irritation, denial, etc.

nut·shell (nut'shel), *n.* the shell around a nut kernel.

nut·ty (nut'i), *adj.* -ti·er, -ti·est, 1. abounding in or tasting like nuts. 2. [Slang], zealous. 3. [Slang], crazy.

nux vom·i·ca (nuks' vom'i-kă), the flat, poisonous seed of an Asiatic tree, yielding

---

ŏ in drag*o*n, ōō in cr*u*de, oo in w*oo*l, u in c*u*p, ū in c*u*re, û in t*u*rn, ŭ in f*o*cus, oi in b*oy,* ou in h*ou*se, th in *th*in, th in shea*th*e, g in *g*et, j in *j*oy, y in *y*et.

several alkaloids, as strychnine. 2. the tree producing the seed.

nuz·zle (nuz'l), v.t. -zled, -zling, 1. to root up with the nose: said of swine. 2. to touch with the muzzle: v.i. 1. to touch with the nose. 2. to nestle.

nyc·ta·lo·pi·a (nik-tā-lō'pi-ā), n. an abnormal condition of vision in which the affected see poorly at night or on dull days.

nyc·tit·ro·pism (nik-tit'rō-pizm), n. the changes of position which the leaves of certain plants undergo during the night.

nyc·to·pho·bi·a (nik-tō-fō'bi-ā), n. a morbid fear of the night or of darkness.

nyl·ghai (nil'gī), n. same as nilgai.

ny·lon (nī'lon), n. 1. an elastic, synthetic substance made into fiber, sheets, etc. 2. pl. stockings produced from nylon.

nymph (nimf), n. 1. in *Greek & Roman Mythology*, a minor goddess of nature inhabiting the mountains, woods, streams, etc. 2. a handsome, graceful young woman. 3. an insect offspring that has not undergone full development.

nym·pha·lid (nim'fā-lid), n. any of a group of butterflies with brightly colored wings.

nym·pho·ma·ni·a (nim-fō-mā'ni-ā), n. abnormal and unmanageable sexual desire in a woman. —**nym·pho·ma'ni·ac** (-ak), adj. & n.

nys·tag·mus (nis-tag'mùs), n. a spasmodic, rapid movement of the eyeball from side to side.

O

O, o (ō), *n., pl.* **O's, o's,** 1. the fifteenth letter of the English alphabet. 2. any of the various sounds of this letter, as in *bone, hot, horse, hoot, book,* and *dragon.* 3. a type or impression of *O* or *o.* 4. a cipher; the numeral zero.

O (ō), *adj.* shaped like *O;* circular or oval: *n.* 1. an object shaped like *O.* 2. a circle or oval.

O (ō), *interj.* 1. an expression of wonder, fear, surprise, annoyance, pain, etc. 2. a word used before a name in direct address: *n., pl.* O's, the use of this interjection. Interchangeable with *oh.*

O' (ō), a prefix to certain Irish proper names, signifying *descendant of,* as *O'Brien.*

o' (ō, ō), *prep.* a contracted form of *of,* as in *o'clock, will-o'-the-wisp.*

oaf (ōf), *n.* 1. originally, a changeling. 2. [Rare] a misshapen or idiotic child. 3. a stupid, clumsy fellow; lout.

oaf-ish ('ish), *adj.* simple; like an oaf; silly; doltish. —**oaf'ish-ly,** *adv.* —**oaf'ish-ness,** *n.*

oak (ōk), *n.* 1. any of various large hardwood trees of the beech family: its hard, small nuts are called *acorns.* 2. the wood of this tree, which is strong, durable, and with a distinctive grain. 3. furniture, woodwork, etc. made of this wood. 4. any of various other shrubs or plants resembling the oak. 5. a garland of oak leaves: *adj.* 1. of or pertaining to oak. 2. made of oak; oaken.

oak apple, an excrescence on the leaf of an oak, produced by an insect, especially the gall wasp.

oak-en (ō'kĕn), *adj.* made of oak wood.

oak-leaf cluster (ōk'lēf), in the *U.S. Army* or *Air Force,* a small metal cluster of oak leaves awarded to the holder of a decoration for additional awards of that decoration.

oa-kum (ō'kŭm), *n.* old ropes untwisted and pulled into loose hemp, used in caulking seams in boats.

oar (ōr), *n.* 1. a light pole with a broad blade, for rowing a boat. 2. an oarsman; rower: *v.t. & v.i.* to row. —**oar'like,** *adj.*

oar-fish (ōr'fish), *n., pl.* **-fish, -fish-es,** any of several fishes, long and narrow, with no caudal fin, but a dorsal fin along the entire length of the back.

oar-lock ('lok), *n.* a usually metal device, often U-shaped, on the gunwale of a rowboat for holding the oar in place.

oars-man (ōrz'mǎn), *n., pl.* **-men,** one who rows or sculls a boat.

oars-man-ship (-ship), *n.* the art or skill of rowing.

o-a-sis (ō-ā'sis), *n., pl.* **-ses** ('sēz), a fertile spot in a barren, sandy desert.

oast (ōst), *n.* a kiln for drying hops or barley.

oat (ōt), *n.* 1. an edible grain or seed of a kind of cereal grass. 2. the plant itself, widely grown for food. 3. any of a number of related grasses, especially the wild oat. 4. *pl.* [Slang], high spirits: in the phrase **feel one's oats.**

oat-cake (ōt'kāk), *n.* a flat cake made from oatmeal.

oat-en ('n), *adj.* of, pertaining to, or made from oats, oatmeal, or oat straw.

oath (ōth), *n., pl.* **oaths** (ōthz, ōths), 1. a solemn declaration that one will tell the truth, keep a vow, etc., with an appeal to God as witness. 2. a blasphemous use of the name of God or of sacred things. 3. a swearword.

oat-meal (ōt'mēl), *n.* 1. ground or rolled oats. 2. a porridge made from either of these: *adj.* made with oatmeal as the main ingredient, as cookies.

ob- (ob, ōb), a prefix signifying *before, against, toward, upon, reversed.*

O-ba-di-ah (ō-bǎ-dī'ǎ), *n.* a book of the Bible.

ob-bli-ga-to (ob-ll-gät'ō), *n., pl.* **-tos, -ti** ('ī), an instrumental musical accompaniment, formerly understood to be indispensable for proper performance of a composition: now usually said of one that can be omitted: *adj.* of or pertaining to such an accompaniment.

ob-du-rate (ob'door-ǎt, 'dyoor-), *adj.* 1. hardened in heart or feelings; unsympathetic. 2. not penitent after wrongdoing. 3. unmoving; unyielding; perverse; stubborn. —**ob'du-ra-cy** (-ǎ-si), *n.* —**ob'du-rate-ly,** *adv.*

o-be-ah (ō'bi-ǎ), *n.* 1. [also O-], a form of African witchcraft. 2. a fetish or magic object used in this.

o-be-di-ence (ō-bē'di-ĕns), *n.* submission to authority; dutifulness.

o-be-di-ent (-ĕnt), *adj.* submissive to authority; dutiful. —**o-be'di-ent-ly,** *adv.*

o-bei-sance (ō-bā'sns, -bē'-), *n.* 1. a bow or curtsy; gesture of reverence or respect. 2. a respectful attitude; deference; homage. —**o-bei'sant,** *adj.*

ob-e-lisk (ob'ē-lisk, ō'bĕ-), *n.* a lofty, four-sided stone pillar gradually tapering as it rises, and terminating in a pyramidal top.

ob-e-lus (ob'ē-lŭs), *n., pl.* **-li** (-lī), a mark (— or ÷) used in old manuscripts to point out questionable passages.

o-bese (ō-bēs'), *adj.* corpulent; stout; very fat. —**o-be'si-ty,** *n.*

o-bey (ō-bā', ō-), *v.t.* 1. to submit to the rule or control of. 2. to comply with the orders or instructions of. 3. to carry out (an order, instruction, etc.): *v.i.* to do as bidden.

ob-fus-cate (ob'fŭs-kāt), *v.t.* **-cat-ed, -cat-ing,** to bewilder; confuse. —**ob-fus-ca'tion,** *n.*

o-bi (ō'bi), *n.* a broad sash worn with a Japanese kimono.

o-bit-u-ar-y (ō-bich'oo-wer-i), *n., pl.* **-ar-ies,** a notice of a person's death, as in a newspa-

ō in drag*o*n, ōō in cr*u*de, oo in w*oo*l, u in c*u*p, ū in c*u*re, ŭ in t*u*rn, ŭ in foc*u*s, oi in b*oy*, ou in h*ou*se, th in *th*in, *th* in shea*th*e, g in ge*t*, j in *j*oy, y in *y*et.

491

per: also **o-bit** (ō'bit): *adj.* pertaining to or recording a death.

ob-ject (ŏb-jekt', ob-), *v.t.* to state or cite in opposition: *v.i.* to express or feel disapproval: *n.* (ob'jikt), 1. a thing that can be seen, touched, or thought about. 2. end; aim. 3. a person or thing to which action or thought is directed. 4. in *Grammar*, a noun or substantive that receives the action of a verb; also, a noun or substantive in a prepositional phrase. —**ob-jec'tor**, *n.*

ob-jec-tion (ŏb-jek'shŭn), *n.* 1. the act of objecting; expression of disapproval., 2. a ground for objecting.

ob-jec-tion-a-ble (-ă-bl), *adj.* 1. liable or open to objection. 2. offensive.

ob-jec-tive (ŏb-jek'tiv, ob-), *adj.* 1. having an existence independent of the mind; real. 2. not subjective; dealing with the realities of the matter at hand rather than thoughts about it. 3. without prejudice. 4. in *Grammar*, of or denoting the case of an object of a verb or preposition: *n.* 1. something aimed at. 2. the lens of a telescope or microscope nearest to the object: also object glass. —**ob-jec'tive-ly**, *adv.* —**ob-jec-tiv'i-ty**, *n.*

ob-jec-tiv-ism ('tiv-izm), *n.* 1. a philosophical doctrine emphasizing the independent existence of what is observed. 2. the practice of writing objectively.

object lesson, an exemplification of a principle; striking example.

ob-jet d'art (ŏb-zhä där'), *pl.* **ob-jets d'art** (ŏb-zhä), a small object of artistic value.

ob-jur-gate (ob'jĕr-gāt), *v.t.* -gat-ed, -gat-ing, to chide or reprove severely. —**ob-jur-ga'tion**, *n.* —**ob-jur'ga-to-ry**, *adj.*

ob-late (ob'lāt), *adj.* depressed or flattened at the poles.

ob-late (ob'lāt), *n.* a person living in a religious community of the Roman Catholic Church.

ob-la-tion (o-blā'shŭn), *n.* an offering or sacrifice presented in religious worship.

ob-li-gate (ob'li-gāt), *v.t.* -gat-ed, -gat-ing, to bind by law, a sense of duty, a promise, etc.

ob-li-ga-tion (ob-li-gā'shŭn), *n.* 1. the binding power of a vow, promise, or contract. 2. a binding contract, promise, etc. 3. the state of being indebted for a favor. 4. in *Law*, an agreement by which one person (the *obligor*) is bound to make payment or do something for another (the *obligee*). —**ob-li-ga'tion-al**, *adj.*

ob-lig-a-to-ry (ŏ-blig'ă-tōr-i), *adj.* morally or legally binding; required.

o-blige (ŏ-blij', ō-), *v.t.* **o-bliged'**, **o-blig'ing**, 1. to constrain by force, morally, legally, or physically. 2. to bind by a particular favor or kindness rendered: *v.i.* to do a favor or service. —**o-blig'er**, *n.*

ob-li-gee (ob-li-jē'), *n.* see obligation.

o-blig-ing (ŏ-blij'jing, ō-), *adj.* willing to do favors; accommodating. —**o-blig'ing-ly**, *adv.*

ob-li-gor (ob-li-gōr'), *n.* see obligation.

o-blique (ŏ-blēk', ō-), *adj.* 1. inclined; slanting. 2. not direct or straightforward. 3. denoting any angle other than a right angle, as one that is acute or obtuse. 4. in *Grammar*, de-

noting any case except the nominative and the vocative. —**o-blique'ly**, *adv.* —**o-blique'-ness**, *n.*

ob-lit-er-ate (ŏ-blit'ĕ-rāt), *v.t.* -at-ed, -at-ing, 1. to efface or blot out. 2. to destroy, leaving no trace. —**ob-lit-er-a'tion**, *n.* —**ob-lit'er-a-tor**, *n.*

ob-liv-i-on (ŏ-bliv'i-ŏn), *n.* 1. forgetfulness. 2. the state of being forgotten.

ob-liv-i-ous (-ŭs), *adj.* forgetful or unaware. —**ob-liv'i-ous-ly**, *adv.*

ob-long (ob'lông), *adj.* longer than broad: *n.* a rectangle having greater length than breadth.

ob-lo-quy (ob'lŏ-kwi), *n., pl.* -quies, 1. severe censure or vituperation of a person or thing, especially when widespread. 2. ill repute resulting from this; infamy.

ob-nox-ious (ŏb-nok'shŭs, ob-), *adj.* extremely offensive or unpleasant.

o-boe (ō'bō), *n.* 1. a woodwind instrument with a reed mouthpiece, with a high, plaintive tone. 2. an organ stop. —**o'bo-ist**, *n.*

ob-o-vate (ob-ō'vāt), *adj.* inversely ovate.

ob-o-void ('void), *adj.* having an ovoid shape with the larger end toward the top.

ob-scene (ŏb-sēn', ŏb-), *adj.* 1. offensive; indecent; lewd. 2. repulsive; disgusting. —**ob-scene'ly**, *adv.*

ob-scen-i-ty (ob-sen'i-ti), *n.* 1. the state of being obscene. 2. *pl.* -ties, an obscene action, expression, etc.

ob-scu-rant (ob-skyoor'ănt, ŏb-), *adj.* tending to obscure: *n.* one who opposes or tends to prevent human progress and enlightenment.

ob-scu-rant-ism (-izm), *n.* 1. opposition to the advancement of knowledge. 2. the practice of being deliberately vague.

ob-scure (ŏb-skyoor'), *adj.* 1. dark; dim. 2. faint; not easy to see. 3. not easily understood; ambiguous. 4. secluded; hidden. 5. not prominent: *v.t.* -scured', -scur'ing, to make obscure. —**ob-scure'ly**, *adv.* —**ob-scu'ri-ty**, *n.*

ob-se-quies (ob'sĕ-kwēz), *n.pl.* funeral rites.

ob-se-qui-ous (ŏb-sē'kwi-ŭs), *adj.* servile; fawning; excessively compliant.

ob-serv-a-ble (ŏb-zûr'vȧ-bl, ob-), *adj.* 1. that can be observed; discernible. 2. worthy of observation; remarkable. —**ob-serv'a-bly**, *adv.*

ob-serv-ance (ŏb-zûr'văns), *n.* 1. the act of observing a rule, custom, law, etc. 2. a customary rite, ceremony, act, etc.

ob-serv-ant ('ănt), *adj.* 1. taking notice; attentive. 2. alert. 3. careful to observe a law, custom, etc.

ob-ser-va-tion (ob-zēr-vā'shŭn), *n.* 1. the act or power of observing. 2. that which is observed. 3. a recording of information, as for research. 4. a remark; comment. —**ob-serva'tion-al**, *adj.*

ob-serv-a-to-ry (ŏb-zûr'vȧ-tōr-i), *n., pl.* -ries, 1. a building equipped for astronomical research. 2. any place or position commanding a wide view.

ob-serve (ŏb-zûrv', ob-), *v.t.* -served', -serv'ing, 1. to take notice of. 2. to celebrate (a holiday, etc.). 3. to mention; remark. 4. to conform to (a law, custom, etc.). 5. to study scientifically: *v.i.* to make observations. —**ob-serv'er**, *n.*

ob·sess (ob-ses′), *v.t.* to preoccupy to an unreasonable degree; haunt. —**ob·ses′sive**, *adj.* —**ob·ses′sive·ly**, *adv.*

ob·ses·sion (-sesh′ŭn), *n.* 1. the state of being obsessed with an idea, desire, etc. 2. such a persistent idea, desire, etc.

ob·sid·i·an (ob-sid′i-ăn), *n.* a black, volcanic glass, often used as a gemstone.

ob·so·lesce (ob-sŏ-les′), *v.i.* -lesced′, -lesc′ing, to be or become obsolescent.

ob·so·les·cent (′nt), *adj.* becoming obsolete. —**ob′so·les·cence**, *n.*

ob·so·lete (ob-sŏ-lēt′), *adj.* 1. out-of-date; outmoded. 2. no longer in use. —**ob·so·lete′ness**, *n.*

ob·sta·cle (ob′sti-kl), *n.* a hindrance; impediment; obstruction.

ob·stet·rics (ob-stet′riks, ob-), *n.* the branch of medicine dealing with pregnancy and childbirth. —**ob·stet′ric, ob·stet′ri·cal**, *adj.* —**ob·ste·tri·cian** (ob-stē-trish′ŭn), *n.*

ob·sti·nate (ob′sti-nit), *adj.* determined to have one's own way; stubborn. —**ob′sti·na·cy** (-nā-si), *n.* —**ob′sti·nate·ly**, *adv.*

ob·strep·er·ous (ŏb-strep′ẽr-ŭs), *adj.* noisy, uncontrollable, defiant, etc. —**ob·strep′er·ous·ly**, *adv.* —**ob·strep′er·ous·ness**, *n.*

ob·struct (ŏb-strukt′), *v.t.* 1. to block up (a passage). 2. to impede; hinder. 3. to block from sight. —**ob·struc′tive**, *adj.* —**ob·struc′tive·ly**, *adv.*

ob·struc·tion (ŏb-struk′shŭn, ob-), *n.* an impediment; hindrance.

ob·struc·tion·ist (-ist), *n.* a member of a legislative assembly who hinders the passage of legislation by parliamentary maneuvers. —**ob·struc′tion·ism**, *n.*

ob·tain (ŏb-tān′), *v.t.* to get possession of by effort; gain; acquire: *v.i.* to be established; prevail. —**ob·tain′a·ble**, *adj.* —**ob·tain′ment**, *n.*

ob·test (ob-test′), *v.t.* to supplicate; beg for. 2. to call to witness. —**ob·tes·ta′tion**, *n.*

ob·trude (ŏb-trōōd′), *v.t.* -trud′ed, -trud′ing, 1. to thrust forward; eject. 2. to force (something) upon another without invitation: *v.i.* to obtrude oneself. —**ob·tru′sion**, *n.* —**ob·tru′sive**, *adj.*

ob·tund (ob-tund′), *v.t.* to make blunt or dull; deaden, as pain.

ob·tuse (ob-tōōs′), *adj.* 1. not pointed or sharp; blunt. 2. denoting an angle greater than a right angle. 3. slow to understand. —**ob·tuse′ly**, *adv.* —**ob·tuse′ness**, *n.*

ob·verse (ob-vũrs′), *adj.* 1. facing the observer. 2. narrower at the base than at the top. 3. forming a counterpart: *n.* (ob′vẽrs), 1. the side of a coin or medal bearing the main design: opposed to reverse. 2. the front surface of anything. 3. a counterpart. —**ob·verse′ly**, *adv.*

ob·vert (ob-vũrt′), *v.t.* to turn so as to show the main or a different surface.

ob·vi·ate (ob′vi-āt), *v.t.* -at·ed, -at·ing, to remove or prevent beforehand; make unnecessary. —**ob·vi·a′tion**, *n.*

ob·vi·ous (ob′vi-ŭs), *adj.* evident; manifest; plain. —**ob′vi·ous·ly**, *adv.*

ob·vo·lute (ob′vŏ-lōōt), *adj.* having margins that overlap, as some petals or leaves.

oc·a·ri·na (ok-ă-rē′nă), *n.* a small wind instrument shaped like a sweet potato.

oc·ca·sion (ŏ-kā′zhŭn), *n.* 1. [O-], an occurrence. 2. an opportunity; suitable time. 3. an incidental cause or need. 4. an event, fact, etc. that makes something else possible. 5. a special event or time: *v.t.* to cause; give rise to.

oc·ca·sion·al (-l), *adj.* 1. happening now and then. 2. used for special occasions. —**oc·ca′sion·al·ly**, *adv.*

oc·ca·sion·al·ism (-l-izm), *n.* the doctrine that God intervenes in each instance of coordination of physical movement and thought.

oc·ci·dent (ok′si-dĕnt), *n.* 1. the countries of the world west of Asia, especially Europe and the Americas. 2. [Poetic], the west.

oc·ci·den·tal (ok-si-den′tl), *adj.* 1. [O-], of the Occident, its people, or their culture. 2. [Poetic], western: *n.* [usually O-], a native of the Occident.

Oc·ci·den·tal·ism (-izm), *n.* the spirit, character, style, manners, customs, etc. of the people of the Occident. —**Oc·ci·den′tal·ist**, *n.*

oc·cip·i·tal (ok-sip′ĭ-tl), *adj.* of the occiput: *n.* the bone that forms the back part of the skull: also occipital bone. —**oc·cip′i·tal·ly**, *adv.*

oc·ci·put (ok′si-put), *n.*, *pl.* **oc·cip′i·ta** (-sip′ĭ-tă), -puts, the back part of the skull or head.

oc·clude (ŏ-klōōd′, o-), *v.t.* -clud′ed, -clud′ing, 1. to close, shut, or block (a passage). 2. to shut in or out. 3. in *Chemistry*, to absorb (a gas, liquid, or solid): *v.i.* to come together with the cusps fitting closely: said of the upper and lower teeth. —**oc·clu′sion**, *n.* —**oc·clu′sive**, *adj.*

oc·cult (ŏ-kult′), *adj.* 1. hidden. 2. secret. 3. mysterious. 4. of or pertaining to magic, alchemy, astrology, etc. —**oc·cult′ly**, *adv.*

oc·cult·ism (ŏ-kul′tizm), *n.* a belief in and study of mysterious and supernatural occurrences and phenomena.

oc·cu·pan·cy (ok′yŭ-păn-si), *n.*, *pl.* -cies, 1. the act of occupying or of taking and holding in possession. 2. the period during which a residence, business, etc. is occupied.

oc·cu·pant (-pănt), *n.* one who occupies.

oc·cu·pa·tion (ok-yŭ-pā′shŭn), *n.* 1. the act or state of occupying. 2. one's business, profession, work, etc. —**oc·cu·pa′tion·al**, *adj.*

oc·cu·py (ok′yŭ-pī), *v.t.* -pied, -py·ing, 1. to take possession of as by invasion or settlement. 2. to be a tenant of; dwell in. 3. to hold (an office or position). 4. to employ, as one's mind. 5. to fill; take up (time or space). —**oc′cu·pi·er**, *n.*

oc·cur (ŏ-kũr′), *v.i.* -curred′, -cur′ring, 1. to happen or take place. 2. to come to mind. 3. to be found or met with.

oc·cur·rence (′ăns), *n.* an event or incident.

o·cean (ō′shŭn), *n.* 1. the vast expanse of salt water covering about 71% of the globe. 2. any one of its five chief divisions: the Atlantic, Pacific, Indian, Arctic, or Antarctic Ocean. 3. an immense expanse. —**o·ce·an·ic** (ō-shi-an′ik), *adj.*

o·cean·aut (-ôt), *n.* same as *aquanaut.*

o·cean-go·ing (-gō-ing), *adj.* used for ocean travel.

o·ce·a·nog·ra·phy (ō-shē-nog'rā-fi, ō-shi-ä-), *n.* the study of ocean environment, including mineral deposits, flora and fauna, the waters, etc. —o·ce·a·nog'ra·pher, *n.*

o·cean-ol·o·gy (nol'ō-ji), *n.* 1. same as oceanography. 2. the study of the ocean in all its aspects, including oceanography, undersea exploration, ocean floor topography, etc. —o·ce·an·ol'o·gist, *n.*

o·cel·lus (ō-sel'ŭs), *n., pl.* -li ('ī), 1. a minute eyespot, as of some invertebrates. 2. a spot of color like an eye, as in a peacock's tail.

o·ce·lot (os'ē-lot, ō'sē-), *n., pl.* -lots, -lot, a spotted wildcat of a medium size, found in North and South America.

o·cher, o·chre (ō'kēr), *n.* 1. a fine yellow or reddish-brown clay, used as a pigment. 2. its color.

och·loc·ra·cy (ok-lok'rā-si), *n.* rule of the multitude; mob rule.

och·one (ō-kōn'), *interj.* [Scottish & Irish], alas!

o'clock (ō-klok', ō-), *adv.* according to the clock.

o·cre·a (ok'ri-ā, ō'kri-ā), *n., pl.* -re·ae (-ē), in *Botany*, a sheath around some stems.

oc·ta-, a combining form meaning *eight.*

oc·ta·gon (ok'tā-gon), *n.* a plane figure of eight sides and eight angles. —oc·tag'o·nal (-tag'ō-nl), *adj.*

oc·ta·he·dron (ok-tā-hē'drŏn), *n., pl.* -drons, -dra ('drä), a solid figure with eight plane surfaces. —oc·ta·he'dral, *adj.*

oc·tam·e·ter (ok-tam'ē-tēr), *adj.* containing eight metrical feet. —*n.* a verse containing eight metrical feet.

oc·tane (ok'tān), *n.* an oily hydrocarbon occurring in petroleum.

octane number, a numerical designation of the antiknock properties of a gasoline or other fuel: also octane rating.

oc·tan·gu·lar (ok-tang'gyŭ-lēr), *adj.* having eight angles.

oc·tant (ok'tănt), *n.* an eighth of a circle; 45° angle or arc.

oc·tarch·y (ok'tär-ki), *n., pl.* -tarch·ies, 1. government by eight rulers. 2. a group of eight kingdoms.

oc·tave (ok'tiv, 'tāv), *n.* 1. a group of eight. 2. the eighth full musical tone above or below a given tone. 3. a musical interval of eight degrees. 4. the series of tones or keys within this interval. 5. the eighth day after a church festival, counting the festival day as the first: *adj.* consisting of eight.

oc·ta·vo (ok-tā'vō, -tä'vō), *n., pl.* -vos, 1. a book made up of pages cut eight to a printer's sheet of paper. 2. the page size of such a book, about 6 by 9 inches.

oc·ten·ni·al (ok-ten'i-ăl), *adj.* 1. comprising eight years. 2. occurring every eight years. —oc·ten'ni·al·ly, *adv.*

oc·tet, oc·tette (ok-tet'), *n.* 1. a musical composition for eight voices or instruments. 2. the eight performers of this.

oc·til·lion (ok-til'yŭn), *n.* 1. in the U.S. and France, the number indicated by 1 followed by 27 zeros. 2. in Great Britain and Germany, the number indicated by 1 followed by 48 zeros. —oc·til'lionth, *adj.* & *n.*

oc·to-, a combining form meaning *eight.*

Oc·to·ber (ok-tō'bēr), *n.* 1. the tenth month of the year, having 31 days. 2. in England, ale brewed in October.

oc·to·dec·i·mo (ok-tō-des'ĭ-mō), *n., pl.* -mos, same as eighteenmo.

oc·to·ge·nar·i·an (ok-tō-ji-ner'i-ăn), *n.* one who is eighty years old or between eighty and ninety: *adj.* of or denoting an octogenarian.

oc·to·pod (ok'tō-pod), *n.* any animal with eight limbs.

oc·to·pus (ok'tō-pŭs), *n., pl.* -pus·es, -pi (-pī), 1. a mollusk with a soft body and eight long arms covered with suckers. 2. an organization with far-reaching influence or power.

oc·to·roon (ok-tō-rōōn'), *n.* a person who is the offspring of a white and a quadroon.

oc·tu·ple (ok'too-pl), *adj.* 1. having eight parts. 2. having eight times as much or as many.

oc·u·lar (ok'yŭ-lēr), *adj.* 1. of or having to do with the eye. 2. known from actual sight.

oc·u·list (-list), *n.* an ophthalmologist: an earlier term.

OD (ō-dē'), *n., pl.* ODs or OD's, [Slang], an overdose, esp. of a narcotic: *v.i.* OD'd or ODed, OD'ing or ODing, [Slang], to take an overdose, esp. a fatal overdose of a narcotic.

o·da·lisque, o·da·lisk (ōd'l-isk), *n.* a female slave or concubine in an Oriental harem.

odd (od), *adj.* 1. not paired or matched with another. 2. not exactly divisible by two. 3. left over after taking a round number. 4. peculiar. 5. eccentric. 6. occasional. 7. with a few more. —odd'ly, *adv.*

odd·ball ('bôl), *n.* [Slang], one who is odd or eccentric.

odd·i·ty ('i-ti), *n.* 1. the state or quality of being odd. 2. *pl.* -ties, a person or thing that is odd.

odds (odz), *n.pl.* 1. the advantage of one side over another. 2. an equalizing allowance given by a competitor or bettor to another in order that both may have an equal chance of winning. 3. a quarrel; dispute: usually in the phrase at odds.

odds and ends, fragments; scraps; remnants.

odds-on (odz-on'), *adj.* having a better than even chance to win.

ode (ōd), *n.* a lyric poem of exalted tone and style.

o·di·ous (ō'di-ŭs), *adj.* offensive; deserving hatred or disgust; loathsome.

o·di·um (ō'di-ŭm), *n.* 1. hatred. 2. the state of being hated; disgrace or stigma.

o·dom·e·ter (ō-dom'ē-tēr), *n.* an instrument for measuring the distance traveled by a vehicle.

o·dont·o-, a combining form meaning *tooth.*

o·don·tol·o·gy (ō-don-tol'ō-ji), *n.* dental science. —o·don·tol'o·gist, *n.*

o·dor (ō'dēr), *n.* a scent; smell; aroma: also, British spelling, odour. —o'dor·less, *adj.* —o'dor·ous, *adj.*

o·dor·if·er·ous (ō-dē-rif'ēr-ŭs), *adj.* giving off an odor, especially a fragrant odor. —o·dor·if'er·ous·ly, *adv.*

Od·ys·sey (od'ĭ-si), *n.* 1. an ancient Greek epic poem ascribed to Homer, telling of the ten years' wandering of Odysseus, a mythical Greek hero. 2. [sometimes o-], pl. -seys, any long, extended journey or series of travels.

oe-de-ma (ē-dē'mȧ), n. chiefly British spelling of edema.

Oed-i-pus (ed'i-pŭs), n. in Greek Mythology, a king who unwittingly killed his father and married his mother.

oe-nol-o-gy (i-nal'ō-ji), n. alternate spelling of enology.

o'er (ôr), prep. & adv. poetic contraction of over.

of (uv, ov, ŏv), prep. 1. from. 2. belonging to. 3. concerning. 4. during. 5. specified as. 6. during. 7. possessing.

off (ôf), adj. 1. more remote. 2. not at work. 3. wrong. 4. in a (specified) situation. 5. not attached, in operation, etc.: adv. 1. away from. 2. so as to be no longer attached, on, in operation, etc. 3. at a distance: prep. 1. not on, attached, etc. 2. away from. 3. distant from. 4. below the usual standard: interj. go away!

off-fal (ôf'l), n. 1. refuse. 2. the waste parts of an animal killed for food; entrails, etc.

off-beat (ôf'bēt), n. a musical note having a weak accent: adj. [Informal], unusual, unconventional, different, etc.

off-col-or ('kul-ẽr), adj. 1. varying from the standard color. 2. risqué; slightly improper.

of-fend (ō-fend'), v.t. 1. to displease or make angry; insult. 2. to affect (the senses) unpleasantly: v.i. 1. to commit a sin or crime; transgress. 2. to do anything displeasing. —of-fend'er, n.

of-fense (ō-fens'), n. 1. a sin or crime. 2. anything that causes displeasure, anger, resentment, etc. 3. an insult. 4. an attack. 5. the side that is attacking or seeking to score. Also, British spelling, offence.

of-fen-sive (ō-fen'siv), adj. 1. causing displeasure; disgusting. 2. insulting. 3. used in attacking. 4. attacking: n. the act or position of attacking (with the). —of-fen'sive-ly, adv. —of-fen'sive-ness, n.

of-fer (ôf'ẽr), v.t. 1. to present for acceptance or refusal; proffer. 2. to present in worship. 3. to bid as a price or reward. 4. to give signs of: v.i. to present itself: n. something offered, as a proposal, bid, etc.

of-fer-ing (-ing), n. something offered or presented, as a gift or presentation in worship.

of-fer-to-ry (-tôr-i), n., pl. -ries, [often O-]. 1. the offering of the bread and wine to God in the Eucharist. 2. the collection of money in a church service, or music played during the collection.

off-hand (ôf'hand'), adv. without forethought: adj. 1. said or done without forethought; unpremeditated. 2. curt, brusque, etc. Also off'hand'ed. —off'hand'ed-ly, adv.

of-fice (ôf'is), n. 1. a place where business affairs are carried on. 2. an assigned function or duty. 3. a position of authority, as in government. 4. a religious rite or ceremony. 5. a service done for another.

of-fice-hold-er (-hōl-dẽr), n. a government official.

of-fi-cer (ôf'i-sẽr), n. 1. a person holding an office in a government, club, business, etc. 2. one in a position of command or authority, especially by commission, in the armed forces. 3. a policeman: v.t. 1. to furnish with officers. 2. to command; manage.

officer of the day, the military officer in charge of the guard and security of his post on a given day.

of-fi-cial (ō-fish'ȧl), adj. 1. pertaining to or holding an office or position of authority. 2. from the proper authority; authorized. 3. formal: n. one holding office, especially public office. —of-fi'cial-dom, n. —of-fi'cial-ly, adv.

of-fi-ci-ant (ō-fish'i-ȧnt), n. an officiating clergyman.

of-fi-ci-ar-y (-er-i), n., pl. -ar-ies, an official body; group of officials.

of-fi-ci-ate (-āt), v.i. -at-ed, -at-ing, 1. to perform the duties of an office. 2. to perform the functions of a clergyman at a religious rite. 3. to act as a sports referee, umpire, etc. —of-fi'ci-a-tor, n.

of-fi-cious (ō-fish'ŭs), adj. too forward in offering advice or services; meddlesome, especially in an overbearing way. —of-fi'cious-ly, adv.

off-ing (ôf'ing), n. 1. the distant part of the sea visible from the shore. 2. some vague time in the future: in the phrase in the offing.

off-key (ôf'kē'), adj. 1. not in the right musical key; sharp or flat. 2. not in harmony.

off-lim-its (-lim'its), adj. denoting a place that may not be entered, visited, etc. by a specified group.

off-put-ting ('poot-ing), adj. [Chiefly British], disconcerting.

off-scour-ing ('skour-ing), n. refuse.

off-set (ôf'set), n. 1. something that is set off or has sprung from something else. 2. a thing that balances or compensates for another. 3. same as offset printing. 4. an impression made by this process: v.t. (ôf-set'), -set', -set'ting, 1. to balance or compensate for. 2. to make (an impression) by offset printing.

offset printing, a lithographic printing process in which the inked impression is made on a rubber roller, then transferred to paper.

off-shoot (ôf'shoot), n. a stem or shoot growing from the main stem of a plant.

off-shore (ôf'shôr'), adj. 1. situated some distance from the shore. 2. moving out from the shore: adv. away from the shore.

off-side (ôf'sid'), adj. in Sports, not in the prescribed area at a specified time, so that play cannot continue.

off-spring (ôf'spring), n., pl. -spring, -springs, a child or children; progeny; young.

off-stage (ôf'stāj'), n. that part of the stage the audience cannot see: adv. 1. to the offstage. 2. away from the view of the public: adj. from the offstage area.

off-white (ôf'hwīt'), adj. grayish-white or yellowish-white.

off year, 1. a year of less production than usual. 2. a year without a major political election.

oft (ôft), adv. [Poetic], often.

ŏ in dragon, ōō in crude, oo in wool, u in cup, ū in cure, û in turn, ŭ in focus, oi in boy, ou in house, th in thin, th in sheathe, g in get, j in joy, y in yet.

of-ten (ôf'n), *adv.* frequently; many times: also of 'ten-times.

o-gee (ō'jĭ), *n.* a molding that has an S-shaped curve.

og-ham (og'ăm), *n.* an ancient Irish alphabet developed in the 5th and 6th centuries A.D.

o-gle (ō'gl, o'gl), *v.i. & v.t.* o'gled, o'gling, to keep looking (at) boldly and fondly: *n.* an ogling look. —o'gler, *n.*

o-gre (ō'gēr), *n.* 1. in folklore, a man-eating monster or giant. 2. a cruel, ugly, frightening man. —o'gress, *n.fem.*

oh (ō), *interj.* see O.

ohm (ōm), *n.* unit of electrical resistance.

-oid (oid), a suffix meaning *resembling, like.*

oil (oil), *n.* 1. any of various unctuous, flammable substances, usually liquid, obtained from animal, vegetable, or mineral matter, soluble in ether, but not in water. 2. same as petroleum. 3. an oil color or oil painting: *v.t.* to lubricate or supply with oil: *adj.* 1. using oil. 2. of or from oil. 3. concerning the production of oil.

oil-bird ('bûrd), *n.* same as guacharo.

oil cake, a cake of crushed cottonseed, rapeseed, linseed, etc. from which the oil has been extracted, used as fertilizer or food for livestock.

oil-cloth ('klôth), *n.* cloth coated usually with heavy coats of paint (formerly with oil), used as a waterproof covering for tables, shelves, etc.

oil color, a paint made by grinding a pigment in oil, usually linseed oil.

oil-er ('ēr), *n.* a ship that transports oil; tanker.

oil painting, 1. a painting done in oil colors. 2. the art of painting in oils.

oil-skin ('skĭn), *n.* 1. cloth treated with oil to make it waterproof. 2. *usually pl.* a garment or outfit made from this.

oil well, a well bored through layers of rock, etc. to reach a bed of petroleum.

oil-y ('ĭ), *adj.* oil'i-er, oil'i-est, 1. containing or like oil. 2. greasy; unctuous. 3. too suave and smooth. —oil'i-ness, *n.*

oink (oink), *n.* the grunt of a pig: *v.i.* to make this sound.

oint-ment (oint'mĕnt), *n.* a fatty substance applied to the skin as a salve, etc.

O-jib-wa (ō-jĭb'wä, 'wä), *n., pl.* -was, -wa, a member of a North American Indian tribe, mainly of the Great Lakes region. Also O-jib'way ('wä).

OK, O.K. (ō'kā'), *interj. & adv. & adj.* all right: *n., pl.* OK's, O.K.'s, approval: *v.t.* OK'd or O.K.'d, OK'ing or O.K.'ing, to approve. Also [Informal], o'kay'.

o-ka-pi (ō-kä'pi), *n., pl.* -pis, -pi, an African animal resembling the giraffe, but smaller and having a shorter neck.

o-kra (ō'krä), *n.* 1. a plant with sticky green pods which are eaten as a cooked vegetable and used in soups, etc. 2. the pods.

old (ōld), *adj.* old'er or eld'er, old'est or eld'est, 1. having lived for a long time; aged. 2. of or having to do with aged people. 3. ancient. 4. decayed or worn out. 5. long-practiced. 6. experienced. 7. former. 8. de-

noting the earlier of two or more. 9. of a certain age: *n.* 1. something old. 2. the ancient past. —old'ish, *adj.*

Old Catholic, a member of a religious sect organized in 1870 by a group of Roman Catholics who refused to accept the doctrine of papal infallibility.

old country, the country from which an immigrant came: said especially of European countries.

old-en (ōl'dn), *adj.* [Poetic], 1. ancient. 2. of former times.

Old English, the Germanic language spoken by the Anglo-Saxons in England from about 400 to about 1100 A.D.

old-fash-ioned (ōld'făsh'ŭnd), *adj.* 1. antiquated; out-of-date. 2. liking or clinging to the old ways, modes of behavior, etc.: *n.* a cocktail made with whiskey, soda, bitters, and bits of fruit.

Old Guard, 1. the imperial guard organized by Napoleon I in 1804. 2. the most conservative faction of a party, group, etc.

old hand, an experienced person.

old hat, [Slang], old-fashioned.

old-ie, old-y ('ĭ), *n., pl.* -ies, [Informal], an old song, movie, motto, etc.

old lady, [Slang], 1. one's mother. 2. one's wife.

old-line (ōld'lĭn'), *adj.* traditional, conservative, well-established, etc.

old maid, 1. an older woman who has never been married. 2. a fussy, prudish person.

old man, [Slang], 1. one's father. 2. one's husband. 3. [usually O- M-], one in authority, as the captain of a ship.

old master, 1. any one of the great European painters before the 18th century. 2. a painting by any of these artists.

Old Nick, the Devil.

old squaw, a sea duck of northern regions with black-and-white plumage and long tail feathers.

old-ster (ōld'stēr), *n.* [Informal], an old person.

Old Testament, the first of the two main divisions of the Christian Bible, made up of the Holy Scriptures of Judaism.

old-time (ōld'tīm'), *adj.* 1. long-standing. 2. of or pertaining to the past.

old-tim-er ('ēr), *n.* [Informal], 1. one who has been employed, in residence, etc. for a long time. 2. an old person.

old-wife (ōld'wīf'), *n., pl.* -wives, any of various sea fishes.

Old World, the Eastern Hemisphere; Europe, Asia, and Africa: often used in reference to European flora and fauna, customs, etc. —old'-world', Old'-World', *adj.*

o-lé (ō-lā'), *interj.* [Spanish], a shout of approval, joy, etc., as at a bullfight.

o-le-ag-i-nous (ō-li-ăj'i-nŭs), *adj.* oily; unctuous.

o-le-an-der (ō'li-an-dēr), *n.* an evergreen shrub with fragrant white or red flowers.

o-le-as-ter (ō-li-as'tēr), *n.* any of several trees or shrubs with silver-gray foliage.

o-le-ate (ō'li-āt), *n.* a salt or ester of oleic acid.

o-le-fin (ō'lĕ-fĭn), *n.* an unsaturated hydrocarbon.

o-le-ic (ō-lē'ĭk), *adj.* pertaining to or obtained from oil.

oleic acid, an oily acid obtained from animal

or vegetable fats and used in making soap, etc.

o-le-in (ō'li-in), n. the liquid part of oil or fat.

o-le-o-, a combining form meaning *oil.*

o-le-o-graph (ō'li-ō-graf), n. a lithograph printed so that it looks like an oil painting on canvas. —**o-le-og-ra-phy** (ō-li-og'rā-fi), n.

o-le-o-mar-ga-rine (ō-li-ō-mär'jă-rin), n. same as margarine: also **o'le-o.**

oleo oil, oil obtained from animal fat.

ol-fac-tion (ol-fak'shŭn, ōl-), n. 1. the sense of smell. 2. the act of smelling.

ol-fac-to-ry (ol-fak'tĕr-i, ōl-), adj. of or pertaining to the sense of smell.

o-lib-a-num (ō-lib'ă-nŭm), n. same as frankincense.

ol-i-garch (ol'i-gärk), n. any one of the rulers of an oligarchy.

ol-i-garch-y (-gär-ki), n., pl. -garch-ies, 1. government in which the ruling power is in the hands of a few. 2. a state so governed. 3. the persons who rule. —**ol-i-gar'chic,** adj.

ol-i-go-, a combining form meaning *small, few, scant.*

Ol-i-go-cene (ol'i-gō-sēn), n. an epoch of the Cenozoic Era, in which many mammals became extinct and the first apes appeared.

ol-i-gu-ri-a (ōl-i-gyŏor'i-ă), n. a condition marked by an abnormally small secretion of urine.

o-li-o (ō'li-ō), n., pl. o'li-os, 1. a highly spiced stew of meat and vegetables. 2. a medley of musical numbers.

ol-i-va-ceous (ol-i-vā'shŭs), adj. olive-green.

ol-ive (ol'iv), n. 1. an evergreen tree of southern Europe and the Near East, cultivated for its wood and fruit. 2. the small, oval, oily fruit. 3. the yellowish-green color of the unripe fruit.

olive branch, 1. a branch of an olive tree, an emblem of peace. 2. any peace offering.

olive oil, a light-yellow oil pressed from ripe olives, used in salad dressing, cooking, soap, cosmetics, etc.

ol-i-vine (ol'i-vēn), n. a silicate of magnesium and iron, usually in the form of green crystals.

ol-la-po-dri-da (ol-ă-pō-drē'dă), n. 1. a meat and vegetable stew. 2. a medley.

O-lym-pi-an (ō-lim'pi-ăn), n. 1. in *Greek Mythology,* any one of the major gods who lived on Mount Olympus. 2. a participant in the Olympic games: adj. 1. of or pertaining to Olympus. 2. exalted; majestic.

O-lym-pic games ('pik), an international athletic competition held every four years: also the **O-lym'pics** ('piks).

O-lym-pus (-pŭs), n. 1. a mountain in Greece: also **Mount Olympus.** 2. in *Greek Mythology,* the home of the gods.

om (ōm, ŏn), n. a mystic incantation intoned as part of a mantra or Indian religious meditation.

om-ber, om-bre (om'bĕr), n. a card game of Spanish origin.

om-buds-man (om'bŭdz-măn), n., pl. -men (-mĕn), a public official appointed to hear and investigate complaints by citizens against government agencies, officials, etc.

o-me-ga (ō-mā'gă, -mē'gă), n. 1. the last letter of the Greek alphabet. 2. the last; end.

om-e-let, om-e-lette (om'lit, om'ĕ-let), n. eggs beaten, often with milk or water, and cooked in a pan without stirring.

o-men (ō'mĕn), n. something supposed to be a sign of some future event: v.t. to portend; augur.

om-i-cron, om-i-kron (om'i-kron, ō'mi-), n. the 15th letter of the Greek alphabet.

om-i-nous (om'i-nŭs), adj. foreboding evil; inauspicious. —**om'i-nous-ly,** adv.

o-mis-sion (ō-mish'ŭn), n. 1. the act of omitting; especially, neglect or failure to do something required. 2. something omitted.

o-mit (ō-mit'), v.t. o-mit'ted, o-mit'ting, 1. to leave out; fail to mention. 2. to neglect; fail to do. —**o-mit'ter,** n.

om-ni-, a combining form meaning *everywhere, all.*

om-ni-bus (om'ni-bŭs), n., pl. -bus-es, 1. same as bus. 2. a large book containing reprinted works of a single author or reprinted works related in theme: adj. providing for many things at once.

om-ni-far-i-ous (om-ni-fer'i-ŭs), adj. of all varieties, kinds, or forms.

om-nip-o-tent (ŏm-nip'ō-tĕnt), adj. having unlimited power; all-powerful: n. [O-], God (with *the*). —**om-nip'o-tence,** n. —**om-nip'o-tent-ly,** adv.

om-ni-pres-ence (om-ni-prez'ns), n. the state of being present in all places at the same time. —**om-ni-pres'ent,** adj.

om-nis-cient (om-nish'ent), adj. having infinite knowledge; knowing all things: n. [O-], God (with *the*). —**om-nis'cience,** n.

om-ni-um-gath-er-um (om'ni-ŭm-gath'ĕr-ŭm), n. a miscellaneous collection of persons or things.

om-niv-o-rous (om-niv'ĕr-ŭs), adj. 1. eating both animal and vegetable food. 2. taking in everything, as with the mind. —**om-niv'o-rous-ly,** adv. —**om-niv'o-rous-ness,** n.

o-soph-a-gia (o-mō-fā'ji-ă, -fā'jă), n. the eating of raw flesh. —**o-moph-a-gist** (ō-mof'ă-jist), n. —**o-moph'a-gous,** adj.

on (on), prep. 1. upon; in contact with the upper part of. 2. near to. 3. in the direction or at the time of. 4. by means of. 5. about; concerning. 6. in a state of. 7. connected with. 8. through the agency of. 9. [Slang], using; addicted to: adv. 1. forward. 2. in a state of touching, covering, or being supported by. 3. in a direction toward. 4. continuously. 5. into operation: adj. in progress or operation.

on-a-ger (on'ă-jĕr), n., pl. -gri (-grī), -gers, 1. a wild ass of central Asia. 2. a catapult for throwing stones, used in ancient warfare.

once (wuns), adv. 1. one time only. 2. ever; at any time. 3. formerly. 4. by one degree of relationship: n. one time: conj. as soon as.

once-o-ver (ō'vĕr), n. [Informal], 1. a quick examination. 2. a fast job.

on-col-o-gy (on-kol'ō-ji), n. the branch of medicine dealing with tumors.

on-com-ing (on'kum-ing), adj. approaching.

one (wun), adj. 1. single in number; individual. 2. some. 3. the same. 4. united. 5. a certain:

n. 1. the first and lowest cardinal number; 1; I. 2. an individual: *pron.* 1. any person or thing. 2. a certain person or thing.

one-horse ('hôrs'), *adj.* 1. drawn by one horse. 2. [Informal], petty; inferior; unimportant.

o·nei·ro·crit·ic (ō-nī-rō-krit'ik), *n.* an interpreter of dreams. —**o·nei·ro·crit'i·cal**, *adj.* —**o·nei·ro·crit'i·cism**, *n.*

o·nei·ro·man·cy (ō-nī'rō-man-si), *n.* the supposed foretelling of the future by the interpretation of dreams.

one·ness (wun'nis), *n.* 1. the state of being one; singleness. 2. unity. 3. sameness.

on·er·ous (on'ēr-ŭs), *adj.* burdensome; weighty; oppressive.

one·self (wun-self'), *pron.* a person's own self: also **one's self**.

one-sid·ed (wun'sīd'id), *adj.* 1. having or concerned with one side only. 2. partial. 3. unequal. —**one'-sid'ed·ness**, *n.*

one-time ('tim), *adj.* earlier; former.

one-track ('trak), *adj.* [Informal], able to think of only one thing at a time, as a *one-track mind.*

one-up ('up), *adj.* having gained an advantage over another. —**one'-up'man·ship**, *n.*

one-way ('wā'), *adj.* 1. moving or allowing movement in one direction only. 2. with no reciprocation.

on·go·ing (on'gō-ing), *adj.* continuing.

on·ion (un'yŭn), *n.* 1. a vegetable plant of the lily family, with green, tubular stalks. 2. its pungent, edible bulb, eaten as a vegetable and used for flavoring.

on·ion-skin (-skin), *n.* a translucent, glossy writing paper, often used for carbon copies.

on·look·er (on'look-ēr), *n.* a spectator.

on·ly (ōn'li), *adj.* 1. single; one and no more. 2. best; finest: *adv.* 1. merely. 2. solely. 3. as a final result: *conj.* [Informal], but.

on·o·mas·tic (on-ō-mas'tik), *adj.* 1. of or pertaining to a name. 2. in *Law,* denoting a signature different from the writing in the body of a document.

on·o·mat·o·poe·ia (on-ō-mat-ō-pē'ā, -mät-), *n.* 1. the forming of words by imitation of a sound, as *whiz.* 2. the use of such words. —**on·o·mat·o·poe'ic, on·o·mat·o·po·et'ic** (-pō-et'ik), *adj.*

on·rush (on'rush), *n.* a rushing forward.

on·set ('set), *n.* 1. a beginning. 2. an attack.

on·slaught ('slôt), *n.* a furious attack.

on·to (on'tōō), *prep.* 1. to a position on. 2. [Slang], aware of. Also **on to**.

on·tog·e·ny (on-toj'ē-ni), *n.* the development of the individual organism from the germ; life cycle: also **on·to·gen'e·sis** (on-tō-jen'ē-sis). —**on·to·ge·net'ic** (-jē-net'ik), *adj.*

on·to·log·i·cal (on-tō-loj'i-kl), *adj.* of or pertaining to ontology; metaphysical.

ontological argument, a metaphysical argument for the existence of God, that asserts that God, the perfect being, must exist because the concept of perfection logically entails existence.

on·tol·o·gy (on-tol'ō-ji), *n.* 1. the branch of metaphysics that studies the nature of exist-

ence. 2. *pl.* **-gies,** a particular theory about existence. —**on·tol'o·gist,** *n.*

o·nus (ō'nŭs), *n.* 1. a burden, duty, obligation, etc. 2. blame.

on·ward (on'wērd), *adj.* advancing: *adv.* forward: also **on'wards**.

on·yx (on'iks), *n.* a variety of agate with layers of varying colors.

oo·dles (ōō'dlz), *n.pl.* [Informal], a great many.

o·o·gen·e·sis (ō-ō-jen'ē-sis), *n.* the origin and development of the ovum. —**o·o·ge·net'ic** (-jē-net'ik), *adj.*

o·o·lite (ō'ō-līt), *n.* a rock composed of tiny, round or oval particles resembling fish roe, formed in agitated seas: also **o'o·lith** (-lith). —**o·o·lit'ic** (-ō-lit'ik), *adj.*

o·ol·o·gy (ō-ol'ō-ji), *n.* the scientific study of birds' eggs. —**o·ol'o·gist,** *n.*

oo·long (ōō'lông), *n.* a dark tea grown in China and Taiwan that is partly fermented before being dried.

oo·mi·ac, oo·mi·ak (ōō'mi-ak), *n.* same as umiak.

o·o·pho·rec·to·my (ō-ō-fē-rek'tō-mi), *n., pl.* **-mies,** the surgical removal of one or both ovaries.

o·o·pho·ri·tis (-rīt'is), *n.* inflammation of one or both ovaries.

o·o·the·ca (ō-ō-thē'kä), *n., pl.* **-cae** ('sē), the egg case of certain mollusks and insects.

ooze (ōōz), *n.* 1. soft mud or slime, as at the bottom of a lake. 2. something that oozes, or flows slowly: *v.i.* oozed, ooz'ing, to flow gently or leak out; seep: *v.t.* to exude. —**oo·zy** (ōō'zi), *adj.* **-zi·er, -zi·est**

op (op), *n.* same as **op art**.

o·pac·i·ty (ō-pas'i-ti), *n.* the state of being opaque.

o·pah (ō'pä), *n.* a very large, brightly colored food fish of the Atlantic and Pacific oceans.

o·pal (ō'pl), *n.* a stone of various colors that reflects light in a play of colors: some milky varieties are semiprecious. —**o·pal·ine** (ō'pl-in, -ēn), *adj.*

o·pal·esce (ō-pä-les'), *v.i.* **-esced', -esc'ing,** to exhibit a play of colors like that of the opal. —**o·pal·es'cence,** *n.* —**o·pal·es'cent,** *adj.*

o·paque (ō-pāk'), *adj.* 1. not transparent. 2. not shining or reflecting light. 3. not lucid; hard to understand. 4. stupid; obtuse. —**o·paque'·ly,** *adv.* —**o·paque'ness,** *n.*

op art, a style of abstract art in which optical illusions are created by the use of geometrical figures.

o·pen (ō'pn), *adj.* 1. not shut; unfastened. 2. uncovered. 3. unsealed. 4. not frozen or frosty. 5. with few or no trees. 6. having holes or gaps. 7. unreserved; frank. 8. public. 9. generous. 10. spread out. 11. not decided. 12. receptive to new ideas. 13. free to be used, entered, etc.: *v.t. & v.i.* 1. to make or become open. 2. to begin. 3. to expand; spread out. 4. to start operating. 5. to make or become accessible or available: *n.* 1. the outdoors (with *the*). 2. public knowledge (with *the*). 3. [usually O-], any one of a number of golf tournaments open to both professionals and amateurs. —**o'pen·er,** *n.* —**o'pen·ly,** *adv.* —**o'pen·ness,** *n.*

---

a in cap, ā in cane, ä in father, ȧ in abet, e in met, ē in be, ē in baker, ē in regent, i in pit, ī in fine, i in manifest, o in hot, ô in horse, ō in bone,

o·pen-air (-er'), *adj.* of, existing in, or occurring outdoors.

o·pen-and-shut (-n-shut'), *adj.* obvious.

o·pen-door (-dôr'), *adj.* of or denoting a policy of unrestricted trade between nations.

o·pen-end·ed (-en'did), *adj.* not limited or restricted.

o·pen-eyed (-īd), *adj.* with the eyes wide open, as in surprise or watchfulness.

o·pen-faced (-fāst'), *adj.* 1. having a face with an honest expression. 2. denoting a sandwich without a slice of bread on top: also o'pen-face'.

o·pen-hand·ed (-han'did), *adj.* generous.

o·pen-hearth (-härth'), *adj.* 1. denoting a furnace used for making steel, with a wide hearth and low roof. 2. using such a furnace.

open heart surgery, surgery on the heart during which the blood is diverted and circulated by mechanical means.

open house, 1. a time when an institution, school, etc. is open for visitors. 2. an informal reception or party at home.

o·pen·ing (-ing), *n.* 1. an aperture. 2. a beginning. 3. an opportunity. 4. a clearing in the woods. 5. an unfilled position or job.

o·pen-mind·ed (-mīn'did), *adj.* 1. without preconceptions. 2. unprejudiced; unbiased.

open sea, the part of the sea away from coastlines.

open sesame, 1. the magic command which opened the robbers' den in the tale of Ali Baba in the "Arabian Nights." 2. something that always enables a person to get what is desired.

open shop, a factory employing either union or nonunion workers.

o·pen-work (-würk), *n.* ornamental work, as in cloth, metal, etc., with openings or spaces in the material.

o·pe·ra (ō'pe-rà, op'ēr-à), *n.* 1. a musical drama; play in which the text is set to music. 2. such works collectively as a branch of the performing arts. 3. an opera house.

op·er·a (op'ēr-à), *n.* plural of opus.

op·er·a·ble (op'ēr-â-bl), *adj.* 1. possible; practicable. 2. able to be treated by surgery.

opera glasses, a small, binocular telescope used at the theater, opera, etc.

opera hat, a man's tall silk hat, made so that it can be collapsed.

opera house, a theater for the performance of operas.

op·er·ate (op'ē-rāt), *v.i.* -at·ed, -at·ing, 1. to work; function. 2. to produce a certain effect. 3. to perform a surgical operation: *v.t.* 1. to put or keep in operation. 2. to conduct or manage.

op·er·at·ic (op·ē-rat'ik), *adj.* of or having to do with the opera. 2. like or suited to opera. —op·er·at'i·cal·ly, *adv.*

op·er·a·tion (-rā'shŭn), *n.* 1. the act or manner of operating. 2. the condition of being in operation or at work. 3. a surgical procedure. 4. a series or any one of a series of military movements, industrial activities, etc.

op·er·a·tion·al (-l), *adj.* 1. of or related to the operation of a machine, system, etc. 2. able to be operated. 3. in use. 4. for use in a military operation. —op·er·a'tion·al·ly, *adv.*

op·er·a·tive (op'ē-rā-tiv, op'ēr-â-), *adj.* 1. working; in operation. 2. effective. 3. having to do with physical work or productive activity: *n.* 1. a skilled industrial worker. 2. a spy or detective. —op'er·a·tive·ly, *adv.*

op·er·a·tor (-rāt-ēr), *n.* 1. one who operates a machine. 2. an owner or manager of a mine, factory, etc.

o·per·cu·late (ō-pûr'kyoo-lit, -lāt), *adj.* having an operculum.

o·per·cu·lum (-lŭm), *n., pl.* -la (-là), -lums, in Botany & Zoology, a cover, flap, lid, calyx, or platelike process.

op·er·et·ta (op·ē-ret'à), *n.* a light musical drama with spoken dialogue.

oph·i·cleide (of'i-klīd), *n.* an early, keyed, brass-wind musical instrument consisting of a long tube bent double.

o·phid·i·an (ō-fid'i-ăn), *adj.* of or like a snake: *n.* a snake or serpent.

oph·i·ol·o·gy (of-i-ol'ō-ji), *n.* the branch of zoology concerned with the study of snakes. —oph·i·ol'o·gist, *n.*

oph·thal·mi·a (of-thal'mi-à), *n.* inflammation of the eyeball or conjunctiva.

oph·thal·mic ('mik), *adj.* of or having to do with the eyes.

oph·thal·mo-, a combining form meaning *the eye or eyes.*

oph·thal·mol·o·gy (of-thăl-mol'ō-ji), *n.* the branch of medicine dealing with the structure, functions, and diseases of the eye. —oph·thal·mo·log'i·cal (-mō-loj'i-kl), *adj.* —oph·thal·mol'o·gist, *n.*

oph·thal·mo·scope (of-thal'mō-skōp), *n.* an instrument for examining the interior of the eye. —oph·thal·mos·co·py (of-thăl-mos'kŏ-pi), *n.*

o·pi·ate (o'pi-it), *n.* 1. any medicine containing opium or any of its derivatives, acting as a narcotic and sedative. 2. anything tending to soothe or quiet: *adj.* narcotic; soothing.

o·pine (ō-pīn'), *v.t. & v.i.* o-pined', o·pin'ing, to deem; think: usually humorous.

o·pin·ion (ō-pin'yŭn), *n.* 1. a belief based on what seems to be true; judgment. 2. an estimation of the value or importance of something. 3. a formal judgment by an expert on some matter.

o·pin·ion·at·ed (-āt-id), *adj.* firm or obstinate in one's opinions.

o·pin·ion·a·tive (-āt-iv), *adj.* 1. of or having the nature of opinion. 2. opinionated.

op·is·thog·na·thous (op-is-thog'nà-thŭs), *adj.* having receding jaws.

o·pi·um (ō'pi-ŭm), *n.* a narcotic drug prepared from the juice expressed from the unripe seeds of the opium poppy.

opium poppy, a tall, Asiatic, annual poppy with grayish-green leaves and white or purple flowers, cultivated as the source of opium.

o·pos·sum (ō-pos'ŭm), *n., pl.* -sums, -sum, 1. a small, tree-dwelling American marsupial, with a prehensile tail: it is active at night. 2. the Australian phalanger.

ō in dragon, ōō in crude, oo in wool, u in cup, ū in cure, û in turn, ă in focus, oi in boy, ou in house, th in thin, th in sheathe, g in get, j in joy, y in yet.

op·pi·dan (op′i-dǎn), n. a person living in a town.

op·po·nent (ŏ-pō′nĕnt), adj. opposing; adverse; antagonistic: n. one who opposes, especially in a fight, argument, debate, etc.; adversary.

op·por·tune (op-ĕr-tōōn′, -tyōōn′), adj. 1. well-timed; seasonable. 2. fitting or suitable: said of time. —op·por·tune′ly, adv. —op·por·tune′-ness, n.

op·por·tun·ism (′izm), n. the sacrifice of principles to circumstances, especially in politics. —op·por·tun′ist, n.

op·por·tun·i·ty (op-ĕr-tōō′nĭ-tĭ), n., pl. -ties, 1. a convenient time or occasion, as for progress. 2. an auspicious combination of circumstances.

op·pos·a·ble (ŏ-pō′zȧ-bl), adj. that can be opposed.

op·pose (ŏ-pōz′), v.t. -posed′, -pos′ing, 1. to act against; to place as an obstacle. 2. to contend with; resist.

op·po·site (op′ŏ-zit), adj. 1. placed or set against; in a contrary direction. 2. exhibiting resistance; hostile. 3. completely different; contrary; antithetical: n. anything opposed: prep. across from. —op′po·site·ly, adv. —op′po·site·ness, n.

op·po·si·tion (op-ŏ-zish′ŭn), n. 1. the state or act of opposing or of being opposite. 2. hostility; resistance; contradiction. 3. something that opposes; specifically, [often O-], a political party opposing the party in power. 4. the situation of two heavenly bodies when their longitudes differ by 180°. —op·po·si′tion·ist, n.

op·press (ŏ-pres′), v.t. 1. to lie heavily upon as a mental or spiritual worry; burden. 2. to subjugate or tyrannize over by the unjust use of power. —op·pres′sor, n.

op·pres·sion (ŏ-presh′ŭn), n. 1. the act of oppressing or the state of being oppressed. 2. that which oppresses. 3. physical weariness or mental depression.

op·pres·sive (ŏ-pres′iv), adj. 1. unreasonably burdensome. 2. unjustly severe; tyrannical. 3. distressing. —op·pres′sive·ly, adv.

op·pro·bri·ous (ŏ-prō′bri-ŭs), adj. expressing opprobrium; contemptuous.

op·pro·bri·um (-ŭm), n. 1. disgrace arising from conduct considered shamefully wrong. 2. contempt.

op·pugn (ŏ-pūn′), v.t. 1. to oppose; contend against. 2. to contradict.

op·so·nin (op′sŏ-nin), n. a substance in blood serum that renders bacteria more susceptible to destruction by phagocytes.

opt (opt), v.i. to make a choice.

op·ta·tive (op′tȧ-tiv), adj. 1. expressing a wish or desire. 2. denoting a grammatical mood, as in Greek, used to express a wish.

op·tic (op′tik), adj. 1. of or pertaining to the eye or to vision.

op·ti·cal (-l), adj. 1. of or pertaining to vision. 2. of or pertaining to optics. 3. designed to aid vision. —op′ti·cal·ly, adv.

op·ti·cian (op-tish′ǎn), n. one who makes or sells lenses, eyeglasses, and other optical instruments.

op·tics (op′tiks), n. the science of the properties of light and vision.

op·ti·mism (op′tǐ-mizm), n. 1. the doctrine that everything in the present state of existence is for the best. 2. the disposition to expect the best outcome. —op′ti·mist, n. —op·ti·mis′tic, adj. —op·ti·mis′ti·cal·ly, adv.

op·ti·mum (-mŭm), n. the most favorable degree, condition, amount, etc.

op·tion (op′shŭn), n. 1. the act of choosing. 2. the right of choice. 3. something that can be selected. 4. the right to buy, sell, or lease something at a specified price during a specified time. —op′tion·al, adj.

op·tom·e·ter (op-tom′ĕ-tĕr), n. an instrument for measuring the eye's refractive power.

op·tom·e·try (-tri), n. 1. measurement of the range of vision. 2. the profession of examining the eyes, measuring errors in refraction, and prescribing corrective lenses. —op·tom′-e·trist, n.

op·u·lent (op′yū-lĕnt), adj. 1. having great wealth; rich. 2. abundant; luxuriant; profuse. —op′u·lence, n. —op′u·lent·ly, adv.

o·pun·ti·a (ŏ-pun′shi-ȧ, ′shä), n. any one of various cactus plants having stems studded with flat joints and red, yellow, or purple flowers, including the prickly pears.

o·pus (ō′pŭs), n., pl. o·pe·ra (ō′pĕ-rȧ, op′ĕr-ȧ), o′pus·es, a work; musical composition.

o·pus·cule (ō-pus′kŭl), n. a small or unimportant work.

or (ŏr), conj. a coordinating conjunction used to indicate: a) an alternative or the last term in a series; b) a word or expression equivalent in meaning.

-or (ĕr), a suffix signifying one that performs or acts, a state, a quality.

or·ach, or·ache (ŏr′äch), n. a garden potherb.

or·a·cle (ŏr′ȧ-kl), n. 1. among the ancients, a) the response of a deity or inspired priest to some inquiry; b) the medium through which a deity was consulted; c) the place where a deity might be consulted. 2. the holy of holies in the ancient Jewish Temple. 3. a prophet or person of wisdom. 4. a prophetic declaration of such a person —o·rac·u·lar (ŏ-rak′yū-lẽr), adj.

o·ral (ŏr′ăl), adj. 1. verbal; spoken. 2. of, at, or near the mouth. —o′ral·ly, adv.

or·ange (ŏr′inj, or′-), n. 1. a round, juicy, citrus fruit with a reddish-yellow rind and sweet pulp. 2. the evergreen tree bearing this fruit. 3. reddish yellow.

or·ange·ade (-ād′), n. a beverage of orange juice, water, and sugar.

Or·ange·ism (ŏr′inj-izm), n. the principles, tenets, or practices of Orangemen.

Or·ange·man (-mǎn), n., pl. -men (-mĕn), any member of a Protestant secret society in northern Ireland.

or·ange·ry (ŏr′inj-ri, or′-) n., pl. -ries, a sheltered place for growing orange trees.

orange stick, a pointed stick of wood from an orange tree, used in manicuring.

o·rang·u·tan (ō-rang′oo-tan, -tang), n. a tree-dwelling anthropoid ape of Borneo and Sumatra, with a shaggy, reddish-brown coat.

o·rate (ō-rāt′, ŏr′āt), v.i. -rat′ed, -rat′ing, to

make an oration; speak with great pomposity.

o·ra·tion (ô-rā'shŭn), *n.* a formal public speech delivered on some special or ceremonial occasion.

or·a·tor (ŏr'ăt-ēr, or'-), *n.* an eloquent speaker.

or·a·tor·i·cal (ŏr-ā-tŏr'ĭ-kǎl), *adj.* of or pertaining to oratory or orators. —**or·a·tor'i·cal·ly,** *adv.*

or·a·tor·i·o (ŏr-ā-tŏr'ĭ-ō, or-), *n.* a musical composition on a sacred theme.

or·a·tor·y (ŏr'ā-tŏr-ĭ, or'-), *n., pl.* **-ries,** 1. the art of public speaking. 2. a small chapel, especially one for private devotions.

orb (ŏrb), *n.* 1. a sphere or globe. 2. any one of the heavenly spheres, as the sun, moon, etc. —**orbed,** *adj.*

or·bic·u·lar (ôr-bik'yoo-lēr), *adj.* spherical.

or·bit (ôr'bĭt), *n.* the path described by a heavenly body, man-made satellite, or spacecraft during its periodical revolution around another body: *v.t. & v.i.* to move in or put into an orbit. —**or'bit·al,** *adj.*

or·chard (ôr'chērd), *n.* 1. an area devoted to the growing of fruit trees. 2. the trees of such an area.

or·ches·tra (ôr'kis-trā, 'kes-), *n.* 1. the space in front of the stage of a theater, occupied by the musicians. 2. the whole main floor of a theater. 3. a group of musicians who play together, especially a large group that plays symphonies. 4. the instruments of such a group. —**or·ches'tral** (-kes'trăl), *adj.*

or·ches·trate (-trāt), *v.t. & v.i.* **-trat·ed, -trat·ing,** to arrange (music) for an orchestra. —**or·ches·tra'tion,** *n.*

or·chid (ôr'kĭd), *n.* 1. any one of numerous plants growing worldwide and often having brightly colored flowers with distinctive shapes. 2. one of these flowers. 3. pale purple.

or·dain (ôr-dān'), *v.t.* 1. to decree; order. 2. to invest with ministerial or priestly functions: *v.i.* to command.

or·deal (-dēl'), *n.* 1. an ancient method of trial by fire, water, combat, etc. to determine the guilt or innocence of the accused. 2. any severe trial or test.

or·der (ôr'dēr), *n.* 1. a method or system of regular arrangement. 2. a settled mode of procedure. 3. a rule; regulation; command. 4. social position or rank. 5. a state of peace and tranquillity. 6. a religious, military, or social fraternity. 7. a condition in which everything is in the proper place and working well. 8. a request or instruction to buy or sell something. 9. that which is bought or sold. 10. in *Architecture,* any one of several classical systems of constructing columns. 11. in *Biology,* a classification of plants or animals ranking above the family and below the class. 12. *pl.* the office of ordained minister or priest: *v.t. & v.i.* 1. to arrange. 2. to command; direct. 3. to request (something to be supplied).

or·der·ly (-lĭ), *adj.* 1. neatly arranged; in good order. 2. peaceful; law-abiding: *adv.* methodically: *n., pl.* **-lies,** 1. in *military usage,* a soldier assigned to perform personal services for an officer. 2. a male hospital attendant. —**or'der·li·ness,** *n.*

or·di·nal (ôr'dn-ăl), *adj.* denoting order in a series: *n.* any number indicating position in a series: in full **ordinal number.**

or·di·nance (ôr'dn-ăns), *n.* 1. an established rule, rite, or law. 2. a statute or regulation, especially one of a local government.

or·di·nar·i·ly (ôr-dn-er'ĭ-lĭ), *adv.* 1. usually. 2. to the usual degree.

or·di·nar·y (ôr'dn-er-ĭ), *adj.* 1. usual; customary. 2. commonplace; mediocre; plain.

or·di·nate (ôr'dn-ĭt, -āt), *n.* in *Mathematics,* the vertical distance of a point from the horizontal axis, represented by a coordinate.

or·di·na·tion (ôr-dn-a'shŭn), *n.* 1. the act of conferring holy orders. 2. the state of being ordained.

ord·nance (ôrd'năns), *n.* 1. artillery. 2. all military stores, weapons, materials, etc.

Or·do·vi·cian (ôr-dō-vĭsh'ăn), *n.* the second period of the Paleozoic Era, during which primitive fish appeared.

or·dure (ôr'jēr, 'dyoor), *n.* filth; dung.

ore (ôr), *n.* a mineral in its natural state, especially one from which a valuable metal can be extracted.

o·re·ad (ôr'ĭ-ad), *n.* in *Greek & Roman Mythology,* a mountain nymph.

o·reg·a·no (ō-rĕg'ä-nō, ŏ-), *n.* a bushy mint whose leaves are dried for seasoning.

or·gan (ôr'găn), *n.* 1. a musical instrument consisting of a number of pipes and a keyboard that, when played, allows compressed air to sound in the pipes. 2. any one of various instruments producing similar sounds, as a reed organ. 3. an instrument of communication. 4. a means through which some action is performed. 5. a part of a living organism, having specialized tissues for the performance of some particular function.

or·gan·die, or·gan·die (ôr'găn-di), *n., pl.* **-dies,** a sheer, crisp fabric of cotton.

or·gan·ic (ôr-găn'ĭk), *adj.* 1. of or pertaining to a bodily organ. 2. innate; inborn. 3. denoting or of carbon compounds. 4. of or obtained from an organism. 5. grown only with natural fertilizers, as manure or compost. —**or·gan'i·cal·ly,** *adv.*

or·gan·ism (ôr'gă-nizm), *n.* any living animal or plant.

or·gan·ist (ôr'gă-nist), *n.* one who plays the organ.

or·gan·i·za·tion (ôr-gă-ni-zā'shŭn), *n.* 1. an act of organizing or a state of being organized. 2. a group of persons united for some purpose.

or·gan·ize (ôr'gă-nīz), *v.t.* **-ized, -iz·ing,** 1. to form or furnish with organs. 2. to systematize. 3. to originate; establish. 4. to induce to join (a cause, union, etc.): *v.i.* to become organized. —**or'gan·iz·er,** *n.*

or·ga·no·gen·e·sis (ôr-gă-nō-jen'ĕ-sis), *n.* in *Biology,* organic development.

or·ga·nog·ra·phy (-nog'ră-fĭ), *n.* scientific description of the organs of plants and animals.

or·ga·nol·o·gy (-nol'ō-jĭ), *n.* the study of plant and animal organs.

or·ga·non (ôr'gă-non), *n., pl.* **-na** (-nă), **-nons,** a system of rules for scientific or philosophical investigation.

or·ga·no·ther·a·py (ôr-gă-nō-ther'ă-pi), *n.* the treatment of disease with extracts from the internal gland secretions of animals.

or·gan·za (ôr-gan'ză), *n.* a sheer, stiff fabric of silk, rayon, etc.

or·gan·zine (ôr'găn-zēn), *n.* a strong silk thread used as a warp thread.

or·gasm (ôr'gazm), *n.* a sexual climax.

or·geat (ôr'zhat), *n.* a sweet syrup used as a flavoring.

or·gy (ôr'ji), *n., pl.* **-gies,** 1. wild, riotous revelry. 2. excessive indulgence in any activity.

o·ri·el (ôr'i-ĕl), *n.* a large bay window.

o·ri·ent (ôr'i-ĕnt), *n.* [O-], 1. the countries of the world east of Europe, especially eastern Asia. 2. [Poetic], the East: *adj.* bright; lustrous: *v.t. & v.i.* (-ent), 1. to locate with reference to the east. 2. to adjust or become adjusted to a situation.

o·ri·en·tal (ôr-i-en'tl), *adj.* 1. [O-], of the Orient, its people, or their culture. 2. [Poetic], eastern: *n.* [usually O-], a native of the Orient.

O·ri·en·tal·izm (-izm), *n.* the spirit, character, customs, style, manners, etc. of the people of the Orient. —**O·ri·en'tal·ist,** *n.*

o·ri·en·tate (ôr'i-en-tāt), *v.t. & v.i.* same as **orient.** —**o·ri·en·ta'tion,** *n.*

or·i·fice (ôr'i-fis), *n.* a mouth or aperture.

o·ri·flamme (ôr'i-flam), *n.* 1. the ancient royal standard of France, a red flag split at one end to form flame-shaped streamers. 2. any battle standard.

o·ri·ga·mi (ô-ri-gä'mi), *n.* a Japanese art of folding paper to make flowers, figures, etc.

or·i·gin (ôr'i-jin, or'-), *n.* 1. a beginning; first existence. 2. ancestry; derivation. 3. source; cause.

o·rig·i·nal (ô-rij'ĭ-nl), *adj.* 1. first in order; earliest. 2. having the power to originate or create. 3. not copied; new. 4. denoting that from which a copy is made: *n.* 1. that from which anything is copied. 2. an archetype. —**o·rig·i·nal'i·ty,** *n.* —**o·rig'i·nal·ly,** *adv.*

original sin, in Christian Theology, the inherent tendency of mankind to sin, derived from Adam and imparted to his descendants.

o·rig·i·nate (ô-rij'ĭ-nāt), *v.t.* **-nat·ed, -nat·ing,** to bring into existence; invent: *v.i.* to commence. —**o·rig·i·na'tion,** *n.* —**o·rig·i·na'tor,** *n.*

o·ri·ole (ôr'i-ōl), *n.* any one of various American birds the males of which are black and orange (or yellow).

O·ri·on (ô-rī'ŏn), *n.* an equatorial constellation near Taurus.

or·lop (ôr'lop), *n.* the lowest deck of a ship.

Or·mazd (ôr'mäzd), *n.* the chief deity of Zoroastrianism.

or·mo·lu (ôr'mō-lōō), *n.* a bronze or copper gilt in imitation of gold.

or·na·ment (ôr'nă-mĕnt), *n.* 1. anything that adorns or beautifies. 2. a person regarded as illustrious because of talent, character, etc.: *v.t.* to adorn. —**or·na·men'tal,** *adj.* —**or·na·men·ta'tion,** *n.*

or·nate (ôr-nāt'), *adj.* elaborately ornamented; showy. —**or·nate'ly,** *adv.* —**or·nate'ness,** *n.*

or·ner·y (ôr'nēr-i), *adj.* 1. having a vile disposition. 2. stubborn. 3. contemptible.

or·nis (ôr'nis), *n.* same as **avifauna.**

or·nith·ic (ôr-nith'ik), *adj.* of or pertaining to birds.

or·nith·o-, a combining form meaning *a bird, birds.*

or·ni·thoid (ôr'ni-thoid), *adj.* birdlike.

or·ni·thol·o·gy (ôr-ni-thol'ŏ-ji), *n.* the scientific study of birds. —**or·ni·thol'o·gist,** *n.*

or·ni·thop·ter (ôr'ni-thop-tẽr), *n.* an airplane that is to be propelled by the flapping of its wings.

or·ni·tho·rhyn·chus (ôr-ni-thō-ring'kŭs), *n.* same as **platypus.**

or·og·e·ny (ô-roj'ĕ-ni), **or·o·gen·e·sis** (ôr-ô-jen'ĕ-sis), *n.* the process of mountain formation.

o·rog·ra·phy (ô-rog'ră-fi), *n.* the branch of physical geography that treats of mountains and mountain systems. —**or·o·graph·ic** (ôr-ô-graf'ik), *adj.*

o·ro·ide (ôr'ô-īd), *n.* an alloy of tin, copper, and zinc, resembling gold and used in cheap jewelry.

o·rol·o·gy (ô-rol'ŏ-ji), *n.* the study of mountains.

o·ro·tund (ôr'ŏ-tund), *adj.* 1. characterized by fullness, clearness, and strength: said of the voice. 2. pompous.

or·phan (ôr'făn), *n.* a child bereft of one or both parents: *adj.* 1. being an orphan. 2. for orphans: *v.t.* to make an orphan of.

or·phan·age (-ij), *n.* 1. the state of being an orphan. 2. an institution serving as a home for orphans.

or·phic (ôr'fik), *adj.* mystic; oracular.

or·phrey (ôr'fri), *n.* an embroidered band of gold or silver on the front of an ecclesiastical vestment.

or·pi·ment (ôr'pi-mĕnt), *n.* a yellow compound of arsenic, used as a pigment.

or·pine (ôr'pin), *n.* a succulent plant with fleshy leaves.

Or·ping·ton (ôr'ping-tŏn), *n.* any one of a breed of chickens with a full breast, single comb, and unfeathered legs.

or·rer·y (ôr'ēr-i), *n., pl.* **-rer·ies,** an apparatus to illustrate by balls mounted on rods the motions, magnitudes, and positions of the planets of the solar system.

or·ris (ôr'is), *n.* any one of several European irises.

or·ris·root (-rōōt), *n.* the dried roots of the orris, used in perfumery when pulverized.

or·tho-, a combining form meaning *straight, upright, correct, perpendicular.*

or·tho·clase (ôr'thō-klās, -klāz), *n.* a potassium feldspar common in igneous and granitic rocks.

or·tho·don·tics (ôr-thô-don'tiks), *n.* the branch of dentistry specializing in correcting irregularities of the teeth and poor occlusion. —**or·tho·don'tist,** *n.*

or·tho·dox (ôr'thô-doks), *adj.* holding or in accordance with the received or established belief, as in religion. —**or'tho·dox·y,** *n.*

Orthodox Eastern Church, the Christian Church dominant in eastern Europe, western Asia, and northern Africa.

or·tho·e·py (ôr-thō'ĕ-pi, ôr'thō-), *n.* 1. the

standard pronunciation of words. 2. the study of pronunciation. —or·tho'e·pist, *n.*

or·tho·gen·e·sis (ôr-thō-jen'ě-sĭs), *n.* the theory that certain organisms evolve in a way predetermined by inherited characters and independent of external factors.

or·thog·na·thous (ôr-thŏg'ná-thŭs), *adj.* having no projecting jaw in the facial profile.

or·thog·o·nal (ôr-thŏg'ô-nl), *adj.* rectangular.

or·tho·grade (ôr'thŏ-grād), *adj.* walking with the body upright.

or·thog·ra·phy (ôr-thŏg'rá-fĭ), *n., pl.* -phies, 1. correct spelling. 2. the study of correct spelling. —or·tho·graph·ic (ôr-thŏ-graf'ĭk), *adj.* —or·thog'ra·pher, *n.*

or·tho·pe·dics (ôr-thŏ-pē'dĭks), *n.* the branch of surgery dealing with deformities, injuries, etc. of the bones and joints. —or·tho·pe'dic, *adj.* —or·tho·pe'dist, *n.*

or·thop·ter·an (ôr-thŏp'tēr-ăn), *n.* any one of a large order of insects which comprises cockroaches, crickets, earwigs, etc.

or·tho·scope (ôr'thŏ-skōp), *n.* an instrument for examining the interior of the eye.

or·to·lan (ôr'tl-ăn), *n.* a bunting of the Old World, esteemed for its flesh.

-o·ry (ôr'ĭ, ôr-ĭ), a suffix meaning *having the nature of, a place or thing for.*

o·ryx (ôr'ĭks), *n.* any one of several large African and Asian antelopes with long, straight horns projecting backward.

os (ŏs), *n., pl.* os'sa ('á), [Latin], a bone.

os (ŏs), *n., pl.* o·ra (ô'rá), [Latin], a mouth.

Os·car (ŏs'kēr), *n.* [Slang], any one of the statuettes given annually in the U.S. for achievement in motion pictures.

os·cil·late (ŏs'ĭ-lāt), *v.i.* -lat·ed, -lat·ing, 1. to swing back and forth. 2. to be indecisive. 3. in *Physics,* to vary between an upper and a lower value, as a sound wave or an electric current. —os·cil·la'tion, *n.* —os·cil·la·tor, *n.* — os'cil·la·to·ry, *adj.*

os·cil·lo·graph (o·sĭl'ô-graf), *n.* an instrument for recording oscillations of electric current.

os·cil·lo·scope (-skōp), *n.* an oscillograph that visually displays an electric wave on a fluorescent screen.

os·cine (ŏs'ĭn), *adj.* denoting or of a large group of perching birds, as the finches, shrikes, etc., with highly developed vocal organs, although some do not sing: a bird of this group.

os·ci·tan·cy (ŏs'ĭ-tăn-sĭ), *n.* 1. drowsiness. 2. apathy.

os·cu·lant (ŏs'kyŭ-lănt), *adj.* 1. in *Biology,* linking: said of a characteristic. 2. in *Zoology,* gripping or adhering together.

os·cu·late (-lāt), *v.t. & v.i.* -lat·ed, -lat·ing, 1. to kiss. 2. to touch closely. —os·cu·la'tion, *n.*

os·cu·la·to·ry (-lá-tôr·ĭ), *adj.* of or pertaining to kissing.

-ose (ōs), a suffix meaning *full of, having the qualities of, like.*

o·sier (ō'zhēr), *n.* 1. any one of various willows with pliable branches and stems used in basket-making and in furniture. 2. one of these branches or stems.

O·si·ris (ō-sī'rĭs), *n.* a god of ancient Egypt, judge of the dead.

-o·sis (ō'sĭs), a suffix meaning *state, action, abnormal condition, diseased condition.*

Os·man·li (oz-man'lĭ, os-), *n., pl.* -lis, a Turk belonging to the western branch of the Turkish peoples.

os·mi·um (ŏz'mĭ-ŭm), *n.* a very hard, bluish-white, metallic chemical element, occurring as an alloy with platinum.

os·mose (ŏs'mōs, oz'mōs), *v.t. & v.i.* -mosed, -mos·ing, to subject to, or to undergo, osmosis.

os·mo·sis (os-mō'sĭs, oz-), *n.* 1. tendency of a solvent to go through a membrane and into a solution that is more highly concentrated, the solutions being thus equalized in concentration on both sides. 2. diffusion of fluids through a membrane or porous partition. —os·mot'ic (-mŏt'ĭk), *adj.*

os·mun·da (oz-mun'dă), *n.* any one of a genus of ferns with specialized fronds bearing dense masses of sporangia.

os·mun·dine (oz'mŭn-dēn), *n.* a fibrous mass of dried fern roots, used as a rooting medium for orchids and other epiphytes.

os·na·burg (ŏz'nă·bŭrg), *n.* a coarse, heavy cloth, originally of linen and now of cotton, used for making sacks, work clothes, etc.

os·prey (os'prĭ), *n., pl.* -preys, a large diving bird belonging to the hawk family and preying solely on fish.

os·sa (ŏs'ă), *n.* [Latin], plural of os (a bone).

os·se·in (os'ĭ-ĭn), *n.* the organic basis of bone, the part remaining after the mineral matter is dissolved by acid.

os·se·ous (-ŭs), *adj.* bony.

os·si·cle (os'ĭ-kl), *n.* a little bone.

os·si·frage (os'ĭ-frĭj), *n.* either one of two birds, a lammergeier or an osprey.

os·si·fy (os'ĭ-fī), *v.t. & v.i.* -fied, -fy·ing, 1. to convert into bone. 2. to harden into set ways. —os·si·fi·ca'tion, *n.*

os·te·i·tis (os-tĭ-ī'tĭs), *n.* bone inflammation.

os·ten·si·ble (os-ten'sĭ-bl), *adj.* 1. apparent; seeming. 2. avowed; alleged. —os·ten'si·bly, *adv.*

os·ten·sive ('sĭv), *adj.* 1. showing clearly or directly. 2. ostensible.

os·ten·so·ri·um (os-těn-sôr'ĭ-ŭm), *n., pl.* -ri·a (-ă), same as monstrance.

os·ten·ta·tion (os-těn-tā'shŭn), *n.* ambitious or vain display; mere show; pretentiousness. — os·ten·ta'tious, *adj.*

os·te·o-, a combining form meaning *bone.*

os·te·o·blast (os'tĭ-ô-blast), *n.* a cell developing into, or producing, bone.

os·te·oc·la·sis (os-tĭ-ok'lá-sĭs), *n.* 1. the breaking down and absorption of bony tissue. 2. the breaking of a bone to correct a deformity.

os·te·oid (os'tĭ-oid), *adj.* bonelike.

os·te·ol·o·gy (os-tĭ-ol'ô-jĭ), *n.* anatomical study of bone. —os·te·ol'o·gist, *n.*

os·te·o·ma (-ō'mă), *n., pl.* -mas, -ma·ta ('mă-tă), a tumor composed of bony tissue.

os·te·o·ma·la·ci·a (os-tĭ-ô-mă-lā'shă), *n.* a softening of the bones as a result of a deficiency in calcium salts.

---

os·te·o·my·e·li·tis (-mĭ-ĕ-līt'ĭs), *n.* infection of bone marrow or bone structure.

os·te·o·path (os'ti-ō-path), *n.* a doctor who practices osteopathy.

os·te·op·a·thy (os-tē-op'ǎ-thi), *n.* a type of medicine and surgery specially emphasizing the interrelationship of the skeletal-muscular system with all other systems of the body. —os·te·o·path·ic (os-ti-ō-path'ik), *adj.*

os·te·o·phyte (os'ti-ō-fīt), *n.* a small bony outgrowth.

os·te·o·plas·tic (os-ti-ō-plas'tik), *adj.* 1. in *Anatomy,* of or pertaining to bone formation. 2. in *Surgery,* of or pertaining to osteoplasty.

os·te·o·plas·ty (-plas'ti), *n.* surgical replacement of bone.

os·te·ot·o·my (os-ti-ot'ō-mi), *n., pl.* -mies, the surgical operation of dividing a bone or of cutting out a piece of bone.

ost·ler (os'lĕr), *n.* same as hostler.

os·tra·cism (os'trǎ-sizm), *n.* 1. in ancient Greece, temporary banishment by popular vote. 2. a forcing out or exclusion of someone from a group by general agreement.

os·tra·cize (-sīz), *v.t.* -cized, -ciz·ing, to subject to ostracism.

os·trich (ôs'trich, os'-), *n.* 1. an extremely large and powerful, long-necked, flightless bird of Africa and the Near East, with very long legs and small, nonfunctional wings. 2. a rhea.

Os·tro·goth (os'trō-goth, -gôth), *n.* a Goth of more easterly regions; especially, a member of a tribe of such Goths that conquered Italy in the 5th century A.D.

o·tal·gi·a (ō-tal'ji-ǎ), *n.* earache.

O·thel·lo (ō-thel'ō), *n.* the title character of a play by Shakespeare: duped into thinking his wife faithless, he kills her.

oth·er (uth'ĕr), *adj.* 1. being the remaining one or ones. 2. different or distinct. 3. being further or in addition. 4. former: *pron.* the other one or some other one: *n.* the opposite: *adv.* otherwise.

oth·er·wise (-wiz), *adv.* 1. in another way. 2. in other respects. 3. in other circumstances: *adj.* different.

oth·er·world·ly (-wûrld'li), *adj.* rising above earthly interests; spiritual.

o·tic (ōt'ik, ot'ik), *adj.* of the ear.

o·ti·ose (ō'shi-ōs, ōt'i-), *adj.* 1. marked by idleness; indolent or at leisure. 2. ineffective; futile. 3. useless; functionless. —o·ti·os·i·ty (-os'ĭ-ti), *n.*

o·ti·tis (ō-tīt'ĭs), *n.* ear inflammation.

o·tol·o·gy (ō-tol'ō-ji), *n.* the medical science treating of the ear and its disorders.

o·to·scope (ōt'ō-skōp), *n.* an instrument to examine the interior of the ear.

ot·ter (ot'ĕr), *n.* 1. any one of a group of furry, flesh-eating, web-footed mammals related to the weasel and mink. 2. its lustrous fur. 3. same as sea otter.

Ot·to·man (ot'ō-mǎn), *adj.* Turkish: *n., pl.* -mans, a Turk.

ot·to·man (ot'ō-mǎn), *n.* 1. a low, cushioned seat that is backless and armless. 2. a kind

of couch or divan. 3. a low, cushioned footstool. 4. a corded fabric of silk, rayon, etc.

ou·bli·ette (ōō-bli-et'), *n.* a dungeon into which the only opening is in the ceiling.

ouch (ouch), *interj.* an exclamation indicating sudden pain.

ought (ôt), *v.aux.* an auxiliary used with infinitives and meaning: *a)* to be bound as by duty; be required; *b)* to be proper, fit, warranted, desirable, etc.; *c)* to be expected or likely: *n.* 1. anything whatever; aught. 2. a cipher; nought.

ought·n't ('nt), ought not.

Oui·ja (wē'jǎ, 'ji), *n.* an occult device consisting of a planchette and a board marked with letters of the alphabet and other symbols, used to get messages and answers often held to be of telepathic, subconscious, or spiritualistic origin: a trademark.

ounce (ouns), *n.* 1. a unit of weight, equal to 1/16 pound avoirdupois or 1/12 pound troy. 2. same as fluid ounce. 3. any small amount. 4. same as snow leopard.

our (our), *adj.* of or belonging to us.

Our Father, same as Lord's Prayer.

Our Lady, the mother of Jesus: a term used chiefly by Roman Catholics.

ours (ourz), *pron.* that or those belonging to us.

our·self (our-self'), *pron.* 1. the emphatic or reflexive form of we, used formally as by a king in reference to himself. 2. our true self: formal use as by a king.

our·selves (-selvz'), *pron.* 1. the emphatic or reflexive form of we. 2. our true selves.

-ous (ŭs), a suffix meaning *having, full of, characterized by.*

ou·sel (ōō'zl), *n.* same as ouzel.

oust (oust), *v.t.* to eject, expel, etc.

oust·er ('ĕr), *n.* an ousting or being ousted.

out (out), *adv.* 1. away from a given place or point. 2. outdoors; outside. 3. so as to be seen or noticed. 4. in a way that is full, complete, developed, etc. 5. [Slang], in or into unconsciousness. 6. in *Baseball,* in a manner producing an out: *adj.* 1. being at or going toward or beyond the outer side, outer limits, etc. 2. being away from a given place. 3. bared, exposed, etc. 4. not effective, feasible, etc. 5. checked from operating or functioning. 6. [Informal], being in a condition of financial loss. 7. [Informal], unfashionable. 8. in *Baseball,* failing or having failed to get on base: *prep.* 1. to the outside by way of. 2. from the inside of. 3. along the way of: *n.* 1. one that is out. 2. [Slang], a means of escape. 3. in *Baseball,* the failure of a player to reach base safely: *v.i.* to become disclosed: *interj.* begone!

out-, a combining form meaning *outer, away, outside, outward, beyond, better than.*

out·age ('ij), *n.* interruption of power supply as because of a damaged generator.

out-and-out (out'n-out'), *adj.* unmitigated; total; complete.

out·back (out'bak), *n.* a remote, wild area, with few settlers; hinterland.

out·bal·ance (out-bal'ǎns), *v.t.* -anced, -anc·ing, to outweigh.

---

a in cap, ā in cane, ä in father, ȧ in abet, e in met, ē in be, ĕ in baker, ė in regent, i in pit, ī in fine, ĭ in manifest, o in hot, ô in horse, ō in bone,

out-bid (-bĭd′), v.t. -bid′, -bid′ding, to surpass the bid or offer of.

out-board (out′bôrd), adj. outside or away from the hull or main body of a ship, boat, aircraft, etc.: n. 1. same as **outboard motor**. 2. a boat with an outboard motor.

outboard motor, a portable gasoline engine mounted outside a boat to propel it.

out-bound ('bound), adj. outward bound.

out-break ('brāk), n. 1. a breaking out; eruption. 2. a revolt; uprising.

out-build-ing ('bĭl-dĭng), n. a shed, barn, etc. separate from the main building.

out-burst ('bûrst), n. a bursting forth, as of joy or activity.

out-cast ('kăst), adj. cast out; rejected: n. one that is cast out, as from society.

out-class (out-klăs′), v.t. to surpass decisively in kind or performance.

out-come (out′kŭm), n. result; consequence.

out-crop ('krŏp), n. 1. protrusion through the soil, as of rock. 2. rock or other mineral material so emerging: v.t. (out-krŏp′), -cropped′, -crop′ping, 1. to emerge thus. 2. to break forth.

out-cry (′krī), n. clamor; tumult.

out-dat-ed (out-dāt′ĭd), adj. no longer current, popular, accepted, etc.; outmoded.

out-dis-tance (-dĭs′tăns), v.t. -tanced, -tanc-ing, to pass, as in a race, or leave behind; outstrip.

out-do (-dōō′), v.t. -did′, -done′, -do′ing, to surpass at doing something.

out-door (out′dôr), adj. of, in, or for the outdoors.

out-doors (-dôrz′), adv. in or to a location outside a building or other shelter: n. 1. a location outside a building or other shelter. 2. the aggregate of natural features found outside houses or other buildings or in parks, rural regions, etc., as fresh air, sunshine, trees, streams, etc. 3. regions abounding in such features, as rural regions or wooded or mountainous areas.

out-er (out′ĕr), adj. 1. being closer to, closest to, or at the exterior; external; exterior. 2. relatively far out.

out-er-most (-mōst), adj. 1. closest to or at the exterior; external; exterior. 2. farthest out or away; most distant.

outer space, space beyond the atmosphere of the earth or outside the solar system.

out-er-wear (-wer), n. apparel worn over the usual clothing, as for extra warmth.

out-field (out′fēld), n. 1. the outlying land of a farm. 2. the playing area of a baseball field beyond the infield. 3. the outfielders as a group.

out-field-er (-ĕr), n. in Baseball, a player whose position is in the outfield.

out-fit (out′fĭt), n. 1. a set of equipment; paraphernalia. 2. a set of clothes to be worn together; ensemble. 3. a group of individuals associated in an activity, as a military unit: v.t. -fit-ted, -fit-ting, to equip; fit out. — **out′fit-ter**, n.

out-flank (out-flăngk′), v.t. to go around and beyond the flank of (enemy troops).

out-flow (out′flō), n. 1. a flowing out. 2. that which flows out.

out-fox (out-fŏks′), v.t. to outwit.

out-go (out′gō), n. expenditure.

out-go-ing ('gō-ĭng), adj. 1. being on the way out; leaving; departing. 2. not withdrawn or introverted; readily associating with or helping others; warm and sympathetic; sociable.

out-grow (out-grō′), v.t. -grew′, -grown′, -grow′-ing, 1. to grow faster or bigger than. 2. to grow or develop to the point of putting aside or ridding oneself of (something seen or thought of as no longer sufficiently mature, sophisticated, etc.). 3. to grow too big for.

out-growth (out′grōth), n. 1. the act of growing out. 2. something growing out of something else. 3. something developing as a consequence of something else; sequence; result.

out-guess (out-ges′), v.t. 1. to guess better than. 2. to gain advantage or victory over by superior conjecture.

out-house (out′hous), n. an outbuilding; specifically, a small, shedlike structure housing a toilet.

out-ing (out′ĭng), n. 1. an outdoor excursion for pleasure and relaxation, as in going on a picnic. 2. the picnicking, games, etc. often forming a central part of such an excursion.

out-land-er (out′lăn-dĕr), n. 1. a person from outlying regions of a country; provincial person; rustic. 2. any stranger; specifically, a foreigner.

out-land-ish (out-lăn′dĭsh), adj. 1. most peculiar; bizarre; grotesque. 2. utterly absurd; idiotic. 3. altogether immoderate; extreme; outrageous. 4. out-of-the-way.

out-last (out-lăst′), v.t. to last longer than.

out-law (out′lô), n. 1. originally, one deprived of legal benefits and protection. 2. a fugitive habitual criminal: v.t. 1. to declare unlawful, illegal, or unenforceable. 2. to ban; bar.

out-lay (out′lā), n. expenditure.

out-let (out′lĕt), n. 1. an opening or passage to allow release or escape of something, as of gas. 2. a means of relieving or discharging pent-up emotions, extra energy, etc. 3. a stream, river, etc. flowing out as from a lake. 4. a market, specifically one for goods of a certain kind or make or from a certain source. 5. in an electrical wiring system, any point at which current may be drawn for consumption by inserting a plug.

out-line (out′lĭn), n. 1. a line bounding an object or figure in such a way as to show its shape. 2. a sketch limited to such a line or lines. 3. also pl. an overall plan, without details. 4. a summary of something, the main points being indicated or presented concisely but systematically: v.t. -lined, -lin-ing, to make an outline of.

out-live (out-lĭv′), v.t. -lived′, -liv-ing, 1. to live longer than. 2. to live beyond the end or disappearance of; survive.

out-look (out′look), n. 1. a place from which to watch for or gaze at something. 2. that which can be seen from such a place; view. 3. alert, careful watching for something. 4. a particular way of looking at things; viewpoint. 5. the way something looks with re-

---

ŏ in dragon, ōō in crude, oo in wool, u in cup, ū in cure, û in turn, ŭ in focus, oi in boy, ou in house, th in thin, th in sheathe, g in get, j in joy, y in yet.

gard to subsequent or future developments; prospect. 6. possibility, probability, or expectation of a given occurrence or development.

out-ly-ing ('lī-ing), *adj.* situated in the outer reaches of a locality; remote.

out-man (out-man'), *v.t.* -**manned'**, -**man'ning**, to exceed in number of men.

out-ma-neu-ver, out-ma-noeu-vre (-mȧ-nōō'vēr), *v.t.* -**vered** or -**vred**, -**ver-ing** or -**vring**, 1. to maneuver better than. 2. to gain advantage or victory over by superior maneuvering.

out-mod-ed (out-mōd'id), *adj.* outdated.

out-most (out'mōst), *adj.* same as outermost.

out-num-ber (out-num'bēr), *v.t.* to exceed in number.

out-of-date (out'ȯv-dāt'), *adj.* outdated.

out-of-door (-dôr'), *adj.* same as outdoor.

out-of-doors (-dôrz'), *adv.* same as outdoors.

out-of-the-way (out'ȯv-thē-wā'), *adj.* 1. situated where there are few people or few visitors; remote. 2. not ordinary; unusual. 3. not conventional or proper.

out-of-town-er (out-ȯv-toun'ēr), *n.* a visitor in a town or city.

out-pa-tient (out'pā-shènt), *n.* a patient who is treated at a hospital but who is not lodged there.

out-play (out-plā'), *v.t.* to play better than. 2. to gain advantage or victory over by superior playing.

out-post (out'pōst), *n.* 1. an observation station at a distance from the main body of a military force. 2. the individuals there. 3. a foreign military base of a country. 4. an outlying settlement.

out-pour (out'pôr), *n.* 1. a pouring out. 2. that which pours out: *v.t. & v.i.* (out-pôr'), to pour out.

out-put (out'poot), *n.* 1. the total of something produced. 2. the act of producing. 3. data transferred or delivered by a computer; also, such transferal or delivery, or a device involved in this. 4. the useful voltage, current, or power delivered as by a generator or by a circuit; also, the terminal delivering this.

out-rage (out'rāj), *n.* 1. open and excessive viciousness or violence, or an instance of this. 2. an extremely grave insult or offense. 3. extreme anger, indignation, etc. prompted by this. 4. rape: *v.t.* -**raged**, -**rag-ing**, 1. to commit outrage or an outrage on or against. 2. to offend, insult, etc. grievously. 3. to rape. 4. to make extremely angry, indignant, etc.; fill with outrage.

out-ra-geous (out-rā'jùs), *adj.* 1. of, like, or involving outrage; extremely offensive, shocking, etc. 2. exceeding all bounds of reason, propriety, etc.; extreme beyond belief.

out-rank (-rangk'), *v.t.* to surpass in rank.

ou-tré (ōō-trā'), *adj.* [French], 1. exaggerated. 2. unconventional; bizarre.

out-reach (out-rēch', out'rēch), *v.t. & v.i.* 1. to reach farther (than). 2. to exceed. 3. to extend: *n.* (out'rēch), a reaching out: *adj.* (out'rēch), designating or of a branch office as of a social agency.

out-rid-er (out'rīd-ēr), *n.* 1. a mounted attendant, as one riding on horseback ahead of or beside a carriage. 2. a cowboy riding about on a range to keep cattle from straying. 3. a trailblazer; forerunner.

out-rig-ger ('rig-ēr), *n.* 1. any one of various frameworks or devices extending out from the main part of something, as a projecting spar or beam to extend sails or ropes. 2. a canoe equipped at either side with a stabilizing, buoyant timber or other float held parallel to and at a distance from the canoe by projecting supports; also, the float itself.

out-right (out'rīt, out'rīt'), *adj.* 1. positive; unqualified; downright. 2. straightforward. 3. complete; whole: *adv.* 1. without reservation; openly. 2. entirely. 3. at one and the same time.

out-run (out-run'), *v.t.* -**run'**, -**run'**, -**run'ning**, 1. to run faster or farther than. 2. to surpass.

out-sell (-sel'), *v.t.* -**sold'**, -**sell'ing**, to sell better or more than.

out-set (out'set), *n.* a setting out; beginning; start.

out-shine (out-shīn'), *v.t.* -**shone'** or -**shined'**, -**shin'ing**, 1. to shine better or brighter than. 2. to excel.

out-shoot (out'shōōt), *n.* 1. a shooting out, gushing forth, etc. 2. an outgrowth, projection, etc.

out-side (out'sīd', out-sīd', out'sīd), *n.* 1. the outer side, part, aspect, etc. 2. a place, area, or location not within a building, other shelter, enclosure, etc. or not at or near the inner side, part, etc. 3. the outdoors: *adj.* 1. of, in, on, to, or from the outside. 2. extreme; maximum. 3. mere; slight: *adv.* 1. in, on, or to the outside. 2. outdoors: *prep.* 1. in, on, or to the outside of. 2. [Informal], except.

out-sid-er (out-sīd'ēr), *n.* 1. one not a member of or participant in a certain group, as by personal choice, or because not qualified, or by reason of exclusion through decision of the group members. 2. a contender thought to have small chance of winning, as in a race.

out-size (out'sīz), *n.* 1. a size notably differing from the usual one or ones; especially, an unusually large size. 2. something of such a size: *adj.* that is of an outsize: also **out'-sized** ('sīzd).

out-skirts ('skûrts), *n.pl.* the outer areas, as of a city.

out-smart (out-smärt'), *v.t.* [Informal], to get the better of by craftiness or cleverness; outwit.

out-spo-ken (out'spō'kn), *adj.* candid; frank.

out-spread ('spred'), *adj.* spread out, as wings; extended; expanded.

out-stand-ing (out-stan'ding), *adj.* 1. sticking out; projecting. 2. prominent; conspicuous. 3. notable; distinguished. 4. not cleared up; remaining unsettled. 5. unpaid; uncollected. 6. that have been issued and sold: said of stocks and bonds.

out-sta-tion (out'stā-shùn), *n.* a far-off station or post, as in an unsettled area.

out-stay (out-stā'), *v.t.* 1. to stay longer than. 2. to stay beyond.

out·stretch (-strech′), *v.t.* 1. to stretch out; extend. 2. to stretch beyond.

out·strip (-strip′), *v.t.* -stripped′, -strip′ping, 1. to go faster than or leave behind. 2. to excel.

out·ward (out′wĕrd), *adj.* 1. external; exterior; outer. 2. going or leading to or toward the outer side, part, etc.: *adv.* 1. to or toward the outer side, part, etc.; away from the center or interior. 2. away from port.

out·ward·ly (out′wĕrd-li), *adv.* 1. with regard to the outside or exterior, the outer appearance, outer indications, etc. 2. same as **outward**.

out·wards (′wĕrdz), *adv.* same as **outward**.

out·wear (out-wer′), *v.t.* -wore′, -worn′, -wear′ing, 1. to wear out by constant use; impair, exhaust, etc. by use. 2. to last longer than; outlast. 3. to outgrow (senses 2 & 3).

out·weigh (-wā′), *v.t.* 1. to surpass in weight; be heavier than. 2. to surpass in importance, value, etc.

out·wit (-wit′), *v.t.* -wit′ted, -wit′ting, to gain advantage or victory over through quicker thinking or through craftiness.

out·work (out′wûrk), *n.* an accessory trench or fortification beyond the main defenses.

o·va (ō′và), *n.* plural of *ovum*.

o·val (ō′vl), *adj.* 1. egglike in form; having the form of an ellipsoid. 2. having the shape of an egg cut in half lengthwise; elliptical: *n.* anything of oval form or shape.

o·var·i·an (ō-ver′i-ån), *adj.* of or pertaining to an ovary or the ovaries.

o·var·i·ec·to·my (ō-ver-i-ek′tō-mi), *n., pl.* -mies, surgical removal of an ovary or ovaries.

o·var·i·ot·o·my (-ot′ō-mi), *n., pl.* -mies, 1. surgical incision into an ovary. 2. ovariectomy.

o·va·ry (ō′vēr-i), *n., pl.* -ries, 1. in *Anatomy & Zoology*, either of the pair of female reproductive glands that produce eggs and, in vertebrates, sex hormones. 2. in pistils, the enlarged, hollow part containing ovules.

o·vate (ō′vāt), *adj.* egg-shaped.

o·va·tion (ō-vā′shŭn), *n.* an enthusiastic demonstration of public esteem, approval, or appreciation, as by applause or cheering.

ov·en (uv′ĕn), *n.* a compartment or structure for baking or roasting meat or other foods or for heating or drying various things.

o·ver (ō′vēr), *prep.* 1. in, at, or to a point or position up from; above. 2. across and down from. 3. on, upon, or down on. 4. during the course of. 5. in a position covering the surface, outline, etc. of. 6. in a condition or state of authority, dignity, quality, etc. superior to. 7. in a course leading along, across, or above. 8. on or to the other side of. 9. beyond. 10. in preference to. 11. with regard to: *adv.* 1. above or across. 2. beyond. 3. throughout; through. 4. from beginning to end; through. 5. down. 6. into an inverted position. 7. once more; again. 8. in or to a specified place: *adj.* 1. upper or outer. 2. superior. 3. extra or excessive. 4. finished; gone; done.

o·ver- a combining form meaning *above, across, beyond, excessive, excessively, etc.*: as

many **over-** compounds are obvious in meaning, they are omitted from the list of definitions.

o·ver·act (ō-vēr-akt′), *v.t. & v.i.* to act in an exaggerated way; specifically, in playing a part, to overdo (facial expressions, gestures, etc.).

o·ver·age (-āj′), *adj.* being beyond a certain age taken as a standard or qualification.

o·ver·age (ō′vēr-ij), *n.* a surplus.

o·ver·all (-ōl), *adj.* taken in totality; viewed as a whole; complete: *adv.* (ō-vēr-ōl′), on the whole; for the most part.

o·ver·alls (ō′vēr-ōlz), *n.pl.* a garment worn over regular clothes to protect them from dirt and wear and consisting of loose trousers with an upper front part supported by shoulder straps.

o·ver·awe (ō-vēr-ô′), *v.t.* -awed′, -aw′ing, to fill with extreme or unreasoning awe.

o·ver·bal·ance (-bal′åns), *v.t.* -anced, -anc·ing, 1. to outweigh. 2. to throw off balance.

o·ver·bear·ing (-ber′ing), *adj.* 1. arrogant; tyrannical. 2. ruling out or dominating all other considerations, reasons, interests, etc.; surpassingly urgent or weighty.

o·ver·board (ō′vēr-bôrd), *adv.* 1. over the side of a ship. 2. over the side of a ship and into the water.

o·ver·cast (-kast), *n.* 1. a covering, especially of clouds. 2. an arch in a mine, supporting an overhead passage: *adj.* marked by an overcast of clouds: said of the sky or the weather.

o·ver·charge (ō-vēr-chärj′), *v.t. & v.i.* -charged′, -charg′ing, 1. to charge too much, as for goods. 2. to load too much on: *n.* 1. an excessive charge. 2. an excessive load.

o·ver·cloud (-kloud′), *v.t. & v.i.* to darken over with or as if with clouds; cloud up.

o·ver·coat (ō′vēr-kōt), *n.* a coat designed for wear over regular outer clothing, especially one for very cold weather.

o·ver·come (ō-vēr-kum′), *v.t.* -came′, -come′, -com′ing, 1. to gain advantage or victory over in a struggle, contest, etc. 2. to deal effectively with or dispose of (a difficulty, obstacle, etc.); surmount. 3. to affect to an incapacitating extent as with laughter, fear, or fatigue: *v.i.* to gain the victory; win; triumph.

o·ver·do (-dōō′), *v.t.* -did′, -done′, -do′ing, 1. to do to excess. 2. to cook beyond the proper amount of time. 3. to push or use to excess, with consequent ineffectiveness, exhaustion, or other ill effects: *v.i.* 1. to do, push, or use something to excess. 2. to drive oneself too hard.

o·ver·dose (ō′vēr-dōs), *n.* an excessive dose of something: *v.t.* (ō-vēr-dōs′), -dosed′, -dos′ing, to dose to excess.

o·ver·draft (-draft), *n.* 1. an overdrawing from a bank account. 2. the amount overdrawn.

o·ver·draw (ō-vēr-drô′), *v.t.* -drew′, -drawn′, -draw′ing, 1. to exaggerate too much in the description, portrayal, or other presentation of. 2. to draw upon (a bank account) beyond the amount on deposit. 3. to draw too far, as a bow.

o·ver·dress (-dres'), *v.t.* & *v.i.* to dress to excess; especially, to dress up too much for a given occasion.

o·ver·due (-dōō', -dū'), *adj.* 1. past the time for payment, delivery, return, etc. 2. past the scheduled or expected time of arrival, accomplishment, effecting, happening, etc. 3. that should have come about sooner.

o·ver·es·ti·mate (-es'ti-māt), *v.t.* -mat·ed, -mat·ing, to set too high an estimate on or for: *n.* (-mit), an estimate that is too high.

o·ver·flight (-flīt), *n.* the flight of an aircraft over a specified area or a foreign territory, as in reconnaissance.

o·ver·flow (o-vēr-flō'), *v.t.* 1. to flow or spread over, across, or into. 2. to flow over the brim or edge of. 3. to make overflow by filling beyond capacity: *v.i.* 1. to flow or spread over, across, or into something. 2. to be so full as to flow over. 3. to be superabundant: *n.* (ō'vēr-flō), 1. an overflowing. 2. that which overflows. 3. an outlet or container for overflowing liquid.

o·ver·grow (-grō'), *v.t.* -grew', -grown', -grow'-ing, 1. to spread over and cover with vegetation or other growth. 2. to grow too big for: *v.i.* to grow too big.

o·ver·grown (-grōn'), *adj.* 1. covered over with growth, as of vegetation. 2. grown to excess, beyond the usual, or to such an extent as to be awkward or disproportionate.

o·ver·growth (ō'vēr-grōth), *n.* a covering growth, as of vegetation.

o·ver·hand (-hand), *adj.* 1. with the hand over the thing grasped by it. 2. done with the hand raised above the elbow or the arm above the shoulder: *adv.* in an overhand manner: *n.* in *Sports*, an overhand stroke.

o·ver·hang (ō-vēr-hang'), *v.t.* & *v.i.* -hung', -hang'ing, 1. to hang over or stick out beyond (something). 2. to threaten or impend: *n.* (ō'vēr-hang), 1. an overhanging projection. 2. the degree of this.

o·ver·haul (-hôl'), *v.t.* 1. to inspect so as to note repairs or adjustments to be made. 2. to make such repairs or adjustments in. 3. to catch up with: *n.* (ō'vēr-hôl), an overhauling.

o·ver·head (ō'vēr-hed), *adj.* 1. above the level of the head. 2. above and connected to related parts. 3. in the sky. 4. relating to the overhead of a business: *n.* the overall, continuing costs of a business, including rent, utilities, taxes, etc.: *adv.* (ō-vēr-hed'), in an overhead position; above.

o·ver·hear (ō-vēr-hir'), *v.t.* -heard', -hear'ing, to hear without being addressed and by or as if by chance, as from an adjoining room; hear accidentally or seemingly so.

o·ver·in·dul·gence (-in-dul'jēns), *n.* excessive indulgence. —o·ver·in·dul'gent, *adj.*

o·ver·joy (-joi'), *v.t.* to make extremely glad; fill with extraordinary joy.

o·ver·kill (ō'vēr-kil), *n.* the capacity of a nuclear weapon stockpile to kill many times the total of an enemy population.

o·ver·land (-land, -länd), *adv.* & *adj.* by, on, or across land.

o·ver·lap (ō-vēr-lap'), *v.t.* & *v.i.* -lapped', -lap'-ping, 1. to extend over and beyond. 2. to coincide in part (with): *n.* (ō'vēr-lap), 1. an overlapping. 2. something overlapping.

o·ver·lay (-lā'), *v.t.* -laid', -lay'ing, to lay or spread over; superimpose: *n.* (ō'vēr-lā), something superimposed.

o·ver·leaf (ō'vēr-lēf), *adj.* & *adv.* on the other side of the page or leaf.

o·ver·lie (ō-vēr-lī'), *v.t.* -lay', -lain', -ly'ing, to lie on or over.

o·ver·load (ō-vēr-lōd'), *v.t.* to load too heavily: *n.* (ō'vēr-lōd), too heavy a load.

o·ver·look (-look'), *v.t.* 1. to look at from above; view from a position higher up. 2. to fail to notice; miss seeing. 3. to choose not to notice or take account of; deliberately pass over. 4. to oversee.

o·ver·lord (ō'vēr-lôrd), *n.* a lord superior to another or others.

o·ver·ly (ō'vēr-li), *adv.* too or too much.

o·ver·mas·ter (ō-vēr-mas'tēr), *v.t.* to get the better of or force into subjection; overcome; overpower; subdue.

o·ver·much (-much'), *adj.* & *adv.* too much.

o·ver·night (-nīt'), *adv.* 1. for, during, or throughout the night. 2. in or as if in a single night: *adj.* (ō'vēr-nīt), 1. of, for, during, or throughout the night. 2. in or as if in a single night.

o·ver·pass (ō'vēr-pas), *n.* an elevated structure, as such a section of a highway or railroad, that bridges a lower-level road, footpath, river, etc.

o·ver·plus (ō'vēr-plus), *n.* an excess.

o·ver·pow·er (ō-vēr-pou'ēr), *v.t.* to bear down or crush by superior force; vanquish.

o·ver·pro·duc·tion (-prō-duk'shŭn), *n.* supply in excess of the demand.

o·ver·qual·i·fied (ō-vēr-kwäl'i-fīd), *adj.* having more knowledge, education, etc. than needed to qualify.

o·ver·rate (-rāt'), *v.t.* -rat'ed, -rat'ing, to attach too high a value to.

o·ver·reach (-rēch'), *v.t.* to reach beyond or above.

o·ver·re·act (-ri-akt'), *v.i.* to react too passionately.

o·ver·ride (-rīd'), *v.t.* -rode', -rid'den, -rid'ing, 1. to ride over. 2. to subdue. 3. to pay no attention to.

o·ver·rule (-rōōl'), *v.t.* -ruled', -rul'ing, 1. to annul. 2. to subdue.

o·ver·run (-run'), *v.t.* -ran', -run', -run'ning, 1. to cover. 2. to infest. 3. to go past.

o·ver·seas (ō'vēr-sēz'), *adv.* abroad: *adj.* 1. of or pertaining to foreign nations. 2. over the sea. Also *o'ver·sea'.*

o·ver·see (ō-vēr-sē'), *v.t.* -saw', -seen', -see'ing, to superintend. —o'ver·se·er, *n.*

o·ver·sexed (ō-vēr-sekst'), *adj.* having exceptional sexual drive or interest.

o·ver·shad·ow (-shad'o), *v.t.* 1. to throw a shadow upon. 2. to hide. 3. to make seem less significant.

o·ver·shoe (ō'vēr-shōō), *n.* a protective boot worn over the shoe.

o·ver·shoot (ō-vēr-shōōt'), *v.t.* -shot', -shoot'ing, to go beyond (an end, limit, etc.).

o·ver·shot wheel (ō'vēr-shot), a water wheel

which is driven by water flowing over its top into buckets in the rim.

o·ver·sight (ō'vẽr·sīt), *n.* a neglectful error.

o·ver·sim·pli·fy (ō·vẽr·sim'pli·fī), *v.t. & v.i.* **-fied, -fy·ing,** to simplify too much and thus bring into misrepresentation. **—o·ver·sim·pli·fi·ca·tion,** *n.*

o·ver·size (ō'vẽr·sīz), *adj.* of a size greater than normal or larger than necessary: also **o'ver·sized.**

o·ver·sleep (ō·vẽr·slēp'), *v.i.* **-slept', -sleep'ing,** to sleep on past the usual waking time.

o·ver·spread (-spred'), *v.t.* **-spread', spread'ing,** to extend all over.

o·ver·state (-stāt'), *v.t.* **-stat'ed, -stat'ing,** to describe in an excessive way. **—o'ver·state'·ment,** *n.*

o·ver·stay (-stā'), *v.t.* to stay beyond.

o·ver·step (-step'), *v.t.* **-stepped', -step'ping,** to go too far or to go beyond.

o·ver·stuff (-stuf'), *v.t.* 1. to stuff too much. 2. to put heavy stuffing in (furniture).

o·vert (ō·vũrt'), *adj.* 1. open. 2. in *Law,* public. **—o·vert'ly,** *adv.*

o·ver·take (ō·vẽr·tāk'), *v.t.* **-took', -tak'en, -tak'ing,** 1. to catch up with by pursuit. 2. to take by surprise.

o·ver·tax (-taks'), *v.t.* 1. to put too great a tax on. 2. to ask too much of.

o·ver-the-count·er (ō'vẽr-thẽ-kount'ẽr), *adj.* 1. designating or of securities sold directly to buyers. 2. sold legally without prescription, as some drugs.

o·ver·throw (-thrō'), *v.t.* **-threw', -thrown', -throw'ing,** 1. to turn upside down. 2. to demolish; vanquish; destroy. 3. to throw a ball, etc. past: *n.* (ō'vẽr·thrō), 1. the act of overthrowing. 2. ruin; defeat.

o·ver·time (ō'vẽr·tīm), *n.* 1. time past the normal period. 2. the amount paid for work done past normal hours: *adj. & adv.* of, pertaining to, for, or in the course of overtime.

o·ver·tone (-tōn), *n.* 1. an accompanying tone produced over the basic tone by a musical instrument. 2. an accompanying hint or suggestion.

o·ver·ture (ō'vẽr·chẽr), *n.* 1. a preliminary offer or proposal. 2. an opening. 3. a musical introduction before the commencement of an opera, etc.

o·ver·turn (ō·vẽr·tũrn'), *v.t.* 1. to throw over. 2. to vanquish: *v.i.* to upset.

o·ver·ween·ing (-wē'ning), *adj.* 1. conceited. 2. exaggerated.

o·ver·weight (ō·vẽr·wāt'), *adj.* weighing beyond the permitted limit.

o·ver·whelm (-hwelm'), *v.t.* 1. to cover completely. 2. to crush or destroy utterly; overpower. **—o·ver·whelm'ing,** *adj.*

o·ver·work (-wũrk'), *v.t.* to utilize too much: *v.i.* to labor excessively: *n.* (ō'vẽr·wũrk), work that is too difficult or taxing.

o·ver·wrought (-rôt'), *adj.* 1. very upset. 2. too decorated.

ov·i·duct (ō'vi·dukt), *n.* a duct or passage for the eggs from an ovary to the uterus or to the exterior.

o·vip·a·rous (ō·vip'ẽr·ũs), *adj.* denoting reproduction by means of eggs that hatch outside the body.

o·void (ō'void), *adj.* egg-shaped: *n.* an ovoid object or body.

o·vo·lo (ō'vô·lō), *n., pl.* **-li** (-lē), a convex molding.

o·vo·vi·vip·a·rous (ō-vō-vi-vip'ẽr·ũs), *adj.* denoting the production of eggs that are hatched within the body, as is the case with certain reptiles and fishes.

o·vu·late (ō'vyū·lāt), *v.i.* **-lat·ed, -lat·ing,** to produce and release ova from the ovary. **—o·vu·la'tion,** *n.*

o·vule (ō'vũl), *n.* 1. the germ borne by the placenta of a plant, and subsequently developing into a seed. 2. the undeveloped ovum. **—o·vu·lar** (ō'vyū·lẽr), *adj.*

o·vum (ō'vũm), *n., pl.* **o·va** (ō'vä), 1. the germ cell which when impregnated develops into a new individual. 2. in *Architecture,* an egg-shaped ornament.

owe (ō), *v.t.* **owed, ow'ing,** 1. to be indebted or under obligation to. 2. to be obliged to pay. 3. to feel an emotional need to do: *v.i.* to be in debt.

ow·ing (ō'ing), *adj.* 1. that owes. 2. due as a debt. 3. ascribable or imputable (with *to*).

owl (oul), *n.* 1. a raptorial, nocturnal bird characterized by its hoot. 2. a person who keeps late hours.

owl·et (oul'it), *n.* a young or small owl.

own (ōn), *adj.* belonging to; peculiar or proper to: *n.* that which belongs to oneself: *v.t.* 1. to possess or hold by right. 2. to concede or acknowledge: *v.i.* to confess (with *to*). **—own'er,** *n.*

own·er·ship (ō'nẽr·ship), *n.* 1. rightful possession. 2. the state or fact of being an owner.

ox (oks), *n., pl.* **ox'en,** 1. a castrated bull. 2. a cud-chewing quadruped mammal related to cattle.

ox·a·late (ok'sä·lāt), *n.* a salt or ester of oxalic acid.

ox·al·ic acid (ok·sal'ik), a poisonous, crystalline acid found in many plant tissues, used in bleaching, dyeing, printing, etc.

ox·a·lis (ok'sä·lis), *n.* any of a large group of plants with compound leaves and white, pink, red, or yellow flowers.

ox·blood (oks'blud), *n.* a dark-red color.

ox·bow ('bō), *n.* a section of an ox yoke passing around and under the neck, shaped like a U.

ox·eye ('ī), *n.* any of various plants, as the yellow daisy.

ox·ford (oks'fẽrd), *n.* [sometimes O-], 1. a low shoe with laces on the instep: also **oxford shoe.** 2. a woven fabric with a basketlike pattern: also **oxford cloth.**

Ox·ford gray, a very dark gray.

Oxford movement, a reform movement in the Church of England seeking to increase the use of ritual, begun in 1833.

ox·i·dant (ok'si·dänt), *n.* that which causes oxidation.

ox·i·da·tion (ok·si·dā'shũn), *n.* the operation of converting into an oxide.

ox·ide (ok'sīd), *n.* a binary compound of oxygen with some other element or a radical.

ox·i·dize (ok'si·dīz), *v.t.* **-dized, -diz·ing,** to convert into an oxide, as in combustion: *v.i.* to be converted into an oxide. **—ox'i·diz·er,** *n.*

ox·lip (ŏks'lĭp), *n.* a plant related to the primrose, with yellow flowers.

Ox·o·ni·an (ŏk-sō'nĭ-ân), *n.* a student or graduate of Oxford University in England.

ox·y-, a combining form meaning: 1. *indicating the presence of oxygen or its compounds.* 2. *sharp, acid.*

ox·y·a·cet·y·lene (ŏk-sĭ-â-sĕt'l-ēn), *adj.* of or pertaining to the use of a combination of acetylene and oxygen to make a hot flame for welding or cutting metals.

ox·y·gen (ŏk'sĭ-jĕn), *n.* a colorless, odorless, gaseous element which constitutes about 1/5 of the earth's atmosphere and in combination with hydrogen forms water.

ox·y·gen·ate (ŏk'sĭ-jĕ-nāt), *v.t.* **-at·ed, -at·ing,** to combine with oxygen: also **ox'y·gen·ize** (-nīz), **-ized, -iz·ing. —ox·y·gen·a'tion,** *n.*

oxygen tent, a device consisting of a transparent curtain with oxygen pumped in, surrounding a patient to help his breathing.

ox·y·hy·dro·gen (ŏk-sĭ-hī'drŏ-jĕn), *adj.* of or consisting of a mixture of oxygen and hydrogen, as for welding.

ox·y·mo·ron (ŏk-sĭ-môr'ŏn), *n., pl.* **-mo'ra** (-môr'â), a figure of speech in which two contradictory words are placed together for effect, as *sad pleasure.*

ox·y·to·cic (ŏk-sĭ-tō'sĭk), *adj.* hastening parturition.

ox·y·tone (ŏk'sĭ-tōn), *adj.* having the last syllable acutely accented: *n.* an oxytone word.

o·yer (ō'yĕr), *n.* a copy of the subject of a suit given to the other party.

o·yez, o·yes (ō'yĕz', ō'yĕs', ō'yā'), *interj.* hear ye!: the cry of an official demanding silence before a public pronouncement.

oys·ter (oi'stĕr), *n.* 1. a marine bivalve mollusk much esteemed as a delicacy. 2. any similar bivalve mollusk. 3. something favorable.

oyster bed, a place where oysters are cultivated.

oyster catcher, a wading bird with thick legs and a strong, wedgelike bill.

oyster plant, same as **salsify.**

o·zo·ke·rite, o·zo·ce·rite (ô-zō'kĕ-rīt), *n.* a waxlike mineral consisting of hydrocarbons, used in making candles.

o·zone (ō'zōn), *n.* 1. an allotropic form of oxygen with a characteristic odor, present in the atmosphere usually after an electrical disturbance. 2. [Slang], clean air.

o·zon·ize (ō'zō-nīz), *v.t.* **-ized, -iz·ing,** to convert into or impregnate with ozone. **—o'zon·iz·er,** *n.*

P

P, p (pē), *n., pl.* **P's, p's,** 1. the sixteenth letter of the English alphabet. 2. the sound of this letter, as in *pace.* 3. a type or impression of *P* or *p.*

P (pē), *adj.* shaped like *P: n.* an object shaped like *P.*

pa (pä), *n.* [Informal], papa; father.

pab·u·lum (pab'yoo-lŭm), *n.* 1. food; nutriment. 2. food for the mind. 3. banalities; oversimplified, superficial thoughts, writings, etc.

pac (pak), *n.* 1. originally, a high moccasin. 2. a high, warm, laced boot.

pa·ca (pä'kä, pak'ä), *n.* a small Central and South American rodent of a dark-brown color spotted with white.

pace (päs), *n.* 1. a step; stride. 2. a manner of walking or running; gait. 3. the length of a stride. 4. the rate of advancement, movement, etc. 5. a horse's gait in which both legs on a side are raised together: *v.t.* **paced, pac'ing,** 1. to measure by steps or paces. 2. to stride or traverse slowly, or back and forth. 3. to regulate or measure the pace of: *v.i.* 1. to take regular steps. 2. to raise both legs on a side: said of a horse.

pace·mak·er (pās'mā-kĕr), *n.* 1. *a)* a runner, horse, motor vehicle, etc. that sets the pace, as in a race; *b)* one who or that which serves as a model for others. Also **pace'set·ter.** 2. an electronic device implanted in the body to regulate the heartbeat. **—pace'mak·ing,** *n.*

pac·er (pā'sĕr), *n.* 1. a horse used for pacing. 2. one who paces. 3. same as **pacemaker** (noun 1).

pa·cha (pä-shä', pä'shä, pash'ä), *n.* variant spelling of **pasha.**

pa·chi·si (pä-chē'zi), *n.* 1. an Indian game for four players in which pieces are moved about on a board. 2. same as **parcheesi.**

pach·y·derm (pak'i-dĕrm), *n.* any of a group of hoofed, thick-skinned animals, including the elephant, rhinoceros, hippopotamus, etc. — **pach·y·der'mal, pach·y·der'mic,** *adj.*

pach·y·der·ma·tous (pak·i-dûr'mä-tŭs), *adj.* 1. thick-skinned, like a pachyderm. 2. insensitive to slights, criticism, etc. Also **pach·y·der'mous. —pach·y·der'ma·tous·ly,** *adv.*

pach·y·san·dra (pak-i-san'drä), *n.* a low-growing evergreen plant often grown as ground cover.

pa·cif·ic (pä-sif'ik), *adj.* 1. conciliatory; making peace. 2. mild; peaceful; not warlike. **—pa·cif'i·cal·ly,** *adv.*

pa·cif·i·cate ('i-kāt), *v.t.* **-cat·ed, -cat·ing,** same as **pacify. —pa·cif'i·ca·tor,** *n.* **—pa·cif'i·ca·to·ry,** *adv.*

pac·i·fi·ca·tion (pas-i-fi-kā'shŭn), *n.* the act of peacemaking; conciliation.

pac·i·fi·er (pas'i-fi-ĕr), *n.* 1. one who pacifies. 2. a teething ring or nipple for a baby to suck or chew on.

pac·i·fism (pas'i-fizm), *n.* opposition to war or any military force. **—pac'i·fist,** *n. & adj.* **—pac·i·fis'tic,** *adj.* **—pac·i·fis'ti·cal·ly,** *adv.*

pac·i·fy (pas'i-fī), *v.t.* **-fied, -fy·ing,** 1. to calm or appease; assuage. 2. to bring to a condition of peacefulness or tranquillity. 3. to subdue. **—pac·i·fi'a·ble,** *adj.*

pack (pak), *n.* 1. a large bundle tied up for carrying; load; burden. 2. a number or quantity. 3. a package of a standard number, as of playing cards. 4. a gang. 5. a group of wild animals that hunt or live together: *v.t.* 1. to bind and press together, as goods for carrying; load. 2. to send (*off*) summarily. 3. to put together. 4. to cram. 5. to fill or press in tightly. 6. to transport as in a pack. 7. [Slang], to carry or wear (a gun, etc.). 8. [Slang], to be able to deliver (a blow) forcefully: *v.i.* 1. to prepare packs. 2. to stow or package clothes or personal effects in luggage for a trip, etc. 3. to become firmly pressed. 4. to crowd together: *adj.* 1. put together in packs. 2. used for carrying loads, as an animal. **—pack·a·bil'i·ty,** *n.* **—pack'a·ble,** *adj.*

pack (pak), *v.t.* to select (a jury, etc.) in such a way as to be sure of the decisions.

pack·age (pak'ij), *n.* 1. a parcel; boxed or wrapped bundle. 2. a combination or group of things put forth as a single unit: *v.t.* **-aged, -ag·ing,** to make into a package. **—pack'ag·er,** *n.*

package store, a store that sells bottles of alcoholic liquor to be consumed off the premises.

pack·er (pak'ĕr), *n.* 1. one who packs. 2. one who packs goods for transportation. 3. a person in charge of a packing house, especially one for meatpacking.

pack·et (pak'it), *n.* 1. a small package or parcel. 2. a boat sailing between two or more ports for the conveyance of passengers, mail, and merchandise at regular intervals: also **packet boat.**

pack·ing (pak'ing), *n.* 1. the operation of packing goods, as for transportation. 2. the packing of foodstuffs on a large scale, especially meatpacking. 3. materials used for packing.

packing house, a large plant where foodstuffs, especially meat, are processed and packaged.

pack rat, a kind of rat found in North America that often carries off small articles to store in its nest.

pack·sad·dle ('sad-l), *n.* a saddle fastened to a pack animal to secure loads.

pact (pakt), *n.* an agreement; compact.

pad (pad), *n.* 1. a cushion. 2. a stuffed seat. 3. a tablet of writing paper. 4. a soft saddle. 5. the thickened skin on the sole of a foot. 6. the footprint of an animal. 7. the leaf of an aquatic plant. 8. the dull sound of a

---

ŏ in drag*o*n, ōō in cr*u*de, oo in w*oo*l, u in c*u*p, ū in c*u*re, ū in t*u*rn, ŭ in foc*u*s, oi in b*o*y, ou in h*ou*se, th in *th*in, th in shea*th*e, g in g*e*t, j in j*o*y, y in y*e*t.

footstep. 9. [Slang], one's living quarters: *v.t.*

pad·ded, pad·ding, 1. to stuff, as a cushion. 2. to put extraneous or unnecessary matter into a composition or writing. 3. to list fraudulent expenses on (an expense account): *v.i.* 1. to travel on foot. 2. to walk with a dull tread.

pad·ding ('ing), *n.* 1. material used for stuffing. 2. inserted matter for filling out a newspaper or magazine article, etc.

pad·dle (pad'l), *v.i.* -dled, -dling, 1. to row slowly. 2. to play in the water: *v.t.* 1. to propel by paddle. 2. to spank: *n.* 1. a short, broad oar. 2. one of the boards on a wheel for propelling a steamship, etc. 3. an oar-shaped instrument for hitting, etc.

pad·dle·fish (-fish), *n., pl.* -fish, -fish-es, a large, scaleless fish of the Mississippi River.

paddle wheel, a wheel with paddles for propelling a steamship.

pad·dock (pad'ŏk), *n.* a small field or enclosure adjacent to a stable, for horses, etc.

pad·dy (pad'i), *n., pl.* -dies, a rice field.

pad·lock (pad'lŏk), *n.* a lock with a link to pass through a staple or eye: *v.t.* to fasten or shut with a padlock.

pa·dre (pä'drā), *n.* 1. father: priestly title in Latin countries. 2. [Slang], a chaplain or priest.

pa·dro·ne (pä-drō'nĭ), *n.* boss; patron.

pae·an (pē'ăn), *n.* a triumphal or joyful song.

pa·gan (pā'găn), *n.* a person who has no religion or one who worships many gods. — **pa'gan·ish,** *adj.* —**pa'gan·ism,** *n.*

page (pāj), *n.* 1. a boy attending on a person of distinction. 2. a bellboy in a hotel. 3. a young attendant on a legislative body. 4. one side of a leaf of a book, etc. 5. a whole leaf. 6. *often pl.* a chronicle: *v.t.* paged, pag'ing, 1. to mark or number in pages. 2. to notify or summon by announcing the name of.

pag·eant (paj'ĕnt), *n.* 1. a theatrical show or outdoor spectacle. 2. anything merely showy.

pag·eant·ry ('ĕn-trĭ), *n., pl.* -ries, 1. pageants collectively. 2. ostentatious display. 3. valueless show.

pag·i·nal (paj'ĭ-nl), *adj.* of or consisting of pages.

pag·i·na·tion (paj-ĭ-nā'shŭn), *n.* the marking, numbering, or making into pages.

pa·go·da (pä-gō'dä), *n.* in India and the Far East, a temple with several stories, in the shape of a pyramid.

paid (pād), past tense and past participle of pay.

pail (pāl), *n.* 1. a vessel in the shape of a cylinder with an open end, furnished with a handle, for carrying water, etc. 2. the quantity that a pail will hold: also **pail'ful** ('fool), *pl.* -fuls.

pain (pān), *n.* 1. physical or mental suffering. 2. *pl.* diligent effort. 3. *pl.* throes of parturition: *v.t.* to cause physical or mental suffering; render uneasy. —**pain'less,** *adj.*

pain·ful (pān'fŭl), *adj.* full of or causing pain. —**pain'ful·ly,** *adv.* —**pain'ful·ness,** *n.*

pains·tak·ing (pānz'tā-king), *adj.* careful; diligent; assiduous. —**pains'tak·ing·ly,** *adv.*

paint (pānt), *v.t.* 1. to construct (a picture, etc.) with colors. 2. to represent by delineation and colors. 3. to depict. 4. to besmear or cover with color: *v.i.* to practice painting: *n.* 1. a coloring substance or pigment. 2. rouge, lipstick, etc. 3. a coat of paint that has dried.

paint·er (pānt'ēr), *n.* 1. one whose occupation is to paint. 2. an artist who is skilled in creating compositions or in depicting subjects in colors. 3. a rope for fastening a boat.

painter's colic, a form of lead poisoning.

paint·ing (pānt'ing), *n.* 1. the act, art, or occupation of laying on colors; representation of objects by delineation and colors. 2. a picture or composition.

pair (per), *n., pl.* pairs, pair, 1. two things of a kind, similar in form, suited to each other, and used together. 2. a whole thing made up of two associated parts. 3. a couple. 4. a married couple: *v.t.* to join in couples: *v.i.* 1. to be joined in couples. 2. to suit or be adapted to each other. 3. in a legislative body, to offset votes.

pais·ley (pās'lĭ), *adj.* [also P-], of or pertaining to a complicated pattern of colorful shapes.

pa·ja·mas (pä-jam'ăz), *n. pl.* 1. in the Orient, loose trousers of silk or cotton. 2. a loose sleeping costume of blouse and trousers.

pal (pal), *n.* [Informal], an intimate friend: *v.i.* **palled, pal'ling,** [Informal], to keep company as pals.

pal·ace (pal'is), *n.* 1. the residence of a sovereign or bishop. 2. a magnificent house or building.

pal·a·din (pal'ä-din), *n.* a knight.

pa·lae·o-, same as **paleo-.**

pa·laes·tra (pä-les'trä), *n., pl.* -trae ('trē), -tras, same as **palestra.**

pal·an·quin, pal·an·keen (pal-ăn-kēn'), *n.* formerly in eastern Asia, a covered conveyance, usually for one passenger, borne on the shoulders of men.

pal·at·a·ble (pal'it-ä-bl), *adj.* agreeable to the taste or intelligence; savory.

pal·a·tal (pal'it-l), *adj.* of, pertaining to, or uttered by means of the palate: *n.* a sound pronounced by means of the palate.

pal·ate (pal'it), *n.* 1. the roof of the mouth. 2. taste. 3. liking.

pa·la·tial (pä-lā'shăl), *adj.* 1. of, pertaining to, or suitable to a palace. 2. magnificent.

pa·lat·i·nate (pä-lat'ĭ-nāt), *n.* the province of a palatine.

pal·a·tine (pal'ä-tīn), *adj.* 1. invested with royal privileges and rights. 2. of or pertaining to a royal palace or its officials. 3. of a count or earl who was sovereign in his own province: *n.* a lord who had sovereign power over a province or territory.

pa·lav·er (pä-lav'ēr), *n.* 1. a conference. 2. superfluous or idle talk; chatter: *v.t.* to deceive by words: *v.i.* 1. to confer. 2. to chatter.

pale (pāl), *adj.* 1. not of a fresh or ruddy complexion; wan. 2. wanting in color; of a faint luster: *n.* 1. a narrow, pointed stake used in

---

a in cap, ā in cane, ä in father, ȧ in abet, e in met, ē in be, ē in baker, ĕ in regent, i in pit, ī in fine, ĭ in manifest, o in hot, ô in horse, ō in bone,

fencing. 2. a limit. 3. a district or territory: *v.i. & v.t.* **paled, pal'ing,** to turn or cause to be pale. —**pale'ly,** *adv.* —**pale'ness,** *n.*

pa·le·eth·nol·o·gy (pā-li-eth-nol'ō-ji), *n.* the science which treats of the earliest races of mankind.

pa·le·o-, a combining form meaning *ancient.*

Pa·le·o·cene (pā'li-ō-sēn), *n.* the first epoch of the Tertiary Period in the Cenozoic Era, characterized by the development of primitive mammals.

pal·i·mo·ny (pal'ĕ-mō-ni), *n.* an allowance or property settlement claimed by or granted to one member of an unmarried couple who separate after having lived together.

pa·le·o·lith (pā'li-ō-lith), *n.* a rude stone object or implement of the early Stone Age.

pa·le·on·tol·o·gy (pā-li-on-tol'ō-ji), *n.* that branch of geology which treats of fossil remains. —**pa·le·on·tol'o·gist,** *n.*

Pa·le·o·zo·ic (pā-li-ō-zō'ik), *n.* the geologic era after the Precambrian and before the Mesozoic, marked by the beginnings of fish, reptiles, land plants, etc.

pa·les·tra (pả-les'trả), *n., pl.* **-trae** ('trē), **-tras,** a place for gymnastic or wrestling exercises in ancient Greece.

pal·ette (pal'it), *n.* a thin board used by artists for mixing and holding colors.

pal·frey (pôl'fri), *n., pl.* **-freys,** [Archaic], a small saddle horse for a lady's use.

pal·imp·sest (pal'imp-sest), *n.* a parchment manuscript, tablet, etc. which, after the writing upon it has been partially erased, is used again, the former writing being more or less discernible.

pal·in·drome (pal'in-drōm), *n.* a word, sentence, etc. which reads the same backward or forward, as "Able was I ere I saw Elba."

pal·ing (pāl'ing), *n.* 1. a fence constructed of pales. 2. materials for a fence of pales.

pal·in·gen·e·sis (pal-in-jen'ĕ-sis), *n.* 1. new birth or regeneration. 2. reproduction of ancestral characteristics.

pal·i·sade (pal-i-sād'), *n.* 1. a fence or fortification formed of stakes driven into the ground and pointed at the top. 2. one of the stakes. 3. *pl.* a line of rocks jutting up in bold relief: *v.t.* **-sad'ed, -sad'ing,** to enclose or fortify with stakes.

pal·ish (pāl'ish), *adj.* somewhat pale.

pall (pôl), *n.* 1. a piece of cardboard covered with cloth for covering the chalice at Mass. 2. something that produces a gloomy effect, as a *pall* of smoke. 3. a coffin covering: *v.i.* **palled, pall'ing,** 1. to become insipid. 2. to have enough of something; become bored.

pal·la·di·um (pả-lā'di-ùm), *n., pl.* **-di·a** (-ả), 1. any safeguard. 2. [P-], the statue of Pallas at Troy, said to have fallen from heaven, on the preservation of which depended the safety of the city. 3. a rare, grayish metallic element.

pall·bear·er (pôl'ber-ēr), *n.* one of the mourners at a funeral who attend or carry the coffin.

pal·let (pal'it), *n.* 1. same as palette. 2. a tool used in smoothing pottery. 3. a tool used for putting letters on book bindings. 4. a

small piece of the mechanism of a watch. 5. a small, rough bed for the floor, as one filled with straw.

pal·li·ate (pal'i-āt), *v.t.* **-at·ed, -at·ing,** 1. to excuse or cover over; extenuate; mitigate. 2. to lessen or abate. —**pal·li·a'tion,** *n.* —**pal'li·a·tive,** *adj. & n.*

pal·lid (pal'id), *adj.* pale; wan.

pal·li·um (pal'i-ùm), *n., pl.* **-li·ums, -li·a** (-ả), 1. a large, loose, rectangular cloak worn by the ancient Romans and Greeks. 2. a white, woolen band with hangings, worn over the shoulders by a pope or archbishop of the Roman Catholic Church.

pall-mall (pel'mel'), *n.* 1. formerly, a game played with a wooden ball which was driven through an iron ring by a mallet. 2. [P- M-], (also pal'mal'), a street in London, celebrated for its clubs.

pal·lor (pal'ēr), *n.* abnormal paleness.

palm (päm), *n.* 1. any of various tropical or subtropical trees or shrubs whose trunks have no branches. 2. a leaf of such a tree carried as a symbol of victory, joy, etc. 3. the inner part of the hand from the wrist to the fingers. 4. a linear measure of from 3 to 4 or 7 to 9 inches: *v.t.* 1. to conceal in the palm of the hand. 2. to impose upon by fraud (with *off*). —**pal·ma·ceous** (pal-mā'-shùs), *adj.*

pal·mar (pal'mēr), *adj.* of or pertaining to the palm of the hand.

pal·mate (pal'māt), *adj.* 1. resembling a hand with fingers outstretched. 2. web-footed.

palm·er (päm'ēr), *n.* a pilgrim.

pal·met·to (pal-met'ō), *n., pl.* **-tos, -toes,** a type of palm tree with the leaves in a fan formation.

palm·is·try (päm'is-tri), *n.* the pretended art of foretelling the future by examination of the lines and marks of a person's hand. —**palm'ist,** *n.*

pal·mi·tin (pal'mi-tin), *n.* a solid, fatty substance found in palm oil and many other fats.

palm oil, a reddish or yellowish fat found in the fruit of several types of palm, used in the manufacture of soap, candles, etc.

Palm Sunday, the Sunday before Easter.

palm·y (päm'i), *adj.* **palm'i·er, palm'i·est,** 1. of or abounding in palms. 2. flourishing; prosperous.

pal·my·ra (pal-mī'rả), *n.* a palm of India and Africa, with fan-shaped leaves and very hard wood.

pal·o·mi·no (pal-ō-mē'nō), *n., pl.* **-nos,** a light-yellow horse whose mane and tail are white.

pal·pa·ble (pal'pả-bl), *adj.* 1. that has physical substance. 2. easily perceived. 3. obvious. —**pal·pa·bil'i·ty,** *n.* —**pal'pa·bly,** *adv.*

pal·pate (pal'pāt), *v.t.* **-pat·ed, -pat·ing,** in *Medicine,* to examine (a body, organ, etc.) by feeling with the fingers.

pal·pe·bral (pal'pĕ-brảl), *adj.* of or relating to the eyelids.

pal·pi·tate (pal'pi-tāt), *v.i.* **-tat·ed, -tat·ing,** 1. to beat, as the heart. 2. to throb; tremble. —**pal'pi·tant** (-tảnt), *adj.* —**pal·pi·ta'tion,** *n.*

---

pal·sy (pôl'zi), *n., pl.* **-sies,** paralysis of voluntary muscles: *v.t.* **-sied, -sy·ing,** to paralyze.

pal·ter (pôl'tĕr), *v.i.* 1. to trifle. 2. to act insecurely.

pal·try (pôl'tri), *adj.* **-tri·er, -tri·est,** nearly worthless; contemptible. **—pal'tri·ness,** *n.*

pa·lu·dal (pā-lōō'dl), *adj.* of or pertaining to marshes; marshy.

pam·pas (pam'pāz), *n.pl.* in South America, vast treeless plains.

pam·per (pam'pĕr), *v.t.* to treat tenderly or with too much leniency.

pam·pe·ro (päm-per'ō), *n., pl.* **-ros,** a strong wind that blows across the pampas of South America from the Andes.

pam·phlet (pam'flit), *n.* a small unbound book, usually on some current topic, of one or more sheets stitched or stapled together.

pam·phlet·eer (pam-flĕ-tir'), *n.* a writer of pamphlets: *v.i.* to write pamphlets.

pan (pan), *n.* 1. a wide, shallow, metallic dish, as for cooking. 2. any similar vessel, as for evaporating salt. 3. a hollow suggesting a pan; natural basin or depression in the land. 4. a hard soil layer. 5. [P-], in *Greek Mythology,* a woodland spirit, god of flocks, and patron of shepherds, represented as a human with the legs, feet, and horns of a goat and playing pipes: *v.t.* & *v.i.* **panned, pan'ning,** 1. [Informal], to give an adverse review (of). 2. to wash (gravel, etc.) in a pan in order to remove gold.

pan-, a combining form meaning: 1. *all.* 2. [P-], *including or joining all.*

pan·a·ce·a (pan-ă-sē'ă), *n.* something claimed as a universal remedy or medicine.

pa·nache (pă-nash'), *n.* 1. a plume of feathers on a helmet. 2. a bold and lively way of behavior.

pa·na·da (pă-nā'dă), *n.* flour boiled in water or milk, used in cooking as a binding agent.

Pan·a·ma hat (pan'ă-mä), a fine, hand-plaited hat made from the thin fibers of a Central and South American palm.

Pan-A·mer·i·can (pan-ă-mer'ĭ-kăn), *adj.* of both the American continents.

Pan-A·mer·i·can·ism (-izm), *n.* advocacy of a political and social alliance of all the Pan-American countries.

pan·a·tel·a, pan·a·tel·la (pan-ă-tel'ă), *n.* a long, slender cigar.

pan·cake (pan'kāk), *n.* a thin cake of batter fried in a pan or on a griddle.

pan·chro·mat·ic (pan-krō-mat'ik), *adj.* responding to light of every color.

pan·cre·as (pan'kri-ăs, pang'kri-), *n.* a large, fleshy gland situated under and behind the stomach, secreting a fluid that assists in the process of digestion. **—pan·cre·at'ic** (-at'ik), *adj.*

pan·cre·a·tin (pan'kri-ă-tin, pang'kri-), *n.* any one of the enzymes secreted by the pancreas.

pan·da (pan'dă), *n.* 1. a large mammal of China with black-and-white coloring and the appearance of a bear. 2. a mammal of the Himalayas with reddish coloring and the appearance of a raccoon.

pan·da·nus (pan-dā'nŭs), *n.* a tree or shrub of southeast Asia with slender leaves and stems supported by roots resembling props.

Pan·de·an (pan-dē'ăn), *adj.* of or pertaining to Pan.

Pandean pipes, a wind instrument consisting of short reeds of varying lengths.

pan·dects (pan'dekts), *n.pl.* 1. any complete code of law. 2. [P-], the digest of the Roman civil law.

pan·dem·ic (pan-dem'ik), *adj.* widely epidemic.

pan·de·mo·ni·um (pan-dĕ-mō'ni-ùm), *n.* 1. the abode of all demons. 2. a place or condition of general disorder.

pan·der (pan'dĕr), *v.i.* to act as an agent for the gratification of the passions, ignoble ambitions, etc.: *n.* 1. a go-between in a sexual intrigue; pimp. 2. one who acts to gratify the passions of others. Also **pan'der·er.**

pan·dow·dy (pan-dou'di), *n., pl.* **-dies,** a dish of baked apples, with only a top crust.

pane (pān), *n.* 1. a square of glass, as in a window. 2. any one of the sides of a gem.

pan·e·gyr·ic (pan-ē-jir'ik), *n.* a speech in praise of a person or event; encomium. **—pan'e·gy·rize** (-ji-rīz), *v.t.* & *v.i.* **-rized, -riz·ing.**

pan·el (pan'l), *n.* 1. a section or division of a wall, ceiling, door, or other surface. 2. a thin board on which a picture is painted. 3. a section of an airplane wing. 4. a board supporting the controls of an electric circuit, etc. 5. a vertical section in a dress. 6. a list containing the names of persons summoned to serve as jurors. 7. the jury. 8. a group chosen for a particular purpose: *v.t.* **-eled** or **-elled, -el·ing** or **-el·ling,** to form or decorate with panels.

pan·el·ing, pan·el·ling (-ing), *n.* 1. a group of panels. 2. thin sections of wood, wallboard, etc. used for panels.

pan·el·ist (-ist), *n.* a person on a panel.

panel truck, a small, covered pickup truck.

pan·e·tel·a, pan·e·tel·la (pan-ē-tel'ă), *n.* same as **panatela.**

pang (pang), *n.* a violent, sudden pain; agony, mental or physical.

pan·go·lin (pang-gō'lin), *n.* the scaly anteater of Asia and Africa.

pan·han·dle (pan'han-dl), *n.* [often P-], a strip of territory resembling the handle of a pan, between two other divisions: *v.t.* & *v.i.* **-dled, -dling,** [Informal], to beg (from) on the public street.

pan·ic (pan'ik), *n.* 1. a sudden fright. 2. a kind of grass, as millet: *adj.* suddenly and violently alarming: *v.t.* **-icked, -ick·ing,** 1. to cause to have panic. 2. [Slang], to cause to shake with laughter, delight etc.: *v.i.* to succumb to panic. **—pan'ick·y,** *adj.*

pan·i·cle (pan'i-kl), *n.* a flower cluster formed by irregular branching.

pan·ic-strick·en (pan'ik-strik-n), *adj.* extremely terrified.

pan·jan·drum (pan-jan'drŭm), *n.* a pompous official.

pan·nier, pan·ier (pan'yĕr), *n.* 1. a basket carries on the back. 2. one of two baskets suspended across the back of a horse, mule, etc. for carrying market produce.

---

a in *cap,* ā in *cane,* ä in *father,* ă in *abet,* e in *met,* ē in *be,* ĕ in *baker,* ĕ in *regent,* i in *pit,* ī in *fine,* ĭ in *manifest,* o in *hot,* ō in *horse,* ō in *bone,*

pan·ni·kin (pan'ĭ-kin), *n.* [Chiefly British], 1. a small saucepan. 2. a metal cup.

pa·no·cha (pä-nō'chä), *n.* 1. a rough Mexican sugar. 2. same as penuche: also **pa·no·che** ('chi).

pan·o·ply (pan'ō-pli), *n., pl.* **-plies**, 1. a complete suit of armor. 2. any magnificent covering or display.

pan·o·ra·ma (pan-ō-ram'ä), *n.* 1. a wide, extended view in every direction; complete outlook on a region. 2. a scene passing continuously before the vision. 3. a picture of objects within a certain area observed from a central point. —**pan·o·ram'ic**, *adj.*

pan·pipe (pan'pīp), *n.* same as Pandean pipes.

pan·soph·ic (pan-sof'ik), *adj.* laying claim to universal knowledge: also **pan·soph'i·cal.**

pan·so·phism (pan'sō-fizm), *n.* a laying claim to universal wisdom or knowledge.

pan·sy (pan'zi), *n., pl.* **-sies**, a garden flower of the violet family with varicolored petals.

pant (pant), *v.i.* 1. to breathe rapidly. 2. to desire ardently (with *for* or *after*): *v.t.* to say with rapid breathing: *n.* rapid breathing.

pan·ta·lets, pan·ta·lettes (pan-tl-ets'), *n.pl.* loose drawers formerly worn by women.

pan·ta·loon (pan-tl-ōōn'), *n.* 1. [P-], a buffoon in a pantomime. 2. *pl.* formerly, a pair of tight trousers.

pan·tech·ni·con (pan-tek'ni-kon), *n.* [British], a furniture van.

pan·the·ism (pan'thi-izm), *n.* the doctrine that the universe in its totality is God. —**pan'the·ist**, *n.* —**pan·the·is'tic**, *adj.*

pan·the·on (pan'thi-on), *n.* 1. a temple dedicated to all the gods. 2. [P-], a particular temple in ancient Rome, now a church. 3. [often P-], a monument memorializing the famous dead of a country.

pan·ther (pan'thēr), *n., pl.* **-thers, -ther**, 1. a black leopard. 2. a jaguar or cougar.

pant·ies (pan'tiz), *n.pl.* short underpants for women or children: also **pant'ie, pant'y.**

pan·tile (pan'tīl), *n.* a curved tile for roofing.

pan·to·graph (pan'tō-graf), *n.* an instrument for copying drawings, designs, etc. on the same, an enlarged, or a reduced scale.

pan·to·mime (pan'tō-mīm), *n.* 1. a drama presented by gesture without speech. 2. gesture without speech. 3. in England, a Christmastime theatrical entertainment: *v.t.* & *v.i.* **-mimed, -mim·ing**, to show or act in pantomime. —**pan·to·mim'ic** (-mim'ik), *adj.* —**pan'to·mim·ist**, *n.*

pan·try (pan'tri), *n., pl.* **-tries**, a closet or small room for storing provisions.

pants (pants), *n.pl.* 1. trousers. 2. panties or drawers.

pant·suit (pant'sōōt), *n.* a combination of pants and jacket for women: also **pants suit.**

panty hose, a combination of panties and hose for women.

pap (pap), *n.* 1. soft food for infants. 2. pulp, as of fruit. 3. writing, ideas, etc. that have been made insipid by simplifying too much. 4. money or largess through political or official patronage. 5. [Archaic], a nipple or teat.

pa·pa (pä'pä), *n.* father.

pa·pa·cy (pä'pä-si), *n., pl.* **-cies**, 1. the office or authority of the Pope. 2. popes collectively. 3. the time during which a pope is in authority. 4. the Roman Catholic Church government.

pa·pal (pä'pàl), *adj.* of or pertaining to the Pope, the papacy, or the Church of Rome.

pa·paw (pô'pô), *n.* 1. same as papaya. 2. a fruit-bearing tree of the central and southern U.S. 3. the oblong, yellow fruit of this tree.

pa·pa·ya (pä-pä'yä), *n.* 1. the large, oblong, yellow-orange fruit of a tropical American tree. 2. this tree.

pa·per (pä'pēr), *n.* 1. a thin, flexible substance made of various materials, as linen or wood pulp, used as a wrapping, to write or print on, etc. 2. a piece of paper. 3. a newspaper. 4. an essay or literary contribution. 5. a document. 6. a bank note. 7. a bill of exchange. 8. wallpaper. 9. *pl.* identifying documents: *adj.* 1. of or made of paper. 2. thin: *v.t.* to cover with or wrap in paper. —**pa'per·y**, *adj.*

pa·per·back (-bak), *n.* a book with a paper cover.

pa·per·boy (-boi), *n.* a male newspaper deliverer or seller.

paper clip, a pliant fastener, as of metal, for attaching sheets of paper together.

pa·per·hang·er (-hang-ēr), *n.* 1. one who is employed to apply wallpaper to walls. 2. [Slang], a forger.

paper mulberry, an Asiatic tree having red fruits used for ornament.

paper nautilus, a mollusk with eight arms, the female of which lives in a thin spiral shell.

pa·per·weight (-wāt), *n.* something small and heavy for holding down loose papers.

paper work, the written work that goes along with some undertaking.

pape·te·rie (pap'ē-tri), *n.* a case containing stationery.

pa·pier-mâ·ché (pä'pēr-mä-shā'), *n.* paper pulp mixed with size, glue, etc. and molded into various shapes for ornament and use.

pa·pil·la (pä-pil'ä), *n., pl.* **-lae** ('ē), a small nipplelike projection, as any one of the minute elevations on the tongue. —**pap·il·lar·y** (pap'ĭ-ler-i), *adj.*

pa·poose (pa-pōōs'), *n.* a young child of North American Indian parents.

pap·pus (pap'ùs), *n., pl.* **pap'pi** ('ī), the feathery substance on the seed of certain plants; the calyx of a composite flower.

pap·py (pap'i), *adj.* **-pi·er, -pi·est**, resembling pap.

pa·pri·ka (pa-prē'kä), *n.* the dried fruit of a pepper plant, prepared as a powder for use as a condiment.

Pap test, a medical examination to determine the presence of cancer in the uterus.

pap·ule (pap'ūl), *n.* a pimple; small elevation of the skin.

pa·py·rus (pä-pī'rùs), *n., pl.* **-ri** ('rī), **-rus·es**, 1. a type of reed found in Egypt, used by the ancients to make paper. 2. this paper. 3. a manuscript on papyrus.

par (pär), *n.* 1. a state of equality: usually in the phrase **on a par** (with). 2. a normal state, level, etc. 3. the set rate of exchange for money in foreign currencies. 4. the nominal value of a stock, etc. 5. in *Golf,* the number of strokes set as requiring a certain level of skill: *adj.* 1. of or at par. 2. normal.

par·a-, a prefix meaning *beyond, beside, diverging.*

par·a·ble (per'ȧ-bl), *n.* an allegorical method of conveying instruction by means of a fable or short fictitious narrative.

pa·rab·o·la (pȧ-rab'ō-lȧ), *n.* one of the conic sections formed by the intersection of the cone by a plane parallel to one of its sides. **—par·a·bol·ic** (per·ȧ-bol'ik), *adj.*

par·a·chute (per'ȧ-shōōt), *n.* an apparatus consisting of a large cloth, umbrella-shaped when open, for descending from an airplane: *v.t. & v.i.* **-chut·ed, -chut·ing,** to drop by parachute. **—par·a·chut·ist,** *n.*

par·a·clete (per'ȧ-klēt), *n.* 1. one who acts on behalf of another. 2. [P-], the Holy Ghost.

pa·rade (pȧ-rād'), *n.* 1. ostentatious display; show. 2. a military display. 3. a place of assembly for exercising troops. 4. a march or procession: *v.t.* **-rad·ed, -rad·ing,** 1. to marshal in military order. 2. to make a display of. 3. to march through: *v.i.* 1. to walk about ostentatiously; show off. 2. to march in a procession.

par·a·digm (per'ȧ-dim, -dīm), *n.* 1. an example or model. 2. in *Grammar,* an example of the inflections of a word.

par·a·dise (per'ȧ-dīs), *n.* 1. [P-], the garden of Eden. 2. same as heaven. 3. any place of great happiness.

par·a·dox (per'ȧ-doks), *n.* 1. something apparently absurd or incredible that may be true in fact. 2. a statement that is false because it goes against itself in fact. **—par·a·dox'i·cal,** *adj.* **—par·a·dox'i·cal·ly,** *adv.*

par·af·fin (per'ȧ-fin), *n.* a white crystalline substance of a waxy consistency, usually obtained from petroleum and used in making candles, sealing preserving jars, etc.: also **par'af·fine** (-fin, -fēn).

par·a·go·ge (per'ȧ-gō-ji), *n.* the addition of a letter or syllable to the end of a word.

par·a·gon (per'ȧ-gon), *n.* something of extraordinary excellence; model or pattern of perfection.

par·a·graph (per'ȧ-graf), *n.* 1. a small subdivision of a written piece, often indented on a new line. 2. a mark showing the beginning of a new paragraph (¶). 3. a short item in a newspaper, magazine, etc.: *v.t.* to organize in paragraphs. **—par'a·graph·er, par'a·graph·ist,** *n* **—par·a·graph'ic,** *adj.*

par·a·keet (per'ȧ-kēt), *n.* a small, thin parrot with a long narrow tail.

par·a·le·gal (par·ȧ-lē'gȧl), *adj.* designating or of persons trained to aid lawyers but not licensed to practice law: *n.* a person doing paralegal work.

par·a·leip·sis (per·ȧ-līp'sis), *n.* a pretended suppression of what one wishes to emphasize, as "I will not call attention to his trickery and deception"; feigned omission.

Par·a·li·pom·e·non (per·ȧ-li·pom'ē·non), *n.* Chronicles in the Douay Bible.

par·al·lax (per'ȧ-laks), *n.* 1. the apparent angular shifting of an object caused by change in the position of the observer. 2. the difference in the apparent position of a heavenly body and its true place.

par·al·lel (per'ȧ-lel), *adj.* 1. extended in the same direction and equidistant at all points. 2. having the same direction or tendency; corresponding: *n.* 1. a line equidistant at all points from another line. 2. a correspondent resemblance or likeness. 3. a person or thing corresponding to another. 4. an imaginary line running parallel to the equator, delineating a degree of latitude: *v.t.* **-leled** or **-lelled, -lel·ing** or **-lel·ling,** 1. to place parallel. 2. to run parallel to. 3. to correspond to; equal. 4. to examine for similarities. **—par'al·lel·ism** (-izm), *n.*

par·al·lel·e·pi·ped (per·ȧ-lel-ē-pī'pid), *n.* a solid figure bounded by six parallelograms: also **par·al·lel·e·pip'e·don** (-pip'ē-don).

par·al·lel·o·gram (per·ȧ-lel'ō-gram), *n.* a plane four-sided figure whose opposite sides are parallel and equal.

pa·ral·o·gism (pa·ral'ō-jizm), *n.* in *Logic,* a fallacy of reasoning.

pa·ral·y·sis (pa·ral'i-sis), *n., pl.* **-ses** (-sēz), 1. loss of the power of sensation or motion in one or more parts of the body. 2. a state of being unable to act.

par·a·lyt·ic (per·ȧ-lit'ik), *adj.* of, pertaining to, affected by, or inclined to paralysis: *n.* one who is affected with paralysis.

par·a·lyze (per'ȧ-līz), *v.t.* **-lyzed, -lyz·ing,** 1. to affect with paralysis. 2. to make unable to act.

par·a·me·ci·um (par·ȧ-mē'sē-ŭm), *n., pl.* **-ci·a** (-sē-ȧ), an elongated protozoan that moves by means of cilia.

par·a·med·ic (par·ȧ-med'ik), *n.* a person doing paramedical work.

par·a·med·i·cal (-med'i-kȧl), *adj.* of auxiliary medical personnel, as midwives, medics, nurses' aides, laboratory technicians, etc.

pa·ram·e·ter (pȧ-ram'ē-tēr), *n.* a constant that varies with the functions of its application.

par·a·mil·i·tar·y (per·ȧ-mil'i-ter-i), *adj.* of or pertaining to an unofficial military group, often operating in secret.

par·a·mor·phism (par·ȧ-môr'fizm), *n.* the change of one mineral type to another having the same chemical composition but a different molecular structure.

par·a·mount (per'ȧ-mount), *adj.* superior to all others; eminent or chief.

par·a·mour (per'ȧ-moor), *n.* an illicit lover.

par·a·noi·a (per·ȧ-noi'ȧ), *n.* a mental disorder characterized by delusions, usually of persecution.

par·a·noid (per'ȧ-noid), *n.* one who has paranoia: *adj.* of, pertaining to, or affected with paranoia. Also **par·a·noi'ac** (-noi'ak).

par·a·pet (per'ȧ-pit, -pet), *n.* 1. a low wall or railing. 2. a rampart to protect troops from the fire of an enemy.

par·a·pher·na·li·a (par·ȧ-fēr-nāl'yȧ), *n.pl.* 1. equipment; trappings. 2. personal property. 3. in *Law,* formerly, the property of a wife which she possesses over and above her dowry.

par·a·phrase (per'ȧ-frāz), *n.* a stating of the meaning of something in different words: *v.t. & v.i.* **-phrased, -phras·ing,** to state in a

---

ă in c*a*p, ā in c*a*ne, ä in f*a*ther, ȧ in *a*bet, e in m*e*t, ē in b*e,* ê in b*a*ker, ê in r*e*gent, i in p*i*t, ī in f*i*ne, ï in man*i*fest, o in h*o*t, ô in h*o*rse, ō in b*o*ne,

paraphrase. —**par·a·phras'tic** (-fras'tik), *adj.* —**par·a·phras'ti·cal·ly,** *adv.*

par·a·ple·gi·a (per-å-plē'ji-å), *n.* paralysis of the lower half of the body on both sides. —**par·a·pleg'ic** (-plē'jik), *adj. & n.*

par·a·site (per'å-sīt), *n.* 1. one, as in ancient Greece, who frequented the table of a rich man and gained his favor by flattery. 2. one who lives at the expense of others. 3. in *Biology,* an animal or plant nourished by another to which it attaches itself. —**par·a·sit'ic** (-sit'ik), *adj.* —**par·a·sit'i·cal·ly,** *adv.*

par·a·sit·ism (per'å-sīt-izm), *n.* the state or behavior of a parasite.

par·a·sol (per'å-sôl), *n.* a lady's sunshade in the form of an umbrella.

par·a·tax·is (per-å-tak'sis), *n.* a loose arrangement of clauses, etc. leaving out connectives.

par·a·thi·on (par-å-thī'on), *n.* a very poisonous liquid insecticide.

par·a·thy·roid (-thī'roid), *adj.* of or pertaining to the area or glands near the thyroid gland: *n.* one of the glands near the thyroid gland.

par·a·troops (per'å-trōōps), *n.pl.* troops that use parachutes to get into a battle area.

par·a·ty·phoid (per-å-tī'foid), *n.* a disease resembling typhoid fever, but less severe.

par·a·vane (per'å-vān), *n.* an apparatus with projecting fins, used for clearing mines, etc. from the course of vessels.

par·boil (pär'boil), *v.t.* to boil partially.

par·buck·le (pär'buk-l), *n.* a rope formed into a double sling for hoisting casks, logs, etc.: *v.t.* to hoist by means of a parbuckle.

Par·cae (pär'si), *n.pl.* in *Roman Mythology,* the three Fates, Clotho, Lachesis, and Atropos, who controlled the destiny of every mortal.

par·cel (pär'sl), *n.* 1. a small bundle or package. 2. a small part (of land): *v.t.* -celed or -celled, -cel·ing or -cel·ling, to divide into parts and allot (with *out*).

par·cel·ing, par·cel·ling (pär'sl-ing), *n.* long, narrow strips of tarred canvas put around ropes to prevent friction.

parcel post, a government mailing system for bulky parcels in which the postal charge is regulated according to distance as well as weight.

par·ce·nar·y (pär'sē-ner-i), *n.* same as **coparcenary.** —**par'ce·ner** (-nēr), *n.*

parch (pärch), *v.t.* 1. to scorch; burn slightly. 2. to cause great thirst in: *v.i.* to dry to excess.

Par·chee·si (pär-chē'zi), *n.* a game in which players move pieces around a board on the throw of dice: a trademark.

parch·ment (pärch'mĕnt), *n.* 1. the skin of a sheep, goat, etc. dressed and prepared for writing upon. 2. paper made to look like parchment. 3. a document on parchment.

par·don (pär'dn), *v.t.* 1. to forgive. 2. to absolve. 3. to remit (a penalty, etc.): *n.* 1. forgiveness. 2. absolution. 3. official remission of a penalty. —**par'don·a·ble,** *adj.* —**par'don·er,** *n.*

pare (per), *v.t.* pared, par'ing, 1. to cut away little by little. 2. to reduce or diminish (often with *down*).

par·e·gor·ic (per-ē-gôr'ik), *n.* a camphorated tincture of opium, used to assuage diarrhea.

pa·rei·ra (på-rer'å), *n.* the root of a South American plant, formerly used in medicine as a diuretic: also **pareira bra·va** (brä'vå).

pa·ren·chy·ma (på-reng'ki-må), *n.* 1. the soft cellular tissue or pith of plants. 2. the soft tissue of the organs of the body. —**pa·ren'chy·mal, par·en·chym·a·tous** (per-eng-kim'å-tŭs), *adj.*

par·ent (per'ĕnt), *n.* 1. a father or mother. 2. origin. 3. any living thing in respect to its offspring. —**pa·ren·tal** (på-ren'tl), *adj.* —**pa·ren'tal·ly,** *adv.* —**par'ent·hood,** *n.*

par·ent·age (per'ĕnt-ij), *n.* extraction; birth.

pa·ren·the·sis (på-ren'thē-sis), *n., pl.* -ses (-sēz), 1. an explanatory word or clause inserted in a sentence which is grammatically complete without it. 2. the marks, ( ), used to indicate such a word or clause.

par·en·thet·i·cal (per-ĕn-thet'i-kl), *adj.* 1. expressed in a parenthesis. 2. using parentheses. Also **par·en·thet'ic.** —**par·en·thet'i·cal·ly,** *adv.*

pa·re·sis (på-rē'sis), *n., pl.* -ses ('sēz), 1. partial paralysis. 2. swelling of the brain resulting from syphilis of the central nervous system. —**pa·ret'ic** (-ret'ik), *adj. & n.*

par·es·the·si·a (per-is-the'zhå), *n.* an abnormal sensation of the skin, as tingling, prickling, burning, etc.

par·fait (pär-fā'), *n.* 1. a frozen dessert of cream, eggs, etc. served in a tall, slender glass. 2. a dessert of ice cream and fruit, syrup, etc. served in a similar glass.

par·fleche (pär'flesh), *n.* a raw hide soaked in lye to remove the hair, and dried.

par·get (pär'jit), *v.t.* -get·ed or -get·ted, -get·ing or -get·ting, to cover with plaster ornamentally: *n.* 1. plaster or coating for a wall. 2. decorative plasterwork in raised figures, formerly used on ceilings and interiors. Also, for *n.,* **par'get·ing, par'get·ting.**

par·he·li·on (pär-hē'li-ŏn), *n., pl.* -li·a (-å), a bright light seen near the sun.

par·i-, a combining form meaning *equal.*

pa·ri·ah (på-rī'å), *n.* 1. a person of the lowest caste of India. 2. an outcast.

Par·i·an (per'i-ån), *adj.* 1. of or pertaining to a white marble found on Paros, a Greek island in the Aegean. 2. denoting a white porcelain like this.

pa·ri·e·tal (på-rī'ē-tl), *adj.* 1. of, pertaining to, or forming the walls of a body cavity. 2. denoting either of the two bones between the occipital and frontal bones of the skull.

par·i·mu·tu·el (per-i-mū'choo-wŭl), *n.* a form of wagering on races, in which the winners divide the part of the pool due to them in relation to the size of their bets.

par·ing (per'ing), *n.* 1. the process of cutting away little by little. 2. that which is pared off.

Paris green (per'is), a poisonous, green powder used as an insecticide.

par·ish (per'ish), *n.* 1. an ecclesiastical district under the particular charge of a priest or minister. 2. a civil district in Louisiana. 3. a church congregation.

ŏ in dragon, ōō in crude, oo in wool, u in cup, ū in cure, û in turn, ů in focus, oi in boy, ou in house, th in thin, th in sheathe, g in get, j in joy, y in yet.

pa·rish·ion·er (pá-rish'ĕ-nẽr), *n.* one who belongs to a parish.

par·i·ty (per'ĭ-tĭ), *n., pl.* -ties, 1. equality. 2. likeness. 3. equivalence in value of one country's currency in terms of another's.

park (pärk), *n.* 1. a wooded area surrounding a mansion. 2. an expanse of public land used for recreation: *v.t. & v.i.* 1. to enclose in a park. 2. to place (an automobile, etc.) in a certain place for a time. 3. to move (an automobile, etc.) into such a space.

par·ka (pär'kȧ), *n.* an outer coat with a hood, as that originally worn by Eskimos.

parking meter, a timer apparatus activated by coins, which registers the amount of time a vehicle may stand in a parking space.

Par·kin·son's disease (pär'kin-sŏnz), a degenerative disease of later life, causing rhythmic tremor and muscular rigidity: after J. *Parkinson* (1755-1824), English physician.

Parkinson's Law, a parody of economic laws, such as that work expands to fill the allotted time: stated by C. *Parkinson* (1909-), British economist.

park·way (pärk'wā), *n.* a wide thoroughfare lined with trees, grass, etc.

parl·ance (pär'lȧns), *n.* an idiom.

par·lay (pär'lā, 'lĭ), *n.* a wager consisting of the winnings from a previous wager and that wager: *v.t. & v.i.* (also pär-lā'), to make (such a wager).

par·ley (pär'lĭ), *n., pl.* -leys, a conference, especially with an enemy: *v.i.* to hold a conference, especially with an enemy with a view to making peace.

par·lia·ment (pär'lȧ-mĕnt), *n.* 1. a public or formal conference. 2. [P-], the supreme legislative assembly of Great Britain, consisting of the House of Lords and the House of Commons. 3. [P-], a legislative assembly in some other countries.

par·lia·men·tar·i·an (pär-lȧ-men-ter'ĭ-ȧn), *n.* one who is versed in parliamentary law and usages.

par·lia·men·ta·ry (pär-lȧ-men'tēr-ĭ), *adj.* of, pertaining to, enacted by, or in accordance with the usages of a parliament.

par·lor (pär'lẽr), *n.* 1. a drawing room. 2. a kind of business establishment with particular accommodations for patrons. Also, British spelling, **parlour.**

parlor car, same as chair car.

par·lous (pär'lŭs), *adj.* [Chiefly Archaic], 1. risky; dangerous. 2. dangerously clever; keen; shrewd.

Par·me·san cheese (pär'mĕ-zän), a hard, dry skim-milk cheese originally from Italy.

Par·nas·si·an (pär-nas'ĭ-ȧn), *adj.* 1. of or pertaining to Mount Parnassus in Greece, the fabled abode of the Muses. 2. of or pertaining to poetry.

pa·ro·chi·al (pá-rō'ki-ȧl), *adj.* 1. of or pertaining to a parish. 2. narrow; limited; confined.

parochial school, a school under jurisdiction of a church or religious body.

par·o·dist (per'ŏ-dist), *n.* one who writes parodies.

par·o·dy (-dĭ), *n., pl.* -dies, a burlesque imitation of a serious poem, piece of music, etc.: *v.t.* -died, -dy·ing, to convert into a parody.

pa·role (pá-rōl'), *n.* 1. a word of honor, especially one given by a prisoner of war that in return for conditional freedom he will not attempt to fight, escape, etc. 2. the granting of freedom to a prisoner on condition of proper behavior for a period of time: *v.t.* -roled', -rol'ing, to set at liberty on parole.

par·o·nym (per'ŏ-nim), *n.* a paronymous word.

pa·ron·y·mous (pá-ron'ŏ-mŭs), *adj.* of the same derivation, but different in spelling and meaning.

pa·rot·id (pá-rot'id), *adj.* situated near the ear: *n.* a salivary gland situated a little below the ear and in front.

par·ox·ysm (per'ŏk-sizm), *n.* 1. a sudden spasm or fit of acute pain, etc. 2. a sudden action or convulsion, as of sneezing. **—par·ox·ys·mal** (per-ŏk-siz'ml), *adj.*

par·quet (pär-kā'), *n.* 1. a flooring of parquetry. 2. the main floor of a theater between the orchestra rail and parquet circle.

parquet circle, the section of a theater underneath the balcony and behind the parquet on the main floor.

par·quet·ry (pär'kĕ-trĭ), *n.* a mosaic woodwork for floors.

par·ra·keet (per'ȧ-kēt), *n.* same as **parakeet.**

par·ri·cide (per'ȧ-sīd), *n.* 1. the act of murdering a father or mother or other near relative. 2. the murderer of a father, mother, etc.

par·rot (per'ŏt), *n.* 1. a tropical bird with a hooked bill and brilliant plumage: some parrots can imitate the human voice. 2. a person who imitates the sayings of others without comprehension: *v.t.* to imitate without comprehension.

parrot fish, a brilliantly colored fish of the tropical seas.

par·ry (per'ĭ), *v.t. & v.i.* -ried, -ry·ing, to ward off or turn aside (a blow, question, etc.): *n., pl.* -ries, a parrying.

parse (pärs), *v.t. & v.i.* parsed, pars'ing, 1. to resolve (a sentence) by grammatical analysis into its component parts, indicating the form and relationship of each part. 2. to indicate the form, part of speech, and function of (a word) in a sentence.

par·sec (pär'sek), *n.* a unit of measure of astronomical distance, equal to well over 19 trillion miles.

Par·see, Par·si (pär'sē), *n.* a member of a Zoroastrian religious group in India, descended from Persian refugees.

par·si·mo·ny (pär'si-mō-ni), *n.* extreme frugality; closeness, stinginess, or miserliness. **—par·si·mo·ni·ous,** *adj.*

pars·ley (pärs'lĭ), *n.* a cultivated plant with aromatic leaves used in garnishing or flavoring soups, stews, etc.

pars·nip (pär'snip), *n.* 1. a biennial plant related to parsley and having a long, white, edible root. 2. the root.

par·son (pär'sn), *n.* a clergyman, specifically the incumbent of a parish.

par·son·age (-ij), *n.* a parson's dwelling.

part (pärt), *n.* 1. something less than the whole; often, any one of several equal

---

pieces, portions, shares, quantities, etc. 2. a particular piece or portion contributing to a whole. 3. a section or organ as of the body. 4. a constituent or ingredient. 5. something detached, cut off, etc. from the whole or main section. 6. a separate division. 7. a character or role as in a play. 8. in a music composition for two or more performers, the portion written for a specified performer or instrument; also, any one of the performers or instruments. 9. a particular side or party as in a transaction or dispute. 10. involvement, interest, or concern. 11. a particular region or area. 12. *usually pl.* a district or section of a country. 13. a dividing line made by combining the hair in different directions. 14. *usually pl.* talent; ability: *v.t.* 1. to divide or separate into two or more pieces, portions, or sections. 2. to break up or put apart. 3. to make a part (sense 13) in: *v.i.* 1. to become parted. 2. to leave each other; separate. 3. to leave another or others and go elsewhere; depart (with *from*): *adj.* of, pertaining to, or involving only a part; partial: *adv.* to some extent or degree; not wholly or entirely.

par·take (pär-tāk′), *v.i.* -took′, -tak′en, -tak′ing, 1. to participate. 2. to eat or drink something, especially with others. 3. to show an admixture or trace (*of* something specified). —**par·tak′er**, *n.*

par·terre (pär-ter′), *n.* 1. an ornamental arrangement of flower beds. 2. same as **parquet circle**.

par·the·no·gen·e·sis (pär-thē-nō-jen′ė-sis), *n.* reproduction by development of an unfertilized ovum, seed, or spore.

Par·the·non (pär′thė-non), *n.* the ancient Doric temple of Athena on the Acropolis.

par·tial (pär′shûl), *adj.* 1. inclined to favor one side, party, etc.; biased. 2. especially fond of something specified: with *to.* 3. of, being, or involving only a part; not complete or entire.

par·ti·al·i·ty (pär-shi·al′i-ti), *n.* 1. favoritism; bias. 2. special fondness, as for a food.

par·tial·ly (pär′shûl-i), *adv.* to some extent or degree; not fully or wholly.

par·tic·i·pant (pär-tis′i-pânt), *adj.* participating: *n.* one that participates.

par·tic·i·pate (pär-tis′i-pāt), *v.i.* -pat·ed, -pat·ing, to take part or share with others in something planned or going on, as a discussion. —**par·tic·i·pa′tion**, *n.*

par·tic·i·pa·tor (-pat-ẽr), *n.* one that participates; participant. —**par·tic′i·pa·to·ry** (-pá-tôr-i), *adj.*

par·ti·cip·i·al (pär-ti-sip′i-âl), *adj.* of, formed from, or used as a participle.

par·ti·ci·ple (pär′ti-sip-l), *n.* a verbal form combining the characteristics and functions of a verb and an adjective.

par·ti·cle (pär′ti-kl), *n.* 1. a very tiny piece; bit. 2. a usually uninflected part of speech, such as *of,* used to show syntactical relationships.

par·ti·col·ored (pär′ti-kul-ẽrd), *adj.* 1. varied in coloration. 2. variegated.

par·tic·u·lar (pẽr-tik′yû-lẽr), *adj.* 1. distinct from others; individual. 2. specific; certain; special. 3. detailed. 4. highly selective; fas-

tidious: *n.* 1. a specific instance, example, etc. 2. a detail.

par·tic·u·lar·i·ty (pẽr-tik-yû-ler′l-ti), *n., pl.* -ties, 1. the quality, condition, or fact of being particular. 2. a detail, attribute, etc.

par·tic·u·lar·ize (-tik′yû-lá-rīz), *v.t. & v.i.* -ized, -iz·ing, to specify one or more particulars, details, characteristics, etc. (of). —**par·tic·u·lar·i·za′tion**, *n.*

par·tic·u·lar·ly (-lẽr-li), *adv.* 1. especially. 2. in such a way as to be specific.

part·ing (pärt′ing), *adj.* said, done, given, etc. at the time of leaving or going away: *n.* 1. a place, line, etc. where separation occurs. 2. a departure.

par·ti·san (pär′ti-zn), *n.* 1. a zealous or fanatical adherent of a given party, faction, etc. 2. a guerrilla fighter: *adj.* of or like a partisan. —**par′ti·san·ship**, *n.*

par·tite (pär′tīt), *adj.* divided into parts.

par·ti·tion (pär-tish′ûn), *n.* 1. separation into parts. 2. something, as an interior wall, separating one part from another. 3. a part so separated; section, compartment, etc. 4. a parting (sense 1): *v.t.* 1. to divide into parts, units, sections, etc. 2. to divide and portion out.

par·ti·tive (pärt′l-tiv), *adj.* 1. effecting division; dividing. 2. in *Grammar,* of or denoting a construction or form indicating limitation to one part of a whole: *n.* in *Grammar,* a partitive term or case.

part·ly (pärt′li), *adv.* to some extent or degree; not wholly or entirely.

part·ner (pärt′nẽr), *n.* 1. one associated with another, especially in business. 2. one dancing with another. 3. in games, one joined with another against two others. 4. a husband or wife.

part·ner·ship (-ship), *n.* 1. association with a partner. 2. those so associated.

part of speech, 1. any one of various categories of the terms of a language, the terms being grouped in one or the other category according to form, function, etc.: in traditional English grammar these categories include noun, verb, adjective, etc. 2. a term viewed as assigned or assignable to such a category.

par·took (pär-took′), past tense of partake.

par·tridge (pär′trij), *n., pl.* -tridg·es, -tridge, 1. a European game bird with an orange-brown head, stout body, and short wings and tail. 2. any one of various similar game birds.

part song, a song usually in four parts, one part carrying the melody and the other parts harmonizing with it.

part-time (pärt′tīm), *adj.* designating of, or doing work, study, etc. for periods of time that are less than a full schedule.

par·tu·ri·en·cy (pär-tūr′i-ėn-si, -toor′-), *n.* the condition of being parturient.

par·tu·ri·ent (-ėnt), *adj.* 1. giving birth or about to give birth. 2. of childbirth.

par·tu·ri·tion (pär-choo-rish′ûn, -tyoo-), *n.* a giving birth; childbirth.

part·way (pärt′wā′), *adv.* as far as part but not all of a distance or extent.

par·ty (pär′ti), *n., pl.* -ties, 1. a group united for a particular purpose, as in politics. 2.

any group acting together, traveling together, meeting, etc. 3. a gathering for social entertainment, recreation, or amusement; also, the entertainment itself, the activities, etc. 4. one participating or otherwise involved in something. 5. the plaintiff or defendant in a lawsuit. 6. [Informal], any person: *v.i.* **-tied, -ty·ing,** to take part in or hold a social party.

par·ty line, 1. a boundary line. 2. the policy line of a political party. 3. a telephone line connecting two or more users by the same circuit with the central office.

par·ty wall, a common wall between two buildings or properties.

par·ve·nu (pär'vē-nōō), *n.* one newly rich or powerful; upstart.

pas (pä), *n., pl.* **pas** (päz, pä), 1. a step or steps in dancing. 2. right to precede.

Pasch (pask), *n.* 1. Passover. 2. Easter.

pas·chal (pas'k!), *adj.* of or pertaining to Passover or Easter.

pa·sha (pä·shä', pä'shà, pash'à), *n.* formerly, in Turkey, 1. a title of rank or honor put after the name. 2. a high civil or military official.

pa·sha·lik, pa·sha·lic (pä·shä'lik), *n.* the jurisdiction of a pasha.

pass (pas), *v.i.* 1. to move along or go, especially forward. 2. to go from one place, condition, etc. to another. 3. to stop; terminate. 4. to go away; depart. 5. to die (especially with *away*). 6. to go by. 7. to elapse. 8. to get by without being rejected or challenged. 9. to gain confirmation or approval. 10. to get through a test successfully. 11. to happen. 12. to give a judgment, decision, etc. 13. in *card games*, to decline bidding, anteing, etc. 14. in *Sports,* to try or complete a pass of the ball, puck, etc.: *v.t.* 1. to go by, beyond, over, through, etc. 2. to get through (a test) successfully. 3. to cause or allow to move onward, through, etc. 4. to give confirmation or approval to. 5. to spend (time). 6. to excrete; void. 7. to make (a judgment, remark, etc.). 8. in *Sports,* to try or complete a pass of (the ball, puck, etc.): *n.* 1. the act of passing. 2. a narrow passage, avenue, or entrance. 3. a condition or situation. 4. a ticket, paper, etc. allowing or authorizing passage, entrance, use, etc.; also, a written leave of absence, as for a soldier. 5. a movement of the hands as by a magician or a hypnotist. 6. a tentative attempt. 7. [Slang], an attempt to touch, embrace, etc., specifically in seeking sexual intimacy. 8. in *card games,* a declining to bid, ante, etc. 9. in *Sports,* an intentional transfer of the ball, puck, etc. to another player during play.

pass·a·ble ('à-bl), *adj.* 1. that can be passed. 2. not very good but meeting minimum standards; tolerable.

pass·a·bly (-bli), *adv.* tolerably.

pass·age (pas'ij), *n.* 1. the act of passing. 2. a course or journey. 3. passenger accommodations, as on a ship, or the charge made. 4. a means of getting in or out of or moving along, as a road, path, duct, or corridor. 5. permission, right, or opportunity to pass. 6. an interchange as of words or blows. 7.

enactment into law. 8. a short section of something written, spoken, sung, played, etc.

pass·age·way (-wā), *n.* a means of getting in or out or of moving along; passage.

pass·book (pas'book), *n.* 1. a bankbook. 2. a customer's record with notations by a seller of items bought on credit.

pas·sé (pa·sā'), *adj.* 1. outmoded. 2. old.

pas·sel (pas'l), *n.* [Informal], a group or collection, especially when quite large.

pas·sen·ger (pas'n·jèr), *n.* one traveling in a car, plane, ship, etc. and usually one not engaged in operating the vehicle.

passenger pigeon, an extinct North American pigeon with an extremely long, narrow tail.

pass·er·by (pas'ēr·bī), *n., pl.* **pass'ers·by,** one going by, as a person out walking.

pas·ser·ine (pas'ēr·in, 'ē·rīn), *adj.* of or pertaining to a large order of chiefly perching songbirds: *n.* such a bird.

pass·ing (pas'ing), *adj.* 1. that passes. 2. not lasting long. 3. casual; incidental. 4. meeting given requirements or, standards: *adv.* [Archaic], exceedingly: *n.* 1. the act of passing. 2. death.

pas·sion (pash'ūn), *n.* 1. originally, suffering. 2. [P-], the agony of Jesus before and during the Crucifixion. 3. an emotion or the emotions. 4. violent emotional agitation. 5. great anger. 6. great liking. 7. intense affection or love. 8. strong or overpowering sexual desire or drive. 9. someone or something that one greatly likes or desires.

pas·sion·ate (-it), *adj.* 1. full of or moved by passion. 2. intense: said of emotion.

pas·sion-flow·er (pash'ūn·flou·ēr), *n.* a tropical climbing plant with flowers that are red or yellow or of other colors and with small, yellow or purple fruits.

pas·sive (pas'iv), *adj.* 1. acted upon rather than acting. 2. submissive. 3. signifying the voice of a verb whose subject is the receiver of the action of the verb.

passive resistance, nonviolent opposition, as by demonstrating, ignoring orders, etc.

pas·siv·ism (-izm), *n.* passive behavior, principles, etc. **—pas'siv·ist,** *adj. & n.*

pas·siv·i·ty (pa·siv'ī·ti), *n.* the state of being passive; inaction, inertia, etc.

pass·key (pas'kē), *n.* 1. a master key or a skeleton key. 2. any private key.

Pass·o·ver (pas'ō·vēr), *n.* 1. a Jewish holiday commemorating the deliverance of the ancient Hebrews from Egyptian slavery: it begins on the 14th of Nisan and lasts eight (or seven) days. 2. among the ancient Hebrews, a lamb killed and eaten at the Passover.

pass·port (pas'pôrt), *n.* 1. a document authorizing one to travel in a foreign country. 2. a document allowing a vessel to enter or leave a port.

pass·through ('thrōō), *n.* a wall aperture for passing food, plates, etc. through.

pass·word ('wûrd), *n.* one or more secret words agreed on for identification.

past (past), *adj.* 1. having been; gone by; completed. 2. indicating a time, condition, or action gone by, as a verb form: *n.* 1. time, life, events, etc. gone by. 2. the past

a in cap, ā in cane, ä in father, å in abet, e in met, ē in be, ẽ in baker, ẽ in regent, i in pit, ī in fine, ï in manifest, o in hot, ô in horse, ō in bone,

tense, or a verb form in this tense: *adv. & prep.* beyond.

pas·ta (päs′tä), *n.* 1. dough, as of durum or semolina, made into spaghetti, macaroni, etc. 2. the spaghetti, macaroni, etc. made.

paste (pāst), *n.* 1. dough for rich pastry. 2. pasta dough. 3. any one of various soft, smooth substances. 4. a jellylike candy. 5. a mixture of flour or starch, water, etc., used to stick pieces of paper or the like together. 6. a hard, brilliant glass used in artificial gems. 7. [Slang], a blow; punch: *v.t.* past′ed, past′ing, 1. to stick together with or as if with paste. 2. to cover with material pasted on. 3. [Slang], to hit; punch.

paste·board (′bôrd), *n.* 1. a stiff material made of layers of paper pasted together or of pressed and dried paper pulp. 2. [Slang], a ticket, card, etc. made of this.

pas·tel (pas-tel′), *n.* 1. ground coloring material, or a crayon of this. 2. a drawing made with such crayons. 3. drawing with pastels as an art form or medium. 4. a light literary sketch. 5. a soft, pale shade of a color: *adj.* 1. soft and pale: said of a color. 2. of pastel. 3. drawn with pastels.

past·er (päs′tēr), *n.* 1. one that pastes. 2. a piece of gummed paper to stick on something; sticker.

pas·tern (pas′tērn), *n.* the part of a horse's foot between the fetlock and hoof.

pas·teur·ize (pas′chŭ-rīz, ′tŭ-), *v.t.* -ized, -iz·ing, to subject (milk, beer, etc.) to a heating process designed to destroy harmful bacteria and check fermentation. —**pas·teur·i·za′tion,** *n.*

pas·tiche (pas-tēsh′), *n.* 1. a literary or other work made up of bits from various sources. 2. a hodgepodge.

pas·tie (pas′ti), *n.* same as pasty (a pie).

pas·tille (pas-tēl′), *n.* 1. a medicated lozenge. 2. an aromatic pellet burned for fumigating or deodorizing. Also **pas·til** (pas′til).

pas·time (pas′tīm), *n.* a pleasant way of spending spare time; diversion.

past·i·ness (päs′ti-nis), *n.* the quality or state of being pasty.

past master, one of long experience and proved skill or knowledge in something.

pas·tor (pas′tēr), *n.* a clergyman in charge of a church or congregation.

pas·to·ral (-ăl), *adj.* 1. of or characteristic of rural life or literature, music, etc. dealing with it. 2. of a pastor or a pastor's duties: *n.* 1. a pastoral poem, play, etc. 2. a letter from a pastor or bishop to those in his charge.

pas·tor·ate (-it), *n.* the rank, duties, or office of a pastor.

past participle, a participle expressing past or completed action, time, or condition and used with auxiliaries or as an adjective.

past perfect, 1. a tense indicating an action or state as completed before a specified or implied time in the past. 2. a verb form in this tense.

pas·tra·mi (pä-strä′mi), *n.* highly spiced, smoked beef, especially from a shoulder cut.

pas·try (päs′tri), *n., pl.* -tries, 1. flour dough made with shortening and used as for pie

crusts. 2. pies, tarts, etc. made with this. 3. any fancy baked goods. 4. a single pie, cake, etc.

pas·tur·age (pas′chēr-ij), *n.* 1. same as pasture. 2. the pasturing of animals.

pas·ture (pas′chēr), *n.* 1. land with herbage for grazing animals; also, a particular plot of such land. 2. grass or other growing plants for grazing: *v.t.* -tured, -tur·ing, 1. to provide with pasture. 2. to put (animals) out to graze in a pasture. 3. to graze (grass or other growing plants): *v.i.* to graze herbage.

past·y (päs′ti), *adj.* past′i·er, past′i·est, of or like paste.

pas·ty (pas′ti, päs′ti), *n., pl.* -ties, [Chiefly British], a pie, especially a meat pie.

pat (pat), *n.* 1. a light, quick blow as with the hand. 2. a small lump as of butter: *v.t.* pat′ted, pat′ting, 1. to strike quickly and lightly as with the hand. 2. to shape or apply so: *adj.* 1. apt. 2. exactly suitable. 3. glib. 4. immovable: in *stand pat: adv.* in a pat way.

pa·ta·gi·um (pä-tā′ji-ŭm), *n., pl.* -gi·a (-å), 1. a fold of skin between the fore and hind limbs of bats, flying squirrels, etc., enabling the animals to fly or glide. 2. a fold of skin between the shoulder and front part of a bird's wing.

patch (pach), *n.* 1. a piece applied to cover a hole or rent. 2. a covering put over a wound or sore. 3. a pad or shield put over an injured eye. 4. a scrap; remnant; specifically, a piece inserted in variegated work; also, any area, spot, or piece suggestive of this. 5. a small plot of ground. 6. a cloth insignia of unit identification, high on the sleeve of a military uniform: *v.t.* 1. to put a patch or patches on. 2. to serve as a patch for. 3. to make out of patches. 4. to mend or repair clumsily.

patch·ou·li, patch·ou·ly (pach′oo-li, pä-chōō′li), *n., pl.* -lis, -lies, 1. an East Indian mint yielding a fragrant oil. 2. a perfume made from this oil.

patch·work (pach′wŭrk), *n.* 1. work made of irregular pieces of cloth of various colors, sewn together. 2. a hodgepodge.

patch·y (′i), *adj.* patch′i·er, patch′i·est, of, like, or full of patches.

pate (pāt), *n.* the head, especially the top of it: now a humorous usage.

pâ·té (pä-tā′), *n.* 1. a pie. 2. a meat paste.

pâ·té de foie gras (pä-tā′ dē fwä′ grä′, pät′ā), a paste made of the livers of fattened geese.

pa·tel·la (på-tel′å), *n., pl.* -las, -lae (′ē), 1. a small, shallow pan. 2. a kneecap. —**pa·tel′lar,** *adj.*

pat·en (pat′n), *n.* a metal plate used for holding the bread in the Eucharist.

pa·ten·cy (pāt′n·si, pat′n-), *n.* the quality or state of being patent, or obvious.

pat·ent (pat′nt), *adj.* 1. open to perusal by all: said of a public document. 2. secured by letters patent. 3. of, pertaining to, or involving a patent or patents. 4. patented. 5. (pāt′nt, pat′nt), unmistakably clear or evident; obvious; altogether apparent: *n.* 1. a public document (*letters patent*) granting a right or privilege, especially one granting exclusive right with regard to an invention, process, etc. 2. the right so granted or the thing so protected: *v.t.* 1. to grant a patent to or for. 2. to get a patent for.

pat-en-tee (pat-n-tē'), *n.* one granted a patent.

patent leather, leather with a hard, glossy finish.

pa-tent-ly (pat'nt-li, pat'nt-), *adv.* in an unmistakably clear or evident way.

patent medicine, a trademarked medical preparation available without prescription.

pat-en-tor (pat'n-tēr), *n.* a patent grantor.

pa-ter (pāt'ēr), *n.* 1. [Chiefly British Informal], father. 2. [P-], (pät'ēr), short for paternoster.

pa-ter-fa-mil-i-as (-fā-mil'i-ăs), *n., pl.* **pa'tres-fa-mil-i-as** (pā'trēz-fä-), the father of a family; male head of a household.

pa-ter-nal (pä-tûr'nl), *adj.* 1. of, like, or from a father. 2. being a specified relative or relatives through the father's side of the family.

pa-ter-nal-ism (-izm), *n.* a way of controlling or managing others that suggests a father's relationship with his children. —**pa-ter-nal-is'-tic,** *adj.*

pa-ter-ni-ty (pä-tûr'ni-ti), *n.* 1. the state or character of being a father; fatherhood or fatherliness. 2. male parentage; paternal origin. 3. origin in general.

pa-ter-nos-ter (pat-ēr-nòs'tēr, pāt-ēr-nos'tēr), *n.* the Lord's Prayer, especially in Latin: often Pater Noster.

path (path), *n.* 1. a footway; track. 2. a course of movement, behavior, etc.

pa-thet-ic (pä-thet'ik), *adj.* 1. eliciting or playing on such emotions as pity or compassion; touching; affecting. 2. so ineffective, unskillful, etc. as to invite a mixture of pity and contempt. —**pa-thet'i-cal-ly,** *adv.*

path-find-er (path'fin-dēr), *n.* one blazing a new path; pioneer.

path-o-gen (path'ō-jĕn), *n.* a disease-causing microorganism or virus.

path-o-gen-ic (path-ō-jen'ik), *adj.* producing disease.

path-o-log-i-cal (-loj'i-kl), *adj.* of, pertaining to, or involving disease.

pa-thol-o-gist (pä-thol'ō-jist), *n.* a specialist in pathology.

pa-thol-o-gy (-ji), *n., pl.* **-gies,** 1. the science treating of the causes, symptoms, and effects of disease. 2. the characteristics of and data on a particular disease. 3. any disease-like condition.

pa-thos (pā'thos), *n.* 1. a quality, as in something seen, that elicits an emotional response of pity, compassion, etc. 2. the emotional response elicited.

path-way (path'wā), *n.* a path.

pa-tience (pā'shēns), *n.* the quality, state, or fact of being patient.

pa-tient (pā'shěnt), *adj.* 1. undergoing pain, hardship, affliction, insult, etc. with calmness and equanimity. 2. persevering in spite of difficulties, delays, or uncertainty; steadfast: *n.* one receiving treatment, especially from a doctor.

pat-i-na (pat'n-ä), *n.* 1. a filmy greenish coating formed naturally by oxidation on bronze and copper. 2. any distinctive coloration or sheen produced as by aging.

pa-ti-o (pat'i-ō, pät'-), *n., pl.* **-ti-os,** 1. a courtyard or unroofed inner area, as in Spanish and Spanish-American architecture. 2. an outdoor area, typically paved, adjacent to a house and used especially for lounging, casual dining, etc.

pa-tois (pat'wä), *n.* a nonstandard form of some language; dialect.

pa-tri-arch (pā'tri-ärk), *n.* 1. the father, founder, or head of a family, tribe, colony, etc. 2. an aged, venerable man. 3. [often P-], any one of various high-ranking bishops. —**pa-tri-arch'al,** *adj.*

pa-tri-ar-chate (-är-kit), *n.* 1. the office, rank, or jurisdiction of a patriarch. 2. a patriarchy.

pa-tri-ar-chy (-är-ki), *n., pl.* **-chies,** 1. social organization recognizing the father or eldest male as head of the family or tribe, with kinship and succession traced through the male line. 2. rule by men.

pa-tri-cian (pä-trish'än), *n.* 1. a nobleman or other high-ranking individual, as in ancient Rome. 2. an aristocrat: *adj.* of or like a patrician.

pat-ri-cide (pat'ri-sīd, pā'tri-), *n.* 1. murder of a father by his son or daughter. 2. the murderer. —**pat-ri-ci'dal,** *adj.*

pat-ri-mo-ny (pat'ri-mō-ni), *n., pl.* **-nies,** 1. an inheritance; heritage; specifically, property inherited from one's father or ancestors. 2. an endowment made as to a church. —**pat-ri-mo'ni-al,** *adj.*

pa-tri-ot (pā'tri-ōt, -ot), *n.* one who loves his country, devotedly supporting and defending it. —**pa-tri-ot'ic** (-ot'ik), *adj.* —**pa-tri-ot'i-cal-ly,** *adv.*

pa-tri-ot-ism (-ō-tizm), *n.* love and devoted support and defense of one's country.

pa-tris-tic (pä-tris'tik), *adj.* of or pertaining to various Christian writers of the earlier centuries of the Christian Church, whose works are viewed by the Church as of special theological value.

pa-trol (pä-trōl'), *v.t. & v.i.* **-trolled',** -trol'ling, to go round (an area, town, etc.) regularly to guard or inspect: *n.* 1. the act of patrolling. 2. one or more individuals or groups patrolling. 3. a small group of soldiers sent on a mission, as to reconnoiter. 4. a group of ships, airplanes, etc. used in guarding.

pa-trol-man ('măn), *n., pl.* **-men** ('měn), a policeman who patrols a certain area.

pa-tron (pā'trŏn), *n.* 1. a protector; guardian. 2. a benefactor; specifically, a sponsor or supporter of a person, institution, etc. 3. a regular customer.

pa-tron-age (pā'trŏn-ij, pat'rŏn-), *n.* 1. sponsorship, support, protection, etc. contributed by a patron or patrons. 2. customers collectively; clientele. 3. business; trade. 4. patronizing treatment; condescension. 5. power to grant political favors; also, the distribution of such favors or the favors themselves.

pa-tron-al (-l), *adj.* of a patron.

pa-tron-ess (pā'trŏn-is), *n.* a woman patron.

pa-tron-ize (pā'trŏ-nīz, pat'rŏ-), *v.t.* **-ized,** -izing, 1. to act as a patron toward; sponsor, support, or guard. 2. to be a regular customer of; buy from regularly. 3. to treat with an air of stooping down to an inferior.

patron saint, a saint viewed as a special guardian of a person, place, etc.

pat·ro·nym·ic (pat-rō-nim'ik), *adj.* formed with or being a prefix or suffix showing descent from an indicated father or paternal ancestor: *n.* 1. such a name or form. 2. any last name; surname.

pa·troon (pä-trōōn'), *n.* one that held a large estate, with special privileges attached, under a grant from the old Dutch governments of New York and New Jersey.

pat·sy (pat'si), *n., pl.* -sies, [Slang], one easily imposed upon or victimized.

pat·ten (pat'n), *n.* a clog or similar shoe.

pat·ter (pat'ēr), *v.i.* 1. to make a quick succession of tapping sounds, as of light footsteps. 2. to move along, making such sounds: *n.* a quick succession of light taps.

pat·ter (pat'ēr), *v.t. & v.i.* to speak, recite, or mumble rapidly: *n.* 1. cant, jargon, or chatter. 2. quick, glib speech, as of a magician or comedian.

pat·tern (pat'ērn), *n.* 1. something to be imitated or copied; model. 2. a sample or specimen. 3. an arrangement of parts, details, etc.; design. 4. a set way of behaving, moving, etc.: *v.t.* to do, produce, shape, etc., following a pattern.

pat·ty (pat'i), *n., pl.* -ties, 1. a small, flat, rounded mass, as of ground meat, usually fried. 2. a small pie; also, a piece of candy, as of chocolate-covered soft peppermint, suggestive of this.

patty shell, a small pastry shell to hold an individual serving, as of creamed fish.

pau·ci·ty (pô'si-ti), *n.* 1. fewness. 2. scarcity; lack; insufficiency.

paunch (pônch), *n.* the belly; abdomen; especially, a large, fat, bloated belly. —**paunch'y,** *adj.*

pau·per (pô'pēr), *n.* an utterly destitute person, especially one living on tax-supported charity. —**pau'per·ism,** *n.*

pau·per·ize (pô'pē-rīz), *v.t.* -ized, -iz·ing, to reduce to the condition of a pauper.

pause (pôz), *n.* a brief stop, delay, interruption, etc.: *v.i.* paused, paus'ing, to make a pause.

pave (pāv), *v.t.* paved, pav'ing, to cover, as a road, with concrete, brick, etc.

pave·ment (pāv'mēnt), *n.* a paved surface.

pa·vil·ion (pä-vil'yūn), *n.* 1. a large tent. 2. a building, as in a park, for exhibits, relaxation, etc. 3. a section or unit in a complex of buildings.

pav·ing (pā'ving), *n.* a pavement.

paw (pô), *n.* the foot of a four-footed animal with claws: *v.t. & v.i.* to touch, manipulate, hit, etc. as with paws.

pawl (pôl), *n.* a mechanical part, as a hinged tongue engaging the notches of a ratchet wheel, allowing only one-way motion.

pawn (pôn), *n.* 1. something given or delivered as security, as for a debt. 2. the act of pawning or the state of being pawned. 3. a chess piece of lowest value. 4. a person or thing callously used or sacrificed to gain

some objective: *v.t.* 1. to give as security, as for a debt; specifically, to deliver to a pawnbroker as security for a loan. 2. to risk or wager.

pawn·bro·ker ('brō-kēr), *n.* one licensed to lend money at interest in exchange for personal property left as security.

pawn·shop ('shop), *n.* a pawnbroker's shop.

paw·paw (pô'pô), *n.* same as **papaw**.

pay (pā), *v.t.* paid or obs. (except sense 7) payed, pay'ing, 1. to give to (someone) what is due, as for goods. 2. to give (what is due). 3. to deposit or transfer (money). 4. to settle (a debt, obligation, etc.). 5. to give (a compliment, attention, etc.); also, to make (a visit, call, etc.). 6. to profit. 7. to let (a rope, cable, etc.) run: with *out*: *v.i.* to make payment: *n.* payment; wages; salary: *adj.* 1. operated by deposit of a coin, as a public telephone. 2. designating a service available as by subscription.

pay·a·ble ('ā-bl), *adj.* 1. that can be paid. 2. that is to be paid (on a date indicated).

pay·check ('chek), *n.* a check in payment of salary or wages.

pay·day ('dā), *n.* a day on which salary or wages are paid.

pay dirt, soil, ore, etc. that can be mined at a profit.

pay·ee (pā-ē'), *n.* one to whom money is payable.

pay·er (pā'ēr), *n.* one that pays or that is to pay.

pay·load ('lōd), *n.* 1. cargo producing income: also pay load. 2. the warhead of a ballistic missile, the spacecraft launched by a rocket, etc.; also, the weight of such.

pay·mas·ter ('mas-tēr), *n.* one in charge of paying salaries or wages.

pay·ment ('mēnt), *n.* 1. a paying or being paid. 2. something paid. 3. reward or penalty.

pay·off ('ôf), *n.* 1. the act or time of payment. 2. settlement; reckoning. 3. recompense; return. 4. [Informal], a bribe. 5. [Informal], something coming as a climax or culmination.

pay·roll ('rōl), *n.* 1. a list of employees and of how much is due each in salary or wages. 2. the total due for a period.

pea (pē), *n., pl.* peas, archaic pease, 1. an annual, leguminous climbing plant with green pods. 2. any one of its small, round seeds, eaten as a vegetable.

peace (pēs), *n.* 1. freedom from or cessation of war. 2. a treaty or agreement to this end. 3. freedom from or cessation of public disturbance; prevailing of law and order. 4. absence or stopping of quarrels, disagreement, etc.; concord. 5. freedom from or cessation of inner conflict; mental, emotional, or spiritual tranquillity. 6. quiet; calm.

peace·a·ble ('ā-bl), *adj.* 1. disposed to or furthering peace. 2. calm; quiet; peaceful. — **peace'a·bly,** *adv.*

peace·ful ('fŭl), *adj.* characterized by or full of peace; free of agitation; calm.

peace·mak·er ('māk-ēr), *n.* one skilled at or given to settling quarrels, disputes, etc. — **peace'mak·ing,** *n. & adj.*

ō in dragon, ōō in crude, oo in wool, u in cup, ū in cure, û in turn, ŭ in focus, oi in boy, ou in house, th in thin, th in sheathe, g in get, j in joy, y in yet.

peace officer, an officer appointed to maintain law and order.

peace pipe, same as calumet.

peace-time ('tīm), *n.* a time of freedom from war: *adj.* of such a time.

peach (pēch), *n.* 1. a small tree bearing edible fruits that are round, fuzzy-skinned, orange-yellow, and juicy and that have a single, rough pit. 2. one of these fruits. 3. the color of these fruits. 4. [Slang], a well-liked person or thing. —**peach'i-ness,** *n.*

peach-y ('ī), *adj.* **peach'i-er, peach'i-est,** of or like a peach. —**peach'i-ness,** *n.*

pea-cock (pē'kok), *n., pl.* **-cocks, -cock,** a bird, specifically the male, of a species of pea-fowls, with a crested head, blue neck and breast, and, in the male, a long train of feathers that can be erected and spread in a fanlike arrangement displaying brilliant iridescent colors marked with glittering eye-like spots.

pea-fowl (pē'foul), *n., pl.* **-fowls, -fowl,** any one of a genus of pheasantlike birds commonly found in wooded areas of southern Asia and the East Indies.

pea-hen ('hen), *n.* a female peafowl.

pea jacket, a heavy, hip-length, double-breasted outdoor coat of wool, worn as by some seamen: also **pea'coat** ('kōt).

peak (pēk), *n.* 1. a sharp-pointed summit, as of a mountain; also, a mountain or hill with such a summit. 2. any pointed top or end. 3. a tapering projection. 4. a point of highest development, activity, energy, etc.; height; pinnacle: *v.t. & v.i.* 1. to bring or come to a peak. 2. to form or cause to form a peak or peaks.

peak-ed (pē'kid), *adj.* of or having wan or drawn facial features indicative of illness.

peal (pēl), *n.* 1. a loud ringing of one or more bells. 2. a set of musical bells, or the ringing of these in various patterns. 3. a sudden, loud, prolonged or reverberating sound, as of laughter or thunder: *v.i. & v.t.* to sound with or in a peal.

pe-an (pē'ăn), *n.* alternate spelling of paean.

pea-nut (pē'nut), *n.* 1. a spreading, annual vine of the legume family, having brittle pods that ripen underground and contain one to three edible seeds. 2. one of these pods or seeds. 3. *pl.* [Slang], a relatively trifling sum of money.

peanut butter, a food paste or spread made of ground roasted peanuts.

pear (per), *n.* 1. a tree bearing juicy, edible fruits that are large and rounded in the basal portion, more narrowly rounded toward the top, and yellow, brown, or red in coloration. 2. one of these fruits.

pearl (pûrl), *n.* 1. a smooth, hard, lustrous, beadlike body, typically white or bluish-gray, formed in layers around a foreign particle within the shell of certain mollusks and valued as a gem. 2. same as mother-of-pearl. 3. something pearllike in appearance, value, etc. 4. the bluish-gray color of some pearls. 5. in *Printing,* a very small size of type. —**pearl'y,** *adj.*

peas-ant (pez'nt), *n.* 1. any person of the class of small farmers and farm laborers, as in Europe and Asia. 2. a person viewed as ignorant, uncouth, etc.

peas-ant-ry ('n-tri), *n.* 1. peasants collectively. 2. peasant status.

peat (pēt), *n.* decayed vegetable matter used as fuel when dried.

pea-vey (pē'vi), *n., pl.* **-veys,** a lever with a metal point and hinged hook, used in logging: also spelled **pea'vy, pl. -vies.**

peb-ble (peb'l), *n.* a small, rounded stone: *v.t.* **-bled, -bling,** to make pebbly.

peb-bly ('li), *adj.* **-bli-er, -bli-est,** 1. full of pebbles. 2. having little bumps suggestive of pebbles.

pe-can (pi-kan', -kǎn'; pē'kan), *n.* 1. an olive-shaped, edible nut with a thin, smooth shell, produced by a North American tree of the walnut family. 2. the tree.

pec-ca-dil-lo (pek-ȧ-dil'ō), *n., pl.* **-loes, -los,** a minor fault.

pec-ca-ry (pek'ēr-i), *n., pl.* **-ries, -ry,** either of two related American piglike animals with sharp tusks.

peck (pek), *n.* 1. a unit of dry measure, equal to 1/4 bushel. 2. a quick, sharp stroke with or as if with a bird's beak; also, a mark so made: *v.t.* to strike, make, or take up by or as if by such a stroke.

pec-tin (pek'tin), *n.* a carbohydrate found in certain ripe fruits, yielding a gelatinous substance used as the basis of jellies and jams. —**pec'tic** ('tik), *adj.*

pec-to-ral (pek'tēr-ȧl), *adj.* of, in, or on the chest or breast.

pec-u-late (pek'yu̇-lāt), *v.t. & v.i.* **-lat-ed, -lat-ing,** to embezzle. —**pec-u-la'tion,** *n.*

pe-cul-iar (pi-kūl'yēr), *adj.* 1. exclusively individual; distinctive. 2. odd; strange.

pe-cu-li-ar-i-ty (-kū-li-er'ĭ-ti), *n.* 1. the quality or state of being peculiar. 2. *pl.* **-ties,** a distinctive characteristic.

pe-cu-ni-ar-y (-kū'ni-er-i), *adj.* monetary.

ped-a-gogue, ped-a-gog (ped'ȧ-gog), *n.* a teacher, often a pedantic one.

ped-a-go-gy (-gō-ji, -goj-i), *n.* teaching or teaching methods. —**ped-a-gog'ic** (-goj'ik, -gō'jik), **ped-a-gog'i-cal,** *adj.*

ped-al (ped'l), *adj.* 1. (also pēd'l), of the foot or feet. 2. of a pedal or pedals: *n.* a foot-operated lever, as on a bicycle or for an organ: *v.t. & v.i.* **-aled** or **-alled, -al-ing** or **-al-ling,** to work the pedal or pedals of (something).

ped-ant (ped'nt), *n.* a teacher or scholar overemphasizing minutiae, rigidly insisting on arbitrary rules, or making a vain display of learning. —**pe-dan-tic** (pi-dan'tik), *adj.* —**ped'ant-ry,** *n.*

ped-dle (ped'l), *v.t. & v.i.* **-dled, -dling,** to carry about (small articles, circulars, etc.) so as to sell or distribute. —**ped'dler,** *n.*

-pede (pēd), a combining form meaning *feet.*

ped-es-tal (ped'is-tl), *n.* the base or support of a pillar, vase, statue, etc.

pe-des-tri-an (pē-des'tri-ȧn), *adj.* 1. on foot; walking. 2. dull; prosaic: *n.* a walker. —**pe-des'tri-an-ism,** *n.*

pe·di·a·tri·cian (pē-di-a-trish'ǝn), *n.* a specialist in pediatrics.

pe·di·at·rics (pē-di-at'riks), *n.* the branch of medicine dealing with the care and treatment of children.

ped·i·cab (ped'i-kab), *n.* a three-wheeled passenger vehicle pedaled like a bicycle by the driver, as in southeastern Asia.

ped·i·cel (ped'i-sl), *n.* in *Botany & Zoology,* a small stalk or stalklike structure.

pe·dic·u·lo·sis (pi-dik-yǔ-lō'sis), *n.* infestation with lice.

ped·i·cure (ped'i-kyoor), *n.* a trimming, polishing, etc. of the toenails.

ped·i·gree (ped'i-grē), *n.* 1. a listing or tracing of ancestors; ancestry; lineage 2. a recorded line of descent, especially of a purebred animal. —**ped'i·greed,** *adj.*

ped·i·ment (ped'i-mĕnt), *n.* 1. in classic architecture, a gable. 2. any decorative gablelike form or part.

ped·lar, ped·ler (ped'lēr), *n.* a peddler.

pe·dom·e·ter (pi-dom'ě-tēr), *n.* a device measuring distance walked.

pe·dun·cle (pi-dung'kl, pē'dung-kl), *n.* in *Botany, Zoology, etc.,* a stalk or stalklike structure.

peek (pēk), *n.* a quick or furtive glance; peep: *v.i.* to glance thus.

peel (pēl), *v.t.* to cut or strip off (the rind, skin, covering, etc.) from (something): *v.i.* 1. to shed skin, bark, etc. 2. to come off in layers or flakes, as old paint: *n.* the rind or skin, as of an orange.

peel·ing ('ing), *n.* a peeled-off strip.

peen (pēn), *n.* in certain hammers, the part opposite the flat striking surface.

peep (pēp), *v.i.* 1. to cheep. 2. to peek: *n.* 1. a cheep. 2. a peek.

peep·hole ('hōl), *n.* a hole to peep through.

peer (pir), *n.* 1. one of the same rank, value, etc.; equal. 2. a noble: *v.i.* to look attentively or searchingly.

peer·age ('ij), *n.* 1. the rank or dignity of a peer. 2. peers collectively. 3. a book or list of peers with their lineage.

peer·ess ('is), *n.* 1. a peer's wife. 2. a woman holding the rank of a peer.

peer·less ('lis), *adj.* without an equal.

peeve (pēv), *v.t.* peeved, peev'ing, [Informal], to make peevish: *n.* [Informal], an irritation.

pee·vish (pē'vish), *adj.* fretful; hard to please; irritable. —**pee'vish·ly,** *adv.* —**pee'vish·ness,** *n.*

pee·wee (pē'wē), *n.* [Informal], a very small person or thing.

peg (peg), *n.* 1. a small, pointed wooden pin. 2. a piece of wood serving as a nail. 3. a prong or claw. 4. a step or degree. 5. [Informal], a throw: *v.t.* pegged, peg'ging, 1. to fasten, mark, etc. with a peg or pegs. 2. [Informal], to throw.

Peg·a·sus (peg'ǝ-sǔs), *n.* in *Greek Mythology,* a horse with wings.

peg·board (peg'bôrd), *n.* 1. a board with holes for holding pegs: used for scoring in cribbage. 2. fibrous or wooden material containing holes for the insertion of pegs or hooks on which to hang tools, displays, etc.

peg leg, [Informal], 1. a wooden leg. 2. one having a wooden leg.

peh (pā), *n.* the 17th letter of the Hebrew alphabet.

peign·oir (pān-wär'), *n.* [French], a woman's loose dressing gown.

pe·jo·ra·tion (pē-jǒ-rā'shǔn, pej-ǒ-), *n.* a worsening. —**pe·jo·ra·tive** (pi-jôr'ǝ-tiv), *adj.*

pe·kin (pē'kin), *n.* a flowered silk fabric.

Pe·king·ese (pē-ki-nēz'), *n., pl.* -ese', a small dog with short legs, a pug nose, and a flowing silky coat: also **Pe·kin·ese'.**

pe·koe (pē'kō), *n.* a black tea made from leaves at the tips of the stem.

pel·age (pel'ij), *n.* the hair, fur, wool, etc. covering a mammal.

pe·lag·ic (pi-laj'ik), *adj.* of or pertaining to the open ocean.

pel·er·ine (pel-ē-rēn'), *n.* a woman's long cape with tapering ends.

pelf (pelf), *n.* money or wealth fraudulently acquired.

pel·i·can (pel'i-kǝn), *n.* any one of several large, fish-eating, web-footed birds, with an expansible pouch under the lower jaw which it uses to capture and store fish.

pe·lisse (pē-lēs'), *n.* a long outer coat, usually of fur or trimmed with fur.

pel·la·gra (pē-lag'rǎ, -lā'grǎ), *n.* a chronic disease caused by a lack of nicotinic acid and characterized by digestive disturbances, skin eruptions, etc.

pel·let (pel'ĕt), *n.* 1. a small ball, as of bread, medicine, etc. 2. a bullet, small piece of shot, etc.

pel·li·cle (pel'i-kl), *n.* a thin skin or film.

pel·li·to·ry (pel'i-tôr-i), *n., pl.* -ries, any one of several plants of the nettle family, formerly used in medicine as a diuretic.

pell-mell, pell-mell (pel'mel'), *adv. & adj.* 1. in confusion. 2. with reckless haste.

pel·lu·cid (pē-lōō'sid), *adj.* 1. clear; transparent. 2. readily understandable.

pe·lo·ta (pē-lōt'ǎ), *n.* same as **jai alai.**

pelt (pelt), *v.t.* 1. to strike by throwing something at. 2. to hit repeatedly: *v.i.* to fall heavily, as rain.

pelt (pelt), *n.* the hide of a fur-bearing animal.

pel·tast (pel'tast), *n.* in ancient Greece, a soldier protected by a light shield.

pel·tate (pel'tāt), *adj.* in *Botany,* having the stalk attached to the lower surface instead of to the margin.

pelt·ry (pel'tri), *n.* pelts collectively.

pel·vis (pel'vis), *n.* 1. the bony cavity in the lower part of the abdomen. 2. the bones forming this. —**pel'vic,** *adj.*

pem·mi·can (pem'i-kǎn), *n.* dried meat, pounded into paste and preserved in cakes.

pem·phi·gus (pem'fi-gǔs), *n.* a disease characterized by serous blotches on the skin.

pen (pen), *n.* a small enclosure for domestic animals: *v.t.* penned or pent, pen'ning, to shut up, as in a pen.

pen (pen), *n.* an instrument for writing with ink: *v.t.* penned, pen'ning, to write with a pen.

pen (pen), *n.* [Slang], a penitentiary.

---

pe·nal (pē'nl), *adj.* of, inflicting, prescribing, or incurring punishment.

pe·nal·ize (pē'nl-īz, pen'l-), *v.t.* -ized, -iz·ing, 1. to render subject to punishment. 2. to impose a penalty on. **—pe·nal·i·za'tion,** *n.*

pen·al·ty (pen'l-ti), *n., pl.* -ties, 1. legal punishment. 2. something, as a sum of money, imposed on an offender as a forfeit or fine. 3. in *Sports,* a disadvantage resulting from the breaking of a rule.

pen·ance (pen'ăns), *n.* 1. self-imposed suffering or privation as an expression of contrition for sin. 2. in the *Roman Catholic Church,* a sacrament demanding sorrow for sin, confession to a priest, acceptance of the satisfaction imposed, and absolution.

pe·na·tes (pi-nāt'ēz), *n.pl.* in the belief of ancient Romans, the household gods who guarded the home and state.

pence (pens), *n.* British plural of **penny.**

pen·chant (pen'chănt), *n.* a strong inclination; taste.

pen·cil (pen'sl), *n.* a cylinder containing graphite, carbon, chalk, etc. that is sharpened to a point for writing, drawing, etc.: *v.t.* -ciled or -cilled, -cil·ing or -cil·ling, to write, draw, etc. with a pencil.

pend (pend), *v.i.* to wait for settlement or disposal.

pend·ant (pen'dănt), *n.* anything hanging for ornamentation, as from a necklace.

pend·ent ('dĕnt), *adj.* 1. hanging down. 2. projecting. 3. undecided.

pend·ing ('ding), *adj.* 1. undecided. 2. impending: *prep.* 1. during. 2. until.

pen·drag·on (pen-drag'ŏn), *n.* in ancient Britain, supreme chief or leader.

pen·du·lous (pen'joo·lŭs), *adj.* 1. hanging loosely. 2. drooping.

pen·du·lum (pen'joo·lŭm), *n.* a body suspended from a fixed point so that it may swing back and forth under the forces of gravity and momentum.

pe·ne·plain, pe·ne·plane (pē'nĕ-plān), *n.* a land surface reduced to base level by erosion.

pen·e·tra·li·a (pen-ĕ-trā'li-ă), *n.pl.* 1. the innermost part of a temple, house, etc. 2. secrets; mysteries.

pen·e·trant (pen'ĕ-trănt), *adj.* penetrating; subtle; acute.

pen·e·trate (-trāt), *v.t.* -trat·ed, -trat·ing, 1. to pierce; enter into. 2. to permeate. 3. to affect deeply. 4. to reach the interior of. 5. to understand. **—pen'e·tra·ble,** *adj.* **—pen·e·tra'tion,** *n.*

pen·e·trat·ing (-trāt·ing), *adj.* 1. piercing; sharp. 2. acute; discerning. 3. that can penetrate. Also **pen'e·tra·tive** (-trāt-iv).

pen·guin (peng'gwin), *n.* any one of various flightless sea birds of the Southern Hemisphere, having webbed feet and paddlelike wings for swimming.

pen·i·cil·lin (pen-i-sil'in), *n.* any one of several antibiotic compounds obtained from certain common molds or made synthetically.

pen·in·su·la (pĕ·nin'sŭ·lă, 'syoo·), *n.* a portion of jutting land nearly surrounded by water and connected with the mainland by an isthmus. **—pen·in'su·lar,** *adj.*

pe·nis (pē'nis), *n., pl.* -nis·es, -nes ('nēz), the male organ of copulation. **—pe'nile** ('nīl), *adj.*

pen·i·tent (pen'i-tĕnt), *adj.* repentant: *n.* one who is penitent. **—pen'i·tence,** *n.* **—pen·i·ten'tial** (-ten'shăl), *adj.* **—pen'i·tent·ly,** *adv.*

pen·i·ten·ti·a·ry (pen-i-ten'shă-ri), *adj.* making one liable to imprisonment: *n., pl.* -ries, a State or Federal prison for persons convicted of serious offenses.

pea·knife (pen'nif), *n., pl.* -knives ('nīvz), a small pocketknife.

pen·man (pen'măn), *n., pl.* -men ('mĕn), 1. an author. 2. one skilled in penmanship.

pen·man·ship (-ship), *n.* the art or skill of handwriting.

pen name, a pseudonym.

pen·nant (pen'ănt), *n.* 1. any long, narrow strip of cloth, used for naval signaling, as a school banner, etc. 2. any similar flag symbolic of a championship in certain sports.

pen·nate (pen'āt), *adj.* same as **pinnate.**

pen·ni·less (pen'i-lis), *adj.* without money.

pen·non (pen'ŏn), *n.* a small, swallow-tailed flag or streamer.

pen·ny (pen'i), *n., pl.* -nies, 1. a coin of the United Kingdom, equal to *a)* 1/12 shilling. *b)* one 100th of a pound as of February, 1971. 2. a U.S. or Canadian cent.

penny arcade, a public amusement center with various coin-operated devices and machines.

penny pincher, a person who is very stingy. **— pen'ny-pinch·ing,** *n. & adj.*

pen·ny·roy·al (pen-i-roi'ăl), *n.* a heavily scented mint that yields an aromatic oil.

pen·ny·weight (pen'i-wāt), *n.* a unit of weight, equal to 1/20 ounce troy weight.

pen·ny·wise (pen'i-wīz'), *adj.* frugal only in small matters.

pe·nol·o·gy (pi-nol'ŏ-ji), *n.* the study of prison management and of the rehabilitation of prisoners. **—pe·nol'o·gist,** *n.*

pen·sile (pen'sil), *adj.* hanging.

pen·sion (pen'shŭn), *n.* a stated amount of money paid regularly to a retired or disabled person: *v.t.* to grant a pension to. **— pen'sion·er,** *n.*

pen·sion (pän-syön'), *n.* [French], a boarding house in continental Europe.

pen·sion·ar·y (pen'shŭn-er-i), *adj.* consisting of or maintained by a pension: *n., pl.* -ar·ies, a person receiving a pension.

pen·sive (pen'siv), *adj.* thoughtful. **—pen'sive·ly,** *adv.* **—pen'sive·ness,** *n.*

pent (pent), alternate past tense and past participle of **pen** (to shut up): *adj.* kept in; confined.

pen·ta-, a combining form meaning *five.*

pen·ta·cle (pen'tă·kl), *n.* a five-pointed star, formerly used in magic.

pen·tad ('tad), *n.* 1. the number five. 2. a group of five. 3. a period of five years.

pen·ta·dac·tyl (pen-tă-dak'tl), *adj.* having five fingers or toes.

pen·ta·gon (pen'tă·gon), *n.* 1. a plane figure of five sides and five angles. 2. [P-], a five-sided building housing the Defense Department, near Washington, D.C. **—pen·tag·o·nal** (pen-tag'ŏ-nl), *adj.*

pen·ta·he·dron (pen-tȧ-hē'dron), *n.* a solid figure having five surfaces. —**pen·ta·he'dral,** *adj.*

pen·tam·er·ous (pen-tam'ẽr-ŭs), *adj.* in *Biology,* consisting of five parts or divisions.

pen·tam·e·ter ('ē-tẽr), *n.* a line of verse containing five metrical feet.

Pen·ta·teuch (pen'tȧ-tōōk), *n.* the first five books of the Bible.

pen·tath·lon (pen-tath'lon), *n.* an athletic contest of five different events in each of which the contestants compete.

Pen·te·cost (pen'tĕ-kŏst), *n.* a Christian festival on the seventh Sunday after Easter.

Pen·te·cos·tal (pen-tĕ-kŏs'tl), *adj.* 1. of or pertaining to Pentecost. 2. denoting or of any one of various Protestant fundamentalist congregations that stress the influence of the Holy Spirit.

pent·house (pent'hous), *n.* an apartment or dwelling located on the roof of a building.

Pen·to·thal Sodium (pen'tȯ-thal), a yellowish powder injected intravenously as a general anesthetic: a trademark.

pent-up (pent'up'), *adj.* not expressed; confined; curbed.

pe·nu·che, pe·nu·chi (pȇ-nōō'chi), *n.* a fudgelike candy.

pe·nult (pȇ'nult), *n.* the next to the last syllable in a word. —**pe·nul·ti·mate** (pi-nul'ti-mit), *adj.*

pen·um·bra (pi-num'brȧ), *n., pl.* **-brae** ('brē), **-bras,** the partly lighted area surrounding the complete shadow of a body that is in eclipse.

pe·nu·ri·ous (pȇ-nyoor'i-ŭs), *adj.* 1. miserly; stingy. 2. needy; impoverished. —**pe·nu'ri·ous·ly,** *adv.* —**pe·nu'ri·ous·ness,** *n.*

pen·u·ry (pen'yū-ri), *n.* want of the necessities of life; poverty.

pe·on (pē'on), *n.* 1. in Latin America, a person of the laboring class. 2. a worker forced into servitude to repay a debt. —**pe'on·age,** *n.*

pe·o·ny (pē'ȯ-ni), *n., pl.* **-nies,** 1. a perennial plant of the buttercup family, often with double flowers of white, red, pink, or yellow. 2. the flower.

peo·ple (pē'pl), *n., pl.* **-ple;** for sense 1 **-ples,** 1. all the persons living in one country or under one government; race, nationality, etc. 2. persons having the same residence, profession, etc. 3. one's relatives; family. 4. the mass of persons without wealth, distinction, etc.; populace. 5. persons in general. 6. human beings, as distinct from lower animals: *v.t.* **-pled, -pling,** to populate.

pep (pep), *n.* [Informal], energy; vim: *v.t.* **pepped, pep'ping,** [Informal], to invigorate (with *up).* —**pep'py,** *adj.* **-pi·er, -pi·est.**

pe·po (pē'pō), *n., pl.* **-pos,** any fleshy gourd fruit with a hard rind, as a melon, squash, etc.

pep·per (pep'ẽr), *n.* 1. a hot pungent spice prepared from the ground berries of an East Indian plant. 2. any one of several varieties of the red pepper plant. 3. the fruit of any of these plants, varying in size, shape, color, and hotness: *v.t.* 1. to sprinkle with pepper. 2. to hit with small missiles.

pep·per·corn (-kôrn), *n.* the small, dried berry of the pepper plant, ground as a spice.

pepper mill, a utensil for grinding peppercorns.

pep·per·mint (-mint, -mĭnt), *n.* 1. an aromatic plant with lance-shaped leaves and white or purplish flowers. 2. the oil from this plant used as flavoring. 3. a candy with this flavoring.

pep·per·o·ni (pep-ĕ-rō'ni), *n., pl.* **-nis, -ni,** a hard, spicy, Italian sausage.

pepper pot, a West Indian stew of meat and vegetables, highly spiced.

pepper shaker, a container from which ground pepper is dispensed.

pepper tree, a South American evergreen tree, grown as a shade tree in mild climates.

pep·per·y (-i), *adj.* 1. of, like, or heavily seasoned with pepper. 2. stinging and fiery, as words. 3. sharp-tempered.

pep·sin (pep'sin), *n.* a digestive enzyme in the gastric juice that assists in the digestion of proteins.

pep·tic ('tik), *adj.* 1. of, pertaining to, or promoting digestion. 2. produced by digestive secretions.

pep·tone ('tōn), *n.* any one of a group of soluble protein compounds formed by the action of enzymes on proteins, as in digestion.

per (pûr), *prep.* 1. through; by means of. 2. for each. 3. [Informal], according to.

per-, a prefix signifying *through, throughout, thoroughly.*

per·ad·ven·ture (pûr-ȧd-ven'chẽr), *adv.* [Archaic], 1. possibly. 2. by chance: *n.* chance; doubt.

per·am·bu·late (pẽr-am'byoo-lāt), *v.t.* **-lat·ed, -lat·ing,** to walk over, around, etc., especially in inspecting: *v.i.* to stroll. —**per·am·bu·la'tion,** *n.*

per·am·bu·la·tor (-lāt-ẽr), *n.* [Chiefly British], a baby carriage.

per an·num (pẽr an'ŭm), annually.

per·cale (pẽr-kāl'), *n.* a closely woven cotton fabric, used for sheets, clothing, etc.

per cap·i·ta (pẽr kap'i-tȧ), for each person.

per·ceive (pẽr-sēv'), *v.t. & v.i.* **-ceived', -ceiv'ing,** 1. to obtain knowledge (of) through the senses. 2. to understand; observe. —**per·ceiv'a·ble,** *adj.* —**per·ceiv'a·bly,** *adv.*

per·cent (pẽr-sent'), *adv. & adj.* in, to, or for every hundred: *n.* [Informal], percentage.

per·cent·age ('ij), *n.* 1. a given amount in every hundred. 2. a portion; share. 3. [Informal], advantage; gain.

per·cen·tile (pẽr-sen'tĭl), *n.* in *Statistics,* a number that represents one of 100 equal divisions in a given series.

per·cept (pûr'sept), *n.* an impression of things received through the senses.

per·cep·ti·ble (pẽr-sep'ti-bl), *adj.* that may be perceived. —**per·cep'ti·bly,** *adv.*

per·cep·tion ('shŭn), *n.* 1. the act, state, or faculty of perceiving. 2. insight; intuition. 3. an idea, concept, etc. gained by perceiving. —**per·cep'tu·al** (-chōō-ȧl), *adj.*

per·cep·tive ('tiv), *adj.* 1. of or pertaining to perception. 2. quick in discerning.

perch (pûrch), *n., pl.* **perch, perch'es,** 1. a spiny-finned, freshwater, food fish. 2. any one of various similar or related fishes.

perch (pûrch), *n.* 1. a horizontal pole, branch, etc. on which birds roost. 2. any place for sitting or resting. 3. a measure of length, equal to 5.5 yards: *v.t. & v.i.* to rest or set on or as on a perch.

per-chance (pẽr-chans'), *adv.* perhaps.

Per-che-ron (pûr'chē-ron), *n.* any one of a breed of large draft horses from France.

per-chlo-rate (pẽr-klôr'āt), *n.* a salt of perchloric acid.

per-chlo-ric acid ('ĭk), a colorless liquid that is a strong oxidant and is explosively unstable under some conditions.

per-chlo-ride ('ĭd), *n.* any chloride having more chlorine than the usual chlorides of the same element.

per-cip-i-ent (pẽr-sip'ĭ-ènt), *adj.* perceiving: *n.* one who perceives. —**per-cip'i-ence,** *n.*

per-co-late (pûr'kô-lāt), *v.t.* -lat-ed, -lat-ing, to pass (a liquid) through small spaces; filter: *v.i.* to seep through a porous substance.

per-co-la-tor (-lāt-ẽr), *n.* 1. a thing that percolates. 2. a coffeepot in which boiling water is forced up a central tube and is repeatedly filtered down through ground coffee held in a perforated basket.

per-cuss (pẽr-kus'), *v.t.* to tap gently but firmly, as in medical diagnosis.

per-cus-sion (pẽr-kush'ŭn), *n.* 1. the collision of two bodies striking against one another. 2. the shock, vibration, noise, etc. produced by such a collision. 3. the impact of sound waves on the ear. 4. in *Medicine,* the gentle tapping of the chest, abdomen, etc. to determine the condition of internal parts by the resultant sound.

percussion cap, a paper or metal container holding an explosive charge.

percussion instrument, a musical instrument, as a drum, triangle, etc., that produces sound when struck.

per-cus-sion-ist (-ist), *n.* one who plays percussion instruments.

per di-em (dē'ĕm, dī'ĕm), [Latin], daily.

per-di-tion (pẽr-dish'ŭn), *n.* in *Theology,* 1. the loss of the soul. 2. same as hell.

per-du, per-due (pẽr-dōō'), *adj.* out of sight; concealed, as in ambush.

per-dure (pẽr-door'), *v.i.* -dured', -dur'ing, to continue long in existence. —**per-dur'a-ble,** *adj.*

père (per), *n.* [French], father.

per-e-gri-nate (per'ē-gri-nāt), *v.t.* -nat-ed, -nat-ing, to travel over or through: *v.i.* to journey or travel. —**per-e-gri-na'tion,** *n.* —**per-e-gri-na'tor,** *n.*

per-e-grine (per'ē-grin, -grēn), *adj.* wandering; migratory.

peregrine falcon, a large, swift, gray-and-white falcon, formerly much used in falconry.

per-emp-to-ry (pé-remp'tẽr-i), *adj.* 1. in *Law,* barring further action; final. 2. precluding discussion or hesitation, as a command. 3. imperious. —**per-emp'to-ri-ly,** *adv.*

per-en-ni-al (pē-ren'i-ăl), *adj.* 1. lasting through the whole year. 2. lasting a long time; perpetual. 3. denoting or of plants that have a life cycle of more than two years: *n.* a perennial plant. —**per-en'ni-al-ly,** *adv.*

per-fect (pûr'fĭkt), *adj.* 1. complete in every

way; without defect or blemish; flawless. 2. completely accurate. 3. pure; sheer. 4. most excellent; faultless. 5. in *Grammar,* of or pertaining to a verb form expressing action completed before a particular time: *v.t.* (pẽr-fekt'), 1. to make perfect. 2. to finish: *n.* 1. the perfect tense. 2. a verb form in this tense. —**per'fect-ly,** *adv.* —**per'fect-ness,** *n.*

per-fect-i-ble (pẽr-fek'tĭ-bl), *adj.* capable of being made perfect. —**per-fect-i-bil'i-ty,** *n.*

per-fec-tion ('shŭn), *n.* 1. the state of being perfect; supreme excellence. 2. the process or act of perfecting.

per-fec-tion-ism (-izm), *n.* 1. the theory that moral, religious, or social perfection can be attained by mortals. 2. excessive striving for perfection in performing a duty, task, etc. —**per-fec'tion-ist,** *n.*

per-fec-to (pẽr-fek'tō), *n., pl.* -tos, a medium-sized cigar tapering at both ends.

per-fer-vid (pẽr-fûr'vid), *adj.* extremely fervid; ardent.

per-fi-dy (pûr'fĭ-di), *n., pl.* -dies, the violation of trust; deliberate breach of faith. —**per-fid-i-ous** (pẽr-fid'i-ŭs), *adj.*

per-fo-rate (pûr'fô-rāt), *v.t. & v.i.* -rat-ed, -rat-ing, 1. to punch or bore a hole or holes through; penetrate. 2. to pierce with rows of holes, as between some postage stamps: *adj.* pierced with rows of holes: also **per'fo-rat-ed.** —**per-fo-ra'tion,** *n.*

per-force (pẽr-fôrs'), *adv.* by or through necessity; necessarily.

per-form (pẽr-fôrm'), *v.t.* 1. to do so as to carry out, complete, etc.; execute. 2. to fulfill (a duty, promise, etc.). 3. to give a public presentation of; to play (a composition, role, etc.): *v.i.* to carry out an action; especially to play a role, a musical work, etc. before an audience. —**per-form'er,** *n.*

per-form-ance (-fôr'mẽns), *n.* 1. the act of performing; execution. 2. the manner in which a machine operates or functions. 3. a deed or feat. 4. a presentation, as of a play, before an audience.

performing arts, arts, such as drama, presented in public.

per-fume (pẽr-fūm'), *v.t.* -fumed', -fum'ing, 1. to impregnate with a pleasant odor; scent. 2. to put perfume on: *n.* (pûr'fūm), 1. a pleasant scent; fragrance. 2. a substance that emits such an odor.

per-fum-er-y (pẽr-fūm'ẽr-i), *n., pl.* -ies, perfumes in general.

per-func-to-ry (pẽr-fungk'tẽr-i), *adj.* 1. done carelessly or negligently. 2. done routinely or indifferently. —**per-func'to-ri-ly,** *adv.* —**per-func'to-ri-ness,** *n.*

per-fuse (pẽr-fūz'), *v.t.* -fused', -fus'ing, 1. to sprinkle or suffuse with or as with a liquid. 2. to pour or spread (a liquid) over or through something. —**per-fu'sion,** *n.*

per-go-la (pûr'gô-lä), *n.* an arbor or latticework covered with climbing plants.

per-haps (pẽr-haps'), *adv.* possibly; maybe.

pe-ri (pir'i), *n.* 1. in *Persian Mythology,* a descendant of a fallen angel, excluded from paradise until penance has been performed. 2. a lovely girl or woman.

per-i-, a prefix meaning *around, about, enclosing, near.*

per-i-anth (per'i-anth), *n.* the floral envelope.

per-i-apt (-apt), *n.* same as **amulet.**

per-i-car-di-tis (per-i-kär-dīt'is), *n.* inflammation of the pericardium.

per-i-car-di-um (-kär'di-ŭm), *n., pl.* -di-a (-ă), the membrane that surrounds the heart. — **per-i-car'di-ac,** *adj.*

per-i-carp (per'i-kärp), *n.* in *Botany*, the wall of a ripened ovary. — **per-i-car'pi-al,** *adj.*

pe-ric-o-pe (pê-rik'ō-pi), *n.* a selection from a book; especially, same as **lection.**

per-i-cra-ni-um (per-i-krā'ni-ŭm), *n.* the membrane that surrounds the skull.

per-i-gee (per'i-jē), *n.* the point nearest the earth in the orbit of the moon or a satellite.

per-i-he-li-on (per-i-hē'li-ŏn), *n., pl.* -li-ons, -li-a (-ă), the point nearest the sun in the orbit of a planet, comet, or man-made satellite.

per-il (per'il), *n.* 1. exposure to injury; danger; jeopardy. 2. something that imperils; risk: *v.t.* -iled or -illed, -il-ing or -il-ling, to expose to danger.

per-il-ous (-ŭs), *adj.* full of peril; hazardous; dangerous.

pe-rim-e-ter (pê-rim'ê-tēr), *n.* 1. the outer boundary of a plane area. 2. the whole length of such a boundary. 3. in *military usage*, a boundary strip fortified to protect a position.

per-i-morph (per'i-môrf), *n.* a mineral that encloses a different mineral.

per-i-ne-um (per-i-nē'ŭm), *n., pl.* -ne'a ('ă), that part of the pelvic region that lies between the genitals and the rectum.

pe-ri-od (pir'i-ŏd), *n.* 1. the interval of time between recurring conditions or events. 2. a subdivision of a geologic era. 3. a length of time marked by certain activities, events, conditions, etc. 4. any set length of time, as the divisions of a school day, a game, etc. 5. the menses. 6. a completion or conclusion. 7. the pause in speaking or the punctuation mark (.) placed at the end of a declarative sentence. 8. the dot (.) after many abbreviations.

pe-ri-od-ic (pir-i-od'ik), *adj.* 1. of or pertaining to a period. 2. occurring at regular intervals. 3. intermittent.

pe-ri-od-i-cal ('i-kl), *adj.* 1. same as **periodic.** 2. published at regular intervals. 3. of or pertaining to a periodical: *n.* a publication issued periodically. —**pe-ri-od'i-cal-ly,** *adv.*

pe-ri-o-dic-i-ty (pir-i-ŏ-dis'i-ti), *n.* the state, quality, or fact of recurring at regular intervals.

per-i-o-don-tal (per-i-ŏ-don'tl), *adj.* of or pertaining to the bone and tissue surrounding and supporting the teeth.

per-i-pa-tet-ic (per-i-pă-tet'ik), *adj.* 1. [P-], of or pertaining to the philosophy of Aristotle who instructed his disciples while walking about the Lyceum. 2. moving from place to place; itinerant: *n.* 1. [P-], a disciple of Aristotle. 2. one given to walking about.

pe-riph-er-y (pê-rif'ēr-i), *n., pl.* -er-ies, 1. the circumference of a circle, ellipse, or similar figure. 2. the perimeter of a polygon. 3. the outermost confines of a region or area.

pe-riph-er-al (pê-rif'ēr-ăl), *adj.* 1. of or forming a periphery. 2. outer; external: *n.* a piece of equipment used with a computer to increase its functional range or efficiency, as a printer, disk, etc.—**pe-riph'er-al-ly,** *adv.*

pe-riph-ra-sis ('rä-sis), *n.* circumlocution; the use of many words to express but little. — **per-i-phras-tic** (per-i-fras'tik), *adj.*

pe-rique (pê-rēk'), *n.* a strong, black tobacco grown in Louisiana.

per-i-scope (per'i-skōp), *n.* an optical instrument containing a series of lenses and mirrors by which an observer can view objects, as from a submarine, not in his direct line of vision. —**per-i-scop'ic** (-skop'ik), *adj.*

per-ish (per'ish), *v.i.* 1. to die, especially in a violent or untimely way. 2. to be destroyed.

per-ish-a-ble (-ă-bl), *adj.* liable to perish, spoil, etc.: *n.* something, especially a food, liable to spoil. —**per-ish-a-bil'i-ty,** *n.*

pe-ris-so-dac-tyl (pê-ris-ô-dak'til), *adj.* having an odd number of toes on each foot: *n.* any one of a group of hoofed mammals with an odd number of toes, including the horses, tapirs, etc.

per-i-stal-sis (per-i-stŏl'sis, -stal'-), *n.* the contracting movements of the intestines by which their contents are forced onward. — **per-i-stal'tic,** *adj.*

per-i-style (per'i-stīl), *n.* an open court surrounded by a row of columns.

per-i-to-ne-um (per-it-n-ē'ŭm), *n.* the thin serous membrane that covers the abdominal viscera. —**per-i-to-ne'al,** *adj.*

per-i-to-ni-tis (-ī'tis), *n.* inflammation of the peritoneum.

per-i-wig (per'i-wig), *n.* a small wig.

per-i-win-kle (per'i-wing-kl), *n.* a perennial creeping plant with evergreen leaves.

per-i-win-kle (per'i-wing-kl), *n.* any one of several small marine snails.

per-jure (pūr'jēr), *v.t.* -jured, -jur-ing, to make (oneself) guilty of perjury.

per-ju-ry ('jēr-i), *n., pl.* -ries, the willful telling of a falsehood while under oath.

perk (pūrk), *v.t.* 1. to make trim or smart in appearance (often with *up*). 2. to lift (the head, ears, etc.) in a brisk or saucy manner (often with *up*). —**perk'y,** *adj.* **perk'i-er, perk'i-est.**

perk (pūrk), *v.t. & v.i.* [Informal], to percolate.

perk (pūrk), *n.* [Informal], a perquisite (sense 1).

per-lite (pūr'līt), *n.* a glassy volcanic rock.

per-ma-frost (pūr'mă-frŏst), *n.* subsoil permanently frozen.

per-ma-nent (pūr'mă-nĕnt), *adj.* lasting; durable; continuing for a long time. —**per'ma-nence,** *n.* —**per'ma-nent-ly,** *adv.*

permanent wave, a wave that is produced in the hair by heat or chemicals and lasts a long time.

per-me-a-ble (pūr'mi-ă-bl), *adj.* that may be passed through. —**per-me-a-bil'i-ty,** *n.*

per-me-ate (-āt), *v.t. & v.i.* -at-ed, -at-ing, to penetrate or pass through; diffuse. —**per-me-a'tion,** *n.*

Per-mi-an (pūr'mi-ăn), *n.* the last period of the Paleozoic Era, in which reptilian life in-

---

ô in dragon, ōō in crude, oo in wool, u in cup, ū in cure, ū in turn, ŭ in focus, oi in boy, ou in house, th in thin, th in sheathe, g in get, j in joy, y in yet.

creased and major mountain building occurred.

per·mis·si·ble (pẽr-mis′ĭ-bl), *adj.* that may be permitted.

per·mis·sion (-mish′ŭn), *n.* the act of permitting; leave; license.

per·mis·sive (-mis′ĭv), *adj.* 1. granting permission or license. 2. tolerant; indulgent. —per·mis′sive·ly, *adv.* —per·mis′sive·ness, *n.*

per·mit (pẽr-mit′), *v.t.* -mit′ted, -mit′ting, 1. to consent to; tolerate. 2. to grant liberty to: *v.i.* to provide opportunity: *n.* (pũr′mit), a written document giving permission to do something; license; warrant. —per·mit′ter, *n.*

per·mit (pũr′mit), *n.* an Atlantic pompano.

per·mu·ta·tion (pũr-myoo-tā′shŭn), *n.* 1. a complete transformation. 2. any one of the arrangements of a group of things in a particular order.

per·ni·cious (pẽr-nish′ŭs), *adj.* highly injurious or hurtful; destructive; fatal. —per·ni′cious·ly, *adv.* —per·ni′cious·ness, *n.*

per·nick·et·y (pẽr-nik′ĕ-ti), *adj.* same as per·snickety.

per·o·rate (per′ŏ-rāt), *v.i.* -rat·ed, -rat·ing, 1. to speak at length; deliver a bombastic oration. 2. to conclude a speech; sum up. —per·o·ra′tion, *n.*

per·ox·ide (pẽ-rok′sīd), *n.* an oxide containing a large proportion of oxygen; especially, a compound, as hydrogen peroxide, in which two oxygen atoms are joined by a single bond.

per·pend (pũr′pĕnd), *n.* a stone built through a wall as a binder, jutting out on either side: also per′pent (′pĕnt).

per·pen·dic·u·lar (pũr-pĕn-dik′yŭ-lẽr), *adj.* 1. standing at right angles to a given line or plane. 2. perfectly upright; vertical: *n.* a line or plane perpendicular to another line or plane.

per·pe·trate (pũr′pĕ-trāt), *v.t.* -trat·ed, -trat·ing, 1. to commit (a crime). 2. to perform; carry out (a deception). —per·pe·tra′tion, *n.* —per′pe·tra·tor, *n.*

per·pet·u·al (pẽr-pech′oo-wǎl), *adj.* 1. never ceasing; constant. 2. enduring permanently or for a long time. —per·pet′u·al·ly, *adv.*

per·pet·u·ate (-wāt), *v.t.* -at·ed, -at·ing, to make perpetual; preserve from extinction or oblivion. —per·pet′u·a′tion, *n.*

per·pe·tu·i·ty (pũr-pĕ-tōō′ĭ-ti), *n., pl.* -ties, 1. the state or quality of being perpetual. 2. endless duration; eternity.

per·plex (pẽr-pleks′), *v.t.* 1. to make (something) difficult to understand. 2. to make (a person) puzzled, embarrassed, or confused. —per·plex′ing, *adj.* —per·plex′i·ty, *n., pl.* -ties.

per·qui·site (pũr′kwi-zit), *n.* 1. a gift or payment received in addition to regular wages or salary. 2. a tip. 3. a privilege claimed as a right; prerogative.

per·ron (per′ŏn), *n.* an outside staircase leading to a platform at a building entrance.

per·ry (per′i), *n.* the fermented juice of pears.

per se (pũr sē′, sā′), [Latin], in or by itself.

per·se·cute (pũr′sĕ-kūt), *v.t.* -cut·ed, -cut·ing, 1. to harass or ill-treat, especially for religious or racial reasons. 2. to annoy persistently. —per·se·cu′tion, *n.* —per′se·cu·tor, *n.*

per·se·vere (pũr-sĕ-vir′), *v.i.* -vered′, -ver′ing, to persist in any enterprise, task, etc. against obstacles, delays, etc.; continue steadfastly. —per·se·ver′ance, *n.*

Per·sian (pũr′zhǎn, ′shǎn), *adj.* same as Iranian: *n.* 1. same as Iranian (n. 1). 2. the Iranian language of Iran.

Persian cat, a type of domestic cat having long, silky fur.

Persian lamb, the pelt of karakul lambs.

per·si·flage (pũr′si-fläzh), *n.* foolish or flippant speech or writing; banter.

per·sim·mon (pẽr-sim′ŏn), *n.* 1. an American hardwood tree with plumlike fruit. 2. the fruit.

per·sist (pẽr-sist′, -zist′), *v.i.* 1. to continue steadily in any course undertaken, especially against obstacles and difficulties. 2. to repeat insistently. 3. to last; endure; remain.

per·sist·ent (-sis′tĕnt, -zis′-), *adj.* 1. continuing, especially against obstacles, interference, etc. 2. lasting continuously. 3. insistently repeated. —per·sist′ence, *n.*

per·snick·e·ty (pẽr-snik′ĕ-ti), *adj.* [Informal], 1. very attentive to details. 2. fussily particular; overly fastidious.

per·son (pũr′sn), *n.* 1. a human being. 2. an individual with his unique personality; self. 3. the human body. 4. any individual or corporation having certain legal rights. 5. in *Grammar*, any one of three particular pronoun forms and corresponding verb inflections: see first person, second person, third person. 6. in *Theology*, any one of the three individual entities, Father, Son, and Holy Spirit, of the triune Godhead.

per·son·a·ble (pũr′sŏn-ǎ-bl), *adj.* attractive in appearance and personality.

per·son·age (-ij), *n.* a person, especially one of distinction; notable.

per·son·al (-ǎl), *adj.* 1. of or pertaining to persons or human beings. 2. of or peculiar to a particular person; private. 3. of or pertaining to the body or external appearance. 4. done in person. 5. directed at the character, personality, etc. of a particular individual. 6. denoting person (sense 5). 7. in *Law*, of property that is movable: *n.* an item or advertisement in a newspaper relating to a personal matter.

personal effects, personal belongings.

personal equation, disparity in reaction time, judgment, etc. between individuals or in relation to a standard.

per·son·al·i·ty (pũr-sŏ-nal′ĭ-ti), *n., pl.* -ties, 1. the state or quality of being a person. 2. those qualities that distinguish the individual as a person. 3. a notable person. 4. *pl.* disparaging remarks aimed at an individual.

per·son·al·ize (pũr′sn-ǎ-līz), *v.t.* -ized, -iz·ing, 1. to take (a retort, observation, etc.) personally. 2. to have marked with one's name or initials.

per·son·al·ly (-li), *adv.* 1. in person. 2. to one's way of thinking. 3. as an individual. 4. as if aimed at oneself.

per·son·al·ty (-ǎl-ti), *n., pl.* -ties, personal property.

per·so·na non gra·ta (pẽr-sō′nǎ non grät′ǎ,

grāt'ā), [Latin], an unacceptable or unwelcome person.

per·son·ate (pûr'sō-nāt), v.t. -at·ed, -at·ing, 1. to act a part; portray. 2. in *Law*, to assume the character of for fraudulent purposes; impersonate.

per·son·i·fi·ca·tion (pēr-son-i-fi-kā'shŭn), n. 1. the act of personifying or state of being personified. 2. a figure of speech endowing animals, plants, objects, or abstractions with human attributes or form. 3. a person or thing regarded as the embodiment of a certain quality or idea.

per·son·i·fy (pēr-son'i-fī), v.t. -fied, -fy·ing, 1. to think of or represent (an object or an abstraction) as a person. 2. to embody; typify.

per·son·nel (pûr-sō-nel'), n. 1. persons employed in any work, service, business, etc. 2. an administrative department concerned with these persons.

per·spec·tive (pēr-spek'tiv), adj. 1. of perspective. 2. drawn in accordance with perspective: n. 1. the art of representing objects and showing depth relationships on a plane surface. 2. the effect of distance and depth upon the appearance of objects to normal vision. 3. the ability to see things in their true relationships.

per·spi·ca·cious (pûr-spi-kā'shŭs), adj. acutely perceptive; discerning. —per·spi·cac'i·ty (-kas'i-ti), n.

per·spic·u·ous (pēr-spik'yoo-wŭs), adj. easily understood; clear. —per·spi·cu·i·ty (pûr-spi-kū'i-ti), n.

per·spi·ra·tion (pûr-spi-rā'shŭn), n. 1. saline moisture excreted by the pores of the skin; sweat. 2. the act of sweating.

per·spire (pēr-spīr'), v.i. -spired', -spir'ing, to excrete (saline moisture) through the pores of the skin; sweat.

per·suade (pēr-swād'), v.t. -suad'ed, -suad'ing, 1. to influence (someone) by argument, advice, entreaty, etc.; win over. 2. to cause (someone) to believe something; convince. —per·sua·si·bil'i·ty, n.

per·sua·sion (pēr-swā'zhŭn), n. 1. the act of persuading or the state of being persuaded. 2. the ability to persuade. 3. settled belief. 4. a particular sect, religious belief, system of religion, etc.

per·sua·sive ('siv), adj. having the power to persuade. —per·sua'sive·ly, adv. —per·sua'sive·ness, n.

pert (pûrt), adj. saucy; forward.

per·tain (pēr-tān'), v.i. 1. to belong; be associated. 2. to have reference; be related. 3. to be fitting.

per·ti·na·cious (pûr-ti-nā'shŭs), adj. 1. unyielding; obstinate. 2. tenacious; resolute. —per·ti·nac'i·ty (-nas'i-ti), n.

per·ti·nent (pûr'tn-ĕnt), adj. fitting or appropriate; relevant. —per'ti·nence, n.

per·turb (pēr-tûrb'), v.t. 1. to agitate; disturb greatly. 2. to confuse; unsettle. 3. in *Astronomy*, to cause an irregularity in the movement of (a heavenly body) in its orbit because of the attraction of one or more bodies beyond its orbit. —per·tur·ba'tion, n.

per·tus·sis (pēr-tus'is), n. same as whooping cough.

pe·ruke (pē-rōōk'), n. same as periwig.

pe·rus·al (pē-rōō'zl), n. the act of perusing.

pe·ruse (pē-rōōz'), v.t. -rused', -rus'ing, 1. to read with care and attention; study. 2. to read.

Pe·ru·vi·an bark (pē-rōō'vi-ăn), same as cinchona (sense 2).

per·vade (pēr-vād'), v.t. -vad'ed, -vad'ing, to permeate; extend or be diffused all over. —per·va'sive (-vā'siv), adj.

per·verse (pēr-vûrs'), adj. 1. turned away from what is right or proper. 2. obstinate; stubborn. 3. contrary; petulant. —per·verse'ly, adv. —per·verse'ness, per·ver'si·ty, n.

per·ver·sion (pēr-vûr'zhŭn), n. 1. the act of perverting or the state of being perverted. 2. any aberrant sexual act. —per·ver'sive ('siv), adj.

per·vert (-vûrt'), v.t. 1. to turn from the true end or proper purpose; corrupt. 2. to misuse. 3. to misapply. 4. to debase: n. (pûr'vērt), one who practices sexual perversion.

per·vert·ed (-vûr'tid), adj. 1. turned from the proper course; corrupted. 2. of or practicing sexual perversion. 3. misconstrued; distorted.

per·vi·ous (pûr'vi-ŭs), adj. 1. admitting passage; permeable. 2. open to ideas, changes, etc.

pe·sade (pē-säd', -zad'), n. in *Horsemanship*, the act or position of a horse when rearing.

pe·se·ta (pē-sāt'ä), n. the monetary unit and a coin of Spain.

pes·ky (pes'ki), adj. -ki·er, -ki·est, [Informal], troublesome; annoying. —pes'ki·ness, n.

pe·so (pā'sō), n., pl. -sos (-'sōz), the monetary unit and a coin of several Spanish-speaking countries.

pes·sa·ry (pes'ēr-i), n., pl. -ries, a device worn in the vagina to support the uterus or prevent conception.

pes·si·mism (pes'i-mizm), n. 1. in *Philosophy*, the doctrine that the present state of existence is essentially evil. 2. the tendency to expect the worst possible outcome. —pes'si·mist, n. —pes·si·mis'tic, adj.

pest (pest), n. 1. [Now Rare], a fatal epidemic disease; plague. 2. a person or thing that is annoying or troublesome; nuisance. 3. an animal or plant that is destructive or is harmful to man.

pes·ter (pes'tēr), v.t. to annoy; bother.

pest·hole (pest'hōl), n. a place subject to or infested with an epidemic disease.

pes·ti·cide (pes'ti-sīd), n. any one of various chemicals used to kill pests, as insects, rodents, weeds, etc.

pes·tif·er·ous (pes-tif'ēr-ŭs), adj. 1. originally, carrying disease or infected with disease. 2. injurious; morally evil. 3. [Informal], mischievous; annoying.

pes·ti·lence (pes'ti-ĕns), n. 1. any contagious or infectious disease that is usually fatal and often epidemic, as bubonic plague. 2. anything considered to be an evil or a harmful influence.

pes·ti·lent (-ĕnt), adj. 1. likely to result in death; fatal. 2. noxious to morals, society, etc.; pernicious. 3. annoying; irritating.

---

pes·ti·len·tial (pes-tǐ-len'shŭl), *adj.* 1. of, pertaining to, or causing pestilence or infection. 2. like a pestilence; deadly. 3. pernicious; destructive.

pes·tle (pes'l), *n.* a club-shaped instrument for pounding or grinding substances in a mortar: *v.t. & v.i.* -tled, -tling, to pound, pulverize, etc. with or as with a pestle.

pet (pet), *n.* 1. an animal that is tame and is kept for companionship or for pleasure. 2. a person who is treated with unusual kindness or indulgence; favorite: *adj.* 1. kept as a pet. 2. particularly cherished. 3. expressing affection: *v.t.* pet'ted, pet'ting, 1. to pat or stroke gently; fondle. 2. to indulge; pamper: *v.i.* [Informal], to kiss, caress, etc. in making love.

pet (pet), *n.* a peevish or sulky state.

pet·al (pet'l), *n.* any one of the parts, or leaves, of a corolla of a flower. —**pet'aled**, ('ld), *adj.*

pet·al·oid (-oid), *adj.* in Botany, resembling a petal.

pe·tard (pi-tärd'), *n.* 1. a bell-shaped metal case containing explosives, formerly used in warfare to break down a wall, gate, door, etc. 2. a kind of firecracker.

pet·cock (pet'käk), *n.* a small valve or faucet for draining pipes, boilers, etc.

Pe·ter (pēt'ẽr), *n.* either of two books of the New Testament, I Peter and II Peter.

pe·ter (pēt'ẽr), *v.i.* [Informal], 1. to become exhausted (with *out*). 2. to become gradually smaller, less abundant, etc. and then cease (with *out*).

pet·i·ole (pet'i-ōl), *n.* in Botany, the stalk connecting a leaf to the stem.

pet·it (pet'i), *adj.* in Law, lesser; minor.

pe·tite (pe-tēt'), *adj.* small and trim of figure: said of a woman or girl.

pe·tit four (pet'i fôr'), *pl.* pe·tits fours, pe·tit fours (pet'i fôrz'), a small cake decorated and frosted.

pe·ti·tion (pē-tish'ŭn), *n.* 1. an earnest supplication or request to a deity or superior authority; prayer; entreaty. 2. a formal written document containing such a request, often supported by many signers and directed to a particular person or group. 3. in Law, a formal written plea asking for a specific action by a court: *v.t.* 1. to request formally. 2. to solicit; ask for: *v.i.* to make an entreaty. —**pe·ti'tion·ar·y**, *adj.* —**pe·ti'tion·er**, *n.*

petit jury, a jury of twelve citizens chosen to hear the evidence and reach a verdict in a court trial.

pet·rel (pet'rẽl), *n.* any one of numerous small oceanic birds with webbed feet, long pointed wings, and oily plumage, seldom found on shore.

pet·ri·fac·tion (pet-rǐ-fak'shŭn), *n.* 1. the process of petrifying. 2. the state of being petrified. 3. something petrified. Also **pet·ri·fi·ca'tion** (-fi-kā'shŭn). —**pet·ri·fac'tive**, *adj.*

pet·ri·fy (pet'rǐ-fī), *v.t.* -fied, -fy·ing, 1. to change (organic matter) into a stony substance by replacing the original structures

with minerals, as silica. 2. to make rigid or stonelike; harden. 3. to stun or stupefy, as with fear.

petro-, a combining form meaning *rock, stone*.

pet·ro·chem·i·cal (pet-rō-kem'i-kl), *n.* any chemical derived from petroleum or natural gas. —**pet·ro·chem'is·try** ('is-tri), *n.*

pet·ro·dol·lars (pe-trō-dol'ẽrs), *n.* revenue from the sale of petroleum.

pet·ro·glyph (pet'rō-glif), *n.* a carving or inscription on rock. —**pe·trog·ly·phy** (pi-trog'li-fi), *n.*

pe·trog·ra·phy (pi-trog'rǎ-fi), *n.* the description and classification of rocks. —**pe·trog'ra·pher**, *n.*

pet·rol (pet'rŏl), *n.* British term for gasoline.

pe·tro·la·tum (pet-rō-lāt'ŭm), *n.* an oily, jellylike substance consisting of various hydrocarbons obtained from petroleum and used as a base in ointments, lubricants, etc.

pe·trol·e·um (pē-trōl'i-ŭm), *n.* an oily, flammable liquid mixture of hydrocarbons, yellow to black in color, found naturally in certain rock formations and distilled to yield paraffin, kerosine, benzine, naphtha, gasoline, fuel oil, etc.

pe·trol·o·gy (pi-trol'ŏ-ji), *n.* the study of the origin, structure, composition, and alteration of rocks. —**pe·trol'o·gist**, *n.*

PET scan (pet), a diagnostic X-raying of the metabolism of the body, esp. the brain, using many single-plane X-rays (*tomograms*) and radioactive tracers.

pet·ti·coat (pet'i-kōt), *n.* a woman's loose underskirt: *adj.* of or by women.

pet·ti·fog·ger (pet'i-fog-ẽr), *n.* 1. a lawyer who practices in petty cases; especially one who uses unscrupulous methods and trickery in his practice. 2. a trickster. 3. a quibbler. —**pet'ti·fog**, *v.i.* -fogged, -fog·ging.

pet·tish (pet'ish), *adj.* fretful; petulant. —**pet'·tish·ly**, *adv.* —**pet'tish·ness** *n.*

pet·ty ('i), *adj.* -ti·er, -ti·est, 1. trifling; small; insignificant. 2. narrow-minded; mean. 3. low in rank; subordinate. —**pet'ti·ly**, *adv.* —**pet'ti·ness**, *n.*

petty cash, a small fund of cash for incidentals, as in an office.

petty officer, a noncommissioned officer in the navy.

pet·u·lant (pech'oo-lãnt), *adj.* peevish; capricious; irritable. —**pet'u·lance**, **pet'u·lan·cy**, *n.* —**pet'u·lant·ly**, *adv.*

pe·tu·ni·a (pē-tōōn'yà), *n.* 1. any one of various ornamental plants native to South America, with funnel-shaped flowers. 2. the flower.

pew (pū), *n.* any of the backed benches placed in rows in a church for the congregation.

pe·wit (pē'wit), *n.* same as **lapwing**.

pew·ter (pūt'ẽr), *n.* 1. a silver-gray alloy of tin with antimony, copper, lead, etc. 2. pewter articles collectively.

pey·o·te (pā-ōt'i), *n.* same as **mescal** (sense 3).

pha·e·ton (fā'ĕt-n), *n.* 1. an open, four-wheeled carriage. 2. an early kind of open automobile.

phag·o·cyte (fag'ŏ-sīt), *n.* a leukocyte that devours hurtful bacteria in the human body.

---

a in cap, ā in cane, ä in father, à in abet, e in met, ē in be, ẽ in baker, ĕ in regent, i in pit, ī in fine, ĭ in manifest, o in hot, ô in horse, ō in bone,

phal-ange (fal'ănj, fāl'-), *n.* same as phalanx (sense 3).

pha-lan-ger (fă-lan'jĕr), *n.* any one of a number of Australian marsupials with a long prehensile tail.

pha-lanx (fā'langks), *n., pl.* -lanx-es or pha-lan-ges (fă-lan'jēz), 1. in ancient Greece, a heavily armed body of infantry drawn up in close, deep ranks. 2. any close compact body. 3. *pl.* phalanges, in *Anatomy*, any bone of a finger or toe.

phal-a-rope (fal'ă-rōp), *n.* any of several small wading birds of fresh and salt waters, having lobed feet for swimming.

phal-lus (fal'ŭs), *n., pl.* -li (ī), -lus-es, a representation of the penis as a symbol of generative power. —phal'lic, *adj.*

phan-er-o-gam (fan'ĕr-ō-gam), *n.* any seed plant or flowering plant.

phan-tasm (fan'tazm), *n.* 1. an illusory vision having no reality; specter. 2. a misleading likeness.

phan-tas-ma-go-ri-a (fan-taz-mă-gôr'i-ă), *n.* 1. an early kind of magic-lantern show, producing optical illusions in which objects appear to dwindle into the distance, rush forward, blend together, increase in size, etc. 2. a continuously shifting sequence of figures or images, as seen in a dream.

phan-ta-sy (fan'tă-si), *n., pl.* -sies, same as fantasy.

phan-tom (fan'tŏm), 1. an apparition; ghost; vision. 2. an image existing only in the mind; illusion: *adj.* of or like a phantom.

Phar-aoh (fer'ō), *n.* the title of the rulers of ancient Egypt.

Phar-i-sa-ic (far-i-sā'ik), *adj.* 1. of, pertaining to, or characteristic of the Pharisees. 2. [p-], formally religious; sanctimonious. 3. [p-], hypocritical. Also **phar-i-sa'i-cal.**

Phar-i-sa-ism (fer'i-sā-izm), *n.* 1. the beliefs and practices of the Pharisees. 2. [p-], pharisaic behavior; sanctimoniousness.

Phar-i-see (fer'i-sē), *n.* 1. any member of an ancient Jewish sect, characterized by strict observance of the letter of the law. 2. [p-], a sanctimonious hypocrite.

phar-ma-ceu-ti-cal (fär-mă-sōōt'i-kl), *adj.* 1. of pharmacy or pharmacists. 2. of or by drugs. Also **phar-ma-ceu'tic.** *n.* a pharmaceutical product or preparation.

phar-ma-ceu-tics (-iks), *n.* same as pharmacy (sense 1).

phar-ma-cist (fär'mă-sist), *n.* a person skilled in pharmacy; druggist.

phar-ma-co-dy-nam-ics (fär-mă-kō-dī-nam'iks), *n.* that branch of pharmacology that deals with the effects of drugs on the human system.

phar-ma-col-o-gy (fär-mă-kol'ō-ji), *n.* the science that treats of drugs and medicines, their composition, nature, administration, and effects. —phar-ma-co-log'i-cal (-kō-loj'i-kl), *adj.* —phar-ma-col'o-gist, *n.*

phar-ma-co-pe-ia, phar-ma-co-poe-ia (fär-mă-kō-pē'ă), *n.* an official publication containing a list of medicinal drugs together with articles describing their composition, uses, side effects, etc.

phar-ma-cy (fär'mă-si), *n., pl.* -cies, 1. the art or profession of preparing and dispensing drugs. 2. a place where drugs are sold; drugstore.

pha-ros (fer'os), *n.* a lighthouse or beacon light.

pha-ryn-ge-al (fă-rin'ji-ăl), *adj.* of, pertaining to, or located in the region of the pharynx: also **pha-ryn'gal** (-ring'găl).

phar-yn-gi-tis (fer-in-jīt'is), *n.* inflammation of the pharynx; sore throat.

phar-yn-gol-o-gy (fer-ing-gol'ō-ji), *n.* the branch of medical science that treats of the pharynx and its diseases.

pha-ryn-go-scope (fă-ring'gō-skōp), *n.* an instrument for viewing the pharynx. —phar-yn-gos-co-py (fer-ing-gos'kō-pi), *n.*

phar-ynx (fer'ingks), *n., pl.* phar'ynx-es, pha-ryn-ges (fă-rin'jēz), the muscular and membranous sac of the digestive tract extending from mouth and nasal cavities to the larynx and esophagus.

phase (fāz), *n.* 1. a recurring change in the illumination of the moon or a planet. 2. an aspect or side.

phase-out (fāz'out), *n.* a gradual ending; a closing out.

pheas-ant (fez'nt), *n.* 1. a gallinaceous bird with brilliant plumage and a long tail, hunted as game. 2. any one of various birds resembling the pheasant, as the ruffed grouse.

phe-nac-e-tin (fi-nas'ĕ-tin), *n.* same as aceto-phenetidin.

phen-a-zine (fen'ă-zēn), *n.* a yellowish crystalline substance that forms the basis of many dyestuffs.

phe-nix (fē'niks), *n.* same as phoenix.

phe-no-bar-bi-tal (fē-nō-bär'bi-tôl), *n.* a white crystalline compound used in medicine as a sedative and hypnotic.

phe-nol (fē'nōl, 'nŏl), *n.* 1. a colorless, crystalline substance obtained by distillation from several organic materials, as coal tar and wood, and used in making explosives, synthetic resins, etc.: it is a powerful, caustic poison and its aqueous solution, popularly called carbolic acid, is used as an antiseptic. 2. any one of a group of hydroxyl derivatives of benzene.

phe-nom-e-nal (fi-nom'ĕ-nl), *adj.* 1. of or like a phenomenon. 2. extraordinary; remarkable. —phe-nom'e-nal-ly, *adv.*

phe-nom-e-nal-ism (-izm), *n.* the metaphysical doctrine that there is no knowledge except through phenomena or no reality except that of phenomena. —phe-nom'e-nal-ist, *n.*

phe-nom-e-nol-o-gy (fi-nom-ĕ-nol'ō-ji), *n.* 1. the scientific study of phenomena, without regard to metaphysics. 2. the branch of metaphysics that treats of phenomena as distinguished from reality.

phe-nom-e-non (fi-nom'ĕ-non, -nŏn), *n., pl.* -na (-nă), -nons, 1. any fact, occurrence, or experience observable to the senses. 2. the appearance of something, as distinguished from reality or the thing itself. 3. something extraordinary or wonderful. 4. [Informal], a remarkable person; prodigy.

phen-yl (fen'il, fē'nil), *n.* a monovalent radical that forms the base of phenol, aniline, benzene, etc.

phen·yl·ene (fen'i-lēn, fē'ni-), *n.* a bivalent radical occurring in some derivatives of benzene.

phew (fū, fyoo), *interj.* an expression of disgust, relief, tiredness, etc.

phi (fī, fē), *n.* the 21st letter of the Greek alphabet.

phi·al (fī'ăl), *n.* a small glass bottle; vial.

phi·lan·der (fi-lan'dēr), *v.i.* to make love lightly or insincerely: said of a man. —**phi·lan'der·er,** *n.*

phil·an·throp·ic (fil-ăn-throp'ik), *adj.* loving mankind; benevolent: also **phil·an·throp'i·cal.** —**phil·an·throp'i·cal·ly,** *adv.*

phi·lan·thro·pist (fi-lan'thrŏ-pist), *n.* one who practices philanthropy, especially a wealthy person who provides endowments, etc.

phi·lan·thro·py (-pi), *n.* 1. love of mankind; benevolence, especially as shown through gifts to institutions, etc. 2. *pl.* -**pies,** *a)* a philanthropic action, gift, etc.; *b)* a philanthropic institution, etc.

phi·lat·e·ly (fi-lat'l-i), *n.* the systematic collection of postage stamps, stamped envelopes, etc., usually as a hobby. —**phil·a·tel·ic** (fil-ă-tel'ik), *adj.* —**phi·lat'e·list,** *n.*

-phile (fīl, fil), a combining form meaning *one who loves.*

Phi·le·mon (fi-lē'mŏn, fī-), *n.* a book of the New Testament.

phil·har·mon·ic (fil-här-mon'ik, fil-ēr-), *adj.* loving music: *n.* 1. a society organized to sponsor a symphony orchestra. 2. [Informal], an orchestra or concert sponsored by such a society.

Phi·lip·pi·ans (fi-lip'i-ănz), *n.* a book of the New Testament.

phi·lip·pic (fi-lip'ik), *n.* a speech of bitter invective.

Phil·ip·pine (fil'i-pēn), *adj.* of the Philippine Islands, a group of islands in the southwest Pacific.

Phil·is·tine (fil'is-tēn, fi-lis'tin), *n.* 1. a member of a non-Semitic people who lived in Philistia, an ancient country at the eastern end of the Mediterranean. 2. [p-], an uncultured person or one of narrow or conventional views: *adj.* [p-], uncultured; smugly conventional; narrow-minded. —**phil'is·tin·ism,** *n.*

phil·o·den·dron (fil-ŏ-den'drŏn), *n.* a tropical American vine with heart-shaped leaves.

phi·log·y·ny (fi-loj'i-ni), *n.* fondness for or love of women. —**phi·log'y·nist,** *n.* —**phi·log'y·nous,** *adj.*

phi·lol·o·gy (fi-lol'ŏ-ji), *n.* 1. originally, the love of learning or of literature. 2. the study of literature to determine meanings, authenticity, etc. 3. an earlier term for **linguistics.** —**phil·o·log·i·cal** (fil-ŏ-loj'i-kl), *adj.* —**phi·lol'o·gist,** *n.*

phil·o·mel (fil'ŏ-mel), *n.* [Poetic], the nightingale.

phil·o·pro·gen·i·tive (fil-ŏ-prŏ-jen'i-tiv), *adj.* loving one's offspring.

phi·los·o·pher (fi-los'ŏ-fēr), *n.* 1. a student of philosophy. 2. one noted for calm judgment and practical wisdom.

philosophers' (or **philosopher's**) **stone,** an imaginary stone or substance believed to have the magic power of transmuting the baser metals into gold.

phil·o·soph·ic (fil-ŏ-sof'ik), *adj.* 1. of or pertaining to philosophers or philosophy. 2. rational, wise, calm, etc. Also **phil·o·soph'i·cal.** —**phil·o·soph'i·cal·ly,** *adv.*

phi·los·o·phism (fi-los'ŏ-fizm), *n.* sophistry; spurious or unsound philosophy.

phi·los·o·phize (-fīz), *v.i.* -**phized,** -**phiz·ing,** 1. to reason like a philosopher. 2. to moralize or speculate in a superficially philosophical manner. —**phi·los'o·phiz·er,** *n.*

phi·los·o·phy (-fi), *n., pl.* -**phies,** 1. study of the principles underlying knowledge, thought, conduct, and the nature of the universe. 2. the basic principles or laws of a specific field of knowledge. 3. a particular philosophic system. 4. calmness of temper; composure.

phil·ter, phil·tre (fil'tēr), *n.* a magic charm or potion to arouse sexual love.

phi·mo·sis (fī-mō'sis), *n.* an abnormal condition in which the foreskin of the penis is so tight that it cannot be drawn back over the glans.

phiz (fiz), *n.* [Old Slang], 1. the face. 2. a facial expression.

phle·bi·tis (fli-bit'is), *n.* inflammation of a vein.

phleb·o-, a combining form meaning *vein.*

phleb·o·scle·ro·sis (fleb-ŏ-skli-rō'sis), *n.* hardening of the walls of the veins.

phle·bot·o·my (fli-bot'ŏ-mi), *n.* the act or practice of drawing off blood as a therapeutic measure.

phlegm (flem), *n.* 1. thick mucus secreted in the air passages and discharged from the throat, as during a cold. 2. sluggishness; dullness. 3. calmness.

phleg·mat·ic (fleg-mat'ik), *adj.* sluggish; dull; stolid. —**phleg·mat'i·cal·ly,** *adv.*

phlo·em (flō'em), *n.* the vascular tissue through which food is conducted in a plant.

phlo·gis·tic (flō-gis'tik), *adj.* 1. of phlogiston. 2. in *Medicine,* inflammatory.

phlo·gis·ton ('ton, 'tŏn), *n.* a supposed principle of fire or of combustible materials; imaginary element formerly believed to start fires.

phlox (floks), *n.* a North American plant with purple, white, or red flowers.

-phobe (fōb), a suffix meaning *one who hates or fears.*

pho·bi·a (fō'bi-ă), *n.* an unreasonable and unwarranted fear or dread of a particular thing or situation. —**pho'bic,** *adj.*

-pho·bi·a (fō'bi-ă), a combining form meaning *hatred, fear.*

Phoe·be (fē'bi), *n.* 1. the moon personified. 2. [p-], a small American flycatcher.

Phoe·bus (fē'bŭs), *n.* the sun personified.

Phoe·ni·cian (fŏ-nish'ŭn, -nē'shŭn), *adj.* of or pertaining to Phoenicia, an ancient region at the eastern end of the Mediterranean: *n.* a native of Phoenicia.

phoe·nix (fē'niks), *n.* a mythical, beautiful bird that lived for hundreds of years, consumed itself in fire, and rose renewed from the ashes: a symbol of immortality.

---

a in cap, ā in cane, ä in father, å in abet, e in met, ē in be, ē in baker, ē in regent, i in pit, ī in fine, i in manifest, o in hot, ô in horse, ō in bone,

phone (fōn), *n. & v.t. & v.i.* phoned, phon'ing, [Informal], telephone.

-phone (fōn), a combining form meaning *transmitting sound, telephone.*

pho·neme (fō'nēm), *n.* a set of similar linguistic sounds that are represented by the same symbol in phonemic transcription. —**pho·ne·mic** (fō-nē'mik), *adj.*

pho·net·ic (fō-net'ik, fō-), *adj.* 1. of or pertaining to speech sounds, their production, or transcription. 2. denoting a set of symbols (phonetic alphabet), one for each distinguishable speech sound. —**pho·net'i·cal·ly,** *adv.*

pho·net·ics ('iks), *n.* 1. the science of speech sounds. 2. the system of sounds of a particular language. —**pho·ne·ti·cian** (fō-nē-tish'ůn), *n.*

phon·ics (fon'iks), *n.* 1. the science of sound; acoustics. 2. a method of teaching reading by phonetics. —**phon'ic,** *adj.* —**phon'i·cal·ly,** *adv.*

pho·no·gram (fō'nō-gram), *n.* a character or symbol representing a word, syllable, or sound, as in shorthand.

pho·no·graph (fō'nō-graf), *n.* an instrument for reproducing sound that has been recorded on a disk or cylinder, by means of a stylus or needle that picks up the sound vibrations from a spiral groove. —**pho·no·graph'ic,** *adj.*

pho·nog·ra·phy (fō-nog'rá-fi), *n.* 1. phonetic spelling or transcription. 2. a system of shorthand by which each sound is represented by a separate character or mark, especially the system invented by Isaac Pitman (1813-97).

pho·nol·o·gy (fō-nol'ō-ji), *n.* 1. the speech sounds of a language. 2. the study of changes in these. —**pho·no·log·i·cal** (fō-nō-loj'i-kl), *adj.* —**pho·nol'o·gist,** *n.*

pho·nom·e·ter (fō-nom'ē-tēr), *n.* an instrument for measuring the intensity of sound and the frequency of vibrations.

pho·no·type (fō'nō-tīp), *n.* a phonetic symbol or character, as used in printing.

pho·ny (fō'ni), *adj.* -ni·er, -ni·est, [Informal], not genuine; sham: *n., pl.* -nies, [Informal], a person or thing that is not what it seems to be; fraud; fake. Also spelled **pho'ney.** —**pho'ni·ness,** *n.*

phooey (fōō'i), *interj.* an expression of disgust, scorn, etc.

phos·gene (fos'jēn), *n.* a colorless, volatile, highly poisonous liquid used as a poison gas, in making dyes, etc.

phos·phate (fos'fāt), *n.* 1. a salt or ester of phosphoric acid. 2. a fertilizer that contains phosphates. 3. a carbonated soft drink.

phos·pha·tu·ri·a (fos-fá-toor'i-á), *n.* an excess of phosphates in the urine.

phos·phene (fos'fēn), *n.* a sensation of light resulting from closing the eye and pressing the eyeball.

phos·phide ('fīd), *n.* a compound of trivalent phosphorus and another element or a radical.

phos·phite ('fīt), *n.* a salt or ester of phosphorous acid.

phos·pho·rate ('fō-rāt), *v.t.* -rat·ed, -rat·ing, to combine or impregnate with phosphorus.

phos·pho·resce (fos-fō-res'), *v.i.* -resced', -resc'-ing, to emit light like phosphorus.

phos·pho·res·cence (-res'ns), *n.* 1. the emission of light from a substance after exposure to light, X-rays, etc. 2. the light. 3. luminescence without heat, as from phosphorus. —**phos·pho·res'cent,** *adj.*

phos·pho·ret·ed, phos·pho·ret·ted (fos'fō-ret-id), *adj.* combined or impregnated with phosphorus.

phos·phor·ic (fos-fôr'ik), *adj.* pertaining to, like, or containing phosphorus, especially with a valence of five.

phosphoric acid, any of several acids obtained by the oxidation of phosphates.

phos·pho·rous (fos'fēr-ůs), *adj.* of, like, or containing phosphorus, especially with a valence of three.

phosphorous acid, a crystalline acid that absorbs oxygen readily: the source of phosphites.

phos·pho·rus (fos'fēr-ůs), *n.* a waxy, nonmetallic chemical element that is luminous and ignites at room temperature.

pho·tic (fōt'ik), *adj.* 1. of light. 2. of or concerning the production of light by, or the effect of light on, organisms.

pho·to (fōt'ō), *n., pl.* -tos, [Informal], a photograph.

pho·to-, a combining form meaning *of or produced by light, photography.*

pho·to·chron·o·graph (fōt-ō-kron'ō-graf), *n.* an apparatus for recording very minute intervals of time.

pho·to·com·po·si·tion (-kom-pō-zish'ůn), *n.* a method of composing printing matter by which light images, as of letters, are projected onto a photosensitive surface, resulting in a negative from which a printing plate is made.

pho·to·cop·y (fōt'ō-kop-i), *n., pl.* -cop·ies, a photographic reproduction, as of a line drawing, document, page of a book, etc. made by a special device (photocopier): *v.t.* -cop·ied, -cop·y·ing, to make a photocopy of.

pho·to·dy·nam·ic (fōt-ō-dī-nam'ik), *adj.* 1. of or pertaining to the energy of light. 2. denoting a fluorescent substance.

pho·to·dy·nam·ics ('iks), *n.* 1. the influence of light on plant development, as in causing phototropism. 2. the science dealing with this.

pho·to·e·lec·tric cell (-i-lek'trik), a device in which light activates an electric circuit which operates a mechanical device, as for opening doors.

pho·to·en·grav·ing (-in-grā'ving), *n.* 1. a process by which photographs are reproduced on relief printing plates. 2. such a printing plate. 3. a print made from such a plate. —**pho·to·en·grave',** *v.t.* -graved', -grav'ing. —**pho·to·en·grav'er,** *n.*

photo finish, the finish of a race so close that the winner can be determined only by photographs taken just as the contestants cross the finish line.

pho·to·flash (fōt'ō-flash), *adj.* denoting a flashbulb electrically synchronized with the shutter of the camera.

pho·to·gen·ic (-jen'ik), *adj.* denoting a person or thing that looks or is likely to look attractive in photographs.

pho·to·graph (fōt'ō-graf), *n.* a picture made by photography: *v.t.* to take a photograph of: *v.i.* to appear (as specified) in a photograph. —**pho·tog·ra·pher** (fō-tog'rá-fēr), *n.*

pho·to·graph·ic (fōt-ō-graf'ik), *adj.* 1. of, like, made by, or used in photography. 2. recalling or able to recall in exact detail. —**pho·to·graph'i·cal·ly,** *adv.*

pho·tog·ra·phy (fō-tog'rá-fi), *n.* the art or process of producing pictures by the action of light on surfaces sensitized by various processes.

pho·to·gra·vure (fōt-ō-grá-vyoor'), *n.* 1. a process by which photographs are reproduced on intaglio printing plates or cylinders. 2. such a printing plate. 3. a print made from such a plate, usually with a satiny finish.

pho·to·lith·o·graph (-lith'ō-graf), *n.* a print made by photolithography. —**pho·to·lith·og'ra·pher** (-li-thog'rá-fēr), *n.*

pho·to·li·thog·ra·phy (-li-thog'rá-fi), *n.* a printing method combining lithography and photography. —**pho·to·lith·o·graph'ic** (-lith-ō-graf'ik), *adj.*

pho·tol·y·sis (fō-tol'i-sis), *n.* chemical decomposition due to the action of light.

pho·tom·e·ter (fō-tom'ĕ-tēr), *n.* an instrument for measuring the intensity of light or comparing the relative intensity of light from different sources.

pho·tom·e·try (-tri), *n.* the art of measuring the intensity of light.

pho·to·mi·crog·ra·phy (fōt-ō-mī-krog'rá-fi), *n.* the art of taking photographs through a microscope. —**pho·to·mi'cro·graph,** *n.*

pho·to·mon·tage (-mon-täzh'), *n.* a montage of photographs.

pho·ton (fō'ton), *n.* a unit of electromagnetic energy.

pho·to·off·set (fōt-ō-ôf'set), *n.* a method of offset printing in which graphic material is transferred photographically to a metal plate from which inked impressions are made on a rubber roller.

pho·toph·i·lous (fō-tof'i-lùs), *adj.* loving light; thriving in strong light. —**pho·toph'i·ly** (-li), *n.*

pho·to·phore (fōt'ō-fōr), *n.* a luminous organ, as found in some marine fish.

pho·to·play (fōt'ō-plā), *n.* a motion picture.

pho·to·re·con·nais·sance (fōt-ō-ri-kon'á-sàns), *n.* military reconnaissance involving aerial photography.

pho·to·sen·si·tive (-sen'si-tiv), *adj.* sensitive to radiant energy, especially to light. —**pho·to·sen·si·tiv'i·ty,** *n.*

pho·to·sphere (fōt'ō-sfir), *n.* the luminous surface of the sun.

Pho·to·stat (-stat), *n.* 1. an apparatus for making photographic copies of graphic material directly as positives on prepared paper: a trademark. 2. [p-], a copy made in this way: *vt.* [p-], -stat·ed or -stat·ted, -stat·ing or

-stat·ting, to make a photostat of. —**pho·to·stat'ic,** *adj.*

pho·to·syn·the·sis (fōt-ō-sin'thē-sis), *n.* the formation of organic materials, especially sugars, in green plants by action of light on chlorophyll.

pho·to·tax·is (-tak'sis), *n.* the movement of an organism due to the influence of light. —**pho·to·tac'tic,** *adj.*

pho·to·te·leg·ra·phy (-tĕ-leg'rá-fi), *n.* 1. communication by light, as by use of a heliograph. 2. same as telephotography.

pho·tot·ro·pism (fō-tot'rō-pizm), *n.* movement of a part of a plant toward or away from a source of light. —**pho·to·trop·ic** (fōt-ō-trop'-ik), *adj.*

phrase (frāz), *n.* 1. a group of words expressing a thought but not containing a subject and predicate. 2. a brief, pithy expression. 3. a short, distinct passage of music: *v.t. & v.i.* phrased, phras'ing, to express in words or in a phrase.

phra·se·ol·o·gy (frā-zi-ol'ō-ji), *n., pl.* -gies, style, manner, or pattern of expression in words.

phre·net·ic (fri-net'ik), *adj.* same as frenetic.

phren·ic (fren'ik), *adj.* 1. of or pertaining to the diaphragm. 2. of or pertaining to the mind.

phre·nol·o·gy (fri-nol'ō-ji), *n.* the study of the shape and protuberances of the skull, formerly supposed to reveal character traits, intelligence, etc. —**phren·o·log·i·cal** (fren-ō-loj'-i-kl), *adj.* —**phre·nol'o·gist,** *n.*

phthi·ri·a·sis (thi-rī'á-sis), *n.* infestation by body lice; pediculosis.

phthi·sis (thī'sis, tī'-), *n.* a wasting disease, especially tuberculosis of the lungs. —**phthis·ic** (tiz'ik), *adj. & n.* —**phthis'i·cal, phthis'ick·y,** *adj.*

phy·lac·ter·y (fi-lak'tēr-i), *n., pl.* -ter·ies, either of two small leather cases containing Scripture texts, worn on the forehead and left arm by orthodox Jewish men at prayer.

phyl·loid (fil'oid), *adj.* resembling a leaf.

phyl·loph·a·gous (fi-lof'á-gùs), *adj.* feeding on leaves.

phyl·lox·e·ra (fil-ôk-sir'á), *n., pl.* -rae ('ē), -ras, any of several related plant lice.

phy·log·e·ny (fi-loj'ĕ-ni), *n., pl.* -nies, the evolution or development of a species, race, or other classification of plants or animals.

phy·lum (fī'lùm), *n., pl.* -la (-'là), any of the major divisions of the animal kingdom, and sometimes of plants.

phys·ic (fiz'ik), *n.* 1. a medicine. 2. a laxative or cathartic medicine: *v.t.* -icked, -ick·ing, to dose with a medicine, especially a laxative or cathartic.

phys·i·cal (fiz'i-kl), *adj.* 1. pertaining to nature or material things. 2. according to the laws of nature. 3. of or relating to physics. 4. of or having to do with the body. —**phys'i·cal·ly,** *adv.*

physical education, instruction in exercises, sports, hygiene, etc., especially a gymnastics course in school.

physical therapy, the treatment of disease or injury by physical means, as hydrotherapy, massage, exercises, heat, etc.

phy·si·cian (fi-zish'ùn), *n.* a doctor of medicine.

phys·ics (fiz'iks), *n.* the science dealing with matter and energy. —**phys'i·cist** ('i-sist), *n.*

phys·i·o-, a combining form meaning *natural, physical.*

phys·i·og·no·my (fiz-i-og'nō-mi), *n.* 1. the practice of trying to judge character by observing facial features. 2. facial expression and features. —**phys·i·og'no·mist,** *n.*

phys·i·og·ra·phy ('rä-fi), *n.* geography having to do with description of natural features of the earth. —**phys·i·o·graph'ic** (-ō-graf'ik), *adj.*

phys·i·ol·o·gy (-ol'ō-ji), *n.* 1. the science dealing with the functions and vital processes of living organisms. 2. the functions of an organ or organism. —**phys·i·o·log'i·cal** (-ō-loj'i-kl), *adj.* —**phys·i·ol'o·gist,** *n.*

phys·i·o·ther·a·py (fiz-i-ō-ther'ā-pi), *n.* same as physical therapy. —**phys·i·o·ther'a·pist,** *n.*

phy·sique (fi-zēk'), *n.* the physical structure, strength, muscular system, etc. of the body.

phy·to-, a combining form meaning *vegetation, a plant.*

phy·to·gen·e·sis (fīt-ō-jen'ē-sis), *n.* the study of the generation and development of plants: also **phy·tog·e·ny** (fī-toj'ē-ni). —**phy·to·ge·net'ic** (-jē-net'ik), *adj.*

phy·to·ge·og·ra·phy (fīt-ō-ji-og'rä-fi), *n.* the branch of botany that treats of the geographical distribution of plants.

phy·tog·ra·phy (fī-tog'rä-fi), *n.* the branch of botany that treats of the description of plants.

phy·to·pa·thol·o·gy (fīt-ō-pa-thol'ō-ji), *n.* the science and study of plant diseases and their control. —**phy·to·path·o·log'ic** (-path-ō-loj'ik), *adj.*

pi (pī), *n., pl.* **pies,** disarranged or jumbled printing type: *v.t.* **pied, pie'ing** or **pi'ing,** to jumble (printing type).

pi (pī), *n.* 1. the 16th letter of the Greek alphabet. 2. the symbol ( ) denoting the ratio of the circumference of a circle to its diameter, about 3.1416.

pi·ac·u·lar (pī-ak'yū-lēr), *adj.* 1. expiatory. 2. calling for sacrifice or atonement.

pi·a ma·ter (pī'ä mät'ēr, pē'ä mät'ēr), a delicate vascular membrane enveloping the brain and spinal cord.

pi·a·nis·si·mo (pi-ä-nis'i-mō), *adj. & adv.* in Music, very soft.

pi·a·nist (pi-an'ist, pyan'-), *n.* one who plays the piano.

pi·an·o (pi-an'ō, pyan'ō), *n., pl.* **-an·os,** a large, stringed, keyboard musical instrument, the notes of which are produced by felt-covered hammers as they strike wires: also **pi·an·o·for·te** (pi-an'ō-fôrt, pyan'ō-fôr'ti).

pi·a·no (pē-ä'nō, pyä'-), *adj. & adv.* in Music, soft.

Pi·a·no·la (pi-ä-nō'lä), *n.* a kind of player piano: a trademark.

pi·as·ter (pi-as'tēr), *n.* 1. the principal monetary unit in South Vietnam. 2. a unit of currency in Turkey, Syria, Egypt, Lebanon, etc.

pi·az·za (pi-at'sä, pyat'-), *n.* 1. in Italy, a public square surrounded by buildings. 2. (pi-az'ä), a veranda.

pi·broch (pē'brok), *n.* the martial music of the Scottish bagpipe.

pi·ca (pī'kä), *n.* 1. a size of type, 12 point. 2. a unit of measure in printing. 3. an abnormal craving for sand, chalk, clay, or other substances not fit for food.

pic·a·dor (pik'ä-dôr), *n.* any one of the horsemen who incite the bull in a bullfight by pricking the neck with a lance.

pic·a·resque (pik-ä-resk'), *adj.* 1. pertaining to rogues or vagabonds. 2. denoting a form of fiction telling adventures of a roguish vagabond.

pic·a·roon (pik-ä-rōōn'), *n.* 1. an adventurous vagabond. 2. a pirate. 3. a pirate ship.

pic·a·yune (pik-i-ōōn', -ä-ūn'), *n.* 1. a small coin of little value. 2. anything small or worthless: *adj.* paltry; of little value; petty; trivial: also **pic·a·yun'ish.**

pic·ca·lil·li (pik'ä-lil-i), *n.* a relish of chopped vegetables and spices.

pic·co·lo (pik'ō-lō), *n., pl.* **-los,** a small flute having notes an octave higher than the ordinary flute.

pic·e·ous (pis'i-ŭs, pī'si-), *adj.* 1. of or like pitch. 2. black as pitch.

pich·i·ci·e·go (pich-i-si-ä'gō), *n., pl.* **-gos,** a small, burrowing South American animal related to the armadillo.

pick (pik), *n.* 1. a sharp, pointed, metal tool, used as in breaking up soil, rocks, etc. 2. a plectrum. 3. a choice or selection. 4. the best: *v.t.* 1. to strike or pierce with a sharp instrument or with the beak. 2. to gather, as flowers. 3. to pluck, as feathers from a fowl. 4. to separate with the fingers, as fibers. 5. to choose; select. 6. to provoke (a quarrel). 7. to pluck (strings of a musical instrument). 8. to pilfer; steal from (a person's pocket). 9. to open (a lock) with a wire or other implement rather than a key: *v.i.* 1. to use a pick. 2. to select in a fussy manner. —**pick'er,** *n.*

pick·a·back (pik'ä-bak), *adv. & adj.* same as piggyback.

pick·ax, pick·axe (pik'aks), *n.* a woodenhandled implement with a pick at one end of the head and a strong, flat blade at the other end.

pick·er·el (pik'ēr-ēl), *n., pl.* **-el, -els,** a small North American freshwater fish.

pick·et (pik'it), *n.* 1. a pointed stake used as a pale of a fence or as a hitching post, etc. 2. a military guard to keep watch for surprise attack. 3. a member of a striking labor union, stationed outside a store, factory, etc. on strike, to dissuade people from entering: *v.t.* 1. to enclose with a picket fence. 2. to fasten to a picket. 3. to post as a military picket. 4. to place pickets, or act as a picket, at (a store, etc.): *v.i.* to go on picket duty. —**pick'et·er,** *n.*

pick·ings (pik'ings), *n.pl.* 1. small scraps; remains. 2. gains gotten dishonestly; spoils.

pick·le (pik'l), *n.* 1. a brine or vinegar used to marinate or preserve food. 2. a vegetable, especially a cucumber, preserved in this solution. 3. [Informal], an embrassment; awkward situation: *v.t.* **-led, -ling,** to preserve in a pickle solution.

pick-lock (pik'lok), *n.* 1. an instrument for picking locks. 2. a thief.

pick-pock-et ('pok-it), *n.* one who steals from the pockets of persons, as in a crowd.

pick-up ('up), *n.* 1. the act of picking up, as a ball. 2. the ability, as of a motor vehicle, to accelerate sharply. 3. a small, open truck. 4. the part of a phonograph apparatus that converts the vibrations picked up by the needle from the record into audio-frequency current. 5. [Informal], an unintroduced acquaintance.

pick-y ('i), *adj.* pick'i-er, pick'i-est, [Informal], very fussy or finicky.

pic-nic (pik'nik), *n.* 1. an informal meal eaten outdoors. 2. an outing at which such a meal is eaten: *v.i.* -nicked, -nick-ing, to have a picnic. —pic'nick-er, *n.*

pic-ric acid (pik'rik), a bitter, poisonous, yellow crystalline acid, used in making explosives and dyes.

pic-ro-tox-in (pik-rō-tok'sin), *n.* a bitter, poisonous, white crystalline compound, used as a stimulant in treating barbiturate poisoning.

pic-to-ri-al (pik-tôr'i-ăl), *adj.* 1. of, pertaining to, or illustrated by pictures. 2. graphic, as a description. —pic-to'ri-al-ly, *adv.*

pic-ture (pik'chẽr), *n.* 1. a painting, drawing, photograph, etc. representing a person, scene, etc. 2. a perfect image. 3. a mental image. 4. a detailed description. 5. a motion picture. 6. the image on a television screen: *v.t.* -tured, -tur-ing, 1. to make a picture of. 2. to show clearly. 3. to form a mental picture of.

pic-tur-esque (pik-chù-resk'), *adj.* 1. having a romantic, charming, or striking appearance. 2. vividly descriptive. —pic-tur-esque'ly, *adv.*

picture window, a large window, as in a living room, that appears to frame the view outside.

pid-dle (pid'l), *v.i.* & *v.t.* -dled, -dling, to dawdle; waste time. —pid'dler, *n.*

pid-dling ('ling), *adj.* of little account; trivial; petty.

pidg-in (pij'in), *n.* a simplified jargon used in trade, that uses the words of one language and syntax of another: **pidgin English**, spoken in the Orient, uses English words and Chinese syntax.

pie (pī), *n.* a baked dish with a pastry crust and fruit or meat filling.

pie-bald (pī'bôld), *adj.* having patches of two colors, especially black and white: *n.* a piebald animal, as a horse.

piece (pēs), *n.* 1. a fragment; part of a whole. 2. one of a group, set, or quantity. 3. a literary or artistic composition. 4. any single thing, specimen, example, etc. 5. a length or amount of some product: *v.t.* pieced, piec'ing, 1. to enlarge by adding a piece. 2. to patch. 3. to join (*together*) the pieces of.

piece de ré-sis-tance (pyes' dè rā-zēs-täns'), [French], 1. the principal dish of a meal. 2. the choicest or most important item.

piece goods, same as yard goods.

piece-meal (pēs'mēl), *adj.* made or done one piece at a time: *adv.* piece by piece.

piece-work ('wûrk), *n.* work paid for by the piece. —piece'work-er, *n.*

pied (pīd), *adj.* variegated; piebald.

pier (pir), *n.* 1. a heavy support for the ends of adjacent spans of a bridge. 2. a structure built out into the water and supported by pillars, used as a landing place, breakwater, etc. 3. a heavy column used to support weight, as at the end of an arch.

pierce (pirs), *v.t.* pierced, pierc'ing, 1. to penetrate, especially with a pointed instrument; stab. 2. to make a hole in. 3. to explore with the sight or mind. 4. to sound sharply through (the air, etc.): *v.i.* to penetrate. —pierc'er, *n.*

pierc-ing ('ing), *adj.* penetrating; keen. —pierc'ing-ly, *adv.*

pier glass, an ornamental mirror placed in a wall section between windows.

Pie-tà (pyä-tä'), *n.* a painting or sculpture of Mary, the mother, weeping over the dead body of Jesus.

pi-e-tism (pī'ĕ-tizm), *n.* 1. a religious movement or system that stresses personal piety. 2. an exaggerated piety. —pi'e-tist, *n.* —pi-e-tis'tic, *adj.*

pi-e-ty (pī'ĕ-ti), *n.* 1. the quality of being pious, or devoted to religious affairs. 2. devotion to parents. 3. *pl.* -ties, a pious act.

pif-fle (pif'l), *n.* [Informal], nonsense.

pig (pig), *n.* 1. *pl.* **pigs**, a domesticated animal with short legs and a fat body; swine; hog. 2. a young swine. 3. a dirty, untidy, or greedy person. 4. an oblong casting of unforged metal poured into a mold from the smelting furnace: *v.i.* pigged, pig'ging, 1. to farrow; bear pigs. 2. to live in filth, like a pig.

pi-geon (pij'ùn), *n.* any one of a number of related birds with a stout body and short legs.

pi-geon-breast-ed (-bres-tid), *adj.* having a deformity of the chest in which the sternum protrudes.

pi-geon-hole (-hōl), *n.* a small, open compartment in a desk or cabinet for papers, etc.: *v.t.* -holed, -hol-ing, 1. to place in a pigeonhole. 2. to put aside indefinitely. 3. to classify.

pi-geon-toed (-tōd), *adj.* having the toes turned inward.

pig-ger-y (pig'ẽr-i), *n.*, *pl.* -ger-ies, chiefly British form for pigpen.

pig-gin (pig'in), *n.* a small wooden pail or tub with one stave extending above the rim as a handle.

pig-gish (pig'ish), *adj.* like a pig; greedy, gluttonous, filthy, etc. —pig'gish-ness, *n.*

pig-gy (pig'i), *n., pl.* -gies, a little pig: *adj.* -gi-er, -gi-est, piggish.

pig-gy-back (-bak), *adv.* & *adj.* 1. on the back or shoulders. 2. denoting a transportation arrangement by which truck trailers are carried on railroad cars.

pig-head-ed (pig'hed-id), *adj.* stubborn; obstinate. —pig'head-ed-ness, *n.*

pig iron, crude iron cast in pigs.

pig-ment (pig'mĕnt), *n.* 1. coloring matter, often a powder, used to make paints. 2. coloring matter in the cells of plants or animals.

pig·men·ta·tion (pig-měn-tā'shŭn), *n.* coloration because of pigments in the tissues.

Pig·my (pig'mi), *adj. & n., pl.* -mies, same as Pygmy.

pi·gno·li·a (pēn-yō'li-ă), *n.* 1. a nut-bearing pine tree, especially one of the western U.S. 2. the edible nut of this tree.

pig·nut (pig'nut), *n.* 1. the bitter nut of a kind of hickory tree. 2. the tree on which this nut grows.

pig·pen (pig'pen), *n.* a pen for keeping pigs: also **pig'sty** ('stī), *pl.* -sties.

pig·skin ('skin), *n.* 1. the skin of a pig. 2. leather made from this. 3. [Informal], a football.

pig·tail ('tāl), *n.* 1. the tail of a pig. 2. hair twisted into a long queue and hanging down the back of the head. 3. tobacco in a long twist.

pi·ka (pī'kä), *n.* any of several small, rabbitlike mammals of Asia and of western North America.

pike (pīk), *n.* 1. a former weapon with shaft and spearhead. 2. *pl.* pike, pikes, a voracious, freshwater fish with a narrow, elongated, pointed head. 3. same as turnpike. 4. [British Dialectal], a mountaintop; peak.

pik·er (pī'kēr), *n.* [Slang], one who does things in a stingy or cheap way.

pi·laf, pi·laff (pi-läf', pē'läf), *n.* rice boiled in a seasoned broth, often served with meat or fish: also **pi·lau'** (-lô').

pi·las·ter (pi-las'tēr), *n.* a square column or pillar inserted partly in a wall.

pil·chard (pil'chērd), *n.* a small marine fish of the herring family; sardine.

pile (pīl), *n.* 1. a large beam driven into the ground to make a firm foundation. 2. a mass or heap. 3. a heap of wood on which something is burned. 4. a covering of hair or down. 5. a velvety surface of looped or clipped yarn, etc., as on a rug or on cloth. 6. a series of plates arranged to produce an electric current. 7. earlier name for nuclear reactor. 8. [Informal], a large amount: *v.t.* piled, pil'ing, 1. to heap up. 2. to collect in a mass (often with *up*). 3. to load: *v.i.* 1. to form in a pile. 2. to crowd (*into, on,* etc.).

pi·le·ate (pī'li-it, pil'i-āt), *adj.* crested, as some birds: also **pi'le·at·ed** (-āt-id).

pileated woodpecker, a North American woodpecker of black-and-white plumage and a red crest.

pile driver, a machine for driving piles into the earth by raising and dropping a heavy weight: also **pile engine.**

piles (pīlz), *n.pl.* same as hemorrhoids: see hemorrhoid.

pi·le·um (pī'li-ŭm, pil'i-), *n., pl.* -le·a (-ă), the top of a bird's head.

pile-up (pīl'up), *n.* 1. an accumulation. 2. [Informal], a collision of several motor vehicles.

pil·fer (pil'fēr), *v.t. & v.i.* to steal in small quantities. —**pil'fer·er**, *n.*

pil·fer·age (-ij), *n.* the act of pilfering.

pil·gar·lic (pil-gär'lik), 1. [Dialectal], a bald-headed man. 2. a contemptible or pitiful fellow.

pil·grim (pil'grim), *n.* 1. a traveler; wanderer. 2. one who travels to visit some sacred place or shrine. 3. [P-], any one of the group of English Puritans who came to America in 1620: the group is sometimes called Pilgrim Fathers.

pil·grim·age (-ij), *n.* 1. a long journey. 2. a journey made to some sacred place.

pil·ing (pī'ling), *n.* 1. a structure or foundation of piles. 2. piles collectively.

pill (pil), *n.* 1. a little ball or tablet of medicine to be swallowed whole. 2. [Informal], any contraceptive drug for women, in pill form: also the **Pill.** 3. something disagreeable that must be accepted: *v.i.* to form into small balls, as down or fluff on fabric.

pil·lage (pil'ij), *n.* 1. the act of plundering. 2. spoils; loot: *v.t. & v.i.* -laged, -lag·ing, to plunder. —**pil'lag·er**, *n.*

pil·lar (pil'ēr), *n.* 1. a column to support a structure. 2. such a column standing alone and used as a monument. 3. something resembling a pillar or affording support.

pill-box (pil'boks), *n.* 1. a small box for holding pills. 2. a low concrete gun emplacement, usually circular.

pil·lion (pil'yŭn), *n.* a seat for a second person behind the saddle of a horse or motorcycle.

pil·lo·ry (pil'ēr-i), *n., pl.* -ries, a wooden frame supported by upright posts, in which petty offenders were formerly held by head and hands for exposure to public scorn: *v.t.* -ried, -ry·ing, 1. to place in a pillory. 2. to expose to public scorn or abuse.

pil·low (pil'ō), *n.* 1. a cloth case filled with feathers, foam rubber, etc., usually used to support the head of a person lying down. 2. the block on which the inner end of a bowsprit is supported: *v.t.* to rest as on a pillow.

pil·low·case (-kās), *n.* a removable cover for a pillow: also **pil'low·slip.**

pillow lace, same as bobbin lace.

pi·lose (pī'lōs), *adj.* covered with hair, especially soft hair. —**pi·los·i·ty** (pī-los'i-ti), *n.*

pi·lot (pī'lŏt), *n.* 1. a person licensed to conduct vessels in or out of a harbor or where navigation is difficult. 2. a person qualified to operate an aircraft. 3. a guide; leader: *v.t.* 1. to act as a pilot on, in, or over. 2. to guide or direct: *adj.* denoting an experimental undertaking.

pi·lot·age (-ij), *n.* 1. the act of piloting. 2. the fee paid to a pilot. 3. navigation of aircraft based on observation of landmarks and use of maps.

pilot engine, a locomotive sent on in front to clear the line.

pi·lot·house (-hous), *n.* an enclosure on the upper deck of a ship for the helmsman.

pilot light, a small gas jet which is kept burning, as on a stove, to light the burners.

Pil·sener, Pil·sner (pilz'nēr, pils'-), *adj.* [often p-], denoting a kind of lager beer.

Pilt·down man (pilt'doun), a supposed type of primitive man whose existence was presumed from bone fragments found in 1911 and exposed as a hoax in 1953.

---

pi·men·to (pi-men′tō), *n., pl.* -tos, a mild, sweet red pepper: also **pi·mien·to** (pi-myen′tō, -men′-).

pimp (pimp), *n.* a man who is an agent for prostitutes; procurer: *v.i.* to act as a pimp.

pim·per·nel (pim′pẽr-nel), *n.* a plant of the primrose family with scarlet, blue, or white flowers that close at the approach of rain.

pimp·ing (pim′ping), *adj.* 1. petty. 2. pitiful; puny.

pim·ple (pim′pl), *n.* a small, inflamed swelling on the skin. —**pim′ply**, *adj.* -pli·er, -pli·est.

pin (pin), *n.* 1. a short piece of wire sharpened at one end and with a head at the other, used for fastening things together. 2. a wooden or metal peg. 3. anything like a pin. 4. an ornament or emblem with a pin by which it is fastened to clothing. 5. any one of the wooden clubs at which the ball is rolled in bowling. 6. a pole with a flag attached, placed in the hole on a golf green: *v.t.* **pinned, pin′ning,** to fasten with or as with a pin.

pi·na·ceous (pi-nā′shŭs), *adj.* of or belonging to the pine family of trees, including the fir, spruce, cedar, etc.

pi·ña cloth (pēn′yä), a cloth made from the fibers of the pineapple leaf.

pin·a·fore (pin′ȧ-fōr), *n.* a sleeveless, protective garment worn over a dress.

pi·nas·ter (pi-nas′tẽr, pi-), *n.* a pine tree of southern Europe with paired needles: also called cluster pine.

pi·ña·ta (pē-nyä′tä), *n.* [Spanish], a Mexican papier-mâché figure, as of an animal, broken by sticks in a festival game, to release toys and candy inside.

pin·ball machine (pin′bôl), a game machine with a sloping board: a spring-driven ball hits pins or rolls into holes, with the score recorded electrically.

pince-nez (panz′nā, pins′-), *n., pl.* **pince′-nez** (′nāz), eyeglasses clipped to the bridge of the nose by a spring.

pin·cers (pin′sẽrz), *n.pl.* 1. a gripping tool with two pivoted parts forming two handles and two grasping jaws. 2. a grasping claw, as of a lobster. —**pin′cer·like,** *adj.*

pinch (pinch), *v.t.* 1. to squeeze between finger and thumb or between two surfaces, etc. 2. to cramp or compress painfully. 3. to make thin or drawn, as hunger does. 4. [Slang], *a)* to steal. *b)* to arrest: *v.i.* 1. to compress painfully. 2. to be niggardly. 3. to economize; be frugal: *n.* 1. a squeeze or nip. 2. a very small amount, as that which may be taken between thumb and finger. 3. an emergency. 4. a trying situation; distress.

pinch·beck (′bek), *n.* 1. an alloy of copper and zinc, used to make cheap jewelry in imitation of gold. 2. anything imitation or cheap: *adj.* 1. made of pinchbeck. 2. cheap; imitation.

pinch·ers (pin′chẽrz), *n.pl.* same as pincers.

pinch-hit (pinch′hit′), *v.i.* -hit′, -hit′ting, 1. to substitute at bat for the baseball player whose turn it is. 2. to take the place of (someone) in an emergency. —**pinch hitter.**

pin curl, a curl of hair held in place by a bobby pin.

pin-cush·ion (pin′koosh-ŭn), *n.* a pad or cushion to stick pins in, to keep when not in use.

pin·dling (pin′dling), *adj.* [Dialectal], puny; sickly; weak and undersized.

pine (pin), *n.* 1. any one of several varieties of cone-bearing tree with needle-shaped evergreen leaves and a sticky resin from which turpentine, tar, etc. are obtained. 2. the wood of such a tree: *v.i.* **pined, pin′ing,** 1. to waste (*away*) from grief, longing, etc. 2. to yearn or long (*for*).

pin·e·al (pin′i-ăl), *adj.* 1. shaped like a pine cone. 2. of or pertaining to the pineal body.

pineal body, a small, cone-shaped body in the back of the brain of all vertebrates having a cranium: its function is undetermined.

pine·ap·ple (pin′ap-l), *n.* 1. the juicy, edible fruit of a tropical plant, shaped somewhat like a pine cone. 2. the plant.

pin·er·y (pi′nẽr-i), *n., pl.* -er·ies, 1. a pine forest. 2. a hothouse or plantation where pineapples are cultivated.

pine tar, a thick brown liquid distilled from pine wood and used in medications, paints, disinfectants, etc.

pi·ne·tum (pi-nēt′ŭm), *n., pl.* -ta (′ä), a place where pine trees are grown for exhibition or study.

pin·ey (pi′ni), *adj.* -i·er, -i·est, 1. having a growth of many pine trees. 2. having the odor of pines.

pin·feath·er (pin′feth-ẽr), *n.* a new feather just emerging from the skin.

pin·fish (′fish), *n., pl.* -fish, -fish·es, any one of several fishes having sharp dorsal spines.

ping (ping), *n.* 1. the sound of a bullet striking sharply. 2. any sound similar to this: *v.i. & v.t.* to strike with a ping.

Ping-Pong (ping′pong), *n.* 1. equipment for playing table tennis: a trademark. 2. [p- p-], the game of table tennis.

pin·head (pin′hed), *n.* 1. the head of a pin. 2. [Slang], a stupid person.

pin·hole (′hōl), *n.* a small hole made by or as by a pin.

pin·ion (pin′yŭn), *n.* 1. the end section of a bird's wing. 2. a wing. 3. the smaller of two geared wheels: *v.t.* 1. to bind or secure, as by binding the wings or arms of. 2. to shackle.

pink (pingk), *n.* 1. a light-red color. 2. a garden plant with sharp-pointed leaves and fragrant light-red, white, or red flowers. 3. this flower. 4. the best condition, finest example, etc.: *adj.* light-red: *v.t.* 1. to stab or prick. 2. to cut a saw-toothed edge on (cloth, etc.). 3. to punch small holes in an ornamental pattern, as in cloth, paper, etc. —**pink′er,** *n.* —**pink′ish,** *adj.*

pink-eye (′i), *n.* an acute, contagious inflammation of the eye.

pink·ie, pink·y (ping′ki), *n., pl.* -ies, the smallest finger.

pink·ing (′king), *n.* a method of ornamenting materials by notching the edges: usually done with shears with notched blades (**pinking shears**).

---

a in cap, ā in cane, ä in father, ȧ in abet, e in met, ē in be, ẽ in baker, ė in regent, i in pit, ī in fine, i in manifest, o in hot, ô in horse, ō in bone,

pink·o ('kō), *n., pl.* **pink'os**, [Slang], one whose political views are more or less radical.

pink·root (pingk'rōōt), *n.* a plant of the southeastern U.S., with showy red flowers.

pin money, 1. originally, money given by a husband to his wife for personal expenses. 2. any small sum for minor expenses.

pin·nace (pin'is), *n.* 1. a small, light sailing ship formerly used as a tender, scout, etc. 2. a ship's boat.

pin·na·cle (pin'ă-kl), *n.* 1. a small turret or elevation above the rest of a building. 2. a high point like a spire, as a mountain peak. 3. the highest point: *v.t.* -cled, -cling, 1. to furnish with pinnacles. 2. to set on a pinnacle.

pin·nate (pin'āt, 'it), *adj.* in *Botany*, having leaflets on each side of a common stem.

pin·ni·ped (pin'ĭ-ped), *n.* any one of a group of aquatic mammals with flippers, including the seals and walruses.

pi·noch·le, pi·noc·le (pē'nuk-l), *n.* a card game played with two of each card above eight, or 48 cards.

pi·ñon (pin'yŏn, 'yŏn), *n.* 1. any one of several small pine trees of western U.S. with large, edible seeds. 2. the seed.

pin·point (pin'point), *v.t.* to locate exactly.

pin·prick ('prik), *n.* 1. a tiny hole as made by a pin. 2. a petty annoyance.

pins and needles, 1. a prickly feeling in a limb recovering from being numb. 2. a state of nervous suspense: used in the phrase on **pins and needles**.

pin·set·ter (pin'set-ēr), *n.* a person or automatic machine that sets up bowling pins: also **pin'spot·ter**.

pin stripe, a pattern of very narrow stripes, as in cloth for some suits.

pint (pīnt), *n.* a measure of capacity, equal to 1/2 quart.

pin·tail (pin'tāl), *n., pl.* -tails, -tail, a kind of duck with a pointed tail.

pin·to (pin'tō), *adj.* piebald; mottled: *n., pl.* -tos, a pinto horse or pony.

pinto bean, a kind of mottled kidney bean cultivated in the southwestern U.S.

pin·up (pin'up), *adj.* 1. designed to be hung up on the wall, as a lamp. 2. [Informal], denoting a pretty girl whose picture is often pinned up on walls.

pin·wheel ('hwēl), *n.* 1. a firework that spins about and throws off colored lights. 2. a small paper or plastic circle of vanes fastened to a stick so as to revolve in the wind.

pin·worm ('wūrm), *n.* a small nematode worm sometimes found as a parasite of the rectum and lower intestine.

pi·o·neer (pī-ŏ-nir'), *n.* one who goes before to prepare the way for others, as an early settler: *v.i.* to be a pioneer; prepare the way: *v.t.* to be a pioneer in or of.

pi·ous (pī'ŭs), *adj.* 1. devout; dutiful to God and religious obligations. 2. pretending religious devotion; sanctimonious. 3. sacred. — **pi'ous·ly**, *adv.*

pip (pip), *n.* 1. a small seed, as of an apple. 2. a contagious disease in fowls. 3. a spot on

a playing card: *v.i.* pipped, pip'ping, to chirp like a young bird.

pipe (pīp), *n.* 1. a hollow tube of wood, metal, etc. for use as, or as part of, a musical instrument. 2. *pl.* the bagpipe. 3. a long tube for the conveyance of gas, water, steam, etc. 4. a tube with a bowl at one end for smoking tobacco. 5. a unit of capacity, equal to about 126 gallons, or a cask of this size. 6. any tubular organ or part: *v.i.* piped, pip'ing, 1. to emit shrill sounds. 2. to play on a pipe: *v.t.* 1. to play (a tune) on a pipe. 2. to call or summon by piping. 3. to utter in a shrill tone. 4. to convey by pipes. — **pip'er**, *n.*

pipe dream, [Informal], an improbable fancy; vain hope or scheme, etc.

pipe fitter, a mechanic who installs or maintains heating or plumbing pipes, etc.

pipe·line ('līn), *n.* 1. a line of pipes for the conveyance of oil, gas, water, etc. 2. a channel for information: *v.t.* -lined, -lin·ing, to convey by pipeline.

pipe organ, an organ with pipes, as distinguished from one with reeds: see organ.

pip·er·ine (pip'ĕ-rēn, 'ĕr-in), *n.* a white, crystalline alkaloid found in pepper.

pipe-stem (pīp'stem), *n.* 1. the stem of a tobacco pipe. 2. something like this in form, as a very thin leg.

pi·pette, pi·pet (pī-pet', pi-), *n.* a small glass tube for drawing up a small portion of fluid by suction: *v.t.* -pet'ted, -pet'ting, to transfer, remove, or measure (fluid) by use of a pipette.

pip·ing (pīp'ing), *adj.* playing on a pipe: *n.* 1. the sound of pipes. 2. a narrow fold of cloth for trimming garments, cushions, etc.

piping hot, very hot.

pip·it (pip'it), *n.* a small North American songbird resembling the lark.

pip·pin (pip'in), *n.* any one of several varieties of apple.

pip·squeak (pip'skwēk), *n.* [Informal], a small or unimportant person.

pi·quant (pē'kānt), *adj.* 1. pleasantly pungent or sharp to the taste. 2. stimulating; exciting. — **pi'quan·cy**, *n.*

pique (pēk), *n.* slight anger or resentment; ruffled vanity or pride: *v.t.* piqued, piqu'ing, 1. to wound the pride of. 2. to excite; provoke.

pi·qué, pi·que (pi-kā'), *n.* [French], a closely woven cloth, usually of cotton, with slight ridges.

pi·quet (pi-ket', -kā'), *n.* a card game for two players, using 32 cards.

pi·ra·cy (pī'ră-si), *n., pl.* -cies, 1. robbery on the high seas. 2. an infringement of copyright or patent.

pi·ra·nha (pi-rän'yă, -ran'-), *n.* any one of several small, voracious, South American fishes, schools of which attack any animal, including man.

pi·rate (pī'răt), *n.* 1. a robber on the high seas. 2. one who infringes the law of copyright or patent: *v.t. & v.i.* -rat·ed, -rat·ing, 1. to take by piracy. 2. to reproduce or copy (a book, recording, etc.) in violation of a copyright. — **pi·rat'i·cal** (-rat'i-kl), *adj.*

ŏ in *dragon*, ōō in *crude*, oo in *wool*, u in *cup*, ū in *cure*, ū in *turn*, ŭ in *focus*, oi in *boy*, ou in *house*, th in *thin*, th in *sheathe*, g in *get*, j in *joy*, y in *yet*.

pi·ro·gi (pi-rō′gi), *n.pl.* small pastry turnovers with a filling of meat, cheese, etc.: also **pi·rosh′ki** (-rosh′ki), **pi·ro′gen** (-rō′gĕn).

pi·rogue (pi-rōg′), *n.* a canoe made of the hollowed trunk of a single tree.

pir·ou·ette (pir-oo-wet′), *n.* a whirling or turning about on the toes or on one foot, as in ballet: *v.i.* **-et′ted, -et′ting,** to execute a pirouette.

pis·ca·to·ri·al (pis-kâ-tôr′i-âl), *adj.* of or pertaining to fishing or fishermen.

Pis·ces (pī′siz, pis′iz), *n.* 1. a northern constellation. 2. the twelfth sign of the zodiac.

pis·cine (pis′īn, pi′sin), *adj.* of, pertaining to, or resembling fish.

pi·si·form (pī′si-fôrm), *adj.* like a pea in size and shape: *n.* a small bone on the inner side of the wrist, shaped like half a pea.

pis·mire (pis′mīr, piz′-), *n.* an ant.

pi·so·lite (pī′sō-līt), *n.* limestone made up of little round concretions the size of a pea, composed of calcium carbonate.

pis·ta·chi·o (pi-stä′shi-ō, -stash′i-ō), *n., pl.* **-chios,** 1. a small tree of southern Europe, of the cashew family. 2. its green, edible seed **(pistachio nut).** 3. the flavor of this nut. 4. a light-green color.

pis·til (pis′tl), *n.* the seed-bearing organ in the center of a flower.

pis·til·late (pis′tl-lit, -lāt), *adj.* having a pistil; specifically, having pistils but no stamens.

pis·tol (pis′tl), *n.* a small firearm designed to be held, aimed, and fired with one hand: *v.t.* **-toled** or **-tolled, -tol·ing** or **-tol·ling,** to shoot with a pistol.

pis·ton (pis′tn), *n.* a short, solid cylinder fitting exactly into, and moving up and down in, another cylinder in order to receive or transmit motion by pressure on a fluid within.

piston ring, a split metal ring placed around a piston to make it fit the cylinder closely so that fluid cannot escape.

piston rod, a rod moving or being moved by a piston.

pit (pit), *n.* the stonelike seed of certain fruits, as of the cherry, date, or plum: *v.t.* **pit′ted, pit′ting,** to remove the pits from.

pit (pit), *n.* 1. a hole in the earth. 2. an abyss. 3. a covered hole for trapping wild animals; pitfall. 4. an enclosed place where animals are kept or made to fight. 5. the section in a theater for the orchestra, in front of the stage. 6. a small hollow on the surface of a body, especially a scar from smallpox. 7. an area for servicing cars: *v.t.* **pit′ted, pit′ting,** 1. to mark with small hollows. 2. to place in a pit. 3. to set in competition (*against*): *v.i.* to become marked with pits.

pi·ta (pĕt′ä), *n.* 1. a fiber of the agave plant from which rope and paper are made. 2. any one of several plants yielding this fiber.

pit·a·pat (pit′ä-pat), *adv.* with quick beating; palpitatingly: *n.* a quick succession of taps or beats.

pitch (pich), *n.* 1. the sticky, black substance obtained from coal tar, etc. and used for roofing, etc. 2. the resinous sap of pine trees. 3. a casting forward; throw or toss. 4.

something that has been pitched. 5. a relative level; degree. 6. degree of inclination. 7. the highness or lowness of a musical tone. 8. [Slang], persuasive talk: *v.t.* 1. to throw or cast headlong. 2. to set to a keynote in music. 3. to set up, as a tent on the ground. 4. in *Baseball, a)* to throw (the ball); *b)* to perform as pitcher for (a game): *v.i.* 1. to fall forward or downward. 2. to rise and fall, as a ship in rough water. 3. to pitch a ball, etc.

pitch-black (′blak), *adj.* very black.

pitch-blende (′blend), *n.* a lustrous, brown to black variety of uraninite, chief ore of uranium.

pitch-dark (′därk), *adj.* very dark.

pitched battle, 1. a battle in which the opposing forces take fixed positions. 2. a closely fought battle.

pitch·er (′ĕr), *n.* 1. a container, usually with a handle and pouring lip, for holding liquids. 2. as much as a pitcher will hold: also **pitch′er·ful.** 3. in *Baseball,* the player who pitches the ball to batters of the opposing team.

pitcher plant, any one of several plants with pitcherlike leaves.

pitch-fork (′fôrk), *n.* a long-handled fork for pitching hay, straw, etc.: *v.t.* to lift or to throw with a pitchfork.

pitch-man (′mân), *n., pl.* **-men,** 1. a hawker, as at a carnival. 2. [Slang], any high-pressure salesman or advertiser.

pitch·y (′i), *adj.* **pitch′i·er, pitch′i·est,** 1. like or smeared with pitch. 2. sticky. 3. black. — **pitch′i·ness,** *n.*

pit·e·ous (pit′i-ŭs), *adj.* deserving or evoking pity. —**pit′e·ous·ly,** *adv.*

pit-fall (pit′fôl), *n.* 1. a covered hole for trapping wild animals. 2. any hidden danger or difficulty.

pith (pith), *n.* 1. the soft, spongy substance in the center of some plant stems. 2. the white, fibrous tissue surrounding the sections in citrus fruits. 3. marrow. 4. the important part; essence.

pith·y (pith′i), *adj.* **pith′i·er, pith′i·est,** 1. of, like, or full of pith. 2. full of meaning; forcible. —**pith′i·ly,** *adv.* —**pith′i·ness,** *n.*

pit·i·a·ble (pit′i-ä-bl), *adj.* deserving pity. —**pit′i·a·bly,** *adv.*

pit·i·ful (-fŭl), *adj.* 1. deserving pity. 2. despicable. —**pit′i·ful·ly,** *adv.*

pit·i·less (-lis), *adj.* without pity or compassion; merciless. —**pit′i·less·ly,** *adv.*

pi·ton (pē′ton), *n.* a spike or peg to drive into ice or rock in mountain climbing, usually with an eye for a rope.

pit·tance (pit′ns), *n.* a small allowance or share, especially of money.

pit·ted (pit′id), *adj.* 1. marked with pits or indentations. 2. with pits removed.

pit·ter-pat·ter (pit′ĕr-pat-ĕr), *n.* a sound as of light, rapid tapping.

pi·tu·i·tar·y (pi-tōō′i-ter-i), *adj.* of or pertaining to a small, oval, endocrine gland (pituitary gland or body) attached to the brain: it secretes hormones that affect metabolism, growth, etc.

---

a in cap, ā in cane, ä in father, â in abet, e in met, ē in be, ê in baker, ê in regent, i in pit, ī in fine, î in manifest, o in hot, ô in horse, ō in bone,

pit viper, any one of several poisonous snakes with a pit on each side of the head.

pit·y (pit′i), *n., pl.* **pit′ies,** 1. sympathy for one in distress; compassion. 2. a cause for sorrow or grief: *v.t. & v.i.* **pit′ied, pit′y·ing,** to feel pity (for).

pit·y·ri·a·sis (pit-i-rī′ā-sis), *n.* 1. a skin disease characterized by irregular scaly patches. 2. a skin disease of domestic animals characterized by dry scales.

piv·ot (piv′ŏt), *n.* 1. the shaft or point on which something revolves. 2. a person or thing on which much depends. 3. the action of pivoting: *v.t. & v.i.* to provide with or turn on a pivot. —**piv′ot·al,** *adj.*

pix·ie, pix·y (pik′si), *n., pl.* **pix′ies,** a fairy. — **pix′ie·ish, pix′y·ish,** *adj.*

piz·za (pēt′sä), *n.* a baked, pie-shaped food made of thin bread dough spread with spiced tomato and cheese, and often with sausage, mushrooms, etc.

piz·zi·ca·to (pit-si-kät′ō), *adj.* in *Music,* plucked, as a violin, guitar, etc.

plac·a·ble (plak′ā-bl, plā′kā-), *adj.* that can be placated or pacified; forgiving. —**plac·a·bil′i·ty,** *n.* —**plac′a·bly,** *adv.*

plac·ard (plak′ärd, ′ärd), *n.* a notice for posting in a public place: *v.t.* to give notice or advertise by placards.

pla·cate (plā′kāt, plak′āt), *v.t.* -**cat·ed, -cat·ing,** to appease; conciliate; mollify. —**pla′cat·er,** *n.* —**pla′ca·to·ry,** *adj.*

place (plās), *n.* 1. a particular spot or locality. 2. a short city street, or square. 3. a position; office. 4. a residence. 5. a city or town. 6. space; room. 7. duty. 8. a passage or page in a magazine, book, etc. 9. a usual position or seat. 10. a step or point in order of progression. 11. a region. 12. situation. 13. second position at the finish of a race: *v.t.* **placed, plac′ing,** 1. to put in any place, situation, etc. 2. to identify. 3. to find work for. 4. to settle. 5. to establish. 6. to finish in (a specified position) in a race: *v.i.* to finish second or among the first three in a race.

pla·ce·bo (plā-sē′bō), *n., pl.* -**bos, -boes,** an unmedicated substance given as a medicine to humor a patient or as a control in an experiment.

place kick, in *Football,* a kick made while the ball is held in place on the ground. — **place′-kick,** *v.i.*

place·ment (plās′mĕnt), *n.* 1. the act of placing. 2. arrangement. 3. location.

pla·cen·ta (plā-sen′tä), *n., pl.* -**tas, -tae** (′tē), 1. the vascular organ attached to the embryo by the umbilical cord and through which the embryo is nourished in the uterus. 2. that part of the carpel of a plant to which the ovules and seeds are attached. —**pla·cen′tal,** *adj.*

plac·er (plās′ẽr), *n.* a mineral deposit of particles that has been built up by erosion or glacial action.

plac·id (plas′id), *adj.* calm; peaceful; mild. — **pla·cid′i·ty,** *n.* —**plac′id·ly,** *adv.*

plack·et (plak′it), *n.* a slit with fasteners in a skirt or dress so that the garment can be put on or taken off.

pla·gia·rism (plā′ji-rizm), *n.* 1. the act of plagiarizing. 2. plagiarized matter. —**pla′gia·rist,** *n.* —**pla·gia·ris′tic,** *adj.*

pla·gia·rize (-rīz), *v.t. & v.i.* -**rized, -riz·ing,** to appropriate (literary material, ideas, etc.) from (someone else) and represent it as one's own work. —**pla′gia·riz·er,** *n.*

plague (plāg), *n.* 1. a contagious, deadly, epidemic disease. 2. anything very troublesome; calamity. 3. [Informal], an annoyance: *v.t.* **plagued, plagu′ing,** 1. to infest with a plague. 2. to trouble; torment; vex. —**plagu′er,** *n.*

pla·guy, pla·guey (plā′gi), *adj.* [Informal], vexatious; annoying.

plaice (plās), *n.* any one of several related American or European flatfishes.

plaid (plad), *n.* 1. a long, checkered, woolen cloth worn over the shoulder by the Scottish Highlanders. 2. cloth with the checkered pattern of a plaid or tartan: *adj.* made with a plaid pattern.

plain (plān), *adj.* 1. evident; easily understood. 2. clear; open. 3. not luxurious. 4. homely. 5. outspoken. 6. simple. 7. unmixed; pure. 8. ordinary: *n.* level ground; a flat expanse: *adv.* clearly. —**plain′ly,** *adv.* —**plain′ness,** *n.*

plain-clothes man (plān′klōz′), a police detective who does not wear a uniform when on duty.

plain·song (′sông), *n.* a kind of early Christian church music sung in unison, in free rhythm and with a limited scale.

plain-spo·ken (′spō′kn), *adj.* speaking bluntly or frankly.

plaint (plānt), *n.* 1. a grievance or complaint. 2. [Poetic], lamentation.

plain·tiff (plān′tif), *n.* one who commences a suit in a court of law.

plain·tive (′tiv), *adj.* expressing grief or sorrow; sad. —**plain′tive·ly,** *adv.* —**plain′tive·ness,** *n.*

plait (plāt), *n.* 1. a pleat; flat fold. 2. a braid of hair, straw, ribbon, etc.: *v.t.* to fold or braid; interweave. —**plait′er,** *n.*

plan (plan), *n.* 1. a diagram or drawing showing the arrangement of a building, plot of land, etc. 2. a scheme or schedule for making or doing something. 3. any outline or sketchy design: *v.t.* **planned, plan′ning,** 1. to make a plan or sketch of. 2. to devise a scheme for doing, making, etc. 3. to think about as a project: *v.i.* to make plans. — **plan′ner,** *n.*

pla·nar·i·an (plā-ner′i-ăn), *n.* a flat, soft, aquatic worm that moves by means of cilia.

plan·chet (plan′chit), *n.* a flat piece of metal prepared for coining.

plan·chette (plan-chet′, -shet′), *n.* a small, heart-shaped board which is supposed to write out a message or, on a Ouija board, point to letters, etc.

plane (plān), *adj.* 1. flat; level. 2. of or having to do with flat surfaces or points and lines on them: *n.* 1. a flat or even surface. 2. a level of progress, character, etc. 3. a wing of an airplane. 4. an airplane. 5. a carpenter's tool for smoothing wood. 6. any of several related trees having bark that peels off: also **plane tree:** *v.t.* **planed, plan′-**

---

ing, to make level or smooth with a plane: *v.i.* to rise up and glide or soar. —**plan'er,** *n.*

plan·et (plan'it), *n.* any one of the heavenly bodies revolving around the sun. —**plan'e·tar·y,** *adj.*

plan·e·tar·i·um (plan-ē-ter'i-ŭm), *n., pl.* **-i·ums, -i·a** (-â), a large room with a dome-shaped ceiling on which moving images of the planets, sun, and stars are projected.

plan·e·tes·i·mal (plan-ē-tes'i-ml), *n.* any one of the minute bodies in space traveling in planetary orbits: *adj.* of these bodies.

plan·et·oid (plan'ē-toid), *n.* same as **asteroid** (*n.* 1).

plan·ish (plan'ish), *v.t.* to polish or smooth (metal) by hammering.

plan·i·sphere (plan'i-sfir), *n.* a sphere or globe projected on a plane surface.

plank (plangk), *n.* 1. a long, broad, thick board. 2. an item in a political policy: *v.t.* 1. to cover with planks. 2. to broil and serve on a board. 3. [Informal], to put (*down*) with emphasis.

plank·ton (plangk'tŏn), *n.* the minute animal and plant life found in bodies of water, used by fish as food.

plant (plant), *n.* 1. an organism that is stationary, makes food from the atmosphere, and has no sense organs. 2. such an organism with a soft stem: *v.t.* 1. to put (seed, plants etc.) into the ground for growth. 2. to fix in the mind. 3. to establish. 4. to put solidly in the ground. 5. [Slang], to conceal; hide. 6. [Slang], to situate so as to entrap, swindle, etc.

plan·tain (plan'tin), *n.* 1. a tropical broad-leaved tree yielding an edible fruit similar to the banana. 2. a common, roadside weed with basal leaves and small flowers.

plan·tar (plan'tēr), *adj.* of or on the sole of the foot.

plan·ta·tion (plan-tā'shŭn), *n.* 1. a place planted with trees. 2. a cultivated estate, as in a tropical climate, with resident workers.

plant·er (plan'tēr), *n.* 1. one who or that which plants. 2. the owner of a plantation. 3. a plant holder, usually with ornamentation.

plan·ti·grade (plan'ti-grād), *adj.* walking on the sole of the foot: *n.* a plantigrade animal, as the bear.

plaque (plak), *n.* 1. an inscribed or decorated plate of metal, wood, etc. for hanging on a wall. 2. a colored patch or spot on the skin. 3. a thin layer of a substance that collects on teeth not properly cleaned.

plash (plash), *n.* 1. a puddle; pool. 2. a splash: *v.t. & v.i.* to splash.

plas·ma (plaz'mà), *n.* 1. the liquid part of whole blood after the red and white corpuscles have been removed. 2. same as **protoplasm.** 3. a very hot, ionized gas that is neither positive nor negative. 4. a green variety of quartz.

plas·ter (plas'tēr), *n.* 1. a composition of lime, sand, and water for coating walls, etc., that hardens when dry. 2. a medicinal application of paste for external use: *v.t.* 1. to overlay or cover with or as with plaster. 2. to put on like a plaster. 3. to flatten or smooth. —**plas'ter·er,** *n.*

plas·ter·board (-bôrd), *n.* a thin board of layered plaster and paper for use in walls.

plaster of Paris (per'is), a heavy white powder obtained by calcining gypsum, which as a thick paste sets quickly, and is thus much used for casts, moldings, etc.

plas·tic (plas'tik), *adj.* 1. capable of being formed or molded. 2. that forms or shapes matter. 3. consisting of a plastic: *n.* 1. a substance, usually produced from organic materials, which, after chemical treatment may be molded into various shapes and hardened for commercial use. 2. an object made of plastic. —**plas·tic'i·ty** (-tis'i-ti), *n.*

plastic surgery, surgery that corrects or renews hurt or disfigured body parts, as by moving skin from one place on the body to another.

plat (plat), *n.* 1. a small area; plot of land. 2. a map of land laid out in plots: *v.t.* **plat'-ted, plat'ting,** to form a map of.

plate (plāt), *n.* 1. a thin piece of metal, etc. 2. an engraved piece of metal. 3. a shallow vessel on which food is placed at a meal; dish. 4. a course of food. 5. a surface of metal, glass, etc. coated with a film sensitized to light. 6. an electrotype cast. 7. a book illustration on a kind of paper different from the paper of the text. 8. a thin section of beef from the forequarter. 9. table utensils, originally coated with gold or silver. 10. a prize given at a race. 11. armor. 12. in *Baseball,* same as **home plate:** *v.t.* **plat'ed, plat'ing,** 1. to coat with gold, silver, etc. 2. to overlay with metal plates.

pla·teau (pla-tō'), *n., pl.* **-teaus', -teaux'** (-tōz'), 1. an elevated, broad, flat land; tableland. 2. a stable period, or a period of little change.

plate glass, a fine kind of glass cast in thick plates.

plat·en (plat'n), *n.* 1. the flat metal part of a printing press by which an impression is made. 2. the rubber-covered cylinder of a typewriter.

plat·form (plat'fôrm), *n.* 1. a flat floor of wood, stone, etc. raised above the level of the ground. 2. a political program or policy.

plat·i·nize (plat'n-iz), *v.t.* **-nized, -niz·ing,** to coat with platinum.

plat·i·noid (plat'n-oid), *n.* an alloy of zinc, nickel, copper, and tungsten, used in electric resistance coils, etc.

plat·i·nous (plat'n-ŭs), *adj.* of or containing platinum.

plat·i·num (plat'n-ŭm), *n.* a grayish-white, malleable, ductile metallic element that stands up well against corrosion.

plat·i·tude (plat'i-tōōd), *n.* 1. insipidity; dullness. 2. a weak, empty, trite remark.

Pla·ton·ic (plâ-ton'ik), *adj.* 1. of or pertaining to Plato, an ancient Greek philosopher, or to his philosophy. 2. [usually p-], pure; not concerned with sexual desire.

Pla·to·nism (plāt'n-izm), *n.* 1. the doctrine taught by Plato (427?-347? B.C.), a Greek philosopher, that reality consists of unchanging forms or ideas of which perceptible things are imitations. 2. a tenet or maxim of Plato. 3. the practice of love between per-

---

a in *cap,* ā in *cane,* ä in *father,* â in *abet,* e in *met,* ē in *be,* ê in *baker,* ê in *regent,* ĭ in *pit,* ī in *fine,* i in *manifest,* o in *hot,* ô in *horse,* ō in *bone,*

sons of the opposite sex, free from sexual feeling or desire. —Pla'to·nist, n.

pla·toon (plȧ-tōōn'), n. two or more groups of soldiers forming a subdivision of a military unit.

plat·ter (plat'ẽr), n. a large, shallow, roundish dish for serving food.

plat·y-, a combining form meaning broad, wide, flat.

plat·y·pus (plat'ĭ-pŭs), n., pl. -pus·es, -pi (-pī), a small, aquatic mammal of Australia and Tasmania with a bill like that of a duck and webbed feet: in full, duckbill platypus.

plat·yr·rhine (plat'ĕ-rīn), n. a broad-nosed animal: adj. broad-nosed.

plau·dit (plô'dĭt), n., usually pl. 1. applause. 2. praise or approval.

plau·si·ble (plô'zĭ-bl), adj. apparently pleasing, genuine, honest, etc.; specious. —plau·si·bil'i·ty, plau'si·ble·ness, n. —plau'si·bly, adv.

play (plā), n. 1. any exercise or occupation for amusement; diversion; pastime. 2. ease of movement. 3. scope for movement. 4. jest. 5. game playing. 6. manner of game playing; style. 7. drama: v.i. 1. to engage in some exercise for amusement. 2. to sport or frolic. 3. to perform upon a musical instrument. 4. to impersonate a character on the stage, in motion pictures, etc. 5. to gamble. 6. to produce sounds. 7. to dally (with). 8. to behave in a particular way. 9. to obtrude unfairly (on): v.t. 1. to engage in (a sport, game, etc.). 2. to be the opponent of in a game. 3. to perform for amusement. 4. to wager on. 5. to use or exercise. 6. to bring about. 7. to perform (music, drama, etc.). 8. to perform on (an instrument). 9. to impersonate the character of.

play·back (plā'bak), n. the reproduction of a tape or disc immediately after recording.

play·bill ('bil), n. a play program.

play·boy ('boi), n. [Informal], a wealthy, profligate man.

play·er ('ẽr), n. 1. one who plays in a game. 2. an actor. 3. a performer on a musical instrument. 4. an automatic device for playing music. 5. a gambler.

player piano, a piano that can play automatically by means of a pneumatic device.

play·ful ('fŭl), adj. 1. sportive; lively. 2. done as a joke. —play'ful·ly, adv. —play'ful·ness, n.

play·go·er ('gō-ẽr), n. a habitual patron of the theater.

play·ground ('ground), n. a place used for recreation, as one adjacent to a school.

play·house ('hous), n. 1. a theater. 2. a small building for children to play in.

playing cards, cards in a deck of four suits, used for playing various games.

play·mate ('māt), n. a companion in play: also play'fel·low.

play·off ('ôf), n. a game or games to decide the final winner or to overcome a tie.

play on words, the act of punning or a pun.

play·pen ('pen), n. a small enclosure for an infant to play in.

play·thing ('thing), n. an object with which to play; toy.

play·wright ('rīt), n. a writer of plays.

pla·za (plä'za), n. 1. an open square or mar-

ketplace. 2. a group of shops. 3. a place along a highway for obtaining food and automobile service.

plea (plē), n. 1. an excuse or apology. 2. an urgent entreaty. 3. in Law, the defendant's answer to the plaintiff's declaration in a lawsuit.

plead (plēd), v.i. plead'ed or (informal) pled or plead (pled), plead'ing, 1. to argue or reason in support of a cause against another; supplicate earnestly. 2. to argue before a court of law: v.t. 1. to discuss or defend by arguments. 2. to offer as an excuse. 3. to state (one's guilt or innocence) in answer to a charge. —plead'er, n.

plead·ings (plēd'ingz), n.pl. the written statements of the two parties in a lawsuit.

pleas·ant (plez'nt), adj. 1. pleasing to the mind or senses; delightful; agreeable. 2. cheerful; jocular. —pleas'ant·ly, adv. —pleas'ant·ness, n.

pleas·ant·ry ('n-trĭ), n., pl. -ries, 1. merriment; lively talk; gaiety. 2. a humorous trick, remark, etc.; joke. 3. a refined or courteous remark.

please (plēz), v.t. pleased, pleas'ing, 1. to gratify; give pleasure to. 2. to be the desire of: v.i. 1. to afford pleasure or gratification. 2. to like or choose.

pleas·ing (plē'zing), adj. affording pleasure; agreeable. —pleas'ing·ly, adv.

pleas·ur·a·ble (plezh'ēr-ȧ-bl), adj. gratifying; delightful. —pleas'ur·a·bly, adv.

pleas·ure (plezh'ẽr), n. 1. gratification; agreeable physical sensations. 2. enjoyment; an agreeable emotional feeling. 3. a liking or choice.

pleat (plēt), n. a flat fold in cloth, doubled over and held in place: v.t. to fold (cloth) in pleats.

ple·be·ian (pli-bē'ȧn), adj. 1. of or pertaining to the lower class of Rome or to the common people anywhere. 2. common or vulgar: n. 1. one of the common people. 2. a rough, vulgar person. —ple·be'ian·ism, n.

pleb·i·scite (pleb'ĭ-sīt), n. a vote taken in an area on some special political matter.

plebs (plebz), n., pl. ple·bes (plē'bĭz), 1. the lower class in ancient Rome. 2. the common people.

plec·trum (plek'trŭm), n., pl. -trums, -tra ('trȧ), a thin piece of plastic, etc. for plucking guitar strings, etc.

pledge (plej), n. 1. anything placed as a security or guarantee; pawn; hostage. 2. the state of being given as security or a guarantee. 3. a toast in drinking. 4. an agreement. 5. that which is agreed to: v.t. pledged, pledg'ing, 1. to give as a security or guarantee; deposit in pawn. 2. to drink to the health of. 3. to obligate by agreement. 4. to agree to donate or give.

pledg·et (plej'it), n. a small piece of cloth placed over a wound.

Ple·ia·des (plē'ȧ-dēz), n.pl. 1. in Greek Mythology, the seven daughters of Atlas and Pleione, fabled to have been placed by Jupiter as a group of stars. 2. in Astronomy, a group of stars in the constellation Taurus, six of which are visible to the naked eye.

Plei·o·cene (plī'ō-sēn), n. same as Pliocene.

ō in dragon, ōō in crude, oo in wool, u in cup, ū in cure, û in turn, ù in focus, oi in boy, ou in house, th in thin, th in sheathe, g in get, j in joy, y in yet.

Pleis·to·cene (plīs'tō-sēn), *n.* an early epoch in the Cenozoic Era, marked by the beginnings of modern man.

ple·na·ry (plē'nȧ-rĭ, plen'ȧ-), *adj.* 1. full; complete. 2. designating a meeting, assembly, etc. to be attended by the entire membership.

plen·i·po·ten·ti·a·ry (plen-i-pō-ten'shi-er-i), *adj.* having or granting full power: *n., pl.* **-ar·ies**, an ambassador, etc. with full powers.

plen·i·tude (plen'i-tōōd), *n.* 1. fullness. 2. copiousness.

plen·te·ous (plen'ti-ŭs), *adj.* abundant; amply sufficient.

plen·ti·ful (plen'ti-fŭl), *adj.* 1. yielding abundance. 2. copious. —**plen'ti·ful·ly,** *adv.*

plen·ty (plen'tĭ), *n.* 1. abundance. 2. an ample supply. 3. many: *adv.* [Informal], abundantly; amply.

ple·num (plē'nŭm), *n., pl.* **-nums, -na** ('nȧ), 1. fullness of matter in space. 2. a body of gas under heavy pressure. 3. a full meeting of a legislative body.

ple·o-, a combining form meaning *more.*

ple·o·nasm (plē'ō-nazm), *n.* the use of more words than necessary in speech or writing. —**ple·o·nas'tic,** *adj.*

ple·si·o·saur (plē'si-ō-sôr), *n.* an extinct, long-necked marine reptile of the Mesozoic Era.

pleth·o·ra (pleth'ō-rȧ), *n.* 1. an excess. 2. an abnormal supply of blood in the system. —**ple·thor·ic** (plē-thôr'ik), *adj.*

pleu·ra (ploor'ȧ), *n., pl.* **-rae** ('ē), a serous membrane covering each lung and the interior of the thorax. —**pleu'ral,** *adj.*

pleu·ri·sy (ploor'i-si), *n.* inflammation of the pleura, with difficulty breathing. —**pleu·rit·ic** (ploo-rit'ik), *adj.*

pleu·ro·pneu·mo·ni·a (ploor-ō-nōō-mōn'yȧ), *n.* inflammation of the pleura and lungs.

plex·i·form (plek'si-fôrm), *adj.* like a network; complicated.

Plex·i·glas (plek'si-glas), *n.* a clear, lightweight plastic, used for lenses, windows, etc.: a trademark.

plex·us (plek'sŭs), *n., pl.* **-us·es, -us,** a network, as of veins, nerves, etc.

pli·a·ble (plī'ȧ-bl), *adj.* 1. easily bent; flexible. 2. easy to be persuaded. 3. easily adjusting. —**pli·a·bil'i·ty,** *n.* —**pli'a·bly,** *adv.*

pli·ant (plī'ȧnt), *adj.* 1. flexible; easily bent. 2. yielding to persuasion. —**pli'an·cy,** *n.*

pli·ca (plī'kȧ), *n., pl.* **-cae** ('sē), a fold of skin, mucous membrane, etc.

pli·cate (plī'kāt), *adj.* 1. plaited. 2. folded in the form of a fan.

pli·ers (plī'ērz), *n.pl.* a kind of small pincers for seizing and bending small articles, wire, etc.

plight (plīt), *n.* a dangerous or distressed condition; predicament: *v.t.* to pledge or hold by a pledge.

plinth (plinth), *n.* 1. the lowest, square-shaped part of the base of a column, pedestal, etc. 2. a projecting section at the bottom of a wall.

Pli·o·cene (plī'ō-sēn), *n.* the last epoch of the Tertiary Period, marked by the beginnings of many modern types of animals and plants.

plod (plod), *v.i.* **plod'ded, plod'ding,** 1. to travel laboriously. 2. to drudge or toil: *n.* 1. a slow, wearied walk. 2. the dull sound of a heavy step. —**plod'der,** *n.*

plop (plop), *v.t. & v.i.* **plopped, plop'ping,** to fall with a sound like that of a flat object hitting the water: *n.* a plopping sound.

plo·sive (plō'siv), *adj.* in *Phonetics,* designating sounds formed by a full stopping and abrupt letting out of the breath, as *k, p,* and *t* at the beginning of a word.

plot (plot), *n.* 1. a secret scheme, conspiracy, or plan; intrigue. 2. a chain of incidents in a play, novel, etc., which are gradually developed. 3. a small area of ground: *v.t.* **plot'ted, plot'ting,** 1. to make a plan or chart of. 2. to mark on a map or chart. 3. to make a secret scheme for: *v.i.* to conspire; form a plan against another. —**plot'ter,** *n.*

plov·er (pluv'ēr, plō'vēr), *n., pl.* **plov'ers, plov'er,** a shore bird with long wings, a short tail, and a small, thick beak.

plow (plou), *n.* 1. an agricultural implement for turning up the soil. 2. a snow plow or other tool like a farm plow: *v.t.* 1. to turn up with a plow. 2. to furrow. 3. to move through as if by plowing: *v.i.* 1. to turn up the soil with a plow. 2. to move (*through, into,* etc.) powerfully. 3. to move forward laboriously. 4. to initiate activity energetically (with *into*). Also, chiefly British spelling, **plough.**

plow·man (plou'mȧn), *n., pl.* **-men** ('mĕn), 1. a man who guides a plow. 2. a rustic.

plow·share ('sher), *n.* the part of a plow that cuts the soil.

ploy (ploi), *n.* a scheme or act the purpose of which is to upset or overcome someone.

pluck (pluk), *v.t.* 1. to pull off, out, or up; pick. 2. to snatch. 3. to tear hair from. 4. to draw and let go quickly (a string of a musical instrument, etc.). 5. [British Slang], to reject as a candidate in an examination: *v.i.* to snatch; pull (with *at*): *n.* 1. a pull. 2. the heart, liver, and lungs of an animal, used for food. 3. courage.

pluck·y (pluk'i), *adj.* **pluck'i·er, pluck'i·est,** having courage or spirit. —**pluck'i·ly,** *adv.* —**pluck'i·ness,** *n.*

plug (plug), *n.* 1. a piece of wood, rubber, etc. used for stopping a hole. 2. same as **spark plug.** 3. a cake of pressed tobacco. 4. a pronged electrical connection. 5. a type of fishing lure. 6. [Informal], an unpaid promotional mention. 7. [Slang], a worn-out, old horse: *v.t.* **plugged, plug'ging,** 1. to stop up with a plug. 2. to insert a plug of. 3. [Informal], to give an unpaid advertisement for. 4. [Slang], to shoot a bullet into: *v.i.* [Informal], to work ploddingly.

plum (plum), *n.* 1. the edible fruit of various trees related to the rose. 2. the tree bearing this. 3. a raisin as used in cooking. 4. a dark purple color. 5. something desirable, as a political appointment.

plum·age (plōō'mij), *n.* a bird's feathers.

plumb (plum), *n.* a heavy lead bob suspended at the extremity of a line to indicate the perpendicularity of a wall, the depth of water, etc.: *adj.* perpendicular: *adv.* **1.** perpendicularly. **2.** [Informal], completely: *v.t.* **1.** to adjust by a plumb line. **2.** to make perpendicular. **3.** to sound (the depth of water) by a plumb bob. **4.** to come to an understanding of.

plum·ba·go (plum-bā'gō), *n., pl.* **-gos,** same as graphite.

plumb bob, a heavy lead bob suspended at the end of a plumb line.

plumb·er (plum'ẽr), *n.* one who is engaged in the business of plumbing.

plumb·ing ('ing), *n.* **1.** the occupation of putting into buildings the pipes, traps, etc. for the conveyance of water, gas, sewage, etc. **2.** the pipes, traps, etc. that a plumber installs and repairs.

plumb line, 1. a line attached to a bob of lead to indicate the perpendicular. **2.** a perpendicular line.

plume (ploom), *n.* **1.** a feather, especially one worn as an ornament. **2.** a crest: *v.t.* **plumed, plum'ing, 1.** to smooth (the feathers). **2.** to adorn with plumes. **3.** to boast; pride (oneself).

plum·met (plum'it), *n.* **1.** a leaden weight attached to a string, used for sounding depths, etc. **2.** anything that bears down like a heavy weight: *v.i.* to plunge.

plump (plump), *adj.* **1.** round with fullness of flesh. **2.** downright; unqualified: *adv.* **1.** with a sudden or heavy fall. **2.** directly downward: *v.i.* **1.** to grow plump. **2.** to fall down heavily. **3.** to vote (*for* a single candidate when one has the right to vote for two or more): *v.t.* **1.** to make plump; fatten. **2.** to let down heavily or abruptly: *n.* **1.** a heavy or abrupt fall. **2.** the sound this makes. — **plump'ness,** *n.*

plum pudding, a pudding composed of flour, suet, raisins, currants, citron, and spices and boiled, as in a linen bag.

plum·ule (ploom'ūl), *n.* in Botany, the first bud of an embryo.

plum·y (ploo'mi), *adj.* **plum'i·er, plum'i·est,** feathered.

plun·der (plun'dẽr), *n.* **1.** pillage. **2.** booty: *v.t. & v.i.* **1.** to take by open force. **2.** to rob.

plun·der·age (-ij), *n.* the embezzlement of goods on board ship.

plunge (plunj), *v.t.* **plunged, plung'ing,** to put suddenly (*into* water or any other liquid, a hole, etc.); immerse: *v.i.* **1.** to sink, fall, or rush, as into water, battle, etc.; dive. **2.** to move abruptly downward and forward. **3.** [Informal], to bet heavily and thoughtlessly: *n.* **1.** the act of plunging. **2.** a sudden fall. **3.** [Informal], a heavy, thoughtless wager.

plung·er (plun'jẽr), *n.* **1.** one who plunges. **2.** a diver. **3.** a long, solid cylinder or piston, as of a pump. **4.** a rubber suction device for freeing blocked drains. **5.** [Informal], one who bets heavily and thoughtlessly.

plunk (plungk), *v.i.* **1.** to play (a guitar, etc.) by picking or strumming. **2.** to lay down heavily: *v.i.* **1.** to produce a sharp, vibrating sound. **2.** to fall heavily: *n.* the sound of plunking.

plu·per·fect (ploo-pûr'fikt), *adj.* denoting an event or action occurring prior to some past event or action: *n.* in Grammar, a tense expressing pluperfect action.

plu·ral (ploor'ăl), *adj.* consisting of more than one: *n.* in Grammar, that form of a word that expresses more than one.

plu·ral·ism (-izm), *n.* **1.** the doctrine that there are two or more causative influences affecting the universe. **2.** the holding of two or more offices at the same time.

plu·ral·i·ty (ploo-ral'ĭ-ti), *n., pl.* **-ties, 1.** the majority. **2.** the state of being a great number. **3.** the excess of votes cast for any one candidate over the candidate who receives the next largest number of votes at an election in which there are three or more candidates for the same office.

plu·ral·ize (ploor'ă-līz), *v.t. & v.i.* **-ized, -iz·ing,** to make or become plural.

plus (plus), *n., pl.* **plus'es, plus'ses, 1.** the sign (+) used to denote addition or a positive amount. **2.** that which is added: *adj.* **1.** denoting increase or addition. **2.** above zero. **3.** more by some amount. **4.** [Informal], and more: *prep.* **1.** combined with. **2.** besides.

plush (plush), *n.* a kind of soft cloth with a deep pile: *adj.* [Slang], rich and comfortable: also **plush'y.**

Plu·to (ploot'ō), *n.* **1.** in Greek and Roman Mythology, the god of the lower world. **2.** the most remote planet of the solar system, ninth in distance from the sun.

plu·toc·ra·cy (ploo-tok'ră-si), *n., pl.* **-cies, 1.** rule or government by the wealthy. **2.** a number of wealthy people who exercise political power or influence.

plu·to·crat (ploot'ō-krat), *n.* **1.** one of a number of wealthy people who rule a country. **2.** one who exercises political power or influence by virtue of wealth.

Plu·to·ni·an (ploo-tō'ni-ăn), *adj.* of or pertaining to Pluto, god of the lower world, or the world of the dead.

plu·ton·ic (ploo-ton'ik), *adj.* of or pertaining to rocks created underneath the earth's surface by great heat and pressure.

plu·to·ni·um (ploo-tō'ni-ŭm), *n.* a radioactive, metallic element.

plu·vi·al (ploo'vi-ăl), *adj.* **1.** of rain. **2.** rainy.

ply (plī), *v.t.* **plied, ply'ing, 1.** to work on energetically. **2.** to be employed at (a trade). **3.** to urge or solicit. **4.** to continue furnishing (*with* gifts), attacking (*with* questions), etc. **5.** to sail on a regular basis across. **6.** to twist or mold: *v.i.* **1.** to continue to be active (*at* a trade). **2.** to work (*with* a tool). **3.** to run regularly between two places, as a ship. **4.** to sail against the wind: *n., pl.* **plies, 1.** a layer or thickness, as of carpet. **2.** a twisted strand, as of rope.

Ply·mouth Rock (plim'ŭth), **1.** a rock at Plymouth, Mass., said to be the first place stepped on by the Pilgrims in landing from the Mayflower. **2.** any one of a breed of American domestic fowl with gray or black feathers.

ply·wood (plī'wood), *n.* a building material consisting of thin layers of wood combined with an adhesive.

pneu·ma (nōō'mä), *n.* the soul; spirit.

pneu·mat·ic (nōō-mat'ik), *adj.* **1.** of, pertaining

ŏ in dra*g*on, ōō in cr*u*de, oo in w*oo*l, u in c*u*p, ū in c*u*re, ū in t*u*rn, ŭ in f*o*cus, oi in b*oy*, ou in h*ou*se, th in *th*in, th in shea*th*e, g in *g*et, j in *j*oy, y in *y*et.

to, or containing air or gases. 2. inflated with or moved by compressed air. —pneu-mat'i-cal-ly, adv.

pneu-mat-ics ('iks), n. the science that treats of the mechanical properties of air and other gases.

pneu-ma-tol-o-gy (nōō-mȧ-tol'ȯ-ji), n. the study of spirits or spiritual phenomena.

pneu-mo-, a combining form meaning lung.

pneu-mo-co-ni-o-sis (nōō-mō-kō-ni-ō'sis), n. a disease of the lungs due to the inhaling of dust or minute metallic particles.

pneu-mo-gas-tric (-gas'trik), adj. of or pertaining to the lungs and stomach.

pneu-mo-ni-a (noo-mōn'yȧ), n. acute inflammation of the lungs. —pneu-mon'ic (-mon'ik), adj.

pneu-mo-tho-rax (nōō-mō-thôr'aks), n. accumulation of air or gas in a pleural cavity.

poach (pōch), v.i. to shoot or steal game while trespassing: v.t. 1. to trespass upon (preserves, etc.) to shoot or steal (game). 2. to cook (eggs without shells, fish, etc.) in boiling water. —poach'er, n.

poach-y (pōch'i), adj. poach'i-er, poach'i-est, swampy; marshy.

po-chard (pō'cherd), n., pl. -chards, -chard, a diving sea duck.

pock (pok), n. 1. a pustule containing eruptive matter. 2. a pit, as that left by smallpox.

pock-et (pok'it), n. 1. a small bag inserted in a garment for carrying small articles. 2. a small net bag in a billiard table for the reception of balls. 3. a small region or unit. 4. a cavity holding or able to hold something. 5. a condition in the atmosphere which causes an airplane to make a sudden drop: also air pocket: adj. 1. small; diminutive. 2. of the size that can fit in a pocket: v.t. 1. to put into a pocket. 2. to appropriate (money, etc.). 3. to accept (an insult, etc.) without retaliation. 4. to furnish with pockets. 5. to surround. 6. to put aside. —pock'et-ful (-fool), n., pl. -fuls.

pock-et-book (-book), n. 1. a handbag carried by a woman. 2. financial assets.

pock-et-knife (-nīf), n., pl. -knives (-nīvz), a knife with blades that fold into the handle.

pock-mark (pok'märk), n. a pit on the skin resulting from a pustule.

pod (pod), n. 1. the covering of the seed of certain plants, as the pea. 2. a group of whales, seals, etc.: v.i. 1. to swell into a pod. 2. to produce pods.

-pod (pod), a combining form meaning foot, feet.

po-dag-ra (pō-dag'rȧ), n. gout, especially in the big toe of the foot.

podg-y (poj'i), adj. podg'i-er, podg'i-est, short and fat.

po-di-a-try (pō-dī'ȧ-tri), n. the act or practice of treating disorders of the feet. —po-di'a-trist, n.

po-di-um (pō'di-ŭm), n. 1. a low wall acting as a base. 2. a small stand, as for a speaker, conductor, etc.

pod-o-phyl-lin (pod-ō-fil'in), n. a purgative resin obtained from the root of the mandrake.

po-em (pō'ĕm), n. 1. a composition, usually metrical, sometimes rhymed, expressing creative imagination. 2. a poetic conception.

po-e-sy (pō'ĕ-si), n., pl. -sies, [Obsolete], same as poetry.

po-et (pō'ĕt), n. 1. the author of poems. 2. one gifted in writing poetry. 3. one who is strongly creative and imaginative. —po'et-ess, n.fem.

po-et-as-ter (pō'ĕ-tas-tēr), n. a dabbler in poetry; one who writes inferior verse.

po-et-ic (pō-et'ik), adj. 1. of, pertaining to, suitable to, or expressed in poetry. 2. sublime. Also po-et'i-cal. —po-et'i-cal-ly, adv.

poetic license, a taking latitude in the creation of art.

po-et-ics (pō-et'iks), n. 1. rules and principles governing poetic composition. 2. a treatise on poetry.

poet laureate, pl. poets laureate, poet laureates, a court poet or official national poet.

po-et-ry (pō'ĕ-tri), n. 1. a collection of poems. 2. the composing of poems. 3. the characteristics of a poem.

po-go stick (pō'gō), a stout stick with projections for the feet and a spring near one end, on which one can jump from place to place.

po-grom (pō-grom', pō'grŏm), n. a massacre and pillage directed against a group, as the Jews in czarist Russia.

po-gy (pō'gi), n., pl. -gies, same as menhaden.

poi (poi), n. a gelatinous food made in Hawaii from the ground root of the taro plant.

poign-ant (poin'yȧnt), adj. 1. having a stimulating smell. 2. irritating, very painful. 3. producing an emotional response. 4. keen; incisive. —poign'an-cy, n.

poin-ci-a-na (poin-si-an'ȧ), n. a small tropical tree or shrub bearing scarlet or orange-yellow flowers.

poin-set-ti-a (poin-set'i-ȧ, -set'ȧ), n. a plant of Mexico and Central America with red leaves and yellow flowers.

point (point), n. 1. the sharp end of any instrument. 2. a tiny mark or dot. 3. a mark in punctuation. 4. that which has position but no magnitude. 5. a spot; exact place. 6. a critical moment. 7. expression or force. 8. the main idea of a joke, epigram, etc. 9. an aim. 10. a cape or promontory. 11. lace wrought with a needle. 12. a level attained. 13. a characteristic. 14. a fixed amount. 15. a striking statement. 16. a useful suggestion. 17. a compass mark indicating direction. 18. a unit of measurement for type bodies, equal to .0138 inch, or one twelfth of a pica: v.t. 1. to sharpen; give a point to. 2. to direct or aim. 3. to mark with points. 4. to give force to. 5. to fill joints of (masonry) with mortar: v.i. 1. to direct one's finger (with at or to). 2. to hint. 3. to aim (with to or toward).

point-blank (point'blangk'), adj. 1. horizontal; straight at a mark. 2. direct: adv. directly.

point-ed (poin'tid), adj. 1. sharpened; having a sharp point. 2. direct; telling; epigrammatic. 3. personal. 4. extremely clear or obvious. —point'ed-ly, adv.

point-er (poin'tēr), n. 1. one who or that which points. 2. a large dog trained to point out game. 3. a long, thin stick used for pointing at something. 4. a needle on a meter, scale, etc. 5. [Informal], an idea presented for consideration.

point lace, same as **needlepoint**.

point-less (point'lis), *adj.* 1. having no point. 2. having no purpose or meaning.

point of view, 1. the manner of viewing something. 2. an attitude.

point-y (poin'ti), *adj.* **point'i-er, point'i-est**, 1. that forms a sharp point. 2. with numerous points.

poise (poiz), *n.* 1. balance; equilibrium. 2. self-possession. 3. posture: *v.t.* & *v.i.* **poised, pois'ing**, to balance or be in a state of equilibrium.

poi-son (poi'zn), *n.* anything noxious or destructive to life, health, or well-being: *v.t.* 1. to infect with or kill by poison. 2. to administer poison to. 3. to corrupt: *adj.* having the qualities of poison.

poison ivy, a plant with leaves having three leaflets, greenish flowers, and white berries, that can produce a painful rash upon contact.

pois-on-ous (poi'zn-ǔs), *adj.* having the qualities of poison; deadly; injurious to health. — **poi'son-ous-ly,** *adv.*

poison sumac, a plant found in swamps with leaves of small leaflets, greenish-white flowers, and small bunches of fruit, that can produce a painful rash upon contact.

poke (pōk), *n.* 1. a thrust or push. 2. [Dialectal], a bag or sack. 3. [Slang], a hitting with the hand clenched: *v.t.* **poked, pok'ing**, 1. to thrust or push against with something pointed. 2. to produce by poking. 3. [Slang], to strike with the hand clenched: *v.i.* 1. to thrust (*at*). 2. to grope or feel; search (*about* or *around*). 3. to dawdle (*along*).

pok-er (pō'kēr), *n.* 1. a metal bar for stirring fires. 2. a card game in which each player bets on the value of the hand he holds.

poker face, [Informal], a face that indicates nothing, as of a poker player attempting to keep the character of his hand to himself.

pok-y (pō'ki), *adj.* **pok'i-er, pok'i-est**, 1. lacking spirit or interest; slow. 2. stuffy; lacking ventilation. Also **pok'ey**.

po-lar (pō'lēr), *adj.* 1. of, pertaining to, or situated near either the North or South Pole. 2. of or pertaining to a pole.

polar bear, a large, white bear of the arctic regions.

Po-la-ris (pō-ler'is), *n.* same as **North Star**.

po-lar-i-scope (pō-ler'i-skōp), *n.* an instrument for showing the polarization of light.

po-lar-i-ty (pō-ler'i-ti), *n., pl.* **-ties**, 1. the property possessed by certain bodies by which they arrange themselves so that their opposite ends point to the earth's two magnetic poles. 2. a contrary inclination.

po-lar-i-za-tion (pō-lēr-i-zā'shǔn), *n.* 1. the act of polarizing. 2. the state of being polarized. 3. in *Optics*, a type of light in which the waves are restricted to one plane.

po-lar-ize (pō'lá-rīz), *v.t.* **-ized, -iz-ing**, to communicate polarity to: *v.i.* 1. to take on polarity. 2. to split into contrary factions.

Po-lar-oid (pō'lá-roid), *n.* 1. a light-polarizing agent consisting of a transparent material covered with crystals. 2. a portable camera that makes prints almost instantly: in full, **Polaroid Land camera**. A trademark.

pole (pōl), *n.* 1. a long staff of wood, metal, etc. 2. a unit of measure, equal to 5 1/2 yards, or in square measure to 30 1/4 square yards. 3. one of the extremities of the imaginary axis of the earth. 4. one of two points, as in a magnet, in which the attractive or repellent force is concentrated. 5. that on which something revolves. 6. the extreme opposite: *v.t.* & *v.i.* **poled, pol'ing**, to make (a boat or raft) move with a pole.

pole-cat (pōl'kat), *n., pl.* **-cats, -cat**, 1. a small carnivorous animal resembling a weasel. 2. a skunk.

po-lem-ic (pō-lem'ik), *n.* 1. controversy. 2. one who likes to take part in controversy. 3. *pl.* the art of controversy; controversial writings, etc.: *adj.* 1. of, pertaining to, or including controversy. 2. liking argument: also **po-lem'i-cal**. —**po-lem'i-cal-ly,** *adv.*

po-lem-i-cist ('i-sist), *n.* an expert in polemics: also **po-lem'ist** ('ist).

pole-star (pōl'stär), *n.* 1. the North Star, Polaris. 2. a guide.

pole vault, a leap for height by vaulting over a bar with the aid of a long pole.

po-lice (pō-lēs'), *n.* 1. in a city, town, or district, an organized force of civil officers for preserving order. 2. those officers belonging to the force: *v.t.* **-liced', -lic'ing**, 1. to guard or preserve order with policemen. 2. to maintain cleanliness and order in (a military location).

police court, in some States, a lower court able to pass judgment on a person charged with a minor offense and hold one charged with a felony for trial in a higher court.

police dog, a dog trained to assist the police.

po-lice-man ('mǎn), *n., pl.* **-men** ('měn), a member of a police force. —**po-lice'wom-an** *n.fem., pl.* **-wom-en**.

police state, a nation or government that utilizes police to squelch political activity.

pol-i-clin-ic (pol-i-klin'ik), *n.* a hospital dispensary where outpatients are treated.

pol-i-cy (pol'i-si), *n., pl.* **-cies**, 1. method of government; system of regulative measures; course of conduct. 2. sagacity in management. 3. a document containing a contract of insurance: in full, **insurance policy**. 4. a gambling game.

pol-i-cy-hold-er (-hōl-dēr), *n.* a person to whom an insurance policy has been granted.

po-li-o-my-e-li-tis (pō-li-ō-mī-ē-līt'is), *n.* an acute infectious disease, usually attacking young children, caused by inflammation of the gray matter of the spinal cord: it is characterized by muscle paralysis and sometimes atrophy that results in deformity.

Po-lish (pō'lish), *adj.* of or pertaining to Poland, a nation in central Europe, or to its inhabitants: *n.* the language of Poland.

pol-ish (pol'ish), *v.t.* 1. to make smooth and glossy by friction. 2. to make polite or refined: *v.i.* to become polished: *n.* 1. a smooth, glossy surface. 2. a preparation for

---

ō in dragon, ōō in crude, oo in wool, u in cup, ū in cure, ŭ in turn, ủ in focus, oi in boy, ou in house, th in thin, th in sheathe, g in get, j in joy, y in yet.

imparting a polish. 3. refinement or elegance of manners.

po·lite (pô-līt′), *adj.* 1. well-bred; refined in manner. 2. courteous or obliging. —**po·lite′ly**, *adv.* —**po·lite′ness**, *n.*

pol·i·tesse (pol-ī-tes′), *n.* politeness.

pol·i·tic (pol′ī-tik), *adj.* 1. shrewd; sagacious. 2. carefully formed; utilizing advantageously; expedient: *v.i.* -**ticked**, -**tick·ing**, to take part in political campaigns.

po·lit·i·cal (pô-lit′i-kl), *adj.* 1. of or pertaining to politics, government, etc. 2. of or like politicians, political parties, etc. —**po·lit′i·cal·ly**, *adv.*

political science, the study of governmental methods, policies, etc. —**political scientist**.

pol·i·ti·cian (pol-i-tish′ûn), *n.* 1. one who is skilled in politics. 2. one who is active in politics, often for self-interest.

po·lit·i·co (pô-lit′i-kō), *n., pl.* -**cos**, same as politician.

pol·i·tics (pol′ī-tiks), *n.pl.* 1. the art of government or the administration of public affairs. 2. political opinions, principles, etc. 3. party management or control. 4. planning for power by groups within a party, organization, etc.

pol·i·ty (pol′ī-ti), *n., pl.* -**ties**, 1. political form of civil government. 2. a state.

pol·ka (pōl′kä), *n.* 1. a fast dance of Bohemian origin, performed by two persons. 2. music suitable for such a dance.

pol·ka dot (pō′kä), 1. any one of the little, round dots forming a pattern on a background of a different color. 2. a pattern formed of these dots.

poll (pōl), *n.* 1. the head, especially the back part of it. 2. a register of persons, especially those entitled to vote. 3. an election. 4. the number of votes recorded at an election. 5. *pl.* a place where votes are cast. 6. a researching of attitudes: *v.t.* 1. to lop, clip, or shear. 2. to remove the horns, wool, etc. of. 3. to take the votes of. 4. to obtain (votes). 5. to cast (a vote). 6. to obtain and evaluate attitudes of.

pol·lack (pol′ăk), *n., pl.* -**lack**, -**lacks**, any of several marine food fishes related to the cod.

pol·lard (pol′ērd), *n.* 1. a tree with the top branches polled. 2. an ox, goat, etc. without horns.

pol·len (pol′ĕn), *n.* the powderlike male fertilizing cells of the anthers of flowers.

pollen count, the frequency of pollen, especially of ragweed, in a given volume of air.

pol·li·nate (pol′ī-nāt), *v.t.* -**nat·ed**, -**nat·ing**, to convey pollen to the pistil of (a flower). —**pol·li·na′tion**, *n.*

pol·li·wog (pol′i-wog), *n.* same as tadpole.

poll·ster (pōl′stēr), *n.* a person employed to obtain polls of public attitudes.

poll tax, a per capita tax.

pol·lute (pô-lōōt′), *v.t.* -**lut′ed**, -**lut′ing**, to defile; render unclean; corrupt; violate. —**pol·lu′tant**, *n.* —**pol·lu′tion**, *n.*

po·lo (pō′lō), *n.* a game played on horseback by two teams attempting to drive a wooden ball through the opponent's goal with long-handled mallets.

po·lo·naise (pol-ô-nāz′), *n.* a very formal Polish dance.

po·lo·ni·um (pô-lō′ni-ûm), *n.* a radioactive chemical element.

pol·ter·geist (pōl′tēr-gīst), *n.* a ghost supposed to cause strange noises and activities.

pol·troon (pol-trōōn′), *n.* a complete coward.

pol·y-, a combining form meaning *many, much.*

pol·y·an·dry (pol′i-an-dri), *n.* the practice of having more than one husband at the same time.

pol·y·an·thus (pol-i-an′thûs), *n.* 1. a kind of primrose. 2. a narcissus.

pol·y·chot·o·mous (pol-i-kot′ô-mûs), *adj.* divided into many parts or branches.

pol·y·chro·mat·ic (-krō-mat′ik), *adj.* exhibiting a play of colors.

pol·y·chrome (pol′i-krōm), *adj.* having many colors: *n.* a work of art executed in many colors.

pol·y·clin·ic (pol-i-klin′ik), *n.* a hospital that is equipped to treat a variety of diseases.

pol·y·es·ter (pol′i-es-tēr), *n.* a resin formed of polymers, used to make plastics, fibers, etc.

pol·y·eth·yl·ene (pol-i-eth′ī-lēn), *n.* a resin that can be heated and molded to make hard, light plastics, films, etc.

po·lyg·a·my (pô-lig′ă-mi), *n.* the practice of having more than one wife or husband at the same time. —**po·lyg′a·mist**, *n.* —**po·lyg′a·mous**, *adj.*

pol·y·gen·e·sis (pol-i-jen′ĕ-sis), *n.* a plurality of origins. —**pol·y·ge·net′ic** (-jĕ-net′ik), *adj.*

pol·y·glot (pol′i-glot), *adj.* 1. containing many languages. 2. versed in many languages: *n.* 1. a book in several languages. 2. one versed in many languages.

pol·y·gon (pol′i-gon), *n.* a plane figure having more than four angles and sides. —**po·lyg·o·nal** (pô-lig′ô-nl), *adj.*

pol·y·graph (-graf), *n.* 1. an early copying machine. 2. a device to register alterations in breathing, pulse, etc., often used on persons suspected of lying.

pol·y·he·dron (pol-i-hē′drŏn), *n., pl.* -**drons**, -**dra** (′drä), a solid figure with more than six plane surfaces. —**pol·y·he′dral**, *adj.*

pol·y·mer (pol′i-mēr), *n.* a material that is composed of very large molecules which are made up of smaller molecules of the same sort.

pol·y·mor·phous (pol-i-môr′fûs), *adj.* assuming various forms.

Pol·y·ne·sian (pol-i-nē′zhûn, ′shûn), *n.* a member of a dark-skinned people native to the islands in the eastern part of the Pacific: *adj.* of this people or region.

pol·y·no·mi·al (pol-i-nō′mi-ăl), *n.* an algebraic expression consisting of two or more terms.

pol·yp (pol′ip), *n.* any one of a group of aquatic animals that have cylindrical bodies and tentacles around the mouth, as the hydra, sea anemone, etc.

pol·y·pha·gi·a (pol-i-fā′ji-ä), *n.* 1. abnormal hunger. 2. the ability to exist on various kinds of foods. —**po·lyph·a·gous** (pô-lif′ā-gûs), *adj.*

po·lyph·o·ny (pô-lif′ô-ni), *n.* 1. multiplicity of sounds, as in an echo. 2. in *Music*, the mixing of harmonious tones. 3. in *Phonetics*, the representation of more than one sound by the same written character. —**pol·y·phon·ic** (pol-i-fon'ik), *adj.* —**pol·y·phon'i·cal·ly**, *adv.*

pol·y·phy·let·ic (pol-i-fī-let'ik), *adj.* derived from more than one ancestral type.

pol·y·syl·lab·ic (-si-lab'ik), *adj.* 1. of, pertaining to, or consisting of four or more syllables. 2. having polysyllabic words. —**pol'y·syl·la·ble** (-sil-ā-bl), *n.*

pol·y·tech·nic (pol-i-tek'nik), *adj.* denoting or imparting instruction in the sciences and technology: *n.* a school for imparting such instruction.

pol·y·the·ism (pol'i-thi-izm), *n.* the doctrine or worship of a plurality of gods. —**pol'y·the·ist**, *adj. & n.* —**pol·y·the·is'tic**, *adj.*

pol·y·un·sat·u·rat·ed (pol-i-un-sach'ū-rāt-id), *adj.* of or denoting various animal and plant oils and fats containing very little cholesterol.

pol·y·u·ri·a (-yoor'i-ā), *n.* excessive secretion and discharge of urine.

pol·y·va·lent (-vā'lĕnt), *adj.* 1. having more than one valence or a valence of more than two. 2. powerful against many infections: said of a vaccine.

pom·ace (pum'is), *n.* the crushed pulp of apples or similar fruits.

po·made (po-mād', pō-; -mäd'), *n.* a perfumed ointment for dressing the hair: also **po·ma·tum** (pō-māt'ŭm): *v.t.* -**mad'ed**, -**mad'ing**, to dress (the hair) with pomade.

pome·gran·ate (pom'gran-it, pom'ē-; pum'-), *n.* 1. a roundish fruit that has a very hard rind enclosing a red, pulpy mass interspersed with many seeds. 2. the tree or bush on which the fruit grows.

Pom·er·a·ni·an (pom-ē-rā'ni-ăn), *n.* one of a breed of small dog with long, silky hair, a foxlike muzzle, and pointed ears.

po·mif·er·ous (pō-mif'ēr-ŭs), *adj.* bearing pomes.

pom·mel (pum'l), *v.t.* -**meled** or -**melled**, -**mel·ing** or -**mel·ling**, to thrash soundly with the fists: *n.* (also **pom'l**), a knob at the front of a saddle or on the hilt of a sword.

po·mol·o·gy (pō-mol'ō-ji), *n.* the science of cultivating fruit and fruit trees.

Po·mo·na (pō-mō'nä), *n.* the Roman goddess presiding over orchards and vineyards.

pomp (pomp), *n.* 1. ostentatious display. 2. grandeur.

pom·pa·dour (pom'pä-dôr), *n.* 1. a style of dressing a woman's hair by drawing it straight back from the front and elevating it with a roll. 2. a mode of arranging a man's hair by combing it straight up from the forehead.

pom·pa·no (pom'pä-nō), *n., pl.* -**no**, -**nos**, a food fish of the waters of the southeastern coast of the U.S., with spiny fins.

pom·pon (pom'pon, 'pom), *n.* 1. a tufted ornament, as on caps. 2. a variety of chrysanthemum, dahlia, etc. with tiny, round flower heads.

pom·pous (pom'pŭs), *adj.* 1. stately; grand. 2. self-important; ostentatious. —**pom·pos'i·ty** (-pos'i-ti), *n.*

pon·cho (pon'chō), *n., pl.* -**chos**, 1. a cloak with a hole for the head, worn in Spanish America. 2. a similar cloak worn as a raincoat.

pond (pond), *n.* a large pool of standing water.

pon·der (pon'dēr), *v.t.* to weigh mentally: *v.i.* to deliberate. —**pon'der·a·ble**, *adj.* —**pon·der·a·bil'i·ty**, *n.*

pon·der·ous (pon'dēr-ŭs), *adj.* 1. very heavy; weighty. 2. dull. 3. difficult to manage. —**pon·der·os'i·ty** (-ti), *n.*

pone (pōn), *n.* [Chiefly Southern], a small, roundish bread made of cornmeal.

pon·gee (pon-jē'), *n.* a kind of soft, sheer silk.

pon·iard (pon'yērd), *n.* a small dagger: *v.t.* to stab with a poniard.

pon·tiff (pon'tif), *n.* 1. a high priest. 2. a bishop. 3. [P-], the Pope.

pon·tif·i·cal (pon-tif'i-kl), *adj.* of or pertaining to a high priest or pope; papal: *n.* 1. a book containing the ecclesiastical rites and ceremonies of a bishop. 2. *pl.* the full dress worn by a pontiff. —**pon·tif'i·cal·ly**, *adv.*

pon·tif·i·cate (-kit), *n.* the office or reign of a high priest or pope: *v.i.* (-kāt), 1. to perform ecclesiastical rites or ceremonies as a pontiff. 2. to talk in an arrogant or self-important manner.

pon·toon (pon-tōōn'), *n.* 1. a buoyant structure supporting a floating bridge. 2. a boat with a flat bottom. 3. the float of an aircraft.

po·ny (pō'ni), *n., pl.* -**nies**, 1. a small horse. 2. a small glass for liqueur. 3. [Informal], a translation of foreign literature, used dishonestly in doing schoolwork: *v.t. & v.i.* -**nied**, -**ny·ing**, [Slang], to pay (with *up*).

pooch (pōōch), *n.* [Slang], a dog.

poo·dle (pōō'dl), *n.* any one of a breed of dog with hair of a solid color in ringlets.

pooh (pōō), *interj.* an exclamation of scorn, skepticism, etc.

pooh-pooh (pōō'pōō'), *v.t.* to be scornful or slighting of.

pool (pōōl), *n.* 1. a small body of water. 2. a small amount of liquid. 3. a puddle. 4. an artificially created tank for swimming. 5. the stakes in certain games. 6. a variety of billiards using a six-pocket table. 7. an aggregate of money, materials, etc. for some common purpose. 8. the members forming such an aggregate: *v.t. & v.i.* to contribute to a common fund.

pool·room (pōōl'rōōm), *n.* a room where pool games are played.

pool table, a kind of billiard table for playing pool.

poop (pōōp), *n.* the raised deck in the stern of a vessel: also **poop deck**: *v.t.* to break heavily over the stern of: said of waves.

poop (pōōp), *v.t.* [Slang], to exhaust; tire.

poor (poor), *adj.* 1. needy; having little or no means; destitute of riches. 2. without strength, beauty, or dignity. 3. dejected; spiritless. 4. insignificant. 5. humble. 6. lean. 7. without fertility. 8. pitiful. 9. without value: *n.* poor persons collectively (preceded by *the*).

poor·house (poor'hous), *n.* formerly, a place supported by taxes for the housing of paupers.

poor·ly (poor'li), *adv.* 1. without adequate

ŏ in dragon, ōō in crude, oo in wool, u in cup, ū in cure, û in turn, ŭ in focus, oi in boy, ou in house, th in thin, th in sheathe, g in get, j in joy, y in yet.

means. **2.** with scant success: *adj.* [Informal], somewhat ill; delicate in health.

pop (pop), *n.* **1.** a short, quick, bursting sound. **2.** a carbonated beverage without alcohol. **3.** a shortened form of *popular.* **4.** [Slang], father or an elderly man: *v.t.* popped, pop'-ping, **1.** to thrust suddenly. **2.** to expose to heat and make expand, as corn kernels: *v.i.* **1.** to make a short, quick, bursting sound. **2.** to move quickly; dart; come suddenly into view. **3.** to protrude: said of the eyes. **4.** in *Baseball,* to strike the ball up into the air in the infield: *adv.* suddenly.

pop art, a style of art based in realism and utilizing subjects and materials from commercial art.

pop-corn (pop'kôrn), *n.* any variety of Indian corn with small ears and small, hard grains which expand, when exposed to heat, with a popping sound.

Pope (pōp), *n.* **1.** the bishop of Rome and head of the Roman Catholic Church. **2.** [p-], a title of priests of the Orthodox Eastern Church. **3.** [p-], a person of much authority. —**pope'dom** ('dŏm), *n.*

pop-eyed (pop'īd), *adj.* having protruding eyes.

pop-gun ('gun), *n.* a toy gun with a cork in the end of the barrel, which pops out when the trigger releases compressed air.

pop-in-jay (pop'in-jā), *n.* a vain, garrulous person.

pop-lar (pop'lêr), *n.* **1.** a tree of rapid growth with a white, soft wood. **2.** the wood of this tree.

pop-lin (pop'lin), *n.* a strong fabric of silk, cotton, etc. with ribbing.

pop-o-ver (pop'ō-vêr), *n.* a very light muffin with a hollow center.

pop-pet (pop'it), *n.* a piece of wood for supporting an oarlock.

pop-py (pop'i), *n., pl.* -**pies,** **1.** a plant with bright, showy flowers of various shades of red, white, and yellow. **2.** the juice of one type, from which opium is prepared. **3.** a vivid scarlet color.

pop-py-cock (pop'i-kok), *n.* [Informal], nonsense.

poppy seed, the tiny, black seed of the poppy, used to flavor or decorate baked goods.

pop-u-lace (pop'yū-lis), *n.* **1.** the common people. **2.** same as **population** (sense 1).

pop-u-lar (pop'yū-lêr), *adj.* **1.** of, pertaining to, suitable for, or pleasing to the common people; plebian. **2.** pleasing to a great number of people. **3.** financially available to most persons. **4.** having the affection of many persons. —**pop-u-lar'i-ty** (-lêr'ĭ-ti), *n.* —**pop'u-lar-ly,** *adv.*

pop-u-lar-ize (pop'yū-lā-rīz), *v.t.* -**ized, -iz-ing,** to render popular. —**pop-u-lar-i-za'tion,** *n.* —**pop'u-lar-iz-er,** *n.*

pop-u-late (pop'yū-lāt), *v.t.* -**lat-ed, -lat-ing,** **1.** to furnish with inhabitants. **2.** to live in.

pop-u-la-tion (pop-yū-lā'shŭn), *n.* **1.** the inhabitants of a country, place, town, etc. collectively. **2.** the total number of inhabitants. **3.** the act of populating. **4.** the state of being populated.

population explosion, a large and mounting growth of population.

pop-u-lous (pop'yū-lŭs), *adj.* thickly peopled.

por-bea-gle (pôr'bē-gl), *n.* a very voracious shark found in the north Atlantic and Pacific.

por-ce-lain (pôr'sl-in), *n.* a fine, white, thin, semi-transparent kind of eathenware: *adj.* of, pertaining to, or made of porcelain.

porch (pôrch), *n.* **1.** a covered entrance to a building, usually projecting from the wall. **2.** an enclosed room attached to the exterior of a building.

por-cine (pôr'sin), *adj.* of or pertaining to swine.

por-cu-pine (pôr'kyū-pīn), *n., pl.* -**pines, -pine,** a large rodent having strong, stiff, sharp, erectile spines interspersed through its hair.

pore (pôr), *n.* a minute hole in the skin, plant leaves, etc. through which liquid is taken in or let out: *v.i.* pored, por'ing, **1.** to look with close and steady attention, as on a book (with *over*). **2.** to consider carefully and completely (with *over*).

por-gy (pôr'gi), *n., pl.* -**gies, -gy,** a marine food fish.

pork (pôrk), *n.* the flesh of swine, especially when used fresh, or uncured.

pork barrel, [Informal], a fund of money obtained from the Federal treasury through Congressional appropriation bills for rivers, harbors, public buildings, etc., which is regarded as the reward for political services.

pork-er (pôr'kêr), *n.* a young hog.

pork-y (pôr'ki), *adj.* pork'i-er, pork'i-est, **1.** of or similar to pork. **2.** fat. **3.** [Slang], impudent; swaggering.

por-nog-ra-phy (pôr-nog'rā-fī), *n.* books, photographs, etc. designed to stimulate sexual desire. —**por-no-graph'ic** (-nō-graf'ik), *adj.*

por-o-mer-ic (pôr-ō-mer'ik), *n.* a man-made substance that has the appearance of leather, used for making shoes, suitcases, etc.

po-rous (pôr'ŭs), *adj.* having pores; permeable by liquid, air, etc. —**po-ros-i-ty** (pō-ros'ĭ-ti), *n.*

por-phy-rit-ic (pôr-fĭ-rit'ik), *adj.* having the appearance or texture of porphyry.

por-phy-ry (pôr'fêr-i), *n., pl.* -**ries,** **1.** originally, a reddish igneous rock found in Egypt, with enclosed crystals of feldspar. **2.** any igneous rock with large feldspar crystals.

por-poise (pôr'pis), *n., pl.* -**pois-es, -poise,** **1.** a small, gregarious whale with a rounded snout. **2.** a dolphin.

por-ridge (pôr'ij), *n.* [Chiefly British], oatmeal or other cereal boiled slowly in water until it thickens.

por-rin-ger ('in-jêr), *n.* a small bowl for porridge, etc.

port (pôrt), *n.* **1.** a harbor. **2.** deportment or carriage. **3.** the left side of a ship when one is facing forward. **4.** a porthole. **5.** a dark-colored, sweet wine. **6.** a city having a harbor. **7.** an aperture in a valve or cylinder face: *v.t. & v.i.* **1.** to turn (the helm) to the port or left side of a ship. **2.** to present (a weapon) on a slant in front for inspection: *adj.* of or on the port.

port·a·ble (pôr'tȧ-bl), *adj.* 1. that may be carried. 2. that may be easily carried by hand or about the person: *n.* that which is portable. —**port·a·bil'i·ty,** *n.*

por·tage (pôr'tij), *n.* 1. carriage. 2. cost of carriage. 3. the act of transporting boats and stores from one waterway to another. 4. the route of such transportation: *v.t. & v.i.* -taged, -tag·ing, to transport (boats, etc.) along a portage.

por·tal (pôr'tl), *n.* a gate, entrance, or doorway.

port·cul·lis (pôrt-kul'is), *n.* a strong grating hung over the doorway of a fortified place and capable of being let down to defend the gate.

por·tend (pôr-tend'), *v.t.* 1. to indicate. 2. to presage; forebode.

por·tent (pôr'tent), *n.* 1. an omen; especially, an ill omen. 2. importance.

por·ten·tous (pôr-ten'tŭs), *adj.* 1. ominous; foreshadowing evil. 2. wondrous. 3. pretentious. —**por·ten'tous·ly,** *adv.*

por·ter (pôr'tẽr), *n.* 1. a doorman or gatekeeper. 2. a dark-colored malt beer. 3. one who carries parcels, luggage, etc. for hire. 4. a man who cleans, does small jobs, etc. in a bank, restaurant, etc. 5. the attendant on a railroad passenger car.

por·ter·age (-ij), *n.* money charged for carriage by a porter.

por·ter·house (-hous), *n.* formerly, a place where beer, malt liquor, etc., and sometimes steaks and chops, were sold.

porterhouse steak, a choice cut of beef from between the sirloin and tenderloin.

port·fo·li·o (pôrt-fō'li-ō), *n., pl.* -li·os, 1. a flat, portable case for loose papers, drawings, etc. 2. the office and functions of a minister of state. 3. an investor's stocks, bonds, etc.

port·hole (pôrt'hōl), *n.* a windowlike hole in the side of a ship.

por·ti·co (pôr'ti-kō), *n., pl.* -coes, -cos, a walk covered by a roof supported on columns; columned porch.

por·tiere, por·tière (pôr-tyer'), *n.* a door curtain.

por·tion (pôr'shŭn), *n.* 1. a piece or part; allotment; dividend. 2. a dowry. 3. the part of an estate descending to an heir. 4. one's final state; destiny: *v.t.* 1. to divide. 2. to allot. 3. to endow.

port·land cement (pôrt'land), [sometimes P-], a cement that solidifies in water, composed of limestone, clay, etc. that has been burned.

port·ly (pôrt'li), *adj.* -li·er, -li·est, 1. large and stately of mien. 2. corpulent. —**port'li·ness,** *n.*

port·man·teau (pôrt-man'tō), *n., pl.* -teaus, -teaux ('tōz), a bag or case in two sections, for carrying clothes.

por·trait (pôr'trit, -trāt), *n.* 1. a picture or representation of an individual or face, painted, photographed, etc. 2. a vivid description, as in words.

por·trai·ture (pôr'tri-chēr), *n.* 1. the art or practice of drawing, painting, etc. portraits. 2. vivid delineation in words.

por·tray (pôr-trā'), *v.t.* 1. to paint, draw, etc.

the likeness of. 2. to describe in words. 3. to perform the role of in a play, film, etc.

por·tray·al ('ăl), *n.* a description.

Por·tu·guese (pôr'chù-gēz), *adj.* of or pertaining to Portugal, a nation in southwestern Europe, or its inhabitants: *n.* 1. *pl.* -guese, a native or inhabitant of Portugal. 2. the language of Portugal and Brazil.

pose (pōz), *n.* 1. an attitude or position, as that maintained for an artist. 2. an affected style: *v.i.* posed, pos'ing, 1. to assume a studied attitude. 2. to affect a certain style. 3. to pretend to be what one is not (with *as*): *v.t.* 1. to lay down; propose. 2. to assert. 3. to place in a studied attitude.

Po·sei·don (pō-sī'dn), *n.* in *Greek Mythology,* the sea god.

pos·er (pō'zẽr), *n.* 1. a puzzling question. 2. one who or that which poses.

po·seur (pō-zūr'), *n.* one who assumes attitudes for effect: also **pos'er.**

posh (posh), *adj.* [Informal], elegant; rich.

po·si·tion (pō-zish'ŭn), *n.* 1. the manner of being set or placed. 2. a situation; location. 3. one's attitude; principles laid down. 4. an office; job. 5. social status. 6. a regular post.

pos·i·tive (poz'ĭ-tiv), *adj.* 1. clearly expressed; direct; explicit. 2. actual; real. 3. overconfident; dogmatic. 4. settled. 5. not admitting of doubt. 6. factual. 7. advancing; formative. 8. of or charged with electricity deficient in electrons. 9. in *Grammar,* denoting the uninflected form of an adjective or adverb. 10. in *Mathematics,* above zero in amount or degree. 11. in *Photography,* having shaded and light portions like those of the subject: *n.* 1. that which may be affirmed. 2. reality. 3. a photograph with the natural lights and shades. 4. in *Grammar,* the positive degree of comparison. 5. in *Mathematics,* a plus quantity. —**pos'i·tive·ly,** *adv.* —**pos'i·tive·ness,** *n.*

pos·i·tiv·ism (pos'ĭ-tiv-izm), *n.* 1. the philosophy of Auguste Comte (1798-1857), which maintains that man can have no knowledge of anything but the phenomena of knowable things and that inquiry into the origin or cause of such phenomena is absolutely useless. 2. the theory that nothing can be discovered or ascertained beyond that which is knowable by the senses. —**pos'i·tiv·ist,** *n. & adj.*

pos·i·tron (pos'ĭ-tron), *n.* an unstable particle possessing the same weight as an electron but having a positive charge.

pos·se (pos'i), *n.* a force or company of persons called on by a sheriff to assist in maintaining order.

pos·sess (pō-zes'), *v.t.* 1. to have as an owner. 2. to have as a characteristic, attribute, etc. 3. to be master of. 4. to seize control over. 5. to control (one's will, emotions, etc.). —**pos·ses'sor,** *n.*

pos·sessed (-zest'), *adj.* 1. owned. 2. controlled by an emotion or as if by an evil spirit; mad.

pos·ses·sion (-zesh'ŭn), *n.* 1. the act of possessing or the state of being possessed. 2. any-

---

ō in dragon, ōō in crude, ᴏᴏ in wool, u in cup, ū in cure, û in turn, ů in focus, ol in boy, ou in house, th in thin, th in sheathe, g in get, j in joy, y in yet.

thing possessed. 3. *pl.* property; wealth. 4. territory held under foreign control.

pos·ses·sive (-zes'iv), *adj.* 1. of or pertaining to possession. 2. exhibiting or demonstrating a desire for control. 3. in *Grammar,* denoting or of a case form showing ownership or a similar relationship: *n.* in *Grammar,* the possessive case, form, etc.

pos·ses·so·ry ('ĕr-i), *adj.* 1. of or pertaining to a possessor. 2. of or depending on possession.

pos·set (pos'ĭt), *n.* hot milk curdled with wine and spiced.

pos·si·bil·i·ty (pos-ĭ-bil'ĭ-ti), *n.* 1. the state or quality of being possible. 2. *pl.* -ties, something possible.

pos·si·ble (pos'ĭ-bl), *adj.* 1. that may happen. 2. that can be or exist. 3. that can be accomplished, chosen, learned, etc. 4. allowable.

pos·si·bly (-bli), *adv.* 1. by any possible methods. 2. perhaps; by some chance.

pos·sum (pos'ŭm), *n.* [Informal], same as *opossum.*

post (pōst), *n.* 1. a piece of timber, metal, etc. set erect, usually to support something else. 2. the starting point of a horse race: *v.t.* 1. to affix (a notice, poster, etc.) to a wall, board, post, etc. 2. to announce by putting up notices. 3. to enter (a name) on a published list.

post (pōst), *n.* 1. a place to which a soldier, sentry, guard, etc. is assigned. 2. a military base where troops are stationed. 3. a place to which anyone is assigned for duty. 4. a job or position: *v.t.* 1. to assign to a post. 2. to put up, as bond.

post (pōst), *n.* [Chiefly British], the mail: *v.i.* to travel rapidly; hasten: *v.t.* 1. to mail (a letter). 2. to inform.

post-, a prefix signifying *behind, after.*

post·age (pōs'tĭj), *n.* the fee for the conveyance of letters, packages, etc. by post, as represented by stamps.

post·al (pōs'tl), *adj.* of or pertaining to the post office or mail service.

postal card, a card with a printed postage stamp, issued and sold by a government for sending messages at a low rate.

post card, an unofficial card, often a picture card, that has space for a postage stamp, an address, and a short message.

post-date (pōst-dāt'), *v.t.* -dat'ed, -dat'ing, 1. to put a date on (a check, letter, etc.) that is a future date rather than the actual date. 2. to happen later than.

post-di·lu·vi·an (pōst-di-lōō'vi-ăn), *adj.* existing or happening after the Biblical Flood: *n.* a person or thing living after this Flood.

post·er (pōs'tĕr), *n.* a large printed card, bill, etc., often illustrated, displayed to advertize or publicize something.

pos·te·ri·or (pos-tir'i-ĕr, pōs-), *adj.* 1. subsequent in time or place; later. 2. at the rear; behind: *n.* the buttocks.

pos·ter·i·ty (pos-ter'i-ti), *n.* 1. all succeeding generations. 2. all of a person's descendants.

pos·tern (pōs'tĕrn, pos'-), *n.* 1. formerly, a small gate or door at the rear. 2. a private entrance at the side or rear: *adj.* rear; private.

post exchange, a general store on a military base, that sells merchandise, refreshments, etc. to military personnel.

post-fix (pōst'fĭks), *n.* a suffix: *v.t.* (pōst-fiks'), to suffix.

post-free (frē'), *adj.* that can be mailed without postal charges.

post-grad-u-ate ('graj'oo-wĭt, -wāt), *adj.* of or pursuing a course of study after having graduated from high school or college: *n.* one who is taking or has completed postgraduate studies.

post-haste (pōst'hāst'), *adv.* with great speed; hurriedly.

post-hu-mous (pos'choo-mŭs, 'tyoo-), *adj.* 1. born after the death of the father. 2. published after the death of the author. —post'-hu-mous-ly, *adv.*

pos-til-ion, pos-til-lion (pōs-til'yŭn, pos-), *n.* the rider on the left leader of a carriage team.

post-im-pres-sion-ism (pōst-im-presh'ŭn-izm), *n.* the practice of a group of late 19th-century artists who turned aside from naturalism and expressed their personal viewpoints in their use of structure and color.

post-lude (pōst'lōōd), *n.* in *Music,* a concluding piece or movement.

post-man ('măn), *n., pl.* -men ('mĕn), same as *mailman.*

post-mark ('märk), *n.* a post-office mark stamped on mail that cancels the stamp and records the date and place of sending or receipt: *v.t.* to stamp with a postmark.

post-mas-ter ('mas-tĕr), *n.* a person in charge of a post office. —post'mis-tress ('mis-tris), *n.fem.*

postmaster general, *pl.* postmasters general, postmaster generals, the head of a government's postal system.

post-me-rid-i-an (pōst-mĕ-rid'i-ăn), *adj.* of or in the afternoon.

post me-ri-di-em ('i-ĕm), [Latin], after noon.

post-mor-tem (-mōr'tĕm), *adj.* 1. after death. 2. of or pertaining to a post-mortem examination: *n.* 1. same as post-mortem examination. 2. an evaluation or discussion of something that has just ended.

post-mortem examination, an examination of a human body after death.

post-na-sal drip (pōst'nā'zl), a dripping of mucus onto the pharyngeal surface from the back of the nasal cavity, usually as the result of a cold or allergy.

post-na-tal (pōst-nāt'l), *adj.* after birth; especially, immediately following birth.

post-nup-tial (-nup'shăl, 'chăl), *adj.* done or occurring after marriage.

post office, 1. the government department for handling mail. 2. a place where mail is received, sorted, and distributed, stamps are sold, etc.

post-op-er-a-tive (pōst-op'ĕr-ă-tiv), *adj.* of or happening after a surgical operation.

post-paid (pōst'pād'), *adj.* having the postage paid in advance.

post-pone (pōst-pōn'), *v.t.* -poned', -pon'ing, to delay; defer until a later time. —post'pone'-ment, *n.*

post-script (pōst'skript), *n.* 1. a paragraph, comment, etc. added to a letter after the writer's signature. 2. an appendix or supplement added to a book, speech, etc. after its original ending.

post time, the time at which a horse race is scheduled to begin.

pos·tu·lant (pos'chŭ-lǎnt), *n.* a petitioner, especially one seeking admission into a religious order.

pos·tu·late (pos'chŭ-lāt), *v.t.* **-lat·ed, -lat·ing,** 1. to assume without proof. 2. to solicit; demand; claim. 3. to assert as self-evident; assume; *n.* 1. something, as a proposition, assumed as self-evident. 2. a necessary condition. 3. a fundamental principle.

pos·ture (pos'chĕr), *n.* 1. the placement or carriage of the body. 2. an attitude or frame of mind. 3. a position assumed in posing. 4. a position or outlook taken in response to an issue or particular state of affairs: *v.i.* **-tured, -tur·ing,** to assume a particular bodily position or mental outlook; especially, to assume an attitude simply for effect; pose: also **pos'tur·ize** (-īz), **-ized, -iz·ing.**

post·war (pōst'wôr'), *adj.* after a particular war.

po·sy (pō'zi), *n., pl.* **-sies,** 1. a flower; bouquet. 2. [Obsolete], a motto or verse sent with a bouquet.

pot (pot), *n.* 1. a metallic or earthenware vessel of a round shape, used for various culinary and domestic purposes. 2. the contents of such a vessel. 3. a mug of liquor; potation. 4. a vessel for holding plants. 5. [Informal], all the money bet at one time. 6. [Slang], same as **marijuana:** *v.t.* **pot'ted, pot'ting,** 1. to place in a pot. 2. to preserve or cook in a pot.

po·ta·ble (pōt'ȧ-bl), *adj.* drinkable: *n.* something fit to drink; beverage. **—po·ta·bil'i·ty,** *n.*

pot·ash (pot'ash), *n.* a powerful alkali obtained from wood ashes; potassium carbonate, used in soaps, fertilizers, etc.

po·tas·si·um (pō-tas'i-ŭm), *n.* a soft, bluish-white, waxy, metallic chemical element, widely distributed in nature, but always combined in compounds: its salts are used in fertilizers, glass, medicine, explosives, etc.

potassium bromide, a white, crystalline compound, used in medicine as a sedative, in photography, etc.

potassium carbonate, a white, crystalline compound that forms a strong alkaline solution: it is used in making soap, glass, medicines, etc.

potassium cyanide, a white, crystalline salt, exceedingly poisonous, used in electroplating, metallurgy, insecticides, etc.

potassium hydroxide, a white, caustic, crystalline compound, used in making soap, glass, etc.

potassium iodide, a colorless, crystalline compound or a white powder, used in medicine, photography, etc.

potassium sulfate, a white, crystalline salt, used in fertilizers, medicine, etc.

po·ta·tion (pō-tā'shŭn), *n.* 1. the act of drinking. 2. a draft or drink, especially an alcoholic one.

po·ta·to (pō-tāt'ō), *n., pl.* **-toes,** 1. the starchy,

edible tuber of a South American plant, widely cultivated as a food crop. 2. this plant.

potato bug, a black-and-yellow beetle that is very destructive to potatoes and other plants.

potato chip, a thin slice of potato fried in deep fat and salted.

pot-au-feu (pô-tō-foo'), *n.* [French], meat and vegetables boiled, then usually strained so that the broth may be served separately.

pot·bel·ly (pot'bel-i), *n., pl.* **-lies,** a protuberant belly. **—pot'bel·lied,** *adj.*

pot·boil·er ('boil-ẽr), *n.* a literary or artistic work hurriedly produced and usually pedestrian and badly done.

po·tent (pōt'nt), *adj.* 1. having great power, authority, or influence. 2. convincing. 3. powerful; effective, as a drug. 4. capable of having sexual intercourse: said of a male. **—po'ten·cy,** *n.*

po·ten·tate ('n-tāt), *n.* one who possesses great power; sovereign; monarch.

po·ten·tial (pō-ten'shŭl), *adj.* 1. existing in possibility, not in reality; latent. 2. in *Grammar,* expressing possibility: *n.* 1. something potential or possible. 2. the potential energy at a point in an electric circuit with respect to some reference point in the same circuit. **—po·ten·ti·al'i·ty** (-shi-al'i-ti), *n., pl.* **-ties.** **—po·ten'tial·ly,** *adv.*

po·ten·ti·ate ('shi-āt), *v.t.* **-at·ed, -at·ing,** to intensify the power (of a drug or toxin) by administering at the same time another drug or toxin. **—po·ten·ti·a'tion,** *n.*

poth·er (poth'ẽr), *n.* confusion; bustle: *v.t. & v.i.* to bother or worry.

pot·herb (pot'ûrb), *n.* any plant that furnishes leaves and stems that are cooked and eaten or used in flavoring.

pot·hold·er ('hōl-dẽr), *n.* a padded piece of cloth or other material, used for handling hot pans, pots, etc.

pot·hook ('hook), *n.* 1. an S-shaped hook on which to hang pots, kettles, etc. over a fire. 2. a curved character used in writing.

pot·house ('hous), *n.* [British], a small public house or tavern.

po·tion (pō'shŭn), *n.* a drink, as of medicine, poison, or some substance reputedly having magic powers.

pot·luck (pot'luk'), *n.* the food or the meal being served to a family as its ordinary fare.

pot·pie (pot'pī'), *n.* 1. a pie made in a deep dish, containing meat and usually vegetables, and topped by a pastry crust. 2. a stew with dumplings, biscuits, etc.

pot·pour·ri (pō-poo-rē'), *n.* 1. a medley of musical airs. 2. an anthology of literary extracts. 3. a dish of meats and vegetables; stew. 4. a mixture or jumble of unrelated things. 5. a mixture of flower petals and spices, kept for its fragrance.

pot·sherd (pot'shûrd), *n.* a fragment of broken pottery, especially one discovered in archaeological diggings.

pot·shot ('shot), *n.* 1. an easy, unsporting shot at game. 2. an aimless shot. 3. a random criticism or uncalled-for assault on a person, policy, etc.

ŏ in drag*o*n, ōō in cr*u*de, oo in w*oo*l, u in c*u*p, ū in c*u*re, ū in t*u*rn, ủ in foc*u*s, oi in b*oy*, ou in h*ou*se, th in *th*in, th in shea*the*, g in *g*et, j in *j*oy, y in *y*et.

pot·tage (pot'ij), *n.* a thick soup or stew made of vegetables, with or without meat.

pot·ter (pot'ēr), *n.* a person who makes earthenware pots, dishes, etc.

potter's field, a place of burial for the destitute or the unknown.

potter's wheel, a flat disk upon which clay is placed and rotated while being molded into vases, bowls, etc.

pot·ter·y (pot'ēr-i), *n., pl.* -ter·ies, 1. earthenware of all kinds formed into shapes and hardened by heat. 2. the place where earthenware is manufactured. 3. the art of a potter.

pot·tle (pot'l), *n.* 1. a former liquid measure, equal to four pints. 2. a container or tankard of this capacity. 3. the contents held by this; especially, wine, ale, etc.

pot·to (pot'ō), *n.* an arboreal, African, slow-moving monkey.

Pott's disease (pots), disintegration of the vertebrae, usually resulting in curvature of the spine: after Percival Pott (1714-88), English surgeon.

pot·val·iant (pot'val'yānt), *adj.* having false courage stimulated by strong drink.

pouch (pouch), *n.* 1. a small bag. 2. a saclike structure in some animals, as the cheek receptacles in gophers or the abdominal pocket in marsupials. 3. a mailbag; especially, one used by diplomatic couriers: *v.t.* to put into a pouch.

pou·lard, pou·larde (pou-lärd'), *n.* 1. a young hen from which the ovaries have been taken in order to fatten the bird. 2. any fat, young hen.

poult (pōlt), *n.* a young chicken, turkey, partridge, or other fowl.

poul·ter·er (pōl'tēr-ēr), *n.* [British], a dealer in poultry and game.

poul·tice (pōl'tis), *n.* a hot, soft preparation of bread, meal, mustard, herbs, etc., usually spread on cloth and applied to warm, moisten, or soothe a sore or inflamed part of the body; cataplasm: *v.t.* to apply a poultice to.

poul·try (pōl'tri), *n.* domestic fowls, as chickens, ducks, geese, or turkeys, raised for meat or eggs.

pounce (pouns), *n.* 1. the talon or claw of a bird of prey. 2. the act of pouncing; swoop, jump, spring, etc.: *v.i.* pounced, pounc'ing, to swoop or jump (*on, upon,* or. *at*) as to seize or attack.

pounce (pouns), *n.* 1. a fine powder formerly used for drying ink on paper or to prepare paper and parchment surfaces for writing. 2. a fine powder sprinkled into holes in paper to make a pattern on the surface below: *v.t.* pounced, pounc'ing, 1. to sprinkle, rub, treat, etc. with pounce. 2. to transfer (a pattern) with pounce.

pound (pound), *n., pl.* pounds, 1. a unit of weight that is equal to 16 ounces avoirdupois or 12 ounces troy. 2. the monetary unit of the United Kingdom, equal to 20 shillings or 100 new pennies. 3. the monetary unit of various other countries.

pound (pound), *v.t.* 1. to pulverize as in a mortar. 2. to strike hard and repeatedly: *v.i.* 1.

to deliver hard, repeated blows (*on* or *at*). 2. to plod. 3. to throb.

pound (pound), *n.* an enclosure for confining stray animals, maintained by a municipality.

pound·age ('ij), *n.* .1. a rate, allowance, etc. of so much in the pound. 2. weight in pounds.

pound·cake ('kāk), *n.* a cake made of equal portions of flour, butter, sugar, and eggs.

pour (pôr), *v.t.* 1. to empty, as a liquid, out of a vessel. 2. to discharge in a continuous stream. 3. to send forth, give vent to, or utter profusely: *v.i.* 1. to stream; rush tumultuously. 2. to rain heavily.

pour·boire (pōōr-bwär'), *n.* [French], a tip: originally money given for drink.

pour·par·ler (pōōr-pär-lā'), *n.* [French], 1. a diplomatic conference preliminary to a treaty. 2. an informal conference.

pousse·ca·fé (pōōs-ka-fā'), *n.* a liqueur or cordial served with after-dinner coffee.

pout (pout), *n.* 1. the act of thrusting out the lips. 2. a fit of sullenness: *v.i.* 1. to thrust out the lips, as in sullenness, contempt, etc. 2. to sulk.

pout (pout), *n., pl.* pout, pouts, any of various marine or freshwater fishes, as the eelpout.

pout·er (pout'ēr), *n.* 1. a person who pouts. 2. any one of a breed of pigeon with long legs, a slender body, and a distensible crop.

pov·er·ty (pov'ēr-ti), *n.* 1. the state or quality of being poor; indigence; penury. 2. deficiency in needed or desirable qualities. 3. paucity; scantiness.

pov·er·ty-strick·en (-strik'n), *adj.* very poor; indigent.

pow·der (pou'dēr), *n.* 1. any dry substance in fine particles. 2. same as gunpowder. 3. face powder. 4. a medicinal preparation in the form of a powder: *v.t.* 1. to pulverize. 2. to sprinkle or cover with or as with powder. —pow'der·y, *adj.*

pow·er (pou'ēr), *n.* 1. the faculty of doing or performing something. 2. ability; energy; force; strength. 3. rule; authority; influence. 4. dominion; government. 5. mental capacity. 6. legal authority. 7. a nation or state having influence over other nations. 8. a force tending to produce motion. 9. the magnifying power of a lens. 10. the product arising from multiplication of a number or quantity by itself: *v.t.* to supply with a source of power: *adj.* 1. operated by electricity, gasoline, etc. 2. supplied by a source of power that reduces effort in operation. 3. transmitting electricity.

power dive, in *Aeronautics,* a dive in which engine power is used to increase the speed. —**pow'er-dive',** *v.i. & v.t.* -dived', -div'ing.

pow·er·ful (-fūl), *adj.* having great power; mighty; forcible; strong; efficacious. —**pow'er·ful·ly,** *adv.* —**pow'er·ful·ness,** *n.*

pow·er·house (-hous), *n.* 1. a building in which electrical energy is generated. 2. [Informal], a person, group, etc. that has great energy, vitality, drive, etc.

pow·er·less (-lis), *adj.* destitute of power; weak; ineffectual. —**pow'er·less·ly,** *adv.*

power of attorney, a written legal statement granting a person the authority to act as another's agent or attorney.

---

a in cap, ā in cane, ä in father, à in abet, e in met, ē in be, ē in baker, ê in regent, i in pit, ī in fine, i in manifest, o in hot, ô in horse, ō in bone,

pow-wow (pou'wou), *n.* 1. a North American Indian priest or conjurer. 2. among North American Indians, an incantation accompanied by dancing, for the cure of diseases, success in war, etc. 3. a conference of or with North American Indians. 4. [Informal], any meeting or gathering: *v.i.* 1. to hold a powwow. 2. [Informal], to hold a conference.

pox (poks), *n.* 1. an eruptive disease characterized by pustules on the skin, as smallpox. 2. same as syphilis.

poz-zuo-la-na (pot-swó-lä'nä), *n.* [Italian], volcanic rock ground and used in hydraulic or Roman cement.

praam (präm), *n.* a flat-bottomed boat or lighter, used in Holland and the Baltic.

prac-ti-ca-ble (prak'ti-ká-bl), *adj.* 1. that can be done or effected; feasible. 2. that can be used; usable. —**prac-ti-ca-bil'i-ty**, *n.* —**prac'ti-ca-bly**, *adv.*

prac-ti-cal (prak'ti-kl), *adj.* 1. of or pertaining to action or practice. 2. useful. 3. capable of applying knowledge or theory to practice. 4. derived from or reduced to practice. 5. that is actually so in practice, if not theory; virtual. —**prac-ti-cal'i-ty** (-kal'ĭ-ti), *n., pl.* -**ties.** —**prac'ti-cal-ness,** *n.*

practical joke, a mischievous or embarrassing trick played on someone to cause him to lose dignity, but meant in fun. —**practical joker.**

prac-ti-cal-ly (prak'tik-li), *adv.* 1. in a practical manner. 2. from a practical way of looking. 3. in all important respects; virtually. 4. [Informal], almost.

prac-tice (prak'tis), *n.* 1. frequent or customary action. 2. dexterity acquired by practice. 3. use. 4. exercise of any profession. 5. systematic exercise: *v.t.* -**ticed, -tic-ing,** 1. to do habitually or repeatedly. 2. to perform as a habit. 3. to exercise, as a profession: *v.i.* 1. to exercise a profession. 2. to drill oneself to obtain skill or proficiency.

prac-ticed ('tist), *adj.* skilled; expert.

prac-tise ('tis), *v.t. & v.i.* -**tised, -tis-ing,** chiefly British spelling of **practice.**

prac-ti-tion-er (prak-tish'ŭ-nêr), *n.* one who is engaged in the practice of any profession, especially medicine or law.

prae-, same as **pre-:** the preferred form in some words.

prae-di-al (prē'di-ăl), *adj.* 1. of the nature of or relating to land or landed property. 2. of or pertaining to land or its products; agrarian.

prae-no-men (prē-nō'měn), *n., pl.* -**no'mens, -nom'i-na** (-nom'ĭ-nä), the first or personal name of an ancient Roman citizen.

prae-tor (prēt'êr), *n.* an ancient Roman magistrate ranking next below a consul.

prag-mat-ic (prag-mat'ik), *adj.* 1. [Rare], meddling; officious. 2. avoiding theory; practical. 3. testing the truth, value, etc. of concepts by their practical consequences.

prag-ma-tism (prag'má-tizm), *n.* 1. the quality or state of being pragmatic. 2. the doctrine that the test and validity of everything depend upon the practical results. 3. the theory that the purpose of thinking should be

to develop beliefs on which to base laws to govern right living and conduct.

prai-rie (prer'i), *n.* an extensive, treeless tract of level or slightly undulating land covered with tall, coarse grass.

prairie chicken, a spotted grouse of the North American prairies and the Gulf coast.

prairie dog, any one of a number of small, burrowing rodents that live in large communities on the prairies.

prairie schooner, a long, canvas-covered wagon in which early pioneers crossed the deserts and plains.

praise (präz), *v.t.* **praised, prais'ing,** 1. to bestow (commendation) upon. 2. to honor; worship; glorify: *n.* 1. approbation; commendation. 2. renown; applause.

praise-wor-thy ('wûr-thi), *adj.* worthy of praise; laudable. —**praise'wor-thi-ly,** *adv.* —**praise'wor-thi-ness,** *n.*

pra-line (prä'lĕn, prä'-), *n.* any of various confections made of boiled sugar and nuts.

prance (prans), *v.i.* **pranced, pranc'ing,** 1. to rear on the hind legs, as a horse. 2. to strut about in a showy manner: *n.* a prancing. —**pranc'er,** *n.* —**pranc'ing-ly,** *adv.*

prank (prangk), *n.* a mischievous trick. —**prank'ster,** *n.*

prank (prangk), *v.t.* to dress up in a showy style.

prate (prät), *v.i.* **prat'ed, prat'ing,** to prattle; talk idly; chatter: *v.t.* to utter without sense or meaning: *n.* trifling talk.

prat-in-cole (prat'ing-kōl), *n.* a shore bird resembling a plover, with long, pointed wings and a forked tail.

pra-tique (pra-tēk'), *n.* a license to a ship to trade after quarantine or after a certificate has been given that the vessel has not come from an infected port.

prat-tle (prat'l), *v.i. & v.t.* -**tled, -tling,** to talk much and lightly; chatter: *n.* childish or empty talk.

prawn (prôn), *n.* a small, edible marine crustacean, allied to the shrimp.

prax-is (prak'sis), *n.* 1. an example or series of examples for exercise, as in grammar. 2. practice of an art, science, etc., as distinguished from theory.

pray (prā), *v.i.* 1. to ask earnestly. 2. to address or petition. 3. to ask with humility and reverence. 4. to supplicate: *v.i.* to make supplication to God. —**pray'er,** *n.*

prayer (prer), *n.* 1. a solemn address to the Supreme Being. 2. an entreaty. 3. a formula for worship. 4. that part of a petition that specifies the request or desire. —**prayer'ful,** *adj.* —**prayer'ful-ly,** *adv.*

prayer-book ('book), *n.* a manual of public or private devotion, containing forms of prayer.

pre-, a prefix signifying *before in time, place, rank:* many words beginning with this particle are self-explanatory and are omitted from the list of definitions.

preach (prēch), *v.i.* 1. to pronounce a public discourse on a sacred subject, especially from a text of Scripture. 2. to give advice in an offensive or obtrusive manner, on religious or moral grounds: *v.t.* 1. to teach

---

ŏ in dragon, ōō in crude, oo in wool, u in cup, ū in cure, û in turn, ŭ in focus, oi in boy, ou in house, th in thin, th in sheathe, g in get, j in joy, y in yet.

publicly. 2. to deliver (a sermon). —preach'-ment, *n.*

preach-er ('ẽr), *n.* a person who preaches, especially a clergyman.

preach-y (prē'chi), *adj.* preach'i-er, preach'i-est, [Informal], indulging in tiresome or pretentious moralizing.

pre-am-ble (prē'am-bl), *n.* 1. an introduction or preface. 2. the opening clauses in a statute, constitution, etc. setting forth the reasons and purposes of the document.

pre-ar-range (pri-ā-rānj'), *v.t.* -ranged', -rang'-ing, to arrange ahead of time. —pre-ar-range'meent, *n.*

preb-end (preb'ĕnd), *n.* 1. the stipend granted to a clergyman out of the estate of a cathedral or collegiate church. 2. same as prebendary.

preb-en-dar-y (preb'ĕn-der-i), *n., pl.* -dar-ies, 1. a clergyman who receives a prebend. 2. in the Anglican Church, a clergyman holding the honorary title of prebend without receiving the stipend.

Pre-cam-bri-an (pri-kam'brĭ-ăn), *n.* the earliest geologic era, preceding the Cambrian Period and characterized by the first evidence of primitive forms of life.

pre-can-cer-ous (-kan'sẽr-ŭs), *adj.* that may or will probably become cancerous.

pre-car-i-ous (pri-ker'ĭ-ŭs), *adj.* 1. depending on the will or pleasure of another. 2. uncertain; insecure. 3. subject to chance; risky. —pre-car'i-ous-ly, *adv.* —pre-car'i-ous-ness, *n.*

prec-a-tive (prek'ā-tiv), *adj.* expressing entreaty or supplication: also prec'a-to-ry (-tôr-i).

pre-cau-tion (pri-kô'shŭn), *n.* 1. caution taken beforehand. 2. a preventive measure taken in advance against possible contingencies. —pre-cau'tion-ar-y, *adj.*

pre-cede (pri-sēd'), *v.t.* -ced'ed, -ced'ing, 1. to go before in time, place, rank, or importance. 2. to preface or introduce.

prec-e-dence (pres'ĕ-dĕns, pri-sēd'ns), *n.* 1. the act, right, or state of going before in time, rank, etc. 2. priority. 3. a relative ranking of dignitaries followed on ceremonial or formal occasions. Also prec'e-den-cy.

prec-ed-ent (pri-cēd'nt), *adj.* going before; anterior: *n.* (pres'ĕ-dĕnt), 1. something previously said or done, serving as an example to be followed. 2. custom or practice.

pre-ced-ing (pri-sēd'ing), *adj.* going before; antecedent; former.

pre-cen-tor (-sen'tẽr), *n.* the leader of a church choir or congregation in singing.

pre-cept (prē'sept), *n.* 1. an authoritative command. 2. a rule of action or moral conduct; maxim. 3. in *Law,* a written mandate; writ.

pre-cep-tor (pri-sep'tẽr), *n.* 1. an instructor or teacher. 2. the head of a preceptory of Knights Templars. —pre-cep'tress, *n.fem.*

pre-cep-to-ry ('tẽr-i), *n., pl.* -ries, 1. a college or religious house of the medieval Knights Templars. 2. its estates.

pre-ces-sion (pri-sesh'ŭn), *n.* 1. the act or condition of coming before; precedence. 2. in *Physics,* a continuous change in the direction of the axis in a body rotating on its axis as the result of a force acting at right angles to it, causing the axis to describe a cone. 3. same as precession of the equinoxes.

precession of the equinoxes, in *Astronomy,* the slow but continuous shifting of the equinoctial points along the ecliptic from east to west as the result of the precession of the earth's axis of rotation: precession is caused by the attraction of the sun and moon upon the bulging part of the earth near the equator.

pre-cinct (prē'singkt), *n.* 1. *usually pl.* an enclosure marked off by limits or definite boundaries. 2. *pl.* neighborhood; environs. 3. a police district. 4. a subdivision of a ward or county. 5. a confined area, as of thought or action. 6. a boundary.

pre-cious (presh'ŭs), *adj.* 1. of great price or value; costly. 2. highly esteemed or valued. 3. dear; beloved. 4. overrefined; affectedly dainty. —pre'cious-ly, *adv.* —pre'cious-ness, *n.*

prec-i-pice (pres'ĭ-pis), *n.* a perpendicular or almost perpendicular overhanging rock mass; steep descent. 2. the edge of a disastrous situation.

pre-cip-i-tance (pri-sip'ĭ-tăns), *n.* great haste in resolving a situation or carrying out a purpose: also pre-cip'i-tan-cy (-tăn-si), *pl.* -cies.

pre-cip-i-tant (-tănt), *adj.* same as precipitate: *n.* any chemical substance that, when added to a solution, causes something to be separated out from the solution.

pre-cip-i-tate (pri-sip'ĭ-tāt), *v.t.* -tat-ed, -tat-ing, 1. to throw headlong; urge on violently. 2. to bring on rashly, thoughtlessly, or unexpectedly; hasten. 3. in *Chemistry,* to cause (a solid substance) to be separated out from a solution: *v.i.* 1. in *Chemistry,* to be precipitated. 2. in *Meteorology,* to condense and fall as rain, snow, etc.: *adj.* (-tit), 1. rushing impetuously; overhasty; rash. 2. falling, flowing, or rushing headlong. 3. occurring suddenly or abruptly: *n.* (-tit), a substance separated out chemically from a solution. —pre-cip'i-tate-ly, *adv.*

pre-cip-i-ta-tion (pri-sip-ĭ-tā'shŭn), *n.* 1. the act of precipitating. 2. rash haste. 3. in *Chemistry,* the production of a precipitate. 4. in *Meteorology,* rain, snow, sleet, etc. falling to the earth's surface. 5. the amount of this.

pre-cip-i-tous (pri-sip'ĭ-tŭs), *adj.* 1. very steep; sheer. 2. rash; hasty.

pré-cis (prā-sē'), *n., pl.* pré-cis (prā-sēz'), a short abridgment; summary; abstract.

pre-cise (pri-sīs'), *adj.* 1. exact. 2. accurately defined; definite. 3. adhering rigidly to rule. 4. punctilious; scrupulous. —pre-cise'ly, *adv.* —pre-cise'ness, *n.*

pre-ci-sion (pri-sizh'ŭn), *n.* the quality of being precise; exactness: *adj.* demanding exactness.

pre-clude (pri-klōōd'), *v.t.* -clud'ed, -clud'ing, 1. to shut out; prevent. 2. to restrain (someone) from access. —pre-clu'sion (-klōō'zhŭn), *n.* —pre-clu'sive ('siv), *adj.*

pre-co-cious (-kō'shŭs), *adj.* 1. prematurely ripe or developed beyond that which is normal. 2. showing mature qualities at an early age. —pre-co'cious-ly, *adv.* —pre-co'cious-ness, pre-coc'i-ty (-kos'ĭ-ti), *n.*

pre-cog-ni-tion (prē-kog-nish'ŭn), *n.* previous

---

a in *cap,* ā in *cane,* ä in *father,* å in *abet,* e in *met,* ē in *be,* ē in *baker,* ĕ in *regent,* ĭ in *pit,* ī in *fine,* ĭ in *manifest,* o in *hot,* ô in *horse,* ō in *bone,*

knowledge or perception of an event, result, etc. before its occurrence.

pre·con·ceive (prē-kŏn-sēv'), *v.t.* -ceived', -ceiv'ing, to form an opinion of beforehand.

pre·con·cep·tion (-sep'shŭn), *n.* 1. the act of preconceiving. 2. an opinion or conception formed before actual knowledge is available. 3. prejudice or bias.

pre·con·di·tion (-kŏn-dish'ŭn), *v.t.* to condition or train (someone or something) to respond or act in a particular manner under certain conditions: *n.* a condition that must exist or be set up before something else can happen, be considered, etc.; requisite.

pre·co·nize (prē'kŏ-nīz), *v.t.* -nized, -niz·ing, 1. to announce or commend in public. 2. to approve and announce (an ecclesiastical preferment or appointment) publicly: said of the Pope.

pre·cur·sor (pri-kûr'sĕr), *n.* 1. one who or that which precedes; forerunner; harbinger. 2. a predecessor, as in office. 3. a substance that precedes and is the source of another substance.

pre·cur·so·ry ('sō-ri), *adj.* 1. indicating something that is to happen or follow; acting as a precursor. 2. preliminary; introductory.

pre·da·cious, pre·da·ceous (pri-dā'shŭs), *adj.* living by preying on other animals.

pre·date (pri-dāt'), *v.t.* -dat'ed, -dat'ing, 1. to date with an earlier date than the actual one. 2. to precede in date; antedate.

pred·a·to·ry (pred'ă-tôr·i), *adj.* 1. of or existing by plundering, pillaging, or robbing. 2. living by preying on other animals, predacious. 3. characterized by exploiting others to one's own benefit. —**pred'a·tor** (-tĕr), *n.*

pred·e·ces·sor (pred'ē-ses-ĕr), *n.* 1. one who has preceded another in the same office, business, position, etc. 2. an ancestor; forefather.

pre·des·ti·nar·i·an (pri-des-ti-ner'i-ăn), *adj.* of or pertaining to predestination: *n.* one who believes in the doctrine of predestination.

pre·des·ti·nate (pri-des'ti-nit), *adj.* foreordained by divine decree: *v.t.* (-nāt), -nat·ed, -nat·ing, 1. in *Theology,* to foreordain by divine decree. 2. same as **predestine**.

pre·des·ti·na·tion (pri-des-ti-nā'shŭn), *n.* 1. the act of foreordaining or the state of being predestined; fate. 2. in *Theology,* the doctrine that God has from all eternity decreed whatever comes to pass and that certain souls are predestined for salvation and the others to damnation.

pre·des·tine (pri-des'tin), *v.t.* -tined, -tin·ing, to destine or decide in advance; foreordain.

pre·de·ter·mine (-di-tûr'min), *v.t.* -mined, -min·ing, to determine beforehand.

pred·i·ca·ble (pred'i-kå-bl), *adj.* capable of being predicated: *n.* 1. something that can be predicated; attribute. 2. in *Logic,* any of several types of predicate relating to a subject, as one of the five general attributes in Aristotelian logic, namely, genus, species, difference, property, and accident. —**pred·i·ca·bil'i·ty,** *n.* —**pred'i·ca·bly,** *adv.*

pre·dic·a·ment (pri-dik'å-mĕnt), *n.* 1. same as category (sense 2). 2. a trying, critical, ludicrous, or embarrassing situation or state.

pred·i·cate (pred'i-kāt), *v.t.* -at·ed, -at·ing, 1. to affirm something of another person or thing. 2. to base (an idea, assertion, etc. *on* or *upon* facts, situations, etc.): *n.* (-kit), 1. in *Logic,* that which is affirmed or denied of a subject. 2. in *Grammar,* the word or words in a sentence or clause that express what is said of the subject: *adj.* (-kit), in *Grammar,* of or belonging to the predicate of a sentence or clause. —**pred·i·ca'tion,** *n.* —**pred·i·ca'tive,** *adj.*

pre·dict (pri-dikt'), *v.t. & v.i.* to foretell (an event or events to come). —**pre·dict'a·ble,** *adj.* —**pre·dic'tion,** *n.*

pre·di·gest (prē-di-jest', -dī-), *v.t.* to treat (food) with enzymes before it is eaten to make it easier to digest. —**pre·di·ges'tion,** *n.*

pre·di·lec·tion (pred-l-ek'shŭn, prēd-), *n.* a preference beforehand; partiality.

pre·dis·pose (prē-dis-pōz'), *v.t.* -posed', -pos'ing, to incline or adapt (someone *to* something) beforehand. —**pre·dis·po·si'tion** (-pō-zi'shŭn), *n.*

pre·dom·i·nant (pri-dom'i-nănt), *adj.* 1. having authority over others; superior. 2. most frequent; prevailing. —**pre·dom'i·nance,** *n.* —**pre·dom'i·nant·ly,** *adv.*

pre·dom·i·nate (-nāt), *v.i.* -nat·ed, -nat·ing, 1. to have authority (*over* other people). 2. to be superior in amount, number, etc.; prevail.

pre·em·i·nent (pri-em'l-nĕnt), *adj.* excelling others; prominent among the eminent; surpassing in quality, state, condition, rank, etc.: also pre·em'i·nent, pre·ĕm'i·nent. —**pre·em'i·nence,** *n.* —**pre·em'i·nent·ly,** *adv.*

pre·empt (pri-empt'), *v.t.* 1. to settle on (public land) in order to establish one's right to buy it. 2. to take as one's own before others can; seize beforehand. 3. to replace (a regularly scheduled program) on radio or television. Also **pre·empt', pre·ĕmpt'.**

pre·emp·tion (-emp'shŭn), *n.* 1. the act or right of preempting. 2. action done to stop other action before it happens. —**pre·emp'tive,** *adj.*

preen (prēn), *v.t.* 1. to clean and trim (the feathers) with the beak, as birds do. 2. to dress (oneself) up. 3. to pride (oneself); be very satisfied with (oneself).

pre·ex·ist (prē-ig-zist'), *v.t. & v.i.* to exist before (another person or thing): also **pre·ex·ist',** **pre·ĕx·ist'.** —**pre·ex·ist·ence,** *n.*

pre·fab (prē'fab'), *n.* [Informal], a prefabricated building.

pre·fab·ri·cate (pri-fab'ri-kāt), *v.t.* -cat·ed, -cat·ing, to build (a house or other structure) in ready-made sections that are then shipped to a site where they can be quickly put together.

pref·ace (pref'is), *n.* an introduction to a book, speech, etc.: *v.t.* -aced, -ac·ing, 1. to introduce with a preface. 2. to introduce. —**pref'a·to·ry** ('å-tôr-i), *adj.*

pre·fect (prē'fekt), *n.* 1. any of various government officials, as the head of a department of France. 2. a senior student chosen to help keep order in certain private schools.

pre·fec·ture ('fek-chēr), *n.* the office, territory, or residence of a prefect.

pre·fer (pri-fûr'), *v.t.* -ferred', -fer'ring, 1. to regard more highly than something else. 2.

---

to present for consideration. 3. to place before something else; promote.

pref·er·a·ble (pref'ēr·a·bl), *adj.* that is preferred over something else. —**pref'er·a·bly,** *adv.*

pref·er·ence (pref'ēr·ēns), *n.* 1. the act of preferring. 2. the thing preferred; first choice. 3. choice of one thing over another. —**pref·er·en'tial** (-ē·ren'shŭl), *adj.*

pre·fer·ment (pri·fûr'mĕnt), *n.* 1. a promotion in rank or office. 2. the rank or office one is promoted to.

pre·fig·ure (-fig'yēr), *v.t.* **-ured, -ur·ing,** to represent beforehand; foreshadow.

pre·fix (prē'fĭks), *n.* a syllable or group of syllables placed before a word to modify its meaning: *v.t.* (pri·fĭks'), to place before or at the beginning of.

preg·nan·cy (preg'nǎn·si), *n., pl.* **-cies,** the state or period of being pregnant.

preg·nant (preg'nǎnt), *adj.* 1. being with child; having an embryo or fetus growing in the uterus. 2. having a fertile or inventive mind. 3. full of importance or meaning. 4. rich *(in)* or filled *(with).*

pre·heat (pri·hēt'), *v.t.* to heat beforehand.

pre·hen·sile (pri·hen'sl), *adj.* adapted for holding or seizing, as a monkey's tail.

pre·his·tor·ic (prē·his·tôr'ĭk), *adj.* of the period of time before history was recorded.

pre·judge (pri·juj'), *v.t.* **-judged', -judg'ing,** to judge without a hearing or investigation; condemn beforehand or hastily. —**pre·judg'ment, pre·judge'ment,** *n.*

prej·u·dice (prej'ŭ·dis), *n.* 1. a judgment or opinion formed without knowing the facts or in spite of the facts; especially, one that is unfavorable. 2. hatred and fear of other races, nations, creeds, etc. 3. harm or injury: *v.t.* **-diced, -dic·ing,** 1. to hurt, impair, or damage in any way. 2. to create a prejudice in the mind of; bias.

prej·u·di·cial (prej·ŭ·dish'ǎl), *adj.* that causes prejudice or harm; injurious.

prel·a·cy (prel'ä·si), *n., pl.* **-cies,** 1. the office or status of a prelate. 2. prelates collectively. 3. government of a church by prelates.

prel·ate ('ĭt), *n.* an ecclesiastic with high rank, as a bishop. —**pre·lat·ic** (pri·lat'ĭk), *adj.*

pre·lim (prē'lĭm, pri·lĭm'), *n.* [Slang], preliminary.

pre·lim·i·nar·y (pri·lĭm'ĭ·ner·ĭ), *adj.* preceding the main action, discussion, or business; introductory: *n., pl.* **-nar·ies,** 1. a preliminary step, test, etc. 2. a contest preceding the main contest.

pre·lit·er·ate (pri·lĭt'er·it), *adj.* of or in a society that has not as yet developed a written language.

prel·ude (prel'ŭd, prā'lōōd), *n.* 1. a preliminary part; preface. 2. in *Music,* a) a section that introduces a suite, fugue, etc.; b) a short composition in romantic style: *v.t. & v.i.* **-ud·ed, -ud·ing,** 1. to serve as a prelude (to). 2. to play (as) a prelude.

pre·mar·i·tal (pri·mer'ĭ·tl), *adj.* before marriage.

pre·ma·ture (prē·mǎ·toor', -choor', -tyoor'), *adj.* arriving, occurring, or done before the proper time; untimely. —**pre·ma·ture'ly,** *adv.*

pre·med (prē'med'), *adj.* [Informal], premedical: *n.* a premedical student.

pre·med·i·cal (pri·med'ĭ·kl), *adj.* designating or of those studies that are taken before the study of medicine.

pre·med·i·tate (pri·med'ĭ·tāt), *v.t. & v.i.* **-tat·ed, -tat·ing,** to conceive or plan beforehand. —**pre·med·i·ta'tion,** *n.*

pre·mier (pri·mir', -myir'), *adj.* first; chief; foremost: *n.* a chief official, as the prime minister in certain countries or the governor of a Canadian province. —**pre·mier'ship,** *n.*

pre·mière (pri·myir', -mir'), *n.* the first performance of a play, motion picture, etc.

prem·ise (prem'is), *n.* 1. a proposition that is assumed as a basis for another that follows it; specifically, in *Logic,* either of the two propositions from which the conclusion of a syllogism is drawn. 2. *pl.* the statements in a deed or lease concerning the conveyance of property. 3. *pl.* a building and the land it is on: *v.t.* (also pri·mīz'), **-ised, -is·ing,** 1. to lay down as a premise. 2. to preface (remarks, a speech, etc.): *v.i.* to formulate a premise.

pre·mi·um (prē'mi·ŭm), *n.* 1. a reward or bonus, especially one given to get someone to do or buy something. 2. an additional amount paid, charged, or in excess of the nominal value. 3. a payment made or to be made for an insurance policy, in one sum or periodically. 4. great value.

pre·mo·ni·tion (prē·mō·nish'n), *n.* 1. a warning ahead of time; forewarning. 2. a feeling that something, usually evil, is about to come or occur; foreboding. —**pre·mon·i·to·ry** (pri·mon'ĭ·tôr·i), *adj.*

pre·na·tal (pri·nāt'l), *adj.* before birth.

pre·nup·tial (pri·nup'shŭl), *adj.* 1. before a marriage or wedding. 2. before mating.

pre·oc·cu·py (-ok'yŭ·pī), *v.t.* **-pied, -py·ing,** 1. to occupy to the exclusion of other matters that may be thought of. 2. to occupy beforehand or take prior possession of. —**pre·oc·cu·pa'tion** (-pā'shŭn), *n.*

pre·or·dain (prē·ôr·dān'), *v.t.* to ordain in advance.

prep (prep), *adj.* [Informal], preparatory: *v.t.* **prepped, prep'ping,** to prepare (especially a patient for a surgical operation).

pre·pack·age (pri·pak'ij), *v.t.* **-aged, -ag·ing,** to package (foods or goods) in certain sizes or amounts before selling.

pre·paid (prē·pād'), past tense and past participle of prepay.

prep·a·ra·tion (prep·ǎ·rā'shŭn), *n.* 1. the act of preparing. 2. the state of being prepared; readiness. 3. something done in advance to make ready. 4. that which is prepared for a particular purpose, as a medicine.

pre·par·a·tive (pri·per'ǎ·tiv), *adj.* preparatory: *n.* 1. that which prepares. 2. a preparation.

pre·par·a·to·ry (-tôr·i), *adj.* 1. that prepares; introductory; preliminary. 2. of or attending a preparatory school.

preparatory school, a private secondary school that prepares students for college.

pre·pare (pri·per'), *v.t.* **-pared', -par'ing,** 1. to make ready or adaptable. 2. to make ready to receive. 3. to fit out; equip. 4. to put together; arrange; construct: *v.i.* 1. to get things ready. 2. to get oneself ready.

pre·par·ed·ness ('id·nis), *n.* a state of readiness, especially of the armed forces in case of attack.

pre·pay (pri·pā'), *v.t.* -**paid'**, -**pay'ing**, to pay in advance or pay for in advance.

pre·pense (pri·pens'), *adj.* planned in advance.

prep·py, prep·pie (prep'ē), *n.*, *pl.* -**pies**, a student or former student at a preparatory school: *adj.* -**pi·er**, -**pi·est**, of or like the clothes worn by such students.

pre·pon·der·ant (pri·pon'dēr·ånt), *adj.* greater in amount, power, etc.; outweighing. —**pre·pon'der·ance**, *n.*

pre·pon·der·ate ('dē·rāt), *v.i.* -**at·ed**, -**at·ing**, 1. to sink downward. 2. to be greater in amount, power, etc.; predominate.

prep·o·si·tion (prep·ō·zish'ûn), *n.* a word used to show the relation of a noun or pronoun to some other word in a sentence. —**prep·o·si'tion·al**, *adj.*

prepositional phrase, a phrase that consists of a preposition followed by its object.

pre·pos·sess (prē·pō·zes'), *v.t.* 1. to prejudice, especially in favor of something. 2. to impress favorably. —**pre·pos·ses'sion** (-zesh'ûn), *n.*

pre·pos·sess·ing ('ing), *adj.* pleasing; attractive.

pre·pos·ter·ous (pri·pos'tēr·ûs), *adj.* contrary to nature or reason; ridiculous; absurd. —**pre·pos'ter·ous·ly**, *adv.*

pre·puce (prē'pūs), *n.* same as **foreskin**.

pre·re·cord (prē·ri·kôrd'), *v.t.* to record (a program) in advance, for later broadcasting on radio or television.

pre·re·cord·ed (prē·ri·kôr'did), *adj.* designating or of a magnetic tape, as in a cassette, on which sound, images, etc. have been recorded before its sale.

pre·req·ui·site (pri·rek'wŭ·zit), *adj.* required in advance as being necessary for something else: *n.* something that is prerequisite.

pre·rog·a·tive (pri·rog'â·tiv), *n.* 1. an exclusive privilege, especially one belonging to a certain rank, class, etc. 2. a superior advantage: *adj.* of or having a prerogative.

pres·age (pres'ij), *n.* 1. an omen; portent. 2. a foreboding: *v.t.* (pri·sāj'), -**aged'**, -**ag'ing**, to forebode; predict.

pres·by·ter (prez'bi·tēr), *n.* 1. in the *Presbyterian Church*, an elder. 2. in the *Episcopal Church*, a priest or minister.

Pres·by·te·ri·an (prez·bi·tir'i·ân), *adj.* denoting or of a church that is Calvinistic, Protestant, and governed by presbyters, or elders: *n.* a member of the Presbyterian Church. —**Pres·by·te'ri·an·ism**, *n.*

pres·by·ter·y (prez'bi·tēr·i), *n.*, *pl.* -**ter·ies**, 1. a body of presbyters. 2. in the *Presbyterian Church*, a governing body made up of all the ministers and a number of elders from all the churches in a district. 3. such a district.

pre·school (prē'skōōl'), *adj.* denoting, of, or for a child not old enough to go to school, usually between the ages of two and five (or six). —**pre·school'er**, *n.*

pre·sci·ence (prē'shi·ēns), *n.* foreknowledge.

pre·sci·ent (-ēnt), *adj.* foreknowing.

pre·scribe (pri·skrīb'), *v.t.* -**scribed'**, -**scrib'ing**, 1. to set down as a rule; order; direct. 2. to order as a medicine or medical treatment: *v.i.* 1. to set down rules; dictate. 2. to write medical directions or prescriptions.

pre·scrip·tion (pri·skrip'shûn), *n.* 1. the act of prescribing. 2. something prescribed. 3. a doctor's written direction for the preparation and use of a medicine. 4. a medicine so prescribed. 5. the right or title to something acquired by long-continued use or possession.

pre·scrip·tive ('tiv), *adj.* 1. that prescribes. 2. prescribed by custom or long use.

pres·ence (prez'ns), *n.* 1. the fact or state of being present. 2. nearby or close surroundings. 3. a person's bearing or personality. 4. impressive bearing or personality. 5. a supernatural or divine spirit that seems to be present.

presence of mind, mental alertness at a critical moment or in time of danger.

pres·ent (prez'nt), *adj.* 1. being in a certain place; at hand or in sight. 2. at this time; being or happening now. 3. indicating the time that is now, as a verb form: *n.* 1. the present time. 2. the present tense or a verb form in this tense. 3. a gift or donation. 4. *pl.* what is written in a document referred to: *v.t.* (pri·zent'), 1. to introduce to another. 2. to display; show. 3. to offer for consideration. 4. to give or hand over. 5. to point or aim. 6. to appoint to an ecclesiastical benefice.

pre·sent·a·ble (pri·zen'tâ·bl), *adj.* 1. suitable to be presented. 2. in proper attire, order, etc. to be seen in public.

pre·sen·ta·tion (prē·zen·tā'shûn, prez'n-), *n.* 1. the act of presenting. 2. something presented.

pres·ent-day (prez'nt·dā), *adj.* of the present time.

pre·sen·ti·ment (pri·zen'tî·mênt), *n.* a feeling that something is about to happen, usually something unfortunate.

pres·ent·ly (prez'nt·li), *adv.* 1. in a little while; soon. 2. at present; now.

pre·sent·ment (pri·zent'mênt), *n.* 1. the act of presenting; presentation. 2. a thing presented.

present participle, a participle expressing present or continuing action, time, or condition and used with auxiliaries or as an adjective.

pres·er·va·tion (prez·ēr·vā'shûn), *n.* 1. the act of preserving. 2. the state of being preserved.

pre·serv·a·tive (pri·zûr'vâ·tiv), *adj.* having the power of preserving: *n.* that which preserves.

pre·serve (pri·zûrv'), *v.t.* -**served'**, -**serv'ing**, 1. to keep from harm or injury; protect. 2. to keep from spoiling. 3. to prepare (food), as by canning, for future use. 4. to keep up; maintain: *v.i.* to preserve fruit: *n.* 1. *usually pl.* fruit preserved by cooking with sugar. 2. a place where game, fish, etc. are preserved, or protected. —**pre·serv'er**, *n.*

pre·set (pri·set'), *v.t.* -**set'**, -**set'ting**, to set beforehand, as the guidance system of a missile.

pre-shrunk (prē'shrungk'), *adj.* shrunk by a special process in manufacture so as to minimize any shrinkage later in washing or dry cleaning.

pre-side (pri-zīd'), *v.i.* -**sid**'ed, -**sid**'ing, to be in charge, especially at a public meeting.

pres-i-den-cy (prez'i-děn-si), *n.*, *pl.* -**cies**, the office, function, or term of a president.

pres-i-dent (prez'i-děnt), *n.* 1. the chief officer of a corporation, club, etc. 2. [often P-], the chief executive of a republic, as in the U.S., or the titular head of a republic, as in France. 3. any officer who presides. —**pres-i-den'tial** (-děn'shŭl), *adj.*

pres-i-dent-e-lect (-i-lekt'), *n.* a president who has been elected but has not yet taken office.

pre-sid-i-o (pri-sid'i-ō), *n.*, *pl.* -**i-os**, a fortified place or a military post.

pre-sid-i-um (pri-sid'i-ŭn), *n.*, *pl.* -**i-a** (-ȧ), -**i-ums**, 1. in the Soviet Union, any one of a number of permanent committees having the power to act for a larger administrative body. 2. [P-], such a committee of the Supreme Soviet. 3. [P-], any similar committee in certain other countries.

press (pres), *v.t.* 1. to exert force or weight on; push against; squeeze; compress. 2. to squeeze (juice) from. 3. to make (cloth or clothes) smooth by ironing. 4. to hug or embrace. 5. to force or compel. 6. to force into service, especially into military or naval service. 7. to urge or entreat. 8. to try to force. 9. to insist upon; emphasize. 10. to trouble or harass. 11. to drive quickly. 12. to shape (a phonograph record, plastic products, etc.) by using a form or matrix: *v.i.* 1. to exert pressure. 2. to move forward forcibly. 3. to crowd or throng. 4. to take pressing or ironing. 5. to iron clothes: *n.* 1. pressure; urgency. 2. a crowd. 3. an instrument or machine for compressing anything. 4. the smooth condition of clothes after being pressed. 5. a printing press. 6. a printing business. 7. the business or practice of printing. 8. newspapers, magazines, etc. or the people who write for them. 9. publicity in newspapers, magazines, etc. 10. a closet for clothes. 11. a lift in weight lifting in which the barbell is lifted to the shoulders and then pushed overhead to the full length of the arms. —**press'er**, *n.*

press agent, a person engaged to obtain publicity in newspapers, magazines, etc. for some institution, enterprise, private individual, etc.

press-ing (pres'ing), *adj.* needing attention; urgent: *n.* 1. the process of stamping, squeezing, etc. with a press. 2. the result of this. —**press'ing-ly**, *adv.*

press-man (-măn), *n.*, *pl.* -**men** ('měn), one who operates a printing press.

press-room ('rōōm), *n.* the room that contains the printing presses of a newspaper or printing business.

pres-sure (presh'ēr), *n.* 1. the act of pressing or

state of being pressed. 2. oppression; affliction. 3. a constraining force or compelling influence. 4. demands for attention; urgency. 5. in *Physics*, force per unit of area, exerted against an opposing body: *v.t.* -**sured**, -**sur-ing**, to put pressure on.

pressure cooker, a container for cooking food quickly by means of steam under pressure.

pressure group, any group that puts pressure on lawmakers and the public, using lobbies and propaganda to try to influence the making of laws or policies.

pressure point, any one of the points on the body where pressure can be applied to an artery near the surface so as to check bleeding from an injured part beyond the point.

pres-sur-ize (presh'ēr-īz), *v.t.* -**ized**, -**iz-ing**, to keep the atmospheric pressure nearly normal inside (an airplane, spacesuit, etc.), as at high altitudes.

press-work (pres'wûrk), *n.* 1. the operation or management of a printing press. 2. the work done by a printing press.

pres-ti-dig-i-ta-tion (pres-ti-dij-i-ta'shŭn), *n.* sleight of hand.

pres-ti-dig-i-ta-tor (-dij'i-tāt-ēr), *n.* an expert at prestidigitation.

pres-tige (pres-tēzh'), *n.* 1. power and influence due to success, wealth, etc. 2. reputation due to achievements, character, etc.; renown.

pres-ti-gious (-tij'ŭs, -tē'jŭs), *adj.* having prestige.

pres-to (pres'tō), *adv. & adj.* at once; fast.

pre-stressed concrete (prē'strest'), concrete with steel cables, wires, etc. fixed in it under pressure in order to make the concrete stronger.

pre-sume (pri-zōōm'), *v.t.* -**sumed'**, -**sum'ing**, 1. to dare or venture. 2. to take for granted; suppose: *v.i.* 1. to behave with presumption or overconfidence. 2. to take liberties in relying (*on* or *upon*). —**pre-sum'a-ble**, *adj.* —**pre-sum'a-bly**, *adv.*

pre-sump-tion (pri-zump'shŭn), *n.* 1. the act of presuming. 2. the thing presumed. 3. arrogance or overconfidence. 4. a reason for presuming something. 5. the assumption of the credibility of certain facts, based on circumstantial evidence.

pre-sump-tive ('tiv), *adj.* 1. that affords reasons for believing something. 2. based on probability.

pre-sump-tu-ous (pri-zump'choo-wŭs), *adj.* overly bold and confident; arrogant; willful.

pre-sup-pose (prē-sŭ-pōz'), *v.t.* -**posed'**, -**pos'ing**, 1. to suppose beforehand; take for granted. 2. to need or imply as an antecedent.

pre-sup-po-si-tion (prē-sup-ō-zish'ŭn), *n.* a supposition previously formed.

pre-tence (pri-tens', prē'tens), *n.* British spelling for pretense.

pre-tend (pri-tend'), *v.t.* 1. to claim or profess. 2. to claim or profess falsely; simulate; feign. 3. to create in the imagination; make believe: *v.i.* 1. to put forward a claim (*to*). 2. to imagine or make believe: *adj.* [Informal], make-believe.

---

pre-tend-ed (pri-ten'did), *adj.* feigned or alleged.

pre-tend-er ('dẽr), *n.* 1. one who pretends. 2. one who lays claim to anything under the guise of a right, as a claimant to a throne.

pre-tense (pri-tens', prē'tens), *n.* 1. a claim, especially an unfounded or unsupported claim. 2. a fake or hypocritical claim. 3. a false show of something. 4. the act of making believe, in play.

pre-ten-sion (pri-ten'shŭn), *n.* 1. a pretext; allegation. 2. a claim as to a right or title. 3. assertion of a claim. 4. pretentiousness.

pre-ten-tious (pri-ten'shŭs), *adj.* 1. making claims to being important, dignified, excellent, etc. 2. assuming an air of superiority; ostentatious. —**pre-ten'tious-ness,** *n.*

pret-er-it, pret-er-ite (pret'ẽr-it), *adj.* expressing past action or state, as a verb form: *n.* the past tense or a verb form in this tense.

pret-er-i-tion (pret-ẽ-rish'ŭn), *n.* 1. the act of passing over; omission. 2. the Calvinistic doctrine that God passes over those who are not chosen.

pre-ter-mit (prēt-ẽr-mit'), *v.t.* -mit'ted, -mit'ting, 1. to omit. 2. to let pass; overlook.

pre-ter-nat-u-ral (prēt-ẽr-nach'ẽr-ȧl), *adj.* 1. beyond what is ordinary and natural, but not supernatural; abnormal; strange. 2. same as supernatural.

pre-test (prē'test), *n.* a preliminary test: *v.t. & v.i.* (prē-test'), to test beforehand.

pre-text (prē'tekst), *n.* 1. an ostensible reason or motive put forward to conceal the real one; excuse. 2. a cover-up; front.

pret-ti-fy (prit'i-fī), *v.t.* -fied, -fy-ing, to make pretty.

pret-ty (prit'i, pûr'ti), *adj.* -ti-er, -ti-est, 1. pleasing without being absolutely beautiful; attractive in a dainty way. 2. fine; nice; good. 3. [Informal], quite large; considerable: *adv.* fairly; moderately: *v.t.* -tied, -ty-ing, to make pretty (with *up*). —**pret'ti-ly,** *adv.* —**pret'ti-ness,** *n.*

pre-typ-i-fy (pri-tip'i-fī), *v.t.* -fied, -fy-ing, to typify beforehand; prefigure.

pret-zel (pret'sl), *n.* a hard, brittle biscuit, heavily salted and baked in the form of a loose knot or as a stick.

pre-vail (pri-vāl'), *v.i.* 1. to gain the advantage (*over* or *against*). 2. to operate effectually; succeed. 3. to become stronger; obtain superiority. 4. to be in use generally. 5. to persuade (with *on* or *upon*).

pre-vail-ing ('ing), *adj.* 1. greater in strength or influence. 2. predominant or prevalent.

prev-a-lent (prev'ȧ-lĕnt), *adj.* generally used, accepted, etc.; widely existing. —**prev'a-lence,** *n.*

pre-var-i-cate (pri-ver'i-kāt), *v.i.* -cat-ed, -cat-ing, 1. to evade the truth; equivocate. 2. to tell a lie or lies. —**pre-var-i-ca'tion,** *n.* —**pre-var'-i-ca-tor,** *n.*

pre-vent (pri-vent'), *v.t.* to keep or stop from happening or doing; hinder. —**pre-vent'a-ble, pre-vent'i-ble,** *adj.*

pre-ven-tion (pri-ven'shŭn), *n.* the act of preventing.

pre-ven-tive ('tiv), *adj.* tending to prevent: *n.*

that which prevents. Also **pre-vent'a-tive** ('tȧ-tiv).

pre-view (prē'vū), *v.t.* to show in advance or in a preview: *n.* 1. a preliminary view. 2. a showing of something, as a motion picture, to a limited number of people before it is shown to the general public. 3. a showing of certain scenes from a motion picture, television show, etc. to advertise the full showing soon to appear.

pre-vi-ous (prē'vi-ŭs), *adj.* going before; prior. —**pre'vi-ous-ly,** *adv.*

pre-vi-sion (pri-vizh'ŭn), *n.* foresight; foreknowledge.

pre-vue (prē'vū), *n.* same as preview.

pre-war (prē'wôr'), *adj.* before any war or before a particular war.

prex-y (prek'si), *n., pl.* **prex'ies,** [Slang], the president, as of a college.

prey (prā), *n.* 1. an animal that may be, or is, seized by another animal for food. 2. a victim. 3. the habit of preying on other animals: *v.i.* 1. to plunder. 2. to seize and feed on other animals. 3. to weigh heavily (*on* or *upon*). 4. to treat as prey or a victim (with *on* or *upon*).

price (pris), *n.* 1. the amount of money paid or asked for something; cost. 2. value or worth. 3. what is required in time, labor, etc. to get something desired: *v.t.* priced, pric'ing, 1. to fix as the price of. 2. [Informal], to inquire about the price of.

price control, the establishing by a government of price limits for certain basic commodities, as in trying to fight inflation.

price fixing, the setting of prices and keeping them at a certain level, as by agreement among competitors.

price-less (pris'lis), *adj.* invaluable.

price support, the support of certain price levels, at or above market values, especially as done by a government agency by buying up surpluses.

price war, competition among rival business companies that keep lowering prices on their products, so as to force one or more out of business.

prick (prik), *n.* 1. a tiny puncture made by something pointed. 2. a sharp, stinging pain: *v.t.* 1. to pierce with, or as with, a prick. 2. to give sharp pain to. 3. to make (one's ears) stick up, as in listening intently (with *up*): *v.i.* 1. to feel a sharp pain. 2. to have a tingling sensation.

prick-et (prik'it), *n.* 1. a small spike on which a candle can be stuck. 2. a candlestick having such a spike.

prick-ing (prik'ing), *n.* 1. the act of one that pricks. 2. a prickly feeling.

prick-le ('l), *n.* 1. a sharp, pointed part growing from a plant; thorn: also prick'er. 2. a tingling sensation: *v.t.* -led, -ling, 1. to prick, as with a thorn. 2. to make tingle.

prick-ly ('lĭ), *adj.* -li-er, -li-est, 1. full of prickles. 2. stinging; tingling. —**prick'li-ness,** *n.*

prickly heat, a skin rash caused when the sweat glands become inflamed.

prickly pear, 1. any one of various cactus plants with cylindrical or oval stem joints and edible fruits. 2. the fruit of such a plant.

pride (prīd), *n.* 1. inordinate self-esteem; high opinion of one's own importance or worth; conceit. 2. arrogance; haughtiness. 3. honorable self-respect; personal dignity. 4. smug pleasure taken in the success of oneself or another. 5. a person or thing in which one takes such pleasure. 6. the best of a group; pick. 7. a group (of lions): *v.t.* prid'ed, prid'ing, to take pride in: used chiefly in pride oneself on. —pride'ful, *adj.*

prie-dieu (prē'dū), *n.* a small desk with a ledge for kneeling on while praying and a shelf for books.

pri-er (prī'ēr), *n.* one that pries.

priest (prēst), *n.* 1. a person who officiates in sacred religious rites, as by offering sacrifices to propitiate a deity. 2. a Christian clergyman ranking next below a bishop. 3. any clergyman. —priest'ess, *n.fem.* —priest'-hood, *n.*

priest-craft ('kraft), *n.* the methods used by priests in performing their duties.

priest-ly ('li), *adj.* -li-er, -li-est, of, like, or befitting a priest or priests. —priest'li-ness, *n.*

priest-rid-den ('rid'n), *adj.* dominated by priests.

prig (prig), *n.* a conceited person whose smug moral attitudes annoy other people. —prig'-gish, *adj.* —prig'gish-ness, *n.*

prill (pril), *n.* a small pellet, like a bead.

prim (prim), *adj.* prim'mer, prim'mest, formal, precise, or moral in a stiff way; very proper: *v.t. & v.i.* primmed, prim'ming, to give (one's face or mouth) a prim appearance. —prim'ly, *adv.* —prim'ness, *n.*

pri-ma ballerina (prē'mä), the principal female dancer in a ballet company.

pri-ma-cy (prī'mä-si), *n., pl.* -cies, 1. the state of being first in time, order, etc. 2. the rank or authority of a primate.

pri-ma don-na (prē'mä don'ä, prim'ä), *pl.* pri'-ma don'nas, 1. the principal female singer in an opera. 2. [Informal] a vain or arrogant person.

pri-ma fa-ci-e (prī'mä fā'shi-ē, fā'shi), at first sight; on first appearance.

prima facie evidence, evidence that is adequate, as in a law court, to establish a fact.

pri-mal (prī'ml), *adj.* 1. first in time; original. 2. first in importance; chief.

pri-ma-quine (prī'mä-kwēn), *n.* a synthetic chemical compound that is used as a cure for malaria.

pri-ma-ri-ly (prī-mer'i-li, prī'mer-), *adv.* 1. mainly. 2. originally.

pri-ma-ry (prī'mer-i, 'mēr-i), *adj.* 1. first in time; original. 2. first in importance; chief; principal. 3. firsthand; direct. 4. from which others are derived; fundamental; basic: *n., pl.* -ries, 1. that which is first in rank, order, importance, etc. 2. an election in which voters cast their votes directly for the candidates, usually to choose those who will run later in a general election. 3. a primary color.

primary accent, the heaviest accent (') in pronouncing a word: also **primary stress.**

primary color, any one of the basic colors, which are, in the spectrum, red, green, and blue, or, in painting, red, yellow, and blue.

pri-mate (prī'māt), *n.* 1. (also 'mit), an archbishop or the highest-ranking bishop in a province, district, etc. 2. any one of an order of mammals, including human beings, that have flexible hands and feet, with five digits on each hand and foot.

prime (prīm), *adj.* 1. first in time; original. 2. first in rank or importance; principal; chief. 3. of first quality; first-rate. 4. fundamental; basic. 5. denoting the most favorable rate of interest on bank loans. 6. denoting a number that can be evenly divided by no other whole number than itself or the number one: *n.* 1. the earliest part. 2. the best or most vigorous period. 3. the best part. 4. the best of several or many: *v.t.* primed, prim'ing, 1. to make ready; prepare. 2. to get (a pump) working by pouring water into it. 3. to put an undercoat on before painting. 4. to supply with facts, answers, etc. in advance.

prime meridian, the meridian at Greenwich, England, from which longitude is measured east and west.

prime minister, the chief executive in certain countries having parliamentary governments.

prime mover, 1. an original or initiating force. 2. any natural source of power, as flowing water. 3. any machine used to convert a natural force into power, as a turbine. 4. the first cause of all movement, that is itself not movable, according to Aristotle's philosophy.

prim-er (prim'ēr), *n.* 1. a simple book for teaching children to read. 2. a textbook giving basic information in some subject.

prim-er (prī'mēr), *n.* 1. one that primes. 2. an explosive cap or tube used to set off a main charge. 3. a first, underlying coat of paint, varnish, etc.

prime ribs, a choice cut of beef that includes the seven ribs just before the loin.

prime time, the hours when the largest audience for radio and television programs is usually available, especially in the evening.

pri-me-val (prī-mē'vl), *adj.* of the earliest times or age; primordial.

prim-ing (prī'ming), *n.* 1. the act of one that primes. 2. the explosive used to set off the charge in a gun or in blasting. 3. the paint, varnish, etc. used as a primer.

pri-mip-a-ra (prī-mip'ä-rä), *pl.* -a-ras, -a-rae ('ä-rē), a woman who has borne but one child or who is pregnant for the first time. —pri-mip'a-rous, *adj.*

prim-i-tive (prim'i-tiv), *adj.* 1. of the earliest times or beginnings; original. 2. crude; simple; rough. 3. not derivative; basic: *n.* 1. a primitive person or thing. 2. an artist or a work of art of an early, often preliterate culture; also, one showing a lack of formal training in art. —prim'i-tive-ly, *adv.* —prim'i-tive-ness, *n.*

prim-i-tiv-ism (-tiv-izm), *n.* 1. primitive ways or

---

a in cap, ā in cane, ä in father, å in abet, e in met, ē in be, ẽ in baker, ê in regent, i in pit, ī in fine, i in manifest, o in hot, ô in horse, ō in bone,

customs, or a belief in them. 2. the qualities of primitive art or artists.

pri-mo-gen-i-tor (prī-mō-jen'ĭ-tẽr), *n.* 1. an ancestor. 2. the earliest ancestor of a family.

pri-mo-gen-i-ture (-chẽr), *n.* 1. seniority of birth, as of the firstborn of the same parents. 2. the legal right of the eldest son to inherit his father's estate.

pri-mor-di-al (prī-môr'di-ăl), *adj.* 1. first in time; primitive. 2. not derivative; fundamental.

primp (primp), *v.t. & v.i.* to dress up or groom in a fastidious way.

prim-rose (prim'rōz), *n.* 1. any one of variously colored plants with tubelike corollas. 2. the flower of such a plant, often yellow in color.

primrose path, a path or course of action that leads, or seems to lead, one to great pleasures, especially those of the senses.

prim-u-la (prim'yoo-lă), *n.* same as primrose.

prince (prins), *n.* 1. a ruler of a principality. 2. a son of a sovereign. 3. a preeminent person in a group. 4. [Informal], a good fellow.

prince consort, the husband of a female sovereign.

prince-ly ('lĭ), *adj.* -li-er, -li-est, 1. of a prince; royal. 2. generous. 3. magnificent. —**prince'-li-ness,** *n.*

prin-cess (prin'sis, 'ses), *n.* 1. a daughter of a sovereign. 2. the wife of a prince.

princess royal, the oldest daughter of a sovereign.

prin-ci-pal (prin'si-păl), *adj.* of the first rank, degree, importance, etc.: *n.* 1. a principal person or thing. 2. an actor who has the leading role, as in a play. 3. the head of a school. 4. the amount of an investment, debt, etc. without the interest. —**prin'ci-pal-ly,** *adv.*

prin-ci-pal-i-ty (prin-si-pal'ĭ-ti), *n., pl.* -ties, the territory of a prince.

principal parts, the principal inflected forms of a verb, the present infinitive, the past tense, and the past participle.

prin-ci-ple (prin'si-păl), *n.* 1. source; origin. 2. a fundamental truth or doctrine. 3. a settled rule of action or conduct. 4. uprightness; integrity. 5. a basic part; element. 6. the law governing a natural action or occurrence. 7. the method in which something operates.

print (print), *n.* 1. a mark or character made by impression. 2. an impression from inked type, blocks, plates, etc. 3. a cloth printed with a pattern. 4. a photograph, especially one made from a negative: *v.t. & v.i.* 1. to stamp (letters, a mark, etc.) on a surface. 2. to produce on (paper, etc.) the impression of inked type, engravings, etc. 3. to produce (a book, etc.). 4. to write in letters that look like printed ones. 5. to make (a print) from a photographic negative. —**print'er,** *n.*

printed circuit, an electrical circuit on an insulating sheet, formed by the application of fine lines of conductive ink, etc.

printer's devil, an errand boy or apprentice in a printing office.

print-ing ('ing), *n.* 1. the art or act of printing. 2. the occupation of printing. 3. something printed. 4. the number of copies printed at one time.

printing press, a machine for printing on paper, etc. from inked type, plates, etc.

print-out ('out), *n.* the printed or typed material from a computer.

pri-or (prī'ẽr), *adj.* 1. coming before in time; earlier. 2. preceding in order; more important: *n.* the head of a priory. —**pri'or-ess,** *n.fem.*

pri-or-i-ty (prī-ôr'ĭ-ti), *n., pl.* -ties, 1. the state of being first in rank, time, or place. 2. first claim; a prior right to do or have something. 3. something given first attention.

pri-o-ry (prī'ẽr-i), *n., pl.* -ries, a religious house governed by a prior or prioress.

prism (priz'm), *n.* 1. a solid figure whose ends are equal and parallel and whose sides are parallelograms. 2. a transparent, three-sided prism that breaks up light into the spectrum. —**pris-mat-ic** (prĭ-mat'ik), *adj.*

prismatic colors, the colors into which a ray of light is dispersed wh. 1 refracted from a prism.

pri-or-i-tize (prī-ôr'ĭ-tīz), *v.t.* -tized, -tiz-ing, to arrange (items) in order of priority; handle in order of importance.

pris-on (priz'n), *n.* a public building for the confinement of criminals or those accused of crimes; jail.

pris-on-er (-ẽr), *n.* 1. one confined in a prison. 2. a captive.

pris-sy (pris'i), *adj.* -si-er, -si-est, [Informal], very fussy or prim.

pris-tine (pris'tin, pris-tēn'), *adj.* 1. pertaining to an early period; primitive. 2. pure; unspoiled. —**pris'tine-ly,** *adv.*

prith-ee (prith'i), *interj.* [Archaic], I pray thee; please.

pri-va-cy (prī'vă-si), *n., pl.* -cies, 1. a place or state of seclusion. 2. secrecy. 3. one's personal affairs.

pri-vate (prī'vit), *adj.* 1. of or for a particular person or group. 2. not public. 3. not in an official position. 4. for just one person. 5. secret: *n.* an enlisted man of one of the lowest ranks in the U.S. Army and Marine Corps. —**pri'vate-ly,** *adv.*

pri-va-teer (prī-vă-tir'), *n.* 1. a private vessel commissioned by a government to attack enemy merchant ships. 2. the captain or a crew member of a privateer.

private eye, [Slang], a private detective.

pri-va-tion (prī-vă'shŭn), *n.* a being deprived of the necessities of life; destitution.

priv-et (priv'it), *n.* an ornamental, bushy, evergreen shrub much used for hedges.

priv-i-lege (priv'l-ij), *n.* a special advantage, right, or immunity granted to an individual or group; favor; prerogative: *v.t.* -leged, -leg-ing, to grant a privilege to.

priv-i-ty (priv'ĭ-ti), *n., pl.* -ties, secret knowledge shared by two or more persons.

priv-y (priv'i), *adj.* 1. private. 2. admitted to the knowledge of something secret (with *to*): *n., pl.* priv'ies, an outhouse. —**priv'i-ly,** *adv.*

---

privy council, the council of confidential advisers of a sovereign.

prize (prīz), *n.* 1. a reward gained in a contest, lottery, etc. 2. something worth striving for. 3. a vessel captured in time of war. 4. [Dialectal], a lever used for prying: *adj.* awarded or worthy of a prize: *v.t.* prized, priz'ing, 1. to value or esteem. 2. to pry with a lever.

prize-fight ('fīt), *n.* a boxing match, usually a professional one. —prize'fight-er, *n.* —prize'fight-ing, *n.*

prize ring, a square platform, enclosed by ropes, for prizefights.

pro (prō), *adv.* in the affirmative: *n., pl.* pros, a vote, position, etc. in the affirmative.

pro (prō), *n., pl.* pros, [Informal], same as professional.

pro-, a prefix signifying *before, forward, in front, in favor of, in substitution of.*

prob-a-bil-i-ty (prob-ǝ-bil'ĭ-tĭ), *n., pl.* -ties, 1. likelihood. 2. something likely or probable. 3. the relative frequency with which something will probably occur.

prob-a-ble (prob'ǝ-bl), *adj.* 1. likely to occur or be true. 2. seeming to be true according to evidence, but not proved. —prob'a-bly, *adv.*

pro-bate (prō'bāt), *n.* the process of officially establishing that a will is valid: *adj.* of or concerning this process or the court with jurisdiction over wills and estates: *v.t.* -bat-ed, -bat-ing, to establish in court that (a will) is valid.

pro-ba-tion (prō-bā'shŭn), *n.* 1. a period during which one is on trial or being tested, as a student with low grades, a new employee, etc. 2. such a testing or trial. 3. a suspension of sentence of a convicted person as long as his behavior is satisfactory. —pro-ba'tion-ar-y, *adj.*

pro-ba-tion-er (-ẽr), *n.* one who is on probation.

probation officer, an official who supervises and guides persons on probation.

probe (prōb), *n.* 1. a surgical instrument for examining a wound. 2. a searching investigation. 3. an instrumented missile used to get information about space, a celestial body, etc. 4. any investigative device: *v.t.* probed, prob'ing, 1. to examine (a wound) with a probe. 2. to investigate thoroughly: *v.i.* to investigate. —prob'er, *n.*

prob-i-ty (prō'bĭ-tĭ, prob'ĭ-), *n.* integrity; sincerity.

prob-lem (prob'lĕm), *n.* 1. a question for solution. 2. a matter causing perplexity; difficulty; trouble.

prob-lem-at-ic (prob-lĕ-mat'ĭk), *adj.* 1. hard to deal with. 2. doubtful; uncertain: also problem-at'i-cal. —prob-lem-at'i-cal-ly, *adv.*

pro-bos-cis (prō-bos'ĭs), *n., pl.* -cis-es, 1. the trunk of an elephant. 2. any similar long, flexible snout or the like.

pro-caine (prō'kān), *n.* a synthetic compound used as a local anesthetic.

pro-ce-dure (prō-sē'jẽr), *n.* 1. a manner of proceeding. 2. an established or particular way of doing something.

pro-ceed (-sēd'), *v.i.* 1. to pass from one step or place to another; advance. 2. to continue

some action. 3. to carry on a legal process. 4. to issue (*from*).

pro-ceed-ing ('ing), *n.* 1. advancement. 2. a course of action. 3. *pl.* a record of business transacted, as by a learned society. 4. *pl.* legal process.

pro-ceeds (prō'sēdz), *n.pl.* money derived from a business venture, sale, etc.

proc-ess (pros'es), *n.* 1. a progressive course. 2. a series of measures or changes. 3. a detailed method of doing something. 4. in *Biology*, an appendage or projection, as on a bone. 5. in *Law*, a writ or summons: *v.t.* to treat or prepare by a special method: *adj.* prepared by a special method.

pro-ces-sion (prō-sesh'ŭn), *n.* a formal train or line of persons or things moving forward.

pro-ces-sion-al (-l), *adj.* of a procession: *n.* a musical composition or hymn played during the procession of clergy at the beginning of a church service.

pro-choice (prō'chois'), *adj.* advocating the right to obtain a legal abortion. —pro'choic'er, *n.*

pro-claim (prō-klām'), *v.t.* to announce officially; make known.

proc-la-ma-tion (prok-lǝ-mā'shŭn), *n.* an official announcement to the public.

pro-clit-ic (prō-klit'ĭk), *adj.* in *Grammar*, dependent for its stress on a following word: *n.* any such word or particle.

pro-cliv-i-ty (prō-kliv'ĭ-tĭ), *n., pl.* -ties, an inclination; tendency.

pro-con-sul (prō-kon'sl), *n.* 1. a Roman official who governed or had military authority in a province. 2. an administrator in an occupied territory, etc. —pro-con'sul-ar, *adj.*

pro-cras-ti-nate (prō-kras'tǐ-nāt, prō-), *v.i. & v.t.* -nat-ed, -nat-ing, to put off to a future time; defer. —pro-cras-ti-na'tion, *n.* —pro-cras'ti-na-tor, *n.*

pro-cre-ate (prō'krĭ-āt), *v.t. & v.i.* -at-ed, -at-ing, to generate and produce (young); beget (offspring). —pro-cre-a'tion, *n.* —pro'cre-a-tor, *n.*

Pro-crus-te-an (prō-krus'tĭ-ǎn), *adj.* determined to secure conformity even if drastic or violent measures must be used.

proc-tor (prok'tẽr), *n.* 1. one employed to manage the affairs of another. 2. a college or university official who supervises examinations, maintains order, etc.: *v.t.* to supervise (an examination). —proc'tor-ship, *n.*

pro-cum-bent (prō-kum'bĕnt), *adj.* 1. lying face down; prostrate. 2. in *Botany*, trailing along the ground.

proc-u-ra-tion (prok-yŭ-rā'shŭn), *n.* 1. the act of procuring. 2. the granting of power of attorney, or the authority conferred by this.

proc-u-ra-tor (prok'yŭ-rāt-ẽr), *n.* 1. a provincial or territorial government official in the Roman Empire. 2. one who manages another's affairs.

pro-cure (prō-kūr'), *v.t.* -cured', -cur'ing, to get or obtain; secure. —pro-cur'a-ble, *adj.* —pro-cure'ment, *n.*

pro-cur-er ('ẽr), *n.* one who obtains women for the purpose of prostitution; pander. —pro-cur'ess, *n.fem.*

prod (prod), *n.* 1. a goad or pointed stick, used in driving cattle. 2. a poke or jab: *v.t.*

prod'ded, prod'ding, 1. to goad; poke; jab. 2. to incite; urge on. —**prod'der,** *n.*

prod-i-gal (prod'i-găl), *adj.* 1. extravagant; recklessly wasteful. 2. very abundant: *n.* a spendthrift; one who is lavish or wasteful. —**prod-i-gal'i-ty** (-găl'i-ti), *n., pl.* -ties. — **prod'i-gal-ly,** *adv.*

pro-di-gious (prō-dij'ŭs), *adj.* 1. enormous. 2. exciting wonder; marvelous. —**pro-di'gious-ly,** *adv.*

prod-i-gy (prod'i-ji), *n., pl.* -gies. 1. something or someone wonderful or extraordinary. 2. a child with extraordinary talent or intelligence.

pro-drome (prō'drōm), *n.* a warning symptom of approaching disease.

pro-duce (prō-dōōs'), *v.t.* -duced', -duc'ing, 1. to exhibit or bring to view. 2. to yield or bring forth. 3. to manufacture. 4. to cause. 5. to prepare (a play, motion picture, etc.) for presentation: *v.i.* to bring forth something: *n.* (prod'ōōs, prō'dōōs), that which is produced; yield; especially, fresh fruits and vegetables. —**pro-duc'er,** *n.* —**pro-duc'i-ble,** *adj.*

prod-uct (prod'ŭkt), *n.* 1. that which is produced by nature, art, or industry. 2. result. 3. in *Mathematics,* the result obtained by multiplying two or more numbers together.

pro-duc-tion (prō-duk'shŭn), *n.* 1. that which is produced, as a dramatic presentation, work of art or literature, etc. 2. the rate or act of producing. 3. the amount produced.

pro-duc-tive ('tiv), *adj.* 1. having the power of producing; fertile. 2. having abundant or effective results. 3. causing (with *of*). —**pro-duc'tive-ly,** *adv.* —**pro-duc'tive-ness,** *n.*

pro-em (prō'em), *n.* a preface or introduction.

prof-a-na-tion (prof-ă-nā'shŭn), *n.* a desecration or defilement. —**pro-fan-a-to-ry** (prō-fan'ă-tōr-i), *adj.*

pro-fane (prō-fān'), *adj.* 1. not concerned with religion; secular. 2. irreverent; disrespectful or contemptuous of sacred things: *v.t.* -faned', -fan'ing, 1. to treat with irreverence. 2. to desecrate; violate (holy things); defile. —**pro-fane'ly,** *adv.* —**pro-fane'ness,** *n.*

pro-fan-i-ty (-fan'i-ti), *n.* 1. the quality of being profane. 2. *pl.* -ties, profane language; swearing.

pro-fess (prō-fes'), *v.t.* 1. to make open declaration of; affirm. 2. to claim to have (knowledge, a feeling, etc.) falsely. 3. to declare one's belief in, especially publicly.

pro-fessed (-fest'), *adj.* 1. openly avowed. 2. avowed falsely; pretended. 3. professing to be fully qualified.

pro-fes-sion (prō-fesh'ŭn), *n.* 1. the act of professing. 2. an open declaration or avowal. 3. a calling or vocation, especially one that requires an advanced academic degree. 4. the collective body of persons in a profession. 5. the formal entrance of a novice into a religious order.

pro-fes-sion-al (-l), *adj.* 1. of or having to do with a profession. 2. practicing some sport, or involved in some occupation, for pay: *n.* one who makes his living by a sport or occupation often taken part in by amateurs. —**pro-fes'sion-al-ly,** *adv.*

pro-fes-sion-al-ism (-izm), *n.* 1. the status of being professional. 2. the using of professional players in organized sports.

pro-fes-sor (prō-fes'ẽr), *n.* a college or university teacher of the highest rank. —**pro-fes-so-ri-al** (prō-fĕ-sōr'i-ăl), *adj.* —**pro-fes'sor-ship,** *n.*

pro-fes-so-ri-ate (prō-fĕ-sōr'i-it), *n.* 1. professors collectively. 2. the position of a professor; professorship.

prof-fer (prof'ẽr), *v.t.* to offer for acceptance; tender: *n.* an offer made.

pro-fi-cien-cy (prō-fish'ĕn-si), *n., pl.* -cies, expertness; skill.

pro-fi-cient ('ĕnt), *adj.* thoroughly qualified or skilled; expert. —**pro-fi'cient-ly,** *adv.*

pro-file (prō'fil), *n.* 1. a face or picture of a face, in side view. 2. an outline or contour. 3. a side elevation of a building. 4. a character sketch: *v.t.* -filed, -fil-ing, to make a profile of.

prof-it (prof'it), *n.* 1. gain; benefit or advantage. 2. *often pl.* monetary gain; especially, the amount remaining after deduction of costs: *v.t. & v.i.* 1. to be of advantage (to). 2. to benefit. —**prof'it-less,** *adj.*

prof-it-a-ble (-â-bl), *adj.* yielding or bringing profit; lucrative. —**prof-it-a-bil'i-ty,** *n.* —**prof'it-a-bly,** *adv.*

prof-i-teer (prof-i-tir'), *n.* one who charges excessively high prices in order to make big profits, especially in time of scarcity: *v.i.* to be a profiteer.

prof-li-gate (prof'li-git), *adj.* 1. dissolute; immoral. 2. recklessly extravagant. —**prof'li-ga-cy** (-gă-si), *n.*

pro-found (prō-found'), *adj.* 1. characterized by depth of thought or intellect. 2. intense. 3. very deep. 4. extensive. —**pro-found'ly,** *adv.* —**pro-found'ness,** *n.*

pro-fun-di-ty (-fun'di-ti), *n., pl.* -ties, 1. the state or quality of being profound. 2. depth of thinking. 3. a profound thought or matter.

pro-fuse (prō-fūs'), *adj.* 1. pouring out abundantly. 2. generous; liberal to excess. —**pro-fuse'ly,** *adv.* —**pro-fu'sion,** *n.*

pro-gen-i-tor (prō-jen'i-tẽr), *n.* 1. an ancestor in a direct line; forefather. 2. an originator.

prog-e-ny (proj'ĕ-ni), *n., pl.* -nies, offspring; descendants; children.

prog-na-thous (prog'nă-thŭs, prog-nā'-), *adj.* having projecting lower jaws.

prog-no-sis (prog-nō'sis), *n., pl.* -no'ses ('sēz), a forecast of the probable course of a disease and of the patient's chance of recovery, based on knowledge of the symptoms.

prog-nos-tic (-nos'tik), *n.* 1. an omen. 2. a prediction.

prog-nos-ti-cate (-nos'ti-kāt), *v.t.* -cat-ed, -cat-ing, to foretell; predict. —**prog-nos-ti-ca'tion,** *n.* —**prog-nos'ti-ca-tor,** *n.*

pro-gram (prō'gram), (-grăm), *n.* 1. an outline of the items to be presented in a public entertainment, ceremony, sports event, etc. 2. a course of action prepared or announced beforehand. 3. a scheduled production on television or radio. 4. a unified sequence of operations for an electronic computer. 5. the coded instructions for this: *v.t.* -grammed or

-gramed, -gram·ming or -gram·ing, 1. to enter in a program. 2. to prepare a program for. British spelling pro'gramme. —pro'gram·mer, pro'gram·er, n.

programmed learning, learning by means of a special textbook rather than an instructor: the pupil works through questions whose answers are elsewhere in the book.

prog·ress (prog'res), n. 1. a moving or going forward. 2. development. 3. advancement; improvement: v.i. (pro-gres'), 1. to move forward. 2. to advance toward completion. 3. to improve.

pro·gres·sion (pro-gresh'un), n. 1. motion onwards. 2. intellectual advance. 3. a series, as of events; sequence. 4. a series of numbers increasing or decreasing by proportional differences.

pro·gres·sive (-gres'iv), adj. 1. moving forward. 2. advocating methods or policies that will promote reform, improvement, etc. 3. passing from one step to the next: n. one who is progressive. —pro·gres'sive·ly, adv. —pro·gres'sive·ness, n.

pro·hib·it (pro-hib'it), v.t. 1. to forbid by law or authority. 2. to hinder. —pro·hib'i·tive, pro·hib'i·to·ry, adj.

pro·hi·bi·tion (-i-bish'un), n. 1. the act of prohibiting. 2. the legal prohibiting of the manufacture, sale, or transportation of alcoholic liquors. —pro·hi·bi'tion·ist, n.

proj·ect (proj'ekt), n. 1. a design or scheme. 2. a planned undertaking: v.t. (pro-jekt'), 1. to throw or cast forward. 2. to plan or scheme. 3. to cause to jut out. 4. to cast (an image, light, shadow, etc.) upon a surface: v.i. to jut out. —pro·jec'tion, n.

pro·jec·tile (pro-jek'til), n. anything shot or hurled forward, especially an object intended for this purpose, as a bullet, shell, missile, etc.

projection booth, the small enclosure in a motion-picture theater from which the films are projected on the screen.

pro·jec·tion·ist (pro-jek'shun-ist), n. one who operates a motion-picture or slide projector.

pro·jec·tor ('ter), n. an apparatus for projecting a film or slides on a screen.

pro·lapse (pro'laps), n. 1. a falling down or out of place of an internal organ of the body, as the uterus or bladder: v.i. (pro-laps'), -lapsed', -laps'ing, to fall down or out of place.

pro·late (pro'lāt), adj. elongated in the direction of the poles: opposed to oblate.

pro·le·gom·e·non (pro-li-gom'e-non), n., pl. -e·na (-nä), 1. a preliminary remark. 2. often pl. a preface or foreword.

pro·lep·sis (pro-lep'sis), n., pl. -ses ('sēz), 1. an anticipation. 2. the answering of an argument, as in debate, before it has been advanced. 3. a mistake in chronology by giving an event a date earlier than it could have happened. —pro·lep'tic, adj.

pro·le·tar·i·at (pro-le-ter'i-åt), n. the working class, especially industrial workers. —pro·le·tar'i·an, adj. & n.

pro·life (pro'lif'), adj. opposing the right to legal abortion. —pro'lif'er, n.

pro·lif·er·ate (pro-lif'e-rāt), v.t. -at·ed, -at·ing, to produce (new cells, buds, or offspring) in quick succession: v.i. to grow or increase rapidly. —pro·lif·er·a'tion, n.

pro·lif·er·ous (-rüs), adj. producing freely, as buds or leafy shoots.

pro·lif·ic (pro-lif'ik), adj. 1. producing many young or much fruit; fertile. 2. turning out many products of the mind; productive. —pro·lif'i·ca·cy ('i-kå-si), n. —pro·lif'i·cal·ly, adv.

pro·lix (pro-liks'), adj. tedious and verbose; not concise. —pro·lix'i·ty, n. —pro·lix'ly, adv.

pro·logue (pro'lôg), n. 1. an introduction or preface to a poem or play, especially lines spoken before a dramatic performance. 2. any introductory event, act, etc.

pro·long (pro-lông'), v.t. to lengthen; extend: also **pro·lon'gate** ('gāt), -gat·ed, -gat·ing. —pro·lon·ga·tion (pro-lông-gā'shün), n.

pro·lu·sion (pro-loo'zhün), n. a prelude, introduction, or introductory essay.

prom (prom), n. [Informal], a formal dance of a class at high school or college.

prom·e·nade (prom-e-nād', -nād'), n. 1. a walk for pleasure, show, or exercise. 2. a public place for walking. 3. a ball, or formal dance: v.i. & v.t. -nad'ed, -nad'ing, to walk for show or pleasure (along or through).

pro·me·thi·um (pro-me'thi-üm), n. a metallic chemical element of the rare-earth group, obtained from neodymium or uranium.

prom·i·nent (prom'i-nent), adj. 1. projecting; protuberant. 2. conspicuous; easy to see. 3. well-known; leading. —prom'i·nence, n. —prom'i·nent·ly, adv.

pro·mis·cu·ous (pro-mis'kyoo-wüs), adj. 1. confused; indiscriminately mingled. 2. indulging in sexual relations with many partners. —prom·is·cu·i·ty (prom-is-kū'i-ti), n., pl. -ties. —pro·mis'cu·ous·ly, adv.

prom·ise (prom'is), n. 1. an agreement to do or not to do something. 2. a basis for expectation. 3. the thing promised: v.i. & v.t. -ised, -is·ing, 1. to make a promise of (something). 2. to afford reason to expect. —prom'is·er, n.

Promised Land, in the Bible, a land promised by God to Abraham and his descendants: Gen. xvii, 8.

prom·i·sor (prom-i-sôr'), n. in Law, a person who makes a legal promise or covenant.

prom·is·so·ry (prom'i-sôr-i), adj. 1. containing a promise. 2. stipulating conditions.

promissory note, a written promise to pay a certain sum on demand or at a specified date to a certain person.

pro·mo (pro'mō), adj. [Informal], of or engaged in the promotion or advertisement of a product, etc.: n., pl. -mos, [Informal], a recorded announcement, radio or TV commercial, etc. used in advertising, etc.

prom·on·to·ry (prom'on-tôr-i), n., pl. -ries, a headland; high peak jutting into the sea.

pro·mote (pro-mōt'), v.t. -mot'ed, -mot'ing, 1. to advance or further. 2. to encourage sales, popularity, etc. of by advertising or publicity. 3. to raise to a higher rank or position. —pro·mo'tion, n. —pro·mo'tion·al, adj.

pro·mot·er ('ẽr), *n.* one who starts, organizes, and advances an enterprise, project, etc.

pro·mo·tive ('iv), *adj.* tending to promote.

prompt (prompt), *adj.* 1. ready and quick to act as the occasion demands; punctual. 2. done without delay: *v.t.* 1. to incite to action. 2. to remind (a person) of something he has forgotten; specifically, to help (an actor when he has forgotten his lines) by giving a cue. 3. to inspire. —**prompt'ly**, *adv.* —**prompt'ness, promp'ti·tude** ('i-tōōd), *n.*

prompt·er ('ẽr), *n.* a person offstage who gives cues or reminds an actor of forgotten lines.

prom·ul·gate (prom'ŭl-gāt), *v.t.* -**gat·ed, -gat·ing,** 1. to set (something) forth officially and publicly. 2. to make widespread. —**prom·ul·ga'tion**, *n.* —**prom'ul·ga·tor**, *n.*

pro·nate (prō'nāt), *v.t. & v.i.* -**nat·ed, -nat·ing,** to move (the hand) so that the palm faces toward the body or down. —**pro·na'tion**, *n.*

prone (prōn), *adj.* 1. lying with the face downward; prostrate. 2. inclined; disposed (*to*). —**prone'ness**, *n.*

prong (prông), *n.* 1. a sharp-pointed instrument or projecting part. 2. a tine of a fork. —**pronged** (prôngd), *adj.*

prong·horn ('hôrn), *n., pl.* **-horns, -horn,** a kind of deer of the western U.S., with a prong on each of its curved horns.

pro·nom·i·nal (prō-nom'i-n'l), *adj.* 1. pertaining to a pronoun. 2. having the function of a pronoun. —**pro·nom'i·nal·ly,** *adv.*

pro·noun (prō'noun), *n.* a word used in place of a noun, as *I, he, it, who,* etc.

pro·nounce (prō-nouns'), *v.t.* -**nounced', -nounc'ing,** 1. to speak or utter distinctly; articulate. 2. to declare formally, authoritatively, or with ceremony. —**pro·nounce'a·ble,** *adj.*

pro·nounced (-nounst'), *adj.* strongly marked or decided.

pro·nounce·ment (-nouns'mĕnt), *n.* a formal or emphatic declaration.

pron·to (pron'tō), *adv.* [Slang], at once; immediately.

pro·nun·ci·a·men·to (prō-nun-si-å-men'tō), *n., pl.* -**tos,** 1. a public proclamation. 2. same as manifesto.

pro·nun·ci·a·tion (prō-nun-si-ā'shŭn), *n.* 1. the act or a manner of articulating words or syllables. 2. a usual way of pronouncing a word, especially as represented by phonetic symbols.

proof (prōōf), *n.* 1. testimony or convincing evidence. 2. a test or experiment. 3. the strength of alcoholic liquor with reference to a standard. 4. an impression taken from type for correction. 5. a first print of a photographic negative, taken as a trial: *adj.* capable of moral or physical resistance.

-proof (prōōf), a suffix meaning *protected from, unaffected by.*

proof·read (prōōf'rēd), *v.t. & v.i.* to read (printer's proofs, etc.) and mark errors for correction. —**proof'read·er,** *n.*

prop (prop), *n.* a support or stay, as a stake, placed under or against something: *v.t.* **propped, prop'ping,** 1. to support by something under or against. 2. to lean (a thing) *against* a support. 3. to sustain.

prop (prop), *n.* 1. a property, as an article of furniture, used in a stage setting. 2. [Informal], a propeller.

pro·pae·deu·tics (prō-pi-dōōt'iks), *n.* 1. preliminary instructions. 2. a preparatory course in any branch of knowledge.

prop·a·ga·ble (prop'å-gå-bl), *adj.* denoting what may be propagated.

prop·a·gan·da (prop-å-gan'då), *n.* 1. [P-], in the *Roman Catholic Church,* a committee of cardinals in charge of foreign missions. 2. a method for the spread of certain ideas, doctrines, etc. 3. the ideas, doctrines, etc. so spread.

prop·a·gan·dism ('dizm), *n.* the art, practice, or a system of using propaganda. —**prop·a·gan'dist,** *n. & adj.*

prop·a·gan·dize ('dīz), *v.t.* -**dized, -diz·ing,** 1. to disseminate (ideas, doctrines, etc.) by propaganda. 2. to subject to propaganda: *v.i.* to disseminate propaganda.

prop·a·gate (prop'å-gāt), *v.t.* -**gat·ed, -gat·ing,** 1. to raise or breed (plants or animals). 2. to reproduce (itself): said of a plant or animal. 3. to extend or spread (principles, ideas, etc.): *v.i.* to multiply; breed, as plants or animals. —**prop·a·ga'tion,** *n.* —**prop'a·ga·tor,** *n.*

pro·pane (prō'pān), *n.* a heavy, colorless, flammable gas obtained from petroleum, used as a fuel, in refrigerants, etc.

pro·pel (prō-pel'), *v.t.* -**pelled', -pel'ling,** to drive or impel onward or forward.

pro·pel·lant, pro·pel·lent ('ănt), *n.* 1. the explosive that fires a bullet from a gun. 2. the fuel for propelling a rocket.

pro·pel·ler ('ẽr), *n.* a device on a ship or aircraft, having a revolving hub with two or more blades for propelling the vehicle.

pro·pen·si·ty (prō-pen'si-ti), *n., pl.* -**ties,** a natural tendency; inclination; bias.

prop·er (prop'ẽr), *adj.* 1. fit or suitable; appropriate. 2. peculiar (*to*). 3. correct; conforming to a standard. 4. respectable; decorous. 5. strictly limited: usually following the noun that it modifies, as the city *proper.* 6. denoting a noun that names a single individual, place, etc., and is capitalized. —**prop'er·ly,** *adv.*

prop·er·ty (prop'ẽr-ti), *n., pl.* -**ties,** 1. a peculiar attribute or characteristic. 2. the right of possession; ownership. 3. the thing owned, especially real estate. 4. any one of the movable objects or articles used in a stage or motion-picture setting, aside from scenery or costumes.

proph·e·cy (prof'ē-si), *n., pl.* -**cies,** 1. a prediction of something in the future, especially a prediction by divine inspiration. 2. something predicted.

proph·e·sy (-sī), *v.t. & v.i.* -**sied, -sy·ing,** 1. to foretell (future events), especially by divine inspiration. 2. to foretell in any way.

proph·et (prof'it), *n.* 1. a religious leader regarded as being divinely inspired. 2. one who predicts the future. 3. [P-], *a)* in *Mohammedanism,* Mohammed; *b)* in *Mormonism,* Joseph Smith, the founder of the Mormon Church. *pl.* [P-]. the prophetic books of the Bible. —**proph'et·ess,** *n.fem.*

ŏ in drag*o*n, ōō in cr*u*de, oo in w*oo*l, u in c*u*p, ū in c*u*re, ū in t*u*rn, ù in f*o*cus, oi in b*o*y, ou in h*ou*se, th in *th*in, th in shea*th*e, g in *g*et, j in *j*oy, y in *y*et.

pro·phet·ic (prō-fet′ik), *adj.* 1. of or pertaining to a prophet. 2. containing a prophecy. 3. that predicts. —**pro·phet′i·cal·ly**, *adv.*

pro·phy·lac·tic (prō-fi-lak′tik), *adj.* guarding against or preventing disease: *n.* a preventive against disease, especially a prophylatic device or medicine.

pro·phy·lax·is (′sis), *n., pl.* **-lax′es** (′sēz), a measure or treatment designed to prevent or guard against disease; specifically, in *Dentistry*, a mechanical cleaning of the teeth.

pro·pin·qui·ty (prō-ping′kwi-ti), *n.* nearness of place, time, or relationship.

pro·pi·ti·ate (prō-pish′i-āt), *v.t.* **-at·ed, -at·ing,** to conciliate; mollify; appease. —**pro·pi·ti·a′tion,** *n.* —**pro·pi′ti·a·to·ry,** *adj.*

pro·pi·tious (prō-pish′ŭs), *adj.* 1. favorable; auspicious. 2. disposed to be gracious or merciful; favorably inclined. —**pro·pi′tious·ly,** *adv.*

prop·jet (prop′jet), *n.* same as turboprop.

pro·po·nent (prō-pō′nĕnt), *n.* 1. one who makes a proposal. 2. an advocate of a principle, cause, etc.

pro·por·tion (prō-pôr′shŭn), *n.* 1. the comparative relation of one thing to another; ratio. 2. the relation of a part to the whole. 3. symmetry; balance. 4. *pl.* measurements; dimensions: *v.t.* 1. to adjust (something) so as to be in proper relation with something else. 2. to arrange the parts of so as to be harmonious. —**pro·por′tion·ment,** *n.*

pro·por·tion·al (-l), *adj.* 1. being in proportion. 2. having the same or a constant ratio: *n.* a quantity or number in proportion. —**pro·por·tion·al′i·ty** (-al′i-ti), *n.* —**pro·por′tion·al·ly,** *adv.*

pro·por·tion·ate (′shŭ-nit), *adj.* in proper proportion to something else; proportional: *v.t.* (-nāt), **-at·ed, -at·ing,** to make proportionate. —**pro·por′tion·ate·ly,** *adv.*

pro·pos·al (prō-pō′zl), *n.* 1. the act of proposing. 2. something offered for consideration or acceptance, as terms, plans, etc. 3. an offer of marriage.

pro·pose (prō-pōz′), *v.t.* **-posed′, -pos′ing,** 1. to put forward or offer for consideration, acceptance, etc. 2. to intend; plan. 3. to suggest as a toast in drinking. 4. to nominate for membership, office, etc.: *v.i.* to offer marriage.

prop·o·si·tion (prop-ō-zish′ŭn), *n.* 1. something proposed; plan. 2. a subject to be discussed or problem to be solved. 3. [Informal], *a)* proposed terms of a business transaction; *b)* a matter to be dealt with; *c)* a proposal of illicit sexual relations. —**prop·o·si′tion·al,** *adj.*

pro·pound (prō-pound′), *v.t.* to offer for consideration; put or set as a question. —**pro·pound′er,** *n.*

pro·pri·e·tar·y (prō-prī′ĕ-ter·i), *adj.* 1. belonging to a proprietor, as a trademark, patent, etc. 2. owned and operated privately: *n., pl.* **-tar·ies,** 1. a possessor in his own right; proprietor or owner. 2. proprietors collectively. 3. a proprietary medicine.

pro·pri·e·tor (prō-prī′ĕ-tẽr), *n.* 1. one who has a legal right or title to some property; owner. 2. the owner and operator of a business establishment. —**pro·pri′e·tor·ship,** *n.* —**pro·pri′e·tress,** *n.fem.*

pro·pri·e·ty (′ĕ-ti), *n., pl.* **-ties,** 1. conformity to established rules or customs; decorum. 2. fitness. 3. *pl.* the standards of behavior in polite society (with *the*).

pro·pul·sion (prō-pul′shŭn), *n.* 1. the act of propelling or state of being propelled. 2. a propelling force. —**pro·pul′sive,** *adj.*

pro ra·ta (prō rāt′ā, rät′ä), [Latin], according to share or liability; in proportion.

pro·rate (prō-rāt′), *v.t. & v.i.* **-rat′ed, -rat′ing,** to divide or distribute proportionally. —**pro·rat′a·ble,** *adj.*

pro·rogue (prō-rōg′), *v.t. & v.i.* **-rogued′, -rogu′ing,** to terminate a session of (a legislative body). —**pro·ro·ga′tion,** *n.*

pro·sa·ic (prō-zā′ik), *adj.* commonplace; uninteresting. —**pro·sa′i·cal·ly,** *adv.* —**pro·sa′ic·ness,** *n.*

pro·sa·ism (prō′zā-izm), *n.* a prosaic expression: also **pro·sa′i·cism** (′i-sizm).

pro·sce·ni·um (prō-sē′ni-ŭm), *n., pl.* **-ni·ums, -ni·a** (-ä), the section of a conventional stage between the main part of the stage and the audience, including the arch (*proscenium arch*) and the curtain.

pro·scribe (prō-skrīb′), *v.t.* **-scribed′, -scrib′ing,** 1. to deprive of legal protection. 2. to banish. 3. to forbid the practice or use of. —**pro·scrip′tion** (-skrip′shŭn), *n.*

prose (prōz), *n.* ordinary spoken or written language, not rhymed or metrical: *v.t. & v.i.* **prosed, pros′ing,** to express (thoughts, etc.) in prose: *adj.* 1. dull; commonplace. 2. of or in prose. —**pros′er,** *n.*

pros·e·cute (pros′ĕ-kūt), *v.t.* **-cut·ed, -cut·ing,** 1. to follow up or pursue (something) to a conclusion. 2. to engage in. 3. to carry on legal proceedings in court against: *v.i.* to carry on a legal suit. —**pros′e·cut·a·ble,** *adj.* —**pros′e·cu·tor,** *n.*

pros·e·cu·tion (pros-ĕ-kū′shŭn), *n.* 1. the act of prosecuting. 2. the instituting and carrying on of a legal suit or of criminal proceedings in court. 3. the State as the party that institutes and carries on criminal proceedings.

pros·e·lyte (pros′ĕ-līt), *n.* a person who has been converted from one sect, religion, etc. to another: *v.t. & v.i.* **-lyt·ed, -lyt·ing,** to try to convert (a person). —**pros′e·lyt·ism** (-li·tizm, -līt-izm), *n.*

pros·e·lyt·ize (-li·tīz), *v.i. & v.t.* **-ized, -iz·ing,** same as proselyte.

pro·sit (prō′zit, ′sit), *interj.* [German], to your health: a toast: also **prost** (prōst).

pro·so (prō′sō), *n.* same as millet.

pros·o·dy (pros′ō-di), *n., pl.* **-dies,** the art or study of versification, including metrical form, rhyme, stanzas, etc.

pro·so·po·poe·ia (prō-sō-pō-pē′ä), *n.* 1. a personification. 2. a figure of speech in which a dead, absent, or imaginary person is represented as speaking.

pros·pect (pros′pekt), *n.* 1. an extensive view; scene. 2. a view from a particular spot; outlook. 3. expectation. 4. that which is expected. 5. a potential customer, candidate, etc. 6. *usually pl.* a possible chance for success. 7. a place where a mineral deposit may be found: *v.t. & v.i.* to explore or search, especially for gold or valuable minerals (followed by *for*).

pro-spec-tive (prŏ-spek'tiv), *adj.* 1. looking forward in time. 2. likely; expected. —**pro-spec'tive-ly,** *adv.*

pros-pec-tor (pros'pek-tẽr), *n.* one who prospects for valuable minerals, oil, etc.

pro-spec-tus (prŏ-spek'tŭs), *n.* an outline of a proposed undertaking, a new work, etc.

pros-per (pros'pẽr), *v.i.* to thrive; succeed: *v.t.* [Archaic], to cause to prosper; favor.

pros-per-i-ty (pro-sper'ĭ-tĭ), *n., pl.* -**ties,** good fortune; a prosperous state; wealth; success.

pros-per-ous (pros'pẽr-ŭs), *adj.* 1. successful; thriving. 2. wealthy. 3. propitious. —**pros'per-ous-ly,** *adv.*

pros-tate (pros'tāt), *adj.* designating a small gland of male mammals at the base of the bladder, surrounding the urethra.

pros-the-sis (pros'thē-sis, pros-thē'-), *n., pl.* -**ses** (-sēz), 1. the replacement of a missing part of the body with an artificial substitute. 2. such a substitute. 3. same as prosthesis (sense 1). —**pros-thet-ic** (pros-thet'ik), *adj.*

pros-thet-ics (pros-thet'iks), *n.* the branch of surgery concerned with the replacement of missing parts of the body, especially limbs, by artificial substitutes. —**pros-the-tist** (pros'thĕ-tist), *n.*

pros-ti-tute (pros'tĭ-tōōt), *v.t.* -**tut-ed,** -**tut-ing,** 1. to hire (oneself or another) out for sexual intercourse. 2. to sell (one's talents or efforts) for unworthy purposes: *n.* 1. a woman who hires herself out for sexual intercourse; whore; harlot. 2. a person, as a writer or artist, who sells his services for unworthy purposes. —**pros'ti-tu-tor,** *n.*

pros-ti-tu-tion (pros-tĭ-tōō'shŭn), *n.* the act or practice of prostituting; especially, the trade of a prostitute.

pros-trate (pros'trāt), *adj.* 1. lying at full length, especially with the face downward. 2. lying in this way in abject humility or submission. 3. laid low; completely overcome, as by grief or exhaustion. 4. in *Botany,* extended on the ground: *v.t.* -**trat-ed,** -**trat-ing,** 1. to put in a prostrate position. 2. to overcome. —**pros-tra'tion,** *n.*

pro-style (prŏ'stīl), *n.* 1. a portico with a range of columns, usually four, across the front. 2. a building, as a Greek temple, with such a portico.

pros-y (prō'zĭ), *adj.* **pros'i-er, pros'i-est,** tedious; dull; prosaic. —**pros'i-ly,** *adv.* —**pros'i-ness,** *n.*

pro-tag-o-nist (prŏ-tag'ŏ-nist), *n.* 1. one who takes the lead or plays an active part in a movement, etc. 2. the leading character in a story, play, motion picture, etc.

prot-a-sis (prot'ă-sis), *n.* in *Grammar,* the introductory clause of a conditional sentence.

pro-te-an (prŏt'ĭ-ăn), *adj.* 1. [P-], of or like Proteus, a Greek sea god who could change form and shape at will. 2. able to change form or shape; changeable.

pro-tect (prŏ-tekt'), *v.t.* to defend or shield from danger, injury, trouble, loss, etc.; guard. —**pro-tec'tor,** *n.*

pro-tec-tion (prŏ-tek'shŭn), *n.* 1. the act of protecting. 2. the state of being protected. 3. something or someone that protects; de-

fense. 4. a system of protecting domestic industry by tariffs on competitive imports.

pro-tec-tion-ism (-izm), *n.* the economic theory or practice of protecting certain domestic industries by taxes on imports. —**pro-tec'-tion-ist,** *n. & adj.*

pro-tec-tive (prŏ-tek'tiv), *adj.* 1. serving to protect. 2. serving to protect domestic industries against foreign competition. —**pro-tec'-tive-ly,** *adv.* —**pro-tec'tive-ness,** *n.*

pro-tec-tor-ate ('tẽr-it), *n.* 1. the relation of a strong state to a weaker one under its control and protection. 2. the state protected in this way. 3. the authority of the controlling state.

pro-té-gé (prŏt'ĕ-zhā), *n.* one who is guided and helped in his career by someone more influential. —**pro'té-gée** (-zhā), *n.fem.*

pro-tein (prŏ'tēn, prŏt'ĭ-in), *n.* any of a class of nitrogenous substances occurring in all animal and vegetable matter and essential to the diet.

pro tem-po-re (prŏ tem'pŏ-ri), for the time (being); temporarily: often shortened to **pro tem.**

pro-te-ol-y-sis (prŏt-ĭ-ol'ĭ-sis), *n.* the breaking down of proteins, as by gastric juices, to form simpler, soluble substances. —**pro-te-o-lyt'ic** (-ŏ-lit'ik), *adj.*

pro-te-ose (prŏt'ĭ-ōs), *n.* any one of a group of water-soluble products formed in the hydrolysis of proteins.

pro-test (prŏ-test'), *v.i.* to object strongly; remonstrate: *v.t.* 1. to declare or affirm positively. 2. to speak strongly against: *n.* (prŏ'test), 1. an objection; remonstrance. 2. a document containing a formal objection to something. —**pro-test'er, pro-tes'tor,** *n.*

Prot-es-tant (prot'is-tănt), *n.* 1. a member of any of the Christian churches derived from the Reformation. 2. any Christian not a member of the Roman Catholic or Orthodox Eastern Church: *adj.* of or pertaining to Protestants or their practices, doctrines, etc.

Protestant Episcopal Church, the church in the U.S. that derived from the Church of England.

Prot-es-tant-ism (-izm), *n.* the belief of, adherence to, or practices, etc. of, a Protestant faith or church.

prot-es-ta-tion (prot-is-tā'shŭn, prŏ-tes-), *n.* 1. the act of protesting. 2. a solemn affirmation. 3. a declaration of dissent; objection.

pro-tha-la-mi-on (prŏ-thă-lā'mĭ-ăn, -on), *n., pl.* -**mi-a** (-ă), a song composed to celebrate a marriage: also **pro-tha-la'mi-um** (-ŭm), *pl.* -**mi-a** (-ă).

proth-e-sis (proth'ĕ-sis), *n.* 1. in *Grammar,* the addition of a letter, syllable, etc. at the beginning of a word. 2. in the *Orthodox Eastern Church,* the preparation of the Eucharistic elements previous to the liturgical service. —**pro-thet'ic** (pro-thet'ik), *adj.*

pro-thon-o-tar-y (prŏ-thon'ŏ-ter-i), *n., pl.* -**tar-ies,** 1. a chief clerk in certain law courts. 2. in the *Roman Catholic Church,* a clerical official who records important pontifical events.

pro-throm-bin (prŏ-throm'bin), *n.* a factor in the blood plasma that takes part in the blood-clotting process: it is a precursor of thrombin.

pro-to-, a combining form meaning *most important, chief, primitive, original*.

pro-to-col (prōt'ō-kôl), *n.* 1. the original draft of a treaty, diplomatic dispatch, etc. 2. any preliminary document or record as a basis of further negotiations. 3. the ceremonial code of diplomatic etiquette.

pro-to-lith-ic (prōt-ō-lith'ik), *adj.* of or pertaining to the earliest Stone Age.

pro-to-mar-tyr (prōt-ō-mär'tēr), *n.* the first martyr in some cause.

pro-ton (prō'ton), *n.* any one of the positively charged elementary particles in the nucleus of an atom, and the atomic nucleus of the most common isotope of hydrogen.

pro-to-plasm (prōt'ō-plazm), *n.* the essential living matter of plant and animal cells, a semifluid colloid. —**pro-to-plas'mic**, *adj.*

pro-to-plast (prōt'ō-plast), *n.* 1. the thing or being that is the first of its kind. 2. the nucleus of a cell. 3. the protoplasm within a single plant cell. —**pro-to-plas'tic**, *adj.*

pro-to-type (prōt'ō-tīp), *n.* 1. the original being or thing of its kind, serving as a model. 2. a perfect example of a certain type. —**pro'to-typ-al** (-tī-pl), *adj.*

pro-tox-ide (prō-tok'sīd), *n.* the oxide in a given series of oxides having the smallest proportion of oxygen.

pro-to-zo-an (prōt-ō-zō'ən), *n.* any one of a large group of usually single-celled animal organisms, mostly aquatic and including some parasites: also **pro-to-zo'on** ('on), *pl.* **-zo'a** ('ə).

pro-tract (prō-trakt'), *v.t.* to draw out or lengthen in time; prolong. —**pro-trac'tion**, *n.*

pro-trac-tile (prō-trak'til), *adj.* capable of being thrust out, as claws.

pro-trac-tor (prō-trak'tēr), *n.* 1. a semicircular instrument marked in degrees, used to construct or measure angles. 2. in *Anatomy*, a muscle that protracts, or extends, a limb.

pro-trude (prō-trōōd'), *v.t. & v.i.* **-trud'ed**, **-trud'ing**, to project; push forward; jut out. —**pro-tru'sion**, *n.*

pro-tru-sile (prō-trōō'sl), *adj.* capable of being protruded, or thrust out, as a tentacle, the tongue of an insectivore, etc.

pro-tru-sive ('siv), *adj.* 1. protruding; jutting out. 2. obtrusive. —**pro-tru'sive-ly**, *adv.*

pro-tu-ber-ance (prō-tōō'bēr-əns), *n.* a thing or part that protrudes; swelling, projection, bulge, etc. —**pro-tu'ber-ant**, *adj.* —**pro-tu'ber-ant-ly**, *adv.*

proud (proud), *adj.* 1. having a proper self-esteem. 2. having excessive self-esteem; haughty. 3. feeling greatly pleased, honored, etc. 4. caused by pride. 5. being a cause of pride. 6. spirited. 7. glorious; stately. —**proud'ly**, *adv.*

prove (prōōv), *v.t.* **proved**, **proved** or **prov'en**, **prov'ing**, 1. to try out or test by experiment or by a standard. 2. to establish as true. 3. to ascertain the validity of. 4. to verify the correctness of (a mathematical calculation): *v.i.* to be shown to be (as specified) by trial or experience. —**prov-a-bil'i-ty**, *n.* —**prov'a-ble**, *adj.*

prov-e-nance (prov'ē-nəns), *n.* derivation; origin.

Pro-ven-cal (prō-vèn-säl'), *n.* a Romance language of southern France.

prov-en-der (prov'ēn-dēr), *n.* 1. dry food, as hay, for livestock; fodder. 2. [Informal], food.

prov-erb (prov'ērb), *n.* a short, familiar, pithy saying, expressing some obvious truth or common fact of experience; adage.

pro-ver-bi-al (prō-vūr'bi-əl), *adj.* 1. of or like a proverb. 2. mentioned in a proverb. 3. well-known because widely spoken of. —**pro-ver'bi-al-ly**, *adv.*

Prov-erbs (prov'ērbz), *n.* a book of the Bible.

pro-vide (prō-vīd'), *v.t.* **-vid'ed**, **-vid'ing**, 1. to arrange for beforehand. 2. to supply. 3. to furnish with. 4. to stipulate as a preliminary condition: *v.i.* 1. to make preparations (*for* or *against*). 2. to furnish support (*for*). —**pro-vid'er**, *n.*

pro-vid-ed ('id), *conj.* on condition (*that*); if; also **pro-vid'ing** ('ing).

prov-i-dence (prov'i-dèns), *n.* 1. timely care or preparation. 2. economy and prudence in management. 3. the care or guidance of God or nature. 4. [P-], God, especially when thought of as providing care or guidance.

prov-i-dent (-dènt), *adj.* 1. acting with foresight in providing for future needs. 2. prudent; economical. —**prov'i-dent-ly**, *adv.*

prov-i-den-tial (prov-i-den'shùl), *adj.* 1. by or as if by divine providence. 2. lucky; fortunate. —**prov-i-den'tial-ly**, *adv.*

prov-ince (prov'ins), *n.* 1. an administrative division of a country, specifically of Canada. 2. a district; region. 3. *pl.* the parts of a country away from the largest cities. 4. the jurisdiction of an archbishop or metropolitan. 5. a branch of knowledge, sphere of work, etc.

pro-vin-cial (prō-vin'shùl), *adj.* 1. of the provinces. 2. having the speech or manners of a particular province. 3. rustic. 4. narrow; not liberal. —**pro-vin'cial-ly**, *adv.*

pro-vin-cial-ism (-izm), *n.* 1. an idiom or dialect peculiar to a certain province. 2. narrowness of outlook; interest only in local affairs. —**pro-vin'cial-ist**, *n.*

proving ground, an area or place for testing something, as new equipment, new theories, etc.

pro-vi-sion (prō-vizh'ùn), *n.* 1. the act of providing. 2. things provided for the future. 3. measures taken beforehand. 4. *pl.* a stock of food. 5. a proviso; stipulation: *v.t.* to supply with provisions.

pro-vi-sion-al (-l), *adj.* for present use; temporary. —**pro-vi'sion-al-ly**, *adv.*

pro-vi-so (prō-vī'zō), *n.*, *pl.* **-sos**, **-soes**, a conditional clause or stipulation, as in a document, law, etc.

pro-vi-so-ry ('zēr-i), *adj.* 1. conditional. 2. provisional. —**pro-vi'so-ri-ly**, *adv.*

prov-o-ca-tion (prov-ō-kā'shùn), *n.* 1. that which provokes to anger or resentment. 2. the act of provoking.

pro-voc-a-tive (prō-vok'ə-tiv), *adj.* tending to provoke to thought, feeling, or action; exciting, stimulating, irritating, erotic, etc. —pro-voc'a·tive·ly, *adv.*

pro·voke (prō-vōk'), *v.t.* -voked', -vok'ing, 1. to excite or stir to action. 2. to enrage or irritate. 3. to arouse; stir up (emotions, activity, etc.). 4. to induce. —pro·vok'er, *n.*

pro·vok·ing (-vō'king), *adj.* tending to arouse annoyance, vexation, etc. —pro·vok'ing·ly, *adv.*

pro·vost (prō'vōst), *n.* 1. an administrative official in some colleges. 2. the chief dignitary of a cathedral, principal church, etc. 3. an official in charge.

provost marshal (prō'vō), an officer in charge of a detail of military police (provost guard).

prow (prou), *n.* the bow of a ship or boat.

prow·ess (prou'is), *n.* 1. bravery; valor. 2. exceptional ability or skill.

prowl (proul), *v.i.* & *v.t.* to wander stealthily, as in search of prey or plunder: *n.* a roving.

prowl car, same as squad car.

prox·i·mal (prok'si-ml), *adj.* in *Anatomy*, nearest to the center of the body or to the point of origin or attachment. —prox'i·mal·ly, *adv.*

prox·i·mate (-mit), *adj.* 1. immediate; next in space or time. 2. approximate. —prox'i·mate·ly, *adv.*

prox·im·i·ty (prok-sim'i-ti), *n.* immediate nearness in place, time, order, relation, etc.

prox·i·mo (prok'si-mō), *adv.* in or of the next or coming month.

prox·y (prok'si), *n., pl.* prox'ies, 1. the agency or authority of a substitute. 2. the document by which one person is authorized to act or vote for another. 3. a person so authorized.

prude (prōōd), *n.* one who affects excessive modesty, propriety, virtue, etc., especially in a way to irritate others. —prud'er·y, *n.*

pru·dence (prōōd'ns), *n.* 1. the quality of being prudent. 2. cautious and provident management; economy.

pru·dent ('nt), *adj.* 1. wise in practical matters. 2. cautious in behavior; discreet. 3. practicing careful management; economical. —pru'dent·ly, *adv.*

pru·den·tial (proo-den'shùl), *adj.* 1. of, characterized by, or resulting from prudence. 2. showing prudence. 3. acting in an advisory capacity. —pru·den'tial·ly, *adv.*

prud·ish (prōōd'ish), *adj.* like a prude; too modest or proper. —prud'ish·ly, *adv.* —prud'ish·ness, *n.*

prune (prōōn), *n.* a dried plum: *v.t.* & *v.i.* pruned, prun'ing, to cut superfluous twigs or branches from (a vine, bush, or tree); trim. —prun'er, *n.*

pru·nel·la (prōō-nel'ä), *n.* a strong, smooth, woolen cloth, formerly much used for shoe uppers, clerical gowns, etc.

pru·ri·ent (proor'i-ént), *adj.* 1. feeling or showing lust. 2. exciting lust; lewd. —pru'ri·ence, pru'ri·en·cy, *n.* —pru'ri·ent·ly, *adv.*

pru·ri·go (proo-rī'gō), *n.* a chronic inflammation of the skin, characterized by eruptive, itching papules. —pru·rig'i·nous (-rij'i-nûs), *adj.*

pru·ri·tus (proo-rīt'ûs), *n.* itching of the skin, especially without eruption. —pru·rit'ic (-rit'ik), *adj.*

Prus·sian (prush'ûn), *adj.* of or pertaining to Prussia, a former kingdom of northern Europe and dominant state of the former German Empire: *n.* an inhabitant of Prussia, or one considered to be like the Prussians in actions or temperament.

Prussian blue, a rich, dark-blue color obtained from ferrocyanide of iron.

Prus·sian·ism (-izm), *n.* the practices and behavior of the Prussian ruling class, characterized by harsh discipline, militarism, and despotism.

prus·si·ate (prus'i-āt, prush'-), *n.* 1. a salt of hydrocyanic acid. 2. a salt of ferrocyanic acid; ferrocyanide.

pry (prī), *n., pl.* pries, a crowbar; lever: *v.t.* pried, pry'ing, 1. to raise up or move with a pry. 2. to draw forth with difficulty: *v.i.* to snoop; inquire or inspect impertinently. —pry'er, *n.*

psalm (säm), *n.* 1. a sacred song or poem. 2. [usually P-], any one of the hymns in the Book of Psalms in the Bible. —psalm'ist, *n.*

psal·mo·dy (säm'ō-di, sal'mä-), *n.* the art or practice of singing psalms or of arranging psalms for singing. —psal'mo·dist, *n.*

Psalms (sämz), *n.* a book of the Bible: also Book of Psalms.

Psal·ter (sôl'tér), *n.* 1. the Book of Psalms. 2. [also p-], a version of the Psalms for devotional or liturgical use.

psal·ter·y (sôl'tér-i, 'tri), *n., pl.* -ter·ies, a stringed musical instrument used by the ancient Hebrews.

psam·mite (sam'īt), *n.* [Rare], same as sandstone. —psam·mit·ic (sa-mit'ik), *adj.*

pseu·de·pig·ra·pha (sōō-dē-pig'rä-fä, sū-), *n.pl.* [also P-], early writings falsely attributed to Biblical characters. —pseu·de·pig'ra·phous (-fûs), *adj.*

pseu·do-, a prefix meaning *false, counterfeit, pretended.*

pseu·do·carp (sōō'dō-kärp, sū'-), *n.* a fruit formed from the uniting of a cluster of flowers, as the raspberry, or from the addition of parts other than the mature ovary, as the apple.

pseu·do·morph (sōō'dō-môrf, sū'-), *n.* 1. an irregular form. 2. a mineral having the external form of another.

pseu·do·nym (sōō'dō-nim, sū'-), *n.* a fictitious name, especially one used by an author; pen name. —pseu·don·y·mous (sōō-don'i-mûs, sū-), *adj.*

pshaw (shô), *interj.* & *n.* an expression of disgust, contempt, exasperation, etc.

psi (sī), *n.* the 23rd letter of the Greek alphabet.

pso·ri·a·sis (sō-rī'ä-sis), *n.* a chronic skin disease characterized by reddish, scaly patches.

psst (pst), *interj.* a vocal sound made to quietly attract the attention of another person.

psych (sīk), *v.t.* psyched, psych'ing, [Slang], to study (someone's) personality so as to be able to outwit him.

psy·che (sī'ki), *n.* 1. the soul. 2. the mind as it governs the total human being. 3. [P-], in *Roman Mythology*, the goddess who personifies the soul.

psy·che·del·ic (sī-kē-del'ik), *adj.* 1. of or having

ô in dragon, ōō in crude, oo in wool, u in cup, ū in cure, û in turn, ŭ in focus, oi in boy, ou in house, th in thin, th in sheathe, g in get, j in joy, y in yet.

to do with hallucinations, intensified sensory perception, etc. 2. denoting various drugs that cause these effects. 3. of or resembling the sounds or visual effects experienced with such drugs.

psy·chi·a·trist (si-kī'ă-trist, sī-), *n.* a doctor of medicine specializing in psychiatry.

psy·chi·a·try (si-kī'ă-tri, sī-), *n.* the branch of medicine concerned with the study and treatment of mental disorders, including psychoses and neuroses. —**psy·chi·at·ric** (sī-ki-at'rik), **psy·chi·at'ri·cal,** *adj.* —**psy·chi·at'ri·cal·ly,** *adv.*

psy·chic (sī'kik), *adj.* 1. of the mind, or psyche. 2. outside of normal physical processes. 3. seeming to be sensitive to supernatural forces. Also **psy'chi·cal.** —**psy'chi·cal·ly,** *adv.*

psy·cho (sī'kō), *n.* [Informal], 1. a psychopath. 2. a psychotic.

psy·cho-, a combining form meaning *the mind.*

psy·cho·a·nal·y·sis (sī-kō-ă-nal'ī-sis), *n.* a procedure for treating neuroses and some other disorders of the mind by investigating the unconscious and dealing with repressions, mental conflicts, etc. —**psy·cho·an'a·lyst** (-an'ăl-ist), *n.*

psy·cho·an·a·lyze (-an'ă-līz), *v.t.* **-lyzed, -lyz·ing,** to treat or investigate by psychoanalysis.

psy·cho·bab·ble (sī'kō-bab-ĕl), *n.* [Informal], talk or writing that uses psychological or psychiatric terms and concepts in a trite or superficial way.

psy·cho·gen·ic (-jen'ik), *adj.* originating in the mind or caused by mental conflicts.

psy·cho·log·i·cal (sī-kō-loj'i-kl), *adj.* 1. of or pertaining to psychology. 2. mental. 3. affecting the mind. Also **psy·cho·log'ic.** —**psy·cho·log'i·cal·ly,** *adv.*

psy·chol·o·gy (sī-kol'ō-ji), *n., pl.* **-gies,** 1. the science that treats of mental and emotional processes and states. 2. the science of human and animal behavior. 3. the sum of the attitudes, modes of behavior, etc. of a person or group. 4. a particular system of psychology. —**psy·chol'o·gist,** *n.*

psy·cho·neu·ro·sis (sī-kō-nŏŏ-rō'sis), *n., pl.* **-ro'ses** (-sēz), same as **neurosis.**

psy·cho·path (sī'kō-path), *n.* a person suffering from a mental or emotional disorder, especially one who is asocial and amoral. —**psy·cho·path'ic,** *adj.*

psy·cho·pa·thol·o·gy (sī-kō-pa-thol'ō-ji), *n.* the branch of science dealing with mental disorders.

psy·cho·phys·i·ol·o·gy (-fiz-i-ol'ō-ji), *n.* the study of the relationship between physical and mental processes.

psy·cho·sex·u·al (-sek'shoo-wăl), *adj.* of or pertaining to the relationship of the physical and psychological aspects of sex. —**psy·cho·sex·u·al'i·ty** (-sek-shoo-wal'ī-ti), *n.*

psy·cho·sis (sī-kō'sis), *n., pl.* **-ses** ('sēz), a serious mental disorder usually characterized by lack of contact with reality and disorganization of the personality.

psy·cho·so·mat·ic (sī-kō-sō-mat'ik), *adj.* designating or of a physical disorder of the body caused or affected by the emotions.

psy·cho·sur·ger·y (-sûr'jĕr-i), *n.* brain surgery in treatment of mental illness.

psy·cho·ther·a·py (-ther'ă-pi), *n.* a system for treating mental disorders by means of counseling, psychoanalysis, suggestion, etc. —**psy·cho·ther'a·pist,** *n.*

psy·chot·ic (sī-kot'ik), *adj.* 1. of or like a psychosis. 2. having a psychosis: *n.* a person who has a psychosis.

psy·cho·trop·ic (sī-kō-trop'ik), *adj.* denoting various drugs that affect mental activity, as hallucinogens, tranquilizers, etc.

Ptah (ptä), *n.* the great god of ancient Egypt, regarded as the father of gods and men.

ptar·mi·gan (tär'mi-găn), *n.* a northern grouse with feathered legs and feet and with plumage whose color changes with the seasons.

pter·o·dac·tyl (ter-ō-dak'tl), *n.* an extinct flying reptile having wings of skin.

pter·o·pod (ter'ō-pod), *n.* any of a number of small, thin-shelled gastropods that swim at or near the surface of the water by small, winglike lobes on the feet.

pto·maine (tō'mān), *n.* an alkaloid substance, often poisonous, found in dead or decaying matter.

pto·sis (tō'sis), *n.* a permanent drooping of the upper eyelid.

pty·a·lin (tī'ă-lin), *n.* an enzyme in saliva that converts starches into dextrins and maltose.

pty·a·lism (-lizm), *n.* an abnormal flow of saliva.

pub (pub), *n.* [Chiefly British Informal], a tavern or bar; public house.

pu·ber·ty (pū'bĕr-ti), *n.* the period of life when sexual reproduction first becomes possible.

pu·bes (pū'bēz), *n.* 1. the hair which grows, at puberty, on the lower part of the abdomen surrounding the external genitals. 2. the lower part of the abdomen. —**pu'bic,** *adj.*

pu·bes·cence (pū-bes'ns), *n.* 1. the state or age of puberty. 2. fine hair or down as found on plants, insects, etc. —**pu·bes'cent,** *adj.*

pub·lic (pub'lik), *adj.* 1. of people in general. 2. generally known. 3. open to general use; especially, financed by the government, as a park. 4. acting officially for the people: *n.* 1. people in general. 2. a group of the people that have something in common. —**pub'lic·ly,** *adv.*

pub·li·can (pub'li-kăn), *n.* 1. in England, the keeper of a public house. 2. in ancient Rome, a tax collector.

pub·li·ca·tion (pub-li-kā'shŭn), *n.* 1. the act of making known to the public. 2. the act of publishing, as the printing and distribution of a book, periodical, etc. 3. any printed work.

public defender, a lawyer employed through public funds to defend indigents accused of crimes.

public domain, 1. public lands. 2. the condition of being available to the public without restrictions of copyright or patent.

public enemy, a criminal who is a menace to society.

public house, in England, a bar or tavern.

pub·li·cist (pub'li-sist), *n.* 1. a writer on international law. 2. a writer on current events. 3. one whose business is publicity.

pub·lic·i·ty (pŭ-blis'ī-ti), *n.* 1. the business or technique of bringing a person, organization, product, etc. to the notice of the public. 2. any material used for this. 3. public notice.

pub·li·cize (pub′li-siz), *v.t.* -cized, -ciz·ing, to give publicity to.

public relations, relations with the public, as by an organization, institution, etc.

public school, 1. in the U.S., a school for primary or secondary education maintained at public expense. 2. in England, a private boarding school for boys.

public servant, a person who is employed by civil service or is a public official.

pub·lic-spir·it·ed (-spir′i-tid), *adj.* caring about or willing to work for the welfare of the general public.

public utility, an establishment that supplies gas, water, transportation, etc. to the general public.

pub·lish (pub′lish), *v.t.* 1. to make known; announce or proclaim. 2. to print and offer for sale; put into circulation: *v.i.* to write books, articles, etc. that are published. — **pub′lish·er,** *n.*

puce (pūs), *adj.* of a brownish-purple color.

puck (puk), *n.* the hard, black disk of vulcanized rubber used in ice hockey.

puck (puk), *n.* a mischievous sprite or elf. — **puck′ish,** *adj.*

puck·er (puk′ĕr), *v.t. & v.i.* to gather into small folds; wrinkle: *n.* a small fold or wrinkle made by puckering. —**puck′er·y,** *adj.*

pud·ding (pood′ing), *n.* a soft, sweet dessert made variously with milk, flour, bread, fruit, eggs, etc.

pud·dle (pud′l), *n.* 1. a small pool of dirty, stagnant, or spilled water. 2. a mixture of clay and water, sometimes with sand: *v.t.* -dled, -dling, 1. to make muddy. 2. to make watertight with puddle. 3. to convert (pig iron) into (wrought iron).

pud·dling (′ling), *n.* the making of wrought iron from pig iron by melting and stirring it in the presence of oxidizing substances.

pu·den·cy (pūd′n-si), *n.* modesty; bashfulness.

pu·den·dum (pū-den′dùm), *n., pl.* -den′da (′dä), the vulva.

pudg·y (puj′i), *adj.* pudg′i·er, pudg′i·est, short and fat; dumpy. —**pudg′i·ness,** *n.*

pueb·lo (pweb′lō), *n., pl.* -los, 1. a village made up of terraced adobe buildings housing many families, made by Indians in the southwestern U.S. 2. [P-], a member of any of a number of Indian tribes inhabiting pueblos.

pu·er·ile (pū′ĕr-il), *adj.* childish; juvenile; trivial. —**pu·er·il·i·ty** (pū-ĕ·ril′ĭ-ti), *n.*

pu·er·per·al (pū-ûr′pẽr-ăl), *adj.* of, pertaining to, or following childbirth.

puff (puf), *n.* 1. a short, quick burst, gust, or expulsion of breath, air, smoke, etc. 2. an inhaling of smoke from a cigarette, etc. 3. a light kind of pastry shell with a filling of cream, custard, etc. 4. a soft pad, coverlet, roll of hair, etc. 5. exaggerated praise, as of a publication: *v.i.* 1. to blow in short, quick gusts, as the wind. 2. to breathe rapidly. 3. to swell or fill (up or out). 4. to inhale smoke from a cigarette, etc.: *v.t.* 1. to blow,

smoke, etc. with puffs. 2. to swell; inflate. 3. to praise in exaggerated terms.

puff adder, a large, venomous snake of South Africa that distends its body and hisses when irritated.

puff·ball (′bôl), *n.* any one of a number of round fungi that burst when mature and scatter a brown powder.

puff·er (′ĕr), *n.* any one of a number of fish that can expand the body by swallowing air or water.

puf·fin (puf′in), *n.* a northern sea bird with a thick, brightly colored, triangular beak.

puff·y (puf′i), *adj.* puff′i·er, puff′i·est, 1. distended with air or other light matter; inflated. 2. panting. 3. windy. 4. obese. — **puff′i·ly,** *adv.* —**puff′i·ness,** *n.*

pug (pug), *n.* 1. a small dog with a wrinkled face and snub nose. 2. [Slang], a pugilist. 3. a wet, plastic clay: *v.t.* pugged, pug′ging, 1. to mix (wet, plastic clay) for making bricks, earthenware, etc. 2. to line or fill in with pug for soundproofing.

pug·ging (′ing), *n.* 1. the act or operation of working up clay for bricks, earthenware, etc. 2. wet clay or the like used for soundproofing.

pugh (pū, pōō), *interj.* an exclamation of disgust.

pu·gil·ism (pū′jĭ-lizm), *n.* the sport of boxing, or fighting with the fists; prizefighting. — **pu′gi·list,** *n.* —**pu·gi·lis′tic,** *adj.*

pug·na·cious (pug-nā′shùs), *adj.* disposed to fight; quarrelsome. —**pug·na′cious·ly,** *adv.* — **pug·nac′i·ty** (-nas′i-ti), *n.*

pug-nosed (pug′nōzd), *adj.* having a short, broad, turned-up nose.

puis·ne (pū′ni), *adj.* [Chiefly British], inferior in rank; junior, as in appointment: said of judges, etc.

pu·is·sance (pū′i-săns), *n.* [Archaic or Poetic], power; strength. —**pu′is·sant,** *adj.* —**pu′is·sant·ly,** *adv.*

puke (pūk), *n. & v.t. & v.i.* puked, puk′ing, [Informal], vomit.

pul·chri·tude (pul′kri-tōōd), *n.* beauty; comeliness.

pule (pūl), *v.i.* puled, pul′ing, to whine.

pull (pool), *v.t.* 1. to exert force so as to draw toward (something or someone). 2. to extract, as a tooth. 3. to rend or tear. 4. to strain, as a muscle, tendon, etc. 5. [Informal], to hold back. 6. [Informal], to put into effect: *v.i.* 1. to exert force in drawing, dragging, attracting, etc. 2. to drive a vehicle (*into, out of,* etc.): *n.* 1. the act or an instance of pulling. 2. the force of pulling. 3. a device for pulling something. 4. a continuous effort. 5. [Informal], *a)* special influence; *b)* appeal; attraction.

pull·back (′bak), *n.* a planned withdrawal of military forces.

pul·let (pool′it), *n.* a young hen.

pul·ley (pool′i), *n., pl.* -leys, a small wheel with a grooved rim in which a belt, rope, chain, etc. passes, used for transmitting motion, guiding or lifting weights, etc.

Pull·man (pool′măn), *n.* a railroad sleeping car with private berths: also **Pullman car.**

pull·out (pool'out), *n.* the act of pulling out; removal or withdrawal.

pull·o·ver ('ō·vĕr), *adj.* denoting a sweater, shirt, etc. that is put on by being drawn over the head: *n.* such a garment.

pul·lu·late (pul'yoo·lāt), *v.i.* -lat·ed, -lat·ing, 1. to germinate; bud. 2. to breed or spring up abundantly. —**pul·lu·la'tion,** *n.*

pull·up ('up), *n.* the act of chinning oneself.

pul·mo·nar·y (pul'mō·ner·i), *adj.* of, pertaining to, or affecting the lungs: also **pul·mon·ic** (pool·mon'ik).

Pul·mo·tor (pool'mōt·ĕr, pul'·), *n.* a device for applying artificial respiration: a trademark.

pulp (pulp), *n.* 1. the soft, fleshy part of fruit. 2. any soft, more or less uniform mass. 3. the soft pith of the stem of a plant. 4. the inner, sensitive part of a tooth. 5. ground-up material, as wood or rags, moistened and used in making paper: *v.t.* to reduce to pulp. —**pulp'y,** *adj.*

pul·pit (pool'pit), *n.* 1. an elevated platform from which a clergyman conducts a church service. 2. clergymen collectively.

pul·que (pool'ki), *n.* a fermented Mexican drink made from the juice of the agave.

pul·sar (pul'sär), *n.* any one of several small celestial objects in the Milky Way that emit radio waves in regular pulsations.

pul·sate (pul'sāt), *v.i.* -sat·ed, -sat·ing, 1. to throb or beat. 2. to vibrate. —**pul·sa'tion,** *n.* —**pul'sa·to·ry,** *adj.*

pulse (puls), *n.* 1. the rhythmic beating of the arteries, caused by the contraction of the heart. 2. any regular vibration or beat. 3. the opinion or feelings of the public or of some group. 4. leguminous plants or their seeds, as peas, beans, etc.; *v.i.* pulsed, puls'ing, to beat or throb.

pul·sim·e·ter (pul·sim'ē·tĕr), *n.* an instrument to measure the force and rate of the pulse.

pul·som·e·ter (pul·som'ē·tĕr), *n.* 1. same as pulsimeter. 2. a kind of pump that raises water by the pulling power of a partial vacuum produced by condensing steam.

pul·ver·ize (pul'vĕ·rīz), *v.t. & v.i.* -ized, -iz·ing, to reduce or be reduced, as by crushing or grinding, into very small particles or powder. —**pul·ver·i·za'tion,** *n.*

pul·vil·lus (pul·vil'ŭs), *n., pl.* -li ('ī), the pad or cushion between the tarsal claws or tarsal segments of some insects. —**pul·vil'lar,** *adj.*

pul·vi·nate (pul'vi·nāt, -nit), *adj.* shaped like or resembling a cushion.

pu·ma (pū'mà), *n.* a cougar; mountain lion.

pum·ice (pum'is), *n.* a light, spongy, volcanic rock, used for smoothing and polishing: also **pumice stone.**

pum·mel (pum'l), *v.t.* -meled or -melled, -mel·ing or -mel·ling, to beat or hit with repeated blows with the fist.

pump (pump), *n.* 1. a machine for forcing a fluid into or out of a confined space by use of suction or pressure. 2. [Informal], the heart. 3. a light, low-cut shoe without ties or straps: *v.t.* 1. to move (fluids) with a pump. 2. to free from water as with a pump. 3. to force air into with a pump. 4. [Informal], to extract (information) from by persistent questioning. —**pump'er,** *n.*

pump·er·nick·el (pum'pĕr·nik·l), *n.* a coarse, dark bread made of unsifted rye.

pump·kin (pum'kin, pung'·), *n.* 1. a large, trailing, hairy vine with heart-shaped leaves and yellow flowers. 2. the large, orange, round, edible fruit of this vine, used in making pies. 3. in England, any one of various kinds of squash.

pun (pun), *n.* a play on words similar in sound but having different meanings: *v.i.* punned, pun'ning, to make puns.

punch (punch), *n.* 1. a tool for stamping or perforating. 2. a sweet drink made with carbonated beverages, fruit juices, etc., often mixed with liquor or wine. 3. a blow or thrust with the fist. 4. [P-], buffoon or clown; punchinello: *v.t.* 1. to perforate with a punch. 2. to strike with the fist. 3. to prod or poke sharply. 4. to herd (cattle) as by prodding.

punch card, a card used in data processing, with holes punched in it to indicate pieces of information that are to be processed.

punch-drunk ('drungk'), *adj.* physically unsteady and mentally dull from many blows to the head, as in boxing.

pun·cheon (pun'chŭn), *n.* a large cask for wine, beer, etc.

pun·chi·nel·lo (pun·chi·nel'ō), *n., pl.* -los, a buffoon; clown.

punch line, a final line that gives the point of a joke, anecdote, advertisement, etc.

punch press, a press using dies for forming, cutting, or stamping metal.

punc·tate (pungk'tāt), *adj.* dotted with small spots, as some plants and animals. —**punc·ta'tion,** *n.*

punc·til·i·o (pungk·til'i·ō), *n., pl.* -i·os, 1. a nice point in conduct or ceremony. 2. formal exactness.

punc·til·i·ous (-ŭs), *adj.* 1. very nice or precise in conduct or ceremony. 2. exact and precise. —**punc·til'i·ous·ly,** *adv.*

punc·tu·al (pungk'choo·wâl), *adj.* prompt; on time; not late. —**punc·tu·al'i·ty** (-wal'l·ti), *n.* —**punc'tu·al·ly,** *adv.*

punc·tu·ate (pungk'choo·wāt), *v.t.* -at·ed, -at·ing, 1. to divide or mark (printed matter) by punctuation marks. 2. to interrupt. 3. to emphasize. —**punc·tu·a'tion,** *n.*

punctuation marks, the standardized marks used in punctuation, as the comma, period, colon, etc.

punc·ture (pungk'chĕr), *n.* 1. a hole or wound made by a sharp point. 2. the act of piercing: *v.t. & v.i.* -tured, -tur·ing, to pierce or be pierced as with a sharp point.

pun·dit (pun'dit), *n.* 1. in India, a learned Brahman; one versed in Sanskrit and Hindu philosophy, law, and religion. 2. one who has, or professes to have, great learning.

pung (pung), *n.* in the northeastern U.S., a sleigh drawn by one horse.

pun·gent (pun'jĕnt), *adj.* 1. sharp or stinging to the taste or smell. 2. biting; keen; stimulating, as wit, language, etc. —**pun'gen·cy,** *n.* —**pun'gent·ly,** *adv.*

Pu·nic (pū'nik), *adj.* 1. of or pertaining to the people of Carthage, an ancient city in northern Africa. 2. characteristic of these people, considered by the Romans to be treacherous and perfidious.

pun·ish (pun'ish), *v.t.* 1. to cause loss or pain to, as a penalty for a crime or fault. 2. to inflict a penalty for (an offense). —**pun'ish·a·ble,** *adj.*

pun·ish·ment (-mĕnt), *n.* 1. the act of punishing. 2. a penalty, as pain or loss, inflicted for a crime or fault. 3. harsh or rough treatment.

pu·ni·tive (pū'ni·tiv), *adj.* pertaining to or inflicting punishment. —**pu'ni·tive·ly,** *adv.* —**pu'ni·tive·ness,** *n.*

punk (pungk), *n.* 1. decayed wood used as tinder. 2. a stick of a fungous substance that smolders when lighted, used to light fireworks, etc. 3. [Slang], a young, presumptuous person; especially, a young hoodlum: *adj.* [Slang], inferior.

pun·ster (pun'stĕr), *n.* a person who is skilled at, or fond of, making puns.

punt (punt), *n.* 1. a flat-bottomed boat with square ends, usually propelled by a long pole. 2. the kicking of a football before it falls to the ground: *v.t. & v.i.* 1. to propel (a boat) with a pole. 2. to kick (a football) in a punt.

pu·ny (pū'ni), *adj.* **-ni·er, -ni·est,** inferior in strength or size; weak; feeble; unimportant. —**pu'ni·ness,** *n.*

pup (pup), *n.* 1. a puppy; young dog. 2. any of the young of some other animals, as the seal and fox.

pu·pa (pū'pä), *n., pl.* **-pae** ('pē), **-pas,** an insect in the stage of growth between the larval and adult forms, when it is usually in a cocoon or cell. —**pu'pal,** *adj.*

pu·pil (pū'pl), *n.* 1. a person who studies under the supervision of a teacher or tutor; learner. 2. the contractile opening in the iris of the eye, through which rays of light pass to the retina.

pu·pil·age, pu·pil·lage (-ij), *n.* the state or period of being a pupil.

pup·pet (pup'it), *n.* 1. a doll. 2. a small figure of a person or animal, moved by strings or manipulated by hand, as in a show. 3. one who is under the influence or control of another.

pup·pet·eer (pup-i-tir'), *n.* a person who operates or designs puppets or puppet shows.

pup·py (pup'i), *n., pl.* **-pies,** 1. a whelp. 2. a young dog. 3. a conceited or silly young man.

pup tent, a small, portable tent.

pur·blind (pûr'blind), *adj.* 1. nearly blind. 2. slow to understand; dull.

pur·chase (pûr'chăs), *v.t.* **-chased, -chas·ing,** 1. to obtain by paying money or an equivalent; buy. 2. to obtain at the expense of some sacrifice, labor, etc. 3. to move or raise by the application of some mechanical power: *n.* 1. the act of buying. 2. the thing bought. 3. a secure grip applied to raise or move something mechanically or to keep it from slipping. —**pur'chas·a·ble,** *adj.* —**pur'chas·er,** *n.*

pure (pyoor), *adj.* 1. free from moral or physical defilement. 2. chaste. 3. free from any taint, pollution, etc. 4. unmixed or unadul-

terated. 5. simple; mere. 6. absolute; sheer. 7. blameless; sinless. 8. concerned with the abstract or theoretical. —**pure'ly,** *adv.* —**pure'ness,** *n.*

pu·rée (pyoo-rā'), *n.* 1. cooked vegetables, fruits, etc. mashed, whipped, or pressed through a sieve to produce a smooth texture. 2. a thick soup made from this: *v.t.* **-réed', -rée'ing,** to make a purée of.

pur·fle (pûr'fl), *v.t.* **-fled, -fling,** 1. to decorate with an ornamental border. 2. to ornament or trim with beads, lace, fur, etc.: *n.* an ornamental border: also **pur'fling.**

pur·ga·tion (pêr-gā'shŭn), *n.* the act of purging or purifying.

pur·ga·tive (pûr'gă·tiv), *adj.* serving to purge: *n.* a purging medicine; cathartic.

pur·ga·to·ri·al (pûr-gă-tôr'i-ăl), *adj.* 1. serving to make reparation for sins; expiatory. 2. of, pertaining to, or resembling purgatory.

pur·ga·to·ry (pûr'gă-tôr-i), *n., pl.* **-ries,** 1. [often P-], an intermediate state or place in the afterlife where, according to Roman Catholic and other Christian doctrine, the souls of the faithful departed suffer for a time in order to atone for their sins and thus gain entrance to heaven. 2. a place of exile or banishment. 3. a state of temporary misery, remorse, etc.

purge (pûrj), *v.t.* **purged, purg'ing,** 1. to cleanse or free from impurities, foreign matter, etc. 2. to rid of sin, guilt, or ceremonial defilement. 3. to rid (a nation, political party, etc.) of persons regarded as undesirable. 4. in *Law,* to clear from an accusation of guilt. 5. to empty (the bowels): *n.* 1. the act of purging. 2. that which purges, as a cathartic medicine. 3. the process of removing, killing, etc. persons regarded as undesirable by a nation, political party, etc.

pu·ri·fi·ca·tor (pyoor'i-fi-kāt-ēr), *n.* in ecclesiastical usage, a linen cloth used to clean the chalice and wipe the fingers and mouth of the celebrant after the Eucharist.

pu·ri·fy (pyoor'i-fi), *v.t.* **-fied, -fy·ing,** 1. to free from impurities; render pure. 2. to free from guilt or ceremonial uncleanness. 3. to free from impure or corrupting elements: *v.i.* to become purified. —**pu·ri·fi·ca'tion,** *n.* —**pu'ri·fi·er,** *n.*

Pu·rim (poor'im), *n.* a Jewish feast, the Feast of Lots, usually observed in March, to commemorate the deliverance of the Jews by Esther from the massacre planned by Haman.

pu·rine (pyoor'in), *n.* 1. a white, crystalline, organic compound regarded as the basic substance of the uric-acid group of compounds. 2. any of several basic substances having a purine-type molecule, as caffeine.

pur·ism (pyoor'izm), *n.* strict observance of or rigid insistence upon traditional rules, correct form, precise usage, etc., as in language, art, etc. —**pur'ist,** *n.* —**pu·ris'tic,** *adj.*

Pu·ri·tan (pyoor'i-tn), *n.* 1. any member of a group of Protestants in England and the American colonies who, in the 16th and 17th centuries, insisted on modifying the traditional and formal ceremonies of the Church of England and who advocated rigid adherence to the letter of the Scriptures in points of doctrine and practice. 2. [p-], a person regarded as extremely strict in moral and religious matters: *adj.* 1. of or pertaining to the Puritans or their doctrines or practices. 2. [p-], same as **puritanical**. —**Pu'ri·tan·ism, pu'ri·tan·ism,** *n.*

pu·ri·tan·i·cal (pyoor-i-tan'i-kl), *adj.* 1. [P-], of the Puritans or Puritanism. 2. excessively strict in moral and religious matters. —**pu·ri·tan'i·cal·ly,** *adv.*

pu·ri·ty (pyoor'i-ti), *n.* 1. the state or quality of being pure. 2. cleanness or clarity. 3. freedom from adulteration. 4. freedom from sin; innocence; chastity. 5. freedom from foreign words, slang, etc. in speech and writing.

purl (pûrl), *n.* the continuous murmuring sound of rippling water: *v.i.* to flow or ripple with a gentle murmur.

purl (pûrl), *n.* 1. an embroidered or puckered border. 2. metal thread used in embroidery. 3. the inversion of a stitch in knitting: *v.t. & v.i.* 1. to edge with lace or embroidery. 2. to invert (a stitch or stitches) in knitting.

pur·lieu (pûr'lōō, pûrl'ū), *n.* 1. a place one visits frequently or regularly; haunt. 2. *pl.* limits; environs. 3. an outlying area, as of a city.

pur·lin, pur·line (pûr'lin), *n.* a piece of timber laid horizontally to support the rafters of a roof.

pur·loin (pêr-loin', pûr'loin), *v.t. & v.i.* to steal; filch.

pur·ple (pûr'pl), *adj.* 1. of the color purple. 2. regal; imperial. 3. elaborate or ornate. 4. marked by profanity: *n.* 1. a deep color that is a blend of blue and red. 2. cloth or clothing of this color, indicative of royal or high rank: *v.t. & v.i.* **-pled, -pling,** to make or become purple.

pur·port (pûr'pôrt), *n.* 1. meaning; sense; signification. 2. design; intention: *v.t.* (pêr-pôrt'), 1. to convey (some particular impression) outwardly. 2. to mean or signify.

pur·pose (pûr'pôs), *n.* 1. design; end or aim desired. 2. object kept in view. 3. determination: *v.t. & v.i.* **-posed, -pos·ing,** to intend, resolve, or design.

pur·pose·ful (-fûl), *adj.* 1. expressly intended. 2. having meaning or purpose.

pur·pose·less (-lis), *adj.* without any purpose; aimless; pointless.

pur·pose·ly (-li), *adv.* with a specific purpose; intentionally.

pur·pu·ra (pûr'pyoo-rá), *n.* a disease characterized by livid spots on the skin or mucous membranes, caused by a flow of blood into the skin.

purr (pûr), *n.* 1. the low, murmuring sound made by a cat when it seems pleased. 2. any sound similar to this: *v.t. & v.i.* to utter or express such a sound.

purse (pûrs), *n.* 1. a small bag or receptacle for carrying money. 2. a sum of money collected as a present for someone. 3. financial resources; money. 4. a woman's handbag: *v.t.* pursed, purs·ing, to contract (the lips or brow) into folds or wrinkles; pucker.

purs·er (pûr'sêr), *n.* an officer having charge of

the provisions, clothing, money, etc. on board a ship.

purs·lane (pûrs'lin, 'lān), *n.* any one of a number of trailing weeds, with pink stems, yellowish flowers, and succulent fleshy leaves that are sometimes used as a potherb and in salads.

pur·su·ance (pêr-sōō'áns, -sū'-), *n.* the carrying out or prosecution of something, as a plan; pursuit.

pur·su·ant ('ánt), *adj.* pursuing: now followed by *to* and meaning "following upon."

pur·sue (pêr-sōō', -sū'), *v.t.* **-sued, -su'ing,** 1. to follow for some purpose, as to capture; chase. 2. to proceed along or follow the course of. 3. to seek after; strive for. 4. to annoy; harass. —**pur·su'er,** *n.*

pur·suit (-sōōt', -sūt'), *n.* 1. the act of pursuing; chase. 2. an occupation, hobby, interest, etc. that one follows.

pur·sui·vant (pûr'si·vánt, 'swi-), *n.* an attendant; follower.

pur·sy (pûr'si), *adj.* **-si·er, -si·est,** 1. shortwinded, especially from being fat. 2. fat; thick. —**pur'si·ness,** *n.*

pu·ru·lent (pyoor'ū-lênt), *adj.* of, pertaining to, or producing pus. —**pu'ru·lence, pu'ru·len·cy,** *n.*

pur·vey (pêr-vā'), *v.t.* to furnish or equip, as with provisions. —**pur·vey'or,** *n.*

pur·vey·ance ('áns), *n.* 1. the act of procuring provisions. 2. provisions provided.

pur·view (pûr'vū), *n.* 1. the extent of sight or comprehension. 2. the body and scope of a statute. 3. the range of authority, operation, or concern.

pus (pus), *n.* the white or yellowish-white liquid matter secreted in sores, infections, etc., containing bacteria, serum, white corpuscles, etc.

push (poosh), *v.t.* 1. to press against with force in order to move. 2. to urge forward; impel. 3. to press hard for the sale, use, etc. of: *v.i.* to put forth great effort: *n.* 1. the act of pushing. 2. a great effort. 3. exigency. 4. persistent endeavor. 5. [Informal], drive; aggressiveness.

push-ball ('bôl), *n.* 1. a game played by two teams of eleven each, in which a large ball about six feet in diameter is to be pushed across the opponents' goal. 2. this ball.

push button, a small knob which, on being pushed, opens or closes an electric circuit and so operates doors, motors, lights, etc. —**push'-but·ton** ('but-n), *adj.*

push-cart ('kärt), *n.* a cart pushed by hand.

push·er ('êr), *n.* 1. a person or thing that pushes. 2. a very energetic person. 3. an airplane having its propellers mounted behind the engines. 4. [Slang], a person who sells narcotics illegally.

push·ing ('ing), *adj.* 1. energetic; enterprising. 2. forward; aggressive.

push·o·ver ('ō-vêr), *n.* [Slang], 1. anything easy to accomplish. 2. a person, group, etc. readily induced, overawed, defeated, etc.

push-up, push·up ('up), *n.* an exercise in which a person prone on the ground alternately raises himself by straightening his arms and lowers himself by bending his arms.

push·y (ʻĭ), *adj.* push'i·er, push'i·est, [Informal], obnoxiously overbearing and persistent. — push'i·ness, *n.*

pu·sil·lan·i·mous (pyoo-sĭ-lan'ĭ-mŭs), *adj.* cowardly; timid or irresolute. —pu·sil·la·nim'i·ty (-ă-nĭm'ĭ-tĭ), *n.* —pu·sil·lan'i·mous·ly, *adv.*

puss (poos), *n.* [Informal], a cat.

pus·sy (pus'ĭ), *adj.* -si·er, -si·est, like or containing pus.

puss·y (poos'ĭ), *n., pl.* puss'ies, same as puss: also puss'y·cat.

puss·y·foot (poos'ĭ-foot), *v.i.* [Informal], 1. to sneak or creep about noiselessly, as a cat does. 2. to avoid taking a position or committing oneself. —puss'y·foot·er, *n.*

pussy willow, any one of several willows having silky, silvery catkins.

pus·tu·lar (pus'chŭ-lẽr), *adj.* 1. covered with pustulelike excrescences. 2. like or resembling pustules.

pus·tule (ʻchōōl), *n.* 1. a small elevation of the skin holding pus. 2. any similar elevation, as a pimple or blister.

put (poot), *v.t.* put, put'ting, 1. to place in or bring into any place or condition. 2. to drive into action; thrust. 3. to impose. 4. to apply. 5. to lay or deposit. 6. to state or express. 7. to attribute. 8. to shoot out or send forth. 9. to bet (money) *on*: *v.i.* to go (*out, in,* etc.): *adj.* [Informal], fixed: *n.* 1. a cast or heave; especially the act of putting the shot. 2. a contract by which one party secures from another the right to sell the other a certain amount of securities at a set price within a stipulated period of time.

pu·ta·men (pū-tā'mĕn), *n.* the hard stone of certain fruits, as the peach, cherry, etc.

pu·ta·tive (pūt'ă-tiv), *adj.* reputed; supposed; thought to be such.

put-down (poot'doun), *n.* [Slang], a slighting remark or curt dismissal.

put·log (poot'lôg), *n.* a short piece of timber used in the floor of a scaffolding.

put-on (poot'än), *n.* the act of misleading someone by trickery; hoax.

pu·tre·fy (pū'trĕ-fī), *v.t. & v.i.* -fied, -fy·ing, to make or become rotten or decayed by the decomposition of organic matter, resulting in the production of foul-smelling matter; decompose. —pu·tre·fac'tive, *adj.* —pu·tre·fac'tion, *n.*

pu·tres·cent (pū-tres'nt), *adj.* 1. of or pertaining to putrefaction. 2. becoming rotten; putrefying. —pu·tres'cence, *n.*

pu·tres·ci·ble (ʻĭ-bl), *adj.* liable to putrefy; tending to become putrid.

pu·trid (pū'trĭd), *adj.* 1. decomposed and foul-smelling. 2. pertaining to, arising from, or displaying decay. 3. morally rotten; corrupt. 4. [Informal], extremely disagreeable; vile. —pu·trid'i·ty, pu'trid·ness, *n.*

putt (put), *n.* in *Golf,* a light stroke made on a putting green in an effort to sink the ball in the hole: *v.t. & v.i.* to hit (the ball) on the green with such a stroke.

put·tee (pu·tē', put'ĭ), *n.* 1. a strip of cloth wound spirally around the leg from ankle to knee for protection. 2. a leather legging going from the knee to the ankle.

putt·er (put'ẽr), *n.* in *Golf,* 1. a club used for putting. 2. one who putts.

put·ter (put'ẽr), *v.i.* to employ oneself in unnecessary activity (often with *along, around, over,* etc.): *v.t.* to dawdle (*away*).

putt·ing green (put'ing), the smooth plot of turf surrounding a golf hole.

put·ty (put'ĭ), *n.* 1. an oxide of tin, or of lead and tin, used for polishing: in full, putty powder. 2. a compound of chalk and linseed oil used in glazing, filling cracks, etc.: *v.t.* to cement or plug up with putty.

put-up (poot'up), *adj.* [Informal], planned or arranged before.

puz·zle (puz'l), *n.* 1. something that tries the ingenuity. 2. something that perplexes: *v.t.* -zled, -zling, to perplex; confuse: *v.i.* 1. to be perplexed. 2. to work mentally over a puzzle.

py·e·mi·a (pī-ē'mĭ-ȧ), *n.* blood poisoning.

pyg·mae·an, pyg·me·an (pĭg-mē'ȧn), *adj.* same as pygmy.

Pyg·my (pĭg'mĭ), *n., pl.* -mies, 1. one of the fabled dwarfish peoples of Asia and Africa mentioned by ancient authors. 2. any one of a dark-skinned, dwarfish people of Africa and southeastern Asia. 3. [p-], any abnormally small person or thing. 4. [p-], an insignificant person or thing: *adj.* 1. of or pertaining to Pygmies. 2. [p-], dwarfish or insignificant.

py·ja·mas (pĭ-jam'ăz), *n.pl.* [British], same as pajamas.

py·lon (pī'lon), *n.* 1. a narrow tower, as that erected on a field of an airport to mark a course for aircraft. 2. a building of a truncated pyramidal form, at the entrance of Egyptian temples. 3. an entrance having a gate.

py·lo·rus (pī-lôr'ŭs), *n., pl.* -ri (ʻī), the opening of the stomach leading to the small intestine. —py·lor'ic, *adj.*

py·o·der·ma (pī-ō-dûr'mȧ), *n.* any suppurative skin disease.

py·o·gen·e·sis (-jen'ĕ-sis), *n.* the formation of pus; suppuration. —py·o·gen'ic, *adj.*

py·oid (pī'oid), *adj.* of the nature of pus.

py·or·rhe·a, py·or·rhoe·a (pī-ō-rē'ȧ), *n.* 1. a discharge of pus. 2. pyorrhea alveolaris.

pyorrhea al·ve·o·la·ris (al-vē-ō-ler'is), a loosening of the teeth accompanied by inflammation of the gums, causing a flow of pus.

pyr·a·can·tha (pir-ă-kan'thȧ), *n.* a plant with flame-colored fruit.

pyr·a·mid (pir'ȧ-mid), *n.* 1. a solid body standing on a polygonal base, having four triangular sides terminating in a point at the apex. 2. a sepulchral monument of such a shape with a square base, as in Egypt. 3. a crystal of three or more planes having a common point of intersection: *v.t. & v.i.* 1. to use the profits on stocks to buy or sell additional amounts on margin. 2. to form as a pyramid. —py·ram·i·dal (pi-ram'ĭ-dl), *adj.*

pyre (pīr), *n.* a pile on which a dead body is burned in a funeral rite.

py·rene (pī'rĕn), *n.* 1. a colorless hydrocarbon occurring in coal tar. 2. the stone of a drupe fruit.

ō in drag*o*n, ōō in cr*u*de, oo in w*oo*l, u in c*u*p, ū in c*u*re, û in t*u*rn, ŭ in f*o*cus, oi in b*oy*, ou in h*ou*se, th in *th*in, *th* in shea*th*e, g in *g*et, j in *j*oy, y in *y*et.

py·ret·ic (pī-ret'ik), *adj.* febrile; affected with fever.

Py·rex (pī'reks), *n.* a kind of glass that withstands heat: a trademark.

py·rex·i·a (pī-rek'si-à), *n.* same as fever. —**py·rex'i·al**, *adj.*

pyr·i·dine (pir'ĭ-dēn), *n.* a colorless liquid compound found in coal tar and bone oil, used for producing drugs, as a solvent, etc.

pyr·i·form (pir'ĭ-fôrm), *adj.* pear-shaped.

py·rite (pī'rīt), *n., pl.* **py·ri·tes** (pī-rīt'iz, pī'rīts), 1. a shiny, yellow disulfide of iron: also **iron pyrites**. 2. *pl.* any of several sulfides, as of iron, copper, or tin.

py·ro-, a combining form meaning *fire*.

py·ro·ma·ni·a (pī-rō-mā'ni-à), *n.* a compulsion to destroy by fire. —**py·ro·ma'ni·ac** ('ni-ak), *n. & adj.*

py·rom·e·ter (pī-rom'ĕ-tēr), *n.* an instrument for measuring degrees of heat higher than those recorded by a mercurial thermometer.

py·ro·pho·bi·a (pī-rō-fō'bi-à), *n.* a morbid dread of fire.

py·ro·sis (pī-rō'sis), *n.* a condition like heartburn, accompanied by the belching of an acrid fluid.

py·ro·tech·nic (pī-rō-tek'nik), *adj.* 1. of or pertaining to fireworks or the art of making them. 2. overpowering; intense.

py·ro·tech·nics ('niks), *n.pl.* 1. fireworks or the art of making them. 2. an overpowering exhibition, as of cleverness. —**py·ro·tech'nist**, *n.*

py·rox·ene (pī-rok'sin), *n.* a mineral composed of calcium and magnesium, occurring in crystals: a chief constituent of igneous rocks.

py·rox·y·lin, py·rox·y·line (pī-rok'sĭ-lin), *n.* a

weakened form of nitrocellulose used to make paints, celluloid, etc.

pyr·rhic (pir'ik), *n.* 1. a metrical foot of two short or unaccented syllables. 2. an ancient Greek military dance: *adj.* of or made up of pyrrhics.

Pyr·rhic victory (pir'ik), a victory gained at enormous cost or loss: after King Pyrrhus of Epirus, an ancient Greek kingdom.

Py·thag·o·re·an (pi-thag-ō-rē'ân), *n.* a follower of Pythagoras, a Greek philosopher of the 6th century B.C., who proposed the doctrine of the transmigration of the soul: *adj.* of or relating to Pythagoras or his philosophy.

Pyth·i·an (pith'i-ân), *adj.* 1. of or pertaining to Apollo in relation to Delphi and the oracle there. 2. of or pertaining to the great national games of ancient Greece celebrated every four years at Delphi in honor of Apollo.

Py·thon (pī'thon), *n.* 1. in *Greek Mythology*, a large serpent slain by Apollo. 2. [**p-**], a large, nonvenomous snake of Africa and southeastern Asia that kills by squeezing its victim to death.

py·tho·ness (pī'thō-nis), *n.* 1. the priestess of Apollo, who gave oracular answers at the temple of Delphi. 2. a female prophet.

py·thon·ic (pī-thon'ik), *adj.* of or pertaining to prophecy; oracular.

py·u·ri·a (pī-yoor'i-à), *n.* a discharging of pus with the urine.

pyx (piks), *n.* 1. in the Roman Catholic Church service, a box or receptacle in which the consecrated wafer is placed. 2. a box in which selected coins are placed at a mint, to be tested prior to their issue as currency.

Q

Q, q (kū), *n., pl.* **Q's, q's,** 1. the seventeenth letter of the English alphabet. 2. any of the sounds of this letter, as in *quack* or *lacquer. Q* is followed by *u* unless the word in which it is used is a borrowing from Arabic. 3. a type or impression of *Q* or *q.*

Q (kū), *adj.* shaped like *Q: n.* an object shaped like *Q.*

qua (kwā, kwä), *adv.* in the character or capacity of.

quack (kwak), *n.* 1. the cry of a duck. 2. a pretender to medical skill. 3. a charlatan: *v.i.* 1. to cry like a duck. 2. to act or practice like a quack: *adj.* pertaining to quacks or fraudulent medical practice. —**quack'er·y,** *n.*

quack·ish ('ish), *adj.* 1. like or acting like a quack. 2. boastful. —**quack'ish·ly,** *adv.*

quad (kwäd), *n.* 1. the quadrangle of a college. 2. a quadruplet. 3. a piece of type metal lower than the type, used to fill spaces in a line, page, etc.; quadrat: *v.t.* **quad'ded, quad'ding,** to fill out (a line) with quads on a printed page.

quad·ra·ge·nar·i·an (kwäd-rä-ji-ner'i-ån), *n.* one who is forty years old, or between forty and fifty: *adj.* of or denoting a quadragenarian.

Quad·ra·ges·i·ma (-jes'i-mä), *n.* 1. the first Sunday in Lent: also **Quadragesima Sunday.** 2. [Obsolete], the forty days of Lent.

quad·ra·ges·i·mal (-mäl), *adj.* 1. consisting of forty days, as Lent. 2. [Q-], pertaining to or used during Lent.

quad·ran·gle (kwäd'rang-gl), *n.* 1. an open area surrounded on its four sides by buildings. 2. a plane figure with four angles and four sides. —**quad·ran'gu·lar** (gyū-lėr), *adj.*

quad·rant (kwäd'ränt), *n.* 1. the fourth part of a circle; an arc of 90˚. 2. a quarter section of a circle. 3. an instrument for measuring elevations, used in surveying and astronomy. —**quad·ran'tal** (-ran'tl), *adj.*

quad·ra·phon·ic (kwäd-rä-fon'ik), *adj.* of or denoting a system of sound reproduction using four channels and four speakers.

quad·rat ('rät), *n.* 1. in *Ecology,* a specimen plot, usually a square meter, in which plant and animal life is observed and studied. 2. in *Printing,* same as **quad.**

quad·rate ('rät), *n.* a square or rectangle, or something shaped like one of these: *adj.* having four equal or nearly equal angles and four equal or nearly equal sides: *v.i.* ('rāt), **-rat·ed, -rat·ing,** to square; agree (*with*): *v.t.* to make square; make correspond.

quad·rat·ic (kwäd-rat'ik), *adj.* in *Algebra,* involving the square but no higher power of a quantity. —**quad·rat'i·cal·ly,** *adv.*

quadratic equation, in *Algebra,* an equation in which the highest power of the unknown quantity is a square.

quad·ra·ture (kwäd'rä-chėr), *n.* 1. the act of squaring. 2. the process of determining a square equal in area to a given surface. 3. the position of a heavenly body when 90˚ distant from another: said especially of the position of the moon from the sun as seen from the earth.

quad·ren·ni·al (kwäd-ren'i-ål), *adj.* 1. comprising four years. 2. occurring every four years: *n.* a quadrennial occurrence, celebration, etc. —**quad·ren'ni·al·ly,** *adv.*

quad·ren·ni·um ('i-ům), *n., pl.* **-ni·ums, -ni·a** ('i-ä), a period of four years.

quadri-, a combining form meaning *four.*

quad·ri·ga (kwäd-rī'gä), *n., pl.* **-gae** ('jē), a Roman chariot drawn by four horses abreast.

quad·ri·lat·er·al (kwäd-rī-lat'ėr-ål), *n.* a plane figure bounded by four straight sides: *adj.* four-sided. —**quad·ri·lat'er·al·ly,** *adv.*

qua·drille (kwä-dril'), *n.* a square dance performed by four couples.

quad·ril·lion (kwäd-ril'yůn), *n.* 1. in the U.S. and France, the number indicated by one followed by 15 zeros. 2. in Great Britain and Germany, the number indicated by one followed by 24 zeros. —**quad·ril'lionth,** *adj. & n.*

quad·ri·no·mi·al (-rī-nō'mi-ål), *n.* an algebraic expression of four terms.

quad·ri·ple·gi·a (-rī-plē'ji-ä), *n.* total paralysis from the neck down. —**quad·ri·ple'gic** (-rī-plē'jik, -rī-plej'ik), *adj. & n.*

quad·ri·syl·la·ble (kwäd'rī-sil-ä-bl), *n.* a word of four syllables. —**quad·ri·syl·lab'ic** (-si-lab'ik), *adj.*

quad·ri·va·lent (kwäd-rī-vä'lént, kwä-driv'ä-), *adj.* 1. having four valences. 2. same as **tetravalent** (*adj.* 1).

quad·riv·i·al (kwäd-riv'i-ål), *adj.* 1. having four roads meeting in a point. 2. of or pertaining to the quadrivium.

quad·riv·i·um (-ům), *n.* the four higher liberal arts of medieval times; namely, arithmetic, geometry, astronomy, and music.

quad·roon (kwä-drōōn'), *n.* the child of a mulatto and a white; a white person of one-fourth Negro blood.

quad·ru·ma·nous (kwä-drōō'mä-nůs), *adj.* 1. with all four feet adapted for use as hands. 2. of or denoting a group of primates with feet like this, including the monkey, baboon, etc. —**quad'ru·mane** ('roo-mān), *n.*

quad·ru·ped (kwäd'roo-ped), *n.* a four-footed animal: *adj.* four-footed. —**quad·ru·pe·dal** (kwä-drōō'pi-dl, kwäd-rů-ped'l), *adj.*

quad·ru·ple (kwä-drōō'pl), *adj.* 1. made up of four. 2. fourfold: *n.* a sum or quantity four times as great: *v.t. & v.i.* **-pled, -pling,** to multiply or increase four times.

quad·ru·plet (kwä-drup'lit, -drōō'plit), *n.* 1. any

of four offspring born at the same time. 2. a collection of four of the same kind.

quaes·tor (kwes′tĕr), *n.* in ancient Rome, a public treasurer.

quaff (kwäf, kwaf), *v.t. & v.i.* to drink or swallow in large quantities or luxuriously: *n.* the act of quaffing.

quag·ga (kwag′ä), *n., pl.* -ga, -gas, a South African striped wild ass resembling the ass and zebra: now extinct.

quag·mire (kwag′mir), *n.* wet, boggy ground, yielding under the feet.

qua·hog, qua·haug (kwô′hŏg, kō′hŏg), *n.* a type of edible clam with a hard shell, found on the eastern coast of North America.

quail (kwāl), *v.i.* to lose heart; cower: *n., pl.* quails, quail, 1. a gallinaceous game bird similar to the partridge. 2. same as bob-white.

quaint (kwānt), *adj.* 1. singular; odd. 2. not expressed or shown in the usual way; pleasingly odd. 3. playfully imaginative. —**quaint′ly**, *adv.* —**quaint′ness**, *n.*

quake (kwāk), *v.i.* **quaked, quak′ing**, 1. to tremble or shake. 2. to shudder: *n.* 1. a tremble or shudder. 2. an earthquake.

Quak·er (kwāk′ĕr), *n.* [Informal], one of a religious sect, the Society of Friends. —**Quak′-er·ism**, *n.*

Quaker gun, a dummy cannon, as of wood.

quak·y (kwā′ki), *adj.* **quak′i·er, quak′i·est**, shaky. —**quak′i·ness**, *n.*

qual·i·fi·ca·tion (kwäl·i·fi·kā′shŭn), *n.* 1. any quality, endowment, experience, etc. which fits a person for an office or occupation. 2. legal power or ability. 3. a limitation; restriction. 4. the act of qualifying.

qual·i·fied (kwäl′i·fid), *adj.* 1. fit; competent. 2. restricted; limited.

qual·i·fi·er (-fi·ĕr), *n.* one who or that which qualifies.

qual·i·fy (-fi), *v.t.* **-fied, -fy·ing**, 1. to render fit or capable for an office, occupation, etc. 2. to render legally capable. 3. to moderate. 4. to limit. 5. in *Grammar*, to limit (a word) in meaning: *v.i.* to be or become qualified.

qual·i·ta·tive (-tāt·iv), *adj.* of or pertaining to quality or qualities. —**qual′i·ta·tive·ly**, *adv.*

qualitative analysis, the chemical process of determining the elements or ingredients in any mixture or compound.

qual·i·ty (kwäl′i·ti), *n., pl.* -ties, 1. a special power or property; attribute. 2. degree of superiority. 3. greatness. 4. [Archaic], superior social status.

qualm (kwäm), *n.* 1. a sudden fit of sickness, nausea, etc. 2. a scruple. 3. an uneasy emotional reaction.

quam·ash (kwäm′ash, kwä-mash′), *n.* an edible bulb of a plant related to the lily.

quan·da·ry (kwän′dri), *n., pl.* -ries, a state of perplexity.

quan·dong, quan·dang (kwän′dong), *n.* a small Australian tree having fruit with sweet, edible kernels.

quan·ti·fy (kwän′ti·fi), *v.t.* **-fied, -fy·ing**, to determine or express the quantity of; indicate the extent of.

quan·ti·ta·tive (kwän′ti·tāt·iv), *adj.* of or pertaining to quantity.

quantitative analysis, a determination of the quantity of ingredients in any substance or compound.

quan·ti·ty (kwän′ti·ti), *n., pl.* -ties, 1. that property of anything that may be increased or diminished. 2. any indeterminate bulk, weight, or number. 3. *also pl.* a large portion, sum, or mass. 4. anything that can be increased, divided, or measured. 5. the symbol or number expressing that increase, measurement, etc. 6. in *Logic*, a general conception. 7. in *Phonetics*, the measure of time in pronouncing a syllable, vowel, etc.

quan·tum (kwän′tŭm), *n., pl.* -ta (′tä), 1. a definite amount; portion; share. 2. the elemental unit of energy.

quantum theory, the theory that energy is intermittently radiated in quanta.

quar·an·tine (kwôr′ăn·tēn), *n.* 1. the time (originally 40 days) during which a vessel is suspected of carrying infectious disease is kept isolated from contact with shore. 2. enforced isolation of a person, animal, plant, etc. having or suspected of having a contagious disease. 3. a place where this is done: *v.t.* -tined, -tin·ing, to place under quarantine.

quark (kwôrk), *n.* one of three hypothetical particles thought to compose matter.

quar·rel (kwôr′ĕl), *n.* 1. an angry dispute; altercation. 2. a ground for dispute: *v.i.* -reled or -relled, -rel·ing or -rel·ling, 1. to dispute violently. 2. to express displeasure. 3. to have a breach in friendship. —**quar′rel·er, quar′rel·ler, n.** —**quar′rel·some (-sŏm), adj.**

quar·ri·er (kwôr′i·ĕr), *n.* one who works in a stone quarry.

quar·ry (kwôr′i), *n., pl.* -ries, 1. a place where stone is excavated for building purposes. 2. game pursued by hawks or dogs. 3. anything being pursued: *v.t.* -ried, -ry·ing, to excavate from a quarry.

quart (kwôrt), *n.* 1. a dry measure, equal to 1/8 peck. 2. a liquid measure, equal to 1/4 gallon.

quar·tan (kwôr′tn), *adj.* occurring every fourth day: said of a fever: *n.* a malarial fever with attacks every fourth day.

quar·ter (kwôr′tĕr), *n.* 1. a fourth part. 2. a fourth part of an hour, year, etc. 3. a term, as in school, of three months. 4. a limb of a slaughtered meat animal. 5. in the U.S., a coin equal to 25 cents. 6. a phase of the moon, one fourth of its revolution of the earth. 7. a part of the earth. 8. a particular region or district of a city. 9. *pl.* lodgings. 10. a specific person, group, etc. that provides something. 11. mercy. 12. the after part of a ship's side. 13. one of the four points of the compass. 14. in *Heraldry*, one of the four divisions of a shield. 15. in the *Military*, life granted to a captive or enemy: *v.t.* 1. to divide into four equal parts. 2. to furnish (soldiers, etc.) with lodgings; station. 3. in *Heraldry*, to bear (a coat of arms) on a division of a shield: *v.i.* 1. to have lodgings (*with* or *at*). 2. to range to and fro:

said of dogs hunting: *adj.* equal to a quarter

quar·ter·back (-bak), *n.* in *Football*, the back who directs the offensive plays and calls the signals.

quarter day, the day regarded as beginning each quarter of the year and on which, it is presumed, rents fall due.

quar·ter·deck, **quar·ter·deck** (-dek), *n.* the part of the upper deck near the rear of a ship, usually for officers.

quar·ter·ing (-ing), *n.* 1. the act of dividing into quarters. 2. the assigning of quarters, as to soldiers. 3. in *Heraldry*, the division of an escutcheon into four compartments.

quar·ter·ly (-li), *adj.* 1. consisting of or containing a quarter. 2. appearing consistently four times each year: *adv.* once each quarter of the year: *n., pl.* -lies, a publication issued every quarter.

quar·ter·mas·ter (-mas-tēr), *n.* 1. an officer whose duty it is to assign quarters and provide food, clothing, equipment, etc. for troops. 2. in the *Navy*, a petty officer or mate who attends to the navigation, signals, etc. of a ship.

quar·tern (kwôr'tērn), *n.* [British], one fourth of a pint, peck, bushel, etc.

quarter note, a note held one fourth as long as a whole note.

quar·ter·saw (-sô), *v.t.* -sawed, -sawed or -sawn, -saw·ing, to saw (a log) into quarters and then into boards, so that the grain of the wood is shown to advantage.

quar·tet, **quar·tette** (kwôr-tet'), *n.* 1. anything in fours. 2. a musical composition for four voices or instruments. 3. the four persons who perform such a composition.

quar·to (kwôr'tō), *n., pl.* -tos, 1. a size of paper made by folding a sheet into four leaves. 2. a book about nine by twelve inches comprised of such leaves: *adj.* having four leaves to the sheet.

quartz (kwôrts), *n.* a mineral compound of silica occurring in transparent crystals.

quartz·ite (kwôrt'sīt), *n.* a firm sandstone.

qua·sar (kwā'sär, 'sēr), *n.* any of various apparently distant objects like stars that send out a great deal of light and radio waves.

quash (kwäsh), *v.t.* 1. to crush; subdue (resistance) completely. 2. in *Law*, to render void; annul (an indictment).

qua·si (kwä'sī, 'zi; kwä'sī), *adv.* as if; to a certain degree; seemingly. *adj.* having a resemblance to. Also used as a prefix with a hyphen.

quas·si·a (kwäsh'i-ä), *n.* the wood of a tropical American tree: its bitter extract was formerly used as a drug.

qua·ter·na·ry (kwät'ēr-ner-i, kwä-tūr'nēr-i), *adj.* consisting of four; in sets of four: *n., pl.* -ries, 1. [Q-], the geological period from the Tertiary to the present time. 2. a group of four.

qua·ter·ni·on (kwä-tūr'ni-ōn), *n.* a set of four.

quat·rain (kwä'trān), *n.* a stanza of four lines.

quat·re·foil (kat'ēr-foil), *n.* 1. a four-petal flower. 2. in *Architecture*, any ornamentation or design in four arcs coming together.

qua·ver (kwā'vēr), *v.i.* 1. to shake or tremble;

vibrate. 2. to sing or play with trills: *n.* 1. a vibration of the voice or a tone. 2. [Chiefly British], a musical eighth note; one half of a crotchet.

quay (kē), *n.* a wharf for loading or unloading vessels, usually made of concrete or stone.

quea·sy (kwē'zi), *adj.* -si·er, -si·est, 1. affected with or causing nausea. 2. squeamish.

que·bra·cho (kā-brä'chō), *n., pl.* -chos, a tropical South American tree having hard wood, whose bark possesses medicinal qualities.

queen (kwēn), *n.* 1. a female sovereign. 2. the consort of a king. 3. a fertile female bee, ant, etc. of a swarm or colony. 4. a playing card with the figure of a queen. 5. the strongest piece in chess. 6. the best or chief of its kind. 7. a woman famous for beauty, intelligence, etc.: *v.i.* to play the queen: *v.t.* in *Chess*, to make a queen of (a pawn at the opposite end of the board).

queen consort, the wife of a reigning king.

queen dowager, the widow of a king.

queen·ly (kwēn'li), *adj.* -li·er, -li·est, of, like, or befitting a queen. **—queen'li·ness,** *n.*

queen post, one of two vertical timbers in a roof rising from a horizontal beam.

queen regnant, a queen in her own right.

queer (kwir), *adj.* 1. odd; singular; strange. 2. unhealthy. 3. [Informal], unconventional: *v.t.* [Slang], to spoil (a chance or opportunity); jeopardize or injure (some enterprise): *n.* [Slang], 1. counterfeit money. 2. an unconventional person. 3. a male homosexual. **—queer'ly,** *adv.*

quell (kwel), *v.t.* 1. to crush or subdue; put an end to. 2. to calm; allay.

quench (kwench), *v.t.* 1. to put out or extinguish. 2. to check. 3. to allay; slake. 4. to reduce heat in (steel, etc.) by placing suddenly in water. **—quench'less,** *adj.*

que·nelle (kĕ-nel'), *n.* a dumpling of finely chopped meat or fish, cooked in boiling water.

quer·cine (kwūr'sin), *adj.* of or pertaining to oaks.

que·rist (kwir'ist), *n.* one who asks questions.

quer·u·lous (kwer'û-lûs), *adj.* 1. complaining. 2. discontented. **—quer'u·lous·ly,** *adv.*

que·ry (kwir'i), *n., pl.* -ries, 1. a question; inquiry to be resolved. 2. a question mark (?): *v.t.* -ried, -ry·ing, 1. to examine by questions. 2. to doubt. 3. to mark with a query: *v.i.* to ask questions.

quest (kwest), *n.* 1. a search; inquiry. 2. a traveling for excitement: *v.t.* to search or seek for.

ques·tion (kwes'chûn), *n.* 1. an inquiry; act of asking. 2. an interrogation; query. 3. doubt. 4. a subject of discussion. 5. a complex or troublesome affair. 6. the subject of legislative debate: *v.t.* 1. to ask or interrogate. 2. to treat as doubtful. 3. to debate or contest: *v.i.* to ask questions. **—ques'tion·er,** *n.*

ques·tion·a·ble (-ä-bl), *adj.* 1. that may be questioned; doubtful. 2. of suspicious moral quality. 3. vague.

question mark, a mark of punctuation (?) placed after a question.

ques·tion·naire (kwes-chû-ner'), *n.* a series of questions submitted to a number of people in order to obtain information on a given subject or subjects.

ques·tor (kwes'tẽr), *n.* same as quaestor.

quet·zal (ket-säl'), *n.* a large, crested bird of Central America with brilliant plumage and very long tail feathers.

queue (kū), *n.* 1. a plait of hair hanging from the back of the head. 2. [Chiefly British], a line of persons, vehicles, etc. waiting as to be served. 3. stored computer data or programs waiting to be processed: *v.i.* **queued, queuing,** [Chiefly British], to form into a line (often with *up*).

quib·ble (kwib'l), *n.* a petty evasion or cavil: *v.i.* **-bled, -bling,** to evade the truth by caviling.

quiche (kēsh), *n.* a custard baked in a pastry shell with various ingredients, as bacon, cheese, or spinach.

quick (kwik), *adj.* 1. rapid; hasty. 2. active; nimble. 3. ready. 4. sharp in discernment. 5. excitable: *adv.* quickly; swiftly: *n.* 1. the living, especially in *the quick and the dead.* 2. the sensitive flesh under a nail. 3. the most sensitive emotions.—**quick'ly,** *adv.* —**quick'ness,** *n.*

quick bread, a bread that can be baked as soon as the batter is mixed due to a leavening of baking soda, baking powder, etc.

quick·en (kwik'ẽn), *v.i.* 1. to become lively. 2. to show signs of life in the womb. 3. to become faster: *v.t.* 1. to increase the speed of. 2. to resuscitate. 3. to stimulate.

quick-freeze (kwik'frēz'), *v.t.* **-froze', -froz'en, -freez'ing,** to subject (food) to sudden freezing so that it can be stored at low temperatures for long periods.

quick·ie (kwik'i), *n.* [Slang], something produced or done rapidly or inexpensively.

quick·lime (-līm), *n.* unslaked lime.

quick·sand ('sand), *n.* 1. a moist, sandy deposit readily yielding to pressure and engulfing an object. 2. anything unreliable or treacherous.

quick·sil·ver (kwik'sil-vẽr), *n.* same as mercury: *v.t.* to overlay with mercury.

quick·step ('step), *n.* a step at the normal rate of marching. 2. a lively dance step.

quick-tem·pered ('tem-pẽrd), *adj.* easily angered; irascible; irritable.

quick-wit·ted ('wit'id), *adj.* keen; of quick discernment.

quid (kwid), *n.* 1. a plug of tobacco for chewing. 2. [British Slang], a sovereign or pound sterling.

quid·nunc (kwid'nungk), *n.* one who is curious to know everything that passes.

qui·es·cent (kwi-es'nt), *adj.* reposing or resting; calm; silent. —**qui·es'cence,** *n.*

qui·et (kwī'ẽt), *adj.* 1. free from motion; calm; still. 2. free from disturbance; gentle. 3. secluded. 4. subdued and modest. 5. not showy. 6. peaceful. 7. without noise. 8. without sound: *n.* 1. a state of being quiet; calmness. 2. freedom from noise or disturbance: *v.t.* to calm or pacify; reduce to a state of rest: *v.i.* to become quiet. —**qui'et·ly,** *adv.*

qui·et·ism (-izm), *n.* 1. peace; tranquillity of mind; calmness. 2. [Q-], a religious mysticism based on withdrawal of the mind from

all worldly concerns and interests and fixing it on a contemplation of God.

qui·e·tude (kwī'ẽ-tōōd), *n.* repose; tranquillity.

qui·e·tus (kwi-ēt'ŭs), *n.* 1. death. 2. final settlement or discharge of a debt, obligation, etc.

quill (kwil), *n.* 1. a large, strong feather of a bird's wing or tail. 2. the hollow stem of such a feather used as a pen, a plectrum, etc. 3. any one of the spines of a porcupine. 4. a weaver's spindle: *v.t.* to plait or form with small quill-like ridges.

quil·lai·a, quil·laj·a (ki-li'ā), *n.* a South American tree, the inner bark of which is used as a soap or detergent.

quill·ing (kwil'ing), *n.* a strip of fabric fluted and joined so as to resemble a row of quills or feathers.

quilt (kwilt), *n.* a kind of heavy coverlet or counterpane consisting of two cloth layers stuffed and stitched together in patterns: *v.t.* to stitch together (two pieces of cloth with a soft material between them): *v.i.* to stitch a quilt.

quilt·ing (kwilt'ing), *n.* 1. the act or process of making a quilt. 2. the material for quilting. 3. quilted work.

qui·na·ry (kwi'nā-ri), *n., pl.* **-ries,** a body or group consisting of five members: *adj.* consisting of or arranged in fives.

quince (kwins), *n.* 1. the hard, apple-shaped fruit of a small tree related to the rose, used in preserves. 2. the tree bearing this fruit.

quin·cunx (kwin'kungks), *n.* an arrangement of five objects in a square with one at each corner and one in the middle.

quin·ic acid (kwin'ik), *n.* a colorless, crystalline compound found in cinchona bark, coffee beans, etc.

qui·nine (kwī'nīn), *n.* a bitter, alkaline substance obtained from the bark of the cinchona tree, used as a febrifuge for malaria.

quin·nat salmon (kwin'at), *n.* a salmon found along both coasts of the Pacific.

quin·qua·ge·nar·i·an (kwin-kwä-jē-ner'i-ăn), *n.* one who is fifty years old, or between fifty and sixty: *adj.* of or denoting a quinquagenarian.

quin·que-, a combining form meaning *five.*

quin·quen·ni·al (kwin-kwen'i-ăl), *adj.* 1. comprising five years. 2. occurring every five years: *n.* a quinquennial occurrence, celebration, etc.

quin·sy (kwin'zi), *n.* inflammation of the tonsils; tonsillitis.

quin·tan (kwin'tn), *adj.* recurring every fifth day: *n.* an intermittent fever which recurs thus.

quin·tes·sence (kwin-tes'ns), *n.* 1. the pure concentrated essence of anything. 2. a flawless example.

quin·tet, quin·tette (kwin-tet'), *n.* 1. anything in fives. 2. a musical composition for five voices or instruments. 3. the five persons singing or playing this composition.

quin·til·lion (kwin-til'yŭn), *n.* 1. in the U.S. and France, the number indicated by one followed by 18 zeros. 2. in Great Britain and Germany, the number indicated by one followed by 30 zeros. —**quin·til'lionth,** *adj.* & *n.*

quin·tu·ple (kwin-tōō'pl), *v.t.* & *v.i.* -pled, -pling, to make or become fivefold: *adj.* fivefold.

quin·tu·plet (kwin-tup'lit, -tōō'-), *n.* 1. one of five offspring born at the same time. 2. a collection of five things of the same kind.

quip (kwip), *n.* 1. a gibe; jest. 2. a droll saying. 3. a quibble; equivocation: *v.i.* **quipped, quip'ping,** to scoff or gibe; utter quips.

quire (kwīr), *n.* twenty-four or twenty-five sheets of paper, equal to 1/20th of a ream.

Qui·ri·tes (kwi-rī'tēz), *n.pl.* the ancient Romans in their civil capacity.

quirt (kwûrt), *n.* a rawhide riding whip with a short handle: *v.t.* to strike with a quirt.

quit (kwit), *v.t.* quit, **quit'ted, quit'ting,** 1. to depart from. 2. to discharge (an obligation). 3. to give up; forsake. 4. to disengage. 5. to cease. 6. to leave (a job): *v.i.* 1. to stop doing something; cease. 2. to leave a job: *adj.* set free.

quit·claim (kwit'klām), *n.* a legal instrument by which a person relinquishes a claim or title to property, a right, etc.: *v.i.* to relinquish a claim or title.

quite (kwīt), *adv.* 1. wholly; completely. 2. truly. 3. somewhat.

quits (kwits), *adj.* balanced, as by a quittance.

quit·tance (kwit'ns), *n.* 1. a discharge from a debt, service, or obligation. 2. a paying back.

quit·ter (kwit'ēr), *n.* [Informal], one who quits without making much effort.

quiv·er (kwiv'ēr), *n.* 1. a case for arrows. 2. a trembling or shivering: *v.i.* to tremble, shake, or shiver.

quix·ot·ic (kwik-sot'ik), *adj.* chivalrous or romantic to extravagance; not practical: from Don Quixote, hero of Cervantes' romance: also **quix·ot'i·cal.** —**quix·ot'i·cal·ly,** *adv.*

quiz (kwiz), *n.*, *pl.* **quiz'zes,** a series of questions, as in a form for testing knowledge:

v.t. **quizzed, quiz'zing,** to question, as in a formal test.

quiz·zi·cal (kwiz'i-kl), *adj.* 1. puzzled. 2. comical. —**quiz'zi·cal·ly,** *adv.*

quod (kwod), *n.* [Chiefly British Slang], prison.

quoin (koin, kwoin), *n.* 1. a wedge used to support or steady something. 2. the external corner of a building, or one of the stones marking it. 3. a wedge-shaped wooden or metal block used to lock up type in a chase.

quoit (kwoit), *n.* 1. a circular ring of metal or rope to be pitched at a fixed object. 2. *pl.* a game played with quoits.

quon·dam (kwon'dåm), *adj.* former.

Quon·set hut (kwon'sit), a small building of standardized manufacture resembling a half cylinder placed on the flat side: a trademark.

quo·rum (kwôr'ûm), *n.* the minimum number of members of a body or corporation needed to transact business by law or constitution.

quo·ta (kwōt'å), *n.* a part or share assigned to each; proportional part or number.

quo·ta·tion (kwō-tā'shun), *n.* 1. the act of quoting. 2. that which is quoted. 3. in *Commerce,* the current price.

quotation mark, a punctuation mark used to denote the beginning (") or end (") of a quotation.

quote (kwōt), *v.t.* **quot'ed, quot'ing,** 1. to repeat (a passage) from some author or speaker for authority or illustration. 2. to present a passage or speech from. 3. in *Commerce,* to give the current price of: *n.* [Informal], 1. a quotation. 2. a quotation mark. —**quot'a·ble,** *adj.*

quoth (kwōth), *v.t.* [Archaic], said; spoke.

quoth·a (kwōth'å), *interj.* [Archaic], indeed!

quo·tid·i·an (kwō-tid'i-ån), *adj.* recurring daily.

quo·tient (kwō'shēnt), *n.* the number resulting from the division of one number by another.

R

R, r (är), *n.*, *pl.* **R's, r's,** 1. the eighteenth letter of the English alphabet. 2. any of the sounds of this letter, as in *run, barrel,* and *car.* 3. a type or impression of *R* or *r.*

R (är), *adj.* shaped like R: *n.* 1. an object shaped like R. 2. one of the elements of education, in the phrase the three R's, reading, (w)riting, and (a)rithmetic.

Ra (rä), *n.* the sun god and principal deity of the ancient Egyptians.

ra·bat (rab'i, rä-bat'), *n.* a short, black shirt front worn with a clerical collar.

ra·ba·to (rä-bät'ō, -bät'-), *n., pl.* **-tos,** a wide collar of the 16th and 17th centuries that lay flat on the shoulders or turned up in the back.

rab·bet (rab'it), *n.* a groove cut in the edge of a plank, etc. so that the edge of another may fit into it: *v.t.* to groove and unite by a rabbet: *v.i.* to be joined by a rabbet.

rab·bi (rab'ī), *n., pl.* **-bis, -bies,** originally, a Jewish scholar and teacher; now, specifically, one ordained for religious leadership.

rab·bin·ate (rab'i-nit), *n.* 1. the office or tenure of a rabbi. 2. rabbis in general.

rab·bin·i·cal (rä-bin'i-kl), **rab·bin·ic** ('ik), *adj.* pertaining to rabbis, their doctrines, learning, or language. —**rab·bin'i·cal·ly,** *adv.*

rab·bit (rab'it), *n., pl.* **-bits, -bit,** 1. a burrowing mammal of the hare family, with long ears and a short, fluffy tail. 2. the soft fur of a rabbit.

rabbit ears, [Informal], an adjustable indoor television antenna with two upright rods.

rabbit fever, same as tularemia.

rabbit punch, a sharp punch to the back of the neck.

rab·bit·ry (rab'i-tri), *n., pl.* **-ries,** a rabbit hutch; a structure for raising and housing rabbits.

rab·ble (rab'l), *n.* 1. a noisy crowd or mob. 2. the common people; masses: *v.t.* **-bled, -bling,** to attack by a mob.

rab·ble-rous·er (-rouz-ēr), *n.* one who tries to stir up a crowd to frenzied action; agitator. —**rab'ble-rous·ing,** *n. & adj.*

rab·id (rab'id), *adj.* 1. mad; violent. 2. excessively enthusiastic; intemperate. 3. afflicted with rabies. —**ra·bid·i·ty** (rä-bid'i-ti), **rab'id·ness,** *n.* —**rab'id·ly,** *adv.*

ra·bies (rä'bēz), *n.* an infectious disease of mammals causing convulsions: it can be transmitted to man by the bite of an infected animal.

rac·coon (ra-kōōn'), *n., pl.* **-coons', -coon',** 1. a small mammal of North America, with a long, black-ringed tail. 2. its yellowish-gray fur.

race (rās), *n.* 1. a rapid course, as of a river, or its channel. 2. a contest of speed, as in running or driving. 3. any competition, as

for elective office. 4. any of the three major groups of mankind, distinguished mainly by color of skin. 5. any ethnic group, as a tribe or nation. 6. any group of people with similar ideas, likes, etc.: *v.i.* **raced, rac'ing,** 1. to move swiftly. 2. to contend in a race: *v.t.* 1. to cause to contend in a race. 2. to compete against in a contest of speed. 3. to cause to move fast. 4. to run (an engine) fast without engaging the gears.

race·horse (rās'hôrs), *n.* a horse bred and kept for racing.

ra·ceme (rā-sēm', rä-), *n.* a flower cluster with single flowers growing on short stems from a single central stem, as the hyacinth. —**rac·e·mose** (ras'ē-mōs), *adj.*

rac·er (rās'ēr), *n.* 1. a person, animal, etc. that competes in races. 2. a vehicle made for, or used for, racing. 3. a slim, harmless snake.

race track, a course constructed and maintained for racing: also **race'course,** *n.*

ra·cial (rā'shŭl), *adj.* 1. pertaining to a race, or ethnic group. 2. of or pertaining to relations between races. —**ra'cial·ly,** *adv.*

ra·cial·ism (-izm), *n.* 1. a claim, unfounded in scientific fact, that any race is superior to another. 2. racial discrimination; racism. —**ra'cial·ist,** *adj. & n.*

rac·i·ly (rā'si-li), *adv.* in a racy manner.

rac·i·ness (rā'si-nis), *n.* the state or quality of being racy.

rac·ism (rā'sizm), *n.* 1. a claim of racial superiority; racialism. 2. the practice of racial discrimination, persecution, segregation, etc., based on racialism. —**rac'ist,** *adj. & n.*

rack (rak), *n.* 1. formerly, an instrument of torture for stretching the limbs. 2. a frame in which or on which various things are placed or arranged. 3. a straight toothed bar meshing in the pinions of a wheel. 4. a heavy device for lifting an automobile for repairs or work to the underside. 5. thin, broken, vapory clouds. 6. entire destruction: now only in go to rack and ruin: *v.t.* 1. to stretch or strain forcibly on the rack. 2. to torment or afflict. 3. to place or arrange on a rack. 4. to decant or strain off.

rack·et (rak'it), *n.* 1. a clattering noise. 2. a hilarious merrymaking. 3. a dishonest, fraudulent, or illegal scheme, practice, or method of obtaining money. 4. any of various network bats used in tennis, squash, badminton, etc. 5. a snowshoe. 6. *pl.* a game like court tennis; racquets: *v.i.* to make a clattering noise.

rack·et·eer (rak-ē-tir'), *n.* a person who gets money from unlawful activities, as by using threats or violence. —**rack·et·eer'ing,** *n.*

rack·et·y (rak'ē-ti), *adj.* uproariously noisy.

rack-rent (rak'rent), *n.* 1. an excessive rent. 2. annual rent almost equal to the value of the property.

---

a in *cap,* ā in *cane,* ä in *father,* à in *abet,* e in *met,* ē in *be,* ē in *baker,* ê in *regent,* i in *pit,* ī in *fine,* i in *manifest,* o in *hot,* ô in *horse,* ō in *bone,*

rac·on·teur (rak-on-tūr'), *n.* an expert teller of anecdotes or stories.

rac·quet·ball (rak'it-bôl), *n.* a game played like handball, but with a racquet.

rac·quets (rak'its), *n.* an indoor game similar to tennis.

rac·y (rā'sĭ), *adj.* **rac'i·er, rac'i·est,** 1. possessing the real characteristics, taste, etc. of something. 2. energetic; active. 3. piquant. 4. daring; suggestive; exciting.

ra·dar (rā'där), *n.* an electronic device using transmitted and reflected radio waves for detecting and locating objects, as aircraft, and determining distance, speed, etc.

ra·dar·scope (-skōp), *n.* an oscilloscope that shows the pattern of reflected radio waves produced by radar.

ra·di·al (rā'di-ăl), *adj.* 1. of, like, or pertaining to a ray. 2. of or like a radius. 3. of or pertaining to the radius of the forearm: *n.* a radiating part or structure.

radial ply tire, a tire for an automobile in which ply cords run at almost right angles to the tread center.

ra·di·an (rā'di-ăn), *n.* an arc of a circle equal to the radius.

ra·di·ant (rā'di-ănt), *adj.* 1. emitting rays of light or heat; shining; brilliant. 2. cheerful; happy. 3. radiated: *n.* 1. the point from which a shower of meteors proceeds. 2. a luminous point from which light emanates. —**ra'di·ance, ra'di·an·cy** (-ăn-si), *n.*

ra·di·ate (rā'di-āt), *v.t.* **-at·ed, -at·ing,** 1. to send out as rays. 2. to disseminate (joy, friendliness, etc.): *v.i.* 1. to emit or issue forth in rays. 2. to extend in lines from a center: *adj.* having rays.

ra·di·a·tion (rā-di-ā'shŭn), *n.* 1. the emission or diffusion of rays of light or heat from a luminous or heated body. 2. the rays emitted. 3. nuclear particles.

radiation sickness, sickness produced by overexposure to X-rays, radioactive matter, etc.

ra·di·a·tor (rā'di-āt-ẽr), *n.* 1. the body from which rays radiate. 2. a chamber, coil, drum, etc. heated by steam, etc. for radiating heat into a room. 3. a water-cooling device used with gasoline motors.

rad·i·cal (rad'i-kl), *adj.* 1. of or pertaining to the root or origin; fundamental; original; underived; extreme. 2. of or proposing a basic transformation of the economy or society: *n.* 1. one who has radical ideas. 2. a simple, underived thing. 3. in *Chemistry,* a group of atoms behaving as one atom. 4. in *Mathematics,* a sign (√) that shows that a root is to be extracted. —**rad'i·cal·ly,** *adv.*

rad·i·cal·ism (-izm), *n.* 1. the state or quality of being radical. 2. the principles and practices of radicals.

ra·di·i (rā'di-ī), *n.* alternate plural of radius.

ra·di·o (rā'di-ō), *n., pl.* **-os,** 1. the science of communication by the transmission or reception of electromagnetic waves through space without wires. 2. apparatus or equipment for transmitting or receiving sounds by means of electromagnetic waves. 3. the business of broadcasting programs by radio: *adj.* of, pertaining to, or operated by radio: *v.t.*

& *v.i.* **-oed, -o·ing,** to transmit, inform, etc. by radio.

ra·di·o-, a combining form meaning *having rays, by radio, using radiant energy.*

ra·di·o·ac·tive (rā-di-ō-ak'tiv), *adj.* emitting atomic radiation. —**ra·di·o·ac·tiv'i·ty** (-ak-tiv'i-ti), *n.*

radio astronomy, the science that treats of radio waves in space, for gathering data concerning outer space.

ra·di·o·chem·is·try (-kem'is-tri), *n.* the study of radioactive phenomena.

radio frequency, a frequency beyond that of normally audible sound and below infrared light, about 10 kilohertz to 1,000,000 megahertz.

ra·di·o·gram (rā'di-ō-gram), *n.* a message transmitted by radio.

ra·di·o·i·so·tope (rā-di-ō-ī'sō-tōp), *n.* a radioactive isotope of an element.

ra·di·ol·o·gy (rā-di-ol'ō-ji), *n.* the branch of science which treats of radiant energy and its applications. —**ra·di·ol'o·gist,** *n.*

ra·di·om·e·ter (ra-di-om'ĕ-tẽr), *n.* an instrument used for measuring the intensity of radiant energy by its mechanical effect.

ra·di·o·paque (rā-di-ō-pāk'), *adj.* not allowing the passage of X-rays.

ra·di·o·phone (rā'di-ō-fōn), *n.* same as **radiotelephone.**

ra·di·os·co·py (rā-di-os'kō-pi), *n.* the examination of bodies by means of X-rays or some other form of radiant energy. —**ra·di·o·scop'ic** (-ō-skop'ik), *adj.*

ra·di·o·tel·e·gram (rā-di-ō-tel'ĕ-gram), *n.* same as **radiogram.**

ra·di·o·tel·e·graph (-tel'ĕ-graf), *n.* same as wireless telegraphy: also **ra·di·o·te·leg'ra·phy** (-tĕ-leg'rä-fi).

ra·di·o·tel·e·phone (-tel'ĕ-fōn), *n.* a telephonic instrument for transmitting and receiving sound waves without wires. —**ra·di·o·te·leph'o·ny** (-tĕ-lef'ō-ni), *n.*

ra·di·o·ther·a·py (-ther'ä-pi), *n.* the treatment of disease by X-rays or with rays of radioactive elements.

rad·ish (rad'ish), *n.* a plant with an edible root, used in salads.

ra·di·um (rā'di-ŭm), *n.* a radioactive element found in pitchblende and some other minerals extracted from uranium, emitting ionizing radiation.

radium therapy, the treatment of various diseases, as cancer, by radium.

ra·di·us (rā'di-ŭs), *n., pl.* **-di·i** (-ī), **-us·es,** 1. a straight line from the center to the circumference of a circle. 2. the area of a circle limited by the sweep of this line. 3. the forearm bone on the thumb side. 4. anything resembling a radius, as the spoke of a wheel.

ra·dix (rā'diks), *n., pl.* **ra·di·ces** (rad'ī-sēz), **ra'dix·es,** 1. a root. 2. a base word. 3. in *Mathematics,* the base of a number system.

ra·don (rā'don), *n.* a radioactive, gaseous chemical element formed in the atomic disintegration of radium.

raf·fi·a (raf'i-ä), *n.* 1. a palm of Madagascar, the leaves of which yield a fiber used in

---

ŏ in dragon, ōō in crude, oo in wool, u in cup, ū in cure, ū in turn, u in focus, oi in boy, ou in house, th in thin, th in sheathe, g in get, j in joy, y in yet.

making baskets, hats, and cordage. 2. this fiber.

raf-fish (raf'ish), *adj.* 1. dissolute; dissipated. 2. vulgar.

raf-fle (raf'l), *n.* a kind of lottery in which each participant pays for the chance of winning a thing: *v.t.* **-fled, -fling,** to dispose of by raffle (often with *off*).

raft (raft), *n.* 1. a float of logs, boards, etc., as for transporting goods by water. 2. a floating wooden framework. 3. a boat of rubber, plastic, etc. filled with air. 4. [Informal], a great number: *v.t.* to carry on a raft.

raft-er (raf'tēr), *n.* an inclined beam supporting the roof of a house.

rag (rag), *n.* 1. a fragment of cloth, as for cleaning. 2. a piece of refuse cloth. 3. *pl.* worn-out or tattered garments. 4. a ragtime composition.

ra-ga (rä'gä), *n.* a traditional melody pattern used for improvisation by Hindu musicians.

rag-a-muf-fin (rag'ä-muf-in), *n.* an unkempt child dressed in tattered clothes.

rag-bag (rag'bag), *n.* 1. a miscellaneous grouping. 2. a sack for rags.

rage (rāj), *n.* 1. excessive and uncontrolled anger; vehemence. 2. extreme violence. 3. great enthusiasm; extreme desire or eagerness: *v.i.* **raged, rag'ing,** 1. to be furious with anger. 2. to spread widely, as a disease. 3. to be violently agitated, as the sea.

rag-ged (rag'id), *adj.* 1. rent or worn into rags. 2. clothed in tattered garments. 3. rough; jagged. 4. unkempt.

rag-ged-y (-i), *adj.* a little tattered.

rag-lan (rag'lan), *n.* a loose overcoat with sleeves having no shoulder seams and continuing in one piece to the collar.

ra-gout (ra-gōō'), *n.* a dish of stewed and highly seasoned meat and vegetables.

rag-time (rag'tim), *n.* strongly syncopated American music from the early part of the 20th century, with a fast, even beat. 2. the rhythmic beat of ragtime.

rag-weed (rag'wēd), *n.* a common garden and field weed with flowers that yield a pollen that is a major cause of hay fever.

rag-wort ('wŭrt), *n.* same as groundsel.

rah (rä), *interj.* hurrah.

raid (rād), *n.* 1. a hostile or predatory incursion. 2. an abrupt entry made by police investigating crimes: *v.t. & v.i.* to make a raid (upon). **—raid'er,** *n.*

rail (rāl), *n.* 1. a bar of timber or metal extending horizontally from one post to another. 2. a fence. 3. a railroad. 4. any one of the parallel metal strips forming railroad tracks. 5. any one of a number of wading birds with short wings and a harsh cry: *v.i.* to use scornful language; scoff: *v.t.* to enclose with rails.

rail-ing (rāl'ing), *n.* 1. material for rails. 2. a fence made of posts and rails.

rail-ler-y (ral'ēr-i), *n., pl.* **-ler-ies,** good-humored irony or satire; banter.

rail-road (rāl'rōd), *n.* 1. a road laid with parallel steel rails along which cars carrying passengers or freight are drawn by locomotives. 2. a complete system of such roads: *v.t.* 1. to carry on a railroad. 2. [Informal],

to hurry (legislation, convictions, etc.) without allowing time for thought or consideration: *v.i.* to be employed by a railroad.

rail-way ('wā), *n.* 1. a railroad for light vehicles. 2. [British], a railroad.

rai-ment (rä'mĕnt), *n.* [Archaic], clothing.

rain (rān), *n.* 1. water in drops discharged from the clouds. 2. the discharging of such drops. 3. a dropping like rain: *v.i.* 1. to fall in drops from the clouds. 2. to drop like rain: *v.t.* 1. to pour down (rain or something like rain). 2. to give in large amounts.

rain-bow (rän'bō), *n.* the bright-colored arc formed in the heavens by the refraction and reflection of the sun's rays falling upon watery particles.

rainbow trout, a trout found in the mountain streams and rivers of the Pacific coast of North America.

rain check, the part of a ticket kept by the purchaser, which allows entry to an event if the original event was postponed.

rain-coat ('cōt), *n.* a waterproof or water-repellent coat for protection from rain.

rain-drop ('drop), *n.* one drop of rain.

rain-fall ('fôl), *n.* 1. the amount of rain that falls on any given area. 2. a shower of rain.

rain forest, a thick forest in a tropical region with plentiful rainfall.

rain gauge, an instrument for measuring the quantity of rain that falls at a given place in a given time.

rain-storm ('stôrm), *n.* a storm with great amounts of rain.

rain-y (rä'ni), *adj.* **rain'i-er, rain'i-est,** abounding with rain.

raise (rāz), *v.t.* **raised, rais'ing,** 1. to cause to rise; lift up; elevate. 2. to originate or produce. 3. to promote. 4. to rouse. 5. to increase. 6. to construct. 7. to levy; collect. 8. to cause to appear. 9. to cause to swell. 10. to suggest. 11. to take away. 12. to cultivate. 13. to bring up: *n.* 1. the act of raising. 2. an increase in price, salary, etc.

raised (rāzd), *adj.* 1. projecting above the surface. 2. having figures in relief. 3. leavened, as bread.

rai-sin (rä'zn), *n.* a dried grape.

ra-jah, ra-ja (rä'jä), *n.* a prince or chief in India.

Raj-put (räj'pŏŏt), *n.* one of a former Hindu ruling group in India.

rake (rāk), *n.* 1. a toothed implement for gathering hay, leaves, etc. 2. any toothed gathering tool. 3. inclination or slope. 4. a dissolute man: *v.t.* **raked, rak'ing,** 1. to gather or smooth with a rake. 2. to collect. 3. to scour. 4. to direct fire upon, so as to sweep horizontally. 5. to make slant: *v.i.* to slope from the perpendicular.

rake-hell (rāk'hel), *n.* a debauchee; rake: *adj.* dissolute; lewd; wild.

rake-off (rāk'ôf), *n.* [Slang], a commission or share of illegal profits.

rak-ish (rä'kish), *adj.* 1. tidy and fast. 2. spirited; striking. 3. dissolute; debauched.

ral-ly (ral'i), *v.t.* **-lied, -ly-ing,** 1. to collect and arrange (troops in confusion); reunite. 2. to call to a meeting. 3. to resuscitate. 4. to attack with raillery; banter or satirize humorously: *v.i.* 1. to return to order. 2. to come together and meet. 3. to recover strength. 4. to exercise raillery: *n., pl.* -lies, 1. the act of recovering order or of regaining strength. 2. a mass meeting.

ram (ram), *n.* 1. the male of sheep. 2. the first sign of the zodiac. 3. a military implement for battering. 4. a hydraulic engine. 5. a ship with a metal beak: *v.t.* rammed, ram'ming, to push or press with force. —ram'mer, *n.*

Ram·a·dan (ram-å-dän'), *n.* the ninth month of the Moslem year, in which fasting and praying take place.

Ra·ma·ya·na (rä-mä'yå-nå), *n.* a great epic of India, written after the Mahabharata.

ram·ble (ram'bl), *v.i.* -bled, -bling, 1. to wander or rove about; visit many places. 2. to be desultory. 3. to extend widely: *n.* a roving or wandering from place to place.

ram·bler (ram'blēr), *n.* 1. one who or that which rambles. 2. a rose that climbs.

ram·bunc·tious (ram-bungk'shŭs), *adj.* exuberant, noisy, wild, etc.

ram·e·kin, ram·e·quin (ram'ē-kin), *n.* a small dish for baking.

ra·men·tum (rå-men'tŭm), *n., pl.* -men'ta (-men'tå), a coating on fern leaves and stems.

ram·ie (ram'i), *n.* a plant related to the nettle, which yields a tough fiber woven into fabric.

ram·i·fi·ca·tion (ram-i-fi-kā'shŭn), *n.* 1. a division or separation into branches. 2. a subdivision; also, an effect. 3. the manner of producing branches.

ram·i·form (ram'i-fôrm), *adj.* branched.

ram·i·fy (-fi), *v.t. & v.i.* -fied, -fy·ing, to divide or become divided into branches or divisions.

ram·mish ('ish), *adj.* like a ram; strongsmelling, lustful, etc.

ra·mose (rä'mōs), *adj.* 1. branching. 2. producing branches.

ramp (ramp), *n.* 1. a slope or incline, as for walking on. 2. a staircase with wheels, for entering or leaving an aircraft.

ram·page (ram-pāj'), *v.i.* -paged', -pag'ing, to dash about with rage or anger; to move furiously: *n.* (ram'pāj), a state of excitement or the act of dashing wildly about in rage or anger: usually in *on the rampage.*

ramp·ant (ram'pånt), *adj.* 1. overleaping restraint or natural bounds; unchecked; widespread. 2. vehement in talk or acts. 3. in *Heraldry,* standing upright on the hind legs.

ram·part (ram'pärt), *n.* 1. a mound or wall surrounding a fortified place. 2. protection from assault or danger: *v.t.* to fortify with a rampart.

ram·pi·on (ram'pi-ŏn), *n.* a plant, the root of which is used in salads.

ram·rod (ram'rod), *n.* a rod used for ramming down the charge of a gun.

ram·shack·le (ram'shak-l), *adj.* loose; shaky; not in repair.

ram·til (ram'til), *n.* a plant, the seeds of which yield a valuable oil used for both food and illumination.

ram·u·lose (ram'yū-lōs), *adj.* having many small branches.

ra·mus (rä'mŭs), *n., pl.* ra·mi (rä'mī), a branch.

ran (ran), past tense of run.

ranch (ranch), *n.* 1. a large farm, with buildings, personnel, etc. for the raising of horses, cattle, etc. 2. a type of house with only one floor: in full, ranch house: *v.i.* to live or work on a ranch.

ranch·er (ran'chēr), *n.* the owner of a ranch or one who helps run it: also ranch'man (ranch'mån), *pl.* -men ('mén).

ran·che·ro (ran-cher'ō), *n., pl.* -ros ('ōz), in the southwestern U.S. and Mexico, same as rancher.

ran·cho (ran'chō, rän'-), *n., pl.* -chos, 1. a cabin or group of cabins where ranchmen are sheltered. 2. same as ranch.

ran·cid (ran'sid), *adj.* having a rank, unpleasant smell; sour or musty. —ran·cid'i·ty (-sid'i-ti), ran'cid·ness, *n.*

ran·cor (rang'kēr), *n.* implacable enmity; deep spite or malice. —ran'cor·ous, *adj.*

rand (rand, ränd), *n., pl.* rand, a monetary unit in South Africa and certain other African countries.

ran·dom (ran'dŏm), *n.* lack of direction or method: in *at random: adj.* 1. haphazard. 2. not uniform.

ran·dy (ran'di), *adj.* -di·er, -di·est, amorous; lustful.

ra·nee (rä'ni), *n.* alternate spelling of rani.

rang (rang), past tense of ring.

range (ränj), *v.t.* ranged, rang'ing, 1. to arrange in order, as in rows. 2. to join with others, as in a cause. 3. to adjust the aim of (a gun, telescope, etc.). 4. to roam over or through. 5. to hold a parallel course to: *v.i.* 1. to extend in a given direction. 2. to roam. 3. to vary between indicated limits: *n.* 1. a row, series, or rank. 2. a class, order, or kind. 3. a mountain chain. 4. the flight distance or path of a missile, rocket, aircraft, etc. 5. a place to practice shooting; also, a place to test the flight of rockets. 6. the extent or scope of something indicated. 7. a roaming. 8. a tract of land for raising cattle, horses, etc. 9. a stove for cooking. 10. habitat.

rang·er (rān'jēr), *n.* 1. a roamer. 2. any one of a group of mounted patrol troops. 3. [often R-], any one of a military group trained for raiding and close combat. 4. a warden patrolling government forests.

rang·y (rän'ji), *adj.* rang'i·er, rang'i·est, 1. ranging widely. 2. tall and lean, or long and slender. 3. open; spacious.

ra·ni (rä'ni), *n.* the wife of a rajah.

rank (rangk), *n.* 1. a row, line, or series; also, any orderly grouping. 2. a set of organ pipes of the same kind. 3. a social class. 4. high social position; eminence. 5. an official grade. 6. a particular degree of quality within a given scale. 7. a line of soldiers, vehicles, etc. side by side. 8. *pl.* an army. 9. *pl.* ordinary soldiers as distinguished from officers. 10. ordinary people: in *the rank and file: v.t.* 1. to group in or assign to a rank or ranks. 2. to rank higher than: *v.i.* to be in a certain rank or position: *adj.* 1.

growing vigorously and often to excess, as wild vegetation. 2. extremely bad in smell or taste, as from decay. 3. offensively coarse or low. 4. complete; thorough; utter; out-and-out.

rank-ing ('ing), *adj.* 1. of the highest rank. 2. outstanding; eminent.

ran-kle (rang'kl), *v.i. & v.t.* **-kled, -kling,** to fill with, undergo, or produce rancor, seething resentment, etc.

ran-sack (ran'sak), *v.t.* 1. to search or search through thoroughly, persistently, and often desperately or wildly. 2. to go through, plundering completely.

ran-som (ran'sŏm), *n.* 1. a freeing from captivity or from seizure by paying a sum demanded or by meeting some other demand. 2. the sum itself or whatever else is demanded for such freeing: *v.t.* to free as from captivity by providing the ransom.

rant (rant), *v.i. & v.t.* to speak or declaim in a blustering, pompous, or feverishly frenzied way: *n.* such speech; raving.

rap (rap), *v.t.* rapped, rap'ping, 1. to strike quickly and sharply. 2. to say sharply (with *out*). 3. [Informal], to criticize sharply: *v.i.* 1. to knock quickly and sharply. 2. [Slang], to talk together; chat: *n.* 1. a quick, sharp knock. 2. [Informal], the least bit: in *not care* (or *give*) *a rap*. 3. [Slang] a talking together; chat. 4. [Slang], *a)* blame; *b)* a criminal charge; *c)* punishment; especially, a prison sentence. —rap'per, *n.*

ra-pa-cious (rā-pā'shŭs), *adj.* 1. greedy; covetous. 2. predatory.

ra-pac-i-ty (-pas'i-ti), *n.* the quality, fact, or practice of being rapacious.

rape (rāp), *n.* 1. the crime of illicit sexual intercourse with a woman against her consent, or with a girl below an age fixed by law. 2. any sexual assault upon a person. 3. any outrageous assault or violation. 4. an annual old-world plant of the mustard family, with leaves used as fodder: *v.t. & v.i.* raped rap'ing, to commit rape (against). —rap'ist, *n.*

rap-id (rap'id), *adj.* swift; speedy: *n.* usually pl. a swift part of a river. —ra-pid-i-ty (rā-pid'i-ti), *n.*

ra-pi-er (rā'pi-ēr), *n.* a long, thin sword used for thrusting.

rap-ine (rap'in), *n.* plundering; pillage.

rap-pel (ra-pel', rā-), *n.* a descent by a mountain climber, as down a sheer cliff, with a double rope so arranged that the climber can control the descent: *v.i.* -pelled', -pel'-ling, to descend thus.

rap-port (ra-pôr'), *n.* harmonious or sympathetic relationship; affinity.

rap-proche-ment (ra-prōsh'môn, ra-prōsh-môn'), *n.* [French], establishment or restoration of friendly relations.

rap-scal-lion (rap-skal'yŭn), *n.* a rascal.

rapt (rapt), *adj.* 1. carried away with joy, love, etc. 2. engrossed.

rap-to-ri-al (rap-tôr'i-ăl), *adj.* 1. of a group of birds of prey with sharp talons and a strong, notched beak, as the eagle. 2. adapted to seizing prey. 3. predacious.

rap-ture (rap'chēr), *n.* 1. a state, feeling, or ex-

perience of extreme joy, pleasure, delight, etc.; ecstasy. 2. an outward indication or expression of this. —rap'tur-ous, *adj.*

rare (rer), *adj.* rar'er, rar'est, 1. scarce; uncommon; unusual. 2. unusually good; excellent. 3. not dense; thinly scattered. 4. not completely cooked; partly raw. —rare'ness, *n.*

rare-bit (rer'bit), *n.* same as Welsh rabbit.

rare earth, 1. any one of certain basic oxides closely resembling each other. 2. any one of the rare-earth metals.

rare-earth metals (rer'ûrth'), a group of rare metallic chemical elements with consecutive atomic numbers of 57 to 71 inclusive: also rare-earth elements.

rar-e-fy (rer'ĕ-fī), *v.t. & v.i.* -fied, -fy-ing, 1. to make or become thinly scattered or less dense. 2. to lift far above what is gross or common. —rar-e-fac'tion (-fak'shŭn), *n.*

rare-ly (rer'li), *adv.* 1. very infrequently; almost never. 2. exceptionally.

rare-ripe (rer'rīp), *adj.* ripening early: *n.* such a fruit or vegetable.

rar-ing (rer'ing), *adj.* [Informal], extremely eager: followed by an infinitive.

rar-i-ty (rer'i-ti), *n.* 1. scarcity; uncommonness. 2. lack of density; tenuousness. 3. *pl.* -ties, an uncommon thing.

ras-cal (ras'kl), *n.* a scoundrel; scamp; rogue: now usually used playfully.

ras-cal-i-ty (ras-kal'i-ti), *n.* 1. rascally quality or conduct. 2. *pl.* -ties, a rascally deed.

ras-cal-ly (ras'kl-i), *adj.* of, like, or typical of a rascal; mean.

rash (rash), *adj.* reckless; incautious: *n.* 1. an eruption of red spots on the skin. 2. a sudden occurrence of many things. —rash'ly, *adv.* —rash'ness, *n.*

rash-er (rash'ēr), *n.* 1. a thin slice of bacon. 2. a serving of such slices.

rasp (rasp), *v.t.* 1. to rub with or as if with a rasp. 2. to utter in a scraping tone. 3. to irritate as if by scraping: *v.i.* 1. to rasp something. 2. to make a scraping noise: *n.* 1. a scraping tool with raised points. 2. a scraping noise.

rasp-ber-ry (raz'ber-i, 'bēr-), *n., pl.* -ries, 1. the small, juicy, red, black, or purple, edible fruit of certain brambles of the rose family. 2. such a bramble. 3. [Slang], a derisive blowing sound.

rasp-y (ras'pi), *adj.* rasp'i-er, rasp'i-est, 1. of a harshly scraping quality, as a sound or texture. 2. easily annoyed; irritable. —rasp'i-ness, *n.*

rat (rat), *n.* 1. any one of several groups of long-tailed rodents that are similar to but larger than mice: rats are destructive pests and carriers of disease. 2. any one of various other rodents of ratlike appearance. 3. [Slang], a despicable person, as a sneak or traitor: *v.i.* rat'ted, rat'ting, 1. to hunt rats. 2. [Slang], *a)* to desert or betray a cause, movement, etc.; *b)* to act as an informer; be a stool pigeon: *v.t.* to tease (the hair).

rat-a-ble (rāt'ā-bl), *adj.* 1. capable of being rated or estimated. 2. made or calculated at a certain rate; proportional. Also spelled rate'a-ble.

---

a in cap, ā in cane, ä in father, å in abet, e in met, ē in be, ē in baker, ĕ in regent, i in pit, ī in fine, i in manifest, o in hot, ô in horse, ō in bone,

rat-a-tat (rat'ă-tat), *n.* a series of quick, sharp, staccato sounds.

rat-chet (rach'it), *n.* 1. a toothed wheel, the teeth being angled so as to engage a pawl. 2. a similarly toothed bar. 3. the pawl itself. 4. the unit made up of the wheel or bar and the pawl.

ratchet wheel, a ratchet (sense 1).

rate (rāt), *n.* 1. the amount, quantity, or degree of one thing in relation to units of another thing. 2. ratio; proportion. 3. a price or value, as the cost per unit of something. 4. a particular speed. 5. class; rank: *v.t.* **rat'ed, rat'ing.** 1. to estimate; appraise; value. 2. to rank; class. 3. to consider; esteem. 4. to set or determine the rates for. 5. [Informal], to deserve: *v.i.* 1. to be classed or ranked. 2. to have value, status, etc.

rate (rāt), *v.t. & v.i.* **rat'ed, rat'ing,** to scold vehemently.

rath-er (ra*th*'ẽr), *adv.* 1. more willingly; preferably. 2. with greater right, justice, logic, etc. 3. more accurately. 4. on the contrary. 5. somewhat.

raths-kel-ler (rät'skel-ẽr, rath'skel-), *n.* a restaurant reminiscent of some German restaurants, typically below street level.

rat-i-fy (rat'i-fī), *v.t.* **-fied, -fy-ing,** to approve or confirm, especially officially. —**rat-i-fi-ca'tion,** *n.* —**rat'i-fi-er,** *n.*

rat-ing (rāt'ing), *n.* 1. a rank, class, or grade. 2. classification into rank or grade, as of military personnel. 3. the effective performance level of an engine, furnace, etc. expressed in units as of horsepower. 4. an evaluation as of credit standing. 5. the degree of popularity of a radio or television program, based on a poll.

ra-tio (rā'shō, 'shi-ō), *n., pl.* **-tios,** a relation in number, degree, etc. between one thing or group of things and another; proportion.

ra-ti-o-ci-nate (rash-i-ō'si-nāt, rat-i-; -os'i-), *v.i.* **-nat-ed, -nat-ing,** to reason, especially formally. —**ra-ti-o-ci-na'tion,** *n.*

ra-tion (rash'ŭn, rā'shŭn), *n.* 1. a fixed share; portion; allowance: especially, a fixed allowance of food or other provisions, often on a daily basis, as for a soldier. 2. *pl.* food or food supply: *v.t.* 1. to supply with a ration or rations. 2. to distribute as rations.

ra-tion-al (rash'ŭn-l), *adj.* 1. of or pertaining to reason. 2. using reason or able to do so. 3. having the faculty of reason. 4. sound in mind; sane. 5. wise; judicious. —**ra'tion-al-ly,** *adv.*

ra-tion-ale (rash-ŭ-nal', -nä'li), *n.* the rational basis advanced in support of something; justification.

ra-tion-al-ism (rash'ŭn-l-izm), *n.* use of or reliance on reason. —**ra'tion-al-ist,** *n. & adj.* —**ra-tion-al-is'tic,** *adj.*

ra-tion-al-i-ty (rash-ŭ-nal'i-ti), *n.* 1. accordance with reason; reasonableness. 2. power to reason.

ra-tion-al-ize (rash'ŭn-ă-līz), *v.t.* **-ized, -iz-ing,** 1. to bring into accordance with reason. 2. to set forth the rational basis of. 3. to seek to justify (actions, beliefs, etc.) on grounds that are only apparently reasonable or only seemingly in accordance with fact, usually

through error or self-deception: *v.i.* to rationalize something. —**ra'tion-al-i-za'tion,** *n.*

rat-line (rat'lin), *n.* any one of the small lengths of rope joining the shrouds of a ship and used as ladder steps to climb the rigging: also **rat'lin.**

rat race, [Slang], a constant, wearisome, competitive struggle, as in business.

rats-bane (rats'bān), *n.* rat poison.

rat-tan (ra-tan'), *n.* 1. a climbing palm tree with long, slender, tough stems. 2. the stems, used as for wickerwork.

rat-ter (rat'ẽr), *n.* a dog or cat good at catching rats.

rat-tle (rat'l), *v.i.* **-tled, -tling,** 1. to produce rapid, sharp noises. 2. to go or move with such noises. 3. to chatter: *v.t.* 1. to cause to make rapid, sharp noises. 2. to say, do, etc. with brisk rapidity. 3. to bewilder; confuse: *n.* 1. rapid, sharp noises. 2. chatter. 3. something that rattles, as a baby's toy.

rat-tle-brain (-brān), *n.* a silly person.

rat-tler (rat'lẽr), *n.* 1. one who or that which rattles. 2. a rattlesnake.

rat-tle-snake (rat'l-snāk), *n.* any one of various poisonous American snakes with horny rings at the tail tip: the snakes rattle the rings when disturbed or about to strike.

rat-tle-trap (-trap), *n.* a worn-out car.

rat-tling (rat'ling), *adj.* 1. that rattles. 2. [Informal], *a)* brisk; *b)* very good: *adv.* [Informal], very: used with *good.*

rat-trap (rat'trap), *n.* a trap for rats.

rat-ty (rat'i), *adj.* **-ti-er, -ti-est,** 1. of or like a rat. 2. infested with rats. 3. shabby. 4. dirty and ramshackle.

rau-cous (rô'kŭs), *adj.* 1. hoarse and loud; strident. 2. noisy; boisterous.

raun-chy (rôn'chi, rän'chi), *adj.* **-chi-er, -chi-est,** [Slang], 1. dirty, slovenly, inferior, etc. 2. lustful, smutty, etc.

rav-age (rav'ij), *v.t.* **-aged, -ag-ing,** 1. to lay waste; devastate; ruin. 2. to pillage; plunder; sack: *v.i.* to ravage something: *n.* devastation; ravaging.

rave (rāv), *v.i.* **raved, rav'ing,** 1. to pour out words wildly or incoherently. 2. to speak volubly and enthusiastically about someone or something: *n.* [Informal], an extraordinarily enthusiastic appraisal or review, as of a play, movie, or book.

rav-el (rav'l), *v.t. & v.i.* **-eled or -elled, -el-ing** or **-el-ling,** same as **unravel.**

ra-ven (rā'vēn), *n.* a large, black bird of the crow family, with a straight, sharp beak: *adj.* of a glossy black color.

rav-en-ing (rav'n-ing), *adj.* rapacious.

rav-e-nous (rav'ē-nŭs), *adj.* 1. voracious. 2. famished. 3. extremely eager for an indicated gratification. 4. rapacious.

ra-vine (ră-vēn'), *n.* a deep, narrow gorge.

rav-ing (rā'ving), *adj.* 1. that raves; frenzied. 2. [Informal], arousing wild admiration: *adv.* to the point of raving.

ra-vi-o-li (rav-i-ō'li), *n.* small pasta cases holding ground meat, cheese, etc., boiled, and usually served in tomato sauce.

rav-ish (rav'ish), *v.t.* 1. to seize and carry off by force. 2. to rape. 3. to transport with rapture. —**rav'ish-ment,** *n.*

ŏ in dragon, ōō in crude, oo in wool, u in cup, ū in cure, û in turn, ŭ in focus, oi in boy, ou in house, th in thin, *th* in sheathe, g in get, j in joy, y in yet.

raw (rô), *adj.* 1. uncooked. 2. unprocessed. 3. inexperienced. 4. open, as a sore. 5. cold and damp. 6. crude, sordid, or obscene. 7. [Informal], unfair or nasty.

raw-boned ('bōnd), *adj.* gaunt.

raw-hide ('hīd), *n.* 1. cattle hide tanned little or not at all. 2. a whip of this.

ray (rā), *n.* 1. a thin beam of light. 2. any similar beam. 3. a raylike line, as a radius. 4. a small, raylike organ or part. 5. any one of several slender-tailed fishes with a cartilaginous, horizontally flat body, both eyes being on the upper surface, and with wide fins at each side.

ray-on (rā'on), *n.* 1. a synthetic textile fiber made from a cellulose solution. 2. a fabric of such fibers.

raze (rāz), *v.t.* **razed, raz'ing,** to level to the ground; tear down; demolish.

ra-zor (rā'zēr), *n.* a cutting device used for shaving, as one consisting of a sharp-edged blade and a handle.

razz (raz), *v.t. & v.i.* [Slang], to ridicule, heckle, etc.

raz-zle-daz-zle (raz'l-daz'l), *n.* [Slang], showiness meant to bewilder or trick.

razz-ma-tazz (raz'mä-taz), *n.* [Slang], 1. liveliness; excitement. 2. flashiness.

re (rā), *n.* in *Music,* the second tone in any major or minor scale of eight tones.

re (rē, rā), *prep.* in the case or matter of.

re-, a prefix meaning *again, back:* such terms are sometimes written with a hyphen, as to distinguish *re-cover* from *recover.*

reach (rēch), *v.i.* 1. to stretch forth (the hand, arm, etc.). 2. to touch, grasp, come against, etc. thus. 3. to touch or hit with or as if with a missile. 4. to pass to another with the hand. 5. to arrive at or attain; get to. 6. to amount to (a total). 7. to affect upon coming into contact with: *v.i.* 1. to stretch forth the hand, arm, etc. 2. to extend. 3. to strain to do or get something: *n.* 1. a stretching forth, or the power or extent of this. 2. a continuous expanse or stretch of something.

re-act (ri-akt'), *v.i.* 1. to act in return, reciprocally, or in opposition. 2. to return to a previous condition. 3. to undergo a change, effect, etc. in response to a stimulus, influence, etc.; specifically, in *Chemistry,* to act with another substance in producing a chemical change: *v.t.* to make react; specifically, to produce a chemical change in.

re-act-ance (-ak'tăns), *n.* opposition to the flow of alternating current, caused by inductance or capacitance.

re-act-ant ('tănt), *n.* a substance involved in a chemical reaction.

re-ac-tion (ri-ak'shŭn), *n.* 1. reverse action. 2. tendency toward, or movement back to, a former or opposed condition. 3. response, as in attitude or action, evoked as by an occurrence. 4. a chemical or medical change or response.

re-ac-tion-ar-y ('shŭ-ner-i), *adj.* of, marked by, or given to reaction, especially in politics: *n., pl.* **-ar-ies,** a reactionary individual.

re-ac-ti-vate (ri-ak'ti-vāt), *v.t. & v.i.* **-vat-ed,**

-vat-ing, to return to an active condition. — **re-ac-ti-va'tion,** *n.*

re-ac-tive ('tiv), *adj.* that reacts.

re-ac-tor ('tēr), *n.* 1. one that reacts. 2. same as **nuclear reactor.**

read (rēd), *v.t.* **read** (red), **read-ing** (rēd'ing), 1. to look at (writing), reproducing mentally or vocally the words or ideas symbolized, especially with comprehension. 2. to subject (other communication devices or symbols, as lip movements or flag signaling) to such observation and reproduction. 3. to touch (raised Braille characters) and achieve such reproduction. 4. to grasp or interpret the nature, content, or meaning of as if by reading. 5. to present, give, or substitute (an indicated word, phrase, etc. as in a given text). 6. to devote oneself to (a given study or course, as of law). 7. to indicate or register, as a thermometer or barometer does. 8. to obtain (information) from (tapes, punched cards, etc.): said of a computer. 9. [Slang], to hear and understand: *v.i.* 1. to read books, other writing, etc. 2. to give a certain meaning when read. 3. to be phrased in a certain way.

read (red), *adj.* informed by reading.

read-a-ble (rēd'ä-bl), *adj.* read easily or with pleasure.

read-er ('ēr), *n.* 1. one that reads. 2. a book for practicing reading. 3. a compilation of selected writings; anthology.

read-er-ship (-ship), *n.* all those reading a particular magazine, newspaper, etc.

read-i-ly (red'l-i), *adv.* in a ready way; willingly, quickly, or easily.

read-i-ness ('i-nis), *n.* 1. the state of being ready. 2. alacrity. 3. ease in doing something; facility.

read-ing (rēd'ing), *adj.* 1. that reads. 2. of or for reading: *n.* 1. the act of reading. 2. a rendition or interpretation. 3. matter read or to be read. 4. a particular wording, word form, etc. in a given source. 5. the registration shown by an instrument or device, as by a thermometer.

read-out (rēd'out), *n.* 1. information fed out by a computer or other equipment, as on tape. 2. the getting of this.

read-y (red'i), *adj.* **read'i-er, read'i-est,** 1. being in a condition proper for action or use; prepared. 2. being on the verge of something; very close to a given action or condition. 3. not holding back; prompt or willing. 4. particularly disposed or inclined; quick; apt. 5. nimble; skilled; dexterous. 6. available easily or at once: *v.t.* **read'ied, read'y-ing,** to cause to be ready; prepare.

read-y-made (-mād'), *adj.* 1. not made just for a certain customer; not made-to-order. 2. lacking originality; commonplace.

re-a-gent (ri-ā'jĕnt), *n.* in *Chemistry,* a substance used to detect or measure another substance or to convert one substance into another by reaction.

re-al (rē'ăl, rēl), *adj.* 1. actually existing or corresponding to fact; not fictitious. 2. genuine; true. 3. designating wages or income as measured by purchasing power. 4. in *Law,* of or pertaining to permanent, immovable things: *adv.* [Informal], very.

real estate, land, including the buildings on it and its natural assets.

re·al·ism (rē'ǎ-lizm), *n.* 1. readiness to confront and adapt to fact. 2. representation, as in literature, of what is fact. 3. in *Philosophy, a)* the doctrine that abstractions are objectively actual; *b)* the doctrine that material objects exist in themselves, not merely in the mind. —re'al·ist, *n.*

re·al·is·tic (rē·ǎ-lis'tik), *adj.* of or marked by realism. —re·al·is'ti·cal·ly, *adv.*

re·al·i·ty (ri-al'ĭ-ti), *n., pl.* -ties, 1. the quality or fact of being real. 2. adherence to what is real; realism. 3. that which is real; fact. 4. one that is real; a real thing.

re·al·ize (rē'ǎ-līz), *v.t.* -ized, -iz·ing, 1. to bring into being; make real. 2. to perceive clearly; make no mistake about. 3. to convert into money. 4. to gain; achieve. 5. to bring (an indicated sale price or profit). —re·al·i·za'tion, *n.*

re·al·ly (rē'ǎ-li), *adv.* indeed; in truth.

realm (relm), *n.* 1. a kingdom. 2. a region; area. 3. a sphere, as of thought.

Re·al·tor (rē'ǎl-tēr), *n.* a real estate broker who is a member of the National Association of Real Estate Boards.

re·al·ty (rē'ǎl-ti), *n.* same as real estate.

ream (rēm), *n.* 1. a quantity of paper, from 480 to 516 sheets. 2. *pl.* [Informal], a great quantity: *v.t.* 1. to enlarge, shape, or clean out (a hole). 2. to juice.

ream·er ('ēr), *n.* a reaming tool or device.

reap (rēp), *v.t. & v.i.* 1. to cut (standing grain) with a machine, scythe, or sickle. 2. to harvest. —reap'er, *n.*

re·ap·por·tion (rē·ǎ-pôr'shŭn), *v.t.* to apportion again; specifically, to adjust (a legislature) for more nearly equalized representation of constituents. —re·ap·por'tion·ment, *n.*

rear (rir), *n.* 1. hind part or area; back. 2. the part of a military force farthest from the fighting zone. 3. [Informal], the buttocks: also rear end: *adj.* of or at the rear; *v.t.* 1. to raise; erect; put up. 2. to grow or breed (animals or plants). 3. to nurture to maturity: *v.i.* 1. to stand on the hind legs, as a horse. 2. to rise (*up*), as in anger. 3. to tower.

rear admiral, a naval officer next in rank above a captain and below a vice admiral.

rea·son (rē'zn), *n.* 1. ability to think. 2. right judgment; sense. 3. sanity. 4. a cause; motive; explanation; justification: *v.i.* 1. to use reason. 2. to think or speak in accordance with reason: *v.t.* 1. to think through or analyze in accordance with reason. 2. to argue, conclude, or infer. 3. to support by giving reasons for.

rea·son·a·ble (-ǎ-bl), *adj.* 1. able to reason. 2. using or conforming to reason; sensible. 3. open to reason; just. 4. balanced; not extreme. 5. not expensive. —rea'son·a·bly, *adv.*

re·as·sure (rē·ǎ-shoor'), *v.t.* -sured', -sur'ing, 1. to assure again. 2. to give confidence or new confidence to.

re·bate (rē'bāt), *n.* a return of part of an amount paid: *v.t.* (also ri-bāt'), -bat·ed,

-bat·ing, 1. to return (part of a payment). 2. to make a deduction from (a bill).

reb·el (reb'l), *n.* one that rebels; one in rebellion: *adj.* of rebels; rebellious.

re·bel (ri-bel'), *v.i.* -belled', -bel'ling, 1. to be in rebellion; be rebellious. 2. to experience a strong dislike; be repelled.

re·bel·lion (ri-bel'yŭn), *n.* resistance to or defiance of authority; specifically, armed resistance to one's government.

re·bel·lious ('yŭs), *adj.* 1. of, typical of, tending toward, or marked by rebellion. 2. resisting easy management or control.

re·birth (rē'bûrth), *n.* 1. a new or second birth. 2. a restoration to vigor.

re·bound (ri-bound'), *v.i. & v.t.* to bound or spring back, or make do so: *n.* (rē'bound), an act or instance of rebounding.

re·bo·zo (ri-bō'zō), *n., pl.* -zos, a long scarf worn as by Mexican women.

re·buff (ri-buf'), *n.* 1. a sharp rejection, as of proffered friendship. 2. a sharp setback: *v.t.* to subject to a rebuff.

re·buke (ri-būk'), *v.t.* -buked', -buk'ing, to reprimand or chide: *n.* a reprimand.

re·bus (rē'bŭs), *n.* an enigmatical representation of a word or phrase by pictured objects, numbers, etc.

re·but (ri-but'), *v.t.* -but'ted, -but'ting, to oppose or refute by argument or proof. —re·but'tal, *n.* —re·but'ter, *n.*

re·cal·ci·trant (ri-kal'si-trǎnt), *adj.* stubbornly contrary; obstinate; refractory. —re·cal'ci·trance, *n.*

re·call (ri-kôl'), *v.t.* 1. to call back. 2. to remember. 3. to revoke; withdraw: *n.* (also rē'kôl), 1. a recalling. 2. memory. 3. removal of an official from office by popular vote, or the right to do this.

re·cant (-kant'), *v.t.* to withdraw or retract; abjure. —re·can·ta'tion, *n.*

re·cap (ri-kap', rē'kap), *v.t.* -capped', -cap'ping, to put a new tread on (a worn pneumatic tire): *n.* (rē'kap), a recapped tire.

re·cap (rē'kap), *n.* recapitulation: *v.i. & v.t.* -capped, -cap·ping, to recapitulate.

re·ca·pit·u·late (rē·kǎ-pich'ŭ-lāt), *v.i. & v.t.* -lat·ed, -lat·ing, to go over (a discourse, argument, etc.) again, giving only the main points. —re·ca·pit·u·la'tion, *n.*

re·cede (ri-sēd'), *v.i.* -ced'ed, -ced'ing, 1. to fall back, as flood waters; retreat. 2. to diminish. 3. to slant back.

re·ceipt (ri-sēt'), *n.* 1. a receiving or being received; reception. 2. a written acknowledgment of something received. 3. *pl.* what is received or taken in, as cash for goods sold. 4. a recipe: old-fashioned term: *v.t.* 1. to mark (a bill) as paid. 2. to sign in acknowledgment of.

re·ceiv·a·ble (ri-sē'vǎ-bl), *adj.* 1. that can be received. 2. to be paid; due.

re·ceive (ri-sēv'), *v.t.* -ceived', -ceiv'ing, 1. to get or take (something given, sent, etc.). 2. to let come in; admit. 3. to undergo: *v.i.* to receive something.

re·ceiv·er (ri-sē'vēr), *n.* 1. one that receives. 2. a device to receive electrical signals sent and to reconvert them into the corresponding sound or image. 3. in *Law,* a person ap-

---

ò in dragon, ōō in crude, oo in wool, u in cup, ū in cure, ũ in turn, ŭ in focus, oi in boy, ou in house, th in thin, th in sheathe, g in get, j in joy, y in yet.

pointed by a court to have custody of property in litigation.

re·ceiv·er·ship (-ship), *n.* in *Law*, 1. the duties or office of a receiver. 2. the state of being in the custody of a receiver.

re·cen·cy (rē'sn-si), *n.* the condition or quality of being recent.

re·cen·sion (ri-sen'shŭn), *n.* a critical revision of the text of an author.

re·cent (rē'snt), *adj.* 1. just previous to the immediate present; existing, occurring, etc. not very long ago; not very far off in time. 2. formed, produced, built, etc. within the present period; contemporary; modern: *n.* [R-], the present epoch of the Cenozoic, marked by the extinction of giant mammals and by the spread of human culture.

re·cep·ta·cle (ri-sep'tă-kl), *n.* 1. a container; vessel. 2. a place or thing, as an electrical outlet, into which something is received. 3. in *Botany*, the enlarged upper end of the stalk of a flowering plant, where the flower parts grow; also, any of various cuplike or disclike structures supporting spores, sex organs, etc.

re·cep·tion (ri-sep'shŭn), *n.* 1. the act of receiving or condition of being received. 2. a festive social function centering about one or more persons being welcomed or specially honored. 3. the receiving of electrical signals being broadcast; also, the performance of a receiver device, as a tuner, in picking up and reconverting such signals.

re·cep·tion·ist (-ist), *n.* an employee assigned to welcoming and assisting clients and visitors, as in an office.

re·cep·tive (ri-sep'tiv), *adj.* 1. having the quality of receiving, especially with ease or tenacity. 2. open to ideas, suggestions, etc. —**re·cep·tiv'i·ty,** *n.*

re·cep·tor ('tĕr), *n.* one that receives; specifically, a nerve structure responding to stimuli and transmitting impulses to the brain.

re·cess (rē'ses, ri-ses'), *n.* 1. a temporary withdrawal from or remission of activity, business, study, etc. 2. an inlet, niche, alcove, etc.: also, in *Anatomy*, a cavity, indentation, etc. in an organ or part. 3. a secluded, inner, or secret place: *v.t.* (usually ri-ses'), 1. to put into a recess. 2. to make a recess in: *v.i.* to take a recess.

re·ces·sion (ri-sesh'ŭn), *n.* 1. a receding; falling back. 2. a going out, leaving, or withdrawal, as of clergy in procession from a service. 3. a receding part. 4. a temporary economic decline in a previously good period.

re·ces·sion·al (-l), *n.* a hymn, organ piece, etc. for use during a recession (sense 2).

re·ces·sive (ri-ses'iv), *adj.* receding.

re·cid·i·vism (ri-sid'i-vizm), *n.* repetition of undesirable behavior, or a tendency toward this, after presumed abandonment of such behavior; especially, a falling back repeatedly into misbehavior or crime. —**re·cid'i·vist,** *n. & adj.*

rec·i·pe (res'i-pi), *n.* 1. a statement of the way to prepare or make some food or drink, giving the ingredients, method of combination, cooking instructions, etc. 2. any similar

statement of the way to do, make, or effect something.

re·cip·i·ent (ri-sip'i-ĕnt), *n.* one that receives: *adj.* receiving.

re·cip·ro·cal (ri-sip'rŏ-kl), *adj.* 1. done, given, etc. in return. 2. mutual. 3. corresponding, but reversed or inverted. 4. complementary or interchangeable: *n.* 1. something reciprocal. 2. in *Mathematics*, a quantity which equals one when multiplied by a given quantity.

re·cip·ro·cate (-kāt), *v.t.* -**cat·ed**, -**cat·ing**, 1. to give and receive, do, etc. reciprocally. 2. to give, do, etc. in return. 3. to make move alternately back and forth: *v.i.* 1. to give, do, etc. in response to a corresponding action. 2. to move alternately back and forth. —**re·cip·ro·ca'tion,** *n.* —**re·cip'ro·ca·tor,** *n.*

rec·i·proc·i·ty (res·i-pros'i-ti), *n.* 1. reciprocal action, condition, or relationship. 2. mutual exchange of favors or privileges, as reduction of tariffs between two countries.

re·cit·al (ri-sit'l), *n.* 1. recitation or narration. 2. what is recited or narrated; account, story, etc. 3. a detailed relating of facts, events, etc. 4. a live presentation, before an audience, of music performed by an individual or group, as by a pianist or string ensemble; also, a similar presentation of dancing.

rec·i·ta·tion (res·i-tā'shŭn), *n.* 1. a reciting; recital. 2. oral delivery, before an audience, of a memorized piece of verse or prose; also, the piece delivered. 3. oral answering by a pupil or pupils in class to questions on material studied; also, a particular class period or time for this.

rec·i·ta·tive (res·i-tă-tēv'), *n.* 1. in an opera or other sung musical work, a line or lines written to be delivered in a way closer to rhetorical speaking than to song. 2. such delivery. 3. any musical passage, part, or work performed or to be performed with such delivery or in a manner suggestive of such delivery.

re·cite (ri-sit'), *v.t.* -**cit·ed**, -**cit·ing**, 1. to repeat aloud from or as if from memory, as in doing a recitation. 2. to relate in detail. 3. to list (reasons, objections, etc.) in detail; enumerate: *v.i.* to recite something.

reck·less (rek'lis), *adj.* careless or heedless, especially to an extreme extent; rash.

reck·on (rek'ŏn), *v.t.* 1. to count, compute, or figure; calculate. 2. to consider or regard as being. 3. to judge; estimate. 4. [Informal], to suppose: *v.i.* 1. to count or figure up something. 2. to take something indicated into account (with *with*). 3. [Informal], to rely (*on* something indicated). 4. [Informal], to suppose.

reck·on·ing (-ing), *n.* 1. the act of one that reckons. 2. a reasoned guess about the future. 3. a bill or account; also, its settlement. 4. an assigning of rewards or penalties. 5. in *nautical usage*, calculation of a ship's position.

re·claim (ri-klām'), *v.t.* 1. to bring back to ways of behavior viewed as right; save or reform. 2. to make (wasteland, desert, etc.) productive or habitable. 3. to get or salvage (useful material) from waste products: *n.* a reclaiming or being reclaimed; reclamation.

rec·la·ma·tion (rek-lá-mã'shŭn), *n.* the act of reclaiming, or the condition or process of being reclaimed.

re·cline (ri-klīn'), *v.i. & v.t.* -clined', -clin'ing, to lean or lie back or down, or to cause to do this.

rec·luse (rek'lōōs, ri-klōōs'), *n.* one living in seclusion; hermit: *adj.* secluded.

rec·og·ni·tion (rek-ŏg-nish'ŭn), *n.* the act of recognizing or state of being recognized.

rec·og·niz·a·ble (-nī'zå-bl), *adj.* capable of being recognized. —**rec·og·niz'a·bly**, *adv.*

re·cog·ni·zance (ri-kog'ni-zăns, -kon'i-), *n.* a legal obligation entered into before a magistrate or court to do or abstain from doing some particular act.

rec·og·nize (rek'ŏg-nīz), *v.t.* -nized, -niz·ing, 1. to perceive as already known. 2. to identify. 3. to acknowledge as existing, real, valid, etc. 4. to signal the right of to speak, as in a meeting. —**rec'og·niz·er**, *n.*

re·coil (ri-koil'), *v.i.* 1. to draw back suddenly; jump back or retreat precipitately; be driven suddenly backward. 2. to return abruptly and with force to the original position, as a released spring. 3. to move back swiftly and hard, as a gun upon being fired: *n.* (also rē'koil), the act of recoiling.

rec·ol·lect (rek-ŏ-lekt') *v.t & v.i.* to remember; recall, especially with effort.

rec·ol·lec·tion (-lek'shŭn), *n.* 1. remembrance; memory. 2. composure.

rec·om·mend (rek-ŏ-mend'), *v.t.* 1. to commit to another; entrust. 2. to suggest as being suitable, desirable, well-qualified, etc.; commend. 3. to make acceptable or desirable. 4. to advise. —**rec·om·mend'a·to·ry**, *adj.*

rec·om·men·da·tion (-měn-dā'shŭn), *n.* 1. a recommending. 2. a recommendatory suggestion. 3. a feature or quality recommending something. 4. a commendatory letter, note, remark, etc.

rec·om·pense (rek'ŏm-pens), *n.* an equivalent given or done in return; remuneration or compensation: *v.t.* -pensed, -pens·ing, to remunerate or compensate.

rec·on·cil·a·ble (rek-ŏn-sil'å-bl), *adj.* capable of being reconciled.

rec·on·cile (rek'ŏn-sīl), *v.t.* -ciled, -cil·ing, 1. to restore to friendliness. 2. to make favorable or receptive. 3. to smooth over or bring into agreement; adjust or harmonize. 4. to bring into acceptance of or resignation to.

rec·on·cil·i·a·tion (rek-ŏn-sil-i-ā'shŭn), *n.* a reconciling or being reconciled: also **rec·on·cile'ment** (-sīl'měnt). —**rec·on·cil'i·a·to·ry** (-sil'i-å-tôr-i), *adj.*

rec·on·dite (rek'ŏn-dīt), *adj.* 1. abstruse; deep. 2. secret; hidden; obscure.

re·con·di·tion (rē-kŏn-dish'ŭn), *v.t.* to put back in good condition as by repairing.

re·con·nais·sance (ri-kon'ĭ-sáns), *n.* the act of reconnoitering; preliminary survey.

rec·on·noi·ter (rē-kŏ-noit'ĕr, rek-ŏ-), *v.t. & v.i.* to make a preliminary exploration, survey, or examination (of), especially for military purposes. —**rec·on·noi'ter·er**, *n.*

rec·on·noi·tre (rē-kŏ-noit'ĕr, rek-ŏ-), *v.t. & v.i.*

-tred ('tĕrd), -tring, chiefly British form for reconnoiter. —**rec·on·noi'trer** ('trēr), *n.*

re·con·sti·tute (rē-kon'sti-tōōt), *v.t.* -tut·ed, -tut·ing, to constitute once more; reconstruct, reorganize, etc.; specifically, to restore (a dehydrated or condensed substance) to full liquid form by the addition of water.

re·con·struct (rē-kŏn-strukt'), *v.t.* 1. to construct again; rebuild. 2. to construct the original or complete form of by combining actual and hypothetical elements.

re·con·struc·tion (-struk'shŭn), *n.* 1. the act of reconstructing or the state of being reconstructed. 2. something reconstructed. 3. [R-], reestablishment (1867-1877) back into the Union, after the U.S. Civil War (1861-1865), of Southern States that had seceded.

re·cord (ri-kôrd'), *v.t.* 1. to register for reading or reference, as by putting into writing. 2. to indicate or give evidence of by registering as on a scale. 3. to register (music, speech, a performing artist or group, etc.) as on a phonograph disc or magnetic tape allowing subsequent reproduction: *v.i.* 1. to record something. 2. to undergo the process of being recorded: *n.* (rek'ĕrd), 1. the state of being recorded. 2. something recorded. 3. a writing, report, etc. recording something. 4. anything, as a monument, serving as witness to something. 5. the known or recorded background of someone or something. 6. a top level of achievement, production, etc. 7. something carrying a recording as of music; especially, a thin, flat, grooved disc for use on a record player: *adj.* (rek'ĕrd), establishing a record (sense 6).

re·cord·er (ri-kôr'dĕr), *n.* 1. one that records, especially officially. 2. a device for recording sound or visual images and, typically, for playing recordings, as a tape recorder. 3. an early kind of flute held vertically for playing.

re·cord·ing ('ding), *n.* 1. something recorded, as on magnetic tape or on a phonograph disc. 2. a tape, disc, etc. carrying this.

record player, a device, especially an electric or electronic one, to play phonograph records.

re·count (ri-kount'), *v.t.* to relate in detail.

re·count (rē-kount'), *v.t.* to count again: *n.* (rē'kount), an additional count, as of votes: also written recount.

re·coup (ri-kōōp'), *v.t.* 1. to make up for (a loss); make good; redeem. 2. to get back again (one's health, fortune, etc.); recover. 3. to reimburse; indemnify.

re·course (rē'kôrs, ri-kôrs'), *n.* 1. a going to someone or something as for help or protection. 2. the person or thing so sought out.

re·cov·er (ri-kuv'ĕr), *v.t.* 1. to get back into one's possession; regain; retrieve. 2. to make good (a loss); redeem; recoup. 3. to obtain as compensation. 4. to get (oneself) back into control, balance, etc.; also, in *Sports*, to get back control over or possession of (a ball, puck, etc.). 5. to get back or out to a usable or improved condition; reclaim, as flooded land, valuable material from waste products, etc.: *v.i.* 1. to become healthy, composed, balanced, etc. again. 2. in *Sports*, to recover a ball, puck, etc.

ŏ in dragon, ōō in crude, oo in wool, u in cup, ū in cure, ŭ in turn, ů in focus, oi in boy, ou in house, th in thin, *th* in sheathe, g in get, j in joy, y in yet.

re·cov·er·y (-ĭ), *n.*, *pl.* **-er·ies,** the act of recovering; regaining of health, getting back something lost, return to a condition of control, composure, or readiness, etc.

rec·re·ant (rĕk'rĭ-ănt), *adj.* 1. cowardly. 2. traitorous: *n.* one that is recreant.

rec·re·ate (rĕk'rĭ-āt), *v.t.* **-at·ed, -at·ing,** to refresh or reinvigorate physically or mentally through play, amusement, or any form of relaxation: *v.i.* to take part in recreation.

rec·re·a·tion (rĕk-rĭ-ā'shŭn), *n.* 1. the act of recreating. 2. something conducive to this. **—rec·re·a'tion·al, rec're·a·tive,** *adj.*

re·crim·i·nate (rĭ-krĭm'ĭ-nāt), *v.i.* **-nat·ed, -nat·ing,** to counter an accusation by making an accusation in return. **—re·crim·i·na'tion,** *n.* **—re·crim'i·na·to·ry** (-nȧ-tōr-ĭ), *adj.*

re·cru·desce (rē-krōō-dĕs'), *v.i.* **-desced', -desc'-ing,** to break out again after being inactive. **—re·cru·des'cence,** *n.*

re·cru·des·cent ('nt), *adj.* recrudescing.

re·cruit (rĭ-krōōt'), *v.t.* 1. to build up, strengthen, or form (a military group or other group) by getting or adding members. 2. to get (members) for a military group or other group: *v.i.* to enlist members: *n.* a newly enlisted member. **—re·cruit'ment,** *n.*

rec·tal (rĕk'tl), *adj.* of the rectum.

rec·tan·gle (rĕk'tăng-gl), *n.* a four-sided plane figure with four right angles. **—rec·tan·gu·lar** (rĕk-tăng'gyu̇-lēr), *adj.*

rec·ti·fi·er (rĕk'tĭ-fī-ēr), *n.* 1. one that rectifies. 2. a device, as a vacuum tube, converting alternating current to direct current.

rec·ti·fy (rĕk'tĭ-fī), *v.t.* **-fied, -fy·ing,** 1. to make or put right; correct, as by amending or adjusting. 2. to convert (alternating current) to direct current. 3. in *Chemistry,* to refine or purify (a liquid) by distillation. 4. in *Mathematics,* to determine the length of a (curve). **—rec·ti·fi'a·ble,** *adj.* **—rec·ti·fi·ca'tion,** *n.*

rec·ti·lin·e·ar (rĕk-tĭ-lĭn'ĭ-ēr), *adj.* 1. moving in, or forming, a straight line. 2. formed or bounded by straight lines. 3. characterized by straight lines. Also **rec·ti·lin'e·al.**

rec·ti·tude (rĕk'tĭ-tōōd, -tūd), *n.* rightness or integrity of principles or behavior.

rec·to (rĕk'tō), *n.*, *pl.* **-tos,** a right-hand page of a book or the front side of a leaf.

rec·tor (rĕk'tēr), *n.* 1. in certain churches, a clergyman heading a parish. 2. one heading certain schools.

rec·to·ry (rĕk'tēr-ĭ), *n.*, *pl.* **-ries,** 1. a rector's house. 2. in a Roman Catholic parish, the house where the pastor lives.

rec·tum (rĕk'tŭm), *n.*, *pl.* **-tums, -ta** ('tȧ), the final segment of the large intestine.

rec·tus ('tŭs), *n.*, *pl.* **rec'ti** ('tī). any one of various straight muscles, as of the thigh.

re·cum·bent (rĭ-kŭm'bĕnt), *adj.* lying down or reclining. **—re·cum'ben·cy,** *n.*

re·cu·per·ate (ĭ-kōō'pē-rāt, -kū'-), *v.t. & v.i.* **-at·ed, -at·ing,** to get back (one's health, energy, losses, etc.); recover. **—re·cu·per·a'-tion,** *n.* **—re·cu'per·a·tive** ('pē-rāt-ĭv, 'pēr-ȧ-tĭv), *adj.*

re·cur (rĭ-kūr'), *v.i.* **-curred', -cur'ring,** 1. to have recourse. 2. to go or come back in speech or thought. 3. to return or keep returning, as a subject of discussion or a problem. 4. to happen again or at intervals. **—re·cur'rence,** *n.* **—re·cur'rent,** *adj.*

re·curved (rĭ-kûrvd'), *adj.* curved back or in.

rec·u·sant (rĕk'yōō-zănt, rĭ-kū'znt), *adj.* refusing compliance with or conformity to some established authority, practice, etc.; dissenting: *n.* a recusant individual. **—rec'u·san·cy,** *n.*

re·cy·cle (rĭ-sī'kl), *v.t.* **-cled, -cling,** 1. to put through a cycle again. 2. to use (a single supply of water) repeatedly for different purposes. 3. to reprocess (used material, as paper) into a form for fresh use.

red (rĕd), *n.* 1. a primary color ranging from the hue of blood to pale rose or pink. 2. a pigment producing this color. 3. something of this color. 4. [often R-], a political radical; specifically, a communist. 5. [often R-], *pl.* North American Indians: *adj.* **red'der, red'dest,** 1. of the color red. 2. [R-], politically radical; specifically, communist.

re·dact (rĭ-dăkt'), *v.t.* 1. to draft or compose (an edict, proclamation, etc.). 2. to edit or revise. **—re·dac'tion,** *n.* **—re·dac'tor,** *n.*

red·bird (rĕd'bûrd), *n.* any one of several chiefly red-colored birds, as the cardinal.

red blood corpuscle, a corpuscle containing hemoglobin and carrying oxygen to the body tissues: also **red blood cell, red corpuscle.**

red-blood·ed ('blŭd'ĭd), *adj.* vigorous, strong, high-spirited, etc.

red·breast ('brĕst), *n.* any one of several birds with a reddish breast, as the robin.

red·cap ('kăp), *n.* one whose work is carrying luggage, as at a railroad station; porter.

red carpet, a very ceremonious or otherwise impressive reception or welcome (with *the*).

red cedar, 1. any one of various junipers with red wood and bluish, berrylike fruit, including a juniper of eastern North America (**eastern red cedar**) noted for its especially fragrant wood. 2. the wood of such a juniper.

red·coat ('kōt), *n.* [Informal], a British soldier, especially during the American Revolution.

Red Cross, an international society aiding victims of war or other calamity.

red deer, 1. a common American deer with a white-spotted red coat in summer. 2. a mooselike deer native to Europe and Asia.

red·den (rĕd'n), *v.t. & v.i.* to turn red.

red·dish (rĕd'ĭsh), *adj.* somewhat red.

re·deem (rĭ-dēm'), *v.t.* 1. to get back, set free, or rescue. specifically by making some kind of payment; release or deliver, as by payment of ransom. often, to deliver from sin and its consequences, as by a sacrifice made for the sinner. 2. to pay off (a mortgage or note). 3. to convert (paper money) into cash. 4. to convert, as stocks, into cash. 5. to turn in (trading stamps or coupons) for something offered in exchange. 6. to do (something promised or pledged). 7. to make up for; compensate or atone for. 8. to get (oneself) back into favor by atonement. 9. to make good use of, as time; make worthwhile. **—re·deem'er,** *n.*

re·demp·tion (rĭ-dĕmp'shŭn), *n.* 1. the act of

redeeming or the state of being redeemed.
2. something that redeems.

re-demp-tive ('tiv), *adj.* 1. of redemption. 2. serving to redeem. Also **re-demp'to-ry.**

re-de-vel-op (rē-di-vel'ŏp), *v.t.* 1. to develop again. 2. to restore (as an impoverished or run-down area) to a better or good condition.

red-hand-ed (red'han'did), *adv. & adj.* in the act of wrongdoing or just at its completion.

red-head ('hed), *n.* one with a head of red hair. **—red'head-ed,** *adj.*

red herring, 1. a smoked herring. 2. something intended to divert attention from the real issue.

red-hot ('hot'), *adj.* 1. very hot; specifically, so hot as to glow red. 2. burning with ardor; passionate; torrid. 3. strongly aroused; driven by excitement; keyed-up. 4. extremely vigorous, powerful, etc.; driving. 5. acclaimed or supported with wild enthusiasm. 6. that has just happened, just been learned, just been made available, etc. and is full of excitement; excitingly fresh or new.

re-dis-trict (ri-dis'trikt), *v.t.* to make a fresh division of into districts, especially so as to reapportion electoral representatives.

red-let-ter (red'let'ẽr), *adj.* designating an outstandingly happy or memorable day or event.

red-lin-ing (red-lī'ning), *n.* the refusal by some lending institutions or insurance companies to issue mortgage loans or insurance on property in certain neighborhoods regarded by them as deteriorating.

re-do (rē-dōō'), *v.t.* **-did', -done', -do'ing,** 1. to do again. 2. to redecorate.

red-o-lent (red'l-ĕnt), *adj.* 1. emitting a sweet smell; fragrant. 2. smelling or suggestive (*of* something specified). **—red'o-lence,** *n.*

re-dou-ble (ri-dub'l), *v.t.* **-bled, -bling,** 1. to double again. 2. to make twice as much. 3. to increase greatly; intensify: *v.i.* 1. to become redoubled. 2. in *Bridge,* to double a bid already doubled by an opponent.

re-doubt (ri-dout'), *n.* 1. a small, usually additional fortification, as a breastwork. 2. a stronghold.

re-doubt-a-ble (ri-dout'â-bl), *adj.* formidable.

re-dound (ri-dound'), *v.i.* 1. to conduce; accrue. 2. to flow back in its effect; return.

red pepper, 1. a plant cultivated in many varieties and producing a mild or pungent red fruit containing many seeds, the fruit and seeds being variously used as a flavoring, condiment, etc. 2. the fruit or seeds, often ground.

re-dress (ri-dres'), *v.t.* to rectify or make up for (evils, wrongs, etc.): *n.* (usually rē'dres), the act of redressing, or the rectification made.

red snapper, a red-colored, deep-water food fish of the Gulf of Mexico and the near Atlantic.

red spider, any one of several kinds of tiny, red mite, destructive to many plants.

red squirrel, a small, reddish North American tree squirrel.

red-start (red'stärt), *n.* 1. a European warbler with a reddish tail. 2. an American warbler

with orange and black feathers on the back of the male.

red tape, 1. tape commonly used for tying official papers. 2. a strict observance of rules and regulations that causes delay.

red tide, sea water discolored by red algae poisonous to marine life.

re-duce (ri-dōōs'), *v.t.* **-duced', -duc'ing,** 1. to bring into a lower state; degrade. 2. to diminish; lessen in size, weight, amount, etc. 3. to conquer. 4. to change the form of. 5. in *Mathematics,* to change in denomination but not in value: *v.i.* to lose weight, as by dieting. **—re-duc'er,** *n.* **—re-duc'i-ble,** *adj.*

re-duc-tion (ri-duk'shŭn), *n.* 1. the act of reducing. 2. the state of being reduced. 3. something made or brought about by reducing. 4. the amount by which something is reduced.

re-duc-tive ('tiv), *adj.* 1. of reduction. 2. tending to reduce. **—re-duc'tive-ly,** *adv.*

re-dun-dant (ri-dun'dånt), *adj.* 1. superfluous; in excess of what is needed. 2. wordy. 3. not necessary to the meaning: said of words or affixes. **—re-dun'dan-cy,** *n.*

re-du-pli-cate (ri-dōō'pli-kāt), *v.t.* **-cat-ed, -cat-ing,** 1. to double again; repeat. 2. to repeat (a sound or syllable) in forming (a word). **—re-du-pli-ca'tion,** *n.*

red-winged blackbird ('wingd), a North American blackbird: the male has a red patch on each wing: also **redwing blackbird.**

red-wood ('wood), *n.* 1. a very large evergreen tree of the Pacific coast. 2. the soft, durable, reddish wood of this tree.

re-ech-o, re-ech-o (rē-ek'ō), *v.t. & v.i.* **-ech'oed, -ech'o-ing,** 1. to echo back or again. 2. to give back an echo: *n., pl.* **-ech'oes,** the echo of an echo.

reed (rēd), *n.* 1. a large, coarse grass with jointed, hollow stems. 2. a musical pipe made from a hollow stem. 3. *a)* a small piece of reed or metal in the mouthpiece of a musical instrument, that is vibrated by the breath; *b)* a similar device in some organs. 4. the comb-shaped part of a loom that guides threads between the separated threads of the warp. 5. [Poetic], an arrow. **—reed'y,** *adj.* **reed'i-er, reed'i-est.**

reed-bird ('bŭrd), *n.* [Dialectal], same as **bobolink.**

reed organ, an organ in which the musical tones are produced by vibrating metal reeds.

reef (rēf), *n.* 1. that part of a sail which can be reduced by being drawn in by small ropes running in eyelet holes. 2. the act of reefing. 3. a ridge of rock, sand, or coral at or near the surface of the water: *v.t.* to reduce the size of (a sail) by means of reefs.

reef-er ('ẽr), *n.* 1. one who reefs. 2. a closefitting, short, double-breasted jacket. 3. [Slang], a marijuana cigarette.

reek (rēk), *n.* 1. fume; vapor. 2. a strong smell, usually disagreeable: *v.i.* to have a strong, disagreeable smell. **—reek'y,** *adj.*

reel (rēl), *n.* 1. a spool or cylinder on which wire, yarn, film, etc. is wound. 2. such a spool on the handle of a fishing rod, for winding or letting out the line. 3. the quan-

---

ô in dra*g*on, ōō in cr*u*de, oo in w*oo*l, u in c*u*p, ū in c*u*re, û in t*u*rn, ù in f*o*cus, oi in b*o*y, ou in h*ou*se, th in *th*in, *th* in shea*th*e, g in *g*et, j in *j*oy, y in *y*et.

tity of film, tape, etc. usually wound upon one reel. **4.** in a lawn mower, a horizontal bar set with spiral blades. **5.** a lively dance: *v.i.* to wind on a reel: *v.i.* 1. to stagger. 2. to whirl. 3. to recoil; fall back. 4. to feel dizzy.

re-en-force, re-en-force (rē-in-fôrs'), *v.t.* -forced', -forc'ing, same as **reinforce.**

re-en-try, re-en-try (rē-en'tri), *n., pl.* -tries, the act of entering again, as a spacecraft returning to the earth's atmosphere.

reeve (rēv), *n.* 1. in England, a bailiff or steward. 2. in Canada, the head of a town council. 3. the female of the ruff (sandpiper): *v.t.* reeved or rove, rove or rov'en, reev'ing, to pass (a rope) through, in, or around something, as a block or pulley on shipboard.

re-ex-am-ine, re-ex-am-ine (rē-ig-zam'in), *v.t.* -ined, -in-ing, 1. to examine again. 2. in *Law*, to question (one's own witness) again in a trial. —**re-ex-am-i-na'tion, re-ex-am-i-na'tion,** *n.*

ref (ref), *n. & v.t. & v.i.* [Informal], same as **referee.**

re-fec-tion (ri-fek'shun), *n.* a light repast.

re-fec-to-ry ('tēr-i), *n., pl.* -ries, an eating room or hall, as in a monastery.

re-fer (ri-fûr'), *v.t.* -ferred', -fer'ring, 1. to submit (a question, quarrel, etc.) to another person for answer or settlement. 2. to send (*to* someone or some thing) for information, help, etc.: *v.i.* 1. to allude (*to*). 2. to relate (*to*). 3. to turn (*to*). —**ref-er-a-ble** (ref'ēr-a-bl, ri-fûr'-),* adj.*

ref-er-ee (ref-ē-rē'), *n.* 1. one to whom something is referred for decision. 2. a sports official who enforces the rules. 3. in *Law*, one appointed by a court to study and report on a matter: *v.t. & v.i.* -eed', -ee'ing, to act as a referee (in).

ref-er-ence (ref'ēr-ēns), *n.* 1. the act of referring. 2. allusion; mention. 3. a direction to some source of information. 4. such a source. 5. a person who can give information or testimony as to one's ability, character, etc. 6. a testimony, usually written, from such a person.

ref-er-en-dum (ref-ē-ren'dum), *n., pl.* -dums or -da ('dä), 1. the referring of a bill or act of the legislature to the people for direct vote. 2. the right of the people to vote directly on such measures.

ref-er-en-tial ('shul), *adj.* 1. referring to something else. 2. used for reference. —**ref-er-en'tial-ly,** *adv.*

re-fer-ral (ri-fûr'al), *n.* 1. the act of referring. 2. the state of being referred. 3. a person who is referred or directed to another person or to an organization, etc.

re-fill (rē-fil'), *v.t. & v.i.* to fill again: *n.* (rē'fil), 1. a filling again of a prescription for medicine. 2. a supply or part for replenishing something used up. —**re-fill'a-ble,** *adj.*

re-fi-nance (rē-fi-nans', rē-fī'nans), *v.t.* -nanced', -nanc'ing, to grant or get a new loan or more capital for.

re-fine (ri-fin'), *v.t. & v.i.* -fined', -fin'ing, 1. to separate or be separated from impurities; clear or be cleared of dross. 2. to make or

become more polished; improve. —**re-fin'er,** *n.*

re-fined (-find'), *adj.* 1. freed from impurities. 2. cultivated; cultured. 3. subtle; more accurate or precise.

re-fine-ment (-fin'mēnt), *n.* 1. the act of refining. 2. the state of being refined. 3. an improvement. 4. elegance; polish, fineness of manners, etc. 5. a fine distinction.

re-fin-er-y (ri-fīn'ēr-i), *n., pl.* -er-ies, an establishment for refining or purifying raw materials such as oil, sugar, etc.

re-fin-ish (rē-fin'ish), *v.t.* to put a new surface on (wood, metal, etc.).

re-fit (rē-fit'), *v.t. & v.i.* -fit'ted, -fit'ting, to make or become fit for use again by replacing equipment, renewing supplies, etc.

re-flect (ri-flekt'), *v.t.* 1. to throw back, especially light, heat, or sound, after striking some surface. 2. to give back an image of. 3. to bring back as a consequence of: *v.i.* 1. to throw back light, heat, or sound. 2. to give back an image. 3. to think deeply; meditate. 4. to cast reproach or censure (*on* or *upon*).

re-flec-tion (ri-flek'shun), *n.* 1. the act of reflecting. 2. the state of being reflected. 3. that which is reflected. 4. an image, as in a mirror. 5. serious thought; contemplation. 6. censure; discredit. 7. a thought or conclusion. British spelling **re-flex'ion.**

re-flec-tive ('tiv), *adj.* 1. reflecting. 2. cast by reflection. 3. given to contemplation. —**re-flec'tive-ly,** *adv.* —**re-flec'tive-ness,** *n.*

re-flec-tor ('tēr), *n.* 1. a person or thing that reflects. 2. an object or surface, especially a highly polished surface, that reflects light, heat, or sound.

re-flex (rē'fleks), *adj.* 1. bent or turned back. 2. reflected back. 3. denoting or of an involuntary action, as sneezing, in which the motor nerves act in response to a stimulus from an impression made on the sensory nerves: *n.* 1. a reflex action. 2. the ability to react quickly: used in the plural. 3. a reflected image. —**re'flex-ly,** *adv.*

re-flex-ive (ri-flek'siv), *adj.* 1. denoting a verb whose subject and direct object refer to the same thing or person. 2. denoting a pronoun used as the object of a reflexive verb: *n.* a reflexive verb or pronoun. —**re-flex'ive-ly,** *adv.*

ref-lu-ent (ref'loo-wēnt), *adj.* flowing back; ebbing, as the tide. —**ref'lu-ence,** *n.*

re-flux (rē'fluks), *n.* a flowing back.

re-for-est (rē-fôr'ist), *v.t. & v.i.* to plant young trees in (a forest area from which the trees have been cut, burned, etc.). —**re-for-est-a'-tion,** *n.*

re-form (ri-fôrm'), *v.t.* 1. to make better by removing faults; correct; amend. 2. to improve by stopping abuses, etc. 3. to persuade (a person) to behave better: *v.i.* to give up misconduct; become better in behavior: *n.* a change for the better; correction; improvement.

re-form (rē-fôrm'), *v.t. & v.i.* to form again or anew.

ref-or-ma-tion (ref-ēr-mā'shun), *n.* 1. the act of reforming. 2. the state of being reformed. 3.

[R-], the great religious movement of the 16th century which resulted in the establishment of the Protestant churches.

re·form·a·tive (ri-fôr′mă-tiv), *adj.* reforming or tending to reform.

re·form·a·to·ry (ri-fôr′mă-tôr-i), *adj.* tending to or intended to reform: *n., pl.* -ries, an institution for the detention and reformation of young offenders against the law.

re·formed (ri-fôrmd′), *adj.* 1. improved, corrected, amended, etc. 2. [R-], denoting certain Protestant churches, especially Calvinist as distinguished from Lutheran.

re·form·er (-fôr′mĕr), *n.* one who advocates or works toward reform, especially social or political reform.

re·fract (ri-frakt′), *v.t.* to subject (rays or waves of light, sound, heat, etc.) to refraction.

re·fract·ing (′ing), *adj.* having the power to change the direction of a ray or wave of light, heat, or sound.

re·frac·tion (ri-frak′shŭn), *n.* the change in direction which a ray or wave of light, heat, or sound assumes when passing from one medium into another.

re·frac·to·ry (ri-frak′tĕr-i), *adj.* 1. sullen; obstinate; hard to manage or control. 2. resisting treatment, as a disease. —**re·frac′to·ri·ly**, *adv.* —**re·frac′to·ri·ness**, *n.*

re·frain (ri-frān′), *v.i.* to forbear; keep oneself (*from* some action): *n.* 1. a verse repeated at the end of each stanza of a song. 2. the music for this.

re·fran·gi·ble (ri-fran′ji-bl), *adj.* capable of being refracted, as light rays. —**re·fran·gi·bil′i·ty**, *n.*

re·fresh (ri-fresh′), *v.t.* 1. to revive after fatigue or being overheated, as by food, drink, sleep, etc. 2. to make fresh by cooling, wetting, etc. 3. to stimulate (the memory). 4. to renew supplies for: *v.i.* to become fresh again. —**re·fresh′er**, *n.*

re·fresh·ing (′ing), *adj.* invigorating; stimulating.

re·fresh·ment (′mĕnt), *n.* 1. the act of refreshing. 2. the state of being refreshed. 3. that which refreshes. 4. *pl.* food or drink; usually, a light meal.

re·frig·er·ant (ri-frij′ĕr-ănt), *adj.* cooling or freezing something: *n.* 1. a medicine used to reduce fever. 2. a substance used in refrigeration; specifically, a liquid used in mechanical refrigeration.

re·frig·er·ate (ri-frij′ĕ-rāt), *v.t.* -at·ed, -at·ing, to cool, or keep cool, as for preserving. —**re·frig·er·a′tion**, *n.*

re·frig·er·a·tor (-rāt-ĕr), *n.* a room, box, cabinet, electrical appliance, etc. in which food, drink, etc. is kept cool.

re·fu·el (rē-fū′ĕl, -fūl′), *v.t.* -fu·eled or -fu·elled, -fu·el·ing or -fu·el·ling, to supply again with fuel: *v.i.* to take on a new supply of fuel.

ref·uge (ref′ŭj), *n.* 1. protection from danger or distress. 2. a shelter; retreat; asylum. 3. a person or thing that gives comfort, help, etc.

ref·u·gee (ref-yoo-jē′), *n.* one who flees for refuge, especially to a foreign country.

re·ful·gent (ri-ful′jĕnt), *adj.* brilliant; splendid; glowing. —**re·ful′gence**, *n.*

re·fund (ri-fund′), *v.t. & v.i.* to give back or pay back (money, etc.); repay: *n.* (rē′fund), 1. the act of paying back. 2. the amount paid back. —**re·fund′a·ble**, *adj.*

re·fur·bish (ri-fûr′bish), *v.t.* to brighten or polish up again; renovate. —**re·fur′bish·ment**, *n.*

re·fus·al (ri-fū′zl), *n.* 1. the act of refusing. 2. the right to accept or refuse something; option.

re·fuse (ri-fūz′), *v.t. & v.i.* -fused′, -fus′ing, 1. to deny or reject, as a demand or request. 2. to decline (*to* do something): *n.* (ref′ūs, ′ūz), waste; trash; rubbish: *adj.* (ref′ūs, ′ūz), thrown away as worthless.

re·fute (ri-fūt′), *v.t.* -fut′ed, -fut′ing, to prove to be false or erroneous. —**ref·u·ta·tion** (ref-yŭ-tā′shŭn), *n.* —**re·fut′er**, *n.*

re·gain (ri-gān′), *v.t.* 1. to recover possession of; get back. 2. to succeed in reaching again; get back to.

re·gal (rē′găl), *adj.* 1. of or pertaining to a king; royal. 2. fit for a king; magnificent, splendid, etc. —**re′gal·ly**, *adv.*

re·gale (ri-gāl′), *v.t.* -galed′, -gal′ing, 1. to entertain by providing a feast. 2. to delight or entertain as with amusement. —**re·gale′ment**, *n.* —**re·gal′er**, *n.*

re·ga·li·a (ri-gāl′yă, -gā′li-ă), *n.pl.* 1. the emblems and insignia of royalty, as the crown, scepter, etc. 2. royal rights or prerogatives. 3. decorations of a society or office. 4. finery.

re·gard (ri-gärd′), *v.t.* 1. to observe attentively. 2. to heed; consider. 3. to think highly of; esteem; respect. 4. to concern; relate to: *n.* 1. a gaze; look. 2. consideration; concern. 3. respect; esteem. 4. reference; relation. 5. *pl.* good wishes.

re·gard·ant (′nt), *adj.* in *Heraldry*, looking backward, with the head in profile.

re·gard·ful (′fŭl), *adj.* 1. taking notice; observant (often with *of*). 2. respectful; considerate. —**re·gard′ful·ly**, *adv.*

re·gard·ing (′ing), *prep.* concerning.

re·gard·less (′lis), *adj.* having no regard for; heedless; negligent: *adv.* [*Informal*], having no regard for warnings, objections, etc.; anyway. —**re·gard′less·ly**, *adv.*

re·gat·ta (ri-găt′ă), *n.* 1. sailing or rowing race. 2. a series of such races.

re·ge·la·tion (rē-jĕ-lā′shŭn), *n.* a freezing or refreezing together of pieces of ice.

re·gen·cy (rē′jĕn-si), *n., pl.* -cies, 1. the office or jurisdiction of a regent. 2. a group of persons serving as regents.

re·gen·er·ate (ri-jen′ĕr-āt), *v.t.* -at·ed, -at·ing, 1. to cause to be born again spiritually. 2. to produce or form anew. 3. to make over completely. 4. in *Biology*, to grow (a new part to replace a lost one): *adj.* (′ĕr-it), renewed; reformed; restored. —**re·gen′er·a·cy**, *n.* —**re·gen′er·ate·ly**, *adv.*

re·gen·er·a·tion (ri-jen-ĕ-rā′shŭn), *n.* 1. the act of regenerating. 2. the state of being regenerated. 3. the formation of new tissue to replace that which has been lost, as the claw of a lobster.

re·gen·er·a·tive (ri-jen′ĕ-rāt-iv), *adj.* 1.

regenerating. 2. characterized by regeneration. —re·gen′er·a·tive·ly, adv.

re·gen·er·a·tor ('ĕ-rāt-ĕr), n. a mechanical device in engines, furnaces, etc., used to heat incoming air or gas by exposure to the heat of exhaust gases.

re·gent (rē′jĕnt), adj. acting in place of a king or ruler: n. 1. one who governs in the absence, minority, disability, etc. of a sovereign. 2. a member of a governing board of a university. —re′gent·ship, n.

reg·i·cide (rej′i-sīd), n. 1. the killing of a king. 2. the killer of a king. —reg·i·ci′dal, adj.

re·gime, ré·gime (rē·zhēm′, rā-), n. 1. a mode of government or rule. 2. a political system. 3. a social system. 4. same as regimen.

reg·i·men (rej′i-mĕn), n. a systematic regulation of diet and exercise for good health.

reg·i·ment (rej′i-mĕnt), n. a military unit of ground forces consisting of two or more battalions: no longer a tactical unit in the U.S. Army: v.t. (-ment), 1. to form into an organized group. 2. to subject to rigid discipline. —reg·i·men·ta′tion, n.

reg·i·men·tal (rej·i-men′tl), adj. of or pertaining to a regiment.

reg·i·men·tals ('tlz), n.pl. 1. the uniform and insignia of a given regiment. 2. military uniform.

re·gi·nal (ri-jī′nl), adj. queenly.

re·gion (rē′jŭn), n. 1. an extensive part or area, as of the earth's surface. 2. any one of the parts or zones into which the sea or atmosphere are thought of as being divided. 3. any part or division, as of an organism. —re′gion·al, adj. —re′gion·al·ly, adv.

re·gion·al·ism (-l·izm), n. 1. concern with one's own geographic region. 2. a word, phrase, pronunciation, custom, etc. peculiar to a given region. 3. the setting of a story, novel, etc. in a particular region, in order to portray regional characteristics or values.

reg·is·ter (rej′is-tĕr), n. 1. an official written list of names, items, events, etc. 2. a book in which this is kept. 3. an official recorder; registrar. 4. a mechanical device for recording money deposited, fares paid, etc. 5. an opening into a room for the passage of heated air, etc. 6. in Music, a part of the range or compass of a voice or instrument. 7. an organ stop: v.t. 1. to show (an emotion) as by facial expression or bodily movement. 2. to make an official entry, as on a list. 3. to record automatically, as a thermometer. 4. to cause (mail) to be recorded when entered at the post office, as a safeguard: v.i. 1. to enter one's name, as on a list of voters, a hotel register, etc. 2. to enroll, as in a school or college. 3. to make an impression.

registered nurse, a graduate nurse who has passed a special State examination and has been licensed to practice nursing.

reg·is·trant (-trănt), n. one who registers.

reg·is·trar (rej′i-strär), n. a college or university official who keeps records.

reg·is·tra·tion (rej·i-strā′shŭn), n. 1. the act of inserting in a register. 2. enrollment, as of voters. 3. the number of persons registered.

reg·is·try (rej′is-tri), n., pl. -tries, 1. a place, as

an office, where registers are kept. 2. an official list of names, etc., or a book for such a list; register.

re·gi·us (rē′ji-ŭs), adj. 1. royal. 2. in England, denoting certain professors holding chairs founded by the sovereign.

reg·let (reg′lit), n. a flat strip of wood used in printing to separate lines of type or to fill blank spaces.

reg·nal (reg′năl), adj. of or pertaining to a reign or to a sovereign.

reg·nant ('nănt), adj. 1. reigning. 2. exercising royal authority; having much power. 3. prevalent. —reg′nan·cy, n.

re·gress (ri-gres′), v.i. to go back; return; move backward. —re·gres′sion, n. —re·gres′sive, adj.

re·gret (ri-gret′), n. sorrow or concern, as for past conduct or negligence; remorse: v.t. -gret′ted, -gret′ting, 1. to remember with sorrow. 2. to bewail the loss or want of. —re·gret′ta·ble, adj. —re·gret′ta·bly, adv.

re·gret·ful ('fûl), adj. full of regret. —re·gret′ful·ly, adv. —re·gret′ful·ness, n.

re·group (rē-groop′), v.t. & v.i. to reorganize (military forces) after a battle.

reg·u·lar (reg′yû-lĕr), adj. 1. according to a rule, order, or established usage. 2. uniform; symmetrical. 3. governed by rule. 4. methodical. 5. consistent. 6. fully qualified. 7. having sides or surfaces composed of equal figures or lines. 8. normal. 9. of or pertaining to the standing army of a country: n. 1. a regular soldier. 2. a member of a religious order. 3. an athlete who plays regularly, not as a substitute. 4. in Politics, one who is loyal to his party. 5. [Informal], one who is regular, as in attendance. —reg′u·lar·ly, adv.

reg·u·lar·i·ty (reg·yû-ler′i-ti), n., pl. -ties, 1. the state, quality, or an instance of being regular. 2. conformity to rule. 3. uniformity. 4. a method or certain order.

reg·u·lar·ize (reg′yû-lă-rīz), v.t. -ized, -iz·ing, to make regular. —reg·u·lar·i·za′tion, n.

reg·u·late (reg′yû-lāt), v.t. -lat·ed, -lat·ing, 1. to put in good order, so as to work accurately. 2. to govern, direct, etc. according to a rule or method. 3. to adjust to a standard. —reg′u·la·tive, reg′u·la·to·ry, adj.

reg·u·la·tion (reg·yû-lā′shŭn), n. 1. the act of regulating. 2. order; method; rule: adj. normal; regular

reg·u·la·tor (reg′yû-lāt-ĕr), n. 1. one who or that which regulates. 2. a mechanism for regulating motion or a flow of liquid, electricity, etc. 3. the part of a watch by which its speed is adjusted. 4. an accurate timepiece used as a standard.

reg·u·lus (reg′yoo-lŭs), n. 1. [R-], a brilliant white star in the constellation Leo. 2. pl. -lus·es, (-lī), an impure or partly purified metal produced by the smelting of various ores.

re·gur·gi·tate (ri-gûr′ji-tāt), v.i. & v.t. -tat·ed, -tat·ing, to surge back or cause to surge back, as to bring (partly digested food) from the stomach back to the mouth. —re·gur·gi·ta′tion, n.

re·ha·bil·i·tate (rē-hă-bil′i-tāt), v.t. -tat·ed, -tat·ing, 1. to restore to a former condition or status. 2. to bring or restore to a condition of health, ability to work, etc. —re-ha-bil-i-ta'tion, n. —re-ha-bil'i-ta-tive, adj.

re-hash (rē-hash'), v.t. 1. to work up (old material) in a new form. 2. to discuss (something) again: n. (rē'hash), something that has been rehashed.

re-hear (-her'), v.t. -heard', -hear'ing, to hear (a law case) again. —re-hear'ing, n.

re-hears-al (ri-hûr'sl), n. a practice performance, usually in private, before a public performance.

re-hearse (ri-hûrs'), v.t. & v.i. -hearsed', -hears'ing, 1. to repeat what has already been said or written; recite. 2. to tell or narrate at great length. 3. to perform (a play, etc.) as practice before its public performance.

reign (rān), v.i. 1. to exercise sovereign authority; rule. 2. to be predominate: n. 1. royal power or influence. 2. the time during which a sovereign rules or a condition, etc. prevails

re-im-burse (rē-im-bûrs'), v.t. -bursed', -burs'ing, to pay back. —re-im-burse'ment, n.

rein (rān), n. 1. the strap of a bridle, held by the driver or rider to control the animal: usually used in the plural. 2. pl. a means of curbing, restraining, or governing: v.t. to restrain or control as with reins.

re-in-car-na-tion (rē-in-kär-nā'shŭn), n. 1. the doctrine or belief that the soul comes back after death in a different bodily form. 2. the rebirth of the soul after death in another body. —re-in-car'nate, v.t. -nat-ed, -nat-ing.

rein-deer (rān'dir), n., pl. -deer, a large deer of northern regions with antlers in both sexes, domesticated as a beast of burden and for meat, leather, etc.

re-in-force (rē-in-fôrs'), v.t. -forced', -forc'ing, 1. to strengthen by addition, as in sending more troops or ships to a military force. 2. to add new material, prop up, patch, etc. —re-in-force'ment, n.

reins (rānz), n.pl. [Archaic], 1. the kidneys, or inner parts. 2. the passions or affections.

re-in-state (rē-in-stāt'), v.t. -stat'ed, -stat'ing, to restore to a former state or condition. —re-in-state'ment, n.

re-it-er-ate (rē-it'ē-rāt), v.t. -at-ed, -at-ing, to repeat; say over again. 2. to do repeatedly. —re-it-er-a'tion, n. —re-it'er-a-tive, adj.

re-ject (ri-jekt'), v.t. 1. to throw away as useless or unsatisfactory. 2. to refuse to believe, accept, make use of, act upon, etc.: n. (rē'jekt), a rejected person or thing. —re-jec'tion, n.

re-joice (ri-jois'), v.i. & v.t. -joiced', -joic'ing, to be or cause to be joyful and glad. —re-joic'ing, n.

re-join (rē-join'), v.t. & v.i. 1. to unite again after separation. 2. to answer. 3. in Law, to answer as the defendant to the plaintiff's replication.

re-join-der (ri-join'dẽr), n. 1. an answer, especially to a reply. 2. in Law, the defendant's answer to the plaintiff's replication.

re-ju-ve-nate (ri-jōō'vě-nāt), v.t. -nat-ed, -nat-ing, to cause to appear, seem, or feel youthful once more. —re-ju-ve-na'tion, n.

re-ju-ve-nes-cence (ri-jōō-vĕ-nes'ns), n. a renewing of youthfulness. —re-ju-ve-nes'cent, adj.

re-lapse (ri-laps'), v.i. -lapsed', -laps'ing, 1. to fall back from a state of convalescence. 2. to return to a former bad state or habit: n. (also rē'laps), 1. the return of an illness after convalescence or partial recovery. 2. a falling into a former bad state or habit.

relapsing fever, an acute, infectious disease transmitted by lice or ticks and characterized by alternating attacks of fever and chills.

re-late (ri-lāt'), v.t. -lat'ed, -lat'ing, 1. to tell; narrate. 2. to show a relation between; connect in meaning or thought: v.i. to refer (to).

re-lat-ed ('id), adj. 1. told or described. 2. of the same family; connected by kinship or marriage. —re-lat'ed-ness, n.

re-la-tion (ri-lā'shŭn), n. 1. a telling, narrating, etc. 2. an account; recital. 3. connection by kinship or marriage. 4. connection, as in meaning or thought. 5. a proportion or ratio. 6. a relative. 7. pl. association or involvement between people, nations, etc. —re-la'tion-ship, n.

rel-a-tive (rel'ă-tiv), adj. 1. related; having to do with each other. 2. pertinent; relevant. 3. comparative. 4. having meaning only in relation to something else. 5. in Grammar, denoting a pronoun or clause that relates to an antecedent: n. a person related by blood or marriage. —rel'a-tive-ness, n.

rel-a-tive-ly (rel'ă-tiv-li), adv. in a relative manner; comparatively.

rel-a-tiv-i-ty (rel-ă-tiv'ĭ-ti), n. 1. the quality of being relative. 2. in Physics, the theory that mass, velocity, and motion are relative rather than absolute, and that time, space, and matter are interdependent.

re-la-tor (ri-lāt'ẽr), n. in Law, a private citizen whose prompting starts a public inquiry regarding the exercise of an office, franchise, etc.

re-lax (ri-laks'), v.t. & v.i. 1. to become or cause to become less tense, rigorous, severe, etc. 2. to rest, as from work.

re-lax-ant ('ănt), adj. pertaining to or causing relaxation of the muscles: n. a drug or other substance that relaxes the muscles.

re-lax-a-tion (rē-lak-sā'shŭn), n. 1. the act of relaxing. 2. the state of being relaxed. 3. a lessening of tension; especially, release or rest from work, worry, etc. 4. recreation.

re-lay (ri-lā', rē'lā), v.t. layed', -lay'ing, to receive and pass on (something) by or as by relays: n. (rē'lā), 1. fresh horses or hunting dogs to replace those that have become tired. 2. a crew of workers relieving others; shift. 3. a race between teams, with each team member going part of the distance: also relay race. 4. an electromagnetic device that actuates other devices.

re-lay (rē-lā'), v.t. -laid', -lay'ing, to lay again: also written relay.

re-lease (ri-lēs'), v.t. -leased', -leas'ing, 1. to set free, as from restraint, imprisonment, pain, etc. 2. to free from obligation or penalty. 3. to let go. 4. to allow to be published, broadcast, etc.: n. 1. a setting free; libera-

tion from restraint, imprisonment, pain, etc.
2. a document authorizing release. 3. a device for letting loose a catch, etc. to start or stop a machine. 4. a news story, film, etc. that has been released to the public. 5. in *Law*, a surrender of a claim.

rel·e·gate (rel'ě-gāt), *v.t.* -gat·ed, -gat·ing, 1. to banish (*to*). 2. to consign, especially to an inferior position. 3. to refer for judgment. —**rel·e·ga'tion**, *n.*

re·lent (ri-lent'), *v.i.* to grow less hard or severe; become more tender; yield.

re·lent·less ('lis), *adj.* 1. pitiless; cruel; harsh. 2. persistent. —**re·lent'less·ly**, *adv.* —**re·lent'-less·ness**, *n.*

rel·e·vant (rel'ě-vǎnt), *adj.* applicable; related; pertinent. —**rel'e·vance, rel'e·van·cy**, *n.* —**rel'e·vant·ly**, *adv.*

re·li·a·ble (ri-li'ǎ-bl), *adj.* trustworthy; dependable. —**re·li·a·bil'i·ty, re·li'a·ble·ness**, *n.* —**re·li'a·bly**, *adv.*

re·li·ance (ri-li'ǎns), *n.* 1. confidence; trust. 2. something relied upon. —**re·li'ant**, *adj.* —**re·li'ant·ly**, *adv.*

rel·ic (rel'ik), *n.* 1. *pl.* that which is left after the loss or decay of the rest. 2. a custom, object, etc. that has survived from the past. 3. a keepsake or souvenir. 4. the body of, or some object associated with, a saint, kept as a religious memorial.

rel·ict (rel'ikt), *n.* 1. [Archaic], a widow or widower. 2. a plant or animal species surviving from an earlier period: *adj.* (ri-likt'), [Archaic], denoting the survivor of a married couple.

re·lief (ri-lef'), *n.* 1. that which mitigates pain, grief, a burden, etc. 2. anything that affords freedom from stress, as a pleasant change. 3. release from some duty or work. 4. those who bring such release by acting as replacement. 5. assistance given to the poor, especially by a public agency. 6. the projection of a sculptured design from a plane surface. 7. redress. 8. elevation of land forms: *adj.* in *Baseball*, denoting a pitcher who acts as replacement for another during a game.

re·lieve (ri-lev'), *v.t.* -lieved', -liev·ing, 1. to free from pain, suffering, grief, etc. 2. to mitigate (pain, distress, etc.). 3. to help. 4. to release from duty or work by replacing. 5. to make more pleasant by providing a change. —**re·liev'a·ble**, *adj.*

re·li·gion (ri-lij'ŭn), *n.* 1. belief in God or gods. 2. manifestation of this by worship, rituals, prayers, devotion, etc. 3. any system of faith or worship, etc. built around God, ethical values, a philosophy, etc. 4. piety. 5. a monastic state or way of life. 6. any object of devotion.

re·li·gi·os·i·ty (ri-lij-i-os'ĭ-ti), *n.* intense fervor in religion; deep religious feeling. —**re·lig'i·ose** (-ōs), *adj.*

re·li·gious (ri-lij'ŭs), *adj.* 1. pertaining to, characteristic of, or set apart for religion. 2. godly; pious; devout. 3. conscientiously exact or strict. 4. bound by monastic vows: *n.* one who is bound by monastic vows; monk or nun. —**re·li'gious·ly**, *adv.* —**re·li'gious·ness**, *n.*

re·lin·quish (ri-ling'kwish), *v.t.* 1. to abandon or

quit (a plan, policy, etc.). 2. to renounce (a claim, right, etc.). 3. to let go (one's hold or grasp). —**re·lin'quish·ment**, *n.*

rel·i·quar·y (rel'ĭ-kwer-i), *n., pl.* -quar·ies, a casket or small chest for holding and displaying relics.

rel·ish (rel'ish), *v.t.* to like; enjoy: *n.* 1. a savory taste; good flavor. 2. zest; enjoyment. 3. a savory dish or condiment eaten with other foods to give flavor.

re·live (rē-liv'), *v.t.* -lived', -liv'ing, to experience (something) once again, as in the imagination.

re·lo·cate (rē-lō'kāt), *v.t. & v.i.* -cat·ed, -cat·ing, to move to another place. —**re·lo·ca'tion**, *n.*

re·lu·cent (ri-lōō'snt), *adj.* reflecting light; glittering; bright.

re·luc·tant (ri-luk'tǎnt), *adj.* 1. unwilling; disinclined. 2. showing unwillingness. —**re·luc'tance**, *n.* —**re·luc'tant·ly**, *adv.*

re·ly (ri-li'), *v.i.* -lied', -ly'ing, to have confidence; trust; depend (with *on* or *upon*).

REM (rem), *n., pl.* REMs, the rapid eye movements under the eyelids during sleep periods associated with dreaming.

rem (rem), *n.* the amount of any ionizing radiation that will have the biological effect about equal to one roentgen of X-ray.

re·main (ri-mān'), *v.i.* 1. to stay. 2. to continue; endure. 3. to be left in a particular state or place. 4. to be left after or out of a greater number.

re·main·der ('dēr), *n.* 1. that which is left after a part has been taken away. 2. those remaining. 3. the number left after subtraction. 4. the part of an edition of a book left unsold and held by the publisher. 5. in *Law*, an estate in expectancy but not in possession.

re·mains (ri-mānz'), *n.pl.* 1. a dead body. 2. parts, fragments, traces, etc. left over; ruins. 3. the works of an author left unpublished at his death.

re·mand (ri-mand'), *v.t.* 1. to send back. 2. to remit (a prisoner) in custody until a future time: *n.* 1. the act of remanding. 2. the state of being remanded.

re·mark (ri-märk'), *v.t. & v.i.* to note or observe; express; say: *n.* a notice or observation; brief comment.

re·mark·a·ble ('ǎ-bl), *adj.* worthy of notice or remark; extraordinary; unusual. —**re·mark'a·bly**, *adv.*

re·me·di·a·ble (ri-mē'di·ǎ-bl), *adj.* that can be remedied. —**re·me'di·a·bly**, *adv.*

re·me·di·al (ri-mē'di·ǎl), *adj.* 1. affording remedy. 2. intended to remedy, correct, improve, etc., as some study courses. —**re·me'di·al·ly**, *adv.*

rem·e·dy (rem'ě-di), *n., pl.* -dies, 1. something, as a medicine or treatment, that cures or relieves an illness, ailment, etc. 2. something that corrects an evil of some kind: *v.t.* -died, -dy·ing, to remove, cure, correct, etc.

re·mem·ber (ri-mem'bēr), *v.t.* 1. to recall to mind. 2. to attend to; keep in mind. 3. to keep in mind with gratitude, regard, or reverence. 4. to convey greetings from (a person): *v.i.* 1. to call something back to mind. 2. to keep in mind.

---

re·mem·brance ('brăns), n. 1. the power of remembering; memory. 2. the length of time through which one's memory extends. 3. a souvenir, gift, keepsake, etc.

re·mem·branc·er ('brăn-sĕr), n. 1. one who reminds another of something, especially someone hired or appointed to do so. 2. a reminder; memento.

rem·i·ges (rem'ĭ-jĕz), n.pl., sing. re·mex (rē'meks), the quill feathers of a bird's wing; flight feathers. —re·mig·i·al (rĭ-mĭj'ĭ-ăl), adj.

re·mind (rĭ-mīnd'), v.t. & v.i. to bring to the remembrance of; put in mind. —re·mind'er, n.

rem·i·nisce (rem-ĭ-nĭs'), v.i. -nisced', -nis'cing, to recall events of the past.

rem·i·nis·cence ('ns), n. 1. the act of remembering. 2. a memory. 3. pl. a narration of remembered experiences. —rem·i·nis'cent, adj.

re·mise (rĭ-mīz'), v.t. -mised', -mis'ing, in Law, to resign or surrender by deed.

re·miss (rĭ-mis'), adj. 1. careless in the performance of duty or business. 2. showing heedlessness or negligence. —re·miss'ly, adv. —re·miss'ness, n.

re·mis·sion (-mish'ŭn), n. 1. pardon; forgiveness. 2. abatement of (pain, a disease, etc.). 3. cancellation of a penalty, debt, etc.

re·mit (rĭ-mit'), v.t. -mit'ted, -mit'ting, 1. to pardon or forgive. 2. to transmit, as money in payment. 3. to abate; relax. 4. to refrain from exacting (a payment), enforcing (a penalty), etc.: v.i. 1. to moderate in force or intensity. 2. to send money in payment. —re·mit'tance, n. —re·mit'tent, adj.

rem·nant (rem'nănt), n. that which is left after a part has been removed, as a piece of cloth, ribbon, etc. at the end of a bolt.

re·mod·el (rē-mod'l), v.t. -eled or -elled, -el·ing or -el·ling, to make over; construct again.

re·mon·e·tize (rē-mon'ĕ-tīz), v.t. -tized, -tiz·ing, to restore to circulation as legal tender. —re·mon·e·ti·za'tion, n.

re·mon·strance (ri-mon'străns), n. 1. a strong protest against something; complaint; expostulation. 2. a document listing grievances, etc. —re·mon'strant (strănt), adj. & n. —re·mon'strant·ly, adv.

re·mon·strate (ri-mon'strāt), v.t. & v.i. -strat·ed, -strat·ing, to urge or put forward strong reasons (against some act or course complained of); protest.

rem·o·ra (rem'ĕr-ă), n. a fish with a sucking disc on the head by which it attaches itself to sharks and other large fishes.

re·morse (ri-môrs'), n. 1. anguish of mind caused by guilt; self-reproach. 2. compassion: now only in without remorse.

re·morse·ful ('fŭl), adj. full of remorse. —re·morse'ful·ly, adv. —re·morse'ful·ness, n.

re·morse·less ('lis), adj. feeling no remorse; pitiless; cruel. —re·morse'less·ly, adv. —re·morse'less·ness, n.

re·mote (ri-mōt'), adj. -mot'er, -mot'est, 1. distant in time or space; far. 2. distant in connection. 3. distantly related by blood or marriage. 4. faint; slight. —re·mote'ly, adv. —re·mote'ness, n.

remote control, the control of aircraft, missiles, spacecraft, or other apparatus, from a distance, as by radio waves.

re·mov·al (ri-mōō'vl), n. 1. the act of removing or displacing. 2. a change of place. 3. dismissal from a position or office.

re·move (ri-mōōv'), v.t. -moved', -mov'ing, 1. to move (something) from its place; lift, push, take, etc. away or off. 2. to dismiss, as from a position or office. 3. to kill. 4. to eliminate: v.i. to change residence: n. 1. a space or interval. 2. a degree; step. —re·mov'a·ble, adj. —re·mov'er, n.

re·moved (-mōōvd'), adj. 1. remote; not connected. 2. distant by a given number of degrees of relationship.

re·mu·ner·ate (ri-mū'nĕ-rāt), v.t. -at·ed, -at·ing, to pay or recompense (someone) for (work, a loss incurred, etc.). —re·mu·ner·a'tion, n.

re·mu·ner·a·tive (-iv), adj. 1. remunerating. 2. lucrative; profitable. —re·mu'ner·a·tive·ly, adv. —re·mu'ner·a·tive·ness, n.

Re·mus (rē'mŭs), see Romulus.

ren·ais·sance (ren'ă-săns), n. 1. [R-], a revival of art and learning in Europe from the 14th to the 16th centuries, marking the transition from medieval to modern. 2. the style of architecture of this period, an adaptation of the classical. 3. any revival or rebirth: adj. [R-]. of or characteristic of the Renaissance.

re·nal (rē'nl), adj. of pertaining to, or near the kidneys.

re·nas·cence (ri-nas'ns, -năs'-), n. [also R-], same as renaissance. —re·nas'cent, adj.

ren·coun·ter (ren-koun'tĕr), n. [French], 1. a hostile meeting, as in conflict or for a contest, debate, etc. 2. a casual meeting, as with a friend. Also ren·con'tre (-kon'tĕr).

rend (rend), v.t. rent, rend'ing, to tear apart with violence; split; lacerate: v.i. to split apart.

ren·der (ren'dĕr), v.t. 1. to return or give back. 2. to give or pay as due. 3. to deliver or submit, as for approval, payment, etc. 4. to provide (aid, a service, etc.). 5. to depict, as by drawing. 6. to present or play, as a stage role, music, etc. 7. to translate. 8. to melt down (fat).

ren·der·ing (-ing), n. 1. a translation; version. 2. an execution, performance, etc. 3. a perspective drawing of a building, etc. 4. a first coat of plaster.

ren·dez·vous (ron'dā-vōō), n., pl. -vous (-vōōz), 1. an appointed place of meeting, as for warships, troops, spacecraft, etc. 2. an agreement to meet. 3. the meeting itself: v.i. & v.i. -voused (-vōōd), -vous·ing, to assemble at a certain time or place.

ren·di·tion (ren-dish'ŭn), n. an interpretation of music, drama, etc.; performance, translation, etc.

ren·e·gade (ren'ĕ-gād), n. one who renounces his party, faith, etc., and goes over to the opposition; traitor; turncoat.

re·nege (ri-nig'), v.i. -neged', -neg'ing, 1. to fail to play a card of the suit led in a card game. 2. to fail to live up to a promise or obligation. —re·neg'er, n.

re·new (ri-nōō'), v.t. 1. to make new again. 2. to restore; renovate. 3. to revive. 4. to take up again; resume. 5. to put in a fresh supply of. —re·new'a·ble, *adj.* —re·new'al, *n.*

ren·i·form (ren'i-fôrm, rē'ni-), *adj.* shaped like a kidney.

re·ni·tent (ri-nīt'nt, ren'i-tĕnt), *adj.* 1. opposed to; recalcitrant. 2. resisting pressure. —re·ni'ten·cy, *n.*

ren·net (ren'it), *n.* 1. the mucous membrane lining the fourth stomach of a calf. 2. an extract of this used in curdling milk.

ren·nin (ren'in), *n.* a coagulating enzyme that can curdle milk, found in rennet.

re·nounce (ri-nouns'), *v.t.* -nounced, -nounc'ing, 1. to give up (a claim, belief, etc.) by formal declaration. 2. to repudiate; disown. 3. to give up (a habit, etc.) voluntarily. —re·nounce'ment, *n.*

ren·o·vate (ren'ô-vāt), *v.t.* -vat·ed, -vat·ing, 1. to make sound again; restore to a good condition; repair. 2. to refresh. —ren·o·va'tion, *n.* —ren'o·va·tor, *n.*

re·nown (ri-noun'), *n.* celebrity; fame; distinction. —re·nowned', *adj.*

rent (rent), *n.* 1. a tear; fissure or rip made by rending. 2. a periodic payment for use of property: *v.t.* to receive or allow use of in exchange for rent: *v.i.* to be let for rent. —rent'er, *n.*

rent·al (ren'tl), *n.* 1. amount of rent. 2. an apartment, appliance, car, etc. for rent. 3. the act of renting: *adj.* of or for rent.

re·nun·ci·a·tion (ri-nun-si-ā'shŭn), *n.* a renouncing or disavowal, as of a claim.

re·or·gan·ize (rē-ôr'gá-nīz), *v.t.* & *v.i.* -ized, -iz·ing, to organize anew, as a business. —re·or·gan·i·za'tion, *n.* —re·or'gan·i·zer, *n.*

rep (rep), *n.* a fabric with a fine, corded surface.

re·paid (rē-pād'), past tense and past participle of repay.

re·pair (ri-per'), *v.i.* to go (*to* a specified place): *v.t.* 1. to restore after injury; mend; renovate. 2. to make amends. *n.* 1. the act of repairing. 2. *usually pl.* an instance of repairing, or the work done. 3. the state, as of a building, in reference to being repaired. —re·pair'a·ble, *adj.*

rep·a·ra·ble (rep'êr-á-bl), *adj.* that can be repaired. —rep'a·ra·bly, *adv.*

rep·a·ra·tion (rep'â-rā'shŭn), *n.* 1. restoration to a good condition. 2. a making of amends. 3. *usually pl.* compensation, as for war damage.

re·par·a·tive (ri-per'á-tiv), *adj.* 1. repairing, mending defects, etc. 2. having to do with reparation.

rep·ar·tee (rep'êr-tē', -tā'), *n.* a ready, witty reply; banter.

re·past (ri-past'), *n.* a meal; food and drink.

re·pa·tri·ate (rē-pā'tri-āt), *v.t.* & *v.i.* -at·ed, -at·ing, to return to a country of birth, citizenship, etc. —re·pa·tri·a'tion, *n.*

re·pay (ri-pā'), *v.t.* -paid', -pay'ing, 1. to pay back. 2. to make some return for. —re·pay'ment, *n.*

re·peal (rē-pēl'), *v.t.* to revoke or abrogate; annul: *n.* revocation; abrogation.

re·peat (ri-pēt'), *v.t.* 1. to say a second time. 2. to recite; as a poem. 3. to quote from

someone else. 4. to tell to someone else. 5. to do, perform, make, etc. again: *v.i.* to say or do again: *n.* 1. repetition. 2. a television or radio program that is broadcast again. 3. in *Music, a)* a sign directing a part to be repeated; *b)* the part.

re·peat·ed ('id), *adj.* recurring or said again and again. —re·peat'ed·ly, *adv.*

re·peat·er ('ēr), *n.* 1. one who or that which repeats. 2. a watch that strikes the time when a spring is pressed. 3. a firearm that can discharge a number of shots without reloading: also **repeating firearm.** 4. a decimal in which the same digit or digits are repeated: also **repeating decimal.** 5. one who illegally votes more than once in the same election.

re·pel (ri-pel'), *v.t.* -pelled', -pel'ling, 1. to drive back; check the advance of. 2. to reject. 3. to disgust. 4. to ward off; be resistant to (water, etc.).

re·pel·lent (ri-pel'ênt), *adj.* that repels: *n.* 1. a substance used to make fabrics help resist water to some extent. 2. a substance that repels insects. Also **re·pel'lant.** —re·pel'lence, *n.*

re·pent (ri-pent'), *v.i.* 1. to feel pain or sorrow for something done or left undone; be contrite. 2. to change one's ways; be penitent: *v.t.* 1. to feel penitent or contrite over (a sin, error, etc.). 2. to feel regret so as to change one's mind about. —re·pent'ance, *n.* —re·pent'ant, *adj.*

re·per·cus·sion (rē-pêr-kush'ŭn), *n.* 1. reverberation. 2. a recoil or rebound. 3. a result or effect, sometimes remote, of some event or action. —re·per·cus'sive, *adj.*

rep·er·toire (rep'êr-twär), *n.* [French], a stock of dramas, songs, etc. that a singer, actor, or group is prepared to present.

rep·er·to·ry (-tôr-i), *n., pl.* -ries, 1. same as repertoire. 2. the system of presenting several plays successively or alternately by a permanent theatrical company.

rep·e·tend (rep'ê-tend), *n.* 1. a repeated word, phrase, or sound. 2. the digit or digits constantly repeated in a repeating decimal.

rep·e·ti·tion (rep-ê-tish'ŭn), *n.* 1. the act of repeating. 2. something repeated. —rep·e·ti'tious, *adj.* —re·pet·i·tive (ri-pet'ǐ-tiv), *adj.*

re·pine (ri-pīn'), *v.i.* -pined', -pin'ing, to complain; feel discontent. —re·pin'er, *n.*

re·place (ri-plās'), *v.t.* -placed', -plac'ing, 1. to restore to a former place. 2. to take the place of. 3. to provide an equivalent for. —re·place'ment, *n.*

re·plen·ish (ri-plen'ish), *v.t.* 1. to fill up again. 2. to make complete again. —re·plen'ish·ment, *n.*

re·plete (ri-plēt'), *adj.* completely filled; filled in abundance. —re·ple'tion, *n.*

re·plev·in (ri-plev'in), *n.* 1. an action at law to recover goods said to be wrongfully seized, upon a promise to try the matter in court. 2. the writ by which this is done: *v.t.* same as replevy.

re·plev·y (ri-plev'i), *v.t.* -plev'ied, -plev'y·ing, to take back (goods) under a writ of replevin: *n.* same as replevin.

rep·li·ca (rep'li-ká), *n.* 1. a copy of an original

picture or statue executed by the same artist or sculptor. 2. a facsimile.

rep·li·cate (rep′li-kit), *adj.* in *Botany,* folded back, as a leaf: *v.t.* (-kāt), **-cat·ed, -cat·ing,** 1. to duplicate. 2. to fold or bend back.

rep·li·ca·tion (rep·li-kā′shŭn), *n.* 1. a folding back. 2. a reply, especially a reply to an answer. 3. an echo; repetition. 4. in *Law,* the plaintiff's answer to the plea of the defendant.

re·ply (ri-plī′), *v.i.* **-plied′, -ply′ing,** to answer; respond: *n., pl.* **-plies′,** an answer; response.

re·port (ri-pôrt′), *v.t.* 1. to give an account of, as for publication. 2. to tell from one to another. 3. to announce publicly. 4. to make known to those in authority: *v.i.* 1. to make a report. 2. to present oneself, as for work: *n.* 1. an official statement of facts. 2. an account, description, etc. 3. rumor; hearsay. 4. the noise of an explosion. **—re·port′ed·ly,** *adv.*

re·port·age (′ij), *n.* 1. the work of reporting news events. 2. writing done in a journalistic manner.

report card, a written record of a pupil's progress and behavior, sent periodically to the parents or guardian.

re·por·ter (′ẽr), *n.* 1. an official in a court or legislative assembly who reports proceedings. 2. one who gathers and writes up news, as for a newspaper. **—rep·or·to·ri·al** (rep·ẽr-tôr′i-ăl), *adj.*

re·pose (ri-pōz′), *v.t.* **-posed′, -pos′ing,** 1. to lay for rest. 2. to place or rest (confidence or trust) in someone. 3. to place (power, control, etc.) *in* the hands of someone: *v.i.* 1. to recline. 2. to sleep or rest. 3. to lie dead: *n.* 1. sleep. 2. rest. 3. tranquillity; calm. 4. composure.

re·pos·i·to·ry (ri-poz′i-tôr′i), *n., pl.* **-ries,** a warehouse, room, box, etc. for the storing and safekeeping of goods.

re·pos·sess (rē-pô-zes′), *v.t.* to take possession of again. **—re·pos·ses′sion,** *n.*

re·pous·sé (rē-pŏŏ-sā′), *n.* [French], 1. ornamental metal work formed in relief and chased. 2. the art of doing this.

rep·re·hend (rep·ri-hend′), *v.t.* to censure, criticize, rebuke, etc.

rep·re·hen·si·ble (-hen′si-bl), *adj.* deserving to be reprehended. **—rep·re·hen′si·bly,** *adv.*

rep·re·hen·sion (-hen′shŭn), *n.* 1. the act of reprehending. 2. censure; reproof. **—rep·re·hen′sive,** *adj.* **—rep·re·hen′sive·ly,** *adv.*

rep·re·sent (rep·ri-zent′), *v.t.* 1. to present an image of. 2. to describe; give an account of. 3. to symbolize. 4. to personate or act the part of. 5. to be the equivalent of. 6. to act in place of, especially by authority. 7. to serve as an example of.

rep·re·sen·ta·tion (-zen-tā′shŭn), *n.* 1. the act of representing. 2. the fact of being represented, as in a legislative assembly. 3. a likeness; image or picture. 4. a dramatic performance. 5. a body of representatives. 6. *often pl.* a statement of claims, reasons, etc. **—rep·re·sen·ta′tion·al,** *adj.*

rep·re·sent·a·tive (rep·rē·zen′tă·tiv), *adj.* 1. representing. 2. typical. 3. founded on or pertaining to representation of the people by

elected legislative members: *n.* 1. one who is authorized to act for another or others; deputy, delegate, agent, salesman, etc. 2. [R-], a member of a State legislature or of the lower house of the Congress. 3. a typical specimen. **—rep·re·sent′a·tive·ly,** *adv.*

re·press (ri-pres′), *v.t.* 1. to check or restrain. 2. to crush; quell; subdue. 3. in *Psychiatry,* to exclude (painful thoughts) from the conscious mind. **—re·pres′sion,** *n.* **—re·pres′sive,** *adj.* **—re·pres′sive·ly,** *adv.*

re·prieve (ri-prēv′), *v.t.* **-prieved′, -priev′ing,** 1. to give a respite to. 2. to postpone the execution of (a condemned person): *n.* 1. a temporary respite, as from pain, trouble, etc. 2. a temporary suspension of a criminal sentence, especially death.

rep·ri·mand (rep′ri-mand), *v.t.* 1. to reprove severely. 2. to reprove publicly and officially: *n.* a severe reproof.

re·pris·al (ri-prī′zl), *n.* something done or seized by way of retaliation for an injury or wrong suffered.

re·prise (ri-prēz′), *n.* in a musical play, the playing or singing again of all or part of a song that was presented earlier.

re·proach (ri-prōch′), *v.t.* to censure severely; upbraid: *n.* 1. blame; rebuke. 2. shame or disgrace. 3. a cause of this.

re·proach·ful (′fŭl), *adj.* 1. full of reproach. 2. expressing reproach. **—re·proach′ful·ly,** *adv.* **—re·proach′ful·ness,** *n.*

rep·ro·bate (rep′rō-bāt), *v.t.* **-bat·ed, -bat·ing,** 1. to condemn strongly. 2. in *Theology,* to abandon; disown: *adj.* 1. depraved; corrupt. 2. abandoned by God; lost in sin: *n.* a depraved person; wretch. **—rep·ro·ba′tion,** *n.*

re·pro·duce (rē-prō-dŏŏs′), *v.t.* **-duced′, -duc′ing,** 1. to produce by generation or propagation. 2. to make a copy of. 3. to repeat: *v.i.* to produce offspring. **—re·pro·duc′i·ble,** *adj.*

re·pro·duc·tion (-duk′shŭn), *n.* 1. the act of reproducing. 2. the process by which animals and plants bring forth their kind. 3. an imitation; copy, duplication, etc. **—re·pro·duc′tive,** *adj.*

re·proof (ri-prŏŏf′), *n.* 1. the act of reproving. 2. a rebuke; censure. Also **re·prov′al** (-prŏŏ′vl).

re·prove (ri-prŏŏv′), *v.t.* **-proved′, -prov′ing,** 1. to rebuke; reprimand; censure. 2. to express disapproval of.

rep·tant (rep′tănt), *adj.* in *Biology,* creeping or crawling.

rep·tile (rep′tl, ′tīl), *n.* 1. a coldblooded vertebrate that creeps or crawls, as a snake, lizard, crocodile, etc. 2. a sneaky or groveling person: *adj.* of or having the nature of a reptile. **—rep·til·i·an** (rep·til′i-ăn), *adj.*

re·pub·lic (ri-pub′lik), *n.* 1. a state or country in which the supreme power is vested in representatives elected by popular vote. 2. a state in which the head of government is a president. 3. a group of persons with some common goal or interest.

re·pub·li·can ('li-kăn), *adj.* 1. of, pertaining to, or like a republic. 2. [R-], of or characteristic of the Republican Party: *n.* 1. an advocate of the republican form of government. 2. [R-], a member of the Republican Party.

ŏ in drag*o*n, ŏŏ in cr*u*de, oo in w*oo*l, u in c*u*p, ū in c*u*re, ũ in t*u*rn, ŭ in f*o*cus, oi in b*o*y, ou in h*ou*se, th in *th*in, *th* in shea*th*e, g in get, j in joy, y in yet.

re-pub-li-can-ism (-izm), *n.* 1. the principles of a republican government. 2. an attachment to such principles.

re-pub-li-can-ize (-īz), *v.t.* -ized, -iz-ing, 1. to form into a republic. 2. to convert to republican ideas and practices.

Republican Party, one of the two chief political parties of the U.S.

re-pub-li-ca-tion (rē-pub-li-kā'shŭn), *n.* 1. the act of republishing. 2. a book or other printed work that is published again.

re-pub-lish (rē-pub'lish), *v.t.* 1. to publish again. 2. in *Law,* to execute (a will formerly revoked) once again.

re-pu-di-ate (ri-pū'di-āt), *v.t.* -at-ed, -at-ing, 1. to disown or disclaim. 2. to refuse to pay or acknowledge. 3. to disavow (a treaty, belief, etc.). —**re-pu-di-a'tion,** *n.* —**re-pu'di-a-tor,** *n.*

re-pug-nant (ri-pug'nănt), *adj.* 1. highly distasteful or offensive. 2. contrary. 3. hostile. —**re-pug'nance,** *n.*

re-pulse (ri-puls'), *v.t.* -pulsed', -puls'ing, 1. to drive back; beat off; repel. 2. to rebuff; reject or deny discourteously: *n.* the state of being driven back or repelled; rebuff; rejection.

re-pul-sion (-pul'shŭn), *n.* 1. the act of driving back. 2. the state of being repelled. 3. the physical force by which bodies or particles of matter tend to repel each other: opposed to *attraction.* 4. a strong aversion.

re-pul-sive ('siv), *adj.* disgusting; causing aversion or strong dislike. —**re-pul'sive-ly,** *adv.* —**re-pul'sive-ness,** *n.*

rep-u-ta-ble (rep'yoo-tă-bl), *adj.* esteemed; in good repute; honorable. —**rep'u-ta-bly,** *adv.*

rep-u-ta-tion (rep-yoo-tā'shŭn), *n.* 1. judgment commonly applied to a person or thing. 2. favorable judgment. 3. renown; fame.

re-pute (ri-pūt'), *v.t.* -put'ed, -put'ing, to estimate; deem: *n.* 1. reputation. 2. fame; renown. —**re-put'ed,** *adj.* —**re-put'ed-ly,** *adv.*

re-quest (ri-kwest'), *n.* 1. the expression of a desire; petition. 2. something asked for. 3. a state of being wanted; demand: *v.t.* 1. to ask for. 2. to make a request to.

Re-qui-em (rek'wi-ăm, rāk'-), *n.* in the *Roman Catholic Church,* 1. a Mass for the repose of the soul of a deceased person. 2. a musical setting for this.

re-quire (ri-kwīr'), *v.t.* -quired', -quir'ing, 1. to ask for or claim as by right or authority; demand; exact. 2. to need. —**re-quire'ment,** *n.*

req-ui-site (rek'wi-zit), *adj.* needful; indispensable; necessary: *n.* anything requisite; something necessary.

req-ui-si-tion (rek-wi-zish'ŭn), *n.* 1. the act of requiring; formal demand. 2. a demand, especially a written order, as for supplies: *v.t.* to demand or take, as by authority.

re-quit-al (ri-kwīt'l), *n.* retaliation; something done or given in return.

re-quite (ri-kwīt'), *v.t.* -quit'ed, -quit'ing, to make return for treatment, good or evil; recompense; retaliate. —**re-quit'er,** *n.*

rere-dos (rir'dŏs), *n.* an ornamental screen behind an altar.

re-run (rē'run), *n.* a showing over again of a film or television program.

re-sale (rē'sāl), *n.* the act of selling once again, especially to a third party.

re-scind (ri-sind'), *v.t.* to annul; revoke. —**re-scis'sion** (-sizh'ŭn), *n.*

re-script (rē'skript), *n.* an edict or decree, as of an emperor or pope, in answer to some question of jurisprudence officially submitted to him.

res-cue (res'kū), *v.t.* -cued, -cu-ing, to free from danger, restraint, or violence; liberate; deliver: *n.* a deliverance from danger, restraint, or violence. —**res'cu-er,** *n.*

re-search (ri-sûrch'), *n.* meticulous, patient inquiry and investigation of some field of knowledge: *v.i. & v.t.* to do research on or in. —**re-search'er,** *n.*

re-sec-tion (ri-sek'shŭn), *n.* the surgical removal of some part of a bone, organ, etc.

re-se-da (ri-sē'dá), *n.* same as **mignonette.**

re-sem-blance (ri-zem'blăns), *n.* a similarity, especially of appearance; likeness.

re-sem-ble (ri-zem'bl), *v.t.* -bled, -bling, to have a likeness to; have similarity to.

re-sent (ri-zent'), *v.t.* to consider as an injury or affront; be angry or bitter because of.

re-sent-ful ('fŭl), *adj.* full of resentment; showing resentment. —**re-sent'ful-ly,** *adv.* —**re-sent'ful-ness,** *n.*

re-sent-ment ('mĕnt), *n.* a deep and bitter sense of injury or offense.

re-ser-pine (ri-sûr'pin, 'pēn), *n.* a crystalline alkaloid, used as a tranquilizer and in the treatment of hypertension.

res-er-va-tion (rez-ēr-vā'shŭn), *n.* 1. anything kept back or reserved. 2. public land set aside for some particular use, as for Indians. 3. a clause, proviso, or limitation. 4. the allotting of space on an airplane or in a theater, hotel, etc.; also, any space so allotted.

re-serve (ri-zûrv'), *v.t.* -served', -serv'ing, 1. to keep in store; hold back for future or special use. 2. to retain for onself: *n.* 1. caution in speaking or acting. 2. taciturnity; silence. 3. something set aside for a particular purpose, as a tract of land. 4. *pl.* troops subject to call, but not on active duty.

re-served (-zûrvd'), *adj.* 1. set apart for some purpose, person, etc.; saved. 2. reticent; silent. —**re-serv'ed-ly** (-zûr'vid-li), *adv.* —**re-serv'ed-ness,** *n.*

re-serv-ist (-zûr'vist), *n.* a member of the military reserves.

res-er-voir (rez'ēr-vwär), *n.* a place where anything, usually fluid, is collected and stored up for use; specifically, a lake or pond.

re-set (rē-set'), *v.t.* -set', -set'ting, to set again, as type, a broken bone, controls, etc.: *n.* (rē'set), that which is set again.

resh (rāsh), *n.* the 20th letter of the Hebrew alphabet.

re-side (ri-zīd'), *v.i.* -sid'ed, -sid'ing, 1. to dwell or inhabit; live (*in*). 2. to be inherent (*in*).

res-i-dence (rez'i-dĕns), *n.* 1. a place of abode; domicile. 2. the act of residing. —**res-i-den'-tial** (-i-den'shŭl), *adj.*

res·i·den·cy (-dĕn-si), *n., pl.* **-cies, 1.** same as **residence. 2.** the residence or territory of a diplomat. **3.** a period of advanced medical or surgical training in a hospital.

res·i·dent (rez´ĭ-dent), *adj.* dwelling in; having a residence in; abiding: *n.* **1.** one who lives in a place, not a visitor. **2.** a doctor serving a residency.

re·sid·u·al (rĭ-zij´oo-wǎl), *adj.* remaining after a part has been taken away: *n.* **1.** a remainder; residue. **2.** *pl.* fees paid for reruns on television, etc. **—re·sid´u·al·ly,** *adv.*

re·sid·u·ar·y (´oo-wer-i), *adj.* **1.** pertaining to or constituting a residue. **2.** in *Law,* denoting the remainder of an estate after specific bequests.

res·i·due (rez´i-dōō), *n.* **1.** that which is left; remainder. **2.** the part of an estate that remains after all claims are satisfied.

re·sid·u·um (ri-zij´oo-wŭm), *n., pl.* **-u·a** (-wǎ), same as **residue.**

re·sign (ri-zīn´), *v.t. & v.i.* **1.** to give up or withdraw from (a claim, office, position, etc.), especially formally. **2.** to submit calmly.

res·ig·na·tion (rez-ig-nā´shŭn), *n.* **1.** the act of resigning. **2.** a formal statement of this. **3.** a calm or patient submission or acquiescence.

re·signed (ri-zīnd´), *adj.* submissive; showing or feeling resignation. **—re·sign´ed·ly** (-zīn´id-li), *adv.*

re·sile (ri-zīl´), *v.i.* **-siled´, -sil´ing,** to spring back; resume original shape or position.

re·sil·ient (ri-zil´yĕnt), *adj.* **1.** springing back; resuming the original form or position; elastic. **2.** recovering from illness, trouble, etc. readily. **—re·sil´ience,** **re·sil´ien·cy,** *n.*

res·in (rez´n), *n.* **1.** a viscous, solid or semisolid, translucent, brownish or yellowish, organic substance which exudes from trees, as pines: it is used in varnishes, plastics, etc. same as **rosin.**

res·in·ous (-ŭs), *adj.* **1.** containing resin. **2.** of or like resin. **3.** obtained from resin. Also **res´in·y.**

re·sist (ri-zist´), *v.t.* **1.** to oppose; strive against. **2.** to withstand; stand firm against. **3.** to keep from yielding to: *v.i.* to make opposition or resistance. **—re·sist´er,** *n.*

re·sist·ance (-zis´tǎns), *n.* **1.** the act of resisting. **2.** the opposition offered by one thing to another. **3.** the ability to resist disease, etc. **4.** the opposition of a conductor to the flow of electric current, resulting in the generation of heat. **5.** **[R-],** an organized underground movement against invaders of a country. **—re·sist´ant,** *adj. & n.*

re·sist·i·ble (´ti-bl), *adj.* capable of being resisted. **—re·sist·i·bil´i·ty,** *n.* **—re·sist´i·bly,** *adv.*

re·sist·less (ri-zist´lis), *adj.* **1.** irresistible. **2.** unresisting. **—re·sist´less·ly,** *adv.*

re·sis·tor (ri-zis´tēr), *n.* a device to provide resistance in an electrical circuit.

re·sole (rē-sōl´), *v.t.* **-soled´, -sol´ing,** to put a new sole on (a shoe, boot, etc.).

re·sol·u·ble (ri-zol´yoo-bl), *adj.* capable of being resolved. **—re·sol·u·bil´i·ty,** *n.*

res·o·lute (rez´ŏ-lōōt), *adj.* determined; having a fixed purpose; decided. **—res´o·lute·ly,** *adv.*

res·o·lu·tion (rez-ŏ-lōō´shŭn), *n.* **1.** the act of resolving. **2.** the state or result of being resolved. **3.** analysis. **4.** fixed determination; constancy of purpose. **5.** a decision regarding future action. **6.** a formal proposal in a legislative assembly or public meeting. **7.** a solution.

re·solv·a·ble (ri-zol´vǎ-bl), *adj.* that can be resolved. **—re·solv·a·bil´i·ty,** *n.*

re·solve (ri-zolv´), *v.t.* **-solved´, -solv´ing, 1.** to reduce to constituent parts; analyze. **2.** to free from (doubt or difficulty). **3.** to explain or make clear. **4.** to solve (a problem). **5.** to determine by vote. **6.** to reach as an opinion or decision. **7.** to convert a musical discord into harmony: *v.i.* **1.** to determine. **2.** to be resolved, as by analysis. **3.** to pass a formal resolution: *n.* **1.** fixed purpose or intention. **2.** a formal resolution.

re·solved (-zolvd´), *adj.* determined; firm. **—re·solv´ed·ly** (-zol´vid-li), *adv.*

re·sol·vent (-zol´vĕnt), *adj.* having power of resolving; causing solution: *n.* **1.** a medicine that can cause swelling to go down. **2.** any solvent.

res·o·nant (rez´ŏ-nǎnt), *adj.* **1.** returning sound; resounding. **2.** deep and vibrant, as a tone, voice, etc. **3.** causing amplification of sound. **—res´o·nance,** *n.* **—res´o·nant·ly,** *adv.*

res·o·nate (-nāt), *v.t. & v.i.* **-nat·ed, -nat·ing,** to echo; resound; be or make resonant.

res·o·na·tor (-nāt-ēr), *n.* **1.** a device for increasing or producing resonance. **2.** an electronic apparatus or circuit that can be activated by another.

re·sorb (ri-sôrb´), *v.t.* to absorb again. **—re·sorp´tion** (-sôrp´shŭn), *n.* **—re·sorp´tive,** *adj.*

res·or·cin·ol (ri-zôr´si-nôl, -nōl), *n.* a colorless, crystalline compound obtained from resin or made synthetically, used in making dyes, medical ointments, etc.: also **res·or´cin** (´sin).

re·sort (ri-zôrt´), *v.i.* to turn (*to*) for help; have recourse: *n.* **1.** a place much frequented, as for vacations. **2.** recourse; source of help, support, etc.

re·sound (ri-zound´), *v.i.* **1.** to reverberate; sound again. **2.** to make a prolonged, echoing sound. **3.** to be renowned or celebrated. **—re·sound´ing,** *adj.* **—re·sound´ing·ly,** *adv.*

re·source (rē´sôrs, ri-zôrs´), *n.* **1.** a source of help or supply; an expedient to which one may resort. **2.** *pl.* money; assets. **3.** *pl.* a source of personal strength: also *inner resources.* **4.** ability to deal with difficulties, problems, etc.

re·source·ful (ri-sôrs´fǔl, -zôrs´-), *adj.* able to deal skillfully with difficulties, problems, etc. **—re·source´ful·ly,** *adv.* **—re·source´ful·ness,** *n.*

re·spect (ri-spekt´), *n.* **1.** regard; esteem. **2.** consideration; courtesy. **3.** a particular point or detail. **4.** relation; reference. **5.** *pl.* expressions of good will or regard: *v.t.* **1.** to honor or esteem. **2.** to be considerate of. **3.** to have reference to.

re·spect·a·ble (´ǎ-bl), *adj.* **1.** worthy of respect. **2.** behaving well; proper. **3.** moderate in quality or number. **4.** fit to be seen, worn, etc. —re·spect·a·bil'i·ty, n. —re·spect'a·bly, adv.

re·spect·ful ('fŭl), adj. showing respect or deference; courteous and considerate. —re·spect'ful·ly, adv. —re·spect'ful·ness, n.

re·spect·ing (ri-spek'ting), prep. concerning.

re·spec·tive ('tiv), adj. relating to or considering each particular person or thing separately.

re·spec·tive·ly ('tiv-li), adv. with respect to each in the order named.

re·spir·a·ble (ri-spīr'å-bl), adj. 1. that may be, or is fit to be, breathed. 2. capable of breathing. —re·spir·a·bil'i·ty, n.

res·pi·ra·tion (res-pĭ-rā'shŭn), n. the act or process of breathing. —res·pi·ra·to·ry (res'-pēr-å-tôr-i), adj.

res·pi·ra·tor (res'pĭ-rāt-ēr), n. 1. a device, as of gauze, for covering the mouth and nose to protect the lungs, throat, etc. from harmful substances, cold air, etc. 2. an apparatus used for giving artificial respiration.

re·spire (ri-spīr'), v.t. & v.i. -spired', -spir'ing, to draw air into the lungs and expel it again; breathe.

res·pite (res'pit), n. 1. a pause or interval of rest. 2. a temporary cessation of anything, as pain; lull: v.t. -pit·ed, -pit·ing, to give a respite to.

re·splend·ent (ri-splen'dĕnt), adj. shining with brilliant luster; dazzling; splendid. —re·splend'ence, re·splend'en·cy, n.

re·spond (ri-spond'), v.i. 1. to answer or reply. 2. to act as if answering. 3. to have a reaction. 4. to be liable legally: n. a response in a church worship service.

re·spond·ent (ri-spon'dĕnt), adj. giving response; answering: n. 1. one who responds. 2. a defendant in a lawsuit, especially in equity, admiralty, appellate, and divorce proceedings.

re·spond·er ('dēr), n. 1. one that responds. 2. an electronic device that indicates that a signal has been received.

re·sponse (ri-spons'), n. 1. something said or done in answering or replying. 2. words or phrases sung or spoken by the congregation or choir in answer to the clergyman. 3. any reaction to a stimulus.

re·spon·si·bil·i·ty (ri-spon-sĭ-bil'ĭ-ti), n., pl. -ties, 1. condition or fact of being responsible; obligation; accountability. 2. a person or thing that one is responsible for.

re·spon·si·ble (ri-spon'sĭ-bl), adj. 1. expected to account (for); answerable (to). 2. involving duties or obligations. 3. rational and able to answer for one's behavior. 4. reliable; dependable. 5. able to pay debts. —re·spon'si·ble·ness, n. —re·spon'si·bly, adv.

re·spon·sive ('siv), adj. 1. serving as an answer or response. 2. reacting readily to a suggestion or an appeal. 3. consisting of responses. —re·spon'sive·ly, adv. —re·spon'sive·ness, n.

re·spon·so·ry ('sō-ri), n., pl. -ries, an anthem or a series of responses sung by a soloist and choir alternately.

rest (rest), n. 1. sleep or a period of sleep. 2. ease or inactivity after having worked. 3. relief from distress, annoyance, etc. 4. cessation of motion; immobility. 5. the repose of

death. 6. a shelter or place for resting or stopping. 7. a thing used for supporting something else. 8. a measured interval of silence between musical tones, or a symbol for such an interval: v.i. 1. to be eased or refreshed by sleeping or by stopping work. 2. to be at ease. 3. to be or become quiet or still. 4. to be supported; lean or lie (in, on, etc.). 5. to be found. 6. to depend; rely: v.t. 1. to cause to rest. 2. to place for ease or comfort. 3. to desist from presenting evidence in a law case.

rest (rest), n. 1. what is left or remains. 2. the others. Used with the: v.i. to continue to be.

re·state (rē-stāt'), v.t. -stat'ed, -stat'ing, to state again, especially in a different way. —re·state'ment, n.

res·tau·rant (res'tå-ränt, -ränt), n. a place where meals are prepared and served to customers for a price.

res·tau·ra·teur (res-tēr-å-tûr'), n. the proprietor of a restaurant.

rest cure, a treatment for persons suffering from nervous exhaustion, fatigue, etc., in which complete rest, special diets, etc. are provided.

rest·ful (rest'fŭl), adj. full of or providing rest; quiet.

rest home, a residence that provides care for aged persons or convalescents.

res·ti·tu·tion (res-tĭ-tōō'shŭn, -tū'-), n. the act of making good any loss, injury, or damage; restoration or reimbursement.

res·tive (res'tiv), adj. 1. balky or unruly. 2. nervous when subjected to restraint; restless. —res'tive·ness, n.

rest·less (rest'lis), adj. 1. unable to rest; uneasy. 2. affording no rest; disturbed. 3. hardly ever quiet; constantly moving. 4. showing discontent. —rest'less·ly, adv. —rest'less·ness, n.

res·to·ra·tion (res-tō-rā'shŭn), n. 1. the act of restoring; repair; renewal; reinstatement; restitution. 2. a restoring of something, as a building, to its original form or structure. 3. something restored.

re·stor·a·tive (ri-stôr'å-tiv), adj. capable of restoring: n. something that restores, as a food or medicine intended to restore health.

re·store (ri-stôr'), v.t. -stored', -stor'ing, 1. to return (something lost or taken). 2. to bring back to a former condition or to a position, rank, etc. formerly held. 3. to bring back to its former strength, health, etc. 4. to reestablish.

re·strain (ri-strān'), v.t. to check; repress; curb; restrict.

re·straint (ri-strānt'), n. 1. the act of restraining. 2. a means of restraining. 3. confinement. 4. constraint.

restraint of trade, the restricting of business competition, as by monopoly, price fixing, etc.

re·strict (ri-strikt'), v.t. to keep within fixed limits; confine or limit.

re·strict·ed (-strik'tid), adj. 1. confined; limited. 2. limited in accessibility to certain authorized personnel, as certain documents. 3. keeping out a specified group or groups: said of certain living areas.

a in cap, ā in cane, ä in father, å in abet, e in met, ē in be, ê in baker, ê in regent, i in pit, ī in fine, ĭ in manifest, o in hot, ô in horse, ō in bone,

re·stric·tion ('shŭn), *n*. 1. the act of restricting. 2. the state of being restricted. 3. something that restricts.

re·stric·tive ('tiv), *adj*. 1. restricting; limiting. 2. in *Grammar*, denoting a clause or phrase that restricts the meaning of the word it modifies and is not set off by commas. —**re·stric'tive·ly**, *adv*.

restrictive covenant, a covenant that restricts the action of a party to an agreement, usually in a way that cannot be enforced legally.

rest·room (rest'rōōm), *n*. a room in a public building in which there are toilets, washbowls, etc.: also **rest room**.

re·struc·ture (rē-struk'chĕr), *v.t.* **-tured, -tur·ing**, to plan a new structure for.

re·sult (ri-zult'), *v.i.* 1. to follow as a consequence. 2. to come to an end (*in* something that is an effect): *n*. 1. anything that follows as a consequence. 2. *pl*. the effect desired. 3. the number or quantity that is the answer to a mathematical problem.

re·sult·ant ('nt), *adj*. that results or follows as a consequence: *n*. something that results.

re·sume (ri-zōōm', -zūm'), *v.t.* **-sumed', -sum'-ing**, 1. to take again. 2. to take up again after interruption: *v.i.* to begin again.

ré·su·mé (rez'oo-mā, rā-zoo-mā'), *n*. a condensed statement; summary.

re·sump·tion (ri-zump'shŭn), *n*. the act of resuming.

re·sur·face (rē-sûr'fis), *v.t.* **-faced, -fac·ing**, to give a new surface to: *v.i.* to rise again to the surface.

re·sur·gent (ri-sûr'jĕnt), *adj*. rising again. —**re·sur'gence**, *n*.

res·ur·rect (rez-ŭ-rekt'), *v.t.* 1. to raise from the dead; restore to life. 2. to bring back into use or notice.

res·ur·rec·tion (rez-ŭ-rek'shŭn), *n*. 1. a rising again from the dead. 2. [R-], the rising of Jesus from the dead: used with *the*. 3. a coming back into use or notice.

re·sus·ci·tate (ri-sus'i-tāt), *v.t. & v.i.* **-tat·ed, -tat·ing**, to revive from a state of apparent death. —**re·sus·ci·ta'tion**, *n*. —**re·sus'ci·ta·tor**, *n*.

ret (ret), *v.t.* **ret'ted, ret'ting**, to steep (hemp, flax, etc.) in water to separate its fibers.

re·tail (rē'tāl), *n*. the sale of goods in small quantities to the consumer directly: *adj*. of or having to do with the sale of goods thus: *adv*. at a retail price or in small quantities: *v.t. & v.i.* to sell or be sold in small quantities or to the consumer directly. —**re'-tail·er**, *n*.

re·tain (ri-tān'), *v.t.* 1. to hold or keep in possession. 2. to engage by paying a fee.

re·tain·er ('ēr), *n*. 1. one that retains. 2. a servant or attendant. 3. a device for holding teeth in a desired position. 4. a fee paid in advance for engaging the services of a lawyer, consultant, etc.

retaining wall, a wall built to keep a bank of earth in place or to prevent water from flooding.

re·take (rē-tāk'), *v.t.* **-took', -tak'en, -tak'ing**, 1. to take again or take back. 2. to photo-

graph again: *n*. (rē'tāk), anything photographed again.

re·tal·i·ate (ri-tal'i-āt), *v.i.* **-at·ed, -at·ing**, to return like for like, or evil for evil: *v.i.* to pay back (a wrong, injury, etc.) in kind. —**re·tal·i·a'tion**, *n*. —**re·tal'i·a·to·ry** ('i-ā-tôr-i), *adj*.

re·tard (ri-tärd'), *v.t.* to keep back; slow down; hinder; delay: *n*. delay; retardation.

re·tard·ant ('nt), *n*. something that retards: *adj*. that tends to retard.

re·tar·date (ri-tär'dāt), *n*. a person who is mentally retarded.

re·tar·da·tion (rē-tär-dā'shŭn), *n*. 1. the act of retarding. 2. something that retards. 3. same as **mental retardation**. 4. the amount by which something is retarded. —**re·tard·a·tive** (ri-tär'dā-tiv), **re·tard'a·to·ry** (-tôr-i), *adj*.

re·tard·ed (ri-tär'did), *adj*. slowed down or delayed in one's development, especially because of mental retardation.

retch (rech), *v.i.* to try to vomit; especially, to strain in vomiting without bringing anything up.

re·ten·tion (ri-ten'shŭn), *n*. 1. the act of retaining or state of being retained. 2. power of retaining. 3. memory, or ability to remember.

re·ten·tive ('tiv), *adj*. 1. that tends to retain. 2. that has the power of retaining. —**re·ten'-tive·ness**, *n*.

re·think (rē-thingk'), *v.t.* **-thought', -think'ing**, to think about or again; consider again.

ret·i·cent (ret'i-snt), *adj*. 1. not inclined to speak; usually keeping silent or quiet; taciturn; reserved. 2. quiet and restrained. —**ret'i·cence**, *n*.

ret·i·cle (ret'i-kl), *n*. a network of very fine lines, wires, etc. in the eyepiece of an optical instrument, for dividing the field of view into small equal squares.

re·tic·u·lar (ri-tik'yoo-lĕr), *adj*. like a net; intricate.

re·tic·u·late (-lit, -lāt), *adj*. formed or resembling network; netlike: also **re·tic'u·lat·ed**: *v.t. & v.i.* (-lāt), **-lat·ed, -lat·ing**, to form to look like network or a net.

ret·i·cule (ret'i-kūl), *n*. 1. a lady's handbag, originally made of network. 2. same as **reti·cle**.

ret·i·na (ret'n-ă), *n., pl.* **-nas** or **-nae** (-ē), the inner coat of the back of the eye, containing cells sensitive to light: images formed on the retina by the lens are carried by the optic nerve to the brain. —**ret'i·nal**, *adj*.

ret·i·ni·tis (ret-n-īt'is), *n*. inflammation of the retina.

ret·i·nue (ret'n-ōō), *n*. all the followers or servants of a person of importance or rank; body of retainers.

re·tire (ri-tīr'), *v.i.* **-tired', -tir'ing**, 1. to go away to a secluded or private place. 2. to go to bed. 3. to retreat or withdraw. 4. to withdraw from business or official life; give up one's work, usually after one has reached a specified age. 5. to move backward, or seem to do so: *v.t.* 1. to make retreat. 2. to remove (money) from circulation. 3. to pay off (stock, bonds, etc.). 4. to make (someone) retire from business, work, etc. 5.

ŏ in drag*o*n, ōō in cr*u*de, oo in w*oo*l, u in c*u*p, ū in c*u*re, ū in t*u*rn, ŭ in f*o*cus, oi in b*o*y, ou in h*ou*se, th in *th*in, th in shea*th*e, g in *g*et, j in *j*oy, y in *y*et.

to stop using. 6. in *Baseball*, to put out (a batter, side, etc.).

re-tired (-tīrd'), *adj.* 1. withdrawn from the society of others; secluded. 2. having given up one's business, work, etc. after having reached a specified age. 3. of or for people who have retired from business, work, etc.

re-tir-ee (-tīr-ē'), *n.* one who has retired from business, work, etc. after reaching a specified age.

re-tire-ment (-tīr'mĕnt), *n.* 1. the act of retiring or state of being retired. 2. withdrawal from business, work, etc. after having reached a specified age. 3. seclusion; privacy. 4. a place of seclusion or privacy.

re-tir-ing (-tīr'ing), *adj.* 1. that retires. 2. inclined to withdraw from society; reserved; shy; modest.

re-tool (rē-tōōl'), *v.t. & v.i.* 1. to change the tools, machinery, etc. used in (a factory) in order to make a different product. 2. to change in order to adapt to new or different conditions.

re-tort (ri-tôrt'), *v.t.* 1. to return (an incivility, insult, etc.) to the person who gave it. 2. to answer (an argument) in a like manner. 3. to say in replying: *v.i.* to make a retort; reply: *n.* 1. a sharp or quick reply, often a witty one. 2. the act of making such a reply. 3. a container with a long tube, used in distilling substances. 4. a vessel in which ore is heated to get metal, coal is heated to get gas, etc.

re-touch (rē-tuch'), *v.t.* to put touches in or on (a work of art, photographic negative, etc.) so as to improve it; touch up or change by adding or removing details: *n.* (also rē'tuch), the act of retouching. —**re-touch'er**, *n.*

re-trace (ri-trās'), *v.t.* -traced', -trac'ing, to go over again or go back over again.

re-trace (rē-trās'), *v.t.* -traced', -trac'ing, to trace (something drawn, engraved, etc.) over again.

re-tract (ri-trakt'), *v.t. & v.i.* 1. to draw back or draw in. 2. to withdraw or disavow (something stated, promised, charged, etc.). —**re-tract'a-ble**, *adj.* —**re-trac'tive**, *adj.*

re-trac-tile (ri-trak'tl, -tĭl), *adj.* capable of being drawn back or drawn in, as the claws of a cat.

re-trac-tion ('shŭn), *n.* 1. the act or power of retracting. 2. the withdrawal of something stated, promised, etc.

re-trac-tor ('tĕr), *n.* one that retracts; especially, a muscle that retracts an organ, or a surgical device for drawing a part or organ back.

re-tread (rē-tred'), *v.t.* to recap (a worn tire): *n.* (rē'tred), a recapped tire.

re-treat (ri-trēt'), *n.* 1. the act of withdrawing, as from danger. 2. a place of privacy; shelter. 3. a period of being secluded, especially for religious contemplation. 4. the withdrawal of a body of troops under attack. 5. a signal for such withdrawal. 6. a signal on bugle or drum for the national flag to be lowered at sunset. 7. the ceremony for this: *v.i.* to make a retreat; go back; withdraw; retire.

re-trench (rē-trench'), *v.t. & v.i.* to cut down or reduce (expenses). —**re-trench'ment**, *n.*

ret-ri-bu-tion (ret-ri-bū'shŭn), *n.* reward or punishment suitable to action done and, in some religions, regarded as deserved in a future life for good or evil deeds in this life. —**re-trib-u-tive** (ri-trib'yoo-tiv), *adj.*

re-triev-al (ri-trē'vl), *n.* the act or process of retrieving.

re-trieve (ri-trēv'), *v.t.* -trieved', -triev'ing, 1. to get back; recover, restore, or rescue. 2. to make right (an error, loss, etc.). 3. to obtain (information) that has been previously stored in a computer. 4. to find and bring back (game animals that have been wounded or killed): said of dogs: *v.i.* to retrieve game animals: *n.* the act of retrieving. —**re-triev'a-ble**, *adj.*

re-triev-er ('ĕr), *n.* 1. one who retrieves. 2. a dog that has been trained to retrieve game animals.

retro-, a combining form meaning *backward, back, behind.*

ret-ro-ac-tive (ret-rō-ak'tiv), *adj.* 1. that has application to things already past: said of certain laws. 2. put into effect as of a specified date in the past, as a salary increase. —**ret-ro-ac'tive-ly**, *adv.*

ret-ro-fire (ret'rō-fīr), *v.t.* -fired, -fir-ing, to ignite (a retrorocket).

ret-ro-flex-ion, **ret-ro-flec-tion** (ret-rō-flek'shŭn), *n.* the bending backward of an organ of the body upon itself.

ret-ro-grade (ret'rō-grād), *adj.* 1. going or moving backwards. 2. going from a better to a worse condition: *v.i.* -grad-ed, -grad-ing, 1. to go or move backwards. 2. to become worse.

ret-ro-gress (ret'rō-gres), *v.i.* to move backward; especially, to return to an earlier or worse condition. —**ret-ro-gres'sion**, *n.* —**ret-ro-gres'sive**, *adj.*

ret-ro-rock-et (ret'rō-rok-it), *n.* a small rocket, as on a spacecraft, used to reduce landing speed, etc. by causing thrust in an opposite direction.

ret-ro-spect (ret'rō-spekt), *n.* contemplation and review of the past.

ret-ro-spec-tion (ret-rō-spek'shŭn), *n.* the act or faculty of looking back on the past.

ret-ro-spec-tive ('tiv), *adj.* 1. looking back on things past. 2. referring to past things: *n.* a representative exhibition of an artist's lifetime work. —**ret-ro-spec'tive-ly**, *adv.*

ret-rous-sé (ret-rōō-sā'), *adj.* turned up at the end: said of a nose.

ret-ro-ver-sion (ret-rō-vūr'zhŭn), *n.* 1. a turning back. 2. a turning backward (of a body part or organ).

ret-si-na, **ret-zi-na** (ret'si-nä), *n.* a white or red Greek wine with the flavor of pine resin.

re-turn (ri-tūrn'), *v.i.* 1. to come or go back again to the same place or state. 2. to reply; answer: *v.t.* 1. to send or put back; restore. 2. to do (something) as a response. 3. to produce (a revenue, profit, etc.). 4. to reply in an official way. 5. to elect or re-elect: *n.* 1. the act of coming or going back. 2. the act of sending or putting back. 3. something returned. 4. a recurrence or reappearance. 5. something done to repay, requite, reciprocate, etc. 6. *often pl.* revenue or profit, as from investments. 7. a reply. 8. *often pl.* an official report, as on the counting of votes, in an election. 9. a form used for reporting income and computing a tax on it: *adj.* 1. of or for a return. 2. done, sent, etc. in return. —re-turn'a-ble, *adj.*

re-turn-ee (ri-tūr-nē'), *n.* one who returns, as after having been away in military service.

re-tuse (ri-tōōs', -tūs'), *adj.* in *Botany*, having a rounded or blunt apex with a small notch.

re-u-ni-fy (rē-ū'ni-fī), *v.t. & v.i.* -fied, -fy-ing, to unify again. —re-u-ni-fi-ca'tion, *n.*

re-un-ion (rē-ūn'yŭn), *n.* 1. the act of reuniting. 2. a gathering of members of a family, a school class, or some other group, after they have been separated for some time.

re-u-nite (rē-yoo-nīt'), *v.t. & v.i.* -nit'ed, -nit'ing, to unite again.

rev (rev), *v.t.* revved, rev'ving, [Informal], to increase the speed of (an engine, motor, etc.): usually with *up.*

re-vamp (rē-vamp'), *v.t.* 1. to provide (a shoe or boot) with a new vamp. 2. to do over; revise.

re-veal (ri-vēl'), *v.t.* 1. to make known (something secret or hidden). 2. to show or display: *n.* the vertical side of a doorway or window.

revealed religion, any religion whose followers believe that divine knowledge and will are revealed to them.

re-veil-le (rev'ē-li), *n.* the beat of a drum or a bugle call at daybreak to awaken soldiers and sailors.

rev-el (rev'l), *v.i.* -eled or -elled, -el-ing or -el-ling, 1. to make merry. 2. to take delight (*in*): *n.* revelry; merrymaking. —rev'el-er, rev'el-ler, *n.*

rev-e-la-tion (rev-ē-lā'shŭn), *n.* 1. the act of revealing or making known. 2. a startling disclosure. 3. that which is revealed, especially by God to man. —rev'e-la-to-ry (-lā-tōr-i), *adj.*

Rev-e-la-tions (rev-ē-lā'shŭnz), *n.* the last book of the New Testament: in full, The Revelation of St. John the Divine.

rev-el-ry (rev'l-ri), *n., pl.* -ries, boisterous festivity; merrymaking.

re-venge (ri-venj'), *v.t.* -venged', -veng'ing, 1. to inflict pain or injury in return for (pain or injury received). 2. to avenge (a person): *n.* 1. the act of revenging. 2. desire for vengeance. 3. a chance for retaliation. —re-venge'ful, *adj.*

rev-e-nue (rev'ē-nōō, -nū), *n.* 1. income or profit from lands, investments, etc. 2. *pl.* all the items of income, as of a nation. 3. the income that a city, state, or nation gets from taxes, licenses, etc. 4. the department of government that collects taxes.

re-ver-ber-ate (ri-vūr'bē-rāt), *v.t. & v.i.* -at-ed, -at-ing, 1. to reecho or cause to reecho. 2. to reflect or be reflected, as light or sound waves. 3. to deflect or be deflected, as heat or flame in a reverberatory furnace. —re-ver-ber-a'tion, *n.*

re-ver-ber-a-to-ry ('bēr-å-tōr-i), *adj.* 1. working or produced by means of reverberation. 2.

deflected, as heat or flame. 3. denoting a furnace or kiln in which the flame is deflected downward from the roof onto the ore, metal, etc. being heated.

re-vere (ri-vir'), *v.t.* -vered', -ver'ing, to regard with respect, affection, and awe; venerate.

rev-er-ence (rev'ēr-ēns, rev'rēns), *n.* 1. a feeling of respect, affection, and awe; veneration. 2. a bow or any gesture showing such feeling. 3. [R-], a title used in addressing members of the clergy (preceded by *His, Her,* or *Your*): *v.t.* -enced, -enc-ing, to regard with reverence.

rev-er-end ('ēr-ēnd), *adj.* worthy of reverence: used [R-], as a title of respect for a member of the clergy: *n.* [Informal], a member of the clergy (preceded by *the*).

rev-er-ent ('ēr-ēnt), *adj.* showing, or expressive of, reverence. —rev'er-ent-ly, *adv.*

rev-er-en-tial (rev-ē-ren'shŭl), *adj.* showing or due to reverence. —rev-er-en'tial-ly, *adv.*

rev-er-ie, rev-er-y (rev'ēr-i), *n., pl.* -er-ies, 1. a state of dreaming while awake; deep musing. 2. time spent in this state; daydream.

re-vers (ri-vir', -ver'), *n., pl.* -vers (-virz', -verz'), a lapel or other part (of a garment) turned back to show the reverse side: also re-vere' (-vir').

re-ver-sal (ri-vūr'sl), *n.* 1. the act of reversing. 2. a change to the opposite. 3. an annulment.

re-verse (ri-vūrs'), *adj.* 1. turned backward; having an opposite or contrary position, direction, or order. 2. causing movement backward: *n.* 1. the contrary or opposite. 2. the back of a coin or medal. 3. a change in fortune; misfortune or defeat. 4. a mechanism used for reversing, as in a motor vehicle: *v.t.* -versed', -vers'ing, 1. to turn upside down, backward, to an opposite position or direction, etc. 2. to change entirely. 3. to annul (a legal decision). —re-vers'i-ble, *adj.*

re-ver-sion (ri-vūr'zhŭn), *n.* the act of reverting, especially to a former condition or type, or to a former owner. —re-ver'sion-ar-y, *adj.*

re-vert (ri-vūrt'), *v.i.* 1. to return to a condition, topic, custom, etc. 2. to return to a former or primitive type: said of an animal or plant. 3. in *Law*, to return to the original owner or his heirs. —re-vert'i-ble, *adj.*

re-vest (rē-vest'), *v.t.* 1. to reinstate (someone). 2. to vest (powers, an office, etc.) again: *v.i.* to become vested (*in*) again.

re-vet-ment (ri-vet'mĕnt), *n.* 1. a strong wall erected to fortify the lower part of a rampart. 2. a retaining wall. 3. a protective facing of stone, cement, etc. for a wall or bank of earth.

re-view (ri-vū'), *v.t.* 1. to look back on. 2. to give a survey of. 3. to examine or evaluate (a book, play, etc.) as a critic. 4. to inspect (troops). 5. to examine or study again: *v.i.* to review books, plays, etc.: *n.* 1. the act of looking back on the past. 2. a survey. 3. an evaluation done by a critic. 4. a periodical containing critical articles on books, plays, etc. 5. an inspection of troops. 6. a reexamination, as of the decision made by a lower court. —re-view'er, *n.*

ô in drag*o*n, ōō in cr*u*de, oo in w*oo*l, u in c*u*p, ū in c*u*re, ū in t*u*rn, ů in f*o*cus, oi in b*o*y, ou in h*ou*se, th in *th*in, *th* in shea*th*e, g in *g*et, j in *j*oy, y in *y*et.

re·vile (ri-vīl'), *v.t. & v.i.* **-viled'**, **-vil'ing**, to call (someone) bad names. **—re·vile'ment**, *n.*

re·vise (ri-vīz'), *v.t.* **-vised'**, **-vis'ing**, 1. to review and amend. 2. to examine with care and correct, improve, rewrite, etc.: *n.* 1. a revision. 2. a printing proof of a revised manuscript.

Revised Standard Version, a mid-20th-century revision of the Bible.

re·vi·sion (ri-vizh'ün), *n.* 1. the act or work of revising. 2. the result of revising.

re·viv·al (ri-vī'vl), *n.* 1. the act of reviving or state of being revived, as in use or existence. 2. a new production, as of a stage play. 3. restoration to a vigorous condition. 4. a religious meeting led by a fervent, usually fundamentalist evangelist. **—re·viv'al·ism**, *n.*

re·viv·al·ist (-ist), *n.* a leader of religious revivals.

re·vive (ri-vīv'), *v.i. & v.t.* **-vived'**, **-viv'ing**, 1. to come or bring back to life. 2. to return to vigor or activity. 3. to come or bring back into use, existence, popularity, etc.

re·viv·i·fy (ri-viv'i-fī), *v.t.* **-fied**, **-fy·ing**, to reanimate; quicken: *v.i.* to revive.

rev·o·ca·ble (rev'ō-kȧ-bl), *adj.* that can be revoked.

rev·o·ca·tion (rev·ō-kā'shŭn), *n.* the act of revoking; repeal; cancellation; annulment.

re·voke (ri-vōk'), *v.t.* **-voked'**, **-vok'ing**, to repeal, cancel, or annul (a law, license, etc.): *v.i.* in card games, to fail to follow suit: *n.* in card games, the act of revoking.

re·volt (ri-vōlt'), *n.* rebellion against any authority or against a government in power; insurrection: *v.i.* 1. to join in a revolt; rebel. 2. to turn (*from* or *against*) in disgust; be disgusted (*at*): *v.t.* to make disgusted.

re·volt·ing ('ing), *adj.* disgusting; repulsive.

rev·o·lute (rev'ō-lōōt), *adj.* rolled backwards, as some leaves at the tip.

rev·o·lu·tion (rev·ō-lōō'shŭn), *n.* 1. the act of revolving; movement in an orbit. 2. the motion of spinning around an axis; rotation. 3. a repeated series of events. 4. any radical change. 5. a sudden and radical change in a country's government, social order, etc., often by use of force.

rev·o·lu·tion·ar·y (-er-i), *adj.* of, characterized by, causing, or constituting a revolution: *n.,* pl. **-ar·ies**, same as **revolutionist**.

rev·o·lu·tion·ist (-ist), *n.* one who organizes or takes part in a revolution.

rev·o·lu·tion·ize (-īz), *v.t.* **-ized**, **-iz·ing**, to bring about a revolution or radical change in.

re·volve (ri-volv'), *v.t.* **-volved'**, **-volv'ing**, 1. to turn over mentally; meditate upon; reflect on. 2. to cause to move in an orbit or circle. 3. to cause to rotate: *v.i.* 1. to move in an orbit or circle. 2. to rotate. 3. to occur again at intervals.

re·volv·er (-vol'vẽr), *n.* 1. one who, or that which, revolves. 2. a handgun with a revolving barrel, which can be fired successively without reloading.

revolving door, a structure consisting of four doorlike sections fastened to a central post and made to turn round when one of the leaves is pushed.

re·vue (ri-vū'), *n.* a musical show with songs and dances and skits, in which events of the day may be parodied.

re·vul·sion (ri-vul'shŭn), *n.* 1. sudden and violent change, especially of feeling. 2. a feeling of great disgust or loathing. **—re·vul'sive**, *adj.*

re·ward (ri-wôrd'), *n.* 1. something given as a return for good or evil. 2. money offered, as for returning a lost article. 3. profit; compensation: *v.t.* to give a reward to (someone) for doing (something).

re·wind (rē-wīnd'), *v.t.* **-wound'**, **-wind'ing**, to wind again: *n.* 1. the act of rewinding. 2. something rewound.

re·wire (-wīr'), *v.t. & v.i.* **-wired'**, **-wir'ing**, to wire again or with new wires or wiring.

re·word (rē-wûrd'), *v.t.* to give a different wording to.

re·work (-wûrk'), *v.t.* 1. to revise or rewrite. 2. to work on (something) so that it can be used again.

re·write (rē-rīt'), *v.t. & v.i.* **-wrote'**, **-writ'ten**, **-writ'ing**, 1. to write again. 2. to revise the written form of. 3. to write (news stories) over again to make them suitable for publication: *n.* (rē'rīt), a news story that has been rewritten.

rhap·sod·ic (rap-sod'ik), *adj.* of, like, or pertaining to rhapsody; highly enthusiastic; ecstatic: also **rhap·sod'i·cal**. **—rhap·sod'i·cal·ly**, *adv.*

rhap·so·dist (rap'sō-dist), *n.* one who rhapsodizes.

rhap·so·dize (-dīz), *v.i. & v.t.* **-dized**, **-diz·ing**, to speak or write in the style of a rhapsody.

rhap·so·dy (-di), *n.,* pl. **-dies**, 1. any utterance expressing great enthusiasm or inspired by high excitement. 2. intense delight; ecstasy. 3. a musical composition in a free form that sounds improvised.

rhat·a·ny (rat'n-i), *n.,* pl. **-nies**, the root of certain South American plants that contains tannins used in tanning leather.

rhe·a (rē'ȧ), *n.* any one of various large South American ostriches that have three toes, and feathers on the head and neck.

Rhen·ish (ren'ish), *adj.* of the Rhine: *n.* [Rare], a Rhine wine.

rhe·ni·um (rē'ni-ŭm), *n.* a rare metallic chemical element similar to manganese.

rhe·o-, a combining form meaning *a flow, current.*

rhe·om·e·ter (ri-om'ê-têr), *n.* an instrument that measures the velocity at which a fluid flows.

rhe·o·stat (rē'ō-stat), *n.* a device for regulating the resistance of an electric circuit, especially for regulating the brightness of an electric light.

rhe·ot·ro·pism (ri-ot'rō-pizm), *n.* the tendency of living plants to turn towards, or away from, a current of water. **—rhe·o·trop·ic** (ri-ō-trop'ik), *adj.*

rhe·sus (rē'sŭs), *n.* a brownish-yellow macaque of India, used widely in medical and biological research: in full, **rhesus monkey**.

rhet·or·ic (ret'ẽr-ik), *n.* 1. the art or skill of speaking or writing, especially of writing prose literary compositions using figurative language. 2. a showy, ornate literary style.

a in cap, ā in cane, ä in father, å in abet, e in met, ē in be, ê in baker, ê in regent, i in pit, ī in fine, i in manifest, o in hot, ō in horse, ō in bone,

rhe·tor·i·cal (ri-tôr'ĭ-kl), *adj.* of or using rhetoric, especially in a showy, ornate style. — **rhe·tor'i·cal·ly**, *adv.*

rhetorical question, a question that has an obvious answer that need not be given, although it may be, so as to stress some point.

rhet·o·ri·cian (ret-ô-rish'ûn), *n.* a teacher of rhetoric or one skilled in the art; orator.

rheum (rōōm), *n.* 1. a watery discharge from the nose, eyes, or mouth, or from any mucous membrane. 2. a cold; rhinitis. — **rheum'y**, *adj.*

rheu·mat·ic (roo-mat'ik), *adj.* of, caused by, or affected by rheumatism: *n.* one suffering from rheumatism. — **rheu·mat'i·cal·ly**, *adv.*

rheumatic fever, a chronic or acute disease accompanied by fever, the painful swelling of joints, etc., usually afflicting children.

rheu·ma·tism (rōō'mä-tizm), *n.* a painful condition of the muscles and joints, characterized by inflammation, stiffness, etc.

rheu·ma·toid (-toid), *adj.* of or like rheumatism.

rheumatoid arthritis, a chronic disease in which the joints become painfully swollen and often deformed.

Rh factor (är'ăch'), a group of antigens found in human blood: people are called **Rh positive** if they have this factor and **Rh negative** if they do not.

rhi·nal (rī'nl), *adj.* of the nose; nasal.

rhine·stone (rīn'stōn), *n.* an imitation gem made of hard glass: it takes a high luster and may be cut to look like a diamond.

rhi·ni·tis (rī-nīt'is), *n.* inflammation of the mucous membranes of the nostrils.

rhi·no (rī'nō), *n.*, *pl.* -nos, -no, same as rhinoceros.

rhi·noc·er·os (rī-nos'ēr-ûs), *n.*, *pl.* -os·es, -os, a large, thick-skinned mammal of Asia and Africa: it has one or two horns on the snout and three toes on each foot.

rhi·no·lar·yn·gol·o·gy (rī-nō-lar-in-gol'ô-ji), *n.* the medical science that treats of the nose and larynx. — **rhi·no·lar·yn·gol'o·gist**, *n.*

rhi·nol·o·gy (rī-nol'ô-ji), *n.* the medical science that treats of the nose and its diseases. — **rhi·nol'o·gist**, *n.*

rhi·no·plas·ty (rī'nô-plas-ti), *n.* plastic surgery as performed on the nose.

rhi·no·scope (rī'nô-skōp), *n.* an instrument equipped with a mirror for examining the passages of the nose. — **rhi·nos·co·py** (rī-nos'kô-pi), *n.*

rhi·zome (rī'zōm), *n.* a thick stem running along or under the soil, producing roots below and shoots or leaves above.

rhi·zo·pod (rī'zô-pod), *n.* any one of a class of one-celled animals, including the amoebas.

Rhodes scholarship (rōdz), any one of many scholarships founded at Oxford University, England, by Cecil John Rhodes, British millionaire, for selected students (**Rhodes scholars**) from the British Commonwealth and the U.S.

rho·di·um (rō'di-ûm), *n.* a whitish-gray metallic chemical element of the platinum group, used in alloys and in electroplating silverware, jewelry, etc.

rho·do·den·dron (rō-dô-den'drûn), *n.* any one

of a group of trees and shrubs, mainly evergreen, with roselike flowers of white, pink, or purple.

rho·do·lite (rōd'l-īt), *n.* a variety of garnet, of pink or rose color, often used as a gem.

rho·dop·sin (rō-dop'sin), *n.* a purplish pigment in the retina of the eye, necessary for seeing in dim light.

rho·do·ra (rō-dôr'ä), *n.* a plant related to the heath, having pink flowers and blossoming in the spring.

rhomb (romb), *n.* same as rhombus.

rhomb·ic (rom'bik), *adj.* of or shaped like a rhombus.

rhom·bo·he·dron (rom-bô-hē'drŭn), *n.*, *pl.* -drons, -dra ('drä), a prism with six sides, each side shaped like a rhombus. — **rhom·bo·he'dral**, *adj.*

rhom·boid (rom'boid), *n.* a four-sided figure having its opposite sides equal and its angles not right angles: *adj.* shaped like a rhomboid.

rhom·bus ('bŭs), *n.* a four-sided figure whose sides are equal and the opposite sides parallel, but which has two of its angles obtuse and two acute.

rho·ta·cism (rōt'ä-sizm), *n.* the substitution of the sound of *r* for *or* by some other sound.

rhu·barb (rōō'bärb), *n.* 1. a plant with long thick stalks that are cooked for making a sauce or pie. 2. [Slang], an angry argument.

rhumb (rum), *n.* any one of the 32 points of a mariner's compass, or the sector between one point and the next.

rhumb line, the course taken by a ship when it keeps to the same compass direction: it can be drawn on a map, chart, etc. as a line cutting across all meridians at the same angle.

rhyme (rīm), *n.* 1. a verse or poem in which there is correspondence of the sound of the last word or syllable of one line to the sound of the last word or syllable of another. 2. such correspondence or a word having such correspondence. 3. poetry: *v.i.* rhymed, rhym'ing, 1. to make verses or rhymes. 2. to form a rhyme: *v.t.* 1. to put into rhymes. 2. to use as a rhyme.

rhym·er (rīm'ēr), *n.* one who makes rhymes or poems.

rhyme·ster ('stēr), *n.* one who makes inferior rhymes or verse; poetaster.

rhythm (rith'm), *n.* 1. movement or flow in which there is a regularly recurring beat, accent, etc. 2. the pattern of such movement in poetry, dancing, music, etc.; specifically, in *poetry*, arrangement of syllables that are long or short, accented or unaccented, according to a basic metrical pattern, or, in *music*, arrangement of successive tones, generally in measures, according to accentuation and time value.

rhyth·mic (rith'mik), *adj.* of or pertaining to rhythm: also rhyth'mi·cal. — **rhyth'mi·cal·ly**, *adv.*

ri·ant (rī'änt), *adj.* laughing; smiling; gay.

rib (rib), *n.* 1. any one of the curved bones attached to the vertebral column and supporting the lateral walls of the thorax. 2. anything resembling a rib in appearance. 3. a

ô in dragon, ōō in crude, oo in wool, u in cup, ū in cure, û in turn, ŭ in focus, oi in boy, ou in house, th in thin, th in sheathe, g in get, j in joy, y in yet.

piece of timber to shape and strengthen the side of a ship. 4. in *Botany*, any one of the main veins in a leaf: *v.t.* **ribbed, rib'bing,** 1. to furnish or enclose with ribs. 2. [Slang], to tease.

rib·ald (rib'ǎld), *adj.* of, pertaining to, or indulging in vulgar, lewd, or licentious humor: *n.* a ribald person.

rib·ald·ry ('ǎl-drī), *n.* ribald language or vulgar joking.

rib·bon (rib'ŏn), *n.* 1. a fillet or narrow strip of silk, velvet, etc. used for decorating or tying. 2. *pl.* tattered shreds. 3. a narrow strip of inked cloth used for printing characters, as in a typewriter.

rib·bon·fish (-fish), *n.*, *pl.* **-fish, -fish·es,** an elongated and very compressed ocean fish with a long dorsal fin.

ri·bo·fla·vin (rī'bō-flā-vin), *n.* a growth-promoting factor in the vitamin B complex, found in milk, leafy vegetables, egg yolks, etc.

ri·bo·nu·cle·ase (rī-bō-nōō'kli-ās), *n.* any one of various enzymes that decompose ribonucleic acid.

ri·bo·nu·cle·ic acid (rī-bō-nōō-klē'ik), a universal component of all living cells, consisting of a long chain of phosphate and ribose units together with four bases that participate in protein synthesis.

ri·bose (rī'bōs), *n.* a sugar occurring in nucleic acids.

rice (rīs), *n.* 1. a cereal grass that is produced extensively in hot climates. 2. the starchy edible grain of this grass: *v.t.* **riced, ric'ing,** to force (food) through small perforations to produce ricelike granules.

rice·bird ('bürd), *n.* in the southern U.S., same as **bobolink.**

rice paper, 1. a thin kind of paper prepared from rice straw. 2. a thin paper made from the pith of the rice-paper tree.

rice-pa·per tree ('pā-pér), a small tree of eastern Asia that yields fiber for rice paper (sense 2).

rich (rich), *adj.* 1. abounding in money or possessions; wealthy. 2. opulent; sumptuous. 3. valuable. 4. fertile; fruitful. 5. full-bodied. 6. deep and mellow. 7. vivid. 8. fragrant. 9. abundant. 10. [Informal], extremely funny. **—rich'ly,** *adv.* **—rich'ness,** *n.*

rich·es (rich'iz), *n.pl.* wealth.

ri·cin (rīs'in), *n.* a violently poisonous protein found in the castor bean.

rick (rik), *n.* a pile or heap of hay, straw, etc. in a field, usually thatched or sheltered from rain: *v.t.* to pile or heap in a rick or ricks.

rick·ets (rik'its), *n.* a deficiency disease in children, caused by lack of vitamin D or sunlight and resulting in softness and, often, curvature of the bones.

rick·ett·si·a (ri-ket'si-à), *n.*, *pl.* **-si·ae** (-ē), **-si·as,** any one of various microorganisms that cause certain diseases in man, as typhus, and that are transmitted by the bite of many lice, fleas, and ticks in which they are parasitic.

rick·et·y (rik'it-i), *adj.* 1. of or afflicted with rickets. 2. feeble in the joints. 3. unsound

and likely to break apart; shaky. **—rick'et·i·ness,** *n.*

rick·rack (rik'rak), *n.* a flat, zigzag braid, used as a trimming.

rick·shaw, rick·sha (rik'shô), *n.* same as **jinriki·sha.**

ric·o·chet (rik'ō-shā), *n.* 1. the rebounding of a bullet, stone, etc. from a surface, as of rock or water. 2. a bullet, stone, etc. that ricochets: *v.i.* **-cheted** (-shād) or **-chet·ted** (-shet-id), **-chet·ing** (-shā-ing), or **-chet·ting** (-shet-ing), to rebound from a surface or surfaces.

rid (rid), *v.t.* **rid** or **rid'ded, rid'ding,** 1. to set free of something undesirable (usually with *of*). 2. [Obs.], to save or deliver; rescue.

rid·dance (rid'ns), *n.* the act of ridding or the state of being rid; a removal or deliverance from something unwanted.

rid·den (rid'n), past participle of **ride:** *adj.* dominated or haunted (by a specified thing): used in compounds, as fear-*ridden.*

rid·dle (rid'l), *n.* 1. a puzzling or seemingly unexplainable person or thing; enigma. 2. a problem or puzzle that requires analysis in order to answer or unravel it; conundrum: *v.t.* **-dled, -dling,** to answer or unravel (a riddle).

rid·dle (rid'l), *n.* a large sieve for separating and grading things, as gravel or grain: *v.t.* 1. to screen through a riddle. 2. to perforate with many holes, as by a shotgun blast. 3. to discover and demonstrate flaws or weaknesses in. 4. to course throughout; spread through.

ride (rīd), *v.i.* **rode, rid'den, rid'ing,** 1. to be borne along as on horseback or in a vehicle. 2. to be supported in motion. 3. to be fit to be ridden. 4. to move or float on the water. 5. [Informal], to continue undisturbed: *v.t.* 1. to ride or sit on or in and control the movement of. 2. to go over, along, or through (a road, region, etc.) by bus, horse, etc. 3. to control, dominate, etc. 4. [Informal], to torment, as with criticism; ridicule: *n.* 1. the act of riding. 2. an excursion on horseback or in some conveyance. 3. a thing to ride at an amusement park.

rid·er (rīd'ér), *n.* 1. a person who rides. 2. an addition or amendment to a document.

ridge (rij), *n.* 1. originally, an animal's back or spine. 2. anything formed like an animal's back, as a range of hills, a wave, etc. 3. any narrow uplifted strip. 4. the horizontal line produced by the joining of two sloping surfaces: *v.t.* & *v.i.* **ridged, ridg'ing,** 1. to mark or be marked with a ridge or ridges. 2. to furnish or form with a ridge or ridges.

ridge·pole ('pōl), *n.* a horizontal beam at the ridge of a roof, to which the rafters are attached.

ridg·y ('i), *adj.* **ridg'i·er, ridg'i·est,** rising in or having ridges.

rid·i·cule (rid'i-kūl), *n.* 1. words or actions designed to make one the butt of laughter or contempt. 2. the act of making someone the object of derision: *v.t.* **-culed, -cul·ing,** to mock, deride, or make fun of; expose to scornful merriment.

ri·dic·u·lous (ri-dik'yū-lŭs), *adj.* deserving of or exciting ridicule; preposterous; absurd; ludi-

---

a in cap, ā in cane, ä in father, å in abet, e in met, ē in be, ê in baker, è in regent, i in pit, ī in fine, i in manifest, o in hot, ô in horse, ō in bone,

crous. —ri·dic'u·lous·ly, adv. —ri·dic'u·lous·ness, n.

rid·ing (rīd'ing), adj. 1. that rides. 2. suitable or designed for riding. 3. designed to be ridden by an operator: n. the act of a person or thing that rides.

rid·ing (rīd'ing), n. an administrative division in Great Britain or an electoral district in Canada.

rife (rīf), adj. 1. widespread; common; prevalent. 2. abundant; replete.

riff (rif), n. in Jazz, a rhythmic phrase constantly repeated: v.i. in Jazz, to perform a riff.

rif·fle (rif'l), n. 1. a shallow stretch just below the surface of a stream. 2. the ruffled surface caused by such shallows. 3. in Mining, a device, as rods or bars, laid on the bottom of a sluice to catch particles of minerals, as gold, washed down with the sands. 4. a way of shuffling cards by splitting the deck, raising the corners of each part, and letting the cards fall alternately in one stack: v.t. & v.i. -fled, -fling, 1. to form or flow over a riffle. 2. to shuffle (playing cards) by using riffles.

riff·raff (rif'raf), n. 1. a worthless or disreputable person. 2. rabble.

ri·fle (rī'fl), n. 1. a firearm with the barrel spirally grooved, designed to be fired from the shoulder. 2. an artillery piece with similar groovings. 3. pl. troops armed with rifles: v.t. -fled, -fling, to cut spiral grooves (in a gun barrel).

ri·fle (rī'fl), v.t. -fled, -fling, 1. to plunder; pillage. 2. to search and rob (a safe, building, etc.).

ri·fle·bird (rī'fl-bûrd), n. any one of several birds of paradise of Australia.

ri·fle·man (-mǎn), n., pl. -men (-měn), 1. a soldier armed with a rifle. 2. a person skilled in the use of a rifle.

rift (rift), n. 1. an opening or split in anything; fissure. 2. a break or disruption of previous friendship: v.t. & v.i. to cleave; split.

rig (rig), v.t. rigged, rig'ging, 1. to equip (a ship) with sails, shrouds, etc. 2. to gather together. 3. to fit out; provide. 4. to manage in a fraudulent way. 5. [Informal], to dress or adorn (with out): n. 1. the way sails, shrouds, etc. are arranged. 2. any special equipment or gear. 3. a tractor-trailer.

rig·a·doon (rig-ă-dōōn'), n. an old-fashioned, lively dance performed by one couple.

rig·a·ma·role (rig'ă-mă-rōl), n. alternate spelling of rigmarole.

rig·ger (rig'ẽr), n. 1. a person who rigs ships. 2. a person who works with hoisting tackle, pulleys, etc.

rig·ging ('ing), n. the cordage or ropes by which the masts of a vessel are supported and the sails extended or furled.

Rigg's disease (rigz), same as pyorrhea: named after J. M. Riggs (1810-85), U.S. dentist.

right (rīt), adj. 1. according to truth, justice, or law; virtuous. 2. correct. 3. fitting; suitable. 4. mentally or physically normal; well. 5. denoting the side opposed to the left. 6. having a straight or perpendicular line: n. 1.

uprightness; justice; rectitude. 2. propriety. 3. a just or legal claim. 4. the right side. 5. the right hand. 6. [often R-], in Politics, a party, faction, etc. upholding conservative or reactionary policies: adv. 1. in a straight line; directly. 2. fittingly. 3. completely. 4. exactly. 5. justly. 6. correctly. 7. toward the right side: v.t. 1. to put in the vertical position. 2. to correct. 3. to make amends to or for: interj. I understand! well done! —right'ly, adv. —right'ness, n.

right-a·bout-face (rīt'ă-bout-fās'), n. same as about-face.

right angle, an angle of 90 degrees, formed by one straight line standing perpendicular to another.

right·eous (rī'chŭs), adj. 1. doing what is right; just; equitable. 2. morally proper; fair. 3. morally justifiable. —right'eous·ly, adv. —right'eous·ness, n.

right·ful (rīt'fŭl), adj. 1. fair or proper; just. 2. having a just claim; accordant with justice. —right'ful·ly, adv. —right'ful·ness, n.

right-hand (rīt'hand'), adj. 1. located on the right. 2. directed toward the right side. 3. of, for, or done by the right hand. 4. helpful; steady; reliable.

right-hand·ed ('han'did), adj. 1. using the right hand more skillfully than the left. 2. done with the right hand. 3. made for use with the right hand: adv. with the right hand.

right·ist (rīt'ist), n. & adj. conservative or reactionary.

right-mind·ed ('mīn'did), adj. having proper views based on what is right.

right of way, 1. the right of one person to pass over the property of another. 2. the strip of land over which a highway, railroad, power line, etc. passes. 3. the customary or legal right of one ship, automobile, etc. to proceed first or pass in front of another.

right-to-life (rīt'tōō-līf'), adj. designating any movement, party, etc. opposed to abortion. —right'-to-lif'er, n.

right whale, any one of several whales characterized by a huge head, long strips of whalebone in the mouth, and the absence of a dorsal fin.

right wing, a division within a large group, as a political party, that holds conservative or reactionary views. —right'-wing', adj. —right'-wing'er, n.

rig·id (rij'id), adj. 1. not pliant or bending; stiff; inflexible. 2. not moving; fixed. 3. strict; stern. 4. exact; not deviating. —ri·gid·i·ty (ri-jid'ĭ-ti), rig'id·ness, n. —rig'id·ly, adv.

rig·ma·role (rig'mă-rōl), n. 1. foolish or disconnected talk. 2. a time-wasting or foolishly complicated set of procedures.

rig·or (rig'ẽr), n. 1. stiffness or severity. 2. exactitude; precision. 3. severity of climate. British spelling rig'our.

rig·or·ism (-izm), n. austerity or severity in principle or practice, as in living style, religious principles, artistic practice, etc. —rig'or·ist, n.

rig·or mor·tis (rig'ẽr môr'tis), the stiffening of the muscles following death.

rig·or·ous (rig'ẽr-ŭs), adj. 1. characterized by or exercising rigor; very stern. 2. full of rigors;

harsh. 3. scrupulously accurate; precise. — **rig'or·ous·ly,** *adv.* **—rig'or·ous·ness,** *n.*

Rigs·dag (rigz'dag), *n.* formerly, the two-chambered legislature of Denmark.

rile (rīl), *v.t.* **riled, ril'ing,** [Informal or Dial.], 1. same as **roil.** 2. to irritate; anger.

rill (ril), *n.* a small stream; rivulet: *v.i.* to flow in a small stream.

rim (rim), *n.* 1. a border or margin. 2. a raised or projecting border. 3. the circular outer part of a wheel. 4. the circular metal flange around an automobile wheel, in which the tire is fitted: *v.t.* **rimmed, rim'ming,** to furnish with a rim; put a rim around.

rime (rīm), *n.* & *v.t.* & *v.i.* **rimed, rim'ing,** same as **rhyme.**

rime (rīm), *n.* hoarfrost.

ri·mose (rī'mōs), *adj.* full of fissures or chinks; having many clefts or crevices, as the bark of a tree.

rim·ple (rim'p'l), *n.* & *v.t.* & *v.i.* **-pled, -pling,** [Now Rare], wrinkle; fold; crease.

rim·y (rīm'i), *adj.* **rim'i·er, rim'i·est,** covered with hoarfrost; frosty.

rind (rīnd), *n.* 1. the tough or hard, natural outer covering of an orange, melon, squash, etc. 2. any outer layer resembling this, as on cheese, bacon, etc.

rin·der·pest (rin'dēr-pest), *n.* a contagious disease of cattle and, often, sheep and goats, characterized by fever and the formation of ulcers in the intestinal tract.

ring (ring), *v.i.* **rang, rung, ring'ing,** 1. to sound clearly and resonantly when struck, as a bell. 2. to seem. 3. to cause a bell to sound. 4. to reverberate. 5. to hear a buzzing in the ears: *v.t.* 1. to cause (a bell, chimes, etc.) to ring. 2. to announce or sound abroad, as by ringing. 3. to call (someone) on the telephone: *n.* 1. the sound made by a bell, metal object, etc. when struck. 2. a particular quality. 3. an act of sounding a bell. 4. a telephone call.

ring (ring), *n.* 1. a circle. 2. anything circular in form, as the rim of a wheel. 3. a small hoop of metal, plastic, etc., sometimes set with gems, worn on a finger. 4. a circular band used for holding something or as a means of attachment. 5. an enclosed area or course of various shapes, used for sports, exhibitions, contests, etc. 6. a group of persons or things in a circle. 7. a group of persons combined to accomplish its private ends. 8. prizefighting (with *the*): *v.t.* **ringed, ring'ing,** 1. to encircle. 2. to form into or supply with a ring or rings.

ring·bone ('bōn), *n.* a bony excrescence on a horse's pastern, often producing lameness.

ring·dove ('duv), *n.* the European wood pigeon with whitish markings on each side of the neck.

ringed (ringd), *adj.* 1. wearing a ring. 2. decorated with a ring. 3. encircled with a ring. 4. shaped like a ring.

rin·gent (rin'jĕnt), *adj.* 1. having the mouth open; gaping. 2. in *Biology,* having gaping, liplike parts, as certain corollas, valves, etc.

ring·er (ring'ēr), *n.* 1. a horseshoe, quoit, etc. thrown so that it surrounds the peg. 2. such a toss.

ring·er (ring'ēr), *n.* 1. one that sounds a bell, chime, etc. 2. [Slang], a person so like another that he can pass for him. 3. [Slang], a person, horse, etc. dishonestly substituted for another in a competition.

ring finger, the third finger on the left hand, on which the wedding ring is worn.

ring·lead·er (ring'lēd-ēr), *n.* a person who leads others, especially in illegal or disruptive activities.

ring·let ('lit), *n.* 1. a little ring. 2. a curl of hair.

ring·mas·ter (ring'mas-tēr), *n.* one who directs the performances in a circus ring.

ring·neck ('nek), *n.* a bird, snake, etc. with a colored ring around the neck.

ring·necked ('nekt), *adj.* in *Zoology,* having a ring or stripes of distinctive color encircling the neck.

ring·necked duck, a North American duck, the male of which has a black head, white belly, and a brownish circlet of feathers around the neck.

ring·necked pheasant, a widely distributed Asian game fowl, the male of which has a white ring around the neck.

ring ouzel, a small European bird with a white band around its throat.

ring·side ('sid), *n.* 1. the space just outside the ring, as at a prizefight or circus. 2. any place from which a close view may be had of something.

ring·worm ('wŭrm), *n.* any of various contagious cutaneous diseases caused by several fungi, characterized by distinct circular patches covered with scales.

rink (ringk), *n.* 1. a smooth, clear expanse of ice, used for the game of curling. 2. a smooth expanse of ice that is prepared for ice-skating or playing hockey. 3. a smooth floor used for roller-skating.

rinse (rins), *v.t.* **rinsed, rins'ing,** 1. to cleanse lightly with water. 2. to wash (soap, dirt, etc.) from by running clean water over or through: *n.* 1. the act of rinsing. 2. the water or the solution used in rinsing. 3. a solution used to condition or tint the hair.

ri·ot (rī'ŏt), *n.* 1. a wild or tumultuous disturbance; uproar; confusion. 2. a violent disturbance of the public peace by three or more persons. 3. [Now Rare], noisy revelry. 4. a profusion, as of colors. 5. [Informal], a very amusing person or thing: *v.i.* to participate in a riot. **—ri'ot·er,** *n.*

ri·ot·ous (rī'ŏt-ŭs), *adj.* 1. of or resembling a riot. 2. participating in or inciting to riot. 3. disorderly; boisterous. 4. dissolute; licentious. 5. luxuriant; abundant.

rip (rip), *v.t.* **ripped, rip'ping,** 1. to divide by cutting or tearing. 2. to cut asunder. 3. to undo the threads of (a seam). 4. to saw (wood) along the grain: *v.i.* 1. to become ripped. 2. [Informal], to hurry; rush: *n.* a rent; tear; split.

rip (rip), *n.* [Informal], a dissolute or disreputable person.

ri·par·i·an (ri-per'i-ăn), *adj.* 1. living or growing along a river bank or, sometimes, a lake, pond, etc. 2. of or pertaining to land along

---

a in cap, ā in cane, ä in father, å in abet, e in met, ē in be, ẽ in baker, ĕ in regent, i in pit, ī in fine, i in manifest, o in hot, ô in horse, ō in bone,

such banks. 3. denoting a right belonging to one who owns riparian land.

rip cord, a cord pulled to release a parachute pack during descent.

ripe (rīp), *adj.* 1. brought to maturity; ready to be harvested. 2. aged sufficiently for use. 3. fully developed by study, experience, etc.; mature. 4. completely prepared; ready for something. —**ripe′ly,** *adv.* —**ripe′ness,** *n.*

rip·en (rī′pĕn), *v.t. & v.i.* to become or make ripe; mature. —**rip′en·er,** *n.*

rip-off (rip′ôf), *n.* [Slang], the act or an instance of stealing, cheating, etc.

ri·poste, ri·post (ri-pōst′), *n.* 1. in *Fencing,* a quick thrust after parrying a lunge. 2. a sharp, quick retort: *v.i.* -**post′ed,** -**post′ing,** to make a riposte.

rip·per (rip′ẽr), *n.* 1. a person who rips. 2. a device or instrument for ripping.

rip·ping (′ing), *adj.* 1. that rips or tears. 2. [Chiefly British Slang], remarkable; excellent; superior.

rip·ple (rip′l), *n.* 1. a small, curling wave, as on the surface of water. 2. a movement or effect suggesting this. 3. a sound like that of rippling water. 4. a small rapid: *v.i. & v.t.* -**pled,** -**pling,** to have or form ripples.

ripple effect, the spreading effects experienced as the result of a single event.

rip·ply (rip′lĭ), *adj.* -**pli·er,** -**pli·est,** having ripples; resembling the sound of ripples.

rip-rap (rip′rap), *n.* 1. a loose foundation or assemblage of broken stones in water or on a soft bottom. 2. the broken stones used for this: *v.t.* -**rapped,** -**rap·ping,** 1. to build a riprap in or on. 2. to strengthen with riprap.

rip-roar·ing (′rôr-ing), *adj.* [Slang], very noisy; lively; boisterous.

rip·saw (′sô), *n.* a coarse-toothed saw for cutting wood in the line of its grain.

rise (rīz), *v.i.* rose, ris·en (riz′n), ris′ing, 1. to go up higher; ascend. 2. to get up from a sitting, kneeling, or recumbent position. 3. to begin; originate. 4. to increase in quantity or extent. 5. to swell or expand. 6. to grow or extend upward. 7. to appear above the horizon. 8. to rebel; revolt. 9. to end an assembly; adjourn. 10. in *Theology,* to ascend from the grave: *n.* 1. the act of rising. 2. upward motion; ascent. 3. an elevated place. 4. an upward slope. 5. an advance in status, position, etc. 6. an increase in degree, amount, etc. 7. origin; source.

ris·er (′ẽr), *n.* 1. a person or thing that rises. 2. something, as a piece of wood, placed under another to elevate it. 3. the vertical parts between the steps in a stairway.

ris·i·bil·i·ty (riz-i-bil′ĭ-ti), *n., pl.* -**ties,** 1. the inclination or ability to laugh. 2. *often pl.* a sense of the ludicrous or the amusing.

ris·i·ble (riz′i-bl), *adj.* 1. having the power or faculty of laughing. 2. of or pertaining to laughter. 3. causing laughter; amusing.

ris·ing (rī′zing), *n.* 1. the act of getting up or ascending. 2. an uprising; insurrection. 3. something that rises, as a prominence. 4. [Dial.], a boil, abscess, etc.: *adj.* 1. ascending; sloping upward; advancing. 2. growing; maturing.

risk (risk), *n.* 1. the possibility of loss, injury, damage, etc.; hazard. 2. peril; danger: *v.t.* 1. to expose to the chance of loss, injury, etc.; hazard. 2. to incur the risk of.

risk·y (ris′ki), *adj.* risk′i·er, risk′i·est, involving risk; dangerous; hazardous. —**risk′i·ness,** *n.*

ri·sot·to (ri-sot′ō), *n.* rice cooked in broth with grated cheese, seasonings, etc.

ris·qué (ris-kā′), *adj.* approaching indelicacy; almost indecent; suggestive.

ris·sole (ris′ōl), *n.* minced meat or fish enclosed in a thin pastry and fried.

rite (rīt), *n.* 1. a solemn or ceremonial act, as in a religious observance. 2. any formal or prescribed practice or procedure.

ri·tor·nel·lo (rĭt-ẽr-nel′ō), *n., pl.* -**los,** in *Music,* 1. an instrumental interlude in early 17th-century opera. 2. the refrain of a rondo.

rit·u·al (rich′oo-wăl), *adj.* of, pertaining to, consisting of, or prescribing rites *n.* 1. a set manner of performing rites, as in a religious or other ceremony. 2. a book of rites. 3. the liturgy used in certain Christian churches.

rit·u·al·ism (-izm), *n.* 1. a system of ritual or prescribed forms in religion. 2. excessive observance of ritual. 3. the use of ritual. —**rit′u·al·ist,** *n. & adj.* —**rit·u·al·is′tic,** *adj.*

ri·val (rī′vl), *n.* one who strives to equal or excel another in some subject or pursuit: competitor: *adj.* acting as a rival; competing: *v.t.* -**valed** or -**valled,** -**val·ing** or -**val·ling,** 1. to strive to equal or excel; compete with. 2. to equal in some respect.

ri·val·ry (-ri), *n., pl.* -**ries,** 1. the act of competing or emulating. 2. the state or condition of being a rival.

rive (rīv), *v.t.* rived, rived or riv′en, riv′ing, 1. to rend asunder; tear apart. 2. to split: *v.i.* to be or become rived.

riv·er (riv′ẽr), *n.* 1. a large, natural stream of running water flowing into a sea, a lake, or another river. 2. any similar stream or abundant flow, as of lava.

river basin, the area of land drained by a river and its tributaries.

riv·er·bed (-bed), *n.* the channel a river occupies or once occupied.

river horse, same as hippopotamus.

riv·er·ine (-in, -in), *adj.* 1. of, pertaining to, or produced by a river. 2. near or located on the banks of a river; riparian.

riv·er·side (-sīd), *n.* the bank of a river: *adj.* on or close to the bank of a river.

riv·et (riv′it), *n.* a metal bolt with a head at one end, used to fasten objects together by inserting the shank through holes in the objects and clinching or hammering down the plain end so as to form a second head: *v.t.* to secure with or as with rivets. —**riv′et·er,** *n.*

ri·vière (rē-vyer′, riv-i-er′), *n.* a necklace of diamonds or other precious stones.

riv·u·let (riv′yoo-lit), *n.* a little stream.

riv·u·lose (riv′yū-lōs), *adj.* marked with sinuous or crooked lines.

RNA, ribonucleic acid.

roach (rōch), *n.* 1. short for cockroach. 2. [Slang], the butt of a marijuana cigarette.

roach (rōch), *n., pl.* roach, roach′es, 1. a freshwater fish of the carp family, found in

---

northern Europe. 2. any one of various similar or related fishes.

roach (rōch), *v.t.* 1. to brush (a person's hair) back from the forehead into a roll. 2. to cut (a horse's mane) so that the bristles left stand straight up.

road (rōd), *n.* 1. a public way for persons, vehicles, or animals to travel between places; highway. 2. a path; way; course. 3. *often pl.* a place near shore where ships may ride safely at anchor.

road-a-bil-i-ty (rōd-ä-bil'ĭ-ti), *n.* the degree of comfort, ease in handling, etc. of an automobile on the road.

road agent, a highwayman, especially one who robbed stagecoaches.

road-bed ('bed), *n.* 1. the foundation on which the ties, rails, and ballast of a railroad are laid. 2. the ballast immediately below the ties. 3. the foundation and surface of a highway or road.

road-block ('blok), *n.* 1. a barricade or block-ade across a road to prevent passage of troops, vehicles, etc. 2. any obstruction or hindrance.

road hog, a driver of an automobile, truck, etc. whose vehicle occupies parts of two lanes.

road-house ('hous), *n.* an inn or nightclub located on a country road.

road runner, a swift-running, crested bird of southwestern North America, with brownish plumage and a long tail.

road-show ('shō), *n.* 1. a theatrical show that goes on tour. 2. the showing of a film at certain theaters with reserved seats.

road-side ('sid), *n.* the side of a road: *adj.* located in the area bordering upon a side of a road.

road-stead ('sted), *n.* same as **road** (sense 3).

road-ster ('stēr), *n.* 1. a horse for riding on a road. 2. an earlier type of open automobile with a single seat for two or three people and, sometimes, a rumble seat.

road-way ('wā), *n.* 1. a road. 2. the part of a road over which vehicles travel.

road-work ('würk), *n.* running or jogging out-doors as an exercise for conditioning an athlete.

roam (rōm), *v.i. & v.t.* to wander about without any definite objective; ramble: *n.* the act of roaming. —**roam'er,** *n.*

roan (rōn), *adj.* having a coat of any solid color thickly interspersed with white or gray hairs: *n.* 1. a roan horse. 2. a roan color.

roan (rōn), *n.* a sheepskin leather grained to resemble morocco.

roar (rôr), *n.* 1. the deep, full cry of a lion, bull, etc. 2. a loud, continuous noise, as of waves, a motor, etc. 3. a loud burst of laughter: *v.i.* 1. to utter a loud, deep, rum-bling sound. 2. to laugh loudly: *v.t.* to ex-press with a roar.

roar-ing ('ing), *n.* 1. the act of an animal or person that roars. 2. the full, deep sound made by an animal that roars. 3. a disease of horses, characterized by difficult, stridu-lous breathing: *adj.* 1. noisy; boisterous. 2. [Informal], very lively; brisk.

roast (rōst), *v.t.* 1. to cook (something) with dry heat, as in an oven, over an open fire, or in hot embers, stones, etc. 2. to dry or brown (coffee, nuts, etc.) by exposure to heat. 3. to expose to intense or excessive heat. 4. to heat (ores) in a furnace to remove impurities, produce oxidation, etc. 5. [Informal], to criticize severely; ridicule: *v.i.* 1. to undergo roasting. 2. to be or become very hot: *adj.* roasted: *n.* 1. roasted meat. 2. a cut of meat ready for roasting. 3. the act of roasting or the state of being roasted. 4. a picnic, meeting, etc. at which food is roasted and eaten.

roast-er (rōs'tēr), *n.* 1. a person or thing that roasts. 2. an apparatus or pan for roasting. 3. something fit for roasting, as a chicken, young pig, etc.

rob (rob), *v.t.* robbed, rob'bing, 1. to take money, property, etc. from (a person) ille-gally by violence or threat; steal from. 2. to plunder; rifle. 3. to deprive (someone) of something due, belonging, or desired. 4. to take unjustly or injuriously. —**rob'ber,** *n.*

robber fly, a large, predacious, two-winged fly resembling a bumblebee.

rob-ber-y (rob'ēr-i), *n., pl.* -ber-ies, 1. the act or practice of robbing. 2. the felonious and forcible taking away of the money or goods of another.

robe (rōb), *n.* 1. a loose outer garment. 2. an official garment worn on formal occasions to show office or rank, as by a judge or church dignitary. 3. a dressing gown or bathrobe: *v.t. & v.i.* robed, rob'ing, to invest with a robe; dress or cover with a robe.

robe-de-cham-bre (rōb-dĕ-shăm'br), *n.* [French], a dressing gown.

rob-in (rob'in), *n.* 1. a large North American thrush with a dull reddish breast. 2. a little European warbler with a yellowish throat and breast.

Robin Hood, in *English Legend,* the leader of an outlaw band that robbed the rich to aid the poor.

Rob-in-son Cru-soe (rob'in-sn krŏŏ'sō), the hero of a Defoe novel (1719), a shipwrecked sailor who survived for years on a tropical island.

ro-ble (rō'blä), *n.* any one of several oak trees of the southwestern U.S.; especially, a white oak of California.

ro-bot (rō'bŏt), *n.* 1. a machine resembling a human being in form, designed to perform mechanical tasks. 2. a person who acts me-chanically. 3. a device that can be operated automatically or by remote control.

ro-bur-ite (rō'bŭ-rīt), *n.* a powerful, flameless explosive, used in mining operations.

ro-bust (rō-bust'), *adj.* 1. hardy; vigorous. 2. muscular; sturdy.

roc (rok), *n.* a fabulous bird of prey of great size and strength.

roc-am-bole (rok'ăm-bōl), *n.* a European plant with bulbous roots like an onion and cloves used like garlic in flavoring.

Ro-chelle salt (rō-shel'), sodium potassium tar-trate, a colorless crystalline compound, used in electronics and as a laxative.

roch-et (roch'it), *n.* a linen vestment resembling a surplice, worn by bishops and other church dignitaries.

---

a ın cap, ā in cane, ä in father, å in abet, e ın met, ē in be, ē ın baker, ê ın regent, i in pit, ī in fine, i in manifest, o ın hot, ô in horse, ō in bone,

rock (rok), *n.* 1. a large mass of stone or stony material. 2. a relatively large, detached piece of this; boulder. 3. a broken piece or fragment of this material. 4. any naturally formed mineral mass in the earth's crust. 5. anything suggesting a rock in stability, firm support, strength, etc. 6. [Informal], a stone.

rock (rok), *v.t. & v.i.* 1. to sway back and forth or from side to side. 2. to move strongly; shake: *n.* 1. a rocking motion. 2. rock-and-roll.

rock-and-roll (rok'n-rōl'), *n.* a kind of popular music having a heavily accented beat and often blues and folk elements.

rock bottom, the lowermost bottom. —**rock-bottom** (rok'bot'ŏm), *adj.*

rock-bound ('bound), *adj.* surrounded or bordered by rocks.

rock candy, sugar in hard, clear, crystalline masses.

rock cod, any of various ocean fishes found around rocks, including a variety of the true cod.

rock·er (rok'ẽr), *n.* 1. a person who rocks a cradle, chair, etc. 2. either of the curved pieces of wood or metal on which a cradle, chair, etc. rocks. 3. a chair with such pieces. 4. any one of various devices that operate with a rocking motion.

rock·et (rok'it), *n.* 1. any one of various devices, usually cylindrical, containing a combustible substance which when ignited produces gases that escape through a vent in the rear and drive the container forward by the principle of reaction. 2. a spacecraft, missile, firework, etc. propelled by a rocket: *v.i.* to move swiftly like a rocket; soar.

rock·et·ry (rok'ě-tri), *n.* the science of designing, constructing, and launching rockets.

rock·fish (rok'fish), *n., pl.* -fish, -fish·es, any of various fishes that live among rocks.

rock garden, a garden planted in a rocky area and in which plants adapted to such a terrain are cultivated.

rock hind, a food fish of West Indian waters, related to the groupers.

rock·i·ness (rok'i-nis), *n.* a rocky state or quality.

rocking horse, a toy horse for a child to ride, mounted on rockers or springs.

rock maple, same as sugar maple.

rock oil, [Chiefly British], petroleum.

rock-ribbed (rok'ribd'), *adj.* 1. having rocky ridges. 2. rigid; unyielding.

rock salt, common salt, occurring in solid masses.

rock wool, a fibrous material resembling spun glass, made from molten rock or slag and used for insulation.

rock·y (rok'i), *adj.* rock'i·er, rock'i·est, 1. containing or consisting of rocks. 2. resembling rock; firm, hard, stony, inflexible, etc. 3. marked by obstructions or difficulties.

rock·y (rok'i), *adj.* rock'i·er, rock'i·est, 1. inclined to sway; unsteady; shaky. 2. [Slang], weak and dizzy.

ro·co·co (rô-kō'kō), *n.* a style of art used especially in architecture and ornamentation, prevalent in the first half of the 18th century and characterized by elaborate designs imitating shells, scrolls, leaves, etc.: *adj.* 1. of or in rococo. 2. overdone; elaborate; florid.

rod (rod), *n.* 1. a slender twig or shoot cut from or growing as part of a woody plant. 2. a straight stick or bar of wood, metal, plastic, etc. 3. a stick used to punish. 4. a scepter symbolizing office or authority. 5. a pole used in fishing. 6. a measure of length, equal to 5.5 yards. 7. [Slang], a pistol.

rode (rōd), past tense of **ride**.

ro·dent (rōd'nt), *adj.* gnawing: *n.* any one of a large group of gnawing mammals, including rats, mice, rabbits, squirrels, beavers, porcupines, etc.

ro·de·o (rō'di-ō), *n.* 1. [Now Rare], a gathering together of cattle on a ranch; roundup. 2. a public entertainment or competition featuring cowboy skills, as riding broncos, lassoing steers, etc.

rod·o·mon·tade (rod-ō-mon-tād'), *n.* vain boasting; ranting talk; empty blustering: *v.i.* -tad'ed, -tad'ing, to boast; rant.

roe (rō). *n.* fish eggs, especially when still enclosed in the ovarian sac.

roe (rō), *n., pl.* roe, roes, a small, delicate Eurasian deer, noted for its agility.

roe·buck (rō'buk), *n., pl.* -bucks, -buck, the male of the roe deer.

roent·gen (rent'gĕn), *n.* the international unit for measuring ionizing radiation, such as X-rays or gamma rays.

roent·gen·ol·o·gy (rent-gĕ-nol'ô-ji), *n.* the use of X-rays for diagnosing and treating disease. —**roent·gen·ol'o·gist,** *n.*

Roent·gen ray (rent'gĕn), [also r-], same as X-ray: after W. K. Roentgen (1845-1923), German physicist.

ro·ga·tion (rō-gā'shŭn), *n.* a formal supplication or prayer, especially as chanted during the ceremonies of the Rogation Days.

Rogation Days, Monday, Tuesday, and Wednesday preceding Ascension Thursday.

Rog·er (roj'ẽr), *interj.* [also r-], 1. received: term used to indicate the reception of a radio message. 2. [Informal], right!

rogue (rōg), *n.* 1. a person without principles; scoundrel. 2. a mischievous person; scamp: *v.i.* rogued, rogu'ing, to live or act like a rogue. —**ro·guer·y** (rō'gĕr-i), *n., pl.* -guer·ies.

rogues' gallery, a collection of photographs of criminals kept by the police and used in identification.

ro·guish (rō'gish), *adj.* 1. dishonest; unprincipled. 2. playfully mischievous. —**ro'guish·ly,** *adv.* —**ro'guish·ness,** *n.*

roil (roil), *v.i.* 1. to make (a liquid) turbid by agitation. 2. to make angry or disturbed; rile; vex.

roist·er (rois'tĕr), *v.i.* 1. to brag; boast. 2. to revel noisily. —**roist'er·er,** *n.* —**roist'er·ous,** *adj.*

role, rôle (rōl), *n.* 1. a part or character in a play, etc. 2. function or part.

roll (rōl), *v.i.* 1. to move by turning on an axis or over and over. 2. to move in a circular direction. 3. to move on rollers or wheels. 4. to rock from side to side. 5. to wallow. 6. to elapse, as time. 7. to make a long, deep sound: *v.t.* 1. to revolve; make move by

ŏ in dragon, ōō in crude, oo in wool. u in cup, ū in cure, û in turn, ŭ in focus, oi in boy, ou in house, th in thin, th in sheathe, g in get, j in joy, y in yet.

turning. 2. to move on wheels or rollers. 3. to utter with a full, continuous sound. 4. to say with a trill. 5. to spread flat with a roller. 6. to move in a circular direction. 7. to wrap (something) around into a rounded shape. 8. to cause to swing or sway: *n.* 1. the act of rolling. 2. a document, paper, etc. that has been rolled up; scroll. 3. a list of names; register. 4. a round piece of bread, cake, etc. 5. a continued, deep sound, as of a drum, thunder, etc. 6. a swaying motion. 7. something in the shape of a cylinder. 8. [Slang], a wad of paper money.

roll·back ('bak), *n.* the act of rolling back; specifically, a lowering of prices to an earlier level by government order.

roll call, 1. the reading aloud of a list of names for checking attendance. 2. a set time for this.

roll·er ('ēr), *n.* 1. one that rolls. 2. a cylinder of wood, metal, etc. used for grinding, smoothing, flattening, etc. 3. a long, heavy wave. 4. a long, broad bandage. 5. a cylinder on which something is wound. 6. any of various kinds of old-world birds that roll in flight. 7. a kind of canary that rolls, or trills, its notes.

roller coaster, a ride as in an amusement park, in which small, open cars move swiftly on tracks that are steeply inclined and curved.

roller skate, a shoe, or frame to fit on a shoe, with two pairs of small wheels, for gliding on a floor or sidewalk. —**roll'er-skate,** *v.i.* -**skat·ed,** -**skat·ing.**

roll·lick (rol'ik), *v.i.* to move or act in a carefree, lively manner. —**rol'lick·ing,** *adj.*

roll·ing (rōl'ing), *adj.* 1. moving on or as on wheels. 2. undulating. 3. used for rolling: *n.* motion, sound, etc. of something that rolls.

rolling pin, a cylindrical piece of wood for flattening dough.

rolling stock, all the engines, flatcars, cars, etc. of a railroad, or the vehicles of a trucking company.

roll·top (rōl'top), *adj.* denoting a flexible cover for the working area of a desk, that slides up.

ro·ly-po·ly (rō'li-pō'li), *n., pl.* -**lies,** 1. a short, pudgy person. 2. [Chiefly British], a kind of pudding made with fruit and pastry: *adj.* short and plump; pudgy.

ro·maine (rō-mān'), *n.* a variety of lettuce with long leaves clustered together in a slender, columnlike head: also **romaine lettuce.**

Ro·man (rō'mǎn), *adj.* 1. of or pertaining to ancient or modern Rome, its people, language, etc. 2. of the Roman Catholic Church. 3. [usually r-], denoting the ordinary upright type used in printing; not italic: *n.* 1. a person of ancient or modern Rome. 2. [usually r-], Roman type or characters.

Roman candle, a firework that shoots off sparks and balls of fire.

Roman Catholic, 1. of or pertaining to the Christian church (**Roman Catholic Church**) that is headed by the Pope. 2. a member of the Roman Catholic Church. —**Roman Catholicism.**

ro·mance (rō-mans'), *n.* 1. a work of fiction, especially a novel, telling of adventure, love, exciting events, etc. 2. excitement, love, etc. of the kind found in such fiction. 3. a love affair: *adj.* [R-], denoting any of the languages derived mainly from Latin, as Italian, French, Spanish, Portuguese, etc.: *v.i. & v.t.* -**manced', -manc'ing,** [Informal], to make love (to).

Ro·man·esque (rō-mǎ-nesk'), *n.* 1. a style of architecture of the 11th and 12th centuries, characterized by heavy masonry, the round arch and vault, etc. 2. a style of ornamentation, sculpture, and painting corresponding to this: *adj.* of or like this style.

Roman numerals, the letters representing numbers in the Roman system of notation, as I, 1; V, 5; X, 10; L, 50; C, 100; D, 500; and M, 1000.

Ro·mans (rō'mǎnz), *n.* a book of the New Testament.

ro·man·tic (rō-man'tik), *adj.* 1. pertaining to, or of the nature of, romance. 2. fanciful; not factual. 3. not practical. 4. idealistic, adventurous, etc. 5. preoccupied with thoughts of love. 6. suited for romance. 7. [often R-], of or pertaining to a style of literature, painting, music, etc. of the 19th century, in which the emphasis was on emotion, freedom of form, and originality: *n.* one who is romantic. —**ro·man'ti·cal·ly,** *adv.* —**ro·man'ti·cism** ('ti-cizm), *n.*

Rom·a·ny (rom'ǎ-ni, rō'mǎ-), *n.* 1. *pl.* -**ny,** -**nies,** a Gypsy. 2. the language of the Gypsies: *adj.* of or pertaining to the Gypsies or their language.

Romany rye, one who is not a Gypsy, but who lives with Gypsies, speaks their language, etc.

Ro·me·o (rō'mi-ō), *n.* 1. the young lover who is hero of Shakespeare's "Romeo and Juliet." 2. *pl.* -**os,** an ardent lover.

romp (romp), *n.* 1. unrestrained, boisterous play. 2. one who plays boisterously, especially a girl. 3. an easy victory in racing: *v.i.* 1. to play in an unrestrained, boisterous way. 2. to win easily in a race.

romp·er ('ēr), *n.* 1. one who romps. 2. *pl.* a loose garment for a baby, with bloomerlike pants.

Rom·u·lus (rom'yoo-lŭs), in *Roman Mythology,* the first king and founder of Rome: he and his twin brother, Remus, were suckled by a she-wolf.

ron·deau (ron'dō), *n., pl.* -**deaux** ('dōz), a poem of usually thirteen lines with only two rhymes and an unrhymed refrain.

ron·del ('dl, 'del), *n.* a kind of rondeau, with fourteen lines, two rhymes, and the first two lines repeated as a refrain.

ron·do (ron'dō), *n., pl.* -**dos,** a musical composition or movement, often the last movement of a sonata.

rood (rōōd), *n.* 1. a measure of area, equal to 40 square rods (1/4 acre). 2. a cross or crucifix.

roof (rōōf, roof), *n., pl.* **roofs,** 1. the top covering of a house or other building. 2. anything like this; covering or shelter. 3. the palate of the mouth: *v.t.* to cover with or as with a roof. —**roof'less,** *adj.*

---

a in cap, ā in cane, ä in father, ȧ in abet, e in met, ē in be, ê in baker, ê in regent, i in pit, ī in fine, i in manifest, o in hot, ô in horse, ō in bone,

roof·er ('ĕr), *n.* a person who repairs or makes roofs.

roof garden, 1. the top floor or roof of a high building, having a restaurant, garden, etc. 2. a garden on the flat top of a building.

roof·ing ('ing), *n.* material used to make or cover roofs.

roof·top ('top), *n.* the roof of a building.

roof·tree ('trē), *n.* 1. the horizontal beam across the main part of a roof; ridgepole. 2. a roof.

rook (rook), *n.* 1. a gregarious European crow with black, glossy feathers. 2. a swindler; cheat. 3. the castle in chess, a piece moving horizontally or vertically: *v.t. & v.i.* to swindle; cheat.

rook·er·y ('ĕr-i), *n., pl.* **-er·ies,** 1. a breeding place or colony of rooks. 2. a breeding place or colony of other gregarious animals or birds.

rook·ie (rook'i), *n.* [Slang], a new recruit, as in the army, a police force, athletic team, etc.

room (rōōm), *n.* 1. unoccupied place or space. 2. a walled or partitioned space within a building. 3. *pl.* lodgings; living quarters. 4. the people in a room. 5. opportunity or scope: *v.t. & v.i.* to have or provide with a room. **—room'ful,** *adj.*

room and board, lodging and meals.

room·er ('ĕr), *n.* a lodger.

room·ette (rōō-met'), *n.* a small compartment in a sleeping car of a train.

rooming house, a house with furnished rooms that are rented.

room·mate (rōōm'māt), *n.* a person who shares one's room or rooms.

room·y ('i), *adj.* **room'i·er, room'i·est,** spacious; having ample room. **—room'i·ness,** *n.*

roor·back, roor·bach (roor'bak), *n.* a fictitious or slanderous report against a candidate for public office, made to influence an election.

roost (rōōst), *n.* 1. a pole or perch upon which birds, especially domestic fowl, may rest. 2. a place, as a building, for birds to perch in. 3. a resting place: *v.i.* 1. to sit or rest on a perch. 2. to stay or settle, as for the night.

roos·ter ('ĕr), *n.* a male chicken; cock.

root (rōōt), *n.* 1. that part of a plant that descends and fixes itself in the earth and by which the plant is nourished. 2. the embedded or attached part of a tooth, nail, hair, etc. 3. a source, cause, origin, etc. 4. a basis or fundamental part. 5. that quantity which multiplied by itself produces a given quantity. 6. the part of a word which expresses its primary or essential meaning, as distinguished from a derivative; base: *v.t.* 1. to fix by the roots in the ground. 2. to implant deeply. 3. to settle. 4. to dig (*up* or *out*), as by using the snout. 5. to eradicate (with *out*): *v.i.* 1. to take root. 2. to rummage about. 3. [Informal], to encourage a contestant or team (with *for*). **—root'er,** *n.*

root beer, a carbonated, nonalcoholic beverage made of extracts from certain roots and herbs.

root canal, the channel in the root of a tooth, that normally contains pulp.

root·less ('lis), *adj.* without a settled place or status in society; feeling no ties to a given environment, place, etc. **—root'less·ly,** *adv.* **—root'less·ness,** *n.*

root·let ('lit), *n.* a radicle; little root.

root·stock ('stok), *n.* 1. same as **rhizome.** 2. a plant onto which another is grafted.

rope (rōp), *n.* 1. a strong, thick cord made of several strands twisted together; small cable. 2. such a cord for hanging a person. 3. death by hanging. 4. a viscous filament in a liquid, as wine. 5. a series of things connected by stringing, twining, etc.: *v.t.* roped, **rop'ing,** 1. to fasten, tie, or draw together with a rope. 2. to catch with a lasso. 3. to enclose or separate with a rope (with *in, off,* or *out*). **—rop'er,** *n.*

rope·walk ('wôk), *n.* a long, narrow shed or building where ropes are made.

rop·y (rō'pi), *adj.* **rop'i·er, rop'i·est,** 1. like a rope. 2. viscous; stringy. Also spelled **rop'ey.** **—rop'i·ness,** *n.*

roque (rōk), *n.* a form of croquet played on a specially constructed court.

Roque·fort (rōk'fĕrt), *n.* a kind of strong cheese with a bluish mold, made in France: also **Roquefort cheese.**

Ror·schach test (rôr'shäk), in *Psychology,* a personality test in which a person's impressions of standard inkblot designs are interpreted.

ro·sa·ceous (rō-zā'shŭs), *adj.* 1. of or pertaining to the rose family of plants. 2. like a rose. 3. rose-colored.

ro·sa·ry (rō'zer-i), *n., pl.* **-ries,** 1. a string of beads by which prayers are counted. 2. the prayers thus counted.

rose (rōz), *n.* 1. a hardy, sometimes climbing, prickly shrub with fragrant, showy flowers of red, pink, yellow, white, etc. 2. any one of these flowers. 3. a pinkish or purplish red. 4. a perforated nozzle for releasing fine jets of water. 5. a rosette: *adj.* 1. scented like a rose. 2. rose-colored. **—rose'like,** *adj.*

rose (rōz), past tense of **rise.**

ro·sé (rō-zā'), *n.* a light, pink wine.

rose·ate (rō'zi-it), *adj.* 1. rose-colored; rosy. 2. cheerful. **—ro'se·ate·ly,** *adv.*

rose·bud (rōz'bud), *n.* the bud of a rose.

rose·bush ('boosh), *n.* a bush that bears roses.

rose·col·ored ('kul-ĕrd), *adj.* 1. pinkish red or purplish red. 2. optimistic; cheerful.

rose·mar·y ('mer-i), *n.* a sweet-smelling evergreen shrub of the mint family, with leaves used in cooking and perfumery.

rose of Sharon (sher'ŏn), 1. a hardy plant of the mallow family, with white, pink, red, or purplish flowers. 2. in England, a species of Saint Johnswort, with large, yellow flowers.

ro·se·o·la (rō-zē'ō-lä, rō-zi-ō'lä), *n.* 1. any rose-colored rash. 2. German measles, or rubella. Also called **rose rash.**

ro·sette (rō-zet'), *n.* a cluster of ribbons arranged like a rose, or an ornament in this shape.

rose water, a mixture of rose water and attar of roses, used as a toilet water.

rose window, a circular window with roselike tracery branching from the center in a symmetrical pattern.

rose·wood (rōz'wood), *n.* 1. a very hard, reddish wood, sometimes with a roselike odor, obtained from several tropical trees and used for making furniture, etc. 2. any one of the trees yielding this wood.

Rosh Ha·sha·na (rŏsh' hä·shō'nä), the Jewish New Year.

Ro·si·cru·cian (rō·zĭ·krōō'shŭn), n. any one of a group with doctrines based on those of a secret society of the 17th and 18th centuries whose members were supposed to be versed in various kinds of occult lore.

ros·in (roz'n), n. the amber residue left after the distillation of crude turpentine, used in varnish, rubbed on violin bows, etc.: v.t. to rub with rosin. —**ros'in·ous, ros'in·y,** adj.

ros·ter (ros'tēr), n. 1. a list of military or naval personnel. 2. any list, as of club members.

ros·tral (ros'trăl), adj. 1. of or pertaining to a rostrum. 2. decorated in a way to resemble rostrums, or beaks of ships.

ros·trate ('trāt), adj. having a rostrum.

ros·trum (ros'trŭm), n., pl. -**trums,** -**tra** ('trä), 1. the beak of a bird. 2. the beak or prow of an ancient war vessel. 3. in ancient Rome, the speakers' platform in the Forum, decorated with the beaks or prows of ships taken from the enemy. 4. any pulpit or platform for public speaking.

ros·y (rō'zi), adj. **ros'i·er, ros'i·est,** 1. like a rose in color. 2. flushed with good health, etc. 3. optimistic, promising, etc. —**ros'i·ly,** adv. —**ros'i·ness,** n.

rot (rot), v.i. **rot'ted, rot'ting,** 1. to decay or decompose by the action of bacteria, etc. 2. to languish, as in prison. 3. to degenerate: v.t. to cause to decay or decompose: n. 1. decomposition. 2. a rotten part, spot, or thing. 3. a disease characterized by rotting and decay. 4. [Slang], nonsense.

ro·ta (rō'tä), n. 1. [Chiefly British], a roster detailing the rotation of duties. 2. [R-], a high tribunal of the Roman Catholic Church, acting chiefly as a court of appeals from lower courts.

ro·ta·ry (rō'tēr·i), adj. 1. turning on an axis, as a wheel. 2. having rotating parts. 3. denoting a lawn mower with blades rotating on a hub rather than a reel.

rotary engine, a type of engine in which rotary motion is produced without reciprocating parts.

ro·tate (rō'tāt), v.i. & v.t. -**tat·ed,** -**tat·ing,** 1. to revolve on or as on an axis. 2. to change in regular succession: adj. shaped like a wheel. —**ro·ta'tion,** n. —**ro'ta·tive,** adj.

ro·ta·tor (rō'tāt·ēr), n. 1. something that rotates. 2. a muscle that rotates some part of the body.

ro·ta·to·ry (rō'tä·tôr·i), adj. 1. that rotates; rotary. 2. of or having to do with rotation. 3. causing or following in rotation.

rote (rōt), n. 1. mechanical repetition or learning without understanding. 2. the noise of the surf on the shore. 3. a medieval stringed instrument somewhat like a lyre or harp.

ro·te·none (rōt'n·ōn), n. a white, crystalline substance derived from certain plant roots and used as an insecticide.

ro·ti·form (rōt'ĭ·fôrm), adj. shaped like a wheel.

ro·tis·ser·ie (rō·tis'ēr·i), n. 1. a shop where meat is roasted and sold. 2. a broiler with an electrically turned spit.

ro·to·gra·vure (rōt·ō·grä·vyoor'), n. 1. a printing process using a press with rotating cylinders etched from plates made photographically. 2. a newspaper section, usually pictorial, printed by this method.

ro·tor (rōt'ēr), n. 1. the rotating hub of a motor, etc. 2. a system of rotating airfoils, as on a helicopter.

rot·ten (rot'n), adj. 1. putrefied; decomposed; decayed. 2. unsound, as if decayed inside. 3. fetid. 4. morally corrupt. 5. [Slang], very bad, inferior, nasty, etc. —**rot'ten·ness,** n.

rot·ten·stone (-stōn), n. a soft, friable limestone, used for polishing metals.

ro·tund (rō·tund'), adj. 1. rounded; plump or stout. 2. sonorous. —**ro·tun'di·ty, ro·tund'ness,** n. —**ro·tund'ly,** adv.

ro·tun·da (rō·tun'dä), n. a circular, domed building, room, or hall.

rou·é (rōō·ā'), n. a man who is dissipated; debauchee; rake.

rouge (rōōzh), n. 1. a reddish cosmetic for coloring the lips and cheeks. 2. a reddish powder used for polishing jewelry, metal, etc.: v.t. & v.i. **rouged, roug'ing,** to use rouge (on).

rough (ruf), adj. 1. not smooth or level on the surface; uneven. 2. uncut; unpolished. 3. harsh to the ear. 4. uncivil; coarse. 5. austere; without comforts and conveniences. 6. boisterous. 7. shaggy. 8. turbulent; stormy. 9. not exact. 10. [Informal], trying; difficult: n. 1. something that is rough, as ground. 2. a preliminary sketch. 3. in Golf, a part of the course with the grass left uncut: adv. in a rough manner: v.t. 1. to make rough. 2. to handle roughly (with up). 3. to form or sketch in a preliminary way (with in or out). —**rough'ly,** adv. —**rough'ness,** n.

rough·age ('ij), n. rough, bulky foods or fodder, as bran, fresh green vegetables, etc.

rough·en ('n), v.t. & v.i. to make or become rough.

rough·hew (ruf·hū'), v.t. -**hewed'** or -**hewn',** -**hew'ing,** 1. to hew or cut roughly and without smoothing. 2. to form crudely. Also **roughhew.**

rough·house (ruf'hous), n. [Slang], rough, noisy playing, or fighting, especially indoors: v.t. & v.i. -**housed,** -**hous·ing,** [Slang], to treat or act roughly.

rough·neck ('nek), n. [Slang], a person who is uncouth and rowdy.

rough·rid·er ('rīd'ēr), n. 1. one who breaks horses so they can be ridden. 2. [R-], a member of a cavalry unit organized during the Spanish-American War (1898).

rough·shod ('shod), adj. shod with horseshoes with rough metal points to prevent slipping: often in ride roughshod over, to treat harshly.

rou·lade (rōō·läd'), n. 1. a musical flourish of tones sung in rapid succession to one syllable. 2. a slice of meat rolled around a filling of minced meat and cooked.

rou·leau (rōō·lō'), n., pl. -**leaux'** (-lōz') or -**leaus',** 1. a roll of coins in a paper wrapper. 2. a piping or fold as for trimming hats, dresses, etc.

rou·lette (rōō·let'), n. 1. a game of chance played with a small ball that whirls in a revolving disk (**roulette wheel**), marked off into red and black numbered sections. 2. a wheeled instrument for making perforated lines, as between postage stamps.

round (round), *adj.* 1. spherical; globular. 2. circular. 3. cylindrical. 4. plump; corpulent. 5. whole; complete. 6. considerable; large. 7. expressed by a whole number, with no fractions, or in even units as tens or hundreds: *n.* 1. something circular, as the rung of a ladder. 2. anything that is round. 3. *often pl.* a circuit or tour. 4. a recurring cycle. 5. *a)* a volley of firearms, or the single firing of one gun; *b)* the ammunition used. 6. one of the periods making up a boxing match. 7. movement in a circular course. 8. a song in which part of those singing join in at successive points. 9. the part of a thigh of beef between the leg and rump: *v.t.* 1. to make round. 2. to travel or pass around. 3. to make plump; fill out. 4. to finish (with *out or off*). 5. to express as a round number: *v.i.* 1. to make the rounds, as a patrol. 2. to grow or become round. 3. to reverse direction: *adv.* 1. on all sides. 2. in a circle. 3. from one side or party to another. 4. throughout a recurring period of time. 5. near. 6. in various places. 7. with a revolving movement: *prep.* 1. all about. 2. on every side of. 3. near. 4. in a circuit or course through. 5. throughout. —**round′ish,** *adj.* —**round′ness,** *n.*

round·a·bout (′ă-bout), *adj.* 1. indirect. 2. encompassing; encircling: *n.* [British], 1. a merry-go-round. 2. a traffic circle.

round dance, 1. any of various dances in which the couples move in revolving or circular movements, as the waltz. 2. a dance in which several dancers form a circle.

roun·del (roun′dl), *n.* 1. same as **roundelay.** 2. a small, ornamental panel, window, plate, etc. 3. a kind of verse; rondel.

roun·de·lay (roun′dĕ-lā), *n.* a simple song or dance in which the passages are repeated.

round·er (roun′dĕr), *n.* 1. a tool for rounding edges. 2. *pl.* in Britain, a game resembling baseball. 3. [Informal], a dissolute person; drunkard.

round hand, penmanship in clear, well-rounded letters.

Round·head (round′hed), *n.* a member of the Parliamentary, or Puritan, party in the civil war in England (1642-52).

round·house (′hous), *n.* 1. the cabin on the after part of a ship's deck. 2. a round building having a turntable and facilities for storing and servicing locomotives.

round·ly (′li), *adv.* 1. in a round form. 2. completely and fully. 3. severely; bluntly; straightforwardly.

round robin, 1. a petition having the signatures written in a circle so as not to show who signed first. 2. a letter going to members of a group in turn, each one of which may add comments, etc.

round-shoul·dered (′shōl-dĕrd), *adj.* stooped in such a way that the shoulders are rounded.

rounds·man (roundz′măn), *n., pl.* **-men,** one who makes rounds, as of inspection.

Round Table, 1. the legendary round table around which King Arthur and his knights gathered. 2. King Arthur and his knights collectively. 3. [r- t-], a gathering, as for informal discussion.

round-the-clock (round′*thĕ*-klok′), *adj.* continuous: *adv.* continuously.

round-trip (′trip), *adj.* denoting arrangements, a ticket, etc. for a trip to a place and back again.

round-up (′up), *n.* 1. the act of herding cattle together by riding around them and driving them in. 2. the cowboys and horses that do this. 3. any similar gathering together. 4. a summary, as of news.

round-worm (′wûrm), *n.* any of several kinds of nematode worms.

rouse (rouz), *v.t. & v.i.* **roused, rous′ing,** 1. to awaken. 2. to stir to thought or action. 3. to rise or cause to rise, as game from cover.

rous·ing (rou′zing), *adj.* 1. stirring; exciting. 2. remarkable. 3. very lively. —**rous′ing·ly,** *adv.*

roust (roust), *v.t.* [Informal], 1. to rouse. 2. to drive (*out*).

roust·a·bout (′ă-bout), *n.* an unskilled laborer, as on the waterfront, in a circus, or on a ranch.

rout (rout), *n.* 1. a total defeat. 2. a disorderly flight, especially following such a defeat. 3. in *Law,* an attempt by two or more persons to start a riot: *v.t.* 1. to defeat totally. 2. to put to flight. 3. to root up; force or gouge out. 4. to make (someone) leave (with *out*).

route (rōōt, rout), *n.* 1. a way or road traveled. 2. a regular course, as for the delivery of milk, mail, etc. 3. a marching order for troops: *v.t.* **rout′ed, rout′ing,** 1. to arrange a route or order of procedure for. 2. to send by a specified route.

rou·tine (rōō-tēn′), *n.* a regular habit or practice, as a course of business or official duties regularly pursued: *adj.* of or by routine. —**rou·tine′ly,** *adv.*

roux (rōō), *n.* a thickening for soups, sauces, etc. of melted butter and flour.

rove (rōv), *v.i.* **roved, rov′ing,** 1. to roam; wander. 2. to look around: said of the eyes: *v.t.* 1. to roam through. 2. to draw (fibers) out before spinning. —**rov′er,** *n.*

row (rō), *n.* 1. a line; file or rank, as of persons or things. 2. a line of seats, etc. 3. an excursion in a rowboat: *v.t. & v.i.* 1. to propel (a boat) with oars. 2. to travel or carry in a rowboat. —**row′er,** *n.*

row (rou), *n.* a brawl; turbulent quarrel; noisy disturbance: *v.i.* to brawl; quarrel.

row·an (rō′ăn, rou′-), *n.* 1. the mountain ash. 2. the orange-red berry of this tree: also **row′an·ber·ry,** *pl.* **-ries.**

row·boat (rō′bōt), *n.* a small boat for rowing.

row·dy (rou′di), *n., pl.* **-dies,** a rough, riotous person: *adj.* **-di·er, -di·est,** rough, riotous, etc. —**row′di·ly,** *adv.* —**row′di·ness,** *n.*

row·el (rou′ĕl), *n.* the small, sharp-pointed wheel of a spur.

row·en (rou'ĕn), *n.* the aftermath; second growth of hay in one season.

row·lock (rŏ'lŏk), *n.* chiefly British form of **oarlock**.

roy·al (roi'ăl), *adj.* 1. of or pertaining to a king or queen. 2. befitting or like a king or queen; majestic, magnificent, etc. 3. of a kingdom or its government: *n.* 1. a large size of paper. 2. a small sail of a ship. — **roy'al·ly,** *adv.*

roy·al·ist (-ist), *n.* an adherent of a monarch or monarchism. —**roy'al·ism,** *n.*

roy·al·ty (roi'ăl-tĭ), *n., pl.* **-ties,** 1. the status or power of a king or queen. 2. a person who is royal. 3. the character or quality of being royal. 4. payment to the crown on the produce of a mine, etc. 5. a percentage of proceeds from a book, patent, etc. paid to the author or owner.

rub (rub), *v.t.* **rubbed, rub'bing,** 1. to apply pressure with motion to the surface of. 2. to move (things) over each other with pressure and motion. 3. to apply (polish) with pressure and motion. 4. to make sore by friction. 5. to erase or remove by pressure and motion (with *out*): *v.i.* 1. to move with pressure (*on*). 2. to make friction: *n.* 1. the act of rubbing. 2. a difficulty or obstruction.

rub-a-dub (rub'ă-dub), *n.* the sound of a drum being beaten.

ru·ba·to (rŏŏ-bät'ō), *adj. & adv.* in *Music,* deliberately played with a slight variation in tempo.

rub·ber (rub'ĕr), *n.* 1. one that rubs. 2. an elastic substance prepared from the juice of several tropical trees or synthetically. 3. a product made of this, as a low-cut overshoe. 4. in *Baseball,* a piece of rubber set into the pitcher's mound. 5. the deciding game in a series, as of card games; also **rubber game:** *adj.* made of rubber. —**rub'ber·y,** *adj.*

rubber band, a thin, continuous strip of rubber used for holding things together.

rubber cement, an adhesive consisting of unvulcanized rubber in a solvent.

rub·ber·ize (-īz), *v.t.* **-ized, -iz·ing,** to impregnate with rubber.

rubber plant, 1. any plant that yields latex, from which crude rubber is formed. 2. an ornamental house plant with leathery leaves.

rubber stamp, 1. a stamp made of rubber, pressed on an inking pad and used to print dates, etc. 2. [Informal], *a*) automatic approval; *b*) a legislature, person, etc. who gives such approval.

rub·bish (rub'ish), *n.* 1. anything that is thrown away as of no value; trash. 2. nonsense.

rub·ble (rub'l), *n.* 1. rough, undressed stone or brick. 2. debris from buildings, walls, etc. as from earthquake or bombing.

rub·down (rub'doun), *n.* a massage.

rube (rŏŏb), *n.* [Slang], a rustic; yokel.

ru·be·fa·cient (rŏŏ-bē-fā'shĕnt), *n.* a medical preparation that causes reddening of the skin.

ru·bel·la (rŏŏ-bel'ă), *n.* an infectious, communicable disease caused by a virus, causing small red spots on the skin; German measles.

ru·be·o·la (rŏŏ-bē'ō-lă), *n.* same as **measles**.

ru·bes·cence (rŏŏ-bes'ns), *n.* 1. the state of becoming red. 2. a blushing or flushing of the face. —**ru·bes'cent,** *adj.*

Ru·bi·con (rŏŏ'bi-kon), *n.* a river which separated Gaul from the Roman Empire: by crossing it, Caesar committed himself to civil war.

ru·bi·cund (rŏŏ'bi-kund), *adj.* inclined to redness; ruddy. —**ru·bi·cun'di·ty,** *n.*

ru·bid·i·um (rŏŏ-bid'i-ŭm), *n.* a soft, silvery, metallic chemical element which ignites spontaneously in air.

ru·bied (rŏŏ'bid), *adj.* ruby-colored; deep-red.

ru·big·i·nous (rŏŏ-bij'i-nŭs), *adj.* rust-colored.

ru·ble (rŏŏ'bl), *n.* the monetary unit of the Soviet Union.

ru·bric (rŏŏ'brik), *n.* 1. one of the directions for liturgical use in prayer books. 2. in early books and manuscripts, a title, initial letter, etc. written or printed in red, ornamental lettering, etc. 3. any title or heading, as of a chapter, a law, etc. 4. a rule or explanatory comment: *adj.* inscribed in red.

ru·bri·cate (rŏŏ'bri-kāt), *v.t.* **-cat·ed, -cat·ing,** to mark, distinguish, or illuminate with red. — **ru·bri·ca'tion,** *n.*

ru·by (rŏŏ'bi), *n., pl.* **-bies,** a clear, deep-red variety of corundum, used as a precious stone: *adj.* deep-red.

ru·by-throat·ed hummingbird (-thrōt'id), a common hummingbird of North America, with a red throat and green back.

ruche (rŏŏsh), *n.* frilled or pleated lace, net, ribbon, etc. used for edging dresses, etc., as at the throat or wrists.

ruch·ing ('ing), *n.* 1. ruches collectively. 2. material for ruches.

ruck (ruk), *v.t. & v.i.* to wrinkle, crease, or pucker: *n.* 1. a wrinkle, crease, or pucker. 2. a heap. 3. the crowd of horses that come in at the end of a race. 4. the large mass of indistinguishable people or things.

ruck·sack (ruk'sak), *n.* a kind of knapsack.

ruck·us (ruk'ŭs), *n.* [Informal], an uproar; noisy commotion or disturbance.

ruc·tion (ruk'shŭn), *n.* [Informal], a riotous uproar; row; disturbance.

rudd (rud), *n.* a red-eyed, freshwater fish with red fins: it belongs to the carp family.

rud·der (rud'ĕr), *n.* the broad, flat, movable blade at the rear of a watercraft or aircraft by which it is steered.

rud·dle (rud'l), *n.* red ocher, a reddish iron ore used as a pigment: *v.t.* **-dled, -dling,** 1. to paint or mark with ruddle, especially to mark (sheep) with this. 2. to cause to flush.

rud·dock (rud'ŏk), *n.* [British Dialectal], same as **robin** (sense 2).

rud·dy (rud'i), *adj.* **-di·er, -di·est,** 1. having a healthy red color. 2. inclined to redness. — **rud'di·ness,** *n.*

ruddy duck, a small, North American duck with brownish-red feathers on the neck and back, and a blue bill.

rude (rŏŏd), *adj.* **rud'er, rud'est,** 1. rough; crude. 2. barbarous. 3. uncultivated; uncouth. 4. impolite; discourteous. 5. primitive. —**rude'ly,** *adv.* —**rude'ness,** *n.*

ru·di·ment (rŏŏ'di-mĕnt), *n.* 1. a first or elementary principle of a subject. 2. anything in its first or undeveloped state.

ru·di·men·ta·ry (rōō-di-men'tēr-i), *adj.* 1. pertaining to or containing first principles; elementary. 2. denoting an undeveloped state. 3. vestigial. —**ru·di·men'ta·ri·ness,** *n.*

rue (rōō), *v.t. & v.i.* rued, ru'ing, 1. to repent (a fault, sin, etc.). 2. to regret (something done): *n.* 1. [Archaic], sorrow, repentance, or regret. 2. an herb of bitter taste and strong odor, formerly used in medicine.

rue·ful ('fŭl), *adj.* 1. regretful. 2. mournful. 3. lamentable. —**rue'ful·ly,** *adv.* —**rue'ful·ness,** *n.*

ru·fes·cent (rōō-fes'nt), *adj.* reddish. —**ru·fes'cence,** *n.*

ruff (ruf), *n.* 1. a large, frilled collar worn in the 16th and 17th centuries. 2. a band of outstanding feathers or fur around the neck of a bird or animal. 3. a small, spotted European freshwater fish: also **ruffe.** 4. a sandpiper of Europe and Asia, the male of which grows a large ruff during the mating season: the female is called a *reeve.* 5. the act of trumping when playing cards: *v.t. & v.i.* to trump when playing cards.

ruffed grouse, a large game bird of North America with neck feathers that can be extended.

ruf·fi·an (ruf'i-ăn), *n.* a violent, brutal person; hoodlum; bully.

ruf·fle (ruf'l), *v.t.* -fled, -fling, 1. to wrinkle, ripple, or disarrange. 2. to gather into ruffles. 3. to adorn with ruffles. 4. to make (feathers, etc.) stand up. 5. to annoy or vex: *v.i.* 1. to become wrinkled, disarranged, etc. 2. to become annoyed or vexed: *n.* 1. a strip of cloth, lace, etc. that has been gathered into pleats or puckers and used for trimming. 2. a ripple. 3. an irritation. 4. a low roll of a drum.

ru·fous (rōō'fŭs), *adj.* rust-colored; brownish-red.

rug (rug), *n.* 1. a piece of a heavy, thick, often napped fabric used as a floor covering. 2. [Chiefly British], a lap robe.

ru·ga (rōō'gă), *n., pl.* -gae ('jē), a wrinkle or fold, as in the lining of the stomach or some other body part: usually used in the plural. —**ru'gate** ('gāt, 'git), *adj.*

Rug·by (rug'bi), *n.* a kind of football that was the forerunner of American football, first played at Rugby, a school for boys in England: also **Rugby football.**

rug·ged (rug'id), *adj.* 1. having an uneven surface; rough. 2. stormy. 3. severe; harsh. 4. sturdy; robust. 5. uncouth; not polished. — **rug'ged·ly,** *adv.* —**rug'ged·ness,** *n.*

ru·gose (rōō'gōs), *adj.* full of wrinkles: also **ru'gous** ('gŭs). —**ru·gos·i·ty** (rōō-gos'i-ti), *n., pl.* -ties.

ru·in (rōō'in), *n.* 1. overthrow, destruction, downfall, etc. 2. a cause of destruction, decay, etc. 3. something destroyed, etc. 4. *pl.* the remains of a building, town, etc. that has been destroyed: *v.t.* to pull down, destroy, subvert, overthrow, impoverish, etc. — **ru·in·a'tion,** *n.* —**ru'in·ous,** *adj.*

rule (rōōl), *n.* 1. a standard or guide; maxim or precept for conduct, procedure, etc. 2. government; reign. 3. a regulation for court

procedures. 4. an established practice. 5. a ruler; straightedge. 6. a set of regulations in a religious order: *v.t. & v.i.* ruled, rul'ing, 1. to govern. 2. to settle officially, as by a rule. 3. to manage, restrain, guide, etc. 4. to mark with lines.

rule of thumb, a rule, procedure, method of estimating, etc. that is based on practical experience and may not be precise or exact.

rul·er (rōō'lēr), *n.* 1. one who rules or governs. 2. a strip of wood, metal, etc. marked off into inches, centimeters, etc., used in drawing lines or measuring; straightedge.

rul·ing ('ling), *adj.* 1. governing. 2. predominant: *n.* a rule or official decision laid down by a judge or court.

rum (rum), *n.* 1. an alcoholic liquor made from fermented molasses, sugar cane, etc. 2. alcoholic liquor in general: *adj.* [Chiefly British Slang], 1. queer; strange. 2. poor, as a *rum* joke.

rum·ba (rum'bă), *n.* 1. a ballroom dance characterized by rhythmic hip movements. 2. the music for this, with strong and complex rhythm: *v.i.* to dance the rumba.

rum·ble (rum'bl), *v.i. & v.t.* -bled, -bling, 1. to make or cause to make a low, heavy, continuous sound. 2. to move with this sound: *n.* 1. a rumbling sound. 2. [Slang], a fight between teen-age gangs. —**rum'bler,** *n.* — rum'bly, *adj.*

ru·men (rōō'min), *n., pl.* -mi·na ('mi·nă), the first stomach of a ruminant.

ru·mi·nant (rōō'mi·nănt), *adj.* 1. chewing the cud. 2. meditative: *n.* an animal that chews the cud, as the cow, buffalo, goat, camel, deer, etc.

ru·mi·nate (-nāt), *v.t. & v.i.* -nat·ed, -nat·ing, 1. to chew (the cud). 2. to meditate (on). —**ru·mi·na'tion,** *n.* —**ru'mi·na·tor,** *n.*

ru·mi·na·tive (-nāt-iv), *adj.* given to rumination. —**ru'mi·na·tive·ly,** *adv.*

rum·mage (rum'ij), *v.t. & v.i.* -maged, -mag·ing, to search through (a place, receptacle, etc.); ransack: *n.* 1. a careful searching. 2. miscellaneous articles.

rummage sale, a sale of contributed items of all sorts, as to raise money for charity.

rum·my (rum'i), *n.* any one of several card games whose object is to match cards in sets or sequences.

ru·mor (rōō'mēr), *n.* 1. gossip or hearsay; general talk. 2. a story or report in general circulation, but without knowledge or proof of its truth: *v.t.* to spread or tell by rumor. British spelling **rumour.**

ru·mor·mon·ger (-mung-gēr), *n.* one who spreads rumors.

rump (rump), *n.* 1. the end of the backbone of an animal, with its adjacent parts. 2. a cut of meat, usually beef, from this part, above the round. 3. the buttocks.

rum·ple (rum'pl), *n.* an uneven fold or crease; wrinkle: *v.t. & v.i.* -pled, -pling, to muss; wrinkle.

rum·pus (rum'pŭs), *n.* [Informal], a noisy disturbance; commotion.

run (run), *v.i.* ran, run, run'ning, 1. to go by moving the legs more rapidly than in walking. 2. to extend in space or continue in

---

ŏ in dragon, ōō in crude, oo in wool, u in cup, ŭ in cure, ū in turn, ů in focus, oi in boy, ou in house, th in thin, *th* in sheathe, g in get, j in joy, y in yet.

time. 3. to move swiftly. 4. to flee. 5. to contend in a race, election, etc. 6. to flow. 7. to melt. 8. to spread, as color on cloth when moistened. 9. to function; operate. 10. to discharge pus, mucus, etc. 11. to pass. 12. to make a casual or quick trip. 13. to ravel, as a stocking: *v.t.* 1. to cause to move swiftly. 2. to push or force. 3. to cover by running, driving, etc. 4. to back as a candidate. 5. to smuggle or get past. 6. to be in charge of (a household, etc.). 7. to be affected by (a fever, etc.). 8. to operate (a machine, etc.). 9. to make pass, go, or flow in a specified place or manner. 10. to subject oneself to (a risk, etc.). 11. to publish (a story) in a newspaper or periodical: *n.* 1. the act or a period of running. 2. a course run. 3. a journey or route. 4. a period of continuous performance. 5. a trend. 6. a sudden, pressing series of demands. 7. a migration. 8. free access. 9. a brook. 10. the usual or normal kind. 11. output during a specific period. 12. an enclosure for animals. 13. a ravel, as in a stocking. 14. in *Baseball*, a scoring point, made by a base runner reaching home.

run·a·bout ('ǎ-bout), *n.* a small, light carriage, car, or motorboat.

run·a·gate ('ǎ-gāt), *n.* [Archaic]. 1. a fugitive. 2. a homeless wanderer.

run·a·round ('ǎ-round), *n.* [Informal]. evasive action, as delays and excuses: usually in the phrase to get (or give) the runaround.

run·a·way ('ǎ-wā), *n.* 1. one who flees, as a fugitive. 2. a horse or other animal that runs away: *adj.* running away, breaking loose from control, escaping, etc.

run·ci·nate (run'si·nit, -nāt), *adj.* denoting a kind of leaf with the lobes curved backward, and the edges irregularly saw-toothed.

run·dle (run'dl), *n.* a rung of a ladder.

rund·let (rund'lit), *n.* [Archaic]. 1. a small barrel. 2. a wine measure of about 18 gallons.

run·down (run'doun), *n.* a summary; report.

run-down (run'doun'), *adj.* 1. not in good repair; dilapidated. 2. in poor health, worn out, weary, etc. 3. not running because unwound, as a clock.

rune (rōōn), *n.* 1. any one of the characters in an ancient Germanic alphabet. 2. a poem, song, or verse. —ru'nic, *adj.*

rung (rung), *n.* 1. a round, sturdy stick or bar used as one of the steps on a ladder. 2. a similar piece of wood used as a support between two legs of a chair, or across the back.

rung (rung), past participle of **ring**.

run-in (run'in), *n.* 1. printed matter added, without indenting for a new paragraph: also **run-on**. 2. [Informal], a fight or quarrel.

run·let (run'lit), *n.* 1. a runnel; little brook. 2. same as **rundlet**.

run·nel (run'l), *n.* a little brook.

run·ner (run'ẽr), *n.* 1. one who runs, as a racer or messenger. 2. either of the long strips of metal, wood, etc. on which a sled or sleigh slides. 3. a long, slender stem that trails along the ground; stolon. 4. a ravel, as in a stocking. 5. a long, narrow rug or cloth.

run·ner-up (-up), *n.* a contestant or team that finishes second, as in a competition, tournament, etc.

run·ning ('ing), *adj.* 1. moving swiftly. 2. continuous. 3. flowing. 4. measured in a straight line: *adv.* in succession: *n.* 1. the act of one that runs. 2. that which runs or flows. 3. the quantity that runs or flows. 4. the condition of a track for racing.

running gear, the chassis of a motor vehicle.

running lights, the lights displayed by an aircraft or ship when traveling at night.

running mate, a candidate for an office connected with, but less important than, a higher office.

run·ny ('i), *adj.* -ni·er, -ni·est, 1. running, especially running too freely. 2. discharging mucus, as the nose. —run'ni·ness, *n.*

run-off ('ôf), *n.* 1. rain that drains off and is not absorbed in the ground. 2. a final contest.

run-of-the-mill ('uv-*the*-mil'), *adj.* average; ordinary; mediocre.

runt (runt), *n.* 1. a stunted or dwarfish animal, plant, thing, etc. 2. the smallest animal of a litter. —runt'y, *adj.*

run-through (run'thrōō), *n.* a complete rehearsal, as of a play.

run·way ('wā), *n.* 1. a channel, track, etc. along which something moves. 2. a landing and takeoff strip for aircraft. 3. a narrow platform extending from a stage into the audience.

ru·pee (rōō-pē'), *n.* the monetary unit of India, Ceylon, Pakistan, etc.

rup·ture (rup'chẽr), *n.* 1. the act of bursting or breaking. 2. the state of being broken or violently burst apart or open. 3. a breach of friendly relations. 4. a hernia: *v.t.* & *v.i.* -tured, -tur·ing, to cause or undergo a rupture.

ru·ral (roor'ǎl), *adj.* 1. of, pertaining to, or characteristic of the country or country life; rustic. 2. living in the country. 3. having to do with farming. —ru'ral·ly, *adv.*

rural delivery, delivery of mail to rural districts: formerly **rural free delivery**.

ru·ral·ist (-ist), *n.* one who leads or advocates a rural life. —ru'ral·ism, *n.*

ru·ral·ize (roor'ǎ-līz), *v.t.* -ized, -iz·ing, to make rural: *v.i.* to live for some time in the country. —ru·ral·i·za'tion, *n.*

ruse (rōōz), *n.* a trick; stratagem.

rush (rush), *v.i.* & *v.t.* 1. to move or press forward with impetuosity. 2. to make a swift assault (on); charge. 3. to enter, go, act, do, etc. with undue haste; hurry: *n.* 1. the act of rushing. 2. a moving forward with eagerness and haste, especially of many people to a specific place. 3. haste. 4. unusual acitivity or press demanding speed or extra effort. 5. a marsh plant with round stems used in making baskets, mats, etc.

rush hour, the time of day when traffic or business is the heaviest.

rusk (rusk), *n.* a piece of sweet, raised bread or cake made brown and crisp in the oven.

rus·set (rus'it), *adj.* yellowish-brown or reddish-brown: *n.* 1. russet color. 2. a homespun cloth of this color, formerly used

a in cap, ā in cane, ä in father, ǎ in abet, e in met, ē in be, ĕ in baker, ĕ in regent, i in pit, ī in fine, i in manifest, o in hot, ô in horse, ō in bone,

for clothing by country people. 3. a kind of winter apple with mottled skin.

Rus·sia leather (rush'ă), a fine, smooth leather, often dyed dark red, originally made in Russia of leather treated with oil from birch bark.

Rus·sian (rush'ăn), *adj.* of or pertaining to the Union of Soviet Socialist Republics, a country of northern Asia and eastern Europe, or its inhabitants: *n.* 1. a native or inhabitant of this country. 2. the Slavic language of the Russians.

rust (rust), *n.* 1. the reddish-brown coating formed on iron and steel exposed to air and moisture. 2. anything resembling this, as a stain or growth. 3. a reddish brown. 4. a fungous disease of plants, characterized by red and brown spots on leaves and stems. 5. a parasitic fungus causing this: *v.i. & v.t.* 1. to form rust (on). 2. to deteriorate or become impaired, as through inactivity or disuse.

rus·tic (rus'tik), *adj.* 1. of or pertaining to the country; rural. 2. artless; simple. 3. unpolished; rough: *n.* a country person. —**rus'ti·cal·ly,** *adv.* —**rus·tic'i·ty** (-tis'ĭ-tĭ), *n.*

rus·ti·cate (rus'tĭ-kāt), *v.i. & v.t.* -cat·ed, -cat·ing, 1. to go or make go to the country. 2. to make or become rustic. —**rus·ti·ca'tion,** *n.*

rus·tle (rus'l), *v.i. & v.t.* -tled, -tling, 1. to make or cause a soft, whispering sound, as the rubbing together of silk or dry leaves. 2. [Informal], to bestir oneself; work or proceed with vigor. 3. [Informal], to steal (cattle, horses, etc.). —**rus'tler,** *n.*

rust-proof ('prōōf), *adj.* protected against rust.

rust·y (rus'tĭ), *adj.* rust'i·er, rust'i·est, 1. covered with rust. 2. impaired by neglect, inaction, etc. 3. out of practice. 4. rust-colored. —**rust'i·ly,** *adv.* —**rust'i·ness,** *n.*

rut (rut), *n.* 1. the period of sexual excitement of certain male mammals, as the deer, corresponding to *estrus* in the female. 2. the track of a wheel. 3. a groove or hollow. 4. a fixed condition or routine, especially one thought of as unpromising or dull: *v.t.* rut'ted, rut'ting, to make a rut or ruts in: *v.i.* to be sexually excited, as a male mammal in rut.

ru·ta·ba·ga (rōōt-ă-bā'gă), *n.* a kind of turnip, larger than the common turnip and of a yellowish color.

Ruth (rōōth), *n.* a book of the Bible.

ruth (rōōth), *n.* [Rare], 1. pity; compassion. 2. sorrow; remorse.

ru·the·ni·um (rōō-thē'nĭ-ŭm), *n.* a hard, brittle, silvery, rare metallic chemical element, extracted from platinum ore.

ruth·ful (rōōth'fŭl), *adj.* [Rare], 1. full of sorrow. 2. causing sorrow.

ruth·less ('lis), *adj.* without ruth; pitiless; cruel. —**ruth'less·ly,** *adv.* —**ruth'less·ness,** *n.*

ru·ti·lant (rōōt'l-ănt), *adj.* [Rare], shining; having a reddish glow.

ru·tile (rōō'tēl, 'tĭl), *n.* red oxide of titanium.

rut·tish (rut'ish), *adj.* sexually excited; in rut; lustful. —**rut'tish·ly,** *adv.* —**rut'tish·ness,** *n.*

rut·ty ('ĭ), *adj.* -ti·er, -ti·est, full of ruts, as a road. —**rut'ti·ness,** *n.*

-ry (rĭ), a short form of the suffix -ery.

ry·a rug (rē'ă), a kind of ornamental, handwoven rug or wall hanging, originally made in Scandinavia, usually with an abstract design.

rye (rī), *n.* 1. a hardy cereal grass. 2. the seeds or grain of this plant. 3. flour made from this grain, used for bread, etc. 4. whiskey distilled wholly or mainly from this grain. 5. a gypsy gentleman.

rye-grass ('gras), *n.* a common grass much used for forage or for quick lawns.

ry·ot (rī'ŏt), *n.* in India, a tenant farmer or peasant.

S

S, s (es), *n., pl.* S's, s's, 1. the nineteenth letter of the English alphabet. 2. any of the various sounds of this letter, as in *sun, buds,* and *version.* 3. a type or impression of S or *s.*

S (es), *adj.* shaped like S: *n.* an object shaped like S.

-s, a suffix used to form some adverbs, as *days;* the third person present tense of most verbs, as *eats;* and the plural of most nouns, as *boys, foes.*

-'s, a suffix used to form the possessive singular of nouns and some pronouns, and the possessive plural of some nouns.

sab-a-dil-la (sab-â-dil'â), *n.* 1. a bulbous-rooted Mexican and Central American plant of the lily family, producing acrid seeds from which various alkaloids are obtained. 2. the seeds.

Sab-a-oth (sab'i-oth, sâ-bā'ōth), *n.pl.* in the *Bible,* armies; hosts: see *Romans ix,* 29.

Sab-ba-tar-i-an (sab-â-ter'i-ân), *adj.* 1. pertaining to the Sabbath. 2. of the practices and beliefs of Sabbatarians: *n.* 1. one who observes the Sabbath on the seventh day of the week. 2. one who favors a rigid observance of Sunday as the Sabbath. —Sab-ba-tar'i-an-ism, *n.*

Sab-bath (sab'âth), *n.* 1. the seventh day of the week (Saturday), observed by the Jews and some Christian sects as a day of rest and worship. 2. Sunday, the usual Christian day of worship: *adj.* of or pertaining to the Sabbath.

Sab-bat-i-cal (sâ-bat'i-kl), Sab-bat-ic, *adj.* 1. of or pertaining to the Sabbath. 2. [s-]. denoting a period of rest that occurs at regular intervals. —Sab-bat'i-cal-ly, *adv.*

sabbatical year, 1. among the ancient Jews, every seventh year, in which the lands remained fallow and debtors were released. 2. a year or lesser period for study or travel, granted every seven years to some college teachers.

sa-ber (sā'bēr), *n.* a heavy cavalry sword with a somewhat curved blade: *v.t.* to cut, wound, or kill with a saber.

sa-ber-toothed tiger (-tōōtht), a fierce, extinct animal of the cat family, about the size of the tiger, found from the Oligocene to the Pleistocene: it had powerful, curved, canine teeth in the upper jaw.

Sa-bine (sā'bīn), *adj.* pertaining to a tribe of ancient Italy, conquered by the Romans in the third century. B.C.: *n.* a member of this tribe, or its language.

Sa-bin vaccine (sā'bin), an oral vaccine to prevent poliomyelitis.

sa-ble (sā'bl), *n.* 1. same as marten. 2. the soft, dark, valuable, luxurious fur of this animal. 3. *pl.* a garment made of this fur. 4. in *Heraldry,* the color black: *adj.* 1. made of sable. 2. black or dark-colored.

sable antelope, a large antelope of South Africa, with very large, curving horns: the adult male is glossy black

sa-bot (sab'ō, sâ-bō'), *n.* a wooden shoe traditionally worn by the peasantry in various parts of Europe.

sab-o-tage (sab'ō-täzh), *n.* destruction of property as by workmen during labor troubles or by foreign or underground agents in time of war: *v.t.* -taged, -tag-ing, to injure or destroy by sabotage: *v.i.* to take part in sabotage.

sab-o-teur (sab-ō-tūr'), *n.* a person who practices sabotage.

sa-bra (sä'brä), *n.* a person born in Israel.

sa-bre (sā'bēr), *n.* & *v.t.* -bred, -bring, same as saber.

sa-bre-tache (sā'bēr-tash), *n.* a leather case worn by cavalrymen, suspended from the sword belt.

sab-u-lous (sab'yoo-lûs), *adj.* sandy; gritty.

sac (sak), *n.* a pouchlike structure of an animal or plant, especially one filled with fluid. —sac'like, *adj.*

sac-char-ic (sâ-ker'ik), *adj.* pertaining to or obtained from a saccharine substance.

sac-cha-ride (sak'â-rīd), *n.* 1. a compound containing sugar. 2. any of the carbohydrates.

sac-cha-rin (sak'â-rin), *n.* a white, crystalline compound derived from coal tar, about 500 times sweeter than cane sugar.

sac-cha-rine (-rin, -rīn), *n.* same as saccharin: *adj.* 1. of, like, or containing sugar. 2. excessively sweet; cloying. —sac'cha-rine-ly, *adv.* —sac-cha-rin'i-ty (-rin'i-ti), *n.*

sac-cha-roi-dal (sak-â-roid'l), *adj.* having a texture resembling loaf sugar; granular and crystalline, as some marble and limestone; also sac'cha-roid.

sac-cha-rom-e-ter (sak-â-rom'ê-tēr), *n.* an instrument for determining the quantity of sugar in a solution.

sac-cha-rose (sak'â-rōs), *n.* same as sucrose.

sac-cu-late (sak'yū-lât), *adj.* divided into saccules or having a series of saclike expansions: also sac'cu-lat-ed. —sac-cu-la'tion, *n.*

sac-cule (sak'ūl), *n.* a little sac; especially, the membranous labyrinth of the ear: also sac'cu-lus ('yoo-lûs). *pl.* -li (-lī).

sac-er-do-tal (sas-ēr-dōt'l, sak-), *adj.* of or pertaining to priests or to priesthood; priestly.

sac-er-do-tal-ism (-izm), *n.* 1. the spirit, system, or practices of the priesthood. 2. an excessive reverence for, or reliance on, the priesthood. —sac-er-do'tal-ist, *n.*

sa-chem (sā'chêm), *n.* a North American Indian chief, as of a tribe or confederation of tribes.

sa-chet (sa-shā'), *n.* 1. a small bag, cushion, pad, etc. filled with a perfumed powder and

---

a in cap, ā in cane, ä in father, å in abet, e in met, ē in be, ê in baker, ê in regent, i in pit, ī in fine, i in manifest, o in hot, ō in horse, ō in bone,

placed in dresser drawers, etc. 2. the powder used for this: also **sachet** powder.

sack (sak), *n.* 1. a bag or pouch, especially a large, coarse bag for holding grain, etc. 2. the quantity contained in a sack. 3. a kind of dry white Spanish wine. 4. a plundering or pillaging of a captured town or city by soldiers. 5. [Slang], dismissal from a job (with *the*). 6. [Slang], bed: *v.t.* 1. to plunder or pillage (a captured town or city). 2. to put into sacks. 3. [Slang], to dismiss from a job.

sack-but (sak'but), *n.* 1. a medieval wind instrument, the forerunner of the trombone. 2. in the *Bible,* a kind of lyre: see *Daniel iii,* 5.

sack-cloth ('klôth), *n.* 1. a coarse material of which sacks are made; sacking. 2. coarse, rough cloth: see **sackcloth and ashes.**

sackcloth and ashes, a state of deep mourning or repentance for sin, as in Biblical times, symbolized by the wearing of sackcloth and the sprinkling of ashes on the head.

sack coat, a man's coat, often part of a business suit, that has a straight back and no seam at the waist.

sack-ful ('fool), *n., pl.* **-fuls,** the quantity a sack will hold.

sack-ing ('ing), *n.* a coarse, cheap material made of jute, hemp, flax, etc. and used for making sacks.

sa-cral (sā'krâl), *adj.* 1. of or pertaining to sacraments, or to religious rites. 2. of or pertaining to the region of the sacrum.

sac-ra-ment (sak'râ-mènt), *n.* 1. in *Christianity,* any one of certain rites instituted by Jesus and regarded as a visible sign of inward grace: baptism, confirmation, the Eucharist, penance, holy orders, matrimony, and anointing of the sick are the sacraments of the Roman Catholic and Orthodox Eastern churches; Protestants usually recognize as sacraments only baptism and Holy Communion, or the Eucharist. 2. something thought of as having a sacred or mysterious significance.

sac-ra-men-tal (sak-râ-men'tl), *adj.* 1. of or used in a sacrament. 2. constituting or like a sacrament. **—sac-ra-men'tal-ly,** *adv.*

sa-cred (sā'krid), *adj.* 1. of or having to do with religion or religious rites. 2. consecrated; holy. 3. hallowed or venerated. 4. inviolate. **—sa'cred-ly,** *adv.* **—sa'cred-ness,** *n.*

Sacred College, same as **College of Cardinals.**

sac-ri-fice (sak'ri-fis), *n.* 1. the act of offering the life of an animal or person, or some object, to a deity. 2. that which is so offered. 3. the destruction or giving up of one thing for another. 4. goods sold at a loss: *v.t.* **-ficed, -fic-ing,** 1. to offer to God or a deity in worship. 2. to destroy or give up for the sake of gaining something of more value. 3. to sell at a loss: *v.i.* to offer a sacrifice.

sac-ri-fi-cial (sak-ri-fish'âl), *adj.* of, pertaining to, consisting in, or offering sacrifice. **—sac-ri-fi'cial-ly,** *adv.*

sac-ri-lege (sak'ri-lij), *n.* 1. the act of appropriating to oneself, or to secular use, what

is consecrated to God or religion. 2. the desecration or profanation of something holy.

sac-ri-le-gious (sak-ri-lij'ûs, -lē'jûs), *adj.* 1. violating sacred things. 2. guilty of sacrilege. **—sac-ri-le'gious-ly,** *adv.* **—sac-ri-le'gious-ness,** *n.*

sa-cring (sā'kring), *n.* [Archaic], the act of consecrating the bread and wine of the Eucharist.

sacring bell, the small bell rung when the bread and wine are elevated during the Mass.

sac-ris-tan (sak'ris-tân), *n.* one who has charge of the sacristy of a church: also **sa-crist** (sā'krist).

sac-ris-ty (-ti), *n., pl.* **-ties,** the small room in a church where the sacred vessels, vestments, etc. are kept; vestry.

sa-cro-il-i-ac (sā-krō-il'i-ak, sak-rō-), *adj.* denoting the joint between the sacrum and the ilium: *n.* this joint.

sac-ro-sanct (sak'rō-sangkt), *adj.* very sacred or inviolable. **—sac-ro-sanc'ti-ty,** *n.*

sa-crum (sā'krûm, sak'rûm), *n., pl.* **-cra** ('krâ, 'râ), a thick, triangular bone at the base of the vertebral column; the dorsal part of the pelvis.

sad (sad), *adj.* **sad'der, sad'dest,** 1. full of grief; mournful; sorrowful. 2. causing sorrow. 3. dark-colored; drab. **—sad'ly,** *adv.* **—sad'ness,** *n.*

sad-den ('n), *v.t. & v.i.* to make or become sad.

sad-dle (sad'l), *n.* 1. a seat, usually of leather, for riding on a horse, bicycle, etc. 2. anything resembling a saddle. 3. a part of the hindquarters of a carcass of lamb, venison, etc. 4. a ridge between two summits or peaks: *v.t.* **-dled, -dling,** 1. to put a saddle upon. 2. to encumber. 3. to impose (a burden, obligation, etc.).

sad-dle-bag (-bag), *n.* 1. either one of a pair of bags slung over the back of a horse, behind the saddle. 2. a similar bag for the back of a bicycle or motorcycle.

sad-dle-bow (-bō), *n.* the bow, or arched front part, of a saddle, the top of which is the pommel.

saddle horse, a kind of horse that has been trained for riding.

sad-dler (sad'lēr), *n.* 1. one who repairs, makes, or sells saddles or harnesses. 2. a breed of American saddle horse.

sad-dler-y (sad'lē-ri), *n., pl.* **-dler-ies,** 1. the business of a saddler. 2. articles made by a saddler. 3. a saddler's shop.

saddle shoes, white oxford shoes with a band of contrasting color across the instep.

Sad-du-cee (saj'oo-sē, sad'yoo-), *n.* a member of an ancient Jewish party that believed only in the written law and rejected the oral, or traditional, law. **—Sad-du-ce'an,** *adj.*

sad-i-ron (sad'i-ērn), *n.* a solid flatiron, pointed at both ends.

sad-ism (sad'izm, sā'dizm), *n.* gratification or pleasure, often sexual, from hurting or humiliating another. **—sad'ist,** *n.* **—sa-dis'tic,** *adj.* **—sa-dis'ti-cal-ly,** *adv.*

sad-o-mas-o-chism (sā-dō-mas'ō-kizm, sad-ō-), *n.* a tendency to sadism and masochism within

---

ȯ in dra**g**on, ōō in cr**u**de, oo in w**oo**l, u in c**u**p, ū in c**u**re, û in t**u**rn, ů in f**o**cus, oi in b**o**y, ou in h**o**use, th in **th**in, ŧh in shea**th**e, g in **g**et, j in **j**oy, y in **y**et.

the same person. —sad·o·mas'o·chist, n. — sad·o·mas·o·chis'tic, adj.

sa·fa·ri (sä·fär'i), n., pl. -ris, a journey or expedition, as for hunting in Africa.

safe (sāf), adj. saf'er, saf'est, 1. free from danger, injury, or damage; secure from harm. 2. providing protection; not dangerous; sound. 3. that can be trusted. 4. cautious: n. a heavy metal box or chest, with a lock, for valuables. —safe'ly, adv. —safe'ness, n.

safe-con·duct ('kon'dukt), n. 1. a written pass giving official permission to travel in an area, as in wartime. 2. such permission.

safe-de·pos·it ('di·poz'it), adj. denoting a vault, box, etc. for keeping valuables, as in a bank: also safety-deposit.

safe·guard ('gärd), n. 1. that which guards or protects. 2. a precaution. 3. a permit for safe passage. 4. a safety device, as on machinery: v.t. to protect or guard.

safe-keep·ing ('kēp'ing), n. custody or protection.

safe·ty ('ti), n., pl. -ties, 1. freedom from danger, injury, or damage. 2. a device for preventing injury or accident. 3. a catch on a firearm that keeps it from firing.

safety glass, glass made to be shatterproof by putting two sheets of glass together with a transparent plastic substance between, that will hold pieces if the glass should be broken.

safety island, same as safety zone.

safety lamp, a former type of miner's lamp made with wire gauze around the flame, to avoid explosion.

safety match, a match that will light only when it is scratched on a specially prepared surface.

safety pin, a pin bent back upon itself, with the point enclosed in a guard.

safety razor, a razor with a replaceable blade held between guards that minimize the danger of cutting the skin.

safety valve, an automatic valve in a boiler, which opens when the steam exceeds a certain pressure.

safety zone, an area or platform marked in a roadway for the safety of pedestrians, as in boarding or leaving buses.

saf·fi·an (saf'i·ăn), n. leather made from goatskin or sheepskin tanned with sumac and dyed a bright color: also saffian leather.

saf·flow·er (saf'lou·ēr), n. 1. a thistlelike annual plant with large, orange flowers. 2. a drug or kind of dye made from the flowers.

safflower oil, an oil expressed from the seeds of the safflower plant, used in cooking, as a salad oil, and in varnishes and medicines.

saf·fron (saf'rŏn), n. 1. a perennial plant of the iris family, with purplish flowers. 2. the orange stigmas of these flowers, dried and used in flavoring and coloring food. 3. orange yellow: also saffron yellow: adj. orange-yellow.

sag (sag), v.i. sagged, sag'ging, 1. to sink or curve downward from weight or pressure, especially in the middle. 2. to droop; hang down unevenly. 3. to weaken or decline, as from age or fatigue. 4. to drift to leeward,

as a ship: v.t. to cause to sag: n. a part that sags.

sa·ga (sä'gá), n. 1. a medieval Scandinavian legend, tale, or story. 2. any long story of events and achievements of a person, family, clan, etc.

sa·ga·cious (sá·gā'shús), adj. mentally quick and discerning; judicious; wise; acute.

sa·gac·i·ty (sá·gas'i·ti), n. the quality of having great wisdom and sound judgment.

sag·a·more (sag'á·môr), n. any one of certain North American Indian chiefs of second rank.

sage (sāj), adj. sag'er, sag'est, 1. wise; discerning. 2. showing wisdom: n. 1. an elderly man held in great respect for his experienced wisdom and sound judgment. 2. an aromatic herb of the mint family, used in seasoning foods. 3. sagebrush. —sage'ly, adv. —sage'ness, n.

sage-brush ('brush), n. a tough, wiry shrub with aromatic leaves, common in the dry, alkaline plains of the western U.S.: it is important as a forage plant.

sage grouse, a large grouse of the sagebrush plains of the western U.S.

sage hen, the female of the sage grouse.

sag·it·tal (saj'i·tl), adj. 1. of or resembling an arrow or arrowhead. 2. denoting a suture in the skull between the parietal bones. —sag'-it·tal·ly, adv.

Sag·it·ta·ri·us (saj·i·ter'i·ŭs), n. 1. a large southern constellation in the brightest part of the Milky Way. 2. the ninth sign of the zodiac.

sa·go (sā'gō), n., pl. -gos, 1. a kind of granulated, edible starch obtained from the pith of various plants of East India, especially palms. 2. any one of several palms that yield sago: also sago palm.

sa·gua·ro (sä·gwä'rō, -wä'-), n., pl. -ros, a giant cactus with a white flower, found in northern Mexico and the southwestern U.S.: also sa·hua'ro (-wä'-).

sa·hib (sä'ib, 'hib, 'ēb), n. master; sir: a term of address formerly used in colonial India in speaking to a European man.

said (sed), past tense and past participle of say.

sai·ga (sī'gá), n. a small, sturdy antelope of the steppes of Russia and Siberia.

sail (sāl), n. 1. a sheet of canvas spread to catch the wind, by means of which a vessel is driven forward in the water. 2. sails collectively. 3. a sailing ship or vessel. 4. an excursion or trip in a ship or boat, especially one moved by sails: v.i. 1. to be moved by a sail or sails. 2. to travel on water. 3. to commence a trip by water. 4. to direct the course of a sailboat. 5. to glide or pass smoothly along: v.t. 1. to pass over in a ship. 2. to navigate; direct the course of.

sail·boat ('bōt), n. a boat with a sail or sails which catch the wind by which it is propelled.

sail·cloth ('klôth), n. 1. a heavy fabric, as canvas, used for sails, tents, etc. 2. a piece of such fabric, used as a covering.

sail·er ('ēr), *n.* a vessel that sails, with reference to its speed or manner of sailing.

sail·fish ('fish), *n.*, *pl.* **-fish, -fish·es**, a large, tropical, ocean fish related to the swordfish but having a large dorsal fin that looks much like a sail.

sail·ing ('ing), *n.* 1. the art of navigation. 2. the act of moving through the water. 3. the sport or pastime of racing or cruising in a sailboat. 4. the commencement of a trip on water.

sail·or ('ēr), *n.* 1. one who makes his living by sailing; mariner; seaman. 2. an enlisted man in the navy. 3. a kind of straw hat with a flat top and wide brim.

sail·or's-choice ('ērz-chois), *n.*, *pl.* **sail·or's-choice**, any one of a number of food fishes; specifically, a kind of small grunt.

sail·plane (sāl'plān), *n.* a kind of light glider designed for soaring by means of air currents: *v.i.* **-planed, -plan·ing,** to soar in a sailplane.

sain·foin (sān'foin), *n.* a cloverlike, leguminous plant, much grown in Europe and Asia for forage.

saint (sānt), *n.* 1. a holy person. 2. a person who is unusually patient, meek, etc. 3. *pl.* those who have died after leading a good life, and are believed to be in heaven. 4. in some Christian churches, a person who has been officially recognized as having lived a life of great holiness; canonized person: 5. [S-], a member of certain religious groups calling themselves *Saints*: *v.t.* to canonize.

Saint An·drew's cross (an'drōōz), a cross shaped like a letter X.

Saint An·tho·ny's fire (an'thō-niz), an earlier name for any one of several skin conditions, as erysipelas.

Saint Ber·nard (bēr-närd'), any one of a breed of large, white and reddish-brown dog once trained in the Swiss Alps to rescue travelers in the snow.

saint·ed (sān'tid), *adj.* 1. of or like a saint; saintly. 2. holy; sacred. 3. venerated as a saint.

Saint El·mo's fire (el'mōz), a ball or streak of flame resulting from an electrical discharge during an electrical storm, as from the tip of a ship's masthead or from the top of a steeple; corona.

saint·hood (sānt'hood), *n.* the status of being a saint.

Saint Johns·wort (jonz'wûrt), a shrub or herb with spotted leaves, usually yellow flowers, and numerous stamens.

saint·ly ('li), *adj.* **-li·er, -li·est,** 1. like or suited to a saint. 2. behaving like a saint. **—saint'-li·ness,** *n.*

Saint Nich·o·las (nik'l-ûs), see **Santa Claus.**

Saint Pat·rick's Day (pat'riks), March 17, observed by the Irish in honor of Saint Patrick, the patron saint of Ireland.

Saint Swith·in's Day (swith'ûnz), July 15: according to legend, the weather on this day sets the pattern for the weather of the succeeding 40 days.

Saint Val·en·tine's Day (val'ēn-tīnz), February 14, observed in honor of Saint Valentine, a 3d-century martyr, and marked by sending valentines.

Saint Vi·tus' dance (vī'tûs), same as chorea.

sake (sāk), *n.* 1. end; purpose; cause. 2. behalf; benefit.

sa·ke (sā-ki), *n.* a Japanese alcoholic beverage made from fermented rice: also spelled **sa'-ki.**

Sak·ti (sāk'ti, sak'-), *n.* same as **Shakti.** — **Sak'tism,** *n.*

sal (sal), *n.* in *Chemistry & Pharmacy,* salt.

sa·laam (sā-läm'), *n.* an Oriental salutation made by placing the right hand on the forehead and bowing very low: *v.t. & v.i.* to make or greet with a salaam.

sal·a·ble (sāl'ā-bl), *adj.* able or likely to be sold; marketable. **—sal·a·bil'i·ty,** *n.*

sa·la·cious (sā-lā'shûs), *adj.* 1. lustful. 2. pornographic; obscene. **—sa·la'cious·ly,** *adv.* **—sa·la'cious·ness, sa·lac'i·ty** (-las'i-ti), *n.*

sal·ad (sal'ād), *n.* any one of various usually cold dishes of vegetables (especially lettuce), fruits, seafood, meat, eggs, etc., usually mixed with salad dressing.

salad days, time of youthful inexperience.

salad dressing, any one of various mixtures, usually with a base of oil, vinegar, and spices, to be used as a sauce on salad.

sal·a·man·der (sal'ā-man-dēr), *n.* 1. an amphibious animal resembling the lizard but without scales. 2. a mythological lizard said to live in fire. **—sal·a·man'drine** ('drin), *adj.*

sa·la·mi (sā-lä'mi), *n.* a highly spiced, salted sausage, of Italian origin.

sal ammoniac, same as **ammonium chloride.**

sal·a·ried (sal'ā-rid), *adj.* producing or receiving a salary.

sal·a·ry (sal'ā-ri), *n.*, *pl.* **-ries,** recompense, usually periodically, for services rendered, especially clerical or professional services; stipend.

sale (sāl), *n.* 1. the act of selling; exchange of a commodity for an agreed price. 2. the opportunity to sell. 3. an auction. 4. a limited presentation of commodities for purchase at lower prices.

sal·e·ra·tus (sal-ē-rāt'ûs), *n.* sodium bicarbonate; baking soda.

sales·clerk (sālz'klûrk), *n.* one whose job is to sell items in a store.

sales·man ('mān), *n.*, *pl.* **-men** ('mēn), 1. a man whose job is to sell goods or services. 2. a salesclerk.

sales·per·son ('pûr-sn), *n.* one whose job is to sell items, as a salesclerk.

sales slip, a receipt from a retail store.

sales talk, 1. speech for the purpose of making a sale. 2. speech for any purpose of persuasion.

sales tax, a tax on the sale of items.

sales·wom·an ('woom-ān), *n.*, *pl.* **-wom·en** ('wim-in), a female salesclerk: also **sales'la·dy** ('lā-di), *pl.* **-dies, sales'girl** ('gûrl).

sal·i·cin (sal'i-sin), *n.* a substance extracted from willow and poplar bark, used as a reagent and, formerly, in medicine.

sal·i·cyl·ic acid (sal-i-sil'ik), a white, crystalline acid used as an ingredient in aspirin, as an antiseptic, for treating rheumatism, etc.

sa·lient (sāl'yēnt), *adj.* 1. leaping. 2. prominent;

conspicuous. 3. projecting: *n.* 1. an advanced position in a battle line. 2. something salient. —sa'lience, *n.*

sa·lif·er·ous (så-lif'ẽr-ùs), *adj.* yielding or impregnated with salt.

sa·lim·e·ter (så-lim'ĕ-tẽr), *n.* an instrument for determining the amount of salt in a solution.

sa·li·na (så-lī'nå), *n.* a salt marsh, pond, etc.

sa·line (sā'līn), *adj.* of, consisting of, containing, or like salt: *n.* a salt spring, marsh, etc. —sa·lin·i·ty (så-lin'ĭ-ti), *n.*

sa·li·va (så-lī'vå), *n.* the watery fluid secreted in the mouth, which is an agent in digestion. —sal·i·var·y (sal'ĭ-ver-i), *adj.*

sal·i·vate (sal'ĭ-vāt), *v.t.* -vat·ed, -vat·ing, to produce an excessive flow of saliva in the mouth of: *v.i.* to produce saliva. —sal·i·va'·tion, *n.*

sal·low (sal'ō), *adj.* of a pale, sickly, yellow color: *n.* a small tree of the willow type.

sal·ly (sal'i), *n., pl.* -lies, 1. a sudden rushing forth of troops to attack besiegers. 2. a sudden outburst of wit or fancy. 3. an excursion: *v.i.* -lied, -ly·ing, 1. to rush out, as troops from a besieged town. 2. to issue or rush forth suddenly.

Sally Lunn (sal'i lun), [also s- l-], a sweetened tea biscuit raised with leaven.

sal·ma·gun·di (sal-må-gun'di), *n.* 1. a compound of chopped meats with other ingredients, seasoning, etc. 2. any medley or potpourri.

sal·mi (sal'mi), *n.* a ragout of roasted game and other ingredients stewed in wine.

salm·on (sam'ŏn), *n., pl.* -on, -ons, 1. a marine fish which ascends freshwater rivers to spawn: its flesh becomes pink or red when cooked. 2. yellowish pink: also **salmon pink.**

sal·mo·nel·la (sal-mŏ-nel'å), *n., pl.* -nel'lae ('ē), -nel'la, -nel'las, any one of a type of disease-producing bacilli that cause typhoid, food poisoning, etc.

sal·ol (sal'ōl), *n.* a colorless, crystalline compound prepared from salicylic acid.

sa·lon (så-lon'), *n.* 1. a large room for a formal reception. 2. a fashionable assembly. 3. a room or gallery where pictures and objects of art are exhibited. 4. a place of business.

sa·loon (så-lōōn'), *n.* 1. a large reception room. 2. a bar for alcoholic drinks.

sal·pin·gi·tis (sal-pin-jīt'is), *n.* inflammation of either a Fallopian or Eustachian tube.

sal·pinx (sal'pingks), *n., pl.* **sal·pin'ges** (-pin'·jēz), 1. a Eustachian tube. 2. a Fallopian tube.

sal·si·fy (sal'sĭ-fē), *n.* a plant which has roots that taste like oysters.

salt (sôlt), *n.* 1. sodium chloride, a white crystalline substance, used for seasoning, preserving meat, etc.: it is obtained from the earth or by the evaporation of sea water. 2. anything like salt. 3. a chemical compound resulting from the replacement in an acid of the hydrogen by a metal. 4. wit; piquancy. 5. *pl.* mineral salts used as a purgative. 6. [*Informal*], a sailor: *v.t.* 1. to sprinkle or season with salt. 2. to scatter minerals or ores in a place barren of such, in or-

der to deceive a prospective purchaser: *adj.* flavored, seasoned, or impregnated with salt. —salt'ed, *adj.*

sal·ta·rel·lo (sal-tå-rel'ō), *n.* 1. a skipping Italian dance. 2. music for such a dance.

sal·ta·tion (sal-tā'shŭn), *n.* a leaping or dancing.

sal·ta·to·ry (sal'tå-tôr-i), *adj.* dancing; leaping.

salt-bush (sôlt'boosh), *n.* a stiff, weedy plant that grows in desert and marsh areas.

salt·cel·lar ('sel-ẽr), *n.* a small receptacle for table salt.

sal·tern ('tẽrn), *n.* a place where salt is manufactured.

salt·ine (sôl-tēn'), *n.* a flat cracker sprinkled with salt granules.

sal·tire (sal'tīr), *n.* in *Heraldry*, an X-shaped cross: also **sal'tier.**

salt·ish (sôl'tish), *adj.* somewhat salty.

salt lick, a block of salt for animals to lick.

salt·pe·ter (sôlt'pēt-ẽr), *n.* same as niter.

salt pork, salt-cured pork.

salt-shak·er (sôlt'shā-kẽr), *n.* a salt dispenser with holes in the top.

salt-wa·ter ('wôt-ẽr), *adj.* of, pertaining to, or living in salt water or the ocean.

salt·y (sôl'ti), *adj.* salt'i-er, salt'i-est, 1. of, containing, or like salt or the sea. 2. witty. 3. vulgar.

sa·lu·bri·ous (så-lōō'bri-ùs), *adj.* healthful; wholesome. —sa·lu'bri·ty ('bri-ti), sa·lu'bri·ous·ness, *n.*

sal·u·tar·y (sal'yoo-ter-i), *adj.* 1. healthful; wholesome. 2. beneficent. —sal'u·tar·i·ly, *adv.* —sal'u·tar·i·ness, *n.*

sal·u·ta·tion (sal-yoo-tā'shŭn), *n.* 1. the act or manner of saluting. 2. a greeting or act of paying respect. 3. the form this takes, as the opening address of a letter.

sa·lu·ta·to·ry (så-lōōt'å-tôr-i), *adj.* saluting; greeting: *n., pl.* -ries, 1. the opening oration at the commencement in schools and colleges. 2. any address of welcome.

sa·lute (så-lōōt'), *n.* 1. a mark of military respect shown by raising the hand to the head, etc. 2. a greeting. 3. a salvo of artillery, lowering of a flag, etc. as a mark of honor: *v.t.* 1. to address with kind wishes. 2. to welcome. 3. to greet with a bow, etc. 4. to honor by a salvo of artillery, lowering a flag, etc. 5. to praise: *v.i.* to make a salute.

sal·va·ble (sal'vå-bl), *adj.* capable of being saved.

sal·vage (sal'vij), *n.* 1. compensation given to those who assist at saving a vessel or cargo at sea. 2. the goods or vessel saved. 3. the act of saving a vessel, cargo, etc. at sea. 4. compensation for any property saved from damage or loss, or the act of saving it. 5. the property so saved: *v.t.* -vaged, -vag·ing, to save (property) from damage or loss.

sal·va·tion (sal-vā'shŭn), *n.* 1. the act of saving. 2. preservation from destruction; rescue. 3. spiritual deliverance from sin and death.

Salvation Army, a religious and charitable organization formed on a quasi-military model, founded in England in 1865 by William Booth: the present title was adopted in 1878. —Sal·va'tion·ist, *n.*

salve (sav), *n.* 1. a healing ointment. 2. a

remedy or soothing application: *v.t.* **salved,** **salv'ing,** to smooth; palliate.

sal·ver (sal'vēr), *n.* a tray on which anything is presented.

sal·vo (sal'vō), *n., pl.* **-vos, -voes,** 1. a discharge of a number of pieces of artillery, intended as a salute or attack. 2. the discharge of several rockets or bombs simultaneously. 3. a simultaneous cheering. 4. a proviso; excuse. 5. in *Law,* an exception.

sal vo·la·ti·le (vō-lat'l-ē), 1. ammonium carbonate. 2. aromatic spirits of ammonium carbonate and ammonium bicarbonate.

sal·vor (sal'vēr), *n.* one who effects the salvage of a ship or its goods.

Sa·mar·i·tan (sä-mer'ī-tn), *n.* 1. a native or inhabitant of Samaria, a region in ancient Palestine. 2. a kind, charitable person.

sam·ba (sam'bä), *n.* a Brazilian dance or the music for it: *v.i.* to dance the samba.

sam·bar (sam'bēr), *n., pl.* **-bars, -bar,** a large, brown Asiatic deer with an erect mane: also **sam'bur.**

sam·buke (sam'būk), *n.* an ancient musical instrument with strings like a harp.

same (sām), *adj.* 1. identical in kind or degree. 2. exactly alike. 3. before-mentioned. 4. without difference: *pron.* the same one: *adv.* in the same way.

sa·mekh, sa·mech (sä'mekh), *n.* the fifteenth letter of the Hebrew alphabet.

same·ness (sām'nis), *n.* identity; similarity.

sam·i·sen (sam'ī-sen), *n.* a Japanese instrument similar to a banjo, having three strings.

sam·ite (sam'īt, sä'mīt), *n.* a rich silk fabric sometimes interwoven with gold or silver.

sam·let (sam'lit), *n.* a young salmon.

sam·o·var (sam'ō-vär), *n.* in Russia, a metal urn used to boil water for tea.

samp (samp), *n.* 1. Indian cornmeal. 2. porridge made from it.

sam·pan (sam'pan), *n.* a small Chinese boat propelled by an oar from the stern.

sam·phire (sam'fīr), *n.* a marine plant growing along the seashore.

sam·ple (sam'pl), *n.* a specimen; model; pattern; part shown as indicative of the whole: *v.t.* **-pled, -pling,** to take a sample of.

sam·pler (sam'plēr), *n.* 1. a person who samples. 2. a piece of ornamental needlework with a variety of stitches, designs, etc.

Sam·son (sam'sn), *n.* 1. in the *Bible,* a very strong Israelite. 2. any very strong man.

Sam·u·el (sam'yoo-wäl, 'yool), *n.* either of two books of the Bible, I Samuel and II Samuel: cf. **Kings.**

sam·u·rai (sam'ū-rī), *n., pl.* **-rai,** one who belonged to a feudal military caste in Japan.

san·a·tive (san'ä-tiv), *adj.* tending to heal or cure.

san·a·to·ri·um (san-ä-tōr'ī-ûm), *n., pl.* **-ri·ums, -ri·a** (-ä), [Chiefly British], same as **sanitarium.**

sanc·ti·fied (sangk'ti-fīd), *adj.* 1. made holy. 2. sanctimonious.

sanc·ti·fy (sangk'ti-fī), *v.t.* **-fied, -fy·ing,** 1. to make holy; consecrate. 2. to make pure. — **sanc·ti·fi·ca'tion,** *n.* —**sanc'ti·fi·er,** *n.*

sanc·ti·mo·ni·ous (sangk-ti-mō'ni-ûs), *adj.* having the appearance of or affecting sanctity; religiously hypocritical.

sanc·ti·mo·ny (sangk'ti-mō-ni), *n.* affected sanctity; religious hypocrisy.

sanc·tion (sangk'shûn), *n.* 1. the act of ratifying or giving authority to; authority. 2. consent; confirmation. 3. *usually pl.* in international law, the punishment inflicted by various nations, upon a nation that has broken a treaty or otherwise transgressed the law, such as the imposition of an embargo: *v.t.* to give sanction to; countenance; approve.

sanc·ti·ty (sangk'ti-ti), *n., pl.* **-ties,** 1. purity; inviolability. 2. sacredness.

sanc·tu·ar·y (sangk'choo-wer-i), *n., pl.* **-ar·ies,** 1. the most sacred part of a temple or church. 2. a consecrated place. 3. a temple or church. 4. the part of a church around the altar. 5. an inviolable asylum. 6. shelter; refuge.

sanc·tum (sangk'tûm), *n., pl.* **-tums, -ta** (-tä), 1. a sacred or private place. 2. a room for personal use.

sanctum sanc·to·rum (sangk-tôr'ûm), 1. same as holy of holies. 2. a place of the utmost privacy.

Sanc·tus bell (sangk'tûs), a bell rung during various parts of the Mass.

sand (sand), *n.* 1. fine particles of crushed or worn rock, as on the desert. 2. *usually pl.* a tract of sand. 3. moments of time: *v.t.* 1. to sprinkle with sand. 2. to smooth or polish with sandpaper, sand, etc. —**sand'er,** *n.*

san·dal (san'dl), *n.* 1. a kind of shoe consisting of a sole fastened by straps to the foot. 2. a low slipper. 3. same as **sandalwood.** — **san'daled, san'dalled,** *adj.*

san·dal·wood (-wood), *n.* 1. a light-colored, closegrained, odoriferous wood of a south Asian tree, used in cabinetmaking. 2. the tree.

san·da·rac (san'dä-rak), *n.* 1. a kind of resin obtained from a North African tree related to the pine, used as a varnish. 2. this tree.

sand·bag (sand'bag), *n.* 1. a small, narrow bag filled with sand and used as a weapon, as by robbers. 2. a bag filled with sand and used for protection, ballast, etc.: *v.t.* **-bagged, -bag·ging,** 1. to stun with a sandbag. 2. to place sandbags in or about. 3. [Informal], to coerce.

sand bar, a narrow mound of sand formed in a river or along a shore by currents or tides: also **sand·bank** (sand'bangk).

sand·blast (sand'blast), *n.* a current of air or steam carrying sand at high velocity, used in etching glass, cleaning surfaces of stone buildings, etc.: *v.t.* to engrave, clean, etc. with a sandblast. —**sand'blast·er,** *n.*

sand·box ('boks), *n.* a large container of sand for playing in.

sand·bur, sand·burr ('bur), *n.* a kind of nightshade growing in the western U.S.

sand dab, a small food fish related to the flounder.

sand·er·ling (san'dēr-ling), *n.* a kind of small sandpiper.

---

sand fly, any one of various dipterous, biting flies.

sand-glass (sand'glas), *n.* an instrument for measuring time by the flowing of sand from one compartment to another; hourglass.

sand grouse, a bird resembling a pigeon, inhabiting arid parts of southern Europe, Asia, and Africa.

sand-hog ('hŏg), *n.* one who works beneath the ground or sea in construction.

sand-lot ('lot), *adj.* of or pertaining to amateur games, as baseball.

sand-man ('man), *n.* a mythical person supposed to make children sleepy.

sand myrtle, a small, evergreen plant of the sandy coast of the southeastern U.S.

sand-pa-per ('pā-pēr), *n.* paper with sand grains stuck to one side, used for polishing and smoothing: *v.t.* to use sandpaper on.

sand-pip-er ('pī-pēr), *n., pl.* -pip-ers, -pip-er, any one of a group of small birds living on the shore and having a long, soft-tipped bill.

sand-stone ('stōn), *n.* a rock composed of sand united by silica or other binding material.

sand-storm ('stôrm), *n.* a storm with heavy winds that blow sand around in the air.

sand-wich (sand'wich), *n.* 1. slices of bread with meat, cheese, etc. between. 2. anything like a sandwich: *v.t.* to place between two other persons, things, etc.

sand-y (san'dĭ), *adj.* sand'i-er, sand'i-est, 1. composed of, abounding in, or covered with sand. 2. of the color of sand; light reddish-yellow. 3. shifting; unstable.

sane (sān), *adj.* 1. mentally sound or healthy. 2. reasonable; intelligent. —sane'ly, *adv.* — sane'ness, *n.*

San-for-ize (san'fô-rīz), *v.t.* -ized, -iz-ing, to shrink (cloth) by a patented process before making it into garments.

sang (sang), alternate past tense of sing.

san-ga-ree (sang-gē-rē'), *n.* a cold beverage of wine that has been spiced.

sang-froid (sang-frwä'), *n.* cool indifference or composure.

san-gui-nar-y (sang'gwi-ner-ĭ), *adj.* 1. attended with much bloodshed. 2. bloodthirsty; murderous; cruel.

san-guine (sang'gwin), *adj.* 1. warm and ardent in temper; hopeful; confident. 2. having the color of blood.

san-guin-e-ous (sang-gwin'ĭ-ŭs), *adj.* 1. of, pertaining to, abounding with, or constituting blood. 2. of a blood color.

San-he-drin (san-hed'rin), *n.* the great judicial council of the ancient Jews.

sa-ni-es (sā'nĭ-ēz), *n.* a thin greenish discharge from a wound or sore.

san-i-tar-i-an (san-i-ter'ĭ-ăn), *adj.* same as sanitary: *n.* one versed in or devoted to sanitary studies; advocate or promoter of sanitary measures.

san-i-tar-i-um ('ĭ-ŭm), *n., pl.* -i-ums, -i-a (-ă), 1. a health retreat. 2. an institution for the care of invalids, the infirm, etc. or the treatment of particular diseases.

san-i-tar-y (san'i-ter-ĭ), *adj.* 1. of, pertaining to, connected with, or promoting health. 2. hygienic.

san-i-ta-tion (san-i-tā'shŭn), *n.* 1. the practice of making sanitary; hygiene. 2. the removal of sewage.

san-i-tize (san'i-tīz), *v.t.* -tized, -tiz-ing, to cause to become sanitary.

san-i-ty (san'i-tĭ), *n.* saneness; mental health.

sank (sangk), past tense of sink.

san-nup (san'up), *n.* a male American Indian who is married.

sans-cu-lotte (sanz-koo-lot'), *n.* 1. a revolutionary: a term of contempt applied to one of the French Revolutionaries. 2. a revolutionary of any sort.

San-skrit (san'skrit), *n.* the ancient literary language of India.

San-ta Claus, San-ta Klaus (san'tă klôz), an imaginary, fat, happy old man in a red suit with a white beard, who brings presents at Christmas: also called *Saint Nicholas.*

sap (sap), *n.* 1. the watery, circulating juice of a plant. 2. a vital fluid. 3. an excavated trench for approaching a fort. 4. power; energy. 5. [Slang], one who is stupid: *v.t.* sapped, sap'ping, 1. to deprive of vitality. 2. to undermine: *v.i.* to proceed by secretly undermining. —sap'less, *adj.*

sap-a-jou (sap'ă-jōō), *n.* same as Capuchin (sense 3).

sap-head (sap'hed), *n.* [Slang], one who is stupid.

sap-id (sap'id), *adj.* savory. —sa-pid-i-ty (să-pid'ĭ-tĭ), *n.*

sa-pi-ent (sā'pi-ĕnt), *adj.* wise; sagacious. —sa'-pi-ence, *n.*

sap-ling (sap'ling), *n.* 1. a young tree. 2. a youthful person.

sap-o-dil-la (sap-ō-dil'ă), *n.* 1. any one of a group of tropical trees yielding chicle. 2. the fruit of any of these trees, having a rough, brown skin and sweet, yellowish pulp.

sap-o-na-ceous (sap-ō-nā'shŭs), *adj.* resembling or having the qualities of soap.

sa-pon-i-fy (să-pon'i-fī), *v.t.* -fied, -fy-ing, to convert into soap by reaction with an alkali. —sa-pon-i-fi-ca'tion (-fi-kā'shŭn), *n.*

sap-o-nin (sap'ō-nin), *n.* a glucoside used as a detergent.

sa-por (sā'pēr), *n.* that which produces or stimulates taste; savor. —sa-po-rif-ic (să-pō-rif'ik), sa-por-ous (să'pēr-ŭs), *adj.*

sa-po-te (să-pōt'ĭ), *n.* a tropical tree that produces a plumlike fruit.

sap-pan-wood (să-pan'wood), *n.* 1. a wood producing a red dye, obtained from an East Indian tree. 2. the tree.

sap-per (sap'ēr), *n.* 1. one who or that which saps. 2. a soldier employed in sapping or digging trenches.

Sap-phic (saf'ik), *adj.* of Sappho, a Greek poet of the 7th century B.C., or like her lyric verses.

sap-phire (saf'īr), *n.* a precious stone of a blue color, a variety of corundum.

sap-py (sap'ĭ), *adj.* -pi-er, -pi-est, 1. full of sap; juicy. 2. [Slang], inane; fatuous.

sap-ro-gen-ic (sap-rō-jen'ik), *adj.* capable of producing or caused by putrefaction: also **sa-prog-e-nous** (să-proj'ĕ-nŭs).

sap-ro-lite (sap'rō-līt), *n.* decomposed rock.

a in cap, ā in cane, ä in father, å in abet, e in met, ē in be, ê in baker, ê in regent, i in pit, ī in fine, i in manifest, o in hot, ô in horse, ō in bone,

sa·proph·a·gous (sa-prof'ǎ-gǔs), *adj.* feeding on decaying matter.

sap·ro·phyte (sap'rō-fīt), *n.* any organism living on decaying or putrefied matter.

sap·suck·er (sap'suk-ẽr), *n.* a small American woodpecker which feeds on insects and tree sap.

sap·wood (sap'wood), *n.* the soft wood that lies just over the innermost wood of a tree and carries water.

sar·a·band (sar'ǎ-band), *n.* 1. a slow Spanish dance in 3/4 time. 2. music for such a dance.

Sar·a·cen (ser'ǎ-sn), *n.* 1. originally, a nomadic Arab. 2. later, any Moslem or Arab in the medieval period. —**Sar·a·cen·ic** (-sen'ik), *adj.*

sar·casm (sär'kazm), *n.* 1. a bitter, cutting, satirical expression. 2. the act of making such an expression. —**sar·cas·tic** (-kas'tik), *adj.* —**sar·cas·tic·al·ly**, *adv.*

sarce·net (särs'net), *n.* a thin, fine kind of woven silk, used for ribbons, linings, etc.

sar·co-, a combining form meaning *flesh.*

sar·co·carp (sär'kō-kärp), *n.* the fleshy part of a fruit having a stone.

sar·col·o·gy (sär-kol'ŏ-ji), *n.* that part of anatomy study that treats of the soft parts of the body.

sar·co·ma (sär-kō'mǎ), *n.*, *pl.* **-mas**, **-ma·ta** ('mǎ-tǎ), a fleshy, malignant tumor. —**sar·co·ma·to·sis** (-tō'sis), *n.* —**sar·co·ma·tous** (-tǔs), *adj.*

sar·coph·a·gus (sär-kof'ǎ-gǔs), *n.*, *pl.* **-gi** (-jī), **-gus·es**, 1. a limestone coffin used by the ancient Greeks and Romans, which quickly disintegrated the dead body within. 2. any stone coffin that may be viewed.

sar·cous (sär'kǔs), *adj.* of, pertaining to, or composed of flesh or muscle.

sard (särd), *n.* a precious stone, a deep orange-red variety of chalcedony.

sar·dine (sär-dēn'), *n.*, *pl.* **-dines**, **-dine**, the pilchard or other small ocean fish preserved in cans for eating.

sar·di·us (sär'di-ǔs), *n.* in the *Bible*, a precious stone in the Jewish high priest's breastplate.

sar·don·ic (sär-don'ik), *adj.* bitter, contemptuous, or sneering, as a sardonic laugh.

sar·do·nyx (sär'dŏ-niks), *n.* a variety of onyx made up of alternate layers of chalcedony and carnelian.

Sar·gas·so Sea (sär-gas'ō), a portion of the North Atlantic covered with a floating mass of seaweed.

sar·gas·sum (sär-gas'ŭm), *n.* a floating brown seaweed in warm seas: also **sar·gas·so** ('ō), *pl.* **-sos.**

sa·ri (sä'ri), *n.* the principal garment of a Hindu woman, consisting of a long piece of fabric wrapped around the waist, with one part thrown over the shoulder and the other hanging down to the feet.

sa·rong (sǎ-rŏng'), *n.* a skirtlike garment worn by both sexes in the East Indies, Malay Archipelago, etc.

sar·sa·pa·ril·la (sas·pǎ-ril'ǎ, särs-), *n.* 1. the dried roots of a tropical American vine. 2. an extract of these roots, used as a beverage. 3. the vine itself.

sarse·net (särs'net), *n.* same as sarcenet.

sar·to·ri·al (sär-tôr'i-ǎl), *adj.* 1. of or pertaining to a tailor or his work. 2. of or pertaining to men's clothing.

sar·to·ri·us (-ǔs), *n.* the muscle of the leg by means of which the legs can be crossed.

sash (sash), *n.* 1. a band, ribbon, or scarf worn around the waist or over the shoulder. 2. a sliding frame for holding panes of glass: *v.t.* to furnish with sashes.

sa·shay (sa-shā'), *v.i.* [Informal], to move in a relaxed, unplanned way.

sass (sas), *n.* [Informal], bold and disrespectful speech: *v.t.* [Informal], to address disrespectfully.

sas·sa·by (sas'ǎ-bi), *n.*, *pl.* **-bies**, a large South African antelope related to the hartebeest.

sas·sa·fras (sas'ǎ-fras), *n.* a tree related to the laurel with a fragrant root, wood, and flowers.

sass·y (sas'i), *adj.* **sass'i·er**, **sass'i·est**, [Informal], disrespectful; rude.

sat (sat), past tense & past participle of *sit.*

Sa·tan (sāt'n), *n.* the Devil.

sa·tan·ic (sǎ-tan'ik, sā-), *adj.* of, pertaining to, or resembling Satan; diabolical; infernal; extremely wicked and cruel; malicious. —**sa·tan'i·cal·ly**, *adv.*

satch·el (sach'ĕl), *n.* a small bag for carrying books, papers, etc.

sate (sāt), *v.t.* **sat'ed**, **sat'ing**, 1. to satisfy the appetites or desires of. 2. to fulfill (a desire, appetite, etc.).

sa·teen (sǎ-tēn'), *n.* a woolen or cotton fabric made in imitation of satin.

sat·el·lite (sat'l-īt), *n.* 1. a small planet revolving around a larger one. 2. a device launched into orbit around the earth, the moon, etc. 3. a small country politically subordinate to and economically reliant upon a larger country. 4. an obsequious attendant.

sa·tia·ble (sā'shǎ-bl), *adj.* capable of being gratified or satiated.

sa·ti·ate (sā'shi-āt), *v.t.* **-at·ed**, **-at·ing**, to fill or gratify fully; surfeit; glut: *adj.* (-it), glutted.

sa·ti·e·ty (sǎ-tī'ĕ-ti), *n.* fullness or gratification beyond desire; repletion.

sat·in (sat'n), *n.* a woven, glossy material of silk, nylon, etc.: *adj.* made of or like satin; glossy. —**sat'in·y**, *adj.*

sat·i·net, **sat·i·nette** (sat-n-et'), *n.* 1. a thin kind of satin. 2. a glossy cloth woven with wool and cotton, made to resemble satin.

sat·in·wood (sat'n-wood), *n.* 1. the hard, smooth wood of various trees, used in making furniture. 2. any of these trees.

sat·ire (sa'tīr), *n.* 1. a type of literary composition in which vice and folly are held up to ridicule. 2. sarcasm, ridicule, etc. of vice and folly.

sa·tir·i·cal (sǎ-tir'i-kl), *adj.* 1. of, pertaining to, or containing satire. 2. addicted to satire. Also **sa·tir'ic.** —**sa·tir'i·cal·ly**, *adv.*

sat·i·rist (sat'i-rist), *n.* 1. a writer of satire. 2. one who likes to satirize.

sat·i·rize (-rīz), *v.t.* **-rized**, **-riz·ing**, to assail or ridicule with satire.

sat·is·fac·tion (sat-is-fak'shŭn), *n.* 1. the act of satisfying. 2. the state of being satisfied. 3. contentment; gratification. 4. payment.

ŏ in dragon, ōō in crude, oo in wool, u in cup, ū in cure, û in turn, ǔ in focus, oi in boy, ou in house, th in thin, *th* in sheathe, g in get, j in joy, y in yet.

sat·is·fac·to·ry (-fak'tō-ri), *adj.* giving satisfaction or content; making redress; relieving the mind from doubt or uncertainty. —**sat·is·fac'to·ri·ly,** *adv.*

sat·is·fy (sat'is-fī), *v.t.* -fied, -fy·ing, 1. to gratify to the fullest degree. 2. to free from doubt or uncertainty. 3. to pay in full; discharge: *v.i.* to give satisfaction; make atonement or payment.

sa·to·ri (sä-tōr'i), *n.* in *Zen Buddhism,* the informing of the spirit.

sa·trap (sā'trap, sat'rap), *n.* 1. a kind of viceroy among the ancient Persians. 2. a despotic subordinate official.

sa·trap·y (sā'trá-pi, sat'rá-), *n., pl.* -trap·ies,' the government or jurisdiction of a satrap.

sat·u·ra·ble (sach'ēr-á-bl), *adj.* capable of being saturated.

sat·u·rant ('ēr-ánt), *adj.* impregnating to the fullest: *n.* a substance that saturates another.

sat·u·rate (sach'ù-rāt), *v.t.* -rat·ed, -rat·ing, 1. to soak or imbue completely. 2. to make as full as possible with. 3. in *Chemistry,* to cause (a compound) to have all the valence bonds between its atoms filled, so that it can combine no further.

sat·u·ra·tion (sach-ù-rá'shŭn), *n.* 1. the act of saturating. 2. the state of being saturated; impregnation of one substance by another until the latter can contain no more.

Sat·ur·day (sat'ēr-di, -dā), *n.* the seventh day of the week.

Sat·urn (sat'ērn), *n.* 1. the sixth planet in distance from the sun and the second largest in the solar system: it has three rings around it. 2. in *Roman Mythology,* the god of agriculture.

Sat·ur·na·li·a (sat-ēr-nā'li-á), *n.* 1. an ancient Roman festival in honor of Saturn in which all classes, including slaves, took part. 2. [s-], unrestrained revelry.

Sat·ur·na·li·an (-án), *adj.* 1. of, pertaining to, or characteristic of the Saturnalia. 2. [s-], riotously merry or bawdy.

sa·tur·ni·id (sä-tūr'ni-id), *n.* any of a group of large, hairy-bodied moths.

sat·ur·nine (sat'ēr-nin), *adj.* 1. in *Astrology,* under the influence of the planet Saturn. 2. dull; morose; gloomy; phlegmatic.

sat·ur·nism (-nizm), *n.* lead poisoning.

sat·yr (sāt'ēr), *n.* 1. in *Greek Mythology,* a lower deity, attendant on Bacchus, represented with long, pointed ears, short horns, a man's body, and the legs of a goat. 2. a lecherous man. 3. a brown or gray butterfly. —**sa·tyr·ic** (sä-tir'ik), *adj.*

sat·y·ri·a·sis (sat-i-rī'á-sis), *n.* abnormal and unmanageable sexual desire in a man.

sauce (sôs), *n.* 1. a liquid condiment or seasoning for food; any mixture used as a relish. 2. fruit that has been stewed or preserved. 3. [Informal], pertness: *v.t.* sauced, sauc'ing, 1. to put sauce on or over. 2. to render pungent. 3. [Informal], to treat with pertness.

sauce·box (sôs'boks), *n.* [Old Informal], a pert, impudent person, especially such a child.

sauce·pan ('pan), *n.* a small metal pot with a handle, used in cooking.

sau·cer (sô'sēr), *n.* 1. a shallow dish designed to hold a cup. 2. anything shaped like a saucer.

sau·cy (sô'si), *adj.* -ci·er, -ci·est, 1. impudent. 2. pert. —**sau'ci·ly,** *adv.* —**sau'ci·ness,** *n.*

sau·er·bra·ten (sour'brät-n, zou'ēr-), *n.* beef that has been soaked in vinegar, spices, etc. previous to cooking.

sau·er·kraut (sour'krout), *n.* chopped cabbage fermented in a brine of its own juice.

sau·ger (sô'gēr), *n.* a freshwater American fish related to the walleye.

Saul (sôl), *n.* in the *Bible,* 1. the first king of Israel: see *I Samuel ix.* 2. the original name of the apostle Paul.

sau·na (sou'ná), *n.* a bath originating in Finland, in which one is subjected to hot, dry air.

saun·ter (sôn'tēr), *v.i.* to wander about idly; loiter; linger: *n.* an idle walk or ramble.

sau·rel (sôr'ĕl), *n.* a saltwater fish related to the scad.

sau·ri·an (sôr'i-án), *n.* any of a group of reptiles including the lizards.

sau·ry (sôr'i), *n., pl.* -ries, a kind of fish with a long beak, inhabiting the temperate parts of the Atlantic.

sau·sage (sô'sij), *n.* seasoned, minced meat, of pork, often stuffed into a casing.

sau·té (sō-tā', sô-), *n.* a dish cooked by rapid frying in a small amount of fat: *adj.* fried quickly in a small amount of fat: *v.t.* -téed', -té'ing, to fry rapidly in a small amount of fat.

sau·terne (sō-tûrn'), *n.* a white table wine.

sav·age (sav'ij), *adj.* 1. uncivilized. 2. uncultivated; wild. 3. cruel; pitiless. 4. fierce. 5. enraged: *n.* 1. a human being in a rude, uncivilized state; barbarian. 2. a fierce, brutal person. —**sav'age·ly,** *adv.* —**sav'age·ness,** *n.*

sav·age·ry (-ri), *n., pl.* -ries, 1. the state of being wild or uncivilized. 2. barbarism; brutal toughness.

sa·van·na, sa·van·nah (sá-van'á), *n.* an extensive open plain or meadow.

sa·vant (sá-vänt', sav'ánt), *n.* a person of learning.

save (sāv), *v.t.* saved, sav'ing, 1. to bring out of danger; preserve from evil; rescue. 2. to prevent. 3. to lay by. 4. to keep from squandering. 5. in *Theology,* to deliver from spiritual punishment: *v.i.* 1. to be economical. 2. to hoard: *prep.* except; not including: *conj.* except.

sav·e·loy (sav'ē-loi), *n.* a kind of highly seasoned sausage made in England.

sav·in, sav·ine (sav'in), *n.* 1. a type of juniper whose young leaves and branches yield a volatile oil used in perfumes. 2. same as red cedar.

sav·ing (sā'ving), *adj.* 1. preserving. 2. frugal; parsimonious. 3. reserving. 4. being a compensation: *n.* 1. an exception or reservation. 2. *often pl.* a lessening of money, time, etc. spent. 3. *pl.* money, time, etc. saved: *prep.* [Now Rare], with the exception of.

---

a in cap, ā in cane, ä in father, á in abet, e in met, ē in be, ē in baker,
ê in regent, i in pit, ī in fine, i in manifest, o in hot, ō in horse, ō in bone,

savings bank, a bank for savings deposits upon which interest is paid.

sav·ior, sav·iour (sāv′yēr), *n.* 1. one who saves or delivers from danger. 2. [S-], Jesus Christ (preceded by *the*).

sa·voir-faire (sav′wär-fer′), *n.* an intuitive knowledge of what is the right thing to do; tact; presence of mind.

sa·vor (sā′vēr), *n.* 1. flavor; taste; relish; scent. 2. characteristic property: *v.i.* 1. to have a particular flavor or smell (with *of*). 2. to exhibit tokens (*of*): *v.t.* to taste or smell with delight. Also, British spelling, **sa′vour**.

sa·vor·y (sā′vēr-i), *adj.* -vor·i·er, -vor·i·est, 1. pleasing to the taste or smell. 2. delightful; pleasing. Also, British spelling, **sa′vour·y.** — **sa′vor·i·ness,** *n.*

sa·vor·y (sā′vēr-i), *n.* an aromatic mint used in cooking.

sa·voy (sā-voi′), *n.* a kind of cabbage with curled leaves.

sav·vy (sav′i), *v.i.* -vied, -vy·ing, [Slang], to comprehend: *n.* [Slang], comprehension or cleverness.

saw (sô), *n.* 1. a cutting steel instrument with a toothed edge. 2. a proverb or wise saying: *v.t.* to cut or form with a saw: *v.i.* 1. to cut with or as with a saw. 2. to be cut with a saw.

saw (sô), past tense of see.

saw·bones (sô′bōnz), *n.* [Slang], a medical doctor or surgeon.

saw·buck (′buk), *n.* 1. a rack on which wood is placed for sawing. 2. [Slang], a ten-dollar bill.

saw·dust (′dust), *n.* very fine particles of wood produced by sawing.

saw·fish (′fish), *n., pl.* -fish, -fish·es, a fish with a long bony snout with teeth on both sides.

saw·fly (′flī), *n., pl.* -flies, a hymenopterous insect, the female of which has sawlike organs with which it pierces plants, forming a place to deposit its eggs.

saw·horse (′hôrs), *n.* a rack on which wood is placed for sawing.

saw·mill (′mil), *n.* 1. a building containing power machinery for sawing logs. 2. the machinery itself.

saw·yer (sô′yēr), *n.* 1. one who saws timber into planks. 2. a tree or log in a river, whose branches, partly above the water, sway up and down by the force of the current. 3. a beetle that bores into wood.

sax·a·tile (sak′sä-til), *adj.* same as saxicolous.

sax·horn (saks′hôrn), *n.* a brass-wind instrument.

sax·ic·o·lous (sak-sik′ō-lûs), *adj.* growing among or inhabiting rocks: also **sax·ic′o·line** (-lin, lin).

sax·i·frage (sak′si-frij), *n.* any of a group of plants chiefly of arctic and temperate climates, having flowers of various colors.

Sax·on (sak′sn), *adj.* 1. of or pertaining to an ancient people formerly inhabiting northern Germany, or their language. 2. Anglo-Saxon: *n.* 1. a member of the Saxon people. 2. the Saxon dialect. 3. an Anglo-Saxon.

sax·o·phone (sak′sō-fōn), *n.* a woodwind instrument with keys, a single reed, and a metal body.

say (sā), *v.t.* said, say′ing, 1. to utter words; declare. 2. to speak; pronounce. 3. to allege. 4. to intone. 5. to set forth with certainty. 6. to suppose: *v.i.* to speak; state: *n.* 1. the opportunity to say something. 2. power to make judgments.

say·ing (sā′ing), *n.* 1. the act of speaking. 2. an expression, saw, or adage.

say-so (sā′sō), *n.* [Informal], 1. guarantee. 2. authority.

scab (skab), *n.* 1. an incrustation formed over a wound. 2. a skin disease, as of sheep. 3. a workman who refuses to join a union or strike, or who takes the place abandoned by a striker: *v.i.* scabbed, scab′bing, 1. to have a scab cover. 2. to behave as a scab.

scab·bard (skab′ērd), *n.* the sheath in which the blade of a sword, dagger, etc. is kept: *v.t.* to put into a scabbard.

scabbard fish, a silver-colored, elongated, compressed ocean fish, usually found in the South Pacific and Indian oceans.

scab·ble (skab′l), *v.t.* -bled, -bling, to shape or dress (stone) roughly.

scab·by (skab′i), *adj.* -bi·er, -bi·est, 1. covered with or full of scabs. 2. affected with scab. 3. mean; low; contemptible. — **scab′bi·ness,** *n.*

sca·bies (skā′biz), *n.* a skin disease caused by a mite and characterized by an intense itch.

scab·rous (skab′rûs), *adj.* 1. rough to the touch; uneven; dotted; scaly. 2. unseemly; offensive.

scad (skad), *n., pl.* scad, scads, any one of several edible fishes of the Atlantic, having a forked tail.

scad (skad), *n. usually pl.* [Informal], a huge quantity.

scaf·fold (skaf′ld, ′ōld), *n.* 1. a temporary wooden stage. 2. a temporary structure for supporting workers while building, painting, etc. 3. an elevated platform for the execution of a criminal: *v.t.* to furnish or support with a scaffold.

scaf·fold·ing (′l-ding), *n.* 1. a scaffold; framework. 2. materials for erecting scaffolds.

scagl·io·la (skal-yō′lä), *n.* an imitation of granite or marble, made up of gypsum and glue streaked with granite or marble dust or chips.

scal·a·ble (skāl′ä-bl), *adj.* capable of being scaled.

sca·lar (skā′lēr), *adj.* in *Mathematics,* of or denoting a quantity that has extent but no direction, as volume.

scal·a·wag (skal′ä-wag), *n.* a scamp; rogue.

scald (skôld), *v.t.* 1. to burn with hot liquid or steam. 2. to nearly boil. 3. to expose to boiling liquid: *n.* 1. a burn or injury to the skin or flesh from a hot liquid or steam. 2. a diseased condition of plants with tissue bleaching taking place.

scald (skôld, skäld), *n.* same as skald. — **scald′ic,** *adj.*

scale (skāl), *n.* 1. the dish or pan of a balance. 2. *often pl.* a balance, or any instrument or machine for weighing. 3. the small bony or horny plate of a fish, reptile, or insect. 4. any thin plate or layer. 5. the thin oxide which forms on the surface of heated metals. 6. incrustation on the interior of a boiler. 7. a series of steps, degrees, etc. 8. a graduated measure. 9. an instrument with such a measure. 10. a series of musical tones varying in pitch according to set intervals. 11. relative dimensions, as of a map. 12. a basis for a numerical system: *v.t.* 1. to strip or clear of scales. 2. to weigh. 3. to climb over, as by a ladder; clamber up. 4. to ascend by steps or climbing. 5. to form in relation to a scale: *v.i.* to separate and come off in thin layers.

sca·lene (skā-lēn', skā'lēn), *adj.* having the sides and angles unequal: said of a triangle.

scal·lion (skal'yun), *n.* 1. a kind of green onion with a nearly bulbless root. 2. a leek.

scal·lop (skal'ŏp), *n.* 1. a marine bivalve mollusk having the edge of its hinged shell curved. 2. the shell of such a mollusk: it was formerly worn by pilgrims. 3. a dish shaped like a mollusk shell. 4. an ornamental edge of curves, etc.: *v.t.* 1. to cut the edge or border of in scallops or curves. 2. to bake with bread crumbs and a sauce of milk.

scalp (skalp), *n.* 1. the skin on the top and back of the head from which hair grows. 2. the skin and hair of the head torn off by some North American Indians in token of victory: *v.t.* 1. to deprive of the scalp. 2. [Informal], to purchase (tickets, etc.) and sell to others at a greater price. 3. [Informal], to make a small, quick profit by slight fluctuations of the market: *v.i.* [Informal], to scalp tickets, etc. —scalp'er, *n.*

scal·pel (skal'pĕl), *n.* a small, keen-edged knife used by surgeons.

scal·y (skā'li), *adj.* scal'i-er, scal'i-est, covered with or like scales.

scam·mo·ny (skam'ŏ-ni), *n., pl.* -nies, a climbing convolvulus of Asia with thick roots, sagittate leaves, and white or purplish flowers. 2. the gum resin exuded by this plant used in medicine.

scamp (skamp), *n.* a rascal; worthless fellow; rogue: *v.t.* to execute or perform in a superficial or careless manner.

scam·per (skam'pĕr), *v.i.* to run with speed; hasten away: *n.* a hasty flight.

scan (skan), *v.t.* scanned, scan'ning, 1. to mark off the metrical structure of (a poem); examine by counting the metrical feet or syllables. 2. to scrutinize or examine carefully. 3. to look at with haste: *v.i.* to fall within a metrical system: said of poetry: *n.* the act of scanning.

scan·dal (skan'dl), *n.* 1. moral offense occasioned by the actions of another. 2. something uttered that is false and injurious to the reputation. 3. opprobrium; defamation; disgrace. 4. that which causes offense, disgrace, etc.

scan·dal·ize (skan'dă-līz), *v.t.* -ized, -iz·ing, to offend by some supposed improper action or conduct.

scan·dal·mon·ger (skan'dăl-mung-gĕr, -mong-), *n.* one who circulates scandal.

scan·dal·ous (-ŭs), *adj.* 1. giving offense to the conscience or moral sense; exciting condemnation or opprobrium. 2. of or circulating scandal. —scan'dal·ous·ly,' *adv.*

Scan·di·na·vi·an (skan-di-nā'vi-ăn), *adj.* of or pertaining to Scandinavia, an area in northern Europe including Norway, Denmark, and Sweden, or its people: *n.* a native or inhabitant of Scandinavia.

scan·di·um (skan'di-ŭm) *n.* a rare metallic chemical element.

scan·sion (skan'shŭn), *n.* the distinguishing of the metrical feet in verse composition.

scant (skant), *adj.* 1. not full or abundant. 2. scarcely sufficient: *v.t.* 1. to stint; limit. 2. to treat insufficiently.

scant·ling (skant'ling), *n.* 1. a piece of timber cut or sawn to a small size. 2. the size to which a piece of timber or other construction material is cut.

scant·y (skan'ti), *adj.* scant'i·er, scant'i·est, 1. narrow. 2. barely sufficient. 3. scant. —scant'i·ly, *adv.* —scant'i·ness, *n.*

scape (skāp), *n.* 1. the shaft of a column where it leaves the base. 2. a peduncle rising from the root: *v.t. & v.i.* scaped, scap'ing, [Archaic], to escape.

scape·goat (skāp'gōt), *n.* 1. in ancient Jewish ritual, a goat, turned loose in the desert, upon which the sins of the people had been symbolically transferred. 2. one who bears the blame for others.

scape·grace (skāp'grās), *n.* a graceless, unprincipled fellow; rogue.

scaph·oid (skaf'oid), *adj.* boat-shaped.

scap·u·la (skap'yoo-lă), *n., pl.* -lae (-lē), -las, the shoulder blade.

scap·u·lar (-lĕr), *adj.* of or pertaining to the scapula or shoulder: *n.* 1. part of the habit of certain religious orders. 2. two pieces of cloth connected by strings, each bearing some sacred representation, worn over the back and chest, usually under the clothes, by pious Roman Catholics as an insignia of faith or mark of devotion. 3. a surgical bandage.

scar (skär), *n.* 1. a mark caused by a wound. 2. a mark or blemish. 3. [British], a precipitous rock or bank: *v.t.* scarred, scar'ring, to mark with or as with a scar: *v.i.* to form a scar.

scar·ab (sker'ăb), *n.* 1. a black beetle that feeds on dung. 2. a gem or seal cut in the form of such a beetle, worn as a charm by the ancient Egyptians.

scar·a·mouch (sker'ă-mōōsh), *n.* a boastful coward; poltroon.

scarce (skers), *adj.* 1. not common. 2. not plentiful; not equal to the demand. —scarce'ness, *n.*

scarce·ly (skers'li), *adv.* 1. barely. 2. unlikely or definitely not.

scar·ci·ty (skers'si-ti), *n., pl.* -ties, 1. an insufficiency. 2. limited availability.

scare (sker), *v.t.* scared, scar'ing, to strike with sudden terror; frighten: *v.i.* to become terrified: *n.* a sudden fright or panic.

scare·crow (sker'krō), *n.* 1. anything, as the representation of a human figure, set up to scare away birds. 2. a vain cause of terror. 3. a person who looks disreputable.

scarf (skärf), *n., pl.* scarfs, scarves (skärvs), 1. a

handkerchief or tie for the neck. 2. a sash. 3. a table runner. 4. a kind of dovetail joint: *v.t.* 1. to dress with a scarf. 2. to unite (two pieces) at the ends by a kind of dovetail.

scarf-skin (skärf'skin), *n.* the cuticle; epidermis.

scar-i-fi-ca-tor (sker'i-fi-kāt'ēr), *n.* a surgical instrument used in scarifying.

scar-i-fy (sker'i-fī), *v.t.* -fied, -fy-ing, 1. to make small incisions in (the skin), as by a scarificator. 2. to stir up and prepare (soil) for planting. —scar'i-fi-er, *n.*

scar-la-ti-na (skär-lā-tē'nä), *n.* scarlet fever of a mild form.

scar-let (skär'lit), *n.* 1. a bright red color. 2. cloth of such a color: *adj.* 1. of a scarlet color. 2. of or pertaining to sin. 3. of or like a whore.

scarlet fever, a contagious febrile disease characterized by a scarlet eruption.

scarlet runner, a climbing bean with large red flowers and purple mottled seeds: also scarlet runner bean.

scarp (skärp), *n.* 1. a slope or declivity, nearly perpendicular. 2. the slope of a ditch at the foot of a rampart: *v.t.* to cut perpendicularly or nearly so.

scar-y (sker'i), *adj.* scar'i-er, scar'i-est, [Informal], causing or subject to sudden fright. —scar'i-ness, *n.*

scat (skat), *v.i.* scat'ted, scat'ting, [Informal], to leave: usually in the form of an order.

scat (skat), *adj.* in *Jazz*, utilizing nonsense syllables in improvised singing: *n.* the use of such singing: *v.i.* scat'ted, scat'ting, to vocalize using scat.

scathe (skā*th*), *v.t.* scathed, scath'ing, [Archaic], to injure or hurt: *n.* [Archaic], injury or harm.

scath-ing (skā'*th*ing), *adj.* injurious; very severe or bitter. —scath'ing-ly, *adv.*

sca-tol-o-gy (skā-tol'ō-ji), *n.* excessive interest in obscenity, especially that having to do with excrement, as in books.

scat-ter (skat'ēr), *v.t.* 1. to strew or throw loosely about. 2. to disperse or dissipate: *v.i.* to be dispersed or dissipated.

scat-ter-brained (-brånd), *adj.* giddy. —scat'ter-brain, *n.*

scaup (skôp), *n.*, *pl.* scaups, scaup, a type of wild duck: also scaup duck.

scav-enge (skav'inj), *v.t.* -enged, -eng-ing, 1. to cleanse (streets) by removing mud, filth, etc. 2. to rescue (abandoned items).

scav-eng-er ('in-jēr), *n.* 1. [Chiefly British], one employed to clean the streets. 2. any animal that devours refuse or any other decaying matter. 3. a person who collects abandoned things.

sce-nar-i-o (si-ner'i-ō), *n.*, *pl.* -i-os, 1. the sketch of a plot or chief incidents of a play, libretto, etc. 2. the script of a moving picture showing its development from beginning to end, with cast of characters and all details to be used in filming. 3. an outline for a proposed or planned series of events.

scene (sēn), *n.* 1. the time, place, or circumstance in which anything occurs. 2. a part of a play, one of the subdivisions of an act.

3. an action section of a motion picture confined to one time and place. 4. the place where the action of a play is supposed to take place. 5. same as scenery (sense 2). 6. a spectacle; exhibition. 7. a display of feeling or passion in the presence of other people. 8. [Informal], the place where a certain pursuit takes place.

scen-er-y (sē'nēr-i), *n.*, *pl.* -ner-ies, 1. the appearance of anything presented to the vision; general aspect; combination of natural views. 2. painted representation on a stage.

sce-nic (sē'nik), *adj.* 1. of or pertaining to the stage; dramatic. 2. of or pertaining to scenery, of the stage or natural. 3. possessing attractive scenery. Also sce'ni-cal. —sce'ni-cal-ly, *adv.*

sce-nog-ra-phy (si-nog'rä-fi), *n.* the art of drawing in perspective. —sce-no-graph-ic (sē-nō-graf'ik, sen-ō-), sce-no-graph'i-cal, *adj.*

scent (sent), *n.* 1. odor. 2. sense of smell. 3. a fragrant liquid. 4. an animal odor followed in a hunt. 5. a clue: *v.t.* 1. to perceive by the olfactory sense; smell. 2. to perfume. 3. to have a suspicion about: *v.i.* to hunt animals by the sense of smell.

scep-ter (sep'tēr), *n.* a staff held by a sovereign as the emblem of authority: *v.t.* to invest with regal authority.

scep-tic (skep'tik), *n. & adj.* chiefly British spelling of skeptic.

scep-tre (sep'tēr), *n. & v.t.* -tred, -tring, chiefly British spelling of scepter.

schat-chen (shät'kēn), *n.* a marriage broker among Jews.

sched-ule (skej'ool), *n.* 1. a written or printed paper containing a list or inventory. 2. a list or document annexed to a larger instrument, as a will. 3. a timetable. 4. a plan arranged according to a list of times: *v.t.* -uled, -ul-ing, 1. to place in a schedule. 2. to give a specific time to.

scheel-ite (shēl'īt), *n.* a calcium salt of tungstic acid, from which tungsten is derived.

sche-ma (skē'mä), *n.*, *pl.* -ma-ta ('mä-tä), an outline; diagram.

sche-mat-ic (ski-mat'ik), *adj.* of or characteristic of a schema, scheme, etc.

sche-ma-tism (skē'mä-tizm), *n.* a set form for classification or exposition; arrangement of parts according to a scheme; design.

scheme (skēm), *n.* 1. a connected combination of things for the attainment of a certain end. 2. a plan; contrivance; plot. 3. a system. 4. a diagram: *v.t.* schemed, schem'ing, 1. to design or plan. 2. to plot: *v.i.* to form a scheme or plan. —schem'er, *n.*

scher-zo (sker'tsō), *n.*, *pl.* -zos, -zi ('tsi), a vigorous movement in waltz time, as of a sonata, symphony, etc.

Schick test (shik), a test to determine immunity to diptheria, made by injecting dilute diptheria toxin under the skin: if an area of inflammation results, the patient is not immune.

schil-ler (shil'ēr), *n.* a peculiar bronzelike luster in certain minerals.

schil-ling (shil'ing), *n.* a coin and the monetary unit of Austria.

ô in dragon, ōō in crude, oo in wool, u in cup, ū in cure, ŭ in turn, ŭ in focus, oi in boy, ou in house, th in thin, *th* in sheathe, g in get, j in joy, y in yet.

schip·per·ke (skip'ēr-ki), *n.* a small, short-haired, black dog of Belgium.

schism (siz'm), *n.* 1. a split or division, as in a church. 2. the offense of causing such a division.

schis·mat·ic (siz-mat'ik), *adj.* of, pertaining to, characteristic of, or causing schism: *n.* one who creates or takes part in a schism.

schist (shist), *n.* any rock that splits into slates or slabs. —**schist'ose** ('ōs), **schist'ous** ('ŭs), *adj.*

schi·zog·o·ny (ski-zog'ō-ni), *n.* a form of asexual reproduction among lower organisms.

schiz·oid (skit'soid), *n.* 1. a person who is introverted, not fully adjusted to his environment, etc. 2. a person who has schizophrenia: *adj.* 1. of or pertaining to a schizoid. 2. having schizophrenia.

schiz·o·my·cete (skiz-ō-mī-sēt'), *n.* any of a group of vegetable bacteria.

schiz·o·my·co·sis (-mī-kō'sis), *n.* any disease caused by schizomycetes.

schiz·o·phre·ni·a (skit-sō-frē'ni-à), *n.* a state or condition of split personality, severe emotional detachment from thinking, etc. as indicated by illusions, delusions, mannerisms, ataxia, etc.

schiz·o·phren·ic (-fren'ik, -frē'nik), *n.* a person having schizophrenia: *adj.* of, pertaining to, or having schizophrenia.

schle·miel (shlē-mēl'), *n.* [Slang], someone who is always clumsily spoiling situations or being taken advantage of.

schlep, schlepp (shlep), *v.t.* schlepped, schlep'ping, [Slang], to haul, drag, etc.: *n.* [Slang], someone who acts indecisively or ineffectually.

schlock (shlok), *n.* [Slang], something worthless or below standard: *adj.* worthless; not up to standard value or quality.

schmaltz (shmälts), *n.* [Slang], excessively sentimental music or writing.

schmo (shmō), *n., pl.* schmoes, schmos, [Slang], a blockhead; dolt: also schmoe.

schnapps (shnäps, shnaps), *n., pl.* schnapps, 1. a Dutch gin. 2. any highly alcoholic liquor. Also schnaps.

schnau·zer (shnou'zēr), *n.* a small terrier with a stiff coat.

schnor·rer (shnôr'ēr), *n.* [Slang], a beggar or human parasite.

schnoz·zle (shnoz'l), *n.* [Slang], the nose: also schnoz.

schol·ar (skol'ēr), *n.* 1. a student. 2. a person of much learning. 2. a student awarded aid by an educational institution, foundation, etc.

schol·ar·ly (-li), *adj.* 1. of or like a scholar. 2. having much learning. 3. studious.

schol·ar·ship (-ship), *n.* 1. the level of attainment of a scholar. 2. learning. 3. erudition. 4. aid for a scholar, awarded by an educational institution, foundation, etc.

scho·las·tic (skò-las'tik), *adj.* 1. of or pertaining to scholars, schools, etc. 2. formal; pedantic. 3. [also S-]. of or characteristic of the medieval schoolmen.

scho·las·ti·cism ('ti-sizm), *n.* [often S-], the philosophy of the university scholars of the Middle Ages, the chief object of which was

the reconciliation of the Christian faith with reason.

scho·li·ast (skō'li-àst), *n.* a commentator or annotator, especially of the classics.

scho·li·um (skō'li-ùm), *n., pl.* -li·a (-à), -li·ums, a marginal or explanatory note, especially on the text of a classical author.

school (skōōl), *n.* 1. a place where instruction is given. 2. the buildings in which instruction takes place. 3. scholars, pupils, teachers, etc. collectively. 4. the set duration of instruction. 5. a medieval seminary for teaching theology, logic, and metaphysics. 6. the disciples of a particular teacher. 7. an organized form of instruction. 8. any means of acquiring knowledge. 9. a subdivision of a university. 10. canon, precepts, or body of opinion; style. 11. a great number of fish moving together: *adj.* of or pertaining to school: *v.t.* 1. to train or instruct. 2. to regulate. 3. [Archaic]. to chide or admonish.

school board, a group of residents who regulate the local public schools.

school·book (skōōl'book), *n.* same as textbook.

school·boy ('boi), *n.* a boy in school. —**school'-girl,** *n.fem.*

school·house ('hous), *n.* a building in which school instruction takes place.

school·ing ('ing), *n.* 1. education. 2. pay for instruction. 3. [Archaic]. discipline.

school·man ('màn), *n., pl.* -men ('mēn), [often S-]. one of the scholastic teachers of the Middle Ages.

school·marm ('märm), *n.* [Informal]. 1. a female schoolteacher. 2. an excessively proper or formal person.

school·mas·ter ('mas-tēr), *n.* 1. a man who teaches in a school: an old-fashioned term. 2. [Chiefly British]. a man who presides over a school. —**school'mis·tress,** *n.fem.*

school·mate ('māt), *n.* one who attends a particular school concurrently with another person: also school'fel·low.

school·room ('rōōm), *n.* a room in which instruction takes place, as in a school.

school·teach·er ('tē-chēr), *n.* one who is employed to teach in a school.

school·yard ('yärd), *n.* the area surrounding a school, used as for recreation.

school year, the portion of a year during which instruction is given.

schoon·er (skōō'nēr), *n.* 1. a vessel with two or more masts rigged fore and aft. 2. a tall beer glass.

schot·tische (shot'ish), *n.* 1. a dance resembling the polka, but in slower tempo. 2. music for this.

schuss (shoos), *n.* a straight run down a hill in skiing: *v.t.* to ski at top speed down a hill.

schwa (shwä), *n.* 1. the neutral vowel sound of most unstressed syllables in English, as of *a* in *awake*. 2. the symbol (ə) for this.

sci·a·mach·y (sī-am'à-ki), *n., pl.* -chies, a battle with shadows or with imaginary opponents.

sci·at·ic (sī-at'ik), *adj.* of, pertaining to, or affecting the hip or its nerves.

sci·at·i·ca (sī-at'i-kà), *n.* any painful condition of the hip and thighs; especially, neuritis down the nerve at the back of the thigh.

sci·ence (sī'ēns), *n.* 1. systematized knowledge

obtained by study, observation, experiment, etc. 2. any branch of knowledge considered as a distinct field for investigation of the facts, laws, etc. that apply to it. 3. skill or ability.

science fiction, a type of fiction treating scientific facts or speculations in a highly imaginative way.

sci·en·tif·ic (sī-ĕn-tif′ik), *adj.* 1. of, pertaining to, or used in science. 2. based on or conforming to the principles and techniques of science; precise and systematic. —**sci·en·tif′i·cal·ly,** *adv.*

sci·en·tism (sī′ĕn-tizm), *n.* the principles, attitudes, and methods of scientists.

sci·en·tist (-tist), *n.* one skilled in science, as in physics, astronomy, etc.

sci-fi (sī′fī′), *adj. & n.* same as **science fiction.**

scim·i·tar, scim·i·ter (sim′i-tĕr), *n.* a short, curved sword having its edge on the convex side.

scin·til·la (sin-til′ă), *n.* 1. a spark. 2. the least trace.

scin·til·late (sin′til-āt), *v.i.* -lat·ed, -lat·ing, 1. to emit sparks, fire, or igneous particles. 2. to sparkle intellectually. 3. to twinkle, as a star. —**scin·til·la′tion,** *n.*

sci·o·lism (sī′ō-lizm), *n.* superficial knowledge or learning. —**sci′o·list,** *n.* —**sci·o·lis′tic,** *adj.*

sci·on (sī′ŏn), *n.* 1. a twig or shoot of a plant. 2. a descendant or child.

scir·rhus (skir′ŭs), *n., pl.* -rhi (′ī), -rhus·es, a hard, malignant tumor containing much fibrous tissue. —**scir′rhous,** *adj.*

scis·sile (sis′il), *adj.* that can be cut, divided, or split smoothly and readily.

scis·sion (sizh′ŭn, sish′-), *n.* the act of cutting, dividing, or splitting or the state of being cut, divided, or split.

scis·sor (siz′ĕr), *v.t.* to cut, cut off, or cut out with scissors or shears: *n.* scissors, esp. in adjectival use.

scis·sors (siz′ĕrz), *n.pl.* a cutting instrument resembling shears, but smaller, having two opposed, pivoted blades that work against each other: also called **pair of scissors.**

scis·sor·tail (siz′ĕr-tāl), *n.* a flycatcher of the southern U.S., with a deeply forked tail.

sci·u·rid (sī-yoor′id), *n.* any one of a group of rodents, including the squirrels, marmots, etc. —**sci·u′roid,** *adj.*

scle·ra (sklir′ă), *n.* the tough, white, fibrous outer envelope covering all the eyeball except the cornea. —**scle′ral,** *adj.*

scle·ro-, a combining form meaning *hard, of the sclera.*

scler·oid (sklir′oid), *adj.* in *Biology,* hard; indurated.

scle·ro·sis (skli-rō′sis), *n., pl.* -ses (′sēz), 1. in *Botany,* a hardening of plant cell walls, usually by the increase of a celluloselike substance. 2. in *Medicine, a)* a hardening of a body part, as the walls of an artery, caused by abnormal growth or disease; *b)* a disease characterized by sclerosis.

scle·rot·ic (-rot′ik), *adj.* 1. hard. 2. of, pertaining to, or affected by sclerosis. 3. of or pertaining to the sclera.

scle·rous (sklir′ŭs), *adj.* hard; indurated.

scoff (skôf, skof), *n.* an expression of scorn, contempt, or derision: *v.t. & v.i.* to mock or jeer (at). —**scoff′er,** *n.* —**scoff′ing·ly,** *adv.*

scoff·law (′lô), *n.* a person who habitually breaks laws, especially liquor or traffic laws.

scold (skōld), *v.i.* 1. to find fault habitually and angrily. 2. to employ abusive language: *v.t.* to chide or rebuke sharply and rudely: *n.* a person who habitually scolds, especially a rude, abusive woman.

sco·lex (skō′leks), *n., pl.* **sco·le·ces** (skō-lē′sēz), the head of a tapeworm, having hooklike parts for attachment in the intestine of a host.

sco·li·o·sis (skō-li-ō′sis), *n.* lateral curvature of the spine. —**sco·li·ot′ic** (-ot′ik), *adj.*

scol·lop (skol′ŏp), *n. & v.t.* same as **scallop.**

sconce (skons), *n.* a fixed, decorative wall bracket for candles or lights.

sconce (skons), *n.* a bulwark, small fort, etc. for defense.

sconce (skons), *v.t.* sconced, sconc′ing, to fine: *n.* a fine.

scone (skōn), *n.* 1. originally, a cake of oatmeal or barley flour baked on a griddle. 2. a plain or sweet baking powder biscuit.

scoop (skōŏp), *n.* 1. a small, shovel-shaped utensil for dipping up sugar, flour, etc. 2. a long-handled utensil ending in a bowl; ladle; dipper. 3. a coal scuttle. 4. the act of scooping. 5. the amount scooped. 6. the bucket on a dredge or steam shovel. 7. [Informal], a big profit from speculation. 8. [Informal], an exclusive news story. 9. [Informal], current, especially confidential, information: *v.t.* 1. to take out or up with or as with a scoop. 2. to ladle or bail out. 3. to make hollow. 4. [Informal], to get ahead of (a rival) in gathering news.

scoop·ful (′fool), *n., pl.* -fuls, as much as a scoop will hold.

scoot (skōŏt), *v.i. & v.t.* [Informal], to move speedily; dart (off); hurry.

scoot·er (′ĕr), *n.* 1. a toy vehicle for children, with a narrow footboard between wheels and an upright handlebar for steering. 2. a two-wheeled vehicle having a seat and powered by a small gasoline engine.

scope (skōp), *n.* 1. room or opportunity for free outlook, action, or thought. 2. the limit of one's intellectual grasp; range of perception. 3. the area covered by an activity, inquiry, etc. 4. [Now Rare], aim or intention. 5. a shortened form for **telescope, microscope,** etc.

-scope (skōp), a combining form meaning *an instrument for viewing or examining.*

sco·pol·a·mine (skō-pol′ă-mēn), *n.* a vegetable alkaloid used in medicine as a sedative, hypnotic, etc.

scop·u·la (skop′yoo-lă), *n., pl.* -las, -lae (-lē), a tuft of dense hairs, as on some insects. —**scop′u·late,** *adj.*

scor·bu·tic (skôr-bū′tik), *adj.* of, pertaining to, or affected by scurvy.

scorch (skôrch), *v.t.* 1. to burn or char slightly. 2. to parch; shrivel by intense heat: *v.i.* to become scorched: *n.* a surface burn.

ŏ in *dragon,* ōŏ in *crude,* oo in *wool,* u in *cup,* ū in *cure,* ũ in *turn,* ŭ in *focus,* oi in *boy,* ou in *house,* th in *thin,* ᵗʰ in *sheathe,* g in *get,* j in *joy,* y in *yet.*

scorch-er ('ẽr), *n.* 1. anything that scorches. 2. [Informal], an extremely hot day.

score (skōr), *n.* 1. a notch or incision. 2. notches or marks used to keep a tally. 3. a set of twenty people or things. 4. an account; debt. 5. a grudge kept in mind for settlement. 6. a reason. 7. the number of points made, as by a team, individual, etc. 8. a result of a test or examination. 9. a copy of a musical work showing the parts for all the instruments or voices. 10. [Informal], the true facts: *v.t.* scored, scor'ing, 1. to mark or notch (furrows, lines, etc.) in. 2. to make (runs, points, etc.) in a game. 3. to record the score of. 4. to accomplish. 5. to grade (a test). 6. in *Music*, to arrange in a score: *v.i.* 1. to make points in a game. 2. to keep the score of a game. 3. to achieve a success. —scor'er, *n.*

score-board ('bôrd), *n.* a large board for displaying scores and other information, as in a stadium.

sco-ri-a (skōr'i-ä), *n., pl.* -ri-ae (-ē), 1. volcanic cinder. 2. the slag left after the fusion of metallic ores. —sco-ri-a'ceous (-ā'shŭs), *adj.*

sco-ri-fy (skōr'i-fī), *v.t.* -fied, -fy-ing, to reduce to slag or dross. —sco-ri-fi-ca'tion, *n.*

scorn (skôrn), *n.* 1. extreme or lofty contempt for someone or something; haughty disdain. 2. the venting of this in speech or behavior. 3. the object of such contempt: *v.t.* 1. to hold in extreme contempt. 2. to reject or refuse because of scorn. —scorn'er, *n.*

scorn-ful ('fool), *adj.* full of scorn; contemptuous; disdainful. —scorn'ful-ly, *adv.*

Scor-pi-o (skôr'pi-ō), *n.* 1. a southern constellation: also Scor'pi-us (-ŭs). 2. the eighth sign of the zodiac.

scor-pi-on (-ŏn), *n.* an arachnid of warm regions, with a long, jointed tail bearing a poisonous sting at the tip.

Scot (skot), *n.* a native or inhabitant of Scotland, the division of the United Kingdom north of England.

Scotch (skoch), *adj.* of Scotland, its people, their language, etc.: see Scottish: *n.* same as 1. Scottish. 2. Scotch whisky.

scotch (skoch), *v.t.* 1. to cut; incise. 2. to wound; maim. 3. to stifle; crush: *n.* a cut or abrasion.

scotch (skoch), *n.* a wedge, block, etc. placed under a wheel, log, etc. to prevent rolling or slipping: *v.t.* to block (a wheel, barrel, etc.) with a wedge, prop, etc. to prevent movement.

Scotch grain, a coarse finish given to leather, especially for men's shoes.

Scotch-man ('măn), *n., pl.* -men ('mĕn), same as Scotsman.

Scotch tape, a transparent adhesive tape: a trademark.

Scotch whisky, whiskey with a smoky flavor, distilled from malted barley in Scotland.

scot-er (skōt'ẽr), *n., pl.* -ters, -ter, any one of several dark-colored sea ducks of northern coasts.

scot-free (skot'frē'), *adj.* 1. untaxed. 2. unpunished; incurring no penalty.

sco-ti-a (skō'shi-ä), *n.* a hollow molding in the base of a column.

Scot-land Yard (skot'lănd), 1. the headquarters of the London police. 2. the London police, especially the criminal investigation department.

sco-to-ma (skô-tō'mä), *n., pl.* -ma-ta ('mä-tä), -mas, an area of defective vision in the visual field; blind spot.

Scots (skots), *adj. & n.* Scottish.

Scots-man ('măn), *n., pl.* -men ('mĕn), a native or inhabitant of Scotland: in Scotland, *Scotsman* or *Scot* is preferred to *Scotchman*. —Scots'wom-an, *n.fem., pl.* -wom-en.

Scot-tie, Scot-ty (skot'i), *n., pl.* -ties, [Informal], same as Scottish terrier.

Scot-tish (skot'ish), *adj.* of Scotland, its people, their English dialect, etc.: *Scottish* is preferred in formal usage; but in some word combinations *Scotch* is used (e.g., whisky), in others *Scots* (e.g., law): *n.* the English dialect spoken in Scotland.

Scottish terrier, any one of a breed of terriers originating in Scotland, with short legs, a rough coat of dark, wiry hair, and erect ears.

scoun-drel (skoun'drĕl), *n.* a man without honor or virtue; villain: *adj.* low; mean; base.

scour (skour), *v.t.* 1. to clean by friction, usually with abrasives; make clean and bright. 2. to cleanse dirt and grease from (wool, cloth, etc.). 3. to purge: *n. usually pl.* dysentery in livestock. —scour'er, *n.*

scour (skour), *v.t.* 1. to pass swiftly over or along. 2. to search thoroughly. —scour'er, *n.*

scourge (skŭrj), *n.* 1. a whip used to give punishment. 2. any cause of affliction, as famine, war, etc.: *v.t.* scourged, scourg'ing, 1. to whip or flog. 2. to afflict, harass, punish, etc. severely. —scourg'er, *n.*

scout (skout), *n.* 1. a person, aircraft, etc. sent out to obtain information about the strength, disposition, defenses, etc. of the enemy. 2. a person sent out to watch an adversary, seek out new talent, etc., as in sports or entertainment. 3. a Boy Scout or Girl Scout: *v.t. & v.i.* 1. to act as a scout; reconnoiter. 2. to go in search of (something).

scout (skout), *v.t.* to reject with disdain or contempt; scoff at.

scout-mas-ter ('mas-tẽr), *n.* the adult leader of a troop of Boy Scouts.

scow (skou), *n.* a large, flat-bottomed boat with square ends, used to transport coal, dredgings, etc.

scowl (skoul), *v.i.* 1. to wrinkle the brows in showing displeasure, irritation, etc.; frown angrily. 2. to have a sullen or threatening look: *n.* a frowning or scowling look.

scrab-ble (skrab'l), *v.i.* -bled, -bling, 1. to scratch or grope about awkwardly or frantically. 2. to struggle. 3. to scribble; scrawl: *v.t.* to mark with irregular, meaningless lines or letters: *n.* 1. the act of scrabbling. 2. a scribble; scrawl.

scrag (skrag), *n.* 1. a thin, lean person or animal. 2. the neck or back of the neck of mutton, veal, etc.: *v.t.* scragged, scrag'ging,

---

a in cap, ā in cane, ä in father, à in abet, e in met, ē in be, ê in baker, ê in regent, i in pit, ī in fine, i in manifest, o in hot, ō in horse, ō in bone,

[Slang], to hang; wring the neck of; strangle.

scrag-gly (skrag'li), *adj.* -gli-er, -gli-est, ragged, irregular, etc. in growth or form. —scrag'gli-ness, *n.*

scrag-gy (skrag'i), *adj.* -gi-er, -gi-est, 1. jagged; rough. 2. bony and lean. —scrag'gi-ly, *adv.* —scrag'gi-ness, *n.*

scram (skram), *v.i.* scrammed, scram'ming, [Slang], to go away or get out at once.

scram-ble (skram'bl), *v.i.* -bled, -bling, 1. to clamber or crawl hurriedly. 2. to vie or struggle for something. 3. to struggle eagerly or roughly for the possession of something prized: *v.t.* 1. to toss together at random; mix in a confused mass. 2. to make (eggs) fluffy by stirring during frying. 3. to garble (a signal) so as to make a transmitted message unintelligible without a special receiver: *n.* 1. the act of scrambling. 2. a rude, eager struggle.

scrap (skrap), *n.* 1. a small or detached piece; fragment; shred. 2. discarded material, as metal, machinery, paper, etc. 3. *pl.* leftover bits of food: *adj.* 1. made up of fragments, remnants, pieces, etc. 2. no longer useful and so discarded: *v.t.* scrapped, scrap'ping, 1. to turn into scrap. 2. to discard as useless; junk.

scrap (skrap), *n. & v.i.* scrapped, scrap'ping, [Informal], fight or quarrel. —scrap'per, *n.*

scrap-book ('book), *n.* a blank book in which to paste newspaper clippings, souvenirs, etc.

scrape (skrāp), *v.t.* scraped, scrap'ing, 1. to make a harsh, grating sound. 2. to rub with something sharp. 3. to clean by rubbing with an abrasive. 4. to remove by rubbing with something rough (with *off, out,* etc.). 5. to abrade. 6. to gather laboriously and slowly: *v.i.* 1. to rub with a harsh, grating noise. 2. to get by barely; manage precariously (with *through, along, by*). 3. to bow awkwardly, drawing back the foot along the floor: *n.* 1. the act of scraping. 2. the harsh, grating noise of scraping. 3. an abrasion or scratch on the skin. 4. a predicament that is awkward or embarrassing. —scrap'er, *n.*

scrap-py ('i), *adj.* -pi-er, -pi-est, [Informal], aggressive; liking to fight or argue. —scrap'pi-ness, *n.*

scratch (skrach), *v.t.* 1. to mark or tear the surface of with something pointed. 2. to tear or dig with the nails or claws. 3. to rub (the skin) lightly to relieve itching. 4. to rub with a grating sound. 5. to write hurriedly or haphazardly. 6. to strike out (a word, phrase, etc.). 7. in *Sports*, to withdraw (an entry) from a contest, especially a horse race: *v.i.* 1. to use the nails or claws in tearing or digging. 2. to make a harsh, grating noise. 3. to rub the skin to relieve itching: *n.* 1. a mark or tear made by scratching. 2. a superficial wound. 3. a harsh sound made by scratching: *adj.* used for tentative or hasty notes, figures, etc.

scratch test, a test for allergic reactions, performed by putting allergens on scratches made in the skin.

scratch-y ('i), *adj.* scratch'i-er, scratch'i-est, 1. roughly or hurriedly made, drawn, etc. 2.

making a scraping noise. 3. that scratches, chafes, itches, etc. —scratch'i-ly, *adv.* —scratch'i-ness, *n.*

scrawl (skrôl), *v.t. & v.i.* to write or draw irregularly or hastily: *n.* 1. hasty, irregular, or illegible handwriting. 2. something scribbled.

scraw-ny (skrô'ni), *adj.* -ni-er, -ni-est, 1. thin and lean; skinny and bony. 2. stunted. —scraw'ni-ness, *n.*

screak (skrēk), *n.* a shriek; screech: *v.i.* to screech.

scream (skrēm), *n.* 1. a sharp, shrill cry, as of fear or pain. 2. [Informal], a person or thing regarded as very funny: *v.i.* 1. to utter a sharp, shrill cry. 2. to shout, laugh, etc. in a hysterical manner: *v.t.* to utter in or as in a screaming voice.

scream-er ('ēr), *n.* 1. a person who screams. 2. [Slang], an exaggerated statement, or extremely funny joke. 3. any one of several South American wading birds with a harsh cry.

screech (skrēch), *n.* a harsh, shrill cry: *v.i. & v.t.* to give, or utter with, such a cry. —screech'y, *adj.* screech'i-er, screech'i-est.

screech owl, any one of several North American owls with erectile ear tufts and a shrill cry rather than a hoot.

screed (skrēd), *n.* 1. a wooden strip, or the like, put on a wall at intervals to gauge the thickness of plaster to be applied. 2. a long harangue or a dull piece of writing. 3. [Scottish], a tear or rent.

screen (skrēn), *n.* 1. a light, movable partition, frame, etc. for protection, separation, concealment, etc. 2. anything acting to protect, shield, etc. 3. a coarse sieve. 4. a frame holding wire or plastic mesh, placed in a window or door to keep out insects. 5. a surface upon which motion pictures are projected. 6. the motion-picture industry: *v.t.* 1. to shelter, conceal, or protect, as with a screen. 2. to pass through a coarse sieve. 3. to separate by examining systematically for background, skills, etc. 4. to project (a motion picture) on a screen.

screen-play ('plā), *n.* a script written or adapted for a motion picture.

screw (skrōō), *n.* 1. a cylindrical or conical piece of metal threaded spirally and usually having a slotted head for turning with a screwdriver. 2. any of various devices shaped like or operating like a screw. 3. anything having a spiral form. 4. [British Informal], a miser. 5. [British Informal], a salary: *v.t.* 1. to fasten, attach, etc. as with a screw. 2. to drive or twist (a screw). 3. to contort. 4. to force or squeeze. 5. [Slang], to cheat; swindle: *v.i.* 1. to put on or take off by being turned like a screw. 2. to twist or turn.

screw-ball ('bôl), *n.* in *Baseball*, a pitch that spins and breaks in a direction opposite to a curve. 2. [Slang], a person who is whimsical, eccentric, or irrational.

screw-driv-er ('drī-vēr), *n.* a tool for turning screws.

screw-y (skrōō'i), *adj.* screw'i-er, screw'i-est, [Slang], 1. insane; crazy. 2. eccentric; confused; absurd; inappropriate.

scrib-ble (skrib'l), *v.t. & v.i.* **-bled, -bling,** 1. to write hastily and carelessly. 2. to cover with marks that are illegible or without meaning. 3. to write hurriedly with no regard for style, form, or correctness: *n.* writing of such character.

scrib-bler ('lĕr), *n.* 1. a person who scribbles. 2. a literary hack or inferior author.

scribe (skrīb), *n.* 1. a person who copied manuscripts and documents before printing came to be used. 2. a writer or journalist. 3. a teacher or copyist of the Jewish law. 4. a pointed tool used to mark lines on brick, wood, etc. to indicate where a cut should be made: also **scrib'er:** *v.t.* scribed, scrib'ing, to mark (stone, wood, etc.) with a scribe: *v.i.* to work as a scribe.

scrim (skrim), *n.* 1. a light fabric of cotton or linen, used for blinds, curtains, etc. 2. a similar fabric used on the stage as a backdrop or curtain.

scrim-mage (skrim'ij), *n.* 1. a general row or tussle; confused melee. 2. in *Football, a)* the play that ensues between two teams after the snap from center and lasts until the ball is no longer in play; *b)* practice play between units of the same team: *v.i.* **-maged, -mag-ing,** to participate in a scrimmage.

scrimp (skrimp), *v.t. & v.i.* to be parsimonious or miserly (with); to economize extensively. —scrimp'i-ness, *n.*

scrim-shaw (skrim'shô), *n.* 1. neatly executed decoration or carving of shells, bone, ivory, etc., done especially by sailors at sea. 2. an article fashioned this way: *v.t. & v.i.* to carve (bone, shells, etc.) into scrimshaw.

scrip (skrip), *n.* [Archaic], a small bag or satchel.

scrip (skrip), *n.* 1. a brief piece of writing, as a note or a schedule. 2. a certificate granting the holder a fractional share of stock. 3. a certificate of indebtedness, issued by a local government for use as currency.

script (skript), *n.* 1. handwriting. 2. a style of handwriting, or a particular way of forming letters, numbers, etc. 3. in *Printing,* a typeface that resembles handwriting. 4. an original document or instrument. 5. the manuscript of a play, film, etc.; especially, a copy of the text used by a performer: *v.t.* [Informal], to write the script for (a play, film, etc.).

scrip-ture (skrip'chĕr), *n.* 1. originally, anything written. 2. [S-], *often pl., a)* the Jewish Bible; Old Testament; *b)* the Christian Bible; Old and New Testaments; *c)* a Biblical passage. 3. any sacred writing or text. 4. any writing considered to be authoritative. —scrip'tur-al, *adj.* —scrip'tur-al-ly, *adv.*

scriv-en-er (skriv'nĕr), *n.* [Archaic], 1. one who draws up contracts, prepares writings, etc.; scribe; clerk. 2. a notary.

scrof-u-la (skrof'yū-là), *n.* a disease caused by the formation and development of tubercles in the organs and tissues of the body, especially in the lymphatic glands of the neck, characterized by swelling of the glands and scar formation. —scrof'u-lous, *adj.*

scroll (skrōl), *n.* 1. a roll of paper or parchment, usually containing writing. 2. a con-

voluted, spiral ornament, as on the capitals of some columns, resembling a partially rolled sheet of paper. 3. a list of names.

scroll saw, a narrow-bladed saw for cutting out circular work.

scroll-work ('wŭrk), *n.* 1. ornamental work having scrolls. 2. work cut out with a scroll saw.

scroop (skrōōp), *n.* [Dial.], a harsh grating or creaking sound: *v.i.* [Dial.], to make such a sound.

scro-tum (skrōt'ŭm), *n., pl.* **-ta** ('à), **-tums,** in most male mammals, the pouch that holds the testicles and related structures. —scro'tal, *adj.*

scrouge (skrouj, skrōōj), *v.t.* scrouged, scroug'-ing, [Dial.], to crowd or squeeze.

scrounge (skrounj), *v.t.* scrounged, scroung'ing, [Informal], 1. to obtain or locate by foraging around. 2. to get by sponging; wheedle; cadge: *v.i.* [Informal], to search (around) for something at no cost; forage. —scroung'er, *n.*

scrub (skrub), *n.* 1. a stunted tree or shrub. 2. a growth of stunted vegetation or an area covered by such growth. 3. any animal, person, or thing smaller than ordinary, or inferior. 4. in *Sports,* a player not on the varsity or first team: *adj.* 1. mean; inferior. 2. undersized; stunted; insignificant.

scrub (skrub), *v.t.* scrubbed, scrub'bing, 1. to rub hard. 2. to wash by rubbing or brushing hard. 3. to remove (dirt, stains, etc.) by brushing or rubbing. 4. to cleanse (a gas). 5. [Informal], *a)* to cancel; call off; *b)* to eliminate; drop: *n.* an act of scrubbing. —scrub'ber, *n.*

scrub-by (skrub'i), *adj.* **-bi-er, -bi-est,** 1. stunted in growth; straggly. 2. covered with brushwood. —scrub'bi-ness, *n.*

scrub-wom-an ('woom-ăn), *n., pl.* **-wom-en,** same as charwoman.

scruff (skruf), *n.* the back of the neck.

scruff-y (skruf'i), *adj.* scruff'i-er, scruff'i-est, shabby; untidy.

scrump-tious (skrump'shŭs), *adj.* [Informal], excellent, elegant, fine, etc.; delectable.

scrunch (skrunch), *v.t. & v.i.* 1. to crunch or crumple. 2. to hunch or squeeze: *n.* a crunching sound.

scru-ple (skrōō'pl), *n.* 1. a minute amount. 2. a measure of apothecary weight that is equal to one third of a dram (20 grains). 3. hesitation motivated by ethical or conscientious considerations about the rightness of a course of action: *v.t. & v.i.* -pled, -pling, to hesitate (at) through the dictates of conscience.

scru-pu-lous ('pyū-lŭs), *adj.* 1. full of or displaying scruples; having a conscientious regard for what is right or proper. 2. exact; careful; precise; strict. —scru-pu-los'i-ty (-los'i-ti), *n.* —scru'pu-lous-ly, *adv.*

scru-ti-nize (skrōōt'n-īz), *v.t.* -nized, -niz-ing, to inspect or examine very closely and carefully.

scru-ti-ny ('n-i), *n., pl.* -nies, 1. a close inspection or examination. 2. a careful watch. 3. a long, penetrating look.

scu-ba (skōō'bà), *n.* an apparatus used for breathing while swimming under water, hav-

a in *cap,* ā in *cane,* ä in *father,* à in *abet,* e in *met,* ē in *be,* ē in *baker,* ĕ in *regent,* i in *pit,* ī in *fine,* ĭ in *manifest,* o in *hot,* ô in *horse,* ō in *bone,*

ing compressed air tanks that feed air through a hose to a mouthpiece.

scud (skud), *v.i.* **scud′ded, scud′ding,** 1. to run quickly; to move or glide rapidly and easily. 2. to run before the wind: *n.* 1. the act of scudding. 2. rain, snow, clouds, etc. driven by the wind.

scuff (skuf), *v.t. & v.i.* 1. to drag (the feet) in walking. 2. to soil and roughen the surface (of). 3. to shuffle (the feet): *n.* 1. a worn or roughened spot. 2. a flat house slipper without a back.

scuf·fle (skuf′l), *v.i.* -**fled, -fling,** 1. to fight or struggle confusedly. 2. to drag the feet; shuffle: *n.* 1. a rough, disorderly fight or struggle. 2. the sound or act of shuffling feet.

scull (skul), *n.* 1. one of a pair of short oars, used by a single rower. 2. a long oar mounted at the stern of a boat and twisted from side to side to propel it forward. 3. a light, narrow racing boat: *v.t. & v.i.* to propel with a scull or sculls.

scul·ler·y (skul′ēr-i), *n., pl.* -**ler·ies,** a room adjoining the kitchen where culinary utensils are kept and cleaned and where rough kitchen chores are done.

scul·lion (skul′yŏn), *n.* [Archaic], a servant employed to do the menial work in a scullery.

scul·pin (skul′pin), *n., pl.* -**pin, -pins,** any one of various spiny, usually scaleless, mostly sea fishes with a big head and wide mouth.

sculpt (skulpt), *v.t. & v.i.* same as sculpture.

sculp·tor (skulp′tēr), *n.* one who practices the art of sculpture. —**sculp′tress,** *n.fem.*

sculp·ture (skulp′chēr), *n.* 1. the art of forming images of men, animals, objects, etc. out of stone, clay, etc. 2. an image or the images so formed: *v.t. & v.i.* -**tured, -tur·ing,** 1. to represent or fashion like sculpture. 2. to carve, cut, hew, cast, mold, weld, etc. into representations, forms, figures, etc. —**sculp′-tur·al,** *adj.* —**sculp′tur·al·ly,** *adv.*

sculp·tur·esque (skulp·chē-resk′), *adj.* resembling, or having the character of, sculpture.

scum (skum), *n.* 1. extraneous matter or impurities which rise to the surface of liquids when boiled or fermented. 2. the refuse on top of metals in a molten state. 3. anything worthless or vile. 4. a contemptible or mean person or persons: *v.i.* **scummed, scum′ming,** to form scum; become covered with scum: *v.t.* [Archaic], to clear impurities from the surface of; skim.

scup (skup), *n., pl.* **scup, scups,** a marine food fish of the eastern coast of the U.S., related to the porgies.

scup·per (skup′ēr), *n.* a hole or tube in the side of a ship to carry off deck water.

scup·per·nong (skup′ēr-nŏng), *n.* 1. a large, yellowish-green grape, cultivated in the southern U.S. 2. a sweet wine made from grapes of this kind.

scurf (skûrf), *n.* 1. minute, white, flaky scales shed by the skin, as dandruff. 2. any scaly coating or loosely adherent matter, especially on a plant. —**scurf′y,** *adj.* **scurf′i·er, scurf′i·est.**

scur·rile, scur·ril (skûr′il), *adj.* [Archaic], same as scurrilous.

scur·ril·i·ty (skŭ-ril′i-ti), *n.* 1. the quality of being scurrilous; vile or indecent language, jocularity, etc. 2. *pl.* -**ties,** a rude or abusive remark.

scur·ril·ous (skûr′i-lŭs), *adj.* 1. using the low, indecent, abusive language of the vulgar; vile; foulmouthed. 2. containing low or indecent language or coarse abuse. —**scur′-ril·ous·ly,** *adv.* —**scur′ril·ous·ness,** *n.*

scur·ry (skûr′i), *v.i.* -**ried, -ry·ing,** to hasten or move rapidly along: *v.t.* to cause to scamper: *n.* the act or noise of scurrying.

scur·vy (skûr′vi), *adj.* -**vi·er, -vi·est,** 1. [Obs.], scurfy. 2. vile; contemptible; mean: *n.* a disease characterized by anemia, prostration, soft gums, bleeding from the mucous membranes, etc., caused by a deficiency of vitamin C. —**scur′vi·ly,** *adv.* —**scur′vi·ness,** *n.*

scut (skut), *n.* 1. a stubby, erect tail of a hare, rabbit, deer, etc. 2. a mean, contemptible person.

scu·tate (skū′tāt), *adj.* 1. in *Zoology,* covered with bones or horny plates. 2. in *Botany,* shaped like a shield.

scutch (skuch), *v.t.* to separate the fibers of (flax, cotton, etc.) from the woody parts by beating: *n.* an implement for scutching: also **scutch′er.**

scutch·eon (skuch′ŭn), *n.* same as escutcheon.

scute (skūt), *n.* 1. any bony or horny external plate, as on some fishes and reptiles. 2. any structure resembling a scale.

scut·tle (skut′l), *n.* 1. a metal pan for holding and carrying coal. 2. a shallow, open basket for carrying flowers, vegetables, etc.

scut·tle (skut′l), *v.i.* -**tled, -tling,** to hasten or hurry away quickly; scurry: *n.* a quick run or pace.

scut·tle (skut′l), *v.t.* -**tled, -tling,** 1. to cut or open holes in the hull (of a ship) in order to sink it. 2. to abandon or discard (an attempt, plan, etc.): *n.* 1. a hole or opening in a roof, wall, etc. covered with a lid. 2. a covered hatchway or opening in the deck of a ship. 3. a lid or cover for closing or covering any such openings.

scut·tle·butt (skut′l-but), *n.* 1. a drinking fountain on shipboard. 2. [Informal], rumor; gossip.

scu·tum (skūt′ŭm), *n., pl.* **scu′ta** (′å), 1. a wooden shield carried by Roman legionaries. 2. in *Zoology,* a horny or bony plate or scale.

scy·phi·form (sī′fi-fôrm), *adj.* in *Biology,* shaped like a cup.

scythe (sīth), *n.* a single-edged, cutting instrument mounted on a long, bent handle, used for mowing, reaping, etc.

sea (sē), *n.* 1. the expanse of salt water covering most of the earth's surface, especially when distinguished from the land and air; ocean. 2. a large body of salt water completely or partially landlocked. 3. a large inland body of fresh water. 4. the condition of the ocean's surface with regard to its calmness, turbulence, etc. 5. a wave or swell. 6. something that resembles or sug-

---

ŏ in dragon, ōō in crude, oo in wool, u in cup, ū in cure, û in turn, ù in focus, oi in boy, ou in house, th in thin, *th* in sheathe, g in get, j in joy, y in yet.

gests the sea in extent, depth, etc.; a large quantity.

sea anchor, a canvas-covered float thrown from a ship to prevent drifting or to keep a heading into the wind.

sea anemone, any one of numerous brilliantly colored, soft-bodied, marine polyps, having flowerlike tentacles and living attached to rocks, pilings, etc.

sea bass, any one of various marine food fishes, especially a large-mouthed, dark-colored fish of the eastern coast of the U.S.

sea-board ('bôrd), n. the land bordering the sea: adj. bordering the sea.

sea calf, same as seal (the sea mammal).

sea-coast ('kōst), n. land bordering the sea.

sea cow, any one of several marine mammals, as the dugong, manatee, walrus, etc.

sea cucumber, any one of various echinoderms having a body shaped like a cucumber.

sea devil, same as devilfish.

sea dog, 1. any one of various seals. 2. an experienced sailor.

sea duck, any one of various diving ducks, found chiefly along coasts.

sea elephant, either one of two very large seals, the males of which have elongated proboscises.

sea-far-er ('fer-ēr), n. a sailor.

sea-far-ing (-ing), adj. following the occupation of a sailor: n. 1. the profession of a sailor. 2. travel by sea.

sea-food ('fōōd), n. edible marine fish and shellfish.

sea-go-ing ('gō-ing), adj. 1. designed for use on the ocean. 2. same as seafaring.

sea gull, a gull living along a seacoast.

sea horse, 1. a small, semitropical fish having the head and foreparts suggestive of the head and neck of a horse. 2. same as walrus. 3. a fabulous sea creature represented as half horse and half fish.

seal (sēl), n. 1. a stamp or die engraved with some device, motto, or emblem, used in making an impression on wax, lead, etc. 2. the impression made. 3. the design, emblem, etc. belonging to a particular person or office. 4. a small disk of wax, piece of paper, etc. impressed with such a design and used to authenticate a document, signature, etc. 5. something that seals or fastens tightly. 6. a small, ornamental sticker: v.t. 1. to close with or as with a seal. 2. to set or affix a seal to, as to certify. 3. to ratify or confirm the truth, accuracy, quality, etc. of. 4. to determine irrevocably.

seal (sēl), n. 1. any one of various carnivorous sea mammals with a sleek, torpedo-shaped body and paddlelike flippers. 2. its fur.

seal-ant ('ànt), n. an agent used for sealing.

sea lawyer, [Informal], an argumentative sailor.

sea legs, the ability to walk on a ship's deck when the vessel is pitching or rolling.

seal-er (sēl'ēr), n. 1. one who or that which seals. 2. an undercoat for sealing a surface in preparation for painting. 3. an official who tests and certifies weights and measures.

seal-er (sēl'ēr), n. a person or ship engaged in hunting seals.

sea level, the level of the surface of the sea at mean tide, taken as a standard when measuring heights or depths.

sea lion, any one of several seals of the northern Pacific, having external ears.

seal ring, same as signet ring.

seal-skin (sēl'skin), n. 1. the skin of the fur seal. 2. a garment made of this skin.

Sea-ly-ham terrier (sē'li-ham), any one of a breed of small terriers with a long body, short legs, and a white coat.

seam (sēm), n. 1. the line formed by the sewing of two pieces of material together. 2. a line of junction or union. 3. a scar, wrinkle, or mark that looks like such a line. 4. a thin layer of coal, ore, etc.: v.t. 1. to form a seam upon or mark with a seam. 2. to join with a seam. 3. to purl in knitting: v.i. [Rare], to crack open.

sea-man (sē'mán), n., pl. -men, 1. a sailor; mariner. 2. in the U.S. Navy, an enlisted man that ranks below a petty officer.

sea-man-ship (-ship), n. skill in navigation or sailing.

sea mew, same as sea gull.

seam-stress (sēm'stris), n. a woman who is skilled at sewing or who earns her living by sewing.

seam-y (sēm'i), adj. seam'i-er, seam'i-est, 1. showing seams, especially on the underside. 2. sordid or unpleasant.

sé-ance (sā'äns), n. a meeting of spiritualists for the purpose of trying to communicate with the dead.

sea nettle, any one of several large jellyfishes with stinging tentacles.

sea otter, a sea mammal of the northern Pacific coast: it has webfeet and very valuable, dark-brown fur.

sea-plane (sē'plān), n. any airplane that can land on water or take off from water.

sea-port ('pôrt), n. a port or harbor that can be used by seagoing vessels.

sear (sir), adj. [Poetic], sere; dried up: v.t. 1. to dry up; wither. 2. to scorch. 3. to brand or cauterize.

sea raven, a spiny fish related to the sculpin, found in the North Atlantic.

search (sûrch), v.t. 1. to look through to find something. 2. to examine (a person), as for a concealed weapon. 3. to examine thoroughly; probe: v.i. to carry out a search: n. an act of searching.

search-ing ('ing), adj. 1. exploring fully; thorough. 2. sharp; penetrating.

search-light ('lit), n. a strong light with a reflector, set in a swivel so that its beam can be sent in various directions.

search warrant, a warrant authorizing a police officer to search a specified person or place for something specified, as stolen goods.

sea robin, a sea fish with large fins like wings.

sea-scape (sē'skāp), n. 1. a view of the sea. 2. a picture representing such a view.

sea serpent, 1. any imaginary animal reputed to resemble a serpent and to have been seen in the sea. 2. same as sea snake.

sea·shell ('shel), *n.* the shell of any mollusk inhabiting salt water.

sea·shore ('shôr), *n.* land on a coast along the sea.

sea·sick ('sik), *adj.* affected by seasickness.

sea·sick·ness ('sik-nis), *n.* a condition of being sick at the stomach, dizzy, etc. produced by the rolling motion of a ship at sea.

sea·side ('sīd), *n.* same as seashore.

sea snake, a poisonous snake of tropical seas, having a tail flat like an oar.

sea·son (sē'zn), *n.* 1. one of the four divisions of the year; spring, summer, fall, or winter. 2. any particular time, as for some recurring activity. 3. the time that is suitable: *v.t.* 1. to add salt, spices, etc. to (food) to give it zest. 2. to make interesting. 3. to make fit for using, as by curing. 4. to make accustomed to: *v.i.* to become seasoned or mature.

sea·son·a·ble (-â-bl), *adj.* 1. proper for the season. 2. occurring or done in good or proper time; opportune. —**sea'son·a·bly,** *adv.*

sea·son·al (-l), *adj.* of or dependent on the season. —**sea'son·al·ly,** *adv.*

sea·son·ing (-ing), *n.* 1. that which is added to give zest or relish to food. 2. anything added to increase enjoyment.

sea squirt, a kind of ascidian with a flabby body that contracts to shoot out jets of water.

seat (sēt), *n.* 1. that on which anyone sits, as a chair. 2. a place for sitting. 3. the buttocks. 4. that part of a chair or garment on which one sits. 5. one's position as a member, as of a council. 6. the site or location, as of a government. 7. a residence or estate. 8. one's posture on horseback: *v.t.* 1. to place on a seat. 2. to cause or help to sit down. 3. to provide seating for. 4. to establish or fix in some position.

seat belt, straps that can be buckled across the hips to protect a passenger in a vehicle in case of an accident.

seat·ing (sēt'ing), *n.* 1. the act of helping to sit down or of providing a seat for. 2. material for covering seats. 3. the way seats are arranged.

sea trout, any one of various saltwater fishes, such as the weakfish.

sea urchin, any echinoderm with a globular body and movable spines.

sea·ward (sē'wârd), *adj. & adv.* toward the sea: also **sea'wards,** *adv.*

sea·way ('wā), *n.* an inland waterway connecting with the sea and used by oceangoing vessels.

sea·weed ('wēd), *n.* any sea plant; especially, any marine alga.

sea·wor·thy ('wûr-*th*i), *adj.* sturdy enough for travel on the open sea: said of a ship. —**sea'wor·thi·ness,** *n.*

se·ba·ceous (si-bā'shŭs), *adj.* 1. of or like fat. 2. that secretes fat, as certain skin glands.

seb·or·rhe·a, seb·or·rhoe·a (seb-ô-rē'â), *n.* an abnormal discharge of a greasy substance from the sebaceous glands, that makes the skin very oily.

se·cant (sē'kânt), *adj.* intersecting: *n.* in *Trigonometry,* the ratio of the hypotenuse in a right triangle to the side adjacent to a given acute angle.

se·cede (si-sēd'), *v.i.* **-ced'ed, -ced'ing,** to withdraw from fellowship or association or from membership in an organized group.

se·ces·sion (si-sesh'ŭn), *n.* 1. the act of seceding. 2. [often S-], the withdrawal by Southern States from the Federal Union at the beginning of the Civil War.

se·ces·sion·ist (-ist), *n.* 1. an upholder of secession. 2. [often S-], an upholder of the Secession of the Southern States.

Seck·el pear (sek'l), a sweet, small, brown pear.

se·clude (si-klōōd'), *v.t.* **-clud'ed, -clud'ing,** 1. to keep away from the company or society of others. 2. to make hidden.

se·clu·sion (si-klōō'zhŭn), *n.* separation or withdrawal from the society of others; isolation; privacy.

se·clu·sive ('siv), *adj.* keeping in seclusion.

Sec·o·nal (sek'ô-nól), *n.* 1. a white, bitter-tasting powder taken as a sedative: a trademark. 2. [also s-], a capsule containing this.

sec·ond (sek'ônd), *adj.* 1. following next after the first in order of place or time. 2. next after the first in value, excellence, merit, dignity, or importance. 3. inferior; subordinate. 4. being of the same kind as another that is the original. 5. lower in musical pitch: *n.* 1. one that is second. 2. an aid, especially to one of the principals in a duel or boxing match. 3. the forward gear that is next after low gear. 4. *pl.* a coarse kind of flour. 5. one sixtieth of a minute of time. 6. one sixtieth of a minute of angular measurement: symbol ("). 7. an instant; moment: *v.t.* 1. to aid or assist. 2. to be a supporter of; reinforce. 3. to say that one gives one's support to (a motion or nomination) as required before it can be discussed or voted on: *adv.* in the second place, rank, etc. — **sec'ond·er,** *n.*

sec·ond·ar·y (sek'ôn-der-i), *adj.* 1. second, or next to the first, in order, importance, sequence, etc.; of second place, rank, etc.; not primary; subordinate; minor. 2. derivative or derived. 3. secondhand: *n., pl.* **-ar·ies,** 1. one that is secondary. 2. a secondary color. — **sec'ond·ar·i·ly,** *adv.*

secondary accent, any accent that is weaker than the primary accent: also **secondary stress.**

secondary color, any color that is produced by mixing together two primary colors.

secondary school, a school, such as a high school, that comes after elementary school.

sec·ond-class (-klas'), *adj.* 1. of secondary rank, quality, etc. 2. denoting or of a class of mail, including newspapers, magazines, etc., requiring lower postage rates than first-class mail. 3. inferior: *adv.* 1. in second-class accommodations. 2. by second-class mail.

Second Coming, in some Christian theologies, the return of Christ, expected to occur at the Last Judgment: also **Second Advent.**

ô in dragon. ōō in crude. oo in wool. u in cup. ū in cure. û in turn. u in focus. oi in boy. ou in house. th in thin. *th* in shea*th*e. g in get. j in joy. y in yet.

second cousin, the child of a first cousin of one's parent.

second growth, a growth of trees on land from which virgin forest has been stripped.

sec-ond-guess (-ges'), *v.t. & v.i.* [Informal], to use hindsight in deciding about or criticizing (something).

sec-ond-hand (-hand'), *adj.* 1. not from the original source. 2. received after having been used by another; not new. 3. of or dealing in secondhand goods: *adv.* not directly.

second hand, the hand (of a watch or clock) that shows the seconds and makes one circuit of the dial every minute.

second lieutenant, a military officer holding the lowest rank of commissioned officer.

sec-ond-ly (sek'ond-li), *adv.* in the second place.

second mate, the officer next in rank below the first mate on a merchant ship.

second nature, acquired habits, traits, etc. so well established as to seem part of one's nature.

second person, the form of a pronoun or verb that denotes the person or persons spoken to.

sec-ond-rate (-rāt'), *adj.* 1. second in rank, quality, etc.; second-class. 2. not of good quality; inferior. —**sec'ond-rat'er,** *n.*

second sight, a supposed supernatural ability to see things not visible to ordinary persons, to foresee future events, etc.

sec-ond-string (-string'), *adj.* [Informal], in *Sports*, being the second choice to play regularly at a particular position.

second thought, any new thought that comes to one who is reconsidering some matter.

second wind, 1. the recovery of a certain ease in breathing after initial fatigue during hard exercise, as while running. 2. a renewed capacity to go on with some endeavor.

se-cre-cy (sē'krē-si), *n., pl.* -cies, 1. the state or quality of being secret or hidden. 2. the habit of keeping secrets or of being secretive.

se-cret (sē'krit), *adj.* 1. concealed or hidden from sight. 2. kept from the knowledge or view of all except those concerned. 3. acting in a secret way. 4. mysterious or esoteric: *n.* something that is secret or kept secret. —**se'cret-ly,** *adv.*

sec-re-tar-i-at (sek-rē-ter'i-ăt), *n.* a staff having secretarial or administrative duties.

sec-re-tar-y (sek'rē-ter-i), *n., pl.* -tar-ies, 1. a person employed to assist another by handling correspondence, records, etc. 2. one who handles similar matters for a company, club, etc. 3. the head of a government department. 4. a desk for writing, especially one with a bookcase on top. —**sec-re-tar'i-al,** *adj.*

secretary bird, a large, African, predatory bird having a crest of penlike feathers at the back of the head.

sec-re-tar-y-ship (-ship). *n.* the office, or term of office, of a secretary.

se-crete (si-krēt'), *v.t.* -cret'ed, -cret'ing, 1. to hide or conceal. 2. to separate (a substance) from the blood or sap and release for separate use by the organism.

se-cre-tin (si-krēt'n), *n.* a hormone secreted in the small intestine: it stimulates secretion of pancreatic juice.

se-cre-tion (si-krē'shun), *n.* 1. the act or process of secreting. 2. a substance that an animal or plant secretes.

se-cre-tive (sē'krē-tiv, si-krēt'iv), *adj.* given to secrecy; not open or frank. —**se'cre-tive-ly,** *adv.* —**se'cre-tive-ness,** *n.*

se-cre-to-ry (si-krēt'ēr-i), *adj.* of, or performing the process of, secretion.

secret service, 1. a government agency engaged in secret investigation. 2. [S- S-], such an agency of the U.S. Treasury Department, for detecting counterfeiters, protecting the President, etc.

sect (sekt), *n.* a group of persons who are the followers of a particular leader and are united by a common attachment to a certain doctrine or doctrines, as of philosophy or religion.

sec-tar-i-an (sek-ter'i-ăn), *adj.* 1. pertaining to, or characteristic of, a certain sect. 2. narrow-minded: *n.* a sectarian person. —**sec-tar'i-an-ism,** *n.*

sec-tar-i-an-ize (-īz), *v.t. & v.i.* -ized, -iz-ing, to imbue (a person or persons) with a sectarian spirit or attitude.

sec-ta-ry (sek'tēr-i), *n., pl.* -ries, a member of a sect.

sec-tile (sek'tl, 'til), *adj.* capable of being cut.

sec-tion (sek'shun), *n.* 1. the act of cutting, or separation by cutting. 2. a part cut away, as a thin slice or portion. 3. a division or subdivision of a chapter or statute. 4. a distinct part of something. 5. any of the squares, containing 640 acres, into which public lands are divided. 6. a plan or view of any structure as it would appear if cut through by an intersecting plane: *v.t.* to cut or divide into sections.

sec-tion-al (-l), *adj.* 1. of or pertaining to a section. 2. made up of sections. —**sec'tion-al-ly,** *adv.*

sec-tion-al-ism (-l-izm), *n.* devotion to a certain section, as of a country.

sec-tor (sek'tēr), *n.* 1. that part of a circle included between two radii and the arc. 2. any district formed by sectioning an area for military operations.

sec-to-ri-al (sek-tôr'i-ăl), *adj.* adapted for cutting or shearing, as a tooth.

sec-u-lar (sek'yu-lēr), *adj.* 1. pertaining to the material world, or to things not sacred; worldly; temporal. 2. extending over a long period of time. 3. not bound by a monastic vow or rule: *n.* 1. one of the secular clergy. 2. a layman.

sec-u-lar-ism (-izm), *n.* 1. a system of principles that discards the forms of religion and maintains that the duties and problems of life should be the primary concern of mankind. 2. a belief in strict separation of church and state, as by prohibiting religious teaching in public schools. —**sec'u-lar-ist,** *n.*

sec·u·lar·i·ty (sek-yū-ler'i-ti), *n.* 1. secular quality or state. 2. same as secularism.

sec·u·lar·ize (sek'yū-lâ-rīz), *v.t.* -ized, -iz·ing, 1. to convert from sacred to secular or common use. 2. to render worldly or unspiritual. 3. to convert from monastic status to secular status. —sec·u·lar·i·za'tion, *n.*

se·cund (sē'kûnd), *adj.* in Botany, growing on only one side of a stalk or stem.

sec·un·dine (sek'ûn-dīn), *n.* 1. the inner coat of an ovule. 2. *pl.* same as afterbirth.

se·cure (si-kyoor'), *adj.* 1. free from fear, worry, etc. 2. free from danger; safe. 3. firm, stable, or dependable: *v.t.* -cured', -cur'ing, 1. to make safe; protect. 2. to make certain; guarantee. 3. to make firm or fast. 4. to confine effectually. 5. to gain possession of; obtain or capture: *v.i.* to give security (with *against*). —se·cure'ly, *adv.*

se·cur·i·ty (-i-ti), *n., pl.* -ties, 1. the state or quality of being secure; freedom from fear or danger. 2. defense or protection. 3. something given to secure the fulfillment of a contract; pledge. 4. one who becomes surety for another. 5. *pl.* stock certificates or bonds.

se·dan (si-dan'), *n.* 1. same as sedan chair. 2. an enclosed automobile having two or four doors, and two seats, front and rear.

sedan chair, a chair inside a compartment for one person, carried by two men by means of poles.

se·date (si-dāt'), *adj.* calm; composed; quiet; serious; unruffled. —se·date'ly, *adv.* —se·date'ness, *n.*

se·date (si-dāt'), *v.t.* -dat'ed, -dat'ing, to dose with a sedative.

se·da·tion (-dā'shûn), *n.* the process or result of using sedatives to calm the nerves or lessen irritation, excitement, etc.

sed·a·tive (sed'â-tiv), *adj.* lessening nervous irritation and irritability; assuaging pain: *n.* a medicine having such an effect.

sed·en·tar·y (sed'n-ter-i), *adj.* 1. characterized by much sitting; keeping one seated much of the time. 2. accustomed to passing much time in a sitting posture. 3. remaining in one place. —sed·en·tar·i·ly, *adv.*

Se·der (sā'dêr), *n.* the Passover Eve service, the central feature being a ceremonial meal.

sedge (sej), *n.* a coarse grass growing in swamps or wet ground.

sedg·y (sej'i), *adj.* sedg'i·er, sedg'i·est, overgrown with sedge.

se·dil·i·a (si-dil'i-â), *n.pl., sing.* se·di'le (-dī'li), seats, usually three of them, along the south side of a church, set apart for the clergy.

sed·i·ment (sed'i-mênt), *n.* 1. the matter which settles at the bottom of a liquid; dregs; lees. 2. in Geology, matter deposited by wind or water.

sed·i·men·ta·ry (sed-i-men'tĕr-i), *adj.* 1. of, consisting of, or containing sediment. 2. formed, as rocks, by deposited sediment.

sed·i·men·ta·tion (sed-i-men-tā'shûn), *n.* the process of forming or depositing sediment.

se·di·tion (si-dish'ûn), *n.* the act of stirring up resistance or rebellion against lawful authority or the government in power.

se·di·tious (-ûs), *adj.* 1. pertaining to or characterized by sedition. 2. engaging in sedition. —se·di'tious·ly, *adv.*

se·duce (si-dōōs', -dūs'), *v.t.* -duced', -duc'ing, 1. to lead astray into wrongdoing. 2. to persuade to have unlawful sexual intercourse, especially for the first time.

se·duce·ment ('mênt), *n.* the act of seducing or the means employed to seduce.

se·duc·er ('ĕr), *n.* one who seduces, especially a man who seduces a woman sexually.

se·duc·i·ble ('i-bl), *adj.* capable of being seduced.

se·duc·tion (si-duk'shûn), *n.* 1. the act of seducing or the state of being seduced. 2. something that seduces.

se·duc·tive ('tiv), *adj.* tending to seduce or lead astray; enticing. —se·duc'tive·ly, *adv.* —se·duc'tive·ness, *n.*

se·duc·tress ('tris), *n.* a woman who seduces, especially a woman who seduces a man sexually.

se·du·li·ty (si-dūl'i-ti, -dōōl'-), *n.* steady diligence or persistence.

sed·u·lous (sej'oo-lûs), *adj.* 1. steadily industrious and persevering; diligent. 2. persistent; constant. —sed'u·lous·ly, *adv.*

see (sē), *n.* 1. the official seat of a bishop. 2. the authority or jurisdiction of a bishop: *v.t.* saw, seen, see'ing, 1. to perceive by the eyes; look at; view. 2. to perceive mentally; understand. 3. to find out; learn. 4. to experience. 5. to make sure. 6. to escort or accompany. 7. to associate with. 8. to encounter. 9. to call on; consult. 10. to receive as a caller: *v.i.* 1. to have the faculty of sight. 2. to understand. 3. to inquire. 4. to think; reflect: *interj.* behold!

seed (sēd), *n., pl.* seeds, seed, 1. that part of a plant that contains the embryo from which a new plant can grow. 2. semen or sperm. 3. the source or origin of anything. 4. ancestry. 5. descendants; offspring: *v.t.* 1. to plant seeds in or on. 2. to extract seeds from. 3. to distribute (the players in a tournament) so as to avoid matching the best ones in the early rounds: *v.i.* 1. to form seeds. 2. to go to seed. 3. to sow seed. — seed'er, *n.* —seed'less, *adj.*

seed·ling (sēd'ling), *n.* 1. a plant grown from a seed. 2. any young plant or tree.

seed money, money made available to get a project started or to get additional funds for it.

seed·pod ('pod), *n.* a carpel or pistil that encloses ovules or seeds.

seed vessel, any dry, hollow fruit with seeds inside.

seed·y (sēd'i), *adj.* seed'i·er, seed'i·est, 1. containing many seeds. 2. gone to seed. 3. shabby; run-down; exhausted; miserable. — seed'i·ness, *n.*

see·ing (sē'ing), *n.* the act or power of sight: *conj.* inasmuch as; considering; since.

seek (sēk), *v.t.* sought, seek'ing, 1. to go in search of; look for. 2. to try to get or find out. 3. to pursue. 4. to try or endeavor (followed by an infinitive).

seem (sēm), *v.i.* 1. to appear to be; look. 2. to have or give the impression (usually fol-

---

ō in dragon, ōō in crude, oo in wool, u in cup, ū in cure, û in turn, ù in focus, oi in boy, ou in house, th in thin, th in sheathe, g in get, j in joy, y in yet.

lowed by an infinitive). 3. to appear to be true.

seem·ing (sēm'ing), *adj.* that seems but may not be; apparent: *n.* what seems to be; appearance; show. —**seem'ing·ly,** *adv.*

seem·ly (sēm'li), *adj.* 1. fair; comely. 2. proper; suitable; fitting; becoming: *adv.* in a seemly manner. —**seem'li·ness,** *n.*

seen (sēn), past participle of **see.**

seep (sēp), *v.i.* to ooze or flow out slowly through pores. —**seep'age,** *n.*

seer (sir), *n.* 1. one who claims to foresee future events; prophet. 2. (sē'ēr), one who sees.

seer·suck·er (sir'suk-ēr), *n.* a thin, crinkled fabric of linen, cotton, etc., usually having a striped pattern.

see-saw (sē'sô), *n.* 1. a plank balanced on some support, enabling children who sit at each end to move up and down alternately. 2. any up-and-down or reciprocating motion: *v.t. & v.i.* to move up and down or back and forth.

seethe (sēth), *v.i.* seethed, seeth'ing, 1. to cook by boiling. 2. to soak or steep in liquid: *v.i.* 1. to boil, bubble, or foam. 2. to be greatly disturbed: *n.* the condition of seething.

seg·ment (seg'mēnt), *n.* 1. any one of the parts into which something is divided or set off; section. 2. in *Geometry,* a part of a circle or sphere cut off by a line or plane: *v.t. & v.i.* ('ment), to divide into segments.

seg·men·tal (seg-men'tl), *adj.* pertaining to, consisting of, or like a segment.

seg·men·ta·tion (-mēn-tā'shŭn), *n.* the act of segmenting or the state of being segmented.

seg·re·gate (seg'rē-gāt), *v.t.* -gat·ed, -gat·ing, 1. to separate from others or from a group. 2. to subject to segregation according to race, sex, etc.: *adj.* (also -git), separated from others.

seg·re·ga·tion (seg-rē-gā'shŭn), *n.* 1. the act of segregating or state of being segregated. 2. the practice of forcing certain racial groups to live separately and use separate schools, facilities, etc. —**seg·re·ga'tion·ist,** *n. & adj.*

se·gue (seg'wā), *v.i.* -gued, -gue·ing, to go without any pause (*to* or *into* the next part): *n.* a transition without any pause into the next part.

sei·del (zī'dl, sī'-), *n., pl.* -dels, -del, a large beer mug.

Seid·litz powders (sed'lits), two powders, one of sodium bicarbonate and Rochelle salt, the other of tartaric acid: they are dissolved separately, combined, and drunk while effervescing, as a laxative: also **Seidlitz powder.**

sei·gnior (sēn'yēr), *n.* 1. a lord or noble. 2. the lord of a fee or manor.

sei·gnior·age (-ij), *n.* 1. something claimed or taken as a prerogative by a sovereign or other superior. 2. any charges or profits made from the minting of gold and silver coins from bullion.

sei·gnio·ri·al, sei·gno·ri·al (sēn-yôr'i-ăl), *adj.* of or pertaining to a seignior.

seine (sān), *n.* a large fishing net with weights along its bottom edge: *v.t. & v.i.* seined, sein'ing, to fish with a seine. —**sein'er,** *n.*

seis·mic (sīz'mik), *adj.* of or produced by an earthquake. —**seis'mi·cal·ly,** *adv.*

seis·mo·graph ('mō-graf), *n.* an instrument for recording the undulatory motions, durations, and direction of earthquakes. —**seis·mo·graph'ic,** *adj.*

seis·mog·ra·phy (sīz-mog'rā-fi), *n.* the use of the seismograph in recording earthquakes.

seis·mol·o·gist (-mol'ō-jist), *n.* one skilled in seismology.

seis·mol·o·gy (-ji), *n.* the scientific study of earthquakes and phenomena related to them. —**seis·mo·log'ic** (-mō-loj'ik), **seis·mo·log'i·cal,** *adj.* —**seis·mo·log'i·cal·ly,** *adv.*

seiz·a·ble (sēz'â-bl), *adj.* capable of being seized.

seize (sēz), *v.t.* seized, seiz'ing, 1. to take legally by force; confiscate. 2. to put under arrest; apprehend. 3. to take quickly by force; grab. 4. to grasp suddenly. 5. to afflict or attack suddenly.

sei·zin, sei·sin (sē'zin), *n.* in *Law,* possession; especially, possession of a freehold estate.

sei·zor ('zōr), *n.* in *Law,* one who takes possession of a freehold estate.

sei·zure (sē'zhēr), *n.* 1. the act of seizing. 2. a sudden attack, as of a disease.

se·lah (sē'lä, sē-lä'), *n.* a Hebrew word that appears at the end of verses in the Psalms: traditionally given the meaning "forever."

sel·dom (sel'dŏm), *adv.* not often; rarely.

se·lect (sē-lekt'), *adj.* 1. chosen or picked out as being excellent. 2. choice; excellent; superior. 3. careful in choosing. 4. exclusive: *v.t. & v.i.* to pick out or choose.

se·lec·tion (-lek'shŭn), *n.* 1. the act of selecting. 2. that which or those which are selected. 3. a variety to choose from.

se·lec·tive ('tiv), *adj.* 1. of or characterized by selection. 2. capable of selecting; tending to select. —**se·lec'tive·ly,** *adv.* —**se·lec·tiv'i·ty,** *n.*

selective service, military training and service that men are compelled by law to undergo.

se·lect·man (sē-lekt'măn), *n., pl.* -men ('mēn, 'men), any one of a board of officials elected in most New England towns to run local or municipal affairs.

se·lec·tor (-lek'tēr), *n.* one that selects.

sel·e·nate (sel'ē-nāt), *n.* a salt or ester of selenic acid.

se·le·nic acid (sē-len'ik, -len'ik), a colorless, crystalline acid resembling sulfuric acid.

sel·e·nite (-nīt), *n.* a variety of gypsum.

se·le·ni·um (sē-lē'ni-ŭm), *n.* a gray, nonmetallic chemical element: used in photoelectric devices.

sel·e·nod·e·sy (sel-ē-nod'ē-si), *n.* the scientific study of the shape and surface features of the moon and the exact location of points on its surface.

sel·e·nog·ra·phy (sel-ē-nog'rā-fi), *n.* the study of the surface and physical features of the moon. —**sel·e·nog'ra·pher,** *n.* —**se·le·no·graph·ic** (sē-lē-nō-graf'ik), *adj.*

sel·e·nol·o·gy (sel-ē-nol'ō-ji), *n.* that branch of astronomy that deals with the moon.

self (self), *n., pl.* selves, 1. identity; character; essence. 2. one's own person as a distinct identity. 3. one's own welfare; personal interest; selfishness: *pron.* [Informal], myself, himself, herself, or yourself: *adj.* of the same kind, material, etc. as the rest.

self-, a prefix meaning: 1. *of oneself or itself.* 2. *by oneself or itself.* 3. *in, to, or with oneself or itself.*

self-ad-dressed (self'á-drest'), *adj.* addressed to oneself. —**self'-as-sured',** *adj.*

self-as-sur-ance ('á-shoor'áns), *n.* confidence in oneself. —**self'-as-sured',** *adj.*

self-cen-tered ('sen'těrd), *adj.* concerned only about oneself; selfish.

self-con-ceit ('kŏn-sēt'), *n.* too high a value of oneself; vanity.

self-con-fi-dence ('kon'fĭ-děns), *n.* confidence in oneself. —**self'-con'fi-dent,** *adj.*

self-con-scious ('kon'shŭs), *adj.* much too conscious of oneself or of being observed; very much ill at ease. —**self'-con'scious-ly,** *adv.* —**self'-con'scious-ness,** *n.*

self-con-tained ('kŏn-tānd'), *adj.* 1. keeping to oneself; reserved. 2. showing self-control. 3. having in oneself or itself all that is needed.

self-con-tra-dic-tion ('kon-trá-dik'shŭn), *n.* 1. contradiction of oneself or itself. 2. any statement containing conflicting ideas. —**self'-con-tra-dic'to-ry,** *adj.*

self-con-trol ('kŏn-trōl'), *n.* control of oneself, one's emotions, etc.

self-de-fense ('di-fens'), *n.* defense of oneself.

self-de-ni-al ('di-nī'ál), *n.* the act of denying oneself pleasures.

self-de-struct ('di-strukt'), *v.i.* same as destruct.

self-de-ter-mi-na-tion ('di-tŭr-mǐ-nā'shŭn), *n.* 1. determination or decision by oneself without outside influence. 2. the right of a people to choose how they will be governed and by whom.

self-ed-u-cat-ed ('ej'ŭ-kāt-ĭd), *adj.* having been educated by one's own efforts, with very little formal schooling.

self-es-teem ('ĕ-stēm'), *n.* 1. belief in oneself. 2. overweening pride in oneself.

self-ev-i-dent ('ev'ĭ-dĕnt), *adj.* evident without having to be explained or proved.

self-ex-plan-a-to-ry ('ik-splan'á-tôr-i), *adj.* obvious, without having to be explained.

self-ex-pres-sion ('ik-spresh'ŭn), *n.* the expression of oneself, one's ideas, etc., especially in the arts.

self-gov-ern-ment ('guv'ěr-mĕnt, 'ẽrn-mĕnt), *n.* government that is carried on by members of a group for the whole group.

self-im-age ('im'ij), *n.* a person's idea of his own worth, importance, character, etc.

self-im-por-tant ('im-pôr'tnt), *adj.* having too high an opinion of one's own importance.

self-in-ter-est ('in'trist, 'in'tēr-ist), *n.* 1. one's own interest or welfare. 2. too great a regard for this.

self-ish (sel'fish), *adj.* having too great concern for one's own welfare and very little concern for others. —**self'ish-ly,** *adv.* —**self'ish-ness,** *n.*

self-less (self'lis), *adj.* devoted to helping others; unselfish.

self-made ('mād'), *adj.* 1. made by oneself or itself. 2. successful due to one's own efforts.

self-pos-ses-sion ('pŏ-zesh'ŭn), *n.* calm control over oneself, one's feelings, etc.; composure. —**self'-pos-sessed',** *adj.*

self-pro-pelled ('prŏ-peld'), *adj.* propelled by its own power or motor.

self-re-li-ance ('ri-lī'áns), *n.* reliance on oneself and one's own efforts.

self-re-spect ('rĭ-spekt'), *n.* due respect for oneself and one's own worth.

self-re-straint ('ri-strānt'), *n.* restraint that one places on oneself; self-control.

self-right-eous ('rī'chŭs), *adj.* convinced that one is more righteous than others, or morally superior. —**self'-right'eous-ly,** *adv.* —**self'-right'eous-ness,** *n.*

self-sac-ri-fice ('sak'rĭ-fīs), *n.* sacrifice of oneself or one's welfare for the good of others.

self-same ('sām), *adj.* exactly the same.

self-sat-is-fied ('sat'is-fid), *adj.* very much satisfied with oneself; smug. —**self'-sat-is-fac'tion,** *n.*

self-seek-er ('sē'kěr), *n.* one who is always trying to further his own interests. —**self'-seek'ing,** *n.* & *adj.*

self-ser-vice ('sŭr'vis), *n.* the act of serving oneself, as in a cafeteria.

self-serv-ing ('sŭr'ving), *adj.* selfishly serving one's own interests.

self-start-er ('stärt'ẽr), *n.* a device for starting an internal-combustion engine automatically.

self-styled ('stīld'), *adj.* so called by oneself.

self-suf-fi-cient ('sŭ-fish'ĕnt), *adj.* able to get along unassisted; independent; not needing another or others. —**self'-suf-fi'cien-cy,** *n.*

self-taught ('tôt'), *adj.* having been taught by one's own efforts, with very little help from others.

self-willed ('wild'), *adj.* obstinate; stubborn.

self-wind-ing ('win'ding), *adj.* that winds itself automatically, as some watches do.

sell (sel), *v.t.* sold, sell'ing, 1. to transfer (goods, property, etc.) to another in exchange for money or an equivalent. 2. to present for sale; deal in. 3. to cause to be sold: *v.i.* 1. to take part in selling. 2. to be sold (*at* or *for*). 3. to be a popular sales item: *n.* [Slang], a hoax or trick. —**sell'er,** *n.*

Selt-zer (selt'sẽr), *n.* 1. effervescing mineral water. 2. [often s-], carbonated water. Also **Seltzer water.**

sel-vage, sel-vedge (sel'vij), *n.* an edge woven on cloth to prevent its raveling.

selves (selvz), *n.* plural of self.

se-man-tics (sē-man'tiks), *n.* the study of the development of words and of changes in their meanings. —**se-man'tic,** *adj.*

sem-a-phore (sem'á-fôr), *n.* 1. any apparatus for signaling, as by means of flags, lights, or mechanical arms. 2. any system using such means: *v.t.* & *v.i.* -phored, -phor-ing, to signal by semaphore.

se-ma-si-ol-o-gy (si-mā-si-ol'ō-ji), *n.* same as semantics. —**se-ma-si-ol'o-gist,** *n.*

se-mat-ic (si-mat'ik), *adj.* serving as a warning of danger, as the color of some poisonous reptiles.

sem-blance (sem'bláns), *n.* 1. outward form: aspect. 2. likeness; resemblance. 3. a copy or likeness.

se-men (sē'mĕn), *n., pl.* **sem-i-na** (sem'ĭ-ná), the whitish fluid secreted by the male reproductive organs, containing the spermatozoa.

se-mes-ter (sē-mes'tẽr), *n.* 1. a half year. 2. either of the two terms which usually make up a school year.

sem-i-, a prefix meaning: 1. *half.* 2. *partly, not completely.* 3. *twice in a (specified) period.*

sem-i-an-nu-al (sem-i-an'yoo-wâl), *adj.* 1. occurring, appearing, etc. every half year. 2. lasting half a year. —**sem'i-an'nu-al-ly,** *adv.*

sem-i-au-to-mat-ic (-ôt-ô-mat'ik), *adj.* partly automatic and partly controlled by hand.

semiautomatic firearm, a firearm designed to fire another round only after the trigger is pulled.

sem-i-breve (sem'i-brev), *n.* [British], in *Music,* a whole note, equal to four crotchets.

sem-i-cir-cle (-sûr-kl), *n.* a half circle. —**sem-i-cir'cu-lar** ('kyû-lêr), *adj.*

sem-i-co-lon (-kō-lôn), *n.* a mark of punctuation (;) used to show greater separation than a comma does and less than a period does.

sem-i-con-duc-tor (sem-i-kôn-duk'tēr), *n.* a substance used, as germanium in transistors, to control flow of electric current.

sem-i-con-scious (-kon'shûs), *adj.* not completely conscious or awake.

sem-i-fi-nal (sem-i-fi'nl), *adj.* coming just before the final match, as of a tournament: *n.* (usually sem'i-fi-nl), a semifinal match.

sem-i-fi-nal-ist (-ist), *n.* a player in a semifinal match or round.

sem-i-flu-id (-flōō'id), *adj.* thick or heavy but capable of flowing; viscous: *n.* a semifluid substance.

sem-i-lu-nar (-lōō'nēr), *adj.* shaped like a half-moon.

sem-i-month-ly (-munth'li), *adj.* 1. occurring, appearing, etc. twice a month: *adv.* twice every month.

sem-i-nal (sem'i-nl), *adj.* 1. of seed or semen. 2. being a source; originative. —**sem'i-nal-ly,** *adv.*

sem-i-nar (sem'i-när), *n.* 1. a group of students doing research under supervision. 2. a course for such students, or any of its meetings. 3. a group discussion like this.

sem-i-nar-i-an (sem-i-ner'i-ăn), *n.* a student at a seminary preparing for the priesthood, ministry, or rabbinate.

sem-i-nar-y (sem'i-ner-i), *n., pl.* -**nar-ies,** 1. a private school for young women: an old-fashioned term. 2. a school or college for training priests, ministers, or rabbis.

sem-i-na-tion (sem-i-nā'shûn), *n.* 1. propagation; dissemination. 2. the act of sowing seed.

Sem-i-nole (sem'i-nōl), *n., pl.* -**noles, -nole,** a member of an American Indian people, now living in Florida and Oklahoma.

sem-i-o-vip-a-rous (sem-i-ō-vip'ēr-ûs), *adj.* giving birth to young not fully developed, as the kangaroo.

sem-i-pre-cious (-presh'ûs), *adj.* denoting gems, as the turquoise and garnet, that have a lower value than precious gems.

sem-i-pri-vate (-pri'vit), *adj.* partially private, as a hospital room with two, three, or sometimes four beds.

sem-i-pro-fes-sion-al (-prō-fesh'ûn-l), *n.* one who takes part in a sport for pay but not to

earn a living: also [Informal], **sem'i-pro** (-prō).

sem-i-qua-ver (sem'i-kwä-vēr), *n.* [Chiefly British], a musical sixteenth note.

sem-i-skilled (sem-i-skild'), *adj.* 1. partly skilled. 2. of or performing manual labor for which one needs to have only limited training.

Sem-ite (sem'it), *n.* a member of any of the peoples that speak a Semitic language.

Se-mit-ic (sê-mit'ik), *adj.* 1. of or pertaining to the Semites. 2. denoting or of a group of Afro-Asiatic languages, including Hebrew, Arabic, Ethiopic, etc.

Sem-i-tism (sem'i-tizm), *n.* 1. a Semitic word or idiom. 2. the ideas, customs, practices, etc. of the Semites, especially those originating with the Jews.

sem-i-trail-er (sem'i-trã-lēr), *n.* a trailer coupled to the rear of a truck cab: it can be detached by unfastening the coupling.

sem-i-trans-par-ent (sem-i-trans-per'ent), *adj.* not fully or perfectly transparent.

sem-i-trop-i-cal (-trop'i-kl), *adj.* partly tropical.

sem-i-week-ly (-wēk'li), *adj.* occurring, appearing, etc. twice a week: *adv.* twice a week.

sem-i-year-ly (-yir'li), *adj.* occurring, appearing, etc. twice a year: *adv.* twice a year.

sem-o-li-na (sem-ô-lē'nä), *n.* meal made of coarsely ground durum, used in making macaroni, spaghetti, etc.

sem-pi-ter-nal (sem-pi-tūr'nl), *adj.* everlasting; never-ending; eternal.

semp-stress (sem'stris, semp'-), *n.* same as seamstress.

sen-ar-y (sen'ēr-i), *adj.* of six or based on six.

sen-ate (sen'it), *n.* 1. in ancient Rome, the supreme council of state. 2. a legislative assembly. 3. [S-], *a)* the upper branch of the U.S. legislature; *b)* the upper branch of most State legislatures; *c)* a similar body in other countries. 4. an advisory council, as in a college.

sen-a-tor (sen'ä-tēr), *n.* a member of a senate.

sen-a-to-ri-al (sen-â-tôr'i-âl), *adj.* 1. of or appropriate to a senator or a senate. 2. made up of senators.

send (send), *v.t.* sent, send'ing, 1. to cause to go; dispatch; transmit. 2. to cause or enable to go. 3. to force to move; impel. 4. to cause to occur, come, etc. 5. [Slang], to excite or thrill: *v.i.* 1. to send a message or messenger (for someone or something). 2. to transmit, as by radio: *n.* the impelling motion of a wave or the sea. —**send'er,** *n.*

sen-dal (sen'dl), *n.* a light silk fabric used in the Middle Ages.

send-off ('ôf), *n.* an expression or demonstration of goodwill and appreciation for one going off on a journey or beginning some new enterprise.

Sen-e-ca (sen'i-kä), *n., pl.* -**cas, -ca,** a member of a North American Indian tribe now living chiefly in New York and Ontario.

se-nes-cent (sē-nes'nt), *adj.* growing old; aging. —**se-nes'cence,** *n.*

sen-es-chal (sen'ê-shâl), *n.* a medieval majordomo or steward who managed the estate of a noble or lord.

se-nile (sē'nil), *adj.* 1. of or caused by old age.

2. showing signs of old age; weak and infirm physically and mentally.

se·nil·i·ty (si-nil'í-ti), *n.* 1. the state or quality of being senile. 2. physical and mental infirmity caused by old age.

sen·ior (sēn'yẽr), *adj.* 1. the older: written as *Sr.* after the name of a father whose son has the same name. 2. of a higher or longer standing: *n.* 1. one who is older or of a higher standing. 2. a student in the last year, as of high school or college.

senior citizen, an elderly person, esp. one who is retired.

sen·ior·i·ty (sēn-yôr'í-ti), *n.* senior rank.

sen·na (sen'à), *n.* 1. any one of a genus of plants with yellow flowers, some having leaflets used dried, especially formerly, as a laxative. 2. the dried leaflets.

se·ñor (se-nyôr'), *n., pl.* **-ñor'es** ('es), a Spanish title, equivalent to *Mr.*

se·ño·ra (-nyô'rä), *n., pl.* **-ras** ('räs), a Spanish title, equivalent to *Mrs.*

se·ño·ri·ta (-nyô-rē'tä), *n., pl.* **-tas** ('täs), a Spanish title, equivalent to *Miss.*

sen·sate (sen'sāt), *adj.* of, perceived by, or endowed with physical sensation.

sen·sa·tion (sen-sá'shùn), *n.* 1. perception by the sense organs of the body. 2. a generalized feeling or reaction. 3. a state or feeling of intense excitement and interest. 4. something causing such excitement and interest.

sen·sa·tion·al (-l), *adj.* 1. of the senses or sensation. 2. intensely exciting and interesting. 3. startling, shocking, etc. 4. [Informal], extraordinarily good; excellent.

sen·sa·tion·al·ism (-izm). *n.* 1. the use of subject matter or techniques designed to startle, shock, etc. writing, speech, etc. characterized by this. 3. in *Philosophy*, the teaching that all knowledge is acquired through the senses.

sense (sens). *n.* 1. the faculty by which nerves and brain respond to physical stimuli; specifically, any one of five faculties (sight, touch, taste, smell, hearing) operating through certain bodily organs. 2. such response or operation. 3. a generalized feeling or awareness. 4. a judgmental ability derived from or related to perception by the senses. 5. capacity to feel, understand, or respond to such things as beauty, honor, or humor. 6. capacity to think; ability to use intelligence and judgment. 7. sound thinking or judgment. or evidence of this. 8. meaning; signification; gist. 9. the general opinion, feeling. or attitude of a group: *v.t.* sensed, sens'ing, 1. to perceive or feel with or as if with a sense or the senses. 2. to understand. 3. to detect automatically. as by sensors.

sense·less ('lis), *adj.* 1. foolish; stupid; nonsensical. 2. devoid of meaning or purpose. 3. incapable of using the senses; unconscious.

sense organ, any organ or structure, as an ear or eye, that receives specific stimuli and transmits them as sensations to the brain.

sen·si·bil·i·ty (sen-si-bil'í-ti), *n.* 1. capacity for physical sensation. 2. *often pl.* capacity for responding intellectually or emotionally; acuteness of perception; sensitivity.

sen·si·ble (sen'si-bl), *adj.* 1. capable of being

perceived by the senses or mind. 2. easily perceptible. 3. endowed with sense faculties. 4. responsive intellectually or emotionally; sensitive. 5. marked by sound thinking or good judgment; intelligent or judicious. — **sen'si·bly**, *adv.*

sen·si·tive (sen'si-tiv), *adj.* 1. of the senses or sensation; sensory. 2. marked by sense perception. 3. keenly perceiving or responsive to given physical stimuli. 4. keenly responsive intellectually or emotionally. 5. easily offended, shocked, annoyed, etc. 6. easily hurt, as the eye. 7. readily actuated or influenced by a given stimulus or condition. 8. responding readily even to weak stimuli. 9. of, concerned with, or designating highly secret or delicate government matters. —**sen·si·tiv'i·ty**, *n.*

sen·si·tize (-tīz), *v.t.* **-tized, -tiz·ing**, to make sensitive.

sen·sor (sen'sẽr, 'sôr), *n.* a device designed to detect, measure, or record something, as heat, and to respond, as by activating a mechanism.

sen·so·ry (sen'sẽr-i), *adj.* 1. of the senses or sensation. 2. receiving and transmitting sense impressions. Also **sen·so'ri·al** (-sôr'i-ál).

sen·su·al (sen'shoo-wàl), *adj.* 1. bodily rather than spiritual; carnal. 2. voluptuous.

sen·su·al·ism (-izm), *n.* 1. indulgence in sensual pleasures. 2. sensationalism (sense 3).

sen·su·al·ist (-ist), *n.* one given to sensualism.

sen·su·al·i·ty (sen-shoo-wal'í-ti), *n.* 1. the condition or quality of being sensual. 2. indulgence in or tendency toward sensualism.

sen·su·ous (sen'shoo-wùs), *adj.* 1. of, from, or directed toward the senses. 2. highly responsive to sense stimulation.

sent (sent), past tense and past participle of **send**.

sen·tence (sen'tns), *n.* 1. a judgment or decision, as of a court; especially, formal declaration by a court of the penalty it has determined to be imposed on a convicted person: also, the penalty itself. 2. in *Grammar*, a word or word group conveying a determinate thought and usually including a subject and predicate: *v.t.* **-tenced, -ten·cing**, to pass judgment on (a convicted individual); condemn.

sen·ten·tious (sen-ten'shùs), *adj.* 1. succinct and pithy; terse. 2. given to or marked by an abundance of maxims, adages, or other such sayings or expressions. 3. annoyingly moralizing.

sen·tience (sen'shèns), *n.* 1. sentient state or quality. 2. awareness or sensation without thought or perception. Also **sen'tien·cy**.

sen·tient ('shènt), *adj.* of or marked by feeling or perception; conscious.

sen·ti·ment (sen'tí-mènt), *n.* 1. a complex of opinions and feelings, with emotion a strongly conditioning or predominant element. 2. *often pl.* a particular thought, opinion, or attitude, or a combination of these, often influenced by emotion. 3. emotional responsiveness; sensibility; sensitivity. 4. a delicately expressed indication of feeling. 5. emotional appeal, as in literature or art. 6. mere emotionalism; sentimentality. 7. a brief statement expressing a thought or wish, as on a birthday card. 8. the real thought or meaning underlying something said, done, etc.

sen·ti·men·tal (sen-ti-men'tl), *adj.* marked by or full of emotion, often to an excessive extent. —**sen·ti·men'tal·ism**, *n.* —**sen·ti·men'tal·ist**, *n.*

sen·ti·men·tal·i·ty (-men-tal'i-ti), *n.* 1. sentimental quality or condition; especially, excessive emotionalism; mawkishness. 2. *pl.* **-ties,** a statement or other expression marked by sentimentality.

sen·ti·men·tal·ize (sen-ti-men'tå-līz), *v.t.* & *v.i.* **-ized, -iz·ing,** to make or be sentimental.

sen·ti·nel (sen'ti-nl), *n.* one who watches or guards; especially, a soldier on watch.

sen·try (sen'tri), *n., pl.* **-tries,** a sentinel.

se·pal (sē'pl), *n.* any one of the leaflike divisions of a calyx.

sep·a·ra·ble (sep'ēr-å-bl), *adj.* capable of being separated. —**sep·a·ra·bil'i·ty,** *n.*

sep·a·rate (sep'å-rāt), *v.t.* **-rat·ed, -rat·ing,** 1. to part or divide; disunite; disconnect. 2. to make out the distinction between; differentiate. 3. to set apart; sort out or take out. 4. to withdraw or dismiss: *v.i.* to become separated: *adj.* ('ēr-it), 1. that is separated; parted, disconnected, set apart, etc. 2. distinct; individual.

sep·a·ra·tion (sep-å-rā'shŭn), *n.* 1. a separating or being separated. 2. the place or line of this. 3. something separated or separating.

sep·a·ra·tism (sep'ēr-å-tizm), *n.* 1. advocacy of separation as from a social, religious, or political group. 2. such separation. —**sep'a·ra·tist,** *n.* & *adj.*

sep·a·ra·tor ('å-rāt-ēr), *n.* one that separates.

se·pi·a (sē'pi-å), *n.* 1. a dark-brown pigment made from the inky secretion of cuttlefish. 2. a dark reddish-brown color: *adj.* 1. of sepia. 2. dark reddish-brown.

se·poy (sē'poi), *n.* formerly, a native of India in a European army, especially the British army.

sep·sis (sep'sis), *n.* a poisoned state resulting from absorption of harmful microorganisms into the blood.

sept (sept), *n.* a clan or similar group.

sep·ta (sep'tå), *n.* alternate plural of septum.

sep·tal ('tl), *adj.* of a septum or septums.

sep·tate ('tāt), *adj.* having or divided by a septum or septums.

Sep·tem·ber (sep-tem'bēr), *n.* the ninth month of the year, having 30 days.

sep·ti-, a combining form meaning *seven.*

sep·tic (sep'tik), *adj.* of or from sepsis or putrefaction. —**sep'ti·cal·ly,** *adv.*

sep·ti·ce·mi·a (sep-ti-sē'mi-å), *n.* a systemic disease caused by harmful microorganisms in the blood.

septic tank, an underground tank for the decomposition of waste products.

sep·til·lion (sep-til'yŭn), *n.* 1. in the U.S. and France, the number indicated by 1 followed by 24 zeros. 2. in Great Britain and Germany, the number indicated by 1 followed by 42 zeros. —**sep·til'lionth,** *adj.* & *n.*

sep·tu·a·ge·nar·i·an (sep-too-wå-jē-ner'i-ån), *n.* one who is seventy years old, or between

seventy and eighty: *adj.* of or denoting a septuagenarian.

Sep·tu·a·gint (sep'too-wå-jint), *n.* an ancient Greek translation of the Old Testament.

sep·tum (sep'tŭm), *n., pl.* **-tums, -ta** ('tå), a part dividing cavities or tissues, as in the nose.

sep·ul·cher (sep'l-kēr), *n.* a tomb.

se·pul·chral (sē-pul'krål), *adj.* 1. of a sepulcher. 2. dismal. 3. deep and hollow in tone.

sep·ul·chre (sep'l-kēr), *n.* British form for sepulcher.

sep·ul·ture (sep'l-chēr), *n.* burial.

se·quel (sē'kwel), *n.* 1. a continuation or succeeding part. 2. an effect; consequence. 3. a literary work complete in itself but continuing the narrative of a preceding work.

se·que·la (si-kwē'lå, -kwel'å), *n., pl.* **-lae** ('lē, 'ē), 1. an effect; consequence. 2. a diseased condition following, and usually resulting from, a previous disease.

se·quence (sē'kwēns), *n.* 1. a series of things following one after the other in a certain order. 2. three or more playing cards of the same suit, each immediately following the other. 3. a consequence; effect. 4. one of the episodes of a movie. 5. a hymn preceding the Gospel in certain Masses.

se·quent ('kwēnt), *adj.* following in a given order or as an effect or consequence: *n.* something that follows, especially as an effect or consequence. —**se·quen·tial** (si-kwen'shŭl), *adj.*

se·ques·ter (si-kwes'tēr), *v.t.* 1. to set apart; separate. 2. to take possession of (property) as until a debt is paid. 3. to confiscate. 4. to withdraw; seclude.

se·ques·tered ('tērd), *adj.* secluded; withdrawn.

se·ques·trate ('trāt), *v.t.* **-trat·ed, -trat·ing,** same as sequester. —**se·ques·tra·tion** (sē-kwes-trā'-shŭn), *n.*

se·ques·tra·tor (sē'kwes-trāt-ēr), *n.* one that sequestrates.

se·quin (sē'kwin), *n.* a small, glittering, ornamental disk, typically one of many sewn onto fabric as of an evening gown.

se·quoi·a (si-kwoi'å), *n.* either one of two extremely large evergreen coniferous trees of the western U.S.

se·ra (sir'å), *n.* alternate plural of serum.

se·rag·lio (si-ral'yō, -räl'yō), *n., pl.* **-lios,** 1. a harem. 2. a Turkish sultan's palace.

se·ra·i (si-rä'i), *n.* 1. an Oriental inn; caravansary. 2. a Turkish palace.

se·ra·pe (sē-rä'pi), *n.* in Spanish-American countries, a blanket, often brightly colored, worn like a cloak by many men.

ser·aph (ser'åf), *n., pl.* **-aphs, -a·phim** ('å-fim), 1. in the *Bible,* any one of certain heavenly spirits surrounding the throne of God. 2. in *Christian Theology,* any one of the highest order of angels. —**se·raph·ic** (sē-raf'ik), *adj.*

Serb (sûrb), *n.* a native or inhabitant of Serbia: *adj.* Serbian.

Ser·bi·an (sûr'bi-ån), *n.* a Serb: *adj.* of Serbia or the Serbs.

sere (sir), *adj.* [Poetic], dry; withered.

ser·e·nade (ser-ē-nād'), *n.* 1. evening music in the open air. 2. such music sung or played by a lover under the window of his sweet-

---

a in cap, ā in cane, ä in father, å in abet, e in met, ē in be, ê in baker, ẽ in regent, i in pit, ī in fine, i in manifest, o in hot, ô in horse, ō in bone,

heart: *v.t. & v.i.* **-nad'ed, -nad'ing,** to sing or play such music (to).

ser·en·dip·i·ty (ser-ĕn-dip'i-tĭ), *n.* an apparent natural gift for making fortunate discoveries by chance. **—ser·en·dip'i·tous,** *adj.*

se·rene (sĕ-rēn'), *adj.* 1. clear and calm; unclouded. 2. placid; unruffled. 3. exalted: in titles of honor. **—se·ren'i·ty,** *n.*

serf (sûrf), *n.* 1. originally, a slave. 2. one in feudal servitude. **—serf'dom,** *n.*

serge (sûrj), *n.* a strong, twilled fabric, as of wool, with a diagonal rib.

ser·gean·cy (sär'jĕn-si), *n., pl.* **-cies,** the position or rank of a sergeant.

ser·geant ('jĕnt), *n.* 1. a noncommissioned officer ranking next above a corporal. 2. a police officer ranking next below a captain.

ser·geant-at-arms (-ăt ärmz'), *n., pl.* **ser'geants-at-arms',** an officer appointed to keep order in an assembly, as of a legislature.

se·ri·al (sir'i-ăl), *adj.* 1. of, in, or forming a series. 2. appearing in continuous parts as in successive issues of a magazine: *n.* 1. a story, movie, etc. appearing at regular intervals in successive parts; also, any one of the parts. 2. a periodical publication. **—se'ri·al·ly,** *adv.*

se·ri·al·ize (-īz), *v.t.* **-ized, -iz·ing,** 1. to make a serial of. 2. to present as a serial. **—se·ri·al·i·za'tion,** *n.*

serial number, a number identifying one of a series.

se·ri·a·tim (sir-i-āt'im), *adv.* in series; one after the other in regular order.

se·ri·ceous (si-rish'ŭs), *adj.* silky.

ser·i·cin (ser'i-sin), *n.* a resinous bonding substance in raw silk.

ser·i·cul·ture (ser'i-kul-chēr), *n.* culture of silkworms.

ser·i·e·ma (ser-i-ē'mă, -i-ā'mă), *n.* a long-legged, long-necked bird of the crane family, found in Brazil and Argentina.

se·ries (sir'iz), *n., pl.* **-ries,** a number of interrelated or like things standing or following one another in a given order; sequence.

ser·if (ser'if), *n.* any one of the fine terminal projections typical of printed characters in type, especially at the top or bottom of the main stroke, as in *T*.

ser·in (ser'in), *n.* a kind of European finch, yellow or yellowish green, related to the canary.

se·rin·ga (sĕ-ring'gä), *n.* any one of several Brazilian trees yielding rubber.

se·ri·o·com·ic (sir-i-ō-kom'ik), *adj.* serious and comic simultaneously.

se·ri·ous (sir'i-ŭs), *adj.* 1. grave; solemn; not trifling. 2. earnest; sincere.

ser·mon (sûr'mŏn), *n.* 1. an exhortatory discourse on religion or morals, specifically by a clergyman during a service. 2. any similar discourse, admonition, etc., especially if long and tedious.

ser·mon·ize (sûr'mŏ-nīz), *v.i. & v.t.* **-ized, -iz·ing,** to preach a sermon (to): lecture.

Sermon on the Mount, one of the discourses of Jesus: see *Matthew v-vii* and *Luke vi,* 20-49.

se·rol·o·gy (si-rol'ŏ-ji), *n.* the science of serums. **—se·rol'o·gist,** *n.*

se·rous (sir'ŭs), *adj.* of, containing, or like serum.

ser·ow (ser'ō), *n.* a dark-colored animal intermediate between the goat and the antelope in characteristics, found in eastern Asia.

ser·pent (sûr'pĕnt), *n.* a snake, especially when large or poisonous.

ser·pen·tine (sûr'pĕn-tēn, -tīn), *adj.* 1. of or like a serpent. 2. coiling; winding: *n.* 1. something coiling or winding. 2. a mineral or rock, chiefly of hydrated magnesium silicate.

ser·rate (ser'āt, -it), *adj.* notched like a saw: also **ser·rat·ed** (sĕ-rāt'id, ser'āt-).

ser·ried (ser'id), *adj.* crowded; pressed close.

ser·ru·late (ser'yoo-lit, ser'ŭ-lit; -lāt), *adj.* finely serrate: also **ser'ru·lat·ed** (-lāt-id).

se·rum (sir'ŭm), *n.* 1. a thin, watery animal fluid, as within the peritoneal region. 2. a clear yellowish fluid separating from blood; also, specifically, such fluid taken from the blood of an inoculated animal and containing agents of immunity, used as an antitoxin and in diagnosis. 3. whey. 4. the thin, watery part of a plant fluid.

ser·val (sûr'vĭ), *n., pl.* **-vals, -val,** a long-legged African wildcat with a tawny, black-spotted coat.

ser·vant (sûr'vănt), *n.* one in the service of another, especially in a household.

serve (sûrv), *v.t.* served, serv'ing, 1. to work for. 2. to perform duties for or in connection with. 3. to yield obedience to. 4. to attend or wait on (customers, clients, etc.). 5. to supply, as food to diners. 6. to pass or spend, as a term of imprisonment or a period of military duty. 7. to assist; help. 8. to offer (food or drink) in a certain way, as at an indicated temperature. 9. to meet the needs or contribute to the advantage of. 10. to treat or requite. 11. to deliver (a legal instrument, as a summons); also, to deliver a legal instrument to. 12. to hit, as a tennis ball, to the opponent to get play started: *v.i.* 1. to serve someone or something. 2. to do service or be of service: *n.* the act or way of serving the ball, as in tennis; also, one's turn to serve the ball.

serv·er (sûr'vĕr), *n.* 1. one that serves. 2. something used in serving, as a tray.

serv·ice (sûr'vis), *n.* 1. the act of serving or the condition of being served. 2. the condition or occupation of a servant. 3. employment, especially public employment; also, a particular branch of this; specifically, the armed forces. 4. a religious ceremony. 5. benefit; advantage; utility; also, help or assistance. 6. *pl.* kind attention to needs, and the aid given for these. 7. *pl.* professional attention to or assistance with needs. 8. a set of articles, as dishes, used in serving. 9. provision of something needed or wanted, as water, heat, repairs, entertainment, etc.; also, an agency or individual professionally attending to this: *adj.* 1. of, for, or attending to service. 2. of or designed for use by servants, tradespeople, etc.: *v.t.* -iced, -ic·ing, 1. to provide with something needed or wanted. 2. to keep in or restore to proper condition, good working order, etc.: used specifically of an individual or group professionally providing such attention.

serv·ice·a·ble (-ə-blĭ), *adj.* 1. capable of being used; usable. 2. providing what is needed or wanted; having utility; useful. 3. lasting long or well in use; durable. —**serv'ice·a·bly,** *adv.*

serv·ice·man (-mən, -mǎn), *n., pl.* **-men** (-men, -mén), 1. a member of the armed forces. 2. one providing maintenance or repair service: also **service man.**

service mark, a symbol, design, word, slogan, etc. used like a trademark by a supplier of a service, as transportation, laundry, etc. to distinguish the service from that of a competitor.

service station, 1. a place providing maintenance service, parts, etc. for mechanical or electrical equipment. 2. same as gas station.

ser·vi·ette (sûr·vi·et'), *n.* a table napkin.

ser·vile (sûr'vĭl, 'vĭl), *adj.* 1. of or suggestive of slaves or servants. 2. slavishly submissive; obsequious. —**ser·vil·i·ty** (sêr·vĭl'ĭ-ti), *n.*

serv·ing (sûr'vĭng), *n.* 1. the act of one that serves. 2. a single portion of food; helping: *adj.* used for serving food.

ser·vi·tor (sûr'vĭ-têr), *n.* a servant; attendant.

ser·vi·tude (sûr'vĭ-tōōd), *n.* slavery; bondage.

ser·vo·mech·a·nism (sûr·vō·mek'ă-nĭzm), *n.* a system automatically gauging output and input so as to achieve desired control.

ser·vo·mo·tor (sûr'vō·mōt·ĕr), *n.* an electric motor or other device controlled by an amplified signal as from a servomechanism.

ses·a·me (ses'ă-mē), *n.* 1. an East Indian plant with flat, edible seeds. 2. the seeds.

ses·qui-, a combining form meaning *one and a half.*

ses·qui·cen·ten·ni·al (ses-kwĭ-sen-ten'ĭ-ăl), *adj.* 1. comprising one hundred and fifty years. 2. ending a period of one hundred and fifty years: *n.* a sesquicentennial celebration, etc. —**ses·qui·cen·ten'ni·al·ly,** *adv.*

ses·qui·pe·da·li·an (-pē·dā'lĭ·ăn), *adj.* 1. measuring a foot and a half. 2. very long: said of words; also, using long words. Also **ses·quip'e·dal** (-kwĭp'ē·dăl): *n.* a very long word.

ses·sion (sesh'ŭn), *n.* 1. a group's coming together and engagement in discussion or other planned activity; assembly; meeting. 2. the period of time of such a meeting or series of meetings. 3. a school term, class period, study period, etc. 4. a period of activity of any kind.

set (set), *v.t.* **set, set'ting,** 1. to make sit; seat. 2. to place or put in any position, location, or condition. 3. to arrange, adjust, lay out, position, etc. so as to make work, be effective, be in proper condition, etc. 4. to cause to be in a firm, immovable, or rigid position or condition. 5. to make move or turn in or toward a particular direction. 6. to appoint, establish, determine, prescribe, etc. 7. in *Bridge,* to keep (opponents) from achieving a bid. 8. in *Music,* to fit (words to music or music to words). 9. in *Printing,* a) to arrange (type) for printing; b) to put (manuscript) into type. 10. in *Theater,* a) to fix (a scene) in a certain place, environ-

ment, etc.; *b*) to put up (scenery) on (the stage): *v.i.* 1. to sit on eggs: said of a fowl. 2. to become firm, as cement, or fast, as a dye. 3. to start going, moving, operating, etc. (with *off, forth, out,* etc.). 4. to go or tend to move in a certain direction. 5. to seem to descend toward or below the horizon, as the sun. 6. to wane; decline. 7. to conform to contours in a certain way, as a jacket; hang. 8. to mend: said of a broken bone. 9. in *Hunting,* to take a position indicating the location of game: said of a dog: *adj.* 1. fixed; established; determined. 2. deliberately settled upon in advance; premeditated. 3. purposeful. 4. not spontaneous; stereotyped. 5. rigid; immovable. 6. resolute. 7. obstinate. 8. ready for action: *n.* 1. a setting or being set. 2. the way something sets or is set. 3. a stem, twig, etc. for planting or grafting; also, a young plant. 4. a number of pieces of scenery and properties for a particular scene in a play, movie, etc. 5. a particular group of individuals or things, as those having similar characteristics, those used together or associated with each other, etc. 6. an assembly of receiving equipment for radio or television. 7. in *Mathematics,* a collection of points, numbers, etc. satisfying a given condition. 8. in *Tennis,* a group of games constituting a complete unit of a match.

se·ta (sē't'ă), *n., pl.* **-tae** ('ē), a stiff hair, bristle, or bristlelike part.

se·ta·ceous (sĭ-tā'shǔs), *adj.* 1. having bristles. 2. bristlelike. —**se·ta'ceous·ly,** *adv.*

set·back (set'bak), *n.* 1. a reversal or interruption in progress. 2. an upper part of a building that has been set back in.

se·ti·form (sēt'ĭ-fôrm), *adj.* having the form, or shape, of a bristle.

se·tose (sē't'ōs), *adj.* same as setaceous.

set·tee (se-tē'), *n.* 1. a bench with a back, usually for two or three people. 2. a small sofa.

set·ter (set'ĕr), *n.* 1. a person or thing that sets. 2. a kind of bird dog trained to follow and point out game by standing rigid.

set·ting ('ĭng), *n.* 1. the act of one that sets. 2. that which sets or holds, as the mounting of a jewel. 3. the number of eggs set in a nest for a single hen to incubate. 4. the position of a dial, clock, etc. that has been set. 5. the background, environment, circumstances, etc. of a story, play, film, etc. 6. the scenery and properties of a play. 7. a musical composition to go with words.

set·tle (set'l). *n.* a long bench or seat, usually of wood, with arms and a high back.

set·tle (set'l), *v.t.* **-tled, -tling,** 1. to place or set in a fixed place. 2. to establish. 3. to colonize. 4. to cause to sink and become more firm. 5. to free from uncertainty; determine (something in doubt). 6. to decide (a quarrel, legal dispute, etc.). 7. to pay (an account, bill, etc.). 8. to clear of dregs. 9. to compose or calm (the stomach, nerves, etc.): *v.i.* 1. to become fixed, stationary, or permanent. 2. to descend or stop. 3. to sink to the bottom. 4. to cease from agitation; stabilize. 5. to establish a home (with *down*); especially, to marry and establish a home.

---

a in *cap,* ā in *cane,* ä in *father,* à in *abet,* e in *met,* ē in *be,* ē in *baker,* ê in *regent,* i in *pit,* ī in *fine,* i in *manifest,* o in *hot,* ō in *horse,* ō in *bone,*

6. to reach an agreement or decision. 7. to become confined to a specific area, as pain.

set·tle·ment (-mĕnt), *n.* 1. the act of settling. 2. the state of being settled. 3. a payment or adjustment. 4. a colony newly settled. 5. a village or community. 6. an agreement. 7. an establishment in an underprivileged area to provide social services: also **settlement house.**

set·tler (set'lĕr), *n.* 1. one that settles. 2. a colonist; one who settles in a new area, country, or colony.

set-to (set'tōō), *n., pl.* **-tos** ('tōōz), [Informal], 1. a fist fight. 2. a brief but vigorous argument or contest.

set-up ('up), *n.* 1. the way in which something is arranged or organized. 2. the details of this. 3. the things necessary for an alcoholic drink, as ice, ginger ale, etc., except for the liquor. 4. [Informal], *a)* a match or contest arranged so that one contestant will easily win; *b)* the contestant who will lose by such an arrangement; *c)* anyone who is easily duped.

sev·en (sev'n), *adj.* one more than six: *n.* the cardinal numeral that is the sum of six and one; 7; VII.

sev·en·fold (-fōld), *adj.* 1. having seven parts. 2. having seven times as much or as many: *adv.* seven times as much or as many.

seven seas, all the oceans of the world.

sev·en·teen (-tēn'), *adj.* one more than 16: *n.* the cardinal numeral that is the sum of 16 and one; 17; XVII.

sev·en·teenth (-tēnth'), *adj.* next after 16th; 17th: *n.* 1. the one after the 16th. 2. one of 17 equal parts.

sev·en·teen-year locust (sev'n-tēn-yir), a cicada which lives in the soil as a larva for up to 17 years before emerging in the adult form.

sev·enth (sev'nth), *adj.* next after sixth; 7th: *n.* 1. the one after the sixth. 2. one of seven equal parts.

sev·enth-day (-dā'), *adj.* [often S- D-], observing the Sabbath on Saturday, as some religious denominations.

seventh heaven, 1. in some ancient religions, the highest heaven, where God and the angels dwell. 2. perfect happiness; bliss.

sev·en·ti·eth ('n-ti-ith), *adj.* next after 69th: *n.* 1. the one after the 69th. 2. one of 70 equal parts.

sev·en·ty (sev'n-ti), *adj.* seven times 10: *n., pl.* **-ties,** 1. the cardinal numeral that is the sum of 69 and one; 70; LXX. 2. *pl.* years or numbers from 70 through 79 (preceded by *the*).

sev·en-up (sev'n-up'), *n.* a card game in which six cards are dealt to each player: seven points win the game.

sev·er (sev'ĕr), *v.t. & v.i.* 1. to separate or divide. 2. to cut or be cut open or through; break, as by force.

sev·er·a·ble (-â-b'l), *adj.* 1. that can be severed. 2. in *Law,* denoting a contract written so that the annulment of one part does not invalidate the whole. —**sev·er·a·bil'i·ty,** *n.*

sev·er·al (sev'ĕr-âl, sev'râl), *adj.* 1. distinct; separate. 2. consisting of more than two,

but not many; few. 3. different; respective: *n.* more than two persons or objects, but not many.

sev·er·al·ly (-i), *adv.* 1. separately; distinctly. 2. respectively.

sev·er·al·ty (-ti), *n.* 1. a state of separation from the rest. 2. the holding of real estate in one's own individual right.

sev·er·ance (sev'ĕr-âns, sev'râns), *n.* 1. the act of severing. 2. the state of being severed. 3. a separation or partition.

se·vere (sĕ-vir'), *adj.* **-ver'er, -ver'est,** 1. strictly adhering to rule; rigid. 2. austere; very plain. 3. harsh; stern; inflexible. 4. grave; serious. 5. painful; intense. 6. critical; grievous. 7. difficult. —**se·vere'ly,** *adv.* —**se·vere'ness,** *n.*

se·ver·i·ty (sĕ-ver'ĭ-ti), *n.* 1. the quality of being severe. 2. harshness; strictness. 3. exactness. 4. gravity. 5. rigor; sternness.

Se·vres (sev'râ), *n.* a fine, highly glazed French porcelain.

sew (sō), *v.t.* **sewed, sewn** or **sewed, sew'ing,** 1. to unite or fasten together with a needle and thread. 2. to make or repair in this way: *v.i.* to work with a needle and thread or at a sewing machine.

sew·age (sōō'ij), *n.* the waste matter carried away by sewers.

sew·er (sōō'ĕr), *n.* a pipe or drain, usually underground, for carrying away water and waste matter.

sew·er (sō'ĕr), *n.* one who sews.

sew·er·age (sōō'ĕr-ij), *n.* 1. sewage. 2. a system of sewers 3. the removal of waste matter and water by sewers.

sew·ing (sō'ing), *n.* 1. articles sewn or to be sewn. 2. the act of one who sews.

sewing machine, a machine operated by a foot treadle or by electricity and used for sewing.

sex (seks), *n.* 1. either of the two divisions into which animals, persons, and plants are divided according to reproductive function; male or female. 2. the character or distinction of being male or female. 3. the attraction of one sex for the other. 4. sexual intercourse.

sex-, a combining form meaning *six.*

sex·a·ge·nar·i·an (sek-sâ-ji-ner'i-ân), *n.* one who is sixty years old, or between sixty and seventy: *adj.* of or denoting a sexagenarian.

sex appeal, the qualities and characteristics that attract members of the opposite sex.

sex·cen·te·nar·y (seks sen'tĕ ner-i), *adj.* pertaining to 600 years: *n., pl.* **-nar·ies,** a 600th anniversary.

sex·en·ni·al (sek-sen'i-âl), *adj.* 1. comprising six years. 2. occurring every six years. —**sex·en'ni·al·ly,** *adv.*

sex hormone, any one of the hormones, as estrogen or testosterone, that affects the reproductive organs and secondary sex characteristics.

sex hygiene, the branch of hygiene that deals with sex and sexual behavior.

sex·ism (sek'sizm), *n.* the subjugation of one sex to the other; specifically, of women to men. —**sex'ist,** *adj. & n.*

sex·less (seks'lis), *adj.* 1. lacking sex; neuter. 2.

ō in dragon, ōō in crude, oo in wool, u in cup, ū in cure, ū in turn, ù in focus, oi in boy, ou in house, th in thin, th in sheathe, g in get, j in joy, y in yet.

lacking normal sexual desire or appeal. — **sex'less·ly**, *adv.* —**sex'less·ness**, *n.*

sex·ol·o·gy (sek-sol'ō-ji), *n.* the study or science of sexual behavior. —**sex·ol'o·gist**, *n.*

sex·tant (seks'tănt), *n.* an instrument for measuring angular distances, as of the sun or a star, from the horizon, used especially at sea to determine latitude and longitude of a ship.

sex·tet, sex·tette (seks-tet'), *n.* 1. a musical composition for six voices or instruments. 2. a company of six performers of such a composition. 3. any group of six.

sex·tile (seks'tl), *adj.* denoting 60°: *n.* the aspect or position of two heavenly bodies 60° apart.

sex·til·lion (seks-til'yŭn), *n.* 1. in the U.S. and France, the number indicated by 1 followed by 21 zeros. 2. in Great Britain and Germany, the number indicated by 1 followed by 36 zeros. —**sex·til'lionth**, *adj. & n.*

sex·to·dec·i·mo (seks-tō-des'ī-mō), *n., pl.* -mos, same as sixteenmo.

sex·ton (seks'tŏn), *n.* 1. a church official charged with maintenance of the church property; formerly, he also dug graves in the yard of the church. 2. an official in a synagogue who tends to everyday matters.

sex·tu·ple (seks-tōō'pl), *adj.* 1. having six parts. 2. having six times as much or as many.

sex·tu·plet (seks-tup'lit), *n.* 1. any one of six offspring born at a single birth. 2. a group of six.

sex·u·al (sek'shōō-wăl), *adj.* 1. of or pertaining to sex. 2. happening between the two sexes. 3. in *Biology*, denoting reproduction that occurs by union of male and female cells. — **sex'u·al·ly**, *adv.*

sex·u·al·i·ty (sek-shoo-wal'ī-ti), *n.* 1. the state of having sexual characteristics. 2. interest in or emphasis on sex. 3. a readiness or drive for sexual activity.

sex·y (sek'si), *adj.* **sex'i·er**, **sex'i·est**, [Informal], 1. erotic; intended to arouse sexual desire. 2. emphasizing sex or sexual activity. 3. arousing sexual desire. —**sex'i·ly**, *adv.* —**sex'i·ness**, *n.*

sgraf·fi·to (skra-fē'tō), *n., pl.* -fi'ti ('ti), 1. ceramic ware, a mural, etc. in which a design has been incised through an outer coating to reveal a ground of different color. 2. the method of producing such work. 3. a design incised on a work of this kind.

sh (sh), *interj.* silence! be quiet!

shab·by (shab'i), *adj.* -bi·er, -bi·est, 1. threadbare or worn, as old clothes. 2. wearing worn clothes. 3. dilapidated. 4. mean or contemptible. —**shab'bi·ly**, *adv.* —**shab'bi·ness**, *n.*

shack (shak), *n.* a small cabin or house that is roughly built and furnished; shanty.

shack·le (shak'l), *n.* 1. something to confine the hands or feet and obstruct free action, as fetters or handcuffs. 2. anything that restrains freedom. 3. any one of various devices for coupling or fastening: *v.t.* -led, -ling, 1. to put shackles on; fetter. 2. to restrain freedom, as of expression. 3. to unite or fasten with a shackle.

shad (shad), *n., pl.* **shad, shads**, a food fish

related to the herring and living in the Atlantic, but ascending rivers to spawn.

shad·dock (shad'ŏk), *n.* 1. a pear-shaped citrus fruit of the size and color of a grapefruit, but having a coarse-grained skin. 2. the tree on which this fruit grows.

shade (shād), *n.* 1. comparative darkness caused by the interception of rays of light. 2. a shady place. 3. gradation of color in regard to its mixture with black. 4. a screen or cover, as a window shade, lamp shade, etc. 5. a small difference or degree. 6. a ghost or phantom. 7. *pl. a)* the spirits of the dead; *b)* the abode of the dead. 8. *pl.* [Slang], sunglasses: *v.t.* **shad'ed**, **shad'ing**, 1. to screen from light or heat. 2. to darken or obscure. 3. to mark with gradations of light or color. 4. to depict shade in (a drawing, photograph, etc.): *v.i.* to vary slightly or by degrees.

shad·ing ('ing), *n.* 1. representation of light and shade. 2. a slight variation. 3. protection against light or heat.

sha·doof (shā-dōōf'), *n.* a bucket hung from a weighted rod, used in countries at the eastern end of the Mediterranean for raising water for irrigation.

shad·ow (shad'ō), *n.* 1. shade within defined limits, as a dark area cast by a body intercepting rays of light. 2. a shaded part of a picture. 3. a feeling of doubt, gloom, etc., or a cause of this. 4. a ghost. 5. a small degree; trace. 6. an inseparable companion. 7. a detective: *v.t.* 1. to darken; cast a shadow upon. 2. to follow and watch closely, as a detective. —**shad'ow·less**, *adj.*

shad·ow-box (-boks), *v.i.* to practice boxing by making motions as if boxing with one's shadow. —**shad'ow-box·ing**, *n.*

shad·ow·graph (-graf), *n.* a picture or silhouette thrown on a lighted surface by interposing an object, the hands, etc. between a source of light and the surface.

shad·ow·y (-i), *adj.* 1. full of shade or shadow. 2. unreal; illusory. 3. dim; obscure. —**shad'ow·i·ness**, *n.*

shad·y (shād'i), *adj.* **shad'i·er**, **shad'i·est**, 1. full of shade; shaded. 2. giving shade. 3. [Informal], dubious; suspected of being dishonest. —**shad'i·ness**, *n.*

shaft (shaft), *n.* 1. an arrow or spear. 2. anything directed with force. 3. a long, narrow passage in the earth, as a mine entrance. 4. either of the parallel poles between which an animal is hitched for drawing a vehicle. 5. a bar that transmits motion to a mechanical part. 6. a column or the main part of a column between the base and capital. 7. a vertical, enclosed space in a building, as for ventilation or for an elevator: *v.t.* [Slang], to cheat, deceive, trick, etc.

shaft·ing (shaf'ting), *n.* a system of shafts for transmitting motion, conveying air, etc.

shag (shag), *n.* 1. coarsely shredded tobacco. 2. a rough, woolly nap, as on some cloth. 3. cloth, carpeting, etc. with such a nap. 4. any bushy, tangled mass: *v.t.* **shagged**, **shag'ging**, to run after and retrieve (baseballs hit while practicing).

shag·gy ('i), *adj.* -gi·er, -gi·est, 1. having long

hair or wool. 2. with a rough nap, as some cloth. 3. untidy; unkempt. 4. straggly. —shag'gi·ly, adv. —shag'gi·ness, n.

sha·green (shā-grēn'), n. 1. the skins of horses, seals, etc. prepared without tanning and having a roughly grained surface. 2. the hard, rough skin of sharks or dogfish, used as a polisher.

shah (shä), n. a title of the sovereign of Iran.

shai·tan (shī-tän'), n. 1. [often S-], among Moslems, Satan. 2. a fiend or evil spirit.

shake (shāk), v.t. & v.i. shook, shak'en, shak'ing, 1. to move back and forth or up and down with a quick, short motion. 2. to mix, force, scatter, etc. by such motion. 3. to shiver or cause to shiver. 4. to make or become disturbed or upset. 5. to become or cause to become unsteady. 6. to clasp (a person's hand) in greeting: n. 1. the act of shaking. 2. a vibration or trembling. 3. a wood shingle. 4. a milkshake. 5. pl. [Informal], a spell of trembling, as from illness, a hangover, fear, etc. 6. [Informal], an instant; jiffy.

shake·down ('doun), n. 1. a thorough search. 2. [Slang], extortion, as by threats or blackmail: adj. denoting a cruise, flight, etc. for testing new equipment, training personnel, etc.

shak·en ('n), past participle of shake.

shak·er (shā'kēr), n. 1. a person or thing that shakes. 2. a device or container for shaking. 3. [S-], a member of a former religious sect that advocated celibacy and community living. —Shak'er·ism, n.

Shake·spear·e·an (shāk-spir'i-ăn), adj. of or like the works or style of William Shakespeare (1564-1616), English playwright and poet: n. a scholar of Shakespeare's works.

shake·up (shāk'up), n. a drastic business reorganization, especially with changes in personnel.

shak·o (shak'ō), n., pl. shak'os, a kind of high, stiff military hat with a visor and plume.

Shak·ti (shuk'ti), n. in Hinduism, the wife of a deity, worshiped as the female divine power. —Shak'tism, n.

shak·y (shā'ki), adj. shak'i·er, shak'i·est, 1. not strong, sound, or steady. 2. trembling. 3. nervous. 4. questionable; dubious. —shak'i·ly, adv. —shak'i·ness, n.

shale (shāl), n. a laminated rock that splits easily and is formed from hardened clay.

shall (shal), v., past tense, should, an auxiliary used in the first person to express simple futurity, and in the second and third persons to express authority, obligation, or compulsion.

shal·loon (shǎ-lōōn'), n. a kind of twilled woolen fabric used for linings.

shal·lop (shal'ŏp), n. any one of various ships or boats formerly used in shallow waters, fitted with oars or sails or both.

shal·lot (shǎ-lot'), n. 1. a plant like the onion, with small clusters of bulbs used for flavoring. 2. a green onion.

shal·low (shal'ō), adj. 1. having little depth. 2. not profound; superficial; trifling: n. a flat place where the water is not deep; shoal: usually used in the plural.

sha·lom (shä-lōm'), n. & interj. [Hebrew], peace: traditional Jewish greeting or farewell.

shalt (shalt), archaic second person singular, present indicative, of shall.

sham (sham), n. 1. a counterfeit or imitation intended to deceive. 2. hypocritical behavior. 3. a person who is a fraud: adj. feigned; false; imitation: v.t. & v.i. shammed, sham'ming, to pretend; feign.

sha·man (shä'mǎn, shā'-), n., pl. sha'mans, a priest or medicine man of shamanism.

sha·man·ism (-izm), n. 1. in northeast Asia, a religion with the belief that the shamans can bring good or evil by their influence with the spirits of these forces. 2. a similar religion of some Eskimos and American Indians. —sha'man·ist, n. —sha·man·is'tic, adj.

Sha·mash (shä'mǎsh), n. the sun god of the Babylonians and Assyrians.

sham·ble (sham'bl), v.i. -bled, -bling, to walk awkwardly and unsteadily; shuffle: n. a shambling gait.

sham·bles (-blz), n.pl. 1. a slaughterhouse. 2. a place or state of great destruction, ruin, or disorder.

shame (shām), n. 1. a painful feeling caused by a sense of guilt, impropriety, or dishonor. 2. that which causes shame. 3. something that is a cause of regret or outrage: v.t. shamed, sham'ing, 1. to cause to feel shame. 2. to disgrace or dishonor. 3. to force or drive by a sense of shame.

shame·faced ('fāst), adj. 1. bashful; modest. 2. ashamed. —shame·fac·ed·ly (shām-fās'id-li), adv. —shame·fac'ed·ness, n.

shame·ful ('fǔl), adj. 1. causing shame; disgraceful. 2. indecent; offensive. —shame'ful·ly, adv. —shame'ful·ness, n.

shame·less ('lis), adj. immodest; impudent; brazen. —shame'less·ly, adv. —shame'less·ness, n.

sham·mer (sham'ēr), n. one who shams.

sham·my (sham'i), n., pl. -mies, same as chamois (senses 2 & 3).

sham·poo (sham-pōō'), v.t. -pooed', -poo'ing, 1. to wash (the hair and scalp), especially with a shampoo. 2. to wash (a carpet, upholstery, etc.) with a shampoo: n. 1. the act of shampooing. 2. a special liquid soap or other substance that produces suds to use for washing. —sham·poo'er, n.

sham·rock (sham'rok), n. a trefoil, cloverlike plant, or a design like this, used as the emblem of Ireland.

shan·dy·gaff (shan'di·gaf), n. a drink made up of a mixture of beer and ginger ale or lemonade: also shan'dy.

shang·hai (shang'hi), v.t. [S-], any one of a breed of poultry with long, feathered legs: v.t. -haied, -hai·ing, to kidnap, usually by drugging, for work as a sailor.

shank (shangk), n. 1. the leg from the knee to the ankle. 2. the whole leg. 3. the long part of an instrument or tool. 4. the body of a piece of type. 5. the narrow part of the sole of a shoe below the instep.

shan't (shant), shall not.

shan·tung (shan'tung'), n. a silk or silky fabric with a nubby surface.

shan·ty (shan'ti), n., pl. -ties, a rude hut; shack; roughly built dwelling.

shape (shāp), n. 1. the physical form or figure of a thing. 2. the human form; figure. 3. a definite pattern. 4. assumed appearance. 5. sort; kind. 6. [Informal], condition of the body: v.t. shaped, shap'ing, 1. to make into a particular form. 2. to arrange or devise. 3. to adapt. 4. to direct; regulate: v.i. to take shape (often with up).

shape·less ('lis), adj. 1. not having a distinct shape; formless. 2. not pleasingly shaped. —shape'less·ly, adv. —shape'less·ness, n.

shape·ly ('li), adj. -li·er, -li·est, having a graceful or pleasing shape: said especially of a woman. —shape'li·ness, n.

shard (shärd), n. 1. a fragment, as of broken pottery. 2. a shell or scale.

share (sher), n. 1. a portion or part allotted or belonging to one. 2. any one of the equal parts of the capital stock of a corporation. 3. a plowshare: v.t. shared, shar'ing, 1. to divide among two or more. 2. to partake of or use with others: v.i. to have a share or part.

share·crop ('krop), v.i. & v.t. -cropped, -cropping, to farm (land) for a share of the crop. —share'crop·per, n.

share·hold·er ('hōl·dēr), n. a person who owns shares of stock in a corporation.

shark (shärk), n. 1. a large, gray, voracious, marine fish with sharp teeth. 2. a swindler. 3. [Slang], an expert.

shark·skin ('skin), n. 1. the skin of a shark or leather made from it. 2. a smooth, silky fabric of wool, rayon, cotton, etc., used for suits and the like.

sharp (shärp), adj. 1. having a very thin edge or fine point. 2. terminating in an edge or point; not rounded. 3. peaked or ridged. 4. keen; perceptive. 5. severe, as a pain. 6. harsh, as temper. 7. having an acid or pungent taste. 8. biting and cold, as a wind. 9. shrewd. 10. active. 11. vigilant. 12. crafty or dishonest. 13. distinct in outline. 14. in Music, above the true pitch. 15. [Slang], welldressed: v.t. & v.i. to make or become sharp: n. 1. in Music, a note one half step higher than another, or the symbol for this. 2. [Informal], an expert: adv. 1. promptly; on the minute. 2. abruptly. 3. acutely. 4. in Music, above the true pitch. —sharp'ly, adv. —sharp'ness, n.

sharp·en ('n), v.t. & v.i. to make or become sharp or sharper. —sharp'en·er, n.

sharp·er (shärp'ēr), n. a cheat; swindler.

sharp·eyed ('īd'), adj. having keen sight: also sharp-sighted.

sharp·ie (shär'pi), n. 1. a New England fishing boat with a flat bottom and one or two sails. 2. [Informal], a swindler; sharper.

sharp·set (shärp'set'), adj. 1. having a very keen appetite. 2. set so as to be sharp.

sharp·shoot·er ('shoot·ēr), n. a skilled marksman. —sharp'shoot·ing, n.

sharp-tongued ('tungd'), adj. caustic; harsh; sarcastic.

sharp-wit·ted ('wit'id), adj. mentally quick and perceptive. —sharp'-wit'ted·ly, adv. —sharp'-wit'ted·ness, n.

shat·ter (shat'ēr), v.t. 1. to break into many pieces, as by a blow. 2. to damage, impair, or destroy: v.i. to be broken, damaged, impaired, etc.

shat·ter·proof (-prōōf), adj. made to resist shattering.

shave (shāv), v.t. shaved, shaved or shav'en, shav'ing, 1. to cut or pare off with a razor or other sharp-edged instrument. 2. to make bare by cutting off (the hair) to the surface. 3. to slice thin sections from. 4. to skim near; barely touch; graze: v.i. to use a razor in removing hair: n. 1. the operation of shaving the beard. 2. a mounted blade used for shaving off thin slices of wood, as a spokeshave.

shav·er ('ēr), n. 1. one who shaves, as a barber. 2. a small electrical device for shaving; electric razor. 3. [Informal], a lad; boy.

shav·ing ('ing), n. 1. the act of one who shaves. 2. a thin slice pared off.

shawl (shôl), n. an oblong or square cloth worn as a loose outer covering for the shoulders and sometimes the head, especially by women.

shawm (shôm), n. an ancient wind instrument of the oboe class.

shay (shā), n. [Dialectal], a light carriage; chaise.

she (shē), pron., pl. they, 1. the female personified; any female person or animal: sometimes used in combination, as she-goat. 2. an object traditionally regarded as of feminine gender, as a ship. 3. the feminine third person singular pronoun: n., pl. shes, a female person or animal.

shea (shē), n. a tropical tree of western Africa that yields a kind of fat or solid oil (shea butter), used as a food, in soap, etc.

sheaf (shēf), n., pl. sheaves (shēvz), 1. a bundle of stalks of grain that have been bound together. 2. enough arrows to fill a quiver, usually 24. 3. a bundle of things bound together, as papers: v.t. to sheave.

shear (shir), v.t. sheared, sheared or shorn, shear'ing, 1. to cut or clip, especially with shears. 2. to cut or clip (hair or wool) from. 3. to wrench or tear off. 4. to divest (of power, etc.): v.i. 1. to use shears. 2. to come apart or break: n. 1. a machine used in cutting sheet metal. 2. the act or result of shearing.

shear·ing ('ing), n. 1. the act or process of cutting with shears. 2. the product from clipping, as the amount of wool cut from sheep.

shears (shirz), n.pl. 1. large scissors: also called pair of shears. 2. an apparatus or machine with opposed blades, used as for cutting metal. 3. an apparatus for raising heavy weights: also shear'legs.

shear·wa·ter (shir'wôt·ēr), n. a black-and-white sea bird related to the albatross, that skims the water in flight.

---

a in cap, ā in cane, ä in father, à in abet, e in met, ē in be, ē in baker, ē in regent, i in pit, ī in fine, i in manifest, o in hot, ô in horse, ō in bone,

sheat-fish (shēt'fish), *n.*, *pl.* **-fish, -fish-es**, a very large freshwater catfish of Europe.

sheath (shēth), *n.*, *pl.* **sheaths** (shēthz, shēths), l. a case for a blade, as of a knife or sword. 2. in *Biology*, any one of several structures, receptacles, or coverings resembling this. 3. a dress that fits closely.

sheath-bill ('bil), *n.* a sea bird of antarctic regions with a horny sheath covering the base of the upper mandible.

sheathe (shē*th*), *v.t.* **sheathed, sheath'ing**, l. to put into a sheath or scabbard. 2. to encase with a protective covering. 3. to retract (claws).

sheath-ing (shē'*th*ing), *n.* l. the coating or covering of a ship on the bottom or hull. 2. the inner boards or waterproof material of the walls or roof of a house. 3. material for any covering like this.

sheave (shēv), *n.* a grooved wheel in a block or pulley over which the rope runs: *v.t.* **sheaved, sheav'ing**, to gather and bind into a sheaf.

she-bang (shē-bang'), *n.* [Informal], a device, event, thing, etc.: in the phrase *the whole shebang*.

she-been (shi-bēn'), *n.* in Ireland or Scotland, a place where intoxicating liquor is sold illegally.

shed (shed), *v.t.* **shed, shed'ding**, l. to pour out; emit. 2. to cause to flow out or off. 3. to diffuse; radiate. 4. to cast off (hair, feathers, etc.) by natural process: *v.i.* to cast off hair, feathers, etc.: *n.* l. that which sheds; specifically, a watershed. 2. a small, rude structure or lean-to, used for storage or shelter. 3. a large, hangarlike building, often with front or sides open.

she'd (shēd), l. she had. 2. she would.

sheen (shēn), *n.* brightness; gloss; luster. — **sheen'y**, *adj.* **sheen'i-er, sheen'i-est**.

sheep (shēp), *n.*, *pl.* **sheep**, l. a ruminant mammal, valued for its wool and for its flesh, called *mutton*. 2. a person who is meek, easily led, etc.

sheep dog, a dog trained to herd sheep.

sheep-ish ('ish), *adj.* l. diffident; backward; shy. 2. embarrassed because of chagrin. — **sheep'ish-ly**, *adv.* —**sheep'ish-ness**, *n.*

sheeps-head (shēps'hed), *n.* a large food fish of the Atlantic coast of the U.S.

sheep-skin (shēp'skin), *n.* l. the skin of a sheep. 2. such a skin dressed with the wool on, as for a coat. 3. parchment made from the skin of a sheep, often used for documents, as diplomas. 4. [Informal], a diploma.

sheer (shir), *adj.* l. unmixed; absolute. 2. very thin or transparent. 3. precipitous: *adv.* l. absolutely; utterly. 2. very steeply: *n.* l. the upward curve of the lines forward of a ship, as viewed from the side. 2. a change in course; deviation: *v.i. & v.t.* to deviate from a course; swerve; turn aside.

sheet (shēt), *n.* l. a large, thin piece of anything, as glass, metal, etc. 2. a broad piece of linen or cotton to cover a bed. 3. a piece of paper. 4. [Informal], a newspaper. 5. a broad expanse or surface, as of ice. 6. a rope or chain attached to a sail to extend

or shorten it. 7. the open space in the bow or stern of a boat.

sheet anchor, a large, heavy anchor for use only in emergency.

sheet-ing ('ing), *n.* l. material for making sheets. 2. thin material for covering or lining a wall or other surface.

sheet metal, metal that has been rolled thin in sheets.

sheet music, music printed on sheets of paper and left unbound.

sheik, sheikh (shēk), *n.* l. the head of an Arab family, clan, tribe, or village. 2. a Moslem high priest, judge, or other official. —**sheik'-dom, sheikh'dom**, *n.*

shek-el (shek'l), *n.* l. an ancient Jewish coin or weight. 2. *pl.* [Slang], money.

shel-drake (shel'drāk), *n.*, *pl.* **-drakes, -drake**, l. a large, Old-World, wild duck, often brightly colored. 2. same as **merganser**.

shelf (shelf), *n.*, *pl.* **shelves**, l. a flat board attached to a wall for holding things. 2. a flat, projecting ledge of rock. 3. a sand bar.

shell (shel), *n.* l. a hard, outside covering, as of an egg, nut, insect, etc. 2. something like this in being hollow, or a covering or framework. 3. a hollow projectile filled with an explosive charge. 4. a cartridge, as for a shotgun. 5. a light, narrow racing boat rowed by a team: *v.t.* l. to strip or remove the shell of. 2. to separate from the ear or cob. 3. to bombard with explosives: *v.i.* to separate from the shell.

she'll (shēl), l. she will. 2. she shall.

shel-lac, shel-lack (shē-lak'), *n.* l. crude resin lac refined and produced in thin sheets or shells. 2. a kind of thin, clear varnish made from this lac and alcohol: *v.t.* **-lacked', -lack'ing**, l. to cover with shellac. 2. [Slang], to beat decisively.

-shelled (sheld), a combining form meaning *having (a particular kind of) shell.*

shell-fish (shel'fish), *n.*, *pl.* **-fish, -fish-es**, a water animal with a shell, as an oyster, crab, etc.

shel-ter (shel'tēr), *n.* l. that which protects or shields, as from danger, the weather, etc. 2. the state of being protected; protection, refuge, etc.: *v.t.* to protect or shield; provide refuge. —**shel'ter-er**, *n.* —**shel'ter-less**, *adj.*

shelve (shelv), *v.t.* **shelved, shelv'ing**, l. to place on a shelf. 2. to furnish with shelves. 3. to postpone indefinitely. 4. to dismiss or retire from active service.

shelves (shelvz), *n.* plural of **shelf**.

shelv-ing (shelv'ing), *n.* l. material for shelves. 2. shelves collectively.

She-ma (shē-mä'), *n.* passages from Deuteronomy declaring the basic principle of Jewish belief, which proclaims the oneness of God.

she-nan-i-gan (shi-nan'i-gn), *n.* usually *pl.* [Informal], mischief; trickery; tricks.

She-ol (shē'ōl), *n.* in the *Bible*, the dwelling place of the dead, in the depths of the earth.

shep-herd (shep'ērd), *n.* l. one who tends sheep. 2. a clergyman; pastor: *v.t.* to tend as a shepherd. —shep'herd-ess, *n.fem.*

Sher-a-ton (sher'à-tŏn), *adj.* denoting a style of

ò in dragon, ōō in crude, oo in wool, u in cup, ū in cure, û in turn, ů in focus, oi in boy, ou in house, th in thin, *th* in shea*th*e, g in get, j in joy, y in yet.

furniture developed in England by Thomas Sheraton (1751-1806), characterized by simplicity, straight lines, etc.

sher·bet (shŭr'bĕt), n. 1. a fruit-flavored, frozen dessert like an ice, but made with egg white, milk, or gelatin. 2. [British], a cold drink made with fruit juice, water, and sugar.

sherd (shŭrd), n. same as shard.

sher·iff (sher'if), n. the chief law-enforcement officer of a county.

Sher·pa (shŭr'pä, sher'-), n., pl. -pas, -pa, one of a Tibetan people famous as mountain climbers.

sher·ry (sher'i), n., pl. -ries, 1. an amber-colored, fortified Spanish wine. 2. any similar wine made elsewhere.

she's (shēz), 1. she is. 2. she has.

Shet·land pony (shet'lănd), any one of a breed of sturdy ponies, originally from the Shetland Islands, off the coast of Scotland.

shew (shō), n. & v.t. & v.i. shewed, shewn or shewed, shew'ing, archaic spelling of show.

shew·bread (shō'brĕd), n. in an ancient Jewish rite, twelve loaves of unleavened bread placed on the altar of the Temple on the Sabbath.

shib·bo·leth (shib'ō-lĕth), n. 1. in the Bible, the test word used to distinguish the enemy: Judges xii, 4-6. 2. any test word or password. 3. any phrase, practice, etc. that distinguishes a certain party, faction, etc.

shied (shīd), past tense and past participle of shy.

shield (shēld), n. 1. a broad piece of defensive armor worn on the forearm to avert blows, weapons, etc. 2. something for defense or protection. 3. an escutcheon. 4. something shaped like a shield: v.t. & v.i. to defend or protect.

shift (shift), n. 1. a turning from one thing to another; change; substitution. 2. an expedient or stratagem. 3. a trick; evasion. 4. a gearshift. 5. a regularly scheduled work period. 6. the persons working during such a period. 7. a change in direction, as of the wind: v.t. 1. to change from one place or person to another. 2. to replace by another. 3. to change the arrangement of (gears): v.i. 1. to alter or change. 2. to get along; manage.

shift·less ('lis), adj. lazy; lacking ambition or desire for betterment. —shift'less·ly, adv.

shift·y ('i), adj. shift'i·er, shift'i·est, tricky; evasive. —shift'i·ly, adv. —shift'i·ness, n.

shill (shil), n. [Slang], one who poses as a customer, bettor, etc. to lure others into participating, as at a gambling house or auction.

shil·le·lagh (shi-lā'li, 'lä), n. [Irish], a cudgel: also spelled shil·la'lah.

shil·ling (shil'ing), n. a British coin and money of account, equal to one twentieth of a pound.

shil·ly-shal·ly (shil'i-shal-i), n. vacillation, especially over trifles: v.i. -lied, -ly·ing, to vacillate, especially over trifles.

shim (shim), n. a thin wedge, as of wood or metal, for filling in or leveling: v.t. shimmed,

shim'ming, to fill in or level with a shim or shims.

shim·mer (shim'ēr), v.i. to shine unsteadily; flicker: n. a tremulous gleam; flicker.

shim·my (shim'i), n. 1. a jazz dance of the 1920's, marked by shaking of the body. 2. a distinct vibration or wobble, as of the front wheels of a car: v.i. -mied, my·ing, 1. to dance the shimmy. 2. to vibrate or wobble.

shin (shin), n. the front of the leg between the ankle and knee: v.t. & v.i. shinned, shin'ning, to climb by means of the hands and legs: also shin'ny.

shin (shēn), n. the 21st letter of the Hebrew alphabet.

shin·bone (shin'bōn), n. same as tibia.

shin·dig (shin'dig), n. [Informal], a party, dance, or other informal social gathering.

shine (shīn), v.i. shone, shin'ing, 1. to emit rays of light. 2. to be bright or beautiful. 3. to be distinguished; excel. 4. to show clearly: v.t. 1. to direct the light of. 2. shined, shin'ing, to make shiny by buffing or polishing: n. 1. the quality of being bright; brightness. 2. a bright polish on shoes, boots, etc. 3. gloss. 4. splendor. 5. [Slang], a liking or fancy.

shin·er ('ēr), n. 1. pl. -ers, -er, a kind of silvery, freshwater minnow, often used as fish bait. 2. [Slang], a black eye.

shin·gle (shing'g'l), n. 1. a thin, wedge-shaped piece of wood, slate, etc. used for roofing. 2. coarse, round, waterworn gravel. 3. a beach or other area covered with this gravel. 4. a short haircut, tapered at the nape of the neck. 5. [Informal], a small signboard, as of a doctor or lawyer: v.t. -gled, -gling, 1. to cover (a roof, etc.) with shingles. 2. to free (puddled iron) from impurities. —shin'gly, adj. -gli·er, -gli·est.

shin·gles ('g'lz), n. an acute, virus skin disease characterized by a skin eruption in which blisters follow the course of a nerve.

shin·guard (shin'gärd), n. a thickly padded protective covering for the shins, worn as by baseball catchers and hockey goalies.

shin·ing (shīn'ing), adj. 1. emitting light; radiant. 2. eminent; distinguished.

shin·splints (shin'splints), n.pl. painful strain of muscles of the lower leg.

Shin·to (shin'tō), n. a religion of Japan, a system of nature and ancestor worship. — Shin'to·ism, n. —Shin'to·ist, n. & adj.

shin·y (shīn'i), adj. shin'i·er, shin'i·est, 1. diffusing light; bright. 2. glossy; polished. — shin'i·ness, n.

ship (ship), n. 1. any large vessel powered by an engine and traveling in deep water. 2. a sailing vessel with at least three square-rigged masts. 3. the crew and officers of a ship. 4. an aircraft: v.t. shipped, ship'ping, 1. to place or take on board a ship. 2. to carry or send by any method of transportation. 3. to take in (water) over the side. 4. to put in proper position: v.i. 1. to engage to serve on board ship. 2. to go on board. —ship'per, n.

-ship (ship), a suffix meaning state, condition, quality; skill, art; all (specified) persons collectively; status, office or position of.

---

a in cap, ā in cane, ä in father, ȧ in abet, e in met, ē in be, ē in baker, ẽ in regent, i in pit, ī in fine, i in manifest, o in hot, ō in horse, ō in bone,

ship-board ('bôrd), *n.* a ship: in the phrase *on shipboard*: *adj.* used or happening on a ship.

ship-build-ing ('bil-ding), *n.* the business of designing and building ships. —**ship'build-er,** *n.*

ship-mate ('māt), *n.* a fellow sailor on the same ship.

ship-ment ('mènt), *n.* 1. goods shipped. 2. a quantity of goods shipped at one time.

ship-ping ('ing), *n.* 1. the act of sending or conveying goods. 2. ships collectively, as those in a port or belonging to a country.

ship-shape ('shāp), *adj.* in good order; neat and trim: *adv.* neatly.

ship-wreck ('rek), *n.* 1. a total or partial loss of a ship at sea, as by storm, collision, etc. 2. a wrecked ship or its remains. 3. ruin; failure: *v.t.* to cause to suffer shipwreck.

ship-wright ('rīt), *n.* a person whose trade is to help build or repair ships.

ship-yard ('yärd), *n.* a place where ships are built or repaired.

shire (shīr), *n.* in Great Britain, a county.

shirk (shûrk), *v.t. & v.i.* to avoid or get out of (duty, work, etc.). —**shirk'er,** *n.*

shirr (shûr), *n.* same as shirring: *v.t.* 1. to gather (material) in shirring. 2. to bake (eggs) in buttered dishes.

shirr-ing ('ing), *n.* a gathering made in material by drawing the cloth together with small stitches.

shirt (shûrt), *n.* 1. a garment worn by men or boys on the upper part of the body, typically with sleeves, a collar, and a buttoned opening in the front. 2. a similar garment for women or girls. 3. an undershirt.

shirt-tail ('tāl), *n.* the part of a shirt below the waist: *adj.* [Informal], only distantly related.

shirt-waist ('wāst), *n.* 1. a woman's blouse made in the style of a shirt. 2. a dress with a bodice in this style: also shirtwaist dress.

shish ke-bab (shish' kĕ-bäb), *n.* a dish of kebabs, often of lamb.

shit-tah (shit'ä), *n., pl.* **shit'tahs, shit'tim** ('im), in the *Bible*, a tree of Palestine, probably the acacia.

shit-tim (shit'im), *n.* in the *Bible*, the fine-grained, yellowish-brown wood of the shittah, used in making the Jewish tabernacle: *Exodus* xxv, 10; 13: also shittim wood.

shiv (shiv), *n.* [Slang], a knife.

shiv-a-ree (shiv-á-rē'), *n.* a mock serenade with horns, pans, and other noisemakers, for a newly married couple.

shiv-er (shiv'ĕr), *n.* 1. a trembling or quivering from fear, cold, etc. 2. a splinter or sliver: *v.i.* 1. to tremble from cold, fear, etc. 2. to splinter or shatter: *v.t.* to cause to splinter or shatter.

shiv-er-y (-i), *adj.* 1. shivering from cold, fear, etc. 2. frightening; terrifying. 3. easily broken or shattered.

shoal (shōl), *n.* 1. a school of fish. 2. a large crowd. 3. a place where the sea or a river is shallow. 4. a sand bar: *v.i.* to become shallow.

shock (shok), *n.* 1. a sudden, violent blow, impact, collision, etc. 2. a strong emotional disturbance. 3. the cause of such a disturbance. 4. the effect caused on the nerves and muscles by the passage of electrical current through the body. 5. body prostration caused by insufficient circulation of the blood and marked by a drop in blood pressure, rapid pulse, etc.: *v.t.* 1. to give a shock to; horrify, distress, etc. 2. to give an electrical shock to.

shock (shok), *n.* 1. a number of sheaves of grain set up in conical form after reaping. 2. a tangled mass of hair.

shock absorber, a device attached to the springs of a motor vehicle to absorb jolts and shocks.

shock-er ('ĕr), *n.* 1. a person or thing that shocks. 2. a sensational novel, play, etc.

shock-ing ('ing), *adj.* 1. causing intense surprise, distress, etc. 2. disgusting; offensive.

shock-proof ('prŏŏf), *adj.* unaffected by shock.

shock therapy, the treatment of certain mental disorders by using electricity, drugs, etc., producing convulsions or coma.

shock troops, troops leading an attack.

shod (shod), past tense and past participle of shoe.

shod-dy (shod'i), *n., pl.* **-dies,** 1. cheap woolen cloth made from fibers shredded from used fabrics and rewoven. 2. anything inferior, especially an inferior imitation: *adj.* **-di-er, -di-est,** 1. made of cheap, inferior material. 2. poorly made. 3. sham. 4. mean. —**shod'di-ly,** *adv.* —**shod'di-ness,** *n.*

shoe (shŏŏ), *n.* 1. a covering for the human foot, usually of leather. 2. a horseshoe. 3. a metal band on the runner of a sled. 4. the casing of a pneumatic tire. 5. the contact plate beneath an electric train by which it picks up current from the third rail. 6. the part of a brake that applies friction to the wheel: *v.t.* shod or shoed, shoe'ing, to furnish or fit with shoes.

shoe-horn ('hôrn), *n.* an implement of metal, plastic, horn, etc. used to slip the heel into a shoe.

shoe-lace ('lās), *n.* a lace or cord used for lacing a shoe.

shoe-mak-er ('māk-ĕr), *n.* a person whose business or trade is making or repairing shoes.

shoe-shine ('shīn), *n.* 1. the act of cleaning and polishing a pair of shoes. 2. the shiny appearance of shoes after polishing.

shoe-string ('string), *n.* 1. a shoelace. 2. a very small amount of money.

shoe tree, a piece of wood or metal put in a shoe to help keep its shape when not being worn.

sho-far (shō'fĕr), *n.* a ram's horn used in ancient times as a trumpet, and now blown in synagogues during Rosh Hashana and Yom Kippur.

sho-gun (shō'gun, 'gŏŏn), *n.* formerly, any one of the military governors of Japan.

shone (shōn), alternate past tense and past participle of shine.

shoo (shŏŏ), *interj.* go away! be off! *v.t.* shooed, shoo'ing, to drive or scare away, as chickens, by crying "shoo."

shook (shook), *n.* 1. a set of pieces for a box, barrel, etc. ready to be assembled. 2. a pile of grain sheaves set up for drying; shock.

shook (shook), past tense of shake.

shoot (shōōt), *v.t.* **shot, shoot'ing,** 1. to let fly or discharge with a sudden force, as a bullet, arrow, etc. 2. to strike, wound, or kill with a shot. 3. to thrust; hurl. 4. to pass swiftly over, along, etc. 5. to photograph. 6. to emit. 7. to variegate (*with* streaks of color, etc.). 8. in *Sports,* to direct (a ball, etc.) toward the objective. 9. to score (points, a goal, etc.): *v.i.* 1. to protrude or project. 2. to discharge bullets, arrows, etc. 3. to rush along. 4. to sprout; grow rapidly. 5. to be felt suddenly, as pain: *n.* 1. a young branch or growth. 2. a shooting match, trip, etc. 3. the launching of a guided missile, rocket, etc.: *interj.* start talking!

shooting star, same as **meteor.**

shoot-out (shōōt'out), *n.* 1. a battle with handguns, etc., as between police and criminals. 2. any confrontation to settle a dispute, conflict, etc.

shop (shop), *n.* 1. a place where goods are sold retail; especially, a small store selling a certain kind of goods. 2. a place where a certain kind of work is done. 3. one's business or profession as a subject of conversation, as to talk *shop:* *v.i.* **shopped, shop'ping,** to visit shops to look over or purchase goods.

shop-keep-er (shop'kē-pēr), *n.* a person who owns or manages a shop, or small store.

shop-lift-er (lif'tēr), *n.* a person who steals goods from a store during shopping hours. —**shop'lift-ing,** *n.*

shop-per ('ēr), *n.* 1. one who shops. 2. a person whose job is shopping for others. 3. a person whose job is comparing prices in different stores.

shopping center, a number of business establishments grouped together and having a common parking area.

shop-talk ('tôk), *n.* 1. conversation about work outside of business hours. 2. a specialized vocabulary of those in the same line of work.

shop-worn (wôrn), *adj.* soiled, frayed, etc. from being handled in a store.

shore (shôr), *n.* 1. the coast or land adjacent to a body of water. 2. a prop or support: *v.t.* shored, shor'ing, to support by a shore or shores.

shore-line ('līn), *n.* the line where a body of water and the shore meet.

shore patrol, military police of the U.S. Navy, Marine Corps, or Coast Guard, on shore.

shorn (shôrn), alternate past participle of **shear.**

short (shôrt), *adj.* 1. not long in space or time. 2. not extending or ranging far. 3. not tall. 4. insufficient or incorrect in amount. 5. not retentive. 6. abrupt. 7. brief. 8. crumbly or flaky, as pastry made with much shortening. 9. brittle: said of metal. 10. not prolonged in sound. 11. not possessing a commodity or security at time of sale: *n.* 1. something that is short. 2. *pl. a)* short trousers. *b)* men's short underpants. 3. a short circuit: *adv.* 1. abruptly. 2. briefly. 3. rudely. 4. lacking in distance: *v.t. & v.i.* 1. to provide less than needed. 2. to short-circuit. —**short'ness,** *n.*

short-age ('ij), *n.* a deficiency.

short-bread ('bred), *n.* a kind of rich cookie made with much shortening.

short-cake ('kāk), *n.* a light biscuit, spongecake, or the like, served with fruit, whipped cream, etc.

short-change ('chānj'), *v.t. & v.i.* **-changed', -chang'ing,** [Informal], to give less money than is due in change.

short circuit, 1. a condition of low resistance between two points in an electric circuit resulting in an excessive flow of current off to one side, often causing damage. 2. [Informal], the disrupted electric circuit caused by this. —**short'-cir'cuit,** *v.t. & v.i.*

short-com-ing ('kum-ing), *n.* a deficiency, fault, failure, etc.

short-cut ('kut), *n.* 1. a shorter way to get to the same place. 2. a method or manner of doing something that will save time or effort.

short-en ('n), *v.t. & v.i.* 1. to make or become short or shorter in time, extent, or measure. 2. to furl, as a sail, so that less canvas is exposed to the wind. 3. to become or cause to become flaky by adding shortening, as some pastry.

short-en-ing ('n-ing, 'ning), *n.* lard, butter, or the like used to make pastry rich and flaky.

short-hand ('hand), *n.* a system of writing by abbreviated symbols.

short-hand-ed ('han'did), *adj.* not having enough workers.

short-horn ('hôrn), *n.* any one of a breed of large cattle with short, curved horns.

short-lived ('līvd', 'livd'), *adj.* living or existing for a short time.

short-ly ('li), *adv.* 1. soon. 2. rudely; curtly. 3. briefly.

short order, any order of food that can be prepared quickly, as at a lunch counter.

short-range ('rānj'), *adj.* extending over a short range of time or distance.

short ribs, the ends of beef ribs from the forequarter.

short shrift, very little attention or time given to a matter.

short-sight-ed ('sīt'id), *adj.* 1. nearsighted; myopic. 2. not having foresight. —**short'sight'ed-ly,** *adv.* —**short'sight'ed-ness,** *n.*

short-spo-ken ('spō'kn), *adj.* curt; rude.

short-stop ('stop), *n.* in *Baseball,* the infield player between second and third base.

short subject, a short film shown along with a feature of regular length.

short-tem-pered ('tem'pērd), *adj.* easily angered.

short-term ('tūrm'), *adj.* of or extending over a relatively short period of time.

short ton, 2,000 pounds: see **ton.**

short-wave ('wāv'), *n.* a radio wave of 60 meters or less.

short-wind-ed ('win'did), *adj.* denoting a person who gets out of breath easily from exertion.

shot (shot), *n.* 1. the act of shooting; discharge of a missile, as from a gun. 2. a missile; especially, a bullet or ball. 3. small pellets of lead for a shotgun. 4. a critical comment. 5. a marksman. 6. the range or path of a missile. 7. a photograph or film sequence. 8. a hypodermic injection. 9. a drink of liquor. 10. an attempt; try.

---

a in cap, ā in cane, ä in father, å in abet, e in met, ē in be, ê in baker, ê in regent, I in pit, ī in fine, i in manifest, o in hot, ô in horse, ō in bone,

shot (shŏt), past tense and past participle of shoot: *adj.* 1. variegated or streaked with another color. 2. [Informal], worn-out.

shot-gun ('gun), *n.* a gun for firing small pellets of lead at short range, as at small game. —**shot'-gun-ter**, *n.*

shot put, an athletic contest in which a heavy metal ball is thrust overhand from the shoulder. —**shot'-put-ter**, *n.*

should (shood), *v.* 1. past tense of **shall**. 2. an auxiliary that expresses duty or obligation, probability, or a future condition.

shoul-der (shōl'dĕr), *n.* 1. the joint connecting the human arm, or the forelimb of a quadruped, with the body. 2. the part of the body including this joint. 3. *pl.* the upper part of the back. 4. a projection. 5. the land along the edge of a paved road: *v.t.* 1. to take or carry upon the shoulder. 2. to assume the responsibility of. 3. to jostle or thrust about with the shoulder.

shoulder blade, either one of the two flat bones in the upper back; scapula.

shoulder harness, a strap fastened across the shoulder as a safety device, as in a car.

shoulder strap, 1. a cloth strap at the shoulder of a uniform to indicate rank. 2. a strap over the shoulder to help support a garment, or to carry a purse, camera, etc.

should-n't (shood'nt), should not.

shout (shout), *n.* a sudden, loud cry, call, or outburst: *v.t. & v.i.* to utter or call out in a shout.

shove (shuv), *n.* a forcible push: *v.t. & v.i.* shoved, shov'ing, 1. to push along. 2. to push roughly; jostle.

shov-el (shuv'l), *n.* an implement with a broad scoop and a handle, for lifting and throwing coal, snow, etc.: *v.t.* -eled or -elled, -el-ing or -el-ling, 1. to take and throw with a shovel. 2. to dig out with a shovel.

shov-el-er, shov-el-ler ('l-ēr, 'lēr), *n.* 1. one who shovels. 2. a freshwater duck with a large, long, broad bill.

show (shō), *v.t.* showed, shown or showed, show'ing, 1. to present to view; display. 2. to disclose, as by behavior. 3. to make clear; prove. 4. to guide or direct. 5. to point out. 6. to confer or bestow, as favor or mercy: *v.i.* 1. to appear; become manifest. 2. to be apparent. 3. to finish third in a horse race: *n.* 1. the act of showing; exposure to sight. 2. ostentatious display. 3. an exhibition or spectacle. 4. a pretense. 5. a presentation of entertainment.

show-boat ('bōt), *n.* a boat with a theater, that travels on a river and stops at towns to give shows.

show-case ('kās), *n.* a display case enclosed in glass, as in a store or museum.

show-down ('doun), *n.* [Informal], 1. the laying down of a poker hand face up to see who wins. 2. anything that settles a matter.

show-er (shou'ēr), *n.* 1. a fall of rain, sleet, etc. of short duration. 2. a sudden, copious fall, as of sparks. 3. a bath in which water is sprayed on the body: also **shower bath**. 4. a party given in order that gifts may be presented to the guest of honor: *v.t.* 1. to

spray or sprinkle, as with water. 2. to pour forth as in a shower: *v.i.* 1. to fall in a shower. 2. to bathe in a shower. —**show'er-y**, *adj.*

show-ing (shō'ing), *n.* 1. a display or exhibition. 2. an appearance or performance.

show-man ('măn), *n., pl.* -men, 1. one whose business is presenting theatrical shows. 2. one with a knack for presenting things in a dramatic manner. —**show'man-ship**, *n.*

shown (shōn), alternate past participle of **show**.

show-off (shō'ôf), *n.* one who likes to attract attention to himself.

show-piece ('pēs), *n.* 1. something put on display. 2. a fine example of something.

show-place ('plās), *n.* a place on display to the public because of its beauty, etc.

show-room ('rōōm), *n.* a room or place where merchandise for sale is displayed.

show window, a store window in which merchandise is displayed.

show-y ('i), *adj.* show'i-er, show'i-est, 1. striking; attractive. 2. ostentatious; gaudy. —**show'i-ly**, *adv.* —**show'i-ness**, *n.*

shrank (shrangk), alternate past tense of **shrink**.

shrap-nel (shrap'nl), *n.* 1. a projectile filled with small metal balls and an explosive charge. 2. the balls or any shell fragments scattered on explosion.

shred (shred), *n.* 1. a long, narrow piece torn or cut off. 2. a fragment; scrap: *v.t.* shred'ded or shred, shred'ding, to cut or tear into small pieces. —**shred'da-ble**, *adj.* —**shred'der**, *n.*

shrew (shrōō), *n.* 1. a scolding, vexatious woman. 2. a small, fierce, burrowing mammal resembling a mouse. —**shrew'ish**, *adj.*

shrewd (shrōōd), *adj.* sharp-witted or clever in practical affairs; astute; clever. —**shrewd'ly**, *adv.* —**shrewd'ness**, *n.*

shriek (shrēk), *v.i.* to make a sharp, shrill cry; screech: *v.t.* to utter with such a cry: *n.* a sharp, shrill cry; screech.

shriev-al-ty (shrēv'l-ti), *n., pl.* -ties, [British], the office or jurisdiction of a sheriff.

shrift (shrift), *n.* [Archaic], confession to a priest and absolution given by him.

shrike (shrīk), *n.* any one of several shrill-voiced birds of prey with hooked beaks: see also **butcherbird**.

shrill (shril), *adj.* sharp and piercing in tone: *v.i. & v.t.* to utter (with) a sharp, piercing sound. —**shrill'ness**, *n.* —**shrill'ly**, *adj.*

shrimp (shrimp), *n.* 1. a small, edible crustacean with a long tail. 2. [Informal], anything very small of its kind.

shrine (shrīn), *n.* 1. a case or box in which sacred relics are kept. 2. any sacred place. 3. a saint's tomb. 4. a place of worship.

shrink (shringk), *v.i.* shrank or shrunk, shrunk or shrunk'en, shrink'ing, 1. to contract, as from cold, heat, wetness, etc. 2. to draw back; cower or flinch. 3. to lessen in amount: *v.t.* to cause to shrink: *n.* 1. shrinkage. 2. [Slang], a psychiatrist.

shrink-age ('ij), *n.* 1. the act of shrinking. 2. the amount of shrinking.

shrinking violet, a person who is very shy.

shrive (shrīv), *v.t.* shrived or shrove (shrōv), shriv-en (shriv'n) or shrived, shriv'ing, [Ar-

---

ŏ in dragon, ōō in crude, oo in wool, u in cup, ū in cure, ū in turn, ů in focus, oi in boy, ou in house, th in thin, th in sheathe, g in get, j in joy, y in yet.

chaic], to hear the confession of and give absolution to.

shriv-el (shriv'l), *v.t. & v.i.* -eled or -elled, -el-ing or -el-ling, to shrink and wither or wrinkle.

shroff (shrof), *v.t.* to sort (coins), separating the genuine from the counterfeit: *n.* 1. an expert in testing coins. 2. a banker.

shroud (shroud), *n.* 1. a cloth for wrapping a corpse for burial. 2. anything that covers or conceals. 3. any one of the large ropes supporting the masts of a ship. 4. any one of the set of lines of a parachute: *v.t.* 1. to wrap (a corpse) in a shroud. 2. to cover or conceal.

Shrove Tuesday (shrōv), the last day before Lent.

shrub (shrub), *n.* 1. a woody plant with several stems, smaller than a tree; bush. 2. a beverage made of a citrus fruit juice, sugar, and usually brandy or rum.

shrub-ber-y ('er-i), *n.* shrubs collectively.

shrub-by ('i), *adj.* -bi-er, -bi-est, 1. like a shrub. 2. abounding in shrubs. —**shrub'bi-ness**, *n.*

shrug (shrug), *v.t. & v.i.* shrugged, shrug'ging, to contract or draw up (the shoulders) to express doubt, contempt, indifference, etc.: *n.* the gesture made.

shrunk (shrungk), alternate past tense and past participle of shrink.

shrunk-en ('n), alternate past participle of shrink: *adj.* having become smaller in size.

shuck (shuk), *n.* a shell, husk, or pod: *v.t.* to remove the shucks of.

shucks (shuks), *interj.* an expression of chagrin, disgust, etc.

shud-der (shud'ēr), *n.* a trembling or shaking, as in fear or horror: *v.i.* to tremble or shake.

shuf-fle (shuf'l), *v.t.* -fled, -fling, 1. to change the relative positions of, as cards in a deck. 2. to jumble. 3. to drag (the feet); walk clumsily: *v.i.* 1. to shuffle playing cards. 2. to act in a deceitful or evasive manner. 3. to drag or scrape the feet in walking or dancing: *n.* the act of shuffling. —**shuf'fler**, *n.*

shuf-fle-board (-bôrd), *n.* a game in which a cue is used to drive wooden disks into marked divisions.

shun (shun), *v.t.* shunned, shun'ning, to avoid; keep clear of; refuse to associate with.

shun-pike ('pīk), *adj.* avoiding turnpikes and major roads.

shunt (shunt), *v.t. & v.i.* 1. to turn to one side. 2. to switch (a train) from one track to another: *n.* 1. the act of shunting. 2. a railroad switch.

shush (shush), *interj.* be quiet! hush! *v.t.* to say "shush" to.

shut (shut), *v.t.* shut, shut'ting, 1. to close so as to prevent entrance or exit. 2. to close (a door, cover, etc.). 3. to close by bringing together the parts of (a book, parasol, etc. or the eyes or mouth). 4. to confine (*in* a cage, etc.): *v.i.* to be or become shut: *adj.* closed.

shut-down ('doun), *n.* a temporary closing or work stoppage, as in a factory.

shut-eye ('ī), *n.* [Slang], sleep.

shut-in ('in), *n.* a person who is confined indoors because of illness; invalid: *adj.* confined indoors.

shut-out ('out), *n.* a game in which the losing team is prevented from scoring at all.

shut-ter ('ēr), *n.* 1. one who or that which shuts. 2. a movable cover for a window. 3. a part in a camera that opens and closes to expose the film or plate: *v.t.* to furnish with shutters.

shut-tle (shut'l), *n.* 1. a holder for thread or yarn that moves or is moved back and forth in weaving or in a sewing machine. 2. a bus, plane, etc. that travels back and forth over a short route: *v.t. & v.i.* -tled, -tling, to move back and forth quickly or often.

shut-tle-cock (-kok), *n.* a cork stuck with feathers and batted back and forth in badminton or in battledore and shuttlecock.

shy (shī), *adj.* shy'er or shi'er, shy'est or shi'-est, 1. timid. 2. bashful. 3. distrustful; suspicious. 4. [Slang], short of a full number or amount: *v.i.* shied, shy'ing, 1. to jerk aside, as when startled. 2. to shrink back; become cautious: *v.t.* to throw sideways with a jerk; fling. —**shy'ly**, *adv.* —**shy'ness**, *n.*

shy-ster (shī'stēr), *n.* [Slang], an unethical lawyer.

si (sē), *n.* in Music, same as ti.

si-al-a-gogue (si-al'å-gog), *n.* any substance that promotes the flow of saliva. —**si-al-a-gog'ic** (-goj'ik), *adj.*

si-a-loid (sī'å-loid), *adj.* resembling saliva.

si-a-mang (sē'å-mang), *n.* the large, black gibbon of Sumatra and the Malay Peninsula.

Si-a-mese (sī-å-mēz'), *adj. & n., pl.* -mese', same as Thai.

Siamese cat, a breed of short-haired cat with blue eyes and a fawn-colored coat.

Siamese twins, any twins who are born joined together.

sib-i-lant (sib'l-ånt), *adj.* making or uttering a hissing sound: *n.* a sibilant letter, as s or z. —**sib'i-lance**, *n.* —**sib'i-lant-ly**, *adv.*

sib-i-late (-āt), *v.t. & v.i.* -lat-ed, -lat-ing, to hiss, or utter with a hissing sound. —**sib-i-la'tion**, *n.*

sib-ling (sib'ling), *n.* a brother or sister.

sib-yl (sib'l), *n.* in ancient Greece and Rome, a woman who was a prophet or seer. —**sib'yl-line** (-in, -ēn), *adj.*

sic (sik), *adj.* [Latin], so; thus: usually printed within brackets [*sic*] to indicate that quoted material has been given verbatim.

sic (sik), *v.t.* sicked, sick'ing, to order or urge (a dog) to attack: also spelled sick.

sic-ca-tive (sik'å-tiv), *adj.* drying; causing to dry: *n.* a substance that promotes drying, especially something added to paints.

sick (sik), *adj.* 1. ill; not well. 2. affected with nausea; inclined to vomit. 3. disgusted, as by an excess. 4. of or for sick people. 5. languishing; grieving. 6. [Informal], morbid: *n.* sick people collectively (with *the*).

sick-bed ('bed), *n.* the bed of a sick person.

---

a in cap, ā in cane, ä in father, å in abet, e in met, ē in be, ē in baker, ē in regent, i in pit, ī in fine, i in manifest, o in hot, ô in horse, ō in bone,

sick·en ('n), v.t. & v.i. to make or become ill, disgusted, etc. —sick'en·ing, adj.

sick·ish ('ish), adj. 1. somewhat sick or nauseated. 2. somewhat sickening or nauseating.

sick·le (sik'l), n. a cutting tool consisting of a crescent-shaped blade and short handle, used for reaping grain, cutting down weeds, etc.

sick leave, leave from work granted because of illness.

sickle cell anemia, an inherited chronic anemia, usually of Negroes, in which the red blood cells become shaped like sickles.

sick·ly ('li), adj. -li·er, -li·est, 1. ailing; in poor health. 2. caused by sickness. 3. pale. 4. insipid; weak. —sick'li·ness, n.

sick·ness ('nis), n. 1. the state of being diseased or in poor health. 2. a malady; illness. 3. nausea.

sick·room ('rōōm), n. a room in which a sick person is confined.

side (sīd), n. 1. one of the surfaces or lines that define or limit a solid. 2. either of the two surfaces of a thing that are not the top, bottom, front, or back. 3. the right or left half, as of the body. 4. a place or position beside one. 5. either of the two surfaces of cloth, paper, a door, etc. 6. the position of one party or person facing another. 7. one party or person facing another in a conflict, contest, etc. 8. a line of descent. 9. an aspect. 10. any area or space in reference to a central point. 11. a slope: v.i. sid'ed, sid'ing, to support one party in a conflict, discussion, etc. (followed by with): adj. 1. from or to one side. 2. of or on a side. 3. subordinate.

side·arm ('ärm), adj. & adv. with a swinging motion of the arm at or below shoulder level.

side arms, weapons, as swords, pistols, etc., worn at the side or in the belt.

side·board ('bôrd), n. a piece of dining-room furniture for holding china, table linens, etc.

side·burns ('bûrnz), n.pl. side whiskers growing on a man's face, just in front of the ears.

side·car ('kär), n. a small car attached to the side of a motorcycle, for carrying a passenger, parcels, etc.

side chain, in Chemistry, a chain of atoms that are attached to a longer chain or to a ring of atoms.

side dish, food served along with the main course in a separate dish.

side·kick ('kik), n. [Slang], 1. a close friend. 2. a confederate.

side·light ('līt), n. 1. light coming from the side. 2. an extra piece of information.

side·line ('līn), n. 1. either of the two lines marking the side limits of a playing field, court, etc. 2. pl. the areas just outside of these lines. 3. a second line of goods or kind of activity in addition to the main line: v.t. -lined, -lin·ing, to remove from activity.

side·long ('lông), adv. obliquely: adj. 1. sloping. 2. to the side, as a glance. 3. subtle; indirect.

side·man ('măn), n., pl. -men ('men), a player in a jazz or dance band other than the leader or soloist.

side·piece ('pēs), n. a piece forming a side of something, or attached to a side.

si·de·re·al (sī-dir'ĭ-ăl), adj. 1. of or pertaining to the stars; astral. 2. expressed in reference to the stars. —si·de're·al·ly, adv.

sidereal year, the exact period of time taken by the earth in completing a revolution of the sun, equal to approximately 365 days, 6 hours.

sid·er·o·sis (sid-ē-rō'sis), n. any disease of the lungs caused by inhaling particles of iron or other metal.

side·sad·dle (sīd'sad-l), n. a saddle, as for a horse, made so that the rider's legs will both be on the same side of the animal: adv. on a sidesaddle.

side·show ('shō), n. a small show in addition to the main show, as at a carnival.

side·slip ('slip), v.i. -slipped, -slip·ping, to slip or skid sideways: v.t. to cause to slip sideways: n. a slip or skid sideways.

side·split·ting ('split-ing), adj. 1. highly amusing. 2. very hearty: said of laughter.

side·step ('step), v.t. & v.i. -stepped, -step·ping, to avoid or dodge by stepping aside.

side·swipe ('swīp), v.t. & v.i. -swiped, -swip·ing, to glance or hit along the side in passing: n. such a sweeping blow.

side·track ('trak), v.t. & v.i. 1. to switch to a siding, as a train. 2. to divert or be diverted from a main task or concern.

side·walk ('wôk), n. a walk, especially a paved walk, at the side of a street.

side·wall ('wôl), n. the side of a tire.

side·ways ('wāz), adj. & adv. 1. with one side toward the front. 2. toward or to one side. 3. from one side. Also side'wise ('wīz).

side·wheel·er ('hwēl-ēr, 'wēl-ēr), n. a steamboat with a paddle wheel on each side.

sid·ing (sīd'ing), n. 1. a railroad track by the side of the main track for switching, unloading, etc. 2. a covering, as of aluminum panels, overlapping wooden shingles, etc. for the outside walls of a frame building.

si·dle (sī'dl), v.i. -dled, -dling, to go or move sideways, especially quietly or stealthily.

siege (sēj), n. 1. the surrounding of a fortified place by an army to force its surrender. 2. a continuing effort to gain control, overcome resistance, etc. 3. a long, difficult spell, as of an illness.

si·en·na (si-en'ă), n. 1. a kind of yellowish-brown clay used as a pigment, that turns red when burnt (burnt sienna). 2. either of these colors.

si·er·ra (si-er'ă), n. a chain of mountains with a serrated appearance.

si·es·ta (si-es'tă), n. a nap or rest after the meal at noon.

sieve (siv), n. a utensil with many tiny holes for separating the finer from the coarser parts of a substance.

sift (sift), v.t. 1. to pass through a sieve so as to separate coarse from fine particles, or to break up lumps. 2. to separate. 3. to scrutinize closely: v.i. to sift something.

sigh (sī), v.i. 1. to inhale and exhale with a long, deep, and audible breath, as in relief,

ŏ in dragon, ōō in crude, ꬴ in wool, u in cup, ū in cure, ū in turn, ů in focus, oi in boy, ou in house, th in thin, th in sheathe, g in get, j in joy, y in yet.

sorrow, etc. 2. to grieve; lament: *v.t.* to express by sighs: *n.* the act or sound of sighing.

sight (sit), *n.* 1. the act of seeing. 2. the faculty of seeing; eyesight; vision. 3. a view. 4. field of vision. 5. mental view; perception. 6. something seen or worth seeing. 7. a small guide on a gun, etc. to aid the eyes in aiming. 8. an observation taken, as on a sextant. 9. [Informal], something that looks outlandish, odd, etc.: *v.t.* 1. to see; observe. 2. to catch sight of. 3. to aim at. 4. to adjust the sight (of): *v.i.* to look carefully.

sight-ed ('id), *adj.* 1. having sight; not blind. 2. having a (certain kind of) sight.

sight-less ('lis), *adj.* blind.

sight-ly ('li), *adj.* -li-er, -li-est, pleasant to the sight. —**sight 'li-ness,** *n.*

sight reading, the ability to perform unfamiliar written music without study.

sight-see-ing ('sē-ing), *n.* the act of visiting places of interest. —**sight 'se-er,** *n.*

sig-il (sij'il), *n.* 1. a seal; signet. 2. a sign in magic, supposedly having power.

sig-ma (sig'mä), *n.* the 18th letter of the Greek alphabet.

sig-moid (sig'moid), *adj.* curved like the letter S.

sign (sin), *n.* 1. a mark or symbol having a particular meaning. 2. that by which anything is known or represented; token. 3. an indication; trace. 4. a division of the zodiac. 5. a motion or gesture that has a meaning. 6. an omen; portent. 7. a signboard, placard, etc. with writing or a picture on it: *v.t.* 1. to affix (one's signature) to a contract, letter, etc. 2. to engage by written agreement: *v.i.* to write one's signature.

sig-nal (sig'nl), *n.* 1. a sign for giving notice or warning, as by gesture, flashing light, etc. 2. a device or object providing such a sign. 3. anything agreed upon as a sign to initiate action. 4. in *Radio, Telegraphy, etc.,* the electrical impulses, sound waves, etc. transmitted or received: *adj.* 1. memorable; remarkable. 2. of or pertaining to signals: *v.t.* -naled or -nalled, -nal-ing or -nal-ling, 1. to convey by signals. 2. to make signals to.

sig-nal-ize (-iz), *v.t.* -ized, -iz-ing, 1. to make especially conspicuous; draw attention to. 2. to make remarkable.

sig-na-to-ry (sig'nä-tôr-i), *adj.* having signed or joined in signing: *n., pl.* -ries, any one of the persons, nations, etc. whose signatures appear on a document.

sig-na-ture (sig'nä-chēr), *n.* 1. the name of a person written by himself. 2. a mark or stamp representing this. 3. in *Music,* a sign on the staff showing the key or time. 4. in *Printing,* a section of a book.

sign-board (sin'bôrd), *n.* a board bearing a sign, as an advertisement, warning, etc.

sig-net (sig'nit), *n.* a seal, as on a ring, used in marking documents as official.

sig-nif-i-cance (sig-nif'i-käns), *n.* 1. meaning; import. 2. consequence; importance. 3. the quality of being significant.

sig-nif-i-cant (-känt), *adj.* 1. expressing a meaning, especially a hidden or special meaning.

2. expressive; meaningful. 3. important. —**sig-nif 'i-cant-ly,** *adv.*

sig-ni-fy (sig'nI-fI), *v.t.* -fied, -fy-ing, 1. to show by a sign, mark, or token. 2. to denote; mean; manifest: *v.i.* to be important. —**sig-ni-fi-ca 'tion,** *n.*

sign language, signs and gestures of the hands used to communicate thoughts and ideas, usually as a substitute for speech.

sign manual, a personal signature, especially that of a sovereign on a state document.

sign of the cross, an outline of a cross made by movements of the fingers and hand.

si-gnor (si-nyôr'), *n., pl.* **si-gno'ri** (-nyô'rē), [Italian], 1. a man; gentleman. 2. [S-], Mister.

si-gno-ra (si-nyô'rä), *n., pl.* **si-gno're** ('re), [Italian], 1. a married woman. 2. [S-], Madam; Mrs.

si-gno-re (si-nyô'rē), *n., pl.* **si-gno'ri** ('rē), [Italian], 1. a man; gentleman. 2. [S-], Sir.

si-gno-ri-na (si-nyô-rē'nä), *n., pl.* **-ri'ne** ('ne), [Italian], 1. an unmarried woman or girl. 2. [S-], Miss.

si-gno-ri-no (si-nyô-rē'nô), *n., pl.* **-ri'ni** ('nē), [Italian], 1. a boy or young man. 2. [S-], Master.

Sikh (sēk), *n.* a person belonging to a religious group in India, which believes in one God and frowns on idolatry and the caste system. —**Sikh'ism,** *n.*

si-lage (si'lij), *n.* same as **ensilage**.

si-lence (si'lēns), *n.* 1. an entire absence of sound; having no sound. 2. taciturnity. 3. obscurity; oblivion: *v.t.* -lenced, -lenc-ing, 1. to make silent. 2. to restrain from exercise of any function. 3. to cause to cease firing: *interj.* become silent!

si-lenc-er ('lēn-sēr), *n.* 1. a person or thing that silences. 2. an object whose purpose is to deaden sound, as a piece fit on the end of a gun.

si-lent (si'lēnt), *adj.* 1. noiseless; quiet. 2. not speaking. 3. not pronounced. 4. taciturn. 5. not spoken. 6. not functioning. —**si'lent-ly,** *adv.*

sil-hou-ette (sil-oo-wet'), *n.* 1. an outline or profile filled in with a color. 2. a likeness or representation cast by a shadow: *v.t.* -et'ted, -et'ting, to represent by a silhouette.

sil-i-ca (sil'i-kä), *n.* silicon dioxide, a hard, smooth, translucent mineral, occurring naturally as quartz, opal, etc.

sil-i-cate (sil'i-kit, -kāt), *n.* a salt or ester of silicic acid or silica.

si-lic-ic (si-lis'ik), *adj.* of, pertaining to, derived from, compounded with, or like silica or silicon.

silicic acid, a gelatinous substance, a hydrated form of silica.

sil-i-co-, a combining form meaning *silica* or *silicon.*

sil-i-con (sil'i-kôn), *n.* a nonmetallic element, next to oxygen the most abundant element in nature: it is always combined with another element.

sil-i-cone (-kôn), *n.* an organic compound of silicon that withstands changes in temperature.

a in cap, ā in cane, ä in father, ȧ in abet, e in met, ē in be, ē in baker, ė in regent, i in pit, ī in fine, i in manifest, o in hot, ô in horse, ō in bone,

sil·i·co·sis (sil-i-kō'sis), *n.* a lung disease caused by inhaling particles of silica.

silk (silk), *n.* 1. a fine, soft thread spun by the larvae of the silk moth to form their cocoons. 2. a thread or fabric made from this. 3. a garment made of this fabric. 4. a similar thread, as that spun by certain arachnids: *adj.* of, pertaining to, or made of silk. —**silk·en** (sil'kn), *adj.* made of or like silk; soft, smooth, etc.

silk-screen process (silk'skrēn), a stencil method of printing a color design through a piece of silk or other fine cloth on which parts of the design not to be printed have been blocked up. —**silk'screen**, *v.t.*

silk·worm (silk'wûrm), *n.* the larva of a certain moth which, before changing to a pupa, constructs itself a dense cocoon of fine threads spun from a viscous secretion in the body glands.

silk·y (sil'ki), *adj.* **silk·i·er**, **silk·i·est**, of, pertaining to, made of, or resembling silk; silken. —**silk·i·ness**, *n.*

sill (sil), *n.* 1. timber or masonry providing a horizontal foundation. 2. a piece placed horizontally at the bottom of a window or door.

sil·la·bub (sil'ă-bub), *n.* same as syllabub.

sil·ly (sil'i), *adj.* **-li·er**, **-li·est**, weak in intellect; foolish: *n., pl.* **-lies**, a silly person. —**sil'li·ly**, *adv.* —**sil'li·ness**, *n.*

si·lo (sī'lō), *n., pl.* **-los**, a storage pit or closed, towerlike structure for packing green fodder.

silt (silt), *n.* a fine sediment of sand and mud deposited by running water: *v.t. & v.i.* to fill up or obstruct with silt.

Si·lu·ri·an (si-loor'i-ăn), *n.* the period of the Paleozoic Era during which invertebrates proliferated.

sil·ver (sil'vêr), *n.* 1. a soft, white, metallic element, used for coins, jewelry, etc. 2. silver coin. 3. money. 4. anything resembling silver in brightness or color. 5. silverware. 6. the shiny, grayish-white color of silver: *adj.* 1. of, pertaining to, having, or made of silver. 2. soft and clear, as a sound. 3. of a silver color: *v.t.* to cover or coat with or as with silver.

sil·ver·fish (-fish), *n., pl.* **-fish**, a silvery insect without wings, that lives in moist and dark places.

sil·ver·ing (-ing), *n.* 1. the process of covering with silver or with a substance like silver in appearance. 2. the film thus laid on.

silver lining, a positive side to a negative situation.

silver nitrate, a colorless, crystalline salt used as an antiseptic, in silver plating, photography, etc.

sil·ver·smith (-smith), *n.* one who produces and fixes things made of silver.

sil·ver·tongued (-tungd'), *adj.* fluent and forceful.

sil·ver·ware (sil'vêr-wer), *n.* 1. things, as table utensils, made of or plated with silver. 2. any table utensils made of a metal.

sil·ver·y (sil'vêr-i), *adj.* 1. of, pertaining to, consisting of, or having silver. 2. having a silver sound. —**sil'ver·i·ness**, *n.*

sil·vics (sil'viks), *n.* the science which treats of the growth and life of forest trees.

sil·vi·cul·ture (sil'vi-kul-chêr), *n.* the branch of arboriculture which treats of the tending of forest trees.

sim·i·an (sim'i-ăn), *adj.* of, pertaining to, characteristic of, or like an ape: *n.* an ape or monkey.

sim·i·lar (sim'i-lêr), *adj.* having a general likeness or correspondence; nearly alike. —**sim'i·lar·ly**, *adv.*

sim·i·lar·i·ty (sim-i-ler'i-ti), *n.* 1. resemblance. 2. *pl.* **-ties**, a similar aspect.

sim·i·le (sim'i-lē), *n.* a figure of speech which draws a comparison between two different objects or things.

si·mil·i·tude (si-mil'i-tōod), *n.* same as similarity.

sim·i·tar (sim'i-tēr), *n.* same as scimitar.

sim·mer (sim'êr), *v.t. & v.i.* 1. to boil gently. 2. to remain or keep at a level just below the outbreak of rage, uprising, etc.: *n.* the condition of simmering.

si·mon-pure (sī'mŏn-pyoor'), *adj.* real; true.

si·mo·ny (sī'mŏ-ni), *n.* the act of buying or selling ecclesiastical offices; traffic in anything sacred.

si·moom (si-mōōm'), *n.* a hot, dry, suffocating wind which blows in the deserts of Africa and Asia.

sim·pa·ti·co (sim-pat'i-kō), *adj.* sympathetic; congenial.

sim·per (sim'pêr), *v.i.* to smile in an affected or silly manner: *n.* an affected or silly smile.

sim·ple (sim'pl), *adj.* **-pler**, **-plest**, 1. single; not complex. 2. undivided. 3. not blended or compounded. 4. pure. 5. plain. 6. unadorned. 7. sincere. 8. natural. 9. unaffected. 10. intelligible; clear. 11. weak in intellect. 12. humble. 13. ordinary: *n.* 1. something unmixed or not compounded. 2. [Archaic] a medicinal herb. —**sim'ple·ness**, *n.*

simple interest, interest figured only on the principal sum, not on that sum with interest.

sim·ple·ton (-tŏn), *n.* one who is foolish or of weak intellect.

sim·plex (sim'pleks), *adj.* denoting a system of telegraphy in which only one message is sent over a wire at a time.

sim·plic·i·ty (sim-plis'i-ti), *n., pl.* **-ties**, 1. the state or quality of being simple. 2. artlessness of mind; innocence. 3. absence of excessive or artificial ornament; clearness. 4. folly.

sim·pli·fy (sim'pli-fī), *v.t.* **-fied**, **-fy·ing**, to make simpler; render less complex; make plain or easy. —**sim·pli·fi·ca'tion**, *n.*

sim·plis·tic (sim-plis'tik), *adj.* simplified to the point that realism is lost. —**sim·plis'ti·cal·ly**, *adv.*

sim·u·la·crum (sim-yoo-lā'krŭm), *n., pl.* **-cra** ('krä), 1. that which is fashioned in the likeness of a being or thing; image. 2. a sham.

sim·u·late (sim'yoo-lāt), *v.t.* **-lat·ed**, **-lat·ing**, 1. to pretend or counterfeit. 2. to assume the likeness of: *adj.* [Archaic], denoting pretension; having a deceptive appearance.

sim·u·la·tion (sim-yoo-lā'shŭn), *n.* 1. the act of

simulating. 2. that which has been simulated or counterfeited.

si-mul-cast (sī'ml-kast), v.t. -cast or -cast-ed, -cast-ing, to transmit (a program, event, etc.) simultaneously by radio and television: n. a program, event, etc. so transmitted.

si-mul-ta-ne-ous (si-ml-tā'ni-ûs), adj. happening, done, or existing at the same time. —si-mul-ta'ne-ous-ly, adv.

sin (sēn), n. a variant of the twenty-first letter of the Hebrew alphabet.

sin (sin), n. 1. willful transgression of divine law; neglect of the laws of morality and religion. 2. violation of propriety; transgression; iniquity: v.i. sinned, sin'ning, 1. to commit a sin. 2. to transgress or offend.

sin-a-pism (sin'ă-pizm), n. a mustard plaster used to relieve congestion, pain, etc.

since (sins), adv. 1. from that time until this time. 2. before this or now. 3. at a time before now but after a previous time: prep. 1. from the time of. 2. after: conj. 1. because; seeing that; considering. 2. following the time when. 3. without interruption from the time when.

sin-cere (sin-sir'), adj. -cer'er, -cer'est, 1. honest; not falsely assumed; frank; upright. 2. genuine; true. 3. [Archaic], pure. —sin-cere'-ly, adv. —sin-cer'i-ty (-ser'i-ti), n.

sin-ci-put (sin'si-put), n. the forehead or the upper part of the skull.

sine (sin), n. in Trigonometry, the ratio of the side opposite a given acute angle in a right triangle and the hypotenuse.

si-ne (sī'ni, sē'nā), prep. [Latin], without.

si-ne-cure (sī'nē-kyoor, sin'ā-), n. an office with compensation in which there is little work to do.

si-ne di-e (sī'ni dī'i, sin'ā dē'ā), without a day being determined, as an adjournment having no day determined for future meetings.

si-ne qua non (sī'ni kwä non', sin'ā kwä non'), something which is indispensable or absolutely necessary to the carrying out of a plan or purpose.

sin-ew (sin'ū), n. 1. a tendon. 2. force. 3. often pl. anything supplying strength: v.t. to supply with or as with sinews; make strong.

sin-ew-y (sin'yoo-wi), adj. 1. of, pertaining to, consisting of, or like sinew; tough. 2. vigorous.

sin-ful (sin'fûl), adj. full of sin; wicked; impious; unholy. —sin'ful-ly, adv.

sing (sing), v.i. sang or rarely sung, sung, sing'ing, 1. to utter melodious sounds. 2. to make a shrill or humming noise. 3. to celebrate in verse or poetry. 4. to produce sounds similar to music. 5. [Slang], to admit to wrongdoing and include others in the telling: v.t. 1. to perform (a song, etc.) by uttering in musical tones. 2. to celebrate, describe, etc. in song. 3. to cause to assume a state or condition by the use of singing. 4. to chant: n. [Informal], singing with a large number of people. —sing'er, n.

sing-a-long (sing'ă-lông), n. [Informal], a casual meeting of people for the purpose of singing.

singe (sinj), v.t. singed, singe'ing, 1. to burn slightly or on the surface. 2. to subject (an animal carcass) to fire in order to remove feathers, bristles, etc.: n. 1. the act of singeing. 2. a slight burn.

sin-gle (sing'gl), adj. 1. consisting of one only. 2. alone. 3. separate. 4. unmarried. 5. performed by one person or one on each side. 6. straightforward; sincere; honest. 7. of or for one only. 8. with only one piece; not compound. 9. complete: v.t. -gled, -gling, to select from others; separate (usually with out): v.i. in Baseball, to make a single: n. 1. a unit. 2. in Baseball, a hit which allows the batter to get as far as first base. 3. pl. in Tennis, a game with only one player on each side.

sin-gle-breast-ed (-bres'tid), adj. going across the body in front only enough so as to attach by a single button or a single line of buttons.

single file, one line of people or things with each behind the one preceding.

sin-gle-hand-ed (-han'did), adj. & adv. 1. with only one hand. 2. accomplished alone.

sin-gle-mind-ed (-min'did), adj. having only a single end or goal.

sin-gle-stick (-stik), n. 1. a stick with a guard near the handle, formerly used for fencing. 2. a fencing game with such sticks.

sin-gle-ton (-ton), n. 1. a single card of any suit held by a player at a deal. 2. that which exists or happens alone.

sin-gle-track (-trak'), adj. [Informal], same as one-track.

sin-gle-tree (-trē), n. the center bar on a plow, wagon, etc. which is attached to the ends of the horse's harness.

sin-gly (sing'gli), adv. 1. without assistance. 2. individually; particularly. 3. separately.

sing-song (sing'sông), n. 1. a climbing and falling tone which does not change when speaking. 2. monotonous song or poetry: adj. unchanging climbing and falling, as in tone.

sin-gu-lar (sing'gyû-lěr), adj. 1. uncommon; unusual; unique. 2. strange; peculiar; odd. 3. extraordinary; eminent. 4. [Archaic], alone. 5. in Grammar, denoting one person or thing: n. in Grammar, the number denoting one person or thing. —sin'gu-lar-ly, adv.

sin-gu-lar-i-ty (sing-gyû-ler'i-ti), n., pl. -ties, 1. the state or quality of being singular. 2. a peculiarity; oddity.

sin-is-ter (sin'is-těr), adj. 1. inauspicious; unlucky. 2. ill-omened. 3. corrupt; dishonest; evil. 4. [Obsolete], on the left-hand side.

sink (singk), v.i. sank or sunk, sunk, sink'ing, 1. to fall or go downward slowly. 2. to fall beneath the surface of water, soft ground, etc. 3. to seem to descend. 4. to go lower, as in value. 5. to abate. 6. to recede. 7. to go from one condition to another little by little (with into). 8. to fail: v.t. 1. to cause to sink. 2. to make by digging. 3. to lower in value or amount. 4. to reduce or extinguish by payment. 5. to put (money, capital, etc.) into for profit. 6. to bring to ruin: n. 1. a basin for receiving waste water, connected with a drain for carrying off such water. 2. a cesspool. 3. a place of immoral or vile character. 4. an area where the land

---

a in cap, ā in cane, ä in father, à in abet, e in met, ē in be, ē in baker, ě in regent, i in pit, ī in fine, ï in manifest, o in hot, ô in horse, ō in bone,

level is depressed below that of the surrounding land.

sink·er (sing'kẽr), *n.* 1. one who or that which sinks. 2. a lead weight for fishing. 3. [Informal], a doughnut.

sinking fund, a reserve of money accumulated in regular amounts, as for retiring a debt.

sin·ner (sin'ẽr), *n.* one who sins; offender; transgressor.

Sinn Fein (shin' fān'), an Irish political society organized in the early 20th century, having for its aim the complete independence of Ireland.

Si·no-, a combining form meaning *Chinese and.*

Si·nol·o·gist (sī-nol'ō-jist, si-), *n.* one versed in Chinese literature, language, etc.: also **Si·no·logue** (sī'nō-lôg, sin'ō-).

Si·nol·o·gy (-ji), *n.* the systematized study of the Chinese language, literature, laws, history, etc.

sin·ter (sin'tẽr), *n.* 1. crystallized rock precipitated from mineral water. 2. a mass of metal particles heated and pressed together without melting: *v.t. & v.i.* to make or become a sinter (sense 2).

sin·u·ate (sin'yoo-wit), *adj.* having the margin alternately curved inward and outward: *v.i.* (-wāt), -at·ed, -at·ing, to curve in and out.

sin·u·os·i·ty (sin-yoo-wäs'l-ti), *n.* 1. *pl.* -ties, a wavy line. 2. the character of being sinuous.

sin·u·ous (sin'yoo-wäs), *adj.* 1. bending in and out; winding. 2. crooked.

si·nus (sī'nŭs), *n.* 1. a bay or recess. 2. a cavity or depression. 3. a skull cavity filled with air, connected to the nasal cavities. 4. a fistula.

si·nus·i·tis (sī-nŭ-sīt'ĭs), *n.* sinus inflammation, as in the skull.

-sion (shŭn, zhŭn), a suffix meaning the *doing, quality, state, or consequence of.*

sip (sip), *v.t. & v.i.* sipped, sip'ping, to imbibe in small quanities; drink a small amount at a time: *n.* 1. the act of sipping. 2. a small amount sipped. —**sip'per,** *n.*

si·phon (sī'fŏn), *n.* 1. a bent pipe or tube having one end longer than the other, used for drawing off liquids from a higher to a lower level. 2. the respiratory tube of certain animals. 3. same as **siphon bottle:** *v.t.* to convey or draw off by a siphon.

siphon bottle, a sealed bottle containing carbonated water which may be released by a nozzle.

Sir (sũr), *n.* 1. the title of a baronet or knight. 2. [often s-], a term of respect for a man.

sir·dar (sẽr-där'), *n.* in India, Pakistan, etc. a chief, captain, etc.

sire (sīr), *n.* 1. a title of respect used in addressing a sovereign. 2. [Poetic], a father. 3. the male parent of an animal: *v.t.* sired, sir'ing, to procreate: used of animals.

si·ren (sī'rĕn), *n.* 1. in *Greek & Roman Mythology,* one of certain fabled nymphs that lured mariners to destruction. 2. a woman dangerous because of her fascinations. 3. a foghorn. 4. a device that produces a loud, wailing sound, usually as a warning signal. 5. an eellike amphibian: *adj.*

of, pertaining to, characteristic of, or like a siren: bewitching.

Sir·i·us (sir'i-ŭs), the Dog Star, brightest of the stars in a southern constellation (*Canis Major*).

sir·loin (sũr'loin), *n.* a choice cut of beef, from the loin end.

si·roc·co (si-rok'ō), *n., pl.* -cos, 1. a hot, uncomfortable wind from the Libyan deserts. 2. any hot, uncomfortable wind.

sir·rah, sir·ra (sir'â), *n.* [Archaic], a term of reproach or contempt, used toward a man.

sir·ree, sir·ee (si-rē'), *interj.* an interjection stressing *yes* or *no.*

sir·up (sir'up, sũr'-up), *n.* same as syrup. —**sir'up·y,** *adj.*

sis (sis), *n.* [Informal], a shortened form of sister.

si·sal (sī'sl), *n.* 1. an agave of southern Mexico and Central America. 2. the fiber made from the leaves of this plant, used for making ropes, insulation, etc. Also **sisal hemp.**

sis·kin (sis'kin), *n.* a small, greenish finch of Europe and Asia.

sis·sy (sis'i), *n., pl.* -sies, [Informal], 1. a man or boy regarded as weak, soft, etc. 2. a coward or fearful person. —**sis'si·fied** ('i-fīd), *adj.*

sis·ter (sis'tẽr), *n.* 1. a female born of the same parents as another person. 2. a female of the same religious society, order, or community. 3. a nun. 4. a friend who is considered to be like a sister. 5. one of the same kind or condition.

sis·ter·hood (-hood), *n.* 1. sisters collectively. 2. a number of females belonging to the same religious society, organization, etc.

sis·ter-in-law (-in-lô), *n., pl.* **sis'ters-in-law,** 1. the sister of one's husband or wife. 2. the wife of one's brother. 3. the wife of the brother of one's husband or wife.

sis·ter·ly (-li), *adj.* 1. of a sister. 2. as becomes a sister; kindly, affectionate, etc.

Sis·tine (sis'tin), *adj.* of or pertaining to any of the Popes who bore the title of Sixtus.

Sistine Chapel, the main chapel in the Vatican: named after Pope Sixtus IV of the 15th century.

Sis·y·phe·an (sis-i-fē'ân), *adj.* 1. of or pertaining to Sisyphus, condemned by Pluto to roll to the top of a hill a stone which incessantly fell back when it had reached the summit. 2. incessantly recurring; vainly toilsome; requiring continual doing.

sit (sit), *v.i.* sat, sit'ting, 1. to rest on the lower part of the trunk of the body. 2. to repose on a seat. 3. to perch. 4. to rest or lie; press or weigh. 5. to occupy a seat officially. 6. to hold a session. 7. to incubate. 8. to be in a place. 9. to assume a position for portrait painting or as a model. 10. same as **baby-sit:** *v.t.* 1. to make sit. 2. to maintain a sitting position upon. —**sit'ter,** *n.*

si·tar (si-tär'), *n.* a musical instrument of India, resembling a lute.

sit-down (sit'doun), *n.* 1. a strike in which workers stay in the building. 2. a form of civil resistance in which the protesters sit down in a public place and refuse to move.

ŏ in drag*o*n, ōō in cr*u*de, oo in w*oo*l, u in c*u*p, ū in c*u*re, ŭ in t*u*rn, ŭ in foc*u*s, oi in b*oy*, ou in h*ou*se, th in *th*in, *th* in shea*th*e, g in *g*et, **J** in *j*oy, y in *y*et.

site (sīt), *n.* 1. a plot of ground for some use. 2. a location.

sit-in (sit'in), *n.* a civil protest in the form of a sit-down within a public area.

situation comedy, a comic television series made up of episodes involving the same group of characters: also sit'com (sit'kom).

sit-ting (sit'ing), *adj.* resting on the haunches; perching; incubating: *n.* 1. the posture or act of one who sits. 2. a session. 3. the time during which one sits. 4. a set of eggs for one incubation.

sitting duck, [Informal], a very vulnerable person or thing.

sit-u-ate (sich'oo-wāt), *v.t.* -at-ed, -at-ing, to place in a particular location.

sit-u-at-ed (-wāt-id), *adj.* 1. placed with respect to any other object. 2. having a position with regard to a particular financial, social, etc. situation.

sit-u-a-tion (sich-oo-wā'shŭn), *n.* 1. position. 2. locality. 3. circumstances. 4. office; employment. 5. the conditions of a particular time.

sit-up, sit-up (sit'up), *n.* an exercise in which a sitting position is achieved from lying flat on the back, without the use of the hands and keeping the legs straight.

sitz bath (sits, zits), a bath for bathing in a sitting position; hip bath.

Si-va (sē'vä, shē'-), *n.* the god of ruin and procreation who forms with Brahma and Vishnu the supreme Hindu trinity.

six (siks), *adj.* one more than five: *n.* the cardinal numeral that is the sum of five and one; 6; VI.

six-fold (siks'fōld), *adj.* 1. containing six parts. 2. containing six times as many or as much: *adv.* six times as many or as much.

six-pack (-'pak), *n.* a container of six items of the same type.

six-pence ('pens), *n.* a former British silver coin, equal to six pence.

six-shoot-er ('shōōt-ẽr), *n.* [Informal], a handgun that may be fired six times in succession without loading again: also six'-gun.

six-teen ('tēn'), *adj.* one more than 15: *n.* the cardinal numeral that is the sum of 15 and one: 16; XVI.

six-teen-mo ('mō), *n., pl.* -mos, 1. the page size (about 4 1/2 by 6 3/4 inches) of a book made by folding printer's sheets into 16 leaves. 2. a book with such pages.

six-teenth ('tēnth'), *adj.* next after 15th; 16th: *n.* 1. the one after the 15th. 2. one of 16 equal parts.

sixth (siksth), *adj.* next after fifth; 6th: *n.* 1. the one after the fifth. 2. one of six equal parts.

sixth sense, an ability to perceive without reasoning.

six-ti-eth (siks'ti-ith), *adj.* next after 59th; 60th: *n.* 1. the one after the 59th. 2. one of 60 equal parts.

six-ty (siks'ti), *adj.* six times 10: *n., pl.* -ties, 1. the cardinal numeral that is the sum of 59 and one; 60; LX. 2. *pl.* years or numbers from 60 through 69 (preceded by *the*).

siz-a-ble (sī'zȧ-bl), *adj.* of considerable or massive size: also size'a-ble.

siz-ar (sī'zẽr), *n.* a student who gets a scholarship at Trinity College (Dublin) or at Cambridge University.

size (sīz), *n.* 1. a kind of thin, weak glue or paste used as a glaze, filler, etc. 2. magnitude or bulk. 3. any one of a group of systematized degrees on a measuring scale, used to separate goods for sale: *v.t.* sized, siz'ing, 1. to prepare or cover with size. 2. to arrange according to size or bulk.

siz-ing (sī'zing), *n.* a glutinous preparation for glazing paper, plaster, etc.; paste.

siz-zle (siz'l), *v.i.* -zled, -zling, 1. to make a hissing sound when heated. 2. to be very hot: *n.* a hissing sound.

skat (skat, skät), *n.* a card game played by three people with a deck of thirty-two cards.

skate (skāt), *n.* 1. a kind of flat fish related to the ray. 2. a metallic runner to slide over ice, for fastening to a boot, or the boot to which it is fastened. 2. a shoe to which rollers are fastened for gliding over a floor, sidewalks, etc.: *v.i.* skat'ed, skat'ing, to slide or glide on skates.

skate-board (skāt'bôrd), *n.* a short, oblong board with two wheels at each end, ridden, as down an incline: *v.i.* -board-ed, -board-ing, to ride on a skateboard.

ske-dad-dle (ski-dad'l), *v.i.* -dled, -dling, [Informal], to run away, especially hastily.

skein (skān), *n.* a quantity of thread, silk, etc. coiled together.

skel-e-ton (skel'ĕ-tn), *n.* 1. the bones of an animal supporting the flesh, musculature, etc. 2. the framework of anything. 3. an outline. —skel'e-tal (-tl), *adj.*

skel-e-ton-ize (-īz), *v.i.* -ized, -iz-ing, to make a skeleton of.

skeleton key, a thin, light key designed to open many kinds of locks as a master key.

skep (skep), *n.* 1. a beehive of plaited straw. 2. a round wooden or wicker basket.

skep-tic (skep'tik), *n.* 1. one who doubts the truth of any doctrine or system. 2. one who doubts the existence of God, the validity of religious doctrines, etc. 3. an adherent of philosophical skepticism: *adj.* same as skeptical.

skep-ti-cal (skep'ti-kl), *adj.* of, pertaining to, or characteristic of a skeptic or skepticism. —skep'ti-cal-ly, *adv.*

skep-ti-cism (-sizm), *n.* 1. incredulity. 2. the doctrine that no facts can be known with certainty. 3. unbelief in any particular doctrine.

sketch (skech), *n.* 1. an outline. 2. a rough draft or drawing. 3. a preliminary study. 4. a brief story, play, etc. lacking detail: *v.t.* to draw the outline or give principal features of; make a sketch of: *v.i.* to make sketches.

sketch-y (skech'i), *adj.* sketch'i-er, sketch'i-est, 1. outlined. 2. unfinished; incomplete. —sketch'i-ly, *adv.* —sketch'i-ness, *n.*

skew (skū), *n.* 1. distortion; twist. 2. an oblique movement; squint sideways: *adj.* oblique; distorted; twisted: *v.i.* 1. to move obliquely.

---

a in c**a**p, ā in c**a**ne, ä in f**a**ther, ȧ in **a**bet, e in m**e**t, ē in b**e**, ẽ in bak**e**r, ė in reg**e**nt, i in p**i**t, ī in f**i**ne, ĭ in man**i**fest, o in h**o**t, ō in h**o**rse, ŏ in b**o**ne,

2. to turn or twist: *v.t.* 1. to distort; pervert.
2. to give an oblique position to.

skew·bald (skū'bôld), *n.* a horse with brown and white spots: *adj.* with brown and white spots.

skew·er (skū'ēr), *n.* a pin of wood or metal for securing meat when roasting: *v.t.* to fasten with or as with a skewer.

ski (skē), *n., pl.* **skis, ski,** a long runner of wood, metal, etc. attached to a boot, for sliding on snow: *v.i.* **skied** (skēd), **ski'ing,** to slide on skis. —ski'er, *n.*

ski·a·graph (skī'á-graf), *n.* same as radiograph.

skid (skid), *n.* 1. the act of skidding. 2. a sliding wedge or drag used to retard the motion of a vehicle by pressure against the wheel. 3. *pl.* a wooden fender to protect the side of a ship. 4. a mobile support for loads. 5. a runner that substitutes for a wheel on airplane landing gear. 6. a set of long wooden pieces forming a track on which to move heavy things: *v.t.* **skid'ded, skid'ding,** 1. to cause to move on a skid. 2. to retard with a skid. 3. to make slip: *v.i.* to slip along obliquely.

skid-doo (ski-dōō'), *v.i.* [Old Slang], to vamoose; beat it; go away: used imperatively.

skid row, a part of a city in which tramps, vagabonds, and other idlers live.

skiff (skif), *n.* 1. a light rowboat. 2. a small boat with a sail.

skil·ful (skil'fŭl), *adj.* same as skillful.

ski lift, a continuous cable with seats suspended, for transporting skiers up a hill.

skill (skil), *n.* 1. expertness in any art or science. 2. power to discern and execute. 3. an art, science, etc. requiring dexterity.

skilled (skild), *adj.* 1. having the knowledge and ability which come from experience. 2. possessing skill.

skil·let (skil'it), *n.* a shallow pan with a handle, used for frying.

skill·ful (skil'fŭl), *adj.* having or displaying skill; expert in any art or science; dexterous.

skim (skim), *v.t.* **skimmed, skim'ming,** 1. to remove (scum, fat, etc.) from (a liquid). 2. to brush the surface of lightly. 3. to read quickly and superficially: *v.i.* 1. to move along lightly. 2. to read superficially: *n.* the act of skimming.

skim·mer (skim'ēr), *n.* 1. one who or that which skims. 2. an implement for skimming liquids. 3. a long-winged marine bird.

skim milk, milk from which the cream has been taken: also skimmed milk.

skimp (skimp), *v.t.* [Informal], 1. to do carelessly or superficially. 2. same as scrimp: *v.i.* [Informal], same as scrimp: *adj.* [Informal], same as scanty.

skimp·y (skim'pi), *adj.* **skimp'i·er, skimp'i·est,** [Informal], same as scanty.

skin (skin), *n.* 1. the external covering of an animal body. 2. a hide or pelt. 3. bark or rind. 4. anything resembling a skin: *v.t.* **skinned, skin'ning,** 1. to remove or strip the skin from. 2. to cover with or as with skin. 3. to damage by an abrasion. 4. [Informal], to cheat: *v.i.* to become covered over with skin. —skin'less, *adj.*

skin-dive (skin'dīv'), *v.i.* **-dived, -div'ing,** to swim underneath the water with the aid of various respiratory devices. —skin'div·er, *n.*

skin-flint (skin'flint), *n.* a miser.

skin·ful (skin'fool), *n., pl.* **-fuls,** [Informal], as much as the stomach can hold.

skink (skingk), *n.* a kind of lizard with short limbs and smooth scales.

skinned (skind), *adj.* possessing skin (of a particular type).

skin·ny (skin'i), *adj.* **-ni·er, -ni·est,** very lean. —skin'ni·ness, *n.*

skin·ny-dip (-dip), *v.i.* **-dipped, -dip·ping,** [Informal], to swim without clothes: *n.* [Informal], the act of swimming without clothes.

skip (skip), *v.t.* **skipped, skip'ping,** 1. to leap lightly over. 2. to omit. 3. to make bounce against at an angle. 4. [Informal], to go away from (a city, country, etc.) with haste: *v.i.* 1. to leap or bound lightly. 2. to pass over something, omitting parts. 3. to bounce at an angle. 4. [Informal], to go away hastily: *n.* 1. a light leap or bound. 2. an omission. 3. a type of walking with hops on each foot in succession.

skip·per (skip'ēr), *n.* 1. one who or that which skips. 2. a ship's captain.

skirl (skūrl), *n.* a shrill cry or sound: *v.t.* & *v.i.* [Dialectal], to make (such a cry or sound), as by the use of bagpipes.

skir·mish (skūr'mish), *n.* 1. a brief combat or irregular fight between two small parties. 2. a contest: *v.i.* to take part in a skirmish; fight.

skirr (skūr), *v.t.* to pass over, as in searching: *n.* a whir.

skirt (skūrt), *n.* 1. the part of a coat, dress, or other garment below the waist. 2. a woman's garment that falls from the waist. 3. *pl.* the outer border, as of a city: *v.t.* 1. to move or sail along the edge of. 2. to be the edge of: *v.i.* to move or sail along the edge.

skit (skit), *n.* 1. a brief satire. 2. a burlesque.

ski tow, a type of ski lift that pulls skiers up a hill on their skis.

skit·ter (skit'ēr), *v.i.* to move along lightly; skim.

skit·tish (skit'ish), *adj.* 1. shy; easily frightened. 2. volatile. 3. vivacious.

skit·tles (skit'lz), *n.* an English game resembling ninepins, using a wooden ball.

skiv·er (ski'vēr), *n.* 1. a paring tool for leather. 2. a leather of split sheepskin, used for hat linings, bookbindings, etc.

skiv·vy (skiv'i), *n., pl.* **-vies,** [Slang], 1. a man's undershirt: usually skivvy shirt. 2. *pl.* men's underwear.

skoal (skōl), *interj.* good health!: a toast.

sku·a (skū'á), *n.* a large gull of the northern seas.

skul·dug·ger·y, skull·dug·ger·y (skul-dug'ēr-i), *n.* [Informal], deception; fraud.

skulk (skulk), *v.i.* 1. to lurk furtively. 2. [Chiefly British], to avoid work: *n.* one who skulks. —skulk'er, *n.*

skull (skul), *n.* 1. the bony case enclosing the brain of a vertebrate animal. 2. the head of a person, considered as the source of thought.

ô in drag*o*n, ōō in cr*u*de, oo in w*oo*l, u in c*u*p, ŭ in c*u*re, ü in t*u*rn, ü in foc*u*s,
oi in b*o*y, ou in h*ou*se, th in *th*in, *th* in shea*th*e, g in *g*et, j in *j*oy, y in *y*et.

skull-cap (skul'kap), *n.* a light, closefitting cap without a brim.

skunk (skungk), *n.* 1. a nocturnal, carnivorous animal, black with a white stripe or spots on the back, which emits a fetid secretion when pursued. 2. the fur of this animal. 3. [Informal], a vile, contemptible person: *v.t.* [Slang], to defeat (an opponent), as in a game.

sky (ski), *n., pl.* skies, 1. the apparent arch of the heavens. 2. *often pl.* the region of clouds, etc. surrounding the earth. 3. climate or weather. 4. the hypothetical abode of the Deity: *v.t.* skied or skyed, sky'ing, [Informal], to cause to rise in the air.

sky blue, the blue color of the clear sky. —**sky'-blue'**, *adj.*

sky-cap (ski'kap), *n.* one who carries luggage at an airport.

sky diving, a sport in which one jumps from an airplane and does acrobatics in the air before opening a parachute.

sky-high (ski'hi'), *adj. & adv.* 1. extremely high. 2. to pieces.

sky-jack ('jak), *v.t.* [Informal], to take over (an aircraft) by force and cause it to be flown to an unscheduled destination.

Sky-lab ('lab), *n.* a U.S. space station orbiting the earth and housing astronauts who conduct scientific experiments.

sky-lark ('lärk), *n.* a type of lark that sings as it soars high in the air: *v.i.* to run about in sport; frolic.

sky-light ('lit), *n.* a ceiling window.

sky-line ('lin), *n.* 1. the line where the sky and earth seem to meet. 2. the outline of a city with the sky as a background.

sky marshal, a Federal officer who guards against the hijacking of commercial airliners.

sky pilot, [Slang], a clergyman; chaplain.

sky-rock-et ('rok-it), *n.* a colorful firework that explodes in the air: *v.i. & v.t.* to go up or make go up quickly.

sky-scrap-er ('skrā-pēr), *n.* a lofty building.

sky-ward ('wêrd), *adv. & adj.* in the direction of the sky: also sky'wards, *adv.*

sky-ways ('wāz), *n.pl.* lanes for air travel.

sky-writ-ing ('rit-ing), *n.* the use of smoke from an airplane to create written messages in the sky. —**sky'writ-er,** *n.*

slab (slab), *n.* 1. a flat, thick piece of something. 2. the first, rough cut of a log: *adj.* [Archaic], thick; viscous: *v.t.* slabbed, slab'bing, to cut into slabs.

slab-ber (slab'ēr), *v.i. & v.t. & n.* same as slobber.

slack (slak), *adj.* 1. relaxed or loose. 2. inattentive. 3. not busy. 4. slow: *n.* 1. that part of anything, as a rope, etc., that hangs loose. 2. flat, unmoving water in a stream. 3. screenings of coal; coal dust. 4. *pl.* trousers. 5. an inactive time. 6. a looseness: *v.t. & v.i.* to make or become slack.

slack-en (slak'n), *v.i.* 1. to become slack or less firm, tense, or rigid. 2. to languish; become slower, less intense, etc.: *v.t.* 1. to make slower. 2. to make less rigid; relax.

slack-er ('ēr), *n.* 1. one who shirks military service. 2. a person who tries to avoid work or duty.

slag (slag), *n.* 1. the dross of metal after smelting. 2. lava that looks like this. —**slag'gy,** *adj.* -gi-er, -gi-est.

slain (slān), past participle of slay.

slain-te (slän'chĕ), *interj.* good health!: a toast.

slake (slāk), *v.t.* slaked, slak'ing, 1. to quench (thirst). 2. to extinguish (a fire). 3. to mix (lime) with water: *v.i.* to become slaked or be subjected to slaking.

sla-lom (slä'lôm), *n.* a ski race that follows a zigzag path down a hill.

slam (slam), *v.t.* slammed, slam'ming, 1. to shut violently and with a loud noise. 2. to put down with force and loud noise. 3. [Informal], to be highly critical of: *v.i.* to strike violently or noisily: *n.* 1. a noisy banging. 2. [Informal], a criticism.

slam-bang (slam'bang'), *adv.* [Informal], 1. quickly or suddenly and carelessly. 2. very noisily: *adj.* animated, noisy, etc.

slan-der (slan'dēr), *n.* 1. a false or malicious report. 2. verbal defamation: *v.t.* to defame; calumniate. —**slan'der-er,** *n.*

slan-der-ous (-ŭs), *adj.* 1. consisting of slander. 2. uttering slander.

slang (slang), *n.* 1. a colloquial language or expression current at any particular period. 2. a jargon of some particular calling or class in society: *v.t.* [Chiefly British], to abuse with vulgar language. —**slang'y,** *adj.* slang'i-er, slang'i-est.

slant (slant), *n.* 1. an inclined plane. 2. an opinion: *v.t. & v.i.* 1. to slope. 2. to express with an opinion: *adj.* inclined from a straight line; oblique.

slap (slap), *n.* 1. a blow given with the open hand or anything broad and flat. 2. an affront: *v.t.* slapped, slap'ping, 1. to strike with the open hand or anything broad. 2. to place forcefully: *adv.* 1. [Informal], directly. 2. [British Informal], suddenly; abruptly.

slap-dash (slap'dash), *n.* rough, careless work: *adj.* rough; careless; unthinking: *adv.* in a careless or random manner.

slap-hap-py ('hap-i), *adj.* [Slang], 1. dizzy; lightheaded. 2. foolish; flighty; silly.

slap-stick ('stik), *n.* 1. a contrivance made up of two pieces of flat board, formerly used by comedians in striking, as the noise made it appear a heavy blow had been dealt. 2. a form of low comedy relying on boisterous activity to produce laughter: *adj.* of or resembling slapstick comedy.

slash (slash), *n.* 1. a long, sweeping movement. 2. a cut; gash. 3. a slit in a garment, fabric, etc. 4. swampy or wet land. 5. the tops and branches of trees cut off in logging: *v.t.* 1. to cut by striking, as with a knife. 2. to cut slits into. 3. to whip. 4. to depress (prices) to an extremely low level: *v.i.* to cut or strike with a sweeping movement or violence. —**slash'er,** *n.*

slash-ing (slash'ing), *adj.* severe: *n.* debris left in a forest after logging.

slash pocket, a pocket in clothing, the opening of which is on a slant.

slat (slat), *n.* a thin, narrow strip of wood, metal, etc.

slate (slāt), *n.* 1. a rock that splits into thin plates. 2. a thin stone for roofing. 3. a tablet of stone for writing upon. 4. a list of candidates prepared for nomination or election. 5. the bluish-gray color of slate rock: *v.t.* slat'ed, slat'ing, 1. to cover with slate. 2. to choose or designate for a particular purpose. 3. [Chiefly British Informal], to criticize sharply.

slath-er (slath'ẽr), *v.t.* [Informal], to cover with a heavy layer.

slat-tern (slat'ẽrn), *n.* a careless, slovenly woman.

slat-tern-ly (-li), *adj.* slovenly; untidy: *adv.* untidily.

slat-ting (slat'ing), *n.* 1. the violent flapping of anything hanging loose in the wind. 2. slats collectively.

slat-y (slāt'i), *adj.* slat'i-er, slat'i-est, of or like slate.

slaugh-ter (slôt'ẽr), *n.* 1. great destruction of life by violence; carnage. 2. the violent killing of a person. 3. the killing of animals for human food: *v.t.* 1. to slay or kill with violence or extensively. 2. to kill (animals) for the market.

slaugh-ter-house (-hous), *n.* a place where animals are slaughtered for human food.

Slav (släv, slav), *n.* a member of one of the various peoples speaking Slavic languages in eastern, southeastern, and central Europe, comprising Russians, Poles, Czechs, Serbs, Slovaks, Croats, Bulgars, etc.

slave (släv), *n.* 1. a human being held as the property of another. 2. a drudge. 3. one under the power or influence of another: *v.i.* slaved, slav'ing, to work like a slave; toil or drudge.

slave driver, 1. a cruel taskmaster. 2. one who directs slaves in their work.

slav-er (slav'ẽr), *n.* saliva or spittle drooling or dribbling from the mouth: *v.i.* to allow spittle to dribble from the mouth: *v.t.* [Archaic], to smear with spittle.

slav-er (slā'vẽr), *n.* a vessel or trader engaged in the transporting and sale of slaves.

slav-er-y (slā'vẽ-ri, slāv'ri), *n.* 1. the state of entire subjugation to the will of another. 2. the condition of a slave. 3. the custom or institution of maintaining slaves.

slav-ey (slā'vi, slav'i), *n., pl.* -eys, [British Informal], a female domestic servant.

Slav-ic (släv'ik, slav'-), *adj.* of or pertaining to the Slavs or to their languages: *n.* the related languages of the Slavs, collectively.

slav-ish (slā'vish), *adj.* 1. of, pertaining to, befitting, or characteristic of a slave. 2. unthinkingly subordinate or imitative. —slav'-ish-ly, *adv.*

Sla-von-ic (slā-von'ik), *adj. & n.* same as Slavic.

slaw (slô), *n.* same as coleslaw.

slay (slā), *v.t.* slew, slain, slay'ing, to kill or put to death with a weapon; destroy suddenly or with violence. —slay'er, *n.*

sleave (slēv), *n.* [Obsolete], the knotted or entangled part of silk or thread; floss.

slea-zy (slē'zi), *adj.* -zi-er, -zi-est, 1. flimsy; lacking firmness of texture. 2. cheap; inferior. —slea'zi-ly, *adv.*

sled (sled), *n.* a carriage or vehicle mounted on runners for traveling over snow and ice: *v.t.*

sled'ded, sled'ding, to carry or transport on a sled: *v.i.* to be carried on a sled.

sled-ding (sled'ing), *n.* 1. the act of transporting on, or conveying by, a sled. 2. the condition of snow for the running of sleds.

sledge (slej) *n.* 1. a large, heavy hammer: also **sledge'ham-mer** ('ham-ẽr). 2. a sled or sleigh: *v.t. & v.i.* sledged, sledg'ing, to convey or travel in a sledge.

sleek (slēk), *adj.* 1. smooth; glossy. 2. looking healthy or clean and neat. 3. smooth and polite; polished in manners: *v.t.* to make smooth; render glossy. —sleek'ness, *n.*

sleep (slēp), *n.* 1. a natural, regular state of rest without conscious thought; slumber. 2. anything similar to this, as death: *v.i.* slept, sleep'ing, 1. to be in a state of sleep. 2. to be motionless or inactive, as in sleep. — sleep'less, *adj.* —sleep'less-ness, *n.*

sleep-er (slē'pẽr), *n.* 1. one who sleeps. 2. a horizontal supporting timber. 3. a railroad car which can accommodate those who wish to sleep: also **sleeping car.** 4. [Chiefly British], a piece of timber supporting a railroad track. 5. something or someone who attains an unforeseen prosperity, importance, etc.

sleeping bag, a large, lined bag for sleeping in, as while camping.

sleeping sickness, 1. a usually fatal disease of the African tropics caused by either of two parasites transmitted by the bite of the tsetse fly: it produces somnolence, trembling, etc. before death. 2. inflammation of the brain due to a virus.

sleep-walk-ing (slēp'wôk-ing), *n.* the practice of walking during sleep. —sleep'walk-er, *n.*

sleep-y (slē'pi), *adj.* sleep'i-er, sleep'i-est, 1. inclined to or overcome by sleep; drowsy. 2. sluggish; lethargic. —sleep'i-ly, *adv.* —sleep'i-ness, *n.*

sleep-y-head (-hed), *n.* one who is sleepy.

sleet (slēt), *n.* 1. rain mingled with snow or hail. 2. freezing rain: *v.i.* to hail or snow with rain mingled. —sleet'y, *adj.* sleet'i-er, sleet'i-est.

sleeve (slēv), *n.* 1. the part of a garment that covers the arm. 2. a part that covers another part by fitting around: *v.t.* sleeved, sleev'ing, to furnish with sleeves.

sleigh (slā), *n.* a light vehicle with runners, for use on snow or ice, usually pulled by horses: *v.i.* to ride on a sleigh.

sleight (slīt), *n.* 1. dexterity. 2. cunning.

sleight of hand, 1. skill in doing magic tricks; legerdemain. 2. the tricks done.

slen-der (slen'dẽr), *adj.* 1. small or narrow in proportion to the length or height. 2. feeble. 3. slim. 4. meager.

slen-der-ize (-īz), *v.t.* -ized, -iz-ing, to make slender: *v.i.* to become slender.

slept (slept), past tense and past participle of sleep.

sleuth (slōōth), *n.* [Informal], a detective.

sleuth-hound (slōōth'hound), *n.* a bloodhound.

slew (slōō), *n.* 1. a boggy, marshy place. 2. [Informal], a great amount or number.

slew (slōō), past tense of slay.

slice (slīs), *n.* 1. a thin, broad piece of anything. 2. a thin, broad knife for taking up or serving food; spatula. 3. a share: *v.t.*

sliced, slic'ing, 1. to cut into thin, broad pieces. 2. to cut into parts. 3. to divide as in slices (with *off, away, from,* etc.). 4. to strike (a ball) so as to make veer off to the side. —**slic'er,** *n.*

slick (slik), *n.* 1. a smooth place on the surface of water. 2. a polishing tool, as a broad, flat chisel: *adj.* 1. smooth. 2. slippery. 3. quick-thinking. 4. [Informal], smoothly deceptive: *v.t.* 1. to brighten up; make smooth. 2. [Informal], to make presentable, trim, etc. (usually with *up*): *adv.* smoothly; smartly. —**slick'ness,** *n.*

slick·er (slik'ẽr), *n.* 1. a waterproof raincoat. 2. [Informal], a deceptive person.

slide (slid), *v.i.* **slid** (slid), **slid'ing,** 1. to pass smoothly over a surface without leaving it. 2. to glide. 3. to pass inadvertently or unobserved. 4. to slip: *v.t.* 1. to thrust along smoothly; cause to slide. 2. to cause to slip dexterously or secretly (*in* or *into*): *n.* 1. a smooth surface for sliding upon; smooth declivity. 2. a picture on glass, plastic, etc. for exhibition on a screen. 3. a small glass plate on which objects are placed for study under a microscope. 4. the act of sliding. 5. a sliding part. 6. the fall of a mass of rock or snow down a mountain. 7. in *Music,* a series of tones merging into one another.

slide fastener, 1. a zipper. 2. a device resembling a zipper, with two parallel plastic tracks connected or separated by a slide.

slid·er (slid'ẽr), *n.* 1. one who or that which slides. 2. in *Baseball,* a pitch that curves only a little.

slide rule, a rulerlike device having two pieces stamped with logarithmic scales, used for quick solving of mathematical problems.

sliding scale, a variable scale of wages, prices, etc. according to the state of trade.

slight (slīt), *adj.* 1. feeble. 2. inconsiderable. 3. unimportant; trifling. 4. not severe. 5. slender: *n.* 1. neglect. 2. rude treatment: *v.t.* 1. to regard as of little value. 2. to neglect. 3. to treat rudely. —**slight'ly,** *adv.*

slim (slim), *adj.* **slim'mer, slim'mest,** 1. of small diameter; small in breadth or thickness in proportion to height; slender. 2. meager; scant: *v.t.* & *v.i.* **slimmed, slim'ming,** to make or become slim. —**slim'ness,** *n.*

slime (slim), *n.* 1. a glutinous or slippery substance, as mud, the exudation from fish, etc. 2. any unpleasant viscous substance.

slim·sy (slim'zi), *adj.* **-si·er, -si·est,** [Informal], frail; flimsy.

slim·y (slī'mi), *adj.* **slim'i·er, slim'i·est,** 1. of, consisting of, covered over with, or like slime. 2. unpleasant. —**slim'i·ly,** *adv.* —**slim'i·ness,** *n.*

sling (sling), *n.* 1. an early instrument for throwing stones. 2. a throw. 3. a cloth looped around the neck and under an injured arm for support. 4. a strap, band, etc. for lifting something heavy. 5. an alcoholic drink containing sugar, lemon juice, etc: *v.t.* **slung, sling'ing,** 1. to hurl with or as with a sling. 2. to hang so as to swing. 3. to hang in a sling.

sling·shot (sling'shot), *n.* a piece of wood,

metal, etc. in the shape of a Y, used with elastic bands to hurl stones.

slink (slingk), *v.i.* **slunk, slink'ing,** to creep away as if ashamed, fearful, etc.; sneak off: *v.t.* slinked or slunk, slink'ing, to cast off (a fetus) prematurely: said of animals: *adj.* produced prematurely: *n.* an animal prematurely born, especially a calf.

slink·y (sling'ki), *adj.* **slink'i·er, slink'i·est,** 1. sneaky; sly. 2. [Slang], sinuous and graceful.

slip (slip), *v.i.* **slipped, slip'ping,** 1. to glide or slide. 2. to miss one's foothold; fall down. 3. to escape observation. 4. to make an oversight. 5. to slide out of place. 6. to depart or escape. 7. to decline or worsen: *v.t.* 1. to convey secretly. 2. to cause to move quickly and smoothly. 3. to pass from (memory): *n.* 1. the act of slipping. 2. an oversight; indiscretion. 3. a strip. 4. a twig from a stock; scion. 5. a loose garment worn under a woman's dress or skirt. 6. liquid potter's clay. 7. an incline for launching ships. 8. the water between wharves, serving as a docking place. 9. a fielder in cricket. 10. a pillowcase. 11. a narrow pew or bench. 12. a small piece of paper. 13. a slender person.

slip-case (slip'kās), *n.* an open box for enclosing a book.

slip-cov·er (-kuv·ẽr), *n.* a chair or couch cover which can be removed.

slip-knot ('not), *n.* a knot which is formed so that it can move.

slip noose, a noose formed with a slipknot.

slip-page (slip'ij), *n.* the act or amount of slipping.

slipped disk, an injured disk that sticks out from the spinal column.

slip-per (slip'ẽr), *n.* a loose shoe, easily slipped on and off the foot.

slip-per·y (slip'ẽ-ri), *adj.* **-per·i·er, -per·i·est,** 1. not adhesive. 2. without firm hold or footing; smooth. 3. unstable; cunning. —**slip'per·i·ness,** *n.*

slip·py (slip'i), *adj.* [Informal or Dialectal], same as slippery.

slip·shod ('shod), *adj.* 1. wearing shoes or slippers that are down at the heel. 2. slovenly; neglectful.

slip-up (slip'up), *n.* [Informal], an oversight.

slit (slit), *v.t.* **slit, slit'ting,** to cut lengthwise or into long strips; split: *n.* 1. a long cut. 2. a narrow opening.

slith·er (slith'ẽr), *v.i.* 1. to slide, glide, etc. 2. to shuffle or slide in walking.

sliv·er (sliv'ẽr), *v.t.* & *v.i.* to cut or separate into long, thin, or very small pieces: *n.* a splinter.

slob (slob), *n.* [Informal], an awkward, clumsy, or slovenly person.

slob·ber (slob'ẽr), *n.* saliva, food, etc. running from the mouth: *v.i.* 1. to dribble at the mouth; drool. 2. to talk in a drooling, insipid manner: *v.t.* 1. to make foul with saliva. 2. to spill (food) in eating. —**slob'-ber·er,** *n.*

sloe (slō), *n.* 1. the fruit of the blackthorn bush. 2. the blackthorn bush. 3. a variety of wild, bitter plum.

sloe-eyed (slō'īd), *adj.* 1. characterized by large,

dark eyes. 2. characterized by eyes resembling almonds in shape.

sloe gin, a reddish liqueur of dry gin with sloe flavoring.

slog (slog), *v.t. & v.i.* 1. to hit hard; slug. 2. to plod. 3. to work with great effort (at).

slo-gan (slō´gán), *n.* 1. originally, the war cry or gathering cry of Scottish Highland and Irish clans. 2. a rallying cry, as of a political party. 3. a phrase used to attract attention, as in advertising.

sloop (slōōp), *n.* a one-masted vessel with a fore-and-aft rig.

slop (slop), *n.* 1. water or other liquid carelessly spilled; puddle. 2. liquid food of a poor quality. 3. dirty water, mud, or slush. 4. *pl.* liquid waste matter, as from a kitchen. 5. *pl.* cheap, ready-made clothing. 6. *pl.* seamen's clothing: *v.i.* slopped, slop´ping to soil by letting liquid fall upon: *v.i.* to splash; spill.

slope (slōp), *n.* 1. ground not in a horizontal plane. 2. an oblique direction. 3. a surface inclining or declining gradually. 4. the degree to which the surface is inclined: *v.t.* sloped, slop´ing, to form with a slope; incline or slant; direct obliquely: *v.i.* 1. to take an oblique direction; slant. 2. [Informal], to run off.

slop-py (slop´i), *adj.* -pi-er, -pi-est, 1. extremely untidy or neglected. 2. wet; muddy. 3. splashed. 4. [Informal], excessively sentimental.

sloppy Joe (jō), a dish of ground meat, tomato sauce, etc. on a bun.

slosh (slosh), *v.i.* 1. to move awkwardly through liquid. 2. to splash: said of a liquid.

slot (slot), *n.* 1. a narrow aperture; groove; opening, as for a coin in an automatic vending machine. 2. a deer's track. 3. [Informal], a place, rank, etc.: *v.t.* slot´ted, slot´ting, 1. to put a slot in; groove. 2. to trace by slot.

sloth (slôth, slōth), *n.* 1. idleness; habitual indolence. 2. a South American arboreal quadruped which hangs from branches, back down, and feeds on leaves and fruits.

sloth bear, a fruit-eating black bear of India and Ceylon.

sloth-ful (slôth´ful, slōth´-), *adj.* lazy; inactive. —**sloth´ful-ly**, *adv.*

slot machine, a vending machine functioning by the insertion of a coin in a slot; specifically, a gambling device.

slouch (slouch), *n.* 1. a hanging down, as of the head or other parts of the body. 2. a poor posture. 3. an awkward, lazy person: *v.i.* to cause to hang down: *v.i.* to walk, sit, etc. in a clumsy, heavy, awkward manner.

slough (sluf), *n.* 1. the cast-off skin of a snake. 2. the part of dead skin that separates from a sore: *v.i.* 1. to separate naturally dead matter from the sound flesh. 2. to come off: *v.t.* to cast off.

slough (slou), *n.* 1. a deep, muddy place. 2. (slōō), a bog. 3. mental depression.

Slo-vak (slō´vak, ´vak), *n.* 1. any one of the Slavic people of eastern Czechoslovakia. 2. the language of the Slovaks: *adj.* of or pertaining to the Slovaks, their language, etc.

Slo-va-ki-an (slō-vä´ki-án, -vak´i-án), *adj. & n.* same as Slovak.

slov-en (sluv´én), *n.* one who is habitually untidy in dress and negligent of cleanliness; one who is negligent of order and neatness.

Slo-vene (slō´vēn, slō-vēn´), *adj. & n.* same as Slovenian.

Slo-ve-ni-an (slō-vē´ni-án, -vēn´yán), *n.* 1. one of the Slavic peoples of northwestern Yugoslavia. 2. the language of these people: *adj.* of or pertaining to the Slovenians or to their language.

slov-en-ly (sluv´én-li), *adj.* -li-er, -li-est, lacking neatness or order; negligent or careless in appearance. —**slov´en-li-ness**, *n.*

slow (slō), *adj.* 1. not quick or rapid in motion. 2. dilatory. 3. not prompt or quick. 4. behind in time. 5. not progressive. 6. dull: *v.t. & v.i.* to make or become slow or slower (often with *up* or *down*): *adv.* in a slow way. —**slow´ly**, *adv.* —**slow´ness**, *n.*

slow burn, [Slang], a slow rise to wrath: often in *do a slow burn.*

slow-down (slō´doun), *n.* a gradual diminishing of the production rate.

slow-mo-tion (´mō´shún), *adj.* 1. functioning at a rate of speed lower than normal. 2. denoting a slowing down of the activity in a scene on film or videotape.

slow-wit-ted (´wit´id), *adj.* mentally dull.

slow-worm (´wûrm), *n.* same as blindworm.

sludge (sluj), *n.* 1. slush, mire, or mud. 2. pasty refuse; slime, as of ore. —**sludg´y**, *adj.* sludg´i-er, sludg´i-est.

slue (slōō), *v.t. & v.i.* slued, slu´ing, to turn about, as around a fixed point.

slug (slug), *n.* 1. a gastropod mollusk that looks like a snail, but has only a rudimentary shell. 2. a strip of metal for spacing type. 3. any small piece of metal, as a bullet. 4. [Informal], a heavy blow, as with the fist. 5. [Slang], one drink of alcoholic liquor: *v.t.* slugged, slug´ging, [Informal], to strike hard, as with the fist.

slug-gard (slug´érd), *n.* one who is habitually lazy and idle.

slug-ger (slug´ér), *n.* [Informal], 1. a hard hitter. 2. a pugilist who hits hard. 3. a batter in baseball who has produced many doubles, triples, and home runs.

slug-gish (´ish), *adj.* 1. habitually lazy and idle; slothful. 2. dull; inactive; slow. 3. not operating at the usual rate. —**slug´gish-ness**, *n.*

sluice (slōōs), *n.* 1. a gate for regulating the flow of water in a canal, stream, etc.; also sluice gate. 2. the stream of water issuing through such a gate. 3. the canal, stream, etc. whose flow the gate is used to regulate. 4. a waterway used to draw off unneeded water. 5. a long, narrow, sloping channel or flume through which water is passed: *v.t.* sluiced, sluic´ing, 1. to remove with a sluice. 2. to wash with water from a sluice. 3. to wet copiously.

slum (slum), *n.* a crowded district of a city or town, characterized by poverty, poor housing, etc.: *v.i.* slummed, slum´ming, to go into the slum areas in a patronizing manner.

slum-ber (slum´bér), *v.i.* 1. to sleep; doze. 2. to

be in a state of inactivity or dormancy: *n.* the state of sleeping or inactivity. —**slum'-ber·er**, *n.*

slum·lord (slum'lôrd), *n.* [Slang], an owner of slum buildings, who lives in another area and takes advantage of the slum occupants.

slump (slump), *n.* a sudden fall, as of prices: *v.i.* 1. to fall or sink suddenly. 2. to have a drooping posture.

slung (slung), past tense and past participle of sling.

slunk (slungk), alternate past tense and past participle of slink.

slur (slûr), *v.t.* slurred, slur'ring, 1. to pass over superficially (often with *over*). 2. to disparage. 3. to pronounce indistinctly. 4. [Dialectal], to sully; soil; contaminate. 5. in *Music*, to sing or perform (notes) by gliding without breaks: *n.* 1. a stain. 2. a reproach; stigma. 3. the act of slurring. 4. an indistinct pronunciation. 5. a blurred spot, as in print. 6. in *Music*, a curve connecting notes that are to be sung or played without a break.

slurp (slûrp), *v.t.* & *v.i.* [Slang], to imbibe, chew, etc. noisily: *n.* [Slang], a loud sound made while ingesting food or drink.

slush (slush), *n.* 1. half-melted snow. 2. a greasy lubricating mixture. 3. mire. 4. effusive talk or writing; gush. —**slush'y**, *adj.* **slush'i·er**, **slush'i·est**.

slut (slut), *n.* 1. a female dog. 2. a slattern. 3. a woman of low sexual morals. —**slut'tish**, *adj.*

sly (slī), *adj.* sli'er or sly'er, sli'est or sly'est, 1. artfully cunning. 2. underhanded and crafty. 3. rascally; teasing. —**sly'ly**, **sli'ly**, *adv.* —**sly'ness**, *n.*

sly·boots (slī'bō̄ots), *n.* a pleasantly crafty person.

smack (smak), *n.* 1. a quick, sharp blow. 2. a loud kiss. 3. a quick, sharp noise with the lips. 4. flavor; taste. 5. a small fishing boat or sailboat. 6. a bit; trace: *v.t.* 1. to kiss with a quick, sharp noise. 2. to strike with a quick, sharp blow. 3. to separate (the lips) in making a quick, sharp noise: *v.i.* 1. to possess a bit (*of*). 2. to make a quick, sharp noise: *adv.* 1. sharply. 2. exactly.

smack·er (smak'ēr), *n.* [Slang], a dollar.

small (smôl), *adj.* 1. little in quantity or degree. 2. inconsiderable; of little worth or ability. 3. not large or extended in dimensions. 4. narrow-minded; mean. 5. in an early period of life. 6. same as lower-case: *n.* 1. the small or slender part of anything. 2. *pl.* small articles. 3. *pl.* [British], underclothes. 4. *pl.* [Archaic], closefitting knee breeches. —**small'ness**, *n.*

small arms, pistols, rifles, etc. of a small caliber.

small-mind·ed (smôl'mīn-did), *adj.* selfish, mean, or narrow-minded.

small·pox (smôl'poks), *n.* a contagious, feverish disease characterized by eruptions upon the skin.

small talk, trivial, commonplace talk or discussion.

smalt (smôlt), *n.* a deep-blue pigment produced from cobalt, potash, and silica.

smart (smärt), *adj.* 1. causing a quick, sharp pain. 2. poignant; sharp. 3. clever; accomplished; brilliant; witty. 4. vivacious; brisk. 5. sharp in practice. 6. spruce. 7. in line with fashion: *n.* a sharp, stinging pain: *v.i.* 1. to feel a sharp, stinging pain. 2. to cause or be a source of such a pain. 3. to endure mental upset. —**smart'ly**, *adv.* —**smart'ness**, *n.*

smart al·eck, **smart al·ec** (al'ik), [Informal], a vain and annoying person.

smart bomb, [Military Slang], a guided missile directed to its target by any of various electronic means.

smart·en (smärt'n), *v.t.* to make smart or spruce (usually with *up*).

smart money, a wager or speculation by informed persons.

smart-weed (smärt'wēd), *n.* a weed with a sharp, bitter juice.

smash (smash), *v.t.* 1. to break into pieces by violence. 2. to crush. 3. to hit solidly: *v.i.* 1. to break into pieces. 2. to be crushed. 3. to be hit solidly: *n.* 1. a violent breaking to pieces. 2. bankruptcy. 3. an alcoholic drink with ice, sugar, and mint flavoring. 4. a solid blow. 5. a very hard impact. 6. a great gain or accomplishment achieving wide acceptance.

smash·er (smash'ēr), *n.* 1. one who or that which smashes. 2. [Chiefly British Informal], a good-looking, pretty, etc. person or thing.

smash-up (smash'up), *n.* 1. a very hard impact. 2. anything completely destroyed.

smat·ter·ing (-ing), *n.* 1. a superficial knowledge. 2. a small amount.

smear (smir), *v.t.* 1. to overspread with anything unctuous, viscous, or adhesive. 2. to daub; streak. 3. to make harmful remarks about: *v.i.* to become smeared: *n.* 1. a blot or stain. 2. something said that is harmful to one's reputation.

smear-case (smir'käs), *n.* same as cottage cheese.

smell (smel), *v.t.* smelled or smelt, smell'ing, 1. to perceive by the nose; obtain the scent of. 2. to perceive the action or state of: *v.i.* 1. to affect the nose or olfactory nerves. 2. to exercise the sense of smell: *n.* 1. that quality of something which affects the sense of smell. 2. any sensation of odor or perfume. 3. the act of smelling. 4. the sense of the body which perceives odors by means of nerves in the nasal cavity.

smell·y (smel'i), *adj.* smell'i·er, smell'i·est, smelling bad.

smelt (smelt), *n.* a small, silvery food fish of northern seas, resembling the salmon: *v.t.* 1. to fuse (ore, etc.) to separate the pure metal. 2. to remove (metal) by fusing.

smelt·er (smel'tēr), *n.* 1. one who smelts for a living. 2. a furnace for smelting.

smew (smū), *n.* the small merganser of northern Europe and Asia.

smidg·en (smij'ēn), *n.* [Informal], a small total; bit: also smidg'in, smidg'eon.

smi·lax (smī'laks), *n.* a climbing plant related to the lily, cultivated widely in greenhouses for its greenish flowers.

smile (smīl), v.i. smiled, smil'ing, 1. to express pleasure, moderate joy, love, or kindness by turning up the edges of the mouth. 2. to look gay, cheerful, or happy. 3. to express slight contempt by a smile. 4. to favor (with *on* or *upon*): v.t. to express by a smile: n. 1. the act of smiling. 2. a look of pleasure, kindness, happiness, or slight contempt. —smil'ing·ly, adv.

smirch (smûrch), v.t. 1. to smear; dirty. 2. to disgrace: n. 1. a smear; stain. 2. a taint, as on one's reputation.

smirk (smûrk), v.i. to smile affectedly or conceitedly: n. an affected smile.

smite (smīt), v.t. smote, smit'ten or smote, smit'ing, 1. [Now Rare], to strike with the hand or a weapon. 2. [Now Rare], to kill; overthrow in battle; chasten; blast. 3. to attack with calamitous results. 4. to affect (*with* an emotion): v.i. [Now Rare], to hit solidly.

smith (smith), n. 1. a blacksmith. 2. a worker in metals.

smith·er·eens (smith-ĕ-rēnz'), n.pl. [Informal], fragments resulting from a blow.

smith·y (smith'i), n., pl. smith'ies, a smith's workshop.

smit·ten (smit'n), alternate past participle of smite.

smock (smok), n. 1. a loose garment worn over the clothes for protection. 2. [Archaic], a chemise.

smog (smôg, smog), n. an unhealthful combination of smoke and fog.

smoke (smōk), n. 1. the vapor that escapes when a substance is burned. 2. any vapor; exhalation. 3. the act of smoking. 4. a pipe, cigar, etc.: v.t. smoked, smok'ing, 1. to apply smoke to. 2. to flavor or cure with smoke. 3. to puff out, and often inhale, the smoke of. 4. to expel or ferret (*out*) by smoke. 5. [Archaic], to detect: v.i. 1. to emit smoke. 2. to puff out, and often inhale, smoke. —smoke'less, adj. —smok'er, n.

smoke detector, a warning device that sets off a loud signal when excessive smoke, heat, etc. are detected.

smoke-house (smōk'hous), n. a farm building where meats, fish, etc. are flavored or cured by smoke.

smoke screen, 1. a dense cloud of smoke sent forth by ships or aircraft over either land or sea to screen an attack or bombardment, or hide movements being made by troops against an enemy. 2. anything intended to conceal, dissemble, or deceive.

smoke-stack ('stak), n. 1. the chimney of a factory or similar building. 2. the vent of a locomotive.

smok·y (smō'ki), adj. smok'i·er, smok'i·est, 1. giving out or filled with smoke. 2. of, characteristic of, or colored like smoke. 3. tarnished or noisome with smoke. —smok'i·ly, adv. —smok'i·ness, n.

smol·der (smōl'dĕr), v.i. 1. to burn slowly or smoke without flame. 2. to exist in a stifled condition.

smooth (smooth), adj. 1. not rough; even-surfaced. 2. gently flowing. 3. bland. 4. having an even consistency. 5. flattering. 6. frictionless. 7. calm. 8. unobstructed. 9. having an easy, gliding rhythm, sound, etc.: v.t. 1. to make smooth. 2. to render easy. 3. to calm. 4. to give an even consistency to. 5. to make more elegant, polished, etc.: v.i. to become smoothed: adv. in a smooth way: n. 1. the act of making smooth. 2. the smooth part of anything. —smooth'ly, adv. —smooth'ness, n.

smor·gas·bord, smör·gås·bord (smôr'gås-bôrd, smûr'-), n. 1. a diversified grouping of foods placed together on a table from which guests may serve themselves. 2. a restaurant serving foods in such a way.

smote (smōt), past tense and alternate past participle of smite.

smoth·er (smuth'ĕr), v.t. 1. to destroy the life of by suffocation. 2. to stifle. 3. to suppress or conceal. 4. to coat to a considerable extent: v.i. to be suffocated: n. stifling smoke or thick dust.

smoul·der (smōl'dĕr), v.i. [British], same as smolder.

smudge (smuj), n. 1. a smear or stain. 2. suffocating smoke. 3. a smoldering fire for keeping off mosquitoes, protecting plants from frost, etc.: v.t. & v.i. smudged, smudg'ing, to smear or stain.

smudg·y (smuj'i), adj. smudg'i·er, smudg'i·est, stained, smeared, etc. —smudg'i·ness, n.

smug (smug), adj. smug'ger, smug'gest, 1. originally, spruce; neat. 2. content or complacent about oneself in such a way as to irritate others. —smug'ly, adv. —smug'ness, n.

smug·gle (smug'l), v.t. -gled, -gling, 1. to import or export secretly without paying custom duties. 2. to convey or introduce clandestinely: v.i. to practice smuggling.

smug·gler (smug'lĕr), n. 1. one who smuggles. 2. a vessel engaged in smuggling.

smut (smut), n. 1. a spot or stain made by soot or similar dirty matter. 2. a piece of soot or dirty matter. 3. obscenity. 4. in Botany, a fungous disease affecting cereal grain: v.t. smut'ted, smut'ting, to soil or blacken with or as with smut: v.i. to be affected with or stained by smut.

smutch (smuch), n. a smudge; stain: v.t. to dirty, as with smoke or soot.

smut·ty (smut'i), adj. -ti·er, -ti·est, 1. soiled or stained with smut. 2. affected with smut. 3. obscene. —smut'ti·ly, adv. —smut'ti·ness, n.

snack (snak), n. a light, hasty meal: v.i. to have a light, hasty meal.

snack bar, a lunch counter, cafeteria, etc. serving snacks.

snaf·fle (snaf'l), n. a bit consisting of a joint in the middle and rings at the ends: v.t. -fled, -fling, to control with a snaffle bit.

snag (snag), n. 1. a short, rough projecting part, as a broken branch. 2. a stump of a tree fixed in the bed of a river. 3. a ripped part in cloth. 4. a looped thread in a knitted fabric, caused by catching on something. 5. an unforeseen impediment: v.t. snagged, snag'ging, 1. to clear of snags. 2.

ŏ in dragon, oo in crude, oo in wool, u in cup, ū in cure, û in turn, ŭ in focus, oi in boy, ou in house, th in thin, th in sheathe, g in get, j in joy, y in yet.

to run upon a snag. 3. to obstruct by a snag.

snail (snāl), *n.* 1. a slow-moving gastropod mollusk with a spiral shell into which it can withdraw for protection. 2. any slow-moving person.

snake (snāk), *n.* a reptile with a limbless, elongated body: some have hollow or grooved fangs through which a deadly poison flows: *v.t.* [Informal], to drag or pull; jerk: *v.i.* to wind around spirally, crawl along, etc. like a snake. —**snake′like,** *adj.*

snake-bird (snāk′bûrd), *n.* a tropical American diving bird with a sharp-pointed bill and long, slender neck.

snake-root (′rōōt), *n.* any of various plants reputed as effective remedies for snake bite.

snak·y (snā′ki), *adj.* snak′i-er, snak′i-est. 1. of, pertaining to, or having the characteristics of a snake. 2. deceitful; sly; cunning. 3. winding around; twisting.

snap (snap), *v.i.* snapped, snap′ping. 1. to break short or instantaneously. 2. to produce a sharp, sudden sound. 3. to utter sharp, angry words (with *at*). 4. to make a sharp, clicking sound. 5. to make a fast closing, as of the jaws, with this sound. 6. to act instantaneously: *v.t.* 1. to break suddenly. 2. to crack. 3. to bite suddenly and unexpectedly. 4. to take a photograph of. 5. to make move quickly. 6. to speak sharply (often with *out*): *n.* 1. the act of snapping. 2. a noise made by snapping. 3. a catch or fastener that closes with a snapping sound. 4. a sudden and sharp spell of cold weather. 5. short and angry words. 6. a flat, hard cookie. 7. [Informal], an energetic condition. 8. [Slang], something that presents no difficulties in execution: *adj.* 1. offhand; made or done hastily. 2. that joins by means of a snap. 3. [Slang], presenting no difficulty in execution.

snap bean, same as green bean or wax bean.

snap·drag·on (snap′drag-ŏn), *n.* 1. a plant with flowers of crimson, purple, etc. having two lips resembling a mouth. 2. a social game in which raisins are snatched from a bowl of burning brandy.

snap·per (′ẽr), *n.* 1. one who or that which snaps. 2. any of several marine food fishes. 3. a snapping turtle.

snapping turtle, a large freshwater turtle of North America, which seizes its prey with a strong snap of the jaws.

snap·pish (snap′ish), *adj.* 1. apt to snap or bite. 2. peevish; irritable.

snap·py (′i), *adj.* -pi-er, -pi-est. 1. snappish. 2. that snaps; snatching, cracking, etc. 3. [Informal], brisk; also, stylish; smart.

snap·shot (snap′shot), *n.* a quick, informal photograph taken by snapping the shutter of a hand-held camera.

snare (sner), *n.* 1. a trap for small animals, typically a noose jerking tight. 2. anything that entangles or traps. 3. a length of wire or gut strung across the bottom of a small, double-headed drum for extra vibration. 4. *pl.* a set of drums so strung; snare drums: *v.t.* snared, snar′ing, to catch or entangle with or as if with a snare.

snare drum, a small, double-headed drum strung with snares.

snarl (snärl), *v.i.* 1. to growl fiercely, showing the teeth, as a hostile dog does. 2. to snap out words in an angry, irritated, or surly way. 3. to become knotted or tangled: *v.t.* 1. to express or indicate by or as if by growling fiercely. 2. to make knotted, tangled, or complicated. 3. to decorate (metal) with a raised design, as by hammering: *n.* 1. a fierce growl, or an utterance suggestive of this. 2. something knotted, tangled, or confusingly complicated. —**snarl′y,** *adj.* **snarl′i-er, snarl′i-est.**

snatch (snach), *v.t.* 1. to take or seize abruptly or without right, permission, etc.; grab. 2. to seize and carry off abruptly or hastily. 3. to take or get hurriedly: *v.i.* to grab or grab at something: *n.* 1. a snatching; grabbing. 2. a brief period; short interval. 3. a fragmentary part; short section, example, etc.

sneak (snēk), *v.i.* to move silently and with extreme caution, on or as if on tiptoe, so as not to be seen or heard and often for some underhanded or otherwise questionable purpose: *v.t.* to take, put, give, etc. in a stealthy way: *n.* 1. the act of sneaking. 2. an obnoxious, sneaking individual. 3. a sneaker (sense 2): *adj.* stealthy; clandestine.

sneak·er (′ẽr), *n.* 1. one that sneaks; sneak. 2. a light shoe typically of canvas with a sole and heel of one piece of soft rubber, worn especially as for handball or tennis.

sneak·ing (′ing), *adj.* 1. of or characteristic of one that sneaks; furtive and typically underhanded. 2. kept from being known; not openly admitted; secret; clandestine. 3. contemptibly unconvincing, as an excuse; weak; lame. 4. slight but not easily dismissed: in *sneaking suspicion.*

sneak·y (′i), *adj.* sneak′i-er, sneak′i-est. of, like, or typical of one that sneaks; furtive and typically underhanded. —**sneak′i-ness,** *n.*

sneer (snir), *v.i.* 1. to express derision or contempt by a contortion of the facial features, typically with a curling of the upper lip. 2. to express derision or contempt in speaking or writing: *v.t.* 1. to utter or give vent to in the manner of one that sneers. 2. to act upon, influence, etc. by or as if by sneering: *n.* 1. the act of sneering. 2. a remark, insinuation, etc. marked by or suggestive of sneering.

sneeze (snēz), *v.i.* sneezed, sneez′ing, to expel breath suddenly and explosively through the nose and mouth, as a reflex action to an irritation or tickling of the mucous membrane of the nose: *n.* a sneezing.

snell (snel), *n.* a short piece of gut, nylon, etc. for attaching a fishhook to a fishing line: *v.t.* to attach (a fishhook) to a snell.

snick·er (snik′ẽr), *n.* a partly suppressed, snorting laugh, typically derisive, embarrassed, or uneasy: *v.i.* to laugh with a snicker or snickers: *v.t.* to utter with a snicker.

snide (snīd), *adj.* derisive or disparaging in a mean, underhanded way.

sniff (snif), *v.i.* 1. to make one or more quick, short, typically audible inhalations through the nose, as in trying to smell something. 2

to express disdain, indignation, etc. thus: *v.t.* to inhale, get the smell of, or detect by or as if by sniffing: *n.* 1. a sniffing. 2. something sniffed.

snif·fle (snif'l), *v.i.* -fled, -fling, to sniff repeatedly, as to keep the nose from running: *n.* 1. a sniffling. 2. *pl.* [Informal], a head cold: usually preceded by *the.*

snif·ter (snif'tēr), *n.* a large goblet with a short stem, the opening being relatively small in circumference to intensify the aroma of the drink, typically brandy, contained.

snig·ger (snig'ēr), *n. & v.i. & v.t.* same as snicker.

snip (snip), *v.t. & v.i.* snipped, snip'ping, to cut or cut off or out with scissors or shears in one or more short, quick clips: *n.* 1. a small cut so made. 2. a small piece snipped off. 3. [Informal], a small individual, or one, especially a young girl, viewed as impudent.

snipe (snip), *n.* 1. any one of several long-billed wading birds found chiefly in marshes. 2. a shot from a hidden position: *v.i.* 1. to hunt snipe. 2. to shoot, as at enemy soldiers, from a hidden position. —snip'er, *n.*

snip·pet (snip'it), *n.* 1. a small piece snipped off. 2. a very short excerpt. 3. a bit or scrap, especially of information.

snip·py (snip'i), *adj.* -pi·er, -pi·est, [Informal], impertinent; impudent.

snitch (snich), *v.t.* [Slang], to pilfer; filch: *v.i.* [Slang], to tattle (*on*): *n.* [Slang], one that tattles; tattletale: also **snitch'er.**

sniv·el (sniv'l), *v.i.* -eled or -elled, -el·ing or -el·ling, 1. to run at the nose. 2. to sniffle. 3. to whimper and sniffle. 4. to complain or lament in a manner suggestive of a fretful, sniveling child; whine: *n.* a sniveling.

snob (snob), *n.* an individual, often a social climber, arrogantly convinced of the superiority of his own tastes and interests. — snob'bish, *adj.*

snob·ber·y ('ēr·i), *n., pl.* -ber·ies, 1. snobbish conduct, pretense, or character. 2. an instance of this.

snood (snōōd), *n.* a baglike net worn at the back of a woman's head to hold the hair.

snook (snook), *n., pl.* snook, snooks, any one of a family of pikelike fishes of warm seas.

snoop (snōōp), *v.i.* [Informal], to pry where one has no business; spy on the affairs of others: *n.* [Informal], one that snoops.

snoop·y ('i), *adj.* snoop'i·er, snoop'i·est, [Informal], marked by or given to snooping.

snoot (snōōt), *n.* [Informal], the nose or face.

snoot·y ('i), *adj.* snoot'i·er, snoot'i·est, [Informal], disdainfully aloof; supercilious.

snooze (snōōz), *v.i.* snoozed, snooz'ing, [Informal], to take a nap; doze: *n.* [Informal], a nap.

snore (snōr), *v.i.* snored, snor'ing, to make harshly vibratory breathing noises in sleep: *n.* a snoring. —snor'er, *n.*

snor·kel (snôr'kl), *n.* a long tube used by a swimmer to breathe while swimming just under the surface of water, one end being held in the mouth and the other projecting into the air.

snort (snôrt), *v.i.* to breathe through the nose in sudden, harsh inhalations or exhalations:

n. 1. a snorting. 2. [Slang], a drink of straight liquor tossed down in one gulp.

snot (snot), *n.* 1. [Vulgar], nasal mucus. 2. [Slang], a young, impudent individual.

snot·ty ('i), *adj.* snot'ti·er, snot'ti·est, 1. [Vulgar], of, full of, or covered with nasal mucus. 2. [Slang], nasty, mean, etc.

snout (snout), *n.* 1. the projecting nose of an animal. 2. a noselike projection. 3. [Informal], the nose of a person.

snow (snō), *n.* 1. white, feathery flakes formed by the freezing of water vapor in the upper air and falling to the ground. 2. an accumulation of these on the ground. 3. a falling of snow, or weather marked by this. 4. something snowlike. 5. a blur of specks on a television screen, resulting from a weak signal: *v.i.* to fall as or like snow: *v.t.* 1. to make fall as or like snow. 2. to blanket, block, etc. with or as if with snow. 3. [Slang], to barrage with much talk in trying to deceive, trick, confuse, convince, etc.

snow·ball ('bôl), *n.* a ball-like mass of packed snow: *v.i.* to increase rapidly in intensity, complexity, etc., as a rapidly rolling snowball.

snow·bank ('bangk), *n.* a long, deep mound or heap of fallen snow.

Snow·belt (snō'belt), *n.* the northeastern and Midwestern U.S. characterized by cold, snowy winters: also **Snow Belt.**

snow·bound ('bound), *adj.* confined or blocked by a heavy fall of snow.

snow·drift ('drift), *n.* a mass of fallen snow blown into a pile by the wind.

snow·drop ('drop), *n.* any one of a Mediterranean species of low-growing plants with small, bell-shaped, white flowers.

snow·fall ('fôl), *n.* a fall of snow.

snow fence, a light fence of lath and wire to control the drifting of snow.

snow·flake ('flāk), *n.* a flake of snow.

snow leopard, a large cat with long, thick, whitish fur blotched with dark spots, found in the mountains of central Asia.

snow line, the lowest limit of a region of perpetual snow: also **snow limit.**

snow·man ('man), *n., pl.* -men ('men), a comical figure fashioned of snow, usually of stacked, large snowballs, and made to resemble a human being.

snow·mo·bile ('mō·bēl), *n.* any one of various motor vehicles designed to travel over snow, usually with steerable runners at the front part and tractor treads at the rear.

snow·plow ('plou), *n.* any one of various plowlike devices, or a vehicle equipped with such a device, for clearing away snow as from roads.

snow·shoe ('shōō), *n.* either one of a pair of typically oval wooden frames strung with a network as of leather strips, worn attached to a shoe to keep a person from sinking in snow.

snow·storm ('stôrm), *n.* a storm characterized by a heavy fall of snow.

snow·suit ('sōōt), *n.* a heavily lined, one-piece or two-piece outer garment, often hooded, designed for wear by children in snowy weather.

---

snow tire, a tire with a special tread, and sometimes studs, for better traction on a surface covered with snow or ice.

snow·y (snō'i), *adj.* snow'i·er, snow'i·est, 1. of, marked by, or full of snow. 2. snowlike, as in whiteness.

snub (snub), *v.t.* snubbed, snub'bing, 1. to ignore, reject, or repress in a contemptuous or scornful way. 2. to pretend not to see, hear, or know (someone), as at a social function, so as to wound; cut. 3. to snub (a cigarette). 4. to stop suddenly the movement of (a rope, cable, etc. being run out) by turning a length of it about a post or fixed object. 5. to bring up short, check, or make fast by or as if by such action: *n.* 1. a disdainful or contemptuous ignoring, rejection, etc. 2. a pretended failure to see, recognize, etc., so as to wound. 3. a snubbing as of a rope: *adj.* short and turned up: said of a nose.

snub·by ('i), *adj.* -bi·er, -bi·est, 1. snub or snub-nosed. 2. of or given to snubbing.

snub-nosed (snub'nōzd'), *adj.* having a snub nose.

snuff (snuf), *n.* the charred part of the wick of a candle: *v.t.* 1. to trim off this part of (the wick of a candle). 2. to extinguish (a candle) with snuffers or by pinching. 3. to bring suddenly to an end; kill (with *out*).

snuff (snuf), *v.t.* 1. to draw in strongly through the nose. 2. to smell or detect by smelling through such strong inhalation; scent; sniff: *v.i.* to snuff something or make snuffing noises; sniff; sniffle: *n.* 1. a snuffing. 2. a powdered tobacco for snuffing into the nose or for applying to the gums. 3. a pinch of this. 4. smell; scent. 5. [Informal], a standard, as of quality or condition: in *up to snuff*.

snuff·box (snuf'boks), *n.* a container, usually ornamental, for holding snuffing tobacco.

snuff·er (snuf'ẽr), *n.* 1. an implement consisting of a handle with a cone at the end, used for extinguishing a candle. 2. *pl.* a scissors-like implement for trimming the charred part of the wick of a candle.

snuf·fle (snuf'l), *v.i. & v.t.* -fled, -fling, to inhale, or inhale and exhale, strongly and audibly through the nose, often with or as if with difficulty: *n.* a snuffling or the sound of this.

snuf·fy (snuf'i), *adj.* snuf'fi·er, snuf'fi·est, 1. suggestive of or stained with snuffing tobacco. 2. habitually using such tobacco.

snug (snug), *adj.* snug'ger, snug'gest, 1. secure and comfortable; cozy. 2. compact and neat; trim. 3. hugging the contours; fitting closely. 4. well-concealed: *adv.* in a snug way.

snug·gle (snug'l), *v.i.* -gled, -gling, to draw oneself together and huddle up closely so as to have warmth, comfort, affection, etc.; nestle; cuddle: *v.t.* 1. to hold or bring close, or move up close to, so as to have warmth, comfort, affection, etc. 2. to make snug.

so (sō), *adv.* 1. in the way shown, indicated, etc. 2. in such a way (followed by *as,* to express purpose). 3. to such a degree or extent. 4. to such a high degree or extent. 5. therefore. 6. likewise: *conj.* 1. in order that

(usually followed by *that*). 2. on condition that. 3. [Informal], with the result that; and consequently: *pron.* such as indicated: *interj.* an exclamation of surprise, indignation, etc.: *adj.* 1. true. 2. properly arranged.

so (sō), *n.* same as **sol** (tone in a musical scale).

soak (sōk), *v.t.* 1. to wet thoroughly; drench. 2. to steep or submerge for a long time in or as if in liquid. 3. to draw in (liquid, warmth, knowledge, etc.) by or as if by absorption. 4. [Informal], to overcharge to an extreme extent. 5. [Slang], to hit hard; sock; slug: *v.i.* 1. to be in a condition of immersion or absorption. 2. to pass into or through something by or as if by absorption: *n.* 1. the action of soaking or the condition of being soaked. 2. a liquid used for soaking. 3. [Slang], a drunkard.

soap (sōp), *n.* a substance, usually consisting chiefly of sodium or potassium salts of fatty acids, used with water to make suds for washing or cleaning: *v.t.* to lather, scrub, etc. with soap.

soap-box ('boks), *n.* 1. a box or crate for soap. 2. a makeshift platform climbed up on as by a haranguer to address passers-by or chance groups.

soap opera, [Informal], a melodramatic, sentimental serial on radio or television.

soap-stone ('stōn), *n.* same as steatite.

soap-suds ('sudz), *n.pl.* 1. soapy, foamy water. 2. the foam formed on such water.

soap·y (sō'pi), *adj.* soap'i·er, soap'i·est, of, like, or covered with soap. —soap'i·ness, *n.*

soar (sōr), *v.i.* 1. to sail along in the air, usually at a lofty altitude, or rise higher and higher in the air, specifically in a swift, smooth, graceful way. 2. to rise high above the usual or ordinary level: *n.* a soaring.

sob (sob), *v.i.* sobbed, sob'bing, to weep in a heartbroken way, with convulsive catching of the breath: *v.t.* to utter while sobbing: *n.* a sobbing or the sound of it.

so·ber (sō'bẽr), *adj.* 1. not drunk; not intoxicated. 2. marked by moderation or restraint, especially in the use of alcoholic liquor; temperate, especially habitually. 3. not flurried; not excited; calm; self-possessed. 4. not ostentatious or obtrusive; quiet; plain; sedate. 5. solemn; grave: *v.i. & v.t.* to make or become sober (often with *up* or *down*).

so·ber-mind·ed (-mīn'did), *adj.* marked by sobriety of attitude and judgment.

so·bri·e·ty (sō-brī'ê-ti, sō-), *n.* the quality or state of being sober.

so·bri·quet (sō'bri-kā, sō-bri-kā'), *n.* 1. an assumed name. 2. a nickname.

soc·cer (sok'ẽr), *n.* a field game played with a round ball by two teams of eleven players each, the ball being moved chiefly by kicking.

so·cia·ble (sō'shä-bl), *adj.* 1. seeking after association with others; disposed to companionship; gregarious. 2. affable; companionable. 3. characterized by pleasant conversation and companionship: *n.* a social. —so·cia·bil'i·ty, *n.* —so'cia·bly, *adv.*

so·cial (sō'shůl), *adj.* 1. of, pertaining to, or involving the association of human beings with each other in matters affecting their common welfare. 2. marked by or disposed toward such association. 3. of or involving society, especially elite society. 4. friendly; affable; sociable. 5. of or involving friends, companionship, or sociability. 6. of or engaged in providing material aid, counseling services, etc., specifically to the needy. 7. living or associating in groups or communities. 8. in *Botany*, growing in clumps or masses: *n.* an informal social gathering or party, public or semipublic, typically featuring a meal or light refreshments, games, etc., sponsored as by a church and often designed as a modest fund-raising event.

social climber, an individual much concerned with rising socially and, in trying to do this, seeking to meet socially prominent persons.

social disease, any venereal disease.

so·cial·ism (sō'shul-izm), *n.* 1. any one of various systems of public ownership of all production, distribution, and communication. 2. [S-], a political movement, or its doctrines, methods, etc., for establishing such a system. —so'cial·ist, *n. & adj.* —so·cial·is'tic, *adj.*

so·cial·ite (sō'shā-līt), *n.* a socially prominent person.

so·ci·al·i·ty (sō-shi-al'ĭ-ti), *n.* the state or quality of being social.

so·cial·ize (sō'shŭ-līz), *v.t.* -ized, -iz·ing, 1. to make social or sociable. 2. to make socialistic: *v.i.* 1. to engage in social activities; associate amiably with others. 2. to converse in a friendly, informal way with others; chat. —so·cial·i·za'tion, *n.*

socialized medicine, any system supplying all medical needs of a society by public funding.

social science, any one of various studies, as sociology or history, centered on the elements, structure, development, or behavior of human society.

social security, any one of various systems provided by a government and designed to protect all its citizens against loss, deprivation, or neglect arising as from old age, disability, or unemployment.

social service, same as **social work.**

social studies, the part of a school curriculum that includes history, civics, and other social sciences.

social welfare, 1. the welfare of society, especially of needy members. 2. same as **social work.**

social work, activity, or any individual service, designed to promote the welfare of society, as material aid or counseling. —**social worker.**

so·ci·e·tal (sō-sī'ĕ-tl), *adj.* of or pertaining to society; social.

so·ci·e·ty (sō-sī'ĕ-ti), *n., pl.* -ties, 1. a number of persons regarded as constituting a single group or community. 2. the complex of factors, as activities, attitudes, and environment, characterizing any such group. 3. the worldwide community made up of all human beings. 4. companionship; company. 5. the totality of an individual's friends or associates. 6. any group of persons organized on the basis of common work, interests, etc.

7. a group of persons viewed as elite in some way, as by reason of distinguished ancestry, wealth, education, etc. 8. a group of animals or plants living together in a single environment and viewed as constituting a homogeneous unit or entity.

Society of Friends, a Christian religious sect founded in England about 1650: it rejects war and all violence and is without formal creed, rites, liturgy, or priesthood.

Society of Jesus, see **Jesuit.**

so·ci·o-, a combining form meaning *social, society, sociological.*

so·ci·o·e·co·nom·ic (sō-si-ō-ē-kō-nom'ik, sō-shi-ō-), *adj.* of or involving both social and economic factors.

so·ci·o·log·i·cal (sō-si-ō-loj'i-kl, sō-shi-ō-), *adj.* 1. of or pertaining to human society. 2. of or pertaining to sociology. Also **so·ci·o·log'ic.**

so·ci·ol·o·gist (sō-si-ol'ō-jist, sō-shi-), *n.* a specialist in sociology.

so·ci·ol·o·gy (sō-si-ol'ō-ji, sō-shi-), *n.* the science or study of human society, specifically of its nature, development, behavior, etc.

so·ci·o·path (sō'si-ō-path, sō'shi-ō-), *n.* an aggressively antisocial psychopath.

sock (sok), *n.* 1. a light shoe worn by classic actors of comedy. 2. *pl.* **socks, sox,** a close-fitting covering, as of cotton, which is drawn over the foot and over which a shoe, boot, etc. is typically worn, usually extending up over the ankle to mid-calf or to just below the knee. 3. [Slang], a heavy blow, especially with the fist: *v.t.* [Slang], 1. to hit hard, especially with the fist. 2. to set aside (money), as in a savings account (followed by *away*): *adv.* [Slang], directly; square.

sock·et (sok'it), *n.* a hollow into which something is fitted.

sock·eye (sok'ī), *n.* a small salmon of the northern Pacific.

so·cle (sok'l, sōk'l), *n.* an architectural piece projecting to support a column, statue, etc.

So·crat·ic (sō-krat'ik), *adj.* of or pertaining to Socrates (470?-399 B.C.), Greek philosopher.

Socratic irony, a feigning of ignorance so as to expose fallacies in an opponent's logic.

Socratic method, a method of leading an individual to a logical conclusion by asking a series of easily answered questions.

sod (sod), *n.* turf; sward; also, a piece of this: *v.t.* **sod'ded, sod'ding,** to cover with sod.

so·da (sō'dá), *n.* 1. an oxide of sodium. 2. same as **sodium bicarbonate, sodium carbonate, sodium hydroxide.** 3. same as **soda water.** 4. a cooling drink made of chilled soda water mixed with a syrup or other flavoring agent and usually containing a ball or two of ice cream.

soda biscuit, 1. a biscuit made with baking soda and sour cream or buttermilk. 2. [Chiefly British], a soda cracker.

soda cracker, a light cracker, originally one leavened with baking soda.

soda fountain, a counter equipped to prepare and serve sodas, sundaes, etc.

soda jerk·er (jûr'kẽr), [Informal], one who prepares and serves sodas, sundaes, etc. at a soda fountain: also **soda jerk.**

so·dal·i·ty (sō-dal'ĭ-ti), *n., pl.* -ties, 1. fellowship. 2. a Roman Catholic lay society for devotional or charitable activity.

soda pop, a flavored, carbonated soft drink.

soda water, water charged with carbon dioxide; carbonated water.

sod·den (sod'n), *adj.* 1. soaked through with water or other liquid; saturated. 2. heavy or soggy, as poorly baked bread. 3. dull or numbed, as from overindulgence in alcoholic liquor. 4. devoid of spirit and vitality; torpid; sluggish; apathetic.

so·di·um (sō'di-ŭm), *n.* an alkaline metallic chemical element, white in color and of a waxy consistency, found in nature only in combined form.

sodium benzoate, a sweet, odorless, white powder, the sodium salt of benzoic acid, used for preserving food, as an antiseptic, etc.

sodium bicarbonate, a certain compound of sodium, white and crystalline, used in baking powder, as an antacid, etc.

sodium carbonate, any one of various hydrated carbonates of sodium; also, the anhydrous sodium salt of carbonic acid.

sodium chloride, common salt.

sodium hydroxide, a compound of sodium, white and strongly caustic, used in chemistry, oil refining, etc.

sodium nitrate, a clear, odorless, crystalline salt, a compound of sodium, used as an oxidizing agent and in making explosives, fertilizers, etc.

sod·om·y (sod'ŏm-i), *n.* any sexual intercourse considered abnormal, especially anal intercourse.

so·ev·er (sō-ev'ẽr), *adv.* 1. in any way; to any extent or degree. 2. at all. Also used as a combining form to emphasize or generalize *who, what, when, where,* etc.

so·fa (sō'fä), *n.* a long seat with stuffed bottom, back, and arms.

sofa bed, a sofa designed to open out and form a double bed.

sof·fit (sof'it), *n.* the underpart of a cornice, lintel, arch, etc.

soft (sôft), *adj.* 1. yielding easily to pressure, friction, etc. 2. easily worked, shaped, etc.; plastic; malleable. 3. smooth to the touch or taste. 4. light; gentle; not rough. 5. not severe or harsh; easy or pleasant to experience, encounter, deal with, etc.; mild or agreeable. 6. not requiring much effort, application, ability, etc.; not at all demanding. 7. easily approached or imposed upon; complaisant. 8. quick to respond emotionally; suggestible. 9. kindhearted or compassionate. 10. gently affectionate; loving; tender. 11. not resistant to something specified; easily acted upon; open or too open as to influences or ideas. 12. lacking proper vigor or hardiness; not in good shape physically or mentally, especially from self-indulgence or lack of discipline; flabby. 13. lacking strength of character; deficient in moral fiber; weak, irresolute, etc. 14. free of mineral salts interfering with the lathering of soap: said of water. 15. nonalcoholic: said of beverages. 16. not sharply angular; rounded. 17. not glaring, bright, or strong; subdued: said of light or color. 18. not marked by sharp

outlines or by sharp contrasts as of light and shadow, as a photograph. 19. not strident, ringing, loud, or harsh; mellow, low, or quiet. 20. made up of easily digested food: said of a diet: *adv.* in a soft way: *n.* something soft; soft part. —**soft'ly,** *adv.* —**soft'ness,** *n.*

soft-ball ('bôl), *n.* 1. a game like baseball but played on a smaller diamond, using a larger and softer ball, and having seven innings instead of the nine innings of baseball. 2. the ball.

soft-boiled ('boild'), *adj.* boiled only a few minutes so that the contents do not become hard: said of an egg.

soft-core ('kôr'), *adj.* approaching but not quite so extreme as what is considered hard-core.

sof·ten (sôf'n), *v.t. & v.i.* to make or become soft or softer. —**sof'ten·er,** *n.*

soft-heart·ed (sôft'här'tid), *adj.* compassionate; tender; gentle. —**soft'heart'ed·ly,** *adv.*

soft-ped·al ('ped'l), *v.t.* -aled or -alled, -al·ing or -al·ling, [Informal]. to make less emphatic, less noticeable, etc.

soft-soap ('sōp'), *v.t.* [Informal]. to use ingratiating terms or flattery in speaking to.

soft·ware ('wer), *n.* whatever is used in a digital computer other than its physical components, as the data fed in.

soft·wood ('wood'), *n.* 1. any light, easily cut wood. 2. any tree yielding such wood.

soft·y (sôf'ti), *n., pl.* **soft'ies,** [Informal]. 1. one given to self-coddling. 2. a weakling. 3. one who gives up too easily. 4. one easily moved by sentiment.

sog·gy (sog'i), *adj.* -gi·er, -gi·est, 1. saturated; soaked; sodden. 2. too moist and heavy, as insufficiently baked cake.

soil (soil), *n.* 1. the top stratum of the earth's surface, where plants grow. 2. any material, environment, etc. in which something can or does take root and flourish. 3. ground; land; country. 4. a dirtied, smudged, or stained area, spot, etc. 5. a dirtying, staining, or sullying. 6. excrement, sewage, refuse, etc. 7. manure used for fertilizing: *v.t. & v.i.* to make or become dirtied, stained, or sullied.

soi·ree, soi·rée (swä-rā'), *n.* an evening party.

so·journ (sō'jûrn, sō-jûrn'), *v.i.* to dwell or stay somewhere for a time: *n.* (sō'jûrn), a sojourning. —**so'journ·er,** *n.*

Sol (sol), *n.* 1. in *Roman Mythology,* the sun god. 2. the sun personified. 3. [s-], (sōl), *pl.* **sols, so'les,** the monetary unit of Peru.

sol (sōl), *n.* 1. the fifth tone in any major or minor musical scale of eight tones. 2. (sol, sōl), a colloid combined with a liquid.

sol·ace (sol'is), *n.* comfort in sorrow; consolation: *v.t.* -aced, -ac·ing, to comfort; console.

so·lan (sō'lán), *n.* same as gannet: also **solan goose.**

so·lar (sō'lẽr), *adj.* 1. of or from the sun. 2. using the light or heat of the sun.

so·lar·i·um (sō-ler'i-ŭm, sō-), *n., pl.* -i·a (-ä), a room or other enclosed area designed to admit much direct sunlight, especially for therapeutic use.

so·lar·ize (sō'lä-rīz), *v.t.* -ized, -iz·ing, 1. to affect by exposure to the sun. 2. to expose (a photographic film or plate) too much or too long to light coming from the sun: *v.i.* to become affected by excessive exposure to light from the sun: said of a photographic film or plate. —**so·lar·i·za'tion,** *n.*

solar plexus, 1. a complex network of nerves behind the stomach. 2. [Informal], the area of the belly just below the breastbone.

solar system, the sun and the heavenly bodies revolving about it.

solar year, same as **tropical year.**

so·la·tium (sō-lā'shi-ùm), *n., pl.* **-ti·a** (-å), compensation claimed or paid, especially for injury to the feelings.

sold (sōld), past tense and past participle of **sell.**

sol·der (sod'ēr), *n.* a metal alloy used· melted for uniting or patching metals: *v.t. & v.i.* to join or become joined with this.

sol·dier (sōl'jēr), *n.* 1. one engaged in military service; specifically, a member of an army: often restricted to an enlisted man, as distinguished from one holding a warrant or commission. 2. one of much· military experience or skill. 3. a persistent, courageous worker for some cause: *v.i.* 1. to serve or act as a soldier. 2. to shirk one's duty, as by merely pretending to work.

sol·dier·ly (-li), *adj.* of, like, or typical of a good soldier. —**sol'dier·li·ness,** *n.*

soldier of fortune, 1. a soldier serving in a foreign army for pay. 2. an individual searching for adventure; adventurer.

sol·dier·y (sōl'jēr·i), *n., pl.* **-dier·ies,** 1. soldiers collectively; also, a group of soldiers. 2. military science.

sole (sōl), *n.* 1. the underside of the.foot; also, the corresponding underside of a shoe, sock, etc. 2. the bottom surface as of a plow or golf club. 3. any one of various flatfishes, especially those of a large family prized as food: *v.t.* soled, sol'ing, to provide, as a shoe, with another sole, especially with a new one: *adj.* 1. that is without another or others; lone; single; solitary. 2. not shared or divided, as rights; exclusive.

sol·e·cism (sol'ê-sizm), *n.* 1. a blunder in using language; specifically, an unidiomatic or ungrammatical use of words. 2. a breach of etiquette. 3. any mistake or impropriety.

sole·ly (sōl'li), *adv.* 1. to the exclusion of any other or others; alone. 2. with no other purpose, intention, etc.

sol·emn (sol'ēm), *adj.* 1. of, marked by, or observed with the full ceremony, ritual, or other detail prescribed, customary, or expected for something viewed as of outstanding importance, as a major religious holiday or the dedication of a national monument. 2. of, marked by, or accomplished with the sanctions or special gravity reserved for or associated with something of extraordinary significance or consequence, as an oath to tell the truth. 3. of, in, or in accordance with, strict form; highly formalized. 4. far removed from all that is superficial, trivial, or flippant; deep and serious. 5. altogether earnest; not flighty, light, or capricious. 6. so deeply impressive as to be awe-inspiring; overwhelmingly stately, majestic, sublime,

etc. 7. not jolly or gay; somber. —**sol'emn·ly,** *adv.*

so·lem·ni·fy (sò-lem'ni-fī), *v.t.* **-fied, -fy·ing,** to make solemn.

so·lem·ni·ty (sò-lem'ni-ti), *n., pl.* **-ties,** 1. the quality or state of being solemn. 2. solemn observance, as of a religious holiday. 3. a solemn occasion, event, remark, etc.

sol·em·nize (sol'ém-nīz), *v.t.* **-nized, -niz·ing,** 1. to celebrate or observe with full ceremony, ritual, etc. 2. to mark, perform, or attend to with due solemnity. 3. to make solemn; solemnify. —**sol·em·ni·za'tion,** *n.*

so·le·noid (sō'lê-noid, sol'ê-), *n.* a coil of wire that carries an electric current and that acts like a magnet. —**so·le·noi'dal,** *adj.*

sole·plate (sōl'plāt), *n.* the bottom surface of a flatiron.

so·les (sō'les), alternate plural of **sol** (monetary unit of Peru).

sol·fa (sōl-fä'), *n.* 1. the syllables *do, re, mi, fa, sol, la, ti, do,* used in singing the tones of an eight-tone musical scale. 2. use of these; solfeggio: *v.t. & v.i.* **-faed' (-fäd'), -fa'ing,** to sing (a scale, song, etc.) using sol-fa.

sol·fa·ta·ra (sōl-fâ-tä'rå), *n.* a volcanic vent emitting only vapors, especially sulfurous gases.

sol·feg·gio (sol-fej'ō), *n., pl.* **-feg'gios, -feg'gi** ('i), use of the sol-fa syllables, especially in voice practice.

so·lic·it (sò-lis'it), *v.t.* 1. to ask or ask for with earnestness or pleas. 2. to entice; lure. 3. to approach for sexual purposes, as a prostitute does; accost: *v.i.* to solicit someone or something. —**so·lic·i·ta'tion,** *n.*

so·lic·i·tor (-ēr), *n.* 1. one that solicits; especially, one asking for contributions, selling subscriptions, etc. 2. in England, a member of the legal profession who is not entitled to plead cases in superior courts. 3. in the U.S., a lawyer serving as official law officer for a city, department, etc.

solicitor general, *pl.* solicitors general, solicitor generals, 1. a law officer serving the national government and ranking next below the attorney general. 2. in some States without an attorney general, the chief law officer.

so·lic·i·tous (sò-lis'ĭ-tùs), *adj.* 1. eagerly or anxiously disposed to help, advise, or comfort others. 2. worriedly concerned; apprehensive; uneasy. 3. anxiously and busily engaged in achieving some aim. 4. conscientious and carefully attentive to detail. 5. of, typical of, or prompted by solicitude.

so·lic·i·tude (-tōōd), *n.* 1. the quality or state of being solicitous. 2. something giving rise to concern, worry, or anxiety.

sol·id (sol'id), *adj.* ·1. wholly or relatively firm, compact, or hard; not fluid or gaseous. 2. not hollow. 3. of, pertaining to, or marked by length, breadth, and thickness. 4. resistant to being moved, shaken, upset, etc.; not flimsy or weak. 5. genuine; true; real. 6. not broken, divided, or scattered. 7. being the same throughout, as in material or color. 8. unified; unanimous: *n.* 1. a substance that is not a liquid or gas. 2. a three-dimensional figure or object. —**sol'id·ly,** *adv.*

ð in dragon, ōō in crude, oo in wool, u in cup, ū in cure, ü in·turn, ŭ in focus, oi in boy, ou in house, th in thin, *th* in sheathe, g in get, j in joy, y in yet.

sol·i·dar·i·ty (sol-i-der'i-ti), *n., pl.* **-ties,** complete, harmonious unity or agreement, as in aims, principles, or ideals.

so·lid·i·fy (sō-lid'i-fī), *v.t. & v.i.* **-fied, -fy·ing,** to make or become solid; make or become firm, strong, unified, etc. **—so·lid·i·fi·ca'tion,** *n.*

so·lid·i·ty (sō-lid'i-ti), *n.* the quality or state of being solid.

sol·id-state (sol'id-stāt), *adj.* designating or of electronic devices controlling current without heated filaments, moving parts, etc.

sol·i·dus (sol'i-dùs), *n., pl.* **-di** (-dī), 1. a gold coin of the Late Roman Empire. 2. a short, slanted line, as a virgule.

so·lil·o·quize (sō-lil'ō-kwīz), *v.i. & v.t.* **-quized, -quiz·ing,** to speak in or as if in a soliloquy. **—so·lil'o·quist,** *n.*

so·lil·o·quy (sō-lil'ō-kwi), *n., pl.* **-quies,** 1. a talking to oneself. 2. an actor's speech designed to reveal to the audience the thoughts of the character being played but delivered as though in solitude or as though not heard by other characters in the drama.

sol·ip·sism (sol'ip-sizm), *n.* the theory that the self alone exists or that the self can know only its own experiences and states.

sol·i·taire (sol'i-ter), 1. a single gem set by itself, as in a ring. 2. a card game or other game played by one person.

sol·i·tar·y (sol'i-ter-i), *adj.* 1. being entirely apart from any other or others; being wholly alone; being by oneself or itself; altogether isolated; lone. 2. being the only one of the kind; unduplicated; unique. 3. done or engaged in by only one or by one that is alone. 4. of, marked by, or suggestive of total isolation, loneliness, or remoteness: *n., pl.* **-tar·ies,** an individual living totally alone; recluse.

sol·i·tude (sol'i-tōōd), *n.* 1. total isolation; complete seclusion. 2. the condition of being far distant from any other or others; remoteness. 3. an isolated, secluded, or remote region or place.

sol·mi·za·tion (sol-mi-zā'shùn), *n.* solfeggio.

so·lo (sō'lō), *n., pl.* **-los,** 1. a performance, presentation, work or section of a work, as of music or dance, done or to be done by just one performer, with or without accompaniment. 2. an airplane flight made by a pilot alone, without an assistant, instructor, etc. 3. a card game for two or more in which no player has a partner: *adj.* 1. designed for or performed by a single voice, instrument, or individual. 2. performing a solo: *adv.* without any other or others; alone: *v.i.* to perform a solo; especially, to make a solo flight.

so·lo·ist (-ist), *n.* a solo performer.

Sol·o·mon (sol'ō-mòn), *n.* 1. in the *Bible,* a son of David and king of Israel, noted for his wisdom. 2. any very wise man.

Solomon's seal, 1. a mystic symbol in the form of a six-pointed star. 2. any one of a genus of perennial plants with greenish flowers.

So·lon, so·lon (sō'lòn), *n.* a wise lawmaker.

so long, [Informal], goodbye.

sol·stice (sol'stis, sōl'stis), *n.* the point in the ecliptic of the sun at which it is either farthest north or farthest south of the equator.

sol·u·ble (sol'yoo-bl), *adj.* 1. capable of being dissolved or of passing into solution. 2. capable of being solved. **—sol·u·bil'i·ty,** *n.*

so·lu·tion (sō-lōō'shùn), *n.* 1. a mixing or combining of a solid, liquid, or gas with another substance, usually a fluid, in such a way that a homogeneous combination is formed. 2. the combination formed. 3. the solving of a problem. 4. the answer to a problem.

solv·a·ble (sol'vȧ-bl), *adj.* capable of being solved. **—solv·a·bil'i·ty,** *n.*

solve (solv), *v.t.* **solved, solv'ing,** 1. to find the correct answer to (a problem as in mathematics). 2. to find a satisfactory answer or explanation for (a mystery, puzzling situation, etc.).

sol·ven·cy (sol'vèn-si), *n.* the quality or state of being solvent.

sol·vent (sol'vènt), *n.* 1. a liquid or other agent that dissolves a substance. 2. that which solves or explains: *adj.* 1. dissolving or capable of dissolving a substance. 2. able to discharge all financial debts or claims.

so·ma (sō'mä), *n.* 1. *pl.* **-ma·ta** ('mä-tä), the whole of any organism, the germ cells excepted. 2. an East Indian plant with a milky juice.

so·mat·ic (sō-mat'ik), *adj.* 1. bodily; physical; corporeal; specifically, of or pertaining to the soma (sense 1). 2. of or pertaining to the framework or outer walls of the body. 3. designating or of the cells differentiating into bodily tissues, organs, etc.

so·ma·tol·o·gy (sō-mä-tol'ō-ji), *n.* 1. the science dealing with the properties of organic bodies. 2. a branch of anthropology dealing with man's physical nature and characteristics.

som·ber (som'bèr), *adj.* 1. dark; gloomy. 2. melancholy; depressed or depressing. 3. not bright, shiny, or gay; devoid of luster; dull. 4. solemn; grave.

som·bre ('bèr), *adj.* chiefly British form for somber.

som·bre·ro (som-brer'ō, sŏm-), *n., pl.* **-ros,** a hat with a broad brim and tall crown, common in the southwestern U.S., Mexico, etc.

some (sum, sùm), *adj.* 1. being one or ones unspecified or unknown. 2. being of an unspecified number, quantity, degree, etc. 3. [Informal], not ordinary; remarkable: *pron.* 1. one or ones unspecified or unknown. 2. an unspecified number, quantity, etc.: *adv.* 1. approximately; about. 2. [Informal], to an unspecified but often considerable extent, degree, etc.

-some (sùm), a suffix meaning *like, tending to, tending to be* or *in* (a specified) *number.*

-some (sōm), a combining form meaning *body, chromosome.*

some·bod·y (sum'bud-i, 'bod-i), *pron.* a person unknown or unnamed: *n., pl.* **-bod·ies,** a person of importance, accomplishment, etc.

some·day ('dā), *adv.* at some future day or time.

some·how ('hou), *adv.* in a way or by a

ā in *cap,* ā in *cane,* ä in *father,* ȧ in *abet,* e in *met,* ē in *be,* ē in *baker,* ē in *regent,* ĭ in *pit,* ī in *fine,* i in *manifest,* o in *hot,* ō in *horse,* ō in *bone,*

method unknown, unspecified, or not understood.

some-one ('wun), *pron.* same as somebody.

som-er-sault (sum'ẽr-sôlt), *n.* a rolling or throwing of the body either forward or backward, end over end, in a complete revolution: *v.i.* to do a somersault.

some-thing (sum'thing), *n.* 1. a thing or things not definitely known, understood, or identified. 2. an unspecified thing or things. 3. a thing or things of unspecified kind, number, degree, etc. 4. a small amount or quantity; a little. 5. [Informal], a thing or things quite significant, important, different, outstanding, etc.: *adv.* to some extent, degree, etc.

some-time ('tīm), *adv.* at a time unknown or unspecified: *adj.* 1. of an earlier time; former. 2. merely occasional; sporadic.

some-times ('tīmz), *adv.* at times; occasionally.

some-way ('wā), *adv.* in some way; somehow.

some-what ('hwut), *n.* some amount, quantity, degree, etc.: *adv.* to some extent or degree.

some-where ('hwer), *adv.* 1. in, to, or at a place unknown or unspecified. 2. at some time, degree, etc. (followed by *about*, *near*, etc.): *n.* a place unknown or unspecified.

som-me-lier (sum-ĕl-yā'), *n.* a wine steward.

som-nam-bu-late (som-nam'byoo-lāt, sŏm-), *v.i.* -lat-ed, -lat-ing, to walk about while asleep. —**som-nam-bu-lant**, *adj.* —**som-nam-bu-la'tion**, *n.*

som-nam-bu-lism (-lizm), *n.* a somnambulating. —**som-nam'bu-list**, *n.*

som-nif-er-ous (som-nif'ẽr-ŭs, sŏm-), *adj.* that induces sleep; soporific: also **som-nif'ic**.

som-no-lent (som'nō-lĕnt), *adj.* 1. sleepy; drowsy. 2. making drowsy. —**som'no-lence**, *n.*

son (sun), *n.* 1. a male child or descendant. 2. a son-in-law. 3. a stepson.

so-nant (sō'nănt), *adj.* sounding; vocal.

so-nar (sō'när), *n.* an apparatus designed to locate underwater objects, find depths, etc. by sending high-frequency sound waves through the water and recording reflected vibrations.

so-na-ta (sō-nät'ä), *n.* an extended musical composition for one or two instruments, usually of from two to five related movements.

song (sông), *n.* 1. the act or art of singing. 2. a musical composition to be sung. 3. something sung or suggestive of singing. 4. poetry. 5. a relatively short poem designed to be sung or suitable for singing, as a ballad.

song-bird ('bŭrd), *n.* a bird that makes sounds suggestive of music.

song-fest ('fest), *n.* an informal gathering of people for singing songs.

Song of Solomon, a book of the Bible: also called **Song of Songs**.

song sparrow, a common North American sparrow that produces melodious notes.

song-ster ('stẽr), *n.* 1. a singer. 2. a song writer or poet. 3. a songbird. —**song'stress** ('stris), *n.fem.*

song thrush, any one of a species of European songbirds with brown wings and white breast.

son-ic (son'ik), *adj.* 1. of or pertaining to sound. 2. designating or as fast as the speed of sound (about 1088 feet per second).

sonic barrier, a sharp increase in aerodynamic resistance encountered by some aircraft upon nearing the speed of sound.

sonic boom, a loud, booming noise heard at ground level and caused by the air-pressure wave generated by an aircraft going as fast as, or faster than, the speed of sound (about 1088 feet per second).

so-nif-er-ous (sō-nif'ẽr-ŭs), *adj.* producing or conveying sound.

son-in-law (sun'in-lô), *n., pl.* **sons'-in-law**, the husband of one's daughter.

son-net (son'it), *n.* a 14-line poem having a single theme and following any one of several fixed verse and rhyme schemes.

son-net-eer (son-i-tir'), *n.* 1. a writer of sonnets. 2. a lesser or inferior poet: term of contempt: *v.i.* to write sonnets.

son-ny (sun'i), *n., pl.* -nies, little son: a familiar term of address often used in speaking to any young boy.

so-nor-i-ty (sō-nôr'i-ti), *n., pl.* -ties, the quality or state of being sonorous, or an instance of this.

so-no-rous (sō-nôr'ŭs, son'ẽr-ŭs), *adj.* 1. marked by, producing, or able to produce sound, especially of a deep and full quality; resonant. 2. impressive in sound; ringing; resounding.

soon (sōōn), *adv.* 1. in a short time; without delay; promptly; quickly. 2. before the expected or usual time; early. 3. willingly.

soot (soot), *n.* a fine, black substance made up chiefly of carbon particles produced by incomplete combustion as of coal or wood. —**soot'y**, *adj.* **soot'i-er**, **soot'i-est**.

sooth (sōōth), *n.* [Archaic], truth; reality: *adj.* [Archaic], true.

soothe (sōōth), *v.t.* soothed, sooth'ing, 1. to calm, mollify, or please, as with soft words or blandishments. 2. to relieve or reduce (pain, discomfort, etc.); assuage: *v.i.* to have an effect of calming, relieving, etc.

sooth-say (sōōth'sā), *v.i.* -said, -say-ing, to predict or profess to predict the future; act as a seer. —**sooth'say-er**, *n.*

sop (sop), *n.* 1. anything steeped, dipped, or softened in a liquid. 2. something given to pacify or influence: *v.t.* sopped, sop'ping, 1. to steep, dip, or soften in a liquid. 2. to draw up (liquid) freely by absorption: *v.i.* to soak (*in*, *into*, or *through*).

soph-ism (sof'izm), *n.* a plausible, often subtle, but fallacious piece of reasoning.

soph-ist (sof'ist), *n.* 1. [often S-], in ancient Greece, any one of a group of teachers of philosophy, rhetoric, etc., some of whom were viewed as given to clever but fallacious reasoning. 2. any individual marked by or given to plausible, often subtle, but fallacious reasoning.

so-phis-ti-cal (sō-fis'ti-kl), *adj.* 1. of, like, or typical of a sophist or sophists. 2. of, marked by, or given to sophisms or sophistry. Also **so-phis'tic**. —**so-phis'ti-cal-ly**, *adv.*

so-phis-ti-cate (sō-fis'ti-kāt), *v.t.* -cat-ed, -cat-ing, 1. to bring from a condition of being simple, naive, inexperienced, untaught, etc. to a condition of being complex, subtle, experienced, knowledgeable, etc. 2. to bring (a technique, process, device, etc.) to a high or higher level of development or refinement: *n.* (-kit), 1. a knowledgeable, polished, experienced individual, especially one wise in the ways of the world. 2. a jaded individual of this kind.

so·phis·ti·cat·ed (-kāt-id), *adj.* 1. knowledgeable, polished, urbane, experienced, perceptive, etc. 2. designed for or appealing to sophisticates. 3. marked by a high level of development or complexity; highly advanced or refined.

so·phis·ti·ca·tion (sô-fis-ti-kā′shŭn), *n.* 1. the act of sophisticating. 2. the quality or state of being sophisticated.

soph·is·try (sof′is-tri), *n., pl.* -tries, 1. a sophism or the use of sophisms. 2. the reasoning typical of a sophist or sophists; plausible, often subtle, but fallacious reasoning.

soph·o·more (sof′ô-môr), *n.* a student in the second year of college or the tenth grade of high school: *adj.* of or for sophomores.

soph·o·mor·ic (sof-ô-môr′ik), *adj.* of, like, or typical of a sophomore or sophomores; specifically, of, marked by, or typical of the intellectual immaturity, superficial knowledge, or brash display of shallow wisdom often associated with sophomores. —soph·o·mor′i·cal·ly, *adv.*

so·por (sô′pêr), *n.* an unnaturally deep sleep.

sop·o·rif·ic (sop-ô-rif′ik, sô-pô-), *adj.* of or inducing sleep or sleepiness: also **sop·o·rif′er·ous** (′er-ŭs): *n.* something, as a drug, that induces sleep.

sop·ping (sop′ing), *adj.* so wet as to be saturated or dripping: *adv.* to such a degree of being wet.

sop·py (sop′i), *adj.* -pi·er, -pi·est, 1. soaked; sopping; very wet. 2. [Informal], maudlin.

so·pra·no (sô-pran′ō, -prä′nō), *n., pl.* -pra′nos, -pra′ni (-prä′nē), 1. the highest singing voice of women or boys. 2. the range of such a voice. 3. an instrument with a similar range: *adj.* of or for such a range.

so·ra (sôr′ä), *n.* a small, short-billed wading bird of the rail family, frequenting marshes of North America: also **sora rail.**

sorb (sôrb), *n.* any one of various European trees of the rose family, as the European mountain ash.

sor·bic acid (sôr′bik), a crystalline solid derived from the berries of the mountain ash or made synthetically, used as in preserving foods.

sor·bi·tol (sôr′bi-tôl, -tōl), *n.* a sweet, crystalline alcohol obtained as from the berries of the mountain ash and used as a moistening agent in lotions and creams, as a sugar substitute, etc.

Sor·bonne (sôr-bon′), *n.* the University of Paris; specifically, the seat of the faculties of letters and science.

sor·cer·er (sôr′sêr- êr), *n.* one that practices sorcery. —sor′cer·ess, *n.fem.*

sor·cer·y (sôr′sêr-i), *n., pl.* -cer·ies, 1. a resorting to a supposed power, evil and supernatural in character, in an attempt to control people and events; witchcraft. 2. any seemingly magical power; enchantment.

sor·did (sôr′did), *adj.* 1. depressingly dirty or squalid; mean; vile; wretched. 2. meanly selfish or avaricious; meanly eager for gain.

sore (sôr), *adj.* sor′er, sor′est, 1. painful or tender to the touch, as a wound. 2. producing or undergoing pain, distress, or discomfort. 3. full of grief or distress; very sad. 4. causing grief or distress; distressing. 5. tending to ruffle the feelings, arouse hostility or animosity, disturb, vex, etc. 6. [Informal], angry, annoyed, resentful, etc.: *n.* a painful or tender area of injury or other lesion on some part of the body, as a cut, bruise, or boil, specifically one in the process of healing or one that is chronic, infected, or symptomatic: *adv.* [Archaic], same as sorely.

sore·head (′hed), *n.* [Informal], 1. one that is easily angered, vexed, or disgruntled; peevish individual. 2. one simmering with resentment or sulking, as a poor loser.

sore·ly (′li), *adv.* to a most distressing degree; very badly.

sore·ness (′nis), *n.* the quality or state of being sore.

sor·gho (sôr′gō), *n., pl.* -ghos, same as sorgo.

sor·ghum (sôr′gŭm), *n.* 1. any one of a genus of tropical old-world grasses with solid stems, grown for grain, syrup, fodder, etc. 2. syrup made from sorgo juice.

sor·go (sôr′gō), *n., pl.* -gos, any one of various sorghums yielding a sweet juice that can be made into syrup.

so·ror·al (sô-rôr′l), *adj.* of or like a sister or sisters; sisterly.

so·ror·i·cide (sô-rôr′i-sīd), *n.* 1. the act of killing one's sister. 2. one doing this.

so·ror·i·ty (sô-rôr′i-ti), *n., pl.* -ties, a group of women or girls joined by common interests.

so·ro·sis (sô-rô′sis), *n., pl.* -ses (′sēz), a fruitlike structure produced by the merging of many flowers into a fleshy mass, as in the mulberry.

sor·rel (sôr′l, sor′l), *n.* 1. a certain coarse weed; dock. 2. same as wood sorrel. 3. a reddish-brown color; also, an animal of this color: *adj.* reddish-brown.

sor·ri·ly (sor′i-li, sôr′-), *adv.* deplorably; wretchedly; miserably.

sor·ri·ness (sor′i-nis, sôr′i-), *n.* the quality or condition of being deplorable; wretchedness.

sor·row (sor′ō, sôr′ō), *n.* 1. mental pain or uneasiness caused by loss, disappointment, etc.; sadness; grief; distress; unhappiness. 2. a source of such a condition, as a particular loss, disappointment, or affliction. 3. the outer expression of reaction to such a condition, as weeping; lamentation. 4. a feeling of guilt and deep grief or earnest regret over sins, wrongs, or faults committed by oneself; contrition: *v.i.* to feel or show grief, sadness, distress, or earnest regret; grieve; lament; mourn.

sor·row·ful (′ô-fŭl), *adj.* 1. of, marked by, or indicative of sorrow. 2. bringing or causing sorrow. —sor′row·ful·ly, *adv.*

sor·ry (sor′i, sôr′i), *adj.* -ri·er, -ri·est, 1. grieved, distressed, or earnestly regretful. 2. feeling commiseration, compassion, or pity. 3. deplorable; wretched; miserable.

sort (sôrt), *n.* 1. a group of individuals or things having some common element or characteristic; a particular kind or class. 2. that which makes a particular kind or class to be what it is; aggregate of distinctive characteristics; distinctive nature or character; type. 3. an individual or thing viewed as having certain characteristics, as being of a certain kind, or as being representative of a certain group. 4. *usually pl.* in *Printing,* any of the kinds of characters in a font: popularly used in *out of sorts,* not feeling one's best, not feeling pleasant, etc.: *v.t.* to separate or group according to kind.

sor·tie (sôr'tï), *n.* 1. a sudden issuing forth, as of besieged troops to attack the besiegers; sally. 2. one mission by a single military plane.

sor·ti·lege (sôr'ti-lij), *n.* 1. divination by casting lots. 2. sorcery.

SOS (es'ō-es'), *n.* a wireless call for help, as from a ship in peril.

so-so (sō'sō), *adv.* in a passable but not particularly good way; not too badly: *adj.* barely acceptable; just fair. Also so so.

sos·te·nu·to (sos-tĕ-nŏŏt'ō), *adj. & adv.* in *Music,* at a slower but sustained tempo, each note being held for its full value.

sot (sot), *n.* a drunkard.

so·te·ri·ol·o·gy (sō-tir-i-ol'ō-ji), *n.* a doctrine of spiritual salvation; specifically, the Christian doctrine of salvation through Jesus.

so·tol (sō-tōl', sō'tōl), *n.* any one of a genus of yuccalike desert plants of the southwestern U.S. and the northern part of Mexico.

sot·tish (sot'ish), *adj.* 1. of or like a sot. 2. stupid or foolish, from or as if from drinking too much alcoholic liquor.

sot·to vo·ce (sot'ō vō'chi), in an undertone.

sou (sŏŏ), *n., pl.* **sous** (sŏŏz, sŏŏ), a former French coin, especially one equal to 5 centimes.

sou·brette (sŏŏ-bret'), *n.* 1. an actress typically playing the role of a flirtatious or frivolous young lady. 2. such a role.

sou·bri·quet (sŏŏ'bri-kā), *n.* same as **sobriquet.**

sou·chong (sŏŏ'shông'), *n.* a large-leaved tea withered and fermented before being dried.

souf·flé (sŏŏ-flā'), *n.* a baked food that is made light and puffy through the addition of beaten egg whites to a combination of such ingredients as white sauce, egg yolks, and cheese: *adj.* made light and puffy in cooking: also **souf·fléed** (-flād').

sough (sou, suf), *n.* a low, indistinct, sighing or rustling sound, as of the wind: *v.i.* to make such a sound.

sought (sôt), past tense and past participle of **seek.**

soul (sōl), *n.* 1. according to many, a nonmaterial entity or animating principle that constitutes the spiritual or immortal part of a person, that is the foundation of thought, will, and emotion, and that is the essential basis of the individual's personality. 2. any vital principle or essence viewed as being that which actuates or controls from within. 3. any inherent central factor giving something aesthetic effectiveness, emotional warmth, etc. 4. the moral or emotional nature of man. 5. a leading or dominating individual, as in an enterprise. 6. any person.

7. the spirit of a deceased person, thought of as continuing to exist though separated from the body. 8. the embodiment or personification of something indicated. 9. [Informal], *a)* among U.S. Negroes, a sense of racial pride and solidarity; *b)* same as **soul food** or **soul music:** *adj.* [Informal], of, for, like, or typical of Negroes, especially U.S. Negroes.

soul food, [Informal], food popular especially among U.S. Negroes, as chitterlings, ham hocks, etc.

soul·ful (sōl'fŭl), *adj.* full of deep feeling.

soul·less ('lis), *adj.* lacking vibrancy, feeling, or spirit; lifeless and robotlike; mechanical.

soul music, [Informal], a form of popular American Negro music, typically marked by a strong beat and developed from or showing the influence of jazz, the blues, and evangelistic singing.

sound (sound), *adj.* 1. being in good condition; not defective, damaged, or decayed. 2. being in good health or in satisfactory condition; not diseased, impaired, or weakened. 3. firm; safe; strong; secure. 4. marked by or conforming to truth, fact, or valid reasoning. 5. not deviating from established belief, doctrine, practice, etc.; orthodox. 6. being to the fullest the thing specified; altogether such; thorough; solid. 7. deep and unbroken: said of sleep. 8. steadfast, loyal, honest, etc. 9. that cannot be contested legally or on other grounds, as a claim: *adv.* deeply; profoundly: *n.* 1. the impression made on the ear by vibrations in air, water, etc. 2. such vibrations. 3. any distinctive, identifiable auditory stimulus, as a particular noise, tone, or vocalization. 4. the distance within which any given stimulus of this kind can be heard. 5. the impression made on the mind by the way something is worded or uttered. 6. noise without signification. 7. a passage or channel of water, as a strait, bay, or inlet of the sea. 8. a gasfilled sac in the body cavity of most bony fishes, giving buoyancy: *v.i.* 1. to produce the vibrations that stimulate the auditory nerves; produce sound. 2. to produce an indicated mental impression from the kind of wording or utterance used. 3. to measure the depth of water or of a body of water as with a weighted line. 4. to examine or sample the bottom of the sea, etc., using a weighted line to bring up particles. 5. to probe into the atmosphere or space so as to get data. 6. to try to get an idea of another's or others' views, feelings, etc. as by indirect questions. 7. to dive suddenly downward through water, as a whale does: *v.t.* 1. to cause (a musical instrument, bell, etc.) to produce sound. 2. to articulate (a given sound) clearly. 3. to proclaim or signal, as the time of day, by producing sound. 4. to make a sounding of (water, the atmosphere, opinion, etc.).

sounding board, 1. a structure, as in a musical instrument or in an auditorium, designed to increase resonance or to reflect sound: also **sound·board.** 2. a person on whom one tests one's ideas, views, plans, etc.

ō in dragon, ōō in crude, oo in wool, u in cup, ū in cure, û in turn, ù in focus, oi in boy, ou in house, th in thin, th in sheathe, g in get, j in joy, y in yet.

sound-proof ('prōōf), *adj.* impervious to sound: *v.t.* to make soundproof.

sound track, a track running along a motion-picture film and carrying the sound recording of the film.

soup (sōōp), *n.* 1. a food consisting wholly or largely of liquid and made by cooking meat, fish, vegetables, etc. as in water or stock. 2. [Slang], a heavy fog. 3. [Slang], nitroglycerin: *v.t.* [Slang], to increase the power, speed capacity, etc. of (an engine, etc.): with *up*.

soup-çon (sōōp-sōn', sōōp'sōn), *n.* a tiny trace of something, as of a flavor or aroma; bit.

soup-spoon (sōōp'spōōn), *n.* a spoon with a large bowl, designed for eating soup.

soup-y (sōō'pi), *adj.* soup'i-er, soup'i-est, 1. of or marked by a consistency so fluid, mushy, or soft as to be suggestive of soup. 2. [Informal], very rainy, foggy, or sloppy. 3. [Slang], dripping with sentimentality; mawkish.

sour (sour), *adj.* 1. acid or sharp in taste. 2. rancid; spoiled. 3. peevish, morose, bitter, etc. 4. unpleasant; disagreeable: *v.t. & v.i.* to make or become sour.

source (sôrs), *n.* 1. that from which anything arises or originates. 2. that which supplies something. 3. an individual, book, document, etc. providing information. 4. a spring, fountain, etc. giving rise to a stream. 5. the thing or point from which rays of light, waves of sound, etc. come.

sour-dough (sour'dō), *n.* 1. [Dialectal], leaven; especially, fermented dough. 2. a prospector living alone in the western U.S. or Canada.

sour grapes, a belittling of something only because it is unattainable.

souse (sous), *n.* 1. anything steeped or preserved in pickle. 2. pickling liquid; brine. 3. a plunging into liquid. 4. [Slang], a drunkard: *v.t. & v.i.* soused, sous'ing, 1. to steep in pickle. 2. to plunge into liquid. 3. to make or become drenched.

south (south), *n.* 1. the part of the sky to the right of where the sun rises. 2. a region or area toward this part. 3. [often S-], the southern part of the earth; antarctic areas: *adj.* of, in, or coming from the south: *adv.* in a southerly direction.

South-down (south'doun), *n.* any one of a breed of English short-wooled sheep bred chiefly for food.

south-east (south-ēst'), *n.* 1. the direction or point halfway between south and east; 45° east of due south. 2. a region or area toward this direction: *adj.* of, in, or coming from the southeast: *adv.* in, to, or from the southeast. —south-east'er-ly, *adj. & adv.* — south-east'ern, *adj.*

south-east-ward ('wērd), *adv. & adj.* toward the southeast: also **south-east'wards**, *adv.*

south-er (sou'thēr), *n.* a gale from the south.

south-er-ly (suth'ēr-li), *adj. & adv.* to or from the south.

south-ern (suth'ērn), *adj.* 1. in, from, or toward the south. 2. [S-], of or pertaining to the South.

south-er-ner (suth'ēr-nēr), *n.* 1. one born or living in the south. 2. [S-], a native or inhabitant of the southern U.S.

southern lights, same as aurora australis.

south-ern-wood (suth'ērn-wood), *n.* a species of European wormwood with fragrant leaves.

south-ing (sou'thing), *n.* the distance traversed by a vessel sailing southward.

south-paw (south'pô), *n.* [Slang], a left-handed person; especially, a left-handed baseball pitcher.

south-ward (south'wērd), *adv. & adj.* toward the south: also **south'wards**, *adv.*

south-west (south-west'), *n.* 1. the direction or point halfway between south and west; 45° west of due south. 2. a region or area toward this direction: *adj.* of, in, or coming from the southwest: *adv.* in, to, or from the southwest. —south-west'er-ly, *adj. & adv.* — south-west'ern; *adj.*

south-west-ward ('wērd), *adv. & adj.* toward the southwest: also **south-west'wards**, *adv.*

sou-ve-nir (sōō-vē-nir'), *n.* a keepsake; memento.

sov-er-eign (sov'rin, 'ēr-in), *adj.* 1. superior to all others. 2. supreme in power or dominion. 3. royal; reigning. 4. independent. 5. excellent. 6. altogether effectual: *n.* 1. one supreme in power or dominion: specifically, a king, emperor, etc. 2. an independent group or state. 3. a British gold coin.

sov-er-eign-ty (-ti), *n., pl.* -ties, 1. the quality or state of being sovereign. 2. a sovereign state or group.

so-vi-et (sō'vi-it, 'vi-et), *n.* 1. a governing body in the Soviet Union. 2. [S-], *pl.* the government officials or the people of the Soviet Union: *adj.* [S-], of the Soviet Union.

sow (sou), *n.* 1. any one of certain adult female mammals; specifically, an adult female pig or hog. 2. a channel running molten metal to molds.

sow (sō), *v.t.* sowed, sown (sōn) or sowed, sow'ing, 1. to scatter or plant (seed) in or on (a field, earth, etc.). 2. to instill, as an idea, or disseminate, as propaganda: *v.i.* to sow seed.

sow bug (sou), any one of a group of small, flat, oval bugs found typically under rocks.

sox (soks), *n.* alternate plural of sock.

soy (soi), *n.* 1. a dark-brown, salty sauce made from the seeds of the soybean plant, used especially with Chinese and Japanese dishes. 2. the soybean plant or its seeds.

soy-bean ('bēn), *n.* 1. a leguminous plant native to China and Japan, widely grown as for fodder and for the edible seeds. 2. the seed.

spa (spä), *n.* 1. a spring yielding natural mineral water. 2. a place with such a spring.

space (spās), *n.* 1. the continuous and either unbounded or indeterminately finite expanse within which all things exist. 2. same as outer space. 3. a delimited extension within continuous space, as that occupied by an object or that between objects. 4. a specified measure of the area or three-dimensional extension needed for, available for, assigned to, or occupied by something, as on a surface or within an enclosure. 5. a period of time; interval. 6. accommodations or an accommodation in a hotel, on a plane, etc.: *v.t.* spaced, spac'ing, to arrange with a certain amount of space or a certain number of spaces in or between.

space-craft (spās'kraft), *n., pl.* -craft, any vehicle or satellite designed for outer space.

space fiction, fiction about space travel.

space-flight ('flīt), *n.* a flight in outer space.

space heater, a small heating unit designed to warm a room or other single confined area.

space-man ('man, -mån), *n., pl.* -men ('men, -mēn), an astronaut or other space traveler.

space platform, a space station.

space-port ('pôrt), *n.* a center for assembling, testing, and launching spacecraft.

space-ship ('ship), *n.* a rocket-propelled vehicle designed for outer space travel.

space station, a structure designed to orbit in outer space and to be used for launching other spacecraft, as an observation post, etc.

space-suit ('sōōt), *n.* a pressurized garment designed for wear especially by outer-space travelers as to counteract the effects of rapid acceleration and deceleration.

space-walk ('wôk), *n.* a moving about in outer space by an astronaut outside his spacecraft: *v.i.* to do a spacewalk. —**space'walk-er**, *n.*

spa-cial (spā'shūl), *adj.* alternate spelling of spatial.

spa-cious (spā'shūs), *adj.* 1. extending far and wide; not at all hemmed in; vast. 2. full of room; not at all cramped; roomy.

spade (spād), *n.* 1. a long-handled digging tool with a flat blade designed to be pressed into earth with the foot. 2. one of a suit of cards marked with a black figure suggestive of the pointed blade of some spades. 3. *pl.* this suit of cards: *v.t.* & *v.i.* spad'ed, spad'ing, to dig with a spade.

spade-work ('wūrk), *n.* work, especially when hard, done as the preparatory part of a project.

spa-dix (spā'diks), *n., pl.* spa'dix-es, spa'di-ces (spā'di-sēz, spā-dī'sēz), a spike of tiny flowers on a fleshy axis, usually in a spathe.

spa-ghet-ti (spā-get'i), *n.* long, thin strings of pasta.

spake (spāk), archaic past tense of speak.

spall (spôl), *n.* a flake or chip, specifically of stone; splinter: *v.t.* & *v.i.* 1. to break up or split. 2. to break off in layers parallel to a surface.

span (span), *n.* 1. a measure of length, equal to nine inches, based on the distance from the tip of the extended thumb to the tip of the extended little finger. 2. the interval, spatial or temporal, between any two points. 3. a part between two supports. 4. a team of two animals: *v.t.* spanned, span'ning, 1. to measure, especially by the hand with thumb and little finger extended. 2. to reach or extend fully across, over, or around, from one point to another.

span-gle (spang'gl), *n.* a small, bright, glittering object; especially, a little piece of shiny metal, used for ornamentation: *v.t.* -gled, -gling, to stud or ornament with spangles.

Span-iard (span'yērd), *n.* a native or inhabitant of Spain.

span-iel (span'yēl), *n.* any one of several breeds of small, short-legged dogs with long, wavy hair and large, drooping ears.

Span-ish (span'ish), *adj.* of or pertaining to Spain, its inhabitants, or its language: *n.* the language of the, people of Spain and of Spanish America.

Span-ish-A-mer-i-can (-ā-mer'ī-kán), *adj.* 1. of or pertaining to both Spain and America. 2. of or pertaining to Spanish America, those countries south of the U.S. in which Spanish is the chief language: *n.* a native or inhabitant of Spanish America.

Spanish fly, 1. a species of beetle, bright green in color, of southern Europe. 2. same as cantharides.

spank (spangk), *v.t.* to strike as with the open hand, especially on the buttocks: *v.i.* to move swiftly: *n.* a blow given in spanking.

spank-ing ('ing), *adj.* 1. moving quickly. 2. brisk: said of a breeze. 3. [Informal], remarkably fine, big, vigorous, etc.: *adv.* [Informal], utterly; wholly: *n.* a series of spanks administered as in punishment.

span-ner (span'ēr), *n.* 1. one that spans. 2. [Chiefly British], a wrench (the tool).

spar (spär), *n.* 1. a lustrous, crystalline, nonmetallic mineral. 2. a mast, yard, boom, etc. of a ship. 3. a lateral part of an airplane wing, supporting the ribs. 4. a jabbing or feinting movement, ordinarily involving no heavy blows, as in boxing practice; also, a match characterized by such movements. 5. a wrangling; dispute: *v.i.* sparred, spar'ring, 1. to jab, feint, etc. in or as if in boxing practice. 2. to wrangle.

spar-a-ble (sper'ā-bl), *n.* a small, headless nail used by shoemakers.

spare (sper), *v.t.* spared, spar'ing, 1. to use frugally or omit using altogether. 2. to part with or give up without inconvenience. 3. to treat gently; avoid killing, hurting, or distressing. 4. to keep or save from (trouble, unwelcome news, etc.): *v.i.* 1. to be frugal or live frugally. 2. to be gentle, as in punishing: *adj.* 1. thin; lean. 2. frugal; parsimonious; scanty. 3. available for use or occupancy because extra, not needed or in use, or vacated. 4. that can be parted with: *n.* 1. something spare (senses 3 & 4). 2. in Bowling, a knocking down of all the pins in two consecutive rolls of the ball.

spare-ribs (sper'ribz), *n.pl.* a closely trimmed rib cut of pork or other meat.

spar-ing (sper'ing), *adj.* 1. that spares. 2. frugal; parsimonious.

spark (spärk), *n.* 1. a small particle of fire or ignited substance thrown off in combustion. 2. any similar small, shining particle or transient light. 3. a tiny start, trace, or particle of something, as of life or interest. 4. liveliness; vivacity: *v.i.* to make sparks: *v.t.* to rouse up; elicit; activate.

spar-kle (spär'kl), *v.i.* -kled, -kling, 1. to emit sparks. 2. to flash or glisten; scintillate; coruscate. 3. to effervesce: *n.* 1. a spark or sparkling. 2. liveliness.

spar-kler ('klēr), *n.* something that sparkles;

ŏ in dragon, ōō in crude, oo in wool, u in cup, ū in cure, û in turn, ū in focus, oi in boy, ou in house, th in thin, *th* in sheathe, g in get, j in joy, y in yet.

specifically, a thin, light rod of a material that burns slowly and throws off little sparks.

spark plug, a device fitted into a cylinder of an internal-combustion engine and designed to spark so as to ignite the fuel mixture.

spar-ling (spär'ling), n., pl. -ling, -lings, a European smelt.

spar-row (spar'ō), n. 1. any one of several weaverbirds. 2. any one of numerous finches, including the song sparrow.

sparrow hawk, 1. a small European hawk with rounded wings. 2. a small North American falcon.

sparse (spärs), adj. thinly scattered; not dense. —sparse'ly, adv. —sparse'ness, spar'si-ty, n.

Spar-tan (spär'tn), adj. 1. of or pertaining to Sparta, a southern city and military power in ancient Greece, its people, or their culture. 2. like the Spartans; bellicose, hardy, severe, etc.: n. a Spartan person.

spasm (spazm), n. 1. a sudden, violent, involuntary contraction of the muscles. 2. any sudden outburst of activity, emotion, etc.

spas-mod-ic (spaz-mod'ik), adj. of, like, or pertaining to spasms; convulsive; intermittent; fitful. —spas-mod'i-cal-ly, adv.

spas-tic (spas'tik), adj. of, pertaining to, or characterized by muscular spasms: n. a person afflicted with a spastic condition.

spat (spat), n. [Informal], a short, petty quarrel: v.i. spat'ted, spat'ting, [Informal], to engage in a spat.

spat (spat), n. a cloth or leather covering worn over the top of the instep and fastened beneath.

spat (spat), alternate past tense and past participle of spit.

spat (spat), n. the spawn of the oyster or similar bivalve shellfish: v.i. spat'ted, spat'ting, to spawn: said of oysters.

spate (spāt), n. 1. [Chiefly British], a sudden flood or heavy rain. 2. a sudden rush or outpouring.

spathe (spāth), n. a large, leaflike sheathing enclosing a flower cluster.

spa-tial (spā'shŭl), adj. of, pertaining to, or happening in space. —spa'tial-ly, adv.

spat-ter (spat'ēr), v.t. & v.i. 1. to scatter or fall in small drops. 2. to splash or soil. 3. to defame or slander: n. 1. an act of spattering. 2. a spot or stain caused by spattering.

spat-ter-dash (-dash), n. a long legging formerly worn as protection against spotting a stocking or trouser leg.

spat-u-la (spach'ū-lā), n. any one of various flat, thin, flexible, knifelike instruments, used for spreading or mixing paint, food, etc.

spat-u-late (-lit, -lāt), adj. formed like a spoon; spatula-shaped.

spav-in (spav'in), n. a disease of horses, characterized by a swelling in the hock joint resulting in lameness.

spawn (spōn), n. 1. the eggs or offspring of fishes, mollusks, etc. 2. something produced in abundance, as progeny. 3. the mycelium of fungi: v.t. & v.i. 1. to produce and deposit (eggs or spawn). 2. to produce in great numbers.

spay (spā), v.t. to remove the ovaries of (a female animal).

speak (spēk), v.i. spoke or archaic spake, spo'ken, speak'ing, 1. to utter articulate sounds; talk. 2. to communicate ideas, opinions, etc. as by talking. 3. to deliver a speech; discourse. 4. to make a request (for). 5. to converse. 6. to give out sound: v.t. 1. to utter articulately by speaking. 2. to use (a particular language) in speaking. 3. to express aloud; declare; pronounce.

speak-eas-y (-ē'zi), n., pl. -eas-ies, [Slang], a place where intoxicating liquors are illegally sold.

speak-er (spē'kēr), n. 1. a person who speaks. 2. one who delivers a discourse in public. 3. the presiding officer of a legislative body, specifically [S-], of the U.S. House of Representatives. 4. same as loudspeaker.

speak-ing ('king), adj. 1. uttering or seeming to utter words; eloquent; expressive. 2. in or for speech: n. 1. the act of uttering words. 2. oratory.

spear (spir), n. 1. a weapon with a long shaft and a sharp point, used for thrusting or throwing. 2. a lance with barbed prongs for spearing fish. 3. a long blade or stalk, as of grass: v.t. to pierce or stab with or as with a spear: v.i. to sprout into a long stem.

spear-fish (-fish), n., pl. -fish, -fish-es, any one of several large ocean fishes with the upper jaw ending in a long, spearlike projection.

spear grass, any one of several long, stiff grasses having sharp-pointed fruits.

spear-head (-hed), n. 1. the sharp head of a spear. 2. the vanguard in a military attack. 3. the person or group acting as the leading force in pursuing a given end.

spear-mint (-mint), n. an aromatic plant of the mint family, used for flavoring.

spe-cial (spesh'ăl), adj. 1. of or pertaining to a kind distinct and different. 2. designed for a particular purpose, occasion, person, etc. 3. uncommon; extraordinary. 4. limited in range; specific: n. a special person or thing. —spe'cial-ly, adv.

special delivery, the delivery of mail, for an additional charge, by a special messenger.

spe-cial-ism (-izm), n. concentration or limitation to a certain branch of knowledge, science, etc.

spe-cial-ist (-ist), n. a person who devotes himself to a particular branch of a field of study, profession, etc.

spe-cial-ize ('ā-līz), v.i. -ized, -iz-ing, to devote one's efforts to a certain branch of study, activity, etc. —spe-cial-i-za'tion, n.

spe-cial-ty ('ăl-ti), n., pl. -ties, 1. a special or distinctive quality, mark, etc. 2. a special study, interest, etc. 3. a product with special features, particular excellence, etc.

spe-cie (spē'shi), n. minted money; coin.

spe-cies ('shiz), n., pl. -cies, 1. a distinct category or sort. 2. in Biology, a basic taxonomic classification, comprising a subdivision of a genus and made up of plants or animals capable of interbreeding. 3. in Logic, a group of individuals or objects agreeing in common attributes and called by a common name.

---

a in cap, ā in cane, ä in father, å in abet, e in met, ē in be, ẽ in baker, ė in regent, i in pit, ī in fine, ĭ in manifest, o in hot, ō in horse, ō in bone,

spe·cif·ic (spi-sif'ik), *adj.* 1. of, pertaining to, or characteristic of a species. 2. definite; precise; particular. 3. characteristic of or peculiar to something. 4. definitely indicated as a remedy for a particular disorder or disease: *n.* 1. a cure for a particular disease. 2. a detail; particular. —**spe·cif'i·cal·ly,** *adv.*

spec·i·fi·ca·tion (spes-i-fi-kā'shŭn), *n.* 1. the act of specifying. 2. *usually pl.* a detailed and precise statement of particulars, as to dimensions, standards, etc. 3. a thing specified.

specific gravity, the ratio of the weight of a given body to another body of equal volume taken as a standard: the standard is usually water for liquids and solids, and air for gases.

spec·i·fy (spes'i-fī), *v.t.* -fied, -fy·ing, 1. to mention or name in particular; state precisely. 2. to include as a condition.

spec·i·men (spes'i-mĕn), *n.* 1. an individual item, part, etc. used as representative of a class, group, whole, etc.; sample. 2. a sample of tissue, urine, etc. used for diagnosis.

spe·cious (spē'shŭs), *adj.* appearing to be true, sound, etc. at first sight, but actually not so; seeming plausible but really false. —**spe'cious·ly,** *adv.* —**spe'cious·ness,** *n.*

speck (spek), *n.* 1. a spot; flaw; blemish. 2. a very small particle: *v.t.* to spot with specks.

speck·le ('l), *n.* a small spot or speck: *v.t.* -led, -ling, to mark with speckles.

specs (speks), *n.pl.* [Informal], 1. spectacles; eyeglasses. 2. specifications.

spec·ta·cle (spek'tä-kl), *n.* 1. something exhibited, especially something unusual or strange. 2. a public exhibition; pageant. 3. *pl.* a pair of eyeglasses.

spec·tac·u·lar (spek-tak'yŭ-lēr), *adj.* 1. of, like, or pertaining to shows or exhibitions. 2. striking; sensational: *n.* an elaborate production or presentation. —**spec·tac'u·lar·ly,** *adv.*

spec·ta·tor (spek'tä-tēr), *n.* a person who views an event, show, etc. as an observer; onlooker.

spec·ter (spek'tēr), *n.* a ghost or apparition: British spelling spec'tre.

spec·tral ('trăl), *adj.* 1. of or resembling a specter; ghostly. 2. of or produced by a spectrum.

spec·tro·gram (spek'trŏ-gram), *n.* a photograph of a spectrum.

spec·tro·graph (-graf), *n.* an apparatus for dispersing radiation into a spectrum and photographing the spectrum.

spec·tro·he·li·o·gram (spek-trŏ-hē'li-ŏ-gram), *n.* a photograph of the sun taken on a selected wavelength.

spec·tro·he·li·o·graph (-graf), *n.* an apparatus for making spectroheliograms.

spec·trom·e·ter (spek-trom'ē-tēr), *n.* 1. an instrument for measuring spectral wavelengths. 2. an instrument for determining the index of refraction.

spec·tro·pho·tom·e·ter (-trŏ-fŏ-tom'ē-tēr), *n.* an instrument for determining the relative color intensities of different spectra.

spec·tro·scope (spek'trŏ-skōp), *n.* an optical instrument for forming and examining spectra. —**spec·tro·scop'ic** (-skop'ik), *adj.*

spec·tros·co·py (spek-tros'kŏ-pi), *n.* the use of the spectroscope to study spectra.

spec·trum (spek'trŭm), *n., pl.* -tra ('trä), 1. the series of colored bands produced when a beam of white light is diffracted, as by passage through a prism, so that the distribution of the bands is arranged according to wavelengths. 2. the distribution of the components of a system arranged in an order corresponding to some variant in the system. 3. a continuous sequence, range, or extent.

spectrum analysis, the investigation of substances or bodies by analysis of their spectra.

spec·u·lar (spek'yŭ-lēr), *adj.* of, like, or produced by a speculum.

spec·u·late (-lāt), *v.i.* -lat·ed, -lat·ing, 1. to consider or meditate upon a particular subject; reflect. 2. to buy or sell stocks, commodities, etc. in the hope of realizing a large profit from future changes in the market. —**spec·u·la'tion,** *n.* —**spec'u·la·tive,** *adj.* —**spec'u·la·tor,** *n.*

spec·u·lum (spek'yŭ-lŭm), *n., pl.* -u·la (-lä), 1. a mirror, especially a polished metal plate used as a reflector in an optical instrument. 2. an instrument for dilating and examining a body cavity or passage. 3. an iridescent patch on the wings of certain birds, especially ducks.

speech (spēch), *n.* 1. the expression of thought or feelings in words; act of speaking. 2. the faculty of uttering articulate sounds or words. 3. that which is spoken; remark, utterance, conversation, etc. 4. a particular language or dialect. 5. a formal address given in public.

speech·i·fy (spē'chi-fī), *v.i.* -fied, -fy·ing, to orate; harangue.

speech·less ('lis), *adj.* 1. unable to speak. 2. temporarily unable to speak, as from shock.

speed (spēd), *n.* 1. the act or state of moving quickly; swiftness; rapidity. 2. a measure of motion; velocity. 3. [Slang] any of various amphetamine compounds. 4. [Archaic] success: *v.i.* sped (spēd) or speed'ed, speed'ing, to move rapidly, especially at an excessive or illegal rate: *v.t.* 1. to aid or promote (an action, project, etc.). 2. to cause to go swiftly. —**speed'er,** *n.*

speed·boat ('bōt), *n.* a fast motorboat.

speed·ing ('ing), *n.* the act of driving a motor vehicle at a speed beyond a legal or safe limit.

speed·om·e·ter (spi-dom'ē-tēr), *n.* an instrument for indicating the speed of a motor vehicle.

speed·ster (spēd'stēr), *n.* a very fast driver, runner, vehicle, etc.

speed·way ('wā), *n.* 1. a track on which automobiles or motorcycles are raced. 2. a road for fast-moving traffic.

speed·well ('wel), *n.* a common garden herb producing clusters of blue flowers.

speed·y ('i), *adj.* speed'i·er, speed'i·est, 1. not dilatory or slow; prompt; quick. 2. moving with speed; rapid; swift.

ŏ in drag*o*n, ōō in cr*u*de, oo in w*oo*l, u in c*u*p, ū in c*u*re, û in t*u*rn, ŭ in f*o*cus, oi in b*oy*, ou in h*ou*se, th in *th*in, *th* in shea*th*e, g in *g*et, j in *j*oy, y in *y*et.

speiss (spīs), *n.* a mixture of arsenides resulting from the smelting of certain ores.

spe·lae·an, spe·le·an (spi-lē'ǎn), *adj.* 1. of or pertaining to a cave. 2. dwelling in a cave.

spe·le·ol·o·gy (spē-li-ol'ŏ-ji), *n.* 1. the scientific study of caves. 2. the exploration of caves. —**spe·le·ol'o·gist**, *n.*

spell (spel), *n.* 1. a word or arrangement of letters supposed to have magic power; incantation. 2. an enchanting or compelling influence; bewitchment; fascination.

spell (spel), *v.t.* spelled or spelt, spell'ing, 1. to name, print, or write in sequence the letters of (a word, syllable, etc.). 2. to be the specified letters of (a word). 3. to mean; signify: *v.i.* 1. to form a word or words with the correct letters.

spell (spel), *v.t.* spelled, spell'ing, [Informal], to take the place of (another) temporarily; relieve: *n.* 1. a period of time spent at an occupation, duty, etc. 2. a period of a particular kind of weather. 3. [Informal], a period of illness, indisposition, agitation, etc.

spell·bind (spel'bīnd), *v.t.* -bound, -bind·ing, to hold as if under a spell; enrapture; fascinate. —**spell'bind·er**, *n.*

spell·bound ('bound), *adj.* fascinated; charmed.

spell·down ('doun), *n.* a spelling match in which a competitor is eliminated for misspelling a word or words.

spell·er ('ẽr), *n.* 1. one who spells words. 2. a book containing spelling lessons.

spell·ing ('ing), *n.* 1. the act of spelling words. 2. the proper forming of letters into words; orthography.

spelt (spelt), alternate past tense and past participle of **spell**.

spelt (spelt), *n.* a kind of wheat.

spel·ter (spel'tẽr), *n.* zinc from the smelter.

spe·lunk·er (spi-lung'kẽr), *n.* one who explores caves as a hobby.

spence (spens), *n.* [Archaic or Dial.], a pantry or buttery.

spen·cer (spen'sẽr), *n.* a kind of short jacket.

spen·cer (spen'sẽr), *n.* a trysail on a gaff.

Spen·ce·ri·an (spen-sir'i-ǎn), *adj.* 1. of or pertaining to the philosophy of Herbert Spencer (1820-1903), English philosopher, that proposes that the evolution of the cosmos passes from relative simplicity to relative complexity. 2. of or pertaining to a system of handwriting using well-formed letters, taught by P. R. Spencer (1800-64), U.S. teacher.

spend (spend), *v.t.* spent, spend'ing, 1. to pay out (money); disburse. 2. to give (time, effort, etc.) for some purpose. 3. to dispose of; consume; drain of force or strength. 4. to pass (time): *v.i.* to pay out or expend money, strength, etc. —**spend'er**, *n.*

spend·thrift ('thrift), *n.* a person who squanders money: *adj.* prodigal.

spent (spent), past tense and past participle of **spend**: *adj.* 1. exhausted; without force or energy. 2. worn out; having no power.

sperm (spũrm), *n.* 1. the male fluid of reproduction; semen. 2. same as **spermatozoon**.

sper·ma·ce·ti (spũr-mǎ-set'i), *n.* a white, waxy substance obtained from the head of the sperm whale, used in cosmetics, candles, etc.

sper·ma·ry (spũr'mǎ-ri), *n., pl.* -ries, an organ in which spermatozoa are developed; testis; male gonad.

sper·mat·ic (spẽr-mat'ik), *adj.* of or pertaining to sperm or a spermary.

sper·ma·tid (spũr'mǎ-tid), *n.* in *Zoology,* any one of the four cells formed during meiosis in the male, each of which becomes a spermatozoon.

sper·ma·ti·um (spẽr-mā'shi-ŭm), *n., pl.* -ti·a (-ǎ), a nonmotile male sex cell found in some lower plants, as in red algae.

sper·mat·o-, a combining form meaning *seed, sperm.*

sper·mat·o·gen·e·sis (spẽr-mat-ŏ-jen'ĕ-sis), *n.* the formation and development of spermatozoa.

sper·mat·o·phyte (-mat'ŏ-fīt), *n.* any seed-bearing plant.

sper·mat·o·zo·on (-mat-ŏ-zō'on), *n., pl.* -zo'a ('ǎ), the motile gamete of a male animal, with a whiplike tail for locomotion.

sper·mo-, same as **spermato-**.

sperm oil, a yellowish lubricating oil from the sperm whale.

sper·mo·phile (spũr'mŏ-fīl), *n.* any one of various burrowing North American rodents.

sperm whale, a large, toothed whale inhabiting warm seas, with a closed cavity in the head containing sperm oil and spermaceti.

spew (spū), *v.t. & v.i.* 1. to eject from the mouth; vomit. 2. to flood forth; gush: *n.* vomit.

sphac·e·late (sfas'ĕ-lāt), *v.t. & v.i.* -lat·ed, -lat·ing, to make or become gangrenous. —**sphac·e·la'tion**, *n.*

sphag·num (sfag'nŭm), *n.* 1. any one of various grayish mosses found in bogs; peat moss. 2. a compacted mass of such mosses used in packing and potting. —**sphag'nous** ('nŭs), *adj.*

sphe·noid (sfē'noid), *adj.* 1. wedge-shaped. 2. in *Anatomy,* of or pertaining to a compound bone at the base of the skull: *n.* the sphenoid bone.

sphere (sfir), *n.* 1. a globe or globelike body or figure. 2. a star or planet. 3. the vault of the heavens; sky. 4. the circuit or range of knowledge, influence, action, etc.; province. 5. social position or rank. 6. in *Geometry,* a solid body under a single surface, each point of which is equidistant from a central point.

spher·i·cal (sfer'i-kl), *adj.* 1. shaped like a sphere; globular. 2. of a sphere or spheres. 3. of or pertaining to heavenly spheres; celestial. Also **spher'ic**. —**spher'i·cal·ly**, *adv.*

spher·ic·i·ty (sfi-ris'i-ti), *n.* roundness.

spher·ics (sfer'iks), *n.* spherical geometry or spherical trigonometry.

sphe·roid (sfir'oid), *n.* a body resembling a sphere but not quite round: *adj.* of this shape: also **sphe·roid'al**.

sphe·rom·e·ter (sfi-rom'ĕ-tẽr), *n.* an instrument for measuring the curvature of a surface.

spher·ule (sfer'ōōl), *n.* a little sphere.

sphinc·ter (sfingk'tẽr), *n.* a muscle that opens or closes a body orifice that it surrounds.

Sphinx (sfingks), *n.* 1. a huge statue with a man's head and lion's body near Cairo, Egypt. 2. in *Greek Mythology,* a winged monster with a woman's head and a lion's body that strangled all who could not solve its riddle. 3. [s-], any enigmatic person.

sphra·gis·tics (sfră-jis'tiks), *n.* the study of engraved seals and signets.

sphyg·mic (sfig'mik), *adj.* of the pulse.

sphyg·mo·gram (sfig'mō-gram), *n.* the record traced by a sphygmograph.

sphyg·mo·graph (-graf), *n.* an instrument for recording the beat, force, and variations of the pulse. —**sphyg·mog'ra·phy,** *n.*

sphyg·mo·ma·nom·e·ter (sfig-mō-mà-nom'ē-tẽr), *n.* an instrument for measuring the pressure of the blood in an artery.

spi·cate (spi'kāt), *adj.* having, or arranged in, the form of a spike.

spice (spis), *n.* 1. any one of various aromatic or pungent herbs or vegetables used to season foods. 2. something that adds zest or piquancy: *v.t.* spiced, spic'ing, 1. to season with spice. 2. to add zest or interest to.

spice·ber·ry ('ber-i), *n., pl.* -ries, 1. a Caribbean tree with orange or black fruit. 2. any one of several aromatic plants.

spice·bush ('boosh), *n.* an aromatic plant of eastern North America, with a red fruit formerly dried and used as a spice.

spick-and-span (spik'n-span'), *adj.* 1. new; fresh. 2. neat and spotless.

spic·u·late (spik'yû-lāt), *adj.* 1. needlelike. 2. covered with spicules. Also **spic'u·lar** (-lẽr).

spic·ule (spik'ūl), *n.* 1. in *Botany,* a small spike. 2. in *Zoology,* a slender, sharp-pointed body, especially of bony material.

spic·u·lum ('yû-lùm), *n., pl.* -u·la, same as spicule.

spic·y (spi'si), *adj.* spic'i·er, spic'i·est, 1. flavored with, containing, or having the qualities of spice; fragrant; aromatic. 2. lively; piquant. 3. risqué. —**spic'i·ly,** *adv.* —**spic'i·ness,** *n.*

spi·der (spi'dẽr), *n.* 1. a small, eight-legged animal that spins webs to ensnare its prey. 2. anything resembling a spider, as a framework. 3. an iron frying pan.

spider crab, any one of various sea crabs having long legs and a somewhat triangular body.

spider monkey, any one of various South or Central American monkeys with long, slender limbs and a long, prehensile tail.

spiel (spēl), *n.* [Slang], a long and extravagant dissertation, as in persuading or selling.

spiff·y (spif'i), *adj.* spiff'i·er, spiff'i·est, [Slang], smart; stylish; dapper.

spig·ot (spig'ŏt, spik'-), *n.* 1. a plug used to stop the vent hole in a cask. 2. a faucet.

spike (spik), *n.* 1. a large nail. 2. a sharp-pointed projection, as from the top of a fence, from the sole of a shoe, etc. 3. the unbranched antler of a young deer: *v.t.* spiked, spik'ing, 1. to fasten with spikes. 2. to pierce or impale with a spike. 3. to render (a cannon) unusable by driving a spike into the vent. 4. to stop or thwart (a plot, rumor, etc.). 5. [Slang], to add liquor to (a drink).

spike (spik), *n.* 1. an ear of grain. 2. a long inflorescence with stalkless flowers attached to the main axis.

spike·let ('lit), *n.* a small spike.

spike·nard ('nârd, 'närd), *n.* 1. an aromatic Asiatic plant. 2. a fragrant ointment used by the ancients, believed to have been derived from this plant.

spik·y (spi'ki), *adj.* spik'i·er, spik'i·est, 1. shaped like a spike. 2. set with spikes.

spile (spil), *n.* 1. a stopper or spigot. 2. a heavy stake driven into the ground as a foundation: *v.t.* spiled, spil'ing, 1. to support with spiles. 2. to plug up or tap with a spile.

spill (spil), *v.t.* spilled or spilt, spill'ing, 1. to cause or allow to run, flow, etc. accidentally. 2. [Informal], to divulge (a secret). 3. [Informal], to cause (a substance, person, etc.) to fall off or out of: *v.i.* to be spilled; run out or over: *n.* 1. an act of spilling. 2. [Informal], a fall. —**spill'age,** *n.*

spill (spil), *n.* 1. a splinter. 2. a slip of paper or wood for lighting a lamp, pipe, etc. 3. a peg or plug; spile.

spill·way (spil'wā), *n.* a channel to carry off water, as from a reservoir.

spin (spin), *v.t.* spun, spin'ning, 1. to draw out and twist (fibers) into thread. 2. to form (thread or yarn) in this way. 3. to make (a thread, web, etc.) by extruding a viscous fluid, as spiders. 4. to draw *out* (a story) tediously; prolong. 5. to cause to whirl rapidly: *v.i.* 1. to make thread or yarn by spinning. 2. to form a web, cocoon, etc. 3. to whirl. 4. to seem to be whirling from dizziness. 5. to move rapidly and smoothly: *n.* 1. the act of spinning. 2. a ride in a motor vehicle, on a bicycle, etc. 3. a spiraling descent of an aircraft with the nose down. — spin'ner, *n.*

spin·ach (spin'ich), *n.* 1. a cultivated plant having succulent, green leaves. 2. the leaves of this plant, usually cooked as a vegetable.

spi·nal (spi'nl), *adj.* of or pertaining to the spine or spinal cord.

spinal column, the articulated series of small bones that form the supporting axis of the body; backbone; spine.

spinal cord, the long cord of nerve tissue in the spinal column.

spin·dle (spin'dl), *n.* 1. a long, thin rod used on a spinning wheel for twisting the thread. 2. any slender revolving part that serves as an axis of revolution. 3. something shaped like a spindle.

spin·dle-leg·ged (-leg-id, -legd), *adj.* having long, thin legs: also **spin'dle-shanked** (-shangkt).

spin·dling (spin'dling), *adj.* same as spindly: *n.* a thin, tall person.

spin·dly (spin'dli), *adj.* -dli·er, -dli·est, disproportionately tall and slender.

spin·drift (spin'drift), *n.* spray blown from waves on the sea.

spine (spin), *n.* 1. same as spinal column. 2. a ray of a fish. 3. a pointed projection or appendage on an animal, as a bristle of a porcupine. 4. a short, sharp, woody process, as a thorn of a cactus. 5. anything resembling a spine, as the back of a book.

spi·nel (spi-nel', spin'l), *n.* a hard, crystalline

mineral occurring in various colors, the red variety of which is used as a gem.

spine·less (spīn'lis), *adj.* 1. lacking a backbone; invertebrate. 2. having a weak backbone. 3. lacking courage or strength of character; vacillating. 4. having no spines or thorny processes.

spin·et (spin'it), *n.* 1. a small, obsolete harpsichord with a single keyboard. 2. a compact upright piano.

spi·nif·er·ous (spī-nif'ēr-ùs), *adj.* bearing spines; thorny.

spin·i·fex (spin'i-feks), *n.* any one of various Australian grasses, with sharp-pointed leaves and spiny seed heads.

spin·na·ker (spin'å-kēr), *n.* a large, triangular sail set on the mainmast opposite the mainsail, used on some racing yachts when running before the wind.

spin·ner·et (spin-ē-ret'), *n.* 1. a posterior organ in spiders, some insect larvae, etc. containing glands for the secretion of filaments used in making webs, cocoons, etc. 2. a device containing tiny holes through which plastic material is extruded in making nylon, rayon, and other synthetic fibers.

spin·ney, spin·ny (spin'i), *n., pl.* -neys, -nies, [British], a small wood; thicket; copse.

spinning jenny, an early form of spinning machine having several spindles for spinning several threads at the same time.

spinning wheel, a machine for spinning yarn or thread, with a large wheel rotated by hand or foot to drive a single spindle.

spin·off (spin'ôf), *n.* an incidental advance, aid, product, breakthrough, process, benefit, etc. resulting from research or activity devoted originally to some seemingly unrelated project.

spi·nose (spī'nōs), *adj.* covered with spines or thorns; prickly.

Spi·no·zism (spi-nō'zizm), *n.* the philosophy of B. Spinoza (1632-77), Dutch philosopher, who proposed that the universe is formed of one substance, God, having an infinite number of attributes of which only thought and extension can be apprehended.

spin·ster (spin'stēr), *n.* an unmarried woman; old maid. —**spin'ster·hood,** *n.*

spin·thar·i·scope (spin-thär'i-skōp), *n.* a device consisting of a fluorescent screen and a magnifying lens for viewing the scintillations produced by the bombardment of alpha rays given off by a radioactive substance.

spin·y (spī'ni), *adj.* **spin'i·er, spin'i·est,** 1. covered with or bearing spines, thorns, etc. 2. troublesome; difficult; thorny. 3. shaped like a spine. —**spin'i·ness,** *n.*

spiny lobster, any one of various edible marine crustaceans lacking the large pincers of the lobster and having a spiny shell.

spi·ra·cle (spī'rå-kl), *n.* in *Zoology,* an aperture for breathing, as one of the external tracheal openings of an insect or spider, or the blowhole of a cetacean.

spi·ral (spī'rål), *adj.* 1. moving around a central point at a constantly increasing or decreasing distance. 2. winding around a central axis, as the thread of a screw; helical: *n.* 1. a spiral curve in one plane. 2. a helix:

v.t. & v.i. -raled or -ralled, -ral·ing or -ral·ling, to form or cause to form a spiral. —**spi'ral·ly,** *adv.*

spi·rant (spī'rånt), *n. & adj.* same as fricative.

spire (spīr), *n.* 1. a slender stalk of a plant, blade of grass, etc. 2. the top part of an object that tapers upward. 3. a structure that tapers to a point at the top, as a steeple: *v.i.* spired, spir'ing, to shoot forth or up in a spire or spires.

spi·re·a (spī-rē'å), *n.* a plant of the rose family, with clusters of small, white or pink flowers: also **spi·rae'a.**

spir·it (spir'it), *n.* 1. same as soul (sense 1). 2. sentience, will, intelligence, life, etc. regarded as immaterial. 3. an apparition, as a ghost, angel, demon, etc. 4. an individual having a specified quality, as courage, energy, vivacity, etc. 5. *pl.* mood; disposition; emotional state. 6. dedication; loyalty. 7. real meaning or intention. 8. the essence; prevailing mood; characteristic quality. 9. *usually pl.* a distilled alcoholic liquor. 10. *often pl.* in *Chemistry,* a) any volatile liquid produced by distillation; b) same as alcohol (sense 1): *v.t.* to carry (*off, away,* etc.) mysteriously or secretly.

spir·it·ed (-id), *adj.* full of spirit or life; animated; vivacious; lively.

spir·it·ism (-izm), *n.* same as spiritualism.

spir·it·less (-lis), *adj.* without spirit; depressed; listless; dejected.

spirit level, an instrument for determining if a surface is horizontal, consisting of a framed, liquid-filled tube containing an air bubble that moves to a central position when the instrument rests on a horizontal plane.

spirits of ammonia, a 10% solution of ammonia in alcohol.

spirits of turpentine, refined turpentine.

spirits of wine, same as alcohol (sense 1).

spir·it·u·al (spir'i-choo-wål, -chool), *adj.* 1. of the spirit or soul; not material. 2. of or possessing the nature of spirit; incorporeal. 3. of or pertaining to the mind or intellect. 4. religious; sacred; not lay or temporal; ecclesiastical: *n.* a religious folk song of U.S. Negro origin. —**spir·it·u·al'i·ty** (-wal'i-ti), *n., pl.* -ties. —**spir'it·u·al·ly,** *adv.*

spir·it·u·al·ism (-izm), *n.* 1. the state of being spiritual. 2. the philosophical doctrine that nothing is real except spirit. 3. the belief that the dead can communicate with the living, usually through a medium, and can manifest their presence by rapping, turning furniture, etc. 4. the doctrines and practices of those subscribing to this belief. —**spir'it·u·al·ist,** *n.* —**spir·it·u·al·is'tic,** *adj.*

spir·it·u·al·ize (-choo-wå-līz, -choo-līz), *v.t.* -ized, -iz·ing, 1. to free from materiality or sensuality; make spiritual. 2. to give a spiritual meaning to. —**spir·it·u·al·i·za'tion,** *n.*

spi·ri·tu·el (spir-i-choo-wel'), *adj.* [French], possessing or displaying a refined nature, especially a sprightly or witty nature. —**spi·ri·tu·elle'** (-wel'), *adj.fem.*

spir·it·u·ous (spir'i-choo-wùs), *adj.* containing or having the nature of alcohol; alcoholic.

spi·ro·chete (spī'rō-kēt), *n.* any one of various slender, spiral-shaped bacteria, including some that cause diseases, as syphilis, relapsing fever, etc.

spi-ro-graph (spī'rō-graf). *n.* an instrument for recording respiratory movements.

spi-rom-e-ter (spī-rom'ĕ-tĕr), *n.* an instrument for measuring the breathing capacity of the lungs.

spit (spit), *n.* 1. a long, pointed rod on which meat is impaled for roasting or broiling. 2. a narrow point of land, or a long narrow shoal, running into a body of water: *v.t.* **spit'ted, spit'ting,** to impale on or as if on a spit.

spit (spit), *v.t.* **spit or spat, spit'ting,** 1. to eject from within the mouth. 2. to eject, throw (*out*), or utter violently: *v.i.* 1. to expectorate. 2. to snow or drizzle lightly. 3. to make a hissing or sputtering noise: *n.* 1. the act of spitting. 2. saliva; spittle. 3. something resembling saliva, as the frothy secretion of certain insects. 4. a flurry of rain or snow. 5. [Informal], an exact likeness, as of a person: used in the phrase *spit and image.*

spit-ball ('bôl), *n.* 1. chewed paper rolled into a ball and thrown as a missile. 2. in *Baseball,* an illegal pitch caused to move erratically by moistening the ball with saliva or some other foreign substance.

spite (spit), *n.* 1. ill will or malice toward another, with the desire to thwart or hurt. 2. a grudge: *v.t.* **spit'ed, spit'ing,** to show spite toward by thwarting, hurting, harassing, etc. **—spite'ful,** *adj.*

spit-fire (spit'fir), *n.* a violent-tempered or very excitable person, especially a woman or girl.

spit-ter ('ĕr), *n.* 1. a person or animal that spits saliva, froth, etc. 2. [Informal], same as spitball (sense 2).

spit-tle ('l), *n.* 1. saliva: sputum. 2. the frothy liquid secreted by larval spittlebugs.

spit-tle-bug (-bug), *n.* any one of various insects whose larvae produce frothy liquid masses on plants: also called **spittle insect.**

spit-toon (spi-tōōn'), *n.* a round, bowllike, earthenware or metal container to spit into; cuspidor.

spitz (spits), *n.* a variety of Pomeranian dog, with a thick, usually white coat, erect ears, and a tail that curls over the back.

splanch-nol-o-gy (splangk-nol'ô-ji), *n.* the branch of anatomy that treats of the structure, functions, and disorders of the viscera.

splash (splash), *v.t.* 1. to splatter or scatter (a liquid) about in flying blobs. 2. to dash mud, grease, water, etc. on, so as to dampen or soil: *v.i.* to spill, strike, or splatter with a splash: *n.* 1. the act or sound of splashing. 2. a blob of splashed mud, water, grease, etc. 3. a spot made by splashing.

splash-board ('bôrd), *n.* 1. a device that protects a vehicle or its riders from being splashed. 2. a screen to prevent water from splashing on the deck of a boat.

splash-down ('doun), *n.* the landing of a spacecraft on water.

splash-y ('i), *adj.* **splash'i-er, splash'i-est,** 1. splashing; making splashes. 2. liable to make splashes; slushy, muddy, etc. 3. covered with splashes of color. 4. [Informal],

striking; showy. **—splash'i-ly,** *adv.* **—splash'i-ness,** *n.*

splat (splat), *n.* a thin slat of wood as in the middle of a chair back.

splat (splat), *n. & interj.* a wet, slapping noise.

splat-ter ('ĕr), *n. & v.t. & v.i.* splash or spatter.

splay (splā), *v.t. & v.i.* 1. to spread out or expand. 2. to bevel or slope: *adj.* 1. spread outward. 2. broad and flat. 3. awkwardly formed; ungainly: *n.* 1. an expansion; spread. 2. a bevel or slope, as of the sides of a window or door.

splay-foot ('foot), *n., pl.* **-feet,** 1. a very flat foot that turns outward. 2. the condition of having feet of this kind.

spleen (splēn), *n.* 1. a soft, vascular organ, lying in the abdominal cavity on the left side below the diaphragm, that stores blood, disposes of cellular debris, etc. 2. spite; ill temper.

splen-dent (splen'dĕnt), *adj.* [Poetic], 1. brilliant, illustrious. 2. shining; very conspicuous.

splen-did (splen'did), *adj.* 1. very bright; brilliant 2. magnificent, imposing. 3 famous; celebrated; illustrious; praiseworthy 4. [Informal]. very good; fine. **—splen'did-ly,** *adv.*

splen-dor (splen'dĕr), *n.* 1. great brightness; brilliance. 2. pomp; magnificence; grandeur. British spelling **splen'dour.**

sple-nec-to-my (spli-nek'tô-mi), *n.* the surgical excision of the spleen.

sple-net-ic (spli-net'ik), *adj.* 1. of the spleen; splenic 2. peevish; fretful; irritable: *n.* a splenetic person.

splen-ic (splen'ik, splēn'-), *adj.* 1. of or pertaining to the spleen. 2. near or in the spleen.

splice (splis), *v.t.* **spliced, splic'ing,** 1 to unite, as two ropes, by interweaving the strands. 2. to connect, as pieces of wood, wire, or film, by overlapping parts and making them fast together 3. [Slang], to unite in marriage *n.* a union or joint made by splicing.

splint (splint), *n.* 1 a thin piece of wood, metal, etc. to keep a broken bone in position. 2. a thin strip of wood, cane, etc. woven with others to make baskets.

splin-ter (splin'tĕr), *n.* a thin piece of wood, bone, etc. split off lengthwise. fragment *v.t. & v.i.* to split or rend into thin, sharp pieces, sliver. **—splin'ter-y,** *adj*

split (split), *v.t. & v.i.* **split, split'ting,** 1 to divide lengthwise into two or more parts. 2. to tear apart; cleave. 3. to disunite 4. to break (a molecule) into atoms. 5 to divide (atoms) by nuclear fission *n.* 1. a crack or break. 2. a division into parts, sections, factions, etc. 3. the act of splitting *adj* 1. separated; divided. 2. divided lengthwise

split-lev-el ('lev'l), *adj.* denoting a house in which a room or section is about a half story above or below the adjacent rooms.

split-ting ('ing), *adj.* very severe, as a headache

splotch (sploch), *n.* an irregular stain, spot, or daub: *v.t. & v.i.* to daub or be daubed with splotches. **—splotch'y,** *adj*

splurge (splûrj), *n.* [Informal], 1 a lavish display 2. an extravagant spending spree *v.i.*

ô in dragon, ōō in crude, oo in wool, u in cup, û in cure, û in turn, û in focus, oi in boy, ou in house, th in thin, th in sheathe, g in get, j in joy, y in ret.

splurged, splurg'ing, [Informal], 1. to spend money extravagantly. 2. to show off.

splut·ter (splut'ẽr), v.i. 1. to speak hastily and confusedly. 2. to sputter. 3. to spatter: n. 1. a spluttering noise or utterance. 2. a spattering; splash. —**splut'ter·y,** adj.

spoil (spoil), v.t. spoiled or spoilt, spoil'ing, 1. to harm or damage so as to make valueless, useless, etc. 2. to impair the enjoyment of. 3. to make expect too much by pampering or overindulgence. 4. [Archaic], to plunder; pillage; rob: v.i. to become spoiled; decay, as food: n. usually pl. plunder; booty. —**spoil'a·ble,** adj. —**spoil'er,** n.

spoil·age ('ij), n. 1. the act of spoiling. 2. the state or condition of being spoiled. 3. something spoiled or the amount spoiled.

spoil·sport ('spōrt), n. a person whose behavior spoils the enjoyment of others.

spoils system, the practice of distributing political appointments as favors to those who have aided the victorious party in an election.

spoke (spōk), n. 1. any one of the bars of a wheel connecting the hub with the rim. 2. a rung of a ladder.

spoke (spōk), past tense of speak.

spo·ken (spō'kn), past participle of speak: adj. 1. oral. 2. having a (specified) kind of voice.

spokes·man (spōks'mǎn), n., pl. -men ('mĕn), one who speaks for others. —**spokes'wom·an,** n.fem., pl. -wom·en.

spokes·per·son (spōks'pûr·sn), n. same as spokes-man: used to avoid the masculine implication of spokesman.

spo·li·ate (spō'li·āt), v.t. -at·ed, -at·ing, to plunder, rob, or pillage.

spo·li·a·tion (spō·li·ā'shŭn), n. 1. the act of plundering or robbery, especially an authorized seizure of neutral ships in wartime. 2. the act of spoiling. 3. in Law, injury done to a document by an unauthorized person.

spon·dee (spon'dī), n. a poetic foot consisting of two heavily accented syllables. —**spon·da·ic** (spon·dā'ik), adj.

spon·dy·li·tis (spon·di·līt'is), n. inflammation of the vertebrae.

sponge (spunj), n. 1. the porous, elastic, fibrous framework of a fixed marine animal. 2. this plantlike animal. 3. a like substance, as of rubber, plastic, cellulose, or cotton, used for scrubbing, absorbing liquids, bathing, etc. 4. yeast dough as it is rising. 5. [Informal], one who lives off others; parasite: also **spong'er:** v.i. sponged, spong'ing, 1. to take in liquid like a sponge. 2. [Informal], to live off others: v.t. 1. to clean, wipe, absorb, dampen, etc. as with a sponge. 2. to erase; eradicate. 3. [Informal], to get without cost, as by begging. —**spon'gi·ness,** n. —**spon'gy,** adj. -gi·er, -gi·est.

sponge bath, a bath taken by washing with a sponge or washcloth, but not getting into water.

sponge-cake ('kāk), n. a light cake made of flour, beaten eggs, sugar, and flavoring, but no shortening: it has a spongy texture.

spon·sion (spon'shŭn), n. 1. a formal pledge made on behalf of another, as by a godparent. 2. something done on behalf of a state or nation by an unauthorized person.

spon·son (spon'sŏn), n. 1. a projecting gun platform on a ship. 2. a winglike piece on the hull of a seaplane.

spon·sor (spon'sẽr), n. 1. one who acts as surety for another. 2. an endorser. 3. a godparent. 4. a company that pays for a radio or television broadcast that advertises its products: v.t. to act as sponsor for. —**spon·so'ri·al** (-sôr'i·ǎl), adj. —**spon'sor·ship,** n.

spon·ta·ne·i·ty (spon·tā·nē'i·ti), n. 1. the quality of being spontaneous. 2. pl. -ties, a spontaneous impulse, action, etc.

spon·ta·ne·ous (spon·tā'ni·ŭs), adj. 1. proceeding or acting from natural disposition or impulse. 2. produced without external intervention. —**spon·ta'ne·ous·ly,** adv.

spontaneous combustion, combustion produced in a substance from heat generated by internal chemical action.

spontaneous generation, the theory, now discredited, that living matter may originate from nonliving matter.

spoof (spoof), v.t. & v.i. [Slang], 1. to mislead; hoax; fool. 2. to satirize lightly: n. [Slang], 1. a hoax or joke. 2. a light satire.

spook (spook), n. [Informal], a ghost: v.t. & v.i. [Informal], to startle or frighten or become startled or frightened.

spook·y ('i), adj. spook'i·er, spook'i·est, [Informal], 1. weird; eerie. 2. easily frightened or startled; jumpy. —**spook'i·ly,** adv. —**spook'i·ness,** n.

spool (spool), n. 1. a cylinder, usually with a hole through the middle and a ridge at each end, on which thread, wire, etc. is wound. 2. the amount that a spool will hold.

spoon (spoon), n. 1. a small implement consisting of a hollow bowl and handle, for eating, stirring, etc. 2. a club used in golf: also called number 3 wood. 3. a shiny, curved fishing lure: v.t. to take up in or as in a spoon.

spoon-bill ('bil), n. a wading bird with a spoonlike bill.

spoon-er·ism (spoon'ẽr·izm), n. an accidental transposition of initial sounds of words that are spoken together.

spoon-ful ('fool), n., pl. -fuls, as much as a spoon will hold.

spoor (spoor), n. the track or trail of a wild animal.

spo·rad·ic (spô·rad'ik), adj. occurring one at a time or apart from others; happening in scattered single instances. —**spo·rad'i·cal·ly,** adv.

spo·ran·gi·um (spô·ran'ji·ŭm, spô-), n., pl. -gi·a (-ǎ), in Botany, a sac or organ producing spores.

spore (spōr), n. a minute reproductive body produced by ferns, mosses, algae, bacteria, etc. and capable of giving rise to a new individual: v.i. spored, spor'ing, to develop or produce spores.

spo·ro·gen·e·sis (spôr·ō·jen'ē·sis), n. reproduction by spores.

spo·ro·phore (spôr'ō-fôr), *n.* an organ or structure that bears spores.

spo·ro·phyll (-fil), *n.* a leaf or leaflike part bearing spores.

spor·ran (spor'ăn, spôr'-), *n.* the furry pouch worn with the Scottish Highland costume in front of the kilt.

sport (spôrt), *n.* 1. a diversion or recreational activity, especially a competition or game requiring physical skill or exertion. 2. play; fun. 3. jest or mockery; thing joked about. 4. [Informal], a sportsmanlike person. 5. [Informal], a flashy, outgoing person. 6. in *Biology*, an animal or plant that deviates from the normal type: *v.i.* 1. to play. 2. to joke: *v.t.* [Informal], to exhibit or wear in public: *adj.* 1. of or for sports. 2. suitable for informal or casual wear. —**sport'ful**, *adj.*

sport·ing ('ing), *adj.* 1. of, pertaining to, or engaging in sports. 2. having to do with gambling. 3. fair; sportsmanlike.

sport·ive ('iv), *adj.* frolicsome; full of or done in fun. —**sport'ive·ly**, *adv.* —**sport'ive·ness**, *n.*

sports car, a small, low car with a powerful engine.

sports·cast (spôrts'cast), *n.* a telecast or radio broadcast of sports news. —**sports'cast·er**, *n.*

sports·man ('măn), *n., pl.* -**men**, 1. one who engages in sports, especially hunting or fishing. 2. one who plays fairly and courteously, and can win or lose gracefully. —**sports'man·like**, *adj.* —**sports'man·ship**, *n.*

sport·y (spôrt'ï), *adj.* **sport'i·er**, **sport'i·est**, [Informal], 1. like or suitable to a sportsman. 2. showy or flashy. —**sport'i·ness**, *n.*

spor·ule (spôr'ül), *n.* a small spore.

spot (spot), *n.* 1. a small area differing in color or texture from the rest of the area of which it is a part. 2. a stain, blot, mark, etc. 3. a blemish or flaw. 4. a locality; place. 5. a food fish of the Atlantic coast of the U.S.: *v.t.* **spot'ted**, **spot'ting**, 1. to mark with spots. 2. to discolor or stain. 3. to locate; place. 4. to mark or note for future consideration. 5. to detect. 6. [Informal], to allow as a handicap: *v.i.* to become spotted: *adj.* 1. on hand; ready. 2. random. 3. made between regular radio or television programs.

spot-check ('chek), *v.t.* to examine or check at random: *n.* a random checking.

spot·less ('lis), *adj.* without a spot or blemish; faultless; pure. —**spot'less·ly**, *adv.* —**spot'less·ness**, *n.*

spot·light ('līt), *n.* 1. a strong beam of light, usually adjustable, that can be focused on a particular person or thing, as on a stage. 2. a lamp for projecting such a beam. 3. a lamp with a strong, focused beam of light, as on the side of a car. 4. public attention or notice: *v.t.* to draw attention to, as by a spotlight.

spot·ted ('id), *adj.* 1. marked with spots. 2. tarnished; sullied.

spotted fever, 1. any one of various diseases characterized by fever and skin eruptions, as typhus. 2. an acute, infectious disease caused by ticks: also called *Rocky Mountain spotted fever.*

spot·ter ('ēr), *n.* an assistant to a football coach stationed in the stands, who watches and reports on the action on the field.

spot·ty ('ï), *adj.* **-ti·er**, **-ti·est**, 1. marked with or full of spots. 2. occasional or irregular; not consistent. —**spot'ti·ly**, *adv.* —**spot'ti·ness**, *n.*

spous·al (spou'zl), *n. often pl.* [Rare], a marriage ceremony; nuptials.

spouse (spous), *n.* a partner in marriage.

spout (spout), *n.* 1. a projecting tube, mouth, pipe, etc. from which a liquid is poured. 2. a stream or gushing forth of liquid from a spout. 3. a chute: *v.t. & v.i.* 1. to throw or gush out forcibly as from a spout. 2. to talk or utter in a loud, pompous manner. —**spout'er**, *n.* —**spout'less**, *adj.*

sprain (sprān), *n.* an excessive strain of the muscles or ligaments of a joint without dislocation: *v.i.* to overstrain (a joint) in this way

sprang (sprang), alternate past tense of **spring**.

sprat (sprat), *n.* a small European fish, a kind of herring.

sprawl (sprôl), *v.i.* 1. to stretch the limbs awkwardly or in an unnatural position. 2. to spread out in an awkward or irregular manner, as handwriting, troops, etc.: *n.* a sprawling posture or movement. —**sprawl'y**, *adj.*

spray (sprā), *n.* 1. a small shoot or branch of a tree or bush, or a collection of them. 2. a mist of fine particles of liquid. 3. a jet of fine medication, perfume, or other fluid, as discharged from an atomizer, aerosol can, etc. 4. anything like a spray: *v.t. & v.i.* 1. to direct a spray (on). 2. to discharge in a spray. —**spray'er**, *n.*

spray can, an aerosol can.

spray gun, a device that shoots out a liquid through a nozzle by air pressure.

spread (spred), *v.t. & v.i.* 1. spread, spread'ing, 1. to extend or be extended over an area. 2. to disseminate; or cause to be widely known. 3. to unfurl, open out, etc. 4. to scatter. 5. to covered or be covered (*with*), as a thin layer. 6. to push or be pushed apart. 7. to set (a table) for a meal: *n.* 1. the act of spreading. 2. the extent of this. 3. an expanse; extent. 4. a cover for a bed, table, etc. 5. butter, jelly, or the like, used on bread. 6. [Informal], a feast. 7. a ranch of the western U.S.

spread-ea·gle ('ē-gl), *adj.* 1. having or like the form of an eagle with wings elevated and legs extended, used as an emblem of the U.S. 2. [Informal], boastful or chauvinistic about the U.S.

spread·sheet (spred'shēt), *n.* a computer program that organizes numerical data into rows and columns on a video screen, for computing desired calculations.

spree (sprē), *n.* 1. a merry frolic. 2. a carousal; drinking bout. 3. an outburst of activity.

sprig (sprig), *n.* 1. a small twig or shoot. 2. a scion. 3. a headless brad or nail. 4. an ornament in the form of a spray: *v.t.* **sprigged**, **sprig'ging**, 1. to decorate with a design of sprigs. 2. to drive brads into.

spright·ly (sprīt'li), *adj.* **-li·er**, **-li·est**, animated;

lively: *adv.* in a sprightly manner. **—spright'-li-ness,** *n.*

spring (spring), *v.i.* **sprang** or **sprung, sprung, spring'ing,** 1. to arise or originate; grow. 2. to appear, come, etc. suddenly. 3. to leap; bound. 4. to bounce. 5. to start or rise up suddenly. 6. to become warped, loose, bent, etc. 7. to rise up above surroundings; tower: *v.t.* 1. to cause to spring up, leap forth, etc. 2. to cause to close suddenly, as a trap. 3. to cause to warp, bend, etc. 4. to leap over. 5. to cause to appear suddenly. 6. [Slang], to get (someone) released from jail: *n.* 1. a leap or bound. 2. the distance covered in a leap. 3. an elastic body or device, as a coil of wire, that returns to its original form after being out of shape. 4. a flying back with elastic force. 5. elasticity. 6. a flow of water from the ground. 7. a source. 8. the season between winter and summer; in the astronomical year, the period beginning in the Northern Hemisphere at the vernal equinox, about March 21, and ending at the summer solstice, about June 21. 9. a period or condition resembling spring, as of beginning or newness: *adj.* 1. of, for, appearing in, or planted in the spring. 2. supported on or by springs. 3. from a spring, as water.

spring-board ('bôrd), *n.* a springy board, used for leaping or diving, as into water.

spring-bok ('bok), *n., pl.* **-bok, -boks,** a South African gazelle.

springe (sprinj), *n.* [Rare], a noose attached to a bent tree branch or the like, used as a snare.

spring-er (spring'ĕr), *n.* 1. the support on which an arch rests; impost. 2. a breed of hunting dog used to spring game: also **springer spaniel.**

spring fever, a listlessness or restlessness often felt in early spring.

spring-time ('tīm), *n.* 1. the spring season. 2. the earliest period of something. Also **spring'tide** ('tīd).

spring-y ('ī), *adj.* **spring'i-er, spring'i-est,** elastic, light, resilient, etc. **—spring'i-ly,** *adv.* **—spring'i-ness,** *n.*

sprin-kle (spring'k'l), *v.t.* **-kled, -kling,** 1. to scatter drops upon. 2. to scatter (a liquid, powder, sand, etc.) in drops or particles: *v.i.* 1. to scatter something or fall in drops or particles. 2. to rain lightly: *n.* 1. the act of sprinkling. 2. a light rain. **—sprin'kler,** *n.*

sprin-kling ('kling), *n.* a small quantity or number distributed or scattered.

sprint (sprint), *n.* a run for a short distance at full speed: *v.i.* to run at full speed. **—sprint'er,** *n.*

sprit (sprit), *n.* a small spar which raises diagonally the peak of the sail of a ship.

sprite (sprīt), *n.* an elf, goblin, pixie, etc.

sprock-et (sprok'it), *n.* 1. a tooth on a wheel rim that fits into the links of a chain. 2. such a wheel: also **sprocket wheel.**

sprout (sprout), *v.i.* to germinate; begin to grow; give off buds or shoots: *n.* a shoot.

spruce (sprōōs), *n.* 1. an evergreen tree of the pine family with cones and slender needles. 2. the wood of this tree: *adj.* **spruc'er, spruc'est,** smart, trim, neat, etc.: *v.t. & v.i.*

spruced, spruc'ing, to make or become spruce (with *up*). **—spruce'ly,** *adv.* **—spruce'-ness,** *n.*

sprue (sprōō), *n.* 1. a chronic, tropical disease characterized by malfunction of the digestive system, anemia, diarrhea, etc. 2. a hole in a mold through which molten metal is poured.

sprung (sprung), past participle and alternate past tense of **spring.**

spry (sprī), *adj.* **spri'er** or **spry'er, spri'est** or **spry'est,** nimble, sharp, lively, etc., even though elderly. **—spry'ly,** *adv.* **—spry'ness,** *n.*

spud (spud), *n.* 1. a sharp, narrow spade. 2. [Informal], a potato.

spume (spūm), *n.* froth; foam: *v.i.* **spumed, spum'ing,** to froth; foam. **—spum'y,** *adj.*

spu-mes-cent (spyoo-mes'nt), *adj.* like froth; foamy. **—spu-mes'cence,** *n.*

spu-mo-ni (spu-mō'ni), *n.* an Italian ice cream in layers that are variously colored and flavored, containing candied fruits and pistachio nuts.

spun (spun), past tense and past participle of **spin.**

spunk (spungk), *n.* [Informal], pluck; courage; mettle. **—spunk'y,** *adj.* **—spunk'i-ness,** *n.*

spur (spur), *n.* 1. a device with sharp points worn on the heel by horse riders and used to urge the animal forward. 2. any incentive to action. 3. a ridge extending from a mountain range. 4. a buttress of a wall. 5. a wooden brace or strut. 6. a spinelike process on a bird's leg. 7. a sharp metal device put on the leg of a gamecock. 8. a stunted branch or shoot. 9. a slender structure on some flowers. 10. a short railroad track off the main track: *v.t.* **spurred, spur'ring,** 1. to prick with spurs. 2. to incite to action: *v.i.* to travel with haste; push on.

spurge (spûrj), *n.* any one of a family of woody plants with milky juice, including the poinsettia and cassava.

spu-ri-ous (spyoor'i-ŭs), *adj.* not genuine; counterfeit; false. **—spu'ri-ous-ly,** *adv.* **—spu'ri-ous-ness,** *n.*

spurn (spûrn), *v.t.* 1. to drive away as with the foot. 2. to reject with contempt or disdain.

spur-ri-er (spûr'i-ĕr), *n.* a spur maker.

spur-ry, spur-rey (spûr'i), *n.* a weed with whorled leaves and small, white flowers.

spurt (spûrt), *v.i.* 1. to issue forth suddenly in a stream or jet. 2. to make a sudden, brief effort: *v.t.* to throw out in a stream or jet; expel suddenly: *n.* 1. a sudden or forcible ejection of a liquid. 2. a sudden, brief effort.

sput-nik (spoot'nik, sput'-), *n.* an artificial satellite of the earth, especially any put into orbit by the Soviet Union.

sput-ter (sput'ĕr), *v.i.* 1. to spit out scattered drops or bits. 2. to speak in a rapid, confused, excited manner. 3. to make sharp, sizzling sounds, as frying fat, burning wood, etc.: *v.t.* 1. to spit out (bits or drops). 2. to utter by sputtering: *n.* the act or noise of sputtering.

spu-tum (spūt'ŭm), *n., pl.* **-ta** ('ă), saliva mixed with mucus, that has been spit out of the mouth.

---

a in cap, ā in cane, ä in father, à in abet, e in met, ē in be, ẽ in baker, ê in regent, i in pit, ī in fine, i in manifest, o in hot, ô in horse, ō in bone,

spy (spī), v.t. **spied, spy'ing,** 1. to discover, especially at a distance; gain sight of. 2. to detect; observe closely and secretly, usually with unfriendly intent: v.i. to act as a spy, observing and watching closely: n., pl. **spies,** 1. a person employed by a government to gain secret information about the affairs, especially military affairs, of another government. 2. one who keeps watch on others; secret agent.

spy-glass ('glas), n. a small telescope.

squab (skwäb), n. 1. a nestling pigeon. 2. a short, fat person.

squab-ble (skwäb'l), v.i. **-bled, -bling,** to wrangle or dispute noisily over a small matter: v.t. to disarrange (type) that has been set up ready for printing: n. a noisy wrangle or dispute. —**squab'bler,** n.

squad (skwäd), n. 1. a small party of soldiers assembled for drill, duty, etc. 2. any small party of persons working or operating together.

squad car, a car in which police patrol city streets.

squad-ron (skwäd'rŏn), n. 1. a unit of military aircraft, usually of the same type. 2. a detachment of warships. 3. a division of cavalry, consisting of two to four troops and auxiliary units. 4. any organized group.

squal-id (skwäl'id), adj. 1. extremely dirty; foul. 2. miserable; wretched. —**squal'id-ness,** n.

squall (skwôl), n. 1. a sudden and violent windstorm, often with rain, sleet, or snow. 2. a harsh, loud scream: v.i. & v.t. to scream or cry loudly or harshly. —**squall'y,** adj.

squal-or (skwäl'ĕr), n. the condition of being squalid; filth and wretchedness.

squa-mate (skwä'māt), adj. covered with scales.

squa-mous (skwä'mŭs), adj. 1. formed of or covered with scales. 2. resembling scales. Also **squa'mose** ('mōs).

squan-der (skwän'dĕr), v.t. to spend or use lavishly or wastefully; dissipate.

square (skwer), n. 1. a plane figure having four equal sides and four right angles. 2. anything nearly resembling this shape. 3. an open area in a city or town into which several streets lead. 4. a city block. 5. any side of a city block. 6. an instrument for drawing or testing right angles. 7. the product of a number multiplied by itself. 8. [Slang], one who is square (adj 8): adj. 1. having four equal sides and four right angles. 2. forming a right angle. 3. straight; even; level. 4. upright; honest. 5. just; fair. 6. stated in terms of a unit of surface measure in the form of a square. 7. [Informal], substantial; hearty. 8. [Slang], highly conservative and conventional; old-fashioned: v.t. **squared, squar'ing,** 1. to form with four equal sides and four equal angles. 2. to multiply (a number) by itself. 3. to make conform. 4. to adjust; regulate. 5. to make straight or even: v.i. 1. to accord or agree (with); fit. 2. to assume a boxing attitude (with off): adv. 1. in a square manner. 2. directly. —**square'ly,** adv. —**square'ness,** n.

square dance, a dance in which couples form a square. —**square'-dance,** v.i.

square-rigged ('rigd'), adj. denoting a ship rigged principally with square sails.

square root, the quantity which when multiplied by itself will produce a given quantity, as 2 is the square root of 4.

square sail, a four-sided sail rigged on a yard suspended horizontally across the mast.

squash (skwäsh), v.t. 1. to crush into a soft, flat mass or pulp. 2. to put down; suppress: v.i. 1. to be mashed to a soft consistency. 2. to make a sound of squashing. n. 1. the act of squashing or the sound of this. 2. something squashed. 3. the fleshy fruit of any one of several plants of the gourd family, eaten as a vegetable. 4. the plant, usually a vine, bearing this fruit. 5. a game played in a court with rackets and a rubber ball.

squash bug, a large insect that attacks squash vines and has an offensive odor

squash-y ('i), adj. **squash'i-er, squash'i-est,** 1. easily crushed; soft. 2. mushy. —**squash'i-ly,** adv. —**squash'i-ness,** n.

squat (skwät), v.i. **squat'ted, squat'ting,** 1. to crouch or sit down on the heels with the knees bent. 2. to cower or lie close, as an animal. 3. to settle on public land, especially to get title. 4. to settle on land without right or title: adj. short and thickset: also **squat'ty:** n. the act or posture of one who squats.

squat-ter ('ĕr), n. 1. one who squats. 2. one who settles on public or unoccupied land.

squaw (skwô), n. a North American Indian woman, especially a wife.

squaw-fish ('fish), n., pl. **-fish, -fish-es,** any one of a number of long, slender fishes found in rivers of the Pacific coast.

squawk (skwôk), v.i. 1. to utter a loud, harsh cry. 2. [Informal], to complain loudly: n. 1. a loud, harsh cry. 2. [Informal], a loud, raucous complaint. 3. the black-crowned night heron.

squaw man, a white man married to a North American Indian woman and living with her tribe.

squeak (skwēk), v.i. to make or utter a sharp, shrill, high-pitched cry or sound. v.t. to say in a squeak. n. a short, shrill, sharp cry or sound. —**squeak'y,** adj. —**squeak'i-ness,** n.

squeal (skwēl), v.i. 1. to utter or make a high, shrill, prolonged cry or sound. 2. [Slang], to act as an informer: n. a sharp, shrill, prolonged cry or sound

squeam-ish (skwēm'ish), adj. 1. easily nauseated. 2. easily disgusted or shocked. 3. fastidious about trifles. —**squeam'ish-ness,** n.

squee-gee (skwē'jī), n. a rubber-edged implement for scraping water or other liquid from a flat surface.

squeez-a-ble (skwēz'ā-bl), adj. able to be squeezed.

squeeze (skwēz), v.t. **squeezed, squeez'ing,** 1. to press hard or closely; compress. 2. to force (into, out, etc.) by compression. 3. to extract (juice, etc.), as from fruit. 4. to hug; embrace closely: v.i. 1. to give way to pressure. 2. to push one's way through or into. 3. to press: n. 1. the act of squeezing. 2. the state

of being closely pressed: crush. 3. a hug;
close embrace 4. a time of scarcity, hardship, etc. —**squeez'er**, *n.*

squelch (skwelch), *v.t* [Informal]. to silence or
subdue completely *n.* 1. the noise of mud
or slush moving under wet boots, shoes, etc.
2. [Informal]. a crushing retort, scolding,
snub, etc. —**squelch'er**, *n.*

squib (skwib), *n.* 1 a kind of firework that
hisses before exploding. 2. a lampoon, sarcastic, witty saying or writing.

squid (skwid), *n.* any one of several long, slender marine mollusks with ten arms, two of
which are longer than the others.

squig·gle (skwig'l), *n.* 1 a short line that twists
or curves. 2. illegible handwriting. *v.t & v.i.*
-gled, -gling, to make or write as a squiggle.
—**squig'gly,** *adj.*

squil·gee (skwē'jī), *n.* in *nautical usage,* same as
squeegee.

squill (skwil), *n.* a bulbous plant of the lily
family, with long racemes of white flowers.

squint (skwint), *v.i.* 1. to see or look obliquely.
2. to peer with the eyes partly shut. 3. to
be cross-eyed: *n.* 1 the act of looking
obliquely or with the eyes partly shut. 2.
the condition of being cross-eyed. 3. [Informal]. a quick look or a sidelong glance.
squint-eyed ('id), *adj.* cross-eyed.

squire (skwir), *n.* 1 a title of respect for a justice of the peace or other local dignitary 2.
in England, the owner of a large farm. 3. a
gentleman escorting a lady *v.t. & v.i.*
squired, squir'ing, to act as a squire (to).

squire·ar·chy ('är-ki), *n.* in England, country
gentry collectively: also **squir'ar·chy.**

squirm (skwurm), *v.i.* 1. to wriggle; twist and
turn. 2. to display distress or embarrassment *n* a wriggling or twisting motion. —
squirm'y, *adj.*

squir·rel (skwur'el), *n.* 1 a small, tree-dwelling
rodent with a long, bushy tail. 2. its thick,
soft fur *v.t.* **-reled** or **-relled, -rel·ing** or
-rel·ling, to hoard or store (*away*).

squirt (skwurt), *v.t. & v.i.* 1 to eject (a liquid)
in a stream from a small orifice; spurt. 2.
to wet with liquid so ejected: *n.* a small
stream or jet.

stab (stab), *v.t & v.i.* **stabbed, stab'bing,** 1. to
pierce with or as with a pointed weapon. 2.
to thrust (a knife, sword, etc.) into something. 3. to pain sharply *n.* 1 a thrust, as
with a pointed weapon. 2. a wound made
by stabbing. 3. a sharp pain. 4. an effort or
attempt

sta·bile (stā'bl), *adj.* stationary; not kept in
motion *n.* ('bēl), a large piece of stationary,
abstract sculpture, often of metal, wire,
wood, etc.

sta·bil·i·ty (stā-bil'i-ti), *n.* 1 the state or quality
of being stable: 2. firmness of
character; strength of purpose or resolution.
3. permanence.

sta·bi·lize (stā'bi-līz), *v.t.* **-lized, -liz·ing,** 1. to
make stable. 2. to keep from changing or
fluctuating, as prices. 3. to secure or maintain equilibrium of (a ship, aircraft, etc.). —
sta·bi·li·za'tion, *n.* —**sta'bi·liz·er,** *n.*

sta·ble (stā'bl), *adj.* **-bler, -blest,** 1. fixed; firm.

2. constant; steadfast. 3. lasting; not likely
to change: *n.* 1. a building in which animals, especially horses, are kept and fed. 2.
the horses of some particular stable or
belonging to one owner *v.t. & v.i.* **-bled,
-bling,** to put, keep, or dwell in a stable. —
sta'ble·man, *n., pl.* **-men.**

sta·bling (stā'bling). *n.* accommodations for
horses, etc in a stable or stables.

stac·ca·to (stä-kät'ō), *adj.* in *Music,* with each
note distinct and separate.

stack (stak), *n.* 1 a large quantity of hay,
wood, etc piled up in a neat, regular form.
2. any orderly pile. 3. a number of chimney
flues standing together 4. a smokestack. 5.
pl. a series of bookshelves in a library *v.t.*
1 to arrange in a stack. 2. to arrange (playing cards in a deck) so as to cheat.

stack-up ('up), *n.* a number of aircraft circling
an airport waiting for a turn to land.

sta·di·um (stā'di-ŭm), *n.* 1 *pl.* **-di·a** (-ä), in ancient Greece and Rome, a unit of linear
measure, equal to about 607 ft. 2. *pl.* **-di·
ums,** a large structure for baseball, football,
etc., surrounded by tiers of seats, usually
for several thousand spectators.

staff (staf), *n., pl.* **staffs,** 1. *pl.* also **staves,** a
stick, rod, or pole, used as a support in
walking, for defense, as a symbol of authority, or as a support for a flag. 2. a group
of officers serving a military or naval commanding officer as advisers. 3. a group of
people serving as assistants to any leader 4.
any group of workers or employees. 5. *pl.*
also **staves,** in *Music,* the five lines and four
spaces between them on which music is
written or printed: *v.t.* to provide with a
staff, as of workers.

stag (stag), *n.* 1. a full-grown male deer; especially, a male European red deer 2. a castrated hog. 3. a man attending a social
gathering without a woman. 4. a social
gathering for men only· *adj.* for men only.

stag beetle, a beetle having, in the male,
mandibles suggestive of a stag's horns.

stage (stāj), *n.* 1 a platform. 2. an area or
platform as in a theater, where plays,
speeches, etc. are presented. 3. the theatrical
profession. 4. a place of rest on a journey.
5. the distance between such places of rest.
6. a stagecoach 7 a degree of progress or
development. 8. any one of the propulsion
units used in succession as the rocket of a
missile or spacecraft: *v.t.* **staged, stag'ing,** 1.
to put on the stage, as a play. 2. to arrange
and carry out.

stage-coach ('kōch), *n.* a horse-drawn coach
that formerly carried passengers, parcels,
etc. over a regular route.

stage·craft ('kraft), *n.* the art or skill of writing
or staging plays.

stage director, one who prepares a theatrical
play, coaches the players, and arranges the
details for presentation.

stage fright, nervousness felt when appearing
before an audience.

stage·hand ('hand), *n.* a worker who sets up
and removes the scenery and furniture for a
play, operates the curtain, etc.

stage manager, an assistant to the stage direc-

a in cap, ä in cane, ä in father, ä in abet, e in met, ē in be, ē in baker,
ē in regent, i in pit, ī in fine, i in manifest, o in hot, ō in horse, ō in bone,

tor, in charge backstage during the performance of a play.

stag·er ('ēr), *n.* a person or animal of much experience.

stage-struck ('struk), *adj.* eager to become an actor or actress.

stag·ger (stag'ēr), *v.i.* to totter or reel, as from weariness or a blow: *v.t.* 1. to cause to stagger, as with a blow. 2. to shock. 3. to set or incline alternately; make zigzag. 4. to arrange so as to come at different times: *n.* 1. a reeling or tottering. 2. *pl.* a disease or toxic condition of horses, cattle, etc. causing staggering.

stag·ing (stā'jing), *n.* 1. a temporary structure of boards and posts; scaffolding. 2. the business of managing stagecoaches. 3. a style of play production.

stag·nant (stag'nänt), *adj.* 1. not flowing or running in a stream. 2. stale or foul from lack of movement: said of water or bodies of water. 3. not brisk; torpid; dull. —**stag'nan·cy**, *n.* —**stag'nant·ly**, *adv*

stag·nate ('nāt), *v.i. & v.t.* -**nat·ed**, -**nat·ing**, to become or make stagnant. —**stag·na'tion**, *n.*

stag·y (stā'ji), *adj.* **stag'i·er, stag'i·est**, 1. theatrical; characteristic of the stage. 2. unreal. —**stag'i·ly**, *adv.* —**stag'i·ness**, *n.*

staid (stād), archaic past tense and past participle of **stay**: *adj.* sober; sedate; steady. —**staid'ly**, *adv.* —**staid'ness**, *n.*

stain (stān), *v.t.* 1. to discolor with streaks or spots of dirt or foreign matter 2. to color (wood, glass, etc.) by applying pigment, stain, etc. 3. to bring shame upon; disgrace: *n.* 1 a spot or blot of color different from the ground; discoloration. 2. a dye for staining wood, etc. 3. dishonor; taint.

stained glass, glass colored by any one of several methods, as baking pigments onto its surface or fusing metallic oxides into it, and used for windows in churches and other buildings.

stain·less steel ('lis), an alloy of steel and chromium that resists rust and corrosion.

stair (ster), *n.* 1. any one of a series of steps for ascending or descending to different levels. 2. *usually pl.* a set of steps between levels.

stair·case ('kās), *n.* a flight of steps with railings: also **stair'way** ('wā).

stair·head ('hed), *n.* the top of a staircase.

stair·well ('wel), *n.* a vertical shaft, as in a building, containing a staircase.

staith, staithe (stāth), *n.* [British Dialectal], a stage or wharf with equipment for loading (coal, etc.) from railroad cars into vessels.

stake (stāk), *n.* 1. a post or strong stick sharpened at one end and fixed in the ground. 2. the post to which a person condemned to be burned was tied. 3. execution by burning. 4. *often pl.* something risked or hazarded, especially money, in a wager, contest, or game. 5. *often pl.* a prize, as in a race. 6. a grubstake: *v.t.* **staked, stak'ing**, 1. to fasten to or support with stakes. 2. to mark out the limits of. 3. to gamble; wager. 4. [Informal], to furnish with money, resources, etc. **stake-hold·er** ('hōl·dēr), *n.* one who holds the

money or other stakes bet by others and pays it to the winner

stake-out ('out), *n.* 1. the stationing of policemen for surveillance of a suspect. 2. the location or area of surveillance.

sta·lac·tite (stâ-lak'tīt), *n.* an icicle-shaped deposit of carbonate of lime hanging from the roof of a cave.

sta·lag·mite (stâ-lag'mīt), *n.* a cone-shaped deposit of carbonate of lime built up on the floor of a cave by drip, often from a stalactite above.

stale (stāl), *adj.* **stal'er, stal'est,** 1. no longer fresh, having become dry, hard, musty, flat, etc from having been kept too long. 2. trite; common, boring. 3. not in condition; enervated, bored, etc —*v.t. & v.i.* **staled, stal'ing,** to make or become stale. —**stale'ness,** *n.*

stale-mate ('māt), *n.* 1. in *Chess,* a situation in which a player cannot move without placing his king in check; it results in a draw 2. any deadlock *v.t.* -**mat·ed,** -**mat·ing,** to subject to a stalemate.

stalk (stôk), *v.t* to pursue stealthily or under cover, so as to kill, as game *v.i.* 1 to walk stiffly or haughtily. 2. to spread grimly *n.* 1. a stiff, haughty, or grim stride 2 the act of stalking. 3. the main stem or axis of a plant. 4. any stemlike part acting as a support, etc

stalk·ing-horse ('stôk'ing-hôrs), *n.* 1. a horse, or figure of a horse, behind which a hunter conceals himself from game 2. something used to conceal one's purpose or intention. 3. in *Politics,* a supposed candidate advanced only to divide opposition or conceal the actual choice until an opportune time.

stall (stôl), *n.* 1 a compartment for one animal in a stable or barn. 2. a table, booth, counter, etc. at a market, where goods are displayed for sale. 3. a seat or pew in the choir or the main part of a church. 4. in England, a seat near the stage in a theater. 5. a stop or standstill, especially the stopping of an engine because of malfunction. 6. [Informal], any evasive action: *v.t. & v.i.* 1. to place or stay in a stall. 2. to bring or come to a standstill, especially unintentionally. 3. to delay, as by speaking or acting evasively.

stall-feed ('fēd), *v.t.* -**fed,** -**feed·ing,** to feed (an animal kept inactive in a stall) for fattening.

stal·lion (stal'yun), *n.* an uncastrated male horse, especially one kept for breeding.

stal·wart (stôl'wērt), *adj.* 1. sturdy; strong. 2. resolute; firm. 3. valiant; brave. —**stal'wart·ly,** *adv.* —**stal'wart·ness,** *n.*

sta·men (stā'mēn), *n., pl.* -**mens, stam·i·na** (stam'i·nâ), the pollen-bearing organ of a flower, which produces the male or fertilizing cell.

stam·i·na (stam'i·nâ), *n.* power of endurance; ability to resist disease, fatigue, hardship, etc.

stam·i·nal (stam'i·nl), *adj.* 1. of or pertaining to stamina. 2. of or pertaining to stamens.

stam·i·nate (-nit, -nāt), *adj.* 1. of or having stamens. 2. bearing stamens but no pistils, as male flowers.

ō in *dragon,* ōō in *crude,* oo in *wool,* u in *cup,* ū in *cure,* ū in *turn,* u in *focus,* oi in *boy,* ou in *house,* th in *thin,* th in *sheathe,* g in *get,* j in *joy,* y in *yet.*

stam·i·nif·er·ous (stam-i-nif'ẽr-ŭs), *adj.* bearing stamens.

stam·mel (stam'l), *n.* 1. a coarse, woolen cloth dyed dull scarlet. 2. this color.

stam·mer (stam'ẽr), *v.t. & v.i.* to speak or utter with hesitation, faltering, and rapid repetitions: *n.* the act or an instance of stammering. —**stam'mer·ing·ly,** *adv.*

stamp (stamp), *v.t.* 1. to thrust (the foot) down forcibly. 2. to crush or strike with the foot. 3. to impress or cut out (a design, mark, etc.). 4. to cut (*out*) by impressing with a die. 5. to affix a stamp to. 6. to distinguish or reveal: 4. to thrust the foot down forcibly. 2. to tread with loud, heavy steps: *n.* 1 the act of stamping. 2. a die. 3. a tool or machine for stamping. 4. a mark or impression made by stamping. 5. a small piece of paper, usually with a distinctive imprint on the front and gum on the back, required by a government to be affixed to a letter, document, etc. 6. any similar seal. 7. type, kind.

stam·pede (stam-pēd'), *n.* a sudden panic, causing a headlong flight or rush, as of a herd of animals: *v.i.* -ped'ed, -ped'ing, to rush off in a stampede: *v.t.* to cause to stampede. —**stam·ped'er,** *n.*

stance (stans), *n.* 1. the position or posture while standing, especially in reference to the feet. 2. the attitude taken toward something.

stanch (stônch), *v.t. & v.i. & adj.* same as **staunch.**

stan·chion (stan'chŭn), *n.* 1. a support or post. 2. a device placed around the neck of a cow to keep it in its stall.

stand (stand), *v.i.* stood, stand'ing, 1. to be upright on the feet; be erect. 2. to occupy a certain position. 3. to cease to move. 4. to be at rest; be stationary. 5. to remain unchanged. 6. to be obstinate or firm; resist. 7. to be supported on a base. 8. to have a (certain) height while standing. 9. to gather and remain, as water: *v.t.* 1. to endure. 2. to sustain; tolerate. 3. to set in an erect position. 4. to pay for. 5. to undergo: *n.* 1. a stop or halt. 2. a reserved parking place along a street for the hire of taxicabs, etc. 3. a raised platform as for spectators, a band, etc. 4. a stall or booth where goods are sold. 5. a place where a theatrical company stops over. 6. a small table, rack, etc. 7. a growth of trees or plants. 8. a position, view, opinion, etc.

stand·ard (stan'dẽrd), *n.* 1. an ensign or flag, especially a banner with a military emblem. 2. something established by authority as a fixed rule or measure; criterion, rule, or model. 3. an upright support. 4. a tree standing alone. 5. a basis of comparison in measuring or judging quantity, value, etc.

stand·ard-bear·er (-bẽr-ẽr), *n.* 1. a soldier or other person who carries a flag. 2. the leader of a movement, cause, political party, etc.

stand·ard·ize (stan'dẽr-dīz), *v.t.* -ized, -iz·ing, to cause to conform to a standard. —**stand·ard·i·za'tion,** *n.*

standard time, the civil time established for a

country or region: the earth is divided into 24 time zones, each one hour apart, determined by distance east or west from Greenwich, England: the zones within the 48 contiguous States of the U.S. are *Eastern, Central, Mountain,* and *Pacific.*

stand·by (stand'bī), *n.,* pl. **-bys,** something which one can depend on, use as a substitute, rely on in emergency, etc.

stand·ee (stan-dē'), *n.* [Informal], one who has to stand, for lack of seats, as in a bus or theater.

stand-in (stand'in), *n.* one who takes the place of another, as for a motion-picture or television actor while lights are being adjusted, etc.

stand·ing ('ing), *n.* 1. duration. 2. reputation, rank, or status. 3. *pl.* a list showing rank or order: *adj.* 1. that stands; erect. 2. stagnant, as water. 3. lasting; permanent. 4. from a standing position. 5. not in use.

stand-off ('ôf), *n.* a tie in a game or contest.

stand-off-ish (stand-ôf'ish), *adj.* reserved; aloof.

stand·pat·ter ('pat-ẽr), *n.* [Informal], one who resists change; conservative.

stand·pipe ('pip), *n.* a large, round tower or vertical pipe for water storage, especially as part of the water-supply system for a community.

stand·point ('point), *n.* point of view.

stand·still ('stil), *n.* a halt or stop.

Stan·ford-Bi·net test (stan'fẽrd bi-nā'), a revision of the Binet-Simon test that covers a wider range.

stan·hope (stan'hŏp), *n.* a light, two-wheeled carriage without a top.

stank (stangk), alternate past tense of **stink.**

stan·na·ry (stan'ẽr-i), *n.,* pl. **-ries,** a region of tin mines.

stan·nic ('ik), *adj.* of or containing tin, especially with a valence of four.

stan·nous ('ŭs), *adj.* of or containing tin, especially with a valence of two.

stan·za (stan'zä), *n.* a group of lines of verse making up a division of a poem or song. —**stan·za'ic** (-zā'ik), *adj.*

sta·pes (stā'pēz), *n.,* pl. **sta'pes, sta·pe·des** (stā-pē'dēz), a small, stirrup-shaped bone of the inner ear.

staph·y·lo·coc·cus (staf-i-lō-kok'ŭs), *n.,* pl. **-coc'ci** (-kok'sī), any one of certain spherical bacteria, generally grouped in clusters or chains: some species are pathogenic, causing pus formation in boils, abscesses, etc. —**staph·y·lo·coc'cal** (-kok'ål), *adj.*

staph·y·lo·plas·ty (staf'i-lō-plas-ti), *n.* the repair of defects of the soft palate by plastic surgery.

staph·y·lor·rha·phy (staf-i-lôr'ä-fi), *n.,* pl. **-phies,** the uniting of a cleft palate by plastic surgery.

sta·ple (stā'pl), *n.* 1. a principal commodity or product made or grown in a country or district. 2. raw material. 3. something for sale that is regularly kept in stock, as flour, sugar, etc. 4. the fiber of wool, cotton, etc. 5. a U-shaped piece of metal with sharp ends, used to fasten papers together or to drive into wood as for holding a hook or wire: *adj.* 1. chief; principal. 2. regularly stocked or produced: *v.t.* **-pled, -pling,** to fasten with a staple —**sta′pler,** *n.*

star (stär), *n.* 1. any one of the luminous heavenly bodies seen as points of light in the night sky: specifically, any one of the self-luminous, gaseous bodies, as the sun, seen (except for the sun) as a point of light. 2. a conventionalized figure with five or six points representing a star. 3. a planet or star regarded as influencing one's destiny. 4. a white spot on the forehead of a horse. 5. an asterisk. 6. one who is prominent in entertainment or sports. 7. an actor or actress taking a leading part: *v.t.* **starred, star′ring,** 1. to mark with stars. 2. to present (a performer) as a star: *v.i.* 1. to appear as a star. 2. to be brilliant; shine as a star: *adj.* 1. of a star. 2. celebrated. —**star′less,** *adj.*

star-board (′bērd, ′bôrd), *n.* the right side of a ship looking toward the bow: *adj.* of or on the starboard.

starch (stärch), *n.* 1. a white, tasteless, odorless, carbohydrate food substance found in potatoes, rice, corn, wheat, beans, and many other vegetable foods: it is used in foods, sizes, adhesives, pharmacy, etc. 2. a powdered form of this substance used to stiffen fabrics in laundering: *v.t.* to stiffen as with starch.

Star Chamber, an English court abolished in 1641 which passed upon civil and criminal cases without a jury: notorious for arbitrary rulings and the use of torture to extort confessions.

starch-y (stär′chi), *adj.* **starch′i-er, starch′i-est,** 1. of or like starch. 2. containing much starch, as some foods. 3. stiffened with starch. 4. stiff; formal; precise. —**starch′i-ness,** *n.*

star-crossed (stär′krôst), *adj.* ill-fated; unlucky.

star-dom (stär′dōm), *n.* the status of a star in the entertainment field.

stare (ster), *n.* a steady, fixed look with wide-open eyes: *v.i.* **stared, star′ing,** to gaze fixedly with eyes wide open: *v.t.* to gaze at fixedly. —**star′er,** *n.*

star-fish (stär′fish), *n., pl.* **-fish, -fish-es,** an echinoderm having a star-shaped body made up of five or more radiating arms or rays.

star-gaz-er (′gāz-ēr), *n.* 1. one who gazes at the stars, as an astronomer. 2. an idealist or daydreamer. 3. any one of several marine fishes with eyes on top of its head.

stark (stärk), *adj.* 1. stiff or rigid, as a corpse. 2. utter; downright. 3. barren; bleak. 4. prominent: *adv.* utterly; completely. —**stark′-ly,** *adv.* —**stark′ness,** *n.*

stark-nak-ed (′nā′kid), *adj.* completely naked.

star-let (stär′lit), *n.* a young actress being publicized as a future star.

star-light (′lit), *n.* the light of the stars. —**star′-lit** (′lit), *adj.*

star-ling (stär′ling), *n.* any one of a family of old-world, passerine birds, especially one with iridescent plumage, now common in the U.S. where it is often a pest.

Star of David, a symbol of Judaism made up of two interlaced triangles, forming a six-pointed star.

starred (stärd), *adj.* 1. decorated with stars. 2. thought to be influenced by the stars, as in astrology. 3. featured as a star in a theatrical presentation.

star-ry (stär′i), *adj.* **-ri-er, -ri-est,** 1. shaped like a star. 2. full of stars. 3. lighted by stars. 4. of or coming from the stars. —**star′ri-ness,** *n.*

star-ry-eyed (-id), *adj.* with sparkling eyes.

Stars and Stripes, the flag of the U.S.

star-span-gled (stär′spang′ld), *adj.* spangled or decorated with stars.

Star-Spangled Banner, 1. the flag of the U.S., with 13 alternating red-and-white stripes and a field in the upper left corner that is blue with 50 white stars, one for each State. 2. the U.S. national anthem, with words written by Francis Scott Key during the War of 1812.

start (stärt), *v.i.* 1. to set out; commence; begin. 2. to give an involuntary move or twitch, as from surprise. 3. to become loose. 4. to spring into action, being, etc.: *v.t.* 1. to originate or set going. 2. to rouse suddenly, as from concealment. 3. to loosen, displace, etc. 4. to begin to perform, do, etc. 5. to cause to be an entrant, as in a race: *n.* 1. the act of starting or beginning. 2. a sudden, startled movement. 3. a place or time of beginning. 4. an advance or lead, as in a race. 5. opportunity or assistance given to one beginning a career. —**start′er,** *n.*

star-tle (stärt′l), *v.t.* **-tled, -tling,** to frighten suddenly; especially, to cause to start or move suddenly in alarm: *v.i.* to be startled.

star-tling (′ling), *adj.* causing a sudden shock of surprise or fright. —**star′tling-ly,** *adv.*

starve (stärv), *v.i.* 1. to **starved, starv′ing,** 1. to suffer from extreme hunger. 2. to die from lack of food. 3. to feel a great need (for): *v.t.* 1. to subdue by depriving of food. 2. to cause to starve. —**star-va-tion** (stär-vā′shŭn), *n.*

starve-ling (′ling), *adj.* hungry; weak; lean: *n.* a thin, weak, starving person or animal.

stash (stash), *v.t. & v.i.* [Informal], to put or store away (money, supplies, etc.).

sta-sis (stā′sis, stas′is), *n., pl.* **-ses** (′sēz), 1. the arrest or slackening of the flow of a fluid in the body, as of the blood. 2. a slackening of peristalsis of the intestines. 3. a state of balance or equilibrium.

-stat (stat), a combining form meaning *stationary.*

state (stāt), *n.* 1. the way that a person or thing is at a given time; circumstances or condition. 2. mode, form, phase, etc. 3. emotional or mental condition. 4. imposing display. 5. [sometimes S-], the whole body of people organized under one government. 6. [usually S-], any one of the political units forming a federal government, as in the U.S. 7. civil government. 8. governmental authority: *adj.* 1. [sometimes S-], of the government or a State. 2. used on state occasions; ceremonial: *v.t.* **stat′ed, stat′ing,** 1. to express in words; tell. 2. to fix by specifying; settle.

state-craft (′kraft), *n.* the management of a state; statesmanship.

stat·ed (stāt'id), *adj.* fixed or regular, as by agreement. —**stat'ed·ly**, *adv.*

State Department, the department of the executive branch of the U.S. government that deals with foreign governments.

State·hood ('hood), *n.* the condition of being a State of the U.S.

state·house (stāt'hous), *n.* [often S-], the official meeting place of the legislature of a State of the U.S.

state·less (stāt'les), *adj.* having no state or nationality.

state·ly ('li), *adj.* -li·er, -li·est, 1. majestic; magnificent. 2. dignified and deliberate, as a manner of walking. —**state'li·ness,** *n.*

state·ment (mėnt), *n.* 1. the act of stating. 2. something stated, as a declaration, assertion, narration, etc. 3. a financial account or bill.

state of the art, the current level of sophistication of a developing technology, as of computer science. —**state'-of-the-art,** *adj.*

state·room (stāt'rōōm), *n.* a private cabin or room on a ship or train.

state·side ('sīd), *adj.* [Informal]. in or of the U.S. used in speaking of the U.S. from abroad: *adv.* [Informal], in or to the U.S.

states·man (stāts'mǎn), *n.*, *pl.* **-men,** one who is skilled in public affairs and the art of government. —**states'man·like, states'man·ly,** *adj.*

states·man·ship (-ship), *n.* skill, wisdom, and vision in the management of public affairs and in the art of government.

States' rights, all of the rights that the Constitution of the U.S. neither reserves to the Federal government nor denies to the State governments: also **State rights.**

state·wide (stāt'wīd'), *adj.* throughout a whole state.

stat·ic (stat'ik), *adj.* 1. of or having to do with bodies at rest or in equilibrium. 2. acting by mere weight without producing motion. 3. inactive; at rest. 4. of or denoting stationary electrical charges, as from friction. 5. in *Radio,* of or having to do with static: *n.* 1. noise on radio or television caused by atmospheric electrical activity. 2. the electrical discharges causing this noise. 3. [Slang], unfavorable criticism. —**stat'i·cal·ly,** *adv.*

stat·ics ('iks), *n.* the branch of mechanics that treats of the equilibrium, pressure, weight, etc. of bodies at rest.

sta·tion (stā'shůn), *n.* 1. the place where a person or thing stands or is located. 2. an assigned post. 3. social rank or order. 4. a place where a train or bus stops regularly for passengers. 5. a building at such a stopping place. 6. a post, building, headquarters, etc. for a service or business. 7. in Australia, a sheep ranch. 8. a place where radio or television broadcasts originate. 9. the frequency assigned to a regular broadcaster: *v.t.* to assign to a station; place.

sta·tion·ar·y (stā'shůn-er-i), *adj.* 1. fixed; not moving. 2. not movable. 3. not migratory. 4. not changing; remaining in the same state.

station break, a pause in a radio or television broadcast for station identification.

sta·tion·er (stā'shů-nēr), *n.* one who sells sta-

tionery, office supplies, and the like.

sta·tion·er·y (-ner-i), *n.* writing materials, especially writing paper and envelopes.

sta·tion·mas·ter (stā'shůn-mas-tēr), *n.* a person in charge of a railroad station.

Stations of the Cross, [also s- c-]. a series of 14 pictures or mural tablets depicting stages of Jesus' suffering, often placed on the walls of a Roman Catholic church, and visited in turn as a devotional exercise.

station wagon, an automobile with rear seats that can be folded down and a tailgate that can be opened for loading packages, etc.

sta·tis·ti·cian (stat-is-tish'ůn), *n.* a person whose work is the compiling or analyzing of statistics.

sta·tis·tics (stå-tis'tiks), *n.pl.* 1. the science of compiling, classifying, and arranging numerical data. 2. such data so arranged and analyzed as to present important information. —**sta·tis'ti·cal,** *adj.* —**sta·tis'ti·cal·ly,** *adv.*

sta·tor (stāt'ēr), *n.* the part of a dynamo, motor, etc. that remains at rest, forming a pivot or housing for a revolving part (*rotor*).

stat·o·scope (stat'ô-skōp), *n.* 1. an aneroid barometer for recording slight changes in atmospheric pressure. 2. an instrument for registering slight variations in the altitude of an aircraft.

stat·u·ar·y (stach' oo-wer-i), *n.* 1. statues collectively. 2. the art of making statues.

stat·ue (stach'ōō), *n.* a representation of a person or animal as carved in stone or wood, cast in plaster or bronze, or modeled in clay.

stat·u·esque (stach-oo-wesk'), *adj.* 1. stately and dignified. 2. tall and well-proportioned: usually said of a woman. —**stat·u·esque'ly,** *adv.*

stat·u·ette (-wet'), *n.* a small statue.

stat·ure (stach'ēr), *n.* 1. the natural height of a person standing. 2. level of achievement or development.

sta·tus (stāt'ůs, stat'-), *n.*, *pl.* **-tus·es,** 1. legal condition. 2. state, as of affairs. 3. social standing or place. 4. prestige.

status quo (kwō), [Latin], the existing state or condition.

status symbol, a possession, article of clothing, action, etc. regarded as a symbol of high social status.

stat·ute (stach'ōōt), *n.* 1. a law enacted by a legislature of a state or country. 2. an established law or rule.

statute book, the record, as in a book, of the statutes of a given jurisdiction.

statute mile, a unit of measure: the legal mile of the U.S., equal to 5,280 feet.

statute of limitations, a statute specifying the time during which legal action may be taken on a given matter.

stat·u·to·ry (stach'oo-tôr-i), *adj.* 1. enacted or authorized by statute. 2. punishable by statute, as an offense.

staunch (stônch, stänch), *v.t.* 1. to stop the flow of (a liquid, as blood, tears, etc.). 2. to stop the flow of blood or a liquid from (a cut, leak, etc.): *v.i.* to cease flowing or draining away: *adj.* 1. watertight, as a ship. 2. solid; strong. 3. firm; trustworthy. —**staunch'ly,** *adv.* —**staunch'ness,** *n.*

---

a in cap, ā in cane, ä in father, å in abet, e in met, ē in be, ê in baker, ê in regent, i in pit, ī in fine, ĭ in manifest, o in hot, ō in horse, ō in bone,

stau·ro·lite (stôr'ō-līt), *n.* an opaque silicate of aluminum and iron of a reddish-brown color, formed in crystals.

stave (stāv), *n.* 1. one of the shaped strips of wood forming the sides of a cask, barrel, etc. 2. any similar slat, rung, etc. 3. a staff or stick. 4. a music staff. 5. a stanza: *v.t.* staved or stove, stav'ing, 1. to break a hole in; puncture; especially, to break or smash in a stave. 2. to hold back; turn aside (followed by *off*). 3. to furnish with staves.

staves (stāvz), *n.* 1. alternate plural of staff. 2. plural of stave.

stay (stā), *n.* 1. a large, strong rope or cable that braces or supports a mast; guy. 2. a prop or support. 3. a strip of material used to stiffen a collar, corset, etc. 4. a stop, halt, or pause. 5. a temporary residence in a place, or the time of this. 6. a delay or postponement of legal action: *v.t.* 1. to hold up or support. 2. to restrain; hinder. 3. to delay or postpone (legal action). 4. to appease (appetite, thirst, etc.) for a time. 5. to remain or last through (a period of time, an event, etc.): *v.i.* 1. to dwell; live. 2. to remain; continue in a condition or place. 3. to stop; halt. 4. to pause. 5. [Informal], to endure.

stead (sted), *n.* 1. the place of someone or something as filled by a substitute or successor. 2. advantage or service: used in the phrase stand (one) in good stead.

stead·fast (·fast), *adj.* 1. firmly fixed or established. 2. steady; constant. —stead'fast·ly, *adv.* —stead'fast·ness, *n.*

stead·y (sted'i), *adj.* stead'i·er, stead'i·est, 1. fixed, regular, or uniform. 2. constant in feeling or purpose; loyal, stable, etc. 3. firm; not shaky. 4. sober; reliable. 5. calm; unwavering: *v.t. & v.i.* stead'ied, stead'y·ing, to make or keep steady: *n.* [Informal], a person whom one dates exclusively; sweetheart. —stead'i·ly, *adv.* —stead'i·ness, *n.*

stead·y-state (-stāt'), *adj.* of or denoting an operation, system, etc. that maintains equilibrium in spite of fluctuations or transformations.

steady-state theory, in *Cosmology*, a theory that the universe is constantly expanding and that new matter is continuously created.

steak (stāk), *n.* a slice of meat, especially beef or fish, for broiling or frying.

steal (stēl), *v.t.* stole, stol'en, steal'ing, 1. to take (the property of another) without leave or right; especially secretly. 2. to gain secretly and gradually. 3. to withdraw, move, put, etc. stealthily (*from, in,* etc.). 4. to take (a peek, look, etc.) slyly. 5. in *Baseball,* to gain (a base) by running without the aid of a hit or an error: *v.i.* 1. to commit theft. 2. to move in or out unperceived: *n.* [Informal], a remarkable bargain.

stealth (stelth), *n.* a secret or underhanded procedure; furtiveness.

stealth·y ('i), *adj.* stealth'i·er, stealth'i·est, done or performed by stealth; sly; furtive. —stealth'i·ly, *adv.* —stealth'i·ness, *n.*

steam (stēm), *n.* 1. vapor into which water is changed when heated to the boiling point. 2. condensed water vapor, seen as mist above boiling water. 3. the power supplied by steam under pressure. 4. [Informal], energy; force: *v.i.* 1. to emit steam. 2. to move by steam power. 3. to become covered with condensed steam (often followed by *up*): *v.t.* to apply steam to, as in cooking: *adj.* 1. operated by steam. 2. containing steam.

steam·boat ('bōt), *n.* a small steamship, as one used on rivers.

steam engine, an engine operated by steam under pressure; specifically, a locomotive.

steam·er ('ēr), *n.* 1. a vessel operated by steam under pressure; steamship. 2. formerly, an automobile operated by steam. 3. a cooking utensil or other apparatus for steaming.

steam fitter, one whose occupation (steam fitting) is the installation or repair of boilers, pipes, etc. in a system operated by steam pressure.

steam·roll·er ('rōl-ēr), *n.* 1. a heavy, steam-powered roller used in building roads. 2. a force or power arbitrarily used to overcome opposition to a policy, etc.

steam·ship ('ship), *n.* a ship driven by steam power

steam shovel, a large excavating machine operated by steam power.

steam table, in restaurants, a table or counter with a metal top and sections holding hot water, the steam from which keeps foods warm.

steam·y (stē'mi), *adj.* steam'i·er, steam'i·est, 1. of or like steam. 2. full of steam. 3. covered with condensed steam. 4. giving off steam. 5. hot and humid. —steam'i·ness, *n.*

ste·a·rate (stē'ȧ-rāt, stir'āt), *n.* a salt or ester of stearic acid.

ste·ar·ic (stē-er'ik, stir'ik), *adj.* 1. of or obtained from stearin. 2. of or pertaining to stearic acid.

stearic acid, a white, fatty acid found in animal and vegetable fats, used in making candles, soaps, etc.

ste·a·rin (stē'ȧ-rin, stir'in), *n.* a white, crystalline substance found in most animal and vegetable fats and used in soaps, sizes, adhesives, etc.: also ste'a·rine (-rin, -rēn, -in, -ēn).

ste·a·tite (stē'ȧ-tīt), *n.* a compact variety of talc, used to make electrical insulators, etc.; soapstone. —ste·a·tit'ic (-tit'ik), *adj.*

steed (stēd), *n.* a horse, especially one that is spirited.

steel (stēl), *n.* 1. iron refined and combined with carbon to form a hard, tough alloy. 2. something made of steel. 3. toughness, strength, etc.: *adj.* of or like steel: *v.t.* 1. to overlay, edge, or tip with steel. 2. to make hard or invulnerable.

steel band, a percussion band of a kind native to Trinidad, using steel oil drums tuned to produce various pitches.

steel·head ('hed), *n., pl.* -head, -heads, a kind of large rainbow trout of the Pacific coast.

steel wool, long, fine steel shavings in a pad or ball, used for scouring, polishing, etc.

steel·work ('wûrk), *n.* 1. a structure or framework made of steel. 2. steel parts or articles. 3. *pl.* a mill where steel is made,

---

ō in dragon, o͞o in crude, o͝o in wool, u in cup, ū in cure, û in turn, ŭ in focus, oi in boy, ou in house, th in thin, th in sheathe, g in get, j in joy, y in yet.

shaped, etc.: also **steel mill**. —**steel'work·er**, *n.*

steel·y ('i), *adj.* **steel'i·er**, **steel'i·est**, 1. made of or like steel. 2. hard; inflexible. 3. of the color of steel. —**steel'i·ness**, *n.*

steel·yard ('yärd), *n.* a kind of balance suspended from above and consisting of a single weight moved along a graduated arm.

steen·bok (stēn'bok, stän'-), *n.* same as steinbok: also **steen'buck** ('buk).

steep (stēp), *adj.* 1. rising or descending with abrupt inclination; precipitous. 2. [Informal], excessive: *n.* 1. a precipitous place; sharp incline. 2. a liquid in which something is steeped: *v.t.* 1. to soak in a liquid, so as to extract the essence of, or to soften, clean, etc. 2. to imbue: *v.i.* to be soaked in liquid, as tea leaves.

steep·en ('n), *v.t.* & *v.i.* to make or become steep or steeper.

stee·ple (stē'p'l), *n.* 1. a tower tapering to a point, especially on a church. 2. a spire.

stee·ple·bush (-boosh), *n.* a bush of the rose family, with pink or purple flowers in steeplelike clusters, native to the eastern U.S.

stee·ple·chase (-chās), *n.* a horse race over a course with obstructions such as ditches, hedges, etc. —**stee'ple·chas·er**, *n.*

stee·pled (stē'p'ld), *adj.* furnished with, like, or adorned with a steeple.

stee·ple·jack (-jak), *n.* one whose work is climbing steeples, towers, smokestacks, etc. to build, paint, or repair them.

steer (stir), *v.t.* 1. to direct the course of (a vessel) by use of various devices, as a rudder. 2. to direct the course of (an automobile). 3. to guide or control. 4. to pursue (a set course): *v.i.* to guide a ship, vehicle, etc.

steer (stir), *n.* a castrated male of the cattle family; bullock.

steer·age (stir'ij), *n.* 1. the act or practice of steering. 2. the response of a ship to the helm. 3. formerly, that part on some passenger ships having inferior accommodations and allotted to passengers paying the lowest fare.

steer·age·way (-wā), *n.* the minimum rate of speed through the water sufficient to make a vessel respond to the helm.

steers·man (stirz'man), *n., pl.* -men, a person who steers a ship or boat; helmsman.

stein (stīn), *n.* 1. a beer mug. 2. the amount that a stein will hold.

stein·bok (stīn'bok), *n.* a brownish antelope of the plains of southern and eastern Africa.

ste·le (stē'li), *n.* 1. an inscribed, upright slab or tablet, used as a grave marker, monument, etc. 2. in *Botany*, the axial cylinder of vascular tissue in the stems and roots of plants.

stel·lar (stel'ēr), *adj.* 1. of or pertaining to a star or stars. 2. shaped like a star. 3. outstanding. 4. leading; chief.

stel·late ('āt), *adj.* shaped like a star; radiating from a center.

stel·li·form ('i-fôrm), *adj.* shaped like a star.

stel·lu·lar ('yoo-lēr), *adj.* 1. shaped like a small star or stars. 2. covered with small stars.

stem (stem), *n.* 1. the principal stalk of a plant. 2. a plant part supporting another

plant part, as a leaf, flower, or fruit. 3. anything resembling a stem, as the tube of a tobacco pipe, the support of a wine glass, etc. 4. the forepart of a ship; prow. 5. *a)* ancestry; lineage; *b)* a branch of a family. 6. the basic part of a word to which inflectional endings are added: *v.t.* **stemmed**, **stem'ming**, 1. to remove the stem or stems of. 2. to move forward against (an obstacle): *v.i.* to derive from or originate.

stem (stem), *v.t.* **stemmed**, **stem'ming**, to resist or check; especially, to dam up (a river, stream, etc.).

stem·mer (stem'ēr), *n.* a person or thing that stems; specifically, one that removes stems from fruit or tobacco.

stem·ware (stem'wer), *n.* glasses, goblets, etc. having stems.

stem-wind·er ('wīn·dēr), *n.* a watch whose inside mechanism can be wound by turning a knurled knob on the outside end of the stem.

stench (stench), *n.* a strong, offensive odor; stink.

sten·cil (sten'sl), *v.t.* **-ciled** or **-cilled**, **-cil·ing** or **-cil·ling**, to make, mark, or color with a stencil: *n.* 1. a thin plate, as of metal or plastic, cut through in a pattern, letters, etc. so that when ink, paint, etc. is applied to the plate the design will be reproduced on the surface beneath. 2. the design so made.

sten·o- (sten'ō), a combining form meaning *narrow, thin, small*.

sten·o·graph (sten'ō-graf), *n.* a machine for reproducing shorthand symbols: *v.t.* to write in shorthand.

ste·nog·ra·pher (stē-nog'rā-fēr), *n.* a person skilled in writing in shorthand.

ste·nog·ra·phy (-fi), *n.* the skill or process of writing down in shorthand dictation, testimony, etc. and transcribing it later. —**sten·o·graph·ic** (sten-ō-graf'ik), *adj.* —**sten·o·graph'i·cal·ly**, *adv.*

sten·tor (sten'tôr), *n.* 1. a person with a very powerful voice. 2. any one of several large, trumpet-shaped protozoans with cilia.

sten·to·ri·an (sten-tôr'i-ăn), *adj.* extremely loud.

step (step), *n.* 1. the act of raising one foot and bringing it down in another spot, as in walking, running, dancing, etc. 2. the distance covered by this complete movement. 3. a very short distance. 4. an impression made by stepping; footprint. 5. any one of a series of actions or procedures toward some goal. 6. a manner of stepping; gait. 7. the sound of stepping; tread. 8. a rest for the foot in climbing or descending, as a stair or ladder rung: *v.i.* **stepped**, **step'ping**, 1. to move by taking a step or steps. 2. to walk a short distance. 3. to move briskly. 4. to move into a new condition. 5. to press down with the foot: *v.t.* 1. to set (the foot) down. 2. to measure by pacing off steps. 3. to furnish with steps.

step-broth·er (step'bruth·ēr), *n.* a son by the previous marriage of a stepparent.

step-child ('chīld), *n.* a child by a previous marriage of one's spouse.

step-daugh·ter ('dôt·ēr), *n.* a female stepchild.

step-fa·ther ('fä·thēr), *n.* a male stepparent.

a in cap, ā in cane, ä in father, á in abet, e in met, ē in be, ê in baker, ê in regent, I in pit, ī in fine, i in manifest, o in hot, ô in horse, ō in bone,

steph·a·no·tis (stef-å-nōt'is), *n.* a twining shrub bearing fragrant white flowers.

step·lad·der ('lăd-êr), *n.* a set of portable steps with a hinged supporting frame.

step·moth·er ('mu*th*-êr), *n.* a female stepparent.

step·par·ent ('per-ênt), *n.* the husband or wife of one's father or mother who remarried after the death or divorce of the other parent; stepfather or stepmother.

steppe (step), *n.* a vast, grassy, usually treeless plain of southeastern Europe or Asia.

step·per (step'êr), *n.* a person or animal that steps in a certain way, as a dancer or horse.

step·ping-stone (step'ing-stōn), *n.* 1. a stone that provides a dry place on which to step, as in crossing a muddy area, stream, etc. 2. something used to further one's progress or advancement.

step·sis·ter (step'sis-têr), *n.* a daughter by the previous marriage of a stepparent.

step·son ('sun), *n.* a male stepchild.

step-up ('up), *adj.* increasing in size, amount, etc.: *n.* an increase in size, activity, etc.

-ster (stêr), a suffix meaning *a person who is, does, makes, is associated with* (something specified).

stere (stir), *n.* a measure of volume, equal to 35.31 cubic feet or 1.308 cubic yards.

ster·e·o (ster'i-ō, stir'-), *n.*, *pl.* **-e·os**, 1. a stereophonic record player, radio, tape, etc. 2. a stereoscopic system, picture, etc.: *adj.* shortened form of **stereophonic**.

ster·e·o, a combining form meaning *hard, solid, firm.*

ster·e·o·gram (ster'i-ō-gram), *n.* a picture or diagram giving an impression of a solid in relief.

ster·e·og·ra·phy (ster-i-og'rå fi), *n.* the art of constructing lines on a plane or flat surface, giving the impression of a solid in relief; specifically, the branch of solid geometry that treats of the construction of regularly defined solids.

ster·e·om·e·try (-om'ĕ-tri), *n.* the art of determining the dimensions and cubic contents of solids.

ster·e·o·phon·ic (-ō-fon'ik), *adj.* having, relating to, or reproducing sound as if from its original directions.

ster·e·op·ti·con (-op'ti-kån), *n.* an instrument for viewing transparent slides, often made double so as to produce dissolving effects.

ster·e·o·scope (ster'i-ō-skōp), *n.* a binocular optical instrument by means of which two pictures appear as one that seems to possess depth. **—ster·e·o·scop'ic** (-skop'ik), *adj.*

ster·e·os·co·py (ster-i-os'kō-pi), *n.* 1. the construction of stereoscopes. 2. the technique of producing stereoscopic effects.

ster·e·ot·o·my (-ot'ō-mi), *n.* the art of cutting solids; especially, stonecutting.

ster·e·o·type (ster'i-ō-tip), *n.* 1. a metal printing plate cast from a mold taken from a printing surface, as from a page of type. 2. an uncritical or formalized conception, notion, or attitude: *v.t.* **-typed**, **-typ·ing**, to make a stereotype of. **—ster'e·o·typed**, *adj.*

ster·e·o·typ·y (-tī-pi), *n.* the process of making stereotype plates.

ster·ile (ster'l), *adj.* 1. incapable of reproducing; barren. 2. producing little or nothing; unfruitful. 3. destitute of ideas, vitality, etc. 4. free from living microorganisms. **—ster'ile·ly**, *adv.* **—ste·ril·i·ty** (stê-ril'i-ti), *n.*

ster·i·lize ('i-līz), *v.t.* **-lized**, **-liz·ing**, to make sterile; specifically, *a*) to deprive of the power of reproduction; *b*) to free from living germs. **—ster·i·li·za·tion** (ster-i-li-zā'shun), *n.* **—ster'i·liz·er**, *n.*

ster·let (stûr'lit), *n.* a small sturgeon used as food and as a source of caviar, found in the Caspian Sea.

ster·ling (stûr'ling), *adj.* 1. of the highest quality; excellent. 2. denoting British money. 3. of silver that is at least 92.5% pure. 4. made of sterling silver: *n.* 1. sterling silver. 2. British money.

stern (stûrn), *adj.* 1. harsh or severe in features or manners. 2. austere; foreboding. 3. unrelenting. 4. steadfast; firm.

stern (stûrn), *n.* 1. the rear part of a vessel. 2. the hindmost part of anything.

ster·nal (stûr'nl), *adj.* of or pertaining to the sternum.

stern sheets, the space at the stern of an open boat.

ster·num (stûr'nùm), *n.*, *pl.* **-nums**, **-na** ('nå), the flat, bony structure at the front of the chest, to which most of the ribs are attached.

ster·nu·ta·tion (stûr-nyoo-tā'shùn), *n.* the act or sound of sneezing.

ster·nu·ta·to·ry (stêr-nût'â-tōr-i), *adj.* causing or tending to cause sneezing: also **ster·nu·ta·tive** (stûr'nyoo-tāt-iv): *n.*, *pl.* **-ries**, a substance that causes sneezing.

stern·way (stûrn'wā), *n.* a movement of a vessel backwards.

ster·ol (stir'ôl, ster'-; 'ōl), *n.* any one of a group of unsaturated alcohols found in plant and animal tissues.

ster·tor (stûr'têr), *n.* labored, noisy breathing, as in sleep, caused by respiratory obstruction. **—ster'to·rous**, *adj.*

stet (stet), let it stand: a printer's mark indicating that something previously marked for omission is to be retained: *v.t.* **stet'ted**, **stet'ting**, to mark with "stet."

steth·o·scope (steth'ō-skōp), *n.* in *Medicine*, an instrument used to carry the sounds of the heart, lungs, etc. to the ear of the examiner. **—steth·o·scop'ic** (-skop'ik), *adj.* **—ste·thos·co·py** (ste-thos'kō-pi), *n.*

ste·ve·dore (stē'vē-dôr), *n.* one who loads or unloads a vessel in port.

stew (stōō, stū), *v.t. & v.i.* 1. to boil slowly or with simmering heat. 2. to worry: *n.* 1. a dish prepared by stewing. 2. a state of worry, excitement, or confusion.

stew·ard (stōō'êrd, stū'-), *n.* 1. one who manages the domestic concerns of a family or estate. 2. an administrator of property or finances for another. 3. one who superintends the kitchen, bar, etc. at a restaurant, hotel, etc. 4. an attendant who is responsible for the comfort of passengers, as on a ship, airplane, etc. **—stew'ard·ship**, *n.*

ŏ in dragon, ōō in crude, oo in wool, u in cup, ū in cure, û in turn, ŭ in focus, oi in boy, ou in house, th in *thin*, *th* in sea*th*e, g in get, j in joy, y in yet.

stew·ard·ess ('ēr-dis), *n.* a woman steward, especially on an airplane.

sthen·ic (sthen'ik), *adj.* denoting or of feelings of excessive energy or unusual excitement.

stich (stik), *n.* a line or verse of poetry.

stick (stik), *n.* 1. a small branch or shoot cut off a tree. 2. a long, slender piece of wood, as a walking stick, staff, etc. 3. something shaped like a stick, as a piece of celery, gum, etc. 4. a thrust with a pointed instrument; stab. 5. [Informal], a dull or spiritless person. 6. [Slang], a marijuana cigarette. 7. in *Printing*, a printer's composing tray or its contents: *v.t.* stuck, stick'ing, 1. to stab, as with a pointed instrument. 2. to thrust (*into, out,* etc.). 3. to pierce with (a pin, knife, etc.). 4. to fasten or attach, as by pinning, gluing, etc. 5. [Informal], to place, put, etc. 6. [Informal], to baffle. 7. [Slang], *a)* to burden with a task, expense, etc.; *b)* to cheat: *v.i.* 1. to be fixed by a sharp point. 2. to adhere; remain. 3. to continue firm and resolute. 4. to become enmeshed. 5. to be puzzled. 6. to hesitate (with *at*). 7. to project (*out, up,* etc.).

stick·er ('ēr), *n.* one that sticks; specifically, an adhesive label.

stick-in-the-mud (stik'n-*th*ē-mud), *n.* [Informal], a person who avoids or rejects new ideas, activities, etc.

stick·le (stik'l), *v.i.* -led, -ling, 1. to wrangle or contend pertinaciously, especially on insufficient grounds, for something of little importance. 2. to scruple (*at*).

stick·le·back (stik'l-bak), *n.* any one of various scaleless, spiny-backed fishes of fresh or salt waters.

stick·ler (stik'lēr), *n.* 1. a person who demands rigid adherence to a particular way of doing things. 2. [Informal], a difficult or baffling problem.

stick·pin (stik'pin), *n.* a decorative pin worn on a necktie.

stick shift, a manual gearshift, as on a car, operated by a lever.

stick-up (stik'up), *n.* [Slang], same as holdup (sense 2).

stick·y ('i), *adj.* stick'i·er, stick'i·est, 1. adhesive. 2. [Informal], hot and humid. 3. [Informal], awkwardly difficult. —stick'i·ness, *n.*

stiff (stif), *adj.* 1. not easily bent; rigid. 2. stubborn; uncompromising. 3. not liquid or fluid. 4. strong; violent. 5. not natural or easy; constrained in movement. 6. severe. 7. formal. 8. [Informal], excessive; high. — stiff'ly, *adv.* —stiff'ness, *n.*

stiff·en (stif'n), *v.t. & v.i.* to make or become stiff or stiffer. —stiff'en·er, *n.*

stiff-necked (stif'nekt'), *adj.* inflexibly obstinate; stubborn.

sti·fle (stif'l), *v.t.* -fled, -fling, 1. to suffocate; smother. 2. to suppress; check: *v.i.* to die or suffer from lack of air.

sti·fle (stif'l), *n.* the joint corresponding to the human knee in the hind leg of a horse, dog, etc.

stig·ma (stig'mä), *n., pl.* -mas, stig·ma·ta (stig-mä'tä), 1. originally, a mark branded into the flesh, as of a slave. 2. a mark of infamy or disgrace. 3. the upper part of the pistil

of a flower on which the pollen that fertilizes it falls. 4. *pl.* the counterparts of the crucifixion wounds in Christ's body, impressed on the bodies of some devout persons. —stig·mat'ic, *adj.*

stig·ma·tize (-tīz), *v.t.* -tized, -tiz·ing, 1. to mark with a stigma or brand. 2. to hold up to disgrace, reproach, or infamy.

stile (stīl), *n.* a series of steps for climbing over a fence or wall.

stile (stīl), *n.* an upright piece of framing or paneling, as in a door.

sti·let·to (sti-let'ō), *n., pl.* -tos, -toes, 1. a small dagger with a thin, rounded, and pointed blade. 2. a pointed instrument for making eyelet holes.

still (stil), *adj.* 1. at rest; without motion. 2. calm; tranquil. 3. silent; soundless. 4. denoting a single photograph from a motion-picture film: *n.* 1. silence. 2. a still photograph: *adv.* 1. at this time. 2. nevertheless. 3. even; yet: *conj.* nevertheless; yet: *v.t. & v.i.* to make or become still. —still'ness, *n.*

still (stil), *n.* an apparatus for distilling liquids, especially alcoholic liquors.

still-born (stil'bôrn), *adj.* dead when born.

still life, a picture of inanimate objects, as fruit, flowers, etc.

stilt (stilt), *n.* 1. either one of a pair of poles with a footrest above its base, used in walking with the feet above the ground. 2. any one of a number of timbers set upright to hold a structure above ground or water.

stilt·ed (stil'tid), *adj.* inflated; pompous.

Stil·ton (stil'tn), *n.* a rich cheese permeated with blue mold when ripe.

stim·u·lant (stim'yū-lânt), *adj.* serving to stimulate: *n.* anything, as a medicine or food, that stimulates.

stim·u·late (-lāt), *v.t.* -lat·ed, -lat·ing, to excite or rouse; animate; goad. —stim·u·la'tion, *n.* —stim'u·la·tive, *adj. & n.*

stim·u·lus (-lûs), *n., pl.* -u·li (-lī), 1. that which stimulates or excites to action. 2. an incentive.

sting (sting), *n.* 1. the act of stinging. 2. anything that gives acute mental or physical pain. 3. a sharp-pointed organ in certain insects, used to wound or poison. 4. any one of the stiff, sharp-pointed, hollow hairs of certain plants: *v.t.* stung, sting'ing, 1. to pierce or wound with or as with a sting. 2. to cause a sudden, acute pain to. 3. to make unhappy mentally. 4. to urge or stimulate sharply; goad. 5. [Slang], to cheat: *v.i.* to produce or suffer sudden, smarting pain. —sting'er, *n.*

sting·a·ree (sting'ä-rē), *n.* variant of stingray.

sting·ray (sting'rā), *n.* any one of several rays having dorsal spines on a whiplike tail that is capable of inflicting painful and dangerous wounds.

stin·gy (stin'ji), *adj.* -gi·er, -gi·est, 1. close and covetous; miserly; niggardly. 2. scanty. — stin'gi·ly, *adv.* —stin'gi·ness, *n.*

stink (stingk), *v.i.* stank or stunk, stunk, stink'-ing, to emit a strong, offensive odor: *n.* a disgusting smell; stench. —stink'er, *n.*

stink·pot ('pot), *n.* 1. a kind of bomb holding malodorous compounds, formerly thrown on the deck of an enemy vessel. 2. a musky turtle of the eastern and southeastern U.S.

stink-weed ('wēd'), *n.* any one of several foul-smelling plants, as the jimson weed.

stint (stint), *v.t.* to restrict within certain limits: *v.i.* 1. to be sparing. 2. [Archaic]. to stop; cease: *n.* 1. a limit; limitation. 2. an assigned period or amount of work.

stipe (stīp), *n.* in *Botany.* 1. the main stem of a fern frond. 2. the stalk of a mushroom.

sti-pend (stī'pend), *n.* a regular payment, as a salary, for services performed.

sti-pen-di-ar-y (stī-pen'di-er-i), *adj.* 1. receiving or rendering services for a stipend. 2. of or pertaining to a stipend: *n., pl.* -ar-ies, a person who receives a stipend.

stip-ple (stip'l), *v.t.* -pled, -pling, 1. to paint, engrave. etc. by means of dots or flecks. 2. to mark with dots or short strokes. —stip'-pler, *n.*

stip-u-late (stip'yū-lāt), *v.t.* -lat-ed, -lat-ing, 1. to arrange or settle definitely; mention specifically. 2. to guarantee in an agreement: *v.i.* to make an express provision (for something) as a requirement in an agreement. —stip'u-la-tor, *n.*

stip-ule (stip'yōōl), *n.* either one of the two small, leaflike appendages at the base of a leaf in certain plants.

stir (stūr), *v.t.* stirred, stir'ring, 1. to put into motion; move. 2. to incite; rouse, animate. 3. to agitate (a liquid) by moving an implement through it to mix the particles. 4. to provoke or instigate. 5. to move strongly; excite the feelings of: *v.i.* 1. to change position slightly. 2. to be in motion and active. 3. to happen; occur. 4. to begin to be active. 5. to be able to be stirred: *n.* 1. the act of stirring. 2. bustle; agitation; tumult. 3. excitement; activity. —stir'rer, *n.*

stir-a-bout (stūr'à-bout), *n.* [British], oatmeal or cornmeal porridge.

stirk (stūrk), *n.* [British Dial.], a young bull or heifer.

stirps (stūrps), *n., pl.* **stir-pes** (stūr'pēz). 1. family; race; stem. 2. in *Law,* a person from whom a family is descended.

stir-ring (stūr'ing), *adj.* 1. busy; bustling. 2. exciting; stimulating.

stir-rup (stūr'ŭp), *n.* 1. an iron hoop suspended from a saddle by a strap, in which a horseman sets his foot in mounting and riding. 2. any of various pieces resembling a stirrup, as a clamp in carpentry. 3. in *nautical usage,* a ship's rope hanging from a yard, having a socket or eye at the end for supporting a wire rope on which sailors stand when furling or reefing sail.

stitch (stich), *n.* 1. a single pass of a needle and thread through anything being sewed. 2. a link of yarn in knitting. 3. a loop made by stitching. 4. a certain kind of stitch. 5. a sudden, sharp, local pain. 6. a very small piece: *v.t.* & *v.i.* to make or decorate with stitches; sew. —stitch'er, *n.*

stith-y (stith'i), *n., pl.* stith'ies, [Archaic]. a smith's anvil or forge.

sti-ver (stī'vēr), *n.* something of trifling value.

sto-a (stō'à), *n., pl.* **sto'ae** ('ē), **sto'as,** an ancient Greek portico.

stoat (stōt), *n., pl.* **stoats, stoat,** the common ermine when its coat assumes a russet brown in the summer.

stock (stok), *n.* 1. the trunk or stem of a tree or plant. 2. a pillar, log, or post. 3. a stem into which a graft is inserted. 4. race; family; descent; lineage. 5. capital invested in a business. 6. shares of corporate capital. 7. a store or supply, as of animals, merchandise, etc. 8. short for **livestock.** 9. a former wide, stiff cravat. 10. a part of a firearm to which the barrel and lock are attached. 11. water in which meat, vegetables, etc. have been cooked, used as a foundation for soups, gravies, etc. 12. *pl.* a former instrument of punishment, consisting of a wooden frame with holes for confining the ankles or wrists of an offender. 13. a frame on which a ship is held during construction. 14. same as **stock company** (sense 2): *v.t.* 1. to provide (a store, farm, etc.) with stock. 2. to store up, as for future sale or use: *v.i.* to take in and store supplies (with *up*): *adj.* 1. kept in stock. 2. ordinary; trite. 3. dealing in stock or merchandise. 4. of or pertaining to a stock company.

stock-ade (sto-kād'), *n.* 1. a line of posts driven into the ground, used as a barrier for defense. 2. any enclosed area, as a fort, used for protection or to confine military prisoners.

stock-bro-ker ('brō-kēr), *n.* one who buys and sells stocks or securities for others.

stock car, a racing car made by modifying a standard automobile.

stock company, 1. a company or corporation whose capital is divided into shares. 2. a theatrical company performing a repertoire under one management.

stock dove, a European pigeon with gray plumage.

stock exchange, 1. a place where stocks, bonds, etc. are put up for sale or purchase. 2. an association of stockbrokers organized under certain rules to buy and sell securities.

stock farm, a farm for breeding livestock.

stock-fish (stok'fish), *n., pl.* -fish, -fish-es, a fish, as cod, haddock, etc., cured by being split and dried without salt in the open air.

stock-hold-er ('hōl-dēr), *n.* one who owns shares in a stock company (sense 1).

stock-i-nette, stock-i-net (stok-i-net'), *n.* an elastic textile fabric, used in making stockings, underwear, etc.

stock-ing (stok'ing), *n.* a closefitting covering for the foot and leg.

stock-job-ber ('job-ēr), *n.* 1. a stockbroker, especially one regarded as unscrupulous. 2. [British], a stock-exchange operator who deals only with brokers and not with the public.

stock market, same as **stock exchange.**

stock-pile ('pīl), *n.* a supply of goods, products, etc. stored against future needs, price increases, emergencies, etc.: *v.t.* & *v.i.* -piled, -pil'ing, to build up a stockpile (of).

stock-still (stok'stil'), *adj.* motionless.

---

stock·y (stok'ĭ), *adj.* **stock'i·er**, **stock'i·est**, thickset; short, but strongly built.

stock·yard (stok'yärd), *n.* an extensive enclosure with pens, stalls, etc. in which cattle, hogs, sheep, etc. are temporarily penned until butchered or shipped elsewhere.

stodg·y (stoj'ĭ), *adj.* **stodg'i·er**, **stodg'i·est**, 1. heavy and indigestible: said of food. 2. stockily built; thickset. 3. dull; narrow; conventional. —**stodg'i·ly**, *adv.* —**stodg'i·ness**, *n.*

sto·gie, **sto·gy** (stō'gĭ), *n.*, *pl.* **-gies**, a cheap cigar rolled in cylindrical form.

Sto·ic (stō'ĭk), *n.* 1. a member of an ancient Greek school of philosophy that taught that the wise man should be governed by reason alone, subdue all passions, and be indifferent to pleasure or pain. 2. [s-], a stoical person: *adj.* 1. of or pertaining to the Stoics. 2. [s-], same as stoical.

sto·i·cal ('ĭ-kl), *adj.* indifferent to pleasure, pain, joy, etc. —**sto'i·cal·ly**, *adv.*

stoi·chi·om·e·try (stoi-kĭ-om'ĕ-trĭ), *n.* the calculation of the weights and amounts of chemical elements or compounds that are involved in chemical reactions. —**stoi·chi·o·met'ric** (-ô-met'rĭk), *adj.*

Sto·i·cism (stō'ĭ-sizm), *n.* 1. the doctrines and maxims of the Stoics. 2. [s-], real or assumed insensibility to pleasure and pain.

stoke (stōk), *v.t.* & *v.i.* **stoked**, **stok'ing**, 1. to stir up and feed fuel to (a fire). 2. to tend and maintain (a furnace, boiler, etc.). —**stok'er**, *n.*

STOL (stōl), *adj.* denoting or of an aircraft capable of a short takeoff or landing run: *n.* a STOL aircraft, runway, etc.

stole (stōl), *n.* 1. a long, loose, outer garment worn by ancient Roman matrons. 2. a long, narrow scarf, worn by various church officials. 3. a woman's cloth or fur scarf, worn around the shoulders.

stole (stōl), past tense of steal.

stol·en (stō'lĕn), past participle of steal.

stol·id (stol'ĭd), *adj.* unemotional; impassive. —**sto·lid·i·ty** (stō-lĭd'ĭ-tĭ), *n.* —**stol'id·ly**, *adv.*

sto·lon (stō'lon), *n.* in *Botany*, a horizontal branch running along or under the ground and rooting at its nodes or tip to produce new plants.

sto·ma (stō'mä), *n.*, *pl.* **-ma·ta** ('mä-tä), **-mas**, 1. in *Botany*, a minute pore in the epidermis of plants, for the passage of gases. 2. in *Zoology*, a mouthlike opening, as in some invertebrates.

stom·ach (stum'ăk), *n.* 1. the principal organ of digestion in vertebrates, connected to the esophagus. 2. the belly; abdomen. 3. an appetite for food. 4. desire; inclination: *v.t.* 1. to put up with; tolerate. 2. to digest.

stom·ach·ache (-āk), *n.* pain in the abdomen.

stom·ach·er (-ĕr), *n.* a decorative covering, formerly worn over the chest and abdomen by women.

sto·mach·ic (stō-mak'ĭk), *adj.* 1. of or pertaining to the stomach. 2. aiding digestion: *n.* a digestive stimulant.

stomach pump, a suction pump with a flexible tube for emptying the stomach.

sto·mat·ic (stō-mat'ĭk), *adj.* 1. of or pertaining to the mouth. 2. of or having a stoma.

sto·ma·ti·tis (stō-mä-tīt'ĭs), *n.* inflammation of the mouth.

sto·ma·tol·o·gy (-tol'ô-jĭ), *n.* the branch of medicine treating of the mouth and its diseases.

stomp (stomp), *v.t.* & *v.i.* same as stamp.

-sto·my (stō-mĭ), a combining form meaning *a surgical opening into* (*a specified organ or part*).

stone (stōn), *n.* 1. a hard mass of earthy or mineral matter; rock. 2. a gemstone. 3. material used for building. 4. a calculus in the kidney or gallbladder. 5. the hard seed of certain fruits. 6. the endocarp of a drupe fruit. 7. *pl.* **stone**, in Great Britain, 14 pounds avoirdupois: *v.t.* **stoned**, **ston'ing**, 1. to pelt or kill with stones. 2. to free from stones, as fruit.

stone-, a combining form meaning *completely*: used in compounds, as *stone-blind*.

Stone Age, the period of civilization when stone weapons, implements, etc. were used.

stone-blind ('blīnd'), *adj.* completely blind.

stone·chat ('chat), *n.* a European singing bird.

stone·crop ('krop), *n.* a mosslike plant with fleshy, pungent leaves and variously colored flowers, growing on rocks and walls.

stone·cut·ter ('kut-ĕr), *n.* a person or machine that hews and dresses stone. —**stone'cut·ting**, *n.*

stoned (stōnd), *adj.* [*Slang*], 1. drunk. 2. under the influence of a drug.

stone marten, same as sable (*n.* 1 & 2).

stone roller, any one of several freshwater suckers.

stone's throw, a short distance.

stone·wall (stōn-wôl'), *v.i.* [Chiefly British Informal], to prolong or obstruct a debate, negotiation, etc.

stone·ware ('wer), *n.* a coarse kind of glazed or unglazed pottery.

ston·y (stō'nĭ), *adj.* **ston'i·er**, **ston'i·est**, 1. of, pertaining to, of the nature of, or like stone. 2. rocky. 3. hard; cruel; inflexible; pitiless. Also **ston'ey**. —**ston'i·ly**, *adv.* —**ston'i·ness**, *n.*

stood (stood), past tense and past participle of stand.

stooge (stōōj), *n.* [Informal], 1. an actor who serves as the target for the jests and pranks of a comedian. 2. anyone who allows himself to be the puppet or foil of another.

stool (stōōl), *n.* 1. a seat having no back or arms, for the use of one person. 2. feces; excrement.

stool pigeon, [Informal], an informer, especially a police spy.

stoop (stōōp), *v.i.* 1. to bend the body downward and forward. 2. to walk with the head and shoulders always bent forward. 3. to descend from rank or dignity; demean oneself: *n.* the act or position of stooping.

stoop (stōōp), *n.* an outside stairway, porch, or platform at the entrance to a house.

stoop labor, work performed while stooping, as in picking crops.

stop (stop), *v.t.* **stopped**, **stop'ping**, 1. to hinder, check, or impede. 2. to intercept; block; render impassable. 3. to close by cutting off.

filling, etc. 4. to desist from; cease: *v.i.* 1. to cease from any motion or action. 2. to put an end to doing something. 3. to reside temporarily: *n.* 1. the act of stopping or the state of being stopped. 2. a termination; end. 3. a short visit. 4. any place stopped at, as on a bus route. 5. a plug. 6. a finger hole for regulating the tone of a wind instrument. 7. a key, lever, etc. for regulating a set of organ pipes.

stop-cock (stop'kok), *n.* a cock or valve with a turning plug for permitting, regulating, or stopping the flow of a liquid or a gas.

stop-gap ('gap), *n.* a temporary expedient; makeshift.

stop-light (stop'līt), *n.* 1. a traffic light, esp. when red to signal vehicles to stop. 2. a light at the rear of a vehicle, that lights up when the brakes are applied.

stop-o-ver ('ō-vēr), *n.* 1. a brief stop or stay in the course of a journey. 2. a place for such a stop.

stop-page ('ij), *n.* 1. the act of stopping or state of being stopped. 2. obstruction; block.

stop-per ('ēr), *n.* one who, or that which, stops; that which closes a vent or hole.

stop-ple ('l), *n.* a stopper, or plug: *v.t.* -pled, -pling, to close with a stopple.

stop-watch (stop'wäch), *n.* a watch with a hand that can be stopped instantly by pressing a knob at the side: used in timing races and other sporting events.

stor-age (stōr'ij), *n.* 1. the safekeeping of goods, as in a warehouse. 2. the price charged for storing goods. 3. space for storing goods. 4. the parts of a computer designed to receive and store information.

storage battery, a battery of cells in which electrical energy that is chemically produced can be stored by running a current through it for a time, after which it is capable of supplying current for a certain period.

store (stōr), *v.t.* stored, stor'ing, 1. to set aside to be used when needed. 2. to furnish or supply with stores. 3. to put in a warehouse or other storage place. 4. to put (information) in a computer storage unit: *v.i.* to undergo storage: *n.* 1. a supply to be used; reserve; stock. 2. *pl.* supplies, as of food or clothing. 3. a place of business where goods are for sale. 4. a storehouse or warehouse. 5. a large number; abundance. —**stor'a-ble**, *adj.*

store-front ('frunt), *n.* a first-floor front room of a building, designed or adapted for use as a retail store.

store-house ('hous), *n.* a place where things are stored.

store-keep-er ('kēp-ēr), *n.* 1. one who has the charge of military or naval supplies. 2. one who runs a retail store.

store-room ('rōōm), *n.* a room for storing things.

sto-rey (stōr'i), *n.*, *pl.* -reys, British form for story (of a building).

sto-ried (stōr'id), *adj.* 1. having stories or floors. 2. historically famous.

stork (stōrk), *n.*, *pl.* storks, stork, a large wading bird with long legs and neck and a pointed bill: it is regarded as a symbol of childbirth, from the story told to children that babies are not born but brought by the stork.

storm (stōrm), *n.* 1. a violent atmospheric disturbance with high winds and usually with rain, snow, hail, or sleet. 2. any heavy fall of rain, snow, or hail. 3. a heavy shower of things. 4. a violent outburst, agitation, or upheaval. 5. a violent assault on a fortified place. 6. a wind whose speed is 64 to 72 miles per hour: *v.i.* 1. to blow violently. 2. to be very angry; rage. 3. to move violently: *v.t.* 1. to attack with violence or in an angry way. 2. to try to capture (a fortified place) with a strong, sudden attack.

storm door, an outside door in addition to the regular entrance door, for protection against winter weather.

storm window, an outside window in addition to the regular window, for protection against winter weather.

storm-y (stōr'mi), *adj.* storm'i-er, storm'i-est, 1. of, or characteristic of, storms. 2. having or characterized by storms. 3. tempestuous; violent; raging. —**storm'i-ly**, *adv.* —**storm'i-ness**, *n.*

stormy petrel, 1. any one of certain small petrels thought to presage storms, especially a black-and-white one of the North Atlantic. 2. one regarded as a bringer of trouble.

Stor-ting, Stor-thing (stōr'ting), *n.* the Norwegian Parliament.

sto-ry (stōr'i), *n.*, *pl.* -ries, 1. the telling of something that happened, as a news event, or that might happen, as a piece of fiction; narration. 2. a fictitious narrative, especially a short story. 3. the plot of a novel, play, etc. 4. a joke or anecdote. 5. a rumor. 6. a news report. 7. [Informal], a fib or falsehood. 8. a division of a building from one floor to the ceiling or roof above it. 9. any horizontal division.

sto-ry-book (-book), *n.* a book of stories, especially one written for children.

sto-ry-tell-er (-tel-ēr), *n.* one who narrates or tells stories. —**sto'ry-tell-ing**, *n.*

stoup (stōōp), *n.* 1. [Archaic], a tankard. 2. a receptacle for holy water in a church.

stout (stout), *adj.* 1. brave; courageous. 2. strong and sturdy in body. 3. strong and firm. 4. forceful; powerful. 5. corpulent; thickset: *n.* a dark-brown brew like porter. —**stout'ly**, *adv.* —**stout'ness**, *n.*

stout-heart-ed ('härt'id), *adj.* brave; courageous. —**stout'heart'ed-ly**, *adv.* —**stout'heart'ed-ness**, *n.*

stove (stōv), *n.* 1. an apparatus for cooking or heating that uses fuel or electricity. 2. any heated room or chamber, as a kiln.

stove (stōv), alternate past tense and past participle of stave.

stove-pipe ('pīp), *n.* 1. a metal pipe used as a chimney or to carry smoke from a stove to a chimney flue. 2. [Informal], a tall silk hat, for men: also stovepipe hat.

stow (stō), *v.t.* 1. to fill by packing closely; pack. 2. to hide (*away*): *v.i.* to be a stowaway (with *away*).

stow-age ('ij), *n.* 1. the act of stowing or state of being stowed. 2. room for stowing things.

3. the amount stowed. 4. charges made for stowing.

stow·a·way ('å-wā), *n.* one who conceals himself on a ship, an aircraft, etc., as to avoid paying passage or fare.

STP, an hallucinogenic drug similar to mescaline.

stra·bis·mus (strå-biz'mŭs), *n.* a condition of the eyes in which they cannot focus on the same point at the same time.

stra·bot·o·my (-bot'ŏ-mi), *n.* a surgical operation to correct strabismus.

Strad (strad), *n.* same as Stradivarius.

strad·dle (strad'l), *v.i.* **-dled, -dling,** 1. to stand or sit astride of. 2. to avoid taking a stand on (an issue): *v.i.* 1. to stand, walk, or sit with the legs wide apart. 2. to straddle an issue: *n.* the act or position of straddling.

Strad·i·var·i·us (strad-i-ver'i-ŭs), *n.* a violin or other string instrument made by Antonio Stradivari (1644-1737).

strafe (stråf), *v.t.* strafed, straf'ing, to attack with gunfire, especially with machine-gun fire from aircraft flying low. —straf'er, *n.*

strag·gle (strag'l), *v.i.* **-gled, -gling,** 1. to wander from the direct course or way. 2. to wander widely; ramble. 3. to arrive, leave, or occur at scattered intervals. 4. to hang in an unkempt fashion, as hair. —strag'gler, *n.*

strag·gly ('li), *adj.* **-gli·er, -gli·est,** spread out or scattered irregularly.

straight (strāt), *adj.* 1. in the same direction along its length; not crooked, curved, bent, etc. 2. upright. 3. level; even. 4. direct; not interrupted. 5. consistent in support of a political candidate or party. 6. in proper order. 7. honest. 8. undiluted. 9. [Slang], normal; conventional: *adv.* 1. in a straight line. 2. upright; erectly. 3. without delay or detour. 4. in a direct, honest, or truthful way: *n.* 1. the part of a race track between the last turn and the winning post. 2. a hand of any five cards in sequence. —straight'ness, *n.*

straight·ar·row ('er-ō), *adj.* [Slang], proper, righteous, conscientious, etc.

straight·en (strāt'n), *v.t.* & *v.i.* to make or become straight. —straight'en·er, *n.*

straight face, a facial expression devoid of any expression of feeling.

straight·for·ward (strāt-fôr'wĕrd), *adj.* 1. straight ahead; direct. 2. honest; open; frank *adv.* directly or openly: also straight·for'wards. —straight·for'ward·ly, *adv.* —straight·for'ward·ness, *n.*

straight·way (strāt'wā), *adv.* at once.

strain (strān), *v.t.* 1. to stretch or draw tight. 2. to use or exert to the fullest extent. 3. to injure by overtaxing. 4. to stretch beyond what is normal. 5. to pass through a sieve, screen, etc.; filter: *v.i.* 1. to make violent efforts. 2. to filter or ooze: *n.* 1. a violent effort. 2. a bodily injury caused by this. 3. force or stress. 4. a great demand on one's energy, emotions, etc. 5. ancestry; descent. 6. race; stock. 7. a line of individuals differing from the species it belongs to. 8. an inherited character. 9. a streak; trace. 10. a musical tune.

strain·er ('ĕr), *n.* 1. one that strains. 2. a device for straining, filtering, or sifting.

strait (strāt), *adj.* [Archaic], narrow; confined; strict; distressing: *n. often pl.* 1. a narrow waterway that connects two larger bodies of water. 2. distress; difficulty.

strait·en ('n), *v.t.* 1. formerly, to make strait or narrow. 2. to put into difficulties, especially financial difficulties: in the phrase *in straitened circumstances.*

strait·jack·et ('jak-it), *n.* a strong canvas jacket that confines the arms: used in restraining persons who are violent.

strait·laced ('lāst), *adj.* 1. laced tightly, as a corset. 2. holding strict moral views.

strake (strāk), *n.* a continuous line of planking or metal plating along the hull of a vessel from stem to stern.

stra·mo·ni·um (strå-mō'ni-ŭm), *n.* the jimson weed or its dried leaves.

strand (strand), *n.* 1. the shore of a sea, ocean, or large lake. 2. any one of the twisted threads, wires, etc. in a length of string, rope, etc. 3. anything like a length of string: *v.t.* & *v.i.* 1. to drive aground or run aground, as a ship. 2. to leave in, or be left in, a helpless situation.

strand·ed ('id), *adj.* left helpless, without funds or money.

strange (strānj), *adj.* **strang'er, strang'est,** 1. foreign; alien. 2. not known, seen, etc. before; unfamiliar. 3. extraordinary; unusual. 4. odd; peculiar. 5. distant or reserved. 6. not accustomed (to). —strange'ly, *adv.* —strange'ness, *n.*

stran·ger (strān'jer), *n.* 1. a foreigner or newcomer. 2. one who is unknown or unacquainted. 3. one not accustomed (to something).

stran·gle (strang'gl), *v.t.* **-gled, -gling,** 1. to choke to death by compressing the throat and windpipe. 2. to choke in any way. 3. to suppress or stifle: *v.i.* to be strangled. —stran'gler, *n.*

stran·gle·hold (-hōld), *n.* 1. an illegal hold in which one wrestler chokes another. 2. any means of suppression.

stran·gles ('glz), *n.* an infectious disease of horses, characterized by an inflamed condition of the membranes inside the respiratory tract.

stran·gu·late (strang'gyŭ-lāt), *v.t.* **-lat·ed, -lat·ing,** 1. to strangle or choke. 2. to constrict (a tube or organ of the body), especially so as to stop the blood from circulating. —stran·gu·la'tion, *n.*

stran·gu·ry (strang'gyŭ-ri), *n.* a painful voiding of the urine, drop by drop.

strap (strap), *n.* 1. a long, narrow piece of leather or cloth. 2. a razor strop: *v.t.* strapped, strap'ping, 1. to fasten with a strap. 2. to beat with a strap.

strap·less ('lis), *adj.* without straps; having no straps.

strap·per ('ĕr), *n.* 1. one that straps. 2. [Informal], a strapping person.

strap·ping ('ing), *adj.* [Informal], tall, well-built, and robust.

strass (stras), *n.* a type of lead glass used in making artifical jewels.

stra·ta (strāt'ā, strat'ā), *n.* alternate plural of stratum.

strat·a·gem (strat'ā-jĕm), *n.* 1. a device or scheme for defeating an enemy, especially in war. 2. a trick or plan for carrying out some deception or for gaining some advantage.

stra·te·gic (strā-tē'jik), *adj.* 1. of or pertaining to strategy. 2. based on or necessary to sound strategy. —stra·te'gi·cal·ly, *adv.*

stra·te·gics (jiks), *n.* same as strategy (sense 1).

strat·e·gy (-ji), *n., pl.* -gies, 1. the science of military warfare, especially in making skillful plans before an actual battle. 2. any such plan. 3. skill in using stratagems. 4. a stratagem; trick or plan. —strat'e·gist, *n.*

strat·i·form (-fôrm), *adj.* 1. formed like a stratum. 2. arranged in a stratus, as clouds.

strat·i·fy (strat'i-fī), *v.t.* & *v.i.* -fied, -fy·ing, to arrange or form in strata or layers. —strat·i·fi·ca'tion, *n.*

strat·o·sphere (strat'ō-sfir), *n.* the zone of the atmosphere that begins about six miles above the earth's surface and extends to fifteen miles.

stra·tum (strāt'ŭm, strat'-), *n., pl.* -ta ('ā), -tums, 1. a horizontal layer; especially, any one of a series of layers, one on top of the other. 2. a single layer of sedimentary rock. 3. any one of the various levels of society.

stra·tus ('ŭs), *n., pl.* stra'ti ('ī), a gray cloud in a long, low layer with a straight base.

straw (strô), *n.* 1. hollow stalks of threshed grain. 2. any one of these stalks. 3. a tube used for sucking up beverages. 4. a mere trifle: *adj.* 1. yellow in color like straw. 2. made of straw. 3. trivial; worthless.

straw·ber·ry ('ber-i), *n., pl.* -ries, 1. the juicy, edible, red fruit of a plant of the rose family. 2. the plant itself.

straw boss, [Informal], an assistant foreman, especially one without the power to enforce his orders.

straw color, a light yellow color, like that of the straw of wheat. —straw'-col·ored, *adj.*

straw vote, a vote or poll taken unofficially in order to get a sample of the general opinion of a group on a particular issue.

straw·worm ('wûrm), *n.* any one of several insect larvae that destroy wheat stalks, etc.

straw·y ('i), *adj.* straw'i·er, straw'i·est, pertaining to, made of, or like straw.

stray (strā), *v.i.* 1. to wander beyond limits or from a direct path; roam. 2. to err; deviate (*from*). 3. to wander in attention; digress: *n.* one that strays, especially a domestic animal that is wandering at large: *adj.* 1. gone astray; lost. 2. isolated; incidental. —stray'er, *n.*

streak (strēk), *n.* 1. a line or stripe usually different in color from the background. 2. a stripe of fat running through meat. 3. a trait or tendency. 4. a spell or period: *v.t.* to mark with streaks: *v.i.* 1. to form streaks. 2. to go fast.

streak·y (strē'ki), *adj.* streak'i·er, streak'i·est, 1. having streaks. 2. uneven; varying.

stream (strēm), *n.* 1. a current of water or other liquid. 2. a small river. 3. any flow of air or other fluid. 4. a steady emanation of light or energy. 5. a series of things: *v.i.* 1. to issue or flow in, or as in, a stream. 2. to move fast; rush.

stream·er (strē'mēr), *n.* 1. a long, narrow flag or pennant. 2. a stream of light, as from the aurora borealis. 3. a headline the full width of a newspaper.

stream·ing ('ming), *adj.* issuing forth in rays or streams, or like wavy lines.

stream·let (strēm'lit), *n.* a little stream; rivulet.

stream·line ('lin), *v.t.* -lined, -lin·ing, to make streamlined: *adj.* same as streamlined.

stream·lined ('lind), *adj.* 1. denoting a contour so constructed as to give unbroken flow to air or water currents with a minimum of resistance, as that of an automobile body. 2. arranged so as to be simple and efficient. 3. having no excess; trim.

stream·y (strē'mi), *adj.* stream'i·er, stream'i·est, 1. abounding in or full of streams. 2. flowing in streams.

street (strēt), *n.* 1. a public road in a city or town. 2. such a road along with the sidewalks and buildings on either side. 3. the people, collectively, living on the same street.

street Arab, a neglected or homeless child who roams the streets; guttersnipe: also street urchin.

street·car ('kär), *n.* a car that runs on a street railway.

street railway, a railway laid on the surface of certain streets, providing transportation for the public.

street·walk·er ('wôk'ēr), *n.* a prostitute who seeks customers while walking along the streets. —street'walk·ing, *n.*

strength (strength), *n.* 1. the state or quality of being strong; power; force; vigor. 2. the power of endurance or resistance; durability; toughness; impregnability. 3. numerical makeup. 4. intensity, as of light or color. 5. legal or moral force. 6. potency, as of liquor.

strength·en ('n), *v.t.* & *v.i.* to make or become stronger. —strength'en·er, *n.*

stren·u·ous (stren'yoo-wŭs), *adj.* 1. requiring a great deal of energy or effort. 2. vigorous; zealous; earnest. —stren'u·ous·ly, *adv.* —stren'u·ous·ness, *n.*

strep (strep), *n.* same as streptococcus.

strep·to·coc·cus (strep-tō-kok'ŭs), *n., pl.* -coc'ci (-kok'sī), any one of various spherical bacteria, generally grouped in chains: some species are pathogenic and cause serious diseases, such as pneumonia. —strep·to·coc'cal (-kok'ăl), *adj.*

strep·to·my·cin (-mī'sin), *n.* an antibiotic drug obtained from soil bacteria and used in treating various diseases.

stress (stres), *n.* 1. strain or force; especially, force that deforms the shape of a body subjected to it. 2. importance; emphasis. 3. any strain or pressure on the body or mind. 4. the force of utterance given to a syllable;

accent: *v.t.* 1. to subject to stress. 2. to place emphasis on.

stretch (strech), *v.t.* 1. to extend or cause to extend. 2. to draw out to a greater length or width. 3. to strain or force. 4. to strain the meaning or scope of; exaggerate: *v.i.* 1. to spread out to a greater length or width. 2. to be extended. 3. to extend one's body to its full length, standing or lying: *n.* 1. the act of stretching. 2. the state of being stretched. 3. a continuous period (of time). 4. a continuous distance, length, etc. 5. the homestretch: *adj.* made of elastic fabric that will stretch, as pants. —**stretch'a·ble**, *adj.*

stretch·er ('ēr), *n.* 1. one that stretches. 2. a frame or litter for carrying the sick, injured, etc. 3. a frame on which cloth, curtains, etc. can be stretched and shaped. 4. a transverse piece.

stretch·y ('ī), *adj.* **stretch'i·er, stretch'i·est,** 1. stretchable; elastic. 2. that may stretch too much.

strew (strōō), *v.t.* **strewed, strewed** or **strewn, strew'ing,** 1. to spread by scattering. 2. to cover as by sprinkling.

stri·a (strī'ä), *n., pl.* **stri'ae** ('ē), 1. a narrow channel or groove. 2. any one of a series of parallel lines, bands, stripes, etc.

stri·ate ('āt), *v.t.* **-at·ed, -at·ing,** to mark with striae: *adj.* ('it), marked with striae: also **stri'at·ed.**

strick·en (strik'n), *adj.* 1. affected by weakness or disease. 2. smitten; wounded.

strict (strikt), *adj.* 1. exact and careful. 2. absolute; perfect. 3. enforcing discipline; severe. 4. observing rules. —**strict'ly,** *adv.* —**strict'·ness,** *n.*

stric·ture (strik'chēr), *n.* 1. censure or adverse criticism. 2. an abnormal contraction of any passage of the body.

stride (strīd), *n.* 1. a long step or the distance it covers. 2. *usually pl.* progress: *v.i. & v.t.* **strode, strid'den** (strid'n), **strid'ing,** 1. to walk with long steps. 2. to take a single long step (over something).

stri·dent (strīd'nt), *adj.* harsh; shrill; grating. —**stri'dence, stri'den·cy,** *n.* —**stri'dent·ly,** *adv.*

stri·dor (strī'dēr), *n.* a shrill, whistling sound in respiration, due to the clogging of an air passage.

strid·u·late (strij'oo-lāt), *v.i.* **-lat·ed, -lat·ing,** to make a grating, high-pitched sound, as certain insects do, by rubbing parts of the body together. —**strid·u·la'tion,** *n.*

strid·u·lous (-lús), *adj.* producing a shrill, harsh, grating sound: also **strid'u·lant** (-länt).

strife (strīf), *n.* 1. contention for superiority; competition. 2. conflict; quarrel; struggle.

stri·ga (strī'gä), *n., pl.* **-gae** ('jē), 1. the fluting of a column. 2. a short, sharp-pointed, stiff hair or scale.

strig·il (strij'il), *n.* an instrument for scraping the skin, used by the ancients during a bath.

stri·gose (strī'gōs), *adj.* covered with strigae; set with bristles, as some leaves.

strike (strīk), *v.t.* **struck, struck** or **strick'en, strik'ing,** 1. to hit with a blow or with force. 2. to give (a blow). 3. to collide with or cause to crash. 4. to affect strongly, as if

by a blow. 5. to produce by a blow or by friction. 6. to coin or mint. 7. to notify by sound or a bell: said of a clock. 8. to light on or fall on. 9. to make (a bargain, agreement, etc.). 10. to find; notice. 11. to attack or afflict. 12. to remove, as *from* a list. 13. to lower or take down (a flag, sail, etc.): *v.i.* 1. to make a quick blow or thrust; hit. 2. to attack. 3. to sound by being struck, as a clock does. 4. to lower a flag or sail to show respect or submission. 5. to fall or light (*on*). 6. to cease work; take part in a strike: *n.* 1. the act of striking. 2. a blow or attack. 3. a cessation of work by employees, especially to try to obtain higher wages and better working conditions. 4. the finding of a large deposit of oil or minerals. 5. in *Baseball,* a pitched ball that is struck at but not hit, across the plate but not struck at, etc. 6. in *Bowling,* the act of knocking down every pin on the first bowl. —**strik'er,** *n.*

strike-break·er ('brā·kēr), *n.* one who tries to break up a strike, as by taking the place of a workman on strike.

strik·ing (ing), *adj.* 1. that strikes. 2. highly impressive; forcible; wonderful; surprising. —**strik'ing·ly,** *adv.*

string (string), *n.* 1. a small cord or line. 2. a series of things on a string. 3. a series of similar things. 4. any one of the cords on a musical instrument. 5. *pl.* the stringed instruments of an orchestra, collectively. 6. an inclined board at either end of stairs, notched to support the treads and risers: *v.t.* **strung, string'ing,** 1. to furnish with strings. 2. to thread on a string. 3. to hang, tie, etc. with a string. 4. to deprive of strings. 5. to arrange or stretch like a string. 6. [Informal], to hoax; fool: *v.i.* to stretch out in a long, irregular line.

string bean, same as green bean or wax bean.

stringed (stringd), *adj.* furnished with strings.

strin·gen·cy (strin'jen-si), *n., pl.* **-cies,** the state or quality of being stringent.

strin·gent ('jent), *adj.* 1. severe; strict; rigid. 2. convincing; compelling. —**strin'gent·ly,** *adv.*

string·er (string'ēr), *n.* 1. one that strings something, as a musical instrument. 2. a heavy piece of timber placed horizontally for the support of other timbers.

string·i·ness ('i-nis), *n.* state of being stringy; condition of being viscid or sticky.

string tie, a narrow necktie.

string·y ('ī), *adj.* **string'i·er, string'i·est,** 1. consisting of strings. 2. like a string or filament. 3. full of tough fibers. 4. viscid; sticky; ropy.

strip (strip), *v.t.* **stripped, strip'ping,** 1. to make naked. 2. to deprive of (a covering, clothing, etc.). 3. to skin; peel. 4. to rob or pillage. 5. to take away (titles, honors, etc.). 6. to damage the teeth of (a gear) or the thread of (a screw or bolt). 7. to milk (a cow) dry: *v.i.* 1. to undress. 2. [Informal], to do a striptease: *n.* 1. a striptease. 2. a long, narrow piece, as of wood or land. 3. a runway for airplanes.

stripe (strip), *v.t.* **striped, strip'ing,** 1. to form stripes upon. 2. to variegate with lines of different colors: *n.* 1. a line or long, narrow division of anything, as of a different color from the background. 2. [Archaic], a stroke or welt made by a whip. 3. a strip of braid or cloth worn by an officer on his sleeve to indicate rank.

striped (strīpt), *adj.* marked with stripes.

striped bass, a large, silvery food and game fish, having dark stripes on the sides, found along the coasts of North America.

striped squirrel, same as **chipmunk.**

strip-ling (strip'ling), *n.* a youth.

strip-per ('ēr), *n.* 1. a person or thing that strips. 2. a cow that is almost dry of milk.

strip-tease ('tēz), *n.* an act in a burlesque show, in which a woman slowly undresses, usually in rhythm to music. —**strip'teas-er,** *n.*

strive (strīv), *v.i.* **strove-** or **strived, striv-en** (striv'n) or **strived, striv'ing,** 1. to make exertions or efforts; labor or try hard. 2. to struggle; contend. —**striv'er,** *n.*

strobe (strōb), *n.* 1. same as **stroboscope.** 2. an electronic tube that emits very brief and bright flashes of light rapidly: also **strobe light:** *adj.* same as **stroboscopic.**

stro-bile (strō'bil, -bil, strob'il), *n.* same as **cone** (*n.* 3).

stro-bo-scope (strō'bō-skōp), *n.* 1. a device that throws very quick flashes of light on a moving body at frequent intervals: used in studying motion. 2. same as **strobe** (*n.* 2).

stro-bo-scop-ic (strō-bō-skop'ik), *adj.* of or pertaining to a stroboscope: also **stro-bo-scop'i-cal.**

strode (strōd), past tense of **stride.**

stroke (strōk), *n.* 1. a knock or blow. 2. a sudden effect or event. 3. an effort by which something is accomplished. 4. a sudden illness, especially one causing paralysis. 5. a forceful effect as if caused by a blow. 6. a movement made with a pen, tool, golf club, etc. 7. the sound made by something striking, as a clock. 8. one full movement of a piston back and forth. 9. one of the repeated motions made in swimming, rowing, etc.: *v.t.* **stroked, strok'ing,** 1. to rub gently with the hand in one direction. 2. to hit (a ball) in tennis, golf, etc.

stroll (strōl), *v.i.* 1. to wander on foot; ramble; saunter. 2. to wander: *n.* a leisurely ramble.

stroll-er ('ēr), *n.* 1. one who strolls. 2. an itinerant actor. 3. a vagrant. 4. a baby carriage built like a chair on wheels.

stro-ma (strō'mä), *n., pl.* **-ma-ta** (-tä), the basis or framework of an organ or cell of the body.

strong (strông), *adj.* 1. having strength; powerful in physique; robust. 2. healthy; hale and hearty. 3. having power of endurance. 4. powerful morally or mentally. 5. powerful in numbers or resources. 6. violent or vigorous. 7. affecting the senses powerfully. 8. well-fortified. 9. intense in odor, flavor, etc. 10. ardent or zealous. 11. rising to higher prices: said of the stock market. 12. in *Grammar,* irregular. —**strong'ly,** *adv.*

strong-arm ('ärm), *adj.* [Informal], using violence or physical force: *v.t.* [Informal], to use violence or physical force on.

strong-box ('boks), *n.* a strongly constructed box or container for the safekeeping of valuables.

strong-hold ('hōld), *n.* a fortress; fortified place.

strong-mind-ed ('mīn'did), *adj.* having a strong, vigorous mind or strong will; determined: also **strong'-willed'** ('wild').

strong-room ('rōōm), *n.* a strongly constructed room in which valuables can be stored for safekeeping.

stron-gyle (stron'jil, 'jīl), *n.* any one of various roundworms, parasitic on man and domestic animals.

stron-ti-a (stron'shi-ä), *n.* the oxide of strontium, a white powder resembling lime.

stron-ti-um ('shi-ŭm), *n.* a yellow metallic chemical element having properties like those of calcium.

strop (strop), *n.* a thick strip of leather on which the blade of a razor can be sharpened: *v.t.* **stropped, strop'ping,** to sharpen on a strop.

stro-phan-thin (strō-fan'thin), *n.* a plant extract used as a heart stimulant.

stro-phe (strō'fi), *n.* 1. in the ancient Greek chorus, the movement in turning from right to left. 2. the part of the song, drama, etc. performed by the chorus during this movement. 3. a stanza; especially, in an ode, the stanza that is answered by the antistrophe. —**stroph-ic** (strof'ik), *adj.*

stroph-u-lus (strof'yoo-lŭs), *n.* a skin disease of children, characterized by a red rash due to inflammation of the sweat glands.

strove (strōv), a past tense of **strive.**

struck (struk), past tense and past participle of **strike:** *adj.* closed, as a factory where the workers are on strike.

struc-tur-al (struk'chēr-ăl), *adj.* 1. of or pertaining to structure. 2. used in construction, as steel. —**struc'tur-al-ly,** *adv.*

struc-ture ('chēr), *n.* 1. an edifice or building. 2. manner or form of building. 3. the arrangement of parts, as in an organism. 4. an organism or organization made up of related parts: *v.t.* **-tured, -tur-ing,** to organize; construct.

stru-del (strōō'd'l), *n.* a thin sheet of dough filled with cherries, cheese, etc., rolled up and baked as a pastry.

strug-gle (strug'l), *v.i.* **-gled, -gling,** 1. to fight with a foe. 2. to try hard; strive. 3. to have trouble getting (*through, over,* etc.): *n.* 1. violent effort or exertion. 2. a contest; conflict.

strum (strum), *v.t.* & *v.i.* **strummed, strum'ming,** to play (a guitar, banjo, etc.) in an amateurish or casual way.

stru-ma (strōō'mä), *n., pl.* **-mae** ('mē), 1. a swelling on a part of a plant. 2. same as goiter.

stru-mose ('mōs), *adj.* having a struma: also **stru-mous** ('mŭs).

strum-pet (strum'pit), *n.* a woman hired for sexual intercourse; prostitute.

strung (strung), past tense and past participle of **string.**

strut (strut), *v.i.* **strut'ted, strut'ting,** to walk with affected dignity; swagger: *n.* 1. a proud, strutting walk. 2. a part of a framework designed to resist pressure in the direction of its length.

strych·nic (strik'nik), *adj.* of or from strychnine.

strych·nine ('nin, 'nīn), *n.* a highly poisonous alkaloid extracted from nux vomica.

stub (stub), *n.* 1. the stump of a tree or plant. 2. a short, leftover piece, as of a cigar. 3. a stub nail. 4. the part of a bank check, ticket, etc. detached to be kept as a record: *v.t.* **stubbed**, **stub'bing**, 1. to pull up by the roots. 2. to strike (one's toe or foot) against some fixed obstacle. 3. to put out (a cigar or cigarette) by pressing it against a surface.

stubbed (stubd), *adj.* short and thick.

stub·bi·ness (stub'i-nis), *n.* the state or quality of being stubby.

stub·ble (stub'l), *n.* 1. short stalks or stumps of grain left in the ground after reaping. 2. any growth of short bristles, as of beard.

stub·born (stub'ern), *adj.* 1. inflexibly headstrong; not yielding; obstinate. 2. done in an obstinate way. 3. hard to manage or cope with. —**stub'born·ly**, *adv.* —**stub'born·ness**, *n.*

stub·by (stub'i), *adj.* 1. abounding in stubs or stubble. 2. short and heavy or thickset.

stub nail, a short, thick nail.

stuc·co (stuk'ō), *n.*, *pl.* -**coes**, -**cos**, 1. plaster or cement used as a coating for walls or for molded decorations. 2. the work involved in this: also **stuc'co·work:** *v.t.* -**coed**, -**co·ing**, to cover or decorate with stucco.

stuck (stuk), past tense and past participle of stick.

stuck-up ('up'), *adj.* [Informal], conceited; snobbish.

stud (stud), *n.* 1. an ornamental knob. 2. any one of several buttonlike devices inserted in the front of a dress shirt. 3. any one of the upright pieces in a wall to which lath or paneling is nailed. 4. any male animal, especially a stallion, used for breeding. 5. a number of such stallions, or the place where they are kept: *v.t.* **stud'ded**, **stud'ding**, 1. to adorn with, or as with, studs. 2. to be scattered over.

stud·ding ('ing), *n.* 1. material for studs in a building. 2. such studs, collectively.

stud·ding-sail (stud'ing-sāl, stun'sl), *n.* a light sail set at the side of a square sail to increase speed: also **studding sail**.

stu·dent (stōōd'nt, stūd'-), *n.* 1. one who is engaged in study; scholar. 2. one who is attending a school, college, etc.

stud·fish (stud'fish), *n.* a minnowlike fish used as bait.

stud·horse ('hôrs), *n.* a stallion for breeding.

stud·ied (stud'ēd), *adj.* 1. qualified by study. 2. premeditated; deliberate.

stu·di·o (stōō'di-ō, stū'-), *n.*, *pl.* -**os**, 1. the workroom of an artist or photographer. 2. a place where lessons, as in dancing, are given. 3. a place where motion pictures are made, or where radio or television programs originate.

studio couch, a kind of couch that can be made into a full-sized bed.

stu·di·ous ('di-ŭs), *adj.* 1. devoted to study or to acquiring knowledge. 2. thoughtful or closely attentive.

stud·y (stud'i), *n.*, *pl.* **stud'ies**, 1. the application of the mind to acquisition of knowledge. 2. any particular branch of learning. 3. a preparatory sketch, as for a painting. 4. *pl.* schooling; education. 5. a room set apart for study, reading, etc.: *v.i.* **stud'ied**, **stud'y·ing**, 1. to apply the mind closely to a subject. 2. to take courses (*at* a school, college, etc.). 3. to ponder. 4. to try hard: *v.t.* 1. to try to learn about (something) by studying. 2. to examine carefully. 3. to prepare (one's lessons) or read (a book) carefully.

stuff (stuf), *n.* 1. materials out of which anything is made. 2. textile fabrics. 3. goods; objects. 4. fundamental character. 5. matter in general. 6. refuse matter; junk: *v.t.* 1. to fill by crowding something into; press or pack. 2. to fill (a fowl, fish, etc.) with bread crumbs, seasoning, etc. before cooking. 3. to fill the skin of (a dead animal) for preservation in its natural form. 4. to fill very full: *v.i.* to eat gluttonously.

stuffed shirt, [Slang], an inane, conceited person.

stuff·ing ('ing), *n.* material used to stuff or fill, as padding for furniture, or a seasoned mixture placed in meat, poultry, etc. before cooking.

stuff·y ('i), *adj.* **stuff'i·er**, **stuff'i·est**, 1. close; badly ventilated. 2. having the nasal passages obstructed. 3. [Informal], dull; conventional. —**stuff'i·ness**, *n.*

stul·ti·fy (stul'ti-fī), *v.t.* -**fied**, -**fy·ing**, 1. to render foolish, ridiculous, etc. 2. to make worthless, ineffectual, or futile. 3. in *Law*, to allege to be of unsound mind. —**stul·ti·fi·ca'tion**, *n.* —**stul'ti·fi·er**, *n.*

stum (stum), *n.* 1. unfermented or partly fermented grape juice. 2. old wine renewed by the addition of stum: *v.t.* **stummed**, **stum'ming**, to renew (wine) by adding stum.

stum·ble (stum'bl), *v.i.* -**bled**, -**bling**, 1. to trip or fall in walking, running, etc. 2. to proceed unsteadily. 3. to act, speak, etc. falteringly. 4. to happen on by accident. 5. to err in conduct; do wrong: *n.* an act of stumbling.

stumbling block, an obstacle.

stump (stump), *n.* 1. that part of a tree that remains in the ground after the trunk has been cut off. 2. the part of a branch, tooth, limb, etc. remaining after the main part is gone. 3. the place, platform, etc. used in making a political speech. 4. in *Cricket*, any one of the three posts of a wicket. 5. *pl.* [Slang], the legs: *v.t.* 1. to lop off; reduce to a stump. 2. to traverse (a region), making political speeches. 3. [Informal], to baffle; puzzle: *v.i.* 1. to walk noisily. 2. to go about making political speeches.

stump·y (stum'pi), *adj.* **stump'i·er**, **stump'i·est**, 1. full of stumps. 2. short and thick.

stun (stun), *v.t.* **stunned**, **stun'ning**, 1. to render senseless, as by a blow. 2. to daze; shock; stupefy; overwhelm. 3. to confuse or bewilder, as by a loud noise.

---

stung (stung), past tense and past participle of sting.

stunk (stungk), past participle and alternate past tense of stink.

stun·ner (stun'ẽr), n. 1. one that stuns. 2. [Informal], an exceptionally attractive, forceful, magnetic, etc. person or thing.

stun·ning ('ing), adj. 1. that stuns. 2. [Informal], exceptionally attractive, striking, etc. —**stun'ning·ly**, adv.

stunt (stunt), v.t. 1. to check the growth or progress of; dwarf. 2. to hinder (growth or development).

stunt (stunt), n. 1. a difficult feat displaying skill, daring, etc. 2. something unusual undertaken for publicity or notoriety: v.i. to perform a stunt.

stupe (stōōp), n. a hot, wet, often medicated compress.

stu·pe·fa·cient (stōō-pē-fā'shĕnt), n. a stupefying agent; narcotic: adj. having the power to stupefy: also **stu·pe·fac'tive** (-fak'tiv).

stu·pe·fac·tion (-fak'shŭn), n. 1. the act of stupefying or the state of being stupefied. 2. utter astonishment; great bewilderment.

stu·pe·fy (stōō'pē-fī), v.t. -fied, -fy·ing, 1. to deprive of sensibility; put into a stupor. 2. to astonish; bewilder. —**stu'pe·fi·er**, n.

stu·pen·dous (stoo-pen'dŭs), adj. 1. of astonishing force, worth, value, etc.; overwhelming. 2. immensely large or great.

stu·pid (stōō'pid), adj. 1. deficient in understanding or intelligence. 2. slow to learn; obtuse. 3. foolish; irrational; nonsensical. 4. dull; dreary; tiresome. —**stu'pid·ly**, adv. — **stu'pid·ness**, n.

stu·pid·i·ty (stoo-pid'i-ti), n. 1. the state or quality of being stupid. 2. pl. -ties, a foolish or irrational action, idea, statement, etc.

stu·por (stōō'pẽr), n. 1. suspension or great diminution of sensibility, as from shock or a drug. 2. mental numbness; intellectual lethargy. —**stu'por·ous**, adj.

stur·dy (stũr'di), adj. -di·er, -di·est, 1. hardy; robust; strong physically. 2. stubborn; unyielding. 3. durable; firmly built. —**stur'di·ly**, adv. —**stur'di·ness**, n.

stur·geon (stũr'jŭn), n., pl. stur'geons, stur'geon, any one of several large, cartilaginous fishes of the Northern Hemisphere, with rows of bony plates on the body: valued as a source of caviar and isinglass.

stut·ter (stut'ẽr), n. & v.t. & v.i. same as stammer. —**stut'ter·er**, n.

sty (stī), n., pl. sties, 1. a pen or enclosure for swine. 2. any filthy or foul place: v.t. stied, sty'ing, to shut up in or as in a sty.

sty (stī), n., pl. sties, inflammation and swelling of a sebaceous gland of an eyelid.

Styg·i·an (stij'i-ăn), adj. 1. of or pertaining to the Styx and the lower world. 2. [also s-], a) hellish; infernal; b) gloomy and dark; c) inviolable.

style (stīl), n. 1. a pointed instrument used by the ancients for writing on waxed tablets. 2. a tool used for etching or engraving. 3. the gnomon of a sundial. 4. a phonograph needle. 5. a manner of expression in writing or speech, as distinguished from the thoughts conveyed. 6. the distinctive or characteristic mode of expression, execution, etc. of an individual, school, period, or people. 7. excellence in artistic or literary expression. 8. the current fashion, as in dress. 9. a method of reckoning time, dates, etc. 10. in Botany, the stalk between the ovary and stigma of a flower: v.t. styled, styl'ing, 1. to designate; name. 2. to give style to.

sty·let (stī'lit), n. 1. a surgeon's probe. 2. a stiletto.

sty·li·form (stī'li-fôrm), adj. shaped like a style or stylus.

styl·ish (stī'lish), adj. fashionable; modish. — **styl'ish·ly**, adv. —**styl'ish·ness**, n.

styl·ist ('list), n. 1. a writer whose work has a distinguished or distinctive style. 2. a designer or adviser on current styles, as of dress, coiffures, etc. —**sty·lis'tic**, adj. —**sty·lis'ti·cal·ly**, adv.

styl·ize (stī'līz), v.t. -ized, -iz·ing, to represent in the formalized pattern of a particular style or convention. —**styl·i·za'tion**, n.

sty·lo·bate (stī'lō-bāt), n. in Architecture, an uninterrupted base below a row of columns.

sty·lo·graph (-graf), n. a fountain pen in which the ink flows through a tubular writing point instead of a nib.

sty·lo·graph·ic (stī-lō-graf'ik), adj. of or pertaining to a stylograph or stylography.

sty·log·ra·phy (stī-log'ră-fi), n. a method of drawing, writing, engraving, etc. with a style or stylus.

sty·loid (stī'loid), adj. resembling a style; styliform; specifically, denoting or of any of various slender, bony processes, as the lower end of the radius or ulna.

sty·lus (stī'lŭs), n., pl. -lus·es, -li ('lī), 1. a style or other sharp-pointed instrument for marking, writing, etc., as on a stencil. 2. a sharp, cutting tool for making grooves in phonograph records. 3. a phonograph needle.

sty·mie (stī'mi), n. a golfing situation that occurs when an opponent's ball lies directly on a line between a player's ball and the hole on a putting green: v.t. -mied, -mie·ing, to obstruct; thwart. Also **sty'my**.

styp·tic (stip'tik), adj. stopping bleeding by causing contraction of tissues; astringent: n. a styptic medicine or substance. —**styp'sis**, n.

styptic pencil, a styptic material, as alum, formed into a stick and applied to stop bleeding, as from razor nicks.

Styx (stiks), n. in Greek Mythology, the river of the underworld over which the souls of the dead were ferried by Charon, the boatman.

su·a·ble (sōō'ă-bl, sū'-), adj. capable of being, or liable to be, sued in court.

sua·sion (swā'zhŭn), n. same as persuasion: now chiefly in moral suasion. —**sua'sive** ('siv), adj.

suave (swäv), adj. ingratiating in manner; urbane. —**suave'ly**, adv. —**suav'i·ty**, n.

sub (sub), n. a shortened form of 1. submarine. 2. substitute: v.i. subbed, sub'bing, [Informal], to act as a substitute (for).

sub-, a prefix meaning under, below; lower, subordinate; to a lesser degree; in Chemistry, having less than the normal amount of. In words borrowed from Latin, sub- becomes suc- before c, suf- before f, sug- before g, *sum-* before *m*, *sup-* before *p*, and *sur-* before *r*: *sub-* sometimes becomes *sus-* before *c*, *p*, and *t*.

sub·ac·id (sub-as'id), *adj.* slightly acid.

sub·al·tern (sub-ôl'tĕrn), *n.* [British], a commissioned officer under the rank of captain: *adj.* lower in rank; subordinate.

sub·a·que·ous (sub-ā'kwi-ŭs), *adj.* 1. happening or living below the surface of the water. 2. adapted for use under water.

sub·branch (sub'branch), *n.* a division of a branch.

sub·class ('klas), *n.* a taxonomic category between a class and an order.

sub·com·mit·tee ('kŏ-mit-i), *n.* a small committee whose members are appointed from a main committee.

sub·com·pact (sub-kom'pakt), *n.* a model of car smaller than a compact.

sub·con·scious (-kon'shŭs), *adj.* dimly conscious or aware. —**sub·con'scious·ly,** *adv.*

sub·con·ti·nent (-kon'ti-nĕnt), *n.* a large land mass, usually part of a continent but distinct from it in some geographical respect.

sub·con·tract (-kon'trakt), *n.* a subsidiary contract obligating a third party to perform all or part of the requirements of the original contract: *v.t. & v.i.* to make a subcontract (for). —**sub·con'trac·tor** (-ĕr), *n.*

sub·cul·ture (sub'kul-chēr), *n.* 1. an ethnic, economic, religious, etc. group within a predominant culture, differentiated by mutual bonds, interests, activities, etc. from the encompassing society. 2. its cultural patterns.

sub·cu·ta·ne·ous (sub-kyoo-tā'ni-ŭs), *adj.* beneath the skin.

sub·dea·con (-dē'kn), *n.* a cleric ranking below a deacon.

sub·deb (sub'deb), *n.* 1. a girl just before she becomes a debutante. 2. a girl in her middle teens.

sub·dis·trict ('dis-trikt), *n.* a subdivision of a district.

sub·di·vide (sub-di-vīd'), *v.t. & v.i.* -vid·ed, -vid'ing, 1. to divide (a part or parts) into smaller parts. 2. to divide (land) into small lots. —**sub·di·vi'sion,** *n.*

sub·dom·i·nant (-dom'i-nänt), *n.* in *Music,* a tone next below the dominant.

sub·due (-dōō', -dū'), *v.t.* -dued', -du'ing, 1. to overcome; conquer. 2. to control; restrain. 3. to reduce; tone down; diminish.

su·be·re·ous (soo-bir'i-ŭs), *adj.* in *Botany,* of or pertaining to cork: also **su'ber·ose** ('bĕ-rōs).

su·ber·ic acid (soo-ber'ik), a crystalline acid obtained from cork, various fatty oils, etc.

sub·fusc (sub-fusk'), *adj.* [Chiefly British], having little color; drab; dull.

sub·ge·nus (-jē'nŭs), *n., pl.* -**gen'er·a** (-jen'ēr-ä), -**ge'nus·es,** a taxonomic category between a genus and a species.

sub·ja·cent (-jā'snt), *adj.* 1. lying directly under or below. 2. situated lower but not directly underneath.

sub·ject (sub'jikt), *adj.* 1. under the power or control of another; vassal. 2. disposed; liable (*to*). 3. exposed. 4. dependent or contingent upon: *n.* 1. one who is under the

power or control of another. 2. one made the object of treatment, study, dissection, etc. 3. that which is treated in writing, painting, speaking, etc.; theme; topic. 4. any one of the courses of study in a school. 5. in *Grammar,* the word or phrase in a sentence concerning which something is said or done: *v.t.* (sŭb-jekt'), 1. to bring under the power or control of. 2. to render liable. 3. to make undergo or experience something. —**sub·jec'tion,** *n.*

sub·jec·tive (sŭb-jek'tiv), *adj.* 1. of or pertaining to the subject of a sentence. 2. of or derived from the mind or the inner feelings of a person; not objective. —**sub·jec'tive·ly,** *adv.* —**sub·jec·tiv·i·ty** (sub-jek-tiv'i-ti), *n.*

sub·jec·tiv·ism (-izm), *n.* the philosophical doctrine that knowledge is relative and purely subjective.

sub·join (sŭb-joiň', *v.t.* same as append.

sub·ju·gate (sub'jŭ-gāt), *v.t.* -gat·ed, -gat·ing, 1. to conquer by force; bring under dominion. 2. to make servile; subdue. —**sub·ju·ga'tion,** *n.*

sub·junc·tive (sŭb-jungk'tiv), *adj.* denoting or of that mood of a verb expressive of contingency, desire, hypothesis, etc.: *n.* 1. the subjunctive mood. 2. a verb in this mood.

sub·lap·sar·i·an (sub-lap-ser'i-än), *n. & adj.* same as infralapsarian. —**sub·lap·sar'i·an·ism,** *n.*

sub·lease (sub'lēs), *n.* a lease granted by a lessee: *v.t.* (sub-lēs'), -**leased'**, -**leas'ing,** 1. to give a sublease of. 2. to get a sublease of.

sub·let (sub-let'), *v.t.* -**let'**, -**let'ting,** 1. to rent or lease (leased or rented property) to another. 2. to subcontract (work).

sub·li·mate (sub'li-māt), *v.t.* -mat·ed, -mat·ing, 1. to sublime (a solid). 2. to change unconsciously (an unacceptable impulse) into a personally and socially acceptable form. —**sub·li·ma'tion,** *n.*

sub·lime (sŭ-blīm'), *adj.* 1. awakening feelings of awe and reverence. 2. exalted; grand; majestic. 3. supreme; unexcelled: *v.t.* -**limed'**, -**lim'ing,** 1. to render sublime or noble. 2. in *Chemistry,* to cause (a solid) to change directly into a vapor by heat and then condense directly back to a solid state: *v.i.* to undergo this change of states. —**sub·lime'ly,** *adv.* —**sub·lim'i·ty** (-blim'i-ti), *n.*

sub·lim·i·nal (sub-lim'i-nl), *adj.* below the threshold of consciousness: said of stimuli. —**sub·lim'i·nal·ly,** *adv.*

sub·lin·gual (sub-ling'gwäl), *adj.* located beneath the tongue.

sub·lu·nar·y (sub'lōō-ner-i), *adj.* 1. terrestrial; situated beneath the moon. 2. mundane; of this earth: also **sub·lu'nar.**

sub·ma·chine gun (sub-mä-shēn'), a portable, lightweight, automatic or semiautomatic gun.

sub·mar·gin·al (sub-mär'ji-nl), *adj.* 1. below minimum standards. 2. unproductive.

sub·ma·rine (sub-mä-rēn'), *adj.* located or found under the sea: *n.* (sub'mä-rēn), a ship that can operate under water; especially, a warship armed with torpedoes, missiles, etc.: *v.t.* -rined, -rin·ing, to attack with a submarine.

submarine sandwich, same as hero sandwich.

---

a in cap, ä in cane, ä in father, â in abet, e in met, ē in be, ē in baker, ê in regent, i in pit, ī in fine, i in manifest, o in hot, ō in horse, ō in bone,

sub-max-il-la (sub-mak-sil'ä), *n., pl.* -lae ('ē), -las, the lower jaw.

sub-max-il-lar-y (mak'si-ler-i), *adj.* denoting of, or beneath the lower jaw; specifically, denoting or of either one of the two salivary glands located there.

sub-merge (sŭb-mŭrj'), *v.t.* -merged', -merg'ing, 1. to place under water or other liquid. 2. to cover with water; inundate. —sub-mer'-gence, *n.*

sub-merse (-mŭrs'), *v.t.* -mersed', -mers'ing, same as submerge. —sub-mer'sion, *n.*

sub-mers-i-ble (-mŭr'si-bl), *adj.* of or pertaining to a substance that can be submerged and continue to function.

sub-mis-sion (-mish'ŭn), *n.* 1. the act of submitting, yielding, or surrendering. 2. obedience; meekness. —sub-mis'sive, *adj.*

sub-mit (-mit'), *v.t.* -mit'ted, -mit'ting, 1. to yield to the authority, power, etc. of another. 2. to present (something) to the judgment, discretion, etc. of another. 3. to offer as a belief, evaluation, etc.; suggest: *v.i.* to yield; acquiesce.

sub-mul-ti-ple (sub-mul'ti-pl), *n.* a number that is an exact divisor of another number.

sub-nor-mal (-nôr'ml), *adj.* below average, especially in intelligence.

sub-or-bit-al (-ôr'bit-l), *adj.* denoting or of a space flight on a limited trajectory instead of full orbit.

sub-or-der (sub'ôr-dèr), *n.* a taxonomic category between an order and a family.

sub-or-di-nate (sŭ-bôr'di-nit), *adj.* 1. inferior in rank, value, power, importance, etc. 2. subject to the authority of another. 3. in *Grammar,* that cannot stand alone: *n.* one that is subordinate: *v.t.* (-nāt), -nat-ed, -nat-ing, to place in a lower or subject position. —sub-or-di-na'tion, *n.*

sub-orn (sŭ-bôrn'), *v.t.* 1. to accomplish through unlawful means. 2. to induce (someone) to commit perjury. —sub-or-na-tion (sub-ôr-nā'shŭn), *n.*

sub-plot (sub'plot), *n.* a subordinate plot in a play, novel, etc.

sub-poe-na (sŭ-pē'nä), *n.* a writ commanding the attendance of a person in court to testify: *v.t.* -naed, -na-ing, to serve or summon with such a legal writ. Also **sub-pe'na**.

sub-rep-tion (sŭ-rep'shŭn), *n.* the act of obtaining a favor by fraud or misrepresentation.

sub-ro-gate (sub'rō-gāt), *v.t.* -gat-ed, -gat-ing, to substitute (one person) for another.

sub ro-sa (sub rō'zä), in secret, privately.

sub-scribe (sub-skrīb'), *v.t. & v.i.* -scrib'ed, -scrib'ing, 1. to write or annex (one's name) to a paper or document. 2. to give one's approval or sanction (to). 3. to promise to give (a sum of money). 4. to consent to accept and pay for a periodical, product, etc. (with *to*). —sub-scrib'er, *n.*

sub-script (sub'skript), *adj.* written beneath: *n.* a figure, letter, etc. written at the lower right side of another.

sub-scrip-tion (sŭb-skrip'shŭn), *n.* 1. the act of subscribing. 2. something subscribed, as a signature. 3. a sum of money subscribed. 4. a contract to accept and pay for a periodical, books, etc. for a certain time.

sub-se-quence (sub'si-kwens), *n.* the act or state of being subsequent.

sub-se-quent (-kwěnt), *adj.* following or coming after in time or order. —sub'se-quent-ly, *adv.*

sub-serve (sŭb-sŭrv'), *v.t.* -served', -serv'ing, to be subservient to; promote; serve instrumentally.

sub-ser-vi-ent (-sŭr'vi-ěnt), *adj.* 1. that helps in a subordinate way. 2. fawningly servile; truckling. —sub-ser'vi-ence, *n.*

sub-side (sŭb-sīd'), *v.i.* -sid'ed, -sid'ing, 1. to sink or fall to the bottom. 2. to settle to a lower level. 3. to abate; become tranquil or calm. —sub-sid'ence, *n.*

sub-sid-i-ar-y (-sid'i-er-i), *adj.* 1. furnishing assistance; auxiliary. 2. tributary. 3. of the nature of a subsidy: *n., pl.* -ar-ies, one that is subsidiary; specifically, a company whose controlling interest is owned by another company.

sub-si-dize (sub'si-dīz), *v.t.* -dized, -diz-ing, to furnish with a subsidy. —sub-si-di-za'tion, *n.*

sub-si-dy (sub'si-di), *n., pl.* -dies, 1. pecuniary aid granted by one government to another. 2. a public grant to aid a private enterprise for public benefits.

sub-sist (sŭb-sist'), *v.i.* 1. to have existence. 2. to retain the present state. 3. to inhere (*in*). 4. to remain alive (*on* or *by*).

sub-sist-ence (-sis'těns), *n.* 1. existence. 2. the act of providing support. 3. means of support or maintenance. 4. inherent quality. —**sub-sist'ent**, *adj.*

sub-soil (sub'soil), *n.* the stratum of earth immediately below the surface: *v.t.* to turn up the subsoil of.

sub-son-ic (sub-son'ik), *adj.* denoting or of a speed less than that of sound in a given medium.

sub-stance (sub'stăns), *n.* 1. physical matter; material. 2. the basic or essential part of anything. 3. the meaning or purport of what is written or said. 4. wealth; property; possessions.

sub-stand-ard (sub-stan'dèrd), *adj.* falling below a standard.

sub-stan-tial (sŭb-stan'shŭl), *adj.* 1. belonging to, or having, substance. 2. containing the essential parts. 3. solid; strong. 4. not imaginary; material; corporeal. 5. ample. 6. important. 7. having considerable wealth. —sub-stan'tial-ly, *adv.*

sub-stan-ti-ate (-'shi-āt), *v.t.* -at-ed, -at-ing, to establish the truth of by proof or competent evidence. —sub-stan-ti-a'tion, *n.*

sub-stan-ti-val (sub-stăn-tī'vl), *adj.* of, pertaining to, or of the nature of a substantive. —sub-stan-ti'val-ly, *adv.*

sub-stan-tive (sub'stăn-tiv), *adj.* 1. having existence; real. 2. substantial. 3. essential: *n.* in *Grammar,* a noun or any group of words that functions as a noun. —sub'stan-tive-ly, *adv.*

sub-sta-tion (sub'stā-shŭn), *n.* a subsidiary station, as of a post office.

sub-sti-tute (sub'sti-tōōt), *v.t.* -tut-ed, -tut-ing, to put or employ in the place of another: *n.* one who, or that which, is put or used in the place of another. —sub-sti-tu'tion, *n.*

sub-stra-tum (sub'strāt-ŭm), *n., pl.* -ta (-ä), -tums, a

ŏ in dragon, ōō in crude, oo in wool, u in cup, ū in cure, ŭ in turn, ŭ in focus, oi in boy, ou in house, th in thin, th in sheathe, g in get, j in joy, y in yet.

layer, part, material, etc. underlying and supporting something.

sub·struc·ture ('struk-chĕr), *n.* a base, foundation, etc. serving as a support.

sub·sume (sŭb-sōōm', -sŭm'), *v.t.* **-sumed', -sum'ing,** to place in a more extensive class or under a general principle.

sub·tan·gent (sub-tan'jĕnt), *n.* the part of the axis of a curve intercepted between the tangent and the ordinate.

sub·teen (sub'tēn'), *n.* a child nearly of teen age.

sub·ten·ant (sub-ten'ănt), *n.* one who rents from a tenant. —**sub·ten'an·cy,** *n.*

sub·ter-, a prefix signifying *below, beneath, less than.*

sub·ter·fuge (sub'tĕr-fūj), *n.* an evasion or artifice; trick.

sub·ter·ra·ne·an (sub-tĕ-rā'ni-ăn), *adj.* **1.** below the earth's surface. **2.** secret; clandestine.

sub·tile (sut'l, sub'til), *adj.* [Rare], same as **subtle** —**sub'tile·ly,** *adv.*

sub·ti·tle (sub'tīt-l), *n.* **1.** a secondary or explanatory title. **2.** a line or portion of dialogue shown on a movie screen or TV tube: *v.t.* **-tled,** to add a subtitle to.

sub·tle (sut'l), *adj.* **-tler, -tlest. 1.** not dense; thin. **2.** mentally acute; keen. **3.** artfully skillful; deft. **4.** crafty; cunning. **5.** hidden; concealed. —**sub'tly,** *adv.*

sub·tle·ty (-ti), *n.* **1.** the quality or condition of being subtle. **2.** the ability to make fine distinctions. **3.** *pl.* **-ties,** something that is subtle.

sub·to·tal (sub'tōt-l), *n.* a total that is part of a final, complete total: *v.t. & v.i.* **-taled** or **-talled, -tal·ing** or **-tal·ling,** to add up part of a final total.

sub·tract (sub-trakt'), *v.t. & v.i.* to withdraw or take away, as a part from a whole; deduct. —**sub·trac'tion,** *n.*

sub·trac·tive (-trak'tiv), *adj.* **1.** tending to subtract. **2.** having the power to subtract.

sub·tra·hend (sub'trå-hend), *n.* a quantity or number to be subtracted from another.

sub·treas·ur·y (sub'trezh-ĕr-i), *n., pl.* **-ur·ies,** a branch treasury.

sub·trop·i·cal (sub-trop'ĭ-kl), *adj.* denoting, of, or characteristic of areas bordering on the tropics.

su·bu·late (sōō'byoo-lāt), *adj.* in *Biology,* awl-shaped; tapering to a point.

sub·urb (sub'ĕrb), *n.* **1.** an outlying district of a city or town, often residential. **2.** *pl.* city environs. —**sub·ur·ban** (sŭ-bûr'bǎn), *adj.*

sub·ur·ban·ite (sŭ-bûr'bǎn-īt), *n.* one who lives in a suburb.

sub·ur·bi·a (sŭ-bûr'bi-å), *n.* suburbs or suburbanites collectively.

sub·ven·tion (sŭb-ven'shŭn), *n.* a grant of financial aid; subsidy.

sub·ver·sive (-vûr'siv), *adj.* tending to subvert: *n.* one who is subversive.

sub·vert (-vûrt'), *v.t.* **1.** to overthrow or ruin (an established government, institution, etc.). **2.** to corrupt, as in allegiance. —**sub·ver'sion** (-vûr'zhŭn), *n.*

sub·way (sub'wā), *n.* **1.** an underground passage. **2.** an underground urban railway, usually electric.

suc-, same as **sub-:** used before *c.*

suc·ceed (sŭk-sēd'), *v.t.* **1.** to take the place of. **2.** to come after; follow: *v.i.* **1.** to come next in time; ensue. **2.** to replace another in office, ownership, etc. (often with *to*). **3.** to be successful. **4.** to achieve something intended. **5.** to have success; prosper.

suc·cess (sŭk-ses'), *n.* **1.** a favorable termination of some enterprise, as the gaining of fame, prosperity, etc. **2.** the degree of such achievement. **3.** one that is successful.

suc·cess·ful ('fŭl), *adj.* **1.** ending in success. **2.** having gained success. —**suc·cess'ful·ly,** *adv.*

suc·ces·sion (-sesh'ŭn), *n.* **1.** the act of following in order to a title, inheritance, etc. **2.** the right to succeed to a title, estate, etc. **3.** a group of persons or things following in sequence. —**suc·ces'sion·al,** *adj.*

suc·ces·sive (-ses'iv), *adj.* following in uninterrupted order; consecutive. —**suc·ces'sive·ly,** *adv.*

suc·ces·sor ('ĕr), *n.* one who succeeds another, as to a title.

suc·cinct (sŭk-singkt'), *adj.* tersely expressed; clear and brief. —**suc·cinct'ly,** *adv.* —**suc·cinct'ness,** *n.*

suc·cin·ic acid (sŭk-sin'ik), a white crystalline acid, found in amber, lignite, and some plants, or produced synthetically.

suc·cor (sŭk'ĕr), *v.t.* to help or relieve when in difficulty or distress; aid: *n.* relief; aid. British spelling **suc'cour.**

suc·cor·y (sŭk'ĕr-i), *n.* same as **chicory.**

suc·co·tash (sŭk'ō-tash), *n.* lima beans and kernels of corn cooked together.

suc·cu·lent (yoo-lĕnt), *adj.* full of juice; juicy. —**suc'cu·lence, suc'cu·len·cy,** *n.*

suc·cumb (sŭ-kum'), *v.i.* **1.** to yield; submit. **2.** to die.

suc·cus·sion (sŭ-kush'ŭn), *n.* the act of shaking violently or the state of being shaken violently. —**suc·cus'sive** (-kus'iv), *adj.*

such (such), *adj.* **1.** of the same or like kind. **2.** of the kind most recently referred to. **3.** certain but not defined. **4.** so great, so extreme, etc.: *pron.* **1.** such a person or thing. **2.** that one implied or indicated: *adv.* to so great an extent.

such and such, not yet determined or specified.

such-like (such'līk), *adj.* of a like kind: *n.* persons or things of such a kind.

suck (suk), *v.t.* **1.** to draw (liquid) into the mouth. **2.** to draw in by or as if by sucking. **3.** to draw liquid from (a breast, orange, etc.). **4.** to dissolve (a sweet) in the mouth by moistening and licking: *v.i.* **1.** to draw in by or as if by a vacuum. **2.** to draw nourishment; suckle: *n.* the act of sucking.

suck·er ('ĕr), *n.* **1.** one that sucks. **2.** any one of various freshwater fishes having thick-lipped, sucking mouths. **3.** a structure, part, or organ adapted for sucking. **4.** a piston, as in a suction pump. **5.** a tube through which something is drawn. **6.** a shoot from the lower stem or roots of a plant. **7.** a lollipop. **8.** [Slang], one who is easily deceived or cheated; dupe.

---

a in *cap,* ā in *cane,* ä in *father,* å in *abet,* e in *met,* ē in *be,* ē in *baker,* ĕ in *regent,* i in *pit,* ī in *fine,* i in *manifest,* o in *hot,* ô in *horse,* ō in *bone,*

suck·le (´l), *v.t. & v.i.* -led, -ling. 1. to nurse at the breast or udder. 2. to rear; nourish.

suck·ling (´ling), *n.* an unweaned child or animal.

·su·cre (sōō´kre), *n.* the monetary unit of Ecuador.

su·crose (sōō´krōs), *n.* in *Chemistry*, a white, crystalline sugar, obtained from sugar cane or sugar beets.

suc·tion (suk´shun), *n.* 1. the act or process of sucking. 2. the production of a difference between internal and external air pressure in a fluid or solid, forcing an inward flow or an adherence to a surface.

suction pump, a pump in which liquid is raised by atmospheric pressure that forces the liquid into the partial vacuum created by drawing a valved piston upward in a cylinder.

suc·to·ri·al (suk-tôr´i-ål), *adj.* 1. adapted for sucking or suction. 2. having suctorial organs. 3. feeding by sucking blood or juices.

su·da·to·ri·um (sōō-då-tôr´i-ûm), *n., pl.* -ri·a (-å), a hot-air room in a sweat bath.

sud·den (sud´n), *adj.* 1. happening unexpectedly. 2. abrupt; rash. 3. instantaneous; quick. —**sud´den·ly,** *adv.* —**sud´den·ness,** *n.*

sudden death, in *Sports,* a period of play after a tied game that ends when one side scores.

su·dor·if·er·ous (sōō-dô-rif´ër-ûs), *adj.* secreting perspiration.

su·dor·if·ic (-rif´ik), *adj.* causing perspiration: *n.* a sudorific medicine.

Su·dra (sōō´drä), *n.* a member of the lowest of the four major Hindu castes, formerly assigned menial tasks.

suds (sudz), *n.pl.* 1. soapy water. 2. froth. 3. [Slang], beer or ale.

suds·y (sud´zi), *adj.* suds´i·er, suds´i·est, like suds; frothy; foamy.

sue (sōō), *v.t.* sued, su´ing, 1. to petition; entreat. 2. to prosecute at law in seeking justice or redress.

suede, suède (swād), *n.* 1. leather having a napped surface on the flesh side. 2. a fabric made to resemble this leather.

su·et (sōō´it), *n.* the hard fat around the kidneys and loins of cattle and sheep, used in cooking and making tallow.

suf-, same as *sub-:* used before *f.*

suf·fer (suf´ër), *v.t. & v.i.* 1. to feel pain; endure (hardship, loss, etc.). 2. to undergo or experience. 3. to bear or stand up under. 4. to allow; tolerate. —**suf´fer·er,** *n.*

suf·fer·a·ble (-å-bl), *adj.* that can be suffered, endured, or permitted.

suf·fer·ance (suf´ër-åns), *n.* 1. the ability to endure pain, suffering, etc. patiently. 2. consent or permission implied by failure to prevent; toleration.

suf·fer·ing (-ing), *n.* 1. the state or condition of enduring mental or physical pain. 2. loss, pain, distress, etc. endured.

suf·fice (sù-fis´, -fiz´), *v.i.* -ficed, -fic´ing, to be sufficient or adequate.

suf·fi·cient (-fish´nt), *adj.* equal to what is needed; enough. —**suf·fi´cien·cy,** *n.* —**suf·fi´cient·ly,** *adv.*

suf·fix (suf´iks), *n.* a syllable or syllables added at the end of a word or stem to alter its meaning, make a new word, etc.: *v.t.* (sù-fiks´), to add as a suffix.

suf·fo·cate (suf´ô-kāt), *v.t.* -cat·ed, -cat·ing, 1. to kill by depriving the lungs, gills, etc. of oxygen. 2. to hinder the respiration of by cutting off fresh air; stifle; choke: *v.i.* 1. to die from suffocation. 2. to smother; stifle. —**suf·fo·ca´tion,** *n.*

Suf·folk (suf´ôk), *n.* 1. any one of a breed of heavy-bodied English workhorses. 2. any one of a breed of hornless English sheep with a black face and black feet.

suf·fra·gan (suf´rå-gån), *n.* a bishop appointed to assist a diocesan bishop: *adj.* denoting or of such a bishop.

suf·frage (´rij), *n.* 1. the right to vote; franchise. 2. a vote in favor of some question or candidate.

suf·fra·gette (suf-rå-jet´), *n.* a woman who advocates suffrage for women.

suf·fra·gist (suf´rå-jist), *n.* one who advocates extending political suffrage, as to women.

suf·fuse (sù-fūz´), *v.t.* -fused, -fus´ing, to spread over or through, as a glow, light, or fluid does. —**suf·fu´sion** (-fū´zhûn), *n.*

Su·fi (sōō´fi), *n.* an adherent of Sufism.

Su·fism (´fizm), *n.* a system of Moslem mysticism originated in Persia.

sug·ar (shoog´ër), *n.* 1. a sweet, crystalline substance obtained from sugar cane and sugar beets. 2. any one of a number of other sweet, soluble carbohydrates. 3. flattery. 4. [Slang], money: *v.t.* 1. to cover with sugar. 2. to sweeten with sugar: *v.i.* to form crystals of sugar.

sugar beet, a variety of beet widely cultivated for the high amount of sugar it contains.

sugar cane, a tropical grass with very tall, thick stems, widely cultivated for the sugar it yields.

sug·ar·coat (-kōt), *v.t.* 1. to cover with sugar. 2. to make seem more pleasant.

sugar gum, a low gum tree of Australia with sweetish leaves browsed on by livestock.

sugar maple, the hard maple, from the sap of which maple syrup and maple sugar are made.

sugar of lead, a crystalline substance obtained by dissolving lead in acetic acid and used as a mordant in dyeing.

sug·ar·plum (-plum), *n.* a piece of sugary candy; bonbon.

sug·ar·y (-i), *adj.* 1. of, like, or containing sugar, sweet, granular, etc. 2. cloyingly or mawkishly sweet.

sug·gest (sùg-jest´), *v.t.* 1. to introduce to the mind intentionally, as by way of a hint or a proposal, or indirectly, as through association of ideas. 2. to show indirectly; imply.

sug·gest·i·ble (-jes´ti-bl), *adj.* readily influenced by suggestion. —**sug·gest·i·bil´i·ty,** *n.*

sug·ges·tion (-jes´chûn), *n.* 1. the act of suggesting. 2. the thing suggested. 3. a hint or trace.

sug·ges·tive (-jes´tiv), *adj.* 1. tending to recall or bring to mind various related ideas. 2. suggesting something considered improper or lewd. —**sug·ges´tive·ly,** *adv.* —**sug·ges´tive·ness,** *n.*

ô in dragon, ōō in crude, oo in wool, u in cup, ū in cure, û in turn, ù in focus, oi in boy, ou in house, th in thin, th in sheathe, g in get, j in joy, y in yet.

su·i·ci·dal (sōō-i-sīd'l), *adj.* of, pertaining to, or tending to suicide. —**su·i·ci'dal·ly**, *adv.*

su·i·cide (sōō'i-sīd), *n.* 1. the intentional killing of oneself. 2. a person who kills himself. 3. ruin of one's own interests.

su·i ge·ne·ris (sōō'i jen'ēr-is), of his, her, or its own kind; unique.

su·int (sōō'int, swint), *n.* the greasy substance found in sheep's wool.

suit (sōōt, sūt), *n.* 1. a coat and trousers (or skirt) of the same material. 2. an outfit worn by a person for a particular purpose. 3. any one of the four sets making up a pack of cards. 4. an action in a court of law to recover a right, be awarded damages, etc. 5. a suing or pleading for something. 6. courtship: *v.t.* 1. to make or be appropriate to; fit or befit. 2. to satisfy or please.

suit·a·ble ('ā-bl), *adj.* fitting; appropriate. — **suit·a·bil'i·ty**, *n.* —**suit'a·bly**, *adv.*

suit·case ('kās), *n.* a firm, box-shaped case for carrying clothes when traveling.

suite (swēt), *n.* 1. a company of attendants; retinue. 2. a set, as of rooms, furniture, etc.

suit·ing (sōōt'ing, sūt'-), *n.* cloth used for making suits.

suit·or ('ēr), *n.* a man who is courting a woman.

su·ki·ya·ki (sōō'ki-yā-ki), *n.* [Japanese], a dish of thinly sliced meat, ·onions, and other vegetables cooked, often at the table, in soy sauce, sake, etc.

Suk·kot, Suk·koth (soo-kōt', sook'ōs), *n.* a Jewish fall festival commemorating the wandering in the desert after the Exodus.

sul·cate (sul'kāt), *adj.* grooved; furrowed.

sul·cus (sul'kus), *n.* 1. a groove or furrow. 2. any of the grooves on the surface of the brain.

sul·fa (sul'fä), *adj.* of or denoting drugs of the sulfanilamide type used in treating certain bacterial infections.

sul·fa·nil·a·mide (sul-fä-nil'ä-mīd), *n.* a white crystalline substance formerly used against certain infectious bacteria.

sul·fate (sul'fāt), *n.* a salt or ester of sulfuric acid.

sul·fide ('fīd), *n.* a compound of sulfur with another element or a radical. ·

sul·fite ('fīt), *n.* a salt or ester of sulfurous acid.

sul·fur (sul'fēr), *n.* a pale-yellow chemical element found in crystalline or amorphous form and used in vulcanizing rubber, making matches, etc.

sul·fu·rate ('fyoo-rāt), *v.t.* -rat·ed, -rat·ing, same as sulfurize.

sulfur dioxide, a colorless, suffocating gas easily liquefied and used as a bleach, refrigerant, preservative, etc.

sul·fu·re·ous (sul-fyoor'i-us), *adj.* of, like, or containing sulfur.

sul·fu·ret (sul'fyoo-ret), *v.t.* -ret·ed or -ret·ted, -ret·ing or -ret·ting, same as sulfurize.

sul·fu·ric (sul-fyoor'ik), *adj.* of or containing sulfur, especially in its highest valence.

sulfuric acid, a strong liquid acid much used in chemistry and industry, composed of hydrogen, sulfur, and oxygen.

sul·fu·rize (sul'fyoo-rīz), *v.t.* -rized, -riz·ing, to treat or combine with sulfur or a compound of sulfur.

sul·fu·rous (sul-fyoor'us), *adj.* 1. of or containing sulfur. 2. (usually sul'fēr-us), like burning sulfur in odor, color, etc.

sulfurous acid, a colorless acid containing sulfur, known only in solution and by its salts.

sul·fur·y (sul'fēr-i), *adj.* like sulfur.

sulk (sulk), *v.i.* to be sulky: *n. often pl.* a sulky mood (with *the*).

sulk·y (sul'ki), *adj.* sulk'i·er, sulk'i·est, peevishly sullen: *n., pl.* sulk'ies, a light, two-wheeled carriage for one person. —**sulk'i·ly**, *adv.* —**sulk'i·ness**, *n.*

sul·len (sul'ēn), *adj.* showing resentment by silence, withdrawal, etc.; gloomily angry. — **sul'len·ly**, *adv.* —**sul'len·ness**, *n.*

sul·ly (sul'i), *v.t.* -lied, -ly·ing, to tarnish or soil (one's honor, reputation, etc.).

sul·phur (sul'fēr), *n.* the chiefly British form for sulfur.

sul·tan (sul'tn), *n.* a Moslem ruler, especially the ruler of Turkey in earlier times.

sul·tan·a (sul-tan'ä), *n.* 1. the wife, mother, sister, or daughter of a sultan. 2. the mistress of a king, prince, etc. 3. a variety of seedless grape.

sul·tan·ate (sul'tn-it, -āt), *n.* the rule, office, or dominion of a sultan.

sul·try (sul'tri), *adj.* -tri·er, -tri·est, 1. very hot, humid, and oppressive; sweltering. 2. passionate; voluptuous. —**sul'tri·ness**, *n.*

sum (sum), *n.* 1. the whole amount of two or more things or numbers added together; total. 2. a problem in arithmetic presented for solution. 3. an amount of money. 4. summary or substance. 5. the utmost or highest degree: *v.t.* summed, sum'ming, 1. to add into one amount. 2. to condense into a few words: *v.i.* to recapitulate (with *up*).

su·mac, su·mach (shōō'mak, sōō'-), *n.* any of a number of related plants with compound leaves which, when dried and powdered, are used in tanning and dyeing: some sumacs can cause a severe itching skin rash on contact.

sum·mar·i·ly (su·mer'i-li, sum'ä-ri-li), *adv.* in a summary manner; quickly and without formality.

sum·ma·rize (sum'ä-rīz), *v.t.* -rized, -riz·ing, to make or constitute a summary of; state concisely.

sum·ma·ry ('ä-ri), *adj.* 1. that gives the substance briefly; summarizing. 2. done quickly with little regard to form or details: *n., pl.* -ries, a brief account stating the main points.

sum·ma·tion (su-mā'shun), *n.* the act of summing up, as of arguments in a court trial.

sum·mer (sum'ēr), *n.* 1. the season between spring and autumn; in the astronomical year, the period beginning in the Northern Hemisphere at the summer solstice, about June 21, and ending at the autumnal equinox, about September 22. 2. a period or condition resembling summer, as a time of flowering or fulfillment: *adj.* of, like, or for summer: *v.i.* to pass the summer: *v.t.* to feed or keep during the summer.

---

a in cap, ā in cane, ä in father, å in abet, e in met, ē in be, ê in baker, ê in regent, i in pit, ī in fine, i in manifest, o in hot, ô in horse, ō in bone,

sum·mer·house (-hous), *n.* a small, roofed, open shelter in a park or garden.

summer sausage, a type of hard, dried and smoked sausage that does not spoil easily.

sum·mer·time (-tīm), *n.* the season of summer.

sum·mer·y (-i), *adj.* of, pertaining to, or like summer.

sum·mit (sum'it), *n.* the top or highest point, state, level, etc.

sum·mit·ry (sum'i-tri), *n.*, *pl.* -tries, the use of conferences between heads of state to resolve problems of diplomacy.

sum·mon (sum'ŏn), *v.t.* 1. to call together by authority; send for or call. 2. to order to appear in court. 3. to rouse to activity; call forth. —sum'mon·er, *n.*

sum·mons (sum'ŏnz), *n.*, *pl.* -mons·es, 1. an order to come or attend. 2. an official order to appear in court on a certain day.

su·mo (sōō'mō), *n.* [Japanese], [sometimes S-], a Japanese form of wrestling engaged in by large, very heavy men.

sump (sump), *n.* a pit for draining or collecting liquids; cistern, reservoir, cesspool, etc.

sump pump, a pump for removing liquid that has collected in a sump.

sump·tu·ar·y (sump'choo-wer-i), *adj.* of, pertaining to, or regulating expenses or expenditures.

sumptuary laws, laws to limit expenditure on extravagant dress or other luxuries.

sump·tu·ous (sump'choo-wŭs), *adj.* 1. expensive; costly; lavish. 2. luxurious; magnificent. —sump'tu·ous·ly, *adv.* —sump'tu·ous·ness, *n.*

sun (sun), *n.* 1. the luminous body around which the earth and other planets revolve; it is the source of light, heat, and energy in the solar system. 2. any star having a system of planets around it. 3. anything like the sun in splendor or power. 4. sunshine: *v.t.* sunned, sun'ning, to expose to the sun's rays; warm, dry, tan, etc. in the sun. —sun'less, *adj.*

sun bath, exposure of the body to the rays of the sun.

sun·bathe ('bā*th*), *v.i.* -bathed, -bath·ing, to expose the body to the rays of the sun.

sun·beam ('bēm), *n.* a beam or shaft of sunlight.

Sun·belt (sun'belt), in the U.S., the southern and southwestern States having a sunny climate and an expanding economy.

sun·bird ('bûrd), *n.* a small, brightly colored tropical songbird that resembles the hummingbird.

sun·bon·net ('bon-it), *n.* a woman's bonnet with a large brim and a back flap that protect the face and neck from the sun.

sun·burn ('bûrn), *n.* an inflamed condition of the skin from too much exposure to the sun: *v.i. & v.t.* -burned or -burnt, -burn·ing, to give or get sunburn.

sun·burst ('bûrst), *n.* 1. a burst of sunlight, as through a break in clouds. 2. a decoration representing the sun with spreading rays.

sun·dae (sun'di, 'dā), *n.* a dish of ice cream and syrup, fruit, nuts, etc.

Sun·day (sun'di, 'dā), *n.* the first day of the week; it is the usual Christian day of worship.

Sunday school, a school held on Sunday, as at a church or synagogue, for teaching religion.

sun·der (sun'dēr), *v.t. & v.i.* to split apart; rend.

sun·di·al (sun'dī-âl, 'dīl), *n.* a device for measuring time by the shadow of a pointer cast by the sun on the face of a dial marked in hours.

sun·dog ('dôg), *n.* a bright spot on a halo that appears to be around the sun when seen through crystals in the air.

sun·down ('doun), *n.* same as sunset.

sun·down·er ('doun-ēr), *n.* [Australian Informal], a tramp, originally one who comes to a stock farm too late for work but early enough to get a night's lodging and food.

sun·dries (sun'driz), *n.pl.* numerous small or miscellaneous articles or matters.

sun·drops (sun'drops), *n.*, *pl.* -drops, any of several plants having yellow flowers that stay open during the sunlight hours.

sun·dry (sun'dri), *adj.* various; miscellaneous.

sun·fish (sun'fish), *n.*, *pl.* -fish, -fish·es, 1. an ocean fish with a shortened tail. 2. a North American freshwater fish resembling a perch.

sun·flow·er ('flou-ēr), *n.* a tall plant with a large, yellow-rayed flower head.

sung (sung), past participle and rare past tense of sing.

sun·glass·es (sun'glas-iz), *n.* eyeglasses with tinted lenses to protect the eyes from the sun's glare.

sun·glow ('glō), *n.* the rosy glow seen in the sky just before sunrise or just after sunset.

sunk (sungk), past participle and alternative past tense of sink.

sunk·en (sungk'n), *adj.* 1. sunk in water or other liquid. 2. below the surrounding surface or usual level. 3. in a hollow.

sun·lamp (sun'lamp), *n.* a lamp radiating ultraviolet rays, used as a substitute for sunlight as in getting a tan.

sun·light ('līt), *n.* the light of the sun.

sun·lit ('līt), *adj.* lighted by the sun.

sunn (sun), *n.* an East Indian plant the fiber of which has many uses similar to hemp; also sunn hemp.

Sun·na, Sun·nah (soon'â), *n.* Moslem law based, according to tradition, on the precepts and teachings of Mohammed and fully accepted by the Sunnites.

Sun·nite (soon'īt), *n.* an orthodox Moslem who regards the Sunna as equally binding with the Koran: also Sun'ni (soon'i), *pl.* Sun'ni.

sun·ny (sun'i), *adj.* -ni·er, -ni·est, 1. of, pertaining to, like, or from the sun. 2. full of sunlight. 3. bright; warm; cheerful.

sunny side, 1. the side exposed to the sun. 2. the more favorable aspect.

sun·rise ('rīz), *n.* the rising of the sun above the eastern horizon; early morning.

sun·roof (sun'rōōf, -roof), *n.* a car roof with a panel that opens to let in air and light: also sun roof.

sun·set ('set), *n.* the setting of the sun below the western horizon; twilight.

sun·shine ('shīn), *n.* the light or rays of the sun; brightness; sunny brightness, warmth, etc. —sun'shin·y, *adj.*

sun·spot ('spot), *n.* any of the dark, irregular

ŏ in dragon, ōō in crude, oo in wool, u in cup, ū in cure, û in turn, ŭ in focus, oi in boy, ou in house, th in thin, *th* in sheathe, g in get, j in joy, y in yet.

spots that appear on the sun from time to time and are believed to cause terrestrial magnetic disturbances.

sun star, a starfish with many rays.

sun·stroke ('strōk), *n.* a form of heatstroke caused by being out in the hot sun too long.

sun·tan ('tan), *n.* a darkened condition of the skin caused by exposure to the sun.

sun·up ('up), *n.* same as **sunrise**.

sup (sup), *v.i.* **supped, sup'ping,** to have supper: *v.t.* to take into with the lips; sip.

su·per (sōō'pėr), *n.* 1. same as **supernumerary**, especially in the theater. 2. same as **superintendent:** *adj.* of very large size, high quality, etc.; much above average.

su·per-, a prefix meaning *above, over, very, very much, very large, in excess.*

su·per·a·ble (sōō'pėr-ȧ-b'l), *adj.* capable of being overcome or conquered. —**su'per·a·bly,** *adv.*

su·per·a·bun·dant (sōō-pėr-ȧ-bun'dȧnt), *adj.* abundant to a great, unusual, or excessive degree. —**su·per·a·bun'dance,** *n.* —**su·per·a·bun'dant·ly,** *adv.*

su·per·an·nu·ate (-an'ū-āt), *v.t. & v.i.* **-at·ed, -at·ing,** to retire on account of old age or infirmity. —**su·per·an·nu·a'tion,** *n.*

su·perb (soo-pûrb', sŏŏ-), *adj.* 1. grand, majestic, splendid, etc. 2. first-rate; excellent. —**su·perb'ly,** *adv.* —**su·perb'ness,** *n.*

su·per·car·go (sōō'pėr-kär-gō, sū'-), *n., pl.* **-goes, -gos,** an officer on a merchant ship who has charge of the cargo and commercial affairs of a ship.

su·per·charge (-chärj), *v.t.* **-charged, -charg·ing,** to increase the power of (an engine), as by using a supercharger.

su·per·charg·er (-chärj-ėr), *n.* a blower or compressor that is used to increase the power of an internal-combustion engine by forcing more air into the cylinders.

su·per·cil·i·ar·y (sōō-pėr-sil'i-er-i), *adj.* of, pertaining to, or situated above the eyebrow.

su·per·cil·i·ous (-sil'i-ŭs), *adj.* proud and scornful; haughty; disdainful.

su·per·con·duc·tiv·i·ty (-kon-duk-tiv'ī-tĭ), *n.* the ability that some metals have of conducting electricity without resistance when cooled to near absolute zero.

su·per·e·go (-ē'gō), *n., pl.* **-gos,** in *Psychoanalysis,* that part of the ego which is self-critical and influences behavior on a moral basis.

su·per·em·i·nent (-em'i-nėnt), *adj.* eminent above all others. —**su·per·em'i·nent·ly,** *adv.*

su·per·e·ro·ga·tion (-er-ō-gā'shŭn), *n.* the performance of more than is required. —**su·per·e·rog·a·to·ry** (-i-rog'ȧ-tôr-i), *adj.*

su·per·fe·cun·da·tion (-fē-kŭn-dā'shŭn, -fek-ŭn-), *n.* the fertilization of two ova at separate times during the same ovulation period.

su·per·fe·ta·tion (-fē-tā'shŭn), *n.* the impregnation of a female already pregnant.

su·per·fi·cial (-fish'ăl), *adj.* 1. of, pertaining to, or on the surface. 2. shallow, slight, cursory, etc. —**su·per·fi'cial·ly,** *adj.*

su·per·fi·ci·al·i·ty (-fish-i-al'ī-ti), *n., pl.* **-ties,** the state or quality of being superficial.

su·per·fi·ci·es (-fish'i-ēz, -fish'ēz), *n., pl.* **su·per·fi'ci·es,** 1. the outer surface. 2. the outward form or aspect.

su·per·fine (-fin'), *adj.* 1. too subtle or refined. 2. very fine or excellent. 3. very fine-grained.

su·per·flu·ous (soo-pûr'flōō-ŭs), *adj.* more than enough or necessary; excessive. —**su·per·flu·i·ty,** *n., pl.* **-ties.**

su·per·high·way (sōō'pėr-hī'wā), *n.* an expressway for high-speed traffic with divided lanes, and overpasses and underpasses at most intersections.

su·per·hu·man (sōō-pėr-hū'mȧn), *adj.* 1. regarded as having a nature above that of man; divine. 2. greater than that of a normal human being.

su·per·im·pose (-im-pōz'), *v.t.* **-posed, -pos'ing,** to lay or impose on something else.

su·per·in·cum·bent (-in-kum'bėnt), *adj.* lying or resting on something else.

su·per·in·duce (-in-dōōs', -dūs'), *v.t.* **-duced, -duc'ing,** to bring in as an addition to something else.

su·per·in·tend (-in-tend'), *v.t.* to have or exercise charge or oversight of; supervise.

su·per·in·tend·ence (-ten'dėns), *n.* supervision; oversight; control.

su·per·in·tend·ent ('dėnt), *n.* 1. a person in charge of a department, organization, etc.; director. 2. a person whose work is to take care of a building; custodian.

su·pe·ri·or (sú-pir'i-ėr), *adj.* 1. higher in place, position, rank, etc. 2. greater, better, etc. than (with *to*). 3. above average in quality, value, skill, etc.; excellent. 4. indifferent (*to* something painful or unpleasant). 5. making a show of being better than others; haughty: *n.* 1. one who is superior to others; one of a higher rank or position. 2. the head of a monastery, convent, etc.

su·pe·ri·or·i·ty (sú-pir-i-ôr'ī-ti), *n.* the state or quality of being superior, or higher, greater, better, etc.

su·per·la·tive (sú-pûr'lȧ-tiv), *adj.* 1. superior to all others; of the highest kind. 2. denoting the greatest degree of comparison of adjectives or adverbs: *n.* 1. the highest degree; height. 2. the superlative degree in grammar.

su·per·man (sōō'pėr-man, sū'-), *n.* a man who seems to have superhuman powers.

su·per·mar·ket (-mär-kit), *n.* a large food store of the self-service type.

su·per·nal (sōō-pûr'n'l), *adj.* in, from, or pertaining to a higher place or region; celestial. —**su·per'nal·ly,** *adv.*

su·per·nat·u·ral (sōō-pėr-nach'ēr-ȧl), *adj.* 1. beyond or exceeding the powers or laws of nature. 2. of or pertaining to God or ghosts, spirits, etc. —**su·per·nat'u·ral·ly,** *adv.*

su·per·nat·u·ral·ism (-izm), *n.* 1. the state or quality of being supernatural. 2. belief in a supernatural or divine force in the universe. —**su·per·nat'u·ral·ist,** *n.*

su·per·nu·mer·ar·y (-nōō'mėr-er-i, -nū'-), *n., pl.* **-ar·ies,** 1. a person or thing beyond the stated or required number. 2. a performer in a show who has a small, nonspeaking part, as in a mob scene.

su·per·phos·phate (-fos'fāt), *n.* a phosphate containing the greatest quantity of phosphoric acid entering into combination with the base.

su·per·pose (-pōz'), *v.t.* -posed', -pos'ing, to put on or over something else. —**su·per·pos'a·ble**, *adj.*

su·per·sat·u·rate (-sach'ŭ-rāt), *v.t.* -rat·ed, -rat·ing, to make more highly concentrated than in normal saturation at a given temperature.

su·per·scribe (-skrīb'), *v.t.* -scribed', -scrib'ing, to write (words, numbers, etc.) on the outside or at the top. —**su·per·scrip'tion** (-skrip'shŭn), *n.*

su·per·script (sōō'pẽr-skript, sū'-), *n.* a number, letter, etc. written above and to the side of another.

su·per·sede (sōō-pẽr-sēd'), *v.t.* -sed'ed, -sed'ing, to replace or supplant because superior, more up-to-date, etc.

su·per·son·ic (-son'ik), *adj.* 1. of or denoting a speed greater than the speed of sound. 2. same as **ultrasonic**.

su·per·star (sōō'pẽr-stär, sū'-), *n.* an outstanding performer, as in sports or show business, considered to have exceptional skill and talent.

su·per·sti·tion (sōō-pẽr-stish'ŭn), *n.* a belief or practice that is based on fear and ignorance and that is against the known laws of science, as a belief in omens.

su·per·sti·tious ('ŭs), *adj.* of, pertaining to, caused by, or believing in superstitions. —**su·per·sti'tious·ly**, *adv.*

su·per·struc·ture (sōō'pẽr-struk-chẽr, sū'-), *n.* a structure built on top of another.

su·per·tax (-taks), *n.* an additional tax on income above a certain amount.

su·per·ton·ic (sōō-pẽr-ton'ik), *n.* the note next above the keynote of a musical scale.

su·per·vene (-vēn'), *v.i.* -vened', -ven'ing, to come or occur as something additional or unexpected.

su·per·vise (sōō'pẽr-vīz), *v.t. & v.i.* -vised, -vis·ing, to oversee or be in charge of (work, a group of workers, etc.); direct.

su·per·vi·sion (sōō-pẽr-vizh'ŭn), *n.* the act of supervising; direction.

su·per·vi·sor (sōō'pẽr-vī-zẽr), *n.* a person who supervises; head of a department, organization, etc.

su·per·vi·so·ry (sōō-pẽr-vī'zẽr-i), *adj.* of, pertaining to, or exercising supervision.

su·pi·nate (sōō'pi-nāt, sū'-), *v.t. & v.i.* -nat·ed, -nat·ing, to rotate (the hand or forearm) so that the palm faces upward or outward.

su·pine (sōō-pīn'), *adj.* 1. lying on the back with the face up. 2. inactive; listless; passive. —**su·pine'ly**, *adv.* —**su·pine'ness**, *n.*

sup·per (sup'ẽr), *n.* an evening meal.

supper club, an expensive nightclub.

sup·plant (sŭ-plant'), *v.t.* 1. to take the place of, as by force or craft. 2. to remove and replace with something else.

sup·ple (sup'l), *adj.* -pler, -plest, 1. bending easily; flexible. 2. lithe or limber. 3. easily

changed or easily changing; adaptable. —**sup'ple·ly, sup'ply,** *adv.* —**sup'ple·ness,** *n.*

sup·ple·ment (sup'lê-mênt), *n.* 1. something added to supply what is lacking, deficient, etc. 2. a section with special articles or features, more up-to-date information, etc. added to a book, newspaper, etc.: *v.t.* (-ment), to be or give a supplement to.

sup·ple·men·ta·ry (sup-lê-men'tẽr-i), *adj.* serving as a supplement; additional: also **sup·ple·men'tal** ('tal).

sup·pli·ance (sup'li-ăns), *n.* supplication; entreaty.

sup·pli·ant ('li-ănt), *adj.* supplicating; beseeching; entreating.

sup·pli·cant ('li-kănt), *adj.* asking with humility: *n.* one who asks humbly.

sup·pli·cate ('li-kāt), *v.t. & v.i.* -cat·ed, -cat·ing, to ask or beg (someone) humbly to do or give (something); pray; implore.

sup·pli·ca·tion (sup-li-kā'shŭn), *n.* the act of supplicating; humble and earnest prayer or entreaty.

sup·pli·er (sŭ-plī'ẽr), *n.* one who or that which supplies.

sup·ply (sŭ-plī'), *v.t.* -plied', -ply'ing, 1. to provide (a person, group, etc.) with (the things required). 2. to make up for; fill: *n., pl.* -plies', 1. the act of supplying. 2. the amount at hand; stock. 3. *pl.* things required; materials; provisions.

sup·port (sŭ-pôrt'), *v.t.* 1. to bear the weight of; hold in place. 2. to encourage or help. 3. to uphold or favor. 4. to provide the means of existence for; maintain. 5. to help prove; show to be right. 6. to bear; endure: *n.* 1. the act of supporting. 2. that which supports. 3. maintenance; livelihood. —**sup·port'a·ble,** *adj.* —**sup·por'tive,** *adj.*

sup·port·er ('ẽr), *n.* 1. a person who supports; advocate; adherent. 2. a thing that supports, as a band or truss for the abdomen, an elastic belt with a groin pouch for men, etc.

sup·pose (sŭ-pōz'), *v.t.* -posed', -pos'ing, 1. to assume as true although not yet proved. 2. to believe, guess, think, or imagine. 3. to propose or weigh as a possibility. 4. to expect: always in the passive: —*v.i.* to conjecture. —**sup·posed'**, *adj.* —**sup·pos'ed·ly**, *adv.*

sup·po·si·tion (sup-ō-zish'ŭn), *n.* 1. the act of supposing. 2. the thing supposed; assumption. —**sup·po·si'tion·al**, *adj.*

sup·pos·i·ti·tious (sŭ-poz-i-tish'ŭs), *adj.* 1. supposed or imaginary. 2. not genuine; counterfeit.

sup·pos·i·tive ('i-tiv), *adj.* based on or involving supposition. —**sup·pos'i·tive·ly**, *adv.*

sup·pos·i·to·ry (sŭ-poz'i-tôr-i), *n., pl.* -ries, a small, medicated mass, usually in the form of a cone, for insertion into the rectum, vagina, etc., where it dissolves.

sup·press (sŭ-pres'), *v.t.* 1. to put down by force; subdue; quell. 2. to prevent from being known, published, etc. 3. to hold back; restrain; check. 4. to arrest the normal secretion of. 5. in *Psychiatry,* to dismiss from the mind (that which is unacceptable) by a conscious effort. —**sup·pres'sive**, *adj.* —**sup·pres'sor**, *n.*

---

sup·pres·sion (-presh'ŭn), *n.* the act of suppressing; stoppage, subduing, etc.

sup·pu·rate (sup'yoo-rāt), *v.i.* -rat·ed, -rat·ing, to form pus; fester. —**sup'pu·ra·tive,** *adj.*

sup·pu·ra·tion (sup-yoo-rā'shŭn), *n.* 1. the formation of pus. 2. pus.

su·pra-, a prefix meaning *above, over, beyond.*

su·pra·lap·sar·i·an (sōō-prá-lap-ser'i-ăn), *adj.* of or pertaining to supralapsarianism: *n.* a believer in supralapsarianism.

su·pra·lap·sar·i·an·ism (-izm), *n.* the doctrine held by some Calvinists that the divine decrees of election and predestination preceded the fall of man from grace.

su·pra·na·tion·al (-nash'ŭn-ăl), *adj.* of, pertaining to, or over all or a number of nations.

su·pra·re·nal (-rē'nl), *adj.* situated on or above the kidney: *n.* an adrenal gland.

su·prem·a·cist (sŭ-prem'ă-sist), *n.* one who believes in the supremacy of one group over others.

su·prem·a·cy (-prem'ă-si). *n., pl.* -cies, 1. the state or quality of being supreme. 2. supreme power or authority.

su·preme (sŭ-prēm', soo-), *adj.* 1. highest in power or authority. 2. most excellent. 3. extreme; utmost. —**su·preme'ly,** *adv.*

Supreme Being, God.

Supreme Court, 1. the highest Federal court. 2. the highest court in most States.

Supreme Soviet, the parliament of the Soviet Union.

sur-, a prefix meaning *over, beyond.*

su·ra (soor'ā), *n.* any one of the sections of the Koran.

su·rah (soor'ā), *n.* a soft, twilled silk fabric.

su·ral (soor'ăl, syoor'ăl), *n.* of or pertaining to the calf of the leg.

sur·base (sŭr'bās), *n.* a molding or cornice along the top of the base of a pedestal, baseboard, etc.

sur·cease (sŭr'sēs), *n.* cessation; end.

sur·charge (sŭr'chärj), *n.* 1. an extra or excessive charge, burden, or load. 2. a new value overprinted on a postage stamp: *v.t.* (sŭr-chärj'), -charged', -charg'ing, to put a surcharge on or in (something).

sur·cin·gle (sŭr'sing-gl), *n.* 1. a belt or strap for passing around the body of a horse and securing the saddle, pack, etc. 2. the girdle of a cassock.

sur·coat (sŭr'kōt), *n.* an outer coat; especially, a loose, short cloak worn over a knight's armor.

surd (sŭrd), *n.* 1. an irrational number or quantity; a root, as $\sqrt{3}$, that can be expressed only approximately. 2. in *Phonetics,* a voiceless sound.

sure (shoor), *adj.* 1. fit to be depended on; safe, unfailing, etc. or reliable, dependable, etc. 2. without doubt; certain, positive, etc. 3. firm or steady, as a footing. 4. certain to be, do, happen, etc.: *adv.* [Informal], surely; certainly.

sure-fire ('fīr), *adj.* [Informal], sure to be successful or as expected.

sure-foot·ed ('foot'ĕd), *adj.* not likely to slip, stumble, or fall. —**sure'foot'ed·ly,** *adv.* — **sure'foot'ed·ness,** *n.*

sure·ly ('li), *adv.* in a sure way; certainly, firmly, steadily, etc.

sure·ty (shoor'ē-ti), *n., pl.* -ties, 1. sureness; certainty. 2. security against loss or damage. 3. one who makes himself responsible for another; specifically, in *Law,* one responsible for another's debts and obligations. —**sure'ty·ship,** *n.*

surf (sŭrf), *n.* the swell of the sea that breaks and foams on the shore or rocks: *v.i.* to engage in surfing. —**surf'er,** *n.*

sur·face (sŭr'fis), *n.* 1. the exterior part or upper face of anything. 2. any of the faces of a solid. 3. superficial features: *adj.* 1. of, at, or on the surface. 2. of or via land or sea, as distinguished from air or undersea. 3. apparent; superficial: *v.t.* -faced, -fac·ing, 1. to give a surface to, as a road. 2. to polish, smooth, or level a surface: *v.i.* 1. to rise to the surface of the water. 2. to work at or near the surface of a mine. 3. to become known. —**sur'fac·er,** *n.*

surf-bird ('bŭrd), *n.* a shore bird of the sandpiper family, found on the Pacific coast.

surf·board ('bōrd), *n.* a long, narrow board used in surfing.

surf·boat ('bōt), *n.* a strong, light boat used in heavy surf.

sur·feit (sŭr'fit), *n.* 1. too much. 2. excess in eating or drinking. 3. sickness or nausea caused by such excess: *v.t.* to feed or supply to excess.

surf·ing (sŭr'fing), *n.* the sport of riding the crest of a wave in toward shore while standing, lying, or kneeling on a surfboard.

surge (sŭrj), *n.* 1. a large wave or billow; swell. 2. a movement like that of a large wave or rush of water. 3. a sudden, strong increase, as of electric current, energy, power, etc.: *v.i.* surged, surg'ing, to rush forward; move as in a rolling swell.

sur·geon (sŭr'jŭn), *n.* a doctor of medicine who specializes in surgery.

sur·ger·y (sŭr'jēr-i), *n., pl.* -ger·ies, 1. the act and art of treating injuries or diseases by manual or instrumental operations. 2. the place where a surgeon operates; operating room. 3. [British], a doctor's office.

sur·gi·cal ('ji-kl), *adj.* of or having to do with surgeons or surgery. —**sur'gi·cal·ly,** *adv.*

su·ri·cate (soor'i-kāt), *n.* any one of a number of small, four-toed, burrowing mammals of South Africa, related to the mongoose.

sur·ly (sŭr'li), *adj.* -li·er, -li·est, uncivil; churlish; ill-natured; rude. —**sur'li·ly,** *adv.* —**sur'-li·ness,** *n.*

sur·mise (sĕr-mīz'), *n.* a guess or conjecture; suspicion: *v.t. & v.i.* -mised', -mis'ing, to guess; conjecture.

sur·mount (sĕr-mount'), *v.t.* 1. originally, to exceed. 2. to rise above; be at the top of. 3. to overcome; conquer. 4. to climb up and across. —**sur·mount'a·ble,** *adj.*

sur·name (sŭr'nām), *n.* 1. the family name, or last name, as distinguished from a given name. 2. a name or epithet added to a person's given name: *v.t.* -named, -nam·ing, to give a surname to.

sur·pass (sĕr-pas'), *v.t.* 1. to excel; be better

than. 2. to go beyond the range or capacity of. 3. to exceed in quantity, amount, etc.

sur-pass-ing ('ing), *adj.* 1. excellent. 2. of a large amount: *adv.* [Archaic], exceedingly. —**sur-pass'ing-ly,** *adv.*

sur-plice (sûr'plis), *n.* a white outer vestment with wide sleeves, worn by the clergy or choir in some churches.

sur-plus (sûr'plus), *n.* a quantity above what is required or used; excess: *adj.* exceeding what is required.

sur-plus-age (-ij), *n.* 1. excess; surplus. 2. in *Law*, matter that is irrelevant or superfluous in the pleading of a case.

sur-prise (sĕr-prīz'), *n.* 1. the act of taking unawares. 2. the state of being aroused by something unexpected; astonishment; wonder. 3. something that causes astonishment or wonder: *v.t.* -**prised', -pris'ing,** 1. to take unawares; come upon unexpectedly. 2. to assail without warning. 3. to astonish; amaze.

sur-re-al-ism (sû-rē'ā-lizm), *n.* a modern movement in the arts that attempts to portray the subconscious mind through nonrational, unconventional juxtapositions of material. —**sur-re'al-ist,** *adj. & n.* —**sur-re-al-is'tic,** *adj.*

sur-ren-der (sû-ren'dĕr), *v.t.* 1. to yield to the power of another; give up on compulsion. 2. to abandon; cede; resign: *v.i.* to yield; give oneself up into the power of another, especially as a prisoner: *n.* the act of surrendering.

sur-rep-ti-tious (sûr-ĕp-tish'ŭs), *adj.* 1. done or obtained by stealth. 2. acting in a stealthy, secret manner. —**sur-rep-ti'tious-ly,** *adv.*

sur-rey (sûr'i), *n., pl.* -**reys,** a light, four-wheeled carriage with two seats, and usually a flat top.

sur-ro-gate (sûr'ō-gāt, -git), *n.* 1. in some States of the U.S., a judge in probate court. 2. a substitute or deputy.

sur-round (sû-round'), *v.t.* to enclose or encircle on all sides or nearly all sides; encompass.

sur-round-ings (-roun'dingz), *n.pl.* the things, circumstances, conditions, etc. that surround a person or thing; environment.

sur-tax (sûr'taks), *n.* an additional tax on something already taxed; especially, an additional income tax levied on the amount the income exceeds a certain sum: *v.t.* (sĕr-taks'), to impose a surtax on.

sur-tout (sĕr-tōō', -tōōt'), *n.* a man's closefitting overcoat reaching below the knees, worn in the late 19th century.

sur-veil-lance (sĕr-vā'lāns), *n.* 1. watch kept over a person, especially a suspect or prisoner. 2. supervision.

sur-vey (sĕr-vā'), *v.t.* 1. to inspect, examine, or consider comprehensively; view in detail. 2. to measure and determine boundaries, area, form, etc. of (a tract of land): *n., pl.* -**veys,** 1. the act or process of surveying an area. 2. a written description, or a diagram or plan of an area surveyed. 3. a general view. 4. a detailed study, examination, inspection, etc. —**sur-vey'or,** *n.*

sur-vey-ing ('ing), *n.* the art or business of surveying land.

sur-viv-al (sĕr-vī'vl), *n.* 1. the act or fact of surviving. 2. any ancient use, custom, or belief continuing to the present day.

survival of the fittest, same as natural selection.

sur-vive (sĕr-vīv'), *v.t.* -**vived', -viv'ing,** to outlive; continue to live or exist after: *v.i.* to continue living or existing after another's death or after an event. —**sur-vi'vor,** *n.*

sur-vi-vor-ship (-vī'vĕr-ship), *n.* 1. the state of outliving another. 2. in *Law*, the right of a surviving joint owner or owners to the share of an owner who dies.

sus-cep-ti-bil-i-ty (sû-sep-ti-bil'i-ti), *n., pl.* -**ties,** 1. the state or quality of being susceptible. 2. *pl.* feelings. 3. capacity for receiving impressions.

sus-cep-ti-ble (sû-sep'ti-bl), *adj.* 1. having little resistance (to). 2. easily influenced or affected; sensitive. —**sus-cep'ti-bly,** *adv.*

sus-lik (sus'lik), *n.* a small ground squirrel of northern Europe and Asia.

sus-pect (sû-spekt'), *v.t.* 1. to distrust; believe to be wrong or bad. 2. to believe to be guilty on little or no evidence. 3. to conjecture; guess: *v.i.* to be suspicious: *adj.* (sus'-pekt), regarded with suspicion: *n.* (sus'pekt), one suspected of a crime.

sus-pend (sû-spend'), *v.t.* 1. to cause to hang by a support from above. 2. to defer; hold back. 3. to interrupt; cause to cease for a time. 4. to exclude temporarily, as from school or an office, as a penalty. 5. to keep (particles) in suspension: *v.i.* to stop temporarily.

sus-pend-ers ('ĕrz), *n.pl.* 1. adjustable straps or bands worn over the shoulders to hold up trousers. 2. [British], garters.

sus-pense (sû-spens'), *n.* 1. a state of uncertainty, doubt, or anxiety. 2. the interest and excitement that grows as one nears the climax or denouement of a play, novel, etc. —**sus-pense'ful,** *adj.*

sus-pen-sion (sû-spen'shŭn), *n.* 1. the act of suspending. 2. the state of being suspended. 3. the condition of a liquid or gas that has minute particles dispersed throughout it. 4. a delay; interruption; temporary stoppage. 5. in *Music*, the continuing of a note from one chord to another.

suspension bridge, any bridge held up by cables anchored at either end and supported by towers at intervals.

sus-pen-sive (sû-spen'siv), *adj.* 1. tending to stop activity. 2. hesitating; indecisive. 3. in suspense. —**sus-pen'sive-ly,** *adv.*

sus-pen-so-ry (-sō'ri), *adj.* 1. suspending or sustaining, as a muscle or ligament that supports a body organ. 2. suspending or delaying, thus allowing something to remain undecided. Also **sus-pen'sor** ('sĕr): *n., pl.* -**ries,** 1. a suspensory muscle, bandage, etc. 2. a fabric pouch for supporting the scrotum.

sus-pi-cion (sû-spish'ŭn), *n.* 1. the act or an instance of suspecting wrong, guilt, evil, etc. with little or no evidence. 2. distrust; the feeling of one who suspects. 3. a hint; very small amount: *v.t.* [Dialectal], to suspect.

ô in drag*o*n, ōō in cr*u*de, oo in w*oo*l, u in c*u*p, ū in c*u*re, u̇ in t*u*rn, ŭ in foc*u*s, oi in b*oy*, ou in h*ou*se, th in *th*in, t͟h in shea*th*e, g in *g*et, j in *j*oy, y in *y*et.

sus·pi·cious ('ŭs), *adj.* 1. full of doubt, suspicion, distrust, etc. 2. open to or exciting suspicion. 3. inclined to suspect evil. —**sus·pi'cious·ly,** *adv.* —**sus·pi'cious·ness,** *n.*

sus·tain (sŭ-stān'), *v.t.* 1. to hold up or support. 2. to maintain; keep in existence. 3. to keep; support; provide nourishment for. 4. to bear; endure. 5. to suffer (a loss, injury, etc.). 6. to support as legal or valid. 7. to confirm. —**sus·tain'a·ble,** *adj.* —**sus·tain'ment,** *n.*

sus·te·nance (sus'ti-năns), *n.* 1. the act of sustaining. 2. the state of being sustained. 3. a way of earning one's living. 4. that which supports life; food.

sus·ten·ta·tion (sus-ten-tā'shŭn), *n.* 1. maintenance; support. 2. that which sustains or supports; sustenance.

su·sur·rus (soo-sûr'ŭs), *n.* a light whispering, humming, or gentle sighing, as of the wind.

sut·ler (sut'lēr), *n.* formerly, a person who followed an army and sold provisions, liquor, etc. to the troops.

su·tra (sōō'trä), 1. in *Brahmanism,* an aphorism or maxim, or a collection of these. 2. in *Buddhism,* any one of the sermons of the Buddha. Also **sut·ta** (soot'ä).

sut·tee (su-tē'), *n.* 1. a Hindu widow who immolated herself on the funeral pyre of her deceased husband. 2. the former Hindu custom by which this was done.

su·ture (sōō'chēr), *n.* 1. the stitching together of the two edges of a wound or incision. 2. the thread, wire, gut, etc. used for this. 3. any one of the individual stitches. 4. the line of junction between two parts, especially the bones of the skull. 5. the line of junction between parts of a plant: *v.t.* **-tured, -tur·ing,** to unite by or as by sutures. —**su'tur·al,** *adj.*

su·ze·rain (sōō'zĕ·rin, -rān), *n.* 1. a feudal lord. 2. a state that exercises political control over a dependent state. —**su'ze·rain·ty,** *n.*

svelte (svelt), *adj.* 1. suave. 2. lithe and slender.

swab (swäb), *n.* 1. a mop for cleaning decks, floors, etc. 2. a small piece of sponge or cotton, often on a stick, used to medicate or cleanse the throat, mouth, etc. 3. [Slang], *a)* a clumsy lout; *b)* a sailor: also **swab'ble** ('i): *v.t.* **swabbed, swab'bing,** to rub or clean with a swab. —**swab'ber,** *n.*

swad·dle (swäd'l), *v.t.* **-dled, -dling,** formerly, to swathe (a newborn baby) in long, narrow bands of cloth.

swaddling clothes, the long, narrow bands formerly swathed around a newborn baby: also **swaddling bands.**

swag (swag), *v.i.* **swagged, swag'ging,** to sink down by its own weight; sag: *v.t.* to hang in a swag: *n.* 1. a valance, festoon, chain, etc. hanging in a curve or loop for decoration. 2. in Australia, a pack or bundle carried or worn on the shoulders by an itinerant worker. 3. [Slang], loot; booty.

swage (swāj), *n.* 1. a grooved tool used for bending and shaping metal. 2. a die or stamp for shaping metal by hammering: *v.t.* **swaged, swag'ing,** to shape or bend with a swage.

swage block, a perforated and grooved steel

block, used as a mold in hammering out the heads of bolts, etc.

swag·ger (swag'ēr), *v.i.* 1. to strut haughtily; walk boldly and arrogantly. 2. to boast loudly: *n.* 1. a swaggering manner or walk. 2. noisy boastfulness. —**swag'ger·er,** *n.*

Swa·hi·li (swä-hē'li), *n.* 1. *pl.* **-lis, -li,** a member of a Bantu people of the east coast of Africa. 2. their language.

swain (swān), *n.* [Poetic], 1. a country lad. 2. a sweetheart or lover.

swal·low (swäl'ō), *n.* 1. a small, migratory, passerine bird with a forked tail. 2. a kind of swift resembling the swallow. 3. the act of swallowing. 4. as much as can be swallowed at one time. 5. the groove or hole in a block or pulley on board ship, through which the rope runs: *v.t.* 1. to take (food, drink, etc.) into the stomach through the esophagus. 2. to absorb or engulf. 3. to retract (words said). 4. to put up with. 5. to suppress (pride, a laugh, etc.). 6. [Informal], to accept as true without question: *v.i.* to perform the actions of swallowing.

swal·low·tail (-tāl), *n.* 1. something shaped like a swallow's tail. 2. a brightly colored butterfly with hind wings extended in points.

swal·low·tailed (-tāld'), *adj.* 1. having a forked tail. 2. of or denoting a man's full-dress coat, with long, tapering tails at the back.

swam (swam), past tense of **swim.**

swamp (swämp, swômp), *n.* wet or boggy land; soft, low land saturated with water: *v.t.* 1. to plunge or sink in a swamp or deep water. 2. to flood as with water. 3. to sink (a boat) by filling with water. 4. to overwhelm; ruin: *v.i.* to become swamped. —**swamp'ish,** *adj.*

swamp buggy, a vehicle, often amphibious, for traveling over swampy ground or in shallow water.

swamp·y ('i), *adj.* **swamp'i·er, swamp'i·est,** 1. consisting of a swamp or swamps. 2. like a swamp; wet; marshy; boggy. —**swamp'i·ness,** *n.*

swan (swän, swôn), *n.* 1. *pl.* **swans, swan,** a large, graceful, web-footed water bird, usually white but sometimes black, with a long, curved neck. 2. a sweet singer or fine poet.

swan dive, a dive in which the arms are stretched out to the sides, then brought forward over the head just before entering the water.

swank (swangk), *n.* [Informal], 1. swaggering behavior. 2. pretentious stylishness in dress: *adj.* [Informal], pretentiously stylish.

swank·y ('i), *adj.* **swank'i·er, swank'i·est,** [Informal], pretentiously stylish; expensive and showy. —**swank'i·ly,** *adv.* —**swank'i·ness,** *n.*

swan's-down (swänz'doun, swônz'-), *n.* 1. the soft, fine down of a swan. 2. a soft, thick fabric of mixed wool and cotton, rayon, or silk, used as for baby clothes. 3. a very soft cotton flannel. Also **swansdown.**

swan-skin (swän'skin, swôn'-), *n.* a kind of soft, fine, twilled flannel, used for work clothes.

swan song, a last song, utterance, or work of a dying poet or composer: from the myth that the swan sings before dying.

---

swap (swäp, swôp), *v.t. & v.i.* **swapped, swap'-ping,** [Informal], to trade or barter: *n.* [Informal], a trade or barter. —**swap'per,** *n.*

swa·raj (swä·räj'), *n.* in India, self-government; home rule. —**swa·raj'ist,** *n.*

sward (swôrd), *n.* a grassy surface of land; turf: *v.t.* to cover with turf.

swarm (swôrm), *v.i.* 1. to throng together in a crowd; abound. 2. to be crowded; teem. 3. to collect, rise, and fly from the hive: said of bees. 4. to climb a tree, mast, etc. by grasping it with the arms and legs alternately; shin [up]: *n.* 1. a large number of bees with a queen, leaving a hive to start a new colony. 2. a hive of bees. 3. a crowd or multitude in motion. —**swarm'er,** *n.*

swarth·y (swôr'*thi*, 'thi), *adj.* **swarth'i·er, swarth'i·est,** dark-skinned. —**swarth'i·ness,** *n.*

swash (swäsh, swôsh), *n.* a dashing or splashing of water, or the sound of this: *v.i.* to dash or splash water about.

swash·buck·ler ('buk·lēr), *n.* a swaggering swordsman or adventurer; blustering braggart. —**swash'buck·ling,** *n. & adj.*

swash·ing ('ing), *adj.* 1. swaggering; swashbuckling. 2. splashing or dashing. —**swash'ing·ly,** *adv.*

swas·ti·ka (swäs'ti·kȧ), *n.* 1. an ancient ornament, still used as a design, consisting of a cross with arms of equal length bent in a right angle 2. this design with the arms bent clockwise: used as a Nazi emblem.

swat (swät), *v.t.* **swat'ted, swat'ting,** [Informal], to hit sharply; slap; smack: *n.* [Informal], a sharp hit, as with a swatter or bat.

swatch (swäch), *n.* a sample piece of cloth or other material.

swath (swäth, swôth), *n.* 1. a line or ridge of grass or grain as cut down by the mower. 2. the sweep of a scythe or other mowing device in mowing.

swathe (swä*th*), *v.t.* **swathed, swath'ing,** 1. to wrap up in a bandage or strips of cloth. 2. to enclose or envelop: *n.* a bandage or wrapping.

swat·ter (swät'ēr), *n.* a device with which to swat flies, as a piece of wire mesh at the end of a stick: also **fly swatter.**

sway (swä), *v.i.* 1. to cause to move to and fro. 2. to influence or cause to swerve: *v.i.* 1. to incline to one side; veer. 2. to swing or move to and fro. 3. to incline or be drawn as in opinion or judgment: *n.* 1. a movement to the side; swinging, fluctuation, etc. 2. influence or control. 3. sovereign rule, dominion, or authority.

sway·backed ('bakt), *adj.* having an abnormal sagging of the spine, as some horses. —**sway'back,** *n.*

swear (swer), *v.i.* **swore, sworn, swear'ing,** 1. to make a solemn declaration by appealing to God for the truth of what is affirmed. 2. to give evidence on oath. 3. to make a solemn promise; vow. 4. to use profane language; curse: *v.t.* 1. to utter or affirm on oath. 2. to administer a legal oath to. —**swear'er,** *n.*

swear·word ('wûrd), *n.* a profane or obscene word or phrase.

sweat (swet), *n.* 1. the salty liquid that exudes from the pores of the skin; perspiration. 2. toil; hard work. 3. exertion or exercise. 4. the act or condition of sweating or being sweated. 5. a condition of apprehension, eagerness, impatience, etc. 6. droplets of moisture collected on a surface: *v.i. & v.t.* **sweat or sweat'ed, sweat'ing,** 1. to exude or cause to exude a salty liquid through the pores of the skin; perspire. 2. to work hard or cause to work hard. 3. to collect or give forth (moisture) on a surface. —**sweat'i·ness,** *n.* —**sweat'y,** *adj.*

sweat·band ('band), *n.* a leather band inside a hat to absorb sweat from the brow.

sweat box, 1. a box in which hides, dried fruits, etc. are sweated. 2. a hot, confined place.

sweat·er ('ēr), *n.* 1. a person or thing that sweats. 2. an outer garment for the upper part of the body, knitted or crocheted and with or without sleeves.

sweat gland, any one of the very numerous, tiny, coiled glands in the skin that secrete sweat.

sweating sickness, a rapidly fatal disease characterized by fever and profuse sweating, epidemic in Europe in the 15th and 16th centuries.

sweat shirt, a heavy, usually long-sleeved, cotton jersey worn to absorb sweat while or after exercising.

sweat-shop ('shop), *n.* a place with poor working conditions, where employees are overworked and paid low wages.

Swede (swed), *n.* a native or inhabitant of Sweden.

Swe·den·bor·gi·an (swed-n-bôr'ji·ȧn), *n.* any one of the followers of Emanuel Swedenborg (1688-1772), Swedish mystic and religious philosopher, founder of the Church of the New Jerusalem. —**Swe·den·bor'gi·an·ism,** *n.*

Swed·ish (swe'dish), *adj.* of Sweden, a country of northern Europe, its people, or language: *n.* the Germanic language of the Swedes.

sweep (swep), *v.t.* **swept, sweep'ing,** 1. to brush or clean (a floor, sidewalk, etc.) as with a broom. 2. to remove (dirt or debris) as with a broom. 3. to drive or carry along with force. 4. to touch in passing. 5. to pass swiftly over. 6. to win a complete victory: *v.i.* 1. to clean a floor or other surface as with a broom. 2. to pass steadily with speed, force, and stateliness. 3. to extend in a wide curve or long line: *n.* 1. the act of sweeping. 2. range; compass. 3. extent, as of land. 4. a wide or gentle curve. 5. a steady, sweeping movement. 6. the extent of a stroke. 7. a long oar. 8. one whose work is sweeping. 9. a complete victory or success. —**sweep'er,** *n.* —**sweep'ing,** *adj.*

sweep·ings ('ingz), *n.pl.* things swept up, as dirt or debris swept up from a floor.

sweep·stakes ('stāks), *n., pl.* **-stakes,** 1. a lottery in which each bettor puts money in a fund which is awarded to the winner or winners of a horse race. 2. the race. 3. the prize or prizes won. 4. any one of various other lotteries.

sweet (swet), *adj.* 1. pleasing to the senses, as smell, taste, sound, etc. 2. tasting like sugar.

---

3. soft and gentle. **4.** kind; obliging. **5.** not stale or sour. **6.** not salty or salted: *n.* a food that is sweet. —**sweet'ish,** *adj.* —**sweet'-ly,** *adv.* —**sweet'ness,** *n.*

sweet alyssum, a short garden plant with small spikes of tiny flowers.

sweet bay, 1. a North American magnolia with fragrant white flowers. **2.** same as laurel.

sweet-bread ('bred), *n.* the thymus or sometimes the pancreas of an animal, especially the calf or lamb, as used for food.

sweet-bri-er, sweet-bri-ar ('brī-ẽr), *n.* same as eglantine.

sweet cherry, a European wild cherry with small, black fruit that is very sweet: many varieties have been derived from it.

sweet clover, any one of a genus of leguminous plants with small flowers and leaflets in groups of three.

sweet corn, 1. Indian corn eaten as a vegetable in the unripe stage, when it is sweet and milky. **2.** an ear of this corn.

sweet-en ('n), *v.t.* **1.** to make sweet or sweeter, as with sugar. **2.** to make pleasant or agreeable.

sweet-en-er (-ẽr), *n.* a substance used to sweeten foods, especially a synthetic substance such as saccharin.

sweet-flag (swēt'flag), *n.* an aromatic marsh plant with sword-shaped leaves; calamus.

sweet-heart ('härt), *n.* one who is beloved; lover.

sweet-meat ('mēt), *n.* a sweet food made with sugar, honey, or the like; confection or candy.

sweet oil, any mild, edible oil, such as olive oil.

sweet pea, a climbing plant with fragrant flowers of various colors.

sweet pepper, 1. a red pepper with a bell-shaped, mild fruit. **2.** the fruit.

sweet potato, 1. a twining vine of tropical America, bearing purplish flowers. **2.** the thick, fleshy, orange root of this plant, eaten as a vegetable.

sweet-talk ('tôk), *v.t.* & *v.i.* [Informal], to flatter; cajole.

sweet tooth, [Informal], a craving for sweet foods.

sweet wil-liam, sweet Wil-liam (wil'yŭm), a perennial plant of the pink family, with flat clusters of showy, fragrant flowers.

swell (swel), *v.i.* & *v.i.* **swelled, swelled** or **swol'len, swell'ing, 1.** to expand or puff up because of pressure from within. **2.** to increase in bulk, intensity, force, etc. **3.** to bulge. **4.** to fill (*with* pride, indignation, etc.): *n.* **1.** a gradual increase of sound; crescendo. **2.** a large, rolling wave. **3.** a part that swells; bulge, curve, etc. **4.** a gradual elevation of land; rounded hill. **5.** [Informal], *a*) a distinguished person; *b*) one who is stylishly dressed: *adj.* **1.** [Informal], stylish. **2.** [Slang], excellent.

swell-fish ('fish), *n.*, *pl.* -**fish,** -**fish-es,** any one of a number of fishes that can expand the body; globefish, puffer, etc.

swell-head ('hed), *n.* one who is vain or conceited. —**swell'head-ed,** *adj.* —**swell'head-ed-ness,** *n.*

swell-ing ('ing), *n.* **1.** an expansion; increase in size or volume. **2.** a part of the body that is abnormally swollen.

swel-ter (swel'tẽr), *v.i.* to feel oppressed and sweat profusely from great heat.

swel-ter-ing (-ing), *adj.* **1.** suffering from great heat. **2.** sultry; oppressive. Also **swel'try** ('tri). —**swel'ter-ing-ly,** *adv.*

swept (swept), past tense and past participle of sweep.

swept-back ('bak), *adj.* slanting backward, as the wings of an aircraft.

swerve (swûrv), *v.i.* & *v.i.* swerved, swerv'ing, to turn aside from a straight line or course, or from a resolution, duty, etc.; deviate: *n.* the act of swerving. —**swerv'er,** *n.*

swift (swift), *adj.* **1.** moving far in a short time; rapid; quick. **2.** sudden: *adv.* in a swift manner: *n.* **1.** a swift-flying bird related to the swallows. **2.** a kind of North American lizard. **3.** a cylinder in a carding machine. —**swift'ly,** *adv.* —**swift'ness,** *n.*

swift-er (swif'tẽr), *n.* any one of various ropes used on shipboard to fasten a sail, tighten bars in a capstan, etc.

swig (swig), *v.i.* & *v.i.* swigged, swig'ging, [Informal], to gulp; swallow in long drafts: *n.* [Informal], a long, deep draft, especially of liquor. —**swig'ger,** *n.*

swill (swil), *v.t.* & *v.i.* **1.** to drink greedily or grossly. **2.** to feed swill to (hogs, etc.): *n.* **1.** garbage. **2.** garbage mixed with liquid as feed for hogs.

swim (swim), *v.i.* swam, swum, swim'ming, **1.** to float on or in water or other liquid. **2.** to move progressively in the water by movements of the arms, legs, fins, etc. **3.** to glide smoothly. **4.** to overflow. **5.** to be dizzy. **6.** to appear to whirl: *v.t.* to swim across or in: *n.* **1.** the act or a period of swimming. **2.** a distance swum. **3.** a gas-filled sac in some fishes, giving buoyancy: also **swim bladder.** —**swim'mer,** *n.* —**swim'ming,** *n.*

swimming hole, a deep place in a creek, river, etc. used for swimming.

swim-ming-ly ('ing-li), *adv.* in an easy, smooth manner and with success.

swim-suit ('sōōt), *n.* a garment worn for swimming.

swin-dle (swin'dl), *v.t.* & *v.i.* -dled, -dling, to cheat grossly and deliberately under false pretenses; defraud: *n.* an act of swindling; fraud; cheat. —**swin'dler,** *n.*

swine (swin), *n.*, *pl.* **swine, 1.** a hog or pig. **2.** a disgusting, contemptible person. —**swin'ish,** *adj.*

swing (swing), *v.i.* swung, swing'ing, **1.** to sway or move to and fro; oscillate. **2.** to walk or move along in a relaxed manner. **3.** to turn, as on a hinge or pivot. **4.** to be suspended; hang. **5.** to move in a curve or arc. **6.** [Informal], to be hanged. **7.** [Slang], to be sophisticated and uninhibited in seeking pleasure: *v.t.* **1.** to cause to move to and fro. **2.** to brandish. **3.** to cause to turn, as on a hinge or pivot. **4.** to suspend; hang. **5.** to move in a curve or arc. **6.** [Informal], to manage successfully: *n.* **1.** the act or state of swinging. **2.** the curve or arc through which something swings. **3.** a manner of swinging a baseball bat, golf club, etc. 4. a stroke or blow. 5. the progression of some activity. 6. a relaxed manner of walking. 7. rhythm, as in music or poetry. 8. a tour. 9. a seat hanging from ropes or chains, on which a person can swing to and fro for recreation. 10. a kind of jazz music marked by strong rhythms.

swinge (swinj), *v.t.* swinged, swinge'ing, [Archaic], to punish by whipping or thrashing.

swing-er (swing' gĕr), *n.* 1. one that swings. 2. [Slang], one who is sophisticated and uninhibited in seeking pleasure.

swin-gle (swing'gl), *v.t.* -gled, -gling, to clean (flax or hemp) by beating or scraping: *n.* 1. the part of a flail that strikes the grain; swiple. 2. a flat, wooden tool for cleaning flax or hemp by beating or scraping.

swin-gle-tree (-trē), *n.* same as singletree.

swing shift, [Informal], a work shift from midafternoon until about midnight.

swink (swingk), *v.i.* [Archaic], to toil; drudge.

swipe (swip), *n.* [Informal], a vigorous, sweeping blow: *v.t.* swiped, swip'ing, 1. [Informal], to hit with a sweeping blow: 2. [Slang], to steal.

swi-ple, **swip-ple** (swip'l), *n.* the part of a flail that strikes the grain in threshing.

swirl (swûrl), *v.i.* & *v.t.* to move or cause to move along or around with a whirling motion: *n.* 1. a whirling motion. 2. a whirl; eddy. 3. a curl or twist.

swish (swish), *v.i.* 1. to make a rustling sound, as a silk skirt. 2. to move through the air with a sharp, hissing sound, as a stick being swung: *v.t.* 1. to cause to swish. 2. to whip or flog: *n.* a swishing sound or movement.

Swiss (swis), *adj.* of Switzerland, a country in central Europe, or its people: *n.*, *pl.* **Swiss**, a native or inhabitant of Switzerland.

Swiss cheese, a hard, pale-yellow cheese made with skim milk and having many large holes.

Swiss steak, a cut of round steak pounded with flour, browned, and cooked by braising.

switch (swich), *n.* 1. a thin, flexible rod used for whipping. 2. a device for shifting a railroad train from one track to another. 3. a device for opening, closing, or redirecting an electric circuit. 4. a change or shift. 5. a tress of long hair used as part of a woman's coiffure: *v.t.* 1. to lash or flog. 2. to shunt (a train) from one track to another. 3. to swing sharply; lash. 4. to change or shift. 5. to turn (an electric appliance, lamp, etc.) *off* or *on* by operating a switch. 6. [Informal], to exchange: *v.i.* to shift. —switch'er, *n.*

switch-back ('bak), *n.* 1. a road or railroad that follows a zigzag course on a steep incline. 2. in England, a roller coaster.

switch-blade knife ('blād'), a large pocketknife with a spring-held blade that is released when a button on the handle is pushed.

switch-board ('bôrd), *n.* a board or panel with a number of switches for connecting or disconnecting the electric circuits of a system, as of a telephone exchange.

switch-hit-ter ('hit-ĕr), *n.* a baseball player who can bat either left-handed or right-handed.

swiv-el (swiv'l), *n.* a fastening or coupling device that allows the parts attached to it to turn freely; especially, a chain link with two parts, one of which fits below the bolt head of the other and rotates freely: *v.i.* & *v.t.* -eled or -elled, -el-ing or -el-ling, to turn or pivot on or as on a swivel.

swiz-zle stick (swiz'l), a small rod, as of plastic, for stirring mixed drinks.

swol-len (swō'lĕn), alternate past participle of swell: *adj.* enlarged or distended by swelling; bulging.

swoon (swoōn), *v.i.* 1. to faint. 2. to exhibit rapture, especially in a theatrical way: *n.* the act or an instance of swooning. — swoon'er, *n.* —swoon'ing-ly, *adv.*

swoop (swoōp), *v.t.* to snatch (*up*), as prey: *v.i.* to pounce or sweep down through the air, as a bird of prey in hunting: *n.* the act of swooping.

sword (sôrd), *n.* 1. a hand weapon with a long, keen blade for cutting or thrusting, that is set in a hilt. 2. this weapon as an emblem of military power, war, or vengeance. — sword'like, *adj.*

sword cane, a hollow cane which conceals a sword or dagger.

sword dance, a dance performed, especially by men, over bare swords laid in a cross on the ground.

sword-fish ('fish), *n.*, *pl.* -fish, -fish-es, a large ocean food fish with the bone of the upper jaw extended into a swordlike process.

sword knot, a loop of ribbon, gold braid, or leather attached to the hilt of a sword.

sword-play ('plā), *n.* the art or skill of using a sword in fencing or fighting.

swords-man (sôrdz'mån), *n.*, *pl.* -men, one who fences or fights with a sword, especially skillfully.

swore (swôr), past tense of swear.

sworn (swôrn), past participle of swear: *adj.* pledged or bound by an oath.

swum (swum), past participle of swim.

swung (swung), past participle and past tense of swing.

syb-a-rite (sib'å-rīt), *n.* a self-indulgent person who enjoys luxury and idle pleasure. —syb-a-rit'ic (-rit'ik), *adj.*

syc-a-mine (sik'å-min, -mīn), *n.* a tree mentioned in the Bible (Luke *xvii*, 6), believed to be a kind of mulberry.

syc-a-more (sik'å-môr), *n.* 1. a maple tree with yellow flowers, of Asia and Europe. 2. an American tree with bark that comes off in patches: also called plane (*tree*).

sy-cee (sī'sē'), *n.* formerly, silver cast into small ingots and used in China as currency.

sy-co-ni-um (sī-kō'ni-ûm), *n.*, *pl.* -ni-a (-å), a multiple fruit on which many flowers are borne on a hollow, fleshy receptacle, as of the fig.

syc-o-phant (sik'ô-fånt), *n.* one who seeks favors by fawning on wealthy or influential people; servile flatterer. —syc'o-phan-cy, *n.*

sy-co-sis (si-kō'sis), *n.* an inflammatory disease of the hair follicles, especially of the beard, characterized by pustules and papules.

ŏ in dragon, ōō in crude, oo in wool, u in cup, ū in cure, ū in turn, û in focus, oi in boy, ou in house, th in thin, th in sheathe, g in get, j in joy, y in yet.

sy·e·nite (sī'ē-nīt), *n.* a granular, igneous rock composed chiefly of feldspar, with hornblende and some silicates. —**sy·e·nit·ic** (-nit'ik), *adj.*

syl·lab·ic (si-lab'ik), *adj.* 1. of or consisting of a syllable or syllables. 2. pronounced with the syllables distinct. —**syl·lab'i·cal·ly,** *adv.*

syl·lab·i·cate (si-lab'i-kāt), *v.t.* -cat·ed, -cat·ing, same as **syllabify.** —**syl·lab·i·ca'tion,** *n.*

syl·lab·i·fy (si-lab'i-fī), *v.t.* -fied, -fy·ing, to divide or form into syllables. —**syl·lab·i·fi·ca'tion,** *n.*

syl·la·ble (sil'ȧ-bl), *n.* 1. a word or part of a word that can be uttered distinctly by a single effort of the voice. 2. one or more letters written or printed to represent such an element of speech.

syl·la·bub (sil'ȧ-bub), *n.* a frothy drink or dessert of sweetened milk or cream mixed with wine or cider.

syl·la·bus (sil'ȧ-bùs), *n., pl.* -bus·es, -bi (-bī), a summary or list of the main points of a course of study.

syl·lo·gism (sil'ō-jizm), *n.* an argument stated in logical form, with two premises from which a conclusion is reached. —**syl·lo·gis'tic,** *adj.* —**syl·lo·gis'ti·cal·ly,** *adv.*

sylph (silf), *n.* 1. an imaginary being inhabiting the air; fairy. 2. a graceful, slender girl or woman.

syl·van (sil'vȧn), *adj.* 1. of, pertaining to, inhabiting, or growing in the woods or forest. 2. wooded. 3. shady.

syl·vite (sil'vīt), *n.* native potassium chloride, used as a source of potash for fertilizers.

sym·bi·o·sis (sim-bi-ō'sis, -bi-), *n.* 1. in *Biology,* the more or less permanent living together of two dissimilar organisms, usually to their mutual advantage. 2. a kind of mutual interdependence between persons or groups. —**sym·bi·ot'ic** (-ot'ik), *adj.*

sym·bol (sim'bl), *n.* 1. something that represents something else; especially, an object that stands for something abstract; emblem. 2. a mark, printed character, abbreviation, etc. used to represent a process, object, quantity, etc., as in chemistry, mathematics, or music. —**sym·bol'ic** (-bol'ik), **sym·bol'i·cal,** *adj.* —**sym·bol'i·cal·ly,** *adv.*

sym·bol·ism (-izm), *n.* 1. representation by symbols. 2. a system of symbols. 3. symbolic meaning. 4. the theories and practices of a school of French and Belgian artists and authors of the late 19th century, who attempted to express emotions or ideas through symbolic words, objects, images, etc.

sym·bol·ist (-ist), *n.* 1. one who uses symbols. 2. a student or expert in interpreting symbols. 3. one who practices symbolism, as in art or literature. —**sym·bol·is'tic,** *adj.* —**sym·bol·is'ti·cal·ly,** *adv.*

sym·bol·ize (-īz), *v.t.* -ized, -iz·ing, 1. to be a symbol of; stand for. 2. to represent by symbols: *v.i.* to use symbols. —**sym·bol·i·za'tion,** *n.* —**sym'bol·iz·er,** *n.*

sym·bol·o·gy (sim-bol'ō-ji), *n.* 1. the art of expressing or representing by symbols. 2. the study or interpretation of symbols.

sym·met·al·lism (sim-met'l-izm), *n.* a system of coinage in which the unit of currency is a combination of two or more metals.

sym·met·ri·cal (si-met'ri-kl), *adj.* 1. characterized by symmetry; well-proportioned; regular in form. 2. in *Botany,* divisible into two similar parts by a plane passing through the center. 3. in *Chemistry,* having a regular pattern repeated in the structure of a compound. 4. in *Medicine,* having the same effect on corresponding parts of the body, as some diseases. Also **sym·met'ric.** —**sym·met'ri·cal·ly,** *adv.*

sym·me·trize (sim'ē-trīz), *v.t.* -trized, -triz·ing, to make symmetrical. —**sym·me·tri·za'tion,** *n.*

sym·me·try (sim'ē-tri), *n., pl.* -tries, 1. the due proportion of the several parts of a body to each other. 2. similarity of size, form, and arrangement on opposite sides of a line, axis, point, etc. 3. balance or harmony of form resulting from this.

sym·pa·thet·ic (sim-pȧ-thet'ik), *adj.* 1. of, showing, or feeling sympathy; compassionate. 2. sharing one's feelings, tastes, etc.; congenial. 3. showing approval. —**sym·pa·thet'i·cal·ly,** *adv.*

sym·pa·thize (sim'pȧ-thīz), *v.i.* -thized, -thiz·ing, 1. to feel or express sympathy; be compassionate. 2. to have a mutual feeling with another. —**sym'pa·thiz·er,** *n.*

sym·pa·thy (sim'pȧ-thi), *n., pl.* -thies, 1. a mutual feeling of pleasure, pain, etc. 2. harmony; accord. 3. a mutual liking or understanding. 4. a sharing of another's troubles; pity; compassion.

symphonic poem, a musical composition for a symphony orchestra that interprets a poetic story or concept in music: it is free in form and not divided into movements: also called *tone poem.*

sym·pho·ny (sim'fō-ni), *n., pl.* -nies, 1. harmony of sounds, especially of musical instruments. 2. harmony of any kind. 3. a long composition for a full orchestra, having several movements. 4. a large orchestra of wind, string, and percussion instruments: also **symphony orchestra.** 5. [Informal], a symphony concert. —**sym·phon'ic** (-fon'ik), *adj.* —**symphon'i·cal·ly,** *adv.*

sym·phy·sis (sim'fi-sis), *n., pl.* -ses (-sēz), 1. the union of two or more bones of the body by growing together or by cartilage, as the sacrum and ilium. 2. the line of fusion or cartilage of such bones. 3. a coalescence of parts of a plant. —**sym·phys'i·al** (-fiz'i-ȧl), *adj.*

sym·po·si·ac (sim-pō'zi-ak), *adj.* of or suitable for a symposium.

sym·po·si·um (sim-pō'zi-ùm), *n., pl.* -si·ums, -si·a (-ȧ), 1. in ancient Greece, a drinking party, with intellectual discussion. 2. a gathering or conference for a serious discussion of some subject. 3. an article, as in a magazine or journal, in which several writers express their views on some given topic.

symp·tom (simp'tȯm), *n.* 1. an indication or sign of something. 2. in *Medicine,* a condition, change in bodily function, or the like that accompanies or is caused by some disease, and serves as a sign of it. —**symp·to·mat'ic** (-tȯ-mat'ik), *adj.*

---

a in cap, ā in cane, ä in father, ȧ in abet, e in met, ē in be, ē in baker, ė in regent, i in pit, ī in fine, i in manifest, o in hot, ô in horse, ō in bone,

symp·tom·a·tize ('tŏ-mä-tīz), *v.t.* -tized, -tiz·ing, to be a symptom or sign of: also symp'-tom·ize.

symp·tom·a·tol·o·gy (simp-tŏ-mä-tol'ŏ-ji), *n.* 1. the study of symptoms. 2. symptoms of disease, collectively. 3. all of the symptoms of a given disease or patient.

syn-, a prefix signifying *with, together, at the same time*: it becomes *sym-* before *p, b,* and *m*; *syl-* before *l*; and *sys-* before *s* and aspirate *h*.

syn·a·gogue (sin'ä-gäg, -gŏg), *n.* 1. a religious assembly of Jews for worship and study. 2. a building or place for this. —syn·a·gog'al, *adj.*

syn·a·loe·pha, syn·a·le·pha (sin-ä-lē'fä), *n.* a blending into one syllable of two vowels of adjacent syllables, usually by elision.

syn·apse (si·naps'), *n.* the point of contact where nerve impulses are passed from one neuron to another.

syn·ar·thro·sis (sin-är-thrō'sis), *n., pl.* -ses ('sēz), any one of the immovable articulations of bones in the body.

syn·carp (sin'kärp), *n.* a fused cluster of the ovaries of several flowers, forming a fruit such as the pineapple: also called *multiple fruit.*

syn·car·pous (sin-kär'pŭs), *adj.* 1. of or pertaining to a syncarp. 2. made up of carpels growing together. —syn'car·py, *n.*

syn·chro·nism (sing'krŏ-nizm), *n.* 1. a concurrence in time of two or more events. 2. a tabular arrangement of contemporary historical events. —syn·chro·nis'tic, *adj.*

syn·chro·nize (sing'krŏ-niz), *v.t.* -nized, -niz·ing, 1. to set, as clocks so as to agree or a flash bulb and camera so as to be activated at the same time. 2. to show or to be simultaneous; assign to the same time or period in history. 3. in *Motion Pictures,* to adjust (the picture and sound of a film) so as to come together perfectly: *v.i.* 1. to happen simultaneously. 2. to move at the same rate or rhythm. —syn·chro·ni·za'tion, *n.* —syn'chro·niz·er, *n.*

syn·chro·nous (-nŭs), *adj.* 1. happening at the same time; simultaneous. 2. having the same rate or rhythm. —syn'chro·nous·ly, *adv.* —syn'chro·nous·ness, *n.*

syn·chro·tron (sing'krŏ-tron), *n.* a machine for accelerating charged particles to very high energies.

syn·cline (sing'klin), *n.* a curved fold of stratified rock with the central part down and the sides rising upward and outward in opposite directions: opposed to *anticline.* —syn·cli·nal (sin-klī'nl), *adj.*

syn·co·pate (sing'kŏ-pāt), *v.t.* -pat·ed, -pat·ing, 1. to shorten a word by syncope. 2. in *Music,* to shift a regular accent by continuing (a tone) from an unaccented beat through the next accented beat. —syn·co·pa'tion, *n.* —syn'co·pa·tor, *n.*

syn·co·pe (sing'kŏ-pi), *n.* 1. the omission of letters or sounds from the middle of a word. 2. faintness or loss of consciousness, caused by a decrease of blood supply to the brain. —syn'co·pal, *adj.*

syn·cre·tism (sing'krĕ-tizm), *n.* 1. an attempt to

compromise or reconciliate different religious or philosophical beliefs or practices. 2. the merging of two or more differently inflected linguistic forms into one. —syn·cret·ic (sin-kret'ik), syn·cre·tis·tic (sing-krĕ-tis'tik), *adj.* —syn'cre·tist, *n.*

syn·cre·tize (sing'krĕ-tiz), *v.t. & v.i.* -tized, -tiz·ing, to reconcile, compromise, or merge.

syn·dac·tyl (sin-dak'tl), *adj.* having two or more digits united or partly united, as by webbing: *n.* a syndactyl bird or mammal.

syn·des·mo·sis (sin-des-mō'sis), *n., pl.* -ses ('sēz), the articulation of bones by ligaments.

syn·det·ic (sin-det'ik), *adj.* serving to connect or unite; connective.

syn·dic (sin'dik), *n.* 1. any one of various government officials, as a chief magistrate or municipal official. 2. [British], a business agent or manager, especially of a university.

syn·di·cal·ism (sin'di-kl-izm), *n.* a movement of trade unionism advocating federations of labor unions controlling the means of production and distribution.

syn·di·cate (sin'di-kit), *n.* 1. a council of syndics. 2. a group of individuals or organizations associated for a project requiring much capital. 3. any group, as of criminals, set up to control or further some enterprise. 4. an organization that sells features or articles to many newspapers or periodicals: *v.t.* (-kāt), -cat·ed, -cat·ing, 1. to combine or form into a syndicate. 2. to control or manage as a syndicate. 3. to sell (a feature, article, etc.) through a syndicate: *v.i.* to form a syndicate. —syn·di·ca'tion, *n.* —syn'di·ca·tor, *n.*

syn·drome (sin'drōm), *n.* a number of symptoms that together are characteristic of a certain disease or condition.

syne (sin), *prep. & conj. & adv.* [Scottish], since; ago.

syn·ec·do·che (si-nek'dŏ-ki), *n.* a figure of speech in which the whole is used for a part, or the general for the particular, or the reverse of either of these.

syn·er·gism (sin'ër-jizm), *n.* 1. the joint action, as of drugs, greater in total effect than the sum of their effects if taken separately. 2. a combined or cooperative action of parts of the body, as muscles working together. —syn·er·gis'tic, *adj.* —syn·er·gis'ti·cal·ly, *adv.*

syn·er·gy (sin'ër-ji), *n.* joint action or force; synergism. —syn·er·gic (sin-ŭr'jik), *adj.*

syn·e·sis (sin'ĕ-sis), *n.* a grammatical construction in which the sense is considered more important than strict syntactical agreement or reference.

syn·gen·e·sis (sin-jen'ĕ-sis), *n.* sexual reproduction. —syn·ge·net·ic (sin-jĕ-net'ik), *adj.*

syn·od (sin'ŏd), *n.* a council of churches or church officials; ecclesiastical council. —syn'od·al (-l), syn·od·i·cal (si-nod'i-kl), *adj.*

syn·oe·cious (si-nē'shŭs), *adj.* in *Botany,* having male and female flowers in the same inflorescence.

syn·o·nym (sin'ŏ-nim), *n.* a word having the same or nearly the same meaning as another word in the language. —syn·on·y·mous (si-non'i-mŭs), *adj.*

---

syn·on·y·my (si-non'l-mi), *n.* 1. the quality of being synonymous. 2. *pl.* **-mies**, a list of synonyms.

syn·op·sis (si-nop'sis), *n., pl.* **-ses** ('sēz), 1. a brief, general view of some subject; summary. 2. an outline, as of the plot of a story.

syn·op·tic ('tik), *adj.* 1. giving a general view of the whole or principal parts of a thing. 2. [often S-], of or pertaining to the first three Gospels, thought of as having a common point of view. —**syn·op'ti·cal·ly,** *adv.*

syn·o·vi·a (si-nō'vi-ā), *n.* an albuminous fluid secreted in joints, tendon sheaths, and at articulation points where lubrication is necessary. —**syn·o'vi·al,** *adj.*

syn·o·vi·tis (sin-ō-vit'us), *n.* inflammation of a synovial membrane.

syn·tax (sin'taks), *n.* the branch of grammar dealing with the arrangement of words in a sentence and their relationship and organization. —**syn·tac·tic** (-tak'tik), **syn·tac'ti·cal,** *adj.* —**syn·tac'ti·cal·ly,** *adv.*

syn·the·sis (sin'thē-sis), *n., pl.* **-ses** (-sēz), 1. a combining of two or more elements or parts into a whole. 2. a whole made up of elements or parts combined. 3. in *Chemistry,* the combining of two or more elements, radicals, or simple compounds to form a complex compound.

syn·the·size (-sīz), *v.t.* **-sized, -siz·ing,** 1. to form a whole from separate parts. 2. in *Chemistry,* to combine (elements, radicals, or simple compounds) to produce a complex compound, as distinguished from producing a substance by extraction or refinement.

syn·the·siz·er (-ēr), *n.* an electronic musical instrument with amplifiers, oscillators, etc. that operate together to produce sounds different from those of ordinary musical instruments.

syn·thet·ic (sin-thet'ik), *adj.* 1. of or having to do with synthesis. 2. produced by chemical synthesis, rather than of natural origin. 3. artificial; not genuine. Also **syn·thet'i·cal:** *n.* a substance produced by chemical synthesis.

syn·ton·ic (sin-ton'ik), *adj.* psychologically in harmony with one's environment.

syph·i·lis (sif'ǐ-lis), *n.* an infectious venereal disease, caused by a spirochete: it may be congenital or transmitted by sexual intercourse. —**syph·i·lit'ic,** *adj. & n.*

syph·i·loid (-loid), *adj.* resembling syphilis.

sy·phon (sī'fŏn), *n. & v.t.* same as **siphon.**

Syr·i·an (sir'i-ǎn), *adj.* of or pertaining to Syria, a country at the eastern end of the Mediterranean, or its people, language, etc.: *n.* a native or inhabitant of Syria.

sy·rin·ga (si-ring'gā), *n.* 1. a small genus of ornamental shrubs, the lilacs. 2. a shrub with fragrant white blossoms: also called *mock orange.*

sy·ringe (si-rinj'), *n.* a device consisting of a tube connected with a rubber bulb or piston by which liquids may be drawn in and then ejected in a stream or spray: used to draw fluids from or inject fluids into body cavities, wounds, etc.: *v.t.* **-ringed', -ring'ing,** to wash, inject, etc. by using a syringe.

syr·inx (sir'ingks), *n., pl.* **sy·rin·ges** (si-rin'jēz), **syr'inx·es,** the vocal organ of a songbird.

syr·phus fly (sûr'fŭs), a large fly, widely distributed, somewhat resembling the wasp or bee: the larvae feed on aphids and plants.

syr·up (sir'ŭp, sûr'-), *n.* 1. a solution made by boiling sugar in water, often flavored. 2. any sweet, thick liquid. 3. the liquid obtained in processing cane sugar. 4. in *Pharmacy,* a sugar solution used as a vehicle for medication. —**syr'up·y,** *adj.*

sys·tal·tic (sis-tôl'tik, -tal'-), *adj.* contracting and dilating alternately, as heart movements.

sys·tem (sis'tĕm), *n.* 1. a combination or arrangement of parts to form a whole. 2. an orderly arrangement according to some common principles. 3. a collection of rules and principles. 4. a plan or method of doing something. 5. a number of bodily organs, or the body itself, functioning as a unit.

sys·tem·at·ic (sis-tĕ-mat'ik), *adj.* 1. methodical; according to a system. 2. making up a system. Also **sys·tem·at'i·cal.** —**sys·tem·at'i·cal·ly,** *adv.*

sys·tem·at·ics ('iks), *n.* 1. a method of classification, such as taxonomy. 2. the science or work of classification.

sys·tem·a·tism (sis'tĕm-ā-tizm), *n.* the process or work of systematizing. —**sys'tem·a·tist,** *n.*

sys·tem·a·tize (-tīz), *v.t.* **-tized, -tiz·ing,** to arrange according to a system; make systematic. —**sys·tem·a·ti·za'tion,** *n.* —**sys'tem·a·tiz·er,** *n.*

sys·tem·ic (sis-tem'ik), *adj.* of or affecting an entire organism or bodily system: *n.* any one of a number of insecticides that are absorbed into plant tissues, which are then poisonous to insects and other animals that feed on them. —**sys·tem'i·cal·ly,** *adv.*

sys·tem·ize (sis'tĕ-mīz), *v.t.* **-ized, -iz·ing,** same as **systematize.** —**sys'tem·i·za'tion,** *n.*

sys·to·le (sis'tō-li), *n.* 1. the rhythmical contraction of the heart in beating. 2. the shortening of a long syllable, as in Latin. —**sys·tol'ic** (-tol'ik), *adj.*

T

T, t (tē), *n.*, *pl.* **T's, t's. 1.** the twentieth letter of the English alphabet. **2.** the sound of this letter, as in *tag, little,* or *boot.* **3.** a type or impression of *T* or *t.*

T (tē), *adj.* shaped like *T*: *n.* an object shaped like *T.*

ta (tä), *interj.* [British Informal], thank you.

tab (tab), *n.* **1.** a small tag, strap, or flap fastened on something, used for hanging, pulling, etc. or for decoration. **2.** a small projection on a card or the page of a book for locating things quickly. **3.** [Informal], a bill or check, especially for total expenses. **4.** [Informal], close watch: only in the phrase **keep tab** (or **tabs**) **on**: *v.t.* **tabbed, tab'bing,** **1.** to select. **2.** to put a tab or tabs on.

tab·ard (tab'ērd), *n.* **1.** a loose garment or mantle worn over armor. **2.** a herald's coat, emblazoned with the arms of his lord or king. **3.** a short, heavy coat for rough weather, formerly worn by peasants.

Ta·bas·co (tā-bas'kō), *n.* a very hot, pungent sauce made from a variety of red pepper: a trademark.

tab·by (tab'i), *adj.* **1.** brindled. **2.** having a variegated or wavy appearance: *n., pl.* **-bies, 1.** a kind of wavy or watered silk. **2.** a brown or gray cat with dark stripes. **3.** a pet cat, especially a female.

tab·er·nac·le (tab'ēr-nak-l), *n.* **1.** formerly, a temporary dwelling, movable residence, or tent. **2.** the human body considered to be the temporary dwelling place of the soul. **3.** [T-], *a)* the movable sanctuary carried by the Israelites in the wilderness; *b)* later, the Jewish Temple. **4.** a large house of worship. **5.** a receptacle near the back of an altar for consecrated elements of the Eucharist: *v.i.* **-led, -ling,** to sojourn; take up temporary residence.

ta·bes (tā'bēz), *n.* any gradual wasting away or atrophy of the body due to disease. **—ta·bet·ic** (tā-bet'ik), *adj.*

ta·bes·cent (tā-bes'nt), *adj.* wasting away; declining. **—ta·bes'cence,** *n.*

tabes dor·sa·lis (dôr-sā'lis, -sal'is), a disease of the nervous system, usually caused by syphilis of the spine, marked by loss of muscular control, sensory disturbances, etc.

tab·la·ture (tab'lā-choor), *n.* **1.** a system of musical notation for stringed instruments in which the lines represent the strings, and the notes or letters on them represent the finger placement. **2.** [Archaic], a painting, design, etc. on walls or ceiling, a table, or other flat surface.

ta·ble (tā'bl), *n.* **1.** originally, a tablet. **2.** a piece of furniture with a flat, smooth top supported by legs. **3.** a group of people seated around a table for a meal. **4.** the food served. **5.** same as **tableland.** **6.** a collection of numbers or facts methodically arranged. **7.** an orderly list, as an index, syllabus, etc. **8.** any of various flat surfaces, as the upper facet of a gem: *adj.* of, pertaining to, or for use on a table: *v.t.* **-bled, -bling, 1.** to put on a table. **2.** to put aside (a proposal, bill, etc.) for future consideration.

tab·leau (tab'lō, ta-blō'), *n., pl.* **-leaux** ('lōz, -blōz'), a striking and vivid representation.

tab·leau vi·vant (ta-blō vi-vän'), *pl.* **tab·leaux vi·vants'** ('-blō vi-vän'), [French], a living picture; a picturesque representation by one or more silent and motionless performers suitably costumed and posed.

ta·ble·cloth (tā'bl-klôth), *n.* a cloth used to cover a table, especially for a meal.

ta·ble d'hôte (tā'bl-dōt'), *pl.* **ta'bles d'hôte'** ('blz), a complete meal, with courses predetermined, served at a restaurant or hotel dining room at a fixed price.

ta·ble-hop (tā'bl-hop), *v.i.* **-hopped, -hop·ping,** [Informal], to leave one's own table and talk to people at various other tables in a restaurant or nightclub. **—ta'ble-hop·per,** *n.*

ta·ble·land (-land), *n.* a high, flat stretch of country; plateau.

ta·ble·spoon (-spōōn), *n.* **1.** a large spoon used for serving food at table. **2.** a spoon used as a unit of measure in cooking, equal to three teaspoonfuls. **3.** as much as a tablespoon will hold: also **ta'ble·spoon·ful** (-fool), *pl.* **-fuls.**

tab·let (tab'lit), *n.* **1.** a small, flat piece of metal, ivory, wood, stone, etc. **2.** such a piece with an inscription; plaque. **3.** a set of sheets of paper glued together at one side, as for a writing pad. **4.** a small, compressed cake of some substance, as medicine, soap, etc.

table tennis, a game somewhat like tennis, played on a large table with a small hollow ball and paddles.

ta·ble·ware (tā'bl-wer), *n.* the dishes, glassware, and eating utensils used at meals.

tab·loid (tab'loid), *n.* **1.** [T-], a small tablet of medicine: a trademark. **2.** a newspaper, usually half the size of a regular newspaper page, with many pictures and, often, sensational treatment of news stories: *adj.* small; condensed.

ta·boo, ta·bu (ta-bōō'), *n.* **1.** among some peoples of the South Pacific, a sacred ban or prohibition put upon some persons or things, making them untouchable or unacceptable. **2.** the set of rules and rites governing this. **3.** any conventional social restriction: *adj.* **1.** prohibited by taboo. **2.** of or denoting certain words or terms considered improper and unacceptable by polite society: *v.t.* **1.** to put under taboo. **2.** to forbid or prohibit.

ta·bor, ta·bour (tā'bēr), *n.* a small drum, for-

ō in drag*o*n, ōō in cr*u*de, oo in w*oo*l, u in c*u*p, ū in c*u*re, ŭ in t*u*rn, ŭ in f*o*cus, oi in b*oy*, ou in h*ou*se, th in *th*in, th in shea*th*e, g in *g*et, j in *j*oy, y in *y*et.

737

merly beaten by a fife player to accompany his fifing: *v.i.* to beat on a tabor.

tab·o·ret, tab·ou·ret (tab'ẽr-it), *n.* 1. a small tabor. 2. a cushioned stool.

tab·o·rin (tab'ẽr-in), *n.* a small tabor played with only one stick: also **tab·o·rine'** (-ẽ-rēn').

tab·u·lar (tab'yŭ-lẽr), *adj.* 1. having the form of a table; flat. 2. set down, computed, or arranged in tables or columns. —**tab'u·lar·ly,** *adv.*

tab·u·late (-lāt), *v.t.* **-lat·ed, -lat·ing,** to set down or arrange in tables or columns. —**tab·u·la'tion,** *n.*

tab·u·la·tor (-ẽr), *n.* 1. a machine for making lists or tabulations from information recorded from punch cards. 2. a typewriter key for moving the carriage a set number of spaces.

tac·a·ma·hac (tak'ă-mă-hak), *n.* 1. a yellowish gum resin, with a strong odor used in incense and ointments. 2. any one of several trees from which this resin is obtained. Also **tac·a·ma·hac'a** ('ă), **tac'ma·hack.**

tach·i·na fly (tak'i-nă), a two-winged fly whose larvae are parasitic on caterpillars, beetles, etc.: also **tach'i·nid** (-nid), *n.*

ta·chis·to·scope (tă-kis'tō-skōp), *n.* an apparatus that exposes pictures, words, etc. briefly on a screen, used in memory tests or to increase reading speed. —**ta·chis·to·scop'ic** (-skōp'ik), *adj.*

ta·chom·e·ter (tă-kom'ē-tẽr), *n.* an instrument that indicates or measures the revolutions per minute of a revolving shaft, as in an engine.

tach·y-, a combining form meaning *swift, rapid.*

tach·y·car·di·a (tak-i-kär'di-ă), *n.* excessively rapid heartbeat.

tach·y·graph (tak'i-graf), *n.* 1. something written in tachygraphy. 2. one who is skilled in writing tachygraphy: also **ta·chyg·ra·pher** (ta-kig'ră-fẽr).

ta·chyg·ra·phy (ta-kig'ră-fi), *n.* an ancient system of shorthand, as of the early Greeks and Romans. —**tach·y·graph·ic** (tak-i-graf'ik), **tach·y·graph'i·cal,** *adj.*

ta·chym·e·ter (ta-kim'ē-tẽr), *n.* a surveyor's instrument for making determinations of elevation, distance, or the like.

tac·it (tas'it), *adj.* 1. implied, but not expressed openly. 2. silent; unspoken. —**tac'it·ly,** *adv.*

tac·i·turn (tas'i-tũrn), *adj.* habitually silent; not liking to talk. —**tac·i·tur'ni·ty,** *n.*

tack (tak), *n.* 1. a small, flat-headed nail. 2. a temporary stitch, as for holding seams or darts until they are sewed more securely. 3. the direction of a vessel in relation to the trim of her sails. 4. a change of a ship's direction. 5. a zigzag course. 6. a course of action. 7. foodstuff; food in general. 8. a horse's equipment: *v.t.* 1. to fasten with tacks. 2. to fasten slightly. 3. to attach. 4. to change the course of (a ship): *v.i.* 1. to tack a ship. 2. to zigzag. 3. to change courses suddenly. —**tack'er,** *n.*

tack·le (tak'l), *n.* 1. the running and rigging that operate a ship's sails. 2. apparatus consisting of pulleys and ropes for moving heavy weights. 3. implements or gear. 4. ei-

ther of two players in football stationed between the guard and end: *v.t.* **-led, -ling,** 1. to seize or take hold of. 2. to try to do, as something difficult; begin to deal with. 3. to harness (a horse). 4. in *Football,* to seize or throw down (the ball carrier). —**tack'ler,** *n.*

tack·y (tak'i), *adj.* **tack'i·er, tack'i·est,** 1. sticky, as paint, glue, etc. before completely dry. 2. [Informal], grubby or shabby in appearance. —**tack'i·ness,** *n.*

ta·co (tä'kō), *n., pl.* **-cos,** a folded tortilla filled with meat, shredded lettuce, etc. and fried.

tact (takt), *n.* delicate skill in saying and doing exactly what is suitable in given circumstances, especially in dealing with awkward situations without offending.

tact·ful ('fŭl), *adj.* having or exhibiting tact. —**tact'ful·ly,** *adv.* —**tact'ful·ness,** *n.*

tac·ti·cal (tak'ti-kl), *adj.* 1. of or pertaining to tactics, especially in naval or military maneuvers. 2. skillful and adroit in tactics. —**tac'ti·cal·ly,** *adv.*

tac·ti·cian (tak-tish'ŭn), *n.* one skilled in tactics.

tac·tics (tak'tiks), *n.pl.* 1. the science of disposing and maneuvering naval and military forces in action, especially in regard to short-range objectives. 2. maneuvers or actions taken according to this science. 3. any skillful procedures taken to gain an end.

tac·tile (tak'tl), *adj.* 1. perceptible to the touch; tangible. 2. of or related to the sense of touch. —**tac·til'i·ty** (-til'i-ti), *n.*

tact·less (takt'lis), *adj.* not having or exhibiting tact. —**tact'less·ly,** *adv.* —**tact'less·ness,** *n.*

tac·tu·al (tak'choo-wăl), *adj.* 1. of or pertaining to the organs or sense of touch. 2. causing a sensation of touch. —**tac'tu·al·ly,** *adv.*

tad (tad), *n.* a small child; especially, a little boy.

tad·pole (tad'pōl), *n.* the aquatic larva of a frog or toad, having gills and a tail.

tael (tāl), *n.* 1. formerly, a Chinese unit of money. 2. any one of various units of weight of eastern Asia.

tae·ni·a (tē'ni-ă), *n., pl.* **-ni·ae** (-ē), 1. an ancient Greek headband, ribbon, fillet, or the like. 2. a tapeworm.

tae·ni·a·cide (-sīd), *n.* a drug or preparation for destroying tapeworms.

tae·ni·a·sis (ti-ni'ă-sis), *n.* ill health due to tapeworms.

taf·fe·ta (taf'i-tă), *n.* a fine, firm, glossy fabric of silk, rayon, etc.

taff·rail (taf'rāl), *n.* the rail around a ship's stern.

taf·fy (taf'i), *n.* 1. a sugar or molasses candy which must be chewed. 2. [Old Slang], flattery.

taf·i·a, taf·fi·a (taf'i-ă), *n.* an inferior rum produced in the West Indies.

tag (tag), *n.* 1. a hard point, as of metal, at the end of a string or lace. 2. something small attached to another thing. 3. a piece of paper, metal, etc. attached to something for identification. 4. a name added on, as to a proper name, for identification or in contempt. 5. the final passage of a story, speech, etc. 6. a children's game in which a player designated as "it" pursues others in

---

a in *cap,* ä in *cane,* ä in *father,* â in *abet,* e in *met,* ē in *be,* ë in *baker,* ê in *regent,* i in *pit,* ï in *fine,* i in *manifest,* o in *hot,* ō in *horse,* ō in *bone,*

order to touch one of them and make the one touched "it." 7. a hanging part: *v.t.* tagged, tag'ging, 1. to fix a tag to; append or tack on. 2. to touch in the game of tag. 3. to pick out. 4. [Informal], to follow closely and persistently: *v.i.* [Informal], to follow closely (with *after, along*, etc.).

Ta-ga-log (tä-gä'log), *n.* 1. *pl.* -logs, -log, one of a Malayan people constituting the main group in the Philippine Islands. 2. the main native language of the Philippine Islands.

tag day, a day upon which contributions are publicly solicited for some charitable purpose, each contributor being pinned with a tag.

tag-ger (tag'ĕr), *n.* 1. one who or that which tags. 2. *pl.* very thin sheets of metal, usually tin-coated.

Ta-hi-tian (tä-hēsh'ûn), *adj.* of or pertaining to Tahiti, a French island in the South Pacific, or its inhabitants: *n.* a native or inhabitant of Tahiti.

tai-ga (tī'gä), *n.* the vast stretch of pine forests in Europe, Asia, and North America.

tail (tāl), *n.* 1. the end of the backbone of an animal's body, especially when forming a distinct and flexible part. 2. the hinder or inferior part of anything. 3. anything pendent. 4. one of the horizontal or vertical surfaces of an airplane placed near the rear. 5. the luminous appendage of the nucleus of a comet. 6. a limitation placed on inheritance. 7. *often pl.* the back side of a coin. 8. *pl.* [Informal], formal clothes for men. 9. [Informal], one who follows and watches another: *adj.* at or from the back end: *v.i.* [Informal], to pursue at a close proximity: *v.t.* 1. to supply with a tail. 2. to hang on like a tail. 3. to join (a brick, board, etc.) as to a wall (with *on* or *in*). 4. [Informal], to follow without the other being aware. —tail'less, *adj.*

tail-gate (tāl'gāt), *n.* a movable board at the rear of a cart, truck, etc.; also tail'board: *v.i. & v.t.* -gat-ed, -gat-ing, to follow (another vehicle) too closely.

tail-ing (tāl'ing), *n.* 1. the part of a projecting stone or brick inserted in a wall. 2. *pl.* refuse, as of ore.

tail-light ('līt), *n.* a red warning light on the back end of a vehicle.

tai-lor (tā'lĕr), *n.* one whose business is to make, change, or mend clothes: *v.t.* 1. to make or mend (garments, slipcovers, etc.). 2. to shape or change to suit a certain requirement: *v.i.* to work as a tailor.

tai-lor-bird (-bûrd), *n.* an Asian or African bird that stitches leaves together to hide its nest.

tai-lor-ing (-ing), *n.* 1. the work of a tailor. 2. the quality of something tailored.

tai-lor-made (-mād'), *adj.* 1. designating garments made by a tailor. 2. designating something shaped to fit a certain requirement. 3. designating closefitting garments.

tail-piece (tāl'pēs), *n.* 1. a piece added at the end; appendage. 2. an illustration or ornament put at the bottom of a page or end of a chapter. 3. a piece at the lower end of a violin, for holding the strings. 4. a short plank in a wall.

tail-pipe ('pīp), *n.* a pipe at the back end of a vehicle, for letting out exhaust fumes.

tail-spin ('spin), *n.* same as spin (*n.* 3).

taint (tānt), *n.* 1. corruption; disgrace. 2. infection. 3. [Obsolete], a spot or stain: *v.t.* 1. to imbue or impregnate with anything noxious; infect. 2. to corrupt: *v.i.* 1. to become corrupted. 2. to become infected.

take (tāk), *v.t.* took, tak'en, tak'ing, 1. to lay or seize hold of. 2. to catch. 3. to obtain; assume. 4. to receive mentally. 5. to capture, engage, or interest. 6. to choose. 7. to use. 8. to require. 9. to conduct or lead. 10. to transport. 11. to swallow. 12. to note or measure. 13. to make or perform (an action). 14. to purchase, rent, etc. 15. to join with (a group, etc., as in a disagreement). 16. to journey by means of. 17. to ponder. 18. to sit or stand in. 19. to draw from. 20. to select (a part). 21. to execute (a photograph, picture, etc.). 22. to be registered as a student of. 23. to be subjected to. 24. to enter into. 25. to agree to. 26. to incur. 27. to believe or imagine. 28. to experience. 29. to appropriate unlawfully. 30. to subtract. 31. [Slang], to deceive or swindle. 32. in *Grammar*, to be used with according to construction: *v.i.* 1. to obtain possession. 2. to proceed. 3. to be made to be taken (with *up, down, apart*, etc.). 4. to have the intended effect. 5. to please. 6. to start growing. 7. to get hold. 8. [Informal], to become (ill). 9. in *Law*, to receive title to property: *n.* 1. the act of taking. 2. the amount or quantity received or caught, as of fish. 3. [Slang], money received, as from the sale of tickets. 4. in *Printing*, the portion of copy given to a compositor to set at one time.

take-off (tāk'ôf), *n.* 1. the act of rising from the ground. 2. [Informal], a humorous or derisive imitation.

take-o-ver (ō'vĕr), *n.* the forcible seizure of power in a country, group, etc.

tak-er (tāk'ĕr), *n.* 1. one who takes, seizes, or captures. 2. one who accepts a bet.

ta-kin (tä'kin, tä'-), *n.* a Tibetan mammal resembling the goat.

tak-ing (tāk'ing), *adj.* 1. attractive; alluring; pleasing. 2. [Obsolete], infectious: *n.* 1. the act of gaining possession; seizure. 2. *pl.* receipts. 3. [British Informal], agitation.

tal-a-poin (tal'ä-poin), *n.* 1. a Buddhist monk. 2. a small, long-tailed West African monkey.

ta-la-ri-a (tä-ler'i-ä), *n.pl.* the small wings attached to the ankles of Mercury or Hermes.

talc (talk), *n.* 1. a hydrous silicate of magnesium, that is soft with a soapy feel, used to produce talcum powder. 2. same as talcum powder.

tal-cum powder (talk'ûm), a body and face powder produced from talc that has been pulverized and made pure.

tale (tāl), *n.* 1. a narrative or story; fable. 2. an anecdote. 3. malicious gossip. 4. an untruth. 5. [Archaic], a reckoning or the number reckoned.

tale-bear-er (tāl'ber-ĕr), *n.* a gossip; one who willfully and maliciously spreads scandal.

tal-ent (tal'ĕnt), *n.* 1. among the ancients, a weight, coin, or sum of money of varying

---

ô in drag*o*n, ōō in cr*u*de, oo in w*oo*l, u in c*u*p, ū in c*u*re, û in t*u*rn, ŭ in f*o*cus, oi in b*o*y, ou in h*ou*se, th in *th*in, th in shea*th*e, g in *g*et, j in *j*oy, y in *y*et.

value. 2. mental capacity; eminent ability; skill; cleverness. 3. a natural gift. 4. the artists collectively who have ability, skills, etc. in performing or creating. —tal'ent·ed, *adj.*

ta·les (tā'lēz), *n.* in *Law,* 1. persons called in to make up a jury deficiency. 2. a writ summoning jurors.

ta·les·man (tālz'mǎn, tā'lĭz-), *n., pl.* ta'les·men (-mĕn), one summoned on the panel of a jury.

tal·i·pot (tal'ǐ-pot), *n.* the gigantic fan palm of Ceylon and India.

tal·is·man (tal'ĭs·mǎn), *n., pl.* -mans, 1. a figure cut in metal or stone, supposed to possess magical virtues in averting evil, bringing good luck, etc.; amulet. 2. something supposed to produce an extraordinary effect; charm. —tal·is·man'ic, tal·is·man'i·cal, *adj.*

talk (tôk), *v.i.* 1. to utter words; speak; converse. 2. to show thoughts by making signs, etc. 3. to prattle. 4. to confer. 5. to report secrets: *v.t.* 1. to utter. 2. to make a subject of conversation. 3. to utilize when making utterances. 4. to bring into a particular state by talking: *n.* 1. the act of talking. 2. familiar conversation. 3. a colloquy; conference. 4. a subject of discourse. 5. a rumor. 6. an informal speech. 7. a specific form of speech; dialect.

talk·a·tive (tôk'ǎ-tiv), *adj.* addicted to much talking: also talk'y ('ĭ). —talk'a·tive·ness, *n.*

talk·ing (tôk'ing), *n.* the act of conversing: *adj.* that talks; loquacious.

talking book, an audio recording of a book, produced for the blind.

talk show, in *Radio & Television,* a program in which a host or hostess talks with guest celebrities, experts, etc.

talk·ing·to (tôk'ing-tōō), *n.* [Informal], a sharp reprimand.

tall (tôl), *adj.* 1. high in stature. 2. of a particular height. 3. [Informal], extravagant. 4. [Informal], lofty.

tall·boy (tôl'boi), *n.* [British], same as highboy.

tal·lit (tä-lēt', täl'ĭs), *n.* a tasseled shawl worn over the shoulders or head by Jewish men when at morning prayer.

tal·low (tal'ō), *n.* the solid fat produced from the animal fat of cattle, sheep, etc., used for candles, soap, etc.

tal·ly (tal'ĭ), *n., pl.* -lies, 1. originally, a stick notched to match another stick, used for keeping accounts. 2. an account; score. 3. anything on which an account is kept. 4. one thing made to match or suit another. 5. a label; tag: *v.t.* -lied, -ly·ing, 1. to put on a tally. 2. to count (usually with *up*). 3. to label. 4. [Archaic], to make correspond: *v.i.* 1. to make a tally. 2. to score. 3. to be fitted; match.

tal·ly·ho (tal·i·hō'), *interj.* the huntsman's cry to incite his hounds: *n.* (tal'i·hō), *pl.* -hos, 1. the cry of "tallyho." 2. a four-horse coach.

Tal·mud (täl'mood), *n.* the book which contains the whole body of the Jewish civil and religious law. —Tal·mud'ic, Tal·mud'i·cal, *adj.* —Tal'mud·ism, *n.*

Tal·mud·ist (-ist), *n.* one learned in the Talmud.

tal·on (tal'ŏn), *n.* 1. the claw of a bird of prey. 2. an S-shaped molding.

tam (tam), *n.* same as tam-o'-shanter.

tam·a·ble (tǎm'ǎ-bl), *adj.* capable of being tamed.

ta·ma·le (tǎ-mä'li), *n.* a kind of steamed or baked Mexican food made of minced meat and cornmeal seasoned with red peppers and wrapped in corn husks.

ta·man·dua (tä-män-dwä'), *n.* an arboreal anteater of tropical America.

tam·a·rack (tam'ǎ-rak), *n.* 1. the American larch. 2. its wood.

tam·a·rin (tam'ǎ-rin), *n.* a South American marmoset with silky hair.

tam·a·rind (tam'ǎ-rind), *n.* 1. a leguminous tropical tree having red and yellow flowers and brown pods with a soft, acid pulp. 2. the fruit of this tree, which can be eaten.

tam·a·risk (tam'ǎ-risk), *n.* a tree or shrub with small flowers and feathery branches, found near oceans.

tam·bour (tam'boor), *n.* 1. a drumlike frame on which a kind of embroidery is worked. 2. the embroidery so worked. 3. a drum: *v.t. & v.i.* to embroider with or upon a tambour.

tam·bou·rin (tam'bĕr-in), *n.* a sprightly French dance.

tam·bou·rine (tam-bŏ-rēn'), *n.* a small hand drum with one head and little cymbals inserted in the hoop.

tame (tām), *adj.* 1. domesticated. 2. spiritless; insipid. 3. easily handled or controlled: *v.t.* tamed, tam'ing, 1. to bring from a wild to a domesticated state. 2. to subdue. —tame'ly, *adv.* —tame'ness, *n.* —tam'er, *n.*

tame·a·ble (tǎm'ǎ-bl), *adj.* same as tamable.

tame·less (lĭs), *adj.* 1. wild. 2. not capable of being tamed.

Tam·il (tam'l, tum'-), *n.* 1. one of a people of southern India and northern Ceylon. 2. the language spoken by the Tamils.

tam-o'-shan·ter (tam'ŏ-shan'tēr), *n.* a broad, circular cap with a tassel in the middle, worn in Scotland.

tamp (tamp), *v.t.* 1. to block up (the blast hole in rock) with clay or similar material. 2. to drive (*down*) by repeated gentle strokes.

tamp·er (tam'pĕr), *v.i.* 1. to meddle so as to injure or alter anything (with *with*). 2. to use bribery or other illegal methods (with *with*).

tam·pi·on (tam'pi-ŏn), *n.* a stopper for the mouthpiece of a gun in storage.

tam·pon (tam'pon), *n.* a wad of cotton used to stop a wound, hole, or cavity: *v.t.* to plug with a tampon.

tan (tan), *n.* 1. same as tanbark. 2. the color brown with a yellowish tinge. 3. the color imparted to skin by exposure to the sun's rays: *adj.* tan'ner, tan'nest, yellowish-brown: *v.t.* tanned, tan'ning, 1. to convert (a hide) into leather by steeping it in an infusion of tannin. 2. to make yellowish-brown by exposure to the sun. 3. [Informal], to beat: *v.i.* to become tanned.

tan·a·ger (tan'ǎ-jēr), *n.* a North American bird

---

a in cap, ā in cane, ä in father, ȧ in abet, e in met, ē in be, ē in baker, ē in regent, ĭ in pit, ī in fine, ǐ in manifest, o in hot, ô in horse, ō in bone,

of brilliant scarlet plumage, closely allied to the finch.

tan·bark (tan'bärk), *n.* a bark of tannin, crushed for tanning purposes.

tan·dem (tan'dĕm), *n.* 1. a vehicle with two horses harnessed one before the other. 2. a bicycle for two, one riding before the other: *adj.* arranged one before the other: *adv.* one before another.

tang (tang), *n.* 1. a strong taste or odor. 2. a taste, quality, etc. peculiar to itself. 3. that part of a knife, fork, tool, etc. inserted into the handle. 4. a ringing sound or tone: *v.i.* to make a ringing sound.

tan·ge·lo (tan'jĕ-lō), *n., pl.* **-los,** a hybrid fruit between a tangerine and a grapefruit.

tan·gent (tan'jĕnt), *adj.* 1. touching. 2. in *Geometry,* meeting or touching a circle or curve, but not cutting it: *n.* 1. in *Geometry,* a line, curve, etc. that is tangent. 2. in *Trigonometry,* the ratio of the side opposite a given acute angle in a right triangle to the side adjacent to the angle.

tan·gen·tial (tan-jen'shŭl), *adj.* of, pertaining to, or in the direction of a tangent.

tan·ge·rine (tan-jĕ-rēn'), *n.* a small orange of a deep reddish-yellow color, with segments that are easily separated.

tan·gi·ble (tan'ji-bl), *adj.* 1. perceptible to the touch. 2. capable of being possessed or realized: evident: real: *n. pl.* real things with value. **—tan·gi·bil'i·ty,** *n.*

tan·gle (tang'gl), *v.t.* **-gled, -gling,** 1. to interweave so as to render difficult to unravel. 2. to entrap: *v.i.* 1. to become tangled. 2. [Informal], to contest or dispute: *n.* 1. an interwoven snarl. 2. a disordered condition.

tan·go (tang'gō), *n., pl.* **-gos,** 1. a South American dance in 2/4 or 4/4 time, performed with long, gliding steps. 2. the music for this dance: *v.i.* to perform the tango.

tan·gram (tang'grăm), *n.* a Chinese toy consisting of cardboard cut into squares, triangles, etc. for forming combinations of figures.

tang·y (tang'i), *adj.* **tang'i·er, tang'i·est,** flavorful.

tan·is·try (-ri), *n.* a system among the old Irish tribes according to which a successor was elected chief before his predecessor died.

tank (tangk), *n.* 1. a large cistern or reservoir for storing water or other liquid, gas, etc. 2. a land vehicle of destruction in time of war, encased in heavy steel plates, furnished with machine guns, and mounted on tractor treads, capable of traversing very rough ground and crashing over heavy obstacles.

tank·ard (tang'kĕrd), *n.* a large drinking vessel that often has a lid.

tank·er ('kĕr), *n.* 1. a vessel for carrying liquids such as oil. 2. an airplane for supplying fuel to other airplanes while flying.

tank farming, same as **hydroponics.**

tank top, a casual shirt like an undershirt but with wider shoulder straps.

tank truck, a truck for carrying gasoline, oil, etc.

tan·nate (tan'āt), *n.* a salt of tannic acid.

tan·ner (tan'ĕr), *n.* one who tans hides.

tan·ner·y (-i), *n., pl.* **-ner·ies,** a place where hides are tanned.

tan·nic (tan'ik), *adj.* of, pertaining to, or obtained from tanbark.

tannic acid, an astringent element in oak bark, gallnuts, etc.

tan·nin (tan'in), *n.* same as **tannic acid.**

tan·ning ('ing), *n.* the process of converting hides into leather.

tan·ta·lize (tan'tă-līz), *v.t.* **-lized, -liz·ing,** to tease or torment by exciting hopes or fears which will not be realized.

tan·ta·lum (tan'tă-lŭm), *n.* a rare, bluish-gray, metallic chemical element.

Tan·ta·lus (tan'tă-lŭs), *n.* in *Greek Mythology,* a son of Zeus, punished in the underworld by being plunged to the neck in water with luscious fruit above his head, both of which receded when he attempted to drink or eat.

tan·ta·mount (tan'tă-mount), *adj.* equal in value or significance (with *to*).

tan·ta·ra (tan'tă-rā), *n.* the blare of a horn.

tan·tiv·y (tan-tiv'i), *n., pl.* **-tiv'ies,** a gallop: *adv.* swiftly.

tan·tra (tun'tră, tăn'-), *n.* [often T-], any of a group of mystical Hindu or Buddhist religious writings. **—tan'tric,** *adj.*

tan·trum (tan'trŭm), *n.* a sudden outburst of temper or anger.

Tao·ism (dou'ism), *n.* a religion and philosophy originating in China of which the chief concept is leading a simple, unselfish life. **—Tao'ist,** *n. & adj.*

tap (tap), *v.t.* **tapped, tap'ping,** 1. to strike or touch lightly. 2. to broach (a vessel) to let out a fluid. 3. to add material to the sole or heel of. 4. to find a new outlet for. 5. to produce by tapping. 6. to select or appoint, as for a candidacy. 7. to remove (fluid) from a container. 8. to join or couple with (a pipe, electric circuit, etc.), as in wiretapping. 9. to wiretap: *v.i.* to strike lightly and quickly: *n.* 1. a gentle blow or touch. 2. a taproom. 3. a contrivance for controlling the movement of fluid from a container. 4. a stopper on a vessel containing a fluid. 5. an implement for cutting threads on a female screw. 6. in *Electricity,* a place for a connection in a circuit.

ta·pa (tä'pä), *n.* the bark of the paper mulberry made into a cloth by people of the Pacific islands.

tap-dance (tap'dans), *v.i.* **-danced, -danc·ing,** to perform a tap dance. **—tap'-danc·er,** *n.*

tap dance, a dance in which the steps consist of quick, loud taps of the toe, heel, or whole foot.

tape (tāp), *n.* 1. a narrow band of linen or cotton cloth. 2. a tape measure. 3. magnetic tape: *v.t.* **taped, tap'ing,** 1. to fasten, bind, or cover with tape. 2. to measure with a tape. 3. to record on a magnetic tape.

tape deck, a component of an audio system that records and plays back magnetic tapes.

tape measure, a tape with graduated divisions, used for measuring.

ta·per (tā'pĕr), *n.* 1. a long, wax candle. 2. a small light. 3. a gradual narrowing in breadth: *adj.* growing smaller or regularly narrowed toward an end: *v.t. & v.i.* 1. to

---

ō in drag**o**n, ōō in cr**u**de, oo in w**oo**l, u in c**u**p, ū in c**u**re, ū in t**u**rn, ŭ in f**o**cus, oi in b**o**y, ou in h**ou**se, th in **th**in, th in sh**ea**the, g in **g**et, j in **j**oy, y in **y**et.

make or become gradually more slender: often with *off.* 2. to make or become smaller: often with *off.*

tape recorder, 1. a contrivance for magnetic recording on tape. 2. this contrivance in combination with another contrivance for playing back the recorded material.

tap·es·try (tap'is-tri), *n., pl.* **-tries,** a sturdy textile fabric ornamented with designs, figures, etc., used for hangings: *v.t.* **-tried, -try·ing,** to hang or adorn with tapestry: usually in the past participle.

tape·worm (tāp'wûrm), *n.* a flat, ribbonlike worm, parasitic in the intestines of man and animals.

tap·house (tap'hous), *n.* an inn.

tap·i·o·ca (tap·i-ō'kȧ), *n.* a starchy food obtained from the root of the cassava, used in making pudding.

ta·pir (tā'pẽr), *n., pl.* **ta'pirs, ta'pir,** a large, herbivorous ungulate with short, stout legs and a flexible proboscis, found in Central and South America, and in the Malayan peninsula.

tap·is (tap'i, 'is), *n.* tapestry formerly used to cover a table, as a carpet, etc.: now used only in *on the tapis,* under consideration.

tap·pet (tap'it), *n.* a small lever or projection for changing or regulating motion.

tap·ping (tap'ing), *n.* the act of tapping.

tap·room (tap'room), *n.* a place where alcoholic liquor is sold; barroom.

tap·root ('rōōt), *n.* the main root of a plant.

taps (taps), *n.* a bugle call sounded in camp at night, signifying "lights out": also sounded at a military burial.

tar (tär), *n.* 1. a thick, dark-brown, oily, viscous substance obtained by distillation of wood, coal, etc. 2. any of the solids in smoke, especially tobacco smoke. 3. [Informal], a sailor: *v.t.* **tarred, tar'ring,** to smear with or as with tar.

ta·ran·tass (tä-rän-täs'), *n.* a large, four-wheeled, springless Russian carriage.

tar·an·tel·la (ter-ĕn-tel'ȧ), *n.* 1. a swirling, rapid Neapolitan dance. 2. music for such a dance.

tar·ant·ism (ter'ĕn-tizm), *n.* a nervous affliction characterized by outbursts of wild, uncontrolled behavior.

ta·ran·tu·la (tä-ran'choo-lȧ), *n., pl.* **-las, -lae** (-lē), 1. a large, hairy spider of southern Europe. 2. a poisonous spider of the southwestern U.S., Mexico, etc.

tar·boosh (tär-bōōsh'), *n.* a cap without a brim, tapering to a flat top, worn by Moslem men.

tar·dy (tär'di), *adj.* **-di·er, -di·est,** 1. moving with a slow pace or motion. 2. dilatory; late. **—tar'di·ly,** *adv.* **—tar'di·ness,** *n.*

tare (ter), *n.* 1. an allowance made for the weight of the container or receptacle in which goods are delivered. 2. a type of vetch. 3. in the *Bible,* a harmful weed: *v.t.* **tared, tar'ing,** to mark the tare or tares; weigh so as to determine the tare.

tar·get (tär'git), *n.* 1. originally, a small shield. 2. an object set up for rifle and artillery practice. 3. a surface upon which a stream of nuclear particles is sent. 4. an end; goal.

5. that which receives much criticism, jeering, etc.

tar·iff (ter'if), *n.* 1. a schedule or list of dutiable goods, specifying the customs, rates, etc. to be paid or allowed on articles exported or imported. 2. a duty levied according to such a schedule. 3. any similar schedule or list, as of prices. 4. [Informal], any price: *v.t.* to fix a duty on.

tar·la·tan, tar·le·tan (tär'lȧ-tȧn), *n.* a thin, transparent muslin.

tarn (tärn), *n.* a small mountain lake.

tar·nish (tär'nish), *v.t.* 1. a being dulled. 2. a stain; blemish: *v.t.* 1. to diminish the luster of. 2. to sully: *v.i.* 1. to lose luster; become dull. 2. to become dirty.

ta·ro (tä'rō), *n., pl.* **-ros,** a tropical plant allied to the arum, the edible root of which forms a staple food of the Polynesians and is made into poi.

ta·rot (ter'ō, -ōt), *n.* [often T-], a pack of cards used to tell fortunes.

tar·pau·lin (tär-pô'lin), *n.* a stout, waterproof canvas.

tar·pon (tär'pŏn), *n., pl.* **-pons, -pon,** a large game fish of the western Atlantic.

tar·ra·gon (ter'ȧ-gon), *n.* a European wormwood whose aromatic leaves are used for seasoning.

tar·ry (ter'i), *v.i.* **-ried, -ry·ing,** 1. to stay behind. 2. to linger. 3. to remain without permanence.

tar·ry (tär'i), *adj.* **-ri·er, -ri·est,** covered or smeared with tar.

tar·sus (tär'sŭs), *n., pl.* **tar'si** ('sī), 1. the ankle, consisting of seven bones. 2. the shank of a bird's leg. 3. the connective cartilage of the eyelid. 4. part of the leg of an insect. — **tar'sal,** *adj.*

tart (tärt), *adj.* 1. sharp to the taste; acid. 2. severe; keen: *n.* 1. a small piece of pastry containing fruit, custard, etc. 2. a loose woman.

tar·tan (tär'tn), *n.* 1. a woolen cloth with a colored pattern of vertical and horizontal lines crossing each other at right angles. 2. a small Mediterranean vessel with one mast: *adj.* made from or like tartan.

Tar·tar (tär'tẽr), *n.* 1. same as **Tatar.** 2. [usually t-], a person of irritable temper. 3. [t-], one who proves stronger than an assailant suspects.

tar·tar (tär'tẽr), *n.* 1. a deposit from the juice of grapes. 2. a phosphate concretion which gathers on the teeth.

Tar·tar·e·an (tär-ter'i-ȧn), *adj.* of or pertaining to Tartarus or hell; infernal.

tartar emetic, antimony combined with potassium and tartaric acid, used as a sudorific and, in dyeing, as a mordant.

tar·tar·ic (tär-ter'ik), *adj.* of or pertaining to tartar or tartaric acid.

tartaric acid, an acid found in the juice of grapes, berries, etc., used in dyeing, photography, medicinal preparations, etc.

tartar sauce, a sauce of mayonnaise, pieces of pickle, olives, etc.: also **tartare sauce.**

Tar·ta·rus (tär'tẽr-ŭs), *n.* in Greek Mythology, 1. the deep and sunless abyss of the infernal regions. 2. same as **Hades.**

ta·sim·e·ter (tǎ-sǐm'ě-tēr), *n.* an electrical instrument for measuring minute movements in solid bodies and recording temperature by the changes in pressure. —**ta·sim'e·try,** *n.*

task (task), *n.* 1. work or study imposed by another. 2. a burdensome employment: *v.t.* to impose a task upon.

task force, a number of people, as in a military section, assigned particular work to do.

task·mas·ter ('mas-tēr), *n.* 1. one who assigns tasks; overseer. 2. one who imposes hard work on an employee.

Tas·ma·ni·an devil (taz-mā'ni-ǎn), a fierce, carnivorous, burrowing marsupial of Tasmania, with coarse, intensely black fur.

tas·sel (tas'l), *n.* 1. a pendent ornament of silk, wool, etc. with strings or threads hanging loosely from it. 2. the pendent flower or head of certain plants, as corn: *v.t.* -seled or -selled, -sel·ing or -sel·ling, to adorn with tassels.

taste (tāst), *v.t.* tast'ed, tast'ing, 1. to perceive by the tongue and palate. 2. to test by eating or sipping a little. 3. to participate in; experience. 4. to eat lightly of. 5. [Archaic], to obtain pleasure from: *v.i.* 1. to try by the palate. 2. to have a flavor (*of*). 3. to enjoy moderately (with *of*): *n.* 1. the sensation produced on the tongue and palate by something taken into the mouth. 2. quality or flavor. 3. discernment of the sublime or beautiful. 4. a relish. 5. a sample. 6. intellectual relish; bent. 7. a choice of pleasures, pursuits, etc. 8. [Obsolete]; trial; experiment. —**taste'less,** *adj.*

taste bud, one of the cells of the tongue that provides taste sensation.

taste·ful ('fŭl), *adj.* savory; characterized by or showing good taste. —**taste'ful·ly,** *adv.* — **taste'ful·ness,** *n.*

tast·y (tās'ti), *adj.* tast'i·er, tast'i·est, 1. savory. 2. [Now Rare], showing good taste. —**tast'i·ly,** *adv.* —**tast'i·ness,** *n.*

tat (tat), *v.t.* tat'ted, tat'ting, to make by tatting: *v.i.* to perform tatting.

ta·ta (tā-tā'), *interj.* [British], goodbye; farewell.

Ta·tar (tät'ēr), *n.* 1. one of a tribal people of Mongolia, Turkey, etc. who entered western Asia and eastern Europe in medieval times. 2. one of their Turkic languages.

tat·ter (tat'ēr), *n.* 1. a loose, hanging rag. 2. *pl.* rags: *v.t.* to make ragged; rend: *v.i.* to become ragged. —**tat'tered,** *adj.*

tat·ter·de·mal·ion (tat-ēr-di-māl'yŭn), *n.* a ragged person.

tat·ting (tat'ing), *n.* 1. a kind of narrow lace for edging, made with a small hand shuttle. 2. the act of making such a kind of lace.

tat·tle (tat'l), *v.i.* -tled, -tling, 1. to talk idly or triflingly; prate. 2. to tell tales or secrets: *v.t.* to tell (a secret) by idle talk: *n.* trifling or idle talk. —**tat'tler,** *n.*

tat·tle·tale (tat'l-tāl), *n.* one who tells secrets or tells tales.

tat·too (ta-tōō'), *n., pl.* -toos', 1. a beat of a drum, especially for warning soldiers to retire to their quarters. 2. a noise made by repeated tapping. 3. a mark or figure made by puncturing the skin with a needle and rubbing a stain or dye into the wounds: *v.t.*

1. to mark (the skin) permanently with designs by puncturing it and staining the wounds. 2. to mark (designs) on the skin in this way.

tau (tô, tou), *n.* the nineteenth letter of the Greek alphabet.

taught (tôt), past tense and past participle of **teach.**

taunt (tônt), *adj.* lofty: *n.* a bitter or sarcastic reproach; scoff; insulting invective: *v.t.* to reproach with bitter, sarcastic, or insulting language; revile.

taupe (tōp), *adj.* of a moleskin color; dark brownish-gray: *n.* the color of moleskin.

tau·rine (tôr'īn), *adj.* of or pertaining to a bull: *n.* ('in), a colorless, crystalline compound found in the bile of mammals and certain invertebrates.

tau·ro·cho·lic acid (tôr-ô-kō'lik), a crystalline compound found in the bile of mammals: it promotes the absorption of cholesterol.

Tau·rus (tôr'ŭs), *n.* 1. a northern constellation between Aries and Orion. 2. the second sign of the zodiac.

taut (tôt), *adj.* 1. tight; stretched. 2. under emotional strain. 3. orderly; efficient. — **taut'ly,** *adv.* —**taut'ness,** *n.*

taut·en (tôt'n), *v.t.* to make taut: *v.i.* to become taut.

tau·tog (tô-tog'), *n.* a thick, black, edible fish of the Atlantic coast of the U.S.

tau·tol·o·gy (tô-tol'ô-ji), *n., pl.* -gies, repetition of the same thing or idea in different words; sameness of words or of meaning. —**tau·to·log·i·cal** (tôt-ô-loj'i-kl), *adj.* —**tau·to·log'i·cal·ly,** *adv.*

tau·to·nym (tôt'ô-nim), *n.* in Biology, a scientific name of three terms in which the species name is repeated in the third term.

tav (tāf, tāv), *n.* the twenty-third letter of the Hebrew alphabet: also **taw.**

tav·ern (tav'ērn), *n.* an inn or bar.

taw (tô), *v.t.* to prepare (hides) by imbuing them with alum or salt to soften and bleach them: *n.* 1. a game at marbles. 2. a decorative marble to be played with.

taw·dry (tô'dri), *adj.* -dri·er, -dri·est, showy or fine without elegance; gaudy. —**taw'dri·ly,** *adv.* —**taw'dri·ness,** *n.*

taw·ny (tô'ni), *adj.* -ni·er, -ni·est, yellowish-brown. —**taw'ni·ness,** *n.*

taws (tôz), *n., pl.* taws, [British], a leather strap with one end cut into fringes, used as an instrument of punishment: also **tawse.**

tax (taks), *n.* 1. a compulsory payment or duty on income, property, etc.; excise; impost. 2. a burdensome or oppressive duty: *v.t.* 1. to impose a payment or duty upon for state or municipal purposes. 2. to burden or oppress. 3. to accuse. —**tax·a·bil'i·ty,** *n.* —**tax'a·ble,** *adj.*

tax·a·tion (tak-sā'shŭn), *n.* 1. the act of taxing. 2. the rate or tax imposed. 3. the system of raising revenues.

tax·i (tak'si), *n., pl.* tax'is, same as taxicab: *v.i.* tax'ied, tax'i·ing or tax'y·ing, 1. to ride in a taxicab. 2. to move slowly on the ground, or on the water, in an airplane or seaplane in preparing to take off or after landing.

tax·i·cab (-kab), *n.* an automobile carrying

passengers for a fee, usually computed by a device that records the time and length of trip.

tax·i·der·my (tak'si-dûr-mi), *n.* the art of stuffing the skins of animals and arranging them for exhibition. —**tax'i·der·mist,** *n.*

tax·i·me·ter (tak'si-mēt-ēr), *n.* the recording device used in a taxicab.

tax·on·o·my (tak-son'ô-mi), *n.* 1. that science which treats of the laws and principles of classification. 2. the department of natural history which treats of the classification of animals and plants according to natural relationship. —**tax·on'o·mist,** *n.*

tax·pay·er (taks'pā-ēr), *n.* one who pays a tax of any kind.

tax shelter, any financial investment made for the purpose of acquiring expenses which can be deducted from taxable income.

tax·us (tak'sŭs), *n., pl.* **tax'us,** same as yew (evergreen tree).

T-bone steak (tē'bōn), a steak having a T-shaped bone, cut from the loin and having some tenderloin.

T cell, any of the lymphatic leukocytes affected by the thymus, that regulate immunity, control the production of antibodies, etc.

tea (tē), *n.* 1. an evergreen shrub indigenous to China, India, Japan, etc. 2. a drink made from the dried leaves of this shrub. 3. a similar drink made from other substances, as beef. 4. [Chiefly British]. an afternoon repast at which tea is served. 5. a social occasion at which tea is served, as in the afternoon.

tea·ber·ry (tē'ber-i), *n., pl.* **-ries,** 1. same as wintergreen (sense 1). 2. the berry of the wintergreen.

teach (tēch), *v.t.* **taught, teach'ing,** 1. to impart knowledge to; inform. 2. to instruct. 3. to cause to learn or acquire skill in: *v.i.* to work as a teacher.

teach·er (tē'chēr), *n.* one who teaches others; instructor.

teach·ing (tē'ching), *n.* instruction.

tea·cup (tē'kup), *n.* a cup from which tea is drunk. —**tea'cup·ful,** *n., pl.* **-fuls.**

teak (tēk), *n.* 1. a large East Indian tree that yields a very hard, durable timber much prized for shipbuilding. 2. the wood of the teak· also **teak'wood.**

tea·ket·tle (tē'ket-l), *n.* a kettle for boiling water for tea.

teal (tēl), *n.* 1. *pl.* **teals, teal,** a type of small, wild freshwater duck. 2. the color blue with a gray or green tinge: also **teal blue.**

team (tēm), *n.* 1. two or more horses or other animals harnessed to the same vehicle for drawing. 2. [Dialectal], a litter; brood. 3. a number of persons associated together to form a side in a game, or to perform a certain piece of work: *v.i.* to unite in shared work, play, etc. (often with *up*).

team·mate ('māt), *n.* another person on the same team.

team·ster ('stēr), *n.* the driver of a team or truck in carrying freight.

team·work ('wŭrk), *n.* combined activity by a number of people working or playing together.

tea·pot (tē'pot), *n.* a vessel with a spout for the brewing and serving of tea.

tear (ter), *n.* 1. the act of tearing. 2. a rent. 3. [Slang], a spree: *v.t.* **tore, torn, tear'ing.** 1. to separate by violence; rend. 2. to disrupt. 3. to lacerate. 4. to produce by rending. 5. to cause uncertainty in. 6. to extract with effort (with *out, up, off,* etc.); *v.i.* 1. to be torn. 2. to act with violence. 3. to rave or rant.

tear (tir), *n.* 1. a small drop of the watery fluid secreted by the lacrimal gland of the eye. 2. anything tearlike or shaped like a tear.

tear·drop (tir'drop), *n.* a tear or something with that shape or form.

tear·ful (fŭl), *adj.* shedding tears. —**tear'ful·ly,** *adv.*

tear gas (tir), a gas that blinds the eyes with tears. —**tear'-gas,** *v.t.* **-gassed, -gas·sing.**

tea·room (tē'rōōm), *n.* a place where one may buy and eat small meals, drink tea or coffee, etc.

tea rose, a hybrid, hardy garden rose with the scent of tea blossoms.

tear·y (tir'i), *adj.* **tear'i·er, tear'i·est,** of, pertaining to, or shedding tears. —**tear'i·ly,** *adv.* —**tear'i·ness,** *n.*

tease (tēz), *v.t.* **teased, teas'ing,** 1. to comb or unravel (wool, flax, etc.): separate the fibers of. 2. to fluff (the hair) by combing toward the scalp. 3. to teasel. 4. to vex by petty requests or raillery. 5. to upset with unfulfilled promises: *v.i.* to give oneself up to teasing: *n.* one who teases.

tea·sel (tē'zl), *n.* 1. a plant with hooked burrs, which are used for raising the nap of cloth. 2. a burr or flower head of this plant. 3. anything used to raise the nap on cloth: *v.t.* -**seled** or -**selled, -sel·ing** or -**sel·ling,** to raise a nap on (cloth) with teasels.

teas·er (tē'zēr), *n.* 1. one that teases. 2. a perplexing puzzle.

tea·spoon (tē'spōōn), *n.* 1. a small spoon used at table. 2. the quantity that a teaspoon will hold, equal to 1 1/3 fluid drams: also **tea'-spoon·ful** (-fool), *pl.* **-fuls.**

teat (tēt, tit), *n.* the nipple of the female breast; fleshy protuberance through which milk is drawn from the udder or breast of a mammal.

tea·zel, tea·zle (tē'zl), *n. & v.t.* same as teasel.

tech·nic (tek'nik), *adj.* same as technical.

tech·ni·cal (tek'ni-kl), *adj.* 1. of or pertaining to the mechanical arts. 2. of or relating to a particular art or science. 3. suited or adapted to a particular trade or art. 4. of or demonstrating the way of doing something. 5. utilizing small details of technique. —**tech'ni·cal·ly,** *adv.*

tech·ni·cal·i·ty (tek-ni-kal'i-ti), *n., pl.* **-ties,** 1. something peculiar to a trade, calling, art, or manner of performance. 2. the condition of being technical. 3. a small detail applied to a larger matter.

tech·ni·cian (tek-nish'ŭn), *n.* one skilled in the mechanical aspects of an art or trade.

Tech·ni·col·or (tek'ni-kul-ēr), *n.* a method of photographing motion pictures in color: a trademark.

a in cap, ā in cane, ä in father, ȧ in abet, e in met, ē in be, ė in baker, ḗ in regent, I in pit, ī in fine, i in manifest, o in hot, ô in horse, ō in bone,

tech·nics (tek'niks), *n.pl.* those branches of learning which relate to the arts.

tech·nique (tek-nēk'), *n.* 1. the system used in an art, science, etc. 2. the quality of skill in execution of some artistic or scientific work.

tech·noc·ra·cy (tek-nok'rȧ-si), *n.* a modern philosophy advocating control of economic activity by technicians. —**tech'no·crat** ('nŏ-krat), *n.*

tech·nol·o·gy (tek-nol'ō-ji), *n.* 1. the science of the industrial arts. 2. science used in a practical way. —**tech·no·log'i·cal** (-nŏ-loj'i-kl), *c.lj.*

tech·y (tech'i), *adj.* **tech'i·er**, **tech'i·est**, same as tetchy.

tec·ton·ics (tek-ton'iks), *n.* the science or art of construction.

tec·trix (tek'triks), *n.*, *pl.* **-tri·ces** ('trī-sēz), a wing covert of a bird.

ted (ted), *v.t.* **ted'ded**, **ted'ding**, to turn or spread (new-mown grass) for drying. —**ted'der**, *n.*

ted·dy bear (ted'i), a miniature of a bear, made as a stuffed toy for children.

Te De·um (tē dē'ûm), 1 an ancient hymn of the Christian Church. 2. a thanksgiving service.

te·di·ous (tē'di-ûs), *adj.* wearisome by continuance or repetition; tiresome. —**te'di·ous·ly**, *adv*

te·di·um ('di-ûm), *n.* wearisomeness.

tee (tē), *n.* 1. the mark aimed at in quoits and curling. 2. an object shaped like a T. 3. in *Golf, a)* a plastic or wooden holder from which the ball is struck. *b)* the place at the beginning of each hole from which a player makes his first stroke: *v.t* & *v.i.* **teed**, **tee'ing**, to put (a ball) on a tee

tee·hee (tē'hē'), *interj.* & *n.* a titter: *v.i.* **-heed'**, **-hee'ing**, to titter

teem (tēm), *v.t.* 1 originally, to be prolific. 2. to be full: to be stocked to overflowing.

teen (tēn), *n.* 1. [Archaic], sorrow 2 *pl* the years from thirteen to nineteen of a person's age 3 a person between the ages of thirteen and nineteen: also **teen'-ag·er** ('āj-ẽr).

teen-age (tēn'āj), *adj.* of. pertaining to, for, or in the years of a person's life between thirteen and nineteen also **teen'age**.

tee·ny (tē'ni), *adj.* **-ni·er**, **-ni·est**, [Informal], very small: tiny also **teen'sy**, **tee'ny-wee'ny** (-wē'ni), **teen'sy-ween'sy** (tēn'si-wēn'si).

teen·y-bop·per (tē'ni-bŏp-ẽr), *n.* [Slang]. in the 1960's. a young female teenager attempting to follow the changing fashions.

tee·pee (tē'pi), *n.* same as tepee.

tee shirt, same as T-shirt.

tee·ter (tē'tẽr), *v.i.* to move up and down or from side to side: *v.i.* to make teeter· *n.* same as seesaw.

tee·ter-tot·ter (-tot-ẽr), *n.* & *v.i.* same as seesaw.

teeth (tēth), *n.* plural of tooth.

teethe (tēth), *v.i.* **teethed**, **teeth'ing**, to have teeth grow.

tee·to·tal (tı̄-tōt'l, tē'tōt-l), *adj.* of or pertaining to teetotalers or teetotalism.

tee·to·tal·er (-ẽr), *n.* a total abstainer from intoxicating liquors.

tee·to·tal·ism (-izm), *n.* entire abstinence from intoxicating liquors.

Tef·lon (tef'lon), *n.* a hard substance which resists sticking. used as a coating for cooking utensils. machinery, etc.: a trademark.

teg·men (teg'mĕn), *n.*, *pl.* **teg'mi·na** ('mi-nȧ), 1. a covering. 2. in *Botany*, the inner layer of the coating of a seed.

teg·u·ment (teg'yoo-mĕnt), *n.* same as integument. —**teg·u·men'ta·ry** (-men'tȧ-ri), *adj.*

te·hee (tē'hē'), *interj.* & *n.* & *v.i.* **-heed'**, **-hee'ing**, same as tee-hee.

tek·tite (tek'tīt), *n.* a dark, smooth, glasslike rock, thought to have come from outer space.

tel·a·mon (tel'ȧ-mon), *n.*, *pl.* **tel·a·mo'nes** (-mō'nēz), a figure of a man, used as a column or pilaster.

Tel·Au·to·graph (tel-ôt'ō-graf), *n.* a telegraphic instrument for reproducing writings or drawings at a distance: a trademark.

tel·e-, a combining form meaning: 1. *far.* 2. *of* or *relating to television.*

tel·e·cast (tel'ē-kast), *v.t.* & *v.i.* **-cast** or **-cast·ed**, **-cast·ing**, to transmit by television: *n.* a television transmission. —**tel'e·cast·er**, *n.*

tel·e·con·fer·ence (tel'ē-kon-fẽr-ĕns), *n.* a conference of persons in different locations, as by telephone, TV, etc.

tel·e·du (tel'ē-dōō), *n.* a badgerlike animal of Java and Sumatra which secretes a malodorous fluid and ejects it when aroused.

te·leg·o·ny (tē-leg'ō-ni), *n.* the supposed influence of a previous sire on offspring subsequently borne to a second male by the same female

tel·e·gram (tel'ē-gram), *n.* a telegraphic communication

tel·e·graph (-graf), *n.* an instrument or apparatus for communicating intelligence rapidly between certain points by means of electricity over wires or by radio waves *v.t.* 1 to convey by telegraph. 2. [Informal]. to signal inadvertently *v.i.* to send a telegraphic message —**te·leg·ra·pher** (tē-leg'rȧ-fẽr). **te·leg'ra·phist**, *n.*

tel·e·graph·ic (tel-ē-graf'ik). *adj.* of. pertaining to. done by means of. or communicated by telegraph.

tel·e·mar·ket·ing (tel'ē-mär'ket-ing), *n.* the use of the telephone in marketing for sales research, promotion, etc.

te·leg·ra·phy (tē-leg'rȧ-fi), *n.* the science or art of constructing and working telegraphs.

tel·e·ki·ne·sis (tel-ē-ki-nē'sis), *n.* the apparent causing of movement in a body by unexplained means

tel·e·me·ter (tel'ē-mĕt-ẽr), *n.* 1 an instrument for determining distances. 2. a similar instrument for transmitting to a distance records and impressions of natural phenomena.

te·le·ol·o·gy (tē-li-ol'ō-ji). *n.* the doctrine that everything is to be understood in terms of its ultimate goal or purpose.

te·lep·a·thy (tē-lep'ȧ-thi), *n.* the supposed transference of thought from one person to another by means other than the usual

---

ō in dragon. ōō in crude. oo in wool. u in cup. ū in cure. ū in turn. ŭ in focus. oi in boy. ou in house. th in thin. *th* in sheathe. g in get. j in joy. y in yet.

senses. —**tel·e·path·ic** (tel-ē-path'ik), *adj.* — **te·lep'a·thist,** *n.*

tel·e·phone (tel'ē-fōn), *n.* an instrument for reproducing sound at a distance by means of converting it to electricity and sending it through a wire: *v.t.* -**phoned, -phon·ing,** to send (a message) by telephone to (someone): *v.i.* to communicate by telephone. — **tel·e·phon'ic** (-fon'ik), *adj.*

te·leph·o·ny (tē-lef'ō-ni), *n.* 1. the process of conducting sounds over a distance by means of a wire. 2. the act of communicating by telephone.

tel·e·pho·to (tel'ē-fōt-ō), *adj.* designating a combination of lenses which give a large image of a distant object in a camera of short focus.

tel·e·pho·to·graph (tel-ē-fōt'ō-graf), *n.* 1. a photograph made by using a telephoto lens. 2. a photograph sent by electricity over wires or by radio: *v.t. & v.i.* 1. to make (photographs) by means of a telephoto lens. 2. to send (telephotographs) over a wire or by radio waves.

tel·e·pho·tog·ra·phy (-fō-tog'rā-fi), *n.* 1. reproduction of photographs by transmitting images by radio or telegraph. 2. the making of photographs of distant objects by using a telephoto lens.

tel·e·scope (tel'ē-skōp), *n.* an optical instrument for viewing and magnifying objects at a distance: *v.i.* -**scoped, -scop·ing,** to fit or move into one another, as the parts of a compact telescope: *v.t.* to cause to telescope, or move into one another.

tel·e·scop·ic (tel-ē-skop'ik), *adj.* of, pertaining to, visible by, or like a telescope.

te·les·co·py (tē-les'kō-pi), *n.* the art or science of using or constructing a telescope. —**te·les'co·pist,** *n.*

tel·e·sis (tel'ē-sis), *n.* progress clearly planned and accomplished by consciously directed effort.

tel·e·spec·tro·scope (tel-ē-spek'trō-skōp), *n.* a combination of telescope and spectroscope for obtaining the spectrum of a heavenly body.

tel·es·the·si·a (tel-ēs-thē'zhä), *n.* a mental impression received at a distance without any conscious thought on the part of the receiver; telepathic impression.

tel·e·thon (tel'ē-thon), *n.* a long television program the purpose of which is to gain charitable contributions, give publicity to a candidate for office, etc.

Tel·e·type (-tīp), *n.* a kind of typewriter which transmits messages by wire to another typewriter at a distance: a trademark.

tel·e·vise (tel'ē-vīz), *v.t. & v.i.* -**vised, -vis·ing,** to broadcast by television.

tel·e·vi·sion (-vizh-ŭn), *n.* 1. an electronic system of sending pictures by radio waves. 2. the business of sending such pictures. 3. an apparatus for receiving television pictures.

tell (tel), *v.t.* **told, tell'ing,** 1. originally, to enumerate. 2. to express or make known by words. 3. to narrate. 4. to explain to. 5. to order. 6. to separate mentally: *v.i.* 1. to give an account; report (with *of*). 2. to play the informer. 3. to act effectively.

tell·er (tel'ēr), *n.* 1. one who tells, narrates, or communicates. 2. a bank clerk who receives or pays out money. 3. one who counts ballots, as in a legislative body.

tell·ing ('ing), *adj.* effective. —**tell'ing·ly,** *adv.*

tell·tale ('tāl), *adj.* talebearing; tattling; betraying: *n.* 1. a person who officiously or maliciously divulges the private conversations of others. 2. an automatic device for counting or indicating. 3. a row of dangling cords above a railroad track to give warning that the train is approaching a low bridge, tunnel, etc.

tel·lu·ri·an (te-loor'i-ăn), *adj.* of or pertaining to the earth: *n.* a dweller upon the earth.

tel·lu·ric (te-loor'ik), *adj.* of, pertaining to, or derived from the earth or tellurium.

tel·lu·ride (tel'yū-rīd), *n.* a compound of tellurium with another element or a radical.

tel·lu·ri·um (te-loor'i-ŭm), *n.* a rare nonmetallic element, often used in making alloys.

tel·ly (tel'i), *n.* [British Informal], same as television.

tel·pher (tel'fēr), *n.* an electric car running on cables suspended in the air.

tel·pher·age (-ij), *n.* a system of electric transport through the air by means of cars suspended from cables.

tem·blor (tem'blôr, 'blēr), *n.* same as earthquake.

tem·er·ar·i·ous (tem-ē-rer'i-ŭs), *adj.* foolhardy; rash; impetuous; heedless.

te·mer·i·ty (tē-mer'i-ti), *n.* foolhardiness; rashness; precipitancy.

tem·per (tem'pēr), *v.t.* 1. to moderate; assuage; calm. 2. to bring to a proper proportion or to a proper degree of elasticity or hardness. 3. to make hard or strong: *n.* 1. formerly, proper proportion of different qualities or ingredients. 2. the state of a metal as to its hardness or elasticity. 3. mental disposition; mood. 4. equanimity: now only in *keep one's temper, lose one's temper.* 5. heat of mind or passion.

tem·per·a (tem'pēr-ä), *n.* 1. a painting method utilizing eggs, size, etc. mixed in with the colors. 2. this kind of paint. 3. an opaque, water-base paint.

tem·per·a·ment (tem'pēr-mĕnt), *n.* 1. originally, the proportionate mixture of opposite or different qualities. 2. natural inclinations or disposition. 3. a passionate or changeable disposition. —**tem·per·a·men'tal,** *adj.*

tem·per·ance (tem'pēr-ĕns), *n.* 1. moderation in respect to the appetite or passions. 2. moderation in or total abstinence from drinking intoxicating liquor.

tem·per·ate (tem'pēr-it), *adj.* 1. moderate. 2. not characterized by passion or indulgence of the appetite; abstemious. 3. calm. 4. not liable to excess of heat or cold. —**tem'per·ate·ly,** *adv.* —**tem'per·ate·ness,** *n.*

Temperate Zone, either of two geographical zones of the earth between the polar circles and the tropics.

tem·per·a·ture (tem'prá-chēr), *n.* 1. the state of a living body with respect to heat; degree of hot or cold. 2. the amount of heat beyond the normal amount in a body.

tem·pered (tem'pērd), *adj.* 1. brought to a par-

---

a in *cap,* **ã** in *cane,* **ä** in *father,* **à** in *abet,* **e** in *met,* **ē** in *be,* **ē** in *baker,* **ē** in *regent,* **i** in *pit,* **ī** in *fine,* **i** in *manifest,* **o** in *hot,* **ô** in *horse,* **ō** in *bone,*

ticular hardness. 2. constitutionally disposed in a particular way.

tem·pest (tem'pist), *n.* 1. wind rushing with great violence, usually accompanied by rain, hail, etc. 2. tumult.

tem·pes·tu·ous (tem-pes'choo-wŭs), *adj.* 1. very stormy; of, pertaining to, or like a tempest. 2. violent.

Tem·plar (tem'plẽr), *n.* 1. same as **Knight Templar**. 2. [t-], in London, a law student or barrister located in a special area of legal buildings.

tem·plate (tem'plit), *n.* 1. a mold or pattern. 2. a piece of stone or wood put under a beam or girder to help distribute the weight equally.

tem·ple (tem'pl), *n.* 1. an edifice for the worship of a deity or deities. 2. a place of public worship. 3. a large edifice for a particular public or private use. 4. [T-], the series of buildings used by the ancient Jews in Jerusalem, for worship of Jehovah. 5. the flat part of either side of the head above the cheekbones. 6. either of the two parts of a pair of eyeglasses that go across this area of the head.

tem·plet (tem'plit), *n.* same as **template**.

tem·po (tem'pō), *n., pl.* **-pos, -pi** ('pi), 1. the pace of a musical piece. 2. any pace.

tem·po·ral (tem'pẽr-ăl), *adj.* 1. of or pertaining to time. 2. secular. 3. measured or restricted by time. 4. civil or political. 5. not lasting forever. 6. of or in the vicinity of the temples of the head.

tem·po·rar·y (tem'pō-rer-i), *adj.* existing or continuing for a limited time or some special purpose. **—tem'po·rar·i·ly,** *adv.* **—tem'po·rar·i·ness,** *n.*

tem·po·rize (tem'pō-rīz), *v.i.* **-rized, -riz·ing,** 1. to comply with the times; yield to current opinion. 2. to parley. 3. to delay.

tempt (tempt), *v.t.* 1. originally, to put to trial; test. 2. to persuade to evil. 3. to defy. 4. to allure; entice. 5. to be highly disposed to.

temp·ta·tion (temp-tā'shŭn), *n.* 1. the state of being tempted. 2. enticement, especially to evil.

tempt·er (temp'tẽr), *n.* 1. one who tempts. 2. [T-], the Devil (preceded by *the*).

tempt·ing ('ting), *adj.* alluring; seductive.

tempt·ress ('tris), *n.* a woman who tempts.

tem·pu·ra (tem'poo-rä), *n.* a Japanese dish of deep-fried fish, shrimp, vegetables, etc.

ten (ten), *adj.* one more than nine: *n.* the cardinal number that is the sum of nine and one; 10; X.

ten·a·ble (ten'ă-bl), *adj.* capable of being held, maintained, or defended. **—ten·a·bil'i·ty,** *n.*

ten·ace (ten'ās), *n.* in *Bridge,* the holding of two out of three high cards in a suit, with one of the sequence missing.

te·na·cious (tě-nā'shŭs), *adj.* 1. holding fast or firmly. 2. cohesive; tough. 3. obstinate. 4. adhesive. **—te·na'cious·ly,** *adv.* **—te·nac'i·ty** (-nas'i-ti), *n.*

te·nac·u·lum (tě-nak'yoo-lŭm), *n., pl.* **-la** (-lă), a surgical instrument with a sharp-pointed hook for lifting up a divided artery for the purpose of tying it.

ten·an·cy (ten'ăn-si), *n., pl.* **-cies,** 1. the holding of land or buildings on certain conditions and for a specified time. 2. tenure of any sort.

ten·ant (ten'ănt), *n.* 1. one who holds land or buildings on certain conditions and for a specified time. 2. an occupant: *v.t.* to hold as a tenant.

tenant farmer, a farmer who rents the land that he cultivates.

ten·ant·ry ('ăn-tri), *n., pl.* **-ries,** tenants collectively.

tench (tench), *n., pl.* **tench'es, tench,** a freshwater fish related to the carp.

Ten Commandments, in the *Bible,* the ten moral laws given by God to Moses on Mount Sinai.

tend (tend), *v.t.* 1. to care for; attend; watch over or protect. 2. to direct: *v.i.* 1. to move in a particular direction. 2. to be disposed. 3. to be directed (*to* any end or purpose).

tend·en·cy (ten'děn-si), *n., pl.* **-cies,** 1. an inclination. 2. an aim; direction or course.

ten·den·tious (ten-den'shŭs), *adj.* having a specific aim in mind. **—ten·den'tious·ly,** *adv.*

ten·der (ten'dẽr), *adj.* 1. easily impressed or injured. 2. sensitive. 3. soft. 4. not hard, rough, etc.; gentle. 5. weak and feeble. 6. easily influenced by love, pity, etc.; compassionate. 7. careful. 8. needing care in treatment. 9. young: *n.* 1. a vehicle attached to a locomotive, containing coal and water. 2. a smaller vessel attending a larger one. 3. an offer or proposal for acceptance. 4. an offer of a sum of money under specified legal conditions. 5. the sum of money offered. 6. a person who tends: *v.t.* to offer for acceptance. **—ten'der·ly,** *adv.* **—ten'der·ness,** *n.*

ten·der·foot (-foot), *n., pl.* **-foots, -feet,** 1. one who is new to life in a mining region or frontier district of the West. 2. one who is new to something, as a job.

ten·der·heart·ed (-härt'id), *adj.* susceptible to emotions; prone to pity.

ten·der·ize (ten'dě-rīz), *v.t.* **-ized, -iz·ing,** to cause (meat) to become tender.

ten·der·loin ('dẽr-loin), *n.* a choice cut of beef, pork, etc. from the loin.

ten·di·nous (ten'di-nŭs), *adj.* 1. of or pertaining to a tendon. 2. sinewy.

ten·don (ten'dŏn), *n.* the hard bundle of fibers which connect the muscles to the bones.

ten·dril (ten'drĭl), *n.* the slender, twining part of a plant, which attaches itself to a supporting body.

Ten·e·brae (ten'ě-brā), *n.pl.* in the *Roman Catholic Church,* the matins and lauds sung Wednesday through Friday of Holy Week in commemoration of the Savior's passion and death.

ten·e·brif·ic (ten·ě-brif'ik), *adj.* dark; gloomy.

ten·e·brous (ten'ě-brŭs), *adj.* gloomy.

ten·e·ment (ten'ě-měnt), *n.* 1. in *Law,* a house, shop, land, etc. held by a tenant. 2. a dwelling house. 3. a suite of rooms. 4. a building consisting of a number of suites of rooms, usually in shabby condition: also **tenement house.**

---

ten·et (ten′it), *n.* a doctrine, opinion, or belief held or maintained as true.

ten·fold (′fōld), *adj.* 1. having ten parts. 2. having ten times as much or as many: *adv.* ten times as much or as many.

ten·nis (ten′is), *n.* 1. a game in which players stroke a ball with rackets back and forth over a net stretched across a marked court. 2. see court tennis.

tennis shoe, a sneaker.

ten·on (ten′ŏn), *n.* a projection on the end of a piece of wood, cut wedge-shaped for insertion into a mortise: *v.t. & v.i.* 1. to form a tenon (on). 2. to unite by a tenon.

ten·or (ten′ẽr), *n.* 1. a continuance in a course, action, etc. 2. general sense; drift; purport. 3. *a)* the highest natural adult male singing voice; *b)* a part for this voice; *c)* any wind instrument with this range; *d)* a singer of a tenor part. 4. in *Law,* the exact wording or an exact copy of a writing: *adj.* of, pertaining to, or for a tenor.

tenor clef, the C clef when placed on the fourth line of the staff.

te·nor·rha·phy (tĕ-nôr′ȧ-fi), *n., pl.* -phies, in *Surgery,* the suturing together of the ends of a severed tendon.

te·not·o·my (tĕ-not′ō-mi), *n., pl.* -mies, in *Surgery,* the cutting of a tendon.

ten·pen·ny (ten′pen-i), *adj.* denoting a nail of large size (three inches long).

ten·pins (′pinz), *n.* 1. a bowling game using ten pins. 2. the pins.

ten·pound·er (′poun′dẽr), *n.* a large food and game fish of tropical seas, related to the tarpon.

ten·rec (ten′rek), *n.* any one of various mammals of Madagascar, resembling a hedgehog.

tense (tens), *adj.* tens′er, tens′est, 1. drawn tightly; rigid. 2. feeling or showing nervous tension; jittery: *v.t. & v.i.* tensed, tens′ing, to make or become tense. —tense′ly, *adv.* — tense′ness, *n.*

tense (tens), *n.* any one of the inflectional forms of a verb expressing time of action or of being.

ten·si·ble (ten′si-bl), *adj.* same as tensile (sense 2).

ten·sile (ten′sl), *adj.* 1. of or pertaining to tension. 2. capable of being stretched.

ten·sim·e·ter (ten-sim′ĕ-tẽr), *n.* an instrument for measuring slight changes in gas or vapor pressure.

ten·si·om·e·ter (ten-si-om′ĕ-tẽr), *n.* an instrument for measuring tension, as of wire, yarn, etc.

ten·sion (ten′shŭn), *n.* 1. the act of stretching or the state of being stretched. 2. mental or emotional strain. 3. a state of suppressed hostility between persons or groups. 4. a force tending to cause elongation or extension. 5. voltage.

ten·si·ty (ten′si-ti), *n.* a tense state or condition.

ten·sive (′siv), *adj.* of or causing tension.

ten·sor (ten′sẽr), *n.* a muscle that stretches a part of the body.

ten·strike (ten′strik), *n.* 1. in *Bowling,* same as strike. 2. [Informal], any successful move, act, or accomplishment.

tent (tent), *n.* a movable shelter usually of canvas supported by poles and anchored by stakes: *v.t. & v.i.* to live in a tent or tents.

tent (tent), *n.* in *Medicine,* a plug or roll of lint, gauze, etc. placed in a wound or orifice for dilating or probing.

ten·ta·cle (ten′tȧ-kl), *n.* any one of various appendages or organs around the head or mouth of certain invertebrate animals, used for feeling, grasping, locomotion, etc. —tentac·u·lar (ten-tak′ū-lẽr), *adj.*

ten·ta·tive (ten′tȧ-tiv), *adj.* 1. experimental; provisional. 2. hesitant; uncertain. —ten′tative·ly, *adv.*

ten·ter (ten′tẽr), *n.* a frame for stretching milled cloth to avoid shrinkage in drying: *v.t.* to stretch (cloth) on a tenter or tenters.

ten·ter·hook (-hook), *n.* a sharp, hooked nail for fastening cloth on a tenter.

tenth (tenth), *adj.* next after ninth; 10th: 1. the one after the ninth. 2. one of ten equal parts. 3. a tenth of a gallon.

te·nu·i·ty (tĕ-nōō′i-ti), *n., pl.* -ties, 1. thinness. 2. rarity. 3. meagerness.

ten·u·ous (ten′yoo-wŭs), *adj.* 1. slender or fine. 2. not dense; rare. 3. flimsy; unsubstantial.

ten·ure (ten′yẽr), *n.* 1. the conditions under which something is held. 2. the act, right, manner, etc. of holding property, an office, etc. 3. the length of time something is held.

te·o·sin·te (tĕ-ō-sin′ti), *n.* a tall grass of Mexico and Central America, related to maize and used for fodder.

te·pee (tĕ′pi), *n.* a conical tent of skins, used by North American Indians.

tep·e·fy (tep′ĕ-fi), *v.t. & v.i.* -fied, -fy·ing, to make or become tepid. —tep·e·fac′tion (-fak′shŭn), *n.*

tep·id (tep′id), *adj.* 1. lukewarm. 2. wanting enthusiasm. —te·pid·i·ty (tĕ-pid′i-ti), tep′id·ness, *n.*

tep·i·dar·i·um (tep-i-der′i-ŭm), *n., pl.* -i·a (-ȧ), in an ancient Roman bath, the warm room.

te·qui·la (tĕ-kē′lä), *n.* 1. a century plant of Mexico. 2. an alcoholic liquor made from this plant.

ter·aph (ter′ȧf), *n., pl.* ter′a·phim (′ȧ-fim), a tutelary household god or image among ancient Semitic peoples.

ter·a·tism (ter′ȧ-tizm), *n.* a monstrosity.

ter·a·to-, a combining form meaning *monster, monstrosity.*

ter·a·toid (ter′ȧ-toid), *adj.* resembling a monster.

ter·a·tol·o·gy (ter-ȧ-tol′ō-ji), *n.* the study of malformations and monstrosities in organisms.

ter·bi·um (tūr′bi-ŭm), *n.* a metallic chemical element of the rare-earth group.

ter·cel (tūr′sl), *n.* a variant of tiercel.

ter·cen·te·nar·y (tūr-sen-ten′ẽr-i, -sen′tĕ-ner-i), *adj. & n., pl.* -nar·ies, tricentennial.

ter·e·binth (ter′ĕ-binth), *n.* a small European tree that yields a turpentine. —ter·e·bin′thine (-bin′thin), *adj.*

te·re·do (tĕ-rē′dō), *n., pl.* -dos, -di·nes (′di-nēz), any one of various wormlike marine mollusks that bore into and damage wood pilings and wooden ship hulls.

te·rete (tĕ-rēt', ter'it), *adj.* cylindrical but usually tapering at the ends.

ter·gal (tûr'gl), *adj.* of or pertaining to the back or tergum; dorsal.

ter·gi·ver·sate (tûr'ji-vĕr-sāt), *v.i.* -sat·ed, -sat·ing, 1. to defect from a party, cause, etc. 2. to employ subterfuges; equivocate. —ter·gi·ver·sa'tion, *n.*

ter·gum (tûr'gŭm), *n., pl.* -ga ('gå), the upper surface of a body segment of most arthropods.

term (tûrm), *n.* 1. a limited period of time, as for holding an office. 2. a specified time, as for making a payment. 3. in *Logic*, the subject or predicate of a proposition. 4. in *Mathematics*, a member of a fraction, series, equation, etc. 5. *pl.* conditions stipulated in a contract or agreement. 6. *pl.* relations between persons or groups. 7. a word or expression having a precise meaning in a particular science, art, etc. 8. *pl.* words or manner of speech. 9. in *Law*, the time during which the courts are in session; *v.t.* to name; designate.

ter·ma·gant (tûr'må-gånt), *n.* a noisy, scolding woman; shrew. *adj.* nagging; abusive.

ter·mi·na·ble (tûr'mi-nå-bl), *adj.* 1. that which can be ended. 2. ceasing after a designated time.

ter·mi·nal ('mi-nl), *adj.* 1. of, pertaining to, or situated at the end or extremity. 2. ending; concluding. 3. in *Biology*, growing or occurring at the end of a structure, stem, branch, etc. 4. at the point of causing death: *n.* 1. a limit; boundary; end; extremity. 2. a device attached to an electric circuit for convenience in making connections. 3. either one of the ends of a transportation line. 4. a station at one of these ends or at a main junction of a transportation line. 5. a device, usually with a typewriter keyboard and a video screen, for putting data in, or getting it from, a computer.

ter·mi·nate ('mi-nāt), *v.t.* -nat·ed, -nat·ing, 1. to end; stop. 2. to form the conclusion of; limit; bound: *v.i.* 1. to come to an end. 2. to have its end (*in* something). —ter·mi·na'tion, *n.*

ter·mi·na·tor (-nāt-ēr), *n.* 1. one that terminates. 2. the dividing line between the illuminated and dark regions of the disk of the moon or of a planet.

ter·mi·nol·o·gy (tûr-mi-nol'ŏ-ji), *n., pl.* -gies, the technical terms used in any trade, art, or profession.

term insurance, insurance coverage in effect for a specified time only after which it becomes void.

ter·mi·nus (tûr'mi-nŭs), *n., pl.* -ni (-nī), -nus·es, 1. a limit or boundary. 2. an end. 3. a station at either end of a transportation line.

ter·mite (tûr'mīt), *n.* any one of various antlike insects, very destructive to wood.

tern (tûrn), *n.* any one of several sea birds related to the gulls.

ter·nar·y (tûr'nĕr-i), *adj.* proceeding by or consisting of threes; triple.

terne·plate (tûrn'plāt), *n.* sheet iron or steel plated with an alloy of lead and tin.

Terp·sich·o·re (tĕrp-sik'ŏ-ri), *n.* in *Greek Mythology*, the Muse of dancing.

Terp·si·cho·re·an (tûrp-si-kŏ-rē'ån), *adj.* 1. of or pertaining to Terpsichore. 2. [t-], of or pertaining to dancing.

ter·ra (ter'å), *n.* [Latin], the earth.

terra al·ba (al'bå), any one of several white substances, as magnesia, ground gypsum, etc.

ter·race (ter'ås), *n.* 1. a level space or platform of earth with sloping sides. 2. an open, paved area adjacent to a house; patio. 3. a flat roof, as on an Oriental house. 4. a large open balcony or gallery. 5. a row of houses: *v.t.* -raced, -rac·ing, to form into a terrace.

ter·ra cot·ta (ter'å kot'å), 1. a composition of fine clay and sand, used for statues, pottery, etc. 2. its reddish-brown tint.

terra fir·ma (fûr'må), solid earth.

ter·rain (tĕ-rān', ter'ān), *n.* a tract or expanse of land, especially when suited for some use.

ter·ra in·cog·ni·ta (ter'å in-kog'ni-tå), an unknown or unexplored land.

Ter·ra·my·cin (ter-å-mi'sn), *n.* an antibiotic drug: a trademark.

ter·rane (tĕ-rān', ter'ān), *n.* a series of geologic formations.

ter·ra·pin (ter'å-pin). *n.* any one of several aquatic turtles of North America.

ter·ra·que·ous (tĕr-å'kwi-ŭs), *adj.* consisting of land and water.

ter·rar·i·um (tĕr-âr'i-ŭm), *n., pl.* -i·ums, -i·a (-å), a small enclosure, as of glass or wire mesh, in which small plants or land animals are kept.

ter·raz·zo (tĕ-raz'ō, -rät'sō), *n.* flooring of stone chips, as of marble, cemented in place and polished when dry.

ter·rene (tĕ-rēn'), *adj.* 1. earthy. 2. mundane: *n.* the earth.

ter·res·tri·al (tĕ-res'tri-ål), *adj.* 1. of this world; mundane. 2. of or pertaining to the earth. 3. living or growing on land. 4. consisting of land as distinct from water. —ter·res'tri·al·ly, *adv.*

ter·ret (ter'it), *n.* 1. a ring, as on a dog collar, for fastening a leash. 2. any one of the rings on a harness, through which the driving reins pass.

ter·ri·ble (ter'i-bl), *adj.* 1. exciting awe; causing fear. 2. extreme; severe. 3. [Informal], unpleasant; disagreeable. —ter'ri·ble·ness, *n.* —ter'ri·bly, *adv.*

ter·ri·er (ter'i-ēr), *n.* any one of various breeds of active, usually small dog, originally bred to hunt burrowing animals.

ter·rif·ic (tĕ-rif'ik), *adj.* 1. arousing great fear or terror; dreadful. 2. [Informal], very great; astounding; particularly fine.

ter·ri·fy (ter'i-fī), *v.t.* -fied, -fy·ing, to frighten or alarm exceedingly; fill with dread.

ter·rig·e·nous (te-rij'ē-nŭs), *adj.* produced by the earth; earthborn.

ter·rine (te-rēn'), *n.* an earthenware jar containing some table delicacy.

ter·ri·to·ri·al (ter-i-tôr'i-ål), *adj.* 1. of or pertaining to a territory or to land. 2. of or restricted to a particular territory, district, etc.

---

3. [T-], of a Territory or Territories. 4. [often T-], organized for home defense: *n.* a member of a territorial force. —ter·ri·to'ri·al·ly, *adv.*

ter·ri·to·ri·al·ism (-izm), *n.* any territorial system.

ter·ri·to·ry (ter'ĭ-tôr·ĭ), *n., pl.* -ries, 1. the extent of land under the jurisdiction of a state, sovereign, city, etc. 2. any large tract of land. 3. a part or possession of a country that does not have full status; specifically, [T-], formerly, a part of the United States not yet granted statehood and having an appointed governor and its own legislature. 4. an area assigned to a salesman, agent, etc. 5. a field of action, interest, knowledge, etc.

ter·ror (ter'ēr), *n.* 1. extreme fear. 2. one who excites extreme fear. 3. the ability to cause such fear. 4. the systematic use of violence, as murder, by a party or faction to maintain power, promote political policies, etc.

ter·ror·ism (-izm), *n.* the use of violence, intimidation, etc. to gain an end; especially, a system of government ruling by terror. — ter'ror·ist, *n.*

ter·ror·ize (-īz), *v.t.* -ized, -iz·ing, 1. to fill with dread or terror; terrify. 2. to intimidate or coerce by terror or by threats of terror.

ter·ry (ter'ĭ), *n., pl.* -ries, a heavy corded fabric having a pile of uncut loops; especially, a woven cotton used for towels, robes, etc.: also terry cloth.

terse (tũrs), *adj.* ters'er, ters'est, effectively concise; free of superfluous words; succinct. —terse'ly, *adv.* —terse'ness, *n.*

ter·tial (tũr'shŭl), *adj.* denoting or of the flight feathers on the basal joint of a wing of a bird: *n.* a tertial feather.

ter·tian (tũr'shŭn), *adj.* occurring every other day: usually applied to an intermittent fever or the disease producing it, as a form of malaria: *n.* a tertian fever or disease.

ter·ti·ar·y (tũr'shĭ-er·ĭ), *adj.* third in order, rank, or formation: *n.* 1. a tertial feather. 2. [T-], the first period of the Cenozoic Era, marked by the predominance of land mammals.

ter·va·lent (tẽr-vā'lènt), *adj.* 1. having three valences. 2. same as trivalent (sense 1).

tes·sel·late (tes'é-lāt), *v.t.* -lat·ed, -lat·ing, to lay out, as pavement, in squares or checkered work.

tes·ser·a (tes'ēr·à), *n., pl.* -ser·ae (-ē), any one of the small squares of marble, glass, etc. used in mosaic work.

test (test), *n.* 1. an investigation or trial to ascertain the true character of a person or thing. 2. a method or trial used in such an examination. 3. in *Chemistry,* a reaction by which the constituents of a compound or substance are determined. 4. a series of questions, tasks, etc. to ascertain a person's knowledge, aptitudes, etc.; examination: *v.t.* to put to the proof; try: *v.i.* to undergo a test.

test (test), *n.* a hard outer case or covering, as of mollusks and certain other invertebrates.

tes·ta (tes'tà), *n., pl.* -tae ('tē), the hard outer integument or covering of a seed.

tes·ta·ceous (tes·tā'shŭs), *adj.* consisting of or having a hard shell.

tes·ta·cy (tes'tà·si), *n.* the state or fact of leaving a valid will.

tes·ta·ment (tes'tà·mènt), *n.* 1. a solemn, authentic instrument in writing disposing of the estate of a person deceased; will. 2. a statement of beliefs. 3. [T-], either one of the two divisions of the Bible, the *Old Testament* and the *New Testament.*

tes·ta·men·ta·ry (tes·tà-men'tà·ri), *adj.* of, pertaining to, bequeathed by, or done by a will.

tes·tate (tes'tāt), *adj.* having made and left a valid will.

tes·ta·tor (-ēr), *n.* a person who has made a will. —tes·ta'trix (-tā'triks), *n.fem., pl.* -tri·ces ('trĭ·sēz).

test·er (tes'tēr), *n.* a person or thing that tests.

tes·ter (tes'tēr), *n.* a flat canopy over a bed, pulpit, or tomb.

tes·ter (tes'tēr), *n.* an English coin of the 16th century.

tes·tes (tes'tēz), *n.* plural of testis.

tes·ti·cle (tes'ti·kl), *n.* either one of two oval reproductive glands in the male that lie in the scrotum and secrete spermatozoa; testis.

tes·ti·fy (tes'ti·fī), *v.i.* -fied, -fy·ing, 1. to make a solemn declaration to verify a fact; bear witness or give evidence under oath, usually in court. 2. to serve as evidence: *v.t.* 1. to affirm or declare solemnly on oath. 2. to afford evidence of; indicate.

tes·ti·mo·ni·al (tes·ti-mō'ni·âl), *n.* 1. a writing or statement bearing testimony to a person's character, proficiency, etc. 2. a present, dinner, etc. given as a token of respect, appreciation, etc.

tes·ti·mo·ny (tes'ti·mō·ni), *n., pl.* -nies, 1. any type of evidence; proof. 2. a solemn declaration made on oath to establish a fact. 3. a public profession, as of faith. 4. in the *Bible, a)* the two tablets containing the Mosaic law; *b)* divine revelation.

tes·tis (tes'tis), *n., pl.* -tes ('tēz), same as testicle.

tes·tos·ter·one (tes·tos'tē·rōn), *n.* a male sex hormone.

test tube, a thin, hollow, clear tube, made of glass and closed at one end, used in laboratories.

tes·tu·di·nal (tes·tōōd'n·âl), *adj.* like a tortoise or its shell.

tes·tu·di·nate (-it), *adj.* 1. arched like a tortoise shell. 2. covered by a bony, protective shell, as a turtle.

tes·tu·do (tes·tōō'dō, -tū'-), *n., pl.* -di·nes ('dī·nēz), 1. a protective screen or shelter with a vaulted roof, used by ancient Roman soldiers in besieging a city. 2. among ancient Roman soldiers, a protective covering formed by overlapping their shields over their heads.

tes·ty (tes'ti), *adj.* -ti·er, -ti·est, peevish; morose; irritable. —tes'ti·ly, *adv.* —tes'ti·ness, *n.*

te·tan·ic (ti·tan'ik), *adj.* of, pertaining to, or producing tetanus: *n.* any substance, as nux

---

vomica, that is able to produce tetanic muscle spasms.

tet·a·nus (tet'n-ŭs), *n.* 1. an acute infectious disease caused by the specific toxin of a certain bacillus and characterized by severe spasms and rigidity of voluntary muscles, especially of the jaw and neck; lockjaw. 2. in *Physiology,* the condition of continuous muscle spasm, as excited by shock, stimuli, etc.

tetch·y (tech'i), *adj.* **tetch'i·er, tetch'i·est,** touchy; morose; irritable. **—tetch'i·ly,** *adv.*

tête-à-tête (tāt'ȧ-tāt), *n.* 1. private or confidential conversation between two people. 2. a type of sofa, usually S-shaped, that allows two people to sit facing each other: *adv.* face to face; privately.

teth, tet (tet), *n.* the ninth letter of the Hebrew alphabet.

teth·er (teth'ĕr), *n.* 1. a rope or chain attached to an animal for confining it within certain limits. 2. the scope or limit of one's abilities or resources: *v.t.* to confine or restrict with or as with a tether.

tet·ra (tet'rȧ), *n.* any one of various brilliantly colored, tropical American fishes.

tet·ra- (tet'rȧ), a combining form meaning *four.*

tet·ra·chord (tet'rȧ-kôrd), *n.* in *Music,* half of the octave scale.

tet·rad ('rad), *n.* 1. a group or set of four. 2. in *Chemistry,* an atom, element, or radical with a combining power of four.

tet·ra·eth·yl lead (tet-rȧ-eth'l), a colorless, poisonous compound of lead, used in gasoline to prevent engine knock.

tet·ra·gon (tet'rȧ-gon), *n.* a plane figure with four sides and four angles; quadrangle.

Tet·ra·gram·ma·ton (tet-rȧ-gram'ȧ-ton), *n.* the four consonants of the ancient Hebrew name for God (variously written JHVH, JHWH, YHWH, etc.), regarded as ineffable because of its sacredness.

tet·ra·he·dral (tet-rȧ-hē'drȧl), *adj.* 1. having four faces. 2. of or pertaining to a tetrahedron.

tet·ra·he·dron (-hē'dron), *n., pl.* **-drons, -dra** ('drȧ), a solid figure having four triangular faces.

tet·tram·er·ous (te-tram'ēr-ŭs), *adj.* in *Biology,* having the parts arranged in four similar structures.

te·tram·e·ter (te-tram'ē-tĕr), *n.* 1. a line of verse having four feet or measures. 2. a verse consisting of such lines.

tet·ra·pod (tet'rȧ-pod), *n.* any object having four feet, legs, projections, etc.

te·trap·ter·ous (te-trap'tēr-ŭs), *adj.* in *Zoology,* having four wings.

te·trarch (te'trärk, tet'-), *n.* 1. an ancient Roman governor whose jurisdiction extended over a part (originally a fourth part) of a province. 2. a petty or subordinate prince, governor, etc.

te·trarch·y ('trär-ki), *n., pl.* **-trarch·ies,** 1. the office or jurisdiction of a tetrarch. 2. rule by four persons jointly. 3. a group of four such persons. Also **te'trarch·ate** (-kȧt, -kit).

tet·ra·stich (tet'rȧ-stik), *n.* a poem or stanza of four verses or lines.

tet·ra·syl·la·ble (tet'rȧ-sil-ȧ-bl), *n.* a word of four syllables.

tet·ra·va·lent (tet-rȧ-vā'lĕnt), *adj.* 1. having a valence of four. 2. same as **quadrivalent** (sense 1).

tet·ter (tet'ĕr), *n.* any one of various cutaneous diseases, as herpes and eczema, characterized by itching and eruptions.

Teu·ton (tōōt'n, tūt'-), *n.* 1. any member of an ancient people, variously regarded as Germanic or Celtic, that lived in Jutland, a peninsula in northern Europe. 2. any one of these peoples speaking a Germanic language; especially, a German.

Teu·ton·ic (tōō-ton'ik, tū-), *adj.* 1. of or pertaining to the ancient Teutons. 2. of or pertaining to the Germans. 3. denoting or of a group of north European peoples speaking a Germanic language.

Teu·ton·ism (tōōt'n-izm, tūt'-), *n.* 1. Teutonic life, character, customs, etc. 2. a Germanic idiom.

tex·as (tek'sȧs), *n.* the pilothouse together with the officers' quarters, housed in a structure on the hurricane deck of a steamboat.

Tex·as fever (tek'sȧs), an infectious disease of cattle, transmitted by a tick and caused by a protozoan that invades the blood, destroying the red blood corpuscles.

Texas leaguer, in *Baseball,* a fly ball that drops between the infield and the outfield for a hit.

text (tekst), *n.* 1. the original words of a written or printed work. 2. the actual words of an author, as distinct from notes, emendations, translation, etc. 3. a verse or passage from Scripture forming the subject of a sermon. 4. any topic or subject. 5. a textbook. 6. same as **text hand.**

text·book ('book), *n.* a standard book of instruction in the principles of a particular subject.

text hand, large handwriting.

tex·tile (teks'til, 'til), *adj.* 1. of, pertaining to, or formed by weaving. 2. woven or capable of being woven: *n.* 1. a woven or knitted fabric. 2. material, as fiber or yarn, for weaving or knitting into fabric.

tex·tu·al (teks'choo-wȧl), *adj.* 1. of, pertaining to, or contained in a text. 2. literal; word-for-word. **—tex'tu·al·ly,** *adv.*

tex·tu·al·ism (-izm), *n.* 1. exact adherence to the letter of a text, especially of the Scriptures. 2. textual criticism. **—tex'tu·al·ist,** *n.*

tex·ture (teks'chēr), *n.* 1. the structure produced by the interwoven filaments or fibers of a fabric. 2. the disposition or arrangement of the parts or structures of a body or substance. 3. underlying character. **—tex'tur·al,** *adj.*

-th, a suffix meaning *the act of, the condition or quality of being or possessing.*

-th, a suffix used in forming ordinal numerals, as *fourth, sixth.*

Thai (tī), *adj.* of or pertaining to Thailand, a country in southeast Asia, or its inhabitants, culture, etc.: *n.* 1. *pl.* **Thais, Thai,** a native or inhabitant of Thailand. 2. the official language of Thailand.

thal·a·mus (thal'á-mǔs), *n., pl.* **-mi** (-mī), 1. in *Anatomy,* an oval mass of gray matter at the base of the brain that relays certain stimuli. 2. same as **receptacle** (sense 3).

tha·las·sic (thá-las'ik), *adj.* 1. of, pertaining to, or formed in the seas or oceans; marine. 2. of or pertaining to seas or gulfs, as distinct from oceans.

tha·ler (tä'lẽr), *n., pl.* **tha'ler,** a silver coin of the former German empire.

thal·li·um (thal'i-ǔm), *n.* a rare, poisonous, metallic chemical element, used in photoelectric cells, rat poisons, etc.

thal·lus (thal'ǔs), *n., pl.* **-li** ('ī), **-lus·es** (-iz), a plant body, as of the bacteria, having no distinctive roots, stem, or leaves.

than (*than, then*), *conj.* a particle used to indicate comparison: used after an adjective or adverb in the comparative degree.

than·age (thän'ij), *n.* the land, rank, or jurisdiction of a thane.

than·a·to-, a combining form meaning *death.*

than·a·to·pho·bi·a (than-á-tô-fô'bi-à), *n.* a morbid dread or fear of death.

than·a·top·sis (-top'sis), *n.* a meditation upon death.

Than·a·tos (than'á-tos), *n.* in *Greek Mythology,* the personification of death.

thane (thän), *n.* 1. in early England, any member of a class of freemen holding land from the king by virtue of military service. 2. in early Scotland, a member of the nobility, often a chief of a clan, holding land from the king.

thank (thangk), *v.t.* 1. to express gratitude or obligation to. 2. to blame; hold responsible: an ironic usage.

thank·ful ('fǔl), *adj.* feeling gratitude; grateful. —**thank'ful·ly,** *adv.*

thank·less ('lis), *adj.* 1. not feeling gratitude; ungrateful. 2. not deserving or obtaining thanks; unappreciated. —**thank'less·ly,** *adv.*

thanks (thangks), *n.pl.* an expression of gratitude or obligation: *interj.* I thank you.

thanks·giv·ing (thangks-giv'ing), *n.* 1. the act of expressing gratitude. 2. a formal public celebration expressing thanks to God. 3. [T-], the fourth Thursday of November set aside annually in the U.S. as a public holiday for giving thanks and feasting.

that (*that*), *pron., pl.* **those,** 1. the person or thing mentioned. 2. the one more remote or the other one. 3. who, whom, or which. 4. where. 5. when: *adj.: pl.* **those,** 1. denoting the person or thing mentioned, indicated, or understood. 2. denoting the one more remote or the other one: *conj., used to introduce* 1. a noun clause. 2. an adverbial clause expressing reason, purpose, result, or cause. 3. an elliptical sentence or exclamatory clause expressing desire, indignation, etc.: *adv.* to such a degree; so.

thatch (thach), *n.* 1. material, as straw, reeds, leaves, etc. used for covering roofs: also **thatch'ing.** 2. such a roof: *v.t.* to cover with or as with thatch.

thau·ma·tol·o·gy (thô-má-tol'ô-ji), *n.* the study of miracles; lore of wonder-working.

thau·ma·trope (thô'má-trōp), *n.* an optical device for showing the persistence of an impression on the eye, consisting of a circular card or disk with different figures on each side that appear to blend into one when the card or disk is twirled rapidly.

thau·ma·turge (-tûrj), *n.* a magician; conjurer; supposed worker of miracles.

thaw (thô), *v.i.* 1. to melt or become liquid, as ice or snow. 2. to become less frozen: said of frozen foods. 3. to become warm enough to melt ice and snow. 4. to become milder or more genial in manner: *v.t.* to make thaw: *n.* 1. the act of thawing. 2. a rise in temperature bringing weather warm enough to melt ice and snow.

the (*the*; before vowels *thi, thē*), *adj. & definite article* (as distinct from *a, an*) pertaining to 1. a particular person, object, or thing. 2. a person or thing regarded as a class or understood generically: *adv.* 1. by how much. 2. to that extent.

the·ar·chy (thē'är-ki), *n., pl.* **-chies,** 1. government by God or by deities. 2. an order of ruling deities.

the·a·ter, the·a·tre (thē'á-tẽr), *n.* 1. a public building, room, or other place where dramatic representations, motion pictures, etc. are presented. 2. any similar place, as a lecture hall, surgical arena, etc. having raised rows of seats. 3. any scene or sphere of action. 4. *a)* drama as art; *b)* the world of the theater:

the·at·ri·cal (thi-at'ri-kl), *adj.* 1. of or pertaining to the theater, the dramatic arts, actors, etc. 2. affected; pompous; artificially dramatic; histrionic. —**the·at'ri·cal·ly,** *adv.*

the·at·ri·cals (-klz), *n.pl.* dramatic presentations, especially as given by amateurs.

the·ba·ine (thē'bá-ēn, thi-bá'in), *n.* a colorless, crystalline, poisonous alkaloid, found in opium and used in medicine.

The·ban (thē'bán), *adj.* 1. of or pertaining to Thebes, an ancient city on the Nile and capital of ancient Egypt in the period of its greatest glory. 2. of or pertaining to Thebes, the chief city of a powerful state of ancient Greece. 3. of or pertaining to the people inhabiting these cities.

the·ca (thē'ká), *n., pl.* **-cae** ('sē), 1. in *Botany,* a spore case, sac, or capsule. 2. in *Zoology,* a sheath or case enclosing an animal structure or an organism, as the horny covering of an insect pupa.

thee (thē), *pron.* the objective case of **thou.**

theft (theft), *n.* the act or an instance of stealing; larceny.

the·ine (thē'in, 'ēn), *n.* same as **caffeine.**

their (*ther*), *adj.* of or belonging to them.

theirs (*therz*), *pron.* that or those belonging to them.

the·ism (thē'izm), *n.* 1. belief in the existence of a god or gods. 2. monotheism. —**the'ist,** *n. & adj.* —**the·is'tic,** *adj.*

them (*them*), *pron.* the objective case of **they.**

theme (thēm), *n.* 1. the subject or topic of a discourse or dissertation. 2. a short essay. 3. a series of notes selected as the subject of a musical composition. 4. a song repeated in a movie, play, etc. or associated with a radio show, TV series, etc.: also **theme song.** —**the·mat·ic** (thē-mat'ik), *adj.*

them·selves (them-selvz'), *pron.* 1. the emphatic or reflexive form of they. 2. their true selves.

then (then), *conj.* therefore; in that case: *adv.* 1. next. 2. at that or another time. 3. further; besides: *adj.* of that time: *n.* that time.

the·nar (thē'när), *n.* 1. the palm of the hand. 2. the ball of the thumb: *adj.* of or pertaining to the thenar.

thence (thens, thens), *adv.* 1. from that place. 2. from that time. 3. therefore.

thence·forth ('fōrth'), *adv.* after that time; thereafter: also **thence·for'ward, thence·for'wards.**

the·o·bro·mine (thē-ô-brō'mēn), *n.* an alkaloid derived from the cacao plant, used in medicine.

the·oc·ra·cy (thi·ok'rá-si), *n.* 1. rule by priests. 2. a country so ruled. —**the·o·crat·ic** (thē-ô-krat'ik), *adj.*

the·o·cra·sy (thi·ok'rá-si), *n.* 1. a worship in which originally distinct deities are worshiped as a single deity. 2. the union of the soul with God.

the·od·i·cy (thi·od'i-si), *n., pl.* **-cies,** a philosophical vindication of divine justice.

the·od·o·lite (thi·od'ô-līt), *n.* an instrument for measuring horizontal and vertical angles and ascertaining distances and heights.

the·og·o·ny (thi·og'ô-ni), *n., pl.* **-nies,** that branch of mythology which treats of the origin or genealogy of ancient deities.

the·o·lo·gi·an (thē-ô-lō'jàn, 'ji-àn), *n.* one versed in theology.

the·o·log·i·cal (thē-ô-loj'i-kl), *adj.* of or pertaining to theology.

theological virtues, faith, hope, and charity.

the·ol·o·gy (thi·ol'ô-ji), *n., pl.* **-gies,** the study of the existence, nature, and attributes of God.

the·om·a·chy (thi·om'á-ki), *n., pl.* **-chies,** a battle against or among the gods.

the·o·mor·phic (thē-ô-môr'fik), *adj.* having the form of God. —**the·o·mor'phism,** *n.*

the·op·a·thy (thi·op'á-thi), *n., pl.* **-thies,** intense emotion aroused by contemplation of God.

the·oph·a·ny (thi·of'á-ni), *n., pl.* **-nies,** a visible manifestation of God to man.

the·o·rem (thē'ô-rêm), *n.* 1. a proposition to be proved. 2. a proposition that is regarded as an established principle.

the·o·ret·i·cal (thē-ô-ret'i-kl), *adj.* 1. of, pertaining to, or depending on theory; not practical. 2. given to speculation. Also **the·o·ret'ic.** —**the·o·ret'i·cal·ly,** *adv.*

the·o·ret·ics (thē-ô-ret'iks), *n.* the speculative part of a science.

the·o·rize (thē'ô-rīz), *v.i.* **-rized, -riz·ing,** to form a theory or theories; speculate. —**the·o·re·ti'cian** (-rē-tish'ân), the 'o·rist (-rist), *n.*

the·o·ry (thē'ô-ri, thir'i), *n., pl.* **-ries,** 1. the principles of a science or art considered apart from practice. 2. a systematic statement, partly validated, of the apparent relationships of certain phenomena. 3. a supposition; guess. 4. a speculative plan.

the·o·soph·ic (thē-ô-sof'ik), *adj.* of or pertaining to theosophy or theosophists. —**the·o·soph'i·cal·ly,** *adv.*

the·os·o·phy (thi·os'ô-fi), *n., pl.* **-phies,** 1. any one of various religious systems which profess to show how to attain direct, mystical knowledge of God. 2. [also T-], the doctrines of a modern sect of this kind based more or less on Brahmanism and Buddhism. —**the·os'o·phist,** *n.*

ther·a·peu·tic (ther-â-pūt'ik), *adj.* curative; of or pertaining to the healing art.

ther·a·peu·tics ('iks), *n.* the part of medical science that treats of the application of remedies for the cure of diseases.

ther·a·py (ther'â-pi), *n., pl.* **-pies,** the treatment of diseases by medical or physical means, —**ther'a·pist,** *n.*

there (ther), *adv.* 1. in or at that place. 2. at that point or state. 3. to or into that place. 4. in that respect: *n.* that place: *interj.* an exclamation expressing alarm, triumph, encouragement, sympathy, etc.

there·a·bouts ('â-bouts), *adv.* 1. near that place. 2. near that time, degree, number, etc. Also **there'a·bout.**

there·af·ter (ther-af'tēr), *adv.* after that.

there·at (-at'), *adv.* 1. there; at that place. 2. at that time. 3. for that reason.

there·by (-bī'), *adv.* 1. by that means. 2. connected with that.

there·for (-fōr'), *adv.* for this or that.

there·fore (ther'fôr), *adv. & conj.* for that or this reason; as a result.

there·in (ther-in'), *adv.* 1. in that place. 2. in that respect.

there·of (-uv'), *adv.* 1. of that. 2. from that as a cause.

there·on (-on'), *adv.* 1. on that or it. 2. just after that.

there·to (-tōō'), *adv.* to that place, thing, etc.: also **there·un'to** (-un'tōō).

there·to·fore (-tô-fôr'), *adv.* until then.

there·up·on (-û-pän'), *adv.* 1. immediately after that. 2. on account of that. 3. upon that or this.

there·with (-with'), *adv.* 1. along with that. 2. immediately after that.

the·ri·an·throp·ic (thir-i-an-throp'ik), *adj.* combining the form of man and beast.

the·ri·o·mor·phic (thir-i-ô-môr'fik), *adj.* having the form of an animal.

ther·mae (thūr'mē), *n.pl.* 1. the public baths of ancient Rome. 2. hot springs or baths.

ther·mal (thūr'ml), *adj.* 1. of or pertaining to heat. 2. warm or hot. 3. denoting a fabric containing pockets of air for insulation.

ther·mic (thūr'mik), *adj.* of, pertaining to, or due to heat.

thermo-, a combining form meaning *heat.*

ther·mo·chem·is·try (thūr-mô-kem'is-tri), *n.* that branch of chemistry which treats of the relations between heat and chemical activity.

ther·mo·dy·nam·ics (thūr-mô-di-nam'iks), *n.* the science which treats of the relation between heat and mechanical energy. —**ther·mo·dy·nam'ic,** *adj.*

ther·mo·e·lec·tric·i·ty (thūr-mô-i-lek-tris'i-ti), *n.* electricity produced by the direct action of heat.

ō in dragon, ōō in crude, oo in wool, u in cup, ū in cure, û in turn, ů in focus, oi in boy, ou in house, th in thin, th in sheathe, g in get, j in joy, y in yet.

ther·mo·gen·e·sis (thûr·mō·jen'ĕ·sis), *n.* the production of heat in an animal body, as by organic action.

ther·mol·y·sis (thêr·mol'ĭ·sis), *n.* 1. loss of body heat. 2. in *Chemistry,* dissociation of a compound into its elements by heat.

ther·mom·e·ter (thêr·mom'ĕ·têr), *n.* an instrument for measuring temperature. —ther·mo·met'ric (-mō·met'rik), *adj.*

ther·mom·e·try (thêr·mom'ĕ·tri), *n.* 1. the measurement of heat or cold. 2. the science treating of the use of thermometers.

ther·mo·nu·cle·ar (thûr·mō·nōō'kli·êr, -nū'-), *adj.* in *Physics,* 1. denoting a reaction in which isotopes of a light element fuse into heavier nuclei. 2. of or using the heat from such a reaction.

ther·mo·plas·tic (thûr·mō·plas'tik), *adj.* soft and malleable when exposed to heat: *n.* a thermoplastic substance.

ther·mos (thûr'mŏs), *n.* a bottle or jug in which a liquid retains its temperature for several hours: also called thermos bottle, thermos jug.

ther·mo·scope (thûr'mō·skōp), *n.* an instrument that indicates differences in temperature without measuring them.

ther·mo·stat (thûr'mō·stat), *n.* an apparatus for regulating temperature automatically. —ther·mo·stat'ic, *adj.*

ther·mot·ro·pism (thêr·mot'rō·pizm), *n.* the phenomenon exhibited by some plants of moving toward or away from a source of heat.

the·roid (thir'oid), *adj.* resembling a beast in nature or manner of living.

ther·sit·i·cal (thêr·sit'i·kl), *adj.* scurrilous and loud-mouthed; abusive: from Thersites, a scurrilous Greek in the *Iliad.*

the·sau·rus (thi·sôr'ŭs), *n., pl.* -sau·ri ('ī), -sau·rus·es, 1. a storehouse or treasury. 2. a book of synonyms and antonyms.

these (thēz), *pron. & adj.* plural of this.

The·seus (thē'sōōs, 'si·ŭs), *n.* in *Greek Mythology,* a hero who killed the Minotaur.

the·sis (thē'sis), *n., pl.* the·ses ('sēz), 1. a proposition defended, as in debating. 2. an essay based on research, especially one a student must write before being granted a master's degree. 3. in *Logic,* a postulate.

Thes·pi·an (thes'pi·ǎn), *adj.* of or pertaining to drama; dramatic: from Thespis, the founder of Greek drama: *n.* [often t-], an actor.

Thes·sa·lo·ni·ans (thes·ǎ·lō'ni·ǎnz), *n.* either of two books of the New Testament, I Thessalonians and II Thessalonians.

the·ta (thā'tǎ, thět'ǎ), *n.* the eighth letter of the Greek alphabet.

thet·ic (thet'ik), *adj.* arbitrary; prescribed.

the·ur·gy (thē'êr·ji), *n.* 1. magic supposedly produced by supernatural agency. 2. divine intervention in worldly affairs. —the·ur·gic (thi·ûr'jik), *adj.* —the'ur·gist, *n.*

thews (thūz), *n.pl., sing.* thew, 1. muscles. 2. strength. —thew'y, *adj.* thew'i·er, thew'i·est.

they (thā), *pron., sing.* he, she, it, 1. the ones previously mentioned. 2. people in general: used indefinitely. 3. the third personal plural pronoun.

they'd (thād), 1. they had. 2. they would.

they'll (thāl), 1. they will. 2. they shall.

they're (ther), they are.

they've (thāv), they have.

thi·a·mine (thī'ǎ·mēn, -min), *n.* a white, crystalline substance, part of the vitamin B complex, found in beans, egg yolk, liver, etc.; vitamin B1: also thi'a·min (-min).

thick (thik), *adj.* 1. of relatively great extent from side to side; not thin. 2. measured from side to side. 3. growing, found, etc. in close proximity and in profusion; dense, compact, etc. 4. not clear or transparent. 5. indistinct, muffled, etc. 6. closely set; crowded. 7. [Informal], dull; stupid. 8. [Informal], very intimate: *adv.* in a thick way: *n.* the thickest part. —thick'ly, *adv.*

thick·en ('ĕn), *v.t. & v.i.* 1. to make or become thick or thicker. 2. to make or become more complex.

thick·en·ing (-ing), *n.* something added to a liquid mass to make it thicker.

thick·et (thik'it), *n.* a thick growth or cluster of shrubs or small trees.

thick·head (thik'hed), *n.* a dull, stupid person.

thick·ness ('nis), *n.* 1. the condition of being thick. 2. measurement in the third dimension. 3. a layer, stratum, etc.

thick·set ('set'), *adj.* 1. closely planted. 2. having a thick body; stocky: *n.* [Archaic], a close, thick hedge.

thick·skinned ('skind'), *adj.* 1. having a thick skin. 2. lacking sensitiveness; callous to insults.

thick·skulled ('skuld'), *adj.* dull; stupid.

thief (thēf), *n., pl.* thieves (thēvz), one who takes unlawfully what is not his own.

thieve (thēv), *v.t. & v.i.* thieved, thiev'ing, to steal.

thiev·er·y (thēv'êr·i), *n., pl.* -er·ies, the act or an instance of stealing; theft.

thiev·ish (thēv'ish), *adj.* addicted to theft; dishonest.

thigh (thī), *n.* the thick, muscular part of the leg between the knee and the hip.

thigh·bone ('bōn), *n.* the bone extending from the hip to the knee.

thill (thil), *n.* either of the two shafts for hitching a horse to a cart or wagon.

thim·ble (thim'bl), *n.* 1. a small cap of plastic, metal, etc. that fits over the finger to protect it in sewing. 2. anything like a thimble. 3. a metal ring in a sail, through which a rope is passed. —thim'ble·ful, *n., pl.* -fuls.

thim·ble·rig (-rig), *n.* a sleight-of-hand game played with three small cups (*thimbles*) and a pea which is shifted from cup to cup: *v.t. & v.i.* -rigged, -rig·ging, to cheat or swindle, as by means of this game.

thim·ble·weed (-wēd), *n.* any one of several anemones with long, thimble-shaped heads.

thin (thin), *adj.* thin'ner, thin'nest, 1. of relatively little extent from side to side. 2. slim; slender. 3. not dense or thick. 4. not close or crowded. 5. watery. 6. high in pitch and lacking volume. 7. sheer. 8. not persuasive or convincing. 9. slight, weak, etc.: *adv.* in a thin way: *v.t. & v.i.* thinned, thin'ning, to make or become thin. —thin'ly, *adv.* —thin'ness, *n.*

thine (thin), *adj.* [Archaic or Poetic], of or

belonging to thee: *pron.* [Archaic or Poetic], that or those belonging to thee.

thing (thing), *n.* 1. anything that exists or is supposed to exist. 2. a discrete, tangible object. 3. an inanimate object. 4. a part, item, detail, etc. 5. any matter, affair, etc. 6. an act, happening, event, etc. 7. *pl.* personal belongings; also, clothes. 8. a garment. 9. an object of pity or contempt. 10. [Informal], a matter for argument; issue. 11. [Informal], an irrational craving, dislike, etc. 12. [Informal], something one wants to do or does very well.

think (thingk), *v.i.* thought, think'ing, 1. to use the mind; reason, ponder, or reflect. 2. to have an opinion. 3. to recollect (with *of* or *about*). 4. to consider the well-being of another or others (with *of* or *about*). 5. to conceive (*of*): *v.t.* 1. to form or have in the mind. 2. to hold as an opinion; consider. 3. to conceive as possible; believe; surmise. 4. to call to mind. 5. to use reason in working out. —think'er, *n.*

think-a-ble ('ǝ-bl), *adj.* conceivable.

think-ing ('ing), *adj.* 1. having the faculty of thought. 2. given to thinking; reflective: *n.* the act or result of thinking.

think tank, [Slang], a group or place established for doing research, making long-range plans, etc.: also **think factory**.

thin-ner (thin'ǝr), *n.* something mixed with paint, varnish, etc. to thin it.

thin-skinned ('skind'), *adj.* 1. having a thin skin. 2. sensitive; easily offended.

thi-ol (thī'ōl), *n.* any one of a class of brown, strong-smelling chemical compounds containing sulfur.

thi-on-ic (thī-on'ik), *adj.* of, pertaining to, or containing sulfur.

thi-o-nyl (thī'ō-nil), *n.* a bivalent radical of oxygen and sulfur.

thi-o-phene (thī'ō-fēn), *n.* a colorless liquid occurring in coal tar, resembling benzene.

third (thûrd), *adj.* next after second; 3d or 3rd: *n.* 1. the one after the second. 2. one of three equal parts. 3. the third forward gear ratio of an automotive vehicle.

third-class ('klas'), *adj.* 1. of the class, rank, etc. next below the second. 2. denoting a less-expensive class of mail used as for advertisements: *adv.* by third-class mail or travel accommodations.

third degree, [Informal], harsh grilling, physical punishment, etc. used to get a confession from a prisoner.

third dimension, 1. the quality of having or seeming to have depth. 2. the quality of seeming real.

third person, the form of a pronoun or verb that denotes the person or thing spoken of.

third rail, an additional rail used in some electric railroads to supply power.

third-rate ('rāt'), *adj.* 1. third in quality. 2. not very good; inferior.

third world, [often T- W-], the underdeveloped countries of the world.

thirst (thûrst), *n.* 1. a sensation of dryness in the throat and mouth. 2. a great desire for

drink. 3. a strong craving for anything: *v.i.* 1. to have a desire for drink. 2. to have a strong craving.

thirst-y (thûrs'ti), *adj.* thirst'i-er, thirst'i-est, feeling thirst; dry. —thirst'i-ly, *adv.* —thirst'i-ness, *n.*

thir-teen (thûr'tēn'), *adj.* one more than 12: *n.* the cardinal numeral that is the sum of 12 and one; 13; XIII.

thir-teenth ('tēnth'), *adj.* next after 12th; 13th: *n.* 1. the one after the 12th. 2. one of 12 equal parts.

thir-ti-eth (thûr'ti-ith), *adj.* next after 29th; 30th: *n.* 1. the one after the 29th. 2. one of 30 equal parts.

thir-ty (thûr'ti), *adj.* three times 10: *n.*, *pl.* -ties, 1. the cardinal numeral that is the sum of 29 and one; 30; XXX. 2. *pl.* years or numbers from 30 through 39 (preceded by *the*). 3. the numeral 30, used to signify the end of a newspaper story, etc.

this (this), *pron.*, *pl.* these, 1. the person or thing that is nearer in place, time, or thought. 2. the person or thing that is present. 3. the person or thing that is just now or was last mentioned: *adj.*, *pl.* these, 1. denoting the person or thing that is nearer in place, time, or thought. 2. denoting the person or thing that is present. 3. denoting the person or thing that is just now or was last mentioned: *adv.* to this degree.

this-tle (this'l), *n.* a strong, prickly plant with purple, white, etc. flowers.

this-tle-down (-doun), *n.* the down growing on the flower of a thistle.

thith-er (thith'ẽr, *thith'*-), *adv.* to or toward that place or end.

tho, tho' (*thō*), *conj. & adv.* though.

thole (thōl), *n.* a pin set in the gunwale of a boat to serve as a fulcrum for the oar.

Tho-mism (tō'mizm), *n.* the doctrine of St. Thomas Aquinas, a 13th-century Italian philosopher, who held that theology and philosophy, faith and reason, are compatible.

thong (thông), *n.* 1. a thin leather strap or string for fastening something. 2. the striking part of a whip.

Thor (thôr), *n.* in *Norse Mythology*, the god of thunder and of war.

tho-rac-ic (thō-ras'ik), *adj.* of or pertaining to the thorax.

thoracic duct, the main canal of the lymphatic system, passing along the front of the spinal column.

tho-rax (thôr'aks), *n.*, *pl.* -rax-es, -ra-ces ('ǝ-sēz), 1. the part of the body between the neck and abdomen; specifically, the cavity containing the heart and lungs; chest. 2. the middle division of an insect.

tho-rite (thôr'īt), *n.* a dark-colored mineral, a silicate of thorium.

tho-ri-um (thôr'i-ŭm), *n.* a rare, radioactive chemical element found in certain minerals.

thorn (thôrn), *n.* 1. a very short, leafless branch with a sharp point. 2. any tree or shrub with thorns. 3. something sharp and pointed growing on an animal; spine. 4. anything that troubles or annoys.

ŏ in dragon, ōō in crude, oo in wool, u in cup, ū in cure, ŭ in turn, ŭ in focus, oi in boy, ou in house, th in thin, th in sheathe, g in get, j in joy, y in yet.

thorn apple, 1. a hawthorn. **2.** the fruit of the hawthorn.

thorn-back ('bak), *n.* **1.** any one of several spiny European rays. **2.** a large spider crab.

thorn-y (thôr'ni), *adj.* **thorn'i-er, thorn'i-est, 1.** full of thorns. **2.** full of difficulties, annoyances, etc.

thor-ough (thûr'ō), *adj.* **1.** originally, passing through. **2.** proceeding through to the end; complete. **3.** in every way; absolute. **4.** very careful or exact. —**thor'ough-ly,** *adv.* —**thor'ough-ness,** *n.*

thorough bass, in *Music,* **1.** loosely, the theory of harmony. **2.** an old method used to indicate accompanying chords by means of small marks, as numerals, placed below the bass notes.

thor-ough-bred (thûr'ō-bred), *adj.* **1.** of pure and unmixed breed; pedigreed. **2.** completely instructed, trained, etc.; accomplished: *n.* a thoroughbred animal; specifically, [T-], any one of a breed of horses kept for racing.

thor-ough-fare (-fer), *n.* **1.** a passage through. **2.** a public street open at both ends. **3.** a principal highway.

thor-ough-go-ing (-gō'ing), *adj.* very thorough.

thor-ough-paced (-pāst), *adj.* **1.** able to perform all gaits. **2.** thoroughgoing.

those (thōz), *pron. & adj.* plural of that.

Thoth (thōth, tōt), *n.* the god of wisdom and magic of the ancient Egyptians, represented with the body of a man and the head of an ibis or a dog.

thou (thou), *pron.* the second personal singular pronoun in the nominative case: now only in poetic and religious use.

though (thō), *conj.* **1.** supposing that; if. **2.** notwithstanding that. **3.** nevertheless; however: *adv.* nevertheless; however.

thought (thôt), *n.* **1.** the act of thinking; meditation; reflection. **2.** that which the mind thinks; an idea, opinion, etc. **3.** care; heed. **4.** the ability to think. **5.** a slight amount; trifle.

thought (thôt), past tense and past participle of think.

thought-ful ('fūl), *adj.* **1.** full of thought; contemplative. **2.** considerate of others; kind. —**thought'ful-ly,** *adv.* —**thought'ful-ness,** *n.*

thought-less ('lis), *adj.* **1.** unthinking; careless, heedless, rash, etc. **2.** inconsiderate. —**thought'less-ly,** *adv.* —**thought'less-ness,** *n.*

thou-sand (thou'znd), *adj.* consisting of ten hundred, or 1000: *n.* **1.** the number of ten hundred. **2.** any large but indefinite number.

thou-sandth ('zndth), *adj.* next in order after 999th; 1000th: *n.* **1.** the one after the 999th. **2.** one of 1000 equal parts.

thrall (thrôl), *n.* **1.** a slave. **2.** slavery.

thrall-dom, thral-dom ('dôm), *n.* the condition of being a thrall; slavery.

thrash (thrash), *v.t.* **1.** same as thresh. **2.** to beat; flog. **3.** to make move wildly. **4.** to defeat soundly. **5.** to discuss until settled (with *out*): *v.i.* **1.** same as thresh. **2.** to move about wildly.

thrash-er ('ēr), *n.* **1.** one that thrashes. **2.** any one of a group of brownish American songbirds somewhat like the thrush.

thrash-ing ('ing), *n.* a sound beating.

thread (thred), *n.* **1.** a very thin line or cord of flax, cotton, or other fibrous -substance twisted and drawn out. **2.** a filament, as from a spider. **3.** any thin line, vein, ray, etc. **4.** something continued in a long course. **5.** the spiral ridge of a screw, nut, etc.: *v.t.* **1.** to pass a thread through the eye of. **2.** to walk carefully through the intricacies of. **3.** to fashion a spiral ridge on or in.

thread-bare ('ber), *adj.* **1.** so worn down that the threads can be seen. **2.** wearing old, worn clothes; shabby. **3.** hackneyed; stale.

threat (thret), *n.* **1.** an indication or source of impending danger, evil, etc. **2.** a declaration of an intention to harm, injure, etc.

threat-en ('n), *v.t.* **1.** to make threats against. **2.** to be a menacing indication of. **3.** to be a danger to: *v.i.* **1.** to use threats. **2.** to be an indication or source of impending danger, evil, etc.

three (thrē), *adj.* one more than two: *n.* the cardinal numeral that is the sum of two and one; 3; III.

three-deck-er ('dek'ēr), *n.* **1.** formerly, a warship with guns mounted on three decks. **2.** anything with three levels, layers, etc.

three-di-men-sion-al ('di-men'shūn-l), *adj.* **1.** having or looking as if it has thickness or depth as well as width and height. **2.** lifelike.

three-fold ('fōld), *adj.* **1.** having three parts. **2.** having three times as much or as many: *adv.* three times as much or as many.

three-mile limit ('mil'), a distance of three miles from shore, sometimes considered the limit of a country's territorial jurisdiction.

three-score ('skôr'), *adj.* sixty.

thren-o-dy (thren'ō-di), *n., pl.* **-dies,** a song of lamentation; dirge.

thresh (thresh), *v.t.* **1.** to beat out (grain) from the husk. **2.** same as thrash: *v.i.* **1.** to thresh grain. **2.** same as thrash. —**thresh'er,** *n.*

thresh-old (thresh'ōld, 'hōld), *n.* **1.** the sill of a door. **2.** the place or point of entrance or beginning. **3.** in *Psychology & Physiology,* the point at which a stimulus becomes strong enough to produce a response.

threw (thrōō), past tense of throw.

thrice (thris), *adv.* **1.** three times. **2.** three-fold. **3.** highly; greatly.

thrift (thrift), *n.* **1.** frugality; economical management. **2.** any one of a group of small, evergreen plants with pink or white flowers.

thrift shop, a store where discarded clothing, housewares, etc. are sold, as for charity.

thrift-y ('i), *adj.* **thrift'i-er, thrift'i-est,** characterized by economy and good management; showing thrift. —**thrift'i-ly,** *adv.* —**thrift'i-ness,** *n.*

thrill (thril), *v.t.* **1.** to cause to have a shivering, tingling, excited feeling. **2.** to make vibrate or quiver: *v.i.* **1.** to shiver or tingle with excitement. **2.** to vibrate or quiver: *n.* **1.** a thrilling or being thrilled. **2.** something that causes a thrill. **3.** a vibration or quiver.

thrill-er ('ēr), *n.* one that thrills; specifically, a suspenseful novel, motion picture, etc.

---

a in *cap,* ā in *cane,* ä in *father,* å in *abet,* e in *met,* ē in *be,* ē in *baker,* ê in *regent,* i in *pit,* ī in *fine,* i in *manifest,* o in *hot,* ô in *horse,* ō in *bone,*

thrips (thrips), *n.* any one of numerous small insects which feed on the juice of plants.

thrive (thrīv), *v.i.* thrived or throve, thrived or thriv·en (thriv'n), thriv'ing, 1. to prosper or flourish; be successful, as through good management. 2. to grow vigorously or luxuriantly.

throat (thrōt), *n.* 1. the front part of the neck. 2. the upper part of the passage leading from the mouth to the stomach and lungs. 3. any narrow passage.

throat·y ('ĭ), *adj.* throat'i·er, throat'i·est, guttural or husky. —throat'i·ness, *n.*

throb (throb), *v.i.* throbbed, throb'bing, 1. to beat, pulsate, etc. with more than usual force. 2. to be excited: —*n.* 1. the act of throbbing. 2. a strong pulsation.

throe (thrō), *n.* 1. a sharp sensation of pain. 2. *pl.* agonies.

throm·bin (throm'bĭn), *n.* the enzyme of the blood which forms fibrin from the soluble protein known as fibrinogen, causing coagulation.

throm·bo·sis (throm-bō'sĭs), *n.* coagulation of the blood in the heart or a blood vessel, forming a clot.

throm·bus (throm'bŭs), *n.* the clot formed in thrombosis.

throne (thrōn), *n.* 1. a chair on which a king, cardinal, etc. sits on state occasions. 2. sovereign power or dignity. 3. a sovereign, ruler, etc.: *v.t. & v.i.* to place or be placed on a throne; put or be in power.

throng (thrông), *n.* a great number of people or things gathered together; crowd or multitude: *v.t.* 1. to crowd into. 2. to press upon in large numbers: *v.i.* to come or move together in a throng.

thros·tle (thros'l), *n.* 1. same as song thrush. 2. a machine for spinning wool, cotton, etc.

throt·tle (throt'l), *n.* 1. [Rare], the trachea. 2. the valve for controlling the amount of fuel vapor that enters an internal-combustion engine or the flow of steam in a steam line: also throttle valve: *v.t.* -tled, -tling, 1. to strangle or choke. 2. to censor or suppress. 3. to reduce the flow of, or lessen the speed of, by means of a throttle.

through (thrōō), *adj.* 1. unobstructed; admitting free passage. 2. not stopping along the way. 3. finished: *adv.* 1. from end to end. 2. from beginning to end. 3. to a conclusion. 4. thoroughly; completely: *prep.* 1. from end to end of; between the sides of. 2. in the midst of; among. 3. by the agency of. 4. by way of; via. 5. to various places in. 6. from beginning to end of. 7. up to and including. 8. because of.

through·out (thrōō-out'), *prep.* in every part of: *adv.* in every part; right through.

through·way (thrōō'wā), *n.* an expressway.

throve (thrōv), past tense of thrive.

throw (thrō), *v.t.* threw, thrown, throw'ing, 1. to fling or hurl. 2. to cast to a distance. 3. to cast in any manner. 4. to overturn; upset. 5. to put on hastily or carelessly. 6. to cast off; shed. 7. to form or make roughly. 8. to produce. 9. to twist or wind. 10. to send hurriedly. 11. to put suddenly into a certain state or condition. 12. to move (a lever,

switch, etc.). 13. [Informal], to lose (a game, race, etc.) deliberately. 14. [Informal], to give (a party, dance, etc.). 15. [Informal], to confuse, fluster, etc.: *v.i.* to cast or fling something: *n.* 1. the act of flinging or hurling. 2. a cast of dice. 3. the distance something can be or is thrown. 4. a spread for a bed, sofa, etc. 5. the motion of a moving machine part.

thrum (thrum), *n.* 1. the end of a weaver's thread. 2. *pl.* in *nautical usage,* short pieces of rope yarn. 3. a strumming or drumming: *v.t.* thrummed, thrum'ming, 1. to fringe. 2. in *nautical usage,* to put thrums in (canvas). 3. to strum or drum on: *v.i.* to strum or drum.

thrush (thrush), *n.* 1. any one of a large family of songbirds that includes the robin. 2. a fungous infection affecting the mouth and throat and producing whitish patches.

thrust (thrust), *v.t.* thrust, thrust'ing, 1. to push or drive with or as if with force. 2. to intrude or impose (oneself). 3. to pierce or stab: *v.i.* 1. to move with or as if with force toward, against, or into something; push hard. 2. to move suddenly as or as if as to pierce or stab something: *n.* 1. a thrusting. 2. driving force, specifically of gases from a jet or rocket engine. 3. the ultimate direction or objective of a remark, speech, activity, etc.

thru·way (thrōō'wā), *n.* an expressway.

thud (thud), *v.i.* thud'ded, thud'ding, to strike or fall heavily, making a dull or muffled sound on impact: *n.* such a sound.

thug (thug), *n.* a ruffian, gangster, etc.

thu·li·um (thōō'li·ŭm), *n.* a metallic chemical element of the rare-earth group.

thumb (thum), *n.* the short, thick digit of the hand, nearest the wrist: *v.t.* 1. to handle, turn, soil, etc. with or as if with the thumb. 2. [Informal], to get or try to get (a ride) in hitchhiking by signaling with the thumb.

thumb·nail ('nāl), *n.* the nail of the thumb: *adj.* diminutive or very brief.

thumb·screw ('skrōō), *n.* 1. a screw to turn with the thumb and forefinger. 2. an old instrument of torture, squeezing the thumbs.

thumb·tack ('tak), *n.* a tack with a large, flat head, designed to be pressed into a surface with the thumb.

Thum·mim (thum'im), *n.* see Urim and Thummim.

thump (thump), *n.* a fairly heavy blow with or as if with something blunt, making a thudding sound on impact; knock; rap. 2. the sound so made: *v.t. & v.i.* to strike, beat, or fall with a thump or thumps.

thump·ing ('ing), *adj.* 1. that thumps. 2. [Informal], very great, big, or decisive.

thun·der (thun'dẽr), *n.* 1. the loud crack, boom, or rumble following a flash of lightning, caused by sudden air expansion produced by the electrical discharge. 2. any similar noise. 3. talk, procedures, etc. designed to intimidate, overwhelm, impress, gain advantage, etc.: *v.i.* 1. to produce thunder. 2. to move along with or as if with thunderous noise: *v.t.* to voice or otherwise express with extreme loudness or vehemence.

ŏ in drag*on,* ōō in crude, oo in wool, u in cup, ū in cure, û in turn, ŭ in foc*us,* oi in boy, ou in house, th in thin, th in sheathe, g in get, j in joy, y in yet.

thun·der·bird (-bûrd), *n.* in some North American Indian mythologies, a huge bird producing thunder, lightning, and rain.

thun·der·bolt (-bōlt), *n.* 1. a flash of lightning, together with the thunder accompanying it. 2. such a flash, or a supposed missile accompanied by such a flash, viewed as directed from the heavens toward a target. 3. something, as a piece of news, that is totally unexpected and that amazes or utterly dismays.

thun·der·clap (-klap), *n.* a loud crash of thunder.

thun·der·cloud (-kloud), *n.* a large cloud with great vertical development, charged with electricity and producing lightning and thunder.

thun·der·head (-hed), *n.* a round mass of clouds with dark bottoms and domed tops, portending a thunderstorm.

thun·der·ing (-ing), *adj.* 1. that thunders. 2. [Informal], very great, big, or impressive.

thun·der·ous (-ŭs), *adj.* 1. of, suggestive of, or marked by thunder; thundering. 2. as loud as thunder; booming or reverberating like thunder.

thun·der·show·er (-shou-ĕr), *n.* a shower of rain, together with thunder and lightning.

thun·der·squall (-skwôl), *n.* a squall characterized by rain and thunder and lightning.

thun·der·storm (-stôrm), *n.* a storm marked by thunder and lightning.

thun·der·struck (-struk), *adj.* suddenly struck by and overcome with complete amazement.

thu·ri·ble (thoor'ĭ-bl, thyoor'-), *n.* same as censer.

thu·ri·fer ('ĭ-fēr), *n.* one assisting in a religious rite and bearing a thurible.

Thurs·day (thûrz'dĭ, 'dā), *n.* the fifth day of the week.

thus (*th*us), *adv.* 1. in this or that manner. 2. to this or that degree or extent; so. 3. consequently; therefore. 4. for example.

thwack (thwak), *v.t.* to strike with something flat; whack: *n.* a blow so struck.

thwart (thwôrt), *adj.* extending across; transverse: *n.* 1. a seat for a rower, extending from one side to the other of a boat. 2. a transverse brace in a canoe: *v.t.* to hinder, check, or foil.

thy (*th*ī), *adj.* of or belonging to thee.

thyme (tīm), *n.* 1. a shrubby plant or aromatic herb of a genus of the mint family. 2. the fragrant leaves, used for seasoning.

thy·mol (thī'môl, 'mōl), *n.* an aromatic crystalline compound derived from thyme or made synthetically, used in antiseptics, perfumes, etc.

thy·mus (thī'mŭs), *n.* a ductless, glandlike body in the upper part of the chest, near the throat, disappearing or vestigial in the adult and of unknown function.

thy·roid (thī'roid), *adj.* 1. designating or of a large ductless gland in the neck, regulating body growth and metabolism. 2. designating or of the principal cartilage of the larynx: *n.* 1. the thyroid gland or cartilage. 2. a medical preparation made from an animal thyroid gland.

thyr·sus (thûr'sŭs), *n., pl.* **-si** ('sī), 1. a staff

tipped with a pine cone, represented as being carried in Bacchic revels. 2. in *Botany*, a mixed inflorescence made up of a racemose main axis and branched secondary axes.

thy·self (*th*ī-self'), *pron.* 1. the emphatic or reflexive form of thou. 2. thy true self.

ti (tē), *n.* the seventh tone in any major or minor musical scale of eight tones.

ti·ar·a (ti-er'å, tī-), *n.* 1. a triple crown worn by the Pope. 2. a woman's crownlike head-dress of jewels or flowers.

Ti·bet·an (ti-bet'n), *adj.* of or pertaining to Tibet, an autonomous region of southwestern China, or its inhabitants: *n.* a native or inhabitant of Tibet.

tib·i·a (tib'ĭ-å), *n., pl.* **-i·ae** ('ĭ-ē), **-i·as**, the inner and larger of the two lower leg bones. —**tib'i·al**, *adj.*

tic (tik), *n.* a regularly repeating spasmodic muscular contraction.

tick (tik), *n.* 1. any one of an extensive group of wingless arachnids that suck the blood of both animals and man and that are larger than the related mites. 2. the cloth case of a pillow, mattress, etc. 3. a little mark made as in checking off items. 4. a light clicking or tapping sound, or a series of these, characteristically made by the functioning of the escapement of a wound clock or watch. 5. [Chiefly British Informal], credit extended to allow buying something: *v.i.* 1. to produce the tick or ticks characteristic of a wound clock or watch. 2. [Informal], to function; run; operate: *v.t.* 1. to make a little mark before, after, etc., as in checking off items. 2. to tabulate or count by or as if by doing this.

tick·er ('ēr), *n.* 1. one that ticks; specifically, a telegraphic device recording stock-market quotations, etc. on paper tape. 2. [Slang], the heart.

tick·et (tik'it), *n.* 1. a piece of paper or a card indicating that the holder can do or have something specified, as one giving admission to a theater, entitling one to a ride, showing one's right to pick up a purchased article, etc. 2. a label or tag, as on an article in a store, indicating price, size, etc. 3. the list of candidates nominated by a political party in an election. 4. [Informal], a summons to appear in court because of a traffic violation: *v.t.* 1. to put a ticket on, as to indicate the price. 2. to label, tag, or classify by or as if by putting a ticket on. 3. to provide a ticket or tickets for. 4. [Informal], to issue or attach a ticket (sense 4) to.

tick·ing (tik'ing), *n.* strong, heavy cloth used for making a tick (sense 2).

tick·le (tik'l), *v.t.* **-led, -ling**, 1. to touch lightly as with a feather or with wiggling movements of the fingers in such a way as to produce in the individual so touched a pleasant surface sensation or a reaction of annoyance, uncontrollable laughter, etc. 2. to make chuckle, smile, etc. by reason of being funny; amuse. 3. to gratify, please, etc.: *v.i.* 1. to undergo or be especially subject to the sensation of being tickled as with a feather. 2. to produce such a sensation: *n.* 1. a tickling or a being tickled. 2.

the sensation of being tickled as with a feather.

tick·ler (tik'lēr), *n.* 1. one that tickles. 2. a notebook, reference file, etc. holding reminders to do something at a certain time.

tick·lish ('lish), *adj.* 1. marked by a tickling sensation. 2. reacting quickly or easily to the sensation of being tickled. 3. being of such a kind as to require great delicacy of approach or treatment; difficult. 4. easily disturbed or upset; touchy; sensitive.

tick-tack-toe (tik-tak-tō'), *n.* a game for two, one player marking X and the other O in turn in a nine-square block and each trying to be first to complete a three-square row of the mark chosen: also **tic-tac-toe'**.

tick·tock (tik'tok), *n.* a ticking sound, as of a large, wound clock: *v.i.* to sound thus.

tid·al (tīd'l), *adj.* of, produced, or governed by a tide or tides.

tidal wave, 1. popularly, a huge ocean wave produced as by an earthquake. 2. an enormous surge of feeling, emotion, widespread opinion, support, etc.

tid·bit (tid'bit), *n.* a tasty morsel; delicacy.

tid·dly-winks (tid'li-wingks), *n.* a game in which little disks are pressed down with another disk to snap them into a cup.

tide (tīd), *n.* 1. the regular rising and falling of oceans, seas, and bodies of water connected with them: it is caused by the attraction of the moon and sun and occurs twice every 24 hours and 50 minutes. 2. any rising and falling suggestive of the tide. 3. a stream, current, trend, etc., as of public opinion. 4. the point marking the fullest or highest development of something. 5. a particular time or season: now used only in combination: *adj.* same as **tidal**: *v.i.* **tid'ed, tid'ing,** to move or surge in a tidelike manner: *v.t.* 1. to carry along with or as if with the tide. 2. to help along or through temporarily (with *over*).

tide-land ('land, 'länd), *n.* land alternately covered and uncovered by tide.

tide-wa·ter ('wôt-ēr), *n.* 1. water produced or acted upon by the tide. 2. the adjacent land area: *adj.* of a tidewater.

ti·dings (tī'dingz), *n.pl.* news.

ti·dy (tī'di), *adj.* **-di-er, -di-est,** 1. neat; trim; orderly. 2. [Informal], quite good; satisfactory; also, quite large: *v.t. & v.i.* **-died, -dying,** to make (things) tidy: *n., pl.* **-dies,** same as **antimacassar.** —**tid'i-ness,** *n.*

tie (tī), *n.* 1. a string, cord, etc. for fastening. 2. a binding or joining connection; bond. 3. same as **necktie.** 4. a beam, rod, etc. for holding parts of a building together. 5. any one of the parallel pieces laid across a railroad bed to support the rails. 6. an equality of scores, votes, etc.; also, a game or other contest marked by such equality. 7. in *Music*, a curved line joining two notes of the same pitch to show that the first note is to be held for the duration of the two: *adj.* marked by a tie (sense 6): *v.t.* **tied, ty'ing,** 1. to fasten, bind, etc. as with string or cord. 2. to make (a knot or bow) in. 3. to restrain, restrict, etc. 4. to join together by

some bond. 5. to bring into relationship, consistency, harmony, etc. with something else (with *in*). 6. to moor as to a dock (with *up*). 7. to occupy or engage in such a way as to make unavailable for anything else (with *up*). 8. to equal the score, achievement, total, etc. of: *v.i.* 1. to undergo being tied. 2. to equal the score, achievement, etc. of another or others.

tie clasp, an ornamental clasp to hold the lower part of a necktie in place at the shirt front: also **tie clip, tie bar.**

tie-in (tī'in), *n.* a connection; relationship.

tie-pin (tī'pin), *n.* same as **stickpin.**

tier (tir), *n.* 1. a row, grouping, or level, as of theater seats, especially one situated higher or lower than another or others. 2. a layer, as of cake, or a stratum or the like, especially when above or below another: *v.t. & v.i.* to set or be set in tiers.

tier·cel (tir'sěl), *n.* in *Falconry*, a male hawk.

tie tack, an ornamental pin with a short point to go through a necktie and into a snap so as to hold the lower part of the necktie in place on a shirt front.

tie-up (tī'up), *n.* 1. a snarling or blocking of the flow of traffic, production, etc. 2. a connection, relationship, or involvement.

tiff (tif), *n.* 1. a slight fit of anger or irritableness. 2. a slight quarrel: *v.i.* to have a tiff.

tif·fa·ny (tif'ā-ni), *n., pl.* **-nies,** a thin gauze of silk or muslin.

tif·fin (tif'in), *n. & v.i.* [British], lunch.

ti·ger (tī'gēr), *n., pl.* **-gers, -ger,** 1. a large, fierce, flesh-eating animal with wavy black stripes on its tawny coat: tigers constitute a certain species of the cat family and are native to Asia. 2. any one of certain similar animals, as the jaguar. 3. an individual characterized by extraordinary drive or fierceness.

tiger beetle, any one of a family of brightly colored, often striped beetles, the larvae of which feed on other insects.

tiger cat, 1. any one of various wildcats, as the ocelot, suggestive of but smaller than the tiger. 2. a domestic cat with markings suggestive of those of a tiger.

tiger lily, a species of lily: the flowers are orange in color and have purplish-black spots.

tiger's eye, an ornamental, semiprecious, yellow-brown stone: also **tiger eye.**

tight (tīt), *adj.* 1. compact and not leaky. 2. close together. 3. securely joined; not loose; firm. 4. stretched out completely so as to be taut; not slack. 5. close or too close in fit; very snug. 6. rigid; strict; severe. 7. constrictive and hazardous. 8. tense; strained. 9. so close as to be uncertain in outcome, as a race. 10. short in radius, as a turn or curve; sharp. 11. not easily obtained, as money for borrowers or as a commodity; not freely available; also, marked by such scarcity, as the market for capital to be loaned. 12. concise or condensed: said of the use of words. 13. [Informal], stingy; parsimonious. 14. [Slang], drunk: *adv.* in a tight way; firmly, securely, etc.

tight·en (tīt'n), *v.t. & v.i.* to make or become tight or tighter.

tight·fist·ed (tīt'fis'tid), *adj.* parsimonious.

tight·fit·ting ('fit-ing), *adj.* fitting very tight.

tight-lipped ('lipt'), *adj.* saying little; taciturn or secretive.

tight·rope ('rōp'), *n.* a rope or cable which is stretched tight, as above a circus ring, and on which acrobats walk or do balancing acts.

tights (tīts), *n.pl.* a tightly fitting garment covering the legs and lower part of the trunk and worn as by acrobats.

tight ship, [Informal], an organization as efficient as a well-run ship.

tight-wad (tīt'wäd), *n.* [Slang], a stingy person.

ti·gress (tī'gris), *n.* a female tiger.

tike (tīk), *n.* same as tyke.

til·bu·ry (til'bēr-i), *n., pl.* -ries, a light, two-wheeled carriage for two persons.

til·de (til'dē), *n.* a mark (˜) used typically over the *n* of some Spanish words to indicate an *ny* sound, over vowels of some Portuguese words to indicate nasalization, or as a special symbol in some pronunciation systems.

tile (tīl), *n.* 1. a thin, typically rectangular piece of baked clay or of stone, rubber, plastic, etc., used as to cover roofs, floors, walls, etc. 2. tiles collectively; tiling. 3. a drain made of baked clay or of concrete. 4. one of the small pieces used in playing certain table games: *v.t.* tiled, til'ing, to cover with tiles.

til·ing (tīl'ing), *n.* 1. tiles collectively. 2. a covering or structure of tiles.

till (til), *n.* 1. a drawer, as in a store, in which money is kept. 2. an unstratified mass of intermingled clay, sand, gravel, etc. pushed or deposited by a glacier: *prep. & conj.* same as **until**: *v.t.* to put and maintain (land) in proper condition for raising crops, as by plowing and fertilizing; cultivate.

till·age (til'ij), *n.* 1. tilled land. 2. the work of tilling land.

till·er ('ēr), *n.* 1. one that tills land. 2. a machine to till land. 3. a bar or handle to turn the rudder of a boat. 4. a shoot from the lower part of a plant.

tilt (tilt), *n.* 1. a rooflike cloth covering put up over a wagon, stall, boat, etc. 2. a thrusting or parrying movement made as with a lance. 3. same as **joust**. 4. the act of tilting. 5. the degree of an incline or slant; also, the condition of being at an inclined angle: *v.t.* 1. to cover (a wagon, stall, etc.) with a tilt. 2. to poise or thrust (a lance), as in jousting; also, to charge at (a jousting opponent). 3. to cause to tip or slant. 4. to forge or hammer with a tilt hammer: *v.i.* 1. to joust; also, to make a jousting movement or charge. 2. to undergo tipping; slant; incline.

tilth (tilth), *n.* 1. a tilling or being tilled. 2. tilled land.

tilt hammer, a machine that pounds metal into shape by dropping a heavy weight onto the metal.

tilt-top (tilt'top), *adj.* denoting a table, stand, etc. with a top that can be tilted to a vertical position.

tim·bale (tim'bl), *n.* 1. a dish consisting of a creamy preparation, as of chicken, baked in a small drum-shaped mold or served in a small pastry shell of various shapes. 2. the shell.

tim·ber (tim'bēr), *n.* 1. wood suitable for houses, ships, etc. 2. a large, heavy piece of such wood, readied for use in building. 3. trees or forests collectively; also, wooded land. 4. one of the wooden ribs of a ship. 5. kind; character; type: *v.t.* to furnish, build, or prop up with timbers.

tim·ber·line (-lin), *n.* a line of demarcation, as along the side of a mountain, above or beyond which trees do not grow.

timber wolf, a large wolf, gray in color, formerly common as in northern North America.

tim·bre (tam'bēr, tim'bēr), *n.* a quality of sound distinguishing one voice, musical instrument, or vowel sound from another.

tim·brel (tim'brĕl), *n.* a kind of tambourine or drum anciently in use.

time (tīm), *n.* 1. measure of duration, whether past, present, or future, or a particular period of this. 2. a system of reckoning duration. 3. *usually pl.* conditions characterizing a particular period of time; also, an age, era, epoch, etc. 4. rate of speed; tempo. 5. a particular instant, moment, occasion, etc. 6. same as **timeout**: *v.t.* timed, tim'ing, 1. to regulate or measure the time of. 2. to adjust or adapt the time of: *adj.* of, pertaining to, or regulated according to time or a particular period or moment of time.

time clock, a clock devised to record the arrival and departure time of an employee.

time-hon·ored ('on'ērd), *adj.* revered by reason of long usage or existence.

time-keep·er ('kē-pēr), *n.* 1. one keeping time, as of employees' hours. 2. a timepiece.

time·less ('lis), *adj.* unending; eternal.

time·ly (tīm'li), *adj.* -li·er, -li·est, opportune. — time'li·ness, *n.*

time-out (tīm'out'), *n.* an interval of temporary suspension of activity, as of play in a game.

time·piece ('pēs), *n.* a device to measure time, as a clock or watch.

tim·er (tīm'ēr), *n.* 1. a timekeeper. 2. a stopwatch. 3. a clocklike controlling device.

times (tīmz), *prep.* multiplied by.

time-serv·er (tīm'sûr-vēr), *n.* one cynically or obsequiously conforming merely for personal advantage; opportunist. —**time'serv·ing,** *n. & adj.*

time sharing, 1. a system for simultaneous computer use at many remote sites. 2. a system for sharing ownership of a vacation home, condominium, etc., with each joint purchaser occupying the unit at a specific time each year: also **time share.**

time·ta·ble ('tā-bl), *n.* a time schedule.

time-worn ('wôrn'), *adj.* worn out by time.

tim·id (tim'id), *adj.* lacking courage.

ti·mid·i·ty (ti-mid'ĭ-ti), *n.* lack of courage.

tim·ing (tīm'ing), *n.* regulation of speed or occurrence for most effective results.

tim·or·ous (tim'ēr-ŭs), *adj.* timid.

Tim·o·thy (tim'ō-thi), *n.* either of two books of

the New Testament, I Timothy and II Timothy.

tim·o·thy (tim'ô-thi), *n.* a bristly European grass widely grown for hay.

tim·pa·ni (tim'pä-ni), *n.pl.* kettledrums.

tin (tin), *n.* 1. a soft, silvery-white, metallic chemical element. 2. same as **tin plate**. 3. a pan, box, etc. made of tin plate; also, [Chiefly British], a can (senses 1 & 3): *v.t.* **tinned, tin'ning,** 1. to cover or plate with tin. 2. [Chiefly British], to can.

tin·a·mou (tin'â-mōō). *n.* any one of a family of birds that look like partridges but are related to the ostrich, found in Central and South America.

tin·cal (ting'kâl, 'kôl), *n.* crude borax.

tin can, same as **can** (sense 1).

tinc·to·ri·al (tingk-tôr'i-âl), *adj.* of, pertaining to, or involving color, coloring, dyeing, or staining.

tinc·ture (tingk'chēr), *n.* 1. a tinge or shade of color 2. a hint or trace of something. 3. an alcoholic solution of a medicinal substance: *v.t* **-tured, -tur·ing,** to tint or tinge.

tin·der (tin'dēr), *n.* easily ignitable material.

tin·der·box (-boks), *n.* 1. originally, a box for tinder 2. something dangerously subject to the risk of fire, as a rickety old wooden building. 3. any place or situation likely to flare up into rebellion, warfare, etc.

tine (tin), *n.* a pointed projection; prong.

tin·foil (tin'foil), *n.* tin or a tin alloy beaten into thin sheets used as for wrapping.

ting (ting), *n.* a single light, clear sound made as by flicking the fingernail against a wine glass: *v.i.* & *v.t.* to ring with such a sound.

tinge (tinj), *v.t.* **tinged, tinge'ing** or **ting'ing,** 1. to color lightly; tint. 2. to touch lightly or imbue with a trace of something indicated: *n.* 1 a slight coloring; tint. 2. a light touch of something; trace; hint.

tin·gle (ting'gl), *v.i.* **-gled, -gling,** to have or produce a diffused sensation of light pricking or stinging, often accompanied by a spreading warmth or glow *v.t.* to cause to have or produce this sensation. *n.* this sensation.

ti·ni·ness (ti'ni-nis), *n.* the quality or state of being tiny

tin·ker (ting'kēr), *v.i.* 1. to work at repairing or adjusting something, especially in an experimental or superficial way or without much attention or skill. 2. to meddle. 3 to do the work of a tinker (sense 1): *v.t.* 1. to work at or upon, repair, or adjust, especially experimentally, superficially, etc. 2. to meddle with. 3. to repair (pots, kettles, etc.) as a tinker (sense 1) does: *n.* 1. an itinerant repairer of pots, kettles, etc. 2. one that tinkers (senses 1 & 2). 3. a young mackerel.

tin·kle (ting'kl), *n.* a light, high, short, nonresonant sound, as of a tiny bell; jingle *v.i.* & *v.t.* **-kled, -kling,** to make or cause to make such a sound, jingle.

tin·ny (tin'i), *adj.* **-ni·er, -ni·est,** 1. of, like, or suggestive of tin. 2. lacking solidity or value; flimsy, cheap, etc. 3. lacking richness of tone; thin, shrill, etc.

tin plate, thin sheets of iron or steel plated with tin.

tin·sel (tin'sl), *n.* 1. formerly, cloth interwoven with lustrous metallic material. 2. thin sheets, strips, etc. of inexpensive glittering material, as of metal foil, used for decoration. 3. anything showy but of little value: *adj.* 1. of or decorated with tinsel. 2. showy but worthless; gaudy: *v.t.* **-seled** or **-selled, -sel·ing** or **-sel·ling,** 1. to decorate with or as if with tinsel. 2. to make gaudy.

tin·smith (tin'smith), *n.* a worker in tin or in tin plate; maker of tinware.

tint (tint), *n.* 1. a very light coloring; pale color; tinge. 2. a particular color or a variety of it; especially, a gradation of a color in regard to its mixture with white. 3. a hair dye: *v.t.* to give a tint to.

tin·tin·nab·u·la·tion (tin-ti-nab-yoo-lā'shŭn), *n.* the ringing or sound of or as if of bells.

tin·type (tin'tip), *n.* same as **ferrotype.**

tin·ware ('wer), *n.* pots, pans, or other articles made of tin plate.

ti·ny (ti'ni), *adj.* **-ni·er, -ni·est,** very small.

-tion (shŭn), a suffix meaning *act of, state of being, thing that is.*

-tious (shŭs), an adjectival suffix corresponding to **-tion.**

tip (tip), *n.* 1. the pointed or rounded extremity or top of something, as of a finger or mountain peak. 2. something attached to the extremity of a thing, as a metal cap or ring at the end of a cane. 3. a light blow; tap. 4. a gratuity 5 a confidential or advance piece of information meant to be helpful; also, a hint, warning, etc 6. a tilt; slant. *v.t.* **tipped, tip'ping,** 1. to form or constitute the tip or a tip (senses 1 & 2) of 2. to put a tip or tips (senses 1 & 2) on, or cover the tip or tips of. 3. to strike lightly or glancingly 4. to give a gratuity to. 5. to give a tip (sense 5) to. 6. to tilt; slant. 7 to raise up slightly or touch (one's hat brim) in salutation. 8. to overturn or upset by or as if by first making tilt or slant *v.t.* 1 to give a gratuity or gratuities. 2. to strike something lightly or glancingly 3. to become tilted or slanted 4. to become overturned or toppled from being tilted.

tip-off (tip'ôf), *n.* same as **tip** (sense 5).

tip·pet (tip'it), *n.* a narrow cape or covering, as of fur or wool, for the neck or shoulders.

tip·ple (tip'l), *v.i.* & *v.t.* **-pled, -pling,** to sip or imbibe (alcoholic liquor) repeatedly or habitually *n.* alcoholic liquor **—tip'pler,** *n.*

tip·ster (tip'stēr), *n.* [Informal], one providing tips, as to bettors, usually for a fee

tip·sy (tip'si), *adj.* **-si·er, -si·est,** 1 somewhat intoxicated; befuddled 2. apt to tip over; also, askew **—tip'si·ness,** *n.*

tip·toe (tip'tō), *n.* a toe tip or the toe tips: *adv.* & *adj.* on the toe tips. *v.i.* **-toed, -toe·ing,** to go along on the toe tips, as in stealth.

tip·top (tip'top), *n.* the highest point or degree: *adj.* & *adv* at tiptop, in excellent condition.

ti·rade (ti'rād, ti-rād'), *n.* a long, vehement speech, as of denunciation, harangue

tire (tir), *n.* 1 a continuous strip of metal or rubber tightly encircling the outside of the rim of a **vehicle** wheel and constituting the tread of the wheel. 2. a shock-absorbing inflatable tube of rubber or of rubber and fabric, etc. so encircling a vehicle wheel. 3. a heavy, hooplike casing of such material designed to enclose a shock-absorbing inflatable tube of rubber and so to encircle a vehicle wheel: *v.t.* **tired, tir'ing,** 1. to lessen or exhaust the energy or strength of (the body, a bodily part, or an individual); fatigue. 2. to lessen or destroy the interest or patience of, as because of repetition or boring details: *v.i.* to become fatigued, weary, bored, etc.

tired (tīrd), *adj.* 1. fatigued; weary. 2. lacking originality, freshness, etc., stale.

tire-less (tīr'lis), *adj.* not tiring.

tire-some ('sŏm), *adj.* 1. fatiguing; wearisome; tedious. 2. vexing; annoying.

'tis (tiz), it is.

tis-sue (tish'ōō), *n.* 1. a thin, light, delicate fabric, as gauze. 2. an intricately interconnected aggregate of events, things said or done, etc.; weblike complex. 3. soft absorbent paper, as that used for disposable handkerchiefs; also, a piece or sheet of this. 4. same as **tissue paper**; also, a piece or sheet of such paper. 5. in *Biology,* the aggregate of cells and connective material forming an organic body or bodily part.

tissue paper, unsized, very thin, translucent paper used as for tracing, wrapping, etc.

tit (tit), *n.* 1. a teat; nipple. 2. a breast: now vulgar. 3. a titmouse.

Ti-tan (tīt'n), *n.* 1. in *Greek Mythology,* any one of a race of giant deities overthrown by the Olympian gods. 2. [t-], a person or thing of great size or power.

Ti-tan-ic (tī-tan'ik), *adj.* 1. of or like the Titans. 2. [t-], great in size or power.

ti-ta-ni-um (tī-tā'ni-ŭm, ti-), *n.* a silvery or gray, lustrous, metallic chemical element.

tit for tat (tit' fer tat'), exact retaliation.

tithe (tīth), *n.* 1. a tenth of one's annual income, paid as a tax or given as a contribution to a church. 2. any tax or levy: *v.i.* **tithed, tith'ing,** to pay or give a tithe: *v.t.* 1. to pay a tithe of 2. to levy a tithe on or collect a tithe from.

ti-tian (tish'ăn), *n.* reddish yellow; auburn: *adj.* of this color

tit-il-late (tit'l-āt), *v.t.* **-lat-ed, -lat-ing,** 1. to stimulate or arouse pleasurably. 2. to tickle. —tit-il-la'tion, *n.*

tit-i-vate (tit'i-vāt), *v.t. & v.i.* **-vat-ed, -vat-ing,** to spruce up.

tit-lark (tit'lärk), *n.* same as **pipit.**

ti-tle (tīt'l), *n.* 1. the name given a book, poem, play, musical work, painting, etc. 2. an epithet. 3. an appellation of rank, distinction, etc. 4. a claim, right. 5. a larger division of a law book, statute, etc. 6. a championship, as in sports. 7. in a movie or TV production, any one of the written acknowledgments shown of work done or assistance given; also, a subtitle: *v.t.* **-tled, -tling,** to give a title to; entitle.

ti-tle-hold-er (-hōl-dĕr), *n.* a champion, as in sports.

tit-mouse (tit'mous), *n., pl.* **-mice** ('mīs), any one of a family of common, small songbirds.

ti-trate (tī'trāt), *v.t. & v.i.* **-trat-ed, -trat-ing,** to test by or be subjected to titration.

ti-tra-tion (tī-trā'shŭn), *n.* in *Chemistry,* volumetric analysis indicating how much of a certain substance is in a solution.

tit-ter (tit'ēr), *v.i.* to giggle: *n.* a giggling.

tit-tle (tit'l), *n.* a tiny particle; iota; jot.

tit-tle-tat-tle (tit'l-tat-l), *n.* idle, trifling talk.

tit-u-ba-tion (tich-oo-bā'shŭn), *n.* a stumbling or staggering gait, characteristic of persons suffering from spinal or cerebral afflictions.

tit-u-lar (tich'ŭ-lēr), *adj.* 1. of, pertaining to, or possessing a title. 2. existing in name or title only; nominal: *n.* one who is invested with a title to an office, but does not possess the power and authority appertaining to it.

Ti-tus (tīt'ŭs), *n.* a book of the New Testament.

tiz-zy (tiz'i), *n., pl.* **-zies,** [Informal] an agitated condition brought on by something insignificant.

tme-sis (tē-mē'sis), *n.* the separation of the parts of a compound word by the intervention of another word or words.

TNT (tē'en-tē'), *n.* a powerful substance used for exploding, blasting, etc.; trinitrotoluene.

to (tōō), *prep.* 1. toward. 2. in accordance with. 3. in a direction understood. 4. in respect of. 5. in comparison with. 6. close in; against. 7. up to the limit of. 8. up to the time of. 9. for. 10. with. 11. making up; in. 12. in celebration of: *adv.* 1. toward the thing to be done. 2. into place; into a normal state. 3. forward. 4. shut. *To* is also used as the sign of the infinitive.

toad (tōd), *n.* a jumping, tailless amphibian resembling the frog.

toad-eat-er ('ēt-ēr), *n.* a sycophant.

toad-fish ('fish), *n., pl.* **-fish, -fish-es,** a fish with a large head and wide mouth.

toad-stone ('stōn), *n.* a material supposed to have originated in the stomach of a toad, sometimes worn as a pendant.

toad-stool ('stool), *n.* 1. an umbrella-shaped fungus. 2. a poisonous mushroom.

toad-y (tōd'i), *n., pl.* **toad'ies,** a sycophant: *v.t. & v.i.* **toad'ied, toad'y-ing,** to fawn upon as a sycophant; to play the sycophant. —toad'-y-ism, *n.*

toast (tōst), *n.* 1. bread browned by heat. 2. the act of drinking to one's health, or to some sentiment or popular appeal. 3. a sentiment proposed at a banquet or the like to which the company responds by drinking: *v.t.* 1. to brown or heat (bread, cheese, etc.). 2. to heat completely. 3. to show honor to in drinking by making a toast: *v.i.* 1. to make a toast in drinking. 2. to become toasted, browned, etc.

toast-mas-ter ('mas-tēr), *n.* one who presides at a public dinner or banquet, announces the toasts, and calls upon the speakers.

to-bac-co (tō-bak'ō), *n., pl.* **-cos,** 1. a plant allied to the nightshade with white, purple, or

---

a in cap, ā in cane, ä in father, å in abet, e in met, ē in be, ē in baker, è in regent, i in pit, ī in fine, i in manifest, o in hot, ô in horse, ō in bone,

yellow flowers, and leaves which are prepared in various ways for smoking, chewing,
and snuffing. 2. cigarettes, cigars, snuff, etc.

to·bac·co·nist (tŏ-bak'ŏ-nist), *n.* [Chiefly Brit-
ish], a dealer in tobacco, cigars, etc.

tobacco worm moth, a greenish caterpillar with
white stripes, which feeds on the tobacco
plant.

to·bog·gan (tŏ-bog'ăn), *n.* a kind of runnerless
sled in which one or more persons sit, for
sliding down snow-covered hills or inclines:
v.i. 1. to slide downhill by means of a
toboggan. 2. to go down quickly

To·by (tŏ'bi), *n., pl.* **-bies**, a drinking mug used
for beer or ale, shaped like a fat man with
a cocked hat which forms the brim.

to·col·o·gy (tŏ-kol'ŏ-ji), *n.* same as **obstetrics**.

toc·sin (tok'sin), *n.* 1. an alarm bell. 2. the
ringing of a bell to sound an alarm.

tod (tod), *n.* [Scottish], a fox.

to·day (tŏ-dā'), *n.* 1. the present day. 2. the
present time or age: *adv.* 1. on this day. 2.
at the present time.

tod·dle (tod'l), *v.i.* **-dled, -dling**, to walk with
short, tottering steps like a child. **—tod'dler,**
n.

tod·dy (tod'i), *n., pl.* **-dies**, 1. a sweet juice obtained from certain palms. 2. a sweetened
mixture of hot water, brandy, whiskey, etc.:
also **hot toddy**.

to·do (tŏ-dōō'), *n.* [Informal], a noisy confusion; tumult.

to·dy (tŏ'di), *n., pl.* **-dies**, a small, insect-eating
bird of the West Indies, green in color with
a crimson throat.

toe (tŏ), *n.* 1. one of the terminal members of
the foot of a man or animal. 2. the forepart
of a man's foot, animal's hoof, etc. 3. a
projection: *v.t.* **toed, toe'ing**, to touch, reach,
or strike with the toe or toes.

toed (tŏd), *adj.* possessing (a particular type or
number of) toes.

toe·hold ('hŏld), *n.* 1. sufficient room to place
the toe in ascending. 2. a small position
leading to a greater one.

toe·nail ('nāl), *n.* the nail of a toe.

toff (tof), *n.* [British Slang], a dandy.

tof·fee, tof·fy (tof'i), *n.* a taffy.

tog (tog), *v.t. & v.i.* **togged, tog'ging**, [Informal],
to dress; put on togs: *n. pl.* [Informal],
dress; clothing of a particular kind.

to·ga (tŏ'gă), *n., pl.* **-gas, -gae** ('jē), the loose
outer garment worn by the ancient Romans.

toga vi·ri·lis (vi-rī'lis), [Latin], the toga assumed by Roman youths at the age of four-
teen.

to·geth·er (tŏ-geth'ẽr), *adv.* 1. in company or
association. 2. mutually. 3. in union or concert. 4. uninterruptedly. 5. in a single location or group. 6. thought of as a group. 7.
following one after another. 8. in accordance: *adj.* [Slang], being a well-adjusted person.

to·geth·er·ness (-nis), *n.* the devoting of time
and effort to being in close association in
order to encourage the growth of solid relationships.

tog·ger·y (tog'ẽr-i), *n.* [Informal], clothing.

tog·gle (tog'l), *n.* a small pin, rod, etc. for

keeping the strands of a rope, parts of a
chain, etc. from loosening.

toggle joint, a mechanical device consisting of
a frame with two bars joined together in
the center like an elbow: power is applied
at the joint, changing the direction of motion.

toggle switch, a switch with a small movable
bar that turns on or shuts off an electrical
circuit.

toil (toil), *n.* 1. labor oppressive to mind or
body; fatiguing exertion. 2. *pl.* a snare; net:
v.i. 1. to labor or work with pain or fatigue.
2. to move with a great deal of effort: *v.t.*
[Now Rare], to accomplish by toil.

toi·let (toi'lit), *n.* 1. formerly, a dressing table.
2. style or manner of dressing. 3. attire. 4. a
room containing a device for the disposal of
bodily waste matter. 5. the device in such a
room.

toilet paper, a thin paper for use in toilets:
also **toilet tissue**.

toi·let·ry (toi'lĕ-tri), *n., pl.* **-ries**, an agent, as
soap, used in dressing and preparing for
outside appearance.

toi·lette (two-let'), *n.* 1. the procedure of cleaning and preparing oneself for outside appearance. 2. attire.

toilet water, a scent for the skin, containing a
small amount of alcohol.

toil·some (toil'sŭm), *adj.* laborious; wearisome.
—toil'some·ness, *n.*

To·kay (tŏ-kā'), *n.* 1. a rich Hungarian wine.
2. a large, sweet, purplish grape.

toke (tŏk), *n.* [Slang], one draw on a cigarette
or pipe of marijuana or hashish: *v.i.* **toked,
tok'ing**, [Slang], to take a draw on (a cigarette or pipe of such a substance).

to·ken (tŏ'kn), *n.* 1. a mark or sign. 2. a
memorial of affection; keepsake. 3. a sign
of authority or identity. 4. a distinguishing
mark. 5. a piece of metal issued for currency with a face value much above its real
value: *adj.* giving only a small appearance
or indication.

to·ken·ism (-izm), *n.* the making of a small
gesture of compliance, as by hiring members
of minority groups, in yielding to requirements.

to·la (tŏ'lä), *n.* in India, a unit of weight,
equal to 180 grains.

told (tŏld), past tense and past participle of
tell.

To·le·do (tŏ-lē'dō), *n., pl.* **-does**, a sword or
sword blade of the finest temper, made at
Toledo, Spain.

tol·er·a·ble (tol'ẽr-ă-bl), *adj.* 1 endurable; sup-
portable. 2. fairly good. **—tol'er·a·ble·ness,** *n.*
—tol'er·a·bly, *adv.*

tol·er·ance (-ăns), *n.* 1. endurance; toleration.
2. the range of deviation permitted from a
criterion. 3. in *Medicine*, the capability for
withstanding certain levels of drug use.

tol·er·ant (-ănt), *adj.* disposed to or favoring
toleration.

tol·er·ate (tol'ĕ-rāt), *v.t.* **-at·ed, -at·ing**, 1. to endure. 2. to permit; allow so as not to hin-
der or prohibit. 3. to be considerate of (the
ideas, behavior, etc. of others) while not
wholly approving. 4. in *Medicine*, to be ca-

ŏ in dragon, ōō in crude, oo in wool, u in cup, ū in cure, ū in turn, ŭ in focus,
oi in boy, ou in house, th in thin, th in sheathe, g in get, j in joy, y in yet.

pable of withstanding (drugs, treatments, etc.).

tol·er·a·tion (tol-ĕ-rā'shŭn), *n.* 1. the act of tolerating. 2. allowance of that which is not wholly approved. 3. recognition of the right of private judgment in religious opinions and modes of worship differing from those of the established church. 4. freedom from bigotry.

toll (tōl), *n.* 1. the sound of a bell slowly repeated at short intervals. 2. a duty or tax on travelers or goods passing along a public road or bridge. 3. a tax or duty paid for some privilege. 4. a charge for the transportation of goods, distant telephone communication, etc. 5. the amount demanded, destroyed, etc.: *v.i.* to sound or ring slowly: used of a bell: *v.t.* 1. [Now Rare], to take or exact (a toll). 2. to cause (a bell) to ring slowly and repeatedly. 3. to declare or proclaim by the sound of a bell.

toll·gate ('gāt), *n.* a gate at which a toll is demanded, after which travel may continue.

to·lu (tō-lōō'), *n.* an oily resin produced by a tree of South America: also **tolu balsam.**

tol·u·ene (tol'yoo-wĕn), *n.* a hydrocarbon obtained as a colorless liquid by distilling coal tar, tolu balsam, etc.

to·lu·ic acid (tō-lōō'ik), any of four isomeric acids, derivatives of toluene.

tolu tree, a large tree related to the bean, indigenous to South America.

tom (tom), *n.* the male of various animals, especially the cat: *adj.* male.

tom·a·hawk (tom'ȧ-hôk), *n.* a hatchet used by the North American Indians in war and as an implement: *v.t.* to strike or kill with a tomahawk.

to·ma·to (tō-māt'ō), *n., pl.* **-toes,** 1. the pulpy, edible fruit of a plant related to the nightshade. 2. the plant on which it grows.

tomb (tōōm), *n.* 1. a grave or vault. 2. a monument erected to the memory of the dead: *v.t.* [Rare], to entomb.

tom·bac, tom·bak (tom'bak), *n.* an alloy of copper and zinc, used in cheap jewelry.

tom·boy (tom'boi), *n.* a girl who acts in a boyish way.

tomb·stone (tōōm'stōn), *n.* a stone or slab erected over a grave in memory of the person buried there.

tom·cat (tom'kat), *n.* a full-grown male cat.

tom·cod ('kod), *n.* a small, codlike, edible fish.

tome (tōm), *n.* a large book.

to·men·tose (tō-men'tōs), *adj.* in *Biology,* covered very closely with matted hairs.

to·men·tum (tō-men'tŭm), *n., pl.* **-ta** ('tȧ), the closely matted down on leaves or stems of certain plants.

tom·fool (tom'fōōl'), *n.* a great fool; silly trifler.

tom·fool·er·y ('ĕr-i), *n., pl.* **-er·ies,** nonsense; silly behavior.

to·mor·row (tŏ-mor'ō), *n.* the day after the present: *adv.* on the day after today.

tom·pi·on (tom'pi-ŏn), *n.* same as **tampion.**

Tom Thumb, a legendary dwarf of English literature.

tom·tit (tom'tit'), *n.* [Chiefly British], the titmouse.

tom-tom (tom'tom), *n.* a drum struck with the hands, as those used in Africa and by American Indians.

-to·my (tō-mi), a combining form meaning *a separating, surgery.*

ton (tun), *n.* 1. a unit of weight that is equal to 2,000 pounds avoirdupois in the U.S.: also *short ton.* 2. a unit of weight that is equal to 2,240 pounds avoirdupois in Great Britain: also *long ton.* 3. a unit of capacity for ship freight equivalent to 40 cubic feet. 4. a unit of capacity for reckoning the displacement of vessels, equal to about 35 cubic feet.

ton (tōn), *n.* [French], fashion; style.

ton·al (tō'nl), *adj.* of or pertaining to a tone or tonality.

to·nal·i·ty (tō-nal'i-ti), *n., pl.* **-ties,** 1. in *Art,* the general color scheme of a picture. 2. in *Music, a)* key relationship; *b)* quality of tone.

tone (tōn), *n.* 1. sound or character of sound. 2. a quality of the voice indicating expression, emotion, etc. 3. prevailing style or character. 4. individual style; grace. 5. the state of the body with reference to the healthy performance of its functions. 6. shade; tint. 7. the harmony of the colors, shades, etc. of a painting. 8. in *Music, a)* a particular sound; note; *b)* an interval of sound; *c)* a chant: *v.t.* **toned, ton'ing,** 1. to bring to a required shade of color. 2. to tune (an instrument). 3. [Rare], to intone or utter in a monotonous, recitative manner. 4. to mitigate (with *down*): *v.i.* to take on a tone.

tone arm, the movable bar holding the phonograph pickup.

tone-deaf ('def), *adj.* not capable of differentiating distinct pitches in music.

tone row, see **twelve-tone.**

tong (tông), *n.* a Chinese secret society: *v.t.* to take or gather with tongs.

ton·ga (tong'gä), *n.* a two-wheeled vehicle used in India.

tongs (tongz), *n.pl.* an instrument consisting usually of a pair of arms on a swivel or hinge, used for grasping objects, as hot coal, ice, etc.

tongue (tung), *n.* 1. a fleshy, movable, protrusile organ on the floor of the mouth of most vertebrates. 2. the chief organ of speech. 3. the power of speech. 4. the manner of speaking. 5. dialect; idiom. 6. discourse. 7. the clapper of a bell. 8. anything resembling a tongue. 9. a promontory: *v.t.* **tongued, tongu'ing,** 1. to modulate or modify with the tongue. 2. [Archaic], to scold: *v.i.* to talk; prate.

tongue-and-groove joint, a joint with a projecting part on one piece that slips into a groove on a second piece.

tongue-lash·ing ('lash-ing), *n.* [Informal], a severe rebuke.

tongue-tied ('tīd), *adj.* unable to speak because of shame or surprise.

ton·ic (ton'ik), *adj.* 1. increasing muscle tension; strengthening. 2. in *Music,* of, pertaining to, or based on the keynote: *n.* 1. a strengthening medicine. 2. carbonated water flavored with quinine, for adding to alcohol to make mixed drinks. 3. in *Music*, the keynote.

to·nic·i·ty (tō-nis'ĭ-tĭ), *n.* 1. the state of being in tone. 2. a strong, healthy condition.

tonic sol-fa, a system of music writing and reading which emphasizes the tonal relations of the key elements and which has for its scale the syllables *do, re, mi, fa,* etc.

to·night (tǒ-nīt'), *n.* the night of the present day, or the present night: *adv.* on this present night or the night of this day.

ton·ka bean (tong'kä), one of the aromatic kernels of the fruit of a tree of South America, used for scenting and flavoring.

ton·nage (tun'ij), *n.* 1. the carrying capacity of a vessel. 2. the duty or toll on vessels. 3. the collective shipping of any port or country.

ton·neau (tu-nō'), *n., pl.* **-neaus', -neaux'** (-nōz'). the part of an automobile body behind the chauffeur's seat, arranged for passengers.

to·nom·e·ter (tō-nǒm'ĕ-tēr), *n.* a tuning fork.

ton·sil (ton'sĭl), *n.* an almond-shaped structure situated at the sides of the fauces of the throat.

ton·sil·lec·to·my (ton-sĭ-lek'tō-mĭ), *n., pl.* **-mies,** the operation of removing the tonsils.

ton·sil·li·tis (-līt'ĭs), *n.* inflammation of the tonsils.

ton·so·ri·al (ton-sōr'ĭ-ăl), *adj.* of or pertaining to a barber.

ton·sure (ton'shēr), *n.* 1. the shaving of a round spot on the crown of the head, practiced by certain Roman Catholic ecclesiastics to denote the priestly office or order to which they belong. 2. the part of the head thus bared: *v.t.* **-sured, -sur·ing,** to shave the head in giving the tonsure to.

ton·tine (ton'tĭn), *n.* a system of life insurance or annuities, the profits of which increase as the number of those insured diminish, the whole amount accruing to the last survivor.

to·ny (tō'nĭ), *adj.* **ton'i·er, ton'i·est,** [Slang], foppish; high-toned.

too (tōō), *adv.* 1. more than enough; over and above. 2. in addition; also. 3. to a high degree.

took (took), past tense of take.

tool (tōōl), *n.* 1. an instrument of manual operation. 2. a part of a machine like this, or the machine itself. 3. an agency for accomplishing something. 4. one who acts as the instrument of another. 5. a person who carries out the designs of another: *v.t.* 1. to shape with a tool. 2. to drive (a coach, car, etc.). 3. to mark (leather) with ornamentation: *v.i.* to obtain and install necessary tools (often with *up*).

tool·ing ('ing), *n.* 1. workmanship performed with a tool. 2. ornamental handwork on stone, wood, metal, ivory, or other substances.

toon (tōōn), *n.* the valuable dark wood of a large tree of the East Indies and Australia.

toot (tōōt), *v.i. & v.t.* to sound (a horn, flute, etc.) with short bursts: *n.* a brief blast on a horn.

tooth (tōōth), *n., pl.* **teeth** (tēth), 1. one of the hard bony processes growing in the jaws, which serve for biting and chewing. 2. any projection resembling a tooth. 3. palate or taste. 4. *pl.* a strong agency for enforcing rules: *v.t.* to indent or form into teeth.

tooth·ache ('āk), *n.* a pain in a tooth.

tooth·brush ('brush), *n.* a stiff, bristly brush for cleaning the teeth.

toothed (tōōtht), *adj.* provided with teeth; dentate.

tooth·paste ('pāst), *n.* a paste used for cleaning the teeth.

tooth·pick ('pik), *n.* a pointed sliver for removing particles from between the teeth.

tooth powder, a powder used for cleaning the teeth.

tooth·some ('sŏm), *adj.* palatable; tasty.

tooth·wort ('wŭrt), *n.* 1. a plant with toothlike roots. 2. a plant with roots covered with toothlike scales.

tooth·y ('i), *adj.* **tooth'i·er, tooth'i·est,** having or showing prominent teeth. —**tooth'i·ly,** *adv.*

too·tle (tōō't'l), *v.i.* **-tled, -tling,** to toot repeatedly: *n.* the act of tootling.

top (tŏp), *n.* 1. the head, or the crown of the head. 2. the highest part; summit. 3. the part of a plant growing above ground. 4. the upper part, side, or surface. 5. the highest person, thing, rank, etc. 6. a platform around the head of the lower mast. 7. a child's toy in the shape of a cone, that can be spun on its pointed apex: *adj.* of, at, or being the top: *v.t.* **topped, top'ping,** 1. to cut off the top of. 2. to cover with a top. 3. to place on the top of. 4. to be a top for. 5. to rise to the top of. 6. to be larger, better, etc. than; surpass.

top·arch·y ('är-kĭ), *n.* a small state or a country province.

to·paz (tō'paz), *n.* any one of various yellow gems; especially, a variety of aluminum silicate.

to·paz·o·lite (tō-paz'ō-līt), *n.* a variety of garnet, yellow to green in color.

top boot, a high boot reaching just below the knee, usually with different material in the top part.

top brass, the more important officials or officers.

top·coat (top'kōt), *n.* a lightweight overcoat.

top·drawer ('drôr'), *adj.* first in importance.

tope (tōp), *n.* 1. a dome-shaped Buddhist shrine. 2. a small, gray European shark: *v.t. & v.i.* **toped, top'ing,** [Archaic], to drink (alcoholic liquor) habitually and excessively.

to·pee (tō-pē', tō'pi), *n.* a pith helmet worn in India as a sunshade.

top·er (tō'pēr), *n.* a drunkard.

top·flight (top'flīt'), *adj.* [Informal], first-rate; best.

top·gal·lant ('gal'ănt), *adj.* situated above the topmost: *n.* a topgallant mast, sail, etc.

top·ham·per ('ham-pēr), *n.* a ship's rigging, spars, etc.

ŏ in dragon, ōō in crude, oo in wool, u in cup, ū in cure, û in turn, ů in focus, oi in boy, ou in house, th in thin, th in sheathe, g in get, j in joy, y in yet.

top hat, a man's tall, black hat of cylindrical shape, worn on formal occasions.

top-heav-y ('hev'i), *adj.* having the top part too heavy for the lower, so as to be unsteady.

To-phet, To-pheth (tō'fit), *n.* 1. in the *Bible,* a place near Jerusalem where human beings were sacrificed to Moloch. 2. hell.

to-phus (tō'fus), *n.* a calcareous deposit on the teeth and about the joints of persons having the gout.

to-pi (tō'pi), *n.* a brown antelope of eastern Africa.

top-ic (top'ik), *n.* a subject of discourse, conversation, or argument; theme.

top-i-cal ('i-kl), *adj.* 1. relating to a particular place; local. 2. of, pertaining to, or consisting of a topic or topics. 3. of local or current interest.

top-knot (top'not), *n.* a tuft of feathers or hair on the top of the head.

top-less ('lis), *adj.* 1. having no top or top part, as a garment which exposes the breasts. 2. wearing such a garment.

top-lev-el ('lev'l), *adj.* of or by those holding the highest rank or office.

top-mast ('mast), *n.* the second mast from the deck of a ship.

top-most ('mōst), *adj.* uppermost.

top-notch ('noch'), *adj.* [Informal], first-rate.

to-pog-ra-pher (tō-pog'rà-fēr), *n.* 1. an expert in topography. 2. one who describes the surface features of a place or region.

to-pog-ra-phy (tō-pog'rà-fi), *n., pl.* **-phies,** the scientific description of the surface features of a region; also, the surface features. — **top-o-graph-i-cal** (top-ō-graf'i-kl), **top-o-graph'ic,** *adj.*

top-o-nym (top'ō-nim), *n.* 1. a place name. 2. a name based on or derived from the location of the object named.

top-ping (top'ing), *adj.* rising above; surpassing: *n.* 1. the act of one that tops. 2. something forming a top for something else.

top-ple ('l), *v.t.* -**pled,** -**pling,** to overturn: *v.i.* to fall forward; tumble down.

top-sail ('sl, 'sāl), *n.* the sail second from the deck of a ship.

top-se-cret ('sē'krit), *adj.* denoting or of information of the most secret sort.

top-soil ('soil), *n.* the uppermost layer of soil.

top-sy-tur-vy (top'si-tûr'vi), *adv.* in an inverted position; in confusion: *adj.* disordered; chaotic.

toque (tōk), *n.* a woman's small, closefitting hat, with or without a brim.

tor (tôr), *n.* a high, pointed hill; crag.

to-rah, to-ra (tō'rà, tō-rä'), *n.* in *Judaism,* 1. instruction, law, etc. 2. [also T-], all the Jewish religious writings, including the Scripture, the Talmud, etc. 3. [usually T-], the Pentateuch or a scroll containing it.

torch (tôrch), *n.* 1. a flaming light, as from one end of a resinous piece of wood, carried in the hand; flambeau. 2. any source that illuminates or inspires. 3. a portable device for making a very hot flame. 4. [British], a flashlight.

torch-bear-er ('ber-ēr), *n.* 1. the bearer of a torch. 2. one who brings illumination, inspi-

ration, etc. to others. 3. a leader who inspires the others in a movement.

torch-light ('līt), *n.* the light from a torch.

tore (tōr), alternate past tense of **tear** (to rend).

tor-e-a-dor (tôr'i-à-dôr), *n.* a bullfighter.

to-reu-tic (tō-rōōt'ik), *adj.* of or pertaining to work done in metal or other material by embossing or chasing.

to-reu-tics ('iks), *n.* the art of doing toreutic work.

to-ri-i (tōr'i-ē), *n., pl.* **-ri-i,** the arched gateway of a Japanese Shinto temple, topped by a curved lintel just above a straight crosspiece.

tor-ment (tôr'ment), *n.* extreme pain; torture; anguish; *v.t.* (tôr-ment'), to put to extreme pain, physical or mental; torture; harass. — **tor-men'tor, tor-ment'er,** *n.*

tor-men-til (tôr'men-til), *n.* a European cinquefoil with yellow flowers: the root extract is used in dyeing and tanning.

torn (tôrn), alternate past participle of **tear** (to rend).

tor-na-do (tôr-nā'dō), *n., pl.* **-does, -dos,** a violent tempest or whirlwind.

to-rose (tōr'ōs), *adj.* swelling in knobs; bulging; knobbed, etc.: also **to'rous** ('us). —**to-ros-i-ty** (tō-ros'i-ti), *n.*

tor-pe-do (tôr-pē'dō), *n., pl.* **-does,** 1. a cigar-shaped projectile that propels itself underwater after being fired, as from a submarine, against enemy ships: it explodes on contact. 2. any one of various explosive devices, as a small firework that makes a loud explosion or an underwater mine: *v.t.* -**doed, -do-ing,** to attack or destroy as with a torpedo. —

torpedo boat, a fast, small warship easily maneuvered for attacking with torpedoes.

tor-pid (tôr'pid), *adj.* 1. dormant, as a hibernating animal. 2. dull and slow or sluggish. —**tor-pid'i-ty, tor'pid-ness,** *n.* —**tor'pid-ly,** *adv.*

tor-pi-fy ('pi-fī), *v.t.* -**fied, -fy-ing,** to make torpid.

tor-por ('pēr), *n.* the condition of being torpid.

tor-por-if-ic (tôr-pō-rif'ik), *adj.* producing torpor.

tor-quate (tôr'kwāt), *adj.* having a ring, as of color or feathers, around the neck.

torque (tôrk), *n.* 1. a twisted metal collar or necklace worn by ancient Gauls and Britons. 2. the force that produces a twisting or rotating effect.

tor-re-fy (tôr'è-fī), *v.t.* -**fied, -fy-ing,** to dry by fire; roast (ores or drugs); subject to great heat.

tor-rent (tôr'ènt, tor'-), *n.* 1. a violent and rapid stream, as of water. 2. a heavy fall of rain. 3. a strong current, rising suddenly and rushing rapidly along.

tor-ren-tial (tō-ren'shàl), *adj.* of the nature of, or suggestive of, a torrent.

tor-rid (tôr'id, tor'-), *adj.* 1. dried with heat; scorched. 2. extremely hot; scorching. 3. very ardent, passionate, etc. —**tor'rid-ly,** *adv.*

Torrid Zone, the broad area of the earth's surface lying between the two tropics and divided by the equator.

tor-sade (tôr-sād'), *n.* 1. a molding or ornamentation resembling a length of rope. 2. a twisted cord used for draperies, etc.

---

a in cap, ā in cane, ä in father, à in abet, e in met, ē in be, ê in baker, ê in regent, i in pit, ī in fine, i in manifest, o in hot, ô in horse, ō in bone,

tor·sel (tôr'sĕl), *n.* a piece of iron, stone, wood, or the like, used for supporting the end of a joist or beam.

tor·sion (tôr'shŭn), *n.* 1. the act of turning or twisting. 2. the strain resulting when a wire, rod, etc. is twisted at one end and held firm or twisted in the opposite direction at the other end.

torsion bar, a metal bar that shows resilience when subject to torsion.

tor·so (tôr'sō), *n., pl.* **-sos, -si** ('sī), 1. the trunk of a human body. 2. the trunk of a statue of a nude person, especially of a statue with the head and limbs missing. 3. something incomplete.

tort (tôrt), *n.* in *Law,* any wrong, injury, or damage not involving breach of contract.

torte (tôrt), *n.* a rich cake made of eggs, crumbs, finely chopped nuts, etc.

tor·ti·col·lis (tôr-ti-kol'ĭs), *n.* a contraction, or spasm, of the muscles of the neck, which draws the head to one side.

tor·tile (tôr'tĭl, 'tīl), *adj.* bent; twisted.

tor·til·la (tôr-tē'ä), *n.* a thin unleavened cake of cornmeal or flour, baked on a griddle or, originally, on a hot, flat stone: a staple Mexican food.

tor·toise (tôr'tŭs), *n.* a turtle; especially, a land turtle.

tortoise shell, 1. the hard, yellow-and-brown shell of some turtles. 2. a synthetic substance made to look like this. **—tor'toise·shell,** *adj.*

tor·to·ni (tôr-tō'nī), *n.* an ice cream containing maraschino cherries, almonds, etc.

tor·tu·ous (tôr'choo-wŭs), *adj.* 1. having many twists and turns; crooked. 2. deceitful; underhanded.

tor·ture ('chĕr), *n.* 1. agony of mind or body; any excruciating pain. 2. the inflicting of such pain, as a punishment or as a means of extorting a confession: *v.t.* **-tured, -turing,** 1. to punish with, or as with, torture. 2. to wrest from the true meaning. **—tor'tur·er,** *n.*

to·rus (tôr'ŭs), *n., pl.* **-ri** ('ī), 1. a large, convex molding in the base of a column. 2. same as receptacle (sense 3). 3. in *Anatomy,* any rounded protuberance.

To·ry (tôr'ī), *n., pl.* **-ries,** 1. a member of the British Conservative Party. 2. one who remained loyal to Great Britain during the American Revolution: *adj.* of or pertaining to Tories. **—To'ry·ism,** *n.*

toss (tôs), *v.t.* 1. to throw with the hand. 2. to throw upward; jerk. 3. to put into violent motion; cause to rise and fall: *v.i.* 1. to be tossed about. 2. to roll or tumble: *n.* the act of tossing or the state of being tossed.

toss·ing ('ing), *n.* the act of one who tosses.

toss-up ('ŭp), *n.* 1. the act of tossing a coin to decide a matter according to which side shows when it lands. 2. an even or fair chance.

tot (tot), *n.* 1. a young child: a term of endearment. 2. [Chiefly British], anything small or insignificant: *v.t.* **tot'ted, tot'ting,** [Chiefly British], to add (*up*); total.

to·tal (tōt'l), *adj.* 1. not divided; whole; entire.

2. complete; utter: *n.* the whole sum or amount: *v.t.* **-taled** or **-talled, -taling** or **-talling,** 1. to arrive at the total of. 2. to 'add up to: *v.i.* to come (*to*) as a whole. **—to'tal·ly,** *adv.*

to·tal·i·tar·i·an (tō-tal-ĭ-ter'ĭ-ăn), *adj.* of or relating to a system of government which is greatly centralized and is controlled by a political group which prohibits the existence of other political parties: *n.* one favoring such a government.

to·tal·i·ty (tō-tal'ĭ-ti), *n., pl.* **-ties,** the entire quantity, amount, or sum.

to·tal·i·za·tor (tōt'l-ĭ-zāt-ĕr), *n.* a machine for recording the bets at race tracks where the parimutuel system prevails.

to·ta·ra (tōd'ä-rä), *n.* a valuable timber tree of New Zealand: its durable, hard wood is used for furniture.

tote (tōt), *v.t.* **tot'ed, tot'ing,** [Informal], to carry; haul.

to·tem (tōt'ĕm), *n.* 1. an animal, plant, or object adopted as a symbol by a particular group of primitive people in the belief that there is an affinity or natural relationship between them and this symbol. 2. an image of such an animal, plant, etc.

to·tem·ism (-izm), *n.* 1. belief in totems. 2. the use of totems. 3. the customs based on such belief or use. **—to'tem·ist,** *n.*

totem pole, a pole with carved and painted totems on it, set up by Indian tribes of northwestern North America.

tot·ter (tot'ĕr), *v.i.* to shake as if about to fall; be unsteady; stagger; reel.

tot·ter·y (-ĭ), *adj.* shaking, as if about to fall; unsteady.

tou·can (tōō'kan), *n.* a fruit-eating tropical bird having an enormous beak and plumage of blue, yellow, red, and black.

touch (tuch), *v.t.* 1. to perceive by feeling. 2. to handle slightly. 3. to attain to; reach. 4. to meddle with; molest. 5. to treat of in a superficial manner. 6. to add a light stroke to. 7. to affect the senses or sensibility of. 8. [Slang], to ask for and get a gift of money from, or borrow from: *v.i.* 1. to be in contact. 2. to touch someone or something. 3. to verge (*on*). 4. to bear (*on*). 5. to comment (*on*): *n.* 1. the act of touching or the state of being touched. 2. the sense of feeling. 3. a special quality. 4. a slight change or addition in a painting, story, etc. 5. a slight trace, case, etc. (of something). 6. [Slang], the act of touching someone for money. 7. the way in which one uses one's fingers on a musical instrument.

touch and go, a situation that is uncertain or risky. **—touch'-and-go',** *adj.*

touch·down ('doun), *n.* 1. a point scored in football by grounding the ball on or past the opponent's goal line. 2. the act of making such a point.

tou·ché (tōō-shā'), *interj.* touched: a word spoken in recognition of a point scored by one's opponent in fencing, or of a point made in debating, arguing, etc.

touched (tucht), *adj.* 1. moved emotionally. 2. somewhat insane.

---

touch·i·ness (tuch'i-nis), *n.* the state of being touchy.

touch·ing ('ing), *adj.* pathetic; moving: *prep.* with respect to; concerning.

touch·stone ('stōn), *n.* 1. a black stone used in earlier times to test the purity of gold or silver by the streak made on it by the metal. 2. a criterion.

touch-type ('tīp), *v.i.* -typed, -typ·ing, to type without looking at the keys of a typewriter, always using the same finger on any given key.

touch·wood ('wood), *n.* any decayed wood or dried fungus which ignites easily and burns slowly.

touch·y ('i), *adj.* touch'i·er, touch'i·est, 1. overly sensitive; irritable; peevish. 2. full of risk; uncertain.

tough (tuf), *adj.* 1. flexible without being brittle; not easily broken. 2. able to endure hardship; strong; firm. 3. tenacious; stubborn. 4. rough or brutal. 5. difficult; requiring effort. 6. not easy to masticate: *n.* a pugnacious fellow; rowdy; thug.

tough·en ('n), *v.t. & v.i.* to make or become tough.

tough·ie, tough·y ('i), *n., pl.* tough'ies, [Informal], 1. a tough; rowdy; ruffian. 2. a situation full of difficulties.

tou·pee (tōō-pā'), *n.* a man's small wig.

tour (toor), *n.* 1. a period of military duty. 2. a trip or journey, as one for sightseeing or for presenting theatrical performances: *v.t. & v.i.* 1. to make a tour (of). 2. to take (a play) on a tour.

tou·ra·co (toor'ȧ-kō), *n.* an African bird with brightly colored plumage and a white crest.

tour·bil·lion (toor-bil'yŭn), *n.* a firework that spirals upward.

tour de force (toor dĕ fôrs'), *pl.* tours de force' (toor), a very skillful or clever performance.

touring car, a large, open automobile of an early type.

tour·ism (toor'izm), *n.* travel by tourists; especially, such travel that provides income for a country.

tour·ist ('ist), *n.* one who takes tours or trips: *adj.* of or for tourists.

tour·ma·line (toor'mȧ-lin, -lēn), *n.* a mineral that is a silicate of aluminum and boron: it occurs in black, colored, or transparent varieties and is often used as a gem.

tour·na·ment (toor'nȧ-mĕnt, tûr'-), *n.* 1. a mock fight by knights on horseback. 2. a series of contests in some sport or game, as to decide a championship.

tour·ney ('ni), *n., pl.* -neys, a tournament.

tour·ni·quet (toor'ni-kit, tûr'-), *n.* a device for compressing a blood vessel and arresting hemorrhage.

tou·sle (tou'zl), *v.t.* -sled, -sling, to put in disorder; muss; dishevel: also touzle.

tout (tout), *v.i. & v.t.* [Informal], 1. to recommend highly. 2. to sell private information to those betting on (racehorses): *n.* [Informal], one who touts, especially one who makes a business of touting racehorses: —tout'er, *n.*

tout en·sem·ble (tōō tän-sän'bl), [French]. 1. all together. 2. the general effect, as of a work of art or a costume, regarded as a whole.

tow (tō), *v.t.* to drag or pull, as a vessel, by means of a rope or chain: *n.* 1. the act of towing or the state of being towed. 2. that which is towed. 3. a towline. 4. coarse fibers of hemp, flax, etc.

tow·age ('ij), *n.* 1. the act of towing. 2. the price paid for towing.

to·ward (tôrd, tô-wôrd'), *prep.* 1. in the direction of. 2. having the face to. 3. with a tendency to. 4. with respect to. 5. close to; just before. 6. so as to get; for. Also towards (tôrdz, tô-wôrdz').

tow·el (tou'l), *n.* a piece of cloth for wiping or drying the hands, dishes, etc. after washing: *v.t.* -eled or -elled, -el·ing or -el·ling, to wipe or dry with a towel.

tow·el·ing, tow·el·ling (-ing), *n.* material for towels.

tow·er (tou'ẽr), *n.* 1. a lofty structure, especially one that is the top part of another building. 2. a fortress: *v.i.* to rise above other objects; be lofty or high.

tow·er·ing (-ing), *adj.* 1. very high; soaring. 2. violent; outrageous.

tow·head (tō'hed), *n.* 1. a head of hair that is pale yellow. 2. one having such hair. —tow'head·ed, *adj.*

tow·hee (tou'hē, tō'-), *n.* a small North American bird related to the sparrow.

tow·line (tō'līn), *n.* a rope or chain for towing.

town (toun), *n.* 1. a collection of houses larger than a village. 2. a city. 3. a township. 4. a unit of local government, as in New England, controlled by a town meeting. 5. the inhabitants of a town.

town crier, one who, in earlier times, walked the streets of a town, calling out public announcements.

town hall, a building in a town, in which the town officers transact their business.

town house, 1. a dwelling in town, as distinguished from one's dwelling in the country. 2. a two-story dwelling in a complex of such dwellings.

town meeting, 1. a meeting of the inhabitants of a town. 2. a meeting, as in New England, of the voters in a town to conduct town business.

town·ship ('ship), *n.* 1. in the U.S., a subdivision of a county that is a unit of local government and controls the schools, roads, etc. 2. same as **town** (sense 4). 3. a unit in the U.S. land survey that is generally six miles square.

towns·man (tounz'mȧn), *n., pl.* -men ('mĕn), 1. one who lives in, or has been brought up in, a town. 2. someone who lives in the same town as oneself.

towns·peo·ple ('pē-pl), *n.pl.* the people living in a town: also towns'folk ('fōk).

tow·path (tō'path), *n.* a path alongside a canal, used by men or animals towing boats.

tow·rope ('rōp), *n.* a rope for towing.

tox·e·mi·a (tok-sē'mi-ȧ), *n.* a condition in which poisonous substances, especially toxins, are present in the bloodstream. —tox·e'mic ('mik), *adj.*

---

tox·ic (tok'sik), *adj.* 1. of or caused by a toxin. 2. poisonous. —**tox·ic'i·ty** (-sis'i-ti), *n.*

tox·i·col·o·gy (tok-si-kol'ō-ji), *n.* the science that treats of poisons, their effects, antidotes, etc. —**tox·i·col'o·gist,** *n.*

tox·i·co·sis (-kō'sis), *n.* any diseased condition due to the action of poison in the body.

tox·in (tok'sin), *n.* 1. any one of various poisons that form in certain plants or are secreted by certain animals. 2. any one of various poisonous compounds that are produced by microorganisms and that cause certain diseases.

tox·oph·i·lite (tok-sof'i-līt), *n.* a lover of archery.

toy (toi), *n.* 1. a child's plaything. 2. something of no real value. 3. a bauble: *adj.* used or intended to be used as a toy: *v.i.* 1. to dally amorously; flirt. 2. to play (*with* something).

trace (trās), *n.* 1. a mark left by anything passing, as a footprint. 2. a small quantity. 3. either of the two straps, etc. by which a vehicle is attached to the harness of a horse: *v.t.* **traced, trac'ing,** 1. to follow the traces or marks of. 2. to follow the course of. 3. to discover (the origin of something). 4. to make a sketch or outline of. 5. to copy the lines of (a drawing) on a clear sheet placed over it.

trace·a·ble ('â-bl), *adj.* capable of being traced.

trace element, a chemical element, as iron, copper, etc., essential to nutrition, but only in very small quantities.

trac·er ('ēr), *n.* 1. one who traces drawings. 2. any one of various devices for tracing or copying. 3. one who tries to find persons or things that are lost or missing. 4. a letter of inquiry sent out for a missing letter or piece of mail.

trac·er·y ('ēr-i), *n., pl.* **-er·ies,** the ornamentation produced by interlacing lines, as in Gothic windows.

tra·che·a (trā'ki-â), *n., pl.* **-ae** (-ē), **-as,** 1. the tube through which air passes from the larynx to the bronchi. 2. any one of the small tubes in the body of insects, used in breathing. —**tra'che·al,** *adj.*

tra·che·i·tis (trā-ki-ī'tis), *n.* inflammation of the trachea.

tra·che·ot·o·my (-ot'ō-mi), *n., pl.* **-mies,** the surgical operation of making an opening into the trachea.

tra·cho·ma (trâ-kō'mâ), *n.* an inflamed condition of the eyes, characterized by hard, granular growths on the conjunctiva and cornea: it is caused by a virus.

tra·chyte (trā'kīt, trak'īt), *n.* a fine-grained, igneous rock, consisting chiefly of feldspars.

tra·chyt·ic (trâ-kit'ik), *adj.* pertaining to, consisting of, or resembling trachyte.

trac·ing (trā'sing), *n.* 1. the act of one who traces. 2. something traced, as a copy made by tracing a drawing.

track (trak), *n.* 1. a mark or impression left, as by the foot or a wheel, in passing. 2. a beaten path. 3. any sequence, as of events. 4. a course or circuit laid out for racing. 5. a pair of rails laid out parallel for a railroad train to run on. 6. those sports, as running or hurdling, performed on a track; also, these sports along with such sports, like jumping, as are performed on a field. 7. any one of the separate recording surfaces running along a magnetic tape: *v.t.* 1. to follow the track of. 2. to follow or record the path taken by (an aircraft or spacecraft). 3. to leave tracks, as of mud on a floor.

track·age ('ij), *n.* 1. the tracks of a railroad, collectively. 2. the privilege of one railroad to use the tracks of another; also, the charge for this.

track·less ('lis), *adj.* 1. having no track or path. 2. not running on tracks or rails, as a trolley.

track·walk·er ('wô-kēr), *n.* a person whose work is inspecting railroad tracks for needed repairs.

tract (trakt), *n.* 1. a pamphlet containing propaganda, usually on a religious or political subject. 2. a region of indefinite extent; expanse. 3. a system of organs or parts having some body function.

trac·ta·ble (trak'tâ-bl), *adj.* 1. easily taught or managed; docile. 2. malleable. —**trac·ta·bil'i·ty,** *n.*

Trac·tar·i·an·ism (trak-ter'i-ân-izm), *n.* the principles of the Oxford Movement, promoting a revival of early Catholic doctrines and practices in the Church of England. —**Tractar'i·an,** *n. & adj.*

trac·tate (trak'tāt), *n.* a small book or treatise.

trac·tile (trak'til), *adj.* ductile; tensile.

trac·tion (trak'shûn), *n.* 1. the act of pulling or drawing. 2. the state of being pulled or drawn. 3. the sort of power that a locomotive or a street railway uses. 4. adhesive friction, as of automobile tires on pavement.

trac·tive ('tiv), *adj.* serving or used to draw along; pulling.

trac·tor ('tēr), *n.* 1. a vehicle powered by a motor and used for pulling farm machinery or hauling loads. 2. a truck with a cab for the driver but no body: a large trailer or trailers can be attached to it to be hauled.

trade (trād), *n.* 1. any kind of work requiring some skill. 2. buying and selling; commerce; business. 3. all the persons engaged in a particular business. 4. customers. 5. a sale; purchase. 6. an exchange: *v.i.* **trad'ed, trad'ing,** 1. to carry on commerce. 2. to do business (*with*). 3. to exchange (*with* someone). 4. [Informal], to buy goods (*at* a certain store): *v.t.* to barter; exchange; swap.

trade acceptance, a bill of exchange drawn by a seller on a buyer for the purchase price of goods: the buyer guarantees to pay the bill at a specified time.

trade-in ('in), *n.* a thing the value of which is used as part of the payment for something else.

trade·mark ('märk), *n.* a distinguishing word, symbol, etc. affixed by a manufacturer or dealer to his product to show his exclusive right: usually protected by law.

trade name, 1. the name by which a commodity is commonly known among traders. 2. a name adopted by a company to identify a product or service that it sells; often, a name that is a trademark. 3. the name under which a business or firm operates.

trade-off ('ôf), *n.* an exchange, especially one in which something is given up for a more desirable or less objectionable alternative.

trad-er ('ēr), *n.* 1. one who trades, or is engaged in commerce; merchant. 2. a ship used in any particular trade.

trade school, a school in which a trade or trades are taught.

trades-man (trādz'măn), *n.*, *pl.* **-men** ('mĕn), [Chiefly British], a storekeeper.

trades-peo-ple ('pē-pl), *n.pl.* people engaged in trade or commerce; especially, shopkeepers.

trades union, [Chiefly British], same as labor union.

trade union, same as **labor union**. **—trade'-un-ion**, *adj.* **—trade unionism**.

trade wind, a wind which blows steadily toward the equator from either side of it.

trad-ing (trād'ing), *adj.* of or pertaining to trade: *n.* the action of one who trades.

trading post, a store in a settlement, outpost, etc. where trading is done, as with natives.

trading stamp, a stamp that can be redeemed for specified merchandise, given as a premium by some merchants.

tra-di-tion (trā-dish'ŭn), *n.* 1. the oral transmission of opinions, doctrines, customs, etc. through successive generations. 2. a doctrine, custom, etc. that is so handed down. 3. an old, well-established custom.

tra-di-tion-al (-l), *adj.* of, pertaining to, derived from, or handed down by tradition. **—tra-di'tion-al-ly**, *adv.*

tra-duce (trā-dōōs', -dūs'), *v.t.* **-duced'**, **-duc'ing**, to slander.

traf-fic (traf'ik), *n.* 1. business or trade; commerce. 2. business or dealings (with someone). 3. the number of automobiles, pedestrians, etc. moving along a street; also, their movement along a street. 4. the business done by a company that transports persons or goods by rail, bus, etc.: *adj.* of or pertaining to the control of traffic: *v.i.* **-ficked**, **-fick-ing**, 1. to carry on traffic (*in* an article of commerce). 2. to have dealings (*with* someone).

traffic circle, a street in the form of a circle, into which several streets feed traffic that moves in one direction only.

traffic light, an apparatus with lights, usually set to change, from red to yellow to green and back, as signals to control traffic at street intersections: also **traffic signal**.

trag-a-canth (trag'ā-kanth), *n.* 1. a reddish or white gum, used in pharmacy. 2. any one of various leguminous plants yielding this gum.

tra-ge-di-an (trā-jē'di-ăn), *n.* an actor or writer of tragedies.

tra-ge-di-enne (-jē-di-en'), *n.* an actress of tragedy.

trag-e-dy (traj'ē-di), *n.*, *pl.* **-dies**, 1. a dramatic representation of a series of human events, usually leading to an unhappy ending brought on by fate or by some moral weakness in the central character. 2. a tragic or melancholy event.

trag-ic ('ik), *adj.* 1. of or pertaining to tragedy.

2. like tragedy; calamitous; fatal; terrible. Also **trag'i-cal**: *n.* the tragic part of life. **—trag'i-cal-ly**, *adv.*

trag-i-com-e-dy (traj-ĭ-kom'ē-di), *n.*, *pl.* **-dies**, 1. a drama in which tragic and comic elements are combined. 2. a situation in real life resembling this.

trag-o-pan (trag'ō-pan), *n.* an Asiatic pheasant having two hornlike growths on the head and brilliant plumage.

tra-gus (trā'gŭs), *n.*, *pl.* **-gi** ('jī), the fleshy protuberance that partly covers the opening of the ear.

trail (trāl), *v.t.* 1. to draw or drag along the ground. 2. to follow or hunt by tracking. 3. to follow behind. 4. to lag behind: *v.i.* 1. to fall or hang down behind. 2. to be drawn out at length. 3. to grow at length, as some plants along the ground. 4. to flow in a stream behind. 5. to straggle or lay behind. 6. to grow dimmer, weaker, etc. (with *away* or *off*): *n.* 1. the track followed by a hunter. 2. the scent left by a track. 3. a path made, as through a wilderness. 4. something that is dragged behind.

trail-blaz-er ('blā-zēr), *n.* 1. one who blazes a trail. 2. a pioneer or innovator.

trail-er ('ēr), *n.* 1. one that trails. 2. a cart, van, etc. designed for being pulled by an automobile, truck, etc. 3. a vehicle designed to be pulled by an automobile and used as a home.

trailer park, an area, usually having facilities for water, electricity, etc., for trailers and mobile homes: also **trailer camp**, **trailer court**.

train (trān), *n.* 1. something drawn or dragged behind, as the trailing part of a dress. 2. a retinue or suite. 3. a procession or caravan. 4. a connected series or sequence. 5. a line of connected railroad cars with one or more locomotives. 6. a line of gunpowder laid to fire a charge: *v.t.* 1. to guide (a plant) in its growth. 2. to educate, instruct, or drill, as with exercises. 3. to discipline or tame for use. 4. to prepare and make ready, as for athletic contests or horse racing. 5. to aim (a gun or binoculars) *on* something: *v.i.* to receive training.

train-ee (trān-ē'), *n.* one who is receiving training.

train-er (trān'ēr), *n.* one who trains; specifically, one who prepares animals for shows or races, or athletes for sports contests.

train-ing ('ing), *n.* 1. the action of one that trains. 2. the process of being trained.

train-man ('măn), *n.*, *pl.* **-men**, one who works on a railroad train; especially, a brakeman.

train oil, oil obtained from whales.

traipse (trāps), *v.i. & v.t.* **traipsed**, **traips'ing**, [Informal], to walk or wander.

trait (trāt), *n.* a quality or characteristic that distinguishes one individual from another.

trai-tor (trāt'ēr), *n.* 1. one who is guilty of treason or the betrayal of his country. 2. one who betrays his friends, a cause, etc. **—trai-tress** (trā'tris), *n.fem.*

trai-tor-ous (-ŭs), *adj.* 1. of a traitor; treacherous. 2. involving treason.

tra·ject (trá-jekt'), *v.t.* [Rare], to transport or transmit. —**tra·jec'tion,** *n.*

tra·jec·to·ry (trá-jek'tô-ri), *n., pl.* **-ries,** 1. the curve described by something hurtling through space, especially by a projectile after it leaves the muzzle of a gun. 2. in *Mathematics,* a curve that passes through all the curves of a given system at the same angle.

tram (tram), *n.* 1. an open car that runs on a railway in a mine. 2. [British], a streetcar. Also **tram'car.**

tram·mel (tram'l), *n.* 1. a net used for fowling or fishing. 2. a shackle for horses. 3. *usually pl.* anything that impedes progress, action, or freedom: *v.t.* **-meled** or **-melled, -mel·ing** or **-mel·ling,** to impede or hinder; shackle.

tra·mon·ta·na (trä-mon-tä'nä), *n.* the north wind; especially, a cold northerly wind, often violent, which blows across the Adriatic.

tra·mon·tane (trá-mon'tān), *adj.* located or coming from beyond the mountains: *n.* 1. one who comes from beyond the mountains. 2. a foreigner; barbarian.

tramp (tramp), *v.t.* 1. to walk through. 2. to tread upon heavily: *v.i.* 1. to wander or travel about on foot. 2. to step or walk heavily: *n.* 1. a wandering foot traveler; hobo; vagrant. 2. a journey on foot. 3. the sound of heavy steps. 4. a freight ship not engaged in regular trade, but taking on cargo when offered. 5. [Slang], a loose woman.

tram·ple (tram'pl), *v.t.* **-pled, -pling,** to crush by treading under the feet: *v.i.* to tread roughly.

tram·po·line (tram'pô-lēn, -lin), *n.* a sheet of heavy canvas stretched on a frame and used in tumbling.

tram·way (tram'wā), *n.* [British], a streetcar line.

trance (trans), *n.* 1. a stupor; daze. 2. a state somewhat like sleep, as in hypnosis. 3. a state of complete mental absorption. 4. a state in which a spiritualistic medium is supposedly under the control of an outside force, as in attempting to communicate with the dead.

tran·quil (trang'kwil), *adj.* calm; quiet; not agitated; serene. —**tran·quil'li·ty, tran·quil'i·ty** (-kwil'l-ti), *n.* —**tran'quil·ly,** *adv.*

tran·quil·ize, tran·quil·lize (-īz), *v.t. & v.i.* **-ized** or **-lized, -iz·lug** or **-liz·ing,** to make or become tranquil or calm. —**tran·quil·i·za'tiou, tran·quil·li·za'tion,** *n.*

tran·quil·iz·er, tran·quil·liz·er (-ī-zēr), *n.* a drug, often in pill form, used as a medication to relieve emotional stress, anxiety, etc.

trans-, a prefix signifying *beyond, over, across, through.*

trans·act (tran-sakt', -zakt'), *v.t.* to manage, as business; carry through; negotiate. —**trans·ac'tor,** *n.*

trans·ac·tion (-sak'shŭn, -zak'-), *n.* 1. the process of transacting something. 2. something transacted, especially a business deal. 3. *pl.* a record or report of the proceedings of a society, convention, etc.

trans·al·pine (trans-al'pin, tranz-), *adj.* on the other side of the Alps with regard to Rome; north of the Alps.

trans·at·lan·tic (-ât-lan'tik), *adj.* on the other side of the Atlantic Ocean.

trans·ceiv·er (tran-sē'vēr), *n.* a radio transmitter and receiver in a single unit.

tran·scend (tran-send'), *v.t.* 1. to rise above; surpass; excel. 2. to exceed; go beyond. —**tran·scend'ent,** *adj.*

tran·scend·ence (-sen'dĕns), *n.* the state or quality of being transcendent: also **tran·scend'en·cy.**

tran·scen·den·tal (tran-sen-den'tl), *adj.* 1. noting that which lies beyond sense experience but not knowledge. 2. supernatural. 3. metaphysical; abstract. —**tran·scen·den'tal·ly,** *adv.*

tran·scen·den·tal·ism (-izm), *n.* 1. any one of various philosophies, as that of Immanuel Kant (1724-1804), based on a doctrine that the nature of reality is best determined by a study of the process of thought. 2. a philosophy of a school of 19th-century New Englanders, as Ralph Waldo Emerson (1803-82), emphasizing the search for reality through intuition. 3. any vague or visionary idealism or thinking. —**tran·scen·den'tal·ist,** *n.*

trans·con·ti·nen·tal (trans-kon-ti-nen'tl), *adj.* 1. passing across a continent. 2. on the other side of a continent.

tran·scribe (tran-skrīb'), *v.t.* **-scribed', -scrib'ing,** 1. to write out or type out (material taken in shorthand, notes of a lecture, etc.). 2. to arrange (a piece of music) for a different instrument, range of voice, etc. than that for which it was originally intended. 3. to record a radio or television program, commercial, etc. for replay at a later time. —**tran·scrib'er,** *n.*

tran·script (tran'skript), *n.* 1. a written or typewritten copy, as of notes, shorthand, etc. 2. a copy; especially, an official copy.

tran·scrip·tion (tran-skrip'shŭn), *n.* 1. the act of transcribing. 2. a transcript. 3. an arrangement of a piece of music for a different instrument or voice. 4. a recording for radio or television.

tran·sept (tran'sept), *n.* that part of a cross-shaped church at right angles on either side to the nave.

trans·fer (trans-fûr'), *v.t.* **-ferred', -fer'ring,** 1. to convey from one person or place to another. 2. to make over (a legal right, title, etc.) to another. 3. to produce (a picture, design, etc.) by impressing or imprinting from one surface to another: *v.i.* to change from one bus, school, etc. to another: *n.* (trans'fĕr), 1. the act of transferring. 2. the fact of being transferred. 3. one that is transferred. 4. a ticket entitling one to change to another bus, streetcar, etc. 5. a picture transferred or to be transferred from one surface to another. —**trans·fer'al, trans·fer'ral,** *n.*

trans·fer·a·ble, trans·fer·ra·ble ('á-bl), *adj.* capable of being transferred. —**trans·fer·a·bil'i·ty,** *n.*

trans·fer·ee (trans-fēr-ē'), *n.* 1. a person to whom something is transferred, especially in law. 2. a person who is transferred.

---

trans·fer·ence (trans-fŭr'ĕns), *n*. 1. the act of transferring. 2. the fact of being transferred. 3. in *Psychoanalysis*, the transfer of emotions having to do with an early experience from the original object to the psychoanalyst.

trans·fig·u·ra·tion (trans-fig-yoo-rā'shŭn), *n*. 1. a change of form or appearance. 2. in the *Bible*, [T-], the supernatural change in the personal appearance of Jesus on the mountain: *Matthew xvii*. 3. [T-], a church festival commemorating this, celebrated on August 6.

trans·fig·ure (trans-fig'yĕr), *v.t.* -ured, -ur·ing, 1. to change the outward form or appearance of. 2. to change so as to idealize or glorify.

trans·fix (trans-fiks'), *v.t.* 1. to pierce through. 2. to make or hold motionless with horror, fascination, etc. —trans·fix'ion (-fik'shŭn), *n*.

trans·form (trans-fôrm'), *v.t.* 1. to change the shape or appearance of. 2. to change the character of. 3. to change the nature or function of; metamorphose. 4. to change the form of (an algebraic equation) to another having the same value. —trans·form'a·ble, *adj*. —trans·for·ma'tion, *n*.

trans·form·er (trans-fôr'mĕr), *n*. 1. one that transforms. 2. an electrical device consisting of induction coils that transform current to a different voltage.

trans·fuse (trans-fūz'), *v.t.* -fused', -fus'ing, 1. to instill; impart. 2. to transfer or introduce (blood, a saline solution, etc.) into a blood vessel. —trans·fu'sion, *n*.

trans·gress (trans-gres', tranz-), *v.t. & v.i.* 1. to pass over or go beyond (a boundary, limit, etc.). 2. to offend by the violation or infraction of (a law, commandment, etc.); sin (against). —trans·gres'sion (-gresh'ŭn), *n*. —trans·gres'sor, *n*.

tran·sient (tran'shĕnt), *adj*. 1. fleeting; brief. 2. temporary: *n*. a person who stays temporarily, as in a hotel or lodging house. —tran'sience, tran'sien·cy, *n*. —tran'sient·ly, *adv*.

tran·sis·tor (tran-zis'tĕr, -sis'-), *n*. 1. a compact, solid-state, electronic device made of semiconductor material. 2. [Informal], a transistorized radio.

tran·sis·tor·ize (-tō-rīz), *v.t.* -ized, -iz·ing, to equip with or convert to transistors.

trans·it (tran'sit, 'zit), *n*. 1. a passage through or over. 2. the conveyance, as of goods, through or across. 3. a system of public transportation. 4. such a system using electric trains: often called **rapid transit**. 5. a surveying instrument for measuring horizontal angles. 6. the apparent passage of a heavenly body across a given meridian or the field of a telescope. 7. the apparent passage of a smaller heavenly body across the disk of a larger one, as a planet across the sun.

tran·si·tion (tran-zish'ŭn), *n*. 1. a passage from one place or state to another. 2. a change of key in music; modulation. 3. the connecting words, phrases, sentences, etc. marking the change from one subject or scene to another in a piece of writing. —tran·si'tion·al, *adj*.

tran·si·tive (tran'si-tiv), *adj*. of or denoting a verb that takes a direct object to complete the meaning. —tran'si·tive·ly, *adv*. —tran'si·tive·ness, *n*.

tran·si·to·ry (tran'si-tôr-i), *adj*. of brief duration; continuing but a short time; fleeting. —tran'si·to·ri·ly, *adv*. —tran'si·to·ri·ness, *n*.

trans·late (trans-lāt', tranz-), *v.t.* -lat'ed, -lat'ing, 1. to change (something written or spoken) from one language into another. 2. to interpret; put into different words. 3. to change from one place, form, condition, etc. to another. 4. in *Theology*, to convey to heaven, originally without death. —trans·lat'a·ble, *adj*. —trans·la'tor, *n*.

trans·la·tion (-lā'shŭn), *n*. 1. the act of translating. 2. that which is translated; especially, written or spoken material that has been translated into a different language.

trans·lit·er·ate (trans-lit'ĕ-rāt, tranz-), *v.t.* -at·ed, -at·ing, to change (letters or words) into the corresponding characters of a different alphabet. —trans·lit·er·a'tion, *n*.

trans·lu·cent (trans-lōō'snt, tranz-), *adj*. partially transparent; letting light pass through. —trans·lu'cence, trans·lu'cen·cy, *n*. —trans·lu'cent·ly, *adv*.

trans·mi·grate (trans-mī'grāt, tranz-), *v.i.* -grat·ed, -grat·ing, 1. to move from one place of habitation to another. 2. to migrate to another country. 3. in some religions, to pass from one body to another at death: said of the soul. —trans·mi·gra'tion, *n*.

trans·mis·si·ble (trans-mis'i-bl, tranz-), *adj*. capable of being transmitted. —trans·mis·si·bil'i·ty, *n*.

trans·mis·sion (-mish'ŭn), *n*. 1. the act of transmitting. 2. the things transmitted. 3. the part of an automotive vehicle that transmits motive force from the engine to the wheels, as by gears.

trans·mit (-mit'), *v.t.* -mit'ted, -mit'ting, 1. to send from one person or place to another. 2. to pass (heat, light, etc.) through some medium. 3. to conduct. 4. to send out (radio or television signals). 5. to pass on by heredity, as from parent to child. 6. to pass along, as a disease. —trans·mit'tal, trans·mit'tance, *n*.

trans·mit·ter (-mit'ĕr), *n*. 1. one that transmits. 2. an apparatus for transmitting signals, as for telephone, radio, etc.

trans·mog·ri·fy (trans-mog'ri-fī, tranz-), *v.t.* -fied, -fy·ing, to change into a different shape, especially to one that is grotesque; transform. —trans·mog·ri·fi·ca'tion, *n*.

trans·mute (trans-mūt', tranz-), *v.t. & v.i* -mut'ed, -mut'ing, to change from one form, nature, or substance to another. —trans·mu·ta'tion, *n*.

trans·na·tion·al (-nash'ŭ-nl), *adj*. going beyond the interests or boundaries of a single nation.

trans·o·ce·an·ic (-ō-shi-an'ik), *adj*. across the ocean.

tran·som (tran'sŏm), *n*. 1. a beam or bar over a door or window, or over the sternpost of a ship. 2. a horizontal mullion in a window. 3. a small window just above a door or another window.

trans·pa·cif·ic (trans-pā-sif′ik), *adj.* on the other side of the Pacific Ocean.

trans·par·en·cy (trans-per′ēn-si), *n.* 1. the state or quality of being transparent: also **trans·par′ence**. 2. *pl.* **-cies**, a positive film or slide bearing a picture or design that can be viewed when light shines through or when projected on a screen.

trans·par·ent (′ēnt), *adj.* 1. having the property of transmitting rays of light so that objects on the other side may be seen; clear. 2. sheer; diaphanous. 3. obvious; easily understood. **—trans·par′ent·ly**, *adv.*

tran·spire (tran-spīr′), *v.i.* **-spired′, -spir′ing**, 1. to be exhaled or passed through the pores of the skin or the surface of leaves, etc. 2. to become known. 3. to come to pass; occur: *v.t.* to cause (vapor, moisture, etc.) to pass through (skin, tissues, leaves, etc.). **—tran·spi·ra′tion** (-spi-rā′shŭn).

trans·plant (trans-plant′), *v.t.* 1. to remove and plant or settle in another place. 2. in *Medicine*, to transfer (an organ or tissue) from one part of the body to another or from one person to another; graft. **—trans·plan·ta′tion**, *n.*

tran·spon·der (tran-spon′dēr), *n.* a transceiver that automatically transmits radio or radar signals in response to those received.

trans·port (trans-pōrt′), *v.t.* 1. to carry across or from one place to another. 2. to banish as a criminal. 3. to carry away by emotion: *n.* (trans′pōrt), 1. the act of transporting. 2. conveyance; transportation. 3. a ship, train, aircraft, etc. used for transporting troops, stores, etc. 4. rapture; ecstasy.

trans·por·ta·tion (-pēr-tā′shŭn), *n.* 1. the act of transporting. 2. the state of being transported. 3. a means or system of conveyance. 4. price, fare, or a ticket for public transportation.

trans·pose (trans-pōz′), *v.t. & v.i.* **-posed′, -pos′ing**, 1. to change the place or order of by putting each in the place of the other; interchange. 2. to change the key of (a piece of music) in writing or playing. 3. to transfer (an algebraic term) from one side of an equation to the other by changing the sign. **—trans·po·si′tion** (-pō-zish′ŭn), *n.*

tran·sub·stan·ti·a·tion (tran-sub-stan-shi-ā′shŭn), *n.* in the *Roman Catholic & Orthodox Eastern Churches*, the doctrine that, in the Eucharist, the bread and wine are changed into the body and blood of Christ.

tran·sude (tran-sōōd′), *v.i.* **-sud′ed, -sud′ing**, to pass or ooze through pores or interstices, as blood through vessel walls.

trans·verse (trans-vûrs′), *adj.* lying or being across or crosswise: *n.* (trans′vûrs), a transverse part. **—trans·verse′ly**, *adv.*

trans·ves·tite (trans-ves′tīt, tranz-), *n.* one who receives sexual pleasure from wearing clothes appropriate to the opposite sex. **—trans·ves′tism**, *n.*

trap (trap), *n.* 1. a device, as one that shuts suddenly with a spring, for catching animals; snare. 2. an ambush or stratagem to trick or catch. 3. any one of various devices in a drain to prevent the escape of sewer gas. 4. any one of several dark, heavy, igneous rocks, such as basalt: also **trap′rock**. 5. a light, two-wheeled carriage on springs. 6. *pl.* percussion devices attached to a drum, as in a jazz band. 7. *pl.* [Informal], one's clothes or personal possessions: *v.t.* **trapped, trap′ping**, 1. to catch as in a trap; ensnare. 2. to cover or adorn with trappings: *v.i.* 1. to set traps for game. 2. to trap animals, as for their fur.

trap·door (′dör), *n.* a hinged or sliding door in a roof, ceiling, floor, or theater stage.

tra·peze (tra-pēz′), *n.* a swinging horizontal bar suspended by ropes for gymnasts and circus aerialists.

tra·pe·zi·um (trā-pē′zi-ŭm), *n., pl.* **-zi·ums, -zi·a** (-â), 1. a plane figure with four sides, no two of which are parallel to each other. 2. a small bone of the wrist on the side toward the thumb.

trap·e·zoid (trap′ē-zoid), *n.* 1. a plane figure with four sides, two of which are parallel to each other. 2. a small bone of the wrist near the base of the index finger: *adj.* shaped like a trapezoid: also **trap·e·zoi′dal**.

trap·per (trap′ēr), *n.* one who traps animals, especially to obtain the furs.

trap·pings (′ingz), *n.pl.* 1. ornamental articles of dress. 2. an ornamental covering for a horse.

Trap·pist (trap′ist), *n.* [Informal], a monk of a strict branch of the Cistercian order.

trap·shoot·ing (trap′shōōt-ing), *n.* the sport of shooting at clay disks suddenly released into the air by throwing devices (*traps*). **—trap′·shoot·er**, *n.*

trash (trash), *n.* 1. worthless or useless matter; rubbish. 2. plant trimmings; parts, as limbs or leaves, that have been broken or trimmed off. 3. the refuse of sugar cane after the juice has been expressed. 4. a worthless person or people. **—trash′y**, *adj.*

trass (tras), *n.* a volcanic rock used in preparing hydraulic cement.

trau·ma (trou′mà, trô′-), *n., pl.* **-mas, -ma·ta** (′mä-tà), 1. a bodily wound, injury, or shock caused by an external agent. 2. an emotional experience causing shock, with sometimes lasting psychological effects. **—trau·mat′ic** (-mat′ik), *adj.* **—trau·mat′i·cal·ly**, *adv.*

trau·ma·tism (-tizm), *n.* 1. a trauma. 2. an abnormal condition caused by trauma.

trav·ail (trav′āl, trà-vāl′), *n.* 1. exceedingly hard labor. 2. the pains of childbirth. 3. agony; intense pain: *v.i.* 1. to labor very hard. 2. to suffer the pains of childbirth.

trave (trāv), *n.* [Rare], 1. a wooden frame for confining a horse while being shod. 2. a section between beams in a ceiling. 3. a beam going crosswise.

trav·el (trav′l), *v.i.* **-eled or -elled, -el·ing or -el·ling**, 1. to go from one place to another; especially, to visit foreign or distant places. 2. to proceed or move: *v.t.* to move or pass over or through: *n.* 1. the act or process of traveling. 2. *pl.* trips or tours taken, or an account of these. 3. traffic through a given place.

trav·eled, trav·elled (′ld), *adj.* 1. having traveled

ŏ in dragon, ōō in crude, oo in wool, u in cup, ū in cure, û in turn, ŭ in focus, oi in boy, ou in house, th in thin, th in sheathe, g in get, j in joy, y in yet.

a great deal. 2. much used by travelers, as a road.

trav·el·er, trav·el·ler ('l-ẽr), *n.* 1. one who travels. 2. a traveling salesman. 3. a metal ring that slides along a rope or spar.

traveler's check, a check, usually one of a set, issued by a bank and sold to a traveler who signs it when issued and again when cashing it.

traveling salesman, a salesman who travels from one place to another soliciting orders for his company.

trav·e·logue, trav·e·log (trav'ẽ-lŏg), *n.* a lecture on travels, usually illustrated.

trav·erse (trav'ẽrs), *adj.* 1. lying or extending across. 2. denoting drapes drawn together or apart by pulling a cord at the side: *n.* 1. a cross piece; something lying or placed across something else. 2. a gallery or loft crossing a building. 3. a parapet or wall of earth across a trench. 4. a formal denial of the pleadings of the opposite party in a lawsuit. 5. an instance of traversing, as an oblique or zigzag movement: *v.t.* (tra·vũrs'), -ersed', -ers'ing, 1. to travel or pass over, across, or through. 2. to oppose or thwart. 3. to survey carefully. 4. to deny formally: *v.i.* 1. to turn, as on a pivot. 2. to cross over. 3. to move across a hill or slope obliquely, as in skiing.—**trav·ers'a·ble,** *adj.*

trav·es·ty (trav'is-ti), *n., pl.* -ties, 1. a burlesque or parody for ridicule. 2. a debased imitation: *v.t.* -tied, -ty·ing, to make a travesty of.

trawl (trôl), *n.* 1. a large fishing net dragged along the sea bottom: also called **trawl·net.** 2. a long line held up by buoys, with many short fishing lines hung from it: also **trawl line:** *v.t. & v.i.* to fish with a trawl.

trawl·er ('ẽr), *n.* a fishing boat used in trawling.

tray (trā), *n.* a flat, shallow container, usually with raised edges, for holding and carrying things.—**tray'ful,** *n.*

treach·er·ous (trech'ẽr-ŭs), *adj.* 1. betraying a trust; perfidious; faithless. 2. insecure; not safe.—**treach'er·ous·ly,** *adv.*

treach·er·y ('i), *n., pl.* -er·ies, 1. violation of allegiance; treason. 2. perfidious conduct; betrayal of trust.

trea·cle (trē'kl), *n.* [British], molasses.

tread (tred), *v.i.* trod, trod'den or trod, tread'ing, 1. to step or walk, especially to walk with a more or less measured step. 2. to put one's foot or feet (*upon, on,* etc.). 3. to copulate, as birds: *v.t.* 1. to walk on, along, about, or in. 2. to crush or beat with the feet. 3. to perform by walking or dancing. 4. past tense **tread'ed,** to keep the head above water by moving the legs up and down: only in **tread water.** 5. to oppress or subdue: *n.* 1. a step or manner of stepping. 2. the sound of stepping. 3. the part of something on which a person or thing treads or moves, as the horizontal surface of a stair, wheel rim, shoe sole, etc. 4. the outer layer of a rubber tire, or the pattern or thickness of this.

trea·dle (tred'l), *n.* a lever, as on a loom or other machine, moved by the foot so as to

turn a wheel or other moving part: *v.i.* -dled, -dling, to work a treadle.

tread·mill ('mil), *n.* 1. a mill wheel turned by animals treading an endless belt. 2. any wearisome routine, as of the same work.

trea·son (trē'zn), *n.* the betrayal of one's country to an enemy.—**trea'son·a·ble, trea'son·ous,** *adj.*

treas·ure (trezh'ẽr), *n.* 1. accumulated wealth, as money, gold or silver, jewels, etc. 2. any person or thing that is highly valued: *v.t.* -ured, -ur·ing, 1. to lay up or collect for future use; hoard; accumulate. 2. to value highly; cherish.

treas·ur·er (-ẽr), *n.* an officer in charge of the funds of a club, government, corporation, etc.—**treas'ur·er·ship,** *n.*

treas·ure-trove (-trōv), *n.* money, jewels, or other valuables found hidden, the original owner being unknown.

treas·ur·y (-i), *n., pl.* -ur·ies, 1. a place or building where a treasure or funds are kept. 2. the funds of a state, corporation, etc. 3. [T-], the department of a state or country that has charge of finances. 4. a collection of treasures in verse, art, etc.

treasury note, any one of the interest-bearing notes of the U.S. Treasury which become due at periods between one and five years.

treat (trēt), *v.t.* 1. to handle or manage in a particular manner. 2. to behave toward. 3. to pay for the food, drink, or entertainment of (a guest). 4. to discuss or deal with (a subject) in speech, writing, music, etc. 5. to give medical or surgical care to (someone) or for (some disorder): *v.i.* 1. to discuss terms; negotiate. 2. to deal with a subject in speech or writing (with *of*). 3. to bear the expense of entertaining a guest: *n.* 1. a meal, drink, etc. paid for by another. 2. anything that gives great enjoyment.

trea·tise (trēt'is), *n.* a formal, systematic article or book on some subject, as one that gives information about it or discusses its principles.

treat·ment (trēt'mẽnt), *n.* 1. an act, manner, or procedure of treating something. 2. medical or surgical care.

trea·ty (trēt'i), *n., pl.* -ties, a formal agreement between two or more nations, usually arrived at by negotiation and concerning peace, trade, alliances, etc.

tre·ble (treb'l), *n.* 1. the singing voice of the highest range; soprano. 2. the range of such a voice. 3. any instrument with this range. 4. a high-pitched sound: *adj.* 1. of, for, or having the range of a treble. 2. threefold; triple: *v.t. & v.i.* -bled, -bling, to make or become threefold.—**tre'bly,** *adv.*

treb·u·chet (treb'yoo-shet), *n.* a medieval catapult for hurling large stones in warfare: also **tre·buck·et** (trē'buk·it).

tree (trē), *n.* 1. a large, woody, perennial plant with one main trunk and many branches at some height from the ground. 2. any one of various shrubs resembling a tree. 3. a chart or diagram showing family descent: also 'family tree. 4. anything resembling a tree: *v.t.* treed, tree'ing, to chase up a tree.—**tree'less,** *adj.*

tree fern, any one of various giant tropical ferns with a long, trunklike stem and fronds at the top.

tree-nail (trē'nāl; tren'l, trun'-), *n.* a wooden pin used for fastening timbers together, as in shipbuilding: it swells after immersion in water to fit tightly.

tref (trāf), *adj.* not clean or fit to eat according to Jewish dietary laws; not kosher.

tre-foil (trē'foil), *n.* 1. any one of a number of plants with leaves divided into three leaflets, as the clover. 2. an ornamental design resembling a leaf like this, as used in architecture.

trek (trek), *v.i.* **trekked, trek'king,** 1. in South Africa, to travel or migrate by ox wagon. 2. to travel slowly or with difficulty. 3. [Informal], to go, especially on foot: *n.* 1. a journey or leg of a journey. 2. a migration. 3. [Informal], a short walk.

trel-lis (trel'is), *n.* a structure or frame of latticework on which vines are trained.

trel-lis-work (-wûrk), *n.* small strips or bars nailed together crosswise.

trem-ble (trem'bl), *v.i.* **-bled, -bling,** 1. to shake involuntarily, as from fear, cold, weakness, etc. 2. to shudder, quiver, vibrate, etc. 3. to quaver, as sound. 4. to be apprehensive, afraid, etc.: *n.* 1. an involuntary shaking; shiver. 2. *pl.* a state or spell of trembling.

trem-bling ('bling), *adj.* shaking as with fear; quivering: also **trem'bly.** —**trem'bling-ly,** *adv.*

tre-men-dous (tri-men'dùs), *adj.* 1. exciting fear or terror; dreadful. 2. great, powerful, or very large. 3. [Informal], wonderful, excellent, etc. —**tre-men'dous-ly,** *adv.*

trem-o-lite (trem'ò-līt), *n.* a white or gray variety of hornblende.

trem-o-lo (trem'ò-lō), *n., pl.* **-los,** 1. a tremulous or fluttering effect in vocal or instrumental music. 2. a mechanical device in an organ by which a tremolo is produced.

trem-or (trem'ēr), *n.* 1. an involuntary trembling. 2. a quivering or vibratory motion. 3. a feeling of tingling excitement. —**trem'or-ous,** *adj.*

trem-u-lous (trem'yoo-lùs), *adj.* 1. trembling; quivering. 2. fearful; timid. —**trem'u-lous-ly,** *adv.* —**trem'u-lous-ness,** *n.*

trench (trench), *n.* 1. a long, narrow cut or ditch excavated in the earth. 2. such a ditch with earth thrown up in front as a parapet, used in battle. 3. a deep furrow in the ocean floor: *v.t.* to dig or form a ditch in: *v.i.* 1. to dig a ditch or ditches, as for fortification. 2. to encroach.

trench-ant (tren'chànt), *adj.* 1. sharp; keen; penetrating. 2. forceful; vigorous. —**trench'-an-cy,** *n.* —**trench'ant-ly,** *adv.*

trench coat, a waterproof, often double-breasted, belted coat with straps on the shoulders.

trench-er (tren'chēr), *n.* [Archaic], 1. a wooden platter. 2. meat served on such a platter.

trench-er-man (-màn), *n., pl.* **-men** (-mèn), one who enjoys eating; especially, a hearty eater.

trench fever, an infectious disease transmitted by body lice, common among soldiers in trenches in World War I.

trench foot, a disease of the feet due to exposure to wet and cold and circulatory problems from inactivity, formerly common to soldiers in trenches.

trench mouth, an infectious disease of the mucuous membranes of the mouth, caused by a bacterium.

trend (trend), *n.* 1. an inclination in a general direction, as of a river, road, etc. 2. a general tendency or course; drift. 3. a current vogue in fashions.

trend-y ('i), *adj.* **trend'i-er, trend'i-est,** of or in the latest trend or vogue.

tre-pan (tri-pan'), *n.* 1. an early form of the trephine. 2. a heavy boring tool used as in sinking shafts: *v.t.* **-panned', -pan'ning,** 1. to trephine. 2. to cut a disk out of (a metal plate, etc.). —**tre-pan-a'tion,** *n.*

tre-pang (tri-pang'), *n.* smoked, dried sea cucumber used in the Orient for making soup.

tre-phine (tri-fīn', -fēn'), *n.* a surgical instrument for removing disks of bone from the skull: *v.t.* **-phined', -phin'ing,** to operate on with a trephine. —**treph-i-na-tion** (tref-i-nā'shùn), *n.*

trep-i-da-tion (trep-i-dā'shùn), *n.* 1. trembling movement; shaking. 2. a state of terror or alarm. 3. confusion or apprehension.

tres-pass (tres'pàs, 'pas), *v.i.* 1. to commit any offense; sin; do wrong. 2. to enter upon the land or property of another without right or permission: *n.* a wrong, sin, or offense, especially a moral offense. —**tres'pass-er,** *n.*

tress (tres), *n.* 1. originally, a braid of hair. 2. a lock of hair. 3. *pl.* a woman's or girl's long hair, falling loosely.

tres-sure (tresh'ēr), *n.* an ornamental border around the edge of a heraldic shield, often with fleurs-de-lis.

tres-tle (tres'l), *n.* 1. a movable frame consisting of a horizontal piece of wood with a set of spreading legs at each end. 2. a braced framework of wood or steel supporting a bridge, as over a valley and river. 3. a bridge supported by this kind of framework.

tres-tle-work (-wûrk), *n.* a structure or system of trestles.

trey (trā), *n.* a playing card with three spots.

tri-, a prefix meaning *three, three times, in three ways, every third.*

tri-a-ble (trī'à-bl), *adj.* 1. subject to trial in a court of law. 2. that can be tested.

tri-ac-id (trī-as'id), *adj.* 1. capable of combining with three molecules of a monobasic acid. 2. having three replaceable hydrogen atoms: said of an acid.

tri-ad (trī'ad), *n.* 1. a group of three persons or things. 2. the common musical chord of a tone together with the third and fifth tones above it on the diatonic scale. —**tri-ad'ic,** *adj.*

tri-age (trē-äzh'), *n.* a system of establishing the order in which acts of esp. medical assistance are to be carried out in an emergency.

tri-al (trī'àl), *n.* 1. an attempt or endeavor. 2. the act of trying or testing; test. 3. an experiment. 4. a state of being tried by suffering, temptation, hardship, etc. 5. an irritation; source of annoyance. 6. a judicial ex-

---

ò in dragon, ōō in crude, oo in wool, u in cup, ü in cure, û in turn, ù in focus, oi in boy, ou in house, th in thin, th in sheathe, g in get, j in joy, y in yet.

amination of the facts and law of a case in court.

trial and error, a method of finding a solution or arriving at a conclusion by making a series of experiments, or trials.

trial jury, a jury impaneled to try a civil or criminal case; petit jury.

tri·an·gle (trī'ang-gl), *n.* 1. a plane figure having three angles and three sides. 2. any three-sided or three-cornered object, piece of land, figure, etc. 3. a triangular percussion instrument that produces a high, clear sound. 4. a situation involving three people. —**tri·an'gu·lar** (-gyŭ-lēr), *adj.*

tri·an·gu·late ('gyŭ-lāt), *v.t.* -lat·ed, -lat·ing, 1. to divide into triangles. 2. to survey by means of triangles. —**tri·an·gu·la'tion,** *n.*

tri·arch·y (trī'är-ki), *n.*, *pl.* **-arch·ies,** 1. government by three rulers; triumvirate. 2. a country or state under three rulers.

Tri·as·sic (trī-as'ik), *n.* the first period of the Mesozoic Era, in which the dinosaurs appeared.

tri·a·tom·ic (trī-ǎ-tom'ik), *adj.* 1. denoting a molecule consisting of three atoms. 2. denoting a molecule having three replaceable atoms or groups.

trib·al·ism (trī'bl-izm), *n.* 1. the state of existing in tribes. 2. tribal culture. 3. a strong loyalty or feeling of identification with one's tribe or group. —**trib'al·ist,** *n. & adj.* —**trib·al·is'tic,** *adj.*

tri·bas·ic (trī-bā'sik), *adj.* denoting an acid that has in its molecule three hydrogen atoms that are replaceable by basic atoms or radicals.

tribe (trīb), *n.* 1. a group of persons, families, or clans descended from a common ancestor and living under a chief or leader. 2. a natural group of plants or animals. —**trib'al,** *adj.* —**trib'al·ly,** *adv.*

tribes·man (trībz'măn), *n.*, *pl.* **-men** ('měn), a member of a tribe.

tri·bo·e·lec·tric·i·ty (trī-bō-i-lek-tris'ī-ti), *n.* electricity on a surface, that is generated by friction, as by rubbing nylon on glass. —**tri·bo·e·lec'tric** (trik), *adj.*

tri·bo·lu·mi·nes·cence (-lōō-mi-nes'ns), *n.* luminescence caused by friction.

tri·brach (trī'brak, trib'rak), *n.* a poetic foot of three short syllables.

trib·u·la·tion (trib-yŭ-lā'shŭn), *n.* 1. deep sorrow; severe distress. 2. a cause of this; affliction.

tri·bu·nal (trī-bū'nl), *n.* 1. the seat of a judge. 2. a court of justice.

trib·une (trib'ūn, tri-būn'), *n.* 1. an ancient Roman official elected by the people to safeguard their rights. 2. a champion of the people: often used in newspaper names. 3. a raised stand or rostrum for public speakers. —**trib'une·ship,** *n.*

trib·u·tar·y (trib'yoo-ter-i), *adj.* 1. paying tribute. 2. under another's control, as a nation. 3. contributing to make up a greater object of the same kind: *n., pl.* **-tar·ies,** 1. a tributary nation. 2. a tributary stream or river.

trib·ute (trib'ūt), *n.* 1. a regular payment of money from a subject nation to the nation

that controls it, as for peace or protection. 2. something said, given, or done as in praise, gratitude, esteem, or honor.

trice (trīs), *n.* an instant: now only in the phrase **in a trice.**

tri·cen·ten·ni·al (trī-sen-ten'i-ǎl), *adj.* marking a period or duration of three hundred years: *n.* a tricentennial anniversary or its celebration. —**tri·cen·ten'ni·al·ly,** *adv.*

tri·ceps (trī'seps), *n.*, *pl.* **-ceps, -ceps·es,** a muscle having three points of origin; especially, the extensor muscle of the arm.

tri·cer·a·tops (trī-ser'ǎ-tops), *n.* a kind of plant-eating dinosaur with a bony crest over the neck and horns above the eyes.

tri·chi·a·sis (tri-kī'ǎ-sis), *n.* an abnormal condition in which the eyelashes grow inward.

tri·chi·na (tri-kī'nǎ), *n.*, *pl.* **-nae** ('nē), a parasitic nematode worm which infests the intestines and voluntary muscles of hogs and human beings, causing trichinosis.

trich·i·no·sis (trik-i-nō'sis), *n.* a disease caused by the presence of trichinae in the muscles and intestines, characterized by fever, diarrhea, and muscular pains: it is usually acquired by eating pork from infested hogs.

trich·i·nous (trik'i-nŭs), *adj.* 1. of or suffering from trichinosis. 2. infested with trichinae.

trich·ite (trik'īt), *n.* a crystallite resembling a mass of hairs, found in volcanic rocks.

trich·o-, a combining form meaning *hair:* also, before a vowel, **trich-.**

tri·choid (trik'oid), *adj.* hairlike.

tri·chol·o·gy (tri-kol'ō-ji), *n.* the science dealing with the hair and its diseases. —**tri·chol'o·gist,** *n.*

tri·chome (trī'kōm), *n.* any hairlike growth from a plant, as a prickle, bristle, or the like.

tri·cho·sis (tri-kō'sis), *n.* any disease of the hair.

tri·chot·o·my (trī-kot'ō-mi), *n.* division into three parts, groups, categories, etc. —**tri·chot'o·mous,** *adj.* —**tri·chot'o·mous·ly,** *adv.*

tri·chro·ism (trī'krō-izm), *n.* the . property of certain crystals of transmitting three colors when viewed from three different directions. —**tri·chro'ic,** *adj.*

tri·chro·mat·ic (trī-krō-mat'ik), *adj.* 1. of or using three colors, as in color photography. 2. of, pertaining to, or having normal vision, in which the three primary colors are seen clearly. Also **tri·chro'mic.** —**tri·chro'ma·tism** (-krō'mǎ-tizm), *n.*

trick (trik), *n.* 1. a stratagem or artifice intended to deceive, cheat, etc. 2. a deception or illusion. 3. a prank; practical joke. 4. an act of legerdemain. 5. a clever act or skillful feat intended to amuse. 6. a peculiarity or mannerism. 7. a work shift or turn at duty. 8. the playing cards taken in by the winner in a single round: *v.t.* to cheat; impose upon; deceive: *adj.* 1. having to do with a trick. 2. denoting something that may fail to function properly, as a faulty knee joint.

trick·er·y ('er-i), *n.*, *pl.* **-er·ies,** deception; cheating; fraud; the use of artifice.

trick·le (trik'l), *v.i.* **-led, -ling,** 1. to flow gently in a small stream; run down in drops. 2. to move slowly: *n.* a small, gentle flow.

---

a in cap, ā in cane, ä in father, ȧ in abet, e in met, ē in be, ē in baker, ė in regent, i in pit, ī in fine, ĭ in manifest, o in hot, ô in horse, ō in bone,

trick·le-down (trik'l-doun), *adj.* of an economic theory holding that government aid to big business, such as loans and tax abatement, will ultimately benefit the poor.

trick·ster (trik'stēr), *n.* 1. one who likes to play tricks. 2. a cheater.

trick·y ('ï), *adj.* **trick'i·er**, **trick'i·est**, 1. given to tricks; artful; cunning. 2. difficult; hard to deal with. —**trick'i·ly**, *adv.* —**trick'i·ness**, *n.*

tri·clin·ic (trī-klin'ik), *adj.* having three unequal axes intersecting at oblique angles, as some crystals.

tri·clin·i·um ('i-ŭm), *n.*, *pl.* **-i·a** (-å), in ancient Rome, 1. a couch extending around three sides of a dining table, for reclining at meals. 2. a dining room with such a couch.

tri·col·or (trī'kul-ēr): *n.* a flag of three colors, especially, the flag of France, with broad, vertical bands of blue, white, and red: *adj.* having three colors.

tri·corn ('kôrn), *n.* a hat with the brim folded up on its three sides.

tri·cot (trē'kō), *n.* 1. a soft, thin fabric that is knitted, or woven to resemble knitting. 2. a kind of ribbed cloth.

tri·cus·pid (trī-kus'pid), *adj.* having three cusps, or points, as some teeth: *n.* a tooth with three cusps.

tri·cy·cle (trī'si-kl), *n.* a vehicle, especially a small one for children, consisting of three wheels, one in front and two in back, connected by a tubular frame that supports a saddle for the rider: it is propelled by pedals and has handlebars for steering.

tri·dent (trīd'nt), *n.* 1. a three-pronged spear, as one used for fishing. 2. in *Roman & Greek Mythology*, a three-pronged spear used as a scepter by the sea god, Neptune (or Poseidon): *adj.* three-pronged.

tri·den·tate (trī-den'tāt), *adj.* having three teeth or prongs.

tried (trīd), past tense and past participle of **try**: *adj.* 1. proved; tested. 2. trustworthy; faithful. 3. having suffered and endured.

tri·en·ni·al (trī-en'i-ål), *adj.* 1. comprising three years. 2. occurring every three years: *n.* a triennial occurrence, celebration, etc. —**tri·en'ni·al·ly**, *adv.*

tri·er (trī'ēr), *n.* a person or thing that tries.

tri·fle (trī'fl), *n.* 1. anything of little value or importance. 2. a small amount of something. 3. [British], a dessert made of spongecake soaked in wine, spread with jam, and covered with cream or custard: *v.i.* **tri·fled**, **-fling**, 1. to act or talk with levity; joke. 2. to toy (with): *v.t.* to waste (time, etc.). —**tri'fler**, *n.*

tri·fling ('fling), *adj.* 1. of small value or importance; trivial. 2. frivolous.

tri·fo·cal (trī-fō'kl), *adj.* denoting a lens with three parts, the lower part ground for near focus, a narrow band in the center for intermediate focus, and the upper part for distant focus: *n.* 1. a lens made like this. 2. *pl.* (trī'fō-klz), eyeglasses fitted with trifocal lenses.

tri·fo·li·ate (trī-fō'li-it, -āt), *adj.* in *Botany*, having three leaves.

tri·fo·li·o·late (trī-fō'li-ô-lāt), *adj.* in *Botany*, di-vided into three leaflets, as the leaf of a clover.

tri·fo·ri·um (-fōr'i-ŭm), *n.*, *pl.* **-ri·a** (-å), an arcade or gallery in the wall above the arches of a church, separating the nave arches from the choir or transept.

tri·fur·cate (trī-fūr'kit, 'kåt), *adj.* divided into three branches or forks. —**tri·fur·ca'tion**, *n.*

trig (trig), *adj.* [Chiefly British], 1. trim; neat. 2. in good condition: *n.* [Chiefly Dialectal], a stone or wedge placed under a wheel to keep it from rolling: *v.t.* **trigged**, **trig'ging**, [Chiefly Dialectal], to stop (a wheel) from rolling by placing a trig under it.

trig (trig), *n.* [Informal], trigonometry.

tri·gem·i·nal (trī-jem'i-nl), *adj.* denoting or of either of a pair of cranial nerves that divide into three branches on the head and extend down into the face: *n.* a trigeminal nerve.

trig·ger (trig'ēr), *n.* 1. a lever which, when pulled, releases the hammer of a firearm. 2. any catch or lever that is pulled or pressed to release a pawl, spring, etc. 3. an act or incident that starts a series of events or actions: *v.t.* 1. to fire or put into action by pulling a trigger. 2. to set off (an action).

trig·ger·fish (-fish), *n.*, *pl.* **-fish**, **-fish·es**, any one of a number of brightly colored tropical fish.

tri·glyph (trī'glif), *n.* an ornament of the Doric frieze, placed directly over each column and at equal distances.

trig·o·nal (trig'ô-nl), *adj.* three-cornered; triangular.

trig·o·nom·e·try (trig-ô-nom'ï-tri), *n.* the branch of mathematics dealing with the relations between the sides and angles of triangles, used in surveying, engineering, navigation, etc. —**trig·o·no·met'ric** (-nô-met'rik), *adj.* —**trig·o·no·met'ri·cal·ly**, *adv.*

tri·graph (trī'graf), *n.* a combination of three letters representing one sound.

tri·he·dral (trī-hē'drål), *adj.* having three sides or faces.

tri·hy·drate (-hī'drāt), *n.* a chemical compound having three molecules of water.

tri·ju·gate (trī'joo-gāt), *adj.* having three pairs of leaflets.

tri·lat·er·al (trī-lat'ēr-ål), *adj.* three-sided. —**tri·lat'er·al·ly**, *adv.*

tri·lin·e·ar (-lin'i-ēr), *adj.* of or having three lines.

tri·lin·gual (-ling'gwål), *adj.* 1. able to use three languages equally well. 2. of or in three languages. —**tri·lin'gual·ly**, *adv.*

trill (tril), *n.* 1. a rapid alternation of a musical tone with that immediately adjacent. 2. a warble. 3. a rapid vibration of one of the speech organs, as of the tongue against the inside of the front upper teeth. 4. a speech sound made by such a vibration.

tril·lion (tril'yŭn), *n.* 1. in the U.S. and France, the number indicated by 1 followed by 12 zeros. 2. in Great Britain and Germany, the number indicated by 1 followed by 18 zeros. —**tril'lionth**, *adj. & n.*

tril·li·um (tril'i-ŭm), *n.* a kind of spring plant with three leaves and one flower with three petals, usually white.

ŏ in dragon, ōō in crude, oo in wool, u in cup, ū in cure, ū in turn, ŭ in focus, oi in boy, ou in house, th in thin, th in sheathe, g in get, j in joy, y in yet.

tri·lo·bate (trī-lō'bāt), *adj.* having three lobes, as some leaves.

tri·lo·bite (trī'lō-bīt), *n.* an extinct arthropod with a body divided by two clefts into three parts: its fossils are found in Paleozoic rocks. —**tri·lo·bit'ic** (-bit'ik), *adj.*

tril·o·gy (tril'ò-ji), *n., pl.* **-gies,** a series of three dramas, novels, etc. each complete in itself, but forming one extended, unified work.

trim (trim), *adj.* **trim'mer, trim'mest,** 1. neat; orderly. 2. smart; attractive. 3. in good condition: *v.t.* trimmed, trim'ming, 1. to decorate or adorn. 2. to make neat or smooth. 3. to clip or cut. 4. to balance (a ship) by shifting cargo, etc. 5. to adjust (sails) for sailing according to the wind, etc. 6. to adjust (an aircraft) for steady and smooth flight. 7. [Informal], to thrash, defeat, beat, etc., *v.i.* to compromise or adjust one's approach or viewpoint to satisfy opposing parties or factions: *n.* 1. order; adjustment. 2. good condition. 3. the state of a ship in regard to cargo, sailing capacity, etc. 4. the framing, moldings, etc. around a window or door. 5. ornaments or edgings on garments or household articles. —**trim'ly,** *adv.* —**trim'ness,** *n.*

tri·ma·ran (trī'mâ-ran), *n.* a boat with three parallel hulls.

tri·mes·ter (tri-mes'tēr), *n.* 1. a period of three months. 2. in some colleges, any one of the three periods of the academic year.

tri·met·ric (trī-met'rik), *adj.* 1. having three metrical feet. 2. having three unequal axes intersecting at right angles, as some crystals. Also **tri·met'ri·cal.**

trim·mer (trim'ēr), *n.* 1. a person, device, machine, etc. that trims. 2. a floor joist to which beams are fastened.

trim·ming ('ing), *n.* 1. something used to decorate. 2. *pl.* the accompaniments or side dishes of the main dish of a meal. 3. *pl.* parts trimmed off. 4. [Informal], *a)* a thrashing; *b)* a cheating.

tri·month·ly (tri-munth'li), *adj. & adv.* once every three months.

tri·morph (trī'môrf), *n.* 1. a substance that crystallizes in three forms. 2. any one of these forms.

tri·mor·phism (trī-môr'fizm), *n.* 1. the property of crystallizing in three forms. 2. the existence of three distinct forms within the same species. —**tri·mor'phic, tri·mor'phous,** *adj.*

tri·nal (trī'nl), *adj.* threefold: triple.

trine (trīn), *adj.* 1. threefold. 2. in *Astrology,* favorable: *n.* 1. a triad. 2. [T-], the Trinity. 3. in *Astrology,* the aspect of two planets 120° apart, considered to be favorable.

Trin·i·tar·i·an (trin-i-ter'i-ân), *adj.* 1 pertaining to the Trinity or the doctrine of the Trinity. 2. believing in this doctrine. 3. [t-], threefold. *n.* a believer in the doctrine of the Trinity. —**Trin·i·tar'i·an·ism,** *n.*

tri·ni·tro·tol·u·ene (trī-ni-trō-tol'yoo-wēn), *n.* a high-powered explosive, a derivative of toluene, used for blasting and in warfare: commonly called TNT: also **tri·ni·tro·tol'u·ol** (-ōl).

trin·i·ty (trin'i-ti), *n., pl.* **-ties,** 1 a set of three that form a unit. 2. [T-], in *Christian*

Theology, the union of the Father, Son, and Holy Ghost in one Godhead.

Trinity Sunday, the Sunday next after Whitsunday.

trin·ket (tring'kit), *n.* 1. anything small or of little value. 2. a small ornament or jewel.

tri·no·mi·al (trī-nō'mi-âl), *adj.* consisting of three terms: *n.* 1. a mathematical expression consisting of three terms connected by plus or minus signs. 2. in *Biology,* a name consisting of three words denoting the genus, species, and subspecies or variety.

tri·o (trē'ō), *n., pl.* **tri'os,** 1. a set or group of three. 2. a musical composition for three singers or players. 3. the performers of such a composition.

trip (trip), *v.i.* **tripped, trip'ping,** 1. to run or step lightly or nimbly; take short, quick steps. 2. to stumble. 3. to err: *v.t.* 1 to cause to stumble, especially by catching the foot. 2. to cause to err. 3. to release (a spring, catch, etc.): *n.* 1. a quick, light step. 2. an excursion, jaunt, journey, etc. 3. a stumble, especially one caused by catching the foot. 4. [Slang], the sensations, period, or experience of being under the influence of a psychedelic drug. —**trip'per,** *n.*

tri·par·tite (tri-pär'tīt), *adj.* 1 having three parts. 2. made by three parties, nations, etc., as an agreement.

tri·par·ti·tion (tri-pär-tish'ûn), *n.* division into three parts.

tripe (trīp), *n.* 1. part of the stomach of a ruminant, especially the ox, used for food. 2. [Slang], anything worthless; nonsense.

trip·ham·mer (trip'ham-ēr), *n.* a heavy hammer that is raised and then allowed to fall by means of a tripping device: also **trip hammer.**

tri·plane (trī'plān), *n.* an early kind of airplane with three sets of wings, one above the other

tri·ple (trip'l), *adj.* 1. made up of three. 2. threefold. 3. in *Music,* containing three, or a multiple of three, beats to the measure: *n.* 1 a sum or quantity three times as great. 2. in *Baseball,* a hit in which the batter reaches third base *v.t. & v.i.* **-pled, -pling,** 1. to multiply or increase three times. 2. in *Baseball,* to hit a triple. —**tri'ply,** *adv*

tri·plet (trip'lit), *n.* 1 any one of three offspring born at the same time. 2. a collection of three things of the same kind.

tri·ple-tail (trip'l-tāl), *n.* a large food fish found in the western Atlantic: it has long fins that extend backward and give the effect of a tail with three parts.

tri·plex (trip'leks), *adj.* triple; threefold: *n.* something that is triplex.

trip·li·cate (trip'li-kit), *adj.* 1 threefold. 2. denoting the last of three identical copies *n.* the last of three identical copies *v.t.* (-kāt), **-cat·ed, -cat·ing,** to make three copies of. —**trip·li·ca'tion,** *n.*

tri·plic·i·ty (tri-plis'i-ti), *n., pl.* **-ties,** 1 the state of being triple. 2. a group of three.

tri·pod (trī'pod), *n.* 1. a three-legged stool or table 2. a three-legged stand for a camera, theodolite, etc., often adjustable. —**trip·o·dal** (trip'ō-dl), **tri·pod·ic** (tri-pod'ik), *adj*

---

a in *cap,* *ā* in *cane,* *ä* in *father,* *ə* in *abet,* *e* in *met,* *ē* in *be,* *ē* in *baker,* *ê* in *regent,* *i* in *pit,* *ī* in *fine,* *i* in *manifest,* *o* in *hot,* *ô* in *horse,* *ō* in *bone,*

trip·o·li (trĭp′ō-lĭ), *n.* a light-colored, earthy substance that consists chiefly of silica and is used for polishing: also called **trip′o·lite** (-līt).

trip·tych (trĭp′tĭk), *n.* an altarpiece consisting of three hinged panels with paintings, designs, etc., two of them folding over the middle one which is fixed in place.

tri·reme (trī′rēm), *n.* an ancient galley with three banks of oars on each side.

tri·sect (trī-sĕkt′), *v.t.* to cut or divide into three equal parts. **—tri·sec′tion,** *n.* **—tri·sec′tor,** *n.*

tris·kel·i·on (tris-kĕl′ĭ-ŏn), *n., pl.* **-i·a** (-ă), a symbol or design consisting of three bent legs or arms or three curved branches radiating from a common center: also **tris·kele** (tris′kĕl).

tris·mus (trĭz′mŭs, tris′-), *n.* a spasm or contraction of the jaw muscle, specifically as a symptom of lockjaw.

tris·tich (tris′tĭk), *n.* a stanza of three lines.

tris·tich·ous (′tĭ-kŭs), *adj.* arranged in three vertical rows.

tri·syl·la·ble (trī-sĭl′ă-bl), *n.* a word of three syllables. **—tri·syl·lab·ic** (trī-si-lăb′ĭk), *adj.*

trite (trīt), *adj.* trit′er, trit′est, worn-out; stale; hackneyed. **—trite′ly,** *adv.* **—trite′ness,** *n.*

tri·the·ism (trī′thē-ĭzm), *n.* the doctrine that the three making up the Trinity (Father, Son, and Holy Ghost) are three separate Gods. **—tri′the·ist,** *n.*

Tri·ton (trīt′n), *n.* 1. in *Greek Mythology,* a sea god, son of Poseidon. 2. [t-], any one of several large sea snails. 3. [t-], the long, colorful, spiral shell of this snail.

trit·u·rate (trĭch′ŭ-rāt), *v.t.* **-rat·ed, -rat·ing,** to rub, grind, or crush to a powder; pulverize. **—trit·u·ra′tion,** *n.*

tri·umph (trī′ŭmf), *n.* 1. a major success; victory. 2. great joy at victory or success. 3. a procession celebrating a conquest or victory: *v.i.* 1. to rejoice over success. 2. to obtain a victory. **—tri·um′phal** (-um′fl), *adj.*

tri·um·phant (trī-um′fănt), *adj.* 1. rejoicing for victory. 2. victorious. **—tri·um′phant·ly,** *adv.*

tri·um·vir (trī-um′vēr), *n., pl.* **-virs, -vir·i** (′vi-rī), in ancient Rome, any one of three men sharing administrative authority in government.

tri·um·vi·rate (-ĭt), *n.* 1. government by a group of three men. 2. the office or term of a triumvir or triumvirs.

tri·une (trī′ūn), *adj.* denoting three in one: said of the Godhead: n. a triad. 2. [T-], same as **Trinity. —tri·u′ni·ty,** *n.*

tri·va·lent (trī-vā′lĕnt), *adj.* 1. having a valence of three. 2. same as **tervalent** (*adj.* 1).

triv·et (triv′ĭt), *n.* 1. a three-legged stand for holding a kettle or pot near a fire. 2. a small metal or ceramic plate with short legs, on which to place a hot platter or dish on a table.

triv·i·a (triv′ĭ-ă), *n.pl.* trivial matters; unimportant trifles.

triv·i·al (triv′ĭ-ăl), *adj.* trifling; commonplace; unimportant. **—triv·i·al′i·ty** (-al′ĭ-tĭ), *n., pl.* **-ties.**

-trix (triks), *pl.* **-trix′es, -tri·ces′** (trī-sēz′, trī′-**

siz), a suffix used in forming certain feminine nouns of agent, as *aviatrix.*

tro·car (trō′kär), *n.* a surgical instrument with a sharp point, used for inserting drainage tubes: also spelled **tro′char.**

tro·cha·ic (trō-kā′ĭk), *adj.* of or relating to verse made up of trochees: *n.* 1. a trochaic verse. 2. a trochee.

tro·che (trō′kĭ), *n.* a small, usually round, medicinal lozenge, used especially for. sore throat.

tro·chee (trō′kĭ), *n.* a metrical foot of two syllables, the first accented, the second unaccented.

troch·i·lus (trok′ĭ-lŭs), *n., pl.* **-li** (-lī), a hummingbird.

troch·le·ar (trok′lĭ-ēr), *adj.* 1. shaped like a pulley, as being circular and contracted in the middle. 2. acting like a pulley, as certain muscles, bones, etc.

trod (trod), past tense and alternate past participle of **tread.**

trod·den (′n), alternate past participle of **tread.**

trog·lo·dyte (trog′lŏ-dīt), *n.* 1. a cave dweller; especially, one of the prehistoric people who lived in caves. 2. an anthropoid ape. **—trog·lo·dyt′ic** (-dĭt′ĭk), *adj.*

troi·ka (troi′kă), *n.* 1. a Russian carriage or sleigh drawn by three horses abreast. 2. any group of three, especially three people in authority.

Tro·jan (trō′jăn), *adj.* of or pertaining to ancient Troy, a city in northwest Asia Minor, or its inhabitants: *n.* 1. a native or inhabitant of Troy. 2. one who works doggedly or very hard.

Trojan horse, in *Greek Mythology,* a huge, hollow, wooden horse full of Greek soldiers, left at the gates of Troy: when it was brought into the city, the soldiers opened the gates to the Greek army which destroyed the city.

troll (trōl), *n.* 1. in *Scandinavian Folklore,* any one of various supernatural creatures, as a giant or a dwarf, that lives in a cave. 2. *a)* the method of trolling in fishing; *b)* a fishing lure and line used in trolling. 3. a song with parts sung in succession; round: *v.t.* & *v.i.* 1. to sing the parts of (a round) in succession. 2. to sing lustily. 3. to fish (for) with a lure and line running on a reel, as from a moving boat. **—troll′er,** *n.*

trol·ley (trol′ĭ), *n., pl.* **-leys,** 1. a wheeled container running suspended from an overhead track. 2. a grooved wheel, as at the end of a pole, that collects electric current from an overhead wire and transmits it to a motor of a streetcar. 3. a trolley car. 4. [British], any one of a number of low carts or trucks: *v.t.* & *v.i.* **-leyed, -ley·ing,** to transport or ride in a trolley car.

trolley car, a streetcar run by electricity collected from overhead wires by means of a trolley.

trol·lop (trol′ŏp), *n.* a prostitute.

trom·bone (trom-bōn′), *n.* a large, brass-wind instrument in which the tones are produced by moving a slide, or movable section of its tube: also **slide trombone:** another kind is played like a trumpet, with valves: also valve trombone.

troop (trōōp), n. 1. a group of persons or animals; band; company. 2. a unit of cavalry. 3. pl. soldiers. 4. a unit of Boy Scouts or Girl Scouts: v.i. 1. to form in a troop. 2. to go as a troop.

troop·er (trōō'pẽr), n. 1. a cavalryman. 2. a mounted policeman. 3. [Informal], a State policeman.

trope (trōp), n. 1. a word or expression used figuratively. 2. figurative language.

troph·ic (trof'ik), adj. pertaining to nourishment or nutrition.

tro·phy (trō'fi), n., pl. -phies, 1. a memorial of a victory in war. 2. a prize, as a silver cup, received in a sports contest or other competition. 3. the head, skin, etc. of wild game displayed by a hunter.

trop·ic (trop'ik), n. 1. either of the two parallels of latitude, one 23.5° north of the equator (Tropic of Cancer), and one 23.5° south of the equator (Tropic of Capricorn). 2. pl. [also T-], the region between these two parallels of latitude: adj. of the tropics; tropical.

trop·i·cal ('i-kl), adj. 1. of, pertaining to, or situated in the tropics. 2. suitable to the tropics. 3. very hot; torrid. —**trop'i·cal·ly,** adv.

tropical fish, any one of numerous, usually brightly colored, small fish, originally from the tropics, kept in heated aquariums.

tropical year, the period of time consisting of 365 days, 6 hours, 9 minutes, and 46 seconds, from vernal equinox to vernal equinox.

Tropical Zone, same as **Torrid Zone.**

tropic bird, a sea bird resembling the tern, having white feathers with black markings, and two long tail feathers.

tro·pism (trō'pizm), n. the tendency of any living thing to grow or turn in response to external stimulus, as plants to light.

tro·pol·o·gy (tro-pol'ō-ji), n. 1. the use of tropes, or figurative language. 2. interpretation of the figurative language of the Bible.

trop·o·pause (trop'ō-pôz), n. a zone between the troposphere and the stratosphere.

tro·poph·i·lous (trō-pof'i-lŭs), adj. adapted to either heat or cold, dryness or moisture: said of some plants.

trop·o·phyte (trop'ō-fīt), n. a tropophilous plant, especially a deciduous tree. —**trop·o·phyt'ic** (-fit'ik), adj.

trop·o·sphere (trop'ō-sfir), n. the atmosphere from the surface of the earth to about twelve miles up at the equator and about six miles at the poles. —**trop·o·spher'ic** (-sfir'ik), adj.

trot (trot), n. 1. the gait of a horse or other quadruped in which the legs leave the ground in alternating diagonal pairs. 2. the sound of a horse trotting. 3. a gait of a person, between a walk and a run; jog: v.t. & v.i. trot'ted, trot'ting, 1. to move or cause to move at a trot. 2. to hurry.

troth (trôth), n. [Archaic], 1. fidelity; loyalty. 2. truth. 3. a promise to marry.

trot·ter (trot'ẽr), n. 1. a horse that trots in races. 2. the foot of a hog or sheep used for food.

trou·ba·dour (trōō'bá-dôr), n. any one of a class of poet-musicians who flourished in southern France and northern Italy from the 11th to the 13th centuries.

trou·ble (trub'l), n. 1. mental agitation, worry, or distress. 2. calamity; misfortune. 3. a cause of distress or calamity. 4. a public disorder or disturbance. 5. bother; pains. 6. illness; ailment: v.t. -bled, -bling, 1. to agitate, worry, or distress. 2. to cause difficulty to: v.i. to bother; take pains.

trou·ble·mak·er (-mā-kẽr), n. one who causes trouble for others, especially one who stirs up quarrels, rebellion, etc. —**trou'ble·mak·ing,** n.

trou·ble·shoot·er (-shōōt-ẽr), n. 1. one whose work is searching out and repairing mechanical troubles. 2. an expert in solving work holdups, settling quarrels, resolving impasses, etc.

trou·ble·some ('sŏm), adj. 1. causing trouble. 2. irritating, aggravating, inconvenient, etc. — **trou'ble·some·ness,** n.

trou·blous (trub'lŭs), adj. [Archaic], 1. agitated; troubled; upset. 2. causing trouble.

trough (trôf), n. 1. a long, hollow, open container for holding water or food for animals. 2. a gutter for carrying off rain water. 3. a long depression, as between waves. 4. a long, narrow area of relatively low barometric pressure.

trounce (trouns), v.t. trounced, trounc'ing, 1. to beat soundly; thrash. 2. [Informal], to defeat. —**trounc'er,** n.

troupe (trōōp), n. a company of theatrical performers: v.i. trouped, troup'ing, to travel as a member of such a company. —**troup'er,** n.

trou·sers (trou'zẽrz), n.pl. a garment worn, especially by men and boys, from the waist to the ankles, and covering each leg separately.

trous·seau (trōō'sō), n., pl. -seaux ('sōz), -seaus, a bride's outfit of clothes, linens, etc.

trout (trout), n., pl. trout, trouts, any one of a number of mostly freshwater food and game fishes of the salmon family.

tro·ver (trō'vẽr), n. an action at law to recover goods wrongfully withheld.

trow (trō, trou), v.i. & v.t. [Archaic], to think or suppose.

trow·el (trou'ĕl), n. 1. a flat hand tool for spreading mortar, smoothing plaster, etc. 2. a gardening tool for digging, loosening soil, etc.

troy (troi), adj. by or in troy weight.

troy weight, a system of weights for gold, silver, precious stones, etc. in which 12 ounces equals one pound: see **Weights & Measures** in Supplements.

tru·an·cy (trōō'ăn-si), n. 1. the state or habit of being truant. 2. pl. -cies, an act or instance of being truant.

tru·ant (trōō'ănt), n. 1. a student who stays out of school without permission. 2. an idler; one who neglects his work: adj. 1. out of school

---

a in cap, ā in cane, ä in father, á in abet, e in met, ē in be, ê in baker, ê in regent, i in pit, ī in fine, i in manifest, o in hot, ō in horse, ō in bone,

without permission. 2. neglecting one's work. 3. errant.

truce (trōōs), *n.* 1. a temporary peace or cessation of hostilities. 2. a brief cessation or respite, as from trouble.

truck (truk), *n.* 1. a heavy automotive vehicle for carrying loads. 2. a low, wheeled frame for carrying heavy goods. 3. a small, solid wheel or roller. 4. a kind of barrow used to carry trunks, crates, and the like. 5. a wheeled frame at each end of a streetcar, railroad car, etc. 6. vegetables raised for market. 7. small goods or merchandise. 8. [Informal], rubbish: *v.t. & v.i.* 1. to transport on or drive a truck. 2. to barter; exchange.

truck·er ('ẽr), *n.* 1. a truck driver. 2. a person or company engaged in trucking. 3. a truck farmer.

truck farm, a farm where vegetables are grown to be marketed.

truck·ing ('ing), *n.* the business of carrying goods by truck.

truck·le ('l), *n.* 1. a small wheel or caster. 2. same as trundle bed: also **truckle bed**: *v.i.* -led, -ling, to yield obsequiously to the will of another; be submissive.

.truck·man ('măn), *n., pl.* -men ('mĕn), same as trucker.

truck system, the system of paying wages in goods instead of money.

truc·u·lence (truk'yoo-lĕns), *n.* fierceness, meanness, belligerence, etc.: also **truc'u·len·cy,** *n.*

truc·u·lent (-lĕnt), *adj.* fierce, savage, mean, scathing, belligerent, etc. —**truc'u·lent·ly,** *adv.*

trudge (truj), *v.i.* trudged, trudg'ing, to travel on foot, especially with effort or fatigue: *n.* a long or fatiguing walk. —**trudg'er,** *n.*

true (trōō), *adj.* tru'er, tru'est, 1. conforming to fact; not false. 2. faithful or loyal. 3. exact, accurate, or correct. 4. genuine; real. 5. rightful. 6. right in form, fit, etc.: *adv.* truly; exactly: *v.t.* trued, tru'ing or true'ing, to fit form, etc. accurately: *n.* that which is true. —**true'ness,** *n.*

true bill, a bill of indictment endorsed by a grand jury.

true-blue ('blōō'), *adj.* unswerving loyalty.

true-heart·ed ('härt'id), *adj.* honest; faithful; sincere. —**true'heart'ed·ness,** *n.*

truf·fle (truf'l), *n.* a fleshy underground fungus much esteemed as a delicacy.

tru·ism (trōō'izm), *n.* a self-evident truth.

tru·ly ('li), *adv.* in a way that is true; exactly, accurately, really, sincerely, etc.

trump (trump), *n.* 1. any one of a suit of cards that ranks higher than any of the other suits. 2. this suit: *v.t.* 1. to take with a trump card. 2. to devise fraudulently (with *up*): *v.i.* to play a trump card.

trump·er·y (trum'pẽr-i), *n., pl.* -er·ies, 1. something showy but useless. 2. nonsense.

trum·pet (trum'pit), *n.* 1. a brass-wind musical instrument formed of an oblong, looped tube flared at the end. 2. something shaped like a trumpet. 3. a sound like that of a trumpet: *v.i.* to make the sound of a trumpet: *v.t.* to herald or proclaim by or as by the sound of a trumpet.

trump·et·er (-ẽr), *n.* 1. a person who plays the

trumpet or one who signals on a trumpet. 2. a person who heralds or proclaims something. 3. same as trumpeter swan. 4. a variety of pigeon. 5. a long-legged, cranelike, South American bird having a loud cry.

trumpeter swan, a pure-white wild swan of western North America: now rare.

trun·cate (trung'kāt), *v.t.* -cat·ed, -cat·ing, to shorten by cutting off a part. —**trun·ca'tion,** *n.*

trun·cat·ed (-id), *adj.* cut off short.

trun·cheon (trun'chŭn), *n.* 1. a short, thick stick or club; cudgel. 2. a baton or staff of authority: *v.t.* to beat with a truncheon.

trun·dle (trun'dl), *v.t. & v.i.* -dled, -dling, to roll along; roll, as on small wheels: *n.* 1. a small wheel or caster. 2. same as trundle bed.

trundle bed, a low bed on small wheels or casters, that can be rolled out from under another bed for use.

trunk (trungk), *n.* 1. the main stem of a tree. 2. a body, as distinguished from the head and limbs. 3. the main stem or line of anything. 4. a long snout or proboscis, as of an elephant. 5. a large chest for holding a traveler's clothes, etc. 6. *pl.* shorts worn by men for boxing, swimming, etc. 7. a storage compartment in an automobile, usually in the rear.

trunk-fish ('fish), *n.* a large fish of tropical waters, the angular body of which is covered with bony plates.

trunk hose, full, baggy breeches reaching about halfway to the knee, worn by men in the 16th and 17th centuries.

trunk line, the main line of a railroad, telephone system, etc.

trun·nion (trun'yŭn), *n.* either of two projecting gudgeons or pins on each side of a cannon, on which it pivots.

truss (trus), *n.* 1. a bundle or pack. 2. a rigid framework of beams, girders, struts, etc. supporting a roof, bridge, etc. 3. a belt with a padded part for giving support in cases of hernia: *v.t.* 1. to bind or pack close. 2. to bind the arms or wings of to the sides.

truss·ing ('ing), *n.* 1. trusses in general. 2. bracing by or as by trusses.

trust (trust), *n.* 1. strong reliance on the integrity, honesty, dependability, etc. of some person or thing; confidence; faith. 2. the one trusted. 3. something put in one's care or keeping; responsibility. 4. confidence in a person's ability to pay later; credit. 5. property held and managed for the benefit of another. 6. a combination of businesses joined together to secure a monopoly: *v.t.* 1. to place or have confidence in; rely on; count on. 2. to commit to someone's care. 3. to permit to do something without fear of the outcome. 4. to expect; hope. 5. to believe. 6. to give credit to on purchases: *v.i.* to have trust or confidence: *adj.* 1. of, pertaining to, or held in trust. 2. serving as trustee. —**trust'er,** *n.*

trus·tee (trus-tē'), *n.* a person to whom property or the management of property is entrusted for the benefit of others.

ŏ in dragon, ōō in crude, oo in wool, u in cup, ū in cure, ü in turn, ŭ in focus, oi in boy, ou in house, th in thin, th in sheathe, g in get, j in joy, y in yet.

trus-tee-ship ('ship), *n.* the office or functions of a trustee.

trust-ful (trust'fŭl), *adj.* full of trust or confidence in others; trusting. —**trust'ful-ly**, *adv.* —**trust'ful-ness**, *n.*

trust fund, money, stock, etc. held in trust.

trust-ing ('ing), *adj.* that trusts; trustful. —**trust'ing-ly**, *adv.*

trust territory, a territory placed under the administration of a country by the United Nations.

trust-wor-thy ('wûr-*th*i), *adj.* worthy of trust; dependable; reliable. —**trust'wor-thi-ness**, *n.*

trust-y (trus'ti), *adj.* **trust'i-er**, **trust'i-est**, that can be relied on; dependable; reliable: *n.*, *pl.* **trust'ies**, a convict allowed special privileges on account of good conduct. —**trust'i-ness**, *n.*

truth (trōōth), *n.* 1. the quality or fact of being true, honest, sincere, accurate, etc.; agreement with fact or reality. 2. something that is true; a true statement or the real facts. 3. an established or verified principle, as in science. 4. a belief, religion, etc. regarded by the speaker as the true one.

truth-ful ('fŭl), *adj.* according to, adhering to, or telling the truth; honest, accurate, etc. —**truth'ful-ly**, *adv.* —**truth'ful-ness**, *n.*

try (trī), *v.t.* **tried**, **try'ing**, 1. to prove by test or experiment. 2. to subject to a trial in a court of law. 3. to subject to strain or severe trial. 4. to render or melt out (fat). 5. to test the working or effect of; experiment with. 6. to make an effort at; attempt: *v.i.* to make an attempt: *n.*, *pl.* **tries**, an attempt or trial.

try-ing ('ing), *adj.* hard to bear; annoying.

try-out ('out), *n.* a trial or test, especially one to determine fitness, chances for success, etc.

tryp-a-no-some (trip'ă-nō-sōm), *n.* any of a genus of parasitic protozoans that can infest the blood of man and other vertebrates, causing sleeping sickness and other diseases.

try-sail (trī'sl, 'sāl), *n.* a small, stout, fore-and-aft sail hoisted to keep a vessel's head to the wind in a storm.

tryst (trist), *n.* 1. an appointment to meet, especially one made secretly by lovers. 2. a meeting in accordance with such an appointment. 3. the place of such a meeting: also **trysting place**.

tsa-di (tsä'di), *n.* the eighteenth letter of the Hebrew alphabet.

tsar (tsär, zär), *n.* same as **czar**.

tset-se fly (tset'si, tsĕt'-), a small fly of central and southern Africa that carries the trypanosomes causing sleeping sickness.

T-shirt (tē'shûrt), *n.* a knitted, pullover shirt or undershirt with short sleeves and no collar.

T square, a T-shaped ruler for drawing parallel lines.

tsu-na-mi (tsŏō-nä'mi), *n.* a huge sea wave caused by an undersea disturbance, as an earthquake or volcanic eruption.

tub (tub), *n.* 1. a round, broad, wooden container, open at the top, usually formed of staves and hoops around a flat bottom. 2. any large, open container, as one of metal for washing clothes. 3. the amount a tub

will hold. 4. same as **bathtub**. 5. [British], a bath: *v.t.* & *v.i.* **tubbed**, **tub'bing**, [Informal], to wash or bathe in a tub.

tu-ba (tōō'bä, tū'-), *n.* 1. *pl.* **-bas**, a large, deep-toned, brass-wind instrument. 2. *pl.* **-bae** ('bē), an ancient Roman war trumpet.

tub-by (tub'i), *adj.* **-bi-er**, **-bi-est**, 1. tub-shaped. 2. short and fat.

tube (tōōb, tūb), *n.* 1. a long, slender, hollow cylinder for conveying or holding fluids. 2. a tubelike part or organ. 3. a tubelike container with a screw cap at one end, from which toothpaste, glue, etc. can be squeezed. 4. same as **electron tube**, **vacuum tube**. 5. [Informal], television (with *the*). 6. [British], a subway: *v.t.* **tubed**, **tub'ing**, to furnish with, put in, or pass through a tube.

tu-ber (tōō'bẽr, tū'bẽr), *n.* 1. a thickened, roundish, underground stem, as a potato. 2. in *Anatomy*, a tubercle or swelling.

tu-ber-cle ('kl), *n.* 1. a small, rounded or knob-like protuberance on a plant root, bone, etc. 2. a hard nodule or swelling, as a lesion formed in tuberculosis.

tubercle bacillus, the bacterium that causes tuberculosis.

tu-ber-cu-lar (too-bûr'kyoo-lẽr), *adj.* 1. full of small knobs or tubercles. 2. of, pertaining to, or having tuberculosis.

tu-ber-cu-lin (-lin), *n.* a liquid preparation derived from cultures of the tubercle bacillus and injected into the skin as a test for tuberculosis.

tu-ber-cu-lo-sis (too-bûr-kyoo-lō'sis), *n.* an infectious disease in which small tubercles are formed in the body tissues; specifically, this disease when it attacks the lungs.

tu-ber-cu-lous (too-bûr'kyoo-lŭs), *adj.* same as **tubercular**.

tube-rose (tōōb'rōz, tūb'-), *n.* a Mexican plant with a tuberous root and fragrant white flowers.

tu-ber-ous (tōō'bẽr-ŭs, tū'-), *adj.* 1. covered with knoblike swellings. 2. in *Botany*, of, resembling, or having a tuber or tubers.

tub-ing (tōōb'ing, tūb'-), *n.* 1. tubes or a series of tubes. 2. material made up in the shape of a tube. 3. a length of tube.

tu-bu-lar (tōō'byoo-lẽr, tū'-), *adj.* 1. tube-shaped. 2. consisting of a tube or tubes.

tu-bu-late (-lāt), *adj.* having the form of, or provided with, a tube.

tu-bule (tōōb'yool, tūb'-), *n.* a small tube.

tuck (tuk), *n.* 1. a sewed fold in a garment. 2. the part of a ship where the ends of the bottom planks meet under the stern. 3. [British Slang], food: *v.t.* 1. to pull up in folds so as to shorten. 2. to sew tucks in (a garment). 3. to push the edges of (a sheet, napkin, etc.) in or under to keep in place. 4. to cover snugly. 5. to press snugly into a small space.

tuck-a-hoe ('ă-hō), *n.* any of various roots, tubers, or underground fungi used as food by American Indians.

tuck-er ('ẽr), *n.* 1. a device for making tucks. 2. formerly, a piece of lace or cloth worn by women to cover the neck or shoulders. 3. [Australian Slang], food: *v.t.* [Informal], to tire; weary (usually with *out*).

---

a in cap, ā in cane, ä in father, å in abet, e in met, ē in be, ê in baker, ê in regent, i in pit, ī in fine, i in manifest, o in hot, ō in horse, ō in bone,

-tude (tōōd, tūd), a suffix meaning *state or quality of being.*

Tues·day (tōōz'dĭ, tūz'-; 'dā), *n.* the third day of the week.

tu·fa (tōō'fá, tū'fá), *n.* soft or porous stone formed by the carbonate of lime deposited near the mouth of a mineral spring, geyser, etc.

tuft (tuft), *n.* a bunch of hairs, grass, threads, etc. growing or tied together: *v.t.* 1. to provide or decorate with tufts. 2. to hold the padding of (a mattress, quilt, etc.) in place by tightly tying tufts of thread drawn through at regularly spaced points.

tuft·ed (tuf'tĭd), *adj.* 1. provided or decorated with tufts. 2. formed into or growing in a tuft.

tufted coquette, a hummingbird of Central America.

tuft·er ('tēr), *n.* 1. one that tufts. 2. a hound dog that scents and drives a deer from cover.

tuft·hunt·er (tuft'hunt-ēr), *n.* one who courts the acquaintance of persons of rank; toady; sycophant.

tug (tug), *n.* 1. a hard pull. 2. same as **tugboat:** *v.t. & v.t.* **tugged, tug'ging,** 1. to pull or draw with continued effort; to strain at (something). 2. to tow with a tugboat.

tug·boat ('bōt), *n.* a sturdily built, powerful boat used for towing or pushing ships, barges, etc.

tug of war, a contest in which two teams pull at opposite ends of a rope. 2. any power struggle between two persons, groups, etc.

tuille (twēl), *n.* hinged plates of armor for covering the thigh.

tu·i·tion (tōō-ĭsh'ŭn, tū-), *n.* 1. the fee for instruction, as at a college or private school. 2. the act of teaching; instruction.

tu·la·re·mi·a (tōō-lá-rē'mĭ-á, tū-), *n.* an infectious disease of rabbits that can be transmitted to human beings.

tu·lip (tōō'lĭp, tū'-), *n.* a bulb plant bearing a large, cup-shaped flower.

tulip tree, a tall tree of North America with lobed leaves and tulip-shaped, greenish-yellow flowers.

tulle (tōōl), *n.* a thin, fine netting of silk, nylon, etc., used for veils.

tum·ble (tum'bl), *v.i.* **-bled, -bling,** 1. to fall in a sudden or helpless way, 2. to roll or toss about. 3. to move in a quick, disorderly way. 4. to do somersaults, handsprings, and the like: *v.t.* 1. to throw down. 2. to roll or toss about: *n.* 1. a fall. 2. a confused state or heap.

tum·ble·down (-doun), *adj.* broken down; ramshackle.

tum·bler (tum'blēr), *n.* 1. an acrobat or gymnast who tumbles. 2. a kind of drinking glass. 3. a variety of pigeon. 4. a part of a lock that must be moved by a key to release the bolt.

tum·ble·weed ('bl-wēd), *n.* any of various plants that break away from their roots in autumn and are blown about in the wind.

tum·brel, tum·bril ('brĕl), *n.* a cart, as one that can be tilted up.

tu·me·fa·cient (tōō-mē-fā'shĕnt), *adj.* causing or tending to cause swelling.

tu·me·fac·tion (-fak'shŭn), *n.* 1. a swelling up. 2. a swollen part.

tu·me·fy (tōō'mē-fī, tū'-), *v.t. & v.i.* **fied, -fy·ing,** to make or become swollen.

tu·mes·cence (tōō-mes'ns), *n.* 1. a swelling or distention. 2. a swollen or distended part.

tu·mes·cent ('nt), *adj.* swelling or somewhat swollen.

tu·mid (tōō'mĭd, tū'-), *adj.* 1. swollen; distended. 2. bombastic; pompous. —**tu·mid'i·ty,** *n.*

tum·my (tum'ĭ), *n., pl.* **-mies,** a child's word for stomach.

tu·mor (tōō'mēr, tū'-), *n.* an abnormal growth of extra tissue on or in some part of the body.

tu·mu·lar (tōō'myoo-lēr, tū'-), *adj.* of, pertaining to, or formed like a tumulus.

tu·mu·lose (-lōs), *adj.* full of mounds or little hills: also **tu'mu·lous** (-lŭs).

tu·mult (tōō'mult, tū'-), *n.* 1. the noisy commotion of a number of people; uproar. 2. great confusion or disturbance of the mind or emotions.

tu·mul·tu·ous (tōō-mul'chōō-ŭs), *adj.* characterized by or full of tumult; uproarious, agitated, etc. —**tu·mul'tu·ous·ly,** *adv.*

tu·mu·lus (tōō'myoo-lŭs, tū'-), *n., pl.* **-li** (-lī), **-lus·es,** an artificial mound raised over a grave.

tun (tun), *n.* a large cask, as for wine or beer, holding 252 gallons: *v.t.* **tunned, tun'ning,** to put into a tun or tuns.

tu·na (tōō'ná, tū'-), *n., pl.* **-na, -nas,** 1. any one of a group of large ocean fishes. 2. the flesh of the tuna used as food, usually canned: also **tuna fish.**

tun·a·ble (tōō'ná-bl, tū'-), *adj.* 1. capable of being tuned. 2. [Archaic], harmonious; melodious.

tun·dra (tun'drá), *n.* a stretch of treeless, flat or undulating plain in the arctic regions.

tune (tōōn, tūn), *n.* 1. a series of musical tones forming a melody. 2. the condition of having correct musical pitch. 3. harmony; agreement; concord: *v.t.* **tuned, tun'ing,** 1. to put (a musical instrument) in tune. 2. to adapt to the prevailing conditions, mood, etc. 3. to adjust (an engine, etc.) so it will work well. 4. to set radio or television dials for (a particular station, program, etc.) (with *in*).

tune·ful ('fŭl), *adj.* containing melody; melodious. —**tune'ful·ly,** *adv.*

tun·er ('ēr), *n.* 1. a person who tunes musical instruments. 2. a device for tuning an organ pipe. 3. an instrument for tuning an electric circuit, detecting radio signals, etc.

tune·up, tune·up ('up), *n.* an adjusting, as of an engine, to good condition.

tung·sten (tung'stĕn), *n.* a hard, heavy metal that is a chemical element and is used in steel, lamp filaments, etc.

ŏ in dragon, ōō in crude, oo in wool, u in cup, ū in cure, û in turn, ù in focus,
oi in boy, ou in house, th in thin, th in sheathe, g in get, j in joy, y in yet.

tungsten lamp, an incandescent electric lamp with a filament of tungsten.

tu·nic (tōō'nik, tū'-), *n.* 1. a loose, gownlike garment worn by persons of both sexes in ancient Greece and Rome. 2. a blouselike garment that reaches to the hips, often worn with a belt. 3. covering tissue or membrane, as of a seed.

tu·ni·cate ('ni·kāt), *adj.* 1. in *Botany*, of or covered with concentric layers, as an onion. 2. in *Zoology*, having a tunic or covering: also **tu'ni·cat·ed**.

tuning fork, a steel instrument with two prongs, that sounds a certain fixed tone when struck.

tun·nel (tun'l), *n.* 1. a vaulted, underground passage cut through a mountain or under a river. 2. any underground passage: *v.t. & v.i.* -neled or -nelled, -nel·ing or -nel·ling, to make a tunnel through or under (a place).

tunnel vision, a narrow outlook, as on a particular problem without regard for possible consequences, alternative approaches, etc.

tun·ny (tun'i), *n., pl.* -nies, -ny, same as **tuna** (sense 1).

tup (tup), *n.* 1. a male sheep. 2. the striking part of a pile driver or drop hammer: *v.t.* **tupped, tup'ping,** to copulate with (a ewe): said of a ram.

tu·pe·lo (tōō'pe·lō), *n., pl.* -los, 1. a North American gum tree having purple fruits. 2. its wood.

tur·ban (tūr'bán), *n.* 1. a Moslem headdress consisting of a band of cloth wound around the head, sometimes over a cap. 2. any similar head covering or hat.

tur·ba·ry (tūr'bēr·i), *n., pl.* -ries, land where turf or peat is dug.

tur·bid (tūr'bid), *adj.* 1. not clear; muddy or cloudy. 2. confused or muddled. —**tur·bid'i·ty, tur'bid·ness,** *n.*

tur·bi·nate (tūr'bi·nit, -nāt), *adj.* 1. shaped like a top or inverted cone. 2. shaped like a scroll or spiral, as certain spongy bones in the nasal passages. Also **tur'bi·nat·ed** (-nāt·id). **tur'bi·nal** (-nl): *n.* 1. a turbinate shell. 2. a turbinate bone.

tur·bine (tūr'bin, 'bīn), *n.* an engine driven by the pressure of steam, water, air, etc. against the curved vanes of a wheel.

tur·bit (tūr'bit), *n.* a variety of pigeon.

tur·bo·jet (tūr'bō·jet), *n.* a jet engine having a turbine that drives the air compressor supplying compressed air for fuel combustion: the hot exhaust gases provide thrust: in full, **turbojet engine.**

tur·bo·prop (-prop), *n.* a jet engine having a turbine that drives a propeller: in full, **turboprop engine.**

tur·bot (tūr'bŏt), *n., pl.* -bot, -bots, a large European flatfish, esteemed as food.

tur·bu·lent (-lĕnt), *adj.* full of commotion, turmoil, wild disorder, etc.; violently agitated, upset, etc. —**tur'bu·lence** (-lĕns), *n.*

tu·reen (tú·rēn'), *n.* a large, deep, covered dish from which soup is served at table.

turf (tūrf), *n.* 1. a surface layer of earth with grass and its roots, or a piece of this. 2. peat. 3. a track for horse racing; hence,

horse racing (usually with *the*). *v.t.* to cover with turf.

turf·man ('mán), *n., pl.* -men ('mĕn), an owner, trainer, etc. of racehorses.

turf·y ('i), *adj.* **turf'i·er, turf'i·est,** of, resembling, or covered with turf.

tur·ges·cent (tūr·jes'nt), *adj.* becoming turgid or swollen. —**tur·ges'cence,** *n.*

tur·gid (tūr'jid), *adj.* 1 swollen; distended. 2. bombastic; grandiloquent. —**tur·gid'i·ty,** *n.*

Turk (tūrk), *n.* a native or inhabitant of Turkey, a country of Asia Minor and part of the Balkan Peninsula.

tur·key (tūr'ki), *n., pl.* -keys, -key, 1. a large North American bird with a spreading tail. 2. its flesh, used as food.

turkey buzzard, a large, brownish-black vulture of southern North America and South America.

Tur·kic (tūr'kik), *adj.* of or denoting a group of languages that includes Turkish, Tatar, etc.

Tur·kish (tūr'kish), *adj.* of Turkey, a country of Asia Minor and part of the Balkan Peninsula, or its people, culture, etc.: *n.* the language of Turkey.

Turkish bath, a bath having steam rooms, showers, massage facilities, etc.

Turkish towel, a cotton cloth with a heavy, thick nap.

tur·mer·ic (tūr'mēr·ik), *n.* the root of an East Indian plant, ground into a spicy powder used as a seasoning.

tur·moil (tūr'moil), *n.* commotion; confusion; tumult.

turn (tūrn), *v.t* 1. to cause to go around or partly around. 2. to do by a revolving motion. 3. to change the position or direction of. 4. to reverse. 5. to change (a person or thing) in condition, actions, feelings, beliefs, etc. 6. to wrench (an ankle). 7. to make (one's stomach) nauseated. 8. to shape on or as on a lathe. 9. to convert or transform from one form to another. 10. to deflect or divert. 11. to reach or pass (a particular age, amount, etc.). 12. to drive, set, let go, etc. in a specified way. 13. to stop or repel (an attack). 14. to direct; aim. 15. to put to a specified use: *v.i.* 1. to rotate, revolve, or pivot. 2. to change or reverse direction. 3. to change in feelings, attitudes, interests, etc. 4. to seem to be whirling. 5. to become nauseated: said of the stomach. 6. to be deflected. 7. to go (*to*) for help, support, corroboration, etc. 8. to make a sudden attack (*on*). 9. to depend (*on* or *upon* something uncertain). 10. to change in form or condition. 11. to become sour or rancid: *n.* 1. the act of turning; movement in a circular direction. 2. a twist, coil, bend, or curve. 3. a change of direction or course. 4. a change in condition. 5. a fright or shock. 6. a (good or bad) deed. 7. a change in regular order. 8. a short walk or ride. 9. phrasing of a specified kind.

turn·a·bout ('å·bout), *n.* 1. the act of turning about. 2. a reversal or shift of opinion, allegiance, etc.

turn·a·round ('å·round), *n.* 1. same as **turn-**

---

a in cap, ā in cane, ä in father, å in abet, e in met, ē in be, ẽ in baker, ė in regent, i in pit, ī in fine, ĭ in manifest, o in hot, ô in horse, ō in bone,

about. 2. a wide area to allow for turning a vehicle around.

turn·buck·le ('buk-l), n. a metal sleeve with opposite internal threads at each end, used as a coupling.

turn·coat ('kōt), n. one who deserts his church, his party, or his cause; renegade.

turn·er (tûr'nêr), n. 1. one who or that which turns. 2. a person who operates a lathe.

turn·er·y ('i), n., pl. -er·ies, the work, product, or workshop of a lathe operator.

turn·ing ('ning), n. 1. the act of one who or that which turns. 2. a turn, deviation, winding, etc.

turning point, the point at which there is a decisive change.

tur·nip (tûr'nip), n. 1. a plant having a roundish, white root that is eaten as a vegetable. 2. same as rutabaga. 3. the root of either of these plants.

turn·key (tûrn'kē), n., pl. -keys, a jailer.

turn·off ('ôf), n. a turning off or the place where one turns off.

turn·out ('out), n. 1. a gathering of people, as for a meeting. 2. a wider part of a narrow road, enabling vehicles to pass one another.

turn·o·ver ('ō-vêr), n. 1. the act of turning over or reversing, upsetting, etc. 2. the amount of business done, especially as shown by the rate at which a stock of goods is sold and replaced. 3. the rate at which workers are replaced. 4. a small pie with the crust turned over, enclosing the fruit.

turn·pike ('pīk), n. a road having tollgates.

turn·sole ('sōl), n. any of several plants whose flowers turn to face the sun, as the sunflower and heliotrope.

turn·stile ('stīl), n. a post with four crossbars working on a pivot that turns to let one person through an entrance or exit at a time.

turn·stone ('stōn), n. a migratory shore bird related to the sandpiper.

turn·ta·ble ('tā-bl), n. a round, rotating platform, as for playing phonograph records.

tur·pen·tine (tûr'pĕn-tīn), n. the resinous or viscid juice of pines and certain other trees, or the oil extracted from this and used in paints and varnishes.

tur·pi·tude (tûr'pi-tōōd), n. baseness; depravity.

tur·quoise (tûr'koiz, 'kwoiz), n. 1. a greenish-blue semiprecious stone. 2. its color.

tur·ret (tûr'ĭt), n. 1. a small tower on a building, usually on a corner. 2. a low, armored, usually revolving structure for guns, as on a warship, tank, or airplane. 3. a part of a lathe, drill, etc., that holds several cutting tools and can be rotated to change the tool in use.

tur·ret·ed (-id), adj. provided with turrets.

tur·tle (tûr'tl), n., pl. -tles, -tle, 1. any of a large group of land and water reptiles having a broad, soft body covered by a hard shell. 2. [Archaic], same as turtledove.

tur·tle·dove (-duv), n. a wild dove noted for its gentleness and plaintive cooing.

tur·tle·neck (-nek), n. 1. a high collar that turns down and fits snugly around the neck. 2. a sweater, shirt, etc. with such a collar.

Tus·can (tus'kǎn), adj. denoting a classic Roman order of architecture characterized by unfluted columns with plain, ringlike capitals.

Tus·ca·ro·ra (tus-kå-rôr'å), n. 1. pl. -ras, -ra, a member of a North American Indian tribe living in New York and Ontario. 2. the Iroquoian language of this tribe.

tush (tush), interj. an exclamation expressing impatience, rebuke, contempt, etc.

tusk (tusk), n. a very long, pointed tooth, usually one of a pair, that projects outside the mouth, as in elephants, walruses, etc.

tusk·er (tus'kêr), n. an animal with tusks.

tus·sah (tus'å), n. 1. an Asiatic silkworm that produces a strong, coarse silk. 2. this silk or the cloth woven from it.

tus·sis (tus'is), n. a cough.

tus·sive ('iv), adj. pertaining to a cough.

tus·sle (tus'l), v.i. -sled, -sling, to scuffle or struggle: n. a scuffle or struggle.

tus·sock (tus'ŏk), n. a tuft or clump of grass, sedge, or the like.

tut (tut), interj. a sound one makes to show impatience, annoyance, etc.

tu·te·lage (tōō'tl-ij, tū'tl-), n. 1. care and protection under a guardian. 2. teaching; instruction.

tu·te·la·ry (-er-i), adj. 1. protecting as a guardian. 2. of, pertaining to, or serving as a guardian.

tu·tor (tōō'tér, tū'-), n. a private teacher; instructor: v.t. & v.i. to teach or instruct as a tutor. —tu'tor·ship (-ship), n.

tu·tor·i·al (tōō-tôr'i-ǎl), adj. of or pertaining to a tutor.

tut·ti-frut·ti (tōō'ti-frōō'ti), n. ice cream or other confection containing bits of candied fruits.

tu·tu (tōō'tōō), n. a very short skirt that puffs out, worn by ballerinas.

tu-whit tu-who (tōō-hwit' tōō-whōō'), a representation of the cry of the owl.

tux (tuks), n. same as tuxedo.

tux·e·do (tuk-sē'dō), n., pl. -dos, a man's formal suit with a tailless jacket.

tu·yere (twē-yer', twir), n. the pipe or nozzle through which air is forced into a blast furnace.

TV (tē'vē'), n., pl. TVs, TV's, television or a television set.

TV dinner, a frozen, precooked dinner that is to be heated and served in the compartmented tray it is packaged in.

twad·dle (twäd'l), n. silly or foolish talk or writing.

twain (twān), n. & adj. [Archaic], two.

twang (twang), n. 1. a sharp, vibrating sound, as of a plucked banjo string. 2. a nasal tone of voice: v.i. to sound or speak with a twang.

tweak (twēk), v.t. to pinch (the nose, ear, etc.) with a twisting motion: n. such a pinch.

tweed (twēd), n. 1. a wool fabric with a rough surface. 2. pl. clothing of tweed.

twee·dle·dum and twee·dle·dee (twē-dl-dum'n-twē-dl-dē'), any two things almost identical.

tweet (twēt), n. a thin, chirping sound, as of a bird: v.i. to utter such a sound.

tweez·ers (twē'zērz), n.pl. small pincers for

ŏ in dragon, ōō in crude, oo in wool, u in cup, ū in cure, ū in turn, ù in focus, oi in boy, ou in house, th in thin, th in sheathe, g in get, j in joy, y in yet.

pulling out hairs, handling small objects, etc.

twelfth (twelfth), *adj.* next after 11th; 12th: *n.* 1. the one after the 11th. 2. one of 12 equal parts.

Twelfth Day, same as **Epiphany.**

twelve (twelv), *adj.* one more than 11: *n.* the cardinal numeral that is the sum of 11 and one; 12; XII.

twelve-mo ('mō), *n.* same as **duodecimo.**

twelve-tone ('tōn'), *adj.* in *Music,* of or pertaining to composition in which the twelve tones of the chromatic scale are used without reference to a keynote but in some arbitrary, fixed succession (*tone row*).

twen-ti-eth (twen'ti-ith), *adj.* next after 19th; 20th: *n.* 1. the one after the 19th. 2. one of twenty equal parts.

twen-ty (twen'ti), *adj.* two times 10: *n., pl.* **-ties,** 1. the cardinal numeral that is the sum of 19 and one; 20; XX. 2. *pl.* years or numbers from 20 through 29 (preceded by *the*).

twen-ty-one (-wun'), *n.* a gambling game at cards, the object of which is to total as many as but no more than twenty-one points.

twerp (twûrp), *n.* [Slang], one who is thought of as ridiculous, contemptible, etc.

twice (twis), *adv.* two times; doubly.

twid-dle (twid'l), *v.t. & v.i.* to twirl or play with (something) in a light manner: *n.* a twirling, as of the thumbs.

twig (twig), *n.* a small shoot or branch of a tree or shrub: *v.t.* [British Slang], to observe, notice, or understand.

twi-light (twi'lit), *n.* 1. the faint light just after sunset or just before sunrise. 2. the period from sunset to dark. 3. a period of gradual decline.

twilight sleep, a condition of partial anesthesia induced by the injection of a drug, formerly used to lessen the pains of childbirth.

twill (twil), *n.* 1. a pattern of parallel diagonal lines in textile fabrics, formed in the weaving. 2. fabric woven with this pattern.

twin (twin), *n.* 1. one of two born at the same birth. 2. one of two persons or things very much alike or forming a pair. 3. a crystal formed by two crystals having a common face but in reversed position with respect to each other: *adj.* being a twin or twins.

twine (twin), *v.t. & v.i.* **twined, twin'ing,** 1. to twist together, or unite or form by twisting together; interlace. 2. to wind around: *n.* a strong string or cord of strands twisted together.

twinge (twinj), *v.t. & v.i.* **twinged, twing'ing,** to affect with or suffer a sudden, sharp pain: *n.* a sudden, sharp pain.

twi-night, twi-night (twi'nit), *adj.* denoting a baseball double-header starting in the late afternoon and running into the evening.

twin-kle (twing'kl), *n.* 1. a flicker or glint of the eye. 2. a short, tremulous light; sparkle. 3. an instant: *v.i.* **-kled, -kling,** 1. to flicker or sparkle, as with amusement: said of the eyes. 2. to shine with a tremulous, sparkling light. 3. to move about quickly, as a dancer's feet.

twin-kling (twing'kling), *n.* 1. a twinkle. 2. an instant.

twirl (twûrl), *v.t. & v.i.* to move or turn around rapidly; spin, whirl, etc.: *n.* 1. a quick, twirling motion. 2. a twist, coil, etc. — **twirl'er,** *n.*

twist (twist), *v.t.* 1. to wind or twine together, or form by doing this. 2. to wind (rope, wire, etc.) around something. 3. to turn (a bottle cap, etc.) around sharply. 4. to force out of shape or position. 5. to distort the meaning of. 6. to contort or writhe. 7. to bend in a spiral or curve. 8. to break off by turning the end: *v.i.* 1. to undergo twisting. 2. to curve, wind, etc. or spiral, coil, etc. 3. to turn to one side. 4. to squirm or writhe: *n.* 1. the act or manner of twisting. 2. something twisted, as a roll of tobacco, strands of thread or cord, etc. 3. a twisting stress; contortion, wrench, sprain, etc. 4. a special meaning or slant.

twist-er (twis'tẽr), *n.* 1. one who or that which twists. 2. a tornado or cyclone.

twit (twit), *v.t.* **twit'ted, twit'ting,** to annoy by reminding of a fault, mistake, etc.; taunt: *n.* a taunt.

twitch (twich), *v.t.* to pull with a sudden jerk: *v.i.* to contract spasmodically; move in jerks: *n.* a sudden jerk or pull; spasmodic contraction.

twit-ter (twit'ẽr), *v.i.* 1. to make a succession of small, tremulous sounds, as a bird. 2. to tremble with excitement: *n.* 1. the act or sound of twittering. 2. a state of tremulous excitement.

two (tōō), *adj.* one more than one: *n.* 1. the cardinal numeral that is the sum of one and one; 2; II. 2. a pair; couple.

two-bit ('bit'), *adj.* [Slang], cheap, inferior, etc.

two bits, [Informal], twenty-five cents.

two-by-four (tōō'bī-fôr), *n.* any length of lumber two inches thick and four inches wide.

two-faced ('fāst'), *adj.* 1. having two faces. 2. hypocritical; deceitful.

two-fer ('fẽr), *n. usually pl.* [Informal], two tickets, etc. for the price of one.

two-fist-ed ('fist'id), *adj.* 1. using both fists. 2. vigorous; virile.

two-fold ('fōld'), *adj.* 1. having two parts; double. 2. having twice as much or as many: *adv.* twice as much or as many.

two-hand-ed (tōō-han'did), *adj.* 1. requiring the use of both hands. 2. played by two persons. 3. having two hands.

two-pence (tup'ns), *n.* two pence.

two-pen-ny (tup'ẽn-i), *adj.* 1. of the value of twopence. 2. cheap; worthless: 3. (tōō'pen-i), denoting a size of nails one inch long.

two-ply (tōō'plī), *adj.* composed of two layers, strands, etc.

two-some ('sôm), *n.* 1. two people together; couple. 2. a golf match for two.

two-step ('step), *n.* 1. a ballroom dance in 2/4 time. 2. a piece of music for this dance.

two-time ('tim), *v.t.* **-timed, -tim-ing,** [Slang], to be unfaithful to.

two-way ('wā'), *adj.* 1. that moves or allows movement in either direction. 2. that involves two or is used in two ways.

-ty (-tĭ), a suffix meaning. *quality of; condition of.*

ty·coon (tī-kōōn'), *n.* a wealthy, powerful industrialist, financier, etc.

ty·ing (tī'ing), present participle of **tie.**

tyke (tīk), *n.* [Informal], a small child.

ty·lo·sis (tī-lō'sĭs), *n.* 1. a thickening of the skin. 2. in *Botany,* a growth from one cell into the cavity of another.

tym·pan (tĭm'păn), *n.* the paper, cardboard, etc. stretched over the platen or the impression cylinder of a printing press as a cushion or to equalize type pressure.

tym·pa·ni (tĭm'pä-nǐ), *n.pl.* same as **timpani.** — **tym'pa·nist,** *n.*

tym·pan·ic membrane (tĭm-păn'ĭk), the eardrum.

tym·pa·num (tĭm'pä-nŭm), *n., pl.* **-nums, -na** (-nä), 1. same as **middle ear.** 2. the eardrum. 3. the diaphragm of a telephone.

tym·pa·ny (-nĭ), *n.* a distended condition, as of the abdomen.

typ·al (tīp'l), *adj.* relating to or serving as a type.

type (tīp), *n.* 1. the general form, structure, style, etc. characterizing a class or group of people or things. 2. a class or group having distinguishing characteristics in common; kind; sort. 3. a person, animal, or thing representative of a class or group; typical individual or example. 4. a perfect example; model or pattern. 5. a symbol; token; sign. 6. a piece of metal, wood, etc. with a raised letter, figure, etc. in reverse on it, used in printing. 7. a set of such pieces. 8. printed letters, figures, etc.: *v.t.* typed, typ'ing, 1. to classify according to type. 2. to typewrite: *v.i.* to typewrite.

-type (tīp), a combining form meaning: 1. *type, example.* 2. *stamp, print, printing type.*

type·cast (tīp'kast), *v.t.* **-cast, -cast·ing,** to cast (an actor or actress) repeatedly in the same type of role.

type·face ('fās), *n.* 1. the printing part of a letter or plate. 2. the design of type.

type metal, an alloy of lead, antimony, and tin, used for casting type.

type·script ('skript), *n.* typewritten matter or copy.

type·set ('set), *v.t.* **-set, -set·ting,** to set in type.

type·set·ter ('set-ēr), *n.* 1. a person who sets type. 2. a machine for setting type.

type·write ('rīt), *v.t. & v.i.* **-wrote, -writ·ten, -writ·ing,** to write with a typewriter; now usually shortened to *type.*

type·writ·er ('rīt-ēr), *n.* a machine with a keyboard for producing printed letters or figures on paper by means of an inked ribbon and types pressed down when the keys are struck.

ty·phoid (tī'foid), *n.* an acute infectious disease spread by contaminated food or water and causing fever, intestinal disorders, etc.: also called **typhoid fever.**

ty·phoon (tī-fōōn'), *n.* a tropical cyclone occurring in the western Pacific.

ty·phus (tī'fŭs), *n.* an acute infectious disease transmitted by the bite of fleas, lice, etc. and causing fever, headache, and a red rash over the entire body: also called **typhus fever.**

typ·i·cal (tĭp'i-kl), *adj.* 1. being a true or representative example of its kind. 2. usual for the type; characteristic. 3. serving as a type; symbolic. —**typ'i·cal·ly,** *adv.*

typ·i·fy ('i-fī), *v.t.* **-fied, -fy·ing,** 1. to have all the usual qualities or features of; be typical of. 2. to be a type, or symbol, of.

typ·ist (tīp'ist), *n.* a person who uses a typewriter or whose work is typewriting.

ty·po (tī'pō), *n., pl.* **-pos,** [Informal], a mechanical error made in setting type or in typing.

ty·pog·ra·pher (tī-pog'rä-fēr), *n.* a person skilled in typography; printer, compositor, etc.

ty·po·graph·i·cal (tī,pō-graf'i-kl), *adj.* of typography; pertaining to the setting of type, printing, etc.: also **ty·po·graph'ic.** —**ty·po·graph'i·cal·ly,** *adv.*

ty·pog·ra·phy (tī-pog'rä-fĭ), *n.* 1. the art or process of setting type and printing with type. 2. the style, design, etc. of matter printed from type.

ty·pol·o·gy (tī-pol'ō-jĭ), *n.* 1. the study of types, symbols, or symbolism. 2. symbolism.

ty·ran·ni·cal (ti-ran'i-kl), *adj.* of, pertaining to, or characteristic of a tyrant; despotic, cruel, harsh, etc. —**ty·ran'ni·cal·ly,** *adv.*

ty·ran·ni·cide ('i-sīd), *n.* 1. the act of killing a tyrant. 2. one who kills a tyrant.

tyr·an·nize (tir'ä-nīz), *v.i.* **-nized, -niz·ing,** to rule as a tyrant or be tyrannical; use power in a despotic or harsh way: *v.t.* to treat tyrannically.

ty·ran·no·saur (ti-ran'ō-sôr), *n.* a huge, two-footed, flesh-eating dinosaur of North America: also **ty·ran·no·saur'us** (-ùs).

tyr·an·nous (tir'ä-nùs), *adj.* tyrannical; despotic, oppressive, unjust, etc.

tyr·an·ny (-nĭ), *n., pl.* **-nies,** 1. the government of a tyrant; despotic rule. 2. very harsh and unjust use of power.

ty·rant (tī'rănt), *n.* 1. an absolute ruler, especially one who is oppressive, cruel, etc. 2. a person who treats others he has authority over in a cruel or oppressive way.

Tyr·i·an purple (tir'i-ăn), a purple or crimson dye used by the ancient Greeks and Romans: it was made from a secretion of certain mollusks, originally at Tyre, a Phoenician seaport: also **Tyrian dye**

ty·ro (tī'rō), *n., pl.* **-ros,** a beginner; novice.

ty·ro·sine (tī'rō-sēn, -sin), *n.* a white, crystalline amino acid formed by the decomposition of proteins, as in the putrefaction of cheese.

tzar (tsär, zär), *n.* same as **czar.** —**tza·ri·na** (tsä-rē'nä, zä-), *n.fem.*

Tzi·gane (tsē-gän'), *n.* [Hungarian], a gypsy; especially, a Hungarian gypsy.

ŏ in drag*o*n, ōō in cr*u*de, oo in w*oo*l, u in c*u*p, ū in c*u*re, ü in t*u*rn, ù in f*o*cus, oi in b*oy*, ou in h*ou*se, th in *thin,* th in shea*th*e, g in g*e*t, j in *j*oy, y in *y*et.

U

U, u (ū), *n., pl.* **U's, u's,** 1. the twenty-first letter of the English alphabet. 2. any one of the various sounds of this letter, as in *crude, cup, cure, turn,* or *focus.* 3. a type or impression of *U* or *u.*

U (ū), *adj.* shaped like *U*: *n.* an object shaped like *U.*

u-bi-e-ty (ū-bī'ĕ-ti), *n.* [Rare], the state of being in a particular place.

u-biq-ui-tous (ū-bik'wi-tûs), *adj.* existing or being present everywhere at the same time; omnipresent. —**u-biq'ui-tous-ly,** *adv.*

u-biq-ui-ty (-ti), *n.* omnipresence.

U-boat (ū'bōt), *n.* a German submarine.

ud-der (ud'ĕr), *n.* a large, pendulous mammary gland with two or more teats, as in cows.

UFO (ū'fō, ū-ef-ō'), *n., pl.* **UFOs, UFO's,** an unidentified flying object.

u-fol-o-gist (ū-fol'ō-jist), *n.* one who believes UFOs to be spacecraft from outer space and takes a special interest in reports about them. —**u-fol'o-gy,** *n.*

ugh (ug), *interj.* an exclamation of disgust or horror.

ug-li (ug'li), *n.* a citrus fruit that is a cross between an orange, grapefruit, and tangerine.

ug-ly (ug'li), *adj.* **-li-er, -li-est,** 1. offensive to the eye; unpleasant to look at. 2. repulsive; revolting. 3. dangerous; threatening. 4. [Informal], cross; ill-tempered. —**ug'li-ly,** *adv.* —**ug'li-ness,** *n.*

uh (u), *interj.* 1. a vocal sound indicating hesitation. 2. same as **huh.**

uh-lan (ōō'län, ū'-), *n.* formerly, a cavalryman in Poland, Prussia, etc.

u-kase (ū'kās, ū-kāz'), *n.* 1. in Czarist Russia, an imperial décree having the force of a law. 2. any official decree, especially one considered somewhat dictatorial.

u-ku-le-le (ū-kǔ-lā'li), *n.* a small musical instrument with four strings, somewhat like a guitar.

ul-cer (ul'sĕr), *n.* 1. an open sore on the skin or mucous membrane, with a secretion of pus. 2. a corrupting influence or condition. —**ul'cer-ous,** *adj.*

ul-cer-ate (ul'sĕ-rāt), *v.t. & v.i.* **-at-ed, -at-ing,** to make or become ulcerous. —**ul-cer-a'tion,** *n.*

u-le-ma (ōō-lĕ-mä'), *n.* 1. Moslem scholars or leaders who interpret the Koran and the laws, especially in Turkey. 2. a council of such men.

ull-age (ul'ij), *n.* the amount of liquid a container, as a cask, lacks of being full.

ul-na (ul'nä), *n., pl.* **-nae** ('nē), **-nas,** 1. the larger of the two bones in the forearm of man. 2. the inner bone of the forelimb of other land vertebrates. —**ul'nar,** *adj.*

u-lot-ri-chous (yoo-lät'ri-kǔs), *adj.* having woolly or crisply curly hair.

ul-ster (ul'stĕr), *n.* a long, loose, heavy overcoat, usually with a belt.

ul-te-ri-or (ul-tir'i-ĕr), *adj.* 1. lying beyond or on the farther side. 2. beyond what is expressed or implied. —**ul-te'ri-or-ly,** *adv.*

ul-ti-ma (ul'ti-mä), *n.* the last syllable of a word.

ul-ti-mate (ul'ti-mit), *adj.* 1. being the last; final. 2. farthest. 3. primary; elemental. 4. maximum; utmost. —**ul'ti-ma-cy** (-mä-si), *n.*

ul-ti-mate-ly (-li), *adv.* finally; at last.

ultima Thu-le (thōō'li), 1. among the ancients, the northernmost parts of the earth. 2. the uttermost point, limit, or goal.

ul-ti-ma-tum (ul-ti-māt'ûm), *n., pl.* **-tums, -ta** ('ä), a final condition offered as the basis of an agreement: if the condition is rejected, force, hostilities etc. may ensue.

ul-ti-mo (ul'ti-mō), *adv.* in the month preceding the present.

ul-tra (ul'trä), *adj.* extreme: *n.* an extremist.

ul-tra-, a prefix meaning *beyond, excessively.*

ul-tra-high frequency (ul'trä-hī'), any radio frequency between 300 and 3,000 megahertz.

ul-tra-ma-rine (ul-trä-mä-rēn'), *adj.* deep-blue: *n.* a permanent blue pigment, originally obtained by grinding lapis lazuli.

ul-tra-mon-tane (-mon'tän), *adj.* 1. being beyond the mountains, specifically the Alps. 2. of, pertaining to, or advocating the doctrine that the Pope has supreme authority and is superior to all councils and national churches. —**ul-tra-mon'ta-nism** ('tä-nizm), *n.*

ul-tra-son-ic (-son'ik), *adj.* above the range of sound audible to the human ear.

ul-tra-sound (ul'trä-sound), *n.* ultrasonic waves, used in medicine, surgery, etc.

ul-tra-vi-o-let rays (ul-trä-vī'ō-lit), the very short light rays lying just beyond the violet end of the visible spectrum.

u-lu-lant (ūl'yoo-länt, ul'-), *adj.* howling; wailing.

u-lu-late (ūl'yoo-lāt, ul'-), *v.i.* **-lat-ed, -lat-ing,** 1. to howl or hoot. 2. to wail. —**ul-u-la'tion,** *n.*

um-bel (um'bl), *n.* an umbrellalike inflorescence radiating from a common center.

um-bel-lif-er-ous (um-bĕ-lif'ĕr-ûs), *adj.* producing or bearing umbels.

um-ber (um'bĕr), *n.* 1. a brownish earth used as a pigment. 2. a brownish color. 3. a grayling: *adj.* of the color of umber: *v.t.* to color with umber.

um-bil-i-cal (um-bil'i-kl), *adj.* of, pertaining to, or like a navel or an umbilical cord.

umbilical cord, a cordlike structure joining a fetus with the placenta and conveying food to the fetus.

um-bil-i-cate (-kit, -kāt), *adj.* like a navel in shape or form.

um-bil-i-cus (-kûs, um-bi-lī'kûs), *n.* the navel.

---

a in cap, ä in cane, ä in father, å in abet, e in met, ē in be, ě in baker, ĕ in regent, i in pit, ī in fine, ì in manifest, o in hot, ô in horse, ō in bone,

um·bil·i·form (um-bil'ĭ-fôrm), *adj.* shaped like a navel.

um·bo (um'bō), *n., pl.* **um·bo·nes** (um-bō'nēz), **um'bos** ('bōz), 1. the boss of a shield. 2. the raised point on each half of a bivalve shell beside the hinge.

um·bra (um'brä), *n., pl.* **-brae** ('brē), **-bras,** 1. shade or a shadow. 2. the dark cone of shadow projected from a planet or satellite on the side opposite to the sun. 3. the dark central part of a sunspot.

um·brage (um'brij), *n.* 1. trees or foliage providing shade. 2. offense or resentment.

um·bra·geous (um-brā'jùs), *adj.* 1. shady; shaded. 2. feeling or taking umbrage readily.

um·brel·la (um-brel'ä), *n.* 1. a cloth or plastic cover on a sliding frame, carried as a screen against rain or sun. 2. any inclusive protective device, arrangement, etc.

umbrella tree, any one of a number of trees, as an American magnolia, with leaves that suggest an umbrella in shape or arrangement.

um·brette (um-bret'), *n.* a large, brown, crested, African wading bird allied to the stork.

u·mi·ak (ōō'mi-ak), *n.* a boat fashioned by Eskimos, having the frame covered with skins.

um·laut (oom'lout), *n.* 1. a change in the sound of a vowel that came about through the influence on it of another vowel. 2. the two dots placed over a vowel to indicate this change.

ump (ump), *n. & v.i. & v.t.* same as umpire.

um·pire (um'pīr), *n.* 1. a third party to whom a dispute is referred for settlement. 2. one chosen in certain sports to see that the rules are observed: *v.i.* **-pired, -pir·ing,** to act as umpire: *v.t.* to act as umpire in or of.

ump·teen (ump'tēn'), *adj.* [Slang], very many. **—ump'teenth',** *adj.*

un-, a prefix meaning: 1. *not, lack of, the opposite of.* 2. *back:* used to indicate a reversal of action. As many words carrying this prefix are self-explanatory, such words are omitted from the list of definitions.

un·a·bridged (un-ä-brijd'), *adj.* not shortened or condensed.

un·ac·count·a·ble (-ä-koun'tä-bl), *adj.* 1. that cannot be accounted for; mysterious. 2. not responsible.

un·ac·cus·tomed (-ä-kus'tômd), *adj.* 1. not accustomed (*to*). 2. unusual; not expected.

un·a·dorned (-ä-dôrnd'), *adj.* without adornment; plain; simple.

un·ad·vised (-äd-vīzd'), *adj.* 1. without guidance or advice. 2. foolish and hasty; rash.

un·A·mer·i·can (-ä-mer'ĭ-kän), *adj.* thought of as being opposed to the U.S., its goals, institutions, etc.

un·nan·i·mous (yoo-nan'ĭ-mùs), *adj.* completely in agreement. **—u·na·nim·i·ty** (yōō-nä-nim'ĭ-tĭ), *n.* **—u·nan'i·mous·ly,** *adv.*

un·ap·proach·a·ble (un-ä-prōch'ä-bl), *adj.* 1. impossible to reach, talk to, etc. 2. without an equal; unmatched.

un·armed (-ärmd'), *adj.* without weapons.

un·as·sum·ing (-ä-sōōm'ing), *adj.* without pretense; modest.

un·at·tached (-ä-tacht'), *adj.* 1. not attached or fastened. 2. not engaged or married.

un·at·tend·ed (-ä-ten'did), *adj.* 1. not waited on. 2. not accompanied (*by* or *with*). 3. neglected.

u·nau (yoo-nô', ōō-nou'), *n.* the two-toed sloth of South America.

un·a·vail·ing (un-ä-vāl'ing), *adj.* not effective; useless; futile.

un·a·ware (-ä-wer'), *adj.* not aware: *adv.* same as unawares.

un·a·wares (-ä-werz'), *adv.* 1. without intending to. 2. without warning; unexpectedly.

un·bal·anced (-bal'änst), *adj.* 1. out of balance. 2. unsound in mind.

un·bar (-bär'), *v.t.* **-barred', -bar'ring,** to remove bars from; unfasten; throw open.

un·bear·a·ble (-ber'ä-bl), *adj.* that cannot be endured.

un·be·com·ing (-bi·kum'ing), *adj.* not suited to one's appearance, character, etc.; unattractive, unseemly, etc.

un·be·lief (-bē·lēf'), *n.* lack of belief, especially in religion. **—un·be·liev'er,** *n.*

un·be·liev·a·ble (-lēv'ä-bl), *adj.* impossible to believe; incredible.

un·bend (-bend'), *v.t.* **-bent'** or **-bend'ed, -bend'ing,** 1. to release from flexure. 2. to relax from strain. 3. to straighten. 4. in *nautical usage,* to unfasten or untie: *v.i.* 1. to become straight. 2. to relax and be less formal.

un·bend·ing (-ben'ding), *adj.* 1. rigid; stiff. 2. resolute; inflexible. 3. aloof.

un·bi·ased (-bī'äst), *adj.* without bias; unprejudiced; impartial.

un·bid·den (-bid'n), *adj.* uninvited; unasked.

un·blush·ing (-blush'ing), *adj.* 1. not blushing. 2. unashamed; shameless.

un·bolt (-bōlt'), *v.t. & v.i.* to withdraw the bolt or bolts of (a door, etc.); open.

un·born (-bôrn'), *adj.* 1. not born. 2. still in the mother's womb. 3. still to be; future.

un·bos·om (-booz'ôm, -bōō'zôm), *v.t. & v.i.* to tell or confess (secrets, feelings, etc.).

un·bound·ed (-boun'did), *adj.* 1. unlimited; boundless. 2. unrestrained.

un·bri·dled (-brī'dld), *adj.* 1. with no bridle on. 2. unrestrained; unhampered.

un·bro·ken (-brō'kn), *adj.* 1. whole. 2. untamed. 3. uninterrupted. 4. not interfered with.

un·bur·den (-bûrd'n), *v.t.* 1. to remove a burden from. 2. to free (one's conscience, mind, etc.) from anxiety by confessing or revealing (guilt, difficulties, etc.).

un·called-for (-kôld'fôr), *adj.* 1. not called for or needed. 2. gratuitous; impertinent.

un·can·ny (-kan'ĭ), *adj.* 1. weird; eerie. 2. far beyond what is normal.

un·ceas·ing (-sēs'ing), *adj.* without stopping; incessant. **—un·ceas'ing·ly,** *adv.*

un·cer·e·mo·ni·ous (-ser-ē-mō'ni-ùs), *adj.* 1. informal; casual. 2. curt or abrupt.

un·cer·tain (-sûrt'n), *adj.* 1. doubtful; not sure. 2. subject to change. 3. not definite; vague. 4. unreliable. **—un·cer'tain·ty,** *n., pl.* **-ties.**

un·char·i·ta·ble (-cher'ĭ-tä-bl), *adj.* without

charity; harsh, unkind, etc. **—un·char'i·ta·bly,** *adv.*

un·chart·ed (-chär'tid), *adj.* not marked on a chart or map.

un·checked (-chekt'), *adj.* without restraint; unhindered.

un·chris·tian (-kris'chǔn), *adj.* 1. not of the Christian faith. 2. not in keeping with the spirit of Christianity. 3. uncivilized.

un·ci·al (un'shi-ǎl), *adj.* denoting or of a style of letters used in Greek and Latin manuscripts from the 4th through the 9th century, somewhat resembling modern capitals but more rounded: *n.* an uncial letter or manuscript.

un·ci·nate (un'si-nit, -nāt), *adj.* bent like a hook; hooklike.

un·cir·cum·cised (un-sûr'kǔm-sīzd), *adj.* 1. not circumcised. 2. not of the Jewish faith; gentile. 3. [Archaic]. heathen.

un·civ·il (-siv'l), *adj.* rude; impolite.

un·cle (ung'kl), *n.* 1. the brother of one's father or mother. 2. the husband of one's aunt.

Uncle Sam (sam), [Informal], the US. government or people, represented as a tall man with whiskers.

Uncle Tom (tom), 1. the principal character in H. B. Stowe's novel, "Uncle Tom's Cabin" (1852), a faithful, pious Negro slave. 2. [Informal], a Negro regarded as servile toward whites.

un·cloak (un-klōk'), *v.t.* 1. to remove a cloak from. 2. to reveal; expose: *v.i.* to remove one's cloak.

un·clothe (-klōth'), *v.t.* **-clothed'** or **-clad'**, **-cloth'ing,** to undress, divest, etc.

un·coil (-koil'), *v.t. & v.i.* to unwind.

un·com·fort·a·ble (kumf'tēr-bl, -kum'fēr-tǎ-bl), *adj.* 1. not comfortable. 2. causing discomfort. 3. uneasy. **—un·com'fort·a·bly,** *adv.*

un·com·mit·ted (-kô-mit'id), *adj.* 1. not committed or done. 2. not bound or pledged. 3. not taking a stand; neutral.

un·com·mon (-kom'ŏn), *adj.* 1. not common; rare. 2. strange or extraordinary.

un·com·mu·ni·ca·tive (-kô-mū'ni-kāt-iv, -ni-kǎ-tiv), *adj.* tending not to express one's ideas, feelings, etc.; reserved.

un·com·pro·mis·ing (-kom'prô-mī-zing), *adj.* unyielding; firm.

un·con·cern (-kŏn-sûrn'), *n.* 1. lack of interest; indifference. 2. lack of worry.

un·con·cerned (-kŏn-sûrnd'), *adj.* 1. not interested; indifferent. 2. not anxious or worried.

un·con·di·tion·al (-kŏn-dish'ǔn-l), *adj.* without conditions or reservations; absolute.

un·con·scion·a·ble (-kon'shǔn-ǎ-bl), *adj.* 1. not governed by conscience; unscrupulous. 2. out of all reason or expectation; unreasonable, excessive, etc. **—un·con'scion·a·bly,** *adv.*

un·con·scious (-kon'shǔs), *adj.* 1. without consciousness. 2. not aware (*of*). 3. not deliberately intended: *n.* in *Psychoanalysis*, the elements and functionings of the mind of which the individual is not conscious.

un·con·sti·tu·tion·al (-kon-sti-tōō'shǔn-l, -tū'-), *adj.* in conflict with a constitution.

un·con·ven·tion·al (-kŏn-ven'shǔn-l), *adj.* not according to form or custom.

un·cork (-kôrk'), *v.t.* to pull the cork out of.

un·count·ed (-koun'tid), *adj.* 1. not counted. 2. too many to be counted; countless.

un·cou·ple (-kup'l), *v.t.* **-pled, -pling,** to unfasten (things coupled together); disconnect.

un·couth (-kōōth'), *adj.* 1. clumsy; awkward. 2. unrefined; boorish.

un·cov·er (-kuv'ēr), *v.t.* 1. to take away the cover of. 2. to expose or bring to light. 3. to remove the hat, cap, etc. from (the head): *v.i.* to remove the hat, cap, etc. from the head, as in showing respect.

unc·tion (ungk'shǔn), *n.* 1. the act of anointing, as in a religious rite. 2. the ointment or oil used for this. 3. anything soothing. 4. fervor or earnestness, especially when sham.

unc·tu·ous (ungk'choo-wǔs), *adj.* 1. oily. 2. marked by a smooth, hypocritical show of fervor or earnestness. **—unc'tu·ous·ness,** *n.*

un·cut (un-kut'), *adj.* 1. not shaped by grinding: said of a gem. 2. not shortened or abridged.

un·daunt·ed (-dôn'tid, -dän'-), *adj.* bold; fearless; unafraid.

un·de·ceive (-di-sēv'), *v.t.* **-ceived', -ceiv'ing,** to cause to be no longer deceived or deluded.

un·de·cid·ed (-di-sīd'id), *adj.* 1. not decided. 2. lacking resolution; not having come to a decision.

un·de·filed (-di-fīld'), *adj.* unstrained; pure; spotless.

un·de·mon·stra·tive (-di-mon'strǎ-tiv), *adj.* not showing one's feelings; reserved. **—un·de·mon'stra·tive·ly,** *adv.*

un·de·ni·a·ble (-di-ni'ǎ-bl), *adj.* 1. not to be denied; beyond dispute. 2. unquestionably good. **—un·de·ni'a·bly,** *adv.*

un·der (un'dēr), *prep.* 1. lower than; below. 2. beneath the surface of. 3. below and to the other side of. 4. covered by. 5. subordinate to. 6. less than. 7. during the time of. 8. lower than the required degree of. 9. subject to control by. 10. undergoing. 11. with the disguise of. 12. included in (the designated category, class, etc.). 13. being the subject of. 14. because of. 15. validated by: *adv.* 1. in a lower or subordinate position or capacity. 2. so as to be covered, hidden, etc.: *adj.* 1. lower in position. 2. subordinate.

un·der-, a prefix meaning: 1. *in, on, to,* or *from a lower place; beneath.* 2. *in a subordinate position.* 3. *too little, not enough.* As many words carrying this prefix are self-explanatory, such words are omitted from the list of definitions.

un·der·a·chieve (un-dēr-ǎ-chēv'), *v.i.* **-chieved', -chiev'ing,** to fail to realize one's potential, as in school studies.

un·der·act (-akt'), *v.t. & v.i.* to act (a part) with great, often too great, restraint.

un·der·age (-āj'), *adj.* 1. not of mature age. 2. below the legal age.

un·der·arm (un'dēr-ärm), *adj.* 1. of, for, or in the area under the arm, or the armpit. 2. same as **underhand** (sense 1): *adv.* same as **underhand** (sense 1).

un·der·bel·ly (-bel-i), *n.* 1. the lower, posterior

part of an animal's belly. 2. any place, point, etc. that is poorly protected.

un·der·bid (un-dĕr-bid'), *v.t.* -bid', -bid'ding, 1. to offer less than (another person). 2. to bid less than the value of.

un·der·bred (-bred'), *adj.* lacking refinement.

un·der·brush (un'dĕr-brush), *n.* small trees or shrubs growing closely together beneath large trees in woods or forests.

un·der·car·riage (-ker'ij), *n.* a supporting frame, as of an automobile.

un·der·charge (un-dĕr-chärj'), *v.t. & v.i.* -charged', -charg'ing, to charge (someone) too low a price: *n.* (un'dĕr-chärj), an insufficient charge.

un·der·class·man (un-dĕr-klas'măn), *n., pl.* -men ('mĕn), a freshman or sophomore.

un·der·clothes (un'dĕr-klōz, -klōthz), *n.pl.* same as underwear: also un'der·cloth·ing.

un·der·coat (-kōt), *n.* 1. a tarlike coating applied to the underside of a motor vehicle to hinder rusting and corrosion. 2. a coat of paint, shellac, etc. applied before the final coat. Also un'der·coat·ing: *v.t.* to apply an undercoat to.

un·der·cov·er (un-dĕr-kuv'ĕr), *adj.* acting or carried out in secret.

un·der·cur·rent (un'dĕr-kûr-ĕnt), *n.* 1. a current flowing under the surface. 2. a general tendency, feeling, etc. that is not apparent or openly expressed.

un·der·cut (un-dĕr-kut'), *v.t.* -cut', -cut'ting, 1. to cut away beneath so as to leave an overhanging part. 2. to undersell or work for lower wages than. 3. in *Sports*, to strike (a ball) in such a way as to impart backspin.

un·der·de·vel·oped (-di-vel'ŏpt), *adj.* lacking adequate economic and industrial development.

un·der·dog (un'dĕr-dôg), *n.* a person who is losing, expected to lose, handicapped, underprivileged, etc.

un·der·done (un-dĕr-dun'), *adj.* insufficiently cooked.

un·der·es·ti·mate (-es'ti-māt), *v.t.* -mat·ed, -mat·ing, to estimate at less than proper value, amount, etc.

un·der·foot (-foot'), *adv. & adj.* 1. under the foot or feet. 2. in the way.

un·der·gar·ment (un'dĕr-gär-mĕnt), *n.* an item of underwear.

un·der·go (un-dĕr-gō'), *v.t.* -went', -gone', -go'ing, to pass through, experience, or suffer.

un·der·grad·u·ate (-graj'oo-wit), *n.* a student at a college or university who does not have a degree.

un·der·ground (un'dĕr-ground'), *adj.* 1. under the surface of the ground. 2. secret; surreptitious. 3. unconventional, experimental, etc.: *adv.* 1. under the surface of the ground. 2. in or into secrecy: *n.* (-ground), 1. the region beneath the surface of the earth. 2. a secret movement in a country, organized to oppose those in authority. 3. [British], a subway.

un·der·growth (-grōth), *n.* same as underbrush.

un·der·hand (-hand), *adj.* 1. performed with the hand below the level of the elbow or shoulder. 2. same as underhanded: *adv.* 1. with an underhand motion. 2. underhandedly.

un·der·hand·ed (un-dĕr-han'did), *adj.* clandestine, deceitful, etc. —un·der·hand'ed·ly, *adv.*

un·der·lie (-lī'), *v.t.* -lay', -lain', -ly'ing, 1. to lie beneath. 2. to form the basis or foundation of.

un·der·line (un'dĕr-līn), *v.t.* -lined, -lin·ing, 1. to make a line under. 2. to emphasize.

un·der·ling (-ling), *n.* a subordinate; inferior.

un·der·mine (un-dĕr-mīn'), *v.t.* -mined', -min'ing, 1. to dig under, so as to form a tunnel or mine. 2. to wear away the foundations of. 3. to weaken in secret or insidious ways.

un·der·most (un'dĕr-mōst), *adj. & adv.* lowest in position, rank, etc.

un·der·neath (un-dĕr-nēth'), *adv. & prep.* beneath; under.

un·der·pants (un'dĕr-pants), *n.pl.* an undergarment consisting of long or short pants.

un·der·pass (-pas), *n.* a passageway, road, etc. that goes under something, as a railway or highway.

un·der·pin·ning (-pin-ing), *n.* 1. a support; prop. 2. *pl.* [Informal], the legs.

un·der·priv·i·leged (un-dĕr-priv'l-ijd, -priv'lijd), *adj.* living in poverty, discriminated against, etc.

un·der·pro·duce (-prō-dōōs', -dūs'), *v.t. & v.i.* -duced', -duc'ing, to produce less than is required or desired.

un·der·rate (-rāt'), *v.t.* -rat'ed, -rat'ing, to estimate below the true value.

un·der·score (-skôr'), *v.t.* -scored', -scor'ing, same as underline.

un·der·sea (-sē'), *adj. & adv.* below the surface of the sea.

un·der·sec·re·tar·y (-sek'rĕ-ter-i), *n., pl.* -tar·ies, an assistant secretary.

un·der·sell (-sel'), *v.t.* -sold', -sell'ing, to sell at a lower price than.

un·der·shirt (un'dĕr-shûrt), *n.* an undergarment without a collar, worn under an outer shirt.

un·der·shorts (-shôrts), *n.pl.* short underpants for men and boys.

un·der·shot (-shot), *adj.* 1. with the lower part projecting farther than the upper part. 2. operated by water moving against the lower part.

un·der·side (-sīd), *n.* the side or surface that is underneath.

un·der·signed (-sīnd'), *adj.* 1. signed at the end. 2. whose name or names are signed at the end: *n.* the person or persons whose name or names are signed at the end.

un·der·stand (un-dĕr-stand'), *v.t.* -stood' (-stood'), -stand'ing, 1. to perceive by the mind. 2. to assume or infer. 3. to interpret as having a certain meaning. 4. to take for granted. 5. to learn. 6. to know by experience. 7. to have a sympathetic relationship with: *v.i.* 1. to have understanding, awareness, etc. 2. to be informed; believe. —un·der·stand'a·ble, *adj.*

un·der·stand·ing (-ing), *n.* 1. comprehension, knowledge, etc. 2. the ability to think or learn; intelligence. 3. a specific interpretation. 4. mutual agreement: *adj.* that understands; sympathetic.

un·der·state (-stāt'), *v.t.* -stat'ed, -stat'ing, 1. to state with insufficient force. 2. to state in an unemotional, unhyperbolic way. —under-state'ment, n.

un·der·strap·per (un'dĕr-strap-ĕr), n. an underling; subordinate.

un·der·stud·y (-stud-i), n., pl. -stud·ies, an actor who learns another actor's part so as to be able to substitute for him if necessary: v.t. & v.i. -stud·ied, -stud·y·ing, to learn (a part) as an understudy (to).

un·der·take (un·dĕr-tāk'), v.t. -took', -tak'en, -tak'ing, 1. to take upon oneself. 2. to guarantee; promise.

un·der·tak·er (un'dĕr-tāk-ĕr), n. 1. one who undertakes a task, project, etc. 2. [Rare], same as funeral director.

un·der·tak·ing (un-dĕr-tāk'ing), n. 1. a task, project, etc. a person undertakes. 2. a guarantee; promise.

un·der-the-count·er (un'dĕr-thĕ-koun'tĕr), adj. [Informal], secret and illegal or unethical: also un'der-the-ta'ble (-tā'b'l).

un·der·things (-thingz), n.pl. underwear for women or girls.

un·der·tone (-tōn), n. 1. a low tone of voice; murmur. 2. a faint color. 3. an underlying factor, tendency, etc.

un·der·tow (-tō), n. a current flowing beneath the surface water and in a direction opposite to its movement.

un·der·waist (-wāst), n. [Rare], a woman's undergarment for wear under a blouse.

un·der·wa·ter (-wŏt'ĕr), adj. 1. existing, done, etc. beneath the surface of the water. 2. for use under water: adv. beneath the surface of the water.

un·der·wear (-wer), n. clothes worn next to the skin beneath outer clothing.

un·der·weight (-wāt), adj. weighing less than the normal or permitted weight.

un·der·world (-wûrld), n. 1. Hades. 2. criminals regarded as an organized social group.

un·der·write (-rīt'), v.t. -wrote', -writ'ten, -writ'-ing, 1. to guarantee the sale of (as an issue of securities). 2. to agree to finance, as a business venture. 3. to affix one's signature to (an insurance policy), thus assuming liability. —un'der·writ'er, n.

un·de·sir·a·ble (un-di-zīr'â-b'l), adj. not desirable; objectionable.

un·dies (un'diz), n.pl. [Informal], underwear for women or girls.

un·dine (un-dēn', un'dēn, 'dīn), n. in Folklore, a female water spirit.

un·do (un-dōō'), v.t. -did', -done', -do'ing, 1. to loosen, untie. 2. to do away with (that which has been done); cancel. 3. to put an end to; ruin.

un·do·ing ('ing), n. 1. a canceling or reversing. 2. a ruining. 3. the cause of ruin.

un·done (-dun'), adj. 1. not performed, completed, etc. 2. ruined, disgraced, etc.

un·doubt·ed (-dout'id), adj. that cannot be doubted; certain. —un·doubt'ed·ly, adv.

un·dress (-dres'), v.t. to remove the clothing of: v.i. to remove one's clothes.

un·due (-dōō', -dū'), adj. 1. improper; inappropriate. 2. excessive; immoderate.

un·du·lant (un'joo-lănt, 'dyoo-), adj. moving in waves; undulating.

undulant fever, a disease contracted by man from domestic animals, characterized by an undulating, or recurrent, fever.

un·du·late (-lāt), v.i. & v.t. -lat·ed, -lat·ing, 1. to move or cause to move like waves. 2. to have or cause to have a wavy form or surface. —un·du·la'tion, n.

un·du·la·to·ry (un'joo-lâ-tôr-i, 'dyoo-), adj. undulating; wavelike

un·du·ly (un-dōō'li, -dū'-), adv. 1. excessively. 2. improperly.

un·dy·ing (-dī'ing), adj. imperishable; possessing immortality.

un·earned (-ûrnd'), adj. not earned by work or effort.

unearned increment, an increase in the value of land or other property without labor or expenditure on the part of the owner.

un·earth (-ûrth'), v.t. 1. to dig out of the earth. 2. to uncover; reveal.

un·earth·ly (-ûrth'li), adj. 1. supernatural. 2. weird or bloodcurdling. 3. [Informal], fantastic, ridiculous, etc.

un·eas·y (-ē'zi), adj. -eas'i·er, -eas'i·est, 1. without ease; anxious, unquiet, uncomfortable, etc. 2. awkward; forced. —un·eas'i·ly, adv. —un·eas'i·ness, n.

un·em·ployed (-im-ploid'), adj. 1. not employed; without a job. 2. not in use; idle. —un·em·ploy'ment, n.

un·e·qual (-ē'kwâl), adj. 1. not equal, as in size, strength, worth, etc. 2. not regular, uniform, balanced, etc. 3. not equal or adequate (to).

un·e·qualed, un·e·qualled (-ē'kwâld), adj. not equaled; unmatched; supreme.

un·e·quiv·o·cal (-i-kwiv'ō-k'l), adj. clear; not ambiguous; unmistakable.

un·err·ing (-ûr'ing, -er'-), adj. 1. making no mistake; without error. 2. not missing or failing; sure; certain. —un·err'ing·ly, adv.

un·es·sen·tial (-i-sen'shûl), adj. not entirely necessary; not of vital importance.

un·e·ven (-ē'vĕn), adj. 1. not level, smooth, etc.; rough. 2. not equal. 3. in Mathematics, odd. —un·e'ven·ly, adv.

un·e·vent·ful (-i-vent'fûl), adj. with no remarkable event; routine.

un·ex·am·pled (-ig-zam'pld), adj. without precedent or parallel.

un·ex·cep·tion·a·ble (-ik-sep'shûn-â-b'l), adj. which cannot be objected to or criticized. —un·ex·cep'tion·a·bly, adv.

un·ex·pect·ed (-ik-spek'tid), adj. not expected; unforeseen. —un·ex·pect'ed·ly, adv.

un·fail·ing (-fāl'ing), adj. 1. not failing. 2. never running short; inexhaustible. 3. certain; sure.

un·fair (-fer'), adj. 1. showing prejudice; biased. 2. dishonest or unethical.

un·faith·ful (-fāth'fûl), adj. 1. not observing a vow, promise, duty, etc.; disloyal. 2. not accurate or reliable. 3. guilty of adultery.

un·fa·mil·iar (-fâ-mil'yĕr), adj. 1. not well-known; strange. 2. not acquainted (with).

un·fas·ten (-fas'n), v.t. to loosen, untie, undo, etc.

un·fa·vor·a·ble (-fā'vēr-â-bl). *adj.* not favorable; disadvantageous, discouraging, etc.

un·feel·ing (-fēl'ing). *adj.* 1. unable to feel; insensible. 2. unsympathetic; hardhearted. —**un·feel'ing·ly,** *adv.*

un·feigned (-fānd'). *adj.* genuine; not feigned.

un·fet·ter (-fet'ēr), *v.t.* to free from fetters; place at liberty.

un·fil·i·al (-fil'i·âl). *adj.* not showing love and respect to a parent.

un·fin·ished (-fin'isht), *adj.* 1. not finished; incomplete. 2. without a finish or final coat.

un·fix (-fiks'), *v.t.* to detach; unfasten.

un·flag·ging (-flag'ing), *adj.* not drooping; unwearied.

un·flap·pa·ble (-flap'â·bl), *adj.* [Informal], not easily excited; calm.

un·flinch·ing (-flin'ching), *adj.* not flinching; unshrinking; steadfast.

un·fold (-fōld'), *v.t.* 1. to open out. 2. to disclose, explain, etc.; *v.i.* 1. to spread out. 2. to develop.

un·forced (-fōrst'), *adj.* not forced; uncompelled; willing.

un·for·get·ta·ble (-fēr·get'â·bl), *adj.* impossible to forget because so important, striking, etc.

un·formed (-fôrmd'), *adj.* 1. without definite shape. 2. not organized.

un·for·tu·nate (-fôr'chû·nit), *adj.* 1. unlucky. 2. unsuccessful: *n.* an unfortunate person.

un·found·ed (-foun'did), *adj.* 1. without foundation in fact or truth. 2. not established.

un·friend·ly (-frend'li), *adj.* 1. not friendly. 2. not favorable.

un·frock (-frok'), *v.t.* to divest (a priest or minister) of rank and privileges.

un·fruit·ful (-frōōt'fûl), *adj.* 1. barren of fruit; unproductive. 2. without results.

un·furl (-fûrl'), *v.t. & v.i.* to open or spread out from a furled state; unfold.

un·gain·ly (-gān'li), *adj.* clumsy or awkward.

un·gen·er·ous (-jen'ēr·ûs), *adj.* 1. stingy; mean. 2. not tolerant or charitable.

un·gird (-gûrd'), *v.t.* 1. to remove the belt or girdle of. 2. to remove by unfastening a belt.

un·girt (-gûrt'), *adj.* 1. not girded; unbelted. 2. slack; loose.

un·god·ly (-god'li), *adj.* 1. not devoted to God; not religious; impious or profane. 2. [Informal], dreadful. —**un·god'li·ness,** *n.*

un·gov·ern·a·ble (-guv'ēr·nâ·bl), *adj.* impossible to govern or control; wild.

un·gra·cious (-grā'shûs), *adj.* 1. rude; impolite. 2. unpleasant or unattractive.

un·gram·mat·i·cal (-grâ·mat'i·kl), *adj.* not in accordance with the rules of grammar.

un·grate·ful (-grāt'fûl), *adj.* 1. without gratitude. 2. irksome; unpleasing.

un·gual (ung'gwâl), *adj.* of, pertaining to, or having a nail, claw, or hoof.

un·guard·ed (-gärd'id), *adj.* 1. without protection. 2. without guile; open. 3. careless; incautious.

un·guent (ung'gwênt), *n.* an ointment or salve.

un·guis (ung'gwis), *n., pl.* **un'gues** ('gwēz), a hoof, claw, talon, or nail.

un·gu·la (ung'gyoo·lâ), *n., pl.* **-lae** (-lē), same as **unguis.**

un·gu·late (-lit, -lāt), *adj.* 1. having hoofs. 2. shaped like a hoof: *n.* a mammal having hoofs.

un·hal·lowed (un·hal'ōd), *adj.* 1. not hallowed; unholy. 2. profane; wicked.

un·hand (-hand'), *v.t.* to release from the hand or hands; let go of.

un·hap·py (-hap'i), *adj.* **-pi·er, -pi·est,** 1. not happy; wretched. 2. unlucky. 3. not suitable or appropriate. —**un·hap'pi·ly,** *adv.*

un·har·ness (-här'nis), *v.t.* 1. to remove the harness from. 2. to remove the armor from.

un·health·y (-hel'thi), *adj.* **-health'i·er, -health'i·est,** 1. sickly; subject to disease. 2. not conducive to good health. 3. harmful to character. 4. dangerous; risky.

un·heard (-hûrd'), *adj.* 1. not perceived by the ear. 2. not listened to.

un·heard-of ('uv), *adj.* 1. not heard of before; unprecedented. 2. outrageous.

un·hinge (-hinj'), *v.t.* **-hinged', -hing'ing,** 1. to remove from the hinges. 2. to loosen or dislodge. 3. to render wavering or unsound, as the mind.

un·ho·ly (-hō'li), *adj.* **-li·er, -li·est,** 1. profane; wicked. 2. not hallowed, sanctified, or sacred. 3. [Informal], terrible; dreadful.

un·hoped-for (-hōpt'fôr), *adj.* not hoped for; unlooked for; unexpected.

un·horse (-hôrs'), *v.t.* **-horsed', -hors'ing,** to throw from a horse.

u·ni-, a prefix meaning *having only one.*

u·ni·cam·er·al (û·ni·kam'ēr·âl), *adj.* having only one chamber: said of a legislative assembly.

u·ni·cel·lu·lar (-sel'yoo·lēr), *adj.* having only one cell, as the protozoa.

u·ni·corn (û'ni·kôrn), *n.* a mythical animal resembling a horse but with a straight horn projecting from its forehead.

u·ni·cy·cle (û'ni·sī·kl), *n.* a vehicle with only one wheel, used chiefly by acrobats, clowns, etc.

u·ni·fi·ca·tion (û·ni·fi·kā'shûn), *n.* the act of unifying or the state of being unified.

u·ni·fo·li·ate (-fō'li·it), *adj.* in *Botany,* having only one leaf.

u·ni·form (û'ni·fôrm), *adj.* 1. always the same in form, manner, degree, etc. 2. conforming to a common standard: *n.* the prescribed clothing of a certain group, as soldiers: *v.t.* to furnish with a uniform. —**u·ni·form·i·ty** (û·ni·fôr'mi·ti), *n.* —**u'ni·form·ly,** *adv.*

u·ni·form·i·tar·i·an (û·ni·fôr·mi·ter'i·ân), *adj.* relating to or holding the doctrine of uniformitarianism: *n.* one who believes in uniformitarianism.

u·ni·form·i·tar·i·an·ism (-izm), *n.* the doctrine that all geologic changes are explicable in terms of physical and chemical processes that were essentially the same in the past as they are now.

u·ni·fy (û'ni·fī), *v.t. & v.i.* **-fied, -fy·ing,** to make or become united.

u·ni·lat·er·al (û·ni·lat'ēr·âl), *adj.* 1. having, occurring on, or affecting one side only. 2. involving or binding one only of several parties. —**u·ni·lat'er·al·ly,** *adv.*

---

u·ni·loc·u·lar (-lok'yŭ-lêr), *adj.* having or consisting of only one cell or chamber.

un·i·mag·i·na·ble (un-i-maj'i-nâ-bl), *adj.* inconceivable.

un·im·pas·sioned (-im-pash'ŭnd), *adj.* without passion; calm, cool, reasonable, etc.

un·im·peach·a·ble (-im-pēch'â-bl), *adj.* not liable to doubt or blame; irreproachable.

un·in·sured (-in-shoord'), *adj.* not insured, especially against loss of life or property.

un·in·tel·li·gent (-in·tel'i-jênt), *adj.* lacking, or deficient in, intelligence.

un·in·ten·tion·al (-in-ten'shŭn-l), *adj.* not intentional; not deliberate.

un·in·ter·est·ed (-in'trist-id, -in'tēr-ist-id), *adj.* not interested; indifferent.

un·in·vit·ed (-in·vīt'id), *adj.* 1. not invited; not asked to come. 2. not requested; unsolicited.

un·ion (ŭn'yŭn), *n.* 1. the act of uniting or the state of being united; combination. 2. a grouping together of nations, parties, etc. for some purpose. 3. marriage. 4. a whole formed from united parts, as a coalition of various individuals or groups. 5. that part of a flag or ensign symbolizing political union. 6. a device for connecting parts, as in a machine. 7. same as **labor union.** 8. in England, formerly, a parish workhouse.

un·ion·ize (-īz), *v.t.* -ized, -iz·ing, to form into a union, especially a labor union; *v.i.* to organize a labor union.

Union Jack, 1. the flag of the United Kingdom, combining features of the flags of England, Scotland, and Ireland. 2. [u- j-], a flag or jack consisting of a union only.

u·nip·a·rous (yoo-nip'â-rŭs), *adj.* denoting a female animal that produces only one egg or offspring at a time.

u·ni·per·son·al (ŭ-ni·pûr'sn-âl), *adj.* manifested in, or existing in, one person.

un·i·po·lar (-pō'lêr), *adj.* showing one kind of polarity; operating by one pole.

u·nique (ŭ-nēk'), *adj.* 1. without another of the same kind. 2. unparalleled. 3. extremely uncommon.

u·ni·sex (ŭ'ni-seks), *adj.* [Informal], of or pertaining to styles of clothing, hair, etc. that are the same for both sexes.

u·ni·sex·u·al (ŭ-ni-sek'shoo-wâl), *adj.* showing but one sex; denoting either male or female.

u·ni·son (ŭ'ni-sòn), *n.* 1. sameness of pitch of two or more musical sounds. 2. concord; harmony.

u·nit (ŭ'nit), *n.* 1. one. 2. a single person or thing. 3. a standard amount or quantity. 4. a particular section or thing.

U·ni·tar·i·an (ŭ-ni·ter'i-ân), *n.* any one of a denomination of Christians who deny the doctrine of the Trinity, regarding God as unipersonal; *adj.* of or pertaining to Unitarians. —**U·ni·tar'i·an·ism,** *n.*

u·nite (yoo-nīt'), *v.t.* -nit'ed, -nit'ing, 1. to incorporate into one. 2. to make agree or adhere. 3. to join by a legal or moral bond; *v.i.* to become one; combine; commingle.

u·ni·tive (ŭ'ni-tiv), *adj.* 1. tending to unite. 2. having the power to unite.

u·nit·ize (ŭ'ni-tīz), *v.t.* -ized, -iz·ing, to cause to become a unit.

unit pricing, a system of showing prices in terms of standard units.

u·ni·ty (ŭ'ni-ti), *n., pl.* -ties, 1. the state of being one. 2. concord; uniformity; agreement; harmony. 3. a distinct unit. 4. a whole consisting of associated sections. 5. a concordant composition, as of an artistic nature. 6. constancy of purpose or action. 7. in *Mathematics,* a unit quantity; one; 1.

u·ni·va·lent (ŭ-ni-vā'lênt), *adj.* in *Chemistry,* having one valence or having a valence of one.

u·ni·valve (ŭ'ni-valv), *n.* 1. a gastropod. 2. the shell of a mollusk, consisting of one piece.

u·ni·ver·sal (ŭ-ni-vûr'sl), *adj.* 1. all-pervading. 2. embracing or comprehending the whole. 3. general: *n.* in *Logic,* a proposition not restricted in application, belonging to the whole of the subject. —**u·ni·ver·sal'i·ty** (-vêr'sal'i-ti), *n.*

U·ni·ver·sal·ism (-izm), *n.* the doctrine that all mankind will ultimately be saved. —**U·ni·ver'sal·ist,** *n.*

u·ni·ver·sal·ize ('sâ-līz), *v.t.* -ized, -iz·ing, to cause to become universal.

universal joint, a mechanical joint allowing restricted movement in all directions: also **universal coupling.**

Universal Product Code, a patterned series of vertical bars printed on consumer products: it can be read by computerized electronic devices for pricing, etc.

u·ni·ver·sal·ly ('sl-i), *adv.* 1. without exception. 2. everywhere.

u·ni·verse (ŭ'ni-vûrs), *n.* 1. the whole system of created things. 2. the earth and its inhabitants.

u·ni·ver·si·ty (ŭ-ni-vûr'si-ti), *n., pl.* -ties, 1. an assemblage of colleges or incorporated institutions, at both the undergraduate and graduate level, for instruction in the higher branches of art, science, etc., and empowered to confer degrees. 2. the students, faculty, etc. of such an institution.

u·niv·o·cal (yoo-niv'i-kl), *adj.* having but one meaning.

un·just (un-just'), *adj.* not just; unfair.

un·kempt (-kempt'), *adj.* 1. not combed. 2. rough. 3. not neat or tidy.

un·kind (-kīnd'), *adj.* 1. not thoughtful of others. 2. rough; mean. —**un·kind'ness,** *n.*

un·kind·ly ('li), *adj.* same as **unkind:** *adv.* in an unkind manner.

un·known (-nōn'), *adj.* not known; especially, not often encountered or not within one's scope.

un·law·ful (-lô'fŭl), *adj.* in violation of the law or moral standards. —**un·law'ful·ly,** *adv.* —**un·law'ful·ness,** *n.*

un·lead·ed (-led'id), *adj.* not containing lead compounds: said of gasoline.

un·learn (-lûrn'), *v.t. & v.i.* to try to forget (something learned).

un·learn·ed (-lûr'nid), *adj.* 1. ignorant; uneducated. 2. (-lûrnd'), not learned.

un·leash (-lēsh'), *v.t.* to let go.

un·leav·ened (-lev'nd), *adj.* not leavened.

un·less (ûn-les'), *conj.* except if; if not.

---

a in cap, ā in cane, ä in father, å in abet, e in met, ē in be, ê in baker, è in regent, i in pit, ī in fine, i in manifest, o in hot, ô in horse, ō in bone,

un·let·tered (un-let'ĕrd), *adj.* 1. not able to read. 2. not having an education.

un·like (-līk'), *adj.* not similar: *prep.* having no similarity to.

un·like·ly (-līk'li), *adj.* 1. not reasonably expected. 2. not having a basis for favorable expectation.

un·lim·ber (-lim'bĕr), *v.t. & v.i.* to prepare for activity.

un·lim·it·ed (-lim'it-id), *adj.* 1. without limit. 2. boundless.

un·load (-lōd'), *v.t. & v.i.* 1. to take off or out (a load). 2. to take away a load from. 3. to communicate (one's problems). 4. to get rid of the burden of one's difficulties. 5. to extract the explosive charge of. 6. to free of.

un·lock (-lok'), *v.t.* 1. to unfasten (a lock). 2. to unfasten (a door, window, etc.). 3. to loosen. 4. to make known.

un·looked-for (-lookt'fôr), *adj.* not known beforehand.

un·loose (-lōōs'), *v.t.* **-loosed', -loos'ing,** to free, let go, etc.

un·luck·y (-luk'i), *adj.* **-luck'i·er, -luck'i·est,** unfortunate; subject to bad luck.

un·make (-māk'), *v.t.* **-made', -mak'ing,** 1. to make go back to a former state. 2. to crush; ruin. 3. to take away the rank or office of.

un·man (-man'), *v.t.* **-manned', -man'ning,** 1. to deprive of courage or fortitude. 2. to emasculate. **—un·man'ly,** *adv.*

un·man·age·a·ble (-man'ij-ă-bl), *adj.* beyond control.

un·manned (-mand'), *adj.* controlled automatically from another location; without human beings in direct control.

un·mask (-mask'), *v.t. & v.i.* 1. to take away a mask (from). 2. to reveal the actual quality (of).

un·mean·ing (-mēn'ing), *adj.* without meaning or importance.

un·men·tion·a·ble (un-men'shŭn-ă-bl), *adj.* not to be mentioned; disgusting.

un·mer·ci·ful (-mûr'si-fŭl), *adj.* without mercy, pity, etc.

un·mis·tak·a·ble (-mis-tāk'ă-bl), *adj.* not capable of being misunderstood; plain. **—un·mis·tak'a·bly,** *adv.*

un·mit·i·gat·ed (-mit'ĭ-gāt·id), *adj.* 1. unabated. 2. complete.

un·mor·al (-môr'ăl), *adj.* same as **amoral.**

un·nat·u·ral (-nach'ĕr-ăl), *adj.* 1. not in accordance with the laws of nature. 2. extremely wicked. 3. forced. **—un·nat'u·ral·ly,** *adv.*

un·nec·es·sar·y (-nes'ĕ-ser·i), *adj.* without need. **—un·nec·es·sar'i·ly,** *adv.*

un·nerve (-nûrv'), *v.t.* **-nerved', -nerv'ing,** to deprive of strength or confidence; weaken.

un·num·bered (-num'bĕrd), *adj.* 1. not included in counting. 2. lacking a number. 3. beyond count.

un·ob·tru·sive (-ŏb-trōō'siv), *adj.* not obtrusive; modest.

un·or·gan·ized (-ôr'gă-nīzd), *adj.* 1. lacking organization. 2. not affiliated with a labor union.

un·pack (-pak'), *v.t. & v.i.* 1. to take out (that which is within a suitcase, parcel, etc.). 2. to take out items from (a suitcase, parcel, etc.).

un·par·al·leled (-per'ă-leld), *adj.* without parallel; unrivaled.

un·placed (-plāst'), *adj.* 1. not placed. 2. not holding an office. 3. not among the first three at the end of a race.

un·pleas·ant (un-plez'nt), *adj.* disagreeable; objectionable; not pleasing to the feelings.

un·plumbed (-plumd'), *adj.* 1. not reckoned by means of a plumb. 2. not completely comprehended.

un·pop·u·lar (-pop'yŭ-lĕr), *adj.* not accepted by most people. **—un·pop·u·lar'i·ty** (-ler'ĭ-ti), *n.*

un·prac·ticed (-prak'tist), *adj.* 1. not expert. 2. not performed often.

un·prec·e·dent·ed (-pres'ĕ-den-tid), *adj.* new; lacking precedent.

un·pre·med·i·tat·ed (-pri-med'ĭ-tāt-id), *adj.* not arranged or thought of beforehand.

un·pre·ten·tious (-pri-ten'shŭs), *adj.* without pretense; modest in action or demeanor.

un·prin·ci·pled (-prin'si-pld), *adj.* with no principles; without scruple.

un·print·a·ble (-print'ă-bl), *adj.* obscene or slanderous.

un·pro·fes·sion·al (-prŏ-fesh'ŭn-l), *adj.* not according to the ethics of a profession.

un·pro·pi·tious (-prŏ-pish'ŭs), *adj.* not propitious; unfavorable.

un·pub·lished (-pub'lisht), *adj.* not printed or published; still in manuscript.

un·qual·i·fied (-kwäl'ĭ-fīd), *adj.* 1. not fulfilling the requirements for something. 2. without restriction.

un·quench·a·ble (-kwench'ă-bl), *adj.* that which cannot be subdued or extinguished.

un·ques·tion·a·ble (-kwes'chŭn-ă-bl), *adj.* that which should not be challenged or queried; definite. **—un·ques'tion·a·bly,** *adv.*

un·quote (un'kwōt), *interj.* the quotation is completed.

un·rav·el (un-rav'l), *v.t.* **-eled** or **-elled, -el·ing** or **-el·ling,** 1. to undo (something woven or tangled); untangle. 2. to divest of mystery: *v.i.* to become unraveled.

un·read (-red'), *adj.* 1. not having read much. 2. not having been read.

un·re·al (-rē'ăl), *adj.* not real; whimsical, false, etc.

un·rea·son·a·ble (un-rē'zn-ă-bl), *adj.* 1. acting contrary to reason; irrational. 2. without restraint or moderation.

un·rea·son·ing (-ing), *adj.* not rational.

un·re·gen·er·ate (-ri-jen'ĕr-it), *adj.* 1. remaining at enmity with God. 2. not converted. 3. stubborn. Also **un·re·gen'er·at·ed.**

un·re·lent·ing (-ri-len'ting), *adj.* 1. not relenting; determined. 2. pitiless. 3. not reducing intensity, force, etc.

un·re·mit·ting (-ri-mit'ing), *adj.* continuous; without interruption.

un·re·served (-ri-zûrvd'), *adj.* 1. unrestrained. 2. without reserve in manner. **—un·re·serv'ed·ly** (-zûr'vid-li), *adv.*

un·rest (-rest'), *n.* 1. an agitated condition. 2. dissatisfaction and dissent that may lead to revolution or resistance.

un·right·eous (-rī'chŭs), *adj.* 1. unholy; sinful. 2. unjust.

ŏ in drag*o*n, ōō in cr*u*de, oo in w*oo*l, u in c*u*p, ū in c*u*re, û in t*u*rn, ú in foc*u*s, oi in b*oy,* ou in h*ou*se, th in *th*in, t͟h in shea*th*e, g in g*e*t, j in *j*oy, y in *y*et.

un·ri·valed, un·ri·valled (-rī'vld), *adj.* without a rival; alone in a class.

un-roll (-rōl'), *v.t.* 1. to roll out or uncoil. 2. to show; exhibit: *v.i.* to be unrolled.

un-ruf·fled (un-ruf'ld), *adj.* not ruffled; reserved; calm.

un-rul·y (-rōō'li), *adj.* -rul'i·er, -rul'i·est, disregarding restraint or authority; ungovernable; turbulent. —**un-rul'i·ness,** *n.*

un-sad·dle (-sad'l), *v.t.* -dled, -dling, to remove the saddle from (a horse, donkey, etc.).

un-said (-sed'), *adj.* not uttered.

un·sat·u·rat·ed (-sach'ū-rāt·id), *adj.* in *Chemistry,* denoting an organic substance having a double or triple bond of carbon atoms.

un·sa·vor·y (-sā'vēr·i), *adj.* 1. displeasing to the taste or smell. 2. displeasing to one's moral sense.

un-scathed (-skāt̸hd'), *adj.* uninjured; without harm.

un-schooled (-skōōld'), *adj.* not having a formal education.

un-scram·ble (-skram'bl), *v.t.* -bled, -bling, to clear up or organize (a jumble, confused arrangement, etc.).

un-screw (-skrōō'), *v.t.* to unfasten by taking away the screws, or by turning.

un-scru·pu·lous (-skrōōp'yū-lŭs), *adj.* without principles or scruples.

un-seal (-sēl'), *v.t.* 1. to remove or destroy the seal of. 2. to open (that which is sealed) by destroying the seal.

un·sea·son·a·ble (-sē'zn-ȧ-bl), *adj.* 1. not fitting the season. 2. not opportune.

un-seat (-sēt'), *v.t.* 1. to remove from a seat. 2. to eject from an office.

un-seem·ly (-sēm'li), *adj.* not seemly; unbecoming.

un-seen (-sēn'), *adj.* invisible.

un-self·ish (-sel'fish), *adj.* not influenced by personal interests; having regard for others; broad; liberal; humane.

un-set·tle (-set'l), *v.t.* -tled, -tling, to cause uncertainty, confusion, etc. in: *v.i.* to become unsettled or confused.

un-sex (-seks'), *v.t.* 1. to deprive of the attributes of one's sex. 2. to make unfeminine or deprive (a woman) of her characteristic qualities.

un-shack·le (-shak'l), *v.t.* -led, -ling, 1. to remove the bonds from. 2. to give freedom to.

un-sheathe (-shēt̸h'), *v.t.* -sheathed', -sheath'ing, to remove from the scabbard or sheath.

un-shorn (-shôrn'), *adj.* not sheared or clipped.

un-sight·ly (-sīt'li), *adj.* unpleasant to the eye; disagreeable in appearance.

un-skilled (-skild'), *adj.* needing or possessing no technical skill or education.

un-skill·ful (-skil'fŭl), *adj.* not skillful; without grace.

un-snap (-snap'), *v.t.* -snapped', -snap'ping, to unfasten by releasing the snaps.

un-snarl (-snärl'), *v.t.* to remove tangles from.

un-so·cial (-sō'shŭl), *adj.* having an aversion for the company of others.

un·so·phis·ti·cat·ed (-sō-fis'ti-kāt-id), *adj.* without experience; innocent.

un-sound (-sound'), *adj.* 1. weak in a material sense; decayed; rotten. 2. in poor health. 3. erroneous in doctrine or religion.

un-spar·ing (-sper'ing), *adj.* 1. pitiless; harsh. 2. not holding back in giving; profuse.

un-speak·a·ble (-spēk'ȧ-bl), *adj.* 1. not to be mentioned or spoken of. 2. incapable of description; vile; wicked; loathsome.

un-sta·ble (-stā'bl), *adj.* 1. not firm. 2. not reliable. 3. varying; changing. 4. having confused emotions. 5. in *Chemistry,* breaking down into components or changing to new compounds.

un-stead·y (-sted'i), *adj.* 1. not fixed or firm. 2. not constant in feeling or purpose. 3. wavering.

un-stop (-stop'), *v.t.* -stopped, stop'ping, 1. to take out the stopper from. 2. to unblock (a pipe, drain, etc.).

un-struc·tured (-struk'chērd), *adj.* informally arranged; free.

un-strung (-strung'), *adj.* 1. having the strings loose or unfastened. 2. emotionally disturbed.

un-stud·ied (-stud'id), *adj.* 1. without study; without preparation. 2. natural.

un·sub·stan·tial (-sub-stan'shŭl), *adj.* 1. not real. 2. not having materiality. 3. unstable; lacking firmness.

un-suit·a·ble (-sōōt'ȧ-bl, -sūt'-), *adj.* not suited to; inadequate.

un-sung (-sung'), *adj.* not recognized or memorialized, as in literature.

un·sus·pect·ed (-sŭ-spek'tid), *adj.* 1. not suspected. 2. not foreseen.

un-tam·a·ble (-tām'ȧ-bl), *adj.* wild; that cannot be tamed.

un-tan·gle (-tang'gl), *v.t.* -gled, -gling, to extricate from a tangle, disorder, etc.

un-taught (-tôt'), *adj.* 1. natural. 2. ignorant.

un-ten·a·ble (-ten'ȧ-bl), *adj.* not tenable; incapable of defense.

un-think·a·ble (-thingk'ȧ-bl), *adj.* 1. not conceivable. 2. not possible.

un-think·ing ('ing), *adj.* 1. not rational. 2. not considerate or thoughtful.

un-ti·dy (-tī'di), *adj.* -di·er, -di·est, not neat; disordered.

un-tie (-tī'), *v.t.* -tied', -ty'ing or -tie'ing, 1. to release (a knot). 2. to release from chains, bonds, etc.

un-til (un-til'), *prep.* 1. till; up to the time of. 2. ahead of: *conj.* 1. ahead of the time. 2. as far as the time that. 3. to the extent, intensity, or location that.

un-time·ly (-tīm'li), *adj.* 1. coming too soon. 2. coming at an improper time: *adv.* 1. too soon. 2. improperly. —**un-time'li·ness,** *n.*

un-to (un'tōō), *prep.* [Archaic], 1. to. 2. until.

un-told (-tōld'), *adj.* 1. not told. 2. not capable of being measured.

un-touch·a·ble (-tuch'ȧ-bl), *adj.* not able or allowed to be touched: *n.* in India, formerly, one belonging to the lowest caste.

un-to·ward (-tō'ērd), *adj.* 1. not fitting. 2. unlucky. 3. [Archaic], obstinate.

un-trimmed (-trimd'), *adj.* without trimming or adornment.

---

un-truth (-trōōth'), *n.* 1. a falsehood. 2. the state of being false. —**un-truth'ful,** *adj.*

un-tu-tored (-tōōt'ĕrd), *adj.* 1. untaught. 2. ignorant.

un-used (-ūzd'), *adj.* 1. not being used. 2. never having been used. 3. not in the habit of (with *to*).

un-u-su-al (-ū'zhoo-wăl), *adj.* not ordinary. — **un-u'su-al-ly,** *adv.*

un-ut-ter-a-ble (-ut'ĕr-ă-bl), *adj.* denoting that which cannot be uttered or expressed in language; ineffable.

un-var-nished (-vär'nisht), *adj.* 1. not varnished. 2. without embellishment.

un-veil (-vāl'), *v.t.* 1. to take the veil from. 2. to cause to be revealed: *v.i.* to take off a veil.

un-war-rant-ed (-wôr'ăn-tid), *adj.* 1. without warrant. 2. unauthorized. 3. unguaranteed.

un-war-y (-wer'i), *adj.* incautious; careless.

un-well (-wel'), *adj.* ill.

un-whole-some (-hōl'sŭm), *adj.* 1. not wholesome. 2. unhealthy. 3. unhealthful. 4. detrimental to morality. —**un-whole'some-ly,** *adv.*

un-wield-y (-wēl'di), *adj.* 1. difficult to move. 2. [Now Rare], awkward.

un-will-ing (-wil'ing), *adj.* 1. averse. 2. performed aversely. —**un-will'ing-ly,** *adv.*

un-wind (-wīnd'), *v.t.* -**wound'**, -**wind'ing,** 1. to release (something wound). 2. to bring (something mixed up) into order: *v.i.* 1. to become loose. 2. to become less tense.

un-wise (-wīz'), *adj.* not wise or prudent.

un-wit-ting (-wit'ing), *adj.* 1. not aware; without knowledge. 2. without purpose.

un-wom-an-ly (-woom'ăn-li), *adv.* not becoming to the female sex.

un-wont-ed (-wun'tid), *adj.* 1. not common; strange. 2. [Archaic], unaccustomed (usually with *to*).

un-world-ly (-wûrld'li), *adj.* beyond worldly consideration.

un-wor-thy (-wûr'thi), *adj.* -**thi-er,** -**thi-est,** 1. of no value or worth. 2. not fitting (with *of*). 3. not warranted (with *of*). —**un-wor'thi-ness,** *n.*

un-wrap (-rap'), *v.t.* -**wrapped'**, -**wrap'ping,** to remove the wrapping from.

un-writ-ten (-rit'n), *adj.* 1. not written. 2. not statutory.

unwritten law, 1. a law or rule established by general usage. 2. a custom whereby immunity is granted to, or but slight sentence passed on, one who has attacked or murdered another who has raped or seduced the former's wife or daughter.

un-yield-ing (-yēl'ding), *adj.* not yielding; obstinate.

un-yoke (-yōk'), *v.t.* -**yoked'**, -**yok'ing,** 1. to remove the yoke from. 2. to sever.

up (up), *adj.* 1. moving or sloping upward. 2. in a lofty place, state, etc. 3. of a higher level, number, etc. 4. upright. 5. agitated, functioning, etc. 6. finished; at the end. 7. at stake. 8. [Informal], happening. 9. in Baseball, having one's position for batting -**come around.** 10. in Sports, *a)* before, or in advance of, an opponent; *b)* necessary to

win: said of the points in a game: *adv.* 1. toward or in a higher place. 2. to a higher price, number, level, etc. 3. to a greater degree. 4. to a larger size. 5. in an upright position. 6. so as to be even with. 7. in commotion. 8. in progress, consideration, etc. 9. into a state of preservation. 10. to a subsequent time. 11. in such a way as to be firmly sealed, tied, etc. 12. completely. 13. in Baseball, to one's position for batting. 14, in nautical usage, denoting a movement or shift of the bow toward the wind: *prep.* 1. from a lower to a higher point; on a line of ascent. 2. from the mouth to the source of a river. 3. at or near a higher place. 4. from the coast to the interior: *n.* 1. the state of being or moving up. 2. a state of prosperity. 3. that which is up: *v.i.* upped, up'ping, [Informal], to move upward: *v.t.* [Informal], 1. to cause to go upward. 2. to cause to go higher.

U-pan-i-shad (ōō-pan'i-shad), *n.* one of the many books of Vedic literature, dealing with the origin of the universe and its relationship to man.

u-pas (ū'păs), *n.* a tree common in Java, yielding an exceedingly poisonous juice like milk.

up-beat (up'bēt), *n.* in Music, a beat that is not accented and usually is the final note of a bar: *adj.* gay; lively.

up-braid (up-brād'), *v.t.* to reproach harshly.

up-bring-ing (up'bring-ing), *n.* a bringing up; rearing.

up-cast (up'kast), *n.* 1. the ventilating shaft of a mine, through which the air passes after circulating below. 2. something cast up: *adj.* 1. cast up. 2. directed up.

up-com-ing (-kum'ing), *adj.* appearing soon.

up-coun-try (kun'tri), *adj.* & *adv.* & *n.* inland.

up-date (up-dāt'), *v.t.* -**dat'ed,** -**dat'ing,** to fit into current trends, systems, etc.

up-end (-end'), *v.t.* & *v.i.* to place on its end.

up-grade (up'grād), *n.* an ascending incline: *adj.* & *adv.* toward a higher place: *v.t.* (up-grād'), -**grad'ed,** -**grad'ing,** to cause to take on a higher level, degree, character, etc.

up-heav-al (up-hē'vl), *n.* 1. a lifting from below, as of strata by some internal force. 2. an abrupt, intense alteration of a condition.

up-heave (-hēv'), *v.t.* -**heaved'** or -**hove',** -**heav'ing,** to lift up from beneath.

up-hill (up'hil'), *adj.* 1. rising. 2. difficult: *adv.* 1. in a rising direction. 2. with considerable difficulty.

up-hold (up-hōld'), *v.t.* -**held'**, -**hold'ing,** 1. to hold up. 2. to sustain; maintain; defend. 3. to praise; encourage. —**up-hold'er,** *n.*

up-hol-ster (up-hōl'stĕr), *v.t.* to furnish (furniture) with covers, cushions, tassels, hangings, etc.; stuff or pad and cover (cushions, mattresses, etc.).

up-hol-ster-er (-ĕr), *n.* one who upholsters or supplies upholstery.

up-hol-ster-y (-i), *n.,* *pl.* -**ster-ies,** 1. the business of an upholsterer. 2. materials used in upholstering.

up-keep (up'kēp), *n.* 1. maintenance. 2. cost of maintenance. 3. condition of maintenance.

up-land ('land), *n.* elevated land as distinguished from land between hills or along the seashore or rivers: *adj.* of or located in upland.

upland cotton, cotton with a short fiber.

up-lift (up-lift'), *v.t.* 1. to lift up or elevate. 2. to elevate in rank or state: *n.* (up'lift), 1. the act of lifting up. 2. spiritual or social elevation, or activity intended to achieve this.

up-on (ŭ-pon'), *prep.* on; resting on: almost identical with *on*, being used for the latter for the sake of euphony or when motion into position is involved.

up-per (up'ĕr), *adj.* higher in place, rank, or dignity: *n.* 1. the part of the shoe above the sole. 2. [Slang], any drug that is a stimulant; esp., an amphetamine.

upper case, type consisting of capital letters. — up'per-case, *adj.*

upper class, the highest social or economic class. —up'per-class, *adj.*

up-per-class-man (up-ĕr-klas'man), *n., pl.* -men ('mĕn), a person of the junior or senior class of a high school or college.

up-per-cut (up'ĕr-kut), *n.* in *Boxing*, a short arm swing directed upward, as to the jaw of an opponent: *v.t. & v.i.* -cut, -cut-ting, to hit with an uppercut.

upper hand, a favorable or commanding situation or place.

up-per-most (-mōst), *adj.* of the superior position of power, command, etc.: *adv.* in the superior level, location, etc.; first.

up-pish (up'ish), *adj.* [Informal], arrogant; contemptuous: also **up'pi-ty** ('i-ti).

up-raise (up-rāz'), *v.t.* -raised', -rais'ing, to lift up; elevate.

up-rear (-rir'), *v.t.* 1. to elevate. 2. to rear. 3. to raise in position.

up-right (up'rīt), *adj.* 1. erect. 2. just; honest; equitable: *adv.* (also up-rīt'), erectly: *n.* an erect or vertical part.

upright piano, a piano with the body in a vertical position.

up-ris-ing (up'rīz-ing), *n.* 1. a popular movement against authority. 2. a rising up.

up-roar ('rōr), *n.* 1. a noisy disturbance. 2. bustle and clamor.

up-roar-i-ous (up-rōr'i-ŭs), *adj.* 1. making great noise and tumult. 2. noisy and lively.

up-root (-rōōt'), *v.t.* 1. to take up by the roots. 2. to eradicate.

up-scale (up'skāl), *adj.* of or for people who are affluent, stylish, etc.

up-set (up-set'), *v.t.* -set', -set'ting, 1. to overthrow. 2. to put out of normal condition: *v.i.* to be overthrown or upset: *n.* (up'set), 1. the act of upsetting. 2. the state of being upset. 3. an overthrowing by surprise. 4. a disordered condition: *adj.* 1. overthrown. 2. not in order. 3. [Rare], fixed.

up-shot (up'shot), *n.* the result; conclusion.

up-side ('sīd), *n.* the side on top.

upside down, 1. having the upper side below. 2. in a state of confusion. —up'side-down', *adj.*

up-si-lon (ūp'si-lon), *n.* the twentieth letter of the Greek alphabet.

up-stage (up'stāj'), *adv. & adj.* in the direction

of or at the back part of a stage: *v.t.* -staged', -stag'ing, to draw attention to oneself and thus attract attention from (someone else).

up-stairs ('sterz'), *adv.* 1. at or to the top of the stairs. 2. to or upon a higher floor, level, etc.: *adj.* located on a higher floor: *n.* a higher floor.

up-stand-ing (up-stan'ding), *adj.* upright in position, character, etc.

up-start (up'stärt), *n.* one who suddenly rises from a humble position to wealth or influence and behaves arrogantly or boldly: *adj.* suddenly raised to a position of wealth and influence.

up-state (up'stāt'), *adj. & adv.* in, from, or to the northern section of a State.

up-stream ('strēm'), *adv. & adj.* toward the direction from which a stream flows.

up-surge (up'sûrj), *n.* a surge upward.

up-swing ('swing), *n.* a shift or tendency in an upward direction.

up-take ('tāk), *n.* 1. the act of taking up. 2. [Informal], ability to understand.

up-tight, up-tight ('tīt'), *adj.* [Slang], extremely apprehensive, jittery, etc.

up-to-date ('tō-dāt'), *adj.* 1. current. 2. in accordance with the latest custom or fashion.

up-town ('toun'), *adj. & adv.* of, situated in, or in the direction of that part of town away from the main business district.

up-turn (up-tûrn'), *v.t. & v.i.* to turn up: *n.* (up'tûrn), a move or tendency in an upward direction. —up'turned', *adj.*

up-ward (up'wĕrd), *adv. & adj.* toward a higher place, level, etc.: also up'wards, *adv.* —up'ward-ly, *adv.*

upward mobility, movement from a lower to a higher social and economic status.

u-rae-us (yoo-rē'ŭs), *n., pl.* -rae'i ('ī), the emblem or symbol of the sacred asp on the headdress of an Egyptian Pharaoh.

u-ran-ic (yoo-ran'ik), *adj.* 1. of or pertaining to the heavens. 2. of or pertaining to uranium.

u-ran-i-nite (yoo-ran'i-nīt), *n.* a black mineral consisting of uranium, thorium, and other metals.

u-ra-ni-um (yoo-rā'ni-ŭm), *n.* a radioactive, metallic element found in combination with pitchblende and other rare minerals: the isotope of uranium known as *uranium 235* has been used in producing atomic energy.

U-ra-nus (yoor'à-nŭs, yoo-rā'nŭs), *n.* a planet in the solar system, seventh in distance from the sun.

ur-ban (ûr'bǎn), *adj.* of, pertaining to, like, or in a city or town.

ur-bane (ûr-bān'), *adj.* polite; refined. —urban'i-ty (-ban'i-ti), *n.*

ur-ban-ize (ûr'bǎ-nīz), *v.t.* -ized, -iz-ing, to change from rural to urban in character. —ur-ban-i-za'tion, *n.*

ur-ban-ol-o-gist (ûr-ban-ol'ō-jist), *n.* a specialist in urban problems. —ur-ban-ol'o-gy, *n.*

urban renewal, rebuilding of rundown city areas.

urban sprawl, the spread of urban congestion into adjoining suburbs and rural sections.

ur-chin (ûr'chin), *n.* 1. a small boy. 2. [Obs.], a hedgehog.

---

a in cap, ā in cane, ä in father, à in abet, e in met, ē in be, ê in baker, ê in regent, i in pit, ī in fine, ì in manifest, o in hot, ô in horse, ō in bone,

-ure (ēr), a suffix meaning *product of being, instrument of, condition of being.*

u·re·a (yoo-rē'á), *n.* the chief solid constituent of the urine of mammals.

u·re·do (yoo-rē'dō), *n.* same as **urticaria**.

u·re·mi·a ('mi-á), *n.* poisoning of the blood by the presence of waste products normally eliminated in the urine. **—u·re'mic,** *adj.*

u·re·ter (yoo-rēt'ẽr), *n.* the duct through which the urine flows from the kidney to the bladder.

u·re·thra (-rē'thrá), *n., pl.* **-thrae** ('thrē), **-thras,** the canal or duct through which the urine is discharged from the bladder.

u·re·thri·tis (yoor-i-thrī'tis), *n.* inflammation of the urethra.

u·re·thro·scope (yoo-rē'thrá-skōp), *n.* an instrument for viewing the interior of the urethra.

u·ret·ic (yoo-ret'ik), *adj.* of or pertaining to urine.

urge (ûrj), *v.t.* **urged, urg'ing,** 1. to incite; provoke. 2. to impel. 3. to press earnestly: *v.i.* to act with earnestness; insist upon: *n.* 1. the act of urging. 2. an impelling force.

ur·gen·cy (ûr'jĕn-si), *n., pl.* **-cies,** 1. the pressure of necessity. 2. importunity.

ur·gent ('jĕnt), *adj.* 1. pressing; calling for immediate attention. 2. importunate. **—ur'gent·ly,** *adv.*

-ur·gy (ûr'ji), a suffix meaning *the way of operating with* or *with (something) as an agent for.*

u·ric (yoor'ik), *adj.* of, pertaining to, or obtained from urine.

uric acid, a crystalline compound found in the excrement of birds and snakes, human urine, etc.

U·rim and Thum·mim (yoor'im-n-thum'im), objects in the breastplate of the high priest of Israel: see *Exodus* xxviii, 30.

u·ri·nal (yoor'i-nl), *n.* 1. a receptacle for urine. 2. a place for urinating.

u·ri·nal·y·sis (yoor'i-nal'i-sis), *n., pl.* **-ses** (-sēz), scientific analysis of urine.

u·ri·nar·y (yoor'i-ner-i), *adj.* 1. of, pertaining to, or like urine. 2. of or pertaining to the organs producing and emitting urine.

u·ri·nate (-nāt), *v.i.* **-nat·ed, -nat·ing,** to discharge urine; make water. **—u·ri·na'tion,** *n.*

u·rine (yoor'in), *n.* a fluid excretion from the kidneys into the bladder, from which it is voided through the urethra.

u·ri·no·gen·i·tal (yoor-i-nō-jen'i-tl), *adj.* same as **urogenital.**

urn (ûrn), *n.* 1. a roundish vessel of various materials, usually with a foot or pedestal. 2. a vessel in which the ashes of the dead are preserved. 3. a vessel with a spigot for dispensing hot beverages.

u·ro·dele (yoor'ō-dēl), *n.* any of a group of amphibians, as salamanders, newts, etc.

u·ro·gen·i·tal (yoor-ō-jen'i-tl), *adj.* of or pertaining to the organs of urinary excretion and of reproduction.

u·rol·o·gy (yoo-rol'ō-ji), *n.* that branch of medical science which treats of urine, the urinary and genital organs, and related diseases. **—u·rol'o·gist,** *n.*

Ursa Major (ûr'sá), the Great Bear, the most conspicuous of the northern constellations.

Ursa Minor, the Little Bear, the constellation which includes the North Star.

ur·sine (ûr'sīn), *adj.* of, pertaining to, or resembling a bear.

Ur·su·line (ûr'su̇-lin), *n.* one of an order of Roman Catholic nuns.

ur·ti·car·i·a (ûr-ti-ker'i-á), *n.* an inflammatory skin disease, characterized by red pimples and a burning or stinging sensation.

ur·ti·cate (ûr'ti-kāt), *v.t. & v.i.* **-cat·ed, -cat·ing,** to sting with or as with nettles.

ur·ti·ca·tion (ûr-ti-kā'shŭn), *n.* 1. formerly, the act of stinging with nettles. 2. a prickly irritation.

us (us), *pron.* objective case of **we.**

us·a·ble, use·a·ble (ū'zȧ-bl), *adj.* denoting that which can be used. **—us·a·bil'i·ty, use·a·bil'-i·ty** (-bil'i̇-ti), *n.*

us·age (ū'sij), *n.* 1. the act or mode of using; treatment. 2. habitual or long-continued use or custom. 3. the mode of expression in a language, used to communicate concepts.

use (ūs), *n.* 1. the act of using. 2. the state of being used. 3. application of anything to a particular purpose. 4. habitual employment; custom or practice. 5. treatment. 6. permission for using. 7. capability of using. 8. help. 9. necessity or purpose for use. 10. worth: *v.t.* (ūz), **used, us'ing,** 1. to apply to a particular purpose; employ. 2. to avail oneself of. 3. to possess or enjoy for a time. 4. to habituate (*to*). 5. to exhaust (with *up*): *v.i.* to be accustomed. **—us'er,** *n.*

used (ūzd), *adj.* 1. that has been used. 2. same as **secondhand.**

use·ful (ūs'fu̇l), *adj.* full of use, profit, or advantage; beneficial. **—use'ful·ly,** *adv.* **—use'-ful·ness,** *n.*

use·less ('lis), *adj.* 1. having or being of no use. 2. of no avail. **—use'less·ly,** *adv.* **—use'-less·ness,** *n.*

us·er-friend·ly (ūs'ẽr-friend'li), *adj.* easy to use or understand: said esp. of computer hardware, programs, etc.

ush·er (ush'ẽr), *n.* 1. a doorkeeper. 2. a person who introduces strangers or walks before persons of rank. 3. a person whose job is to escort patrons to their seats, as in a theater. 4. an attendant to the bridegroom in a wedding. 5. [Obs.], in Great Britain, an assistant schoolteacher for boys: *v.t.* 1. to escort, as to seats. 2. to introduce (often with *in*).

us·que·baugh (us'kwi-bô), *n.* [Irish & Scottish], same as **whiskey.**

u·su·al (ū'zhoo-wȧl), *adj.* habitual; customary; ordinary. **—u'su·al·ly,** *adv.*

u·su·fruct (ū'zyoo-frukt), *n.* in *Roman & Civil Law,* the temporary use and enjoyment of lands and buildings belonging to another.

u·surp (ū-sûrp', -zûrp'), *v.t. & v.i.* to take possession of (an office, functions, powers, rights, etc.) by force or, without right. **—u·surp'er,** *n.*

u·sur·pa·tion (ū-sẽr-pā'shŭn, -zẽr-), *n.* 1. the act of usurping. 2. the unlawful seizure of regal or other power.

u·su·ry (ū'zhoo-ri), *n., pl.* **-ries,** 1. interest on money beyond the legal rate of interest. 2.

the practice of lending money at exorbitant rates of interest. —u'su·rer, *n.* —u·su·ri·ous (ū-zhoor'i-ŭs), *adj.*

Ute (ūt), *n.* one of a tribe of North American Indians living in the western U.S.

u·ten·sil (ū-ten'sĭl), *n.* an implement, especially one used for domestic or culinary purposes.

u·ter·ine (ūt'ĕr-ĭn), *adj.* 1. of or pertaining to the uterus. 2. born of the same mother, but by a different father.

u·ter·us (-ŭs), *n., pl.* u'ter·i (-ī), the organ of a female in which a fetus forms; womb.

u·til·i·tar·i·an (yoo-tĭl-ĭ-ter'ĭ-ăn), *adj.* 1. of, pertaining to, or aiming at utility. 2. emphasizing utility over aesthetic considerations: *n.* one who holds the doctrine of utilitarianism.

u·til·i·tar·i·an·ism (-ĭzm), *n.* the doctrine that virtue is defined and achieved by its tendency to promote the highest happiness of mankind.

u·til·i·ty (yoo-tĭl'ĭ-tĭ), *n., pl.* -ties, 1. usefulness. 2. that which is useful. 3. a public service, as the supplying of electricity. 4. a business which supplies this service.

u·ti·lize (ū'tĭ-īz), *v.t.* -lized, -liz·ing, to make useful or profitable. —u·ti·li·za'tion, *n.*

ut·most (ut'mōst), *adj.* 1. in the greatest degree. 2. most distant; furthest; extreme: *n.* the extreme limit or extent.

U·to·pi·a (yoo-tō'pi-ă), *n.* 1. an imaginary island described by Sir Thomas More as the place of perfect moral and social conditions. 2. [u-], any place of perfection. 3. [u-], any visionary plan for a perfect system of living.

U·to·pi·an (-ăn), *adj.* 1. of or pertaining to Utopia. 2. [often u-], ideal; visionary: *n.* 1. one who lives in Utopia. 2. [often u-], a visionary.

u·to·pi·an·ism (-ĭzm), *n.* schemes for social happiness or perfection.

u·tri·cle (ū'trĭ-kl), *n.* a little sac; vesicle: also **u·tric·u·lus** (yoo-trĭk'yŭ-lŭs), *pl.* -li (-lī). —u·tric·u·lar (yoo-trĭk'yŭ-lĕr), *adj.*

ut·ter (ut'ĕr), *adj.* 1. entire; total. 2. absolute; unqualified: *v.t.* 1. to speak; pronounce. 2. to express. 3. to circulate (counterfeit coins or notes). 4. [Obs.], to publish.

ut·ter·ance (ut'ĕr-ăns), *n.* 1. vocal expression; speech. 2. style of speaking. 3. that which is spoken, written, etc.

ut·ter·most (ut'ĕr-mōst), *adj. & n.* same as **ut·most**.

u·va·rov·ite (ōō-vä'rŏf-īt), *n.* a kind of garnet of an emerald-green color.

u·ve·a (ū'vĭ-ă), *n.* the posterior, dark-colored layer of the iris.

u·ve·i·tis (ū-vi-ĭt'ĭs), *n.* inflammation of the uvea.

u·vu·la (ū'vyă-lă), *n., pl.* -las, -lae (-lē), the fleshy, conical body, attached to the soft palate, hanging above the back of the tongue. —u'vu·lar, *adj.*

ux·or·i·cide (ŭk-sŏr'ĭ-sīd), *n.* 1. one who murders his wife. 2. the murder of a wife by her husband.

ux·o·ri·ous ('ĭ-ŭs), *adj.* foolishly or excessively fond of one's wife; foolishly submissive to one's wife. —ux·o'ri·ous·ness, *n.*

---

a in cap, ā in cane, ä in father, ȧ in abet, e in met, ē in be, ē in baker, ē in regent, i in pit, ī in fine, ĭ in manifest, o in hot, ō in horse, ō in bone,

V

V, v (vē), *n., pl.* **V's, v's,** 1. the twenty-second letter of the English alphabet. 2. the usual sound of this letter, as in *vale.* 3. a type or impression of *V* or *v.*

V (vē), *adj.* shaped like *V: n.* 1. an object shaped like *V.* 2. a Roman numeral denoting 5. 3. [Informal], a five-dollar bill.

va·can·cy (vā'kǎn-si), *n., pl.* **-cies,** 1. the state of being vacant, or empty. 2. lack of thought or intelligence; vacuity. 3. an unfilled position, office, job, etc. 4. an unoccupied building, apartment, hotel room, etc. 5. empty or open space.

va·cant (vā'kǎnt), *adj.* 1. empty. 2. lacking in thought or intelligence. 3. not held, in use, filled, etc., as a chair, house, position, etc. —**va'cant·ly,** *adv.*

va·cate ('kāt), *v.t.* **-cat·ed, -cat·ing,** 1. to make vacant, as a house, chair, office, etc. 2. to annul; make void.

va·ca·tion (vǎ-kā'shǔn, vā-), *n.* 1. a period of rest from work, school, etc. 2. a recess between terms of a court of law: *v.i.* to take one's vacation. —**va·ca'tion·er, va·ca'tion·ist,** *n.*

vac·ci·nate (vak'si-nāt), *v.t. & v.i.* **-nat·ed, -nat·ing,** to inoculate with a vaccine to prevent a disease, specifically smallpox. —**vac·ci·na'tion,** *n.* —**vac'ci·na·tor,** *n.*

vac·cine (vak-sēn'), *n.* 1. a substance containing the virus of cowpox, used in vaccination against smallpox. 2. any substance used to produce immunity to a particular disease.

vac·cin·i·a (vak-sin'i-å), *n.* same as cowpox.

vac·il·late (vas'i-lāt), *v.i.* **-lat·ed, -lat·ing,** 1. to be indecisive; waver in opinion. 2. to fluctuate. 3. to be unsteady; waver. —**vac·il·la'tion,** *n.* —**vac'il·la·tor,** *n.*

vac·il·lat·ing (-ing), *adj.* wavering; unsteady; indecisive. —**vac'il·lat·ing·ly,** *adv.*

va·cu·i·ty (va-kū'i-ti), *n., pl.* **-ties,** 1. emptiness. 2. an empty space. 3. lack of thought or intelligence. 4. a foolish or inane remark, action, etc.

vac·u·ole (vak'yoo-wōl), *n.* in *Biology,* a clear, fluid-filled cavity within the plasma membrane of a cell. —**vac'u·o·lar,** *adj.*

vac·u·ous (vak'yoo-wǔs), *adj.* 1. empty. 2. showing a lack of thought or intelligence; inane; senseless. 3. purposeless; idle. —**vac'u·ous·ly,** *adv.* —**vac'u·ous·ness,** *n.*

vac·u·um (vak'yoo-wǔm, vak'yoom), *n., pl.* **-ums, -a** (-å), 1. space devoid of all matter. 2. space from which all air or gas has been exhausted, as by a pump. 3. any void: *adj.* 1. of or producing a vacuum. 2. almost entirely exhausted of air or gas. 3. using a vacuum to operate: *v.t. & v.i.* to clean with a vacuum cleaner.

vacuum bottle, same as thermos: also **vacuum flask** or **vacuum jug.**

vacuum cleaner, a device for cleaning floors, carpets, upholstery, etc. by suction: also **vacuum sweeper.**

vacuum-packed (-pakt'), *adj.* packed in a sealed container from which most of the air has been exhausted.

vacuum pump, 1. same as pulsometer. 2. a pump used to exhaust air or gas from an enclosed space.

vacuum tube, an electron tube from which nearly all the air has been exhausted, containing grids and used as an amplifier, rectifier, etc.

va·de me·cum (vā'di mē'kǔm, vā'-), something a person carries with him constantly, as a reference book, manual, etc.

vag·a·bond (vag'å-bond), *adj.* 1. without fixed habitation; wandering. 2. drifting; vagrant; unsettled. 3. idle; worthless: *n.* 1. one who wanders from place to place. 2. a tramp or vagrant. —**vag'a·bond·ish,** *adj.*

vag·a·bond·age (-ij), *n.* the state or condition of being a vagabond.

va·gar·i·ous (vå-ger'i-ǔs), *adj.* whimsical; capricious; given to vagaries.

va·gar·y (vå-ger'i, vā'gēr-i), *n., pl.* **-gar'ies,** 1. a freakish idea; whim. 2. an odd, freakish, or unexpected action; caprice.

va·gi·na (vå-ji'nå), *n., pl.* **-nas, -nae** ('nē), in female mammals, the canal between the uterus and the vulva. —**vag·i·nal** (vaj'i-nl), *adj.*

vag·i·nate (vaj'i-nit, -nāt), *adj.* having or like a sheath.

vag·i·ni·tis (vaj·i-nīt'is), *n.* inflammation of the vagina.

va·gran·cy (vā'grǎn-si), *n., pl.* **-cies,** 1. a state of wandering without a settled home. 2. the habits and life of a vagrant. 3. a wandering in mind or thought.

va·grant ('grǎnt), *adj.* 1. wandering from place to place; nomadic. 2. pursuing the life of a rover. 3. of or like a vagrant. 4. random; erratic: *n.* one who wanders from place to place without means of support and lives by begging, odd jobs, etc.

vague (vāg), *adj.* 1. not distinctly outlined; hazy; indefinite. 2. inexact in thought or expression; imprecise. —**vague'ly,** *adv.* —**vague'ness,** *n.*

va·gus (vā'gǔs), *n.* either one of the tenth pair of cranial nerves, passing into the abdomen and supplying, mostly to the viscera, motor and sensory impulses.

vain (vān), *adj.* 1. empty; fruitless; worthless. 2. producing no desired results; futile. 3. having or exhibiting an undue preoccupation or regard for one's looks, achievements, etc.; conceited. —**vain'ly,** *adv.*

vain·glo·ry (vān-glôr'i), *n.* 1. excessive vanity;

ŏ in drag*o*n, ōō in cr*u*de, *oo* in w*oo*l, **u** in c*u*p, ū in c*u*re, ū in t*u*rn, û in f*o*cus, *oi* in b*oy*, *ou* in h*ou*se, th in *th*in, *th* in shea*th*e, g in g*e*t, j in *j*oy, y in *y*et.

ostentatious pride. 2. foolish pomp or display. —vain·glo′ri·ous, *adj.*

val·ance (val′ăns, vāl′-), *n.* a short drapery running across the top of a window, hanging from a bed, etc.

vale (vāl), *n.* poetic variant of valley.

va·le (vă′lē, wä′lā), *interj.* & *n.* [Latin], farewell.

val·e·dic·tion (val-ē-dik′shŭn), *n.* 1. the act of bidding farewell. 2. a speech or utterance made at parting.

val·e·dic·to·ri·an (-dik-tōr′i-ăn), *n.* the student, usually the one ranking highest in scholastic standing, who delivers the valedictory at commencement.

val·e·dic·to·ry (-dik′tēr-i), *adj.* given or done in bidding farewell: *n., pl.* -ries, a farewell address, especially one given at graduation.

va·lence (vā′lĕns), *n.* in *Chemistry,* 1. the degree of combining power of an element or radical, indicated by the number of atoms of hydrogen or chlorine which one atom of the element or one radical can combine with or can replace. 2. any of the units of valence, often one of several, that a given element may possess. Also **va′len·cy,** *pl.* -cies.

Va·len·ci·ennes (vă-len-si-enz′), *n.* a rich bobbin lace having a floral pattern: also Valenciennes lace.

val·en·tine (val′ĕn-tīn), *n.* 1. a sweetheart chosen or complimented on St. Valentine's Day, February 14th. 2. a greeting card or present sent on this day, especially to a sweetheart.

va·le·ri·an (vă-lir′i-ăn), *n.* 1. any one of various plants having clusters of small, white or pinkish flowers. 2. a drug consisting of the dried rootstock and roots of a garden variety of valerian, formerly used as a sedative.

val·et (val′it, val′ā), *n.* 1. a man's personal attendant who performs services, as caring for clothes. 2. an employee, as of a hotel, who performs personal services for patrons, as pressing clothes, shining shoes, etc.: *v.i.* & *v.i.* to serve as a valet.

va·let de cham·bre (vă-lā dĕ shăm′br), *pl.* va·lets de cham′bre (vă-lā), [French], same as valet (sense 1).

val·e·tu·di·nar·i·an (val-ē-tōō-di-ner′i-ăn), *adj.* 1. chronically sick; in poor health. 2. overanxious about one's health: *n.* 1. a chronic invalid. 2. a person continuously alarmed or anxious about his health.

Val·hal·la (val-hal′ă), *n.* in *Norse Mythology,* the palace of immortality in which the souls of warriors valiantly fallen in battle were received by Odin.

val·iant (val′yănt), *adj.* possessing or marked by valor; brave; courageous; stouthearted. —val′iance, *n.* —val′iant·ly, *adv.*

val·id (val′id), *adj.* 1. carrying legal force; binding at law. 2. not weak or defective; sound; well-grounded. —val′id·ly, *adv.* —val′id·ness, *n.*

val·i·date (val′i-dāt), *v.t.* -dat·ed, -dat·ing, 1. to give legal form or force to; render legally binding. 2. to verify or substantiate the validity of. —val·i·da′tion, *n.*

va·lid·i·ty (vă-lid′i-ti), *n.* the state or quality of being valid in law, reasoning, etc.

va·lise (vă-lēs′), *n.* a small piece of hand luggage.

Val·i·um (val′ē-ŭm), *n.* a tranquilizing drug: a trademark.

Val·kyr·ie (val-kir′i, val′ki-ri), *n.* in *Norse Mythology,* any one of the handmaidens of Odin who select the warriors who will fall in battle and conduct their souls to Valhalla.

val·ley (val′i), *n., pl.* -leys. 1. a tract of land situated between ranges of hills or mountains and usually traversed by a river or stream. 2. the large land area drained or watered by an extensive river system. 3. any depression, dip, or hollow suggesting a valley.

val·or (val′ēr), *n.* exemplary courage or intrepidity; bravery: British spelling **val′our.** —**val′or·ous,** *adj.*

val·u·a·ble (val′yoo-bl, ′yoo-wă-bl), *adj.* 1. possessing qualities useful for a particular purpose. 2. having value and worth. 3. having great material value; costly: *n.* a thing or possession of value, as a piece of jewelry: *usually used in pl.* —val′u·a·bly, *adv.*

val·u·ate (val′yoo-wāt), *v.t.* -at·ed, -at·ing, to put a value on; appraise.

val·u·a·tion (val-yoo-wā′shŭn), *n.* 1. the act or process of deciding the worth or price of something; appraisal. 2. estimated or set worth or price on the market. 3. estimation of the value, merit, character, etc. of something.

val·ue·add·ed tax (val′ū-ad-id), a tax based and paid on products, etc. at each stage of production or distribution, and included in the cost to the consumer.

val·ue (val′ū), *n.* 1. that quality which renders something useful, estimable, etc. 2. the equivalent of something in goods or services. 3. the worth of something in money; market price. 4. something intrinsically useful or desirable. 5. *pl.* principles or standards. 6. relative intensity, duration, etc.: *v.t.* -ued, -u·ing, 1. to estimate the worth of; appraise. 2. to rate the relative worth of; evaluate. 3. to prize greatly; regard highly; esteem. —val′ue·less, *adj.*

val·ued (′ŭd), *adj.* highly esteemed or prized.

val·vate (val′vāt), *adj.* 1. having or marked by valves or valvelike parts. 2. in *Botany,* meeting at the edges, but not overlapping.

valve (valv), *n.* 1. in *Anatomy,* a membranous structure in an orifice or hollow tube, as a vein, that opens and closes a passage or allows the flow of body fluids in only one direction. 2. any one of various devices that regulate the movement of liquids, gases, etc. through a pipe, aperture, etc. by opening, closing, or partially blocking passage. 3. in *Music,* a device in a brass-wind instrument that rapidly varies the tube length in order to change the pitch. 4. in *Zoology,* one of the hinged divisions of the shell of a mollusk, clam, etc.

val·vu·lar (val′vyŭ-lēr), *adj.* 1. having the shape or action of a valve. 2. of or pertaining to a valve, especially of the heart.

val·vu·li·tis (valv-yŭ-līt'ĭs), *n.* inflammation of a valve, especially of the heart.

va·moose (va-mōōs'), *v.i.* -moosed', -moos'ing, [Old Slang], to depart hurriedly.

vamp (vamp), *n.* 1. the part of the upper of a boot or shoe that covers the instep and sometimes the toes. 2. a piece added to something old to give it a new appearance. 3. in *Music*, an improvised accompaniment: *v.t.* 1. to furnish or patch with a vamp. 2. in *Music*, to improvise.

vamp (vamp), shortened form of *vampire* (sense 3): *v.t.* to seduce or entrap (a man) by using the wiles of a vamp.

vam·pire (vam'pīr), *n.* 1. in *Folklore*, a corpse that can return from the dead at night to suck the blood of sleeping persons. 2. one who preys unscrupulously on others, as an extortionist. 3. a seductive woman who uses her charms to exploit and ruin men. 4. shortened form of *vampire bat*.

vampire bat, any one of various bats of the American tropics that bite vertebrates, especially stock animals, and drink the blood.

vam·pir·ism (-izm), *n.* 1. belief in vampires. 2. the actions of vampires in folklore; specifically, the sucking of blood. 3. the act of beguiling or preying upon other people.

van (van), *n.* same as vanguard.

van (van), *n.* 1. a large closed truck or wagon for moving household goods, freight, etc. 2. [British], a closed railroad baggage or freight car.

va·na·di·um (va-nā'di-ŭm), *n.* a ductile metallic chemical element found in combination with several minerals and used as a catalyst, in some steel alloys, etc.

vanadium steel, steel that is alloyed with vanadium to harden and strengthen it.

Van Al·len radiation belt (van al'ĕn), a zone of ionizing radiation trapped by the earth's magnetic field and encircling the earth in the outer atmosphere: after J. *Van Allen* (1914-), U.S. physicist.

Van·dal (van'dl), *n.* 1. any member of a Germanic people that overran and pillaged Gaul, Spain, and northern Africa, and sacked Rome in 455 A.D. 2. [v-], a person who ruthlessly and wantonly destroys or defaces public or private property, especially property that is beautiful or venerable.

van·dal·ism (-izm), *n.* the actions or attitudes of the Vandals or a vandal; wanton and deliberate destruction of public or private property.

van·dal·ize (-īz), *v.t.* -ized, -iz·ing, to destroy or deface (public or private property) maliciously.

Van·dyke beard (van-dīk'), a beard trimmed to a point: after A. *Vandyke* (1599-1641), Flemish painter, in England after 1632.

Vandyke brown, a deep-brown pigment.

Vandyke collar, a large lace or linen collar with a deeply indented edge.

vane (vān), *n.* 1. a thin piece of metal, wood, etc. that turns on a spindle attached to a spire, tower, etc. and shows the direction of the wind. 2. any one of several rigid, flat or curved pieces that are rotated about an axis by a moving fluid or that rotate to move a fluid.

van·guard (van'gärd), *n.* 1. the advance guard of an army, that precedes the main body. 2. the foremost position or persons in a movement.

va·nil·la (va-nil'ä), *n.* 1. any one of various tropical American orchids with greenish flowers. 2. the podlike, aromatic capsule of some of these plants. 3. a flavoring extract made from these capsules, used in cooking, baking, etc.

va·nil·lin ('in), *n.* a fragrant constituent of vanilla capsules, extracted from the pods as a white, crystalline compound and used in flavorings, perfumes, etc.

van·ish (van'ish), *v.i.* 1. to disappear; pass quickly from sight. 2. to pass away; pass out of existence.

van·i·ty (van'i-ti), *n., pl.* -ties, 1. the quality or condition of being vain; excessive pride in one's appearance, abilities, etc.; conceit. 2. empty show; worthlessness. 3. anything that is fruitless or futile. 4. a low table with a mirror for use when dressing, applying cosmetics, etc.

vanity case, a small case used by women for carrying cosmetics, toiletries, etc.

Vanity Fair, any place where vanity, folly, frivolity, etc. exist: after the fair in Bunyan's "Pilgrim's Progress."

van·quish (vang'kwish, van'-), *v.t.* 1. to conquer; subdue. 2. to defeat in any contest or competition, as in debate.

van·tage (van'tij), *n.* 1. an advantageous position. 2. a position providing a wider or comprehensive outlook or perspective: also vantage point.

vap·id (vap'id), *adj.* 1. lacking taste; flat; stale. 2. lacking zest; dull; insipid. —vap'id·ly, *adv.* —vap'id·ness, *n.*

va·pid·i·ty (va-pid'i-ti), *n.* the state or quality of being vapid; dullness.

va·por (vā'pẽr), *n.* 1. barely perceptible droplets of moisture suspended in the air, as mist, steam, etc. 2. smoke; fumes. 3. a substance in the gaseous state as opposed to its usually liquid or solid form. 4. *pl.* [Archaic], *a)* exhalations from the stomach believed injurious to mental or physical health; *b)* hysteria or hypochondria. British spelling va'pour.

va·por·if·ic (vā-pô-rif'ik), *adj.* same as vaporous.

va·por·im·e·ter (vā-pô-rim'ê-tẽr), *n.* an instrument for determining vapor pressure or volume.

va·por·ing (vā'pẽr-ing), *adj.* bragging; boasting: *n.* bombastic or high-flown speech or behavior.

va·por·ize (vā'pô-rīz), *v.t.* & *v.i.* -ized, -iz·ing, to convert into vapor, as by heating. —va·por·i·za'tion, *n.*

va·por·i·zer (-ri-zẽr), *n.* a device used to vaporize liquids, as an atomizer, a fuel jet, etc.

va·por·ous ('pẽr-ŭs), *adj.* 1. full of or like vapor. 2. releasing vapor. 3. unsubstantial; unreal.

ō in dragon, ōō in crude, oo in wool, u in cup, ŭ in cure, û in turn, ù in focus, oi in boy, ou in house, th in thin, th in sheathe, g in get, j in joy, y in yet.

vapor pressure, the pressure exerted by a vapor in equilibrium with its liquid or solid phase.

vapor trail, same as contrail.

va·por·y (vā'pēr-ĭ), adj. same as vaporous.

va·que·ro (vä-ker'ō), n., pl. -ros, in the southwestern U.S., a herdsman of cattle; cowboy.

var·i·a·ble (ver'ĭ-à-bl), adj. 1. changeable; inconstant; fickle. 2. in Biology, tending not to run true to type; aberrant: n. 1. anything that changes or varies. 2. in Mathematics, a quantity capable of having any one of a set of values. 3. a shifting wind. —var·i·a·bil'i·ty, n.

var·i·ance (-åns), n. 1. the condition, fact, or state of being variant or variable. 2. a degree of difference or change; divergence.

var·i·ant (-ånt), adj. variable; different in some way from the usual form: n. 1. a different form of substantially the same thing, as a different spelling or pronunciation of the same word. 2. in Biology, an organism that displays variation from a type.

var·i·ate (-ĭt), n. same as variant.

var·i·a·tion (ver-ĭ-ā'shŭn), n. 1. the condition, act, or process of varying; change or divergence in form, character, etc. 2. extent of such a modification. 3. in Music, the repetition of a theme with embellishments. 4. a change in the mean motion or orbit of a heavenly body. 5. in Biology, a change in structure or function from the type or parental source. 6. the deviation of a magnetic needle from true north.

var·i·cel·la (var-ĭ-sel'å), n. same as chicken pox.

var·i·co·cele (var'ĭ-kō-sēl), n. a swelling of the veins of the spermatic cord.

var·i·col·ored (ver'ĭ-kul-ērd), adj. having various colors.

var·i·cose (var'ĭ-kōs), adj. abnormally swollen or enlarged: said of veins.

var·ied (ver'ĭd), adj. 1. altered; partially changed. 2. of different forms or kinds; various.

var·i·e·gate (ver'ĭ-ē-gāt), v.t. -gat·ed, -gat·ing, 1. to give a different appearance to, as by marking with colors. 2. to diversify.

var·i·e·gat·ed (-ĭd), adj. 1. having spots, marks, or streaks of different colors. 2. characterized by variety; diversified.

var·i·e·ga·tion (ver-ĭ-ē-gā'shŭn), n. 1. the act of variegating or the state of being variegated. 2. variety in appearance, form, etc.; especially, diversity of colors.

va·ri·e·ty (vå-rī'ē-tĭ), n., pl. -ties, 1. the state or quality of being various or varied. 2. an intermixture or collection of different things. 3. a diverse form, sort, etc. of something. 4. in Biology, a subdivision of a species.

variety store, a retail store stocking an extensive variety of merchandise, usually items of low cost.

va·ri·o·la (vå-rī'ō-là), n. any one of several viral diseases, as smallpox, cowpox, etc., marked by pustular eruptions.

var·i·o·loid (var'ĭ-ō-loid), n. a mild form of variola occurring in persons who have previously had the disease or have been vaccinated.

var·i·o·rum (ver-ĭ-ôr'ŭm), n. 1. an edition of a literary work having notes by various schol-

ars, editors, etc. 2. an edition having variant versions of a text: adj. of or pertaining to such an edition or text.

var·i·ous (ver'ĭ-ŭs), adj. 1. different; of diverse kinds. 2. several; numerous. 3. individual and separate. —var'i·ous·ly, adv.

var·ix (ver'iks), n., pl. var'i·ces ('ĭ-sēz), in Medicine, a swollen or distorted vein or lymph vessel; especially, a varicose vein.

var·let (vär'lĭt), n. [Archaic], a rascal; knave; scoundrel.

var·mint, var·ment (vär'mĭnt), n. [Dial.], a person or animal considered obnoxious or troublesome.

var·nish (vär'nĭsh), n. 1. a viscid, resinous liquid, used for giving a glossy surface to wood, metal, etc. 2. the glaze imparted to a surface by the application of varnish. 3. a smooth, external appearance, as of manner: v.t. 1. to cover with varnish. 2. to make deceptively attractive.

var·si·ty (vär'sĭ-tĭ), n., pl. -ties, the primary team representing a school, university, etc. in competitions, as in sports.

Var·u·na (vŭr'oo-nà), n. the Hindu god of the cosmos.

var·us (ver'ŭs), n. a malformation of a bone; especially, a condition in which the foot is abnormally bent inward.

var·y (ver'ĭ), v.t. var'ied, var'y·ing, 1. to change; alter in form, attributes, etc. 2. to make distinct from another. 3. to make varied; diversify: v.i. 1. to undergo a change. 2. to be distinct. 3. to depart (from).

vas·cu·lar (vas'kyū-lēr), adj. of, marked by, or containing vessels for the transmission of blood, lymph, sap, etc.

vase (vās, vāz), n. an ornamental vessel open at one end, used for displaying flowers, for decoration, etc.

vas·ec·to·my (vas-ek'tō-mĭ), n., pl. -mies, the surgical excision of part of the sperm duct to produce sterility.

Vas·e·line (vas'ē-lēn), n. 1. petrolatum: a trademark. 2. [v-], petrolatum.

vas·o·con·stric·tor (vàs-ō-kŏn-strik'tēr), adj. in Physiology, causing constriction of the blood vessels: n. a nerve or drug causing such constriction. —vas·o·con·stric'tion, n.

vas·o·di·la·tor (-dī-lāt'ēr), adj. in Physiology, causing dilatation of the blood vessels: n. a nerve or drug causing such dilatation. —vas·o·di·la·ta'tion (-dil·à-tā'shŭn), vas·o·di·la'tion (-dĭ-lā'shŭn), n.

vas·o·mo·tor (-mōt'ēr), adj. in Physiology, of, pertaining to, or being a nerve or drug that controls the contraction or expansion of blood vessels.

vas·sal (vas'l), n. 1. in the Middle Ages, a person who held land from a feudal lord, paying homage and allegiance in return for protection. 2. a subordinate, bondsman, slave, etc.: adj. of, pertaining to, or being a vassal.

vas·sal·age (-ĭj), n. 1. the state of being a vassal. 2. fealty and service required of a vassal. 3. dependence; servitude. 4. vassals collectively. 5. land held by a vassal; fief.

vast (vast), adj. 1. of great extent; immense. 2. very great in number, degree, intensity, etc.:

a in cap, ā in cane, ä in father, å in abet, e in met, ē in be, ĕ in baker, ê in regent, i in pit, ī in fine, ĭ in manifest, o in hot, ô in horse, ō in bone,

n. [Archaic]. a boundless space. —**vast′ly**, *adv.* —**vast′ness**, *n.*

vat (vat), *n.* a large container, as a tub, barrel, etc., for holding or storing liquids: *v.t.* **vat′‐ted**, **vat′ting**, to place or treat in a vat.

vat‐ic (vat′ik), *adj.* of or pertaining to a prophet; oracular.

Vat‐i‐can (vat′i‐kn), *n.* 1. the palace of the Pope at Rome. 2. the papal government or authority.

va‐tic‐i‐nal (va‐tis′ĭ‐nl), *adj.* prophetic.

va‐tic‐i‐nate (‐nāt), *v.t. & v.i.* ‐**nat‐ed**, ‐**nat‐ing**, to prophesy; foretell. —**vat‐i‐ci‐na‐tion** (vat‐i‐si‐nā′shŭn), *n.*

vaude‐ville (vôd′vil, vôd′‐; ‐ĕ‐vil), *n.* 1. a stage entertainment presenting a variety of short acts, as songs, dances, impersonations, etc. 2. [Now Rare], a comic play, frequently including dancing, pantomime, and songs.

vault (vôlt), *n.* 1. an arched roof or ceiling, usually of masonry. 2. a covering resembling this, as the sky. 3. an arched room or space, especially when underground, as a cellar storeroom. 4. a burial chamber. 5. a room or compartment designed to keep valuables safe, as in a bank: *v.t.* to cover with, or construct as, a vault.

vault (vôlt), *v.i. & v.t.* to leap, spring, or bound, as over an obstacle, with the hands holding onto the obstacle or onto a long pole: *n.* an act of vaulting. —**vault′er**, *n.*

vault‐ed (vôl′tid), *adj.* 1. arched. 2. having a vault.

vault‐ing (′ting), *adj.* 1. leaping. 2. overreaching.

vaunt (vônt), *v.t. & v.i. & n.* same as boast. —**vaunt′ed**, *adj.*

vav (väv, vôv), *n.* the sixth letter of the Hebrew alphabet.

VD, V.D., venereal disease.

Ve‐a‐dar (vā‐ä‐där′), *n.* an intercalary month of the Jewish year, occurring in leap years between Adar and Nisan.

veal (vēl), *n.* calf's flesh used as food.

vec‐tor (vek′tĕr), *n.* 1. in *Biology*, an organism, as an insect, that transmits pathogens from host to host. 2. in *Mathematics*, a quantity that has a fixed direction and definite magnitude.

Ve‐da (vā′dä, vē′‐), *n.* 1. any one of the oldest sacred writings of the Hindus, collected into four books of hymns, chants, etc. 2. these books collectively. —**Ve‐da‐ic** (vi‐dā′ik), *adj.*

Ve‐dan‐ta (vi‐dän′tä), *n.* a Hindu system of philosophy based on the Vedas. —**Ve‐dan′tic**, *adj.*

ve‐dette (vi‐det′), *n.* 1. formerly, a mounted sentinel stationed in advance of the pickets. 2. a famous personality, especially a luminary of the entertainment world.

Ve‐dic (vā′dik), *n.* the language in which the Vedas are written: *adj.* of the Vedas.

veer (vir), *v.i. & v.t.* to change direction; swing; turn: *n.* a change of direction.

veg‐e‐ta‐ble (vej′ĕ‐tȧ‐bl, vej′ĕ‐tä‐), *adj.* 1. of or pertaining to plants. 2. of, having the nature of, produced by, or consisting of plants: *n.* 1. any plant as distinct from animal or inorganic matter. 2. a plant that is cul‐

tivated for an edible part or parts, as the leaves, roots, etc.

vegetable ivory, the ivorylike seed of a South American palm, used to make small objects, as buttons.

vegetable marrow, [Chiefly British], any one of various long, egg‐shaped summer squashes with tender flesh.

veg‐e‐tal (vej′ĕ‐tl), *adj.* 1. same as vegetable. 2. same as vegetative.

veg‐e‐tar‐i‐an (vej‐ĕ‐ter′i‐ȧn), *n.* one who abstains from a meat diet, usually for reasons of health or principle, and lives solely on fruit, vegetables, nuts, and farinaceous food: *adj.* 1. of or pertaining to vegetarians. 2. consisting of vegetables.

veg‐e‐tar‐i‐an‐ism (‐izm), *n.* the theory or practice of vegetarians.

veg‐e‐tate (vej′ĕ‐tāt), *v.i.* ‐**tat‐ed**, ‐**tat‐ing**, 1. to grow as a plant does. 2. to live a useless, indolent life. —**veg′e‐ta‐tive**, *adj.*

veg‐e‐ta‐tion (vej‐ĕ‐tā′shŭn), *n.* 1. the act or process of vegetating. 2. plants collectively or an area of plant life.

ve‐he‐ment (vē′ĕ‐mĕnt), *adj.* 1. very violent or forcible. 2. passionate; ardent; energetic. —**ve′he‐mence, ve′he‐men‐cy**, *n.* —**ve′he‐ment‐ly**, *adv.*

ve‐hi‐cle (vē′i‐kl), *n.* 1. any conveyance for transporting or carrying persons or objects. 2. a medium in which some other thing is mixed or administered. 3. a medium through which something, as thought, emotion, etc., is communicated, displayed, achieved, etc. —**ve‐hic′u‐lar** (‐hik′yoo‐lẽr), *adj.*

veil (vāl), *n.* 1. a covering, more or less transparent, for the face. 2. a part of a nun's headdress. 3. the religious state or vows of a nun. 4. a curtain or covering for concealment or separation. 5. anything that conceals or obscures like a veil: *v.t.* 1. to cover with a veil. 2. to conceal or disguise.

veiled (vāld), *adj.* 1. wearing or covered with a veil. 2. hidden; obscured. 3. not flatly stated; disguised.

vein (vān), *n.* 1. any one of the vessels that convey blood to the heart. 2. any one of the riblike structures forming a supporting framework in a leaf blade or insect wing. 3. a lode. 4. a fissure in the earth containing a body of minerals. 5. a streak of color in wood or marble. 6. a pervasive quality or tendency in one's expression, thought, action, etc. 7. a transient attitude or frame of mind; mood: *v.t.* to fill or mark as with veins.

vein‐y (vā′ni), *adj.* **vein′i‐er, vein′i‐est**, 1. full of or displaying veins. 2. patterned or streaked with veins, as marble.

ve‐lar‐i‐um (vē‐ler′i‐ŭm), *n., pl.* ‐**i‐a** (‐ä). in ancient Rome, a great awning stretched over an open theater.

veld, veldt (velt), *n.* in South Africa, open, grassy country.

ve‐li‐tes (vē′li‐tēz), *n.pl.* in ancient Rome, lightly armed foot soldiers.

vel‐le‐i‐ty (vĕ‐lē′i‐ti), *n., pl.* ‐**ties**, 1. mere inclination unsupported by an action or effort. 2. the lowest degree of desire.

vel‐li‐cate (vel′i‐kāt), *v.t. & v.i.* ‐**cat‐ed**, ‐**cat‐ing**,

[Now Rare], to twitch, pluck, etc. —vel·li·ca'tion, n.

vel·lum (vel'ŭm), n. 1. a fine parchment made from calfskin, lambskin, etc. and used for writing material and book bindings. 2. a strong paper made to resemble vellum.

ve·loc·i·pede (vē-läs'i-pēd), n. 1. any one of various early, light, wheeled vehicles propelled by the rider's feet. 2. [Rare], same as tricycle.

ve·loc·i·ty (-ti), n., pl. -ties, 1. rapidity or quickness of motion; speed. 2. rate of movement of a body.

ve·lo·drome (vē'lō-drōm, vel'ō-), n. a building containing a depressed bowl designed for bicycle racing.

ve·lour, ve·lours (vē-loor'), n., pl. ve·lours', a plushlike fabric with a short nap, used for draperies, clothing, etc.

ve·lou·té (vē-lōō-tā'), n. a rich white sauce made with flour, butter, and fish or meat stock.

ve·lum (vē'lŭm), n., pl. ve'la ('lȧ), in Biology, a thin, membranous covering like a veil or curtain; especially, the soft palate. —ve'lar, adj.

ve·lure (vē-loor'), n. velvet or a heavy fabric of linen, silk, jute, etc. resembling velvet.

ve·lu·ti·nous (vē-lōōt'n-ŭs), adj. in Biology, covered with fine, silky hairs; velvety and soft.

vel·vet (vel'vit), n. 1. a fabric, usually made of silk, rayon, or nylon, with a short, soft, thick pile. 2. anything like velvet in texture or surface. 3. the soft, vascular skin on the newly growing antlers of a deer: adj. 1. made of or covered with velvet. 2. like or resembling velvet. —vel'vet·y, adj.

vel·vet·een (vel-vē-tēn'), n. a velvetlike fabric with a dense, short pile, usually made of cotton.

ve·na (vē'nȧ), n., pl. ve'nae ('nē), [Latin], a vein.

ve·nal (vē'nl), adj. 1. capable of being readily bought, bribed, or corrupted. 2. marked by corruption, bribery, mercenary dealings, etc. —ve·nal'i·ty, n. —ve'nal·ly, adv.

ve·nat·ic (vi-nat'ik), adj. [Now Rare], of, pertaining to, used in, fond of, or living by hunting: also ve·nat'i·cal.

ve·na·tion (vi-nā'shŭn), n. 1. an arrangement or distribution of veins, as in an animal structure, a leaf blade, or an insect's wing. 2. such veins collectively.

vend (vend), v.t. & v.i. to sell (goods). —vend'or, vend'er, n.

ven·dace (ven'dās), n., pl. -dace, -dac·es, a freshwater whitefish found in a few English and Scottish lakes.

vend·ee (ven-dē'), n. the buyer.

ven·det·ta (ven-det'tȧ), n. 1. a feud in which the relatives of a person who has been murdered or wronged exact blood vengeance upon the perpetrator or members of his family. 2. any continued quarrel or retaliatory feud.

vend·i·ble (ven'di-bl), adj. that can be sold: also vend'a·ble.

vending machine, a slot machine for dispensing certain foods, drinks, articles, etc.

ve·neer (vē-nir'), v.t. 1. to overlay with a thin layer of ornamental or more valuable material; especially, to cover (a surface) with a fine-quality wood. 2. to conceal (a flaw, defect, etc.) by superimposing an attractive but superficial appearance or gloss. 3. to glue together (thin layers of wood) to make plywood: n. 1. a thin layer of wood or more valuable material bonded to a common or inferior base. 2. any one of the thin layers forming plywood. 3. an outward display that camouflages that which underlies it; pretense.

ven·er·a·ble (ven'ēr-ȧ-bl), adj. 1. worthy of being respected or revered by virtue of age, position, etc. 2. rendered sacred by religious or historic association. 3. deserving veneration: used as a title for an Anglican archdeacon or for a Roman Catholic who has reached the lowest of the three degrees of sanctity. —ven·er·a·bil'i·ty, n.

ven·er·ate (ven'ēr-āt), v.t. -at·ed, -at·ing, to regard with the highest respect; esteem as sacred; revere.

ven·er·a·tion (ven-ēr-ā'shŭn), n. 1. the act of venerating or the state of being venerated. 2. profound respect and reverence. 3. an act displaying this.

ve·ne·re·al (vē-nir'i-ȧl), adj. 1. of or pertaining to sexual intercourse. 2. contracted during sexual intercourse. 3. of, pertaining to, or infected with a venereal disease.

ven·er·y (ven'ēr-i), n. [Archaic]. 1. the pursuit of sexual gratification. 2. sexual intercourse.

ven·er·y (ven'ēr-i), n. [Archaic], the act, skill, or sport of hunting game; the chase.

ven·e·sec·tion (ven-ē-sek'shŭn), n. same as phlebotomy.

Ve·ne·tian (vē-nē'shŭn), adj. of or pertaining to Venice, a seaport in northern Italy, its inhabitants, culture, etc.: n. a native or inhabitant of Venice.

Venetian blind, [also v- b-], a window blind formed of thin, parallel slats that can be raised or lowered with one cord and can be set at various angles with another, thus controlling the admission of light.

venge·ance (ven'jȧns), n. the infliction of punishment on another as satisfaction for an injury or offense; retribution.

venge·ful (venj'fŭl), adj. desirous of vengeance; vindictive. —venge'ful·ly, adv.

ve·ni·al (vē'ni-ȧl, vēn'yȧl), adj. 1. that may be forgiven; pardonable. 2. in Theology, denoting a sin that is not a serious offense, is committed without sufficient reflection or full consent, and does not cause the full loss of sanctifying grace. —ve'ni·al·ly, adv.

ve·ni·re (vē-ni'rē), n. [Latin]. 1. a judicial writ issued to a sheriff or coroner, directing him to summon prospective jurors. 2. the panel from which a jury is selected.

ve·ni·re·man (-măn), n., pl. -men (-mĕn), a member of a venire.

ven·i·son (ven'i-sn, -zn), n. deer flesh used as food.

ven·om (ven'ŏm), n. 1. a poisonous secretion of certain snakes, spiders, fishes, etc., chiefly transmitted by a bite or sting. 2. malice; spite.

ven·om·ous (-ŭs), *adj.* 1. full of venom; poisonous. 2. malignant; spiteful. —ven′om·ous·ly, *adv.*

ve·nous (vē′nŭs), *adj.* 1. of or pertaining to veins. 2. in *Physiology*, denoting blood being returned to the heart through the veins.

vent (vent), *n.* 1. a means of escape; outlet; exit. 2. expression; utterance. 3. a small opening for the escape of gases, fumes, etc.: *v.t.* 1. to make an opening in or for. 2. to give expression to; let out.

vent (vent), *n.* a slit in a garment.

ven·ti·late (ven′tĭ-lāt), *v.t.* -lat·ed, -lat·ing, 1. to allow fresh air to enter so as to replace stale air. 2. to provide with an opening for the escape or circulation of air, gas, etc. 3. to expose to open and free discussion. —ven·ti·la′tion, *n.*

ven·ti·la·tor (ven′tĭ-lāt-ēr), *n.* one that ventilates; especially, a contrivance for removing stale air and drawing in and circulating fresh air.

ven·tral (ven′trăl), *adj.* of, pertaining to, on, or toward the belly.

ven·tri·cle (ven′trĭ-kl), *n.* in *Anatomy* & *Zoology*, any one of various cavities in an animal body or organ; especially, either one of the two lower chambers of the heart from which the blood is forced into the arteries.

ven·tri·cose (-kōs), *adj.* inflated; swollen; distended.

ven·tric·u·lar (ven-trik′yŭ-lēr), *adj.* of, pertaining to, or being a ventricle.

ven·tril·o·quism (ven-tril′ō-kwizm), *n.* the act or art of speaking so that vocal sounds appear to originate in a source other than the speaker.

ven·tril·o·quist (-kwist), *n.* a person who is expert in ventriloquism; specifically, an entertainer who carries on a supposed conversation with a dummy by the use of ventriloquism.

ven·ture (ven′chēr), *n.* 1. an undertaking that is risky or dangerous. 2. something on which a gamble is taken, as an investment in stocks, a stake in games of chance, etc.: *v.t.* -tured, -tur·ing, 1. to expose to risk; chance. 2. to express at the risk of criticism, rebuff, etc.: *v.i.* to dare; take a chance.

ven·ture·some (-sŭm), *adj.* 1. disposed to take risks; bold; daring. 2. hazardous; dangerous. —ven′ture·some·ly, *adv.*

ven·tur·ous (-ŭs), *adj.* same as **venturesome.**

ven·ue (ven′ū, ′ōō), *n.* 1. the country or place where a crime has been committed or where grounds for legal action has taken place. 2. the locality from which a jury is drawn and trial is held.

Ve·nus (vē′nŭs), *n.* 1. in *Roman Mythology*, the goddess of love, and beauty. 2. the most brilliant planet in the solar system, second in distance from the sun: as the morning star this planet was called Lucifer by the ancients and as the evening star, Hesperus.

Ve·nus′ fly-trap (vē′nŭs-iz flī′trap), a plant found in swampy areas of the southeastern U.S., having hinged leaf blades that close to trap insects.

ve·ra·cious (vē·rā′shŭs), *adj.* 1. truthful; honest. 2. precise; accurate.

ve·rac·i·ty (vē·ras′ĭ-tĭ), *n.* 1. truthfulness; honesty. 2. conformity with truth. 3. accuracy; precision. 4. truth.

ve·ran·da, ve·ran·dah (vē·ran′dă), *n.* a balcony, porch, or open portico, usually covered, extending along the outside of a building.

ver·a·trine (ver′ă-trēn), *n.* an extremely poisonous mixture of colorless alkaloids extracted from sabadilla seeds, formerly used as a counterirritant.

verb (vŭrb), *n.* that part of speech that expresses action, being, or a state of being.

ver·bal (vŭr′bl), *adj.* 1. expressed in words; oral. 2. of, in, or pertaining to words. 3. [Now Rare], verbatim. 4. of, having the function of, or derived from a verb. —ver′bal·ly, *adv.*

ver·bal·ism (-izm), *n.* 1. something expressed verbally; a word or phrase. 2. wordiness; verbiage.

ver·bal·ize (vŭr′bă-līz), *v.i.* -ized, -iz·ing, to communicate or express in words: *v.t.* to name or describe in words.

verbal noun, in *Grammar*, a noun derived from a verb and in some uses functioning like a verb.

ver·ba·tim (vēr-bā′tĭm), *adv.* & *adj.* word for word.

ver·be·na (vēr-bē′nă), *n.* any one of a group of ornamental, fragrant plants, with dense terminal clusters or spikes of sweet-scented red, white, or purple flowers.

ver·bi·age (vŭr′bi-ij), *n.* wordiness; verbosity.

ver·bose (vēr-bōs′), *adj.* wordy; prolix. —verbose′ly, *adv.* —ver·bos′i·ty (-bos′i-ti), *n.*

ver·dant (vŭr′dnt), *adj.* 1. green. 2. covered with green, growing plants. 3. inexperienced; callow. —ver′dan·cy (′dn-si), *n.* —ver′dant·ly, *adv.*

verd antique, 1. a green mottled or veined marble, used for interior decoration. 2. a dark-green, volcanic porphyry containing embedded crystals of feldspar.

ver·der·er, ver·der·or (vŭr′dēr-ēr), *n.* in medieval England, an official who had charge of the royal forests.

ver·dict (vŭr′dikt), *n.* 1. in *Law*, the finding of a jury on the matter submitted to them in trial. 2. decision; judgment.

ver·di·gris (vŭr′di-grēs), *n.* 1. the blue-green substance that forms a coating on copper, bronze, or brass. 2. a poisonous blue or green pigment prepared by the action of acetic acid on copper.

ver·di·ter (vŭr′di-tēr), *n.* either one of two copper carbonates, used as a blue or green pigment.

ver·dure (vŭr′jēr), *n.* 1. the fresh green color of growing vegetation; greenness. 2. green vegetation.

verge (vŭrj), *n.* 1. a rod, staff, mace, etc. carried in processions as an emblem of office or authority. 2. the spindle of a balance wheel in a clock or watch. 3. the border, limit, or edge (*of* something); brink: *v.i.* verged, verg′ing, to approach the verge; border (with *on* or *upon*).

verge (vŭrj), *v.i.* verged, verg′ing, 1. to slope or

ŏ in dragon, ōō in crude, ōō in wool, ŭ in cup, ū in cure, ū in turn, ŭ in focus, oi in boy, ou in house, th in thin, th in sheathe, g in get, j in joy, y in yet.

íncline (*toward* or *to*). 2. to be tending toward, or changing slowly into, something else.

verg·er (vür'jēr), *n.* 1. a person who carries a verge before a bishop, justice, etc. in a procession. 2. a church official who serves as a caretaker or usher.

ve·rid·i·cal (vē·rid'i·k'l), *adj.* 1. truthful; veracious. 2. real; genuine.

ver·i·fy (ver'i·fī), *v.t.* -fied, -fy·ing, 1. to prove to be true by evidence, testimony, etc.; substantiate. 2. to test the truth or accuracy of, as by examination, comparison, or reference to the facts. —ver'i·fi·a·ble, *adj.* —ver·i·fi·ca'tion, *n.*

ver·i·ly (ver'i·li), *adv.* [Archaic], in truth; certainly.

ver·i·si·mil·i·tude (ver·i·si·mil'i·tōōd, -tūd), *n.* 1. the appearance of truth or reality. 2. something that has this appearance.

ver·i·ta·ble (ver'i·tä·bl), *adj.* true; genuine.

ver·i·ty (ver'i·ti), *n., pl.* -ties, 1. agreement with fact; truth; reality. 2. a belief, doctrine, etc. regarded as basic, unchangeable truth.

ver·juice (vür'jōōs), *n.* 1. an acid liquor expressed from green or unripe fruit, as grapes, apples, etc. 2. sourness of disposition, manner, etc.

ver·meil (vür'mil), *n.* gilded copper, bronze, or silver: *adj.* [Obs.], bright-red.

ver·mi·cel·li (vür·mi·sel'i, -chel'i), *n.* a stiff paste of fine flour made into long strands like spaghetti, but thinner in diameter.

ver·mi·cide (vür'mi·sīd), *n.* any substance that kills worms, especially a drug that destroys intestinal worms.

ver·mic·u·lar (ver·mik'yū·lēr), *adj.* 1. having the shape or motion of a worm. 2. covered with irregular markings resembling the tracks of a worm. 3. of or pertaining to worms. 4. made or caused by worms.

ver·mic·u·late (ver·mik'yū·lāt), *v.t.* -lat·ed, -lat·ing, to ornament with markings or tracery resembling the tracks of a worm: *adj.* (-mik'yū·lit, -lāt), same as **vermiculate**.

ver·mic·u·la·tion (ver·mik·yū·lā'shūn), *n.* 1. vermicular ornamentation or design. 2. the act of vermiculating or the state of being vermiculated. 3. wormlike movement, as the wavelike contractions of the intestine; peristalsis.

ver·mi·form (vür'mi·fôrm), *adj.* resembling a worm in shape.

vermiform appendix, same as **appendix** (appendage of the intestine).

ver·mi·fuge (vür'mi·fūj), *n.* any agent that destroys or expels intestinal worms.

ver·mil·ion (ver·mil'yūn), *n.* 1. a bright-red mercuric sulfide, used as a pigment. 2. brilliant red or scarlet: *adj.* of a vermilion color.

ver·min (vür'min), *n., pl.* -min, 1. any one of various small animals or insects, as rats, fleas, etc., that are injurious to property or health. 2. a low, despicable person.

ver·mi·na·tion (vür·mi·nā'shūn), *n.* [Archaic], 1. the state of being infested with worms or vermin. 2. the breeding or spreading of worms or vermin.

ver·min·ous ('mi·nûs), *adj.* 1. of or pertaining to vermin. 2. infested with vermin. 3. having the nature of vermin.

ver·mouth (ver·mōōth'), *n.* a white wine flavored with aromatic herbs, served as an aperitif or in mixed drinks.

ver·nac·u·lar (ver·nak'yū·lēr), *adj.* 1. using the native language of a country or region as distinguished from literary language. 2. commonly spoken by the inhabitants of a specific country or region. 3. of, pertaining to, or written in the native language: *n.* 1. the native language or dialect of a country or region. 2. the everyday language commonly used by a people. 3. the specialized vocabulary and idioms of a trade or profession.

ver·nac·u·lar·ism (-izm), *n.* 1. a vernacular word, phrase, or idiom. 2. the use of vernacular language.

ver·nal (vür'nl), *adj.* 1. of, pertaining to, or appearing in the spring. 2. springlike; fresh. 3. young; youthful.

vernal equinox, see **equinox**.

ver·na·tion (ver·nā'shūn), *n.* in *Botany*, the arrangement of foliage leaves within a bud.

ver·ni·er (vür'ni·ēr), *n.* a small, graduated scale that slides along a main, graduated scale to indicate fractional parts of the subdivisions of the main scale.

Ver·o·nal (ver'ō·nl), *n.* same as **barbital**: a trademark.

ve·ron·i·ca (vē·ron'i·kä), *n.* 1. a cloth or handkerchief bearing a representation of the face of Christ. 2. in *Bullfighting*, a maneuver in which the cape is passed before the charging bull by the matador, who pivots slowly.

ver·ru·ca (vē·rōō'kä), *n., pl.* -cae ('sē), 1. same as **wart**. 2. in *Biology*, a wartlike projection, as on a toad's back or on some leaves. — **ver·ru·cose** (ver'oo·kōs), **ver'ru·cous** (-kûs), *adj.*

ver·sant (vür'sânt), *n.* 1. the slope of a mountain or chain of mountains. 2. the general slope of any region.

ver·sa·tile (vür'sä·tl), *adj.* 1. turning with ease from one subject, field, occupation, etc. to another; many-sided. 2. capable of many uses or serving varied functions. —**ver'sa·tile·ly**, *adv.* —**ver·sa·til'i·ty** (-til'i·ti), *n.*

verse (vürs), *n.* 1. a metrical line of words; line of poetry. 2. a stanza or other subdivision of a metrical composition. 3. poetry in general. 4. a specific type of poetry. 5. a poem. 6. in the *Bible*, any one of the numbered subdivisions of a chapter.

versed (vürst), *adj.* skilled; conversant.

ver·si·cle (vür'si·kl), *n.* 1. a short verse. 2. a short sentence said or chanted by a priest, to which the congregation responds.

ver·si·fy (vür'si·fī), *v.i.* -fied, -fy·ing, to compose verses: *v.t.* 1. to relate or treat of in verse. 2. to turn into verse. —**ver·si·fi·ca'tion** (-fi·kä'shûn), *n.* —**ver'si·fi·er**, *n.*

ver·sion (zhûn), *n.* 1. a translation from one language into another. 2. a translation of the Bible or a part thereof. 3. a particular account or description by one or several persons. 4. a variation or modification of something. 5. in *Medicine*, the act of turning the fetus during childbirth for easier delivery.

ver·so (vûr'sō), *n., pl.* **-sos**, in *Printing*, any left-hand page of a book; the opposite side of a leaf.

verst (vûrst), *n.* a former Russian unit of linear measure, equal to about 3,500 feet.

ver·sus (vûr'sûs), *prep.* 1. against. 2. as compared to or contrasted with.

vert (vûrt), *n.* 1. [British], thick green vegetation in a forest, as cover for deer. 2. in *Heraldry*, the color green.

ver·te·bra (vûr'tê-brà), *n., pl.* **-brae** (-brē), **-bras**, any one of the single bones of the spinal column.

ver·te·bral (-brăl), *adj.* 1. of, pertaining to, or having the nature of a vertebra or vertebrae. 2. forming or composed of vertebrae.

ver·te·brate (-brit, -brāt), *adj.* 1. having a backbone or spinal column. 2. of or pertaining to the vertebrates: *n.* any one of a large group of animals having a spinal column, including mammals, birds, fishes, reptiles, and amphibians.

ver·te·bra·tion (vûr'tê-brā'shûn), *n.* formation into vertebrae; segmentation into vertebrae.

ver·tex (vûr'teks), *n., pl.* **-tex·es**, **-ti·ces** ('tï-sēz), 1. the highest point; top; summit; apex. 2. same as zenith. 3. in *Anatomy & Zoology*, the crown of the head. 4. in *Geometry*, the point where the two sides of an angle intersect.

ver·ti·cal (vûr'ti-kl), *adj.* 1. of, pertaining to, or situated at the vertex; directly overhead. 2. perpendicular to the plane of the horizon: *n.* a vertical line, circle, etc. —**ver'ti·cal·ly**, *adv.*

vertical circle, any great circle that passes through the zenith or nadir of an imaginary sphere which contains the whole universe.

ver·ti·cil (vûr'ti-sil), *n.* in *Botany*, a whorl of leaves or flowers around a stem.

ver·tig·i·nous (vûr-tij'ï-nùs), *adj.* 1. affected by or causing vertigo; dizzy. 2. revolving; spinning.

ver·ti·go (vûr'ti-gō), *n.* a sickening feeling of dizziness.

ver·tu (vêr-tōō'), *n.* same as virtu.

ver·vain (vûr'vän), *n.* any one of a number of verbenas.

verve (vûrv), *n.* 1. vivacity or liveliness, as in action, expression, etc. 2. animation, enthusiasm; spirit.

ver·vet (vûr'vit), *n.* a small monkey of eastern and southern Africa, having a reddish-brown patch at the base of the tail.

ver·y (ver'i), *adj.* **ver'i·er**, **ver'i·est**, 1. complete. 2. identical; same. 3. suitable; precise. 4. actual: *adv.* 1. extremely; to a high degree. 2. actually; truly.

very high frequency, any radio frequency ranging between 30 and 300 megahertz.

very low frequency, any radio frequency ranging between 10 and 30 kilohertz.

ves·i·cant (ves'i-kânt), *adj.* causing blisters: *n.* something that causes blisters, as any one of various poisonous gases used in chemical

warfare. Also **ves'i·ca·to·ry** (-kâ-tôr-i), *adj. & n., pl.* **-ries.**

ves·i·cate (-kät), *v.t. & v.i.* **-cat·ed**, **-cat·ing**, to blister. —**ves·i·ca'tion**, *n.*

ves·i·cle (ves'i-kl), *n.* a small bladderlike sac, cavity, or cyst. —**ve·sic·u·lar** (vê-sik'yû-lêr), **ve·sic'u·late** (-lit), *adj.*

ves·per (ves'pêr), *adj.* of or pertaining to the evening: *n.* 1. originally, evening. 2. [Poetic], [V-], same as evening star. 3. any one of various evening prayers or services. 4. *pl.* [often V-]. *a)* in the *Roman Catholic Church*, the sixth of the daily canonical hours, recited in the late afternoon; *b)* in the *Anglican Church*, same as evensong (sense 2).

ves·per·tine (ves'pêr-tin, -tin), *adj.* 1. of or happening in the evening. 2. in *Botany*, blossoming in the evening. 3. in *Zoology*, appearing or flying in the early evening. Also **ves·per·ti·nal** (ves-pêr-tï'nl).

ves·pi·ar·y (ves'pi-er-i), *n., pl.* **-ar·ies**, a nest or colony of social wasps.

ves·pid (ves'pid), *n.* any one of a worldwide group of social wasps, including the hornets and yellow jackets, that live in colonies: *adj.* of or pertaining to these wasps.

ves·sel (ves'l), *n.* 1. a utensil for holding something, as a bowl, kettle, etc. 2. a boat or ship. 3. a tube or canal of the body, as a vein, in which fluids are contained or transported. 4. [Chiefly Biblical], a person regarded as the recipient or instrument of some quality, spirit, etc.

vest (vest), *n.* a short garment without sleeves, worn, especially under a suit or sport coat, by men; waistcoat: *v.t.* 1. to clothe with a garment; dress, as in clerical robes. 2. to place or settle in the control of a person (with *in*). 3. to endow (a person or group) with something, as power, authority, etc.: *v.i.* to become vested (*in* a person or persons), as a right, property, etc.

Ves·ta (ves'tà), *n.* 1. the Roman goddess of hearth, home, and culinary arts. 2. [v-], formerly, a short wax or wooden friction match.

ves·tal (ves'tl), *adj.* 1. of, pertaining to, or sacred to the goddess Vesta. 2. of vestal virgins. 3. chaste; pure: *n.* 1. short form of vestal virgin. 2. a chaste woman; virgin.

vestal virgin, any one of the small group of virgin priestesses who tended the sacred fire on the altar of the temple of Vesta in ancient Rome.

vest·ed (ves'tid), *adj.* 1. clothed, especially in clerical vestments. 2. in *Law*, permanent; inalienable; absolute.

ves·ti·ar·y (ves'ti-er-i), *adj.* [Rare], of or pertaining to vestments or clothes.

ves·ti·bule (ves'ti-būl), *n.* 1. a small entrance hall, as to a building. 2. in *Anatomy & Zoology*, a cavity or hollow acting as an entrance to another cavity, as to the inner ear.

ves·tige (ves'tij), *n.* 1. a mark left in the passing of something that no longer exists; trace; sign. 2. in *Biology*, the remains of an organ or part that had a function in an earlier stage. —**ves·tig'i·al** (-tij'i-âl, -tij'âl), *adj.*

vest·ing (vest'ing), *n.* the retention by an employee of all or part of pension rights regardless of change of employers, early retirement, etc.

vest·ment (vest'mĕnt), *n.* a garment or robe, especially an official or clerical gown.

vest-pock·et (vest'pok·it), *adj.* very small, or unusually small for its kind.

ves·try (ves'tri), *n., pl.* -tries, 1. a room in a church, where ecclesiastical vestments, vessels, etc. are kept; sacristy. 2. a room in a church, where meetings, Sunday school lessons, etc. are held. 3. a group of laymen who manage the temporal affairs of certain churches.

ves·try-man (-măn), *n., pl.* -men, any member of a vestry.

vet (vet), *n.* same as veterinarian.

vet (vet), *n.* same as veteran.

vetch (vech), *n.* any one of several leguminous plants, grown for green fodder.

vet·er·an (vet'ẽr·ăn, vet'răn), *adj.* 1. long-practiced or experienced. 2. of or pertaining to veterans: *n.* 1. a person of long service or experience, as in the army, navy, etc. 2. any person who has had military service.

vet·er·i·nar·i·an (vet-ẽr-ĭ-ner'ĭ-ăn), *n.* one who is licensed to practice veterinary medicine.

vet·er·i·nar·y (vet'ẽr-ĭ-ner-i), *adj.* denoting or of the branch of medicine dealing with the prevention and treatment of diseases in animals, especially domestic animals: *n., adj.* -nar·ies, same as veterinarian.

ve·to (vē'tō), *n., pl.* -toes, 1. the power of stopping or preventing some act. 2. an order putting such a prohibition into effect. 3. the right of one branch of a government to reject bills passed by another. 4. the use of this right: *v.t.* -toed, -to·ing, 1. to reject (a bill) by use of a veto. 2. to refuse assent to; prohibit.

vex (veks), *v.t.* 1. to irritate by small annoyances or provocations. 2. to harass; afflict.

vex·a·tion (vek-sā'shŭn), *n.* 1. an act of vexing or state of being vexed. 2. something that vexes; annoyance. —vex·a'tious ('shŭs), *adj.*

vi·a (vī'ă, vē'ă), *prep.* [Latin], by way of.

vi·a·ble (vī'ă-bl), *adj.* 1. capable of existing outside the uterus. 2. practicable; workable.

vi·a·duct (vī'ă-dukt), *n.* a long bridge supported on arches and piers, for conveying a railway, road, etc. over a valley, a gorge, etc.

vi·al (vī'ăl), *n.* a small vessel or bottle, usually of glass, for holding liquids, as medicines: *v.t.* -aled or -alled, -al·ing or -al·ling, to put into or keep in a vial.

vi·and (vī'ănd), *n.* 1. an article of food. 2. *pl.* food of different kinds; especially, delicacies.

vi·at·i·cum (vī-at'ĭ-kŭm), *n., pl.* -ca (-kă) -cums, [often V-], the Eucharist administered to a person in danger of death.

vi·a·tor (vī-āt'ẽr), *n., pl.* -tor·es (-ă-tŏr'ĕz), [Latin], a traveler; wayfarer.

vibes (vībz), *n.pl.* 1. [Informal], same as vibraphone. 2. [Slang], qualities, as in a person, thought of as being like vibrations which produce an emotional reaction.

vi·brant (vī'brănt), *adj.* 1. vibrating; quivering. 2. made by vibration; resonant: said of sound. 3. vivacious; full of energy. —vi'brant·ly, *adv.*

vi·bra·phone (vī'bră-fōn), *n.* a musical instrument similar to the marimba, but having a set of electrically operated resonant tubes for creating a gentle vibrato.

vi·brate (vī'brāt), *v.t.* -brat·ed, -brat·ing, 1. to cause to quiver. 2. to set in back-and-forth motion: *v.i.* 1. to swing back and forth; oscillate. 2. to quiver. 3. to resonate. 4. to thrill; be emotionally moved. 5. to waver; vacillate. —vi·bra'tion, *n.* —vi'bra·tor, *n.*

vi·bra·tile (vī'bră-til, -tĭl), *adj.* 1. characterized by vibration. 2. capable of vibration. 3. capable of or employing vibratory motion.

vi·bra·to (vi-brăt'ō), *n., pl.* -tos, in *Music,* a pulsating effect produced by minute and rapid variations in pitch.

vi·bris·sa (vi-bris'ă), *n., pl.* -sae ('ē), in *Anatomy & Zoology,* 1. any one of the stiff hairs that grow in or near the nostrils of certain animals and often serve as sensory organs. 2. any one of the hairlike feathers that grow near the beak of certain insectivorous birds.

vic·ar (vik'ẽr), *n.* 1. one authorized to perform the functions of another who holds higher office; deputy. 2. in the *Roman Catholic Church,* a clergyman who acts as a deputy of a bishop. 3. in the *Anglican Church,* a parish priest who receives a stipend or salary. 4. in the *Protestant Episcopal Church,* a minister in charge of a chapel, as deputy of another clergyman.

vic·ar·age (-ij), *n.* 1. the residence of a vicar. 2. the benefice or salary of a vicar. 3. the office or duties of a vicar.

vicar apostolic, *pl.* vicars apostolic, in the *Roman Catholic Church,* 1. a titular bishop acting in a missionary region as a representative of the Holy See. 2. a titular bishop administering a vacant see.

vic·ar-gen·er·al (vik'ẽr-jen'ẽr-ăl), *n., pl.* vic'ars-gen'er·al, 1. in the *Roman Catholic Church,* a priest acting as a deputy to a bishop to help in the administration of the diocese. 2. in the *Anglican Church,* a layman who serves as a deputy to an archbishop or bishop in the performance of administrative duties.

vi·car·i·ous (vī-ker'ĭ-ŭs), *adj.* 1. substituting for another person or thing. 2. performed or suffered by one person in the place of another. 3. experienced or shared by sympathetic or imagined participation in the experiences of another. —vi·car'i·ous·ly, *adv.*

vice (vīs), *n.* 1. a fault, defect, failing, etc. 2. an immoral practice or habit. 3. evil conduct; depravity. 4. prostitution.

vi·ce (vī'sē), *prep.* in the place of.

vice-, a prefix meaning *substituting, subordinate.*

vice admiral, a naval officer next in rank above a rear admiral and below an admiral.

vice-chan·cel·lor (vīs'chan'sĕ-lẽr), *n.* 1. an official next in rank below a chancellor; as in a university. 2. in *Law,* a judge in an equity court, subordinate to a chancellor.

vice-ge·rent (vīs-jir'ĕnt), *n.* a person appointed by a superior, especially by a ruler, to exercise the authority of the latter as his deputy: *adj.* of or pertaining to a vicegerent.

vice-pres·i·dent (vīs'prez'i-dĕnt), *n.* 1. one who acts in place of a president in case of the absence, death, incapacity, or removal of the latter: for the U.S. official, usually Vice President. 2. any one of several officers of a corporation, club, etc., each in charge of a department. —**vice'-pres'i·den·cy,** *n.*

vice-re·gal (vīs-rē'gl), *adj.* of or pertaining to a viceroy.

vice·roy (vīs'roi), *n.* one who rules a country, province, etc. in the name of, and by the authority of, the sovereign.

vice·roy·al·ty (vīs-roi'ăl-ti), *n., pl.* -ties, the office, dignity, or jurisdiction of a viceroy.

vi·ce ver·sa (vī'sē vûr'să, vīs' vûr'să), the order or relations being reversed.

vi·chy·ssoise (vē-shi-swäz', vish-i-), *n.* a cream soup of potatoes, onions, etc., usually served cold.

vi·cin·i·ty (vi-sin'ĭ-ti), *n., pl.* -ties, 1. nearness in place; proximity. 2. an adjacent place or region.

vi·cious (vish'ŭs), *adj.* 1. characterized by vice; morally corrupt or depraved. 2. faulty or flawed. 3. unruly. 4. spiteful; mean. 5. very forceful, intense, etc. —**vi'cious·ly,** *adv.* —**vi'cious·ness,** *n.*

vicious circle, a situation in which the solving of one problem only leads to another and then in turn to another and, eventually, back to the original problem.

vi·cis·si·tude (vi-sis'ĭ-tōōd, -tūd), *n.* 1. constant change or alternation. 2. *pl.* the constant changes in one's life or fortunes that seem unpredictable; ups and downs.

vic·tim (vik'tĭm), *n.* 1. a living being, usually some animal, sacrificed to a deity. 2. some person or thing destroyed or injured by some action, accident, circumstance, etc. 3. one who is swindled; dupe.

vic·tim·ize ('tĭ-mīz), *v.t.* -ized, -iz·ing, to make a victim of.

vic·tor (vik'tĕr), *n.* one who wins in a battle, struggle, etc.; conqueror.

vic·to·ri·a (vik-tôr'ĭ-ă), *n.* 1. a four-wheeled carriage for two persons, with a folding top. 2. an early type of touring automobile, with a folding top over the rear seat. 3. any one of a group of South American waterlilies with leaves like platters, up to seven feet wide.

Vic·to·ri·an (-ăn), *adj.* of or pertaining to the period when Victoria was queen of England (1837-1901).

vic·to·ri·ous (-tôr'ĭ-ŭs), *adj.* 1. having conquered in a battle or contest; triumphant. 2. of or contributing to victory. —**vic·to'ri·ous·ly,** *adv.*

vic·to·ry (vik'tĕr-i, 'tri), *n., pl.* -ries, 1. defeat of an enemy in battle or war. 2. success in any contest or struggle.

vict·ual (vit'l), *v.t.* -ualed or -ualled, -ual·ing or -ual·ling, to supply with food as provisions: *n.* 1. [Archaic], food. 2. *pl.* [Informal], articles of food prepared for use.

vict·ual·er, **vict·ual·ler** (-ēr), *n.* 1. formerly, a sutler. 2. [British], an innkeeper.

vi·cu·ña (vī-kōōn'yă, -kōōn'ă), *n., pl.* -ñas, -ña, 1. an animal of the South American Andes,

related to the llama, with soft, shaggy wool. 2. its wool or a fabric made from its wool.

vi·de (vī'dē), [Latin], see; refer to: used to direct the reader's attention to a certain page, book, etc.

vi·de·li·cet (vī-del'i-sit), *adv.* that is; to wit.

vid·e·o (vid'ĭ-ō), *adj.* 1. of or used in television. 2. of or pertaining to the picture portion of a telecast: distinguished from *audio.* 3. of or pertaining to data display on a computer terminal: *n.* 1. same as television. 2. same as videocassette, videotape, etc.

vid·e·o·cas·sette (vid'ĭ-ō-ka-set', -kă-set'), *n.* a cassette containing videotape.

videocassette recorder, a device for recording on and playing back videocassettes: also **video recorder.**

vid·e·o·disc (vid'ĭ-ō-disk), *n.* a disc on which images and sound can be recorded for reproduction on a television set.

vid·e·o·phone (vid'ĭ-ō-fōn), *n.* a telephone hooked into a television system so that pictures as well as voices are transmitted and received.

vid·e·o·tape (vid'ĭ-ō-tāp), *n.* a magnetic tape on which images and sounds can be recorded for reproduction on television: *v.t.* -taped, -tap·ing, to record on videotape.

vie (vī), *v.i.* vied, vy'ing, to strive for superiority (with someone); compete.

Vi·et·nam·ese (vē-ĕt-nă-mēz', vyet-nă-mēs'), *adj.* of or pertaining to Vietnam, a divided country in southeast Asia, or its people: *n.* 1. *pl.* -ese', a native or inhabitant of Vietnam. 2. the language of Vietnam.

view (vū), *n.* 1. the act of seeing. 2. vision; sight. 3. mental or intellectual perception. 4. a prospect or scene. 5. a picture of a scene. 6. a way of looking at something; opinion. 7. purpose; goal: *v.t.* 1. to look upon; see; behold. 2. to survey mentally; consider. 3. to examine; inspect. —**view'er,** *n.*

view·find·er ('fīn-dĕr), *n.* same as finder (camera device).

view·point ('point), *n.* the way in which something is viewed; point of view.

vig·il (vij'l), *n.* 1. the act of staying awake during the usual hours of sleeping. 2. the keeping of a watch. 3. the eve preceding a feast of the church.

vig·i·lance ('i-lăns), *n.* the state of being vigilant; watchfulness.

vigilance committee, a group that takes upon itself the authority to maintain order and punish crime while alleging that the usual law-enforcement agencies are ineffective or lacking.

vig·i·lant (vij'i-lănt), *adj.* alert and attentive to discover and avoid danger.

vig·i·lan·te (vij-i-lan'ti), *n.* one who belongs to a vigilance committee.

vi·gnette (vin-yet'), *n.* 1. a decorative design on a page of a book, as at the beginning or end of a chapter. 2. a picture or photograph shading off so that the border is indefinite. 3. a short literary sketch.

vig·or (vig'ĕr), *n.* physical or mental strength and energy; force.

vig·or·ous (-ŭs), *adj.* full of physical or mental

ō in dragon, ōō in crude, oo in wool, u in cup, ū in cure, û in turn, ŭ in focus, oi in boy, ou in house, th in thin, th in sheathe, g in get, j in joy, y in yet.

strength and energy; robust; forcible. —**vig′-**
or·ous·ly, *adv.*

vig·our (′ẽr), *n.* British form for vigor.

vik·ing (vī′king), *n.* [also V-], any one of the
Scandinavian pirates who ravaged the coasts
of Europe from the 8th to 10th centuries.

vi·la·yet (vē-lä-yet′), *n.* an administrative division of Turkey.

vile (vīl), *adj.* 1. morally base or depraved;
wicked. 2. despicable; disgusting. 3. low; degrading. 4. most unpleasant; very bad. —
vile′ly, *adv.* —**vile′ness,** *n.*

vil·i·fy (vil′i-fī), *v.t.* -fied, -fy·ing, to make slanderous statements about; revile; defame. —
vil·i·fi·ca′tion, *n.* —**vil′i·fi·er,** *n.*

vil·la (vil′ä), *n.* a country estate, especially one
with a large house used mostly in the sum-
mer.

vil·lage (vil′ij), *n.* an assemblage of houses,
smaller than a town but larger than a ham-
let.

vil·lag·er (-ẽr), *n.* an inhabitant of a village.

vil·lain (vil′ŭn), *n.* 1. an evil or wicked person.
2. an evil or wicked character in a novel,
play, etc. 3. same as villein.

vil·lain·ous (-ŭs), *adj.* 1. of or like a villain;
evil or wicked. 2. very unpleasant or bad.

vil·lain·y (-i), *n., pl.* -lain·ies, 1. extreme
wickedness or depravity. 2. a villainous act.

vil·lein (vil′ŭn), *n.* any one of a class of serfs
in feudal England.

vil·lein·age or **vil·len·age** (-ij), *n.* 1. the condition
of being a villein. 2. the form of tenure by
which a villein held his lands.

vil·li (vil′ī), *n.* plural of villus.

vil·li·form (′i-fôrm), *adj.* 1. having the form of
villi. 2. resembling the pile of velvet.

vil·los·i·ty (vi-läs′i-ti), *n., pl.* -ties, 1. the state
of being villous. 2. a surface covered with
villi.

vil·lous (vil′ŭs), *adj.* covered with long, thin,
soft hairs: also **vil′lose** (′ōs).

vil·lus (vil′ŭs), *n., pl.* **vil′li** (′ī), 1. any one of the
minute, hairlike processes on certain
mucous membranes, as of the small intestine or of the placenta of mammals. 2. any
one of the long, thin, soft hairs on certain
plants.

vim (vim), *n.* energy; vigor.

vi·ma·na (vi-mä′nä), *n.* a pyramidal tower
above the center of a Buddhist temple.

vi·men (vī′men), *n., pl.* **vim·i·na** (vim′i-nä), in
Botany, a long, flexible twig or shoot. —**vi-**
min·e·ous (vi-min′i-ŭs), **vim·i·nal** (vim′i-nål),
adj.

vin (van, vin), *n.* [French], wine.

vi·na (vē′nä), *n.* a musical instrument of India,
having seven strings, a long, fretted fingerboard, and one to three gourds attached as
resonators.

vi·na·ceous (vī-nä′shŭs), *adj.* 1. of or like
grapes or wine. 2. wine-colored; red.

vin·ai·grette (vin-i-gret′), *n.* a small decorative
box with a perforated lid, used for holding
aromatic vinegar or smelling salts.

vin·ci·ble (vin′si-bl), *adj.* capable of being conquered or overcome.

vin·cu·lum (ving′kyoo-lŭm), *n., pl.* -cu·la (-lä),
1. a bond of union; tie. 2. a line drawn

over two or more algebraic quantities to indicate they are to be treated together.

vin·di·cate (vin′di-kāt), *v.t.* -cat·ed, -cat·ing, 1.
to remove blame, guilt, etc. from. 2. to defend successfully. 3. to assert a right to. 4.
to justify. —**vin′di·ca·tor,** *n.*

vin·di·ca·tion (vin-di-kā′shŭn), *n.* 1. the act of
vindicating or state of being vindicated. 2.
something that serves to vindicate.

vin·di·ca·to·ry (vin′di-kä-tôr-i), *adj.* 1. serving to
vindicate or justify. 2. punitive.

vin·dic·tive (vin-dik′tiv), *adj.* given to, or
prompted by, revenge. —**vin·dic′tive·ly,** *adv.*
—**vin·dic′tive·ness,** *n.*

vine (vīn), *n.* 1. a plant with a thin, long stem
that climbs a support or grows along the
ground. 2. a grapevine.

vin·e·gar (vin′i-gẽr), *n.* 1. a sour liquid containing acetic acid and obtained by fermenta-
tion of wine, cider, etc. 2. anything sour.

vin·er·y (vīn′ẽr-i), *n., pl.* -er·ies, 1. a greenhouse in which grapes are grown. 2. a mass
of vines.

vine·yard (vin′yẽrd), *n.* 1. a plantation of
grapevines. 2. a field of endeavor.

vingt-et-un (van-tā-un′), *n.* [French], same as
twenty-one.

vi·nic (vī′nik, vin′ik), *adj.* of or derived from
wine.

vin·i·cul·ture (vin′i-kul-chẽr), *n.* the cultivation
of wine-producing grapes.

vi·nif·er·ous (vī-nif′ẽr-ŭs), *adj.* producing wine.

vin·i·fi·ca·tion (vin-i-fi-kā′shŭn), *n.* the conversion of fruit juices into alcohol by fermentation.

vin or·di·naire (ôr-dē-ner′), [French], any inexpensive wine commonly served with meals.

vi·nous (vī′nŭs), *adj.* of, pertaining to, having
the qualities of, or like wine.

vin ro·sé (rō-zā′), [French], same as rosé.

vin·tage (vin′tij), *n.* 1. the grape crop of a single season. 2. the wine of a certain region
and year. 3. an earlier type: *adj.* 1. of a
fine vintage. 2. of a period long past.

vint·ner (vint′nẽr), *n.* a wine merchant.

vin·y (vī′ni), *adj.* **vin′i·er, vin′i·est,** 1. of or like
vines. 2. covered or filled with vines.

vi·nyl (vī′nl), *n.* any one of various compounds
that are changed into polymers to form
plastics and resins.

vi·ol (vī′ŏl), *n.* any one of a family of stringed
instruments, usually having a flat back,
frets, and six strings.

vi·o·la (vi-ō′lä, vī-), *n.* a stringed instrument
slightly larger than a violin, tuned a fifth
lower.

vi·o·la·ble (vī′ō-lä-bl), *adj.* capable of being violated or broken.

vi·o·late (vī′ō-lāt), *v.t.* -lat·ed, -lat·ing, 1. to
break (a law, rule, etc.). 2. to assault sexually; rape. 3. to profane (something holy). 4.
to disturb; interrupt. —**vi′o·la·tor,** *n.*

vi·o·la·tion (vī-ō-lā′shŭn), *n.* the act of violating
or state of being violated.

vi·o·lence (vī′ō-lĕns), *n.* 1. physical force used
to do injury. 2. unjust strength applied to
any purpose. 3. powerful force or strength.
4. any violent act, as rape or assault. 5. any
infringement of rights.

vi·o·lent (-lĕnt), *adj.* 1. using, or driven by,

great physical force. 2. caused by violence. 3. furious; vehement; impetuous. 4. severe; intense; extreme. —vi'o·lent·ly, *adv.*

vi·o·let (vī'ō-lit), *n.* 1. a low-growing plant with blue, purple, white, or yellow flowers. 2. a bluish-purple color: *adj.* bluish-purple.

vi·o·lin (vī-ō-lin'), *n.* any one of a family of four-stringed instruments played with a bow; specifically, the instrument of this family that is the smallest and has the highest pitch.

vi·o·lin·ist ('ist). *n.* a violin player.

vi·ol·ist (vī'ōl-ist), *n.* 1. a viol player. 2. (vi·ō'-list), a viola player.

vi·o·lon·cel·list (vē-ō-län-chel'ist, vī-ō-län-), *n.* a cello player; cellist.

vi·o·lon·cel·lo (-chel'ō), *n., pl.* -los, same as cello.

vio·lo·ne (vyō-lō'nā), *n.* same as double bass.

vi·per (vī'pèr), *n.* 1. any one of various venomous snakes. 2. a malicious or treacherous person.

vi·per·ous (-ŭs), *adj.* of or like a viper; venomous: also vi'per·ish.

vi·ra·go (vī-rā'gō, vī-rā'-), *n., pl.* -goes, -gos, a bad-tempered, quarrelsome woman; scold.

vi·ral (vī'ral), *adj.* of, pertaining to, or caused by a virus.

vir·e·o (vir'i-ō), *n., pl.* -e·os, a small American songbird with green or gray feathers.

vir·gin (vûr'jin), *n.* one who has never engaged in sexual intercourse, especially a young woman: *adj.* 1. that is a virgin. 2. chaste; modest. 3. pure, new, unused. etc.

vir·gi·nal ('ji·nl), *adj.* 1. chaste; modest. 2. pure, new, unused, etc.: *n.* a harpsichord, especially a small one of the 16th century.

Vir·gin·ia creeper (vêr-jin'yá), same as woodbine (sense 2).

Virginia reel, an American reel danced by a number of couples facing in two parallel lines.

vir·gin·i·ty (vêr-jin'i-ti), *n.* 1. the state of being a virgin; chastity. 2. the state of being virgin, pure, new, etc.

Vir·go (vûr'gō), *n.* 1. a large constellation between Leo and Libra. 2. the sixth sign of the zodiac.

vir·gule (vûr'gŭl), *n.* a short diagonal line (/) inserted in dates or fractions (3/8) or between two words (and/or), etc.

vir·ile (vir'll), *adj.* 1. of, pertaining to, or characteristic of mature manhood; masculine. 2. manly; forceful. 3. potent sexually; procreative.

vi·ril·i·ty (vi-ril'i-ti), *n.* the state or quality of being virile; manhood; potency.

vi·rol·o·gy (vī-rol'ō-ji), *n.* the study of viruses and of diseases caused by viruses.

vir·tu (vêr-tōō', vûr'tōō), *n.* 1. a love of antiques, curios, etc. 2. all such objects, or their attraction for collectors.

vir·tu·al (vûr'choo-wàl), *adj.* being such for all practical purposes, but not in actual fact or name.

vir·tu·al·ly (-i), *adv.* practically; in effect but not in fact.

vir·tue (vûr'chōō), *n.* 1. moral goodness or excellence. 2. any moral quality believed to be good. 3. chastity. 4. any sort of excellence.

5. any good quality. 6. power or potency, as in healing.

vir·tu·o·so (vûr-choo-wō'sō), *n., pl.* -sos, -si ('si), one who displays great skill in one of the fine arts, especially in playing music. —vir·tu·os'i·ty (-wos'i-ti), *n.*

vir·tu·ous (vûr'choo-wŭs), *adj.* 1. possessing or displaying virtue; morally good. 2. chaste: said of a woman. —vir'tu·ous·ly, *adv.*

vir·u·lent (vir'yoo-lênt, 'oo-), *adj.* 1. very poisonous; deadly. 2. full of hate; bitter in enmity. 3. very malignant: said of a disease. 4. highly infectious. —vir'u·lence, *n.*

vi·rus (vī'rŭs), *n.* 1. any one of a group of minute infective agents that cause certain diseases, as measles. 2. a harmful or evil influence.

vi·sa (vē'zā), *n.* an endorsement on a passport showing that it has been examined and granting entry into a certain country: *v.t.* -saed, -sa·ing, 1. to put a visa on (a passport). 2. to give a visa to (someone).

vis·age (viz'ij), *n.* 1. the countenance; face. 2. aspect; appearance.

vis·à·vis (vē-zà-vē'), *adj. & adv.* face to face; opposite: *prep.* 1. face to face with. 2. in comparison with: *n., pl.* vis·à·vis (-vēz', -vē'), 1. one who is opposite another. 2. one's counterpart. 3. a carriage with the seats facing.

vis·ca·cha (vis-kä'chä), *n.* a burrowing rodent of South America, with long, gray fur, related to the chinchilla.

vis·cer·a (vis'ēr-ä), *n.pl.* the internal body organs, as the heart, lungs, liver, intestines, etc.

vis·cer·al (-ål), *adj.* 1. of or pertaining to the viscera. 2. emotional, intuitive, etc. rather than intellectual.

vis·cid (vis'id), *adj.* thick, sticky, and syrupy. —vis·cid·i·ty (vi-sid'i-ti), *n.*

vis·coid (vis'koid), *adj.* somewhat viscous.

vis·cose (vis'kōs), *adj.* 1. same as viscous. 2. of or made of viscose: *n.* a syruplike solution prepared by treating cellulose with sodium hydroxide and carbon disulfide, used in making rayon.

vis·cos·i·ty (vis-kos'i-ti), *n., pl.* -ties, 1. the quality of being viscous. 2. the friction within a fluid resulting from molecular attraction and making the fluid resistant to flowing.

vis·count (vī'kount), *n.* a nobleman next in rank below an earl or count and above a baron. —vis'count·ess, *n.fem.*

vis·cous (vis'kŭs), *adj.* 1. thick, sticky, and syrupy. 2. having viscosity.

vis·cus (vis'kŭs), *n.* [Rare], a visceral organ.

vise (vīs), *n.* a device with two jaws operated by a screw or lever: used for holding articles in filing, shaping, etc.

vi·sé (vē'zā, vē·zā'), *n. & v.t.* -séed, -sé·ing, same as visa.

Vish·nu (vish'nōō), *n.* the second god of the Hindu trinity, called "the Preserver."

vis·i·bil·i·ty (viz·i-bil'i-ti), *n., pl.* -ties, 1. the condition of being visible. 2. the degree to which something can be seen under certain conditions of light, distance, etc. 3. range or scope of vision.

vis·i·ble (viz´ĭ-bl), *adj.* 1. perceptible by the eye; capable of being seen. 2. obvious; evident. —**vis´i·bly,** *adv.*

Vis·i·goth (viz´ĭ-goth, -gŏth), *n.* any one of the western Goths: they set up a kingdom in France and Spain. —**Vis·i·goth´ic,** *adj.*

vi·sion (vizh´ŭn), *n.* 1. the act or sense of seeing; sight. 2. something seen in a trance, dream, etc. 3. a creation of the imagination; an image in the mind. 4. keen foresight. 5. a beautiful person or thing.

vi·sion·al (-ăl), *adj.* 1. of or like a vision. 2. seen as if in a vision; unreal.

vi·sion·ar·y (-er-ĭ), *adj.* 1. of or like a vision. 2. existing only in the imagination; not real. 3. not realistic; impractical: *n., pl.* -ar·ies, 1. one who sees visions; seer. 2. an impractical, idealistic person; dreamer.

vis·it (viz´ĭt), *v.t.* 1. to come or go to see. 2. to stay as a guest with. 3. to trouble or afflict: *v.i.* 1. to visit someone or something; especially, to make a social call. 2. [Informal], to have a conversation; chat: *n.* the act of visiting, in making a call socially or professionally or in inspecting officially.

vis·it·ant (-ănt), *n.* a visitor.

vis·it·a·tion (viz-ĭ-tā´shŭn), *n.* 1. the act of visiting. 2. an official visit. 3. the bringing about of good or, especially, evil. 4. any retributive affliction.

vi·site (vi-zēt´), *n.* a light lace or silk cape formerly worn by women in the summer.

vis·i·tor (viz´it-ẽr), *n.* one who visits.

vis·or (vī´zẽr), *n.* 1. the upper movable part of a helmet. 2. a front brim, as of a cap, that sticks out and shades the eyes.

vis·ta (vis´tä), *n.* 1. a view, especially through a long passage. 2. a mental view of a series of events.

vis·u·al (vizh´oo-wăl), *adj.* 1. of sight or used in seeing. 2. intended for the use of sight. 3. visible; capable of being seen. —**vis´u·al·ly,** *adv.*

vis·u·al·ize (-wä-līz), *v.t. & v.i.* -ized, -iz·ing, to form a mental image of (something not before the eyes). —**vis·u·al·i·za´tion,** *n.*

vi·tal (vī´tl), *adj.* 1. of or pertaining to life. 2. necessary to or supporting life. 3. mortal; fatal. 4. indispensable; essential. 5. of great importance. 6. full of energy or life: *n. pl.* 1. the organs of the body essential to life, as the heart, lungs, etc. 2. any parts considered to be essential. —**vi´tal·ly,** *adv.*

vi·tal·ism (-izm), *n.* the theory that the basic principle of life and all living things is a vital force, distinct from all physical or chemical forces.

vi·tal·i·ty (vī-tal´ĭ-tĭ), *n., pl.* -ties, 1. power to go on living or to survive. 2. physical or mental vigor.

vi·tal·ize (vīt´l-īz), *v.t.* -ized, -iz·ing, to endow with life; make vital.

vital statistics, data concerning births, deaths, marriages, etc.

vi·ta·min (vīt´ă-min), *n.* any one of various complex substances found in certain foods or produced synthetically and essential, in small quantities, to good health: the following are important vitamins: —**vitamin A,** an alcohol found in egg yolk, carrots, etc. —**vitamin B complex,** a group of substances including *a)* **vitamin B1** (see **thiamine**); *b)* **vitamin B2** (see **riboflavin**); *c)* **vitamin B12,** a vitamin containing cobalt: see also **nicotinic acid.** —**vitamin C,** a compound occurring in citrus fruits, tomatoes, etc. —**vitamin D,** any of several vitamins found in fish-liver oils, milk, etc. —**vitamin K,** a substance occurring in fish meal, green vegetables, etc.

vi·tel·lin (vi-tel´in), *n.* a protein combined with a phosphorous compound, occurring in the yolk of eggs.

vi·tel·line (´in, ´ēn), *adj.* 1. of or pertaining to egg yolk. 2. yellow like egg yolk.

vi·tel·lus (´ŭs), *n.* the yolk of an egg.

vi·ti·ate (vish´i-āt), *v.t.* -at·ed, -at·ing, 1. to render faulty or defective; spoil. 2. to pervert; debase. 3. to invalidate (a contract). —**vi·ti·a´tion,** *n.*

vit·i·cul·ture (vit´ĭ-kul-chẽr, vīt´-), *n.* the art or science of grape-growing.

vit·i·li·go (vit-ĭ-lī´gō), *n.* a condition of the skin in which white patches appear due to loss of pigment in the skin.

vit·re·ous (vit´rĭ-ŭs), *adj.* consisting of, like, or obtained from glass.

vitreous body, the transparent, jellylike substance filling the inside of the eyeball between the retina and lens: also **vitreous humor.**

vit·res·cent (vi-tres´nt), *adj.* 1. capable of being formed into glass. 2. becoming glass or becoming like glass. —**vit·res´cence,** *n.*

vit·ric (vit´rik), *adj.* of or like glass.

vit·ri·form (vit´rĭ-fôrm), *adj.* having the form or appearance of glass.

vit·ri·fy (-fī), *v.t. & v.i.* -fied, -fy·ing, to make or become vitreous; change into glass or a glasslike material by means of heat. —**vit·ri·fi·ca´tion** (-fi-kä´shŭn), **vit·ri·fac´tion** (-fak´-shŭn), *n.*

vit·rine (vi-trēn´), *n.* a display case of glass or having glass panels.

vit·ri·ol (vit´ri-ŏl, -ōl), *n.* 1. any one of several sulfates of metals, as copper sulfate (**blue vitriol**) or iron sulfate (**green vitriol**). 2. same as **sulfuric acid.** 3. bitterness or sharpness in speaking or writing.

vit·ri·ol·ic (vit-ri-ol´ik), *adj.* 1. of or derived from a vitriol. 2. sarcastic; caustic.

vit·u·line (vich´oo-lĭn, -lĭn), *adj.* of or like a calf or veal.

vi·tu·per·ate (vī-tōō´pẽ-rāt, -tū´-), *v.t.* -at·ed, -at·ing, to censure abusively; berate. —**vi·tu·per·a´tion,** *n.*

vi·tu·per·a·tive (-rä´tiv), *adj.* characterized by or containing abusive censure.

vi·va (vē´vä), *interj.* [Italian & Spanish], long life or success to (someone specified).

vi·va·cious (vi-vä´shŭs, vī-), *adj.* lively; gay. —**vi·va´cious·ly,** *adv.* —**vi·vac´i·ty** (-vas´ĭ-tĭ), **vi·va´cious·ness,** *n.*

vi·var·i·um (vī-ver´i-ŭm), *n., pl.* -i·ums, -i·a (-ä), a place for the keeping of animals in an environment similar to their natural state.

vi·va vo·ce (vī´vä vō´si), by word of mouth.

vive (vēv), *interj.* [French], long life or success to (someone specified).

viv·id (viv´id), *adj.* 1. full of life; lively. 2. intense or bright, as some colors. 3. clear and strong. —viv'id·ly, adv. —viv'id·ness, n.

viv·i·fy (viv'i-fī), v.t. -fied, -fy·ing, to endue with life; animate.

vi·vip·a·rous (vī-vip'ẽr-ŭs), adj. denoting reproduction by bearing living young instead of by laying eggs.

viv·i·sect (viv'i-sekt), v.t. & v.i. to perform vivisection on (living animals).

viv·i·sec·tion (viv-i-sek'shŭn), n. research in medicine by means of surgical operations performed on living animals.

viv·i·sec·tion·ist (-ist), n. one who practices or advocates vivisection.

vix·en (vik'sn), n. 1. a female fox. 2. a quarrelsome, ill-tempered woman. —vix'en·ish, adj. —vix'en·ish·ly, adv.

viz·ard (viz'ẽrd), n. same as visor.

vi·zier, vi·zir (vi-zir'), n. a high officer or councilor of state in Moslem countries.

viz·or (vī'zẽr), n. same as visor.

vo·ca·ble (vō'kā-bl), n. a word, especially a word considered only as a unit of sounds or letters.

vo·cab·u·lar·y (vō-kab'yủ-ler-i), n., pl. -lar·ies, 1. a collection of words, phrases, etc. arranged alphabetically and usually defined, as in a dictionary. 2. all the words used by a person or group, or used in a language.

vo·cal (vō'kl), adj. 1. uttered by the voice; spoken; oral. 2. that is sung. 3. that can speak or utter sounds. 4. used in speaking. 5. speaking without restraint. —vo'cal·ly, adv.

vocal cords, folds of membrane in the larynx, the vibrations of which produce voice.

vo·cal·ic (vō-kal'ik), adj. of, like, or consisting of a vowel or vowels.

vo·cal·ist (vō'kl-ist), n. a singer.

vo·cal·ize (-īz), v.t. & v.i. -ized, -iz·ing, to speak, utter, or sing.

vo·ca·tion (vō-kā'shŭn), n. 1. the career that one feels one has been called to pursue. 2. any occupation, profession, etc.

vo·ca·tion·al (-l), adj. 1. of a vocation or occupation. 2. denoting or of education or training meant to prepare one to carry on a cer· tain occupation, trade, etc.

vocational guidance, any program for testing and questioning persons with a view to helping them choose a suitable vocation or get the proper training for it.

voc·a·tive (vok'ä-tiv), adj. in Grammar, denoting the case that indicates the person or thing addressed: n. the vocative case.

vo·cif·er·ant (vō-sif'ẽr-ânt), adj. vociferating; shouting.

vo·cif·er·ate ('ē-rāt), v.t. & v.i. -at·ed, -at·ing, to shout in a loud voice; clamor. —vo·cif·er·a'·tion, n.

vo·cif·er·ous ('ẽr-ŭs), adj. clamorous; noisy.

vod·ka (vod'kä), n. an alcoholic liquor distilled from wheat, rye, etc.

vogue (vōg), n. 1. the fashion or style that is accepted at a certain time. 2. popularity.

voice (vois), n. 1. sound uttered by the mouth, especially by a human being. 2. the faculty of speech. 3. anything thought of as like vocal utterance. 4. an expressed opinion or

wish. 5. the right to express oneself, as by voting. 6. expression or utterance. 7. in Grammar, the form of a verb that shows it to be active or passive. 8. in Music, a) ability in singing; b) any of the vocal or instrumental parts performed together in a composition: v.t. voiced, voic'ing, to give utterance or expression to.

voiced (voist), adj. 1. having a voice. 2. having (a specified kind of) voice. 3. in Phonetics, made by vibrating the vocal cords.

voice·less (vois'lis), adj. 1. having no voice. 2. silent. 3. in Phonetics, uttered without vibrating the vocal cords.

void (void), adj. 1. holding nothing. 2. destitute or devoid (of). 3. useless; ineffective. 4. legally invalid; null: n. 1. an empty space; vacuum. 2. a feeling of being empty: v.t. 1. to make empty. 2. to evacuate (feces or urine). 3. to make void; nullify.

voi·là (vwä-lä'), [French], behold! there it is!

voile (voil), n. a sheer, thin fabric of cotton, silk, etc.

vo·lant (vō'lânt), adj. flying; nimble.

vo·lar (vō'lẽr), adj. of or pertaining to the palm of the hand or the sole of the foot.

vol·a·tile (vol'ä-til), adj. 1. that evaporates quickly. 2. fickle or unstable.

vol·a·til·i·ty (vol-ä-til'ĭ-ti), n. the state or quality of being volatile.

vol·a·til·ize (vol'ä-tl-īz), v.t. & v.i. -ized, -iz·ing, to make or become volatile; turn to vapor.

vol·can·ic (vol-kan'ik), adj. 1. of or produced by a volcano. 2. like a volcano; explosive.

volcanic glass, natural glass, as obsidian, produced by molten lava as it rapidly cools.

vol·can·ism (vol'kä-nizm), n. volcanic activity.

vol·can·ize (vol'kä-nīz), v.t. -ized, -iz·ing, to subject to volcanic heat.

vol·ca·no (vol-kā'nō), n., pl. -noes, -nos, 1. a vent in the earth's crust through which rocks, earth, etc. are ejected with violent force in a molten state. 2. a mountain or hill formed in a cone shape by the material ejected.

vol·can·ol·o·gy (vol-kä-nol'ō-ji), n. the scientific study of volcanoes and volcanic phenomena.

vole (vōl), n. any one of various small rodents with a short tail.

vo·li·tion (vō-lish'ŭn), n. the act or power of willing, or exerting choice. —vo·li'tion·al, adj.

vol·i·tive (vol'ĭ-tiv), adj. 1. of or pertaining to the will. 2. in Grammar, expressing a wish, as a verb or mood.

vol·ley (vol'i), n., pl. -leys, 1. the simultaneous discharge of a number of small arms or weapons. 2. the bullets, stones, etc. so discharged. 3. any explosive burst, as of words. 4. the return of a ball, etc., as in tennis or badminton, before it reaches the ground: v.t. & v.i. -leyed, -ley·ing, 1. to discharge as in a volley. 2. to return (a ball) as a volley.

vol·ley·ball (-bôl), n. 1. a game played by two teams who hit a large, light ball inflated with air back and forth over a net, using the hands. 2. the ball.

vol·plane (vol'plān), v.i. -planed, -plan·ing, to make a downward glide, as an airplane with the engine turned off.

volt (vōlt), n. 1. the unit of electromotive force,

ȯ in dragon, ōō in crude, oo in wool, u in cup, ū in cure, ū in turn, ů in focus, oi in boy, ou in house, th in thin, th in sheathe, g in get, j in joy, y in yet.

2. in *Fencing*, a sudden leap to avoid a thrust.

volt-age (vōl'tij), *n.* difference in electrical potential, expressed in volts.

vol-ta-ic (vol-tā'ik), *adj.* of or pertaining to electricity generated by chemical action.

vol-ta-ism (vol'tā-izm), *n.* same as galvanism.

vol-tam-e-ter (vol-tam'ē-tēr), *n.* an instrument for measuring the amount of electricity in a current by the amount of electrolysis produced.

volt-am-me-ter (vōlt'am'mēt-ēr), *n.* an instrument that can be used to measure either voltage or amperage.

volt-me-ter (vōlt'mēt-ēr), *n.* an instrument for measuring voltage.

vol-u-ble (vol'yoo-bl), *adj.* fluent in speech; very talkative. —**vol-u-bil'i-ty,** *n.* —**vol'u-bly,** *adv.*

vol-ume (vol'yoom), *n.* 1. a book. 2. one of a set of books. 3. the amount of space occupied, measured in cubic units. 4. mass, quantity, or bulk. 5. the degree of loudness of sound.

vol-u-met-ric (vol-yoo-met'rik), *adj.* of or pertaining to the measurement of volume: also **vol-u-met'ri-cal.** —**vol-u-met'ri-cal-ly,** *adv.*

vo-lu-mi-nous (vō-lōō'mi-nŭs), *adj.* 1. enough to fill volumes. 2. extensive; copious. —**vo-lu-mi-nos'i-ty** (-nos'i-ti), *n.*

vol-un-ta-rism (vol'ŭn-tēr-izm), *n.* 1. any philosophical theory holding that the will is the dominant factor in experience and reality. 2. voluntary action in any course. 3. a system based on this.

vol-un-tar-y (-ter-i), *adj.* 1. acting from choice or free will. 2. given or done without compulsion. 3. not accidental; intentional. 4. controlled by the will. 5. supported by individual contributions rather than by the state: *n., pl.* -tar-ies, an organ solo played before, during, or after a church service. —**vol'un-tar-i-ly,** *adv.*

vol-un-tar-y-ism (-izm), *n.* the system of supporting schools by voluntary contributions.

vol-un-teer (vol-ŭn-tir'), *n.* one who enters into any service of his own free will, especially military service: *v.i.* 1. to offer to do something without being asked. 2. to enlist in a military service: *v.t.* to offer or bestow without constraint or compulsion: *adj.* 1. of or pertaining to volunteers. 2. voluntary.

Volunteers of America, an organization similar to the Salvation Army, established in 1896.

vo-lup-tu-ar-y (vō-lup'choo-wer-i), *n., pl.* -ar-ies, one devoted to sensual pleasures or luxury: *adj.* devoted to pleasure or luxury.

vo-lup-tu-ous ('choo-wŭs), *adj.* 1. concerned with or producing sensual pleasures and enjoyment. 2. arising from gratification of the senses. 3. sexually exciting or attractive. —**vo-lup'tu-ous-ly,** *adv.* —**vo-lup'tu-ous-ness,** *n.*

vo-lute (vō-lōōt'), *n.* 1. a spiral scroll forming one of the chief features of Ionic and Corinthian capitals. 2. a whorl. —**vo-lut'ed,** *adj.*

vo-lu-tion (vō-lōō'shŭn), *n.* 1. a revolving or twisting. 2. a convolution. 3. a whorl, as of a shell.

vol-vu-lus (vol'vyoo-lŭs), *n.* a spasm or twisting of the intestines, causing intestinal obstruction.

vo-mer (vō'mēr), *n.* the thin, slender bone forming most of the partition between the nostrils.

vom-it (vom'it), *v.i.* to eject the contents of the stomach through the mouth; throw up: *v.t.* 1. to throw up (food) from the stomach. 2. to discharge with violence: *n.* matter ejected from the stomach through the mouth.

vom-i-to-ry (vom'i-tôr-i), *n., pl.* -ries, 1. originally, an emetic. 2. an opening through which matter is discharged.

vom-i-tu-ri-tion (vom-i-choo-rish'ŭn), *n.* retching.

voo-doo (vōō'dōō), *n., pl.* -doos, 1. a primitive religion of the West Indies, based on a belief in sorcery, charms, fetishes, etc. 2. a fetish, charm, etc. used in voodooism. 3. sorcery; black magic: *v.t.* to affect by or as if by voodoo.

voo-doo-ism (-izm), *n.* the system of voodoo rites, practices, and beliefs. —**voo'doo-ist,** *n.*

vo-ra-cious (vô-rā'shŭs), *adj.* 1. greedy in eating; ravenous. 2. insatiable. —**vo-ra'cious-ly,** *adv.* —**vo-rac'i-ty** (-ras'i-ti), *n.*

vor-tex (vôr'teks), *n., pl.* -tex-es, -ti-ces ('ti-sēz), 1. the hollow and circular form assumed by a liquid in rotation; whirlpool. 2. a whirlwind. 3. any condition or situation suggestive of a vortex.

vo-ta-ry (vōt'à-ri), *n., pl.* -ries, 1. one bound by a vow or promise. 2. a devoted follower or adherent.

vote (vōt), *n.* 1. an expression of choice or preference, as with regard to a candidate or proposal, indicated by ballot or in some other way; also, the right to indicate such a choice or preference. 2. the ballot or other method used. 3. votes collectively: *v.i.* vot'-ed, vot'ing, to indicate such choice or preference, as by ballot: *v.t.* to choose, decide, support, etc. by vote. —**vot'er,** *n.*

voting machine, a machine on which election votes are registered and counted.

vo-tive (vōt'iv), *adj.* given, consecrated, or promised by a vow or pledge.

vouch (vouch), *v.i.* to give, provide, or function as a guarantee or assurance (with *for*): *v.t.* to substantiate; verify.

vouch-er ('ēr), *n.* one that vouches; specifically, a paper attesting to the accuracy of something, as of an expenditure.

vouch-safe (vouch-sāf'), *v.t.* -safed', -saf'ing, to condescend to grant; concede.

vous-soir (vōō-swär'), *n.* one of the wedge-shaped stones forming the arch of a bridge or vault.

vow (vou), *n.* 1. a solemn promise or pledge, especially one made to God. 2. a pledge of fidelity and love. 3. a solemn declaration: *v.t.* to promise or declare solemnly: *v.i.* to make a vow.

vow-el (vou'ĕl), *n.* 1. a single open speech sound uttered without much constriction of the vocal organs. 2. a letter representing such a sound, as a, e, i, o, u: *adj.* of a vowel or vowels.

vox (voks), *n., pl.* vo-ces (vō'sēz), [Latin], voice.

voy-age (voi'ij), *n.* 1. a long journey by water.

---

a in cap, ā in cane, ä in father, å in abet, e in met, ē in be, ē in baker, ê in regent, i in pit, ī in fine, ĭ in manifest, o in hot, ō in horse, ō in bone,

2. a journey by aircraft or spacecraft: *v.i.* -aged, -ag·ing, to make a voyage; travel: *v.t.* to travel or sail over or on. —**voy'ag·er,** *n.*

vo·ya·geur (vwä-yä-zhŭr'), *n., pl.* **-geurs'** (-zhŭr'), [French], a boatman or woodman of the Canadian wilds.

vo·yeur (vwä-yŭr'), *n.* one who takes an abnormal and excessive interest in viewing sexual objects or activities. —**vo·yeur'ism,** *n.* —**voyeur·is'tic,** *adj.*

VTOL, an aircraft that can take off or land vertically.

vug, vugg, vugh (vug, voog). *n.* an opening or cavity in a rock or mineral vein, often with a crystalline lining or layer.

Vul·can (vul'kn), *n.* the ancient Roman god of fire.

vul·ca·ni·an (vul-kā'ni-ăn), *adj.* 1. of or pertaining to the art or craft of working with metal. 2. volcanic.

vul·can·ite (vul'kā-nīt), *n.* a hard rubber made by vulcanization and used for combs, buttons, and electric insulation; ebonite.

vul·can·i·za·tion (vul-kan-i-zā'shŭn), *n.* the process of treating crude rubber with sulfur or sulfides, under heat, in order to make the rubber harder and more durable.

vul·can·ize (vul'kā-nīz), *v.t. & v.i.* -ized, -iz·ing, to subject to or undergo vulcanization. —**vul'can·iz·er,** *n.*

vul·gar (vul'gĕr), *adj.* 1. of, characteristic of, or used by, the multitude or common people; general; popular. 2. vernacular. 3. unrefined; coarse; boorish. 4. indecent or obscene. —**vul'gar·ly,** *adv.*

vul·gar·i·an (vul-gĕr'i-ăn), *n.* a rich person with vulgar, coarse tastes.

vul·gar·ism (vul'gĕr-izm), *n.* 1. a vulgar phrase or expression, regarded as nonstandard, obscene, or coarse. 2. vulgarity.

vul·gar·i·ty (vul-gĕr'ĭ-ti), *n.* 1. the state or quality of being unrefined, coarse, or boorish. 2. *pl.* -ties, something that is vulgar, as an act, habit, or expression.

vul·gar·ize (vul'gă-rīz), *v.t.* -ized, -iz·ing, 1. to make more widely known; popularize. 2. to make coarse, debased, etc. —**vul·gar·i·za'tion,** *n.*

Vulgar Latin, the form of Latin used in everyday speech by the ancient Romans, as distinguished from standard written Latin.

Vul·gate (vul'gāt), *n.* 1. a Latin version of the Bible used in the Roman Catholic Church. 2. [v-], common speech; vernacular: *adj.* 1. of or contained in the Vulgate. 2. [v-], of or in the vernacular.

vul·ner·a·ble (vul'nĕr-å-bl), *adj.* 1. capable of being wounded or injured; susceptible of wounds or injury. 2. easily hurt by criticism. 3. that can be tempted, bribed, influenced, etc. 4. open to attack by hostile forces. 5. in *Bridge,* liable to increased penalties. —**vul·ner·a·bil'i·ty,** *n.* —**vul'ner·a·bly,** *adv.*

vul·ner·ar·y (vul'nĕ-rer-i), *adj.* used for healing wounds.

vul·pine (vul'pīn, 'pin), *adj.* of, pertaining to, or like a fox.

vul·ture (vul'chĕr), *n.* 1. a large bird, related to the hawks, that lives chiefly on carrion. 2. any ruthless person who preys on others. —**vul'tur·ine** (-īn, -in), **vul'tur·ous** (-ŭs), *adj.*

vul·va (vul'vă), *n., pl.* **-vae** ('vē), -vas, the external sexual organs of the female. —**vul'val, vul'var,** *adj.*

vul·vi·form ('vĭ-fôrm), *adj.* shaped like the vulva.

vul·vi·tis (vul-vīt'ĭs), *n.* inflammation of the vulva.

vul·vo·vag·i·ni·tis (vul-vō-vaj-ĭ-nīt'ĭs), *n.* inflammation of the vulva and the vagina.

vy·ing (vī'ing), *adj.* that vies; competing.

W

W, w (dub'l-ū), *n., pl.* **W's, w's,** 1. the twenty-third letter of the English alphabet. 2. the sound of this letter, as in *wet.* 3. a type or impression of *W* or *w.*

W (dub'l-ū), *adj.* shaped like *W*: *n.* an object shaped like *W.*

wab·ble (wäb'l), *n., v.t. & v.i.* same as **wobble.** —**wab'bler,** *n.*

Wac (wak), *n.* a member of the Women's Army Corps.

wack·y (wak'i), *adj.* **wack'i·er, wack'i·est,** [Slang], crazy; eccentric; odd. —**wack'i·ly,** *adv.* —**wack'i·ness,** *n.*

wad (wäd), *n.* 1. a mass of soft or flexible material, as paper or cotton. 2. a lump or plug. 3. a soft mass of fibrous material, used for padding, stuffing, etc. 4. [Informal], a roll of paper money: *v.t.* **wad'ded, wad'ding,** 1. to form into a wad. 2. to pad or plug with a wad. 3. to crowd or stuff a wad of into something.

wad·ding ('ing), *n.* soft material used for padding, stuffing, etc.

wad·dle (wäd'l), *v.i.* **-dled, -dling,** to sway from side to side in walking, as a duck does: *n.* 1. the act of waddling. 2. a waddling gait. —**wad'dler,** *n.*

wad·dy (wä'di), *n., pl.* **-dies,** a thick club used by Australian aborigines as a weapon: *v.t.* **-died, -dy·ing,** to strike with a waddy.

wade (wäd), *v.i.* **wad'ed, wad'ing,** 1. to walk through any substance, as water, snow, mud, etc. that is somewhat resistant. 2. to go through (a dull book, mass of details, etc.) laboriously but with determination. 3. [Informal], to move forcefully into action against something (with *into* or *in*): *v.t.* to cross by wading, as a stream.

wad·er ('ēr), *n.* 1. one who wades. 2. same as **wading bird.** 3. *pl.* high, waterproof boots, often with trousers, as worn by fishermen.

wa·di (wä'di), *n., pl.* **-dis, -dies,** in Arabia, northern Africa, etc., the channel of a watercourse that is dry except in the rainy season; also, the rush of water that flows through it. Also spelled **wa'dy,** *pl.* **-dies.**

wading bird, any one of various long-legged birds, as cranes, that wade in water for food.

wa·fer (wä'fēr), *n.* 1. a thin, crisp cracker or cookie. 2. a flat disk of Eucharistic bread. 3. a small disk used as a seal on letters, documents, etc. 4. any small, flat disk.

waf·fle (wäf'l), *n.* a somewhat crisp cake made from batter resembling pancake batter but baked in a waffle iron: *adj.* having an indented, gridlike surface like that of a waffle: also **waf'fled.**

waffle iron, a hinged utensil consisting of two indented plates, between which the waffle bakes.

waft (waft, wäft), *v.t.* to bear (sounds, odors, etc.) along lightly, as through the air or over water: *v.i.* 1. to float or drift along, as on the wind. 2. to blow gently, as a breeze: *n.* 1. a slight current, as of air. 2. a sound, odor, etc. wafted along. 3. a movement of wafting.

wag (wag), *v.i. & v.t.* **wagged, wag'ging,** to move up and down or back and forth: *n.* 1. the act of wagging. 2. a witty individual.

wage (wäj), *v.t.* **waged, wag'ing,** to engage in or carry on (a war, campaign, etc.): *n.* 1. *often pl.* payment for work done. 2. *usually pl.* recompense; requital.

wa·ger (wä'jēr), *n.* something risked on an uncertainty or contingency; bet: *v.t. & v.i.* to bet.

wag·ger·y (wag'ēr-i), *n., pl.* **-ger·ies,** 1. mischievous merriment. 2. a joke or jest.

wag·gish ('ish), *adj.* humorous; sportive.

wag·gle (wag'l), *v.t. & v.i.* **-gled, -gling,** to move with a quick, wagging motion: *n.* a quick, wagging motion.

wag·on (wag'ŏn), *n.* 1. any one of various kinds of four-wheeled vehicles for transporting goods or passengers, including both those drawn as by animals or tractors and many that are automotive. 2. a small cart designed for use by children at play.

wag·on·er (-ēr), *n.* the driver of a wagon.

wag·on·ette (wag-ŏ-net'), *n.* a light, open, four-wheeled carriage with two seats facing each other behind the driver.

wag·tail (wag'tāl), *n.* a small bird with a long tail that wags up and down.

wa·hoo (wä'hōō), *n.* 1. any one of several American shrubs having bright red fruits or leaves. 2. a small elm tree of the southern U.S. 3. a large game and food fish related to the mackerel.

waif (wäf), *n.* 1. anything found by chance that is without an owner. 2. a homeless child.

wail (wāl), *v.i. & v.t.* to express (sorrow or pain) with long, loud, sad cries: *n.* 1. a long, loud, sad cry of sorrow or pain. 2. a sound resembling this. 3. the act of wailing.

wain (wān), *n.* [Archaic], a wagon.

wain·scot (wän'skŏt, 'skot), *n.* a panel as of wood on the walls of a room, often on the lower part only: *v.t.* **-scot·ed** or **-scot·ted, -scot·ing** or **-scot·ting,** to panel as with wood.

wain·scot·ing, wain·scot·ting (-ing), *n.* 1. wainscot. 2. material used to wainscot.

wain·wright (wän'rīt), *n.* a maker of wagons.

waist (wāst), *n.* 1. the narrowest part of the body, between the ribs and the hips. 2. the part of a garment that covers the body from the waist to the shoulders, as the bodice of a dress. 3. a blouse. 4. a child's undershirt. 5. the middle section of anything

---

a in cap, ā in cane, ä in father, å in abet, e in met, ē in be, ē in baker, ē in regent, i in pit, ī in fine, i in manifest, o in hot, ô in horse, ō in bone,

that is wider at the ends, as a violin. 6. the middle part of a ship.

waist-band ('band), *n.* a band fitting around the waist, as at the top of trousers or a skirt.

waist-coat (wes'kŏt, wāst'kŏt), *n.* [British], a man's vest.

waist-line (wāst'līn), *n.* 1. the line of the waist, between the ribs and the hips. 2. the line where the waist and skirt of a dress join. 3. the distance around the waist.

wait (wāt), *v.i.* 1. to stay in expectation. 2. to have oneself ready (*for*). 3. to be delayed or temporarily neglected. 4. to act as a waiter or waitress; serve food (with *at* or *on*). 5. to attend to someone's needs (with *on*, *upon*): *v.t.* 1. to await. 2. [Informal], to delay (a meal): *n.* 1. the act of waiting. 2. a period of waiting.

wait-a-bit ('ă-bit), *n.* any one of several plants with sharp, hooked thorns.

wait-er ('ēr), *n.* a man who waits on table, as in a restaurant.

wait-ing ('ing), *adj.* 1. that waits. 2. of or for a wait. 3. in attendance, as on a sovereign or other royal person. 4. serving; attendant: *n.* 1. the act of one who waits. 2. the length of time one waits.

waiting list, a list of those waiting for something, as an item, service, or position, usually in the order of application.

waiting room, a room, as in a bus terminal or doctor's office, in which people wait.

wait-ress (wā'tris), *n.* a woman or girl who waits on table, as in a restaurant.

waive (wāv), *v.t.* waived, waiv'ing, 1. to give up or forgo (a claim); relinquish (that which one has a right to). 2. to postpone.

waiv-er (wā'vēr), *n.* in *Law*, the relinquishing of a claim, privilege, or right.

wake (wāk), *v.i.* woke or waked, waked or wok'en, wak'ing, 1. to cease to sleep; awake. 2. to be or stay awake. 3. to become active. 4. to realize (followed by *to*): *v.t.* 1. to rouse from sleep (often followed by *up*). 2. to arouse or revive (thoughts, emotions, etc.): *n.* 1. an all-night vigil over a dead body before its burial. 2. the track left in the water by a moving ship or boat.

wake-ful ('fŭl), *adj.* 1. watchful; vigilant. 2. not able to sleep. —wake'ful-ly, *adv.* —wake'ful-ness, *n.*

wak-en ('n), *v.t. & v.i.* to wake.

wake-rob-in ('rob-in), *n.* 1. the trillium. 2. [British], any one of several plants of the arum family, especially one similar to the jack-in-the-pulpit.

Wal-den-ses (wăl-den'sēz), *n.pl.* a sect of dissenters from the Roman Catholic Church in southern France, organized in 1170.

wale (wāl), *n.* 1. a mark made on the skin by a rod or whip; welt. 2. a raised ridge on cloth. 3. the texture or weave of a cloth with such ridges: *v.t.* waled, wal'ing, to mark with wales.

walk (wôk), *v.i.* 1. to advance by alternate steps. 2. to go on foot at a moderate pace. 3. to go on foot for pleasure or exercise. 4. to pursue a certain course. 5. in *Baseball*, to

be advanced to first base on four balls: *v.t.* 1. to traverse on foot. 2. to cause to walk. 3. to go along with on a walk or stroll. 4. in *Baseball*, to advance (a batter) to first base by pitching four balls: *n.* 1. the act or a manner of walking. 2. a stroll or hike for pleasure or exercise. 3. a distance to be walked. 4. a path for walking. 5. a course of life or action. 6. in *Baseball*, the act of walking or being walked.

walk-er ('ēr), *n.* 1. a person or animal that walks. 2. a framework on wheels for a baby learning to walk. 3. a tubular framework used as a support by convalescents when walking.

walk-ie-talk-ie (wôk'i-tôk'i), *n.* a small, portable radio that contains both receiver and transmitter.

walk-ing (wôk'ing), *adj.* 1. that walks or moves in a manner suggestive of walking. 2. for use by walkers, hikers, etc. 3. characterized by walking, as a *walking* tour.

walking stick, 1. a cane or staff carried in the hand as an aid to walking. 2. a slender-bodied insect that looks like a twig: also **walk'ing-stick**, *n.*

walk-on ('on), *n.* a minor role in which an actor or actress has few or no lines.

walk-out ('out), *n.* 1. a labor strike. 2. the act of leaving a meeting, in protest.

walk-o-ver ('ō-vēr), *n.* an easy triumph; success gained without much effort.

walk-up ('up), *n.* an apartment house without an elevator.

wall (wôl), *n.* 1. an upright structure of stone, brick, wood, etc. that supports, encloses, protects, or divides. 2. a structure like this forming the side of a building or an inner partition. 3. *usually pl.* ramparts or fortifications as used in military defense. 4. something like a wall in looks or function, as the side of a container, body cavity, biological cell, etc.: *v.t.* 1. to enclose with or as with a wall. 2. to fill up (an opening) with a wall (often followed by *up*).

wal-la-by (wäl'ă-bǐ), *n.*, *pl.* -bies, -by, a small marsupial related to the kangaroo.

wall-board (wôl'bôrd), *n.* a fibrous material, often made with gypsum, prepared in large sheets for making or covering walls and ceilings in place of plaster or paneling.

wal-let (wôl'it, wol'-), *n.* a flat case, usually of leather or a leatherlike material, for holding money, cards, etc.; billfold.

wall-eye (wôl'ī), *n.* 1. an eye, as of a horse, with a white iris. 2. an eye that turns outward, showing much white. 3. a large, staring eye. 4. any one of several kinds of fish with large, staring eyes.

wall-eyed pike ('īd), a large, freshwater food fish of North America, that has prominent, staring eyes.

wall-flow-er (wôl'flou-ēr), *n.* 1. a hardy garden plant of the mustard family, bearing orange or yellow flowers in clusters. 2. [Informal], a person, especially a girl, who merely looks on at a dance because shy or without a partner.

Wal-loon (wä-lōōn'), *n.* any member of a people of chiefly Celtic ancestry dwelling in the southeastern part of Belgium and nearby France.

wal·lop (wäl'ŏp, wôl'-), v.i. [Informal], 1. to boil with a continued bubbling. 2. to move quickly but with much effort. 3. to move clumsily: v.t. [Informal], 1. to defeat soundly. 2. to thrash. 3. to hit hard: n. [Informal], 1. a clumsy, laborious movement. 2. a hard blow. 3. a powerful impact, or the ability to create this. 4. a thrill.

wal·low (wäl'ō, wôl'-), v.i. 1. to roll about, as in mud, water, dust, etc. 2. to pitch and roll, as a ship. 3. to indulge oneself excessively (*in* something): n. 1. the act of wallowing. 2. a muddy or dusty place where animals wallow. —wal'low·er, n.

wall·pa·per (wôl'pā-pēr), n. paper for covering walls, ceilings, etc.: v.t. to put wallpaper on.

wall plate, a horizontal timber laid along a wall to support the ends of joists.

Wall Street, a street in New York City that is the financial center of the U.S.

wal·nut (wôl'nut, 'nŭt), n. 1. any one of a genus of trees valued for their nuts and wood and as shade trees. 2. the nut of this tree, with a two-lobed kernel. 3. the wood, used for furniture, paneling, etc. 4. the brown color of this wood.

Wal·pur·gis Night (väl-poor'gis), the eve of May Day (April 30), when witches allegedly hold revels.

wal·rus (wôl'rŭs, wäl'-), n., pl. -rus·es, -rus, a large, marine mammal related to the seal, with two tusks, a thick hide, and a drooping mustache: adj. of or like a walrus.

waltz (wôlts, wôls), n. 1. a ballroom dance for couples, in moderately fast triple rhythm. 2. music for this: v.i. 1. to dance a waltz. 2. to move deftly and lightly. 3. [Informal], to progress with ease.

wam·ble (wäm'l, 'bl), v.i. -bled, -bling, [Chiefly Dialectal], 1. to writhe, wiggle, or twist. 2. to be unsteady; stagger. 3. to feel unsettled or nauseated: said of the stomach. —wam'bly, adj. -bli·er, -bli·est.

wam·pum (wäm'pŭm), n. beads made of shells, formerly used by North American Indians as money and for ornaments.

wan (wän, wŏn), adj. wan'ner, wan'nest, 1. sickly pale; pallid. 2. faint or feeble, as a wan smile. —wan'ly, adv. —wan'ness, n.

wand (wänd, wŏnd), n. 1. a long, slender rod with supposed magical power, as one carried by a magician or a fairy. 2. a staff of authority.

wan·der (wän'dēr, wŏn'-), v.i. 1. to ramble about aimlessly; stroll. 2. to depart (*from* a path, course, etc.). 3. to be incoherent. 4. to meander, as a stream: v.t. to ramble or roam over or in. —wan'der·er, n.

wan·der·ing (-ing), adj. 1. rambling; going about from place to place. 2. meandering or winding: said of streams or roads. 3. nomadic; roving.

Wandering Jew, 1. in *Medieval Folklore,* a Jew unkind to Christ and condemned to wander until the Second Coming. 2. [w- J-], any one of several trailing plants, especially one with purplish leaves.

wan·der·lust (wän'dēr·lust), n. an urge to travel.

wane (wän), v.i. waned, wan'ing, 1. to become less, as the moon after it is full. 2. to decrease in intensity, as light. 3. to decline in power, influence, prosperity, etc. 4. to draw near the close, as a period of time: n. a waning.

wan·gle (wang'gl), v.i. -gled, -gling, [Informal], to get or accomplish by trickery, persuasion, or teasing. —wan'gler, n.

wan·i·gan (wän'i·gän), n. 1. a chest, trunk, etc. for storing clothing and supplies, as in a lumber camp. 2. a small, rough shelter, as for cooking or sleeping. Also spelled **wan'ni·gan.**

Wan·kel engine (väng'kl, wang'-), a rotary combustion engine with a spinning piston, used as in some automobiles: named after its German inventor, F. Wankel.

want (wänt, wŏnt), n. 1. an absence or scarcity of what is needed or desired. 2. the thing lacking or desired. 3. poverty; destitution. 4. a craving; desire: v.t. 1. to lack. 2. to desire. 3. to crave. 4. to wish to see, speak to, interrogate, etc. 5. [Chiefly British], to require: v.i. 1. to have need (with *for*). 2. to be destitute.

want ad, [Informal], an advertisement, as in a newspaper classified section, for something wanted.

want·ing ('ing), adj. deficient; inadequate; absent; lacking: prep. with lack of.

wan·ton (wän'tn, wŏn'-), adj. 1. sexually unrestrained. 2. malicious. 3. arrogantly disregarding fairness or justice. 4. [Poetic], frolicsome: n. one who is wanton; especially, a woman who is sexually unrestrained: v.i. to be wanton. —wan'ton·ly, adv. —wan'ton·ness, n.

wap·i·ti (wäp'ĭ-ti), n., pl. -ti, -ties, the largest North American deer, with wide antlers: also called *elk*.

war (wôr), n. 1. a state of open, armed hostilities between nations or factions within a nation. 2. any struggle, combat, conflict, etc. 3. the science or profession of military operations: adj. of, from, or used in war: v.i. warred, war'ring, 1. to engage in military conflict. 2. to struggle; contend.

war·ble (wôr'bl), v.t. & v.i. -bled, -bling, to sing in a trilling and quavering manner, as birds: n. a flow of melodious sounds, as by warbling; trill.

war·bler ('blēr), n. 1. one that warbles. 2. any one of many small, often brightly colored songbirds.

war cry, a shout used as a rallying call to charge or battle.

ward (wôrd), v.t. to turn aside; repel (usually followed by *off*): n. 1. the state of being under guard or in care or custody. 2. a division of a city or town for representation, voting, etc. 3. a division of a prison, hospital, etc. 4. a person under the care of a guardian or court.

-ward (wērd), a suffix meaning in or. toward a specified direction or course: also **-wards** (wērdz).

war-den (wôr'dn), *n.* 1. a guardian; keeper. 2. the head official of a prison.

ward-er (wôr'dẽr), *n.* a guard; watchman.

ward heeler, a minor local politician.

ward-robe (wôrd'rōb), *n.* 1. a closet, cabinet, etc for clothes. 2. wearing apparel; especially, one's supply of clothes.

ward-room ('rōom), *n.* a room in a warship for commissioned officers other than the captain, for use as a dining room and lounge.

ware (wer), *n.* 1. a thing or things for sale: usually used in the plural. 2. pottery.

ware-house ('hous), *n.* a building for storing goods: *v.t.* ('houz), -housed, -hous-ing, to deposit in a warehouse.

war-fare (wôr'fer), *n.* 1. hostilities; war; armed conflict. 2. any kind of conflict.

war-head ('hed), *n.* the front part of a guided missile, torpedo, etc. containing the charge.

war horse, 1. a spirited horse for military service; charger. 2. [Informal], a veteran of many conflicts and struggles: now usually **war'horse,** *n.*

war-i-ly (wer'i-li), *adv.* in a wary manner.

war-i-ness (-nis), *n.* wary quality or condition.

war-like (wôr'līk), *adj.* bellicose; martial.

war-lock (wôr'lok), *n.* a male witch.

war-lord (wôr'lôrd), *n.* 1. a high military leader, especially of a warlike state. 2. a tyrannical local leader, often a bandit, as formerly in China.

warm (wôrm), *adj.* 1. having or giving off heat in a moderate degree. 2. hot. 3. preserving warmth or body heat. 4. zealous; excited. 5. lively; animated. 6. irascible; easily angered. 7. cordial. 8. sympathetic. 9. fresh, as a trail. 10. suggestive of warmth, as the color tones of red, orange, or yellow. 11. [Informal], close to a thing for which one is searching: *v.i.* & *v.i.* to become or cause to become warm. —warm'ly, *adv.* —warm'ness, *n.*

warm-blood-ed ('blud'id), *adj.* having warm blood; specifically, denoting animals, as birds and mammals, that maintain a uniform and relatively high body temperature.

warmed-o-ver (wôrmd'ō'ver), *adj.* 1. that has been reheated, as food. 2. presented again.

warm-heart-ed (wôrm'härt'id), *adj.* of a friendly disposition; kind; affectionate.

war-mon-ger (wôr'mung-gẽr), *n.* one who wants or tries to incite war.

warmth (wôrmth), *n.* 1. moderate heat. 2. the quality or state of being moderately warm. 3. enthusiasm, eagerness, etc. 4. affection, kindliness, friendliness, etc.

warn (wôrn), *v.t.* & *v.i.* 1. to let know of possible or impending danger, evil, etc. 2. to advise to be cautious. 3. to notify in advance.

warn-ing ('ing), *n.* 1. the act of one that warns. 2. the condition of being warned. 3. something, as a notice, that warns: *adj.* that warns.

warp (wôrp), *n.* 1. the threads extending lengthwise in the loom and crossed by the weft or woof. 2. a towing rope run as from a ship to a dock, anchor, etc. and used to haul the vessel. 3. a twist out of true shape: *v.t.* 1. to turn or twist out of shape. 2. to

pervert; distort. 3. to tow or move (a vessel) with a warp. 4. to arrange (threads) lengthwise on the loom: *v.i.* to become bent or twisted; deviate. —warp'er, *n.*

war-path (wôr'path), *n.* 1. among North American Indians, a route or course followed in making an attack. 2. any hostile course or condition.

warp beam, the roller of a loom on which the warp is wound.

war-plane (wôr'plān), *n.* an airplane used in warfare.

war-rant (wôr'ắnt, wär'-), *v.t.* 1. to guarantee; give assurance to. 2. to authorize. 3. to give adequate reason for; justify: *n.* 1. a legal authorization. 2. a legal writ authorizing a search, arrest, etc. 3. a guarantee. 4. a reason or justification for something. —war'rant-a-ble, *adj.*

warrant officer, an officer in the U.S. armed forces ranking above an enlisted man but below a commissioned officer.

war-ran-ty (wôr'ắn-ti, wär'-), *n., pl.* -ties, same as guarantee (noun 2).

war-ren (wôr'ẽn, wär'-), *n.* 1. a place where rabbits breed or are numerous. 2. a congested district or building.

war-ri-or (wôr'i-ẽr, wär'-), *n.* a fighting man; soldier.

war-saw (wôr'sô), *n.* a very large, black grouper that is found in the Atlantic off Florida.

war-ship (wôr'ship), *n.* a ship used in war.

wart (wôrt), *n.* a small, usually hard excrescence or protuberance. —wart'y, *adj.*

wart hog, an African wild hog with large, protruding tusks and a warty face.

war whoop, a yell by North American Indians making an attack.

war-y (wer'i), *adj.* war'i-er, war'i-est, cautious; watchful; on guard.

was (wuz, wäz), first and third person singular of the past tense of be.

wash (wösh, wäsh), *v.t.* 1. to clean with water or other liquid. 2. to moisten. 3. to flow along or against, as waves on the shore. 4. to wear or erode by the action of water. 5. to carry or flush by water. 6. to purify. 7. to overlay with thin metal. 8. to cover with a thin coat of color: *v.i.* 1. to bear washing. 2. to wash oneself. 3. to wash clothes. 4. to be removed by washing (followed by *out* or *away*): *n.* 1. the act of washing. 2. a surge of water. 3. an eddy of water or air caused as by a propeller. 4. a quantity of things, especially clothes, to be washed together. 5. alluvial matter, as silt or mud. 6. a shallow part of an arm of a sea or river. 7. a thin coating of metal or paint. 8. a cosmetic lotion or medicinal liquid: *adj.* able to be washed without harm. —wash'a-ble, *adj.* & *n.*

wash-and-wear ('n-wer'), *adj.* denoting clothes or material needing little or no ironing after washing.

wash-board ('bôrd), *n.* a board with a corrugated surface as of metal or glass on which clothes are scrubbed.

wash-bowl ('bōl), *n.* a bowl with water faucets and drain, used as in washing the face and hands: also **wash'ba-sin** ('bās-n).

ō in dragon, ōō in crude, oo in wool, u in cup, ū in cure, ũ in turn, ŭ in focus, oi in boy, ou in house, th in thin, th in sheathe, g in get, j in joy, y in yet.

wash-cloth ('klôth), n. a small cloth used for washing the face or body.

washed-out (wôsht'out'), adj. 1. faded. 2. [Informal], exhausted; weary.

wash-er (wôsh'ēr), n. 1. one that washes. 2. a machine to wash something, as dishes or clothes. 3. a flat disk or ring, as of rubber or metal, used to seat a bolt or nut securely, prevent leaking, check friction, etc.

wash-er-wom-an (-woom-ăn), n., pl. -wom-en, a woman whose work is washing clothes.

wash-ing (wôsh'ing), n. 1. the act of one that washes. 2. clothes washed or to be washed.

washing machine, a machine for washing clothes.

wash-out ('out), n. 1. a ditch or gap caused by a sudden, strong current of water. 2. the flow of water causing this. 3. [Slang], a failure.

wash-room ('rōōm), n. 1. a room for washing. 2. a public restroom.

wash-stand ('stand), n. 1. a stand with a bowl, pitcher, etc. for washing oneself. 2. a washbowl fixture.

wash-tub ('tub), n. a tub for washing clothes.

wash-y ('i), adj. wash'i-er, wash'i-est. 1. watery; diluted too much. 2. pale in color. 3. insipid.

was-n't (wuz'nt, wäz'nt), was not.

WASP, Wasp (wäsp, wôsp), n. a white Anglo-Saxon Protestant.

wasp (wäsp, wôsp), n. any one of a large group of winged insects with a slender body, the abdomen being attached by a narrow stalk, and with biting mouths and, in the females and workers, a vicious sting.

wasp-ish ('ish), adj. 1. like a wasp. 2. petulant and irritable.

was-sail (wäs'l, 'āl), n. 1. a merrymaking; drinking party, especially at Christmas time. 2. spiced ale or other drink served at such a party. 3. a toast drunk at such a time: v.i. & v.t. to drink a wassail (to).

Was-ser-mann test (wäs'ēr-män), a blood test for the detection of syphilis: after August von Wassermann (1866-1925), German bacteriologist who devised it: also **Wassermann reaction**.

wast (wäst), archaic second person singular of the past indicative of be: used with thou.

wast-age (wäs'tij), n. 1. loss by use, wearing away, etc. 2. the amount lost in this way.

waste (wäst), v.t. wast'ed, wast'ing. 1. to destroy wantonly; devastate. 2. to diminish; wear away. 3. to squander; use carelessly or futilely. 4. to impair; make weak or feeble. 5. to neglect to take advantage of: v.i. 1. to be diminished, worn out, or used up slowly. 2. to become weak or feeble: adj. 1. lying unused, untilled, uninhabited, etc. 2. devastated. 3. left over. 4. excreted as of no further use to an animal or plant. 5. used to hold or carry off waste: n. 1. untilled or uninhabited land. 2. an area that has been devastated. 3. the act of wasting. 4. dissipation of resources; useless expenditure. 5. excretions from the body, as urine or feces. 6. discarded material, as garbage, sewage, or ashes; refuse.

waste-bas-ket ('bas-kit), n. a basket or other container for wastepaper and other trash: also **wastepaper basket**.

waste-ful ('ful), adj. spending money or using things extravagantly or uselessly; squandering. —**waste'ful-ly**, adv. —**waste'ful-ness**, n.

waste-land ('land), n. desolate or barren land.

waste-pa-per ('pā-pēr), n. paper discarded after use or as useless: also **waste paper**.

waste pipe, an outlet pipe, as to carry off waste water, excess steam, etc.

wast-er (wās'tēr), n. one who wastes; especially, a prodigal, spendthrift, loafer, etc.

wast-rel (wās'trēl), n. 1. one who wastes; especially, a spendthrift. 2. a shiftless person.

watch (wäch, wôch), n. 1. close observation for a time. 2. a keeping awake so as to guard. 3. a watchman, or a period of duty of a watchman. 4. a period during which part of a ship's crew are on duty, usually four hours. 5. the part of the crew on duty during such a period. 6. a small timepiece to be kept in the pocket or worn on the wrist: v.i. 1. to stay awake; keep guard. 2. to be alert. 3. to observe over a period of time. 4. to wait attentively (for): v.t. 1. to tend; guard. 2. to observe carefully. 3. to look and wait for expectantly. —**watch'er**, n.

watch-band ('band), n. a band, as of leather or metal, to keep a watch on the wrist.

watch-case ('kās), n. the case or outer covering of a watch, especially a pocket watch.

watch-dog ('dôg), n. 1. a dog kept for guarding property. 2. one who keeps watch, as to discover and expose instances of waste or poor management.

watch-ful ('ful), adj. vigilant; wary; keeping close watch. —**watch'ful-ly**, adv. —**watch'ful-ness**, n.

watch-mak-er ('mā-kēr), n. one who makes or mends watches. —**watch'mak-ing**, n.

watch-man ('măn), n., pl. -men, a guard; one who guards a building, residence, or other property, especially at night.

watch night, a religious service held on New Year's Eve: also **watch-night service**.

watch-tow-er ('tou-ēr), n. a high tower from which a sentinel keeps watch.

watch-word ('würd), n. 1. a password. 2. a rallying cry, slogan, etc.

wa-ter (wôt'er, wät'-), n. 1. the colorless, transparent liquid found in the sea, lakes, rivers, etc. and falling as rain: water is a compound of two parts of hydrogen to one part of oxygen, freezes at 32°F (0°C), and boils at 212°F (100°C). 2. the sea or other large body of water. 3. the surface of water. 4. a given level, depth, or displacement of water. 5. a secretion of the body, as urine or saliva; also, a fluid retained abnormally in a joint, organ, etc. 6. the transparency and luster of a diamond or other precious stone. 7. a lustrous, wavy surface given to silk, metal, etc.: v.t. 1. to supply (crops or plants) with water. 2. to give (animals) water to drink. 3. to wet with water. 4. to dilute with water. 5. to give a lustrous, wavy surface to (silk, metal, etc.): v.i. 1. to get or take in a supply of water. 2. to fill with tears, as the eyes. 3. to secrete saliva, as the mouth. 4. to drink water: adj. 1. in, on, or near water, as certain plants and animals. 2. of or for water. 3. operated by water power.

water bed, a bed having as a mattress a heavy plastic casing filled with water, the casing being set in a specially constructed frame: also **wa'ter-bed,** *n.*

water bird, a bird living on or near water.

water brash, same as pyrosis.

wa·ter·buck ('buk), *n., pl.* -buck, -bucks, a long-haired, African antelope with lyre-shaped horns and a reddish or grayish coat.

water buffalo, a strong, oxlike animal of southern Asia and the Philippine Islands, domesticated for use as a draft animal.

water bug, 1. a small cockroach; Croton bug. 2. any one of a number of hemipterous insects that live in fresh waters.

water chestnut, 1. an aquatic Chinese sedge that produces an edible tuber. 2. this tuber, used in Chinese cooking.

water clock, a mechanism measuring time by the flow or fall of water.

water closet, same as toilet (senses 4 & 5).

wa·ter·col·or (-kul-ẽr), *n.* 1. a pigment ground and applied with water as a paint. 2. a painting made with such pigment. 3. the art of painting with watercolors. —**wa'ter·col·or·ist,** *n.*

wa·ter·cooled (-kōōld), *adj.* cooled by water circulating around or through.

wa·ter·course (-kôrs), *n.* a channel or bed in which water runs, as a stream, river, or canal.

wa·ter·craft (-kraft), *n., pl.* -craft, a water vehicle, as a ship or boat.

wa·ter·cress (-kres), *n.* an edible, aquatic, perennial plant of the mustard family, with leaves that are used in salads.

water cure, the cure of disease by water treatment, externally or internally; hydropathy or hydrotherapy.

wa·tered (wôt'ẽrd), *adj.* 1. sprinkled with water. 2. supplied with water: said of land. 3. having a lustrous, wavy surface: said of metal, silk, etc.

watered stock, stock issued without corresponding assets being acquired, thus producing a face value beyond its worth.

wa·ter·fall (-fôl), *n.* water, as of a river, falling perpendicularly from a height; cascade.

wa·ter·fowl (-foul), *n., pl.* -fowl, a water bird, especially one that swims.

wa·ter·front (-frunt), *n.* 1. land abutting on a body of water. 2. the area of a city or town on such land; dock or wharf area.

water gap, a pass between hills or mountains, through which a stream flows.

water gas, a fuel gas formed by passing steam over incandescent coke or coal: it is a poisonous mixture of carbon dioxide, carbon monoxide, nitrogen, and hydrogen.

water gauge, 1. a gauge used to measure the level or flow of water in a stream or channel. 2. a device showing the water level in a boiler, tank, or the like.

water glass, 1. a substance composed of silicate of sodium or potassium, dissolved in water to form a syrupy liquid used to preserve eggs, as a waterproofing coat, etc. 2. a

drinking glass. 3. a glass tube used as a water gauge on a boiler, tank, or the like. 4. a water clock. Also **wa'ter·glass,** *n.*

water hemlock, a perennial plant of the parsley family, growing in moist places in the Northern Hemisphere: its tuberous roots are poisonous.

water hen, 1. the American coot. 2. any one of various birds of the rail family.

water hole, 1. any natural hollow containing water, especially in an arid region. 2. such a hole in the dry bed of an intermittent river. 3. a hole in a sheet of ice.

water hyacinth, a tropical American aquatic plant with showy lavender flowers and thick, floating stalks.

water ice, 1. ice formed directly from the freezing of fresh or salt water rather than from compacted snow. 2. [British], a dessert ice made from water, sugar, and fruit juice or other flavoring.

wa·ter·i·ness (-i-nis), *n.* the state or quality of being watery.

watering place, 1. a place at a body of water where animals go to drink. 2. [Chiefly British], a resort frequented for its natural mineral water or for its beaches, boating activities, etc.

water jacket, an outer casing containing water to keep cylinders, machinery, etc. cool or at a constant temperature.

water level, 1. the surface of smooth water. 2. the height of this. 3. an instrument containing water in a glass tube, used to ascertain whether a surface is level. 3. a waterline.

wa·ter·lil·y (-lil-i), *n., pl.* -lil·ies, 1. an aquatic plant with showy flowers and broad leaves that float on the surface of the water. 2. a flower of this plant.

wa·ter·line (-līn), *n.* the line to which the water rises on the hull of a ship.

wa·ter·logged (-lôgd), *adj.* heavily saturated with water, as the hull of a ship.

Wa·ter·loo (wôt'ẽr-lōō), *n.* a decisive or disastrous defeat or reversal: in reference to Napoleon's final defeat at Waterloo, Belgium, in 1815.

water main, a main pipe, usually underground, in a water system for a town, city, etc.

wa·ter·mark (wôt'ẽr-märk), *n.* 1. a mark indicating the height to which water has risen. 2. a design impressed on paper in the making to indicate trademark, quality, etc.: *v.t.* to impress (paper) with a watermark.

wa·ter·mel·on (-mel-ŏn), *n.* a large, round or oblong, edible fruit of a trailing plant of the gourd family, with a thick, hard, green rind and a sweet, red, watery pulp containing many black seeds.

water moccasin, a poisonous snake, olive-brown with transverse dark stripes, found along or in rivers and swamps of the southeastern U.S.

water ouzel, any one of several birds of America, Europe, and Asia; especially, the American dipper, that dives and swims in Western mountain streams.

water pipe, 1. a pipe for conveying water. 2. a hookah; narghile.

ŏ in dragon, ōō in crude, oo in wool, u in cup, ū in cure, ü in turn, ŭ in focus, oi in boy, ou in house, th in thin, th in sheathe, g in get, j in joy, y in yet,

water polo, a team game played by swimmers with a ball.

water power, power used to drive machinery by utilizing the weight or force of water.

wa·ter·proof (-prŏof), *adj.* impervious to water, as from being treated with rubber, plastic, etc.: *n.* 1. waterproof material. 2. [Chiefly British], a raincoat: *v.t.* to make waterproof. —**wa'ter·proof·er,** *n.*

water rat, 1. any one of various rodents that live along streams or ponds. 2. same as muskrat (sense 1).

wa·ter·re·pel·lent (-ri-pel-ĕnt) *adj.* having a finish that repels water but is not completely waterproof.

wa·ter·shed (-shed), *n.* 1. a region drained by a river or rivers. 2. a ridge dividing such regions from each other.

wa·ter·side (-sīd), *n.* land bordering a body·of water; shore.

wa·ter·ski (-skē), *v.i.* -skied, -ski·ing, to ride on boards like skis (water skis) while holding a towrope attached to a speedboat. —**wa'ter·ski·er,** *n.*

water snake, any one of numerous nonpoisonous snakes found chiefly in rivers and lakes.

water softener, 1. a tank containing any of various chemicals through which water is filtered for softening. 2. a chemical compound added to hard water to soften it, as for bathing or for washing clothes.

wa·ter·sol·u·ble (-sol-yoo-bl), *adj.* able to be dissolved in water.

water spaniel, either of two curly-haired breeds of spaniel used to retrieve waterfowl in hunting.

wa·ter·spout (-spout), *n.* 1. a funnel-shaped or tubelike whirlwind filled with spray; tornado over a body of water. 2. a spout from which water runs.

water table, the level below which the ground is saturated with water.

wa·ter·tight (-tīt), *adj.* 1. so tight as to keep out water altogether. 2. that cannot be refuted, denied, etc.; flawless.

water tower, 1. a portable apparatus used to elevate hoses and nozzles to great heights for fighting fires. 2. a large water tank elevated to maintain pressure in a water system.

wa·ter·way (-wā), *n.* 1. any body of water on which boats and ships can travel. 2. a channel through which water runs.

water wheel, 1. a wheel turned by the flow or fall of water, as to produce power. 2. a wheel that lifts water by buckets fastened to its rim.

water wings, a pair of small, inflatable, balloonlike floats attached together and worn under the arms to keep an inexperienced swimmer afloat in the water.

wa·ter·works (-wŭrks), *n.pl.* a system of pipes, machinery, pumps, tanks, etc. for supplying water to a community.

wa·ter·worn (-wôrn), *adj.* smoothed or worn by the action of moving water.

wa·ter·y (-i), *adj.* 1. pertaining to or like water. 2. moist. 3. thin; diluted. 4. tearful. 5. in water. 6. soft and soggy. 7. discharging or filled with water. —**wa'ter·i·ness,** *n.*

watt (wăt, wŏt), *n.* a unit of electrical power equal to the power developed in a circuit by a current of one ampere flowing through a potential difference of one volt.

watt·age ('ij), *n.* 1. electric power expressed in watts. 2. the number of watts necessary to operate an appliance or device.

wat·tle (wăt'l, wŏt'l), *n.* 1. originally, a stick or twig, or a hurdle made of these. 2. a network of twigs and branches interwoven with sticks or rods to make fences, walls, or roofs. 3. in Australia, any one of various acacias, whose flexible branches were formerly used to make wattles. 4. a fleshy lobe, often brightly colored, under the throat of some birds, as a turkey or rooster, or some lizards: *adj.* made of or having a roof of wattle: *v.t.* -tled, -tling, 1. to interweave (twigs and sticks). 2. to make (a roof, wall, etc.) of wattle.

wat·tle·bird (-bŭrd), *n.* any one of a number of honey eaters of Australia and Tasmania, having a wattle on each side of the throat.

Wa·tu·si (wä-tōō'si), *n., pl.* -sis, -si, any member of a group of tall, slender, African people.

waul (wôl), *n.* a cry or squall, as of a cat or tiny baby: *v.i.* to cry or squall.

Wave (wāv), *n.* a member of the women's branch of the U.S. Navy.

wave (wāv), *n.* 1. an undulation of water above and below its natural level along the surface of a body of water; ridge or swell. 2. a state of vibration propagated through a system of particles or through an elastic medium. 3. a signal made by moving a hand, arm, etc. 4. a curve, as in the hair. 5. something like a wave in effect, as an upsurge, rise, or mass movement: *v.i.* waved, wav'ing, 1. to swing, sway, or flutter to and fro. 2. to signal by moving the hand, arm, etc. 3. to curve up and down: *v.t.* 1. to cause to wave. 2. to brandish. 3. to signal or beckon by waving. 4. to swing (something) as a signal. 5. to form in a series of curves, as hair. —**wave'less,** *adj.* —**wav'er,** *n.*

wave·length ('length), *n.* in *Physics,* the distance between corresponding points on two consecutive waves.

wave·let ('lit), *n.* a little wave; ripple.

wa·ver (wā'vĕr), *v.i.* 1. to move or sway to and fro. 2. to vacillate; hesitate or be undecided. 3. to flicker or quiver: *n.* the act of wavering. —**wa'ver·er,** *n.*

wa·ver·ing (-ing), *adj.* hesitating; undecided. —**wa'ver·ing·ly,** *adv.*

wa·vy (wā'vi). *adj.* wav'i·er, wav'i·est, 1. rising and swelling in waves; undulating. 2. full of or characterized by waves. 3. resembling waves. —**wav'i·ly,** *adv.* —**wav'i·ness,** *n.*

wax (waks), *n.* 1. a plastic, yellowish substance secreted by bees; beeswax. 2. a substance resembling this, as paraffin. 3. the cerumen of the ear; earwax: *v.t.* to rub, polish, treat, cover, or smear with wax: *v.i.* 1. to increase in size, extent, power, etc. 2. to gradually become full: said of the moon. 3. to become.

---

a in *cap,* ā in *cane,* ä in *father,* ȧ in *abet,* e in *met,* ē in *be,* ē in *baker,* ẽ in *regent,* ĭ in *pit,* ī in *fine,* ĭ in *manifest,* o in *hot,* ô in *horse,* ō in *bone,*

wax bean, a variety of kidney bean with long, yellow pods, eaten when immature.

wax-bill ('bil), *n.* a bird resembling the finch and having a waxy bill of a red, pink, or white color, sometimes kept as a cage bird.

wax-en (wak'sn), *adj.* made of, like, or consisting of wax.

wax myrtle, a kind of bayberry that bears grayish-white berries coated with wax.

wax paper, a kind of paper coated with wax or paraffin, used as a wrapping paper, as to keep food fresh: also **waxed paper.**

wax-wing ('wing), *n.* a small bird of the Northern Hemisphere that has brown plumage, a crest, and waxy feather tips.

wax-works ('wûrks), *n.pl.* an exhibition of wax figures: also **wax museum.**

wax-y (wak'si), *adj.* **wax'i-er, wax'i-est,** of, consisting of, or resembling wax. —**wax'i-ness,** *n.*

way (wā), *n.* **1.** a road, street, lane, etc. **2.** a route; course. **3.** progression; forward movement. **4.** distance. **5.** an opening, as in a crowd. **6.** direction of action or motion. **7.** a path in life; course of conduct. **8.** a manner or method of doing something. **9.** respect; feature. **10.** wish; will. **11.** *pl.* a wooden framework on which a ship is built and from which it is launched. **12.** a ship's momentum through the water. **13.** [Informal], a locality; area: *adv.* [Informal], away; far.

way-far-er (-fer-ẽr), *n.* a traveler on foot.

way-lay (wā-lā'), *v.t.* **-laid', -lay'ing, 1.** to attack from ambush. **2.** to accost by surprise.

way-out (wā'out'), *adj.* [Informal], very unconventional, advanced, exotic, etc.

-ways (wāz), a suffix meaning *in a (given) manner or direction:* equivalent to **-wise.**

way-side (wā'sīd), *n.* the area along the edge of a road: *adv.* at, on, or along the side of a road.

way station, a small station between principal stations on a railroad.

way-ward (wẽrd), *adj.* **1.** perverse, headstrong, disobedient, etc. **2.** capricious; unpredictable. —**way'ward-ness,** *n.*

way-worn (wôrn), *adj.* tired from traveling.

we (wē), *pron.* **1.** the ones speaking or writing; sometimes used by a person in speaking of a group that includes himself, or by a sovereign, editor, etc. in place of *I.* **2.** the first person plural pronoun.

weak (wēk), *adj.* **1.** lacking strength or vigor; feeble; frail. **2.** lacking will power. **3.** lacking discernment, good judgment, or wisdom. **4.** lacking authority or force. **5.** easily broken, bent, etc. **6.** lacking in volume; faint. **7.** diluted. **8.** faulty or unconvincing. **9.** not secure; unfortified. **10.** in *Grammar,* denoting a verb that has its past tense formed by the addition of *-ed* or *-d* to the present tense.

weak-en ('n), *v.t. & v.i.* to make or become weak or weaker; reduce in quality or strength.

weak-fish ('fish), *n., pl.* **-fish, -fish-es,** a marine food fish found off the eastern coast of the U.S.

weak-kneed ('nēd'), *adj.* lacking willpower, courage, or determination; irresolute.

weak-ling ('ling), *n.* a person weak in moral or physical strength.

weak-ly ('li), *adj.* **-li-er, -li-est,** not strong; feeble; sickly: *adv.* in a weak manner.

weak-mind-ed ('mīn'did), *adj.* **1.** mentally deficient; feebleminded. **2.** indecisive; irresolute. **3.** indicating lack of resolve or initiative. — **weak'-mind'ed-ness,** *n.*

weak-ness ('nis), *n.* **1.** the quality of being weak. **2.** a fault; weak point. **3.** a special fondness (*for* something).

weal (wēl), *n.* **1.** welfare; prosperity. **2.** a wale or stripe; welt, as from a blow.

weald (wēld), *n.* [Poetic] **1.** a wood or forest. **2.** a stretch of open country that was once forest.

wealth (welth), *n.* **1.** much money; riches; affluence. **2.** an abundance. **3.** worldly possessions. **4.** valuable products or derivatives. **5.** everything having economic value.

wealth-y ('i), *adj.* **wealth'i-er, wealth'i-est,** rich; affluent. —**wealth'i-ly,** *adv.* —**wealth'i-ness,** *n.*

wean (wēn), *v.t.* **1.** to accustom (a child or other young mammal) to food other than its mother's milk or milk taken from a bottle with nipple. **2.** to withdraw (a person) from an object of affection, habit, etc.: *n.* [Scottish], a child or baby.

weap-on (wep'ŏn), *n.* **1.** any instrument of offense or defense in fighting. **2.** anything used against an opponent. —**weap'on-less,** *adj.*

wear (wer), *v.t.* **wore, worn, wear'ing, 1.** to impair or waste by time, usage, friction, etc. **2.** to cause or produce by friction, flowing, etc. **3.** to carry (clothes, jewelry, etc.) on the person. **4.** to show in one's appearance. **5.** to weaken or fatigue (a person): *v.i.* **1.** to be impaired or wasted by time, usage, friction, etc. **2.** to last under use. **3.** to have a tiring effect (*on*): *n.* **1.** the act of wearing. **2.** the state of being worn. **3.** clothes. **4.** diminution or loss from usage, friction, etc. — **wear'a-ble,** *adj.* —**wear'er,** *n.*

wea-ri-some (wir'i-sŏm), *adj.* fatiguing; tiresome or tedious.

wea-ry ('i), *adj.* **-ri-er, -ri-est, 1.** worn out physically or mentally. **2.** having one's patience exhausted or enthusiasm diminished. **3.** causing weariness; fatiguing. **4.** irksome: *v.t.* **-ried, -ry-ing, 1.** to wear out or make weary. **2.** to harass by something irksome: *v.i.* **1.** to become weary, tired, or fatigued. **2.** to become impatient. —**wea'ri-ly,** *adv.* — **wea'ri-ness,** *n.*

wea-sand (wē'znd), *n.* the esophagus; gullet.

wea-sel (wē'zl), *n.* a small, carnivorous mammal with short legs and a long, slender body.

weath-er (weth'ẽr), *n.* **1.** the state of the atmosphere with respect to cold, heat, moisture, etc. **2.** an unpleasant atmospheric state, as rain, a storm, etc.: *v.t.* **1.** to expose to, or season by exposure to, the weather. **2.** to sail to the windward of. **3.** to endure; survive: *v.i.* to undergo change by the action of the weather.

weath-er-beat-en (-bēt-n), *adj.* **1.** worn, tanned,

toughened, etc. by the weather, as a person or his face. 2. damaged, discolored, or worn down by the action of weather.

weath·er·cock (-kok), *n.* 1. a weather vane in the form of a cock. 2. a person who is fickle or changeable.

weath·er·glass (-glas), *n.* same as **barometer** (sense 1).

weath·er·ing (-ing), *n.* the action or effect of sun, air, rain, etc. on material objects, specifically on rock surfaces, as in forming sand, gravel, soil, etc.

weath·er·man (-man), *n., pl.* **-men** (-men), a weather forecaster, especially one who reports forecasts, as on television.

weather map, a map or chart showing the meteorological conditions over a given area at a given time, as temperature, humidity, barometric pressure, etc.

weath·er·proof (-prōōf), *adj.* able to withstand exposure to the weather without harm: *v.t.* to make weatherproof.

weath·er·strip (-strip), *n.* a strip of thin material, as metal, felt, rubber, etc. for inserting in the joints of doors and windows to exclude rain, frost, cold winds, etc.: also **weath·er·strip·ping:** *v.t.* -stripped, -strip·ping, to apply weatherstrips to.

weather vane, a vane that swings with the wind to show the direction of the wind.

weave (wēv), *v.t.* wove, wo'ven or wove, weav'ing, 1. to interlace (threads). 2. to form (cloth) by such interlacing, as on a loom. 3. to twist or interlace (reeds, twigs, etc.). 4. to form (a basket) by such interweaving. 5. to compose or fabricate in the mind. 6. to spin (a web): said of spiders or some larvae. 7. past tense weaved, past participle weaved, to move (someone or something) along in a winding or zigzag course: *v.i.* 1. to practice weaving; work with a loom. 2. to become interlaced. 3. past tense weaved, past participle weaved, to move along in a winding or zigzag course: *n.* a method or pattern of weaving. —weav'er, *n.*

weav·er·bird (wē'vēr-bûrd), *n.* a finchlike bird of the Old World, that constructs a large, dome-shaped nest of interlaced grass and vegetable stalks.

web (web), *n.* 1. a texture or fabric of threads or threadlike material. 2. the woven or spun network of a spider. 3. a carefully contrived trap or snare. 4. a network of tissue. 5. a large roll of paper for a kind of printing press. 6. a membrane uniting the digits of various water birds, amphibians, etc.: *v.t.* **webbed, web'bing,** 1. to join by a web. 2. to surround with or as with a web. 3. to entangle or snare as in a web. —web'like, *adj.*

webbed (webd), *adj.* 1. having fingers or toes joined by webs. 2. made of webbing or formed like a web. ·

web·bing (web'ing), *n.* 1. a strong fabric, as of cotton or jute, woven in strips or tape and used as for belts or straps. 2. a membrane between fingers and toes, or uniting the digits of various animals.

web-foot ('foot), *n., pl.* **-feet,** 1. a foot having the toes connected by a membrane. 2. an animal or bird with feet having membranes between the toes. —web'-foot·ed, *adj.*

wed (wed), *v.t. & v.i.* wed'ded, wed'ded or wed, wed'ding, 1. to marry. 2. to unite; join.

we'd (wēd), 1. we had. 2. we should. 3. we would.

wed·ding (wed'ing), *n.* 1. marriage; nuptial ceremony or festivities. 2. a marriage anniversary.

wedge (wej), *n.* 1. a piece of wood or metal, thick at one end and thin at the other, used to split wood, hold a door in place, lift a weight, etc. 2. anything shaped like a wedge, as a formation of troops, a piece of pie, etc. 3. an act, event, etc. that opens the way to change, intrusion, etc.: *v.t.* wedged, wedg'ing, 1. to cleave, force, drive, or fasten with a wedge. 2. to press closely; pack: *v.i.* to be forced as a wedge.

Wedg·wood (wej'wood), *n.* a fine English pottery having white figures in relief on a tinted background: a trademark: also **Wedgwood ware.**

wed·lock (wed'lok), *n.* matrimony.

Wednes·day (wenz'di, ·dā), *n.* the fourth day of the week.

wee (wē), *adj.* we'er, we'est, 1. very small. 2. very early, as the *wee* hours of the morning.

weed (wēd), *n.* 1. a useless or noxious uncultivated plant that crowds out desired plants. 2. *pl.* a widow's black mourning garments: *v.t. & v.i.* 1. to remove (weeds) from (a garden, lawn, etc.). 2. to remove as being undesirable or troublesome (often followed by *out*). —weed'er, *n.*

weed·y ('i), *adj.* weed'i·er, weed'i·est, 1. full of weeds. 2. of or resembling a weed. 3. thin and lank. —weed'i·ness, *n.*

week (wēk), *n.* 1. a period of seven days, especially the days from Sunday through Saturday. 2. the days of work or school during this period.

week·day ('dā), *n.* any day of the week except Sunday, and, often, Saturday.

week·end, week·end ('end), *n.* the period from Friday night or Saturday until Monday morning: also **week end:** *v.i.* to spend a weekend (*in* or *at*).

week·ly ('li), *adj.* 1. continuing or lasting for a week. 2. occurring, done, payable, etc. once a week: *adv.* once each week: *n., pl.* -lies, a periodical published once a week.

ween (wēn), *v.i. & v.t.* [Archaic], to think; fancy; suppose.

weep (wēp), *v.i.* wept, weep'ing, 1. to express grief by shedding tears. 2. to lament or mourn (followed by *for*). 3. to exude or drip liquid: *v.t.* 1. to lament; bewail. 2. to shed (tears or other drops of liquid). —weep'er, *n.*

weep·ing ('ing), *n.* the act of weeping: *adj.* 1. that weeps. 2. having slender, drooping branches.

weeping willow, a Chinese willow tree with slender, drooping branches: it is grown as an ornamental.

weep·y ('i), *adj.* weep'i·er, weep'i·est, 1. crying; tearful. 2. easily moved to tears. —weep'i·ness, *n.*

---

a in cap, ā in cane, ä in father, å in abet, e in met, ē in be, ẽ in baker, ë in regent, i in pit, ī in fine, i in manifest, o in hot, ô in horse, ō in bone,

wee·ver (wē'vēr), n. an edible marine fish with poisonous spines and a broad nose.

wee·vil (wē'vil), n. a small beetle, the larvae of which are very destructive to grain.

weft (weft), n. the woof of cloth; the threads crossing the warp.

weigh (wā), v.t. 1. to ascertain the weight of. 2. to have (a certain weight). 3. to reflect on and choose carefully. 4. to lift, or hoist (an anchor): v.i. 1. to bear heavily; be a burden. 2. to be important; have influence. 3. to hoist anchor.

weight (wāt), n. 1. the quality of being heavy; especially, the force exerted on a mass by gravity. 2. a quantity of matter weighing a certain amount. 3. the amount of heaviness. 4. a system of units for expressing heaviness. 5. any one of these units. 6. a piece of metal or other substance of a specific standard heaviness, used on a scale. 7. an object used for its heaviness. 8. something oppressive, as sorrow or responsibility. 9. power or importance: v.t. 1. to make heavy or heavier. 2. to oppress; load down.

weight·less ('lis), adj. being without apparent weight, as a body subjected to a force that neutralizes gravity. —**weight'less·ly**, adv. — **weight'less·ness**, n.

weight lifting, the act or sport of lifting heavy weights as in a competition.

weight·y ('i), adj. **weight'i·er**, **weight'i·est**, 1. very heavy. 2. troublesome. 3. momentous; important. —**weight'i·ness**, n.

weir (wir), n. 1. a dam across a stream to raise the level of the water, as for use at a mill. 2. a fence, as of stakes or brushwood, set in a stream for catching fish.

weird (wird), adj. 1. unearthly, mysterious, etc.; seemingly connected with spirits or other supernatural things. 2. very odd; queer; bizarre.

weird·o (wir'dō), n., pl. **weird'os**, [Slang], a very odd person; one who is strange, bizarre, etc.

Weird Sisters, the three Fates.

we·ka (wā'kä, wē'kä), n. a large, flightless bird of New Zealand, one of a group of rails.

wel·come (wel'kúm), adj. 1. received with gladness or hospitality. 2. given permission (to do, use, go, etc.). 3. without obligation: n. a kind reception to a guest or newcomer: v.t. -**comed, -com·ing**, 1. to greet with hospitality. 2. to receive with pleasure. —**wel'com·er**, n.

weld (weld), v.t. 1. to unite by hammering or fusion, as two pieces of heated metal. 2. to join together closely: v.i. to be welded: n. 1. the act of welding. 2. the state of being welded. 3. a joint formed by welding. — **weld'er**, n.

wel·fare (wel'fer), n. 1. a state of well-being; prosperity, comfort, health, etc. 2. the government agencies that provide aid to the poor, the unemployed, etc.

well (wel), n. 1. a natural spring or fountain. 2. a deep hole or shaft sunk into the earth to reach a supply of water, oil, gas, etc. 3. something resembling a well in shape. 4. a source or supply that can be drawn upon. 5. a container for holding liquid, as an ink-

well: v.t. & v.i. to flow or issue forth as from a well.

well (wel), adv. bet'ter, best, 1. in a satisfactory or pleasing manner. 2. affluently. 3. justly; properly. 4. to a great extent or degree. 5. completely; thoroughly. 6. certainly. definitely. 7. closely; intimately. 8. favorably: adj. 1. satisfactory, right, etc. 2. not sick; healthy. 3. fortunate; favorable· interj. an exclamation of surprise, remonstration, etc.

we'll (wel), 1. we shall. 2. we will.

well-ap·point·ed (wel'ă-poin'tid), adj. finely furnished.

well-bal·anced ('bal'ănst), adj. 1. nicely balanced. 2. mentally sound; sensible

well-be·haved ('bi-hāvd'), adj. behaving well; polite; decorous.

well-be·ing ('bē'ing), n. the state of being well, happy, or prosperous; welfare.

well-bred ('bred'), adj. refined in manners; cultivated; considerate.

well-dis·posed ('dis-pōzd'), adj. disposed to be kindly, friendly, or sympathetic.

well-done ('dun'), adj. 1 accomplished efficiently. 2. thoroughly cooked.

well-fed ('fed'), adj. corpulent. fat.

well-fixed ('fikst'), adj. [Informal]. rich.

well-found·ed ('foun'did), adj. based on solid evidence, good judgment. or facts.

well-groomed ('grōōmd'), adj. clean and tidy.

well-ground·ed ('groun'did), adj. having a sound, extensive knowledge of fundamentals.

well-heeled ('hēld'), adj. [Slang]. rich.

well-in·formed ('in-fôrmd'), adj. having extensive knowledge of a subject or many subjects.

Wel·ling·ton (wel'ing-tŏn), n. a long-legged boot.

well-in·ten·tioned (wel'in-ten'shŭnd), adj. having or displaying good intentions; meant to be helpful.

well-knit ('nit'), adj. 1. firmly constructed. 2. sturdy of build.

well-known ('nōn'), adj. 1. generally known; famous. 2. completely known.

well-made ('mād'), adj. skillfully and soundly constructed.

well-man·nered ('man'ērd), adj. polite; courteous.

well-mean·ing ('mē'ning), adj. 1. having good intentions. 2. prompted by good intentions; also **well'-meant'** ('ment').

well-nigh ('ni'), adv. almost; nearly.

well-off ('ôf'), adj. 1. in a favorable circumstance. 2. wealthy; prosperous.

well-read ('red'), adj. well informed through having read extensively.

well-round·ed ('roun'did), adj. 1. well-balanced. 2. displaying many interests or talents. 3. shapely.

well-spo·ken ('spō'kn), adj. 1. speaking fluently, courteously, etc. 2. expressed with precision or fitness.

well-spring (wel'spring), n. 1. the origin of a spring, stream, etc.; fountainhead. 2. a source of uninterrupted supply.

well-thought-of (wel'thôt'uv), adj. respected; admired.

well-to-do ('tŏ-dōō'), adj. wealthy; affluent.

ŏ in dragon, ōō in crude, oo in wool. u in cup. ū in cure. ū in turn. ŭ in focus, oi in boy, ou in house, th in thin, **th** in sheathe, g in get, j in joy, y in yet.

well-wish-er ('wish-ẽr), *n.* one who offers good wishes to another, an undertaking, etc.

well-worn ('wôrn'), *adj.* 1. much used or worn. 2. trite; hackneyed.

Wels-bach burner (welz'bäk), a gas burner having a gauze mantle that, when lighted, gives off a bright light: a trademark: after C. von *Welsbach* (1858-1929), Austrian chemist.

Welsh (welsh), *adj.* of Wales, a division of the United Kingdom located on a peninsula of west central Great Britain, its people, their language, etc.: *n.* 1. the people of Wales. 2. the Celtic language of Wales. —**Welsh'man** ('mán), *n., pl.* -men ('mĕn).

welsh (welsh), *v.i.* [Slang], to avoid paying a debt, obligation, etc. (often with *on*). — **welsh'er,** *n.*

Welsh rabbit, a dish of melted cheese, seasoning, etc., served on crackers or toast: also **Welsh rarebit.**

welt (welt), *n.* 1. a strip of leather stitched between the sole and upper of a shoe. 2. a ridge raised on the flesh by a blow: *v.t.* 1. to furnish with a welt. 2. [Informal], to flog so as to cause welts.

wel-ter (wel'tẽr), *v.i.* to tumble, writhe, or wallow: *n.* 1. turbulence. 2. turmoil.

wel-ter-weight (wel'tẽr-wāt), *n.* a boxer, wrestler, etc. between a lightweight and a middleweight.

wen (wen), *n.* a cyst containing sebaceous matter.

wench (wench), *n.* 1. a young woman: derogatory term. 2. [Archaic], a female servant.

wend (wend), *v.t.* to proceed on (one's way): *v.i.* [Archaic], to go; journey.

went (went), past tense of go.

wept (wept), past tense and past participle of weep.

were (wûr), plural and second person singular, past indicative, and the past subjunctive, of be.

we're (wir), we are.

weren't (wûrnt), were not.

were-wolf (wir'woolf, wûr'-), *n., pl.* -wolves ('woolvz), in *Folklore,* a person transformed into a wolf: also **wer'wolf.**

Wes-ley-an (wes'li-án), *adj.* of or pertaining to John Wesley or the Methodist Church: *n.* same as Methodist. —**Wes'ley-an-ism,** *n.*

west (west), *n.* 1. that part of the sky where the sun appears to set. 2. a region or area toward this part. 3. [W-], the western part of the earth; Occident: *adj.* of, in, or coming from the west: *adv.* in a westerly direction.

west-er-ly (wes'tẽr-li), *adj.* 1. situated in, or moving toward, the west. 2. coming from the west: *adv.* in the direction of the west.

west-ern ('tẽrn), *adj.* 1. situated toward, or lying in, the west. 2. from the west. 3. [W-], of or pertaining to the West.

Western Church, the Roman Catholic Church.

west-ern-er (-ẽr), *n.* 1. a person who resides in the western part of any country. 2. [W-], a native of, or one who lives in, the western U.S.

west-ing (wes'ting), *n.* the distance traversed by a vessel sailing westward.

west-ward (west'wẽrd), *adv. & adj.* toward the west: also **west'wards,** *adv.*

wet (wet), *adj.* wet'ter, wet'test, 1. containing, consisting of, or soaked with water or some other liquid. 2. very damp; rainy; misty. 3. not yet dry. 4. allowing or advocating the sale of alcoholic liquor: *n.* 1. water; moisture. 2. rain or misty weather. 3. a person who favors the sale of alcoholic liquor: *v.t. & v.i.* wet or wet'ted, wet'ting, to make or become wet. —wet'ly, *adv.* —wet'ness, *n.*

wet-back (wet'bak), *n.* [Informal], a Mexican agricultural worker who illegally crosses the U.S. border to work.

wet blanket, a person who is staid and reserved, dampening the enthusiasm and enjoyment of others.

weth-er (weth'ẽr), *n.* a castrated male sheep.

wet nurse, a woman who suckles the child of another. —**wet-nurse** (wet'nûrs), *v.t.* -nursed, -nurs-ing.

we've (wēv), we have.

whack (hwak), *n.* [Informal], 1. a sharp, resounding blow or the sound it makes. 2. a share. 3. a try: *v.t. & v.i.* [Informal], to strike with a sharp, resounding blow. — whack'er, *n.*

whack-ing ('ing), *adj.* [Informal], very large.

whale (hwāl), *n.* a very large sea mammal that is fishlike in form, breathes air, and suckles its young: *v.i.* whaled, whal'ing, to hunt for whales: *v.t.* to flog; thrash; beat soundly.

whale-bone ('bōn), *n.* the horny substance that hangs in plates from the upper jaw or palate of certain whales, formerly used for corset stays and the like.

whal-er ('ẽr), *n.* 1. a ship used in hunting and killing whales. 2. one who works on such a ship.

wham (hwam), *interj.* a sound like that heard with a heavy blow or explosion:. *n.* a heavy blow or impact: *v.t. & v.i.* whammed, wham'ming, to strike or explode with a loud sound.

wham-my ('i), *n., pl.* -mies, [Slang], a jinx or the evil eye.

whang (hwang), *n.* [Dial.], 1. a thong or whip of leather. 2. a lashing blow or its sound.

wharf (hwôrf), *n., pl.* wharves, wharfs, a structure built along, or out from, a shore so that ships can dock beside it to load and unload.

wharf-ing-er ('in-jẽr), *n.* the owner or manager of a wharf.

what (hwut, hwät), *pron.* 1. which thing, happening, condition, etc.? 2. that which; the thing that: *adj.* 1. which kind of; which. 2. as much as or as many as. 3. how great; so much: *adv.* 1. in which way? how? 2. in some way; partly (usually followed by *with*). 3. to so great a degree: *conj.* that: used in *but what: interj.* an exclamation of surprise, anger, etc.

what-ev-er (hwut-ev'ẽr), *pron.* 1. what: used for emphasis. 2. anything that. 3. no matter what: *adj.* 1. of any type or kind. 2. no matter what.

the wind. **3.** to blow a whistle: *v.t.* **1.** to produce (a tune, notes, etc.) by whistling. **2.** to summon, signal, etc. by whistling: *n.* **1.** a device for making whistling sounds. **2.** the act or sound of whistling.

whis·tler ('lẽr), *n.* **1.** a person, animal, or thing that whistles. **2.** a horse breathing in a forced way because of respiratory disease.

whistle stop, **1.** a small town. **2.** a brief stop in a small town, as during a political campaign.

whit (hwit), *n.* the smallest particle.

white (hwit), *adj.* **1.** being without color or of the color of pure snow. **2.** pure or innocent. **3.** light or pale in color. **4.** pallid, wan, or ashen. **5.** having a light-colored skin; Caucasoid: *n.* **1.** white color, paint, etc. **2.** a white or light-colored part, as the albumen of an egg. **3.** a person with a light-colored skin. —**white'ness**, *n.*

white blood corpuscle, an anti-infection blood cell; leukocyte: also **white blood cell**, **white corpuscle**.

white book, an official government report bound in white, fuller in detail than a *white paper*.

white·cap ('kap), *n.* a wave with a crest of foam.

white-col·lar ('kol'ẽr), *adj.* of or pertaining to clerical or professional workers.

white-collar crime, fraud, embezzlement, etc., committed by a person in business, government, or a profession.

white elephant, **1.** an albino elephant, regarded as sacred in Thailand, Burma, etc. **2.** something of little use that is costly to maintain. **3.** any object that its owner no longer wants, but that might be wanted by someone else.

white feather, a symbol of cowardice.

white·fish ('fish), *n., pl.* **-fish, -fish·es, 1.** a white or silvery freshwater food fish found in the lakes of northern U.S. and Canada. **2.** any of various similar fishes.

white flag, a white banner held up as a signal of truce or surrender.

White Friar, a Carmelite monk.

white gold, a gold alloy that looks like platinum.

white goods, household linens; sheets, pillowcases, towels, etc.

white-hot ('hot), *adj.* **1.** glowing white with heat. **2.** intensely angry, excited, enthusiastic, etc.

White House, the 1. the executive mansion of the President of the U.S., in Washington, D.C. **2.** the executive branch of the U.S. government.

white lead, a poisonous lead compound that is a white powder, used in making paint.

white lie, a lie about something trivial, told out of politeness, to avoid hurt feelings, etc.

white-liv·ered ('liv'ẽrd), *adj.* cowardly.

white metal, any of various light-colored alloys containing much lead or tin, as pewter.

whit·en (hwit'n), *v.t. & v.i.* to make or become white. —**whit'en·er**, *n.* —**whit'en·ing**, *n.*

white oak, a very strong oak of eastern North America, with light-colored bark and hard wood that is used in furniture, barrels, etc.

white pine, a pine of eastern North America with soft, light wood that is much used in construction, shelving, etc.

white sale, a sale of household linens.

white sauce, a cooked sauce for vegetables, meat, fish, etc., made of fat or butter, flour, milk or stock, and seasoning.

white slave, a woman forced into prostitution for the profit of others. —**white slavery**.

white-smith (hwit'smith), *n.* a worker in white metals; especially, a tinsmith.

white squall, a squall at sea not preceded by clouds.

white-throat ('thrōt), *n.* any of several old-world warblers with a whitish throat and belly.

white vitriol, sulfate of zinc.

white-wall ('wôl), *adj.* denoting a tire with a circular white band on the outer sidewall: *n.* a whitewall tire.

white·wash ('wôsh), *n.* **1.** a mixture of lime, chalk, water, etc., used to whiten walls. **2.** the glossing over or covering up of faults so as to exonerate: *v.t.* **1.** to cover with whitewash. **2.** to cover up the faults of. **3.** [Informal], in *Sports*, to defeat (an opponent) in a shutout.

white wine, wine of a clear, light-yellow to amber color.

white-wood ('wood), *n.* any of various white or light-colored woods, as of the tulip tree, cottonwood, etc.

whith·er (hwith'ẽr), *adv. & conj.* to what place, condition, etc.; where; wherever.

whit·ing (hwit'ing), *n.* **1.** powdered chalk used in whitewash, etc. **2.** any of various ocean fishes used for food.

whit·ish ('ish), *adj.* somewhat white.

whit·low (hwit'lō), *n.* a painful infection near a fingernail or toenail.

Whit·sun (hwit'sn), *adj.* of, pertaining to, or observed on Whitsunday or the season of Pentecost.

Whit·sun·day ('sun'di), *n.* Pentecost, the seventh Sunday after Easter.

whit·tle (hwit'l), *v.t.* **-tled, -tling, 1.** to cut small bits or thin slices from (wood) with a knife. **2.** to make or form (an object) in this manner. **3.** to reduce bit by bit: *v.i.* to whittle wood.

whiz, whizz (hwiz), *v.i.* **whizzed, whiz'zing, 1.** to make the buzzing or hissing sound of something rushing through the air. **2.** to rush by with this sound: *n.* **1.** a whizzing sound. **2.** [Slang], an expert.

who (hōō), *pron.* objective **whom**, possessive **whose**, **1.** which or what person or persons. **2.** that.

whoa (hwō), *interj.* stop!: a word used by drivers of horses or oxen.

who·dun·it (hōō-dun'it), *n.* [Informal], a novel, play, etc. about solving a secret crime; murder mystery.

who·ev·er (-ev'ẽr), *pron.* **1.** any person that. **2.** whatever person. **3.** who?: used for emphasis.

whole (hōl), *adj.* **1.** containing all of its elements or parts; complete. **2.** not divided up; entire. **3.** not a fraction or mixed number. **4.** not broken, injured, defective, etc.;

---

sound: *n.* 1. the sum of all the parts; the total; entirety. 2. that which is complete in itself. —**whole′ness,** *n.*

whole-heart-ed (′här′tid), *adj.* with all one's interest and energy; sincere. —**whole′heart′ed-ly,** *adv.* —**whole′heart′ed-ness,** *n.*

whole milk, milk with none of the butterfat or other elements removed.

whole note, a musical note having four times the duration of a quarter note.

whole-sale (′sāl), *n.* the sale of goods in large quantities at lower prices, especially to retail merchants; *adj.* 1. of or pertaining to such sale of goods. 2. widespread; extensive; sweeping; *adv.* 1. at wholesale prices. 2. extensively; sweepingly; *v.t. & v.i.* -saled, -sal-ing, to sell wholesale. —**whole′sal-er,** *n.*

whole-some (′sŏm), *adj.* 1. conducive to good health or well-being; healthful. 2. having a good moral or social influence. 3. characterized by or showing health and vigor. — **whole′some-ly,** *adv.* —**whole′some-ness,** *n.*

whole-wheat (′hwēt), *adj.* 1. made from the entire kernels of wheat, as flour. 2. made with whole-wheat flour, as bread.

whol-ly (hō′li), *adv.* to the whole amount or extent; totally.

whom (hōōm), *pron.* the objective case of who.

whom-ev-er (hōōm-ev′ĕr), *pron.* the objective case of whoever.

whom-so-ev-er (-sō-ev′ĕr), *pron.* the objective case of whosoever.

whoop (hōōp), *n.* 1. a loud shout or cry of joy, surprise, ferocity, etc. 2. a long, gasping breath after a fit of coughing; *v.t. & v.i.* to shout with whoops.

whoop-ing cough (′ing), a children's disease in which there are fits of coughing that end in a whoop.

whooping crane, a large, white North American crane noted for its whooping call: it is now nearly extinct.

whoop-la (hōōp′lä), *n.* same as hoopla.

whop (hwop), *v.t. & v.i.* whopped, whop′ping, [Informal], 1. to hit, strike, or beat. 2. to defeat decisively; *n.* [Informal], a sharp blow, thump, etc.

whop-per (hwop′ĕr), *n.* [Informal], 1. something unusually large. 2. a big lie. —**whop′ping,** *adj.*

whore (hōr), *n.* a prostitute. —**whor′ish,** *adj.*

whorl (hwôrl, hwûrl), *n.* anything in a coiled or circular arrangement, as the ridges that form a fingerprint or the leaves or petals around the same point on a stem.

whorled (hwôrld, hwûrld), *adj.* having whorls.

whor-tle-ber-ry (hwûr′tl-ber-i), *n., pl.* -ries, 1. any of various blueberry plants. 2. the berries of any of these plants.

who's (hōōz), 1. who is. 2. who has.

whose (hōōz), *pron.* which person's or persons'?: used without a following noun; *adj.* of whom or of which.

who-so-ev-er (hōō-sō-ev′ĕr), *pron.* whoever: used for emphasis.

why (hwi), *adv.* for what cause, reason, or purpose?; *conj.* 1. because of which. 2. the reason for which; *n., pl.* whys, the reason, cause, etc.; *interj.* an exclamation of surprise, annoyance, etc.

whyd-ah bird (hwid′ä), any of several dark-colored weaverbirds.

wick (wik), *n.* a length of cord or tape, as in a candle, oil lamp, etc., that absorbs the fuel and burns with a steady flame when lighted.

wick-ed (′id), *adj.* 1. morally bad; evil. 2. causing pain, trouble, distress, etc. 3. full of mischief. 4. [Slang], showing great skill. — **wick′ed-ly,** *adv.* —**wick′ed-ness,** *n.*

wick-er (wik′ĕr), *n.* 1. thin twigs or long, woody strips that are flexible and are woven together to make baskets, furniture, etc. 2. articles made of wicker; *adj.* made of wicker.

wick-er-work (-wûrk), *n.* articles made of wicker; woven wicker.

wick-et (wik′it), *n.* 1. a small gate, especially one set in a larger one. 2. a small window, as at a ticket office. 3. a set of sticks at which the ball is thrown in cricket. 4. any one of the small wire arches through which the balls must be hit in croquet.

wick-i-up (wik′i-up), *n.* a hut having an oval-shaped frame covered with grass, brush, etc., built by the nomadic Indians of the southwestern U.S.

wide (wid), *adj.* wid′er, wid′est, 1. extending over a large area; especially, measuring much from side to side; broad. 2. of a specified measurement from side to side. 3. extensive in kinds, amount, degree, etc. 4. far from the point or goal aimed at; *adv.* 1. over a large area. 2. so as to be wide. — **wide′ly,** *adv.* —**wide′ness,** *n.*

-wide (wid), a prefix meaning *extending throughout.*

wide-a-wake (wid′ä-wāk′), *adj.* 1. fully awake. 2. watchful and ready; alert.

wide-eyed (′īd′), *adj.* with the eyes fully open, as in wonder or surprise.

wid-en (wid′n), *v.t. & v.i.* to make or become wide or wider.

wide-spread (wid′spred′), *adj.* widely extended; spread out.

widg-eon (wij′ûn), *n., pl.* -eons, -eon, any one of a group of wild freshwater ducks having a cream-colored or white crown.

wid-ow (wid′ō), *n.* a woman whose husband has died and who remains unmarried; *v.t.* to cause to become a widow. —**wid′ow-hood,** *n.*

wid-ow-er (-ĕr), *n.* a man whose wife has died and who remains unmarried.

width (width), *n.* 1. extent of something from side to side; breadth. 2. a piece of a certain width.

wield (wēld), *v.t.* 1. to handle (a tool, weapon, etc.). 2. to exercise (power, influence, etc.).

wie-ner (wē′nĕr), *n.* a smoked sausage of a kind made in narrow links a few inches long; frankfurter.

wife (wif), *n.* a married woman; a woman in relationship to her husband.

wife-ly (′li), *adj.* of, like, or fit for a wife.

wig (wig), *n.* a false covering of hair for the head; *v.t.* wigged, wig′ging, 1. to furnish with a wig. 2. [Slang], to annoy, upset, excite, craze, etc.; *v.i.* [Slang], to become upset, excited, etc.

---

wig-an (wig'ǎn), *n.* a canvaslike cotton fabric used as stiffening, as in lapels.

wi-geon (wij'ǔn), *n.* same as widgeon.

wigged (wigd), *adj.* wearing a wig.

wig-ging (wig'ing), *n.* [British Informal], a scolding.

wig-gle (wig'l), *v.t. & v.i.* -gled, -gling, to twist and turn from side to side. —wig'gler, *n.*

wig-gly ('li), *adj.* -gli-er, -gli-est, 1. that wiggles. 2. having a twisting or wavy form.

wight (wīt), *n.* [Archaic], a human being; person.

wig-let (wig'lit), *n.* a small wig.

wig-wag (wig'wag), *v.t. & v.i.* -wagged, -wagging, 1. to wave back and forth. 2. to communicate by waving flags, lights, etc. in accordance with a code: *n.* the act or practice of sending messages in this way.

wig-wam (wig'wäm), *n.* a shelter made by some North American Indians in the form of a dome or cone covered with bark.

wild (wīld), *adj.* 1. living or growing in nature; untamed; uncultivated. 2. not lived in or used for farming, etc.; waste. 3. uncivilized; savage. 4. not easy to control; disorderly, unruly, etc. 5. not restrained socially or morally; dissolute, orgiastic, etc. 6. violent, rough, stormy, etc. 7. extremely excited. 8. reckless, fantastic, crazy, etc. 9. going wide of the target. 10. having any value specified by the holder: said of a card in some poker games: *adv.* in a wild manner: *n. usually pl.* wilderness or wasteland. —wild'ly, *adv.* —wild'ness, *n.*

wild-cat ('kat), *n.* 1. a fierce, wild animal of the cat family, of medium size, as the lynx. 2. a person who has a fierce temper and is always ready to fight. 3. a successful oil well drilled in an area not known to yield oil: *adj.* 1. wildly speculative. 2. unauthorized or illegal: *v.i.* -cat-ted, -cat-ting, to drill for oil in an area not known to yield oil.

wil-der-ness (wil'dẽr-nis), *n.* a wild region; wasteland or overgrown land with no people settled on it.

wild-eyed (wīld'īd), *adj.* 1. staring in a wild manner. 2. fantastically foolish, impractical, etc.

wild-fire ('fīr), *n.* a fire that spreads rapidly and is hard to put out.

wild-flow-er ('flou-ẽr), *n.* any flowering plant growing without cultivation in fields, woods, etc.: also wild flower.

wild-fowl ('foul), *n.* a wild bird, especially a game bird: also wild fowl.

wild goose, any undomesticated goose, especially the common, wild species of Canada and the northern U.S.

wild-goose chase ('gōōs), any search, pursuit, etc. as futile as trying to catch a wild goose by chasing it.

wild lettuce, a wild, weedy species of lettuce having small, dandelionlike flower heads and, often, prickly foliage.

wild-life ('līf), *n.* wild mammals, birds, etc.

wild oats, 1. a wild, oatlike grass. 2. youthful sexual promiscuity: used in the phrase *sow one's wild oats.*

wild rice, 1. a tall, aquatic grass of Canada and the northern U.S. 2. its edible grain.

wild vanilla, a plant with vanilla-scented leaves, found in the southeastern U.S.

Wild West, the western U.S. in its early frontier period of lawlessness.

wile (wīl), *n.* 1. a sly artifice or trick. 2. a beguiling or coquettish trick: *usually used in pl.*: *v.t.* wiled, wil'ing, 1. to beguile or lure. 2. same as while.

will (wil), *n.* 1. the faculty of the mind by which one chooses, determines one's actions, etc. 2. determination. 3. one's feeling toward others. 4. choice; desire. 5. expressed wish or command. 6. a legal document in which a person directs the disposal of his property after death: *v.t.* 1. to desire; want. 2. to influence or control by the power of the will. 3. to bequeath to someone by a will: *v.i.* to desire, choose, wish, etc.

will (wil), *v.* past tense would, an auxiliary used to express simple futurity in all persons: in formal speech, *will* is used in the first person to express determination, obligation, etc.: see shall.

wil-let (wil'it), *n., pl.* -lets, -let, a gray-and-white, long-legged wading bird of North and South America.

will-ful (wil'fŭl), *adj.* 1. following one's own will in a stubborn and unreasonable way. 2. done or said deliberately. Also wil'ful. —will'ful-ly, *adv.* —will'ful-ness, *n.*

wil-lies (wil'iz), *n.pl.* [Slang], a state of nervousness; jitters (with *the*).

will-ing (wil'ing), *adj.* 1. inclined or consenting to do a particular thing. 2. doing, giving, etc. or done, given, etc. freely or gladly. —will'ing-ly, *adv.* —will'ing-ness, *n.*

wil-li-waw, wil-ly-waw (wil'i-wô), *n.* a sudden, violent cold wind blowing from mountain to coast in far northern or southern latitudes.

will-o'-the-wisp (wil-ô-thẽ-wisp'), *n.* 1. a shifting light seen over marshes at night: see ignis fatuus. 2. any hope or goal luring one to a vain pursuit.

wil-low (wil'ô), *n.* a tree or shrub with long, slender twigs that are tough and pliable: used much in basketry and wickerwork.

willow pattern, a design for china picturing a river, pagodas, willow trees, etc., usually blue on white.

wil-low-y (-i), *adj.* 1. full of or shaded with willows. 2. slender and graceful, lithe, etc.

will-pow-er (wil'pou-ẽr), *n.* strength of will or determination; self-control.

wil-ly-nil-ly (wil'i-nil'i), *adv.* whether wanted or not: *adj.* being or happening whether wanted or not.

wilt (wilt), *v.t.* 1. to cause to droop or wither. 2. to lower in energy or strength: *v.i.* 1. to droop or wither, as a plant. 2. to lose energy or strength; become weak; languish: *n.* 1. the act or an instance of wilting. 2. a plant disease caused by bacteria or fungi, characterized by wilting of the leaves.

Wil-ton (wil'tn), *n.* a kind of carpet having a velvety pile of cut loops: also Wilton carpet, Wilton rug.

Wilt-shire (wilt'shir, 'shẽr), *n.* any one of an

ô in dragon, ōō in crude, oo in wool, u in cup, ū in cure, ũ in turn, ŭ in focus, oi in boy, ou in house, th in thin, th in sheathe, g in get, j in joy, y in yet.

old breed of sheep with pure-white wool, originating in England.

wi·ly (wī'li), *adj.* **-li·er, -li·est,** full of wiles, or sly tricks; cunning; crafty. **—wi'li·ness,** *n.*

wim·ble (wim'bl), *n.* a gimlet, auger, or similar tool for boring: *v.t.* **-bled, -bling,** to bore with a wimble.

wim·ple (wim'pl), *n.* a kind of head covering for women that is draped around the head and neck so that only the face shows: worn in earlier times but now only by some orders of nuns: *v.t.* **-pled, -pling,** 1. to cover with a wimple. 2. to arrange in folds. 3. to cause to ripple: *v.i.* 1. to lie in folds. 2. to ripple.

win (win), *v.t.* won, win'ning, 1. to gain by superiority in a contest or competition. 2. to finish first in (a contest, etc.). 3. to gain or obtain by effort or struggle. 4. to influence or persuade (often with *over*). 5. to gain (the sympathy, friendship, etc.) of a person. 6. to persuade to marry one: *v.i.* 1. to gain a victory; triumph. 2. to finish first in a contest: *n.* [Informal], a victory, as in a game.

wince (wins), *v.i.* winced, winc'ing, to shrink back or flinch slightly with a grimace, as in pain: *n.* the act of wincing.

winch (winch), *n.* 1. a crank with a handle, used to transmit motion. 2. a machine for hoisting or pulling, with a cylinder on which a rope or chain tied to the load is wound.

wind (wind), *v.t.* wound, wind'ing, 1. to turn, or cause to revolve. 2. to coil around itself or around something else. 3. to cover or wrap by encircling with something. 4. to make (one's way) or cause to move in a twisting course. 5. to tighten the spring of (a clock, etc.) by turning a stem or key. 6. to bring to an end (with *up*): *v.i.* 1. to move or go in a twisting or sinuous course. 2. to coil (*around* or *about* an object): *n.* 1. the act of winding. 2. a turn or twist.

wind (wind), *n.* 1. air that is moving. 2. a strong air current; gale. 3. air carrying a scent, as in hunting. 4. breath or power of breathing. 5. air thought of as carrying information. 6. idle or boastful talk. 7. flatulence. 8. *pl.* the wind instruments in an orchestra: *v.t.* 1. to cause to be out of breath. 2. to scent with the nose, as hounds. 3. to allow (a horse) to rest so as to recover breath.

wind·break (wind'brāk), *n.* a hedge, fence, etc. serving as a shield from the wind.

wind·chill factor ('chil), the estimated measurement of the combined effect of low temperatures and high winds on exposed skin.

wind·ed (win'did), *adj.* out of breath.

wind·fall (wind'fôl), *n.* 1. fruit blown down by the wind. 2. unexpected good fortune.

wind·flow·er ('flou·ẽr), *n.* same as **anemone** (sense 1).

wind shear, a sudden change in wind direction, esp., dangerous vertical wind shifts encountered by aircraft.

wind·ing sheet (wīn'ding), a shroud for a corpse.

wind instrument (wind), any musical instrument

sounded by the breath or wind, **as a clarinet.**

wind·jam·mer (wind'jam-ẽr), *n.* a large ship with sails; also, one of its crew.

wind·lass (wind'lás), *n.* a winch, usually cranked.

wind·mill (wind'mil), *n.* a structure with sails or contrivances revolved by the wind to generate power, as for grinding.

win·dow (win'dō), *n.* 1. an aperture, as in a wall, typically having a pane of glass to let light in, see through, etc. 2. the pane or its frame. 3. any windowlike opening.

win·dow-pane (-pān), *n.* the pane of a window.

win·dow-shop (-shop), *v.i.* **-shopped, -shop·ping,** to look at goods in store windows but not buy.

win·dow-sill (-sil), *n.* the sill of a window.

wind·pipe (wind'pip), *n.* same as **trachea** (sense 1).

wind·row (wind'rō), *n.* 1. a swath as of grass or grain, left lying to dry. 2. a row as of fallen dry leaves swept together by wind.

wind·shield ('shēld), *n.* a broad piece of glass or the like shielding from the wind, as the broad front window of a car.

wind·sock ('sok), *n.* a tapering, tubelike piece of cloth, open at both ends to let wind blow through, pivoting and so showing wind direction.

Wind·sor knot (win'zẽr), a bulky double knot in a four-in-hand necktie.

wind·storm (wind'stôrm), *n.* a storm marked by strong wind but by little rain, hail, etc.

wind·up (wind'up), *n.* 1. a concluding part. 2. in *Baseball,* a pitcher's swinging of the arm in preparing to throw the ball.

wind·ward (wind'wẽrd), *n.* the side from which the wind blows: *adj.* of or pertaining to this side.

wind·y (win'di), *adj.* wind'i·er, wind'i·est, 1. of or like the wind. 2. marked by or full of wind. 3. blustering, ranting, etc. 4. boastful, pompous, etc. 5. lacking substance; empty. **—wind'i·ly,** *adv.* **—wind'i·ness,** *n.*

wine (win), *n.* 1. the fermented juice of grapes or of other fruits or plants. 2. anything that intoxicates or exhilarates. 3. a dark, purplish red: *v.t.* & *v.i.* wined, win'ing, to treat with or partake of wine.

wine-col·ored ('kul-ẽrd), *adj.* dark purplish-red.

wine press, an apparatus for crushing grapes to extract the juice.

win·er·y (win'ẽr-i), *n., pl.* **-er·ies,** a place where wine is made.

wing (wing), *n.* 1. either one of the two anterior limbs of a bird, used for flying or, as when less developed, for balance in running or for swimming. 2. either one of certain other paired, winglike structures, as the flight organs of an insect. 3. anything winglike; especially, a (or the) chief lateral supporting surface of an airplane. 4. a subsidiary part attached to the side of a building, fortification, etc. 5. a similar part of an army, fleet, etc. 6. a section or faction, as of a political party. 7. any group branching from or subsidiary to a main group. 8. either one of the inner side areas of a theater stage that are outside the view of the audience; also, a piece of scenery set up at either side of the stage. 9. in certain goal games, a position forward and to either side of center; also, a player so positioned. 10. a certain unit in an air force. 11. movement on or as if on wings; flight. 12. care, protection, patronage, etc.: *v.t.* 1. to furnish with or as if with wings. 2. to make fly, soar, or go swiftly on or as if on wings. 3. to make (one's way) by flying. 4. to go through or over by or as if by flying. 5. to transport by or as if by flight. 6. to hit or wound, as with a bullet, in the wing, arm, etc.: *v.i.* to move swiftly on or as if on wings.

winged (wingd; poetical also wing'id), *adj.* 1. having wings. 2. moving on or as if on wings. 3. lofty; sublime.

wing-span (wing'span), *n.* 1. the distance from the tip of one wing of an airplane to the tip of the other. 2. same as **wingspread**.

wing-spread ('spred), *n.* 1. the distance from the tip of one wing of a pair of fully spread wings, as of a bird, to the tip of the other. 2. same as **wingspan**.

wink (wingk), *v.i.* 1. to close and open an eyelid quickly, as in signaling. 2. same as **blink**: *v.t.* 1. to make (an eye) wink. 2. to make (the eyes) blink: *n.* 1. a winking. 2. a tiny interval; instant.

win-kle (wing'k'l), *n.* 1. any one of several small marine snails; periwinkle. 2. any one of many large marine snails that are very destructive to oysters and clams.

win-ner (win'ēr), *n.* one that wins.

win-ning ('ing), *adj.* 1. that wins. 2. attractive; charming: *n.* 1. victory. 2. *pl.* money or other things won.

win-now (win'ō), *v.t.* 1. to separate and drive (chaff) from (grain) by wind or forced air. 2. to blow away; scatter. 3. to separate out by or as if by winnowing or sifting: *v.i.* to separate chaff from grain: *n.* 1. a winnowing. 2. an apparatus for winnowing.

win-o (wī'nō), *n.*, *pl.* win'os, [Slang], an individual, especially a derelict, habitually drunk on cheap wine.

win-some (win'sôm), *adj.* charmingly attractive.

win-ter (win'tēr), *n.* 1. the season between autumn and spring; in the astronomical year, the period beginning in the Northern Hemisphere at the winter solstice, about December 22, and ending at the vernal equinox, about March 21; the coldest season of the year. 2. a year as reckoned by this season. 3. a period or condition resembling winter, as in being a time of checked activity, dreariness, etc.: *adj.* of or like winter: *v.i.* 1. to pass the winter. 2. to be supplied with food and shelter in the winter: *v.t.* to feed or maintain during winter.

win-ter-ber-ry (-ber-i), *n.*, *pl.* -ries, any one of several hollies of the eastern part of North America that bear brilliant red, black, yellow, or purple berries persisting over the winter.

win-ter-green (-grēn), *n.* any one of several evergreen shrubs of the heath family; especially, a shrubby evergreen with white, bell-like flowers, red, edible berries, and leaves yielding an aromatic oil used as a flavoring or in medicine; also, this oil or its flavor.

win-ter-ize (īz), *v.t.* -ized, -iz-ing, to put into condition or equip for winter.

win-ter-time (-tīm), *n.* the winter season.

win-try (win'tri), *adj.* -tri-er, -tri-est, of or like winter; frigid, bleak, etc.

win-y (wī'ni), *adj.* win'i-er, win'i-est, like wine in taste, color, stimulating effect, etc.

wipe (wīp), *v.t.* **wiped, wip'ing,** 1. to move (a cloth, tissue, etc.) over the surface of (something) as in cleansing or drying. 2. to cleanse, dry, etc. thus. 3. to apply or remove, as oil, with a wiping movement. 4. to destroy or obliterate (with *out*): *n.* a wiping. —wip'er, *n.*

wire (wīr), *n.* 1. metal drawn into lengths suggestive of string, cord, etc. 2. such a length; also, a cable, netting, mesh, etc. of wire. 3. a telegraph or telegram. 4. in *Horse Racing,* a wire stretched above the finish line of a race track: *adj.* of wire: *v.t.* **wired, wir'ing,** 1. to join, bind, etc. with wire. 2. to provide with wires or wiring, as to bring in an electric current. 3. to telegraph: *v.i.* to telegraph.

wire-hair ('her), *n.* a fox terrier with a wiry coat: also ~~wire-haired terrier~~ ('herd).

wire-less ('lis), *adj.* 1. without wire or wires; specifically, operating with electromagnetic waves rather than with conducting wire. 2. [Chiefly British], same as **radio**: *n.* 1. same as: *a)* **wireless telegraphy;** *b)* **wireless telephony;** *c)* [Chiefly British], **radio.** 2. a message sent by wireless: *v.t.* & *v.i.* to communicate (with) by wireless.

wireless telegraphy, telegraphy by radio-transmitted signals: also **wireless telegraph.**

wireless telephone, a telephone operating by radio-transmitted signals.

wireless telephony, use of the wireless telephone.

Wire-pho-to (wīr'fōt-ō), *n.* 1. a system of photographic reproduction at a distance by wire-transmitted electric impulses. 2. a photograph so reproduced. A trademark.

wire-pull-er (wīr'pool-ēr), *n.* one using private or secret influence to gain an objective.

wire service, a business organization providing directly telegraphed news stories, features, etc. to subscribers.

wire-tap ('tap), *v.i.* & *v.t.* **-tapped, -tap-ping,** to tap, as a telephone wire, so as to get messages, data, etc. secretly or underhandedly: *n.* 1. a wiretapping. 2. a device used for this.

wire-work ('wûrk), *n.* wire netting, mesh, etc.

wir-ing (wir'ing), *n.* a wire system, as for providing electricity.

wir-y (wir'i), *adj.* wir'i-er, wir'i-est, 1. of, like, or suggestive of wire. 2. lean, sinewy, and strong. —wir'i-ness, *n.*

wis (wis), *v.t.* [Archaic], to think; suppose.

wis-dom (wiz'dôm), *n.* 1. the ability to make sound choices and decisions based upon knowledge of what is right, true, enduring, etc.; sagacity. 2. learning; erudition. 3. sayings or teachings marked by wisdom.

wisdom tooth, any one of four molars farthest

back on each side of the upper and lower jaws.

wise (wiz), *adj.* **wis'er, wis'est,** 1. possessing or marked by wisdom; discerning, sagacious, erudite, etc. 2. informed. 3. [Slang], aware or knowing in a smug or conceited way; also, brash or impudent.

wise (wiz), *n.* method; way.

-wise (wiz), a suffix meaning *in a (specified) way, with regard to.*

wise-a-cre (wiz'ā-kēr), *n.* one making a shallow pretense of wisdom, knowledge, or insight.

wise-crack ('krak), *n.* [Slang], a sarcastic or flippant remark or retort; gibe: *v.i.* [Slang], to make wisecracks.

wi-sent (vē'zĕnt), *n.* a nearly extinct bison of Europe.

wish (wish), *v.t.* 1. to desire; want; long for. 2. to desire (something specified, as luck) to come to someone or something. 3. to request. 4. to impose (something unwanted) *on* someone: *v.i.* 1. to desire something; yearn; long. 2. to make a wish: *n.* 1. a wishing. 2. a thing wished. 3. *pl.* one's expressed hopes for something for another or others.

wish-bone (wish'bōn), *n.* the forked bone at the front of the breastbone of most birds.

wish-ful (wish'fŭl), *adj.* marked, prompted, or guided by wishing. **—wish'ful-ly,** *adv.*

wish-y-wash-y (wish'i-wôsh'i), *adj.* [Informal], 1. weak; insipid. 2. indecisive.

wisp (wisp), *n.* 1. a thin piece, slight trace, etc. 2. something delicate, frail, etc. 3. a little bunch, as of hair or grass.

wisp-y ('i), *adj.* wisp'i-er, wisp'i-est, of or like a wisp. **—wisp'i-ness,** *n.*

wis-ter-i-a (wis-tir'i-ā), *n.* any one of a genus of twining woody vines or shrubs with white, pink, or bluish flowers, native to the eastern part of the U.S. and the eastern part of Asia: also **wis-tar'i-a** (-ter'i-ā).

wist-ful (wist'fŭl), *adj.* marked by or indicative of vague or pensive yearning; musing or sadly longing. **—wist'ful-ly,** *adv.*

wit (wit), *n.* 1. originally, the mind. 2. *pl.* powers of thinking; mental faculties, specifically in their normal condition of sanity. 3. good sense. 4. ability to make cleverly amusing remarks, especially in a terse, arresting way. 5. an individual having this ability. 6. writing or speech manifesting such ability: *v.t. & v.i.* wist, wit'ting, [Archaic], to know or learn: now only in the phrase to wit, namely.

witch (wich), *n.* 1. a woman supposedly having supernatural powers through the aid of the devil or other evil spirits. 2. an ugly or spiteful old woman; hag. 3. [Informal], a bewitching woman.

witch-craft ('kraft), *n.* supernatural powers or practices of or like those of witches: also **witch'er-y** ('ēr-i), *pl.* **-er-ies.**

witch hazel, 1. a tall shrub of eastern North America, yielding an extract used in a lotion for bruises, inflammations, etc. 2. the lotion.

with (with, with), *prep.* 1. against. 2. near; at the side of. 3. in the company or presence of. 4. into or among. 5. as a member of. 6. in regard to. 7. compared to. 8. in the opinion of. 9. in consequence of. 10. through the medium of. 11. in reception of. 12. having the attribute, possession, etc. of. 13. in the guardianship, care, etc. of. 14. in spite of. 15. in the course of. 16. to or onto. 17. from. 18. after.

with-, a prefix meaning *away, against, back, from.*

with-al (with-ôl', with-), *adv.* 1. also; in addition. 2. nevertheless; notwithstanding.

with-draw (-drô'), *v.t.* -drew', -drawn', -draw'ing, 1. to draw back; take away; remove. 2. to retract; recall: *v.i.* 1. to go back, off, or away from something. 2. to remove oneself, as from an activity or group. **—with-draw'al,** *n.*

with-drawn (-drôn'), *adj.* shy, introverted, etc.

withe (with, with, with), *n.* a tough, flexible twig.

with-er (with'ēr), *v.i.* to become completely dried up, shriveled, etc.: *v.t.* to make wither.

with-ers (with'ērz), *n.pl.* the top part of a horse's back between the shoulder blades.

with-hold (with-hōld', with-), *v.t.* -held', -hold'-ing, 1. to keep back; restrain. 2. to take out (taxes or other deductions) from wages or salary. 3. to refuse to give, permit, etc.

withholding tax, the amount of income tax withheld from employees' wages or salaries.

with-in (with-in', with-), *adv.* 1. inside. 2. inwardly: *prep.* 1. inside. 2. not beyond.

with-out (-out'), *adv.* outside: *prep.* 1. outside. 2. with avoidance of. 3. lacking.

with-stand (with-stand', with-), *v.t. & v.i.* to resist or endure.

with-y (with'i, with'i), *n., pl.* **with'ies,** a large withe: *adj.* tough and flexible.

wit-less (wit'lis), *adj.* unintelligent; stupid.

wit-ness (wit'nis), *n.* 1. attestation, as of a fact or event; testimony; evidence. 2. one having direct knowledge of something, as through having seen it. 3. one testifying in court. 4. one observing a transaction, a signing, etc. so as to be ready to attest to the fact. 5. something sufficient as evidence: *v.t.* 1. to testify to; attest. 2. to constitute evidence of. 3. to serve as witness of. 4. to see; behold: *v.i.* to testify.

wit-ti-cism (wit'i-sizm), *n.* a witty remark.

wit-ting ('ing), *adj.* deliberate; intentional.

wit-ty (wit'i), *adj.* -ti-er, -ti-est, cleverly amusing; full of wit. **—wit'ti-ness,** *n.*

wive (wiv), *v.t.* wived, wiv'ing, [Archaic], 1. to provide with a wife. 2. to take for a wife: *v.i.* [Archaic], to take a wife.

wi-vern (wi'vērn), *n.* same as wyvern.

wives (wivz), *n.* plural of wife.

wiz-ard (wiz'ērd), *n.* 1. a magician or sorcerer. 2. [Informal], one highly skilled at something indicated: *adj.* 1. of wizards. 2. magic. 3. [Chiefly British], excellent. **—wiz'ard-ry,** *n.*

wiz-en (wiz'n, wēz'n), *v.t. & v.i.* to wither; shrivel: *adj.* same as wizened.

wiz-ened ('nd), *adj.* withered; shriveled.

woad (wōd), *n.* any one of a genus of plants of the mustard family.

wob-ble (wob'l), *n.* an unsteady motion or gait marked specifically by an irregular swaying, bobbing, shaking, etc.: *v.i.* -bled, -bling, to cause to have a wobble: *v.i.* 1. to move with a wobble. 2. to vacillate. —**wob′bler,** *n.*

wob·bly ('li), *adj.* **-bli·er, -bli·est,** that wobbles. —**wob′bli·ness,** *n.*

woe (wō), *n.* great sorrow: grief: *interj.* alas!

woe·be·gone ('bi-gôn), *adj.* looking beset with woe.

woe·ful ('fŭl), *adj.* full of woe; miserable; wretched. —**woe′ful·ly,** *adv.*

woke (wōk), alternate past tense of wake.

wold (wōld), *n.* a treeless, rolling plain.

wolf (woolf), *n., pl.* **wolves,** 1. any one of a large group of wild, flesh-eating, doglike mammals of the Northern Hemisphere. 2. a rapacious or cruel individual. 3. [Slang], a man who flirts with many women: *v.t.* to devour ravenously.

wolf·hound ('hound), *n.* any one of several breeds of large dogs once used for hunting wolves.

wolf·ram ('răm), *n.* same as tungsten.

wolfs·bane (woolfs'bān), *n.* an aconite plant, especially a species of Europe and Asia.

wol·ver·ene (wool·vě-rēn', wool'vě-rēn), *n.* British form for wolverine.

wol·ver·ine (wool·vě-rēn', wool'vě-rēn), *n., pl.* **-ines′, -ine′,** a ferocious, stout-bodied carnivore of northern regions.

wom·an (woom'ăn), *n., pl.* **wom·en** (wim'in), 1. an adult human female. 2. an adult female servant, employee, etc. 3. a wife.

wom·an·hood (-hood), *n.* 1. the state of being a woman. 2. womanly qualities. 3. womankind.

wom·an·ish (-ish), *adj.* feminine or effeminate.

wom·an·ize (-īz), *v.t.* **-ized, -iz·ing,** to make effeminate: *v.i.* [Informal], to philander. — **wom′an·iz·er,** *n.*

wom·an·kind (-kīnd), *n.* women collectively.

wom·an·like (-līk), *adj.* like or fit for a woman; womanly.

wom·an·ly (-li), *adj.* 1. characteristic of or fit for a woman. 2. like a woman: womanish.

woman suffrage, women's right to vote.

womb (woom), *n.* 1. the uterus of a female. 2. any place where something is produced.

wom·bat (wom'bat), *n.* a nocturnal, burrowing Australian marsupial resembling a small bear.

wom·en (wim'in), *n.* plural of woman.

wom·en·folk (-fōk), *n.pl.* [Dial. or Informal], same as womankind: also wom′en·folks.

wom·er·a (wom'ĕr-ă), *n.* a device for throwing spears, used by Australian aborigines.

won (wun), past tense and past participle of win.

won·der (wun'dĕr), *n.* 1. the state of mind produced by anything strange, unexpected, surprising, etc.; astonishment. 2. a cause of wonder; marvel; prodigy: *v.i.* 1. to feel wonder; be astonished. 2. to feel curiosity, sometimes mixed with doubt: *v.t.* to feel curiosity or doubt about.

won·der·ful (-fŭl), *adj.* 1. exciting wonder; marvelous. 2. [Informal], excellent, fine, etc. — **won′der·ful·ly,** *adv.*

won·der·land (-land), *n.* 1. an imaginary land

full of wonderful things. 2. a real place that is surprisingly beautiful, fertile, etc.

won·der·ment (-mĕnt), *n.* 1. astonishment; amazement; surprise. 2. a marvel.

won·drous (wun'drŭs), *adj.* exciting wonder; wonderful: *adv.* in a wonderful manner or to a wonderful degree. —**won′drous·ly,** *adv.*

wont (wônt, wŏnt, wunt), *adj.* accustomed: followed by an infinitive: *n.* habit; custom: *v.t.* **wont, wont** or **wont′ed, wont′ing,** to accustom: usually in the passive: *v.i.* to be accustomed.

won't (wōnt), will not.

wont·ed (wôn'tid, wŏn'-, wun'-), *adj.* habitual; accustomed.

won ton (wän' tän), a Chinese dish consisting of noodles filled with ground meat, often served in a broth (called **won·ton soup).**

woo (woo), *v.t.* 1. to seek the love of, usually in order to marry; court. 2. to try to obtain; seek: *v.i.* to woo a person.

wood (wood), *n.* 1. *usually pl.* a large, dense growth of trees; forest. 2. the solid part of trees, beneath the bark. 3. trees cut for use. 4. any one of various golf clubs with wooden heads: *adj.* 1. made of wood; wooden. 2. living or growing in woods. — **wood′ed,** *adj.*

wood alcohol, a colorless, volatile, poisonous liquid obtained by the distillation of wood: used in chemical manufactures and as a solvent, fuel, etc.

wood·bine (wood'bīn), *n.* 1. a European climbing honeysuckle. 2. a vine of the grape family, with dark-blue berries.

wood block, a block of wood, especially one used in making a woodcut.

wood·carv·ing ('kär·ving), *n.* 1. the art of carving wood by hand. 2. an object of wood so carved. —**wood′carv·er,** *n.*

wood·chat ('chat), *n.* 1. any one of several Asiatic birds of the thrush family. 2. a European shrike.

wood·chuck ('chuk), *n.* a thickset, reddish-brown North American burrowing marmot.

wood·cock ('kok), *n.* a wild fowl related to the snipe.

wood·craft ('kraft), *n.* 1. skill in hunting, trapping, camping, and other matters concerning the woods. 2. same as woodworking.

wood·cut ('kut), *n.* 1. a block of hard wood on which a design or picture is engraved. 2. a print or picture made from this.

wood·cut·ter ('kut·ĕr), *n.* a person who fells trees, cuts wood, etc. —**wood′cut·ting,** *n.*

wood duck, a large North American duck with brightly colored plumage: the male has a large crest.

wood·en ('n), *adj.* 1. made or consisting of wood. 2. stiff, expressionless, etc. 3. lacking vitality, sensitivity, etc. —**wood′en·ly,** *adv.*

wood engraving, the art or process of engraving designs or pictures upon wood for printing. —**wood engraver.**

wood hen, 1. same as woodcock. 2. a nonflying rail of New Zealand.

wood ibis, a large, white wading bird of the stork family, frequenting swamps from the southern U.S. to South America.

ŏ in dragon, ōō in crude, ōō in wool, u in cup, ū in cure, û in turn, ŭ in focus, oi in boy, ou in house, th in thin, th in sheathe, g in get, j in joy, y in yet.

wood·i·ness ('ĭ-nĭs), *n.* the state or quality of being woody.

wood·land ('land, 'lănd), *n.* land covered with trees: *adj.* of or pertaining to the woods.

wood lark, a small European lark that sings while soaring.

wood louse, any one of several small crustaceans with flat, oval, segmented bodies, found in damp soil, decaying wood, etc.

wood·man ('măn), *n., pl.* -men ('měn), same as **woodsman.**

wood nymph, 1. a nymph that lives in the woods; dryad. 2. any one of several moths with larvae that are brightly colored. 3. any one of several South American hummingbirds, the male of which is green and blue.

wood·peck·er ('pek-ẽr), *n.* a bird that pecks holes in the bark of trees to get insects.

wood·pile ('pīl), *n.* a pile of wood, especially firewood.

wood pulp, pulp made from wood fiber, used chiefly in making paper.

wood·ruff ('ruf), *n.* a European plant with fragrant leaves, used for flavoring wines and in sachets.

wood screw, a metal screw for use in wood.

wood·shed ('shed), *n.* a shed for storing wood.

woods·man (woodz'măn), *n., pl.* -men ('měn), 1. one who lives or works in the woods. 2. a skillful hunter, trapper, camper, etc.

wood sorrel, any one of a group of creeping plants with cloverlike leaves and flowers with five petals, found in dense, damp woods.

wood spirit, same as **wood alcohol.**

wood·sy (wood'zi), *adj.* -si·er, -si·est, of or characteristic of the woods. —**wood'si·ness,** *n.*

wood thrush, a large, rusty-brown North American thrush with a loud, clear song.

wood·wind (wood'wĭnd), *n.* any one of the wind instruments of an orchestra that were originally, and still are often, made of wood.

wood·work ('wûrk), *n.* things made of wood, especially the interior fittings of a house, as wainscoting, moldings, stairways, etc.

wood·work·ing ('wûr-kĭng), *n.* the art or process of making things out of wood.

wood·y ('ĭ), *adj.* wood'i·er, wood'i·est, 1. covered with trees. 2. consisting of or like wood. —**wood'i·ness,** *n.*

woo·er (wōō'ẽr), *n.* one who woos.

woof (woof, wōōf), *n.* the threads which cross the warp horizontally in weaving.

wool (wool), *n.* 1. the soft, curly hair which covers sheep and some other allied animals. 2. woolen yarn, cloth, etc. 3. anything resembling wool in appearance or texture.

wool·en, wool·len (wool'ěn), *adj.* 1. made of wool. 2. pertaining to wool or woolen cloth: *n. pl.* woolen goods.

wool·gath·er·ing ('găth-ẽr-ĭng), *n.* absentmindedness or daydreaming.

wool·ly ('ĭ), *adj.* -li·er, -li·est, 1. consisting of or like wool. 2. covered with wool. 3. coarse; uncivilized. 4. not clear or precise; confused. —**wool'li·ness,** *n.*

wool·pack ('pak), *n.* 1. a bale of wool, especially, formerly, one weighing 240 pounds. 2. a round cumulus cloud.

wool·shed ('shed), *n.* a building where sheep are sheared and the wool is prepared for market.

wool·y ('ĭ), *adj.* wool'i·er, wool'i·est, same as woolly. —**wool'i·ness,** *n.*

wooz·y (wōō'zĭ), *adj.* wooz'i·er, wooz'i·est, [Informal], befuddled or dazed, as from liquor. —**wooz'i·ness,** *n.*

word (wûrd), *n.* 1. an articulate sound or combination of sounds expressing an idea; constituent part of a sentence. 2. the representation of such a sound or sounds in writing. 3. a brief comment or communication. 4. a promise. 5. tidings; news. 6. a password. 7. a command; order. 8. *pl.* language; speech. 9. *pl.* lyrics; a libretto. 10. *pl.* a dispute; quarrel. 11. [W-], the Bible: *v.t.* to express in words; phrase.

word·book (wûrd'book), *n.* a dictionary.

word·ing ('ĭng), *n.* choice and arrangement of words in expressing ideas.

word processor, a computerized device consisting of an electronic typewriter, video screen, printer, etc., used to generate, edit, store, or duplicate documents, as letters, etc. for a business. —**word processing.**

word·y (wûr'dĭ), *adj.* word'i·er, word'i·est, containing or using more words than are needed; verbose. —**word'i·ness,** *n.*

wore (wôr), past tense of wear.

work (wûrk), *n.* 1. physical or mental effort directed to some end; labor. 2. employment; a job. 3. something one is making or doing. 4. the result of work; something made or done. 5. an act or deed: *usually used in pl.* 6. *pl.* collected writings. 7. *pl.* structures in civil or military engineering. 8. *pl.* the moving parts of a mechanism. 9. *pl.* an industrial manufacturing establishment; factory. 10. workmanship. 11. in *Mechanics,* the transference of force from one body or system to another. 12. *pl.* in *Theology,* moral duties or actions as external to faith: *adj.* of, for, or used in work: *v.i.* worked or wrought, work'ing, 1. to be occupied in work; labor. 2. to be employed. 3. to perform as required; function. 4. to move as with difficulty. 5. to undergo fermentation. 6. to come slowly into a specified condition, as by repeated movement: *v.t.* 1. to effect; bring about. 2. to influence. 3. to excite; provoke. 4. to cause to function; manage. 5. to sew or embroider. 6. to shape; form. 7. to solve, as a problem in mathematics. 8. to knead. 9. to bring slowly into a specified condition, as by movement back and forth. 10. to cultivate (soil). 11. to cause to work. 12. to make (one's way) by exertion.

work·a·ble (wûr'kă-bl), *adj.* 1. that can be worked. 2. practicable; feasible.

work·a·day ('kă-dā), *adj.* 1. of or pertaining to workdays. 2. commonplace; prosaic.

work·a·hol·ic (wûrk-ă-hôl'ĭk, -hol'-), *n.* a person having a compulsive need to work.

work·bench ('bench), *n.* a table where work is done, as by a carpenter or mechanic.

work·book ('book), *n.* a book containing exercises and questions for use by students.

work·day ('dā), *n.* 1. a day on which work is

done. 2. the part of a day during which work is done.

work·er (wûr'kĕr), *n.* 1. one who works for a living. 2. one who works for a cause, campaign, etc. 3. any one of the sterile members of a hive of bees, colony of ants, etc.

work·horse (wûrk'hôrs), *n.* 1. a horse used for working. 2. a steady, reliable worker.

work·ing (wûr'king), *adj.* 1. that works. 2. of, for, or used in work. 3. enough to carry on work.

work·ing·man (-man), *n.,* *pl.* **-men** (-men), a worker; especially, an industrial or manual worker.

work·man (wûrk'măn), *n.,* *pl.* **-men** ('mĕn), 1. same as **workingman**. 2. a craftsman.

work·man·like (-lik), *adj.* worthy of a good workman; skillful.

work·man·ship (-ship), *n.* a workman's skill or the quality of the work he produces.

work·out (wûrk'out), *n.* 1. a session of physical exercises, as to improve one's skill in a sport. 2. any period of strenuous exercise, work, etc.

work·place ('plās), *n.* the office, factory, etc. where one works.

work sheet, a sheet of paper on which work records, working notes, etc. are kept.

work·shop ('shop), *n.* 1. a room or building where work is done. 2. a meeting or series of meetings for study, discussion, etc.

work·sta·tion (-stā'shŭn), *n.* a person's work area, including furniture, appliances, etc. and often, a microcomputer.

work·up (wûrk'up), *n.* a complete medical study of a patient, including tests.

work·week (wĕk), *n.* the total number of hours or days worked in a week.

world-class ('klas'), *adj.* of the highest class, as in international competition.

world (wûrld), *n.* 1. the earth. 2. the whole system of created things; universe. 3. the human race. 4. people generally. 5. public life or society. 6. secular life and interests or the people involved in them. 7. [also W-], some part of the earth. 8. any sphere or domain. 9. individual experience, point of view, etc. 10. *often pl.* a very large quantity.

world·ly ('li), *adj.* **-li·er, -li·est,** 1. of or pertaining to this world; secular. 2. devoted to the pleasures, affairs, etc. of this world: also **world'ly-mind·ed.** 3. same as **worldly-wise.** —**world'li·ness,** *n.*

world·ly·wise (-wiz'), *adj.* knowledgeable concerning the ways of the world; sophisticated.

world power, a country or organization which wields a worldwide influence.

World War I, the war (1914-18) which involved Great Britain, France, Russia, the U.S., etc. on the one side and Germany, Austria-Hungary, etc. on the other.

World War II, the war (1939-45) which involved Great Britain, France, the Soviet Union, the U.S., etc. on the one side and Germany, Italy, Japan, etc. on the other.

world·wide ('wid'), *adj.* extended throughout the world.

worm (wûrm), *n.* 1. a long, slender, legless, soft-bodied invertebrate. 2. something

suggestive of a worm, as in shape. 3. the thread of a screw. 4. a servile or debased person. 5. anything that gnaws or torments the mind. 6. the spiral pipe in a still. 7. *pl.* any disease caused by the presence of parasitic worms in the intestines: *v.i.* to work or move slowly, secretly, deviously, circuitously, etc.: *v.t.* 1. to bring about, make, etc. by devious or circuitous means. 2. to extract (information, secrets, etc.) by means of flattery, subtle questioning, etc. 3. to remove intestinal worms from.

worm-eat·en (wûrm'ēt-n), *adj.* 1. eaten into by worms, termites, etc. 2. impaired, worn-out, outmoded, etc.

worm gear, a gear formed by a spiral, rotating screw meshed with a toothed wheel.

worm·hole ('hōl), *n.* a cavity left, as in wood, by the boring of a worm, termite, etc.

worm wheel, a toothed wheel designed to mesh with the spiral of a screw.

worm·wood ('wood), *n.* 1. a strong-smelling plant that yields a very bitter-tasting oil used in making absinthe. 2. something causing bitter anguish, humiliation, etc.

worm·y (wûr'mi), *adj.* **worm'i·er, worm'i·est,** 1. abounding in worms. 2. like a worm. 3. groveling; debased. 4. same as **worm-eaten.**

worn (wôrn), past participle of **wear:** *adj.* 1. adversely affected by use, wear, etc. 2. weary; exhausted.

worn-out (wôrn'out'), *adj.* 1. used up, made ineffectual, etc. by much wear. 2. tired out; exhausted.

wor·ri·ment (wûr'i·mĕnt), *n.* 1. the act of worrying or state of being worried; anxiety. 2. a cause of worry.

wor·ri·some (-sôm), *adj.* 1. causing worry. 2. given to worrying. —**wor'ri·some·ly,** *adv.*

wor·ry (wûr'i), *v.t.* **-ried, -ry·ing,** 1. to chew or mangle with the teeth. 2. to vex, annoy, etc. 3. to cause to feel anxiety or care; distress: *v.i.* 1. to bite or pull (at something) with the teeth. 2. to feel anxious or fretful: *n., pl.* **-ries,** 1. a troubled state of mind; anxiety. 2. something that causes anxiety. —**wor'ri·er,** *n.*

wor·ry·wart (-wôrt), *n.* a person given to worrying, especially about trivial matters.

worse (wûrs), *adj.* comparative of **bad & ill:** 1. bad or evil in a greater degree. 2. of inferior quality. 3. in poorer health; more ill. 4. in a less satisfactory condition: *adv.* comparative of **badly & ill:** in a worse way; to a worse degree: *n.* a worse thing or condition.

wors·en (wûr'sn), *v.t. & v.i.* to make or become worse.

wor·ship (wûr'ship), *n.* 1. a rite showing reverence for a deity. 2. a feeling of great respect, reverence, admiration, etc. 3. [Chiefly British], a title of respect addressed to magistrates and others of high rank. 4. [Archaic], dignity; worth: *v.t.* **-shiped** or **shipped, -ship·ing** or **-ship·ping,** 1. to show religious devotion for. 2. to have great reverence, admiration, etc. for: *v.i.* to perform acts of religious devotion. —**wor'ship·er,** *n.*

wor·ship·ful (-fŭl), *adj.* 1. [Chiefly British],

worthy of respect or honor: used as a title of respect for certain officials. 2. feeling or offering great devotion or respect.

worst (wûrst), *adj.* superlative of **bad & ill**: 1. bad or evil in the highest degree. 2. of the lowest quality. 3. in the least satisfactory condition: *adv.* superlative of **badly & ill**: in the worst way; to the worst degree: *n.* the worst thing or condition: *v.t.* to get the advantage of as in a contest; defeat.

wor·sted (woos'tid, wûr'stid), *n.* 1. a smooth, firm thread or yarn made from wool. 2. fabric made from this: *adj.* made of worsted.

wort (wûrt), *n.* 1. a saccharine infusion of malt which, after fermentation, becomes beer, ale, etc. 2. a plant or herb: now usually in compounds, as *figwort, liverwort*, etc.

worth (wûrth), *n.* 1. material value, especially in monetary terms. 2. the importance, value, or merit of a person or thing. 3. the amount of something to be had for a specified sum: *adj.* 1. equal in value to. 2. having wealth to the value of. 3. deserving of.

worth·less (wûrth'lis), *adj.* having no value, virtue, or excellence; useless, contemptible, etc. —**worth'less·ness**, *n.*

worth·while ('hwîl'), *adj.* worth the time or effort required: of true value.

wor·thy (wûr'thi), *adj.* -thi·er, -thi·est, 1. having worth or excellence; estimable. 2. deserving; meriting: *n. pl.* -thies, a person of eminent worth. —**wor'thi·ly**, *adv.* —**wor'thi·ness**, *n.*

would (wood), *v.* 1. past tense of **will**. 2. an auxiliary that expresses condition, futurity, habitual action, or a request. 3. I wish.

would-be (wood'bē), *adj.* 1. pretending or wishing to be. 2. meant to be.

would-n't ('nt), would not.

wound (woond), *n.* 1. an injury to the body in which the skin and flesh are cut, torn, etc. 2. an injury to the feelings, honor, etc.: *v.t. & v.i.* to make a wound (on or in); injure; hurt.

wound (wound), past tense and past participle of **wind**.

wove (wōv), past tense and a past participle of **weave**.

wo·ven (wōv'n), a past participle of **weave**.

wow (wou), *interj.* an exclamation of delight, surprise, etc.: *v.t.* to cause to feel great pleasure, enthusiasm, etc.

wrack (rak), *n.* 1. seaweed cast up on shore. 2. ruin; destruction. 3. a broken mass of clouds or other vapor blown by the wind.

wraith (rāth), *n.* the supposed ghost of a person in his exact likeness, seen immediately before his death.

wran·gle (rang'gl), *v.i.* -gled, -gling, to dispute angrily or noisily: *n.* an angry or noisy dispute: *v.t.* to drive (cattle, horses, etc.) in a herd. —**wran'gler**, *n.*

wrap (rap), *v.t.* **wrapped** or **wrapt, wrap'ping**, 1. to roll up or wind together. 2. to wind (a covering) around (something). 3. to involve. 4. to conceal by enveloping: *n.* 1. a wrapper, shawl, or blanket. 2. *pl.* concealment.

wrap·per ('ēr), *n.* 1. one who or that which wraps. 2. that in which anything is enclosed or wrapped. 3. a loose garment.

wrap·ping ('ing), *n. often pl.* that in which something is wrapped.

wrap-up ('up), *n.* [Informal], a declaration, account, etc. that ends a report, etc.

wrasse (ras), *n., pl.* **wrass'es, wrasse**, a brilliantly colored food fish of tropical waters.

wrath (rath), *n.* 1. violent anger; indignation; extreme passion. 2. a passionate act of punishment.

wrath·ful ('fûl), *adj.* violently angry. —**wrath'ful·ly**, *adv.*

wreak (rēk), *v.t.* 1. to release (one's anger). 2. to inflict (vengeance).

wreath (rēth), *n., pl.* **wreaths** (rēthz), 1. anything curled or twisted. 2. a garland or chaplet.

wreathe (rēth), *v.t.* **wreathed, wreath'ing**, 1. to twist into a wreath. 2. to intertwine. 3. to adorn with wreaths: *v.i.* to be interwoven.

wreck (rek), *n.* 1. the destruction of a ship at sea, or by being driven ashore or on a rock, etc. 2. the ruins of a ship so destroyed. 3. the remains of anything ruined. 4. a person who has wasted his strength in dissipation. 5. the victim of a wasting disease. 6. violent destruction: *v.t.* 1. to cause the wreck of (a ship, etc.). 2. to ruin or destroy. 3. to demolish.

wreck·age ('ij), *n.* 1. the remains of a wrecked vessel or of anything wrecked. 2. the act of wrecking. 3. the state of being wrecked.

wreck·er ('ēr), *n.* 1. one who plunders or causes wrecks. 2. one who removes the cargo from a wrecked vessel. 3. one who takes away wrecks, demolishes buildings, etc.

wren (ren), *n.* 1. any one of numerous small singing birds of a dark-brown color mottled with black, having a short tail and round, short wings. 2. [W-], [Informal], a member of the (British) Women's Royal Naval Service.

wrench (rench), *v.t.* 1. to wring or pull with a twist. 2. to strain. 3. to harm (an arm, leg, etc.) with a twist: *n.* 1. a violent twist. 2. harm to the body from a twist. 3. a painful emotional experience. 4. an instrument for turning or loosening nuts, bolts, pipe joints, etc.

wrest (rest), *v.t.* 1. to twist, wrench, or force away by violence. 2. to distort; turn from its natural meaning; pervert: *n.* violent twisting or pulling; perversion. —**wrest'er**, *n.*

wres·tle (res'l), *v.i.* -tled, -tling, 1. to contend by grappling with or striving to trip or throw down another. 2. to strive earnestly: *v.t.* to contend with by wrestling: *n.* 1. the act of one who wrestles. 2. a struggle. —**wres'tler**, *n.*

wres·tling ('ling), *n.* a sport consisting of a hand-to-hand encounter between two persons, each of whom endeavors to throw down the other.

wretch (rech), *n.* 1. a despicable or worthless person; profligate; blackguard. 2. one sunk in the deepest woe.

wretch·ed ('id), *adj.* 1. miserable; unhappy; sunk in deep misery or woe. 2. worthless; of miserable quality or character. 3. causing woe or gloom. —**wretch'ed·ly**, *adv.* —**wretch'ed·ness**, *n.*

---

a in cap. ā in cane. ä in father. å in abet. e in met. ē in be. ē in baker. ē in regent. i in pit. ī in fine. ĭ in manifest. o in hot. ô in horse. ō in bone.

wrig-gle (rig'l), *v.i.* **-gled, -gling,** 1. to twist to and fro. 2. to move by or as by wriggling; dodge: *v.t.* to make wriggle: *n.* a wriggling motion. **—wrig'gly,** *adj.* **-gli-er, -gli-est.**

wrig-gler ('lēr), *n.* 1. one who or that which wriggles. 2. the larva of a mosquito.

wright (rīt), *n.* one occupied in some mechanical operation: used mostly in compounds.

wring (ring), *v.t.* **wrung, wring'ing,** 1. to twist. 2. to turn and strain. 3. to force or compress (usually with *out*). 4. to extort. 5. to clasp (the hands) with a twisting motion, as in distress. 6. to grasp and press hard (another's hand) in salutation: *n.* a forcible twist.

wring-er ('ēr), *n.* 1. one who or that which wrings. 2. a machine for pressing water out of clothes after washing.

wrin-kle (ring'kl), *n.* 1. a small ridge or furrow on a smooth surface. 2. a crease. 3. [Informal], a new or useful idea, trick, or device: *v.t.* **-kled, -kling,** to form or cause wrinkles in: crease: *v.i.* to become wrinkled. **—wrin'kly,** *adj.* **-kli-er, -kli-est.**

wrist (rist), *n.* the joint uniting the hand to the arm.

wrist-band ('band), *n.* the band of a sleeve, as of a shirt, for covering the wrist.

wrist-let ('lit), *n.* 1. a band for keeping the wrist warm. 2. a bracelet.

wrist-watch ('wäch), *n.* a small watch set in a bracelet or attached to a strap around the wrist for the purpose of determining the time easily and quickly.

writ (rit), *n.* 1. a written legal mandate enjoining obedience to an order of a court of justice. 2. [Archaic], that which is written.

write (rīt), *v.t.* **wrote, writ'ten, writ'ing,** 1. to form (letters, words, etc.) with a pen or other suitable instrument, as on paper. 2. to express in letters or words so formed. 3. to produce or both produce and send (a message or messages thus expressed). 4. to compose (literature, music, etc.). 5. to record (data) on computer tape, cards, etc.: *v.i.* to write something.

write-in ('in), *n.* 1. a balloting by writing the name of a candidate not listed. 2. the candidate voted for in such a way.

writ-er ('ēr), *n.* one that writes; specifically, an author, journalist, etc.

write-up ('up), *n.* [Informal], a written account of something, as in a newspaper.

writhe (rīth), *v.i.* **writhed, writh'ing,** 1. to twist the body, a bodily part, etc. 2. to experience emotional upset or distress: *v.t.* to contort (the body, a bodily part, etc.): *n.* the act of writhing.

writ-ing (rīt'ing), *n.* 1. the act of one who writes. 2. that which is written; specifically, a literary production, as a book. 3. handwriting; script. 4. written form.

writ-ten (rit'n), past participle of **write**.

wrong (rông), *n.* 1. that which is contrary to right, justice, morality, etc. 2. in *Law*, an act of disobedience to lawful authority; crime: *adj.* 1. contrary to right, justice, morality, etc. 2. incorrect; false. 3. mistaken. 4. not fit or suitable. 5. out of order. 6. designating the under side: *adv.* in a wrong way: *v.t.* to do wrong to. **—wrong'ly,** *adv.*

wrong-do-er ('dōō-ēr), *n.* one who does wrong. **—wrong'do-ing,** *n.*

wrong-ful ('fūl), *adj.* 1. contrary to right, justice, morality, etc. 2. contrary to law. **—wrong'ful-ly,** *adv.* **—wrong'ful-ness,** *n.*

wrong-head-ed ('hed'id), *adj.* stubbornly holding a wrong attitude, opinion, etc.; perverse.

wrote (rōt), past tense of **write**.

wroth (rôth), *adj.* full of wrath; very angry.

wrought (rôt), past tense and past participle of **work.** *adj.* 1. formed; fashioned. 2. shaped by hammering or beating: said of metals. 3. elaborated. 4. ornamented.

wrought iron, a hard, malleable iron with some slag but little carbon. **—wrought'-i'ron,** *adj.*

wrought-up ('up'), *adj.* 1. tense; excited. 2. emotionally upset.

wrung (rung), past tense and past participle of **wring**.

wry (rī), *adj.* **wri'er, wri'est,** 1. distorted. 2. twisted; turned to one side. 3. perverse. 4. showing distaste, disgust, impatience, etc. 5. ironic, sardonic, etc.: *v.t.* & *v.i.* **wried, wry'ing,** to twist or turn aside; distort; wrest. **—wry'ly,** *adv.* **—wry'ness,** *n.*

wry-neck ('nek), *n.* 1. same as **torticollis**. 2. a kind of bird that writhes its head and neck: it is related to the woodpecker.

wul-fen-ite (wool'fē-nīt), *n.* a lustrous mineral that is a compound of lead and molybdenum and that usually occurs as yellow, tetragonal crystals.

wych-elm (wich'elm), *n.* an elm of Europe and northern Asia.

wy-vern (wī'vērn), *n.* in *Heraldry*, a winged dragon with a knotted, forked tail.

X

X, x (eks), *n., pl.* **X's, x's, 1.** the twenty-fourth letter of the English alphabet. **2.** any of the various sounds of this letter, as in *flex, exempt, anxious, luxurious,* or *xylophone.* **3.** a type or impression of *X* or *x.*

X (eks), *adj.* shaped like X: *n.* **1.** an object shaped like X. **2.** a Roman numeral denoting 10. **3.** a symbol or mark representing a kiss, the signature of a person who cannot write, an unknown quantity, person, or thing, or the word "by" in dimensions or "times" in multiplication. **4.** a symbol for Christ, often in combination, as *Xmas: v.t.* **x-ed** or **x'd, x-ing** or **x'ing, 1.** to cross (*out*) (words or letters) with a series of x's. **2.** to indicate (one's choice or answer) by marking with an X.

xan·thene (zan'thēn), *n.* a yellowish, crystalline compound found in some dyes.

xan·thic (zan'thik), *adj.* **1.** yellow or yellowish in color **2.** of or pertaining to xanthine.

xan·thine (thēn, 'thin), *n.* a white nitrogenous compound resembling uric acid, present in blood, urine, and some plants.

Xan·thip·pe (zan-tip'i), *n.* a shrewish, scolding woman.

xan·tho-, a combining form meaning *yellow.*

xan·tho·ma (zan-thō'má), *n., pl.* **-mas, -ma·ta** ('má-tá), a tiny, soft, yellowish tumor of the skin, often on the eyelids. —**xan·tho'ma·tous** (-thom'á-tûs, -thō'má-), *adj.*

xan·tho·phyll (zan'thō-fil), *n.* the yellow coloring matter seen in some plants and autumn leaves.

xan·thous ('thûs), *adj.* yellow or yellowish.

xe·bec (zē'bek), *n.* a small three-masted vessel with lateen and square sails, once common on the Mediterranean.

xe·ni·a (zē'ni-á), *n.* in *Botany,* the direct hybridizing influence of pollen upon endosperm.

xen·o-, a prefix meaning *foreign, strange.*

xe·nog·a·my (zi-nog'á-mi), *n.* in *Botany,* cross-fertilization between different plants of the same species.

xen·o·gen·e·sis (zen-ō-jen'é-sis), *n.* the fancied production of an organism unlike either of its parents.

xe·non (zē'non), *n.* a heavy, gaseous chemical element occurring in minute quantities in the air

xen·o·pho·bi·a (zen-ō-fō'bi-á), *n.* dread of foreigners or strangers. —**xen'o·phobe** (-fōb), *n.* —**xen·o·pho'bic** (-fō'bik, -fob'ik), *adj.*

xe·ro-, a prefix meaning *dry.*

xe·ro·der·ma (zir-ō-dūr'má), *n.* same as **ichthyosis.**

xe·rog·ra·phy (zi-rog'rá-fi), *n.* a process for copying printed material, pictures, etc., a negative image being transferred by light to an electrically charged surface and there attracting oppositely charged dry ink particles.

xe·roph·i·lous (zi-rof'i-lús), *adj.* able to withstand the absence of moisture.

xe·roph·thal·mi·a (zir-of-thal'mi-á), *n.* abnormal dryness and dullness of the eyeball.

xe·ro·phyte (zir'ō-fit), *n.* a xerophilous plant.

xe·ro·sis (zi-rō'sis), *n.* in *Medicine,* abnormal dryness, as of the eyeball or skin.

Xe·rox (zir'oks), *n.* a copying process involving xerography: a trademark: *v.t. & v.i.* to copy thus.

xi (zī, sī, ksē), *n.* the fourteenth letter of the Greek alphabet.

xiph·i·ster·num (zif-i-stûr'nûm), *n., pl.* **-ster'na** ('ná), the bottom extremity of the sternum.

xiph·oid (zif'oid), *adj.* sword-shaped.

X-ray (eks'rā), *n.* **1.** a nonluminous electromagnetic ray or radiation capable of penetrating opaque or solid substances and used in medicine for the study, diagnosis, and treatment of certain organic disorders. **2.** a photograph made by X-rays: *adj.* of, by means of, or involving X-rays: *v.t.* to examine, treat, or photograph with X-rays. Also **X ray, x-ray, x ray.**

xy·lan (zī'lan), *n.* a gummy substance in wood tissue.

xy·lem (zī'lěm), *n.* the woody vascular tissue of a plant.

xy·lene (zi'lēn), *n.* any one of three colorless hydrocarbons that have the characteristics of benzene and that are derived from coal tar, wood tar, and petroleum.

xy·lo-, a prefix meaning *wood.*

xy·loid (zi'loid), *adj.* of or like wood.

xy·loph·a·gous (zi-lof'á-gús), *adj.* that eat or bore into wood, as certain mollusks do.

xy·lo·phone (zi'lō-fōn), *n.* a musical instrument that consists of a graduated series of wooden bars and that is played with small wooden hammers. —**xy'lo·phon·ist** (-fō-nist, zi-lof'ō-nist), *n.*

xy·lose (zi'lōs), *n.* a sugar obtained from vegetable fiber.

---

a in cap, ā in cane, ä in father, á in abet, e in met, ē in be, ê in baker, ê in regent, i in pit, ī in fine, i in manifest, o in hot, ô in horse, ō in bone,

Y

Y, y (wī), *n., pl.* **Y's, y's,** 1. the twenty-fifth letter of the English alphabet. 2. any of the sounds of this letter, as in *yet, hysteria,* or *fly.* 3. a type or impression of Y or y.

Y (wī), *adj.* shaped like Y: *n.* an object shaped like Y.

-y (i), a suffix meaning *quality* or *condition; action of; group, shop,* etc.; *dear* or *little; like, full of,* etc.; *rather, inclined to, suggestive of.*

yacht (yät), *n.* a light, fast sailing ship used for pleasure or racing.

yacht-ing ('ing), *n.* the sport of sailing a yacht.

yachts-man (yäts'mǎn), *n., pl.* **-men,** one who owns or sails a yacht.

ya-hoo (yā'hōō), *n.* a loutish, ignorant individual.

Yah-weh, Yah-we (yä'we), *n.* God: a form of the Hebrew name in the Old Testament.

yak (yak), *n., pl.* **yaks, yak,** a large, long-haired wild ox of Tibet and central Asia, often domesticated as a beast of burden.

yak (yak), *v.i.* **yakked, yak'king,** [Slang], to talk constantly or idly; chatter: *n.* [Slang], 1. constant or idle chatter. 2. a loud laugh. 3. a joke that evokes such a laugh.

yam (yam), *n.* 1. an edible, starchy, tuberous root of a tropical climbing plant. 2. a large variety of sweet potato.

ya-mal-ka, ya-mul-ka (yäm'ǎl-kǎ), *n.* variants of yarmulke.

yam-mer (yam'ẽr), *v.i.* 1. to shout or yell. 2. to whimper or complain: *v.t.* to whine (a complaint): *n.* a yammering.

yang (yang), *n.* in Chinese philosophy, the positive, male principle in the universe: cf. **yin.**

Yank (yangk), *n.* [Slang], 1. a Yankee. 2. a U.S. soldier of World Wars I and II: *adj.* [Slang], of or like a Yankee.

yank (yangk), *n. & v.t. & v.i.* [Informal], jerk.

Yan-kee (yang'ki), *n.* 1. a person who lives in New England. 2. a native of one of the northern States of the U.S. 3. a citizen of the U.S.: *adj.* of or like a Yankee.

Yankee Doo-dle (dōō'dl), title of a nationalistic American song especially popular during the Revolutionary War.

Yan-kee-ism (-izm), *n.* 1. Yankee spirit or characteristics. 2. a Yankee idiom, custom, etc.

yap (yap), *v.i.* **yapped, yap'ping,** 1. to yelp or bark. 2. [Slang], to jabber; talk nonsensically: *n.* 1. a yelp or bark. 2. [Slang], silly talk; nonsense. 3. [Slang], the mouth. — **yap'py,** *adj.* **-pi-er, -pi-est.**

ya-pok, ya-pock (yä-pok'), *n.* a small, aquatic marsupial of South and Central America.

yard (yärd), *n.* 1. a measure of length, equal to three feet. 2. a long piece of timber on a mast for supporting a sail. 3. an area of ground adjoining or attached to a house or other building. 4. an enclosed area for an activity, business, etc. 5. a central point where trains are serviced, switched, etc.

yard-age (yär'dij), *n.* measurement, extent, or distance of something as calculated in yards.

yard-arm (yärd'ärm), *n.* one of the two ends of a yard of a ship.

yard goods, textiles in widths usually sold by the yard.

yard-man ('mǎn), *n., pl.* **-men,** a man employed in a yard, as in a railroad yard.

yard-stick ('stik), *n.* 1. a measuring stick of three feet in length. 2. a standard for testing.

yar-mul-ke (yär'mǔl-kè), *n.* a closefitting brimless cap worn by Jewish men at prayer, meals, etc.: also **yar'mal-ke, yar'mel-ke.**

yarn (yärn), *n.* 1. spun fiber as of wool or cotton. 2. coarse fibers in strands for use in making ropes. 3. [Informal], a story or tale, particularly one hard to believe.

yar-row (yer'ō), *n.* a strong-scented herb of the composite family.

yash-mak, yash-mac (yäsh-mäk'), *n.* a double veil worn by Moslem women in public.

yat-a-ghan, yat-a-gan (yat'ǎ-gan), *n.* a Turkish double-curved knife or short saber.

yaup (yôp), *v.i. & n.* same as yawp.

yaw (yô), *v.i.* 1. to swing away from the intended course: said as of a ship buffeted by heavy seas. 2. to swing away from the normal line of flight: said as of an aircraft or projectile driven by strong winds: *v.t.* to make yaw: *n.* a yawing, or the extent of this.

yawl (yôl), *n.* 1. a ship's boat. 2. a light, two-masted sailboat.

yawn (yôn), *n.* 1. an opening of the mouth, as from drowsiness. 2. any wide opening, as a chasm: *v.i.* 1. to gape open. 2. to open the mouth in a yawn.

yawp (yôp), *v.i.* 1. to make a loud cry. 2. [Informal], to yawn noisily: *n.* 1. the act of yawping. 2. a loud cry.

yaws (yôz), *n.pl.* an infectious tropical disease marked by raspberrylike skin eruptions and sometimes by subsequent destructive lesions of the skin and bones.

y-clept, y-clept (i-klept'), *past participle* [Archaic], named; known as: also spelled **ycleped, y-cleped.**

ye (thē, *thi,* thē; incorrectly yē), *adj.* [Archaic], same as the.

ye (yē), *pron.* [Archaic], same as you.

yea (yā), *adv.* 1. yes. 2. truly. 3. [Archaic], not only so but indeed: *n.* 1. an affirmative reply. 2. a vote in the affirmative. 3. a person who votes in the affirmative.

yeah (ye'ǎ, ye), *adv.* [Informal], yes.

ô in dragon, ōō in crude, oo in wool, u in cup, ū in cure, ũ in turn, ů in focus, oi in boy, ou in house, th in *thin,* *th* in shea*th*e, g in get, j in joy, y in yet.

yean (yēn), *v.t. & v.i.* to bring forth (young): said of sheep or goats.

yean·ling ('ling), *n.* a lamb or kid.

year (yir), *n.* 1. the period during which the earth makes one complete revolution around the sun, equivalent to 365 1/4 days. 2. the period of 365 days (in leap year, 366) from January 1 through December 31. 3. any period of 12 calendar months. 4. a designated period shorter than 365 days. 5. *pl.* age or time.

year·book ('book), *n.* 1. an annual publication carrying statistics and other information about the preceding year. 2. an annual book or magazine brought out by a senior class in a school or college and carrying pictures of the graduating students, articles about student activities, etc.

year·ling ('ling), *n.* an animal one year old or in its second year.

year·ly ('li), *adj.* 1. of or by the year. 2. occurring once a year. 3. lasting a year: *adv.* every year; annually.

yearn (yûrn), *v.i.* 1. to be filled with eager longing or desire. 2. to be filled with tender emotion.

yearn·ing (yûr'ning), *n.* strong desire; longing with emotion.

yeast (yēst), *n.* 1. any one of various tiny fungi causing fermentation and used together as a leavening in baking and also in the making of beer, wine, etc. 2. a yellowish, moist mass of these that occurs as a froth on fermenting solutions; also, such a mass when dried and formed into cakes or made into flakes or granules. 3. anything fermenting in a manner suggestive of yeast or working as a yeastlike leaven. 4. ferment; agitation. 5. froth; foam; spume. *n.*

yeast·y (yēs'ti), *adj.* yeast'i·er, yeast'i·est, 1. of, like, or containing yeast. 2. frothy. —**yeast'i·ness,** *n.*

yegg (yeg), *n.* [Slang], a criminal; specifically, a burglar or safecracker: also **yegg'man** ('man), *pl.* **-men.**

yell (yel), *n.* 1. a sharp, discordant cry. 2. a cheer in unison: *v.i.* to make a yell: *v.t.* to utter with a yell.

yel·low (yel'ō), *adj.* 1. of the color yellow. 2. jaundiced. 3. [Informal], cowardly. 4. sensational: said of some newspapers: *n.* 1. the color resembling the color of gold and occurring between green and orange in the spectrum. 2. a pigment of or producing this color. 3. the yolk of an egg. 4. *pl.* jaundice in animals. 5. *pl.* a plant disease that makes leaves yellow: *v.t. & v.i.* to make or become yellow.

yel·low·bel·ly (-bel·i), *n., pl.* **-lies,** [Slang], a mean coward. —**yel'low·bel·lied,** *adj.*

yel·low·bird ('bûrd), *n.* a bird having a yellow color, as an American goldfinch.

yellow fever, an acute, infectious tropical disease marked by fever, jaundice, vomiting, etc.; it is transmitted by the bite of a certain mosquito.

yel·low·ham·mer (-ham·ēr), *n.* 1. a European finch with a yellow head, neck, and breast: also **yellow bunting.** 2. a woodpecker, the flicker.

yel·low·ish (yel'ō·wish). *adj.* somewhat yellow.

yellow jack, same as **yellow fever.**

yellow jacket, a bright-yellow wasp or hornet.

yel·low·legs (-legz), *n., pl.* **-legs,** a sandpiper with long, yellow legs, found in North and South America.

yel·low·tail (-tāl), *n., pl.* **-tails, -tail,** any one of various species of fish having a yellow tail.

yel·low·throat (-thrōt), *n.* any one of several American warblers with a yellow neck and breast.

yel·low·weed (-wēd), *n.* any one of various weedy plants with yellow flowers.

yel·low·wood (-wood), *n.* 1. any one of various trees producing a yellow wood, as a certain tree with white flowers that is native to the southeastern U.S. 2. such wood.

yelp (yelp), *v.i. & v.t.* 1. to cry out sharply. 2. to bark sharply: *n.* a sharp cry or bark.

yen (yen), *n., pl.* **yen,** the monetary unit of Japan.

yen (yen), *n.* [Informal], an urge; impulse; drive: *v.i.* yenned, yen'ning, [Informal], to have a yen.

yeo·man (yō'mǝn), *n., pl.* **-men,** 1. originally, an attendant or assistant, or a small proprietor. 2. [British], a small landowner: also, a yeoman of the guard or a member of the yeomanry (sense 2). 3. in the *U.S. Navy,* a petty officer assigned to clerical work: *adj.* of or characteristic of a yeoman; specifically, steadfast, staunch, loyal, etc.

yeo·man·ly (-li), *adj.* of or characteristic of a yeoman; staunch, sturdy, solidly useful, etc.: *adv.* in a yeomanly manner.

yeoman of the guard, any one of 100 men constituting a ceremonial guard for the English royal family.

yeo·man·ry (-ri), *n.* 1. yeomen collectively. 2. a British volunteer cavalry force.

yeoman's service, yeomanly service or assistance.

yer·ba bue·na (yer'bä bwä'nä, yûr'-), a trailing evergreen plant of the mint family, native to the coast of western North America.

yes (yes), *adv.* 1. aye; yea; it is so: used for agreement, acceptance, or confirmation. 2. not only but indeed: *n., pl.* yes'es, 1. an affirmative reply. 2. an affirmative vote: *v.t. & v.i.* yessed, yes'sing, to say or indicate *yes* (to).

yes man, [Slang], a slavish toady.

yes·ter (yes'tēr), *adj.* 1. of yesterday. 2. previous to this. Usually in combination.

yes·ter·day (yes'tēr·di, -dā), *n.* 1. the day before today. 2. a recent time: *adv.* 1. on the day before today. 2. within recent time.

yet (yet), *adv.* 1. in addition; moreover. 2. still. 3. to this time. 4. now. 5. however: *conj.* nevertheless; however.

yew (ū), *n.* 1. an evergreen coniferous tree with needles, yielding a fine-grained, elastic wood. 2. the wood.

Yid·dish (yid'ish), *n.* a language of medieval German derivation, used by Jews of eastern Europe: it includes many words from German, Russian, Hebrew, etc. and is written in Hebrew characters: *adj.* of or in this language.

yield (yēld), *v.t.* 1. to submit. 2. to produce. 3.

---

a in cap, ā in cane, ä in father, ȧ in abet, e in met, ē in be, ē in baker, ė in regent, i in pit, ī in fine, i in manifest, o in hot, ô in horse, ō in bone,

to concede: *v.t.* 1. to assent; comply. 2. to give way; cease opposition (*to*). 3. to give a return or produce. 4. to give in physically: *n.* product; return. —yield´er, *n.*

yield-ing (yēl´ding), *adj.* inclined to give way or comply; accommodating.

yin (yin), *n.* in Chinese philosophy, the negative, female principle in the universe: cf. yang.

yip (yip), *n.* [Informal], a sharp cry or bark: *v.i.* yipped, yip´ping, [Informal], to make a short cry or bark.

yod (yōd, yood), *n.* the tenth letter of the Hebrew alphabet: also spelled yodh.

yo-del (yō´dl), *n.* 1. the act of yodeling. 2. a song or refrain sung in a partially falsetto voice, after the manner of Swiss mountaineers: *v.t.* & *v.i.* -deled or -delled, -del-ing or -del-ling, to sing thus.

yo-ga (yō´gä), *n.* a Hindu discipline or system involving mental concentration and certain bodily postures, methods of breathing, etc. designed to bring the mind and body under perfect control so as to achieve liberation of the spirit.

yo-gi (yō´gi), *n.,* *pl.* -gis, one, especially an adept, practicing yoga: also yo´gin (´gin).

yo-gurt (yō´gĕrt), *n.* a thick, semisolid food made from fermented milk: also yo´ghurt, yo´ghourt.

yoke (yōk), *n.* 1. a piece of hollowed timber for connecting two oxen or other animals together. 2. a frame of wood fitted to a person's shoulder for carrying a pail, etc. 3. a bond, tie, or link. 4. a pair of yoked oxen or other animals. 5. a coupling. 6. servitude. 7. a mark of slavery. 8. a bar attached to the rudder to which the steering lines are fastened. 9. a part of a garment holding other parts below: *v.t.* yoked, yok´ing, 1. to join together. 2. to attach (a draft animal) to (a wagon, plow, etc.). 3. to couple. 4. to place a yoke on. 5. [Rare], to enslave; confine.

yoke-fel-low (´fel-ō), *n.* a partner, especially in marriage.

yo-kel (yō´kl), *n.* a rustic: used scornfully.

yolk (yōk), *n.* 1. the yellow part of an egg. 2. natural grease found in sheep's wool.

Yom Kip-pur (yom kip´ĕr, yōm´ ki-pōōr´), the Jewish Day of Atonement, a time of fasting.

yon (yon), *pron.* [Archaic], that or those yonder: *adj.* & *adv.* [Archaic], yonder.

yon-der (yon´dĕr), *adj.* 1. farther away. 2. at a distance but in view: *adv.* in that place; over there.

yore (yōr), *n.* olden times: now only in *of yore.*

you (ū), *pron.* 1. the person or persons addressed. 2. a person or people generally; one: used indefinitely. 3. the second personal singular and plural pronoun.

you'd (ūd), 1. you would. 2. you had.

you'll (ūl), 1. you shall. 2. you will.

young (yung), *adj.* 1. being in the early part of life or growth. 2. inexperienced; not matured; raw. 3. of youthful appearance; vigorous; fresh. 4. of or pertaining to youth.

5. started only recently: *n.* 1. offspring collectively. 2. young persons.

young blood, 1. young people; youth. 2. youthful strength, vigor, etc.

young-ish (´ish), *adj.* somewhat young.

young-ster (yung´stĕr), *n.* a young individual.

your (yoor, yōr), *adj.* of or belonging to you.

you're (yoor, yōōr), you are.

yours (yoorz, yōrz), *pron.* that or those belonging to you.

your-self (yĕr-self´, yoor-), *pron., pl.* -selves´ (-selvz´), 1. the emphatic or reflexive form of you. 2. your true self.

yours truly, 1. a phrase used in ending a letter. 2. [Informal], I or me.

youth (ūth), *n., pl.* youths (ūths, ū*th*z), 1. the state or quality of being young. 2. adolescence. 3. early existence or growth. 4. a young individual; especially, a young man. 5. young individuals collectively.

youth-ful (´fúl), *adj.* 1. young; not old. 2. of, typical of, or fit for youth. 3. vigorous; active; fresh. 4. in an early stage. —youth´ful-ly, *adv.* —youth´ful-ness, *n.*

you've, (ūv), you have.

yowl (youl), *n.* & *v.i.* howl; wail.

yo-yo (yō´yō), *n.* a spoollike toy attached to a string upon which it may be made to spin up and down.

yt-ter-bi-a (i-tûr´bi-ä), *n.* a colorless oxide of ytterbium.

yt-ter-bi-um (-ŭm), *n.* a scarce metallic chemical element of the rare-earth group, resembling and occurring with yttrium.

yt-tri-a (it´ri-ä), *n.* yttrium oxide, a heavy, white powder.

yt-tri-um (it´ri-ŭm), *n.* a rare, silvery metallic element occurring in combination in certain minerals.

yuc-ca (yuk´ä), *n.* 1. any one of a genus of plants of the agave family, having white flowers and stiff, sword-shaped leaves and found in the U.S. and Latin America. 2. one of its flowers.

Yu-go-slav (ū´gō-släv, ´gô-), *adj.* of or pertaining to Yugoslavia, a country in the northwestern part of the Balkan Peninsula, bordering the Adriatic: *n.* a member of any one of certain Slavic peoples living in Yugoslavia. Also Yu-go-sla´vi-an (-slä´vi-än).

yuk (yuk), *n.* [Slang], something unpleasant, disgusting, etc.: *interj.* an expression of distaste, disgust, etc.

yule (ūl), *n.* Christmas or yuletide.

yule log, a large log traditionally used as the foundation of a ceremonial fire on Christmas Eve.

yule-tide (´tīd), *n.* Christmas time.

Yu-ma (ū´mä), *n., pl.* -mas, -ma, one of a tribe of American Indians of the southwestern U.S. —Yu´man (´män), *adj.*

yum-my (yum´i), *adj.* -mi-er, -mi-est, [Informal], having a very good taste or flavor; delicious.

yup-pie (yup´ē), *n.* [Informal], any of those young professionals regarded as affluent, ambitious, materialistic, etc.

ŏ in dragon, ōō in crude, oo in wool, u in cup, ū in cure, û in turn, ù in focus, oi in boy, ou in house, th in thin, *th* in shea*th*e, g in get, j in joy, y in yet.

Z

Z, z (zē), *n., pl.* **Z's, z's,** 1. the twenty-sixth and last letter of the English alphabet. 2. the usual sound of this letter, as in *gaze, zeal.* 3. a type or impression of Z or z.

Z (zē), *adj.* shaped like Z: *n.* an object shaped like Z.

zaf·fer, zaf·fre (zaf'ēr), *n.* a mixture of impure oxides and arsenates of cobalt, used as a blue pigment in pottery glazes, glassmaking, etc.

zaf·tig (zäf'tig), *adj.* [Slang], buxom and shapely: said of a woman.

za·min·dar (zȧ-mēn-där'), *n.* formerly, in India, a landowner, especially one who paid revenue.

za·ny (zā'ni), *n., pl.* **-nies,** 1. a buffoon; clown. 2. a foolish or silly person: *adj.* **-ni·er, -ni·est,** 1. wildly comical. 2. foolish. **—za'ni·ness,** *n.*

zap (zap), *v.t. & v.i.* **zapped, zap'ping,** [Slang], to move, strike, kill, etc. quickly and suddenly: *n.* [Slang], vigor: *interj.* an exclamation indicating fast action.

zarf (zärf), *n.* a holder for a hot coffee cup.

za·yin (zā'yin), *n.* the seventh letter of the Hebrew alphabet.

zeal (zēl), *n.* ardor; enthusiasm; fervor.

zeal·ot (zel'ŏt), *n.* 1. one who is zealous; especially, one fanatically devoted to a cause. 2. [Z-], in ancient times, one of a fanatical sect of Jews who bitterly opposed Roman rule in Palestine. **—zeal'ot·ry,** *n.*

zeal·ous (zel'ŭs), *adj.* filled with zeal; ardent; enthusiastic. **—zeal'ous·ly,** *adv.*

ze·bec, ze·beck (zē'bek), *n.* same as xebec.

ze·bra (zē'brȧ), *n., pl.* **-bras, -bra,** a wild, equine animal of Africa, with dark stripes on a light body. **—ze'brine** ('brīn, 'brin), *adj.*

ze·bra·wood (-wood), *n.* the hard and striped wood of a tree of Guiana, used in making furniture.

ze·bu (zē'bū), *n., pl.* **-bus, -bu,** an oxlike domestic animal of Asia and parts of Africa, with long, pendulous ears and with a large hump on the shoulders.

Zech·a·ri·ah (zek-ȧ-rī'ȧ), *n.* a book of the Bible.

zed (zed), *n.* [British], the letter Z, z.

Zeit·geist (tsīt'gīst), *n.* [German], the prevailing spirit of a time or age in history.

Zen (zen), *n.* 1. a sect of Buddhism that seeks enlightenment through meditation and intuition rather than through study of Buddhist scriptures. 2. the practices and beliefs of this sect.

ze·na·na (zē-nä'nȧ), *n.* in India and Persia, the part of the house that is reserved for the women.

Zend-A·ves·ta (zen-dȧ-ves'tȧ), *n.* the sacred writings of the Zoroastrians.

ze·nith (zē'nith), *n.* 1. the point in the heavens directly over the head of the observer. 2. the greatest height; summit.

ze·o·lite (zē'ō-līt), *n.* 1. any one of a large group of minerals, consisting of hydrated silicates. 2. a similar silicate, used to soften water.

Zeph·a·ni·ah (zef-ȧ-nī'ȧ), *n.* a book of the Bible.

zeph·yr (zef'ēr), *n.* 1. the west wind. 2. a soft, gentle breeze. 3. a soft, fine yarn or cloth.

zep·pe·lin (zep'ĕ-lin), *n.* [often Z-], an early type of dirigible airship, first designed around 1900 by Count von Zeppelin, a German general.

ze·ro (zir'ō), *n., pl.* **-ros, -roes,** 1. the numeral 0; cipher; naught. 2. the point, marked 0, from which measures or degrees are counted on a graduated scale. 3. nothing. 4. the lowest point in a standard of comparison: *adj.* at zero or of zero.

zero hour, 1. the time at which a military attack, which has been previously planned, is begun. 2. a moment of crisis.

zero (population) growth, a condition in a given population in which the birthrate equals the death rate.

ze·ro·sum (zir'ō-sum), *adj.* of or being a situation, competition, etc. in which a gain for one must result in a loss for another or others.

zest (zest), *n.* 1. a piquant quality; relish. 2. keen enjoyment; gusto (often with *for*). **—zest'ful,** *adj.* **—zest'ful·ly,** *adv.*

ze·ta (zāt'ȧ), *n.* the sixth letter of the Greek alphabet.

ze·tet·ic (zi-tet'ik), *adj.* seeking; inquiring: *n.* a seeker; inquirer; skeptic.

zeug·ma (zōōg'mȧ), *n.* a figure of speech in which a verb or adjective, or other part of speech, is related grammatically to two or more words but is logically related to only one of them.

Zeus (zōōs), *n.* the chief god in Greek mythology.

zig·gu·rat (zig'oo-rat), *n.* any one of the temples built by the ancient Babylonians and Assyrians in the form of a pyramid with terraces: also **zik'ku·rat** (zik'-).

zig·zag (zig'zag), *n.* 1. a series of short, sharp turns. 2. something, as a design, having such a series of turns: *adj.* having such a series of turns: *adv.* in a zigzag: *v.t. & v.i.* **-zagged, -zag·ging,** to form.. or move in a zigzag.

zilch (zilch), *n.* [Slang], zero; nothing.

zil·lion (zil'yŭn), *n.* [Informal], any very large number.

zinc (zingk), *n.* a bluish-white metallic element, used in certain alloys, as a coating to protect iron, etc.: *v.t.* **zincked** or **zinced, zinck'ing** or **zinc'ing,** to treat or coat with zinc.

---

a in cap, ā in cane, ä in father, ȧ in abet, e in met, ē in be, ē in baker, ĕ in regent, ĭ in pit, ī in fine, i in manifest, o in hot, ô in horse, ō in bone,

zinc·ic ('ik), *adj.* of or containing zinc: also **zinc'ous** ('ŭs).

zinc·if·er·ous (zing-kif'ēr-ŭs, zin-sif'-), *adj.* yielding or containing zinc.

zinc·i·fy (zing'ki-fī), *v.t.* **-fied, -fy·ing,** to impregnate or cover with zinc.

zin·co·graph (zing'kō-graf), *n.* an impression made from a zinc plate.

zin·cog·ra·pher (zing-kog'rä-fēr), *n.* one who works in zincography.

zin·cog·ra·phy (-fi), *n.* the art of etching or engraving on zinc plates and printing from them.

zinc·oid (zing'koid), *adj.* of or like zinc.

zinc ointment, an ointment made with zinc oxide.

zinc oxide, a white, powdery zinc compound used in ointments, paints, glass, etc.

zing (zing), *n.* [Slang]. 1. a shrill sound, as of something whizzing. 2. vigor, zest, etc.

zin·ga·no (tsing'gä-nō), *n.* a gypsy: also **zin'ga·ro** (-rō).

zing·el (tsing'ĕl), *n.* a perch found in European waters.

zin·ken·ite (zing'kĕ-nīt), *n.* a steel-gray metallic mineral.

zin·ni·a (zin'i-ä, zin'yä), *n.* a plant of the composite family with colorful flower heads.

Zi·on (zī'ŏn), *n.* 1. a symbol for Jewish national life: after the name of a hill in Jerusalem. 2. the Jewish people. 3. the city of God; heaven.

Zi·on·ism (-izm), *n.* a movement that led to the reestablishment of the Jewish national state of Israel. —**Zi'on·ist,** *n. & adj.*

zip (zip), *n.* 1. a sharp, short hissing sound, as of a whizzing bullet. 2. [Informal]. vim; vigor; energy: *v.i.* **zipped, zip'ping,** 1. to move with a zip. 2. [Informal], to move with energy or speed: *v.t.* to fasten with a zipper.

ZIP code, a system for speeding the delivery of mail, by using code numbers for zones, or regions.

zip·per (zip'ēr), *n.* a device used for fastening and unfastening two edges of a piece of material: it has interlocking tabs that are worked by a part that slides: *v.t. & v.i.* to fasten by means of a zipper.

zip·py ('i), *adj.* **-pi·er, -pi·est,** [Informal], full of zip, or vim; brisk.

zir·con (zūr'kon), *n.* a heavy, hard, crystalline mineral, often used as a gem.

zir·co·ni·a (zēr-kō'ni·ä), *n.* same as **zirconium oxide.**

zir·co·ni·um (-ŭm), *n.* a gray or black metallic element, used in alloys, nuclear reactors, etc.

zirconium oxide, zirconium dioxide, a white powder used in making pigments, crucibles, incandescent burners, etc.

zith·er (zith'ēr, zith'-), *n.* a musical instrument having 30 to 40 strings stretched across a sounding board and played with the fingers and a plectrum.

zi·zit (tsi-tsēt', tsi'tsis), *n.pl.* the fringes or tassels on the four corners of the prayer shawl worn by orthodox Jewish men: also spelled **zizith.**

zo·an·thro·py (zō-an'thrō-pi), *n.* a kind of men-

tal illness in which the patient believes himself to be transformed into an animal.

zo·bo (zō'bō), *n., pl.* **-bos,** an oxlike animal of India: said to be a hybrid from the yak and zebu.

zo·di·ac (zō'di·ak), *n.* 1. an imaginary broad belt in the heavens divided into twelve equal parts, or signs, named after certain constellations: the belt extends on either side of the apparent path of the sun. 2. a diagram showing this belt: used in astrology. —**zo·di'a·cal** (-dī'ä-kl), *adj.*

zodiacal light, a faintly luminous, triangular tract of sky sometimes seen in the west during or after twilight and in the east before dawn.

Zoll·ver·ein (tsōl'fer-īn), *n.* [German]. the customs union formed by German states during the 19th century to establish uniform rates.

zom·bie, zom·bi (zom'bi), *n.* 1. in West Indian superstition, a supernatural power by which a dead body can be brought to a trancelike state of animation. 2. a dead body brought to such a state.

zon·al (zōn'l), *adj.* 1. of or pertaining to a zone or zones. 2. formed of or divided into zones.

zon·ate (zōn'āt), *adj.* ringed or belted; marked with zones or bands.

zo·na·tion (zō-nā'shŭn), *n.* arrangement in zones.

zone (zōn), *n.* 1. any one of the five great belts into which the surface of the earth is divided with respect to latitude and temperature: see **Torrid Zone, Temperate Zone,** and **Frigid Zone.** 2. a district or region distinct from others because of its special animal or plant life, restrictions placed on its use, etc. 3. an encircling belt, stripe, band, etc. 4. any one of a number of districts set up to facilitate mail delivery: *v.t.* **zoned, zon'ing,** 1. to encircle with or as with a zone. 2. to mark off into zones to suit governmental or other purposes. —**zoned,** *adj.*

zoo (zōō), *n.* a park or other large enclosed area where live animals are kept for public exhibition.

zoo-, a prefix meaning *animal, animals:* also **zoö-.**

zo·o·chem·is·try (zō-ō-kem'is-tri), *n.* the chemistry of the solid and fluid constituents of animal bodies.

zo·o·gen·ic (zō-ō-jen'ik), *adj.* of animal origin; acquired by man from the lower animals, as certain diseases: also **zo·og·e·nous** (zō-oj'ē-nŭs).

zo·o·ge·og·ra·phy (zō-ō-ji-og'rä-fi), *n.* the science dealing with the distribution of animals throughout the world; specifically, the study of the relationship between specific groups of animals and the regions in which they live. —**zo·o·ge·o·graph·ic** (-jē-ō-graf'ik), **zo·o·ge·o·graph'i·cal,** *adj.*

zo·o·gloe·a (zō-ō-glē'ä), *n.* a colony of bacteria forming a gelatinous mass due to the swelling of the cell membranes as a consequence of the absorption of water.

zo·og·ra·phy (zō-og'rä-fi), *n.* the branch of zoology dealing with the description of ani-

---

ŏ in drag*o*n, ōō in cr*u*de, oo in w*oo*l, u in c*u*p, ū in c*u*re, ū in t*u*rn, u in f*o*cus, oi in b*o*y, ou in h*ou*se, th in *th*in, *th* in shea*th*e, g in *g*et, j in *j*oy, y in *y*et.

mals, their forms and habits. **—zo·o·graph·ic**
(zō-ō-graf′ik), *adj.*

zo·oid (zō′oid), *adj.* of or having the nature of an animal: *n.* 1. an animal organism produced by a nonsexual method, as fission. 2. any one of the individual members of a compound or colonial animal organization.

zo·ol·a·try (zō-ol′ă-tri), *n.* worship of animals.

zo·o·log·i·cal (zō-ō-loj′i-kl), *adj.* of or pertaining to zoology. **—zo·o·log′i·cal·ly,** *adv.*

zo·ol·o·gy (zō-ol′ō-ji), *n.* the branch of biology that treats of animals, their structure, classification, habits, and distribution. **—zo·ol′o·gist,** *n.*

zoom (zōōm), *v.i.* 1. to make a loud, low-pitched, humming sound. 2. to climb quickly and at a steep angle in an airplane. 3. to rise rapidly. 4. to focus a camera by means of a zoom lens: *v.t.* to cause to zoom: *n.* 1. the act of zooming. 2. a zooming sound.

zo·om·e·try (zō-om′ĕ-tri), *n.* the scientific measurement of the different parts of animals.

zoom lens, a system of lenses, as in a motion-picture camera, which makes it possible to keep the image in focus while adjusting rapidly for close-up or distance shots.

zo·o·mor·phism (zō-ō-môr′fizm), *n.* 1. the representation or conception of a deity in the form, or with the attributes, of an animal. 2. the use of animal forms for ornamentation.

zo·on (zō′on), *n., pl.* **zo′a** (′ă). same as zooid (sense 2).

zo·on·o·sis (zō-on′ō-sis, zō-ō-nō′sis), *n., pl.* **-on′o·ses** (-on′ō-sēz, -ō-nō′sēz), any disease that can be communicated to human beings by vertebrate animals. **—zo·o·not′ic** (-ō-not′ik), *adj.*

zo·o·par·a·site (zō-ō-per′ă-sīt), *n.* any animal that is parasitic.

zo·o·pa·thol·o·gy (zō-ō-pă-thol′ō-ji), *n., pl.* **-gies,** the study of the diseases of the lower animals.

zo·oph·a·gous (zō-of′ă-gŭs), *adj.* eating flesh; carnivorous.

zo·oph·i·lism (-lizm), *n.* 1. love of animals. 2. an abnormal sexual attraction of human beings to animals. Also **zo·oph′i·ly, zo·o·phil·i·a** (zō-ō-fil′i-ă).

zo·oph·i·list (zō-of′i-list), *n.* a lover of animals; one who has zoophilism.

zo·oph·i·lous (-lŭs), *adj.* 1. having zoophilism. 2. that is adapted to pollination by animals: said of plants.

zo·o·pho·bi·a (zō-ō-fō′bi-ă), *n.* an abnormal fear or dread of animals.

zo·o·phys·ics (zō-ō-fiz′iks), *n.* a branch of zoology which treats of the physical structure and functions of the organs of animals.

zo·o·phyte (zō′ō-fīt), *n.* any animal, as a sponge or coral, having some external resemblance to a plant.

zo·o·plas·ty (zō′ō-plas-ti), *n.* the operation or process of grafting animal tissue into human bodies.

zo·o·sperm (zō′ō-spŭrm), *n.* same as spermatozoon.

zo·o·spore (-spōr), *n.* 1. an asexual spore, espe-

cially of certain algae or fungi, able to move independently usually by means of cilia. 2. a motile reproductive cell in certain protozoans.

zo·os·ter·ol (zō-os′tĕ-rôl, -rōl), *n.* any one of certain sterol alcohols found in animals.

zo·o·the·ism (zō′ō-thi-ism), *n.* a belief in animal gods. **—zo′o·the·ist,** *n.* **—zo·o·the·is′tic,** *adj.*

zo·o·ther·a·py (zō-ō-ther′ă-pi), *n.* veterinary therapeutics.

zo·ot·o·my (zō-ot′ō-mi), *n.* the dissection or anatomy of animals other than man. **—zo·ot′o·mist,** *n.*

zo·o·troph·ic (zō-ō-trof′ik), *adj.* of or pertaining to the nourishment of animals.

zo·ri (zôr′i), *n., pl.* **zo′ris, zo′ri,** a Japanese sandal that consists of a flat sole secured to the foot by a thong passed between the big toe and the next toe.

zor·ille (zôr′il, zor′-), *n.* a small, black and white, striped mammal of Africa: it resembles the American skunk and emits a very offensive odor: also spelled zoril.

Zo·ro·as·tri·an (zō-rō-as′tri-ăn), *adj.* of or pertaining to Zoroaster, a Persian religious teacher of the 6th or 7th century B.C., who reputedly founded Zoroastrianism: *n.* a follower of Zoroaster.

Zo·ro·as·tri·an·ism (-izm), *n.* the religious system, contained in the Zend-Avesta, said to have been founded by Zoroaster: it was the religion of the Persians previous to their conversion to Islam.

zos·ter (zos′tĕr), *n.* the shingles; herpes.

Zou·ave (zōō-äv′), *n.* 1. a member of a former French infantry unit having a colorful Oriental uniform. 2. a member of any military group like this.

zounds (zoundz), *interj.* [Archaic], a mild oath, used in showing surprise or anger.

zow·ie (zou′i), *interj.* an exclamation that expresses enthusiasm, excitement, approval, etc.

zuc·chet·to (zōō-ket′ō), *n., pl.* **-tos, -ti** (′ti), a skullcap worn by Roman Catholic ecclesiastics: it is black for priests, purple for bishops, red for cardinals, and white for the Pope.

zuc·chi·ni (zōō-kē′ni), *n., pl.* **-ni, -nis,** a green-skinned summer squash shaped somewhat like a cucumber.

Zu·lu (zōō′lōō), *n., pl.* **-lus, -lu,** any member of a people native to South Africa: *adj.* of the Zulus.

zum·boo·ruk (zum-bōō′ruk), *n.* a small swivel cannon used in the Near East, fired from the back of a camel.

Zu·ñi (zōō′nyi), *n., pl.* **-ñis, -ñi,** a member of an Indian tribe of New Mexico that lives in a pueblo.

zwie·back (swē′bak, swī′-), *n.* a type of biscuit that is baked and then sliced and toasted.

Zwing·li·an (zwing′gli-ăn, tsving′-), *adj.* of or pertaining to Ulrich Zwingli (1484-1531), a Swiss Protestant reformer, who taught that the service of Holy Communion is but a symbolic memorial of the death of Jesus and that the body of Christ is not actually present in the elements of the Eucharist: *n.* a follower of Zwingli. **—Zwing′li·an·ism,** *n.*

---

a in *cap,* ā in *cane,* ä in *father,* å in *abet,* e in *met,* ē in *be,* ē in *baker,* ĕ in *regent,* i in *pit,* ī in *fine,* i in *manifest,* o in *hot,* ō in *horse,* ō in *bone,*

zy·go-, a combining form meaning *yoke* or *yoked, pair* or *paired.*

zy·go·dac·tyl (zī-gō-dak'tl), *adj.* having two toes behind and two in front, as the parrot: *n.* a zygodactyl bird.

zy·goid (zī'goid), *adj.* of or pertaining to a zygote.

zy·go·ma (zī-gō'må), *n., pl.* **-ma·ta** ('må-tå), **-mas**, 1. the cheekbone. 2. a bony arch consisting of a cheekbone along with another bone that connects it with the side of the skull. —**zy·go·mat'ic** (-gō-mat'ik), *adj.*

zygomatic bone, the cheekbone.

zy·go·mor·phic (zī-gō-môr'fik), *adj.* bilaterally symmetrical; capable of being divided into two identical halves: said of organs, organisms, or parts: also **zy·go·mor·phous** (-fŭs).

zy·go·spore (zī'gō-spôr), *n.* a thick-walled spore formed by the conjugation of two similar gametes.

zy·gote (zī'gōt), *n.* a cell formed by the union of male and female gametes; a fertilized egg cell that has not undergone cleavage. —**zy·got'ic** (-got'ik), *adj.*

zy·mase (zī'mās), *n.* an enzyme, present in yeast, which produces fermentation by breaking down glucose and other carbohydrates into alcohol and carbon dioxide.

zy·mo-, a combining form meaning *fermentation.*

zy·mo·gen (zī'mō-jĕn), *n.* an inactive form of an enzyme that can be reactivated by the effect on it of any one of several activators.

zy·mo·gen·e·sis (zī-mō-jen'ĕ-sis), *n.* the transformation of a zymogen into an enzyme.

zy·mo·gen·ic (-jen'ik), *adj.* 1. of or pertaining to a zymogen. 2. causing fermentation.

zy·mol·o·gy (zī-mol'ō-ji), *n.* the science which deals with fermentation. —**zy·mo·log'ic** (-mō-loj'ik), **zy·mo·log'i·cal**, *adj.* —**zy·mol'o·gist**, *n.*

zy·mol·y·sis (zī-mol'ĭ-sis), *n.* 1. the action of enzymes involved in fermentation. 2. fermentation or other changes that result from such action. —**zy·mo·lyt'ic** (-mō-lit'ik), *adj.*

zy·mom·e·ter (zī-mom'ĕ-tēr), *n.* an instrument for measuring the degree of fermentation.

zy·mot·ic (zī-mot'ik), *adj.* of, pertaining to, or produced by fermentation.

zy·mur·gy (zī'mēr-ji), *n.* the branch of chemistry which deals with the processes of fermentation, as in brewing, wine making, etc.

A Dictionary of Geography

ABBREVIATIONS: **cap.** capital; **E** eastern; **EC** east central; **ft.** feet; **Mt.** Mount; **N** northern; **NC** north central; **NE** northeastern; **NW** northwestern; **pop.** population; **R.S.F.S.R.** Russian Soviet Federated Socialist Republic; **S** southern; **SC** south central; **SE** southeastern; **sq.mi.** square miles; **S.S.R.** Soviet Socialist Republic; **SW** southwestern; **U.S.S.R.** Union of Soviet Socialist Republics; **W** western; **WC** west central

A·bu Dha·bi (ä′bōō dä′bi), the largest emirate in the United Arab Emirates, on the Persian Gulf: area, c.26,000 sq.mi.

Ab·ys·sin·i·a (ab-i-sin′i-å), same as Ethiopia.

A·con·ca·gua (ä-kôn-kä′gwä), a mountain of the Andes, in W Argentina: highest peak in the Western Hemisphere: height, 22,835 ft.

A·den (äd′n, ād′n), 1. a former British colony and protectorate in SW Arabia, on the Gulf of Aden: now, part of the People's Democratic Republic of Yemen. 2. **Gulf of**, gulf of the Arabian Sea, between the S coast of Arabia and E Africa.

Ad·i·ron·dack Mountains (ad-i-ron′dak), a mountain range of the Appalachians, in NE New York: highest peak, 5,344 ft.: also **Adirondacks**.

Ad·dri·at·ic (ā-dri-at′ik), a sea between Italy and Yugoslavia: an arm of the Mediterranean: also **Adriatic Sea**.

Ae·ge·an (i-jē′än), a sea between Greece and Turkey: an arm of the Mediterranean: also **Aegean Sea**.

Aegean Islands, the islands in the Aegean Sea; specifically, an administrative division of Greece, including Lesbos, Samos, Khíos, the Cyclades, and the Dodecanese.

Ae·o·lis (ē′ô-lis), an ancient region on the NW coast of Asia Minor, settled by the Greeks: also **Ae·o·li·a** (i-ō′li-å).

Af·ghan·i·stan (af-gan′i-stan), a country in SW Asia, between Iran and Pakistan: area, c.250,000 sq.mi.; pop., 15,425,000; cap., Kabul.

Af·ri·ca (af′ri-kå), the second largest continent, situated in the Eastern Hemisphere, south of Europe, between the Atlantic and Indian oceans: area, 11,677,000 sq.mi.; pop., c.484,000,000.

Aisne (ān), a river in N France, flowing into the Oise: length, 175 mi.

Al·a·bam·a (al-å-bam′å), a Southern State of the SE United States, on the Gulf of Mexico: area, 51,609 sq.mi.; pop., 3,890,000; cap., Montgomery.

A·lai Mountains (ä-lī′), a mountain range in the S Kirghiz S.S.R.: highest peaks, c.16,500 ft.

A·las·ka (å-las′kå), 1. a State of the United States in NW North America, separated from Asia by the Bering Strait: area, 586,400 sq.mi.; pop., 400,000; cap., Juneau. 2. **Gulf of**, an inlet of the Pacific in the S coast of Alaska between the Alaska Peninsula and the Alexander Archipelago.

Alaska Peninsula, a peninsula extending southwestward from the mainland of Alaska.

Alaska Range, a mountain range in SC Alaska; highest peak, Mt. McKinley.

Al·ba·ni·a (al-bā′ni-å, -bān′yå), a country in the W Balkan Peninsula, on the Adriatic: area, 11,099 sq.mi.; pop., 3,020,000; cap., Tirana.

Al·bert, Lake (al′bērt), a lake in W Uganda, bordering on Zaire: area, 2,064 sq.mi.: also **Albert Ny·an·za** (nī-an′zå).

Al·ber·ta (al-bûr′tå), a province of SW Canada: area, 255,285 sq.mi.; pop., 2,366,000; cap., Edmonton.

Al·dan (äl-dän′), a river in the EC R.S.F.S.R., flowing north and east into the Lena River: length, c.1,700 mi.

A·leu·tian Islands (å-lōō′shŭn), a chain of islands extending c.1,200 mi. southwestward from the tip of the Alaska Peninsula: part of the State of Alaska.

Al·ex·an·der Archipelago (al-ig-zan′dēr), a group of c.1,100 islands off the coast of SE Alaska.

Al·ge·ri·a (al-jir′i-å), a country in N Africa, on the Mediterranean: area, c.919,000 sq.mi.; pop., 22,817.000; cap., Algiers.

Al·le·ghe·ny (al-ê-gā′ni), a river in W Pennsylvania, joining the Monongahela at Pittsburgh to form the Ohio: length, 325 mi.

Allegheny Mountains, a mountain range of the Appalachian system, in central Pennsylvania, Maryland, West Virginia, and Virginia: highest peaks, over 4,800 ft.: also **Alleghenies**.

Alps (alps), a mountain system in SC Europe

a in cap, ä in cane, ä in father, å in abet, e in met, ē in be, ê in baker, ê in regent, i in pit, ī in fine, i in manifest, o in hot, ô in horse, ō in bone,

850

extending from S France through Switzerland, Italy, Germany, and Austria into Yugoslavia and Albania: highest peak, Mont Blanc.

Al·sace (al-sās', -sas'; al'sas), a former province of NE France.

Al·sace-Lor·raine (-lō-rän'), a region in NE France consisting of the former provinces of Alsace and Lorraine: since 1945, divided into three departments of France.

Al·tai Mountains (al'tī, al-tī'), a mountain system in SC R.S.F.S.R., NW China, and W Mongolia: highest peak, c.15,000 ft.

Am·a·zon (am'ȧ-zon, -zŏn), a river in South America, flowing from the Andes in Peru across N Brazil into the Atlantic: length, c.3,300 mi.

A·mer·i·ca (ȧ-mer'i-kȧ), 1. North America and South America considered together: also the Americas. 2. North America. 3. South America. 4. the United States of America.

American Samoa, a possession of the United States, consisting of seven islands in the S Pacific, north of Tonga: area, 76 sq.mi.; pop., 32,000; cap., Pago Pago on Tutuila Island.

A·mu Dar·ya (ä-mōō' där'yä), a river in central Asia rising in the Hindu Kush and flowing into the Aral Sea: length, c.1,500 mi.

A·mund·sen Sea (ä'mŭn-sn), a part of the Pacific Ocean bordering on Antarctica, east of the Ross Sea.

A·mur (ä-moor'), a river in NE Asia, flowing along the U.S.S.R.-China border across E Siberia into Tatar Strait: length, c.2,700 mi.

A·na·dyr, A·na·dir (ä-nä-dir'), a river in NE Siberia, flowing into the Bering Sea: length, c.700 mi.

An·a·to·li·a (an-ȧ-tō'li-ȧ), 1. formerly, Asia Minor. 2. the part of modern Turkey that is in Asia.

An·da·lu·sia (an-dȧ-lōō'zhȧ, 'shȧ), a region, formerly a province, of S Spain.

An·da·man Islands (an'dȧ-mȧn), a group of islands in the Bay of Bengal, southwest of Burma: with the Nicobar Islands, constituting a territory of India (Andaman and Nicobar Islands), area, 3,215 sq.mi.; pop., 188,000.

Andaman Sea, a part of the Indian Ocean, west of the Malay Peninsula and east of the Andaman and Nicobar Islands.

An·des (an'dēz), a mountain system extending the length of W South America: highest peak, Aconcagua: also **Andes Mountains.**

An·dor·ra (an-dôr'ȧ, -dor'-) a republic in the E Pyrenees, between Spain and France: area, c.180 sq.mi.; pop., 49,000; cap., Andorra.

A·ne·to, Pi·co de (pē'kô the ä-ne'tô), the highest mountain in the Pyrenees, in Spain: 11,168 ft.

An·ga·ra (än-gä-rä'), a river in SC Siberia, flowing from Lake Baikal to the Yenisei River: length, 1,100 mi.

An·gel Falls (än'jĕl), a waterfall in SE Venezuela: height, over 3,200 ft.: also **Angel Fall.**

Ang·kor (ang'kôr), an accumulation of ruins in NW Khmer Republic, consisting mainly of

Angkor Thom (tôm), the capital of the Khmer civilization of the Middle Ages.

An·go·la (ang-gō'lȧ), a Portuguese territory on the SW coast of Africa: area, 481,351 sq.mi.; pop., 8,164,000; cap., Luanda.

An·guil·la (ang-gwil'ȧ), a British island in the Leeward group of the West Indies: area, 35 sq.mi.; pop., 7,000.

An·jou (an'jōō), a former province of W France: Anjou gave rise to the Plantagenet house of England through Henry II, son of Geoffrey (IV) Plantagenet, Count of Anjou.

An·nam (an-am', an'am), a region and former French protectorate in EC Indochina: the central part of Vietnam.

An·na·pur·na (än-ȧ-poor'nȧ, an-ȧ-pûr'nȧ), a mountain mass of the Himalayas, in central Nepal: highest peak, c.26,500 ft.

Ant·arc·ti·ca (ant-ärk'ti-kȧ, -är'-), a land area about the South Pole, completely covered by an ice shelf: c.5,000,000 sq.mi.: it is almost entirely within the Antarctic Circle.

Ant·arc·tic Ocean (ant-ärk'tik, -är'-), the parts of the Atlantic, Pacific, and Indian oceans surrounding Antarctica.

Antarctic Peninsula, a peninsula in Antarctica, extending toward South America.

An·ti·cos·ti (an-ti-kos'ti), an island at the mouth of the St. Lawrence River, in the province of Quebec, Canada: area, c.3,000 sq.mi.

An·ti·gua (an-tē'gȧ, 'gwä) **and Barbuda**, country in the E West Indies, consisting of three islands, including Antigua and Barbuda: formerly a British colony: area, 171 sq.mi.; pop., 82,000.

An·ti-Leb·a·non (an-ti-leb'ȧ-nŏn), a mountain range in W Syria, east of and parallel to the Lebanon Mountains: highest peak, Mt. Hermon.

An·til·les (an-til'ēz), the main island group of the West Indies, including all but the Bahamas.

An·ti·och (an'ti-ok), the capital of ancient Syria (until 64 B.C.): now, a city in S Turkey.

An·ti·sa·na (än-ti-sä'nȧ), a volcanic mountain of the Andes, in NC Ecuador: height, c.18,800 ft.

Ap·en·nines (ap'ē-nīnz), a mountain range along the length of central Italy: highest peak, 9,560 ft.

Ap·pa·la·chi·an Mountains (ap-ȧ-lā'chi-ȧn, -lach'ȧn), a mountain system in E North America, extending from S Quebec to N Alabama: highest peak, 6,684 ft.: also **Appalachians.**

A·qa·ba, Gulf of (ä'kȧ-bä), an arm of the Red Sea, between the Sinai Peninsula and NW Saudi Arabia.

Aq·ui·taine (ak-wi-tān'), a lowland region of SW France: originally, a division of Gaul.

A·ra·bi·a (ȧ-rā'bi-ȧ), a peninsula in SW Asia, between the Red Sea and the Persian Gulf, largely a desert region: area, c.1,000,000 sq.mi.

A·ra·bi·an Desert (-ȧn), a desert in E Egypt, between the Nile valley and the Red Sea.

Arabian Sea, a part of the Indian Ocean, between India and Arabia.

ȯ in dragon, ōō in crude, oo in wool, u in cup, ū in cure, û in turn, ŭ in focus, oi in boy, ou in house, th in thin, th in sheathe, g in get, j in joy, y in yet.

A·ra·fu·ra Sea (ä-rä-fōō'rä), a part of the South Pacific Ocean, between Australia and New Guinea.

Ar·a·gon (er'ä-gon, -gŏn), a region in NE Spain: from the 11th to the 15th cent., a kingdom which at various times included the Balearic Islands, Sardinia, Sicily, and the kingdom of Naples.

A·ra·gua·ia (ä-rä-gwä'yä), a river in central Brazil, flowing north into the Tocantins: length, c.1,500 mi.

Ar·al sea (er'ăl), an inland body of salt water in the SW Asiatic U.S.S.R., east of the Caspian Sea: also Lake Aral.

Ar·a·rat (er'ä-rat), a mountain in E Turkey, near the Armenian and Iranian borders: highest of its two peaks, c.17,000 ft.

Ar·ca·di·a (är-kā'di-ä), an ancient pastoral district of the central Peloponnesus.

Arc·tic Ocean (ärk'tik, är'-), an ocean surrounding the North Pole, north of the Arctic Circle.

Ar·gen·ti·na (är-jěn-tē'nä), a country in S South America: area, 1,084,120 sq.mi.; pop., 31,186,000; cap., Buenos Aires.

Ar·i·zo·na (er-i-zō'nä), a State of the SW United States, on the Mexican border: area, 113,909 sq.mi.; pop., 2,718,000; cap., Phoenix.

Ar·kan·sas (är'kn-sô; *also, for 2* är-kan'zäs), 1. a Southern State of the SC United States: area, 53,104 sq.mi.; pop., 2,286,000; cap., Little Rock. 2. a river flowing from Colorado southeast into the Mississippi: length, 1,450 mi.

Ar·me·ni·a (är-mēn'i-ä, -mēn'yä), 1. a former kingdom of SW Asia, south of the Caucasus Mountains: now divided between the U.S.S.R., Turkey, and Iran. 2. a republic of the U.S.S.R., in Transcaucasia: area, 11,500 sq.mi.; pop., 3,320,000; cap., Yerevan: in full, Armenian Soviet Socialist Republic.

A·ru·ba (ä-rōō'bä), an island of the Netherlands Antilles, north of the coast of Venezuela: area, 73 sq.mi.; pop., 67,000.

A·shur (ä'shoor), an ancient city on the upper Tigris River: the original capital of Assyria. Also sp. Asshur, Assur, Asur.

A·sia (ā'zhä), the largest continent: situated in the Eastern Hemisphere and separated from N Europe by the Ural Mountains: area, c.17,140,000; pop., c.2,633,000,000.

Asia Minor, a large peninsula in W Asia, between the Black Sea and the Mediterranean, including most of Asiatic Turkey.

As·sin·i·boine (ä-sin'i-boin), a river in SC Canada, flowing from E Saskatchewan through S Manitoba into the Red River: length, c.600 mi.

As·syr·i·a (ä-sir'i-ä), an ancient empire in SW Asia in the region of the upper Tigris River: original cap., Ashur; later cap., Nineveh.

Ath·a·bas·ca, Ath·a·bas·ka (ath-ä-bas'kä), 1. a river rising in the Rocky Mountains of SW Alberta, Canada, and flowing northeast into Lake Athabasca: length, 765 mi. 2. a lake extending across the N Alberta-Saskatchewan border.

At·lan·tic (at-lan'tik), the ocean touching the American continents to the west and Europe and Africa to the east.

At·las Mountains (at'lås), a mountain system in NW Africa, extending across Algeria, Morocco, and Tunisia: highest peak, c.13,600 ft.

At·ti·ca (at'i-kä), an ancient region in SE Greece, dominated by Athens, its chief city: now, a province of Greece.

Aus·tral·a·sia (ôs-trä-lā'zhä), the islands of the SW Pacific; specifically, 1) Australia and New Zealand and adjacent islands; 2) Australia, New Zealand, New Guinea, the Malay Archipelago, and all islands south of the equator between E longitudes 100 and 180; 3) Oceania.

Aus·tral·ia (ô-strāl'yä), 1. an island continent in the S Hemisphere between the S Pacific and Indian oceans. 2. a country comprising this continent and Tasmania: area, 2,971,081 sq.mi.; pop., 15,793,000; cap., Canberra.

Aus·tral·ian Alps (ô-strāl'yŭn), a mountain range in SE Australia, in the states of Victoria and New South Wales: highest peak, 7,316 ft.

Aus·tri·a (ôs'tri-ä), a country in central Europe: area, 32,375 sq.mi.; pop., 7,546,000; cap., Vienna.

Austria-Hungary, a former monarchy in central Europe (1867-1918) consisting of territory that became Austria, Hungary, and Czechoslovakia, as well as parts of Poland, Romania, Yugoslavia, and Italy: dissolved by the Versailles Treaty: area, in 1910, c.260,000 sq.mi.

Az·er·bai·jan (äz-ěr-bī-jän', az-), 1. a region of NW Iran: chief city, Tabriz. 2. a republic of the U.S.S.R., on the Caspian Sea, in Transcaucasia: area, 33,436 sq.mi.; pop., 6,614,000; cap., Baku: in full, Azerbaijan Soviet Socialist Republic.

A·zores (ä-zôrz', ā'zôrz), a group of Portuguese islands in the N Atlantic, west of Portugal: area, 890 sq.mi.; pop., 251,000.

A·zov, Sea of (ä'zôf), a N arm of the Black Sea, in S European U.S.S.R.

Bab·y·lon (bab'l-ŏn, -i-lon), an ancient city on the lower Euphrates River, the capital of Babylonia.

Bab·y·lo·ni·a (bab-i-ō'ni-ä), an ancient empire in SW Asia, in the lower valley of the Tigris and Euphrates rivers.

Baf·fin Bay (baf'in), an arm of the N Atlantic, between Greenland and Baffin Island.

Baffin Island, a large island off the NE coast of Canada, in Franklin District of Northwest Territories: area, c.200,000 sq.mi.

Ba·ha·mas (bä-hä'mäz, -mäz), a country on a group of islands (Bahama Islands) in the West Indies, southeast of Florida and north of Cuba: area, 4,404 sq.mi.; pop., 235,000; cap., Nassau.

Bah·rain, Bah·rein (bä-rān'), country on a group of islands in the Persian Gulf, off the Arabian coast: area, 231 sq.mi.; pop., 422,000.

---

a in c*a*p, ä in c*a*ne, ä in f*a*ther, à in *a*bet, e in m*e*t, ē in b*e*, ê in bak*e*r, ế in regent, i in p*i*t, ī in f*i*ne, î in man*i*fest, o in h*o*t, ô in h*o*rse, ō in b*o*ne,

Bai·kal, Lake (bī-käl′), a large lake in SE Siberia, near the Mongolian border.

Ba·ja Ca·li·for·nia (bä′hä kä-li-fôr′nyä), a peninsula in Mexico, between the Pacific and the Gulf of California.

Bal·e·ar·ic Islands (bal-i-er′ik), a group of islands in the Mediterranean, off the E coast of Spain.

Ba·li (bä′li, bal′i), an island of Indonesia, east of Java: area, c.2,100 sq.mi.

Bal·kan Mountains (bôl′kăn), a mountain range extending across central Bulgaria, from the Yugoslav border to the Black Sea: highest peak, c.7,800 ft.

Balkan Peninsula, a peninsula in SE Europe, between the Adriatic and the Black seas.

Bal·kans (bôl′kănz), the countries of the Balkan Peninsula (Yugoslavia, Bulgaria, Albania, Greece, and the European part of Turkey) and Romania: also **Balkan States**.

Bal·khash, Lake (bäl-khäsh′), a large salt lake in the SE Kazakh S.S.R.

Bal·tic Sea (bôl′tik), a sea in N Europe, south and east of the Scandinavian Peninsula and west of the U.S.S.R., joining the North Sea.

Baltic States, the former independent countries of Latvia, Lithuania, and Estonia.

Ban·gla·desh, Ban·gla Desh (bang′glä-desh′), a country in S Asia, at the head of the Bay of Bengal: area, 55,134 sq.mi.; pop., 104,205,000; cap., Dacca.

Bar·ba·dos (bär-bā′dōz, ′dōs), a country on the easternmost island of the West Indies: area, 166 sq.mi.; pop., 253,000; cap., Bridgetown.

Bar·ba·ry (bär′běr-i), a region in N Africa, between Egypt and the Atlantic.

Barbary Coast, the coastal region of Barbary.

Barbary States, the North African states of Tripolitania, Tunisia, Algeria, and Morocco when they were semi-independent under Turkish rule.

Bar·ents Sea (ber′ĕnts, bär′-), a part of the Arctic Ocean, north of Europe and south of Spitsbergen and Franz Josef Land.

Bar·row, Point (ber′ō), the northernmost point of Alaska; cape on the Arctic Ocean.

Basque Provinces (bask), a region comprising three provinces in N Spain.

Ba·su·to·land (bä-sōōt′ō-land), a former British protectorate in SE Africa: now, the country of Lesotho.

Ba·var·i·a (bä-ver′i-å), a state of S West Germany: formerly a duchy, a kingdom, and a republic: cap., Munich: German name, **Bay·ern** (bī′ẽrn).

Beau·fort Sea (bō′fẽrt), a part of the Arctic Ocean, north of Alaska and northwest of Canada.

Bech·u·a·na·land (bech-oo-wän′å-land), a former British protectorate in S Africa: now, the country of Botswana.

Bel·gian Congo (bel′jån), a former Belgian colony in central Africa: now, the country of Zaire.

Bel·gium (bel′jŭm), a kingdom in W Europe, on the North Sea: area, 11,779 sq.mi.; pop., 9,868,000; cap., Brussels: French name, **Bel·gique** (bel-zhēk′); Flemish name, **Bel·gi·ë** (bel′gi-ä).

Be·lize (bě-lēz′), country in Central America, formerly British Honduras: area, 8,862 sq.mi.; pop., 160,000; cap., Belmopan.

Bell·ings·hau·sen Sea (bel′ingz-hou-zn), a part of the Pacific Ocean bordering Antarctica, west of the Antarctic Peninsula.

Be·lo·rus·sia (bye-lô-rush′ä), same as **Byelorussian Soviet Socialist Republic.**

Ben·gal (ben-gôl′, beng-; beng′gål), 1. a region in the NE part of the Indian peninsula: divided (1947) into a state of India (called *West Bengal*) and a province of Pakistan (called *East Bengal*, changed to *East Pakistan*; now, the country of Bangladesh). 2. **Bay of,** a part of the Indian Ocean, east of India and west of Burma and the Malay Peninsula.

Be·ni (bā′ni), a river in NW Bolivia, joining the Mamoré to form the Madeira: length, c.1,000 mi.

Be·nin (be-nēn′), 1. a former native kingdom in W Africa, now a province of Nigeria. 2. country in W Africa, on the Bight of Benin: area, 43,484 sq.mi.; pop., 4,141,000. 3. **Bight of**, the N part of the Gulf of Guinea, west of the Niger delta.

Ben Ne·vis (ben ně′vis; nev′is), a mountain in WC Scotland: highest peak in the British Isles, 4,406 ft.

Be·nue (bā′nwä), a river in W Africa, a tributary of the Niger, flowing through Cameroun and Nigeria: length, 870 mi.

Ber·ing Sea (ber′ing), a part of the N Pacific, between NE Siberia and Alaska.

Bering Strait, a strait between Siberia and Alaska, joining the Pacific and Arctic oceans.

Ber·me·jo (ber-me′hô), a river in N Argentina, flowing into the Paraguay River: length, c.1,000 mi.

Ber·mu·da (bẽr-mū′då), a self-governing British colony on a group of islands in the W Atlantic, c.580 mi. southeast of North Carolina: area, 20.5 sq.mi.; pop., 55,000; cap., Hamilton.

Bes·sa·ra·bi·a (bes-å-rā′bi-å), a region in SW European Russia, mostly in the Moldavian S.S.R.

Bha·rat (bu′rut), the republic of India: the Hindi name.

Bhu·tan (bōō-tän′), an independent monarchy in the Himalayas, on the northeastern border of India: area, c.18,000 sq.mi.; pop., 1,446,000; cap., Thimphu.

Bi·a·fra (bi-äf′rä), 1. a region in E Nigeria: fought an unsuccessful war for independence (1967-70). 2. **Bight of**, the eastern part of the Gulf of Guinea, on the W coast of Africa.

Big·horn (big′hôrn), a river flowing from NW Wyoming into the Yellowstone River in S Montana: length, c.450 mi.: also **Big Horn**.

Bis·cay, Bay of (bis′kā, -ki), a part of the Atlantic, north of Spain and west of France.

Bis·marck Archipelago (biz′märk), a group of islands northeast of Guinea: area, 19,800 sq.mi.

Black·burn, Mount (blak′běrn), a mountain in the Wrangell Range, SE Alaska: height, 16,523 ft.

Black Hills, a mountainous region in SW South Dakota and NE Wyoming: highest peak, 7,242 ft.

Black Mountains, the highest range of the Ap-

ŏ in drag*o*n, ōō in cr*u*de, oo in w*oo*l, u in c*u*p, û in c*u*re, û in t*u*rn, ŭ in foc*u*s, oi in b*o*y, ou in h*ou*se, th in *th*in, *th* in shea*the*, g in get, j in joy, y in yet.

palachians, in W North Carolina: highest peak, 6,684 ft.

Black Sea, a sea surrounded by European U.S.S.R., Asia Minor, and the Balkan Peninsula.

Blanc, Mont (môn blän'), a mountain in E France: highest peak in the Alps, 15,781 ft.

Blue Ridge Mountains, the easternmost range of the Appalachians, extending from S Pennsylvania to N Georgia.

Boe·o·tia (bi-ō'shà), an ancient region northwest of Attica, dominated by the city of Thebes: now, a province of Greece.

Bo·he·mi·a (bō-hē'mi-à), a region, formerly a province, of W Czechoslovakia: earlier, a kingdom and (after 1526) a province of Austria-Hungary.

Bo·liv·i·a (bô-liv'i-à), an inland country in WC South America: area, 424,000 sq.mi.; pop., 6,350,000; caps., La Paz and Sucre.

Bor·ne·o (bôr'ni-ô), a large island in the Malay Archipelago, southwest of the Philippines: the S portion (called *Kalimantan*) is a part of Indonesia; the N portion is composed of Brunei and the Malaysian states of Sabah and Sarawak: total area, 288,000 sq.mi.

Bos·ni·a and Hercegovina (boz'ni-à), a republic of Yugoslavia, in the central part: area, 19,745 sq.mi; pop., 4,124,000; cap., Sarajevo: Bosnia, formerly an independent kingdom, annexed Hercegovina from Serbia in the late 14th cent.

Bos·po·rus (bos'pô-rŭs), a strait between the Black Sea and the Sea of Marmara: also **Bos·pho·rus** ('fô-rŭs).

Bot·swa·na (bot-swä'nä), a country in S Africa, north of South Africa: area, 222,000 sq.mi.; pop., 1,104,000; cap., Gaborone.

Bou·gain·ville (bōō'gin-vil), the largest of the Solomon Islands: area, 3,880 sq.mi.

Brah·ma·pu·tra (brä-mà-pōō'trà), a river flowing through Tibet, India, and Bangladesh to join the Ganges in forming a vast delta at the head of the Bay of Bengal: length, c.1,800 mi.

Bran·den·burg (bran'dĕn-bûrg), a region and former state of East Germany: earlier, a province of Prussia which became the kingdom of Prussia in 1701.

Bra·zil (brà-zil'), a country in central and NE South America, on the Atlantic: area, c.3,287,000 sq.mi.; pop., 143,277,000; cap., Brasília: Portuguese name, **Bra·sil** (brä-sēl').

Bra·zos (brä'zôs, braz'ôs), a river in central and SE Texas, flowing into the Gulf of Mexico: length, 870 mi.

Bris·tol Bay (bris'tl), an arm of the Bering Sea between the SW Alaska mainland and the Alaska Peninsula.

Bristol Channel, an arm of the Atlantic, between S Wales and SW England.

British Borneo, Brunei and two former British colonies on the N part of Borneo: the name used before the colonies became part of Malaysia.

British Columbia, a province of SW Canada, on the Pacific: area, 366,255 sq.mi.; pop., 2,884,000; cap., Victoria.

British Commonwealth of Nations, a confederation of independent nations, all former parts of the British Empire, united under the British crown.

British East Africa, the former British territories of Kenya, Zanzibar, Tanganyika, and Uganda.

British Empire, formerly, the United Kingdom and the British dominions, colonies, etc.

British Guiana, a former British colony in NE South America: now, the country of Guyana.

British India, the part of India formerly under direct British rule.

British Isles, a group of islands consisting of Great Britain, Ireland, and adjacent islands.

British Malaya, the former British territories in the Malay Peninsula and the Malay Archipelago.

British North America, the former name of Canada.

British Somaliland, a former British protectorate in E Africa: merged with Italian Somaliland to form the republic of Somalia.

British West Africa, the former British possessions in W Africa.

British West Indies, the British possessions in the West Indies, including the British Virgin Islands and the British colonies in the Leeward and Windward groups.

Brit·ta·ny (brit'n-i), a peninsula and former province of NW France, between the English Channel and the Bay of Biscay.

Brooks Range (brooks), a mountain range extending across N Alaska: highest peak, 9,239 ft.

Bru·nei (broo-nī'), a British protected sultanate on the NW coast of Borneo, consisting of two enclaves in the Malaysian state of Sarawak: area, 2,226 sq.mi.; pop., 240,000; cap., Brunei.

Bul·gar·i·a (bul-ger'i-à, bool-), a country in SE Europe, on the Black Sea: area, 42,796 sq.mi.; pop., 8,990,000; cap., Sofia.

Bur·gun·dy (bûr'gŭn-di), 1. a region in EC France: formerly a province and, originally, a kingdom. 2. a former duchy including, at its height, Belgium, Netherlands, Luxemburg, and E France.

Burkina Fhaso, a country in W Africa, north of Ghana: area, 105,870 sq.mi.; pop., 7,094,000; cap., Ouagadougou.

Bur·ma (bûr'mä), a country in SE Asia, on the Indochinese peninsula: area, 261,789 sq.mi.; pop., 37,651,000; cap., Rangoon.

Bu·run·di (Boo-roon'di, -run'-), a country in EC Africa, east of Zaire: area, 10,745 sq.mi.; pop., 4,807,000; cap., Bujumbura.

Bu·tung (bōō'tŏong), an island of Indonesia, southeast of Celebes: area, c.1,700 sq.mi.; also **Bu·ton** (bōō'ton).

Bye·lo·rus·sian Soviet Socialist Republic (bye-lô-rush'ùn), a republic of the U.S.S.R., in the W European part: area, 80,154 sq.mi.; pop., 9,900,000; cap., Minsk: also called Belorussia.

By·zan·tine Empire (biz'n-tēn, -tīn, bi-zan'tin), an empire (395-1453 A.D.) in SE Europe

Ca·bin·da (kȧ-bin'dȧ), a territory of Angola, on the W Coast of Africa at the mouth of the Congo River, north and east of Zaire: area, 2,800 sq.mi.

Cal·i·for·ni·a (kal-i-fôr'nyȧ, 'ni-ȧ), 1. a State of the SW United States, on the Pacific: area, 158,693 sq.mi.; pop., 23,669,000; cap., Sacramento. 2. Gulf of, an arm of the Pacific between Baja California and the Mexican mainland.

Cambodia (kam-bō'dē-ȧ), a country in the S Indochinese peninsula: area, 69,884 sq.mi.; pop., 6,388,000; cap., Phnom Penh.

Cam·e·roons (kam-ê-rōōnz'), a former region in WC Africa consisting of two trust territories, French Cameroons (now, the country of Cameroun) and British Cameroons (divided between Cameroun and Nigeria).

Cam·e·roun, Cam·e·roon (kam-ê-rōōn'), 1 a country in WC Africa, on the Gulf of Guinea: area, c.183,000 sq.mi.; pop., 10,009,000; cap., Yaoundé. 2. a mountain in W Cameroun: height, 13,350 ft.

Cam·pe·che, Gulf (or Bay) of (kam-pē'chi), an arm of the Gulf of Mexico, west of the Yucatán peninsula.

Ca·naan (ka'nȧn), the Promised Land of the Israelites, a region between the Jordan and the Mediterranean.

Ca·na·da (kan'ȧ-dȧ), a country in N North America: area, 3,852,000 sq.mi.; pop., 25,310,000; cap., Ottawa.

Ca·na·di·an River (kȧ-nā'di-ȧn), a river flowing eastward from N New Mexico to the Arkansas River in E Oklahoma: length, 906 mi.

Canal Zone, a strip of land in Panama under lease to the United States: it extends about five miles on either side of the Panama Canal, excluding the cities of Panama and Colón: area, 362 sq.mi. (land area); pop., 45,000.

Ca·nar·y Islands (kȧ-ner'i), a group of islands in the Atlantic, off NW Africa, forming two provinces of Spain: area, 2,808 sq.mi.; pop., 1,445,000: Spanish name, Is·las Ca·na·ri·as (ēs'läs kȧ-nä'ri-äs).

Cape Bret·on Island (bret'n), an island constituting the NE part of Nova Scotia, Canada: area, 3,975 sq.mi.

Cape Province, the province of the Cape of Good Hope.

Cape Verde Islands, country on a group of islands in the E Atlantic, west of Cape Verde, Senegal: area, 1,557 sq.mi.; pop., 318,000.

Ca·pri (kä'pri, kȧ-prē'), an island in the Tyrrhenian Sea, near the entrance to the Bay of Naples: area, 5 sq.mi.

Car·ib·be·an Sea (ker-i-bē'ȧn, kȧ-rib'i-ȧn), a part of the Atlantic, bounded by the West Indies, Central America, and the N coast of South America.

Car·o·li·na (kar-ô-li'nȧ), an English colony (1663-1729) including what is now North Carolina, South Carolina, Georgia, and N Florida.

Car·o·line Islands (ker'ô-līn, -lin), a group of islands in Micronesia: part of the Trust Territory of the Pacific Islands.

Car·pa·thi·an Mountains (kär-pā'thi-ȧn), a mountain system in central Europe, extending southeast from S Poland into NE Romania: highest peak, 8,737 ft.: also **Carpathians**.

Car·pen·tar·i·a, Gulf of (kär-pen-ter'i-ȧ), a large arm of the Arafura Sea, on the N coast of Australia.

Car·thage (kär'thij), an ancient city-state in N Africa, founded by the Phoenicians near the site of modern Tunis and destroyed by the Romans in 146 B.C.: rebuilt by the Caesars and finally destroyed by Arab conquerors in 698 A.D.

Cas·cade Range (kas-kād'), a mountain range extending from N California, through W Oregon and Washington, into S British Columbia: highest peak, Mt. Rainier.

Cas·pi·an Sea (kas'pi-ȧn), an inland sea between Caucasus and Asiatic U.S.S.R.

Cas·tile (kas-tēl'), a region and former kingdom in north and central Spain: divided into Old Castile (to the north) and New Castile (to the south): Spanish name, Cas·til·la (käs-tēl'yä).

Cat·a·lo·ni·a (kat-l-ō'ni-ȧ), a region on NE Spain, on the Mediterranean: Spanish name, Ca·ta·luña (kä-tä-lōō'nyä).

Cats·kill Mountains (kats'kil), a mountain range of the Appalachian system, in SE New York: highest peak, c.4,200 ft.: also **Catskills**.

Cau·ca·sus (kô'kȧ-sŭs), 1. a region in SE European U.S.S.R., between the Black Sea and the Caspian: also **Cau·ca·sia** (kô-kā'zhȧ, 'shȧ). 2. a mountain range in the Caucasus: highest peak, Mt. Elbrus: in full, **Caucasus Mountains**.

Cay·man Islands (kā'mȧn, kī-mȧn'), a group of three British islands south of Cuba: area, c.100 sq.mi.; pop., 22,000.

Ca·yu·ga Lake (kā-ū'gȧ, kī-), a lake in WC New York, one of the Finger Lakes.

Ce·bu (sā-bōō'), an island in the SC Philippines, between Negros and Leyte: area, 1,703 sq.mi.

Cel·e·bes (sel'ê-bēz, sĕ-lē'bēz), an island of Indonesia, east of Borneo: area, with small near-by islands, 72,986 sq.mi.

Celebes Sea, a part of the South Pacific Ocean, north of Celebes and south of the Philippines.

Ce·nis, Mont (môn sê-nē'), a mountain in SE France, near the Italian border: height, c.11,700 ft.

Central African Republic, a country in central Africa, north of the Congo and Zaire: area, 238,224 sq.mi., pop., 2,744,000; cap., Bangui.

Central America, a part of North America between Mexico and South America, sometimes considered to extend as far north as the Isthmus of Tehuantepec.

Ceph·a·lo·ni·a (sef-ȧ-lō'ni-ȧ), the largest of the Ionian Islands, off the W coast of Greece: area, 289 sq.mi.

Ce·ram (si-ram'), one of the Molucca Islands, in Indonesia: area, 6,622 sq.mi.

ô in dragon, ōō in crude, oo in wool, u in cup, û in cure, û in turn, û in focus, oi in boy, ou in house, th in thin, th in sheathe, g in get, j in joy, y in yet.

Cey·lon (sē-lon′, sā-), former name of Sri Lanka.

Cha·co (chä′kō), an extensive lowland plain in Argentina, Paraguay, and Bolivia.

Chad (chad), 1. a country of NC Africa, south of Libya: area, c.495,000 sq.mi.; pop., 5,231,000; cap., Fort Lamy. 2. **Lake**, a lake at the juncture of the Chad, Niger, and Nigeria borders.

Chal·cid·i·ce (kal-sid′ĭ-sē), a peninsula in NE Greece, extending into the Aegean Sea in three prongs.

Chal·de·a, Chal·dae·a (kal-dē′à), 1. an ancient province of Babylonia, in the region of the lower courses of the Tigris and Euphrates rivers. 2. Babylonia: so called during the period when the people of Chaldea dominated the region, c.6th cent. B.C.

Cham·plain, Lake (sham-plān′), a lake between N New York and Vermont.

Chan·nel Islands (chan′l), a group of British islands in the English Channel, off the coast of Normandy: area, 75 sq.mi.; pop., 133,000.

Chao Phra·ya (chou′ prä-yä′), the principal river of Thailand, in the W part, flowing into the Gulf of Thailand: length, c.160 mi.

Chau·tau·qua (shà-tô′kwà), a lake in SW New York.

Che·nab (chi-näb′), a river rising in Kashmir and flowing southwest into the Sutlej River in Pakistan: length, c.675 mi.

Ches·a·peake Bay (ches′à-pēk), an arm of the Atlantic, extending north into Virginia and Maryland.

Chil·e (chil′i; Sp. chē′le), a country on the SW coast of South America: area, 286,397 sq.mi.; pop 12,261,000; cap., Santiago.

Chi·na (chī′nà), a country in E Asia, south and east of the U.S.S.R. and northeast of India: area, 3,691,000 sq.mi.; pop., 1,045,537,000; cap., Peking. See also **Taiwan**.

Cho·sen (chō′sen′), the Japanese name for Korea.

Christ·mas Island (kris′màs), 1. an island in the Indian Ocean, south of Java: under Australian administration: area, 55 sq.mi. 2. a British island in the central Pacific, in the Gilbert and Ellice Islands: area, 222 sq.mi.

Chuk·chi Sea (chuk′chi), a part of the Arctic Ocean, north of the Bering Strait.

Chu Kiang (chōō′ jyäng′), a river in SE China, forming an estuary between Macao and Hong Kong: length, c.100 mi.

Church·ill (chûrch′il), a river in Canada flowing through N Saskatchewan and N Manitoba into Hudson Bay: length, 1,000 mi.

Cim·ar·ron (sim′à-rōn, -ron), a river flowing from E New Mexico eastward to the Arkansas River near Tulsa: length, 600 mi.

Clark Fork (klärk), a river in W Montana flowing northwest into Pend Oreille Lake, in N Idaho: length, with Pend Oreille River, 505 mi.

Coast Mountains (kōst), a mountain range in W British Columbia and S Alaska: highest peak, 13,260 ft.

Coast Ranges, a series of mountain ranges

along the W coast of North America, extending from Alaska to Baja California: highest peak, Mt. Logan.

Co·chin China, Co·chin-China (kō′chin′), a region and former French colony in S. Indochina, on the South China Sea: now part of South Vietnam.

Co·cos Islands (lō′kōs), a group of small coral islands in the Indian Ocean, south of Sumatra: an Australian-administered territory: area, 5.5 sq.mi.; pop., 1,000.

Cod, Cape (kod), a hook-shaped peninsula in E Massachusetts, extending eastward into the Atlantic.

Co·lom·bi·a (kô-lum′bi-à), a country in NW South America, on the Pacific Ocean and the Caribbean Sea: area, 455,335 sq.mi.; pop., 29,956,000; cap., Bogotá.

Col·o·rad·o (kol-ô-rad′ō, -rä′dō), 1. a State of the W United States: area, 104,247 sq.mi.; pop., 2,889,000; cap., Denver. 2. a river in the SW United States, flowing from N Colorado southwest through Utah and Arizona into the Gulf of California: length, 1,450 mi. 3. a river in Texas, flowing from the NW part southeast into the Gulf of Mexico: length, 840 mi.

Co·lum·bi·a (kô-lum′bi-à, ′byà), a river flowing from SE British·Columbia, through Washington, and along the Washington-Oregon border into the Pacific: length, 1,214 mi.

Cem·o·ro Islands (or Archipelago), (kom′ô-rō), country on a group of islands in the Indian Ocean, at the head of the Mozambique Channel: area, 838 sq.mi.; pop., 420,000.

Con·go (kong′gō), 1. a river in central Africa flowing through Zaire into the Atlantic: length, c.2,900 mi. 2. a country in WC Africa, west of Zaire: area, 132,046 sq.mi.; pop., 1,853,000; cap., Brazzaville. 3. the former name of Zaire.

Con·nect·i·cut (kô-net′i-kùt), 1. a New England State of the United States: area, 5,009 sq.mi.; pop., 3,108,000; cap., Hartford. 2. a river in the NE United States, flowing from N New Hampshire across Massachusetts and Connecticut into Long Island Sound: length, 407 mi.

Cook, Mount (kook), a mountain of the Southern Alps, New Zealand: height, 12,349 ft.

Cop·per·mine (kop′ĕr-min), a river in Mackenzie District of Northwest Territories, Canada, flowing northwest into the Arctic Ocean: length, 525 mi.

Cor·al Sea (kôr′àl, kor′-), a part of the S Pacific, northeast of Australia and south of the Solomon Islands.

Cor·dil·le·ras (kôr-dil′ĕr-àz, kôr-dil-yer′àz), 1. a mountain system of W North America, including all mountains between the E Rockies and the Pacific coast. 2. the Andes.

Cor·fu (kôr′fōō, kôr-fōō′), one of the Ionian Islands, off the W coast of Greece: area, 229 sq.mi.

Cor·inth (kôr′inth, kor′-), 1. an ancient city in the NE Peloponnesus, at the head of the Gulf of Corinth. 2. **Gulf of**, an arm of the Ionian Sea, between the Peloponnesus and central Greece.

Cor·o·man·del Coast (kôr-ô-man'dl, kor-), a coastal region in SE India.

Cor·si·ca (kôr'si-kâ), a French island in the Mediterranean, north of Sardinia and south of Genoa, Italy: area, 3,367 sq.mi.: French name, **Corse** (kôrs).

Cos·ta Ri·ca (kos'tâ rē'kâ, kôs'-, kōs'-), a country in Central America, northwest of Panama: area, 19,575 sq.mi.; pop., 2,714,000; cap., San José.

Co·to·pax·i (kō-tô-pak'si), a volcanic mountain in the Andes, in N Ecuador: height, 19,344 ft.

Crete (krēt), 1. a Greek island in the E Mediterranean, at the S limits of the Aegean Sea: area, 3,218 sq.mi. 2. **Sea of,** the S section of the Aegean Sea, between Crete and the Cyclades.

Cri·me·a (krī-mē'â, kri-), a peninsula in SW U.S.S.R., extending into the Black Sea, west of the Sea of Azov.

Cro·a·tia (krô-ā'shâ), a republic of Yugoslavia, in the NW part: area, 21,830 sq.mi.; pop., 4,602,000; cap., Zagreb.

Cu·ba (kū'bâ), 1. an island in the West Indies, south of Florida. 2. a country comprising this island and several small nearby islands: area, 44,218 sq.mi.; pop., 10,221,000; cap., Havana.

Cum·ber·land (kum'bēr-lând), a river in S Kentucky and N Tennessee, flowing west into the Ohio: length, 687 mi.

Cumberland Plateau, a division of the W Appalachians, extending from S West Virginia to N Alabama: highest peak, 4,150 ft.: also **Cumberland Mountains.**

Cu·ra·çao (kyoor-â-sō', kōō-râ-sou'), the largest island of the Netherlands Antilles, just north of the coast of Venezuela: area, 171 sq.mi.; pop., 165,000.

Cyc·la·des (sik'lâ-dēz), a group of islands in the S Aegean, forming a department of Greece: area, 995 sq.mi.

Cy·prus (sī'prûs), a country coextensive with an island at the E end of the Mediterranean, south of Turkey: area 3,572 sq.mi.; pop., 673,000; cap., Nicosia.

Cyr·e·na·i·ca (sir-ê-nā'i-kâ, si-rê-), 1. a region, formerly a province, of E Libya. 2. an ancient Greek kingdom in the same general region.

Czech·o·slo·va·ki·a (chek-ô-slô-vā'ki-â), a country in central Europe, south of Poland and east of Germany: area, 49,367 sq.mi.; pop., 15,542,000; cap., Prague.

Da·ho·mey (dâ-hō'mi), former name of Benin.

Da·ko·ta (dâ-kō'tâ), a former territory of the United States from which North Dakota and South Dakota were formed as States in 1889.

Dal·ma·tia (dal-mā'shâ), a region along the Adriatic coast of Yugoslavia, including numerous offshore islands: part of the republic of Croatia.

Dan·ube (dan'ūb), a river in S Europe, flowing from SW Germany southward and eastward into the Black Sea: length, 1,770 mi.

Dan·zig, Free City of (dan'tsig, 'sig), a former autonomous state in N Europe, on the Baltic, including the city of Danzig (now *Gdańsk*) and its surrounding area: annexed by Germany (1939-45), it is now part of Poland.

Dar·da·nelles (där-dâ-nelz'), a strait between the Sea of Marmara and the Aegean Sea.

Dar·i·en, Gulf of (der'i-ên, der-e-en'), a wedge-shaped extension of the Caribbean, between N Colombia and E Panama.

Dar·ling (där'ling), a river in SE Australia, flowing southwest into the Murray River: length, 1,760 mi.

Dead Sea (ded), an inland body of salt water between Israel and Jordan.

Death Valley (deth), a dry, hot, desert basin in E California and S Nevada: contains the lowest point in the Western Hemisphere, 282 ft. below sea level.

Dec·can Plateau (dek'ân), a triangular tableland occupying most of the peninsula of India, between the Eastern Ghats and the Western Ghats.

Del·a·ware (del'â-wer), 1. an Eastern State of the United States, on the Atlantic: area, 2,057 sq.mi.; pop, 595,000; cap., Dover. 2. a river flowing from S New York along the Pennsylvania-New York and the Pennsylvania-New Jersey borders into the Atlantic: length, c.300 mi.

Del·mar·va Peninsula (del-mär'vâ), a peninsula in the E United States, between Chesapeake Bay and the Atlantic.

Del·phi (del'fi), an ancient city in central Greece, on the slopes of Mount Parnassus.

Den·mark (den'märk), a country in Europe, occupying most of the peninsula of Jutland and several nearby islands in the North and Baltic seas: area, 16,615 sq.mi.; pop., 5,124,000; cap., Copenhagen.

Dev·il's Island (dev'lz), a French island off the coast of French Guiana: site of a former penal colony (1851-1951).

Dhau·la·gi·ri (dou-lâ-gir'i), a mountain of the Himalayas, in NC Nepal: height, 26,810 ft.

Di·o·mede Islands (dī'ô-mēd), an island group in the Bering Strait, between Siberia and Alaska: the U.S.-U.S.S.R. boundary passes between the two main islands, **Big Diomede** (U.S.S.R.) and **Little Diomede** (U.S.).

District of Columbia, a federal district of the United States, on the Potomac River: an enclave in Maryland: area, 69 sq.mi.; pop., 638,000.

Djibouti (ji-bōōt'-ē), country in E Africa, on the Gulf of Aden: area, 8,500 sq.mi.; pop., 430,000.

Dne·pr (nē'pēr), a river in W U.S.S.R., flowing south and southwest into the Black Sea: length, 1,420 mi.

Dnes·tr (nēs'tēr), a river in SW U.S.S.R., flowing from the Carpathian Mountains southeast into the Black Sea: length, c.850 mi.

Do·dec·a·nese (dō-dek-â-nēs', -nēz'), a group of Greek islands in the Aegean, off the SW coast of Turkey: area, 1,050 sq.mi.

Dom·i·ni·ca (dom-i-nē'kâ, dô-min'i-kâ), a country that is an island of the Windward group of the West Indies: area,

290 sq. mi.; pop., 74,000; chief town, Roseau.

Do·min·i·can Republic (dō-min′i-kǎn), a country occupying the E two-thirds of the island of Hispaniola, in the West Indies: area, 18,816 sq. mi.; pop., 6,785,000; cap., Santo Domingo.

Don (don), a river of the central European R.S.F.S.R., flowing south into the Sea of Azov: length, c.1,200 mi.

Do·nets (dō-nets′), a river in SW European U.S.S.R., mostly in the Ukraine, flowing southeast into the Don: length, c.650 mi.

Dor·dogne (dôr-dôn′y), a river in SW France, flowing west to unite with the Garonne and form the Gironde estuary: length, c.300 mi.

Dou·ro (dō′roo), a river flowing from NC Spain west across N Portugal into the Atlantic: length, c.500 mi.

Do·ver, Strait (or **Straits**) **of** (dō′vĕr), a strait between France and England, joining the North Sea and the English Channel.

Drake Passage (drāk), a strait between Cape Horn and the South Shetland Islands.

Dry Tor·tu·gas (tôr-tōō′gäz), a group of small islands of Florida in the Gulf of Mexico, west of Key West.

Dutch Guiana, the former name of **Surinam**.

Dutch West Indies, the former name of the **Netherlands Antilles**.

East China Sea, part of the Pacific Ocean east of China and west of Kyushu, Japan, and the Ryukyu Islands, connected with the South China Sea by Taiwan Strait.

East·er Island (ēs′tĕr), a Chilean island in the South Pacific, c.2,000 mi. west of Chile: area, 64 sq. mi.; pop., c.850.

Eastern Roman Empire, the Byzantine Empire, especially so called from 395 A.D., when the Roman Empire was divided, until 476 A.D., when the Western Roman emperor was deposed.

East Indies, 1. the Malay Archipelago; especially, the islands of Indonesia. 2. formerly, India, the Indochinese peninsula, the Malay Peninsula, and the Malay Archipelago.

East Pakistan, a former province of Pakistan: now, the country of Bangladesh.

East Prussia, a former province of NE Germany, on the Baltic Sea, separated from Prussia proper by a narrow strip of land (called the *Polish Corridor*): divided (1945) between Poland and the U.S.S.R.

East River, a strait in SE New York, connecting Long Island Sound with Upper New York Bay and separating Manhattan Island from Long Island.

E·bro (ē′brō), a river in N Spain, flowing southeastward into the Mediterranean: length, c.575 mi.

Ec·ua·dor (ek′wä-dôr), a country on the NW coast of South America: area, 104,506 sq. mi.; pop., 9,647,000; cap., Quito.

E·dom (ē′dom), an ancient kingdom in SW Asia, between the Dead Sea and the Gulf of Aqaba.

Ed·ward, Lake (ed′wĕrd), a lake in EC Africa, between Zaire and Uganda.

E·gypt (ē′jipt), a country in NE Africa, on the Mediterranean and Red seas: area, c.386,000 sq. mi.; pop., 50,525,000; cap., Cairo.

Eir·e (er′ĕ), the Gaelic name of **Ireland** (the country).

E·lam (ē′lăm), an ancient kingdom of SW Asia, at the head of the Persian Gulf.

El·ba (el′bä), an Italian island in the Tyrrhenian Sea, between Corsica and Tuscany: area, 86 sq. mi.

El·be (el′bĕ, elb), a river in central Europe, flowing from NW Czechoslovakia northwest through Germany into the North Sea: length, c.720 mi.

El·bert, Mount (el′bĕrt), a mountain in central Colorado: height, 14,431 ft.

El·brus, Mount (el′broos), a mountain of the Caucasus range, in the Georgian S.S.R.: height, 18,481 ft.: also sp. **El′brus.**

El·burz Mountains (el-bŏŏrz′), mountains in N Iran, along the S coast of the Caspian Sea: highest peak, 18,934 ft.

Elles·mere Island (elz′mir), an island in the Arctic Ocean, in Northwest Territories, Canada, west of NW Greenland: area, 82,119 sq. mi.

El·lice Islands (el′is), a group of islands in the South Pacific, between the Gilbert and the Fiji islands: part of the British colony of Gilbert and Ellice Islands: area, 9.5 sq. mi.

El Sal·va·dor (el sal′vä-dôr), a country in Central America, southwest of Honduras, on the Pacific: area, 8,260 sq. mi.; pop., 5,105,000; cap., San Salvador.

Eng·land (ing′gländ), 1. a division of the United Kingdom, occupying most of the S half of the island of Great Britain: area, 50,331 sq. mi.; pop., 46,363,000; cap., London. 2. England and Wales, considered an administrative unit. 3. the United Kingdom.

Eng·lish Channel (ing′glish), an arm of the Atlantic, between England and France.

Eph·e·sus (ef′ĕ-sŭs), an ancient Greek city in W Asia Minor.

E·pi·rus (i-pī′rŭs), an ancient kingdom on the E coast of the Ionian Sea, in what is now S Albania and NW Greece.

E·qua·to·ri·al Guinea (ē-kwä-tôr′i-äl, ek-wä-), a country in central Africa, consisting of a mainland section and two islands in the Gulf of Guinea: area, 10,832 sq. mi.; pop., 359,000; cap., Malabo.

Er·e·bus, Mount (er′ĕ-bŭs), a volcanic mountain on an island just off the coast of Victoria Land, Antarctica: height, over 13,000 ft.

Er·ie, Lake (ir′i), one of the Great Lakes, between Lake Huron and Lake Ontario.

Er·i·tre·a (er-i-trē′ä), a former Italian colony in NE Africa, on the Red Sea: now part of Ethiopia.

Es·to·ni·a (es-tō′ni-ä), a republic of the U.S.S.R., in NE Europe, on the Baltic Sea: area, 17,410 sq. mi.; pop., 1,500,000; cap., Tallinn: in full, **Estonian Soviet Socialist Republic.**

a in cap, ä in cane, ä in father, ă in abet, e in met, ē in be, ē in baker, ē in regent, i in pit, ī in fine, î in manifest, o in hot, ō in horse, ô in bone,

E·thi·o·pi·a (ē-thi-ō'pi-à), 1. an ancient kingdom in NE Africa, on the Red Sea, corresponding to modern Sudan and the N part of modern Ethiopia. 2. a country in E Africa, on the Red Sea: area, 457,000 sq.mi.; pop., 43,882,000; cap., Addis Ababa.

Et·na (et'nà), a volcanic mountain in E Sicily: height, 10,705 ft.

E·tru·ri·a (i-troor'i-à), an ancient country occupying what is now Tuscany and part of Umbria, on the WC coast of Italy.

Eu·phra·tes (ū-frā'tēz), a river flowing from EC Turkey through Syria and Iraq, joining the Tigris to form the Shatt al Arab: length, c. 1,700 mi.

Eur·a·sia (yoo-rā'zhà, 'shà), a land mass made up of the continents of Europe and Asia.

Eu·rope (yoor'ŏp), a continent between Asia and the Atlantic Ocean: the Ural Mountains are generally considered the E boundary: area, 4,000,000 sq.mi.; pop., c.688,000,000.

Eux·ine Sea (ūk'sin, 'sīn), the ancient name of the **Black Sea**.

Ev·er·est, Mount (ev'ēr-ist, ev'rist), a peak of the Himalayas, on the border of Nepal and Tibet: highest mountain in the world, 29,028 ft.

Ev·voi·a (ev'i-à), a large Greek island in the Aegean Sea, off the E coast of Greece: area, 1,492 sq.mi.

Eyre, Lake (er), a shallow salt lake in SC Australia, varying from occasionally dry to c.4,000 sq.mi.

Faer·oe Islands (fer'ō), a group of Danish islands in the N Atlantic, between Iceland and the Shetland Islands: area, 540 sq.mi.; pop., 45,000: also **Faeroes.**

Falk·land Islands (fôk'lànd), 1. a group of islands in the South Atlantic, east of the tip of South America. 2. a British crown colony consisting of this group and two island dependencies (**Falkland Island Dependencies**) to the southeast: area, 6,200 sq.mi.; pop., 2,000.

Far East, the countries of E Asia, including China, Japan, Korea, and Mongolia, and, sometimes, the countries of SE Asia and the Malay Archipelago.

Fer·nan·do Pó·o (fer-nän'dō pō'ō), an island in the Gulf of Guinea, off the coast of Cameroun, forming with another island a province of Equatorial Guinea: area, 770 sq.mi.: English name, **Fernando Po** (fēr-nan'dō pō').

Fi·ji (fē'jē), 1. a group of islands in the SW Pacific, north of New Zealand: also called **Fiji Islands.** 2. a country made up of these islands: area, c.7,000 sq.mi.; pop., 672,000; cap., Suva.

Fin·ger Lakes (fing'gēr), a group of long, narrow glacial lakes in WC New York.

Fin·land (fin'lànd), 1. a country in N Europe, northeast of the Baltic Sea: area, 130,119 sq.mi.; pop., 5,099,000; cap., Helsinki. 2. **Gulf of,** an arm of the Baltic Sea, extending

eastward between Finland and the Estonian S.S.R.

Fin·ster·aar·horn (fin-stēr-är'hôrn), a mountain in SC Switzerland: height, 14,026 ft.

Flan·ders (flan'dērz), a region in NW Europe, on the North Sea, including a part of NW France, two provinces of Belgium, and a part of SW Netherlands.

Flo·res (flô'res), an island of Indonesia, west of Timor: area, 5,500 sq.mi.

Flor·i·da (flôr'i-dà, flor'-), 1. a State of the SE United States, mostly on a peninsula between the Atlantic and the Gulf of Mexico: area, 58,560 sq.mi.; pop., 9,740,000; cap., Tallahassee. 2. **Straits of,** a strait between the S tip of Florida and Cuba on the south and the Bahamas on the southeast: also called **Florida Strait.**

Florida Keys, a chain of small islands extending southwest from the S tip of Florida.

For·mo·sa (fôr-mō'sà), the former (Portuguese) name of **Taiwan.**

France (frans, fräns), a country in W Europe, on the Atlantic and the Mediterranean: area, 212,821 sq.mi.; pop., 54,335,000; cap., Paris.

Frank·lin (frangk'lin), the N district of the Northwest Territories, Canada, including the Arctic islands: area, 549,253 sq.mi.

Franz Jo·sef Land (fränts yō'zef), a group of islands of the U.S.S.R., in the Arctic Ocean: area, c.8,000 sq.mi.

Fra·ser (frā'zēr), a river in British Columbia, Canada, flowing from the Rocky Mountains south into the Pacific: length, 850 mi.

French Community (french), a political union comprising France, its overseas departments and territories, and six fully independent member states.

French Equatorial Africa, a former French overseas territory in central Africa: the region is now occupied by the independent countries of Central African Republic, Chad, Congo, and Gabon.

French Guiana, a French overseas department in NE South America, on the Atlantic: area, 35,135 sq.mi.; pop., 73,000; chief town, Cayenne.

French Guinea, Guinea when it was under French control.

French India, a former French territory consisting of five scattered settlements in India, mostly on the E coast: absorbed by India.

French Indochina, a former union of French protectorates and colonies in SE Asia: the region is now occupied by the Khmer Republic, Laos, and Vietnam.

French Morocco, the former French zone of Morocco, comprising most of the country: with Spanish Morocco and Tangier, it became the country of Morocco.

French Polynesia, a French overseas territory in the E South Pacific, consisting principally of five archipelagoes: area, 1,545 sq.mi.; pop., 138,000; cap., Papeete.

French Sudan, a former French overseas territory in W Africa: now, the country of Mali.

French West Africa, a former French overseas

territory in W Africa: the region now includes the countries of Senegal, Mali, Mauritania, Guinea, Ivory Coast, Upper Volta, Dahomey, and Niger.

French West Indies, two overseas departments of France, in the West Indies, including Martinique and Guadeloupe and the dependencies of Guadeloupe.

Fri·sian Islands (frizh'ǎn, 'i-ǎn), an island chain in the North Sea, extending along the coast of NW Europe: it is divided into three groups, one belonging to the Netherlands (**West Frisian Islands**), one belonging to West Germany (**East Frisian Islands**), and one divided between West Germany and Denmark (**North Frisian Islands**).

Fu·ji (fōō'jē), an extinct volcano on Honshu island, Japan, southwest of Tokyo: height, 12,388 ft.: also **Fu·ji·ya·ma** (fōō-ji-yä'mä), **Fu·ji·san** (-sän).

Fun·dy, Bay of (fun'dì), an arm of the Atlantic, between New Brunswick and Nova Scotia, Canada.

Ga·bon (gä-bōn'), a country in WC Africa, on the Gulf of Guinea: area, 103,089 sq.mi.; pop., 1,017,000; cap., Libreville.

Ga·la·pa·gos Islands (gä-lä'pä·gōs), a group of islands in the Pacific on the equator, belonging to Ecuador: area, 3,028 sq.mi.

Ga·la·tia (gȧ-lā'shȧ), an ancient kingdom, and later a Roman province, in central Asia Minor in the region of Ankara, modern Turkey.

Ga·li·cia (gȧ-lish'ȧ), 1. a region in SE Poland and NW Ukrainian S.S.R., northeast of the Carpathian Mountains: formerly, an Austrian crown land and a Polish province. 2. a region and former kingdom in NW Spain, on the Atlantic.

Gal·i·lee (gal'i-lē), 1. a region of N Israel, north and west of the Sea of Galilee. 2. **Sea of,** a lake in NE Israel, on the Syria border.

Gam·bi·a (gam'bi-ȧ), 1. a country on the W coast of Africa, on both sides of the Gambia River and surrounded on three sides by Senegal: area, c.3,450 sq.mi.; pop., 695,800; cap., Banjul. 2. a river in W Africa, flowing from N Guinea, through Senegal and Gambia, into the Atlantic: length, c.700 mi.

Gan·ges (gan'jēz), a river in northern and eastern India and in Bangladesh, flowing from the Himalayas southeast to join the Brahmaputra in forming a vast delta at the head of the Bay of Bengal: length, c.1,560 mi.

Ga·ronne (gä-rôn'), a river in SW France, flowing from the Pyrenees northwest into the Gironde: length, c.400 mi.

Gas·pé Peninsula (gas-pā'), a peninsula in S Quebec, Canada, extending into the Gulf of St. Lawrence, south of the St. Lawrence River.

Gaul (gôl), 1. an ancient region in W Europe, consisting of what is now France and Belgium: after 5th cent. B.C., also called **Transalpine Gaul.** 2. an ancient region in N Italy, occupied by the Gauls (5th cent. B.C.): in full, **Cisalpine Gaul.** 3. an ancient division of the Roman Empire, including Cisalpine Gaul and Transalpine Gaul.

Ga·za Strip (gäz'ȧ, gaz'ȧ), a strip of land in SW Palestine, along the Mediterranean, surrounding the city of Gaza (in ancient times, one of the chief cities of the Philistines).

Ge·ne·va, Lake (of) (jē-nē'vȧ), a lake in SW Switzerland on the border of France.

Gen·o·a (jen'ō-ȧ), 1. a former republic including what is today the region of Liguria and the island of Corsica. 2. **Gulf of,** the N part of the Ligurian Sea, off the NW coast of Italy.

Geor·gia (jôr'jȧ), 1. a Southern State of the SE United States, on the Atlantic: area, 58,876 sq.mi.; pop., 5,464,000; cap., Atlanta. 2. a republic of the U.S.S.R., in Transcaucasia, on the Black Sea: area, 26,900 sq.mi.; pop., 5,200,000; cap., Tbilisi: in full, **Georgian Soviet Socialist Republic.**

Georgian Bay, a NE arm of Lake Huron, along the S coast of Ontario, Canada.

German East Africa, a former colony of the German Empire, in E Africa: now occupied mostly by Tanzania, Rwanda, and Burundi.

German Empire, an empire (1871-1919) consisting of a unification of German states (a group of territorial sovereignties) under the domination of Prussia.

German Southwest Africa, a former German colony in SW Africa: now, the territory of South West Africa.

Ger·ma·ny (jûr'mȧ·ni), a former country in NC Europe, on the North and Baltic seas: divided (1945) into four zones of occupation, administered respectively by France, the United Kingdom, the United States, and the U.S.S.R., and (1949) partitioned into 1) the **Federal Republic of Germany,** a country made up of the three W zones (British, French, and U.S.): area, 95,735 sq.mi.; pop., 61,175,000; cap., Bonn: also called **West Germany.** 2) the **German Democratic Republic,** a country comprising the E (U.S.S.R.) zone: area, c.41,800 sq.mi.; pop., 16,700,000; cap., East Berlin: also called **East Germany.**

Gha·na (gä'nä), a country in W Africa, on the Gulf of Guinea: area, 92,010 sq.mi.; pop., 12,200,000; cap., Accra.

Ghats (gôts, gots), two mountain ranges forming the eastern and western edges of the Deccan Plateau, India, uniting near the S tip of India: highest peak, 8,841 ft.: the **Eastern Ghats** are parallel to the Coromandel Coast and the **Western Ghats** are parallel to the Malabar Coast.

Gi·bral·tar (ji-brôl'tẽr), 1. a small peninsula at the S tip of Spain, extending into the Mediterranean: area, 2.5 sq.mi.: it consists mostly of a rocky hill (**Rock of Gibraltar**), height, 1,396 ft. 2. a self-governing British possession on this peninsula: pop., 29,000. 3. **Strait of,** a strait between Spain and Morocco, joining the Mediterranean and the Atlantic.

Gi·la (hē'lä), a river in S Arizona, flowing southwest into the Colorado: length, 630 mi.

a in cap, ā in cane, ä in father, ȧ in abet, e in met, ē in be, ẽ in baker, ė in regent, i in pit, ī in fine, ï in manifest, o in hot, ô in horse, ō in bone,

Gilbert Islands, a group of islands in the WC Pacific which in 1979 became the independent nation of Kiribati.

Gil·e·ad (gil′i-åd), a mountainous region of ancient Palestine, east of the Jordan, between the Dead Sea and the Sea of Galilee.

Gi·ronde (ji-rond′), an estuary in SW France, formed by the juncture of the Garonne and Dordogne rivers and flowing into the Bay of Biscay.

Go·a (gō′ä), a small region on the SW coast of India: formerly part of Portuguese India.

Go·bi (gō′bi), a desert plateau in E Asia, in the S Mongolian People's Republic and N China.

God·win Aus·ten (god′win ôs′tin), a mountain in N Jammu and Kashmir, near the Chinese border: height, 28,250 ft.

Gold Coast (gōld), a former British territory in W Africa: now part of Ghana.

Good Hope, Cape of (good hōp), 1. a cape at the SW tip of Africa, on the Atlantic. 2. a province of South Africa, in the southernmost part.

Got·land (got′länd), a Swedish island in the Baltic Sea, SE of Sweden: area, 1,167 sq. mi.

Gram·pi·an Mountains (gram′pi-ån), a mountain range extending across central and N Scotland, dividing the Highlands from the Lowlands: highest peak, Ben Nevis: also called **Grampian Hills, Grampians.**

Gra·na·da (grä-nä′dä), a former Moorish kingdom in S Spain.

Great Australian Bight, a wide bay of the Indian Ocean, on the S coast of Australia.

Great Bear Lake, a lake in central Mackenzie District, Northwest Territories, Canada.

Great Britain, 1. the principal island of the United Kingdom, including England, Scotland, and Wales. 2. popularly, the United Kingdom of Great Britain and Northern Ireland.

Great Dividing Range, a series of mountain ranges and plateaus that parallel the E coast of Australia: highest peak, 7,316 ft.

Greater Antilles, a group of islands in the West Indies, made up of the N and W Antilles, including the islands of Cuba, Jamaica, Hispaniola, and Puerto Rico.

Great Lakes, a chain of fresh-water lakes in EC North America, emptying into the St. Lawrence River; Lakes Superior, Huron, Michigan, Erie, and Ontario.

Great Plains, a sloping region of valleys and plains in WC North America, extending from Texas north to S Alberta, Canada, and stretching east from the base of the Rockies for c.400 mi.

Great Salt Lake, a shallow salt-water lake in NW Utah.

Great Slave lake, a lake in S Mackenzie District, Northwest Territories, Canada.

Great Smoky Mountains, a mountain range of the Appalachians, along the Tennessee-North Carolina border: highest peak, 6,642 ft.

Greece (grēs), a country in the S Balkan Peninsula, including many islands in the

Aegean, Ionian, and Mediterranean seas: area, 50,919 sq. mi.; pop., 9,900,000; cap., Athens: in ancient *times,* the region was comprised of a number of *small* monarchies and republics and had no political *unity* until conquered by the Romans in the 2nd cent. B.C.

Green·land (grēn′länd), a large island in the North Atlantic, northeast of North America, constituting an integral part of Denmark: area, 840,000 sq.mi.; pop., 53,000; cap., Godthaab.

Green Mountains (grēn), a range of the Appalachians, extending the length of Vermont: highest peak, 4,393 ft.

Green River, a river flowing from W Wyoming south into the Colorado River in SE Utah: length, 730 mi.

Gre·na·da (grē-nä′dä), 1. the southernmost island of the Windward group in the West Indies: area, 120 sq.mi. 2. a country consisting of this island and a chain of small adjacent islands: formerly a British territory: area, 133 sq.mi.; pop., 92,000; cap., St. George's.

Gua·dal·ca·nal (gwä-dl-kå-nal′), the largest island of the British Solomon Islands Protectorate, in the SW Pacific: area, c.2,500 sq.mi.

Gua·de·loupe (gwä-dĕ-lōōp′, gô-dl-ōōp′), an overseas department of France, consisting of two major islands and five island dependencies, in the Leeward group of the West Indies: area, 688 sq.mi.; pop., 328,000; cap., Basse-Terre.

Guam (gwäm), the largest of the Mariana Islands, in the W Pacific: a possession of the U.S.: area, 209 sq.mi.; pop., 105,800; cap., Agaña.

Gua·po·ré (gwä-pô-rĕ′), a river in central South America, flowing from central Brazil northwest along the Brazil-Bolivia border into the Mamoré: length, c.750 mi.

Gua·te·ma·la (gwä-tĕ-mä′lå), a country in Central America, south and east of Mexico: area, 42,042 sq.mi.; pop., 8,335,000; cap., Guatemala.

Guern·sey (gûrn′zi), the second largest of the Channel Islands: area, 25 sq.mi.; pop., 53,000.

Gui·a·na (gi-an′å, -ä′nå), 1. a region in N South America, including Guyana, Surinam, and French Guiana. 2. an area including this region, SE Venezuela, and part of N Brazil, bounded by the Orinoco, Negro, and Amazon rivers and the Atlantic Ocean.

Guin·ea (gin′i), 1. a coastal region of W Africa, extending from S Senegal to E Nigeria. 2. a country in the NW part of this region: area, 94,925 sq.mi.; pop., 5,400,000; cap., Conakry. 3. **Gulf of,** a part of the Atlantic, off the W coast of Africa.

Guin·ea-Bis·sau (-bi-sou′), a country in W Africa, on the Atlantic between Senegal and Guinea: formerly a Portuguese overseas territory: area, 13,948 sq.mi.; pop., 544,000; cap., Bissau.

Gulf Stream (gulf), a warm ocean current

ô in dragon, ōō in crude, oo in wool, u in cup, û in cure, û in turn, û in focus, oi in boy, ou in house, th in thin, th in sheathe, g in get, j in joy, y in yet.

flowing from the Gulf of Mexico along the E coast of the United States, and turning eastward in the North Atlantic toward Europe.

Guy·a·na (gī-än′ȧ, -än′ȧ), a country in NE South America, on the Atlantic: area, 83,000 sq.mi.; pop., 965,000; cap., Georgetown.

Hai·nan (hī′nän′), an island off the S coast of China, in the South China Sea: area, c.13,000 sq.mi.

Hai·ti (hā′ti), a country occupying the W portion of the island of Hispaniola, in the West Indies: area, 10,714 sq.mi.; pop., 5,250,000; cap., Port-au-Prince.

Hal·i·car·nas·sus (hal-i-kär-nas′ŭs), an ancient city in SW Asia Minor, on the Aegean.

Hal·ma·he·ra (häl-mä-her′ä), the largest island of the Molucca Islands, Indonesia, east of Celebes: area, 6,870 sq.mi.

Han (hän), a river in central China, flowing southeast into the Yangtze: length, c.900 mi.

Han·o·ver (han′ō-vēr), a former province of Prussia, in NW Germany: earlier, an electorate and a kingdom and now a part of West Germany: German name, **Han·no·ver** (hä-nō′vēr)..

Har·lem River (här′lĕm), a river in SE New York, separating NE Manhattan from the Bronx and connecting the East River with the Hudson: length, c.8 mi.

Harz Mountains (härts), a mountain range in central Germany: highest peak, 3,747 ft.

Hat·ter·as, Cape (hat′ēr-ȧs), a cape on an island (**Hatteras Island**) off the coast of North Carolina.

Ha·wai·i (hȧ-wä′ē, -wä′yi), 1. a State of the United States, consisting of a group of islands (**Hawaiian Islands**) in the North Pacific, over 2,000 mi. southwest of California: area, 6,424 sq.mi.; pop., 965,000; cap., Honolulu. 2. the largest and southernmost of the islands of Hawaii: area, 4,021 sq.mi.

Heb·ri·des (heb′ri-dēz), a group of islands off the W coast of Scotland: divided between the **Inner Hebrides**, nearer the mainland, and the **Outer Hebrides**: area, c.2,800 sq.mi.

Hel·les·pont (hel′ĕs-pont), the ancient name of the **Dardanelles**.

Her·ce·go·vi·na (her-tsi-gō-vē′nȧ), a former independent duchy in SE Europe: now, with Bosnia, a republic of Yugoslavia: also **Her·ze·go·vi′na**.

Hermon, Mount (hŭr′mŏn), a mountain on the Syria-Lebanon border, in the Anti-Lebanon mountains: height, 9,232 ft.

High·lands, the (hī′lȧndz), the mountainous region occupying nearly all of the N half of Scotland, extending as far south as the Grampian Mountains.

Hi·ma·la·yas (hi-mäl′yȧz, him-ȧ-lā′yȧz), a mountain system of SC Asia, extending along the India-China border and through Pakistan, Nepal, and Bhutan: highest peak, Mt. Everest: also **Himalaya Mountains**.

Hin·du Kush (hin′dŏŏ kŏŏsh), a mountain range mostly in NE Afghanistan: highest peak, 25,230 ft.

Hin·du·stan (hin-doo-stan′, -stän′), 1. a kingdom in N India in the 15th and 16th cent. 2. variously, *a*) a region in N India, south of the Himalayas, where Hindi is spoken. *b*) the entire Indian peninsula. *c*) the country of India.

His·pan·io·la (his-pȧn-yō′lȧ), an island in the West Indies, between Cuba and Puerto Rico: divided between Haiti and the Dominican Republic: area, 29,530 sq.mi.

Hok·kai·do (hôk′kī-dô, hō-kī′dô), one of the four main islands of Japan, north of Honshu: area, 30,364 sq.mi.

Hol·land (hol′ȧnd), 1. a former county of the Holy Roman Empire, on the North Sea: now divided into two provinces of the Netherlands. 2. the Netherlands.

Holy Roman Empire, and empire of WC Europe, comprising the German-speaking peoples and N Italy: it was established in 800 A.D. (or, in an alternate view, 962) and lasted until 1806.

Holy See, same as **Vatican City**.

Hon·du·ras (hon-door′ȧs, -dyoor′-), 1. a country in Central America, with coast lines on the Pacific and the Caribbean: area, 43,227 sq.mi.; pop., 4,092,000; cap., Tegucigalpa. 2. **Gulf of**, an arm of the Caribbean, on the coasts of British Honduras, Guatemala, and Honduras.

Hong Kong (hong′kong′, hông′kông′), a British crown colony in SE China, on the South China Sea: it consists of one principal island (**Hong Kong Island**), nearby islands, and an area of adjacent mainland leased from China: area, 398 sq.mi.; pop., 5,109,000; cap., Victoria.

Hon·shu (hon′shŏŏ′), the largest of the islands forming Japan: area, 88,946 sq.mi.

Hood, Mount (hood), a mountain of the Cascade Range, in N Oregon: height, 11,245 ft.

Horn, Cape (hôrn), the southernmost point of South America; on an island (**Horn Island**) in Tierra del Fuego, Chile.

Huas·ca·rán (wäs-kä-rän′), a mountain of the Andes, in WC Peru: height, 22,205 ft.

Hud·son (hud′sn), a river in E New York, flowing south into Upper New York Bay: length, c.315 mi.

Hudson Bay, an inland sea in NE Canada; arm of the Atlantic.

Hun·ga·ry (hung′gēr-i), a country in SC Europe: area, 35,919 sq.mi.; pop., 10,700,000; cap., Budapest.

Hu·ron, Lake (hyoor′ŏn), the second largest of the Great Lakes, between Michigan and Ontario, Canada.

Hwang Ho (hwäng′ hō′), a river in N China, flowing from Tibet into the gulf of Po Hai: length, c.2,900 mi.

I·be·ri·a (ī-bir′i-ȧ), a peninsula in SW Europe, occupied by Spain and Portugal: in full, **Iberian Peninsula**.

Ice·land (īs′lȧnd), 1. an island in the North Atlantic, southeast of Greenland. 2. a country including this island and a few small nearby islands: area, 39,768 sq.mi.; pop., 240,000; cap., Reykjavik.

I·da·ho (ī'dä-hō), a State of the NW United States: area, 83,557 sq.mi.; pop., 944,000; cap., Boise.

Il·lam·pu (i-yäm'pōō), a mountain of the Andes, in WC Bolivia, consisting of two peaks (highest, c.21,500 ft.).

Il·li·ma·ni (ē-yi-mä'ni), a mountain of the Andes, in WC Bolivia: height, c.21,200 ft.

Il·li·nois (il-i-noi'), a Middle Western State of east NC United States: area, 56,400 sq.mi.; pop., 11,418,000; cap., Springfield.

Il·lyr·i·a (i-lir'i-ä), an ancient region along the E coast of the Adriatic, occupying what is now Yugoslavia and Albania.

In·di·a (in'di-ä), 1. a region in S Asia, south of the Himalayas, including a large peninsula between the Arabian Sea and the Bay of Bengal: it contains the countries of India, Pakistan, Nepal, Bhutan, and Bangladesh. 2. a republic in central and S India: area, 1,269,000 sq.mi.; pop., 783,940,000; cap., New Delhi.

In·di·an·a (in-di-an'ä), a Middle Western State of east NC United States: area, 36,291 sq.mi.; pop., 5,490,000; cap., Indianapolis.

Indian Ocean, the ocean south of Asia, between Africa and Australia.

In·dies (in'dēz), 1. the East Indies. 2. the West Indies. 3. formerly, SE Asia and the Malay Archipelago.

In·do·chi·na (in'dō-chī'nä), 1. a large peninsula south of China, including Burma, most of Thailand, Indochina (sense 2), and Malaya. 2. the E part of this peninsula, formerly under French control, consisting of Laos, the Khmer Republic, and Vietnam. Also sp. **Indo-China, Indo China.**

In·do·ne·sia (in-dō-nē'zhä, 'shä), a country in the Malay Archipelago, consisting of Java, Sumatra, most of Borneo, West Irian, Celebes, and many smaller nearby islands: area, 736,510 sq.mi.; pop., 176,764,000; cap., Jakarta.

In·dus (in'dûs), a river in S Asia, flowing from SW Tibet through Kashmir and Pakistan into the Arabian Sea: length, c.1,900 mi.

In·land Sea (in'länd), an arm of the Pacific surrounded by the Japanese islands of Honshu, Shikoku, and Kyushu.

I·o·ni·a (ī-ō'ni-ä), an ancient region in W Asia Minor, including a narrow coastal strip and the islands of Samos and Khios: colonized by the Greeks in the 11th cent. B.C.

I·o·ni·an Islands (i-ō'ni-än), a group of islands along the W coast of Greece, forming an administrative division of Greece: area, 873 sq.mi.

Ionian Sea, a section of the Mediterranean, between Greece, Sicily, and the S part of the Italian peninsula.

I·o·wa (ī'ō-wä), a Middle Western State of west NC United States: area, 56,290 sq.mi.; pop., 2,913,000; cap., Des Moines.

I·ran (i-rän', ī-ran'), 1. a country in SW Asia, between the Caspian Sea and the Persian Gulf: area, 636,000 sq.mi.; pop., 46,604,000; cap., Tehrán. 2. **Plateau of,** a broad table-

land extending from the Tigris River to the Indus River, mostly in Iran and Afghanistan.

I·raq (i-räk', i-rak'), a country in SW Asia, at the head of the Persian Gulf: area, 171,599 sq.mi; pop., 16,019,000; cap., Baghdad: also sp. **Irak.**

Ire·land (īr'länd), 1. an island of the British Isles, west of Great Britain. 2. a republic occupying nearly three-quarters of this island: area, 27,136 sq.mi.; pop., 3,624,000; cap., Dublin. Cf. **Northern Ireland.**

Ir·i·an (ir-i-än'), the Indonesian name of New Guinea.

Irish Sea (ī'rish), an arm of the Atlantic between Ireland and Great Britain.

Ir·ra·wad·dy (ir-ä-wä'di, -wô'-), a river flowing from N Burma south into the Andaman Sea: length, c.1,000 mi.

Ir·tysh (ir-tish'), a river in central Asia, flowing from NW China, northwestward into the Ob River: length, c.1,850 mi.: also sp. **Irtish.**

I·shim (i-shēm'), a river flowing from the Kazakh S.S.R. northward into the Irtysh in W R.S.F.S.R.: length, c.1,120 mi.

Is·ra·el (iz'ri-êl, 'rä-), 1. the ancient land of the Hebrews, at the SE end of the Mediterranean. 2. a kingdom in the N part of this region, formed by the ten tribes of Israel that broke with Judah and Benjamin. 3. a country between the Mediterranean Sea and the country of Jordan: established by the United Nations as a Jewish state: area, 7,992 sq.mi.; pop., 4,208,000; cap., Jerusalem.

I·tal·ian East Africa (i-tal'yän), a former Italian colony in E Africa, consisting of Ethiopia, Eritrea, and Italian Somaliland.

Italian Somaliland, a former Italian colony on the E coast of Africa: merged with British Somaliland to form the republic of Somalia.

It·a·ly (it'l-i), a country in S Europe mostly on a peninsula extending into the Mediterranean and including the islands of Sicily and Sardinia: area, 116,304 sq.mi.; pop., 57,226,000; cap., Rome.

Ith·a·ca (ith'ä-kä), one of the Ionian Islands, off the W coast of Greece: area, 37 sq.mi.

I·vo·ry Coast (ī'vêr-i), 1. a country in WC Africa, on the Gulf of Guinea, west of Ghana: area, 124,500 sq.mi.; pop., 10,500,000; cap., Abidjan. 2. formerly, the African coast in this region.

Ix·ta·ci·huatl (ēs-tä-sē'wätl), a volcanic mountain in central Mexico, southeast of Mexico City: height; 17,343 ft.: also sp. **Ixtaccihuatl, Iztaccihuatl.**

Ja·mai·ca (jä-mä'kä), a country on an island in the West Indies, south of Cuba: area, 4,243 sq.mi.; pop., 2,288,000; cap., Kingston.

James (jämz), 1. a river in Virginia, flowing from the W part southeast into Chesapeake Bay: length, 340 mi. 2. a river in E North Dakota and E South Dakota, flowing south into the Missouri: length, 710 mi.

Jam·mu and Kashmir (jum'ōō), a state of N

India: its control is disputed by Pakistan which occupies c.27,000 sq.mi. in the NW part: area, 85,805 sq.mi.; pop., in the part controlled by India, 5,987,000; caps., Srinagar and Jammu.

Jan May·en (yän mī'ěn), a Norwegian island in the Arctic Ocean, between Greenland and N Norway: area, 145 sq.mi.

Ja·pan (jâ-pan'), 1. an island country in the Pacific, off the E coast of Asia, including Hokkaido, Honshu, Kyushu, Shikoku, and many smaller islands: area, 143,750 sq.mi.; pop., 121,402,000; cap., Tokyo. 2. Sea of, an arm of the Pacific, between Japan and E Asia.

Ja·pu·rá (zhä-poo-rä'), a river in S Colombia and NW Brazil, flowing southeast into the Amazon: length, c.1,500 mi.

Ja·va (jä'və, jav'ə), a large island of Indonesia, southeast of Sumatra: area, 48,842 sq.mi.

Jer·sey (jûr'zi), the largest of the Channel Islands: area, 45 sq.mi.; pop., 77,000.

Jor·dan (jôr'dn), 1. a river in the Near East, flowing from the Anti-Lebanon mountains south through the Sea of Galilee through Jordan, into the Dead Sea: length, 200 mi. 2. a country in the Near East, east of Israel: area, 35,000 sq.mi.; pop., 2,756,000; cap., Amman.

Juan Fer·nán·dez Islands (hwän fer-nän'des), a group of three islands in the South Pacific, c.400 mi. west of, and belonging to, Chile: area, c.70 sq.mi.

Ju·de·a, Ju·dae·a (jōō-dē'ə), an ancient region at the E end of the Mediterranean, west of the Jordan and the Dead Sea: it corresponded roughly to the Biblical Judah.

Ju·go·sla·vi·a (ū-gō-slä'vi-ə), same as Yugoslavia.

Jum·na (jum'nə), a river in N India, flowing from the Himalayas southwest into the Ganges: length, 860 mi.

Jung·frau (yoong'frou), a mountain of the Alps, in S Switzerland: height, 13,642 ft.

Ju·ra Mountains (joor'ə), a mountain range extending along the border between France and Switzerland: highest peak, 5,652 ft.

Ju·ruá (zhoor-wä'), a river flowing from the Andes in Peru northeast across NW Brazil into the Amazon: length, c.1,200 mi.

Jut·land (jut'länd), a large peninsula in N Europe, forming the mainland of Denmark and the N part of West Germany.

Ka·hoo·la·we (kä-hōō-lä'wē), an island of Hawaii, southwest of Maui: area, 45 sq.mi.

Ka·la·ha·ri (kä-lä-hä'ri), a desert plateau in S Africa, mostly in Botswana.

Ka·ma (kä'mä), a river in European R.S.F.S.R., flowing from the Urals southwest into the Volga: length, 1,262 mi.

Kam·chat·ka (kam-chat'kä), a peninsula in NE Siberia, between the Sea of Okhotsk and the Bering Sea.

Kan·chen·jun·ga (kän'chěn-joong'gä), a mountain in the E Himalayas, on the Nepal-Sikkim border: height, 28,146 ft.

Kan·sas (kan'zǎs), a Middle Western State of west NC United States: area, 82,264 sq.mi.; pop., 2,363,000; cap., Topeka.

Ka·ra Kum (kä-rä' kōōm'), a desert in the Turkmen S.S.R., east of the Caspian Sea.

Ka·ra Sea (kä'rä), an arm of the Arctic Ocean, northwest of Siberia.

Ka·sai (kä-sī'), a river in SC Africa, flowing from Angola northwest across Zaire into the Congo River: length, c.1,100 mi.

Kat·te·gat (kat'i-gat), a strait between SW Sweden and E Jutland, Denmark.

Ka·u·a·i (kä-ōō-ä'ē, kou'ī), an island of Hawaii, northwest of Oahu: area, 551 sq.mi.

Ka·zak(h) Soviet Socialist Republic (kä-zäk'), a republic of the U.S.S.R., in W Asia: area, 1,048,000 sq.mi.; pop., 15,000,000; cap., Alma-Ata: also **Ka·zakh·stan** (kä-zäk-stän').

Kee·wa·tin (ki-wä'tin), a district of Northwest Territories, Canada, on Hudson Bay: area, 228,160 sq.mi.

Ken·tuck·y (kěn-tuk'i, ken-), an east SC State of the United States: area, 40,395 sq.mi.; pop., 3,661,000; cap., Frankfort.

Ken·ya (ken'yä, kēn'-), 1. a country in EC Africa, on the Indian Ocean: area, 224,960 sq.mi.; pop., 21,044,000; cap., Nairobi. 2. Mount, a mountain in central Kenya: height, 17,040 ft.

Ker·gue·len Islands (kûr'gě-lěn), a group of French islands in the S Indian Ocean, consisting of one large island and over 300 small ones: area, 2,700 sq.mi.

Key Lar·go (kē lär'gō), the largest island of the Florida Keys, off the SE tip of Florida: area, c.40 sq.mi.

Key West, the westernmost island of the Florida Keys.

Khí·os (khē'ŏs), a Greek island in the Aegean, off the W coast of Turkey.

Kil·i·man·ja·ro (kil-i-män-jä'rō), a mountain in NE Tanzania: height, 19,340 ft.

Kir·ghiz Soviet Socialist Republic (kir-gēz'), a republic of the U.S.S.R., in SC Asia: area, 76,460 sq.mi.; pop., 4,000,000; cap., Frunze: also **Kir·ghi·zia** (kir-gē'zhä, 'zhi-ä).

Kiribati (kir'ä-bas'), a country in the WC Pacific, formerly a British territory: pop., 63,000; cap., Tarawa.

Kist·na (kist'nä), a river in S. India, flowing from the Western Ghats eastward into the Bay of Bengal: length, c.800 mi.

Ki·vu, Lake (kē'vōō), a lake in EC Africa, on the border of E Zaire and Rwanda.

Klon·dike (klon'dīk), 1. a river in W Yukon Territory, Canada, flowing west into the Yukon River: length, c.100 mi. 2. a gold-mining region surrounding this river.

Ko·di·ak Island (kō'di-ak), an island off the SW coast of Alaska, in the Gulf of Alaska: part of the State of Alaska.

Ko·ly·ma, Ko·li·ma (ko-li-mä'), a river in E R.S.F.S.R., flowing north into the Arctic Ocean: length, c.1,300 mi.

Koo·te·nay (kōōt'n-ä), 1. a river flowing from SE British Columbia, through Montana and Idaho into Kootenay Lake, and then into the Columbia River: length, 407 mi.: also sp. **Kootenai.** 2. an elongated lake in the valley of this river, SE British Columbia.

Ko·re·a (kô-rē'â, kō-) a peninsula and former country in E Asia, extending south from NE China: now divided into two portions: 1) **Korean People's Democratic Republic,** a country occupying the N half of the peninsula: area, 47,255 sq.mi.; pop., 20,543,000; cap., Pyongyang: also called **North Korea.** 2) **Republic of Korea,** a country occupying the S half of the peninsula: area, 38,030 sq.mi.; pop., 43,285,000; cap., Seoul: also called **South Korea.**

Korea Strait, a strait between Korea and Japan, connecting the Sea of Japan and the East China Sea.

Kos (kos, kôs), a Greek island in the Dodecanese, off the SW coast of Turkey: area, 111 sq.mi.

Koy·u·kuk (kī'ŭ-kuk, koi'-), a river in NC Alaska, flowing from the Brooks Range southwest into the Yukon River: length, c.500 mi.

Kra·ka·tau (krä-kä-tou'), a small volcanic island in Indonesia, between Java and Sumatra: height, 2,667 ft.: also **Kra·ka·to·a** (krä-kä-tō'â)

Ku·ra (koo-rä'), a river flowing from NE Turkey west across Transcaucasia, into the Caspian Sea: length, c.940 mi.

Ku·ril Islands (kōō'ril, kōō-rēl'), a chain of islands belonging to the U.S.S.R., between N Hokkaido, Japan, and Kamchatka Peninsula: area, c.6,000 sq.mi. Also spelled **Kurile.**

Kus·ko·kwim (kus'kô-kwim), a river in SW Alaska, flowing from the Alaska Range southwest into the Bering Sea: length, 550 mi.

Ku·wait (kōō-wīt', -wāt'), an independent Arab state in E Arabia, on the Persian Gulf between Iraq and Saudi Arabia: area, 7,000 sq.mi.; pop., 1,771,000; cap., Kuwait.

Kyu·shu (kū'shōō'), one of the four main islands of Japan, south of Honshu: area, 16,223 sq.mi.

Lab·ra·dor (lab'râ-dôr), 1. a region along the Atlantic coast of NE Canada, constituting the mainland part of the province of Newfoundland. 2. a large peninsula between the Atlantic and Hudson Bay, consisting of Quebec and the region of Labrador.

La·do·ga, Lake (lä'dô-gä), a lake in NW R.S.F.S.R., near the border of Finland.

La Man·cha (lä män'chä), a flat region in SC Spain.

La·na·i (lä-nä'ē), an island of Hawaii, west of Maui: area, 141 sq.mi.

La·os (lä'ôs, lous, lā'os), a country in the NW part of the Indochinese peninsula: area, 91,429 sq.mi.; pop., 3,679,000; cap., Vientiane.

Lap·land (lap'land), a region of N Europe, on the Arctic Ocean, including the N parts of Norway, Sweden, and Finland, and the NW extremity of the U.S.S.R., inhabited by the Lapps.

Lap·tev Sea (läp'tef), an arm of the Arctic Ocean, north of Siberia.

Lat·in America (lat'n), that part of the Western Hemisphere south of the United States, in Mexico, Central America, the West Indies, and South America, where Spanish, Portuguese, and French are the official languages.

Lat·vi·a (lat'vi-â), a republic of the U.S.S.R., in NE Europe, on the Baltic Sea: area, 24,594 sq.mi.; pop., 2,600,000; cap., Riga: in full, **Latvian Soviet Socialist Republic.**

Lau·ren·tian Mountains (lô-ren'shi-ân, 'shăn), a mountain range in S Quebec, Canada, extending along the St. Lawrence River valley: highest peak, 3,905 ft.: also **Laurentian Highlands.**

Leb·a·non (leb'â-nôn), 1. a country in SW Asia, at the E end of the Mediterranean: area, c.4,000 sq.mi.; pop., 2,675,000; cap., Beirut. 2. a mountain range extending nearly the entire length of Lebanon: highest peak, 10,131 ft.

Lee·ward Islands (lē'wêrd), the N group of islands in the Lesser Antilles of the West Indies, extending from Puerto Rico southeast to the Windward Islands.

Lem·nos (lem'nos, 'nōs), a Greek island in the N Aegean: area, 186 sq.mi.

Le·na (lē'nä), a river in EC Siberian R.S.F.S.R., flowing northeast into the Laptev Sea: length, c.2,860 mi.

Len·in Peak (len'in), a mountain in S U.S.S.R., on the border between the Kirghiz S.S.R. and the Tadzhik S.S.R.: height, c. 23,400 ft.

Le·ón (le-ôn'), a region in NW Spain: formerly a kingdom.

Les·bos (lez'bos, 'bos), a Greek island in the Aegean, off the coast of Asia Minor: area, 630 sq.mi.

Le·sot·ho (le-sut'hô, -sō'thô), a country in SE Africa, surrounded by South Africa: area, 11,716 sq.mi.; pop., 1,552,000; cap., Maseru.

Lesser Antilles, a group of islands in the West Indies, southeast of Puerto Rico, including the Leeward Islands, the Windward Islands, and the islands off the N coast of Venezuela.

Le·vant (lê-vant'), the region at the E end of the Mediterranean, including all countries bordering the sea between Greece and Egypt.

Ley·te (lā'ti), an island of the EC Philippines, between Luzon and Mindanao: area, 2,785 sq.mi.

Liao (lyou), a river in NE China, flowing southwest into the Yellow Sea: length, c.900 mi.

Li·ard (lē'ärd, li-är'), a river in W Canada, flowing from S Yukon, through N British Columbia, into the Mackenzie River: length, 755 mi.

Li·be·ri·a (lī-bir'i-â), a country on the W coast of Africa: founded by freed U.S. slaves: area, 43,000 sq.mi.; pop., 2,307,000; cap., Monrovia.

Lib·y·a (lib'i-â), a country in N Africa, on the Mediterranean: area, 679,359 sq.mi.; pop., 3,876,000; cap., Tripoli.

Liech·ten·stein (lēch'těn-shtīn), a country in WC Europe, on the Rhine, between Switzerland and Austria: area, 61 sq.mi.; pop., 27,000; cap., Vaduz.

Li·gu·ri·a (li-gyoor'i-ȧ), a region of NW Italy, on the Ligurian Sea: formerly, a republic (**Ligurian Republic**) set up by Napoleon under French control: area, 2,091 sq.mi.; pop., 1,778,000.

Li·gu·ri·an Sea (li-gyoor'i-ȧn), a part of the Mediterranean, between Corsica and NW Italy.

Lith·u·a·ni·a (lith-oo-wā'ni-ȧ), a republic of the U.S.S.R., in NE Europe, on the Baltic Sea: area, 25,170 sq.mi.; pop., 3,572,000; cap., Vilnius: in full, **Lithuanian Soviet Socialist Republic.**

Little Missouri, a river in the NW United States, flowing from NE Wyoming northeast into the Missouri in W North Dakota: length, 560 mi.

Lo·gan, Mount (lō'gȧn), a mountain in the St. Elias range, SW Yukon, Canada: height, 19,850 ft.

Loire (lwȧr), a river flowing from S France north and west into the Bay of Biscay: length, 625 mi.

Long Island, an island in SE New York, across an arm (**Long Island Sound**) of the Atlantic from S Connecticut: area, 1,411 sq.mi.

Lor·raine (lô-rān'), a former province of NE France: see **Alsace-Lorraine.**

Lou·i·si·an·a (lōō-i-zi-an'ȧ, loo-wē-zi-, lōō-zi-), a Southern State of the west SC United States, on the Gulf of Mexico: area, 48,523 sq.mi.; pop., 4,204,000; cap., Baton Rouge.

Low Countries, the Netherlands, Belgium, and Luxembourg.

Lower California, same as **Baja California.**

Low·lands, the (lō'lȧndz), the lowland region of SC Scotland, south of the Highlands.

Lu·cerne, Lake (of) (lōō-sûrn'), a lake in central Switzerland.

Lu·si·ta·ni·a (lōō-si-tā'ni-ȧ), an ancient Roman province in the Iberian Peninsula, corresponding to most of modern Portugal and part of W Spain.

Lux·em·bourg (luk'sěm-bûrg), a grand duchy in W Europe, bounded by Belgium, West Germany, and France: area, 998 sq.mi.; pop., 366,000; cap., Luxembourg: also sp. **Luxemburg.**

Lu·zon (lōō-zon'), the main island of the Philippines: area, 40,420 sq.mi.

Ma·cao (mȧ-kou'), a Chinese territory under Portuguese administration in SE China, at the mouth of the Chu Kiang River, opposite Hong Kong: it consists of the peninsula of an island belonging to China and two small adjacent islands: area, 6 sq.mi.; pop., 343,000: Portuguese sp. **Macau.**

Mac·e·do·ni·a (mas-ě-dō'ni-ȧ), 1. an ancient kingdom in SE Europe, in the S Balkan Peninsula: now divided among Greece, Bulgaria, and Yugoslavia: also called **Mac·e·don** (mas'ě-don). 2. a republic of Yugoslavia, in the SE part of the country: area, 9,928 sq.mi.; pop., 1,909,000; cap., Skopje.

Mac·ken·zie (mȧ-ken'zi), 1. a river in W

Mackenzie district, flowing from the Great Slave Lake northwest into the Beaufort Sea: length, 2,635 mi. 2. a district of Northwest Territories, Canada, in the W part: area, 527,490 sq.mi.

Mack·i·nac, Straits of (mak'ĭ-nô), a strait connecting Lake Huron and Lake Michigan, separating the upper and lower peninsulas of Michigan.

Mad·a·gas·car (mad-ě-gas'kẽr), a country comprised of the large island of Madagascar and nearby islands in the Indian Ocean, off the SE coast of Africa: area, 228,919 sq.mi., pop., 7,604,000; cap., Antananarivo.

Ma·deir·a (mȧ-dir'ȧ), 1. a group of Portuguese islands in the Atlantic, off the W coast of Morocco. 2. the largest island of this group: area, 286 sq.mi. 3. a river in NW Brazil, formed in Bolivia by the Beni and Mamoré rivers, and flowing northeast into the Amazon: length, with the Mamoré, 2,100 mi.

Ma·du·ra (mä-dōō'rä), an island of Indonesia, just off the NE coast of Java: area, 1,770 sq.mi.

Mag·da·le·na (mäg-dä-le'nä), a river in W Colombia, flowing north into the Caribbean: length, c.1,000 mi.

Ma·gel·lan, Strait of (mȧ-jel'ȧn), a channel between the South American mainland and Tierra del Fuego.

Main (mān), a river in S West Germany, flowing west into the Rhine: length, 307 mi.

Maine (mān), a New England State of the United States: area, 33,215 sq.mi.; pop., 1,125,000.

Ma·jor·ca (mȧ-jôr'kȧ), the largest of the Balearic Islands: area, 1,405 sq.mi.

Ma·kas·sar Strait (mȧ-kas'ẽr), a strait between Borneo and Celebes.

Mal·a·bar Coast (mal'ȧ-bär), a coastal region in SW India, extending from the S tip of India to Goa and inland to the Western Ghats.

Ma·lac·ca, Strait of (mȧ-lak'ȧ), a strait between Sumatra and the Malay Peninsula, connecting the Andaman Sea with the South China Sea.

Mal·a·gas·y Republic, the former name of Madagascar.

Ma·la·wi (mäl-ȧ-wē'), a country in SE Africa, on Lake Nyasa: area, 46,066 sq.mi.; pop., 7,293,000; cap., Lilongwe.

Ma·lay·a (mȧ-lā'ȧ), 1. the Malay Peninsula. 2. a group of eleven states at the S end of the Malay Peninsula: formerly (as the **Federation of Malaya**) an independent state, it is now a part of Malaysia, called *West Malaysia*: area, 50,700 sq.mi.

Malay Archipelago (mā'lā;, mȧ-lā'), a large group of islands between SE Asia and Australia, including Indonesia, the Philippines, and, sometimes, New Guinea.

Malay Peninsula, a peninsula in SE Asia, extending from Singapore to the base of the Indochinese peninsula: it includes the states of Malaya and part of Thailand.

Ma·lay·sia (mȧ-lā'zhȧ, -'shȧ), 1. the Malay archipelago. 2. a country in SE Asia, consisting of the states of Malaya (*West Malaysia*)

a in *cap*, ā in *cane*, ä in *father*, ȧ in *abet*, e in *met*, ē in *be*, ẽ in *baker*, ě in *regent*, i in *pit*, ī in *fine*, ĭ in *manifest*, o in *hot*, ô in *horse*, ō in *bone*,

and Sabah and Sarawak (*East Malaysia*): area, 128,654 sq.mi.; pop., 15,270,000; cap., Kuala Lumpur.

Mal·dives (mal'dīvz), a country on a group of islands in the Indian Ocean, southwest of Sri Lanka: 115 sq.mi.; pop., 110,000; cap., Malé: also called **Maldive Islands.**

Ma·li (mä'li), a country in W Africa, south and east of Mauritania: area, 478,786 sq.mi.: pop., 7,898,000; cap., Bamako.

Mal·ta (môl'tä), 1. a country on a group of islands in the Mediterranean, south of Sicily: area, 122 sq.mi.; pop., 354,000; cap., Valletta. 2. the principal island of this group: area, 95 sq.mi.

Ma·mo·ré (mä-mô-re'), a river in NC Bolivia, flowing north to join the Beni and form the Madeira: length, c.1,200 mi.

Man, Isle of (man), one of the British Isles, in the Irish Sea, between Northern Ireland and England: area, 227 sq.mi.; pop., 60,000; cap., Douglas.

Man·chu·kuo (man-chōō-kwō', man-chōō'kwō), a former country (1932-45) consisting mostly of Manchuria: it was a Japanese puppet state.

Man·chu·ri·a (man-choor'i-ä), a region and former administrative division of NE China.

Man·hat·tan (man-hat'n), an island in SE New York, between the Hudson and East rivers, forming part of New York City: also **Manhattan Island.**

Man·i·to·ba (man-i-tō'bä), 1. a province of SC Canada: area, 251,000 sq.mi.; pop., 1,064,000: cap., Winnipeg. 2. **Lake,** a lake in S Manitoba.

Ma·ra·jó (mä-rä-zhô'), a large island in the Amazon delta, Brazil, dividing the river into the Amazon proper and the Pará River: area, c.18,500 sq.mi.

Ma·ra·ñón (mä-rä-nyôn'), a river in western and northern Peru that joins the Ucayali to form the Amazon: length, c.1,000 mi.

Ma·ri·an·a Islands (mer-i-an'ä), a group of islands in the W Pacific, east of the Philippines: a part, excluding Guam, of the Trust Territory of the Pacific Islands: also **Marianas Islands.**

Mar·i·time Provinces (mer'i-tīm), the Canadian provinces of Nova Scotia, New Brunswick, and Prince Edward Island.

Mar·ma·ra, Sea of (mer'mä-rä), a sea between European and Asiatic Turkey, connected with the Black Sea by the Bosporus and with the Aegean by the Dardanelles: also sp. **Marmora.**

Marne (märn), a river in NE France, flowing northwest into the Seine: length, 325 mi.

Mar·que·sas Islands (mär-kā'zäs, -säs), a group of islands in French Polynesia, in the E South Pacific: area, 492 sq.mi.

Mar·shall Islands (mär'shäl), a group of islands in the W Pacific, east of the Caroline Islands: a part of the Trust Territory of the Pacific Islands.

Mar·tha's Vineyard (mär'thäz), an island off the SE coast of Massachusetts, south of Cape Cod: area, c.100 sq.mi.

Mar·ti·nique (mär-tn-ēk'), an island in the Windward group of the West Indies: over-

seas department of France: area, 420 sq.mi.; pop., 378,000; cap., Fort-de-France.

Mar·y·land (mer'i-länd), an Eastern State of the United States, on the Atlantic: area, 10,577 sq.mi.; pop., 4,216,000: cap., Annapolis.

Mas·sa·chu·setts (mas-ä-chōō'sits), a New England State of the United States: area, 8,257 sq.mi.; pop., 5,737,000; cap., Boston.

Massachusetts Bay, an inlet of the Atlantic, on the E coast of Massachusetts.

Mat·ter·horn (mat'ēr-hôrn), a mountain of the Alps, on the Swiss-Italian border: height, c.14,700 ft.

Mau·i (mou'ē), an island of Hawaii, southeast of Oahu: area, 728 sq.mi.

Mau·na Lo·a (mou'nä lo'ä), an active volcano on the island of Hawaii: height, 13,680 ft.

Mau·re·ta·ni·a (môr-ē-tā'ni-ä), an ancient country and Roman province in NW Africa, including areas now in NE Morocco and W Algeria.

Mau·ri·ta·ni·a (môr-ī-tā'ni-ä), a country in W Africa, on the Atlantic: area, 419,230 sq.mi.; pop., 1,690,000; cap., Nouakchott.

Mau·ri·ti·us (mô-rish'i-ŭs, -rish'ŭs), 1. an island in the Indian Ocean, east of Madagascar: area, 720 sq.mi. 2. a country consisting of this island and several nearby islands: area, 787 sq.mi.; pop., 851,000; cap., Port Louis.

Mc·Kin·ley, Mount (mi-kin'li), a mountain of the Alaska Range, SC Alaska: height, 20,320 ft.

Me·di·a (mē'di-ä), an ancient kingdom in the part of SW Asia that is now NW Iran.

Med·i·ter·ra·ne·an Sea (med-i-tē-rā'ni-än), a large sea surrounded by Europe, Asia, and Africa.

Me·kong (mā'kong'), a river in SE Asia, flowing from Tibet through China and the Indochinese peninsula into the South China Sea: length, c.2,600 mi.

Mel·a·ne·sia (mel-ä-nē'zhä, 'shä), one of the three major divisions of the Pacific islands, south of the equator, including groups from the Bismarck Archipelago to Fiji.

Mem·phis (mem'fis), a city in ancient Egypt, on the Nile, just south of Cairo.

Mes·o·po·ta·mi·a (mes-ô-pô-tä'mi-ä), an ancient country in SW Asia, between the lower Tigris and Euphrates rivers: now part of modern Iraq.

Mes·si·na, Strait of (mē-sē'nä, me-), the strait between Sicily and Italy.

Meuse (mūz), a river flowing from NE France, through Belgium and the Netherlands into the North Sea: length, c.575 mi.

Mex·i·co (mek'si-kō), 1. a country in North America, south of the United States: area, 760,373 sq.mi.; pop., 66,846,000; cap., Mexico City. 2. **Gulf of,** an arm of the Atlantic, east of Mexico and south of the United States.

Mich·i·gan (mish'i-gän), 1. a Middle Western State of the east NC United States: area, 58,216 sq.mi.; pop., 9,262,000; cap., Lansing. 2. **Lake,** one of the Great Lakes, between Michigan and Wisconsin.

Mi·cro·ne·sia (mī-krô-nē'zhä, 'shä), one of the three major divisions of the Pacific islands, north of the equator, east of the Philippines, and west of the international date line.

Middle East, 1. originally, those regions between the Far East and the Near East. 2. the area from Afghanistan to Egypt, including the Arabian Peninsula, Cyprus, and Asiatic Turkey. 3. the Near East, excluding the Balkans.

Middle West, that region of the NC United States between the Rocky Mountains and the E border of Ohio, north of the Ohio River and the S borders of Kansas and Missouri.

Mid·way Islands (mid′wā), a territory of the United States, in the North Pacific, northwest of Hawaii, consisting of a coral atoll and two islets: area, 2 sq.mi.

Milk River (milk), a river in N Montana and S Alberta, Canada, flowing east into the Missouri: length, 625 mi.

Mi·los (mē′lŏs), a Greek island in the SW Cyclades, in the Aegean Sea: area, 61 sq.mi.

Min·da·na·o (min-dă-nou′, -dă-nä′ō), the second largest island of the Philippines, at the S end of the group: area, 36,906 sq.mi.

Min·do·ro (min-dô′rō, -dôr′ō), an island of the Philippines, south of Luzon: area, 3,759 sq.mi.

Min·ne·so·ta ((min-i-sō′tă), a Middle Western State of the west NC United States: area, 84,068 sq.mi.; pop., 4,077,000; cap., St. Paul.

Mi·nor·ca (mi-nôr′kă), the second largest island of the Balearic Islands, east of Majorca: area, 264 sq.mi.

Mi·que·lon (mik-ĕ-lon′), an island in the Atlantic, off the French overseas territory of St. Pierre and Miquelon: area, 83 sq.mi.

Mis·sis·sip·pi (mis-i-sip′i), 1. a river in the central United States, flowing from N Minnesota south into the Gulf of Mexico: length, 2,348 mi. (with the Missouri, its principal tributary, 3,860 mi.). 2. a Southern State of the SE United States, on the Gulf of Mexico: area, 47,716 sq.mi.; pop., 2,521,000; cap., Jackson.

Mis·sour·i (mi-zoor′i, ′i), 1. a river in the WC United States, flowing from NW Montana southeast into the Mississippi: length, 2,466 mi. 2. a Middle Western State of the west NC United States: area, 69,686 sq.mi.; pop., 4,917,000; cap., Jefferson City.

Mo·ab (mō′ab), an ancient kingdom east and south of the Dead Sea, in what is now SW Jordan.

Mo·ja·ve Desert (mō-hä′vi), a desert in SE California: also sp. **Mohave Desert.**

Mol·da·vi·a (mol-dā′vi-ă), a region in E Romania, east of the Carpathian Mountains: formerly, with the Moldavian S.S.R., a Turkish-controlled principality.

Mol·da·vi·an Soviet Socialist Republic (mol-dā′vi-ăn), a republic of the U.S.S.R., on the border of Romania: area, 13,000 sq.mi.; pop., 4,100,000; cap., Kishinev.

Mo·lo·kai (mō-lō-kī′), an island of Hawaii, southeast of Oahu: area, 259 sq.mi.

Mo·luc·cas (mō-luk′ăz), a group of islands of Indonesia, between Celebes and New Guinea: area, c.32,000 sq.mi.: also **Molucca Islands.**

Mon·a·co (mon′ă-kō), an independent principality on the Mediterranean; enclave in SE France: area, 1/2 sq.mi.; pop., 27,000.

Mon·gol Empire (mon′gŏl, ′gōl), the vast 13th-cent. empire of Genghis Khan and Kublai Khan, extending from the Pacific to the Caspian Sea.

Mon·go·li·a (mong-gō′li-ă, mon-gōl′yă), 1. a region in EC Asia, consisting of a section of NE China (called *Inner Mongolia*) and the Mongolian People's Republic. 2. the Mongolian People's Republic.

Mon·go·li·an People's Republic (mong-gō′li-ăn, mon-gōl′yăn), a country in EC Asia, north of China: area, 592,600 sq.mi.; pop., 1,942,000; cap., Ulan Bator.

Mo·non·ga·he·la (mŏ-nong-gă-hē′lă), a river in N West Virginia and SW Pennsylvania, flowing north to join the Allegheny and form the Ohio: length, 128 mi.

Mon·tan·a (mon-tan′ă), a State of the NW United States: area, 147,138 sq.mi.; pop., 787,000; cap., Helena.

Mon·te·ne·gro (mon-tĕ-nē′grō), a republic of Yugoslavia, in the S part on the Albanian border: area, 5,333 sq.mi.; pop., 584,000; cap., Titograd.

Mont·ser·rat (mont-sĕ-rat′), an island of the Leeward group, in the West Indies: it is a self-governing territory under British protection: area, 33 sq.mi.; pop., 12,000; cap., Plymouth.

Mo·ra·vi·a (mō-rā′vi-ă), a region, formerly a province, of central Czechoslovakia: before 1918, a province of Austria-Hungary.

Mo·roc·co (mă-rok′ō), a kingdom on the NW coast of Africa: area, c.254,815 sq.mi.; pop., 23,667,000; cap., Rabat.

Mo·selle (mō-zel′), a river in NE France and W West Germany, flowing north into the Rhine: length, c.320 mi.

Mountain State, any of the eight States of the W United States through which the Rocky Mountains pass; Montana, Idaho, Wyoming, Utah, Colorado, Nevada, Arizona, and New Mexico.

Mo·zam·bique (mō-zăm-bēk′), a country in SE Africa, on Mozambique Channel: area, c.302,300 sq.mi.; pop., 14,022,000; cap., Maputo.

Mozambique Channel, a part of the Indian Ocean, between Mozambique and Madagascar.

Mur·ray (mūr′i), a river in SE Australia, flowing from the Australian Alps west into the Indian Ocean: length, 1,596 mi.

Mur·rum·bidg·ee (mūr-ŭm-bij′i), a river in S New South Wales, Australia, flowing west into the Murray: length, c.1,000 mi.

Mus·cat and Oman (mis-kat′), the former name of **Oman** (the country).

Mus·co·vy (mus′kō-vi), 1. a former grand duchy surrounding and including Moscow: it expanded into the Russian Empire under Ivan IV. 2. the former name of **Russia.**

---

a in cap, ā in cane, ä in father, ȧ in abet, e in met, ē in be, ê in baker, ê in regent, i in pit, ī in fine, ï in manifest, o in hot, ō in horse, ô in bone,

Na·mib·i·a (nä-mib′i-å), the official (United Nations) name of **South West Africa.**

Nan Shan (nän′ shän′), a mountain system in NW China: highest peak, c.20,000 ft.

Nan·tuck·et (nan-tuk′it), an island of Massachusetts, south of Cape Cod: area, 46 sq.mi.

Na·ples (nä′plz), 1. a former kingdom occupying the S half of the Italian peninsula. 2. **Bay of,** an inlet of the Tyrrhenian Sea, on the S coast of Italy.

Nar·bad·a (nûr-bud′å), a river in central India, flowing west into the Arabian Sea: length, c.800 mi.

Nar·ra·gan·sett Bay (ner-å-gan′sit), an inlet of the Atlantic, extending into SE Rhode Island.

Na·u·ru (nä-ōō′rōō), a country on an island in the W Pacific, just south of the equator: area, 8 sq.mi.; pop., 7,254.

Na·varre (nä-vär′), a region in NE Spain and SW France: formerly a kingdom.

Near East, 1. the countries near the E end of the Mediterranean, including those of SW Asia, the Arabian Peninsula, NE Africa, and, sometimes, the Balkans. 2. formerly, the lands occupied by the Ottoman Empire, including the Balkans.

Ne·bras·ka (nė-bras′kå), a Middle Western State of the west NC United States: area, 77,227 sq.mi.; pop., 1,570,000; cap., Lincoln.

Ne·gev (neg′ev), a region in S Israel of partially reclaimed desert: also **Ne·geb** (neg′eb).

Ne·gro (nä′grō), 1. a river in N Brazil, flowing southeast into the Amazon: length, c.1,400 mi. 2. a river in SC Argentina, flowing east into the Atlantic: length, c.700 mi.

Ne·gros (nä′grōs), an island of the central Philippines, between Cebu and Panay: area, 4,905 sq.mi.

Neis·se (ni′sė), a river in N Europe, flowing from NW Czechoslovakia into the Oder River on the Polish-German border: length, c.140 mi.

Ne·pal (ni-pôl′, ne-pol′), a country in the Himalayas, between India and Tibet: area, 54,362 sq.mi.; pop., 17,422,000; cap., Katmandu.

Neth·er·lands (neth′ér-låndz), 1. a country in W Europe, on the North Sea: area, 15,770 sq.mi.; pop., 14,536,000; cap., Amsterdam; seat of government, The Hague. 2. a kingdom consisting of the independent states of the Netherlands and the Netherlands Antilles.

Netherlands Antilles, a part of the kingdom of the Netherlands, consisting of two islands and part of another in the Leeward group of the West Indies, and three islands off the coast of Venezuela: area, 394 sq.mi.; pop., 260,000; cap., Willemstad.

Ne·va·da (nė-vad′å, -vä′då), a State of the W United States: area, 110,540 sq.mi.; pop., 799,000; cap., Carson City.

Ne·vis (nē′vis, nev′is), a British island in the Leeward group of the West Indies: area, 50 sq.mi.; pop., 9,500.

New Bruns·wick (brunz′wik), a province of SE Canada, on the Gulf of St. Lawrence: area,

28,354 sq.mi.; pop., 709,000; cap., Fredericton.

New Cal·e·do·ni·a (kal′ė-dō′ni-å, -dōn′yå), a French island in the SW Pacific, west of Australia: area, 7,218 sq.mi.; pop., 145,000: with nearby island dependencies it constitutes an overseas department of France, cap., Nouméa.

New England, the six NE States of the United States; Maine, Vermont, New Hampshire, Massachusetts, Rhode Island, and Connecticut.

New·found·land (nōō′fûnd-land, nū′fûnd-lånd, nū-found′land), 1. an island of Canada, off the E coast: area, 42,734 sq.mi. 2. a province of Canada, including this island and Labrador: area, 156,185 sq.mi.; pop., 568,000; cap., St. John's.

New Georgia, 1. a group of islands in the British Solomon Islands Protectorate, in the SW Pacific: area, c.2,500 sq.mi. 2. the largest island of this group: area, c.1,300 sq.mi.

New Guinea, a large island in the East Indies, north of Australia: it is divided between Indonesia and a territory under Australian protection: area, c.330,000 sq.mi.

New Hamp·shire (hamp′shir, ham′-), a New England State of the United States: area, 9,304 sq.mi.; pop., 921,000; cap., Concord.

New Hebrides, a group of islands in the SW Pacific, west of Fiji: a British and French condominium: area, 5,700 sq.mi.; pop., 80,000.

New Jersey, an Eastern State of the United States on the Atlantic: area, 7,836 sq.mi.; pop., 7,364,000; cap., Trenton.

New Mexico, a State of the SW United States, on the Mexican border: area, 121,666 sq.mi.; pop., 1,300,000; cap., Santa Fe.

New York, a State of the NE United States, on the Atlantic: area, 49,576 sq.mi.; pop., 17,557,000; cap., Albany.

New York Bay, an inlet of the Atlantic, south of Manhattan: divided by a strait (called *the Narrows*) into a N section (**Upper Bay**) and a S Section (**Lower Bay**).

New Zealand, a country made up of two large islands and several small ones in the S Pacific, southeast of Australia: area, 103,736 sq.mi.; pop., 3,305,000; cap., Wellington.

Nic·a·ra·gua (nik-å-rä′gwä), 1. a country in Central America, on the Caribbean and the Pacific: area, 54,342 sq.mi.; pop., 3,342,000; cap., Managua. 2. **Lake,** a lake in S Nicaragua.

Nic·o·bar Islands (nik′ō-bär, nik-ō-bär′), a group of islands in the Indian Ocean, south of the Andaman Islands: area, 635 sq.mi. See **Andaman Islands.**

Ni·ger (ni′jėr), 1. a river in W Africa, flowing from Guinea eastward in an arc through Mali, Niger, and Nigeria into the Gulf of Guinea: length, c.2,600 mi. 2. a country in WC Africa, north of Nigeria: area, c.489,191 sq.mi.; pop., 6,715,000; cap., Niamey.

Ni·ger·i·a (ni-jir′i-å), a country in WC Africa, on the Gulf of Guinea: area, 356,668 sq.mi.; pop., 105,448,000; cap., Lagos.

ô in dragon, ōō in crude, oo in wool, u in cup, ū in cure, û in turn, ŭ in focus, oi in boy, ou in house, th in thin, th in sheathe, g in get, j in joy, y in yet.

Ni·i·ha·u (nē-ē-hä′ōō, nē′hou), an island of Hawaii, west of Kauni: area, 72 sq.mi.

Nile (nīl), a river in NE Africa, formed in NE Sudan by the juncture of the Blue Nile (which flows from N Ethiopia, c.1,000 mi.) and the White Nile (which flows from Lake Victoria, c.1,650 mi.), and flowing north through Egypt into the Mediterranean: length, with the White Nile and a head-stream south of Lake Victoria, over 4,000 mi.

Nin·e·veh (nin′ē·vĕ), the capital of ancient Assyria, on the Tigris, in what is now N Iraq.

Nip·pon (nip′on, ni·pon′), a Japanese name for Japan.

Nor·man·dy (nôr′măn-di), a region and former province in NW France, on the English Channel.

North America, the N continent in the Western Hemisphere: area, c.9,366,000 sq.mi. (excluding adjacent islands, c.8,400,000 sq.mi.); pop., 366,628,000.

North Ca·na·di·an River (kă-na′di-ăn), a river flowing from NE New Mexico east and southeast into the Canadian River in E Oklahoma: length, 760 mi.

North Carolina, a Southern State of the SE United States, on the Atlantic: area, 52,712 sq.mi.; pop., 5,881,000; cap., Raleigh.

North Channel, a strait between Northern Ireland and SW Scotland, connecting the Irish Sea and the Atlantic.

North Dakota, a Middle Western State of the west NC United States: area, 70,665 sq.mi.; pop., 653,000; cap., Bismarck.

Northern Ireland, a division of the United Kingdom, in the NE part of the island of Ireland: area, 5,462 sq.mi.; pop., 1,573,000; cap., Belfast.

Northern Rhodesia, a former British protectorate in S Africa: now, the country of Zambia.

North Platte, a river flowing from N Colorado north into Wyoming and then southeast through W Nebraska, joining the South Platte to form the Platte: length, 618 mi.

North Saskatchewan, a river flowing from SW Alberta east through Saskatchewan, joining the South Saskatchewan to form the Saskatchewan: length, 760 mi.

North Sea, an arm of the Atlantic, between Great Britain and the European mainland, especially Norway and Denmark.

Northwest Territories, a division of N Canada, subdivided into the Districts of Mackenzie, Keewatin, and Franklin: area, 1,304,903 sq.mi.; pop., 52,000; cap., Yellowknife.

Northwest Territory, a region north of the Ohio River, between Pennsylvania and the Mississippi (established 1787): it now forms the States of Ohio, Indiana, Illinois, Michigan, Wisconsin, and part of Minnesota.

Nor·way (nôr′wā), a country in N Europe, occupying the W and N parts of the Scandinavian Peninsula: area, 125,064 sq.mi.; pop., 4,165,000; cap., Oslo.

No·va Sco·tia (nō′và skō′shä), a province of SE Canada, consisting of a peninsula and Cape Breton Island: area, 21,425 sq.mi.; pop., 873,000; cap., Halifax.

Nu·bi·a (nōō′bi-à, nū′-), a region and former kingdom in NE Africa, between the Red Sea and the Sahara, in Egypt and Sudan.

Nu·bi·an Desert (nōō′bi-ăn), a desert in NE Sudan, between the Nile and the Red Sea.

Nya·sa, Lake (nyä′sä, nī-as′à), a lake in SE Africa, between Malawi and Mozambique.

Nya·sa·land (-land), a former British protectorate in SE Africa: now, the country of Malawi.

O·a·hu (ō-ä′hōō), the chief island of Hawaii: area, 598 sq.mi.

Ob (ŏb), 1. a river in W Siberia, flowing from the Altai Mountains northwest and north into the Gulf of Ob: length, 2,495 mi. 2. **Gulf of,** an arm of the Kara Sea, in NW Siberia.

O·ce·an·i·a (ō-shi-an′i-à), the islands in the south, central, and western Pacific, including Melanesia, Micronesia, and Polynesia and, sometimes, Australia, New Zealand, and the Malay Archipelago.

O·der (ō′dĕr), a river in central Europe, flowing northeast through Czechoslovakia and Poland into the Baltic Sea: length, c.560 mi.: it forms, with the Neisse, the boundary **(Oder-Neisse Line)** between East Germany and Poland.

O·hi·o (ō-hi′ō), 1. a Middle Western State of the east NC United States: area, 41,222 sq.mi.; pop., 10,797,000; cap., Columbus. 2. a river formed by the junction of the Monongahela and the Allegheny in SW Pennsylvania, flowing southwest into the Mississippi: length, 981 mi.

Oise (wäz), a river flowing from S Belgium southwest through N France into the Seine: length, 186 mi.

O·ke·fe·no·kee Swamp (ō-kĕ-fē-nō′ki), a swamp in SE Georgia and NE Florida.

O·khotsk, Sea of (ō-kotsk′), an arm of the Pacific off the E coast of Siberia, west of the Kamachatka Peninsula.

O·ki·na·wa (ō-ki-nä′wä), the largest island of the Ryukyus, in the W Pacific northeast of Taiwan: area, 454 sq.mi.

O·kla·ho·ma (ō-klá-hō′mà), a Southern State of the west SC United States: area, 69,919 sq.mi.; pop., 3,025,000; cap., Oklahoma City.

O·lym·pus, Mount (ō-lim′pŭs, ô-), a mountain in N Greece, on the border between Thessaly and Macedonia: height, c.9,800 ft.

O·man (ō-män′), 1. the SE coastal region of Arabia, south of Qatar. 2. a country occupying most of this region: area, 82,000 sq.mi.; pop., 1,270,000; cap., Muscat. 3. **Gulf of,** an arm of the Arabian Sea, between Iran and Oman.

On·tar·i·o (on-ter′i-ō), 1. a province of SC Canada, between the Great Lakes and Hudson Bay: area, 412,582 sq.mi.; pop., 9,102,000; cap., Toronto. 2. **Lake,** the smallest and easternmost of the Great Lakes, between New York and Ontario.

Or·ange (ôr′ănj, or′inj), 1. a river in S Africa, flowing from NE Lesotho west through

a in cap, ā in cane, ä in father, å in abet, e in met, ē in be, ē in baker, ė in regent, i in pit ī in fine, ι in manifest, o in hot, ô in horse, ō in bone,

South Africa into the Atlantic: length, c.1,300 mi. 2. a former principality in W Europe, in what is now SE France.

Or·e·gon (ôr'i-gǝn, or'i-gǒn), a NW state of the United States, on the Pacific: area, 96,981 sq.mi.; pop., 2,663,000; cap., Salem.

Ö·re·sund (ô-rě-sund'), a strait between Sweden and the Danish island of Zealand.

O·ri·no·co (ôr-i-nô'kō), a river in Venezuela, flowing from the Brazil border northward into the Atlantic: length, c.1,700 mi.

Ork·ney Islands (ôrk'ni), a group of islands north of Scotland, constituting a country of Scotland.

O·sage River (ō'sāj, ō-sāj'), a river in central Missouri, flowing east into the Missouri: length, with its major headstream in E Kansas, c.500 mi.

Ot·ta·wa (ot'ǎ-wǎ, -wä), a river in SE Canada, forming the border between Ontario and Quebec, flowing southeast into the St. Lawrence: length, 696 mi.

Ot·to·man Empire (ot'ô-mǎn), the empire of the Turks, which included at its peak (16th cent.) much of SE Europe, SW Asia, and NE Africa.

Ouach·i·ta (wôsh'i-tô, wäsh'-), a river flowing from W Arkansas southeast and south into the Red River in Louisiana: length, 605 mi.

O·zark Mountains (ō'zärk), a highland region in NW Arkansas, SW Missouri, and NE Oklahoma.

Pa·cif·ic (pǎ-sif'ik), the largest of the earth's oceans, between Asia and the American continents.

Pacific Islands, Trust Territory of the, a United States trust territory in the W Pacific, consisting of the Caroline and Marshall islands.

Pa·ki·stan (pä-ki-stän', pak'i-stan), a country in S Asia, on the Arabian Sea: it formerly included this region (called the province of *West Pakistan*) and an E region (called the province of *East Pakistan*, now *Bangladesh*): area, 310,403 sq.mi.; pop., 101,855,000; cap., Islamabad.

Pal·es·tine (pal'ěs-tīn), 1. a region on the E coast of the Mediterranean, the country of the Jews in Biblical times. 2. a British mandated territory in this region, west of the Jordan River, from 1923 to the establishment of the state of Israel in 1948 by the United Nations.

Pa·mirs (pä-mirz'), a mountain system in SC Asia, mostly in the Tadzhik S.S.R., with fringes in Afghanistan and NW China: highest peak, c.25,000 ft.: also **Pamir**.

Pan·a·ma (pan'ǎ-mä, pan-ǎ-mô'), 1. a country in Central America, on the Isthmus of Panama: area, 29,201 sq.mi.; pop., 2,227,000; cap., Panama. 2. **Isthmus of,** a strip of land connecting South America and Central America.

Panama Canal, a ship canal across the Isthmus of Panama, connecting the Caribbean Sea and the Pacific Ocean.

Pa·nay (pä-nī'), an island of the central Philippines, between Mindoro and Negros: area, 4,446 sq.mi.

Pa·pal States (pä'pl) a former territory in central and north central Italy, ruled by the papacy from the 8th cent. until annexed by Italy in 1870.

Pa·pu·a (pap'yoo-wǎ, pä'pōō-ä), same as **New Guinea.**

Papua-New Guinea, a country occupying the E part of the island of New Guinea: area, 183,540 sq.mi.; pop., 3,395,000; cap., Port Moresby.

Pa·ra (pä-rä'), a river in NE Brazil, forming the estuary of the Tocantins and a S estuary of the Amazon: length, c.200 mi.

Par·a·guay (per'ǎ-gwā, -gwī), 1. an inland country in SC South America: area, 157,042 sq.mi.; pop., 4,119,000; cap., Asunción. 2. a river in SC South America, flowing from S Brazil south through Paraguay into the Paraná: length, c.1,500 mi.

Pa·ra·ná (pä-rä-nä'), a river in S South America, flowing from S Brazil along the SE border of Paraguay, through NE Argentina into the Rio de la Plata: length, c.2,000 mi.

Pa·ri·cu·tin (pä-rē-kōō-tēn'), a volcanic mountain in WC Mexico: height, c.9,000 ft.: also **Pa·ri·cu·tin** (pä-rē'kōō-tēn).

Par·ma (pär'mä), a former duchy in NC Italy.

Par·nas·sus (pär-nas'ǔs), a mountain in central Greece, near the Gulf of Corinth.

Pat·a·go·ni·a (pat-ǎ-gō'ni-ǎ, -gōn'yǎ), a dry grassy region in S South America, east of the Andes, including the S parts of Argentina and Chile.

Peace River (pēs), a river in W Canada, flowing from N British Columbia east and northeast into NE Alberta: length, 1,195 mi.

Pe·cos (pä'kôs, 'kòs), a river in SW United States, flowing from N New Mexico through Texas into the Rio Grande: length, 735 mi.

Pel·o·pon·ne·sus (pel-ô-pô-nē'sǔs), the peninsula forming the S part of the mainland of Greece: also sp. **Peloponnesos.**

Pem·ba (pem'bä), an island of Tanzania in the Indian Ocean, off the E coast of Africa: area, 380 sq.mi.

Pend O·reille (pän-dô-rā'), 1. a river in N Idaho and NE Washington, flowing from Pend Oreille Lake into the Columbia River: see **Clark Fork.** 2. a lake in N Idaho.

Pen·nine Alps (pen'īn, 'in), a division of the W Alps, along the Swiss-Italian border: highest peak, c.15,200 ft.

Penn·syl·va·ni·a (pen-sl-vān'yǎ, -vā'ni-ǎ), an Eastern State of the NE United States: area, 45,333 sq.mi.; pop., 11,867,000; cap., Harrisburg.

Per·sia (pûr'zhǎ, 'shǎ), 1. the former official name of **Iran.** 2. the Persian Empire.

Persian Empire, an ancient empire in SW Asia, including at its peak the area from the Indus River to the W borders of Asia Minor and Egypt.

Persian Gulf, an arm of the Arabian Sea, between SW Iran and Arabia.

Persian Gulf States, the Arab sheikdoms along the Persian Gulf, formerly under British

---

ǒ in dragon, ōō in wool, oo in house, u in cup, û in cure, ü in turn, ü in focus, oi in boy, ou in house, th in thin, th in sheathe, g in get, j in joy, v in vet.

protection, including Bahrain, Qatar, and the United Arab Emirates.

Pe·ru (pẽ-rōō'), a country in W South America, on the Pacific: area, 496,222 sq.mi.; pop., 58,000,000; cap., Lima.

Pes·ca·do·res (pes-kȧ-dôr'iz, 'is), a group of islands in Taiwan Strait, a dependency of Taiwan: area, c.50 sq.mi.

Phi·lip·pi (fi-lip'ī), an ancient city in Macedonia, near the N end of the Aegean Sea.

Phil·ip·pines (fil'i-pēnz) a country occupying a group of c.7,100 islands (**Philippine Islands**) in the SW Pacific off the SE coast of Asia, northeast of Borneo: area, 114,830 sq.mi.; pop., 58,000,000; cap., Manila.

Phi·lis·ti·a (fi-lis'ti-ȧ), the country of the Philistines, in ancient SW Palestine, on the Mediterranean.

Phoe·ni·cia (fē-nish'ȧ, -nē'shȧ), an ancient region of city-states at the E end of the Mediterranean, west of the Anti-Lebanon mountains.

Phryg·i·a (frij'i-ȧ), an ancient kingdom in WC Asia Minor.

Pied·mont (pēd'mont), 1. a hilly, upland region of the E United States, between the Atlantic coastal plain and the Appalachians, stretching from SE New York to central Alabama. 2. a region of NW Italy, on the borders of Switzerland and France: area, 9,807 sq.mi.; pop., 4,479,000: Italian name, **Pie·mon·te** (pye-môn'te).

Pikes Peak (pīks), a mountain of the E Rocky Mountains, central Colorado: height, 14,110 ft.

Pil·co·ma·yo (pēl-kô-mä'yô), a river flowing from S Bolivia along the Argentine-Paraguay border into the Paraguay River: length, c.1,000 mi.

Pines, Isle of (pīnz), an island of Cuba, south of the W end of the Main Island: area, c.1,200 sq.mi.

Pit·cairn Island (pit'kern), an island in Polynesia, South Pacific: area, 1.75 sq.mi.; pop., 67: with three nearby uninhabited islands, it constitutes a dependent territory of the United Kingdom, total area, c.18 sq.mi.

Pia·ta, Rí·o de la (rē'ô de lä plä'tä), the estuary of the Paraná and Uruguay rivers, between Argentina and Uruguay: English name, **River Plate**.

Platte (plat), a river formed in central Nebraska by the junction of the North Platte and the South Platte, and flowing eastward into the Missouri: length, 310 mi.

Po (pô), a river in N Italy, flowing from the Alps east into the Adriatic: length, 405 mi.

Po·land (pô'lȧnd), a country in central Europe, on the Baltic Sea: area, 120,625 sq.mi.; pop., 37,546,000; cap., Warsaw.

Pol·y·ne·sia ()pol-ȧ-nē'zhȧ, 'shȧ), one of the three major divisions of the Pacific islands, east of the international date line, including Hawaii, Samoa, Tonga, the Marquesas Islands, the Gilbert and Ellice Islands, etc.

Pom·er·a·ni·a (pom-ē-rä'ni-ȧ), a region in central Europe, on the Baltic, stretching from the Vistula River westward into NE East Germany.

Pom·pei·i (pom-pā'i, -pā'), an ancient city in S Italy, near the Bay of Naples.

Pont·char·train, Lake (pon'chĕr-trān), a shallow, salt-water lake in SE Louisiana.

Po·po·ca·té·petl (pô-pô-kat'ĕ-petl), a volcano in SC Mexico, height, 17,887 ft.

Por·cu·pine River (pôr'kyoo-pīn), a river in N Yukon, Canada, flowing north and then southwest into the Yukon River in NE Alaska: length, 590 mi.

Por·tu·gal (pôr'chŭ-gȧl), a country on the Iberian Peninsula, SW Europe, on the Atlantic: with the Azores and Madeira, area, 35,509 sq.mi.; pop., 9,834,000; cap., Lisbon

Por·tu·guese East Africa (pôr'chŭ-gēz), same as **Mozambique**.

Portuguese Guinea, former name of **Guinea-Bissau**.

Portuguese India, a former Portuguese overseas territory consisting of three enclaves (including *Goa*) on the W coast of India.

Portuguese Timor, a former Portuguese overseas territory in the Malay Archipelago, consisting of the E half of Timor, an enclave of Indonesian Timor, and two offshore islands: since 1976, a province of Indonesia.

Portuguese West Africa, same as **Angola**.

Po·to·mac (pô-tô'mȧk), a river in the E United States, forming a boundary of West Virginia, Maryland, and Virginia, and flowing into Chesapeake Bay: length, 285 mi.

Prai·rie Provinces (prer'i), the Canadian provinces of Manitoba, Saskatchewan, and Alberta.

Prince Edward Island, an island province of SE Canada, in the S Gulf of St. Lawrence: area, 2,184 sq.mi.; pop., 127,000; cap., Charlottetown.

Prince of Wales Island, an island of SE Alaska; largest in the Alexander Archipelago: area, 2,230 sq.mi.

Prín·ci·pe (prin'si-pē), a Portuguese island in the Gulf of Guinea, off the W coast of Africa: area, 54 sq.mi. See **São Tomé**.

Pro·vence (prô-väns'), a region and former province of SE France, on the Mediterranean between the Rhone River and the Italian border.

Prus·sia (prush'ȧ), a former kingdom in N Europe (1701-1871) and the dominant state of the German Empire (1871-1919); joined the Weimar Republic in 1919 and was formally dissolved in 1947.

Puer·to Ri·co (pwer-tô rē'kô, pôr-), an island in the West Indies which, with small nearby islands, constitutes a commonwealth associated with the United States: area, 3,421 sq.mi.; pop., 3,196,000; cap., San Juan.

Pu·get Sound (pū'jit), an inlet of the Pacific in NW Washington.

Pun·jab (pun-jäb', pun'jäb, 'jab), a region in NW India and NE Pakistan, between the Indus and Jumna rivers.

Pu·rús (pŏō-rōōs'), a river in South America, flowing from E Peru northeast through NW Brazil into the Amazon: length, c.2,000 mi.

Pu·tu·ma·yo (pŏō-tōō-mä'yô), a river in NW

---

a in cap, ā in cane, ä in father, ȧ in abet, e in met, ē in be, ê in baker, ĕ in regent, i in pit, ī in fine, ĭ in manifest, o in hot, ô in horse, ô in bone,

South America, flowing southeast along the Colombia-Peru border into the Amazon in NW Brazil: length, c.1,000 mi.

Pyr·e·nees (pir'ĕ-nēz') a mountain range in SW Europe, along the border between France and Spain: highest peak, 11,168 ft.

Q

Qa·tar (gut'ăr, kä'tär), a country occupying a peninsula on the E coast of Arabia, extending into the Persian Gulf: area, 8,500 sq.mi.; pop., 305,000; cap., Doha.

Que·bec (kwi-bek'), a province of E Canada, between Hudson Bay and the Gulf of St. Lawrence: area, 594,860 sq.mi.; pop., 6,530,000; cap., Quebec.

Queen Char·lotte Islands (kwĕn shär'lŏt), a group of islands in British Columbia, off the W coast: area, 3,970 sq.mi.

Queen E·liz·a·beth Islands (i-liz'ă-bĕth), a group of islands in the Franklin District of Northwest Territories, Canada.

Queen Maud Range (môd), a mountain range in Antarctica, south of the Ross Ice Shelf: highest peaks, over 13,000 ft.

Que·moy (kē'moi'), 1. a group of islands in Taiwan Strait, just off the E coast of China: held by the Chinese Nationalist government on Taiwan: area, 68 sq.mi. 2. the chief island of this group: area, 62 sq.mi.

Qum·ran (koom-rän'), a region in E Palestine, near the NW shore of the Dead Sea.

R

Rai·nier, Mount (rā-nir', rā'nir), a mountain of the Cascade Range, in WC Washington: height, 14,410 ft.

Red River (red), 1. a river flowing southeast along the Texas-Oklahoma border, through SW Arkansas and central Louisiana into the Mississippi: length, 1,018 mi. 2. a river flowing north along the North Dakota-Minnesota border into Lake Winnipeg in Manitoba, Canada: length, 545 mi.: in full, **Red River of the North**. 3. a river in SE Asia, flowing from S China, southeast across North Vietnam into the Gulf of Tonkin: length, c.500 mi.

Red Sea, a sea between NE Africa and W Arabia, connected with the Mediterranean Sea by the Suez Canal and with the Indian Ocean by the Gulf of Aden.

Re·pub·li·can River (ri-pub'li-kăn), a river flowing from E Colorado east and southeast through S Nebraska and NE Kansas, joining the Smoky Hill River to form the Kansas River: length, 445 mi.

Ré·un·ion (ri-ūn'yŏn), an island in the W Indian Ocean; overseas department of France: area, 969 sq.mi.; pop., 515,000; cap., St-Denis.

Rhine (rīn), a river in W Europe, flowing from E Switzerland north through Germany, then west through the Netherlands into the North Sea: length, c.820 mi.

Rhode Island (rōd), a New England State of the United States: area, 1,214 sq.mi.; pop., 947,000; cap., Providence.

Rhodes (rōdz), the largest island of the Dodecanese, in the Aegean off the SW coast of Turkey: area, 545 sq.mi.

Rho·de·si·a (rō-dē'zhi-ă, -'zhä), 1. a former region in S Africa, including **Northern Rhodesia** (now *Zambia*) and **Southern Rhodesia** (now *Zimbabwe*).

Rhone, Rhône (rōn), a river flowing from SW Switzerland west through Lake Geneva and south through France into the Mediterranean: length, 505 mi.

Rif (rif), a mountain range along the NE coast of Morocco, extending from the Strait of Gibraltar to the Algerian border: highest peak, c.8,000 ft.: also **Er Rif** (er), **Riff**.

Ri·ga, Gulf of (rē'gä), an inlet of the Baltic Sea, in NW Latvian S.S.R. and SW Estonian S.S.R.

Ri·o Gran·de (rē'ō grand', gran'di, grän'dä), a river flowing from S Colorado south through New Mexico, then southeast along the Texas-Mexico border into the Gulf of Mexico: length, 1,885 mi.

Ri·o Mu·ni (rē'ō mōō'ni), the continental province of Equatorial Guinea, on the central coast of Africa, now called Mbini.

Ri·vi·er·a (riv-e-er'ä), a narrow coastal strip along the Mediterranean, in SE France and NW Italy.

Rock·y Mountains (rok'i), a mountain system in W North America, extending from central New Mexico northwestward to W Canada and N Alaska: highest peak, Mt. McKinley: also called **Rockies**.

Ro·man Empire (rō'măn), the empire established (27 B.C.) by Augustus, succeeding the Roman Republic: at its peak it included W Europe, S Europe south of the Danube, Great Britain, Asia Minor, N Africa, and the lands of the E Mediterranean: divided (395 A.D.) into the *Eastern Roman Empire* and the *Western Roman Empire*.

Ro·ma·ni·a (rō-mā'ni-ă, -măn'-yă), a country in SE Europe, on the Black Sea: area, 91,700 sq.mi.; pop., 22,830,000; cap., Bucharest: also **România, Roumania, Rumania**.

Roman Republic, the territory ruled by Rome from c.500 B.C. to 27 B.C., a period marked by Rome's vast territorial expansion: succeeded by the Roman Empire.

Ross Ice Shelf (rôs), the frozen S section of the Ross Sea, east of Victoria Land: also called **Ross Shelf Ice**.

Ross Sea, an arm of the Pacific, along the coast of Antarctica, east of Victoria Land.

Ru·an·da-U·run·di (rōō-än'dä-oo-roon'di, roo-wän'dä-), a former Belgian-administered United Nations trust territory in EC Africa: divided into the independent countries of Rwanda and Burundi.

Rub' al Kha·li (roob äl khä'li), a large desert of S and SE Arabia;

Ru·dolf, Lake (rōō'dolf, -'dôlf), a lake in NW Kenya, on the border of Ethiopia.

Ruhr (roor), a river in Central West Germany, flowing west into the Rhine: length, 145 mi.

ō in dragon, ōō in crude, oo in wool, u in cup, û in cure, û in turn, ŭ in focus, oi in boy, ou in house, th in thin, th in sheathe, g in get, j in joy, y in yet.

Ru·ma·ni·a (rōō-mā′ni-ā, -mān′yā), same as Romania.

Rus·sia (rush′ā), 1. a former empire (**Russian Empire**) in E Europe and N Asia, 1547-1917. 2. the popular name for the **Union of Soviet Socialist Republics.** 3. the Russian Soviet Federated Socialist Republic, especially the European part.

Rus·sian Soviet Federated Socialist Republic (rush′ān), the largest republic of the U.S.S.R., extending from the Baltic Sea to the Pacific and from the Arctic Ocean to the Chinese border: area, 6,592,000 sq.mi.; pop., 143,078,000; cap., Moscow.

Rwan·da (ûr-wän′dä, roo-wän′dä), a country in EC Africa, east of Zaire: area, 10,169 sq.mi.; pop., 4,819,000; cap., Kigali.

Kyu·kyu Islands (rū′kū′), a chain of Japanese islands in the W Pacific, between Kyushu and Taiwan: area, c.1,800 sq.mi.

Saar (sär), a river flowing from NE France, north into the Moselle River, SW West Germany: length, c.150 mi.

Sa·bah (sä′bä), a state of Malaysia, occupying NE Borneo and several offshore islands: area, 29,388 sq.mi.; pop., 1,012,000.

Sa·bine (sä-bēn′), a river flowing from E Texas south along the Texas-Louisiana border into the Gulf of Mexico: length, c.550 mi.

Sa·ha·ra (sā-her′ā, -hä′rä), a vast desert region in N Africa, extending from the Atlantic to the Nile (the Red Sea is sometimes considered to be its E extent), north of the Sudan.

Sa·kha·lin (sak′ā-lēn), a long, narrow island of the U.S.S.R., off the E coast of Siberia, north of Hokkaido, Japan.

Sa·la·do (sä-lä′thô), a river in N Argentina, flowing from the Andes southeast into the Parana: length, c.1,100 mi.

Sal·ween (sal-wēn′), a river in SE Asia, flowing from E Tibet through E Burma into the Bay of Bengal: length, c.1,750 mi.

Sa·mar (sä′mär), an island of the E Philippines, southeast of Luzon: area, 5,181 sq.mi.

Sa·mar·i·a (sä-mer′i-ā), 1. a region at the E end of the Mediterranean, west of the Jordan River. 2. in ancient times, *a)* the N kingdom of the Hebrews; Israel. *b)* a district of Palestine between Galilee and Judea, later a part of the Roman province of Judea.

Sa·mo·a (sā-mō′ā), a group of islands in the S Pacific, north of Tonga: divided into two groups, *American Samoa* and *Western Samoa.*

Sa·mos (sä′mos), a Greek island in the Aegean, off the W coast of Turkey: area, c.180 sq.mi.

San Ber·nar·di·no Mountains (san′ bûr-nėr-dē′nō), a mountain range in S California, south of the Mojave Desert: highest peak, 11,502 ft.

Sand·wich Islands (sand′wich, san′-), the former name of the **Hawaiian Islands.**

San Fer·nan·do Valley (san fēr-nan′dō), a valley in SW California, partly in the city of Los Angeles.

San Fran·cis·co Bay (san frän-sis′kō), an inlet of the Pacific, on the coast of central California, separating the cities of San Francisco and Oakland.

San Ma·ri·no (san mā-rē′nō), an independent country in the Apennines, within E Italy: area, 23 sq.mi.; pop., 21,000; cap., San Marino.

São Fran·cis·co (soun′ frän-sēs′koo), a river in E Brazil, flowing northeast and east into the Atlantic: length, c.1,800 mi.

Saône (sōn), a river in E France, flowing south into the Rhone: length, c.280 mi.

São To·mé (soun tô-me′), a country in the Gulf of Guinea, off the W coast of Africa: area, 318 sq.mi.: with the nearby island of Principe, it was, until 1975, an overseas province (São Tomé e Principe) of Portugal: area, 372 sq.mi.; pop., 74,000.

Sa·ra·wak (sā-rä′wäk), a state of Malaysia, occupying NC and NW Borneo: area, 48,250 sq.mi.; pop., 1,295,000.

Sar·din·i·a (sär-din′i-ā, -din′yā), 1. an Italian island in the Mediterranean, south of Corsica: area, c.9,196 sq.mi. 2. a former kingdom including this island, several dependencies on the Italian mainland, Nice, and the duchy of Savoy (by which the kingdom was ruled).

Sas·katch·e·wan (sas-kach′ė-wän, -wän), 1. a province of SC Canada: area, 251,700 sq.mi.; pop., 1,010,000; cap., Regina. 2. a river formed in central Saskatchewan by the junction of the North Saskatchewan and South Saskatchewan rivers and flowing east into Lake Winnipeg: length, 340 mi. (with its principal headstream, 1,205 mi.).

Sa·u·di Arabia (sä-ōō′di), a kingdom occupying most of Arabia: area, c.849,400 sq.mi.; pop., 12,400,000; cap., Riyadh.

Sa·voy (sä-voi′), a region in SE France, on the borders of Italy and Switzerland: formerly a duchy and then a part of the kingdom of Sardinia.

Sax·o·ny (sak′sō-ni), 1. a region in S East Germany: formerly an electorate and a kingdom most of which became a Prussian province, and then a state of the Weimar Republic. 2. a former duchy at the base of the Jutland peninsula in what is now West Germany.

Sa·yan Mountains (sä-yän′), a mountain system in central Asia, partially along the Mongolian-R.S.F.S.R. border: highest peak, 11,453 ft.

Scan·di·na·vi·a (skan-di-nä′vi-ā), 1. a region in N Europe, including Norway, Sweden, and Denmark and, sometimes, Iceland and the Faeroe Islands. 2. the Scandinavian Peninsula.

Scan·di·na·vi·an Peninsula (′vi-ān), a large peninsula in N Europe, containing Norway and Sweden.

Scot·land (skot′lånd), a division of the United

---

a in c*a*p, ä in c*a*ne, ä in f*a*ther, å in *a*bet, e in m*e*t, ē in b*e*, ē in bak*e*r, ė in reg*e*nt, i in p*i*t, ī in f*i*ne, î in man*i*fest, o in h*o*t, ô in h*o*rse, ō in b*o*ne,

Kingdom, occupying the N half of Great Britain and many nearby islands: area, 30,405 sq.mi.; pop., 5,130,000; cap., Edinburgh.

Seine (sān), a river in N France, flowing northwest through Paris into the English Channel: length, 482 mi.

Sen·e·gal (sen·i·gôl'), 1. a country in W Africa, on the Atlantic: area, 76,124 sq.mi.; pop., 6,540,000; cap., Dakar. 2. a river flowing from W Mali northwest along the Senegal-Mauritania border into the Atlantic: length, c.1,000 mi.

Ser·bi·a (sūr'bi·ä), a republic of Yugoslavia, in the E part: area, 21,580 sq.mi.; pop., 9,320,000; cap., Belgrade.

Say·chelles (sā-shel', -shelz'), a country on a group of islands in the Indian Ocean, northeast of Madagascar: area, c.156 sq.mi.; pop., 64,000; cap., Victoria.

Shas·ta, Mount (shas'tả), a volcanic mountain in the Cascade Range, N California: height, 14,162 ft.

Shatt al A·rab (shat ăl ä'räb), a river in SE Iraq, formed by the confluence of the Tigris and Euphrates rivers, and flowing southeast into the Persian Gulf: length, 120 mi.: also **Shatt-al-Arab.**

Shet·land Islands (shet'lănd), a group of islands in the Atlantic, northeast of the Orkney Islands, constituting a county of Scotland.

Shi·ko·ku (shē'kô-kōō), the smallest of the four major islands of Japan, south of Honshu: area, c.6,860 sq.mi.

Si·am (sī-am'), the former name of **Thailand.**

Si·ber·i·a (sī-bir'i·ä), a region in N Asia, between the Urals and the Pacific, north of Kazakh S.S.R. and Mongolia; Asiatic section of the R.S.F.S.R.

Sic·i·ly (sis'l-i), an island of Italy, off its S tip: area, 9,926 sq.mi.

Si·er·ra Le·one (si-er'ả lē-ôn'), a country in W Africa, on the Atlantic between Guinea and Liberia: area, 27,925 sq.mi.; pop., 3,354,000; cap., Freetown.

Si·er·ra Ma·dre (si-er·ả mä'drä), a mountain system of Mexico bordering the central plateau: highest peak, 18,700 ft.

Sierra Nevada, a mountain range in E California: highest peak, Mt. Whitney.

Si Kiang (sē' kyäng'), a river in S China, flowing into the South China Sea: length, with main headstream, 1,250 mi.

Sik·kim (sik'im), state, formerly a protectorate of India, in the E Himalayas, east of Nepal: area, 2,818 sq.mi.; pop., 316,000; cap., Gangtok.

Si·le·sia (sī-lē'shi-ä, sī-lē'shả, 'zhả), a region in E Europe, on both sides of the upper Oder, mostly in what is now SW Poland.

Si·nai Peninsula (sī'nī), a broad peninsula in NE Africa, extending from the Mediterranean to the Red Sea, between the Gulf of Suez and the Gulf of Aqaba.

Sin·ga·pore (sing'gả-pôr), 1. an island off the S tip of the Malay Peninsula. 2. a country comprising this island and nearby islets: area, 225 sq.mi.; pop., 2,558,000; cap., Singapore. 3. **Strait of,** a channel between Sin-

gapore and a group of Indonesian islands to the south: also **Singapore Strait.**

Slo·va·ki·a (slō-vä'ki·ả -vak'i-ả), a region comprising the E half of Czechoslovakia: before 1918, a part of Austria-Hungary.

Slo·ve·ni·a (slō-vē'ni-ả), a republic of Yugoslavia, in the NW part: area, 7,896 sq.mi.; pop., 1,920,000; cap., Ljubljana.

Smok·y Hill (smōk'i), a river flowing from E Colorado east through Kansas, joining the Republican River to form the Kansas River: length, 540 mi.

Snake River (snāk), a river in the NW United States, flowing from NW Wyoming west through Idaho and north along the Oregon-Idaho border into the Columbia River in Washington: length, 1,038 mi.

So·ci·e·ty Islands (sō-si'ē-ti), a group of islands in the South Pacific, in French Polynesia: area, c.650 sq.mi.: also called **Society Archipelago.**

So·co·tra (sō-kō'trả), an island of the People's Democratic Republic of Yemen, in the Indian Ocean off the E tip of Africa: area, 1,400 sq.mi.

Sol·o·mon Islands (sol'ô-mồn), a country on a group of islands in the SW Pacific, east of New Guinea: formerly a British protectorate **(British Solomon Islands Protectorate):** area, c.11,500 sq.mi.; pop. 283,000:

So·ma·li·a (sō-mä'li-ả, sô-), a country on the E coast of Africa, on the Indian Ocean and the Gulf of Aden: area, 246,201 sq.mi.; pop., 7,825,000; cap., Mogadishu.

So·ma·li·land (sō-mä'li-land), a region in E Africa, including Somalia, the French Territory of the Afars and the Issas, and SE Ethiopia.

Soo (sōō), a region in N Michigan and S Ontario, Canada, including three ship canals **(St. Marys Falls Canals)** which bypass a rapids of the St. Marys River, a river flowing from Lake Superior into Lake Huron, between Michigan and Ontario.

South Africa, a country in southernmost Africa: area, 472,358 sq.mi.; pop., 33,241,000; caps., Cape Town, Pretoria, Bloemfontein: former name, the **Union of South Africa.**

South America, the S continent in the Western Hemisphere: area, c.6,864,000 sq.mi.; pop., 241,000,000.

South·amp·ton Island (sou-thamp'tồn, southhamp'-), an island in N Hudson Bay, Canada: area, 15,700 sq.mi.

South Carolina, a Southern State of the SE United States, on the Atlantic: area, 31,055 sq.mi.; pop., 3,121,000; cap., Columbia.

South China Sea, an arm of the Pacific, touching Taiwan, the Philippines, Borneo, the Malay Peninsula, Indochina, and China.

South Dakota, a Middle Western State of the west NC United States: area, 77,047 sq.mi.; pop., 690,000; cap., Pierre.

Southern Rhodesia, see **Rhodesia.**

South Georgia, an island dependency of the Falkland Islands in the South Atlantic, east of the Falkland Islands: area, 1,600 sq.mi.

South Platte, a river flowing from central

ồ in drag*o*n, ōō in cr*u*de, ***oo*** in w*oo*l, **u** in c*u*p, **ū** in c*u*re, **ū** in t*u*rn, **ů** in foc*u*s, **oi** in b*oy*, **ou** in h*ou*se, **th** in *th*in, ***th*** in shea*the*, **g** in g*e*t, **j** in *j*oy, **y** in y*e*t.

Colorado, northeast through W Nebraska, joining the North Platte to form the Platte: length, 424 mi.

South Saskatchewan, a river flowing from SW Alberta east and northeast through Saskatchewan, joining the North Saskatchewan to form the Saskatchewan: length, 865 mi.

South Sea Islands, the islands in the temperate and tropical parts of the South Pacific.

South Seas, 1. the South Pacific. 2. all the seas located south of the equator.

South West Africa, a country in S Africa, on the Atlantic, administered by South Africa under provisions of a mandate of the League of Nations: South Africa's rights to the territory were terminated by the United Nations in 1966 but South Africa refused to accept the United Nations authority: area, 318,261 sq.mi.; pop., 1,033,000; cap., Windhoek: also **South-West Africa.** Cf. **Namibia.**

Soviet Union, same as the **Union of Soviet Socialist Republics:** also **Soviet Russia.**

Spain (spān), a country in SW Europe, on the Iberian Peninsula: area, 194,346 sq.mi.; pop., 39,000,000; cap., Madrid.

Span·ish America (span'ish), Mexico and those countries in Central and South America and islands in the Caribbean in which Spanish is the chief language.

Spanish Main, 1. originally, the coastal region of the Americas along the Caribbean Sea; especially, the N coast of South America between the Isthmus of Panama and the mouth of the Orinoco. 2. later, the Caribbean Sea itself, or that part of it adjacent to the N coast of South America.

Spanish Morocco, the former Spanish zone of Morocco, constituting a coastal strip along the Mediterranean. See **French Morocco.**

Spar·ta (spär'tȧ), an ancient city in the S Peloponnesus.

Spits·ber·gen (spits'bûr-gĕn), 1. a group of Norwegian islands in the Arctic Ocean, constituting the major part of Svalbard: area, 23,658 sq.mi. 2. Svalbard.

Spor·a·des (spŏr'ȧ-dēz), 1. formerly, all of the Greek islands in the Aegean Sea except the Cyclades. 2. sometimes, the Greek islands along the W coast of Asia Minor, especially the Dodecanese and Samos.

Sri Lan·ka (srē läng'kȧ), a country on an island off the SE tip of India: area, 25,332 sq.mi.; pop., 14,850,000; cap., Colombo.

Stat·en Island (stat'n), an island in New York Bay, near the New Jersey shore, comprising, with small nearby islands, a borough (called *Richmond*) of New York City: area, of the borough, 60 sq.mi.

St. Chris·to·pher (kris'tō-fēr), an island in the Leeward group of the West Indies: area, 65 sq.mi.; pop., 45,000.

St. É·li·as (ĭ-lī'ȧs), 1. a range of the Coast Ranges, in SW Yukon and SE Alaska: highest peak, Mt. Logan; in full, **St. Elias Mountains.** 2. **Mount,** a mountain in this range, on the Canada-Alaska border: height, 18,008 ft.

St. George's Channel, a strait between Ireland

and Wales, connecting the Irish Sea with the Atlantic.

St. He·le·na (he-lame'nȧ, hel'i-nȧ), 1. a British island in the S Atlantic, c.1,200 mi. from the coast of Africa: area, 47 sq.mi. 2. a British colony including this island, another island, and the Tristan da Cunha group: area, c. 120 sq.mi.; pop., 5,800.

St. Kitts (kits), same as **St. Christopher.**

St. Law·rence (lôr'ĕns, lär'-), 1. a river flowing from Lake Ontario northeast into the Gulf of St. Lawrence: length, c.750 mi. 2. **Gulf of,** a large inlet of the Atlantic in E Canada, surrounded by Quebec, Newfoundland, Nova Scotia, and New Brunswick.

St. Lawrence Seaway, an inland waterway for ocean-going ships, connecting the Great Lakes with the Atlantic: it consists of the Welland Canal, the St. Lawrence River, and several locks and canals northeast of Lake Ontario.

St. Lu·ci·a (lōō'shi-ȧ, 'shȧ; lōō-sē'ȧ), country on an island of the Windward group, in the West Indies, south of Martinique: area, 238 sq.mi.; pop., 120,000; cap., Castries.

St. Mar·tin (mär'tĭn), an island of the Leeward group, in the West Indies, south of Anguila: the N part is a dependency of Guadeloupe and the S part is in the Netherlands Antilles: area, 13 sq.mi.; pop., 23,000. French name, **St-Mar·tin** (san-mär-tan'); Dutch name, **St. Maar·ten** (sint mär'tĕn).

St. Pierre and Miquelon (san pyer'), a French overseas territory in the Atlantic, south of Newfoundland, consisting of the islands of St. Pierre (c.10 sq.mi.), and Miquelon, and six islets: area, 93 sq.mi.; pop., 6,000.

St. Vin·cent (vin'snt), 1. an island of the Windward group, in the West Indies, south of St. Lucia: area, 133 sq.mi. 2. country consisting of this island and a nearby group, area, 150 sq.mi.; pop., 123,000.

Su·dan (sōō-dan'), 1. a vast semiarid region in NC Africa, extending from the Atlantic to the Ethiopian highlands and the Red Sea. 2. a country in the E part of this region, south of Egypt: area, 967,500 sq.mi.; pop., 20,000,000; cap., Khartoum.

Su·de·ten·land (sōō-dā'tn-land), a mountainous region in N Czechoslovakia.

Su·ez, Gulf of (sōō-ez', sōō'ez), an arm of the Red Sea, in NE Egypt, between the Sinai Peninsula and the Arabian Desert.

Suez, Isthmus of, a strip of land connecting Asia and Africa, between the Mediterranean and the Gulf of Suez.

Suez Canal, a ship canal across the Isthmus of Suez, joining the Mediterranean and the Gulf of Suez.

Su·lu Archipelago (sōō'lōō), a group of islands in the Philippines, between Mindanao and NE Borneo: area, 1,038 sq.mi.

Su·ma·tra (soo-mä'trȧ), a large island of indonesia, just south of the Malay Peninsula: area, c.165,000 sq.mi.

Sum·ba (sōōm'bȧ), an island of Indonesia, west of Timor and south of Flores: area, c.4,300 sq.mi.

---

a in cap, ă in cane, ä in father, ȧ in abet, e in met, ē in be, ē in baker, ē in regent, ĭ in pit, ī in fine, ĭ in manifest, o in hot, ô in horse, ō in bone,

Sum·ba·wa (sŏŏm-bä′wä), an island of Indonesia, between Lombok and Flores: area, c.5,500 sq.mi.

Sun·da Islands (sun′då), a group of islands in the Malay Archipelago, consisting of two smaller groups: 1) **Greater Sunda Islands,** Sumatra, Java, Borneo, Celebes, and small nearby islands; 2) **Lesser Sunda Islands,** Bali and islands extending east to and including Timor.

Sun·ga·ri (sŏŏng′gä-rē′), a river in Manchuria, NE China, flowing northward into the Amur River: length, c.1,150 mi.

Su·pe·ri·or, Lake (sů-pir′i-ĕr, soo-), the largest and westernmost of the Great Lakes, between Michigan and Ontario, Canada.

Su·ri·name (soor-i-näm′, -nam′), a country in N South America, on the Atlantic: area, 63,036 sq.mi.; pop., 381,000; cap., Paramaribo.

Sus·que·han·na (sus-kwi-han′å), a river flowing from central New York south through Pennsylvania and Maryland into Chesapeake Bay: length, 444 mi.

Sut·lej (sut′lej), a river flowing from SW Tibet southwest into the Indus River in Pakistan: length, c.900 mi.

Sval·bard (sväl′bär), a group of Norwegian islands in the Arctic Ocean, between Greenland and Franz Josef Land: area, 23,979 sq.mi.

Swa·zi·land (swä′zi-land), a country in SE Africa, surrounded on three sides by South Africa: area, 6,705 sq.mi.; pop., 626,000; cap., Mbabane.

Swe·den (swē′dn), a country in N Europe, occupying the E part of the Scandinavian Peninsula: area, 173,620 sq.mi.; pop., 8,320,000; cap., Stockholm.

Switz·er·land (swit′sĕr-lånd), a country in WC Europe, in the Alps: area, 15,941 sq.mi.; pop., 6,365,000; cap., Bern.

Syr Dar·ya (sir där′yä), a river in central U.S.S.R., flowing from Uzbek S.S.R. northwest through Kazakh S.S.R. into the Aral Sea: length, c.1,700 mi.

Syr·i·a (sir′i-å), 1. an ancient region at the E end of the Mediterranean, including what is now Israel, Jordan, Lebanon, modern Syria, and part of Iraq. 2. a country in the NW part of this region, south of Turkey: area, 71,227 sq.mi.; pop., 10,900,000; cap., Damascus.

Ta·dzhik Soviet Socialist Republic (tä′jik), a republic of the U.S.S.R., in central Asia, north of Afghanistan: area, 55,250 sq.mi.; pop., 4,400,000; cap., Dushanbe: also **Ta·dzhik·i·stan** (tä-jĕk-i-stän′).

Ta·gus (tä′gůs), a river flowing west across central Spain and Portugal into the Atlantic through a broad estuary: length, c.600 mi.

Ta·hi·ti (tä-hē′ti, tå-), one of the Society Islands of French Polynesia, in the South Pacific: area, c.600 sq.mi.

Tai·wan (tī′wän′), an island province of China, off the SE coast: the seat of the Kuomintang (Nationalist) government since 1949: area, 13,885 sq.mi.; pop., 14,118,000; cap., Taipei.

Taiwan Strait, a strait between Taiwan and mainland China, joining the East China Sea and the South China Sea.

Ta·na·na (tan′ä-nä), a river in E Alaska, flowing northwest into the Yukon River: length, 800 mi.

Tan·gan·yi·ka (tang-gan-yē′kå), 1. the mainland region of Tanzania, on the E coast of Africa: formerly, 1961-64, an independent country and, before 1961, a British trust territory: area, 361,800 sq.mi. 2. **Lake,** a lake in EC Africa, between Tanganyika and Zaire.

Tan·gier (tan-jir′), a former international zone in NW Africa, on the Strait of Gibraltar, surrounding the city of Tangier: it is now part of Morocco: area, 147 sq.mi.

Tan·za·ni·a (tan-zå-nē′å, tän-), a country in E Africa, consisting of the mainland region of Tanganyika and the offshore islands of Zanzibar and Pemba: area, 362,820 sq.mi.; pop., 19,730,000; cap., Dar es Salaam.

Ta·ra·wa (tä-rä′wä, tä′rä-wä), a coral atoll in the WC Pacific: capital of Kiribati: area, 7.5 sq.mi.

Ta·rim River (tä′rēm′, dä′-), a river in NW China, flowing from the Tien Shan Mountains eastward into a marshy depression: length, c.1,300 mi.

Tas·ma·ni·a (taz-mä′ni-å, -mån′yå), an island south of Australia, constituting a part of Australia: area, c.24,450 sq.mi.

Tas·man Sea (taz′mån), a section of the South Pacific, between SE Australia and New Zealand.

Ta·tar Strait (tä′tĕr), a strait between Sakhalin Island and the Asia mainland, connecting the Sea of Okhotsk with the Sea of Japan.

Ta·ta·ry (tä′tå-ri), a vast region in Europe and Asia under the control of Tatar tribes in the Middle Ages: its greatest extent was from SW Russia to the Pacific.

Tau·rus Mountains (tôr′ůs), a mountain range along the S coast of Asia Minor, Turkey: highest peak, c.12,250 ft.

Te·huan·te·pec, Gulf of (te-wän′tĕ-pek, -wän-tĕ-pek′), an arm of the Pacific, on the coast of S Mexico.

Tehuantepec, Isthmus of, the narrowest part of Mexico, between the Gulf of Tehuantepec and the Gulf of Campeche.

Ten·nes·see (ten-ĕ-sē′), 1. a State of the east SC United States: area, 42,244 sq.mi.; pop., 4,591,000; cap., Nashville. 2. a river flowing from NE Tennessee in a U-shaped course through N Alabama and W Tennessee into the Ohio River: length, 652 mi.

Tex·as (tek′sås), 1. a State of the west SC United States, on the Gulf of Mexico and the Mexican border: area, 267,339 sq.mi.; pop., 14,228,000; cap., Austin. 2. formerly (1836-45), an independent country occupying this region.

Thai·land (tī′lånd, ′land), 1. a country in SE Asia, on the Indochinese and Malay penin-

sulas: area, 198,456 sq.mi.; pop., 50,100,000; cap., Bangkok. 2. **Gulf of,** an arm of the South China Sea, between the Malay and Indochinese Peninsulas.

Thames (temz), a river in S England, flowing into the North Sea: length, 210 mi.

Thebes (thēbz), 1. an ancient city in S Egypt, on the Nile. 2. the chief city of ancient Boeotia, EC Greece.

Thes·sa·ly (thes'ȧ-li), a division of E Greece, along the Aegean Sea.

Thou·sand Islands (thou'znd), a group of over 1,500 islands in the St. Lawrence River at the outlet of Lake Ontario: some are part of New York State and some are part of Ontario, Canada.

Thrace (thrās), 1. an ancient region in the E Balkan Peninsula, on the Black Sea, between the Danube and the Aegean Sea. 2. a region in the SE Balkan Peninsula, at the N end of the Aegean, including a division of Greece and European Turkey.

Thu·rin·gi·a (thoo-rin'ji-ȧ), a region of SW East Germany: formerly, a state of the Weimar Republic.

Ti·ber (tī'bẽr), a river in central Italy, flowing from the Apennines south into the Tyrrhenian Sea: Length, c.250 mi.

Ti·bet (ti-bet'), an autonomous region of SW China, occupying a high plateau area north of the Himalayas: area, 471,660 sq.mi.; pop., c.1,892,000; cap., Lhasa.

Tien Shan (tyen shän), a mountain system in central Asia, extending from the Pamirs across the Kirghiz S.S.R., and Sinkiang, China, to the Altai Mountains: highest peak, 24,406 ft.

Tier·ra del Fue·go (ti-er'ȧ del fū-ā'gō, fōō-), 1. a group of islands at the tip of South America, separated from the mainland by the Strait of Magellan and divided between Argentina and Chile: area, c.27,500 sq.mi. 2. the chief island of this group, divided between Argentina and Chile: area, c.18,500 sq.mi.

Ti·gris (tī'gris), a river flowing from EC Turkey through Iraq, to join the Euphrates: length, 1,150 mi.

Ti·mor (tē'môr, ti-môr'), 1. an island in the SE Malay Archipelago, divided between Portugal (*Portuguese Timor*) and Indonesia: area, c.13,000 sq.mi. 2. the W portion of this island, in Indonesia: area, c.5,800 sq.mi.

Tir·ol (tir'ol, ti-rōl'), an E Alpine region in W Austria and N Italy.

Ti·ti·ca·ca, Lake (tit-i-kä'kȧ), the largest lake in South America, on the border of SE Peru and W Bolivia.

To·ba·go (tō-bā'gō, tō-), an island in the West Indies, northeast of Trinidad: area, 116 sq.mi. See **Trinidad and Tobago.**

To·bol (tō-bôl'y), a river flowing from the S Urals northeast through N Kazakh S.S.R. and W R.S.F.S.R. into the Irtysh: length, 1,042 mi.

To·can·tins (tō-kän-tēns'), a river flowing from central Brazil north into the Pará River in the Amazon delta: length, c.1,700 mi.

To·go (tō'gō), a country in W Africa, on the Gulf of Guinea, east of Ghana: area, 21,853 sq.mi.; pop., 2,700,000; cap., Lomé.

To·go·land (tō'gō-land), a region in W Africa, on the Gulf of Guinea: formerly a German colony, it was divided (1922) between France and Great Britain: the W portion became part of Ghana and the E (French) portion became independent as Togo.

Ton·ga (tong'gȧ), 1. a group of islands in the South Pacific, east of Fiji: also **Tonga Islands.** 2. an independent kingdom occupying these islands: area, 270 sq.mi.; pop., 98,700; cap., Nuku'alofa.

Ton·kin (ton'kin, tong'-), 1. a region and former French protectorate in N Indochina: now, part of North Vietnam. 2. **Gulf of,** an arm of the South China Sea between Hainan Island and the coasts of S China and NE Indochina.

Trans·cau·ca·sia (trans-kô-kā'zhȧ, 'shȧ), that part of the Caucasus south of the Caucasus Mountains, containing the republics of Armenia, Azerbaijan, and Georgia.

Trans·jor·dan (trans-jôr'dn, tranz-), a British mandated territory (1923-46) in the Near East, east of the Jordan River: now, part of the country of Jordan: also **Trans·jor·da·ni·a** (trans-jôr-dā'ni-ȧ).

Trans·syl·va·ni·a (tran-sil-vā'ni-ȧ, -vñ'yȧ), a plateau region in central Romania.

Treb·i·zond (treb'i-zond), an empire (1204-1461) on the SE coast of the Black Sea.

Tri·este, Free Territory of (tri-est'), a former region (1947-54) in NE Italy, surrounding the city of Trieste: administered by the United Nations until divided between Italy and Yugoslavia in 1954.

Trin·i·dad (trin'i-dad), an island in the West Indies, off the NE coast of Venezuela: area, 1,864 sq.mi. See **Trinidad and Tobago.**

Trinidad and Tobago, a country in the West Indies, comprising the islands of Trinidad and Tobago: area, 1,980 sq.mi.; pop., 1,055,000; cap., Port-of-Spain.

Trip·ol·i·ta·ni·a (trip-ol-i-tā'ni-ȧ), a region of NW Libya, on the Mediterranean: formerly, a province of Libya and, in the 18th and 19th cent., a Barbary State.

Tris·tan da Cun·ha (tris'tän dȧ kōōn'yȧ), a group of four small islands in the South Atlantic: part of the British colony of St. Helena: area, 38 sq.mi.

Troy (troi), an ancient Phrygian city in NW Asia Minor.

Tru·cial States (trōō'shȧl), a former group of seven semi-independent Arab sheikdoms in SE Arabia, under British protection: they now constitute the United Arab Emirates.

Tu·nis (tōō'nis, tū'-), 1. a former Barbary State: now, the country of Tunisia. 2. **Gulf of,** an inlet of the Mediterranean, on the NE coast of Tunisia.

Tu·ni·sia (tōō-nish'i-ȧ, tū-nish'ȧ, -nē'zhȧ), a country in N Africa, on the Mediterranean: area, 48,332 sq.mi.; pop., 7,424,000; cap., Tunis.

Tur·ke·stan (tūr-ki-stan', -stän'), a region in central Asia, extending from the Caspian Sea to the Gobi Desert: generally divided

---

a in *cap*, ä in *cane*, ä in *father*, ȧ in *abet*, e in *met*, ē in *be*, ẽ in *baker*, ė in *regent*, i in *pit*, ī in *fine*, î in *manifest*, o in *hot*, ô in *horse*, ō in *bone,*

by the Tien Shan into two divisions, Western (or Russian) **Turkestan** and **Eastern** (or Chinese) **Turkestan.**

Tur·key (tûr′ki), a country mostly in W Asia, including Asia Minor, the SW part of the former kingdom of Armenia, and a SE section of the Balkan Peninsula: area, 301,381 sq.mi.; pop., 51,819,000; cap., Ankara.

Turk·men Soviet Socialist Republic (tûrk′men), a republic of the U.S.S.R., in central Asia, on the Caspian Sea, north of Iran: area, 188,400 sq.mi.; pop., 3,192,000; cap., Ashkhabad: also **Turk·men·i·stan** (tûrk-men-i-stan′, -stän′), **Turk·me·ni·a** (tûrk-mē′ni-ȧ).

Turks and Cai·cos Islands (tûrks / kā′kōs), a British territory in the West Indies, consisting of two groups of small islands southeast of the Bahamas: area, 166 sq.mi.; pop., 7,500.

Tus·ca·ny (tus′kȧ-ni), a region of Central Italy, on the Tyrrhenian and Ligurian seas: area, 8,876 sq.mi.; pop., 3,581,000.

Tu·tu·i·la (tōō-tōō-ē′lä), the chief island of American Samoa, in the South Pacific: area, with nearby islets, 53 sq.mi.

Two Sic·i·lies (sis′l-iz), a former kingdom including Sicily and the kingdom of Naples.

Tyr·ol (tir′ol, tī-rōl′), same as **Tirol.**

Tyr·rhe·ni·an Sea (ti-rē′ni-ȧn), a part of the Mediterranean, between the W coast of Italy and the islands of Corsica, Sardinia, and Sicily.

U·ban·gi (ōō-bäng′gi, ū-bang′-) a river in central Africa flowing from N Zaire west and south into the Congo River: length, c.700 mi.

U·ban·gi-Sha·ri (-shä′ri), a former French territory in central Africa: now, the country of Central African Republic.

U·ca·ya·li (ōō-kä-yä′li), a river in E Peru, flowing north to join the Marañón and form the Amazon: length, c.1,200 mi.

U·gan·da (ū-gan′dȧ, ōō-gän′dä), a country in EC Africa, on Lake Victoria: area, 93,981 sq.mi.; pop., 15,158,000; cap., Kampala.

U·krain·i·an Soviet Socialist Republic (ū-krā′ni-ȧn, -krī′-), a republic of the U.S.S.R., in the SW European part: area, 231,990 sq.mi.; pop., 50,000,000; cap., Kiev: also **the U·kraine** (ū′krān, ū-krān′, ū-krīn′).

Ul·ster (ul′stēr), a former province of N Ireland: in 1920, six of its counties separated to form Northern Ireland and three counties remained with Ireland as "Part of Ulster Province," area, 3,094 sq.mi.; pop., 230,000.

Union of South Africa, the former name of **South Africa.**

Union of Soviet Socialist Republics, a country in E Europe and N Asia, extending from the Arctic Ocean to the Black Sea and from the Baltic Sea to the Pacific: area, 8,649,000 sq.mi.; pop., 280,000,000; cap., Moscow.

United Arab Emirates, a country consisting of seven Arab sheikdoms in SE Arabia: area, 32,000 sq.mi.; pop., c.1,326,000.

United Arab Republic, 1. the former name of Egypt and Syria when united as a single nation (1958-61). 2. the former name of Egypt (1961-71).

United Kingdom, 1. a country in W Europe, consisting of Great Britain, Northern Ireland, the Isle of Man, and the Channel Islands: area, 94,217 sq.mi.; pop., 56,458,000; cap., London: in full, **United Kingdom of Great Britain and Northern Ireland.** 2. formerly (1801-1922), a country consisting of Great Britain and Ireland: in full, **United Kingdom of Great Britain and Ireland.**

United States of America, a country made up of the North American area extending from the Atlantic Ocean to the Pacific Ocean between Canada and Mexico, and including Alaska and Hawaii: area, 3,615,211 sq.mi.; pop., 240,856,000; cap., Washington: also called **United States.**

Ur (ûr), an ancient Sumerian city on the Euphrates River, in what is now S Iraq.

U·ral (yoor′ȧl), a river flowing from the S Urals southwest into the N end of the Caspian Sea: length, 1,575 mi.

U·rals (yoor′ȧlz), a mountain system in the W R.S.F.S.R., extending from the Arctic Ocean south to the N border of Kazakh S.S.R.: traditionally regarded as the boundary between Europe and Asia: highest peak, c.6,180 ft.: also **Ural Mountains.**

U·ru·guay (yoor′ŭ-gwā, -gwī), 1. a country in SE South America, on the Atlantic: area, 72,171 sq.mi.; pop., 2,974,000; cap., Montevideo. 2. a river in SE South America flowing from S Brazil along the Brazil-Argentina and Uruguay-Argentina borders and then joining the Paraná to form the Rio de la Plata: length, c.1,000 mi.

U·tah (ū′tô, ū′tä), a State of the W United States: area, 84,916 sq.mi.; pop., 1,461,000; cap., Salt Lake City.

Uz·bek Soviet Socialist Republic (ooz-bek′, uz′bek), a republic of the U.S.S.R., in central Asia, between the Turkmen S.S.R. and the Tadzhik S.S.R.: area, 172,741 sq.mi.; pop., 17,989,000; cap., Tashkent: also **Uz·bek·i·stan** (ooz-bek-i-stan′, -stän′).

Va·len·ci·a (vȧ-len′shi-ȧ, ′shä), a region and former kingdom in E Spain, on the Mediterranean.

Van·cou·ver (van-kōō′vēr), an island of British Columbia, Canada, off the SW coast: area, 12,408 sq.mi.

Vat·i·can City (vat′i-kȧn), an independent papal state constituting an enclave in Rome: area, 108 acres; pop., c.1,000.

Ven·e·zue·la (ven-ē-zwē′lȧ, -i-zwä′-), 1. a country in N South America, on the Caribbean: area, 352,143 sq.mi.; pop., 17,791,000; cap., Caracas. 2. **Gulf of,** an inlet of the Caribbean, on the NW coast of Venezuela.

Verde, Cape (vûrd), a peninsula on the Atlantic coast of Senegal.

Ver·mont (vēr-mont′), a New England State of

the United States: area, 9,609 sq.mi.; pop., 511,000; cap., Montpelier.

Ve·su·vi·us (vĕ-sōō'vĭ-ŭs), an active volcano in S. Italy, on the Bay of Naples: height, c.4,000 ft.

Vic·to·ri·a, Lake (vik-tôr'ĭ-â, -tōr'yâ), a lake in E Africa, bounded by Kenya, Uganda, and Tanzania.

Victoria Island, an island in the Arctic Ocean, Northwest Territories, Canada: area, 81,930 sq.mi.

Victoria Land, a mainland region of Antarctica, along the Ross Sea.

Vi·et·nam (vē'ĕt-năm', vĕt'-, vyet'-; -nam'), a country on the E coast of the Indochinese peninsula: formed (1945) by the union of the French territories of Annam, Tonkin, and Cochin China: partitioned into two republics (**North Vietnam** and **South Vietnam**) in 1954, and reunified in 1976 under the name of **Socialist Republic of Vietnam;** 127,300 sq.mi.; pop. 61,994,000; cap., Hanoi.

Vil·yu·y, Vil·yu·i (vil-ū'ĭ), a river in EC R.S.F.S.R., flowing east into the Lena: length, c.1,500 mi.

Vir·gin·ia (vēr-jin'yâ, 'ĭ-â), A Southern State of the United States, on the Atlantic: area, 40,815 sq.mi.; pop., 5,346,000; cap., Richmond.

Vir·gin Islands (vûr'jin), a group of islands of the Leeward group in the West Indies, east of Puerto Rico, divided into 1) **British Virgin Islands,** the easternmost islands of this group, constituting a British territory, area, 59 sq.mi.; pop., 12,000. 2) **Virgin Islands of the United States,** the islands of this group closest to Puerto Rico, constituting a territory of the United States, area, 132 sq.mi.; pop., 63,000; cap., Charlotte Amalie.

Vis·tu·la (vis'choo-lâ), a river in Poland, flowing from the Carpathian Mountains north into the Baltic Sea: length, 677 mi.

Vol·ga (vol'gâ, vôl'-), a river in W R.S.F.S.R., flowing into the Caspian Sea: length, 2,290 mi.

Vol·ta (vol'tâ), a river in Ghana, flowing south into the Bight of Benin: length, c.300 mi.: it is formed in central Ghana by the confluence of the **Black Volta** (length, c.500 mi.) and the **White Volta** (length, c.550 mi.).

W **a·bash** (wô'bash), a river flowing from W Ohio across Indiana and along the Indiana-Illinois border into the Ohio River: length, 475 mi.

Wake Island (wāk), a coral atoll consisting of three islets in the N Pacific, between the Midway Islands and Guam: a possession of the United States: area, 3 sq.mi.

Wales (wālz), a division of the United Kingdom, occupying a peninsula of WC Great Britain: area, 8,016 sq.mi.; pop., 2,792,000.

Wal·lis and Fu·tu·na (wôl'is / fŭ-tōō'nâ), a French overseas territory in the W South Pacific, northeast of Fiji: area, c.105 sq.mi.; pop., 12,000.

Wal·vis Bay (wôl'vis), a small enclave on the coast of South West Africa, surrounding an inlet (**Walvis Bay**) of the Atlantic: it is a part of Cape of Good Hope province, South Africa, but is administered by South West Africa: area, 434 sq.mi.

Wash·ing·ton (wôsh'ing-tòn, wäsh'-), a NW State of the United States, on the Pacific: area, 68,192 sq.mi.; pop., 4,130,000; cap., Olympia.

Wed·dell Sea (wed'ĕl, wĕ-del'), a section of the Atlantic, on the coast of Antarctica, east of Antarctica Peninsula.

Wei·mar Republic (wī'mär), the republic of Germany, created by a constitutional assembly in 1919 (at the city of Weimar) and dissolved in 1934.

Wel·land Canal (wel'ånd), a ship canal of the St. Lawrence Seaway, in Ontario, Canada, between Lake Ontario and Lake Erie.

Western Reserve, a section of the Northwest Territory, on Lake Erie: reserved by the State of Connecticut for settlers when its other W lands were ceded to the Federal government in 1786: incorporated into the territory of Ohio in 1800.

Western Roman Empire, the W part of the Roman Empire, after it was divided in 395 A.D. until it was overthrown in 476 A.D.

Western Samoa, a country in the South Pacific, consisting of two large islands and several small ones: area, 1,130 sq.mi.; pop., 165,000; cap., Apia.

West Indies, a large group of islands between North America and South America, separating the Caribbean Sea from the Atlantic Ocean: it includes the Greater Antilles, Lesser Antilles, and Bahamas.

West Irian, a province of Indonesia, occupying the W half of the island of New Guinea: area, c.160,000 sq.mi.; pop., 1,174,000; cap., Jayapura.

West Pakistan, formerly, one of the two provinces of Pakistan: since the province of East Pakistan declared its independence as the country of Bangladesh, the region formerly constituting the province of West Pakistan is now the country of Pakistan.

West·pha·li·a (west-fā'li-â, -fāl'yâ), a region in West Germany, on the Rhine: formerly, a duchy, a kingdom, and a province of Prussia.

West Virginia, an Eastern State of the United States, northwest of Virginia: area, 24,181 sq.mi.; pop., 1,950,000; cap., Charleston.

White River, a river flowing from NW Arkansas through S Missouri then south through Arkansas into the Mississippi: length, 690 mi.

White Russia, same as the **Byelorussian Soviet Socialist Republic.**

Whit·ney, Mount (hwit'ni), a mountain of the Sierra Nevada range, EC California: height, 14,495 ft.

Wind·ward Islands (wind'wērd), the S group of islands in the Lesser Antilles of the West Indies, extending from the Leeward Islands south to Trinidad, but often excluding Barbados.

Win·ni·peg, Lake (win'i-peg), a large lake in SC Manitoba.

Wis·con·sin (wis-lin′sn), a Middle Western State of the east NC United States: area, 56,154 sq.mi.; pop., 4,705,000; cap., Madison.

Wit·wa·ters·rand (wit-wôt′ẽrz-rand, -wät′-; -ränt), a region in NE South Africa, consisting of ranges of hills which contain rich gold fields.

Wran·gell (rang′gl), a mountain range in SE Alaska, northwest of the St. Elias Mountains: highest peak, 16,523 ft.: in full, **Wrangell Mountains.**

Würt·tem·berg (würt′ĕm-bûrg), a region in SW West Germany, on the Swiss border: formerly, a duchy, a kingdom, and a state of Germany.

Wy·o·ming (wī-ō′ming), a Western State of the United States: area, 97,914 sq.mi.; pop., 471,000; cap., Cheyenne.

Xin·gu (shing-gōō′), a river in NC Brazil, flowing north into the Amazon: length, c.1,200 mi.

Ya·lu (yä′lōō), a river flowing from NE China southwest along the Manchuria-North Korea border into the Yellow Sea: length, c.500 mi.

Yang·tze (yang′sĕ), a river in central China, flowing from the Tibetan highlands east into the East China Sea: length, c.3,400 mi.

Yel·low River (yel′ō), same as **Hwang Ho.**

Yellow Sea, an arm of the East China Sea, between China and Korea.

Yel·low·stone (yel′ō-stōn), a river flowing from NW Wyoming North and northeast through Montana into the Missouri River: length, 671 mi.

Yem·en, People's Democratic Republic of (yem′ĕn), a country in SW Arabia, on the Gulf of Aden, including a former group of Arab states under British protection: area, c.124,698 sq.mi.; pop., 2,275,000; cap., Aden.

Yemen Arab Republic, a country in the S Arabian Peninsula, on the Red Sea: area, c.75,000 sq.mi.; pop., 6,339,000; cap., San'a.

Ye·ni·sei, Ye·ni·sey (ye-ni-sā′), a river in central Siberian R.S.F.S.R., flowing from the Sayan Mountains north into the Kara Sea: length, c.2,600 mi.

Yu·ca·tán, Yu·ca·tan (ū-kå-tan′), a peninsula occupied by SE Mexico, British Honduras, and part of N Guatemala: it extends north, separating the Gulf of Mexico from the Caribbean.

Yu·go·sla·vi·a (ū-gō-slä′vi-å, ū-go-släv′yå), a country in the NW Balkan Peninsula, on the Adriatic: area, 98,766 sq.mi.; pop., 23,284,000; cap., Belgrade.

Yu·kon (ū′kon), 1. a territory of NW Canada, east of Alaska: area, 207,076 sq.mi.; pop., 22,000; cap., Whitehorse: in full, **Yukon Territory.** 2. a river flowing northwest through this territory and west and southwest through Alaska into the Bering Sea: length, 1,979 mi.

Za·ire, Za·ïre (zä-ir′, zä′ir), 1. a country in central Africa, on the equator: area, 905,563 sq.mi.; pop., 31,330,000; cap., Kinshasa. 2. the Congo River.

Zam·be·zi (zam-bē′zi), a river in S Africa, flowing from NW Zambia south and southeast through Mozambique into the Mozambique Channel: length, c.1,600 mi.

Zam·bi·a (zam′bi-å), a country in S Africa, south of Zaire: area, 290,323 sq.mi.; pop., 7,054,000; cap., Lusaka.

Zan·zi·bar (zan′zi-bär), 1. an island just off the E coast of Africa: area, 640 sq.mi. 2. formerly, (before 1963) a British protectorate and (1963-64) a country including this island, Pemba, and small nearby islands: merged with Tanganyika (1964) to form the country of Tanzania.

Zea·land (zē′lånd), the largest island of Denmark, between Jutland and Sweden: area, 2,912 sq.mi.

Zim·ba·bwe (zim-bä′bwe), the Bantu name of **Rhodesia.**

Zui·der Zee, Zuy·der Zee (zī′dẽr zē′), a former arm of the North Sea, which extended into the Netherlands: its S section was shut off from the North Sea by a dam.

Zu·lu·land (zōō′lōō-land), a region, formerly a Zulu kingdom, in E South Africa, on the Indian Ocean.

ō in drag*o*n, ōō in cr*u*de, oo in w*oo*l, u in c*u*p, ū in c*u*re, û in t*u*rn, ŭ in foc*u*s, oi in b*o*y, ou in h*ou*se, th in *th*in, *th* in shea*th*e, g in *g*et, j in *j*oy, y in *y*et.

LARGEST CITIES IN THE UNITED STATES

City	Population 1980	1970	1960
New York, N.Y.	7,071,639	7,895,563	7,781,984
Los Angeles, Cal.	2,966,850	2,811,801	2,479,015
Chicago, Ill.	3,005,072	3,369,357	3,550,404
Houston, Tex.	1,595,138	1,233,535	938,219
Philadelphia, Pa.	1,688,210	1,949,996	2,002,512
Detroit, Mich.	1,203,339	1,514,063	1,670,144
San Diego, Cal.	875,538	697,471	573,224
Dallas, Tex.	904,078	844,401	679,684
San Antonio, Tex.	785,880	654,153	587,718
Phoenix, Ariz.	789,704	584,303	439,170
Baltimore, Md.	786,775	905,787	939,024
San Francisco, Cal.	678,974	715,674	740,316
Indianapolis, Ind.	700,807	736,856	476,258
San Jose, Cal.	629,442	459,913	204,196
Memphis, Tenn.	646,356	623,988	497,524
Washington, D.C.	638,333	756,668	763,956
Jacksonville, Fla.	540,920	504,265	201,030
Milwaukee, Wis.	636,212	717,372	741,324
Boston, Mass.	562,994	641,071	697,197
Columbus, Oh.	564,871	540,025	471,316
New Orleans, La.	557,515	593,471	627,525
Cleveland, Oh.	573,822	750,879	876,050
Denver, Col.	492,365	514,678	493,887
El Paso, Tex.	425,259	322,261	276,687
Seattle, Wash.	493,846	530,831	557,087
Nashville-Davidson, Tenn.	455,651	426,029	170,874
Austin, Tex.	345,496	253,539	186,545
Oklahoma City, Okla.	403,213	368,164	324,253
Kansas City, Mo.	448,159	507,330	475,539
Fort Worth, Tex.	335,164	393,455	356,268
St. Louis, Mo.	453,085	622,236	750,026
Atlanta, Ga.	425,022	495,039	487,455
Long Beach, Cal.	361,334	358,879	344,168
Portland, Ore.	366,383	379,967	372,676
Pittsburgh, Pa.	423,938	520,089	604,332
Miami, Fla.	346,865	334,859	291,688
Tulsa, Okla.	360,919	330,350	261,685
Honolulu, Ha.	762,874	630,528	294,194
Cincinnati, Oh.	385,457	453,514	502,550
Albuquerque, N.M.	331,767	244,501	201,189
Tucson, Ariz.	330,537	262,933	212,892
Oakland, Cal.	339,337	361,561	367,548
Minneapolis, Minn.	370,951	434,400	482,872
Charlotte, N.C.	314,447	241,420	201,564
Omaha, Neb.	314,255	346,929	301,598
Toledo, Oh.	354,635	383,062	318,003
Virginia Beach, Va.	262,199	172,106	8,091
Buffalo, N.Y.	357,870	462,768	532,759
Sacramento, Cal.	275,741	257,105	191,667
Newark, N.J.	329,248	381,930	405,220
Wichita, Kan.	279,272	276,554	254,698
Louisville, Ky.	298,451	361,706	390,639
Fresno, Cal.	218,202	165,655	133,929
Tampa, Fla.	271,523	277,714	274,970
Birmingham, Ala.	284,413	300,910	340,887
Norfolk, Va.	266,979	307,951	304,869
Colorado Springs, Col.	215,150	135,517	70,194
Corpus Christi, Tex.	231,999	204,525	167,690
St. Paul, Minn.	270,230	309,866	313,411
Mesa, Ariz.	152,453	63,049	33,772
Arlington, Tex.	160,113	90,229	44,775
Baton Rouge, La.	346,029	165,921	152,419
Anaheim, Cal.	219,311	166,408	104,184
St. Petersburg, Fla.	238,647	216,159	181,298
Santa Ana, Cal.	203,713	155,710	100,350
Rochester, N.Y.	241,741	295,011	318,611
Anchorage, Alas.	174,431	48,081	44,237
Akron, Oh.	237,177	275,425	290,351
Shreveport, La.	205,820	182,064	164,372
Jersey City, N.J.	223,532	260,350	276,101

LARGEST CITIES IN THE UNITED STATES (con.)

City	Population		
	1980	1970	1960
Aurora, Col.	158,588	74,974	48,548
Richmond, Va.	219,214	249,332	219,958
Lexington-Fayette, Ky.	204,165	108,137	62,810
Jackson, Miss.	202,895	153,968	144,422
Mobile, Ala.	200,452	190,026	194,856
Riverside, Cal.	170,876	140,089	84,332
Montgomery, Ala.	177,857	133,386	134,393
Des Moines, Ia.	191,003	201,404	208,982
Las Vegas, Nev.	164,674	125,787	64,405
Grand Rapids, Mich.	181,843	197,649	177,313
Lubbock, Tex.	173,979	149,101	126,691
Yonkers, N.Y.	195,351	204,297	190,634
Huntington Beach, Cal.	170,505	115,960	11,492
Stockton, Cal.	149,779	109,963	86,321
Lincoln, Neb.	171,932	149,518	128,521
Little Rock, Ark.	158,461	132,483	107,813
Raleigh, NC	150,255	122,830	93,931
Columbus, Ga.	169,441	155,028	116,779
Dayton, Oh.	203,371	243,023	262,332
Greensboro, N.C.	170,279	144,076	119,574
Garland, Tex.	138,857	81,437	38,501
Madison, Wis.	170,616	171,809	126,706
Knoxville, Tenn.	175,030	174,587	111,827
Fort Wayne, Ind.	172,196	178,269	161,776
Spokane, Wash.	171,300	170,516	181,608
Amarillo, Tex.	149,230	127,010	137,969
Huntsville, Ala.	142,513	139,282	72,365
Chattanooga, Tenn.	169,565	119,923	130,009
Kansas City, Kans	161,087	168,213	121,901
Hialeah, Fla.	145,254	102,452	66,972

LARGEST METROPOLITAN AREAS IN THE UNITED STATES

Metro Area	Population
	1980
New York-Northern New Jersey-Long Island, NY-NJ-CT.	17,539,532
Los Angeles-Anaheim-Riverside, CA	11,497,549
Chicago, IL	7,937,307
San Francisco-Oakland-San Jose, CA	5,367,900
Philadelphia, PA	5,680,509
Detroit-Ann Arbor, MI.	4,752,764
Boston, MA	3,971,792
Dallas-Fort Worth, TX.	2,930,568
Houston, TX.	3,099,942
Washington, DC-MD-VA	3,250,921
Miami-Fort Lauderdale, FL	2,643,766
Cleveland-Akron, OH	2,834,062
Atlanta, GA	2,138,143
St. Louis, MO-IL	2,376,971
Pittsburgh, PA	2,423,311
Minneapolis-St. Paul, MN-WI	2,137,133
Seattle-Tacoma, WA	2,093,285
Baltimore, MD	2,199,497
San Diego, CA	1,861,846
Tampa-St. Petersburg-Clearwater, FL	1,613,600
Phoenix, AZ	1,509,227
Denver-Boulder, CO	1,618,461
Cincinnati-Hamilton, OH-KY-IN	1,660,258
Milwaukee-Racine, WI	1,570,152
Kansas City, MO-KS	1,433,464
Portland-Vancouver, OR-WA.	1,297,977
New Orleans, LA	1,256,668
Norfolk-Virginia Beach-Newport News, VA.	1,160,311
Columbus, OH	1,243,827
Sacramento, CA	1,099,814
San Antonio, TX	1,072,125
Indianapolis, IN	1,166,575
Buffalo-Niagara Falls, NY	1,242,826
Providence-Pawtucket, RI	1,083,139
Charlotte, NC	971,447

PRINCIPAL FOREIGN CITIES

City	Population
Accra, Ghana	954,000
Addis Ababa, Ethiopia	1,413,000
Adelaide, Australia	969,000
Ahmedabad, India	2,515,000
Alexandria, Egypt	2,318,000
Algiers, Algeria	2,400,000
Allahabad, India	642,000
Alma-Ata, USSR	1,068,000
Amagasaki, Japan	506,000
Amsterdam, Netherlands	676,000
Ankara, Turkey	2,800,000
Anshan, China	1,500,000
Antwerp, Belgium	1,583,000
Astrakhan, USSR	493,000
Athens, Greece	886,000
Baghdad, Iraq	2,184,000
Baku, USSR	1,693,000
Bandung, Indonesia	1,463,000
Bangalore, India	2,914,000
Bangkok, Thailand	5,175,000
Barcelona, Spain	1,757,000
Barnaul, USSR	578,000
Barranquilla, Colombia	1,121,000
Beijing, China	9,500,000
Beirut, Lebanon	702,000
Belém, Brazil	756,000
Belfast, Northern Ireland	319,000
Belgrade, Yugoslavia	1,470,000
Belo Horizonte, Brazil	1,442,000
Bilbao, Spain	433,000
Birmingham, England	1,116,000
Bogotá, Colombia	3,968,000
Bologna, Italy	459,000
Bombay, India	8,227,000
Brasilia, Brazil	1,579,000
Bremen, West Germany	672,000
Brisbane, Australia	942,000
Bristol, England	434,000
Brussels, Belgium	980,000
Bucharest, Romania	1,834,000
Budapest, Hungary	2,072,000
Buenos Aires, Argentina	2,923,000
Cairo, Egypt	5,074,000
Calcutta, India	9,166,000
Cali, Colombia	1,398,000
Cape Town, South Africa	214,000
Caracas, Venezuela	1,163,000
Casablanca, Morocco	2,158,000
Catania, Italy	380,000
Changchun, China	1,740,000
Chelyabinsk, USSR	1,096,000
Chengdu, China	2,470,000
Chongqing, China	2,650,000
Cologne, West Germany	932,000
Colombo, Sri Lanka	588,000
Copenhagen, Denmark	633,000
Córdoba, Argentina	969,000
Dakar, Senegal	979,000
Damascus, Syria	1,251,000
Delhi, India	5,714,000
Dhaka, Bangladesh	3,440,000
Dnepropetrovsk, USSR	1,153,000
Donetsk, USSR	1,073,000
Dortmund, West Germany	585,000
Dresden, East Germany	520,000
Dublin, Ireland	526,000
Duisburg, West Germany	528,000
Durban, South Africa	506,000
Düsseldorf, West Germany	571,000
East Berlin, East Germany	1,197,000
Edinburgh, Scotland	419,000
Esfahán, Iran	927,000
Essen, West Germany	629,000
Florence, Italy	430,000
Fortaleza, Brazil	649,000
Frankfurt, West Germany	604,000
Frunze, USSR	617,000
Fukuoka, Japan	1,160,000
Fushun, China	1,019,000
Gdánsk, Poland	464,000
Genoa, Italy	738,000
Gifu, Japan	408,000
Glasgow, Scotland	762,000
Goiânia, Brazil	703,000
Gorki, USSR	1,400,000
Gotëborg, Sweden	424,000
Guadalajara, Mexico	2,244,000
Guatemala City, Guatemala	1,300,000
Guayaquil, Ecuador	1,300,000
Hague, Netherlands	872,000
Hamamatsu, Japan	510,000
Hamburg, West Germany	1,600,000
Hangzhou, China	4,020,000
Hanoi, North Vietnam	1,440,000
Hanover, West Germany	517,000
Harbin, China	2,550,000
Havana, Cuba	1,950,000
Helsinki, Finland	485,000
Higashiosaka, Japan	502,000
Hiroshima, Japan	907,000
Hohhot, China	748,000
Ho Chi Minh City, S. Vietnam	4,000,000
Howrah, India	745,000
Hyderabad, India	2,500,000
Ibadan, Nigeria	847,000
Irkutsk, USSR	597,000
Istanbul, Turkey	2,773,000
Ivanovo, USSR	474,000
Izmir, Turkey	750,000
Jakarta, Indonesia	6,500,000
Jinan, China	1,333,000
Johannesburg, South Africa	1,156,000
Kanpur, India	1,688,000
Kaohsiung, Taiwan	1,290,000
Karachi, Pakistan	5,103,000
Karaganda, USSR	617,000
Kawasaki, Japan	1,050,000
Kazan, USSR	1,048,000
Kharkov, USSR	1,554,000
Kiev, USSR	2,448,000
Kinshasa, Zaire	2,444,000
Kitakyushu, Japan	1,052,000
Kobe, Japan	1,381,000
Kraków, Poland	735,000
Krasnodar, USSR	609,000
Krasnoyarsk, USSR	872,000
Krivoi Rog, USSR	684,000
Kuibyshev, USSR	1,257,000
Kumamoto, Japan	527,000
Kunming, China	1,430,000

Kyoto, Japan	1,464,000
Lagos, Nigeria	1,061,000
Lahore, Pakistan	2,922,000
La Paz, Bolivia	881,000
Leeds, England	442,000
Leipzig, East Germany	556,000
Leningrad, USSR	4,867,000
León, Mexico	656,000
Lima, Peru	5,257,000
Lisbon, Portugal	817,000
Liverpool, England	497,000
Łódź, Poland	845,000
London, England	6,754,000
Lucknow, India	1,007,000
Lvov, USSR	742,000
Lyon, France	418,000
Madras, India	4,277,000
Madrid, Spain	3,200,000
Madurai, India	904,000
Manchester, England	458,000
Manila, Philippines	1,630,000
Mannheim, West Germany	297,000
Maracaibo, Venezuela	929,000
Marseille, France	879,000
Medan, Indonesia	1,379,000
Medellin, Colombia	2,069,000
Melbourne, Australia	2,864,000
Mexico City, Mexico	9,377,000
Milan, Italy	1,520,000
Minsk, USSR	1,472,000
Monterrey, Mexico	1,006,000
Montevideo, Uruguay	1,360,000
Montreal, Canada	980,000
Moscow, USSR	8,642,000
Nagasaki, Japan	446,000
Nagoya, Japan	2,066,000
Nagpur, India	1,298,000
Nairobi, Kenya	828,000
Nanjing, China	2,000,000
Naples, Italy	1,212,000
Novokuznetsk, USSR	577,000
Novosibirsk, USSR	1,393,000
Nuremberg, West Germany	472,000
Odessa, USSR	1,126,000
Omsk, USSR	1,108,000
Osaka, Japan	2,648,000
Oslo, Norway	447,000
Palembang, Indonesia	787,000
Palermo, Italy	700,000
Panama City, Panama	386,000
Paris, France	2,189,000
Perm, USSR	1,056,000
Phnom Penh, Cambodia	1,500,000
Pôrto Alegre, Brazil	1,115,000
Poznań, Poland	571,000
Prague, Czechoslovakia	1,186,000
Pretoria, South Africa	574,000
Poona, India	1,685,000
Pusan, South Korea	3,495,000
Pyongyang, North Korea	1,280,000
Qingdoo, China	1,144,000
Quito, Ecuador	1,110,000
Rangoon, Burma	2,458,000
Recife, Brazil	1,183,000
Riga, USSR	883,000
Rio de Janeiro, Brazil	5,090,000
Rome, Italy	2,840,000
Rosario, Argentina	935,000
Rostov-on-Don, USSR	986,000
Rotterdam, Netherlands	571,000
Sakai, Japan	810,000
Salvador, Brazil	1,490,000
Santiago, Chile	3,615,000
Santo Domingo, Dominican Republic	1,313,000
São Paulo, Brazil	7,032,000
Sapporo, Japan	1,479,000
Semarang, Indonesia	1,027,000
Sendai, Japan	663,000
Seoul, South Korea	9,500,000
Seville, Spain	654,000
Shanghai, China	6,270,000
Sheffield, England	477,000
Shenyang, China	4,020,000
Singapore, Singapore	7,000,000
Sofia, Bulgaria	1,173,000
Stockholm, Sweden	635,000
Stuttgart, West Germany	563,000
Surabaja, Indonesia	2,028,000
Suzhou, China	635,000
Sverdlovsk, USSR	1,300,000
Sydney, Australia	3,300,000
Tabriz, Iran	598,000
Taipei, Taiwan	2,500,000
Taiyüan, China	1,750,000
Tangshan, China	1,200,000
Tashkent, USSR	2,030,000
Tbilisi, USSR	1,158,000
Tehran, Iran	4,530,000
Thonburi, Thailand	628,000
Tianjin, China	5,100,000
Tokyo, Japan	8,991,000
Toronto, Canada	633,000
Tunis, Tunisia	557,000
Turin, Italy	1,117,000
Ufa, USSR	1,064,000
Valencia, Spain	752,000
Vancouver, Canada	410,000
Varanasi, India	794,000
Victoria, Hong Kong	1,000,000
Vienna, Austria	1,531,000
Vladivostok, USSR	600,000
Volgograd, USSR	720,000
Voronezh, USSR	850,000
Warsaw, Poland	1,628,000
West Berlin, West Germany	1,852,000
Wroclaw, Poland	627,000
Wuhan, China	3,200,000
Wuppertal, West Germany	382,000
Xi'an, China	2,800,000
Xuzhou, China	773,000
Yaroslavl, USSR	626,000
Yerevan, USSR	1,133,000
Yokohama, Japan	2,915,000
Zagreb, Yugoslavia	1,174,000
Zaporozhe, USSR	852,000
Zaragoza, Spain	590,000
Zhdanov, USSR	522,000
Zibo, China	927,000
Zurich, Switzerland	440,000

HOLIDAYS
CHIEF LEGAL OR PUBLIC HOLIDAYS

Each State has jurisdiction over holidays that will be observed in that State. They are designated either by the State legislature or by executive proclamation and, therefore, may be changed with each new State executive or legislature. There are no national holidays in the United States. The President and Congress designate holidays only for the District of Columbia and for Federal employees throughout the nation.

A holiday falling on Sunday is usually observed on the Monday following it.

January—January 1. *New Year's Day.* All the States.

Third Monday. *Martin Luther King Day.* In some states, combined with Robert E. Lee Day.

January 20. *Inauguration Day.* Begun in 1937. It is observed every fourth year in the District of Columbia only.

February—February 12. *Lincoln's Birthday.* All the States except Ala., Ark., Ga., Hawaii, Ida., Ky., La., Me., Mass., Miss., Nev., N.H., N.C.., Ohio, Okla., R.I., S.C., Tenn., Tex., Va., and Wis.

Third Monday. *Washington's Birthday.* It is called *President's Day* in Hawaii, and *Washington-Lincoln Day* in Minn.

March or **April**—Friday before Easter. *Good Friday.* Observed in all States. A legal holiday in Conn., Del., Fla., Hawaii, Ind., La., N.J., N.D., Penn., and Tenn. In Calif. and Wis., observed part of the day.

May—Last Monday. *Memorial Day.* All the States except Ala., Miss.,

and S.C. In Va., observed as *Confederate Memorial Day.* In La., observed on May 30 and in Ariz. on May 31.

July—July 4. *Independence Day.* All the States.

September—First Monday. *Labor Day.* All the States.

October—Second Monday. *Columbus Day.* All the States except Ala., Iowa, Md., Mich., Miss., Nev., N.C., N.D., Ore., S.C., Wash., P.R. In Hawaii, Called *Discoverer's Day.* In Ind. and N.D., celebrated as *Discovery Day,* and in Wis. *as Landing Day.* In La. and Wis., celebrated on Oct. 12.

November—Fourth Thursday. *Thanksgiving Day.* All the States. Neb., Ill., and N.H. also observe the day after Thanksgiving.

November 11. *Veterans' Day.*

December—December 25. *Christmas Day.* All the States. Ky. and S.C. observe the day after Christmas. Oklahoma observes December 24.

CANADIAN HOLIDAYS

January—January 1. *New Year's Day.*
April—*Good Friday, Easter Monday.*
May—Monday before May 25. *Queen's Birthday or Victoria Day.*
July—July 1. *Dominion Day.*
August—First Monday. *Civic Holiday.* Declared by municipalities.

September—First Monday. *Labor Day.*
October—Second Monday. *Thanksgiving Day.*
November—November 11. *Remembrance Day.*
December—December 25. *Christmas Day.*

JEWISH HOLIDAYS

All Holidays begin on sunset of the previous day. ‡Observances extending over several days, only the first day of the celebration is noted here.

Rosh Hashana (New Year)‡—Tishri 1.
Yom Kippur (Day of Atonement)—Tishri 10.
Sukkoth (Feast of Tabernacles)‡—Tishri 15.
Simhat Torah (Rejoicing of the Law)—Tishri 23.

Hanuka (Feast of Lights)—Kislev 25.
Purim (Feast of Lots)—Adar 14.
Pesach (Passover)‡—Nisan 15.
Lag b'Omer—Iyar 18.
Shavuot (Feast of Weeks)‡—Sivan 6.
Tishah b'Ab (Fast of Ab)—Av 9.

The months of the Jewish Calendar are: *Tishri, Heshvan, Kislev, Tebet, Shebat, Adar, Nisan, Iyar, Sivan, Tammuz, Ab,* and *Elul.* The month *Tishri* begins in late September or early October.

PERPETUAL CALENDAR: 1 A.D.—2400 A.D.

To find calendar for any year, first find Dominical letter for the year in the upper section of table. Two letters are given for leap year, the first for January and February, the second for other months. In the lower section of table, find column in which the Dominical letter for the year is in the same line with the month for which the calendar is desired; this column gives the days of the week that are to be used with the month.

For example, in the table of Dominical Letters we find that the letter for 1960, a leap year, is CB; in the line with July, the letter B occurs in the third column; hence July 4, 1960, is Monday.

DOMINICAL LETTERS

Century / Year	0 700 1400	100 800 1500†	200 900	300 1000	400 1100	500 1200	600 1300	1500‡ 2000	1600 2100	1700 2200	1800 2300	1900
0	DC	ED	FE	GF	AG	BA	CB	—	BA	C	E	G
1 29 57 85	B	C	D	E	F	G	A	F	G	B	D	F
2 30 58 86	A	B	C	D	E	F	G	E	F	A	C	E
3 31 59 87	G	A	B	C	D	E	F	D	E	G	B	D
4 32 60 88	FE	GF	AG	BA	CB	DC	ED	CB	DC	FE	AG	CB
5 33 61 89	D	E	F	G	A	B	C	A	B	D	F	A
6 34 62 90	C	D	E	F	G	A	B	G	A	C	E	G
7 35 63 91	B	C	D	E	F	G	A	F	G	B	D	F
8 36 64 92	AG	BA	CB	DC	ED	FE	GF	ED	FE	AG	CB	ED
9 37 65 93	F	G	A	B	C	D	E	C	D	F	A	C
10 38 66 94	E	F	G	A	B	C	D	B	C	E	G	B
11 39 67 95	D	E	F	G	A	B	C	A	B	D	F	A
12 40 68 96	CB	DC	ED	FE	GF	AG	BA	GF	AG	CB	ED	GF
13 41 69 97	A	B	C	D	E	F	G	E	F	A	C	E
14 42 70 98	G	A	B	C	D	E	F	D	E	G	B	D
15 43 71 99	F	G	A	B	C	D	E	C	D	F	A	C
16 44 72	ED	FE	GF	AG	BA	CB	DC	BA	CB	ED	GF	BA
17 45 73	C	D	E	F	G	A	B	G	A	C	E	G
18 46 74	B	C	D	E	F	G	A	F	G	B	D	F
19 47 75	A	B	C	D	E	F	G	E	F	A	C	E
20 48 76	GF	AG	BA	CB	DC	ED	FE	DC	ED	GF	BA	DC
21 49 77	E	F	G	A	B	C	D	B	C	E	G	B
22 50 78	D	E	F	G	A	B	C	A	B	D	F	A
23 51 79	C	D	E	F	G	A	B	G	A	C	E	G
24 52 80	BA	CB	DC	ED	FE	GF	AG	FE	GF	BA	DC	FE
25 53 81	G	A	B	C	D	E	F	D	E	G	B	D
26 54 82	F	G	A	B	C	D	E	C	D	F	A	C
27 55 83	E	F	G	A	B	C	D	B	C	E	G	B
28 56 84	DC	ED	FE	GF	AG	BA	CB	AG	BA	DC	FE	AG

Month	Dominical letter						
Jan., Oct.	A	B	C	D	E	F	G
Feb., Mar., Nov.	D	E	F	G	A	B	C
Apr., July	G	A	B	C	D	E	F
May	B	C	D	E	F	G	A
June	E	F	G	A	B	C	D
Aug.	C	D	E	F	G	A	B
Sept., Dec.	F	G	A	B	C	D	E

Day											
1	8	15	22	29	Sun.	Sat.	Fri.	Thurs.	Wed.	Tues.	Mon.
2	9	16	23	30	Mon.	Sun.	Sat.	Fri.	Thurs.	Wed.	Tues.
3	10	17	24	31	Tues.	Mon.	Sun.	Sat.	Fri.	Thurs.	Wed.
4	11	18	25		Wed.	Tues.	Mon.	Sun.	Sat.	Fri.	Thurs.
5	12	19	26		Thurs.	Wed.	Tues.	Mon.	Sun.	Sat.	Fri.
6	13	20	27		Fri.	Thurs.	Wed.	Tues.	Mon.	Sun.	Sat.
7	14	21	28		Sat.	Fri.	Thurs.	Wed.	Tues.	Mon.	Sun.

†On and before 1582, Oct. 4 only.   ‡On and after 1582, Oct. 15 only.

This calendar was prepared by G. M. Clemence, U. S. Naval Observatory, and is reprinted from the Smithsonian Physical Tables, Ninth Edition, by permission of the Smithsonian Institution.

WEIGHTS & MEASURES

METRIC SYSTEM
LENGTH

1 kilometer	1,000 meters	3,280 feet. 10 inches
1 hectometer	100 meters	328 feet. 1 inch
1 meter	1 meter	39 37 inches
1 centimeter	.01 meter	.3937 inch
1 millimeter	.001 meter	.0394 inch
1 micron	.000001 meter	.000039 inch
1 millimicron	.000000001 meter	.000000039 inch

SURFACE

1 sq. kilometer	1,000,000 sq. meters	= .3861 sq. mile
1 hectare	10,000 sq. meters	= 2.47 acres
1 are	100 sq. meters	= 119.6 sq. yards
1 centiare	1 sq. meter	= 1,550 sq. inches
1 sq. centimeter	.0001 sq. meter	= .155 sq. inch
1 sq. millimeter	.000001 sq. meter	= .00155 sq. inch

VOLUME

		Dry	Liquid
1 kiloliter	= 1,000 liters	= 1.308 cu yards or	264.18 gallons
1 hectoliter	100 liters	= 2.838 bushels or	26.418 gallons
1 liter	= 1 liter	= .908 quart or	1.057 quarts
1 centiliter	= .01 liter	= .610 cu. inch or	.338 fl ounce
1 milliliter	= .001 liter	= .061 cu. inch or	.271 fl. dram

WEIGHT

1 kilogram	= 1,000 grams	= 2.205 pounds
1 hectogram	= 100 grams	= 3.527 ounces
1 gram	= 1 gram	= .035 ounce
1 centigram	= .01 gram	= .154 grain (Troy)
1 milligram	= .001 gram	= .015 grain (Troy)

DOMESTIC WEIGHTS AND MEASURES
MEASURE

Linear		Square		Liquid	
12 inches	= 1 foot	144 sq. inches	= 1 sq. foot	4 gills	= 1 pint
3 feet	= 1 yard	9 sq feet	= 1 sq. yard	2 pints	= 1 quart
5½ yards	= 1 rod	30¼ sq yards	1 sq rod	4 quarts	= 1 gallon
40 rods	= 1 furlong	160 sq. rods	= 1 acre	31½ gallons	= 1 barrel
8 furlongs	= 1 mile	640 acres	1 sq. mile	2 barrels	= 1 hogshead
	(5,280 ft.)				

WEIGHT

Avoirdupois		Troy		Apothecaries'	
16 drams	= 1 ounce	24 grains	= 1 penny-weight	20 grains	= 1 scruple
16 ounces	= 1 pound	20 penny-weights	= 1 ounce	3 scruples	= 1 dram
100 pounds	= 1 short hundred-weight	12 ounces	= 1 pound	8 drams	= 1 ounce
112 pounds	= 1 long hundred-weight			12 ounces	= 1 pound
20 hundred-weight	= 1 ton				